THE DICTIONARY OF

Human Geography

To the memory of

GRAHAM SMITH

THE DICTIONARY OF

Human Geography

Fourth Edition

Edited by

R.J. Johnston
Derek Gregory
Geraldine Pratt
and Michael Watts

David M. Smith
Consultant Editor

First edition published 1981
First paperback edition 1983
Reprinted 1985
Second edition 1986
Reprinted 1988
Second paperback edition 1988
Reprinted 1989, 1990, 1991

Third edition, revised and updated, 1994
Third paperback edition 1994
Reprinted in paperback 1994 (twice), 1995, 1996 (twice), 1997, 1998
Fourth edition published 2000

2 4 6 8 10 9 7 5 3 1

Blackwell Publishers Ltd
108 Cowley Road
Oxford OX4 1JF
UK

Blackwell Publishers Inc.
350 Main Street
Malden, Massachusetts 02148
USA

British Library Cataloguing in Publication Data
A CIP catalogue record for this book is available from the British Library

Library of Congress Cataloging-in-Publication Data has been applied for

ISBN 0–631–20560–8 (hbk)
ISBN 0–631–20561–6 (pbk)

Typeset in 9 on 10 pt by Kolam Information Services Pvt Ltd, Pondicherry, India.
Printed in Great Britain by TJ International, Padstow, Cornwall

This book is printed on acid-free paper.

Contents

Preface to the Fourth Edition

Geographical dictionaries have a long history. A number were published in the seventeenth and eighteenth centuries: a few – mostly those with greater pretensions to providing conceptual order – were described as 'Geographical Grammars'. The majority were compendia of geographical information, or gazetteers, some of which were truly astonishing in their scope. For example, Laurence Echard noted with some asperity in his 1691 *Compendium of Geography* that the geographer was by then more or less required to be 'an *Entomologist*, an *Astronomer*, a *Geometrician*, a *Natural Philosopher*, a *Husbandman*, an *Herbalist*, a *Mechanick*, a *Physician*, a *Merchant*, an *Architect*, a *Linguist*, a *Divine*, a *Politician*, one that understands *Laws* and *Military Affairs*, an *Herald* [and] an *Historian*'. Marguerita Bowen, commenting in 1981 on what she took to be geography's isolation from the scientific mainstream in Echard's time, suggested that 'the prospect of adding epistemology and the skills of the philosopher' to such a list might well have precipitated its Cambridge author into the River Cam!

It was in large measure the addition of those skills to the necessary accomplishments of a human geographer which prompted the first edition (1981) of *The Dictionary of Human Geography*. The editors noted then that the changes in human geography since the Second World War had generated a 'linguistic explosion' within the discipline. Part of the *Dictionary*'s purpose – then as now – was to provide students and others with a general series of theoretical frameworks for situating, understanding and interrogating the modern lexicon. The implicit model was something closer to Raymond Williams's marvellous compilation of *Keywords* than to any 'Geographical Grammar'. Certainly the intention was always to provide something more than a collection of annotated reading-lists. Individual entries were located within a web of cross-references to other entries, which enabled readers to follow their own paths through the *Dictionary*, sometimes to encounter unexpected parallels and convergences, sometimes to encounter creative tensions and contradictions. But the major entries were intended to be comprehensible on their own, and many of them not only provided lucid representations of key issues but also made powerful contributions to subsequent debates.

This sense of *The Dictionary of Human Geography* as both mirror and goad, as both reflecting and provoking work in our field, has been retained in all subsequent editions. The pace of change within human geography was such that a second edition (1986) was produced only five years after the first, incorporating significant revisions and additions. For the third edition (1994) yet more extensive revisions and major additions to the text were made. This fourth edition (2000) continues that restless tradition; it has been comprehensively redesigned and rewritten and is a vastly different book from the original. The first edition had over 500 entries written by 18 contributors, whereas the present volume has over 900 entries written by 57 contributors. But it is also considerably different from the second and third editions too: over 200 entries appear for the first time, and virtually all of the others have been fully revised and reworked. With this fourth edition we have thus been able to chart the emergence of new themes, new approaches and new concerns within human geography, and we have also sought to anticipate fresh avenues of inquiry and new links with other disciplines.

The first edition was planned at the height of the critique of spatial science within geography, and for that reason most of the entries were concerned with either analytical methods and formal spatial models or with alternative concepts and approaches drawn from the (other) social sciences. We have taken new developments in analytical methods into account in subsequent editions, and this edition is no exception. We pay particular attention to the continuing stream of innovations in Geographical Information Systems (philosophies, technologies and applications) both inside and outside the discipline and we have included new entries on both technical terms and developments in geocomputation, geodemographics, and Global Positioning Systems. By no means are all of these developments associated with spatial analysis and the emergence of new technical skills and capabilities. In the last edition we provided enhanced coverage of developments in the humanities as well as the social sciences and we have taken this still further in the fourth edition. Human geographers have been particularly assiduous in unpicking the seams between the humanities and the social sciences. Particularly significant has been the incorporation of ideas and approaches informed by what has come to be known as 'post-structuralism'. Like all of the other 'posts' that have recently marked human geography, this is a label that identifies highly variable baggage, including the work of Jacques Derrida, Michel Foucault, Jacques Lacan and others. Its travels through human geography have brought a renewed interest in close and critical reading (surely vital for any dictionary!), a greatly expanded sense of the range of methodological possibilities, and a heightened awareness of the significance of empirical specificity. All of these are registered in this edition, which includes revised entries on deconstruction and post-structuralism, and new entries on keywords like anti-humanism, biopower, episteme, genealogy, governmentality, heterotopia, psychoanalytic theory, and vision and visuality. As this selective listing indicates, the theoretical sensibilities of post-war human geography have certainly not diminished, but they have sustained a much more open and porous culture of geographical inquiry. We are now more aware than ever before of the slipperiness of our geographical 'keywords': of the claims they silently make, the privileges they surreptitiously install, and of the wider web of meaning and practice within which they do their work. Indeed, it seems clear to us that human geographers are now moving with considerable critical intelligence in a transdisciplinary, even a post-disciplinary space. They are engaged with an astonishing range of issues across the whole field of the humanities, the social sciences and the sciences (so much so that these distinctions are themselves increasingly seen as problematic and even counter-productive). Equally, many of the most characteristic concerns of human geography have engaged the attention of scholars in other fields, where issues of place and landscape, of space and nature, are increasingly seen as being of central importance. This is reflected in the countless bibliographic references that appear for the first time in this edition and in the inclusion of new entries on (for example) the relations between geography and film, media, music, performance and travel writing. The fourth edition of *The Dictionary of Human Geography* at once maps and moves within this interdisciplinary topography with an unprecedented precision and range.

As we have noted, that topography extends beyond the humanities and the social sciences. Human geography has long displayed a particular interest in science – in its philosophies, protocols and procedures – and this has been heightened by new developments in the history and sociology of science and, perhaps most of all, by the rise of cultural studies of science and so-called 'science studies'. This has not been without controversy, and the fourth edition of *The Dictionary of Human Geography* engages directly with many of these debates. The critical interest in science and its privileges has contributed to a revitalized interest in ethics and epistemology – and in both these areas new entries have been provided – and to an intensified scrutiny of the politics of the academy itself: witness, for example, new entries on activism in the academy and on critical human geography. The interrogation of science as a series of situated social practices seems to have had relatively little impact on physical geography, and in this sense has done little to develop a dialogue between the two geographical solitudes, but this fourth edition shows that there are other ways in which human geography has moved much closer to the terrain of physical geography. The last several years have seen a much more general interest in the culture and politics of nature emerge within human geography, and this accounts for the inclusion of new entries on (for example) biodiversity, the geography of animals, deep ecology, ecofeminism, ecological imperialism, environmental justice and political ecology. The reinstatement of 'nature' on the agenda of human geography has also been informed by the continued development of historical materialism, with its insistent focus on the production of nature and the production of space, and, more recently still, by the rise of actor–network theory and its attempt to overcome the sedimented partitions between 'culture' and 'nature': many entries now clearly reflect the vitality of – and the *va-et-vient* between – these collective projects.

We continue to pay considerable attention to the importance of feminist perspectives. This is reflected in the language used (the only sexist writing appears in quotations), in the increased space devoted to feminist theory and politics, and in new entries on the body, homophobia and heterosexism, and queer theory. We do not confine issues of gender and sexuality to any separate subdiscipline, however, and they properly appear throughout the *Dictionary* as they now appear throughout the discipline. The significance of feminist work to key debates within human geography cannot be underestimated; we hope that it will have a similar impact on the day-to-day practices of scholars and students, and on the production of human geographies outside the academy.

If the work that is contained within this edition of *The Dictionary of Human Geography* takes place on a far larger intellectual landscape than ever before, however, we also must recognize that this edition continues to be concerned almost entirely with English-language words, terms and literatures. There are of course cautionary observations to be made about the power-laden diffusion of English as a 'global language', and we know that there are severe limitations to working within a single-language tradition (especially in a field like human geography). The vitality of other geographical traditions should be neither overlooked nor minimized. We certainly do not believe that human geography conducted in English somehow constitutes the 'authorized' version of the discipline, though it would be equally foolish to ignore the powers and privileges it has arrogated to itself in the unequal world of the international academy. Neither should one discount the privileges that can be attached to learning other languages, or minimize the perils of translation: all linguistic competences exact their price. But to offer some (limited) protection against an unreflective ethnocentrism we have widened our coverage of issues bound up with colonialism and Eurocentrism, imperialism and Orientalism – all of these in the past and in the present, where they are often considered under the troubled sign of 'postcolonialism' – and we have engaged still more directly with the politics of 'race', racism and representation: see, for example, the new entries on hybridity, otherness, transculturation, transnationalism, and whiteness. All of this makes it impossible for us to present *The Dictionary of Human Geography* as an Archimedean overview, a performance of what Donna Haraway calls 'the God-trick'. The entries are all 'situated knowledges' written by scholars working in Australia, Canada, the United Kingdom and the United States of America. None of them is detached, and all of them are actively involved in the debates which they write about. More than this: the authors write from a diversity of subject-positions, so that this edition succeeds perhaps better than any of its predecessors in conveying a real sense of diversity and debate within the discipline. Even so, we are conscious of at least some of its partialities and limitations, and we invite our readers to consider how these voices might be heard from other positions, other places, and indeed other periods, and to think about the voices that are – deliberately or unconsciously – silenced or marginalized.

None of these changes (and none of these questions) is a purely intellectual matter, of course, for they do not take place in a vacuum: the world has changed dramatically since the first edition, and this is reflected both in the concerns addressed by human geographers and in their approaches to understanding. New entries include (for example) the geography of AIDS, critical geopolitics, ethnic cleansing, globalization, human rights, identity politics, immigration, post-Soviet states and the risk society.

In these various ways the fourth edition of *The Dictionary of Human Geography* is, like its predecessors, a series of reports from scholars occupying different positions inside a crowded and complicated landscape. When the other Johnson planned his great *Dictionary* in 1747 he told his patron: 'When I survey the plan which I have laid before you, I cannot, my Lord, but confess that I am frightened at its extent, and like the soldiers of Caesar, look on Britain as a new world, which it is almost madness to invade. But I hope, though I should not complete the conquest, I shall at least discover the coast, civilize part of the inhabitants, and make it easier for some other adventurer to proceed farther, to reduce them wholly to subjection, and to settle them under laws.' As this implies, there is probably a covert colonialism to any lexicographical project. But this edition of *The Dictionary of Human Geography*, like its predecessors, is marked by struggles and debates and we make no secret of the differences – in position, in orientation, in politics – among our various contributors. They do not speak with a single voice and this is not a work of bland and arbitrary systematization produced by a committee. If, to return to Samuel Johnson, the coast of human geography seems to become longer with each edition of our own *Dictionary*, the editors have no wish to 'civilize' its inhabitants. And there seems no prospect, fortunately, of the multiple worlds of human geography ever being stabilized, ordered and regulated.

Ron Johnston
Derek Gregory
Geraldine Pratt
Michael Watts

How to Use This Dictionary

Keywords are listed alphabetically and appear on the page in **bold type**: in most cases users of the *Dictionary* should begin their searches there. Within each entry, cross-references to other entries are shown in CAPITAL LETTERS (these include the plural and adjectival versions of many of the terms). Readers may trace other connections through the comprehensive index at the back of the book.

Acknowledgements

In the production of this edition, we are again indebted to a large number of people. The entire project was first conceived by John Davey in 1978: he saw the first three editions through the complete process from commissioning to publication, and convinced us to undertake a fourth, as a millennium project. We miss his benign presence, his intellectual vitality and his constant friendship and support, but have been delighted to work with Jill Landeryou in the long process of bringing the project to completion. We are also grateful to the many others at Blackwell Publishers who have been involved in the management and implementation of this project, to Anthony Grahame for the superb copy-editing, and to Ann Barham for another excellent index. (Her skill was recognized by the UK Library Association when the index for the third edition was short-listed as one of the best three indexes to an academic book published in 1994.)

The preparation of a large multi-author volume such as this is dependent on the co-operation of a large number of colleagues, who have accepted our encouragement to contribute, our cajoling to produce the material, our prompts over deadlines, and our editorial whims: we are immensely grateful to them for their tolerance and patience, but above all for the excellence of their work – yet again the parts are superb, and the whole is even greater than their sum. Sadly, one of them – Graham Smith – died in April 1999, and we dedicate this edition of the *Dictionary* to his memory.

We are also indebted to a number of others – to Peter Haggett and David Stoddart who were in the editorial teams for the early editions and helped to shape the *Dictionary*; to David Smith, who after full involvement with the first three editions acted as a consultant editor for this one; and to David Demerritt and John-Paul Jones III for going through our table of contents with a fine tooth-comb and making many valuable suggestions.

The authors, editors and publishers thank the following for permission to reproduce the copyright material indicated.

Martin Cadwallader for the figure reproduced in the entry for **Alonso model** from *Analytical Urban Geography*, 1985.

Blackwell Publishers for the figure reproduced in the entry for **applied geography** from *Tijdschrift voor Economische en Sociale Geographie*, 1990.

Blackwell Publishers Ltd with The University of Chicago Press for the figure reproduced in the entry **capitalism** from D. Harvey, *The Limits to Capital*, 1982.

Lyn Collins for the figures reproduced in the entry for **catastrophe theory** from *The Use of Models in the Social Sciences*, 1976.

John Urry for the figure reproduced in the entry for **civil society** from *The Anatomy of Capitalist Societies*, 1991.

Blackwell Publishers Ltd for the figure reproduced in the entry **crisis** from D. Gregory, *Geographical Imaginations*, 1993.

Blackwell Publishers Ltd for figure 4 reproduced in the entry for **critical theory**, based on Jürgen Habermas, *The Theory of Communicative Action*, Vol. 2, Polity Press.

University of California Press for the figure reproduced in the entry **cultural landscape** from Carl O. Sauer, *The Morphology of Landscape*, 1925. Copyright © 1925 The Regents of the University of California.

Routledge for the figure reproduced in the entry **cycle of poverty** from R.J. Johnston, *City and Society: An Outline of Urban Geography*, 1984, Hutchinson.

Peter Haggett for the figure reproduced in the entry for **demographic transition** from *Geography: A Modern Synthesis*, 1975.

Ohio State University Press Macmillan Publishers Ltd for the figure reproduced in the entry **distance decay** from Peter J. Taylor, 'Distance transformation and distance decay functions', *Geographical Analysis*, Vol. 3, 3 July 1971. Copyright © Ohio State University Press.

Routledge for the figure reproduced in the entry for **dual economy** from Santos, *The Shared Space*, 1979, Methuen & Co.

Routledge for the figure reproduced in the entry for **environmentalism** from *New Models in Geography*, 1989.

Edward Arnold for the figure reproduced in the entry for **feedback**, from J. Langton, 'Potentialities and problems of adopting a systems approach to the study of change in human geography', in *Progress in Geography*, Vol. 4, 1972: 127–79.

The University of New Mexico Press for the figure reproduced in the entry **form of economic integration** from P. Wheatley in J.A. Sabloff and C. Lamberg-Karlovsky, eds, *Ancient Civilisation and Trade*, 1973.

Blackwell Publishers Ltd for the figure reproduced in the entry **human agency** from A. Giddens, *The Constitution of Society*, Polity Press, 1984.

Royal Geographical Society for the figure reproduced in the entry for **indices of segregation** from *Transactions of the IBG* 21, 1996: 224. Table IX showing indices of segregation of the Bangladeshi ethnic population, 1991 in a paper by C. Peach.

Andrew Sayer for the figure reproduced in the entry for **intensive research** from *Method in Social Science*, 1984.

Routledge for the figure reproduced in the entry **internal relations** from Andrew Sayer, *Method in Social Sciences: A Realist Approach*, 1992, 1984, Hutchinson.

Hodder & Stoughton Publishers Ltd for the figure reproduced in the entry **krondratieff cycle** based on Marshall, 1987, from P. Knox and J. Agnew, Geography of the World-Economy, 1989.

Macmillan Publishers Ltd with St. Martin's Press for the figure reproduced in the entry **krondratieff** cycle from Knox and Agnew, adapted from M. Marshall, *Long Waves of Regional Development*, 1987.

Derek Gregory for the figure reproduced in the entry for **layers of investment** from *Horizons in Human Geography*, 1989.

Thomas Nelson and Sons Ltd for the figure reproduced in the entry for **law of the sea** from *The Law of the Sea*, 1978.

Macmillan Publishers Ltd for the figure reproduced in the entry **locale** from A. Giddens, *Power, Property and the State*, Vol. I, 1981.

Peter Haggett for the figure reproduced in the entry for **locational analysis**, from *Locational Analysis in Human Geography*, 1977.

John Libbey Eurotext Ltd for the figure reproduced in the entry **mortality** from J.L. Rallu and A. Blum, eds, *European Population: I country Analysis*, 1991.

Andrew Sayer for the figure reproduced in the entry for **ontology** from *Method in Social Science*, 1984.

Blackwell Publishers Ltd for figures 1 and 2 reproduced in the entry **production of space** from D. Gregory, *Geographical Imaginations*, 1993.

Cambridge University Press and The University of Chicago Press for the figure reproduced in the entry for **multiple nuclei model** from Harris and Ullman in H.M. Mayer and C.F. Kohn, eds, *Readings in Urban Geography*, 1959.

Peter Taylor for the figure reproduced in the entry for **quantitative revolution** from *Quantitative Methods in Geography*, 1977.

Paul Cloke for the figure reproduced in the entry for **realism** from *Approaching Human Geography*, 1991.

Macmillan Publishers Ltd for the figure reproduced in the entry **resource** from J. Rees in D. Gregory and R. Walford, eds, *Horizons in Human Geography*, 1989.

Routledge for the figure reproduced in the entry for **Rostow model** from *Models in Geography*, 1967, Methuen & Co.

Macmillan Publishers Ltd for the figure reproduced in the entry **space-economy** from D. Gregory in D. Gregory and R. Walford, eds, *Horizons in Human Geography*, 1989.

Blackwell Publishers Ltd for the figure reproduced in the entry **spatiality** from D. Gregory, *Geographical Imaginations*, 1993.

Routledge for the figure reproduced in the entry **stages of growth** from D.E. Keeble in R.J. Chorley and P. Haggett, eds, *New Models in Geography*, Methuen & Co.

Blackwell Publishers for the figure reproduced in the entry for **time-space convergence** from *The Professional Geographer*, 1968.

Edinburgh University Press for figures 1 and 2 reproduced in the entry **urban origins** from P. Wheatley, *The Pivot of the Quarters*, 1971.

The University of Chicago Press for the figure reproduced in the entry **zonal model** from R.E. Park, E.N. Burgess and R.D. McKenzie, *The City*, 1925.

Every effort has been made to trace all the copyright holders: if any have been inadvertently overlooked the publishers will be pleased to make the necessary arrangements at the first opportunity.

Contributors

AGH Tony Hoare
University of Bristol

AL Andrew Leyshon
University of Nottingham

AMH Alan Hay
Canterbury Christ Church University College, Canterbury

CP Chris Philo
University of Glasgow

CWJW Charles Withers
University of Edinburgh

DC Dan Clayton University of St Andrews

DEC Denis Cosgrove
Royal Holloway, University of London

DG Derek Gregory
University of British Columbia, Vancouver

DH Daniel Hiebert
University of British Columbia, Vancouver

DL David Ley
University of British Columbia, Vancouver

DM David Matless
University of Nottingham

DMS David M. Smith
Queen Mary and Westfield College, University of London

DNL David Livingstone
Queen's University of Belfast

DW David Woodward
University of Wisconsin, Madison

GES Graham Smith
University of Cambridge

GP Geraldine Pratt
University of British Columbia, Vancouver

GR Gillian Rose
The Open University

GV Gill Valentine
University of Sheffield

JAA John Agnew
University of California, Los Angeles

JM John Mohan
University of Portsmouth

JMCC James McCarthy
Pennsylvania State University

JP Joe Painter
University of Durham

JS Joni Seager
University of Vermont, Burlington

JSD Jim Duncan
University of Cambridge

JW Jennifer Wolch
University of Southern California, Los Angeles

KM Katharyne Mitchell
University of Washington, Seattle

LP Laura Pulido
University of Southern California, Los Angeles

LWH Les Hepple
University of Bristol

MB Mark Blacksell
University of Plymouth

MG Michael Goodchild
University of California, Santa Barbara

MJD Michael Dear
University of Southern California, Los Angeles

MM Mark Monmonier
Syracuse University

MO Mark Overton
Department of History, University of Exeter

MPB Michael Brown
University of Washington, Seattle

MSG Meric Gertler
University of Toronto

MW Michael Watts
University of California, Berkeley

NB Nick Blomley
Simon Fraser University, British Columbia

NC Noel Castree
University of Liverpool

NJT Nigel Thrift
University of Bristol

NRF Nick Fyfe
University of Strathclyde, Glasgow

NS Neil Smith
City University of New York

PAJ Peter Jackson
University of Sheffield

PAL Paul Longley
University of Bristol

PC Phil Crang
University College London

PD Peter Dicken
University of Manchester

PDG Paul Glennie
University of Bristol

PEO Philip Ogden
Queen Mary and Westfield College, University of London

PJC Paul Cloke
University of Bristol

PJT Peter Taylor
Loughborough University

PM Phil McManus
University of Sydney

RI Rob Imrie
Royal Holloway, University of London

RJJ Ron Johnston
University of Bristol

RL Roger Lee
Queen Mary and Westfield College, University of London

RMK Rob Kitchin
National University of Ireland, Maynooth

SJS Susan Smith
University of Edinburgh

SW Sarah Whatmore
University of Bristol

TJB Trevor Barnes
University of British Columbia, Vancouver

A

abstraction Methodologically, 'abstraction' involves the conceptual isolation of (a partial aspect of) an object. Its principles and procedures depend on the philosophy or EPISTEMOLOGY under whose sign it is conducted.

For those geographies committed to POSITIVISM, abstraction represents the starting-point of conventional MODEL-building. Chorley (1964) emphasized both its basic importance and its peculiar difficulty: 'In developing a simplified but appropriate model for a given object system or segment of the real world... huge amounts of available information are being discarded... and therefore much noise is being potentially introduced.' In consequence, Chorley believed that 'in geography most attempts at model-building by abstraction have met with minimal success'. Those which had fared best 'exposed fundamental symmetries and relationships' while avoiding 'excessive simplification'. But he was unable to offer very precise guidelines for their construction, appealing to the 'creative ability and vision of the model-builder'.

For those geographies committed to various forms of IDEALISM, and particularly those whose procedures draw upon Max Weber's interpretative sociology, abstraction usually involves the construction of so-called IDEAL TYPES: 'one-sided' idealizations of reality seen from particular points of view. There is nothing especially 'scientific' about them, Weber claimed, because this kind of selective structuring is something that we all do all the time. But since it is perfectly possible to construct quite different ideal types of the same phenomenon, depending on one's point of view, the critical moment comes when the ideal type is compared with 'empirical reality'. Even so, commentators differ on just how precisely such comparisons are to be made and on how revealing they are likely to be (see Parkin, 1982, pp. 28–32).

For those geographies committed to REALISM, however, both of these versions of abstraction are inadequate because they are supposed to be based on 'an arbitrary attitude to ONTOLOGY' (Sayer, 1984, p. 216). According to Sayer, abstractions should identify essential characteristics of objects and should be concerned with 'substantial' relations of connection rather than merely 'formal' relations of similarity. It is especially important to identify those INTERNAL RELATIONS which necessarily enter into the constitution of specific structures. Hence Sayer distinguishes a rational abstraction, i.e. 'one which isolates a significant element of the world which has some unity and autonomous force', from what Marx called a CHAOTIC CONCEPTION, i.e. one whose definition is more or less arbitrary because it rests on relations of similarity. So, for example, Allen (1983) provided a careful typology of landlords within the housing market, whose classifications 'bestow a degree of coherence upon certain groupings, that is, a structure which enables them to act... in [distinctive] ways depending upon the spatial and temporal circumstances'. From this perspective, it is equally important to recognize the existence of different levels of abstraction. Marx's own writings are usually cited here because they move between the general and the historically specific (see Johnson, 1982) and a number of workers have sought to elucidate, and indeed to refine, the connections between them (see Gibson and Horvarth, 1983; Cox and Mair, 1989).

Other writers have drawn attention to the ways in which these ostensibly analytical processes of selection and dissection spiral out into the constitution of everyday life. Seen thus, 'abstraction' also has substantive implications for the heightened rationalization of everyday life – what Jürgen Habermas (1987) called the 'colonization of the life-world' – and for the production of an abstract space, 'one-sided' and 'incomplete', that Henri Lefebvre (1991) identified as the dominant spatial condition of MODERNITY (see also PRODUCTION OF SPACE). DG

References

Allen, J. 1983: Property relations and landlordism – a realist approach. *Environment and Planning D: Society and Space* 1: 191–203. · Chorley, R.J. 1964: Geography and analogue theory. *Annals of the Association of American Geographers* 54: 127–37. · Cox, K. and Mair, A. 1989: Levels of abstraction in locality studies. *Antipode* 21: 121–32. · Gibson, K. and Horvarth, R. 1983: Marx's method of abstraction. *Antipode* 16: 23–36. · Habermas, J. 1987: *The theory of communicative action.*

Vol. 2: The critique of functionalist reason. Cambridge: Polity Press. · Johnson, R. 1982: Reading for the best Marx: history-writing and abstraction. In Centre for Contemporary Cultural Studies, *Making histories: studies in history-writing and politics*. London: Hutchinson, 153–201. · Lefebvre, H. 1991: *The production of space*, trans. D. Nicholson-Smith. Oxford and Cambridge, MA: Blackwell. · Parkin, F. 1982: *Max Weber*. London: Tavistock. · Sayer, A. 1984: *Method in social science: a realist approach*. London: Hutchinson (2nd edn, 1992. London: Routledge).

Suggested Reading

Allen (1983). · Sayer (1992), 85–92 and 138–40.

accessibility At its simplest, the ease with which one place can be reached from another. It may be measured in terms of geodetic distance, topological distance (see NETWORKS AND GRAPH THEORY), journey distance, journey time or monetary cost (see TRANSPORT COSTS). The concept has been broadened in a number of ways. First general accessibility may be calculated from a single location to all other locations in the study region (cf. POPULATION POTENTIAL). Second, access may be related to the geographical content of other areas in the study region: access to employment, access to markets, access to educational or health facilities etc. Third, some authors have recognized that accessibility to certain activities and facilities is modified by barriers other than geographical distance (e.g. the effects of income, ethnicity, and social class) and therefore attempt to incorporate these effects into measures of accessibility. In all of these applications accessibility is seen to combine at least three elements: the location of a place within a study region; the location within the study region of the activities to which access is being measured; and the form of the transport and communication system. It is generally argued that long-term improvements in transport and communications technology have improved accessibility (especially the access to information) and therefore reduced spatial differences in the degree to which locations are accessible (see COMMUNICATIONS, GEOGRAPHY OF; TIME–SPACE CONVERGENCE). AMH

accumulation The process by which CAPITAL is reproduced at an ever-increasing scale through continued reinvestment of surplus value. In Marx's words: 'Employing *surplus value* as capital, reconverting it into capital, is called the accumulation of capital' (1987, p. 543).

Accumulation is a definitive condition of CAPITALISM. To remain in business, the ordinary capitalist must at least preserve the value of capital advanced ('simple reproduction'), but to continue as a *capitalist* he or she must continually augment the value of invested capital ('expanded reproduction', or accumulation). Capital accumulation becomes a central driving force in capitalist society, influencing broader political, social, demographic and cultural change. More than anything else, Marx attributed the dynamism of capitalist society to the imperative of accumulation (see also MARXIAN ECONOMICS).

The imperative of accumulation presupposes capitalist RELATIONS OF PRODUCTION; on the one side, a CLASS of capitalists who own the means of production, and on the other side, a class of workers who are 'freed' from ownership of the means of production and who are also free to perform labour for the capitalist. The survival of the individual capitalist is dependent on the ability to sell commodities profitably in the market, and this has the effect of institutionalizing technological change as a means of competition between individual capitals. The imperative for accumulation at the individual level thereby translates into the social imperative for economic growth and technological change. In his 'general law of capitalist accumulation', Marx argued that the imperative of accumulation

> implied a second imperative, the relative immiseration of the working class that produces the expanding wealth – a fundamental social relation of capitalism. (Marx, 1987, ch. 25)

The social relations of capitalism are themselves the result of an historical process whereby workers are separated from the land and from the means of production, largely agricultural. This process, known as *primitive accumulation*, forces workers to sell their labour power for a monetary wage, and is best exemplified by the history of the ENCLOSURES in England and the subsequent PRIVATIZATION of land ownership.

The geography of capitalist accumulation (Harvey, 1977) is central to the fortunes of the capitalist mode of production (Harvey, 1982) and results in specific patterns of UNEVEN DEVELOPMENT at different spatial SCALES (Smith, 1990). Equally, accumulation is uneven according to time. The process of accumulation is punctuated by recessions and crises of differing intensities, and these in turn become moments in which the established patterns of economic expansion and the whole social organization of the economy are put in question (Arrighi, 1994). NS

References

Arrighi, G. 1994: *The long twentieth century: money, power, and the origins of our times*. London: Verso. · Gramsci, A. 1971: *Selections from the prison notebooks*, ed. and trans. by Q. Hoare and G. Nowell Smith. London: Lawrence and Wishart; New York: International Publishers, 277–316. · Harvey, D. 1977: The geography of capitalist accumulation: a reconstruction of the Marxian theory. In R. Peet, ed., *Radical geography*. Chicago: Maaroufa, 263–92. · Harvey, D. 1982: *The limits to capital*. Oxford: Blackwell. · Marx, K. 1987: *Capital*, volume I. New York: International Publishers. · Smith, N. 1990: *Uneven Development: nature, capital and the production of space*, 2nd edn. Oxford: Blackwell.

Suggested Reading

Marx (1987), esp. Part VII, 'The accumulation of capital' and Part VIII, 'The so-called primitive accumulation'.

acid rain The deposition of sulphuric and nitric acids onto land or water by rainwater. Acid rain is one form of acid precipitation, which also includes acid snow, acid hail, dry deposition and acid fog condensation. On a pH scale of 14, a substance with a pH value of less than 7 is considered acidic, while a pH value greater than 7 is considered alkaline. Rainwater is naturally slightly acidic with a pH value of about 5.6 due to the formation of weak carbonic acids. Acid rain generally has an average pH range of 3–5, although higher levels of acidity have been recorded. Acidity is greatest near the base of clouds, and is diluted by a factor of 0.5 to 1 pH during rainfall (Pickering and Owen, 1994).

The English chemist R.A. Smith discovered a link between industrial POLLUTION and acid rain in Manchester as early as 1852, although it was known in the twelfth century that burning coal caused air pollution (Turco, 1997). Although Smith first used the term acid rain in 1872, it is only since the late 1950s that Smith's ideas have been treated seriously. The concern expressed in Sweden, generated through the studies of soil scientist Svente Oden, focused attention on this international issue. In 1972 the Swedish Government presented its case at the United Nations Conference on the Human Environment in Stockholm. The term acid rain has been used extensively in recent decades.

Acid rain is caused primarily by the cumulative release of nitrogen and sulphur from the burning of fossil fuels. These are commonly in the form of coal for power, heating and industry, and petrol in automobiles. While acid rain may occur through natural processes such as volcanic activity, it is the cumulative impact of human activities that have caused a marked increase in acid rain over the past decades.

Acid rain is a major concern in western Europe and North America because of the higher generation rates there and because the process crosses international boundaries (see McCormick, 1997). It is a controversial process because acid rain deposition may occur several hundred kilometres from the source of pollution, especially when tall smokestacks are built to displace pollution from its source area. The areas most affected by acid rain tend to be downwind of dense concentrations of power stations, smelters and cities. They are often upland areas which receive high levels of precipitation. They also tend to be forest areas that are dissected by rivers and lakes (Park, 1987). Acid rain kills forests when acidic particles directly damage leaves and/or when the soil becomes acidified and the metals bound in the soil are freed; the nutrients necessary for plant growth are then leached by the water. Acid rain also lowers the pH value of lakes and other water bodies, which kills fish and other aquatic forms of life and may corrode buildings and other structures. PM

References

McCormick, J. 1997: *Acid earth: the politics of acid pollution*, 3rd edn. London: Earthscan. · Park, C. 1987: *Acid rain: rhetoric and reality*. London: Methuen. · Pickering, K. and Owen, L. 1994: *An introduction to global environmental issues*. London and New York: Routledge. · Turco, R. 1997: *Earth under siege: from air pollution to global change*. Oxford and New York: Oxford University Press.

action space A concept used in BEHAVIOURAL GEOGRAPHY to define the area within which an individual makes locational decisions, such as where to shop, which house to purchase, and which church to attend. The relevant locations within that space are evaluated and assigned PLACE UTILITIES; if none of the utility values is high enough to meet the individual's threshold satisfaction level, then the action space within which SEARCH BEHAVIOUR occurs may be extended or the threshold revised (cf. ACTIVITY SPACE; MENTAL MAP). RJJ

activism and the academy Refers to both debates over, and the practice of, political activism within academic geography. The question of geographical activism is old, stretching back to anarchist geographer Peter Kropotkin (1899) and his *Fields, factories and workshops*. However, in the modern era SPATIAL SCIENCE instituted a separation between facts and VALUES which encouraged geographers to consider questions of politics and personal intervention beyond the scope of their inquiries and actions. The advent of RADICAL GEOGRAPHY in the late 1960s thus marked the return of a 'dissenting tradition' (Blaut, 1979) in geography. However, it was a return with two differences from Kropotkin's time. First, geography was by the late 1960s a well established university discipline, part of the settled fabric of 'normal' educational life in most western countries. By contrast though, and secondly, the real world was anything but settled because the late 1960s was an era of civil unrest, environmental protests, student riots, anti-war campaigns and anti-colonial struggles in and against the US, France, Britain and other countries. It was this disjuncture between academic geography and real world socio-economic problems and struggles that inspired the early radical geographers like William Bunge, James Blaut and Richard Peet to call for a *people's geography* in which geographers would (i) study crucial social, economic and environmental problems with (ii) an eye to devising viable solutions in (iii) a way that included the ordinary people subject to those problems and solutions. This, then, was a form of geographical activism in which (i) research was focused on politically charged questions and solutions and (ii) in which geographers actively involved themselves with the peoples and COMMUNITIES studied. Bunge's (1971, 1977) 'Geographical Expeditions' in Detroit and elsewhere were perhaps the most original and unique examples.

Radical geography was the impetus for two subsequent developments regarding activism and the academy. The first was the emergence of a less radical WELFARE GEOGRAPHY which sought to use existing scientific geographical theories and methods in a more socially relevant and useful way (Smith, 1977). The second was the development, in the 1970s and 1980s, of a number of full-blown critical PARADIGMS like MARXIST and FEMINIST GEOGRAPHY. However, what is ironic is that these paradigms, notwithstanding their critical nature, became far more academic and less practically engaged than their radical geography forebears. Thus, by the early 1990s, some leftist geographers were once more complaining of a chasm between geographical 'activism and the academy' (Blomley, 1994). In response some, like Blomley, advocated a return to grass-roots involvement, while others, like Tickell (1995), argued that geographers should more actively involve themselves in the local and national STATE APPARATUS in order to influence PUBLIC POLICY. More recently, Castree (2000) has suggested that much of the activism and the academy debate in geography is overly preoccupied with *reaching out* from the university to intervene in the so-called 'real world', as if intervening *within* the university system itself is somehow a less worthy form of activism. As professional geographers are subject to increased pressures to teach more students and publish more research in countries like the UK and the US, such 'in here' activism is likely to increase. (See also APPLIED GEOGRAPHY; RELEVANCE.) NC

References

Blaut, J. 1979: The dissenting tradition. *Annals of the Association of American Geographers* 69: 157–64. · Blomley, N. 1994: Activism and the academy. *Environment and Planning D: Society and Space* 12: 383–5. · Bunge, W. 1971: *Fitzgerald: geography of a revolution*. Cambridge, MA: Schenkman. · Bunge, W. 1977: The first years of the Detroit Geographical Expedition: a personal report. In R. Peet, ed., *Radical geography*. London: Methuen, 31–9. · Castree, N. 2000: 'In here', 'out there?' Domesticating critical geography. *Area* 31: 81–6. · Kropotkin, P. 1899: *Fields, factories and workshops*. Boston: Houghton Mifflin. · Smith, D.M. 1977: *Human geography: a welfare approach*. London: Edward Arnold. · Tickell, A. 1995: Reflections on 'Activism and the academy'. *Environment and Planning D: Society and Space* 13: 235–7.

activity space The area within which the majority of an individual's day-to-day activities are carried out; it contains, but may be more extensive than, the ACTION SPACE(s) within which particular locational decisions are made. Chombart de Lauwe (1952) suggested a hierarchy of such spaces – familial, NEIGHBOURHOOD, economic, and urban sector – within which different activities are conducted. Many, especially those at the larger spatial scales, may be discontinuous, comprising points linked by known routes but separated by areas that are virtually unknown to the individuals concerned (cf. BEHAVIOURAL GEOGRAPHY; MENTAL MAP). RJJ

Reference

Chombart de Lauwe, P.H. 1952: *Paris et l'agglomeratione Parisienne*. Paris: Presses Universitaires de France.

actor–network theory The study of heterogeneous engineering: 'heterogeneous' because it is concerned with a vision of the world as a multiplicity of different connections (translations, associations, mediations); and 'engineering' because it sees these connections as fabricated out of a diverse range of materials. Actor–network theory is the uneasy progeny of the work of the French philosopher of science, Michel Serres, and the French engineer, Bruno Latour (Serres and Latour, 1995), as well as a host of other writers who initially grouped under the banner of the sociology of science but have now moved into many other areas (e.g. Callon, 1986; Law, 1994: cf. SCIENCE, GEOGRAPHY AND).

Actor–network theory has become a major force in the social sciences just as many of its originators have began to disown not so much the project as the idea that there was ever a project at all. Yet it is no surprise that commentators have produced such an interpretation for, like another ascetic approach, TIME-GEOGRAPHY, actor–network theory is an attempt to write the world anew, by starting from first principles. But, also like time-geography, actor–network theory is quietly ambitious: its aim is nothing less than an attempt to rewrite the 'constitution' of western knowledge (see EPISTEMOLOGY).

The new constitution proposed by actor–network theory is based on four main principles.

The first is that all the usual boundaries from which and with which western knowledge is constituted – between humans and things, NATURE and CULTURE, tradition and MODERNITY, inside and outside – must be put aside. These divides have made it impossible to see the world for what it really is: a collection of heterogeneous activities which are constantly in formation.

The second is that the world is a series of acts of 'heterogenous engineering', by which is meant that the world is made up of diverse networks of association which are constituted by that association – by the links rather than the nodes of the network and, more than this, by the traffic through the links. The network is, in other words, constituted in 'the passing'. It is these diverse 'actor–networks' which are the source of 'agency' in the world. But this is an agency of partial connection which means that Latour prefers to use the word '*actant*' rather than 'actor' to describe this hesitant but still potent status (cf. HUMAN AGENCY). Of course, this might suggest that networks are so hesitant, so flimsy, that they cannot hold. But this is where the third principle bites.

Because the existence of actor–networks depends so heavily on circulation, their continuation relies on a whole series of 'immutable mobiles' – devices, types of people, animals, money, and so on, which can be transported from one location to another without changing form – which allow those networks to become *durable*: 'technology is society made durable' as Latour (1991) would have it. These immutable mobiles harden and anneal the networks, making it possible for them to last.

The fourth principle is a result of the previous three: the stress laid on *mediaries and intermediaries*. Taking a leaf from the work of Michel Serres (1995, 1996), the most important elements of the world are counted as the *messengers* which do the work of keeping networks connected and folding networks into each other. These most prominent performers of association stitch the world together.

Geographers have become very interested in actor–network theory (for reviews see Murdoch, 1997a, 1997b) because it offers them three important points of connection. First, it can be used as a means of producing a better understanding of the twists and turns of both technology and nature (Bingham, 1996; Whatmore, 1999). Second, it problematizes the act of REPRESENTATION; representation becomes a kaleidoscope of different representational modes which can only be briefly stabilized and constantly interfere with each other (see NON-REPRESENTATIONAL THEORY). Third, it provides a means of understanding SPACE as an order of partial connection and in doing so suggests new means of understanding space and PLACE (Thrift, 1996; Hetherington and Law, 1999) as folds in constantly evolving topologies since 'time and space are the consequences of the way in which bodies relate to one another' (Latour, 1997, p. 174). In this depiction, it shares many similarities with the work of Deleuze and Guattari (see, for example, Deleuze, 1993). Indeed, Latour has often suggested that actor–network theory should be known as 'actant-RHIZOME' theory.

NJT

References

Bingham, N. 1996: Object-ions: From technological determinisms towards geographies of relations. *Environment and Planning D: Society and Space* 14: 635–58. · Bingham, N. and Thrift, N.J. 1999: Some new instructions for travellers: the geography of Bruno Latour and Michael Series. In M. Crang and N.J. Thrift, eds, *Thinking space*. London: Routledge. · Callon, M. 1986: Some elements of a sociology of translation: domestication of the scallops and the fishermen of St Brieuc Bay. In J. Law, ed., *Power, action and belief. A new sociology of knowledge*? London: Routledge and Kegan Paul, 234–65. · Deleuze, G. 1993: *The Fold. Leibniz and the baroque*. Minneapolis: University of Minnesota Press. · Hetherington, K. and Law, J., eds, 1999: Special issue on actor–network theory and spatiality. *Environment and Planning D: Society and Space* 17. · Latour, B. 1991: Technology is society made durable. In J. Law, ed., *A sociology of monsters. Essays on power, technology and domination*. London: Routledge, 103–30. · Latour, B. 1993:

We have never been modern. Hassocks: Harvester. · Latour, B. 1997: Trains of thought: Piaget, formalism, and the fifth dimension. *Common Knowledge* 6: 170–91. · Latour, B. and Powers, R. 1998: Two writers face one Turing test. A dialogue in honour of HAL. *Common Knowledge* 7: 177–91. · Law, J. 1994: *Organising modernity.* Oxford: Blackwell. · Murdoch, J. 1997a: Towards a geography of heterogeneous associations. *Progress in Human Geography* 21: 321–37. · Murdoch, J. 1997b: Inhuman/non human/human: actor–network theory and the prospects for a non-dualistic and symmetrical perspective on nature and society. *Environment and Planning D: Society and Space* 15: 731–56. · Powers, R. 1994: *Galatea 2.2.* London. · Serres, M. 1995: *Genesis.* Ann Arbor, MI: University of Michigan Press. · Serres, M. 1996: *Angels. A modern myth.* Paris: Flammarion. · Serres, M. and Latour, B. 1995: *Conversations on science, culture, time.* Ann Arbor, MI: University of Michigan Press. · Thrift, N.J. 1996: *Spatial formations.* London: Sage. · Whatmore, S.J. 1999: Hybrid geographies. Rethinking the human in human geography. In D. Massey, J. Allen and P. Sarre, eds, *Human geography today.* Cambridge: Polity Press.

adaptation Derived from Darwinian and evolutionary theory (cf. DARWINISM; LAMARCKISM), adaptation is an enormously influential metaphor for thinking about the relations between populations (human and non-human) and their environment (Sayer, 1979). It is a concept with a long and robust life in the biological and social sciences. Adaptation is rooted in the question of survival, and specifically of populations in relation to the biological environments which they inhabit (Holling, 1975). Adaptation refers to the changes in gene frequencies that confer reproductive advantage to a population in specific environments, and to physiological and sociocultural changes that enhance individual fitness and well-being. The means by which populations survive and reproduce speaks to processes of adaptation and their mechanisms to the existence of adaptive structure.

Adaptation has a currency in the social sciences through the organic analogy – the idea that social systems are forms of living systems in which processes of adaptation inhere (Slobodkin and Rappaport, 1974). In geography, CULTURAL and HUMAN ECOLOGY drew heavily on biological and adaptive thinking by seeing social development in terms of human niches, adaptive radiation and human ecological succession (see Watts, 1983). Some of the more sophisticated work in cultural ecology (Nietschmann, 1973) drew upon the work of Rappaport (1979), Wilden (1972) and Bateson (1972) who employed systems theory (cf. SYSTEMS ANALYSIS), cybernetics and ECOSYSTEMS modelling as a way of describing the structure of adaptation in PEASANT and tribal societies. Here adaptation refers to the 'processes by which living systems maintain homeostasis in the face of short-term environmental fluctuations and by transforming their own structures through long-term non-reversing changes in the composition and structure of their environments as well' (Rappaport, 1979, p. 145). Cultural ecology and ecological anthropology focused especially on rural societies in the THIRD WORLD to demonstrate that various aspects of their cultural and religious life fulfilled adaptive functions. Adaptation has also been employed however by sociologists, geographers and ETHNOGRAPHERS in contemporary urban settings as a way of describing how individuals, households and communities respond to and cope with new experiences (MIGRATION, POVERTY, violence) and settings (the city, the prison). In the human sciences, the term adaptation has however always been saddled with the baggage of structural FUNCTIONALISM on the one hand and of biological reductionism on the other (Watts, 1983). MW

References

Bateson, G. 1972: *Steps to an ecology of mind.* New York: Ballantine. · Holling, C. 1973: Resilience and stability in ecological systems. *Annual Review of Ecology and Systematics* 4: 1–23. · Nietschmann, B. 1973: *Between land and water.* New York: Academic. · Rappaport, R. 1979: *Ecology, meaning and religion.* Richmond: North Atlantic Books. · Sayer, A. 1979: Epistemology and conceptions of people and nature in geography. *Geoforum* 10: 19–43. · Slobodkin, A. and Rappaport, R. 1974: An optimal strategy of evolution, *Quarterly Review of Biology* 49: 181–200. · Watts, M. 1983: The poverty of theory. In K. Hewitt, ed., *Interpretations of calamity.* London: Allen and Unwin, 231–63. · Wilden, A. 1972: *System and structure.* London: Tavistock.

age and sex structure The composition of a population according to age and/or sex. These universal characteristics of human populations are fundamental to understanding demographic processes of FERTILITY, MORTALITY and MIGRATION. *Age composition* is often summarized in terms of age groups – e.g. 0–15 years, 15–64, and 65 or over: the *sex ratio* is most commonly expressed as the number of males per 100 females. Characteristics of both age and sex may be expressed in the POPULATION PYRAMID and may vary markedly both among and within countries. Age and sex structures reflect past demographic behaviour, give some indication of likely future trends and are of great significance in, for example, social policy. PEO

Suggested Reading

Daugherty, H.G. and Kammeyer, K.C.W. 1995: *An introduction to population*, 2nd edn. New York and London: The Guilford Press, ch. 5. · Petersen, W. 1975: *Population*, 3rd edn. New York and London: Collier-Macmillan, ch. 3.

ageism Discrimination on the basis of age has been identified as a problem in and for geography (Chouinard and Grant, 1996). It is a problem *in* geography because so little geographical research examines the experiences of those other than middle-aged people; both the young and old are largely ignored. It is problem *for* geography because there is a range of geographical themes that should and is beginning to be pursued: the production and regulation of public space as adult space, for example, and age-specific experiences and creation of spaces (including the home: Katz and Monk, 1993; Skelton and Valentine, 1998; see CHILDREN, GEOGRAPHY AND). GP

References

Chouinard, V. and Grant, A. 1996: On being not even anywhere near 'the project': ways of putting ourselves in the picture. In N. Duncan, ed., *Bodyspace*. New York: Routledge, 170–93. · Katz, C. and Monk, J., eds, 1993: *Full circles: geographies of women over the life course*. New York: Routledge. · Skelton, T. and Valentine, G. 1998. *Cool places: geographies of youth cultures*. London: Routledge.

agglomeration The association of productive activities in close proximity to one another. Agglomeration typically gives rise to EXTERNAL ECONOMIES associated with the collective use of the INFRASTRUCTURE of transportation, communication facilities and other services. Historically, there has been a tendency for economic activity to concentrate spatially, the large markets associated with metropolitan areas adding to the external cost advantages. Agglomeration also facilitates the rapid circulation of capital, commodities and labour. In some circumstances, DECENTRALIZATION may counter agglomerative tendencies, for example if land costs and those associated with congestion in the central area are very high. (See also CONCENTRATION AND CENTRALIZATION; ECONOMIES OF SCALE; ECONOMIES OF SCOPE.) DMS

Suggested Reading

Malmberg, A. 1996: Industrial geography: agglomeration and local milieu. *Progress in Human Geography* 20: 392–403.

aggregate travel model A device for estimating the total coverage of distance involved in serving the market from alternative locations. In its more general form this model can be applied to any situation where it is necessary to aggregate all trips made by individual participants in some activity, but the most common context is industrial location.

The aggregate travel model is related to the MARKET POTENTIAL MODEL (see also CENTROGRAPHY; POPULATION POTENTIAL), in that they both compare the advantage of alternative locations with respect to the market, but under different assumptions. The aggregate travel model assumes a market of varying size in different places, but one that is not sensitive to delivered price or distance from the production location. The model seeks the point of minimum coverage of distance, given by:

$$A_i = \sum_{j=1}^{n} Q_j T_{ij}$$

where Ai is aggregate distance travelled to serve the market from plant location i to all n points or areas comprising the market; Q_j is sales expected at market j; and T_{ij} is the distance or transport cost between i and j. The market size Q may be assumed to be proportional to some alternative measure, such as per capita income or retail sales, as in the market potential model. Similarly, T_{ij} may be linear distance, actual cost, or distance raised to some power to reflect the actual cost–distance relationship in the prevailing freight rates (see DISTANCE DECAY; TRANSPORT COSTS).

The aggregate travel model usually provides figures for the relative advantage of alternative locations. Only if Q actually represents volume of sales and T the real transport cost will the calculation of A give total transport costs for serving the market. As with the market potential concept, figures for aggregate travel can be mapped in the form of a surface. Comparison with a market potential surface derived from the same data reveals differences between the spatial patterns of advantage with respect to serving the market, arising from alternative assumptions as to the nature of the demand situation. DMS

Suggested Reading

Smith, D.M. 1981: *Industrial location: an economic geographical analysis*, 2nd edn. New York: John Wiley, 272–4.

agrarian question Refers to the forms in which capitalist relations transform the agrarian sector and the political alliances, struggles and compromises which emerge around different trajectories of change. The founding theoretical text in studies of the agrarian question is Karl Kautsky's magnificent book *The agrarian* *question* of 1899. Kautsky's focus on the agrarian question in western Europe rested on a striking paradox: agriculture (and the rural) came to assume a political gravity precisely at a moment when its weight in the economy was waning. Agriculture's curious political and strategic significance was framed by two key processes: the first was the growth and integration of a world market in agricultural commodities (especially STAPLES) and the international competition which was its handmaiden; and the second was the birth and extension into the countryside of various forms of parliamentary DEMOCRACY. Both forces originated outside the agrarian sector but lent to agriculture its particular political and economic visibility. International competition in grains was driven not only by the extension of the agricultural FRONTIER in the US, in Argentina, in Russia and eastern Europe (what Kautsky called the 'colonies' and the 'Oriental despotisms'), but also by improvements in long-distance shipping, by changes in taste (for example from rye to wheat) and by the inability of domestic grain production to keep up with demand. As a consequence of massive new supplies, grain prices (and rents and profits) fell more or less steadily from the mid-1870s to 1896 (Konig, 1994). It was precisely during the last quarter of the nineteenth century when a series of protectionist and TARIFF policies in France (1885), Germany (1879) and elsewhere were implemented to insulate the farming sector. New World grain exports were but one expression of the headlong integration of world commodity and capital markets on a scale and with an intensity then without precedent and, some would suggest, unrivalled since that period.

Kautsky devoted much time to the Prussian Junkers and their efforts to protect their farm interests. But in reality the structure of protection only biased the composition of production in favour of grains (and rye in particular) grown on the East Elbian estates. Tariffs provided limited insulation in the protectionist countries, while the likes of England, The Netherlands and Denmark actually adopted free TRADE (Konig, 1994). Protection did not, and could not, save landlordism but was rather a limited buffer for a newly enfranchised PEASANT agriculture threatened by the world market. The competition from overseas producers ushered in the first wave of agricultural protectionism, and in so doing established the foundations of the European 'farm problem' whose political economic repercussions continue to resonate in the halls of the European Commission, the GATT/WTO, and trade ministries around the world (Fennell, 1997).

The agrarian question was a product of a particular political economic conjuncture but was made to speak to a number of key theoretical concerns which arose from Kautsky's careful analysis of the consequences of the European farm crisis: falling prices, rents and profits coupled with global market integration and international competition. In brief he discovered that: (i) there was no tendency for the size distribution of farms to change over time (capitalist enterprises were not simply displacing peasant farms, indeed German statistics showed that middle peasants were increasing their command of the cultivated area); (ii) technical efficiency is not a precondition for survivorship (but self-exploitation might be); and (iii) changes driven by competition and market integration did transform agriculture but largely by shaping the production mix of different enterprises, and by deepening debt-burdens and patterns of out-MIGRATION rather than by radically reconfiguring the size distribution of farms. The crisis of European peasants and landlords in the late nineteenth century was 'resolved' by intensification (cattle and dairying in particular in a new ecological complex) and by the appropriation of some farming functions by capital in processing and agro-industry (see also Goodman et al., 1987) (see AGRO-FOOD SYSTEM).

Kautsky concluded that industry was the motor of agricultural development – or more properly agro-industrial capital was – but that the peculiarities of agriculture, its biological character and rhythms (see Wells, 1996; Mann, 1990), coupled with the capacity for family farms to survive through self-exploitation (i.e. working longer and harder to in effect depress 'wage levels'), might hinder some tendencies, namely, the development of classical agrarian capitalism. Indeed agro-industry – which Kautsky saw in the increasing application of science, technology and capital to the food processing, farm input and farm finance systems – might prefer a non-capitalist farm sector. In all of these respects – whether his observations on land and part-time farming, of the folly of land redistribution, his commentary on international competition and its consequences, or on the means by which industry does or does not take hold of land-based production – Kautsky's book was remarkably forward-looking and prescient.

Terry Byres (1996) has suggested that there are three agrarian questions. The first, posed by Engels, refers to the *politics of the agrarian transition* in which peasants constitute the dominant class: what, in other words, are the politics of the development of agrarian CAPITALISM? The second is about *production and the ways in which market competition drives the forces of production* toward increased yields (surplus creation on the land in short). And the third *speaks to* ACCUMULATION *and the flows of surplus* and specifically inter-sectoral linkages between agriculture and manufacture. The latter Byres calls 'agrarian transition' and embraces a number of key moments, namely growth, TERMS OF TRADE, demand for agrarian products, proletarianization, surplus appropriation and surplus transfer. Byres is concerned to show that agriculture can contribute to industry without the first two senses of the agrarian question being, as it were, activated, and to assert the multiplicity of agrarian transitions (the diversity of ways in which agriculture contributes to capitalist INDUSTRIALIZATION with or without 'full' development of capitalism in the countryside). While Byres' approach has much to offer, it suffers from a peculiar narrowness. On the one hand, it is focused on the internal dynamics of change at the expense of what we now refer to as GLOBALIZATION. On the other, the agrarian question for Byres is something that can be 'resolved' (see also Bernstein, 1996). Resolved seems to imply that once capitalism in agriculture has 'matured', or if capitalist industrialization can proceed without agrarian capitalism ('the social formation is dominated by industry and the urban bourgeoisie'), then the agrarian question is somehow dead. This seems curious on a number of counts, not the least of which is that the three senses of the agrarian question are constantly renewed by the contradictory and UNEVEN DEVELOPMENT of capitalism itself. It is for this reason that we return to Kautsky since his analysis embraced all three dimensions of the agrarian question (something seemingly not acknowledged by Byres) and because he focused so clearly on substantive issues central to the current landscape of agro-food systems: globalization, vertical INTEGRATION, the importance of biology in food provisioning, the application of science, the shifts of POWER off farm, the intensification of land-based activities, and the new dynamisms associated with agro-processing (Goodman and Watts, 1997; McMichael, 1996). Of course Kautsky could not have predicted the molecular revolution and its implications or the role of intellectual property rights and so on. But it is an engagement with his work that remains so central.

Kautsky was of course writing toward the close of an era of protracted crisis for European agriculture, roughly a quarter of a century after the incorporation of New World agricultural frontiers into the world grain market had provoked the great agrarian depressions of the 1870s and 1880s. A century later, during a period in which farming and transportation technologies, diet and agricultural commodity markets are all in flux, the questions of competition, shifting terms of trade for agriculture, and subsidies remain politically central in the debates over the European Union, GATT and the NEO-LIBERAL reforms currently sweeping through the THIRD WORLD. Like the 1870s and 1880s, the current phase of agricultural RESTRUCTURING in the periphery is also marked (sometimes exaggeratedly so) by a phase of 'democratization' (Kohli, 1994; Fox, 1995: cf. CORE–PERIPHERY MODEL). Agrarian parallels at the 'centre' can be found in agriculture's reluctant initiation into the GATT/WTO trade liberalization agreement, albeit with a welter of safeguards, and, relatedly, the dogged rearguard action being fought by western European farmers against further attempts to renegotiate the post-war agricultural settlement, which reached its protectionist apotheosis in the Common Agricultural Policy (CAP) during the 1980s. It is a picture clouded, however, by the strange bedfellows that the CAP has joined in opposition, including environmentalists, food safety activists, animal liberationists, bird watchers, rural preservationists, and neo-conservative free marketeers. All of which is to say that if agrarian restructuring has taken on global dimensions, it is riddled with unevenness and inequalities (and here claims that the agrarian question is 'dead' appear rather curious). The rules of the game may be changing, but the WTO playing field is tilted heavily in favour of the OECD sponsors of this neo-liberal spectacle. MW

References

Bernstein, H. 1996: Agrarian questions then and now. *Journal of Peasant Studies* 24 (1/2): 22–49. · Byres, T. 1996: *Capitalism from above and below.* London: Macmillan. · Fennell, R. 1997: *The Common Agricultural Policy.* Oxford: Oxford University Press. · Fox, J. 1995: Government and rural development in rural Mexico. *Journal of Development Studies* 29: 610–44. · Goodman, Sorj, B. and Wilkinson, J. 1987: *From farming to biotechnology.* Oxford: Blackwell. · Goodman, D. and Watts, M., eds, 1997: *Globalizing food.* London: Routledge. · Kautsky K. 1899: *The agrarian question.* London: Zwan (1988). · Kohli, A. 1994: A democracy of economic orthodoxy. *Third World Quarterly* 14: 671–89. · Konig, H. 1994: *The failure of agricultural capitalism.* London: Routledge. · Mann, S. 1990: *Agrarian capitalism.* Durham: University of North Carolina Press. · McMichael, P., ed., 1996: *Food and agrarian orders in the world economy*. New York: Praeger. · Wells, M. 1996: *Strawberry fields*. Ithaca: Cornell University Press.

agribusiness The term agribusiness was coined by economists Davis and Goldberg (1957, 3) at the Harvard Business School who defined it as

> the sum total of all operations involved in the manufacture and distribution of farm supplies; production operations on the farm; storage; processing and distribution of farm commodities and items made from them.

The term emphasizes the increasingly *systemic* character of food production in which the activities of farming are integrated into a much larger industrial complex, including the manufacture and marketing of technological inputs and of processed food products, under highly concentrated forms of corporate ownership and management. Agribusiness has since become used in much looser and more ideologically loaded ways as a shorthand, on the left, for the domination of capitalist corporations in the agro-food industry and, on the right, for the role of *TRANSNATIONAL* companies in the modernization of food production capacities and practices (Wallace, 1985). In this looser sense it has become a synonym for the industrialization of the AGRO-FOOD SYSTEM.

The classic model of agribusiness centres on the *vertical* INTEGRATION of all stages in the food production process, in which the manufacture and marketing of technological farm inputs, farming and food processing are controlled by a single agro-food corporation. This model was based largely on the US experience, where corporations like Cargill and Tenneco gained control of particular *COMMODITY CHAINS* through a combination of direct investment, subsidiary companies and contracting relationships. Numerous studies in the 1970s drew attention to its significance for commodities like fresh fruit and vegetables; broiler chickens and sugarcane (e.g. Friedland et al., 1981). But it should be noted that a rival term '*la complexe agro-alimentaire*', coined contemporaneously in the French research literature, proposed a much more diffuse model of the industrial development of the agro-food complex (e.g. Allaire and Boyer, 1995).

The 'US school' of agribusiness research had considerable influence over the development of AGRICULTURAL GEOGRAPHY in the English-speaking world, particularly in the 1980s. But it has increasingly attracted criticism both because of a disenchantment with its theoretical debt to systems theory, and because vertical integration proved too empirically specific to support the larger claims of agribusiness as a general model of food production today (Whatmore, 1995). SW

References

Allaire, G. and Boyer, R., eds, 1995: *La grande transformation*. Paris: Institute Nationale de Recherche Agronomique (INRA). · Barkin, D. 1982: The impact of agribusiness on rural development. *Current perspectives in social theory* 3: 1–25. · Davis, J. and Goldberg, R. 1957: *A concept of agribusiness*. Boston: Harvard Business School. · Friedland, W., Barton, A. and Thomas, R. 1981: *Manufacturing green gold*. Cambridge: Cambridge University Press. · Wallace, I. 1985: Towards a geography of agribusiness. *Progress in Human Geography*, 9: 491–514. · Whatmore, S. 1995: From farming to agribusiness: the global agro-food system. In R.J. Johnston, P.J. Taylor and M.J. Watts, eds, *Geographies of global change*. Oxford: Basil Blackwell, 36–49.

agricultural geography Agricultural geography, like agriculture itself, has undergone profound changes in the second half of the twentieth century. Until the 1950s agricultural geography was a specialist sub-set of ECONOMIC GEOGRAPHY, concerned with the 'spatial distribution of agricultural activity' (*Dictionary of Human Geography*, 1985). Its traditional focus had been variations and changes in the pattern of agricultural land-use and their classification at a variety of scales (Grigg, 1984; see also FARMING, TYPES OF). As the economic significance of agriculture declined in terms of the sector's contribution to GDP and employment, particularly in advanced industrial countries, so interest in the subject diminished in the geographical research community. Thus, in 1987 two of its leading UK practitioners were moved to declare that the 'traditional field of agricultural geography... shows every sign of diminishing returns (and requires) a new stimulus to maintain its development and vitality' (Bowler and Ilbery, p. 327). Others went further: Atkins (1988, p. 282), for example, advocated the end of agricultural geography and the dawn of a 'geography of food'.

The stimulus which Bowler and Ilbery, and many other geographers, identified centred on importing theoretical concepts from POLITICAL ECONOMY and turning the substantive focus of study away from farming as a self-contained activity to its complex relationships with off-farm agencies which, taken together, could be said to constitute an 'agro-food chain'. Research agendas framed in these terms, for example those by Wallace (1985) in the North America; Marsden et al., (1986) in the UK and Le Heron (1988) in New Zealand, set the parameters for a new phase of geographical interest in the agro-food sector which could no longer be confined to the narrow disciplinary specialism that had been agricultural geography. Its initial momentum came from encounters with inter-disciplinary networks and ideas, notably those of rural sociology and international political economy, as much as with closer contacts with the broader community of economic geographers.

By the early 1990s, attention had turned beyond the farmgate in two directions. First, to look at the wider organization of capital accumulation in the AGRO-FOOD SYSTEM, focusing on the social, economic and technological ties between three sets of industrial activities, those of food raising (i.e. farming); agricultural technology products and services; and food processing and retailing. Secondly to look at the regulatory INFRASTRUCTURE of this system, focusing on the political and policy processes by which national and supranational STATE agencies underpin agricultural markets. Efforts to comprehend these expanded parameters of agro-food production and regulation led to the development of several new concepts, such as *COMMODITY CHAINS* (see also AGRIBUSINESS) and *food regimes* (see Friedmann and McMichael, 1989).

A composite of these various perspectives and concepts describes the contemporary agro-food system (see, for example, Goodman and Redclift, 1991; Tansey and Worsley, 1995). The figure on p. 13 depicts this enlargement of the scope of agricultural geography from a focus primarily on activities taking place on the farm itself (B) to one spanning the diverse sites and activities of food production and consumption (A–D). In addition to emulating Economic Geography's enduring emphasis on Transnational Corporations, this broadening of the focus of agricultural geography has seen particular attention being paid to the regulatory agencies and processes which are so prominent in the organization of advanced industrial agriculture (see, for example, Ufkes, 1993; Le Heron, 1993; Marsden and Wrigley, 1996).

Research within this political economy tradition has been driven by two contradictory impulses (Goodman and Watts, 1994). On the one hand, it has sought to treat agriculture and food production as just another industrial sector, like cars or steel, so aligning it much more closely with the broader community of INDUSTRIAL GEOGRAPHY and its concerns with GLOBALIZATION; corporate CAPITALISM and the so-called transition from FORDISM to POST-FORDISM (see, for example, Page and Walker, 1991; Kim and Curry, 1993; Jarosz, 1996). Indeed, many of the concerns associated with the AGRARIAN QUESTION, such as the uneven process of capitalist development, anticipated some of those which have come to preoccupy industrial geographers in the last decade. On the other hand, researchers have sought to make sense of the distinctive features of the industrial organization of farming which continue to persist, particularly the predominance of family and PEASANT forms of production (see, for example, Whatmore, 1991; Moran et al., 1993; Watts, 1994; Roberts, 1996) and their significance in the social and political landscapes of late twentieth-century agriculture.

The tensions between these two impulses have proved potentially creative and efforts to recognize and work through them mark out one of the major contributions of geographers to the development of the highly interdisciplinary field of agro-food analysis. These efforts centre on bringing quite different levels of analysis into common focus to examine the social and economic connections between, for example, global *and* local SCALES; corporate *and* household arenas; production *and* regulatory processes. This is best exemplified by the influential collection of essays *Globalizing food* edited by David Goodman and Michael Watts (1997). But, as this same volume indicates, the tensions between these two impulses as they have been embraced by agricultural geographers have also generated some significant analytical disagreements and silences.

Two recent overviews of the field prepared for a special issue of the journal *Economic Geography*, for example, show up some interesting divergences in terms of theoretical influence and substantive concern between North American (Page, 1996) and European (Marsden et al., 1996) work over the last decade or so. Crudely put, these revolve around the extent to which social, political and cultural diversity of food production and consumption processes are admitted into the compass and terms of analysis. But there is arguably a more widely shared sense emerging amongst geographers, and others, about the need to direct attention to (at least) three critical issues which have been eclipsed or marginalized by the terms of political economic analysis.

The first of these is the *question of* NATURE (Fitzsimmons and Goodman, 1998). Agriculture, and many of the distinctive features of the organization of food production, is derived from its biological base in the processes of plant and animal growth and reproduction and in the land. The industrialization of agriculture has seen the radical transformation of these processes, through mechanical, chemical and genetic technologies, with potent consequences for the rural environment, animal welfare and human health. Public anxieties on all these fronts are being registered by important changes in food consumption habits, agricultural policies and land-use practices throughout the advanced industrial world (Lowe et al., 1998).

The second new research direction is the question of *food consumption*. Until very recently, the last 'link in the chain' of the agro-food system illustrated in the figure opposite has been paid remarkably little attention by agricultural geographers, not least those working in the political economy tradition. It has tended to be treated by default as an analytically unproblematic and socially undifferentiated process – after all everyone has to eat. At least two lines of inquiry are emerging to redress this serious oversight. One concerns the issue of social construction of food quality – the idea that what constitutes 'wholesome', or even 'sufficient', food is by no means standard or unchanging in human societies but is the outcome of complex cultural processes in particular times and places (Marsden and Arce, 1995; Allaire and Boyer, 1995). The second explores the cultural meanings and practices which make food consumption much more than a question of nutrition or sustenance; for example, in terms of the social capital derived from culinary knowledges amongst affluent social groups (Cook and Crang, 1996) (see also FOOD, GEOGRAPHY OF).

The third direction takes us into perhaps the most intimate of geographical spaces whose contours are intricately bound up with the question of food, namely the body (see also BODY, GEOGRAPHY AND). These micro-spaces in the geographies of agro-food link the material and experiential worlds of people and animals variously positioned in the food production and consumption processes in intricate and multiple ways (Bell and Valentine, 1997). These include the engineered bodies of the industrial pig or cow made larger and leaner by genetic engineering, and hormone supplements; the chemically induced illnesses of farm workers routinely handling crop and livestock treatments; and the food-related illnesses experienced by consumers from food poisoning to eating disorders (Lupton, 1996).

These themes point to important new directions for geographical research which are refiguring the field of agricultural geography yet again as we enter the new millennium. (cf. ANIMALS, GEOGRAPHY OF) SW

References

Allaire, G. and Boyer, R. 1995. *La grande transformation*. Paris: Institute Nationale de Recherche Agronomique (INRA). · Atkins, P. 1988: Redefining agricultural geography as the geography of food. *Area* 20 (3): 281–3. · Bell, D. and Valentine, G. 1997: *Consuming places. We are where we eat*. London: Routledge. · Bowler, I. and Ilbery, B. 1987: Redefining agricultural geography. *Area* 19: 327–32. · Cook, I. and Crang, P. 1996: The world on a plate: culinary culture, displacement and geographical knowledges. *Journal of Material Culture* 1: 131–54. · Fitzsimmons, M. and Goodman, D. 1998: Incorporating nature: environmental narratives and the reproduction of food. In N. Castree and B. Willems-Braun, eds, *The production of nature at the end of the twentieth century*. London: Routledge. · Friedmann, H. and McMichael, P. 1989: Agriculture and the state system: the rise and decline of national agricultures. *Sociologia Ruralis* 29: 73–117. · Goodman, D. and Redclift, M. 1991. *Refashioning nature: food, ecology and nature*. London: Routledge. · Goodman, D. and Watts, M. 1994: Reconfiguring the rural or Fording the divide: capitalist restructuring and the global agro-food system. *Journal of Peasant Studies* 22: 1–49. · Goodman, D. and Watts, M., eds, 1997: *Globalising food*. London: Routledge. · Grigg, D. 1984: *An introduction to agricultural geography*. London: Hutchinson. · Jarosz, L. 1996: Working in the global food system: a focus for international comparative analysis. *Progress in Human Geography* 20 (1): 41–55. · Kim, C. and Curry, J. 1993: Fordism, flexible specialization and agri-industrial restructuring. *Sociologia Ruralis* 33: 61–80. · Le Heron, R. 1988: Food and fibre production under capitalism: a conceptual agenda. *Progress in Human Geography* 12 (3): 409–30. · Le Heron, R., 1993: *Globalised agriculture. Political choice*. Oxford: Pergamon Press. · Lowe, P., Clark, J., Seymour, S. and Ward, N. 1998: *Moralizing the environment*. London: UCL Press. · Lupton, D. 1996: *Food, the body and the self*. London: Sage. · Marsden, T. and Arce, A. 1995: Constructing quality: emerging food networks in the rural transition. *Environment and Planning A* 27: 1261–79. · Marsden, T. and Wrigley, N. 1996: Retailing, the food system and the regulatory state. In N. Wrigley and M. Lowe, eds, *Retailing, consumption and capital: towards a new retail geography*. London: Longman, 33–47. · Marsden, T., Munton, R., Whatmore, S. and Little, J. 1986: Towards a political economy of capitalist agriculture: a British perspective. *International Journal of Urban and Regional Research* 10: 498–521. · Marsden, T., Munton, R., Ward, N. and Whatmore, S. 1996: Agricultural geography and the political economy approach: a review. *Economic Geography* 72: 361–75. · Moran, W., Blunden, G. and Greenwood, J. 1993: The role of family farming in agrarian change. *Progress in Human Geography* 17 (1): 22–42. · Page, B. 1996: Across the great divide: agriculture and industrial geography. *Economic Geography* 72 (4): 376–97. · Page, B. and Walker, R. 1991: From settlement to Fordism: the agro-industrial revolution in the American Mid-West. *Economic Geography* 67: 281–315. · Roberts, R. 1996: Recasting the agrarian question: the reproduction of family farming in the southern High Plains. *Economic Geography*: 398–415. · Tansey and Worsley, 1995: *The food system*. London: Earthscan. · Ufkes, F.,

1993: Trade liberalization, agro-food politics and the globalization of agriculture. *Political Geography* 12 (3): 215–31. · Wallace, I. 1985: Towards a geography of agribusiness. *Progress in Human Geography* 9: 481–514. · Watts, M. 1994: Life under contract: contract farming, agrarian restructuring and flexible accumulation. In P. Little and M. Watts, eds, *Living under contract: contract farming and agrarian transformation in sub-Saharan Africa*. Madison, University of Wisconsin Press, 21–73. · Whatmore, S. 1991: *Farming women: gender, work and family enterprise*. London: Macmillan. · Whatmore S., 1995. From farming to agribusiness: the global agro-food system. In R.J. Johnston, P.J. Taylor and M.J. Watts, eds, 1995. *Geographies of global change*. Oxford: Blackwell, 36–49.

Suggested Reading

Bell and Valentine (1997). · Goodman and Watts (1997). · Lowe, Clark, Seymour and Ward (1998).

agricultural involution A term coined by Geertz (1963) to describe the over-elaboration of labour-intensive methods of agricultural production. Under conditions of population pressure, agricultural output is maintained by increasing the input of labour, so that while output per hectare rises output per capita remains the same. No new methods are introduced, as known methods of production are endlessly elaborated and intensified, while social and economic structures also remain unchanged. This leads to a vicious circle, since there is little incentive for technological innovation in the agricultural sector which could raise output per capita.

Geertz developed his model in a study of the impact of COLONIALISM on Java, where he identified a DUAL ECONOMY: an agricultural sector impoverished through agricultural involution, while in the industrial sector labour productivity continued to grow in response to capital investment. He found a 'sharing of poverty' in the agricultural sector, in that access to land and the opportunities for wage work were shared out, whereas inequality increased in the industrial sector.

Although White (1982) has argued that 'there is room for doubt whether involution and shared poverty as Geertz defined them were ever adequate characterizations of the political economy of Javanese village life', the generalized notion of agricultural involution is a useful ecological model which counters the more optimistic BOSERUP THESIS on the relationship between population growth and agrarian change. (See also the use of involution in writings on PROTOINDUSTRIALIZATION.)

MO

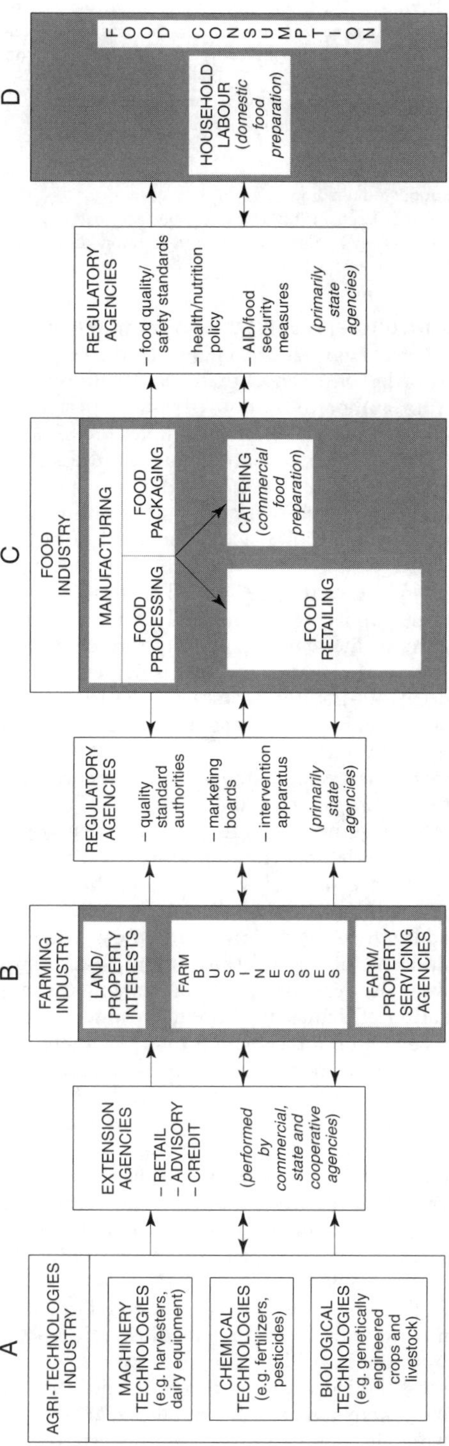

agricultural geography (reproduced from Whatmore, 1995, p. 40)

References

Geertz, C. 1963: *Agricultural involution: the process of ecological change in Indonesia*. Berkeley and Los Angeles: University of California Press. · White, B. 1982: Population, involution and employment in rural Java. In J. Harriss, ed., *Rural development: theories of peasant economy and agrarian change*. London: Hutchinson Library for Africa.

Suggested Reading

Harriss, J., ed., 1982: *Rural development: theories of peasant economy and agrarian change*. London: Hutchinson Library for Africa.

agricultural revolution A term applied to a period of agricultural change held to be significant in some sense: that 'sense' varies widely from author to author, period to period and place to place (see, for example, GREEN REVOLUTION). The standard MODEL of the agricultural revolution is usually taken to imply a dramatic increase in both output and productivity which took place in England during the century after 1750 (Chambers and Mingay, 1966. · Overton, 1996a). The term has also been applied to agricultural changes in other parts of the world, especially France. Output increased through the intensification of land use (e.g. draining marshland, clearing woodland, and improving pastures), while land productivity increased through the DIFFUSION of mixed farming systems which incorporated fodder crops into arable rotations. Clover and other legumes (such as peas and beans) were particularly important in raising land productivity since they converted atmospheric nitrogen into soil nitrogen and thus made a net addition to the supply of the most important nutrient for arable crops. Turnips and clover were also responsible for intensifying the cultivation of light land. Labour productivity also rose at an unprecedented rate, but there is no obvious technological explanation for this before the mid-nineteenth century; it is likely therefore that changes in the organization of labour were responsible, together with an improvement in the energy available to English farmers. From the mid-nineteenth century the introduction of machines for harvesting and threshing grain improved labour productivity dramatically.

Technological change was facilitated by institutional changes including ENCLOSURE, from the 1740s by parliamentary act, whereby the subdivided arable fields of midland England were replaced by smaller regular fields, while in many northern and western areas rough pasture or waste was physically enclosed for the first time. Private property rights replaced common property rights thus removing the right to use a tract of land, e.g. for grazing animals, from those not actually owning the land. The complicated arrangements of feudal tenure, whereby the money paid by the holder of land to a landlord did not necessarily reflect the true value of the holding (see FEUDALISM), were replaced by leases for a period of years at market values. Other institutional changes included the establishment of large farms, usually rented from a landlord by a capitalist tenant farmer who would be employing proletarianized labour (see CAPITALISM).

This standard model of an agricultural revolution has been challenged by a number of authors. Kerrridge (1967) argues that the agricultural revolution took place between 1560 and 1767 with most achieved before 1673; Jones (1974) avoids the term 'agricultural revolution' but nevertheless considers the century after 1650 as particularly significant for agricultural advance. Claims have been advanced for 'agricultural revolutions' in the nineteenth century based on the underdraining of heavy land, and on the import of feedstuffs and fertilizers from abroad (Thompson, 1968). More recent contributions to the debate have also argued that decisive change took place before 1750. Allen (1991) argues for two 'agricultural revolutions': the first in the seventeenth century which saw an increase in crop yields, and a second in the eighteenth century when enclosure transferred income from farmers and labourers to landlords. Finally, Clark (1993) considers, 'there was no agricultural revolution between the early eighteenth and mid-nineteenth centuries'.

With so many definitions the phrase 'agricultural revolution' is in danger of losing its meaning altogether (Overton, 1984). Measuring agricultural performance before national statistics were collected in 1866 is difficult, but recent work tends to re-emphasize the century after 1750 as the period of most decisive and rapid change (Campbell and Overton, 1993, Overton 1996a, 1996b). From the mid-eighteenth century English agriculture was able to feed an unprecedented rise in population (see MALTHUSIAN MODEL). The rise in labour productivity meant that a smaller proportion of the workforce was engaged in farming and therefore a larger proportion was available to work in industry. This facilitated the process of INDUSTRIALIZATION during the INDUSTRIAL REVOLUTION. Institutional changes were responsible for a transformation in the social relations of agricultural production leading to the development of a full-fledged agrarian capitalism (Tribe, 1981; see CAPITALISM). MO

References

Allen, R.C. 1991: The two English agricultural revolutions, 1459–1850. In B.M.S. Campbell and M. Overton, eds, *Land, labour and livestock: historical studies in European agricultural productivity*. Manchester: Manchester University Press, 236–54. · Campbell, B.M.S. and Overton, M. 1993: A new perspective on medieval and early modern agriculture: six centuries of Norfolk farming, *c.*1250–*c.*1850, *Past and Present* 141: 38–105. · Chambers, J.D. and Mingay, G.E. 1966: *The agricultural revolution, 1750–1880*. London: Batsford; New York: Schocken. · Clark, G. 1993: Agriculture and the industrial revolution, 1700–1850. In J. Mokyr, *The British industrial revolution: an economic perspective*. Oxford: Westview Press, 27–266. · Jones, E.L. 1974: *Agriculture and the industrial revolution*. Oxford: Basil Blackwell; New York: Halsted. · Kerridge, E. 1967: *The agricultural revolution*. London: Allen & Unwin. · Overton, M. 1984: Agricultural revolution? Development of the agrarian economy in Early Modern England. In A.R.H. Baker and D. Gregory, eds, *Explorations in historical geography: interpretative essays*. Cambridge: Cambridge University Press, 118–39. · Overton, M. 1996a: *Agricultural revolution in England: the transformation of the agrarian economy 1500–1850* Cambridge: Cambridge University Press. · Overton, M. 1996b: Re-establishing the English agricultural revolution, *Agricultural History Review* 43: 1–20. · Thompson, F.M.L. 1968: The second agricultural revolution, 1815–1880. *Economic History Review* 21: 62–77. · Tribe, K. 1981: *Genealogies of capitalism*. London: Macmillan; Atlantic Highlands, NJ: Humanities Press, 35–100.

Suggested Reading

Beckett, J.V. 1990: *The agricultural revolution*, Oxford: Basil Blackwell. · Overton (1996a). · Overton (1996b).

agro-food system Food is a basic condition of human life and the manner in which interlinked and increasingly globalized networks of knowledge production, on- and off-farm technologies, production, consumption and regulatory systems are bound together is the center-piece of any local, national or transnational agro-food system. According to the Organisation for Economic Cooperation and Development (OECD), the agro-food system is defined as 'the set of activities and relationships that interact to determine what, and much, by what method and for whom food is produced and distributed' (Fine, 1998, p. 3). Sarah Whatmore (1995, p. 40) has provided a simple diagrammatic representation of the agro-food system, a complex unity of four sectors: the agri-technology industry, the farming industry, the food industry, and food consumption. These four components linking knowledge, production and consumption, and agro-food production and processing have also been referred to as an agrofood regime (Friedmann, 1993), an agro-food COMMODITY CHAIN (Friedland, 1994), and as a food provisioning system (Fine and Leopold, 1993). Food-systems have specific properties and characteristics distinctive from industry and manufacture, may exhibit sectoral forms of coordination and integration (Allaire and Boyer, 1995), and may on occasion break down and collapse (FAMINE). The dynamics and developmental tendencies of this agro-food system has obvious overlaps with the AGRARIAN QUESTION (cf. AGRICULTURAL GEOGRAPHY; FOOD, GEOGRAPHY OF; FOODWAYS).

A central dynamic in twentieth-century and especially post-Second World War agro-food systems has been the simultaneous INDUSTRIALIZATION and GLOBALIZATION of the food chain. The genesis of a TRANSNATIONAL fast-food industry – the MacDonaldization thesis as it has been dubbed (Ritzer, 1998) – as a particularly aggressive form of AGRIBUSINESS in the era of NEO-LIBERAL reforms is simply one obvious expression of these twin dynamics. The GREEN REVOLUTION is a compelling case of the industrialization process at work on a global scale. Forged in the 1940s by US philanthropic foundations and the US government, the genesis of high-yielding varieties of wheat and rice, sensitive to petroleum-based chemical inputs and forms of irrigation-based mechanization, is a textbook illustration of how various aspects of the farm production process – seeds, herbicides, pump sets – were appropriated by larger transnational companies (the seed and pharmaceutical companies in particular). This form of world-wide industrialization based on the US petro-chemical model involved the appropriation of various on-farm processes by capital (Goodman, Sorj and Wilkinson, 1987). In the second phase of the Green Revolution, precipitated by the molecular revolution and recombinant DNA, the process of industrialization has been deepened through new forms of appropriation (germ plasm, genetically modified seeds that are 'programmed' for particular inputs – the 'Round-Up Ready' syndrome) and the prospect of substitution (i.e. substituting land-based crops with synthetic and manufactured alternatives).

Industrialization of the agro-food system has its own peculiarities, however, which turn on the distinctiveness of agriculture rooted in the biological foundations of production (Mann, 1990; Kautsky, 1906). These natural and biological processes have resisted the standardization and normalization typically associated with CAPITALIST production. As a result, capitalist enterprises have often found direct on-farm production too risky or unprofitable. As a consequence, the processes of APPROPRIATIONISM and SUBSTITUTIONISM have proceeded apace without necessarily any involvement in production on the land by large capitals. As Kautsky (1906) noted a century ago, industrialization and capitalization occurs in the realm of credit, of processing and of value added after it leaves the farm gate. The expansion and control of these off-farm sectors – seed, fertilizers, machinery, processing – is often striking: in the UK, for example, just four companies control three-quarters of the farm machinery market, a level of concentration replicated in both American poultry processing and the French hog sector. Various forms of contracting in the First and Third Worlds, in which agribusiness contracts to small or medium growers to produce under tightly regulated conditions for specialized niche markets, have proliferated since the 1960s (Watts, 1994). The rise of a massive fresh fruit and vegetable industry which services the retail supermarkets has been synonymous with contract production and what one might called POST-FORDIST agricultural commodities (McMichael, 1995: cf. RETAILING, GEOGRAPHY OF). French researchers working on the agro-food commodity chain (filière) see the genesis of new niche markets as an index of a new 'quality' based agro-food system (Allaire and Boyer, 1995).

While the globalization of the agro-food system proceeds, it is clear that the fast-food chains are in no sense representative of the food system as a whole. Indeed, there is no real equivalent to the 'world car' in the realm of agrifood (Goodman and Watts, 1997). The world steer or the world chicken, while international in character, does not resemble the multi-site, decentralized production and assemblages of the Ford Escort or the Nike's Air Jordan. In some respects, the agribusinesses, while global actors, resemble the 'Sloanist' enterprises rather than the iconic Toyota post-Fordism companies of the world car (Bonnano et al., 1995). Nonetheless, within the agro-food sector, there are important parallels between the JUST-IN-TIME PRODUCTION systems and INDUSTRIAL DISTRICTS which have concerned industrial geographers who study the changing contemporary landscape of industrial manufacture (see Boyd and Watts, 1997: cf. INDUSTRIAL GEOGRAPHY). Indeed, FLEXIBLE ACCUMULATION has been a trademark of agrarian capitalism, and many of the trademarks of the new industrial geography – contracting, SEGMENTED LABOUR MARKETS, outworking, non-traded INTERDEPENDENCIES – can be traced in the workings of the pig sector in the US, and in Brazilian fresh fruit and vegetable growing (Goodman and Watts, 1997).

One of the distinctive features of national agro-food systems is their protected character. A combination of the power of agrarian constituencies coupled with the political premium placed on national food self-sufficiency has produced, in the case of the North Atlantic economies, enormously complex state-regulated forms of protection, TARIFFS and subsidies. Typically the effects of the technological treadmill and the emphasis of increased PRODUCTIVITY has produced an agro-food system in which surplus management (e.g. the butter mountain in the European Union, or grain surpluses in the US) has been paramount. The GATT reforms of 1992 plus twenty years of neo-liberal reforms world-wide have left their mark on First and Third World agro-food systems alike, however, which, as at the end of the nineteenth century, have stimulated new forms of deregulation and tariff reduction. The aggressive role of the World Trade Organization has raised the spectre for many critics of unprecedented competition in agriculture with the result that Third World producers will be outcompeted by American or European growers and transnational agribusinesses will control ever larger parts of the agro-food chain. This RESTRUCTURING of various national agro-food systems is a politically fraught process (McMichael, 1995) and has led Friedmann (1993) to see the emergence of a new international food regime in the wake of the collapse of the Cold War state-managed system, what she calls 'private global regulation'.

One of the paradoxes of the unrelenting industrialization of the agro-food system – whether the rise of fast food, of genetically modified crops, of high-technology food processing, of truly global commodity markets shuttling cut flowers and strawberries around the globe – is the limits to which the process can proceed by virtue of the biological basis of the sector itself. Food carries enormous social, cultural, symbolic and nutritional significance for all human societies (Fox, 1997). Our biological, spiritual and ethical health rests on food in complex ways. Health concerns, coupled with a growing sensitivity to green and organic issues, have presented obstacles to the industrialization process typically associated with productivist or FORDIST agriculture. Food scares (*E. coli* and Mad Cow disease, for example), a growing clamour for organic certification, and the fierce debates over genetically modified crops – in short, consumer concerns over health and sustainability – have both exposed the frailty of hyper-industrialized industries like poultry and beef, and initiated new concerns with 'quality'. In this sense, the recent and quite radical institutional reforms of the 1930s state-regulated agricultural model – for example the New Deal pact in the US – in the name of liberalization and deregulation, has produced new concerns with quality, standards and health, all of which re-regulate the agro-food system. Out of this contradiction between industrialization and health/sustainability emerge new spaces for alternative agro-food networks – grower cooperatives, green worth, local community-based food networks – and for a serious debate over the politics of food (Whatmore, 1995). The outbreak of Mad Cow disease and its impact on the beef industry in the European Union perhaps marks a watershed, and a CRISIS, in the Fordist agro-food system. MW

References

Allaire, G. and Boyer, R., eds, 1995: *La grand transformation.* Paris: Institute Nationale de Recherche Agronomique (INRA). · Bonnano A. et al., eds, 1995: *From Columbus to ConAgra.* Lawrence: University of Kansas Press. · Boyd, W. and Watts, M. 1997: Agro-industrial just-in-time. In Goodman, D. and Watts, M., eds, *Globalising food.* London: Routledge, 192–225. · Fine, B. 1998: The Political Economy of Diet, Health and Food Policy. London: Routledge. · Fine, B. and Leopold, E. 1993: *The World of Consumption*, London: Routledge. · Fox, R. 1997: *Spoiled.* New York: Basic Books. · Friedland, W. 1994: The new globalization: the case of fresh produce. In A. Bonnano et al., eds, *From Columbus to Conagra.* Lawrence: University of Kansas Press, 210–31. · Friedmann, H. 1993: The political economy of food. *New Left Review* 197: 29–57. · Goodman, D., Sorj, B. and Wilkinson, J. 1987: *From farming to biotechnology.* Oxford: Blackwell. · Goodman, D. and Watts, M., eds, 1997: *Globalising food.* London: Routledge. · Kautsky, K. 1906: *La question agraire.* Paris: Maspero. · Mann, S. 1990: *Agrarian capitalism.* Durham: University of North Carolina Press. · McMichael, P., ed., 1995: *The global restructuring of agro-food systems.* Ithaca: Cornell University Press. · Ritzer, G. 1998: *The MacDonaldization thesis.* London: Sage. · Watts, M. 1994: Life under contract. In Little, P. and Watts, M. eds, *Living under contract.* Madison: University of Wisconsin Press, 21–77. · Whatmore, S. 1995: From farming to agribusiness. In Johnston, R.J., Taylor P.J. and Watts, M.J., eds, *Geographies of global change.* Oxford: Blackwell, 36–49.

Suggested Reading

Goodman, D. and Redclift, M. 1990: *Refashioning nature.* London: Routledge. · Torres, G. 1997: *The force of irony.* Oxford: Berg.

aid Limited, conditional and generally highly-targeted flows of resources aimed ostensibly at encouraging economic DEVELOPMENT or alleviating shorter-term crises of SOCIAL REPRODUCTION. An example of the latter was the response to the crisis in South-East Asia during 1997–8 in which the International Monetary Fund (IMF) and various of its member governments intervened to limit the extent of the crisis and to force RESTRUCTURING, especially of financial systems, within the countries caught up in the crisis. These objectives were widely criticized at the time for attempting to impose anti-inflationary policies on a crisis that required reflation.

Official Development Aid (ODA) is financed largely through contributions from donor governments. Such aid is normally offered on financially discretionary but politically restrictive terms. Aid may also be privately financed through mechanisms such as the increasingly popular microcredit. This usually comprises small loans to small businesses, often charging very high rates of interest to cover the risks of lack of collateral but on temporarily flexible terms which allows for the rapid turn around of the loan. Aid may be arranged on bilateral terms and flow directly between two countries or between specified donors and receivers. Flows of resources (capital, technology, expertise), food, export credits, educational and training scholarships and government-to-government lending may be generated in this way. More widely targeted flows may also move on a multilateral basis from donors to recipients using criteria such as levels of income or specific identifiable problems and crises. Attempts such as those advocated by the United Nations Conference on Trade and Development (UNCTAD) with respect to adverse shifts in TERMS OF TRADE to offset the deleterious effects of TRADE relations between developed and underdeveloped economic geographies represent a further form of multilateral aid through the social control of markets.

The origins of the contemporary large-scale flows of aid within the world ECONOMIC GEOGRAPHY lie in the European Recovery Programme of 1948 under which Marshall Aid from the USA was designed to offset balance of payments and liquidity crises in western Europe after the Second World War, thereby sustaining European demand – not least for US products and investments – and subverting the prospect of communist influence in the region. In addition, multilateral agencies may coordinate aid. Such agencies include: semi-official bodies, such as the World Bank (International Bank for Reconstruction and Development) agencies of the UN; more commercial institutions, like the European Bank for Reconstruction and Development (EBRD) set up to aid the process of social and economic transformation in eastern Europe after the events of 1989; the Inter-American, African and Asian Development Banks along with their development funds; and more spatially and temporally-specific organizations which may involve both public and private sources of funding such as the International Fund for Agricultural Development. Regional programmes of aid are exemplified by the Lomé Conventions of the European Union. In addition, charitable organizations, such as Oxfam, War on Want and Live Aid, also collect and redistribute aid.

In 1996 only Denmark (which donated 1.04 per cent of GNP to ODA), Norway, Sweden and the Netherlands (which each gave around 0.8 per cent of GNP) committed more than the minimum 0.7 per cent of GNP recommended by the United Nations. The average level of contribution from developed countries was 0.22 per cent – the lowest figure since records began and well down on the 0.35 per cent contributed during the early 1980s. The USA committed only 0.08 per cent, down from 0.12 per cent in 1986; a major factor in this decline was that Israel – a major recipient of US aid – is no longer considered to be a developing country. In all low and middle income countries taken together, official development assistance amounted to 3.3 per cent of GNP – a figure which hides the range from 16.3 per cent in sub-Saharan Africa to 0.9 per cent in Europe and Central Asia. Official development assistance accounted for over 100 per cent of Mozambique's GNP.

The ideological justification for aid is that it promotes DEVELOPMENT and so may be justified both in terms of the self-interest of the donors and through its appeal to notions of distributive justice (see, for example, Brandt Commission 1980, 1983: see also JUSTICE, GEOGRAPHY AND) Here there are a number of criteria that might be used to assess the quality of aid: does it reach the most needy and does it contribute to their basic needs?; does it help to promote HUMAN RIGHTS and DEMOCRACY?; does it promote SUSTAINABLE DEVELOPMENT?; does it enable autonomous development or increase DEPENDENCE?

But aid is not only limited in amount, it extracts a price which may be met directly – to service interest payments on debt for example – or indirectly in the form of markets for the exports of donors and access to the resources of the receiver. Aid may also facilitate an extension of the donor's global economic and strategic influence – in a very direct way in the case of military aid – or purchase the support of sympathetic political regimes or economic policies. In such ways, aid may intensify relations of economic dependence upon the donor economy, shape local elites through educational assistance and, in the case of food aid, disrupt local prices and supply systems. Aid is, in short, a powerful means of spreading and sustaining particular DISCOURSES of development and forms of social reproduction.

Arguments such as these have been used by those opposed to aid (e.g. Bauer, 1991). They may be extended to suggest that aid actually creates the THIRD WORLD in tying recipients more closely into the economic and geographical dynamics of donors as it addresses limited economic problems such as deficiencies in the local availability of savings, or a need to bridge a technology gap, or lack of foreign currency – all arguments which were significant in the case for Marshall Aid – which may more readily and effectively be retrieved by market forces. Such arguments may be bolstered by the observation that the flow of aid is also highly selective. It is directed mainly towards the middle-income rather than towards the poorest countries. Some indication of this selectivity is given in the following data which show the amount in US dollars of aid received per head in various regions of the world:

Asia	7.2
Americas	16.8
Europe	26.8
Africa	33.3
Oceania	269.0

It is difficult to resist the conclusion that the geography of the flow of aid is directed by the economic ability rather than the social need of the recipients and so serves as a means of maintaining and strengthening current relations of political and economic power in the world economic geography.

However, as ever, the geography of development is far more complex than is allowed for in abstract discussions for and against flows of aid. For example, against the Bauerian argument that the historical geographies of the already developed economies were not based on aid – and, by extension therefore, that aid is not a precondition of development – should be counterposed the point that the global economic geographies in which these regions developed were quite different in terms of absolute and relative inequalities in the distribution of economic and political power and institutional control, and that they too relied on a form of aid in the form of the plunder of the worlds 'discovered' by expansionist European countries (cf. INEQUALITY, SPATIAL). An argument pointing to the greater effectiveness of aid and to its justification in terms of SOCIAL JUSTICE has been made by Riddell (1987) whilst David Smith (1998) has begun to address the moral philosophical questions related to the concern – as represented, for example, in the complex motives for aid-giving – for distant others. RL

References

Bauer, P. 1991: *The development frontier essays in applied economics*. Hemel Hempstead: Harvester Wheatsheaf. · Brandt Commission, 1980: *North–south: a programme for survival*. London: Pan Books. · Brandt Commission, 1983: *Common crisis: North–South cooperation for world recovery*. London: Pan Books. · Cambridge, MA: MIT Press. · Riddell, R. 1987: *Foreign aid reconsidered*. London: James Curry/ODI. · Smith, D.M. 1998: How far should we care? On the spatial scope of beneficence. *Progress in Human Geography* 22: 15–38.

Suggested Reading

Bell, M. 1994: Images, myths and alternative geographies of the third world. In D. Gregory, R. Martin and G. Smith, eds, *Human geography: society, space and social science*, ch. 7. Houndmills and London: Macmillan, 174–99. · Corbridge, S. 1995: *Development studies: a reader*. London: Arnold, section 5. · United Nations Development Programme, annual: *Human development report*. New York and Oxford: Oxford University Press.

AIDS, geography of Geographic perspectives on Acquired Immune Deficiency Syndrome, its causes and consequences, have taken three rather distinct, though obviously related, tacks. The first, and earliest, is from the discipline's SPATIAL SCIENCE tradition (Shannon, Pyle and Bashshur, 1991; Gould, 1993; Williams and Rees, 1994). This tradition has mapped and modelled the spread of AIDS and HIV historically, and developed predictive, future geographies of the epidemic. It began in the 1980s and continues presently.

The second approach has been from POLITICAL and CULTURAL GEOGRAPHY, and has examined the social meanings of the epidemic, as well as its implications for issues of equity and social justice, in particular places (Murray and Robinson, 1996; Wilton, 1996; Brown, 1997). Rather than conceptualizing the virus as a biological entity (as spatial science had), this strand of research emphasizes the virus' thoroughly social existence, showing how various discourses (like hetero-normativity, scientific HEGEMONY, PATRIARCHY and RACISM) in places disempower people living with HIV. This scholarship also signals how new spaces of politics are fashioned by people responding to the pandemic. (See also SEXUALITY, GEOGRAPHY AND.)

The third, and thinner, strand of research comes from an interest in health provision. It examines how various national and local health-care systems have responded to the AIDS crisis, and includes research on funding, as well as the mobility and MIGRATION of people living with HIV and/or AIDS (Davis and Stapleton, 1991; Ellis, 1996). This strand of AIDS geography is often practised outside the discipline proper, but nonetheless carries a geographic perspective (cf. HEALTH AND HEALTH CARE, GEOGRAPHY OF).

Despite the debate that has gone on between these different perspectives on methodological and philosophical grounds (Brown, 1996), there seems to be an emerging appreciation of the contribution each can make, and there have even been attempts to integrate them (Boyle, 1998). MPB

References

Boyle, P. 1998: *Migration and health*. London: Routledge. · Brown, M. 1996: Ironies of distance: an ongoing critique of the geographies of AIDS, *Environment and Planning D: Society and Space* 13: 159–83. · Brown, M. 1997: *RePlacing citizenship: AIDS activism and radical democracy*. New York: Guilford Press. · Davis, K. and Stapleton, J. 1991: Migration to rural areas by HIV patients: impacts on HIV-related health care use. *Infection Control and Hospital Epidemiology* 12: 540–43. · Ellis, M. 1996: The post-diagnosis mobility of people with AIDS. *Environment and Planning A* 28: 999–1017. · Gould, P. 1993: *The slow plague*. Oxford: Blackwell. · Murray, A. and Robinson, T. 1996: Minding your peers and queers: female sex workers in the AIDS discourse in Australia and Southeast Asia. *Gender, Place, and Culture* 3: 43–59. · Shannon, G., Pyle, G. and Bashshur, R. 1991: *The geography of AIDS*. New York: Guilford Press. · Williams, J. and Rees, P. 1994: A simulation of the transmission of HIV and AIDS in regional populations in the United Kingdom. *Transactions, Institute of British Geographers* NS 19: 311–30. · Wilton, R. 1996: Diminished worlds?: The geography of everyday life with HIV/AIDS. *Health and Place* 2: 69–83.

alienation To be estranged from oneself, others or the product of one's labour. Originally used in philosophical and theological discourse, the sociological origins of the term date back to Rousseau (1712–78) and Hegel (1770–1831). Rousseau believed that individuals give up (alienate) their individual liberty in order to participate in CIVIL SOCIETY. Hegel deployed the term differently, asserting that human consciousness is naturally estranged from the physical world surrounding it, and that this alienation can be overcome only when people recognize that external reality is a projection of human consciousness. Resonances of both definitions can be found in the early work of Marx (which many characterize as humanist rather than materialist), and it is his use of the term that motivates much contemporary thought on the subject (cf. MARXIST GEOGRAPHY).

For Marx, alienation is not an intrinsic aspect of the human condition but is a specific result of capitalist social relations. In notes in which he first outlined his approach to the study of CAPITALISM, Marx (1844) began with the assumption that humans 'objectify' their creativity through human labour as they transform the natural world into valued products. Within most social systems this process is straightforward, and one can discern connections between workers and the objects they produce (e.g. artisans produce goods that incorporate their individual character and talent). Under capitalism, however, workers are disconnected, or alienated, from the products of their labour, for two reasons. First, workers in a capitalist system do not choose when to work, what to produce, how to organize production, or what to do with the products of their labour – these decisions are made by capitalists. Second, workers are paid only a portion of the value they add to the goods they produce. Workers therefore cannot recognize themselves in the objects they make. For capitalists, the distinction between worker and product is blurred: workers are seen as 'input costs' in precisely the same way as raw materials, and both are viewed as interchangeable elements in the rational calculus of commodity prices and profit rates. Moreover, the worth of individual workers is determined by the output they are capable of producing, not by their personal characteristics or non-work-related achievements. To obtain and retain employment, workers must demonstrate their 'value' through PRODUCTIVITY, and relations between individual workers become competitive rather than cooperative. Using this logic, Marx concluded that workers, not the products of their labour, are 'objectified' under capitalism. In so doing he attempted to show the relationship between the structural features of capitalism and the subjective feelings of exploited workers.

Since Marx, the concept of alienation has taken on a host of different meanings as it has been redefined by other authors, notably Durkheim (see ANOMIE), Simmel, Lukács, Sartre, Marcuse and Habermas. Increasingly, with some exceptions, the subjective aspects of alienation have been emphasized. In North America, the radical political content of the term was largely purged as it entered the mainstream of American sociology. Blauner (1964), for example, sought to quantify the degree of alienation experienced by workers in different jobs in an effort to formulate new shop-floor policies and ease capital–labour CONFLICT. Obviously, such research was far removed from Marx's ideas.

Human geographers began to incorporate a Marxist definition of alienation into their work in the 1970s (cf. Harvey, 1973), and the concept was particularly engaged during the late 1970s and early 1980s when geographers following HUMANISTIC and Marxist traditions attempted to discover common ground. However, the term is now rarely used, indicating the profound shift in the terrain of debate in recent years as various issues raised within feminism, POST-STRUCTURALISM, POST-COLONIALISM and cultural theory have come to the fore. In particular, the turn towards seeing individual subjects as decentred, as situated within a web of multiple and overlapping relations of power (Smith, 1988; Gregory, 1994), renders the concept of alienation (arising from a single source – the workplace) problematic. DH

References

Blauner, B. 1964: *Alienation and freedom: the factory worker and his industry*. Chicago: University of Chicago Press. · Gregory, D. 1994: *Geographical imaginations*. Cambridge, MA and Oxford: Blackwell. · Harvey, D. 1973: *Social justice and the city*. Baltimore: Johns Hopkins University Press. · Marx, K. 1844: *Economic and philosophical manuscripts*. In *Karl Marx: Early writings*. New York: Vantage Books. · Smith, P. 1988: *Discerning the subject*. Minneapolis: University of Minnesota Press.

Suggested Reading

Giddens, A. 1971: *Capitalism and modern social theory*. Cambridge: Cambridge University Press. · Ollman, B. 1971: *Alienation: Marx's conception of man in capitalist society*. Cambridge: Cambridge University Press. · Rinehart, J.W. 1987: *The tyranny of work: alienation and the labour process*, 2nd edn. Toronto: Harcourt Brace Jovanovich.

Alonso model A model developed by William Alonso (1964), building on the VON THÜNEN MODEL of agricultural land-use patterns, to account for intra-urban variations in land values, land use, and land-use intensity in modern capitalist cities.

The model's key components are ACCESSIBILITY and its relationship to TRANSPORT COSTS. Its simplest form assumes that all journeys from residential to non-residential areas focus on the city centre so that, assuming that households have fixed budgets, the further that a household lives from the city centre the more it will need to spend on COMMUTING and other journeys (such as to shops) and the less it will have available to spend on land and property.

All land users benefit from increased accessibility, according to the model, and thus bid to be at or close to the city centre: among commercial and industrial users, for example, the closer they are to the city centre the nearer they are to their suppliers and customers, the lower their transport costs and the greater their profit margins (all other things being equal); then they will be prepared to pay more for such advantageous locations. In general, these users benefit more from greater accessibility than do households (with commercial users benefiting more than industrial); they can outbid residential users for city centre land, which produces a zonal distribution of land uses around the centre (as shown in the figure). Because land is more expensive close to the centre, it tends to be used more intensively (e.g. buildings are on average higher and occupy more of their site).

The closer that a household or firm locates to the central point the higher the rent that must be paid. There is a DISTANCE-DECAY relationship away from the city centre in the value of locational rents. Each land use has an INDIFFERENCE CURVE which represents the relative priority given to accessibility (and high density locations) over travel costs from lower density locations. (The amount of land available increases with the square of the distance from the centre, increasing its supply relative to demand.) At the centre, accessibility has the greatest priority and travel costs the least, so rents are highest there; further out, as travel costs increase so rents fall to compensate for the greater costs of movement. According to Alonso, all individual location decision-makers have their own BID-RENT CURVES indicating their relative priorities for rent and travel costs: the point at which each bid-rent curve touches the indifference curve identifies that individual's preferred location.

Alonso's model of a unicentric city is readily modified to accommodate more than one centre (several shopping centres, for example)

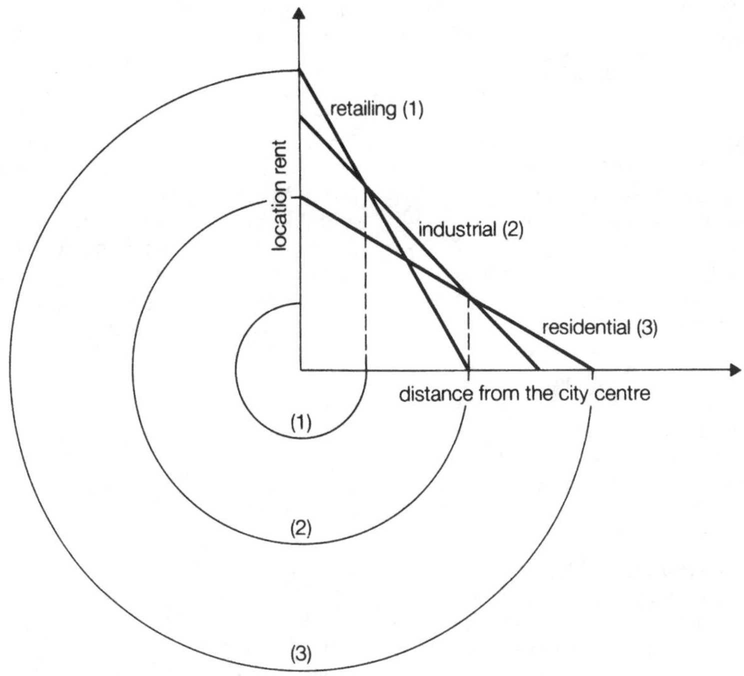

Alonso model *Concentric land-use zones generated by the bid-rent curves for retailing, industrial and residential land use* (Cadwallader, 1985)

and differential patterns of accessibility (such as fast and slow routes to and from the centres). Its hypotheses of declining land rents, values and use intensities away from the defined centres have been largely validated in a substantial number of empirical studies although, as a classic study of Boston illustrated (Firey, 1947), such a model cannot account for the high prices that some people will pay for locations on the basis of criteria like 'sentiment and symbolism'.

Alonso's model provides an economic rationale for the ZONAL MODEL of urban land uses identified by American sociologists in the 1920s. It also shows why those with higher incomes will tend to favour suburban locations within the residential portion of the city, leaving the INNER CITY to be occupied by lower-income groups at higher densities (thereby maximizing the returns on expensive land): this implies that the higher-income groups have different indifference curves from the less well-off, although GENTRIFICATION processes emerge where the richer residents prefer accessibility to the lower densities of the suburbs. RJJ

References

Alonso, W. 1964: *Location and land use: toward a general theory of land rent*. Cambridge, MA: Harvard University Press. · Cadwallader, M. 1985: *Analytical urban geography: spatial patterns and theories*. Englewood Cliffs, NJ: Prentice-Hall. · Firey, W. 1947: *Land use in central Boston*. Cambridge, MA: Harvard University Press.

analogue A scaled representation of some aspect of the world. A paper MAP is an analogue representation of part of the Earth's surface that is additionally distorted to make it lie flat through the use of a map PROJECTION. Photographs and the architect's scale models are other examples. Traditional telephone circuits and radio represent sound by scaled electrical signals. Analogue representations are increasingly being replaced by digital ones, which instead use combinations of symbols in some alphabet that are understood by both the creator and the user of the representation (cf. SYMBOLIZATION). MG

analysis of variance (ANOVA) A PARAMETRIC statistical test associated with the GENERAL LINEAR MODEL in which the dependent variable has either interval or ratio MEASUREMENT and the independent variables are measured at the nominal scale. The sample of individuals is divided into categories and ANOVA tests whether there are significant differences among the means for those categories on the dependent variable. RJJ

Suggested Reading

Johnston, R.J. 1978: *Multivariate statistical analysis in geography*. London and New York: Longman.

analytical Marxism, geography and A school of POLITICAL ECONOMY and social theory originating during the 1980s, and concerned with sorting Marxism into a distinct set of claims that are then analytically scrutinized for their meaning, coherence, plausibility, and truth. More generally, the school eschews any form of dogmatic Marxism, or even a close, interpretive reading of Marx's texts. Marx is treated as an innovative thinker, but one whose ideas require careful dissection and development in the light of intervening history, and with the analytical tools available in contemporary philosophy and social sciences.

Analytical Marxism (or *rational-choice Marxism*) has proponents across a wide range of disciplines, and as a consequence the type of analytical methods employed vary. In economics the favoured starting point is the rational choice assumption of NEO-CLASSICAL ECONOMICS, the idea that making individuals tick is only the maximization of economic gain (Roemer, 1981). In philosophy, the guiding method is the logical syllogism (Cohen, 1978). And in sociology the preferred approach is based on the rigours of statistical analysis (Wright, 1985). In each case, analytical Marxists strive for unblemished clarity and logical impeccability. The principal task is always to cleanse and purify Marx's chronic obscurantism so that the usefulness of his ideas can be critically assessed in understanding the issues of our own time and place.

The antecedents of analytical Marxism are with the Canadian philosopher Gerald Cohen and his book *Karl Marx's theory of history: a defence* (1978); a work that is painstaking in its logic, and '. . . chock-a-block with nice distinctions other people hadn't dreamt were there' (Carling, 1986, p. 25). In particular, Cohen sought to avoid the naive FUNCTIONALISM of some Marxists who believe that by merely pointing to the beneficial consequences of a given event, in their case to its role in furthering capitalism, necessarily serves to explain it. Cohen's solution is to provide an alternative, logically consistent definition of functionalism based on 'consequence laws'. Although Cohen's revamped functional approach has been rejected by many analytical Marxists, the formal character of his argument established the tone and style for the school.

The American economist John Roemer (1981, 1982) brought analytical Marxism to wider attention following the publication of two pioneering monographs. Rejecting all vestiges of functionalism, Roemer argued that Marxists should provide explanations of events and actions at the micro-level using 'rational choice models: general equilibrium theory, game theory, and the arsenal of modelling techniques developed by Neo-classical economics' (Roemer, 1986, p. 192).

In particular, the postulate of RATIONAL CHOICE, and the attendant position of METHODOLOGICAL INDIVIDUALISM, form the twin foundations of much of the constructive analytical work that followed. Both are seen in Roemer's two theories of CLASS and exploitation which lie at the core of analytical Marxism. The beginning point for both theories is a set of rational individuals who are endowed with given but unequal shares of society's economic resources, and are intent on maximizing UTILITY. From these two axioms, Roemer *endogenously* derives the existence of exploitation and class; that is, exploitation and class are not a priori givens, but the logical consequence of any social system whose members are rational and that divides wealth unequally.

The details of the derivations are complex (see Sheppard and Barnes, 1990, ch. 1), but important commonalities connect Roemer's two theories.

- Both make differences in resource (wealth) ownership the basis of exploitation and class membership;
- Both are based on a bastardized LABOUR THEORY OF VALUE because, as Roemer demonstrates mathematically, there are logical incongruities in Marx's original version;
- Both are used to understand the distinctiveness of different historical epochs, from FEUDALISM to COMMUNISM (Wright, 1985, ch. 2); and
- Both suggest that individuals choose their class positions – this is not a choice, of course, that individuals necessarily like making, but they do so because of the constraints that they are under (their society's share of assets) along with their desire to maximize.

With the technical details of analytical Marxism laid bare, proponents of the movement have recently turned to general issues of philosophy and method in the social sciences (Wright et al., 1992), including the nature of freedom, morality and JUSTICE (Cohen, 1988; Roemer, 1988). In this endeavour, as in others, 'analytical Marxism tends to blur received understandings of what distinguishes Marxism from 'bourgeois' theory' (Wright et al., 1992, p. 7).

For this reason, those who are most unhappy with analytical Marxists tend to be other Marxists. Known as *fundamental Marxists*, they strive to uphold Marx's original word against what they think is analytical Marxism's perverse reading (Meiksins-Wood, 1989). Their criticisms include: that the preferences, and social contexts, of rational individuals are never explained by analytical Marxists, with the consequence that everything that is important to social analysis must be done *before* applying the rational choice model; that there is no explanation of historical change other than as unintended consequence; that it rests on an economistic, market view of human nature, thereby aligning analytical Marxism intellectually with the resurgence of interest in right-wing thought; and finally, that its prosecution of METHODOLOGICAL INDIVIDUALISM renders analytical Marxism philosophically and politically bankrupt. It was the arch-conservative British Prime Minister, Margaret Thatcher, after all, who said, 'There is no such thing as society'.

In addition to critique, fundamental Marxists have also demonstrated that they are as adroit as Roemer et al. in mobilizing mathematics, and especially statistics. In their case, though, it is to show the continued relevance of an unadulterated Marx. Following the arguments of Farjoun and Machover (1983), fundamental Marxists, such as Shaikh and Tonak (1994), argue that Marx's labour theory of value is highly tractable and robust in the statistical calculation of such basic classical Marxist variables as rates of ACCUMULATION, exploitation, and the falling rate of profit.

There has been only limited use of the analytical Marxist framework by economic geographers. Sheppard and Barnes (1990) provide the most systematic treatment, and, although sympathetic to analytical arguments, they argue that the incorporation of geography into both Roemer's work on class and exploitation, and Elster's (1985) on class formation, fundamentally disturbs their respective aspatial conclusions. Roemer's central claims about the relationship between exploitation and resource ownership is vitiated in a SPACE-ECONOMY because of the possibility of negative exploitation (Sheppard and Barnes, 1990, chs 8 and 11), while Elster's conclusions about class formation based upon the rationality postulate and accompanying methodological individualism are upset once his scheme is set in a geographical world. For Elster collective action is a puzzle; it is not something in which rational individuals should engage even though they do. Sheppard and Barnes (1990, ch. 10) argue, however, that once such individuals are embedded in the geographical world of space and place, collective action is no longer a puzzle but is the norm (see GAME THEORY).

Paralleling Sheppard and Barnes, but from a fundamental Marxist slant, has been Webber and Rigby's work culminating in their tome, *The golden age illusion* (1996). Less interested in theoretical critique, Webber and Rigby carry out a heroic set of mathematical and statistical calculations based upon Marxian labour values to interpret the recent historical geography of post-war capitalism. Although the framework is different, their conclusion is remarkably similar to Sheppard and Barnes's, and in fact David Harvey's (1982). The introduction of SPACE and PLACE fundamentally disturb the conclusions of aspatial social theory, including such variants of POLITICAL ECONOMY as analytical Marxism. The rigours of the rational choice assumption, logical deduction and statistical analysis cannot protect analytical Marxism from this geographical critique; indeed, they show only its power and force.

TJB

References

Carling, A. 1986: Rational choice Marxism. *New Left Review* 160: 24–62. · Cohen, G.A. 1978: *Karl Marx's theory of history: a defence*. Oxford: Oxford University Press. · Cohen, G.A. 1988: *History, labour and freedom: themes from Marx*. Oxford: Clarendon Press. · Elster, J. 1985: *Making sense of Marx*. Cambridge: Cambridge University Press. · Farjoun, E. and Machover, M. 1983: *Laws of chaos: a probablistic approach to political economy*. London: Verso. · Harvey, D. 1992: *The limits to capital*. Chicago: Chicago University Press. · Meiksins-Wood, E. 1989: Rational choice Marxism: is the game worth the candle? *New Left Review* 177: 41–88. · Roemer, J. 1981: *Analytical foundations of Marxian economic theory*. Cambridge: Cambridge University Press. · Roemer, J. 1982: *A general theory of exploitation and class*. Cambridge, MA: Harvard University Press. · Roemer, J., ed., 1986: *Analytical Marxism*. Cambridge: Cambridge University Press. · Roemer, J. 1988: *Free to lose. An introduction to Marxist economic philosophy*. Cambridge, MA: Harvard University Press. · Shaikh, A. and Tonak, E.A. 1994: *Measuring the wealth of nations: a political economy of national accounts*. Cambridge: Cambridge University Press. · Sheppard, E. and Barnes, T.J. 1990: *The capitalist space economy: geographical analysis after Ricardo, Marx and Sraffa*. London: Unwin Hyman. · Webber, M.J. and Rigby, D.L. 1996: *The golden age illusion: rethinking postwar capitalism*. New York: Guilford. · Wright, E.O. 1985: *Classes*. London: Verso. · Wright, E.O., Levine, A. and Sober, E. 1992: *Reconstructing Marxism: essays on explanation and the theory of history*. London and New York: Verso.

Suggested Reading

Carling (1986). · Ruccio, D.F. 1988: The merchant of Venice or Marxism in the mathematical mode. *Rethinking Marxism* 1: 36–68. · Sheppard and Barnes (1990).

anarchism A political philosophy which advocates elimination of the STATE and its replacement by voluntary groups of individuals who can sustain social order without any external authority. Such a social order may emphasize either individualism (and thus is a logical conclusion of LIBERALISM, stressing the importance of individual liberty) or SOCIALISM (some versions of which reject private property as well as the state): Cook (1990) identified five different forms of anarchism – individualism; collectivism; anarchist communism; anarcho-syndicalism; and pacifism.

The early proponents of anarchist COMMUNISM included Peter Kropotkin and Elisée Reclus, whose geographical writings (especially Kropotkin's) were rediscovered by some of the early advocates of RADICAL GEOGRAPHY: a special issue of the journal *Antipode* promoted the anarcho-communist cause, stressing 'the essential interdependence of personal autonomy and community' (Breitbart, 1979, p. 1). In his seminal essay, 'What geography ought to be' (reprinted in that issue of *Antipode*), Kropotkin argues that its role in early childhood was 'to interest the child in the great phenomena of nature, to awaken the desire of knowing and explaining them', but geography's task more generally was to 'teach us, from our earliest childhood, that we are all brethren, whatever our nationality . . . geography must be . . . a means of dissipating . . . prejudices and creating other feelings more worthy of humanity'. Peet (1979) built on this by promoting a 'geography of human liberation' in which 'people are free to collectively make of themselves what they want within the limit of not damaging others . . . [which] can come only from controlling their own means of production based on their own piece of earth environment' with the latter involving 'an advance to scientific, creative humans *in* nature'. Elsewhere, he argued that 'Anarchism implies a decentralized spatial arrangement of production and people, because the individual can only fully develop in a close community of others' (Peet, 1977,

p. 24): there was little further interest, however, and a decade later Peet (in Peet and Thrift, 1989, p. 7) saw the late 1970s writings on this anarchism as 'the last bursts of colour in the fall of 1960s-style radicalism' – from then on radical geography became 'more sober'. RJJ

References and Suggested Reading

Breitbart, M. 1979: Introduction. *Antipode* 10 (3): 1–5. · Breitbart, M. 1981: Peter Kropotkin, the anarchist geographer. In D.R. Stoddart, ed., *Geography, ideology and social concern*. Oxford: Basil Blackwell, 134–53. · Cook, I. 1990: Anarchistic alternatives: an introduction. In I. Cook and D. Pepper, eds, *Anarchism and geography. Contemporary issues in geography and education.* 3 (2): 9–21. · Peet, R. 1977: The development of radical geography in the United States. In R. Peet, ed., *Radical geography: alternative viewpoints on contemporary social issues.* London: Methuen, 6–31. · Peet, R. 1979: The geography of human liberation. *Antipode* 10 (3): 119–34. · Peet, R. and Thrift, N.J. 1989: Political economy and human geography. In R. Peet and J. Thrift, eds, *New models in geography: the political economy perspective, volume one.* London: Methuen, 3–29. · Stoddart, D.R. 1975: Kropotkin, Reclus and 'relevant' geography. *Area* 7: 180–90.

androcentricity To view the world from a male perspective. Eichler (1988) outlines six types of androcentricity: male frame of reference – locating men as agents and women as objects; female invisibility; maintaining male over female interests; misogyny; and defending male dominance – and traces five manifestations of androcentricity in the research process. (See MASCULINISM.) GP

Reference

Eichler, M. 1988: *Nonsexist research methods: a practical guide.* Winchester, MA: Unwin Hyman.

animals, geography of Animal geography is a newly coined term used to describe a body of work in human geography which has taken shape since the mid-1990s and is concerned with the material well-being and cultural meaning of non-human animals in the geographies of social life. A landmark in the emergence of this new research focus was the publication of a special issue of the journal *Society and Space* in 1995 which makes the case for 'bring(ing) the animals back in' to the compass of human geography (Wolch and Emel, 1995, p. 632). The issue is a controversial one because it challenges entrenched assumptions about the status of animals in modern society and social science and the exclusively human terms in which these have come to be defined. At its most radical, then, animal geography opens up the 'human' in human geography to unprecedented critical scrutiny (Elder et al., 1998; Whatmore, 1999).

Animals have been long relegated to the margins of geographical study, as components in the composition of biogeographical systems or as resources in the social organization of food production. In neither case do animals emerge as active agents fashioning the environments they inhabit or as experiential subjects in the social relationships which bind them in different ways to people. The partial exception to this generalization is a fragile and unfashionable strand of work at the interface between archaeology, anthropology and traditional cultural geography which has been concerned with the process of domestication and the production of cultural landscapes (see, for example, Sauer, 1952; Donkin, 1989; see also CULTURAL ECOLOGY). The animal geography that is now emerging picks up some of these threads but, as Anderson's review (1997) of the domestication literature suggests, it is framed by the more critical intellectual impulses of POST-STRUCTURALISM and broader shifts in the social and political landscape associated with POSTMODERNITY. In this sense, it has been described as a 'thought experiment' (Philo, 1995: 67) to see what happens when animals are treated as another, radically different, social group.

Amongst the several lines of enquiry so far addressed by this new animal geography, the influence of these broader intellectual and social impulses can be traced in three main ways.

First, in studies of the *social practices and meanings* which have shaped relationships between humans and other animals in different times and places (Ingold, 1988). Attention here is focused on the changing geographies of human and animal interaction. For example, the living spaces of 'wild' creatures which have been refashioned by a range of social practices including their systematic eradication from areas of human settlement by hunting (Emel, 1995) and captive display in the exhibition spaces of city zoos (Anderson, 1995; see also WILDERNESS).

Second, in research attuned to the awakening of wider social concerns about the *treatment of animals* and the growth of new political movements around animal liberation, welfare and protection (e.g. Whatmore and Thorne, 1998). Working against the analytical grain which is content to treat animals as things, such work endeavours to extend the compass of ethical concern beyond 'humanity' and explore more environmental, or biocentric, conceptions of moral community (Lynn, 1998; see also ETHICS, GEOGRAPHY AND).

Thirdly, animal geography has been encouraged by developments in social theory which acknowledge a wider range of actors and their effects than people in the *practical business of everyday social life* (see, in particular, ACTOR–NETWORK THEORY and NON-REPRESENTATIONAL THEORY). Here, categorical distinctions between humans, animals and machines are seen to be uncertain as their properties are blurred by a proliferation of hybrid entities and networks, from genetically modified organisms to the simulant creatures of virtual reality (Luke, 1998; see also CYBORGS). SW

References

Anderson, K. 1995: Culture and nature at the Adelaide Zoo: at the frontiers of 'human' geography. *Transactions, Institute of British Geographers* NS 20 (3): 275–94. · Anderson, K. 1997: A walk on the wildside: a critical geography of domestication. *Progress in Human Geography* 21 (4): 463–85. · Donkin, R. 1989: *The Muscovy Duck, Cairina Moschata Domestica: origins, dispersals and associated aspects of the geography of domestication*. Rotterdam: AA Balkema. · Elder, G., Wolch, J. and Emel, J. 1998: Race, place and the bounds of humanity. *Society and Animals* 6/2: 183–202. · Emel, J. 1995: Are you man enough, big and bad enough? Ecofeminism and wolf eradication in the USA. *Society and Space* 13 (4): 707–34. · Ingold, T. ed., 1988: *What is an animal?* London: Routledge. · Luke, T. 1998: *Cyborg ecologies*. London: Routledge. · Lynn, W. 1998: Animals, ethics and geography. In J. Wolch and J. Emel, eds, *Animal geographies*. London: Verso, ch. 13. · Philo, C. 1995: Animals, geography and the city: notes on inclusions and exclusions. *Society and Space* 13 (4): 655–81. · Sauer, C. 1952: *Seeds, spades, hearths and herds*. American Geographical Society; reprinted in 1969, Cambridge, MA: MIT Press. · Whatmore, S. and Thorne, L. 1998: Wild(er)-ness: reconfiguring the geographies of wildlife. *Transactions of the Institute of British Geographers* NS 23 (4). · Whatmore, S. 1999: Rethinking the 'human' in human geography. In D. Massey, J. Allen and P. Sarre, eds, *Human geography today*. Cambridge: Polity Press. · Wolch, J. and Emel, J., eds, 1995: Special issue an 'animal geographies'. *Society and Space* 13 (4).

Suggested Reading

Wolch J. and J. Emel, eds, 1998: *Animal geographies*. London: Verso.

***Annales* school** A school of French historians distinctive in their interest in environmental and social topics, linked through the journal *Annales d'histoire économique et sociale*, founded in 1929 by Marc Bloch and Lucien Febvre (Now *Annales Économies, Sociétés, Civilisations*). Together with Fernand Braudel and others, these authors advocated 'total history' as a synthesizing discipline underlying the human and social sciences in general, integrating long-run changes in ways of life and the short-term political events with which they argued history was preoccupied.

Although often criticized for having, in practice, fallen short of successfully integrating the different 'levels' of time that they had identified, their ideas have continued to influence studies of long-run socio-economic change, of cultural change and mentalities, and of environmental change, especially where induced by human activity (Clark, 1985; Burke, 1990). Numerous geographers have drawn on this tradition, both through explicit application of the long-/medium-/short-run framework of presentation and explanation, and through *Annalistes'* discussions of relationships between social organization and spatial organization (Baker, 1984).

Annales school history continues to be a dominant element within the social sciences in France, and *Annales* historians have been at the forefront of work in cultural history, especially touching on cultures of everyday life (Hunt, 1989). Inter-disciplinary approaches have again been important, but in this case embracing cultural anthropology and literary criticism, in addition to geography and economics (Revel and Hunt, 1995). This long-standing openness to other disciplines helps to explain why the impact of POSTMODERNISM on history and the social sciences in France has been less confrontational than among Anglophone scholars. PG

References

Baker, A.R.H. 1984: Reflections on the relations of historical geography and the *Annales* school of history. In A.R.H. Baker et al., eds, *Explorations in historical geography: interpretative essays*. Cambridge: Cambridge University Press, 1–27; Burke, P. 1990: *The French historical revolution: The Annales school, 1929–1989*. Oxford: Clarendon Press; Clark, S., 1985: The *Annales* historians. In Q. Skinner, ed., *The return of grand theory in the human sciences*. Cambridge: Cambridge University Press, 177–98; Hunt, L., ed., 1989: *The new cultural history*. Berkeley: University of California Press; Revel, J. and Hunt, L., eds, 1995: *Histories: French constructions of the past*. New York: The New Press; Smith, D., 1991: *The rise of historical sociology*. Philadelphia: Temple University Press, 104–20.

anomie A term introduced by the French sociologist Emile Durkheim (1858–1917) to denote a societal condition in which normative standards are absent. Individuals have no widely-accepted behavioural guidelines in such contexts and may be faced by two or more very contrasting, even contradictory, sets of norms which create confusion and stimulate problems of IDENTITY. (Anomie is sometimes mistakenly equated with ALIENATION, a state of individual estrangement which may exist outside an anomic society). According to the adherents of the CHICAGO SCHOOL, behaviours characteristic of social disorganization (such as crime, violence and suicide) are likely to be present where anomie exists, notably in INNER-CITY and SLUM areas (cf. ZONAL MODEL). RJJ

anthropogeography A school of human geography closely associated with the work of the German geographer Friedrich Ratzel (1844–1904). It was inaugurated by his *Anthropogeographie*. This was published in two volumes, in 1882 and 1891, and there were several differences in emphasis between them. To Hartshorne (1939), Ratzel organized his materials in the first volume 'largely in terms of the natural conditions of the earth, which he studied in their relation to human culture', thereby reworking the ideas of Karl Ritter, whereas in the second volume 'Ratzel himself largely reversed the process'; to Dickinson (1969), the first volume was essentially dynamic, 'an application of geography to history', whereas the second was static and treated 'the geographical distribution of man'. Both volumes have to be placed in the context of the contemporary debates within the German intellectual commmunity over the place of the cultural sciences and their relation to the natural sciences (Smith, 1991; see also DIFFUSION). For Ratzel, writing in the middle of what Bassin (1987a) describes as an 'imperialist frenzy', and indeed contributing to it, the cultural development of a STATE could not be separated from its spatial growth. His project was not an ENVIRONMENTAL DETERMINISM, as some later commentators have suggested, but it was distinguished by the attempt to conduct a nominally scientific study of the relations between society and NATURE through the elaboration of a system of concepts.

In many ways Ratzel's *Politische Geographie*, published in 1897, represented the culmination of these ideals. There, Ratzel described the state as 'a living body which has extended itself over a part of the earth and has differentiated itself from other bodies which have similarly expanded'. The object of these extensions and expansions, Ratzel argued, was always 'the conquest of space', and it was this which became formalized in the concept of LEBENSRAUM ('living space'): 'the geographical area within which living organisms develop'. He was keenly aware of the dangers of organicism but, even so, insisted that: 'Just as the struggle for existence in the plant and animal world always centres about a matter of space, so the conflicts of nations are in great part only struggles for territory' (see GEOPOLITICS; TERRITORIALITY). Wanklyn (1961) treats *Lebensraum* as 'a fundamental geographical concept', therefore, in her eyes, Ratzel's writings were directed primarily towards 'thinking out the scope and content of biogeography'. There is certainly a distinguished tradition of biogeographic reflection within human geography, and in this sense there are important continuities between Ratzel's *Lebensraum*, Vidal de la Blache's *GENRE DE VIE* and the concept of *rum* ('room') developed in Hägerstrand's TIME-GEOGRAPHY. If these continuities are recognized, then Dickinson's (1969) view of Ratzel's original formulation, stripped of its subsequent distortions by the Third Reich, as 'one of the most original and fruitful of all concepts in modern geography' becomes peculiarly prescient. But such a purely 'biogeographical' or 'scientific' reading does scant justice to the context in which Ratzel was working and, in particular, ignores the fact that his vision of human geography not only had political implications but also rested on – and was indeed made possible by – a series of political assumptions (Bassin, 1987a, 1987b; Smith, 1991). (See also LAMARCKIANISM.) DG

References

Bassin, M. 1987a: Imperialism and the nation-state in Friedrich Ratzel's political geography. *Progress in Human Geography* 11: 473–95. · Bassin, M. 1987b: Race contra space: the conflict between German Geopolitik and National Socialism. *Political Geography Quarterly* 6: 115–34. · Dickinson, R. 1969: *The makers of modern geography*. London: Routledge and Kegan Paul; New York: Praeger. · Hartshorne, R. 1939: *The nature of geography: a critical survey of current thought in the light of the past*. Lancaster, PA: Association of American Geographers. · Smith, Woodruff. 1991: *Politics and the sciences of culture in Germany 1840–1920*. New York: Oxford University Press. · Wanklyn, H. 1961: *Friedrich Ratzel: biographical memoir and bibliography*. Cambridge: Cambridge University Press.

Suggested Reading

Bassin (1987a and b). · Dickinson (1969), 64–76.

anti-humanism A critique of humanism that seeks to displace 'the human subject' from its central place within conventional projects of interpretation and understanding by raising questions about consciousness, the constitution of subjectivity and the production of agency. 'Anti-humanism' is an umbrella term for a series of often radically different positions, but in philosophical terms all of them object to the twin humanist assumptions that valid knowledge has to be organized around the intellectual capacities of the rational subject (a subject-centred EPISTEMOLOGY) and that social life is the product of creative and conscious human agency (a subject-constituted history). Two politico-intellectual movements have been particularly prominent in the critique of these assumptions and in the formation of what is sometimes called 'theoretical anti-humanism': STRUCTURALISM and POST-STRUCTURALISM. Drawing from each of these movements, more substantive objections have been registered to humanism. In particular, 'the rational subject' around which humanism revolves is not the product of a pure and abstract logic, its critics argue, but of a fractious history (or historical geography) of Reason; the figure of the human subject which lies at its heart turns out to be white, heterosexual and masculine, so that the complex ways in which the play of power and desire enter into the constitution of different subject-positions (and different capacities for action) are erased; and the privileges accorded to intentions occlude the significance of the unconscious for the production of social life. All that having been said, where these critical interventions leave authorial responsibility and political practice remains an open and urgent question. And yet, as Barrett (1991, p. 166) concluded, if the 'anti-humanist abandonment of individual agency and responsibility is ultimately no answer, it has at least effectively undermined the assumption of correctness and universal applicability in its predecessors'.

Anti-humanism has been instrumental in the critique of HUMANISTIC GEOGRAPHY and in the formation of a broadly conceived post-humanist geography. This is a heterogeneous body of work that draws on a wide range of overlapping and contending ideas; consistent with the 'theoretical' sensibilities of anti-humanism, the most important sources have been FEMINIST theory, POST-COLONIAL theory, post-structuralism, PSYCHOANALYTIC THEORY and QUEER THEORY. Perhaps the most innovative contributions of post-humanist geography to date lie in the exploration of the connections between the production of subjectivities and the production of spatialities (see, for example, Pile and Thrift, 1995). (See also MASCULINISM; PHALLOCENTRISM.) DG

References

Barrett, M. 1991: *The politics of truth: from Marx to Foucault*. Stanford: Stanford University Press. · Pile, S. and Thrift, N.J., eds, 1995: *Mapping the subject: geographies of cultural transformation*. London and New York: Routledge.

Suggested Reading

Soper, K. 1986: *Humanism and anti-humanism*. London: Hutchinson.

apartheid The policy of spatial separation of the races, as applied in South Africa after the National Party assumed political control in 1948, but now dismantled. Under the *Population Registration Act*, all South Africans were classified as members of one of four race groups: black (population almost 30 million in the early 1990s before the end of apartheid), white (5 million), coloured (3.5 million) and asian (1 million). RACE provided the basis for separate political institutions, in both national and local government and racial discrimination resulted in marked inequalities in levels of living, with whites better-off overall, blacks worst-off, and, between them, Asians generally faring better than coloureds. (See also RACISM.)

Apartheid, as originally implemented, operated at three spatial scales: personal, within residential space in towns and cities, and at the national level. Personal discrimination with respect to use of such public facilities as parks, theatres, transportation and lavatories was generally referred to as 'petty apartheid'. The extent of this form of discrimination had been reduced in the 1980s, before the abolition of the *Separate Amenities Act* removed its legal basis. Apartheid at the town or city level was implemented via the *Group Areas Act*, under which each portion of urban residential space was allocated for the exclusive occupation of a single race group. This ensured the perpetuation of almost complete residential SEGREGATION by race. However, integration was taking place in so-called 'grey areas' of the larger cities for some years before the repeal of the *Group Areas Act*.

The most important aspect of apartheid was at the national level, where ten so-called 'homelands' (or 'Bantustans') were designated for the occupation of the major black or African tribal groups. All blacks were supposed to exercise their 'political rights' in their respective homelands, which were ultimately to become independent states. Bophuthatswana, Ciskei, Transkei and Venda were granted 'independence', though this was not recognized by the United Nations or any government outside South Africa. The homelands were reincorporated into the post-apartheid South African state.

The South African government originally claimed that apartheid (sometimes known as 'separate development' or 'multi-nationalism') enabled racial harmony and the rights of all groups to be protected in a heterogeneous, pluralistic society (see PLURAL SOCIETY; PLURALISM). The homelands were supposed to give blacks their independence from white rule, and the same rights that the whites enjoyed in their (white) residual Republic. A more plausible explanation was that apartheid enabled the whites to maintain their cultural identity, political power and exploitation of black labour, by associating race with separation, externalizing the black franchise and using the homelands as cheap labour reserves.

International economic sanctions played a part in the eventual abandonment of apartheid. However, the system was already breaking down from within, well before the release of the African National Congress leader Nelson Mandela in February 1990 and the legalization of the ANC and other opposition groups. Erosion of petty apartheid and residential segregation was accelerating, and the distinction between the homelands and white South Africa had always been artificial from an economic point of view (half the black population lived in 'White South Africa', mainly in the cities where the jobs were, and large numbers were also drawn from the homelands as migrant workers or commuters). By the early 1980s it was clear that restrictions known as 'influx control' could not prevent increasing numbers of blacks settling in and around the metropolitan areas, especially the Witwatersrand (centred on Johannesburg), Cape Town and Durban. Millions came to live in informal 'shack' settlements on the peri-urban fringe as well as in the older townships (see also SQUATTER SETTLEMENT). Thus the legitimacy of the homelands as providing for the political rights of blacks was increasingly called into question. And rising tension in the cities expressed in violent unrest made apartheid society increasingly difficult to control.

The first non-racial elections in 1994 replaced the Nationalist Party (NP) rule by a government in which the ANC were in the majority. Nelson Mandela became President. Initially the ANC operated in partnership with the NP, but the latter subsequently withdrew from the coalition which had helped to ensure a peaceful transfer of power under which the white population enjoyed protection from the large-scale redistribution of property which many of them had feared at the hands of a black majority government. Negotiations were set in motion for the design of a new constitution, with a bill of rights, under which further elections would take place in 1999.

Whatever the final outcome of this process, the legacy of apartheid will take decades to eradicate. South Africa's towns and cities remain highly segregated, as few blacks can afford to move into white areas. However, black residential space is becoming increasingly differentiated by CLASS, in a process originally referred to as 'deracialized apartheid'. Whites, along with the better-off members of other race groups, have been able to protect some of their privileges on a neighbourhood basis, while the best a growing number of the black population can hope for is to build houses of their own, with some state subsidy, in one of the 'shack cities'.

The decade since the release of Nelson Mandela has thus been somewhat of a disappointment for those expecting the rapid erosion of the geography of apartheid. When the ANC came to power, they adopted a comprehensive development strategy set out in the *Reconstruction and Development Programme* (RDP for short), which quickly became an almost unchallenged orthodoxy. This prioritized the basic needs of the poor (mainly black) population, who had suffered such discrimination under apartheid. Ambitious targets were set for the construction of new houses, along with improvements in infrastructure and in the provision of education and health services for the poor. However, despite some successes (e.g. in the provision of rural water supply and a school nutrition programme in some areas), the implementation of the RDP was from the outset frustrated by resource constraints exacerbated by so many competing programmes, and by administrative inefficiency accompanied by some corrupt practices. One of the major failures was in housing, with the further growth of informal settlements substituting for what was originally hoped to be formal housing for all.

The latter part of the 1990s saw the downgrading and effective abandonment of the RDP, in favour of a new macro-economic strategy set out in a document *Growth, Employment, and Redistribution* (GEAR) published in 1996. This is much more in tune with the neo-liberal policies of such agencies as the World Bank and International Monetary Fund, with their preference for free-market solutions involving competition, deregulation, flexible labour markets, restrictions on public spending, and other policies thought to be attractive to foreign capital. This strategy contrasts with the more pro-active state involvement required by the RDP. Post-apartheid South Africa has thus adopted a new development orthodoxy, which might increase the country's attraction to international investors in the competitive global economy, but which seems unlikely to generate the kind of benefits for the poor which were supposed to accompany the end of apartheid. In this sense, post-apartheid South Africa increasingly resembles so-called underdeveloped countries with highly unequal distributions of income and wealth – albeit incorporating distinctive features inherited from the apartheid era. The main uncertainties are how fast the economy can grow, to keep up with population growth and assist redistribution, and how much of the post-apartheid political freedom will survive the control of unfulfilled material expectations on the part of the majority poor (and black) population. DMS

Suggested Reading

Lemon, A., ed., 1991: *Homes apart: South Africa's divided cities*. London: Paul Chapman. · Lemon, A., ed., 1995: *The geography of change in South Africa*. Chichester: John Wiley. · Parnell, S. 1997: South African cities: perspectives from the ivory tower of urban studies. *Urban Studies* 35: 891–906. · Pickles, J. and Weiner, D., eds, 1991: *Rural and regional restructuring in South Africa*. Special issue of *Antipode*, 23 (1). · Simon, D. 1990: Crisis and change in South Africa: implications for the apartheid city. *Transactions, Institute of British Geographers* NS14: 198–206. · Smith, D.M. 1990: *Apartheid in South Africa*, 3rd edn. Cambridge: Cambridge University Press (*Update* series, Department of Geography, Queen Mary and Westfield College, University of London). · Smith, D.M., ed, 1992: *The apartheid city and beyond: urbanization in contemporary South Africa*. London: Routledge. · Smith, D.M. 1994: *Geography and social justice*. Oxford: Blackwell Publishers, ch. 8. · Smith, D.M. 1995: Geography, social justice and the new South Africa. *South African Geographical Journal* 77: 1–5. · Robinson, J. 1995: *The power of the apartheid state: power and space in South African cities*. Oxford: Butterworth-Heinemann. · Rogerson, C.M. and Rogerson, J.M. 1997: The changing post-apartheid city: emergent black-owned enterprise in Johannesburg. *Urban Studies* 34: 85–103.

applied geography The application of geographical knowledge and skills to the solution or resolution of problems within society. Geography has been applied for as long as it has been practised – early cartography was very utilitarian – but the specific usage of the term applied geography has been relatively narrow during the last fifty years, reflecting the influence of its main proponent in that form – Dudley Stamp.

Following Stamp's lead, most applied geography in capitalist economies until recently has been undertaken for the public sector, most specifically in the area of physical planning. (This was how Stamp (1951) defined it in his inaugural professorial lecture at the London School of Economics; see also House, 1973.) Geographers now obtain contracts and employment from private sector firms in a wide variety of business types, however, especially marketing. In socialist countries, especially those of eastern Europe and the former USSR, most work by academic geographers was directed by the STATE APPARATUS (of which they were a part) towards the solution of economic and environmental problems: applied geography was relatively more important there than in most of the capitalist world, where Taylor (1985) suggested that pressure for greater concentration on 'applied' (as against 'pure') geography increases during periods of major recession in the capitalist world-economy (see KONDRATIEFF CYCLES).

Stamp's major statement, *Applied geography* (1960), presented the geographer's unique contribution as 'the holistic approach in which he sees the relationship between man and his environment, with its attendant problems, as a whole'; Kenzer (1989, 1992) claims that this synthesizing ability is being lost in the current expansion of applied geography associated with narrow, technocratic specialisms. According to Stamp, the relationship is discerned 'by survey in the field, and the gathering of facts systematically and objectively', with the twin goals of survey and analysis 'achieved fully only when studied cartographically'. Such surveys and analyses were relevant to many of the world's pressing problems, like population pressure on land, economic development, and improvement of living conditions. Stamp's own focus on the use and misuse of land in Great Britain – notably through the first Land Utilization Survey (Stamp, 1946) – led to his involvement in the development of the country's town and country planning legislation after the Second World War, whereas others made major contributions to specific issues, such as Alfred Steers' work on coastal protection.

Stamp presented geographers as information gatherers and synthesisers who stood outside the political processes within which planning goals were formulated and pursued (see also Chisholm, 1971; Gregory, 1978). Geographers were employed in central and local government planning offices, where their skills were relevant to the focus on land use survey and plan, and were also called upon by national government agencies, notably in wartime when information about environments was needed as part of military intelligence (many still are employed in the United States' CIA): in the United Kingdom, they played a major role in the preparation of the Second World War *Admiralty Handbooks*, which summarized knowledge about many theatres of war, and in the interpretation of aerial photographs, out of which has grown the discipline's expertise in REMOTE SENSING.

Later work has gone well beyond information-gathering and synthesizing. Changes in geographical approaches and techniques, notably the QUANTITATIVE REVOLUTION and then GEOGRAPHIC INFORMATION SYSTEMS, enhanced the range of available contributions. *Predictive models* were developed, as in the study of traffic flows: the GRAVITY MODEL was used to predict likely flows between areas according to their land uses and distance apart (from which forecasts of, for example, the likely success of shopping centre developments were derived); more sophisticated procedures, such as the Lowry Model and ENTROPY-MAXIMIZING MODELS, were later adapted to provide more comprehensive information (though see Batty, 1989, on the extent of their use). Such analyses were closely associated with those in REGIONAL SCIENCE: the initial goal was to produce efficient patterns of land use which minimized movement costs (see LOCATION–ALLOCATION MODELS); more recently, they have been used to suggest optimal locations for a range of business operations, such as automobile dealerships (Clarke and Clarke, 1995).

A second strand of work focused on *society–environment interactions*. Geographers in the USA were employed in the public agencies seeking to revive agriculture in the 1930s, for example (Kollmorgen, 1979), and the Australian Commonwealth Scientific and Industrial Research Organisation combined the work of physical and human geographers in evaluations of land suitability for various uses. The developing field of HAZARD studies also led to geographers advising on a wide range of projects concerned with environmental use and rehabilitation (Burton et al., 1978): the journal *Applied Geography*, founded in 1981, carries reports of such studies. (The *Journal of Applied Geographic Studies* – launched in 1997 – concentrates on the work in the first strand.)

A third strand of work, largely developed in the 1990s, has mobilized geography's recent technical advances. Geographers have been presented as not only collectors and collators of material but also able to *'add value' to information* (e.g. Openshaw, 1989, 1991; Rhind, 1989). GEODEMOGRAPHICS involves integrating spatially-referenced data about areas and the individuals living there to assist marketing campaigns devised to focus on particular types of consumer; they build on work in FACTORIAL ECOLOGY and are widely used by market research companies as efficient ways of targeting market segments (as illustrated in Longley and Clarke, 1995).

Despite this categorization of work into three strands, the practice of applied geography lacks a coherent structure and is characterized by pragmatism – as in Berry's (1973) classification of approaches to planning problems. There is no theoretical core or corpus of techniques but rather *ad hoc* approaches to the problems posed, drawing on perceived relevant skills and information. (Kenzer, 1989, for example, wrote that 'regrettably the current spate of applied geography research (at least in North America) does not seem to have any philosophical or theoretical basis in being, other than its understood application to social needs' and, in 1992, that 'the connection between applied and "pure research" was blurred by hazy, nebulous definitions and haughty, unrealistic expectations of what an autonomous, self-reliant applied geography could and could not achieve'.) Pacione (1990) suggested nine 'principles or guidelines' for the conduct of applied work, however, and Clark (1982) – stressing that academic applied geographers cannot be value-free in their work – offered four propositions to guide those who wished to be involved in policy analysis: (1) academics should recognize their own values when tackling problems and formulating solutions; (2) policy advocates should promote particular cases rather than seeking to be independent and objective adjudicators of competing formulations (see also Clark, 1991); (3) policy scientists should be critical of the status quo; and (4) sponsors of applied work should make the reports that they receive publicly available. (Kenzer, 1992, also called for applied geographers to be more 'openly self-critical'.)

Despite the range of applied work in which geographers were involved, some senior academics were concerned in the 1970s that the discipline's expertise was insufficiently called-upon, especially relative to that of other social and environmental scientists. The theme of 'geography and public policy' was taken up in both the Association of American Geographers (Ginsburg, 1972; White, 1972) and the Institute of British Geographers (Coppock, 1974), although some were concerned about its implications, not least because they felt that geographers were insufficiently prepared to perform the role being promoted for them (see Hare, 1974; Zelinsky, 1975).

Pressures on geographers to become more involved in applied work increased during the 1980s (Briggs, 1981, claimed that many already were). This reflected growing political requirements on higher education institutions to make greater contributions to tackling perceived problems and to earn larger proportions of their incomes from such research and consultancy activity, linked to a recognition among some geographers of their responsibility to contribute to the resolution of an increasing range of perceived problems and of students' requirements for a relevant training rather than a general education. Taylor (1985) suggested that this concentration on applied work, which continues in the 1990s, has been enhanced because of the emphasis – in the agenda of both the 'New Right' who dominated politics in the 1980s and the 'New Social Democrats' who have succeeded them – on reducing the role of the state and increasing the importance of market mechanisms in economic, and hence social, revival (Johnston, 1992a). The 'business of geography' has been very significantly changed as a consequence (Johnston, 1995).

Applied geography as practised by geographers working outside academia is less apparent in the United Kingdom than in North America, where there is much greater recognition of a graduate profession of geography and willingness among practitioners to join and participate in the meetings of the main professional society, the Association of American Geographers, which has a large and active Applied Geography Specialty Group. (It was the ninth largest of the Association's 48 groups in 1998; see Sherwood, 1995, however, on the difficulties American geographers have faced.) Some leading American geographers have argued that promotion of the applied value of a geography degree is a necessary route to disciplinary survival, in which technical skills (such as those associated with spatial analysis and GIS) play a major role (NRC, 1997): British geographers have presented similar clarion calls, arguing that the discipline's future lies in developing such approaches, as in (Longley, 1995):

> Social science that does not show interest in real world issues of popular concern is doomed to remain on the sidelines of academic respectability and perceived social relevance, and reinvigorated spatial analysis is central to the measurement and modelling of economic and social aspects of human behaviour.

Not all geographers have accepted this call for a particular form of applied geography, perceiving it as either or both of a narrow presentation of their discipline's expertise (especially the emphasis on technical skills; what Kenzer (1992) refers to as students 'being trained mainly to push buttons and learn software programs') and a value-laden approach to tackling societal problems. Some recognize three types of geography, each of which has its own applied goal, if not programme (Johnston, 1992b; see also Gregory, 1978, pp. 147–52): (1) those areas of study, such as SPATIAL ANALYSIS, which adopt the tenets of POSITIVISM and seek technical solutions to problems within an accepted political economy – sometimes termed socio-spatial engineering; (2) that activity – initially termed HUMANISTIC GEOGRAPHY but now much wider (cf. HUMAN GEOGRAPHY) – which seeks to broaden individuals' understanding of themselves and others, thereby promoting greater tolerance; and (3) the branch of geography – often termed radical – whose goal is to emancipate people by helping them to clarify the nature of the society in which they live, thereby enabling them to participate in its restructuring. Buttimer (1993), for example, identified four 'vocational meanings' in geographers' career trajectories:

- *poesis*, which involves 'the evoking of geographic awareness', eliciting 'curiosity and insight' and addressing 'critical and emancipatory interests';
- *paiedia*, or the circulation of information through teaching and learning strategies;
- *logos*, which seeks explanation, developing generalizations through 'analytical rigor, objectivity, and science making'; and
- *ergon*, efforts to 'render geography relevant to the education and solution of social and environmental problems' with issues assuming central importance and practitioners 'less concerned about disciplinary orthodoxy than about problem solving'.

All four are equally valid and valuable as applied roles within society, but most applied geographers argue for *ergon* – perhaps underpinned by generalizations from *logos* – with Buttimer noting that in Sweden ('as indeed in most major schools in other countries') 'the increasing demand for scientific research or practical applications of geography since The Second World War has certainly diminished the perceived status of teaching and critical reflection'.

Debates over applied geography have involved conflicts between protagonists of the 'radical cause' and those promoting 'socio-spatial engineering'. Harvey (1974), for example, posed the question 'what kind of geography for what kind of public policy?', and exposed the value judgements underpinning much applied geography, against which he set his emancipatory 'people's geography' (Harvey, 1984). Stoddart (1987), on the other hand, criticized much work for concentrating on relatively transient and trivial issues and contended that members of the discipline should instead 'do some real Geography' and focus on the large issue of people–environment relationships.

Harvey's critique and Buttimer's classification draw attention to a much wider issue regarding the use, and abuse, of information and knowledge. All knowledge is power and once created can potentially be used in a variety of ways, which may be less acceptable to some people than others – as exemplified by the use of GIS technology in the 1991 Gulf War. Furthermore, knowledge can be 'produced' to promote particular political projects, a task in which geographers have been far from innocent, as with Jovan Cvijic's cartographic attempts to justify Serbia's claims to Macedonia in the first decades of this century (Wilkinson, 1951) and Isaiah Bowman's involvement in the redrawing of the world political map at the end of the First World War. Indeed, in some places the subject was itself created and promoted because of such perceived 'utility': Jackson (1997) reports that the study of geography was promoted in Sheffield at the start of the twentieth century because of the geographical ignorance which hampered British efforts in the Boer War ('Geography should be taught on thoroughly Imperialist grounds'), for example, and in the Netherlands the first academic appointments were in 'colonial geography'.

The activities designated as applied geography are but a part of a pervasive triangle of power, knowledge, and academic life, therefore. Geographers have always been involved in the production of 'useful knowledge' that has been both applicable and applied – the distinction between 'applied' and, often by implication, 'pure' geography is false. What has been promoted as applied geography from Stamp onwards is a particular form of knowledge-production and application closely linked to the interests of the capitalist state and a wide range of interests therein: within that context, applied work has often been presented as 'neutral' and 'value-free' (on which see Sayer, 1981), allowing those who call themselves applied geographers to claim detachment from the conflicts which underpin all knowledge production and use – a claim now being challenged in great depth in the context of widespread adoption of GIS (Pickles, 1995). RJJ

References and Suggested Reading

Abler, R.F. 1993: Desiderata for geography: an institutional view from the United States. In R.J. Johnston, ed., *The challenge for geography: a changing world; a changing discipline*. Oxford and Cambridge, MA, Basil Blackwell. · Batty, M. 1989: Urban modelling and planning: reflections, retrodictions and predictions. In B. Macmillan, ed., *Remodelling geography*. Oxford and Cambridge, MA: Basil Blackwell, 147–69. · Berry, B.J.L. 1973: *The human consequences of urbanization*. New York: St. Martin's Press; London: Macmillan. · Briggs, D.J. 1981: The principles and practice of applied geography. *Applied Geography* 1: 1–8. · Burton, I., Kates, R.W. and White, G.F. 1978: *The environment as hazard*. New York and Oxford: Oxford University Press. · Buttimer, A. 1993: *Geography and the human spirit*. Baltimore: Johns Hopkins University Press. · Chisholm, M. 1971: Geography and the question of relevance. *Area* 3: 65–8. · Clark, G.L. 1982: Instrumental reason and policy analysis. In D.T. Herbert and R.J. Johnston, eds, *Geography and the urban environment: progress in research and applications, volume 5*. Chichester and New York: John Wiley, 41–62. · Clark, W.A.V. 1991: Geography in court: expertise in adversarial settings. *Transactions, Institute of British Geographers* NS 16: 5–20. · Clarke, G. and Clarke, M. 1995: The development and benefits of customized spatial decision support systems. In P. Longley and G. Clarke, eds, *GIS for business and service planning*. Cambridge: GeoInformation International, 227–46. · Coppock, J.T. 1974: Geography and public policy: challenges and opportunities. *Transactions, Institute of British Geographers* 63: 1–16. · Ginsburg, N.S. 1972: The mission of a scholarly society. *Professional Geographer* 24: 1–6. · Gregory, D. 1978: *Ideology, science and human geography*. London: Hutchinson. · Hare, F.K. 1974: Geography and public policy: a Canadian view. *Transactions, Institute of British Geographers* 63: 25–28. · Harvey, D. 1974: What kind of geography for what kind of public policy? *Transactions, Institute of British Geographers* 63: 18–24. · Harvey, D. 1984: On the history and present condition of geography: an historical materialist manifesto. *Professional Geographer* 36: 1–11. · House, J.W. 1973: Geographers, decision takers and policy makers. In M. Chisholm and B. Rodgers, eds, *Studies in human geography*. London: Heinemann. · Jackson, P. 1997: Geography and the cultural turn. *Scottish Geographical Magazine* 113: 186–8. · Johnston, R.J. 1992a: The internal operations of the state. In P.J. Taylor, ed., *The political geography of the twentieth century*. London: Belhaven Press. · Johnston, R.J. 1992b: Face the challenge: make the change. In R.J. Johnston, ed., *The challenge for geography: a changing world; a changing discipline*. Oxford and Cambridge, MA: Basil Blackwell. · Johnston, R.J. 1995: The business of British geography. In A.D. Cliff, P.R. Gould, A.G. Hoare and N.J. Thrift, eds, *Diffusing geography: essays for Peter Haggett*. Oxford: Blackwell Publishers, 317–41. · Kenzer, M.S. 1989: Applied geography: overview and introduction. In M.S. Kenzer, ed., *Applied geography: issues, questions, and concerns*. Dordrecht, Boston and London: Kluwer Academic Publishers, 1–14. · Kenzer, M.S. 1992: Applied and academic geography and the remainder of the twentieth century. *Applied Geography* 12: 207–10. · Kollmorgen, W. 1979: Kollmorgen as bureaucrat. *Annal of the Association of American Geographers* 69: 77–89. · Longley, P. 1995: GIS planning for businesses and services. *Environment and Planning B* 22: 127–9. · Longley, P. and Clarke, G., eds, 1995: *GIS for business and service planning*. Cambridge: GeoInformation International; NRC 1997: *Rethinking geography: new relevance for science and society*. Washington, D.C.: National Research Council. · Openshaw, S. 1989: Computer modelling in human geography. In B. Macmillan, ed., *Remodelling geography*. Oxford and Cambridge, MA: Basil Blackwell, 70–88. · Openshaw, S. 1991: A view on the GIS crisis in geography, or, using GIS to put Humpty Dumpty back together again. *Environment and Planning A* 23: 621–8. · Pacione, M. 1990: Conceptual issues in applied urban geography. *Tijdschift voor Economische en Sociale Geografie* 81: 1–13. · Pickles, J., ed., 1995: *Ground truth: the social implications of geographical information systems*. New York: The Guilford Press. · Rhind, D.W. 1989: Computing, academic geography, and the world outside. In B. Macmillan, ed., *Remodelling geography*. Oxford and Cambridge, MA: Basil Blackwell: 177–90. · Rundstrom, R.A. and Kenzer, M.S. 1989: The decline of fieldwork in human geography. *Professional Geographer* 41: 294–303. · Sayer, A. 1981: Defensible values in geography: can values be science-free? In D.T. Herbert and R.J. Johnston, eds, *Geography and the urban environment: progress in research and applications, volume 4*. Chichester: John Wiley, 29–56. · Sherwood, N. 1995: 'Business geographers: a US perspective'. In P. Longley and G. Clarke, eds, *GIS for business and service planning*. Cambridge: GeoInformation International, 250–70. · Stamp, L.D. 1946: *The land of Britain and how it is used*. London: Longman. · Stamp, L.D. 1951: Applied geography. In L.D. Stamp and S.W. Wooldridge, *London essays in geography: Rodwell Jones memorial volume*. London: Longman Green. · Stamp, L.D. 1960: *Applied geography*. London: Penguin Books. · Stoddart, D.R. 1987: To claim the high ground: geography for the end of the century. *Transactions Institute of British Geographers* NS 12: 327–36. · Taylor, P.J. 1985: The value of a geographical perspective. In R.J. Johnston, ed., *The future of geography*. London and New York: Methuen, 92–110. · Taylor, P.J. and Johnston, R.J. 1995: GIS and geography. In J. Pickles, ed., *Ground truth: the social implications of geographical information systems*. New York: The Guilford Press, 51–67. · White, G.F. 1972: Geography and public policy. *Professional Geographer* 24: 101–4. · Wilkinson, H.R. 1951: *Maps and politics*. Liverpool: Liverpool University Press. · Zelinsky, W. 1975: The demigod's dilemma. *Annals of the Association of American Geographers* 65: 123–43.

appropriationism A term first employed by Goodman, Sorj and Wilkinson (1987) in relation to the forms in which agriculture is industrialized. Agriculture is a natural production process that cannot be directly transformed into a branch of industrial production. The INDUSTRIALIZATION of agriculture confronts its natural characteristics in the form of the biological conversion of energy, biological time in plant growth and the rigidities of space in land-based activities (see AGRARIAN QUESTION; SUBSTITUTIONISM). Within these constraints which are defined by technological change, discrete elements of the production process in agriculture are taken over by industry (for example the horse by the tractor, organic manure by synthetic alternatives). The persistent but discontinuous undermining of discrete operations and elements of the agricultural production process, their transformation into industrial activities, and their reincorporation into agriculture as inputs is designated by Goodman, Sorj and Wilkinson (1987, p. 2) as appropriationism. MW

References

Goodman, D., Sorj, B. and Wilkinson, J. 1987: *From farming to biotechnology*. Oxford: Blackwell.

areal differentiation The study of the spatial distribution of physical and human phenomena as they relate to other spatially proximate and causally linked phenomena in REGIONS or other spatial units. Along with SPATIAL ANALYSIS and LANDSCAPE approaches, this is often seen as one of the three major approaches to understanding in human geography. It is indeed the oldest western tradition of geographical inquiry, tracing its beginnings to the Greeks Hecateus of Miletus and Strabo. The geographer, in Strabo's words, is 'the person who describes the parts of the Earth'. But description was never simply taking inventory of the various characteristics of different regions. The purpose was to understand those features of parts of the Earth that were of greatest political and military significance. This understanding was to wax and wane in relative importance down the years. But it never completely faded away, even if revived under different circumstances and using different concepts and language.

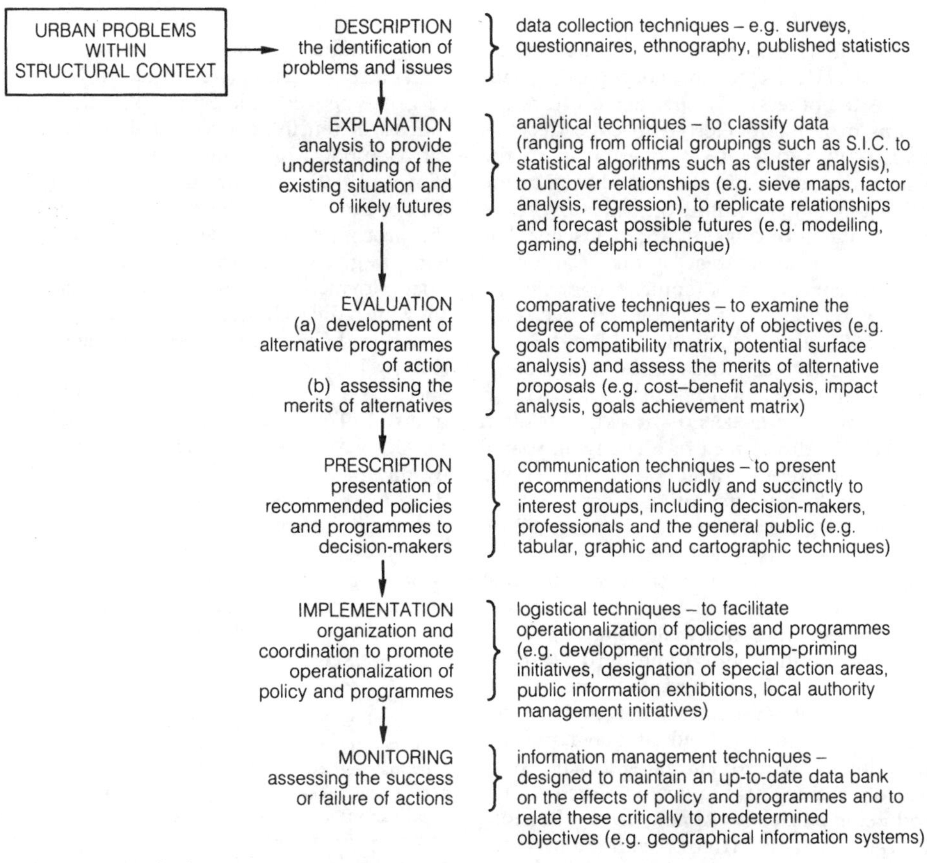
URBAN PROBLEMS WITHIN STRUCTURAL CONTEXT
DESCRIPTION the identification of problems and issues
data collection techniques – e.g. surveys, questionnaires, ethnography, published statistics
EXPLANATION analysis to provide understanding of the existing situation and of likely futures
analytical techniques – to classify data (ranging from official groupings such as S.I.C. to statistical algorithms such as cluster analysis), to uncover relationships (e.g. sieve maps, factor analysis, regression), to replicate relationships and forecast possible futures (e.g. modelling, gaming, delphi technique)
EVALUATION (a) development of alternative programmes of action (b) assessing the merits of alternatives
comparative techniques – to examine the degree of complementarity of objectives (e.g. goals compatibility matrix, potential surface analysis) and assess the merits of alternative proposals (e.g. cost–benefit analysis, impact analysis, goals achievement matrix)
PRESCRIPTION presentation of recommended policies and programmes to decision-makers
communication techniques – to present recommendations lucidly and succinctly to interest groups, including decision-makers, professionals and the general public (e.g. tabular, graphic and cartographic techniques)
IMPLEMENTATION organization and coordination to promote operationalization of policy and programmes
logistical techniques – to facilitate operationalization of policies and programmes (e.g. development controls, pump-priming initiatives, designation of special action areas, public information exhibitions, local authority management initiatives)
MONITORING assessing the success or failure of actions
information management techniques – designed to maintain an up-to-date data bank on the effects of policy and programmes and to relate these critically to predetermined objectives (e.g. geographical information systems)

applied geography *The practice of applied urban geography* (Pacione, 1990)

The 'classic' epoch of regional geography, to use Paul Claval's (1993, p. 15) phrase, was reached in the late nineteenth and early twentieth centuries when much of the conceptual debate in geography was devoted to the concept of the region. Such geographers as Paul Vidal de la Blache and Alfred Hettner were leading exponents of regional perspectives. An influential modern statement of geography as areal differentiation, drawing from the arguments of Hettner in particular, was made in Richard Hartshorne's *The nature of geography* (1939). This is usually seen as claiming that geography is about showing how unique regions reveal the co-variation of phenomena that can only be understood through identifying regions. Hartshorne's repeated use of the term areal *differentiation* and his avowed indifference to the 'phenomena themselves' could well lead to such an IDIOGRAPHIC interpretation. The logic of the presentation, however, suggests that recognizing regions requires investigation of similarities as well as differences over space. Areal differentiation, therefore, is about establishing degrees of sameness as well as difference between regions (Agnew, 1989). Hartshorne's critics (principally exponents of the spatial-analysis view of the field) accused him of seeing locations as unique and justifying a traditional REGIONAL GEOGRAPHY in which 'areal differentiation dominated geography at the expense of areal integration' (Haggett, 1965). This led to the association of areal differentiation with the particularity of regions at the expense of attention to more extensive geographical patterns and to the causes of such spatial distributions. Defining geography as a SPATIAL SCIENCE thus moved the field away from a central concern with regions as spatial clusters of linked phenomena.

In the 1980s areal differentiation made something of a comeback as a central perspective for human geography. The revival is neither directly connected to older debates such as those between Hartshorne and his critics nor is it monolithic. Indeed, there are at least three specific intellectual positions in the revival, none of which uses the same concepts or vocabulary as the others. The first derives from the streams of thought referred to collectively as HUMANISTIC GEOGRAPHY. Their focus on the social construction of spaces, on PLACE as the setting for human action, on SENSE OF PLACE and on the ICONOGRAPHY of landscape has given rise to an interest in the relationship between specific geographical contexts or LOCALES and social life in general (see, e.g., Tuan, 1977; Entrikin, 1990; Feld and Basso, 1996). The second source of revival has come from the analysis of UNEVEN DEVELOPMENT and the geography of LAYERS OF INVESTMENT often associated with the idea of a changing spatial DIVISION OF LABOUR. Rejecting the model of a geographically undifferentiated capitalism, a number of geographers have attempted to infuse into MARXIST GEOGRAPHY a concern for conjoining 'general processes' with 'particular circumstances' to explain spatial variations in economic activities and well-being (e.g. Massey, 1984; Smith, 1990). The third source of influence comes from attempts to create CONTEXTUAL THEORY in social science, in which the place or region is viewed as geographically mediating between HUMAN AGENCY and social structure and is thus implicated directly in the production of society (Agnew, 1987). Versions of STRUCTURATION THEORY and TIME-GEOGRAPHY have been particularly influential in defining this strand of revival in the tradition of areal differentiation (see Giddens, 1984).

The third strand could be seen as potentially integrative of the other two, in that it is at the same time concerned with both the subjective experience and the objective determinants of regions. But there are important philosophical differences between the three directions that limit the possibility of synthesis between them. (Although, for a recent magnificent attempt at engaging with all three simultaneously, see Sack, 1997.) The first direction tends to privilege the human subjective experience of place whereas the other two view the division of space in terms of objective socio-spatial processes with, for the third direction, sense of place arising out of the conditions created by such processes. The second and third part company over the second's insistence on associating general processes with the abstract and local contingencies with the concrete (Smith, 1987). The third rejects the conflation of the general with the abstract and the local with the concrete (see ABSTRACTION), preferring to see places and regions as contexts in which no single geographical scale is necessarily dominant a priori in their production.

Persisting dilemmas continue to limit convergence between the elements of the revival. One is the tension between analytical and narrative modes of thought and presentation (Sayer, 1989). Another has been the general lack of attention to the multi-scalar nature of the processes producing areal differentiation, with a given phenomenon (e.g. new jobs, unemployment, or votes for a political party) showing a different geographical level of aggregation in different time periods because of the shifting balance of local and extra-local influences (see SCALE) (Agnew, 1996; Swyngedouw, 1997). This is a particular problem for those LOCALITY studies that remain transfixed by the local. The final and most challenging dilemma remains that of how to achieve neat BOUNDARY delimitation when the TERRITORIALITY of social groups is dynamic and flows of people, goods, and investment change the character of regions and places from one era to another (e.g. McDowell, 1997). (See also CHOROGRAPHY.) JAA

References

Agnew, J.A. 1987: *Place and politics: the geographical mediation of state and society*. London: Allen and Unwin. · Agnew, J.A. 1989: Sameness and difference: Hartshorne's *The nature of geography* and geography as areal variation. In J.N. Entrikin and S.D. Brunn, eds, *Reflections on Richard Hartshorne's The nature of geography*. Washington, D.C.: Association of American Geographers, 121–39. · Agnew, J.A. 1996: Mapping politics: how context counts in electoral geography. *Political Geography* 15: 129–46. · Claval, P. 1993: *Initiation à la géographie régionale*. Paris: Editions Nathan (English translation by Ian Thompson published by Blackwell: Oxford, 1998). · Entrikin, J.N. 1990: *The betweenness of place: towards a geography of modernity*. Baltimore, MD: Johns Hopkins University Press. · Feld, S. and Basso, K.H. 1996: *Senses of place*. Santa Fe, NM: School of American Research Press. · Giddens, A. 1984: *The constitution of society*. Cambridge: Polity Press. · Haggett, P. 1965: *Locational analysis in human geography*. London: Edward Arnold. · Hartshorne, R. 1939: *The nature of geography: a critical survey of current thought in the light of the past*. Lancaster, PA: Association of American Geographers. · Massey, D. 1984: *Spatial divisions of labour: social structures and the geography of production*. London: Macmillan. · McDowell, L., ed., 1997: *Undoing place? a geographical reader*. London: Edward Arnold. · Sack, R.D. 1997: *Homo geographicus: a framework for action. awareness and moral concern*. Baltimore, MD: Johns Hopkins University Press. · Sayer, R.A. 1989: The 'new' regional geography and problems of narrative. *Environments and Planning D: Society and Space* 7: 23–76. · Smith, N. 1987: Dangers of the empirical turn: some comments on the CURS initiative. *Antipode* 19: 59–68. · Smith, N.

1990: *Uneven development: nature, capital, and the production of space*, 2nd edn. Oxford: Blackwell. · Swyngedouw, E. 1997: Excluding the Other: the production of scale and scaled politics. In R. Lee and J. Wills, eds, *Geographies of economies*. London: Edward Arnold, 167–76. · Tuan, Y.-F. 1977: *Space and place: the perspective of experience*. Minneapolis: University of Minnesota Press.

Suggested Reading

Agnew, J., Livingstone, D.N. and Rogers, A., eds, 1996: *Human geography: an essential anthology*. Oxford: Blackwell, 366–512. · Entrikin, J.N. and Brunn, S.D., eds, 1989: *Reflections on Richard Hartshorne's The nature of geography*. Washington, D.C.: Association of American Geographers. · Hartshorne (1939). · McDowell (1997).

art, geography and A relationship with art is implicit in the meaning of 'geography' – earth description (*graphos*) – although this begs the question of art as practical skill and art as imaginative creation. Claudius Ptolemy, whose first-century text *The Geography* so influenced early modern geographical thinking, distinguished 'geography' from 'CHOROGRAPHY' – the former a mathematical science, the latter, which incorporated REGIONAL description, more closely related to art in its embrace of pictorial REPRESENTATION and imaginative appeal. Ptolemy's claim that chorography required the skills of the painter provided theoretical grounds for chorographies in early modern Europe, which combined written topographical and historical description with graphic images of LANDSCAPE (Cosgrove, 1999). Written chorography is a source for literary celebration of regional character, for example in poetry and novels, while chorographic art developed into both TOPOGRAPHICAL MAPPING and landscape painting. At the regional and local level, therefore, geography has always been closely connected to artistic representation. While the closest links remain with graphic arts, contemporary geographers are exploring other arts, including literature, music and dance (see PERFORMANCE).

As a cultural expression of MODERNITY, geography since the fifteenth century has shared the EPISTEMOLOGICAL fixation with optics and accurate graphic representation on which western art and science have converged (Kemp, 1990). During the period of European oceanic EXPLORATION and NATION-building, geographical knowledge was closely dependent upon graphic skills: visual survey and recording through sketching and draughting; eighteenth-century military topographers and surveyors such as Paul Sandby were also artists of merit (Smith, 1985; Stafford, 1984). Landscape gardening and architecture offer another field of contact between geographical science and design in which aesthetics is prominent. Nineteenth-century critics and designers such as John Ruskin in Britain, Violet-le-Duc in France, Andrew Jackson Downing and Frederick Olmstead in the USA studied landscape as a moral and aesthetic expression of socio-environmental relations, sharing the foundational problem of disciplinary geography at that time (Cosgrove, 1998 [1984], pp. 241–53). For their part, the German scientists Alexander von Humboldt and Friedrich Ratzel, important architects of the modern geographical discipline, regarded landscape aesthetics as a central intellectual concern. As Humboldt's study of landscape art in *Kosmos* (1849) indicates, the Romantic imagination was fundamentally geographical, transferring aesthetic sublimity from God to the physical world: to mountains, oceans, and wild places (cf. WILDERNESS), although geography's Romantic inheritance has only recently been subjected to critical reflection, with studies of landscape painting, literature and MUSIC in the construction and expression of nineteenth-century Romantic NATIONALISM and TERRITORIALITIES (Daniels, 1993). In the early twentieth century, artists maintained close association with many aspects of geographical enquiry, education and representation. In Germany an 'aesthetic geography' was promoted by Ewald Banse, in the USA Carl Sauer (1925) acknowledged an aesthetic dimension – 'beyond science' – to his landscape studies, while in Britain, the *Geographical Magazine* carried an inter-war series on British landscape painting. The chorographic connection between MAP and painting was revived in popular editions of national topographic surveys catering for the boom in outdoor leisure activity. In Italy the publications of the *Touring Club Italiano* exploited art photography to promote TOURISM and popular geographical appreciation of the strategic Alpine borderlands, while in Britain the illustrator Martin Ellis designed iconic images of English landscape for popular Ordnance Survey map sheets (cf. CARTOGRAPHY; CARTOGRAPHY, HISTORY OF). The widely influential Regional Survey movement of the interwar years emphasized observation and sketching in geographical education for CITIZENSHIP, graphic techniques closely associated with landscape art (Matless, 1991). Training in such skills, as in the aesthetic appreciation of cartographic images, remained part of geographical education into the 1960s.

Post-war redefinition of geography as a SPATIAL SCIENCE based on POSITIVISM weakened disciplinary links to the humanities generally and to art in particular, despite occasional pleas for the study of imaginative geographies in literature and painting and such contributions as the Italian Emilio Sereni's 1960s use of painting as the principal source for his historical geography of landscape, establishing a tradition represented in Greppi's recent studies of Tuscany (Greppi, 1990, 1991, 1993). Connecting this approach to a broader humanist critique of spatial science, Cosgrove (1998 [1984]) used painting as a medium through which CULTURAL GEOGRAPHY could trace the interconnections of landscape change and modernity in the West. Others have reconsidered the artistic expression of local and regional consciousness, for example 'Common Ground' parish maps in Britain or minority cultures in the United States such as the Hispanic tradition of mural art. Theoretical study of relations between art and geography has led to consideration of the virtual spaces of painting itself, for studies of linear perspective, and of relations between representational and actual spaces. Critique of vision and representational strategies developed within recent art history, film and media studies, especially from FEMINIST perspectives, has been pursued also within geography. The implications of the *gaze* as a distanciated mode of establishing authority over space and its occupants have been systematically examined and criticized (Deutsche, 1991; Rose, 1993). Modernist attempts by various twentieth-century art movements to collapse the boundaries between art and everyday life, especially French SITUATIONIST interest in subversive forms of 'mapping' the streets and spaces of the modern metropolis, offer an obvious theme for geographical investigation (Pinder, 1996).

The radical claims of contemporary art and the attachment of many artists to ideals of community art and involvement have also attracted the interest of geographers. While occasional geographers, such as S. Quoniam (1988), have been practising artists, more have begun to work closely with professional artists in mounting exhibitions and writing catalogue essays or commentaries (Prendergast, 1997; Nash, 1998; Matless and Revill, 1995). From a different political standpoint, both commercial enterprises and public authorities have placed increasing emphasis on public art in the form of landscaping, commissioned murals and sculpture, and have recognized the significance of visual images in advertising, promotion and place selling. These strategies and the resulting artistic images have been the subject of critical geographical investigation of POSTMODERNISM. David Harvey's (1989) analysis of POSTMODERNITY opened a lively debate within geography and beyond on the increasing significance of style and decoration in contemporary architectural and urban discourse.

The ICONOGRAPHY of individual art works has been examined geographically in order to pursue themes of place making and negotiating spatial meanings and IDENTITIES. Initially such interpretations tended to focus on architecture and painted images, but there has been a marked concentration more recently on MONUMENTS and memorials in studies of the role of art in constructing and identifying spaces and SPATIALITIES within the public realm. Geographers studying the visual arts are also giving increased attention to photography, cinema and advertising, previously neglected in favour of a concentration on fine art oil and watercolour images. The place of visual representations, past and present, from maps to computer images, in the construction of geographical knowledge is a subject of critical concern to many geographers today while the dissolution of disciplinary boundaries has encouraged increased dialogue between practising artists and geographers over matters of spatial experience, mapping and imaging.

Current focus on geography and art reflects the broader 'CULTURAL TURN' within geography (see CULTURAL GEOGRAPHY) and its emphasis on the critical examination of representation and representational strategies for understanding geographical space and spatialities. At the same time, the enormously expanded significance both of the arts and arts-related industries within the post-industrial economy and of graphic images in a media society provide ample external justification for increased research attention to geography and art. DEC

References

Cosgrove, D. 1998 [1984]: *Social formation and symbolic landscape*, 2nd edn. Madison, WI: University of Wisconsin University Press. · Cosgrove, D., ed., 1999: *Mappings*. London: Reaktion Books. · Daniels, S. 1993: *Fields of vision: landscape imagery and national identity in England and the United States*. Cambridge: Polity Press. · Deutsche, R. 1991: Boys Town. *Environment and Planning D: Society and Space* 9: 5–30. · Greppi, C., ed., 1990, 1991, 1993: *Paesaggi dell'Appennino toscano*; *Paesaggi delle colline toscane*; *Paesaggi della costa toscana*. Venezia: Marsilio. · Harvey, D. 1989: *The condition of postmodernity: an enquiry into the origins of cultural change*. Oxford: Blackwell. · Humboldt, A. von 1849: *Kosmos: a sketch of a physical description of the universe*, vol. 2, trans. E.C. Otte. London: Henry G. Bolin. · Kemp, M. 1990: *The science of art: optical themes in western art from*

Brunelleschi to Seurat. New Haven and London: Yale University Press. · Matless, D. 1991: Nature, the modern and the mystic: tales from early twentieth-century geography. *Transactions, Institute of British Geographers* 16: 272–86. · Matless, D. and Revill, G. 1995: A solo ecology: the erratic art of Andy Goldsworthy. *Ecumene* 2: 432–48. · Nash, C. 1998: Mapping emotion. *Environment and Planning D: Society and Space* 16: 1–9. · Pinder, D. 1996: Subverting cartography: the situationists and maps of the city. *Environment and Planning A: Society and Space* 28: 405–27. · Prendergast, K. 1997: Lost. *Environment and Planning D: Society and Space* 15: 663–80. · Quoniam, S. 1988: A painter, geographer of Arizona. *Environment and Planning D: Society and Space* 6: 3–14. · Rose, G. 1993: *Feminism and geography: the limits of geographical knowledge*. Cambridge: Polity Press. · Sauer, C.O. 1925: The morphology of landscape. *University of California Publications in Geography* 2: 19–54. · Smith, B. 1985: *European vision and the South Pacific*, 2nd edn. New Haven and London: Yale University Press. · Stafford, B. 1984: *Voyage into substance: art, science, nature and the illustrated travel account, 1760–1840*. Cambridge, MA and London: MIT Press; von Humboldt, A. 1848–58: *Kosmos: a sketch of a physical description of the universe*, 5 vols. London: Henry G. Bohn.

Suggested Reading

Cosgrove (1998). · Harvey (1989). · Nash (1998). · Ryan, J. 1997: *Picturing Empire: photography and the visualization of the British Empire*. London: Reaktion Books. · Pinder (1996).

artificial intelligence Emulation of the intelligence of the human mind in a computing system. Since the earliest days of computing parallels have been drawn between the operation of a computer and that of the mind, and efforts have been made to find parallels at the neurophysiological level. Artificial intelligence has been advanced as a means of relieving humanity of many of its less demanding mental tasks; of making the abilities of highly talented individuals more widely available; and of capturing sophisticated human expertise in the form of a set of rules that can be applied routinely by a computer; EXPERT SYSTEMS are a form of artificial intelligence.

Many attempts have been made to apply methods of artificial intelligence to problems in human geography. Dobson (1983) wrote of 'automated geography', implying that many forms of routine geographical analysis, such as search for patterns or detection of anomalies, might be turned over to automated experts. Information on incidences of a disease might be analysed continuously with such 'geographical analysis machines', as soon as the data became available, allowing outbreaks to be detected much more rapidly. Today, the term *data mining* is often applied to this concept of rapid automated search through the masses of geographic data that are becoming available through REMOTE SENSING and other programmes. Stan Openshaw has been a staunch advocate of the use of artificial intelligence in geographical analysis (Openshaw and Openshaw, 1997).

Two recent developments in artificial intelligence have attracted particular attention in human geography. *Neural networks* are computer applications in which input data are assigned to a layer of simple processors. The output of these processors then becomes input to a second layer; some applications may include many such layers until finally the last layer provides the outputs. Because of the complex network of connections between processors, it is possible for a set of inputs to produce virtually any output. By modifying the internal connections a sufficiently large number of times, a neural network can be 'trained' to produce a required set of outputs from a given set of inputs. Neural networks have been applied to the automated classification of remotely sensed images, for example in assigning land-use classes to images based on the radiation received by the sensor. This is an extremely complex task even for a human, and there is very little THEORY available to guide the development of automated procedures. They have been used to build models of complex behavioural systems, such as shopping by consumers. Thus neural networks are appealing because of their ability to learn from a few observed instances, and because of the inherent flexibility in the nature of the connections that can be built between inputs and outputs. Neural networks are popular in other areas where the lack of theory makes this extremely general approach to modelling worthwhile (Fischer and Gopal, 1994; Miller et al., 1995).

Genetic algorithms also provide extremely rapid search capabilities over complex functional spaces, but use an analogy to biological evolution rather than to brain function, since evolution can be conceptualized as the process by which a population optimizes itself for an environment, driven by survival as the measure of success. Possible solutions are represented by strings in a suitable alphabet; at each iteration, pairs of solutions 'breed' other solutions by exchanging parts of their strings. In each iteration only the best solutions are retained, and over time the set of solutions steadily improves. Genetic algorithms have been applied to the solution of certain difficult problems in spatial OPTIMIZATION MODELS

(Hosage and Goodchild, 1986), where more conventional methods of search for optimum solutions prove unable to handle the complexity of the problem. For example, they can be used to search for suitable locations for several retail stores in a city, over possibly thousands of available sites, or for optimal tours through a set of destinations minimizing travel distance. MG

References

Dobson, J.E. 1983: Automated geography. *The Professional Geographer* 35 (2): 135–43. · Fischer, M.M. and Gopal, S. 1994: Artificial neural networks: a new approach to modeling inter-regional telecommunication flows. *Journal of Regional Science* 34 (4): 503–27. · Hosage, C.M. and Goodchild, M.F. 1986: Discrete space location-allocation solutions from genetic algorithms. *Annals of Operations Research* 6: 35–46. · Miller, D.M., Kaminsky, E.J. and Rana, S. 1995: Neural network classification of remote-sensing data. *Computers and Geosciences* 21 (3): 377–86. · Openshaw, S. and Openshaw, C. 1997: *Artificial intelligence in geography*. New York: Wiley.

Asiatic mode of production A MODE OF PRODUCTION involving a form of 'communal appropriation' which Marx and Engels believed to be especially characteristic of 'Asiatic societies'. In the most general terms it was supposed to be characterized by three absences:

- *the absence of private property* (especially in land, which was owned by a grossly engorged STATE);
- *the absence of a bourgeoisie*, whose role was replaced by a STATE APPARATUS that was able to appropriate a surplus from direct producers in the form of rents and taxes, by virtue of its centralized and often 'despotic' control over large-scale irrigation works on which communal subsistence depended (so-called 'hydraulic society'); and
- *the absence of a generative city*: direct producers lived in village communities which were 'self-sustaining' and 'compact wholes' with no developed social division of labour between them; any cities which did exist were essentially 'parasitic' creatures of the state with no direct involvement in production.

The primary purpose of this scheme was to account for the genesis of CAPITALISM in Europe. If these absences could explain what Marx and Engels (and many subsequent scholars) took to be the 'unchangeability' of non-capitalist societies in the East then it was assumed that their presence would explain the dynamism of capitalist societies in the West.

The key to the supposed stasis of the Asiatic mode of production was the relation between the state and the local community: between the self-reproducing villages 'below' and the hypertrophied state 'above' dwelt no intermediate forces. The impact of the state on the mosaic of villages beneath it was purely external and tributary; its consolidation or destruction alike left rural society untouched (Anderson, 1974, p. 483).

Hence, as Marx himself wrote: 'The structure of the economic elements of society remains untouched by the storm clouds of the political sky'. Theoretically, however, a major problem is precisely the place this accords to the state, for it presupposes yet does not explain 'a state which already exists and the imposition of state rule on a hitherto stateless people' (Hindess and Hirst, 1975, p. 201). But in his later writings Marx shifted his emphasis from 'above' to 'below', from the state to the local COMMUNITY, and in doing so sought to extend the concept of the Asiatic mode of production beyond the confines of Asia (Anderson, 1974). Empirically, even so, its application there is every bit as questionable as on its original terrain: 'The image of Asia stagnating for millennia in an unfinished transition from classless to class society, from barbarism to civilisation, has not stood up to the findings of archaeology and history in the East and the New World' (Godelier, 1978, p. 214).

Marx was right to emphasize the specificity of non-western societies, and hence in some part to qualify the unilinear view of social evolution which some commentators have seen in his work. But it is also clear that Marx's scheme was constructed on the ground-plan of EUROCENTRISM, and that his characterization of eastern societies as not merely different from western societies but as lacking something – as a mirror image of the positivities of western societies – was entirely typical of nineteenth-century ORIENTALISM. DG

References

Anderson, P. 1974: *Lineages of the absolutist state*. London: Verso. · Godelier, M. 1978: The concept of the 'Asiatic mode of production' and Marxist models of social evolution. In D. Seddon, ed., *Relations of production: Marxist approaches to economic anthropology*. London: Cass, 209–57. · Hindess, B. and Hirst, P.Q. 1975: *Pre-capitalist modes of production*. London: Routledge, ch. 4.

Suggested Reading

Anderson (1974), 462–549.

assimilation The process by which NATIONS or COMMUNITIES and the sub-nations or minorities within them intermix and became more similar. Terms with loosely comparable meaning include acculturation, adjustment and INTEGRATION. The degree of assimilation is a vital influence on the level of residential SEGREGATION and geographers have frequently studied the two processes as they relate to urban immigrants. Factors influencing the rate of assimilation include ETHNICITY, RELIGION, economic status, attitudes, EDUCATION and intermarriage. A distinction may be made between: *behavioural assimilation*, implying a process whereby the members of a group acquire the memories, sentiments and attitudes of other groups and, by sharing their experience and history, are incorporated with them in a common cultural life; and *structural assimilation*, referring to the distribution of migrant ethnics through the groups and social systems of a SOCIETY, including its system of occupational stratification. Differing political IDEOLOGIES may underlie notions of assimilation (see also MULTICULTURALISM). PEO

Suggested Reading

Boal, F.W. 1976: Ethnic residential segregation. In D.T. Herbert and R.J. Johnston, eds, *Social areas in cities*, volume I, *Spatial processes and forms*. Chichester: John Wiley, ch. 2; Drudy, P.J., ed., 1985: *The Irish in America: emigration, assimilation and impact*. Cambridge: Cambridge University Press; Gordon, M.M. 1964: *Assimilation in American life*. New York: Oxford University Press; Petersen, W. 1975: *Population*, 3rd edn. New York and London: Collier-Macmillan, ch. 4.

audience Those people watching or reading an IMAGE or TEXT. In a key paper, Burgess (1990) argues that there are four interconnected sites at which their meanings are made or remade: the *sites of the production*, where meanings are encoded; the *symbolic language* of the text or image; the *sites of CONSUMPTION* where audiences decode those meanings; and the *audiences' everyday lives*. Burgess (1990, p. 140) insists that 'there is no necessary equivalence between . . . sets of encodings and decodings', because, despite the structuring constraints of production and language, audiences bring their own understandings to an image or a text and may renegotiate the meanings made at other sites.

This emphasis is stressed in much work with television audiences. Morley (1986), for example, shows the ways in which specific audiences, themselves produced by relations of social IDENTITY such as CLASS, GENDER, RACE and SEXUALITY, as well as by the specific circumstances of their viewing or reading of a particular text or image, actively engage with televisual representations of those identities, sometimes affirming them and sometimes contesting them. Many studies of film audiences, however, have placed less emphasis on the social identity brought to the film and more on the subjectivity produced by it. Often drawing on aspects of semiotic and PSYCHOANALYTIC THEORY, discussions of film have examined the psychic pleasures and horrors offered to particular spectators by a film's visual and aural organization. However, more recently these two emphases have converged somewhat. Some writers are attempting to specify more carefully the socio-cultural specificity of psychic processes, while others advocate a theoretical concern with questions of subjective desire and fantasy as an antidote to the reification and reproduction of existing categories of social difference (Mayne, 1993). Geographers and others drawing on these debates have considered audiences' complex and sometimes contradictory engagement with the geographies represented by a text or image (Lutz and Collins, 1993), as well as the geographies through which the text or image is encountered (Friedberg, 1993). Some geographers have also considered the implications of these arguments for their own production of texts (Keith, 1992), arguing the need both to consider to which audiences a piece of work is addressed and to remember that the reactions of those audiences are not under the author's control. Nevertheless, Burgess's (1990) demand that geographers pay more attention to the audiences of texts and images still remains valid. (See also MEDIA, GEOGRAPHY OF; HERMENEUTICS; PERFORMANCE.) GR

References

Burgess, J. 1990: The production and consumption of environmental meanings in the mass media. *Transactions, Institute of British Geographers* NS 15: 139–61; Friedberg, A. 1993: *Window shopping: cinema and spectatorship*. Berkeley: University of California Press; Keith, M. 1992: Angry writing: (re)presenting the unethical world of the ethnographer. *Environment and Planning D: Society and Space* 10: 551–68; Lutz, C.A. and Collins, J.L. 1993: *Reading National Geographic*. Chicago: University of Chicago Press; Mayne, J. 1993: *Cinema and spectatorship*. London: Routledge; Morley, D. 1986: *Family television: cultural power and domestic leisure*. London: Comedia.

B

Balkanization The geopolitical fragmentation of a larger polity into increasingly smaller units that are hostile to one another (cf. GEOPOLITICS). The concept originates with the so-called nineteenth-century Balkan 'Great Game'. It involved both local STATES and continental powers in a geopolitical rivalry that became more global in its geopolitical implications, eventually plunging Europe into a world war and leading to the subsequent fragmentation of both the Ottoman and Hapsburg Empires. Contemporary analogies have been made with the break-up of post-1990 Yugoslavia and its ensuing civil and regional wars and with rival geopolitical interests in post-Soviet Transcaucasia. The term has also been used more loosely as a political METAPHOR to describe the disintegration of geopolitical alliances following the end of the Cold War and the possible fragmentation of polities into smaller territorial parts as a result of local demands for autonomy (cf. SELF-DETERMINATION). GES

Suggested Reading

Denitch, B. 1994: *Ethnic nationalism. The tragic death of Yugoslavia*. Minneapolis: University of Minnesota Press. · Mestrovic, S. 1994: *The Balkanization of the West. The consequences of postmodernism and postcommunism*. London and New York: Routledge.

barrio The Spanish term widely used in Latin America for SQUATTER SETTLEMENTS. RJJ

base/superstructure The dualism of base and superstructure was popularized by Stalin as a simplistic means of explaining the distinction between a society's ECONOMY (the 'base') and the political, legal, religious and artistic institutions and IDEOLOGIES that corresponded to a particular economic base (the 'superstructure').

The question of base and superstructure has been a favourite target for critics of Marxism. In its crudest forms, the base/superstructure distinction encouraged an economic determinism whereby the shape of social, political and cultural relations was narrowly determined by economics. This critique is widely accepted today, among Marxists and non-Marxists, perhaps because such a crude conceptual distinction has little if any basis in Marx's writing or that of most Marxist scholars. This distinction has never had a significant effect in geography. Although he never referred to base and superstructure, Marx did argue that in capitalist societies the economic logic of capital ACCUMULATION held considerable sway over the direction of social, political and cultural change. This becomes especially clear during periods of economic CRISIS, or among THIRD WORLD populations in perpetual crisis, where the social and political possibilities of many peoples' lives are severely circumscribed by economic constraints. But the relationship between economy and society is not causal or deterministic but dialectical, and it is precisely the point of Marx's critique that the economic logic of capitalist expansion has to be suspended as any kind of determinant of social relations. NS

behavioural geography An emphasis upon the psychology underpinning individual spatial behaviour that has emphasized the role of cognitive and decision-making factors that intervene in the relations between a multidimensional environment and human action; cognition in this sense is understood as the active mental process of learning about places (Downs and Stea, 1977). The development of SPATIAL ANALYSIS included initially some simple and deterministic assumptions concerning human behaviour. People were assumed to be both rational and optimizers in their actions (see RATIONAL CHOICE THEORY); translated to a spatial surface, this meant that they were above all concerned with the geographical law of least effort, distance minimization (cf. DISTANCE DECAY). With increasing empirical work, the simplicity of this fundamental postulate was steadily relaxed. First, STOCHASTIC or probabilistic processes were admitted to the analysis, as in Hägerstrand's (1968) seminal experiments with SIMULATION models that introduced a random variable into the distance parameters governing an otherwise deterministic spatial process of innovation DIFFUSION. A second modification was the replacement of the random variable by a set of cognitive variables. This advance gave rise to the wide-ranging subfield of behavioural geography.

Not the least interesting aspect of this development was geography's new-found affinity with psychology, an association anticipated in David Lowenthal's (1961) enormously influential paper on geographical experience and imagination. The association was nurtured at both ends, with the simultaneous rise of environmental psychology which found the traditional geographical commitment to fieldwork to be a valuable precedent as it grappled with behaviour outside strictly controlled laboratory settings (Spencer and Blades, 1986; Garling and Golledge, 1993). During the 1970s this productive interdisciplinary relationship developed through the annual meetings of the Environmental Design Research Association in the United States and in the pages of the new journal, *Environment and Behavior*. Only in the 1980s, as human geography turned beyond individual to social contexts of action, and to disciplinary links with sociology, did this relationship wane.

Research in behavioural geography advanced around several more or less independent themes. In LOCATIONAL ANALYSIS the influential research of organizational behaviour theorists such as Simon (1957) and Cyert and March (1963) introduced a more grounded emphasis on DECISION-MAKING to geographical studies. In an important paper, Wolpert (1964) showed that, for a sample of Swedish farmers, optimal farming practices were not attainable. He tested whether the farmers were indeed maximizing their utility functions, and were in possession of a complete stock of knowledge about available economic opportunities (cf. UTILITY THEORY). Finding that neither of these conditions was met, he concluded that the farmers were not optimizers but, in Simon's term, *satisficers* (see SATISFICING BEHAVIOUR). Not only did they lack complete knowledge and a perfect capacity for processing information, but there were other, and competing, VALUES and aspirations which they held, as well as the force of habit that diverted them from new opportunities. A related study of industrial location (Pred, 1967) struck even closer to the core of conventional spatial analysis, Once again, the conclusion was that satisficing, the art (as well as the science) of making do, provided the most appropriate description of corporate decision-making, and thus of subsequent geographical patterns.

The extent to which behavioural geography departed from the PARADIGM of spatial analysis was contested. For some authors, LOCATION THEORY was powerful enough to account for all but a 'residual domain' of spatial events, and 'this domain will presumably be colonised by a cognitive-behavioural location theory' (Harvey, 1969). But other authors saw the development of a cognitive-behavioural perspective in more substantial terms. In Olsson's (1969) oft-cited words, 'the earlier stress on the geometric outcome of the spatial game has lessened in favor of analyses of the rules which govern the moves of the actors who populate the gaming table'. Certainly, the decision-making rules of the actors were the major concern of a second influential body of research which examined the geography of ENVIRONMENTAL HAZARDS. For in this domain, non-rational behaviour was palpable, as residents and businesses chose locations that placed them at risk from such environmental hazards as river or sea floods, avalanches, and earthquakes. Why did such seemingly irrational locational behaviour occur? In some instances, site selection was the product of incomplete information as, for example, homeowners who had purchased property in seismically sensitive areas of California (Palm, 1981). In other instances it seemed that geographical information was interpreted through the filter of distinctive personality dispositions. Here, behavioural research was closest to psychology, and drew upon such personality measures as the thematic apperception test (TAT), skilfully employed by Saarinen (1966) in his study of Great Plains wheat farmers operating in a region of marginal drought conditions. (See also HAZARDS, HUMAN-MADE.)

The TAT was one of a battery of paper and pencil tests used to assess attitudes, a practice that has been a distinctive methodological feature of behavioural geography. The third major field of research, ENVIRONMENTAL PERCEPTION, employed a range of attitudinal scales including repertory grids and the semantic differential to evaluate the meaning of PLACES. The structured QUESTIONNAIRE was the fundamental research instrument. In his seminal study of MENTAL MAPS, for example, Gould asked college students to write down in rank order their residential preferences among different American states (Gould and White, 1974). More usually, geographers took their questionnaires out of the classroom and into the field as they probed the perceptions of such disparate phenomena as shopping centres, recreational sites, or dangerous streets.

Since the 1970s behavioural research in human geography and related interdisciplinary fields has multiplied in such traditional domains as COGNITIVE MAPPING (Kitchin,

1994), environmental learning (Golledge et al., 1995), spatial SEARCH BEHAVIOUR (Clark, 1993) and developmental issues in spatial cognition (Kirasic, 1991), and CARTOGRAPHY (Liben and Downs, 1989), as well as contributing to new research fields including wayfinding among the disabled (Golledge 1993), on which a review collected some 600 citations (Golledge and Timmermans, 1990; Timmermans and Golledge, 1990; also Golledge and Stimson, 1997 – cf. DISABILITY, GEOGRAPHY AND). But in certain respects, despite its range, behavioural geography has become increasingly homogeneous, at least methodologically. Early contributions maintained considerable methodological diversity, employing techniques that included such qualitative methods as PARTICIPANT OBSERVATION (Brookfield, 1969). In such a cognitive-behavioural approach, Mercer and Powell (1972) anticipated a contribution that would 'preserve and foster a "humanist" alternative to the popular mechanistic explanation'. That diversity has given way to a more squarely analytical methodology predicated upon a POSITIVIST philosophy of science favoured by both spatial analysis and psychology (but see Couclelis and Golledge, 1983). As Harvey (1969) predicted, behavioural geography became 'an appendage' of the locational school and as such was irreversibly shaped by the QUANTITATIVE REVOLUTION, developing a preoccupation with MEASUREMENT, statistical analysis and a highly formalized methodology.

But does such a repertoire deal adequately with the realm of human consciousness and intersubjective realms (Ley, 1981; Lowenthal, 1987)? For, as Olsson (1974) has observed, in the realm of hopes and fears, two times two is not always equal to four. A second criticism has been directed against the intrusive nature of behavioural methodology, which either operates in a simplified quasi-laboratory format or else disrupts the flow of spontaneous action in the field and controls the nature of response in its use of formalized research instruments. Such intrusion systematically removes the contexts which give meaning to events and actions. Perhaps the most serious severance of context is the manner in which questionnaires, administered to individuals, remove the social context in which decisions are made, and where actions originate.

As human geography shares something of a post-positivist scepticism of highly formal scientific methods, the criticisms of behavioural geography have assumed greater weight. To earlier criticisms another may be advanced: To what extent is research that is predicated upon a philosophy of observation able to discern realities which are not directly observable? Where do the contextual forces of IDEOLOGY and social structure fit in a research programme concerned with the behaviour of individuals? These questions (and others) extend also to allusions by some geographers to PSYCHOANALYTIC THEORY, which would seem to represent a more structural approach to individual behaviour. An attempt to address some of these questions appears in Golledge and Stimson's (1997) massive codification of behavioural geography. The book's ambitious range and detail guarantee that this entry is far from an obituary. Besides leaving the discipline with some significant concepts like mental maps, MEAN INFORMATION FIELDS, TIME-GEOGRAPHY and spatial search, behavioural geography continues its task to clarify 'the decision-making processes of individuals, groups, and institutions in a spatial context' (Golledge and Stimson, 1997, p. 1). (See also HUMAN AGENCY; HUMANISTIC GEOGRAPHY.)

DL

References

Brookfield, H. 1969: On the environment as perceived. *Progress in Human Geography* 1: 51–80. · Clark, W.A.V. 1993: Search and choice in urban housing markets. In T. Garling and R.G. Golledge, eds, *Behaviour and environment: psychological and geographical approaches*. Amsterdam: Elsevier, 298–316. · Couclelis, H. and Golledge, R.G. 1983: Analytic research, positivism and behavioral geography. *Annals of the Association of American Geographers*. 73: 531–9. · Cyert, R. and March, J. 1963: *A behavioral theory of the firm*. Englewood Cliffs, NJ: Prentice-Hall. · Downs, R. and Stea, D. 1977: *Maps in minds: reflections on cognitive mapping*. New York: Harper and Row. · Garling, T. and Golledge, R.G., eds, 1993: *Behavior and environment: psychological and geographical approaches*. Amsterdam: Elsevier. · Golledge, R.G. 1993: Geography and the disabled: a survey with special reference to vision impaired and blind populations. *Transactions, Institute of British Geographers* NS 18: 63–85. · Golledge, R.G. and Stimson, R. 1997: *Spatial behavior: a geographic perspective*. New York: Guilford Press. · Golledge, R.G. and Timmermans, H. 1990: Applications of behavioral research on spatial problems I: cognition, *Progress in Human Geography* 14: 57–99. · Golledge, R.G., Dougherty, V. and Bell, S. 1995: Acquiring spatial knowledge: survey versus route-based knowledge in unfamiliar environments. *Annals Association American Geographers* 85: 134–58. · Gould, P.R. and White, R. 1974: *Mental maps*. London: Penguin. · Hägerstrand, T. 1968: *Innovation diffusion as a spatial process*. Chicago: University of Chicago Press. · Harvey, D. 1969: Conceptual and measurement problems in the cognitive-behavioral approach to location theory. In K.R. Cox and R.G. Golledge, eds, *Behavioral problems in geography*. Evanston, Ill.: Northwestern Studies in Geography no. 17: 35–67. · Kirasic, K.

1991: Spatial cognition and behavior in young and elderly adults: implications for learning new environments. *Psychology and Aging* 6: 1–18. · Kitchin, R. 1994: Cognitive maps: what are they and why study them? *Journal of Environmental Psychology* 14: 1–19. · Ley, D. 1981: Behavioral geography and the philosophies of meaning. In K.R. Cox, and R.G. Golledge, eds, *Behavioral problems in geography revisited*. London: Methuen, 209–30. · Liben, L. and Downs, R.M. 1989: Understanding maps as symbols: the development of map concepts in children. *Advances in Child Development and Behavior* 22: 145–201. · Lowenthal, D. 1961: Geography, experience and imagination: towards a geographical epistemology. *Annals of Association of American Geographers* 51: 241–60. · Lowenthal, D. 1987: Environmental perception: an odyssey of ideas. *Journal of Environmental Psychology* 7: 337–46. · Mercer, D. and Powell, J.M. 1972: *Phenomenology and related non-positivistic approaches in the social sciences*. Department of Geography, Monash University, Publications no. 1. · Olsson, G. 1969: Inference problems in locational analysis. In K.R. Cox, and R.G. Golledge, eds, pp. 14–34. · Olsson, G. 1974: The dialectics of spatial analysis. *Antipode* 6 (3): 50–62. · Palm, R. 1981: Public response to earthquake hazard information. *Annals Association of American Geographers* 71: 389–99. · Pred, A. 1967: *Behavior and location*. Lund Studies in Geography, Series B, no. 27. · Saarinen, T. 1966: *Perception of drought hazard on the Great Plains*. University of Chicago, Department of Geography, Research paper no. 106. · Simon, H. 1957: *Models of man*. New York: John Wiley. · Spencer C. and Blades, M. 1986: Pattern and process: a review essay on the relationship between behavioural geography and environmental psychology. *Progress in Human Geography* 10: 230–48. · Timmermans, H. and Golledge, R.G. 1990: Applications of behavioural research on spatial problems II: preference and choice. *Progress in Human Geography* 14: 311–54. · Wolpert, J. 1964: The decision process in spatial context. *Annals of the Association of American Geographers* 54: 537–58.

Suggested Reading

Cox, F. and Golledge, R., eds, 1981: *Behavioral problems in geography revisited*. London: Methuen. · Golledge and Stimson (1997). · Spencer and Blades (1986).

Berkeley School Although there has been some dispute about whether it constitutes a school of CULTURAL GEOGRAPHY, there is little question that American cultural geography was dominated until the 1980s by Carl Sauer, his colleagues at Berkeley and their students. It was most certainly a school in the sense that there existed a coherent set of interests and approaches to research. While this type of cultural geography is no longer important in Berkeley, it remains a research tradition carried on by former Berkeley students and their students scattered throughout the world. Among the better known of Sauer's students are Andrew Clark, William Denevan, Fred Kniffen, Marvin Mikesell, James Parsons, David Sopher, Philip Wagner, and Wilbur Zelinsky.

Arguably no geographer had more influence on American geography in the twentieth century than Carl Sauer. He received his Ph.D. in 1915 from the University of Chicago, where he came under the influence of the ENVIRONMENTAL DETERMINISM of Ellen Churchill Semple. In 1923 he moved to Berkeley and under the influence of the anthropologists A.L. Kroeber and R.H. Lowie was exposed to a concept of CULTURE which was to replace his earlier environmentalist ideas (Leighley, 1976). In 1925 Sauer (1963) wrote what is perhaps his best-known work, 'The MORPHOLOGY of LANDSCAPE', which strongly denounced environmental determinism and suggested a method by which cultural geographers should proceed in their field studies.

Shortly after arriving at Berkeley, Sauer developed what was to become a life-long interest in Latin America, and there remains a strong connection with that region in the work of subsequent generations of his students. During the 1930s he also developed increasingly strong ties with biological scientists, describing himself as 'an earth scientist with a slant towards biogeography of which man is a part' (Leighley, 1976). These interests culminated in his monograph, *Agricultural origins and dispersals* (1952).

During the last twenty years of his life, Sauer pursued two broad, rather speculative historical themes. The first was palaeographic and focused on such questions as early human's use of fire, the seashore as a primeval habitat, and primeval man as a peaceful gatherer rather than exclusively a hunter. The second theme was the condition of America when the Europeans encountered it. He published four books on this theme, of which the best known is *The early Spanish main* (1966).

While giving Sauer his due as a creative scholar and founder of American cultural geography, it must be remembered that most of the ideas that he introduced into the field: historical reconstruction, CULTURE AREA, DIFFUSION, were current at the time in German geography and American cultural anthropology. His intellectual debt to Ratzel, Schluter, Hahn and Kroeber was immense. Sauer and his students placed a greater emphasis upon human relationships with the physical environment than did the anthropologists, whose interests not only included human–environment relations but also behaviour more generally.

Wagner and Mikesell (1962) provide what is still thought of as the most useful summation of the nature of Berkeley cultural geography: they define cultural geography as 'the application of the idea of culture to geographic problems'. One can identify three principal themes which define the work of the Berkeley school.

The first is *the diffusion of culture traits*. Cultural geographers, like cultural anthropologists from the 1920s through the 1940s, favoured explanation in terms of the diffusion of culture traits rather than independent invention to account for the development of cultures. Sauer was particularly interested in tracing the spread of plants and animals while others have examined such things as house types, names, and ideas as indicators of the diffusion of cultural traits (Kniffen, 1965).

The second theme is *the identification of culture regions* through material and non-material traits (cf. SEQUENT OCCUPANCE). This theme enjoyed great popularity in American anthropology until the 1940s and continued to be important in cultural geography to the present. CULTURE AREAS were identified by plotting the distribution of material and non-material traits such as building types, ploughs, animals, magazine subscriptions, language, religion and ethnicity (Zelinsky, 1973).

The third theme is *CULTURAL ECOLOGY*, usually studied in historical perspective. Attention was focused on how perception and use of the environment is culturally conditioned.

It has been argued that the Berkeley School adopted a reified superorganic conception of culture from the anthropologist A.L. Kroeber (Duncan, 1980; but see Price and Lewis, 1993). Because of such a REIFIED notion of culture, the Berkeley geographers rarely felt the need to examine in detail the social or political organization of the societies they studied. JD

References

Duncan, J. 1980: The superorganic in American cultural geography. *Annals of the Association of American Geographers* 70: 181–98. · Duncan, J. 1994: After the civil war: reconstructing cultural geography as heterotopia. In K. Foote et al., eds, *Re-reading cultural geography*. Austin: University of Texas Press. · Kniffen, F.B. 1965: Folk housing: key to diffusion. *Annals of the Association of American Geographers* 55: 549–77. · Leighley, J. 1976: Carl Ortwin Sauer, 1889–1975. *Annals of the Association of American Geographers* 66: 337–48. · Price, M. and Lewis, M. 1993: The reinvention of cultural geography. *Annals of the Association of American Geographers* 83: 1–17. · Sauer, C.O. 1952: *Agricultural origins and dispersals*. New York: American Geographical Society. · Sauer, C.O. 1963: The morphology of landscape. In J. Leighley, ed., *Land and life: selections from the writings of Carl Ortwin Sauer*. Berkeley: University of California Press, 315–50. · Sauer, C.O. 1966: *The early Spanish main*. Berkeley: University of California Press. · Wagner, P.L. and Mikesell, M.W., eds, 1962: *Readings in cultural geography*. Chicago: University of Chicago Press. · Zelinsky, W. 1973: *The cultural geography of the United States*. Englewood Cliffs, NJ: Prentice-Hall.

Suggested Reading

Sauer (1963). · Wagner and Mikesell (1962).

bid-rent curve A plot of the rent which people are prepared to pay against distance from some point, usually the city centre. Rent bids generally decrease with increasing distance from a city or its centre where land values are highest, so a bid-rent curve slopes down in a diagram with rent on the vertical axis and distance displayed horizontally (see Alonso model, p. 21). The curve is sometimes shown as convex to the origin of the graph, to reflect sharp decreases in rent with short distances from the city (centre), levelling off with increasing distance. Bid-rent curves are an important element in the ALONSO MODEL of urban land use and in the VON THÜNEN MODEL of agricultural land use. DMS

bifurcation A change in the solution to a differential or difference equation at a critical value of a MODEL's parameter. Three types of change are common (see figure): (a) a 'jump' in the relationship between x and t at a critical value of $t(t_c)$, shown in the figure as a discontinuous 'step function'; (b) a shift from a linear relationship at t_c to a periodic one; and (c) a shift at t_c from a linear to a chaotic relationship. (See also CHAOS and CATASTROPHE THEORY: the latter covers a special case of the general features of bifurcation.)

Bifurcations are common in models of SYSTEMS involving interdependence among the variables, especially if those interrelationships are nonlinear. These are common in environmental science but are also typical of some aspects of human geography: 'jumps' may characterize the crossing of critical thresholds in the relationship between the percentage of the votes cast and the percentage of the seats won by a political party in first-past-the-post electoral systems, for example, whereas transitions to chaos may occur in the process of population change over time in a society which has reached the CARRYING CAPACITY of its land. RJJ

Suggested Reading

Wilson, A.G. 1981: *Catastrophe theory and bifurcation: applications to urban and regional systems.*

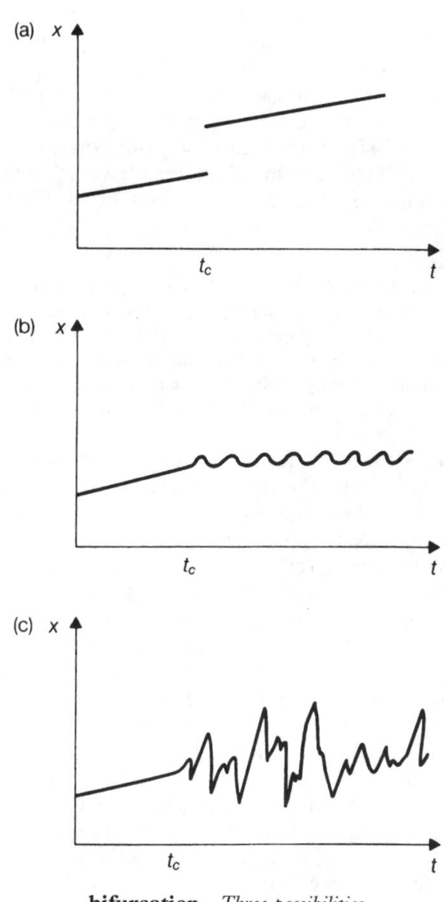

bifurcation *Three possibilities*

London: Croom Helm; Berkeley: University of California Press

biodiversity Biodiversity is an abbreviation of 'biological diversity'; it is generally understood simply as conserving genes, species and ecosystems (Beder, 1996; Diesendorf, 1997).

The Convention on Biological Diversity, presented at the United Nations Conference on Environment and Development (UNCED) in 1992 (see SUSTAINABLE DEVELOPMENT), defined biological diversity as (see Shiva, 1993, p. 163):

> the variability among living organisms from all sources including, inter alia, terrestrial, marine and other aquatic ecosystems and the ecological complexes of which they are a part; this includes diversity within species, between species and of ecosystems.

This convention was signed by 153 countries at UNCED in Rio de Janeiro. The then President of the USA, George Bush, refused to sign the convention because of apparent concern about property rights from biotechnology companies in the USA, but his successor, Clinton, did sign. The convention has now been signed by 163 states (Osborn and Bigg, 1998) and quickly received the necessary thirty signatures for ratification; it came into effect in December 1993 (McConnell, 1997).

Biodiversity is a concern because of awareness of our limited knowledge of the earth's biological diversity, but realization that it is being destroyed. Extinctions are now occurring at a faster rate than in the past due to contemporary agricultural and forestry practices, the destruction of habitats, POLLUTION in ECOSYSTEMS and the introduction of non-native species which eradicate an area's indigenous species.

Biodiversity is important for a number of reasons. ECOLOGICALLY, it focuses attention on habitat CONSERVATION, ecosystems and the importance of all plants and animals. It directs attention away from viewing 'charismatic megafauna' (e.g. pandas) out of their ecological context. Maintaining biological and cultural diversity is seen as increasing the chances of survival, whereas monoculture is perceived as being vulnerable to disease and other threats (Shiva, 1993, 1995). Tropical rainforests and coral reefs are particularly 'rich' in biological diversity, thereby justifying their conservation and PRESERVATION through measures such as NATIONAL PARKS.

Scientifically, focusing on biodiversity helps conserve 'genetic material' for future generations to learn about life on earth. However, economically this is often conflated with corporations taking the biological resources from one part of the world to a science laboratory located elsewhere, and then patenting the 'new' product they claim to have created via biotechnology. It is sometimes claimed that the growth of biotechnology enhances biodiversity, but Shiva (1993, 1995) argues that it reduces it by introducing a common gene into many species, or by marginalizing less economically profitable species in favour of the genetically engineered variety (e.g. apples, cattle breeds).

Politically, biodiversity is controversial because most of the 'biological wealth' is located in the so-called developing countries, while most of the corporations, science laboratories and existing gene pools are located in the richer so-called developed countries. The 1992 Convention of Biological Diversity failed to address the 'theft' of biological resources that developing countries claim has occurred since colonialism. In contrast, developed countries have argued that biodiversity is part of the 'global commons' for the benefit of humankind, regardless of where it is located (cf. TRAGEDY OF THE COMMONS). PM

References

Beder, S. 1996: *The nature of sustainable development*, 2nd edn. Newham (Australia): Scribe Publications. · Diesendorf, M. 1997: Principles of ecological sustainability. In M. Diesendorf and C. Hamilton, eds, *Human ecology, human economy*. St. Leonards (Sydney): Allen and Unwin, 64–97. · McConnell, F. 1997: The Convention on Biodiversity. In F. Dodds, ed., *The way forward: beyond Agenda 21*. London: Earthscan, 47–54. · Osborn, D. and Bigg, T. 1998: *Earth Summit II: outcomes and analysis*. London: Earthscan. · Shiva, V. 1993: *Monocultures of the mind: perspectives on biodiversity and biotechnology*. London and New Jersey/Penang (Malaysia): Zed Books/Third World Network. · Shiva, V. 1995: Biotechnological development and the conservation of biodiversity. In V. Shiva and I. Moser, eds, *Biopolitics: a feminist and ecological reader on biotechnology*. London and New Jersey/Penang (Malaysia): Zed Books/Third World Network, 193–213.

Suggested Reading

Dobson, A. 1996: *Conservation and biodiversity*. New York: Scientific American Library Book. · Shiva, V. 1997: *Biopiracy: the plunder of nature and knowledge*. Boston/Toronto: South End Press/Between the Lines.

biopower A neologism coined by the French thinker Michel Foucault (1926–84) in his book *The history of sexuality, volume 1* (1978) to describe a new 'power over life' which emerged in Europe between the seventeenth and nineteenth centuries. Biopower consists of 'diverse techniques for achieving the subjugation of bodies and the control of populations'. Foucault examined disciplinary – 'micro-physical' – techniques that accustomed the body and mind to SURVEILLANCE, self-regulation and the 'anatomical performances' required by the factory system. He also discussed biological, economic and political – 'macro-physical' – configurations of the 'species-body' (the necessities, aptitudes and rhythms of populations), and STATE intervention in the fields of economic production and consumption, demography, public health and sexual behaviour. Foucault was especially interested in how moral–political questions about what it means 'to be a living species in a living world' were turned into instrumental-scientific ones about physical and mental needs and capacities. Foucault's account of biopower should be considered in relation to his broader thesis that power *produces individuals* and *places* them within webs of subjugation and regulation, rather than cages or represses some 'real' self that might be liberated from power (see GENEALOGY; GOVERNMENTALITY). Foucault worked in Europe and discussed biopower largely through the lexicons of SEXUALITY and CLASS, but commentators suggest that his arguments have a critical purchase in regard to questions of RACE and COLONIALISM (see Stoler, 1995). DC

References

Foucault, M. 1978: *The history of sexuality, vol. 1: An introduction*. Trans. Robert Hurley. New York: Random House, 133–59 (Orig. pub. Fr. 1976, *La volonté de savoir*). · Stoler, A. 1995: *Race and the education of desire: Foucault's* History of Sexuality *and the colonial order of things*. Durham and London: Duke University Press.

blockbusting An American term for the process whereby the racial composition of a residential block changes from white to black, usually as a consequence of actions by real estate agents (cf. INVASION AND SUCCESSION). Agents or speculators may trigger change by introducing a small number of black households to a block when vacancies arise, thereby putting pressure on the remaining white households, many of which may not welcome the prospect of a 'mixed neighbourhood'. Some may be panicked into selling their homes relatively cheaply, which the agents can then resell at higher prices to incoming blacks, making large profits through stimulating rapid neighbourhood change on the bases of fear and prejudice. RJJ

Suggested Reading

Ley, D.F. 1983: *A social geography of the city*. New York and London: Harper and Row.

body, geography and Whether TIME-GEOGRAPHY actually dealt with the body is a matter of dispute (Rose, 1993; Pile and Thrift, 1995). Certainly the body became an object of fascination in the 1990s – 'the body as a surface to be mapped, a surface for inscription, as a boundary between the individual subject and that which is Other to it, as the container of individual identity, but also as a permeable boundary which leaks and bleeds and is penetrable' (McDowell and Sharpe, 1997, p. 3). The reasons for this fascination are diverse: Martin (1992, 121) speculates that the roots are socio-economic, reflecting a 'dramatic transition in body percept and practice', which she locates in the transition from FORDIST mass production to the era of FLEXIBLE ACCUMULATION (and might also be located at the increasingly flexible boundary between body and machine: see CYBERSPACE; CYBORG).

But 'the body' is also at the centre of a number of contemporary theoretical and methodological influences and debates. It figures in Lefebvre's theorizing of the PRODUCTION OF SPACE: abstract space and practices of VISION AND VISUALITY diminish bodily experience and desire but the body is a key site for the continual disruption of abstract space. Foucault's theorizing of BIOPOWER and discourses of SEXUALITY articulate the body as a site and filter for diverse POWER relations. PSYCHOANALYTIC THEORY locates gender formation in the body (i.e. sexual difference) and IDENTITY formation in the stabilization of a bodily boundary; geographers have extended this psychoanalytic theorizing of boundary formation to understand processes of SOCIAL EXCLUSION (Pile, 1996; Sibley, 1995; see SUBJECT FORMATION, GEOGRAPHIES OF).

As a site of speculation, the body has enabled theorists to negotiate a range of troubling dualisms. Notions of biopower blur the distinction between the individual and the social. Feminist theorists have used the body to disrupt the dualisms between sex and gender; mind and body; and subject and object. By understanding the sexed body (either male or female) as discursively constructed out of polymorphous bodies, feminists such as Butler have unsettled a biological understanding of sex and the body (see PERFORMATIVITY and QUEER THEORY), and consequently the distinction between sex and gender (see GENDER AND GEOGRAPHY). Challenging the distinctions between mind and body, and between subject and object, has been one avenue for criticizing the MASCULINISM of the discipline of geography (Longhurst, 1997; Rose, 1993) and has led to methodological prescriptions for embodied or SITUATED KNOWLEDGE.

A point of debate focuses around whether or how to theorize a residual beyond DISCOURSE (and hence the relations between materiality and discourse). Theorists drawing on Merleau Ponty's philosophy frame the body as prediscursive (Young, 1990). Butler (1990) has criticized Foucault for reserving a prediscursive, unregulated body as a site of pleasure. Butler (1993) theorizes a residual in other terms; she argues that some part of subjectivity exceeds the surface of the body (is 'corporeally illegible'). Grosz (1995) opens up some analytical space by drawing on Deleuze's theorizing of the body as movement, arguing that this reverses the Foucauldian links between knowledge–power–bodies such that bodies can be seen as opening new knowledges (see NON-REPRESENTATIONAL THEORY).

These discussions only obliquely address a problem identified by Seager (1997), namely a seeming disregard for 'real' as opposed to representations of bodies; in levelling this criticism, Seager articulates a continuing point of tension between cultural and POLITICAL ECONOMY perspectives. We do, however, see attempts to mediate these tensions in geography: in discussions of how (raced) bodies define new oppositional spaces (e.g. Stewart, 1995), of how spaces constitute sexed bodies (e.g. McDowell and Court (1994) on the City of London; Nast and Pile, 1998), on the geopolitical effects of representations of masculinities and femininities (Nast, 1998) and in efforts to open what has been labelled an 'ableist' discipline to geographies of DISABILITY (Chouinard, 1997). GP

References

Butler, J. 1990: *Gender trouble: feminism and the subversion of identity.* New York: Routledge. · Butler, J. 1993: Critically queer. *GLQ* 1: 17–32. · Chouinard, V. 1997: Making space for disabling differences: challenging ableist geographies. *Environment and Planning D: Society and Space* 15: 379–87. · Grosz, L. 1995: *Space, time, and perversion.* New York: Routledge. · Longhurst, R. 1997: (Dis)embodied geographies. *Progress in Human Geography* 21: 486–501. · Martin, E. 1992: The end of the body? *American Ethnologist* 19: 121–40. · McDowell, L. and Court, G. 1994: Performing work: bodily representations in merchant banks. *Environment and Planning D: Society and Space* 12: 727–50. · McDowell, L. and Sharpe, J., eds, 1997: *Space, gender, knowledge.* London: Arnold. · Nast, H. 1998: Unsexy geographies. *Gender Place and Culture* 5: 191–206. · Nast, H. and Pile, S. 1998: *Places through the body.* London: Routledge. · Pile, S. 1996: *The body and the city: psychoanalysis, space and subjectivity.* London: Routledge. · Pile, S. and Thrift, N., eds, 1995: *Mapping the subject: geographies of cultural transformation.* London: Routledge. · Rose, G. 1993: *Feminism and Geography: the limits of geographical knowledge.* Cambridge: Polity Press. · Seager, J. 1997: Reading the morning paper, and on throwing out the body with the bathwater. *Environment and Planning A* 29: 1521–23. · Sibley, D. 1995: *Geographies of exclusion.* London: Routledge. · Stewart, L. 1995: Louisiana subjects: power, space and the slave body. *Ecumene: A Journal of Environment, Culture and Meaning* 2: 227–46. · Young, I. 1990: *Throwing like a girl and other essays in feminist philosophy and social thought.* Indianapolis, IN: Indiana University Press.

borderland This has been identified as 'the governing trope of the postmodern' (Welchman, 1996, p. 175). It is a site for the production and disruption of 'difference' – especially between NATION-STATES, first and THIRD WORLDS, colonizer and colonized (see COLONIALISM and POSTCOLONIALISM). A number of influences focus attention on border construction, border crossing and border theory. These include: poststructural theories that stress the formation of identity at the border and through the construction of inside and outside (see ORIENTALISM; POST-STRUCTURALISM; SUBJECT FORMATION, GEOGRAPHIES OF), and shifting borders resulting from emerging REGIONALISMS, supranational organizations, and GLOBALIZATION and TRANSNATIONALISM.

The border of the NATION can be a site where displays of NATIONALISM are intensified to consolidate the nation-state (Radcliffe, 1998). The periphery may also be a place where state control is less stable (cf. CORE–PERIPHERY MODEL). In the Indonesian context, Tsing (1993) explores the simultaneous and contradictory production of the periphery of the nation (as marginal and primitive) as a means of consolidating the Javanese centre, and the instability of centralized STATE control in this periphery. Alternatively, or simultaneously, borderlands between nations 'tend historically to be zones of cultural overlap and political instability where the national identity and loyalties of the people often become blurred' (Augelli, 1980, p. 19) and can be places where regional cross-national identities dominate, for example: 'Mex-America is a distinct region. LA is the capital city of Mex-America' (Avalos and Welchman, 1996, p. 197). Anzaldua (1987) describes the dual perspective of the 'consciousness of the Borderlands', but holds the imaginative potential of borderlands (to produce hybridized *mestiza* – literally, mixed American Indian and Spanish ancestry – identities (see HYBRIDITY; THIRD SPACE) in close tension with histories of legal and illegal immigration and unequal relations between the US and Mexico, as well as other exclusions.

The supervision of national borders, and the borderlands of home and exile, of belonging and not belonging, are experienced and enacted at different SCALES and in different places – not just at the boundary of the nation; Harlow (1994) traces instances of border patrol through the prisons and racially-segregated neighbourhoods of the US, a patrol that speaks to the blurring of the boundary between US citizens and third-world populations, even as it re-enacts it.

Attempts have been made to rethink the meaning and potential of borders. Mouffe (1995) envisions the project of RADICAL DEMOCRACY as a perpetual questioning of borders that necessarily exclude; Haraway (1990) urges border wars that both take 'pleasure in the confusion of boundaries and . . . responsibility in their construction (p. 191) . . . We are responsible for boundaries; we are they' (p. 222). Emerging from these reconceptualizations is the border as 'a place of feedback, exchange and process. The border is not univocal, or only polymorphous. Its breaks are not fetishized as a final cut: they are instead, or they may be, re-sutured, re-circulated or re-bonded' (Welchman, 1996, p. 178). In joining these border wars, academics are advised that 'border controls . . . govern national boundaries and university disciplines alike' (Harlow, 1994, p. 123); strategies to exceed these boundaries include PARTICIPATORY ACTION RESEARCH, among others (see ACTIVISM AND THE ACADEMY).

References

Anzaldua, G. 1987: Borderlands/*La Frontera*: the new mestiza. San Francisco: Aunt Lute Books. · Augelli, J. 1980: Nationalization of Dominican borderlands. *The Geographical Review* 70: 19–35. · Avalos, D. and Welchman, J. 1996: Response to The Philosophical Brothel. In Welchman, J., ed., *Rethinking borders*. Minneapolis: University of Minnesota Press, 187–99. · Haraway, D. 1990: A manifesto for cyborgs: science, technology, and socialist feminism in the 1980s. In L., Nicholson, ed., *Feminism/Postmodernism*. New York: Routledge, 190–233. · Harlow, B. 1994: Sites of struggle: immigration, deportation, prison, and exile. In Higonnet, M. and Templeton, J., eds, *Reconfigured spheres: feminist explorations of literary space*. Amherst: University of Massachusetts Press, 108–24. · Mouffe, C. 1995: Post-Marxism: democracy and identity. *Environment and Planning D: Society and Space* 13: 259–66. · Radcliffe, S. 1998: Frontiers and popular nationhood: geographies of identity in the 1995 Ecuador–Peru border dispute. *Political Geography* 17: 273–93. · Tsing, A.L. 1993: *In the realm of the diamond queen*. Princeton: University of Princeton Press. · Welchman, J., ed., 1996: *Rethinking borders*. Minneapolis: University of Minnesota Press.

Boserup thesis Classical political economists, and Malthus and Ricardo in particular, developed in the early stages of the DEMOGRAPHIC TRANSITION in Europe a macroeconomic theory of the relations between population growth and agriculture. Ricardo (1817) distinguished between intensive and extensive agricultural expansion: *extensive expansion* presumed the extension of cultivation into new lands which were marginal and therefore subject to diminishing returns to labour and capital whereas *intensive expansion* enhanced the output of existing lands through the application of better weeding, fertilizer, drainage and so on, which was also subject to diminishing returns to labour and capital. Ricardo, like Malthus (1803), assumed that population increase would be arrested by a decline in real wages, by increases in rents and by per capita food decline.

There is a third form of intensification which rests upon the deployment of the increasing labour force to crop farmland more frequently (i.e. to increase the cropping intensity or to reduce the fallow). The *reduction of the period of fallow* (the period of non-cultivation or recovery in which land is allowed to regenerate its fertility and soil capacities) was a major way in which European agriculture increased its output during periods of population growth, as observed at the time when Ricardo and Malthus were writing. Fallowing does not imply poorer or more distant land but as the fallow length is reduced greater capital and labour inputs are required to prevent the gradual decline in crop yields and the loss of fodder for animals. Esther Boserup (1965, 1981) made the fallow reduction a central plank of her important work on agrarian intensification. While fallow reduction is also likely to yield diminishing returns, these are more than compensated for by the additions to total output conferred by increased cropping frequency.

In the eighth century the two-field system predominated in western Europe but by the twelfth and thirteenth centuries the three-field system had come to displace its two-field counterpart in high density regions. By the eighteenth and nineteenth centuries the fallow had begun to disappear entirely. Boserup (1965) saw this fallowing reduction as the central theme in agrarian history and the centrepiece around which the Malthusian debates over overpopulation and famine ultimately turned (cf. MALTHUSIAN MODEL). In her view, output per man hour is highest in the long fallow systems – for example the shifting or swiddening systems of the humid tropical forest zone in which diverse polycropping of plots for one or two seasons is then followed by a fallow of 15–25 years (depending on local ecological circumstances: cf. SHIFTING CULTIVATION) – and population growth is the stimulus both for reduction in fallow and the innovations associated with intensified land use.

Boserup envisages a progressive series of fallow reductions driven by the pressure of population (and the threat of exceeding CARRYING CAPACITY). Long fallow systems which are technologically simple (associated only with the digging stick and the axe) are displaced by bush fallow (6–10 year fallow) and short fallowing (2–3 year fallow) in which the plough is a prerequisite. Annual and finally multiple cropping appear as responses to continued population pressure. Across this progression of intensification is a reduction in output per man hour but a vast increase in total output. The shift to annual and multiple cropping also requires substantially new forms of skill and investment, however, which typically demands STATE organized forms of investment and surplus mobilization. Boserup saw much of Africa and Latin America as occupying an early position in the linear model of intensification in which output could be expanded by fallow reduction. The "Boserup thesis" refers to the relationship between population growth and agrarian intensification measured through fallow reduction and a decreasing output per man hour.

Implicit in the Boserup thesis, though she did not develop these implications, is the changing role of LAND TENURE, the increasing capitalization of the land, and more complex forms of state–society interaction. Indeed, Boserup's work has been taken up by a number of archaeologists and anthropologists who have charted patterns of state formation and social development in terms of agrarian intensification.

Boserup's anti-Malthusian theory lays itself open to all manner of charges, including a unilinear form of techno-demographic determinism and a general lack of attention to the ECOLOGICAL limits of forms of intensification (Grigg, 1980: cf. TELEOLOGY). It is not at all clear how or whether Boserup's thesis can be applied to market economies. Indeed, her thesis does not seem to be much help for example in the English case: in its essentials the agricultural technology of the eighteenth century (the Norfolk four-course rotation) had been available since the Middle Ages, and although the eighteenth century was a period of population growth, the previous period of sustained demographic growth from the mid sixteenth century had witnessed no intensification as such (Overton, 1996). Processes of intensification are naturally on the historical record and the reduction of fallowing in the Third World – whether driven by demographic growth or not – has been and continues to be documented (see Guyer, 1997). But intensification is a socially, culturally and politically complex process. To the extent that fallow reduction involves someone working harder and differently, the question of who works, when and for what return (a question played out in terms of age, gender and CLASS in the PEASANT household) is not posed by Boserup. Here the newer work on household dynamics has more to offer (Carney and Watts, 1990). MW

References

Boserup, E. 1965: *The conditions of agricultural growth*. London: Allen and Unwin. · Boserup, E. 1981: *Population and technological change*. Chicago: University of Chicago Press. · Carney, J. and Watts, M. 1990: Disciplining women? *Signs* 16 (4): 654–81. · Grigg, D.B. 1980: *Population and agrarian change*. Cambridge: Cambridge University Press. · Guyer, J. 1997: *An African niche economy*. Edinburgh: Edinburgh University Press. · Malthus, T.R. 1803: *An essay on population*. New York: Dutton. · Overton, M. 1996: *Agricultural revolution in England*. Cambridge: Cambridge University Press. · Ricardo, D. 1817: *The principles of political economy and taxation*. Cambridge: Cambridge University Press.

boundary The dividing line between one spatial unit or group and another. Human spatial boundaries are defined by social activities and range from the precise to the fuzzy, depending on the nature of the social activity in question. For example, political boundaries drawn to delimit the TERRITORY of a STATE mark the precise limits of the state's claim to jurisdiction or SOVEREIGNTY. The boundaries of governmental units within a state serve to demarcate areas of legal responsibility for public-service delivery and revenue collection. Under FEDERALISM boundaries between the basic spatial units (Provinces, States, Cantons, etc.) are of special political importance, representing the authority exercised by separate units within the overall system of units. Social and cultural boundary-making are no less universal, and in certain circumstances the results show up vividly in the CULTURAL LANDSCAPE, as in, for example, contrasts in agricultural practices and building styles between English-settled and French-settled Quebec. More frequently, however, social and cultural boundaries are dynamic and fluid, responding to shifts in patterns of social solidarity and mobilization. As a result, they appear more like moving gradients than precise, linear borders. Moreover, linguistic, religious and economic boundaries are often cross-cutting and permeable rather than mutually reinforcing and impermeable (Weiss, 1962). With increased population MOBILITY, social and cultural boundaries become complex and less susceptible to simple cartographic representation (Harley, 1989).

The terms border and FRONTIER are sometimes used as if they were equivalents to boundary, which they are in popular English-language usage. But they seem more 'matter of fact', referring to legal or official boundary lines and zonal areas, respectively. Boundaries involve perceptions by one or other parties of features that distinguish them from one another (Cohen, 1994, p. 122). In geographical usage this is the most general concept designating definite social, cultural or political differences between contiguous areas or populations. Professional usage, however, is sometimes much less clear. For example, some writers reserve the term boundary for the specific case of a boundary-line, preferring border as a zone or line and frontier as a line, zone of demarcation or zone of settlement. This makes boundary the most specific and the others more general. Throughout the social sciences, however, the term boundary has the greatest importance as a concept signifying material and symbolic divisions between social groups (e.g. men and women, rich and poor), areas of knowledge (e.g. disciplinary boundaries) and sets of social practices (e.g. moral boundaries), so it seems best to endorse this practical usage rather than arbitrarily give border and frontier the greater scope. Boundary also has importance in anthropology and sociology as a metaphor for the relational character of group formation and differentiation (Cohen, 1994; Silber, 1995). One group always forms by creating boundaries between itself and others.

Human spatial boundaries are defined when, in the process of social interaction, groups form geographically and differentiate themselves from one another (Simmel, 1971). Socialization into group membership, therefore, is intrinsically spatial. A boundary between two groups is the result of distinctive patterns of behaviour and systems of symbols that are formed geographically (Cohen, 1974). CONFLICT arises when boundaries are ill-defined or there is contested territory. Although imprinted into consciousness in the process of learning, there is always an ambiguity about the meaning of symbols and the differences that they signify, so that the 'traditions' associated with a group are rarely static but constantly reinterpreted (Hobsbawm and Ranger, 1983). Ambiguity is particularly evident when a social group, such as an ethnic group (ETHNICITY), is deeply stratified by caste or CLASS or when large-scale social change challenges the maintenance of existing political and social boundaries.

The practice of TERRITORIALITY by groups is reinforced when social and economic differences between adjacent groups are perceived by them as relatively great. Boundaries then are not so much inclusionary as exclusionary in nature. Distancing and SEGREGATION between ethnic groups and classes become pervasive. Physical barriers and legal devices are used to exclude those who threaten the security and material interests of those groups with sufficient power to exclude. Space is never readily available for expropriation. It is always occupied, guarded and bounded by those who have the power to do so. The real existence of spatial boundaries testifies to the degree to which space is never a totally 'fluid medium in which mobile subjects dwell' (Pile and Thrift, 1995, p. 374), something that is lost on those philosophers and social scientists who use spatial metaphors (such as that of 'boundary') to indicate social oppositions and contrasts without understanding the social significance of a boundary's real spatial content. Important social boundaries are rarely just latent in TEXTS or social categorizations but are found in the landscapes of everyday life.

States and other forms of socio-political organization (such as hierarchical churches and businesses) exercise their power in part through their ability to draw and redraw boundaries inside and around their territories (Sack, 1986). Controlling and managing territory necessitates the demarcation of definite boundaries. These can be formal, as with the delegation of authority to local government units, or informal, as when national governments implement policies to favour their electoral constituencies or specific ethnic or regional groups within the national territory (e.g. on Northern Ireland, see MacLaughlin and Agnew, 1986).

The external boundaries of states have received the most attention from geographers, usually without much discussion of their genesis in social processes. The tendency has been to tie them to physical features, as if the physical world was somehow responsible for their definition, or, more realistically, to see them as the outcome of frontier settlement/development and inter-state conflict. Interest in the historical specificity of boundary-making by states and how this affects the IDENTITY of different national groups is very recent (see, e.g., Sahlins, 1989; Krishna, 1994; Paasi, 1996). There is evidence that the rulers of the ancient empires, such as those of Rome and the early Chinese dynasties, did not share the modern predilection for defining the edges of their empires in terms of fixed boundaries: 'Ancient IMPERIALISM saw control over peoples and towns as the essence of sovereignty . . . in antiquity territory was not a factor constituting the essence of the state as it is in our times' (Isaac, 1990, p. 417). In medieval Europe the hierarchical subordination of different strata by the preceding one (e.g. monarch, nobles, peasants) and the importance of local feudal links encouraged a plurality of social bonds without an exclusive identity based on membership in the 'imagined community' (Anderson, 1983) of the NATION-STATE. Rigid spatial boundaries became important only when the sovereignty of the state and CITIZENSHIP within its territory displaced that of a monarch in a rigid social order as the main source of political legitimacy (Connolly, 1988). JAA

References

Anderson, B. 1983: *Imagined communities: reflections on the origins and spread of nationalism.* London: Verso. · Cohen, A. 1974: *Two-dimensional man: an essay on the anthropology of power and symbolism in complex society.* Berkeley and Los Angeles: University of California Press. · Cohen, A.P. 1994: *Self consciousness: an alternative anthropology of identity.* London: Routledge. · Connolly, W. 1988: *Political theory and modernity.* Oxford: Blackwell. · Harley, J.B. 1989: Historical geography and the cartographic illusion. *Journal of Historical Geography.* 15: 80–91. · Hobsbawm, E. and Ranger, T., eds, 1983: *The invention of tradition.* Cambridge: Cambridge University Press. · Isaac, B. 1990: *The limits of empire: the Roman army in the East.* Oxford: Oxford University Press. · Krishna, S. 1994: Cartographic anxiety: mapping the body politic in India. *Alternatives* 19: 507–21. · MacLaughlin, J. and Agnew, J.A. 1986: Hegemony and the regional question: the political geography of regional industrial policy in Northern Ireland, 1945–1972. *Annals of the Association of American Geographers,* 76: 247–61. · Paasi, A. 1996: *Territories, boundaries and consciousness: the changing geographies of the Finnish–Russian border.* London: Belhaven Press. · Pile, S. and Thrift, N. 1995: Conclusions: spacing and the subject. In S. Pile, and N. Thrift, eds, *Mapping the subject: geographies of cultural transformation.* London: Routledge, 371–80. · Sack, R.D. 1986: *Human territoriality: its theory and history.* Cambridge: Cambridge University Press. · Sahlins, P. 1989: *Boundaries: the making of France and Spain in the Pyrenees.* Berkeley and Los Angeles: University of California Press. · Silber, I.F. 1995: Space, fields, boundaries: the rise of spatial metaphors in contemporary sociological theory. *Social Research* 62: 323–55. · Simmel, G. 1971: *On individuality and social forms.* Chicago: University of Chicago Press. · Weiss, R. 1962: Cultural boundaries and ethnographic maps. In P. Wagner, and M.Mikesell, eds, *Readings in cultural geography.* Chicago: University of Chicago Press, 62–74.

Suggested Reading

Cohen (1994), 118–32. · Paasi (1996). · Sack (1986). · Sahlins (1989).

Brenner debate One of the longest-running debates in the social sciences has concerned the causes and geography of the transition from FEUDALISM to CAPITALISM in medieval and early modern Europe (Hilton, 1975; Holton, 1985). In the mid-1970s the 'transition debate' entered a new phase stimulated by an American historian Robert Brenner (1976,

1982). Brenner reworked an older argument (Dobb, 1946) that the structure of class POWER and CLASS relations (rather than demographic or commercial change) determined long-run patterns of European economic development, explaining the emergence of CAPITALISM in England. The editors of the journal *Past and Present*, in which Brenner's argument appeared, invited several responses, and a rejoinder from Brenner (all reprinted in Aston and Philpin, 1985). Subsequent debate spilled over into historical, historical geographical and social theory literatures (Tribe, 1981; Heller, 1985).

Brenner rejected the notion that European medieval society underwent an ecological crisis from *c.*1300, produced by an underlying ecological dynamic (see POSTAN THESIS), reasserting the Marxian position that agrarian crises were socially precipitated. The legally dependent position of feudal tenants enabled lords to exact surplus above that produced by 'market' forces. Ever-greater surplus extraction from agricultural producers by feudal lords (to finance competition for political status), the Church and the Crown precipitated a crisis of reproduction in peasant agriculture, and threatened peasant subsistence. On this reading, 'the late-medieval crisis in seigneurial revenues was not a mere concomitant of a more general crisis in the economy: it was the very eye of the storm' (B. Harvey in Campbell, 1991, p. 17).

However, class relations varied across Europe, causing demographic decline to have differing effects. Brenner claims that agrarian capitalism appeared in England because of the particular way in which in English feudal society decayed during the later Middle Ages. Central to his argument are two geographical comparisons of social relations. The first comparison is between western Europe (where lords lost their political control of feudal tenants) and eastern Europe (where manorial lords strengthened their control over land and dependant PEASANTRIES). The second comparison is between France (where absolute peasant property rights became entrenched) and England (where peasants failed to establish absolute property rights, but achieved more flexible tenures). English tenants' initiatives rebounded on them when demographic expansion resumed after 1500; landlords now evicted peasant producers and installed entrepreneurial tenants, thereby producing agrarian capitalism.

The main points of dispute between Brenner and his critics, on both the theoretical right and left, involved the extent to which he treated demographic and social causes of long-run change as mutually exclusive, rather than as interactive; and the extent to which he conflated exogenous and endogenous components of demographic and economic change (Hilton, 1978; Postan and Hatcher, 1978; Aston and Philpin, 1985). Within Marxist approaches, the most noteworthy skirmishing involved Wallerstein's WORLD-SYSTEMS view of the emergent European world economy (Wallerstein, 1974, 1980; Brenner, 1977). Brenner's rejoinder (1982) was more a clarified restatement than a sustained response to critics, and failed to problematize the relationship amongst the various components of 'agrarian capitalism' (Holton, 1985; Glennie, 1987).

Brenner's account of emergent agrarian capitalism has fared badly in recent years: 'There is mounting evidence to show that there was not a coordinated relationship between landlord power, tenure, ownership, farm size and capitalistic farming' (Overton, 1996, p. 205).

Most landlords were much less powerful than Brenner claims, and the law more protective of tenants' property rights (Searle, 1986). Much economic differentiation occurred amongst tenants, rather than being engineered by landlords exploiting their class power (Glennie, 1988; Poos, 1991). The main pioneers of new farming methods were middling farmers (owner-occupiers as well as tenants) not the great landowners, who showed little interest either in organizing their estates for capitalist tenant farming or in farming innovations (Allen, 1992). The most dramatic advances in output and land PRODUCTIVITY came where lordship was relatively weak – the opposite of the pattern envisaged by Brenner, who has himself made further important contributions to debates on politics and commerce (Brenner, 1993, see especially part 3).

Brenner's ideas on the decline of feudalism have been more influential (though unfortunately ignored in some key works on medieval agrarian history, see Hallam, 1990). Recent attention to geographies of manorialization, alongside work on medieval commercialization, has produced several new avenues of debate, not least in questioning the POSTAN THESIS, and in stimulating more geographically sensitive accounts of medieval England (Campbell, 1991; Dyer, 1993; Britnell, 1996).

Analogous debates have been amongst the liveliest areas of contemporary agrarian geography and of development studies, and comparative geographical work has much to offer in linking historical and contemporary work. PG

References

Allen, R.C. 1992: *Enclosure and the yeomen* Oxford: Clarendon Press. · Aston, T.H. and Philpin, C.E., eds, 1985: *The Brenner debate: agrarian class structure and economic development in pre-industrial Europe*. Cambridge: Cambridge University Press. · Brenner, R. 1976: Agrarian class structure and economic development in pre-industrial England. *Past and Present* 70: 30–75. · Brenner, R. 1977: The origins of capitalist development: a critique of neo-Smithian Marxism. *New Left Review* 104: 25–92. · Brenner, R. 1982: The agrarian roots of European capitalism. *Past and Present* 97: 20–97. · Brenner, R. 1993: *Merchants and revolution: commercial change, political conflict and London's overseas traders, 1550–1653*. Princeton: Princeton University Press. · Britnell, R. 1996: *Commercialisation in medieval England*, 2nd edn. Manchester: Manchester University Press. · Campbell, B.M.S., ed., 1991: *Before the Black Death: studies in the 'crisis' of the early fourteenth century*. Manchester: Manchester University Press. · Dobb, M. 1946: Studies in the development of capitalism. London: Routledge and Kegan Paul. · Dyer, C. 1993: *Standards of living in the later middle ages: social change in England c.1200–1500*, 2nd edn. Cambridge: Cambridge University Press. · Glennie, P.D. 1987: The transition from feudalism to capitalism as a problem for historical geography. *Journal of Historical Geography* 13: 296–302. · Glennie, P.D. 1988: In search of agrarian capitalism: manorial land markets and the acquisition of land in the Lea valley, *c*.1450–*c*.1560'. *Continuity and Change* 3: 11–40. · Hallam, H.E., ed., 1990: *The agrarian history of England and Wales, volume II 1042–1348*. Cambridge: Cambridge University Press. · Heller, H. 1985: The transition debate in historical perspective. *Science and Society* 49: 208–13. · Hilton, R.H., ed., 1975: *The transition from feudalism to capitalism*. London: Verso. · Hilton, R.H. 1978: A crisis of feudalism. *Past and Present* 80: 3–19. · Holton, R. J. 1985: *The transition from feudalism to capitalism*. London: Macmillan. · Overton, M. 1996: *Agricultural revolution in England: the transformation of the agrarian economy 1500–1850*, ch. 4. Cambridge: Cambridge University Press. · Poos, L. 1991: *A rural society after the Black Death: late-medieval Essex*. Cambridge: Cambridge University Press. · Postan, M. and Hatcher, J. 1978: Population and class structure in feudal society. *Past and Present* 78: 24–37. · Searle, C. 1986: Custom, class conflict and agrarian capitalism: the Cumbrian customary economy in the eighteenth century. *Past and Present* 110: 106–30. · Tribe, K. 1981: The problem of transition and the question of origin. Ch. 1 in his *Genealogies of Capitalism*. London: Routledge. · Wallerstein, I. 1974: *The modern world system I: capitalist agriculture and the origins of the European world-economy in the sixteenth century*. London: Academic Press. · Wallerstein, I. 1980: *The modern world system II: mercantilism and the consolidation of the European world-economy*. London: Academic Press.

Suggested reading

Aston and Philpin, eds (1985). · Campbell, B.M.S. 1990: People and land in the middle ages, 1066–1500. In R. Butlin, and R. Dodgshon, eds, *An historical geography of England and Wales*, 2nd edn. London: Academic Press, 69–122. · Dyer (1993). · Glennie (1987). · Overton (1996).

C

capital Although commonly treated by orthodox economists as a factor of production or more simply as 'money', capital is better understood as 'expanding social value'. The latter conception, derived from Marx, has occupied the attention of critical theorists in ECONOMIC GEOGRAPHY since the early 1970s (see Harvey, 1973). Capital is a social relation rather than a thing, and it can take various material forms; it can be invested as MONEY, consumed as raw material, expended as wages for labour, operated as machinery and other means of production, or sold as commodities. Most succinctly, capital is 'value in motion' (Marx, 1987, p. 149), insofar as it is social value that expands in the production process (see ACCUMULATION). Marx (1987, ch. 4) describes the cyclical conversion from money into labour power, raw materials and commodities, and then back into money again, as the 'general formula of capital' (cf. MARXIAN ECONOMICS). In all its forms, capital is the product of social labour performed in the production of commodities. Increasingly though, some have argued that the production of capital has recently become more distanced from the actual production of commodities as certain technologies enable whole sub-economies to form around the manipulation of information (Castells, 1996).

Historically, capital came to define the MODE OF PRODUCTION at the point when labour itself became commodified as a form of capital. Thereafter the production of surplus value and the reproduction of capital was organized first and foremost as an economic result of market exchange rather than directly through social and political means. In the resulting capitalist society (see CAPITALISM), capital is owned and controlled by a specific social CLASS, the capitalist class, which profits from the expansion of capital and, by dint of its ownership of capital, forms a ruling class.

Different individual capitals (i.e. firms, individual capitalists, etc.) occupy different niches in the cynical reproduction of capital (see CIRCUIT OF CAPITAL) and are associated with different factions of the capitalist class. Financial, industrial, and rentier capital all represent specific interests within the capitalist class, and the role of the STATE is in part to mediate these intra-capitalist interests as well as to regulate class conflict between capital and labour.

Geographical research on capital has largely focused on the ways in which the social power and economic rationale of capital translate into systematic geographical patterns of DEVELOPMENT and UNDERDEVELOPMENT (see UNEVEN DEVELOPMENT), environmental degradation, and diverse experiences of local change (Harvey, 1982; Dunford and Perrins, 1983). NS

References

Castells, M. 1996: *The rise of the network society. Volume 1.* Oxford: Blackwell. · Dunford, M. and Perrins, D. 1983: *The arena of capital.* London: Macmillan. · Harvey, D. 1973: *Social justice and the city.* London: Edward Arnold. · Harvey, D. 1982: *The limits to capital.* Oxford: Blackwell. · Marx, K. 1987: *Capital,* volume I. New York: International Publishers, see esp. ch. IV.

capitalism An historically specific form of economic and social organization which is theorized in different ways by different political and intellectual traditions. It is important to understand the weight placed upon 'theorized' in the preceding sentence because it has practical implications. Theorizations of capitalism are 'regulatory fictions' in the sense that they are conceptual constructions which enter into – shape, inform, delimit – both the reproduction and transformation of capitalism and the development of radical critiques of capitalism. On one side, for example, Thrift (1997) has argued that changes in the international DISCOURSE of management and managerialism have helped produce so-called *soft capitalism,* while on the other side Gibson-Graham (1996) have insisted that the reconceptualization of capitalism has a doubly important part to play in 'the end of capitalism (as we knew it)'.

Conceptions of capitalism typically fasten on the singularity and centrality of its ECONOMY within which:

(a) the direct producer is separated from ownership of the means of production and the product of the LABOUR PROCESS; and where

(b) this separation is effected through the transformation of labour power into a COMMODITY to be bought and sold on a LABOUR MARKET regulated by price signals.

These claims are then elaborated in radically different ways, some of which are closed around the economy while others identify a more comprehensive cultural, social and political 'architecture' that is built around (and on) the capitalist economy.

In NEO-CLASSICAL ECONOMICS, for example, exchanges within the labour market are treated as identical to the price transactions that occur within and between all commodity markets, i.e. as an 'exchange of equivalents', so that the general structure of commodity exchange is sufficient to characterize the entire economy. Buyers and sellers freely enter the frictionless spaces of markets, invested with perfect rationality and perfect knowledge, and respond to the price signals generated by supply and demand schedules to produce a general equilibrium. This scenario is scripted by historical accounts of the generalization of commodity exchange in the course of the eighteenth and nineteenth centuries in western Europe and North America (including, crucially, the commodification of labour) which supposedly ensured that 'the market mode of economic integration gradually bound society into one cohesive economic system' (Harvey, 1973; see MARKET EXCHANGE).

Neoclassical economics is confined to the economy, however, and its social and political counterpart is provided by sociologist Max Weber's (1864–1920) description of the institutional foundations of the market (Collins, 1980; Clarke, 1982). Weber emphasized the importance of the legal and political framework established by the NATION-STATE 'which afforded to capitalism its chance for development', and drew attention to the importance of what he called formal rationality, i.e. the calculability of action, within the capitalist economy. Rationality was the guiding thread of Weber's work. In his view, the generalization of formal rationality, its intrusion into all aspects of everyday life in the West, had as its climax the constitution of a generic industrial society 'characterised by large-scale industrial production, the inexorable power of material goods, bureaucratic administration', and a pervasive 'calculating attitude' (Bottomore, 1985). But where Neo-classical economics can be read as a vindication – even a celebration – of formal rationality and the 'free market economy', Weber's writings were much more ambivalent:

> In no sphere of human life, according to Weber, has rationalization unambiguously advanced human well-being. The rationalization of economic production, for example, has created the 'iron cage' of capitalism, a 'tremendous cosmos' that constrains individuals from without, determining their lives 'with irresistible force'. (Brubaker, 1984)

This occurred, so Weber argued, because there was a disjuncture between formal rationality and substantive rationality: 'While capitalism is rational in the sense of enhancing the calculability of economic action, its rationality may well be problematic in terms of the [substantive] ends it promotes or the [substantive] conditions of life which it imposes' (Bottomore, 1985). Weber's vision was thus profoundly pessimistic:

> Consuming and replacing other forms of life, bourgeois rationalization processes tend to become an end in themselves. Under their monopolistic sway, contemporary capitalist societies knit themselves into a self-enslaving 'iron cage' of bondage. All spheres of daily life tend to become chronically dependent upon disciplined hierarchy, rational specialisation and the continuous deployment of impersonal systems of abstract-general rules. Bureaucratic domination is the fate of the present, whose future is likely to be more of the same. A 'polar night of icy darkness and hardness' is the spectre that haunts the modern world. (Keane, 1984)

The spectre of a 'totally administered society' (see also SURVEILLANCE) confronts capitalism and SOCIALISM alike, so Weber argued, and it is the same spectre that post-Weberian CRITICAL THEORY sought to lay. But its starting-point has usually been Marx rather than Weber.

Karl Marx (1818–83) recognized that capitalism is more than a system of generalized commodity exchange: it is also a generalized system of commodity production. It is this insight which acts as the lever for the characterization of capitalism provided by MARXIAN ECONOMICS and Marxian POLITICAL ECONOMY. From this perspective, capitalism is seen as an historically specific MODE OF PRODUCTION in which 'the reproduction of daily life depends upon the production of commodities produced through a system of circulation that has profit-seeking as its direct and socially accepted goal' (Harvey, 1985). Harvey provides a sketch map of the main circuits of capital (see figure on p. 59). He emphasizes that such differentiated forms of circulation not only 'enable capitalism to shape its historical geography in accordance with the dictates of [capital] ACCUMULATION' but also 'increase immeasurably the possibilities for CRISIS formation'. Far from sustaining the general equilibrium posited by Neo-classical, economics, therefore, the dynamics of capital circulation are seen to generate a crisis-ridden historical geography of 'long waves' and spasmodic perturbations in time and of UNEVEN DEVELOPMENT in space (Harvey, 1982: cf. KONDRAFTIEFF CYCLES). One of the primary concerns of MARXIST GEOGRAPHY has been to bring into view the SPACE ECONOMY of capitalism and to disclose its 'inconstant geography', therefore, as a way of showing that the PRODUCTION OF SPACE is integral rather than merely incidental to the production of commodities and the circulation of capital (see Massey, 1984; Harvey, 1985; Storper and Walker, 1989; see also LOCATION THEORY).

Although Marx himself focused on what he called the 'economic base', other writers have built complex architectures on these foundations that have served two main purposes. Many of them have been concerned to illuminate the relations between economy, society, CULTURE and politics (see, for example, REGULATION SCHOOL; STRUCTURAL MARXISM). These are more than abstract topologies: they have informed empirical analyses of the structure of the capitalist STATE and the STATE APPARATUS, the location and operation of the law and other modes of capitalist regulation, and the significance of cultural formations and cultural politics in the legitimation and contestation of contemporary capitalisms. Other writers have drawn on these active architectures to tease out the intricate connections between capitalism, CLASS and other subject-positions. Particular attention has been paid to the constitution of gendered, racialized and sexualized subjects and their entanglements with capitalism through its historical imbrications with (e.g.) COLONIALISM; PATRIARCHY and RACISM (see GENDER AND GEOGRAPHY; RACE; SEXUALITY AND GEOGRAPHY).

Virtually all the standard theorizations of capitalism emphasize the history of capitalism and thus agree that it is not an ever-present and unchanging system. Both Weber and Marx paid particular attention to the European transition from FEUDALISM to capitalism (see Holton, 1985), and historical typologies of different capitalisms have since proliferated: the conventional Marxian distinction between *merchant capitalism*, *industrial capitalism* and *finance capitalism* has been elaborated in the late twentieth century through the recognition of an 'organized' capitalism that was successively dominated by TAYLORISM and FORDISM and a subsequent DISORGANIZED CAPITALISM dominated by regimes of FLEXIBLE ACCUMULATION (see Lash and Urry, 1987; Harvey, 1989). But these different capitalisms are usually constructed as successive moments in the historical evolution, expansion and exorbitation of what Gibson-Graham (1996) have called 'Capitalism-with-a-capital-C'. Approaches of this sort, so they argue, usually entail a number of characteristic assumptions:

- Capitalism is situated at the heart of the narrative as the central generating mechanism of historical change ('capitalocentrism');
- Non-capitalist forms and practices are cast as backward, traditional, inward-looking;
- Non-capitalist sites are thus sites of a 'lack', always and everywhere impending targets of invasion, submission and colonization, eventually to be eliminated by the inexorable penetrations of a globalizing capitalism (a scenario dramatized in the dominant 'rape script' of GLOBALIZATION);
- Capitalism is thus constructed as a *totality*: 'We cannot get outside Capitalism: it has no outside'.

Against this, Gibson-Graham prefer to speak not of Capitalism but of the co-existence in time and space of multiple capitalisms. Perhaps their most important proposal is to conceptualize 'the economy' not as 'a bounded and unified space with a fixed capitalist identity' – a structure with an essential and invariant 'inside' – but as a plurality and heterogeneity of forms and practices that 'is constituted by its continually changing and contradictory 'outsides' (1996, pp. 15–16). These are trenchant reformulations, which accentuate the importance of not only the history but also the geography of capitalist processes, practices and forms. While it is unclear how much of conventional political economy these proposals leave intact, they intersect with recent studies that accentuate the specificity of different capitalisms presently emerging in (for example) East Asia and eastern Europe. DG

References

Bottomore, T. 1985: *Theories of modern capitalism*. London: Allen and Unwin. · Brubaker, R. 1984: *The limits of rationality*. London: Allen and Unwin. · Clarke, S. 1982: *Marx, marginalism and modern sociology*. London: Macmillan. · Collins, R. 1980: Weber's last theory of capitalism: a systematization. *American Sociological Review* 45: 925–42. · Gibson-Graham, J.-K. 1996: *The end of capitalism (as we knew it)*. Oxford, UK and Cambridge, MA: Blackwell. · Harvey, D. 1973: *Social justice and the city*. London: Edward Arnold; reprinted, Oxford, UK and Cambridge, MA: Blackwell. · Harvey, D. 1982: *The limits to capital*. Oxford, UK and Cambridge, MA: Blackwell. · Harvey, D. 1985: *The urbanization of capital*. Oxford, UK and Cambridge, MA: Blackwell.

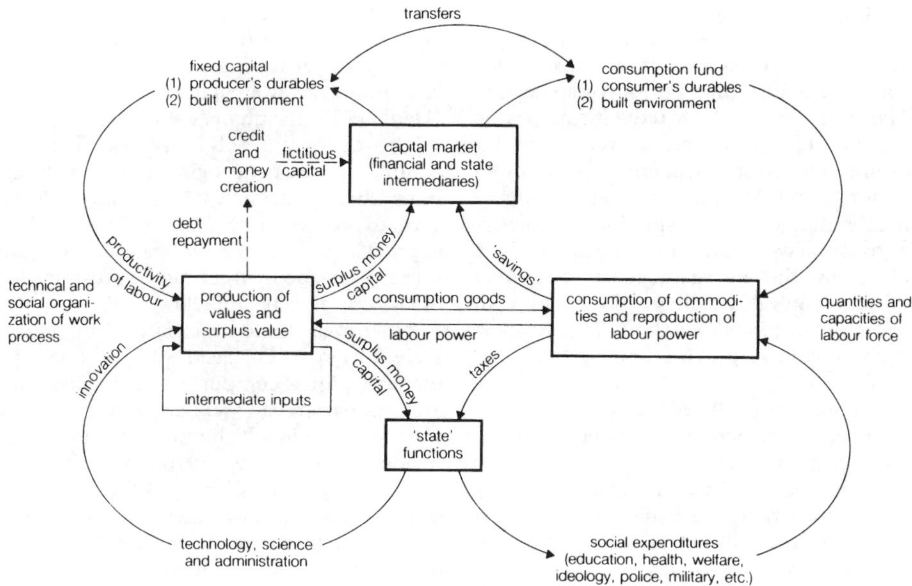

capitalism *Paths of capital flow* (Harvey, 1982)

· Harvey, D. 1989: *The condition of postmodernity: an enquiry into the origins of cultural change*. Oxford, UK and Cambridge, MA: Blackwell. · Holton, R.J. 1985: *The transition from feudalism to capitalism*. London: Macmillan. · Keane, J. 1984: *Public life and late capitalism*. Cambridge: Cambridge University Press. · Lash, S. and Urry, J. 1987: *The end of organized capitalism*. Cambridge: Polity. · Massey, D. 1984: *Spatial divisions of labour*. London: Macmillan. · Storper, M. and Walker, R. 1989: *The capitalist imperative: territory, technology and industrial growth*. Oxford, UK and Cambridge, MA: Blackwell. · Thrift, N. 1997: Soft capitalism. *Cultural Values* 1: 29–57.

Suggested Reading

Bottomore (1985). · Gibson-Graham (1996).

carrying capacity The optimum population of plants, animals or, more controversially, people that can be sustained on a given area of land (see also MALTHUSIAN MODEL). The concept originated in ecological studies to refer to the numbers of different species compatible with particular environmental conditions. It has become a staple, but much criticized, tool of environmental management for quantifying the sustainable limit of different land-use practices. Geographers have used it, for example, to gauge the numbers of livestock or crop plants that can be supported by a given farming system, or the number of visitors compatible with protecting species or habitats in a designated area. (cf. ECOLOGY; SUSTAINABLE DEVELOPMENT.) SW

Reference

Warren, A. 1995: Changing understandings of African pastoralism and the nature of environmental paradigms. *Transactions, Institute of British Geographers* NS 20: 193–203.

cartogram A highly tailored map projection that distorts area or distance either to promote legibility or to reveal patterns not readily apparent on a more traditional base map. Coined around 1860 to describe comparatively abstract small-scale maps of statistical data, the word cartogram acquired the connotation of a purposeful non-conventional map projection in the 1960s, after Waldo Tobler applied the mathematics of equal-area map projection to maps on which the size of areal units represents a transforming variable such as population or wealth (Snyder, 1993, pp. 262–4).

Among the earliest cartograms were nineteenth-century railroad maps deliberately distorted to make room for the names of closely spaced stations. By blatantly stretching political boundaries and rivers, these maps conveniently portrayed the sponsoring company's routes as less contorted and more direct than competing railways (Modelski, 1984, p. xviii). Purposeful stretching is also apparent in the maps of urban mass transit systems, which imitate the London Underground map devised by Harry Beck in 1933. By reducing map scale in the suburbs, where routes diverge and stations are more widely separated, Beck found room for greater detail in the inner city, where stations are more closely spaced and converging routes have complex connections. In a similar vein, the enlargement of very small areal units on a 'visibility base map' can promote the accurate decoding of all symbols on a choropleth map (Monmonier, 1993, pp. 178–80).

The most widely used cartogram is the 'value-by-area cartogram', on which the size of each areal unit represents its population or relative importance. As a base map for choropleth symbolization, the value-by-area cartogram avoids the misinterpretation that can occur when the dark or light tones of large but relatively unimportant areal units with extraordinarily high or low rates overshadow the symbols of smaller but markedly more important areal units. A classic example is the electoral cartogram, which provides a more reliable cartographic portrait of national elections than conventional maps, easily dominated by rural trends. By adjusting for geographic variation in population density, the 'demographic base map' often affords a clearer, more meaningful view of political, economic and mortality data.

Early value-by-area cartograms were so geographically crude that Erwin Raisz (1934), a prominent advocate, chose not to call them maps. As implied by the title of his seminal article, 'The rectangular statistical cartogram', Raisz drew all areal units – the 48 conterminous United States – as rectangles that abutted along vertical and horizontal boundaries. With few visual cues, the map-reader eager to find a specific state or identify a particular rectangle had to rely on abbreviated names, relative position (interior or periphery) and neighbours.

As Tobler (1963) later pointed out, the value-by-area cartogram is a graphic-geometric problem with many mathematical-computational solutions not constrained by horizontal and vertical lines. Although some solutions are more visually pleasing than others, a multiplicity of areal units and wide variation in density can easily thwart a visually pleasing result (see examples in Tobler, 1973). Because of difficulties in finding aesthetically satisfying computational solutions, map authors eager for a cartogram base map typically have adopted an iterative, largely manual trial-and-error strategy of preserving the readily identifiable caricatures of key areal units wherever possible (Dent, 1972; Eastman et al., 1981).

The cartograms of Raisz and Tobler are contiguous area cartograms in which areal units sharing a common boundary are not allowed to separate. A markedly different approach, the noncontiguous area cartogram, preserves shape by freezing the areal unit with the largest density and allowing the perimeters of other areas to contract inward by reducing scale (Olson, 1976; Jackel, 1997). Easily programmed for a computer, the noncontiguous area cartogram can yield an aesthetically awkward solution in which numerous tiny, scarcely identifiable icons surround a few large, easily recognized shapes. Although moving distant area symbols together can provide a more efficient use of the space, abbreviations might be needed to identify areas lacking a distinct shape or detached from a better-known neighbour. Even so, area cartograms with widely separated icons or badly distorted shapes might be useful if the map author supplements the display with a more familiar reference map.

A similar special-purpose projection is the distance cartogram, which portrays geographic distortions resulting from transportation or telecommunication rates (Monmonier, 1993, pp. 198–200). A tailored variation of the azimuthal equidistant projection, the distance cartogram describes relative accessibility to a focal place by moving interacting places closer together or farther apart in accord with telecommunication rates, travel time, frequency of service, migration rates or some other measure of accessibility or interaction. Distance cartograms are especially useful in pairs, to compare different modes of interaction or to illustrate the 'before and after' effects of new regulations. MM

References

Dent, B.D. 1972: A note on the importance of shape in cartogram communication. *Journal of Geography* 71: 393–401. · Eastman, J.R., Nelson, W. and Shields, G. 1981: Production considerations in isodensity mapping. *Cartographica* 18 (1): 24–30. · Jackel, C.B. 1997: Using ArcView to create contiguous and noncontiguous area cartograms. *Cartography and Geographic Information Systems* 24: 101–9. · Modelski, A.M. 1984: *Railroad maps of North America: the first hundred years*. Washington, D.C.: Library of Congress. · Monmonier, M. 1993: *Mapping it out: expository cartography for the humanities and social sciences*. Chicago: University of Chicago Press. · Olson,

J.M. 1976: Noncontiguous area cartograms. *The Professional Geographer* 28: 371–80. · Raisz, E. 1934. The rectangular statistical cartogram. *Geographical Review* 24: 282–96. · Snyder, J.P. 1993: *Flattening the earth: two thousand years of map projection*. Chicago: University of Chicago Press. · Tobler, W.R. 1963: Geographic area and map projections. *Geographical Review* 53: 59–78. · Tobler, W.R. 1973: A continuous transformation useful for districting. *Annals, New York Academy of Sciences* 219: 215–20.

Suggested Reading

Dent, B.D. 1996: The cartogram: value-by-area mapping. In *Cartography: thematic map design*, 4th edn. Dubuque, Iowa: William C. Brown, 202–16. · Dorling, D. 1994: Cartograms for visualizing human geography. In H.M. Hearnshaw, and D. J. Unwin, eds. *Visualization in geographical information systems*. Chichester: John Wiley and Sons, 85–102.

cartography (1) The study of maps and their use (see MAP IMAGE AND MAP), and (2) the art, science and technology of mapmaking. Portuguese scholar Manuel Francisco de Barros e Sousa, Viscount of Santarém, coined the term in 1839 as a rubric for map study, analogous to the use in history of the term historiography (Wolter, 1975). Although Santarém referred only to early maps, the word evolved in the nineteenth century to include contemporary maps and mapping as well as ancient artifacts (Harley, 1987, p. 12). Its popular association with the practice of making maps reflects lexical roots in carte (French for map) and graphie (Greek for writing).

At present, cartography has several shades of meaning. In an inclusive sense, the word refers broadly to mapmaking by governments, private firms and individual map authors. In this context, it includes not only the compilation, design, production and distribution of maps but also the collection of basic data through surveying, remote sensing and census enumeration. More narrowly, the term connotes map design and production: the final stages of mapmaking are sometimes called 'map finishing'. In the 1990s, humanists and other devotees of postmodern critique appropriated the term – often used in its plural, cartographies – as a metaphor for the interpretation, rhetorical power and cultural relations of maps, diagrams and other graphical representations. In academia, though, a cartographer is a person who either creates maps or studies them.

The art in cartography is most apparent in the map's adaptation of emotive symbols and colours, its interpretation and graphic representation of the physical landscape, and its use of/as decoration. This latter context accounts for the collector's interest in old maps that are both aesthetically intriguing and historically significant. Although modern maps are less overtly decorative than their predecessors, any map, no matter how stylistically bland or marginally creative, reflects its author's exercise of judgement, skill and taste – qualities shared with 'works of art' of all kinds. In a still broader sense, cartography has four distinct links with visual aesthetics and art history: art in maps, art as maps, maps in art, and maps as art (Woodward, 1987).

However objective in appearance or reputation, all maps are at least partly subjective, as John K. Wright (1942) eloquently pointed out in his essay 'Mapmakers are human'. Subjectivity gives rise to bias, especially in politics, journalism and even so-called objective science, in which maps are often persuasive communications, designed consciously to support a particular hypothesis, viewpoint or political agenda (Black, 1997; Tyner, 1982). Some of these maps are clearly social constructions, mediated by producers and users or imposed by force or guile on the less powerful. Examples abound in environmental planning and emergency management (cf. HAZARD). In floodplain management, for example, hydrologists and public officials, who agree on the need for flood insurance and restrictions on private use of beaches and flood plains, willingly overlook the uncertainty inherent in delineating flood zones on flood-insurance rate maps (Monmonier, 1997, pp. 105–26). In similar contexts concerned with human safety, scientists and citizens tolerate flawed maps on which crisp, convincing lines portray environmental regulations as essential or emergency evacuation as feasible.

Subjectivity has its price. Public ignorance of cartographic generalization often allows ill-informed designs, not-so-subtle propaganda, blatant mistakes and unwarranted verbal interpretations to go unchallenged. Although cartographic scholars have been remiss to survey the opinions, attitudes and experiences of map users, conventional wisdom suggests that many map viewers attribute to small-scale maps the comparative precision and relative truthfulness of large-scale representations less subject to the imprecision and uncertainty arising from the need to suppress, smooth, displace and classify features. Geographers and cartographers have yet to effect two obvious and complementary solutions: more appropriately fuzzy map symbols and increased emphasis on graphic literacy in public education.

Similar to diverse links between art and maps, the science in cartography refers both to the use of maps as analytical tools in the physical and social sciences and to the application of scientific principles in studying how the map's symbolic codes affect the viewer's comprehension of data values, spatial patterns and geographic relationships (MacEachren, 1995). Subject testing modelled after controlled experiments in perceptual and cognitive psychology has proven an effective approach to evaluating the legibility of type, the relative accuracy and efficiency with which map symbols (see SYMBOLIZATION) help viewers locate features and places, and the reliability of graytones and colour for portraying differences in quantity and quality (Brewer et al., 1997). In their efforts to understand and improve map communication, cartographic researchers employ scientific strategies ranging from computer SIMULATION and mathematical derivation to QUESTIONNAIRES, structured interviewing, content analysis and qualitative data-collection techniques like PARTICIPANT OBSERVATION and ETHNOGRAPHY.

Contemporary cartography is more a technology than an art or a science. In compiling and displaying maps, mapmakers have had to master, adapt or develop a broad variety of electronic, mechanical and photographic techniques for capturing, storing, retrieving, selecting, smoothing and enhancing geographical information. Electronic scanning and plotting have not only displaced pen-and-ink drawing and other traditional techniques but also blurred distinctions between computer-assisted cartography and geographical information systems. Computer programming became an important tool in cartography in the 1960s, as opportunities for creative design expanded to include geographic databases, mapping software, interfaces for high-interaction map viewing and algorithms for automated map analysis. Perhaps the most revolutionary challenge of the new 'digital cartography' was the need to design maps to be read efficiently by machines, not humans.

Computers have taken much of the drudgery out of the expository cartography practised in geography, earth science, journalism and commercial map publishing. Illustration, presentation and image-processing software as well as specialized packages for animation and map projection foster heretofore extraordinary levels of experimentation and customization. Ironically perhaps, map authorship in this era of the keyboard and mouse depends heavily on hand-eye coordination and the skilful point-and-click manipulation of lines, polygons and other cartographic objects sorted into layers and assigned styles. Although positioning labels, correcting mistakes and experimenting with design are markedly faster than a few decades ago, manual dexterity and at least a rudimentary sense of aesthetics are essential to the successful application of software tools.

Despite its challenges and pitfalls, new technology has opened myriad opportunities for innovation, especially in the development of dynamic and interactive software for making and viewing maps. Especially promising are applications of hypertext, multimedia and narrative graphics – including the integration of sound with sequenced graphics – as well as applications of the Internet and the World Wide Web to map compilation, map analysis, map publishing and cartographic education (Peterson, 1997). However promising, apparent improvements in display technology raise equally if not more enigmatic research questions about the utility, philosophical meaning and social impact of new technology. Cartography's rich history demonstrates that progress is neither inherently linear nor necessarily beneficial (Edney, 1993).

In making the tools and data of map authorship widely accessible, personal computers and mapping software have fostered an unprecedented democratization of cartography. Empowered by 'user-friendly' graphical interfaces and laser printers, untrained amateurs can now produce maps with the crisp type, sharp lines and convincing keys – once the hallmark of the professional mapmaker. The consequences of this empowerment are at once encouraging and alarming. Cartographic purists rightly condemn the misinformation promulgated by software developers ignorant of basic principles of cartographic design – instead of promoting graphic logic, software manuals and default symbols often endorse conceptually flawed multi-hue CHOROPLETH MAPS of count data. Equally intriguing are the prospects of a devaluation of maps as symbols of authority and a 'demassification' of cartographic publishing through the World Wide Web, which provides individual map authors direct access to small, specialized markets.

Because of the importance of government as both a producer and user of maps, cartography is also concerned with the impacts of public policy on coverage, appearance and reliability; with technical standards for accuracy, data quality and terminology; and with legal issues such as access, copyright, liability and privacy

(Curry, 1997; Monmonier, 1982). As an institutional enterprise, mapping depends heavily on the interaction of its public and commercial sectors for the development of navigation aids, atlases and other consumer products as well as for the TOPOGRAPHIC MAPS and geographic inventories essential to national defence, economic development, growth management and environmental protection. Other institutional issues that warrant scholarly investigation are marketing strategies (McGrath, 1986; Petchenik, 1985), cost recovery (Rhind, 1992), and the cartographic relations between government and indigenous peoples (Rundstrom, 1993).

As an academic discipline, cartography is largely a subfield of geography. Although mapmaking is studied and taught in departments of landscape architecture, photogrammetry, planning, surveying and other related fields, most scholars of cartography are affiliated with geography departments, in which students are taught the compilation, design and analysis of maps as a basic research skill. The history of cartography (see CARTOGRAPHY, HISTORY OF) is a recognizable but more loosely organized discipline that includes geographers as well as historians, art historians, historians of science and technology, map collectors and map librarians.

Cartography acquired the trappings of a scholarly specialty in the latter half of the twentieth century (Wolter, 1975). Although still tied in most countries to the parent discipline, geography, cartographers developed their own national scholarly-professional societies, largely in the 1950s and 1960s, as well as their own scholarly and technical journals, principally in the 1960s and 1970s. Even so, separate academic departments of cartography are rare in the English-speaking world, and the field is smaller and less visible than the newer, more vigorous interdisciplinary specialty 'geographical information science' (Goodchild, 1992), which focuses less on mapping and map design than on GEOGRAPHICAL INFORMATION SYSTEMS. The International Cartographic Association, founded in 1960, fosters international collaborative research and the transfer of mapping technology to lesser developed nations. At both international and national levels, technology and education are key concerns.

Few links between cartography and geography are as strong as the authorship of atlases addressing a particular theme or region. As a cartographic synthesis, the carefully crafted atlas is the epitome of geographic scholarship: a comprehensive reference work offering ready retrieval as well as serendipitous insight. Because the genre demands knowledge of both subject matter and map design, the atlas is often a collaborative endeavour of a cartographer responsible for designing pages and producing artwork and a researcher who collects source materials and writes the accompanying text. Careful integration of maps, statistical graphs, photographs and interpretative text is essential. For national, provincial or state atlases, which demand a broad range of specialized knowledge, a general editor might recruit subject-matter experts to compile maps for specific sections, write descriptions and interact with the cartographic editor, who coordinates design and layout.

A promising late twentieth-century development is the electronic atlas, distributed on CD-ROM or over the Internet. Although computer display has yet to match the graphic resolution of the printed page, multimedia distribution can offer readers access to basic data and the author's detailed notes as well as provide animated displays describing physical processes or sequences of historical events (Keller, 1995). An essential element is a highly interactive interface that helps readers search for specific facts, explore data and navigate freely among the atlas's varied representations. The two formats are easily integrated in a hybrid electronic atlas, in which CD-ROM storage provides smooth animations and rapid retrieval, while the Internet offers timely access to new information (Crampton, 1995).

In addition to coping with computers and institutional issues, cartographic scholars have shown an increased interest in map use, especially in navigation, scientific analysis, land-use planning and journalism. Even so, the field has yet to adopt interviewing and other ethnographic methods (see ETHNOGRAPHY) with the fervour once used to explore the effectiveness and reliability of graytones and graduated circles. Despite intriguing conjecture about the power and influence of maps, cartography at the turn of the century lacks the empirical foundation necessary for more than a superficial understanding of the map's role in society. MM

References

Black, J. 1997: *Maps and politics*. London: Reaktion Books. · Brewer, C.A. et al. 1997: Mapping mortality: evaluating color schemes for choropleth maps. *Annals of the Association of American Geographers* 87: 411–38. · Crampton, J. 1995: Cartography resources on the World Wide Web. *Cartographic Perspectives* 22: 3–11. ·

Curry, M.R. 1997: The digital individual and the private realm. *Annals of the Association of American Geographers* 87: 681–99. · Edney, M.H. 1993: Cartography without 'progress': reinterpreting the nature and historical development of mapmaking. *Cartographica* 30 (2&3): 504–68. · Goodchild, M.F. 1992: Geographical information science. *International Journal of Geographical Information Systems* 6: 31–45. · Harley, J.B. 1987: The map and the development of the history of cartography. In J.B. Harley, and D. Woodward, eds, *The history of cartography, vol. 1: Cartography in prehistoric, ancient and medieval Europe and the Mediterranean.* Chicago: University of Chicago Press, 1–42. · Keller, C.P. 1995: Visualizing digital atlas information products and the user perspective. *Cartographic Perspectives* 20: 21–8. · MacEachren, A.M. 1995: *How maps work: representation, visualization, and design.* New York: Guilford Press. · McGrath, G. 1986: Measuring the size of the Canadian market for maps, atlases and related products. *Cartographica* 23 (3): 42–53. · Monmonier, M. 1982: Cartography, geographic information, and public policy. *Journal of Geography in Higher Education* 6: 99–107. · Monmonier, M. 1997: *Cartographies of danger: mapping hazards in America.* Chicago: University of Chicago Press. · Petchenik, B.B. 1985: Maps, markets and money: a look at the economic underpinnings of cartography. *Cartographica* 22 (3): 7–19. · Peterson, M.P. 1997: Cartography and the Internet: introduction and research agenda. *Cartographic Perspectives* 26: 3–12. · Rhind, D. 1992: Data access, charging and copyright and their implications for geographical information systems. *International Journal of Geographical Information Systems* 6: 13–30. · Rundstrom, R.A. 1993: The role of ethics, mapping, and the meaning of place in relations between Indians and whites in the United States. *Cartographica* 30 (1): 21–8. · Tyner, J.A. 1982: Persuasive cartography. *Journal of Geography* 81: 140–4. · Wolter, J.A. 1975: Cartography – an emerging discipline. *Canadian Cartographer* 12: 210–16. · Woodward, D. 1987: Introduction. In D. Woodward, ed., *Art and cartography: six historical essays.* Chicago: University of Chicago Press, 1–9. · Wright, J.K. 1942: Mapmakers are human: comments on the subjective in maps. *Geographical Review* 32: 527–44;

Suggested Reading

Monmonier, M. 1993: *Mapping it out: expository cartography for the humanities and social sciences.* Chicago: University of Chicago Press. · Perkins, C.R. and Parry, R.B., eds, 1990: *Information sources in cartography.* London: Bowker-Saur. · Robinson, A.H. et al. 1995: *Elements of cartography*, 6th edn. New York: John Wiley and Sons. · Thrower, N.J.W. 1996: *Maps and civilization: cartography in culture and society.* Chicago: University of Chicago Press. · Wood, C.H. and Keller, C.P., eds, 1996: *Cartographic design: theoretical and practical perspectives.* Chichester: John Wiley and Sons.

cartography, history of The history of cartography documents and explanation of the motives for making maps, the agents and processes used to make them, their functions, and their role in forming society's views of SPACE and PLACE. Maps may be broadly regarded as codified images of all kinds by which humans formally articulate, represent, or construct their spatial knowledge of the world (cf. MAP IMAGE AND MAP). They are thus one of the primary agents of human geography.

The field of study may be distinguished from three other highly related activities: historical cartography (the compilation of maps showing historical events); HISTORICAL GEOGRAPHY (the reconstruction of past geographies); and the history of geography (the intellectual history of the discipline of geography: Skelton, 1972 – see GEOGRAPHY, HISTORY OF). Another, secondary, meaning of the 'history of cartography' is the history of the subject of CARTOGRAPHY itself from the word's coining in 1839 to mean the historical study of maps to its present rapidly changing relationship with the field of GEOGRAPHICAL INFORMATION SYSTEMS.

The history of cartography seeks to understand how maps function under two broad and often conflicting assumptions. The first assumes that there is a positive structural likeness between the map and the TERRITORY, an affinity from which it derives its meaning. In this view, the map is seen as a natural system. The second assumes that maps can be understood only as self-referential systems. They are still REPRESENTATIONS, not of an independent 'real' world but of relativistic human knowledge, 'constructed according to culturally defined semiotic codes; the knowledge is constructed using various intellectual and instrumental technologies; the knowledge and its representation are both constructed by individuals who work for and within various social institutions' (Edney, 1996; cf. RELATIVISM). In this view, the 'natural' and objective appearance of maps is seen as a mask covering what is mostly a cultural and social agenda favoring those in positions of POWER in a variety of ideological contexts (Harley, 1988). Between these two assumptions and interacting with both is the idea that maps can provide evidence of both human cognitive spatial thought and technological and material culture. The concepts and artefacts thus created have been studied along the REALIST/constructivist spectrum. Few students of the subject place themselves at either extreme of it.

Early maps have been used successfully as sources of documentary evidence to reconstruct where things were. Maps have helped to reconstruct FIELD SYSTEMS, land-use change, changing urban MORPHOLOGY (see TOWNSCAPE), PLACE NAMES, or simply to locate lost settlements, roads, vessels, or buildings in connection with studies of local history, historical geography, archaeology, or historical reconstruction (Blakemore and Harley, 1980); they have provided legal evidence in BOUNDARY disputes (De Vorsey, 1982) and as records of geographical EXPLORATION (Skelton, 1970; Harley, 1990; de Vorsey, 1992). Physical changes in the LANDSCAPE, such as coastal change, migrating meanders, ecological and vegetation change, have also employed early maps.

When maps are seen as part of the story of human technological and material CULTURE, the lens focuses more on the artifact itself and less on the content of the image, in what might be called the internal 'cartographic' aspects of technique and style. Some studies have examined how maps have been physically produced at various stages of SURVEYING, drafting and printing, publishing and consumption (Woodward, 1974; cf. MAP IMAGE AND MAP). The technical processes of surveying and the associated art of navigation have been well documented; indeed, the histories of these two activities have their respective professional organizations and literature. The traditional approach has been to develop objective methods of measuring the accuracy of maps derived from such survey data or the precision of various survey and navigation instruments and methods (Blakemore and Harley, 1980). More recently, however, interest has extended to the social construction or RHETORIC of accuracy in the development of a profession of technical practitioners (Fletcher, 1995). Early maps may also be studied in order to trace the changing elements of cartographic style, whether with the semantic elements of map signs (Delano Smith, 1985), colour (Ehrensvdrd, 1987), and lettering (Woodward, 1987), or their syntactic transformation through generalization and PROJECTION (Snyder, 1993). In this, they inform the relationship between geography and art (see also ART, GEOGRAPHY AND). The study of the physical form of maps – maps as paper, ink, pigment, etc. together with the associated technology of drafting, printing, or publishing paraphernalia – is part of the technical history of printing (Woodward, 1975). Their relevance to the history of cartography lies in the effect that style and physical format have on our understanding of the content of maps. Thus, studies have focused on analysing the chemical composition of the ink or paper of single maps or groups of maps, often to answer questions regarding authenticity (Skelton et al., 1995) or the workshop economics and practices behind their production (Woodward, 1996).

Maps may also be seen as bearing evidence of cognitive systems of human spatial thought and communication. Such activities include wayfinding or navigating from one point to another, spatial reckoning of generalized distances and directions (as in an awareness of the cardinal directions), often expressed in the intuitively attractive but multi-faceted term 'cognitive map' (cf. COGNITIVE MAPPING). The most prevalent theory of cognitive development as applied to the history of cartography is that of Wood (1977), who postulated that the development of hill signs on maps followed a similar path to the Piagetian stages in the development of a child's conceptions of space, a progression of types of relief representation from abstract profiles of hills, pictorial depictions, to formlines, to commensurable contours. This theory was expressed in more general terms by Harvey (1980), who saw 'maps' as being a third, more advanced, stage following 'symbols' and 'pictures' – drawing his evidence particularly from a comparison of the mathematical structure of maps in the medieval and Renaissance periods. The problems in both interpretations of maps as indicators of cognitive growth lie in their inability to account for the changing functions needed by – and consequent different needs for precision among – societies in the past and present.

When early maps are historically situated in the societies that made them, their value as evidence of a culture's 'world view' becomes apparent. Examples at global SCALES include the medieval *mappaemundi*, which have been studied for the secular and religious sources of their expression (Edson, 1997) or the concept of creating world maps using coordinates (Woodward, 1991). At local scales, maps have been used as indicators of how the character of landscapes and places has been visualized by different cultures (Woodward and Lewis, 1998).

In the last twenty years, attention has increasingly been paid to the function of maps as expressions of political and economic power in a variety of ideological contexts. This approach was pioneered by Brian Harley and others as an alternative EPISTEMOLOGY to the self-referencing 'cartographic' approach to the field stressing the 'accuracy model'. Harley's goal was 'to search for the social forces that have structured cartography and to locate the presence of power – and its effects – in all map knowledge' (Harley, 1989). These articulations of spatial power and control include the documentation of property boundaries, the SURVEILLANCE of empire and the NATION-STATE, as well as the subliminal geometry of maps expressed in the structure of the grid, centering, and orientation. They also include elements extraneous to the map frame, such as the role of iconographic decoration in reinforcing imperial and nationalist claims and stereotypes (Harley and Zandvliet, 1992). These elements are revealed not only by critically examining what was shown on maps, but reading 'between the lines... to discover the silences and contradictions that challenge the apparent honesty of the image' (Harley, 1989). In challenging the model of the development of maps as progressively producing better delineations of reality, however, insufficient emphasis was paid to the importance of 'accuracy' or at least 'perceived accuracy' in theories of maps as expressions of power.

Until recently, in what could be termed an observation and comparative phase, historians of cartography often focused on individuals in a biographical approach without offering more widely applicable generalizations. They also encouraged the emphasis on the 'lone genius' model that has long been abandoned in the history of science in recognition of a far more complex interwoven story of technological development. Associated with the biographical approach was an emphasis on reference carto-bibliographies and facsimile atlases (*monumenta*) for the national centres of cartography: recent multi-volume examples concern the Netherlands (Schilder, 1986–; van der Krogt, 1997–). These map descriptions and biographies are an invaluable legacy and, despite the frequently voiced ideal of basing such studies on less rigid divisions to reflect the constant interaction between national groups in early modern Europe, organization of major projects by national traditions – constrained by language, library and archival sources, and national interest, expertise, and funds – is likely to continue. Nevertheless, new trends have sought to supplement the observation/comparative phase by searching for a set of connected statements explaining how a world system of cartography was structured and how it functioned in history. These include a movement from studies driven by personal interests to more broadly-based interdisciplinary links, especially with the history of art and the history of science.

There has also been an enlargement of scope from Euro-American cartography to a more global diversity of cartographic representation, resulting partly from a broad definition of map for the University of Wisconsin History of Cartography Project that includes any graphic representation that facilitates spatial understanding of the world. This definition includes depictions of metaphysical as well as physical landscapes and thus addresses maps of concepts (for example, POPULATION DENSITY), events (such as traditional creation myths or founding histories), as well as of the tangible terrain (as in TOPOGRAPHIC MAPS). Since a goal of the multi-volume History is to interpret the maps of each culture within that culture's own frame of reference, this has required devoting three books to the traditional cartography of non-western societies (Harley and Woodward, 1992, 1994; Woodward and Lewis, 1998).

Associated with the trend to broaden the definition of map away from the accepted Euro-American norms, there has been a tendency to think of the map less as a planimetrically accurate replication and more as a socially-constructed representation. The prevailing PARADIGM has been that mapmaking has followed a steady progression toward planimetric accuracy. This statement is broadly true when confined to the precise measurement of abstract position, yet there have been other functions of maps that have had very little to do with measured location and more with how the world is culturally constructed (Edney, 1993). For example, the paucity of sources in the Ancient and Medieval worlds has resulted in a controversy over the technical sophistication signalled by the possible uses of maps in everyday life. Some authors argue the position that maps were used more frequently than the evidence suggests. Others more sceptically challenge any suggestion that evidence points to the common use of maps in social administration. Thus, Dilke's implicitly generous view that the Roman Empire depended on such developed concepts as a 'map library' (Dilke, 1987) has been challenged by other classicists who claim that there is very little evidence to support the notion of extensive military or administrative use of maps in the Roman Empire, and that the process of government (especially on the fringes of the empire) was far more ad hoc than has been supposed (Talbert, 1990; Brodersen, 1995).

In the context of China, where researchers have often assumed technological primacy in cartography (Needham, 1954), it is now more fruitful to regard the development of cartography in the Asian societies as more closely associated with the pursuit of general culture than with the cultivation of a specialized technique of measured mapping (Yee, 1994). What was communicated in maps – as in landscape paintings – did not have to be measurable. Thus, to view the development of Chinese cartography in terms only of maps drawn to scale with ever increasing verisimilitude was to tell only part – and perhaps not the most important part – of the story.

By enlarging the definition of maps to include representations of these non-metric worlds, the study of the history of cartography shows that this dual function of maps – the measured and the symbolic – has existed at every period from prehistory to the present day and in almost all cultures (Harley and Woodward, 1987). The field has thus been more open to social concerns, such as ETHICS, IDEOLOGY, and COLONIALISM, and writers in CRITICAL THEORY and literary criticism have been attracted to its subject matter (Conley, 1996; Helgerson, 1992; Mignolo, 1995; Tomasch and Gilles, 1998).

In general, the emphasis has also moved from the mapmaker to other agents in the cartographic process – attempting to answer the question why maps were made in the first place. These include an interest in the role of the patron, the role of maps in promoting world trade (Brotton, 1997), the role of the market for maps as prints as well as for geographical information made possible by the economies afforded by map printing (Eisenstein, 1979; Mukerji, 1983), and a broad interest in the extent to which maps became used as part of everyday life (Woodward, 1987).

Four reference gateways to the subject are recommended. For a general current guide on practitioners, literature, and general information about the field, the reader is referred to *Who's Who in the History of Cartography* (Lowenthal, 1998). The primary journal of the field is *Imago Mundi* (1935–). Internet resources can best be accessed through http://ihr.sas.ac.uk/maps/. Finally, the multi-volume History of Cartography redefines and expands the canon of early maps while providing a comprehensive work of reference (Harley and Woodward, 1987). DW

References

Blakemore, M.J. and Harley, J.B. 1980: Concepts in the history of cartography: a review and perspective. *Cartographica*, 17: 4. Monograph 26. · Brodersen, K. 1995: *Terra Cognita. Studien zur raumischen Raumerfassung.* Spudasmata 59. Hildesheim: G. Olms. · Brotton, J. 1997: *Trading territories: mapping the early modern world.* London: Reaktion Books. · Conley, T. 1996: *The self-made map: cartographic writing in early modern France.* Minneapolis: University of Minnesota Press. · De Vorsey, L., Jr. 1982: *The Georgia–South Carolina boundary: a problem in historical geography.* Athens: University of Georgia Press. · Delano Smith, C. 1985: Cartographic signs on European maps and their explanation before 1700. *Imago Mundi* 37: 9–29. · Dilke, O.A.W. 1987: Itineraries and geographical maps in the early and late Roman Empire. In J.B. Harley, and P. Woodward, eds, *The History of Cartography: Cartography in Prehistoric, Ancient, and Medieval Europe and the Mediterranean*, 1. Chicago: University of Chicago Press, 234–57. · Edney, M.H. 1993: Cartography without 'progress:' reinterpreting the nature and historical development of mapmaking. *Cartographica* 30: 54–68. · Edney, M.H. 1996: Theory and the history of cartography. *Imago Mundi* 48: 185–91. · Edson, E. 1997: *Mapping time and space: how medieval thinkers viewed their world.* London: British Library. · Ehrensvdrd, U. 1987: Color in cartography: a historical survey. In D. Woodward, ed., *Art and Cartography: Six Historical Essays*, Chicago: University of Chicago Press, 123–46. · Eisenstein, E. 1979: *The printing press as an agent of change.* Cambridge: Cambridge University Press. · Fletcher, D. 1995: *The emergence of estate maps: Christ Church, Oxford, 1600 to 1840.* Oxford: Clarendon Press. · Harley, J.B. 1988: Maps, knowledge and power. In D. Cosgrove and S. Daniels, eds, *The iconography of landscape: essays on the symbolic representation, design and use of past environments.* Cambridge: Cambridge University Press, 277–312. · Harley, J.B. 1989: Decarconstructing the Map. *Cartographica* 26 (2): 1–20. · Harley, J.B. 1990: *Maps and the Columbian encounter.* Milwaukee: Golda Meir Library. · Harley, J.B. 1992: Deconstructing the map. In T.J. Barnes, and J.S. Duncan, eds, *Writing worlds: discourse, text and metaphor.* London, 231–47. · Harley, J.B. and Woodward, D. 1992: The history of Cartography, volume 2, book 1: Cartography in the Islamic and South Asian Societies. Chicago: University of Chicago Press. · Harley, J.B. and Woodward, D. 1994: *History of Cartography. Vol. 1.* Chicago: University of Chicago Press. · Harley, J.B. and Zandvliet, K. 1992: Art, science, and power in 16th-century Dutch cartography. *Cartographica* 29 (2): 10–19. · Harvey, P.D.A. 1980: *The history of topographical maps: symbols, pictures and surveys.* London: Thames & Hudson. · Helgerson, R. 1986: *The land speaks: cartography, chorography, and subversion in renaissance England.* Representations 16: 50–85. · Helgersan, R. 1992: *Forms of nationhood: The Elizabethan writing of England.* Chicago: University of Chicago Press. · Krogt, P. van der. 1997: *Koeman's Atlantes Neerlandici, vol. 1* – Utrecht: H & S. · Lowenthal, M.A., ed., 1998: *Who's who in the history of cartography: the international guide to the subject.* (D9) Map Collector Publications Ltd for Imago Mundi Ltd. · Mignolo, W. 1995: *The darker side of the Renaissance: literacy, territoriality, and colonization.* Ann Arbor: University of Michigan Press. · Mukerji, C. 1983: *From graven images: patterns of modern materialism.* New York: Columbia University Press. · Needham, J. 1954: *Science and civilisation in China.* Cambridge: Cambridge University Press, esp. vol. 3. · Schilder, G. 1986: *Monumenta Cartographica Neerlandica* (Alphen aan den Rijn: Uitgeverij 'Canaletto,'), vols 1–5. · Skelton, R.A. 1970: *Explorers' maps: chapters in the cartographic record of geographical discovery.* Feltham, New

York, Spring Books. · Skelton, R.A. 1972: *Maps: a historical survey of their study and collecting*. Chicago: University of Chicago Press. · Skelton, R.A. et al. 1995: *The Vinland Map and the Tartar relation*. New Haven, CT.: Yale University Press. · Snyder, J. 1993: *Flattening the earth: two thousand years of map projections*. Chicago: University of Chicago Press. · Talbert, R. 1990: Rome's empire and beyond: the spatial aspect. In Gouvernants et Gouvernis dans l'Imperium Romanum, *Cahiers des Etudes Anciennes* XXVI. Universiti Laval, Departement d'histoire, 215–23. · Tomasch, S. and Gilles, S. 1998: *Text and territory: geographical imagination in the European Middle Ages*. Philadelphia: University of Pennsylvania Press. · Wood, D. 1977: Now and then: comparisons of ordinary Americans' Symbol conventions with those of past cartographers. *Prologue: The Journal of the National Archives* 9: 151–61. · Woodward, D. 1974: The study of the history of cartography: a suggested framework. *American Cartographer* 1: 101–15. · Woodward, D ed. 1975: *Five centuries of map-printing*. Chicago: University of Chicago Press. · Woodward, D. 1987: The manuscript, engraved, and typographic traditions of map lettering. *In Art and Cartography: Six Historical Essays*. Chicago: University of Chicago Press. · Woodward, D. 1991: Maps and the rationalization of geographic space. In J.A. Levensan, ed., *Circa 1492: Art in the Age of Exploration*. New Haven: Yale University Press, 83–7. · Woodward, D. 1996: *Maps as prints in the Italian Renaissance: Makers, Distributors & Consumers*. London: British Library. · Woodward, D. and Lewis. G.M., eds, 1998: *The History of Cartography: Cartography in the Traditional African, American, Arctic, Australian, and Pacific Societies*. Chicago: University of Chicago Press. · Yee, C.D.K. 1994: Taking the world's measure: Chinese maps between observation and text. In J. B. Harley and D. Woodward, *The History of Cartography, Volume 2, Book 2: Cartography in the Traditional East and Southeast Asian Societies*. Chicago: University of Chicago Press, 96–127.

Suggested Reading

Blakemore, M.J. and Harley, J.B. (1980). · Harley, J.B. 1987: The map and the development of the history of cartography. In J.B. Harley, and D., Woodward, eds, *The History of Cartography*. Chicago: University of Chicago Press, 1: 1–42. · Harley, J.B. and Woodward, D. 1989: Why cartography needs its history. *American Cartographer* 16: 5–15.

catastrophe theory A branch of mathematics, developed by Rene Thom (1975), concerned with discontinuous relationships (see also BIFURCATION). In a two-dimensional situation, as in figure 1, there is a portion of the relationship between the two variables (the end-points of which – A and B – are called the *fold-points*) where the value of a is associated with two separate values of x. Isnard and Zeeman (1976) illustrated this with the relationship between threat and military action, their graph showing that although in general as the intensity of a threat increases so does the probability of military action between the fold-points there are two values for the probability of a military action (i.e. at a_0 the probability may be either x_4 or x_6). These represent two reactions to the threat – of the dove and of the hawk. There is both an upper level of threat (B on the graph) beyond which public opinion will not accept the doveish option and a lower level (A) below which it will not accept the hawkish reaction. Where

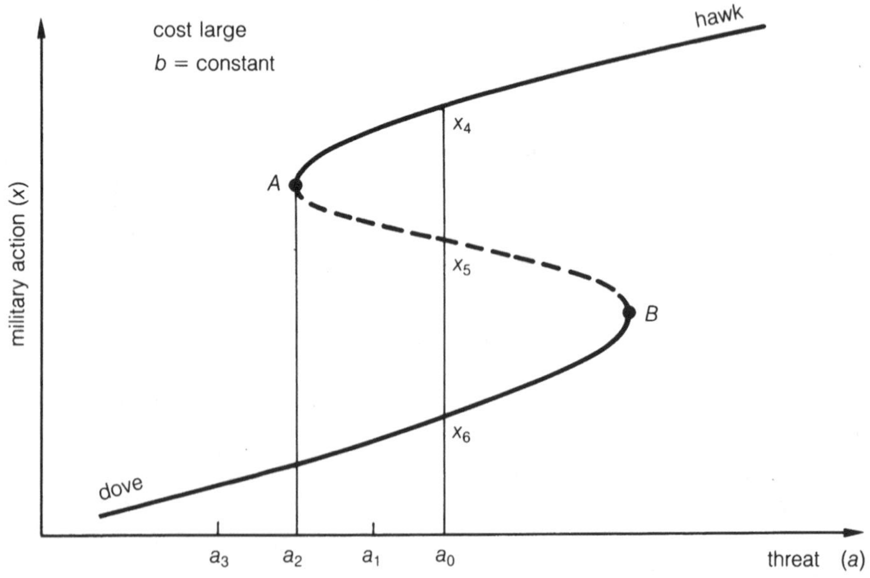

catastrophe theory *1: A threat–action graph for high cost* (Isnard and Zeeman, 1976)

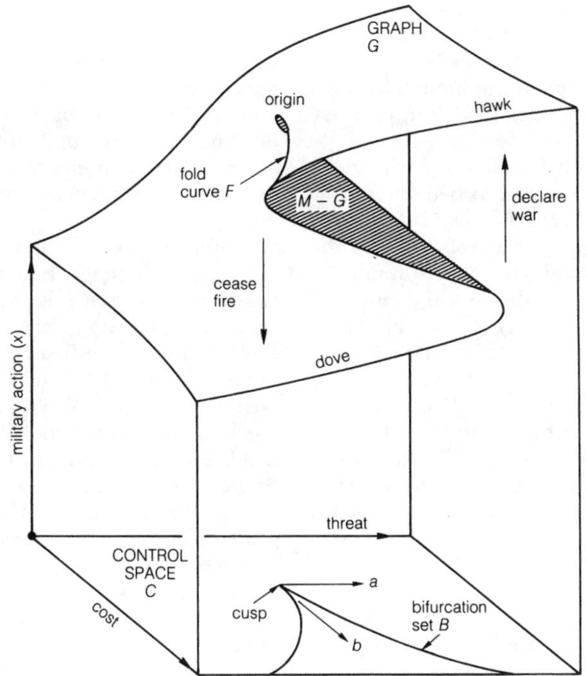

catastrophe theory *2: The cusp catastrophe* (Isnard and Zeeman, 1976)

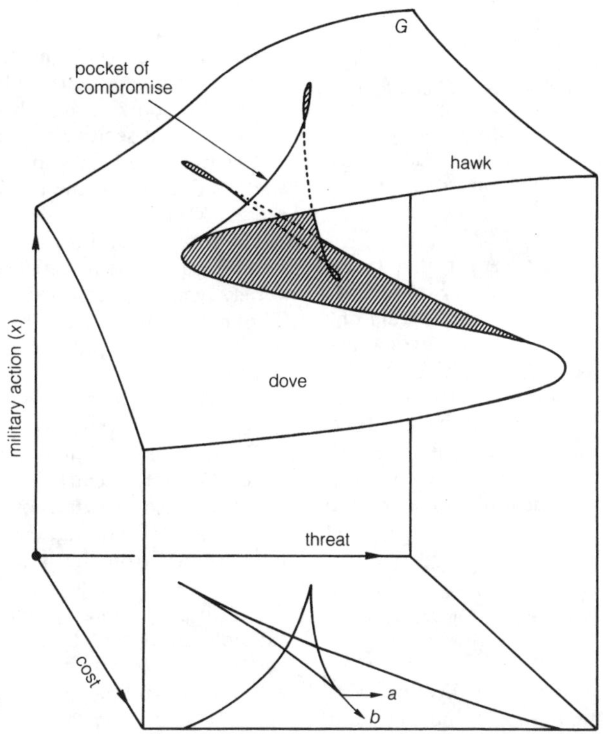

catastrophe theory *3: A section of the butterfly catastrophe* (Isnard and Zeeman, 1976)

the two overlap is what is termed a *hysteresis*, indicating a range of threat levels within which the likely response is not readily predicted, and the shift from one relationship to the other can be understood in qualitative terms only.

In three-dimensional situations, where the response variable is related to two stimuli (as in figure 2), there is a *fold curve* (the area shown by *M–G*) where the probability of the response is indeterminate; the stimuli are the degree of threat and the cost of countering it by military action, the response variable is the probability of military action, and within the cusp the probability of a military action can take several values. The fold curve can take various forms: figure 3 shows a *butterfly catastrophe* which Isnard and Zeeman identify as a 'pocket of compromise' for those promoting the hawkish and doveish responses.

The existence of catastrophes creates difficulties in modelling SYSTEMS, especially in predictive work, since the same conditions can produce different outcomes. Wilson (1981) has illustrated this with examples of the internal structure of cities. RJJ

References and Suggested Reading

Isnard, C.A. and Zeeman, E.C. 1976: Some models from catastrophe theory in the social sciences. In L. Collins, ed., *The use of models in the social sciences*. London: Tavistock Publications, 44–99. · Thom, R. 1975: *Structural stability and morphogenesis*. Reading, MA: W.A. Benjamin. · Wilson, A.G. 1981: *Catastrophe theory and bifurcation: applications to urban and regional systems*. London. Croom Helm; Berkeley: University of California Press.

categorical data analysis A set of statistical procedures employed when one or more of the variables is measured at a nominal scale only (see MEASUREMENT). Standard REGRESSION methods cannot be used with such data because they violate several of the statistical assumptions underlying the GENERAL LINEAR MODEL. Categorical data analysis methods avoid those problems and provide robust procedures for estimating linear relationships with nominal data. RJJ

Suggested Reading

Wrigley, N. 1985: *Categorical data analysis for geographers and environmental scientists*. London and New York: Longman.

census The total process of collecting, compiling and publishing demographic, economic and social data pertaining to all persons in a defined territory at a specified time. The census may thus provide a primary source of information about the population of a country; given its legal status, its coverage, the scale of the operation and resources devoted to it, and that it takes place under the auspices of some governmental authority, it permits a far greater content and depth of analysis than can normally be produced by other methods.

Enumerations of population were carried out in ancient times, but the earliest modern censuses took place in Scandinavia and in some Germanic and Italian states in the eighteenth century. The first census of Iceland, for example, was in 1703, of Sweden in 1749 and Denmark in 1769. The first general census of the USA took place in 1790, although there had been earlier state censuses. In Britain and France the first censuses were held in 1801 and during the nineteenth century all European countries initiated periodic population censuses (Willigan and Lynch, 1982). Governmental attitudes to census-taking varied: some countries equated population numbers with military or economic strength, while others saw the census as a basis for the distribution of resources. In the USA, a specific provision for a population count was made in the Constitution as state populations were to be used to apportion the members of the House of Representatives (Daugherty and Kammeyer, 1995). Aggregate census data are usually in the public domain, though an example of the sensitivity and secrecy surrounding the census comes from the USSR in 1937 when a census was conducted but the results treated as state secrets. During the present century, and especially since 1945, most countries of the world have begun to take censuses, although with widely varying frequency and reliability. Though critiques have been relatively little developed by population geographers, census-taking may be seen as part of the wider monitoring by STATES of human activity (see, for example, SURVEILLANCE).

The census has sometimes proved controversial not only because it is generally compulsory but also because of the sensitivity of questions surrounding, for example, religion or ETHNICITY (on the latter in the 1991 UK census, see Coleman and Salt, 1996; Peach 1996). It may also be prone to inaccuracy, for example in the recording of age. The categories it adopts may be rather inflexible for the understanding of social structure and change, and may themselves represent a particular view of society. Questions asked need to be adapted to changing population behaviour and structure (for example to take account of cohabitation or divorce or changing ethnicity).

Two qualities in a census are particularly important: periodicity and universality – i.e. the need to hold regular censuses and to include every individual in a given area: the UK, for example, has held regular censuses at ten-year intervals. SAMPLING is also used in many countries to establish certain categories of information within a full census, or to replace that census. There is also a general distinction in census method between a *de facto* approach, as in the UK, where individuals are recorded at the place where they were found at the time of the census, and a *de jure* approach, as in the USA, where people are recorded according to their usual place of residence. Census data provide a cross-sectional view of a population at a particular moment and may be distinguished from longitudinal data (cf. LONGITUDINAL DATA ANALYSIS). Attempts to bridge this gap, where individuals are traced from one census to another and where other demographic data relating to the individual may be incorporated, include the Longitudinal Study in Britain or the *Echantillon Démographique Permanent* in France. Access to, and use of, the census in many countries has been much improved through computerization and computer mapping (see COMPUTER-ASSISTED CARTOGRAPHY; GEOGRAPHICAL INFORMATION SYSTEMS). More detailed information has been made available to researchers through samples such as the SARS (Samples of Anonymised Records) in the UK or the PUMS (Public Use Microdata Samples) in the USA. Previous censuses provide invaluable material for historical geography, both the published tables and (subject to time limits that may be imposed to protect confidentiality) individual census returns. Thus, the census enumerators' books – the manuscript recording of information on individuals and households on which the aggregate tables were based – are a valuable source for understanding the social geography of nineteenth-century Britain and other countries where census-taking is well established.

Types of data collected by censuses vary enormously from country to country. The United Nations, in an attempt to foster comparability, has suggested that each census should include: total population; sex, age and marital status; place of birth, citizenship or nationality; first language, literacy and educational qualifications; economic status; urban or rural domicile; household or family structure; and fertility. PEO

References

Coleman, D. and Salt, J., eds, 1996: *Ethnicity in the 1991 census. Volume 1: Demographic characteristics of the ethnic minority populations*. London: HMSO. · Daughtery, H.G. and Kammeyer, K.C.W. 1995: *An introduction to population*, 2nd edn. New York and London: The Guilford Press, ch. 4. · Peach, C., ed, 1996: *Ethnicity in the 1991 census. Volume 2. The ethnic minority populations of Great Britain*. London: HMSO. · Willigan, J.D. and Lynch, K.A. 1982: *Sources and methods of historical demography*. New York and London: Academic Press, ch. 4.

Suggested Reading

Benjamin, B. 1970: *The population census*. London: Heinemann. · Cox, P.R. 1976: *Demography*, 5th edn, Cambridge and New York: Cambridge University Press. · Dale, A. and Marsh, C., eds, 1993: *The 1991 census user's guide*. London: HMSO. · Hakim, C. 1982: *Secondary analysis in social research: a guide to data sources and methods with examples*. London: George Allen and Unwin, Part One, 25–94. · Lawton, R., ed., 1978: *The census and social structure*. London: Frank Cass. · Openshaw, S., ed., 1995: *The census users' handbook*. Cambridge: GeoInformation International. · Petersen, W. 1975: *Population*, 3rd edn. New York and London: Collier-Macmillan, ch. 2.

census tract A small areal unit used in collecting and reporting CENSUS data. The first tracts were defined by the US Bureau of the Census in 1920 to approximate NATURAL AREAS or NEIGHBOURHOODS wherever possible, thereby providing valuable data for analysing city district characteristics (see SOCIAL AREA ANALYSIS). Many census authorities report data for similar small areas (the UK term is enumeration district) but they are generally constructed on logistical grounds (ease of administration) rather than to meet analytical purposes. RJJ

Suggested Reading

Openshaw, S., ed., 1992: *A census users' handbook*, 2nd edition. London: Longman.

central business district (CBD) The nucleus of an urban area, containing the main concentration of commercial land uses (shops, offices and warehouses). This is associated – as both cause and effect – with both the most accessible point in modern capitalist cities and its peak land value (see ALONSO MODEL). The CBD typically contains the urban area's densest concentration of land uses and tallest non-residential buildings and is spatially structured internally, with different use categories (e.g. clothing shops) concentrated in certain areas to benefit from the EXTERNAL ECONOMIES associated with AGGLOMERATION. (There is commonly vertical segregation too, with uses that can afford the highest rents on the ground floors of high-rise buildings.)

Most CBDs are in relative if not absolute decline as their characteristic uses are increasingly decentralized to suburban and exurban locations, as with the growth of planned shopping centres and office parks close to major highway intersections. (See CENTRIFUGAL AND CENTRIPETAL FORCES; RETAILING, GEOGRAPHY OF.) RJJ

Suggested Reading

Carter, H. 1995: *The study of urban geography*, 4th edn. London: Arnold.

central place theory A theoretical account of the size and distribution of settlements within an URBAN SYSTEM in which marketing is the predominant urban function. The theory assumes that both buyers (customers) and sellers (shopowners) make utility-maximizing decisions: the theory is NORMATIVE, showing what might appear in certain idealized circumstances.

The two main approaches to central place theory were developed by German economic geographers – Walter Christaller and August Lösch. Christaller dealt only with retailing functions, and based his theory on two concepts: the *range of a good* (the maximum distance a consumer will travel to purchase that good alone); and the *threshold for a good* (the minimum volume of business necessary for an establishment selling that good alone to be commercially viable). He assumed constant utilities across all consumers and all shopowners and also that different goods would have different ranges and thresholds, which would determine both the number and distribution of establishments – providing a good in an area with a given population.

Christaller (1966) grouped retail establishments into seven orders, with similar thresholds and ranges within each. To derive the geography of the location of the different orders, he argued that shopowners locate their establishments as close to customers as possible, to minimize travelling costs and so maximize both shop turnover and consumer satisfaction: shops are located centrally within their HINTERLANDS.

If population is uniformly distributed across an area where movement in all directions is unimpeded, then meeting this centrality requirement produces a hexagonal network of shop locations in central places. (Hexagons are the most efficient geometrical figures for the exhaustion of a territory without overlap.) Central places with the lowest order functions (having the smallest thresholds and ranges) have the densest network, those in the next order have a less dense hexagonal network, and so forth. All central places of a particular order also contain all of the characteristic functions of the lower order centres (so that if first order central places are characterized by grocers' shops, second order places by butchers' shops, and third order places by hardware stores, then every third order central place will contain grocers' and butchers' shops as well as one or more hardware stores). This produces a hierarchy of central places – with seven levels according to the original theory (whose details were influenced by Christaller's empirical observations in southern Germany).

Christaller suggested three ways in which that hierarchical spatial structure could be organized. The first (a in the figure) minimizes the number of settlements serving an area by having each at the meeting point of three hexagons. This is his $k = 3$ (or marketing principle) model, in which the number of settlements at each level of the hierarchy below the second is three times the number at the next highest. (Thus, with one at the highest, seventh, order, the numbers are 1, 2, 6, 18, 54, 162, 486.) The figure (a) illustrates this arrangement with a three-level hierarchy only.

In Christaller's $k = 4$ (or transport principle) model the goal is to minimize the length of roads needed to join all adjacent pairs of central places. As shown in (b), each settlement is centrally located on each side of a hexagon, at the boundary of two rather than three hinterlands. The number of settlements is thus greater than in the $k = 3$ model (in the ratio 1, 2, 8, 32, 128, 512, 2048). Finally, he suggested a $k = 7$ (or administrative principle) model (c in the figure) in which each lower order hinterland nested exclusively within that of a single higher-order central place only – producing a sequence of 1, 6, 42, 294, 2058, 14,406, and 100,842 settlements.

Lösch's (1954) model was less restrictive than Christaller's because rather than bundle functions into orders he treated each as having a separate range, threshold and hexagonal hinterland. Wherever feasible, establishments in these functions were clustered in the same settlements but in his system all central places with a function having a particular threshold need not contain examples of all functions

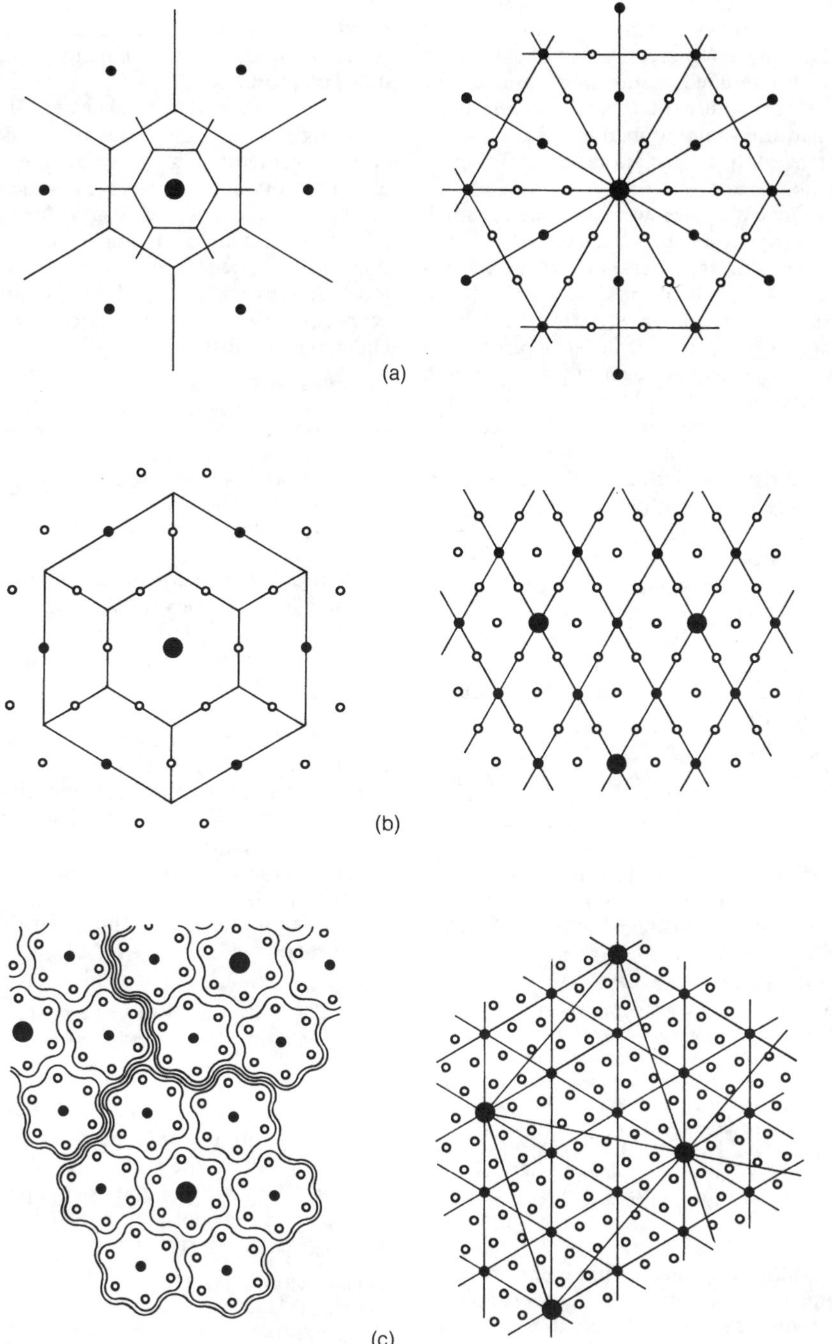

central place theory *The size and spacing of central places, plus their hinterlands (left) and routes (right), according to three variants of Christaller's model: (a) the market principle, which minimum of the number of centres: (b) the transport principle, which minimizes the road length: and (c) the administrative principle, in which hinterlands are nested hierarchically* with smaller thresholds. The result is a more complicated pattern of central places than in Christaller's presentation, and Lösch also incorporated other urban functions (such as manufacturing). Whereas Christaller's theory predicted a stepped hierarchical form to the CITY-SIZE DISTRIBUTION (i.e. all places in an order had the same population), Losch's was consistent with a continuous distribution of population sizes.

These two theories were central to much of the early work on SPATIAL STRUCTURES undertaken during geography's QUANTITATIVE REVOLUTION in the 1960s. Christaller's, in particular, was used many times as the basis for searches for hierarchically structured, hexagonal arrangements of central places, both in rural areas and within cities (see also RETAILING, GEOGRAPHY OF), and for distance-minimizing patterns of consumer shopping choice. Christaller's was used also as the basis for planning settlement patterns, in a variety of contexts. The 'marketing principle' was used in the newly-settled polders of the Netherlands, for example, whereas the 'adminisrative principle' was employed under the Nazis in the 'resolution' of the 'Eastern Question': Christaller was an expert adviser in the 'Reich Commissariat for the Strengthening of Germany' (Freeman, 1987). RJJ

References

Christaller, W. 1966: *Central places in Southern Germany*, trans. C. W. Baskin. Englewood Cliffs, NJ and London: Prentice-Hall (first German edition, 1933). · Freeman, M.J. 1987: *Atlas of Nazi Germany*. London: Croom Helm. · Lösch, A. 1954: *The economics of location*. New Haven, CT: Yale University Press; Oxford: Oxford University Press (first German edition, 1940);

Suggested Reading

Beavon, K.S.O. 1977: *Central place theory: a reinterpretation*. London and New York: Longman. · Berry, B.J.L. 1967: *Geography of market centers and retail distribution*. Englewood Cliffs, NJ and London: Prentice-Hall. · Berry, B.J.L and Parr, J.B. 1988: *Geography of market centers and retail distribution*, 2nd edn. Englewood Cliffs, NJ: Prentice-Hall. · Preston, R.E. 1985: Christaller's neglected contribution to the study of the evolution of central places. *Progress in Human Geography* 9: 177–93.

central planning An omnipotent form of economic and social planning, associated with STATE centralized control and direction over both the SPACE-ECONOMY and SOCIETY. It is a type of planning associated particularly with state SOCIALISM, based on the Marxist supposition that central planning enables society to overcome both the anarchy of production and the CLASS conflict that is inherent in the capitalist mode of production. Under state socialism it is considered the only way of achieving rapid economic growth, an egalitarian income distribution and a strong defence against capitalist countries.

One of the major weaknesses of central planning has been the problem of calculating and implementing a plan for the efficient allocation of national resources in the absence of effective and realistic cost/profit criteria to guide investment decisions. Over-centralization of DECISION-MAKING also tends to stultify local initiative and the ability of grassroots economic decision-makers to respond to changing circumstances. GES

Suggested Reading

Ellman, M. 1979: *Socialist planning*. Cambridge: Cambridge University Press. · Pickles, A. and Smith, A., eds, 1998: *Theorising transition. The political economy of post-communist transformation*. London, Routledge. · Smith, G.E. 1989: *Planned development in the socialist world*. Cambridge: Cambridge University Press.

centrifugal and centripetal forces Term adapted from physics by C.C. Colby (1932) to describe two counteracting forces generating patterns of land use change within urban areas. Centrifugal forces push households and businesses away from the congested, polluted, high density and expensive inner city areas towards the suburbs and beyond (see also COUNTERURBANIZATION; DECENTRALIZATION; SPRAWL); centripetal forces attract them towards the centre for the benefits of ACCESSIBILITY and AGGLOMERATION (see GENTRIFICATION). The balance of these two forces at any period determines the evolution of the urban MORPHOLOGY. RJJ

Reference

Colby, C.C. 1932: Centripetal and centrifugal forces in urban geography. *Annals of the Association of American Geographics* 23: 1–20.

centrography The descriptive statistics for spatially-distributed point patterns, developed in Leningrad in the 1920s to identify, for example, the centre of gravity of a population and its mean dispersal around that point (see also POPULATION POTENTIAL). RJJ

Suggested Reading

Kellerman, A. 1981: *Centrographic methods in geography. Concepts and techniques in modern geography 32*. Norwich: GeoBooks.

chain migration The process whereby migratory movements are sustained through kinship or other links. An initial MIGRATION stream of innovators who make the first moves from home may be followed by others, as information is passed back from destination to point of origin so that, for example, a village may be linked to a particular residential area of a city by this process. Thus, a primary stream of migrants may be dominated by younger adults in search of better employment or a better standard of living, while the secondary stream may include their dependants, children or parents, as well as neighbours and other members of the home COMMUNITY. Occupational specialization as well as kin may be a powerful link in the migration chain. The creation of distinct ethnic residential areas, e.g. by Italians or Chinese in North American cities, may be aided by this process (see SEGREGATION; SOCIAL AREA ANALYSIS). Chain migration is particularly evident in international movements over long distances where information about opportunities for intending migrants is available mainly through the experiences of those who have already moved. PEO

Suggested Reading

Daugherty, H.G. and Kammeyer, K.C.W. 1995: *An introduction to population*. 2nd edn. New York and London: The Guilford Press, ch. 6. · Dinnerstein, L., Nichols, R.L. and Reimers, D.M. 1996: *Natives and strangers. A multicultural history of Americans*. Oxford: Oxford University Press. · Ogden, P.E. 1984: *Migration and geographical change*. Cambridge: Cambridge University Press. · White, P.E. and Woods, R.I., eds, 1980: *The geographical impact of migration*. London: Longman; Seattle: University of Washington Press.

chaos A mathematical term for relationships between variables which show no order, with oscillations displaying periodicity in neither their frequency nor their amplitude (see figure (c) under BIFURCATION). Empirical and theoretical studies are producing increasing evidence of chaotic relationships (cf. CATASTROPHE THEORY), which makes forecasting and prediction of future SYSTEM states extremely difficult. Within geography this is particularly the case in modelling aspects of the physical environment and its changes, such as climate, which is creating substantial difficulties in developing strategies to cope with the assumed impacts of, for example, global warming. RJJ

Suggested Reading

Gleick, J. 1988: *Chaos: making a new science*. London: Cardinal Books.

chaotic conception A term associated with REALISM as a philosophy of science for an arbitrary abstraction from a whole. Most scientific analyses focus on some components of a SYSTEM only. If these have some unity and autonomous existence, their separation for study is a rational ABSTRACTION. If, however, the selection either divides one or more wholes or amalgamates unrelated parts of separate wholes, then it is a chaotic conception whose study has little value. Sayer (1992) argued that many geographical studies deal with chaotic conceptions, such as service industries, which cover a very wide range of dissimilar activities and about which few, if any, useful generalizations can be made. RJJ

Reference

Sayer, A. 1992: *Method in social science: a realist approach*, 2nd edn. London: Routledge.

chi square (χ^2) A widely-used NON-PARAMETRIC STATISTIC for the analysis of nominal data (see MEASUREMENT). SIGNIFICANCE TESTS employing chi square are of two main types:

1 Comparisons of two empirical frequency distributions, such as the number of people in each of five separate ethnic categories in two city districts, to see if they are probably drawn from (i.e. are representative of) the same population. A significant difference between the two would imply that they are unlikely to be separate random SAMPLES from the same population, stimulating the conclusion that the two districts almost certainly have populations with different ethnic profiles.

2 An empirical frequency distribution is compared with another (which may be either theoretically- or empirically-derived) to identify the probability of the former being a random sample of the latter, as with the comparison of the age structure of one town in Wales to that of the total Welsh population. A significant difference between the two would indicate that the town's age structure is not the same as that of the entire country – i.e. the town is not a random sample of the country's population on that characteristic. RJJ

Suggested Reading

O'Brien, L. 1992: *Introducing quantitative geography: measurement, methods and generalised linear models*. London and New York: Routledge. · Walford, N. 1995: *Geographical data analysis*. Chichester and New York: John Wiley.

Chicago school Members of the Department of Sociology at the University of Chicago who activated a major research programme on the American city during the early twentieth century. Many academics over several generations have been associated with the school, but

William Thomas (1863–1947), Robert Park (1864–1944), Ernest Burgess (1886–1966), and Louis Wirth (1897–1952) stand out, as their collective work established and sustained a new direction for American sociology (Bulmer, 1984). Drawing, paradoxically, on both PRAGMATISM and SOCIAL DARWINISM, Chicago School sociologists combined painstaking ETHNOGRAPHIC research with sweeping generalizations, steeped in physical METAPHORS and evolutionary logic, about urban SOCIETY. The legacy of their work is complex and ambiguous, and contemporary authors range in their assessment of it from outright rejection, through a selective incorporation of certain insights and methodologies, to a celebration of the Chicago School as progenitor of humanistic social science.

Thomas introduced many issues that motivated subsequent research within the Chicago sociology department. *The Polish peasant in Europe and America*, published in 1918 (the year Thomas was dismissed over allegations of an extra-marital affair; Deegan, 1988), is a key early text, where Thomas and Znaniecki investigate both sides of a transatlantic flow of IMMIGRANTS: conditions in rural Poland that led to emigration and the settlement of Poles in American cities. This four-volume work set the tone for scores of dense ethnographic studies done by faculty and graduate students at the University of Chicago. In each case researchers acquired new languages where appropriate, conducted social surveys (cf. SURVEY ANALYSIS), and engaged in PARTICIPANT OBSERVATION in an effort to chart the forces that bound COMMUNITIES together. Thomas and Znaniecki initiated perhaps the most enduring theme in Chicago School research: the dynamic between cultural retention among immigrants versus the pull to ASSIMILATE to American social mores. The residential clustering of Poles in American cities was seen as instrumental in allowing these immigrants to retain valued elements of their cultural heritage while, gradually but inevitably, assimilating to the society around them (cf. SEGREGATION). The dual nature of 'ghettoized' neighbourhoods was further elaborated by Wirth (1928) in his seminal study of Chicago's Jewish community (see GHETTO).

Park, who became the dominant intellectual figure in the department after the departure of Thomas, provided a formal theoretical backdrop for Chicago research by adapting principles of plant ECOLOGY to human society (Park, in Turner, 1967; also see McKenzie, in Hawley, 1968; Matthews, 1977; and Cortese, 1995). HUMAN ECOLOGY likens society to an organism, with each constituent part symbiotically related to all others in a web of relations that form around competitive and cooperative behaviour. On one level, which Park labelled biotic (sub-social), human activities at all times are the product of an innate urge to compete in the struggle for survival, a struggle most clearly discernible in the ECONOMY where individuals pursue their own ends. Competition over limited rewards sorts individuals based upon their given level of abilities. Those with similar abilities are 'naturally' channelled into groups that find appropriate occupational and residential niches in society, in much the same way that plant species proliferate in (and eventually dominate) places where environmental qualities favour their particular genetic composition. Within these ecological groups, or communities, individuals discover that it is in their interest to cooperate and regularize their relations with one another. Thus a 'MORAL ORDER' emerges reflecting the principle of cooperation, which Park saw as a necessary complement to competition. Humans, in contrast to plant communities, temper the demands of the biotic level by developing a cultural SUPERSTRUCTURE where rules are established to modify and control competition. Otherwise, Park believed, society would lack the basis to continue its existence, leading to a 'war of all against all'. Armed with these conceptualizations, Park's students set about defining 'natural' communities, such as immigrant groups, hobos, taxi dancers and street gangs, and documenting the moral orders shared by their members (e.g. see Anderson, 1961). These investigations are invariably rich in ethnographic detail but the zeal of researchers to fit their data into the confines of ecological theory often seems forced.

Burgess was instrumental in transcribing the theory of human ecology to the urban arena, deriving a concentric model of the city based on the sorting behaviour of competition (Park, Burgess and McKenzie, 1925: see ZONAL MODEL and the figure there). In his model, commercial and industrial activities capture the city centre (the CENTRAL BUSINESS DISTRICT [CBD]) because of their ability to generate profit and outbid other land uses for locations of highest spatial mobility. A *Zone in Transition* surrounds the city centre, where landlords allow their residential building stock to deteriorate in anticipation of the unearned profits they will reap as the CBD expands. This district houses those least able to pay rent, typically recent immigrants and other racialized minorities, in ghettos. Beyond the Zone in Transition lies a belt of NEIGHBOURHOODS housing the more settled working class, both American-born and immigrants who have achieved a modest level of social mobility. The middle class resides in manicured suburbs, or exurbs, on the periphery of the urbanized area, where they enjoy ample space and easy access to the countryside. Burgess set his model in motion by adding the concept of 'invasion-succession', based on his assumptions that cities, as organisms, must grow, and that individuals are almost universally able to achieve upward social mobility. According to Burgess, as new commercial enterprises are established and new immigrants arrive, the CBD and Zone in Transition expand, pushing into the *Zone of Workers' Homes*. At the same time, new jobs are generated, allowing working-class individuals to move up the occupational hierarchy and attain higher incomes, thereby opening new opportunities for immigrants to fill the jobs left behind. Working-class families direct their elevated incomes to the housing market and 'invade' middle-class suburbs, expanding their zone of the city outward until they dominate the area that was once exclusive to middle-class residents. INVASION AND SUCCESSION therefore follows the cascading effect generated by the relentless growth of the CBD.

It is deeply ironic that the Burgess model continues to inform URBAN PLANNING policy in most North American cities. Planners often reproduce the zonal pattern described above by fostering the development of homogeneous land uses in specified areas of the city. The city centre is therefore scheduled to house the commercial core of the urban economy, surrounded by progressively lower densities of residential land uses. Burgess, however, believed that land uses sorted themselves into a concentric pattern at the biotic level through competition and 'natural' selection. Within the rubric of human ecology theory, planning would be seen as part of the cultural superstructure of society, where the negative effects of excessive competition are muted. Yet planners step in to reinforce (at times even force) a concentric pattern because processes that are supposed to develop 'naturally' do not; instead, the concentric pattern is 'naturalized' within a bureaucracy that operates at the cultural level.

Criticisms of human ecology have been numerous and comprehensive, although the Chicago School is not without its apologists. Early commentators focused on empirical inaccuracies of the Burgess model; of these Homer Hoyt's (1939: cf. SECTORAL MODEL – see also MULTIPLE NUCLEI MODEL) demonstration that urban land values vary more within concentric zones than between them is the most significant. Assessments published during the 1940–65 period were part of a larger project to replace human ecology with structural functionalism as the basic PARADIGM for American sociology. Walter Firey (1947), for example, asserted that the distinction between the biotic and cultural levels of society is overdrawn within Chicago School research. Gideon Sjoberg (1960) focused his criticisms on the tendency for Park and Burgess to UNIVERSALIZE from the American experience, producing GRAND THEORIES that in actuality reflect time- and place-bound experiences. In particular, he argues that the Burgess model of urban land use only applies in the context of industrial capitalist societies (see SJOBERG MODEL). Recent authors have extended this criticism, arguing that the theories presented by the Chicago sociologists contain a substantial normative content – that they legitimate the competition characteristic of CAPITALISM and the melting-pot IDEOLOGY of American society (Harvey, 1973; Castells, 1977). Still others have shown that the Chicago sociologists were incorrect in portraying European immigrants and African-Americans as similar types of ethnic communities, and that they disregarded the depth of colour-based discrimination in American society (Philpott, 1978; Persons, 1987). Finally, feminist criticism has raised an equally serious charge. Deegan (1988) has documented the collaboration between members of the Chicago School and women social critics in the opening decades of the twentieth century. By the late 1910s, however, members of the Chicago sociology department sought to distance themselves from the pioneering social surveys and intellectual insights made by Jane Addams and other women residents of Hull House. In particular, Burgess and Park advocated a sharp distinction between social work (which they deemed an appropriate pursuit for women) and sociology (seen as a manly, intellectual subject, rather than an emotional one), and thereby trivialized the work of their former collaborators (Sibley 1995). Thus, in his introduction to her book, Park characterized Frances Donovan's (1929) study of saleswomen in Chicago as '. . . impressionistic and descriptive rather than systematic and formal . . . ' and '. . . more interested in the history than in the sociology of contemporary life . . . ', despite the fact that Donovan utilized the same ethnographic methodologies as male researchers.

Yet there are those who wish to salvage elements of Chicago School thought, and they too have presented cogent arguments. While it is true that Park and his colleagues portrayed African-Americans too simply (as one ethnic group among many), this fault was related to Park's critique of a biologically-determined conception of RACE. Generally, Park emphasized the socially constructed aspects of race relations, stressing that ethnic groups (including blacks) eventually would be part of mainstream American society as they attained upward social mobility (Jackson and Smith, 1984; Persons, 1987; Farber, 1995). Jackson has also argued that the grand theories produced by Chicago sociologists are overemphasized by critics while the influences of pragmatism in Chicago School research have been ignored. He further suggests that the participant observation studies characteristic of HUMANISTIC sociology and GEOGRAPHY have their roots in the ethnography practised by students of Thomas, Park, and Wirth (Jackson, 1984; also see Lal, 1990; and Burns, 1996). Ultimately, the work of the Chicago School must be judged within its own context, early twentieth-century American thought; in that light it probably led to as many significant advances as strategic oversights. DH

References

Anderson, N. 1961 [orig. pub. 1923]: *The hobo*. Chicago: University of Chicago Press. · Bulmer, M. 1984: *The Chicago School of sociology: institutionalization, diversity and the role of sociological research*. Chicago: University of Chicago Press. · Burns, T. 1996: The theoretical underpinnings of Chicago Sociology in the 1920s and 30s, *Sociological Review* 44: 474–94. · Castells, M. 1977: *The urban question: A marxist approach*, trans. Alan Sheridan. London: Edward Arnold. · Cortese, A.J. 1995: The rise, hegemony, and decline of the Chicago School of sociology, 1892–1945. *Social Science Journal* 32: 235–54. · Deegan, M.J. 1988: *Jane Addams and the men of the Chicago School, 1892–1918*. New Brunswick NJ: Transaction Books. · Donovan, F.R. 1929: *The saleslady*. Chicago: University of Chicago Press. · Farber, N. 1995: Charles S. Johnson's *The Negro in Chicago. American Sociologist* 26: 78–88. · Firey, W. 1947: *Land use in central Boston*. Cambridge, MA: MIT Press. · Harvey, D. 1973: *Social justice and the city*. Baltimore: Johns Hopkins University Press. · Hawley, A.H. 1968: *Roderick D. McKenzie on human ecology*. Chicago: University of Chicago Press. · Hoyt, H. 1939: *The structure and growth of residential neighborhoods in American cities*. Washington, D.C.: Federal Housing Administration. · Jackson, P. 1984: Social disorganisation and moral order in the city, *Transactions, Institute of British Geographers* NS 9: 168–180. · Jackson, P. and Smith S.J. 1984: *Exploring social geography*. London: George Allen and Unwin. · Lal, B.B. 1990: *The romance of culture in an urban civilization: Robert E. Park on race and ethnic relations*. London: Routledge. · Matthews, F.H. 1977: *Quest for an American sociology: Robert E. Park and the Chicago School*. Montreal and London: McGill–Queen's University Press. · Park, R.E, Burgess, E.W. and McKenzie, R.D. 1925: *The city*. Chicago: University of Chicago Press. · Persons, S. 1987: *Ethnic studies at Chicago, 1905–45*. Urbana, IL: University of Illinois Press. · Philpott, T.L. 1978: *The slum and the ghetto: neighborhood deterioration and middle-class reform, Chicago, 1880–1930*. New York: Oxford University Press. · Saunders, P. 1986: *Social theory and the urban question*, 2nd edn. London: Hutchinson. · Sibley, D. 1995: Gender, science, politics and geographies of the city, *Gender, Place and Culture* 2: 37–49. · Sjoberg, G. 1960: *The pre-industrial city, past and present*. New York: The Free Press. · Turner, R.H., ed., 1967: *Robert E. Park: On social control and collective behaviour*. Chicago: University of Chicago Press. · Thomas W.I. and Znaniecki, F. 1918: *The Polish peasant in Europe and America, Vols I and II*. Chicago: University of Chicago Press (Vols III and IV were published two years later by Richard G. Badger, Boston). · Wirth, L. 1928: *The ghetto*. Chicago: University of Chicago Press.

children, geography and A sub-disciplinary area which focuses on how children's perceptions, experiences and opportunities are socially and spatially structured, and which examines the reproduction of culture and social life through children (Aitken, 1994). Two studies (Bunge, 1973; Blaut and Stea, 1971) in the early 1970s were pivotal in the development of this field. Bunge's (1973) research in Detroit and Toronto exposed the ways in which children are oppressed by the built environment. This recognition inspired him to advocate that working-class children should be the focus of academic and political activities. Blaut and Stea's *Place Perception Project* initiated a significant collection of studies on children's COGNITIVE MAPPING skills.

Subsequently the geography of children has ranged widely in subject matter, methodology and philosophical approach. For example, Bunge's research had its roots in RADICAL GEOGRAPHY, whereas Blaut and Stea's work and similar scientific studies are located within POSITIVIST or BEHAVIOURAL schools of thought. Geographers and environmental psychologists (e.g. Hart, 1979) have adopted a HUMANISTIC approach to explore children's imaginative and creative play, attachment to place, and use of space (cf. SENSE OF PLACE). There are WELFARE GEOGRAPHIES which consider how variables such as education, health, housing, poverty, environmental factors such as POLLUTION,

HAZARDS and war, and inequalities in the distribution of resources, affect children's well-being at local, national, and global scales (e.g. Pinch, 1984). Research on young people has also been influenced by FEMINIST and POSTMODERN thought, which has stimulated work promoting the voice of children as a marginal or 'OTHERED' social group, and a sensitivity to DIFFERENCE (for example in terms of gender, age, mobility impairment: see DISABILITY, GEOGRAPHY AND) in relation to children's geographies (e.g. Aitken and Wingate, 1993). Katz's (1993) comparative study of children in the Sudan and US provides a good example of work which recognizes that what it means to be a child, and indeed the point at which childhood begins and ends, varies widely in different cultural and geographical contexts.

Influenced by the extensive body of research on the sociology of childhood, geographers are now reflecting on the particular methodological and ethical problems that arise when working with children and are attempting to develop more child-centred methodologies (cf. ETHICS, GEOGRAPHY AND). The work of psychologists, and psychoanalytical insights, have also been important in shaping the development of geographical research on children and their environments (cf. PSYCHOANALYTIC THEORY). For example, Piaget's theory that a child's intelligence is not innate but develops in complex ways as a result of its participation in its environment, has been employed – and criticized – by a number of geographers studying children's cognition and perception of space. A psychoanalytical notion of 'transitional space' – the space of play – has also been used by geographers to understand how children learn to distinguish between self and other.

Children's lives are strongly defined by adults. The geography of children therefore includes studies of the adult-mediated environments (such as the home and NEIGHBOURHOOD) and institutions (including child-care and day-care centres, schools, hospitals, and homeless shelters) which circumscribe young people's lives and through which young people learn values and ways of living that reproduce cultural and social relations (Aitken, 1994; Sibley, 1995). Some of this work suggests that contemporary concerns in modern western societies about children's safety from traffic and violent strangers, the growth of institutional forms of play, and the development of home-centred forms of entertainment (such as computer games), alongside a deterioration in urban space and the contemporary loss of rural space and woods to agricultural land, may be eroding children's independent access to and use of outdoor space, thus producing so-called 'public space' as adult space (Valentine, 1997).

Rather than passively accepting adults' exclusionary productions of domestic, institutional, urban and rural space, children actively resist and subvert adult definitions of their lives. The concepts of competence and agency form the basis of a body of work on the way children both appropriate adult public space, for example through environmental activism and public art, and develop ingenious ways of adapting everyday environments to make their own space (Ward, 1988). GV

References

Aitken, S. 1994: *Putting children in their place.* Washington, D.C.: Association of American Geographers. · Aitken, S. and Wingate, J. 1993: A preliminary study of the self-directed photography of middle-class, homeless, and mobility impaired children. *The Professional Geographer* 45: 65–72. · Blaut, J. and Stea, D. 1971: Studies of geographic learning. *Annals of the Association of American Geographers* 61: 387–449. · Bunge, W. 1973: The point of reproduction: a second front. *Antipode* 9: 60–76. · Hart, R. 1979: *Children's experience of place.* New York: Irvington. · Katz, C. 1993: Growing girls/closing circles: limits on the spaces of knowing. In C. Katz and J. Monk, eds, *Full circles: geographies of women over the lifecourse.* London: Routledge. · Pinch, S. 1984: Inequalities in pre-school provision: a geographical perspective. In A. Kirby, P. Knox, and S. Pinch, eds, *Public service provision and urban development.* London: Croom Helm. · Sibley, D. 1995: Families and domestic routines: constructing the boundaries of childhood. In S. Pile and N. Thrift, eds, *Mapping the subject.* London: Routledge. · Valentine, G. 1997: 'My son's a bit dizzy'. 'My wife's a bit soft.': Gender, children and cultures of parenting. *Gender, Place and Culture* 4: 37–62. · Ward, C. 1988: *The child in the country.* London: Bedford Square Press.

Suggested Reading

Aitken, S (1994). · Matthews, M.H. 1992: *Making sense of space.* Hemel Hempstead: Harvester Wheatsheaf.

chorology (or chorography) The study of the AREAL DIFFERENTIATION of the earth's surface. Chorology represents the oldest tradition of western geographical inquiry. It was first set forth by Hecataeus of Miletus in the sixth century BC and codified most elegantly by Strabo in the 17 books of his *Geography* written sometime between 8 BC and AD 18. The geographer, he declared, is 'the person who attempts to describe the parts of the earth' (in Greek, *chorographein*). The two key words were 'describe' and 'parts': in effect, Strabo was recommending what would now be called REGIONAL GEOGRAPHY as the core of geographical reflection. He was not interested in chorography for its own sake but intended it to serve a higher purpose. 'If there is one science which is worthy to be practised by a "philosopher",' he argued, 'then it is geographical science'. For Strabo, geography described those worthwhile things from which one could learn about truth, nobility and virtue: it was 'a complement to political and ethical philosophy'. It was, in the original sense of the term, a practical activity. For this reason Strabo's geography was fundamentally concerned with human activities. It was directed towards social and political ends and paid considerable attention to the interests of the military commander and the political ruler. Chorography was not supposed to provide a comprehensive gazeteer or a regional inventory. It was partial and purposive. 'I am neither required to enumerate all the many inhabited places nor to fix all the phenomena', Strabo insisted, and he said he began 'with Europe, because it is admirably adapted by nature for the development of excellence in men and governments' (van Paassen, 1957, pp. 1–32).

Strabo's conception of geography was challenged by Claudius Ptolemaeus (or Ptolemy) round about AD 150. In his view, the purpose of geography was to provide 'a view of the whole, analogous to the drawing of the whole head' and this meant that he separated geography from chorography which, so he said, 'has the purpose of describing the parts, as if one were to draw only an ear or an eye'. As this passage implies, for Ptolemy *graphein* did not mean describing but drawing and, specifically, mapping.

Ptolemy's 'geography' is geodesy and CARTOGRAPHY and he preferred to leave out everything which had no direct connection with that aim: 'We shall expand our "guide" for so far as this is useful for the knowledge of the location of places and their setting upon the map, but we shall leave out of consideration all the many details about the peculiarities of the peoples' (van Paassen, 1957, p. 2).

The distance between Strabo and Ptolemy could not be plainer, and it is indelibly present in the constitution of a distinctively modern geography too. As late as the seventeenth century, Strabo and Ptolemy continued to provide the main models for European geography. The usual distinction was between a special geography, devoted to the description of particular regions (including a study of the human population) and a general geography, mathematically oriented and concerned with the globe as a whole. The premier illustration is provided by Bernhard Varenius who published both studies in special geography and his famous *Geographia Generalis* in which, for the first time, geography sought to engage with the ideas of Descartes, Bacon and Galileo (Bowen, 1981).

The modern case for geography as a 'chorographic science' was argued most forcefully by Richard Hartshorne in *The nature of geography* (1939), and ever since the subsequent debate over EXCEPTIONALISM in geography – and despite the nuances and qualifications which Hartshorne had registered – chorology has often been used in polemical opposition to SPATIAL SCIENCE (cf. Sack, 1974). But the temper of the original version, with its acknowledgement of the importance of political power and philosophical reflection, is a forceful reminder of the continuing need to attend to the politics of geographical inquiry. DG

References

Bowen, M. 1981: *Empiricism and geographical thought: from Francis Bacon to Alexander von Humboldt.* Cambridge: Cambridge University Press. · Hartshorne, R. 1939: *The nature of geography: a critical survey of current thought in the light of the past.* Lancaster, PA: Association of American Geographers. · Sack, R. 1974: Chrology and spatial analysis. *Annals of the Association of American Geographers.* 64: 439–52. · van Paassen, C. 1957: *The classical tradition of geography.* Groningen: J.B. Walters.

Suggested Reading

van Paassen (1957) pp. 1–32.

choropleth A map (see MAP IMAGE AND MAP) that portrays a single distribution for CENSUS TRACTS, counties or other areal units; presents each areal unit as homogeneous; divides the data into discrete categories; and typically describes spatial variation with graytones ordered according to a darker-means-more scheme (see figure). Although most choropleth maps depict quantitative distributions like population density, median income or the percentage rate of population growth, qualitative choropleth maps are useful for showing distributions like dominant religion or form of government.

Easily created with mapping software, the quantitative choropleth map is widely misused (Monmonier, 1993, pp. 160–2). Desktop mapping packages typically offer the choropleth map as the 'default' display: unless a user specifies otherwise, the software generates a choropleth map, usually with five categories, each in a different colour. Lacking an easily and consistently decoded sequence, highly varied hues require frequent reference to the map key. While statistical mapping packages usually organize hues according to wavelength – as on temperature maps, which describe

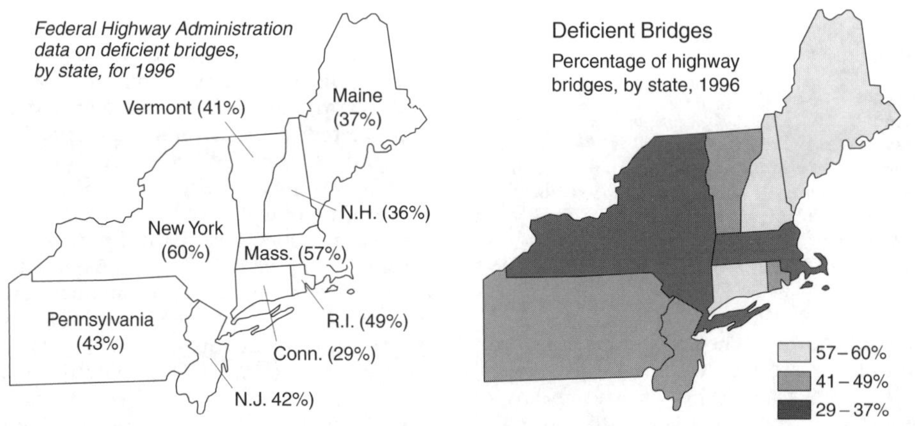

choropleth *map (right) user classification and gray tone area symbols to describe geographic pattern of percentage data (left)*

gradations from cold to hot with a blue–green–yellow–orange–red sequence – choropleth maps in newspapers and popular magazines might reflect the whim of an artist who prefers orange–blue–yellow–red–green. By contrast, a graphically logical light-to-dark sequence of graytones promotes convenient, reliable decoding based on the readily understood darker-means-more metaphor.

When used to portray population size and other count data, choropleth maps are potentially misleading, especially when areal units vary widely in size or population. For example, a choropleth map of population requires division by land area, so that graytones (an intensity symbol) represent population density (an intensity measure). Moreover, a choropleth map of the number of aged residents becomes a pale shadow of population because higher counts occur in comparatively populous enumeration areas. To make the mapped distribution informative, the map author must convert each area's count to a percentage of its total population.

The reliability of a choropleth map depends on the homogeneity of its areal units, the graphic logic of its symbols, and the class intervals that assign places to symbols (Wright, 1942). Although computer-plotted symbols that vary continuously from light to dark obviate classification (Tobler, 1973), 'unclassed' choropleth maps are not easy to reproduce consistently or decode (Mak and Coulson, 1991).

Although choropleth maps usually describe a single distribution, bivariate choropleth maps (Olson, 1981) use a comparatively complex system of colours or patterns to describe simultaneously a pair of variables and their CORRELATION. The key is a square array in which the rows represent categories for one variable and the columns show divisions of the other variable. Typically the cell at the upper right represents the highest category for both variables, whereas the cell at the lower left represents coincidence of lowest values. Sometimes called a cross map because of its focus on cross-correlation, or covariation, these complex maps can repay careful study by readers who understand the technique. MM

References

Mak, K. and Coulson, M.R.C. 1991: Map-user response to computer-generated choropleth maps: comparative experiments in classification and symbolization. *Cartography and Geographic Information Systems* 18: 109–24. · Monmonier, M. 1993: *Mapping it out: expository cartography for the humanities and social sciences*. Chicago: University of Chicago Press. · Olson, J.M. 1981: Spectrally encoded two-variable maps. *Annals of the Association of American Geographers* 71: 259–76. · Tobler, W. 1973: Choropleth maps without class intervals? *Geographical Analysis* 5: 262–5. · Wright, J.K. 1942: Map makers are human: comments on the subjective in maps. *Geographical Review* 32: 527–44.

chronotope A term borrowed from Einstein's physics by Mikhail Bakhtin in order to describe the prototypical cultural formations of time–space found in specific narrative genres such as the romance, the idyll, the folktale, the picaresque novel, the historical novel, and so on. The chronotope is, in other words, 'an optic for reading texts as x-rays of the forces at work in the culture system from which they spring' (Bakhtin, 1981, p. 426). In recent years, the term has been broadened out to describe almost any cultural formation of time–space as in, for example, the work of Paul Gilroy (1993). NJT

Reference

Bakhtin, M. 1981: *The dialogic imagination*. Austin: University of Texas Press. · Gilroy, P. 1993: *The Black Atlantic: modernity and double consciousness*. London: Verso. · Holloway, J. and Kneale, J. 1999: Bakhtin's geographies. In M. Crang, and N.J. Thrift, eds, *Thinking space*. London: Routledge. · Morson, G.S. 1996. *Narrative and freedom. The shadows of time*. New Haven, CT: Yale University Press.

circuit of capital The continuous transformation of CAPITAL into various forms: money, COMMODITIES, labour power, and means of production. Capital circulates into and out of the means of production and labour power in order to generate surplus value (see ACCUMULATION). As money, capital is advanced to purchase raw materials, the means of production (machinery, physical plant, etc.), and labour power which, when combined in production, results in a commodity that can then be exchanged back for money capital. Marx (1987, ch. 4) summarized the circulation of capital as the 'expanded general formula of capital', which he denoted symbolically as follows:

$$M - C\begin{matrix} LP \\ MP \end{matrix} - P - C' - M' \begin{cases} \Delta M \\ M \end{cases}$$

where M is the money capital advanced, C represents the commodities purchased for productive consumption (LP = labour power, MP = means of production), P is the production processes, C' are the commodities produced for sale, M' is the money received in exchange for commodities C', and $\Delta M = M' - M$ (i.e. the surplus value: cf. MARXIAN ECONOMICS).

Capital investment involves a circuit insofar as some of the M' redeemed after the first production period is reinvested in a second round of production. To the degree that the quantity of advanced capital increases with each circuit of capital, accumulation takes place. In practice the circulation of capital is quite complex and at times regionally specific, but as Leyshon and Thrift (1997) have argued, the mores governing its circulation in the form of money have become more similar across geographical boundaries (cf. MONEY AND FINANCE, GEOGRAPHY OF). Generally speaking, the circulation of money capital can be theorized as follows. In addition to direct investment in production, money capital may be: exchanged in a capital market; 'diverted' towards STATE functions of regulation and control; invested in the development of technology and science; or devoted to social expenditures such as education, health, welfare, and the military (cf. WELFARE STATE). All of these activities help in different ways to reproduce capital in its expanded form. Although circulating in economic terms, capital may necessarily be 'fixed' in the built environment, for example, as factories, roads, or fields; or it may be deployed in the 'consumption fund' to produce commodities for the reproduction of labour power, whether spatially fixed, as in houses, or not, as in cars.

The circulation of capital presupposes the specific social relations of CAPITALISM, i.e. labour and capital, or competitions between individual capitals. Economic CRISIS arises when the circulation of capital is halted or circumscribed. This can occur at any point in the circuit: money capital or labour power may be scarce or too expensive; existing means of production may be no longer competitive; final commodities may not sell in sufficient quantities or at a sufficient price (overproduction); or the rate of profit may have fallen too low to allow sufficient reinvestment. Where the circuit of capital is broken, this may lead to a 'switching crisis', in which capitalists switch investment from one circuit to another; for example, from industrial production to the built environment. To the extent that specific circuits of capital dominate certain regional economies, this can lead to regional crises. Crisis becomes global when insufficient profitable circuits exist for capital switching (Harvey, 1982).

The circuit of capital is central to understanding the geography of capitalism. Circuits of capital both produce the geographical structure of circulation and are at the same time constrained by it (Harvey, 1982; Lefebvre, 1991; Smith, 1990). NS

References

Castells, M. 1996: *The rise of the network society. Volume 1*. Oxford: Blackwell. · Harvey, D. 1982: *The limits to capital*. Oxford: Blackwell. · Lefebvre, H. 1991: *The production of space*, trans. D. Nicholson-Smith. Oxford: Blackwell. · Leyshon, A. and Thrift, N. 1997: *Money/ Space: geographies of monetary transformation*. London: Routledge. · Marx, K. 1987: *Capital*, volume I. New York: International Publishers. · Smith, N. 1990: *Uneven Development: nature capital and the production of space*, 2nd edn. Oxford: Blackwell.

citizenship The terms of membership of a political unit (usually the NATION-STATE) which secure certain rights and privileges to those who fulfil particular obligations. Citizenship is a concept, rather than a theory, which formalizes the conditions for full participation in a community. In modern times, the idea owes most to the work of T.H. Marshall whose writings on the civil, social and political rights of citizenship laid the foundations of the European WELFARE STATES.

Painter and Philo (1995) distinguish 'political' forms of citizenship which are 'anchored in questions about the individual's position *vis-à-vis* an overarching political body', from 'socio-cultural' forms of citizenship, which are 'wrapped up in questions about who is accepted as a worthy, valuable and responsible member of an everyday community of living and working' (p. 115). The concept of citizenship thus marks a point of contact between SOCIAL, CULTURAL and POLITICAL GEOGRAPHY, as well as a lens through which to view the history of the discipline (Driver and Maddrell, 1996). It refers to the range of formal and informal processes which determine people's inclusion in, and exclusion from, a variety of symbolic and material spaces and resources. Geography's distinctive contribution has been to draw attention to how SPACE is implicated in the negotiation of the entitlements, obligations, meanings and effectiveness of citizenship. There are at least two broad ways of engaging with this (Smith, 1990).

First, the concept of citizenship can be used analytically, to expose differences in the *de jure* and *de facto* rights of different groups within and between nation-states. Formal citizenship is neither a necessary nor sufficient guarantee that rights and entitlements are extended to those who need them (Garcia, 1996). Changing patterns of eligibility are due not only to economic RESTRUCTURING and cultural transformation but also to political realignments. These realignments have renegotiated the boundaries between CIVIL SOCIETY and the STATE in ways which vary through time and over space. In charting these geographies of citizenship, analysts have: mapped variations in the patriarchal assumptions which underpin the social contracts of most developed societies (see PATRIARCHY); examined the racist and EUROCENTRIC character of many countries' immigration and nationality laws (see ETHNOCENTRISM; RACISM); and specified some key inequalities between LOCALITIES and COMMUNITIES in the extent to which residents' or members' social, economic and political entitlements can be mobilized (Marston, 1990; Smith and Blanc, 1996; Swyngedouw, 1996).

Second, the concept of citizenship can be used normatively, as the basis for ideas about what a SOCIETY that is sensitive to individual rights as well as to SOCIAL JUSTICE should look like (cf. HUMAN RIGHTS). The quest for citizenship entitlements therefore provides a vision of, and a catalyst for, social transformation at a local, national, supranational and global SCALE. One project for political geographers will be to explore the tensions between local and national states and between national and supranational units arising from the struggle to win both the political POWER required to define citizenship rights and the fiscal powers required to guarantee them.

The prescriptive content of the idea of citizenship is not, however, something that is simply imposed on passive citizens by powerful politicians. It is true that one kind of 'active citizenship' is about extracting obligations – requiring friends and relatives to provide caring services that were once extended by the state, expecting citizens to volunteer time and expertise to run operations previously staffed by local governments, and so on (Kearns, 1992). However, as Bell (1995) shows in his discussion of how citizenship is constructed through sexuality, and as several papers in the collection edited by Marston and Staeheli (1994) illustrate, people can create their own, alternative, geographies of citizenship which challenge the inconsistences and inequalities built into prevailing political norms.

What citizenship *should be* is therefore hotly disputed. One argument, usually associated with the political Right, is that the condition of full participation in society is the protection of property rights and personal wealth. The opportunity to participate in the ECONOMY is seen as the gateway to and guarantor of all other rights and entitlements within a market democracy, on the grounds that free markets are the fairest means of exchanging and distributing RESOURCES.

An opposing view argues that market INEQUALITIES deny some individuals their wider range of citizenship entitlements. The democratic Left favours state intervention to offset market inequalities, so ensuring that those without property rights or personal wealth have not only the opportunity but also the right – uncompromised by obligations – to participate in the full range of social affairs. SJS

References

Bell, D. 1995: Pleasure and danger: the paradoxical spaces of sexual citizenship. *Political Geography* 14: 139–54. · Driver, F. and Maddrell, A.M.C., eds, 1996: Geographical education and citizenship. *Journal of Historical Geography* 22, special section: 371–442. · Garcia, S., ed., 1996: Cities and Citizenship. *International Journal of Urban and Regional Research* 20 (special issue). · Kearns, G. 1992: Active citizenship and urban governance. *Transactions, Institute of British Geographers* NS 17: 20–34. · Marston, S. 1990: Who are 'the people'? Gender, citizenship and the making of the American nation. *Environment and Planning D: Society and Space* 8: 449–58. · Marston, S. and Staeheli, L.A., eds, 1994: Restructuring citizenship. *Environment and Planning* A 26 (special issue). · Painter, J. and Philo, C., eds, 1995: Spaces of citizenship. *Political Geography* 14 (special issue). · Smith, S.J. 1990: Society, space and citizenship: a human geography for the 'new times'. *Transactions, Institute of British Geographers* NS 14: 144–56. · Smith, D.M. and Blanc, M. 1996: Citizenship, nationality and ethnic minorities in three European nations. *International Journal of Urban and Regional Research* 20: 66–82. · Swyngedouw, E. 1996: Reconstructing citizenship, the re-shaping of the state and the new authoritarianism: closing the Belgian mines. *Urban Studies* 33: 1499–521.

Suggested Reading

Kofman, E. and England, K., eds, 1997: Citizenship and international migration. *Environment and Planning* A 29 (special issue). · Marston and Staeheli (1994). · Painter and Philo (1995).

city Originally the British term for an urban settlement containing a cathedral and the seat of a bishop, city is now generally applied to large urban places. The criteria for distinguishing cities from towns vary between countries: in some, population size is the determining factor; in others, the status of city implies an administrative rank and carries with it certain rights and privileges. RJJ

city-size distribution The FREQUENCY DISTRIBUTION of settlements of different sizes (or size categories). The observed distribution for an URBAN SYSTEM can be compared with a theoretical model, such as those provided by CENTRAL PLACE THEORY, the RANK-SIZE RULE, and the law of THE PRIMATE CITY. RJJ

Suggested Reading

Carroll, G.R. 1982: National city-size distributions: what do we know after 67 years of research? *Progress in Human Geography* 6: 1–43.

civil society Those segments of a capitalist society which lie outside both the sphere of production and the STATE (alternative terms for civil society are the *sphere of consumption* and the *sphere of struggle*). It involves divisions on a number of criteria, such as gender, RACE, ETHNICITY, religion, and age, between which

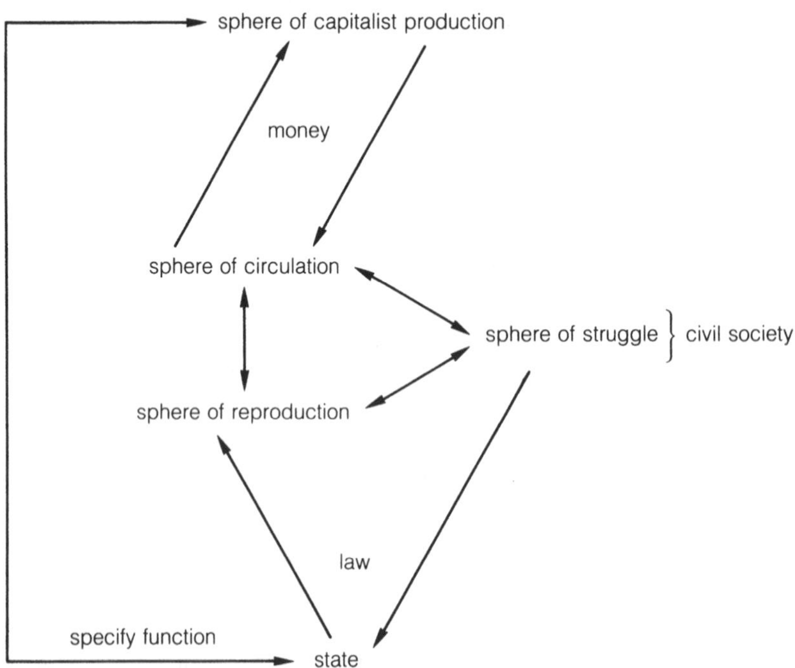

civil society *The basic structure of capitalist social formations* (Urry)

there may be CONFLICT (cf. CLEAVAGE). To Hall (1998) it is 'a form of societal self-organization which allows for co-operation with the state whilst enabling individualism' (see also Taylor, 1990, for a discussion on the idea's origins).

The reproduction of society, both individually and inter-generationally, biologically and culturally, is organized within civil society. Struggles over existence under CAPITALISM involve intersections with both the sphere of production, through the sphere of circulation (money earned in the sphere of production is expended on reproduction), and the state (reproduction is regulated by the state and enhanced by it, through the provision of PUBLIC GOODS – see WELFARE STATE). These intersections define the 'sphere of struggle' (Urry, 1981: see figure). The existence of capitalism does not ensure a civil society, however: many capitalist societies have authoritarian states and other social forces 'which cage and control the individual, limiting room for moral autonomy' over many aspects of life, such as the choice of clothing and marriage partner, whereas in civil societies 'individuals have the chance of at least trying to create their own selves' (Hall, 1998, p. 33) because of the existence of a range of strong, autonomous social groups which can both influence the state and protect individuals from it.

Some of the defences of European COLONIALISM argued that the areas colonized lacked a civil society, and part of the colonial heritage was its creation and development. But civil societies in the western European mode – characterized by a 'special type of societal self-organization, moderate, co-operative and permeable' (Hall, 1998, p. 41) – are not readily transported to other cultural contexts. Hall claims that they are unlikely to be created in many regions outside western Europe and North America, with the exceptions of parts of Central Europe and Latin America. Elsewhere, moves to establish civil society on the European model are strongly contested – as in India, where the ideal is popular among some sectors, including the elite, but which still practises the caste system that 'cages huge numbers with awful efficiency', and the Middle East and North Africa, where religious fundamentalism sustains 'a social world utterly foreign to that whose contours' characterize western liberal democracies. Whereas the latter accepts 'a shared world within which DIFFERENCES are accepted' the former resists difference and diversity (see also McIlwaine, 1998). RJJ

Reference and Suggested Reading

Hall, J.A. 1998: The nature of civil society. *Society* 35: 32–41. · Johnston, R.J. 1991: *A question of place: exploring the practice of human geography*. Oxford and Boston: Basil Blackwell. · McIlwaine, C. 1998: Civil society and development geography. *Progress in Human* Geography 22: 415–24. · Taylor, C. 1990: Modes of civil society. *Public Culture* 3: 95–118. · Urry, J. 1981: *The anatomy of capitalist societies: the economy, civil society and the state*. London: Macmillan; Atlantic Highland, NJ: Humanities Press.

class A concept that describes systems of stratification derived from social relations of property and work. Class is central to theoretical accounts of CAPITALISM but there is a wide range of views as to its meaning. There is also debate as to whether classes exist in non-capitalist societies (see Giddens, 1987, p. 62; Gibson-Graham, 1996).

Geographers use a range of class definitions, drawn from different theoretical traditions. In gradational approaches, classes are measured by attributes such as income, status, and education and tend to be descriptive rather than explanatory categories. With relational approaches, the social relations *between* classes are definitive and gradations in income and status taken as outcomes rather than defining characteristics of class position. David Harvey's book *Social justice and the city* marks the transition from the use of gradational to relational approaches to class in geography, in Harvey's case to MARXIST class theory.

There is a variety of relational approaches to class. A conception of class based on market relations is associated with Weberian theory. Max Weber used the term class to refer to 'objective' market interests that influence 'life-chances' (access to economic and cultural goods). He contrasts this to the concept of *status* groups, which are COMMUNITIES based on common 'styles of life', and *perceptions* of similarity. Although Weber restricts the notion of class to 'pure' economic relations, he presents a pluralistic model, distinguishing between:

- *property classes*, whose membership is based on command over forms of property that can be used to realize income in the market;
- *acquisition classes* with membership determined by marketable skills or services; and
- *social classes* that refer to clusters of class situations linked by common mobility chances (see Giddens, 1973 for a description and critique).

Weber's definition of property classes has been used to argue that classes also emerge out of urban housing markets to form an important basis for conflict in the city and within national politics (Saunders, 1984: see HOUSING CLASS; HOUSING STUDIES).

Other approaches ground class exclusively within the relations of production but, once again, these relations are conceived in different ways. For some theorists, production relations are equivalent to occupation and industrial sector. This interpretation of class has been used by Ley (1996), for example, to explain the gentrification of inner cities in terms of the expansion of professional occupations and the service sector. Marxist theorists conceive of the DIVISION OF LABOUR (the organization of work into occupations, industrial sectors and firms) as distinct from class (Walker, 1985) and usually define the latter in terms of ownership of the means of production, domination (control over labour) and exploitation (appropriation of surplus value). Sheppard and Barnes (1990) and Gibson-Graham (1996) provide critical discussions of the controversies within Marxism surrounding the centrality of each of these factors to the definition of class. As Gibson-Graham note, various concepts of class co-exist in Marxian POLITICAL ECONOMY, 'often within the writings of the same person' (1996, p. 49). At the most abstract level of theory, the three criteria lead to the identification of two classes (capitalist and working), although considerable effort has been made over the last decade to revise Marxist class theory so as to theorize the middle classes in contemporary industrial societies (see Wright, 1985; 1993). In one of the most influential accounts, Wright theorizes the middle class through a more complex conception of exploitation, loosely defined as a process by which one group is able to appropriate part of the social surplus produced by another group. Without owning the means of production, the middle classes nonetheless appropriate part of the surplus through skill exploitation (by which owners of scarce skills extract wages beyond the costs of producing and reproducing the skills) and organization exploitation (through the power managers command within bureaucratic structures of capitalist production).

Debates about and the use of class theory have shifted within geography over the last decade. Theoretical debates between Weberian and Marxist theorists, perspectives once considered irreconcilable, now assume less importance. Weberians now tend to contain their use of the class concept to market relations within the production sphere, using different terminology to analyse distributive- and consumption-based exchange relations (Saunders, 1984). Similarly, Marxist theorists tend to use the concept more specifically, and admit the importance of other dimensions of power and social division (e.g. gender- and race-based forms of oppression). This creates the opportunity to explore the ways that class and other relations and identities are intertwined. Without reducing one set of relations to another, it is argued that gender relations are central to the restructuring of class relations; for example, the increase in contingent forms of labour (e.g. part-time, temporary, and other short-term contractual workers) is intrinsically linked to an increased female labour supply and to gender relations within households.

Some debate between Weberian-inspired and Marxist class analyses persists in studies of GENTRIFICATION. Ley (1996) explains gentrification in terms of the growth of a generational cohort of what he terms the cultural new class comprising college-educated professionals and managers in private and, especially, public sector employment who were influential in and influenced by the countercultural youth movements of the 1960s (see CULTURAL POLITICS) and came to reject the SUBURBS as conservative, homogeneous and alienating places (cf. ALIENATION). Smith (1996) continues to prioritize the RENT GAP in the production of gentrification and sees the production of gentrifiers (consumers) as secondary; he argues that we require analytical tools other than class analysis to understand consumption processes. Bridge (1995) draws upon the notion of levels of ABSTRACTION (moving from MODE OF PRODUCTION, through SOCIAL FORMATION to conjunction) as a means of reconciling these different approaches.

A theoretical issue that continues to perplex many class theorists (both Marxist and Weberian) is how to move between abstractions about class structure to analyses of class *structure, consciousness* and *formation* in concrete societies. Walker (1985) reviews various attempts to resolve this difficulty and argues that the abstract definition of class must be 'recast' in each historical context. Most theorists, including Marxists, no longer expect a direct link between position in the class structure and class consciousness and action, and interpret the constitution of class identity as a highly contingent socio-political activity. More attention is now given to the interrelations between different social identities; an early example is Willis's (1977) discussion of the links between masculinity, RACE, and an affirmative manual, white working-class culture.

There are, however, different strategies for theorizing this contingency and a sharp point of debate has emerged between what have been labelled 'essentialist' and 'anti-essentialist' Marxist theorists. In their influential critique of marxist ESSENTIALISM, Laclau and Mouffe (1985) criticized marxist class analyses for positing class as an objective and foundational social location that should come to consciousness if not distorted by processes of mystification and false consciousness. Laclau and Mouffe displaced the economy from its founding and unifying role within SOCIETY and theorized the social as open and constituted within multiple DISCOURSES (see POST-STRUCTURALISM; RADICAL DEMOCRACY). Drawing on this, and Resnick and Wolff's (1987) class theory, Gibson-Graham (1996) have elaborated an anti-essentialist marxist perspective in geography in which the economy in capitalist societies is not seen to exhaust the social and is conceived as complex combinations of capitalist and non-capitalist processes (e.g. feudal, communal, slave, independent: see FEUDALISM; SLAVERY). Class is represented not as a grouping but as processes of producing, appropriating and distributing social labour. Class processes are constituted by every other aspect of social life; what distinguishes class from gender analysis, for instance, is the point of analytical departure, the fact that class analysis theorizes society and subjectivity from the entry point of class. Class processes occur wherever surplus labour is produced, appropriated and distributed; the household (and not just the workplace) is thus a major site of class processes. Individuals are conceived as contradictory and fragmented social sites, as the intersection of a multiplicity of class and non-class processes (see SUBJECT FORMATION, GEOGRAPHIES OF). It is thus unlikely that an individual will be located in one class position; to search for a 'true and singular class identity in this complex and shifting intersection would involve a quest for the type of "regulatory fiction" that Butler sees gender coherence to be' (1996, p. 63: see GENDER AND GEOGRAPHY; PERFORMATIVITY. This method of conceiving class allows Gibson-Graham a way out of a perennial problem for class analysis: how to theorize individual in relation to household class location.)

Gibson-Graham pursue an anti-essentialist position because it suggests new political possibilities; they make no exhaustive claims to knowledge (see MASCULINISM) and credit Wright (1993) for opening other political options with his more traditional marxist class analysis. Gibson-Graham are reacting to the RESTRUCTURING literature in geography which posits a dissolution in traditional working-class politics with the restructuring of the economy (e.g. the growth of the service sector and contingent forms of work, the feminization of the labour force). Their re-theorization allows class transformation wherever there is an attempt to change the ways that surplus labour is produced, appropriated and distributed (in, for example, the redistribution of domestic work within the household). Their anti-essentialist Marxism has provoked critical commentary and debate (Graham, 1992; Peet, 1992) but should be distinguished from the IDENTITY POLITICS that Harvey (1996) criticizes for displacing class politics.

Another important development involves the spatialization of class theory (Thrift and Williams, 1987). In the mid-1980s, Walker (1985) complained that geographical analyses of class suffered from 'the fallacy of sequential ordering' (i.e. class theory was applied to geographical problems but the role of space in the constitution of classes was usually ignored). The linkages between SPACE, PLACE and class have since been expanded and there is a vast literature, not only on the constitutive role of class in the production of space and places (see Pratt, 1989, for a review at the urban scale and Corbridge, 1989, for a review at the international scale), but also the place-specificity of class relations and the role that space plays in class formation and the development of class consciousness and class practices (Massey, 1984; Peck, 1996). Sheppard and Barnes (1990, pp. 209–10) argue that the insertion of abstract Marxist theories of *class structure* into a spatial (as opposed to aspatial) economy disrupts some of these theories' central conclusions. Focusing on *class politics*, Herod (1991) argues that spatial immobility leads some class actors to take up positions that are opposite to those that an aspatial class analysis would predict. Architecture and landscape status markers are thought to be especially significant in the formation of an otherwise ambiguous middle-class identity (see Pratt, 1989 for review of this literature). GP

References

Bridge, G. 1995: The space for class? On class analysis in the study of gentrification. *Transactions Institute of British Geographers* NS 20: 236–47. · Corbridge, S. 1989: Marxism, post-Marxism, and geography of development. In N. Thrift and R. Peet, eds, *New models in geography, volume 1.* Boston and London: Unwin Hyman, 224–54. · Harvey, D. 1996: *Justice, nature and the geography of difference.* Cambridge, MA and Oxford: Blackwell Publishers. · Herod, A. 1991: Local political practice in response to a manufacturing plant closure: how geography complicates class analysis. *Antipode* 23 (4): 385–402. · Gibson-Graham, J.-K. 1996: *Capitalism (as we knew it): a feminist critique of political economy.* Cambridge, MA and Oxford: Blackwell Publishers. · Giddens, A. 1987: *The nation-state and violence.* Cambridge: Polity Press and Berkeley: University of California Press. · Graham, J. 1992: Anti-essentialism and overdetermination – a response to Dick Peet. *Antipode* 24: 141–56. · Laclau, E. and Mouffe, C. 1985: *Hegemony and socialist strategy: towards a radical democratic politics.* London: Verso. · Ley, D. 1996: *The new middle class and the remaking of the central city.* Oxford: Oxford University Press. · Massey, D. 1984: *Spatial divisions of labour.* London and New York: Methuen. · Peck, J. 1996: *Work-place: the social regulation of labour markets.* New York: Guilford. · Peet, R. 1992: Some critical questions for anti-essentialism. *Antipode* 24: 113–30. · Pratt, G. 1989: Reproduction, class and the spatial structure of the city. In N. Thrift, and R. Peet, *New models in geography, volume 2.* Boston and London: Unwin and Hyman, 84–108. · Resnick, S. and Wolff, R. 1987: *Knowledge and class: a Marxian critique of political economy.* Chicago: University of Chicago Press. · Saunders, P. 1984: Beyond housing classes: the sociological significance of private property rights in the means of consumption. *International Journal of Urban and Regional Research* 8: 201–27. · Sheppard E. and Barnes, T. 1990: *The capitalist space economy: geographical analysis after Ricardo, Marx and Sraffa.* Boston and London: Unwin Hyman. · Smith, N. 1996: *The new urban frontier: gentrification and the revanchist city.* London and New York: Routledge. · Thrift, N. and Williams, P. 1987: *Class and Space: the making of Urban Society.* London: Routledge and Kegan Paul. · Walker, R. 1985: Class, division of labour and employment in space. In D. Gregory and J. Urry, eds, *social relations and spatial structures.* New York: St. Martin's Press, 164–89. · Willis, P. 1977: *Learning to labour.* Farnborough: Saxon House. · Wright, E.O. 1979: *Class structure and income determination.* New York: Academic Press. · Wright, E.O. 1985: *Classes.* London: Verso. · Wright, E.O. 1993: Class analysis, history and emancipation. *New Left Review* 202: 15–35.

Suggested Reading

Giddens, A. 1973: *The class structure of the advanced societies.* London: Hutchinson. · Gibson-Graham, J.K. (1996).

class interval A central element in the design and generalization of a quantitative map that partitions the range of data values into discrete categories, each assigned a unique symbol. Typically a map key links the class intervals to their respective symbols, which may vary in size, graytone value or colour. Especially common on CHOROPLETH maps, which portray data for CENSUS TRACTS and other areal units, class intervals are also used for maps of linear and point phenomena. Although not always apparent in a map key, class intervals are embedded in contour and other maps on which isolines divide the data into categories or layers (Jenks, 1963).

The number of categories and their divisions can have a decisive influence on the mapped pattern (Monmonier, 1996, pp. 40–3; see figure). For example, a map of mortality or poverty can overstate a threat if its classification assigns many places to the highest, most ominous category. Similarly, another map of the same data might present a markedly more optimistic view by placing far fewer areas in the upper category. Moreover, different sets of class intervals suggest or deny similarity to another distribution. Because the map author can influence interpretation by manipulating a map's class intervals, wary viewers might question the author's motives.

Deliberate bias is no less worrisome than ignorance. All too often users of desktop mapping software accept blindly an automatic, 'default' classification that divides the range into five equal intervals. Easily programmed for a computer, an equal-intervals classification is no better or more natural than any other standardized scheme. Moreover, if the data contain one or more extraordinarily high or low values called outliers (cf. RESIDUAL), an equal-intervals classification might yield empty categories or assign almost all places to a single category. A less outrageous default is the quantile scheme, which assigns an approximately equal number of places to each category. Although a five-category map identifying places in the upper and lower fifths can be meaningful to some viewers, the resulting regions are often less homogeneous than the map suggests (Evans, 1977).

Because a choropleth map is a REGIONALIZATION based on a single variable, map authors often examine a univariate scatterplot, or number line, for 'natural breaks' (Jenks and Caspall, 1971). Although readily apparent homogeneous categories merit consideration, map viewers might prefer inherently meaningful breaks such as zero or the variable's national or world average. On a map of population growth rates, for instance, a category break at zero differentiates places that gained from those that lost, and a category break at the national average affords a convenient assessment of relative growth.

Conscientious map authors have several options: provide viewers with a univariate scatterplot that relates class intervals to the

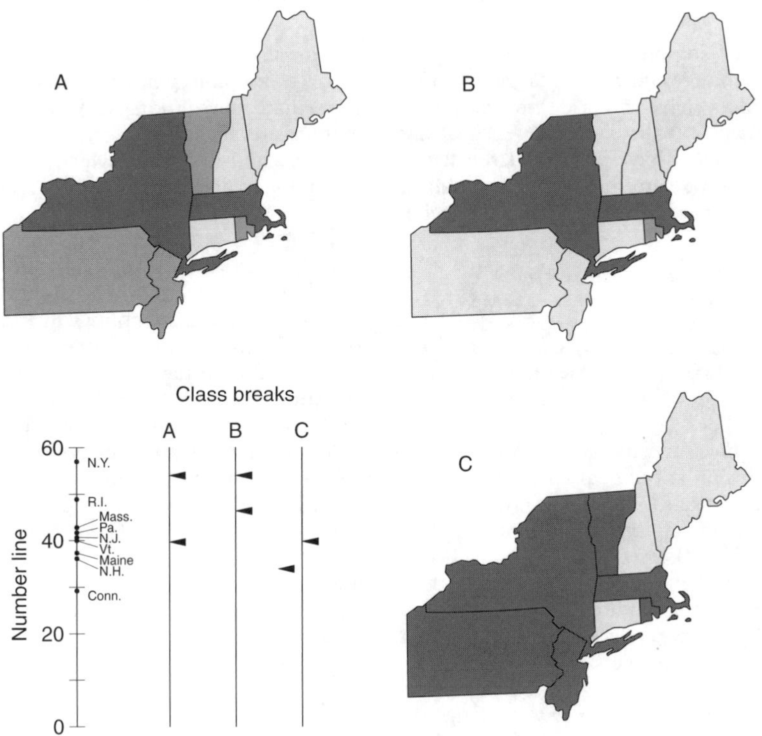

class interval *Three different sets of category breaks (lower left) yield different map patterns*

distribution of data values; use and identify inherently meaningful breaks; or explore the effects of various class-intervals schemes and show whatever radically different alternative views might emerge. Better still is a multimedia VISUALIZATION system in which a dynamic map presents multiple regionalizations and invites the viewer to verify their stability (Egbert and Slocum, 1992). MM

References

Egbert, S.L. and Slocum, T.A. 1992: EXPLOREMAP: an exploration system for choropleth maps. *Annals of the Association of American Geographers* 82: 275–88. · Evans, I.S. 1977: The selection of class intervals. *Transactions, Institute of British Geographers* NS 2: 98–124. · Jenks, G.F. 1963: Generalization in statistical mapping. *Annals of the Association of American Geographers* 53: 15–26. · Jenks, G.F. and Caspall, F.C. 1971. Error on choropleth maps: definition, measurement, reduction. *Annals of the Association of American Geographers* 61: 218–44. · Monmonier, M. 1996: How to lie with maps, 2nd edn. Chicago: University of Chicago Press.

classification and regionalization Procedures for combining individual observations into categories. *Classification* involves splitting a population into mutually exclusive categories on predetermined criteria, either deductively (using a previously determined set of classes) or inductively (finding the best set of classes for the particular data set). Some procedures take the entire population and divide it into classes whereas others begin with the individuals and group them into classes: in both cases, the outcome is a hierarchy of classes (e.g. all people divided by gender; each gender group divided by ethnic origin; each gender and ethnic group divided by age; etc.) With inductive classifications, the guideline is usually that each member of a class should be more like all of the other members of that class than it is like the members of any other: the classes are thus internally homogeneous and externally heterogeneous.

Regionalization (see REGION AND REGIONAL GEOGRAPHY) is a special case of the more general procedure of classification. The individuals comprising the population to be classified are areas and the resulting classes (regions) must form contiguous spatial units. Because of this additional criterion, regions defined for a population of areas may not be as internally homogeneous as a classification of the same areas without the contiguity constraint.

A range of computer algorithms has been devised to produce classifications and regionalizations. Most have precise inter-class and inter-region BOUNDARIES, but Openshaw and Openshaw (1997) have suggested the use of fuzzy logic to indicate the probability that an individual is a member of any particular class. RJJ

References and Suggested Reading

Johnston, R.J. 1976: *Classification in geography. Concepts and techniques in modern geography 6*. Norwich: Geo-Books. · Openshaw, S. and Openshaw, C. 1997: *Artificial intelligence in geography*. Chichester and New York: John Wiley.

cleavage The division of a society into groups with similar political attitudes and partisan identifications. The classic study of west European political systems identified four main cleavages (Lipset and Rokkan, 1967); two related to the growth of the NATION-STATE (subject versus dominant CULTURE; church(es) versus state) and two related to the INDUSTRIAL REVOLUTION (primary versus secondary economy; workers versus employers). Other cleavages have been identified elsewhere (e.g. the sectional – see SECTION – cleavage in the USA and the POST-INDUSTRIAL in many 'advanced industrial' societies: Harrop and Miller, 1987). Cleavages are produced by political parties mobilizing electors on different sides of a social, economic or cultural conflict and are reflected in the geography of voting there (see ELECTORAL GEOGRAPHY). Some argue that with weaker levels of links between parties and specified social groups within contemporary societies (termed partisan and class dealignment) parties are having to develop 'catch-all' characteristics in their competition for votes and power. RJJ

References

Harrop, M.L. and Miller, W.L. 1987: *Electors and voters: a comparative perspective*. London: Macmillan. · Lipset, S.M. and Rokkan, S.E. 1967: Cleavage structures, party systems, and voter alignments: an introduction. In S.M. Lipset and S.E. Rokkan, eds, *Party systems and voter alignments*. New York: The Free Press, 1–64.

cognitive mapping A term first used in geography (see MENTAL MAP) and in planning (Lynch, 1966), then taken up and adopted by the literary theorist, Fredric Jameson, as a METAPHOR to describe both one of the chief symptoms of, and a possible solution to, the cultural condition of late CAPITALISM. For Jameson, this latest global form of capitalism has produced a state of radical unrepresentability. Our situation as individual subjects within this new global network leaves us shorn of the ability to grasp any but our most immediate surroundings. We are unable to extrapolate from these surroundings to any larger spatial imaginary which might allow us to represent and understand the new relations of domination.

What we therefore need are 'cognitive maps', a term that stands for a new aesthetic which is an essential precondition for the renewal of SOCIALIST politics in POSTMODERNISM. With these mental maps we will once again be able to navigate the totality in which we find ourselves, thereby heightening our sense of our place in the global system and consequently boosting our political passions.

The notion is not without its critics. It seems to rely on a misappropriation of the work of both Kevin Lynch and Henri Lefebvre, an all-or-nothing reduction of time to space, and an implicit denigration of the political understandings of ordinary people (see Homer, 1998). NJT

References

Homer, S. 1998: *Fredric Jameson. Marxism, hermeneutics, postmodernism*. Cambridge, Polity Press. · Jameson, F. 1991: *Postmodernism, or the cultural logic of late capitalism*. London: Verso. · Jameson, F. 1994: *The seeds of time*. New York: Columbia University Press. · Lynch, K. 1966: *The image of the city*. Cambridge, MA: The MIT Press.

cohort A group of individuals who enter on some stage in the LIFE-CYCLE simultaneously and are analysed as a unit throughout their lifetime. For example, 1000 babies all born in the same calendar year are a 'birth cohort', and 1000 couples all married for the first time in the same year are a 'marriage cohort'. Cohort or LONGITUDINAL DATA ANALYSIS is much used in demography, for example in comparing FERTILITY behaviour in different generations. If cohorts are not the subject of study, but instead the experiences of particular periods of time are considered, then rates of change are termed *period rates*. The description *secular analysis* is also sometimes employed. PEO

Suggested Reading

Cox, P.R. 1976: *Demography*, 5th edn. Cambridge and New York: Cambridge University Press, ch. 3. · Plane, D.A. and Rogerson, P.A. 1994: *The geographical analysis of population*. New York and Chichester: John Wiley, ch. 3.

collective A form of farm organization associated with socialist countries in which the

STATE retains ownership of land but leases it on a permanent basis to the members of the collective as an institutional unit. In theory each collective is self-governing, but in practice production quotas are invariably determined by the state as part of CENTRAL PLANNING. However, the collective is responsible for paying its employees and financing inputs (e.g. fertilizers or new machinery). Both former Soviet (*kolkhoz*) and Chinese (commune) forms of rural collectivism are being replaced by private forms of farm organization, in China since 1978, and in the former Soviet bloc countries and in Vietnam since the late 1980s. (See also KIBBUTZ.) GES

Suggested Reading

Pallot, J. 1997: Continuity and change in the post-Soviet countryside. In M. Bradshaw, ed., *Geography and transition in the Post-Soviet Republics*. London: Wiley, 109–28. · Smith, G.E. 1989: *Planned development in the socialist world*. Cambridge: Cambridge University Press, 82–97. · Watts, M. 1998: Recombinant capitalism: state, de-collectivisation and the agrarian question in Vietnam. In A. Pickles and A. Smith, eds, *Theorising transition. The political economy of post-communist transformation*. London: Routledge, 450–505.

collective consumption The consumption of services (see PUBLIC SERVICES, GEOGRAPHY OF) produced, managed and distributed on a public/collective basis (see Dunleavy, 1980, pp. 52–3; Pinch, 1985, pp. 12–14; Pinch, 1989, pp. 42–8). This notion of collective consumption – associated especially with the French school of urban sociology and in particular with the writings of Manuel Castells and Jean Lojkine (see Pickvance, 1976) – is becoming increasingly *displaced* by systems of the targeted provision of 'public' services often provided by private agencies operating within a market framework (Mohan, 1995; Pinch, 1996), *challenged* by 'consumers' not buying into the discourse of development promulgated by the state and its agencies (e.g. Routledge, 1997), and *reformulated* in the light of the heterogeneity of the economic, social, cultural and institutional assets of the contemporary city (Amin and Graham, 1997).

Collective consumption 'takes place not through the market but through the STATE APPARATUS' (Castells, 1977, p. 460). It involves the provision of the collective means of consumption of commodities, the production of which is not assured by capital because of their 'lower than average profit rate' but which is, nevertheless, 'necessary to the reproduction of labour power and/or to the reproduction of social relations' (Castells, 1977, pp. 460, 461). The collective means of consumption 'refers today to the totality of medical, sports, educational, cultural and public transport facilities' (Lojkine, 1976, p. 121). A noticeable absentee from this list is public housing which, for Lojkine, is not collective as housing is not consumed collectively (cf. HOUSING CLASS; HOUSING STUDIES). This criterion is not so significant for Castells who is concerned mainly with STATE, i.e. collective, provision.

For Lojkine, the social expenses involved in the provision of collective means of consumption have the effect of lowering the rate of profit. Conversely, for Castells (1977, p. 461) the production of collective means of consumption 'plays a fundamental role in the struggle of capital against the tendency of the profit rate to fall', as unprofitable investments are taken over by the state which thereby 'helps to raise proportionately the rate of profit attributed to social capital as a whole'. In fact, both effects may well occur simultaneously, the net effect on the rate of profit being an empirical matter affected by specific sets of circumstances. Both accounts are, in any case, highly functionalist (cf. FUNCTIONALISM) and imply acceptance of the notion that the activities of the state are simply determined by the demands of capital. Nevertheless, the shift to privatized provision and targeting arises from the IDEOLOGY of individualism and a belief in the superiority of markets and, in material terms, from the alleged effects of taxation (through which funds for collective consumption are raised) on profitability, and of public expenditure on interest rate differentials in global bond markets (cf. PRIVATIZATION).

The notion of collective consumption raises a range of issues for urban analysis. It has given rise to a number of attempts to classify the expenditure of the state, especially at the local level, but it has proved very difficult in practice to make theoretical categories of state expenditure (social investment, social consumption and social expenses) fit the concrete categories of state expenditure in precise terms. Nevertheless, the attempt to do so has produced some helpful insights into the role of the state and trends in its activities (e.g. Saunders, 1980; Dunleavy, 1984).

At a conceptual level the process of collective consumption has been used to define the city. For Castells (1976, p. 148) 'the "city" is a residential unit of labour power... defined as... a unit of collective consumption corresponding more or less to the daily organisation of a section of labour power' which might be defined by patterns of COMMUTING.

This view of the city tends, however, to impose a one-dimensional unity founded solely on CLASS relations.

The concept of collective consumption raises a range of political questions which, in Castells' formulation, are central to the urban question. If the state assumes more and more responsibility for the provision of the means of collective consumption, rationality and fiscal crises affecting the provision become increasingly politicized and so involve sections of the population well beyond the working class alone (cf. CRISIS; CRITICAL THEORY). Crises in state provision therefore generate widely-based urban struggles from which URBAN SOCIAL MOVEMENTS (e.g. Lowe, 1991) may arise to challenge capitalist social relations and/or the legitimacy of the current political order.

Two difficulties are immediately apparent in this account: the translation of contradiction and crisis into struggle; and the translation of struggle into an urban social movement. The individual consumption of services provided collectively may well undermine the development of a social consciousness of crisis, while divisions of collective interest in services provided both by the state and by private capital (e.g. housing, education and health care) will tend to fragment rather than to coalesce class interests. Such an argument lies behind the so-called DUAL THEORY OF THE STATE (Saunders, 1981, 1984). Furthermore, the broadening of the field of potential conflict with the increasing importance of collective means of consumption also complicates the relationships between individuals, groups and political action. Formal political activity may well become increasingly significant and possibly destructive of more radical political challenges (e.g. Pickvance, 1976, 1977).

Indeed, Castells (1983) shifts attention away from the structural generation of crisis and conflict towards a concern for the diverse role of consciousness and social action in the transformation of the conditions of everyday life (Smith and Tardanico, 1987). This shift is prescient as it reflects the emergence of 'the multiplex city' (Amin and Graham, 1997, p. 417) but it also opens up the possibility of displacing SOCIAL JUSTICE from the agenda – especially as the search for capital investment dominates the discourse of development in the contemporary city under conditions of intensifying globalization. For Ash Amin and Stephen Graham (1997) then

> a project seeking unity or solidarity across the diverse fragments and complex relational webs of the contemporary city needs to do much more than this. It has to be a project of restoring social justice in the city in such a way that it responds to genuine social needs and, at the same time, unlocks social capabilities through the empowerment of autonomous groups. This makes it a much more far-reaching project centred around reforms including the democratization of the state, an associationism that expects democratic practice from intermediate organizations, and projects of civic empowerment that are not confined to Machiavellian republican ideals.

The presumption of class relations dominating the social relations of cities and so shaping collective consumption can no longer be sustained but neither can they be displaced. Deregulation, individualism and globalization (Castells, 1997) – exposing not only state agencies but also economic geographies to fierce and increasingly deregulated competition – and the growth of the multiplex city pose questions not only for the concept of collective consumption itself but for the trajectory of urban development in an increasingly polarized society under conditions of intensified inter-urban competition. RL

References

Amin, A. and Graham, S. 1997: The ordinary city. *Transactions of the Institute of British Geographers* NS 22 4: 411–29. · Castells, M. 1976: Theoretical propositions for an experimental study of urban social movements. In C.G. Pickvance, ed., *Urban sociology: critical essays*. London: Methuen, 147–73. · Castells, M. 1977 [orig. pub. 1972]: *The urban question: a Marxist approach*. London: Edward Arnold, 437–71. · Castells, M. 1983: *The city and the grassroots: a cross-cultural theory of urban social movements*. London: Edward Arnold. · Castells, M. 1997: *End of millennium The information age: economy, society and culture*, volume III. Cambridge, MA and Oxford: Blackwell Publishers. · Dunleavy, P. 1980: *Urban political analysis*. London: Macmillan. · Dunleavy, P. 1984: The limits to local government. In M. Boddy, and C. Fudge, eds, *Local socialism?* London and Basingstoke: Macmillan, 49–81. · Lojkine, J. 1976: Contribution to a Marxist theory of urbanization. In C.G. Pickvance, ed., *Urban sociology: critical essays*. London: Methuen, 119–46. · Lowe, S. 1991: *Urban social movements: the city after Castells*. London: Macmillan. · Mohan, J. 1995: *A national health service? The restructuring of health care in Britain since 1979*. London: St. Martin's Press. · Pickvance, C.G., ed., 1976: *Urban sociology: critical essays*. London: Methuen; New York: St. Martin's Press, 1–32; 198–218. · Pickvance, C.G. 1977: Marxist approaches to the study of urban politics. *International Journal of Urban and Regional Research* 1: 218–55. · Pinch, S.P. 1985: *Cities and services: the geography of collective consumption*. London: Routledge and Kegan Paul. · Pinch, S.P. 1989: Collective consumption. In J. Wolch, and M. Dear, eds, *The power of Geography*. Winchester, MA. and London: Unwin Hyman, 41–60. · Pinch, S.P. 1996: *Worlds of welfare*. London: Routledge. · Routledge, P. 1997: The imagineering of resistance: Pollock Free State and the practice of post-modern politics. *Transactions of the Institute of British Geographers* NS 22 (3): 359–76. · Saunders, P. 1980: *Urban politics*. Harmondsworth: Penguin, 103–97. · Saunders, P. 1981: *Social theory and the urban question*. London: Hutchinson; New York: Holmes and Meier, ch. 8. · Saunders, P. 1984: Rethinking local politics. In M. Boddy and C. Fudge, eds, *Local socialism?* London and Basingstoke: Macmillan. · Smith, M.P. and Tardanico, R. 1987: Urban theory reconsidered: Production, reproduction and collective action. In M.P. Smith and J.R. Feagin, eds, *The capitalist city*. Oxford and New York: Blackwell, ch. 4.

Suggested Reading

Amin and Graham (1997). · Pinch (1989).

collinearity A statistical problem in applications of the GENERAL LINEAR MODEL, especially multiple REGRESSION analysis. If two or more of the independent variables are substantially inter-correlated, the resulting regression coefficients are biased and provide inefficient statements of the true relationships. RJJ

colonialism The establishment and maintenance of rule, for an extended period of time, by a SOVEREIGN power over a subordinate and alien people that is separate from the ruling POWER. Colonialism has been associated with *colonization*, which involves the physical settlement of people (i.e. settlers) from the imperial centre to the colonial periphery (for example the ancient Greek colonies, and British settlers in Kenya). Characteristic features of the colonial situation include political and legal domination over an alien SOCIETY, relations of economic and political DEPENDENCE and exploitation between imperial power and colony, and racial and cultural inequality (Fanon, 1966).

Colonialism is a variant of IMPERIALISM, the latter understood as unequal territorial relationships among STATES based on subordination and domination, and typically associated with a distinct forms of contemporary CAPITALISM such as the emergence of monopolies and TRANSNATIONAL CORPORATIONS. As a form of territorial expansion, colonialism is intimately related to UNEVEN DEVELOPMENT within a developing global capitalist system and with new configurations of the international DIVISION OF LABOUR (see DEVELOPMENT; GLOBALIZATION; Barratt-Brown, 1974). In the modern period (since 1870), colonialism emerged as a general description of the state of subjection of non-European societies as a result of specific forms of European, American and Japanese imperial expansion, organization and rule (Fieldhouse, 1981). Colonialism and anti-colonialism have been fundamental forces in the making of the THIRD WORLD and in the shaping of the modern world system (cf. WORLD-SYSTEMS ANALYSIS).

Modern colonialisms can be classified according to the timing and the manner in which alien territories were incorporated, usually through violent conquest and plunder, into a world system. More precisely, variations in colonial experience arise from the specific combination of: (i) the *form of capitalist political economy* at specific moments in world time; (ii) *different forms of colonial state* and interests which they represented; and (iii) the *diversity of pre-colonial societies* upon which European domination was imposed. In the context of a geographical separation of colonizer and colonized, all colonialisms must confront the critical questions of how the colonies are to be administered, financed and made profitable. Colonial states were central to the establishment of conditions by which revenue could be raised (i.e. taxation, customs), labour regimes instituted to promote commodity production (based on various forms of free or servile labour), and political alliances sealed to maintain the fiction of local participation and yet ensure imperial HEGEMONY.

The age of colonialism began in the fifteenth century with the European expansion in Africa, Asia and the New World. Led by Spain and Portugal, and secondarily other west European powers, colonialism expanded by violent conquest and settlement after a period of extensive EXPLORATION. The most ambitious colonial project was established under Spanish auspices in the 'New World' involving complex forms of direct and indirect rule and administration, Spanish settlement through land and labour grants (the *encomienda* and the *repartimiento* system), and new forms of economic exploitation associated with PLANTATIONS and *haciendas*, and labour-intensive mining for bullion (Wallerstein, 1974). This first phase of colonialism is usually assumed to reflect the search for wealth in the form of gold, ivory and slaves (see SLAVERY) but the origins of European expansion also lie in the complex evolution of European mercantile competition, and in regional political developments associated with the crisis of European FEUDALISM (Wolf, 1982). Colonialism emerged in the context of both limited technological capability (the colonies were often geographically distant from the imperial centre and hence relatively autonomous) and at a specific moment in world time (late feudalism). While early colonialism is often seen as mercantile in nature, promoted by European states through merchant companies, its impact on production and international political economy generally was not simply confined to the promotion of exchange. For example, millions of slaves were forcibly taken from Africa to work on plantations in the Caribbean and the US South while mining and ranching enterprises linked the New World into new circuits of international trade in mass commodities (Stavrianos, 1980).

The old colonial system erupted from the contradictions of European feudalism and lasted for three centuries. It was disrupted in the eighteenth century by the rapid advance of industrial capitalism in England and ushered in a second phase of colonialism, much shorter in duration and rooted in an expansionary world capitalism. The century between 1820 and the First World War (1914–18) saw the growth of a modern colonial order backed by complete European hegemony over world TRADE, finance and shipping and by new forms of political and military authority sustained by technology, applied science and information systems. Between 1870 and 1918, the colonial powers added an average of 240,000 sq. miles each year to their possessions; between 1875 and 1915 one-quarter of the globe's land surface was distributed or redistributed as colonies among half a dozen states (Hobsbawm, 1987) – Britain, France, and Germany increased their colonies by 4 million, 3.5 million, and 1 million sq. miles respectively; Belgium and Italy, and the USA and Japan, each increased their holdings by roughly 1 million and 100,000 square miles respectively. This phase of 'classical imperialism' was no longer cast in terms of laissez faire and mercantilism but was rooted in a new phase of capitalist development and of inter-imperial rivalry (cf. MERCANTILIST MODEL).

Modern colonialism took a variety of forms. A useful taxonomy employs the coordinates of forms of commodity production, labour regime and political rule (Hicks, 1969). In the case of Africa there are three broad forms (Amin, 1974): *settler colonies* (e.g. Kenya and Mozambique) in which direct rule by a settler class was associated with plantation-based export commodity production (for example cotton, tea, sugar); *trade or trading post economies* (e.g. Nigeria and Senegal) characterized by indirect rule (Britain's Dual Mandate) through local ruling classes, who acted as colonial bureaucrats, and peasant-based production of export commodities such as palm oil and peanuts; and *mine concessions* (e.g. South Africa) in which transnational capital dominated the national economy and *migrant labour*, recruited, often by direct compulsion in the first instance, from 'native reserves' for work in the mines, overdetermined the shape of the local political economy.

Efforts to explain the origins and timing, and the character and consequences of modern colonialism has produced a vast literature. Colonialism has been seen as a benign force of economic MODERNIZATION and social advancement (the so-called *mission civilatrice*) ensuring law and order, private property and contract, basic INFRASTRUCTURE and modern politico-legal institutions (Bauer, 1976). It has also been posited within the Marxist theoretical tradition as an instrument of wholesale destruction, DEPENDENCY and systematic exploitation producing distorted economies, socio-psychological disorientation, massive POVERTY and neo-colonial dependency (Frank, 1969; Baran, 1957; Rodney, 1972). Some lines of neo-Marxist thinking have posited that colonial capitalism was 'progressive', acting as a powerful engine of social change (Warren, 1980); other, equally controversial, Marxist research has posited a distinctive colonial MODE OF PRODUCTION (Alavi, 1975). What is clear, however, is that the shift from informal spheres of influence to formal colonial rule in the nineteenth century is rooted in a new phase of capitalist transformation (sometimes called the 'second' INDUSTRIAL REVOLUTION) in which inter-capitalist rivalry and the growth of transnational forms of industrial and finance capital promoted a search for raw materials, new markets and new investment opportunities.

The colonial experience involved both resistance and adaptation to colonial rule. Western education and missionary activity, while introduced as a means to train lower-order civil servants and as the civilizing arm of the colonial state, had contradictory consequences. The first generation of anti-colonial nationalist leaders were often products of the civil service (clerks, teachers) and mission schools who continued their education beyond the limits set by their colonial teachers (see NATIONALISM; SELF-DETERMINATION). In the period after 1945, the rise of anti-colonial movements in the colonies and the economic crises within an ageing imperial system both contributed towards the rapid process of DECOLONIZATION. The colonial system was found to be expensive by the imperial powers and increasingly ungovernable. Colonialism was politically and IDEOLOGICALLY discredited by emergent nationalist movements, often actively supported by the United States as well as the Socialist bloc. Independence from colonial rule came quickly in the post-war period though white settler colonies were especially resistant to any notion of indigenous rule. Independence was only achieved in such cases through organized insurrection (e.g. Mau Mau in Kenya) or through a long guerrilla war of liberation (e.g. Mozambique, Angola and Zimbabwe). There is a general sense throughout much of the Third World that decolonization has not resulted in meaningful economic or political independence. The persistence of primary export production and of dependent political elites linked to former colonial powers suggests that colonialism has been transformed into *perpetual Neo-colonialism* (Abdel-Fadil, 1989). MW

References

Abdel-Fadil, M. 1989: Colonialism. In J. Eatwell, M. Milgate, and P. Newmans, eds, *Economic development.* Oxford: Blackwell, 61–7. · Alavi, H. 1975: India and the colonial mode of production. In R. Miliband, and J. Saville, eds, *The socialist register.* London: Merlin, 167–87. · Amin, S. 1974: *Accumulation on a World Scale.* New York: Monthly Review Press · Baran, P. 1957: *The political economy of growth.* New York: Monthly Review. · Barratt-Brown, M. 1974: *The economics of imperialism.* London: Penguin. · Bauer, P.T. 1976: *Dissent on Development.* Cambridge, MA: Harvard University Press. · Fanon, F. 1966: *The wretched of the earth.* Harmondsworth: Penguin. · Fieldhouse, D. 1981: *Colonialism 1870–1945.* London: Weidenfeld and Nicolson. · Frank, A.G. 1969: *Development and underdevelopment in Latin America.* New York: Monthly Review Press. · Hicks, J. 1969: *A theory of economic history.* Oxford: Clarendon. · Hobsbawm, E. 1987: *Age of Empire 1875–1914.* New York: Pantheon. · Rodney, W. 1972: *How Europe underdeveloped Africa.* London: Bogle. · Stavrianos, G. 1980: *Global rift.* New York: Free Press. · Wallerstein, I. 1974: *The modern world-system. Volume 1.* New York: Academic Press. · Warren, B. 1980: *Imperialism: pioneer of capitalism.* London: Verso. · Wolf, E. 1982: *Europe and the people without history.* Berkeley: University of California Press.

Suggested Reading

Brewer, A. 1980: *Marxist theories of imperialism.* London: Routledge and Kegan Paul. · Etherington, N. 1984: *Theories of imperialism.* London: Croom Helm.

command economy An economy in which the means of production are owned and controlled by the STATE and in which CENTRAL PLANNING prevails. The term is used to distinguish economies such as those found until recently in eastern Europe from either CAPITALISM or a MIXED ECONOMY. The dismantling of command economies in eastern Europe in the early 1990s reflected their inability to produce goods in the quantities people had come to expect, as a result of difficulties of coordination and the lack of efficiency incentives. However, the economies which replaced them have their own imperfections, including large-scale criminalization, reflecting the difficulty of creating market-regulated economies in former socialist states (cf. SOCIALISM). DMS

commercial geography A predecessor of ECONOMIC GEOGRAPHY, mainly concerned with presenting factual material about economic activity in various parts of the world. Such compilations – of which the many editions of G.G. Chisholm's *Handbook of commercial geography* (1889) was the most famous – characterized an era in which geography was promoted as a major vehicle for informing colonial policies. Chisholm's book had two main parts, the first detailing the geography of production of various commodities and the second providing a world regional catalogue of what was produced where. RJJ

References and Suggested Reading

Chisholm, G.G. 1889: *Handbook of commercial geography.* London: Longman. · Wise, M.J. 1975: A university teacher of geography. *Transactions, Institute of British Geographers* 66: 1–16.

commodity Commodities are objects that are produced for the purpose of being exchanged. This has not always been the case: for example in many subsistence societies objects are produced simply so that people can carry out their everyday lives, without thought of exchange (see SUBSISTENCE AGRICULTURE). But in a society driven by the production of commodities an entrepreneur chooses both the commodity and the method by which it is produced according to whether she expects that the commodity will sell at a high enough price to realize an adequate profit on the money that must be invested in its production. The mechanism of MARKET EXCHANGE is left to match up to the hunt by commodity producers to realize a profit and the presumed needs of consumers.

Marx (1977, p. 163) stated that 'a commodity at first sight is an extremely obvious, trivial thing'. Thus, for some commentators, the market exchange of commodities defines what commodities are. But for others, including Ricardo and Marx, this view does not go far enough. It *is* obvious and trivial. They want to look behind the mechanism of exchanging commodities at the value created in producing the commodity in order to fully understand what commodities are (Sheppard and Barnes, 1990). In particular, these commentators distinguish between a commodity's use value, exchange value and labour value. *Use value* is simply the usefulness of a product to an individual. *Exchange value* is defined as the number of units of another commodity for which a commodity is exchanged in the market place. Finally, *labour value* is a general measure of the value created in the process of producing a commodity (see MARXIAN ECONOMICS).

In fact, not all commodities are equal. Two types of commodity hold a special place in most economic theories. The first of these is *labour* itself; one of the abiding principles of capitalist societies is that people who work must themselves become commodities, exchanged in LABOUR MARKETS. The second special commodity is *money* which has multiple functions, as a measure of value, a medium of exchange, a store of value and a means of payment (Harvey, 1982; Leyshon and Thrift, 1997: cf MONEY AND FINANCE, GEOGRAPHY OF).

Money is also a good example of *commodity fetishism*, in which social relations appear as things. Thus, in the case of money, social relations with others are secured by the money form. Similarly, RENT transforms land into a commodity with a price on it and makes it seem as though money comes from the soil.

What is certain is that the process of *commodification* has reached into every nook and cranny of modern life (see MODERNITY). Practically every human activity in western countries either relies on or has certain commodities associated with it, from births to weddings to funerals, at work or in the home, in peace or in war. Increasingly, the process of commodification has also taken hold in non-western societies, leading to notions of a global culture based, in part, on the ubiquity of certain commodities and commodity meaning (see GLOBALIZATION).

In some accounts of modern life, the commodity has travelled even deeper, burrowing into the human psyche. Thus the need to make commodities as attractive as possible, so that they will sell in large quantities (and make large profits), leads to the practice of *commodity aesthetics*. Commodities are fashioned that will, as near as possible, mirror consumers' desires. In turn, the potent combination of mass production and the mass media has lead to attempts to *create* desire for commodities, through design, advertising and market research (see CONSUMPTION, GEOGRAPHY OF). No wonder that Richards (1991, p. 13) has argued that 'the commodity is the focal point and, increasingly, the arbiter of all REPRESENTATION in capitalist societies'.

Some commentators would go further again. They would have it that the images and signs used to create desire for commodities have become more important than the commodities themselves; people buy commodities because of the images and signs associated with them, rather than vice versa: 'The surface (of the commodity) has been detached and becomes its second skin, which as a rule is incomparably more perfect than the first; it becomes completely disembodied and drifts unencumbered like a multicoloured spirit into every household, preparing the way for the real distribution of the commodity' (Haug, 1986, p. 50). This description of the modern world, one in which the *simulation* of commodities has become its own reality (or 'hyper-reality'), in which the consumption of the images and signs of commodities has become more important than the consumption of commodities, reaches its zenith in the work of Baudrillard. In turn, Baudrillard's description of a world of simulation and hyper-reality (see HYPERSPACE) has been a key component of work on POSTMODERNISM (Baudrillard, 1988; Gane, 1991a, 1991b; Jameson, 1991). NJT

References

Baudrillard, J. 1988: *Jean Baudrillard. Selected writings*. Cambridge: Polity Press. · Gane, M. 1991a: *Baudrillard: critical and fatal theory*. London: Routledge. · Gane, M. 1991b: *Baudrillard's bestiary*. London: Routledge. · Harvey, D. 1982: *The limits to capital*. Oxford: Basil Blackwell. · Haug, W.F. 1986: *Critique of commodity aesthetics/ Appearances, sexuality and advertising in capitalistic society*. Cambridge: Polity Press. · Jameson, F. 1991: *Postmodernism, or the cultural logic of late capitalism*. London: Verso. · Leyshon, A. and Thrift, N.J. 1997: *Money/ Space. Geographies of monetary transformation*. London: Routledge. · Marx, K. 1977: *Capital, Volume One*. New York: Viking; Richards, T. 1991: *The commodity culture of Victorian England*. London: Verso. · Sheppard, E. and Barnes, T.J. 1990: *The capitalist space economy. Geographical analysis after Ricardo, Marx and Sraffa*. London: Unwin Hyman.

Suggested Reading

Stallybrass, P. 1998: Marx's coat. In P. Spyer, ed., *Border fetishisms*. London: Routledge.

commodity chain/*filière* A collection of interrelated economic activities or industries required for the production of a particular kind of good or service. This meso-level concept – above the microscale of the individual firm but below that of the macroeconomy as a whole – originates in French industrial economics (Montfort and Dutailly, 1983), where it has been used to understand and describe the organizational structure of an economy as a collection of constituent commodity chains or *filières*. Although the concept bears at least a superficial similarity to the more familiar Anglo-American idea of the industrial sector – Storper (1997, p. 196) for example, makes reference to *filières* such as motor vehicles, electronics, chemicals and textiles – it connotes not simply a collection of firms making similar kinds of products, but also the existence of vertical (buyer–supplier) and horizontal (inter-competitor) linkages or interrelations binding firms together (cf. INTEGRATION). Hence, Walker and Storper (1989, p. 133) assert: '"filière" captures the idea of a connecting filament among technologically related activities'. Moreover, such relations are likely to take two different forms: traded relationships such as those accounted for in INPUT–OUTPUT analysis which are achieved through MARKET EXCHANGE; and extra-market interactions of a more informal nature – what Storper and others refer to as 'untraded interdependencies'.

The latter form of inter-firm relations is most significant in giving the commodity chain its distinctive character since close, repeated interaction between member firms creates and reinforces shared conventions and norms that facilitate the development and diffusion of innovative ideas and practices (Groeneweyen and Beije, 1989). Because this kind of exchange is often best achieved through face-to-face interaction facilitated by spatial proximity, many of the most technologically dynamic commodity chains exhibit strong degrees of geographical concentration of their constituent firms (cf. AGGLOMERATION). Storper (1997) gives the example of high-technology industries such as aerospace and electronics, which are concentrated in the Île-de-France region centred on Paris. He also notes that French industrial planners have used the concept of the *filière* to develop national technological competence. When the state initiates a purchase of a particular technology-intensive commodity, it may assist the prime contractor in meeting this order by providing an analysis of the existing structure and competence of the relevant *filière* and by offering direct assistance to firms in the commodity chain in order to augment key technological capabilities. As Storper notes (p. 152), 'This differs from the American defense contracting system, where the development of the filière (through subcontracting or in-house divisions) is left up to the prime contractors themselves'.

The concept of commodity chain has also been applied to the study of food and apparel retailing, where large retailers situated at the market end have taken to managing the entire chain, working closely with suppliers on product design, process innovation, quality monitoring and distribution logistics (Lowe and Wrigley, 1996; cf. RETAILING, GEOGRAPHY OF). Such 'buyer-driven' commodity chains differ from those in sectors such as automotive, computing and aerospace, where *filières* are strongly 'producer-driven' (Gereffi, 1994). In either case, this literature emphasizes the extensive international scale on which commodity chains are often organized and managed by MULTINATIONAL CORPORATIONS. (See also INDUSTRIAL DISTRICT; JUST-IN-TIME PRODUCTION; PRODUCTION COMPLEX.) MSG

References

Gereffi, G. 1994: The organization of buyer-driven global commodity chains: how US retailers shape overseas production networks. In G. Gereffi and M. Korzeniewicz, eds, *Commodity chains and global capitalism*. Westport, CT: Praeger, ch. 5. · Groeneweyen, J. and Beije, P.R. 1989: The French communication industry defined and analyzed through the social fabric matrix, the filière approach, and network analysis. *Journal of Economic Issues* 23: 1059–74. · Lowe, M. and Wrigley, N. 1996: Towards the new retail geography. In N. Wrigley and M. Lowe, eds, *Retailing, consumption and capital*. Harlow: Longman, 3–30. · Montfort, M.J. and Dutailly, J.C. 1983: *Les filières de production*. Paris: INSEE, Archives et Documents no. 67. · Storper, M. 1997: *The regional world: territorial development in a global economy*. New York: Guilford Press. · Storper, M. and Walker, R. 1989: *The capitalist imperative*. Oxford: Blackwell.

common market One of the forms and stages of formal INTEGRATION between separate national economic geographies. All restrictions on the movement of goods, labour, CAPITAL and enterprise should be removed within a common market which is, therefore, a product of negative integration. But a common market also involves positive integration in the creation of a common TRADE policy towards third countries – usually in the form of a common external TARIFF – and the harmonization of other trading regulations over exports as well as imports. The most ambitious attempt to create a common market remains that of the European Union (EU) which set the Single European Market in place between its twelve member states at the end of December 1992. Other examples include the less well-developed central American, east African, Andean and Caribbean common markets.

As a stage in the process of international economic integration, common markets involve the further development of more loosely integrated FREE TRADE AREAS (for example, the North American Free Trade

Agreement – NAFTA) and customs unions (for example Benelux). It may lead on to the creation of closer forms of integration such as monetary union (e.g. European Economic and Monetary Union – EMU) and full economic (fiscal, monetary, policy) union which involve substantial elements of positive as well as negative integration.

Alternative forms of integration include trade preference associations (e.g. the Association of south east Asian nations – ASEAN) in which a full free trade regime between partners may form simply one element of integration between them. This is intended to enable the more limited participation of those countries which would otherwise be encumbered by severe problems of UNEVEN DEVELOPMENT if exposed in their entirety to the rigours of free trade in all commodities and on the terms prevailing between more highly-developed members.

The logics behind the creation of a common market include:

- the release of static (e.g. increased trade) and dynamic (e.g. ECONOMIES OF SCALE) gains and multiplier effects (see MULTIPLIERS) from the geographical extension of the operation of nationally-unencumbered markets; and
- the extension over a wider geographical area of market-based forces and disciplines on economic action operating through the principle of COMPARATIVE ADVANTAGE so generating increased levels of TRADE and competition.

The consequences of common markets also include:

- the loss of local (national) economic SOVEREIGNTY;
- the exposure of geographical diversity to such competition; and
- the intensification of geographically-UNEVEN DEVELOPMENT.

In general terms, then, common markets – like other forms of economic integration – promote the disembedding of economic geographies through their exposure to geographically-extended and market-based processes of evaluation. They represent a shift upwards from the NATION-STATE in the level of GOVERNANCE and so present issues of local and national sovereignty. The formation of economic and monetary union (EMU) in Europe in 1999 – a form of integration going well beyond that of a common market – poses this question in especially insistent terms. When placed alongside the decentralization of government and governance from central to regional and local bodies, this represents a highly significant shift in the political economic geography of power. Urban and regional localities are likely to become increasingly engaged in competitive relations within the context of a geographically-widened framework of economic evaluation founded on the neo-liberal prescriptions of a powerful central bank. RL

Suggested reading

Knox, P. and Agnew, J. 1994: *The geography of the world economy*. London: Edward Arnold; New York: Routledge, Chapman and Hall, 2nd edn, ch. 12. · Lee, R. 1990: Making Europe: towards a geography of European integration. In M. Chisholm and D.M. Smith, eds, *Shared space: divided space*. London and New York: Unwin Hyman, 235–59. · Williams A.M. 1996: *The European Community: contradictions of integration*, 2nd edn. Oxford and New York: Blackwell Publishers.

common pool resources Natural or other resources which are in common ownership. The resource pool is usually so large, as with oceanic fishing areas, that it is extremely difficult to exclude potential beneficiaries from exploiting them, which raises problems of RESOURCE MANAGEMENT undertaken to ensure that the pool is not depleted (cf. TRAGEDY OF THE COMMONS). RJJ

Suggested Reading

Ostrom, E. 1990: *Governing the commons: illustrating the evolution of institutions for collective action*. Cambridge and New York: Cambridge University Press.

communications, geography of The geography of messages and messengers. For a long time, communications were a topic of only secondary interest in human geography. Often subsumed under categories like TRANSPORT GEOGRAPHY, they were seen as simply the threads which drew societies together. But now, communications are seen as central to what societies are and how they can be. As communications have come to be seen as a vital part of the process of social relations (see also MEDIA, GEOGRAPHY OF), so they are now becoming of immense interest to human geographers since they show how SOCIETIES are geographically constructed.

The realization that COMMUNITIES are a crucial element of social relations has many forebears. There is the work of nineteenth-century writers like Baudelaire, for whom one of the chief characteristics of modern life was speed, and in the earlier part of the twentieth century there is the work of sociologists like Lazarsfeld and Sorokin and political scientists like Lasswell and Lerner who, in their very different ways, were keen to inject notions of time and space into their accounts of the media and communications.

But it was not until the mid-twentieth century that the study of communication really started to become central to social science because of the work of two Canadian writers, Harold Innis and Marshall McLuhan. Innis held that communication technology was the basis of political and economic processes, a thesis he set out in *Empire and communications* (1950) and *The bias of communication* (1951). Innis argued that POWER involved the control of space and time and that communication systems therefore shape social organization. Marshall McLuhan made such insights into something approaching a fetish by insisting that the communications medium itself determines the nature of what is communicated and that new communications media will lead to new forms of civilization. McLuhan's technological determinism has been taken up in recent years by writers like Paul Virilio, for whom the speed of modern communications determines the form of civilization we will live in. In Virilio's case this means that the near-instantaneous speed of urban communications produces inertia; what in times past would have appeared as the sign of a handicap or infirmity – the inability to move in order to act – becomes a symbol of progress and ability to command the environment. Instead of the movement of the body, a complex of screens. For a humanist writer like Virilio, this is a profound threat to civilization since it undermines the notion of the human.

There are, however, three less heady approaches to the study of communication. One can be usefully counterpoised to approaches based on technological determinism. It attempts to understand the way in which technologies of communication can be understood as a part of more general practices. Such interchanges between the technology of communication and practices can be understood in numerous ways: through careful ETHNOGRAPHIES of the use of communications devices in everyday life (e.g. Silverstone, 1994); through more general theoretical approaches like ACTOR–NETWORK THEORY, and Debray's (1995) 'mediology'; or even, at the most abstract level, through the work of philosophers like Derrida, who writes of a general and proliferating structure of communication which is based on a scriptural model founded on the new sciences of communication like molecular biology, information theory and cybernetics, and Serres, who wants to write the space–time of communications as a topology of message-bearing systems.

Two other approaches are also important. One is the POLITICAL ECONOMY of communications, which considers the extent to which the ownership and control of communications is a crucial element in the unbalanced flows of information and cultural products between countries. The other is a more practical empirical orientation to communications which is manifested in the results of QUESTIONNAIRE surveys, focus groups and the like and which probably still accounts for the bulk of research on communications.

Given the heritage of the work of geographers like Innis, and the inherent SPATIALITY of communications, it is surprising how little attention has been given by geographers to these issues. There are exceptions, however. In the 1960s, work on TIME–SPACE CONVERGENCE was often conducted around communications (e.g. Jannelle, 1969) and Harvey's subsequent work on TIME–SPACE COMPRESSION might be thought of as in the grandiose tradition of Innis, McLuhan and Virilio. More generally, historical geographers have spent considerable time and effort excavating a geography of communications which is of considerable interest (cf. Pred, 1977; Gregory, 1987; Thrift, 1990; Brayshay et al., 1998; see also Schivelsbuch, 1986).

The issue of communications is, of course, only underlined by the growth of the Internet since the 1980s (Kitchin, 1998). After all, in certain senses, the Internet is nothing more that the telegraph writ large. In another sense, though, it seems to presage new and radically different senses of space and time. In a literature which thrives on exaggeration the answer, no doubt, will lie somewhere between. NJT

References

Brayshay, M., Harrison, P. and Chalkley, B. 1998: Knowledge, nationhood and governance. The speed of the Royal Mail in early-modern England, *Journal of Historical Geography* 24: 265–88. · Debray, R. 1995: *Mediologies*. London: Verso; Frictian of distance? Information circulation and the mails in early nineteenth-century England. · Gregory, D. 1987: *Journal of Historical Geography* 13: 130–54. · Harvey, D. 1989: *The condition of postmodernity*. Oxford: Blackwell. · Innis, M. 1950: *Empire and communications*. Toronto: University of Toronto Press. · Innis, M. 1951: *The bias of communication*. Toronto: University of Toronto Press. · Janelle, D.G. 1969: Spatial reorganisation: a model and a concept. *Annals of the Association of American Geographers* 59: 348–64. · Kitchin, R.M. 1998: *Cyberspace*. Chichester: John Wiley. · Mattelart, A. 1996: *The invention of communication*. Minneapolis: University of Minnesota Press. · Matterlart, A. and Mattelart, M. 1998: *Theories of communication. A short introduction*. London: Sage. · McLuhan, M. 1962: *The Gutenberg galaxy*. Toronto: University of Toronto Press. · McLuhan, M. 1964: *Understanding media*. New York: McGraw-Hill. · Pred, A. 1977: *City systems in advanced economies*. London: Hutchinson. · Schivelsbuch, W. 1986: *The railway journey. The industrialisation of space and time*. Berkeley: University of California Press. · Serres, M. 1995: *Angels. A modern myth*. Paris: Flannmarion. · Silverstone, R. 1994: *Television and everyday life*. London: Routledge. · Thrift, N.J. 1990: Transport and Communications, 1730–194. In R.A. Dodgshon and R.A. Butlin, eds, *A new historical geography of England and Wales*, 2nd edn. London: Academic Press, 453–86. · Virilio, P. 1995: *The art of the motor*. Minneapolis: University of Minnesota Press. · Virilio, P. 1997: *Open sky*. London: Verso.

Suggested Reading

Matterlart, A. and Mattelart, M. (1998).

communism A body of ideas united by a common IDEOLOGICAL tradition which, in modern form, can be traced back to the works of Karl Marx, and which takes as its point of reference the principle of communal ownership of all property. Marx identified two such classless societies (see CLASS): *primitive communism*, usually associated with tribal societies, in which basic economic resources (land and simple technology) were communally owned; and *full communism*, based on common ownership of the means of production, which could only come about in fully industrialized societies where goods were no longer scarce. According to Marx and his followers, such an end-stage society is preceded by a transitional period of SOCIALISM, characterized by the so-called 'dictatorship of the [industrial] proletariat'. With full communism, the STATE will 'wither away', while differences between town and country, between mental and physical labour, between nationality grouping (cf. NATIONALISM), and between state and collective property will disappear, and social relations will be regulated by the principle 'from each according to his ability, to each according to his needs'. However, not all nineteenth-century Marxists agreed with the necessity of a socialist stage. For instance, the Russian anarchist (see ANARCHISM) and geographer, Peter Kropotkin, saw the driving forces of history in terms of *competition* and *cooperation*, and believed them to be analogous to laws of NATURE; he saw no need for any post-revolutionary state, regardless of its purpose or social composition, for he argued that, whatever the MODE OF PRODUCTION, the state would always be a primary source of exploitation. These views aside, historically, state socialist countries have derived their support and legitimation from the claim that they are implementing communist ideas. GES

Suggested Reading

Breibart, M. 1981: Peter Kropotkin, the anarchist geographer. In D.R. Stoddart, ed, *Geography, ideology and social concern*. Oxford: Blackwell; New York: Barnes and Noble, 134–53. · Evans, M. 1975: *Karl Marx*. London: Allen and Unwin; Bloomington: Indiana University Press. · Wright, T 1996: *Socialism: old and new*. London: Routledge.

communitarianism A moral and political philosophy which argues for the good of COMMUNITY, and that this should be preserved and extended. Communitarians challenge liberalism, which they see as too individualistic, insufficiently sensitive to the social sources of self-hood, too much concerned with rights and too little with duty, and failing to grasp the historical contextuality of human life (see MacIntyre, 1985). They also assert that liberalism devalues community and political participation therein.

Three principle elements of communitarianism are recognized by Kymlicka (1993). The first is that the virtues of benevolence or solidarity characteristic of communities render justice a remedial virtue (see Sandel, 1982), rather than the first virtue of social life as claimed by liberals. The second is that justice arises from particular community understandings of social goods (see Walzer, 1983), which are local and historically specific, not from external universal criteria. The third is that the common good of the community comes before individual rights, including the freedom to pursue personal conceptions of the good life.

In such a community, people are supposed to live in harmony, sharing a CULTURE and system of values. While the model is sometimes found in a traditional form of local community life (see RURAL–URBAN CONTINUUM), the family is often considered the ideal case – involving mutual selfless generosity, with no role for the notion of fair shares. Other examples are universities, trade unions, and various ethnic, religious, and cultural groups. While communities might be associated with a particular locality, those valued by communitarians are not necessarily territorially defined.

Central to communitarianism is a relational identity or social self, expressed as a focus on 'we' rather that 'I'. This goes beyond the recognition of community as instrumental in the pursuit of individual ends, and as subject of purely sentimental attachment. Persons are seen as embedded or situated in a particular societal milieu, in contrast to the autonomous self-determination of agents floating free of context in the idealized liberal formulation.

Communitarianism has recently (re)surfaced as a political project with explicit moral content. On both sides of the Atlantic and at different points on the political spectrum, there have been calls for a return to values associated with community, loss of which is thought to be implicated in various contemporary ills. Hence the claim by Amitai Etzioni (1995) of a social movement aiming at shoring up the moral, social and political environment.

Critics of communitarianism point out that its advocates are trying to turn the clock back to a lost form of human society, which was not as harmonious as they claim. Actual communities could (and still can) be intolerant of dissent, and oppressive towards minorities and women. There are also great difficulties facing the recreation of communities which may depend to some extent on face-to-face relationships among persons, in a world of increasingly remote communications. (See also ETHICS, GEOGRAPHY AND; SOCIAL JUSTICE). DMS

References

Etzioni, A. 1995: *The spirit of community: rights, responsibilities and the communitarian agenda*. London: Fontana Press. · Kymlicka, W. 1993: Community. In R. E. Goodin and P. Pettit, eds, *A Companion to Contemporary Political Philosophy*. Oxford: Blackwell, 366–78. · MacIntyre, A. 1985: *After virtue: a study in moral theory*, 2nd edn. London: Duckworth. · Sandel, M. 1982: *Liberalism and the limits of justice*. Cambridge: Cambridge University Press. · Walzer, M. 1983: *Spheres of justice: a defence of pluralism and equality*. Oxford: Blackwell.

Suggested Reading

Kymlicka, W. 1990: *Contemporary political philosophy: an introduction*. Oxford: Clarendon Press, ch. 6. · Mulhall, S. and Swift, A. 1996: *Liberals and communitarians*, 2nd edn. Oxford: Blackwell. · Selznick, P. 1992: *The moral commonwealth: social theory and the promise of community*. Berkeley: University of California Press. · Smith, D.M. 1998: Geography, community, and morality. *Environment and Planning A*, 31, 19–35.

community A SOCIAL NETWORK of interacting individuals, usually concentrated into a defined TERRITORY. The term is widely used in a wide range of both academic and vernacular contexts generating a large number of separate (often implicit) definitions (Stacey, 1969). As a consequence 'What community means has been disputed for even longer than the effects of place' (Bell and Newby, 1978): in the UK, for example, ETHNIC groups are often referred to as communities, irrespective of whether they occupy separately identifiable territories.

Bell and Newby follow Schmalenbach's (1961) definition of community as something more than the sense of belonging to an active social network – which they term *communion*. Community membership involves 'a matter of custom and of shared modes of thought or expression, all of which have no other sanction than tradition': one belongs to a community, but may only be conscious of that when it is threatened. Thus a community does not involve emotional ties, which characterize communion: a community may stimulate such experiences, providing the context within which they can develop, but all communities are not necessarily in communion.

Interest in communities in sociology and SOCIAL GEOGRAPHY developed from the work of the CHICAGO SCHOOL, in particular its evaluation of the social and behavioural consequences of URBANIZATION (cf. URBANISM). Tönnies's original concept of *gemeinschaft* identified communities as particular types of social networks (i.e. community as a form of human association), and was not concerned with community as either a local social system or a finite, bounded physical location (i.e. a territorially-defined social whole). Later workers brought the three together into an all-embracing definition, stimulating the term's wide range of usages.

For the Chicago sociologists and their followers the enhanced definition of community was consistent with their contrast of the (assumed) impersonality and social disorganization of urban life with the (also assumed) closely-integrated social networks characteristic of rural areas, as expressed in their concept of a RURAL–URBAN CONTINUUM. Rural communities were presented not only as the norm against which urban societies could be compared (see URBAN VILLAGE) but also as the desirable condition: rural communities were integrated and stable and so not conducive to individual ALIENATION and social problems, whereas urban societies were much more disorganized, and potentially characterized by ANOMIE and widespread social disorganization. This glorification of the rural was associated with anti-urban sentiments, as in the GARDEN CITY movement in late nineteenth–early twentieth-century Britain (see Pepper, 1990): rural societies were perceived as desirable because their communities were in communion, whereas those in urban areas were not. Later studies argued that whereas urban areas may lack certain positive characteristics relative to rural counterparts they may also have their own positive features which are absent from rural areas (see Frankenberg, 1966).

Community studies declined in popularity throughout the social sciences (except social anthropology) from the 1960s on. The introduction of the concept of LOCALITY in the 1980s suggested a renewed interest in local social systems among some observers, but Giddens (1984) nowhere equates LOCALE with community in his presentation of the former as central to STRUCTURATION THEORY (cf. CONTEXTUAL THEORY). Further, developments in TIME–SPACE COMPRESSION have increased the potential for close interaction among people separated by substantial distances, creating what some term 'community without propinquity' and the rapid expansion of the Internet and the World Wide Web has enhanced this, with the creation of 'virtual communities' (Kitchin, 1998) of people able to interact constantly, and in 'real time', by electronic media which can transmit a wide variety of TEXTS.

RJJ

References and Suggested Reading

Bell, C. and Newby, H. 1978: Community, communion, class and community action: the social sources of the new urban politics. In D.T. Herbert and R.J. Johnston, eds, *Social areas in cities: processes, patterns and problems*. Chichester and New York: John Wiley, 283–302. · Frankenberg, R. 1966: *Communities in Britain: social life in town and country*. London: Penguin Books. · Giddens, A. 1984: *The constitution of society*. Cambridge: Polity Press. · Kitchin, R. 1998: *Cyberspace: the world in the wires*. Chichester and New York: John Wiley. · Pepper, D. 1990: Geography and landscapes of anarchistic visions of Britain: the examples of Morris and Kropotkin. In I. Cook and D. Pepper, eds, *Anarchism and geography. Contemporary issues in geography and education* 3 (2), 63–79. · Schmalenbach, H. 1961: The sociological category of communion. In T. Parsons et al., eds, *Theories of society* 1, 331–47. · Stacey, M. 1969: The myth of community studies. *British Journal of Sociology* 20: 134–47.

commuting The technical term for journeys-to-work. Because these are major generators of traffic flows within cities, models of commuting patterns have been developed to aid transport planning and decisions on the location of new residential and employment areas. RJJ

comparative advantage The principle where-by individuals (or territories) produce those goods or services for which they have the greatest cost or efficiency advantage over others, or for which they have the least disadvantage. The outcome tends to be specialization. A gifted individual or resource-rich region may be able to produce everything more efficiently than others less well-endowed, but as long as some comparative advantage exists specialization may benefit all. An example is that of the best lawyer in town who is also the best typist: it pays the lawyer to concentrate on the lucrative practice of the law and to hire a typist (who has a comparative advantage in typing relative to knowledge of the law). One region may be able to produce two goods more efficiently than another region, but it pays to concentrate on the good for which there is greatest comparative advantage and buy the other from the second region.

The notion of comparative advantage is important in understanding regional specialization, whereby all regions gain from the interchange of products even if they could satisfy their own needs. A condition for realizing the benefits of comparative advantage is free trade. At the international scale, market imperfections such as tariff barriers to free trade can impede specialization based on comparative advantage, protecting domestic production of goods which could not withstand open competition. The objective may be to ensure more 'balanced' economic development and to avoid problems associated with narrow product specialization. DMS

comparative cost analysis The practice of evaluating the COMPARATIVE ADVANTAGE of alternative locations with respect to the cost of production. Comparative cost analysis can serve both to judge the efficiency of existing locations and to assist with the choice of site for a new facility. The theoretical foundations are derived from VARIABLE COST ANALYSIS.

Comparative cost analysis is generally adopted when there are relatively few locations to evaluate and where the inputs involved are also few. Primary metal manufacturing lends itself to this approach. Alternative locations are identified, the cost of each of the inputs in each location is found, and these are aggregated into a figure for total cost. The COST STRUCTURE of the industry can provide initial guidance on which inputs are likely to be of greatest importance to total cost. Inputs that are insignificant in the general cost structure can be omitted with little effect on the final result unless there is evidence that they may be unusually expensive in some of the locations to be considered. Inputs with constant costs in geographical space can be omitted, unless there is a subsequent analysis in which sales or revenue are considered sensitive to the total cost of production (see VARIABLE REVENUE ANALYSIS).

Comparative cost analysis is the most common practical means of making an informed choice among alternative locations. The major drawbacks are the difficulty of calculating total cost when more than a few inputs are involved, the problem of evaluating the effect of linkages and other EXTERNAL ECONOMIES, and failure to incorporate the demand factor. DMS

Suggested Reading

Smith, D.M. 1981: *Industrial location: an economic geographical analysis*, 2nd edn. New York: John Wiley.

complementarity Complementarity between region A and region B implies that A produces (or has the potential to produce) goods or services of which B has a deficit (or potential deficit). The term was used by Ullman (1956) to describe one of the bases of SPATIAL INTERACTION. He argued that complementarity may arise either from AREAL DIFFERENTIATION (in resource endowment, or in social, economic and cultural conditions) or as a result of ECONOMIES OF SCALE. In broader usage complementarity implies that regions produce, or could produce, quite different mixes of goods and services which are, or could be, exchanged between them: in this way complementarity is related to the economic concept of COMPARATIVE ADVANTAGE. AMH

Reference

Ullman, E.L. 1956: The role of transportation and the bases for interaction. In W.L. Thomas, ed., *Man's role in changing the face of the Earth*. Chicago: University of Chicago Press, 862–80.

components of change An accounting framework for studying the changing distribution of various components of a population, most commonly employment in different industries and/or occupations. Changes across the constituent areas of a larger spatial unit (such as regions of a country) over a defined time period are separated into three components:

- *in situ changes*, reflecting the growth or decline of employment at industrial plants since the start of the period;
- *birth and death changes*, resulting from the opening of new plants during the period and the closure of others; and
- *migration changes*, the outcome of some plants being moved to an area and others from it.

The net change in an area (in its industrial employment in this example) is thus represented by the equation:

Net change in employment = (employment in new plants opened during the period) – (employment in plants closed during the period) + (net change in employment in plants surviving through the period) + (employment in plants moved to the area from elsewhere) – (employment in plants moved away from the area).

Studies of more than one area subdivide the migration change component into plants which shed employment during the move, plants which increase their employment during the move, and plants which experience no change. (See also SHIFT-SHARE MODEL.) RJJ

Suggested Reading

Mason, C.M. 1980: Industrial change in Greater Manchester 1966–1975: a components of change approach. *Urban Studies* 17: 173–84.

compositional theory Forms of inquiry that proceed by breaking down their object into general categories based on principles of similarity. The basic idea has a long history: the German philosopher Immanuel Kant (1724–1804) claimed that virtually all major fields of study proceed on the basis of such a logical CLASSIFICATION (see KANTIANISM); the twin exceptions, significantly, were history and geography. And in modern geography the term 'compositional theory' was developed by Hägerstrand (1974) precisely in order to establish the vital difference between such formal-logical approaches – which he thought held sway in much of geography too – and his own TIME-GEOGRAPHY, which he described as a CONTEXTUAL APPROACH based instead on principles of time–space contiguity and connection (see Thrift, 1983). DG

References

Hägerstrand, T. 1974: Tidgeografisk beskrivning – syfte och postulat. *Svensk Geograpisk Årsbok* 50: 86–94. · Thrift, N.J. 1983: On the determination of social action in space and time. *Environment and Planning D: Society and Space* 1: 23–58.

computer-assisted cartography The use of digital computers, mapping software and computer-driven display units to design or produce maps as well as to develop databases employed in map production. Computer-assisted cartography (also called digital cartography) is somewhat older than GEOGRAPHICAL INFORMATION SYSTEMS, a technological specialty concerned more with the storage, retrieval and analysis of spatial data than with cartographic display per se. Because computers are used widely in all phases of cartographic design and production, the adjective computer-assisted has become somewhat redundant insofar as almost all contemporary map production is at least partly computer-assisted.

Map projections, which often require repeated evaluation of complex mathematical formulae, were among the earliest cartographic applications of the computer (Snyder, 1985). Calculation of projected coordinates preceded by several years the automatic plotting of grid lines, boundaries and other geographical features. In the 1950s geographers and planners discovered that a computer could generate a crude map on an electric typewriter or line printer designed to print alphanumeric characters aligned in six or eight rows per inch down the page and in ten columns per inch across (Tobler, 1959). Despite this coarse resolution, the widely available high-speed line printer promoted inexpensive experimentation with CHOROPLETH maps as well as the convenient display of TREND SURFACES and other computationally demanding isoline maps.

Display quality improved markedly in the late 1960s and early 1970s with the introduction of plotters able to raise or lower a ballpoint or liquid-ink pen and draft curved lines by moving it simultaneously in the X and Y directions. Adept at drawing lines and labels, pen-plotters could also produce crude line-pattern area symbols for choropleth and land-use maps (Monmonier, 1982). Although the digital plotter never rivaled the ink pen or engraving tool in the hand of a skilled drafter, development of high-resolution large-format film plotters in the late 1970s provided efficient machine-controlled generation of photographic negatives used in colour printing. Government agencies and large commercial mapping firms that could afford the massive investment began to abandon drafting pens in favour of the digitizers and electronic scanners required for the 'capture' or 'conversion' (see DIGITIZING) of digital cartographic data. Despite high initial costs, cartographic databases promised less expensive production of updated editions as well as increased cost recovery through secondary uses (Morrison, 1980).

Further advances in display technology in the 1980s encouraged university cartographic laboratories and other small map producers to abandon manual, non-electronic drafting. Improved cathode ray tubes and highly interactive illustration software allowed rapid placement of symbols and labels as well as efficient map editing. Toner replaced ink with the advent of high-resolution laser printers able to integrate precise, aesthetically pleasing type with crisp linework and carefully controlled graytones. Page-layout software and ultra-high-resolution imagesetters revolutionized publication design and pre-press production in the 1990s, when publishers began to require electronic versions of authors' text and graphics. Further change is inevitable as a consequence of colour monitors, inexpensive colour printers and the World Wide Web, which supports broad dissemination without the expense and delay of printing.

Digital computing and electronic display challenged cartographers to automate two basic operations: label placement and line generalization. Label placement proved more straightforward: priority rankings describing preferred locations for feature-and place-names allowed algorithms to not only avoid overlapping labels but also provide aesthetically acceptable solutions that maximized the number of labeled features (Jones, 1997, pp. 259–62). By contrast, line generalization proved an enigmatic problem with many facets and richly varied solutions. Although computerized strategies allow mapmakers to smooth and simplify line symbols, eliminate inconsequential point and area features, purge extraneous points from the list of coordinates, consolidate nearby polygons and exaggerate details for clarity, manual intervention is almost always necessary when a substantial reduction in SCALE demands lateral displacement of close, similarly aligned features (McMaster and Shea, 1992).

Other noteworthy developments include specialized data structures for the efficient storage and ready retrieval of spatial data (Laurini and Thompson, 1992); GEOCODING schemes for representing the topological structure of the urban street grid and census enumeration units (Trainor, 1990); more efficient methods for displaying and analysing terrain (Raper, 1989) and tools for automated line-following, edge-matching and other aspects of developing and maintaining a geographical database. Also important are graphical interfaces that promote the integration of mapping with a variety of computational processes, including automated recognition of disease clusters (Openshaw et al., 1987), simulation of toxic plumes in groundwater or atmosphere, and identification of shortest-path highway routes. Optimal routing is a particularly useful addition to automated highway navigation systems that continually update a detailed local street map showing the vehicle's current location. By introducing time and motion as visual variables, interactive computer graphics and animated mapping have vastly enhanced cartographic reconstructions and simulations of complex events and processes. MM

References

Jones, C.B. 1997: *Geographical information systems and computer cartography*. London: Longman. · Laurini, R. and Thompson, D. 1992: *Fundamentals of spatial information systems*. London: Academic Press. · McMaster, R.B. and Shea, K.S. 1992: *Generalization in digital cartography*. Washington, D.C.: Association of American Geographers. · Monmonier, M. 1982: *Computer-assisted cartography: principles and prospects*. Englewood Cliffs, NJ: Prentice-Hall. · Morrison, J.L. 1980: Computer technology and cartographic change. In D.R.F. Taylor, ed., *The computer in contemporary cartography*. New York: John Wiley and Sons, 5–23. · Openshaw, S. et al. 1987: A Mark 1 Geographical Analysis Machine for the automated analysis of point data sets. *International Journal of Geographical Information Systems* 1: 335–58. · Raper, J., ed., 1989: *Three-dimensional applications in geographical information systems*. London: Taylor and Francis. · Snyder, J.P. 1985: *Computer-assisted map projection research, Bulletin 1629*. Reston, Virginia: US Geological Survey. · Tobler, W.R. 1959: Automation and cartography. *Geographical Review* 49: 526–34. · Trainor, T.F. 1990: Fully automated cartography: a major transition at the Census Bureau. *Cartography and Geographic Information Systems* 17: 27–38.

Suggested Reading

Masser, I. and Blakemore, M., eds, 1991: *Handling geographical information: methodology and potential applications*. Harlow, Essex: Longman. · Monmonier, M. 1985: *Technological transition in cartography*. Madison, WI: University of Wisconsin Press.

concentration and centralization The tendency towards localization of economic activity in and around a relatively small number of urban centres. This condition is also referred to as polarization or AGGLOMERATION. It arises from the spatial concentration of the market, sources of information, bases for control and decision making, interactivity linkages and other EXTERNAL ECONOMIES. Concentration and centralization increase the disadvantages of peripheral locations and contribute to the economic and social deprivation commonly found with greater distance from the core (see CORE–PERIPHERY MODEL).

Spatial concentration and centralization are associated with the tendency for economic activity to be organized in units of increasing size and within a hierarchical organizational structure. The growing concentration of ownership of capitalist business activity was evident during the nineteenth century, decades before the contemporary emergence of the MULTINATIONAL or TRANSNATIONAL CORPORATION. The large capitalist corporation of today may have productive capacity and sales outlets in many different nations, but ownership and control remain vested in the headquarters that are usually located within one of the major financial centres of Europe or North America. Concentration of capital in a non-spatial sense, i.e. in the hands of fewer larger owners, is an important feature of advanced capitalism and a source of concentration of political, as well as economic, POWER which transcends that of NATION-STATES. The associated geographical concentration of certain kinds of economic activity facilitates the flow of CAPITAL between different uses and the pace of circulation and turnover on which profits depend. DMS

confirmatory data analysis The use of statistical procedures, including SIGNIFICANCE TESTS, to evaluate HYPOTHESES (cf. EXPLORATORY DATA ANALYSIS). RJJ

conflict A situation involving struggle among two or more protagonists. Within geography, studies of struggles characterize not only POLITICAL GEOGRAPHY but also much SOCIAL and ECONOMIC GEOGRAPHY; many of the patterns that geographers analyse are the outcome of conflicts, which then provide the context for further conflicts.

Much study of conflict focuses on the activities of the STATE, which fall into three main types. First, those controlling the STATE APPARATUS operate the *'police power'*, which enables them to restrict individual freedoms in order to promote what they identify as the 'general good'. (In some arguments, this is a necessary state function, since individuals operating freely are unlikely to achieve what is in their own, let alone society's, best interests: see TRAGEDY OF THE COMMONS.) Urban land-use ZONING is a good example of the police power in operation, whereby an individual owner's freedom to use a piece of land for any purpose is constrained to those purposes considered best for the community as a whole.

Secondly, the state is frequently called upon to *arbitrate* in conflicts and to identify and ensure a resolution. Those which are resolved – usually through its quasi-independent judicial apparatus (see LAW, GEOGRAPHY OF) – involve either two or more parties who claim a legal transgression (such as breach of contract) or the state itself claiming that individuals have violated a law or regulation.

Finally the state acts to *defend* its sovereign TERRITORY (see SOVEREIGNTY; TERRITORIALITY) against external aggressors and, in certain circumstances, to extend it, which will probably involve military activity: the description and analysis of such conflicts is at the core of the study of GEOPOLITICS.

Many of the conflicts involving the state are over the occupation and use of land, including concerns over SUSTAINABLE DEVELOPMENT: issues of CONSERVATION and PRESERVATION are central to many such conflicts at all spatial scales (see LAW OF THE SEA, for example). Land use is also a source of conflicts among neighbours – for example between the residents of a district who wish to protect its character and those promoting alterations to it, with potential EXTERNALITIES that could affect people's properties and levels of living (see Cox and Johnston, 1982).

Empirical studies of conflicts and their outcomes tend to focus on their appearance only, with little appreciation of the contexts in which they have emerged. Increasingly, however, conflicts over the environment and land use are being studied within a theoretical structure provided by the understanding of CAPITALISM in which the fundamental conflict is between the two main economic CLASSES, the bourgeoisie and the proletariat, but within which there are many others involving fractions of the two classes and even fractions of the same class. Many conflicts involve the manipulation of space and the use of NATURE to promote wealth accumulation, as illustrated by Massey's (1996) study of the conflicts between employers and their labour forces in the restructuring of British industry and Clark's (1988) analysis of the role of trades unions in the reorganization of the American space economy.

At the international scale, the growing intersection of studies in political geography and international relations is providing a structure for analysing the geography of conflicts between countries. Taylor (1989, 1996), for example, has linked the changing geography of UNEVEN DEVELOPMENT to the rise and fall of particular nation-states as world powers and has related the pattern of conflicts, and the geopolitical transitions that may follow their resolution, to the KONDRATIEFF CYCLES which characterize the operation of the capitalist economy (see WORLD-SYSTEMS ANALYSIS; on international conflict resolution, see REGIME THEORY). RJJ

References and Suggested Reading

Clark, G.L. 1988: *Unions and communities under siege*. Cambridge: Cambridge University Press. · Cox, K.R. and Johnston, R.J., eds, 1982: *Conflict, politics and the urban scene*. London and New York: Longman. · Massey, D. 1996: *Spatial divisions of labour: social structures and the geography of production*. London: Macmillan. · Taylor, P.J. 1989: *Political geography: world-economy, nation-state and community*, 2nd edn. London and New York: Longman. · Taylor, P.J. 1996: *The way the modern world works: world hegemony to world impasse*. Chichester and New York: John Wiley.

conservation In some contexts, the efficient and non-wasteful use of NATURAL RESOURCES; in others, any form of environmental protection. It is useful to distinguish between conservation and PRESERVATION, plus the different uses of these terms in various countries. In the North American context, an early advocate of conservation, Gifford Pinchot, wrote in 1901 that conservation (Wall, 1994):

> demands the complete and orderly development of all our resources for the benefit of all people [and] recognises fully the right of the present generation to use what it needs and all it needs of the natural resources now available, but it recognises equally our obligation so to use what we need that our descendants shall not be deprived of what they need.

This definition of conservation was an important foundation for the later idea of SUSTAINABLE DEVELOPMENT.

In the 1890s American ENVIRONMENTALISM, which had emerged from the work of George Perkins Marsh, Henry David Thoreau, John James Audubon and George Catlin, divided into two approaches. Gifford Pinchot and other advocates of conservation argued with John Muir and other advocates of preservation about what values the environmental movement of the time should adopt. Conservationists saw NATURE as natural resources that were available for human use, while preservationists attributed inherent value to nature and WILDERNESS. The conservationists emerged victorious, and since that time preservation in the USA has effectively ceased as a movement. However, preservationist ideas continue through the writing of Aldo Leopold (1949) and the contemporary DEEP ECOLOGY movement. Many of the older preservationist groups (as opposed to a movement) tend to be species- or site-specific. Some of the newer, and more radical, preservationist inspired groups, such as Earth First!, advocate the preservation of the idea of wilderness and then campaign for its protection at specific sites.

Glacken (1967) and Grove (1995) both recognized that the literature which influenced conservation in the USA, including the 1864 publication of George Perkins Marsh's book *Man and Nature* (Lowenthal, 1965), is a history of conservation that is specific to the

North American setting. Marsh's work was important as a synthesis of ideas. It recognized the human impact upon nature, that some forms of environmental degradation may be irreversible and that environmental degradation may result in human extinction.

Grove (1995) argued that prior to Marsh's work in the USA, conservation arose virtually simultaneously with colonial trade and expansion by the Venetians, Dutch, French and English in the seventeenth century. Environmental damage, and sometimes repair, was most easily documented in colonial settings, particularly islands (cf. COLONIALISM; ECOLOGICAL IMPERIALISM). The promotion of conservation ideas was aided by some religious beliefs, the adoption of indigenous knowledge and practices, and the perception of threats to climate resulting from land (mis)management practices. In the French colony of Mauritius, distance from the central power's constraints and the emergence of Physiocracy (agricultural economics that cared for the land), aided conservation.

In the UK, *nature conservation* is similar to preservation in the USA, while *resource conservation* is similar to the ideas of American conservationists: the term *preservation* often means the saving of human-made, rather than natural, features of the UK LANDSCAPE, whereas the preservation of human-made structures is often known as *historic preservation* in the USA, and *heritage planning* in Australia. In the UK, conservation of the human-made environment has become an important aspect of urban planning; the *Civic Amenities Act* of 1967 enshrined the notion of *conservation areas*. Conservation Planning has become an important sub-area of URBAN PLANNING in many countries, especially when connected to economic development through the reuse of older built environments with potential to attract tourists.

The term conservation became more accepted across the world as people understood that it usually meant protection, but also use. In 1948, the International Union for the Protection of Nature (IUPN) was established but in 1956, largely at US insistence, its name was changed to the International Union for the Conservation of Nature and Natural Resources (IUCN; McCormick, 1995). In 1980, the IUCN, the World Wildlife Fund (WWF) and the United Nations Environment Programme (UNEP) launched the *World Conservation Strategy* (IUCN, 1980), which introduced the term sustainable development.

Conservation is an aim of many people because to waste nature or natural resources is unacceptable from most economic and environmental perspectives (cf. ENVIRONMENTAL ECONOMICS). However, there is significant disagreement about the appropriate approach that should be taken to conserve species, sites, habitats or even ways of life. While this has often been understood as a failure of market-mechanisms to prevent the destruction of nature, some contemporary approaches advocate conservation through market mechanisms, rather than through approaches such as creating NATIONAL PARKS. These market-oriented approaches include the private ownership of nature (as advocated by the Wise Use movement in western USA and Canada, and self-labelled Free Market Environmentalist authors such as Anderson and Leal, 1991), applying market values to protect the environment (as advocated by Turner, Pearce and Bateman, 1994) through to various government management plans, financial assistance, and penalties for non-compliance. The relative merits of each approach are debatable, and usually depend upon the specific situation. If the intended conservation effort is successful, this very success may generate new conservation issues. Efforts to conserve some species through limiting hunting or fishing, or by eliminating their predators, may result in massive increases in numbers of that species, with detrimental cumulative impacts upon habitats and other species.

Decisions to conserve, how to conserve, what to conserve, when to conserve, and so on, are political decisions that represent value-judgements. Ideally they should be based on an understanding of ECOLOGY and ECOSYSTEMS, but it should be recognized that they are also based upon political expediency.

PM

References

Anderson, T. and Leal D. 1991: *Free market environmentalism*. Boulder: Westview Press. · Glacken, C. 1967: *Traces on the Rhodian Shore*. Berkeley and Los Angeles: University of California Press. · Grove, R. 1995: *Green imperialism: colonial expansion, tropical island Edens and the origins of environmentalism, 1600–1860*. Cambridge: Cambridge University Press. · IUCN, 1980: *World conservation strategy*. Geneva: International Union for the Conservation of Nature and Natural Resources, United Nations Environment Programme, World Wildlife Fund. · Leopold, A. 1968 (1949): *A Sand County almanac*. Oxford: Oxford University Press. · Lowenthal, D., ed., 1965: *George Perkins Marsh: man and nature*. Cambridge, MA: Belknap Press. · McCormick, J. 1995: *The global environmental movement*, 2nd edn. Chichester: John Wiley and Sons. · Pinchot, G. 1901: An extract from *The fight for conservation*. In D. Wall, 1994: *Green history: a reader in environmental literature, philosophy and politics*. London and New York: Routledge. · Turner, R.K., Pearce, D. and Bateman, I. 1994: *Environmental economics: an elementary introduction*. Hemel Hempstead: Harvester Wheatsheaf.

consociationalism A concept and practice of GOVERNANCE based on the idea of working towards political consent among leaders drawn from differing political communities of a polity, based on linguistic, religious or regional differences, in which the overriding objective is to ensure a politically stable and effectively functioning DEMOCRACY. As a form of spatial governance, it has at one time or another been most closely associated with the politics of managing difference in Belgium, Bosnia, Holland, Northern Ireland and Switzerland. To succeed, political elites must possess the ability to accommodate divergent interests, transcend the most salient cultural CLEAVAGES, be committed to STATE cohesion, and reflect support both from and within each sector of their divergent COMMUNITIES. The politicization of ethnoregional and other cultural divisions, however, questions the effectiveness of consociationalism as a form of CONFLICT management. (See also GEO-GOVERNANCE; LANGUAGE AND DIALECT, GEOGRAPHY OF; MULTICULTURALISM; PLURALISM; RELIGION, GEOGRAPHY OF.) GES

Suggested Reading

Barry, B. 1995: Political accommodation and consociational democracy. In *Democracy and power: essays in political theory 1*. Oxford: Oxford University Press, 100–35. · McGarry, J. and O'Leary, B. 1993: *The politics of ethnic conflict regulation* London: Routledge. · Lijphart, A. 1977: *Democracy in plural societies*. New Haven: Yale University Press.

consumer services Services which are ordinarily supplied to individual consumers (cf. PRODUCER SERVICES). This definition encompasses a large array of quite different economic activities. Until recently, precisely for this reason, the study of the geography of consumer services was nearly always subsumed under a whole set of different headings such as the geography of retailing, the geography of public services, and the geography of tourism. However, the geography of consumer services is now more likely to be approached under one heading because of an increasing interest in the geography of the workings of private consumer markets. In particular, as researchers have become more interested in the possibility of a 'third way' between STATE and market provision, so interest has stirred in how markets for consumer services are 'embedded' in state regulatory structures and in the phenomenon of *'quasi-markets'* in which public services are supplied on partly marketized lines. (See also COLLECTIVE CONSUMPTION; CONSUMPTION, GEOGRAPHY OF; MONEY AND FINANCE, GEOGRAPHY OF; RETAILING, GEOGRAPHY OF; SERVICES, GEOGRAPHY OF; TOURISM, GEOGRAPHY OF.) NJT

References

Williams, C. 1997: *Consumer services and economic development*. London: Routledge. · Wrigley, N. and Lowe, M., eds, 1996: *Retailing, consumption and capital. The new retail geography*. London: Longman.

consumption, geography of The study of the geography of consumption of commodities (see COMMODITY). Until quite recently, the study of the geography of consumption had only a fitful history in geography: the BERKELEY SCHOOL of cultural geography had shown an interest in certain issues to do with consumption, most notably food taboos and diets, and the geographies of RECREATION and RETAILING sometimes showed a tangential concern; but in the 1970s and early 1980s most interest in consumption was, in effect, focused on one commodity only – housing (see HOUSING STUDIES). In the middle 1980s, this narrow focus began to broaden out, especially through work on 'consumption sectors', but it was not until the early 1990s that consumption started to become an important point of attention in and for itself, for example through work in SOCIAL and CULTURAL GEOGRAPHY on the 'service class' (see CLASS: Thrift, 1987). That consumption should have remained undiscovered for so long as an object of human geographical enquiry was certainly remarkable because of its ubiquity in everyday life, its massive economic importance and the efforts that had gone into its understanding elsewhere in the social sciences and humanities (e.g. Campbell, 1987; Miller, 1987; McCracken, 1990; Willis, 1990; Richards, 1991). It was all the more remarkable because the LANDSCAPE of consumption is such an integral and obtrusive part of late twentieth-century MODERNITY whether in the form of the shopping mall, the supermarket, the theme park, the heritage centre, or the humble shop on the main street (Knox, 1991; Shields, 1989). Yet, in the space of just ten years, human geographers have turned this story of neglect into a thriving area of research: work in human geography on consumption is now at the forefront of work in the social sciences and humanities

(Gregson, 1995; Jackson and Thrift, 1995, *Environment and Planning A*, 1995/96).

Currently, the geography of consumption is fixed on a series of social-cum-cultural issues to do with the way that commodities and their meanings have become intertwined. The first of these is an interest in the HISTORICAL GEOGRAPHY of consumption and the lessons it holds for modern consumption (Glennie and Thrift, 1992, 1996; Miller, 1991). The second issue is the symbolic work that is done on commodities which invests them with rich and geographically variable meanings – by producers (through the design of commodities), by advertisers (Leslie, 1999), by retailers, and by consumers themselves. Special attention has been paid to how commodities interweave with particular kinds of social activity in specialized spaces, in the process producing new forms of IDENTITY (Shields, 1992; Mort, 1996). In particular, detailed ETHNOGRAPHIC research has been carried out on the various forms of shopping; in shopping malls, at car boot sales (Crewe and Gregson, 1997a, 1997b), or from news stands (Jackson, 1999a). A third issue has been the extent to which a common global capitalist culture has been created by the ever-increasing circulation of commodities and commodity meanings around the world, especially as chains of production and consumption seem to get ever-longer and more complex (as in the cases of 'exotic' fruits and flowers; see FOOD, GEOGRAPHY OF: cf. GLOBALIZATION). In other words, does the spread of McDonald's burgers, Coca-Cola cans, Celine Dion CDs, and the like mean that local cultures will become homogenized and sanitized? The consensus seems to be that what is happening instead is that new forms of local culture are being produced, along with new meanings of what counts as 'local' (Watson, 1998; Jackson, 1999b). A fourth issue is the increasing extent of *commodification*. New forms of commodity are constantly being produced and marketed as new means of making the world saleable are invented. For example, geographers have studied the increasing commodification of knowledge, as manifested in the copyrighting of genetic material (Whatmore, 1999). Again, as they increase in number and sophistication, so commodities seem to take on a life of their own, calling for new modes of understanding like ACTOR–NETWORK THEORY and NON-REPRESENTATIONAL THEORY. Finally, interest in the geography of consumption must be seen as part and parcel of a fascination with POSTMODERNISM. In the most apocalyptic of postmodern pronouncements, the chief reason for existence has become consumption; signs of the commodity have become more important than the commodity itself and people have begun to lose their identity in the melée of consumption (Baudrillard, 1998; Bauman, 1993; Clarke, 1997). But the careful empirical research carried out by geographers over the course of the 1990s (e.g. Miller, Jackson, Thrift, Holbrook and Rowlands, 1998) must give considerable pause to this kind of depiction. NJT

References

Baudrillard, J. 1998: *The consumer society: myths and structures*. London: Sage. · Bauman, Z. 1993: From pilgrim to tourist – or a short history of identity. In S. Hall and P. du Gay, eds, *Questions of cultural identity*. London: Sage, 18–36. · Campbell, C. 1987: *The romantic ethic and the spirit of modern consumerism*. Oxford: Blackwell. · Clarke, D. 1997. *International Journal of Urban and Regional Research*. Environment and Planning A, 1995/1996. Special issue on changing geographies of consumption. *Environment and Planning A* 11: 1875–930, and 12: 10–68. · Crewe, L. and Gregson, N. 1997a: The bargain, the knowledge and the spectacle: making sense of consumption in the space of the car boot sale. *Environment and Planning D: Society and Space* 18: 219–46. · Crewe, L. and Gregson, N. 1997b: Excluded spaces of regulation: car boot sales as an enterprise culture out of control. *Environment and Planning A* 29: 1717–37. · Glennie, P. and Thrift, N.J. 1992: Modernity, urbanism and modern consumption. *Environment and Planning D. Society and Space* 10: 423–44. · Glennie, P. and Thrift, N.J. 1996: Consumers, identities, and consumption spaces in early modern England. *Environment and Planning A* 28: 25–96. · Gregson, N. 1995: And now it's all consumption? *Progress in Human Geography* 19. · Jackson, P., Stevenson, N. and Brooks, K. 1999a. *Environment and Planning D. Society and Space* 17, 353–68. · Jackson, P. 1999b. Commodity Culture: the traffic in things. *Transactions* IBG, NS 24, 95–108. · Jackson, P. and Thrift, N.J. 1995: Geographies of consumption. In D. Miller, ed., *Acknowledging consumption. A review of new studies*. London: Routledge, 204–37. · Knox, P. 1991: The restless urban landscape: economic and social cultural change and the transformation of metropolitan Washington, D.C. *Annals of the Association of American Geographers* 81: 181–209. · Leslie, D. 1997: Flexing specialised agencies? Reflexity, identity and the advertising industry. *Environment and Planning A* 29: 1017–38. · Leslie, D. 1999: Consumer subjectivity, space, and advertising research. *Environment and Planning A* 31: 1443–58. · McCracken, G. 1990: *Culture and consumption*. Bloomington: Indiana University Press. · McKendrick, N., Brewer, J. and Plumb, J. 1978: *The birth of consumer society*. London: Hutchinson. · Miller, D. 1987: *Mass consumption and material culture*. Oxford: Basil Blackwell. · Miller, D., ed., 1995: *Acknowledging consumption: a review of new studies*. London: Routledge. · Miller, D., Jackson, P., Thrift, N.J., Holbrook, B., and Rowlands, M. 1998: *Shopping, place and identity*. London, Routledge. ·

Miller, R. 1991: Selling Mrs Consumer: advertising and the creation of suburban socio-spatial relations, 1910–1930. *Antipode* 23: 263–301. · Mort, F. 1996: *Cultures of consumption: masculinities and social space*. London: Routledge. · Richards, T. 1991: *The commodity culture of Victorian England*. London: Verso. · Sack, R.D. 1988: The consumer's world: place as context. *Annals of the Association of American Geographers* 78: 642–64. · Shields, R. 1989: Social spatialisation and the built environment. The West Edmonton Mall. *Environment and Planning D: Society and Space* 7: 147–64. · Shields, R., ed., 1992: *Lifestyle shopping. The subject of consumption*. London: Routledge. · Thrift, N.J. 1987: The geography of late twentieth century class formation. In N.J. Thrift and P. Williams, eds, *Class and space*. London: Routledge and Kegan Paul, 207–53. · Watson, J., ed., 1998: *Golden Arches East. McDonalds in East Asia*. Cambridge: Cambridge University Press. · Whatmore, S.J. 1999: Elephants on the move. Spatial formations of wildlife exchange. *Environment and Planning D: Society and Space* 17. · Willis, P. 1990: *Common culture*. Milton Keynes: Open University Press.

Suggested Reading
Jackson and Thrift (1995)

contextual approach Forms of inquiry which approach the world as a series of associations and entanglements in time–space, and which seek both to retain and to explicate those interlacings as the central moment of their interpretations and explanations. In so far as contextual approaches depend upon identifying relations of co-existence, connection or 'togetherness' they might seem to find a common ground in REGIONAL GEOGRAPHY. But Thrift (1983) has argued that the classical regional monograph provided little more than a detailed inventory of 'physical' and 'cultural' elements, proceeding category by category (geology, soils and vegetation through to economic activities, settlements and the like), so that in fact it severed the associations and entanglements that are at the heart of a properly contextual approach and separated them into compartments. In this sense, then, the ordering scheme of the regional monograph was predicated on relations of identity or 'similarity' – splitting each region into components assigned to different physical and cultural categories – which is characteristic of a COMPOSITIONAL approach. More than this: traditional regional geography tacitly operated with an absolute conception of SPACE, in which time and space were treated as external containers or frameworks ('neutral grids') within which the world could be divided into its regional 'boxes'. For those committed to a contextual approach, however, this marks the site of a conceptual and an analytical failure: it makes it impossible to disclose the ways in which time and space are folded into the conduct of life on earth. For Thrift (1999), in contrast, a contextual approach registers time and space as productive elaborations: as 'what we labour to produce as we go along', constantly and differentially folded into streams of action and activity.

Seen like this, contextual approaches have had several points of entry into the contemporary discipline. In the first phase of their development, two were particularly important:

The first is TIME-GEOGRAPHY. Its creator, the Swedish geographer Torsten Hägerstrand, defined a contextual approach as one that 'encloses' a 'pocket' of the world 'as it is found, with its mixed assortment of beings', and contrasted this with conventional, compositional approaches that remove different classes of beings 'from their habitats and place them in a classification system' (Hägerstrand, 1984). This distinction had something in common with the distinction between physical and logical classifications proposed by the German philosopher Immanuel Kant, but KANTIANISM treated time and space as external coordinates whereas the central point of Hägerstrand's ('physical') project was to show how time and space were drawn into actions and activities. How successful he was remains a subject for debate: Hägerstrand conceived of time and space as resources that had to be 'drawn upon' in the conduct of social life, but his graphical illustrations retained a strong sense of time and space as external frameworks. Even so, Hägerstrand's commitment to a sort of time–space ecology – to the recovery of what he once called 'collateral processes' that 'cannot unfold freely' but which 'have to accommodate themselves under the pressures and opportunities which follow from their common existence in terrestrial space and time' (Hägerstrand, 1976) – turned out to be a central motif of contextual approaches more generally.

Hägerstrand's ideas intersected with a number of threads spun in modern social theory and social philosophy that all tried to capture a complex dialectic of 'presence' and 'absence' at the heart of social life. In developing his STRUCTURATION THEORY, for example, the British sociologist Anthony Giddens (1984) sought to show how direct face-to-face interaction with those co-present in time and/or space ('social integration') is wired to systems of mediated interaction with those who are absent in time and/or space ('system integration') through the continuous 'binding' of time and space into the conduct of social life. For many geographers this registered an important advance over the typically more localized scenarios of time-geography: even as they were 'folded into' social life, time and space were simultaneously 'opened out' to allow for much more extended networks of co-existence and connection (cf. Simonsen, 1991). In contrast to Hägerstrand's predilections, however, many human geographers came to doubt whether Giddens's rather grandiose and abstract formulations could provide much empirical purchase on the concrete specificities and particularities to which a contextual approach was supposed to be sensitive.

In the second phase of development different contextual approaches have (appropriately) overlapped and intertwined, so that it is now difficult to identify distinctive intellectual topographies. Many human geographers have been drawn to the work of those philosophers who have paid special attention to the spatializations inherent within the production of social life. Michel Foucault's elaborations of the historical connections between POWER, space and subjectivity – his strong belief that it is impossible to make sense of the operation of power or the constitution of subjectivity without seeing how such social productions also entail productions of space – have been of seminal importance. It would be thoroughly misleading to trace all developments back to Foucault – Heidegger's PHENOMENOLOGY has been of great importance in thinking about many of these issues too, for example (Schatzki, 1991), though there are significant connections between Heidegger and Foucault – but these writings can be read as a pivot for the development of two streams of inquiry that increasingly seem to braid into one another.

The first thematic roughly corresponds to EPISTEMOLOGY. One of Foucault's constant concerns was the connective imperative between power and knowledge, which he treated as the historically constituted and intrinsically spatial formation of 'power-knowledge'. Drawing in some part on these ideas, an interest in the avowedly contextual production and reception of what has come to be called SITUATED KNOWLEDGE has animated a revived history of GEOGRAPHY. From this perspective, the production of geographical knowledge is no longer to be narrated as the achievement of a succession of authority figures or intellectual schools. The production of 'TEXTS' is now seen as an irredeemably practical activity that literally takes place within and intervenes within specific 'contexts'. If the critical interpretation of texts thus crucially depends on the recovery of their contexts, however, this is far from straightforward: there has been a vigorous debate about the dangers of reductively 'reading off' texts from contexts and about the identification of the myriad networks that spiral out from and fold back into texts (see also DISCOURSE).

The second thematic roughly corresponds to ONTOLOGY. Foucault worked with a range of spatial formations, but one of his central figures was that of the network, and in some respects ACTOR–NETWORK THEORY can be seen as a radical extension of his ideas. It radicalizes the sense of 'ECOLOGY' implicit within time-geography by providing what Thrift (1999) calls an 'irreducible ontology' in which the world is made up of the intersection of myriad encounters between 'actants' – people and things – and wherein the conventional separations between 'CULTURE' and 'NATURE' are called into question. Such an ontology – which Thrift describes as at once 'sensuous' by virtue of its fibrous physicality and 'spectral' by virtue of its entanglements of absence and presence – underwrites an expansive sense of the time–space configurations through which life on earth goes forward.

Taken together, these recent developments seem to have induced a much more modest sense of THEORY's powers. On the one side, theoretical speculation and elucidation is seen as an intrinsic and vital moment in politico-intellectual inquiry – not least because it functions as a way of clarifying the conditions and consequences of inquiry itself – and yet, on the other side, a sensitivity to context means that all theories are limited and partial – they are all marked by the contexts from which they emerged and the circumstances to which they are made to respond – so that it is now widely accepted that the particularities of any situation cannot be read off from the formulations of any GRAND THEORY (Thrift, 1996).

DG

References

Giddens, A. 1984: *The constitution of society*. Cambridge: Polity Press. · Hägerstrand, T. 1976: Geography and the study of interaction between nature and society. *Geoforum* 7: 329–34. · Hägerstrand, T. 1984: Presences and absences: a look at conceptual choices and bodily necessities. *Regional Studies* 8: 373–80. · Schatzki, T. 1991: Spatial ontology and explanation. *Annals of the Association of American Geographers* 81: 650–70. · Simonsen, K. 1991: Towards an understanding of the contextuality of social life. *Environment and Planning D: Society and Space* 9: 417–32. · Thrift, N. 1983: On the determination of social action in space and time. *Environment and Planning D: Society and Space* D 1: 23–57. · Thrift, N. 1996: *Spatial formations*. London: Sage. · Thrift, N. 1999: Steps to an ecology of place. In

D. Massey, J. Allen, and P. Sarre, eds, *Human geography today*. Cambridge: Polity Press, 295–322.

Suggested Reading

Hägerstrand (1984). · Schatzki (1991). · Simonsen (1991). · Thrift (1999).

contextual effect A concept used in ELECTORAL GEOGRAPHY to account for spatial variations in voting patterns. Most studies of electoral behaviour present voters as mobilized to support particular parties (and their candidates) according to perceptions of self-interest. The result is one or more electoral CLEAVAGES in each society, of which the most common are those based on economic CLASS. Attempts based on those cleavages to predict how people vote (both individually and in aggregate) often fail, however (Miller, 1977: Johnston, Pattie and Allsopp, 1988), because some (perhaps many) people's voting decisions are influenced by others with whom they are in contact – such as their neighbours and workmates (cf. NEIGHBOURHOOD EFFECT). Thus socio-spatial contexts are important influences on how voters interpret their social positions and translate those interpretations into support for particular political parties.

Cox (1969) identified two processes that produce contextual effects. According to the *acquaintance-circle process*, individuals are influenced by the weight of opinion in their contact networks, so that in any area some of those who might – from knowledge of their individual characteristics – be expected to support the minority view are 'converted' to the prevailing majority view by the dominant information flows. (It is assumed that information spreads through a network like a rumour or a disease: see DIFFUSION.) Secondly, according to the *forced-field process* a local political culture is established in an area by the political parties; these mobilize opinions in a particular way – perhaps around local issues. In some places a singular local culture develops which results in a voting pattern that deviates substantially from the national trend – as illustrated by Agnew's (1987) studies of nationalist voting in Scotland.

Many geographical studies have produced evidence of voting patterns that are consistent with the contextual effect hypothesis although the great majority of them use aggregate data only and so face the problems of the ECOLOGICAL FALLACY. Recent developments in MULTI-LEVEL MODELLING have produced clearer circumstantial evidence of contextual effects (Jones, Johnston and Pattie, 1992), however.

Agnew (1996) presented a strong case for contextual effects that:

> the hierarchical-geographical context or place channels the flow of interests, influence and identity out of which political activities emanate . . . political behaviour is inevitably structured by a changing configuration of social-geographical influences

It is based on the following claims:

- Class and community affiliations take on different meanings according to the nature of individual places within the spatial division of labour.
- Communication systems limit interaction across space in some situations, leading to separate networks within which politically relevant information flows and is interpreted.
- There are continuing tensions between local areas and their encompassing national states, which foster spatial variations in political mobilization.
- All cleavages – class, gender, race, age etc. – have local as well as national histories within which the structuration of political movements occurs.
- Many political parties claim local roots and policy directions in their electoral manifestos, which can result in spatially varying support.
- The micro-geography of everyday settings – home, work, leisure etc. – can stimulate local distinctiveness that is reflected in voting patterns.

Nevertheless, some critics have argued that these usually come about because of underspecified models which omit important compositional variables: when such variables are incorporated, contextual effects are, at most, minimal in their importance: thus King (1996), in responding to Agnew's (1996) strong argument for why context matters, contended that 'political geographers should not be so concerned with demonstrating that context matters'. RJJ

References and Suggested Reading

Agnew, J.A. 1987: *Place and politics: the geographical mediation of state and society*. Boston: Allen and Unwin. · Agnew, J.A. 1996: Mapping politics: how context counts in electoral geography. *Political Geography* 15: 129–46. · Cox, K.R. 1969: The voting decision in a spatial context. In C. Board, et al., eds, *Progress in geography Volume 1*. London: Edward Arnold, 81–117. · Eagles, M., ed., 1995: Spatial and contextual models of political behaviour. Special issue of *Political Geography* 14 (6/7): 499–635. · Johnston, R.J., Pattie, C.J. and Allsopp, J.G. 1988: *A nation dividing? The electoral map of Great Britain 1979–1987*. London: Longman. ·

Jones, K., Johnston, R.J. and Pattie, C.J. 1992: People, places and regions: exploring the use of multi-level modelling in the analysis of electoral data. *British Journal of Political Science* 22. · King, G. 1996: Why context should not count. *Political Geography* 15: 159–64. · Miller, W.L. 1977: *Electoral Dynamics*. London: Macmillan.

contiguous zone An area of the high sea, beyond the TERRITORIAL SEA, and extending up to 24 nautical miles from the baseline delimiting the internal waters of a state and within which it may apply customs and other national regulations. The zone was first defined in the 1958 UN Convention on the Territorial Sea and the contiguous zone as extending up to 12 nautical miles from the baseline, but this was replaced by the present definition under the 1982 third UN Convention on the Law of the Sea, which eventually came into force in 1994. At the time the convention was being drawn up, there was some debate as to whether it was still necessary to define a contiguous zone. It was eventually decided to retain it, because of its importance for states when enforcing their domestic law, even against foreign vessels, although the concept has little standing in international law (see LAW OF THE SEA). MB

continental shelf The area of submerged continental rock forming the continental margin lying closest to the shore. It terminates abruptly at varying depths and distances out to sea, but is everywhere relatively clearly defined physically. The political significance of the continental shelf has increased rapidly during the second half of the twentieth century as the exploitation of underwater resources, in addition to fisheries, has become a realistic prospect. The earliest claim was made by Argentina in 1944, when it asserted rights over offshore mineral resources. A year later President Truman issued Proclamation 2667, claiming USA SOVEREIGNTY over the sea bed and the subsoil of the continental shelf, although not over the waters above. Other states were quick to follow suit, but in the absence of any clear definition of the continental shelf much confusion ensued. In 1958 the UN Convention on the Continental Shelf gave states the right to exploit the mineral resources of their coastal waters to a depth of 200 m or beyond if exploitation were technically feasible. In the furtherance of such exploitation, STATES were permitted to build (or agree to the construction of) permanent structures, such as oil wells, as long as they were not accorded the status of islands with territorial waters of their own, and provided that they did not pose an undue hazard for shipping. The convention also gave states rights to sedentary species of living things on the sea bed, such as shellfish and crustacea, but not fish. The changes to the LAW OF THE SEA which came into force in 1994 under the terms of the 1982 UN Convention have radically revised this definition. In legal terms, the continental shelf is now deemed to extend for 200 nautical miles from the coastal baseline of a state, and in a few instances further, up to 350 nautical miles, providing such an extension is agreed by the newly established Commission on the Limits of the Continental Shelf. Within this area states have exclusive rights to explore and exploit the natural resources. MB

Suggested Reading

Juda, L. 1996: *International law and ocean use management. The evolution of ocean governance*. London and New York: Routledge.

contingent valuation A technique associated with ENVIRONMENTAL ECONOMICS which seeks to determine how much consumers of a particular environment are willing to pay to protect it. Environmental economics trades on the difference between *price* and *value*, arguing that many economic activities under-value the environment by either under-pricing it or failing to price it at all. Environmental economists thus undertake a two-stage process of environmental valuation. First, theoretical prices for the full cost of environmental protection are imputed by constructing supply and demand curves. The supply curve consists of the direct costs of the measures required to protect an environment plus the indirect effects (e.g. other economic activities foregone as a result of protection). The demand curve consists of users' 'willingness-to-pay' for a particular level of environmental protection. Second, these imputed supply–demand prices are then turned into real life prices which will yield an appropriate level of environmental protection. Contingent valuation methods belong to the demand-side of the first stage (Bateman, 1995; see also NEO-CLASSICAL ECONOMICS).

Demand-side valuation consists of so-called 'revealed' and 'expressed preference methods' (cf. REVEALED PREFERENCE ANALYSIS). The former consists of methods which 'reveal' user preferences for environmental protection by examining what users pay for *associated* goods (e.g. how much they pay in petrol costs to visit a WILDERNESS area threatened with DEVELOPMENT). The latter, by contrast, investigates what the user would be willing to pay for environmental protection *per se* – it is a 'direct' valuation method. Contingent valuations use either direct or expressed preference methods.

Contingent valuations usually take a representative SAMPLE of the relevant environmental user groups (cf. SURVEY ANALYSIS). Those selected are asked a series of questions which reveal how much they would pay to enjoy a specific type and level of environmental amenity. Broad-based contingent evaluations base their questions upon the recognition of three kinds of environmental value: *economic value*, *option value* (the value of an environment not presently used by a given person but which might be used by them or their family in the future) and *existence value* (the value an individual places on preserving an environment in its own right, like a wetland or upland). This can lead to very complex contingent valuation surveys which yield expressed preferences for a complex range of possible scenarios for a given environment (see Willis and Garrod, 1993).

NC

References

Bateman, I. 1995: Environment and economic appraisal. In T. O'Riordan, ed., *Environmental science for environmental management*. Harlow: Longman, 47–65. · Willis, K.G. and Garrod, G.G. 1993: Valuing landscape: a contingent valuation approach. *Journal of Environmental Management* 37: 1–22.

conurbation A term coined by Patrick Geddes (1854–1932) to describe a built-up area created by the coalescence of several once-separate urban settlements, initially through RIBBON DEVELOPMENT along the main inter-urban routes. With greater urban SPRAWL the term has now largely been replaced by concepts such as MEGALOPOLIS, METROPOLITAN AREA and METROPOLITAN LABOUR AREA. RJJ

convergence, regional The tendency for regional incomes or levels of living within a nation to become more equal over time. That this should be the case is a prediction derived from NEO-CLASSICAL ECONOMICS, which portrays labour, CAPITAL and other FACTORS OF PRODUCTION moving from one region to another seeking the best possible returns (in the form of wages or profits), until there is nothing to gain from further movement because returns are the same in all regions. Thus a competitive free-market economy under CAPITALISM should tend towards regional equality, subject to constraints on the spatial mobility of factors of production.

Evidence for individual nations shows that this prediction does not necessarily hold true. For example, regional incomes in the United States show steady convergence from the latter part of the nineteenth century up to the 1970s. However, individual regions had their own trajectory, reflecting their own historical experience of greater or lesser movement towards the national average income, which complicates a simple picture of regular convergence. In addition, the convergence thesis depends on the geographical scale adopted: the trend towards reduced inequality at a broad regional scale can be contradicted more locally, e.g. between core and periphery and within the city. Thus in the United States convergence at a broad regional scale has been accompanied by local divergence between city and countryside and among neighbourhoods.

Regional convergence is not confined to capitalist economies. Indeed, this trend may be more marked under a SOCIALIST system which has the equalization of regional living standards as an explicit objective. For example, a strong convergence tendency could be observed among the republics of the former Soviet Union, although this may have been reversed during the so-called 'era of stagnation' which preceded *perestroika* and the eventual collapse of COMMUNISM.

There is evidence also of reversals of convergence in the capitalist world, including the United States, with inter-regional inequality increasing since the 1970s. In Britain, divergence can be observed among regions since the early 1980s in GDP per capita and other measures of income. The fact that this has ocurred during an era of dedication to the free market suggests limits to the extent of regional convergence towards perfect equality under capitalism, in practice if not in theory. Indeed, the earlier era of more positive regional planning may have taken the country further in the direction of EQUALITY than would have been the case under less restrained market forces. This suggests that, after a certain level in the convergence process has been reached, state intervention in the form of REGIONAL POLICY is a necessary if not sufficient condition for further convergence. DMS

Suggested Reading

Hudson, R. and Williams, A. 1994: *Divided Britain*, 2nd edn. Chichester: Bellhaven. · Smith, D.M. 1987: *Geography, Inequality and Society*. Cambridge: Cambridge University Press. · Williamson, J.G. 1966: Regional inequality and the process of national development: a description of the patterns. *Economic Development and Cultural Change* 13: 3–45.

cooperative An enterprise formed by an association of members with the aim of promoting their common economic interests. Cooperatives are particularly significant in the farming sector because it is characterized by independent, family producers whose market influence is fragmented in terms of purchasing technological inputs and selling farm produce. Farmers' market vulnerability is exacerbated by the increasingly corporate structure of the agro-technology and food processing sectors with whom they deal (see also AGRICULTURAL GEOGRAPHY). By organizing themselves into cooperatives, farmers aim to improve their negotiating position *vis-à-vis* these corporate players in the agro-food complex whilst securing their operational independence (Moran et al., 1996). It should be noted that this strategy is by no means restricted to small-scale producers and can be adopted by large-scale producers as, for example, in California.

Purchasing cooperatives enable farmers to reduce the cost of technological inputs by bulk purchasing and sharing major capital items, such as farm machinery. Processing cooperatives undertake some or all of produce processing, such as tomato pulping, to increase and retain more of its market value. Marketing cooperatives, such as those for milk, enable farmers to negotiate better product prices by bulk trading. In many cases, farmers' cooperatives cover several of these different functions (Cobia, 1989). Cooperatives have become a staple institutional feature of the agricultural policy process in some countries, for example in Norway and Italy. In other cases their relationship with the state has been much more precarious, buffeted by ideological shifts in the political landscape as, for example, in Peru or Portugal (Cleary, 1989).

In recent years producer cooperatives have become a staple feature of 'Fair trade' initiatives sponsored by western development agencies as a means of improving the working conditions and incomes of peasant producers of commodities like coffee and tea (Barrett-Brown, 1993). SW

References

Barrett-Brown, M. 1993: *Fair trade*. London: Zed Books. · Cleary, M. 1989: *Peasants, politicians and producers*. Cambridge: Cambridge University Press. · Cobia, D., ed., 1989: *Cooperatives in agriculture*. Englewood Cliffs, NJ: Prentice-Hall. · Moran, W., Blunden, G. and Bradly, A. 1996: Empowering family farms through cooperatives and producer marketing boards. *Economic Geography* 72 (2): 161–77.

core area A loose term frequently used to refer to some area within a STATE, or group of states, that acts as the mainspring for its subsequent economic growth. The Manufacturing Belt, stretching from the northeastern seaboard of the USA to the heart of the Midwest, was one such, though its significance is now much diminished. In Europe, the EU's industrial belt, the so-called 'blue banana' extending from southeast England through the Low Countries, France and Germany, and into northern Italy, is another example. Some argue that the continued vitality of a state, or economically linked group of states, depends on whether its core area functions efficiently as a central focus. Others disagree, pointing to the many instances, particularly in Africa and South America, where states have been established without reference to a core area and the territory has subsequently been coherently organized through the creation of a socio-economic infrastructure (see also BOUNDARY; FRONTIER). MB

core–periphery model A model of the geography of human activity based upon the unequal distribution of POWER in ECONOMY, SOCIETY and polity. The core dominates (although it in turn may be dominated from outside) whilst the periphery is dependent. This DEPENDENCE may be structured through the relations of exchange, production or evaluation (see ECONOMIC GEOGRAPHY; MODE OF PRODUCTION) between core and periphery. The power of the core was put down by Wallerstein (1974) to the strength of the state and to the links between the state and CAPITAL through which the processes of surplus extraction might be directed towards the core. In this, Wallerstein was following similar lines of argument on the significance of geographies of power to those of Amin (1976) on tributary modes of production in which tributes flow from producers to the ruling class – somehow understood (often on the basis of magical or religious claims) to be central to SOCIAL REPRODUCTION (see, e.g., Godelier, 1988).

Although it uses similar terms to those adopted in WORLD-SYSTEMS ANALYSIS and accepts that geographically UNEVEN DEVELOPMENT is a long-term process, exchange-based core–periphery models tend, nevertheless, to expect long-term spatial equilibrium if market forces are allowed to work their equilibrating effects. Thus core–periphery relations were seen by John Friedmann (1966), with whom the model is most closely associated, as the second in a four-stage sequence of the development of the space economy. The stages outlined by Friedmann are: (a) *pre-industrial society* with localized economies; (b) *core–periphery*; (c) *dispersion of economic activity* and, to a lesser extent, control into certain parts of the periphery; and (d) the emergence of *spatial* INTEGRATION; in which the various and now more or less fully developed spatial parts of the economy relate in a more truly interdependent manner (see INTERDEPENDENCE).

From such a spatially evolutionist perspective, exchange-based spatial equilibrium may serve as a reasonable policy goal. But such a policy fails to recognize the structurally uneven development of the DIVISION OF LABOUR in the capitalist world-economy and the constraints on equilibrium stemming from market interaction. Unequal exchange (see TRADE), the concentration of economic power, technical progress and productive activity at the core, and the emanation of productive innovations from the core, help to maintain the flow of surplus value (see MARXIAN ECONOMICS) from periphery to core.

For example, increases in PRODUCTIVITY in the core may, with an effective labour movement, be translated into higher wages. At the same time a more plentiful supply of unorganized labour in the periphery may serve to sustain a downward pressure on wages. If wage levels are reflected in the relative prices of the products exchanged between core and periphery, the consequence of higher wages in the core will either be to generate a balance of payments crisis in the periphery or to enforce increased exports from the periphery to finance the increased cost of imports. In either case autonomous development in the periphery is made more difficult and may, indeed, be subverted. Such unequal relations may also be maintained by the implementation of economic and commercial policies favouring the core at the expense of the periphery (see COLONIALISM; NEO-COLONIALISM) and may be reinforced by MIGRATION and capital flows from periphery to core.

Although it implies inter-regional conflict rather than equilibrium and so emphasizes the uneven nature of economic DEVELOPMENT, the core–periphery model has several deficiencies stemming, in the main, from its reliance upon exchange relations (see Brenner, 1977) and the abstract nature of power in the model. Critics argue that it is false to assume that the social concentration of power necessarily leads to spatial concentration. A redistribution of power need not, therefore, be associated with more even development and the emergence of an integrated SPACE-ECONOMY. Many insist that the spatial arrangement and transformation of a capitalist economy reflect, above all, the current geographical requirements of accumulation and the historical legacy of a landscape created by previous rounds of accumulation and LAYERS OF INVESTMENT. Storper and Walker (1989, p. 183), for example, argue that 'the main shape of territorial development in capitalist societies' is a product of the 'spatial expansion, integration, and division of growing industries and industrial ensembles'. They stress that it is the geography of production rather than exchange that acts as the dynamic of geographically uneven development.

Thus Paul Krugman (1991) argues that increasing returns to scale in a particular location based upon geographies of production and demand may, through the mechanisms of cumulative causation and imperfect competition (see NEO-CLASSICAL ECONOMICS), serve to sustain and intensify uneven development. But, Krugman argues, new conditions or even aggressive policies of local economic development may disturb the geographical concentration of growth and allow new sites of development to emerge.

By the same token, these new conditions also constantly expand and diversify the geographies over and through which such competitive relations of growth may operate. They thereby challenge the notion that inter-regional competition is structured merely by existing geographies of development in those regions. Thus the decline of a region like the Ruhr relative to, say, Bavaria in Germany, for example, is explicable in terms of new geographies of production, the influence of an attractive environment on mobile capital and a discriminating and mobile labour force, alternative – but locally embedded and, to a certain degree inevitably, path-dependent – industrial policies and the increasingly sophisticated potential within a globalizing economic geography for the evaluation (including the inter-regional evaluation) by capital of alternative conditions for profitable accumulation.

It may be argued that economic power stems less from its location than from the locus of control over the means of production and that it derives its specific historical characteristics from the nature of this control and the objectives to which it is put. Thus, although the spatial redistribution of productive activity and the decentralization of DECISION-MAKING over the productive process may generate what appears to be a more highly integrated form of spatial organization, it does not necessarily shift power over the means of production to a more democratic base. Nor does it imply that the spatial location of control over the means of production has been decentralized. In fact, the concentration of control is more likely to be intensified (within financial centres, for example, located within global cities) rather than reduced as the economy becomes more highly integrated – and complex.

The second and third stages of Friedmann's model and the policies of regional development with which they may be associated (see GROWTH POLE) could lead to a less unequal exchange between core and periphery. But, within an integrated global economic geography, they offer the means of extracting the surplus more effectively from the economic geography as a whole rather than acting as a means of diffusing development more evenly across it. A more genuine redistribution of development would, necessarily, involve a transformation of the objectives of capitalist development involving – at the least – an effective form of regulation over the practice of power in order to ensure more equitable outcomes. But such an intervention would have to come to terms with the 'continual state of reconstitution' (Knox and Agnew, 1994, p. 85) of the world economic geography, a reconstitution which affects not only the dynamics of its spatial structure (exemplified over *la longue durée* by the changing geography of WORLD CITIES and, more recently, by the dramatic but crisis-ridden rise of the newly industrializing countries, for example), but the spread of prevailing economic norms and representations (the prevalence of the discourse of free markets and associated liberal economic policies during the last two decades or so of the twentieth century) and the disembedding that accompanies them. Cores and peripheries are social products and reflect the circumstances of their construction. RL

References

Amin, S. 1976: *Unequal development*. New York and London: Monthly Review Press. · Agnew, J. 1987: *The United States in the world-economy: a regional geography*. Cambridge and New York: Cambridge University Press, 89–127. · Brenner, R. 1977: The origins of capitalist development: a critique of neo-Smithian Marxism. *New Left Review* 104: 25–92. · Dicken, P.E. and Lloyd, P. 1990: *Location in space: theoretical perspectives in economic geography*, 3rd edn. London and New York: Harper and Row, 239–46. · Friedmann, J. 1966: *Regional development policy: a case study of Venezuela*. Cambridge, MA and London: MIT Press. · Godelier, M. 1988: *The mental and the material*. London and New York: Verso. · Keeble, D.E. 1989: Core–periphery disparities, recession and new regional dynamisms in the European Community. *Geography* 74: 1–11. · Knox, P. and Agnew, J. 1994: *The geography of the world economy*, 2nd edn. London: Edward Arnold; New York: Routledge, Chapman and Hall, ch. 3. · Krugman, P. 1991: *Geography and trade*, Cambridge, MA: MIT Press. · Perloff, H.S., Dunn, E.S., Lampard, E.E., and Muth, R.F. 1960: *Regions, resources and economic growth*. Lincoln, NE: University of Nebraska Press; Baltimore: Johns Hopkins University Press. · Storper, M. and Walker, R. 1989: *The capitalist imperative*. New York and Oxford: Basil Blackwell. · Wallerstein, I. 1974: *The modern world system*. New York and London: Academic Press.

Suggested reading

Agnew, J. (1987). · Dicken, P.E. and Lloyd, P. (1990).

corporatism A model of capitalist STATE APPARATUS operation in which major interest groups – notably those representing capital and labour – share power with the elected representative government. Politicians compete for power through the electoral process, as in PLURALISM, but then, under corporatism, they share that power with unelected representatives of functional interest groups. Corporatism is especially strong in some western European countries (notably Austria and Germany), where employers' groups and trades unions are routinely consulted on major issues of economic policy: it is much weaker in the United Kingdom and the United States. RJJ

Suggested Reading

Cawson, A. 1986: *Corporatism and political theory*. Oxford: Blackwell. · Johnston, R.J. 1992: The internal operations of the state. In P.J. Taylor, ed., *The political geography of the twentieth century*. London: Belhaven Press.

correlation The degree of association between two or more variables, mainly used in the statistical analysis of interval and ratio data. In the GENERAL LINEAR MODEL a correlation coefficient measures the goodness-of-fit of a REGRESSION line to a scatter of points. Its value ranges from +1.0 through 0.0 to −1.0: a value of (1.0 indicates that all of the points lie on the regression line; a positive value indicates that the line slopes upwards to the right and a negative value indicates the converse (i.e. as the values of one variable increase, those of the other decrease). Usually represented by r, the square of the correlation coefficient (r^2) is interpreted as the proportion of the variation in one variable that can be accounted for by the variation in the other.

For multiple regression equations, the multiple correlation coefficient is R. RJJ

Suggested Reading

Johnston, R.J. 1978: *Multivariate statistical analysis in geography*. London and New York: Longman.

cost structure The division of the total cost of production into its constituent parts, or cost of individual inputs. For example, the cost structure of the iron and steel industry would indicate absolute (or relative) amounts of expenditure on iron ore, coking coal, limestone, labour, capital equipment and so on. The cost structure thus reveals whether a particular activity is material-intensive, capital-intensive, labour-intensive, etc., with respect to expenditure on inputs. This information can provide an initial clue to the inputs likely to have the greatest bearing on the location of the activity in question. DMS

cost–benefit analysis An analytical procedure for the comprehensive, often pre-construction, economic evaluation of major public investment projects, embracing their full positive and negative societal consequences over the range of investment options. As such, cost–benefit analysis covers a wider range of considerations than does the profit-and-loss accounting of private-sector investment decision-making. Originally applied to public river and harbour projects in the USA, its contemporary uses extend to such diverse issues as urban air quality, dam and irrigation schemes, refuse recycling, transport deregulation, roadway maintenance, disposal of hazardous waste, choices among electricity generation systems, and job creation by regional policy (Armstrong and Taylor, 1993; see also Walshe and Daffern, 1990).

Cost-benefit analysis involves three stages. First, costs and benefits associated with public projects have to be identified, including intangible EXTERNALITIES such as noise and POLLUTION. Second, these must be quantified, including their discounting to a common base date, since the various costs and benefits are often experienced over very different time periods. Finally, the resulting cost–benefit ratios are incorporated into the decision-making, or project-evaluation, stage, alongside political and other judgemental inputs.

Economists differ as to the appropriate ways to apply these general principles, and over the validity of the exercise as a whole. Defining all costs and benefits is one such: it is difficult to be comprehensive without double-counting. Not all variables have an easily determined market value, and some estimates may be little more than guesses. The discount value can be crucial to the outcome, and endangers undervaluing the welfare of future generations. Finally, distributional issues are important – a $1 million benefit to poor residents from one freeway route should outweigh a $1 million gain to rich citizens from an alternative one.

Recent extensions of cost–benefit analysis to large-scale environmental issues, such as GLOBAL WARMING, have attracted considerable interest (e.g. Harley and Spash, 1993) but also raise particularly challenging difficulties. Not only are such potential environmental changes irreversible but the cost and benefits vary internationally, raise sharp ethical valuing judgements (e.g. over landscape and wildlife) and questions of intergenerational fairness – future generations will feel the sharp end of global changes, but may also have the necessary technology to combat them. AGH

References

Armstrong, H.W. and Taylor, J. 1993: *Regional economics and policy*, 2nd edn. New York: Harvester Wheatsheaf. · Harley, N. and Spash, C.L. 1993: *Cost-benefit analysis and the environment*. Aldershot: Edward Elgar. · Walshe, G. and Daffern, P. 1990: *Managing cost–benefit analysis*. London: Macmillan.

Suggested Reading

Schofield, J. 1987: *Cost-benefit analysis in urban and regional planning*. London: Allen and Unwin.

counterfactual explanation An extension of the comparative method which seeks to check 'hypothetical reconstructions' of what might have happened in the past 'against the record of what actually took place' (Prince, 1971). While there is nothing especially novel about counterfactuals as such – indeed, Cohen (1953) argued that 'the significance of historical fact [is] revealed by asking what might have happened if things had been different', which would make the construction of counterfactuals intrinsic to historical method – they nevertheless played a prominent part in the so-called *New Economic History* (or *econometric history*) in which their supposed success encouraged calls for their formal deployment in HISTORICAL GEOGRAPHY. The emphasis on a formal methodology is important, because what is distinctive about counterfactual explanation in econometric history is its connection with formal MODEL-building: its commitment to 'the efficacy of theory in specifying useful counterfactuals and to quantitative methods in implementing them' in such a way that they indicate 'the latent tendencies of the system being studied' (Fishlow and Fogel, 1971):

both authors provided classic demonstrations of the method (Fogel, 1964; Fishlow, 1965). While counterfactuals restore an essential contingency to historical eventuation, within this framework their viability depends on the specification of adequate theoretical systems and on the use of sufficiently powerful techniques of SIMULATION or SPACE–TIME FORECASTING. But critics have complained that their interpretation is riddled with difficulties, since historical processes are contextual: this means that 'we cannot [readily] decide what we must subtract from the real past' along with the event or process under investigation, and so we cannot readily decide whether the counterfactual construction is legitimate (Gould, 1969). These difficulties proved so formidable that many historical geographers implicitly endorsed economic historian M.M. Postan's claim that 'the might-have-beens of history are not a profitable subject for discussion'. More recently, however, the rise of POSTMODERNISM has underwritten a new scepticism about the possibility of cleaving apart the 'factual' and 'the fictional' as cleanly as Gould, Postan and others supposed, and outside the formal frameworks of econometric history there have been several 'thought-experiments' in the possible outcomes of historical events.

DG

References

Cohen, M.R. 1953: *Reason and nature: essay on the meaning of scientific method*, 2nd edn. Glencoe, IL: Free Press. · Fishlow, A. 1965: *American railroads and the transformation of the antebellum economy*. Cambridge, MA: Harvard University Press; Oxford: Oxford University Press. · Fishlow, A. and Fogel, R. 1971: Quantitative economic history: an interim evaluation. *Journal of Economic History* 21: 15–42. · Fogel, R. 1964: *Railroads and American economic growth: essays in econometric history*. Baltimore: Johns Hopkins University Press. · Gould, J.D. 1969: Hypothetical history. *Economic History Review* 22: 195–207. · Prince, H.C. 1971: Real, imagined and abstract worlds of the past. *Progress in Geography* 3: 1–86.

Suggested Reading

Gould (1969).

counterurbanization A process of population deconcentration away from large URBAN settlements first identified in the USA in the 1970s where METROPOLITAN AREAS, especially the largest and oldest, were losing population by net migration to non-metropolitan areas. The number of places experiencing such decline increased in the following years as people and jobs moved: (a) beyond the SUBURBS to smaller settlements within METROPOLITAN LABOUR AREAS; and (b) to the smaller, rapidly growing metropolitan centres of the sunbelt (see SUNBELT/SNOWBELT). Evidence suggested that counterurbanization was widespread in the advanced industrial countries during the 1980s, but large cities are beginning to grow again in some countries, suggesting that counterurbanization as a dominant trend was but a brief episode.

Attempted explanations for the decline of large and the growth of smaller cities focus on the latter's attractions and the disadvantages of the former for both employers and householders. Smaller towns offer cheaper, more extensive tracts of land and more pliant labour forces lacking strong traditions of militant trade unionism, and these advantages more than counter the greater costs of movement of goods, which in any case are reducing with the trend to higher value, less bulky goods and better road transport. For many households, the smaller places are more attractive than the congested and polluted cities, even for commuters who are prepared to trade longer, more expensive journeys for the pleasanter but remoter living environments. And in ageing populations with an increased percentage of retired healthy and relatively affluent people, the smaller towns (and even the remoter rural areas) offer a better perceived quality of life to many, usually at lower cost, than the large cities (cf. CENTRIFUGAL AND CENTRIPETAL FORCES).

RJJ

Suggested Reading

Berry, B.J.L., ed., 1976: *Urbanization and counterurbanization*. Beverly Hills and London: Sage Publications. · Champion, A.G. 1991: *Counterurbanization*. London: Edward Arnold.

creative destruction The process by which relatively sudden bouts of CAPITAL disinvestment and devaluation destroy invested value in such a way as to establish the opportunity for new rounds of investment.

Marx was the first to argue that creative destruction was endemic to CAPITALISM. The destruction of value amidst CRISES accomplished several things to Marx. It drove down the price of labour through mass unemployment, reduced the price of raw materials insofar as these were unused, and destroyed value invested in fixed capital insofar as production is idled. This in turn readjusts the organic composition of capital and recalibrates the rate of profit upward. In this sense the wholesale destruction of social value establishes the conditions for new rounds of capital investment. But Marx also understood creative destruction in a broader social sense. Of necessity, the bourgeoisie continually revolutionizes the technical as well as social conditions of capitalism in search of profit; he writes in the *Communist Manifesto*: 'All that is solid melts into air'. And yet by so doing, the bourgeoisie also produces 'its own gravediggers' (Marx and Engels, 1955, pp. 13, 22).

This argument was developed by the socialist economist Joseph Schumpeter in the 1930s and 1940s as he reflected on the global depression that came after 1929. Schumpeter believed that capitalism would inevitably self-destruct and the creative destruction internal to capitalist society would lead to the creation of socialism. 'The opening up of new markets, foreign or domestic', and the periodic reorganization of capitalist production amidst crises, 'incessantly revolutionizes the economic structure *from within*, incessantly destroying the old one, incessantly creating a new one. This process of Creative Destruction is the essential fact about capitalism' (Schumpeter, 1975, p. 83; see Hall, 1998).

The importance of this argument for geographers is that the built environment is subject to creative destruction according to the rhythms of the capitalist economy. Major building booms are followed by periods of dramatic or incipient destruction, whether at the local SCALE or the global. The economic obsolescence of even relatively new buildings, the destruction of neighbourhoods for highways, and the emergence of GHETTOES are as much instances of creative destruction as are major economic crises such as that which engulfed East Asia then Russia after 1997. As a history of the Marshall Plan suggests, war, whatever its other motivation, also serves this creative destruction insofar as it obliges an economic reconstruction. NS

References

Hall, P. 1998: *Cities in civilization*. London: Weidenfeld and Nicolson. · Schumpeter, J.A. 1975: *Capitalism, Socialism and Democracy*. New York: Harper Torchbook. · Marx, K. and Engels, F. 1955: *The Communist Manifesto*. New York: Appleton, Century Crofts.

crime, geography of A sub-discipline focused around understanding the interplay between crime, space and society through analyses of offences, offenders and the effects of crime. Studies of the geography of crime have their roots in the mid-nineteenth-century work of European 'cartographic criminologists' who sought to link regional patterns of crime and offender residence to the social and physical environment. At a local level, the mid-nineteenth century also witnessed the city become firmly connected in the popular imagination with notions of danger and crime, vividly portrayed, for example, in Henry Mayhew's ETHNOGRAPHY of London's underworld. The urban focus of the geography of crime was sustained in the 1920s through the seminal contribution of the CHICAGO SCHOOL and, in particular, Clifford Shaw and Henry McKay's meticulous mapping of the residences of juvenile delinquents. Shaw and McKay drew upon both HUMAN ECOLOGY and Burgess's ZONAL MODEL to help explain the spatial regularities and temporal stability of juvenile delinquent residence in the city.

These early studies helped establish a broad distinction between analyses of where criminals live and where crimes occur, a distinction which has informed much subsequent work on the geography of crime and the cognate field of environmental criminology (see Bottoms and Wiles, 1997). Research on where criminals live repeatedly reveals the clustering of offender residences in the INNER CITY and (in the UK) on some peripheral public-sector housing estates. Explanations for these patterns have focused around two main themes.

The *'social disorganization' thesis* advanced by the Chicago School links delinquency residence to the interrelations between economic deprivation, physical deterioration, high population turnover and cultural fragmentation. Although critics argue that this thesis fails to take account of relationships between neighbourhoods and the wider society, the so-called 'New Chicagoans' address this weakness through their 'systemic theory of neighbourhood organization' (see Bursik and Grasmick, 1993). According to this theory neighbourhood social control operates at the 'primary level', via families and friendship networks; the 'parochial level' of schools, businesses and voluntary groups; and the 'public level' of external agencies like the police. Failure to integrate these levels of social control due to high population turnover will, it is argued, contribute to high offender rates.

Critics of the social disorganization perspective maintain, however, that high offender rates are also found in areas with low population turnover, suggesting that other influences are important. The *'Sheffield School'* focuses on how the operation of local housing markets may directly and indirectly contribute to the localization of offender residence. The argument is that residential communities, like individuals, can have 'careers in crime' (i.e. an area may go from having low to high numbers of offenders living there) and that it is the allocative processes of the public and private housing markets that may initiate a clustering of people with a propensity to offend in particular residential areas. The effects of the housing market then interact with other processes, including the socialization of children, the work of social control agencies and the physical design of an area, to create differences between residential areas in their offender rates (see Bottoms, Claytor and Wiles, 1992).

Areas with high numbers of offenders are not necessarily the same as areas with high numbers of offences, given that offenders do not necessarily commit offences close to their homes. A second strand of the geography of crime has therefore focused on where crime occurs, involving both the mapping of offences (areal analysis) and more sophisticated efforts to link the distribution of offences to other socio-economic and environmental variables (ecological analysis). Rooted in POSITIVISM, these approaches have until relatively recently had to rely largely on official (police-recorded) statistics despite the acknowledged limitations of these data as an index of the occurrence of crime because of differential public reporting and police recording practices (see POLICING, GEOGRAPHY OF). With the development of national and local crime surveys (also known as victim surveys) in the 1970s, greater precision is now possible in mapping the contours of crime. These surveys ask samples of the public to describe the crimes committed against them within a specified time period, so avoiding the vagaries of public reporting and police recording practices. At the local level such surveys consistently reveal marked intra-urban variations in crime RISK. High-risk neighbourhoods tend to be located both in the inner city and on the poorest council estates located in inner-city and peripheral locations. Low-risk neighbourhoods include agricultural areas, affluent suburbs and retirement areas. Explanations for this localization of victimization at the neighbourhood level have focused around four main themes:

The *'lifestyle-exposure-to-risk'* hypothesis (also referred to as the 'routine activities theory') proposes that the differential risks of crime in time and space are a function of the convergence of likely offenders and suitable targets in the absence of so-called 'capable guardians'. Two lifestyle variables are particularly important indices of risk: the size of a household because it is a measure of the extent to which capable guardians are able to provide protective SURVEILLANCE of people and property; and spare-time activities because these connect with behaviour patterns at times (evenings and weekends) and in places (streets, clubs and pubs) when high levels of offending occur.

Environmental design may contribute to differences in crime risk via the impact of physical features of the built environment on opportunities for offenders and the capacity for informal, communal surveillance. Associated particularly with Newman's (1972) ideas about TERRITORIALITY and the defensibility of space, research in this field has sparked an important debate over the relative importance of 'architectural determinism' and 'social engineering' on neighbourhood problems (see Coleman, 1985; Smith, 1987a).

Neighbourhood decline may contribute to increasing levels of crime according to proponents of the so-called *'broken windows' hypothesis* (Wilson and Kelling, 1982). A dynamic model is proposed in which initial signs of disorder in an area (such as broken windows, litter and graffiti) may be sufficient to initiate a spiral of decline, with residents retreating from these incivilities into their private, domestic space, so undermining those informal processes whereby communities maintain social control in public space leading, in turn, to more serious crimes occurring. In the US, this combination of physical and social disintegration of neighbourhoods has been linked not only to rising violent crime and drug abuse but also to deteriorating public health, homelessness and other pathologies to create an interacting 'synergism of plagues' which, via DIFFUSION, can spread rapidly beyond inner-city neighbourhoods to create regional problems of disease and violent crime (Wallace et al., 1997).

Offenders' use of space might also contribute to the localization of crime given the findings of research which has drawn on insights from BEHAVIOURAL GEOGRAPHY and work with offenders' images of the city (see MENTAL MAP), to show important relationships between the location of offences and offenders' routine use of space (see Rengert, 1992).

Many of the more recent studies of offence data have used the technology of GEOGRAPHICAL INFORMATION SYSTEMS as a means of revealing patterns in crime statistics and the socio-demographic characteristics of areas with high levels of criminal activity (see Hirschfield et al., 1995). This technology has helped narrow the spatial SCALE of crime pattern analysis to pinpoint so-called crime 'hot spots', particular locations such as street intersections, retail outlets and residential dwellings, which generate a disproportionate number of calls for police attention. The idea of hot spots is also of relevance to studies of repeat victimization (where the same person or property is the subject of more than one offence) which have shown that for crimes such as burglary and assault the rate of repeat victimization is far higher than would be expected under a random distribution. This indicates that crime is not only highly concentrated by neighbourhood area but is also focused on particular dwellings and individuals (see Johnson et al., 1997).

The use of crime surveys to measure the extent of crime has also provided access to information on the effects of crime and, in particular, the importance of fear (see Smith, 1987b). Like crime itself, the fear of crime shows strong geographical variations but these cannot be accounted for only by differences in the incidence of victimization. Fear is also related to features of the physical and social environment, ranging from poor street lighting to vandalism and youths loitering on street corners. Studies of the effects of fear have highlighted its contribution to inhibiting spatial mobility, particular among women who, because of their fear of crime, are much more likely than men to avoid going out alone after dark, to avoid certain streets, and to rely on men as escorts (Painter, 1992). Moreover, research in FEMINIST GEOGRAPHY on women's fear of sexual violence has identified the so-called 'spatial paradox' of women tending to fear strangers in 'public' spaces despite sexual attacks being more common in 'private' spaces (see PRIVATE AND PUBLIC SPHERES) by people known to the victim (Pain, 1992).

An understanding of spatial patterns of victimization and the fear of crime places researchers in a strong position to contribute to public policy (see PUBLIC POLICY, GEOGRAPHY AND) via the development and evaluation of crime prevention and fear-reducing measures. Particular attention has focused on 'situational crime prevention' which aims at reducing opportunities for, and the fear of, crime via the management, design or manipulation of the built environment. Examples of situational prevention include neighbourhood or block watch (Bennett, 1992), improved street lighting (Ditton et al., 1993) and the use of closed-circuit television surveillance (Fyfe and Bannister, 1996). Critics of situational strategies argue, however, that while they may reduce crime in one area they carry the possibility of displacing crime to other, unprotected areas.

Despite the impetus given to studies of the geography of crime by national and local governments struggling to cope with spiralling crime rates, the future development of the sub-discipline needs to address several broader issues. First, ever since the nineteenth-century studies of crime have focused overwhelmingly on urban environments and the local, neighbourhood scale. Not only is there therefore considerable scope for examining crime in non-metropolitan environments (see Duncan, 1997) but also for recognizing the increasing importance of the LOCAL–GLOBAL DIALECTIC in contemporary forms of criminal activity. The geography of illegal drugs, for example, involves large international networks of producers, distributors and consumers (see Rengert, 1996) while much corporate or 'white-collar' crime exploits differences in regulatory regimes across the globe. Second, the politicization of law and order policy raises important questions about how governments regulate the social and political life of society by using the law (see LAW, GEOGRAPHY OF) to criminalize the use of space by particular social groups (Fyfe, 1995). Finally, a key theme to emerge from the analysis of POSTMODERNISM and the city is the way urban 'form follows fear' (Ellin, 1996, p. 145). Gated and walled residential communities, video surveillance systems and the prevalence of the 'fortress impulse' in urban design are increasingly common features of contemporary urban environments. Whether these developments give people a greater sense of security or accentuate their fears by 'increasing paranoia and distrust' (ibid., p. 153) remains unclear but point to the continuing significance of crime and the fear of crime for an understanding of urban society and space. NRF

References

Bennett, T. 1992: Themes and variations in neighbourhood watch. In D.J. Evans, N.R. Fyfe, and D.T. Herbert, eds, *Crime, Policing and Place: Essays in Environmental Criminology*. London: Routledge, 272–85. · Bottoms, A.E. and Wiles, P. 1997: Environmental criminology. In M. Maguire, R. Morgan, and R. Reiner, eds, *The Oxford Handbook of Criminology*, 2nd edn. Oxford: Clarendon Press, 305–59. · Bottoms, A.E., Claytor, A. and Wiles, P. 1992: Housing markets and residential community crime careers: a case study from Sheffield. In D.J. Evans, N.R. Fyfe and D.T. Herbert, eds, *Crime, Policing and Place: Essays in Environmental Criminology*. London: Routledge, 118–44. · Bursik, R.J. and Grasmick, H.G. 1993: *Neighbourhoods and Crime*. New York: Lexington. · Coleman, A. 1985: *Utopia on Trial*. London: Hilary Shipman. · Ditton, J., Nair, G. and Phillips, S. 1993: Crime in the dark: a case study of the relationship between street lighting and crime. In

H. Jones, ed., *Crime and the Urban Environment: the Scottish experience*. Aldershot: Avebury. · Duncan, C.J. 1997: Victimisation beyond the metropolis: an Australian case study. *Area* 29: 119–28. · Ellin, N. 1996: *Postmodern Urbanism*. Oxford: Blackwell. · Fyfe, N.R. 1995: Law and order policy and the spaces of citizenship in contemporary Britain. *Political Geography* 14: 177–89. · Fyfe, N. R. and Bannister, J. 1996: City watching: closed circuit television surveillance in public space. *Area* 28 (1): 37–46. · Hirschfield, A., Brown, P. and Todd, P. 1995: GIS and the analysis of spatially-referenced crime data: experiences in Merseyside. *International Journal of Geographical Information Systems*, 9 (2): 191–210. · Johnson, S.D., Bowers, K., and Hirschfield, A. 1997: New insights into the spatial and temporal distribution of repeat victimization. *British Journal of Criminology*, 32 (2): 224–41. · Newman, O. 1972: *Defensible Space*. New York: Macmillan. · Pain, R. 1992: Space, sexual violence and social control: integrating geographical and feminist analyses of women's fear of crime. *Progress in Human Geography* 15: 415–31. · Painter, K. 1992: Different worlds: the spatial, temporal and social dimensions of female victimization. In D.J. Evans, N.R. Fyfe, and D.T. Herbert, eds, *Crime, Policing and Place: Essays in Environmental Criminology*. London: Routledge, 164–95. · Rengert, G.F. 1992: The journey to crime: conceptual foundations and policy implications. In D.J. Evans, N. R. Fyfe and D.T. Herbert, eds, *Crime, Policing and Place: Essays in Environmental Criminology*. London: Routledge, 109–17. · Rengert, G.F., 1996: *The Geography of Illegal Drugs*. Boulder: Westview Press. · Smith, S.J. 1987a: Design against crime? Beyond the rhetoric of residential crime prevention. *Journal of Property Management* 5: 146–50. · Smith, S.J. 1987b: Fear of crime: beyond a geography of deviance. *Progress in Human Geography* 11: 1–23. · Wallace, R., Wallace, D. and Andrews, H. 1997: AIDS, tuberculosis, violent crime, and low birthweight in eight US metropolitan areas: public policy, stochastic resonance, and the regional diffusion of inner city markers. *Environment and Planning A* 29: 525–55. · Wilson, J.Q. and Kelling, G.I. 1982: Broken windows: the police and neighbourhood safety. *Atlantic Monthly*, March: 29–38.

Suggested Reading

Bottoms, A.E. and Wiles, P. 1997: Environmental criminology. In M. Maguire, R. Morgan and R. Reiner, eds., *The Oxford Handbook of Criminology*, 2nd edn. Oxford: Clarendon Press, 305–59. · Evans, D.J. Fyfe, N. R. and Herbert, D.T., eds, 1992: *Crime, Policing and Place: Essays in Environmental Criminology*. London: Routledge. · Herbert, D.T. 1982: *The Geography of Urban Crime*. London: Longman. · Lowman, J. 1986: Conceptual issues in the geography of crime: toward a geography of social control. *Annals of the Association of American Geographers* 76 (1): 81–94. · Smith, S.J. 1986: *Crime, Space and Society*. Cambridge: Cambridge University Press.

crisis An interruption in the reproduction of economic, cultural, social and/or political life.

The most systematic theories of crisis and crisis formation are provided by HISTORICAL MATERIALISM, which contends that social life is underwritten by the operation of opposing principles of societal organization ('contradictions'; see DIALECTIC). A number of Marxist historians have spoken of a crisis of FEUDALISM in these terms (though in different ways), but most discussion in human geography has centred on crisis in CAPITALISM conceived as a MODE OF PRODUCTION: indeed, in conventional MARXIAN ECONOMICS a crisis is an objective interruption in the ACCUMULATION of capital. There is, however, no single (let alone simple) theory of crisis in Marx's writings, and in *The limits to capital* (1982) D. Harvey went some way beyond Marx to distinguish the following:

A 'first-cut' theory of crisis. Here, so Harvey claims, Marx sought to disclose the *underlying rationale for the instability of capitalist production*. This is usually exemplified by the falling rate of profit, and in particular by the tendency for capitalism to produce both a surplus of capital ('overaccumulation') and a surplus of labour power (unemployment and underemployment).

A 'second-cut' theory of crisis which focuses on *temporal displacement*: on the ways in which surpluses of capital and labour power can be absorbed through new forms of *circulation* and, in particular, through financial and monetary arrangements which are themselves structurally implicated in subsequent financial and monetary crises. This second cut enabled Harvey to differentiate 'between periodic crashes . . . and long-run problems . . . [which] are strongly affected by the increasing socialization of capital itself, first via the agency of the credit system and ultimately through socially necessary interventions on the part of the state' (Harvey, 1982).

The introduction of the STATE into the analysis is of considerable importance since, Harvey emphasizes, once 'we drop the assumption of a closed system and consider international aspects to crisis formation, then it becomes clear that the struggle to export inflation, unemployment, idle productive capacity, excess commodities, etc., becomes the pivot of national policy. The costs of crises are spread differentially according to the financial, economic, political and military power of rival states' (Harvey, 1982). This leads directly to:

A 'third-cut' theory of crisis which focuses not only on 'temporal dynamics' but on the possibility of a *spatial fix*: that is, the ways in which surpluses of capital and labour power might be inscribed in the built environment and, still more important, 'be disposed of and

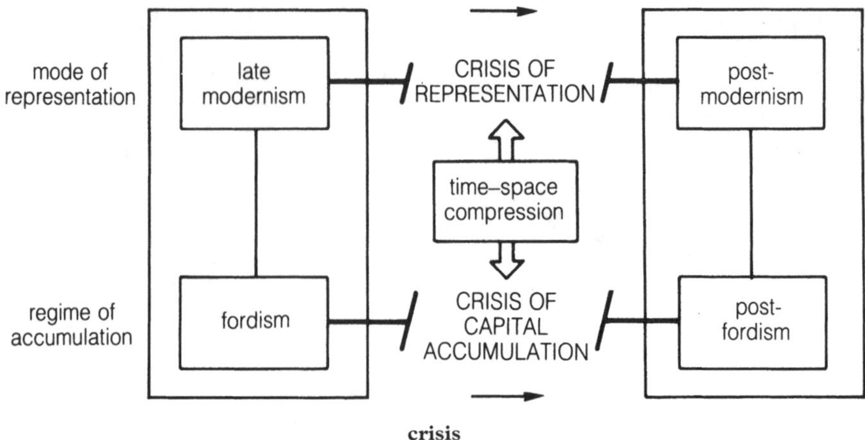

crisis

remunerated by entering into external relations with other regions'. This is one of Harvey's central insights; Marx's formulations, in his view, are 'powerful with respect to time but weak with respect to space' and Marx's political vision is thus 'undermined by his failure to build a systematic and distinctively geographical and spatial dimension into his thought' (Harvey, 1985a; see also MARXIST GEOGRAPHY). Harvey has therefore been concerned, first, to integrate the geography of UNEVEN DEVELOPMENT into crisis theory (Harvey, 1982, 1985b) and, second, to incorporate the state into crisis theory through an analysis of the GEOPOLITICS of capitalism (Harvey, 1985a).

In these discussions capitalism is held to be *both crisis-ridden and crisis-dependent*. Insofar as this understands crisis as a mechanism of auto-regulation, however, there is undoubtedly danger of a covert FUNCTIONALISM in some of these formulations. To blunt the force of these objections, J. O'Connor (1981; see also 1984) insisted that crises are not limited to system integration but also threaten *social integration*. Such a claim evidently owes something to J. Habermas's programmatic reformulation of historical materialism which treats not only economic crises but also (and more particularly) 'rationality crises' and 'legitimation crises' (Habermas, 1976). But O'Connor argued that Habermas did not break sufficiently with classical Marxism. In his view, crises 'originate in the emancipatory practices of human beings': 'the essence of crisis is not social disintegration but social struggle'. In fact, although Habermas has used a model of crisis formation and resolution to account for the evolution of modern societies, he subsequently argued that contemporary social struggles are provoked not only (or even primarily) by spasmodic economic or political crises but by the *colonization* of the LIFEWORLD by economic and political-administrative systems (see CRITICAL THEORY). In any event, it seems clear that these various struggles have their own geographies whose contours cannot be read directly from a map of economic crisis. It is equally clear that social struggles are not always automatically translated into political or even para-political forms because, as Morgan (1983) accentuated, 'formidable integrative mechanisms [can] prevail within the most radical restructuring process [to produce] what might be called a subdued social crisis'. And, as Morgan showed, one of the most powerful ways in which such struggles can be contained is through their fragmentation and localization (see also Massey, 1984).

Other attempts to theorize crisis-formation and -resolution in both economic and social terms have been made by the REGULATION SCHOOL, whose work was very influential in economic geography during the 1980s and 1990s. From this perspective, capitalism's crisis tendencies are managed by a *mode of regulation* – a unique set of social and political norms, rules and regulations – that stabilizes and maintains a particular combination of consumption and investment (a *regime of accumulation*). Thus the FORDISM that dominated western economies between 1945 and 1970 was made viable through the installation of a mode of regulation defined by Keynesian economic policies and the WELFARE STATE. Crises can still occur when the mode of regulation and the regime of accumulation are no longer appropriate to one another: hence the transition to so-called FLEXIBLE ACCUMULATION and its stabilization through a neo-liberal mode of regulation. There is a danger of functionalism in these formulations too, however, and several proposals have been made to guard against it. Hence Webber and Rigby (1996) insist that the so-called 'golden age' of Fordism was an illusion, and that its stereotypical stability was in fact pock-marked by a series of crises that were time- and place-specific. Schoenberger (1997) moves the analysis away from the usual identifications between the NATION-STATE and the SPACE-ECONOMY to understand the internal logics – and above all the cultures – of the large corporations that dominate capitalist economies. When those organizational cultures fail, she argues, then crisis unfolds in complex ways. Other studies have explored the international elaborations of crisis, in particular as these are expressed through the fractured geographies of the international debt crisis (Corbridge, 1992) and within systems of monetary exchange and transformation (Leyshon and Thrift, 1997; cf. MONEY AND FINANCE, GEOGRAPHY OF): here, too, questions of culture (and the politics of culture) loom large. Indeed, Harvey (1989) has himself sought to explore the political and cultural implications of the contemporary crisis of capital accumulation by connecting it to a crisis of representation brought about by TIME–SPACE COMPRESSION (see figure; see also Gregory, 1994).

Whatever one makes of these particular claims, however, they thread out into a wider discussion of MODERNITY and its constant, 'creative destruction' of a world in which, as Marx put it, 'all that is solid melts into air' (see Berman, 1982; Gregory, 1989). Marx's own concerns were the economic and political crises of nineteenth-century capitalism, of course, but the multiple crises which have been inscribed within the trembling foundations of our own *fin-de-siècle* world have such vitally important cultural and ecological dimensions (Emel, 1991; Jackson, 1991) that they pose considerable challenges both to our established ways of thinking and to our established forms of political practice. DG

References

Berman, M. 1982: *All that is solid melts into air: the experience of modernity*. London: Verso. · Corbridge, S. 1992: *Debt and development*. Oxford: Blackwell. · Emel, J. 1991: Ecological crisis and provocative pragmatism. *Environment and Planning D: Society and Space* 9: 384–90. · Gregory, D. 1989: The crisis of modernity? Human geography and critical social theory. In R. Peet and N. Thrift, eds, *New models in geography, volume 2*. London: Unwin Hyman, 348–85. · Gregory, D. 1994: *Geographical imaginations*. Oxford and Cambridge, MA: Blackwell. · Habermas, J. 1976: *Legitimation crisis*. London: Heinemann. · Harvey, D. 1982: *The limits to capital*. Oxford: Basil Blackwell. · Harvey, D. 1985a: The geopolitics of capitalism. In D. Gregory and J. Urry, eds, *Social relations and spatial structures*. London: Macmillan, 128–63. · Harvey, D. 1985b: *The urbanization of capital*. Oxford: Basil Blackwell. · Harvey, D. 1989: *The condition of postmodernity: an enquiry into the origins of cultural change*. Oxford: Blackwell. · Jackson, P. 1991: The crisis of representation and the politics of position. *Environment and Planning D: Society and Space* 9: 131–4. · Leyshon, A. and Thrift, N. 1997: *Money/Space: geographies of monetary transformation*. London: Routledge. · Massey, D. 1984: *Spatial divisions of labour: social structures and the geography of production*. London: Macmillan. · Morgan, K. 1983: The crises of labour and locality in Britain. *International Journal of Urban and Regional Research* 7: 175–201. · O'Connor, J. 1981: The meaning of crisis. *International Journal of Urban and Regional Research* 5: 301–25. · O'Connor, J. 1984: *Accumulation crisis*. Oxford: Basil Blackwell. · Schoenberger, E. 1997: *The cultural crisis of the firm*. Oxford, UK and Cambridge, MA: Blackwell. · Webber, M. and Rigby, D. 1996: *The golden age of illusion*. New York: Guilford.

Suggested Reading

Gregory (1989). · Harvey (1985a). · Schoenberger (1997).

critical geopolitics The bringing together of this adjective and noun represents a neat linguistic amalgam to problematize the least problematized part of twentieth-century geographical knowledge. As such it defies easy definition. One leading writer in the field insists that critical geopolitics is neither developing nor negating theory, rather it is 'parasitical' on other knowledge making tactical interventions instead of indulging in grander strategic thinking (O'Tuathail, 1996, p. 59). Critical geopolitics has not evolved as an integrated cluster of ideas but is represented as a 'constellation', a juxtapositioning of studies impossible to reduce to any core set of ideas (Dalby and O'Tuathail, 1996b, pp. 451–2). The result has been that studies of critical geopolitics 'follow varying research trajectories and engage diverse theoretical enterprises' (ibid., p. 452). The best way to understand such a motley crew of geographers is to investigate their origins.

GEOPOLITICS as an unproblematized set of ideas has surfaced sporadically in the twentieth century to promote political projects of domination. Simple and easy to understand, such a geopolitics emerged to underpin the 'second' Cold War stoked up by US President Reagan and his advisors in the early 1980s. Rather than simply dismissing this geopolitics as right-wing propaganda to be distinguished from 'objective' political geography as done previously, geographers interrogated the latest rediscovery of HEARTLANDS and backyards to create a critical geopolitics. This was not, of course, the first radical critique of geopolitics but it is the first to produce a large and cumulative body of such studies. Although more traditional RADICAL GEOGRAPHY critiques, focusing on the neglect of the economic in geopolitics, emerged as a 'new geopolitics' (e.g. Agnew and Corbridge, 1989), the prime intellectual stimulus to critical geopolitics came from outside the discipline. The mid-1980s saw the development of a dissident international relations school which explicitly problematized the spatial basis of their own discipline (Ashley, 1988; Walker, 1988). It was from this source that POSTCOLONIAL and POSTMODERN ideas informed the new critical geopolitics (e.g. Dalby, 1990). Hence, as well as being concerned for spatial practices, representations of space, and their meanings for the practices, were brought to centre stage. Foucault's ideas on POWER/knowledge and space, Derrida's deconstructing TEXTS (cf. DECONSTRUCTION), and Said's concern for the spatial Other (see ORIENTALISM) have each been crucial to critical geopolitics (O'Tuathail, 1996). Recently there has been an important debate on whether this focus upon political discourse has been at the expense of considering POLITICAL ECONOMY, thus putting the emancipatory credentials of critical geopolitics in doubt (O'Tuathail and Dalby, 1996). However, Agnew and Corbridge (1995) have been successful in setting their critical geopolitics within a world political economy context.

Although eschewing any 'essence' in content, method or theory, critical geopolitics can be seen to be arranged around three basic ideas. First, *there is a politics to all geographical knowledge*. Second, *there is a geography to all political practice*. Third, *the first two ideas can only be uncovered by challenging the taken-for-granted*. The corollary of these is that although most critical geopolitics might continue to problematize questions of international relations and foreign policy, the logic of the position is not to recognize the taken-for-granted separation of the 'international' from other politics. This is reflected in the content of a *Political Geography* special double issue on critical geopolitics (Dalby and O'Tuathail, 1996a) which while dealing mostly with STATE and SPACE, is concerned also with SOCIAL MOVEMENTS, environmental politics and gender. PJT

References

Agnew J and Corbridge, S. 1989: The new geopolitics: the dynamics of global disorder. In R.J. Johnston and P.J. Taylor, eds, *A world in crisis?* Oxford: Blackwell. · Agnew J and Corbridge, S. 1995: *Mastering Space*. London: Routledge. · Ashley, R. 1988: Untying the sovereign state: a double reading of the anarchy problematique. *Millennium* 17: 227–62. · Dalby, S. 1990: *Creating the Second Cold War*. London: Pinter. · Dalby, S. and O'Tuathail, G., eds, 1996a: Special Issue: Critical Geopolitics. *Political Geography* 15 (6/7): 451–6. · Dalby, S. and O'Tuathail, G. 1996b: Editorial introduction. The critical geopolitics constellation: problematizing fusions of geographical knowledge and power, *Political Geography* 15 (6/7): 451–65. · O'Tuathail, G. 1996: *Critical geopolitics*. Minneapolis: University of Minneapolis Press. · O'Tuathail, G. and Dalby, S. 1996: Debate and review essay: dissident IR and writing critical geopolitics. *Political Geography* 15 (6/7): 447–65. · Walker, R.B.J. 1988: *One world, many worlds*. Boulder, CO: Lynne Rienner.

critical human geography A diverse and rapidly changing set of ideas and practices within human geography linked by a shared commitment to emancipatory politics within and beyond the discipline, to the promotion of progressive social change and to the development of a broad range of critical theories and their application in geographical research and political practice. Those who use the term to describe their activity usually do so self-consciously and deliberately to signal their adoption of one or more of these positions. In more detail, critical human geography involves:

Opposition to unequal and oppressive power relations. Critical human geographers emphasize the roles played by social relations of domination and resistance in the production and reproduction of PLACE, SPACE, and LANDSCAPE, and the reciprocal impact of place, space and landscape on the production, reproduction and legitimation of relations of domination and resistance. Among others, unequal relations of CLASS, RACE, ETHNICITY, gender (see GENDER AND GEOGRAPHY), disability (see DISABILITY AND GEOGRAPHY), sexuality (see SEXUALITY AND GEOGRAPHY), and age have all been the focus of empirical and theoretical investigation and critique by geographers, as have the related practices of ACCUMULATION, COLONIALISM, RACISM and PATRIARCHY.

Development and application of critical theories. Critical human geography in the late 1990s is marked by conceptual PLURALISM and an openness to a wide range of critical theoretical approaches, including ANARCHISM, ENVIRONMENTALISM, FEMINISM, MARXISM, POST-MARXISM, POST-COLONIALISM, POST-STRUCTURALISM, PSYCHOANALYSIS as well as CRITICAL THEORY in the strict sense. In each case geographical scholarship has interrogated and developed the relationships between critical theory and SPATIALITY. The enormous diversity within and between these different traditions has ensured that critical human geography is both a highly dynamic and a highly contested terrain. There is no consensus among critical human geographers about the respective merits of different approaches, whether two or more of them can be fruitfully combined, and if so how this should be done. While most critical human geographers resist attempts to prescribe a single theoretical orthodoxy, some seek to develop, extend and work within just one or two theoretical traditions, while others draw on a range of different approaches.

Commitment to social justice and transformative politics. Critical human geographers typically espouse political commitments within and beyond the academy that emphasize resistance to the unequal power relations mentioned above and seek to contribute to political struggles and SOCIAL MOVEMENTS that aim to promote SOCIAL JUSTICE and to transform the social structures and practices that reproduce domination (cf. JUSTICE, GEOGRAPHY AND).

Critical human geography is related to and in large part overlaps a more established tradition of RADICAL GEOGRAPHY. Though there is no sharp distinction to be drawn between the two, critical geography appears at present to be more diffuse, less institutionalized, more theoretically eclectic and, some would argue, less focused politically.

Four key issues have generated much debate within critical human geography and are likely to be crucial to its further development.

The relationship between theory and practice. While emphasizing that theoretically informed political practice is a vital goal, critical human geographers have often been cautious about translating theoretical insights into political engagement. This seems to be due in part because of doubts among some critical human geographers about the possibility of reading off immediate political strategies from critical theories and in part because the scope for radical political action appears to have been eroded by the dominance of neo-conservative and NEO-LIBERAL politics during the 1980s and early 1990s. However, while there is much scepticism about the possibility of building a unitary political project around critical human geography, individuals and groups do participate in a wide range of grassroots political movements, community organizations and practices of resistance (e.g. Routledge, 1997).

Politics inside and outside the academy. Critical human geography recognizes that the western academy and academic life are not as egalitarian as they sometimes purport to be, but are themselves shot through with unequal power relations. For example, many feminist geographers have stressed the extent to which women have been marginalized within the academic institutions of geography. The merger of the Institute of British Geographers with the Royal Geographical Society in 1995 was opposed by many critical human geographers who objected to the continuing effects of the RGS's IMPERIALIST legacy (cf. GEOGRAPHICAL SOCIETIES). The financial patronage of the RGS by the Shell oil company was a further source of conflict arising from both Shell's status as a MULTINATIONAL CORPORATION (and thus deeply implicated in process of capital ACCUMULATION) and its role in environmental conflicts and struggles over HUMAN RIGHTS in less developed countries (notably Nigeria). Although most critical human geographers share this commitment to political action within the academic world, there is clearly some danger that it may lead to the neglect of issues of social justice beyond the academy. On the other hand, critical human geography also involves a critique of the view that the academy is an ivory tower divorced from the 'real world'.

POSITIONALITY/*reflexivity.* Most critical human geography is self-consciously reflexive. That is, it turns critical theory on itself in a process of self-critique, raising a series of uncomfortable questions for critical human geography itself. For example, to what extent, if at all, can academic geographers speak 'on behalf of' marginalized social groups? Does the development of highly sophisticated theory sometimes impede, rather than enable, the pluralist networks of communication on which radical democratic political activity depends? Is it the case that 'the self-reflexivity and respect for DIFFERENCE we have learned to cultivate [themselves] threaten to be debilitating'? (Katz et al., 1998, p. 258).

Internationalism. Notwithstanding its sincere commitments to inclusion, POST-COLONIALISM and anti-RACISM, critical human geography has to date been largely (though by no means exclusively) an Anglo-American affair. There is, though, a wide recognition of the vital necessity of involving a much broader range of participants. Critical human geography is now marked by an emerging, if still hesitant, internationalism. The Inaugural International Conference of Critical Geographers (IICCG) held in August 1997 in Vancouver, Canada, attracted participation from thirty countries

(Katz et al., 1998, p. 257). Widespread use is made of electronic communications media, particularly the Internet, to enable wider international involvement (though it is recognized that access to such facilities is also highly unequal). One of the most interesting and exciting aspects of the further development of critical human geography will be to see how such wider involvement changes theory and practice, and the relationship between them.

JP

References

Katz, C. et al. 1998: Lost and found in the posts: addressing critical human geography. *Environment and Planning D: Society and Space* 16: 257–78. · Routledge, P. 1997: The imagineering of resistance: Pollock Free State and the practice of postmodern politics. *Transactions, Institute of British Geographers* NS 22: 359–76.

Suggested Reading

Katz et al. (1998); Critical Geography electronic mailing list: http://www.mailbase.ac.uk/lists/crit-geog-forum/.

critical rationalism A philosophy of science developed by Karl Popper, originally as a critical response to the LOGICAL POSITIVISM of the Vienna Circle. (Neurath, a member of the Circle, nicknamed Popper 'the Official Opposition'; see Popper, 1976.) Popper's philosophy is wide-ranging, and detailed discussions have been provided by Burke (1983) and O'Hear (1980), but two connected components have been of special significance for human geography.

The principle of falsification. In *The logic of scientific discovery* (1934; translated into English in 1959) Popper challenged the 'principle of verification' which was at the heart of logical positivism by suggesting that 'not the verifiability but the falsifiability of a [theoretical] system' should be taken as a 'criterion of demarcation' between the empirical sciences on the one hand and mathematics, logic and metaphysics on the other. This was not the same as a criterion of meaning, Popper emphasized, because 'falsifiability separates two kinds of perfectly meaningful statements': a view which made him still further at odds with the Vienna Circle who regarded metaphysics as scientifically meaningless. Within human geography, Wilson's (1972, p. 32) programme for a 'theoretical geography' was explicitly based on Popper's procedures:

> The essence of the scientific method is the construction of theories and the continual testing of these by comparing them with observation. The essence of such testing is an attempt to disprove a THEORY – to marshall observations which contradict the predictions of the theory. In this sense, theories are never proved to be generally true. The ones in which we believe represent the best approximations to truth at any one time... We expect, then, that theories will be subject to constant development and refinement: sometimes a falsified theory can be patched up; sometimes, radically different theory is needed.

As the last sentence implies, Popper's principle is often methodologically intractable, whatever its logical attractions. Even though Popper himself recognized this and attempted to stipulate a number of safeguards against ad hoc tinkering, Sayer (1992) dismisses the principle of FALSIFICATION as 'virtually impossible to put into practice' (cf. Marshall, 1982 and Hay, 1985). It is certainly the case that the principle has rarely been used in human geography, even at the height of SPATIAL SCIENCE, but, as Wilson (1972) noted, this was as much a result of the inductivist bias of the QUANTITATIVE REVOLUTION as any considered rejection of critical rationalism. (This never prevented some quantitative geographers from using Popper to object to Marxism because, according to Popper (1945), it either cannot be falsified, or has been falsified and hence loses any claim to be a 'science'.)

The progress of science. Popper used the iterative sequence described by Wilson (above) to argue, further, that 'the growth of knowledge' depends upon a method of 'rational criticism'. He usually represented it like this:

$$P_1 \rightarrow TS \rightarrow EE \rightarrow P_2$$

Thus, we are supposed to start from a problem (P_1), then formulate a trial solution (TS) 'which we then subject to the severest possible test [that is, falsification] in a process of error elimination' (EE), which in turn leads to the creative formulation of a new problem (P_2). Hence, in Popper's view, the progress of science depends upon a creative response to error – upon what he called *Conjectures and refutations* (1963). Many commentators, and Popper too, have contrasted this normative model with Kuhn's account of the changing structure of scientific knowledge (see PARADIGM). So, for example, Bird (1975) correctly recognized that 'the implications for geography to be drawn from Popper's works are quite different from those to be drawn from the writings of Thomas Kuhn'. And Marshall (1982), although he mistakenly assumes Kuhn to stand 'in the mainstream of the logical positivist tradition' by virtue of the very tactic which Popper (1976) rejects (namely judging books 'by their covers or editors'), urged geographers 'to look elsewhere if [they] are concerned to understand the logic of the process by which knowledge advances' (i.e. Popper) rather than 'the sociology of academic life' (i.e. Kuhn). Kuhn's whole object was indeed to confront what Barnes (1985) terms 'the myth of rationalism' on which Popper's project is founded. Barnes provides a number of general reasons why rationalism might properly be called a 'myth'; but perhaps the most telling specific objection comes from Sayer (1992, p. 230): 'What do we learn when a deductive theory is legitimately falsified? . . . Only that we must try a different deductive theory . . . only that something is wrong and not what is wrong'. The essential weakness, Sayer contends, is that – unlike Sayer's preferred philosophy of REALISM – Popper's strategy 'ignores the content of theory' and so is incapable of distinguishing causal explanation from instrumentalist 'deviation' (see INSTRUMENTALISM).

But Chouinard, Fincher and Webber (1984) used Imre Lakatos's critique and reformulation of Popper's proposals to argue that it is possible to conduct scientific research programmes in human geography in ways which are none the less conformable with realism. Lakatos (1978) believed that Popper was too ready to reject theories and argued for a more cautious, 'conservative' strategy: in his view, scientific progress ought to depend on the careful evaluation of what he called problem-shifts. A series of scientific theories is to be counted as theoretically progressive 'if each new theory has some excess empirical content over its predecessor, that is, if it predicts some novel, hitherto unexpected fact', and as empirically progressive if some of this excess empirical content is also corroborated, that is, if each new theory leads us to the actual discovery of some new fact'. Unless a problem-shift satisfies both of these conditions it will be degenerating rather than progressive and ought not to replace the existing formulation (Lakatos, 1979). In much the same way, Chouinard, Fincher and Webber (1984, p. 375) argued that:

> It does not make sense, when dealing with an open SYSTEM and therefore with a reality without invariant cause and effect relationships, to reject one's core propositions about causal mechanisms and processes only because of apparently disconfirming empirical evidence. Instead, the criteria for accepting or rejecting a particular research tradition in human geography must be programmatic, that is, they must evaluate the coherence and creativity of a particular approach in terms of expansion in the conceptual and empirical scope of explanation.

Be that as it may, Lakatos's proposals are not immune to objection (Barnes, 1982) and it is by no means clear that, even in this revised form, 'the critical rationalist viewpoint can provide a new and welcome coherence' in human geography (Marshall, 1982; cf. Bird, 1989). DG

References

Barnes, B. 1982: *T. S. Kuhn and social science*. London: Macmillan. · Barnes, B. 1985: Thomas Kuhn. In Q. Skinner, ed., *The return of grand theory to the human sciences*. Cambridge: Cambridge University Press, 83–100. · Bird, J.H. 1975: Methodological implications for geography from the philosophy of K.R. Popper. *Scottish Geographical Magazine* 91: 153–63. · Bird, J.H. 1989: *The changing worlds of geography*. Oxford: Clarendon Press. · Burke, T. 1983: *The philosophy of Popper*. Manchester: Manchester University Press. · Chouinard, V., Fincher, R. and Webber, M. 1984: Empirical research in scientific human geography. *Progress in Human Geography* 8: 346–80. · Hay, A.M. 1985: Scientific method in geography. In R.J. Johnston, ed., *The future of geography*. London: Methuen, 129–42. · Lakatos, I. 1978: *The methodology of scientific research programmes*. Cambridge: Cambridge University Press. · Lakatos, I. 1979: Falsification and the methodology of scientific research programmes. In I. Lakatos and A. Musgrave, eds, *Criticism and the growth of knowledge*. Cambridge: Cambridge University Press, 91–196. · Marshall, J. 1982: Geography and critical rationalism. In J.D. Wood, ed., *Rethinking geographical inquiry*. Downsview, Ontario: Department of Geography, Atkinson College, York University, 73–171. · O'Hear, A. 1980: *Karl Popper*. London: Routledge and Kegan Paul. · Popper, K. 1945: *The open society and its enemies*. London: Routledge and Kegan Paul. · Popper, K. 1959: *The logic of scientific discovery*. London: Hutchinson; New York: Basic Books. · Popper, K. 1963: *Conjectures and refutations: the growth of scientific knowledge*. London: Routledge and Kegan Paul. · Popper, K. 1976: Reason or revolution? In D. Frisby, ed., *The positivist dispute in German sociology*. London: Heinemann; New York: Harper and Row, 288–300. · Sayer, A. 1992: *Method in social science: a realist approach*, 2nd edn. London: Routledge. · Wilson, A.G. 1972: Theoretical geography: some speculations. *Transactions, Institution of British Geographers* 57: 31–44.

Suggested Reading

Bird (1975). · Chouinard et al. (1984). · Sayer (1992), ch. 8.

critical theory A European tradition of social and political thought, which is centrally concerned with the historicity of social action: in particular, the connections between HUMAN AGENCY and social structure which exist under CAPITALISM and which can be recognized and restructured through a process of critical reflection. Critical theory owed its inspiration to classical Marxism, but it was also a vital presence within the critical

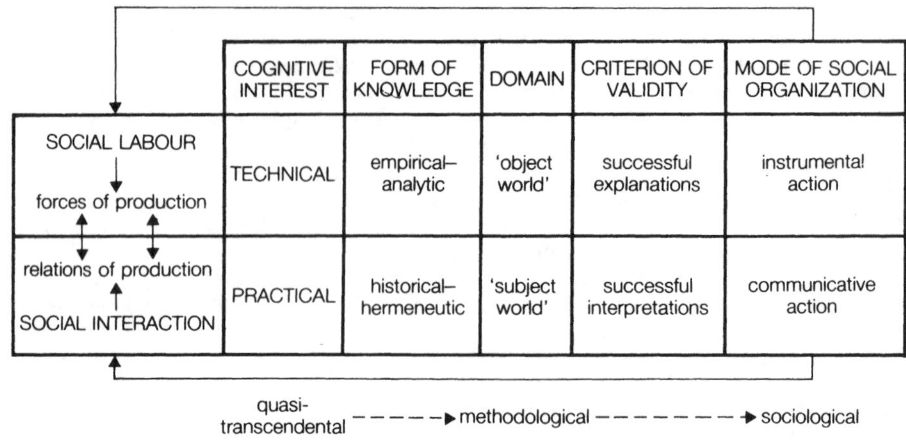

critical theory *1: Cognitive interests*

reformulations and extensions of HISTORICAL MATERIALISM associated with so-called 'Western Marxism': that is to say, it sought to move away from the priorities of POLITICAL ECONOMY in order to address, in full and equal measure, the concerns of philosophy, aesthetics and CULTURE (cf. Merquior, 1986).

It is usual to distinguish between two main schools (although there are connections and continuities between them): (i) the original FRANKFURT SCHOOL; and (ii) the later work of Jürgen Habermas, the focus of attention here, which includes and is variously described as a 'reconstruction of historical materialism' and a 'theory of communicative action' (see Held, 1980). There are three main planks to Habermas's platform.

(a) In his early writings Habermas argued that critical theory had to reflect on the conditions that made it possible: more specifically, he claimed that a critique of EPISTEMOLOGY is only possible as a social theory. To that end, he developed a concept of cognitive (or 'knowledge-constitutive') interests. In his view, any society necessarily entails both (i) social labour, which is organized through a system of *instrumental action*, and (ii) social interaction, which is organized through a system of *communicative action*. The first of these involves the realization of a *technical interest*, so Habermas claimed, because any labour process has to have some means of achieving control over its materials and components (including human beings considered as objects); the second involves the realization of a *practical interest*, because any communication process requires some means of ensuring that the participants understand one another. These two interests, which are supposed to be deep-seated or 'quasi-transcendental' structural rules, thus constitute two different but dependent forms of knowledge by specifying their domains of study and the criteria for making valid statements about them: the *empirical-analytical sciences*, which deal with a world of objects and make predictions about their interactions; and the *historical-hermeneutic sciences*, which deal with a world of subjects and provide interpretations of their interactions (Habermas, 1972). These twin trajectories are summarized in figure 1. At the time, Habermas suggested that a *critical science* would be directed towards the realization of a third, *emancipatory* interest which would necessarily involve the considered conjunction of both forms of knowledge – neither of them was self-sufficient. This scheme has been used in human geography to advance the critique of POSITIVISM and, in particular, to argue for the development of a CRITICAL HUMAN GEOGRAPHY that would be committed neither to the 'objectivist' analysis of spatial systems and SPATIAL STRUCTURES nor to the 'subjectivist' construction of PLACE, but would use and rework both traditions together (Gregory, 1978).

(b) Habermas subsequently proposed that a critical social theory is possible only as a theory of social evolution, and his reconstruction of historical materialism depends on the 'argumentation sketch' summarized in figure 2 (Habermas, 1975, 1979). There, different forms of society are supposed to be characterized by different 'organizational principles', each of which is vulnerable to a distinctive

Type of society	Organization principle ⟶	Characteristic form of crisis
PRIMITIVE	kinship relations	ecological–demographic crisis
TRADITIONAL	class domination through the state	political crisis
EARLY CAPITALISM	class domination through capital–labour relation	economic crisis
LATE CAPITALISM	class domination through state mediation of (corporate) capital–labour relation	sociocultural crisis

critical theory *2: Society, organization principle and crisis in Habermas*

form of CRISIS. Habermas's central claim is that a crisis is both 'objective' and 'subjective', both caused and 'experienced', so that a crisis is caused by an interruption in the prevailing mode of system integration but will only be realized (in the fullest sense of the term) if it is consciously *experienced*; in other words, if human subjects 'feel their social identity threatened'. Habermas's argument is that the resolution of successive crises depends on an evolutionary learning process which takes place in two dimensions: technically useful knowledge and moral-practical consciousness. It is that 'learning process' which Habermas sees inscribed within the ENLIGHTENMENT project of MODERNITY and which has prompted a number of critics to charge him with ETHNOCENTRISM. Habermas's major concern, however, is with the distortion of the project of modernity by the development of capitalism – through the intrusion of domination into labour (ALIENATION) and interaction ('systematically distorted communication') – in such a way that the possibilities of informed democratic debate within a genuinely public sphere have been foreshortened: issues are increasingly constructed as purely technical matters which may be decided without the involvement of a moral-practical consciousness (Habermas, 1989; see also Gregory, 1980). Here too Habermas is vulnerable to criticism, and feminist scholars in particular have objected to his failure to recognize the significance of GENDER as an axis of discrimination and domination; it is also necessary to offer an historically and geographically more nuanced account than Habermas was able to provide at the time (see Fraser, 1987; Calhoun, 1992). But Habermas's commitment to the project of modernity is unwavering and has generated sharp criticism of POSTMODERNISM and POSTSTRUCTURALISM (see Habermas, 1981, 1987b; Bernstein, 1985).

(c) In the early 1970s Habermas focused on the involvement of the STATE in mediating and managing the various crises of so-called *late capitalism*, and he paid particular attention to its propensity for sociocultural crisis or *legitimation crisis* (figure 3; see also Habermas, 1975; McCarthy, 1978). This model was widely if informally used in POLITICAL GEOGRAPHY. Although Harvey and Scott (1989) have implied that it was subsequently overtaken by events – notably by what they saw as the shift from FORDISM to FLEXIBLE ACCUMULATION – Habermas has since revised his account in the direction of a *theory of communicative action*. In the late twentieth-century world, he now argues, the instrumental and strategic rationalities of social systems (the domains of technically useful knowledge) have been overextended: the economic system and the politico-administrative system have encroached on the LIFEWORLD through processes of monetization and bureaucratization (figure 4). At the limit, Habermas suggests, this amounts to a *colonization of the lifeworld*, which occurs as soon as those processes reach 'beyond their mediating roles and penetrate those spheres of the lifeworld which are responsible for cultural transmission, socialization and the formation of personal identity'. When the scope of communicative action is confined in this way, Habermas concludes, people are made to

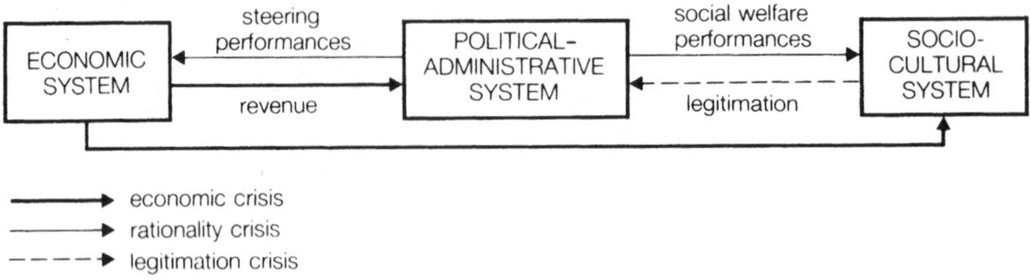

critical theory *3: Crises in late capitalism*

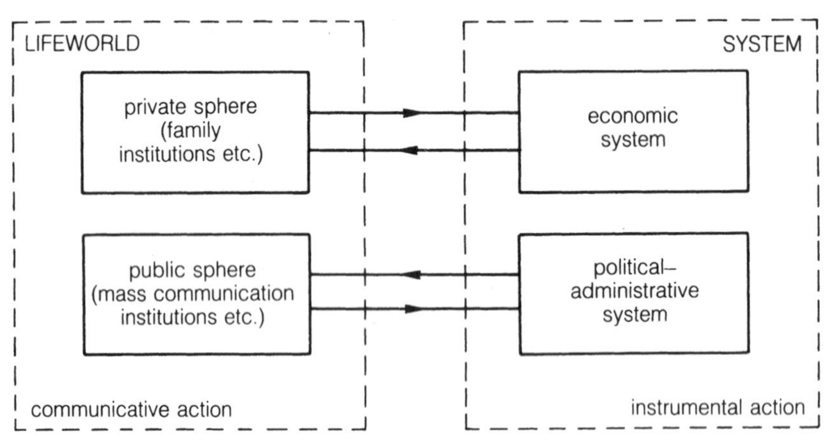

critical theory *4: Lifeworld and system*

feel less like persons and more like things. New conflicts may arise at the seam between system and lifeworld, around 'the grammar of forms of life', where they are articulated by new SOCIAL MOVEMENTS which overlie the traditional politics of economic, social and military security, and revolve around the symbolic reproduction of the lifeworld itself (Habermas, 1984, 1987a; see also Ingram, 1987; White, 1988).

These are important and provocative suggestions, and as such they have been subject to considerable critical scrutiny (see Honneth and Joas, 1991). Oddly, however, neither Habermas nor his critics have paid much attention to the different spatialities involved: although the theory of communicative action is plainly deeply embedded in the dilemmas of post-war Germany, it is none the less a GRAND THEORY (Giddens, 1985) which pays no attention to the significance of webs of difference and connection over space. But it is possible to bring Habermas's project into dialogue with human geography, in particular with concepts of SPACE and place (Gregory, 1989), to chart the territoriality of social struggles (Miller, 1992), and to explore some of the parallels and contrasts between Habermas's advance of the system into the lifeworld and Lefebvre's account of the superimposition of abstract space over concrete space (Lefebvre, 1992; Gregory, 1993). It may even be possible to turn the ethnocentrism of Habermas's project against itself, and to examine the imposition of colonial systems and spatialities on the lifeworlds of native peoples (Harris, 1991). DG

References

Bernstein, R.J., ed., 1985: *Habermas and modernity.* Cambridge: Polity Press. · Calhoun, C. 1992: *Habermas and the public sphere.* Cambridge, MA: MIT Press. · Fraser, N. 1987: What's critical about critical theory? Habermas and gender. In S. Benhabib and D. Cornell, eds, *Feminism as critique: essays on the politics of gender in late-capitalist societies.* Cambridge: Polity Press, 31–56. · Giddens, A. 1985: Jürgen Habermas. In Q. Skinner, *The return of grand theory in the human sciences.* Cambridge: Cambridge University Press, 121–39. · Gregory, D. 1978: *Ideology, science and human geography.* London: Hutchinson. · Gregory, D. 1980: The ideology of control: systems theory and geography. *Tijdschrift voor Economische en Sociale Geographie* 71: 327–42. · Gregory, D. 1989: The crisis of modernity? Human geography and critical social theory. In R. Peet and N. Thrift, eds, *New models in geography, volume 2*. London: Unwin Hyman, 348–85. · Gregory, D. 1993: *Geographical imaginations*. Oxford: Blackwell. · Habermas, J. 1972: *Knowledge and human interests*. London: Heinemann. · Habermas, J. 1975: *Legitimation crisis*. London: Heinemann. · Habermas, J. 1979:*Communication and the evolution of society*. London: Heinemann. · Habermas, J. 1981: Modernity versus postmodernity. *New German Critique* 22: 3–14. · Habermas, J. 1984: *The theory of communicative action, volume 1: Reason and the rationalization of society*. London: Heinemann. · Habermas, J. 1987a: *The theory of communicative action, volume 2: The critique of functionalist reason*. Cambridge: Polity Press. · Habermas, J. 1987b: *The philosophical discourse of modernity*. Cambridge: Polity Press. · Habermas, J. 1989: *The structural transformation of the public sphere*. Cambridge, MA: MIT Press. · Harris, C. 1991: Power, modernity and historical geography. *Annals of the Association of American Geographers* 81: 671–83. · Harvey, D. and Scott, A. 1989: The practice of human geography. In B. Macmillan, ed., *Remodelling geography*. Oxford: Blackwell, 217–29. · Held, D. 1980: *Introduction to critical theory: Horkheimer to Habermas*. London: Hutchinson. · Honneth, A. and Joas, H. 1991: *Communicative action: essays on Jürgen Habermas's* The theory of communicative action. Cambridge, MA: MIT Press. · Ingram, D. 1987: *Habermas and the dialectic of reason*. New Haven: Yale University Press. · Lefebvre, H. 1992: *The production of space*, trans. D. Nicholson-Smith. Oxford: Blackwell. · McCarthy, T. 1978: *The critical theory of Jürgen Habermas*. London: Hutchinson. · Merquior, J. 1986: *Western Marxism*. London: Paladin. · Miller, B. 1992: Collective action and rational choice: place, community and the limits to individual self-interest. *Economic Geography* 68: 22–42. · White, S. 1988: *The recent work of Jürgen Habermas: power, justice and modernity*. Cambridge: Cambridge University Press.

Suggested Reading

Giddens (1985). · Gregory (1989). · Holub, R. 1991: *Jürgen Habermas: critic in the public sphere*. London: Routledge. · Ingram, D. 1990: *Critical theory and philosophy*. New York: Paragon House, chs 1 and 7.

cross-section A description of a CULTURAL LANDSCAPE at a particular point in time: in effect, a horizontal 'slice'. The use of cross-sections as a working methodology in HISTORICAL GEOGRAPHY was popularized by H.C. Darby's classic *Historical geography of England before* AD *1800* (1936), which used 'a sequence of cross-sections taken at successive periods' to represent 'reconstructions of past geographies', a device which owed much to Macaulay's famous description of the landscape of England in 1685 in his *History of England* (1849). At the time, Darby subsequently recalled, 'the method of cross-sections [was] hailed as being essentially geographical as opposed to historical' – largely because it so clearly lent itself to CARTOGRAPHIC representation – but drawing such boundaries soon became problematic since, as Darby himself recognized, 'the moment we ask "Why does this landscape look like it does?" that moment we are committed to something more than mere description or mere cross-section' (see Darby, in Finberg, 1962). Hence in his later compilation, *A new historical geography of England* (1973), Darby employed an intercalation of cross-section and VERTICAL THEME to try to capture stabilities and transformations and to combine description and explanation (see also SEQUENT OCCUPANCE).

But this pragmatic response raises many more questions than it answers. Darby's approach and its derivatives assumed a homogeneous time – and, indeed, treated time as an external system of coordinates such that changes in LANDSCAPES at successive points 'in' time could be organized into a chronological sequence 'authored' by vertical themes – whereas more recent arguments about the social construction of time (and space) and the co-existence of multiple temporalities within cultural landscapes strongly suggest that the cutting of cross-sections (and the identification of vertical themes) is a much more complex and contentious manoeuvre. At the very least, 'cross-sections' ought not to be treated as equilibrium states: cultural landscapes contain forms and traces of residual, dominant and emergent processes, so that their interpretation requires a heterogeneous concept of time capable of recovering these different process-domains and their varying scales of operation (see TIME, GEOGRAPHY AND). DG

References

Darby, H.C., ed., 1936: *Historical geography of England before* AD *1800*. Cambridge: Cambridge University Press. · Darby, H.C., ed., 1973: A *new historical geography of England*. Cambridge: Cambridge University Press. · Finberg, H.P.R., ed., 1962: *Approaches to history: a symposium*. London: Routledge and Kegan Paul; Toronto: University of Toronto Press. · Macaulay, T.B. 1849: *The history of England from the accession of James II*. London: Longman Green.

cultural capital Coined by Pierre Bourdieu, the term refers to the acquisition of social status through cultural practices which involve the exercise of taste or judgement (cf. CULTURE). Originally applied in the context of educational research in France, the concept has been extended to a wider field of social distinctions (Bourdieu, 1984), where tastes and aesthetic judgements (in art and literature, for example) function as markers of CLASS

(Bourdieu, 1993). Cultural (or symbolic) capital can sometimes be exchanged or converted into economic capital and vice versa. Following Bourdieu, sociologists and geographers have distinguished various forms of social, economic and cultural capital, employing these ideas in studies of GENTRIFICATION and middle-class formation (e.g. Savage et al.; 1993, Ley, 1996). PAJ

References

Bourdieu, P. 1984: *Distinction: a social critique of the judgement of taste*. London: Routledge and Kegan Paul. · Bourdieu, P. 1993: *The field of cultural production: essays on art and literature*. Cambridge: Polity Press. · Ley, D. 1996: *The new middle class and the remaking of the central city*. Oxford: Oxford University Press. · Savage, M., Barlow, J., Dickens, P. and Fielding, T. 1993: *Property, bureaucracy and culture: middle-class formation in contemporary Britain*. London: Routledge.

cultural ecology An approach to the study of the relations between a cultural group (a mode of life associated with specific material and symbolic practices) and its natural environment. It is most closely associated with the work of Julian Steward (1955) and with the study of THIRD WORLD PEASANTRIES, PASTORALISTS, hunter-gatherers and tribal peoples (see SUBSISTENCE AGRICULTURE). Cultural ecology proposes that similar configurations of environment and technology tend to be functionally and causally related to similar social organizations: it is therefore the study of the adaptive processes by which human SOCIETIES and CULTURES adjust through subsistence patterns to the specific parameters of their local habitat (see ECOLOGY; ENVIRONMENTAL PERCEPTION). Steward emphasized that adaptive processes could be explored through a 'cultural core' of human activities; social evolution was not a series of stages through which all societies passed but a multilinear process of differing patterns of environmental adaptation. Cultural ecology can thus be seen as a subset of HUMAN ECOLOGY, an approach which attempts to link culture as a material and symbolic realm and Darwinist evolutionary theory (see SOCIAL DARWINISM).

Cultural ecology since Steward's time has developed in two directions. First, to see it as a variant of Marx's materialism in which 'techno-environmental determinism' becomes the motor of history (see MARXIST GEOGRAPHY). The second refines the concept of ecology by introducing notions drawn from SYSTEMS analysis and systems theory (cf. ECOSYSTEM). Cultural practices are related to wider movements of energy, matter and information and fulfil homeostatic or regulatory functions to ensure environmental SUSTAINABILITY. In this latter view, cultural ecology is strongly influenced by cybernetics and ecological theory such that human populations are seen conceptually as like any other animal population struggling for survival amidst the complex webs of ecosystemic relations. Many geographers and anthropologists attempted to develop this theory of ADAPTATION in which culture (for example pig-killing rituals in highland New Guinea or cosmological beliefs in the Kalahari) functions as a self-regulating adaptive mechanism with respect to local environmental systems (CARRYING CAPACITY). Cultural ecology has been heavily criticized for its functionalism and teleology, its heavy reliance on organic analogies, and its incapacity to take account of political economic processes of surplus extraction and appropriation (cf. MARXIAN ECONOMICS). MW

Reference

Steward, J. 1955: *The theory of culture change*. Urban: University of Illinois Press.

cultural geography Currently one of the most vibrant and contested sub-fields within human geography, 'cultural geography' has both a long scholarly tradition and multiple contemporary expressions. While much of human geography today might be characterized as 'cultural' in focus and content, any single or univocal definition of 'cultural geography' would be misleading. Despite attempts to resolve recent scholarly disagreement over its scope and methods (Foote et al., 1994) cultural geography today is marked by quite distinct theoretical positions and methodologies.

In Anglophone scholarship, the dominant theoretical tradition within cultural geography has until recently been American, dating from the early decades of the twentieth century; deeper origins may be traced to late nineteenth-century German ANTHROPOGEOGRAPHY, such as geographer Friedrich Ratzel's (1844–1904) interest in ECOLOGICAL relations between the physical surface of the earth and human cultures combined with the more ETHNOGRAPHIC interest in localized human COMMUNITIES promoted by the anthropologist Franz Boas (1858–1942). The outcome in American geography was a scholarly project emphasizing the active role of human groups in transforming natural environments, interpreting and mapping the cultural ecologies which resulted. Thus, Cultural Geography in many American geography teaching programmes remained synonymous with Human Geography as a whole. The dominant early figure in this North American tradition was undoubtedly Carl O. Sauer whose own writings together with those of subsequent generations of students at BERKELEY and other American universities, especially in the west and south, have dealt with a range of human interventions and transformations within the natural world, across regions at various spatial scales on the earth's surface.

Conventional themes of cultural geography have included plant and animal domestication; the spatial DIFFUSION of domesticates, technologies and material practices; ecologies of fire and water engineering; modes of agrarian life and human conduct of all kinds that bears upon human occupancy and geographical diversity apparent in landscapes. Strongly critical of a prevailing ENVIRONMENTAL DETERMINISM, Sauer's early work was significantly influenced by studies of Native American and Hispanic cultures in the experience and aftermath of Anglo occupation in the American Southwest. From German geography Sauer adopted the concept of *Landschaft*, which he translated as LANDSCAPE, outlining a methodology for cultural geography in his 1925 paper 'The morphology of landscape' (Leighly, 1963). Working empirically and historically mainly in those parts of the Americas strongly influenced by Iberian COLONIALISM, Sauer established strong traditions of field study, language learning and commitment to rural, traditional societies still strongly upheld within CULTURAL ECOLOGY research.

Highlighting the impacts of MODERNIZATION on traditional lifeways, the Sauerian project inevitably raised ethical questions about the impacts of human use of the Earth as a significant theme in cultural geography (cf. ETHICS AND GEOGRAPHY). Sauer himself increasingly came to believe that MODERNITY made such impacts more and more destructive, both to what he took to be long-standing and relatively stable folk cultures and to natural environments themselves, and thus to sustainable cultural ecologies. His concern found expression in the conceptually adventurous and hugely influential *Man's role in changing the face of the Earth* (Thomas, 1956), which emerged from a conference for which Sauer had been the guiding spirit. Its essays and discussion pieces demonstrate the breadth of this American conception of cultural geography, its global commitment and Sauer's own resistance to many aspects of modern, urbanized life. Revivals of environmental concern in the early 1970s and again in the late 1980s have seen writers within geography and beyond turning to Sauer as a pioneer figure in global and local ENVIRONMENTALISM, while the continued significance of this ecological concern is evidenced in a 1990 re-examination of the issues raised in *Man's role*... (Turner et al., 1990).

Despite the criticism from a 'new cultural geography', the ecological and ethnographic tradition in American cultural geography has been reinvigorated by two streams of thinking in the 1990s. These are a recasting of the epistemological dualism of NATURE and CULTURE upon which so much of the geographical tradition has conventionally been constructed (Livingstone, 1992), and the influence of POST-COLONIAL theory. The first of these impacts, strongly influenced by FEMINIST theory, recognizes both the inevitable cultural appropriation and mediation of the natural world, and that human beings are themselves embodied agents through whom an active nature constantly works. Agency cannot therefore be securely divided between nature and culture, so that all environments and landscapes are co-productions of nature–culture (Latour, 1993; Demeritt, 1994), although conventional ecological theory is but one of a number of METAPHORS for examining such co-production. This insight is reinforced by the empirical recognition that virtually no ecology has remained uninfluenced by significant human activity, and that the global environmental impact of humans long predates modernity, extending over the Holocene (Roberts, 1998 [1989]; Simmons, 1989), raising questions of judgement that are more political and moral than objectively scientific (Lewis and Wigen, 1997; cf. MORAL GEOGRAPHIES). This in turn may be related to the second recent influence on cultural ecology, insofar as a significant dimension of post-colonial theory is the belief that to represent colonized and supposedly 'aboriginal peoples' within the language of stable, pre-modern 'folk cultures' subsisting in ecological harmony with 'nature', is itself a colonialist manoeuvre, effectively maintaining their status as passive victims of a continued cultural colonization (Gregory, 1994; Harris, 1996) rather than active agents in the evolution and contestation of their own cultural worlds.

Criticism of Sauerian concepts of culture and landscape was a starting point for what has come to be termed '*new cultural geography*' since the 1980s. Influenced by sociological critique within a British 'cultural studies' tradition more concerned with SPACE and SPATIALITY than with environment and material landscapes, a number of geographers sought to ground a geographical concept of culture in social relations of production and reproduction (Cosgrove, 1983; Cosgrove and Jackson, 1987; Duncan, 1994). In fact, a series of texts in the late 1960s titled *Foundations of Cultural Geography* (Wagner, 1972) had already begun to address a number of issues such as culture and communication, symbolism and meaning in CULTURAL LANDSCAPES, and IDENTITY and TERRITORY which 'new' cultural geographers were calling for in the 1980s, while Glacken's *Traces on the Rhodian Shore* (1967), an intellectual history of European ideas of environmental determinism, a designed earth and HUMAN AGENCY in nature, anticipated current scholarly interest in cultural histories of geography and environmental thought (Livingstone, 1992). Nonetheless, much current work in cultural geography is more closely aligned to theory in the social sciences and humanities than to biology and the earth sciences. And while matters of critical contemporary concern are much more evident in cultural geography today, recognition of the importance of the past and the bias towards historically sensitive explanation remain common ground between its different traditions.

The 'CULTURAL TURN' which has not only come to dominate social science and the humanities in the 1990s, but also penetrated ONTOLOGICAL and EPISTEMOLOGICAL debates within natural science itself, has encouraged a focus on culture as a signifying process of self, of social group formation, the creation of 'OTHERS' and of worlds of experience. In this formulation, meaning is actively constructed, negotiated and contested, always constituted through the shared DISCOURSES of human and non-human agents. Such claims, closely aligned to POSTMODERNIST philosophies, challenge many of the conceptual categories of more conventional cultural geography, which has sometimes thus been figured as conservative and theoretically naive. The debate within cultural geography in the early 1990s produced powerful polemics between upholders of a Sauerian tradition which its defenders felt to have been maligned and misrepresented, and those promoting a more explicitly theorized and 'political' cultural geography (Price and Lewis, 1993; Duncan, 1994). *Re-reading cultural geography*, modelled on the collection edited by Wagner and Mikesell in 1962, which had defined the scope of cultural geography for its time, sought to give expression to both sides of this debate and to secure a resolution to what Duncan (1994) called the 'civil war' in American cultural geography. The evidence of substantive scholarship rather than theoretical position papers in recent cultural geography suggests that the critique of 'master narratives' of nature and culture has in fact significantly reconstituted the Sauerian project itself, while pure SOCIAL CONSTRUCTION in its turn has been undermined by arguments about non-human agency and a revived interest in the physicality and embodiment of human agency itself (cf. BODY, GEOGRAPHY AND). A convergence of practice, if not of rhetoric, is thus apparent, and while the American *Journal of Cultural Geography* retains a strong commitment to the research agenda initially set within the Berkeley school, *Ecumene*, one of a number of cultural geography journals launched in the early 1990s, has styled itself a journal of 'environment, culture and meaning', thus making clear its commitment to an inclusive cultural geography and inviting theoretically informed, substantive contributions while avoiding explicit political positioning. A parallel French publication, *Géographie et Cultures*, also established in 1993, carries a broadly similar range of contributions to *Ecumene*, in each case extending from traditional studies of the visible form and MORPHOLOGY of cultural landscapes or the environmental impact of material cultural practices, to newer themes such as the representation of space and spatialities in literature, ICONOGRAPHIC interpretations of topographic forms, memorialization in landscape and cultural hybridity and identity formation in the context of globalization.

New cultural geography has responded to an increasingly self-conscious CULTURAL POLITICS within contemporary social life, especially that of globalized western cities with their vibrantly mixed and hybrid populations, and to the growing demands from formerly SUBALTERN groups that 'voices' formerly excluded from consideration should find expression and effect. The view of culture as a relatively uniform and normative set of beliefs, values, attitudes, behaviours and artefacts has been revealed as sectionally biased by GENDER, CLASS, ETHNICITY, age and bodily facility (cf. DISABILITY, GEOGRAPHY AND) in favour of specific groups, with a consequent shift in the geographies of culture and the cultural questions to be addressed by geographers. Since 1993, the journal *Gender, Place and Culture* has been a forum for research on gender-connected questions in cultural geography. Like *Ecumene*, the journal does not confine its contributions to geography, but is actively interdisciplinary within the scope of Cultural Studies, which themselves have shown increased sensitivity to matters of space and geographical context. At the same time, the vastly increased significance of CONSUMPTION as an activity shaping individual and social life in the modern world allows growing numbers of individuals increased freedom to shape and reshape their identities in different times and places, for example through bodily appearance, SEXUALITY, FOOD or fashion choices, taste in MUSIC, entertainment or lifestyle, and to form voluntary associations with others who share such cultural identity. While geographically uneven in their impacts and socially unequal in their consequences, these same processes have led to increased transgression of cultural boundaries previously regarded as relatively fixed in space and stable over time and a growing experience and recognition of cultural HYBRIDITY. Cultural geography thus engages with transgressive and hybrid spaces in which cultures are negotiated, fluid and permeable, for example those of HOMELESS, transient, sexually transgressive or post-NATIONALIST groups whose spatialities may be quite liminal within the dominant cultural realms previously the focus of geographical concern (Bell and Valentine, 1995; Pile and Thrift, 1995; Cresswell, 1996). Inevitably, such attributes to culture in the contemporary world have stimulated re-evaluation of past cultural geographies too, so that HISTORICAL GEOGRAPHY has also strongly embraced the 'cultural turn'. This has involved recognizing the contextual, provisional and representational nature of historical sources, stimulating ICONOGRAPHIC analysis of past places and landscapes and their representation, especially in maps, thus revitalizing the history of CARTOGRAPHY. Emphasis on 'cultures of history' has led to studies of public memory and heritage and some replacement of historical geography by 'geographies of the past' (cf. MONUMENTS). Geographers' re-evaluations of past cultural geographies have also been profoundly influenced by post-colonial theory, drawing upon ideas of 'ORIENTALISM,' 'IMAGINATIVE GEOGRAPHIES,' and 'TRANSCULTURATION' (Pratt, 1992) to complicate traditional narratives of cultural dominance and succession during the period of western IMPERIAL expansion (Driver, 1992; Gregory, 1994, 1995).

It could almost be argued that the 'cultural turn' and the influence of postmodernism have so impacted upon human geography that 'all is cultural now'. Some indeed have expressed concern that through its emphasis on cultural interpretation HUMAN GEOGRAPHY risks losing sight of its former explicit concerns with economic, political and social questions. Yet contemporary trends in economy and society such as GLOBALIZATION, bringing peoples into ever closer and more immediate contact with one another, the growth and economic significance of such 'culture industries' as advertising, the arts, sport and media in many economies, the social impacts of virtual space and information technologies, and the end of GEOPOLITICAL domination by socio-economic IDEOLOGIES, have all contributed to a material increase in the significance of cultural matters within human affairs at the turn of the millennium and account for the significant increase of interest in geographical questions of space, PLACE and TERRITORIALITY within Cultural Studies more broadly, promoting a two-way exchange of ideas and findings with cultural geography. Formal recognition by the International Geographical Union of the renewed significance of cultural geography was signalled in 1996 by the establishment of a Study Group to promote international scholarship in this area. The current pertinence of cultural questions in all parts of the world, for example in a western Europe dealing with issues of unification, non-European immigration and multicultural urban society (Claval, 1995), a former communist Eastern bloc dealing with revived ethnic Nationalism, or Islamic regions facing cultural critiques of modernity from religious groups, provides ample justification for this move, and evidence that cultural geography is a vital and productive expression of current geographical imagination and concern. DEC

References

Bell, D. and Valentine, G., eds, 1995: *Mapping desire: geographies of sexualities*. London and New York: Routledge. · Claval, P. 1995: *La géographie culturelle*. Paris: Nathan. · Cosgrove, D. 1983: Towards a radical cultural geography: problems of theory *Antipode* 15: 1–11. · Cosgrove, D. and Jackson, P. 1987: New directions in cultural geography. *Area* 19: 95–101. · Cresswell, T. 1996: *In place, out of place: geography, ideology and transgression*. Minneapolis and London: University of Minnesota Press. · Demeritt, D. 1994: The nature of metaphors in cultural geography and environmental history. *Progress in Human Geography* 18: 163–85. · Driver, F. 1992: Geography's empire: histories of geographical knowledge; *Environment and Planning D: Society and Space* 10: 23–40. · Duncan, J. 1994: After the civil war: reconstructing cultural geography as heterotopia. In K. Foote et al., eds, *Re-reading cultural geography*, Austin: University of Texas Press, 401–8. · Foote, K.,

Hugill, P., Mathewson, K. and Smith, J., eds, 1994: *Rereading cultural geography*, Austin: University of Texas Press. · Glacken, C. 1967: *Traces on the Rhodian shore: nature and culture in western thought from ancient times to the end of the eighteenth century*. Berkeley and Los Angeles: University of California Press. · Gregory, D. 1994: *Geographical imaginations*. Cambridge, MA and Oxford: Blackwell. · Gregory, D. 1995: Imaginative geographies. *Progress in Human Geography* 19: 447–85. · Harris, C. 1996: *The resettlement of British Columbia: essays on colonialism and geographical change*. Vancouver: University of British Columbia Press. · Latour, B. 1993: *We have never been modern*. New York and London: Harvester Wheatsheaf. · Leighly, J. 1963. *Land and life: a selection from the writings of Carl Ortwin Sauer*. Berkeley and Los Angeles: University of California Press. · Lewis, M. and Wigen, K. 1997: *The myth of continents: a critique of metageography*. Berkeley and London: University of California Press. · Livingstone, D. 1992: *The geographical tradition: episodes in the history of a contested enterprise*. Oxford: Blackwell. · Pile, S. and Thrift, N. 1995: *Mapping the subject: geographies of cultural transformation*. London and New York: Routledge. · Pratt. M. 1992 : *Imperial eyes: studies in travel writing and transculturation*. London and New York: Routledge. · Price, M. and Lewis, M. 1993: The reinvention of cultural geography. *Annals, Association of American Geographers* 83: 1–17. · Roberts, N. 1998 [1989]: *The Holocene: an environmental history*, 2nd edn. Oxford: Blackwell. · Simmons, I.G. 1989: *Changing the face of the earth: culture, environment, history*. Oxford: Blackwell. · Thomas, W.L. 1956: *Man's role in changing the face of the earth*. Chicago: University of Chicago Press. · Turner, B.L. II et al., eds, 1990: *The earth as transformed by human action: global and regional changes in the biosphere over the past 300 years*. Cambridge: Cambridge University Press. · Wagner, P. 1972: *Environments and peoples. Foundations of cultural geography series*. Englewood Cliffs, NJ: Prentice-Hall. · Wagner, P. and Mikesell, M., eds, 1962: *Readings in Cultural Geography*. Chicago and London: University of Chicago Press.

Reading:

Duncan, J. and Ley, D., eds, 1993: *Place/Culture/Representation*. London: Routledge. · Claval (1995). · Cresswell (1996). · Foote et al. (1994). · Pile and Thrift (1995).

cultural hearth The area of origin of a cultural group involved in creating a CULTURAL LANDSCAPE. The concept is associated with Carl Sauer (1969) and the BERKELEY SCHOOL: the hearth is the core area in a DIFFUSION process whereby new cultural practices are spread, through HUMAN AGENCY, to create new cultural regions. Sauer (1952) argued that cultural hearths emerge through a combination of especially favourable circumstances, reflecting the local natural resources, and that such locations were very few, and hence of critical importance in the evolution of cultural landscapes:

> In the history of man, unless I misread it greatly, diffusion of ideas from a few hearths has been the rule: independent, parallel invention the exception.

RJJ

References

Sauer, C.O. 1952: *Agricultural origins and dispersal*. New York: American Geographical Society. · Sauer, C.O. 1969: *Seeds, spades, hearths and herds: the domestication of animals and foodstuffs*. Cambridge, MA: The MIT Press.

cultural landscape Conventionally, a principal object of study in CULTURAL GEOGRAPHY and still the subject of intense debate among cultural geographers; the classic definition is Carl Sauer's (1925; see the figure):

> The cultural landscape is fashioned from a natural landscape by a cultural group. Culture is the agent, the natural area the medium, the cultural landscape is the result. Under the influence of a given culture, itself changing through time, the landscape undergoes development, passing through phases, and probably reaching ultimately the end of its cycle of development. With the introduction of a different – that is – alien culture, a rejuvenation of the cultural landscape sets in, or a new landscape is superimposed on remnants of an older one.

Several aspects of this frequently quoted passage are worth examining, for they reflect not only the intellectual context in which Sauer was working and his own scholarly concerns, but also theoretical issues which have remained critical to discussions of cultural landscape to the present.

There is a clear parallel in conceptual language between Sauer's description of cultural landscape as subject to evolutionary change over time, and W.M Davis's normal cycle of natural landscape evolution (Livingstone, 1992). Each scholar was strongly influenced by biological and ecological metaphors then current in the American academy. But Sauer was explicitly concerned to counter an ENVIRONMENTAL DETERMINISM which had dominated the American geography of Davis's generation, within which HUMAN AGENCY was given scant autonomy in the shaping of the visible landscape. Sauer was determined to stress the agency of CULTURE as a force in shaping the visible features of the Earth's surface in delimited areas, and his own landscape studies and methods came to dominate the BERKELEY SCHOOL of cultural geography. Yet the physical environment retains within his definition a central significance, as the medium with and through which human cultures act (see CULTURE AREA). Thus, elements of the physical environment, such as topography, soils, watercourses, plants and animals are to

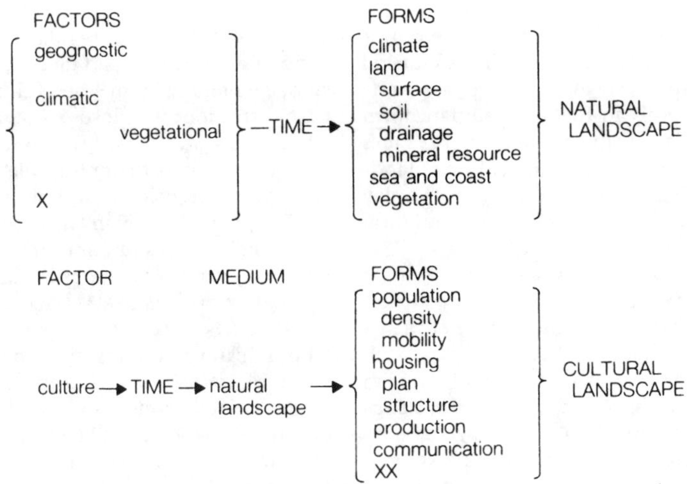

cultural landscape *Natural landscape and cultural landscape* (after Sauer, 1925)

be incorporated into studies of the cultural landscape insofar as they evoke human responses and adaptations, or have themselves been altered by human activity, for example forest clearance, hydrological management or plant and animal domestication (cf. ANIMALS, GEOGRAPHY OF). Sauer's definition is grounded in a neat distinction between NATURE and culture, reflected in the structure of his diagram, a distinction which few cultural geographers would be so willing to uphold or defend today. Not only is there broad acceptance that the *tabula rasa* of 'natural landscape' upon which 'culture' inscribes itself has probably never existed, since its own features are subject to constant change through geophysical, climatic, hydrological and other processes of change, but 'nature' itself and the boundaries which separate it from the human are culturally contrived in radically different ways by different groups in different historical contexts (Cronon, 1995). Thus, both nature and culture are best regarded together, as co-productions (see CULTURE). All landscapes are thus equally natural landscapes and cultural landscapes, according to the questions we ask of them and the processes we choose to examine in relation to them. It is clear also from the model that Sauer laid greatest emphasis on the visible forms of cultural landscape as the principal features for geographic study, as implied also by the term 'MORPHOLOGY' in the title of his essay, and this attention to visible form rather than process has been a matter of some debate in recent discussions of LANDSCAPE and cultural geography.

Sauer's reference to the introduction into a cultural landscape of a different – 'alien' – culture is more than a mere reflection of the Davisian idea of erosional rejuvenation with uplift of physical landscapes, but reflects Sauer's interest in the cultural impacts of COLONIZATION and MODERNIZATION on pre-Columbian cultural landscapes in Hispanic America which manifested visibly the imposition of colonial cultures upon pre-existing cultures, and which many American cultural geographers in the Sauerian tradition have sought to reconstruct. The southwest United States and Mexico, whose stark physical environments have been radically and violently reshaped more than once in recorded historical time by a succession of distinct cultural groups (Native American farmers, Spanish colonial missionaries, Anglo ranchers, water engineers), may offer a more ready medium for Sauer's approach to cultural landscape than the more subtly and slowly modified regions of western Europe or Southeast Asia. More recent studies in CULTURAL ECOLOGY of colonial impacts and exchanges over the past half millennium have deepened our understanding of the complexities of cultural landscape change (Crosby, 1986; Butzer, 1992), while POST-COLONIAL theory has prompted significant re-evaluation of those 'alien' introductions into the existing cultural landscapes, for example in the Pacific North West or Malaysia (Willems-Braun, 1997; Sioh, 1998).

In both these revisions, greater attention is given to 'POLITICAL ECOLOGY' and to the active role played by the subjects of colonization, so that Sauer's idea of a climax cultural landscape swept away by a rejuvenated one and remaining only in relict or remnant form has been replaced by notions of a more mediated, HYBRID and trans-cultural landscape in which various protagonists play active roles in shaping a distinctive cultural geography.

Such studies of cultural landscape may be genealogically related to the Sauerian concept, but they demonstrate also the impact of theoretical criticisms made of the Sauerian model. Writers such as Cosgrove (1992) and Duncan (1990) sought to introduce a more fluid conception of landscape into cultural geography by emphasizing SOCIAL CONSTRUCTION and REPRESENTATION, POWER and contestation as significant considerations. Daniels and Cosgrove (1988, p. 1) claimed that

> a landscape is a cultural image, a pictorial way of representing, structuring or symbolising surroundings. This is not to say that landscapes are immaterial. They may be represented in a variety of materials and on many surfaces – in paint on canvas, in writing on paper, in earth, stone, water and vegetation on the ground.

Here the emphasis remains on the visual character of landscapes, but is not restricted to morphological consideration and visible features: all aspects of landscape are regarded as representational, thus cultural signifiers, the interpretation of which reveals social attitudes and material processes (see ICONOGRAPHY). This approach to cultural landscape draws upon British and European SOCIAL and cultural THEORY with minor concern for ecological and environmental considerations. It also bears comparison with the approach to vernacular cultural landscapes in the United States pioneered by Jackson (1984) and discussed by Meinig (1979), which also emphasized the communicative and representational rather than the ECOLOGICAL aspects of cultural landscapes. A semiotic, and often explicitly political, approach to cultural landscape (Walker, 1995) finds its most extreme expression in the treatment of cultural landscapes as TEXTS and their discursive consideration through the language and methods of literary analysis (Duncan, 1990; Mondada et al., 1992).

Some geographers have been concerned that the emphasis on representational and semiotic qualities of landscape has led to the disappearance of the 'substantive' aspects of landscape, its materialities and roots in the LIFEWORLDS of COMMUNITIES whose local attachments and TERRITORIALITIES are regularly expressed in activities and rituals and given distinct expression, remaining a meaningful term in local administration in Nordic countries for example (Olwig, 1996). By contrast, Mitchell (1994) examines the cultural landscape as an expression of colonialist power, referring to landscape as the 'dreamwork of empire' insofar as its picturesque appropriation acted to naturalize massive social and economic inequalities (cf. IMPERIALISM), while Mitchell (1996) makes the same point in terms of labour history, arguing that the visible landscape of California's fruit farms and irrigated fields is mendacious, its visible Arcadian scene obscuring the social and cultural struggles over exploitation of the surplus labour that went into its production. Schein (1997), while seeking to retain the identification of cultural landscape with the 'tangible, visible scene' (Lewis, 1979), draws upon Massey's (1991) idea of places as 'moments' in a continuing networked process of social relations that stretch across space (see SENSE OF PLACE): 'Landscapes are always in the process of "becoming", no longer reified or concretized – inert and there – but continually under scrutiny, at once manipulable, always subject to change, and everywhere implicated in the ongoing formulation of social life' (Schein, 1997, p. 662). This moves beyond the claim that cultural landscapes are purely discursive: they are materialized, as Schein seeks to demonstrate in an examination of an American suburban landscape in Lexington Kentucky.

In the aftermath of often heated debate over the definition and methods for studying cultural landscape within geography, the concept itself has been rejuvenated; a wealth of substantive cultural landscape studies are appearing, and while the genealogy of the Sauerian concept remains fertile, the usage of the term cultural landscape within cultural geography no longer implies filial attachment to a narrow Berkeleyan model. DEC

References

Butzer, K., ed., 1992 The Americas before and after 1492: current geographical research. *Annals, Association of American Geographers* 82: 343–565. · Cosgrove, D. 1992: *The Palladian landscape: geographical change and its cultural representations in sixteenth-century Italy*. Leicester: Leicester University Press. · Cronon, W., ed., 1995: *Uncommon ground: toward reinventing nature*. New York: Norton. · Crosby, W. 1986: *Ecological imperialism: the biological expansion of Europe 900–1900*. Cambridge: Cambridge University Press. · Daniels, S. and Cosgrove, D., eds, 1988: Iconography and landscape. In idem, *The iconography of landscape: essays on the symbolic representation, design and use of past environments*. Cambridge: Cambridge University Press, 1–10. · Duncan, J. 1990: *The city as text: the politics of landscape interpretation in the Kandyan kingdom*. Cambridge: Cambridge University Press. · Jackson, J.B. 1984: *Discovering the vernacular landscape*. New Haven and London: Yale University Press. · Lewis, P. 1979: Axioms for reading the landscape: some guides to the American scene. In D. Meinig, ed., *The interpretation of ordinary landscapes*. Oxford and New York: Oxford University Press, 11–32. · Livingstone, D. 1992: *The geographical tradition: episodes in the history of a contested enterprise*. Oxford: Blackwell. · Massey, D. 1991: A global sense of place. *Marxism Today*, June: 24–29. · Meinig, D. 1979: *The interpretation of ordinary landscapes: geographical essays*. Oxford and New York: Oxford University Press. · Mitchell, D. 1996: *The lie of the land: migrant workers and the California landscape*. Minneapolis: Minnesota University Press. · Mitchell, W.J.T., ed., 1994: Landscape and power. Chicago and London: University of Chicago Press. · Mondada, L., Panese, F., Söderstrom, O., eds, 1992: *Paysage et crise de la lisibilité*. Lausanne: Institut de Géographie. · Olwig, K. 1996: Rediscovering the substantive meaning of landscape. *Annals, Association of American Geographers* 86: 630–53. · Sauer, C. 1925: The morphology of landscape. Reprinted in J. Leighly, ed., 1963: *Land and life: selections from the writings of Carl Ortwin Sauer*. Berkeley and Los Angeles: University of California Press, 315–50. · Schein, R. 1997: The place of landscape: a conceptual framework for the American scene. *Annals, Association of American Geographers* 87: 660–80. · Sioh, M. 1998: Authorising the Malaysian rainforest: *Ecumene* 5: 144–66. · Walker, R. 1995: Landscape and city life: four ecologies of residence in the San Francisco Bay Area. *Ecumene* 2: 33–64. · Willems-Braun B. 1997: Buried epistemologies: the politics of nature in (post)colonial British Columbia. *Annals, Association of American Geographers* 87: 3–31.

Suggested Reading

Béguin, H. 1995: *Le paysage*. Paris: Flammarion. · Olwig (1996). · Schein (1997).

cultural politics Deriving from the interdisciplinary field of cultural studies, 'cultural politics' refers to the complex processes through which meanings are constructed and negotiated and to the analysis of how relations of dominance and subordination are defined and contested. Rather than separating 'culture' from 'politics', the term insists that the cultural *is* political in the sense that cultural distinctions are rarely made on purely aesthetic grounds but frequently involve conflicting material interests. This politicization of CULTURE has been accompanied by the rise of IDENTITY POLITICS whereby various forms of social DIFFERENCE have formed the basis for political mobilization. New SOCIAL MOVEMENTS (including feminism, anti-RACISM, gay rights and environmental protest: cf. FEMINIST GEOGRAPHIES) have arisen alongside social CLASS as the basis for political action (e.g. Hall and Jacques, 1989; hooks, 1990).

Cultural politics refers to the abstract *maps of meaning* (Jackson, 1992) through which people make sense of the world, attaching value and significance to their material and social environment, and to the ways that those abstractions are objectified in concrete social practices and spatial forms (Hall and Henderson, 1977, p. 10). The term demands a plural definition of culture as 'whole ways of life' associated with various forms of social difference, including those that are articulated through RACE, GENDER and SEXUALITY. Cultural politics draws attention to the diverse ways that cultural constructions help to perpetuate inequalities of POWER within society. Geographical interest in 'cultural politics' coincided with the wider CULTURAL TURN in the social sciences and the humanities, focusing on questions of REPRESENTATION and identity, particularly in relation to the politics of PLACE and SPACE (Duncan and Ley, 1993; Keith and Pile, 1993). In turn, geographers have made other social scientists more aware of the role of space and place in the constitution of social life (Bird et al., 1993; Carter et al., 1993). PAJ

References

Bird, J., Curtis, B., Putnam, T., Robertson, G. and Tickner, L., eds, 1993: *Mapping the futures: local culture, global change*. London: Routledge. · Carter, E., Donald, J. and Squires, J., eds, 1993: *Space and place: theories of identity and location*. London: Lawrence and Wishart. · Duncan, J. and Ley, D., eds, 1993: *Place/culture/representation*. London: Routledge. · Hall, S. and Henderson, J., eds, 1977: *Resistance through rituals*. London: Hutchinson/Centre for Contemporary Cultural Studies. · Hall, S. and Jacques, M. eds, 1989: *New times: the changing face of politics in the 1980s*. London: Lawrence and Wishart; hooks, b. 1990: *Yearning: race, gender, and cultural politics*. Toronto: Between the Lines. · Jackson, P. 1992. *Maps of meaning*. London: Routledge. · Keith, M. and Pile, S., eds, 1993: *Place and the politics of identity*. London: Routledge.

cultural turn An intellectual shift which has brought questions of CULTURE to the forefront of contemporary debates within both human geography and the human sciences more generally.

Within geography, this notion of a cultural turn has been used in three interrelated ways (see also Chaney, 1994, for a parallel view from Sociology).

First, it has signalled and promoted shifting disciplinary landscapes. At the sub-disciplinary level it highlights the growth of CULTURAL GEOGRAPHY over the last decade, especially pronounced in British geography, and its intellectual influence within the discipline more generally. At the super-disciplinary level it points to the emergence of Cultural Studies as a vibrant trans-disciplinary nexus of intellectual inspiration and debate (for a history of Cultural Studies see Brantlinger, 1990; for a sense of its remit and intellectual styles see Grossberg et al., 1994; and for an example of Cultural Studies writings on geographical issues see Carter et al., 1993).

Secondly, a cultural turn has been diagnosed on the basis of the growing preoccupation with culture-related concepts across all the sub-disciplines of human geography. This is seen as a shift from the focus on issues of POLITICAL ECONOMY that emerged strongly in the 1970s and became dominant in the human geography of the 1980s. Geographers' definitions and conceptualizations of cultural processes have always been complex and contested (see CULTURAL POLITICS), and hence a number of different notions of culture have been turned to. Nonetheless, some concerns have been seen as especially symptomatic of a cultural turn, including emphases on the discursive constitution of social life (see DISCOURSE), geographical REPRESENTATION, IMAGINATIVE GEOGRAPHIES, identity and IDENTITY POLITICS, and the embedding of all human activities (whether economic, political, medical, demographic or whatever) within culturally differentiated ways of life.

Thirdly, a cultural turn has been identified beyond the academy, in so far as the intellectual preoccupation with questions of culture is related to wider transformations that make culture a pressing concern in the contemporary world. For example, ECONOMIC GEOGRAPHY has examined so-called 'cultural industries' on the basis of their role within informational and service-based advanced capitalist economies (for an example see Sadler, 1997); and more generally RADICAL GEOGRAPHY has been influenced by a shift in radical political culture away from broadly Marxist emancipatory CLASS politics towards identity-based, post-colonial and environmental social movements (see IDENTITY POLITICS; POST-COLONIALISM and ENVIRONMENTAL MOVEMENT).

In assessing these developments, some human geographers have welcomed the cultural turn, arguing that it rectifies a prior neglect of the cultural dimensions of social, economic and political processes (for an example of this argument see Jackson, 1991 on urban and regional studies). Others, however, view it as deeply problematic, especially insofar as it leads to the abandonment of many of the strengths of the political-economic approaches previously dominant within human geography (see, for example, Sayer, 1994; and for a less apocalyptic assessment, Barnes, 1995).

In order to move beyond this stalemate of polarized assessments of gains and losses it is perhaps helpful to scrutinize critically the very notion of a 'cultural turn'. For instance, it should already be apparent that it operates as a shorthand description for a vast number of different and sometimes incommensurable trends within human geography, united only by their diverse appeals to concepts of culture and to the intellectual field of cultural studies. The cultural turn is not a coherent theoretical development within the subject. Instead it has both evoked and shaped looser shifts in subject matters, approaches, sub-disciplinary and inter-disciplinary affiliations, and intellectual politics. Therefore, just what it is that is cultural about these cultural turns needs to be unpacked, disaggregated and explicitly debated by proponents and opponents alike. Failure to do this runs the dangers of either over-simplifying the intellectual shifts occurring and/or increasingly moulding them into simplistic and under-theorized forms (Barnett, 1998).

Moreover, the idea of an intellectual 'turn' needs just as much unpacking as its 'cultural' destination. Implicit within it is often a very particular mapping of intellectual space, structured in terms of distinct areas of concern: the cultural, the economic, the political, the social and so on. Thus, advocates praise a turn to the cultural, and critics lament the turning away from these other areas of enquiry. Underlying this is a definition of the cultural in opposition to other intellectual concerns and realms of life. However, this emphasis on oppositional definition – for example the cultural as meaningful, imaginative, and intrinsically valuable in contrast to the economic as material, real, and instrumentally essential – actually runs counter to much of the best work on cultural processes, which emphasizes the transcendence of such dichotomies (Crang, 1997). In consequence, it would perhaps be more profitable to pursue the cultural turn not as an absolute change in the direction and destination of geographical inquiry – a turn away from the 'non-cultural', whatever that might be – but as a complex and varied set of changes in human geographers' means of transport, travelling companions and favourite guidebooks.

In summary, the cultural turn is a shorthand highlighting how human geography in the 1990s has seen a number of attempts to address the neglect of cultural processes apparent in the political-economic approaches of the 1980s. Any assessment of these attempts to enculturate human geography, however, is better made in terms of the qualities of the more specific developments referred to by the cultural turn rubric, rather than through summary judgments on the cultural turn *in toto*. PC

References

Barnes, T.J. 1995: Political economy 1: the culture, stupid. *Progress in Human Geography* 19: 423–31. · Barnett, C. 1998: Cultural twists and turns. *Environment and Planning D: Society and Space* 16: 631–4. · Brantlinger, P. 1990: *Crusoe's footprints: cultural studies in Britain and America*. London: Routledge. · Carter, E., Donald, J. and Squires, J., eds, 1993: *Space and place: theories of identity and location*. London: Lawrence and Wishart. · Chaney, D. 1994: *The cultural turn: scene-setting essays on cultural history*. London: Routledge. · Crang, P. 1997: Cultural turns and the (re)constitution of economic geography. In R. Lee and J. Wills, eds, *Geographies of economies*. London: Arnold, 3–15. · Grossberg, L., Nelson, C. and Treichler, P., eds, 1994: *Cultural studies*. New York: Routledge. · Jackson, P. 1991: Mapping meanings: a cultural critique of locality studies. *Environment and Planning A* 23: 215–28. · Sadler, D. 1997: The global music business as an information industry: reinterpreting economies of culture. *Environment and Planning A* 29: 1919–36. · Sayer, A. 1994: Cultural studies and 'the economy, stupid'. *Environment and Planning D: Society and Space* 12, 635–7.

culture A complex and increasingly important concept within the humanities and social sciences, it is widely recognized that culture is best understood contextually and historically. It is broadly accepted that the idea of a 'superorganic' culture as an active force, working through people and possessing existence or agency beyond its specific and contingent historical and geographical expressions, is untenable. However, to restrict cultural expressions to discourse and textuality alone or narrowing their scope to the exercise and contestation of power, as Mitchell (1995) has suggested, seems unduly to confine the purchase of the concept.

The British literary critic Raymond Williams (1976), whose writing strongly influenced critical CULTURAL GEOGRAPHY, attributed the contemporary meaning of 'culture' in popular usage to the social context of eighteenth-century ENLIGHTENMENT, pointing out that its meaning has evolved over historic time, and in close connection with processes of MODERNIZATION. Initially, culture referred to skilled human activities through which non-human nature is encompassed and transformed. Thus *agri*-culture, *horti*-culture, *viti*-culture and *api*-culture, for example, refer to domestication and productive human use of fields, gardens, grape vines and bees respectively. Contact between Europeans and 'other' peoples whose technological skills and modes of life displayed differences from their own, allowed the term culture to be applied to human groups themselves as in 'Carib culture' or 'primitive culture', thus making culture a term of human *difference* and differentiation. Enlightenment belief in human progress prompted attribution of such culture to the human mind itself. Thus 'natural' human conduct could be cultivated, as it were, through 'civilizing' acts, so that the childish or uncouth mind was believed to progress from an aboriginal, 'wild' state of nature and become progressively cultured. Finally 'culture' came to be applied to the activities themselves deemed necessary or helpful in producing this cultivation of human sensibility and conduct, thus to fine art, music, poetry, literature and dance, for example (cf. PERFORMANCE). Culture therefore became attached to 'the human spirit' and appropriated as a mark of refinement: 'cultural capital', available for exploitation in struggles for status. This is the idea of culture that famously impelled the fascist Hermann Goering to reach for his revolver. This semantic history helps clarify many of the debates that have circulated around culture within Human Geography.

A primary and consistent dimension of culture's conceptual history is its opposition to NATURE. Indeed, it is arguable that these two concepts can meaningfully exist only within a dialectical relationship; neither can denote without the other's opposition. FEMINIST writers have been to the fore in pointing out that this opposition has strong GENDER correlates in the western intellectual tradition, in that Nature is conventionally feminized and rendered passive to an active, male-gendered Culture, and each term thereby is differently evaluated according to PATRIARCHAL assumptions which privilege the latter over the former (Merchant, 1980; Haraway, 1991; Nesmith and Radcliffe, 1993; cf. ECOFEMINISM; PHALLOCENTRISM). Recent thinkers both within geography and beyond have sought to challenge such an opposition, on theoretical, political and substantive grounds. Theoretically, boundaries between nature and culture cannot be sustained when physical human activities are the materialized outcomes of mental acts which are themselves increasingly explicable neurologically and biologically (undermining any remaining belief in the idea of an immaterial human 'spirit' which underpinned the nineteenth-century meaning of culture), and when nature can become known to us only within and through discourse, and thus is always cultural (Demeritt, 1994; Castree, 1995; Willems-Braun, 1997). Politically, the POWER and authority implications of such conventional gendering of nature and culture are increasingly unacceptable, while substantively many have pointed out that late twentieth-century technologies such as robotics, virtual reality, genetic engineering and organ transplantation have materially disrupted any boundaries between nature and culture – even within the human body itself (Light, 1997; cf. BODY, GEOGRAPHY AND). In response to this recognition, a number of writers have reached for concepts which acknowledge the collapse of a nature/culture DIALECTIC, for example HYBRIDITY and 'natures-cultures' (Haraway, 1991; Latour, 1993), and studied spaces and places where neat divisions of nature and culture are problematized, for example the zoo (Anderson, 1995), natural parks (Neumann, 1995) and computer-simulated WILDERNESS areas (cf. ANIMALS, GEOGRAPHY OF).

A second important dimension of culture's conceptual evolution is its association with ETHNOGRAPHIC interest in 'OTHER' peoples. Closely connected with the nature and gender DISCOURSES discussed above has been the consistent COLONIALIST use of culture as a strategy of differentiation wherein non-European peoples whose modes of life diverge from those familiar to westerners have been characterized as having different and implicitly inferior (because more 'natural') cultures. The cultural sciences of Ethnography and Anthropology, and through their influence much of CULTURAL GEOGRAPHY, were founded on such assumptions which were widely popularized by such publications as *National Geographic Magazine* (Lutz and Collins, 1993). Peoples were regarded as having distinct 'cultures' which could be described morphologically, explained functionally or structurally, and represented disinterestedly in texts and images. Geography's task was to relate these cultures to the physical environments in which they had evolved. By the same reasoning, the lifeways of spatially or socially marginalized groups within western societies could be described as 'sub'-cultures, within an implicit (and often explicit) hierarchy which reflected the mobilization of cultural capital within social negotiation for status, esteem and material resources. Such considerations lie behind geographical studies of elite and popular, dominant and SUBALTERN, establishment and marginal cultures. These have often operated within a formulation of culture as a field of political contestation between defined human groups, coming to consciousness through their experience of shared productive activity, a formulation which draws upon Hegelian and Marxian notions of collective consciousness, rooted in the same Enlightenment thinking as the culture/nature dialectic itself.

The ultimate historical refinement of the concept of culture which attached it to artistic and associated intellectual activities, initially restricted to a canon of 'official' culture such as opera, oil painting, sculpture, epic poetry and Classical literature, also finds expression within geographical usage. Interpreting geographical meaning and expression in cultural products is a well-established procedure within Human Geography, characteristically using ICONOGRAPHY and other HERMENEUTIC methods. In HUMANISTIC GEOGRAPHY there is often an implicit assumption that such studies allow access to some essential features of the human attachment to PLACE or LANDSCAPE and these have characteristically concentrated in the fields of 'high culture' (Cosgrove and Daniels, 1988), whereas a more explicitly critical approach to interpreting cultural productions and activities has tended to concentrate on more popular expressions such as television soap operas, advertising, graffiti, popular music and community arts, adopting the terminology of CULTURAL POLITICS: power, resistance, conflict (Miller, 1991; Leyshon, Matless and Revill, 1995; Thornton, 1995).

Cultural geography traditionally paid attention primarily to *material culture*, as opposed to the social heritage of collective mental and spiritual products and expressive forms of human conduct. Explicit theorizing of culture was rare in geography as elsewhere during a time when the western, patriarchal norm of culture seemed secure. Thus geographers in the traditions of cultural study developed by Carl Sauer, Paul Vidal de la Blache, H.J. Fleure and Estyn Evans concentrated on relations between apparently static folkways and the physical environments in which they were to be observed, placing emphasis on their visible expressions in LANDSCAPE (see CULTURAL

LANDSCAPE). In the post-war years geographical concentration on economy as foundational in social explanation rendered culture a weak and epiphenomenal concept in studies of human occupance, although Sauer, the most influential English-language geographer writing on culture until the 1970s, recognized that even market ECONOMIES are culturally encompassed (Sauer, 1941). Collapse of faith in economistic explanation as part of a general dissolution of MODERNITY has yielded a concentration on how power and authority are negotiated between human individuals and groups. Within this framework, all human activities may be regarded as mobilized within a constant struggle for differentiation, recognition and status between individuals and groups, and thus cultural. Activities and productions falling within the traditional domain of culture come to be seen as active within social reproduction, the negotiated process and product of the discourses through which humans signify themselves, their experiences, their desires and projects. Thus the realm of culture is extended well beyond the conventional canons of cultural concern and threatens to encompass all human geography, in the opinion of some, dulling the conceptual edge of culture as a useful analytic concept.

The breadth and penetration of culture and cultural questions within human geography today is exemplified by their appearance in specialized sub-fields formerly dominated by economic, social and political theory, such as URBAN STUDIES and ECONOMIC GEOGRAPHY. Themes such as 'selling the city', urban 'aura' and urban-architectural aesthetics or the role of cultural production and cultures of production in urban economic life and regional regeneration, vie with analyses of land rent distributions or household formation in research journals (Harvey, 1989; Imrie, 1996). In DEVELOPMENT GEOGRAPHY, attention to local needs and SUSTAINABILITY has placed emphasis on cultural reception of modernity and outside interventions or plans. These examples reflect significant features of culture within contemporary life. One is the dominance of CONSUMPTION in post-industrial economies whose flexible production modes and labour demands have reduced the need for large, locally based and stable workforces whose association in and with production promoted a degree of solidarity which found expression in shared LIFEWORLDS (cultures), while simultaneously promoting among employees who may move through many different activities over the course of a working life, a more self-conscious and individualized choice of self-representation through customized acts of consumption. The phenomenon is intimately connected to GLOBALIZATION, the complex processes whereby production and consumption and the modes of existence and experience they generate serve to undermine some aspects of local cultural distinctiveness, while reinforcing others. Global culture finds its most immediate expression in forms of commercialized consumption, such as Coca Cola, Disney, MacDonald's, popular MUSIC, dress fashions and cosmetics (Morley and Robins, 1995). The phenomenon has generated a renewed interest in questions of material culture, stimulated by the enormously expanded role in advanced economies of what the Frankfurt school of cultural criticism called the 'cultural' industries: those commercial activities catering to the leisure and recreational demands formerly associated with culture as the 'cultivation' of mind and body. Thus, employment in such activities as television, media, music, sports and the 'arts' expands to occupy ever greater numbers of people in advanced economies, while activities such as agriculture or manufacturing industry, in which humans undertake the oldest cultural activities of transforming the natural world, contract. In less developed regions and economies, in the aftermath of the Cold War and in the context of globalization, increased attention is widely given (even if only RHETORICALLY) to the rights and responsibilities of local groups and COMMUNITIES to formulate their own ways of shaping their environments and futures, both on moral and on practical grounds. This means increased attention to local customs and traditions, and thus again to the realm of culture. Culture's dominance in contemporary geographical study is thus a response to actual changes in material life. But the apparent emphasis on voluntaristic human agency which the turn to culture within geography has produced has led some to challenge its apparent theoretical reification as an active agent in social processes (Mitchell, 1995), and others to call for a refocus upon structural constraints upon human activity which would make culture more a product rather than a process within geographical explanation. DEC

References

Anderson, K. 1995: Culture and nature at the Adelaide Zoo: at the frontiers of 'human' geography. *Transactions, Institute of British Geographers* NS 20: 275–94. · Castree, N. 1995: The nature of produced natures: materiality and knowledge construction in Marxism. *Antipode* 27: 12–48. · Cosgrove, D. and Daniels, S., eds, 1988: *The iconography of landscape: essays on the symbolic representation, design and use of past environments.* Cambridge: Cambridge University Press. · Demeritt, D. 1994: The nature of metaphors in cultural geography and environmental history. *Progress in Human Geography* 18: 163–85. · Haraway, D. 1991: *Simians, cyborgs and women: the reinvention of nature.* London: Free Association. · Harvey, D. 1989: *The condition of postmodernity: an enquiry into the origins of cultural change.* Oxford: Blackwell. · Imrie, R. 1996: Ableist geographers, disabled spaces. *Transactions, Institute of British Geographers* 21: 397–403. · Latour, B. 1993: *We have never been modern.* New York: Harvester Wheatsheaf. · Leyshon, A., Matless D. and Revill, G. 1995: The place of music. *Transactions, Institute of British Geographers* NS 20: 423–33. · Light, J. 1997: The changing nature of nature. *Ecumene* 4: 181–95. · Lutz, C. and Collins J. 1993: *Reading National Geographic.* Chicago and London: University of Chicago Press. · Merchant, C. 1980: *The death of nature: women, ecology and the scientific revolution.* New York: Harper and Row. · Miller, R. 1991: Selling Mrs. Consumer: advertising and the creation of suburban socio-spatial relations 1910–1930. *Antipode* 23: 263–301. · Mitchell, D. 1995: There's no such thing as culture: towards a reconceptualization of the idea of culture in geography. *Transactions, Institute of British Geographers* NS 20: 102–16. · Morley, D. and Robins, K. 1995: *Spaces of identity: global media, electronic landscapes and cultural boundaries.* London and New York: Routledge. · Nesmith, C. and Radcliffe, S. 1993: (Re)mapping Mother Earth: a geographical perspective on environmental feminisms. *Environment and Planning D: Society and Space* 11: 379–94. · Neumann, R. 1995: Ways of seeing Africa: colonial recasting of African society and landscape in the Serengeti National Park. *Ecumene* 2: 149–69. · Sauer, C.O. 1941: Foreword to historical geography. Reprinted in J. Leighley, ed., *Land and life: selections from the writings of Carl Ortwin Sauer.* Berkeley and Los Angeles: California University Press, 351–79. · Thornton, S. 1995: *Club cultures.* London: Routledge. · Willems-Braun, B. 1997: Buried epistemologies: the politics of nature in (post)colonial British Columbia. *Annals, Association of American Geographers* 87: 3–31. · Williams, R. 1976: *Keywords: a vocabulary of culture and society.* London: Croom Helm.

Suggested Reading

Williams (1976). · Mitchell (1995). · Morley and Robins (1995).

culture area A concept derived from CULTURAL ECOLOGY, referring to the geographical REGION over which a degree of homogeneity in measurable cultural traits may be identified (see also CULTURE). The concept's origins lie in Ratzel's notions of a *Kulturprovinz,* and to the concern among German geographers in the late nineteenth and early twentieth centuries to delimit the boundaries of the German *Reich* by means of such cultural indicators as LANGUAGE, settlement form, and *LANDSCHAFT.* The influence of German geographic thought on inter-war American anthropological and geographical studies of native American cultures (Benedict, 1935), seeking to differentiate these groups CARTOGRAPHICALLY, brought the concept into Anglophone geography. Recognizing the absence in such cases of clear boundaries similar to those between NATION-STATES, students using the culture area concept frequently subclassified them into three contiguous zones:

- the *core,* the area over which the culture in question has exclusive or quasi-exclusive influence;
- the *domain,* over which the identifying traits are dominant but not exclusive; and the *realm,* over which such traits may be found but in which they are sub-dominant to those of other culture groups.

A classic example of such study is Meinig's (1965) identification of a Mormon culture area centred on the Great Basin of Utah. The organismic dimension given to the original concept by Ratzel's biologically based ENVIRONMENTAL DETERMINISM, and notions of expansion and conflict between culture areas struggling for life are absent from such MORPHOLOGICAL studies (Jordan, 1973).

Today the concept of culture area is little used in its classic form as culture is identified much more with process, connection and network than with areal extent, and because geographical interest has turned from questions of homogeneity and bounding of cultures towards those of connections, interaction and contestation between groups for whom culture is a mode of self-signification, and to matters of transculturation and cultural HYBRIDITY. Such questions neither assume a necessary connection between culture and TERRITORY nor lend themselves to the cartographic CORRELATION techniques which underpinned the concept of culture area, although the horrors of 'ETHNIC CLEANSING' during the Bosnian War of the early 1990s, when different religious and NATIONALIST groups sought to produce homogeneous culture areas through warfare, civil violence and forced MIGRATION, demonstrate the continued power of blood-soil attachments in certain contexts. Studies of other contemporary cultural conflicts, such as that in Northern Ireland (Graham, 1994), have examined the use of visible LANDSCAPE markers such as graffiti, flags and murals to identify and claim defined areas for culturally defined groups (cf. TERRITORIALITY). In a less directly conflictual context, small, mainly urban, areas dominated by specific sub-cultural lifestyles, such as COMMUNITIES based on ETHNICITY or SEXUALITY, have been examined in San Francisco and London (Forest, 1997), and artificially delimited parts of metropolitan cities where an *erzatz* culture is officially celebrated, such as Chinatowns (Anderson and Gale, 1992), have attracted the attention of CULTURAL GEOGRAPHERS. Although the term culture area may be absent in such studies, they often use visible landscape indicators to record the existence, extent and changing nature of such areas, as for example David Ley's discussion of the fate of suburban sequoias in Vancouver as traditionally Anglo-dominated streets passed to new Asian owners (Ley, 1995). DEC

References

Anderson, K. and Gale, F., eds, 1992: *Inventing places: studies in cultural geography*. London: Longman Cheshire. · Benedict, R. 1935: *Patterns of culture*. London: Routledge. · Forest, B. 1997: West Hollywood as symbol: the significance of place in the construction of gay identity. In L. McDowell, ed., *Undoing place? a geographical reader*. London: Arnold, 112–30. · Graham, B. 1994: No place of the mind: contested Protestant representations of Ulster. *Ecumene* 1: 257–81. · Jordan, T. 1973: *The European culture area: a systematic geography*. New York and London: Harper and Row. · Ley. D. 1995: Between Europe and Asia: the case of the missing sequoias. *Ecumene* 2: 185–210. · Meinig, D. 1965: The Mormon culture region: strategies and patterns in the American West. *Annals, Association of American Geographers* 55: 191–220.

cyberspace Alternative worlds generated by computers. The term cyberspace was first used quite casually by the science fiction writer, William Gibson, in his 1984 novel, *Neuromancer* (Gibson, 1984: see also Gibson 1986, 1988). In the book, cyberspace was a there that was not there, an alternative world conjured up by a computer in which people could cruise like disembodied spirits amongst virtual computer-generated landscapes; 'all the data in the world stacked up like one big neon city, so that you could cruise around and have a kind of grip on it, visually anyway, because if you didn't, it was too complicated, trying to find your way to a particular piece of data you needed' (Gibson, 1988, p. 13). The term rapidly became part of common usage, reflecting more of a cultural longing for such a world than its actual existence (Benedikt, 1992; Bukataman, 1993a, 1993b; Crang and May, 1999). Taken up by an odd alliance of the computer industry, artists, and cultural studies academics, the term has spawned a large number of books and papers which are as likely to be general disquisitions on western society as they are careful empirical studies (see VIRTUAL GEOGRAPHIES). NJT

References

Benedikt, M., ed., 1992: *Cyberspace. First steps*. Cambridge, MA: MIT Press. · Bukatman, S. 1993a: *Terminal identity*. Durham, NC: Duke University Press. · Bukatman, S. 1993b: Gibson's typewriter. *South Atlantic Quarterly* 92: 627–43. · Crang, M. and May, J., eds, 1999: *Virtual geographies*. London: Routledge. · Gibson, W. 1984: *Neuromancer*. New York: Ace Science Fiction. · Gibson, W. 1986: *Count zero*. London: Grafton Books. · Gibson, W. 1988: *Mona Lisa overdrive*. London: Grafton Books.

cyborg A term from science fiction used by Donna Haraway (1985) in her famous paper 'Manifesto for cyborgs: science, technology and socialist-feminism in the 1980s'. Haraway was looking for a METAPHOR that could redefine the potentialities of both embodiment and technology by relating each to the other in more positive way and, for her, 'cyborg' signalled some of the 'ways that the things many feminists have feared most can and must be refigured and put back to work for life not death' (Haraway, 1991, p. 4; see FEMINIST GEOGRAPHY).

The term has since moved into fairly general circulation in fields of research like the study of gender and SEXUALITY, and of technological cultures, as a means of imagining new subject positions which hint at new modes of living together with others (see BODY, GEOGRAPHY AND; SUBJECT FORMATION, GEOGRAPHIES OF). NJT

References

Downey, G., Dumit, J., eds, 1997: *Cyborgs and citadels: anthropological interventions in emerging sciences and technologies*. Santa Fe: School of American Research Press. · Gray, C. H., ed., 1995: *The cyborg handbook*. New York, Routledge. · Haraway, D. 1985: Manifesto for cyborgs: science, technology, and socialist-feminism in the 1980s. *Socialist Review* 80: 65–108 (reprinted in Haraway, 1991 as 'A Cyborg manifesto: science, technology and socialist feminism in the late twentieth century'). · Haraway, D.J. 1991. *Simians, cyborgs and women. The re-invention of nature*. London: Free Association Books. · Haraway, D. 1997: *Modest-Witness@second-millennium. FemaleMan©Meets_OncoMouse TM: Feminism and Technoscience*. New York: Routledge.

Suggested Reading

Pile, S. and Thrift, N.J., eds, 1995: *Mapping the subject. Geographies of cultural transformation*. London: Routledge.

cycle of poverty Self-perpetuating poverty and deprivation transmitted inter-generationally (see figure). Whereas some of the causes of this process lie in a child's home background, others reflect spatial variations in life chances, as with the quality of local schools, the quantity and quality of jobs available locally, health and crime problems in the NEIGHBOURHOOD, and so forth. Thus the cycle of poverty is particularly associated with the INNER CITY in many urban areas. Cycles of poverty operate in a wide variety of contexts, however, both rural and suburban, wherever disadvantaged members of society are concentrated in areas in which the local situation harms their life chances (cf. UNDERCLASS). In some presentations, drawing on the work of Oscar Lewis (e.g. 1969), the victims of the cycle are presented as contributing to their own situation. RJJ

References and Suggested Reading

Lewis, O. 1969: The possessions of the poor. *Scientific American* 221: 114–24. · Rutter, M. and Madge, N. 1976: *Cycles of disadvantage*. London: Heinemann. · Walker A. and Walker, C., eds, 1997: *Britain divided: the growth of social exclusion in the 1980s and 1990s*. London: Child Poverty Action Group.

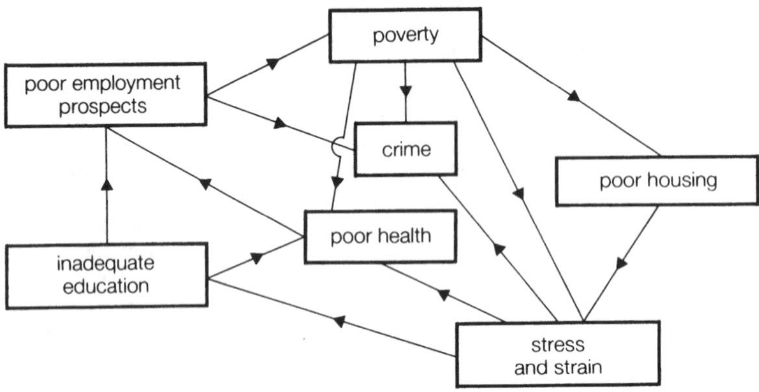

cycle of poverty (after Johnston, 1984)

D

Darwinism While it certainly can be said that Darwinism refers to the version of evolutionary theory originating with Charles Darwin (1809–82), providing any more precise definition is actually extraordinarily difficult. The reasons are manifold. For one thing Darwin's theory of evolution (which involved also commitments to common organic descent, gradualism, and the multiplication of species) encompassed a range of mechanisms for effecting organic transformation; as well as natural selection, Darwin also spoke of sexual selection, family selection, correlative variation, use inheritance and directed variation (Mayr, 1985; Provine 1985). Besides this there is much to be said for the view that Darwinism is itself a historical entity that has evolved over time (Hull, 1985). What it was to be a Darwinian was different for different people at different times and in different places – and all of these Darwinisms bear different relationships to Darwin's own theories. Indeed on some readings, Darwin himself would not qualify as a Darwinian! (see La Vergata, 1985). Evidently Darwinism is a group or system of ideas more related by family resemblance than by genetic identity. For all that, in the *Origin of species* (1859) Darwin did specify one major mechanism – natural selection – by which the transmutation of species could be effected. (A similar theory was simultaneously put forward by Alfred Russel Wallace (1823–1913).) Here Darwin showed how the multitude of living things in our world, so finely adapted to their environments, could have come into being without any recourse to a divine master-plan, in a plain, causal, naturalistic way. Given the self-evident facts of heredity and variation among organisms, and the MALTHUSIAN parameters of population increase, Darwin argued that a struggle for existence must take place; it followed that those who survived were better adapted to their environments than competitors (Young, 1969). This was essentially a theory of reproductive success in which relatively superior adaptations increase while relatively inferior ones are steadily eliminated. As Gould (1980, p. 11) summarizes Darwin's insight:

(a) Organisms vary, and these variations are inherited (at least in part) by their offspring;

(b) Organisms produce more offspring than can possibly survive; and

(c) On average, offspring that vary most strongly in directions favoured by the environment will survive and propagate: favourable variations will therefore accumulate in populations by natural selection.

The implications of Darwin's theory of natural selection were far-reaching. It was, for example, a non-progressivist account of organic change. It assumed that variations in animals were random (or at least obeyed laws as yet unknown) and therefore that there was no inevitable movement of evolutionary history towards some ultimate goal. In this way the older teleological conception of nature was profoundly challenged (cf. TELEOLOGY). Additionally, Darwin had come to the realization that the real units of organic history were populations, not types or species. The change from one species to another was simply the by-product of the process of a population becoming increasingly adapted to its particular environment. Here then was an explanation of population change that accounted in naturalistic terms for differential reproductive success among organic groups.

And yet, in its mode of expression, Darwinian evolution was hardly conveyed in a neutral style. Janet Browne (1996), for example, has disclosed the profoundly imperial tone that pervaded much biogeographical writing in the Darwinian frame, a perhaps not surprising state of affairs given that a vast array of bio- and zoo-geographical data were gathered by colonial officials (see also Ritvo, 1987; Mackenzie, 1990; cf. IMPERIALISM). Besides, Darwin's theory of natural selection was replete with METAPHOR, perhaps the most significant of which was the analogy he developed between the selective activity of breeders and natural selection (Young, 1971; Secord, 1981). To him, Nature was translated into the idioms of breeding, into the language of management husbandry. Indeed it was precisely this species of conceptual manoeuvre that allowed critics to urge that Darwin had simply transferred the attributes of Paley's God to NATURE.

The network of Darwinian commitments, of course, had repercussions beyond biology and biogeography. Disciplines from anthropology to zoology registered at least some of the currents of the Darwinian vision. At the same time, Darwinism had a considerable cultural impact, although interpreting the significance of this 'revolution' has proved to be an infernally stubborn problem (Bowler, 1988). Some have seen its significance as the triumph of science over religion, the substitution of natural law for natural theology, or the shift from a creationist to a positivist EPISTEME (see POSITIVISM). Others, like R.M. Young, stress the ideological continuity between religion and science, regarding both as socially sanctioned IDEOLOGIES (see discussions in Gillespie, 1979; Moore, 1982; Young, 1985; Brooke, 1991). Recent biographies of key figures in the drama – notably Huxley (Desmond, 1994; 1997) and Darwin himself (Desmond and Moore, 1991) – have disclosed a network of Victorian scientists intent on wresting cultural authority from the church (see also Barton, 1983).

Given the ambiguities over the term 'Darwinism' and the fact that it cannot be reduced just to an acceptance of the natural selection mechanism, it is understandable that the percolation of Darwinian themes into geography did not take place in any systematic way. Notions like change through time, interrelationships between organism and environment, organic analogies and selection and struggle certainly became commonplace in the geographical literature (Stoddart, 1966; 1981). But these, as often as not, were derived from the LAMARCKIAN version of evolution which emphasized that organisms could consciously adapt themselves to their surroundings and pass on acquired characteristics to offspring. Still, whatever the sources, aspects of the evolutionary PARADIGM found expression in almost every subdisciplinary specialism of geography. Davis's cycle of erosion expressed his interpretation of LANDSCAPE evolution, though hardly in any specifically Darwinian sense given the absence of sexual reproduction; Clements's plant geography displayed his fascination with organic modes of thought; the Russian geographer and ichthyologist Lev Semyonovich Berg developed a Darwinian theory of 'nomogenesis' which, by emphasizing mutations, allowed for evolutionary 'jumps'; Ratzel's ANTHROPOGEOGRAPHY disclosed his organismic conception of the STATE and provided a human geographical articulation of Moritz Wagner's Lamarckian-based MIGRATION theory; Whittlesey's scheme of SEQUENT OCCUPANCE and Fleure's geographical anthropology and anthropometric CARTOGRAPHY were also evidently imbued with evolutionary thinking. Besides these individuals a variety of key issues within the geographical tradition drew heavily on evolutionary motifs. Statements of ENVIRONMENTAL DETERMINISM by figures like Semple, Huntington and Taylor were invariably couched in evolutionary categories (Livingstone 1987); the transference of ideas about COMMUNITY between sociology and ECOLOGY, and expressed within geography in the tradition of HUMAN ECOLOGY, disclosed an evolutionary political economy (Mitman, 1992); debates about acclimatization were similarly connected up to questions about heredity and adaptation (Anderson, 1992; Livingstone, 1992a); and early theoretical statements about REGIONAL GEOGRAPHY, such as those of Herbertson and Geddes, were supported by appeals to the need for elucidating evolutionary mechanisms in specific contexts (Livingstone 1992b). DNL

References

Anderson, W. 1992: Climates of opinion: acclimatization in nineteenth-century France and England. *Victorian Studies* 35: 135–57. · Barton, R. 1983: Evolution: the Whitworth gun in Huxley's war for the liberation of science from theology. In D. Oldroyd and I. Langham, eds, *The wider domain of evolutionary thought*. Dordrecht: Reidel, 261–87. · Bowler, P. 1988: *The non-Darwinian revolution: reinterpreting a historical myth*. Baltimore: Johns Hopkins University Press. · Brooke, J.H. 1991: *Science and religion*. Cambridge: Cambridge University Press. · Browne, J. 1996: Biogeography and empire. In N. Jardine, J.A. Secord and E.C. Spary, eds, *Cultures of natural history*. Cambridge: Cambridge University Press, 305–21. · Desmond, A. 1994: *Huxley: the devil's disciple*. London: Michael Joseph. · Desmond, A. 1997: *Huxley: evolution's high priest*. London: Michael Joseph. · Desmond, A. and Moore, J. 1991: *Darwin*. London: Michael Joseph. · Gillespie, N.C. 1979: *Charles Darwin and the problem of creation*. Chicago: University of Chicago Press. · Gould, S.J. 1980: *Ever since Darwin; reflections in natural history*. Harmondsworth: Penguin. · Hull, D.L. 1985: Darwinism as a historical entity: a historiographical proposal. In D. Kohn, ed., *The Darwinian heritage*. Princeton: Princeton University Press, 773–812. · La Vergata, A. 1985. Images of Darwin. A historiographic overview. In D. Kohn, ed., *The Darwinian heritage*. Princeton: Princeton University Press, 901–75. · Livingstone, D.N. 1987: Human acclimatization: perspectives on a contested field of inquiry in science, medicine and geography. *History of Science* 25: 359–94. · Livingstone, D.N. 1992a: 'Never shall ye make the crab walk straight': an inquiry into the scientific sources of racial geography. In F. Driver and G. Rose, eds, *Nature and science: essays in the history of geographical knowledge*. Historical Geography Research Series, no. 28: 37–48. · Livingstone, D.N. 1992b: *The geographical tradition*.

Episodes in the history of a contested enterprise. Oxford: Blackwell. · Mackenzie, J.M., ed., 1990: *Imperialism and the natural world*. Manchester: Manchester University Press. · Mayr, E. 1985: Darwin's five theories of evolution. In D. Kohn, ed., *The Darwinian heritage*. Princeton: Princeton University Press, 755–72. · Mitman, G. 1992: *The state of nature: ecology, community, and American social thought, 1900–1950*. Chicago, University of Chicago Press. · Moore, J.R. 1982: 1859 and all that: Remaking the story of evolution-and-religion. In R. Chapman, and C.T. Duval, eds, *Charles Darwin. A centennial commemorative*. Wellington, NZ: Nova Pacifica, 167–94. · Provine, W.P. 1985: Adaptation and mechanisms of evolution after Darwin: a study in persistent controversies. In D. Kohn, ed., *The Darwinian heritage*. Princeton: Princeton University Press, 825–66. · Ritvo, H. 1987: *The animal estate: the English and other creatures in the Victorian age*. Cambridge, MA: Harvard University Press. · Secord, J.A. 1981: Nature's fancy: Charles Darwin and the breeding of pigeons. *Isis* 72: 163–86. · Stoddart, D.R. 1966: Darwin's impact on geography. *Annals of the Association of American Geographers* 56: 683–98. · Stoddart, D.R. 1981: Darwin's influence on the development of geography in the United States, 1859–1914. In B.W. Blouet, ed., *The origins of academic geography in the United States*. Hamden, CT: Archon Books, 265–78. · Young, R.M. 1969: Malthus and the evolutionists: the common context of biological and social theory. *Past and Present* 43: 109–45. · Young, R.M. 1971: Darwin's metaphor: does nature select? *The Monist* 55: 442–503. · Young, R.M. 1985: *Darwin's metaphor. Nature's place in Victorian culture*. Cambridge: Cambridge University Press.

Suggested Reading

Bowler, P.J. 1984: *Evolution. The history of an idea*. Berkeley, Los Angeles and London: University of California Press. · Kohn, D., ed., 1985. *The Darwinian heritage*. Princeton, NJ: Princeton University Press. · Oldroyd, D.R. 1980: *Darwinian impacts. An introduction to the Darwinian revolution*. Milton Keynes: Open University Press; Atlantic Highlands, NJ: Humanities Press. · Ruse, M. 1979: *The Darwinian revolution. Science red in tooth and claw*. Chicago and London: University of Chicago Press.

databases Collections of information records in digital form. A database will probably contain more than one type of record, with information on the linkages or relationships between different types, since the term 'file' implies a simpler collection of only one type of record. To qualify as a database, there is often some degree of 'transparency', a term implying that access to the records does not require detailed knowledge of how they are stored. Transparency is provided by a Database Management System (DBMS), which contains the necessary information on formats and coding schemes and handles requests expressed by the user in convenient terms.

Databases are used to store data and to respond to various kinds of requests from users. For example, an airline maintains a database containing its reservations, information on each of its flights, on its crews and employees, on its aircraft, and many more types of records. The database is accessed whenever information must be updated, and also whenever information is needed in response to a query, such as 'when does my flight arrive?' Databases form one of the fundamental components of most GEOGRAPHIC INFORMATION SYSTEMS (GIS), in which they are used to store records about the attributes and locations of the different kinds of features on the Earth's surface, and the connections that may exist between them. For example, a GIS database might store information on the street network of a city, including its links, intersections, directions of traffic, state of repair, traffic lights, levels of congestion etc.

Many DBMS have adopted the common query language SQL (Structured or Standard Query Language) which allows the user to formulate queries in a simple English-like syntax, and to switch freely from one manufacturer's DBMS to another without the need to learn a new command language. Some widely known DBMS include Oracle, INGRES, INFO, DBase, Access and FileMaker. The database approach is being used increasingly to handle, distribute and access the large collections of social and economic data maintained by national CENSUS and other agencies, and to make them available to researchers.

MG

decentralization A process of spatial change generated by centrifugal forces (see CENTRIFUGAL AND CENTRIPETAL FORCES). Within urban areas, demands for space and the desire to escape the congestion, POLLUTION and high land values of the CENTRAL BUSINESS DISTRICT and surrounding areas are encouraging commercial and industrial businesses to move their premises to the SUBURBS and beyond, where custom-built, accessible industrial estates, office parks and shopping complexes are common. At a larger scale, the negative EXTERNALITIES of big cities encourage movement of both businesses and population to smaller settlements (a process also known as deconcentration: see also COUNTERURBANIZATION). RJJ

decision-making The process whereby alternative courses of action are evaluated and a decision taken. The decision-making perspective attracted great interest after it was introduced to geography during the 1960s as part of the behavioural movement (see

BEHAVIOURAL GEOGRAPHY). It broadened the traditional perspectives, making them more realistic with respect to actual human practice.

The crux of the decision-making perspective is the recognition that real-world location decisions are seldom if ever optimal in the sense of maximizing profits or minimizing RESOURCES used. Similarly, consumer behaviour hardly ever accords with the rational calculus of utilities assumed in conventional economic formulations. The all-knowing and perfectly able ECONOMIC man of NEO-CLASSICAL ECONOMICS bears only slight resemblance to actual human beings.

Sub-optimal location decision-making may be incorporated into conventional location theory by the use of spatial margins to profitability (see VARIABLE COST ANALYSIS), within which some profit is possible anywhere and the business is free to locate away from the optimal (profit-maximizing) location at some pecuniary cost. However, this tells us nothing about how actual choice of location is arrived at within the economically determined constraints.

A step further was taken by Allen Pred (1967, 1969) in his concept of the behavioural matrix. According to this, decision-makers have a position in a matrix with the information available on one axis and the ability to use it on the other. The more information and the greater the ability, the higher the probability of a 'good' location within the spatial margin, i.e. near the optimal location on cost/revenue grounds. Decision-makers with very limited ability and information are more likely to locate beyond the margins and fail, but a good location could still be chosen by chance.

Pred was greatly influenced by H.A. Simon's (1957) concept of satisficing behaviour, as an alternative to the unrealistic optimizing capacity attributed to 'economic man' (sic). Decision-makers were viewed by Simon as considering only a limited number of alternatives, choosing one that is broadly satisfactory rather than optimal. Introduction of a more realistic perspective on location decision-making corresponded with a similar move in the study of business behaviour in general, within a broad context of industrial organization.

The decision-making perspective in location analysis followed two routes: theoretical and empirical. The search for a theoretical framework for studies of location behaviour under conditions of RISK and UNCERTAINTY led geographers and regional scientists into such fields as GAME THEORY and organization theory. The light shed on actual decision-making was very limited, however.

An empirical approach promised more, in a field where the emphasis is so much on individual practice. There was a tradition of SURVEY ANALYSIS in industrial location studies well before the behavioural movements penetrated the subject. Such research often revealed the importance of 'purely personal' factors. Later, empirical research preferred to take sets of firms and examine the actual process of decision-making. Some perceived problem (such as undercapacity) sets in motion a sequence of decisions beginning with whether to expand *in situ*, to set up a branch or to acquire an existing plant; the sequence continues with the process of searching for a site, the evaluation of alternatives, the final decision and the feedback of the learning experience into some subsequent decision of a similar nature. This empirical approach held out the prospect of generalizations that relate the process of location decision-making to the nature of the organization concerned (cf. SEARCH BEHAVIOUR).

After many years of behavioural studies of industrial location decision-making, the findings seemed to promise more than it was able to deliver. A critique was mounted by Doreen Massey (1979), who pointed to objections on epistemological grounds (see EPISTEMOLOGY) to the practice of adopting IDEAL TYPE constructs (whether 'economic man' or some 'satisficing man') and of making a distinction between behaviour that accords with the ideal type and that which must be attributed to other factors. Massey argued that the focus on individual decision-making distracts attention from the structural features of the economy to which firms react, and that what firms actually do with respect to the setting up or closure of plants is best understood in this broader context of POLITICAL ECONOMY. There has recently been a revival of interest in aspects of location decision-making, however, including the learning process and corporate strategy with respect to restructuring. The work of Schoenberger (1997) emphasizes recognition of the significance of cultural factors in the the operation of the firm.

Other aspects of human geography in which the decision-making perspective assumed importance include response to environmental hazards (e.g. Kates, 1962), residential choice (e.g. Brown and Moore, 1970), shopping behaviour (e.g. Rushton, 1969; see also REVEALED PREFERENCE ANALYSIS), and the decision to migrate (e.g. Wolpert, 1965). Again, NEO-CLASSICAL ECONOMICS was originally influential, the concept of PLACE UTILITY being an obvious geographical extension of the theory of consumer behaviour. While qualities of place as people evaluate them do influence decisions including locational choice or movement, there are many other considerations of a fortuitous and seemingly irrational nature. Indeed, geographers can easily exaggerate the spatial element in decision-making.

More recent research involving QUALITATIVE METHODS has sought a more sensitive understanding of how people assign meaning to various aspects of life and how decisions follow from this. For example, the decision to seek health care, involving the coverage of distance, is influenced by culturally specific conceptions of the meaning of illness, personal and shared experience of being ill, assessment of the benefit likely to be derived from the doctor's advice based on past contacts, the felt need for treatment or reassurance, and so on. Such work helps to set the spatial aspects of decision-making and taking in a broader context, getting away from crude notions of human behaviour as some stimulus–response mechanism and allowing greater scope for the way meaning is interpreted and translated into action. Work in the earlier tradition is now part of the discipline's history rather than important to contemporary practice. DMS

References

Brown, L.A. and Moore, E.G. 1970: The intra-urban migration process: a perspectice. *Geogrrafiska Annaler* 52B: 1–13. · Kates, R.W. 1962: *Hazard and choice perception in flood plain management*. Chicago: University of Chicago, Department of Geography, Research Paper 78. · Massey, D.B. 1979: A critical evaluation of industrial location theory. In F.E.I. Hamilton and G.J.R. Linge, eds, *Spatial analysis, industry and the industrial environment, volume I. Industrial systems*. New York and Chichester: John Wiley, 57–72. · Pred, A. 1967, 1969: *Behavior and localion: foundations for a geographic and dynamic location theory*. Parts 1 and 2. Lund studies in geography, series B, 27 and 28. Lund: Gleerup. · Rushton, G. 1969: Analysis of spatial behavior by revealed space preference. *Annals of the Association of American Geographers* 59: 391–400. · Schoenberger, E. 1997: *The cultural crisis of the firm*. Oxford: Blackwell. · Simon, H.A. 1957: *Models of man: social and rational*. New York: John Wiley. · Wolpert, J. 1965: Behavioral aspects of the decision to migrate. *Papers [and Proceedings] of the Regional Science Association* 15: 159–72.

Suggested Reading

Chapman, K. and Walker, D. 1991: *Industrial location: principles and policies*, 2nd edn. Oxford: Basil Blackwell. · Hayter, R. 1997: *The dynamics of industrial location*. New York: John Wiley. · Malmberg, A. 1997: Industrial geography: location and learning. *Progress in Human Geography* 21: 573–82. · Smith, D.M. 1981: *Industrial location: an economic geographical analysis*, 2nd edn. New York: John Wiley, ch. 5. · Wolpert, J. 1964. The decision process in a spatial context. *Annals of the Association of American Geographers* 54: 337–58.

decolonization The process, often long, tortuous and violent, by which colonies achieve their national aspirations for political independence from the colonial metropolitan POWER (cf. NATIONALISM). Decolonization can be understood as the period of late colonialism (Chamberlain, 1985). COLONIALISM covers the period from the fifteenth to the twentieth centuries and hence decolonization is uneven in its geography and history. In the New World, which had been subjected to Spanish, French, Portuguese and Dutch colonial rule in the *First Age of Colonialism*, the first wave of decolonization occurred in the eighteenth century. In this regard, the so-called *Classical Age of Imperialism* in the last quarter of the nineteenth century was short, the first decolonizations of the second wave being achieved after the end of the Second World War. The two cycles of imperialism both concluded with a limited phase of decolonization followed by the rapid collapse of empires and an irresistible push to political independence (Taylor, 1994).

The first challenge to the first wave of IMPERIALISM came in 1776 as British North American colonies declared independence. While Britain maintained its Caribbean and Canadian colonies, the Napoleonic upheavals in Europe so weakened Spain and Portugal that European settlers from Mexico to Chile expelled their imperial masters. By 1825 the Spanish and Portuguese empires were dead. In the subsequent 115 years up to the Second World War, decolonization was limited to Cuba in 1898 and two groups of British colonies: the white settler colonies (Canada, Australia, New Zealand and South Africa) granted internal autonomy and finally full sovereignty in 1931, and Egypt and Iraq after the First World War. The Second World War marked the death knell for European colonization: India's separation from the British, Indonesia from the Dutch, the remaining Arab mandated territories and Indo-China from the French. The independence of Ghana in 1957 marked an avalanche of liberations in Africa, though the process was not complete until 1990 (Namibia). Between 1945 and 1989 over one hundred new independent STATES were created.

Decolonization is a process marked by the achievement of political independence but the duration, depth and character of decolonization movements vary substantially. In some

African colonies, colonization was barely accomplished and resistance movements of varying degrees of organization and institutionalization attended the entire colonial project. In other cases, an organized anti-colonial and nationalist movement came late, accompanied by a rapid and hastily assembled set of political negotiations in which it is clear that the metropolitan power wished to hand over the reigns of power with utmost expediency (Nigeria). In others it took a war of liberation, a bloody armed struggle by leftist guerrillas or nationalist agitators pitted against white settlers or intransigent colonial states (as in Laos, Vietnam and Zimbabwe).

One of the problems of analysing decolonization, as Fred Cooper notes (1997, p. 6), is that the story 'lends itself to be read backwards and to privilege the process of ending colonial rule over anything else that was happening in those years'. It should also be said that any account of decolonization presumes an account, or a THEORY, of colonialism itself: top-down interpretations take colonial projects at face value whereas the nationalist account denies any reality to the goal of MODERNIZATION which the colonial state purported to bring. In general, decolonization is seen as either (i) *self-government as an outcome of negotiated preparation and vision from above* by a colonial state apparatus, or (ii) as a *nationalist triumph from below* in which power is wrested (violently or otherwise) from recalcitrant colonizers. In practice decolonization was an enormously complex process involving something of each, and shaped both by the peculiarities of colonialism itself and the particular setting in world time in which the nationalist drive began.

There are two forms of decolonization which rest on what one might call nationalist triumph. The first is built upon social mobilization in which a patchwork of anticolonial resistances and movements (many of which are synonymous with colonial conquest itself) are sown together into a unified nationalist movement by a western-educated elite (Malaysia, Ghana or Aden). Mobilization occurred across a wide and eclectic range of organizations – trade unions, professional groups, ethnic associations – bringing them into political parties and propelled by a leadership focused on RACISM, on liberation and the sense of national identity of the colony given its own history and CULTURE. The second is revolutionary – Franz Fanon (1967) is its most powerful and articulate spokesman – in which the vanguard is not western-educated elites or indeed workers, but the PEASANTS and lumpenproletariat. It rested upon violence and upon the rejection of any semblance of NEO-COLONIALISM. Decolonization rejected bourgeois nationalism (of the first sort); rather, as Fanon put it, 'the last shall be first and the first last. Decolonization is the putting into practice of this sentence' (1967, p. 30).

Both views depict nationalism as subsuming all other struggles and hence obscures and misses much history; both posit a True Cause, as Cooper (1997, p. 7) puts it, in which there is little truck with opposition. Equally the nationalist road to self-government tends to take for granted the depth and appeal of a national identity (cf. IDENTITY POLITICS). It is precisely the shallowness of these nationalisms in the post-colonial period which reveals how limited is the simple nationalist account of decolonization itself. In practice decolonization occurred in the context of all manner of contradictions and tensions between the national question and other social questions.

There is also a narrative of decolonization which has a singular vision but from the side of the colonial state. It was the colonial bureaucracy, long before nationalist parties arose, which shaped self-government on a calculus of interest and power derived from an older conception of colonial rule (New Zealand and Canada) as a stepping stone to Independence. In this view Africa by 1947 had already been set on the road to decolonization – this is a classic instant of Whig history – in spite of the fact that the Colonial Offices typically saw early African leaders as schoolboys or demagogues (Cooper, 1997). Another version of the dirigiste theory is rendered through the cold calculation of money and cost. It was the decision-making rationale of accountants estimating costs and gains – and who in particular gained – against the backdrop of imperial power's economic performance after the Second World War which sealed the fate of the colonies.

In all of these accounts – for India as much as Indonesia or Iraq – colonialism is as monolithic as the explanations themselves. There is a reduction involved in seeing Indians or Kenyans as colonial subjects or as national or proto-nationalist actors. An alternative approach pursued by the so-called Subaltern School (Guha and Spivak, 1988; cf. SUBALTERN STUDIES) sees colonialism as a contra-metropolitan project, moving against trends to exercise power under universal social practices and norms. It was 'dominance without HEGEMONY'. In other words the hegemonic project of colonialism fragmented as colonial rule attached itself to local idioms of power. From this experience characterized by hybrid forms of identity, of blurred boundaries, and contradictory practices, the process of decolonization must necessarily look more complex than simply self-rule managed from above by the colonial state or mobilized from below by nationalist forces (cf. HYBRIDITY).

MW

References

Chamberlain, M. 1985: *Decolonization*. Oxford: Blackwell. · Cooper, F. 1997: *Decolonization and African society*. Cambridge: Cambrdige University Press. · Fanon, F. 1967: *Black skins, white masks*. Boston: Grove. · Guha, S. and Spivak, G., eds, 1988: *Subaltern studies*. Oxford: Oxford University Press. · Taylor, P.J. 1994: Decolonization. In T., Unwin, *Atlas of world development*. Chichester: John Wiley, 22–3.

Suggested Reading

Grimal, H. 1978: *Decolonization*. London: Routledge.

deconstruction A type of literary method most associated with the French philosopher Jacques Derrida (1930–), and used to destabilize and undercut the truth claims of any written TEXT. On the surface, most writing appears coherent, consistent, unequivocal and about something real. Derrida's argument is that it is not. Applying the method of deconstruction, he shows that every written work, from the most celebrated to the most mundane, is inherently contradictory with neither final meaning nor external reference. Such problems are not the result of *ad hoc* bits of sloppy writing, but subsist in the very construction of all texts. In this sense, deconstruction subversively reveals what is always internally hidden, 'revers[ing] the imposing tapestry [of a text] in order to expose in all its unglamorously dishevelled tangle the threads constituting the well-heeled image it presents to the world' (Eagleton, 1986, p. 80).

For Derrida, carrying out such subversion is necessary for philosophical and ethical reasons. The history of western philosophy, Derrida thinks, is the quest for clarity, certainty, and above all, order. It is the hope that there is some foundation to knowledge beyond which we need not go, such as rationality, logic or truth (cf. FOUNDATIONALISM). Derrida calls any philosophical system that has such aspirations *logocentric*, literally meaning 'reason centred'. At the core of any logocentric system such as, say, POSITIVISM or PHENOMENOLOGY or STRUCTURALISM, is some 'metaphysics of presence', as Derrida calls it.

By metaphysics or metaphysical system is meant a set of abstract principles that allow us to address questions that cannot be answered by addressing the known empirical world using traditional scientific methods. For example, questions like 'what is essential truth?', or 'what is the meaning of life?', or 'what is goodness?' are all metaphysical questions. Typically the metaphysical principles used to address those questions are messy, debatable, and subject to modification. Derrida thinks, however, that the task of western philosophy has been to sort through such metaphysical messiness to find the one principle that is self-evident, clear, and constant, that is, to find a 'metaphysics of presence'. As Lawson (1985, p. 96) puts it, a metaphysics of presence is an 'immediately available arena of certainty', an anchor of stability in the choppy seas of metaphysical life. In turn, it is that belief in an arena of certainty that then provides philosophers with a warrant for making claims to finality and the truth. To use the examples above: for positivists 'facts' are the 'metaphysics of presence', they ensure certainty and finality; for phenomenologists, though, it is interior consciousness; and yet again for structuralists it is the relationship among elements within a wider structure. Derrida's argument, however, is that because of the dislocating effects of LANGUAGE, one can always show through deconstruction that these claimed 'presences' are not present, with the consequence that logocentric systems are left without foundation.

The details of Derrida's argument are complex, but the gist is that within any metaphysical system, as in the examples above, the assertion of a presence relies upon the suppression (absence) of its opposite (which together as a pair are called a *binary*). To assert 'facts' as primary within positivism, for example, means denying 'values' (its antonym), and in this case its subordinate. Now, it is quite easy to reverse this binary, and instead of asserting facts to assert values as primary. While producing a different metaphysical system, with a new 'presence', it would nevertheless remain a metaphysical system, just a different metaphysical system. Derrida's goal through deconstruction, though, is more seditious than turning around binaries. It is to destabilize both parts of the binary from within, rendering any metaphysical system based upon either part problematic. To use Derrida's language, it is always possible to 'overturn' any binary because of 'undecidability' at its core. Undecidability involves finding key terms within the metaphysical system that fit neither half of the binary (the primary or the subordinate). Because such terms slip across both sides of the binary, but fit neither, the very coherence of the binary is questioned, and more generally any metaphysic constructed upon it.

Take, for example, the fact–value binary. During the 1920s and 1930s a group of philosophers (the Vienna Circle) primarily based in Vienna attempted to construct a philosophical system based upon that very binary, LOGICAL POSITIVISM. All meaningful *scientific statements* were either *empirical (or synthetic)*, and could be verified against the facts of the world, or were *analytical*, that is, true by definition such as logic and formal mathematical theorems. Statements that were neither empirical nor analytical were metaphysical, and simply meaningless. Here, then, is a classic case of asserting the presence of one side of the binary, the part representing facts and logic, over its subordinate, the part which is absent and which represents values and metaphysics. An immediate criticism of logical positivism, though, was the justification of the empirical-analytical distinction that defined the limits of meaningful scientific statements. It was itself neither a strictly empirical statement, nor an analytical one. But it wasn't a metaphysical statement either because it would then be meaningless, whereas its purpose is precisely one of delimiting the meaningful from the meaningless. In short, it lies betwixt and between the binary of facts and values, between science and metaphysics, thereby rendering that very distinction problematic.

More generally, Derrida's strategy is always the same: to find the critical binary, and to demonstrate that it never fully determines meaning. In Derrida's vocabulary, signifiers are never fully structurally determined. Instead, there is only endless displacement and deferment of meaning, an eternal 'play of signifiers' (Lawson, 1985), which consequently provide no fixed meaning. To use Derrida's invented term, there is only *différance*: a complicated word, but at its most basic denoting the ultimate undeniability of meaning of all signifiers.

It is important to note that in carrying out deconstruction, Derrida unsettles from within. As Lawson (1985, p. 93) writes, in deconstruction 'the text is seen to fall by its own criteria – the standards or definitions which the text sets up are used reflexively to unsettle and shatter the original distinctions'. In this way, too, Derrida circumvents the charge that he is simply substituting his own metaphysical system for another; for he offers none. Second, in carrying out deconstruction Derrida necessarily adopts an unorthodox style of philosophical argument and writing. Traditional philosophers are not enamoured. Barry Smith, editor of the *Monist*, for example, in writing to *The Times* (6 May 1992) about the nomination of Derrida for an honorary degree from Cambridge University (which, after controversy, he was awarded), says that Derrida has made 'a career out of translating into the academic sphere tricks and gimmicks' with a resulting 'written style that defies comprehension'. For Derrida, though, the reason traditional philosophy has problems is a direct consequence of its style of writing and argument. Any critique, such as his, must be expressed in different terms. Derrida writes as he does for a reason, and not because he can't write.

Derrida's ethical reason for deconstruction is to undermine any metaphysical presence that posits itself as the centre, and which in so doing necessarily creates marginality. Here, as Bernstein (1992, ch. 6) argues, it is tempting to see Derrida's work in autobiographical terms. As an exile, an Algerian Sephardic Jew living in France, Derrida has a personal interest in showing that 'the tactics and strategies designed to exclude, outcast, [and] silence. . . . have never been quite successful' (Bernstein, 1992, p. 180). This is one of the purposes of deconstruction. It demonstrates that all assertions of a metaphysical centre necessarily unravel from within; that the distinction between centre and margin, presence and absence, is not sustainable. The implication, though, is not that all distinctions, boundaries and hierarchies are then dissolved. As Derrida recognizes, we are all implicated in logocentric projects, including him. We can struggle against them, but they can never be completely overthrown. The best we can do is maintain a perpetual state of uneasiness, of continual questioning of what we take to be our centre, our home, our PLACE. That also is the purpose of deconstruction: to decentre, to throw off kilter any all-encompassing logocentric project that claims certainty, determinateness, and the moral privilege of a specific CLASS, GENDER or RACE.

Deconstruction has made significant inroads across a wide range of social sciences and humanities over the last decade, and while clearly found in literary studies (Cullen, 1997), it is also carried out in economics (Amariglio and Ruccio, 1994), political science (Laclau and Mouffe, 1985), and POST-

COLONIAL studies (Young, 1990). The recent interest in POST-STRUCTURALISM within geography has also resulted in a number of references to Derrida's work, and deconstruction in particular, but there are few examples of either being worked through systematically. In many ways Olsson's (1976) iconoclastic *Birds in egg*, written long before post-structuralism was ever mentioned in geography, is an exemplary deconstructive work; in his case unravelling from within the 'threads of the tapestry' of SPATIAL SCIENCE. Harley's (1989) paper on 'Deconstructing the map' is also well-known, although Belyea (1992) doubts whether he really does what he claims in his title. Doel's (1993, 1994) writings are perhaps the most self-consciously Derridean of anyone's in the discipline but, maybe inevitably, like Olsson, he has met charges of obscurantism. And recently, Barnes (1996) attempts to deconstruct geography's QUANTITATIVE REVOLUTION, although he maintains doubts about the success of his own project. This goes to the issue of the difficulty of carrying out deconstruction, which even extends to Derrida (1991, 209) himself who once said: 'deconstruction loses nothing from admitting it is impossible'. TJB

References

Amariglio, J. and Ruccio, D. 1994: Postmodernism, Marxism and the critique of modern economic thought. *Rethinking Marxism* 7 (3): 7–35. · Barnes, T.J. 1994: Probable writing: Derrida, deconstruction and the quantitative revolution in human geography. *Environment and Planning A* 26: 1021–40. · Belyea, B. 1992: Images of power: Derrida/ Foucault/ Harley. *Cartographica* 29: 1–19. · Bernstein, R.J. 1992: *The new constellation: the ethical-political horizons of modernity/ postmodernity*. Cambridge, MA: MIT Press. · Cullen, J. 1997: *Literary theory: a very short introduction*. Oxford: Oxford University Press. · Derrida, J. 1991: *The Derrida reader: between the blinds*. Hemel Hempstead: Harvester Wheatsheaf. · Doel, M.A. 1993: Proverbs for paranoids: writing geography on hollowed ground. *Transactions, Institute of British Geographers* NS 18: 377–94. · Doel, M.A. 1994: Something resist: reading-deconstruction as ontological infestation (departures from the texts of Jacques Derrida). In P. Cloke, M. Doel, D. Matless, M. Phillips and N. Thrift, eds, *Writing country: five cultural geographies*. London: Paul Chapman, 127–48. · Eagleton. T. 1986: *Against the grain*. London: Verso. · Harley, B. 1989: Deconstructing the map. *Cartographica* 26: 1–20. · Laclau, E. and Mouffe, C. 1985: *Hegemony and socialist strategy: towards a radical democratic politics*. London: Verso. · Lawson, H. 1985: *On reflexivity: the postmodern predicament*. London: Hutchinson. · Olsson, G. 1975: *Birds in egg*. Ann Arbor, MI: Department of Geography, University of Michigan. · Young, R. 1990: *White mythologies: writing history and the west*. London: Routledge.

Suggested Reading

Barnes (1994). · Norris, C. 1987: *Derrida*. Cambridge, MA: Harvard University Press.

deep ecology A radical form of ENVIRONMENTALISM which argues that NATURE has inherent rights to existence which are as, if not more, important than those of humans. Deep ecology is both a philosophy and a practice associated with the western ENVIRONMENTAL MOVEMENT. It emerged in the early 1970s when ecologist Arne Naess (1973) made a distinction between 'shallow' and 'deep ecology', although it draws upon much older traditions of thought. For Naess the outpouring of government, business and government concern over the environment in the late 1960s and early 1970s amounted to a *shallow ecology*, or what Luke (1988, p. 66) calls 'reform environmentalism'. Reform environmentalism was fundamentally *technocentric* – it sought managerial solutions to environmental problems within existing socio-economic frameworks – and also *anthropocentric* – in that it both saw human values as the source of all values and saw nature and environment as but means to human ends. Against this, *deep ecology* is *ecocentric* and also advocates *dismantling* the dominant socio-economic systems through which humans appropriate nature. As Naess (1973, p. 100, italics added) put it, deep ecology calls for a post-anthropocentric 'biospherical egalitarianism' to create 'an awareness of the equal right (of *all* things) to live and blossom'. Subsequently, Bill Devall and George Sessions (1985) laid out the philosophical tenets of deep ecology in much more detail.

Contemporary deep ecology is not a singular body of thought but rather a plurality of interrelated perspectives. Philosophically, these perspectives draw upon everything from eastern religions (e.g. Taoism, Buddhism), western process philosophy (e.g. Baruch Spinoza and Alfred North Whitehead) and European literary romanticism (e.g. Blake, Goethe, Wordsworth) to Indian American culture, American preservationism (e.g. John Muir, Walt Whitman) and 'beat philosophy' (e.g. Ginsberg and Kerouac). Practically, deep ecology finds expression in environmental organizations of a more or less broad and a more or less radical kind. For instance, a single-issue based and very radical deep ecology organization is the British Animal Liberation Front, dedicated to animal welfare through violence and other means; by contrast, a broad-based and less radical deep ecology organization was the early Greenpeace of the 1970s. However, notwithstanding these different philosophical and organizational strands, deep ecologists share a number of common characteristics. First, they reject the dualistic worldview of technocentrists and anthropocentrists to argue instead that humanity is a *part* of nature. Second, they argue that *all* parts of nature – humans and non-humans – have an equal right to existence. Finally, they argue that natural systems – again, including humans and non-humans – have limits and thresholds which must be respected if life is to continue on a sustainable basis.

Deep ecology has come in for considerable criticism. First, some doubt that non-human parts of nature have *intrinsic* value (Harvey, 1996, ch. 7): the argument here is that it is not possible to value nature other than through human judgements and assumptions. Second, some worry that deep ecology's ecocentrism shades into *anti-humanism* in which humans' rights are subordinated (Luke, 1988). Third, some argue that deep ecology is *sociologically naive*. This has two dimensions. First, it is claimed that deep ecology lacks a coherent theory of the existing socio-economic systems – particularly CAPITALISM – through which nature is exploited (Pepper, 1993). Second, it is also claimed that by blaming an undifferentiated 'humanity' for the despoliation of nature, deep ecology also fails to discriminate between the different relations to nature and environment of the rich and the poor, men and women, and of different ethnic groups (Bradford, 1989: cf. ECOFEMINISM). Finally, some suggest that deep ecology is also *politically naive* because it lacks a realistic appreciation of the structural difficulties of moving towards a future state of 'harmony' with nature. However, these criticisms aside, deep ecology has undoubtedly been important in encouraging a wider appreciation of the value of nature and of modern humanity's often destructive relations with it.

NC

References

Bradford, G. 1989: *How deep is deep ecology?* Haley, MA: Times Change Press. · Devall, B. and Sessions, G. 1985: *Deep ecology*. Layton, Utah: Peregrine Smith Books. · Harvey, D. 1996: *Justice, nature and the geography of difference*. Oxford: Blackwell. · Luke, T. 1988: The dreams of deep ecology. *Telos* 76: 65–92. · Naess, A. 1973: The shallow and the deep long-range ecology movement: a summary. *Inquiry* 16: 95–100. · Pepper, D. 1993: *Ecosocialism*. London: Routledge.

deindustrialization A sustained decline in industrial (especially manufacturing) activity and capacity (cf. INDUSTRIALIZATION). It may involve the absolute and/or relative decline of industrial output, employment and means of production. Such changes are quite normal in the course of economic DEVELOPMENT. However, when they are linked to the declining competitiveness of industrial production to meet extra-regional, domestic and international demand within reasonable levels of employment and a sustainable balance of payments, deindustrialization represents a process of UNDERDEVELOPMENT. The causes of deindustrialization are complex. In the contemporary global economy, they lie in a combination of local circumstance and locational adjustment to global conditions. In a CAPITALIST economy, the rate of profit and its determinants must lie at the centre of any explanation.

RL

Suggested Reading

Bluestone, B. and Harrison, B. 1982: *The deindustrialization of America*. New York: Basic Books. · Martin, R. and Rowthorn, B., eds, 1986: *The geography of deindustrialization*. Basingstoke: Macmillan.

democracy A form of GOVERNANCE in which rule is by and for the people. Discussions of democracy usually assume the territorial STATE as the frame and opportunity for its execution and practice (cf. TERRITORIALITY). What is democracy, however, is highly contested. Reinvented during the eighteenth-century European ENLIGHTENMENT, it has spawned a series of debates, many of which have their origins and practices in the classical Greek city-state. Since then, three sets of debates have emerged as especially focal in the making of modern and late modern democracies.

First, *who should be included within the citizen-polity* (cf. CITIZENSHIP)? Athenian democracy restricted this to male citizens. But it is only recently that the modern NATION-STATE has evolved an inclusive conception: up until the 1920s, women did not have the franchise in Britain and it was only in the 1960s that the vote was extended to blacks in the United States.

Secondly, there is *the nature of a participatory democracy*. The Athenian city-state enabled citizens to partake in an extraordinary rich and engaged political life, in which all citizens participated in the development of laws in an open forum. Every citizen had an equal vote on each issue, and in true participatory democratic style, the topics for discussion were often introduced by the voters themselves. In modern-day liberal democracies, democratic theory tends to stress as adequate the equal rights to vote through electing representatives.

Thus for Max Weber, democracy is viewed as essentially a means of selecting competent leaders. Arguments against a more Athenian-style democracy tend to focus on two points: (a) citizens were freed to participate in politics by a vast army of women, slaves and foreigners – the very notion of the active citizen, as feminist theory notes, presumes someone is taking care of the children and doing the necessary maintenance of everyday life. Moreover, besides individual, modern TIME-GEOGRAPHIES not necessarily being compatible with direct rule, as a number of observers have noted, there are other good things in life – play, work, sex – than participating directly in politics; and (b) citizen assemblies and rotation of duties work only in the context of tiny small-scale geographic COMMUNITIES like the city-state in which such practices do not easily translate into the modern nation-state which counts its citizens by the millions. Referenda, however, provide one way in which direct Athenian-style rule is often maintained in modern democracies.

Thirdly, there is *the question of rule by the majority*. While most theorists of democracy subscribe to the view that the majority principle of citizen votes is an effective and desirable way of protecting individuals from arbitrary government, how this is to be realized will depend on how electoral systems are spatially organized and how votes are translated into parliamentary seats (see ELECTORAL GEOGRAPHY). In late-modern democracies, much debate has focused on what is known as 'the tyranny of the majority'. Thus while J.S. Mill, one of the founding fathers of liberal democracy, argued for a more inclusive definition of citizenship, he proposed to weight political votes of the more educated, presumably to prevent an enfranchised urban industrial working CLASS from dominating and shaping the political agenda. Today, however, the focus of concern is on how best to protect minority interests. For one school of thought, this can best be achieved by treating toleration, entrenchment of rights as preconditions for democracy but not as constitutive of either democracy itself or by negating the principle of majority rule (cf. HUMAN RIGHTS). Others argue that DIFFERENCE needs to be respected, and that the only way of securing representation by minorities – ethnic, aboriginal, women – is by designing political and electoral systems to include an in-built bias. Thus both Spain and Britain have legislation which enables certain of their ethnic regions – Catalonia, The Basque Country, Scotland, Wales – to have greater representation than others. The problem, however, of ensuring that minority identities are respected, at whatever geographical SCALE of governance – has also given rise to the notion of deliberative democracy (Elster, 1998). Here it is argued that democracy is best achieved through public deliberation over policy issues in which differing voices, rationalities and positions form part of the DECISION-MAKING process. By emphasizing the importance of dialogue, deliberative democracy can enable multiple voices to be heard.

In the light of important current globalizing and technological change, political theorists are calling for ways in which our democratic imagination should be reformulated and retheorized to take into account three developments in particular.

The first concerns *the growth in importance of common global issues and the prominent rise of global institutions of governance* (see GLOBALIZATION; REGIME THEORY). In particular, there is a need to ensure that such forms of governance are democratically rooted and accountable. As Archiburgi, Held and Kohler (1998) argue, one of the major projects faced is to develop a theory of *cosmopolitan democracy*, of ensuring that not only are global institutions accountable but also that there is greater equality between its major participants, including nation-states. Cosmopolitan democracy also raises the thorny issue of whether it is legitimate to continue to export western conceptions of democracy to the democratizing world.

Second, there has been a growing interest in *the role of regions and city regions in the exercise and practice of democracy*. Not only are LOCALITIES becoming more assertive within the global arena and citizens reforming their IDENTITIES in relation to their LOCALE of everyday life, but in the process regions require democratic institutions which celebrate the growing plurality of such REGIONS and WORLD CITIES (cf. PLURALISM). As Hirst (1994) argues, one way of realizing this is by working towards a model of *associational democracy*, in which POWER and authority is delegated to localities, but which ensures that the local institutions combine citizen choice with public welfare provision (see WELFARE STATE).

Finally, while the relationship between geographic scale and democracy needs to be reimagined, so too do *the consequences of the impact of the communications revolution on our understanding of democracy*. The opportunities opened up by electronic communication have not only changed the way in which politics is conducted and practised, but also raise questions of whether CYBERSPACE is empowering or limiting citizen freedoms (cf. COMMUNICATIONS, GEOGRAPHY OF). Most certainly, parallels can be drawn between the new politics mediated by cyberspace and Athenian democracy. On the one hand, while cyberspace has changed the nature of political interaction in which democracy no longer occurs in particular places (the Greek agora, nineteenth-century municipal town hall or public square), but is exchanged amongst non-territorial communities, it can facilitate citizen participation, interaction and even the prospects of mass citizen voting. On the other hand, like the Greek city-state, it is exclusionary, restricted to a political community of technocratic and educated elites, in which there exists large parts of the world that have not been spatially included in this cosmopolitan community of citizens: the INNER-CITY poor, the THIRD WORLD, and those living under authoritarian regimes. GES

References and Suggested Reading

Archiburgi, D., Held, D. and Kohler, M., eds, 1998: *Re-imagining political community: studies in cosmopolitan democracy.* Oxford: Polity Press. · Castells, M. 1997: *The power of identity.* Oxford: Basil Blackwell. · Elster, J. 1998: *Deliberative democracy.* Cambridge: Cambridge University Press. · Hirst, P. 1994: *Associative democracy.* Oxford: Polity Press. · Linz, J. and Stepan, A. 1996: *Problems of democratic transition and consolidation. Southern Europe, South America and Post-Communist Europe.* Baltimore and London: The Johns Hopkins University Press. · Painter, J. 1999: New geographies of democracy in contemporary Europe. In A. Williams and R. Hudson, eds, *Divided Europe: society and territory.* London: Sage. · Przeworski, A. 1996: *Sustainable democracy.* Oxford: Polity Press. · Smith, G. 1994: Political theory and human geography. In D. Gregory, R. Martin and Smith, G., eds, *Human geography: society, space and social science.* London: Macmillan, 54–77. · Sorensen, G. 1993: *Democracy and democratization.* Boulder: Westview. · Touraine, A. 1996: *What is democracy?* Oxford: Polity Press.

demographic transition A general model describing the evolution of levels of FERTILITY and MORTALITY over time. It was devised with particular reference to the experience of developed countries which have passed through the process of INDUSTRIALIZATION and URBANIZATION, and it has attracted considerable criticism as a general model. The first formulation in the demographic literature was by Warren Thompson in 1929, with further significant restatements by Adolphe Landry in 1934 and Frank Notestein in 1945 (Kirk, 1996).

The model suggests four highly stylized phases in the process (see figure). In the first, *high stationary phase*, both birth and death rates are high. Deaths, due to famines, diseases or wars, are said to be the most important influence on population growth, which tends to be at a low level. In the second, *early expanding phase*, the population begins to grow, as a result of a stable birth rate and a rapidly declining death rate. The latter falls as a result of improved nutrition, sanitation and medicine. The third, *late expanding phase*, is characterized by a slowing in the growth rate as the death rate stabilizes at a low level and the birth rate declines. This decline may be associated with the growth of an urban/industrial society, with changing attitudes to family formation, with changing patterns of marriage and with the use of contraceptive methods. In the final, *low stationary phase* birth and death rates have stabilized at a low level, population growth is very slow, and the birth rate is more likely to fluctuate than the death rate.

There is much variety in the way in which demographic transition applies to individual countries and, indeed, widespread doubt about the model's validity and applicability. Most countries of Europe, North America and the rest of the developed world now have very low rates of fertility and mortality, with low levels of population growth, for example, whereas by contrast, many countries of the THIRD WORLD are experiencing high rates of growth, as the decline in mortality has not been fully matched by a reduction in fertility, though the latter is declining in many countries. Great care must be taken in applying the model of demographic transition to individual countries, however: recent research has shown that the first stage of the model is rather oversimplified for the currently developed world, for example, with fluctuating NUPTIALITY and fertility having a greater influence on population growth than previously recognized. The work of the Princeton European Fertility Project (Coale and Watkins, 1986; Watkins, 1991) has demonstrated the complexity of fertility decline in the nineteenth and twentieth centuries, in terms of its geography, periodicity and causality. In addition, post-1945 fluctuations in the birth rates of the developed world are more complex than the model implies, as the role of marriage and attitudes to family formation have proved more variable, for example amongst European countries, than envisaged in the model. Moreover, it is far from certain that the currently developing world will follow the form of transition depicted in the figure

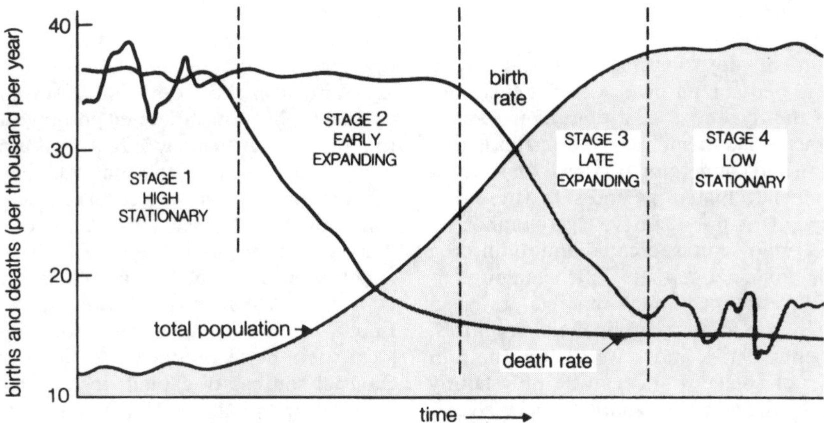

Demographic transition (Haggett, 1975)

(see, for example, Leete, 1996). Demographic transition remains an important, if contested, idea in POPULATION GEOGRAPHY and geographers have sought to match it with a similar model of the mobility transition (see MIGRATION) in order to understand long-term trends in population change. PEO

References

Coale, A.J. and Watkins, S.C., eds, 1986: *The decline of fertility in Europe*. Princeton: Princeton University Press. · Haggett, P. 1983: *Geography: a modern synthesis*, rev. 3rd edn. New York and London: Harper and Row. · Kirk, D. 1996: Demographic transition theory, *Population Studies* 50, 3: 361–87. · Leete, R. 1996: *Malaysia's demographic transition: rapid development, culture and politics*. Kuala Lumpur and Oxford: Oxford University Press. · Watkins, S.C. 1991: *From provinces into nations. Demographic integration in western Europe, 1870–1960*. Princeton, New Jersey: Princeton University Press.

Suggested Reading

Chesnais, J.-C. 1992: *Demographic transition. Stages, patterns and economic implications*, trans. by P. Kreager Oxford: Oxford University Press. · Davis, K., Bernstam, M.S., and R. Ricardo-Campbell, eds, 1986: *Below replacement fertility in industrial societies. Causes, consequences, policies*. (Supplement to *Population and Development Review*, vol. 12). New York: The Population Council. · Day, L.H. 1992: *The future of low-birthrate populations*. London and New York: Routledge. · Livi-Bacci, M. 1997: *A concise history of world population*, 2nd edn. Oxford: Blackwell. · Szreter, S. 1993: The idea of the demographic transition and the study of fertility change: a critical intellectual history. *Population and Development Review* 19 (4): 659–701. · Woods, R. and P. Rees, 1986: *Population structures and models. Developments in spatial demography*. London: Allen and Unwin, ch. 3.

density gradient The rate of falling-off of land-use intensity (or population density etc.) with distance from a central point, as in the DISTANCE DECAY relationship identified in the ALONSO and VON THÜNEN MODELS of land-use distributions. Colin Clark (1951) noted that population density declines exponentially with distance from the CENTRAL BUSINESS DISTRICT, and further empirical studies have replicated his findings: in general the younger the city, the shallower the gradient. RJJ

Reference

Clark, C. 1951: Urban population densities. *Journal of the Royal Statistical Society* 114: 110–16.

deontology Having to do with what is right in a moral sense. Thus a deontological theory of ETHICS or SOCIAL JUSTICE will be concerned with the right conduct, with something right in itself rather than with design or purpose in the pursuit of some ultimate good (cf. TELEOLOGY). The emphasis is on individual duty, like telling the truth, keeping promises or acting justly. Critics point out that doing the right thing can sometimes have bad consequences: telling the truth may not always be the best thing to do, and the Holocaust was perpetrated by people who thought they were doing their duty.

DMS

dependence A dependent relationship between two or more societies. Dependence implies that the ability of a society to survive and to reproduce itself derives, in large measure, from its links with other dominant societies. Without such links (manifest, for example, in flows of value, POWER, technology, AID, political influence and control) a dependent society may be unable to sustain the conditions for its own continued existence.

For Dos Santos (1973), dominant societies are able to achieve self-sustaining growth whilst dependent societies grow only as a reflection of the dominant. A dependent society is tied for its own SOCIAL REPRODUCTION to the dynamics of a dominant society. A good example of such a relationship is that of the so-called 'emerging markets' for security investments evaluated by, and so harnessed to and dependent upon, uneven geographies of financial opportunities created and monitored by global financial markets. The changing criteria of investment in such markets are given entirely by conditions (e.g. financial surpluses, assessments of risk and reward) prevailing in the investor societies and can be only faintly affected by the emerging markets themselves – and then only in ways which gain approval in the investor societies (e.g. through the PRIVATIZATION of choice STATE assets).

Before relations of dependence can develop it is necessary for the means of communication between societies to exist. It follows that dependence cannot be an original condition and must, therefore, relate to the development of such means of communication. For Keith Griffin (1969) the origins of dependence are to be found in the expansion of European influence. He stresses the symbiotic relationship between the development of dependence and the development of UNDERDEVELOPMENT:

> Nearly all of the people in today's underdeveloped areas were members of viable societies which could satisfy the economic needs of the community. Yet these societies were shattered when they came into contact with an expanding Europe. Europe did not 'discover' the underdeveloped countries, on the contrary it created them. In many cases, in fact, the societies with which Europe came into contact were sophisticated, cultured and wealthy.

According to this view, relations of dependence are produced by the disintegration of viable societies resulting from their contact with a powerful external social influence. For some, such as the analyses made by Raoul Prebisch (1950) for the UN Economic Commission for Latin America (ECLA), this contact was related to dependent trade relations (see TERMS OF TRADE) and could be transformed by import and/or export substituting industrial investment. But, for others, much more was involved in dependence (see Peet, 1991, ch. 4).

Following Baran's (1973) argument that UNDERDEVELOPMENT in the periphery is caused by the loss of surplus to the core, André Gunder Frank (1989) argued that DEVELOPMENT and underdevelopment are flip sides of the same coin and that dependence is closely related to the process of ACCUMULATION and development in core capitalist societies. CAPITALISM involves the production of surplus value by the application of labour power (including the application of knowledge) to the production (of material and non-material values) and the extraction and concentration of surplus value by capital (see MARXIAN ECONOMICS). The incorporation of regions such as Latin America into the globalizing capitalist world ECONOMIC GEOGRAPHY involves, according to Frank, a flow of surplus value from satellites – local, peripheral producers, dependent upon external sources of capital, to metropolises – regional, national and global centres of accumulation (see GLOBALIZATION). The surplus may be extracted either directly – through relations of ownership and control – or indirectly through mechanisms like unequal exchange (Emmanuel, 1972) whereby large amounts of (cheap) labour power in the periphery have to be expended on primary and agricultural production, for example, to enable the import of relatively small quantities of (expensive) labour power embodied in industrial products from the core. As a result, the course of economic and social change in the peripheral satellites – articulated by a local ruling class sustained by their involvement in directing the flow of surplus value – is shaped, constrained and governed by their dependence upon the dynamic (or motive force) of the capitalist metropolis (see NEW INTERNATIONAL DIVISION OF LABOUR) and its regulatory (see REGULATION SCHOOL) institutions like national and international state systems and multilateral institutions of GOVERNANCE like the IMF. At the same time, development in the core is dependent upon underdevelopment in the periphery.

The more determinist versions of dependency theory imply that development within dependent societies can come only from outside – indeed they counter the opposite assumption in theories of MODERNIZATION – and that the distinction between metropolis and satellites is permanent and structurally determined with little room for contextual variation or local action (Foster-Carter, 1985). Given the prevalence of capitalism in globalizing economic geographies, the only possibility of development lies in isolation from the world-economy, and yet the dramatic growth of the newly industrializing countries, for example, suggests that it is the combination of internal and external factors which condition economic growth (see THIRD WORLD).

Arguments such as these, as well as a dismissal of the theoretical bases of dependency theory, have been made most notably by Booth (1985). Responding to such critiques, Richard Peet (1991, p. 54) recognizes certain analytical limitations of dependency theory but suggests that it 'opened our eyes and made us see the world from the perspective of the oppressed masses living in its "distant" corners. This is quite a contribution' and it offsets theoretical and empirical limitations without necessarily invalidating them. Furthermore, the crisis experienced by many of the Asian NICs during the late 1990s reflected in part the effect of destabilizing externally controlled financial investment strategies.

Thus, dependence is as much a social as a geographical relationship. It is based on flows of value and so genuine INTERDEPENDENCE (see Brookfield, 1975 for an early statement) will necessarily also involve the creation and realization of non-exploitative relations of production. The transformation of exchange relations is hardly sufficient (Brenner, 1977). Although dependent economies may develop through structural transformation (by import substitution, for example, or export-led growth) their degree of dependency will remain a function of the geographies of the social relations of production and of evaluation shaping such structural transformations. The question of evaluation points to a further limitation of dependency as an explanation of underdevelopment – its stress on unequal power relations manifest in the criteria which shape flows of value around the world economic geography.

However, as Michael Storper (1997) has argued, exchange relations cannot be reduced merely to those of quantities – prices and flows. Within 'network production systems' such traded linkages are 'underpinned by a complex structure of interrelations . . . which allows learning [and is dependent] on the conventions and relations underneath transactional linkages, as well as . . . untraded interdependencies'. However, the political economy of power in the contemporary globalizing ECONOMIC GEOGRAPHY inscribes the one-way relations of dependence all too clearly whilst its evaluations restrict the positive possibilities in Storper's reflexivities.

So dependency is not merely material. Prevailing discourses of evaluation played out in the major financial centres of the world economic geography condition the scope of local action and force compliance with the economic and financial norms articulated through these centres. Such relations of power work very directly in, for example, the dynamic and turbulent geographies of 'emerging markets' as a category of portfolio investment defined and evaluated by the agents of financial capital.

Dependency does not, therefore, necessarily refer only to material inequalities of power but is framed by the prevailing DISCOURSES though which the global economic geography is understood and directed. (See also DEVELOPMENT; DUAL ECONOMY; SUBALTERN STUDIES; WORLD-SYSTEMS ANALYSIS.) RL

References

Baran, P. 1973: *The political economy of growth*. Harmondsworth: Penguin. · Booth, D. 1985: Marxism and development sociology: interpreting the impasse. *World Development* 13 (7): 761–87. · Brenner, R. 1977: The origins of capitalist development: a critique of neo-Smithian Marxism. *New Left Review* 104: 25–92. · Brookfield, H. 1975: *Interdependent development*. London: Methuen; Pittsburgh, PA: University of Pittsburgh Press. · Dos Santos, T. 1973: The crisis of development theory and the problem of dependency in Latin America. In H. Bernstein, ed., *Underdevelopment and development*. Harmondsworth: Penguin. · Emmanuel, A. 1972: *Unequal exchange: a study of the imperialism of trade*. New York: Monthly Review Press. · Foster-Carter, A. 1985: *The sociology of development*. Ormskirk: Causeway. · Frank, A.G. 1989: The development of underdevelopment. *Monthly Review* 41 (July): 37–51. · Griffin, K. 1969: *Underdevelopment in Spanish America*. London: Allen & Unwin; Cambridge, MA: MIT Press. · Peet, R. 1991: *Global capitalism*. London: Routledge. · Prebisch, R. 1950: *The economic development of Latin America and its principal problems*. New York: UN ECLA. · Storper, M. 1997: Regional economies as relational assets. Ch. 19 in R. Lee and J. Wills, eds, *Geographies of economies*. London: Arnold, 248–58.

Suggested reading

Corbridge, S. 1986: *Capitalist world development*. London: Macmillan, ch. 2. · Corbridge, S., ed., 1996: *Development studies: a reader*. London: Arnold, section one. · Kitching, G. 1982: *Development and underdevelopment in historical perspective*. London and New York: Methuen, ch. 6. · Peet (1991) chs 4, 9 and 10.

dependency ratio The number of children (aged 0–14) and old people (aged 65 or over) in a population as a ratio of the number of adults (aged 15–64). The dependency ratio is a useful comparative indicator of the average number of people that each member of the active or potentially active (i.e. employed) population has to support. The definitions by age group are to an extent arbitrary and may be varied to take account of, for example, changes in retirement or school-leaving age. The general definition of adults as aged 15–64 tends to overstate the actual size of the active population in a typical western society.

Changes in the dependency ratio may have profound implications for social and economic policy, for example the provision of schools and pensions. (See also AGE AND SEX STRUCTURE; POPULATION PYRAMID.) PEO

Suggested Reading

Clarke, J.I. 1972: *Population geography*, 2nd edn. Oxford and New York: Pergamon.

dependency theory A complex body of THEORY with STRUCTURALIST, Marxist and Latin American roots which explains the blocked or 'distorted' character of THIRD WORLD development through the powers of external (colonial or post-colonial) metropolitan powers to exploit peripheral satellites (see ACCUMULATION; COLONIALISM; CORE–PERIPHERY MODEL; DEVELOPMENT; UNDER-DEVELOPMENT; UNEVEN DEVELOPMENT). Dependency emerged as a critique of MODERNIZATION theory and economic dualism, arguing that Third World POVERTY was not a function of local failure but rather was a function of the history of the dialectical relations between metropole and satellite. At the heart of the theory stands a claim about the dominant role of external (i.e. global) powers and the super-exploitation by which the metropole subordinates the satellite. The peripheries supplied primary products and low-technology manufactures for the First World in exchange for high technology, high value-added goods. Economic dependency was further expressed through political and cultural *neo-colonialism*. This process is captured in Gunder Frank's (1967) notion of *the development of underdevelopment*. Dependency as a concept implies that the pace, character and timing of national accumulation is determined by non-local (external) forces (Santos 1970). To the extent that accumulation does occur in the periphery it is located in satellite regions which are directly linked to, and regulated by, the metropole.

Dependency theory has strong Latin American roots (the *dependistas*) which can be traced to the debates surrounding TRADE and the global market in the 1950s. Like other parts of the periphery, the colonial experience in Latin America had produced economic trajectories based on outward-oriented primary commodity exploitation. During the 1930s exports of primary products collapsed and Latin American governments often turned to import-substituting INDUSTRIALIZATION. After the Second World War, however, Latin America lost US$13.4 billion due to the deterioration in relative prices. The structuralist approach of Raul Prebisch (1950) at the Economic Commission for Latin America (ECLA: founded in 1948) addressed the problems of primary export dependency, and the problems of specialization within a Ricardian theory of trade (see NEO-RICARDIAN ECONOMICS). The *Prebisch thesis* claimed that the global system was not a uniform marketplace but was divided structurally between rich and poor economies (cf. NORTH–SOUTH). ECLA focused on the self-contained nature of the US economy, on TERMS OF TRADE, the post-1945 dollar shortage and global finance. From this emerged a two-prong development strategy: the need for regional cooperation in Latin America and the need for more liberal trade and financial policies by the capitalist powers.

The emphasis on structural constraints paved the way for Keynesian and Marxist-inspired intellectuals such as André Gunder Frank, Celso Furtado and Henrique Cardoso (the President of Brazil) to formulate a full-blown theory of dependency. Furtado's (1965) account of the Brazilian crisis is an exemplary text. He points to the importance of studying the forms of colonial and post-colonial incorporation into the world economy. He shows the contradictions and limits of both import-substitution and primary export orientation, and the centrality of what he calls institutional arrangements – CLASS relations – in explaining the truncated forms of accumulation and industrialization. Cardoso and Faletto (1970) provide a powerful historical and political analysis of dependency effectively employing the categories of class to make a strong normative argument for the role of a developmental STATE, the regulation of transnational capital flows, and for regional cooperation. An important study of the contemporary forms of *dependent development* was undertaken by Peter Evans (1979) who showed, in the case of Brazil, how key sectors were dominated by transnational capital and who exercised control through direct foreign investment and through the control of production technologies (cf. TRANSNATIONAL CORPORATIONS). Dependency is seen to increase both geographical uneven development – the *islands of development thesis* – and also internal social stratification. Dependency theory was stagnationist, an argument about class (its non-bourgeois character) and state (its neo-colonial character), and a case for the non-dynamic role of agriculture and the centrality of mechanisms of surplus transfer (cf. MARXIAN ECONOMICS).

Dependency theory was heavily criticized in the 1970s, a critique driven in part by the changing realities of the world economy (Palma, 1978). If the terms of trade crisis of the 1950s provided the ether in which Prebisch developed his incipient *dependista* position, the 1970s of the Asian tigers framed the critique. Warren (1974) argued that dependency was in practice the theory of the national bourgeoisie and argued that capitalism was indeed a progressive and radical force which *dependista*-inspired theories of autarky or delinking (or import-substitution) ignored at their peril. Like POPULISM, dependency theory gave primacy to exploitation in the realm of exchange (Kitching, 1982). While dependency theory reached its apogee during the 1960s and 1970s – as many of its intellectual leaders were compelled to flee the region in the face of the militarization there – it has nonetheless continued to be a rich source of ideas. Enriched by theories of IMPERIALISM, and by debates over MODES OF PRODUCTION, it also provided fuel for WORLD-SYSTEMS ANALYSIS. Indeed dependency theory has been 'regionalized' in a number of ways as its ideas were taken up, appropriated and made to speak to the specificities of Africa (Amin, 1976), India and elsewhere (Preston, 1996). In the context of the increasing polarity between North and South in the late twentieth century, *dependista* concerns with uneven development, technological polarization, and trade have experienced a new lease of life (Blaney, 1996). MW

References

Amin, S. 1976: *Unequal development*. New York: Monthly Review. · Blaney, N. 1996: Reconceptualising autonomy. *Review of International Political Economy* 4 (4): 459–97. · Cardoso, F.H. and Faletto, E. 1970: *Dependency and development*. Berkeley: University of California Press. · Evans, P. 1979: *Dependent development*. Princeton: Princeton University Press. · Furtado, C. 1965: *Diagnosis of the Brazilian crisis*. Berkeley: University of California Press. · Gunder Frank, A. 1967: *Capitalism and underdevelopment in Latin America*. New York: Monthly Review. · Kitching, G. 1982: *Development and underdevelopment in historical perspective*. London: Methuen. · Palma, G. 1978: Dependency and imperialism. *World Development* 8. · Prebisch, R. 1950: *The economic development of Latin America*. New York: United Nations. · Preston, P. 1996: *Development theory*. Oxford: Blackwell. · Santos, T. 1970: *Imperialismo y dependencia*. Mexico City: Ediciones Era. · Warren, B. 1974: *Imperialism: pioneer of capitalism*. London: Verso.

desertification Desertification (sometimes referred to as *desertization*) is one of the most serious environmental problems confronting the world in the late twentieth century. Drylands cover more than one-third of the earth's surface, large parts of which are being heavily, and perhaps irreversibly, degraded. Desertification refers to the degradation of lands in these dry areas and conventionally, following the United Nations Conference on Desertification (UNCOD; held in Nairobi in 1977), and is defined as 'the diminution or destruction of the biological potential of the land [which] can lead ultimately to desert-like conditions'. Desertification is thus a global problem characterized by the deterioration and degradation of soil and vegetative cover, and is not confined to deserts *per se* but can occur in any dryland region (Glantz, 1977): according to the United Nations Environment Program (UNEP), drylands denote an area with rainfall up to 600 mm per year. While desertification was implicitly understood by UNCOD to be restricted to dry areas, some scientists have expanded the definition to subsume the impoverishment of any terrestrial ECOSYSTEM which can be measured in reduced productivity of desirable plants, undesirable alterations in biomass and plant and fauna diversity, and accelerated soil erosion (Dregne, 1985).

Processes of desertification are of great antiquity. The Sumerian civilization which exploited the Tigris and Euphrates river basin suffered the consequences of poor irrigation and salinity-induced desertification six thousand years ago; the deforestation and proliferation of desert-like conditions was noted by Plato 2500 years ago in his account of Attica. Desertification reached the world stage in the 1970s, however, in the aftermath of the great Sahelian drought/FAMINE (1968–73) and the prospect of a global food crisis.

UNCOD brought together scientists, policy-makers, activists and government representatives from more than 100 countries to design a Plan of Action to combat desertification. Their scientific investigations not only suggested that the Sahelian tragedy was not a natural disaster caused by drought but also estimated that 20 million square miles of the earth's surface and 281 million people were affected by at least 'moderate desertification'. UNCOD called desertification 'an aspect of the widespread deterioration of ecosystems under the combined pressure of adverse and fluctuating climate and excessive exploitation' (cited in Grainger, 1990, p. 33).

Insofar as drylands are in some measure defined by scarcity of water, highly variable precipitation and limited biomass, they are, from the vantage point of human use, always potentially fragile and vulnerable. The causes of desertification are, however, complex both in terms of the physical and biological sciences and in terms of SOCIAL THEORY. On the climatic front, there is no question that cycles of drought have a long history in the arid zones. But the nature and impact of global climate change, the impact of biophysical feedback (albedo), the consequences of dust storms and GREENHOUSE effects remain the subject of intense debate and dispute (Grainger, 1990). It is clear, for example, that the Sahelian zone has experienced a decline in annual precipitation since the 1950s but this downturn may still fall within the bounds of statistical expectation. Similarly the ECOLOGY of desertification (and its purported irreversibility) is also a subject of debate. Some of the new studies of Sahelian rangelands, for example, suggest that the resiliency and stability of semi-arid savannas may be quite substantial (Leach and Mearns, 1987). In view of the problems over the definition of desertification – there are over 100 – the scale of desertification is itself a thorny question: two recent studies by Mabbutt and Dregne differ by an order of magnitude of 50 per cent! (see Grainger 1990, pp. 141–2). The UNCOD map of desertification estimates 37.6 million sq. km to be at serious risk of desertification (two-thirds of which are in Africa and Asia).

It is widely understood that desertification can only be understood in relation to human practice but there is no agreement on the weighting of social processes which include: agricultural production in marginal areas (overcultivation), overgrazing, poor irrigation practice, deforestation, population growth/migration, state policies, and surplus extraction/exploitation (Glantz, 1987). In order to avoid a shopping list approach to questions of desertification dynamics it is important to engage in a sophisticated POLITICAL ECOLOGY which examines the patterns of livelihood (political economy) and ecology in specific places (Watts, 1983, 1987). The revisionist work on desertification among Sahelian pastoral communities is instructive in this regard (Turner, 1993; Watts, 1987; Leach and Mearns, 1997; cf. PASTORALISM). This scholarship suggests that certain narratives of desertification became dominant (and were encapsulated in the UNCOD report) which were alarmist in their predictions, rooted in limited research, and rested on simple-minded presumptions of drought causality, poor local resource management by farmers and pastoralists, and unregulated population growth. New research starts from a more sophisticated and fine-grained analysis of the ecology of rangelands (which complexifies alarmist positions), and starts from the paradox of why farmers and pastoralists who know a great deal about their environment should self-consciously overexploit it. The starting point here is POVERTY and the ways in which access to and control over local resources is changing in such a way that SUSTAINABILITY and CONSERVATION are undermined, and how situationally rational decisions may induce desertification. Poor pastoralist COMMUNITIES, which are increasingly differentiated economically, are subject to patterns of outmigration, changing TERMS OF TRADE, and agricultural and STATE encroachment which produce excessive animal densities around some dry season wells. Degradation is associated therefore with some locations (public access wells) and some places and some seasons. Whether this represents long-term desertification is another matter. The UNCED Conference in Rio in 1992 (Agenda 21) discussed desertification in much less alarmist terms. MW

References

Dregne, H. 1985: Aridity and land degradation, *Environment* 27 (8): 18–33. · Grainger, A. 1990: *The threatening desert*. London: Earthscan. · Glantz, M. 1977: *Desertification*. Boulder: Westview. · Glantz, M., ed., 1987: *Drought and famine in Africa*. Cambridge: Cambridge University Press. · Leach, M. and Mearns, R. 1997: *The lie of the land*. London: Currey. · Turner, M. 1993: Overstocking the range, *Economic Geography* 69 (4): 402–22. · Watts, M. 1983: *Silent violence*. Berkeley: University of California Press. · Watts, M. 1987: Drought, environment and food security. In M. Glantz, ed., *Drought and famine in Africa*. Cambridge: Cambridge University Press, 171–212.

development Development is one of the most complex words in the English language. In his book *Keywords*, Raymond Williams (1976, pp. 104–6) notes that the historically complex genealogy of development in western thinking can 'limit and confuse virtually any generalising description of the current world order': rather it is in the analysis of the 'real practices subsumed by development that more specific recognitions are necessary and possible'. The history of these real practices is, however, long and their meanings unstable and labile. Development came into the English language in the eighteenth century with its root sense of unfolding and was granted a new lease of life by the evolutionary ideas of the nineteenth century (Parajuli, 1991; Watts, 1995; cf. DARWINISM; LAMARCKISM). As a consequence, development has rarely broken from organicist notions of growth or from a close affinity with TELEOLOGICAL views of history, science and progress in the West. By the end of the nineteenth century, for example, it was possible to talk of societies in a state of 'frozen development'. There is another aspect to the genealogy, however, traced by Cowen and Shenton (1996) to eighteenth-and nineteenth-century notions of *Progress*, and specifically to development as a sort of theological discourse set against the disorder and disjunctures of capitalist growth. Classical POLITICAL ECONOMY – including the work of Smith, Ricardo, Malthus (cf. NEO-CLASSICAL ECONOMICS; NEO-RICARDIAN ECONOMICS; MALTHUSIAN MODEL) – is suffused with the tensions between the desire for unfettered ACCUMULATION on the one hand and unregulated desire as the origin of misery and vice on the other (Herbert, 1990). Development in Victorian England emerged in part, then, as a cultural and theological response to *Progress*. Christopher Lasch (1990), for example, has described a late nineteenth-century obsessed by cultural instability and cataclysm. Saint-Simon himself devoted himself in his last years to a new creed of Christianity to accompany his industrial and scientific vision of capitalist progress. Accordingly, trusteeship, mission and faith were, according to Cowen and Shenton (1996), the nineteenth-century touchstones of development.

There is a body of development theory of much more recent provenance, dominated by the profession of economics, however, which began to emerge between the two world wars. This is a complex story to tell since this THEORY is not simply an invention of western economics or political economy, but has been shaped and profoundly contributed to by various THIRD WORLD intellectual traditions (for example Maoism from China, DEPENDENCY THEORY from Latin America, Tier Mondism from Africa and so on). To simplify an enormously complex field, one can identify four broad conventional streams of development theory:

- one is broadly *Keynesian or neo-Keynesian* (see GROWTH THEORY);
- one draws upon *neo-classical economics* (see NEO-LIBERALISM);
- one is *Marxist* (including dependency theory, MODES OF PRODUCTION, WORLD SYSTEMS ANALYSIS: cf. MARXIAN ECONOMICS); and
- one is *institutional* (for example TRANSACTION COST approaches).

Each of these four has complex genealogies and histories which privilege the STATE, the market and CIVIL SOCIETY in different ways; each is in addition shaped historically by the conditions to which they are made to speak (Peet and Watts, 1995). The broad outlines of these 'conventional' development theories have been reviewed in a number of texts (see Preston, 1996; Cypher and Dietz, 1997).

There is a sense in which Third World development – in its specific forms of state and multilateral policy harnessed to the tasks of championing economic growth, 'catching up', improving welfare and producing governable subjects – is of more recent provenance. It has been argued that development was invented or discovered by President Truman in his famous 1949 speech on 'fair dealing' and undeveloped areas (Sachs, 1992). The key conjuncture is the decade after the end of the Second World War (Escobar, 1995), in spite of the fact that the Third World was seemingly of marginal concern in relation to the reconstruction of Europe, the revivification of the world financial system and the threat of COMMUNISM. These origins of development theory and practice as an academic and governmental enterprise – and of development economics as its HEGEMONIC expression – are inseparable from the process by which the 'colonial world' was reconfigured into a 'developing world' beginning in the 1930s but especially in the aftermath of the Second World War (see COLONIALISM): Africa, for example, became a serious object of planned development after the Great Depression of the 1930s. The British Colonial Development and Welfare Act (1940) and the French Investment Fund for Economic and Social Development (1946) both represented responses to the crises and challenges which IMPERIAL powers confronted in Africa, providing a means by which they could negotiate the perils of independence movements on the one hand and a perpetuation of the colonial mission on the other. But the process by which this produces 'development as a historically singular process' (Escobar, 1995, p. 9) requires a sensitivity to regions, political economy and politics. The significance of this misreading resides not only in the production of poor (and impoverished) history but also in its failure to realize a much more complex and nuanced way in which global DISCOURSE and local POWER, and local discourse and global power, intersect and reproduce particular regional formations. Development was necessarily Eurocentric because its origins lay in the European efforts to deal with the essential fact of CAPITALISM as Schumpeter put it, the tragedy of UNDERDEVELOPMENT and the paradoxical unity of MODERN-

ITY (Berman, 1982). In the same way that Polanyi (1944) saw the later eighteenth-century welfare debates in England as the discovery of the 'social', so the invention of development in nineteenth-century Britain was about the 'failure' of free market capitalism. Within the belly of Modernization has always resided its utopian alternatives.

In his important book *Encountering development* (1995), Arturo Escobar begins from the premise of development as a particular sort of social imaginary. Development, in his view, 'relies on setting up the world as a *picture*, so that the whole system can be grasped in some orderly fashion as forming a structure or system' (p. 56) [emphasis added]. His book purports to show how this picture was painted, what acts of imagination were entailed in its depiction, and how this IMAGE came to be held as a sort of blueprint for a panoply of institutions, a diverse community of planners, politicians and bureaucrats, and for a battery of technologies harnessed for social engineering on a global scale. In short, Escobar portrays how the hegemonic vision of post-war development was institutionalized and with what consequences. Escobar necessarily starts with the fundamental position occupied by economics in the knowledge and practice of development, but posits the economy as an institution composed of production, power and signification. The economic sphere in this rendering is as much cultural as material, and hence as much about the production of social order, truth and forms of subjectivity as child mortality, GNP and high-yielding varieties of rice and wheat (cf. GREEN REVOLUTION).

Escobar finds modern development discourse to be the latest insidious chapter of the larger history of the expansion of western reason. In his diagnosis, development was an invention – more properly a 'historically produced discourse' (p. 6) – of the post-1945 era. This discourse is governed by the same principles as colonial discourse but has its own regimes of truth and forms of REPRESENTATION (pp. 9–10). Development is about forms of knowledge, the power that regulates its practices, and the forms of subjectivity fostered by its impulses. Hegemonic development discourse appropriates societal practices and meanings into the modern realm of explicit calculation, thereby subjecting them to western forms of power-knowledge. It ensures the conformity of peoples to First World economic and cultural practices. Development has in short penetrated, integrated, managed and controlled large parts of the globe in increasingly pernicious and intractable ways. It has produced underdevelopment, a condition politically and economically manageable through normalization, the regulation of knowledges, and the moralization and technification of POVERTY and exploitation as political and material problems. The new space of the Third World, carved out of the vast surface of global societies, is a new field of power dominated by development sciences replete with their own truth claims and constructed subjectivity. The political technologies of development practice which sought to erase underdevelopment from the face of the earth have, to employ Escobar's language, converted a 'dream into a nightmare' (p. 4).

In keeping with a number of other southern activists and hybrid intellectuals – perhaps most notably those associated with the Delhi Center for Developing Societies, including Rajni Kothari, Ashish Nandy and Shiv Vishvanathan – Escobar sees poverty as invented and globalized with the creation of a battery of transnational 'welfare' institutions at Bretton Woods and in San Francisco following the signing of the United Nations charter. The discourse of national and international planning and development agencies was able to constitute a reality by the way it was able to form systematically the objects of which it spoke, to group and arrange them in certain ways, and to give them a unity. PATRIARCHY, ETHNOCENTRISM, GENDER, RACE and NATIONALITY were embraced in this discourse, at the same time that economists were privileged within its ranks. This rule-governed system has remained unchanged at the level of practice, although the discursive formations have been unstable. In all of this modernity's objectifying regime of visuality turned people of the South into spectacles, and the panoptic gaze of development became an apparatus of social control. Institutions such as the World Bank thus embody what Donna Haraway (1991) calls the 'God trick' of seeing everything from nowhere. Development is constructed in large part through keywords – 'toxic words' – which really mean something else: 'planning' normalizes people; RESOURCES desacralize NATURE; poverty is an invention; science is violence; basic needs are CYBORGS, and so forth (see Sachs, 1992). In all of this the Third World came to believe what the First World promulgated: development as a technical project, as rational decision-making, as specialized knowledge, and as normalization (see GOVERNMENTALITY).

There is a complex and differentiated body of work gradually emerging since the 1970s which represents an effort to imagine alternatives, which sees development as a seriously flawed, many would say a disastrously failed, MODERNIST project (Pieterse, 1996). The intellectual and theoretical origins of this critique of what one might call conventional or mainstream development theory and practice – of both neo-classical economics, the new institutionalism and Marxist political economy – is complex, but sheds much light on both the imaginative geography of development, and its imaginary alternatives. In general it needs to be said that the entire field of POST-DEVELOPMENT stands uneasily with respect to modernity – in some cases as a reactionary anti-modernism, in some cases as anti-modernist cultural RELATIVISM, in others as a celebration of 'critical traditionalism' (the language is Ashish Nandy's (1988)). But it is also curious that this flowering of IMAGINATIVE GEOGRAPHIES attached to anti-modernist sentiment – of thinking about alternatives, of alterity and of OTHERNESS – occur precisely at the apogee of two variants of what might be called ultra- or hyper modernism. One is the forging of *the so-called Washington consensus: the triumphalism of the neo-classical counter-revolution* (see NEO-LIBERALISM; STRUCTURAL ADJUSTMENT), the very idea in the wake of 1989 that – to employ the language of the World Bank – there are no alternatives to capitalism and free markets. The other is the *Euro-American vision of modernity* – the object of the post-development community's wrath – which is, in some quarters, seen to be unstable, differentiated and internally reconstituting itself. Ulrick Beck's (1994) notion of 'reflexive modernization' (of new and variegated modernities driven by industrial capitalism's ability to undercut itself, to generate life-threatening RISKS; cf. RISK SOCIETY) and Anthony Giddens's (1994) post-traditionalism and post-scarcity (GLOBALIZED forms of decentred autonomy, emotional DEMOCRACY and debureaucratization) posits another sort of post-development at the capitalist core. In both of these 'alternatives' within the West, some of the attributes which so enrage the likes of Kothari, Alvares or Escobar – developmental linearity, faith in progress, functional autonomization, instrumental rationality and mass politics – are themselves seen to be under threat by the very dynamism and achievements of modernization itself.

What then is the particular genealogy of post-development thinking?

The crisis of needs in the 1970s: one thread surfaces from the 1970s' disillusion with the world economic order and with the fact that the poorest 40 per cent had somehow missed the boat. It is from this pessimism, disenchantment with growth and trickle down that the Dag Hammarskjöld Foundation called for 'Another Development' geared to need satisfaction, self-reliance, and endogeneity (cf. GROWTH POLE). Bjorne Hettne's important book *Three worlds of development* (1990) is the pivotal text in the reaction to failed modernization, and offers a rejection of the 'Eurocentric model' and a plea for egalitarian, participatory ecological, self-reliant and ethno-development strategies.

The 'impasse' of Marxian political economy: another thread emerges from the debates within Marxism, and the sense, articulated in Booth (1994), that Marxian political economy had entered an epistemological, practical, and theoretical cul-de-sac. In order to jettison its economism, reductionism, totalizing history, and CLASS determinism – as it were the worst of the Althusserian revolution – political economy had to encompass diversity, agency, local initiatives, and heterogeneity. Much of this work turns to networks, local institutions, and COMMUNITY institutions – that is to say to the SUBALTERN communities and knowledges invoked by Escobar – as a way of rethinking rural development.

Post-colonialism and the ur history of development: development theory was driven in radically new directions by the POST-STRUCTURAL turn, and specifically by the twin themes of post-coloniality and discourse. In the latter, the *ur* history of the doctrines of development are excavated, and development texts examined as particular forms of text and storytelling (Roe, 1991; Shenton and Cowen, 1996). In the latter, POST-COLONIALISM signals the proliferation of histories, temporalities and spatialities and, to quote Stuart Hall (1996, p. 248), 'the intrusion of DIFFERENCE and specificity into the generalising and Eurocentric post-ENLIGHTENMENT grand narratives .... [to emphasize] the multiplicity of lateral and decentred cultural connections, movements and migrations which make up the world today' (1996, p. 248; cf. GRAND THEORY).

Rediscovering civil society and the new social movements: however subject to hyperbole and exaggeration, the gradual 'democratization' of the post-socialist bloc and the bureaucratic authoritarian states of the South unquestionably provided a new breathing space for CIVIL

SOCIETY – what Cohen and Arato (1992, p. 29) call the 'resurrection, re-emergence and rebirth of civil society'. Indeed, the contraction of the state under (imposed) economic austerity, created opportunities for all manner of Non-Governmental Organizations, SOCIAL MOVEMENTS, and associational networks to flourish as never before. It is this renewed concern with civil society – with communities, popular movements, and social networks – which represents in some quarters the prospect of a new way of doing politics, and the possibility of alternative (grassroots, participatory, subaltern) visions of development outside of the horizon of both state and market (cf. NEW SOCIAL MOVEMENTS).

Indigenous knowledge and global threats: ecological concerns pushed the anti-development agenda in two senses. First, the environmental toll of rapid INDUSTRIALIZATION in the NICs and within the SOCIALIST bloc, coupled with potentially catastrophic forms of *global* degradation (ozone depletion, GLOBAL WARMING), fuelled new concerns over the sustainability of mainstream development. And second, the growing theoretical interest within POLITICAL ECOLOGY over local RESOURCE MANAGEMENT and the repositories of local knowledge (for example forms of 'PEASANT science' as alternatives to 'western expertise' documented by Paul Richards (1985) in *Indigenous agricultural revolution*), reaffirmed the salience of subaltern knowledge and indigenous local practice – typically embodied in the proliferation of all manner of southern green movements – as a counterweight to big science and multilateral greening of the World Bank sort (Routledge, 1994).

Globalization and its malcontents: finally, the rapidity with which the neo-liberal orthodoxy was adopted – through a mixture of coercion and consent – throughout the Second and Third Worlds (keywords which themselves became increasingly inadequate as ways of classifying geographic space), inevitably triggered a counter-reaction against the disruptive social, economic and political consequences of 'globalization' (the dominance of market forces, the integration of the global economy, the genesis of world-wide consumerism and media integration, and the transformation of production and labour markets). To take one example, the United Nations Research Institute for Social Development (UNRISD: one of the UN agencies no less), refers to the 'states of disarray' produced by the 'painful adjustment' of market INTEGRATION and globalization (UNRISD, 1996).

The post-development PARADIGM can be understood in part, then, as a reaction to and a product of a particular congeries of theoretical development (knowledge production) and political economic transformations. The *évenements* of 1989, the unprecedented dislocative effects of globalization and market integration, a deepening sense of global ecological CRISIS, the flowering of civil society and social movements intersected with what one might call with some hesitancy the post-structural turn in its panoply of guises. There is of course a polyphony of voices within this post-development community – Vandana Shiva, Wolfgang Sachs, Arturo Escobar, Gustavo Esteva and Ashish Nandy, for example, occupy quite different intellectual and political locations. But it is striking how intellectuals, activists, practitioners and academics within this diverse community participated in a global debate. The journal *Alternatives* is in some sense its institutionalized mouth-piece, and some sites (in India and Mexico for example) have emerged as its intellectual flagships (the Delhi Center has even been referred to as the new Frankfurt School; see Dallmayr, 1996).

What then can be said about the turn to discourse and the deployment of post-structural tools in the critique of development as capitalist modernity? On the one hand it is important to examine the *ur* history of development and to take seriously the ways in which what passes as development knowledge and practice are institutionalized and with what effects. The language of development is not neutral and neither are its institutions. To deconstruct SUSTAINABLE DEVELOPMENT – to interrogate the assumptions of particular institutionalized visions of green development – is useful on many counts (cf. DECONSTRUCTION). To see how and with what consequences 'ecological economics' has been employed by the Global Environmental Facility might shed much light on the sorts of projects funded by the World Bank and the consequences of specific types of large multilateral programmes. Conducting ETHNOGRAPHIES of development institutions, as Ferguson effectively does in his account of a project in Botswana (1990), is singularly helpful in understanding how particular places and problems are constructed and legitimated by experts and managers. But a singular focus on the discursive aspects of knowledge/power, on populist senses of empowerment and resistance, and on cultural diversity and difference carries its own freight.

Some of these new critical approaches to development ironically have similarities with earlier forms of radical development thinking, notably 1960s' DEPENDENCY THEORY, a perspective largely discredited on the grounds of its simplistic theory of power and crude sense of political economy. Like the Latin American *dependentistas*, it confers enormous power on an external world system, privileges local autonomy and cultural identity, and sees SOVEREIGNTY as a central plank of its own vision of development (Cardoso and Faletto, 1979). Like dependency theory, the nature of external power is often crudely articulated in bold outline – which in Escobar's case is ironic insofar as he employs Foucault to express an alternative theory of capillary power. Escobar's account of the World Bank as an instrument of modernity's power, for example, reads like Third World NATIONALISM of old. No attempt is made to lay out the complex internal divisions within the Bank or the important reversals made by the Bank around some environmental and dam projects (Fox, 1995), or (on the basis of data he himself provides) the relative insignificance of World Bank resources in relation to other capital flows to the South. Indeed, the anti-development communities' focus on keywords and the representation of the Third World could be pulled from a cursory reading of Che Guevara's meditation on the condition of underdevelopment (the Third World as a 'stunted child') penned at least thirty years ago.

It is surely incontestable that knowledge can be a source of power but the danger of a turn to discourse is that development ideas simply become (and remain) narratives or stories. Development narratives remain, in other words, only narratives. In Roe's (1991) work, for example, development problems are converted into stories or folk tales. Stories underwrite or stabilize the assumptions of policy makers. What is required in narrative policy analysis is, then, good, better or different stories. Development as narrative or story telling (see Watts, 1995 for a review of this literature) runs the risk of excluding politics, interest, institutionalized authority and legitimacy and putting in their place a naive sense of sitting around the campfire telling each other stories.

MW

References

Alvarez, C. 1992: *Science, Development and Violence*. Delhi: Oxford University Press. · Beck, U. 1994: The reinvention of politics. In U. Beck, A. Giddens and S. Lash, *Reflexive modernization*. Cambridge: Polity, 1–55. · Berman, M. 1982: *All that is solid melts into air: the experience of modernity*. New York: Penguin. · Booth, D., ed., 1994: *Rethinking social development*. London: Methuen. · Cardoso, H. and Faletto, E. 1979: *Dependency and development in Latin America*. Berkeley: University of California Press. · Cohen, J. and Arato, A. 1992: *Civil society and political theory*. Cambridge, MA: MIT Press. · Cowen, M. and Sherton, R. 1996: *Doctrine of development*. London: Routledge. · Cypher, J. and Dietz, J. 1997: *The process of economic development*. London: Routledge. · Dallmayr, F. 1996: Global development? *Alternatives* 21: 259–82. · Escobar, Arturo. 1995: *Encountering development*. Princeton: Princeton University Press. · Esteva, G. 1992: Development. In Wolfgang Sachs, ed., *The development dictionary: a guide to knowledge as power*. London: Zed Books, 6–25. · Ferguson, J. 1990: *The antipolitics machine*. Cambridge: Cambridge University Press. · Fox, J. 1995: Governance and development in Mexico, *Journal of Development Studies* 34: 610–44. · Giddens, A. 1994: Living in a post traditional society. In U. Beck, A. Giddens and S. Lash, *Reflexive modernization*. Cambridge: Polity, 56–109. · Hall, S. 1996: When was the post-colonial? In I. Chambers and L. Curti, eds, *The post-colonial question*. London: Routledge, 242–60. · Harkwag, D. 1991: *Simians, cyborgs and women*. London: Routledge. · Herbert, C. 1990: *Culture and anomie*. Chicago: University of Chicago Press. · Hettne, B. 1985: *Three worlds of development*. London: Methuen. · Hettne, B. 1990: *Three worlds of development*. London: Methuen. · Kothari, R. 1989: *Rethinking development*. New York: Horizons. · Lasch, C. 1991: *The true and only heaven*. London: Norton. · Nandy, A. 1987: Cultural frames for social transformation. *Alternatives* 12 (1): 101–23. · Nandy, A. 1998: Culture, state and the rediscovery of Irdion politics. *Interculture* 21: 2–17. · Parajuli, P. 1991: Power and knowledge in development discourse. *International Social Science Journal* 127: 173–90. · Peet, R. and Watts, M. 1995: Introduction. In R. Peet and M. Watts, eds, *Liberation ecologies*. London: Routledge. · Pieterse, J. 1996: *My paradigm or yours?* The Hague: Working Paper #229, Institute of Social Studies. · Polanyi, K. 1944: *The great transformation*. Boston: Beacon. · Preston, D. 1996: *Development theory*. Oxford: Blackwell. · Richards, P. 1985: *African agricultural revolution*. London: Methuen. · Roe, E. 1991: Development narratives. *World Development* 19: 287–300. · Routledge, P. 1994: *Resisting and shaping the modern*. London: Routledge. · Sachs, W. (ed.) 1992: *The development dictionary*. London: 2ed. · Shiva, V. 1993: The greening of the global reach. In W. Sachs, ed., *Global ecology: a new arena of political conflict*. London: Zed Books. · Shiva, V. 1989: *Staying alive*. London: Zed Books. · UNRISD, 1995: *States of disarray*. Geneva: United Nations Research Institute for Social Development. · Watts, M. 1995: A new deal for the emotions. In J. Crush, ed., *The power of development*. London: Routledge, 44–62. · Willams, R. 1976: *Keywords*. Oxford: Oxford University Press.

Suggested Reading

Crush, J., ed., 1995: *The power of development*. London: Routledge. · Rahnema, M. and Bawtree, V., eds, 1997: *The post-development reader*. London: Zed Press.

devolution The process of devolving power from central to more local levels of government. This can frequently involve the creation of regional assemblies with limited law-making and tax-raising powers. Devolution has emerged as a key issue in Europe in recent years with the growing size and political influence of the European Union. Linguistic and cultural minorities have increasingly begun to assert their independence more strongly and to demand that they be afforded formal political recognition (see NATIONALISM). This change has been further encouraged by the European Union itself, as it is obliged to work to the principle of SUBSIDIARITY, whereby all decisions are taken as close as possible to those directly affected, thus making devolution a practical necessity.

All states devolve power to some degree, either because they are constitutionally required to do so, as in the case of Germany and the USA, or for reasons of practical management. In Europe, since Spain reverted to democracy in 1977 its government has devolved considerable regional autonomy to the Basques, the Catalans and the Andalusians. In the UK, Northern Ireland elected a new Assembly in 1998 and since 1999 Scotland has a Parliament with tax-raising powers, and complete control over many areas of political decision-making, while Wales has an Assembly with somewhat lesser powers. It would seem that, in Europe at least, the late twentieth-century trend towards supra-national political government has been paralleled by local demands for greater self-determination, often at the expense of the NATION-STATE. MB

Suggested Reading

Bradbury, J. 1996: New Labour. New Devolution? The Labour Party and the politics of English regional reform. *Regional Studies* 30: 704–12. · Deacon, R. 1996: New Labour and the Welsh Assembly: 'Preparing for a new Wales' or updating the Wales Act 1978? *Regional Studies* 30: 689–93. · Garside, P.L. and Hebbert, M. 1989: *British regionalism 1900–2000*. London: Mansell.

dialectic(s) The perpetual resolution of binary oppositions: a metaphysics most closely associated in European philosophy and social thought with G.W.F. Hegel (1770–1813) and Karl Marx (1818–83). In human geography, a simple example would be the following, essentially Hegelian reading of August Lösch's LOCATION THEORY. There:

> a perfectly homogeneous landscape with identical customers, working inside the framework of perfect competition, would necessarily develop, from its inner rules of change, into a heterogeneous landscape with both rich, active sectors and poor, depressed regions. The homogeneous regional system negates itself and generates dialectically its contradiction as regional inequalities appear. (Marchand, 1978, emphasis added).

This is a helpful first approximation, but the dialectic is usually deployed outside the framework of NEO-CLASSICAL ECONOMICS that contains conventional location theory. In fact it is a characteristic of the Löschian system that once the heterogeneous landscape has emerged it is 'frozen' in equilibrium rather than convulsed through transformation. As such, it is really an example of a categorical PARADIGM – one in which change is simply the kaleidoscopic recombination of the same and ever-present, fixed and precise categories and elements (Gregory, 1978) – rather than a fully dialectical paradigm.

The most developed dialectical paradigms in geography are derived from Marx's HISTORICAL MATERIALISM, and they have been deployed to elucidate the contradictory constitution and restless transformation of CAPITALISM as a MODE OF PRODUCTION. A formal statement of the principles of dialectics within historical materialism has been provided by Harvey (1996, pp. 48–57; cf. 1973, pp. 286–302). Its key propositions include the following:

- Dialectical thinking emphasizes processes, flows and relations.
- The formation and duration of systems and structures is not the point of departure (these 'things' are not treated as 'givens') but rather a problem for analysis: processes, flows and relations constitute – form, shape, give rise to – systems and structures.
- The operation of these processes, flows and relations is contradictory, and it is these contradictions that feed into the transformation of systems and structures. All systems and structures thus contain possibilities for change.
- Spaces and times (or, rather, 'space–times') are not external coordinates but are contained within – or 'implicated in' – different processes that effectively 'produce' their own forms of space and time.

Within this scheme, particular analytical importance is attached to the identification of contradictions. Formally, a contradiction is a principle that both (i) enters into the constitution of a SYSTEM or structure and (ii) whose operation negates, opposes ('contradicts') the stability or integrity of that system or structure. A vivid example is provided by one standard model of PROTOINDUSTRIALIZATION which identifies two circuits: a circuit of petty commodity production, in which independent artisans work at home or in their workshops to produce cloth; and a circuit of MARKET EXCHANGE in which merchants buy the cloth from the artisans to sell on domestic or overseas markets. The circuit of petty commodity production is supposed to be organized around use values (meeting the consumption and cultural needs of the artisan) while the circuit of market exchange is organized around exchange values (the strictly commercial search for the highest profits). Seen thus, the protoindustrial system both (i) depends on the articulation of both circuits – it is constituted through the activities of artisans producing cloth and merchants buying and selling cloth; and yet (ii) is constantly subject to disruption and dislocation through the operation of a system of use values (which encourages artisans to step up production when prices tumble, in order to meet their consumption needs, and to slow down production when prices soar, since they can meet those needs much more quickly) in concert with a system of exchange values (which means that merchants want production cut back when prices tumble and increased when prices soar to enhance their search for the highest profits). According to this model of protoindustrialization, the contradiction is 'resolved' through the transformation of the domestic system into a factory system.

Harvey's statement sets out principles; Castree (1996) has provided a rigorous reading of Harvey's practice. In doing so, he raises important questions about reflexivity and, in particular, about the relations of POWER that inhere within Harvey's claims to knowledge. One of Castree's central theses is that in Harvey's writings, as elsewhere, dialectics functions as both a mode of explanation and a mode of representation. It was once said that Marx's words are 'like bats: one can see in them both birds and mice'. And this attentiveness to the slippery subtleties of LANGUAGE and to the powers released by words has occasioned a series of reflections in and around human geography that have taken some writers a considerable distance from Harvey's own base in historical materialism. Thus Gunnar Olsson argues that the categorical paradigm which rules conventional modes of analysis fails to recognize the interpenetration of form and process, subject and object: as a result, its propositions reveal more about the language we are talking in, whereas 'statements in dialectics will say more about the worlds we are talking about'. To be sure, 'words' and 'worlds' are connected, and for this reason Olsson insists on the importance of attending to 'the dialectics of spatial analysis' (Olsson, 1974, 1980, 1991). He too makes much of the play of power through language, although it is by no means clear that his writing is any more reflexive than Harvey's (Sparke, 1994). A similar interest in language and its system of differences has nonetheless impelled some writers to follow the so-called 'linguistic turn' in the humanities and social sciences still further. In particular, those who have been persuaded by the claims of DECONSTRUCTION have set dialectics aside, challenging the metaphysics of binary opposition on which dialectics depends and refusing to conceive of difference as contradiction (Doel, 1992). (See also TRIALECTICS.) DG

References

Castree, N. 1996: Birds, mice and geography: Marxisms and dialectics. *Transactions, Institute of British Geographers* NS 21: 342–62. · Doel, M.A. 1992: In stalling deconstruction: striking out the postmodern. *Environment and Planning D: Society and Space* 10: 163–79. · Gregory, D. 1978: *Ideology, science and human geography*. London: Hutchinson. · Harvey, D. 1973: Social justice and the city. London: Edward Arnold; reprinted 1988. Oxford and Cambridge, MA: Blackwell. · Harvey, D. 1996: *Justice, nature and the geography of difference*. Oxford and Cambridge, MA: Blackwell. · Marchand, B. 1978: A dialectic approach in geography. *Geographical Analysis* 10: 105–19. · Olsson, G. 1974: The dialectics of spatial analysis. *Antipode* 6:3: 50–62. · Olsson, G. 1980: *Birds in egg/Eggs in bird*. London: Pion. · Olsson, G. 1991: *Lines of power, limits of language*. Minneapolis: University of Minnesota Press. · Sparke, M. 1994: Escaping the herbarium: a critique of Gunnar Olsson's chiasm of thought and action. *Environment and Planning D: Society and Space* 12: 207–20.

Suggested Reading

Castree (1996). · Harvey (1996), 48–57. · Olsson (1991), 66–77.

diaspora Literally the scattering of a population, diaspora was originally applied to the dispersal of the Jews following the Roman conquest of Palestine and the destruction of Jerusalem in AD 70 (Keller, 1971). The term is now applied more widely to other non-voluntary population dispersals such as the Black diaspora that resulted from the slave trade (cf. SLAVERY). Several types of diaspora have been distinguished including victim, labour, trade, imperial and cultural diasporas (Cohen, 1997). Within cultural studies, attention has focused on the transnational connections and hybrid cultures that have developed across such diasporic communities (Chow, 1993; Gilroy, 1995; Brah, 1996), ideas which are now being debated within geography (Mitchell, 1997). PAJ

References

Brah, A. 1996: *Cartographies of diaspora*. London: Routledge. · Chow, R. 1993: *Writing diaspora*. Bloomington: University of Indiana Press. · Cohen, R. 1997: *Global diasporas: an introduction*. London: UCL Press. · Gilroy,

P. 1995: *The Black Atlantic*. London: Verso. · Keller, W. 1971: *Diaspora: the post-Biblical history of the Jews*. London: Pitman. · Mitchell, K. 1997: Different diasporas and the hype of hybridity. *Environment and Planning D: Society and Space* 15: 533–53.

difference Poststructuralist social theory has challenged the singular (class-based) logic of Marxist analysis (see POST-STRUCTURALISM), advancing a more complex understanding of social differentiation which encompasses a wider range of human differences associated with culturally constructed notions of GENDER, RACE and SEXUALITY (among other bases of inequality, identification and social action). Geographers have contributed to these debates by showing how this world of DIFFERENCE is articulated through ideas of SPACE and PLACE, including notions of DIASPORA, borderlands, centres and margins.

Exploring the geography of difference radically destabilizes the relationship between place and IDENTITY, emphasizing cultural differences *within* as well as between places (from the SCALE of the NATION to the NEIGHBOURHOOD). In a world of increasing multiculturality, where transnational connections are rapidly proliferating, the boundaries of the NATION-STATE are increasingly porous (Appadurai, 1996). Likewise, at the neighbourhood scale, places can no longer be represented as stable, bounded and inward-looking COMMUNITIES. Rather, places are constantly in flux, requiring new ways of theorizing their external connections in the development of an increasingly global SENSE OF PLACE (Massey, 1995). From this perspective, understanding the connections between places is crucial to understanding the *production* of difference. A sense of 'Englishness', for example, clearly exceeds the boundaries of the nation and cannot be understood apart from the history of British IMPERIALISM which established a range of connections between people and places across the globe whose many traces persist to this day (in commodity flows, MIGRATION patterns, cultural tastes etc.).

The production of difference involves a complex geography of displacement and juxtaposition, where the stable ties of people and place (often exaggerated in the past) are radically disrupted (but see Pratt and Hanson, 1994, on the persistence of place-based identities). The regimes of FLEXIBLE ACCUMULATION and TIME–SPACE COMPRESSION that characterize the 'postmodern condition' (Harvey, 1989) have produced a new and ever-changing set of territorializations where difference is commodified and re-presented to a voracious consumer public (see TERRITORIALITY). In such a world of difference, ideas of depth and authenticity lose their purchase, to be replaced by a language of displacement and dislocation (Crang, 1996).

The play of difference is a pervasive feature of POSTMODERN society, unsettling all kinds of apparent certainties and problematizing any stable sense of identity. But the politics of difference also involve material inequalities. Consumer culture provides a powerful illustration of this process in the commodification of 'exotic' food, for example, which affords those with sufficient economic and CULTURAL CAPITAL the opportunity to 'eat the other' (hooks, 1992), engaging with OTHERNESS in a purely commercial way and entirely on its own terms.

The anthropological recognition that cultural difference is also present 'here at home', and that 'the other' need not be exotic or far away (Gupta and Ferguson, 1992) led to a 'crisis of REPRESENTATION' across the human sciences. How to 'cross the divide' between cultures in our increasingly POST-COLONIAL world has generated complex debates about POSITIONALITY as social scientists are forced to reconsider their right to interpret cultures that are, in significant ways, different from their own. That these differences have been produced (through COLONIALISM, through the work of Transnational Corporations or through earlier generations of scholarship) provides a critical 'handle' in approaching the politics of difference. For 'difference' does not exist in an *a priori* way; it is produced and reproduced through specific historical and political processes that are amenable to critical investigation. As Gupta and Ferguson assert: 'cultural difference is produced and maintained in a field of power relations in a world [that is] always already spatially interconnected' (1992, p. 17).

Informed by recent work in FEMINIST GEOGRAPHIES, a new vocabulary has been evolved to explore this complex world of diversity and difference (Rose, 1993; WGSG, 1997). Rejecting all forms of ESSENTIALISM, geographers and other social scientists have focused on places 'in between': margins rather than centres, interstitial spaces and borderlands with their hybrid cultures, associated with migrants, refugees and displaced people (Anzaldúa, 1987; Bhabha, 1994). Indeed, in mapping the geography of difference, it has also become increasingly clear that the 'margins' can be a very effective place from which to understand what is ostensibly at the 'centre', though the use of such geographical METAPHORS is itself contentious (Pratt, 1992). Serious questions remain about whether it is possible to have a respect for difference while maintaining a commitment to EQUALITY (Young, 1990). PAJ

References

Anzaldúa, G. 1987: *Borderlands/La Frontera: the new mestiza*. San Francisco: Spinsters/Aunt Lute. · Appadurai, A. 1996: *Modernity at large: cultural dimensions of globalization*. Minneapolis: University of Minnesota Press. · Bhabha, H.K. 1994: *The location of culture*. London: Routledge. · Crang, P. 1996: Displacement, consumption and identity. *Environment and Planning A* 28: 47–67. · Gupta, A. and Ferguson, J. 1992: Beyond 'culture': space, identity, and the politics of difference. *Cultural Anthropology* 7: 6–23. · Harvey, D. 1989: *The condition of postmodernity*. Oxford: Blackwell. · hooks, b. 1992: Eating the other. In *Black looks: race and representation*. London: Turnaround, 21–39. · Massey, D. 1995: *Space, place and gender*. Cambridge: Polity Press. · Pratt, G. 1992: Spatial metaphors and speaking positions. *Environment and Planning D: Society and Space* 10: 241–4. · Pratt, G. and Hanson, S. 1994: Geography and the construction of difference. *Gender, Place and Culture* 1: 5–29. · Rose, G. 1993: *Feminism and geography*. Cambridge: Polity Press. · Women and Geography Study Group 1997: *Feminist geographies: explorations in diversity and difference*. London: Longman. · Young, I.M. 1990: *Justice and the politics of difference*. Princeton, NJ: University of Princeton Press.

Suggested reading

Fincher, R. and Jacobs, J.M., eds, 1998: *Cities of difference*. New York: Guilford. · Sibley, D. 1995: *Geographies of exclusion*. London: Routledge.

diffusion The spread of a phenomenon over space and through time. There is a long and distinguished tradition of diffusion studies in CULTURAL GEOGRAPHY. According to Sauer (1941), it was Ratzel who 'founded the study of the diffusion of cultural traits, presented in the nearly forgotten second volume of his *Anthropogeographie*' (see ANTHROPOGEOGRAPHY). In Sauer's view, diffusion – 'the filling of the spaces of the earth' – was a 'general problem of social science': 'A new crop, craft or technique is introduced to a CULTURE AREA. Does it spread, or diffuse vigorously or does its acceptance meet resistance?' The *specific* contribution of geography, so Sauer argued, was to reconstruct diffusion pathways and to evaluate the influence of (physical) barriers (see Sauer, 1952; more generally, Wagner and Mikesell, 1962). Both of these tasks were pursued energetically by various members of the BERKELEY SCHOOL, but they reappeared in a starkly different guise in Hägerstrand's much more formal study of INNOVATION diffusion. In fact, Hägerstrand's original Swedish monograph was introduced to Anglo-American geography in a short note by Leighly (1954), himself an associate of Sauer. 'No one who essays in the future to interpret the distribution of culture elements in the process of diffusion can afford to ignore Hägerstrand's methods and conclusions', Leighly declared, and he drew particular attention to Hägerstrand's emphasis on the importance of 'chance' (see STOCHASTIC PROCESS). Even so, it was some 14 years before an English translation of Hägerstrand's *Innovation diffusion as a spatial process* appeared (1968), although in the interim his basic ideas had already become better known (see Duncan, 1974). The theoretical structure behind Hägerstrand's MODEL is summarized in the figure. An interaction matrix suggests the contours of a generalized or MEAN INFORMATION FIELD, which structures the way in which information circulates through a regional system; these flows are modulated by both physical barriers and individual resistances which together check the transformation of information into innovation and so shape successive diffusion waves which break onto the adoption surface (Gregory, 1985; see also Haggett et al., 1977). Most discussion has been about the operationalization of the model – about Hägerstrand's use of Monte Carlo SIMULATION methods, the comparison of 'observed' and 'predicted' patterns of adoption, and the detection of a NEIGHBOURHOOD EFFECT – rather than about its theoretical basis (but see below). Within the modelling tradition initiated by Hägerstrand, the most important developments have included:

- a formalization of the mathematical relations between the structure of the mean information field and the form and velocity of diffusion waves, indicating the connections between different DISTANCE DECAY curves and the classic neighborhood effect (although it is, of course, scarcely surprising that a distance-bound mean information field should generate a broadly contagious pattern of adoptions);
- a demonstration that the Hägerstrand model is only a special instance of the simple epidemic model, and the subsequent derivation of more complex *epidemic models* – particularly through the remarkable contributions of Haggett, Cliff and Ord (see Haggett et al., 1977, ch. 7), whose replication of a range of supposedly 'spatial processes' (see PROCESS) has confirmed;

- the recognition of *hierarchical diffusion*, typically through central place systems (see CENTRAL PLACE THEORY) and frequently operating alongside the distance-bound, *contagious* processes of the classical model (see Hudson, 1969; Pedersen, 1970);
- the incorporation of rejection and removal processes and the modelling of competitive diffusions (see Webber, 1972).

These changes have entailed a move away from simulation techniques towards the use of more analytical methods, which Agnew (1979) sees as a shift from EMPIRICISM and INSTRUMENTALISM towards REALISM. But to some critics outside the abstract domains of LOCATION THEORY or MEDICAL GEOGRAPHY (where these advances have been immensely important: see Cliff et al., 1981) the move towards a post-positivist formulation remains strategically incomplete. Blaikie (1978) even spoke of a 'crisis' in diffusion research, which he attributed to a reluctance to reverse out from a 'spacious cul-de-sac' – by which he meant a preoccupation with spatial form and space–time sequence – and Gregory (1985) attributed the 'stasis' of diffusion theory to an unwillingness to engage with social theory and social history in ways which clarified both the *conditions* and the consequences of diffusion processes. In the most general terms, this critique notes that the spatial circulation of information is the strategic element in most applications of the Hägerstrand model and its derivatives to human geography. Although the flow of information through different 'propagation structures' and contact networks has been exposed in more detail (e.g. Blaikie, 1973, 1975; Brown, 1975), most critics claim that the primacy accorded to the pattern of these pathways obscures two other, more fundamental, elements (cf. the critique of BEHAVIOURAL GEOGRAPHY).

The Hägerstrand model 'is concerned with the locational attributes and communication habits of potential adopters' and 'does not explicate the process by which potential adopters are identified' (Yapa and Mayfield, 1978). The alternative is a model of *biased innovation* which takes as primary the ways in which 'social access to the means of production' can be closed off through (for example) the CLASS structure of the MODE OF PRODUCTION. In this perspective, 'non-diffusion is not to be equated with the passive state of lack of adoption due to low levels of awareness [or] apathy.... It is an active state arising out of the structural arrangements of the economic [base of] society' (Yapa, 1977; see also Blaikie, 1978 and Gregory, 1985). Claims of this sort carry with them a demand for diffusion theory to be located within a more general POLITICAL ECONOMY, although it is clearly not necessary to endorse the economic reductionism of classical Marxism implicit in Yapa's commentary. At the very least, the significance of ETHNICITY and GENDER needs to be admitted alongside that of CLASS (see Blaikie, 1975).

The Hägerstrand model postulates 'a uniform cognitive region' and does not explicate the selective social processes through which information flows are differentially constituted as socially meaningful. Hence Blaut (1977) has called for the forging of closer links with the older tradition of cultural diffusion, which is capable of treating diffusion in what Blaut takes to be 'its broadest, most adequate sense' by locating diffusion theory within a more general cultural geography. Such a manoeuvre is not the return to Sauer which it seems to be, however, for it is clear from Blaut's other writings that here too the model is to be Marx (see Blaut, 1980). Whatever one thinks of this – and there is certainly a vibrant cultural perspective within HISTORICAL MATERIALISM – no model of biased innovation can equate 'resistance' with ignorance or insufficient information. Access to information, like any other means of production, is indeed socially structured, but resistance equally (and, one might say, usually) connotes a process of sustained struggle: considered and collective action on the part of people whose evaluation of the available information may be strikingly different to that of the 'potential adopters' (see Gregory, 1985).

Hägerstrand has himself conceded the force of some of these objections; rather than explore the claims of contemporary Marxism, however, he has returned to some of those themes which exercised him before he constructed his diffusion model, and he has developed them beyond the confines of its spatial formalism into TIME-GEOGRAPHY.

Many of the continuing tensions within diffusion studies are exemplified by the recent interest in the diffusion of AIDS. Mapping and modelling the spread of the disease has been the major focus of geographical inquiry (see, e.g., Shannon and Pyle, 1989; Casetti and Fan, 1991; Shannon, Pyle and Bashshur, 1991; Smallman-Raynor, Cliff and Haggett, 1992). Where this work has referred to the Hägerstrand model at all, it has usually been to its capacity to describe patterns of spread:

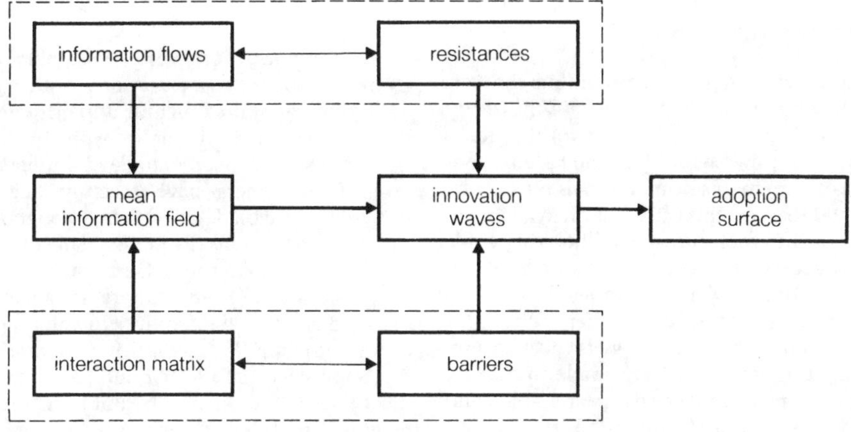

diffusion *The structure of Hägerstrand's diffusion model*

their spatial analysis has involved epidemiological modeling. An interest in the cultural, social and political geography of AIDS diffusion has been much slower to develop – and even then it has often been subordinated to the objectivist logics of spatial science (see, e.g., Wallace and Fullilove, 1991) – but there have been many relevant studies outside the discipline (Shilts, 1987; Crimp, 1988; Patton, 1990), and, laterally, studies within the discipline that have been based on a vigorous critique of spatial science (Brown, 1995). DG

References

Agnew, J.A. 1979: Instrumentalism, realism and research on diffusion of innovation. *Professional Geographer* 31: 364–70. · Blaikie, P. 1973: The spatial structure of information networks and innovative behavior in the Ziz valley, S. Morocco. *Geografisker Annaler* B55: 83–105. · Blaikie, P. 1975: *Family planning in India: a sociogeographical approach.* London: Edward Arnold; New York: Holmes and Meier. · Blaikie, P. 1978: The theory of the spatial diffusion of innovations: a spacious cul-de-sac. *Progress in Human Geography* 2: 268–95. · Blaut, J. 1977: Two views of diffusion. *Annals of the Association of American Geographers* 67: 343–9; Blaut, J. 1980: A radical critique of cultural geography. *Antipode* 12: 25–9. · Brown, L.A. 1975: The market and infrastructure context of adoption: a spatial perspective on the diffusion of innovation. *Economic Geography* 51: 185–216. · Brown, M. 1995: Ironies of distance: an ongoing critique of the geographies of AIDS. *Environment and Planning D: Society and Space* 13: 159–83. · Casetti, E. and Fan, C. 1991: The spatial spread of the AIDS epidemic in Ohio: empirical analyses using the expansion method. *Environment and Planning A* 23: 1589–608. · Cliff, A.D., Haggett, P., Ord, J.K. and Versey, G.R. 1981: *Spatial diffusion: an historical geography of epidemics in an island community.* Cambridge: Cambridge University Press. · Crimp, D., ed., 1988: *AIDS, cultural analysis, cultural criticism.* Cambridge, MA: MIT Press. · Duncan, S.S. 1974: The isolation of scientific discovery: indifference and resistance to a new idea. *Science Studies* 4: 109–34. · Gregory, D. 1985: Suspended animation: the stasis of diffusion theory. In Gregory, D. and Urry, J., eds, *Social relations and spatial structures.* London: Macmillan, 296–336. · Hägerstrand, T. 1968: *Innovation diffusion as a spatial process,* trans. A. Pred. Chicago: University of Chicago Press. · Haggett, P., Cliff, A.D. and Frey, A.E. 1977: *Locational analysis in human geography,* 2nd edn. London: Edward Arnold; New York: John Wiley. · Hudson, J.C. 1969: Diffusion in a central place system. *Geographical Analysis* 1: 45–58. · Leighly, J. 1954: Innovation and area. *Geographical Review* 44: 439–41. · Patton, C. 1990: *Inventing AIDS.* London: Routledge. · Pedersen, P.O. 1970: Innovation diffusion within and between national urban systems. *Geographical Analysis* 2: 203–54. · Sauer, C. 1941: Foreword to historical geography. *Annals of the Association of American Geographers* 31: 1–24. · Sauer, C. 1952: *Agricultural origins and dispersals.* New York: American Geographical Society. · Shannon, G.W. and Pyle, G.F. 1989: The origin and diffusion of AIDS: a view from medical geography. *Annals of the Association of American Geographers* 79: 1–24. · Shannon, G.W., Pyle, G.F. and Bashshur, R.L. 1991: *The geography of AIDS: origins and course of an epidemic.* New York: Guilford Press. · Shilts, R. 1987: *And the band played on: politics, people and the AIDS epidemic.* New York: Penguin. · Smallman-Raynor, M., Cliff, A.D., and Haggett, P. 1992: *London international atlas of AIDS.* Oxford: Blackwell. · Wagner, P.L. and Mikesell, M.W., eds, 1962: *Readings in cultural geography.* Chicago: University of Chicago Press. · Wallace, R. and Fullilove, M. 1991: AIDS deaths in the Bronx 1983–1988: spatiotemporal analysis from a sociogeographic perspective. *Environment and Planning A* 23: 1701–23. · Webber, M.J. 1972: *The impact of uncertainty on location.* Cambridge, MA: MIT Press. · Yapa, L.S. 1977: The green revolution: a diffusion model. *Annals of the Association of American Geographers* 67: 350–9. · Yapa, L.S. and Mayfield, R.C. 1978: Non-adoption of innovations. *Economic Geography* 54: 145–56.

Suggested Reading

Blaikie (1978); Cliff et al. (1981). · Gregory (1985); Wagner and Mikesell (1962), part 3.

digital library A system providing the services of a library in digital form. With recent advances in computing and networking technologies it is now possible in principle to convert all of humanity's printed *corpus* into digital form, and to make this information available to all over the Internet, allowing millions of people to find, access and read millions of books at the same time. Digital libraries have been quickest to develop in areas where funding is greatest, and where technology is most accessible; rapid progress has been made in making medical library collections searchable and readable digitally, and the same is true of collections in computer science. Many electronic journals have emerged in recent years, and the catalogues of research libraries are now almost universally digital. In a related development, bookstores have been among the earliest of businesses to exploit network technology, and it is increasingly possible to acquire printed publications via the World Wide Web.

The digital library concept has also been applied to MAP and imagery libraries, in an effort to make geographic data sets more widely accessible. Many governments and agencies now provide some form of central digital repository or clearing-house for geographic information, allowing users to search, browse and retrieve information that may be of use to them. Imagery from commercial satellites is available for purchase and acquisition over the Internet using very similar technology. Several standards have been devised for cataloging maps and images, of which the US Federal Geographic Data Committee's Content Standards for Digital Geospatial Metadata (FGDC, 1993) are the best known. MG

References

Federal Geographic Data Committee 1993: *Content Standards for Digital Geospatial Metadata*. Washington, D.C.

digitizing A process by which information is converted from ANALOGUE to digital form. The term is frequently applied to the information shown on paper MAPS. In this process, the map is fixed to a special table, and an operator positions a pointing device or 'puck' over selected locations on the map; the coordinates of each selected location are then stored automatically in digital form. 'Scanning' is another form of digitizing of importance in geography; here, the capture of information from a document is automatic. MG

disability, geography and Disability is the study of society's interactions with people with physical and/or mental impairments and the effects of such interactions on the capacities of disabled people to lead independent lives. Geographers have recently begun to research disabled people's geographical experiences and a distinctive sub-discipline can now be discerned. Such studies range from Gleeson's (1998) materialist account of disabled people's hidden lives in colonial Melbourne, to Imrie's (1996a) documentation of the oppressive nature of building design and the built environment in inhibiting disabled people's mobility. Some researchers have documented systemic processes of geographical exclusion of disabled people, such as their GHETTOization in asylums and special zones set aside in cities (Dear, 1981), while others have considered the particular difficulties of people with specific impairments, such as the vision-impaired, in moving around the environment or gaining access to employment (Butler and Bowlby, 1997).

The impetus for studies in disability and geography stems largely from the work of Mike Oliver (1990) and his associates (Abberley, 1987; Barton, 1989; Shakespeare, 1998). They distinguish between two broad approaches to the study of disability and society: the *medical model of disability* and the *social model of disability*. The former conceives of disability as an individual medical or physiological condition which can be overcome by the application of medical knowledge and rehabilitation. The latter sees disability as societal and/or attitudinal or environmental restrictions placed upon people with physical and/or mental impairments to the point whereby they are 'disabled' or prevented from exercising their civil liberties.

The medical model of disability has dominated studies of disability and is still widely used by the medical profession. The medical model sees disability as 'not normal' and disabled people as 'deviant others'. It has been discredited by Oliver (1990) and others, however, because it reduces disability to the specificities of an individual impairment and implies that victims are to blame for their inability to function. In contrast, the social model sees disability as a function of oppressive interpersonal and institutional relations, whereby people with impairments are defined, categorized, and marked out as disabled and different by prejudicial and pejorative social attitudes, values and practices. A third perspective has recently emerged which seeks to connect the medical and social models of disability in ways which recognize the interrelationships between a person's physiological capacity and the wider environment (Bury, 1996).

Geographical studies of disability are largely derived from these contrasting sociological accounts and disputations concerning disability and society. In particular, there are at least five, often overlapping, ways in which disability and geography is studied (see Park et al., 1998, for a thorough overview of the diverse approaches). First, *bio-medical models* of disability are evident in medical geography where disability is conceived as a disease to be treated medically followed by a period of rehabilitation. Such studies range from epidemiological mapping exercises of diseases to the description of the demographic characteristics of disabled people (Foster, 1988). The MOBILITY needs of disabled people also feature within this tradition, including the spatial analysis of disabled people's travel patterns and needs (Gant, 1992).

Second, *behavioural perspectives* on disability have been pioneered by Golledge (1993) with the focus on the spatial cognition, mobility and the spatial competencies of vision-impaired and blind populations (see also BEHAVIOURAL GEOGRAPHY). Golledge's research is particularly concerned with the development of navigational aids and other technical devices, to enable people with vision impairments to move around their environments. Such studies have much in common with the bio-medical tradition and have been criticized by Gleeson (1996) and Imrie (1996b), amongst others, for what they see as its descriptive and reductionist content. Likewise, a third approach, the *geography of psychiatric impairments* or mental health, has a long POSITIVIST tradition with a focus on the distribution of psychiatric conditions (Giggs, 1973) and the location of mental health-care facilities (Hunter, 1987). In contrast, the deinstitutionalization (Dear and Wolch, 1987) of mental care, as part of the psychiatric tradition, considers social-institutional attitudes and practices towards people with mental impairments and, in particular, emphasizes processes of geographic containment and exclusion of those seen as 'deviant'.

Socio-political (or materialist) perspectives are a fourth approach to disability and geography which emphasize the historical and material conditions of disabled people's lives and the contrasting ways in which STATES and SOCIETIES have sought to categorize, define, and control the lives of disabled people. For materialists, disability is neither a fixed category nor end state, but a transformative and contested domain. Such perspectives see geography as a constitutive part of disabled people's oppression and marginalization in society. Gleeson's (1998) work, for example, emphasizes the importance of spatial and temporal perspectives in understanding the diverse states of disability from one society to another. Others emphasize the role of institutions and agents, within the wider context of socio-political structures, in conditioning the experiences of disabled people (Imrie, 1996a; Butler and Bowlby, 1997).

Finally, *bio-sociological approaches* to disability and geography are in their infancy but are an attempt to move beyond the duality of the social and medical models of disability by seeking to interconnect them in ways which recognize the complex interactions between physiology, culture, and wider socio-economic and political relationships (see, for example, Butler and Bowlby, 1997). Few studies in geography have, as yet, adopted such approaches although the collection of papers in Butler and Parr (1999) suggest that this will be the next significant development in the sub-discipline. Dyck's (1995) study of the life-worlds of women with multiple sclerosis complements these new directions by considering the interrelationships between biology, the body and disabled people, particularly disabled women. Such studies have opened up potentially fruitful avenues between feminism and disability studies with the potential to produce new insights into disabled people's oppression and marginalization (see Park et al., 1998).

The study of disability and geography indicates that place and physical and/or mental impairments are closely connected. Like issues of RACE and PLACE, and GENDER AND GEOGRAPHY, disabled people are seeking to assert themselves in recognizing that spatial or geographical processes are potentially disablist and disabling, that geography is not neutral with regards to their mobility, access and other needs. Disabled people are also involved in IDENTITY POLITICS in seeking to assert their needs, but in ways which give them control over their lives. This is important for geographers researching and teaching disability studies because many disabled people have argued that knowledge about them should not be produced or disseminated without their consent or involvement in research and pedagogic processes. Such messages strike to the heart of the discipline in asking geography tutors, for example, to question how far their degree programmes facilitate disabled people's involvement; for instance, are field courses designed with the needs of vision-impaired or wheelchair users in mind and how accessible is the lecture theatre? RI

References

Abberley, P. 1987: The concept of oppression and the development of a social theory of disability. *Disability, Handicap and Society* 2 (1): 5–21. · Barton, L., ed., 1989: *Disability and dependence*. Lewes: Falmer Press. · Bury, M. 1996: Defining and researching disability: challenges and responses. In C. Barnes and G. Mercer, eds, *Exploring the divide: illness and disability*. Leeds: The Disability Press. · Butler, R. and Bowlby, S. 1997: Bodies and spaces: an exploration of disabled people's use of public space. *Environment and Planning D: Society and Space* 15: 411–33. · Butler, R. and Parr, H., eds, 1999: *Mind and body spaces: geographies of disability, illness and impairment*. London: Routledge. · Dear, M. 1981: Social and spatial reproduction of the mentally ill. In M. Dear and A.J. Scott, eds, *Urbanisation and urban planning in a capitalist society*. London: Methuen, 481–97. · Dear, M. and Wolch, J. 1987: *Landscapes of despair: from deinstitutionalisation to homelessness* Princeton, NJ: Princeton University Press. · Dyck, I. 1995: Hidden geographies: the changing lifeworlds of women with multiple sclerosis. *Social Science and Medicine* 40 (3): 307–20. · Foster, H. 1988: Reducing the incidence of multiple sclerosis. *Environments* 19 (3): 14–34. · Gant, R. 1992: Transport for the disabled. *Geography* 77 (1): 88–91. · Giggs, J. 1973: The distribution of schizophrenics in Nottingham. *Transactions, Institute of British Geographers* 59: 55–75. · Gleeson, B. 1996: A geography for disabled people? *Transactions, Institute of British Geographers*, NS21 2: 387–96. · Gleeson, B. 1998: *Geographies of disability*. London: Routledge; Golledge, R. 1993: Geography and the disabled: a survey with special reference to vision impaired and blind populations. *Transactions, Institute of British Geographers* NS 18: 63–85. · Hunter, J. 1987: Need and demand for mental health care. *The Geographical Review* 77 (2): 139–56. · Imrie, R. 1996a: *Disability and the city: international perspectives*. London: Paul Chapman Publishing; New York: St. Martin's Press. · Imrie, R. 1996b: Ableist geographies, disablist spaces: towards a reconstruction of Golledge's geography and the disabled. *Transactions, Institute of British Geographers* NS 21 2: 397–403. · Oliver, M. 1990: *The politics of disablement*. London: Macmillan; Park, D., Radford, J. and Vickers, M. 1998: Disability studies in human geography. *Progress in Human Geography* 22: 208–23. · Shakespeare, T., ed., 1998: *A disability reader: social science perspectives*. London: Cassell.

Suggested Reading

Butler, R. and Parr, H. (1999). · Gleeson, B. (1998). · Imrie, R. (1996a). · Oliver, M. (1990). · Park, D. et al. (1998). · Shakespeare, T. (1998).

discourse A specific series of REPRESENTATIONS, practices and PERFORMANCES through which meanings are produced, connected into networks and legitimized. Different fields and disciplines have worked with different, usually more detailed definitions of 'discourse' (see Mills, 1997), but in the most general terms something like this definition seems to have the most currency within human geography. The following, more particular, characterizations can be derived from it (though by no means all scholars would accept every one of them):

Discourses are heterogeneous: discourses are not the product of a single author, and neither are they confined to (for example) literary TEXTS, or archives, or scientific statements, but instead travel through different domains and registers and carry multiple meanings and implications.

Discourses are regulated: discourses have coherence and systematicity, though they may be (and usually are) contradictory, and are marked through their own 'regimes of truth' that police the boundaries between inside and outside – to legislate inclusions and exclusions – and to establish criteria of acceptability.

Discourses are embedded: discourses are not free-floating constructions but are materially implicated in the conduct of social life; they are embedded in institutions and subject-positions but typically cut across and circulate through multiple institutions and subject-positions.

Discourses are situated: discourses always provide partial, SITUATED KNOWLEDGES, and as such they are always characterized by particular constellations of power and knowledge and are always open to contestation and negotiation.

Discourses are performative: discourses have (variable) meaning, force and effect; they constitute the 'objects' of which they speak and enter into the (variable) constitution of 'the social' and 'the self' (cf. PERFORMATIVITY).

Most of these characterizations derive from POST-STRUCTURALISM. Taken together, they enable us to understand 'how what is said fits into a network that has its own history and conditions of existence' (Barrett, 1992). Such a discursive network also has its own geography and a central concern of CRITICAL HUMAN GEOGRAPHY is to elucidate the connections between POWER, knowledge and SPATIALITY.

These ideas have been particularly helpful for a revivified history of geography. No longer content with a recitation of 'founding figures', a succession of 'schools' or a parade of PARA-

DIGMS, some scholars have sought to recover the production of geographical knowledges as discourses. This has allowed a much more heterogeneous conception of the field to emerge. There has been a lively debate about intellectual histories that limited their accounts to a nominally 'scientific' view of geography and excluded TRAVEL WRITING, for example, even though these discourses intersected with 'scientific' discourse in complex ways (Blunt, 1995). There has also been considerable interest in specifying the complicity of human geography in the discourses of COLONIALISM and IMPERIALISM (see POST-COLONIALISM) and in exposing the ways in which the most powerful, socially sanctioned and institutionalized geographical knowledges (those that constituted 'the discipline') virtually effaced the part played by non-western subjects in their production and erased the traces of their supposedly 'marginal' knowledges (Barnett, 1998). These are matters of more than historical interest, however, and theories of discourse have played an important part in exposing the asymmetries of power that are inscribed within contemporary geographical discourses (notably ETHNOCENTRISM and PHALLOCENTRISM), elucidating the role of RHETORIC – and of POETICS more generally – in legitimizing intellectual practice (Crush, 1991) and in allowing IDEOLOGY to congeal as 'unexamined discourse' (Gregory, 1978).

These are also matters of more than academic interest. Discourses shape the contours of the TAKEN-FOR-GRANTED WORLD: they 'naturalize' and often implicitly universalize a particular view of the world and position subjects differentially within it. Theories of discourse have thus greatly enlarged the interpretative horizon of human geography, where they have been used to explore (for example) the performative function of representations of space within legal discourse (Blomley, 1994) or the ways in which rival discourses about work and the workplace shape local LABOUR MARKETS and economic landscapes (Herod, 1998). They also occupy a central place within studies of subject-formation (see SUBJECT-FORMATION, GEOGRAPHIES OF). DG

References

Barrett, M. 1992: *The politics of truth: from Marx to Foucault*. Stanford, CA: Stanford University Press. · Barnett, C. 1998: Impure and worldly geography: the Africanist discourse of the Royal Geographical Society, 1831–73. *Transactions, Institute of British Geographers* NS 23: 239–52. · Blomley, N. 1994: *Law, space and geographies of power*. New York: Guilford Press. · Blunt, A. 1995: *Travel, gender and imperialism*. New York: Guilford Press. · Crush, J. 1991: The discourse of progressive human geography. *Progress in Human Geography* 15: 395–414. · Driver, F. 1992: Geography's empire: histories of geographical knowledge. *Environment and Planning D: Society and Space* 10: 23–40. · Gregory, D. 1978: *Ideology, science and human geography*. London: Hutchinson; New York: St. Martin's Press. · Herod, A. 1998: Discourse on the docks: containerization and inter-union work disputes in US ports, 1955–1985. *Transactions, Institute of British Geographers* NS 23: 177–91. · Mills, S. 1997: *Discourse*. London and New York: Routledge.

Suggested Reading

Barnett (1998). · Mills (1997).

disorganized capitalism A term used by Lash and Urry (1987) to describe a new form of CAPITALISM that came into existence in the 1960s and 1970s. Disorganized capitalism is the result of the demise of *organized capitalism* (Kocka, 1974), a mature form of capitalism which began to evolve out of so-called 'liberal capitalism' in the final decades of the nineteenth century and became dominant in many western countries in the early and middle parts of the twentieth century. Organized capitalism was characterized by the growth of large bureaucratic organizations in the ECONOMY, the STATE, and CIVIL SOCIETY; by the growth of a middle class employed in these organizations; by a form of partnership (or 'CORPORATIST agreement') between companies, states and workers; and by MODERNIST cultural forms. In contrast, *disorganized capitalism* is a process of disorganization and RESTRUCTURING typified by large, global MULTINATIONAL and TRANSNATIONAL CORPORATIONS striving to become less bureaucratized, by NATION-STATES which find it increasingly difficult to make economic interventions, by the growth of a '*service class*' of managers and professionals (see CLASS), by the breakdown of corporatist agreements, and by POSTMODERN cultural forms.

Put baldly like this, the distinction between organized and disorganized capitalism might seem to be simply a way of synthesizing distinctions that are often made – between FORDISM and POST-FORDISM in the case of the economy, between industrial and POST-INDUSTRIAL SOCIETY, and, in the sphere of culture, between modernism and postmodernism. To some extent, this is true. But the idea of disorganized capitalism has more bite than this. In particular, it can be distinguished from these formulations by three important emphases. First, it is particularly attentive to the importance of geography; changing spatial forms are clearly implicated in the shift from organized to disorganized capitalism. Second, it stresses that disorganized capitalism is a process that moves hesitantly rather than triumphantly. Third, it is methodologically catholic; Lash and Urry are not willing to declare a fixed allegiance to any 'ism' but instead offer a list of diagnostic elements which cannot be reduced to any single, central generating mechanism.

Since their 1987 book, Lash and Urry have developed their thesis in a number of different directions, especially through work on CULTURE and the cultural industries (Lash, 1990), TOURISM (Urry, 1991), travel (Lash and Urry, 1992), and the environment (McNaghten and Urry, 1998). NJT

References

Kocka, J. 1974: *Organiserter Kapitalismus*. Gottingen: Vandenhock and Ruprecht. · Lash, S. 1990: *Sociology of postmodernism*. London, Routledge. · Lash, S. and Urry, J. 1987: *The end of organised capitalism*. Cambridge: Polity Press. · Lash, S. and Urry, J. 1992: *Economies of signs and space: after organised capitalism*. Cambridge: Polity Press. · MacNaghten, P. and Urry, J. 1998: *Contested natures*. London: Sage. · Urry, J. 1991: *The tourist gaze*. London: Sage.

distance decay The attenuation of a pattern or process with distance. Distance was one of the 'fundamental spatial concepts' identified by Nystuen (in Berry and Marble, 1968) and the importance of distance decay (sometimes called a distance lapse rate) was enshrined in Tobler's famous 'first law of geography: everything is related to everything else, but near things are more related than distant things' (Tobler, 1970). The empirical significance of this had of course been recognized in the early formulations of SOCIAL PHYSICS, but only achieved wider formal significance within geography with the emergence of the search for general theorems of spatial organization. Underlying many of the classical models of SPATIAL STRUCTURE, for example, the CENTRAL PLACE models of Christaller and Lösch and the DIFFUSION models of Hägerstrand, are assumptions about SPATIAL INTERACTION which, in the typical GRAVITY MODEL form, postulate a definite inverse 'distance effect', which is capable of a series of mathematical expressions (see the figure). These various transformations have such a powerful effect on the lapse rate that Olsson (1980) argued that the identification of a distance decay 'may reveal as much about the language I am talking in as it does about the phenomena I am talking about'. But in any event the lapse rate is evidently not independent of the geometry of the system within which interaction takes place, and in some locational models this is partially recognized through a parallel discussion of the accessibility of points arrayed on a movement surface (or network) around some hypothetical centre; for example, the VON THÜNEN MODEL of agricultural land use or the density gradients of

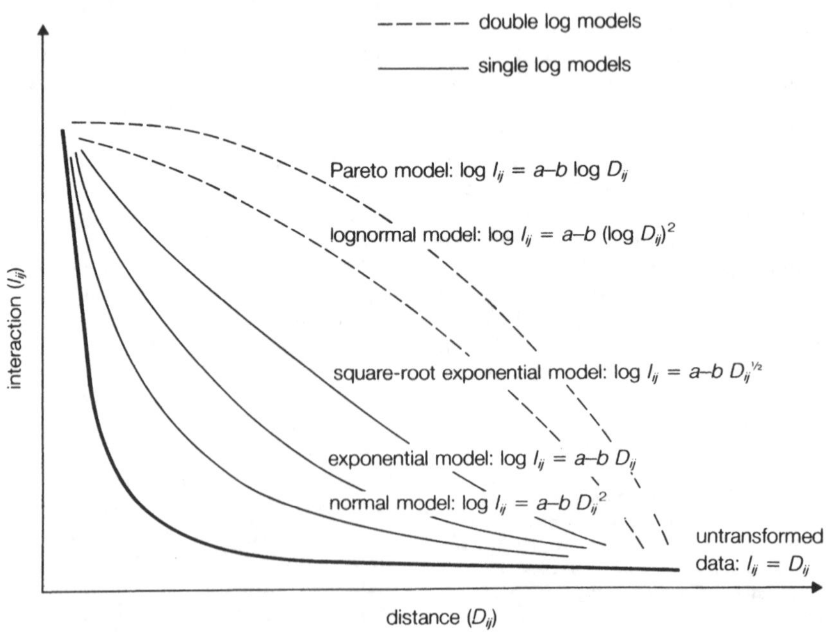

distance decay *Distance decay curves and transformations* (Taylor, 1971)

conventional urban land-use models. Because of these logical connections Bunge (1962) represented interaction and geometry as 'the inseparable duals of geographic theory'; but the matter clearly does not end there, because such interdependence poses formidable interpretative difficulties (e.g., see Curry, 1972; Cliff et al., 1975, 1976). Hence, while distance-decay curves can be identified empirically it is by no means clear how far their form depends on the model structures used to replicate them; nor to what extent their parameters can be given substantive meaning. DG

References

Berry, B.J.L. and Marble, D.F., eds, 1968: *Spatial analysis: a reader in statistical geography*. Englewood Cliffs, NJ: Prentice-Hall. · Bunge, W. 1962: *Theoretical geography*. Lund: C.W.K. Gleerup. · Cliff, A., Martin, R.L., and Ord, J.K. 1975 and 1976: Map pattern and friction of distance parameters. *Regional Studies* 9: 285–8 and 10: 341–2. · Curry, L. 1972: A spatial analysis of gravity flows. *Regional Studies* 6: 131–47. · Olsson, G. 1980: *Birds in eggs/eggs in bird*. London: Pion; New York: Methuen. · Taylor, P.J. 1971: Distance transformation and distance decay functions. *Geographical Analysis* 3: 221–38. · Tobler, W. 1970: A computer movie. *Economic Geography* 46: 234–40.

Suggested Reading

Olsson (1980), ch. 13; Sheppard, E.S. 1984: The distance decay gravity model debate. In G.L. Gaile and C.J. Willmott, eds, *Spatial statistics and models*. Dordrecht: D. Reidel, 367–88.

districting algorithm A procedure, usually programmed for a computer, for defining the boundaries of electoral constituencies. Such algorithms became popular in the USA after the Supreme Court outlawed MALAPPORTIONMENT in the 1960s; they are used to produce constituencies (such as a Congressional District) which conform to the equal-population requirement. RJJ

division of labour An aspect of the RELATIONS OF PRODUCTION of society which involves the separation of tasks within the LABOUR PROCESS and their allocation to different groups of workers. Two forms are commonly identified:

- *Social division of labour* – the division of workers between product sectors (e.g. 'car workers' or 'textile workers').
- *Technical division of labour* – the division of the production process into tasks, and the specialization of workers in one or a small number of these (e.g. managers, supervisors and assembly workers).

To these we may add the following:

- *Gender division of labour* – in which specific jobs are assigned to men or women: in western societies nurses tend to be women, and coal miners men. This extends beyond paid employment, so that unwaged domestic labour is largely performed by women (see GENDER AND GEOGRAPHY; PATRIARCHY).
- *Cultural division of labour* – according to the theory of internal colonialism (Hechter, 1975) regional minorities bear the same relationship to the majority as a colony does to the metropolitan power under COLONIALISM. The periphery supplies the core with raw materials and labour, forming a division of labour between the minority and majority cultures (see CORE–PERIPHERY MODEL).
- *International division of labour* – characteristically, less-developed countries produce raw materials and developed countries produce manufactured goods. More recently, a NEW INTERNATIONAL DIVISION OF LABOUR has involved the development by MULTINATIONAL CORPORATIONS of production facilities in less-developed countries, although normally at the routine and low-skill end of the production process. This is a special case of:
- *Spatial division of labour* – a concept proposed by Massey (1984), which involves the concentration of particular sectors and/ or production tasks in specific geographical areas.

According to Sayer (1995), geographers and other social scientists, particularly those working in the Marxian tradition, have underestimated the significance of the division of labour in the organization of economic activity. Sayer argues that the complexities of modern industrial economies are such that they cannot feasibly be centrally planned (cf. CENTRAL PLANNING), and nor can the social division of labour be abolished. For Sayer, this means that traditional Marxist approaches to geographical change must be rethought to recognize that the political challenges posed by the division of labour would not disappear with the transition to a post-capitalist society. (See also Sayer and Walker, 1992.) JP

References

Hechter, M. 1975: *Internal colonialism*. London: Routledge. · Massey, D. 1984: *Spatial divisions of labour*. London: Macmillan. · Sayer, A. 1995: *Radical political economy: a critique*. Oxford: Blackwell. · Sayer, A. and Walker, R. 1992: *The new social economy: reworking the division of labour*. Oxford: Blackwell.

domino theory A GEOPOLITICS theory adopted by United States' governments in the 1950s to justify their policies of military and political involvement in other countries. They contended that if one country fell into the Soviet Union's sphere of influence its neighbours could well follow, setting up a ripple effect similar to that of a toppling line of dominoes, and this analogy (propounded by President Eisenhower in 1953) was used to justify American involvement in Southeastern Asia. It continues to influence American foreign policy, as in attitudes toward governments in Central America. RJJ

Suggested Reading

O'Sullivan, P. 1982: Antidomino. *Political Geography Quarterly* 1: 57–64.

dry farming A farming technique for crop cultivation without irrigation in areas of low and variable rainfall. Most common is fallowing in which two seasons' rainfall is reserved for one crop, with mulching and frequent weeding. Low-rainfall areas are vulnerable to erosion, and thus soil conservation methods are essential. Dry farming areas can have only a narrow range of crops and low yields. Dry farming is a long established practice in the Near East, North Africa, and north-west India. These methods were instrumental in the extension of crop cultivation into the semi-arid areas of North (and South) America and Australia by European settlers in the nineteenth century. SW

References

Heathcote, R. 1983: *The arid lands: their use and abuse*. London: Longman.

dual economy An ECONOMIC GEOGRAPHY which appears to consist of two separate parts, each having a distinctive history and dynamic.

J.H. Boeke (see Furnivall, 1939; Boeke, 1953) argued that Indonesian society was divided into two separate CULTURES – a western and an eastern. These cultures were considered to be structurally and behaviourally so different that western principles of social analysis were quite inappropriate for an understanding of eastern culture or, indeed, for an understanding of the dual whole. Insofar as western culture is highly organized along lines which facilitate the fulfilment of material objectives by rational means of production (production for gain) and eastern culture is loosely organized, fatalistic, passive and concerned with production for use, the central problem of DEVELOPMENT in dual economies (the context in which they have, in the main, been analysed) is the relationship between the two cultures and, especially, the transformation of the latter by the former. In short, dualistic thinking implies a view of development as MODERNIZATION – a view, rejected by, for example, Frank (1989).

Such an emphasis upon development generates an economistic and universal view of the world and so legitimates dualist thinking by imposing a particular and singular developmental western view of the world on all 'others' (see ETHNOCENTRISM). It thereby encourages the simplistic division of the world in dualist terms (see Said (1985) for a critique of such a manoeuvre: cf. ORIENTALISM). This fails to recognize either the dualities of social interactions or the heterogeneous nature of societies and the multiple circuits of SOCIAL REPRODUCTION which sustain them. There may be two or more driven by very different logics; sensitive social dissection would reveal the variety of social discontinuities and interactions. Even generalizing at the global level, two particularly influential accounts of the world economy (Wallerstein, 1979; Braudel, 1985; see WORLD-SYSTEMS ANALYSIS) identify three, rather different, underlying structures. But to look for two is to find two – to generalize in such a way that the classification which results is binary in form. In developed industrial economies, for example, distinctions are sometimes drawn between the small number of very large firms which dominate economies and the large number of small firms whose conditions of existence are set by the former group.

Nevertheless Harold Brookfield (1975) asserts that 'it is a matter of simple observation that the economies of a great many developing countries are organized in two parts ... the point must be emphasized that a phenomenon called "dualism" exists ...'. The question is whether 'simple observation' is an adequate basis for such an assertion. On the basis of evidence on the complexity, recency and incompleteness of CLASS structures in the underdeveloped world (Roxborough, 1979, chs 6 and 7) the answer must be that it is not.

An alternative but associated conception of dualism – elucidated most explicitly in the writings of Milton Santos (1979; see Chatterjee, 1989 for a critical evaluation) – is that of the emergence of two circuits of production and exchange. Santos (p. 18) refers to these circuits as the 'upper circuit' and the 'lower circuit' (see figure):

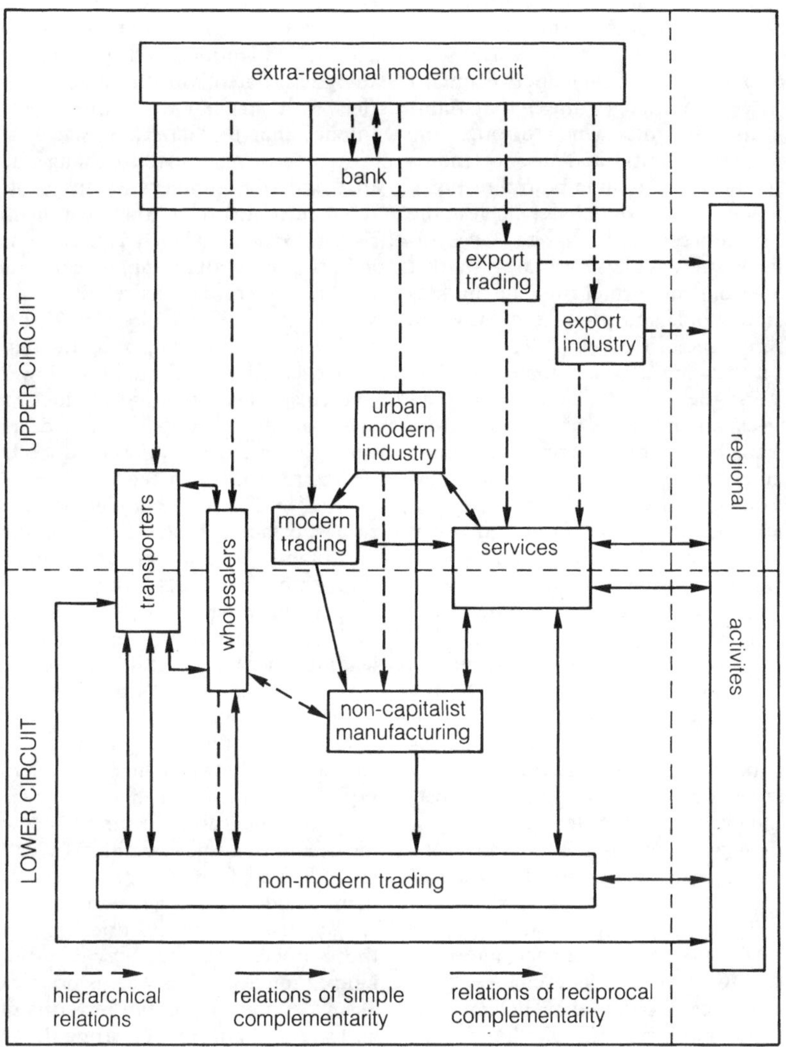

dual economy (after Santos, 1979)

In simple terms, the upper circuit consists of banking, export trade and industry, modern urban industry, trade and services, and wholesaling and trucking. The lower circuit is essentially made up of non-capitalist-intensive forms of manufacturing, non-modern services generally provided at the 'retail' level and non-modern and small-scale trade.

The circuits correspond to what Geertz (1963, p. 34) speaks of as the 'firm-centred economy' and the 'bazaar economy' and the distinction between them is based primarily upon the non-modern/modern cleavage. Thus, whereas the upper circuit is characterized by modern capital-intensive industry, extensive trade and complex commercial flows, the lower circuit involves labour-intensive manufacturing, local services and limited trade. Access by the individual to the products of the upper circuit is restricted by income – the distribution of which is increasingly polarized as the landless and jobless live alongside those productively involved in, and highly remunerated for, their participation in the upper circuit. And yet the poor and dispossessed must somehow create the conditions of their own existence; they do so through their participation in a lower circuit (see INFORMAL SECTOR).

Simple and reciprocal forms of complementarity (inputs and outputs) form the material relationships between the circuits but, insofar as the upper circuit is based upon capitalist production and exchange, the two circuits may be constantly intertwined through the activities of merchants and moneylenders facilitating a flow of capital in both directions. However, in terms of material linkages, the relationship between the circuits is asymmetric: the lower circuit serves as a market for the upper but the former finds its markets amongst households and producers elsewhere in the informal sector (Lubell, 1991).

A view of the circuits based upon the informal sector and the differentiation both of CAPITAL as self-expanding value, and of its sources of expansion, begins to undermine a simple dualism embodied in the dual circuit. This dualism is based on the notion that the hegemony of the upper circuit is reproduced by an inherent process of quantitative expansion (see CAPITALISM) and provides not only the context to which the lower circuit must constantly adapt but the very reason for its existence.

The notion of dualism serves a significant ideological purpose (see IDEOLOGY). On the one hand, and stemming from the work of Ragnar Nurske (1953) and W.A. Lewis (1954), economists have tried to build a theory of development based upon the assumed existence of dualism. Such theories, operating under various assumptions such as the abundance of unemployed labour power in the traditional sector, try to uncover the implications of economic growth and structural change for both parts of the economy, for their interrelationship and for economy-wide change. As a result the dominant sector may be imposed upon the subdominant and the latter may well disintegrate and be transformed into the image of its dominant partner (see DEPENDENCE).

Leaving aside the question of whether or not dualism is an adequate description of the economy in question, problems arise over the nature of the two parts. The solution is to set up IDEAL TYPES which correspond more or less to observed characteristics. But such problems are intensified when such more or less unreal ideal types are brought into interrelationship with each other. Without a detailed social specification of the two parts – which would, in any case, serve to break down a simplistic dualism – it is difficult to build an operational model.

On the other hand, the sustenance of the ideology of dualism may serve the interests of those who promote modernization on the grounds that everything associated with change is identified with progress and everything associated with the status quo is identified with stagnation. Furthermore, dualism implies that UNDERDEVELOPMENT is the consequence of resistance to change. It suggests that underdevelopment is caused by development-restrictive conditions within the underdeveloped society (such as may be manifest in a backward-sloping supply curve of labour) rather than through its relationships with the world outside. For Santos (1979) the objective of development is to open up the upper circuit to participation by those in the lower in order to increase their skills and productivity. This is classical dualist thinking and, despite assertions to the contrary, implies a 'dichotomized or fragmented urban economy'.

Dualism is a powerful idea. It has given rise to a substantial body of development theory and practice and insofar as it emphasizes the UNEVEN nature of DEVELOPMENT and the barriers to its progress, it is useful. The major problem is that it imposes a simplistic, misleading and teleological predefinition of the world (see TELEOLOGY) into two parts (development-facilitative and development-restrictive) rather than emphasizing either the causal links between them or offering a critique of the universalism and implicit assumptions of modernization embodied within the idea. The dualism is defined by external criteria derived from the processes of development under advocacy and are seen as exogenous to the historical geography of those processes. In this way dualism acts as a kind of intellectual as well as practical imperialism defining one entity in terms of another and so simultaneously asserting the superiority of the 'self' and denying both the integrity of the 'other' and any responsibility for its underdevelopment. RL

References

Boeke, J.H. 1953: *Economics and economic policy of dual societies, as exemplified by Indonesia*. Haarlem: H.D. Tjeenk Willink and Zoon; New York: Institute of Pacific Relations (reprinted 1976, New York: AMS Press). · Braudel, F. 1985: *Civilization and capitalism 15th–18th Century*, vol. I: *The perspective of the world*. London: Fontana Press. · Brookfield, H. 1975: *Interdependent development*. London: Methuen; Pittsburgh, PA: University of Pittsburgh Press, ch. 3. · Chatterjee, L. 1989: Third world cities. In R. Peet and N. Thrift, eds, *New models in geography*, vol. II. London and Winchester MA: Unwin Hyman, ch. 6, 127–46. · Frank, A.G. 1989 The development of underdevelopment. *Monthly Review* 41 July: 37–51. · Furnivall, J.S. 1939: *Netherlands India: a study of plural economy*. Cambridge: Cambridge University Press (1944 edition reprinted 1977, New York: AMS Press). · Geertz, C. 1963: *Peddlers and princes*. Chicago: Chicago University Press. ·Lewis, W.A. 1954: Economic development with unlimited supplies of labour. *Manchester School of Economics and Social Studies* 22: 139–91. · Lubell, H. 1991: *The informal sector in the 1980s and 1990s*. OECD Development Centre. Paris: OECD. · Nurske, R. 1953: *Problems of capital formation in underdeveloped countries*. New York: Oxford University Press. · Roxborough, I. 1979: *Theories of underdevelopment*. London: Macmillan; Atlantic Highlands, NJ: Humanities Press. · Said, E.W. 1985 [orig. 1978]: *Orientalism*. London and New York: Penguin Books; Santos, M. 1979: *The shared space*. London and New York: Methuen. · Wallerstein, I. 1979: *The capitalist world economy*. Cambridge: Cambridge University Press and Editions de la Maison des Sciences de l'Homme.

Suggested reading

Brookfield (1975); Frank (1989); Santos (1979).

dual theory of the state A theory developed by Peter Saunders (1986) which analytically separates the STATE's role in promoting production and wealth creation in a capitalist society from that of ensuring satisfactory levels of consumption for its resident population. Saunders argued that these functions involved separate, though overlapping, arenas of CONFLICT – the 'politics of production' and the 'politics of consumption' – in which the actors are differently mobilized. Conflicts in the *politics of production* are largely CLASS-based (involving, for example, employers' organizations and trades unions in conflict with each other and with the state); in the *politics of consumption* the interested parties are sectoral groups – such as those reliant on different sources for housing, transport, health services, education and so forth – which may not be mobilized across a class CLEAVAGE.

The main geographical component of Saunders' theory is his claim that whereas the politics of production are largely organized at the national or regional level, the politics of consumption are played out locally (see LOCAL STATE). Major contentious issues over which conflicts might threaten the rate of capital ACCUMULATION are focused on the national state, where capitalists' interests can best be safeguarded. Other issues, which are subnational in their impact and carry less threat to the capitalist imperative, remain at the local level: most are concerned with consumption issues, with conflict over relative access to PUBLIC GOODS rather than over shares of the national wealth, and these can be relatively safely left to the more pluralist political ethos of local governments (see PLURALISM) whilst production issues are handled in the national government which is more influenced by CORPORATISM.

A simple reading of this theory suggests a clear distinction between central and local governments in their respective roles within the STATE APPARATUS, although the relative allocation of functions varies over time and between places. RJJ

Reference

Saunders, P. 1986: *Social theory and the urban question*, 2nd edn. London: Hutchinson.

E

ecofeminism An umbrella term for a wide variety of approaches to environmental analysis that integrate feminist and environmental perspectives. Ecofeminism is both THEORY and praxis, built on the intellectual foundations of ecology and feminism, and on the populist strength of women's rights and women's health movements, peace, anti-nuclear, socialist, labour, ecological, ENVIRONMENTAL JUSTICE, and animal rights movements. There are varying claims about the origin of the term itself, although most attribute it to French author Françoise D'Eaubonne (1980).

A wide range of scholarly and popular writing is often designated as ecofeminist; there is, however, some ambivalence about the use of this term and not all feminists working on ecological or environmental matters identify their work as ecofeminism, many employing instead designations such as *ecological feminism* (Warren, 1994), *feminist political ecology* (Rocheleau et al., 1996), or simply *feminist* ENVIRONMENTALISM (Seager, 1993a).

The (putative) woman–nature connection is a thematic backdrop that shapes much ecofeminist discourse and may be used as a touchstone for distinguishing among schools of thought in ecofeminism. The notion that women are 'closer' to NATURE is woven into the intellectual, religious and social fabric of many CULTURES. But there is considerable disagreement on how this association is to be interpreted. Much of the academic writing on ecofeminism argues that this association is an artifice of patriarchal ideology, designed primarily to distance women from cultural loci of POWER and to prop up male domination of both women and nature. Much of the populist and more spiritually grounded ecofeminist writing, in contrast, embraces a woman–nature connection, interpreting this as a distinctively 'womanist' claim to strength, a connection perhaps to a long historical lineage of matriarchal power, which also gives women a distinctive voice and position from which to critique the dominant male culture. (See Griffin, 1978; Merchant, 1980; Warren, 1994; cf. PHALLOCENTRISM.) A corollary debate among ecofeminists is the extent to which consideration of a woman–nature connection presumes (and promotes) an essentialized view of 'women'. An emerging middle ground between these schools of thought may be glimpsed in the renewed appreciation among feminist theorists of the uses of 'strategic essentialism'; there is more and more agreement that politically motivated feminist theory perhaps can accommodate 'contingent foundations', moments of toleration for certain UNIVERSALISMS and ESSENTIALISMS (Sturgeon, 1997, p. 10).

Differences aside, there are common analytical and conceptual interests that cut across the plurality of ecofeminist positions, and that frame much of the feminist scholarship and activism in this field. These include:

First, a *commitment to illuminating the ways in which* GENDER, CLASS *and* RACE *mediate the ways in which people live in and with local environments*. Because ecofeminism is both a political stance and an academic inquiry, much of the literature – even the most theoretical writings – pivot around a central interest in the 'real' lives of women and their relationships to the environment. Women everywhere have a different relationship to resources and environmental technics from their male counterparts: because of their social location and socially assigned gender roles, women and men seldom have the same environmental relationships or responsibilities, nor do they enjoy the same access to environmentally constituted power and wealth; women and men live differently in their environments, and are affected differently by ecological change and crisis; large-scale 'DEVELOPMENT' processes or decisions that affect environmental sustainability reverberate differently in women's and men's lives, and among women and men across divides of class and race.

It was primarily THIRD WORLD feminist theorists and activists who forged, in the 1980s, a unified ecofeminist theory and praxis around questions such as: 'How are RESOURCES defined?'; 'Who controls them?'; 'How does ecologic crisis manifest itself?'; 'What are the relationships between local environments and global processes, and who controls them?'; 'How is environmental activism defined?'; 'How does women's involvement in environmental movements change them, change the movements and change the definition of what an environmental problem is?'; and 'Who speaks for the environment?' Because environmental matters are survival matters – literally – these ecofeminist questions take on a certain urgency. The *lived environment* ecofeminist literature overlaps to some extent with the *women in development* literature, but the emphasis on environmental relations is distinctive. (See Rocheleau et al., 1996; Shiva, 1989; Agarwal, 1992.)

Secondly, there is an interest in *examining the ways in which human–environment perceptions and values may be mediated through 'gendered' lenses and shaped by gender roles and assumptions.* Among feminist geographers, this interest has been explored primarily in an extensive scholarship on the gendered dimensions of environmental perception, landscape assessment and Wiegman, and hazards assessment (Norwood and Monk, 1987; Gutteling and Wiegman, 1993). A related scholarship explores the extent to which human theorizing *about* nature, ECOLOGY and environment may reflect gendered imprints. It can be argued that the dominant (western) discourse about nature, including the DISCOURSE of environmental ETHICS and rights, reflects a gender-embedded consciousness, if only opaquely; as many eco feministspointout,'aheavilymasculinepresence has inhabited most accounts of environmental philosophy' (Plumwood, 1993, p. 3; cf. ETHICS, GEOGRAPHY AND). The very distinction between human and non-human realms, the creation of the chasm between human and nature, has been interpreted by some ecofeminists as a product of a distinctly 'MASCULINST' culture. More broadly, much of the (western, contemporary) ethical and philosophical environmental writing is steeped in a masculinist worldview about the hierarchical and utilitarian relationship of humans and nature, or about the role of 'management' of nature and wildlife; much environmental and nature writing presents views of environmental history that reflect only or mostly male activities, thoughts, and priorities; similarly, priorities and assumptions embedded in the ethos, policies and activities of many of the large environmental organizations show a gendered imprint.

Among the more provocative ecofeminist analyses of the insidiousness of 'the masculinist worldview' in environmental analysis are DECONSTRUCTIONS of the imagery of the planet (see, for example, Garb, 1990). That such imagery is 'gendered' might be demonstrated by the wide appeal of representations of earth as 'mother,' and the representations of nature as, variously, a nurturing female or as a vengeful feminized out-of-control force. The most controversial of this literature explores the gendered dimensions of the popular earth-from-space imagery and the distant-view images of place made ubiquitous through GEOGRAPHICAL INFORMATIONAL SYSTEMS and satellite technologies (see REMOTE SENSING), which have been interpreted as products of a masculinist impulse, creating distanced, voyeuristic, almost pornographic representations of PLACE (Garb, 1990; see also Cosgrove, 1994).

Third is an interest in *examining the gendered nature of the constellation of political, economic and ecological power in institutions which are instrumental players in the state of the environment.* Environmental relations are largely shaped by and mediated by bureaucracies and institutions: on a global SCALE by entities such as governments, militaries, multinational corporations, and multilateral organizations such as the World Bank (cf. GLOBALIZATION); on a smaller scale, by organizations such as, in the US for example, the Forestry Service and the Army Corps of Engineers. A gendered analysis of the institutional logic of, the 'culture' of, and the exercise of power by these institutional entities can shed light on environmental agency, causality, and consequences (Seager, 1993a, 1993b; Shiva, 1993; Rocheleau et al., 1996).

Finally there is the interest in *exploring the interconnectedness of systems of oppression and domination.* One organizing premise of this ecofeminist literature is that the abuse and exploitation of natural environments may be read as being ideologically continuous with – even derivative of – structures of oppression and domination in human relations. Many authors argue, in particular, that the domination of women and the domination of nature are ideologically intertwined; the *feminization of nature* and the *naturalization of women* are linked conceptualizations that devalue both (see Merchant, 1980; Warren, 1994; Sturgeon, 1997). In the more self-consciously philosophical scholarship, this relationship is explored through analysis of the construction of the mutually referential 'meta-dualities' of nature:culture and female:male (see Plumwood, 1993; Warren, 1994).

More broadly, ecofeminist analysis points to linkages between environmental oppressions of many kinds (such as species-ist hierarchies, for example, or the hierarchy of value established through the commodification of nature) and human social oppressions of many kinds (such as those based on class, or race-ist, gender and sexuality classifications, or judgements made about 'value' as mediated by physical ability). The ENVIRONMENTAL JUSTICE movement derives, in part, from such an analysis of multiple and overlapping oppressions.

It is also at this analytical point that environmentalism, feminism and animal rights converge, including recent work by geographers (see Donovan, 1990; Gaard, 1993; Wolch and Emel, 1998). Over several centuries, at least in western Europe and North America, women have been the primary supporters of animal rights movements and among the most influential theorists of the rights of animals; most of this literature is grounded in an *overlapping oppressions* analysis (cf. ANIMALS, GEOGRAPHY AND).

The critical feminist scholarship on the construction of science has exerted a strong influence on much of the ecofeminist literature (see for example Harding, 1986; Shiva, 1989, 1993; Sardar, 1988; Merchant, 1980). The intellectual history of western science is intertwined with the development of ideologies and technologies for achieving 'mastery' over nature. The widespread export of these technologies and ideologies, whether as part of an eighteenth-century colonial enterprise or a twentieth-century export of RESOURCE MANAGEMENT and 'development' strategies, has been a strong determinant of the state of the global environment. Around the world, challenges to destructive technologies and to the scientific rationality of environmental 'management' have sparked a robust environmental activism, and especially women's and ecofeminist activism (see Sardar, 1988; Shiva, 1989, 1993; Agarwal, 1992).

Ecofeminist activism typically takes the form of small-scale, grassroots-led movements informed by an analysis of the role of PATRIARCHY in establishing fragmented and exploitative relationships between humans and their environment. Many ecofeminists focus particularly on the contradictions between production (especially the imperatives of capitalist industrialism) and reproduction (the necessity for environments that can sustain healthy life), since it is in women's bodies and women's social roles that these contradictions become the most apparent. (See also BODY, GEOGRAPHY AND; FEMINIST GEOGRAPHIES: GENDER AND GEOGRAPHY.) JS

References

Agarwal, B. 1992. The gender and environment debate: lessons from India. *Feminist Studies* 18 (1). · Cosgrove, D. 1994. Contested global visions: one-world, whole-earth, and the Apollo space photographs. *Annals of the Association of American Geographers* 84 (2): 270–94. · D'Eaubonne, F. 1980: Feminism or death. In E. Marks, and I. de Courtivron, eds, *New French feminisms: an anthology*. Amherst: Amherst University Press. · Donovan, J. 1990: Animal rights and feminist theory. *Signs: Journal of Women in Culture and Society* 15 (2): 350–75. · Gaard, G., ed., 1993: *Ecofeminism: women, animals, nature*. Philadelphia: Temple University Press. · Garb, Y.J. 1990: Perspective or escape? Ecofeminist musings on contemporary earth imagery. In I. Diamond and G. Orenstein, eds, *Reweaving the world: the emergence of ecofeminism*. San Francisco: Sierra Club Books, 264–78. · Griffin, S. 1978: *Woman and nature*. New York: Harper & Row. · Gutteling, J. and Wiegman, O. 1993: Gender-specific reactions to environmental hazards in the Netherlands. *Sex Roles* 28 (7/8): 433–47. · Harding, S. 1986: *The science question in feminism*. Ithaca: Cornell University Press. · Merchant, C. 1980: *The death of nature: women, ecology, and the scientific revolution*. New York: Harper & Row. · Norwood, V. and Monk, J., eds, 1987: *The Desert Is No Lady: Southwestern landscapes in women's writing and art*. New Haven: Yale University Press. · Plumwood, V. 1993: *Feminism and the mastery of nature*. New York and London: Routledge. · Rocheleau, D., Thomas-Slayter, B. and Wangari, E., eds, 1996: *Feminist political ecology: global issues and local experiences*. New York and London: Routledge. · Sardar, Z., ed., 1988: *The revenge of Athena: science, exploitation and the Third World*. London: Mansell Publishing; Seager, J. 1993a: *Earth follies: coming to feminist terms with the global environmental crisis*. New York and London: Routledge. · Seager, J. 1993b: A not-so-natural disaster: militaries, technology and the floods of 1993. *MS Magazine* 4 (3): 26–7. · Shiva, V. 1989: *Staying alive: women, ecology & development*. London: Zed Books. · Shiva, V. 1993: Colonialism and the evolution of masculinist forestry. In S. Harding, ed., *The racial economy of science*. Bloomington: Indiana University Press. · Sturgeon, N. 1997: *Ecofeminist natures*. New York: Routledge. · Warren, K.J., ed., 1994: *Ecological feminism*. London and New York: Rout'-ledge. · Wolch, J. and Emel, J., eds, 1998: *Animal geographies: place, politics and identity in the nature-culture borderlands*. New York: Verso.

Suggested Reading

Mies, M, and Shiva, V. 1993: *Ecofeminism*. London: Zed Books. · Nesmith, C. and Radcliffe, S. 1993: (Re)mapping Mother Earth: a geographical perspective on environmental feminisms. *Environment and Planning D: Society and Space* 11: 379–94. · Rocheleau, Thomas-Slayter and Wangari (1996). · Seager (1993a and b); Sturgeon (1997).

ecological fallacy A problem that can arise when inferring characteristics of individuals from aggregate data referring to a population of which they are members. Such aggregate data are frequently used in geographical work, referring to the populations of defined areas (hence they are often termed ecological data), so the problem is potentially serious for some forms of geographical analysis.

The fallacy was initially highlighted by W.S. Robinson (1950). Using 1930 US CENSUS data, he obtained a high CORRELATION coefficient of 0.773 from a REGRESSION of the percentage of each state's population who were illiterate on the percentage who were black. It could be inferred from this that blacks were much more likely to be illiterate than were non-blacks but using data on individuals from the same source, he found a correlation of only 0.203: there was a higher level of illiteracy among blacks than non-blacks, but much less than the state-level (ecological) analysis suggested. The lesson was clear: just because blacks were concentrated in the states with the highest levels of illiteracy did not necessarily mean a much higher level of illiteracy among blacks.

Alker (1969) extended the ecological fallacy (of identifying spurious individual-level correlations from analyses of aggregate data) by identifying five others:

- *the individualistic fallacy* which assumes that the whole is no more than the sum of its parts (see REGIONALISM) – many societies are more than mere aggregations of their individual members;
- *the cross-level fallacy* assumes that a relationship observed in one aggregation of a population – i.e. one set of spatial units – applies to all others, and is thus a universal feature of that population: research on the MODIFIABLE AREAL UNIT PROBLEM has demonstrated that this is invalid;
- *the universal fallacy* assumes that the pattern observed in a selection of individuals – often not randomly selected according to the principles of SAMPLING – holds for its population;
- *the selective fallacy* in which data from carefully chosen cases are used to 'prove' a point; and
- *the cross-sectional fallacy* is the assumption that what is observed at one point in time applies to other times.

Recognition of these fallacies and their associated pitfalls indicates a need for careful interpretation of the results of studies based on aggregate data. An observed relationship may be consistent with a HYPOTHESIS, but a causal relationship should never be assumed: as Robinson's example showed, wrong conclusions can be drawn by attempts to move from the particular to the general.

The problem of drawing conclusions about individual-level correlations from aggregate data has long concerned social statisticians. Most attempts to resolve it have failed, because they cannot avoid the possibility of producing 'nonsense' answers, such as a population in which 120 per cent of the members are illiterate. King (1997) has solved it for a particular situation, however. If one has information on, for example, the number of black people and the number of illiterates in each sub-area of a larger area for which the inference is to be drawn, then using the 'method of bounds' it is possible to produce robust estimates of the number of blacks who are illiterate, the number of non-blacks who are literate etc. in that larger area as well as in each of the sub-areas. RJJ

References

Alker, H.R. 1969: A typology of ecological fallacies. In M. Dogan, and S. Rokkan, eds, *Quantitative ecological analysis in the social sciences*. Cambridge, MA and London: The MIT Press, 69–86. · King, G. 1997: *A solution to the ecological inference problem: reconstructing individual behavior from aggregate data*. Princeton, NJ: Princeton University Press. · Robinson, W.S. 1950: Ecological correlations and the behavior of individuals. *American Sociological Review* 15: 351–7.

Suggested Reading

Duncan, O.D., Cuzzort, R.P. and Duncan, B. 1961: *Statistical geography*. Glencoe, IL: The Free Press.

ecological imperialism A term which attempts to link environmental ideas, practices and processes – for example ENVIRONMENTAL DETERMINISM, CONSERVATION and deforestation – with the genesis of a world system (beginning with the European expansion of the fifteenth century) and the proliferation of IMPERIALISM in its multiplicity of forms. Ecological imperialism was employed by Alfred Crosby (1986) to describe the traffic in crops, diseases and environmental destruction associated with mercantile expansionism. However, *green imperialism* has been employed by a number of authors to understand the complex relations between environmental change, COLONIALISM, conservation and GLOBALIZATION broadly construed (Grove, 1995).

There are two main strands to the thesis of ecological imperialism that ecological destruction and conservation has attended colonial expansion and the genesis of the European-dominated world system. The first is that *European mercantile expansion represented and facilitated the transnational movement of plants, animals and disease*. The Great Dying which accompanied the first age of Iberian imperialism in the New World was in some senses ecological in character (the accidental introduction of Old-World pathogens for which the absence of local resistance and patterns of vulnerability generated by the dislocations of forms of livelihood at the hands of the Spanish and Portuguese conquerors, produced enormously high mortality rates in indigenous communities). The global traffic in plants and animals – for example, the introduction of New World maize into Africa, of Southeast Asian rubber into Brazil – had tremendous ecological as well as social consequences, often unintentional in their extent and scope (for example, the diffusion and proliferation of New World grasses). Indeed, as Grove (1995) has pointed out, the earliest EXPLORATIONS were Edenic (and therefore green) in impetus (see Prest, 1981). The origins of the botanical garden as a storehouse of tropical germ plasm is not only a form of imperialist plunder and collection but also rooted in the European notion that the gardens and rivers of Eden might be found in the East. In this sense the 'commercial and utilitarian purposes of European expansion produced a situation in which the tropical environment was increasingly utilised as the symbolic location for idealised LANDSCAPES and aspirations of the western imagination' (Grove, 1995, p. 3). This is as true for the significance of the hunt in colonial (and post-colonial) Africa as it is for the power of island paradises in the European imaginary (Prest, 1981; McKenzie, 1988; Miller and Reil, 1996). The green imperialism by which Kew Gardens became a botanical collecting station for Britain has now been displaced by the world-wide collection of germ plasm by seed and bio-technology companies and the United Nations global seed banks (Shiva, 1996; Perkins, 1997). The GREEN REVOLUTION which developed high-yielding varieties on the basis of germ plasm collected globally – often from local varieties invented and reproduced over millennia by local PEASANTS and farmers – is an instance of twentieth-century green imperialism in the sense of First World corporations (in tandem with multilateral development institutions) simultaneously developing profitable 'miracle seeds' and perpetrating ecological destruction through genetic erosion and loss of BIODIVERSITY (Kloppenberg, 1988; Shiva, 1991).

A second theme concerns *conservation and its relationship to the imperial mission.* Grove (1995) has shown how western conservation is 'imperial' in several senses (see also Prest, 1981). On the one hand, the global expansion of trade and economic exploitation after 1500 had direct and deleterious consequences for tropical environments. But on the other, the very idea of western conservation can be traced to the sixteenth- and seventeenth-century destruction of tropical habitats, particularly on islands such as Mauritius, St Helena, the West Indies and the Canary islands, and to the complex scientific, colonial and indigenous amalgam of ideas – what Grove (1995, p. 12) calls 'a highly heterogeneous mixture of indigenous, Romantic, Orientalist and other elements' – which went into the formation of the first conservationist ideology 400 years ago. Processes of deforestation in the island COMMUNITIES, and subsequently in India, figured centrally as indeed did some incongruous scientific communities (for example, the medical services of the East India Company). Of course these colonial conservation movements were complex and contradictory, constrained by the needs of the colonial STATE and later, in the nineteenth century, became the basis for authoritarian and coercive regulation of local communities. The ways in which the colonial state in Africa, for example, used conservation as a way of legitimating land seizures, of compelling forced resettlement, and of promulgating neo-Malthusian views of the inept African farmers is now well documented (Beinart, 1984; cf. MALTHUSIAN MODEL). Conservation in turn became an object of struggle and conflict for subjugated colonial peoples (Guha, 1988).

Green or ecological imperialism should not therefore be understood in terms of the untrammelled powers of colonialism or globalization (in its late twentieth-century incarnation). Ecological destruction and conservation involved a two-way trafficking of ideas, knowledge and practice. Western mercantile expansionism and the first Age of Imperialism was capable of generating an incipient western sense of conservation at the same time that the same colonial presence unleashed ecologically destructive forces. The colonial state embodied the contradictory tendencies of wanting both to exploit *and* to conserve, of wishing both to facilitate resource extraction for imperialist companies and to ensure political stability of colonized communities which ecological destruction and authoritarian conservation strategies did little to promote (cf. HEGEMONY). Neumann's (1998) account of the National Park system in Africa is an instructive instance of the global and local forces and resistances surrounding green imperialism. He shows both the global origins of the very idea of the National Park as it was imposed in Tanzania (for laudable goals), the imagery, politics and practices which entered into its constitution in Africa, and the frictions and struggles which went into the appropriation of the National Park itself. The question of LAND RIGHTS among communities who were expelled from the Arusha National Park and the ways in which the state and the Park Service attempt to police the park's borders are central to any understanding of why parks in Africa have so often failed in their attempt both to preserve endangered species and to elicit the support of peasants and communities along the borders of the park itself. MW

References

Beinart, W. 1984: Soil erosion, conservation and ideas about development. *Journal of Southern African Studies* 11 (1): 52–83. · Cosby, A. 1986: *Biological imperialism*. Cambridge: Cambridge University Press. · Grove, R. 1995: *Green imperialism*. Cambridge: Cambridge University Press. · Guha, R. 1988: *Unquiet woods*. Berkeley: University of California Press. · Kloppenberg, J. 1988: *First the seed*. Cambridge: Cambridge University Press. · Mackenzie, J., ed., 1988: *The empire of nature*. Manchester: Manchester University Press. · Miller, D. and Reill, P., eds, 1996: *Visions of empire*. Cambridge: Cambridge University Press. · Neumann, R. 1998: *Imposing wilderness*. Berkeley: University of California Press. · Perkins, J. 1997: *Geopolitics and the green revolution*. London: Oxford University Press. · Prest, J. 1981: *The garden of Eden*. New Haven: Yale University Press. · Shiva, V. 1991: *The violence of the green revolution*. London: Zed Books. · Shiva, V. 1996: *Biopiracy*. London: Zed Book.

ecology A term coined in 1866 by the German biologist Ernst Haeckel as '*oecologie*'. The Greek word '*oikonomia*' is the root of both 'economy' and 'ecology'; the former means 'management of the household' and the latter means 'science of the household' (Hayward, 1994). When Haeckel coined the term 'oecologie', he had in mind the metaphor of 'nature's economy' (Worster, 1977, p. 192).

Ecology has three distinct, but related, meanings. The first is the interactions of organisms with each other, with their biotic and abiotic environments, and the outcomes of these interactions, (i.e. their ecology). The second, often labelled 'scientific ecology' or 'professional ecology', is an area of academic inquiry that constitutes a sub-discipline of biology. This use of the term 'ecology' is the study of the interactions outlined in the first definition. The third meaning perceives ecology to be the most politically engaged, critical and normative of the traditional sciences (see Merchant, 1994). This politicization of ecology dates from the late 1960s. In 1970, a professional ecologist told a US Congressional Committee that 'ecology is no longer a scientific discipline – it's an attitude of mind' (in McCormick, 1995, p. 57). This definition of ecology is similar to Sachs' perception of ecology as 'the philosophy of a social movement' (Sachs, 1993, p. xv). The tension *within* this third definition is the perceived need to justify normative ideas (see NORMATIVE THEORY) with a scientific basis. Ecology may simultaneously become the attitude of mind (i.e. reverence for the earth, ecological processes and communities), the normative project (i.e. protection for the earth, ecological processes and communities) and the scientific justification that is considered necessary for the normative project.

The tensions *between* scientific/professional ecology and what may be called 'normative ecology' are situated in EPISTEMOLOGY and ONTOLOGY. Epistemologically, scientific ecology claims to be objective. It follows traditional scientific approaches to knowledge, such as quantification and experimentation. Normative ecology is an attitude of mind that focuses on reverence for the earth which comes from intimate contact with the earth as subject. Ontologically, scientific ecology perceives both competition and cooperation, but often implicitly emphasizes competition for food, habitats and light. Nature is perceived to be dynamic, with no sense of 'balance'. Ecologists in the scientific ecology approach often present the findings of scientific studies to political decision-makers. In contrast, normative ecologists often identify a 'balance of nature', although it is recognized that NATURE is dynamic. Normative ecologists generally critique political institutions, and are more likely to take direct action against existing institutions to achieve their normative project. This approach stems largely from an ontological position that believes nature is based largely on cooperation, with competition occurring within limited domains. The cooperation in nature includes humans cooperating in political action. This approach is often equated with ENVIRONMENTALISM or the ENVIRONMENTAL MOVEMENT. However, some authors (e.g. Dobson, 1996) distinguish between 'ecologism' and 'environmentalism', where the former is more radical in its critique of existing society and approaches. This distinction is maintained in the use of the term 'ecology' to distinguish between 'ecological economics' and 'ENVIRONMENTAL ECONOMICS'.

Within the 'normative ecology' approach, there are a number of major distinctions. Bramwell (1989) highlighted their range as being from Left to Right on the traditional IDEOLOGICAL spectrum, which may also be understood as being from strongly anthropocentric to ecocentric (after Dobson, 1996), from romantic to technocratic and from anarchist to authoritarian. Three influential traditions within 'ecologism' are 'social ecology', 'global ecology' and 'political ecology'. *Social ecology* is associated with the eco-anarchist work of Murray Bookchin (1990). In this approach, there are no hierarchies in nature that serve as a natural foundation and justification for the existing hierarchies in human society. Instead, nature is a 'web of life'. However, according to Bookchin, human domination of nature will persist as long as hierarchies within human society are maintained. *Global ecology*, which includes the work of Wolfgang Sachs, is the radical political critique of global and international institutions, and events that are perceived as mildly reformist 'environmentalism'. The question of SCALE is crucial here because although these authors adopt a global focus, they are very concerned with the links between local and global representations and impacts. *Political ecology* is a term that has been used by ANARCHIST authors (Roussopoulos, 1993), 'green' authors (Lipietz, 1995) and Marxist-inspired authors in international development (Blaikie and Brookfield, 1987; Black, 1990; Peet and Watts, 1993; Bryant, 1997). To date, the latter use of POLITICAL ECOLOGY has been the most influential of these approaches within geography.

Geographers have also used work from within the scientific ecology tradition. *Community ecology*, defined as the composition or structure of communities and the movement of energy and matter through them, was developed by Cowles and Clements in the early twentieth century, who studied plant communities and were themselves influenced by geographers such as Humboldt, de Candolle, Engler, Gray and Kerner. The work of Hutchinson and H.T. and E.P. Odum in the 1950s on energy flow and energy budgets has also been used in geography. There have been numerous instances of ecological concepts being borrowed from geographers, economists and anthropologists by ecologists, and vice versa. The fields of HUMAN ECOLOGY, URBAN ECOLOGY, industrial ecology and landscape ecology are attempts to link the separate disciplines and/or to overcome the binary between human and nature. For instance, *urban ecology* challenges the dualism between 'natural' and 'built' environments, but still tends to emphasize biophysical structures and processes relative to social structures and processes. Recent work in human ecology by contributors to Steiner and Nauser (1993) emphasizes STRUCTURATION THEORY as a way to develop an integrative theoretical framework to understand 'ecological issues'. *Industrial ecology* is increasingly being seen as a way to move towards SUSTAINABLE DEVELOPMENT by analysing industries not as isolated entities but as part of an industrial system. Outputs from one industry become inputs into another industry, a process which closes waste loops and conserves RESOURCES and ENERGY (Graedel and Allenby, 1995).

Cronon (1993) noted the historical dimension of ecology. He recognized that the first generation of white American ecologists, such as Frederic Clements, understood natural systems as progressing towards a 'climax'. Once achieved, this was the 'balance of nature' that humans should not disturb. While this approach to ecology underpins some normative ecology positions, it has been thoroughly critiqued from a scientific ecology basis by A.G. Tansley, who coined the term ECOSYSTEM, and more recently by Daniel Botkin (1990) and the Non Equilibrium Thermodynamic ecologists who stress dynamism and change in ecosystems (Reice, 1994). Its implications of a pristine nature prior to human 'disturbance' have also been critiqued because they often associate 'human' with colonial people, rather than indigenous people who have been part of the ecology for thousands of years (Willems-Braun, 1997).

These tensions between normative and scientific ecology, and within various normative ecologies, are deep divides based on ontological and epistemological differences, perceptions of nature and normative projects. Within these tensions is the question of the similarities between processes and structures in human society and those of animals, plants and the earth. Geographers potentially have an important role in moving debates beyond ENVIRONMENTAL DETERMINISM, and dualisms of human and nature, to focus on the ongoing processes that constitute humans as part of nature. PM

References

Black, R. 1990: Regional political ecology in theory and practice: a case study from northern Portugal. *Transactions, Institute of British Geographers* NS 15: 35–47. · Blaikie, P. and Brookfield, H. 1987: *Land degradation and society*. London: Methuen; Bookchin, M. 1990: *Remaking society: pathways to a green future*. Boston: South End Press. · Botkin, D. 1990: *Discordant harmonies: a new ecology for the twenty-first century*. Oxford: Oxford University Press. · Bramwell, A. 1989: *Ecology in the 20th century*. New Haven and London: Yale University Press. · Bryant, R. 1997: Beyond the impasse: the power of political ecology in Third World environmental research. *Area* 29 1: 5–19. · Cronon, W. 1993: Foreword: The turn toward history. In M. McDonnell and S. Pickett, eds, *Humans as components of ecosystems: the ecology of subtle human effects and populated areas*. New York: Springer-Verlag. · Dobson, A. 1996: *Green political thought*, 2nd edn. London: HarperCollins Academic; Graedel, T. and Allenby, B. 1995: *Industrial ecology*. Englewood Cliffs, NJ: Prentice-Hall. · Grove, R. 1995: *Green imperialism*. Cambridge: Cambridge University Press. · Hayward, T., 1994: *Ecological thought: an introduction*. Cambridge: Polity Press. · Lipietz, A. 1995: *Green Hopes: The Future of Political Ecology*. Cambridge: Polity Press. · Merchant, C., ed., 1994: *Ecology*. New Jersey: Humanities Press. · McCormick, J. 1995: *The global environmental movement*, 2nd edn. Chichester: Wiley. · Peet, R. and Watts. M. 1993: Introduction: development theory and environment in an age of market triumphalism. *Economic Geography* 69: 227–53. · Reice, S. 1994: Nonequilibrium determinants of biological community structure. *American Scientist* 82: 424–35. · Roussopoulos, D. 1993: *Political ecology: beyond environmentalism*. Montreal: Black Rose Books. · Sachs, W. 1993: Introduction. In W. Sachs, ed., *Global ecology – a new arena of political conflict*. London and New Jersey: Zed Books, xv–xviii. · Steiner, D. and Nauser, E., eds, 1993: *Human ecology: fragments of anti-fragmentary views of the world*. London and New York: Routledge. · Willems-Braun, B. 1997: Buried epistemologies: the politics of nature in (post)colonial British Columbia. *Annals of the Association of American Geographers* 87 1: 3–31. · Worster, D. 1977: *Nature's economy: a history of ecological ideas*. Cambridge: Cambridge University Press.

Suggested Reading

Graedel and Allenby (1995). · McDonnell, M. and Pickett, S. 1993: *Humans as components of ecosystems: the ecology of subtle human effects and populated areas*. New York: Springer-Verlag.

economic base theory A theory that explains urban and regional growth in terms of a division of employment into basic and non-basic sectors. The *basic sector* (*B*) comprises those industries that meet external or export demand, and the location and growth of this sector is viewed as a function of national and international forces. The *non-basic sector* (*S*) is locally oriented employment, servicing the total local population (*P*). The total population is a function of total employment (*E*) and the economic base relationships are:

$$E = S + B, \quad P = \alpha E, \quad S = \beta P.$$

The coefficients α and β can be obtained by REGRESSION using observations for a SAMPLE of cities or for one city or region over time. Growth (or decline) in local population and employment is controlled by changes in the basic sector, and the impacts (MULTIPLIERS) of such changes can be calculated from the economic base equations:

$$E = (1 - \alpha\beta)^{-1}B$$

$$P = \alpha(1 - \alpha\beta)^{-1}B$$

$$S = \alpha\beta(1 - \alpha\beta)^{-1}B$$

A unit increase in B generates $\alpha/(1 - \alpha\beta)$ units of additional local population.

Economic base theory is very simplistic in its assumptions, but because its data demands are simple it has been widely employed in regional economic analysis. It is used, for example, in activity allocation models and Lowry models (cf. LOCATION–ALLOCATION MODELS). Correct identification of the basic sector is crucial, and LOCATION QUOTIENTS are frequently used for this purpose. Either industries with high indices of specialization are defined as basic industries, or the quotient is used to define a proportion of employment in an industry as basic; so that, for example, one-third of employment in an industry with a quotient of 1.5 is designated as basic employment. A more sophisticated approach is to use INPUT–OUTPUT analysis to trace actual inter-industrial linkages, but this is very data-demanding and expensive.

The major limitations of economic base theory spring from its aggregative nature: the difficulties of sector definition; the dubious assumption that the aggregate multipliers will remain constant; and an inability to trace the impact of particular basic sector shifts, such as a rise in oil exports, on specific sectors of the local economy. LWH

Suggested Reading

Glickman, N.J. 1997: *Econometric analysis of regional systems: explorations in model building and policy analysis*. New York and London: Academic Press, 15–27.

economic geography The geography (or, rather, geographies) of people's struggle to make a living. Economic geographies are simultaneously:

- fields of enquiry: analytical and representational investigations of the geographies of circuits of SOCIAL REPRODUCTION such as the CIRCUIT OF CAPITAL through which people struggle to make a living; and
- substantive practices: the geographies created and destroyed in the struggles to construct such circuits across space and time and to sustain/subvert/displace them.

Although the stress here is upon the path-dependent (reproduction), integrative (circuits) and social (CAPITALISM) nature of economic geographies, economic geography as a field of enquiry has traditionally tended to follow economics in focusing less on *reproduction* than on moments of *consumption*, *production* and *exchange* (a practice recognized in the distinction drawn, for example, by Knox and Agnew (1998) between static and dynamic models). It has also followed economics in tending to represent economies as asocial mechanisms susceptible to purely economic trajectories and logics of analysis (see Sayer, 1994). This supplication was based initially on the gradual incorporation of NEO-CLASSICAL ECONOMICS into economic geography (e.g. Chisholm, 1966; Hodder and Lee, 1974). It is apparent in the many detailed studies of particular economic activities in which the definitional categories used and the causal mechanisms analysed are derived directly from neo-classical economic theory as well as from critiques (e.g. Dicken and Lloyd, 1990; Sheppard and Barnes 1990; Martin 1994) of the social and other limitations of neo-classical analyses and, indeed, of the 'economic' more widely.

Defining economic geographies in terms of social reproduction forces attention onto the inseparability of CULTURE and ECONOMY, no matter how distinct they may be (Sayer, 1997). As early as 1935, in a study of *The pastoral industries of New Zealand*, R.O. Buchanan pointed out that 'geographical conditions . . . are dependent on the precise nature of the economic conditions'. But he went on to suggest that such a relationship 'will be recognized as merely specifying one type of instance of the generally accepted view that geographical values are not absolute, but are relative to the cultural stage [see CULTURE; CULTURAL GEOGRAPHY] achieved by the human actors'. The appearance of David Harvey's *Social justice and the city* in 1973 – nearly 40 years after R.O. Buchanan's comments on the definitive relations between culture and economy – brought such issues, and an EPISTEMOLOGY with which they could be handled, to the attention of geographers. The later chapters of Harvey's (1973) book represent a first attempt to interpret the structure and functioning of economic geographies as cultural, social and historic entities, while his *The limits to capital* (1982) presents a review of, and remarkable response to, criticisms of Marxist economic theory which, whilst widely criticized for determinism and closure, represents a sustained incorporation of social and cultural practices into the analysis of the economic. Working close to the centre of what might once have been conceived of as the heartland of economic geography – its concern with production – Erica Schoenberger (1997) demonstrates the power of a cultural understanding of the economic in her investigation of corporate culture and behaviour and its contribution to 'the failure of American firms to act in their own best interests' (p. 7). Such a 'reversal' or 'dislocation' (Barnes, 1996) of economic logic begins not merely to add the culture to the economic but to question the economic as a process of value (see, e.g., Gertler, 1997).

So, it is not surprising to find that, as Nigel Thrift and Kris Olds (1996, p. 311) put it, the full complexity of modern economies becomes apparent only 'when we move outside what are often still considered to be the "normal" territories of economic inquiry. Then a whole new world moves into view'. Taking economies seriously, it seems, requires the transcendence of economics (see, e.g., Lee and Wills, 1997). Thrift and Olds suggest that new economic geography will be polycentric (Martin, 1994, p. 46 refers similarly to a 'multivocal' economic geography) in recognizing multiple and contested economic geographies, open to influences from well beyond economic theory (Martin's 'multiperspectival' economic geography) and will be driven by the refiguring of conventional notions of the economic.

Substantive economic geographies are irreducibly practical, irreducibly material, irreducibly social, and irreducibly geographical, none of which implies, however, that they are not also discursive notions and practices informed and shaped by prevailing power/knowledge (see, e.g., Crang, 1997). Economic geographies are *practical* or instrumental as they require the workable means through which the interrelated practices of consumption, production and exchange may be articulated (see, e.g., Thrift and Olds (1996) on the social nature of economies and on networks) and they are *material* in that they involve the engagement of people with nature (including their own – Smith, 1984) in the production and consumption of the means of material life (see SUSTAINABLE DEVELOPMENT).

Economic geographies are *social* not merely because they depend upon more, or less, developed social DIVISIONS OF LABOUR or practices of social interaction (Thrift and Olds, 1996) but, more fundamentally, because circuits of social reproduction are shaped by social relations (Lee, 1989). Social relations are themselves a product of the historical geographies of social struggle and discourse (Peet, 1997) through which they come to be shaped. They provide the contested means of communication and frameworks of understanding and conflict and offer purpose and direction to, and evaluative criteria of, circuits of social reproduction (Brenner, 1977).

Although social relations of production are central to understanding in economic geography, they may hide more than they reveal. If their provenance is seen merely in the social struggle over control of production and of the means of production, an oppressively economic domination of society and of its investigation may result. The massive but frequently contested – or worse, ignored – contribution of FEMINIST GEOGRAPHY (see, e.g., McDowell and Sharp, 1997) and of the geography of RACE and, more pertinently, of RACISM has not been merely to reveal gender blindness by adding women to the economic landscape or to recognize discrimination and even oppression but, far more fundamentally, to challenge the very social bases on which the economy, society and the individual are constituted and develop. The division of labour combines with CLASS, GENDER, RACE and RACISM in a complex interaction of multiple structures (Sayer and Walker, 1992; Massey, 1995). More generally, Trevor Barnes (1996), in a quite brilliant intervention, has begun to unpick the (often unspoken) logics of economic geographies to show that 'there is not one economic geography but many economic geographies, not one complete story but a set of fragmented stories' (p. 250).

Economic geographies are *geographical* in that circuits of social reproduction are shaped and decisively influenced by the geographies through which they take place. As Michael Storper and Allen Scott (1986, p. 13) put it:

> the historical dynamics of socioeconomic systems can only (sic) be fully comprehended in geographical context, for the possibilities and limitations of human action are intrinsically constructed in spatially specific circumstances.

For Scott and Storper (1986, p. 310) the 'salient feature' of such circumstances is their 'status as an assemblage of territorial complexes of human labor and emergent social activity':

> Territorial production complexes form the material bases of the relative positions of nations within the world economy, and so they are integral to the evolution of world political relations. They are also the framework within which specific urbanization and regional development processes unfold. Further, it is in these complexes that social reproduction occurs, and thus the creation of or resistance to new forms of domination that appear on the historical scene can be discerned through the window of territorial dynamics.

Geography could hardly be more central to economy, but there is a danger here of overstressing the formative geographies of territorial complexes (e.g. Storper and Walker, 1989) and so devaluing similarly formative geographies such as those of GLOBALIZATION (e.g. Hamnett, 1995; Dicken, Peck and Tickell, 1997), world systems (see WORLD-SYSTEMS ANALYSIS), corporate geographies (e.g. Dicken and Thrift, 1992) and the intersections of local and global (e.g. Amin and Thrift, 1997). Thus, although it is right to claim that 'the question of the geographical anatomy of industrial capitalism is likely to become rapidly of major significance throughout the social sciences at large' (Scott and Storper, 1986, p. 311), such geographies are more complex and multi-layered than those associated with territorial production complexes, no matter how powerful the latter may be. It is this complexity of the continuing and formative interpenetration of geographical scales (see, e.g., Cox, 1997) that matters rather than a simplistic either/or conception of SCALE.

These LANDSCAPES are constituted out of the rules of order – the social relations – of, in the contemporary world, capitalist society. They are manifestations of the 'locational *cum* spatial processes' (Scott and Storper, 1986, p. 310) which shape the material geographies of consumption, production and exchange and they find their immediate phenomenal form in the communities incorporated within and disconnected from processes of social reproduction (e.g. Hudson, 1989). An inclusive economic geography would include the study of:

- constructions of POWER/knowledge which shape discursive practice and arbitrate – forcibly or otherwise – between competing DISCOURSES (see, e.g., Watts, 1992/1996);
- cultural and material origins of social relations of reproduction and the distanciated geographies of struggles, including those involved in the intersections within and between different sets of social relations, to establish/sustain/overthrow particular forms and geographies of such relations (e.g. Peet, 1997);
- conceptualizations of NATURE within particular sets of social relations and forms of social reproduction (e.g. Harvey, 1996; Watts and McCarthy, 1997);
- forms of the calculation and measurement of VALUE and of the evaluation of circuits of social reproduction (e.g. Harvey, 1989, ch.

14; Harvey, 1996, Introduction; Swyngedouw, 1996);

- forms of STATE (e.g. Martin and Sunley, 1997; O'Neill, 1997) and politics and REGULATION which support and legitimize particular social relations and circuits of social reproduction (e.g. Tickell and Peck, 1992);
- means of coordination and exchange through the use of MONEY (e.g. Leyshon and Thrift, 1997, Introduction) and various mechanisms of coordination (e.g. Thompson et al., 1991);
- spaces, such as financial centres, of regulation and evaluation and switching (here/there, direct/indirect investment, inter-sectorial) of productive resources into/from alternative spaces of (re/dis)incorporation (e.g. Sassen, 1991, chs 1–4);
- spaces of (re/dis)incorporation including those of labour power articulated primarily through LABOUR MARKETS (e.g. Hanson and Pratt, 1995; Peck, 1996) and of other commodities, including the construction of the built environment (e.g. Fainstein, 1994), involved in production;
- processes and forms of production. Just as production is one moment of social reproduction, so too production itself is space- and time-dependent. It is, therefore, not simply a singular geographical or temporal moment but consists of a series of chains of production. These may be defined as 'transactionally linked sequence[s] of functions in which each stage adds value to the process of production . . . ' (Dicken, 1998, p. 7). The complex geographies (ranging from the local to the global) of chains of production are coordinated and regulated through processes of collaboration and competition articulated through firms and states;
- processes and forms of consumption and realization – including geographies of TRADE, wholesale and retail (e.g. Wrigley and Lowe, 1996; see RETAILING, GEOGRAPHY OF), and their constitutive processes of production as well as the construction of complex spaces and processes of consumption through which the meaning of commodities may be negotiated (Jackson and Thrift, 1995; Crewe and Gregson, 1998; see CONSUMPTION, GEOGRAPHY OF); and
- the developmental dynamics, geographical intersections and transformations of circuits of social reproduction (see DEVELOPMENT; UNEVEN DEVELOPMENT; FORDISM; POST-FORDISM).

The contemporary world economic geography 'ratifies and glorifies the rule of what we call the financial markets, a return to a radical capitalism answering to no law except that of maximum profit' (Bourdieu, 1998, p. 125). For Altvater (1996), it is a 'geo-economy' and for Castells (1996, p. 428) a *space of flows*: 'because function and power in our societies are organised in the space of flows, the structural domination of its logic essentially alters the meaning and dynamic of places'. Under such circumstances, as Peter Dicken (1998, ch. 13) reminds us, the concern for 'making a living in the global economy' is always and should always be present in any economic geography which insists upon the subordination of the merely economic for the richly human. Keith Buchanan's (1970) assertion that the contribution of this world economy 'to alleviating the lot of the damned of the earth is derisory' should remain as the first item to be addressed on the agenda – substantive and analytical – of economic geography.

RL

References

Altvater, A. 1996: The geo-economy. *Journal of Area Studies*. · Amin, A. and Thrift, N. 1997: Globalization, socio-economics, territoriality. In R. Lee and J. Wills, eds, *Geographies of economies*, ch. 11. London and New York: Arnold, 147–57. · Barnes, T.J. 1996: *Logics of dislocation*. New York and London: Guilford Press; Bourdieu, P. 1998: A reasoned utopia and economic fatalism. *New Left Review* 227: 125–30. · Brenner, R. 1977: The origins of capitalist development: a critique of neo-Smithian Marxism. *New Left Review* 104: 25–92. · Buchanan, K.M. 1970: *The transformation of the Chinese earth*. London: Bell; New York: Praeger. · Buchanan, R.O. 1935: *The pastoral industries of New Zealand: a study in economic geography*. Institute of British Geographers publications 2. London: G. Philip. · Castells, M. 1996: *The rise of the network society, volume I. The information age: Economy, Society and culture*. Oxford and Cambridge, MA: Blackwell. · Chisholm, M. 1966: *Geography and economics*. London: Bell; Boulder, Col.: Westview Press. · Cox, K., ed., 1997: *Spaces of globalization; reasserting the power of the local*. New York and London: Guilford. · Crang, P. 1997: Cultural turns and the (re)constitution of economic geography. In R. Lee, and J. Wills, eds, *Geographies of economies*, section 1. London and New York: Arnold, 3–15. · Crewe, L. and Gregson, N. 1998: Tales of the unexpected: exploring car-boot sales as marginal spaces of contemporary consumption. *Transactions of the Institute of British Geographers* NS 23: 39–53. · Dicken, P. 1998: *Global shift: The transformation of the world economy*, 3rd edn. London: Paul Chapman Publishing. · Dicken, P. and Lloyd, P. 1990: *Location in space: theoretical perspectives in economic geography*, 3rd edn. London and New York: Harper and Row. · Dicken, P. and Thrift, N. 1992: The organization of production and the production of organization: why business enterprises matter in the study of geographical industrialization. *Transactions, Institute of British Geographers* NS 17 (3): 279–91. · Dicken, P., Peck, J. and Tickell, A. 1997: Unpacking the global. In R. Lee and J. Wills, eds, *Geographies of economies*, ch. 12. London and New York: Arnold, 158–66. · Fainstein, S.S. 1994: *The city builders: property, politics and planning in London and New York*. Cambridge, MA and Oxford: Blackwell. · Gertler, M. 1997: The invention of regional culture. In R. Lee, and J. Wills, eds, *Geographies of economies*, ch. 4. London and New York: Arnold, 47–58. · Hamnett, C. 1995: Controlling space: global cities. In J. Allen and C. Hamnett, eds, *A shrinking world?* ch. 3. Oxford and Milton Keynes: Oxford University Press/Open University, 103–42. · Hanson, S. and Pratt, G. 1995: *Gender, work and space*. London and New York: Routledge. · Harvey, D. 1973: *Social justice and the city*. London: Edward Arnold; Baltimore: Johns Hopkins University Press. · Harvey, D. 1982: *The limits to capital*. Oxford: Basil Blackwell; Chicago: Chicago University Press. · Harvey, D. 1989: *The condition of postmodernity*. Oxford and Cambridge, MA: Basil Blackwell. · Harvey, D. 1996: *Justice, nature and the geography of difference*. Cambridge, MA and Oxford: Blackwell. · Hodder, B.W. and Lee, R. 1974: *Economic geography*. London: Methuen; New York: St. Martin's Press. · Hudson, R. 1989: *Wrecking a region*. London: Pion. · Jackson, P. and Thrift, N. 1995: Geographies of consumption. In D. Miller, ed., *Acknowledging consumption*, ch. 6. London and New York: Routledge, 204–37. · Knox, P. and Agnew, J. 1998: *The geography of the world-economy*, 3rd edn. London and New York: Edward Arnold. · Lee, R. 1989: Social relations and the geography of material life. In D. Gregory, and R. Walford, *Horizons in human geography*, ch. 2.4. London: Macmillan; New York: St. Martin's Press. · Lee, R. and Wills, J., eds, 1997: *Geographies of economies*. London and New York: Arnold. · Leyshon, A. and Thrift, N. 1997: *Money/space: geographies of monetary transformation*. London and New York: Routledge. · Martin, R. 1994: Economic theory and human geography. In D. Gregory, R. Martin and G. Smith, eds, *Human geography: society, space and social science*, ch. 2. London: Macmillan, 21–53. · Martin, R. and Sunley, P. 1997: The post-Keynesian state and the space economy. In R. Lee and J. Wills, eds, *Geographies of economies*, ch. 21. London and New York: Arnold, 278–89. · Massey, D. 1995: *Spatial divisions of labour*, 2nd edn. London: Macmillan. · McDowell, L. and Sharp, J.P. 1997: *Space, gender, knowledge; feminist readings*. London and New York: Arnold. · O'Neill, P.M. 1997: Bringing the qualitative state into economic geography. In R. Lee and J. Wills, eds, *Geographies of economies*, ch. 22. London and New York: Arnold, 290–301. · Peck, J. 1996: *Workplace; the social regulation of labor markets*. New York: Guilford. · Peet, R. 1991: *Global capitalism: theories of societal development*. London and New York: Routledge. · Peet, R. 1997: The cultural production of economic forms. In R. Lee and J. Wills, eds, *Geographies of economies*, ch. 3. London and New York: Arnold. · Sassen, S. 1991: *The global city*. Princeton: Princeton University Press. · Sayer, A. 1994: Cultural studies and 'the economy stupid'. *Environment and Planning D: Society and Space* 12: 635–7. · Sayer, A. 1997: The dialectic of culture and economy. In R. Lee and J. Wills, eds, *Geographies of economies*, ch. 1. London and New York: Arnold, 16–26. · Sayer, A. and Walker, R. 1992: *The social economy; reworking the division of labour*. Cambridge, MA. and Oxford: Blackwell. · Scott, A.J. and Storper, M., eds, 1986: *Production, work, territory: the geographical anatomy of industrial capitalism*. London: Allen and Unwin. · Schoenberger, E. 1997: *The cultural crisis of the firm*. Cambridge, MA and Oxford: Blackwell. · Sheppard, E. and Barnes, T.J. 1990: *The capitalist space economy: Geographical analysis after Ricardo, Marx and Sraffra*. London and Cambridge, MA: Unwin Hyman. · Smith, N. 1984: *Uneven development*. Oxford and New York: Basil Blackwell. · Storper, M. and Scott, A.J. 1986: Production, work, territory: contemporary realities and theoretical tasks. In A.J. Scott and M. Storper, eds, *Production, work, territory. The geographical anatomy of industrial capitalism*, ch. 1. London: Allen and Unwin, 3–15. · Storper, M. and Walker, R. 1989: *The capitalist imperative*. New York and Oxford: Basil Blackwell. · Swyngedouw, E. 1996: Producing futures: international finance as a geographical project. In P. Daniels and W. Lever, eds, *The global economy in transition*, ch. 8. Harlow: Longman, 135–63. · Thompson, G., Frances, J., Levacic, R. and Mitchell, J., eds, 1991: *Markets, hierarchies and networks: the co-ordination of social life*. London and Newbury Park, CA: Sage/Open University. · Thrift, N. and Olds, K. 1996: Refiguring the economic in economic geography. *Progress in Human Geography* 20: 311–37. · Tickell, A. and Peck, J. 1992: Accumulation, regulation and the geographies of post-Fordism: missing links in regulationist research. *Progress in Human Geography* 16: 190–218. · Watts, M. 1992: The shock of modernity; petroleum, protest, and fast capitalism in an industrializing society. In A. Pred and M.J. Watts, *Reworking modernity: capitalisms and symbolic discontent*, ch. 2. New Brunswick, NJ; Rutgers University Press. Reprinted in S. Daniels and R. Lee, eds, 1996: *Exploring human geography: a reader*, ch. 6. London and New York: Arnold, 120–52. · Watts, M.J. and McCarthy, J. 1997: Nature as artifice, nature as artefact: Development, environment and modernity in the late twentieth century. In R. Lee and J. Wills, eds, *Geographies of economies*, ch. 6. London and New York: Arnold, 71–86. · Wrigley, N. and Lowe, M., eds, 1996: *Retailing, consumption and capital: towards the new retail geography*. Harlow: Longman.

Suggested reading

Barnes (1996). · Lee and Wills (1997). · Martin (1994). · Thrift and Olds (1996).

economies of scale The cost advantages gained by large-scale production, as the average cost of production falls with increasing output. Total production costs usually increase less than proportionately with output, up to a point where diseconomies of scale (cost disadvantages) set in.

Economies of scale generally arise from conditions internal to the operation of the plant in question. Some important internal sources of scale economies are: (a) *indivisibilities*, where plant is built to a certain capacity below which the average cost of production will be higher than at full capacity, and the plant cannot be divided up into smaller units working with the same efficiency as the larger one; (b) *specialization and division of labour* associated with expansion of scale, which can increase efficiency and hence lower costs; and (c) *overhead processes*, such as the design of a product, which must be undertaken and paid for irrespective of scale so that the larger the output the lower the overhead cost per unit. Certain EXTERNAL ECONOMIES may also be associated with expansion of scale of output, e.g. if the growth of an entire industry reduces costs in each individual firm.

The existence of economies of scale encourages the expansion of productive capacity up to the point where diseconomies eventually pull the cost of the additional (marginal) unit above the price that it will fetch. In some modern industry it may be that this point is reached only at a very high volume of output; thus average cost continues to fall with rising output well beyond the level at which diseconomies might be expected to arise. However, in other activities a trend towards more flexible and differentiated production may lead to diseconomies at relatively small scale of output. (See also ECONOMIES OF SCOPE.) DMS

economies of scope The cost advantages that may arise when performing two or more activities together within a single firm rather than performing them separately. When economies of scope exist, firms have an incentive to internalize (that is, perform in-house) the production of goods or services that otherwise would be acquired through transactions with external suppliers (see TRANSACTIONAL ANALYSIS). This incentive is normally expressed in terms of reductions in production costs as a result of internalization (see TRANSACTION COSTS). Hence, economies of scope may arise where the goods or services in question share inputs to their production (e.g. by using excess capacity in power generation or indivisible machinery), are related to one another through INPUT–OUTPUT relations (one good being an input to the production of the other good), draw upon common technical or manual skills for their production, or can be most efficiently produced at roughly the same scale of output. This concept, when combined with the idea of ECONOMIES OF SCALE, provides an understanding of the forces that determine firm size and the nature of inter-firm relations in localized clusters of producers (Scott, 1988). (See PRODUCTION COMPLEX.) MSG

Reference

Scott, A.J. 1988: *New industrial spaces*. London: Pion.

economy The structure or totality of relations of production, distribution, exchange and consumption of goods and services. While the economy as a set of material practices has existed ever since 'Adam delved and Eve span', the economy as an idea, as something that could be spoken about as a separate entity, has existed for only about three hundred years (Dumont, 1977; Tribe, 1978). Mitchell (1998) suggests an even more recent date, arguing that it was only somewhere between 1930 and 1950 'that the economy came to be understood as a self-evident totality' (Mitchell, 1998, p. 88). Whatever the exact date, if there is an exact date, the point is that 'the economy' is the outcome of a particular kind of DISCOURSE of a specific time and place, and does not precede or exist outside that discourse (a point also made by Buck Morss, 1995).

Of course, this doesn't mean that economic activities did not exist before this time, only that they were not recognized as such. Indeed, work carried out by twentieth-century economic historians and anthropologists shows the enormously diverse forms taken by different economies: from hunting and gathering to centrally planned production to market-based industrial POST-FORDISM. An especially important divide is between market and non-market economies, i.e., between economies organized and regulated by the movement of prices, typically but not exclusively found in CAPITALISM, and those that are not. Furthermore, even within, say, the category 'market economy' there is tremendous diversity. Marx, for example, writing in the second half of the nineteenth century, already recognized at least two varieties of industrial capitalism ('manufacture' and 'machinofacture'), while more recently the REGULATION SCHOOL divides market economies according to both their regulatory framework and principal form of manufacturing, producing a plethora of subtypes (Tickell and Peck, 1992). In addition, economies can take on a mixture of both market and non-market characteristics such as the MARKET SOCIALISM of China.

This kind of diversity is not always recognized by economists, a consequence again of the idiomatic origins of 'economy'. The term arose at a particular historical juncture when a market-based economy predicated upon principles of profit-maximization and rational DECISION-MAKING emerged for the first time. Those principles, in turn, were taken by first the classical economists, and later the neo-classical ones, as the defining features of all economies rather than the particular one in which they happened to live. Even now the 'formalist' school of economic anthropology explains the operation of tribal economies on the basis of rational economic choice. In contrast, since the work of Karl Polanyi (1886–1964), and the substantive or institutionalist school he pioneered, that UNIVERSALISM has been challenged. Polanyi (1968), for example, argued that principles other than the market have organized economies; for example, 'reciprocation' and 'redistribution' (see also Sahlin's (1972) important statement about 'stone age economics'). In addition, Polanyi was also keen to show that even market economies are maintained by, and depend upon, non-market social relations. As a result, the very distinction between things economic and things non-economic is called into question. This is a point with both practical and theoretical import.

Practically, the issue is one of knowing what (literally) counts as part of the economy. Even in market economies where goods and services are numerically valued difficulties and anomalies can arise. For example, current procedures of economic accounting would not include the time a parent spends looking after their child during the day as part of the economy, while the same amount of time spent by a paid baby-sitter would count. This definitional problem is further exacerbated by the existence of underground economies either based upon barter and unofficial currencies (Lee, 1996) or deliberately designed to avoid official detection (for example, illegal drug trade), both of which would not appear in official statistics. The point is that even as an empirical entity the economy is difficult to fix. It seems as much based on the kind of information that the STATE can collect as it is on any general principles. (Mitchell, 1998, sees this problem as endemic to any project that attempts to set irrevocable boundaries between one social sphere, in this case the economy, and any other.)

Theoretically the issue turns on the autonomy and causative POWER accorded the economy. Ever since the economy was recognized as a separate entity there has been discussion about its relationship to things non-economic. NEO-CLASSICAL ECONOMICS tends to portray the economy as a separate realm, imbuing it with an independent logic based upon economic rationality and the power of the market (cf. RATIONAL CHOICE THEORY). Similarly, classical forms of MARXIAN ECONOMICS promulgate 'economism', the idea that all the social and political relations are determined by the economy. In contrast, Polanyi's argument, which has been taken up by contemporary sociologists and recently also by some economic geographers (see NEW INSTITUTIONAL ECONOMICS), is that the economy is an integral component of a broader set of social, political and cultural relations. In this view the economy depends upon those relations for its continued existence, and as a consequence cannot be treated as an isolated, prime cause.

Geographers' interest in the economy stems from its spatial embeddedness and variation. Initially, economic geographers, such as George Chisholm at Edinburgh University writing in the first part of the twentieth century, were content to document in meticulous detail the kinds of commodities produced in different places around the world, and the peculiar local conditions found in them (cf. COMMERCIAL GEOGRAPHY). Later there were attempts (often from a neo-classical economic perspective) at more systematic explanation which reached their peak in the 1960s as SPATIAL SCIENCE, and which understood economic geographical variation on the basis of a few, general assumptions. More recently, economic geographers have focused on the often subtle relations that tie particular places to specific economic forms. They have also become more interested in the relationship between the economy and other social relations, say, around GENDER or RACE or social IDENTITY, and in this sense have moved closer to Polanyi's theoretical sensibility. Throughout this entire period, however, economic geographers of all theoretical stripes have consistently highlighted the geographically variable nature of the economy; that economies come in all shapes and sizes, and are not all cut from the same pattern. Geography matters. TJB

References

Buck Morss, S. 1995: Envisioning capital: political economy on display. *Cultural Inquiry* 21: 434–68. · Dumont, L. 1977: *From Mandeville to Marx: the genesis and triumph of economic ideology*. Chicago: University of Chicago Press. · Lee, R. 1996: Moral money? LETS and the social construction of local economic geographies in Southeastern England. *Environment and Planning A* 28: 1377–94. · Mitchell, T. 1998: Fixing the economy. *Cultural Studies* 12: 82–101. · Polanyi, K. 1968: *Primitive, archaic and modern economies*, ed. G. Dalton. Boston: Beacon Press. · Sahlins, M. 1972: *Stone age economics*. New York: Aldine. · Tickell, A. and Peck, J. 1992: Accumulation, regulation and the geographies of post-Fordism: missing links in regulationist research. *Progress in Human Geography* 16: 196–218. · Tribe, K. 1978: *Land, labour and economic discourse*. London: Routledge & Kegan Paul.

Suggested Reading

Mitchell (1998). · Polanyi (1968).

ecosystem One well-known definition is that of E.P. Odum (1969) who defined an ecosystem as 'any unit that includes all of the organisms in a given area interacting with the physical environment so that a flow of energy leads to . . . exchange of materials between living and non-living parts of the system'. The term was introduced by A.G. Tansley in 1935, but the idea is much older. It derives from Haeckel's use of the term ECOLOGY, which itself echoes the ideas of Alexander von Humboldt who wrote on plant geography in 1807 that 'in the great chain of causes and effects no thing and no activity should be regarded in isolation' (Major, 1969, p. 11). Tansley linked ecology and SYSTEM as ecosystem.

Identifying an ecosystem is challenging because of overlapping ecosystems and because of the issue of SCALE, which may range from the micro-organisms within a drop of water, through to the entire planet Earth. In practice, the term is generally reserved for units below the scale of the major world units, the *biomes*. However, the term has been used outside traditional understandings of ecology, as in Mardh's 1991 article, 'The vaginal ecosystem', a use of the word that is compatible with a definition of ecosystems as being interactions and interdependence between living organisms and their physical, chemical and biological environment, regardless of scale.

An ecosystem refers to a COMMUNITY of organisms interacting with each other and their physical surroundings. Ecosystems may be defined by their dominant features (e.g. tropical rainforest ecosystem), but are more likely to be defined on the basis of scientific and economic interest. Setting boundaries for ecosystems implicitly involves value judgements about what is considered important, and what is considered 'outside' the ecosystem. Sometimes ecosystems are studied without regard to the influence of humans, but those impacts need to be considered as part of ecosystems in ways other than as 'interference' or 'disturbance'. This may be represented through terms such as 'agroecosystem' and 'urban ecosystem' to describe the major modifications of previous ecosystems and the functioning of new ecosystems respectively.

While it is possible to characterize ecosystems by an inventory of their living and nonliving components, the essential feature of an ecosystem is the dynamic relationship between its components. These relationships cannot be understood from knowledge of the constituent parts. The relationship between component parts of an ecosystem involves the flow of ENERGY which originates from the sun, without which life on earth in its present form would not be possible.

The study of functional relationships in ecosystems has often concentrated on phenomena that can be measured, e.g. energy, water and mineral nutrients (see Likens and Bormann, 1995). The temporal dimensions of the system are also studied, e.g. by tracing changes in population numbers through time. For most species each ecosystem has a CARRYING CAPACITY which may be a simple number or subject to fluctuation due to seasonal and other factors. This optimum level is where the number of members of a species within the ecosystem does not change significantly. The temporal dimensions of ecosystems also includes the idea of a succession of species, which is said to reach a mature or climax ecosystem when there is no possibility for change from within the ecosystem. However, factors such as climate change (including GLOBAL WARMING) and sea level change have ensured that so-called climax ecosystems are subjected to major changes over time, and the theory of climax is no longer treated seriously by many scientific ecologists.

Recognition that these changes have resulted from past human activity (e.g. clearing of forests in the Mediterranean region and in Scotland, followed by the introduction of goats and sheep respectively), and are being increasingly generated by contemporary human activities, has been important for geography. It links with work in HUMAN ECOLOGY, URBAN ECOLOGY and ENVIRONMENTAL IMPACT ASSESSMENT. It links geography with SYSTEMS THEORY, SYSTEMS ANALYSIS and ENVIRONMENTALISM. Geographers have been important in introducing considerations of CULTURE and POLITICAL ECONOMY to overcome the reductionist tendencies of quantifying NATURE that is found in some work on ecosystems. Increasingly this work is highlighting the importance of indigenous people as part of the ecosystem (Willems-Braun, 1997).

Ecosystems are gaining increased recognition as part of SUSTAINABLE DEVELOPMENT. One way of moving towards sustainability is to maintain or promote 'ecosystem health'.

The 'ecosystem approach' is being increasingly used in URBAN AND REGIONAL PLANNING, and other applied fields. 'Ecosystem diversity', i.e. differences between groups or communities of different species, also fits in with ENVIRONMENTALISM. The idea of a 'web of life' depicts humans as one component of ecosystems, rather than the final consumer of materials and ENERGY in a linear chain. PM

References

Likens, G. and Bormann, H. 1995: *Biogeochemistry of a forested ecosystem*, 2nd edn. New York: Springer-Verlag. · Major, J. 1969: Historical development of the ecosystem concept. In G. Van Dyne, ed., *The ecosystem concept in natural resource management*. New York and London: Academic Press, 9–22. · Mardh, P. 1991: The vaginal ecosystem. *The American Journal of Obstetrics and Gynaecology* 165 (4–2): 1163–8. · Odum, E. 1969: The strategy of ecosystem development. *Science* 164: 262–70. · Willems-Braun, B. 1997: Buried epistemologies: the politics of nature in (post)colonial British Columbia. *Annals of the Association of American Geographers* 87 (1): 3–31.

Suggested Reading

McDonnell, M. and Pickett, S., eds, 1993: *Humans as components of ecosystems: the ecology of subtle human effects and populated areas*. New York: Springer-Verlag. · Barkham, J. 1995: Ecosystem management and environmental ethics. In T. O'Riordan, ed., *Environmental science for environmental management*. Hanlow: Longman, 80–104.

edge city A term coined by an American journalist, Joel Garreau (1991), to describe the new foci of metropolitan life in the USA, as downtowns there (see CENTRAL BUSINESS DISTRICT) have declined not only as centres of consumption – a process that began several decades ago – but also as centres of production: thus

> First we moved our homes out past the traditional idea of what constituted a city... Then we wearied of returning downtown for the necessities of life, so we moved our marketplaces out to where we lived... Today, we have moved our means of creating wealth, the essence of urbanism – our jobs – out to where most of us have lived and shopped for two generations.

These 'new urban complexes' are the edge cities, so-called because they are at the frontiers of urbanized areas:

> Cities, because they contain all the functions a city ever has, albeit in a spread-out form that few have come to recognize for what it is. Edge, because they are a vigorous world of pioneers and immigrants, rising far from the old downtowns, where little save villages or farmland lay only thirty years ago.

Garreau suggested five criteria for identifying an edge city:

- More than 5 million sq. feet of office space – the workplaces of the information age;
- More than 600,000 sq. feet of retail space;
- More jobs than bedrooms;
- Perceived by the population as one place; and
- Less than thirty years old.

He identified more than 200 places meeting these criteria (including 16 fully-fledged edge cities in the Los Angeles area and a further seven 'emerging edge cities' and 15 and seven respectively around Washington, D.C.); they were presented as reflecting the continued transformation of American society, of the continued presence of the 'frontier spirit' which involves continually 'reinventing ourselves' (cf. DECENTRALIZATION). RJJ

Reference

Garreau, J. 1991: *Edge city: life on the new frontier*. New York: Doubleday.

education, geography of The study of spatial variations in the provision, uptake and outputs of educational facilities and resources. The provision of educational resources involves both fixed facilities and the wherewithal to use them. Thus, the location of play-centres, schools and colleges is important not only to the structuring of educational provision but also, because such facilities fall within the class of PUBLIC GOODS, to the structured inequality in provision which characterizes many societies. Linked to this is the pattern of expenditure on education, which varies at many scales and can be used progressively in POSITIVE DISCRIMINATION programmes.

The uptake of facilities reflects a range of factors that operate at a variety of scales, from the individual and the home through the NEIGHBOURHOOD, the school and its classrooms to the authority responsible for provision and even the region and nation. Many studies have shown that students' aspirations and performance reflect not only their parents' aspirations and the nature of their home environment, but also the characteristics of their peers in class and school (and thus the characteristics of the school catchment area), and the quality of the school and its teaching – including the resources available (Bradford, 1991). Thus the concept of the NEIGHBOURHOOD EFFECT (see also CONTEXTUAL EFFECT) has been central to much analysis of the geography of educational outcomes, for which specialist statistical procedures have been adopted (see MULTI-LEVEL MODELLING).

Recent attempts to improve school quality have included arguments that parental choice and preferences will be enhanced by the provision of standardized information on school performance (standardized tests, for example, as well as other indicators, such as truancy rates), and that schools will be forced to improve in response to those preferences and choices. Schools in England are now the subject of published league tables on such matters. RJJ

References

Bradford, M.J. 1991: School performance indicators, the local residential environment, and parental choice. *Environment and Planning A* 23: 319–33.

Suggested Reading

Bondi, L. and Matthews, M.H., eds, 1988: *Education and society: studies in the politics, sociology and geography of education*. London: Routledge. · Coombes, M. and Raybould, S. 1997: Modelling the influence of individual and spatial factors underlying variations in the levels of secondary school examination results. *Environment and Planning A* 29: 641–58.

egalitarianism A moral and political philosophy which calls for EQUALITY, or moves in this direction. Equality in this context means the same, in a morally significant respect, as in standard of living or some of its constituent elements like income, wealth or health. The term equality is easily confused with EQUITY, which refers to fairness, reflecting a long-standing link between equality and SOCIAL JUSTICE. Justice is not always associated with equality, but egalitarians tend to favour equality, or a process of equalization, in the absence of any compelling justification to the contrary (e.g. that inequality benefits the worst-off: see Rawls, 1971).

Equality is taken for granted in most parts of the world, in some limited spheres of life such as 'one person, one vote' and 'equal treatment before the law'. A minimal formulation of egalitarianism would guarantee certain HUMAN RIGHTS, associated with national CITIZENSHIP, leaving inequality in other spheres. A stronger formulation would be that the sameness, or close similarity, of members of humankind justifies equality with respect to a wide range of sources of need satisfaction, on the grounds that all persons have the same basic needs: for food, clothing, shelter, security, and so on. Such an argument might invoke the notion of the equal moral worth of all persons, as ends in themselves entitled to the wherewithal to live a decent human life, which should be upheld universally. The more generous the set of goods or services which should be distributed equally, the less the scope for inequality.

The egalitarian case can also be made without reference to rights, by recognizing the difficulty of finding moral justification for unequal treatment. The accident of birth – to whom, when and where – has a major bearing on individual life chances, yet there are no moral grounds for such an outcome. This is a matter of chance, over which people have no control, like RACE or GENDER which should similarly have no bearing on life chances. The inheritance of wealth or social status (like a title or throne) may not be entirely indefensible as a social practice, but it does not follow that the individuals concerned deserve their advantage. The same could be said of natural aptitudes such as physical strength, dexterity or intelligence which, again, can be viewed as the results of a natural lottery. It could also be argued that advantages derived from socialization, such as learning to value education or to become enterprising, carry no greater moral approval than those derived from biology. Thus, occupational differences arising from natural aptitudes or character formation do not justify any inequality in remuneration.

The geographical extension of this argument is that the advantages some persons get from being born somewhere with either bountiful natural resources or a well-developed social and economic environment, are difficult if not impossible to justify morally. Inequality with a spatial expression should therefore be reduced or eliminated. DMS

Reference

Rawls, J. 1971: *A theory of justice*. Cambridge, MA: Harvard University Press.

Suggested Reading

Arneson, R. 1993: Equality. In R.E. Goodin and P. Pettit, eds, *A companion to political philosophy*. Oxford: Blackwell Publishers, 489–507. · Kymlicka, W. 1990: *Contemporary political philosophy: an introduction*. Oxford: Clarendon Press, ch. 3. · Smith, D.M. 1994: *Geography and social justice*. Oxford: Blackwell Publishers, 54–8 and ch. 5. · Turner, B. 1986: *Equality*. London: Tavistock.

electoral geography The study of geographical aspects of the organization, conduct and results of elections. Pioneering studies (including those by the French geographer André Siegfried: e.g. Siegfried, 1913) were published early in the twentieth century, but most of the small literature dates from the 1960s on: few researchers identify themselves specifically as electoral geographers. Taylor (1989) argued that many empirical investigations of voting patterns have only a relatively weak theoretical base, and criticized electoral geographers for their lack of integration into the expanding field of POLITICAL GEOGRAPHY.

Many aspects of elections are inherently spatial in their form, covering five separate areas of electoral study:

- *The spatial organization of elections*, especially the definition of constituencies (see DISTRICTING ALGORITHM; GERRYMANDERING; MALAPPORTIONMENT);
- *Spatial variations in voting patterns*, plus the relationships between these and other characteristics of the population (see CLEAVAGE);
- *The influence of local factors* on political attitudes and voting decisions (see CONTEXTUAL EFFECT; FRIENDS-AND-NEIGHBOURS EFFECT; NEIGHBOURHOOD EFFECT);
- *Spatial patterns of representation* which result from the translation of votes into seats in a representative body; and
- *The spatial variations in* POWER and policy implementation which reflect the patterns of representation (see PORK BARREL).

Study of the second and third of these was advanced by the adoption of quantitative methods for analysis of spatial data in the 1960s. Voting returns at various spatial scales can be combined with areal data from CENSUSES to investigate the relationships between population characteristics and partisan choices. Greater sophistication in analyses of such data has been achieved recently (in the context of awareness of both the ECOLOGICAL FALLACY and the MODIFIABLE AREAL UNIT PROBLEM), including the integration of survey (QUESTIONNAIRE) and aggregate data (Johnston, Pattie and Allsopp, 1988: see ENTROPY-MAXIMIZING MODELS; MULTI-LEVEL MODELLING). Most of the work focuses on variations in electoral behaviour at a variety of scales, contrasting people in similar social situations but different spatial locations: seminal work in this field was done by Archer and Taylor (1981), who, using FACTOR ANALYSIS, identified critical elections, when the geography of voting (and hence the underlying electoral cleavages) changes in the voting for American Presidents over a period of 150 years.

In most countries the translation of votes into seats involves the use of spatially delimited constituencies. Manipulation of their boundaries can generate electoral bias (favouring one party or interest group over another) away from the 'norm' of proportional representation (a party's percentage of the seats allocated should be consistent with its percentage of the votes cast). This bias may be the result of deliberate strategies, such as MALAPPORTIONMENT and GERRYMANDERING, or it may, as Gudgin and Taylor (1979) demonstrated, be the unintended consequence of the disinterested application of neutrally conceived rules for constituency construction (as illustrated by Rossiter, Johnston and Pattie, 1999; Rossiter et al., 1999).

The links between electoral and political geography are clearly demonstrated in a recent book on the USA (Shelley et al., 1996), much of which relates the geography of voting at Presidential elections to spatial variations in political interests.

The outcome of an election gives power to individuals and groups within the STATE APPARATUS, who may use that to promote their own interests, including their own re-election, through the selective allocation of PUBLIC GOODS to particular areas (Johnston, 1980).

RJJ

References

Archer, J.C. and Taylor, P.J. 1981: *Section and party: a political geography of American Presidential elections from Andrew Jackson to Ronald Reagan*. London and New York: John Wiley. · Gudgin, G. and Taylor, P.J. 1979: *Seats, votes and the spatial organization of elections*. London: Pion. · Johnston, R.J. 1980: *The geography of federal spending in the United States*. Chichester and New York: John Wiley. · Johnston, R.J., Pattie, C.J. and Allsopp, J.G. 1988: *A nation dividing? The electoral map of Great Britain 1979–1987*. London and New York: Longman. · Rossiter, D.J., Johnston, R.J. and Pattie, C.J. 1999: *The Boundary Commissions: redrawing the UK's map of Parliamentary constituencies*. Manchester: Manchester University Press. · Rossiter, D.J., Johnston, R.J., Pattie, C.J., Dorling, D.F., Tunstall, H. and McAllister, I. 1999: Changing biases in the operation of the UK's electoral system, 1950–1997. *British Journal of Politics and International Relations* 1. · Shelley, F.M., Archer, J.C., Davidson, F.M. and Brunn, S.D. 1996: *Political geography of the United States*. New York and London: Guilford Press. · Siegfried, A. 1913: *Tableau politique de la France de l'Ouest*. Paris: A. Colin. · Taylor, P.J. 1989: *Political geography: world-economy, nation-state and community*, 2nd edn. London and New York: Longman.

Suggested Reading

Johnston, R.J. 1979: *Political, electoral and spatial systems*. Oxford: Clarendon Press. · Reynolds, D.R. and Knight, D.B. 1989: Political geography. In G.L. Gaile and C.J. Willmott, eds, *Geography in America*. Columbus, OH: Merrill Publishing Company, 582–618. · Taylor, P.J. and Johnston, R.J. 1979: *Geography of elections*. London: Penguin Books.

empiricism A philosophy of science which accords a double privilege to empirical observations over theoretical statements:

- *ontological privilege* (see ONTOLOGY): empiricism assumes that observational statements are the only ones which make direct reference to phenomena in the real world; and
- *epistemological privilege* (see EPISTEMOLOGY): empiricism assumes that observational statements can be declared true or false without reference to the truth or falsity of theoretical statements.

Empiricism is a fundamental assumption of POSITIVISM and LOGICAL POSITIVISM and is challenged by most modern philosophies of science, which establish connections between theoretical and observation languages in terms which allow for varying degrees of theoretical (co-) determination (see REALISM). Empiricism is also out of sympathy with those versions of POSTMODERNISM that insist on the importance of multiple points of view and with critiques derived from POST-STRUCTURALISM that seek to establish the social construction of different regimes of truth.

It is important, therefore, to distinguish between (a) an *empiricist inquiry*, which assumes that its facts somehow 'speak for themselves' and represses the concepts and technologies that make its observations possible; and (b) an *empirical inquiry*, which is a substantive study that does not necessarily make any assumptions of ontological and epistemological privilege. DG

enclave A small piece of territory lying within a STATE but which does not fall within its jurisdiction. A number are in Europe and are evidence of the continent's confused political history. The microstates of San Marino and the Vatican City in Italy are classical examples. Elsewhere the city territories of Ceuta and Melilla on the northern coast of Africa are Spanish enclaves in Morocco. It is not uncommon for areas in which a minority of one state is actually isolated within the territory of a neighbouring state to be referred to as enclaves. A good example is the region known as Ngorno Kharabach on the isthmus between the Black Sea and the Caspian Sea. It is part of the state of Azerbaijan but the population is overwhelmingly Armenian and would prefer to be part of the neighbouring state of Armenia, even though physically separated from it (see also EXCLAVE). MB

enclosure Land demarcation using BOUNDARIES, usually associated with the restriction of rights of ownership or use on that land, and the processes through which these physical and tenurial restrictions are achieved. However, the physical separation of land parcels and the restriction of use-rights need not change in parallel. Much discussion has involved the social consequences of enclosure: for example, during conversion of cooperative FIELD SYSTEMS to individualistic landownership and control in the emergence of agrarian CAPITALISM (Neeson, 1993). PG

Reference

Neeson, J. 1993. *Commoners: common rights, enclosure and social change in England, 1700–1820.* Cambridge: Cambridge University Press.

energy The capacity of a physical system for doing work. All species harness energy in some form, but the ability of human beings to harness, convert, release and (re)deploy energy to do work and yield goods and services has been the basis for the material evolution of human societies. Energy forms available to humans include mechanical, solar radiant, geothermal, elastic, heat, chemical and nuclear energy. Mechanical energy includes the kinetic energy of a body in motion and the potential energy that is stored and may be converted into free form by movement, friction and the expenditure of heat. Solar radiant energy is energy transferred from the sun, which sustains the biogeochemical cycles of the global ecosphere that maintain life on earth. Geothermal energy is the energy in volcanoes and geysers that is derived from within the earth. Elastic energy is derived from a condition of mechanical strain (i.e. elastic rebound), while heat energy is the internal random motion of molecules. Chemical energy is stored in the molecules of compounds and nuclear energy is contained in the nucleus of an atom, which may be released through either fission or fusion.

Life on earth is ultimately dependent upon the sun. Odum (1971) defines the *primary productivity* of an ECOSYSTEM as the rate at which producer organisms (usually green plants) store radiant energy in forms which may be usable food material for other species. Humans have eaten some of these plants, as well as some of the animals higher up the food chain, to derive energy for life. However, humans have moved from using their own muscle power to satisfy their energy needs (walking, hunting, fishing) through to other sources of energy (initially animals, then machines) to meet their needs, increasing per capita energy use, particularly by exploiting fossil-fuels, to create an energy-intensive economy.

World-wide energy consumption is increasing, partly because of increases in global POPULATION. However, per capita energy consumption varies significantly throughout the world. When considering energy consumption, it is important to recognize patterns of economic activity, e.g. energy is consumed in developing countries to make cheap products for export to wealthier countries. While there have been significant increased efficiencies in energy consumption in most developed countries (see von Weizsacker et al., 1997), there has also been a redistribution, rather than a reduction, in energy consumption. This work is important for geographers working on modelling human ecosystems, AGRICULTURAL GEOGRAPHY, GEOGRAPHY OF FOOD, POLITICAL ECOLOGY and for geographers questioning the high energy use model of DEVELOPMENT that currently operates in, and increasingly for, wealthier countries.

Since the INDUSTRIAL REVOLUTION, energy has increasingly been derived from non-renewable RESOURCES. Recent activities under the rubric of SUSTAINABLE DEVELOPMENT offer the promise of increased use of energy from renewable resources, and a reduction in energy demand which may be achieved through a reduction in consumption, re-using existing materials and RECYCLING. However, in THIRD WORLD countries undergoing DEVELOPMENT, trends are to greater energy use and higher levels of POLLUTION, as countries attempt to rapidly raise their GROSS NATIONAL PRODUCT. This trend in large economies, such as China, is a concern to many countries that previously have been through an extensive phase of capital ACCUMULATION involving high levels of energy expenditure.

Reduction in the use of energy is one of the most achievable aspects of sustainable development, because it reduces economic costs to a corporation or institution. Energy consumption may be reduced by improved design, greater insulation, changes in use patterns and so on, and does not challenge entities in a threatening way. However, some ecological economics work traces the use of energy and materials throughout the production process (i.e. they trace the 'throughput'). Economists such as Herman Daly call for a 'steady state economy' based on the stabilization of 'throughput' (Daly, 1991). This notion was extended by Wackernagel and Rees (1996) to a measurement of the 'ecological footprint' of a particular lifestyle, i.e. the consumption of materials and energy measured in hectares required to provide those materials and energy. The high use of non-renewable fossil fuels, and their throughput, is frequently challenged by the ENVIRONMENTAL MOVEMENT including the high use of energy in road-based transport (Newman and Kenworthy, 1989), the use of nuclear power and the damming of rivers in WILDERNESS areas to generate hydro-electric power.

Business interests have worked together with some parts of the environmental movement on energy efficiency since the oil crises of 1973 and 1979 which signalled the end of cheap, abundant supplies of non-renewable energy forms, such as oil. They highlighted the dependency of highly industrialized countries upon the Organization of Petroleum Exporting Countries (OPEC), and the vulnerability of economies in some developing countries. While concerns about LIMITS TO GROWTH being in the form of a limit of NATURAL RESOURCES, such as oil, have been reduced, there is greater concern now about the cumulative impacts of fossil-fuel consumption (see GLOBAL WARMING). Ironically, OPEC's price rises may have provided the greatest spur towards sustainable development, despite their intention being about economic and political POWER. One concern is the finite character of the earth's sinks, e.g. the atmosphere, to assimilate wastes from energy and material use.

The transitions from non-renewable to renewable forms of energy, from highly polluting to less polluting forms of energy and from an energy-intensive economy to a energy-conserving economy vary over space and time. The reasons for this include availability of resources, capacity to change, the strength of vested interests, political interests (see Pickering and Owen, 1994) and issues of SOCIAL JUSTICE. The availability of cheap energy sources provides an incentive for their use, especially when the environmental issues of resource extraction and POLLUTION (see also ACID RAIN) may be felt in a 'distant elsewhere'. Natural gas is increasing in importance as a source of energy. However, the dependence on fossil fuel inhibits the transition to renewable forms of energy such as solar, wind and wave power. It means that the cost of renewable energy forms is not reduced because of inadequate research funding, and that the energy involved in their construction costs is also disproportionately high, often because they cannot achieve ECONOMIES OF SCALE in their production processes. Total world energy demand is anticipated to grow in the future, therefore, despite some efforts at reduction through greater efficiency, so that sustainable development programmes which encourage the use of appropriate technologies and energy sources in developing countries, transitions to more benign energy sources throughout the world, and reductions in energy use in developed countries, are crucial. PM

References

Daly, H. 1991: *Steady-state economics*, 2nd edn. Washington, D.C. and Covelo, CA: Island Press. · Newman, P. and Kenworthy, J. 1989: *Cities and automobile dependence: An international sourcebook*. Aldershot: Gower. · Odum, E.P. 1971: *Fundamentals of ecology*, 3rd edn. Philadelphia: W.B. Saunders. · Pickering, K. and Owen, L. 1994: *An introduction to global environmental issues*. London and New York: Routledge. · von Weizsacker, E., Lovins, A. and Lovins, L.H. 1997: *Factor 4: doubling wealth – halving resource use*. London: Earthscan; St Leonards: Allen and Unwin. · Wackernagel, M. and Rees, W. 1996: *Our ecological footprint: reducing human impact on the earth*. Gabriola Island, British Columbia: New Society Publishers.

Suggested Reading

Hill, R., O'Keefe, P. and Snape, C. 1995: Energy planning. In J. Kirkby, P. O'Keefe and L. Timberlake, eds, *The Earthscan reader in sustainable development*. London: Earthscan, 78–98. · World Resources Institute, 1994: Energy. In World Resources Institute, *World resources 1994–95*. New York and Oxford: Oxford University Press, 165–80.

Enlightenment, geography and An understanding of the Enlightenment not solely as a distinctive historical and philosophical enterprise defined by the lives of great thinkers as an eighteenth-century European phenomenon, but as a set of situated ideas and practices, including geography. In this sense, it is possible to conceive and write not of the Enlightenment as an essentialist and largely European category, but as ideas that were produced, sited and debated in local as well as national settings. It is further possible to talk of geographies of Enlightenment as embracing the sites and the practices, including geography as a form of knowledge, in which enlightenment as a *means* of rational enquiry took place. There are, therefore, several important differences from the geography of Enlightenment as a matter of national context (cf. ENLIGHTENMENT, GEOGRAPHY OF): recognition of diversity; attention to PROCESS; and a sense of intrinsic SPATIALITY in all enlightenment discourse (see DISCOURSE). These differences are the result of recent work by scholars on the nature of (the) Enlightenment and by historians of geography and of science (Livingstone and Withers, 1999).

In more detail, and recognizing the important contributions made by historians of Enlightenment and the extensive historiographical literature attaching to both terms, it is helpful to distinguish three main strands connecting geography and Enlightenment. First, we may talk of a more strictly disciplinary history of geography, however contemporaries understood it, in 'the Age of Enlightenment' (see also GEOGRAPHY, HISTORY OF). Secondly, we can identify work on geographical knowledges *in* the Enlightenment; of geography not as a defined subject but as a set of situated discursive practices – of mapping, classifying, visualizing and naming (see also CARTOGRAPHY, HISTORY OF). Finally, and in a related sense, there is now widespread interest in the geographies of Enlightenment knowledge: the *sites* in which ideas were produced and contested, the *circulation* of those ideas, and the variant nature of their *reception*.

The idea of the Enlightenment as an eighteenth-century European intellectual movement characterized by an emphasis upon reason, bound by the lives of great thinkers and apparent only at the scale of the nation, has been challenged by a range of recent work (Hulme and Jordanova, 1990; Outram, 1995; Schmidt, 1996; Yolton, 1991). Broadly, Enlightenment historians now consider it more helpful to look at the Enlightenment 'as a series of debates, which necessarily took different shapes and forms in particular national and cultural contexts' (Outram, 1995, p. 3). Work in this regard has considered, for example, science, political culture and the Enlightenment in provincial and national context, including the forms it took in America and on the periphery of Europe, the sexual underworlds of the Enlightenment, medical knowledge and Enlightenment, exoticism, and the anthropological and literary histories of the Enlightenment (for a fuller review, see Livingstone and Withers, 1999). Work on the diversity of Enlightenment knowledge in these terms has also recognized dialectical contradictions at the heart of the Enlightenment: matters of rationality and the emancipatory power of reason are also matters of restraint and the power of some people over others (Horkheimer and Adorno, 1972; Schmidt, 1996). If, then, scholars would agree with Foucault in his view of the Enlightenment as 'unfinished' and in his claim that 'the Enlightenment is an event, or a set of events and complex historical processes, that it is located at a certain point in the development of European societies' (Foucault, 1984, p. 43), there is also a strong case for seeing (the) Enlightenment as a set of complex *geographical* processes. For Hulme and Jordanova, 'The Enlightenment's self-consciousness was to some extent a geographical consciousness based on the distinctiveness of the part of the world that came to be called Europe' (Hulme and Jordanova, 1990, p. 7). Others have shown how Enlightenment ideas resulted not just from the impact on the European mind of the 'enlargement of geographical and celestial space' (Yolton, 1991, p. 3), but from a precise encounter with particular places, such as, for example, Tahiti specifically and the Pacific peoples in general (Outram, 1995) (see also EXPLORATION).

Until the last few years, geographers have been relatively slow to consider the Enlightenment as a subject of geographical enquiry despite considerable interest from other disciplines in the 'Enlightenment Project'. Harvey has reviewed the Enlightenment origins of 'modern' knowledge (Harvey, 1989), and Gregory has noted how 'modern social theory still bears the marks of its Enlightenment origins' (Gregory, 1994, p. 12). Livingstone has discussed geography's place in the Enlightenment in relation to the history of eighteenth-century (and earlier) ideas about the nature of the terraqueous globe, and considered, too, something of geography's engagement with the precepts of natural theology and with Kantianism (Livingstone, 1992, pp. 102–38). More recently, attention has been paid to the character of geographical knowledge during the Enlightenment and to the spatialities of enlightenment knowledge (Livingstone and Withers, 1999). The European geographical 'discovery' of the 'New World' was at once a material and a metaphorical enterprise evoking 'images of marching into new territories, taming what one found there, and giving a coherent account of fresh terrain' (Hulme and Jordanova, 1990, p. 5). That characteristic Enlightenment philosophy of history, the idea (and ideal) of 'progress', was rooted in a fundamentally geographical comparison between the institutions of Europe and those living in 'a state of Nature'.

Enlightenment geographies which encountered civilizations 'beyond Europe' underpinned Enlightenment theorizations about stadial theory (stage-by-stage social development: see ROSTOW MODEL) and the nature of human history which positioned the same peoples as 'before Europe'. In these terms, that fundamental Enlightenment concern with a 'Science of Man' was profoundly a matter of geography, and geographical knowledge contributed greatly to the enlightenment fascination with conjectural history. CWJW

References

Foucault, M. 1984: What is enlightenment? In P. Rabinow, ed., *The Foucault reader*. London: Penguin, 45–56. · Gregory, D. 1994: *Geographical imaginations*. Oxford: Blackwell. · Harvey, D. 1989: *The condition of postmodernity*. Oxford: Blackwell. · Horkheimer, M. and Adorno, T. 1972: *Dialectic of Enlightenment*. New York: Herder and Herder. · Hulme, P. and Jordanova, L., eds, 1990: *The Enlightenment and its shadows*. London: Routledge. · Livingstone, D. 1992: *The geographical tradition: episodes in the history of a contested enterprise*. Oxford: Blackwell. · Livingstone, D. and Withers, C.W.J., eds, 1999: *Geography and Enlightenment*. Chicago: University of Chicago Press. · Outram, D. 1995: *The Enlightenment*. Cambridge: Cambridge University Press. · Schmidt, J., ed., 1996: *What is Enlightenment?: eighteenth-century answers and twentieth-century questions*. Berkeley, CA: University of California Press. · Yolton, J., ed., 1991: *The Blackwell companion to the Enlightenment*. Oxford: Blackwell.

Suggested Reading

Livingstone, D. and Withers, C.W.J. (1999). · Outram, D. (1995).

Enlightenment, geography of Conventionally, an understanding of the Enlightenment as a distinctive European and eighteenth-century philosophical and historical enterprise occurring in national context. In this understanding, the central tenet of the Enlightenment is the public use of reason to change human society and to de-mystify the world, the Enlightenment is treated as almost entirely a European affair, as relatively homogeneous and with quite precise temporal definition between, for example, the 1685 Revocation of the Edict of Nantes and the 1793 guillotining of Louis XVI (Hulme and Jordanova, 1990). Enlightenment philosophers shared a general commitment to criticizing the 'old order', to the emancipation of civil society through knowledge, education and science (what many saw as the 'Science of Man'), and shared, too, a belief in future 'progress', both as a means to understand and manage social transformation and as an end in itself – the perfectibility of the human condition (Porter, 1990). In these terms, Enlightenment scholars have widely debated the 'what' and the 'why' of the Enlightenment. What little attention has been paid to the geography of Enlightenment has largely considered it at the level of the nation-state within Europe with limited attention to the Enlightenment in the Americas. Porter and Teich (1981) is a key work in this respect with its emphasis upon the Enlightenment's geographical, social and political *location* as a cultural movement' [original emphasis], and its attempts 'to grasp the meaning of Enlightenment in thirteen national contexts' (Porter and Teich, 1981, p. vii).

For several reasons, however, this understanding is now no longer widely held, or, at least, is being strongly challenged. The idea of the Enlightenment has been subject to renewed scrutiny (Outram, 1995; Schmidt, 1996). To understand the geography of the Enlightenment as a national matter obscures variation within the nation in the production and reception of Enlightenment ideas, even given the fact that the idea of the nation was uncertain in this period (see NATION; NATION-STATE). Further, conceiving of national Enlightenments tends to essentialize the Enlightenment either in terms of defining characteristics or in relation to the lives of individual philosophers and to treat questions of geography as simply matters of location. Finally, it is now accepted that the European Enlightenment was substantially moulded through encounters with other parts of the world, notably with the Americas and with the Pacific (Hulme and Jordanova, 1990; Outram, 1995). For these reasons, consideration should be given to a more diverse understanding of Enlightenment and its geography (see ENLIGHTENMENT, GEOGRAPHY AND). CWJW

References

Hulme, P. and Jordanova, L., eds, 1990: *The Enlightenment and its shadows.* London: Routledge. · Outram, D. 1995: *The Enlightenment.* Cambridge: Cambridge University Press. · Porter, R. 1990: *The Enlightenment.* London: Macmillan. · Porter, R. and Teich, M., eds, 1981: *The Enlightenment in national context.* Cambridge: Cambridge University Press. · Schmidt, J., ed., 1996: *What is enlightenment?: eighteenth-century answers and twentieth-century questions.* Berkeley, CA: University of California Press.

enterprise zone An area within which special policies apply to encourage economic DEVELOPMENT through private investment. Enterprise zone (EZs) provide tax concessions and reduced planning restrictions for companies establishing facilities. They represent a NEO-LIBERAL approach to the development of declining areas by promoting market solutions to economic problems. Critics argue that their effect is often to move existing jobs rather than to create new ones and that the real impact has involved concentration of POWER in the central STATE and loss of control by the LOCAL STATE over development strategies. Similar areas of deregulation have been established in a number of countries in different forms. Some 30 EZs were established in Britain between 1981 and 1993, whereas in the USA 34 states had active EZ programmes by 1995. The People's Republic of China was a pioneer in declaring 'special economic zones' (most famously in Shen-chen) from 1979 onwards to encourage foreign investment. JP

Suggested Reading

Wilder, M.G. and Rubin, B.M. 1996: Rhetoric versus reality: a review of studies on state enterprise zone programs. *Journal of the American Planning Association* 62: 473–91.

entropy A measure of the amount of UNCERTAINTY in a probability distribution or a SYSTEM subject to constraints. The term originated in thermodynamics, but has been used in a wide variety of contexts, notably in INFORMATION THEORY and as the basis for ENTROPY-MAXIMIZING MODELS of SPATIAL INTERACTION.

The concepts of macrostate and microstate are central to entropy analysis (note that some writers use the term mesostate where macrostate is employed here). Consider the distribution of 100 people into 10 regions: individual B to region 6, individual K to region 4, and so on. A *macrostate* is an aggregate frequency distribution of people across regions. Several different *microstates* may correspond to or give rise to the same macrostate: different individuals go to different regions, but the frequency distributions are the same. Entropy measures the relationship between a macrostate and the possible microstates that correspond to it. At one extreme, one macrostate (all 100 people in one region) has only one associated microstate, whereas the macrostate with ten people in each region corresponds to a large number of different microstates. The number of microstates corresponding to a macrostate is denoted here by W, and finding the entropy measure is a combinatorial calculation, given by:

$$W = N!/\prod_i n_i!$$

the factorial of the total number of individuals N, divided by the product of the factorials for each n_i (the number in each region).

An alternative entropy measure, used in information theory, is the statistic:

$$H = -\sum_i p_i \log(1/p_i)$$

where p_i is the probability (or proportion) in a given region. H is perfectly related to log W. The entropy statistics W and H measure the uncertainty of a macrostate with regard to its microstates. Minimum entropy ($H = 0$)

occurs for one p_i equal to unity and the rest to zero; there is complete certainty because there is only one microstate. H is at a maximum when all the p_i are equal (maximum uncertainty; all microstates equally likely). W and H can then be used to assess either the expected entropy of distributions and allocations, or the actual entropy of empirical patterns.

In geography, the information theory approach has used H to assess and compare entropy levels for settlement patterns and for trends in population and employment distributions. The entropy-maximizing approach uses entropy as the basis for finding the most likely macrostate of a system subject to constraints. LWH

Suggested Reading

Thomas, R.W. and Huggett, R.J. 1980: *Modelling in geography: a mathematical approach*. New York: Harper and Row, 152–66 and 197–200. · Wilson, A.G. and Bennett, R.J. 1986: *Mathematical methods in human geography and planning*. Chichester: John Wiley.

entropy-maximizing models Statistical models for identifying the 'most likely' spatial allocation pattern in a system subject to constraints. The approach was introduced into geographical modelling by A.G. Wilson in 1967 as the basis for a more rigorous interpretation of the GRAVITY MODEL, and has been extensively used since for SPATIAL INTERACTION modelling in urban regions and for modelling inter-regional flows of traffic and commodities. It is based on the concept of ENTROPY, a measure of the uncertainty or 'likelihood' in a probability distribution.

A journey-to-work model illustrates the method. For a city divided into k zones, we wish to calculate the best estimate of interzonal commuting flows T_{ij} without knowing the detailed information of each individual movement. Assume that there are N total commuters. Any specific trip distribution pattern T_{ij}, known as a 'macrostate' (see ENTROPY), can arise from many different sets of individual commuting movements or 'microstates'. Entropy measures the number of different microstates that can give rise to a particular macrostate:

$$W(\{T_{ij}\}) = N!/\sum_{i}^{k}\sum_{j}^{k} T_{ij}!$$

In the absence of detailed microstate data, we assume that each microstate is equally probable, and that the macrostate $\{T_{ij}\}$ with the maximum entropy value is the most probable or most likely overall pattern.

Additional information is also normally available, notably the number of commuters originating from each zone O_i, the total number of jobs available in each zone D_j, and estimates of the average or total travel expenditure for the city, C (usually based on survey data). The entropy-maximizing method then consists of maximizing $W(\{T_{ij}\})$ subject to the constraints

$$\sum_j T_{ij} = O_i, \quad \sum_i T_{ij} = D_j, \quad \sum_i \sum_j T_{ij c_{ij}} = C,$$

where c_{ij} is the travel cost from zone i to zone j. This maximization is a non-linear optimization problem, and must be solved by iterative search methods, systematically trying out different sets of values until the maximum is found.

Entropy-maximizing models not only fit empirical trip-distributions well, but also facilitate easy calculation of the effects of new housing or jobs (altering the O_i and D_j terms), and so have been widely used in more general urban models. Wilson and his Leeds colleagues have extended the model in many ways, making it dynamic, linking it to industrial and urban LOCATION THEORY, and including several types of disaggregation (e.g. by mode of travel). Recent work links the method to GEOGRAPHICAL INFORMATION SYSTEMS (GIS) to provide corporate and public sector location and strategic planning (Birkin et al., 1996). Other (non-transport) applications of the entropy-maximizing approach include its use to predict the most likely 'flows' or changes in votes between parties in English parliamentary constituencies at general elections (Johnston, 1985).

The entropy-maximizing trip distribution, based on given total cost C, can be related to the optimizing minimum-cost distribution generated by the TRANSPORTATION PROBLEM: as C is reduced to its minimum feasible value the entropy-maximizing pattern converges to the linear-programming transportation problem pattern of flows. LWH

References

Birkin, M., Clarke, G., Clark, M. and Wilson, A.G. 1996: *Intelligent GIS. Location decisions and strategic planning*. Cambridge: GeoInformation International. · Johnston, R.J. 1985: *The geography of English politics: the 1983 general election*. London: Croom-Helm. · Wilson, A.G. 1967: A statistical theory of spatial distribution models. *Transport Research* 1: 253–69.

Suggested reading

Wilson, A.G. and Bennett, R.J. 1986: *Mathematical methods in human geography and planning*. Chichester: John Wiley.

environmental audit In its broadest sense, an environmental audit is either the process, or the product that emerges from the process of checking, assessing, testing or verifying an aspect of environmental management. The International Chamber of Commerce (ICC) defined environmental auditing as 'a management tool comprising a systematic, documented, periodic and objective evaluation of how well the environmental organization, management and equipment are performing' (in Ryding, 1992, p. 414). Buckley (1995) notes how the definition of an environmental audit has changed over time: for example, environmental benchmark audits are alternatively known as state-of-the-environment reports, while environmental product audits are often now known as environmental purchasing.

Audits may be either internal to a corporation or undertaken by an outside organization (see ICC, 1991): they may be undertaken either voluntarily or to fulfil legal requirements. Environmental audits have grown in popularity in recent years due to the increase in public concern over environmental issues, the incorporation of environmental issues within business culture and the complementarity of this process with existing business practices. From a European perspective, Eden (1996) identifies this development as a reactive move in anticipation of the then European Commission's legislation which came into effect in 1995 and is popularly known by its acronoym EMAS (*environmental management and audit scheme*). There are also environmental audits at the level of individual countries (e.g. BS 7750 in England) although participation in these schemes is voluntary and is currently at low levels (Eden, 1996). From an American perspective, Cheremisinoff and Cheremisinoff (1993) identify various types of audits, establish when to do an audit and demonstrate the importance of environmental audits in relation to cleaning up environmentally degraded sites.

Environmental audits may be undertaken for governments, aid agencies, financial institutions and community groups. They may assess the predictions of ENVIRONMENTAL IMPACT ASSESSMENTS, compliance with environmental regulations, the performance of equipment, strategies and legislation, the compliance of corporations and government departments with their stated environmental policies and objectives or the effectiveness of an environmental management system. *Environmental planning audits*, or planning environmental audits, may be undertaken to improve environmental or RESOURCE MANAGEMENT practices.

Environmental auditing developed rapidly in the 1980s and 1990s. From a corporate perspective, internal environmental auditing helps companies to meet environmental regulations and their own environmental goals in a cost-effective manner. It also assists them to avoid the rising legal, financial and public relations costs of poor environmental management. Chapter 30 of *Agenda 21* (see SUSTAINABLE DEVELOPMENT) encourages private corporations to report annually on their environmental records (Buckley, 1995). From a STATE or COMMUNITY perspective, mandatory external auditing verifies and encourages compliance with environmental regulations. The questions of who will undertake the environmental audit, and who will have access to the resulting document, are central to the regulation of industry and commerce. Should corporations and government departments be self-regulated, or should there be outside regulation? Thus, the process of environmental auditing is situated within larger debates about how to achieve and maintain high environmental quality. PM

References

Buckley, R. 1995: Environmental auditing. In F. Vanclay and D. Bronstein, eds, *Environmental and social impact assessment*. Chichester: John Wiley and Sons, 283–301. · Cheremisinoff, P. and Cheremisinoff, N. 1993: *Professional environmental auditors guidebook*. Park Ridge, NJ: Noyes Publications. · Eden, S. 1996: *Environmental issues and business: implications of a changing agenda*. Chichester: John Wiley and Sons; International Chamber of Commerce (ICC) 1991: *ICC guide to effective environmental auditing*. Paris: ICC Publishing S.A.. · Ryding, S.-O. 1992: *Environmental management handbook*. Amsterdam and Oxford: IOS Press.

environmental determinism The doctrine that human activities are controlled by the environment (Lewthwaite, 1966). Since ancient times a belief in the moulding power of the physical environment on human CULTURE and constitution has attracted many advocates (Glacken, 1967). Hippocrates, for instance, linked the characteristics of people in particular PLACES to the influence of such environmental factors as humidity, altitude and terrain; while Aristotle believed that the world's climatic zones (frigid, temperate, and torrid) determined global habitability. Later, during the Renaissance, such climatic imperatives were, as in the case of Bodin during the mid-sixteenth century, frequently tied to astrological convictions that linked the microcosm of the body with the macrocosm of the heavens (Wands, 1986). The widespread publicizing of such environmental doctrines during the ENLIGHTENMENT owed much to the writings of Montesquieu, and in particular to his volume on *The spirit of the laws* (1748). To be sure, many others had flirted with the idea, notably the Abbé Dubos and John Arbuthnot; but Montesquieu's project of locating legislative regulation within the framework of the entire social and environmental conditions of which they were a part was exceptionally influential. Thereby contextualizing law and custom, and drawing from a burgeoning travel literature, Montesquieu disclosed how climatic conditions governed both the degeneration and persistence of cultural traits. Because everything from human physiology to social practices, from religious principles to moral judgements, were geographically conditioned, he presented the case for cultural RELATIVISM (Shklar, 1987). Montesquieu's penchant for recounting how religious beliefs mirrored geographical circumstance (Carrithers, 1995) enjoyed a lasting legacy: Ernest Renan's later expression of the tradition in the dictum that 'the desert is monotheist' persisted well into the twentieth century (Deffontaines, 1948). By the same token, his American disciples – such as Samuel Stanhope Smith – used the doctrine of climatic determinism in the New Republic to underwrite a common human nature and the superficiality of racial difference (Livingstone, 1999).

Notwithstanding the critiques of figures like Herder during the second half of the eighteenth century, environmental determinism flourished in the pre-Darwinian period among those like Henry Buckle who sought for a historicist history that subjected human activities to natural law (Bowler, 1989; see HISTORICISM), among regional sociologists like Le Play who causally connected up work, family and place (Brooke, 1970; cf. LE PLAY SOCIETY), and among ethnologists who accounted for racial differentiation in climatic terms (Stocking, 1987). It also found expression in the writings of those espousing a teleological metaphysics like Victor Cousin who, from time to time, gave the impression that national psyche could be read straight off topographic cartography: 'give me the map of a country... and I pledge myself to tell you, a priori, what the man of that country will be, and what part that country will play in history, not by accident, but of necessity' (quoted in Febvre, 1932, p. 10; cf. TELEOLOGY). In the aftermath of the 'Darwinian Revolution' the naturalistic construal of human culture in the categories of natural law received further encouragement (see also DARWINISM; HUMAN ECOLOGY; LAMARCKISM; SOCIAL DARWINISM). It clearly surfaced, for example, among those writers working on the interface of geography, history and anthropology who continued to read the human story through racial lenses (cf. RACISM). The role of environment in shaping racial 'achievement' was thus emphasized in the writings of figures like A.R. Wallace, Sir John Lubbock and A.H. Keane (Stepan, 1982). The doctrine persisted too in the sociological work of writers like Edmond Demolins who reduced ethnic character and the genesis of civilization to patterns of communication routes. Throughout, the assumption was that human culture was ineluctably shaped by NATURE.

These currents of thought were clearly registered within the geographical tradition. After all, Friedrich Ratzel and Oscar Peschel in Germany acquired distinguished reputations in anthropology as well as geography. Yet for all that there is much to be said for the view that evolution's reinforcement of environmental determinism sprang less from classical Darwinism than from the Neo-Lamarckian version (Campbell and Livingstone, 1983; see LAMARCKISM). Ratzel's *Anthropogeographie*, with its cardinal notion of *LEBENSRAUM*, and his organismic conception of the STATE, owed much to the MIGRATION theories of the Lamarckian Moritz Wagner; and while the environmental determinist element in his early work has perhaps been overestimated, the evolutionary outlook of figures like Wagner and Haeckel did much to legitimate any such tendencies in Ratzel's project (Livingstone, 1992; see also ANTHROPOGEOGRAPHY).

The Ratzelian programme, in its more sternly environmental determinist guise, found its American voice largely through the writings of Ellen C. Semple. Her *American history and its geographic conditions* (1903) and *Influences of geographic environment* (1911), while not so crude as some commentators have implied, nevertheless did much to establish environmentalism as the dominant mode of explanation in American geography during the early decades of the twentieth century. And with the reinforcement of earlier works from writers like Shaler and Brigham its scientific stature seemed secured (Livingstone, 1987). Such was also the conviction of Ellsworth Huntington whose voluminous writings on climate and civilization displayed his predilection for racial typecasting and environmentalist explanations. Yet here again we find another victim of the historical stereotype. For even while he advocated human history on the grand environmental scale, Huntington constantly reiterated the importance of genetic constitution and thus threw his weight behind various eugenic enterprises (Spate, 1968).

Elsewhere during the early years of the twentieth century similar conceptual manoeuvres were discernible. Griffith Taylor, for example, advocated what he called 'stop and go' determinism in the attempt to modulate the shrillest tones of inexorable necessitarianism. And in Britain Halford Mackinder who, at one point, insisted that the only rational basis for human geography was as a causal science built upon physical foundations, nevertheless left space for humanity's wresting the initiative from nature through the exercise of what he came to call the *Going Concern* (O'Tuathail, 1992).

Given this sense of equivocation, it is evident that the distinctions between environmental determinism, POSSIBILISM and PROBABILISM turn out to be far from clear cut. To the contrary. Figures widely regarded as PARADIGM cases actually displayed greater ambivalence and conceptual nuance than is usually acknowledged. Vidal de la Blache, for instance, was convinced that *GENRES DE VIE* were themselves reflective of nature even as they transformed it, and it would therefore be mistaken to consider his as an altogether radical voluntarism (Claval, 1993). Never psychologistic, Vidal always conceived of human geography as a *natural*, not a *social*, *science* (Buttimer, 1971; Livingstone, 1992). Similarly, the anthropologist Franz Boas's polemical crusade against an unsophisticated ENVIRONMENTALISM (a campaign that influenced Carl Sauer's repudiation: see BERKELEY SCHOOL) must not be taken to imply an entire dismissal of the conditioning power of environment, as is clearly evident in his celebrated study of the environmental modification of the immigrant headform (Stocking, 1965; Speth, 1978). In the light of such revelations it seems that the labels *determinism* and *possibilism* were retained with a degree of polemical typecasting compatible with the suspicion that other interests were at stake in the controversies.

Considerable debate on the subject also characterized Soviet geography (Matley, 1966). With the official endorsement of Lysenko's Lamarckism, and the stimulus of Plekhanov's revolutionized Marxism that causally connected the forces and relations of production to natural environment, environmental determinism mobilized considerable support among Russian geographers, notwithstanding the early critiques of Karl Wittfogel (Matley, 1966). In this espousal of the doctrine by the far left, Plekhanov's borrowings from Ratzel were decisively significant, and he used it to combat racial theories of social development and to account for what he saw as 'the backwardness and social deformation of his own native Russia' (Bassin, 1992, p. 3). During the second quarter of the century many more came to query environmental determinism in the wake of Stalin's repudiation. Yet despite such spurnings, V. Anuchin felt justified in reasserting the salience of at least a neo-determinism because he was convinced that classical Marxism was implicated in the attempt to trace causal links between the material and the social (see also MARXIST GEOGRAPHY).

Any acceptable account of the intellectual mainsprings of environmental determinism will have to recognize its plural origins and purposes. Among these are the ways in which it was connected up to the philosophy of scientific and social scientific explanation, the place it occupied in politically conservative regimes, its periodic underwriting of cultural PLURALISM, how it articulated the ideological interests of its academic advocates, and the role that it played in bids to control disciplinary identity (Martin, 1951; Montefiore and Williams, 1955; Peet, 1985; Livingstone, 1992). DNL

References

Bassin, M. 1992: Geographical determinism in *fin-de-siècle* Marxism: Georgii Plekhanov and the environmental basis of Russian history. *Annals of the Association of American Geographers* 82: 3–22. · Bowler, P.J. 1989: *The invention of progress. The Victorians and the past* Oxford: Blackwell. · Brooke, M.Z. 1970: *Le Play: engineer and social scientist. The life and work of Frederic le Play.* London: Longman. · Buttimer, A. 1971: *Society and milieu in the French geographic tradition.* Chicago: Rand McNally. · Campbell, J.A. and Livingstone, D.N. 1983: Neo-Lamarckism and the development of geography in the United States and Great Britain. *Transactions, Institute of British Geographers* NS 8: 267–94. · Carrithers, D. 1995: The Enlightenment science of society. In C. Fox, R. Porter and R. Wokler, eds, *Inventing human science: eighteenth-century domains.* Berkeley: University of California Press, 232–70. · Claval, P., ed., 1993: *Autour de Vidal de la Blache: la formation de l'école française de géographie.* Paris: (Centre National de la Recherche Scientifique (CNRS). · Deffontaines, P. 1948: *Géographie et religions.* Paris: Gallimard. · Febvre, L. 1932: *A geographical introduction to history.* London: Kegan Paul; Trench, Trübner. Originally published in 1922 as *La terre et l'évolution humaine.* · Glacken, C.J. 1967: *Traces on the Rhodian shore. Nature and culture in western thought from ancient times to the end of the eighteenth century.*

Berkeley: University of California Press. · Lewthwaite, G. 1966: Environmentalism and determinism: a search for clarification. *Annals of the Association of American Geographers* 56: 1–23. · Livingstone, D.N. 1987: *Nathaniel Southgate Shaler and the culture of American science.* London: University of Alabama Press. · Livingstone, D.N. 1992: *The geographical tradition. Episodes in the history of a contested enterprise.* Oxford: Blackwell. · Livingstone, D.N. 1999: Geographical inquiry, rational religion and moral philosophy: Enlightenment discourses on the human condition. In D.N. Livingstone and C.W.J. Withers, eds, *Geography and enlightenment.* Chicago: University of Chicago Press. · Martin, A.F. 1951: The necessity for determinism. *Transactions, Institute of British Geographers* 17: 1–12. · Mattey, I.M. 1996: The marxist approach to geographical environment. *Annals of the Association of American Geographers* 56: 97–111. · Montefiore, A. and Williams, W. 1955: Determinism and possibilism. *Geographical Studies* 2: 1–11. · O'Tuathail, G. 1992: Putting Mackinder in his place: material transformations and myth. *Political Geography Quarterly* 11: 100–18. · Peet, R. 1985: The social origins of environmental determinism. *Annals of the Association of American Geographers* 75: 309–33. · Shklar, J.N. 1987: *Montesquieu.* Oxford: Oxford University Press. · Spate, O.H.K. 1968: Ellsworth Huntington. In D.L., Sills, ed., *International encyclopaedia of the social sciences.* New York: Macmillan and Free Press, vol. 7, 26–7. · Speth, W. 1978: The anthropogeographic theory of Franz Boas. *Anthropos,* 73: 1–31. · Stepan, N. 1982: *The idea of race in science: Great Britain 1800–1960.* London: Macmillan. · Stocking, G.W. Jr. 1965: From physics to ethnology: Franz Boas Arctic expedition as problem in the historiography of the behavioral sciences. *Journal of the History of the Behavioral Sciences* 1: 211–18. · Stocking, G.W. Jr. 1987: *Victorian anthropology.* New York: Free Press. · Tatham, G. 1951: Environmentalism and possibilism. In G. Taylor, ed., *Geography in the twentieth century.* London: Methuen, 128–64. · Wands, J. 1986: The theory of climate in the English Renaissance and *Mundus alter et idem.* In I.D. McFarlane, ed., *Proceedings of the Fifth International Congress of Neo-Latin Studies.* Binghamton, New York: Medieval & Renaissance Texts & Studies, 519–25.

environmental economics A branch of economics which seeks to prevent or ameliorate environmental problems by using economic instruments. Environmental economics emerged in the late 1960s Europe and North America, although theoretically it can be traced to the earlier work of economists R.H. Coase (1960) and A.C. Pigou (1920). The ENVIRONMENTAL MOVEMENT which emerged at that time argued that western industrial societies were guilty of 'growthmania' (Daly, 1973, p. 5) predicated on a 'cowboy economy' (Boulding, 1966, p. 9) in which the environment and RESOURCES were but means to the end of economic growth. Symptomatically, most academic and government economists prior to the late 1960s worked with theories (neo-classical, institutionalist, Keynesian) which were 'eco-blind', that is, insensitive to the environmental effects of economic growth. By contrast, environmental economics seeks to incorporate environmental considerations into both economic theory and practice. It is founded on two axioms: first, that the economic system, when left unchecked, is a (the?) major cause of contemporary environmental problems; and second, conversely, that when suitably corrected the economy can be a powerful vehicle for ameliorating and even solving these environmental problems. Three decades after its inception, environmental economics is among the dominant approaches to diagnosing and managing environmental problems in the western social sciences, and is most associated with NEO-CLASSICAL ECONOMICS. (See also RESOURCE MANAGEMENT.)

Environmental economics takes two main forms, which diagnose and manage economically induced environmental problems in rather different ways (Turner, 1995).

The *property rights approach* derives from Coase's (1960) seminal essay 'The problem of social cost'. The argument is that environmental problems arise from the absence of well-defined property rights in environmental assets. For instance, an unowned river may be polluted by a company with impunity. However, if ownership of the river is assigned to, say, a local angling association then the company would have to cease polluting the river or else compensate the anglers for the damage done to their fish.

The more influential *pricing approach* derives from Pigou's (1920) *The economics of welfare.* The argument here is that environmental problems arise because the environment is not priced and is thus a 'free good'. From this perspective a problem such as ozone layer destruction would be an 'EXTERNALITY' problem arising from the fact that the release of chlorofluorocarbons (CFCs) into the atmosphere is free and thus not factored into economic decision-making. The solution is thus to price the environment and to thereby amend existing market transactions or else create new markets in environmental assets. For instance, in the case of ozone layer destruction the imposition of a POLLUTION tax on companies releasing CFCs or else a government subsidy to support alternatives to CFCs would be a case of pricing previously unpriced goods in order to amend existing markets in an environmentally friendly way. Alternatively, a government could issue pollution permits which together limit CFC emissions but which could be freely traded between companies so that those less able to reduce CFC emissions can purchase permits from those who are able to do so. This permit solution thus entails creating a new market in environmentally related goods. Decisions as to what level of tax, subsidy or permit ceiling to set are typically determined by COST–BENEFIT ANALYSIS.

Clearly, both forms of environmental economics prioritize the market: environmental problems are seen as cases of 'market failure' and, when suitably corrected, the market is seen as the key mechanism of problem solution. Reflecting its neo-classical origins, the corrected market's environmental economics advocates are seen as more efficient or 'PARETO OPTIMAL' than uncorrected markets. In other words, with environment assets now priced, markets will better reflect the true costs of economic activity and patterns and prices of commodity supply and demand will settle at new equilibria.

Although environmental economics has many lucid academic and governmental advocates (e.g. Helm and Pearce, 1991), it has been subject to considerable criticism. Sympathetic critics point out that its persuasive theoretical logic rarely translates into practice because real markets are complex and imperfect. Additionally, they point out that its concern to fashion more efficient markets is a rather narrow objective which ignores the scientific and ethical questions of environmental quality (Eckersley, 1993). For instance, a pollution tax may simply make pollution more expensive rather than stop it altogether, but environmental economics is not concerned with ECOLOGICAL questions about the absorptive capacities of natural systems or qualitative questions as to the right and wrong of continued pollution (cf. ETHICS, GEOGRAPHY AND). More ecologically minded economists have therefore advocated an 'ecological economics' which pays much more heed to these questions (Martinez-Alier, 1987). Finally, more radical 'ecocentric' critics point out that environmental economics is 'technocentrist' and anthropocentric. In other words, it seeks to tinker with, rather than overhaul, existing economic and social arrangements and to do so with a view to improving human – rather than natural – welfare. On this view, therefore, environmental economics is still ultimately implicated in the economic 'growthmania' causing environmental problems in the first place and is unable to treat the environment as having existence value in its own right. NC

References

Boulding, K. 1966: The economics of the coming spaceship earth. In H. Jarrett, ed., *Environmental quality in a growing economy*. Baltimore: Johns Hopkins University Press, 3–14. · Coase, R.H. 1960: The problem of social cost. *Journal of Law and Economics* 3: 1–44. · Daly, H.E. 1973: Introduction. In H.E. Daly, ed., *Towards a steady state economy*. San Francisco: Freeman, 1–36. · Eckersley, R. 1993: Free market environmentalism: friend or foe? *Environmental Politics* 2: 1–19. · Helm, D. and Pearce, D. 1991: Economic policy towards the environment: an overview. In D. Helm, ed., *Economic policy towards the environment*. Oxford: Blackwell, 1–24. · Martinez-Alier, J. 1987: *Ecological economics*. Oxford: Blackwell. · Pigou, A.C. 1920: *The economics of welfare*. London: Macmillan. · Turner, R.K. 1995: Environmental economics and management. In T. O'Riordan, ed., *Environmental science for environmental management*. Harlow: Longman, 30–40.

Suggested Reading

Eckersley (1993). · Turner, R.K., Pearce, D.W. and Bateman, I.J. 1993: *Environmental economics: an elementary introduction*. Hemel Hempstead: Harvester Wheatsheaf.

environmental hazard Sometimes known as a '*natural hazard*', or popularly as a 'natural disaster', this term generally refers to geophysical events such as earthquakes, volcanoes, bushfires, drought, flooding, lightning and high winds that can potentially cause large-scale economic damage and physical injury or death. Such events have differing impacts depending upon both their magnitude and the character of the receiving environment (e.g. a heavily populated area versus a sparsely settled area). Sometimes the effects may be beneficial, as with the renewal of mineral nutrients to a floodplain soil during flooding (Pickering and Owen, 1994).

Environmental hazards are sometimes known as 'Acts of God'. However, given the long-term involvement of humans as part of NATURE, a detailed analysis of so-called 'environmental hazards' often reveals significant human input. The characteristics of an environmental hazard are: (1) that it was not directly caused by humans (see HAZARD, HUMAN-MADE); (2) that it directly affects humans (unlike an extreme natural event that does not directly affect humans); (3) that it is often accompanied by a violent release of ENERGY (Chapman, 1996); and (4) that it was beyond PREDICTION in the short to medium term. May et al. (1996) extend the notion of RISK in natural hazard to 'public risks', which also includes ozone depletion and sea-level rise (see GLOBAL WARMING). The awareness of hazards was demonstrated by the United Nations declaring the 1990s to be the

'International Decade for Natural Disaster Reduction' (Mauro, 1995), a terminology which perpetuates the often false perception that humans have played no part in these disasters.

Flooding would be a natural event, but not a natural hazard, if human settlement was located away from areas with potential to flood. Similarly, while heavy rainfall may be considered a natural event (this is becoming more debatable with increased human impact on global systems), flooding is often exacerbated by human actions other than settlement patterns. The severe floods in Poland, Germany and the Czech Republic in 1997 were frequently described as a 'natural disaster' but they were worsened by draining marshlands, industrial POLLUTION (which killed trees that once absorbed the water from the floodplain) and diplomatic issues between countries in the early 1980s that resulted in the dykes being lowered in some cases. The drying up of the Aral Sea in Kazakstan and Uzbekistan (former Soviet Central Asia) was caused by the withdrawal of water for irrigated cotton production. This has severely affected the once lucrative fishing industry and the climate of the region (Meyer and Turner, 1995).

The distinction between an environmental hazard and a human-made hazard has blurred. It was only maintained as long as humans were seen as being separate from nature, rather than one species that has been part of nature for thousands of years. What are experienced today are physical events, whose impacts are influenced by the actions of humans and other species, which in turn influence the character of future physical events.

Work in the United States on hazards and disasters emerged in the context of the nuclear threat and the Cold War; much of the early work was funded by the State Department. In geography, the leading school of natural or environmental hazards research developed out of White's work on human adjustment to floods (summarized in White, 1973). He found that despite heavy spending on technological measures (e.g. dams), losses due to floods in the USA were increasing. This experience is replicated in parts of Australia, where engineering solutions such as levee banks (May et al., 1996) also failed to consider the possibility of behavioural change by people.

The critique of environmental hazard research from CRITICAL THEORY, and explicitly MARXIST GEOGRAPHY, has been withering. Smith and O'Keefe (1980, 1985) said that geographers in the tradition of POSITIVISM have displayed three major ways of dealing with nature which they illustrate through 'natural hazards' research: (1) where nature is seen as separate from human activity; (2) where nature is seen as neutral but becomes hazardous when it intersects with human activity (exemplified by Burton et al., 1993); and (3) where humans are dissolved into nature. The first approach focuses attention on 'natural causes' of disasters, rather than human vulnerability; the second is presented as a technocratic agenda to control nature, while the third is seen as Malthusian (see MALTHUSIAN MODEL) because it blames the victims. Watts (1983), analysing FAMINES in Africa, strongly critiqued the individuality, ahistoricity and lack of POLITICAL ECONOMY in environmental hazards research. He noted that the 1976 drought in Britain was neither responsible for, nor accompanied by, thousands of deaths, yet famine in Africa is seen as a natural hazard. Marxist-inspired authors highlight the difference between the natural event (in this case drought, which may be partly caused by human activity) and the consequences (famine). These differences are attributed to the organization and structure of social systems.

PM

References

Burton, I., Kates, R. and White, G. 1993: *The environment as hazard*, 2nd edn. New York: Oxford University Press. · Chapman, D. 1996: *Natural hazards*. Melbourne: Oxford University Press. · Mauro, A. 1995: Stop disasters: the newsletter of the UN International Decade for Natural Disaster Reduction. In T. Horlick-Jones, A. Amendola and R. Casale, eds, *Natural risk and civil protection*. London: E. and F.N. Spon, 511–15. · May, P. et al. 1996: *Environmental management and governance: intergovernmental approaches to hazards and sustainability*. London and New York: Routledge. · Meyer, W. and Turner, B. 1995: The earth transformed: trends, trajectories and patterns. In R. Johnston, P. Taylor and M. Watts, eds, *Geographies of global change: remapping the world in the late twentieth century*. Oxford: Blackwell. · Pickering, K. and Owen, T. 1994: *An introduction to global environmental issues*. London: Routledge. · Smith, N. and O'Keefe, P. 1980: Geography, Marx and the concept of nature. *Antipode* 12 (2): 30–9. · Smith, N. and O'Keefe, P. 1985: Postscript 1985: the production of nature. *Antipode* 17 2/3: 88. · Watts, M. 1983: *Silent violence: food, famine and peasantry in Northern Nigeria*. Berkeley, CA: University of California Press. · White, G. 1973: Natural hazards research. In R.J. Chorley, ed., *Directions in geography*. London: Methuen and Co., 193–216.

Suggested Reading

Chapman (1996). · Pickering and Owen (1994).

environmental impact assessment A process of systematically identifying and assessing anticipated environmental impacts prior to a proposed project, policy, programme or plan being implemented. The identification of significant negative impacts may prevent the proposal (which, in practice, is usually a project) from going ahead. However, more frequently it results in the modification of the original proposal, or the introduction of measures to ameliorate the anticipated negative environmental impacts. It is also possible for a proposal to generate positive environmental impacts, particularly if the site is already severely degraded, and these should also be considered in the process. Meredith (1995, p. 362) wrote that impact assessment (environmental, social and other forms) 'need consist only of two things: the commitment to forethought and some ability to foresee'. This statement raises questions as to whether an EIA merely predicts changes, if the process of EIA is a key part of change through legitimation, or if it should be used as a tool to introduce progressive changes such as SUSTAINABLE DEVELOPMENT.

Environmental Impact Assessment (EIA) was introduced in the US in 1969 under the *National Environmental Policy Act* (Kreske, 1996). It is now a legal requirement in many countries, provinces/states and sometimes at the level of individual cities. International institutions such as The World Bank and international AID agencies also require an EIA process on particular development proposals. Over time the coverage of assessments has broadened from just federal government departments to include provincial/state proposals and private development proposals, depending upon the legislation in a particular location. Wood (1995) provides a comprehensive comparison of EIA systems in six countries, plus the US state of California. EIA has also been adapted from environmental protection to include the idea of sustainable development, a concept that had not been created when EIA was initiated.

Thomas (1996) defined EIA as an Environmental Impact Statement (EIS) plus an Assessment Report. The terminology varies between countries, and often causes confusion. For example, in some places EIA is simply known as 'Impact Assessment' because it is broader than a narrow definition of the physical environment. In other places it is known as Environmental Assessment (EA) because of the perceived negative connotations of the term 'impact'. However, in the USA, an Environmental Assessment is a preliminary study undertaken within the EIA process to identify the likelihood of significant impacts, which then require the preparation of a full EIS (Burris and Canter, 1997).

The process of EIA has become standardized in many countries. Under some legislative frameworks, the EIS document may be required to address issues such as sustainable development, BIODIVERSITY, social impacts and economic considerations. There are also legal requirements for public participation, which may be limited to giving interested people a period of time to provide written comments on the EIS.

Environmental Impact Assessment is sometimes seen as an important process which prevents the worst aspects of proposals from being implemented; it does not necessarily guarantee high-quality development. In contrast, other people perceive the process to be a way of legitimizing controversial development proposals and in their view it does very little to maintain environmental quality. They argue that many of the key decisions have already been taken at the policy level, and that the individual character of EIA often fails to consider the cumulative impacts of each development. These concerns are partly being addressed by Strategic Environmental Assessments (SEA) at the policy and programme level, and Cumulative Impact Assessment (CIA) over longer time-horizons than those of particular projects. PM

References

Burris, R. and Canter, L. 1997: Cumulative impacts are not properly addressed in Environmental Assessments. *Environmental Impact Assessment Review* 17: 5–18. · Kreske, D. 1996: *Environmental impact statements: a practical guide for agencies, citizens and consultants*. New York: John Wiley and Sons. · Meredith, T. 1995: Assessing Environmental Impacts in Canada. In B. Mitchell, ed., *Resource and environmental management in Canada: addressing conflict and uncertainty*. New York and Toronto: Oxford University Press, 360–83. · Thomas, I. 1996: *Environmental impact assessment in Australia: theory and practice*. Sydney: The Federation Press. · Wood, C. 1995: *Environmental impact assessment: a comparative review*: Harlow: Longman.

environmental justice A socio-political movement that seeks to articulate environmental issues from a SOCIAL JUSTICE perspective. Such justice concerns include the well-being and rights of future and past generations, equity considerations based on RACE, gender, CLASS and NATION, and, to a lesser extent, our rights and obligations towards non-human forms of nature. The movement for environmental justice developed in response to the limitations of mainstream environmentalism, in particular its role in reproducing structures of inequality, and is thus considered an oppositional, or counter-hegemonic form of ENVIRONMENTALISM. (See also ECOFEMINISM; ENVIRONMENTAL MOVEMENT; ENVIRONMENTALISM; HEGEMONY.) The movement for environmental justice was born in the 1980s as marginalized COMMUNITIES across the globe confronted various environmental problems and realized that dominant forms of environmentalism were not only unable to address their social and environmental struggles effectively, but also that their solutions and policies often worked to the detriment of such populations in an exclusionary manner. In effect, the environmental justice movement is an attempt to broaden the definition and scope of environmentalism to include the basic needs of poor and politically less powerful groups. Consequently, it locates environmental problems on an explicitly moral terrain, in an effort to resist the economic rationality of mainstream environmentalism, CAPITAL and the STATE (cf. MORAL GEOGRAPHIES). Although the movement is quite heterogeneous, it seeks to build an inclusive movement based on anti-RACIST, anti-corporate, anti-IMPERIALIST and feminist politics.

As a movement, environmental justice gained momentum and coherence during the 1980s, inspired by several distinct but converging political currents. One major impetus was the rise of the anti-toxics movement, which initially began in more industrialized countries, but has since spread throughout the world. The anti-toxic movement consists of communities threatened by various forms of POLLUTION who have united upon realizing that neither the state nor mainstream environmentalism was prepared to address their problem. Activists named their struggle as the movement for environmental justice, as they sought justice against the forces that undermined the well-being of their communities. A second development was the proliferation of ecological/peasant/livelihood struggles in less industrialized countries, including both pollution and RESOURCE-based conflicts (Escobar, 1992). A third influence was the growing trend in SOCIAL THEORY to challenge and unpack hegemonic concepts and institutions, including environmentalism. This has provided a useful framework in which to uncover a whole series of unacknowledged problems with mainstream environmentalism. In turn, environmental justice activists have defined themselves in opposition to the following criticisms: a reliance on 'expert' scientists; a willingness to accept the dominant model of environmental management versus pollution reduction; a tendency to speak on behalf of others; plus the WHITENESS of the environmental movement, its 'insider' status, and its narrow conception of the environment and environmental concerns.

Some of these critiques are similar to those voiced by ecofeminists, another counter-hegemonic form of environmentalism. But while both challenge the IDEOLOGY and practice of mainstream environmentalism, ecofeminism's critique is based largely on gender, whereas environmental justice is centred on community. In many ways, the difference parallels that between 'First' and 'Third' world feminisms (see FEMINIST GEOGRAPHIES; GENDER AND GEOGRAPHY; THIRD WORLD). In short, at times the two converge, and at others they do not.

While the term 'environmental justice' clearly evokes a broad political position, the concept is frequently associated with a somewhat more narrow set of political and scholarly concerns: the inequitable distribution of environmental quality among various human groups. Scholars and activists alike have not only called attention to the fact that native peoples, people of colour, women and children, and the poor are most vulnerable to environmental hazards, but also that they are excluded from institutional DECISION-MAKING. Moreover, while such groups may bear the least responsibility for environmental degradation, they often bear the brunt of its consequences. These insights have been applied to cases as diverse as deforestation in India (Shiva, 1989), pesticide use in Latin America (Perfecto, 1992), the export of hazardous waste to poor countries throughout the world, and the disproportionate exposure of people of colour in the 'First world', including indigenous NATIONS, to various forms of pollution (Bullard, 1993). As a result, activists from across the world have identified the commonality of their struggles, have mobilized, and seek to create a global movement for environmental justice, that is, an environmental movement rooted in the everyday concerns of the poor and marginalized of the world.

The term *Environmental Racism* covers a subset of environmental justice and refers to the environmental struggles of people of colour primarily in the US, but increasingly in other places as well. Environmental racism was coined by Ben Chavis and developed in conjunction with the United Church of Christ's seminal study documenting that people of colour in the US (African-Americans,

American-Indians, Asian-Americans, and Chicanos/Latinos) were disproportionately exposed to various forms of pollution. Their *Toxic waste and race in the United States* (UCC, 1987) was a critical development in that it not only inspired a great deal of research on the part of scholars who sought to investigate claims of environmental racism (Bowen et al., 1995), but it also offered activists a new way of framing their struggle.

Environmental Equity is often used as a synonym for environmental racism. Besides being a less overtly politicized term, it refers to both racial *and* income INEQUALITY in the distribution of pollution. Despite the fact that many activists organize around a racial definition of the problem, almost all research on environmental racism also examines income data, in order to assess whether race or class is a more powerful indicator in the distribution of pollution. While this is the primary thrust of environmental justice research, scholars have also examined these issues from a variety of other perspectives, including questions of justice and EQUITY (Lake, 1996), the legal arena (Been, 1993), urban development (Pulido, Sidawi and Vos, 1996), and in terms of pollution reduction and class politics (Heiman, 1990). Because of the close relationship between research, policy, and grassroots struggles, environmental justice has become an important site for activism and thus presents an opportunity for geographers to make a difference beyond the academy. (See also NIMBY.)

LP

References

Been, V. 1993: What's fairness got to do with it? Environmental justice and the siting of locally undesirable land uses. *Cornell Law Review* 78: 1001–85. · Bowen, W., Salling, M., Haynes, K. and Cyran, E. 1995: Toward Environmental Justice: Spatial Equity in Ohio and Cleveland. *Annals of the Association of American Geographers* 85: 641–63. · Bullard, R., ed., 1993: *Confronting environmental racism: voices from the grassroots.* Boston: South End Press. · Escobar, A. 1992: Imagining a post-development era? Critical thought, development, and social movements. *Social Text* 10: 20–56. · Heiman, M. 1990: From 'Not in my Backyard!' to 'Not in Anybody's Backyard!': grassroots challenge to hazardous waste facility siting. *Journal of the American Planning Association* 56: 359–62. · Lake, R. 1996: Volunteers, NIMBYs, and environmental justice: dilemmas of democratic practice. *Antipode* 28: 160–74. · Perfecto, I. 1992: Pesticide exposure of farm workers and the international connection. In B. Bryant and P. Mohai, eds, *Race and the incidence of environmental hazards.* Boulder: Westview Press, 177–203. · Pulido, L., Sidawi, S. and Vos, R. 1996: An archaeology of environmental racism in Los Angeles. *Urban Geography* 17: 419–39. · Shiva, V. 1989: *Staying alive: women, ecology and development.* London: Zed Books; United Church of Christ, Commission on Racial Justice 1987: *Toxic waste and race in the United States.* New York: United Church of Christ.

Suggested Readings

Bullard, R. 1991: *Dumping in Dixie: race, class, and environmental quality.* Boulder: Westview Press. · Cutter, S. 1995: Race, class, and environmental justice. *Progress in Human Geography* 19: 107–18.

environmental movement The organized political expression of ENVIRONMENTALISM. The modern environmental movement is an important political force today and dates back to late 1960s Europe and North America. There, in the wake of Rachel Carson's (1962) *Silent spring*, the Torrey Canyon oil tanker disaster (1967), Paul Ehrlich's (1968) *The population bomb* and the first Earth Day (1970), concern over human use and abuse of the environment proliferated. In these early years, the environmental movement was the preserve of relatively small numbers of radical activists, such as those associated with the environmental groups Friends of the Earth and Greenpeace (both founded in 1971). Since then, however, it has grown, diversified and also become a more mainstream political concern. It exists today as an extremely large and heterogeneous movement which can be examined in terms of its different constituent groups, their favoured political tactics and the number and scale of their environmental concerns.

In terms of groups, six categories can be distinguished: environmental non-governmental organizations (NGOs), environmental new SOCIAL MOVEMENTS (NSMs), green political parties, governments with environmental sensibilities, ecologically-sensitized businesses, and 'green consumers'. It is important to understand that only the first three are exclusively environmental, whereas the others devote only some of their energy and resources to environmental matters. *Environmental NGOs* were among the founding groups of the modern environmental movement. Created voluntarily by ordinary members of CIVIL SOCIETY, they have become a vital force in raising public, government and business awareness of current environmental problems. Some environmental NGOS – like Greenpeace – are well-established and well-known, while others are newer and ephemeral, like Friends of Clayoquot Sound in British Columbia, Canada. Most are anti-establishment in their political outlook, although some – like the Worldwide Fund for Nature – have close affiliations with mainstream political and economic interests. In addition, there is the

United Nations which, while ostensibly non-governmental, enjoys the unique capacity of being able to convene most of the world's governments, as it did at the 1992 'Earth Summit'. *Environmental NSMs* also arise from civil society, but are usually more informal, local, issue-based and often temporary (see Escobar, 1995). The 1970s Chipko Movement in India is a well-known example, which comprised ordinary rural Indians coming together to protest corporate exploitation of the environment. Some 'dark green' NSMs are conservative and even authoritarian, urging a return to ecological harmony based on a singular cultural identity (Bramwell, 1985). *Green political parties* are more recent phenomena than environmental NGOS, and in the West date from the late 1970s. As public concern over the environment grew, many environmentalists saw the chance to gain formal political power by standing as candidates in DEMOCRATIC political elections. Green parties have been more successful in Europe than in North America, the German Green Party enjoying reasonable representation in the West German Bundestag in the mid-1980s. Until the late 1990s, however, no green party enjoyed a controlling interest in government and most green parties were less popular then than even a decade ago (Bramwell, 1994): in 1998, however, the German Green Party formed a coalition with the country's Social Democrats, occupying several seats in the Federal Cabinet.

The efforts of green parties and environmental NGOs have contributed to making today's *mainstream political parties* and elected governments far more sensitive to environmental issues than heretofore. In addition, many environmental problems – like ACID RAIN and GLOBAL WARMING – have become too pressing for these parties and governments to ignore. Accordingly, most western administrations today have more or less elaborate environmental policies, including international agreements like the Montreal Protocol on CFCs. Even businesses have been convinced that the environment matters. For some this has taken the form of a '*commercial environmentalism*', as in the case of firms producing 'green commodities' like non-detergent washing liquids. For other businesses, like those involved in commercial fishing and forestry, public opposition has forced them (often reluctantly) to alter their environmental practices. This has been assisted by the emergence of an ENVIRONMENTAL ECONOMICS designed to make businesses bear the full economic cost of their environmental impacts. Finally, although not usually organized formally, diverse consumers keen to buy 'eco-friendly' products have helped bolster the environmental movement.

Not surprisingly, the political tactics of these different groups vary. Many environmental NGOs have used physical intervention – for instance, 'tree-hugging' – as well as graphic media campaigns – like Greenpeace's against the Newfoundland seal hunt in the 1980s. Green parties have used the media too, but have also directly influenced political debate through their Parliamentary debating and voting. Governments, of course, have been able to use their enormous economic and legal POWER to effect environmental improvements, as too have many of the larger TRANSNATIONAL CORPORATIONS like Shell Oil and Dow Chemical. The different sizes and powers of the various groups comprising the environmental movement also decisively alter the number and geographical scale of their environmental concerns. Some groups are local, single-issue groups and may be short-lived whereas others are able to consider multiple environmental issues at the international as well as local scale, notably national governments, big businesses and large environmental NGOs.

IDEOLOGICALLY, the environmental movement has both an 'ecocentric' and a 'technocentric' wing (O'Riordan, 1981; cf. ENVIRONMENTALISM). The former is more radical than the latter, puts the environment first and argues for a fundamental alteration in existing economic and social uses of NATURE. It is associated with most environmental NGOs, NSMs and green parties. By contrast, technocentrism is anthropocentric and suggests that the environment can be rationally managed within existing frameworks. It is associated with mainstream government, business and consumer interests. Despite the popularity of ecocentrism, some have worried that environmentalism has been hijacked by these status quo technocentrist groups (Rowell, 1996). Others, however, suggest that the environment offers one of the few possibilities for genuine global economic and political cooperation because it is an issue of common concern to humanity. Equally, though, some radicals believe that it is precisely this commonality of interest that may serve as the foundation for a new global grassroots movement ranged against those in positions of power and authority (McCormick, 1989).

If such a global movement – in either its radical or mainstream forms – is to materialize it will have to negotiate the serious differences of interest between the developed and developing worlds. As the 1992 'Earth Summit' showed, many developing countries cannot afford to put environmental issues first as long as POVERTY endures (see Chaterjee and Finger, 1994). Indeed, many see the notion of 'global ecology' as an excuse for the developed countries to avoid transferring resources to less developed countries while asking them to forego development in the interests of global environmental protection (Shiva, 1993). In this and many other ways, the environmental movement remains as divided as it is heterogeneous. NC

References

Bramwell, A. 1985: *Blood and soil*. Buckinghamshire: Bourne End. · Bramwell, A. 1994: *The fading of the greens*. New Haven: Yale University Press. · Carson, R. 1962: *Silent spring*. Boston: Houghton Mifflin. · Chaterjee, P. and Finger, M. 1994: *The earth brokers*. London: Routledge. · Ehrlich, P. 1968: *The population bomb*. New York: Ballantine Books. · Escobar, A. 1995: *Encountering development*. Princeton: Princeton University Press. · McCormick, J. 1989: *The global environmental movement*. London: Belhaven. · O'Riordan, T. 1981: *Environmentalism*. London: Pion. · Rowell, A. 1996: *Green backlash*. London: Routledge. · Shiva, V. 1993: The greening of the global reach. In W. Sachs, ed., *Global ecology*. London: Zed Books, 149–56.

Suggested Reading

Bowlby, S. and Lowe, M. 1992: Environmental and green movements. In A.M. Mannion and S. Bowlby, eds, *Environmental issues in the 1990s*. Chichester: Wiley, 161–75; McCormick (1989).

environmental perception The process whereby individuals and groups base their actions upon how they perceive their environment. As Brookfield (1969) put it, 'Decision-makers operating in an environment base their decisions on the environment as they perceive it, not as it is. The action resulting from decision, on the other hand, is played out in a real environment.' This contrast between the environment as perceived and as it is indicates the importance of actors' often idiosyncratic understandings of their surroundings in motivating their actions. Accordingly, the study of environmental perception in geography has long been important. Although the term suggests otherwise, environmental perception is not simply perception of the natural environment but includes built environments, other people, VALUES, cognition and aesthetics.

Perception studies in geography can be traced back to several traditions. Drawing upon environmental psychology, authors like Thomas Saarinen working on geographical study of ENVIRONMENTAL HAZARDS in the 1960s and 1970s sought to complicate the notion of the 'rational economic actor' inherited from NEO-CLASSICAL ECONOMIC models (cf. RATIONAL CHOICE THEORY). Apparently 'irrational' behaviour (e.g. occupying floodplains) could thus be seen as a response by occupants to the perceived opportunities and constraints of their environment. A second stream of research developed in HISTORICAL GEOGRAPHY and the study of geographical thought (cf. GEOGRAPHY, HISTORY OF). Here David Lowenthal, John K. Wright and others uncovered the variety of human perceptions of the environment as well as the importance of geographical ideas in explaining past human behaviour. Third, inspired by Kevin Lynch's (1960) *The image of the city*, urban and economic geographers developed a BEHAVIOURAL GEOGRAPHY in which the study of environmental perception was central and in which topics like MIGRATION, COMMUTING, place perception and MENTAL MAPS became important foci of research. Finally, the geographical study of CULTURAL ECOLOGY has long involved examining indigenous and folk perceptions of their environments. This cultural ecology was in part influenced by cross-cultural work by anthropologists on environmental cognition (cf. BERKELEY SCHOOL).

Environmental perception studies have made an important contribution to geographical knowledge. For instance, behavioural geographers, who drew heavily upon environmental psychology and cognition, developed an elaborate array of general categories which can describe and explain environmental perception in a variety of contexts. This was part of their commitment to making geography a SPATIAL SCIENCE, but it also paved the way for less analytical investigations into human perception and into HERMENEUTICS which are associated with HUMANISTIC GEOGRAPHY. Criticisms of perception studies have been methodological, empirical and theoretical. Methodological worries have been expressed about the reliability of techniques designed to elicit accurate representations of actors' perceptions and how those perceptions link to actual behaviour. Empirically, it has been shown that much perception research is overly focused on individuals, over-estimates their free agency and underplays the wider social structures which constrain behaviour, as in Watts' (1983) critique of HAZARD perception studies. This has led, thirdly, to calls for theoretical reconstructions of perception studies in order to integrate them with an appreciation of the STRUCTURATION of everyday thought and behaviour. NC

References
Brookfield, H. 1969: On the environment as perceived. *Progress in Geography* 1: 51–80. · Lynch, K. 1960: *The image of the city*. Cambridge, MA: MIT Press. · Watts. M. 1983: On the poverty of theory: natural hazards research in context. In K. Hewitt, ed., *Interpretations of a calamity*. Boston: Allen and Unwin, 231–60.

Suggested Reading
Aitken, S.C., Cutter, S.L., Foote, K.E. and Sell, J.L. 1989: Environmental perception and behavioural geography. In G.L. Gaile and C.J. Wilmott, eds, *Geography in America*. Columbus: Merrill, 218–38.

environmental psychology A branch of psychology that concerns itself with the interface between human behaviour and the natural and built environment; how people learn, process, store and act upon information relating to an environment. Unlike other areas of psychology which might be defined by their approach, such as cognitive or ecological psychology, environmental psychology is defined by its focus: how we understand the environment around us and REPRESENTATIONS of that environment (e.g. MAPS), and how we formulate and undertake actions within an environment. In this regard, there are strong links between the ideas and practice of environmental psychology and BEHAVIOURAL GEOGRAPHY (Kitchin et al., 1997). Both share a common history, focus of study, and techniques for collecting and analysing data.

Environmental psychology started to grow as a field enquiry in the late 1960s and by 1981 had its own specialist publication, *Journal of Environmental Psychology*. The focus of study relates to ENVIRONMENTAL PERCEPTION, spatial cognition of natural and built environments, and spatial behaviour. Techniques for generating and analysing data are generally POSITIVISTIC in nature, seeking to scientifically measure people's environmental attitudes, behaviours and cognition.

In both environmental psychology and behavioural geography people are seen as an integral part of every problem and the environment is defined and ordered through human actions (Gold, 1980). The most notable differences between the two concerns are: (1) *the* SCALE *of analysis*: environmental psychologists tend to use manageable, small-scale environments in their studies whereas behavioural geographers use environments ranging from the playground to the city-scale; (2) *the exact focus*: environmental psychologists are more likely to focus on identifying and understanding psychological processes whereas behavioural geographers are more interested in the application of those processes; and (3) *their relationship to their parent disciplines*: environmental psychology is an attempt to extend traditional psychological practice to new contexts; behavioural geography, on the other hand, is defined by its philosopical approach and not just its focus (Kitchin et al., 1997).

The links between environmental psychologists and behavioural geographers diminished in the late 1970s and early 1980s after the behavioural geographers largely failed to address criticisms from MARXIST and HUMANISTIC geographers. However, a number of new links and collaborative projects have once again been forged in the 1990s. These links have largely focused around issues of spatial cognition and how people understand spatial relations such as distance, direction, and the layout of objects. It is anticipated that such knowledge will explain people's spatial behaviour, help design geographic representations and technologies (e.g. GEOGRAPHICAL INFORMATION SYSTEMS) that are easier to comprehend, and provide information useful for planners and architects. These links are, however, limited in their scope and it remains to be seen whether links will be re-forged in relation to topics still popular within environmental psychology such as environmental perception, ENVIRONMENTAL HAZARDS, and spatial DECISION-MAKING. RMK

References
Gold, J.R. 1980: *An introduction to behavioural geography*. Oxford: Blackwell. · Kitchin, R.M., Blades, M. and Golledge, R.G. 1997: Relations between psychology and geography. *Environment and Behaviour* 29: 554–73.

Suggested Reading
Bonnes, M. and Secchiaroli, G. 1995: *Environmental psychology*. London: Sage. · Golledge, R.G. and Stimson, R.J. 1997: *Spatial behavior: a geographic perspective*. New York: Guildford Press. · Kitchin et al. (1997); *Readings in Environmental Psychology* (series editor David Canter): volumes on *Urban Cognition; Giving Places Meaning; Perceiving Environmental Risks; Landscape Perception; The Child's Environment*. London: Academic Press. · Stokols, D. and Altman, I. 1987: *Handbook of environmental psychology, volumes 1 and 2*. New York: John Wiley and Sons.

environmentalism '[R]efers to a concern that the environment should be protected, particularly from the harmful effects of human activities' (Milton, 1996, p. 27). Thus focused on human impacts on the environment, environmentalism is often thought to be a recent phenomenon, one particularly associated with the post-1960s era in North America and western Europe. In both continents, the contradictions between environment and economic development became apparent in resource depletion, pollution etc., sparking the rise of an ENVIRONMENTAL MOVEMENT inspired by such cautionary texts as Rachel Carson's *Silent spring* (1962) and Meadows et al.'s (1972) *The limits to growth* (cf. POLLUTION; LIMITS TO GROWTH). However, environmentalism is far older than the recent wave of environmental concern suggests. In fact, 'it is as old as human society itself' (Powell, 1996, p. 274), with societies across the world having long been preoccupied with their environmental impacts. In the West, Glacken (1967) traces this concern with human–environmental relations back to ancient Greece and identifies three modes of characterizing those relations: humanity in harmony with environment; humanity as determined by environment (see ENVIRONMENTAL DETERMINISM); and humanity as modifier of environment. In the modern era, the last of these has been the dominant element in environmentalism. In Europe and North America, this heightened concern over human modifications can be traced to the nineteenth century. In the rapidly industrializing US, 'preservationists' like John Muir and less radical 'conservationists' (see CONSERVATION) like Gifford Pinchot argued for more care in environmental usage, following George Perkins Marsh's germinal (1864) *Man and nature*. In Britain, the Romantics, like Blake and Shelley, early argued that NATURE possessed an inherent beauty and dignity that should be cherished, not destroyed.

Today, environmentalism encompasses a very wide range of ideas and practices and the term is, strictly speaking, 'too all-inclusive a concept' (O'Riordan, 1996, p. 473), and one must discriminate between different *environmentalisms*. O'Riordan (1996) distinguishes 'ecocentric' and 'technocentric' environmentalisms. The former puts the environment first, and suggests that modern societies should, to a greater or lesser degree, alter their economic practices in order to be more eco-friendly. Technocentrists, by contrast, are more human-centred – or anthropocentric – and believe that the environment can and should be rationally managed and controlled for human benefit. Ecocentrism thus poses more of a challenge to existing socio-economic arrangements, and is often associated with non-governmental groups (NGOs) in CIVIL SOCIETY. By contrast, technocentric environmentalism is a more status quo approach and often associated with big-business and government (see also ENERGY).

In practice, there are different types and degrees of eco- and technocentrism, and the most moderate permutations of both forms of environmentalism overlap. O'Riordan (1989) identifies two forms of eco- and technocentrist environmentalism respectively:

Gaianists derive their ideas from James Lovelock's theory that the earth's biosphere operates as if it were a single living organism which he calls Gaia, after the Greek earth goddess. The Gaia hypothesis proposes that organisms actively alter the biosphere, rather than merely adapting to it. Consequently, if humans continue to alter the biosphere too much then it is argued that Gaia will survive, but in a different form in which humans will have no part. This extreme – or 'DEEP ECOLOGY' – environmentalism urges a radical dismantling of existing socio-economic arrangements which are seen as ecologically destructive. A less extreme ecocentrist position is *communalism*, which argues for more harmony with nature in the form of small-scale, decentralized communities. On the technocentric side, *interventionists* – like Simon (1997) – argue that the environment can be successfully transformed for human benefit by science and technology and that any problems

Forms of Environmentalism

Ecocentrism		Technocentrism	
Gaianism	*Communalism*	*Accommodation*	*Intervention*
Faith in the rights of nature and of the essential need for co-evolution of human natural ethics.	Faith in the cooperative capabilities of societies to establish self-reliant communities based on renewable resource-use and appropriate technologies.	Faith in the adaptability of existing institutions and approaches to assessment to accommodate environmental demands.	Faith in the application science, market forces and managerial ingenuity to intervene in nature to create economic growth and overcome environmental problems.
Demand for redistribution of power towards decentralized, federated economy with more emphasis on informal socio-economic interactions and participatory justice.		Belief in the retention of the status quo in the existing structure of economic and political power, but a demand for more responsiveness and accountability in political regulatory, planning and educational institutions.	

Adapted from O'Riordan (1989)

which arise can be managed. *Accomodationists*, by contrast, are more cautious and argue that existing socio-economic arrangements must be adapted to minimize environmental problems.

Ecocentric environmentalism has become immensely influential since the early 1970s and for this reason has been called the 'new environmentalism'. In addition, this and technocentric environmentalism are no longer largely western preoccupations. Instead, they are now found worldwide, as more local and new global environmental problems have arisen.

Geography was defined by Halford Mackinder as the 'bridging science' which could study society–nature relations and, not surprisingly, geographers have made several contributions to modern environmentalism. One is to define and study environmentalism itself as a set of ideas and practices (see, for example, O'Riordan, 1996). Another is to examine the history of human uses of environment (see, for example, Mannion, 1991). A third contribution has been more practical, and linked to examining specific human–environment interactions. Inspired by HUMAN ECOLOGY in the US, RESOURCE MANAGEMENT in geography has long been involved in the formulation of environmental policy. On the whole, environmentalist thought and practice in geography has been broadly technocentric. However, a more radical tradition stretches back to communitarian Kropotkin's (1899) *Fields, factories and workshops*. In recent years, this radicalism has been renewed. In resource management, for example, a less technocentric approach to resource use has emerged (see Blaikie et al., 1994). Additionally, a new 'POLITICAL ECOLOGY' has been advocated by radical DEVELOPMENT geographers, who argue that environmental problems usually impact more on the poor and are caused by wider social and economic power relations. A '*liberation ecology*' (Peet and Watts, 1996), it is argued, should thus be about human, as much as it is about environmental, emancipation. NC

References

Blaikie, P., Cannon, T., Davis, I. and Wisner, B. 1994: *At risk*. London: Routledge. · Carson, R. 1962: *Silent spring*. Boston: Houghton Mifflin. · Glacken, C. 1967: *Traces on the Rhodian shore*. Berkeley, CA: University of California Press. · *Kropotkin, p. 1899: Fields, factories and workshops*. London: Freedom Press. · Meadows, D.H., Meadows, D.L., Randers, J. and Behrens, W. 1972: *The limits to growth*. New York: New American Library. · Powell, J.M. 1996: Origins of environmentalism. In I. Douglas, R. Huggett and M. Robinson, eds, *Companion encyclopaedia of geography*. London: Routledge, 274–92. · Mannion, A.M. 1991: *Global environmental change*. Harlow: Longman. · Marsh, G.P. 1964 [orig. pub. 1864]: *Man and nature*. Cambridge, MA: Harvard University Press; Milton, K. 1996: *Environmentalism and cultural theory*. London: Routledge. · O'Riordan, T. 1989: The challenge for environmentalism. In R. Peet and N. Thrift, eds, *New models in geography*, vol. 1. Boston: Unwin Hyman, 77–101. · O'Riordan, T. 1996: Environmentalism on the move. In I. Douglas, R. Huggett and M. Robinson, eds, *Companion encyclopaedia of geography*. London: Routledge, 449–69. · Peet, R. and Watts, M., eds, 1996: *Liberation ecologies*. Routledge: New York. · Simon, J. 1997: *The ultimate resource II*. Princeton: Princeton University Press.

Suggested Reading

Bowlby, S. and Lowe, M. 1992: Environmental and green movements. In A.M. Mannion and S. Bowlby, eds, *Environmental issues in the 1990s*. Chichester: Wiley, 161–75. · Pepper, D. 1996: *Modern environmentalism*. London: Routledge.

episteme A term coined by the French thinker Michel Foucault (1926–84) in his book *Les mots et les choses* (1966). An episteme is a conceptual grid that delimits the possibility of all knowledge (*savoirs*) in a given period and within which a culture orders the world and construes truth and reality. Foucault argued that knowledge is not built on a universal foundation and that the history of thought should not be written as a 'checklist' of innovations (Foucault, 1991; cf. FOUNDATIONALISM). Rather, he claimed, there are historically discontinuous 'systems of thought', and at any given time there are limits to what can be said, rules that govern what statements are deemed true and what knowledges are legitimate, and sets of links between different DISCOURSES and practices. Epistemes are the unconscious 'conditions of existence' of such limits, rules and links (Foucault, 1972).

On Foucault's account, an episteme is based on a culture's conception of *order* (how connections between words and things are made), *signs* (how knowledge is construed), and especially *language* (how truths are formulated from linguistic signs). Foucault identified three epistemes in western history: *a Renaissance episteme* (sixteenth-century), based on the *resemblances* between words and things, with one sign in the Book of Nature referring to others in a chain; *a Classical episteme* (mid-seventeenth to late eighteenth-century), founded on the *representation* of IDENTITIES and differences between things and the possibility of a 'general science of order' which would locate all natural and human phenomena on an ideal classificatory table; and *a Mod-*

ern episteme (nineteenth to mid-twentieth century), in which the unity of REPRESENTATION and thought 'shattered' and '*man*' was born as an object of knowledge and a knowing subject for whom representation exists. He also famously posited the imminent 'death of man' as the fulcrum of our thought. Foucault was concerned with the history of *western* thought, and when he adopted the labels 'classical' and 'modern' (rather than, say, 'early modern' or 'ENLIGHTENMENT') he had in mind the contrast between Ancien Régime and post-Revolutionary France.

Foucault saw great conceptual breaks in knowledge – especially in science and philosophy – where others had posited continuities, and he made deep – 'epistemic' – connections between disciplines that others had not seen. He was particularly concerned with the historical specificity of 'man' as the centrepiece of the modern episteme. He focused on the moment when, as Canguilhem (1994) aptly summarizes his thesis, 'life, work and language [three 'classical' domains of knowledge] ceased to be attributes of a [homogeneous] nature and became natures themselves, rooted in their own specific history' – natures and histories that could be studied by the empirical sciences (biology, economics and philology). Foucault also explored how modern philosophy, the human sciences (psychology, sociology and linguistics), and STRUCTURALIST 'counter-sciences' such as PSYCHOANALYSIS were founded on the attempt to conceptualize 'man' as a sovereign subject.

Les mots et les choses has caused considerable debate. Some have questioned whether the concept of 'man' is as central to modern thought as Foucault claims, and others have argued that his account of epistemes cannot account for its own objectivity and rationality, for if individual authors cannot see the epistemic arrangements underpinning their thought and LANGUAGE, then on what grounds does Foucault intuit and reconstruct an episteme? (see Habermas, 1987). On the other hand, anthropologists and geographers have drawn on Foucault's tripartite schema to clarify and question the ways in which concepts of NATURE and CULTURE, 'man' and science, entered their disciplines and were implicated in the history of IMPERIALISM and COLONIALISM (see, e.g., Claval, 1980; McGrane, 1989), and Foucault's work has alerted human scientists to the normative agendas embedded in their work – especially how they authorize specific models of the human subject (cf. HUMANISM; POST-STRUCTURALISM). DC

References

Canguilhem, G. 1994: The death of man, or exhaustion of the cogito? In Gutting, G., ed., *The Cambridge companion to Foucault*. Cambridge: Cambridge University Press, 47–70. · Claval P. 1980: Epistemology and the history of geographical thought. *Progress in Human Geography* 4: 371–84. · Foucault, M. 1970: *The order of things: an archaeology of the human sciences*. New York: Random House. Orig. pub. Fr. 1966: *Les mots et les choses*. · Foucault, M. 1972: *The archaeology of knowledge*, trans. A.M. Sheridan Smith. London: Tavistock Publications. Orig. pub. Fr. 1969: *L'Archéologie du savoir*. · Foucault, M. 1991: Politics and the study of discourse. In G. Burchall, C. Gordon and P. Miller, eds, *The Foucault effect: studies in governmentality*. London: Harvester Wheatsheaf, 53–72. Orig. pub. Fr. 1968. · Habermas, J. 1987: *The philosophical discourse of modernity*, trans. F. Lawrence. Cambridge, MA: The MIT Press. · lecture IX. Orig. pub. Ger. 1985: *Der philosophische diskurs der moderne*. · McGrane, B. 1989: *Beyond anthropology: society and the other*. Columbia: Columbia University Press.

Suggested Reading

Gutting, G. 1989: *Michel Foucault's archaeology of scientific reason*. Cambridge: Cambridge University Press.

epistemology Any theory of what constitutes valid knowledge; also the academic study of what constitutes valid knowledge. In the 1960s and 1970s modern human geography invoked 'epistemology' in both a general sense – to examine 'all geographical knowledge, scientific and other: how it is acquired, transmitted, altered and integrated into conceptual systems; and how the horizon of geography varies among individuals and groups' (Lowenthal, 1961) – and in a more particular sense to interrogate the 'claims to know' made by both positivism and non-positivist philosophies (Gregory, 1978). Until recently the dominant epistemologies in human geography were foundational (cf. FOUNDATIONALISM), and, like the critiques of them, both made systematic claims about the conditions that made knowledge possible and used those claims to adjudicate, decisively and unambiguously, between 'legitimate' and 'illegitimate' knowledges. These policing exercises were usually conducted under the authorizing (and authoritarian) sign of the philosophy of science – what Rorty called 'Philosophy with a capital P' (cf. PRAGMATISM) – and they included CRITICAL RATIONALISM, PHENOMENOLOGY, POSITIVISM, and REALISM.

The advance of POST-STRUCTURALISM in human geography has since radically revised discussions of epistemology within the discipline. Many scholars would now accept that (i) ONTOLOGY is 'grounded' in epistemology – that claims about how we know what the world is like underwrite claims about what the world is like; and (ii) that all epistemologies, however formal and abstract they might appear within academic DISCOURSE, are embedded in social practices. Critiques of the dominant epistemologies of human geography have drawn attention to a strategic intersection between VISION AND VISUALITY and the PRODUCTION OF SPACE, and revealed how the epistemological spaces of human geography (i) locate the authoritative position from which the world is to be seen, and (ii) provide the horizon within which it becomes possible for the world to be viewed in particular ('valid', 'intelligible', 'meaningful') ways.

Two examples help to clarify these claims. Rose (1993) suggests that in its HEGEMONIC forms the production of geographical knowledge is made to turn around a distanced and detached observer, constructed as an unmarked and unproblematized sovereign subject, whose rational gaze sweeps across an object world that can be made fully known and hence exhaustively mapped as a transparent space. Drawing in some part on Foucault's archaeologies of knowledge, Rose describes this project as a series of 'epistemic exclusions' which are conducted under the sign of MASCULINISM: they are implicated in the production of a masculinized 'space of the Same' that is constituted through – and hence depends upon – the identification and exclusion of a feminized 'space of the OTHER'. Rose insists that these are more than purely intellectual operations. For these exclusions 'are enacted by and impact on specific people' (and specifically women): thus the inhabitants of the 'space of the Other' are doubly marked as those who are not to know – because they are made to occupy a position outside that of the viewing subject – but who can none the less be known. This critique is a pivotal moment in Rose's construction of a FEMINIST GEOGRAPHY (see also Rose, 1995).

Similar cases have been made in relation to the other ways in which positions and horizons are marked. Thus Gregory (1994, 1998) advances a parallel argument about human geography's complicity in 'the world as exhibition' and its epistemic exclusions that were conducted under the sign of EUROCENTRISM and through the advance of a colonial, intrinsically colonizing MODERNITY. Following Mitchell (1988) – who was also indebted to Foucault – Gregory argues that, within this optic and from its dominant perspective, the certainty of REPRESENTATION that is held to be the guarantee of truth by foundational epistemologies turns on the establishment of a distance between a sovereign subject who is endowed with the authorized power to represent and a 'subject-ed' world which is to be represented. On one side is 'representation': mounted and staged from within the space of the world-as-exhibition, its horizon of possibility is mapped by the positivity of what Heidegger called 'the ground plan', from which the knowing subject is supposed to derive meaning, coherence and order. On the other side is 'reality': formed by 'the things-in-themselves', this is seen as 'a pristine realm existing prior to all representation', 'an external realm of pure existence', distinguished by an essential absence, namely 'the ground plan'. Within this epistemic framework, order not only becomes visible in opposition to the disorder of things: it is made to appear through a traverse from outside that at once reveals and represses its intrinsically colonizing powers (cf. ORIENTALISM). It is through the production of what, within Foucault's system of thought, can be construed as 'a space of constructed visibility' – through the practices that produce and sustain its exclusions, extensions and incursions – that the world is thus made open to a colonizing 'objectivity' that sanctions imperial measurement and regulation. This is not a detached exercise either; it is instead implicated in the epistemic violence of COLONIALISM (cf. POST-COLONIALISM).

Similar arguments could be made in relation to other markings, including the presumed CLASS position of the knowing subject. In every case, contributions like these re-describe the production of knowledge as always the production of a SITUATED KNOWLEDGE: always partial, imperfect, and constitutively implicated in relations of POWER. Dixon and Jones (1998) have generalized this emerging account of epistemology to argue that human geography, like the other mainstream humanities and social sciences, has been triangulated by three epistemologies (whose effects can be traced in the previous paragraphs). They are:

- *Cartesian perspectivalism*, 'which lineates the world with respect to a central point';
- *Ocularcentrism*, 'which privileges vision from an elevated vantage point from which the world may be surveilled in its totality' (cf. SURVEILLANCE); and
- *The epistemology of the grid*, 'a procedure for locating and segmenting social life so that it may be captured, measured and interrogated'.

Dixon and Jones focus on the third because it 'enables what has been lineated and seen to be segmented'. In their view, the 'epistemology of the grid' has generated 'the stable, stratified, hierarchical ontology' of SPATIAL ANALYSIS: indeed, they describe spatial analysis as the culmination of the grid epistemology within geography. The same emphasis on segmentation (cf. ABSTRACTION) and stratification can also be detected in the successor projects to SPATIAL SCIENCE conducted under the sign of REALISM. Dixon and Jones insist that these segmentations and stratifications have been embedded in our 'ways of living', which explains not only the 'success' of spatial analysis – 'the explanatory power of spatial analysis is due precisely to the deployment of the grid in the study of the grid' – but also the insidious powers of a much longer deployment of political technologies of space.

What are the implications of critiques like these for the production and interrogation of geographical knowledge? First, a reappraisal of the privileges that used to be accorded to 'Philosophy with a capital P' for its capacity to adjudicate unambiguously between competing claims to knowledge (Baynes, Bohman and McCarthy, 1987). There is little doubt that the parade of Philosophy through human geography that distinguished the discipline in the 1970s and 1980s seems to have become much less prevalent in the 1990s. Secondly, a suspicion towards totalizing accounts and an attentiveness to the production, proliferation and extension of 'LOCAL KNOWLEDGES' and 'insurgent knowledges' and their regimes of truth (Rouse, 1987; Barrett, 1991). Here too there are clear signs that human geography has responded to the critique of so-called GRAND THEORY and worried away at its own epistemic imperialism. Thirdly, a need to reconstruct the genealogies of segmentation, to question the categories that result, and to prise them open and insist on their contingent, interested and indefinite rather than 'defined', 'detached' and 'calibrated' status (Thrift, 1996). The history of concepts made little headway in human geography until recently, but there is now a much more general realization that 'posing questions to categories' is also posing questions to power: that 'the category is not only the result of power, it is also a condition for its deployment' (Dixon and Jones, 1998). Fourthly, a recognition of the ways in which knowledge is produced by embodied subjects so that it is irredeemably corporeal and not purely cognitive. Human geography's interest in the BODY is thus more than a cultural or political sensibility; it is also profoundly epistemological, and human geographers nurturing the roots of knowledge in embodiment will also require an awareness of those knowledges rooted in the erotic, pleasured body (Binnie, 1997; cf. QUEER THEORY).

Thrift (1996, pp. 32–5) includes most of these desiderata on his check-list of what he calls a weak epistemology for human geography and social inquiry: see NON-REPRESENTATIONAL THEORY. Rose (1997, p. 319) sharpens a similar point in an elegant and concise plea that summarizes the present, predominantly critical attitude towards traditional epistemology:

> We cannot know everything, nor can we survey power as if we can fully understand, control or redistribute it. What we may be able to do is something rather more modest but, perhaps, rather more radical: to inscribe into our research [and teaching] practices some absences and fallibilities, while recognizing that the significance of this does not rest entirely in our own hands.

DG

References

Barrett, M. 1991: *The politics of truth: from Marx to Foucault*. Cambridge: Polity Press; Stanford, CA: Stanford University Press. · Baynes, K., Bohman, J. and McCarthy, T., eds, 1987: *After Philosophy. End or transformation?* Cambridge, MA: MIT Press. · Binnie, J. 1997: Coming out of geography: towards a queer epistemology? *Environment and Planning D: Society and Space* 15: 223–38. · Dixon, D. and Jones, J.P. 1998: My dinner with Derrida, or spatial analysis and post-structuralism do lunch. *Environment and Planning A* 30: 247–60. · Gregory, D. 1978: *Ideology, science and human geography*. London: Hutchinson; New York: St. Martins Press. · Gregory, D. 1994: *Geographical imaginations*. Cambridge, MA and Oxford: Blackwell. · Gregory, D. 1998: Power, knowledge and geography. *Geographische Zeitschrift* 86: 70–93. · Haraway, D. 1991: Situated knowledges: the science question in feminism and the privilege of partial perspective. In her *Simians, cyborgs and women: the reinvention of nature*. London and New York: Routledge, 183–201. · Lowenthal, D. 1961: Geography, experience and imagination: towards a geographical epistemology. *Annals of the Association of American Geographers* 51: 241–60. · Mitchell, T. 1988: *Colonising Egypt*. Cambridge: Cambridge University Press. · Rose, G. 1993: *Feminism and geography: the limits of geographical knowledge*. Cambridge: Polity Press. · Rose, G. 1995: Distance, surface, elsewhere: a feminist critique of the space of phallocentric self/knowledge. *Environment and Planning D: Society and Space* 13: 761–81. · Rose, G. 1997: Situated knowledges: positionality, reflexivities and other tactics. *Progress in Human Geography* 21: 305–20. · Rouse, J. 1987: *Knowledge and power: toward a political philosophy of science*. Ithaca: Cornell University Press. · Thrift, N. 1996: *Spatial formations*. London and New York: Sage.

Suggested Reading

Barrett (1991). · Dixon and Jones (1998).

equality The same, in an arithmetic sense. Individual incomes are equal if people receive the same number of pounds, dollars or whatever in the same period of time. Equality in a geographical context is a more difficult concept because it is dependent on the nature and level of territorial aggregation adopted. For example, a set of regions may have the same income per capita and thus exhibit equality, while differences (inequality) may exist within them at a sub-regional or local level. Furthermore, equality among population aggregates at any spatial scale can obscure inequality among individuals and groups, such as racial minorities. (See also EGALITARIANISM; INEQUALITY, SPATIAL.) DMS

equilibrium A state in which the forces making for change are in balance. This concept is central to NEO-CLASSICAL ECONOMICS, where a free market working perfectly is supposed to tend towards a state of equilibrium. If the forces of supply and demand for all goods and services and all FACTORS OF PRODUCTION are balanced in such a way that all supply is consumed and all demand is met, and no participant(s) in the economy can derive any further income or satisfaction from doing anything other than what is presently done, this would constitute a state of equilibrium which would be maintained until a change took place, response to which would eventually restore equilibrium.

Suppose that, in a perfectly competitive economy in equilibrium, either the extraction of coal becomes more difficult or resources are depleted, and that the coal owners put up the price of coal so as to meet the rising cost of mining. As the consumption of coal is to some extent sensitive to its price, demand for coal is reduced. The mine owners may then find that they have coal unsold and reduce its price a little to get rid of it. Eventually the balance of forces of supply and demand will be regained by these market adjustments, at a point where the prevailing price just clears the stocks of coal supplied. Equilibrium will have been restored. This process may, of course, involve bringing back into balance other elements of the economy disturbed by change in the coal market, e.g. if there is less coal produced than before under the new state of equilibrium this may affect employment in mining, coal delivery and so on, while if the new market price is higher some customers may substitute other sources of fuel for coal.

In reality, an economy will be in a process of perpetual adjustment to change. Equilibrium is an ideal state never achieved in practice but helpful as a concept in the understanding of a market-regulated economy. A distinction is sometimes made between *general equilibrium*, which relates to the entire economy, and *partial equilibrium*, which refers to a single market or limited set of related activities.

Spatial equilibrium refers to balance in a spatially disaggregated economy. Change in such a system can be spatially selective; the rise in the price of coal may be confined to a specific region and restoration of equilibrium involves change and its repercussions working their way from place to place as well as from one market to another. The spatial version of neo-classical economics suggests the equalization of income as a feature of spatial equilibrium, since regional disparities in wages should encourage labour to move to regions where wages are highest and/or CAPITAL to move to regions where wages are lowest until equality is achieved and no advantage is to be obtained from further movement (see CONVERGENCE, REGIONAL). Just as imperfection in market mechanisms can frustrate the achievement of equilibrium in general so, in geographical space, obstacles to the free mobility of labour, capital and so on impede adjustment to wage and price differentials.

The concept of spatial equilibrium has been partly responsible for some misconceptions in regional development theory and planning practice. The terms equilibrium and balance have desirable connotations and the idea of a self-regulating space economy tending towards equalization of incomes encourages a view that market mechanisms are capable of promoting more even development if planners somehow harness them to a public purpose. However, the tendency of market economies under capitalism in reality is more one of CONCENTRATION AND CENTRALIZATION, characterized by UNEVEN DEVELOPMENT and inequality of living standards, especially in the undeveloped world. DMS

equity Fairness or justice. Equity may be manifest in EQUALITY, but the two are not necessarily synonymous. For example, it is widely accepted that payment by results or at different rates for different levels of skill and responsibility is fair. That social services should be distributed according to need is commonly held to be equitable; different levels of need can therefore justify unequal treatment. In a geographical context, equity in distribution among areas is achieved when any differences or departures from equality are proportional to differences in accepted entitlement such as need (see SOCIAL JUSTICE). DMS

error propagation A term applied to the effects of errors or uncertainties in geographic data, when those data are processed in a GEOGRAPHIC INFORMATION SYSTEM (GIS) to obtain useful results. Through analysis of error propagation, it is possible to determine the effects of errors and uncertainties on the results of analysis, in the form of confidence limits or probabilities that the results are correct. Because of the complexity of many forms of geographical analysis, and the widespread propensity to believe that the results of computer-based analysis are inherently right, the analysis of error propagation often leads to surprising and disturbing conclusions. Recent research efforts have concentrated on finding robust methods of error propagation analysis (Openshaw, 1989; Heuvelink, 1993); making results readily understandable by GIS users (Hunter and Goodchild, 1996); finding ways to visualize confidence limits (Ehlschlaeger et al., 1997); and incorporating error propagation into analyses of decision risk. MG

References

Ehlschlaeger, C.R., Shortridge, A.M. and Goodchild, M.F. 1997: Visualizing spatial data uncertainty using animation. *Computers and Geosciences* 23 (4): 387–95. · Heuvelink, G.B.M. 1993: *Error propagation in quantitative spatial modelling*. Utrecht: Faculteit Wetenschappen Universität Utrecht. · Hunter, G.J. and Goodchild, M.F. 1996: Communicating uncertainty in spatial databases. *Transactions in GIS* 1 (1): 13–24. · Openshaw, S. 1989: Learning to live with errors in spatial databases. In M.F. Goodchild and S. Gopal, eds, *Accuracy of spatial databases*. London: Taylor and Francis, 263–76.

essentialism The philosophical idea that all phenomena and events are reducible to fundamental and inviolable properties, *essences*, that determine their character. A failure to refer to those essential properties is a failure to know those phenomena or events at all. For example, one might argue, as Richard Hartshorne (1939) did, that the essence of geography is AREAL DIFFERENTIATION. Any work that makes no reference to areal differentiation, such as Fred Schaefer's (1953) based upon MORPHOLOGICAL laws, is then by definition not geographical, whatever Schaefer or anyone else might say. Rather, such work is economics or geometry or SOCIAL PHYSICS depending upon the respective essentialist definitions of those fields.

In SOCIAL THEORY essentialism is found in the privileging of particular causal factors within an explanation. As Resnick and Wolff (1987, p. 3) put it, 'essentialism is the presumption that among the influences producing any outcome, some can be shown to be *inessential* to its occurrence, while others will be shown to be *essential* causes'. For example, Marxism is often characterized as essentialist because of its economism, the idea that all events are ultimately determined by economic causes however distant they may appear from them. For example, in a memorable phrase, Marx and Engels said that religion is 'the opiate of the masses'. By that they meant that, however unlikely it seems, there is an ultimate economic cause of religious beliefs: to keep the working class in such a stupor that its members would never think of revolution (cf. MARXIAN ECONOMICS; MARXIST GEOGRAPHY).

Essentialism is found throughout geography in characterizations of human subjects (e.g. in HUMANISTIC GEOGRAPHY), geographical objects (e.g. the CITY), geographical concepts (e.g. PLACE and SPACE), spatial explanations (e.g. GRAVITY MODEL), and disciplinary definitions (e.g. areal differentiation). In recent years, under the sway of POST-STRUCTURALIST and anti-FOUNDATIONALIST philosophies (see DECONSTRUCTION), essentialism is criticized for not recognizing that definitions and explanatory theories are social practices reflecting both contingent conditions, and complicated relations of social interests and POWER.

As a result, anti-essentialist approaches are now increasingly found throughout the discipline, but they are especially marked in FEMINIST GEOGRAPHIES where essentialist definitions of GENDER are criticized; in SOCIAL GEOGRAPHY, and especially in studies of ETHNICITY and RACE; in CULTURAL GEOGRAPHY; and, perhaps most improbably, in ECONOMIC GEOGRAPHY, where the work of Gibson-Graham (1996) challenges the essentialism of Marxist CLASS categories, and the very essentialist definition of CAPITALISM itself. In their critique, Gibson-Graham make use of the idea of *overdetermination*, a notion drawn from the French philosopher, Louis Althusser, that holds that every event is caused by every other. In this overdetermined world, where causality has neither a beginning nor an end, economism, or any other 'ism' that starts with essential causes, has no purchase.

In contrast, there have been some writers even within the post-structural movement who argue that some form of essentialism is both inevitable and necessary. Spivak (1993, p. 15), for example, says that given the structure of western DISCOURSE into which we are socialized, essentialism is 'something one cannot

not use'. Furthermore, there can be compelling political reasons to deploy essentialist arguments strategically in order to mobilize support to change the world rather than simply to describe it. As Spivak (1990, p. 12) writes, 'You pick up the universal that will give you the power to fight against the other side, and what you are throwing away by doing that is your theoretical purity'. TJB

References
Gibson-Graham, J.K. 1996: *The end of capitalism (as we knew it). A feminist critique of political economy.* Oxford: Blackwell. · Hartshorne, R. 1939: *The nature of geography: a critical survey of current thought in light of the past.* Lancaster, PA: Association of American Geographers. · Resnick, S. and Wolff, R. 1987: *Knowledge and class: A Marxian critique of political economy.* Chicago: Chicago University Press. · Schaefer, F.K. 1953: Exceptionalism in geography: a methodological examination. *Annals of the Association of American Geographers* 43: 226–49. · Spivak, G.C. 1990: *The post-colonial critics: interviews, strategies, dialogues.* London: Routledge. · Spivak, G.C. 1993: *Outside in the teaching machine.* London: Routledge.

Suggested Reading
Gibson-Graham (1996), ch. 2.

ethics, geography and Ethics (or moral philosophy) is the systematic study of morality, concerned with what it is to make a moral judgement. Moral judgements are evaluative, involving the question of good or bad, better or worse. They are also reasoned, consistent and conclusive, in the sense that what is morally right is what should be done (though not necessarily what will actually be done). All evaluative judgements are not moral judgements and hence the concern of ethics, e.g. to use a knife to eat peas may be judged bad manners but not immoral, whereas to use a knife to kill someone may be judged bad in a moral sense, unless it is a legal execution (in which case some people may still consider it immoral). Similarly, to catch a train I ought to arrive at the station in time (i.e. it is the right thing to do), but this is not a matter of morality (unless missing the train would mean failing to keep a promise to someone, for example). What is a moral or ethical issue is itself an unresolved philosophical question.

Geography has a long-standing concern with ethical or moral issues, including the question of how geography itself should be practised. However, the explicit recognition of normative content to geography, as a major professional preoccupation, may be dated back to the RADICAL GEOGRAPHY of the late 1960s and early 1970s. This concern continued through the era of captivation with Marxism which followed (see MARXIST GEOGRAPHY), and onto the disquiet about the various groups of disadvantaged or marginalized 'others' which built up during the 1980s. However, substantial publications with a strong ethical or moral focus were rare (Harvey, 1973; Buttimer, 1974; Smith, 1977; Mitchell and Draper, 1982; Tuan, 1986, 1989).

The 1990s saw an awakening of interest in the interface between geography and ethics, otherwise known as moral philosophy. This was interpreted as part of a 'normative turn' in social theory more generally (Sayer and Storper, 1997). Indications included special sessions at meetings of the Institute of British Geographers and the Association of American Geographers, and the publication of a new journal *Ethics, Place and Environment.* Sack has incorporated a prominent moral perspective in his framework for understanding *homo geographicus*, claiming that geography is at the foundation of moral judgement: 'Thinking geographically heightens our moral concerns; it makes clear that moral goals must be set and justified by us in places and as inhabitants of a world' (Sack, 1997, p. 24).

What distinguishes the contemporary geography and ethics movement is a much greater determination than in the past to look outwards. This involves a direct engagement with the fields of ethics or moral philosophy, with the 'articulation of the moral and the spatial', first clearly signalled in the proceedings of a conference organized by the Social and Cultural Geography Study Group of the IBG (Philo, 1991).

Differences are sometimes imputed to the meaning of 'ethics' and 'morals' (or 'morality'), associated with different usage conventions. For example, it is customary to refer to professional *ethics* (like medical ethics), but to conduct in some other spheres of life as *morality* (e.g. sexual morality). However, in the present context both terms are taken to mean the same: having to do with evaluation of human conduct, with what is considered right or wrong, good or bad, in the senses of what people ought or ought not to do and the quality of their actions or characters, in contexts which are not merely matters of etiquette or prudence. The ethics of professional practice in geography (and other fields) is somewhat distinct from broader issues of moral conduct, and is treated separately (see PROFESSIONAL ETHICS).

A common division within the academic disciplines or intellectual practices described as ethics or moral philosophy is between *descriptive ethics*, which identifies actual moral beliefs and practices, *normative ethics*, which proposes solutions to moral problems, and *meta-ethics*, concerned what it means to think or practise ethics.

The broadest (and deepest) of these is meta-ethics, sometimes referred to as theoretical as opposed to applied or practical ethics. It concerns questions which it would be helpful to resolve, or at least consider, before solutions are proposed for particular moral problems. Thus, meta-ethics is concerned with the meaning of such terms as good and bad, right and wrong, ought or should, in a moral context, with trying to explain the fact that people hold moral views, and more generally with what moral argument is all about.

There are enormous differences among philosophers writing on meta-ethics. Smith (1994, pp. 3–4) provides a sample:

> We are told that engaging in moral practice presupposes that there exist moral facts, and that this presupposition is an error... And we are told that moral commitment involves no such error...
>
> We are told that moral facts exist, and that these facts are ordinary facts, not different in kind from those that are the subject matter of science... And we are told that moral facts exist, and that these facts are *sui generis* [unique]... We are told that moral facts exist and are part of the causal explanatory network ... And we are told not just that moral facts play no role in the causal explanatory network, but that there are no moral facts at all... We are told that there is an internal and necessary connection between moral judgement and the will... And we are told that there is no such connection, and that the connection between moral judgement and the will is altogether external and contingent... We are told that moral requirements are requirements of reason... And we are told that it is not necessarily irrational to act immorally, that moral evaluation is different in kind from the evaluation of people as rational or irrational... We are told that morality is objective, that there is a single 'true' morality... And we are told that morality is not objective, that there is no single true morality...

The missing text indicated by dots names numerous writers associated with the various positions identified. Theoretical diversity is expressed in competing 'isms', representing divergent and often seemingly incompatible schools of thought. These include REALISM (the view that there is an objective moral reality), *intuitionism* (that we can know moral truth by a kind of intuition), NATURALISM (that moral truth can be known from some other property), *subjectivism* (that moral views are personal opinions and not objective truth), RELATIVISM (that morality is relative to a particular society or culture), and *universal prescriptivism* (which give prominence to reasoning about ethical judgements).

The most obvious meta-ethical question with which geographers can (and do) engage is that of *relativism*. The moral codes which people have devised and observe (or otherwise) vary from place to place – i.e. what is good and what is right is to some extent relative to place (and to time), or specific to a particular CULTURE: examples include inherited titles, differentiated life chances according to ETHNICITY or RACE, women being expected to obey men, and 'arranged' marriages. However, some values do seem to be held very widely, even universally: examples include the virtues of courage and honesty, and of special consideration towards the weak or needy. A major unresolved question is therefore whether it is possible to discover or invent ways of judging some moral code(s) as better or worse than some other(s). In other words, are there some universal, trans-historic (and -geographic) moral standards by which those of particular societies can be compared and ranked? That there are such standards was a fundamental tenet of the ENLIGHTENMENT, which has been challenged in this era of what some consider postmodernity. If there are some grand, universal ideals, like justice and liberty, to which all human beings could be expected to subscribe, then these will be rather vague, or 'thin' (Walzer, 1994). An important task for geography is therefore to examine their contextual thickening, or what they have come to mean to particular people in place and time.

Sack's moral perspective on *homo geographicus* involves adopting a point of view away from local particularity. Transcending partiality is part of growing up, of expanding horizons, of knowing more about the world and its peoples and the consequences of our actions. Thus, his approach is informed by a perspective 'that strives to be rational and realistic, but takes the necessity of our differences and situatedness seriously – navigating between the arrogance of modernity and the relativizing tendencies of postmodernity' (Sack, 1997, p. 7; cf. SITUATED KNOWLEDGE). The most graphic expression of the moral significance of place is in Sack's recurrent image of thick and thin. As boundaries become porous, this changes the thicker places of premodern society, with their strongly partial moral codes. Thus, 'the local and contextual should be thin and porous enough not to interfere with our ability to attain an expanded view, and the local can be understood and accorded respect only if people attain a more objective perspective, enabling them to see beyond their own partiality and to be held responsible for this larger domain' (Sack, 1997, p. 248).

The study of MORAL GEOGRAPHIES has emerged in recent years, covering various kinds of empirical investigations into aspects of spatial patterns and relationships which invite a moral reading. Philo (1991, p. 16) comments on this application of a 'moral lens' to human geography as follows:

> such an investigation will take us towards the moral 'relativists', in that we will seek to establish the geography *of* everyday moralities given by the different moral assumptions and supporting arguments that particular peoples in particular places make about 'good' and 'bad' / 'right' and 'wrong' / 'just' and 'unjust' / 'worthy' and 'unworthy'. There can be little doubt that these assumptions and arguments *do* vary considerably from one nation to the next, from one community to the next, and one street to the next.

Work on moral geographies has become common enough to stimulate sections in *Progress in Human Geography* reviews of both social and cultural geography (Matless, 1995) and political geography (O'Tuathail, 1996). Some writers prefer the terms MORAL LANDSCAPES and MORAL ORDER, or moral terrain' and 'moral location'.

There are links here with the work of Sibley (1995) and others on boundaries, movement and social exclusion. Sibley asks who places are for, who do they exclude, and how are these prohibitions maintained in practice: 'Exclusionary discourse draws particularly on colour, disease, animals, sexuality and nature, but they all come back to the idea of dirt as a signifier of imperfection and inferiority, the reference point being the white, often male, physically and mentally able person'. As mixing carries the threat of contamination, spatial boundaries are in part 'moral boundaries', with spatial separation symbolizing 'moral order' – as in the case of 'ethnic cleansing'. Who belongs is an important moral aspect of community (Smith, 1998b).

Another moral issue in which geography is clearly implicated is whether, and to what extent, distance makes a difference to how people should be treated by others. This is a question which has been considered directly in papers by scholars from outside geography (Vetlesen, 1993; Ginzburg, 1994), as well as less directly in elaborations of an ethic of care. There is a contradiction between what might appear to be the natural human sentiment of care relating which favour our nearest and dearest of family, friends and community members, who are likely to be close geographically as well as emotionally, and the Enlightenment ideal of impartiality which suggests universal beneficence. How these tensions might be resolved has been explored in a discussion of how far (in a literal geographical sense) we should care for others (Smith, 1998a). This issue links into development ethics, which involves responsibility to distant strangers (Corbridge, 1993, 1998).

There are many other issues being explored at the interface of geography and ethics. Ongoing research into questions of RACE, GENDER and SEXUALITY raise moral questions, including what kind of people and interpersonal relationships are considered to belong where. This might be construed as part of the subject of SOCIAL JUSTICE; indeed it is difficult, and ultimately not very fruitful, to try to resolve where the boundary between ethics and social justice in geography should be drawn. Renewed interest in social justice (e.g. Smith, 1994; Harvey, 1996) is part of the broader normative turn which has brought ethical issues to the fore. And the presence of a strong emphasis on environmental ethics (see ENVIRONMENTAL JUSTICE) is ensuring that the almost exclusively human focus of the concern with social justice during the era of radical geography is not repeated.

Among the questions raised by the geography and ethics movement is whether there is a distinctive role for the geographer in the difficult terrain of moral thinking and practice. At the very least, growing familiarity with work in moral philosophy should make geographers circumspect when it comes to their own value judgements, or supporting the judgements of other (in city, regional and development planning, for example). Contributions to meta-ethics may be best left to philosophers, more familiar than any geographer is likely to be with a vast and tortuous literature. The most obvious, and promising, scope for geography is probably in recognizing, emphasizing and seeking to understand something philosophers often appear to overlook: the diversity of humankind, and of the settings in which practical answers have to be found to the problems of conflicting aspirations, and values, in the practice of making a living together. DMS

References

Buttimer, A. 1974: *Values in Geography*. Washington, D.C.: Association of American Geographers, Commission on College Geography, Resource Paper 24. · Corbridge, S. 1993: Marxisms, modernities, and moralities: development praxis and the claims of distant strangers.

Environment and Planning D: Society and Space 11: 449–72. · Corbridge, S. 1998: Development ethics: distance, differenece, plausibility. *Ethics, Place and Environment* 1: 35–53. · Ginzburg, C. 1994: Killing a Chinese mandarin: the moral implications of distance. *New Left Review* 208: 107–20. · Harvey, D. 1973: *Social Justice and the City*, London: Edward Arnold. · Harvey, D. 1996: *Justice, nature and the geography of difference*. Oxford: Blackwell. · Matless, D. 1995: Culture run riot? Work in social and cultural geography, 1994. *Progress in Human Geography* 19: 395–403. · Mitchell, B. and Draper, D. 1982: *Relevance and Ethics in Geography*. London: Longman. · O'Tuathail, G. 1996: Political geography II: (counter) revolutionary times. *Progress in Human Geography* 20: 404–12. · Philo, C., ed., 1991: *New Words, New Worlds: Reconceptualising Social and Cultural Geography*. Lampeter: Department of Geography, St. David's University College. · Proctor, J.D. 1998: Ethics in geography: giving moral form to the geographical imagination. *Area* 30: 8–18. · Sack, R.D. 1997: *Homo geographicus: A framework for action, awareness, and moral concern*. Baltimore and London: The Johns Hopkins University Press. · Sayer, A. and Storper, M. 1997: Ethics unbound: for a normative turn in social theory. *Environment and Planning D: Society and Space* 15: 1–17. · Sibley, D. 1995: *Geographies of exclusion: society and difference in the west*. London: Routledge. · Smith, D.M. 1977: *Human geography: a welfare approach*. London: Edward Arnold. · Smith, D.M. 1994: *Geography and social justice*. Oxford: Blackwell. · Smith, D.M. 1998a: How far should we care? On the spatial scope of beneficence. *Progress in Human Geography* 22: 15–38. · Smith, D.M. 1998b: Geography, morality and community. *Environment and Planning A* 31, 19–35. · Smith, M. 1994: *The Moral Problem*. Oxford: Blackwell. · Tuan, Y.F. 1986: *The Good Life*. Minneapolis, MN: University of Minnesota Press. · Tuan, Y.-F. 1989: *Morality and imagination: paradoxes of progress*. Madison: University of Wisconsin Press. · Vetlesen, A.J. 1993: Why does proximity make a moral difference? Coming to terms with lessons learned from the Holocaust. *Praxis International* 12: 371–86. · Walzer, M. 1994: *Thick and thin: moral argument at home and abroad*. Notre Dame and London: University of Notre Dame Press.

Suggested Reading

Proctor, J.D. 1998: Ethics in geography: giving moral form to the geographical imagination. *Area* 30: 8–18. · Proctor, J.D. and Smith, D.M., eds, 1999: *Geography and ethics: Journeys in a moral terrain*. London and New York: Routledge. · Singer, P., ed. 1991: *A companion to ethics*. Oxford: Blackwell. · Smith, D.M. 1997: Geography and ethics: a moral turn? *Progress in Human Geography* 21: 596–603. · Smith, D.M. 1998c: Geography and moral philosophy: some common ground. *Ethics, Place and Environment* 1: 7–34.

ethnic cleansing A form of mass genocide associated with the violent removal of an ethnic group from a particular political space or homeland in order to secure spatial homogenization and the subsequent colonization by the perpetrating STATE or ethnic group. In the case of the Jewish Holocaust, in which six million European Jews perished as a result of Nazi policies of ethnic cleansing, this end-stage was achieved in three stages: first, the denial of CITIZENSHIP; second, forced ghettoization (see GHETTO) into particular parts of cities; and, finally, transportation to death camps. A distinction should be made between state and FRONTIER ethnic cleansing (McGarry and O'Leary, 1993; Palmer, 1998). The former – *state genocide* – is more likely to occur when: (a) an empire is being constructed and maintained (e.g. Nazi Germany: cf. IMPERIALISM); (b) a racialized ideology can be appropriated in which the ends justify the means; (c) an ethnic COMMUNITY lacks geo-political resources (e.g. Muslims in Bosnia and Kosovo; Jews in Nazi Germany); (d) a subordinate ethnic community is left vulnerable within a disintegrating system of control, whether organized by an empire or authoritarian state (e.g. former Yugoslavia); and (e) the relevant state is not democratic. In contrast, in *frontier genocide* the state or empire may not be directly implicated. Here, settlers possess technologically superior resources to 'clear' victims from their homelands. Besides understanding the rationality of the perpetrators and of how they ethnicize or racialize the victim as 'the other', one other main issue concerns the role that 'bystanders' play in a phenomenon such as the Holocaust (e.g. Cole and Smith, 1995).

GES

References and Suggested Reading

Bauman, Z. 1989: *Modernity and the Holocaust*. Cambridge: Cambridge University Press. · Bell-Fialkoff, A. 1993: A Brief history of ethnic cleansing. *Foreign Affairs*, 72 (3): 110–21. · Cole, T. and Smith. G. 1995: Ghettoisation and the Holocaust. Budapest 1944. *Journal of Historical Geography* 21 (3): 300–18. · Hayden, R. 1996: Imagined communities and real victims of self-determination and ethnic cleansing in Yugoslavia. *American Ethnologist*, 23 (4): 783–801. · McGarry, B. and O'Leary, B., eds, 1993: *The politics of ethnic conflict regulation*. London: Routledge; Palmer, A. 1998: Colonial and modern genocide: explanations and categories. *Ethnic and Racial Studies* 21 (1): 89–115.

ethnic democracy A mode of CONFLICT regulation in which a particular ethnic or national segment of a polity enjoys a HEGEMONIC position and status within a multicultural polity (cf. MULTICULTURALISM), justified on the basis of its claim to have a privileged ancestral relationship to its political homeland, and in which this self-selective group regards minority ethnic groups as having relatively less claim and as not being fully loyal (cf. ETHNICITY). Such a regime also contains elements of DEMOCRACY and should therefore not be confused with a system of social APARTHEID: thus individual civil rights exist universally throughout its TERRITORY, and certain collective rights are extended to ethnic minorities. It also differs from a CONSOCIATIONAL form of ethnic management. Current examples of polities regarded as ethnic democracies include Israel, Estonia, Latvia, and Malaysia. GES

Suggested Reading

Smith, G. 1996: The ethnic democracy thesis and the citizenship question in Estonia and Latvia. *Nationalities Papers* 24 (2): 199–216. · Smooha, S. 1990: Minority status in an ethnic democracy: the status of the Arab minority in Israel. *Ethnic and Racial Studies* 13 (3): 389–413. · Yiftachel, O. 1993: The concept of 'ethnic democracy' and its applicability to the case of Israel. *Ethnic and Racial Studies* 15 (1): 125–36.

ethnicity This is one of the most difficult concepts in the social sciences to define: researchers disagree on the meaning of the term; social groups differ in their expressions of ethnicity; and some theorists challenge the credibility of the concept in the first place (see Banks, 1996). The etymology of this term dates back to ancient Greece, where the word *ethnos* was used to refer to a distinct 'people'. The word ethnic originally entered the English language as an adjective applied to non-Judeo-Christian peoples. The first instance of the word ethnicity used as a noun occurred in the early 1940s, when researchers sought to find a replacement for the word 'RACE' once it had become associated with the genocidal policies of the Nazi party. In contemporary usage, ethnicity is seen as both a way in which individuals define their personal identity and a type of social stratification that emerges when people form groups based on their real or perceived origins. Members of ethnic groups believe that their specific ancestry and CULTURE mark them as different from others. As such, ethnic group formation always entails both inclusionary and exclusionary behaviour, and ethnicity is a classic example of the distinction people make between 'us' and 'them' (cf. OTHER/OTHERNESS).

While much attention was given to theories of ethnicity and the nature of ethnic groups in the early twentieth century, especially in the US (see CHICAGO SCHOOL), interest waned in the post-war period. The LIBERALISM that came to dominate the intellectual climate by mid-century was predicated on a belief in the autonomy of individuals. Within the discourse of liberal individualism, the notion that people modify their actions because of their ethnic loyalties is suspect, and generally considered a fading remnant of pre-modern times. The version of Marxism that challenged liberalism in the late 1960s was equally dismissive of ethnicity, claiming that ethnic attachments were fostered by capitalists and the STATE in order to divide the working class (e.g. Bonacich, 1972). By the 1970s, many leading social theorists had abandoned the study of ethnicity, associating it with antiquated views of society and conservative politics. This dismissive attitude began to change in the 1980s, however, when it became clear ethnicity was not losing its salience; on the contrary, IDENTITY POLITICS were on the rise and ethnic NATIONALISM had become a primary force in the most violent struggles around the world, especially in the post-Cold-War era – a turn of events unanticipated by liberal and marxist scholars alike (Kimmel, 1996). The fact that over 90 per cent of the world's NATION-STATES are poly-ethnic suggests that this type of conflict is likely to continue (see also MULTICULTURALISM).

Still, much confusion surrounds the concept of ethnicity. Two misconceptions are particularly common. First, *many use the term only to refer to minority groups*, assuming that people in the majority are 'normal' while everyone else is 'ethnic'. While this usage of the term was considered acceptable in the nineteenth century, it is no longer correct. In fact, everyone has an ethnic background, whether or not it is acknowledged. In most situations, people can only afford to be unaware of their ethnicity when they are in a privileged position (see WHITENESS).

A second *ambiguity arises when the terms ethnicity and race are used interchangeably*, or when they are seen as variants of the same classification system. For example, it is often thought that the people can be divided into three or four broad racial groups and that each has a number of ethnic sub-divisions (e.g. race = Caucasian, ethnicity = Italian). However, it is exceedingly difficult – many believe impossible – to discern discrete 'races': the genetic mixing of human populations defies such a simplistic classification system. While there are obvious phenotypical and genetic differences between people, there is only one human race, a point emphatically made by the United Nations. Throughout history, though, people have been racialized by others for particular reasons. Most commentators agree that racialization is necessarily a negative process, where one group chooses to define another as morally and/or genetically inferior in order to dominate and oppress it (cf. MORAL ORDER): racialization is always an imposed category. Phenotypical features, such as skin colour or facial structure, are then interpreted as evidence that the two groups are indeed separate 'types' of people and are used strategically to demark the boundaries between groups (cf. APARTHEID). Once defined, such boundaries are extremely difficult to cross. Racialized minorities become ethnic groups when they achieve social solidarity on the basis of their distinct culture and background. Racialization therefore facilitates the development of ethnic consciousness, which may be harnessed by minorities in their struggle against discrimination (e.g. the Black Power movement of the 1960s in the US or the Palestinian Intifadah), but does not necessarily lead to ethnic group formation. While external forces are important in the generation of ethnic consciousness, the most basic difference between race and ethnicity is that ethnic affiliation arises from inside a group; ethnicity is a process of self-definition.

However, ethnicity is not uniformly important to all people: the degree of ethnic identity and attachment varies strongly between and within societies. Many of the most cohesive ethnic groups have emerged after the conquest of a TERRITORY by an external power. In these cases ethnic attachment and nationalism are powerfully fused as people affiliate to ensure the survival of their culture, religious practices, and access to employment opportunities. The goal in these struggles is usually political independence. Occasionally, tensions in poly-ethnic states become so extreme that ethnic loyalty becomes the overriding social force shaping the polity. The genocide of Jews in Nazi Germany is a repugnant example of this tendency, as are the recent attempts at 'ETHNIC CLEANSING' (the forced removal of all minorities from an area) in parts of the former Yugoslavia. MIGRATION is another impetus for the development of heightened ethnic consciousness. Immigrants often face hostility within the societies they enter, and form ethnic bonds and associations to increase their political credibility. Whereas conquered groups tend to fight for independence, diasporic groups fight for the right to be included in their new societies as equal participants.

Acknowledging the variability of ethnic affiliation, theorists have long debated the causes of ethnic identity and division. Two distinct views dominate the literature: ethnicity as primordial, or absolute, vs. ethnicity as constructed, as the outcome of other social processes (Jenkins, 1996). Those advocating the former see ethnicity as a basic form of affiliation that naturally emerges as people are socialized into cultures with long histories; children are born into ethnic groups and develop deep-seated attachments to them. The most extreme primordial position is taken by socio-biologists, who believe that ethnicity is a legacy of the struggle for food and shelter (Van den Berghe, 1981). In this controversial perspective, ethnic solidarity is seen as an extension of the biologically driven feelings that link individuals to their nuclear family and kin. These researchers find it difficult to explain why some people place little value on their ethnic origin and culture while others choose to express their ethnicity even when it is disadvantageous to do so.

Researchers advocating constructionist views, conversely, assert that ethnic attachments arise in specific contexts, for specific reasons. Marxists, as mentioned, often minimize the importance of ethnicity by arguing that it is a displaced form of CLASS consciousness. In its crudest form, this argument implies a rigid INSTRUMENTALISM wherein the STATE, viewed as a tool of the capitalist class, enacts colonial and IMMIGRATION policies designed to create differences within the working class in order to fragment its solidarity (Bonacich, 1994; cf. COLONIALISM). More sophisticated Marxist treatments of ethnicity have emerged in light of growing ethnic and nationalist movements in the late twentieth century; even these, however, tend to portray ethnicity as a regressive force deflecting people from their 'real' material interests (Williams, 1995).

Another variant of the constructionist view emphasizes the relational causes of ethnic identification – that is, ethnic groups acquire their identity not alone, but in relation to one another. For example, early twentieth-century immigrants from the southern Italian peninsula to North America brought the parochial loyalties of their village origins (see CHAIN MIGRATION); in their new, displaced context, however, these local affiliations were united into a broad consciousness of being 'Italian'. This emergent ethnicity was the product of a host of factors, including similar religious expressions, common languages, geopolitical events, occupational segmentation, residential SEGREGATION and the way in which these immigrants were perceived and categorized as Italians by others around them (Yancey et al., 1976). The constructionist view is also best suited to explain the ways that identity shifts as circumstances change. For example, a person can legitimately identify her/himself as English in the United Kingdom, British in other European countries,

European in Asia, and 'white' in Africa. However, while constructionist theories help us understand the variability of ethnic attachments and identities, their very flexibility make it impossible to develop a systematic account of ethnicity. In fact, the very factors that cause ethnic consciousness to emerge in some contexts impede it in others.

Over time, ethnic solidarity may be perpetuated or may dissipate. The processes governing the dynamic between cultural retention vs. ASSIMILATION are exceedingly complex, but researchers generally agree that the nature of the social boundaries between ethnic groups is critical. Boundaries are maintained when individuals maximize their interactions with those within their ethnic group while minimizing their interactions with others. This occurs when separate social, political and educational institutions are established within different groups. According to Fredrik Barth (1969), boundaries created between groups can be resilient even when the cultural practices of the groups are no longer distinctive. In many cases ethnic boundaries become entrenched in space, such as in the formation of ethnic neighbourhoods in cities.

Geographers have shown a long-standing interest in documenting the causes and consequences of urban ethnic segregation. Much of this work stems from the conceptualization of HUMAN ECOLOGY articulated by Robert Park and other members of the CHICAGO SCHOOL in the early twentieth century. During the 1960s, attention focused on plotting ethnic 'GHETTOES', devising ways to measure the degree of ethnic segregation (see INDICES OF SEGREGATION), and formulating PUBLIC POLICY to integrate ethnic and racialized groups across the city. By the end of the decade, a concern for ethnic residential patterns entered the mainstream of urban theory and increasingly sophisticated models of urban land use were devised. This type of work has came under intense criticism since the 1970s. On the one hand, the relationship between the degree of social tolerance and residential patterns is not entirely clear; that is, a high level of segregation is not necessarily the result of discrimination, just as residential mixing does not necessarily indicate the absence of discrimination (see Peach, 1996). On the other hand, studies of segregation have relied almost exclusively on census data. Ethnicity is defined in most censuses by respondents' national or 'racial' origin, and is therefore a poor indicator of ethnic affiliation (e.g. all those of Polish descent are lumped into the same category, whether or not they identify with that cultural heritage; see Petersen, 1997). Furthermore, such classification of people perpetuates the idea that there are distinct races, and the CENSUS itself may be implicated in the racialization of minorities. Given these criticisms, the number and significance of quantitative studies of ethnicity declined in the 1980s. However, this type of work has been somewhat revived in the 1990s as the number of immigrants in European and North American cities has increased and as immigration policy has become more intensely debated.

Geographers have also devoted considerable energy into examining the racialization process, especially as it impinges on people's access to housing and the labour market (e.g. Anderson, 1991; Jacobs, 1996). The regulatory practices of government are highlighted in this work because immigration, housing, employment EQUITY and other policies directly affect the way individuals experience discrimination and ethnic or racial difference. While this research has led to important insights, it has tended to ignore social processes operating within groups; that is, discrimination and racialization are emphasized without a corresponding interest in the agency of individuals to create ethnic consciousness and use this to struggle against domination (Leitner, 1992; also see IDENTITY POLITICS).

Geographers have also begun to examine the intersections between ethnicity and other forms of personal identity and stratification, notably CLASS and GENDER. Here emphasis is placed on which dimension of identity affects all others; for example, MASCULINITY and femininity may well be defined and lived differently in different ethnic groups (cf. FEMINIST GEOGRAPHIES). This type of investigation is both conceptually difficult, since researchers must study many facets of experience and social structure simultaneously, and controversial, since it destabilizes traditional definitions of class and gender. DH

References

Anderson, K.J. 1991: *Vancouver's Chinatown: racial discourse in Canada, 1875–1980.* Montréal and Kingston: McGill–Queen's University Press. · Banks, M. 1996: *Ethnicity: anthropological constructions.* London: Routledge. · Barth, F. 1969: Introduction. In F. Barth, ed., *Ethnic groups and boundaries: the social organization of cultural difference.* Boston: Little, Brown and Co. 9–38. · Bonacich, E. 1972: A theory of ethnic antagonism: The split labor market. In I.L. Horowitz, J.C. Leggett and M. Oppenheimer, eds, *The American Working class: Prospects for the 1980s.* New Brunswick, NJ: Transaction Books, 73–93. · Bonacich, E. 1994: Thoughts on urban unrest. In F.L. Pincus and H.J. Ehrlich, eds, *Race and ethnic conflict*. Boulder: Westview Press, 404–7. · Esman, M.J. 1994: *Ethnic politics*. Ithaca and London: Cornell University Press. · Jacobs, J.M. 1996: *Edge of empire: postcolonialism and the city*. London and New York: Routledge. · Jenkins, R. 1996. Ethnicity etcetera: social anthropological points of view. *Ethnic and Racial Studies* 19: 807–22. · Kimmel, M.S. 1996: Tradition as revolt: the moral and political economy of ethnic nationalism. *Current Perspectives in Social Theory* 16: 71–98. · Leitner, H. 1992: Urban geography: responding to new challenges. *Progress in Human Geography* 16: 105–18. · Peach, C. 1996: Good segregation, bad segregation. *Planning Perspectives* 11: 379–98. · Peterson, W. 1997: *Ethnicity counts*. New Brunswick, NJ and London: Transaction Books. · Van den Berghe, P. 1981: *The ethnic phenomenon*. New York: Elsevier. · Williams, R.M. 1995: Consenting to whiteness: reflections on race and marxian theories of discrimination. In A. Callari et al., eds, *Marxism in the postmodern age: confronting the new world order*. New York: Guilford. · Yancey, W.L., Ericksen, E.P., and Juliani, R.N. 1976: Emergent ethnicity: a review and reformulation. *American Sociological Review* 41: 391–402.

Suggested reading

Mason, D. 1995: *Race and ethnicity in modern Britain*. New York: Oxford University Press. · Peach, C., Robinson, V. and Smith, S.J., eds., 1981: *Ethnic segregation in cities*. London: Croom Helm. · Smaje, C. 1997: Not just a social construct: theorising race and ethnicity. *Sociology* 31: 307–27. · Smith, S.J. 1989: *The politics of 'race' and residence: citizenship, segregation and white supremacy in Britain*. Cambridge: Polity Press. · Sollors, W., ed., 1996: *Theories of ethnicity: a classical reader*. London: Macmillan.

ethnocentrism A form of prejudice or stereotyping that assumes the superiority of one's own CULTURE or ethnic group (see ETHNICITY). An ethnocentric perspective is unreflexive, regarding a particular outlook (its own) as natural and 'unmarked'. Other ways of seeing are regarded not only as different but as inherently inferior. No longer a key term in contemporary social science, ethnocentrism is often used as a polite synonym for harsher terms such as RACISM or xenophobia (a pathological fear of foreigners). Whereas prejudice may be directed against specific groups or individuals, ethnocentrism is directed indiscriminately against everyone who is perceived to belong to a different ethnic group.

Edward Said's (1978) study of ORIENTALISM provides a searching critique of the IMAGINATIVE GEOGRAPHIES that supported the ethnocentric (European) construction of an exotic cultural OTHER (Gregory, 1997). Said's work also reveals the contradictory nature of ethnocentrism, where hostility towards 'Orientals' can be unproblematically maintained alongside a respect for Arab and Islamic cultures as the historical source of European language and 'civilization'. The ethnocentrism of Geography's history, particularly concerning the politics of Empire, has been explored in several recent studies (e.g. Driver, 1992; Godlewska and Smith, 1994) while Mitchell (1997) has argued for a more critical engagement with transnational processes and discourses of globalization as a way of reducing such ethnocentrism. (See also DIFFERENCE; POSITIONALITY; TRANSNATIONALISM.) PAJ

References

Driver, F. 1992: Geography's history: histories of geographical knowledge. *Environment and Planning D: Society and Space* 10: 23–40. · Godlewska, A. and Smith, N., eds, 1994: *Geography and empire*. Oxford: Blackwell. · Gregory, D. 1997: Orientalism reviewed. *History Workshop Journal* 44: 267–78. · Mitchell, K. 1997: Transnational discourse: bringing geography back in. *Antipode* 29: 101–14. · Said, E.W. 1978: *Orientalism*. London: Routledge.

ethnography Based on first-hand FIELDWORK, ethnography employs PARTICIPANT OBSERVATION and other QUALITATIVE METHODS to convey the inner life and texture of a particular social group or LOCALITY. The staple method of social and cultural anthropology, ethnography involves the intensive study of other CULTURES over an extended period of time, whether 'at home' or 'abroad', in rural or urban settings. Through ethnography, anthropologists have shown how apparently 'exotic' social practices and 'irrational' beliefs can be more fully understood when interpreted in a contextual and holistic manner. Demonstrating how other cultures have their own intrinsic logic when approached as whole ways of life, ethnography is characterized by cultural RELATIVISM, opposing the ETHNOCENTRISM of those who regard other cultures as inherently inferior.

Originally focusing on 'traditional' societies in far-off places, ethnographic methods have also been employed in contemporary urban settings (Jackson, 1985). Drawing on the work of the CHICAGO SCHOOL of urban sociology and sharing a commitment to understand the city's moral order as well as its spatial pattern (cf. MORAL GEOGRAPHIES), urban ethnographers have demonstrated the integrity of working CLASS and ethnic minority cultures.

In contrast to QUESTIONNAIRE surveys and similar QUANTITATIVE METHODS of social research (see SURVEY ANALYSIS), ethnography aims for depth rather than coverage. As a result, ethnographic methods are often criticized for their lack of representativity, though this accusation betrays a misunderstanding of the reliance of such methods on logical rather than on statistical inference (Mitchell, 1983). In practice, ethnographers employ a range of strategies including triangulation and negative case analysis (Lincoln and Guba, 1985; Cook and Crang, 1995) to increase the credibility of their research. While 'ethnography' is sometimes used as a synonym for a wide range of qualitative methods (from FOCUS GROUPS to in-depth INTERVIEWING), anthropologists have been critical of those who claim to use an ethnographic approach without taking on board a serious commitment to intensive fieldwork, often extending for a year or more, and frequently requiring the researcher to learn another language.

The ethics of ethnographic research have often been questioned, especially where covert methods of observation are involved. The fact that most ethnographers have chosen to study working class and ethnic minority COMMUNITIES, rather than those of higher social status, also raises ethical issues regarding the POWER of gatekeepers in providing or withholding access to those whom the ethnographer wishes to study (cf. Stacey, 1988; URBAN MANAGERS AND GATEKEEPERS). Given the disciplinary origins of the method, ethnographers have been forced to come to terms with anthropology's involvement in the colonial encounter (Asad, 1973), facing a crisis of REPRESENTATION in relation to those whose cultures they aim to represent (Marcus and Fischer, 1986).

Various alternatives to the traditional monograph or documentary film have been discussed (e.g. Clifford and Marcus, 1986; Behar and Gordon, 1995) as appropriate textual strategies for dealing with these complex issues of ethnographic authority. In some cases, informed by feminist research (see FEMINIST GEOGRAPHIES), these methods have been designed as ways of 'giving voice' to those who have previously been silenced. Whether this can be achieved within the conventions of the western academy without distorting the lives of those who are represented has been the subject of intense debate (Spivak, 1988). Rather than focusing so much attention on 'exotic' societies in far-off countries, ethnographers are now increasingly studying cultures that are closer to home, discovering the strangeness of more 'familiar' locations such as restaurants and advertising agencies (Crang, 1994; Miller, 1997). PAJ

References

Asad, T., ed., 1973: *Anthropology and the colonial encounter*. London: Ithaca Press. · Behar, R. and Gordon, D.A., eds, 1995: *Women writing culture*. Berkeley: University of California Press. · Clifford, J. and Marcus, G.E., eds, 1986: *Writing culture: the poetics and politics of ethnography*. Berkeley, CA: University of California Press. · Cook, I. and Crang, M. 1995: Doing ethnographies. *Concepts and Techniques in Modern Geography* (CATMOG) 58. · Crang, P. 1994: 'It's showtime': on the workplace geographies of display in a restaurant in southeast England. *Environment and Planning D: Society and Space* 12: 675–704. · Jackson, P. 1985: Urban ethnography. *Progress in Human Geography* 9: 157–76. · Lincoln, Y.S. and Guba, E.G. 1985. *Naturalistic inquiry*. London: Sage. · Marcus, G.E. and Fischer, M.M.J. 1986: *Anthropology as cultural critique*. Chicago: University of Chicago Press. · Miller, D. 1997: *Capitalism: an ethnographic approach*. Oxford: Berg. · Mitchell, J.C. 1983: Case and situation analysis. *Sociological Review* 31: 187–211. · Spivak, G.C. 1988: Can the subaltern speak? in C. Nelson, and L. Grossberg, eds, *Marxism and the interpretation of culture*. Urbana, IL: University of Illinois Press, 271–313. · Stacey, J. 1988. Can there be a feminist ethnography? *Women's Studies International Forum* 11: 21–7.

Selected Reading

Atkinson, P. 1990: *The ethnographic imagination: textual constructions of reality*. London: Routledge. · Hammersley, M. and Atkinson, P. 1983: *Ethnography: principles and practice*. London: Tavistock.

ethnomethodology A way of accounting for the organization of SOCIETY that relies on description rather than THEORY, aims for explication rather than explanation, and is concerned with IDEOGRAPHIC detail rather than broad generalization. According to Harold Garfinkel (with whom the idea is most closely associated) the ethnomethodologist's task is to render the familiar strange in order to expose the common-sense understandings and practical reasonings that sustain local social orderings.

Notwithstanding a growing interest in ACTOR–NETWORK THEORY and conversation analysis (two offshoots of ethnomethodological thinking), neither human geographers nor other social scientists concerned with ideas about SPACE, PLACE and IDENTITY have made much self-conscious reference to the ideas and practices of ethnomethodology in the last five years. This reflects at once the marginalization of ethnomethodology in recent social scientific thinking, and the (arguable) success of the project, which is to re-specify social science (and therefore to make it into something else – not geography, not sociology . . .).

Ethnomethodology is not therefore an 'approach' which can readily be combined with, pursued alongside or mixed in with other analytical agendas. It is rather a way of radically rethinking the aims and conduct of social research. It is not, for example, interested in ONTOLOGICAL debates about the status of social phenomena. (Indeed, it is an alleged indifference to 'given' objects of concern – 'race', gender, religion and so on – that has led some social scientists to give ethnomethodology a wide berth.) For the ethnomethodologist, relationships between the world as it 'is' and as it appears to be are not at issue. The question is 'how does the world appear to be, and how do people make it like this?' The answer is derived not only by analysts observing a variety of social settings, events and process in meticulous detail, but also by them observing and reflecting on their own activities. This places the analyst outside disciplinary debates on whether particular methods are appropriate for particular investigations. It turns attention instead towards the processes that lead analysts to generate and use particular methods, and to produce particular kinds of results, in particular contexts.

Ethnomethodology is a diverse and contested undertaking which has been much-debated in sociology, psychology and anthropology. It has inspired research traditions concerned with ETHNOGRAPHY and DISCOURSE analysis, and points the focus of intellectual activity quite squarely on the 'ordinary' activities of everyday life. These 'ordinary' activities may be concerned with how people go shopping, how officials construct records, or how scientists create knowledge. SJS

Suggested Reading

Button, G., ed., 1991: *Ethnomethodology and the human sciences*. Cambridge: Cambridge University Press. · Garfinkel, H. 1967: *Studies in ethnomethodology*. Englewood Cliffs, NJ: Prentice-Hall (republished 1984, Cambridge: Polity Press). · Garfinkel, H. 1996: Ethnomethodology's program. *Social Psychology Quarterly* 59: 5–21. · Laurier, E. 1998: Geographies of talk. *Area* 31: 36–45.

Eurocentrism An attitude that unthinkingly and unproblematically places 'Europe' at the centre of human inquiry, social analysis and political practice. These three spheres are closely interlinked, and revolve around the constitution of 'Europe' as subject and object of inquiry, as architect and arbiter of method, and as exemplar and engineer of progress. Thus 'Europe' is placed at the centre of human inquiry through the assumption that it provides the MODEL and master-narrative of world history: that its histories and geographies are the norm and the rule from which all others learn or deviate. 'Europe' is placed at the centre of social analysis through the assumption that its theoretical formulations and methods of analysis provide the most powerful resources for all explanation and interpretation. And 'Europe' is placed at the centre of political practice through the assumption that its cultural and political systems act as the bearers of a universal Reason that maps out the ideal course of all human history.

'Europe' appears in scare-quotes throughout the preceding paragraph to draw attention to its cultural construction. Indeed, the DISCOURSE of Eurocentrism has a long history (or rather historical geography) through which it has been so closely entwined with the projects of COLONIALISM and IMPERIALISM that it cannot sensibly be confined to the continent of Europe. In the course of its expansions, 'Europe' has turned into 'the West' (see ORIENTALISM) which has more recently been turned into 'the North'. Each of these transitions has been freighted with its own cultural and political baggage, but their general burden is clear: 'Eurocentrism is not merely the ETHNOCENTRISM of people located in the West', Dhareshwar (1990, p. 235) notes, but rather 'permeates the cultural apparatus in which we participate' (see also Shohat and Stam, 1994). It follows from these characterizations that it is in principle possible to study Europe without being Eurocentric, and that it is equally possible to study non-European and indeed non-western societies in thoroughly Eurocentric ways.

Geography has a particular and a general interest in Eurocentrism. Historians of the modern discipline have argued that it is a constitutively 'European science' (Stoddart, 1986). Critics have objected that this erases the contributions of other geographical traditions, and that geography in its modern, transnational and HEGEMONIC forms is more accurately described as a 'Eurocentric science' (Gregory, 1994 p. 33; see also Sidaway, 1997). Recent work in the HISTORY OF GEOGRAPHY has drawn attention to these issues through a critical interrogation of geography's complicity in the adventures of colonialism and imperialism and, in particular, of the reciprocities between the intellectual formation of the discipline and the political trajectory of European expansion, exploitation and dispossession (Driver, 1992). During the nineteenth and early twentieth centuries the discipline invested heavily outside Europe in activities that had considerable instrumental value (and some historians have suggested that it was precisely these practical contributions that secured the formal incorporation of the modern discipline within the western academy). Its strategic contributions included mapping and surveying other territories, compiling resource inventories, and producing IMAGINATIVE GEOGRAPHIES of other peoples and places (see Godlewska and Smith, 1994; Bell, Butlin and Heffernan, 1995). These investments contributed to the formation of the modern (British) discipline as a 'white mythology' that postulated a racially unmarked subject-position as the condition of scientific discourse, effaced alternative subject-positions, and appropriated other forms of knowledge: all three gestures are diagnostics of Eurocentrism (Barnett, 1998; see also WHITENESS).

Although the contemporary Anglo-American discipline has become sensitive to its intellectual formation as a SITUATED KNOWLEDGE, it continues to rely on what Slater (1992) has called a Euro-Americanism that projects its own situations as 'lineages of universalism'. This colonizing gesture was explicit and obvious in the formulations of classical SPATIAL SCIENCE, whose supposedly general models were almost invariably predicated on specifically European and American cases, but Slater is most interested in the dispositions of an ostensibly 'CRITICAL' HUMAN GEOGRAPHY. He argues that its dependence on CRITICAL THEORY, HISTORICAL MATERIALISM and POSTMODERNISM (the list could now usefully be extended: FEMINIST GEOGRAPHY has also been exercised by these questions) continues to license assumptions of 'universal applicability' that conceal 'a particularity based to a large extent on the specific experiences of the USA and the UK'. Geographies written under the sign of POST-COLONIALISM are directly interested in these issues – in the need to 'provincialize' the assumptions of Euro-American geography, to attend to other voices and to 'learn from other regions' – but they also often draw directly on European 'high theory' so that there is no simple solution to the struggle against Eurocentrism (cf. Young, 1990).

Geography is scarcely alone in these predicaments, and in the sense of discourse rather than discipline it has a much more general involvement in Eurocentrism. Gregory (1998) has drawn attention to four conceptual strategies – four 'geo-graphs' – that entered directly into the formation of a colonial modernity: (i) *absolutizing time and space* (the construction of concepts through which European metrics and meanings of History and Geography were taken to be natural and inviolable, as marking the centre around which other histories and other geographies were to be organized); (ii) *exhibiting the world* (the production of a space within which particular objects were made visible in particular ways, and by means of which particular claims to knowledge made by viewing subjects were negotiated and legitimated); (iii) *normalizing the subject* (the production of spaces of inclusion and exclusion that normalized the subject-position of the white, middle-class, heterosexual male); and (iv) *abstracting culture and nature* (the production of an ideology of NATURE that separated modern western CULTURE from 'nature' and represented temperate nature as 'normal' nature). This argumentation-sketch is more than an exercise in historical reconstruction. 'In elucidating the conceptual orders of Eurocentrism', Gregory argues, 'it becomes much more difficult to assume that we have left such predicaments behind, and much more likely that we will be forced to recognize that Eurocentrism and its geo-graphs continue to invest our geographies with their troubling meanings.' DG

References

Barnett, C. 1998: Impure and worldly geography: the Africanist discourse of the Royal Geographical Society, 1831–73. *Transactions, Institute of British Geographers* NS 23: 239–52. · Bell, M., Butlin, R. and Heffernam, M., eds, 1995: *Geography and imperialism 1820–1940.* Manchester: Manchester University Press. · Dhareshwar, V. 1990: *The predicament of Theory.* In M. Kreiswirth and M. Cheetham (eds), Theory between the disciplines: Authority / vision / politics. Ann Arbor: University of Michigan Press, 231–50. · Driver, F. 1992: Geography's empire: histories of geographical knowledge. *Environment and Planning D: Society and Space* 10: 23–40. · Godlewska, A. and Smith, N., eds, 1994: *Geography and Empire.* Oxford and Cambridge, MA: Blackwell. · Gregory, D. 1994: *Geographical imaginations.* Oxford and Cambridge, MA: Blackwell. · Gregory, D. 1998: Power, knowledge and geography. *Geographisches Zeitschrift*, 86: 70–93. · Shohat, E. and Stam, R. 1994: *Unthinking Eurocentrism: Multiculturalism and the media.* London and New York: Routledge. · Sidaway, J. 1997: The (re)making of the western 'geographical tradition': some missing links. *Area* 29: 72–80. · Slater, D. 1992: On the borders of social theory: learning from other regions. *Environment and Planning D: Society and Space* 10: 307–27. · Stoddart, D.R. 1986: *On geography and its history.* Oxford and Cambridge, MA: Blackwell. · Young, R. 1990: *White mythologies: writing History and the West.* London and New York: Routledge.

Suggested Reading

Slater (1992). · Gregory (1998).

exceptionalism The belief that geography and history are methodologically distinct from other fields of inquiry because they are peculiarly concerned with the study of the unique and the particular. The idea is closely associated with KANTIANISM, but in geography the term is usually identified with Schaefer's (1953) posthumous challenge to what he regarded as the IDIOGRAPHIC orthodoxy enshrined in Hartshorne's *The nature of geography* (1939). Schaefer rejected exceptionalism to argue for a NOMOTHETIC geography which would furnish 'morphological LAWS' about spatial patterns. Hartshorne's views were in fact more nuanced than Schaefer maintained, and he never accepted any clear division between the idiographic and the nomothetic because they were both 'present in all branches of science'. But he did insist that any general concepts used in geography should be directed towards the analysis of specific REGIONS, and that its essential task was the study of AREAL DIFFERENTIATION rather than (as Schaefer preferred) the elucidation of the laws of location that were supposed to underpin these regional configurations. DG

References

Hartshorne, R. 1939: *The nature of geography: a critical survey of current thought in the light of the past.* Lancaster, PA: Association of American Geographers. · Schaefer, F.K. 1953: Exceptionalism in geography: a methodological examination. *Annals of the Association of American Geographers* 43: 226–49.

Suggested Reading

Johnston, R.J. 1991: *Geography and geographers: Anglo-American human geography since 1945*, 5th edn. London: Edward Arnold; New York: Halsted, 55–61.

exclave A small part of a STATE, separated from its main territorial unit and surrounded by the land of a neighbour, such as the area of Spain around Llivia on the French side of the Pyrenees. There are several variations on this basic form. *Pene-exclaves* are part of the state which, although not physically separate, can only be reached conveniently via another country. *Quasi-exclaves* are areas that for all practical purposes have ceased to be treated as exclaves. *Virtual exclaves* are the reverse, areas that enjoy the status of an exclave without the legal entitlement. Finally, *temporary exclaves* result from inconclusive territorial arrangements being made after an armistice (see also ENCLAVE). MB

Suggested Reading

Robinson, G.W.S. 1959: Exclaves. *Annals of the Association of American Geographers* 49: 283–95.

existentialism A philosophy, the central concern of which is with the human subject's existential 'being' in the world (which Heidegger called *Dasein*). Existentialism posits that all persons are typically estranged from their intrinsic creativity and live instead in worlds of objects which exist for them only as externalized 'things' – a passive attitude which Tuan (1971, 1972) called ENVIRONMENTALISM – and that any attempt to realize a truly human condition through an active 'openness' to the world necessarily involves a freely entered struggle against estrangement. Following in some part the ideas of Buber, Heidegger and Sartre, Samuels (1978) has argued that this struggle entails an essentially spatial ONTOLOGY: that it is 'a history of human efforts to overcome or eliminate detachment, which is to say, to eliminate distance' through the creation of meaningful, so to speak 'authored' PLACES. Many of the early existentialist explorations in human geography were concerned not so much with the elaboration of a spatial ontology, however, as with a more general assault on those 'technical' conceptions of the subject, usually closely associated with POSITIVISM, which reduced it to a so-called 'scientism'. 'For the existentially aware geographers', Buttimer (1974) suggested, the human being:

> is more than a cultural, 'rational' or dynamically-charged decision maker out there to be observed, analysed and modelled: he [or she] is a 'subject' of lived experience, past, present and future. An existentially aware geographer is thus less interested in establishing intellectual control over [people] through pre-conceived analytical models than ... in encountering people and situations in an open, inter-subjective manner.

(See also Gibson (1978) for the Weberian alternative.)

As Buttimer's remarks indicate, existentialism involves a critique of both rationalism and IDEALISM, which certainly extends to Weber's interpretative sociology – because it (quite literally) regards existence as primary. And while it has important connections with both PHENOMENOLOGY and HISTORICAL MATERIALISM, especially through some of the contributions of Sartre (see Poster, 1975), it can be distinguished from both by its fundamental concern with what Buttimer describes as 'the quality and meaning of life in the everyday world' (cf. TAKEN-FOR-GRANTED WORLD). Hence, Buttimer invokes Heidegger's distinction between *Herrschaftswissen* ('knowledge of meaning and overlordship') and *Bildungswissen* ('knowledge of meaning and creativity') to support her plea for a 'more concerned, caring approach to knowledge and action' which can resist and ultimately transcend the rationalist impulse for technical control, and the estrangement which this entails, and thereby provide for a truly human existence (Buttimer, 1979a, 1979b; cf. CRITICAL THEORY). Not surprisingly, these sorts of criticisms have been applied *a fortiori* to the relations between human geography and planning (e.g. see Cullen and Knox, 1982), but they are clearly intended to have a much more general purchase.

Indeed, Relph (1981) widened the existentialist critique within the subject far beyond the sphere of spatial science to confront what he calls the 'ontological triviality' of HUMANISTIC GEOGRAPHY (p. 155). In his view, too, Heidegger's writings are an indispensable source for a genuinely human geography; but whereas 'Heidegger's philosophy was a form of contemplation', the 'environmental humility' which Relph is concerned to foster must embrace not only 'an openness to Being' – 'allowing things to disclose themselves as they are', 'letting ourselves be claimed by Being' – but also 'a manifest guardianship for the individuality of places and landscapes' (pp. 187–91). Similar ideas were pursued by Samuels (1979, 1981) in his search for 'an existential geography' directed towards the elucidation of what he termed 'the biography of landscape'. They have been developed most rigorously by Pickles (1985), who has drawn upon Heidegger to identify the significance of the 'existential analytic' for the human sciences in general and human geography in particular. He seeks to clarify the fundamental importance of what, following Heidegger, he terms a 'regional ontology' of human SPATIALITY for both enterprises.

Present in virtually all of these discussions is the idea of 'openness to Being', and in a remarkable essay Gould (1981) worked with *Daseinanalysis* to recover the root meaning of the word 'theory' (*theoria*) in a way which connects up to the foregoing. He suggests that *theoria* connotes both openness and 'the reverent paying heed to phenomena'. If we see conventional 'THEORY-building' from this perspective, then Gould believes that 'our deep and legitimate concern for a scientific geography' may have gone astray:

> In attempting to map the description of human phenomena onto the forms of science generated by those who assault the inanimate or nonconscious physical and biological worlds with their questions, we have objectified, cut off, 'templated' the very beings-in-the-world that should be of our deepest concern in any geography where the adjective 'human' is genuinely deserved. There seems to be little 'reverent paying heed' in the everyday research and questioning of the human sciences today, and the old meanings of theoria seldom seem to shine through the methodical, and often mechanistic, processes of inquiry in these realms.

Gould objects to 'con-templation', therefore, because it involves partition and enclosure – the construction of a template – and prefers instead to explore descriptive languages more appropriate to (open to) human spatiality: in particular languages in which we do not project 'the multidimensional character that seems to characterise the complexity of contemporary life onto the traditional space of the geographic map'.

Much of this discussion has evidently been preoccupied with broadly methodological questions – with mobilizing a philosophical literature to displace the assumptions of SPATIAL SCIENCE – but there has recently been a considerable revival of interest in the historical grounding and substantive implications of Heidegger's work across the humanities and the social sciences as a whole. This has followed four interconnected paths, all of which bear directly on work in contemporary human geography:

- the politics of Heidegger's philosophy and, in particular, the complex connections between his intellectual work and his involvement in National Socialism (see Wolin, 1990) – this examination connects with parallel attempts to establish the contextuality of geographical inquiry;
- Heidegger's critique of MODERNITY, and in particular of its technocratic consciousness (Zimmerman, 1990) and its 'enframing' of what Mitchell (1989) calls the world-as-exhibition – these examinations intersect with attempts to explore human geographies of modernity, to think through society's involvement in and responsibility towards NATURE, and to consider the concept of LANDSCAPE as a 'way of seeing';
- the filiations between Heidegger's ethical concerns and those of POSTMODERNISM (White, 1991) – this examination feeds in to contemporary interests in the geographies of postmodernism and 'postmodernity' and, in particular, to processes of 'Othering'; and
- the construction of a spatial ontology (Schatzki, 1991) – this effort contributes directly to attempts to clarify the importance of space and spatiality in the constitution of social life. DG

References

Buttimer, A. 1974: *Values in geography*. Washington, D.C.: Association of American Geographers, Commission on College Geography, Resource Paper 24. · Buttimer, A. 1979a: Erewhon or nowhere land. In S. Gale, and G. Olsson, eds, *Philosophy in geography*. Dordrecht and Boston: D. Reidel; 9–37. · Buttimer, A. 1979b: Reason, rationality and human creativity. *Geografiska*

Annaler 61B: 43–9. · Cullen, J. and Knox, P. 1982: The city, the self and urban society. *Transactions, Institute of British Geographers* NS 7: 276–91. · Gibson, E. 1978: Understanding the subjective meaning of places. In D. Ley and M.S. Samuels, eds, *Humanistic geography: prospects and problems*. London: Croom Helm, 138–54. · Gould, P. 1981: Letting the data speak for themselves. *Annals of the Association of American Geographers* 71: 166–76. · Mitchell, T. 1989: The world as exhibition. *Comparative Studies in Society and History* 31: 217–36. · Pickles, J. 1985: *Phenomenology, science and geography: spatiality and the human sciences*. Cambridge: Cambridge University Press. · Poster, M. 1975: *Existential Marxism: from Sartre to Althusser*. Princeton, NJ: Princeton University Press. · Relph, E. 1981: *Rational landscapes and humanistic geography*. London: Croom Helm; Totowa, NJ: Barnes and Noble. · Samuels, M. 1978: Existentialism and human geography. In D. Ley and M.S. Samuels, eds, *Humanistic geography: prospects and problems*. London: Croom Helm, 22–40. · Samuels, M. 1979: The biography of landscape: cause and culpability. In D. Meinig, ed., *The interpretation of ordinary landscapes*. Oxford: Oxford University Press, 51–88. · Samuels, M. 1981: An existential geography. In M.E. Harvey and B.P. Holly, eds, *Themes in geographic thought*. London: Croom Helm, 115–32. · Schatzki, T. 1991: Spatial ontology and explanation. *Annals of the Association of American Geographers* 81: 650–70. · Tuan, Y.-F. 1971: Geography, phenomenology and the study of human nature. *Canadian Geographer* 15: 181–92. · Tuan, Y.-F. 1972: Structuralism, existentialism and environmental perception. *Environment and Behavior* 4: 319–42. · White, S. 1991: *Political theory and postmodernism*. Cambridge: Cambridge University Press. · Wolin, R. 1990: *The politics of Being: the political thought of Martin Heidegger*. New York: Columbia University Press. · Zimmerman, M. 1990: *Heidegger's confrontation with modernity: technology, politics and art*. Bloomington, IN: Indiana University Press.

Suggested Reading

Samuels (1978, 1981). · Schatzki (1991). · White (1991). · Zimmerman (1990).

exit, voice and loyalty A theory of consumer influence on the quality of PUBLIC GOODS developed by Hirschman (1970), who contended that their quality is likely to be lower in monopoly conditions than in situations where consumers have a range of potential suppliers. Where choice is available, consumers can react to an inefficient and/or ineffective service by taking one of the following options:

- *exit*, transferring their custom to an alternative supplier;
- *voice*, complaining about the quality of provision and threatening exit if it isn't improved; and
- *loyalty*, remaining with the current supplier without either voicing complaints or threatening exit.

The higher the exit costs (i.e. of switching suppliers) the lower the likely impact of voice, because the supplier can assume loyalty. If exit is impossible, as in a monopoly, then loyalty is virtually guaranteed and voice will have little impact.

Several consequences have been deduced from this argument, and some were put into effect by New Right governments during the 1980s. One is that to obtain efficient and effective service-delivery public sector monopolies should be dismantled, either by their PRIVATIZATION in a way which will create competitive situations or by the creation of quasi-market systems within the sector (as with the British National Health Service: Mohan, 1995; see also TIEBOUT MODEL). Another is that although individual voice may be ineffective, collective protest may not, since powerful pressure groups could mobilize effective collective voice and/or exit: against this, it is argued that those with least political POWER to organize are least likely to have effective exit options open to them (e.g. transferring their consumption of such items as education and health care from the public to the private sector). RJJ

References

Hirschman, A.O. 1970: *Exit, voice and loyalty*. Cambridge, MA: Harvard University Press. · Mohan, J.F. 1995: *A national health service? The restructuring of health care in Britain since 1979*. London: Macmillan.

Suggested Reading

Johnston, R.J. 1992: The internal operations of the state. In P.J. Taylor, ed., *The political geography of the twentieth century*. London: Belhaven Press. · Laver, M. 1997: *Private desires, political action: an invitation to the politics of rational choice*. London: Sage Publications. · Pinch, S. 1997: *Worlds of welfare: understanding the changing geographies of social welfare provision*. London: Routledge.

expert systems Software packages that attempt to mimic the behaviour of an expert in a given field. The notion that a computer could emulate an expert is attractive, since it implies that such expert systems could be used to standardize many decision-making processes, reduce errors, and improve the performance of regulatory agencies. An expert system consists of a rule base, containing a digital representation of the known decision rules, and a processor to evaluate the rules in a given instance and reach an appropriate decision. The builder of an expert system will commonly make use of a set of generic tools known as a 'shell', which takes care of the storage of the rule base, and the processing functions. Expert systems have often been coupled with GEOGRAPHIC INFORMATION SYSTEMS (GIS), which provide many of the inputs and may also display and manage the outputs, in supporting DECISION-MAKING in FORESTRY, RESOURCE MANAGEMENT, hydrology, and URBAN AND REGIONAL PLANNING. The success of expert system approaches depends on the degree to which all relevant rules can be expressed in the highly constrained forms required of a rule base, and on the credibility of an expert system's output to its users. Rules are often imprecise or 'fuzzy', and expert systems based on fuzzy reasoning have become popular in many geographic applications. Finally, an expert system can provide a useful formal structure for studying decision-making processes. MG

Suggested Reading

Kim, T.J., Wiggins, L.L. and Wright, J.R., eds, 1990: *Expert systems: applications to urban planning*. New York: Springer-Verlag.

exploration While it is generally taken to refer to the growth of knowledge of the globe that resulted from various voyages of discovery and scientific expeditions, the label 'exploration' disconcerts. Its contested character arises from the clash over the appropriate vocabulary in which to speak of this essentially contested concept. The very terms discovery and exploration, according to revisionists, should be replaced by invasion, conquest, or occupation, for the simple reason that these unmask the pretended innocence and moral neutrality that the standard scientific-sounding idioms convey.

Whatever the allocation of moral accountability, there can be no doubting the significance of exploration on the scientific enterprise in general and the discourse and discipline of geography in particular (see also GEOGRAPHY, HISTORY OF). Traditional chroniclers of these exploits have thus tended towards a progressivist interpretation of scientific knowledge, cartographic history, and global awareness (Baker, 1931). The vast maritime expeditions of Chêng Ho in the early decades of the fifteenth century (1405–33), for example, have been commended for their contributions to Chinese marine CARTOGRAPHY and descriptive geography, though, in contrast to later voyages, the purpose of the mission was neither the garnering of scientific information nor commercial conquest (Needham, 1959; Chang, 1971). In similar vein the writings of the Muslim traveller Ibn Battuta during the late Middle Ages are typically interpreted as an encyclopaedic conspectus of Islamic life and CULTURE in different climatic regimes (Boorstin, 1983; James, 1972).

It is, however, with the European voyages of Reconnaissance during the fifteenth and sixteenth centuries that putative connections between scientific 'progress' and geographical 'exploration' are even more closely associated (see also TRAVEL WRITING, GEOGRAPHY AND). Parry (1981, p. 3), for example, argues that, save for the arts of war and military engineering, geographical exploration was 'almost the only field' in which 'scientific discovery and everyday technique became closely associated before the middle of the seventeenth century'. Similarly Hale (1967) suggests that the first scientific laboratory was the world itself; O'Sullivan (1984, p. 3) proposes that 'the voyages of discovery were in a way large scale experiments, proving or disproving the Renaissance concepts inherited from the ancient world'. In such scenarios the names of Bartholomew Dias, Vasco da Gama, Christopher Columbus, Fernand Magellan, and, perhaps most of all, 'Prince Henry the Navigator' assume heroic status. For these reasons, the Portuguese and Spanish voyages have been interpreted as precursor to the Scientific Revolution (Hooykaas, 1979).

Francis Bacon later reflected in his *Novum Organum* of 1620 that the opening up of the geographical world through the voyages of discovery foreshadowed the expansion of the 'boundaries of the intellectual globe' beyond the confines of 'the narrow discoveries of the ancients'. Support for this interpretation has come from those attaching crucial significance to the Portuguese encouragement of navigational science and mathematical practice through the work of the Jewish map- and instrument-maker Mestre Jacome. This Jewish tradition of Mallorcan cartography, instrumentation and nautical science was perpetuated by Abraham Zacuto and Joseph Vizinho, while Francesco Faleiro, Garcia da Orta and Pedro Nunes did much to further medicinal botany, CARTOGRAPHY and natural history during the first half of the sixteenth century (Goodman, 1991). Such accomplishments, accordingly, have recently been canvassed to substantiate the claim that this *Jewish* style of science practised in sixteenth-century Portugal provided the template for the Scientific Revolution in England and 'the catalyst inducing the emergence of modern science in Western Europe' (Banes, 1988, p. 58).

Nevertheless, even partisan commentators concede that the scientific advances of the

Age of Discovery were by-products of the commercial, evangelistic, and colonial motives that undergirded these expeditionary enterprises. Ostensibly more scientific were the Pacific exploits of Enlightenment figures like Louis Antoine de Bougainville, James Cook, Joseph Banks, the Forsters, Jean François de la Pérouse, and George Vancouver during the eighteenth century (Beaglehole, 1966). And yet with them, too, political factors loomed as large scientific ones: pre-voyage briefings on settlement possibility, resource inventory, and the staking of colonial claims all revealed the strategic significance of everything from cartographic survey to geodesic experiment and ethnographic illustration (Frost, 1988). Still, the scientific achievements were not insubstantial – Cook, for instance, carried with him LANDSCAPE painters, natural history draughtsmen, and professional astronomers, surgeons and naturalists, and successfully completed an accurate recording of the transit of Venus (Goetzmann, 1986). Indeed the Pacific became something of a laboratory for the testing of scientific methodologies and artistic representational styles (Smith, 1960). Precisely the same was true of later explorations in South America and Central Africa. Alexander von Humboldt and Aimé Bonpland, for example, used their South American findings at the turn of the nineteenth century to break the bonds of the static taxonomic system of Linnaeus (which classified each plant and animal and assigned it a single scientific name), and ultimately to create a distinctive mode of scientific investigation – what Cannon labelled 'Humboldtian science' – in which 'the accurate, measured study of widespread but interconnected real phenomena' were interrogated 'in order to find a definite law and a dynamic cause' (Cannon, 1978, p. 105; for a different perspective see Dettelbach, 1996). Again, Roderick Murchison, who has been dubbed England's scientist of empire, virtually orchestrated the British colonial assault on Central Africa in the Victorian period through his oversight of the Royal Geographical Society, and used a variety of explorers to test his own geological theories there (see GEOGRAPHICAL SOCIETIES). In the expansive personage of Murchison, geography's complicity in the colonial project found expression (Stafford, 1989).

There is not space here to delineate, even in outline, the scientific contributions of a host of other exploratory ventures: the Napoleonic survey of Egypt, Baudin's deadly mission to 'New Holland', the succession of Russian voyages into the Pacific by Krusentern, Kotzebue, and Lutke, the Royal Geographical Society's efforts to reduce the Australian outback to cartographic enclosure, Lewis and Clark's western territorial expedition orchestrated by Thomas Jefferson, Darwin's *Beagle* circumnavigation, the United States Exploring Expedition under Charles Wilkes, the voyage of T.H. Huxley on The Rattlesnake, A.R. Wallace's sojourn in Borneo, and the oceanographic survey of *The Challenger*, to name but a very few. Their role in the evolution of geographical knowledge has been so engrained in the discipline's collective memory that various expeditionary ventures continue to receive the sponsorship of institutions like the Royal Geographical Society and the National Geographic Society, and to provide a language in which to speak of geographical excursions into other threatening environments, such as urban ethnic 'no-go' areas (Horvath, 1971).

To interpret the significance of these SURVEILLANCE exploits solely in terms of cognitive 'progress' is highly questionable, however. Moreover, merely stating that the growth of these scientific knowledges was situated within the framework of IMPERIALISM is to pay scant attention to a whole suite of issues to do with the construction of western IDENTITY, the representations of exoticism, the inscription of otherness, the reciprocal constitution of scientific discourse and colonial praxis (see COLONIALISM), and the DECONSTRUCTION of cartographic ICONOGRAPHY.

It was indeed as a consequence of the European Age of Exploration/ Reconnaissance/ Conquest that the idea of the West and western-ness received its baptism. Europe's sense of distinctiveness from the other worlds that the navigators encountered was embedded in a discourse about identity that represented 'the West' and 'the Rest' – to use Stuart Hall's (1992) words – in the categories of superiority–inferiority, power–impotence, enlightenment–ignorance, civilization–barbarism. Seen in these terms, Europe's rendezvous with the 'New World' in the fifteenth and sixteenth centuries was as much a moral event as a commercial or intellectual one, and induced what Pagden (1986) calls a sense of metaphysical unease because it confounded standard conceptions of human nature (see also Pagden, 1993).

The construction of this 'discourse of the West', of course, depended crucially on the idioms in which the new worlds were represented. The categories, vocabularies, assumptions, and instruments which the explorers brought to the encounter were, understandably, thoroughly European, and so the worlds of the other were interrogated, classified and assimilated according to European norms. That the language of the engagement was invariably gendered, moreover, facilitated the representation of new landscapes in the exotic categories of a potent sexual imagery intended to indicate mastery and submissiveness (see GENDER AND GEOGRAPHY).

If the foundations of western DISCOURSE were laid during the fifteenth and sixteenth centuries, they were reinforced during the following centuries when Eurocentric modes of representation actually constituted regional identities. One such construction was what Edward Said has termed ORIENTALISM – a discursive formation through which, he writes, 'European culture was able to manage – and even produce – the Orient politically, sociologically, militarily, ideologically, scientifically and imaginatively during the post-Enlightenment period' (Said, 1978, p. 3). And if the construction of Orientalism was crucially dependent on the scientific, historical and literary crafts of western exploration, its evocation also owed much to the supposedly realist works of visual art later produced by painters like Jean-Léon Gérôme (Nochlin, 1991). Indeed the standard scholarly practices of science, history and comparative literature were themselves profoundly indebted to artistic representation (Smith, 1960; Stafford, 1984). Said's reading, of course, has not gone uncontested (for example, Mackenzie, 1995). But the idea of the Oriental or Asiatic type certainly gripped western imaginations. Lindeborg (1994), for example, has shown how concerns over what was termed 'oriental vice' in the very heart of England – 'heathenism in the inner radius' as it was called – expressed anxieties about the moral authority of Christian England. The danger of the East occupying the West thus animated a variety of home mission activities.

The procedures facilitating the marginalization of the Oriental realm (and – at the same time – its constitutive role in European self-definition) were also perpetuated in other places and in other terms. The variety of representational devices that Cook and his coterie of naturalists and draughtsmen deployed – whether Bank's abstract taxonomics or Parkinson's evocation of anthropological variety – succeeded in encapsulating the Pacific world within the confines of European EPISTEMOLOGIES. Moreover, their penchant for designating names – the naming of places, peoples and individuals – at once invented, brought into cultural circulation and domesticated the very entities that were the subjects of their enquiries (Carter, 1987). That Cook's team was engaged in what Salmond (1991, p. 15) terms 'mirror-image ETHNOGRAPHY' is beyond dispute. But just because their modes of categorization were suffused with the expectations of eighteenth-century society – from descriptions of social status (governors and kings make their appearance) to the evaluation of character (courage, honour and virtue figure prominently) – should not be permitted to gainsay the remarkable accuracy of their accounts of physical phenomena. Their New Zealand portrayals, for example, 'check well against the surviving evidence of the places and objects which they described', Salmond writes (p. 294). So much is this so that Cook's vivid depictions of the 'regional variability of tribal life' (Salmond, p. 431) exposes the ahistorical idealization of pre-European 'traditional Maori society' which in fact only began to be systematically constructed a century later.

Exploratory encounters such as these contributed massively to the generation of global IMAGINATIVE GEOGRAPHIES (Gregory, 1993). Thus the Americas, in one way or another, were constructed according to European predilections (Harley, 1990; Mason, 1990; Greenblatt, 1991); later the Pacific was recomposed as a coherent geographical entity (MacLeod and Rehbock, 1994) – as was 'darkest Africa' (Brantlinger, 1985) – as these toponymic labels were brought into cultural currency. The same can also be said of the tropical world: Arnold (1996) has thus spoken of the invention of *tropicality* – a conceptual space that came into being courtesy of the conjoined forces of geographical exploration, colonial administration, and tropical medicine (Livingstone, 1999). Moreover exploration and exhibition frequently went hand in hand, as in the case of Egypt which found its people and places enframed, ordered and exhibited to suit European curiosity (Mitchell, 1988).

Space does not permit further elucidation of such motifs in other regions. Suffice to note that in the African context, according to the Comaroffs (1991, p. 313), European colonization 'was often less a directly coercive conquest than a persuasive attempt to colonise consciousness, to remake people by redefining the taken-for-granted surfaces of their everyday worlds'. Yet here too the temptation towards 'monolithizing' the encounter must be resisted: the moral significance of African environments became a source of endless debate about the effects of a tropical climate on white constitution and the connections between black racial character, biological make-up, and physical geography (Livingstone, 1991: see ENVIRONMENTAL DETERMINISM). In South America it was Humboldt's 'interweaving of visual and emotive language' that contributed so powerfully towards what Pratt (1992) calls the 'ideological reinvention' of America – reimagining so vivid and so vital that Humboldt's writings provided founding visions for both the older elites of northern Europe and the newer independent elites of Spanish America.

If these machinations, however tangled their genealogies, satisfied a European sense of superiority through constituting the peripheral regions of the globe in its own terms, those self-same arenas were soon to become pivotal laboratories for scrutiny into human prehistory. In this way the threat that resided in 'alien' human natures could be rendered benign if those races turned out to be the persistent remnants of earlier phases in the story of human evolution. Just as earlier Scottish and French Enlightenment thinkers, like Smith, Ferguson and Buffon (see ENLIGHTENMENT, GEOGRAPHY OF), regularly crafted their image of the bestial or noble savage into evolutionary schemes depicting a transition from barbarism to civilization, so early twentieth-century students of human archaeology used 'the peoples defined as living at the uttermost ends of the imperial world as examples of living prehistory' (Gamble, 1992, p. 713). Thereby their identity remained engulfed within the imperatives of western scientific scrutiny. They remained subordinated too in the cartographic representations that invariably accompanied the exploratory process. Whether in their use as military tools, in their advocacy of colonial promotion, in their marginal decorations, in their systems of hierarchical classification, or in their imposition of a regulative geometry that bore little reference to indigenous peoples, maps became the conductors of imperial power and western ideology (Harley, 1988: see CARTOGRAPHY, HISTORY OF).

Imperial readings of exploration, however, can serve to obscure as much as they reveal when presented with monolithic tenacity. Treating ETHNICITY as simply the invention of missionary activity, colonial officialdom, or early anthropology, for example, is insufficiently flexible to take the measure of exploration encounters. Such scenarios are not sufficiently subtle to discern the complex role of the missionary movement – to take one activity too easily typecast as the servant of cultural imperialism – in emerging senses of nationhood (see NATION; NATIONALISM). Thus we are only beginning to appreciate how, in the African context, a missionary passion to render indigenous languages into written form (for the purpose of Bible translation) provided mother tongue cultures with a vernacular literacy that in turn cultivated nascent senses of nationhood. Through translation, written languages were created and a vocabulary for national self-consciousness fostered (see Sanneh, 1990; Hastings, 1997).

The history of 'exploration', then, turns out to be far from antiquarian chronology. Rather it focuses centrally on the IDENTITY of people, the wielding of POWER, and the construction of knowledge; and it is precisely because these are entangled in such complex and intricate ways that their elucidation is of crucial importance to the future course of human history.

DNL

References

Arnold, D. 1996: *The problem of nature: environment, culture and European expansion*. Oxford: Blackwell. · Baker, J.N.L. 1931: *A history of geographical discovery and exploration*. London: Harrap. · Banes, D. 1988: The Portuguese voyages of discovery and the emergence of modern science. *Journal of the Washington Academy of Sciences* 28: 47–58. · Beaglehole, J.C. 1966: *The exploration of the Pacific*, 3rd edn. Stanford: Stanford University Press. · Boorstin, D. 1983: *The discoverers. A history of man's search to know his world and himself*. New York: Random House. · Brantlinger, P. 1985: Victorians and Africans: the genealogy of the myth of the dark continent. *Critical Inquiry* 12: 166–203. · Cannon, S.F. 1978: *Science in culture: the early Victorian period*. New York: Dawson and Science History Publications. · Carter, P. 1987: *The road to Botany Bay: an essay in spatial history*. London: Faber. · Chang, K.-S. 1971: The Ming maritime enterprise and China's knowledge of Africa prior to the age of great discoverers. *Terrae Incognitae* 3: 33–4. · Comaroff, J. and J. 1991: *Of revelation and revolution: Christianity, colonialism, and consciousness in South Africa, volume 1*. Chicago: University of Chicago Press. · Dettelbach, M. 1996: Humboldtian science. In N. Jardine, J.A. Secord and E.C. Spary, eds, *Cultures of natural history*. Cambridge: Cambridge University Press, 287–304. · Frost, A. 1988: Science for political purposes: European explorations of the Pacific Ocean, 1764–1806. In R. MacLeod and P.E. Rehbock, eds, *Nature in its greatest extent: Western science in the Pacific*. Honolulu: University of Hawaii Press, 27–44. · Gamble, C. 1992: Archaeology, history and the uttermost ends of the earth – Tasmania, Tierra del Fuego and the Cape. *Antiquity* 66: 712–20. · Goetzmann, W.H. 1986: *New lands, new men. America and the second great age of discovery*. New York: Viking. · Goodman, D. 1991: Iberian science: navigation, empire and Counter-Reformation. In D. Goodman and C.A. Russell, eds,

The rise of scientific Europe, 1500–1800. Sevenoaks, Kent: Hodder & Stoughton, 117–44. · Greenblatt, S. 1991: *Marvellous possessions: the wonder of the New World*. Chicago: University of Chicago Press. · Gregory, D. 1993: *Geographical imaginations*. Oxford: Blackwell. · Hale, J.R. 1967: A world elsewhere. In D. Hay, ed., *The Age of Renaissance* London: Thames and Hudson. · Hall, S. 1992: The west and the rest: discourse and power. In S. Hall and B. Gieben, eds, *Formations of modernity*. Oxford: Polity Press in association with the Open University. · Harley, J.B. 1988: Maps, knowledge, and power. In D. Cosgrove and S. Daniels, eds, *The iconography of landscape: essays in the representation, design and use of past environments*. Cambridge: Cambridge University Press, 277–312. · Harley, J.B. 1990: *Maps and the Columbian encounter*. Milwaukee: The Golda Meir Library. · Hastings, A. 1997: *The construction of nationhood: ethnicity, religion and nationalism*. Cambridge: Cambridge University Press. · Hooykaas, R. 1979: *Humanism and the voyages of discovery in 16th Century Portuguese science and letters*. Amsterdam: North Holland Publishing Company. · Horvath, R. 1971: The Detroit Geographical Expedition and Institute experience. *Antipode* 3: 73–85. · James, P.E. 1972: *All possible worlds: a history of geographical ideas*. Indianapolis: The Bobbs-Merrill Company. · Lindeborg, R.H. 1994: The Asiatic and the boundaries of Victorian Englishness. *Victorian Studies* 38: 1–24. · Livingstone, D.N. 1991: The moral discourse of climate: historical considerations on race, place and virtue. *Journal of Historical Geography* 17: 413–34. · Livingstone, D.N. 1999: Tropical climate and moral hygiene: the anatomy of a Victorian debate. *British Journal for the History of Science*, 32, 93–110. · Mackenzie, J.M. 1995: *Orientalism: history, theory and the arts*. Manchester: Manchester University Press. · MacLeod, R. and Rehbock, P.H., eds, 1994: *Darwin's laboratory: evolutionary theory and natural history in the Pacific*. Honolulu: University of Hawaii Press. · Mason, P. 1990: *Deconstructing America: representations of the other*. London and New York: Routledge. · Mitchell, T. 1988: *Colonising Egypt*. Cambridge: Cambridge University Press. · Needham, J. 1959: *Science and civilization in China, volume 3*. Cambridge: Cambridge University Press. · Nochlin, L. 1991: The imaginary Orient. In L. Nochlin, *The politics of vision*. London: Thames and Hudson, ch. 3. · O'Sullivan, D. 1984: The *age of discovery 1400–1550*. London and New York: Longman. · Pagden, A. 1986: The impact of the new world on the old: The history of an idea. *Renaissance and Modern Studies* 30: 1–11. · Pagden, A. 1993: *European encounters with the New World*. New Haven: Yale University Press. · Parry, J.H. 1981: *The age of reconnaissance. Discovery, exploration and settlement 1450 to 1650*. Berkeley: University of California Press. · Pratt, M.L. 1992: *Imperial eyes: travel writing and transculturation*. London: Routledge. · Sanneh, L. 1990: *Translating the message: the missionary impact on culture*. Maryknoll, NY: Orbis Books. · Said, E.W. 1978: *Orientalism: Western conceptions of the Orient*. London: Routledge & Kegan Paul. · Salmond, A. 1991: *Twoworlds. First meetings between Maori and Europeans 1642–1772*. Auckland, NZ: Viking. · Smith, B. 1960: *European vision and the South Pacific, 1768–1850: A study in the history of art and ideas*. Oxford: Oxford University Press. · Stafford, B.M. 1984: *Voyage into substance. Art, science, nature and the illustrated travel account, 1760–1840*. Cambridge, MA: The MIT Press. · Stafford, R.A. 1989: *Scientist of empire. Sir Roderick Murchison, scientific exploration and Victorian imperialism*. Cambridge: Cambridge University Press.

Suggested Reading

Brosse, J. 1983: *Great voyages of discovery: circumnavigators and scientists, 1764–1843*, trans. by S. Hochman. New York: Facts on File Publications. · Penrose, B. 1967: *Travel and discovery in the Renaissance 1420–1620*. Cambridge, MA: Harvard University Press. · Van Orman, R.A. 1984: *The explorers: nineteenth century expeditions in Africa and the American West*. Albuquerque: University of New Mexico Press. · Viola, H.J. and Margolis, C., eds, 1985: *Magnificent voyagers: The U.S. exploring expedition, 1838–1842*. Washington, D.C.: Smithsonian Institution Press.

exploratory data analysis Statistical procedures for describing the major features of a data set, from which HYPOTHESES for further testing may be generated. Whereas many statistical analyses follow the rules of scientific INFERENCE in the evaluation of hypotheses (see CONFIRMATORY DATA ANALYSIS), exploratory data analysis makes few initial assumptions about the expected findings.

Exploratory analyses are of particular value in geographical work for two reasons. First, much geographical investigation has a relatively weak theoretical base and its empirical expectations are consequently fairly imprecise in their goals: exploratory data analysis is sympathetic to such situations, because it lacks the constraints of formal hypothesis-testing. Secondly, few of the data sets employed by geographers are specifically collected for their purposes in properly controlled experimental conditions, so that the investigator has an incomplete appreciation of their structure. Exploratory data analysis, with its emphasis on graphical display, allows researchers to penetrate data sets, appreciate their peculiarities, and draw conclusions which are constrained neither by prior expectations nor by the limitations of inferential techniques. RJJ

Suggested Reading

Sibley, D. 1990: *Spatial applications of exploratory data analysis*. Concepts and techniques in modern geography 49. Norwich: Environmental Publications.

export platform A location for industrial activity, the primary purpose of which is to produce for export. The term is usually applied to a location where cheap labour is available and industrial activity is not closely linked with other elements of the local economy. Export platforms are typically found in underdeveloped countries where labour costs are kept down by low living standards and sometimes also by governments which condone poor working conditions and discourage unionization. Because of their external orientation, export platforms often contribute little to the development of the host nation. DMS

References

Back, L. 1993: Reindeer management in conflict and co-operation. *Nomadic peoples* 32: 65–80. · Galaty, J. and Johnson, J., eds, 1991: *The world of pastoralism*. London: Belhaven Press. · Jarrige, R. and Auriol, P. 1992: An outline of world beef production. In R. Jarrige and C. Beranger, eds, *Beef cattle production*. Amsterdam, Elsevier, 42–85. · Mannion, A. 1995: *Agriculture and environmental change*. Chichester, Wiley: ch. 4.

extensive agriculture In opposition to intensive forms of agriculture which involve the repeated cultivation and/or grazing of the same area of land using supplementary energy inputs, extensive forms of agriculture are characterized by seasonal or other temporal patterns of transitory land use over large areas (Mannion, 1995). They are, in other words, land-extensive and tend to be associated with environments considered to be marginal, or inhospitable, for permanent agriculture. Extensive forms of agriculture range from traditional practices like SHIFTING CULTIVATION in tropical regions and various systems of livestock and dairy production such as nomadic pastoralism and transhumance (Galaty and Johnson, 1991) (see also PASTORALISM), to more recently established practices like ranching associated with the European settlement of the USA and Australia (Jarrige and Auriol, 1992).

Nomadic PASTORALISM occurs in arid and semi-arid regions in low and high altitudes and underpins distinctive cultural communities such as the Saami reindeer herders in the Arctic region of northern Europe and Scandinavia (Back, 1993) and the Tuareg camel herders of the Sahel region of Africa. TRANSHUMANCE is practised in montane regions where livestock, usually goats, sheep or dairy cattle, are moved between valley and uplands on a seasonal basis, for example in the Montes de Pas in north-western Spain or the Himalayan foothills in Uttar Pradesh.

While some of these practices date back many centuries they remain the basis of the livelihoods of millions of people around the world. For example, it has been estimated that some 250 million people in Latin America, Africa and Asia rely on shifting cultivation today. These forms of agriculture have faced growing threats from the incursion of settlement; alternative land uses and property systems; and political boundary disputes on their effective range. Such incursions can undermine the social and environmental viability of these agricultural practices (see also AGRICULTURAL GEOGRAPHY; CARRYING CAPACITY; INTENSIVE AGRICULTURE). SW

extensive research Research that is directed towards discovering common properties and empirical regularities and that aims to offer generalizations about them. The term is derived from the philosopher Rom Harré, and in geography would apply to much of the work conducted under the signs of EMPIRICISM and POSITIVISM with SPATIAL SCIENCE and BEHAVIOURAL GEOGRAPHY. Sayer (1992) suggests that extensive research typically relies on QUANTITATIVE METHODS – including descriptive and inferential statistics and numerical analysis – and on large-scale QUESTIONNAIRES and formal INTERVIEWS. The term has been widely used in discussions of REALISM as a more appropriate philosophy for human geography, where it is contrasted with strategies of INTENSIVE RESEARCH (cf. the figure accompanying that entry). 'Extensive studies are weaker for the purpose of explanation not so much because they are a "broad-brush" method lacking in sensitivity to detail', Sayer (1992) argues, 'but because the relations they discover are formal, concerning similarity, dissimilarity, correlation and the like, rather than causal, structural and substantial'. (See also QUALITATIVE METHODS.) DG

Reference and Suggested Reading

Sayer, A. 1992: *Method in social science a realist approach*, 2nd edn. London: Routledge, 241–51.

external economies Cost advantages obtained from sources external to the organization. These comprise reductions in operating costs, associated with such considerations as the local availability of a skilled labour force, workers familiar with the industry in question, a technical college providing appropriate training, research facilities and the existence of ancillary industries providing materials, components, machinery or specialized services. External economies typically develop in a localized concentration of a particular activity (see GROWTH POLE). If not available externally, such facilities have to be provided internally, which increases costs. External economies are especially important to small firms. DMS

externalities The (usually unintended) effects of one person's actions on another, over which the latter has no control: they may be either positive (bringing benefits to the recipients) or negative (creating costs or other disadvantages for them). Good examples are provided by a neighbourhood environment: high quality local schools can generate positive externalities (excellent contexts for child-rearing) whereas noisy households (which hold parties late at night) can create costs for people in the locality. Each type of externality may have an influence on property values locally.

Most externalities have only local impacts, with a DISTANCE-DECAY effect in their extent and intensity. (There is usually a DENSITY GRADIENT in the spread of a negative externality such as noise, for example: the further you are from its source, the less it affects you.) Because they can impact on people's QUALITY OF LIFE and the value of their properties, there is frequently CONFLICT over the location of land uses which generate externalities. People compete – through the pricing system in the property market, for example – to be near sources of positive externalities (as shown in studies of the geography of house values in many cities) and may become involved in political action (often of a collective kind: see NIMBY) to exclude negative externality generators from their neighbourhoods (cf. ENVIRONMENTAL JUSTICE). Because of unequal power in housing markets, the more affluent are usually better able to succeed in the elimination of negative externalities from their home areas, and thus to protect their property values, thereby promoting residential SEGREGATION. RJJ

Suggested Reading

Cox, K.R. 1973: *Conflict, power and politics in the city: a geographic view*. New York: McGraw-Hill. · Saunders, P. 1979: *Urban politics: a sociological interpretation*. London: Penguin Books. · Smith, D.M. 1977: *Human geography: a welfare approach*. London: Edward Arnold.

F

factor analysis A statistical procedure for transforming (observations by variables) a data matrix so that the variables in the new matrix are uncorrelated. Unlike PRINCIPAL COMPONENTS ANALYSIS, which has a similar goal, factor analysis does not identify as many new variables (termed factors) as there are in the original matrix because it ignores that portion of the variance in each of the original variables which is unique to it – i.e. is uncorrelated with any other variable.

The first stage in a factor analysis involves creating a matrix of similarities between the variables in the original data matrix, usually employing CORRELATION coefficients. It then identifies and eliminates the unique variance (that part of each variable which is uncorrelated with any other), and subsequently follows the same general sequence of procedures as in principal components analysis, with the successive extraction of factors that maximize the common variance accounted for. The results – the eigenvalues and the matrices of factor loadings and factor scores – are interpreted in the same way as the comparable matrices of component loadings and scores.

Factor analysis concentrates on identifying the commonalities in the interrelationships among variables. It can be used either *inductively* (as in EXPLORATORY DATA ANALYSIS), to separate groups of variables with common relative distributions across the observations, or *deductively*, to test HYPOTHESES regarding the existence of such groups. Few geographical applications have rigorously followed the second route, because the available theory gives only very general expectations concerning the loadings.

To facilitate the inductive search for groups of related variables (as in applications which fall under the general term FACTORIAL ECOLOGY), the factor loading matrix may be rotated mathematically to maximize the relationship of each of the original variables to just one factor. Of the many rotation procedures available in computer statistical packages, most fall into one of two types: (1) orthogonal rotations (of which the most popular is Varimax), which maintain the uncorrelated nature of the factors; and (2) oblique rotations, which allow correlations among the factors. RJJ

Suggested Reading

Johnston, R.J. 1978: *Multivariate statistical analysis in geography: a primer on the general linear model*. London and New York: Longman.

factorial ecology The application of either FACTOR ANALYSIS or PRINCIPAL COMPONENTS ANALYSIS to matrices of socio-economic, demographic and housing data for small intra-urban districts (see CENSUS TRACT), to test the general hypothesis that the pattern of residential differentiation (see SEGREGATION) can be reduced to a small number of general constructs. SOCIAL AREA ANALYSIS provides the framework within which factorial ecology was developed: it is generally applied inductively, allowing the constructs to emerge from the data rather than testing for the existence of hypothesized relationships (other than in a qualitative sense of expecting certain broad patterns). Factorial ecology is thus a relatively sophisticated technology for describing the main elements of urban socio-spatial structure, whose outputs depend substantially on the nature of the data input – almost invariably obtained from censuses. RJJ

Suggested Reading

Davies, W.K.D. 1984: *Factorial ecology*. Aldershot: Gower.

factors of production The ingredients necessary to the production process, i.e. those things that must be assembled at one place before production can begin. The three broad headings conventionally adopted are land, labour and CAPITAL. Sometimes the fourth factor of 'enterprise' is added, to recognize the contribution of the 'entrepreneur' or risk-taker and the legitimacy of a special return to this particular participant in the productive process. However, in the current complexity of economic organization it is hard to distinguish enterprise from general management functions, so this factor is more appropriately subsumed under labour. The combination of factors of production reflects the state of technology applied in the activity in question, e.g. whether it is capital-intensive or labour-intensive.

Land is necessary for any productive activity, whether it is agriculture, mining, manufacturing or services. Land may be a direct source of a raw material, as is the case with mining, or it may be required for the cultivation of a crop or to support the physical plant of a manufacturing activity. Modern industry requires increasing quantities of land, as factory sites and for such associated uses as storage, roadways and parking.

Labour requirements vary with the nature of the activity in question. Some need numerous unskilled workers while others require more skilled operatives, technicians, office personnel, etc. The availability of particular types of labour can have an important bearing on the location of economic activity. Despite the growing capital intensity of modern industry, cheap labour with a record of stability is still an attraction. That the value of production can ultimately be traced to the factor of labour is central to the LABOUR THEORY OF VALUE.

Capital includes all things deliberately created by humans for the purpose of production. This includes the physical plant, buildings and machinery, i.e. fixed capital, plus the circulating capital in the form of stocks of raw materials, components, semi-finished goods, etc. Private ownership of capital and land is the major distinguishing feature of the capitalist mode of production, which carries with it important implications for the distribution of income and wealth (see MARXIAN ECONOMICS; NEO-CLASSICAL ECONOMICS).

The conventional categories of land, labour and capital (and enterprise) can serve an ideological role in legitimizing the differential rewards of the various contributors to production under capitalism. The concept of PRODUCTIVE FORCES is preferred in SOCIALIST economics. In any event, for practical purposes these broad categories tend to be subdivided into the individual inputs actually required in particular productive activities.

DMS

Suggested Reading

Smith, D.M. 1981: *Industrial location: an economic geographical analysis*, 2nd edn. New York: John Wiley.

falsification The distinguishing principle of an empirical science, according to the philosophy of CRITICAL RATIONALISM. Progress in such a science involves the articulation of a THEORY which is evaluated empirically by a critical test designed to refute it. RJJ

family reconstitution A technique of nominal linkage in demographic analysis. Family reconstitution creates accurate FERTILITY and MORTALITY rates from data about vital events (births, marriages and deaths): such data are sometimes available in cases where the absence of a CENSUS inhibits the calculation of demographic measures. The researcher assembles all information relating to one marriage on a family reconstitution form: date of marriage, birth and death dates of spouses and of children, and socio-economic information (e.g. occupation). A range of measures may then be calculated, including age-at-marriage, proportion of adult males and females ever married, age-at-death, and childbirth patterns among women.

Reconstitution methodologies are intricate, but designed to eliminate ambiguities arising from MIGRATION and other factors which cause people to enter and leave the study area population. Various 'observation rules' determine whether particular individuals are regarded 'in observation' in a parish register at any given time: for example, following a baptism it is necessary to know whether an infant continues to be resident, if that infant is to be used in calculating infant mortality rates, and this is inferred according to the subsequent appearance in the register of other events relating to the same family. The significance of precise rules for establishing an individual's *presence in observation* was first set out by French demographers M. Fleury and L. Henry, and adapted for English parish registers, available from 1538, by E.A. Wrigley (1966).

The interpretation of the demographic measures obtained from reconstitutions has been much-debated. Obviously, measures which require data relating to an individual over many years use fewer data than those which require presence in observation for only a short period. Thus infant mortality rates are typically based upon 80 per cent or more of legitimate births, whereas age-at-marriage calculations rarely involve more than half of marriage partners, and age-specific fertility rates are typically based upon 15 to 20 per cent of legitimate births. Some debate surrounds the representativeness of the immobile population that remains in observation within a single parish, especially for topics requiring long observation periods of individual families (Souden, 1984).

The main application of family reconstitution has been for pre-census Europe and colonial North America, and based on church registers of baptisms, marriages and burials (note that the first and last of these may not equate exactly with births and deaths). The procedures are very time-consuming, but some progress in computerizing them has been made at the ESRC Cambridge Group for the History of Population and Social Structure. Wrigley et al. (1996) analyse completed family reconstitutions for the whole parish register period from 26 English parishes, in conjunction with their previous aggregate analysis of vital events in over 400 parishes (Wrigley and Schofield, 1983). Partial family reconstitutions over shorter time periods have been undertaken for several dozen other parishes.

These studies have indicated the predominance of natural fertility in pre-industrial European and American populations, with only very limited family limitation before the late nineteenth century. They also enable the beginnings of analysis of long-run geographical variations in NUPTIALITY, fertility, and mortality, and comparisons with nineteenth-century census data (Wrigley and Schofield, 1983; Woods and Wilson, 1991, Wrigley et al., 1996). Substantial geographical variations, both within and among countries, have been reported in marriage patterns and timing, in marital fertility, and in infant mortality (Wrigley, 1998). The integration of reconstitution studies with information on migration patterns has begun to produce sophisticated accounts of interrelated economic and demographic change (Galley, 1995). PG

References

Galley, C. 1995: A model of early modern urban demography. *Economic History Review* 48: 448–69. · Knodel, J. 1988: *Demographic behaviour in the past: a study of fourteen German village populations in the eighteenth and nineteenth centuries*. Cambridge: Cambridge University Press. · Souden, D. 1984: Movers and stayers in family reconstitution populations. *Local Population Studies* 33: 11–27. · Woods, R. and Wilson, C. 1991: Fertility in England: a long-term perspective. *Population Studies* 45: 399–415. · Wilson, C. 1986: The proximate determinants of marital fertility in England 1600–1799. In L. Bonfield, ed., *The world we have gained: histories of population and social structure*. Oxford: Basil Blackwell, 203–30. · Wrigley, E.A. 1966: Family reconstitution. In E.A. Wrigley, ed., *An introduction to English historical demography*. London: Weidenfeld and Nicholson, 96–159. · Wrigley, E.A. 1998: Explaining the rise in fertility in England in the 'long' eighteenth century. *Economic History Review* 51: 435–64. · Wrigley, E.A. and Schofield, R.S. 1983: *The population history of England 1541–1871: a reconstruction*. London: Edward Arnold. · Wrigley, E.A., Davies, R., Oeppen, J. and Schofield, R.S. 1996: *English population history from family reconstitution, 1580–1837*. Cambridge: Cambridge University Press.

Suggested Reading

Knodel (1988). · Wrigley, Davies, Oeppen and Schofield (1996).

family types Families are units of kinsfolk within which many decisions of everyday life are made. In almost all human societies, families form significant units of social recognition and social interaction, but the composition of 'the family' varies widely. Different family types vary in the number and proximity of kin involved in prevailing definitions of 'family' (Wall et al., 1983; Plakans, 1984).

An important distinction separates simple *'nuclear' families* (those consisting of one or more parents with their children) from various *'extended' family types* (where a nuclear family unit may be extended upwards or downwards to include three generations, or laterally to include the families of more than one sibling). Besides natural (i.e. biological) kinship, family types vary in respect of the senses in, and degree to, which family members are created: by *affinity* (through marriage or illegitimate carnal unions); by *legal kinship* (adoption); or by *spiritual kinship* (through godparenthood). Debates on family types overlap with debates on household composition, but these debates are not equivalent because family and household unit need not be synonymous (in part depending on INHERITANCE SYSTEMS), and because household composition may vary through the family life-cycle (Flandrin, 1979).

The family also has an important symbolic role in cultural and political systems. Some claim that 'the family is best understood as a moral system' (Casey, 1989), although the household remains central to most conceptions of the family. Some claim that variations in family structure and kinship structure condition geographical variations in social IDEOLOGY and belief (Todd, 1985), while others hold that the emotional or cultural significance of family ideals may not be directly related to prevailing patterns of family or household behaviour (Anderson, 1980). There is no unanimity amongst contemporary demographers, for example, as to whether distinctive family structures in sub-Saharan Africa assist in accounting for the much later reduction of fertility there than in many other less developed countries (Caldwell, 1987; Lesthaeghe, 1989; Ahlberg, 1994). PG

References

Ahlberg, B. 1994: Is there a distinctive African sexuality? A critical response to Caldwell. *Africa* 64: 220–42. · Anderson, M. 1980: *Approaches to the history of the Western family*. London: Macmillan. · Caldwell, J.C. 1987: The cultural context of high fertility in sub-Saharan Africa. *Population and Development Review* 13: 409–37. · Casey, J. 1989: *The history of the family*. Oxford: Basil Blackwell. · Flandrin, J.-L. 1979: *Families in former times: kinship, household and sexuality*. Cambridge: Cambridge University Press. · Lesthaeghe, R. 1989: *Reproduction and social organisation in sub-Saharan Africa*. Berkeley: University of California Press. · Plakans, A. 1984: *Kinship in the past: an anthropology of European family life 1500–1900*. Oxford: Basil Blackwell. · Todd, E. 1985: *The explanation of ideology: family structures and social systems*. Oxford: Basil Blackwell. · Wall, R. et al., ed., 1983: *Family forms in historic Europe*. Cambridge: Cambridge University Press.

famine Famine refers to a relatively sudden event involving mass mortalities from starvation within a short period. Famine is typically distinguished from chronic hunger, understood as endemic nutritional deprivation on a persistent basis (as opposed to seasonal hunger, for example). Definitions of famine are fraught with danger because (i) cultural, as opposed to biological, definitions of starvation vary around diverse, locally defined norms, and (ii) deaths from starvation are frequently impossible to distinguish from those from disease.

Nearly all societies have periodically suffered from the consequences of famine. The earliest recorded famine which occurred in ancient Egypt dates to 4000 BC; famine conditions currently exist (1998) in Sudan and North Korea (1999). The dynamics and characteristics of mass starvation in modern times have similar structural properties however; typically such famines involve sharp price increases for STAPLE foodstuffs, decapitalization of household assets, gathering of wild foods, borrowing and begging, petty crime and occasionally food riots, and out-MIGRATION. According to the Hunger Program at Brown University, the trend in famine casualties has been downward since 1945 but in the late 1980s STATES with a combined population of 200 millions failed to prevent famine within their national borders. Hunger, and famine in particular, is intolerable in the modern world, however, because it is unnecessary and unwarranted (Sen and Dreze, 1989).

Famine causation has often been linked to natural disasters, population growth and war producing a reduction in food supply (Malthus, 1798). But some major famines (for example, Bengal in 1943) were not preceded by a significant decline in food production or absolute availability and in some cases have been associated with food export. Recent analyses have focused on access to and control over food resources – sometimes called the *food availability decline hypothesis*. Sen (1981) argues that what we eat depends on what food we are able to acquire. Famine therefore is a function of the failure of socially specific entitlements through which individuals command bundles of commodities. Entitlements vary in relation to property rights, asset distribution, CLASS and GENDER. Famine is therefore a social phenomenon rooted in the institutional and political economic arrangements which determine the access to food by different classes and strata (Watts, 1983). Mass POVERTY and mass starvation are obviously linked via entitlements. Mass poverty results from long-term changes in entitlements associated with social production and distribution mechanisms; famines arise from short-term changes in these same mechanisms. Famine and endemic deprivation correspond to two forms of public action to eradicate them: famine policy requires entitlement protection ensuring that it does not collapse among vulnerable groups (i.e. landless labourers, women). Chronic hunger demands entitlement promotion to expand the command people have over basic necessities (Sen and Dreze, 1989). Since 1945 India has implemented a successful anti-famine policy yet conspicuously failed to eradicate endemic deprivation; China, conversely, has overcome the hunger problem but failed to prevent massive famine in the 1950s. Africa has witnessed a catastrophic growth in the incidence of both mass starvation and chronic hunger (de Waal, 1997).

The role of state policy and of humanitarian aid figures centrally in discussions of famine and famine causation. While the public sphere is key in understanding how and why the right to food and the right to not be hungry are made effective, the recent history of famine shows clearly how the state can use famine and humanitarian aid for explicitly political purposes. The case against Stalin and the Ukrainian famine is clear in this regard, and the catastrophic Chinese famine of the late 1950s is a compelling instance of how inept state policies to achieve rapid INDUSTRIALIZATION backfired but also how an authoritarian state ignored famine signals and colluded in the deaths of 20 million people (Becker, 1997). Sen (1981) has argued that famines rarely occur in societies in which there is freedom of the press (and in which states are therefore held to be accountable in some way). Humanitarian assistance has also been an object of critique insofar as it itself becomes politicized (and rendered as a business), and often fails to be more than a short-term palliative (rather than assisting in the rehabilitation and reconstruction of famine-devastated

COMMUNITIES: de Waal, 1997). (See also FOOD, GEOGRAPHY OF.) MW

References

Becker, J. 1997: *Hungry ghosts*. London: John Murray. · de Waal, A. 1997: *Famine crimes*. London: Heinemann. · Malthus, T. 1798: *An essay on the principle of population*. London: Harmondsworth. · Sen, A. 1981: *Poverty and famines*. Oxford: Clarendon Press. · Sen, A. and Dreze, J. 1989: *Hunger and public action*. Oxford: Clarendon Press. · Watts, M. 1983: *Silent violence*. Berkeley: University of California Press.

farm fragmentation Discontiguous patterns of landholding, such that a farm is not composed of a single unit of land, but rather a scattering of fields which increases production costs, particularly for highly mechanized forms of agriculture. Historically, fragmentation resulted from the fossilization of medieval field patterns; inheritance practices amongst family and peasant producers, which divided a farm between sons; and the cumulative effect of piecemeal land purchases (King and Burton, 1982; cf. FIELD SYSTEMS; INHERITANCE SYSTEMS). In the twentieth century it also became associated with major political upheavals and the break-up of large estates through programmes of land reform, such as in Portugal or Mexico.

In the post-war period these fragmented patterns of landholding have come to be regarded as a hindrance to agricultural modernization and AGRARIAN capitalism, and become the subject of government policies of land consolidation in advanced industrial and developing countries, or land collectivization in the formerly communist countries. In Europe, for example, France established a regional network of land management banks (SAFERs) in the 1960s to buy up and re-allocate farmland (Jones, 1989).

In the latter part of the twentieth century farm fragmentation has taken on a new meaning, referring to the break-up of farmholdings as a result of land development and road building pressures; the growth of short-term forms of land tenancy and the rising number of small farms being put out of business by competition, foreclosure or lack of a successor (e.g. Kopeva et al., 1994; Pfeffer and Lapping, 1994). While these problems can and do occur in diverse geographical circumstances, they are especially acute in the RURAL–URBAN FRINGE. SW

References

Jones, A. 1989: The role of SAFER in agricultural restructuring: the case of Languedoc-Rousillon, France. *Land Use Policy* 6: 249–61. · King, R. and Burton, S. 1982: Land fragmentation: notes on fundamental rural spatial problems. *Progress in Human Geography* 6: 475–94. · Kopeva, D., Mishev, P. and Jackson, M. 1994: Formation of land market institutions and their impacts on agricultural activity. *Journal of Rural Studies* 10/4: 377–85. · Pfeffer, M. and Lapping, M. 1994: Farmland preservation, development rights and the theory of the growth machine: the view of planners. *Journal of Rural Studies* 10 (3): 233–48.

farming, type of A way of categorizing patterns of farm land-use which has been a staple feature of traditional AGRICULTURAL GEOGRAPHY (Tarrant, 1974). The objective was to produce systematic indices of trends over time and differences across space in agricultural activity, using farm census data to measure and map regional variations (see, for example, Coppock, 1976). Such classifications have been much criticized for the limited attention they pay to the socio-economic processes driving land-use change and, thus, their lack of explanatory grip on the patterns they describe. As a consequence, and despite the refinements brought to these classificatory procedures in the 1980s and 1990s by the application of GEOGRAPHICAL INFORMATION SYSTEMS and REMOTE SENSING techniques (Barnsley et al., 1997), they have become rather marginal to the research concerns of agricultural geography today.

However, under the influence of the POLITICAL ECONOMY approaches which have come to dominate agricultural geography in the last decade or so geographers have put effort into developing more theoretically informed typologies of farm business organization to help explain variations and changes in farming practice. Such efforts engage with a long sociological tradition of farm typologies concerned with the class location of farmers and the relationship between the social organization of farming – land tenure; capital ownership; labour relations and family life-cycle – and the process of rural change (see, for example, Newby et al., 1978; Goss et al., 1980; Ghorayshi, 1986).

Geographical contributions to the development of these alternative theoretical and methodological approaches to farm typologies have emphasized the persistence and variety of forms of family farming and their role in the uneven development of capitalist agriculture (see, for example, Aitchison and Aubrey, 1982; Whatmore et al., 1987; Marsden et al., 1992). SW

References

Aitchison, J. and Aubrey, P. 1982: Part-time farming in Wales: a typological study. *Transactions of the Institute of British Geographers* NS 7: 88–97. · Barnsley, M., Barr, S.

and Tsang, T. 1997: Scaling and generalisation issues in land cover mapping. In P. van Gardingen, G. Foody and P. Curran, eds, *Scaling-up: from cell to landscape*. Cambridge: Cambridge University Press. · Coppock, J.T. 1976: *An agricultural atlas of England and Wales*, 2nd edn. London: Faber and Faber. · Ghorayshi, P. 1986: The identification of capitalist farms. Theoretical and methodological considerations. *Sociologia Ruralis* xxvi/2: 146–69. · Goss, K., Rodefeld, R. and Buttel, F. 1980: The political economy of class structure in US agriculture: a theoretical outline. In F. Buttel and H. Newby, eds, *The rural sociology of advanced societies: critical perspectives*. London: Croom Helm, 83–132. · Marsden, T., Munton, R. and Ward, N. 1992: Incorporating social trajectories into uneven agrarian development: farm businesses in upland and lowland Britain. *Sociologia Ruralis* 32: 408–30. · Newby, H., Bell, C., Rose, C. and Saunders, P. 1978: *Property, paternalism and power*. London: Hutchinson. · Tarrant, J. 1974: *Agricultural geography*. Newton Abbot: David and Charles. · Whatmore, S., Munton, R., Little, J. and Marsden, T. 1987: Towards a typology of farm businesses in contemporary British agriculture. *Sociologia Ruralis* 28 (1): 21–37.

fecundity The biological capacity to reproduce. The term may refer to the biological capacity of males, females or couples, though the focus is usually on women. Apart from temporary periods of sterility, women are generally fecund (i.e. are biologically capable of bearing children) from menarche to menopause. The term is distinct from FERTILITY which refers to the actual childbearing of an individual or population. PEO

Suggested Reading

Daughtery, H.G. and Kammeyer, K.C.W. 1995: *An introduction to population*, 2nd edn. New York and London: Guilford Press, ch. 8.

federalism A form of government in which central and regional authorities divide powers and functions, with the initial aim of maintaining a high degree of autonomy for the regional units (Wheare, 1963). Federal systems usually come into existence to balance between local and ETHNIC interests yet gain the benefits of ECONOMIES OF SCALE in the provision of some functions at the central level. The challenge facing federal systems is to prevent one level from dictating to the other as, at one extreme, with unitary government and, at the other, with confederation. A written constitution is necessary to achieve this aim, although disputes always seem to arise over interpreting the 'original intent' of the writers in later conditions in which economic, technological and social changes make many of their concerns appear anachronistic. This tends to give extremely wide discretionary powers to the federal judiciary, and the highest court (such as the US Supreme Court) in particular, to adjudicate between the competing demands of the two levels of government. Some matters, such as foreign policy, defence and international trade, are usually reserved for the central government with all others, in theory, left in the hands of the regional units. This geographical division of functions is often designed to prevent the concentration of public POWER, particularly when combined, as in the US case, with a divided central government (executive, legislature and judiciary). This leads to charges of a system-wide lack of 'decisional focus' and the usurping of public power by the best organized private interests (Cerny, 1989; Ollman and Birnbaum, 1990). American federalism, with its emphasis on individual citizenship rights, also has difficulty in moving from the purely 'territorial' conception of representation implicit in a fixed balance between levels of government to one based on recognizing the representation claims of minorities, women and other historically disenfranchised groups who live spread out around the country (Agnew, 1995).

In practice, federations vary widely in how they work. Some, such as the former Soviet Union under its 1936 Constitution, have been fictive rather than real although its claim to allow SECESSION was no more fanciful than the fictions about free consent that animate most other federal constitutions. Most of those federations established in former colonies have long-since floundered (e.g. the Central African Federation of Rhodesia and Nyasaland and the West Indian Federation). Interdependence, more than true separation of functions, marks the political complexion of many of the others, if only because of increased collaboration between governments at different levels. Most federal systems have become more centralized over time as citizens themselves have pressured for national redistributive policies (as in the US New Deal of the 1930s) and the enforcement of civil rights in constituent units (as in the US Civil Rights movement in the 1960s). But some, particularly those with geographically concentrated ethnic groups (see ETHNICITY), have become more decentralized (as in Canada) or have broken up (as in the former Yugoslavia). In the US since the late 1970s the regional units (the States) have become more assertive with respect to taking charge of services, revenue collection and economic development. This trend has been reinforced by the election of presidents in the 1980s and 1990s who have been ideologically committed to limiting the general role of the central government and deregulating the national economy. Increasingly, the States have experimented with their own alternatives to federal mandates. One consequence in some policy areas has been pressure on traditional federal preserves such as control over immigration and foreign-economic policy as some States, such as California and Texas, embark on their own immigration-related and economic-development policies without federal involvement. In those federations based around ethnic divisions the dilemma is that regional units legitimize the ethnic divisions and trap politics in a perpetual round of ethnic enmities, yet also provide one way out of the impasse of open conflict that ethnic divisions often generate (Smith, 1995). One thing all federal systems seem to share is a recurring sense of crisis as old divisions of powers encounter new pressures for centralization or decentralization. The continuing appeal of federalism, however, seems to lie in an openness to plurality and multiplicity; features one does not typically associate with most unitary states such as France or China. JAA

References and Suggested Reading

Agnew, J.A. 1995: Postscript: federalism in the post-Cold War era. In G. Smith, ed., *Federalism: the multi-ethnic challenge*. London: Longman, 294–302. · Cerny, P.G. 1989: Political entropy and American decline. *Millennium* 18: 47–63. · Ollman, B. and Birnbaum, J., eds, 1990: *The United States Constitution: 200 years of anti-federalist, abolitionist, feminist, muckraking, progressive, and (especially) socialist criticism*. New York: New York University Press. · Smith, G., ed., 1995: *Federalism: the multiethnic challenge*. London: Longman. · Wheare, K.C. 1963: *Federal government*, 4th edn. London: Oxford University Press.

feedback The reciprocal effect in a SYSTEM, whereby a change in one variable (*A*) influences change in others (*B* and *C*), which in turn influence change in *A*. The feedback influences may be either negative or positive.

With negative feedback the system's EQUILIBRIUM is maintained: in an ECOSYSTEM, for example, an increase in species *A*'s abundance may generate an increase in the number of predators (*B*) which feed on it; as a consequence, the availability of *A* is reduced, the number of *B* predators that can be sustained falls, and the system returns to its former state. Such a system is said to be *morphostatic*, and in a condition of dynamic equilibrium.

With positive feedback an increase in *A* stimulates an increase in *B*, which in turn stimulates a further increase in *A*, as in the MULTIPLIER process central to INPUT–OUTPUT models of economic growth: such a system is termed *morphogenetic*.

The example in the figure shows a system with both morphogenetic and morphostatic feedback loops. The left-hand loop (P–B–G–D) is morphostatic: population growth in a city induces disease through the greater volume and density of waste matter, which subsequently limits population growth. The right-hand loop (P–M–C–P) is morphogenetic:

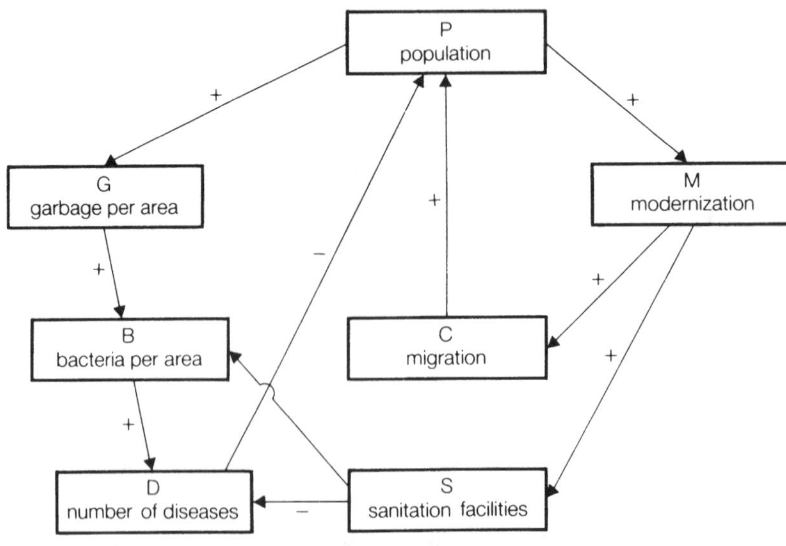

feedback *Urban population change* (Langton, 1972)

a growing city is modernized, attracts more inmigrants, and so grows even further. The two loops are linked via variable S: MODERNIZATION allows greater control over disease and the negative checks are reduced – thereby making the morphogenetic loop dominant and advancing the rate of population growth.

RJJ

Reference

Langton, J. 1972: Potentialities and problems of adopting a systems approach to the study of change in human geography. In C. Board et al., eds, *Progress in geography, volume 4.* London: Edward Arnold, 125–79.

feminist geographies Perspectives that draw on feminist politics and theories to explore how GENDER relations AND GEOGRAPHIES are mutually structured and transformed. The tradition dates from the mid 1970s, drawing inspiration from women's movements of the 1960s. It now has a considerable institutional presence: the journal *Gender Place and Culture* has been published since 1994; there are more than eleven titles in the Routledge *International Studies of Women and Place* series, regular progress reports of feminist geography appear in *Progress in Human Geography* and *Urban Geography*, and three new textbooks appeared in 1997 (Jones, Nast and Roberts, 1997; McDowell and Sharpe, 1997; Women and Geography Study Group, 1997). Although there are distinguishable strands, some common concerns cut across all feminist geographies.

First, they have developed as *critical discourses*, critical not only of women's oppression in society but also of the various ways that this is reproduced in geographical theory. Reflecting their different theoretical and substantive starting points, each refutes a different aspect of geographical theory. This has built towards a comprehensive critique of geographical traditions, for example: POLITICAL GEOGRAPHY (Kofman and Peake, 1990); HISTORICAL GEOGRAPHY (Domosh, 1991); HUMANISTIC GEOGRAPHY (Rose, 1993); SOCIAL AREA ANALYSIS and FACTORIAL ECOLOGY (Pratt and Hanson, 1988); GENTRIFICATION studies inspired by Weberian and MARXIST theory (Rose, 1984); and geographies of MODERNITY and POSTMODERNITY (Deutsche, 1991; Massey, 1991). Rose (1993) extends this critique to the discipline as a whole, cataloguing its various and complementary forms of MASCULINISM. What the relationship between feminist geographies and the discipline now is and should be remain matters of debate: some note the lack of impact that more than a decade of vibrant feminist scholarship has had on the discipline, while others emphasize the increased exchange of ideas between feminist and other strands of critical geography (Women and Geography Study Group, 1997). Feminist geographers' relations with the discipline have been framed through the metaphors of paradoxical and in-between space.

Second, *sexism within geographical institutions* (in the teaching of geography, the staffing of academic departments, and through the publication process) has been a persistent concern (Monk and Hanson, 1982; Rose, 1993).

Third, most feminist geographers share *a commitment to situating knowledge*, to the view that interpretations are context-bound and partial, rather than detached and universal (see PARTICIPATORY ACTION RESEARCH; QUALITATIVE METHODS; SITUATIONISTS). This has produced a large literature on feminist methodologies, including four journal symposia (Moss, 1993; Nast, 1994; Farrow, Moss and Shaw, 1995; Hodge, 1995) and a book (Jones, Nast and Roberts, 1997). It has also led to experimental writing, including various attempts at self-reflexivity (see Rose, 1997 for a critical evaluation of these experiments) and efforts to disrupt the individualist author (for example, the fused subject of Julie Graham and Kathy Gibson as J.K. Gibson-Graham, the Women in Geography Study Group writing collective, and collaborations between academics and community groups).

Fourth, feminist geographies trace the *interconnections between all aspects of daily life*, across the subdisciplinary boundaries of ECONOMIC, SOCIAL, POLITICAL and more recently CULTURAL GEOGRAPHY.

Despite these common themes, there is a great deal of variation among feminist geographers. Bowlby, Lewis, McDowell and Foord (1989) sketch an influential history of feminist geographies, in which they identify two breaks, one in the late 1970s and the other towards the end of the 1980s (see figure on p.260). The first break that they identified was less decisive in the USA, where the influence of the geography of women approach has been stronger than in the UK. (See Monk, 1994, for a more complete map of national variations in feminist geography.) It should be noted, then, that traditions exist simultaneously and there is a great deal of heterogeneity (national and otherwise) within and outside these generalizations.

An important task for feminist geographers has been to make women visible, by developing a geography of women. Two points have been made: women's experiences and perceptions often differ from those of men; and

Three Strands of Feminist Geography

THE GEOGRAPHY OF WOMEN

topical focus:	theoretical influences:	geographical focus:
description of the effects of gender inequality	welfare geography, liberal feminism	constraints of distance and spatial separation

SOCIALIST FEMINIST GEOGRAPHY

topical focus:	theoretical influences:	geographical focus:
explanation of inequality, and relations between capitalism and patriarchy	marxism, socialist feminism	spatial separation, gender place, localities

FEMINIST GEOGRAPHIES OF DIFFERENCE

topical focus:	theoretical influences:	geographical focus
the construction of gendered, heter(sexed) identities; differences among women; gender and constructions of nature; heteropatriarchy and geopolitics	cultural, poststructural, postcolonial, psychoanalytic theories; writings of women of colour, lesbian women, gay men, women from 'developing' countries	micro-geographies of the body; mobile identities; distance, separation and place; imaginative geographies; colonialisms and postcolonialisms; environment/nature

women have restricted access to a range of opportunities, from paid employment to services. This is largely an empirical tradition, loosely influenced by liberal feminism and WELFARE GEOGRAPHY. It has tended to focus on individuals, documenting how women's roles as caregivers and 'housewives', in conjunction with the existing spatial structures, housing design and policy, and patterns of accessibility to transport and other services such as childcare, conspire to constrain women's access to paid employment and other resources. In historical geography, it has taken the form of recovering both the everyday lives of women and the work of women travel writers (Domosh, 1991).

An early criticism of the geography of women approach was that gender inequality is typically explained in terms of the concept of gender roles, especially women's roles as housewives and mothers, in conjunction with some notion of spatial constraint. Foord and Gregson (1986) argued that the concept of gender roles narrows the focus to women (as opposed to male power and the relations between women and men), emerges out of a static social theory, and presents women as victims (as passive recipients of roles). Further, although the geography of women shows how spatial constraint and separation enter into the construction of women's position, it provides a fairly narrow reading of SPACE, conceived almost exclusively as distance (e.g. the journey to work and the separation of SUBURB from paid employment: England, 1993). Little consideration has been given to variations in gender relations across PLACES (although see Momsen and Kinnaird, 1993). There has been, however, a very useful planning component to this literature that outlines, for example, efforts to restructure the city so as to reduce gender inequalities and enhance quality of life (Eichler, 1995; Wekerle and Whitzman, 1995). Both successes and frustrations in attempts to implement some of these reforms have led to critical reconsiderations of the limits of liberal feminism and towards a fuller institutional analysis, confirming Eisenstein's (1981) point that the practical and theoretical limits of LIBERALISM are frequently discovered – in practice – by liberal feminists themselves.

Socialist feminist geographers have reworked Marxian categories and theory to explain the interdependence of geography, gender relations and economic development under CAPITALISM (see MARXIST GEOGRAPHY). One of the key theoretical debates within socialist feminist geography revolved around the question of how best to articulate gender and CLASS analyses. At its most abstract, the question was addressed in terms of PATRIARCHY and capitalism, and the relative autonomy of the two systems.

Socialist feminist geographers first worked primarily at the urban and regional SCALES; arguably, it is now the strand of feminist geography that is most insistent about the material effects of the globalizing forces of capitalism (Katz, 1998). At the urban scale, an early focus of Anglo-American feminist geographers was the social and spatial separation of suburban homes from paid employment; this was seen as crucial to the day-to-day and generational reproduction of workers and the development and continuation of 'traditional' gender relations in capitalist societies (MacKenzie and Rose, 1983). Efforts were made to read these processes in non-functionalist terms and as strategies to manage the effects of a capitalist economy (see FUNCTIONALISM); for example, MacKenzie and Rose argued that the isolation of women as housewives in suburban locations emerged from the combined influence of working-class household strategies, governmental policy and male power within families and trade unions.

Socialist feminist geographers became increasingly attentive to the ways that gender relations differ from place to place and not only reflect but also partially determine local economic changes. At the urban scale, Nelson (1986) argued that employers of clerical workers in the USA began moving to suburban locations in the 1970s to gain access to middle-class, suburban 'house-wives' willing to work for relatively low wages on a part-time basis. Broadly similar arguments, about the importance of local gender relations and the attractions of cheaper, female labour for industrial and geographical restructuring, have been made at the regional (Massey, 1984) and international (Pearson, 1986; Chant and McIlwaine, 1995) scales.

Since the late 1980s, many feminist geographers have moved away from an exclusive focus on gender and class systems. This new phase can be identified as feminist geographies of *difference* (see IDENTITY POLITICS). It has three characteristics.

First, *the category of gender is contested* and expanded beyond the duality: man, woman. Feminist geographers are increasingly attentive to the differences in the construction of gender relations across races, ethnicities, ages, religions, sexualities, and nationalities, and to exploitative relations among women who are positioned in varying ways along these multiple axes of difference.

Second, *feminist geographers are drawing on a broader range of social, and particularly cultural, theory*, including PSYCHOANALYSIS and POST-STRUCTURALISM, in order to develop a fuller understanding of how gender relations and identities are shaped and assumed (see SUBJECT FORMATION, GEOGRAPHIES OF). This has led to fundamental rethinking of the category gender (see GENDER AND GEOGRAPHY), and the contradictions and possibilities presented by the seeming instability and insistent repetitions of gender norms in practice. The focus on multiple identifications and the influence of post-structuralist and psychoanalytic theories have brought feminist geographers into dialogue with other strands of critical geography (see POST-COLONIALISM). But another consequence is that theoretical differences among feminist geographers are more obvious than in the past (and although Monk, 1994, observes that national differences between American and British geographers may be diminishing as both pursue these new directions, divisions between feminist geographers located in 'the north' and 'the south' may be increasing, an institutional schism that repeats geopolitical ones in troubling ways: Katz, 1998).

Third, there has been *a more explicit shift away from objectivist epistemologies* through the espousal of situated knowledge claims (see EPISTEMOLOGY). A key area of discussion concerns the distinction between relativism and SITUATED KNOWLEDGE, and ways to reconcile partial perspectives with commitments to political action and social change. There are now concrete examples of the challenges of creating feminist alliances across differences (e.g. Graham-Gibson, 1994; Jacobs, 1994).

New areas are receiving attention, some of which entail different conceptions of geography and space. A considerable amount of writing has developed around gendered cultural REPRESENTATION, which extends the focus to imaginative and symbolic spaces (see FILM, GEOGRAPHY OF; IMAGINATIVE GEOGRAPHIES; VISION AND VISUALITY). A small but growing number of studies of masculinities (e.g. Sparke, 1994; Phillips, 1997) begin to deliver on the promise of a gender relational approach, by directing the focus away from women to a larger network of heteropatriarchal relations. The influence of identity politics and post-structural theories has refocused attention on SEXUALITY AND GEOGRAPHY, and the scale of the BODY (GEOGRAPHY AND). A theory of PERFORMATIVITY developed within QUEER THEORY, which posits that gender is performed through repetitions and approximations of a normative ideal (rather than existing as a stable identity), suggests the importance of context and contingency; the geographical implications of this are just beginning to be explored. Metaphors of mobility and fluidity, of HYBRIDITY and paradoxical, inbetween spaces have been immensely popular in feminist geography in the 1990s, including Gibson-Graham's (1996) influential retheorizing of capitalism and CLASS processes; it will be interesting to see whether cautionary reactions (e.g. Hanson and Pratt, 1995; Seager, 1997; Katz, 1998) also reinvigorate links with a renewed socialist feminism. GP

References

Bowlby, S., Lewis, J., McDowell, L. and Foord, J. 1989: The geography of gender. In R. Peet and N. Thrift, eds, *New models in geography, volume 1*. Boston and London: Unwin and Hyman, 157–75. · Chant, S. and McIlwaine, C. 1995: Gender and export manufacturing in the Philippines: continuity and change in female employment? The case of the Mactan Export Processing Zone. *Gender Place and Culture* 2: 147–76. · Deutsche, R. 1991: Boy's town. *Environment and Planning D: Society and Space* 9: 5–30. · Domosh, M. 1991: Towards a feminist historiography of geography. *Transactions, Institute of British Geographers* NS 16: 95–104. · Eichler, M. 1995: *Change of plans: Towards a non-sexist sustainable city*. Toronto: Garamond; Eisenstein, Z. 1981: *The radical future of liberal feminism*. London and New York: Longman; England, K. 1993: Suburban pink collar ghettos: the spatial entrapment of women. *Annals of the Association of American Geographers* 83: 225–42. · Farrow, H., Moss, P. and Shaw, B. 1995: Symposium on feminist participatory research. *Antipode* 27: 71–101. · Foord, J. and Gregson, N. 1986: Patriarchy: towards a reconceptualisation. *Antipode* 18:2: 186–211. · Gibson-Graham, J.-K. 1994: 'Stuffed if I know!' Reflections on post-modern feminist social research. *Gender Place and Culture* 1: 205–24. · Gibson-Graham, J.K. 1996: *Capitalism (as we knew it): a feminist critique of political economy*. Oxford and Cambridge, MA: Blackwell. · Hanson, S. and Pratt, G. 1995: *Women, work and space*. London: Routledge. · Hodge, D., ed., 1995: Should women count? the role of quantitative methodology in feminist geographic research. *The Professional Geographer* 47: 426–66. · Jacobs, J. 1994: Earth honoring: western desires and indigenous knowledges. In A. Blunt and G. Rose, eds, *Writing women and space*. New York: Guilford, 169–96. · Jones III, J.-P., Nast, H. and Roberts, S. 1997: *Thresholds in feminist geography*. Lanham: Rowman and Littlefield. · Katz, C. 1998: Lost and found in the posts: addressing critical human geography. *Environment and Planning D: Society and Space* 16: 257–78. · Kofman, E. and Peake, L. 1990: Into the 1990s: a gendered agenda for political geography. *Political Geography Quarterly* 9: 313–36. · MacKenzie, S. and Rose, D. 1983: Industrial change, the domestic economy and home life. In J. Anderson et al., eds, *Redundant spaces in cities and regions*. New York: Academic Press. · McDowell, L. and Sharpe, J. 1997: *Space, gender, knowledge: feminist readings*. London: Arnold; Massey, D. 1984: *Spatial divisions of labour*. London and New York: Methuen; Massey, D. 1991: Flexible sexism. *Environment and Planning D: Society and Space* 9: 31–57. · Momsen, J. and Kinnaird, V., eds, 1993: *Different places, different voices: gender and development in Africa, Asia and Latin America*. London: Routledge. · Monk, J. 1994: Place matters: comparative international perspectives on feminist geography. *The Professional Geographer* 46: 277–88. · Monk, J. and Hanson, S. 1982: On not excluding the other half from human geography. *The Professional Geographer* 32: 11–23. · Moss, P. 1993: Feminism as method. *The Canadian Geographer* 37: 48–61; Nast, H., ed., 1994: Women in the field: critical feminist methodologies and theoretical perspectives. *The Professional Geographer* 46: 54–102. · Nelson, K. 1986: Female labour supply characteristics and the suburbanization of low-wage office work. In A. Scott and M. Storper, eds, *Production, work, territory: the geographical anatomy of industrial capitalism*. Boston and London: Allen and Unwin. · Pearson, R. 1986: Latin American women and the new international division of labour: a reassessment. *Bulletin of Latin American Research* 5: 67–79. · Phillips, R. 1997: *Mapping men and empire*. London: Routledge. · Pratt, G. and Hanson, S. 1988: Gender, class and space. *Environment and Planning D: Society and Space* 6: 15–35. · Rose, D. 1984: Rethinking gentrification: beyond the uneven development of marxist urban theory. *Environment and Planning D: Society and Space* 1: 47–74. · Rose, G. 1993: Feminism and Geography. Minneapolis: University of Minnesota Press. Rose, G. 1997: Situating knowledges: positionality, reflexivities and other tactics. *Progress in Human Geography* 21: 305–20. · Seager, J. 1997: Reading the morning paper, and on throwing out the body with the bathwater. *Environment and Planning A* 29: 1521–3. · Sparke, M. 1994: Writing on patriarchal missiles: the chauvinism of the 'Gulf war' and the limits of critique. *Environment and Planning A* 26: 1061–89. · Wekerle, G. and Whitzman, C. 1995: *Safe cities : guidelines for planning, design, and management*. New York: Van Nostrand Reinhold. · Women and Geography Study Group 1997: *Feminist geographies: explorations in diversity and difference*. Harlow: Addison-Wesley Longman.

fertility The number of live births produced by a woman. Fertility is generally distinguished from FECUNDITY, a biological term for the ability to conceive. Fertility, MORTALITY and MIGRATION are the three fundamental influences on the POPULATION GEOGRAPHY of any area. Although they have recognized the importance of spatial variations in fertility, geographers have made relatively few contributions to research in this field. Demographers, on the other hand, have developed sophisticated measures of fertility and have made considerable progress towards establishing and explaining fertility trends in both developed and developing countries (see DEVELOPMENT). Fertility behaviour is still imperfectly understood, however, and projections are problematic.

Measures of fertility range from the very simple to the very complex. A general distinction is drawn between *period fertility* and *cohort fertility*. The former is the most straightforward and relates to the study of births occurring to all females in their reproductive period – i.e. to groups of females of given ages at a certain point in time or over a relatively short period. The latter is used to trace the reproductive history of a group of females born or married at the same time, so illuminating the ways in which families are built up through time, plus changes in completed family size and the spacing of births. The COHORT approach requires long series of accurate vital statistics and so is most commonly applied to the populations of developed countries in the twentieth century.

The most simple and widely used fertility measure is the *crude birth rate* which expresses the number of live births in a given period as a ratio of the average total population alive during that period in parts per 1000; rates vary from about 10 to 55 per 1000, the latter being an estimate of the biological maximum. The crude birth rate has the advantage of being easy to calculate and is one element in the basic demographic equation of birth, death and migration for any area, but it may be an extremely misleading measure of underlying fertility patterns, because of variations in age structure in the base population (see AGE AND SEX STRUCTURE). Other more sophisticated measures have therefore been devised. The simplest is the *general fertility rate*, or the number of births per 1000 women in the fecund ages (defined variously as 15–49 or 15–44). The *marital fertility rate*, on the other hand, expresses the number of legitimate live births per 1000 married women. These rates are thus useful in relating births to the actual section of the population responsible for them. A further refinement is the *age-specific fertility rate*, defined as the number of births to a specified age-group per 1000 women in those ages, usually taken in five-year periods. This allows more detailed analysis and comparisons of fertility experiences. The *total fertility rate* tells us how many children on average each 1000 women have while passing through their fecund years. In the developed world, a rate of 2.1 children per woman is necessary to ensure replacement of generations (see REPLACEMENT RATES). Replacement may also be measured by

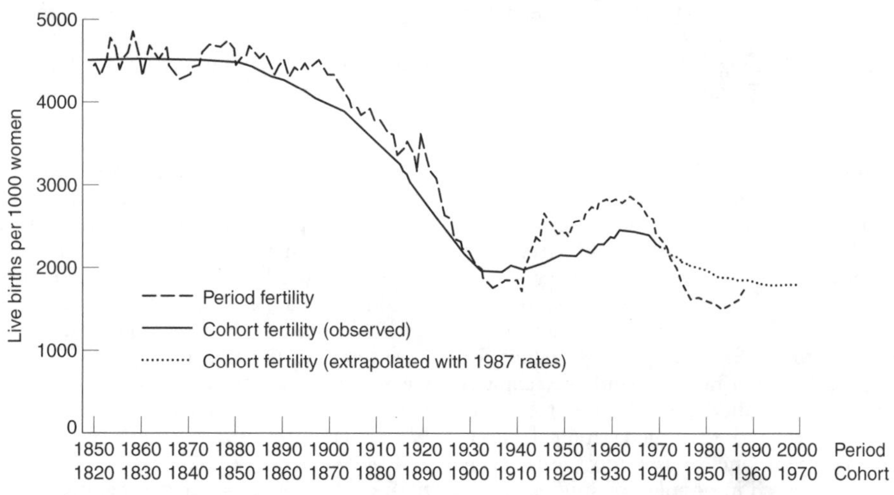

Fertility Period and cohort fertility rates for Norway 1820 to 1973 (Rallu and Blum, 1991)

the *gross reproduction rate*, the average number of daughters produced by a woman during her reproductive lifetime, and the *net reproduction rate*, where mortality is taken into account. A *net reproduction rate* greater than 1.0 ensures replacement of one generation by the next. Of the cohort fertility measures, *completed family size* is the most useful, expressing the average number of children ever born to women currently aged 45 or over.

Factors affecting fertility levels have given rise to much discussion. The general ideas of the DEMOGRAPHIC TRANSITION have been only partially acceptable, given recent fertility behaviour in both developed and developing nations. Explanations have been sought in relation both to the long-term decline of fertility over the last two centuries in much of the developed world (see figure for Norway on p. 263) and to cross-cultural variations in contemporary fertility patterns. Fertility is linked to other aspects of demographic behaviour, to mortality and particularly to marriage patterns, for age at marriage and overall NUPTIALITY are important. Explanations of fertility decline in Europe, which began in France in the later eighteenth century, have been sought in the broad pattern of URBANIZATION, INDUSTRIALIZATION and MODERNIZATION, which changed attitudes to birth control, marriage and family formation and were associated with, for example, higher levels of education and changes in religious attitudes. Interestingly, other links, for example with issues raised in FEMINIST GEOGRAPHY, have attracted relatively little attention, though for a Marxist critique see Seccombe (1983) and for a view of the wider perspective being urged on demographers see Greenhalgh (1996).

Considerable geographical variations in fertility exist within countries today and these too have been related to a very broad series of factors including social and occupational status, rural or urban residence (see RURAL–URBAN CONTINUUM), education, religion and the changing role of women in society. Great care must be taken in analysing fertility trends in the Third World. Because of less complete sources, it is sometimes difficult to estimate accurately even recent trends and there is no guarantee that relationships postulated for developed countries hold true either to explain the past or to predict future trends. Certainly fertility levels, and their geographical variations, represent one of the most important fields for research in population studies.

PEO

References

Greenhalgh, S. 1996: The social construction of population science: an intellectual, institutional and political history of twentieth-century demography. *Comparative Studies in Society and History* 38: 26–66. · Rallu, J.-L. and Blum, A., eds, 1991: *European population. 1. Country analysis*. London: John Libbey, 132. · Seccombe, W. 1983: Marxism and demography. *New Left Review* 137: 22–47.

Suggested Reading

Andorka, R. 1978: *Determinants of fertility in advanced societies*. London: Methuen; New York: Free Press. · Coale, A.J. and Watkins, S.C., eds, 1986: *The decline of fertility in Europe*. Princeton, NJ: Princeton University Press. · Daughtery, H.G. and Kammeyer, K.C.W. 1995: *An introduction to population*, 2nd edn. New York and London: Guilford Press, ch. 8. · Davis, K., Bernstam, M.K., Ricardo-Campbell, R., eds, 1987: *Below-replacement fertility in industrial societies. Causes, consequences, policies*. Population and Development Review. A supplement to Volume 12, 1986. New York: The Population Council; Day, L.H. 1992: *The future of low-birthrate populations*. London: Routledge. · Gillis, J.R., Tilly, L.A. and Levine, D., eds, 1992: *The European experience of declining fertility, 1850–1970. The quiet revolution*. Cambridge, MA and Oxford: Blackwell. · Gould, W.T.S. and Brown, M.S. 1996: Research review 2: fertility in sub-Saharan Africa. *International Journal of Population Geography* 2 1: 1–22. · Greenhalgh, S., ed., 1995: *Situating fertility. Anthropology and demographic enquiry*. Cambridge: Cambridge University Press. · Jones, H.R. 1990: *Population geography*, 2nd edn. London: Paul Chapman; Leete, R. and Alam, I., eds, 1993: *The revolution in Asian fertility. Dimensions, causes and implications*. Oxford: Clarendon Press; Lutz, W., ed., 1990: *Future demographic trends in Europe and North America*. London and New York: Academic Press, part 2. · Tilly, C., ed., 1978: *Historical studies of changing fertility*. Princeton: Princeton University Press.

feudalism A term used in the analysis of pre-capitalist societies, especially in Europe, with senses ranging from a broad type of SOCIAL FORMATION (originating within Marxist analyses, but variously defined therein: cf. MARXIST GEOGRAPHY), to a narrower definition based on legal terminology formulated by nineteenth-century legal historians (Postan, 1983). Indeed, the range of contexts to which this label applied enrages some who advocate its abandonment. The earlier formulations focused on the '*fief*' (see below) and whether notional military obligations were realized, but this focus has largely passed out of use. So too have identifications of feudalism with subsistence society as opposed to capitalist production for profit through MARKET EXCHANGE (e.g. Wallerstein, 1974).

The broadening of definitions reflects twentieth-century interest in comparative history, and has been much stimulated by analyses relating the emergence of agrarian CAPITALISM to the decline of feudalism (Kula, 1976; Martin, 1983; Dodgshon, 1987). Were the decline of feudalism and the rise of agrarian capitalism two separate phenomena, or two facets of a single process (Hilton, 1976; Holton, 1985; Glennie, 1987)?

In its most general sense feudalism possesses, in common with other pre-capitalist social formations, two component social groups. One group are *direct producers* (peasants, broadly speaking), who maintain direct (i.e. non-market) access to the means of production (land, tools, seedcorn, livestock), even though they may not legally own them (especially land). Direct producers are subject to politico-legal domination by a second group, of *social superiors* who form a status hierarchy headed by a monarch. The monarch ultimately owns all land, but landownership is effectively decentralized through Crown land grants to feudal lords, in return for military and political support. Thus social RELATIONS OF PRODUCTION are not defined primarily through MARKETS, as under CAPITALISM, and the means by which direct producers' surplus is extracted by social superiors differs from social formations such as SLAVERY.

The key social relationships in feudalism were vassalage and serfdom. *Vassalage* was an intra-elite relationship by which a subordinate vassal held landed property, the 'fief' (Latin *feodum*, *feudum*, hence feudalism) from a lord, ultimately the Crown, in return for military service required by the Crown. The Crown's vassals were tenants-in-chief, who in turn subinfeudated their estates to raise their own military service. Thus a hierarchy of feudal tenants came to 'own' estates of various sizes, composed of territorial jurisdictions called manors.

Serfdom was the legal subjection of peasant tenants to lords through lords' manorial jurisdictions, of which unfree tenants were legally held to be part. Dependent PEASANT tenants held land from their lord in return for varying combinations of money RENTS and services in kind, especially labour services on the lord's own land, the demesne. The legal dependence of peasant tenants enabled feudal lords both to extract higher than market rents from their tenants, and to impose a range of other dues. These feudal dues included heriot (a tenant's best animal, payable on inheritance), and licenses to marry, to migrate, to mill, or to brew ale. Peasant tenants were fined at a manorial court if these activities were undertaken without appropriate license, and courts also exercised a degree of moral regulation (Bonfield, 1985).

The level of rents and dues, it is held, were set more by lords' income requirements than by market forces, although lords gained from the latter, as population growth made land scarce relative to labour. Seigneurial income requirements progressively increased as lords competed for political status through conspicuous consumption. Moreover, since feudal lords could raise income from intensified surplus-extraction, they were comparatively indifferent to innovations to raise agricultural PRODUCTIVITY, explaining why feudalism was characterized by relatively stagnant technology (see BRENNER DEBATE). Implied here is a strong view about the explanatory value of the geography of manorialism (estate size and fragmentation, seigneurial character), and of lord–tenant struggle, in accounting for geographical diversity in population density, agricultural systems and productivity, and standards of living (Hilton, 1973; Hallam, 1989; Campbell, 1990; Dyer, 1993).

As lordly surplus extraction intensified, and medieval European populations grew (for reasons as yet imperfectly understood), feudal society exhibited certain crisis tendencies because the surplus removal process failed to generate any significant feedback into the productive capacity of agriculture through investment. A crisis of SOCIAL REPRODUCTION was inevitable since:

> In the first place, production for the market and the stimulus of competition only affected a very narrow sector of the economy. Secondly, agricultural and industrial production were based on the household unit and the profits of small peasant and small artisan enterprise were taken by landowners and usurers. Thirdly, the social structure and the habits of the landed nobility did not permit accumulation for investment for the extension of production (Hilton, 1985, p. 244).

Hilton's work remains an important demonstration that towns and TRADE were integral to feudal economies, not exogenous factors that necessarily undermined feudal social relations (the latter view constituting the PIRENNE THESIS). However, recent HISTORICAL GEOGRAPHY has paid far more attention to the extent of commercialization within medieval agrarian economies, and its impact on geographies of manorialism (Campbell and Power, 1992; Campbell, 1995; Britnell, 1996).

While debate continues on the relative importance, as causes of medieval agrarian contraction, of excessive surplus-extraction (see BRENNER DEBATE), and of medieval agriculture's ECOLOGICAL frailties (see POSTAN THESIS), there has been a general move to more sophisticated theorizations, which broaden analysis of feudal society beyond property relations. Greater attention has been paid to ACCUMULATION and differentiation *within* the class of primary producers (Poos, 1991; Razi and Smith, 1996). Important developments in social technologies changed the geographical structuring of feudal society. Over time, status came to be increasingly embodied in property, rather than in interpersonal relations. Notable geographical components stemmed from this shift, including new legal, fiscal and administrative technologies to control time and space (Bean, 1989; Biddick, 1990; Clanchy, 1993). Finally, certain social continuities across the feudalism–capitalism transition, especially in the functioning of geo-demographic and cultural systems, have begun to receive serious attention (Poos, 1991, McIntosh 1998). PG

References

Aston, T.H. and Philpin, C.E., eds, 1985: *The Brenner debate: agrarian class structure and economic development in pre-industrial Europe*. Cambridge: Cambridge University Press. · Bean, J.M.W. 1989: *From lord to patron: lordship in late-medieval England*. Manchester: Manchester University Press. · Biddick, K. 1990: People and things: power in early English development. *Comparative Studies in Society and History* 32: 3–23. · Bois, G. 1984: *The crisis of feudalism: economy and society in eastern Normandy c.1300–1550*. Cambridge: Cambridge University Press. · Bonfield, L. 1985: The nature of customary law in the manor courts of medieval England. *Comparative Studies in Society and History* 31: 514–34. · Britnell, R.H. 1996: *Commercialisation in medieval England*, 2nd edn. Manchester: Manchester University Press. · Campbell, B.M.S. 1990: People and land in the Middle Ages, 1066–1500. In R.A. Butlin and R.A. Dodgshon, eds, *An Historical Geography of England and Wales*, 2nd edn. London: Academic Press, 69–122. · Campbell, B.M.S. 1991: Land, labour, livestock and productivity trends in English seignorial agriculture 1208–1450. In B.M.S. Campbell and M. Overton, eds, *Land, labour and livestock: historical studies in European agricultural productivity*. Manchester: Manchester University Press, 144–82. · Campbell, B.M.S. 1995: Progressiveness and backwardness in thirteenth and early fourteenth century English agriculture: the verdict of recent research. In J-M. Duvosquel and E. Thoen, eds, *Peasants and townsmen in medieval Europe*. Gent: Snoeck-Ducaju & Zoon, 541–59. · Campbell, B.M.S. and Power, J. 1992: Cluster analysis and the classification of medieval demesne-farming systems. *Transactions, Institute of British Geographers* NS 17: 227–45. · Clanchy, M.T. 1993: *From memory to written record: England 1066–1307*, 2nd edn. London: Edward Arnold; Dodgshon, R.A. 1987: *The European past: social evolution and spatial order*. London: Macmillan. · Dyer, C. 1993: *Standards of living in the later middle ages: social change in England c.1200–1520*, 2nd edn. Cambridge: Cambridge University Press; Glennie, P.D. 1987: The transition from feudalism to capitalism as a problem for historical geography. *Journal of Historical Geography* 13: 296–302. · Hallam, H.E., ed., 1989: *The agrarian history of England and Wales, volume II 1042–1350*. Cambridge: Cambridge University Press. · Hilton, R.H. 1973: *Bond men made free: medieval peasant movements and the English rising of 1381*. London: Temple Smith. · Hilton, R.H., ed., 1976: *The transition from feudalism to capitalism*. London: Verso. · Hilton, R.H. 1985: *Class conflict and the crisis of feudalism: essays in medieval social history*. London: Hambledon Press; Holton, R.J. 1985: *The transition from feudalism to capitalism*. London: Macmillan. · Kula, W. 1976: *An economic theory of the feudal system*. London: New Left Books; McIntosh, M. 1998: *Controlling misbehaviour in England, 1370–1600*. Cambridge: Cambridge University Press; Martin, J.E. 1983: *Feudalism to capitalism: peasant and landlord in English agrarian development*. London: Macmillan. · Miller, E., ed., 1991: *The agrarian history of England and Wales, volume III 1348–1500*. Cambridge: Cambridge University Press. · Poos, L. 1991: *A rural society after the Black Death: late-medieval Essex*. Cambridge: Cambridge University Press. · Postan, M. 1983: Feudalism and its decline: a semantic exercise. In T.H. Aston et al., eds, *Social relations and ideas: essays in honour of R.H. Hilton*. Cambridge: Cambridge University Press, 73–87. · Razi, Z. and Smith, R.M., eds, 1996: *Medieval society and the Manorial Court*. Oxford: Clarendon Press. · Wallerstein, I. 1974: *The modern world system I: capitalist agriculture and the origins of the European world-economy in the sixteenth century*. London: Academic Press.

Suggested Reading

Bloch, M. 1961: *Feudal society*. London: Routledge. · Britnell (1996). · Campbell (1990); Dodgshon (1987). · Dyer (1993).

field system The fields and other agricultural lands of a COMMUNITY considered as a functioning whole. Field systems vary in several ways, including the character of LAND TENURE, the sets of rules through which agricultural activities are coordinated, and the physical disposition of landholdings. Particular importance attaches to the relative importance of individual control, and of social coordination, in land ownership, use rights, and agricultural DECISION-MAKING. Many traditional societies have been dominated by complex cooperative systems of rights over both arable land (in 'open field' systems in which the holdings of individuals were scattered) and pasture, and have been much altered by ENCLOSURE which redefined field systems in more individualistic terms. The rise of POLITICAL ECONOMY approaches in human geography has helped to focus attention on field systems as spatial expressions of social power relations.

For historical and contemporary geographers, important debates surround at least five questions about: (1) the origins of different types of field systems, and their connection with familial, social, and territorial forms; (2) their development trajectories, and the extent to which they were flexible and able to evolve, or inflexible and resistant to non-revolutionary change (Allen, 1992); (3) how field systems functioned as channels of social control over agricultural production; (4) the relationship between different types of field system and processes and rates of agricultural change; and (5) connections between field systems and rural standards of living and POVERTY (Neeson, 1993). PG

References

Allen, R.C. 1992: *Enclosure and the yeoman*. Oxford: Clarendon Press; Neeson, J. 1993. *Commoners: common rights, enclosure and social change in England, 1700–1820*. Cambridge: Cambridge University Press.

fieldwork A traditional means of data collection within geography, based on the assumption that reality is present in appearance (see EMPIRICISM) and can therefore be directly apprehended through observation (see REALISM). Its 'traditional' status (which refers to its historic centrality within the discipline) is not unproblematic. Founded uncritically on the ENLIGHTENMENT presupposition that seeing is believing, the idea of fieldwork betrays a bias towards the evidence of the eye (see VISION AND VISUALITY). An implicit emphasis on EXPLORATION and discovery, and on the taming of raw materials into ordered knowledge, has, moreover, earned it the label 'geographical masculinities in action' (Rose, 1993; cf. MASCULINISM; PHALLOCENTRISM). Some feminist responses appear in a theme issue of *The Professional Geographer* (1994, vol. 46).

In quantitative human geography (see QUANTITATIVE METHODS), fieldwork is largely about the implementation of sample QUESTIONNAIRE surveys of people's attributes, attitudes, actions, aspirations and motivations (cf. SURVEY ANALYSIS). Such surveys may be conducted in person or by post, and depend for success on a relatively high response rate from a random sample of households (see SAMPLING). This quantitative approach regards social data as analogous to the raw material of much of natural science: something which is discrete and stable and exists independently of the analyst, and which therefore yields findings which could be replicated and verified by others. Such fieldwork is part of the practical project of empirical-analytical science, and is generally used to establish cause and effect relationships in order to predict and control the future.

There is, however, an alternative view of fieldwork, associated with the advent of HUMANISTIC GEOGRAPHY and with the discovery of meaning. This philosophy requires an approach more akin to the *case study* methods of anthropology than to the statistical generalizations of positivistic social science (cf. LOGICAL POSITIVISM; POSITIVISM). Within this tradition, fieldwork is preoccupied with the project of understanding and communication rather than with the goal of prediction and intervention. Some researchers aim to achieve this depth of understanding by empathizing with their subjects and acquiring knowledge through immersion (for example Crang, 1994), while others prefer to conceptualize fieldwork as a dialogue driven forward precisely because shared understanding cannot be reached (see Folch-Serra, 1990). Either way, these encounter-based approaches to fieldwork are now raising important questions about the politics of REPRESENTATION (Kobayashi, 1994) and the aims of engagement (Katz, 1994).

However achieved, the generalizations arising from qualitative fieldwork are not of a statistical nature, and the validity of the approach does not hinge on the randomness or typicality of the cases selected for study. Such research often takes the form of PARTICIPANT OBSERVATION, written up in the form of ethnographic description (see ETHNOGRAPHY), although it may also include in-depth individual or group INTERVIEWING. These QUALITATIVE METHODS all locate social scientists within, rather than apart from, the social world, and acknowledge that 'reality' is constructed – not uncovered – through the search process. SJS

References

Crang, P. 1994: It's showtime: on the workplace geographies of display in a restaurant in southeast England. *Environment and Planning D: Society and Space* 12: 675–704. · Folch-Serra, M. 1990: Place, voice, space: Mikhail Bakhtin's dialogical landscape. *Environment and Planning D: Society and Space* 8: 255–74. · Katz, C. 1994: Playing the field: questions of fieldwork in geography. *The Professional Geographer* 46: 67–72. · Kobayashi, A. 1994: Coloring the field: gender, 'race' and the politics of fieldwork. *The Professional Geographer* 46: 73–80. · Rose, G. 1993: *Feminism and geography*. Cambridge: Polity Press.

film, geography of Film has been used by geographers as apparently accurate evidence of the appearance of people and places ever since its invention, and in the 1950s the *Geographical Magazine* ran a series of essays on various 'national' cinemas which suggested that a nation's character was reflected in its films. However, the interest in film that developed among some geographers from the mid-1980s has refused to accept the claim that film reflects a reality in any simple way. Indeed, the distinction between the 'real' world and the filmed world has been put into doubt by many geographers' emphasis on 'the importance of cinematic representation to understanding our place in the world' (Aitken and Zonn, 1994, p. 5). These geographers argue that movies provide maps of meaning with which the contemporary world can be navigated, and cinema is thus argued to be one of the most important institutions in constructing an increasingly visualized and spectacularized world (see also SPECTACLE, GEOGRAPHY OF and VISION AND VISUALITY). Nevertheless, these more recent geographies of film have varied greatly in their analytical, methodological and empirical approaches.

Some attention has been paid to the production of films. The film industry based in Los Angeles has been analysed as a highly localized flexible production system, for example, which contributes to a very specific PLACE image: Hollywood (Scott, 1996). It has also been argued that the organization of production processes more generally profoundly shape the places and spaces represented in a film. Harvey (1989, p. 323), for example, claims that the TIME–SPACE COMPRESSION created by contemporary economic processes is reflected 'as in a mirror' in what he sees as the chaotic, depthless and superficial spaces of certain movies made in Hollywood in the 1980s (see also POSTMODERNITY). Morley and Robins (1995), in contrast, although equally concerned with the production of film and other televisual media, pay more attention to the CULTURAL POLITICS shaping that production. In their case study, they argue that in the West these media work to sustain certain dominant visions of western cultural IDENTITY through practices that are simultaneously economic and cultural; both the institutions of film production and the films themselves are the producers of cultural OTHERS.

The most frequent approach taken by geographers to date, however, is through case studies that focus on the geographies shown in particular films. Here, attention has been paid to constructions of SPACE, PLACE, NATURE, LANDSCAPE, the NATION-STATE and the URBAN, and the ways in which specific visions of these serve to sustain or contest particular notions of social DIFFERENCE, especially of CLASS, RACE, GENDER and SEXUALITY (Aitken and Zonn, 1993; Natter and Jones III, 1993; Hopkins, 1994; Natter, 1994; Rose, 1994; Gandy, 1996; Clarke, 1997). The methodologies informing these readings are diverse and often implicit. Emphasis is often placed on the film's narrative – how its story develops and displays relations between characters, environments and events – and some authors (Aitken and Zonn, 1993, 1994) advocate transaction theory as a method for focusing on scenes ('image-events') that disrupt and transform relations between the characters in the film and the environments they inhabit. The use of semiotics has also been advocated (Hopkins, 1994), which entails a careful analysis of the structure of filmic signs and their symbolization of cultural meaning. Another methodological emphasis pays most attention to the formal visual and spatial characteristics of the film in question. This approach considers such filmic geographies to be especially important because it is through them that every film invites the production of only certain kinds of AUDIENCE. A number of film critics have critically explored this intersection between the spaces of particular movies with the spaces of SUBJECT FORMATION (see for example Clover, 1992; de Lauretis, 1994; Kaplan, 1997). Thus far, however, little attention has been paid to the ways in which specific audiences negotiate or refuse the positions offered to them by particular films. Watching a film is a complex experience in which the space in which the film is being seen – the cinema, for example – intersects with both the geographies represented in the film and the senses of space, place, nature and so on that the audience already has. As well as this uninterest in audiences, it is evident too that, so far, geographers have paid most attention to narrative films and to films made in the West. Thus as Aitken and Zonn (1994) remark, many geographies of film remain only partially explored (cf. MEDIA, GEOGRAPHY OF). GR

References

Aitken, S.C. and Zonn, L.E. 1993: Weir(d) sex: the representation of gender-environment relations in Peter Weir's Picnic at Hanging Rock and Gallipoli. *Environment and Planning D: Society and Space* 11: 191–212. · Aitken, S.C. and Zonn, L.E. 1994: Re-presenting the place pastiche. In S.C. Aitken and L.E. Zonn, eds, *Place, power, situation and spectacle: a geography of film*. Lanham: Rowman and Littlefield, 3–26. · Clarke, D.B., ed., 1997: *The cinematic city*. London: Routledge; Clover, C.J. 1992: *Men, women and chainsaws: gender in the modern horror film*. London: British Film Institute. · De Lauretis, T. 1994: *The practice of love: lesbian desire and perverse sexuality*. Bloomington: Indian University Press. · Gandy, M. 1996: Visions of darkness: the representation of nature in the films of Werner Herzog. *Ecumene* 3: 1–21. · Harvey, D. 1989: *The condition of postmodernity: an enquiry into the origins of cultural change*. Oxford: Basil Blackwell. · Hopkins, J. 1994: Mapping of cinematic spaces: icons, ideology, and the power of (mis)representation. In S.C. Aitken and L.E. Zonn, eds, *Place, power, situation and spectacle: a geography of film*. Lanham: Rowman and Littlefield, 47–65. · Kaplan, E.A. 1997: *Looking for the other: nation, woman and desire in film*. London: Routledge. · Morley, D. and Robins, K. 1995: *Spaces of identity: global media, electronic landscapes and cultural boundaries*. London: Routledge. · Natter, W. 1994: The city as cinematic space: modernism and place in Berlin, Symphony of a City. In S.C. Aitken and L.E. Zonn, eds, *Place, power, situation and spectacle: a geography of film*. Lanham: Rowman and Littlefield, 203–28. · Natter, W. and Jones III, J.P. 1993: Pets or meat: class, ideology and space in Roger and Me. Antipode 25: 140–58. · Rose, G. 1994: The cultural politics of place: local representation and oppositional discourse in two films. *Transactions, Institute of British Geographers* NS 19: 46–60. · Scott, A.J. 1996: The craft, fashion and cultural products industries of Los Angeles: competitive dynamics and policy dilemmas in a multisectoral image-producing complex. *Annals of the Association of American Geographers* 86: 306–23.

filtering A process of NEIGHBOURHOOD change that involves its housing passing from one social group to another. Most filtering involves housing in an area moving down the social scale; as the former inhabitants move to better-quality dwellings their previous homes become relatively cheaper and so accessible to lower-income groups. The full filtering process involves the highest income groups moving to new homes, initiating a rippling process whereby all other homes, and thus (to the extent that they are homogeneous) all NEIGHBOURHOODS, move down the income scale: if the rate of new building for the affluent at least equals the total demand for new homes in the system, this should release the lowest quality homes at the end of the process for demolition. If new homes are constructed on the urban periphery, the filtering process ripples in towards the city centre, with every income group moving out one neighbourhood (as proposed in the original SECTORAL MODEL).

Filtering is a continuous process, so that at any time some neighbourhoods are mixed in their composition until the shift from one occupant group to another is complete. It may be 'interrupted' by the construction of new housing for middle-income groups, who release neighbourhoods somewhere in the centre of the idealized sequence, or by the construction of public housing for lower-income groups: it may be initiated by pressure for more housing among the lower-income groups at the centre of the city, as in the INVASION AND SUCCESSION process associated with the ZONAL MODEL.

One widely remarked deviation from the general process of filtering, which associates newer housing with higher income groups, is GENTRIFICATION, whereby higher income groups re-occupy and regenerate older housing in attractive INNER-CITY districts.

Some writers argue that the operation of filtering mechanisms ensures that the housing needs of all are met through market structures, including those of the poor and otherwise disadvantaged. HOMELESSNESS in many cities and poor-quality housing for the less affluent in most cities (see SLUM) leads critics to argue that filtering rarely succeeds in providing adequate housing for all, hence the need for government subsidies and various forms of 'social housing' (see HOUSING STUDIES). RJJ

Suggested Reading

Gray, F. and Boddy, M. 1979: The origins and use of theory in urban geography: household mobility in filtering theory. *Geoforum* 10: 117–27.

financial exclusion The process by which poor and disadvantaged groups are directly and indirectly excluded from the financial system and denied access to mainstream retail financial services. Financial exclusion plays an active part in the production of urban and rural POVERTY, because those who experience the most difficulty gaining access to financial services tend to be experiencing multiple forms of social deprivation (Leyshon, Pratt and Thrift, 1999).

Processes of financial exclusion operate at a range of spatial scales. During the 1980s the less developed countries' debt crisis meant that much of sub-Saharan Africa and most Latin American countries were cut off from the international financial system, so that processes of economic development were stalled or even put into reverse (Corbridge, 1993). Most studies have analysed financial exclusion at lower levels of aggregation, however, and in particular focused on financial exclusion at regional and sub-regional scales within industrialized economies such as the United States and United Kingdom.

Access to mainstream financial services within contemporary capitalist societies is important because many economic exchanges are now mediated through banks and other financial institutions in the form of direct transfers between accounts. Without a bank account, individuals and households may have to pay more for certain services (those provided by utilities, for example), to cover the extra cost and risk incurred by service providers in handling cash. Excluded individuals will also find it difficult to obtain affordable credit, and may be forced to resort to the more expensive credit facilities provided by 'predatory' financial services firms, such as money-lenders (Dymksi and Veitch, 1996; Leyshon and Thrift, 1997). Moreover, an inability to obtain affordable insurance means that households cannot shield themselves from risk, and are forced to bear the full financial consequences if they become victims of criminal action, accidents and environmental hazards (such as floods or storms, for example).

Geographers first became concerned with the equity effects of the retail financial system during the 1970s when, influenced by RADICAL GEOGRAPHY, researchers analysed the role played by financial institutions in the creation of urban and rural poverty. Initial concerns focused on urban housing markets and the ways in which banks and realtors (in the US) and estate agents (in Britain) engaged in RED-LINING urban space to deprive certain communities of mortgage finance, thereby slowing the turnover of housing stock in such areas and locking them into a spiral of social and infrastructure decline (cf. URBAN MANAGERS AND GATEKEEPERS).

Geographical interest in financial exclusion declined during the 1980s. Regulatory reform opened up financial markets to new institutions, and the increase in competition which followed had the effect of forcing financial services firms to seek out new customers to maintain market share. During this inclusionary phase, many individuals and households who previously could not obtain mainstream retail financial services products were signed up as customers.

By the 1990s, financial exclusion was back on the geographical research agenda. The main reason was that retail financial services firms were undertaking extensive branch closure programmes which were spatially uneven, with branches closing fastest in areas of social and economic deprivation, particularly in inner cities with large ethnic minority populations; closure rates were below average in more affluent areas. The programmes were undertaken to cut costs and refocus business on the more profitable parts of the customer base in an increasingly competitive market. In the US, this meant that entire communities were abandoned by the financial services industry, so that large parts of inner cities and many rural areas have lost large parts of their financial infrastructure (Christopherson, 1993). In Britain, where one in five of all bank and building society branches closed during the 1990s, the fastest rate of closure also occurred in socially deprived inner-city areas. Problems of access were exacerbated for the poor, the elderly and those who have physical disabilities, whose mobility over space is constrained, because the thinning out of branch networks increased the average 'journey to bank'. But it is less clear if this decline in physical access led to a decline in absolute levels of access to the retail financial system as a whole, because of the rise of telephone-based financial services which, in theory at least, allowed consumers to gain access to the financial system from the comfort of their homes. Financial services firms reaped considerable economies of scale from such operations, and argued that they served as more than adequate alternatives to branch-based services. Moreover, the proportion of people with access to a bank account in Britain increased over the 1990s (Leyshon, Pratt and Thrift, 1999), while the proportion of the population without any kind of retail financial product made up less than 10 per cent of the total population by the end of the decade.

Such excluded populations are spatially concentrated in poor places, however, and belong to the social groups that are directly excluded by developments such as the rise of telephone banking and Internet banking, because in many socially deprived areas large sections of the population are too poor to even afford a telephone (Graham and Marvin, 1996), let alone a personal computer. Moreover, because they lack the social and economic characteristics that mark them out as 'good' (i.e. profitable) customers, such people have been written out of the databases and credit scoring systems which now control access to the retail financial system (Leyshon, Thrift and Pratt, 1998). AL

References

Christopherson, S. 1993: Market rules and territorial outcomes: the case of the United States. *International Journal of Urban and Regional Research* 17: 274–88. · Corbridge, S. 1993: *Debt and development*. Oxford: Blackwell; Dymski, G. and Veitch, J. 1996: Financial transformation and the metropolis: booms, busts, and banking in Los Angeles. *Environment and Planning A* 28: 1233–60. · Graham, S. and Marvin, S. 1996: *Telecommunications and the city: electronic spaces, urban places*. London: Routledge; Leyshon, A. and Thrift, N. 1996: Financial exclusion and the shifting boundaries of the financial system. *Environment and Planning A* 28: 1150–6. · Leyshon, A. and Thrift, N. 1997: *Money/space: geographies of monetary transformation*. London: Routledge.

· Leyshon, A. Thrift, N. and Pratt, J. 1998: Reading financial services: texts, consumers and financial literacy. *Environment and Planning D: Society and Space* 16: 29–55. · Leyshon, A. Pratt, J. and Thrift, N. 1999: Inside/outside: geographies of financial inclusion and exclusion in Britain. *Urban Studies*.

Suggested Reading

Dymski and Veitch (1996). · Leyshon and Thrift (1997), ch. 7. · Leyshon, Thrift and Pratt (1998).

fiscal crisis The tendency for a government's expenditure to increase more rapidly than its income from taxation and other sources. Any budget deficit could thus be labelled a fiscal crisis, but O'Connor's (1973) classic study argues that a fiscal crisis of the state is a logical consequence of the evolution of monopoly CAPITALISM rather than just the outcome of budgetary mis-management.

According to O'Connor, the STATE has two main functions within a capitalist economy: to promote successful ACCUMULATION strategies for private capitals, and to ensure their legitimation. The former involves it providing social capital, such as the physical INFRASTRUCTURE within which enterprises operate and the trained labour force that they require. For the latter, it promotes social harmony through social expenses on items such as welfare services and the maintenance of law and order (cf. WELFARE STATE). O'Connor argues that under monopoly capitalism an increasing proportion of investment costs must be met by the state while at the same time legitimation of the problems created by monopolies demands greater expenditure too. Thus the state must spend more, relative to GNP. To do so, it must tax more heavily, which, by discouraging investment and enterprise, can counter its pro-accumulation policies. Increasing demands on the state – from both capital (for social capital) and labour (for social expenses) – outpace its ability to meet them, stimulating a fiscal crisis. To counter it, social expenses may be cut (especially on the welfare state) while more is spent on using the ideological and repressive components of the STATE APPARATUS to protect accumulation. (For an extension of these arguments, see Held, 1987.)

In several countries the greatest pressure involved when social expenses are cut in a fiscal crisis is felt at the LOCAL STATE level, which is allocated particular responsibility for welfare service provision (cf. DUAL THEORY OF THE STATE: see also Newton, 1980). This was a major issue in the 1980s – in the United Kingdom and in New Zealand, for example (Johnston, 1992) – when governments tackled the crisis by 'rolling back the frontiers of the state' and promoting PRIVATIZATION and DEREGULATION whilst limiting the powers of the local state apparatus. RJJ

References and Suggested Reading

Held, D. 1987: *Models of democracy*. Cambridge: Polity Press; Johnston, R.J. 1992: The internal operations of the state. In P.J. Taylor, ed., *The political geography of the twentieth century*. London: Belhaven Press. · Newton, K. 1980: *Balancing the books*. London and Beverly Hills: Sage Publications. · O'Connor, J. 1973: *The fiscal crisis of the state*. New York: St. Martin's Press.

fiscal migration MIGRATION undertaken for fiscal advantage, usually to reduce the level of taxation paid. Such migration occurs at all spatial scales. Within an urban area with a fragmented local government structure, for example, the TIEBOUT MODEL argues that land users will move to that administration which optimizes their 'tax/service package'. Internationally, different STATES offer variations in packages whose potentials are realized by the affluent seeking tax havens and by MULTINATIONAL CORPORATIONS. Within countries, the reduction of tax burdens in some areas to stimulate investment can attract firms wishing to reduce their tax bills and for which the costs of the move are far outweighed by the financial advantages gained (cf. ENTERPRISE ZONE). RJJ

flexible accumulation A collection of industrial technologies, labour practices, inter-firm relations, and consumption patterns characterized by the pursuit of greater flexibility. Borrowing from the REGULATION SCHOOL of political economy, Harvey (1988) identifies this idea with a new REGIME OF ACCUMULATION:

> 'Flexible accumulation', as I shall call it, is marked by a direct confrontation with the rigidities of FORDISM. It rests on a startling flexibility with respect to labour processes, labour markets, products, and patterns of consumption. It is characterised by the emergence of entirely new sectors of production, new ways of providing financial services, new markets, and, above all, greatly intensified rates of commercial, technological, and organizational innovation.

Adopted in response to the increasing rigidities of the classical Fordist era (particularly rigid rules for the deployment and remuneration of labour, rigid, dedicated machinery, and the rigid organizational structures of large industrial corporations), these practices are seen by Harvey and others as constituting a set of responses to the productivity slowdown, increasing competition from THIRD WORLD industrialization, and the saturation and fragmentation of home markets that characterized North American and European economies beginning in the late 1960s and early 1970s. Scott (1988) adds that this emergent regime is also 'focused...on the search for external ECONOMIES OF SCALE in the organization of the industrial apparatus'. The desire to circumvent labour market rigidities and to exploit EXTERNAL ECONOMIES has, according to Scott, produced major shifts in the geography of capitalist production, consisting of 'the twofold tendency to (a) a definite spatial re-agglomeration of production in selected areas, combined with (b) active evasion of labor pools dominated now or in the recent past by Fordist industry'. However, while this would imply that flexible accumulation is associated primarily with 'new industrial spaces . . . comprehended as transactions-intensive agglomerations of human labour and social activity' (Scott, 1988), it is also true that some firms in older industrial regions (notably within the automotive industry) are adopting more flexible methods in an attempt to respond to intensified competitive pressures. (See also ECONOMIES OF SCOPE; INDUSTRIAL GEOGRAPHY; JUST-IN-TIME PRODUCTION; LOCATION THEORY; POST-FORDISM; PRODUCTION COMPLEX; SOCIAL CAPITAL; TRANSACTIONAL ANALYSIS.) MSG

References

Harvey, D. 1988: The geographical and geopolitical consequences of the transition from Fordist to flexible accumulation. In G. Sternlieb and J.W. Hughes, eds, *America's new market geography*. New Brunswick, NJ: Rutgers Center for Urban Policy Research, 101–34. · Scott, A.J. 1988: *New industrial spaces*. London: Pion.

focus group A QUALITATIVE METHOD involving a group discussion, usually with six to twelve participants, focused around questions raised by a moderator. The methodology has roots in market research but is now used regularly by human geographers (Goss, 1996). Focus groups typically supplement other methodologies. They can be used at the beginning of a research process: to orient a researcher to a new field; to generate HYPOTHESES that can be tested more systematically; or to identify concepts or themes to be pursued in interviews or QUESTIONNAIRE surveys. Alternatively, focus groups can follow a questionnaire survey, to verify the researcher's interpretation.

The advantages of focus groups over interviews are that they allow meanings to emerge in a less directed way, and they are creative encounters, in which participants share and test their ideas within the group. A researcher doing PARTICIPATORY ACTION RESEARCH may value the opportunity that focus groups provide for participants to learn from and be supported by each other. Concerns about focus groups rest on the representative nature of the SAMPLE and the fact that they are public performances that are both enabled and constrained by social conventions. The former concern confuses the intent of a case study (further, there is no logical reason why focus groups could not be carried out with representative sub-samples). The latter concern generates discussion about whether social differences can be effectively managed within focus groups, whether, for example, men will dominate women, elites will silence non-elites, etc. In Goss's (1996) opinion, an effective moderator can manage these differences and diverse groups and thereby not only elicit a greater variety of perspectives but also offer more potential for members to learn from each other. Nevertheless, variability within each focus group remains a key methodological decision, as is the decision as to how structured the focus group will be. Focus groups can be very structured situations, in which the researcher moves the group through a structured set of questions, or very loosely structured occasions in which the group develops a dynamic of its own and begins to set its own agenda. GP

Reference

Goss, J. 1996: Introduction to focus groups. *Area* 28: 113–14.

food, geography of The study of the spatial and environmental aspects of food production, provision and CONSUMPTION.

Food is a necessity of life, but its importance goes beyond physical nourishment. Its production, distribution and preparation is estimated to account for over half of all the work done in the world today (Grigg, 1995, p. 338). Moreover, food practices are imbued with symbolic significance and are a prime means through which social relationships are developed, as the writings of sociologists and anthropologists have emphasized. Despite this importance, however, food is not the basis of a sub-disciplinary body of research within human geography. There is no single geographical literature on food, with its own coherent themes and problematics. In part this may reflect the very ubiquity of food-related activities. Food is implicated in almost every sort of geography imaginable. It is simultaneously economic, political, cultural, social and biological. It travels through a host of different spaces in its life from farm to fork. It can only be understood in the context of a range of wider social, political and economic relations. Food is not, then, a subject matter that sits easily within neat conceptual and spatial boundaries.

One result of this can be a tendency to view food less in its own terms and more as an illustration of other geographical topics. For instance, Bell and Valentine's survey of writings on food CONSUMPTION, which moves through a series of spatial scales from the BODY up to the WORLD-SYSTEM, is exemplary in its documentation of how a range of geographical issues can be thought about through the example of food (Bell and Valentine, 1997). The positive effect of this is that writings on food have considerable pedagogic potential for the geographer. However, as Fine (1993, p. 670) notes for the social sciences more generally, it can also result in food being 'simply the raw material for applying theories that have nothing as such to do with food', to the extent that food studies comprise 'a disparate set of theoretical and empirical case studies, any one of which, in principle, has more resonance with a similar application to some other non-food item than it does to some other [study of] food'. Certainly, many geographical analyses of food have emerged through its use as an indicator of CULTURE AREAS, as an example of the geographies of CONSUMPTION and/or COMMODITY CHAINS, or through its presence in other more primary concerns such as the geography of RETAILING or AGRICULTURAL GEOGRAPHY. In turn, the more coherent debates on food geographies that do exist, for example those on FOODWAYS or the AGRO-FOOD SYSTEM, operate in isolation from each other with distinct empirical and conceptual concerns.

Nonetheless, past and present studies of the geography of food do cohere around four key issues:

The spatial distribution of foods and dietary practices: the principal concern here 'is how what people eat and drink differs from one part of the earth's surface to another' (Grigg, 1995, p. 339). There is a limited tradition of such work at the regional scale, especially within France (Thouvenot, 1978) and the United States (see FOODWAYS for further details), and this has recently been extended by analyses of international differences in diet (see Grigg, 1995). Variations are emphasized in calorific and nutritional intake, in specific food practices and preferences, and in food institutions such as restaurants (Pillsbury, 1990). The overall effect is to highlight the continuing variations in food habits even in an age of intensified GLOBALIZATION and, to a lesser extent, to identify associated inequalities in dietary intake (see also FAMINE).

The spatial constitution of the food system (see also AGRO-FOOD SYSTEM): here the emphasis is on the changing geographies of the systems linking food production and CONSUMPTION. Generally, the modern food system can be characterized in terms of 'de-localization', with a consequent distinction and distanciation of food producers and consumers. In this light, particular attention has been paid to: the technological, commercial and political factors shaping the 'food regimes' that connect producers and consumers (Friedmann, 1991); the historical transformations in these regimes, especially at the global scale (see for example Bonanno et al., 1994); the POWER relations operating between the different institutions and actors within the food system, especially producers, retailers and consumers; and the environmental and developmental consequences of dominant food regimes.

The PRODUCTION OF SPACE *and place through food*: of central concern are the material and IMAGINATIVE GEOGRAPHIES established through food production, promotion and consumption. For example, studies have emphasized the role of food in establishing gendered experiences of domesticity, urban public spaces of conviviality (Capron, 1997), senses of regional and national identity, and understandings of GLOBALIZATION (Cook and Crang, 1996) (for a fuller review of literature on all these scales see Bell and Valentine, 1997).

The 'refashionings of NATURE*' associated with food* (see Goodman and Redclift, 1991): emphasizing how food practices and attitudes need to be contextualized in terms of broader engagements with NATURE, key geographical issues here include: the HISTORICAL and CULTURAL GEOGRAPHIES of plant and animal cultivation, domestication and CONSUMPTION; the INDUSTRIALIZATION and commodification (see COMMODITY) of the natural world promoted by the modern food system; and the relationships established between external and internal natures through DISCOURSES of health, body and dietary ETHICS.

In summary, food practices are profoundly geographical. In turn, the geographies of food are multi-faceted. However, whilst each of these facets has been the subject of a growing body of geographical research in the last decade there is as yet a paucity of work that ties them together in a sustained fashion. PC

References

Bell, D. and Valentine G. 1997: *Consuming geographies: we are where we eat*. London: Routledge. · Bonanno, A., Busch, L., Friedland, W., Gouveia, L. and Mingione, E., eds, 1994: *From Columbus to ConAgra: the globalization of agriculture and food*. Lawrence: University Press of Kansas. · Capron, G. 1997: Les cafés à Buenos Aires: une analyse historique de la construction sociale et culturelle de l'espace public et de l'urbanité. *Géographie et Cultures* 24: 29–49. · Cook, I. and Crang, P. 1996: The world on a plate: culinary culture, displacement and geographical knowledges. *Journal of Material Culture* 1: 131–53. · Fine, B. 1993: Resolving the diet paradox. *Social Science Information* 32: 669–87. · Friedmann, H. 1991: Changes in the international division of labor: agri-food complexes and export agriculture. In W. Friedland, L. Busch, F. Buttle and A. Rudy, eds, *Towards a new political economy of agriculture*. Boulder: Westview Press, 65–93. · Goodman, D. and Redclift, M. 1991: *Refashioning nature: food, ecology and culture*. London: Routledge. · Grigg, D. 1995: The geography of food consumption: a review. *Progress in Human Geography* 19: 338–54. · Pillsbury, R. 1990: *From boarding house to bistro: the American restaurant then and now*. Boston: Unwin Hyman; Thouvenot, C. 1978: Studies in food geography in France. *Social Science and Medicine* 120: 43–54.

foodways The ways of conceptualizing, evaluating, preparing and consuming foods characteristic of a particular SOCIETY, cultural group or geographical area. The notion of foodways therefore emphasizes how food preferences are solely determined neither by universal human nutritional needs nor by idiosyncratic individual tastes. Rather, food-related activities are understood as part of broader ways of life or GENRES DE VIE (Sorre, 1962) and cultural and geographical variations in food practices and understandings are highlighted. Substantive geographical analyses of foodways are comparatively rare, but are most developed in the United States (see for example Pillsbury, 1998), which is also home to the interdisciplinary journal *Food and Foodways*. Geographers have drawn particular attention to the regional and ethnic diversity of American cuisines (Shortridge and Shortridge, 1998), apparent even in a sector such as fast food which is often assumed to promote culinary and cultural homogenization. More generally, studies of foodways have emphasized cultural and geographical differences in what is recognized as edible, most obviously due to: culturally specific food taboos; locally distinctive recipes and ingredients; and variations in the ways foods are organized into meal occasions, through local conventions of order, combination and social participation.

Explanations for this variety in foodways often view food choices as a reflection of underlying cultural differences. Max Sorre, for example, saw diet as 'one of the most characteristic . . . [if] least simple expressions of CULTURE' (1962, p. 450). In this light, the spatial patterning of foodways can be seen as indicative of more general CULTURE AREAS and histories of cultural DIFFUSION, as well as pointing to the continuing, if diminishing, importance of folk cultures and traditions in the contemporary world. However, in line with theoretical developments in CULTURAL GEOGRAPHY more generally, there is an increasing recognition that diverse foodways are not merely reflections of traditional cultures, under threat in the modern world. For instance, the role food can play in class-based acquisitions of status or CULTURAL CAPITAL has been highlighted, along with the less regionalized, but no less geographically differentiated, patterns of food CONSUMPTION thereby produced. May (1996) has examined the taste for so-called 'exotic' foods amongst fractions of the British middle classes in this way. More generally, such studies are part of a wider trend to conceptualize foodways less as reflections of pre-existing cultures and more as a means through which the cultural IDENTITIES of peoples and PLACES are invented and performed. This is also apparent in research on the public representation of cultural identity through restaurants and food festivals (see for example Lu and Fine, 1995). In consequence, whilst foodways are still often understood as expressions of the culture of a people or place, there is a growing emphasis on seeing how those cultures are themselves in part constructed and contested through food-related activities. PC

References

Lu, S. and Fine, G.A. 1995: The presentation of ethnic authenticity: Chinese food as a social accomplishment. *The Sociological Quarterly* 36 (3): 535–53; May, J. 1996: A little taste of something more exotic: the imaginative geographies of everyday life. *Geography* 81 (1): 57–64. · Pillsbury, R. 1998: *No foreign food: the American diet in time and place*. Boulder: Westview Press. · Shortridge, B.G. and Shortridge, J.R., eds, 1998: *The taste of American place: a reader on regional and ethnic foods*. Lanham: Rowman and Littlefield. · Sorre, M. 1962: The geography of diet. In P.L. Wagner and M.W. Mikesell, eds, *Readings in cultural geography*. Chicago: University of Chicago Press, 445–56.

footloose industry An industry which can locate virtually anywhere because it has no strong MATERIAL ORIENTATION or MARKET ORIENTATION in its locational requirements and very wide spatial margins to profitability; transport usually involves only a small proportion of its total cost structure. RJJ

Fordism A set of industrial and broader societal practices associated with the workplace innovations pioneered by Henry Ford in Detroit, Michigan in the second decade of the twentieth century. In its original usage, Gramsci (1971) wrote of 'Americanism and Fordism' in his description of Ford's strategy to reorganize shopfloor production while at the same time forging a new relationship with his workers. Automobile production was being revolutionized through the use of the mass-production assembly line and application of the principles of TAYLORISM to organize workers' tasks (with higher PRODUCTIVITY and internal ECONOMIES OF SCALE producing a cheaper final product). At the same time, Ford hoped that by paying his workers a high wage commensurate with their enhanced productivity, and by shortening the work day to eight hours, he could create an efficient workforce with a stable family life and incomes large enough to acquire the very products they themselves were producing.

More recently, members of the REGULATION SCHOOL of POLITICAL ECONOMY have used 'Fordism' to describe a broader system of social relations transcending the practices of any single firm. Here, the Fordist REGIME OF ACCUMULATION refers to a period stretching roughly from the end of the Second World War to the mid-1970s. The era was, in this view, characterized by the widespread mass-production of standardized goods using inflexible, dedicated machinery, exploitation of internal scale economies, a Taylorist fragmentation and deskilling of work, and relatively narrow and rigidly defined job descriptions. The key to this regime's sustained success was a unique and unprecedented social compromise struck between workers and owners, manifested in a set of institutions governing wage determination, collective bargaining, and social welfare functions. Collectively, these institutions served to link annual wage increases to the productivity increases being realized from mass-production techniques. Their net result was to distribute sufficient income to workers to support consumption of industrial products on a mass scale. These broad institutional arrangements are said to have prevailed in each of the major industrialized nations of the capitalist world, although the precise form realized may have varied considerably across individual nation-states (Jenson, 1989). Furthermore, these national developments were complemented by a supranational institutional framework set up in the first years after the Second World War to help ensure global economic stability and order through the regulation of currency exchange rates, international trade, financial markets and development assistance. Taken together, the institutional innovations created at these two spatial scales combined to produce the conditions for an unprecedented period of economic growth and stability that has come to be known as the 'Golden Age' of Fordism (Glyn et al., 1991: cf. MONEY AND FINANCE, GEOGRAPHY OF).

Geographers have associated this historical period with the rise of major regional concentrations of mass-production industries in the more developed countries (e.g. automobile manufacturing in the American Midwest, the British West Midlands, northwestern Italy). The later stages of this period have also seen the spatial fragmentation of manufacturing functions, with routinized assembly of standardized products occurring increasingly in branch plants in peripheral regions of industrialized countries, or in Third World production sites. More recent work by economic geographers has raised doubts about many of the basic precepts of the Fordism thesis by questioning the empirical validity of arguments in support of the 'Golden Age' idea (Webber and Rigby, 1996). (See also FLEXIBLE ACCUMULATION; NEW INTERNATIONAL DIVISION OF LABOUR; POST-FORDISM; PRODUCT LIFE CYCLE.) MSG

References

Glyn, A., Hughes, A., Lipietz, A. and Singh, A. 1991: The rise and fall of the Golden Age. In S. Marglin and J.B. Schor, eds, *The golden age of capitalism*. Oxford: Clarendon Press, 39–125. · Gramsci, A. 1971: *Selections from the prison notebooks*. New York: International Publishers; Jenson, J. 1989: 'Different', but not 'exceptional': Canada's permeable Fordism. *Canadian Journal of Sociology and Anthropology* 26: 69–94. · Webber, M.J. and Rigby, D. 1996: *The golden age illusion*. New York: Guilford Press.

Suggested Reading

Harvey, D. 1989: *The condition of postmodernity*. Oxford: Basil Blackwell.

forecast The creation of an estimated value for an observation unit – usually through the application of statistical models such as REGRESSION. Of the two types of estimate, a *forecast* is less certain – because it involves extrapolation from the known to the unknown – than a *prediction*: a forecast is an estimated value for an observation unit not involved in the calibration of the regression equation whereas a prediction is an estimated value for one of the observations used in the calibration. RJJ

forestry The practices of planning, managing and usually harvesting of trees, both as a source of timber and to create or conserve multi-purpose forest environments for CONSERVATION, RECREATION or LANDSCAPE purposes. As Rackham (1986) points out, the word 'forest' in the Germanic origin, probably meant a tract of trees, but throughout Western Europe it came to mean land on which deer were protected. Originally, then, trees were only of secondary importance in forests. Their role was to be a place of food and shelter for animals and people, while the deer were the essential constituent of the forest. Only later did the popular meaning of forest as extensive tracts of timber trees come into popular circulation.

Mather (1990) has suggested three stages in the development of forest resources. The *pre-industrial* forest yields a wide range of localized products, including food and fodder as well as timber/wood for fuel and the making of implements, utensils and weapons. Access to the forest is often on the basis of common-property. The *industrial* forest is characterized by the primary purpose of harvesting timber/wood. Ownership is usually exclusive (either in the private or public sectors) and access is subject to private property rights. In the *post-industrial* forest, the primacy of timber/wood production has been reduced or even removed, and priority is given to recreation and/or conservation alongside or instead of wood production. Here, private property rights may persist, but access is often regulated by public policy or social influence. Although these three stages are perhaps oversimplified, and relate more to developed rather than underdeveloped nations, where forests are often likely to be destroyed by the economic demands of industrialized agriculture, a series of very interesting HISTORICAL GEOGRAPHIES emerge from studies of the diffusion of systematic industrial forestry. For example, Radkan (1996) traces the origins of such forestry to the founding fathers of German forestry, who recognized the twin dangers of increased demand for wood from a growing population and the deterioration of soils from forest exploitation plus loss of communal forests to farmland. Fear of a timber famine in these circumstances led to a systemization of forestry practices based on the concept of controlling nature through precise mathematical design. These ideas were disseminated into colonial forestry enterprises (see Clapp, 1995), and indeed it was from the Indian Forest Service that German practices were adopted in Britain. Moreover, German foresters also went to North America (Rogers, 1991) taking their models of 'sustained yield management' with them. In this way, the WILDERNESS of unmanaged trees of various ages all growing together was often replaced by blocks of same-age trees subjected to cyclical harvesting (Williams, 1989). In turn, some of the 'alien' species from North America were introduced into Europe, forging a significant, and contested, change in some rural landscapes.

Human geographers have studied forests and forestry at a number of different scales. Globally, forests cover more than one quarter of the world's total land area, but some 16 million hectares per annum is thought to be disappearing as forests are cleared by timber producers, or converted to other, usually agricultural, uses (Abramovitz, 1998). A recent report (Bryant et al., 1997) focuses on the 'frontier forests' – areas of large ecologically intact and relatively undisturbed natural forests – concluding that more than 75 per cent are found in Canada/Alaska, Russia, and the Amazon Basin/Guyana Shield. The devastation of deforestation in tropical rainforests has been well publicized, but degradation is also a significant problem elsewhere. For example, it is suggested that some two-thirds of Canada's coastal rainforest has also been degraded by logging and development. Such trends, and the practices behind them, pose very serious questions relating to the upkeep of biodiversity, the practice of SUSTAINABLE DEVELOPMENT and the prevention of global environmental disaster.

Forestry has also been studied at the national and local scales. In Mather's terms, the shift from industrial to post-industrial forests has often been aided by national or federal policies for forestry, which have sought to introduce, or to encourage, management objectives relating to wildlife conservation, recreation and sustainability. The value of some forest environments has thereby increased relative to the value of forests as timber factories, and the shift to multi-purpose objectives has been noted both in old growth native forests in North America and Australasia and also in the smaller European forests such as in Germany and Britain. A new breed of forestry management has emerged in which new values and objectives have grown up alongside the traditional goals of industrial forestry. In some cases a new breed of forests has also emerged, signifying the role of forests in the community (Bishop, 1992) and in the nation (Cloke et al., 1996).

One further fascination with human geographers has been the way in which forests, and trees, have come to signify particular NATURE–SOCIETY relations. The recognition that forests are produced by human activity, creativity and experience, has meant that 'extraordinarily powerful and different myths have come to be woven into the roots and branches of various cultures' (Macnaughton and Urry, 1998, p. 183). For example, Schama (1995) analyses the spirit of militarism represented in German forests, which was deployed as an embodied memory by Nazi modernists, and Daniels (1993) charts the importance of forests as 'greenwood' libertarian spaces in the 'hearts of oak' national identities of England. Forests and forestry, then, are a rich resource for CULTURAL as well as ENVIRONMENTAL and INDUSTRIAL GEOGRAPHIES. PJC

References

Abramovitz, J.N. 1998: Sustaining the world's forests. In Worldwatch Institute, ed., *State of the World 1998.* London: Earthscan. · Bishop, K. 1992: Britain's new forests: dependence on private interest. In A. Gilg, ed., *Restructuring the countryside: environmental policy in practice.* Aldershot: Aveburg. · Bryant, D., Nielson, D. and Tangley, L. 1997: *The last frontier forests: ecosystems and economies on the edge.* Washington, D.C.: World Resource Institute. · Clapp, S. 1995: Creating competitive advantage: forest policy as industrial policy in Chile. *Economic Geography* 71: 273–96. · Cloke, P., Milbourne, P. and Thomas, C. 1996: The English National Forest: local reactions to plans for renegotiated nature–society relations in the countryside. *Transactions, Institute of British Geographers* NS 21: 552–71. · Daniels, S. 1993: *Fields of vision.* Cambridge: Polity. · Mather, A.S. 1990: *Global forest resources.* London: Belhaven. · Macnaughton, P. and Urry, J. 1998: *Contested natures.* London: Sage. · Rackham, O. 1986: *The history of the countryside.* London: Dent. · Radkan, J. 1996: Wood and forestry in German history: in quest of an environmental approach. *Environment and History* 2: 63–76. · Rogers, A. 1991: *Bernhard Eduard Fernow: A story of North American forestry,* 3rd edn. Durham, NC: Forest History Society. · Schama, S. 1995: *Landscape and memory.* London: HarperCollins. · Williams, M. 1989: *Americans and their forests: a historical geography.* Cambridge: Cambridge University Press;

Suggested Reading

European Parliament, 1994: *A global community strategy in the forest sector.* Luxembourg: European Parliament. · Mather, A. 1998: The changing role of forests. In B. Ilbery, ed., *The geography of rural change.* Harlow: Longman. · Rival, L., ed., 1998: *The social life of trees: anthropological perspectives on tree symbolism.* Oxford: Berg.

form of economic integration A concept proposed by Karl Polanyi to describe the means by which an economy 'acquires unity and stability, that is the interdependence and recurrence of its parts' (cf. SYSTEM). Polanyi distinguished three main forms of economic integration: RECIPROCITY, REDISTRIBUTION and MARKET EXCHANGE. 'Since they occur side by side on different levels and in different sectors of the economy', Polanyi argued, 'it may often be possible to select one of them as dominant so that they could be employed for a classification of economies as a whole'. Dominance was to be identified by the degree to which any one of them 'comprises land and labour in a society' (Polanyi in Dalton, 1971, 148–56). Polanyi's purpose was thus to treat the ECONOMY as an instituted process: 'instituted' because coherent structures were imposed on economies through historically specific institutions and 'process' because these various structures were reproduced through transactions across space and over time.

This approach came to be the cornerstone of what Polanyi called substantivist anthropology, whose focus on the historical specificity of different forms of economic integration was in sharp contrast to 'formalist' approaches, the generalizations of which assumed price-fixing markets to be the universal economic mechanism (cf. NEO-CLASSICAL ECONOMICS). 'The error was in equating the human economy in general with its market form', Polanyi wrote, and in assuming that every DIVISION OF LABOUR implied the existence of market exchange. Such a formalism, so he believed, ignored 'the shifting place occupied by the economy in society' and made it impossible to understand the various ways in which pre-capitalist economies were 'embedded' in distinctive social relations (Polanyi in Pearson, 1977, pp. 6 and 104).

Polanyi's ideas have attracted considerable (and sometimes critical) attention within both anthropology and history (see Humphreys, 1969; North, 1977). Within geography, they were used by Wheatley in his seminal investigation of URBAN ORIGINS, which focused on the shift from reciprocity to redistribution (Wheatley, 1971). Wheatley's arguments were extended in different directions by Harvey in his parallel examinations of URBANISM. Although his primary concern was market exchange within contemporary CAPITALISM, he regarded all three concepts of 'reciprocity, redistribution and market exchange [as] simple and effective tools for dissecting the relationship between societies and the urban forms manifest within them'. Indeed, these concepts were treated as both superior to Marx's concept of a MODE OF PRODUCTION, which at the time Harvey thought 'too broad

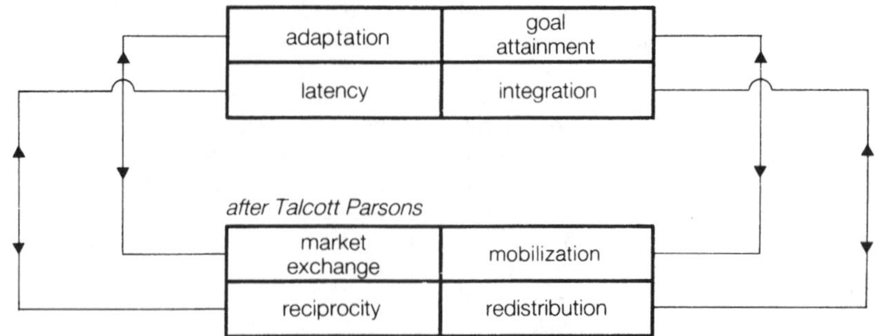

form of economic integration *1: Schemes of form of economic integration* (after Wheatley, 1973)

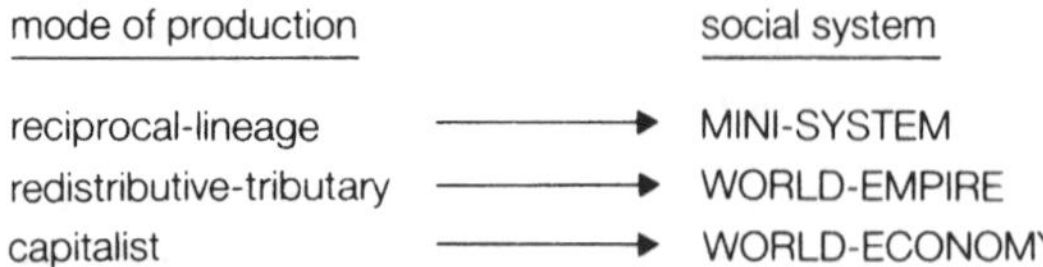

form of economic integration *2: Modes of production and social systems*

and all-embracing' for his purpose, and yet essentially compatible with Marx's views. They offered 'the conceptual means to characterise a social and economic formation' and provided 'consistent threads to trace the transformation from one mode to production to another' (Harvey, 1973, pp. 206–15). But there are important differences between Marx and Polanyi and Polanyi was consistently critical of 'the economistic fallacy' which he considered to be common to both formalist anthropology and HISTORICAL MATERIALISM (Block and Somers, 1984). In his later writings, certainly, Harvey paid little attention to Polanyi and concentrated on Marx (e.g. Harvey, 1982). Even so, the emergence of WORLD-SYSTEMS ANALYSIS has once again brought Polanyi's ideas to the attention of a Marxisant audience. In particular, Wallerstein's (1978, 1984) identification of three distinctive 'social systems' depends upon 'the existence within [each of them] of a division of labour, such that the various sectors or areas with [each one] are dependent upon economic exchange for the smooth and continuous provisioning of the needs of the area'. Wallerstein calls these divisions of labour and systems of exchange 'modes of production' but, as the figure above shows, they are in fact formally equivalent to Polanyi's forms of economic integration and betray a similar emphasis on functionalist constructions (Aronowitz, 1981). DG

References

Aronowitz, S. 1981: A metatheoretical critique of Immanuel Wallerstein's *The modern world system*. *Theory and Society* 9: 503–20. · Block, F. and Somers, M. 1984: Beyond the economistic fallacy: the holistic social science of Karl Polanyi. In T. Skocpol, ed., *Vision and method in historical sociology*. Cambridge: Cambridge University Press, 47–84. · Dalton, G., ed., 1968, 1971: *Primitive, archaic and modern economies: essays of Karl Polanyi*. Boston: Beacon Press; Harvey, D. 1973: *Social justice and the city*. London: Edward Arnold; Baltimore, MD: Johns Hopkins University Press. · Harvey, D. 1982: *The limits to capital*. Oxford: Blackwell; Chicago: Chicago University Press. · Humphreys, S.C. 1969: History, economics and anthropology: the work of Karl Polanyi. *History and Theory* 8: 165–212. · North, D.C. 1977: Markets and other allocation systems in history: the challenge of Karl Polanyi. *Journal of European Economic History* 6: 703–16. · Pearson, H., ed., 1977: *The livelihood of man: essays of Karl Polanyi*. New York: Academic Press; Wallerstein, I. 1978: *The capitalist world-economy*. Cambridge: Cambridge University Press; Wallerstein, I. 1984: *The politics of the world-economy*. Cambridge: Cambridge University Press. · Wheatley, P. 1971: *The pivot of the four quarters*. Edinburgh: Edinburgh University Press; Chicago: Aldine. · Wheatley, P. 1973: Satyantra in Suvarnadvipa: from reciprocity to redistribution in ancient South-East Asia. In J.A. Sabloff and C. Lamberg-Karlovsky, eds, *Ancient civilization and trade*. Albuquerque: University of New Mexico Press, ch. 6.

Suggested Reading

Dalton (1968). · Humphreys (1969). · North (1977).

foundationalism The idea that there exist fixed, indubitable, and final foundations that guarantee the truth of a given claim to knowledge. Foundationalism is most associated with western philosophy, and its historical quest for EPISTEMOLOGICAL certainty; that is, the search for a set of philosophical criteria that if found delineate iron-clad from spurious knowledge. Failure to find such criteria produces, as Bernstein (1983) calls it, the 'Cartesian Anxiety' (after the seventeenth-century French philosopher René Descartes, 1596–1650). This is the fear that by not locating foundations we are doomed to a world of 'intellectual and moral chaos, radical scepticism, and self defeating RELATIVISM' (Bernstein, 1992, p. 17).

Many of philosophy's 'isms', including a large number proposed within the last hundred years or so (e.g. CRITICAL RATIONALISM; LOGICAL POSITIVISM; MARXISM; PHENOMENOLOGY; REALISM; and STRUCTURALISM) are foundationalist in that they designate 'certain sorts of representations, certain expressions, certain processes a[s] "basic", "privileged", and "foundational"' (Rorty, 1979, pp. 318–19). Those foundational terms, in turn, are the touchstones for distinguishing legitimate from illegitimate knowledge: legitimate knowledge makes reference to them, thereby guaranteeing that the acquired knowledge mirrors the world, while illegitimate knowledge does not. For example, under (logical) positivism all meaningful statements are either synthetic or analytic; with these two foundational terms, logical positivists are able to scrutinize any statement and assess its validity. Or again, Marxism in its classical form *reduces* the explanation of all social, cultural and political events to the foundation of economic relations (a position known as *economism*). This second example brings out the close relationship between reductionism and foundationalism. *Reductionism* means the strategy of explaining a phenomenon or event by determining its fundamental cause, which is usually not immediately apparent. In this sense, the cause to which the event of phenomena is reduced is foundational; it is the very basis of the phenomena or event in question.

Running parallel historically to foundationalism has been a counterpunctual movement that in different forms has sought to deflate foundationalism's inflated claims. In brief, the criticism is that all foundational claims to truth are circular because by definition the only guarantor of the foundation selected is the foundation itself. Instead, argue the critics, we should see foundationalist philosophies as no more than particular social practices arising out of given historically and geographically contingent conditions, with no more justification than any other social practice. In recent years, perhaps the best known critic of foundationalism in philosophy is Richard Rorty (1979), although he freely acknowledges his debt to other twentieth-century philosophers, especially those working within the Continental European tradition (cf. PRAGMATISM). For Rorty (1979, Part 3) philosophy should be 'edifying' or 'therapeutic' rather than architectonic – constructing foundationalist systems to know everything. The central task is not to fabricate foolproof methods (for they will always be nothing other than fabrications), but to understand how life is led in the absence of foundations. For Rorty, denying foundations is both scary and liberating: scary because we live life without a safety net, and liberating because it returns us to a Ptolemaic universe where humans are at the centre. We decide our fate.

Rorty's anti-foundationalism resonates with a range of POST-STRUCTURAL and POSTMODERNIST writers who also proffer anti-foundationalism, such as Derrida who makes use of DECONSTRUCTION, and Foucault who practises DISCOURSE analysis. In addition, there are a number of FEMINIST theorists who contend that foundationalism is frequently used as a front for MASCULINIST theory, and therefore represents at best the interests of only half the world. Similarly, many POST-COLONIAL writers argue that foundationalism continues to legitimize various forms of IMPERIALISM and the maintenance of a SUBALTERN class. Given the recent move by some in geography towards a post-structural sensibility, there is increasing awareness of foundationalism as an epistemological issue (Gregory, 1994). Demeritt (1994), though, is one of the few geographers to work it through systematically and substantively, in his case, in writings about ECOLOGY and NATURE. TJB

References

Bernstein, R.J. 1983: *Beyond objectivism and relativism: science, hermeneutics, and praxis*. Philadelphia: University of Pennsylvania Press. · Bernstein, R.J. 1992: *The new constellation: the ethical political horizons of modernity/postmodernity*. Cambridge, MA: MIT Press. · Demeritt, D. 1994: Ecology, objectivity and critique in writings on nature and human societies. *Journal of Historical Geography* 20: 22–37. · Gregory, D. 1994: *Geographical imaginations*. Oxford: Blackwell. · Rorty, R. 1979: *Philosophy and the mirror of nature*. Princeton, NJ: Princeton University Press.

Suggested Reading

Bernstein (1983), ch. 1. · Demeritt (1994).

fractal A geometric form exhibiting the property of 'self-similarity'; that is, a part of the form has the same properties as the form as a whole. If an image is fractal, then any part of the image if suitably enlarged will be indistinguishable from the image as a whole. Certain regular geometric forms have this property, but of greater interest in geography are forms that possess the property in a statistical sense, meaning that a part of the form has the same statistical properties as the whole. Parts of the coastline of Britain, for example, look similarly contorted at different scales, although the exact details are clearly different. If the same or similar forms exist at all levels, it follows that an observer cannot determine the scale at which the form is depicted.

The most important measure of a fractal form is its 'fractional dimension'. A line is normally a one-dimensional object, and if magnified by a factor of 2 its length will double. But a fractal form reveals more detail when magnified, and its length thus grows disproportionately faster. Unlike normal lines, a fractal line has a fractional dimension greater than 1. In the limit an infinitely wiggly line fills the space that contains it and behaves as if it had the dimensions of the space; thus an infinitely wiggly line on a sheet of paper quadruples rather than doubles in length when both dimensions of the paper are doubled. Mandelbrot (1982) argued that geographical LANDSCAPES and many other aspects of natural systems exhibit fractal properties, and demonstrated that such phenomena exhibit regularities across a range of SCALES. He found, for example, a dimension of approximately 1.2 for the west coast of Britain. A large literature has evaluated Mandelbrot's assertion statistically, with mixed results (Xia and Clarke, 1997). Nevertheless, the fractal concept provides a useful framework for many investigations of geographical form. Batty and Longley (1994) have used fractal concepts as the basis for their models of urban form and growth, arguing that cities reveal detail at many scales, and that some aspects of the forms of cities are self-similar. Goodchild and Mark (1987) describe several implementations of fractal concepts within the technical design of GEOGRAPHIC INFORMATION SYSTEMS, including QUADTREES and spatial indexing schemes. MG

References

Batty, M. and Longley, P.A. 1994: *Fractal cities: a geometry of form and function*. London: Academic Press. · Goodchild, M.F., and Mark, D.M. 1987: The fractal nature of geographic phenomena. *Annals of the Association of American Geographers* 77: 265–78. · Mandelbrot, B.B. 1982: *The fractal geometry of nature*. San Francisco: W.H. Freeman. · Xia, Z.-G. and Clarke, K.C. 1997: Approaches to scaling of geo-spatial data. In D.A. Quattrochi and M.F. Goodchild, eds, *Scale in remote sensing and GIS*. Boca Raton: Lewis Publishers.

Frankfurt School A group of radical scholars associated with the Institute of Social Research founded in Frankfurt, Germany in 1923. Their writings established CRITICAL THEORY as a central moment in the wider currents of 'western Marxism' as it emerged in the wake of the Bolshevik Revolution. The label is misleading, however, since the 'Frankfurt School' was only referred to as such after the parent Institute had been closed by the Nazis in 1933 and its members forced to flee the country. Their exile lasted until 1950, but this was arguably the most intellectually productive period for the group as a whole. It was then that their critique of POSITIVISM was developed most forcefully and conjoined to a critique of domination which stressed the relations between THEORY and practice and between material and mental CULTURE. Even then, however, the contributions of the most prominent members of the group – M. Horkheimer, T. Adorno, W. Benjamin, H. Marcuse, L. Lowenthal and F. Pollock – were sufficiently distinctive to require a carefully differentiated analysis rather than the casual attribution of a collective project.

Some critics have regarded their work as being preoccupied with abstract philosophy and aesthetic theory, to such a degree as to represent a radical departure from the concrete historical and economic emphases of orthodox Marxism: Connerton (1980) speaks of an 'enveloping orgy of abstractions' and Bottomore (1984) of the 'extremely limited' range of their interests. Others, by contrast, regard 'the way connections [were] established between apparently disparate fields of inquiry' as one of the features confirming the Frankfurt School as a 'major source for contemporary social and political thought' (Held, 1980). Certainly, its revivification and extension by Habermas, Offe and Schmidt in the 1960s and 1970s had a major impact on all the social sciences, and in geography informed both general discussions, e.g. the RELEVANCE of teaching and research, and specific analyses, e.g. of SOCIAL MOVEMENTS and of the capitalist STATE. DG

References

Bottomore, T. 1984: *The Frankfurt School*. London: Tavistock; Connerton, P. 1980: *The tragedy of enlightenment: an essay of the Frankfurt School*. Cambridge:

Cambridge University Press. · Held, D. 1980: *Introduction to critical theory: Horkheimer to Habermas*. London: Hutchinson.

Suggested Reading

Jay, M. 1973: *The dialectical imagination: a history of the Frankfurt School and the Institute of Social Research 1923–50*. London: Heinemann. · Wiggershaus, R. 1994: *The Frankfurt School: its history, theories and political significance*. Cambridge: Polity Press; Cambridge, MA: MIT Press.

free port A port designed as a FREE TRADE AREA, so that exports are exempt from customs duties and subject to minimal customs regulations. Hong Kong is a significant contemporary example, although its future status is somewhat in doubt since its return by the UK to Chinese rule in 1997. From 1945 to 1954, Trieste in the northern Adriatic Sea was a free port under joint British and American supervision, prior to incorporation into Italy. MB

free trade area A group of STATES that have agreed to remove all artificial barriers to trade between themselves, such as import and export duties, export guarantees and quota restrictions, while at the same time maintaining their own separate policies on trade with other countries. This can cause problems and rules of origin have to be agreed, so that imports from countries outside the free trade area do not flood into all the countries in the group through the member with the lowest duty levels. The European Free Trade Association (EFTA), founded in 1959, has been one of the most successful free trade areas in recent years, though its impact may be rivalled by the North American Free Trade Agreement (NAFTA) which was agreed in 1992. There have also been other similar initiatives in the Caribbean and in Latin America (cf. COMMON MARKET). MB

Suggested Reading

Geiger, T. and Kennedy, D., eds, 1996: *Regional trade blocs, multilateralism and the GATT: complementary paths to free trade?* London: Pinter. · Bulmer-Thomas, V., Craske, N. and Serrano, M., eds, 1994: *Mexico and the North American Free Trade Agreement: who will benefit?* Basingstoke: Macmillan.

freight rates The money charged for the movement of goods by land, sea, or air. Such charges often discriminate between commodities on the basis of handling characteristics; they often taper with distance (i.e. the charge per tonne kilometre falls as distance increases – see DISTANCE DECAY); and they may have a stepped form because it is easier for a transport operator to quote charges for broad distance bands than to have separate charges for every destination or distance. The setting of freight rates may be subject to competitive pressures but is often determined under conditions of monopoly or collusive oligopoly. AMH

frequency distribution A tabulation of the number of occurrences of the values of a variable into classes, which may be arbitrarily defined. An empirical frequency distribution is usually displayed ordinally, as in:

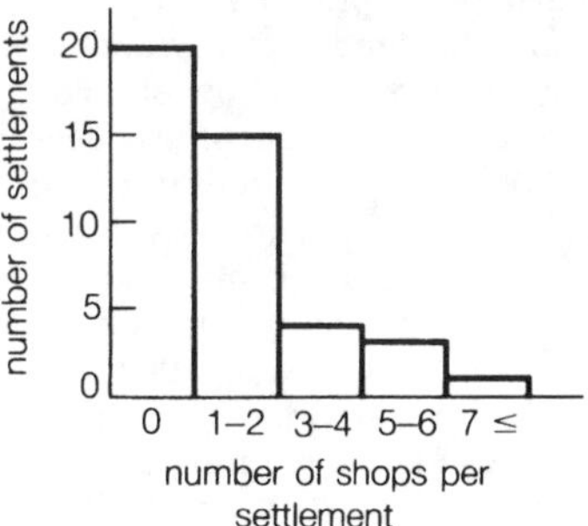

frequency distribution

number of shops per settlement	number of settlements
0	20
1–2	15
3–4	4
5–6	3
7+	1

This information can be displayed graphically as a histogram (see figure).

A theoretical frequency distribution (such as the NORMAL DISTRIBUTION) is a tabulation of the expected number of occurrences in each class according to an algebraic formulation (usually known as the 'generating function'). Most theoretical distributions are smooth because they are based on infinitely large populations: one frequently used is the *Poisson distribution*, which has the special characteristic that its mean is the same as its variance. RJJ

friction of distance The frictional or inhibiting effect of distance on the volume of human interactions of all forms (including MIGRATION, tourist flows, and the movement of goods and information). It is usually seen as a combined effect of the time and cost of overcoming distance and thus linked to TRANSFERABILITY. The friction of distance is geographically variable (being lowest in regions with well-developed transport and communication systems) and is generally believed to have declined as a result of long-term improvements in transport and communication technology (see TIME–SPACE COMPRESSION; TIME–SPACE CONVERGENCE). Empirically its effects are seen in the statistical regularity referred to as DISTANCE DECAY. AMH

friends-and-neighbours effect A particular CONTEXTUAL EFFECT identified in ELECTORAL GEOGRAPHY whereby voters favour local candidates (even if this means abandoning their traditional party preferences) either because they know the candidate personally or in the belief that his/her election should promote local interests. The concept was developed by Key (1949) in the context of intra-party voting in the American South; it was developed and generalized by Cox (1969) and others who related spatially biased information flows within neighbourhoods to patterns of electoral choice. Such voting may be rewarded by the successful candidate winning public expenditure for the area (cf. PORK BARREL). RJJ

References

Cox, K.R. 1969: The voting decision in a spatial context. In C. Board et al., eds, *Progress in geography, volume 1*. London: Edward Arnold, 81–117. · Key, V.O. 1949: *Southern politics in state and nation*. New York: Alfred A. Knopf.

fringe belt A region of mixed land uses at the edge of a built-up area whose heterogeneity reflects the concentration of activities propelled there by centrifugal forces (see CENTRIFUGAL AND CENTRIPETAL FORCES). The study of fringe belts is central to Conzen's method of town-plan analysis, which focuses on TOWNSCAPE morphology (see also EDGE CITY; RURAL–URBAN FRINGE; ZONAL MODEL). RJJ

Suggested Reading

Whitehand, J.W.R. 1967: Fringe belts: a neglected aspect of urban geography. *Transactions, Institute of British Geographers* 41: 223–33.

frontier A zone of varying width that refers either to the political division between two countries or to the settled and uninhabited parts of a country. Prior to the twentieth century, frontiers were a common feature of the political landscape, but most have now disappeared under the global tide of human settlement and economic development, to be replaced by BOUNDARIES, which are lines. In the nineteenth century, land on the frontier was generally regarded as a necessary 'safety valve' for accommodating the populations of fast-growing states, such as the USA (see FRONTIER THESIS). Although this view is now somewhat discredited, the Canadian Northlands and Alaska are still referred to as the last great frontier in North America, and similar descriptions are applied to Russian Siberia and the Australian outback. In reality, however, access to such areas is a luxury open to few states in the modern world, when boundaries on land and sea are so tightly drawn and the legitimacy of colonial territorial claims in the developing world so hotly disputed. MB

Suggested Reading

Prescott, J.V.R. 1987: *Political frontiers and boundaries*. London: Unwin Hyman.

frontier thesis The claim proposed by the American historian Frederick Jackson Turner (1861–1932) that 'the existence of free land, its continuous recession, and the advance of American settlement westward, explain American development' (Turner, 1894). For Turner, the FRONTIER was 'the line of most rapid and most effective Americanization': as it moved westward, so the successive 'primitive' engagements between the colonist and the 'wilderness' entailed 'a steady movement away from the influence of Europe'. That movement could be mapped as a series of settlement 'waves' which corresponded to identifiable evolutionary stages:

> Stand at Cumberland Gap and watch the procession of civilization, marching single file – the Indian, the fur trader and hunter, the cattle raiser, the pioneer farmer – and the frontier has passed by. Stand at South Pass in the Rockies a century later and see the same procession with wider intervals between.

Through these movements, the frontier was supposed to have provided a 'safety valve' for the relief of POVERTY outside the West and, in doing so, to have encouraged a rugged individualism which 'promoted DEMOCRACY'. With the closing of the frontier at the end of the nineteenth century, Turner proclaimed the end of 'the first period of American history': a claim which prompted scholars to describe his thesis – like Mackinder's HEARTLAND thesis – as a 'closed-space doctrine' pregnant with political implications (see Kearns, 1984).

Its intellectual influence was no less powerful. At the turn of the century, from the perspective of his own ANTHROPOGEOGRAPHY, Ratzel regarded Turner's thesis as an important organic theory, conjoining biology and geography to treat the 'struggle for space' as a requirement of the 'social organism'. With the much later emergence of a more clearly defined spatial perspective in geography, Meinig (1960) could still claim that the frontier thesis contained four embryonic concepts – AREAL DIFFERENTIATION, connectivity, cultural succession, and spatial interaction – which were 'undoubtedly the most influential of their type ever to come from American scholarship'; and twenty years later Block (1980) hailed it as 'the classic American essay in speculative historical geography'.

But the frontier thesis was also subject to serious criticism. Within geography, Turner's foremost opponent was C.O. Sauer, who dismissed his thesis as both 'easy and wrong' and reversed its conjectures at virtually every point. Succeeding frontiers were 'a series of secondary CULTURE HEARTHS', Sauer insisted, so 'there was no single type of frontier, neither was there a uniform series of stages'. Insofar as there had been any convergence in frontier development, Sauer believed this to have been the result of 'a growing common political consciousness radiating from the older sections of the country' (reprinted in Leighly, 1963). Other geographers have emphasized similar spatial complications: the economic barriers to frontier settlement, the discontinuous movement of the frontier, and the significance of reverse flows of MIGRATION.

But the most sustained politico-intellectual challenge to the frontier thesis came from scholars who were sharply critical of Turner's studied indifference to the harsh realities of POWER or, more accurately, of his championing of the perspectives of the powerful. Their central charge was that Turner's so-called 'free land' could 'explain' American history only by erasing the claims of native Americans: the frontier thesis was exposed as a rationalization, even a glorification, of conquest and colonial dispossession. Other charges radiated from this core objection. Hofstadter's passionate (1968) indictment censured Turner for his neglect of 'the careless, wasteful and exploitative methods of American agriculture', 'the rapacity and meanness to be found in the petty capitalism of the new towns', the violence and ruthlessness 'to which Indians, Spaniards and Mexicans could testify', and the 'arrogant, flimsy and self-righteous justifications of Manifest Destiny engendered by American expansionism'.

These arguments have been pursued with even greater vigour by proponents of what has come to be called the *new Western history*. Thus Limerick (1987) argues that Turner's thesis is 'entirely irrelevant' to the history of the Trans-Mississippi West. And instead of Turner's TELEOLOGICAL model of a linear, singular frontier process proceeding in lock-step across the continent, three other historians have identified no fewer than six 'frontier processes' that are intended to capture a more complex and more open interplay between productions of power, space and nature in the American West. They are: species-shifting; market-making; land-taking; boundary-setting; state-forming; self-shaping (Cronon, Miles and Gitlin, 1992). DG

References

Block, R. 1980: Frederick Jackson Turner and American geography. *Annals of the Association of American Geographers* 70: 31–42. · Cronon, W., Miles, G. and Gitlin, J. 1992: Becoming West: toward a new meaning for Western history. In W. Cronon, G. Miles and J. Gitlin, eds, *Under an Open Sky: rethinking America's western past*. New York: Norton. · Hofstadter, R. 1968: *The Progressive Historians: Turner, Beard, Parrington*. New York: Knopf. · Kearns, G.P. 1984: Closed space and political practice: Frederick Jackson Turner and Halford Mackinder. *Environment and planning D: Society and Space* 2: 23–34. · Leighly, J., ed., 1963: *Land and life: a selection from the writings of Carl Ortwin Sauer*. Berkeley, CA: University of California Press. · Limerick, P. 1987: *Legacy of Conquest: the unbroken past of the American West*. New York: Norton; Meinig, D.W. 1960: Commentary on W.P. Webb, 'Geographical-historical concepts in American history'. *Annals of the Association of American Geographers* 50: 95–6. · Turner, F.J. 1894: *The significance of the frontier in American history*. Annual Report of the American Historical Association, Washington, D.C.: US Government Printing Office

Suggested Reading

Block (1980). · Cronon, Miles and Gitlin (1992).

functional classification of cities Categorizations of towns and cities according to their economic functions, usually indicated by their occupational and industrial structures. Most classifications are inductive, employing methods such as PRINCIPAL COMPONENTS ANALYSIS (cf. CLASSIFICATION AND REGIONALIZATION). RJJ

functionalism A perspective from which the world is seen as a set of differentiated and interdependent SYSTEMS, whose collective actions and interactions are 'instances of repeatable and predictable regularities in which form and function can be assumed to be related' (Bennett and Chorley, 1978), and which explains these form–function relations in terms of their role in maintaining the continuity or integrity of the system(s). Modern functionalism is usually traced back to advances in evolutionary biology in the nineteenth century (see DARWINISM, SOCIAL DARWINISM), but in geography 'organismic' analogies of the earth, its REGIONS and its STATES pre-dated Darwinian evolutionary theory. Although Darwin provided for the formal articulation of functionalism in many social sciences (as well as the natural sciences), his impact on human geography was, in these terms, less decisive (see Stoddart, 1986): the discipline 'rarely claimed for itself a philosophy of functionalism in the way that anthropology and sociology [did]' and while 'much of the empirical work in geography could be construed as functionalist in form' its precepts 'tended to remain implicit rather than overt in geographical thinking' (Harvey, 1969).

Before the Second World War, the most explicit formulations of functionalism in European geography were found in parts of Ratzel's ANTHROPOGEOGRAPHY, and in the writings of the French school of human geography (particularly the notion of 'terrestrial unity' proposed by Vidal de la Blache: see POSSIBILISM). This was scarcely surprising since Vidal was influenced by the programmatic sociology of Durkheim who was 'without doubt the most important single influence upon the development of functionalism in the [twentieth] century' (Giddens, 1977). In North America Sauer's CULTURAL GEOGRAPHY was also strongly functionalist. He conceived of LANDSCAPE in explicitly functionalist terms as 'a reality as a whole that is not expressed by a consideration of the constituent parts separately', that has 'form, structure and function and hence position in a system, and [which] is subject to development, change and completion' (Leighly, 1963). Similarly, his conception of CULTURE was heavily indebted to Kroeber's functionalist anthropology and was largely responsible for the incorporation of what Duncan (1980) called the 'superorganic' into American cultural geography.

Until the 1970s, however, most of post-war human geography showed little interest in (and even a distrust of) social theory and social science and preferred instead to draw upon MODELS provided by the physical sciences. These provided two principal points of entry for functionalism. The indirect route was through the advance of NEO-CLASSICAL ECONOMICS into ECONOMIC GEOGRAPHY: the so-called 'marginal revolution' of Jevons, Walras and others, with its central concern with the maintenance of an equilibrium between interdependent markets, depended in large measure on a deliberate analogy with statistical mechanics. The more direct route was through SYSTEMS ANALYSIS, whose principles and procedures emerged from control engineering and thermodynamics and which often displayed a similar concern with the maintenance of (dynamic) equilibrium (Bennett and Chorley, 1978). Because of this double history, functionalism advanced in post-war human geography with little or no acknowledgement of parallel developments in social theory. Even in SOCIAL GEOGRAPHY there were no excursions into the STRUCTURAL FUNCTIONALISM proposed by Parsons and others, despite the affinities between some of its formulations and those of the various systems approaches being canvassed within the discipline.

As human geography moved closer to the social sciences, however, functionalism advanced on a broader front. Particularly important was the rapid incorporation of ideas from HISTORICAL MATERIALISM, notably the formal theorization of CAPITALISM as not only a CRISIS-ridden but also crisis-dependent and hence self-regulating MODE OF PRODUCTION (cf. REGULATION THEORY). Functionalism also stalked in the shadows of CRITICAL THEORY: Habermas's theory of communicative action was advertised as 'a critique of functionalist reason', for example, yet Parsons remained a considerable presence in his work (Habermas, 1987; see Joas, 1991; McCarthy, 1991).

Most of these more recent discussions were not burdened with the language of traditional functionalism, however, and their central concern was usually the construction of capitalism as a totality. At the same time many of these formulations were called into question. The critique of functionalism was reopened through a series of major debates over the relations between functionalism and Marxism (see Cohen, 1982; Elster, 1982). The most frequent objections to functionalism were at once logical, e.g. the unintended or unanticipated consequences of a form of social conduct cannot be used to explain its existence in the first place, and substantive, e.g. functionalism characteristically assumes a purpose ('needs' or 'goals') without a purposive agent. Indeed, it was the concern with HUMAN AGENCY that united many of these early critics. Some of them insisted on the importance of METHODOLOGICAL INDIVIDUALISM and refused purely 'structural' explanations (e.g. Duncan and Ley, 1982; Elster, 1982: see HUMANISTIC GEOGRAPHY), while others argued for a bounded conception of human agency within a more inclusive STRUCTURATION THEORY that was advertised as a 'non-functionalist manifesto' (Giddens, 1981). The subsequent rise of POSTMODERNISM, with its suspicion of meta-narratives and J.-F. Lyotard's (1984) injunction to 'wage war on totality' hammered another nail in the coffin of functionalism. The assault was raised to a new intensity by the advance of POST-STRUCTURALISM through human geography and its characteristic strategy of de-centring and dis-placing the social field. Thus Gibson-Graham (1996) objected that dominant conceptions of capitalism 'more often portrayed [it] as a unified entity than as a set of practices scattered over a landscape'. In their view the architectural metaphor of capitalism as a structure conferred upon it an essential integrity, 'a structural and systemic unity' possessing 'qualities of durability, stability and persistence' and hence rendered it more or less 'impervious to ordinary political and cultural interventions' (pp. 254–5). Whatever one makes of this, it is a forceful reminder that the discourse of functionalism has always carried profoundly political implications. DG

References

Bennett, R.J. and Chorley, R.J. 1978: *Environmental systems: philosophy, analysis, control*. London: Methuen; Cohen, G.A. 1982: Functional explanation, consequence explanation and Marxism. *Inquiry* 25: 27–56; Duncan, J.S. 1980: The superorganic in American cultural geography. *Annals of the Association of American Geographers* 70: 181–98; Duncan, J.S. and Ley, D. 1982: Structural Marxism and human geography: a critical assessment. *Annals of the Association of American Geographers* 72: 30–59; Elster, J. 1982: Marxism, functionalism and game theory: the case for methodological individualism. *Theory and society* 11: 453–82; Gibson-Graham, J.K. 1996: *The end of capitalism (as we knew it): a feminist critique of political economy*. Oxford and Cambridge, MA: Blackwell; Giddens, A. 1977: *Studies in social and political theory*. London: Hutchinson; Giddens, A. 1981: *A contemporary critique of historical materialism. Vol. 1: Power, property and the state*. London: Macmillan; Habermas, J. 1987: *The theory of communicative action. Vol. 2: A critique of functionalist reason*. Cambridge: Polity Press; Harvey, D. 1969: *Explanation in geography*. London: Edward Arnold; Joas, H. 1991: The unhappy marriage of hermeneutics and functionalism. In A. Honneth and H. Joas, eds, *Communicative action*. Cambridge: Polity Press, 97–118; Leighly, J., ed., 1963: *Land and life: the writings of Carl Ortwin Sauer*. Berkeley, CA: University of California Press; Luhmann, N. 1981: *The differentiation of society*. New York: Columbia University Press; Lyotard, J.-F. 1984: *The postmodern condition: a report on knowledge*. Minneapolis: University of Minnesota Press; McCarthy, T. 1991: Complexity and democracy: or the seducements of systems theory. In A. Honneth and H. Joas, eds, *Communicative action*. Cambridge: Polity Press, 119–39; Stoddart, D.R. 1986: *On geography and its history*. Oxford and Cambridge, MA: Blackwell.

Suggested Reading

Gibson-Graham (1996), ch. 11; Giddens (1977), ch 2; Harvey (1969), ch. 22.

fuzzy sets Fuzzy sets are sets (categories, classes, types) for which the definitions of set membership are vague or 'fuzzy', and contrast with the sharp, clearly-defined definitions used by standard logic and set theory. Examples include 'cold', 'warm' and 'hot' for the weather: 'cold' is not a precise category, and will overlap with 'warm' and there is no precise boundary between them (e.g. 10 °C), unless we artificially impose one. Similarly 'poor', 'middle-class' and 'rich' are fuzzy categories in everyday life and usage, only converted into precise categories by government or other statistical definitions.

Fuzziness should be distinguished from randomness, and it attempts to represent and model a different type of UNCERTAINTY to that dealt with by probability – Kosko (1992, p. 265) says that:

> Fuzziness describes event ambiguity. It measures the degree to which an event occurs, not whether an event occurs. Randomness describes the uncertainty of event occurrence. An event occurs or not, and you can bet on it. The issue concerns the occurring event: is it uncertain in any way.... Whether an event occurs is 'random'. to what degree it occurs is fuzzy.

There may be a 40 per cent chance of a US citizen being in the 'middle-class' category (if we can define the bounds of the category and 'defuzzy' it), for example, and that would be a probability, whereas the ambiguous, uncertain nature of 'middle-class' is a fuzzy set issue.

Most standard quantitative and mathematical modelling works with non-fuzzy sets and logic, yet much of social life and the environment is represented by fuzzy categories. Engineers such as Zadeh developed 'fuzzy logic' as a new group of methods to allow modelling of such fuzzy problems. The methods require further assumptions (and precision) – ordering the categories; estimating membership shape; and centring (e.g. 'middle-class' centred on $30,000 income with a triangular membership function, with overlap at either side with the other two categories) – but one can test sensitivity to the assumptions. In human geography, the main applications so far have been in the arenas of artificial intelligence (AI) and non-linear systems modelling, such as neural nets. Openshaw and Openshaw (1997) provide examples to SPATIAL INTERACTION modelling using fuzzy distances ('short', 'average', 'big', 'long') and fuzzy trip-frequencies ('some', 'lots', 'massive', etc.), and show how fuzzy systems modelling can perform as well (or better) than many traditional interaction methods.

Fuzzy sets undoubtedly have potential to extend the limits of what can be modelled in socio-economic and spatial systems. Advocates such as Openshaw (1996) see fuzzy logic as the key which will enable 'soft human geography' – all the aspects currently studied by QUALITATIVE and discursive METHODS – to be made 'scientific', but most would paint a much more modest picture. It is notable that most examples come from engineering, systems modelling and AI; the social sciences (including economics) have not made great use of fuzzy sets. Much of human geography is not asking questions of the type that fuzzy logic can help answer, and fuzzy models are likely to be most useful within specialist contexts. LWH

References

Kosko, B. 1992: *Neural networks and fuzzy systems*. Englewood Cliffs, NJ: Prentice-Hall. · Openshaw, S. 1996: Fuzzy logic as a new scientific paradigm for doing geography. *Environment and Planning A* 28: 761–8. · Openshaw, S. and Openshaw C. 1997: *Artificial intelligence in geography*. Chichester: John Wiley.

G

game theory A theory of interdependent DECISION-MAKING where individuals ('players') must choose courses of action ('strategies') while remaining ignorant of other players' choices, but with knowledge of the costs and benefits ('payoffs') of all the resulting potential outcomes. The goal of the theory is to determine through formal reasoning alone the rational course of action for any given player, and the consequences that ensue for the collective. One of game theory's most interesting results, and most familiar incarnations, the PRISONER'S DILEMMA, demonstrates that individual RATIONAL CHOICE produces collective sub-optimality. What appears best for the individual because of interdependent decision-making turns out not to be best for anyone.

Game theory arose at the turn of the century, but was solidified as a sub-discipline in the mid-1940s with the publication of von Neumann's and Morgenstern's (1944) *The theory of games and economic behavior.* Because game theory represents a set of general theorems about behaviour, it is utilized in a swath of disciplines: biology, political science, sociology, philosophy, economics, and human geography (one of the earliest and now classic papers in the geographical literature is Gould's, 1963).

The simplest case is the strictly competitive two-person, zero-sum game. Here there is no potential for cooperation, because whatever one person gains, the other must lose. In geography the classic example is the derivation of the HOTELLING MODEL involving two ice-cream vendors on an elongated beach who must decide where to locate given a uniform distribution of sunbathers. Given the propensity of customers always to buy from the closest vendor, both ice-cream sellers will end up in the middle of the beach, back-to-back. It is a zero-sum game because if one vendor should move even slightly off centre towards one end, s/he will immediately lose some business while the other vendor will correspondingly gain. Under such conditions, the best strategy is one of maximin, that is, acting in such a way that guarantees at least a minimum payoff regardless of the actions of the other player. In the Hotelling case, the maximin solution is always to stand in the middle of the beach because a minimum market of at least half the total customers is always guaranteed irrespective of the actions of the other ice-cream seller. When both vendors adopt a maximin strategy, equilibrium obtains.

More complicated games have been devised that involve non-zero-sum pay-offs, i.e. through interaction all players can potentially gain. Here the bargaining model of John Nash (1950) has proved immensely useful, demonstrating that non-cooperative strategies can be the basis of non-zero-sum games. Other assumptions modified include increasing the number of players, allowing for incomplete information, running a sequence of games ('supergames') rather than assuming each one is a single play, and postulating SATISFICING BEHAVIOUR instead of rational choice. This latter modification has proven particularly difficult to undertake, reinforcing the point that game theory sits squarely within the tradition of RATIONAL CHOICE THEORY, and its concomitant approach of METHODOLOGICAL INDIVIDUALISM.

Some of the more interesting recent work in game theory revolves around the possibility of cooperation. The problem is that usually it is not rational for rational individuals to cooperate in a game, or, more generally, to engage in any form of collective action. At issue is the so-called *free-rider problem*. Associated with collective action are often individual costs if others do not cooperate (for example, being the only industrialist to install expensive anti-pollution equipment in a plant), but large collective gains if they do (for example, clean air and water for everyone). Given this structure of pay-offs, it is individually rational not to engage in collective action, but instead to free-ride on the actions of others (Olson, 1965). By so doing, any losses, such as losing business because of higher costs, are minimized, while any gains, such as an improved environment, can still be obtained, providing others act collectively. Of course, if everyone free-rides then there is no collective action, and as a consequence collective sub-optimality eventuates from individual rational choice.

The free-rider argument has proven powerful. Many political theorists, beginning with Hobbes, have used it to justify the necessity of the STATE – if everyone free-rides, important public goods such as domestic security or even a healthy environment would never be provided (Taylor, 1987). This said, *voluntary* cooperation and collective action clearly do occur: workers go on strike, students defend DEMOCRACY, and environmentalists block bulldozers and logging trucks. In each case, individuals act in a way to benefit collective interests, rather than their narrowly defined self-interest. But why does this happen? Four reasons have been proposed:

- the pay-off structure may not reflect all the incentives impinging on collective action – for example, feelings of guilt or injustice with respect to others;
- the very interactions into which individuals enter can endogenously alter preferences in favour of collective action, for example, being swept up in revolutionary fervour;
- individuals may irrationally believe that if they engage in collective action then others will too; and finally, and most frequently discussed,
- there may be more than a single play to the game, in which case players are able to devise certain meta-strategies that favour cooperation (the most successful of which is 'tit-for-tat', Axelrod, 1984).

In each case because of some form of interdependence among individuals, the norm of free-riding is replaced by one of collective action.

Very little geographical work exists on cooperative game playing. Sheppard and Barnes (1990), however, attempt to ground geographically the four justifications for collective action given above. They argue that the interdependencies among individuals necessary for cooperative behaviour most readily occur in PLACE. This is further justified by Olson's (1965) original work which suggested that free-rider effects are most likely to break down within small groups of people as might be found within specific locales. TJB

References

Axelrod, R. 1984: *The evolution of cooperation*. New York: Basic Books. · Gould, P.R. 1963: Man against his environment: a game-theoretical framework. *Annals of the Association of American Geographers* 53: 290–7. · Nash, J.F. 1950: The bargaining problem. *Econometrica* 18: 155–62. · Olson, M. 1965: *The logic of collective action: public goods and the logic of groups*. Cambridge, MA: Harvard University Press. · Sheppard, E.S. and Barnes, T.J. 1990: *The capitalist space economy: geographical analysis after Ricardo, Marx and Sraffa*. London: Unwin Hyman. · Taylor, M. 1987: *The possibility of cooperation*. Cambridge: Cambridge University Press. · von Neumann, J. and Morgenstern, O. 1944: *Theory of games and economic behavior*. Princeton: Princeton University Press.

Suggested Reading

Axelrod (1984). · Sheppard and Barnes (1990), ch. 10. · Taylor (1987).

garden city A planned and relatively self-contained settlement, developed with an emphasis on spaciousness, environmental quality and 'greenness'. It represents the first successful modern attempt to exploit these planning principles for whole settlements, in turn attributed to the theoretical ideas and practical promotion of a City of London stenographer, Ebenezer Howard (1850–1928).

His own vision, as outlined in his *Garden cities of tomorrow* (1902, first published in 1898 under a different title), saw garden cities combining the social, economic and cultural benefits of big-city living with the advantages to the individual of a more healthy rural environment. Each city would accommodate some 32,000 people on a 6000 acre site, planned according to a concentric land-use pattern in which residential and commercial land were segregated. Openness was injected through wide boulevards, low-density development and public parks within, with farmland and GREEN BELT beyond. On reaching its capacity, additional growth was directed to further garden cities, so creating a system of planned centres around their parent metropolis, the whole being interconnected by efficient rail and road links.

In 1899 Howard founded the Garden City Association which, four years later, bought a site in Hertfordshire on which Barry Parker and Raymond Unwin designed the world's first garden city, Letchworth. A second followed at Welwyn, also in Hertfordshire, in 1920.

The garden city movement showed how DECENTRALIZATION could contribute to the planned improvement of congested urban centres, a theme taken up in Britain's post-war NEW TOWN and URBAN RENEWAL programmes, while the Garden City Association led to the founding of the Town and Country Planning Association in 1918, still a potent pressure group in British planning policy. Thus Howard's ideas, first supported by a fringe grouping of eccentric idealists, have become enshrined in the mainstream professional and political world of urban planning (Hardy, 1991).

They have also been adopted internationally, and although settlements called 'garden cities' outside Britain show variations from the Howard model, high-quality residential environments, low densities and greenness are still central themes. Both in Britain and elsewhere, too, similar ideas have been adopted on a smaller scale in the intra-urban development of garden villages and garden suburbs. The geographical interest in Howard's ideas lies partly in their DIFFUSION and absorption into different cultural contexts, bolstering his claim to be the most important figure in the international history of town planning. While the debt that these adaptations owe to Howard's ideas is an arena of debate, it is clear that Howard in his turn was influenced by the utopian ideas of Victorian urban thinkers and philanthropic industrialists, and by time spent as a young man in the mid-West of the US (Hall, 1996).

AGH

References

Hall, P.G. 1996: *Cities of tomorrow: an intellectual history of urban planning and design in the twentieth century*. Oxford: Blackwell. · Hardy, D. 1991: *From garden cities to new towns: campaigning for town and country planning 1899–1946*. London: Spon.

Suggested Reading

Beevers, R. 1988: *The garden city utopia: a critical biography of Ebenezer Howard*. Basingstoke: Macmillan.

Gastarbeiter The German term for foreign (guest) workers now widely applied to migrant labourers temporarily resident in European cities (cf. MIGRANT LABOUR). RJJ

gateway city A settlement linking two areas whose physical situation means it can command entrance to and exit from its HINTERLAND. As control centres, such settlements often develop into locally dominant PRIMATE CITIES (see also MERCANTILIST MODEL). RJJ

GATT (General Agreement onTariffs and Trade) is the institutional framework established in 1947 to regulate international TRADE in merchandise. It was one of the three international institutions (the others being the International Monetary Fund and the World Bank) created as part of the United States-led 'new international economic order' in the immediate post-war period. Initially 23 countries belonged to the GATT; today there are more than 120 member states. More than 90 per cent of world merchandise trade is now covered by the GATT.

The GATT is a *rule-oriented* approach to multilateral trade cooperation. Its fundamental basis is that of *non-discrimination* which incorporates two principles. The most-favoured nation principle states that a trade concession negotiated between two countries must also apply to all other countries within the GATT. The *national treatment* rule requires that imported goods are treated in the same way as domestic goods. An important development occurred in 1965 with the inclusion of a *generalized system of preferences*, which granted preferential access of developing country products to developed country markets (important exceptions were clothing and textiles).

Negotiations to liberalize international trade have been conducted in a series of 'rounds' which have occurred at irregular intervals. There have been eight such rounds since 1947, the most recent being the protracted and contentious Uruguay Round which began in 1986 and was finally concluded in 1994. The GATT is generally regarded as being instrumental in the progressive lowering of tariff barriers to international trade. In 1940, the average tariff on manufactured products was approximately 40 per cent; in the mid-1990s it was down to 4 per cent. However, the GATT has been far less successful in constraining the proliferation of non-tariff barriers (such as import quotas).

The Uruguay Round was the most ambitious and wide-ranging of all the GATT rounds. For the first time it incorporated agriculture, textiles and clothing into the GATT. Special agreements were concluded in services (GATS – the General Agreement on Trade in Services), intellectual property rights (TRIPS – Trade-Related Aspects of Intellectual Property Rights), and trade related investment (TRIMs – Trade-Related Investment Measures). The major organizational development was the incorporation of the GATT and the other agreements into a new *World Trade Organization* (WTO) which came into being in January 1995, almost 50 years after the original proposal to create an International Trade Organization foundered. During that period, the GATT had continued to be merely a 'temporary framework'.

A number of contentious issues remain in the aftermath of the Uruguay Round to be addressed by the WTO. For example, the GATS is far from being fully agreed. More broadly, there is considerable pressure from a number of developed countries, led by the United States, to incorporate considerations of labour standards and the environment into the WTO's remit on the grounds that labour and environmental differentials distort free trade. This is strongly opposed by developing countries who see such moves as disguised protectionism. PD

Suggested Reading

Bhagwati, J. 1988: *Protectionism*. Cambridge, MA: MIT Press. · Dicken, P. 1998: *Global shift: transforming the world economy*, 3rd edn. London: Sage; New York: Guilford, ch. 3. · Hoekman, B. and Kostecki, M. 1995: *The political economy of the world trading system: from GATT to WTO*. Oxford: Oxford University Press. · Stubbs, R. and Underhill, G.R.D., eds, 1994: *Political economy and the changing global order*. London: Macmillan.

gender and geography The study of the various ways that genders and geographies are mutually constituted. Haraway (1991) provides a thorough discussion of the history and meaning of the term 'gender' within feminist theory through to the mid-1980s. The term has a broadly similar history within geography, with a movement away from theories of gender roles to gender relations and towards a fuller exploration of how gender relations are constructed in all spheres of life (see FEMINIST GEOGRAPHIES).

'Gender' is often contrasted to 'sex' in an effort to remove women from NATURE and place them within CULTURE as constructed and self-constituting social subjects. The treatment of gender within geography is slightly unusual in this regard as it has not been 'quarantined from the infections of biological sex' (Haraway, 1991, p. 134) to the same extent as in other disciplines. In an effort to theorize PATRIARCHY, Foord and Gregson (1986) identified necessary relations that constitute gender relations. Following the analytical procedures of REALISM, they reasoned that two genders, male and female, are the basic characteristics of gender relations. In order to theorize the necessary relations between these basic characteristics, they ask: 'Under what conditions do men and women require each other's existence?', to which they answer, 'for biological reproduction and the practice of heterosexuality'. Foord's and Gregson's analysis was quickly criticized, because it made it difficult to theorize how CAPITALISM structures gender relations (McDowell, 1986) and for its biologism, especially in terms of its portrayal of heterosexuality as biologically or psychologically fixed (Knopp and Lauria, 1987).

The latter criticism signalled important new ways of thinking about the relations between sex and gender. The feminist distinction between sex and gender may save gender from essentialist or naturalizing versions of femininity (see ESSENTIALISM), but it repeats the problems of the NATURE/CULTURE dualism insofar as it posits gender as the (active) social that acts upon the (passive) surface of sex. It is itself thus vulnerable to the charge of MASCULINISM: 'Is sex to gender as feminine to masculine [as nature to culture]?' (Butler, 1993, p. 4). A further problem is that within the terms of the sex/gender dualism sex seems to disappear once it is gendered: gender absorbs and displaces sex (these tendencies within geography are discussed by Nast, 1998). Haraway tackles these criticisms by arguing, through the metaphor of coyote, for the agency of bounded entities, such as sexed bodies (see SITUATED KNOWLEDGE). This is a different, though not necessarily contradictory, strategy to that of Butler who, drawing upon theories of DISCOURSE, DECONSTRUCTION and PSYCHOANALYSIS, argues that the regulatory regime of heterosexuality brings the (hetero)-sexed body (either female or male but never inbetween – she analyses the refusal of intersexed infant bodies as a way of demonstrating this) into being. Sexual determination is an immediate, forcible and reiterative practice. We must be gendered male or female to be human; those who are not properly gendered are threatened by psychosis (unstable bodily and psychic boundaries) and abjection. Neither sex nor gender has ontological status and gender cannot be theorized apart from regimes of (hetero)sexuality (cf. ONTOLOGY). Gender is a truth effect of a discourse of a primary and stable identity; this identity emerges out of repetitive gender performances, instantiations of an ideal/norm (see PERFORMATIVITY; SUBJECT FORMATION, GEOGRAPHIES OF). For Butler, sex is not extra- or pre-discursive; it is brought into being through discourse. She does see opportunities to prise performances of sex and gender apart: subversive potentials of drag performances lie in the disjunction between (a posited interiorized) sex and exteriorized gender performances, and in allowing the sexually disallowed or unperformable (e.g. the figure of femininity for men) to be performed: drag can be read as an effort to negotiate unpermissable cross-gendered identifications.

The implications of this retheorization of gender and sex are far-reaching: gender is recast as derivative of the norms of (hetero)sex and as repetitive and unstable practices enacted in different ways in different places and times. This invites close attention to the persistent deployment of regulatory regimes of heterosexuality, to the sexualities that operate at the margins of and exceed the boundaries of these norms, and to the geographies of both (see QUEER THEORY; SEXUALITY, GEOGRAPHY AND; Bondi, 1998; Nast, 1998) GP

References

Bondi, L. 1998: Sexing the city. In R. Fincher and J. Jacobs, eds, *Cities of difference*. New York: Guilford, 177–200. · Butler, J. 1993: *Bodies that matter: on the discursive limits of 'sex'*. London and New York: Routledge. · Foord, J. and Gregson, N. 1986: Patriarchy: towards a reconceptualisation. *Antipode* 18: 186–211. · Haraway, D. 1991: 'Gender' for a marxist dictionary: the sexual politics of a word. In D. Haraway, *Simians, cyborgs, and women: the reinvention of nature*. London and New York: Routledge, pp. 127–48. · Knopp, L. and Lauria, M. 1987: Gender relations as a particular form of social relations. *Antipode*, 19: 48–53. · McDowell, L. 1986: Beyond patriarchy: a class-based explanation of women's subordination. *Antipode* 18: 311–21. · Nast, H. 1998: Unsexy geographies. *Gender Place and Culture* 5: 191–206.

genealogy An historical reconstruction of the relations between POWER, knowledge and the human subject that aspires to be an immanent critique of the present. The term derives from German philosophy but is usually associated with the French thinker Michel Foucault (1926–84), who sought to illuminate the contingency of our *évidences* (what we take for granted, how we came to recognize ourselves as particular kinds of subjects, and how we came to see some practices and experiences, such as crime, madness and SEXUALITY, as 'problems': cf. TAKEN-FOR-GRANTED WORLD) by tracking their haphazard *descent* from previously unseen historical thresholds. Foucault argued that we have not fully recognized how we became constituted as objects and subjects of 'regimes of power' that have conditioned how we can act. He documented the birth and spread of an anonymous and functional – *disciplinary* – 'technology of power' which is acutely individualizing, fosters obedience by habituating people to practices of examination and SURVEILLANCE, and compares and judges behaviour in terms of norms. The individual is not the 'inert material on which power comes to fasten', Foucault argued (1980a), but 'an effect of power... [and] the element of its articulation'. Disciplinary power was exercised in institutional spaces such as factories, prisons and schools, and it became the 'blueprint' of a 'carceral society' in which our aptitudes and aspirations are subjected to the 'universal reign of the normative' (Foucault, 1977). In Foucault's account, these practices of 'normalization', which proliferated during the nineteenth century, shaped what we came to 'count as being self-evident, universal, and necessary' about history, society and ourselves (e.g. that history is progressive, that criminals should be locked up and reformed, and that we can discover the truth of our being by seeing ourselves as desiring subjects): they 'announce' *our* present, differentiate it from other epochs, and condition our ability to fashion other ways of living and expressing ourselves (Foucault, 1991a). Foucault's histories of the asylum, the clinic, the prison and sexuality describe how general formulas of domination and DISCOURSES on the 'dangers' of madness, sexuality, and so on, emerged from discrete practices and seemingly mundane events.

Critics have complained that Foucault's 'history of the present' is grim and paralysing, and that he draws too many broad and unsubstantiated (epochal) conclusions about the nature of MODERNITY from his local, historical (genealogical) studies (see e.g. Donnelly, 1992). But Foucault stressed that the focus on the individual in modern societies is not completely stifling, and commentators suggest that he magnifies one set of practices – the proliferation of disciplinary power – 'as a [rhetorical] means of moving an audience to vigilance' (Rabinow, 1994). Foucault insisted that the disciplinary make-up of 'our' society rests on a 'hazardous play of dominations' – on minor, accidental and often fragile processes and struggles 'of different origin and scattered location' (Foucault, 1986).

Foucault's genealogies are based on the claim that power is not necessarily concentrated in the hands of a monarch, the STATE, or a particular CLASS, and is not simply imposed on people from on high – this being a premodern, sovereign model of power. He conceptualized power as an incessant, decentred and malleable 'force field' of strategic relations among individuals, groups and institutions that works 'within the social body' and facilitates (rather than reflects) the development of CAPITALISM and the NATION-STATE. Foucault argued that power 'comes from everywhere', has 'a *capillary* form of existence', and is simultaneously constraining and enabling. As such, freedom should not be conceived as a great escape from power or the search for an essential self beyond power. Nor does history have a single objective or potential which we might one day realize. Genealogy, Foucault explained, is 'a form of history which can account for the constitution of knowledges, discourses, domains of objects, etc., without having to make reference to a subject which is either transcendental in relation to the field of events or runs in its empty sameness throughout the course of history' (Foucault, 1980b; cf. ANTI-HUMANISM; BIO-POWER; GOVERNMENTALITY). He saw freedom as a practical and intrinsic – or *strategic* – process of 'insubordination' to the ways in which we are positioned, ongoingly, in relations of domination (see Foucault, 1978, 1982).

Foucault charted the historical lineage and most acute manifestations of what we came to count as normal and abnormal, legitimate and illegitimate, in order to expose the *arbitrariness* of contemporary practices and hint at how they might be surpassed. The genealogist tracks *family associations* between knowledge, power and the self that have an extenuated life in the present, and tries to put the present in an 'agonistic' light rather than offer universal or utopian alternatives to it. Foucault tracked *European* processes of *assujetissement* – disciplinary procedures that have simultaneously turned us into subjects and subjected us to 'a synaptic regime of power' – yet his work is not quintessentially Eurocentric. His deep scepticism towards global narratives of progress, and his meticulous account of the physicality and SPATIALITY of power, informs a range of work on IMPERIALISM and COLONIALISM (see e.g. Arnold, 1994).

Foucault was a remarkably visual and spatial thinker. Rajchman (1991) suggests that he had an 'art of seeing' how 'things were *given* to be seen', how bodies were '"*shown*" to knowledge or to power' through spectacle and surveillance, and how we made the body amenable to discipline by building 'spaces of constructed visibility' such as asylums and prisons. Indeed, Foucault once surmised that 'geography must lie at the centre of my concerns', for he had effectively shown that it is impossible to understand how regimes of power emerge and are deployed without thinking about how they work in and through SPACE (Foucault, 1980c).

Geographers have analysed constellations of disciplinary power and space in a range of European and non-European settings (see Hannah, 1997). They have stressed that genealogy confounds the analytical separation of space and society, and they are now suggesting that Foucault's arguments about normalization give us insights into the discursive constitution of NATURE as well as SOCIETY (see Gregory, 1998). Foucault's ideas also inform recent 'critical histories of geography,' which seek to question the ways in which some geographical ideas, methods, institutions and TEXTS came to be seen as central to the discipline, and others were marginalized (see Driver et al. 1995; cf. GEOGRAPHY, HISTORY OF).

Genealogy is a sensitizing device, and it encourages a style of geographical work that is attentive to a range of problems: (a) the critical purpose of historical perspectives within geography; (b) that the geographies that geographers produce both shape, and are shaped by, relations of power; (c) that the production and representation of space is directly implicated in the exercise of power and formation of identity; (d) that how we think and write about the past has a central bearing on how we ascertain and disclose what is intolerable about the present; and (e) how we might draw out previously unseen spatial dynamics of domination and subjugation, inclusion and exclusion, without entrenching or proliferating their effects. DC

References

Arnold, D. 1994: The colonial prison: power, knowledge and penology in nineteenth-century India. In D. Arnold, and D. Hardiman, eds, *Subaltern studies VIII: essays in honour of Ranajit Guha*. Delhi: Oxford University Press, 148–87. · Donnelly, M. 1992: On Foucault's uses of the notion 'biopower'. In T. Armstrong, ed. and trans., *Michel Foucault: philosopher*. New York: Routledge, 199–203. · Driver, F. et al. 1995: Geographical traditions: rethinking the history of geography. *Transactions of the Institute of British Geographers* NS 20: 403–22. · Foucault, M. 1977: *Discipline and punish: the birth of the prison*, trans. A. Sheridan. London: Allen Lane. Orig. pub. Fr. 1975, *Surveiller et punir* · Foucault M. 1978: *The history of sexuality, vol. 1: an introduction*, trans. Robert Hurley. New York: Random House. Orig. pub. Fr. 1976, *La volonté de savoir*. · Foucault, M. 1980a–c: Two lectures: Truth and power; Questions of geography. In his *Power/knowledge: selected interviews and other writings, 1972–1977*, ed. C. Gordon. New York: Pantheon Books, 78–133, 63–77. · Foucault, M. 1982: The subject and power. In H.L. Dreyfus, and P. Rabinow, *Michel Foucault: beyond structuralism and hermeneutics*. Brighton: The Harvester Press, 208–26. · Foucault, M. 1986: Nietzsche, genealogy, history. In P. Rabinow, ed., *The Foucault reader*. Harmondsworth: Penguin, 76–100. Orig. pub. Fr. 1971. · Foucault, M. 1991a: Questions of method. In G. Burchall, C. Gordon, and Miller, P., eds, *The Foucault effect: studies in governmentality*. London: Harvester Wheatsheaf, 73–86. Orig. pub. Fr. 1980. · Gregory, D. 1998: *Explorations in critical human geography*. Hettner-Lectures, 1. Heidelberg: Department of Geography, University of Heidelberg. · Hannah, M. 1997: Space and the structuring of disciplinary power: an interpretive review. *Geografisker Annaler* 79 B: 171–80. · Rabinow, P. 1994: Modern and counter-modern: Ethos and epoch in Heidegger and Foucault. In G. Gutting, ed., *The Cambridge companion to Foucault*. Cambridge: Cambridge University Press, 197–214. · Rajchman, J. 1991: Foucault's art of seeing. In his *Philosophical events: essays of the '80s*. New York: Columbia University Press, 68–102.

Suggested Reading

Foucault (1977), (1980).

general linear model The collective term for the body of statistical procedures (such as ANALYSIS OF VARIANCE, CORRELATION, FACTOR ANALYSIS, PRINCIPAL COMPONENTS ANALYSIS and REGRESSION) based on the analysis of covariation among variables. Many statistical packages for computer applications of these procedures are available, including GLIM (General Linear Model).

The techniques incorporated within the general linear model are the most widely used of all PARAMETRIC statistical methods. Their application assumes that the data meet a number of criteria, however, of which the most important are that:

- the relationship between any pair of variables should be linear (or can be transformed into a linear relationship: see TRANSFORMATION OF VARIABLES);
- the RESIDUALS from the estimated value of the dependent variable for each value of an independent variable in a regression should have a mean of zero;
- those residuals should be normally distributed and with equal variances (i.e. they should be homoscedastic not heteroscedastic);
- values on each independent variable should not be autocorrelated (i.e. the value at one observation should not determine the value of an adjacent observation – see SPATIAL AUTOCORRELATION); and
- all variables should be measured without error.

In addition, in multiple regression there should be no COLLINEARITY among the independent variables (i.e. they should be uncorrelated).

Where these criteria are not met, use of the methods is inappropriate and potentially misleading: the estimated regression coefficients may be either or both of biased and inefficient, for example, so that forecasts and predictions based on them are unreliable (see ECOLOGICAL FALLACY). A range of other models allows investigators to avoid some of these problems (cf. CATEGORICAL DATA ANALYSIS; LOGISTIC REGRESSION). RJJ

Suggested Reading

Bailey, T.C. and Gatrell, A.C. 1995: *Interactive spatial data analysis*. London: Longman. · Johnston, R.J. 1978: *Multivariate statistical analysis in geography: a primer on the general linear model*. London and New York: Longman. · O'Brien, L. 1992: *Introducing quantitative geography: measurement, methods and generalised linear models*. London and New York: Routledge.

general systems theory An attempt to develop universal statements about the common properties of superficially different SYSTEMS, usually identified with the work of von Bertalanffy (1968). It was introduced to geographers during the 1960s as a structure which could draw together various strands of work undertaken during the discipline's QUANTITATIVE REVOLUTION but dismissed by Chisholm (1967) as an 'irrelevant distraction'.

The search for isomorphisms among different systems focused on three main principles:

- *allometry* – the growth rate of a subsystem is proportional to that of the system as a whole;
- *hierarchical structuring* – as in CENTRAL PLACE THEORY (for isomorphisms see Woldenberg and Berry, 1967); and
- ENTROPY.

Chorley (1962) suggested that appreciation of the common cross-system principles in both human and physical geography would advance their integration – a task promoted in Bennett and Chorley's (1978) *Environmental systems*, whose subtitle – *philosophy, analysis and control* – mimics von Bertalanffy's. Haggett (1965), too, was stimulated by the search for isomorphisms, notably by d'Arcy Thompson's book *On growth and form* (1917), which suggested similarities across subject matter.

Applications of general systems theory principles within human geography made few substantive achievements, however (the early work on MACROGEOGRAPHY was a partial exception), and few geographers now search for such universals (cf. FRACTALS). RJJ

References

Bennett, R.J. and Chorley, R.J. 1978: *Environmental systems: philosophy, analysis and control*. London: Methuen; Princeton, NJ: Princeton University Press. · von Bertalanffy, L. von 1968: *General systems theory: foundation, development, applications*. New York: G. Braziller; London: Allen Lane. · Chisholm, M. 1967: General systems theory and geography. *Transactions, Institute of British Geographers* 42: 45–52. · Chorley, R.J. 1962: *Geomorphology and general systems theory*. Geological Survey Professional Paper 500–B. Washington, D.C.: US Government Printing Office. · Haggett, P.

1965: *Locational analysis in human geography*. London: Arnold. · Thompson, W. d'Arcy 1917: *On growth and form*. Cambridge: Cambridge University Press. · Woldenberg, M.J. and Berry, B.J.L. 1967: Rivers and central places: analogous systems? *Journal of Regional Science* 7: 129–40.

genre de vie Literally translated as a 'mode of life,' or in Anglophone CULTURAL GEOGRAPHY as 'lifeway', the term refers to the connected forms of livelihood functionally characteristic of a human group; for example, transhumants, fishing communities or peasant agriculturalists (see PEASANT; TRANSHUMANCE). Collective human organization for the purposes of producing and sustaining social, economic and religious life within a specific geographical setting is regarded as foundational for an integrated set of environmental, cultural and spiritual practices.

Along with *milieu* (the geographical environment upon which a group depends for its livelihood) and *circulation* (the forms of communication outside its specific setting), *genre de vie* was a pivotal concept in Vidalian human geography (Vidal de la Blache, 1911; see POSSIBILISM). In the early twentieth century it informed the writing of French regional monographs which sought to identify distinct, localized *pays* or CULTURAL LANDSCAPES such as the *pays de Caux* or *pays de Beauce* in the Ile de France, produced by the interaction of these three phenomena. As their common Latin root (*pagus*) implies, *pays, paysage* and *paysan* share the sense of a highly localized, rooted, stable and socially bounded connection between people and land, and this was central to Vidal's admiration of and fears for the mosaic of *genres de vie* that made up the *tableau* of late nineteenth-century French geography. Similar conceptual foundations for geographical studies of livelihood, PLACE and IDENTITY informed Scandinavian geographical studies in the inter-war years (Buttimer, 1994). Conceptual parallels between *genre de vie* and the 'mode of life' (*Lebenssitte*), regarded in Marx's discussion of MODE OF PRODUCTION as the foundation of social consciousness have been noted in discussions of theory within CULTURAL GEOGRAPHY (Cosgrove, 1998 [1984]), as have the nostalgic and folkloric aspects of the concept of *genre de vie* (Claval, 1994). Both sets of connections root the concept in late nineteenth-century critiques of MODERNIZATION and NATIONALIST discourses in early twentieth-century Europe, when the rootedness and solidarity of traditional *genres de vie* were deemed to be threatened and with them the foundations of national identity. Connections between COMMUNITIES and places developed in urban-industrial contexts through shared experiences of FORDIST production and their more recent demise has generated similar fears, although cultural expression of traditional lifeways (*genres de vie*) in collective rituals and practices have been noted in parts of northern Europe (Olwig, 1996). DEC

References

Buttimer, A. 1994: Edgar Kant and Balto-Skandia: *Heimatkunde* and regional identity. In D. Hooson, ed, *Geography and national identity*, Oxford. · Blackwell, 161–83; Claval, P. 1994: From Michelet to Braudel: personality, identity and organization of France. In D. Hooson, ed., *Geography and national identity*. Oxford: Blackwell, 39–57. · Cosgrove, D. 1998 [1984]: *Social Formation and symbolic landscape*, 2nd edn. Madison, WI: University of Wisconsin Press. · Olwig, D. 1996: Recovering the substantive meaning of landscape. *Annals, Association of American Geographers* 86: 630–53. · Vidal de la Blache, P. 1911: Les genres de vie dans la géographie humaine. *Annales de Géographie* 20: 193–212.

gentrification The reinvestment of CAPITAL at the urban centre, which is designed to produce space for a more affluent class of people than currently occupies that space. The term, coined by Ruth Glass in 1964, has mostly been used to describe the residential aspects of this process but this is changing, as gentrification itself evolves.

Gentrification is quintessentially about urban reinvestment. In addition to residential rehabilitation and redevelopment, it now embraces commercial redevelopment and loft conversions (for residence or office) as part of a wider restructuring of urban geographical space. Gentrification proper combines this economic reinvestment with social change insofar as more affluent people – the urban 'gentry' – move in to previously devalued neighbourhoods. Gentrification often involves direct or indirect displacement of poor people.

Following the worldwide economic crisis of the 1930s and the subsequent World War, developed countries, especially the United States and Australia but those in western Europe also, experienced a state-sponsored suburbanization in which capital fled inner cities for more profitable locations usually within the same region (cf. SUBURB). For the next three to four decades this process continued, largely unabated. Deepening disinvestment from INNER CITIES fuelled a crippling devalorization of those land markets by the late 1960s, while at the same time an expanding middle class provided fresh demand for housing. Gentrification of these previously devalorized inner-city spaces was the result.

Early gentrification occurred in large old cities throughout the advanced capitalist world: London (e.g. Islington), New York (e.g. Greenwich Village and Brooklyn Heights), Philadelphia (e.g. Society Hill), and Toronto (e.g. Riverdale). Erroneously boosted as a return of people from the suburbs, it actually involved the more affluent denizens of the city, much more than suburbanites (Smith, 1979). Gentrification-induced displacement became endemic during the 1980s as gentrification spread to cities and neighbourhoods throughout the urban hierarchy. Anti-gentrification protest movements were common in the late 1970s and 1980s, but dissolved after the late 1980s as national economies moved into recession, state welfare was retrenched (see WELFARE STATE), and support for activists eroded. During the early 1990s, gentrification slowed in many cities, prompting some to argue that the process had ended or had been reversed (Bourne, 1993), but by the middle of the decade the process had further expanded into previously unaffected areas and intensified in already pioneered locations. Although it is predominantly observed in the large and medium-sized cities of Europe and North America, similar processes are also beginning to occur elsewhere, in for example Tokyo, São Paulo, Johannesburg, and several eastern European cities as well.

Geographers have played key roles in the burgeoning literature on gentrification. The key debates have focused on: the root cause of gentrification, the probable location of the process, and its future. Consumption-based explanations of gentrification, explicit or implicit, dominated the literature until the 1980s and can be traced to various appropriations of consumer preference theory which is rooted in NEO-CLASSICAL ECONOMICS. According to this approach, gentrification is caused by shifts in demand for housing. It may involve new demand for the aesthetic charm and occupational proximity that only inner-city neighbourhoods can provide, or it may represent a response to the baby boom, or to the economic RESTRUCTURING of the mid-1970s which produced an inflated number of high-paying service jobs while simultaneously undermining the already waning manufacturing base of many cities (Zukin, 1982). This created what some have deemed the 'new middle class' who occupy the high-paying service jobs (Ley, 1996). CULTURE, in this account, outweighed economics as an explanatory variable for inner-city gentrification even though cultural change was expressed through economic change.

But it is difficult for consumption-based explanations to explain why a quantitative shift in economic demand structure resulted in a qualitative spatial shift in the focus of some new development. Thus production-based explanations focused more on the role of capital in the production of gentrified neighbourhoods. Cycles of capital investment and disinvestment lead to the creation of a RENT GAP between capitalized ground rent under current use and potential ground rent under higher and better (gentrified) use. The rent gap becomes an opportunity for capital reinvestment, especially when it coincides with a wider economic shift toward investment in real estate (Smith, 1992). These were the conditions that prevailed in the first two rounds of significant gentrification, prior to 1973 and during the 1980s.

Many researchers have attempted to reconcile these two kinds of explanations (Zukin 1982; Hamnett, 1984; Bondi, 1991; Clark, 1992; Lees, 1994; Smith, 1996). Failed predictions of 'degentrification' in the early 1990s recession, however, and the resurgence of an overtly economic rationale for the process (Badcock, 1993), suggest that gentrification is emerging as an increasingly widespread and trenchant set of processes in the urban landscape embracing culture and economics as well as socio-structural change. NS

References

Badcock, B. 1993. Notwithstanding the exaggerated claims, residential revitalization really is changing the form of some Western cities: a response to Bourne. *Urban Studies* 30: 191–5. · Bondi, L. 1991: Gender divisions and gentrification: a critique. *Transactions, Institute of British Geographers* NS 16: 190–8. · Bourne, L. 1993: The demise of gentrification? A commentary and prospective view. *Urban Geography* 14: 95–107. · Clark, E. 1992: On blindness, centrepieces, and complementarity in gentrification theory. *Transactions, Institute of British Geographers* NS 17: 358–62. · Hamnett, C. 1984: Gentrification and residential location theory: a review and assessment. In D.T. Herbert, and R.J. Johnston, eds, *Geography and the urban environment: progress in research and applications, volume 6*. New York: John Wiley. · Lees, L. 1994: Rethinking Gentrification: beyond the positions of economics or culture. *Progress in Human Geography* 18: 137–50. · Ley, D. 1996: *The new middle class and the remaking of the central city*. Oxford: Oxford University Press. · Smith, N. 1979: Toward a theory of gentrification: a back to the city movement by capital not people. *Journal of the American Planners Association* 45:

538–48. · Smith, N. 1992: Gentrification and uneven development, *Economic Geography* 58: 139–55. · Smith, N. 1996: *The new urban frontier: gentrification and the revanchist city*. New York: Routledge. · Zukin, S. 1982: *Loft living: culture and capital in urban change*. Baltimore: Johns Hopkins University Press.

Suggested Reading

Ley (1996). · Smith (1996).

geocoding The process of assigning a geographical reference to an object or feature. The term is most often applied narrowly to the assignment of latitude and longitude, or coordinates in some similarly general system, to records identified by street address, where it is synonymous with 'address matching'. Geocoding is a necessary stage in mapping the incidence of disease, the customers of a business (see GEODEMOGRAPHICS), or calls to an emergency service. In most countries it is sufficient to know the coordinates of the endpoints of each link in the street network; the coordinates of a specific address can be estimated by interpolation. In some countries this is impossible because addresses are not numbered sequentially. Geocoding is more problematic in rural areas, and numerous other difficulties result in comparatively low success rates. Nevertheless, it is an important function of GEOGRAPHIC INFORMATION SYSTEMS. The implications of widespread use of geocoding for personal privacy and surveillance have been discussed by Goss (1995) and Pickles (1995).

More broadly, geocoding refers to any system for assigning unique references to points on the Earth's surface (DeMers, 1997). In this wider sense it includes coordinate systems, which assign multidimensional identifiers to locations; the most important are latitude and longitude, based on angular measurements to the Equator and the Greenwich Meridian, and Universal Transverse Mercator (UTM) coordinates, based on a system of 60 longitude zones, and widely adopted in the military community. It also includes place-names, which identify location on the Earth to an accuracy depending on the size of the area covered by each place-name. The administrative hierarchy of nation, province, county, township, etc. also provides a system of coarse geocoding. The 'cadastre', or system of land tenure, provides a form of geocoding. In the United States the Public Land Survey System, which is the basis of the cadastre for most of the nation, is the dominant system of geocoding for land management and many primary industries.

MG

References

DeMers, M.N. 1997 *Fundamentals of geographic information systems*. New York: Wiley. · Goss, J.D. 1995: We know where you are and we know where you live. *Economic Geography* 71(2): 171–98. · Pickles, J., ed., 1995: *Ground truth: the social implications of geographic information systems*. New York: Guilford.

geocomputation (sometimes written as GeoComputation) This is the development and application of computationally intensive approaches in geographical analysis. The term was first coined by Openshaw and colleagues working at the University of Leeds in the mid-1990s to describe the inductive approach used in the family of geographical analysis machines (see Openshaw et al., 1988), but has since been used to describe a much wider range of perspectives from a range of disciplines. The approach has been stimulated by precipitous falls in the cost of computer hardware and the proliferation of georeferenced digital data sources, and the environment to geocomputation is provided by GEOGRAPHICAL INFORMATION SYSTEMS (GIS). A distinctive characteristic of geocomputation is the creative and experimental use of GIS that it entails. It presents a broad but research-led approach to problem solving which emphasizes PROCESS over form, dynamics over statics, and interaction over passive response. Geocomputation is being used to devise improved, often application-specific, models of spatial distributions, enhanced VISUALIZATIONS of spatial phenomena and improved specification of spatial process. The spirit of geocomputation is fundamentally about matching technology with environment, process with data model, geometry and configuration with application, analysis with local context, and philosophy of science with practice.

There are some similarities between this approach and quantitative geography (see QUANTITATIVE METHODS) and SPATIAL ANALYSIS: indeed some of the same spatial problems (e.g. the MODIFIABLE AREAL UNIT PROBLEM, non-linear OPTIMIZATION) have been revisited using a geocomputational perspective in order to overcome previous restrictive assumptions and to seek better quality results. Geocomputation is also providing the opportunity to apply new and novel computational tools to problems that previously could not be solved or have more recently become of interest. For some, the development of a grab-bag of techniques and applications under the umbrella term geocomputation is just a manifestation of a secular increase in our dependency upon computers, and is unlikely to exert any unifying effect upon science (see Couclelis, 1998). Yet for others it is much more than just using 'computers in geography': it is at the same time a tool, a scientific paradigm and a whole new integrated way of thinking about spatial data collection, exploration, transformation, visualization and analysis. PAL

References

Couclelis, H. 1998: Geocomputation in context. In P.A. Longley, S.M. Brooks, R. McDonnell and W. Macmillan, eds, *Geocomputation: a primer*. Chichester: John Wiley & Sons, 17–29. · Openshaw, S., Charlton, M., Wymer, C. and Craft, A.W. 1988: A Mark I geographical analysis machine for the automated analysis of point data sets. *International Journal of Geographical Information Systems* 1: 335–58;

Suggested Reading

Couclelis (1998). · Longley, P.A. 1998: Foundations. In P.A. Longley, S.M. Brooks, R. McDonnell and W. Macmillan, eds, *Geocomputation: a primer*. Chichester: John Wiley & Sons, 3–15. · Openshaw, S. and Alvanides, S. 1999: Applying GeoComputation to the analysis of spatial distributions. In P.A. Longley, M.F. Goodchild, D.J. Maguire and D.W. Rhind, eds, *Geographical information systems: principles, techniques, management and applications*. New York: John Wiley, 267–82.

geodemographics A term applied to the analysis of social and economic data in a geographical context for commercial purposes related to marketing, site selection, advertising, and sales forecasting. Geodemographics has emerged as a significant area of application for GEOGRAPHIC INFORMATION SYSTEMS (GIS; see also LOCATIONAL ANALYSIS; LOCATION–ALLOCATION MODELS; MARKET-AREA ANALYSIS; MARKET POTENTIAL MODEL; RETAILING, GEOGRAPHY OF).

In most countries, the socio-economic data collected by the CENSUS every few years are an important source of information on detailed geographical distributions of population. In addition to simple counts, which are needed for purposes such as allocation of central funds and the administration of elections, censuses often include questions on economic status, age, housing quality, migration, and many other topics. GEOCODING of census returns in recent decades has allowed tabulations and cross-tabulations to be made for small areas, for an enormous array of socio-economic characteristics.

When these census tabulations are combined with digital information on the geometric outlines of CENSUS TRACTS and other reporting zones, it is possible for simple and widely available computer mapping packages to be used to create maps indicating areas of high market potential for particular products, suitable locations for businesses, etc. Other data sources can be used to plot the locations of competing businesses, or statistics on sales. But far more valuable insights are available when census data are manipulated within GIS. GEOCODING makes it possible to identify the residents living within a given census reporting zone; a company willing to make the assumption that all of these people have incomes similar to that reported by the census for the zone as a whole can now target mail specifically to those residents. Various techniques of 'clustering' (Weiss, 1988) have been used to generalize the census-reported characteristics of area residents for such purposes. GIS makes it possible to reverse this process, by identifying the census zone containing each of a firm's customers, and thus to impute economic characteristics to customers.

Modern methods of geodemographic analysis go far beyond census-derived data. Retailers use many subtle and not-so-subtle methods to obtain street addresses from their customers, including 'loyalty' cards, prizes, and credit and debit card records. When a customer uses a credit or debit card at a supermarket check-out, a record is created linking the customer, by name and home location, to every item purchased. Imaging systems can read vehicle licence numbers and link them to owners. Database and GIS technologies allow telephone numbers to be linked to street addresses and geocodes, and thus to census records. Geographical location of purchase is also a major factor in detecting likely misuse or theft of stolen credit cards.

Because of widespread commercial use, many governments have moved to recover part of the cost of collecting a census by selling its processed data, rather than distributing data at the cost of reproduction. The USA is now almost alone in maintaining a policy of cost-of-reproduction pricing on all data collected by the Federal government. Moreover the census is collected infrequently, often at ten-year intervals, opening a niche for commercial providers of more recent data, which can have great value to retailers. For all of these reasons commercial production of geodemographic data has grown rapidly in the past decade, and is likely to continue to grow in the future. Geodemographics is increasingly an international industry, gathering information for processing and resale wherever it is economically viable to do so.

Several geographers and others have commented on the privacy implications of geodemographics (Onsrud, 1994; Goss, 1995; Pickles, 1995; Curry, 1997). GIS allows otherwise unrelated data sets to be linked, by name, street address, or geographic location, and thus bypasses the legal constraints that have been built into the use of other unique personal keys, like social security numbers. It is technically straightforward to scan the contents of a telephone book, re-sort it by phone number, and geocode each individual address; the result is little different from painting the occupants' names and telephone number on the outside of each house. Uncontrolled access to such information has been implicated in a small but growing number of cases of stalking, harassment, and other problems. MG

References

Curry, M.R. 1997: The digital individual and the private realm. *Annals of the Association of American Geographers* 87 (4): 681–99. · Goss, J.D. 1995: We know where you are and we know where you live. *Economic Geography* 71 (2): 171–98. · Onsrud, H.J. 1994: Protecting privacy in using geographic information systems. *Photogrammetric Engineering and Remote Sensing* 60 (9): 1083–95. · Pickles, J. 1991: Geography, GIS, and the surveillant society. *Papers and Proceedings of Applied Geography Conferences* 14: 80–91. · Pickles, J., ed., 1995: *Ground truth: the social implications of geographic information systems*. New York: Guilford. · Weiss, M.J. 1988: *The clustering of America*. New York: Harper and Row.

Suggested Reading

Castle, G.H. III, ed., 1993: *Profiting from a geographic information system*. Fort Collins, CO.: GIS World Books.

geo-governance A relatively new term that has two distinct meanings:

According to McGrew geo-governance is synonymous with *global governance*: 'global governance (or geo-governance) is a term which refers to those formal and informal mechanisms for managing, regulating and controlling international activity and international systems of interaction (e.g. the trade system)' (McGrew, 1997, p. 15; cf. REGIME THEORY).

Drawing on the REGULATION SCHOOL and theories of GOVERNANCE, Sum defines geo-governance as 'the governance of social relations qua temporal-spatial practices and relations' (Sum, 1997, p. 161). In this formulation, geo-governance refers to the adoption of governance strategies that are directly oriented towards the spatial and temporal organization of social and economic life. Using the example of cross-border regional networks in East Asia, Sum shows how the time–space embeddedness of such networks is centrally implicated in their governance processes (cf. TRANSNATIONALISM). JP

References

McGrew, A. 1997: Globalization and territorial democracy: an introduction. In A. McGrew, ed., *The transformation of democracy?* Cambridge: Polity, 1–24. · Sum, N.-L. 1997: 'Time–space embeddedness' and 'geo-governance' of cross-border regional modes of growth: their nature and dynamics in East Asian cases. In A. Amin and J. Hausner, eds, *Beyond market and hierarchy: interactive governance and social complexity*. Cheltenham: Edward Elgar, 159–95.

geographical imagination A sensitivity towards the significance of PLACE and SPACE, LANDSCAPE and NATURE in the constitution and conduct of life on earth. As such, a geographical imagination is by no means the exclusive preserve of the academic discipline of geography. Indeed, H.C. Prince (1962) portrayed it as 'a persistent and universal instinct of [humankind]'. The geographical imagination as he saw it was a response to places and landscapes, and above all to their commingling of 'culture' and 'nature', that 'calls into action our powers of sympathetic insight and imaginative understanding' and whose rendering 'is a creative art'. Prince's emphasis on art was, in part, a critical response to the then ongoing reformulation of geography as a SPATIAL SCIENCE. To Prince, these formal abstractions were ingenious and inventive but – 'like abstract painting' – they would always remain indirect approaches to a world to which the freshest, fullest and richest response was (in his view) literary. It was vitally important, Prince believed, to preserve 'a direct experience of landscape' through the art of geographical description.

Some ten years later David Harvey (1973) provided a discussion of the geographical imagination that also recognized the value of the aesthetic, but Harvey departed from Prince's account in two particularly significant ways: Harvey's critique of spatial science was much more open to formal theoretical vocabularies (indeed, it relied on them), and its characteristic emphasis was on place and space rather than landscape and nature (which had occupied a much more prominent position in Prince's discussion). In Harvey's eyes, therefore, the geographical imagination

> enables . . . individual[s] to recognize the role of space and place in [their] own biograph[ies], to relate to the spaces [they] see around [them], and to recognize how transactions between individuals and between organizations are affected by the space

that separates them ... to judge the relevance of events in other places ... to fashion and use space creatively, and to appreciate the meaning of the spatial forms created by others.

Harvey wanted to contrast the 'geographical imagination' with and also to connect it to what sociologist C. Wright Mills (1959) had previously called the 'sociological imagination', a capacity which 'enables us to grasp history and biography and the relations between the two in society'. Neither Harvey nor Mills confined the terms to their own disciplines: they both said they were talking about 'habits of mind' that transcended particular disciplines and spiralled far beyond the discourse of the academy. Nonetheless, much of the discussion that followed more or less directly from Harvey's intervention was concerned with formal questions of theory and method.

A central preoccupation was the articulation between social theory and human geography. 'It has been a fundamental concern of mine for several years now', so Harvey (1973) had written, 'to heal the breach in our thought between what appear to be two distinctive and indeed irreconcilable modes of analysis', and he presented his seminal *Social justice and the city* as (in part) a 'quest to bridge the gap between sociological and geographical imaginations'. It was urgently necessary to *humanize* human geography, and ideas and concepts were drawn in from the humanities and (especially) the social sciences: in particular, from political economy, social theory and cultural studies. En route, however, it became clear that the reverse movement was equally important, sensitizing these other fields to a geographical imagination, because most of them took a COMPOSITIONAL approach that had little interest in place and space. Some ten years after *Social justice*, therefore, Harvey had this to say:

The insertion of space, place, locale and milieu into any social theory has a numbing effect upon that theory's central propositions. ... Marx, Marshall, Weber and Durkheim all have this in common: they prioritize time over space and, where they treat the latter at all, tend to view it unproblematically as the site or context for historical action. Whenever social theorists of whatever stripe actively interrogate the meaning of geographical categories, they are forced either to make so many ad hoc adjustments to their theory that it splinters into incoherence, or else to abandon their theory in favour of some language derived from pure geometry. The insertion of spatial concepts into social theory has not yet been successfully accomplished. Yet social theory that ignores the materialities of actual geographical configurations, relations and processes lacks validity. (Harvey, 1984.)

Subsequent commentators reported considerable progress in sensitizing social theory and social thought more generally to these concerns. There was (and remains) an immensely productive dialogue between MARXIST GEOGRAPHY and HISTORICAL MATERIALISM, especially through urban and regional political economy, and these conversations have spilled over into a number of other politico-intellectual traditions (Harvey, 1990); the rise of POSTMODERNISM was hailed as emblematic of a distinctively geographical (or at any rate 'spatial') imagination (Soja, 1989); and the interest in POSTCOLONIALISM and POST-STRUCTURALISM has contributed in still more radical ways to the critique of abstract and universal models of 'the human subject' and 'society' (cf. CONTEXTUAL APPROACH; GRAND THEORY; see SPACE; HUMAN GEOGRAPHY).

But three other dimensions of the geographical imagination have received closer attention in recent years, and each of them works towards the production of 'impure' geographies that depart considerably from the closures and clinical approaches of Geography-with-a-capital-G.

In the first place, there has been a *renewed interrogation of the 'academic' geographical imagination* and, in particular, of the two versions proposed by Prince and Harvey (above). Influenced by post-structuralism in different ways and to different degrees, and in particular by the thematization of geography as a DISCOURSE, several critics have argued that Geography is not simply framed by or reflective of changes in the 'real' world because its discourses are *constitutive of* that world. For Gregory (1994) and Deutsche (1995), for example, both drawing on Mitchell's (1989) account of the 'world-as-exhibition', human geography is construed as 'a site where images of the city and space more generally are set up as reality', as 'fictions' in the literal sense of 'something made', and hence as 'the *effects rather than the ground* of disciplinary knowledge' (emphasis added). Thus the modern geographical imagination, in its usual hegemonic forms, not only 'stages the world-as-exhibition and at the same time is fabricated by the picture it creates'; it also characteristically disavows its dependence on the image by adopting an objectifying EPISTEMOLOGY which separates itself from the picture as an autonomous, all-seeing 'spectatorial' subject (Deutsche, 1995). Such an epistemology is, as she remarks, a vehicle for 'the silent spatial production' of 'the self-possessed subject of geographical knowledge who, severed from its object, is positioned to perceive an external totality and so avoids the partiality of immersion on the world' (cf. SITUATED KNOWLEDGE). Gillian Rose (1993) emphasizes that this is both an act of *mastery* – hence her critique of 'the MASCULINISM of geographical knowledge' (p. 84) – but also an act which is shot through with *ambivalence*:

> In geography, a controlling, objective distance is not the only relationship which positions the knower in relation to his object of study. There is rather an ambivalence, which produces the restlessness of the signifiers within the discipline's dualistic thinking. On the one hand, there is a fear of the Other, of an involvement with the Other, which does produce a distance and a desire to dominate in order to maintain that distance. This is central to social-scientific masculinism. On the other hand, there is also a desire for knowledge and intimacy, for closeness and humility in order to learn, and this is the desire of aesthetic masculinity to invoke its other. (p. 77)

Rose's critique identifies the first position ('social-scientific masculinity') with projects like Harvey's and the second position ('aesthetic masculinity') with projects like Prince's.

Rose and Deutsche both urged that this recognition of the *limits* (rather than the presumed completeness) of geographical knowledge requires an engagement with PSYCHOANALYTIC THEORY in order to grapple not with the conscious and creative exercise of the 'imagination' – something which concerned Prince (1962) in particular and HUMANISTIC GEOGRAPHY in general – but with the imaginary: in other words, with 'the psychic register in which the subject searches for plenitude, for a reflection of its own completeness'. By this means, Rose (1993, p. 85) suggests, it is possible 'to think about a different kind of geographical imagination which could enable a recognition of radical difference from itself; an imagination sensitive to difference and power which allows others rather than an Other' (see also FEMINIST GEOGRAPHY; POST-COLONIALISM).

In the second place, there has been a *pluralization of geographical imaginations*. Many human geographers have become markedly reluctant to speak of 'the' geographical imagination – unless they are referring to a hegemonic form of geographical inquiry, and then usually as an object of critique – and are correspondingly much more interested in the possibilities and predicaments that arise from working in the spaces *in between* different philosophical and theoretical traditions (see Gregory, 1994). Closely connected to the production of these 'impure' geographies, there has also been a considerable interest in geographical knowledges that are not confined to (indeed, have often been excluded by) the formalizations of the academy. The boundaries of geography have thus been called into question through the recovery of quite other IMAGINATIVE GEOGRAPHIES: by critical readings of TRAVEL WRITING, for example, and by the critical recovery of 'popular' geographical imaginations (see Crowhurst, 1997; Pred, 1997). These studies are not being conducted in some sort of annex to the central structures of Geography. Not only are they informed by contemporary politico-intellectual preoccupations but they also contest the conventional partitions between 'high' and 'low' cultures and imaginations (which explains the scare-quotes around 'popular'). The circulation of discourses in and out of academic institutions is of vital importance to any elucidation of the politics of geographical imaginations. A number of these studies have been informed by post-colonialism, and it is not surprising that there should – at last – be signs of a belated recognition of the 'whiteness' of most western geographical imaginations (Jackson, 1998) and, crucially, of the salience of geographical imaginations outside the western academy (see Slater, 1992; cf. EUROCENTRISM).

Thirdly, there has been *a renewed engagement with nature* within academic geographical imaginations. In the previous paragraphs 'NATURE' has effectively been displaced from the central position it was once accorded within most traditions of geography and its place taken by 'SPACE' (cf. Turner, 1991). The price paid for the articulation of a 'human' geography in the wake of what many critics saw as a de-humanizing spatial science was 'a peculiar silence on the question of nature' (Fitzsimmons, 1989). This was always an issue within MARXIST GEOGRAPHY, though even there it was arguably more honoured in the breach (cf. Smith, 1990), but there has since been a considerable interest in 'rethinking the "human" in human geography' in terms that seek to move beyond the dualisms of 'society' and 'nature' and the DIALECTIC between them that animates HISTORICAL MATERIALISM (Whatmore, 1999; cf. Harvey, 1996). These newer formulations do not eschew the significance of space – on the contrary, informed by ACTOR–NETWORK THEORY they elaborate a topological 'spatial imagination' – but they do so in ways that produce a much more sensuous geographical imagination. For they 'alert us to a world of commotion in which the sites, tracks and contours of social life are constantly in the making through networks of actants-in-relation that are at once local and global, natural and cultural, and always more than human' (Whatmore, 1999, p. 33; see also Braun and Castree, 1998). Such an approach, as Whatmore notes, 'implicates geographical imaginations and practices both in the *purifying logic* which… fragments living fabrics of association and designates the proper places of "nature" and "society", and *in the promise of its refusal*' (p. 34; emphases added). It is in the attempt to fulfil such a promise that critical inquiry will require the production of radically 'impure' geographies. As the philosopher A.N. Whitehead once famously remarked, 'Nature doesn't come as clean as you can think it'. And for the reasons spelled out in the last three paragraphs, many would now agree that geographical imaginations are becoming much dirtier. DG

References

Braun, B. and Castree, N., eds, 1998: *Remaking reality: nature at the millennium*. London and New York: Routledge. · Crowhurst, A. 1997: Empire theatres and the empire: the popular geographical imagination in the age of Empire. *Environment and Planning D: Society and Space* 15: 155–74. · Deutsche, R. 1995: Surprising geography. *Annals of the Association of American Geographers* 85: 168–75. · Fitzsimmons, M. 1989: The matter of nature. *Antipode* 21 (2): 106–20. · Gregory, D. 1994: *Geographical imaginations*. Oxford: Blackwell. · Harvey, D. 1973: *Social justice and the city*. London: Edward Arnold. · Harvey, D. 1984: On the history and present condition of geography: an historical materialist manifesto. *Professional Geographer* 36: 1–11. · Harvey, D. 1990: Between space and time: reflections on the geographical imagination. *Annals of the Association of American Geographers* 80: 418–34. · Harvey, D. 1996: *Justice, nature and the geography of difference*. Oxford UK and Cambridge, MA: Blackwell. · Jackson, P. 1998: Constructions of 'whiteness' in the geographical imagination. *Area* 30: 99–106. · Mills, C.W. 1959: *The sociological imagination*. Oxford and New York: Oxford University Press. · Mitchell, T. 1989: The world-as-exhibition. *Comparative Studies in Society and History* 31: 217–36. · Pred, A. 1997: Somebody else, somewhere else: racisms, racialized spaces and the popular geographical imagination in Sweden. *Antipode* 29: 383–416. · Prince, H.C. 1962: The geographical imagination. Landscape 11: 22–5. · Rose, G. 1993: *Feminism and geography: the limits of geographical knowledge*. Cambridge: Polity; Minneapolis: University of Minnesota Press. · Slater, D. 1992: On the borders of social theory: learning from other regions. *Environment and Planning D: Society and Space* 10: 307–27. · Smith, N. 1990: *Uneven development: nature, capital and the production of space*, 2nd edn. Oxford and Cambridge, MA: Blackwell. · Soja, E. 1989: *Postmodern geographies: the reassertion of space in critical social theory*. London: Verso. · Turner, B.L. et al., eds, 1991: *The earth as transformed by human action*. Cambridge: Cambridge University Press. · Whatmore, S. 1999: Hybrid geographies: rethinking the 'human' in human geography. In D. Massey, J. Allen and P. Sarre, eds, *Human geography today*. Cambridge: Polity Press, 22–39.

Suggested Reading

Gregory (1994), ch. 2. · Harvey (1990). · Rose (1993), ch. 4. · Whatmore (1999).

geographic information systems (GIS) Integrated computer tools for handling, processing and analysing geographic data, that is, data explicitly referenced to the surface of the Earth. They include self-contained software packages for personal computers and workstations, as well as tools for handling and processing geographic information over high-speed networks such as the Internet. Increasingly, the term 'GIS' is used to imply any activity related to geographic information in digital form; hence 'GIS community', 'doing GIS', 'the GIS industry' and 'GIS data'.

Although the first mention of GIS occurred in the literature in the mid-1960s (Foresman, 1998), massive growth began only in 1980 with the introduction of super-minicomputers by manufacturers such as Digital Equipment Corporation and Prime Computer. Growth in the software industry followed, led by Intergraph Corporation and Environmental Systems Research Institute (ESRI), who remain the market leaders today. The technology of GIS found practical applications in RESOURCE MANAGEMENT, particularly FORESTRY, local government, the utility industries and GEODEMOGRAPHICS. More specifically, its uses include the automated measurement and analysis of geographically distributed resources, and the management of distributed facilities. Scientific applications also developed in the 1980s, as GIS was applied to the wide range of sciences and social sciences that deal with geographically distributed data and find value in a spatial perspective. These include epidemiology, archaeology, geology, ecology, geophysics, oceanography, REGIONAL SCIENCE, and of course geography. The methods and concepts of GIS overlap strongly with the concerns of many more established disciplines, including CARTOGRAPHY (particularly COMPUTER-ASSISTED CARTOGRAPHY), REMOTE SENSING, photogrammetry, geodesy and SURVEYING.

Much of the impetus for the initial development of GIS came from the difficulties of analysing data shown on paper MAPS, including such simple tasks as measuring area. To measure areas from a paper map (for example, to measure the amount of Class 1 agricultural land, or to estimate the amount of timber in a forest stand based on the stand's area and the density and size of trees), it is necessary either to use a mechanical device known as a planimeter, or to overlay a transparent sheet of dots and then count them. Both methods are laborious and inaccurate. But if the map can be represented in a computer the calculation is accurate and fast. Today we make such calculations routinely, without realizing how difficult they were before computerization.

Roger Tomlinson was the moving force behind the development in the 1960s of the Canada Geographic Information System, a computer application for the analysis of the data collected by the Canada Land Inventory in the interests of improved land-use policy. Research groups at Harvard (the Laboratory for Computer Graphics and Spatial Analysis, led by William Warntz) and elsewhere conducted basic research into methods for handling geographic data in digital form during the 1960s and 1970s. A significant expansion of research occurred in the late 1980s, after it had become clear that GIS had great potential as a tool to support research and decision-making in a wide range of fields. In the US, the National Center for Geographic Information and Analysis was initiated in 1988 with major funding from the National Science Foundation, based largely on the efforts of Ron Abler, then Director of the NSF Geography and Regional Science Program. The Center exists to conduct basic research in GIS and its applications, particularly in science; funds were awarded to a consortium of the University of California, Santa Barbara; the State University of New York at Buffalo; and the University of Maine. In the UK, the Economic and Social Research Council funded the development of a network of Regional Research Labs, largely based in university Geography departments, to promote GIS applications in a mix of practical and scientific applications, and to build a stronger UK research base. The European Science Foundation launched its GISDATA programme in 1993, under the leadership of Ian Masser, aimed at fostering research collaboration between European countries. Programs similar to these exist in many other countries.

Two major traditions have developed in GIS for representing geographic distributions. The RASTER approach divides the study area into an array of rectangular cells, and describes the content of each cell; the VECTOR approach describes a geographical distribution as a collection of discrete objects (points, lines or areas), and describes the location of each. In essence, the raster approach 'tells what is at every place' and the vector approach 'tells where everything is'. In addition, a GIS database contains information on the attributes of each cell or object, and on various kinds of relationships between objects. Broadly, the continuous view of space embedded in the raster approach is most commonly associated with environmental and physical science applications of GIS, while the view of space as a collection of discrete objects that is implicit in the vector approach has found more applications in the social and policy sciences, in the mapping industry, and in the management of geographically distributed facilities. Most currently available GIS software products can be identified with one approach, although most also provide limited capabilities for handling the other.

The ability to couple the input and output functions of a GIS with its more exploratory functions of browsing and simple statistical analysis, and with more sophisticated confirmatory techniques, has led to many GIS applications in human geography and related disciplines. GIS can be used to 'zoom in' on parts of an area, displaying them at higher resolution, or to 'pan' rapidly across large mapped areas. It can be used to explore statistical relationships between geographical variables, such as the relationship between rainfall and agriculture in arid regions, or between ethnic groups and voting patterns. GIS has been used to implement models of regional economies, transportation systems and urban growth; to develop archaeological hypotheses from complex catalogues of spatially distributed artifacts; to develop understanding from patterns of social deprivation and disease; to analyse voting behaviour; and to understand the sacred meaning many cultures give to space.

For example, GIS has been used to develop reconstructions of Iron Age landscapes in southern England. Three-dimensional models were built and used to gain insights into the criteria for the selection of sites for long barrows, based on intervisibility (Lock and Harris, 1996). GIS have also been used to construct models of pre-Columbian agricultural systems in the US Southwest. Agricultural production models were built using detailed maps of soils, drainage, and rainfall; and used in simulations of production under various climate scenarios. These were linked to data from other sources, such as tree-ring growth, to provide insights into the effects of drought and possible explanations for the catastrophic collapse of early cultures in the centuries before European contact (Van West and Kohler, 1996). Examples of applications can be found in the popular GIS magazines (*GIS World*, *Geo Info Systems*), in the proceedings of GIS conferences, and in introductory texts. In short, GIS has become a powerful tool for automating the geographer's processes of analysis and synthesis, and has been adopted in many other related disciplines.

Currently, GIS remains firmly bound to its cartographic roots; maps continue to be the primary means of input and output. It provides tools for recording and processing the positions of features in space, but has yet to develop much sophistication in its handling of time-dependence (see TIME-GEOGRAPHY), or interaction. In this sense GIS preserves a container-like view of space, and cannot yet deal effectively with the temporal changes and interactions that drive or result from many social processes. However, basic research efforts over the past decade have yielded significant advances in these areas. Moreover, the growth of GIS has led to renewed interest in many of the more fundamental issues of geography and CARTOGRAPHY: the accuracy of abstracted views of geographic distributions; the effects of scale and resolution; languages for describing spatial relations; methods for exploring the spatial perspective; the role of geographic information in empowerment and domination (cf. POWER; SURVEILLANCE); and the importance of geographic information to the DECISION-MAKING process.

A flurry of recent literature has drawn attention to the importance of the social context of GIS, the need to support alternative ways of knowing about the human environment, and the limitations of early GIS technology in that regard (Pickles, 1995; Openshaw, 1997). Although most developers of GIS technology would argue that their contributions are inherently neutral with respect to their social implications, Smith (1992) makes the case that much of GIS development has been driven by military and intelligence applications, which are far from neutral. Others have argued that GIS use in marketing has the potential to invade personal privacy, and that GIS use in environmental decision-making reinforces the power of its users (notably governments and corporations) over those who lack access to it (notably marginalized groups). Other arguments in this social critique of GIS focus on the limited representations that are possible in the digital environment, and how these favour centralized, uniform views over individual, more idiosyncratic ones.

GIS continues to be of great importance to the discipline of Geography, and its popularity has done much to mould the contemporary image of Geography as a discipline in the minds of others. The GIS Specialty Group has been the largest in the Association of American Geographers for many years. The growth of GIS has created a demand for students with GIS skills, and most Geography departments have responded by instituting sequences of courses. Recent surveys suggest that over half of all of University GIS courses worldwide are taught in Geography departments, and 'GIS/remote sensing' was listed most often in a recent survey of US Geography department chairs as the occupation for which students were being prepared (Gober et al., 1995). But debate continues in many departments over the appropriateness of the massive and continuing investments in hardware and software that are needed to support a GIS program; about the intellectual importance of GIS (Wright et al., 1997); and about the importance of the specialty relative to other skills that compete for the attention of students and staff. Geographers have been among the leaders in identifying geographic information science as an important new research field addressing the fundamental issues arising from the use of digital computers to represent, process, and analyse geographic information. In the US, the University Consortium for Geographic Information Science was formed in 1996 in order to act as a national focus for promoting the new field, and now has close to 50 institutional members, including all of the key centres of basic research. MG

References

Foresman, T.W., ed., 1998: *The history of geographic information systems: perspectives from the pioneers*. Upper Saddle River, NJ: Prentice Hall. · Gober, P., Glasmeier A.K., Goodman, J.M., Plane, D.A., Stafford, H.A., and Wood, J.S. 1995: Employment trends in Geography, Part 2: Current demand conditions. *Professional Geographer* 47(3): 329–36. · Lock, G.R. and Harris, T.M. 1996: Danebury revisited: An English Iron Age hillfort in a digital landscape. In M. Aldenderfer, and H.D.G. Maschner, eds, *Anthropology, space, and geographic information systems*. New York: Oxford University Press, 214–40. · Openshaw, S. 1997: The truth about Ground Truth. *Transactions in GIS* 2 (1): 7–24. · Pickles, J. 1995: *Ground truth: the social implications of geographic information systems*. New York: Guilford Press. · Smith, N. 1992: History and philosophy of geography: real wars, theory wars. *Progress in Human Geography* 16 (2): 257–71. · Van West, C, and Kohler, T.A. 1996: A time to rend, a time to sew: New perspectives on Northern Anasazi sociopolitical development in later prehistory. In M. Aldenderfer, and H.D.G. Maschner, eds, *Anthropology, space, and geographic information systems*. New York: Oxford University Press, 107–31. · Wright, D.J., Goodchild, M.F., and Proctor, J.D. 1997: Demystifying the persistent ambiguity of GIS as 'tool' versus 'science'. *Annals of the Association of American Geographers* 87 (2): 346–62.

Suggested Reading

Aldenderfer, M., and Maschner, H.D.G. 1996: *Anthropology, space, and geographic information systems*. New York: Oxford University Press. · Chrisman, N.R. 1997: *Exploring geographic information systems*. New York: John Wiley & Sons. · DeMers, M.N. 1997: *Fundamentals of geographic information systems*. New York: John Wiley & Sons. · Longley, P.A., Goodchild, M.F., Maguire, D.J. and Rhind, D.W., eds, 1998: *Geographical information systems: principles, techniques, management and applications*, 2 vols. Cambridge: GeoInformation International.

geographical societies Institutions established to promote the discipline of geography. Some early societies, both national (e.g. the Royal Geographical Society – RGS – and the American Geographical Society) and regional (e.g. the Manchester Geographical Society), were major forces in the nineteenth-century development of geography and its establishment as a school and university discipline; a number financed major expeditions which extended geographical knowledge (defined widely to incorporate other environmental sciences). They continue to play major roles in promoting geography, both as an academic discipline and as a subject of wider general interest.

Alongside these general societies, a number of professional associations for geographers were established in the late nineteenth and early twentieth century, such as the Geographical Association (GA, for teachers, mainly at school level) in the United Kingdom and the Institute of British Geographers (IBG, mainly for researchers and for teachers in higher education): the National Council for Geographical Education and the Association of American Geographers fulfil comparable roles in the United States. These societies, through conferences, seminars, specialist meetings and publications (including many of the leading academic research journals), participate in the promotion and dissemination of material about research advances and promote the discipline both politically and professionally. In the UK, the members of the RGS and IBG voted in 1993 to merge the two societies.

RJJ

Suggested Reading

Bell, M., Butlin, R.A. and Heffernan, M., eds, 1995: *Geography and imperialism, 1820–1940*. Manchester: Manchester University Press. · Freeman, T.W. 1980: The Royal Geographical Society. In E.H. Brown, ed., *Geography – yesterday and tomorrow*. Oxford: The Clarendon Press. · James, P.E. and Martin, G.J. 1978: *The Association of American Geographers: the first seventy-five years 1904–1979*. Washington, D.C.: Association of American Geographers. · Steel, R.W. 1984: *The Institute of British Geographers: the first fifty years*. London: Institute of British Geographers.

geography, history of Because the term 'geography' means, and has meant, different things to different people in different times and places, there is no agreed-upon consensus on what constitutes the project of writing the history of this enterprise. Moreover, while the story of geography as an independent scholarly discipline is inescapably bound up with the history of the professionalization of academic knowledge since around the middle of the nineteenth century, it is clear that the history of geography as a DISCOURSE not only operates without such constraints but also reaches beyond the historical and institutional confines of the modern-day discipline. Of course geography as discourse and discipline are interrelated in intimate ways – one might even say that the purpose of a discipline is precisely to 'discipline' discourse. Nevertheless there is frequently a considerable difference in both substance and style between those writing the history of these respective geographies.

Although the task of reconstructing geography's history has had its critics, some of whom are suspicious of the interests at stake in the entire enterprise (Barnett, 1995), it would not be unreasonable to suggest that some of the most significant interventions into recent debates on the relationships between knowledge, REPRESENTATION and POWER, have emanated from those concerned with the ways in which geographical knowledge has been socially constituted (Gregory, 1993). Some of these associations will surface below.

So far as the modern *academic discipline* of geography is concerned, those chronicling the course of historical change have conducted their investigations in a variety of ways. Some have concentrated on the subject's institutional expression, and accordingly have produced histories of a range of GEOGRAPHICAL SOCIETIES. Others have organized their material around national traditions or schools, such as the French School (Buttimer, 1971; Berdoulay, 1981), the German tradition (Schultz, 1980), and the British School (Freeman,

1980). Still others have considered the biographies of key professional geographers – Halford Mackinder (Parker, 1982; Blouet, 1987), Isaiah Bowman (Martin, 1980) and Ellsworth Huntington (Martin, 1973) have all been the subject of full-length biographies – while shorter biographical sketches of a wider range of figures have appeared in the serial *Geographers: Biobibliographical Studies*. Biographical treatments are also available of figures looming large in the story of the subject's pre-professional past, such as Humboldt (Botting, 1973), Ritter (Beck, 1979), Reclus (Dunbar, 1978), Marsh (Lowenthal, 1958), and Shaler (Livingstone, 1987).

Of course these emphases do not exhaust the range of work available on the history of geography as a discipline. More specialist treatments of how modern geographical thinking has engaged with wider theoretical currents have been produced (Peet, 1998); histories of sub-disciplines like HISTORICAL GEOGRAPHY have been provided (Butlin, 1995); and the significance of school geography texts and their role in conveying imperial attitudes about race and gender have been scrutinized (Maddrell, 1998). Cumulatively these and similar works have served to demonstrate the immense range of interests and styles expressed by the subject's disciplinary historians embracing philosophy, social theory, intellectual history, and cultural critique.

Inevitably those works dealing with geographical *discourses* come in a variety of guises. Crucial here is the definition of what passes as 'geographical' by the historian in question. Beazley's (1897–1906) *The dawn of modern geography* emphasized the history of medieval travel and exploration, whereas for Eva Taylor (1930) mathematical practice, surveying and navigation assumed greater importance in her investigations into the character of Tudor Geography. J.K. Wright' s (1965) *Geographical lore of the time of the crusades* focused more on earth description with its cartographic and cosmographical correlates, and similarly commented that the project covered 'a wider field than most definitions of geography' (p. 2). Also dealing with the pre-professional past, Glacken's (1967) monumental *Traces on the Rhodian Shore* explored the contact zone between nature and culture, acknowledging that he had thereby to transcend the conventional limits of the modern discipline. More recently, Bowen's (1981) compendious survey of geographical thought from Bacon to Humboldt constitutes a sophisticated historical apologia for an ecological, anti-positivistic vision of the subject. By contrast, in a survey of 'Theoretical Geography', Wilson (1972) presented his own alternative history of geography as SPATIAL SCIENCE in which the names of mathematically inclined economists and sociologists loomed large while the names of geographers were conspicuous by their absence. Alongside these treatments of geographical discourse by geographers is a range of related works by historians of science dealing with allied subjects such as biogeography (Browne, 1983), meteorology (Frisinger, 1977), geology (Laudan, 1987), geomorphology (Davies, n.d.; Tinkler, 1985), HUMAN ECOLOGY (Mitman, 1992), environmental science (Bowler, 1992), and ideas of nature (Merchant, 1980; Marshall, 1992). Voices are also increasingly being heard from historians of cartography (Edney, 1997), of which the first volumes of the projected series spearheaded by Harley and Woodward (1987) promise to be the most comprehensive investigation to date (see CARTOGRAPHY, HISTORY OF).

These relatively specialist studies are supplemented by a number of what Aay (1981) calls 'textbook chronicles' – synthetic treatments designed for student consumption that provide an overview of the field (Dickinson, 1969; James, 1972; Holt-Jensen, 1988). It is now plain, however, that these surveys all too frequently lapsed into apologies for some particular viewpoint – geography as regional interrogation, the study of occupied space, or some such. Moreover, their strategy was typically *presentist*, namely using history to adjudicate present-day controversies; *internalist*, in the sense that they paid scant attention to the broader social and intellectual contexts within which geographical knowledge was produced; and *cumulative*, portraying history in terms of progress towards some perceived contemporary orthodoxy. It is scepticism about precisely these assumptions, however, that a greater sensitivity to currents of historiographical thinking has induced. Accordingly, there have recently been a number of appeals for contextual readings of the tradition (Livingstone, 1979; Stoddart, 1981), and a range of strategies has therefore been deployed in the endeavour to achieve this aim.

Leaving aside their problematic reading of Kuhn, some have turned to his *Structure of scientific revolutions* (1962) to characterize the history of geography as an overlapping succession of PARADIGMS enshrined in a number of key texts: Vidal's POSSIBILISM, Huntington's ENVIRONMENTAL DETERMINISM, Sauer's landscape morphology (cf. LANDSCAPE; MORPHOLOGY), Hartshorne's AREAL DIFFERENTIATION, and Schaefer's EXCEPTIONALISM are typical candidates for paradigm status (Harvey and Holly, 1981; Mair, 1986). In such scenarios, however, a good deal of historical typecasting and editorial management has had to be engaged in. Others have begun to take more seriously the work of the sociologists of scientific knowledge and have examined, for instance, the role of 'invisible colleges' and 'socio-scientific networks' (Lochhead, 1981: see SCIENCE, GEOGRAPHY AND), and the relationships between cognitive claims and institutional arrangements (Capel, 1981). Sociological tools – Bruno Latour's ACTOR–NETWORK THEORY, for example – have been deployed to interpret geography's mid-twentieth century QUANTITATIVE REVOLUTION (Barnes, 1998). At the same time the Marxist HISTORICAL MATERIALIST perspective has been marshalled as a means of elucidating the way in which geographical knowledge and practices have been used to legitimate the social conditions that produced that knowledge in the first place (Harvey, 1984). Still others have seen in the philosophical literature on the cognitive power of METAPHOR a key to unlocking aspects of geography's history (Buttimer, 1982; Barnes and Duncan, 1992), through delineating the different uses of, say, mechanistic, organic, structural, and textual analogies. Thus Barnes (1996) has compellingly shown the relevance of these philosophical manoeuvres for understanding the history and conceptual structure of modern economic geography. The insights of Foucault on the intimate connections between SPACE, SURVEILLANCE, POWER, and knowledge, and of Said on the western construction of 'non-western' realms (see ORIENTALISM, EXPLORATION, TRAVEL-WRITING) have also begun to be mobilized and to open up new vistas to the history of geography by unmasking the pretended neutrality of spatial discourse in a variety of arenas both within and beyond the academy.

Cumulatively, such calls for re-reading geography's history have begun to contribute towards a growing variety of revisionist accounts of particular episodes, among which mention might be made of the links between magic, mysticism and geography at various times (Livingstone, 1988; Matless, 1991), geography's complicity in the shaping of imperial ambitions and national identity in the early modern period (Withers 1995, 1996; Shaw, 1996; Cormack, 1997; see IMPERIALISM), the intimate connections between geography, empire, health and racial theory (Livingstone, 1991; Driver, 1992; Bell, 1993; Godlewska and Smith, 1994; cf. RACISM), the complicity of German geography in the Nazi programme (Sandner, 1988, Rössler, 1989; see GEOPOLITICS), the relations between landscape REPRESENTATION, artistic convention and denominational discourse (Cosgrove and Daniels, 1988; Mayhew, 1996), the circumstances surrounding debates over the boundary between geography and sociology in turn-of-the-century France (Friedman, 1996), the imperial mould in which early ENVIRONMENTALISM was cast (Grove, 1995), the place of geography in a range of enlightenment discourses (Livingstone and Withers, 1999), the relations between geography and travel writing, and calls for feminist readings of the tradition (Domosh, 1991; Rose, 1995; see FEMINIST GEOGRAPHIES). As for practical engagements, Ryan's (1998) account of the connections between geography, photography and racial representation in the Victorian era, and feminist reflections on FIELDWORK have opened up these arenas to theoretically informed interrogation. Embedded within at least some of these accounts is a conviction that 'geography' is a negotiated entity, and that a central task of its historians is to ascertain how and why certain practices and procedures come to be accounted authoritative, and hence normative, at certain moments in time, and in certain spatial settings.

It is plain, then, that the 'history of geography' comprises a variety of enterprises that have been engaged in various ways. Nevertheless, a broad shift can be detected from the 'encyclopaedism' of earlier works (which operated in a cumulative-chronological fashion) towards a more recent 'genealogical' perspective (which aims to disclose the tangled connections between power and knowledge). The subversive character of the latter has been embraced with differing degrees of enthusiasm: some now insist that the idea of History as a single master narrative is a western 'myth' (Young, 1990), while others, either unenamoured of an altogether radical RELATIVISM (in which truth is taken to be relative to circumstance) or suspicious that the genealogist is implicated in an impossible self-referential dilemma (namely that the thesis is self-refuting), suggest that there is more value in thinking of discourses as 'contested traditions' – socially embodied and temporally extended conversations that act as stabilizing constraints on the elucidation of meaning (MacIntyre, 1990). Insofar as 'encyclopaedia', 'genealogy' and 'tradition' as modes of historical interrogation reflect differing attitudes towards what has come to be called the Enlightenment project (see ENLIGHTENMENT, GEOGRAPHY AND), the history of geography has a significant role to play in debates within the discipline over the relations between knowledge, power, representation, and social constitution. Moreover, the recent reassertion of the significance of place and space in historical investigations of human knowing (Livingstone, 1995; Shapin, 1998) suggests that 'the history of geography' as an undertaking could benefit (ironically perhaps) by taking 'geography' more seriously – namely, by reconceptualizing the enterprise as 'the historical geography of geography'.

DNL

References

Aay, H. 1981: Textbook chronicles: disciplinary history and the growth of geographic knowledge. In B.W. Blouet, ed., *The origins of academic geography in the United States*. Hamden, CN.: Archon Books, 291–301. · Barnes, T.J. 1996: *Logics of dislocation: models, metaphors, and meanings of economic space*. New York: Guilford. · Barnes, T.J. 1998: A history of regression: actors, networks, machines, and numbers. *Environmental and Planning A* 30: 203–23. · Barnes, T.J. and Duncan, J.S. 1992: *Writing worlds: discourse, text and metaphor in the representation of landscape*. London: Routledge. · Barnett, C. 1995. Awakening the dead: who needs the history of geography? *Transactions, Institute of British Geographers* NS 20: 417–19. · Beazley, C.R. 1897–1906: *The dawn of modern geography*, 3 vols. Oxford: Clarendon Press. · Beck, H. 1979: *Carl Ritter, Genius der Geographie: Zu Seinem Leben und Werk*. Berlin: Dietrich Reimer Verlag. · Bell, M. 1993: 'The Pestilence that Walketh in Darkness'. Imperial health, gender and images of South Africa c.1880–1910. *Transactions of the Institute of British Geographers* NS 18: 327–41. · Berdoulay, V. 1981: *La Formation de l'École Française de Géographie (1870–1914)*. Paris: Bibliothèque Nationale. · Blouet, B.W. 1987: *Halford Mackinder: a biography*. College Station, Texas: Texas A. & M. University Press. · Botting, D. 1973: *Humboldt and the Cosmos*. London: Sphere Books. · Bowen, M. 1981: *Empiricism and geographical thought: from Francis Bacon to Alexander von Humboldt*. Cambridge: Cambridge University Press. · Bowler, P.J. 1992: *The Fontana history of the environmental sciences*. London: Fontana. · Browne, J. 1983: *The secular ark: studies in the history of biogeography*. New Haven: Yale University Press. · Butlin, R.A. 1995: *Historical geography: through the gates of space and time*. London: Wiley. · Buttimer, A. 1971: *Society and milieu in the French geographic tradition*. Chicago: Rand McNally. · Buttimer, A. 1982: Musing on helicon: root metaphors and geography. *Geografiska Annaler*, Series B, 64: 89–96. · Capel, H. 1981: Institutionalization of geography and strategies of change. In D.R. Stoddart, ed., *Geography, ideology and social concern*. Oxford: Blackwell, 37–69. · Cormack, L.B. 1997: *Charting an empire: geography at the English universities, 1580–1620*. Chicago: University of Chicago Press. · Cosgrove, D. and Daniels, S., eds, 1988: *The iconography of landscape. Essays on the symbolic representation, design and use of past environments*. Cambridge: Cambridge University Press. · Davies, G.L. n.d.: *The earth in decay. A history of British geomorphology 1578 to 1878*. London: MacDonald. · Dickinson, R.E. 1969:*The makers of modern geography*. London: Routledge & Kegan Paul. · Domosh, M. 1991: Towards a feminist historiography of geography. *Transactions, Institute of British Geographers* NS 16: 95–104. · Driver, F. 1992: Geography's empire: histories of geographical knowledge. *Environment and Planning D: Society and Space* 10: 23–40. · Dunbar, G.S. 1978: *Elisée Reclus: historian of nature*. Hamden: Archon Book. · Edney, M. 1997: *Mapping an empire: the geographical construction of British India. 1765–1843*. Chicago: University of Chicago Press. · Freeman, T.W. 1980: *A history of modern British geography*. New York and London: Longman. · Friedman, S.W. 1996: *Marc Bloch, sociology and geography*. Cambridge: Cambridge University Press. · Frisinger, H. 1977: *The history of meteorology to 1800*. New York: Science History Publications. · Glacken, C. 1967: *Traces on the Rhodian Shore: nature and culture in western thought to the end of the eighteenth century*. Berkeley, CA: University of California Press. · Godlewska, A. and Smith, N., eds, 1994: *Geography and empire*. Oxford: Blackwell. · Gregory, D. 1993. *Geographical imaginations*. Oxford: Blackwell. · Grove, R.H. 1995: *Green imperialism: colonial expansion, tropical island Edens and the origins of environmentalism*. Cambridge: Cambridge University Press. · Harley, J.B. and Woodward, D., eds, 1987: *History of cartography. Volume One. Cartography in prehistoric, ancient, and medieval Europe and the Mediterranean*. Chicago: University of Chicago Press. · Harvey, D. 1984: On the history and present condition of geography: an historical materialist manifesto. *Professional Geographer* 36: 1–10. · Harvey, M.E. and Holly, B.P. 1981: Paradigm, philosophy and geographic thought. In M.E. Harvey, and B.P. Holly, eds, *Themes in geographic thought*. London: Croom Helm, 11–37. · Holt-Jensen, A. 1988: *Geography: history and concepts*, 2nd edn. London: Paul Chapman. · James, P.E. 1972: *All possible worlds. a history of geographical ideas*. Indianapolis: Bobbs-Merrill. · Kuhn, T. 1962: The structure of scientific revolutions. Chicago: University of Chicago Press. · Laudan, R. 1987: *From mineralogy to geology. The foundations of a science, 1650–1830*. Chicago: University of Chicago Press. · Livingstone, D.N. 1979: Some methodological problems in the history of geographical thought. *Tijdschrift voor Economische en Sociale Geografie* 70: 226–31. · Livingstone, D.N. 1987: *Nathaniel Southgate Shaler and the culture of American Science*. London: University of Alabama Press. · Livingstone, D.N. 1988: Science, magic and religion: a contextual reassessment of geography in the Sixteenth and Seventeenth Centuries. *History of Science* 26: 269–94. · Livingstone, D.N. 1991: The moral discourse of climate: historical considerations on race, place and virtue. *Journal of Historical Geography* 17: 413–34. · Livingstone, D.N. 1995: The spaces of knowledge: contributions towards a historical geography of science. *Environment and Planning D: Society and Space* 13: 5–34. · Livingstone, D.N. and Withers, C.W.J. eds, 1999: *Geography and enlightenment*. Chicago: University of Chicago Press. · Lochhead, E.

1981: Scotland as the cradle of modern academic geography in Britain. *Scottish Geographical Magazine* 97: 98–109. · Lowenthal, D. 1958: *George Perkins Marsh. Versatile Vermonter.* New York: Columbia University Press. · MacIntyre, A. 1990: *Three rival versions of moral enquiry: encyclopaedia, genealogy, and tradition.* Notre Dame, Ind.: University of Notre Dame Press. · Mayhew, R. 1996: Landscape, religion and knowledge in eighteenth century England. *Ecumene* 3: 454–71. · Maddrell, A.M.C. 1998: Discourses of race and gender and the comparative method in geographical school texts 1830–1918. *Environment and Planning D: Society and Space* 16: 81–103. · Mair, A. 1986: Thomas Kuhn and understanding geography. *Progress in Human Geography* 10: 345–69. · Marshall, P. 1992: *Nature's web: rethinking our place on earth.* London: Simon & Schuster. · Martin, G.J. 1973: *Ellsworth Huntington: his life and thought.* Hamden, CN: Archon Books. · Martin, G.J. 1980: *The life and thought of Isaiah Bowman.* Hamden, CN: Archon Books. · Matless, D. 1991: Nature, the modern and the mystic: tales from early twentieth century geography. *Transactions, Institute of British Geographers* NS 16: 272–86. · Mayhew, R. 1996: Landscape, religion and knowledge in eighteenth century England. *Ecumere* 3: 454–71. · Merchant, C. 1980: *The death of nature: women, ecology and the scientific revolution.* New York: Harper & Row. · Mitman, G. 1992: *The state of nature: ecology, community, and American social thought, 1900–1950.* Chicago: University of Chicago Press. · Parker, W.H. 1982: *Mackinder: geography as an aid to statecraft.* Oxford: Clarendon Press. · Peet, R. 1998: *Modern geographic thought.* Oxford: Blackwell. · Rose, G. 1995: Tradition and paternity: same difference? *Transactions, Institute of British Geographers* NS 20: 414–16. · Rössler, M. 1989: Applied geography and area research in Nazi society: central place theory and planning, 1933 to 1945. *Environment and Planning D: Society and Space* 7: 419–31. · Ryan, J.R. 1998: *Picturing empire: photography and the visualization of the British empire.* Chicago: University of Chicago Press. · Sandner, G. 1988: Recent advances in the history of German geography 1918–1945. A progress report for the Federal Republic of Germany. *Geographische Zeitschrift* 76: 120–33. · Schultz, H.-D. 1980: *Die Deutschsprachige Geographie von 1800 bis 1970: Ein Beitrag zur Geschichte ihrer Methodologie.* Berlin: Geographische Institut der Freien. · Shapin, S. 1998: Placing the view from nowhere: historical and sociological problems in the location of science. *Transactions of the Institute of British Geographers* NS 23: 1–8. · Shaw, D.J.B. 1996: Geographical practice and its significance in Peter the Great's Russia. *Journal of Historical Geography* 22: 160–76. · Stoddart, D.R. ed., 1981: *Geography, ideology and social concern.* Oxford: Blackwell. · Taylor, E.G.R. 1930: *Tudor geography.* London: Methuen. · Tinkler, K.J. 1985: *A short history of geomorphology.* Totowa: Barnes & Noble. · Wilson, A.G. 1972: Theoretical geography. *Transactions, Institute of British Geographers* 57: 31–44. · Withers, C.W.J. 1995: How Scotland came to know itself: geography, national identity and the making of a nation, 1680–1790. *Journal of Historical Geography* 21: 371–97. · Withers, C.W.J. 1996: Geography, science and national identity in early modern Britain: the case of Scotland and the work of Sir Robert Sibbald. *Annals of Science* 53: 29–73. · Wright, J.K. 1965 [orig. pub. 1925]: *The geographical lore of the time of the crusades. A study in the history of medieval science and tradition in western Europe.* New York: Dover Publications. · Young, R. 1990: *White mythologies: writing history and the West.* London: Routledge.

Suggested Reading

Johnston, R.J. 1997: *Geography and geographers: Anglo-American human geography since 1945*, 5th edn. London: Edward Arnold. · Livingstone, D.N. 1992: *The geographical tradition: episodes in the history of a contested enterprise.* Oxford: Blackwell. · Stoddart, D.R. 1986: *On geography and its history.* Oxford: Blackwell.

geopiety A term initially coined by J.K. Wright (1947) to denote the sense of thoughtful piety aroused by human awareness of the natural world and geographical space, and thus closely connected to TOPOPHILIA. Individually, such feelings are commonly associated with the Romantic spirit celebrated in the early nineteenth century and captured, for example, in the LANDSCAPE poetry of William Wordsworth and the paintings of Caspar David Frederick. In the early twentieth century such quasi-religious feelings for NATURE and landscape were expressed by a number of British explorers and geographers such as Francis Younghusband and Vaughan Cornish, and later PHENOMENOLOGICAL writers in geography such as Yi-Fu Tuan (1976) have described similar sentiments relating human consciousness to spaces of care, both natural and constructed or urban. More collectively, such feelings may yield a specific sense of human TERRITORIALITY in which a people (or NATION) develops an almost mystical, organic bond of attachment to its homeland (best expressed by the German term *Heimat*), giving rise to powerful and sometimes violent NATIONALIST sentiments (*Blut und Boden*). More generally, geopiety can refer to sentiments of human attachment to elemental spaces (telluric, aquatic, etc.), dissected by Dardel (1952). The various expressions of geopiety are summarized and discussed by Bishop (1994), who seeks to divorce them from metaphysical considerations and root them in a PSYCHOANALYTIC theory which dissolves *a priori* boundaries between self and world in the construction of human IDENTITY. Late twentieth-century ECOLOGICAL writers, especially those attached to the ideas of 'DEEP ECOLOGY' developed by the Norwegian philosopher Arne Naess, have extended the meaning of geopiety to a quasi-religious belief in an elemental, autochthonous bond between human life and a holistic living Earth and the moral duty of reverential environmental conduct that this entails. Many environmental thinkers and writers who do not subscribe to such a strong position would still support and express a less radical geopiety which requires the granting of agency and thus rights to all forms of life on earth, and the acknowledgement of human responsibilities in this direction (Livingstone, 1995). Such ideas underpin an increased interest in the geographical study of animals and other non-human life forms. DEC

References

Bishop, P. 1994: Residence on Earth: *anima mundi* and a sense of geographical 'belonging'. *Ecumene* 1: 51–64. · Dardel, E. 1952: *L'homme et la terre: nature de la réalité géographique*. Paris: Presses Universitaires de France. · Livingstone, D. 1995: The polity of nature: representation, virtue, strategy. *Ecumene* 2: 353–77. · Tuan, Y.-F. 1976: Geopiety: a theme in man's attachment to nature and to place. In D. Lowenthal, and M. Bowden, eds, *Geographies of the mind: essays in historical geosophy in honor of John Kirtland Wright*. New York: Oxford University Press, 11–39. · Wright, J.K. 1947: *Terrae incognitae:* the place of the imagination in geography. *Annals, Association of American Geographers* 37: 1–15.

geopolitical transition Although international relations is often portrayed as a sphere of anarchy, of innate disorder (see ANARCHISM), political geographers and others have identified patterns in the development of modern international politics which they call *geopolitical world orders*. Geopolitical transitions are the short periods of change from one order to another. A geopolitical order is a relatively stable pattern of international relations such that most STATE behaviour is quite predictable. In a geopolitical transition new options are opened up and predictability is suspended until the new order and its stable political relations have been put into place. Hence geopolitical transitions are crucial periods of world politics around which international relations can be periodized.

Geopolitical transitions are constituted by the disintegration of one set of political practices and representations and the construction of their replacement. The classic case is the period 1944–46 when the grand alliance, which defeated Nazi Germany, collapsed and the Cold War resulted (Taylor, 1990). From the US perspective, the USSR which had so recently been a necessary ally in the fight against tyranny was very quickly converted into the new source of tyranny. Such a turnaround is typical of geopolitical transitions when friends become enemies and *vice versa*. More than any other concept, geopolitical transition challenges the supposed immutability of geopolitical factors in international relations. Contemporary interest in such periods stems from the end of the Cold War interpreted as leading to a contemporary geopolitical transition (Taylor, 1992a; Agnew and Corbridge, 1995).

The number of geopolitical transitions depends upon the identification of geopolitical world orders and this is disputed. No such orders are identified before 1815 because of the fluid nature of early modern international politics. However, the Congress of Vienna established the first international institution to order inter-state relations (the Concert of Europe) thus creating the first geopolitical order. From this time either three or four geopolitical orders are identified. Agnew and Corbridge (1995, pp. 19–23) define three: (i) 1915–75 the Concert of Europe – British Geopolitical Order, (ii) 1875–1945 the Geopolitical Order of Inter-Imperial Rivalry, and (iii) 1945–90 the Cold War Geopolitical Order. Taylor (1992b, pp. 34–6) defines four orders and transitions: (i) transition (1813–15) to World Order of Hegemony and Concert (1815–66), (ii) transition (1866–71) to World Order of Rivalry and Concert (1871–1904), (iii) transition (1904–07) to World Order of the British Succession (1907–44), and (iv) transition (1944–46) to Cold War World Order (1946–89). The specific difference largely revolves over the way in which the political and economic changes around the turn of the twentieth century are interpreted. More basically, this relates to the underlying theories used in the periodizations: Agnew and Corbridge employ a Gramscian approach to define HEGEMONIES, Taylor employs a WORLD-SYSTEMS approach to define world hegemonies. PJT

References

Agnew J. and Corbridge, S. 1995: *Mastering space*. London: Routledge. · Taylor, P.J. 1990: *Britain and the Cold War: 1945 as geopolitical transition*. London: Pinter. · Taylor, P.J. 1992a: Tribulations of transition. *Professional Geographer* 44: 10–3. · Taylor, P.J. 1992b: Geopolitical world orders. In P.J. Taylor, ed., *Political geography of the twentieth century*. London: Belhaven.

geopolitics A long-established area of geographical enquiry which considers SPACE to be important in understanding the constitution of international relations. Its contemporary usage should not be confused with GEOPOLITIK, however, which is a crude form of ENVIRONMENTAL DETERMINISM popularized in foreign-policy circles to legitimize STATE action. In the search for an explanation of the global geopolitical order, four main approaches can be singled out.

Traditional geopolitics has its roots in the early-twentieth-century works of the British geographer, Halford Mackinder who, in an age of British expansion and overseas interests, drew attention to the geostrategic advantages of land power over sea power (cf. COLONIALISM; IMPERIALISM). For Mackinder, the pivotal position of the HEARTLAND within the Eurasian land mass meant that whoever occupied the heartland could exert a dominating influence over world politics. By interpreting European history as a record of struggle to achieve and prevent control over the heartland, Mackinder was arguing that location and the physical environment were important determinants of the global power structure. Like many other geopolitical theoreticians, Mackinder's conception of the geopolitical order was prescriptive and ETHNOCENTRIC, and subject to rapid obsolescence, although it remains one of the most widely read and influential of geographical expositions. It was this heartland thesis, along with Ratzel's organic theory of the state, which was to have a formative influence on *Geopolitik*. The organic theory held that all components of the state 'grow' together into one body which has a 'life' of its own. As a German geographer, Friedrich Ratzel was clearly influenced by the specifically Hegelian concept of the state as a COMMUNITY based on a transcendental spiritual union in which and through which all nationals are bound spiritually into an organic 'oneness'. The biological analogy of state with NATURE was taken further by Otto Maull and Rudolph Kjellen, and later used in inter-war Germany to provide spurious intellectual justifications for national paranoia, territorial claims and geopolitical objectives (see *LEBENSRAUM*; NATIONALISM). This exploitation of political geographical ideas to serve political purposes ensured that *Geopolitik* and geopolitics both became casualties after the Second World War, for anything that even notionally resembled the latter became politically sensitive. By the 1970s, however geopolitics was again undergoing a renaissance amongst US foreign policy analysts focusing on the Cold War. Here containment and DOMINO THEORY were utilized in conjunction with Mackinder's heartland and Spykman's rimland theory to justify the continuing necessity for western geomilitary alliances and interventions in order to prevent COMMUNISM's spatial expansion from the (Soviet) heartland.

The *power-relations* perspective focuses on the hierarchical character of states within the global order by examining a polity's ability to influence or change the behaviour of other states in a desired direction. Drawing in particular upon the realist school of international relations, power relations between states have been conceived in terms of global geopolitical equilibrium or balance of power, by formulating post-war international relations as a model of bipolarity in the late 1940s and early 1950s, loose bipolarity in the late 1950s and 1960s, and the multipolar world of the 1970s, 1980s and 1990s. In the post-Cold War era, however, the geopolitical world order has moved away from one characterized in this approach by an hierarchical, integrated but flexible structure of states, linked in one way or another with the two major geopolitical power blocks of the United States and Soviet Union (Cohen, 1991), to one in which the geopolitical influence of the United States is unrivalled by any other sovereign player. It is, however, hotly debated as to whether the United States can be considered as an unquestioning political hegemon (cf. HEGEMONY). One school of thought argues that Great Powers which over-extend themselves geopolitically, but are unable to innovate and reform at home, become victims of their own 'global overstretch' (Kennedy, 1988) while others argue that having won the Cold War, the United States is now in an unassailable hegemonic position, providing global leadership and international stability to the new world order (see GEOPOLITICAL TRANSITION; KONDRATIEFF CYCLES; WORLD-SYSTEMS ANALYSIS).

The POLITICAL ECONOMY approach is based on the underlying assumption that geopolitics cannot be understood fully without considering the dynamics of the global economy (cf. GLOBALIZATION). By interpreting the state and its external relations as the political organization of the world economy, WORLD-SYSTEMS ANALYSIS moves away from the state-centrism of realist-based accounts. Thus Wallerstein (1984) considers the links between the processes of capital ACCUMULATION, resource competition and foreign policy as part of a singular and interdependent global system in which CAPITALISM determines the character and hierarchical configuration of states. Thus for world-systems theorists the more peripheral location of the former Soviet Union in the world economy helps us to understand why it was unable to compete effectively with the United States during the later stages of the Cold War (e.g. Taylor, 1990). By taking economic forces as, in the last instance, the basis for determining relations between states, there is a tendency to relegate the importance of political and socio-cultural processes at the state level, when both politics and cultural processes can and do play an important and independent part in determining the nature of geopolitics. Such concerns have led Agnew and Corbridge (1995) to advocate a more dynamic and nuanced approach to geopolitics, which moves away from the hypostatization of the world simply into economically differentiated core and periphery states (see CORE–PERIPHERY MODEL). Their call for a new geopolitics based on a *geopolitical economy* perspective focuses on the importance of both economic and political processes shaping post-1945 world orders, in which neither process is simply reducible to the other and in which non-state actors (such as MULTINATIONAL CORPORATIONS and global financial institutions) play a key role.

CRITICAL GEOPOLITICS is a school of thought which explores the meanings, forms of REPRESENTATION and symbolic contestation of the geopolitical world and of the DISCOURSES which underpin the production and reproduction of the meanings of geopolitical spaces. Part of the 1990s CULTURAL TURN in human geography, its practitioners provide fresh insights into how the geopolitical ideas and practices of statecraft constructs global space to reflect and legitimize particular geopolitical interests. GES

References and Suggested Reading

Agnew, J. 1998: *Geopolitics; revisioning world politics*. London: Routledge. · Agnew, J. and Corbridge, S. 1995: *Mastering space: hegemony, territory and international political economy*. London and New York: Routledge. · Cohen, S.B. 1991: Global geopolitical change in the post-Cold War era. *Annals of the Association of American Geographers* 81: 551–80. · Dalby, S. 1991: Critical geopolitics: discourse, difference and dissent. *Environment and Planning D: Society and Space* 9: 261–83. · Dijkink, G. 1996: *National identity and geopolitical visions. Maps of pride and pain*. London: Routledge. · Kennedy, P. 1988: *The rise and fall of the great powers: economic change and military conflict from 1500 to 2000*. London: Unwin Hyman. · O'Tuathail, G. 1996: *Critical geopolitics: the politics of writing global space*. London: Routledge. · O'Tuathail, G. and Dalby, S., eds, 1998: *Rethinking geopolitics*. London: Routledge. · O'Loughlin, J. and van der Wusten, H. 1994: *The political geography of international relations*. London: Frances Pinter. · Parker, G. 1988: *Geopolitics, past, present, future*. London: Pinter. · Smith, G.E. 1993: Ends, geopolitics and transitions. In R.J. Johnston, ed., *The challenge for geography: a changing world, changing discipline*. Oxford: Blackwell, 76–99. · Taylor, P.J. 1990: *Britain and the Cold War: 1945 as a geopolitical transition*. London: Frances Pinter. · Tunander, O., Baev, P., Einagel, V., eds, 1997: *Geopolitics in post-wall Europe, security, territory and identity*. London: Sage. · Wallerstein, I. 1984: *The politics of the world economy*. Cambridge: Cambridge University Press.

Geopolitik A school of POLITICAL GEOGRAPHY developed in inter-war Germany, associated with the geographer, Karl Haushofer, and the journal *Zeitschrift für Geopolitik* (1922–44). The term *Geopolitik* originated with the Swedish political scientist, Rudolph Kjellen, whose ideas, along with Ratzel's organic theory of the STATE and Mackinder's HEARTLAND concept, provided a basis and spurious rationale to justify German expansionism. The state was portrayed as an organism which needed to expand territorially (*LEBENSRAUM*) in order to fulfil its destiny. However, there were important differences between *Geopolitik* and National Socialism, a fact which has not always been appreciated by geographers. Whereas *Geopolitik* was influenced by the significance of natural laws in its understanding of social and political life (cf. SOCIAL DARWINISM), National Socialism saw societies as determined by biological inheritance. Nonetheless, the relationship which undoubtedly existed between *Geopolitik* and 1930s German foreign policy meant that it is only recently that geography, and in particular German geography, has begun to investigate its unhappy past. GES

Suggested Reading

Bassin, M. 1987: Race contra space: the conflict between German *Geopolitik* and national socialism. *Political Geography Quarterly* 6: 115–34. · Sander, G. and Rossler, M. 1994: Geography and empire in Germany, 1871–1945. In A. Godlewska and N. Smith, eds, *Geography and empire*. Oxford: Basil Blackwell, 115–29. · Smith, W. 1980: Friedrich Ratzel and the origins of *Lebensraum*. *German Studies Review* 3: 51–68.

geostrategic regions Large-scale international regions comprising groups of states sharing a common political or economic philosophy. The best-known attempt at devising such a system of world regions is by S.B. Cohen who, in the context of the Cold War, proposed a fundamental twofold division of the globe.

The *Trade-Dependent Maritime World* comprised Western Europe, the Americas and most of Africa and Australasia, and was held together by a complex network of maritime trading links. The *Eurasian Continental World* was a land-based grouping with IDEOLOGY rather than TRADE as the prime cohesive force. Cohen's model was an attempt to provide a more sophisticated and detailed successor to the HEARTLAND theory that was so popular in the early twentieth century, before it too was overtaken by events. The collapse and fragmentation of the Soviet empire in the early 1990s has rendered Cohen's crude two-fold global division virtually meaningless. The emerging new order reflects a more complex pattern of regional trading blocs, such as the enlarged European Union and the ASEAN countries in Southeast Asia. MB

Suggested Reading

Cohen, S.B. 1982: A new map of global geopolitical equilibrium. *Political Geography Quarterly* 1: 223–41. · Cohen, S.B. 1992: Policy prescriptions for the post-Cold War world. *Professional Geographer* 44: 13–15. · Michalak, W. and Gibb, R. 1997: Trading blocs and multilateralism in the world economy. *Annals of the Association of American Geographers* 87: 264–79.

gerrymandering The deliberate drawing of constituency boundaries to produce an electoral advantage for an interested party. The term was coined by the enemies of Republican Governor Elbridge Gerry of Massachusetts, who redrew a district's boundaries to his party's advantage in 1812: that district was shaped like a salamander, hence the neologism and the widespread (though false) belief that gerrymandering necessarily involves odd-shaped district boundaries. Though the widespread practice of gerrymandering has long been appreciated in the US, it has only recently been tackled by the willingness of the Supreme Court to interpret it as a constitutional violation (Grofman, 1990: see also ELECTORAL GEOGRAPHY). RJJ

Reference

Grofman, B., ed., 1990: *Political gerrymandering and the courts*. New York: Agathon Press.

ghetto An extreme form of residential concentration; a cultural, religious, or ethnic group is ghettoized when (a) a high proportion of the group lives in a single area, and (b) when the group accounts for most of the population in that area. Although the practice of ghettoization – forcing a group to live separately within a city – originated in the urban quarters of pre-classical cities, the first use of the term occurred in late medieval Venice, where city authorities required Jews to live on a separate island (called *gheto*) that was sealed behind walls and gates each night (Calimani, 1987). Exclusion was imposed by the dominant CULTURE and, as such, reflected and reinforced the marginalization of the Jewish minority. However, while the ghetto was overcrowded and prone to fire and disease, Jews also gained some benefit from their enforced isolation, especially the right to practise their religion and legal system and, perhaps, a degree of protection from more drastic forms of persecution (Wirth, 1928).

Instances of complete ghettoization have been rare (two modern exceptions are the Warsaw Ghetto of the Second World War and designated areas for black residential settlement in South African cities during the APARTHEID regime). Early in the twentieth century, the term came to be used indiscriminately for almost any residential area identified with a particular group, even when it did not form a majority, and even when SEGREGATION was not the result of discrimination. This ambiguity was especially prevalent in the influential work of the Chicago sociologists (see CHICAGO SCHOOL), who even referred to a wealthy NEIGHBOURHOOD in the city as the 'gilded ghetto'.

Researchers began in the 1970s to call for more analytical precision. Philpott (1979), for example, distinguished between 'SLUMS', areas of poverty that residents (frequently immigrants) leave as they acquire the means to do so, and ghettoes, areas where residents are trapped in permanent poverty (also see Ward, 1989). Also, ghettoes should not be confused with ethnic ENCLAVES, areas dominated by a single cultural group. Ghettoes emerge when political and/or other institutions, such as the housing market, operate to restrict the residential choices of certain groups, channelling them to the most undesirable neighbourhoods. They are the product of racialization (see ETHNICITY; RACE), where particular minority groups are judged by the majority to be genetically and socially inferior. There is always a degree of involuntary behaviour in the formation of ghettoes, whereas ethnic enclaves arise when members of a group choose to live in close proximity (Boal, 1976; Peach, 1996a).

The situation of African-Americans in the US is typically seen as the defining example of contemporary ghettoization (see Darden, 1995). In the 1960s, some American social scientists began to assert that ghetto environments are so debilitating that a 'culture of poverty', associated with high crime rates, substance abuse, broken families, and a reliance on social services, is transmitted from parents to children (cf. CYCLE OF POVERTY). These alarming views were instrumental in the 'war on poverty' declared by the US government, and were important ingredients in the inauguration of urban redevelopment programmes, increased social spending, educational reform, and heightened policing and surveillance of the INNER CITY (cf. URBAN RENEWAL). These initiatives were largely withdrawn in the conservative 1980s, but the argument that ghettoes should be the focus of PUBLIC POLICY was revived later in the decade as part of the UNDERCLASS debate. Again, proponents of this thesis believe that ghettoes are not just places of grinding poverty, but also places where poverty is institutionalized (Wilson, 1987). Similar arguments have surfaced in the United Kingdom (e.g. Rex, 1988; but see Peach, 1996b for an alternate view).

As in the Venetian case, though, ghettoes, once formed, frequently provide a context for the maintenance and development of minority cultures; ironically, these oppositional cultural forms are sometimes embraced by the dominant culture (e.g. the many types of music pioneered by African-Americans).

DH

References

Boal, F.W. 1976: Ethnic residential segregation. In D.T. Herbert, and R.J. Johnston, eds, *Social areas in cities, volume 1: Spatial processes and form*. Chichester: John Wiley, 41–79. · Calimani, R. 1987: *The ghetto of Venice*. New York: M. Evans and Company. · Cross, M. and Keith, M., eds, 1993: *Racism, the city and the state*. London and New York: Routledge. · Darden, J.T. 1995: Black residential segregation since the 1948 Shelly v. Kraemer decision. *Journal of Black Studies* 25: 680–91. · Peach, C. 1996a: Good segregation, bad segregation. *Planning Perspectives* 11: 379–98. · Peach, C. 1996b: Does Britain have ghettos? *Transactions, British Institute of Geographers* NS 22: 216–35. · Philpott, T.L. 1979: *The slum and the ghetto: neighborhood deterioration and middle-class reform*. New York: Oxford University Press. · Rex, J. 1988: *The ghetto and the underclass: essays on race and social policy*. Aldershot: Avebury. · Ward, D. 1989: *Poverty, ethnicity, and the American city, 1840–1925. Changing conceptions of the slum and the ghetto*. New York: Cambridge University Press. · Wilson, W.J. 1987: *The truly disadvantaged: the inner city, the underclass, and public policy*. Chicago: University of Chicago Press. · Wirth, L. 1928: *The ghetto*. Chicago: University of Chicago Press.

global futures Scenarios at a future point in time. These scenarios may be issue-specific (e.g. GLOBAL WARMING) or they may be visions of an entire SOCIETY. They may be global, or they may be given a local setting but with a view to global application (e.g. Callenbach, 1978). The future scenario, whether based in scientific analysis, utopian or dystopian thought, is often a device with which both to explore the future and to make critical comment on, or clarify, the present. To compare the accuracy of these works with actual events at a later date is to often misjudge the author's intentions. If the author is seeking changes to avoid a dystopian scenario, the work may produce the 'Cassandra effect' or the 'self-refuting prophecy' in that it causes behaviour to be altered.

Kates (1995, p. 623) wrote that what is 'so striking about great ideas is how relatively few there are, how powerful their impacts on both science and society, yet how simplified they are in construct and how often wrong in application'. He included in his work the prophet Jeremiah, Thomas Robert Malthus (cf. MALTHUSIAN MODEL), William Vogt's *Road to survival* (1948), LIMITS TO GROWTH work by Meadows et al. (1972, 1992) and the market-based scenario of Julian Simon (1981). The global futures posited in the debates between Meadows et al. and Simon (Simon and Kahn, 1984; Simon, 1994) range from limits to population and RESOURCE use, through to Simon's 'cornucopian' belief that human labour and ingenuity is the ultimate resource that will redefine physical limits. The World Commission on Environment and Development (1987) includes aspects of both of these positions in its notion of SUSTAINABLE DEVELOPMENT.

Contemporary social theory emphasizes contingency of outcomes, cumulative impacts and the futility of PREDICTION. This means that accurate prediction, despite more sophisticated technology, is likely to remain an elusive goal. However, rational action is premised on some form of prediction so that action can be taken to achieve desirable goals or to avoid potential harm (cf. RATIONAL CHOICE THEORY): Kates (1995, p. 631) wrote that 'accuracy may not be a fair test of the prophecy. Instead we can only ask if the prophets' concerns were reasonable for their time and knowledge'. There will continue to be global future scenarios presented in various guises. Depending upon the type of scenario, the most successful work on global futures may be scenarios that induce modifications in human behaviour, and are therefore not accurate in their vision of a future world.

PM

References

Callenbach, E. 1978: *Ecotopia*. London: Pluto Press. · Kates, R. 1995: Labnotes from the Jeremiah Experiment: hope for a sustainable transition. *Annals of the Association of American Geographers* 85 4: 623–40. · Meadows, D.H., Meadows, D.L., Randers, J. and Behrens, W. 1972: *The limits to growth*. London: Earth Island. · Meadows, D.H., Meadows, D.L., Randers, J.

1992: *Beyond the limits: global collapse or a sustainable future*. London: Earthscan. · Simon, J. 1981: *The ultimate resource*. Princetown, NJ: Princetown University Press. · Simon, J. 1994: More people, greater wealth, more resources, healthier environment. *Economic Affairs* 14 (3): 22–9. · Simon, J. and Kahn, H., eds, 1984: *The resourceful earth*. Oxford: Blackwell; World Commission on Environment and Development (WCED) 1987: *Our common future*. Oxford: Oxford University Press.

Suggested Reading
Kates (1995).

Global Positioning System (GPS) A system allowing its users to determine position accurately anywhere on the Earth's surface. A constellation of satellites sends very precisely timed signals to a receiver; by comparing the arrival times of signals from three or more satellites it is possible to determine two-dimensional position; four or more signals can determine three-dimensional position. Two systems were in operation at the time of writing: the US system, known as GPS, and the Russian system, Glonass. GPS consists of a constellation of 24 satellites, and can determine position to 100 m (in 9 cases out of 10) for civilian applications, and 30 m for military applications, which have access to better signals. By comparing the signals received at two stations it is possible to establish relative position much more accurately. GPS is being used in GEOCODING, to monitor locations of vehicles, to aid navigation, and for many other practical purposes. MG

global warming (and greenhouse effect) The increase in global temperature resulting from human activities that enhance the so-called natural 'greenhouse effect'. This phenomenon is often seen as part of 'climate change', a term that is less impelling but recognizes the likely variability of climate changes in different parts of the world.

Greenhouse gases are mostly natural compounds (water vapour, carbon dioxide, methane and nitrous oxide) that allow the earth's atmosphere to trap heat that has been released as longwave energy from the earth's surface. This leads to increases in atmospheric temperature. At an average temperature of fifteen degrees Celsius, the earth is able to support many lifeforms. However, human activity has increased the levels of carbon dioxide (mainly through coal burning, internal combustion engines in transport media and clearing of forests), methane (through burning of natural gas, seepage from landfill sites, rice paddies and from the increased numbers of cattle) and nitrous oxide (mainly through agricultural activities). Artificial gases, such as chlorofluorocarbons (CFCs), have also significantly added to the earth's natural greenhouse effect (see POLLUTION). CFCs are also responsible for a different process, ozone depletion in the earth's atmosphere (see Harries, 1994; Turco, 1997): they are extremely inert, which means they cannot be removed and are not absorbed. The Montreal Protocol (1987) was a significant attempt, followed by amendments in Copenhagen (1992), to phase out CFCs (see Clayton, 1995).

In 1991, eight countries, including three developing countries with large populations, contributed approximately 62 per cent of the world's greenhouse gas emissions (World Resources Institute, 1994). The Intergovernmental Panel on Climate Change (IPCC) provided detailed analyses of various greenhouse scenarios in 1990, 1992, 1994 and 1995 which contributed to the United Nations Framework Convention on Climate Change (1992) at the Rio conference on SUSTAINABLE DEVELOPMENT and to the Climate Change Convention in Kyoto, Japan, in 1997. Unfortunately, at this latter convention it was apparent that individual countries and blocs (e.g. the European Union) were more interested in maintaining economic growth than in taking the ecologically necessary steps to reduce emissions. This was evident in the choice of base year against which reduction in emissions were to be set (1990), which still included pollution from the now inoperational heavy industry in the former East Germany. Under the agreement, the European Union aims to reduce emissions to 8 per cent below their 1990 level by the year 2012; the USA's target is to reduce its emissions by 7 per cent whereas Japan is aiming for a 6 per cent reduction. The role of Australia (a so-called developed country, with high coal exports) in obtaining the right to increase its emissions by 8 per cent to the year 2012, highlighted the lack of environmental commitment by some countries.

Climate change is critical because it highlights human impacts at a global scale. While there have been major cooling and heating periods throughout the earth's history, human input into present changes cannot be ignored. Increased concentrations of greenhouse gases with long lifetimes (Pickering and Owen, 1994), rising sea levels, changes in the location, intensity and frequency of cyclones, drought and flood, and depletion in the earth's ozone layer (particularly over the Antarctic pole) are all important impacts of human activity. These changes are yet to be understood because of the time lag between pollution emission and cumulative impacts. The issues of global warming and ozone depletion have also caused political tensions around consumption lifestyles, ENERGY-use patterns, production methods and deforestation. Global warming has divided the so-called THIRD WORLD countries, more than by wealth alone. Global warming heats the top layer of sea water, which expands in volume (to which is added melting glaciers) and causes sea level rise. Small island states, fearing inundation, want restrictions on fossil-fuel use. Countries that produce and/or consume oil and coal are very reluctant to meet this demand.

The potential for carbon dioxide emissions to affect the earth's radiation balance was suggested as early as 1861 (Pickering and Owen, 1994). Current monitoring of ice sheets, tree rings and other phenomena indicates that human impact has recently altered the earth's radiation system. Computer modelling, otherwise known as General Circulation Models (GCMs), is used to predict possible future changes. Initial predictions of the extent of climate change have been lowered recently by 20 to 30 per cent, due mainly to incorporation of sulphate aerosols emitted by volcanoes which have contributed to stratospheric cooling (Pickering and Owen, 1994) and there is still uncertainty about the significance of clouds and the cumulative impacts of changes.

What is certain is that emissions of carbon dioxide and some other greenhouse gases are increasing, that they have a long lifetime, and that the earth is getting warmer. The lowering of GCM predictions does not dismiss the issue. While the processes are still occurring, it merely means that if the predicted impacts eventuate, they will be delayed by only a few years (see GLOBAL FUTURES). PM

References

Clayton, K. 1995: The threat of global warming. In T. O'Riordan, ed., *Environmental science for environmental management*. Harlow, Essex: Longman, 110–30. · Harries, J. 1994: *Earthwatch – the climate from Space*. Chichester: John Wiley and Sons. · Pickering, K. and Owen, L. 1994: *An introduction to global environmental issues*. London and New York: Routledge. · Turco, R. 1997: *Earth under siege: from air pollution to global change*. Oxford and New York: Oxford University Press. · World Resources Institute 1994: *World resources 1994–95*. New York and Oxford: Oxford University Press.

globalization As a concept this emerged around 1960 when the Canadian media scholar Marshall McLuhan coined the term *global village* to capture the impact of new communications technologies on social and cultural life. TIME–SPACE COMPRESSION, it is argued, has so transformed the structure and scale of human relationships that social, cultural, political, and economic processes now operate at a global SCALE with a consequent reduction in the significance of other geographical scales (national, local, etc.). We live, it is asserted, in a world in which nation-states are no longer significant actors or meaningful economic units; in which consumer tastes and cultures are homogenized and satisfied through the provision of standardized global products created by global corporations with no allegiance to place or community. Within the sphere of the political economy, writers such as Kenichi Ohmae (1990) speak of a *borderless world* in which the NATION-STATE has become rendered impotent by institutions (including the MULTINATIONAL CORPORATION) which, allegedly, operate globally and without any real connections to PLACE.

The global is, thus, claimed to be the natural order of affairs in today's technologically driven world in which time–space has been compressed, the 'end of geography' has arrived and everywhere is becoming the same (cf. PLACELESSNESS). The view of globalization as an inexorable, and virtually unstoppable, force which can only be accommodated, rather than resisted, has become the conventional wisdom in neo-liberal political and business circles and employed as a rhetoric to justify particular kinds of decisions. In fact, globalization consists of a number of distinct, but overlapping, DISCOURSES in which its meaning is highly contested (Waters, 1995, provides a readable general survey).

Although the notion of a globalized world has become pervasive in recent years, there are strong opponents who argue, in effect, that globalization is a mirage or, at the very least, nothing new (see, for example, Hirst and Thompson, 1996). There was, indeed, a substantial debate at the end of the nineteenth century – what might be seen as the 'first globalization debate' – which was concerned with the transformation of economic life by the expansionary forces of capitalism as expressed in the economic theory of IMPERIALISM developed by Lenin and inspired by the work of J.A. Hobson. So, on the one hand, we have the view that we do, indeed, live in a new – globalized – world economy in which our lives are dominated by global forces. On the other hand, we have the view that not all that much has changed; that we still inhabit an international, rather than a globalized, world-economy in which national forces remain highly significant (cf. WORLD-SYSTEMS ANALYSIS).

In fact, neither of these extreme positions can be justified. Although in quantitative terms the world was perhaps at least as open economically before 1913 as it is today – in some respects, even more so (see Kozul-Wright, 1995) – the nature of the integration was qualitatively very different. To argue that the pre-First World War world economy was, in fact, more globalized than now is to conflate what are, in fact, two distinct processes. *Internationalization* involves the simple extension of economic activities across national boundaries. It is, essentially, a quantitative process which leads to a more extensive geographical pattern of economic activity. *Globalization* processes are *qualitatively* different from internationalization processes. They involve not merely the geographical extension of economic activity across national boundaries but also – and more importantly – the functional integration of such internationally dispersed activities.

The pre-1914 world economy was an increasingly internationalizing economy, but the nature of economic integration was essentially 'shallow', based primarily on arm's length trade in goods and services and on flows of portfolio capital. Today's world economy is characterized both by such internationalizing processes and also by a 'deeper' degree of INTEGRATION based upon interconnected configurations of production orchestrated primarily by transnational corporations. Hence, both processes – internationalization and globalization – co-exist. In some cases, what we are seeing is no more than the continuation of long-established international dispersion of activities. In others, however, we are undoubtedly seeing an increasing dispersion and integration of activities across national boundaries. The pervasive internationalization, and growing globalization, of economic life ensure that changes originating in one part of the world are rapidly diffused to others.

McGrew (1992, p. 23) captures the complexity of the current position in a concise and balanced way. He defines globalization as:

> the multiplicity of linkages and interconnections between the states and societies which make up the modern world system. It describes the process by which events, decisions, and activities in one part of the world can come to have significant consequences for individuals and communities in quite distant parts of the globe. Globalization has two distinct dimensions: scope (or stretching) and intensity (or deepening). On the one hand it defines a set of processes which embrace most of the globe or which operate worldwide; the concept therefore has a spatial connotation. Politics and other social activities are becoming stretched across the globe. On the other hand it also implies an intensification in the levels of interaction, interconnectedness or interdependence between the states and societies which constitute the world community. Accordingly, alongside the stretching goes a deepening of global processes.

It must be emphasized, however, that change does not occur everywhere in the same way and at the same rate; the processes of globalization are not geographically uniform. The particular character of individual countries, of regions (see REGIONALISM) and of LOCALITIES interacts with the larger-scale general processes of change to produce quite specific outcomes. LOCALIZATION remains a significant phenomenon. Although there are undoubtedly globalizing forces at work we do not have a fully globalized world. Globalization tendencies can be at work without this resulting in an all-encompassing end-state in which all unevenness and differences are ironed out, market forces are rampant and uncontrollable, and the nation-state merely passive and supine. Hence, globalization should be conceptualized as a complex of interrelated processes, rather than an end-state. Such tendencies are highly uneven in time and space.

PD

Suggested Reading

Dicken, P. 1998: *Global shift: the transformation of the world economy*, 3rd edn. London: Sage; New York: Guilford. · Dicken, P. Peck, J.A. and Tickell, A. 1997: Unpacking the global. In R. Lee, and J. Wills, eds, *Geographies of economies*. London: Arnold, 158–66. · Featherstone, M., ed., 1990: *Global culture*. London: Sage. · Hirst, P. and Thompson, G. 1996: *Globalization in question*. Cambridge: Polity Press. · Kozul-Wright, R. 1995: Transnational corporations and the nation state. In J. Michie, and J. Grieve Smith, eds, *Managing the global economy*. Oxford: Oxford University Press, 135–71. · McGrew, A.G. 1992: Conceptualizing global politics. In A.G. McGrew, and P.G. Lewis, eds, *Global politics: globalization and the nation-state*. Cambridge: Polity Press, 1–28. · Ohmae, K. 1990: *The borderless world: power and strategy in the interlinked economy*. New York: The Free Press. · Waters, M. 1995: *Globalization*. London: Routledge.

governance Governance has become one of the keywords of anglophone social science during the 1990s especially in political theory, political science and HUMAN GEOGRAPHY. The traditional definition is 'the act or process of governing'. Here 'governance' is synonymous with 'government'. However, recent academic usage usually distinguishes governance from government. Two different broad uses of the term can be identified.

The first use refers to *the nature of organizations*. Governance is defined as the involvement of a wide range of institutions and actors in the production of policy outcomes, including non-governmental organizations, quangos, private companies, pressure groups and SOCIAL MOVEMENTS as well as those STATE institutions traditionally regarded as formally part of the government. Here 'governance' is a broader category than 'government', with government being one component of governance among many. To some extent this definition is a belated recognition that the coordination of complex social systems and the steering of societal development have never been the responsibilities of the state alone, but have always involved interaction between a range of state and non-state actors. Most writers, though, go further than this and argue that the state has become less prominent and non-state organizations have become relatively more important within the overall process of governance.

The second use refers to *the nature of the relationships between organizations*. Here governance refers to a particular form of coordination. In contrast with the top-down control in coordination through hierarchy and the individualized relationship in coordination through markets, governance involves coordination through networks and partnerships. Governance refers to 'the "self-organization of inter-organizational relations"' (Jessop, 1997a, p. 59) or to 'self-organizing, interorganizational networks' (Rhodes, 1997, p. 53). Writers adopting this usage commonly refer to a shift in the nature of coordination in contemporary societies from government ('hierarchy') to governance.

Rhodes draws on both the above uses and expands his definition to incorporate four salient features, as follows:

- *Interdependence between organizations*. Governance is broader than government, covering non-state actors. Changing the boundaries of the state meant the boundaries between public, private and voluntary sectors became more shifting and opaque.
- *Continuing interactions between network members*, caused by the need to exchange resources and negotiate shared purposes.
- *Game-like interactions*, rooted in trust and regulated by rules of the game negotiated and agreed upon by network participants.
- *A significant degree of autonomy from the state*. Networks are not accountable to the state; they are self-organizing. Although the state does not occupy a sovereign position, it can indirectly and imperfectly steer networks (Rhodes, 1997, p. 53).

Governance is a rapidly expanding field of both theoretical and empirical enquiry. Four areas of development can be noted.

The use of network theories. A number of different approaches to understanding networks have been drawn on by governance theorists including Rhodes' own 'policy network' approach (Rhodes, 1997) and ACTOR–NETWORK THEORY (e.g. Murdoch and Marsden, 1995).

The implications of social complexity (Amin and Hausner, 1997). Jessop argues (1997b, p. 59) that the recent 'discovery [of governance] could well reflect the dramatic intensification of societal complexity which flows from growing functional differentiation of institutional orders within an increasingly global society, with all that this implies for the widening and deepening of systemic interdependencies across various social, spatial and temporal horizons'. One implication of complexity is that all forms of coordination, including governance, are prone to failure (Jessop, 1997b).

The spatial restructuring of governance. The shift from government to governance has been associated with the hollowing-out of the state (Jessop, 1994): the loss of central state functions to (i) other spatial scales such as the supra-national (e.g. the European Union) and the infra-national (e.g. autonomous regions, local bodies) and (ii) non-state institutions (private companies, voluntary organizations). Much work on governance in human geography has focused on this issue of spatial RESTRUCTURING, including studies of local and urban governance (e.g. Goodwin and Painter, 1996); and rural governance (*Journal of Rural Studies*, 1998).

Empirical research to assess the claims that coordination through network relations is emerging as a core feature of political and economic life. JP

References

Amin, A. and Hausner, J. 1997: Interactive governance and social complexity. In A. Amin, and J. Hausner, eds, *Beyond market and hierarchy: interactive governance and social complexity*. Cheltenham: Edward Elgar, 1–31. · Goodwin, M. and Painter, J. 1996: Local governance, the crises of Fordism and the changing geographies of regulation. *Transactions, Institute of British Geographers* 21: 635–48. · Jessop, B. 1994: Post-Fordism and the state. In A. Amin, ed., *Post-Fordism: a reader.* Oxford: Blackwell, 251–79. · Jessop, B. 1997a: A neo-Gramscian approach to the regulation of urban regimes: accumulation strategies, hegemonic projects and governance. In M. Lauria, ed., *Reconstructing urban regime theory: regulating urban politics in a global economy.* London: Sage, 51–76. · Jessop, B. 1997b: The governance of complexity and the complexity of governance: preliminary remarks on some problems and limits of economic guidance. In A. Amin, and J. Hausner, eds, *Beyond market and hierarchy: interactive governance and social complexity.* Cheltenham: Edward Elgar, 95–128. · *Journal of Rural Studies*, 1998: Special issue on rural governance. *Journal of Rural Studies* 14 (1). · Murdoch, J. and Marsden, T. 1995: The spatialization of politics: local and national actor-spaces in environmental conflict. *Transactions, Institute of British Geographers* NS 20: 368–80. · Rhodes, R. 1997: *Understanding governance*. Buckingham: Open University Press.

governmentality A neologism coined by the French thinker Michel Foucault (1926–84), who used it: (a) as an organizing concept for his work in the late 1970s and early 1980s on 'the government of the self' by the self and by others; and (b) to describe a distinctly 'governmental form of rationality' which emerged in Europe between the fifteenth and eighteenth centuries and was central to the development of BIOPOWER and the human sciences.

Foucault (1989) argued that 'government' is neither identical with political sovereignty nor an intrinsic property of the STATE but is instead *an historically shifting ensemble of practices.* In volumes 2 and 3 of his *History of sexuality*, which deal with late Antiquity, Foucault explores modes of ethical self-conduct, and at the end of his life he suggested that his work could be read as an attempt to analyse the modes of 'governance' through which the human subject is constituted in relation to itself and constellations of POWER (Foucault, 1994).

Foucault discussed a number of *historical ruptures in 'the art of government'* in western societies from Antiquity to the present. He showed how modern (post-1750) systems of government rest on 'micro-physical' – disciplinary – techniques of *individualization* that aim 'to rule [the body and soul] in a continuous and permanent way', and 'macro-physical' strategies of state knowledge-building and regulation – or *totalization* and *centralization* – that deal with people as legal subjects and are concerned with the health and productivity of populations and territories (Foucault, 1988). The former techniques stem from the 'pastoral modality of power' of the Christian Church: 'techniques of examination, confession, guidance, [and] obedience', with the pastor as a shepherd who must consider what *each and every* member of his flock needs, knows and does. The latter stems from doctrines of 'reason of state', which attempted to define how *state* government differed from the government of God and that of the family, and 'theories of police', which mapped 'the objects of the state's rational activity' and fashioned its fields of intervention and instruments of regulation (cf. POLICING, GEOGRAPHY OF).

On Foucault's account, these two processes of 'governmentalization' became intertwined during the sixteenth century and should be understood in relation to the transition from FEUDALISM to CAPITALISM, the growth of administrative states and COLONIAL empires, and the Reformation and Counter-Reformation (Foucault, 1991a). By the eighteenth century, there had been a transition from what Foucault called 'the *étatization* of society' (the advance of the state into more and more areas of life) to 'the 'governmentalization' of the state' (the proliferation of 'apparatuses... institutions, procedures, analyses and calculations' that were both internal and external to the state, and that regarded 'economy' and 'population' as autonomous levels of reality). Foucault focused on Europe, but Scott (1995) draws on his work to sketch shifts in the nature of 'colonial governmentality'.

This modern era of governmentality fostered a 'critical attitude' towards state power which Foucault associated with Kant and adopted as an approximate definition of critique: an 'art of not being governed like that and at that cost' – of finding ways of nestling away from an art of government which 'now reaches the very grain of the individual' (Foucault, 1997). The idea that the state governs too much was one of the founding rationales of western LIBERALISM, and Foucault's sympathetic appreciation of Kant and liberal thought seems at odds with his historical work on the disciplinary cast of MODERNITY and the dark side of ENLIGHTENMENT (see Pizzorno, 1992; cf. GENEALOGY). Yet Foucault drew on this tradition of critique to conceptualize contemporary social protests – particularly the student revolts in Paris and Tunisia of the late 1960s. He argued that it is the recognition that power is now exercised 'within the social body through extremely different channels', and that these channels (the media now being an important one) *produce individuals and solicit compliance*, that lies at the heart of our 'discomfort' about government (Foucault, 1991b).

Foucault worked on these issues with a team of scholars (see Burchall et al., 1991). They have questioned some of his historical generalizations but share his suspicion of cultural and political programmes – most recently NEO-LIBERAL programmes – that claim to speak for *each and all.* Foucault's ideas about governmentality inform recent work in POLITICAL GEOGRAPHY. Ó Tuathail (1996), for instance, tracks the 'modern governmentalization of geography' – by which he means the administration of space by states and other agents of power, and the spatialization of national and political identities by geographers and CARTOGRAPHERS (cf. SPATIALITY) – from the sixteenth century onwards; and Herod et al. (1998) consider the advent of 'geographies of governance' that are no longer organized along strictly 'state-centric' lines (on a model of *étatization*) but work through diverse channels of GLOBALIZATION. Such work elaborates the geographical texture of Foucault's arguments but arguably deflates Foucault's ethical concern with *how* to govern. Foucault's work on 'governmentality' should push geographers into a closer engagement with moral philosophy – particularly the genealogy of western liberalism. DC

References

Burchall, G., Gordon, C. and Miller, P., eds, 1991: *The Foucault effect: studies in governmentality.* London: Harvester Wheatsheaf. · Florence, M. [Foucault, M] 1994: Foucault, Michel, 1926–, trans. C. Porter. In G. Gutting, ed., *The Cambridge companion to Foucault.* Cambridge: Cambridge University Press, 314–19. · Foucault, M. 1988 [orig. pub. 1981]: Politics and reason. In M. Foucault, *Politics, philosophy, culture: interviews and other writings, 1977–1984,* ed. L. Kritzman. London and New York: Routledge, 57–85. · Foucault, M. 1989: *Résumé des cours, 1970–1982.* Paris: Julliard, 99–144. · Foucault, M. 1991a [orig. pub. 1979]: Governmentality. In G. Burchall, C. Gordon, and P. Miller, eds, *The Foucault effect: studies in governmentality.* London: Harvester Wheatsheaf, 87–104. · Foucault, M. 1991b: Between 'words' and 'things' during May '68. In M. Foucault, *Remarks on Marx: conversations with Duccio Trombadori,* trans. R.J. Goldstein and J. Cascaito. New York: Semiotext(e), 131–46. Interview 1978. · Foucault, M. 1997: What is critique? In M. Foucault, *The politics of truth,* ed. S. Lotringer and L. Hochroth. New York: Semiotiext(e), 23–82. Orig. pub. Fr. 1990. · Herod, A., Ó Tuathail, G. and Roberts S., eds, 1998: *Unruly world: globalization, governance and geography.* London and New York: Routledge. · Ó Tuathail, G. 1996: *Critical geopolitics: the politics of writing global space.* London and New York: Routledge. · Pizzorno, A. 1992: Foucault and the liberal view of the individual. In T. Armstrong, ed. and trans., *Michel Foucault: Philosopher.* New York: Routledge, 204–11. · Scott, D. 1995: Colonial governmentality. *Social Text* 43: 191–220.

Suggested reading

Foucault (1988), (1991a).

Grand Theory A term devised by the American sociologist C. Wright Mills (1959) to attack what he took to be the obsessive concern of post-war social science with empty conceptual elaboration ('the associating and dissociating of concepts') at high levels of ABSTRACTION. In his view, Grand Theory was more or less severed from the irredeemably concrete concerns of everyday life and largely indifferent to its immense variety in time and space. His main target was Talcott Parsons, another American sociologist and the architect of STRUCTURAL FUNCTIONALISM, against whom he insisted that 'there is no "grand theory", no one universal scheme in terms of which we can understand the unity of social structure, no one answer to the tired old problem of social order.'

Since Mills wrote this, however, a number of other candidates for the grand prize of Grand Theory have emerged: in such numbers, indeed, that Skinner (1985) could write of 'the return of Grand Theory'. These have included CRITICAL THEORY, STRUCTURALISM, STRUCTURAL MARXISM and STRUCTURATION THEORY, all of which have left their marks on late twentieth-century human geography:

> Much of the history of Anglo-American human geography in the second half of the twentieth century has involved the search for a single or tightly-bounded set of methodological [and theoretical] principles that, once found, would provide unity and intelligibility to the disparate material studied. When located, such principles would function as a kind of philosopher's stone, transmuting the scattered base facts of the world into the pure gold of coherent explanation. No matter the kind of phenomenon investigated, it could always be slotted into a wider theoretical scheme. Nothing would be left out; everything would be explained (Barnes and Gregory, 1997, p. 64).

There have been two sets of responses to such a project, fastening on (i) its theoretical temper; and (ii) its totalizing ambitions.

On the one side, there has been a lively debate about the necessity of THEORY and, indeed, of how 'theory' should be understood and worked with. Few geographers would subscribe to, let alone advocate a return to, the supposedly theory-less world of EMPIRICISM. But Ley (1989), very much in the spirit of Mills's original objections, complained of a fixation upon theory: of the privilege accorded to the 'theorization of theories', second-order abstractions 'doubly removed from the empirical world', whose proliferation threatened to produce a disturbing fragmentation of intellectual inquiry. Set against this, however, Harvey and Scott (1989) were exercised by what they saw as a withdrawal from 'the theoretical imperative' and, in consequence, the dissolution of intellectual inquiry into a host of empirical particulars and fragments. The 'fragmentation' that dismays both sets of writers, in different ways, is itself often a product of theoretical work conducted outside the confines of – and in large measure working against – Grand Theory: see, for example, POSTMODERNISM, POST–STRUCTURALISM, PRAGMATISM.

On the other side, and closely connected to these developments, there has been a more recent and even livelier debate about the capacity of any single theoretical system to know and to represent the world (see also ESSENTIALISM; FOUNDATIONALISM). In consequence of the doubts raised during these discussions many, perhaps most, human geographers now seem to accept: (a) that no single '-ism' or '-ology' can possibly ask all the interesting questions or provide all the satisfying answers; and (b) that scholars necessarily work in the spaces between overlapping, often contending theoretical systems, which redoubles the importance of theoretical critique to clarify dissonances, reveal erasures and evaluate consequences (Gregory, 1994, pp. 100–6; McDowell, 1995).

Intersecting with these calls have been further arguments about the POWERS and politics of grand theory. Thrift (1996, p. 30) has argued that a more 'modest' form of theorizing is necessary to avoid a 'theory-centred' style of research 'which continually avoids the taint of particularity' (Thrift, 1996, p. 30) (see NON-REPRESENTATIONAL THEORY). If Thrift sought to clip the wings of grand theory, Katz (1996) urged human geographers to find other, politically more trenchant ways of letting theory take flight. The metaphor is appropriate since Katz drew upon Deleuze and Guattari (1986) to urge that human geographers learn to work with 'minor theory': to subvert the claims to 'mastery' registered by the projects of Grand Theory by working in the heterogeneous 'spaces-in-between' different traditions, by activating the disjunctures and displacements between different voices and vocabularies, and so ensuring that theoretical work is 'relentlessly transformative' and elaborates 'lines of escape'. DG

References

Barnes, T. and Gregory, D. 1997: Grand Theory and geographical practice. In T. Barnes and D. Gregory, eds, *Reading human geography: the poetics and politics of inquiry*. London: Arnold, 85–91. · Deleuze, G. and Guattari, F. 1986: *Kafka: toward a minor literature*. Minneapolis: University of Minnesota Press. · Gregory, D. 1994: *Geographical imaginations*. Oxford and Cambridge, MA: Blackwell. · Harvey, D. and Scott, A. 1989: The practice of human geography: theory and empirical specificity in the transition from Fordism to flexible accumulation. In B. Macmillan, ed., *Remodelling geography*. Oxford: Blackwell, 217–29. · Katz, C. 1996: Towards minor theory. *Environment and Planning D: Society and Space* 14: 487–99. · Ley, D. 1989: Fragmentation, coherence and limits to theory in human geography. In A. Kobayashi, and S. Mackenzie, eds, *Remaking human geography*. London: Unwin Hyman, 227–44. · McDowell, L. 1995: Understanding diversity: the problem of/for 'theory'. In R.J. Johnston, P.J. Taylor, and M.J. Watts, eds, *Geographies of global change: remapping the world in the twentieth century*. Oxford and Cambridge, MA: Blackwell, 280–94. · Mills, C.W. 1959: *The sociological imagination*. New York: Oxford University Press. · Skinner, Q., ed., 1985: *The return of Grand Theory in the human sciences*. Cambridge: Cambridge University Press. · Thrift, N.J. 1996: *Spatial formations*. London: Sage.

Suggested Reading

Barnes and Gregory (1997). · Katz (1996). · McDowell (1995). · Skinner (1985), ch. 1.

gravity model A mathematical model which was devised to represent a wide range of flow patterns in human geography (MIGRATION, telephone traffic, passenger movements, commodity flow, etc.) and subsequently used and further developed as a planning tool.

The original model, proposed by exponents of SOCIAL PHYSICS, was based on a crude analogy with Newton's gravitational equation (see METAPHOR):

$$G_{ij} = gM_iM_j/{d_{ij}}^2$$

This can be interpreted as follows: the gravitational force (G_{ij}) between two masses (M_i and M_j) is proportional to a gravitational constant (g) and to the product of their masses (M_iM_j) and inversely proportional to the square of the distance between them (${d_{ij}}^2$).

The analogy for migration was therefore given as:

$$F_{ij} = gP_iP_j/d_{ij}^2$$

where the migrant flow (F) from i to j was modelled as being proportional to the product of their populations. In such an application the constant g was empirically determined from the data set by simple arithmetic methods. At a later stage the model was fitted by regression methods in logarithmic form:

$$\log(F_{ij}/P_iP_j) = \log g + b \log d_{ij}$$

In this form both g and the exponent for distance b were empirically determined by calibration with the data set.

Planning applications of these models soon revealed that they gave poor fits to real data sets, so *ad hoc* adjustments were made to the form of the model. Some focused upon the relationship with distance by fitting, for example, the exponential model:

$$F_{ij} = gP_iP_je^{-bdij}$$

where e is the root of Napierian logarithms. Other adjustments were made to the P terms to ensure that the flows predicted by the model either from destinations, or to origins, or both, equalled the actual flow. Where only one of these was attempted the model was described as *origin constrained* or *destination constrained*, but where both were adjusted the model was termed *doubly constrained* and took the form:

$$F_{ij} = A_iP_iB_jP_je^{-bdij}$$

In this form the new symbols A_i and B_j were calibrating constants which had to be empirically determined by an iterative procedure. But such forms were a long way from the original analogy from physics and a stronger rationale was required. There were several attempts to do this in terms of likelihood maximizing, utility maximizing and ENTROPY MAXIMIZING. The last, due to Wilson (1974), has been widely accepted; it has the added advantage that it demonstrates the close links between gravity models on the one hand and competing models based on INTERVENING OPPORTUNITY and the TRANSPORTATION PROBLEM in linear programming.

Despite its problems the gravity model is widely used in transport planning: the great variety of possible mathematical formulations means that an approximate fit to empirical data can nearly always be achieved. On the other hand, those who believe that its theoretical basis is too weak fear that it will be a bad predictive tool and advocate other methods (for example TRANSPORTATION MODELS), and others note that it will lead to a perpetuation or intensification of existing patterns even where these are undesirable in terms of environmental issues or distributional equity (Sayer, 1971). (See also DISTANCE DECAY; FRICTION OF DISTANCE.) AMH

References

Sayer, A. 1971: Gravity Models and spatial autocorrelation, or atrophy in urban and regional modelling. *Area* 9: 183–9. · Wilson, A.G. 1974: *Urban and regional models in geography and planning*. Chichester: John Wiley.

Suggested Reading

Fotheringham, A.S. 1991: Migration and spatial structure: the development of the competing destination model. In J.C. Stilwell and P. Compton, eds, *Migration models*. London: Belhaven, 57–72. · Senior, M.L. 1979: From gravity modelling to entropy maximising: a pedagogic guide. *Progress in Human Geography* 3: 179–211. · Tocalis, T.R. 1978: Changing theoretical foundations for the gravity concept of human interaction. In B.J.L. Berry, ed., *The nature of change in geographic ideas*. De Kalb, IL: Northern Illinois University Press, 66–124.

green belt An area of open, low-density land use surrounding existing major cities and CONURBATIONS whose further extension, including the possible merging of urban areas, is strictly controlled. While occasionally applied elsewhere (e.g. in the Dutch Randstad) the term is more firmly tied to its British roots than planning concepts such as the GARDEN CITY and NEW TOWN, which share a similar historical genesis.

Green belts represent the largest single element in the land-use planning of metropolitan England since the Second World War, and feature prominently in some URBAN AND REGIONAL PLANNING strategies, especially in south-east England. The first such formal proposal appeared in Ebenezer Howard's GARDEN CITY scheme, where the green belt both provided for agriculture and leisure, and acted as a buffer against excessive urban growth. A variety of green belts was advocated around London from the 1890s onwards (Elson, 1986), but land-acquisition costs to local authorities proved prohibitive until the 1947 Town and Country Planning Act. This allowed green belt designations to be proposed under county Development and Structure Plans, a trend encouraged by a central government circular of 1955 extolling their virtues to control conurbation growth and urban coalescence and to maintain the character of historical towns. Their role as providing recreational and amenity space for town dwellers could be added to this rationale although, in practice, most green belt land in Britain remains in private hands.

Green belt designations in England more than doubled between 1979 and 1993, to 12 per cent of the total area – the equivalents in Scotland and Northern Ireland being 2 per cent and 16 per cent, respectively. Controversy over their justification has intensified over the same period. For their opponents (especially in the house-building lobby) green belts are negative devices, preventing development by

'NIMBY'-minded residents and planning authorities, leading to its leap-frogging beyond the green belt with accelerated commuting costs. Costs to the national economy are also increased, by insulating such land from 'normal' development processes (e.g. Simmie, 1993). However, central government, encouraged by conservation lobby groups, has thus far largely resisted calls to relax building restrictions in the green belt, and has recently encouraged local authorities to seek residential land needs for much of the household expansion in Britain within the next century on 'brownfield' sites (i.e. previously under non-rural uses), most of which lie outside the green belts. AGH

References

Elson, M. 1986: *Green belts*. London: Heinemann. · Simmie, J. 1993: *Planning at the crossroads*. London: University College London Press.

Suggested Reading

Munton, R.J.C. 1983: *London's green belt: containment in practice*. London: Allen and Unwin.

green revolution A term coined in the late 1960s to refer to the so-called miracle seeds – the high yielding varieties (HYVs) – especially wheat and rice, which held out the prospect for spectacular increases in cereal production in the Third World. Associated with 1970 Nobel Prize Winner and crop geneticist Norman Borlaug, the term Green Revolution continues to have wide currency 30 years after it was minted. Nonetheless it remains somewhat controversial and indeed there is often little consensus on what Green Revolution actually denotes. The adjective Green implies, at least in our epoch, a sensitivity to SUSTAINABILITY (but ironically the ecological costs of the HYVs has been a purported major failing) and implicitly is opposed to Red in a way in which technical achievements – a technical fix – could banish not simply hunger but also political unrest. In order to understand the origins and genesis of the 'heroic age' (Jirstrom, 1996, p. 15) of the Green Revolution between 1963 and 1970, the miracle seeds must be located on the earlier landscape of the Cold War which embraces American imperialism in Vietnam, a Malthusian view of food shortages in the post-1945 period and the recognition that the Green Revolution was wrapped up with US foreign policy (cf. MALTHUSIAN MODEL).

The meaning of Green Revolution remains a contested issue. The heart of the revolutionary thrust was quite simple: seeds plus nitrogen plus water produced increase yields per unit area. As a consequence there is a narrow and a broad interpretation of the technologies themselves:

> In the narrow sense it consists primarily in the adoption of the new high-yielding varieties of wheat and rice and associated technologies. In the broad sense it includes not only this but all other economic changes as well as the social and cultural changes that either contributed to the technological and ecological changes or were derived from them (Leaf, 1984, p. 23).

The Green Revolution as a set of new production practices for the tropical or subtropical PEASANT or smallholder rested on the development of Mendellian genetics, applied plant breeding (led by the UK and the US), the ability to make inexpensive nitrogen fertilizer (the petro-chemical industry), and water development/irrigation technologies. The coordination between the biochemical, the technological and the social components embraced US philanthropic organizations, the US State Department and Third World governments. What began in the 1940s in Mexico under the auspices of the US government and the Rockefeller Foundation focused on improving wheat has grown in half a century to a massive multi-billion dollar network of international agricultural research centres (the Consultative Group of International Agricultural Research, CGIAR) administered by the World Bank and dealing with virtually all the major food complexes. HYVs are now grown worldwide – for example 100 per cent of rice in China and Korea, and 70 per cent in India and Philippines is miracle rice – and there is no question that the ability of food output to exceed population growth in the Third World since 1950 has been a function of the PRODUCTIVITY gains of the Green Revolution (Lipton, 1989). But the Green Revolution, insofar as it is an example of applied plant breeding, has of course a long history – human history is synonymous with successive Green Revolutions associated with the domestication of plants, with the European agrarian revolutions in the eighteenth century, the Chinese improved rice varieties of 1000 AD and so on – and is a process (still on-going) rather than an event (Rigg, 1989).

If the Green Revolution was facilitated by new practices associated with plant breeding, soil fertility science and hydrologic development, the genesis was stimulated by the activities of the Rockefeller Foundation in conjunction with the Office of Special Operations of the US Government in Mexico during the Second World War (Perkins, 1997). Whatever the intentions of the early plant breeders in Mexico, the combination of Malthusian thinking about food CRISES and the Cold War atmosphere favouring national security and the threat of peasant insurgency contributed mightily to the Green Revolution project and its subsequent backing and support by the Ford Foundation, USAID and the major Western donors. In the first phase of the Green Revolution rice and wheat were the primary crops and Mexico and India its crucibles. The International Rice Research Institute (IRRI) was founded near Manila in 1960 and the Center for Maize and Wheat Improvement (CIMMYT) in Mexico in 1963. Today there are 16 international agricultural research centres focusing on potatoes, germ plasm collection, agro-forestry and tropical agriculture.

The research programme for HYVs brought together in university-type settings transnational congeries of scientists which constituted sophisticated breeding programs. IRRI, for example, built upon rice breeding expertise and dwarf varieties from Taiwan and Japan to produce through hybridization new dwarf HYVs which were resistant to lodging, sensitive to nitrogen fertilizers and which could be double or triple cropped through a reduction in the growing period. Its first success – IR-8 – was released in 1966 and spread rapidly through south and South-East Asia. The DIFFUSION of the seeds and mechanical packages (pumpsets, small tractors) involved a strong STATE intervention typically involving new subsidies, credit, extension services, irrigation development and national breeding programmes. By the mid-1980s more than half of the total rice area of the Third World was planted in HYVs (Lipton, 1989).

There has been considerable disagreement over the productivity increases attributable to HYVs. In one of the best-known and earliest reviews by UNRISD/UNDP, Griffin (1974) painted a bleak picture of the effects of HYVs between 1970 and 1974, arguing that there had been no Green Revolution in rice. A subsequent assessment by Michael Lipton (1989) in the mid-1980s showed that the output increases in wheat and maize were indeed dramatic (at least 4 per cent per year) and that those in rice were slower but no less substantial overall. Lipton pointed however to regional dilemmas – Africa was neglected on balance – and the problems of equity within countries which reflected disparities in irrigation development and water control investment. In the first phase of the Green Revolution a number of important problems emerged: first, increasing pest and weed problems; second, problems of storage and processing; and third, ecological deterioration (especially loss of germ plasm, water depletion and toxicity). All of these direct and indirect consequences initiated a still on-going debate over the consequences of HYVs (see Shiva, 1991, 1996).

At the heart of the impact question are EQUITY, POVERTY and JUSTICE. In the early years, the adoption of HYV packages (and the recognition that the packages were not scale neutral) prompted much speculation about new forms of social differentiation among peasantries, of class conflict between adopters and non-adopters, of deteriorating labour conditions as HYVs were labour-displacing rather than labour-saving: of the 'green revolution turning red'. As the Indian case shows, there was in fact no simple polarization of landholding though there has been the consolidation of a class of increasingly commercialized and organized rich peasants who benefited from the Green Revolution (these are the heart of the New Farmers Movements in India which have changed the face of local and national politics: see SOCIAL MOVEMENTS). The impact on labour markets (new forms of MIGRATION, changing forms of labour permanency and tenancy), on landholding (cf. LAND TENURE), and on social inequality is enormously complex in part because of the linkages between on-farm PRODUCTIVITY increases and off-farm employment (Hazell, 1987). On balance the mechanization which has followed the HYV adoption has been labour-displacing and favoured those with concentrated capital ownership. New forms of inequality have emerged but this is often attributed by the proponents of the HYVs to population growth and state rent seeking rather than technology *per se*. The debate continues.

The Green Revolution has unquestionably increased food output per capita but this has not necessarily increased food availability for the poor (Sen and Dreze, 1989), and neither has it improved the lot of the poor (Lipton, 1989). The first issue turns less on output than on availability and entitlements – in short, the social component of the Green Revolution (including land reform). The second speaks to the problems of both the uneven adoption of HYVs and the biases built into the breeding programmes themselves. The miracle seeds are often not pro-poor and do not speak to circumstances of the land-poor and landless.

There is a debate over whether the Green Revolution has ended in the sense that there are no new seed breakthroughs likely in the world STAPLE crops. The pessimists foresee a Malthusian nightmare of famine and pestilence compounded by the growth of Chinese food imports. Nonetheless the Green Revolution has entered a second phase associated with the breakthroughs of molecular science and recombinant DNA. Here the issue is increasingly the power of large TRANSNATIONAL seed and pharmaceutical companies who develop new crops with built-in requirements for particular inputs, and the intellectual property rights which attend the concentration of power in agribusiness companies (Shiva, 1996). The current debates over farmer breeding rights, over genetically modified crops, and intellectual property rights suggests that the next Green Revolution will be as fraught as the first. MW

References

Griffin, K. 1974: *The political economy of agrarian change*. London: Macmillan. · Grigg, D.B. 1989: *The world food problem*. Cambridge: Cambridge University Press. · Hazell, P., ed., 1987: *The Green Revolution reconsidered*. Baltimore: Johns Hopkins University Press. · Jirstrom, M. 1996: *In the wake of the Green Revolution*. Lund: Lund University Press. · Leaf, M. 1984: *Song of hope*. New Brunswick: Rutgers University Press. · Lipton, M. 1989: *New seeds and poor people*. London: Macmillan. · Perkins, J. 1997: *Geopolitics and the Green Revolution*. Oxford: Oxford University Press. · Rigg, B. 1989: *The green revolution*. Cambridge: Cambridge University Press. · Sen, A. and Dreze, J. 1989: *Hunger and public action*. Oxford: Oxford University Press. · Shiva, V. 1991: *The violence of the Green Revolution*. London: Zed Books. · Shiva, V. 1996: *Biopiracy*. London: Zed Books.

Suggested Reading

Bayliss-Smith, T. and Wanmali, S., eds, 1984: *Understanding Green Revolutions*. Cambridge: Cambridge University Press.

gross domestic product (GDP) A monetary measure of the value at market prices of goods and services produced within a (national) economy over a given period of time, normally a year or a quarter. The value of intermediate products – most notably raw materials – is excluded and incorporated in the market price of goods for final consumption or investment. No allowance is made for expenditure on the replacement of capital assets and the use of market prices incorporates the value of indirect taxes and subsidies. The subtraction of indirect taxes and the addition of subsidies produces GDP at factor cost. GDP may be valued at current prices or in real terms.

GDP provides a better guide to domestic production than GROSS NATIONAL PRODUCT (GNP) and tends to be favoured as a measure of performance by industrial economies because it excludes net income from abroad. In most countries (e.g. USA, UK, Japan), this adjustment makes little difference. But in countries like Kuwait, with large overseas investments, GNP is about 35 per cent greater than GDP, whereas in the Republic of Ireland and Brazil, for example, GNP is about 14 per cent less than GDP.

Like GNP, GDP is seriously deficient as a measure of economic activity and this is true even on its own terms as a numerical measure of the value of output and hence of income. Most seriously, it omits from valuation whole areas of work undertaken in the non-monetary part of the economy (e.g. Waring, 1989; Murgatroyd and Neuberger, 1997) whilst perversely counting as wealth creation what destroys the natural foundations of all productive activity (see, e.g. Anderson, 1991) as well as activities coping with the range of social pathologies treated in contemporary society. Not only that but the measure assumes that quantitative increases imply progress and yet, intuitively, there is a widespread sense that things are in many ways getting worse rather than better. Thus incomes are polarized, people in work are working longer hours (in Britain and the USA especially), unemployment is at historically high levels, the range of work- and stress-related illnesses is increasing, and congestion and pollution are now reaching levels at which serious attention is being given by policy-makers to ways of reducing them at a range of geographical scales from the local to the global.

One problem for such interventions is a lack of adequate data to measure the wider social and economic consequences of quantitative economic growth. Although a CHAOTIC CONCEPTION in measuring 'goods' as well as 'bads', GDP is unambiguous in what it includes and how it values the data included in its calculation. By contrast, alternative measures create problems both of inclusion and valuation. At the global level, the UNDP (annual) *Human development report* incorporates measures of life expectancy, literacy and educational enrolment ratios, for example, and a number of alternative national measures of welfare have been created in the US and the UK. At the local level, communities are creating local measures of QUALITY OF LIFE relevant to their LOCALITIES – so making the point that universal measures like GDP are inadequate as they are disembedded from the geographies in which they may take on meaning.

One of the most systematic attempts to create a more inclusive measure of the state of well-being is the *Index of Sustainable Welfare* (ISEW; New Economics Foundation, 1998). This measure is based on personal consumption but adds to that measures of the value of domestic production, certain forms of public expenditure (such as on education and health) and subtracts from it measures of inequality, private expenditure on health and education, the costs of COMMUTING, measures of POLLUTION and destruction of natural habitats and natural resources and costs of large-scale environmental changes such as those associated with ozone depletion and climatic change. Within the UK the index grew steadily – although not as rapidly as the growth of GDP – from the 1950s to the mid-1970s. Since then it has fallen – so diverging from trends in GDP themselves rather less secure in the consistency of their upward trajectory. Between 1976 and 1996 per capita GDP grew by 44 per cent whereas the ISEW fell, at an accelerating rate, by 25 per cent.

If what GDP measures and the meaning of changes over time are highly problematic, so too is the question of international comparisons. It is very difficult to use GDP to make such comparisons of the value of income or production as fluctuations in exchange rates, determined by the demand for and supply of currency in foreign exchange markets related to a range of processes including balance of payments disequilibria, capital transactions and government policy, are major distortions. One way around such problems (used by the UNDP in its *Human Development Index*, for example) is to modify the GDP measure by using Purchasing Power Parities (PPPs). PPPs adjust GDP by the cost of a given 'basket' of goods and services. Even so, there are problems, not least because of the difficulty in choosing a range of commodities for the 'basket' adequately to reflect the geographically varied nature of SOCIAL REPRODUCTION in different societies and economies around the world and because many goods and especially services do not enter into international TRADE and so do not affect the determination of exchange rates.

Although there are serious problems of data and valuation in the construction of such alternative indices, the problem of reform is less that of data than of DISCOURSE and POWER (see VALUES). As long as GDP (and GNP) are seen as indicators of economic POWER and prestige – especially at the national level – and, as long as the metric of the values flowing around circuits of social reproduction is shaped by a purely economic – and especially capitalist – discourse, other more inclusive and less chaotic indicators must remain, by discursive definition, inferior. RL

References

Anderson, V. 1991: *Alternative economic indicators*. London and New York: Routledge. · Murgatroyd, L. and Neuberger, H. 1997: A household satellite account for the UK. *Economic Trends* 527, October: 63–71. · New Economics Foundation, 1998: *Sustainable economic welfare in the UK*. London: New Economics Foundation; UNDP (United Nations Development Programme) annual: *Human development report*. New York: Oxford University Press. · Waring, M. 1989: *If women counted: a new feminist economics*. London: Macmillan.

gross national product (GNP) This comprises GROSS DOMESTIC PRODUCT (GDP) plus net income from abroad (i.e. GNP equals GDP plus profits, dividends and income earned overseas minus such overseas payments). GNP at factor cost is the market value of GNP net of indirect taxes and subsidies. Although many industrial economies favour GDP as a measure of domestic economic performance, Germany and Japan currently use GNP. International comparisons of GNP avoiding exchange rate fluctuations may be facilitated by the use of purchasing power parities (a measure of the quantity of a 'basket' of goods that nominal GNP will buy in each country) in converting currencies to a common base.

GNP is seriously deficient as a measure of economic activity (see GDP for discussion) as it omits major productive contributions to SOCIAL REPRODUCTION (Murgatroyd and Neuberger, 1997), fails to include the social and environmental consequences of growth as well as including measures which are subtractions from rather than additions to social welfare (e.g. the costs of prisons, defence and the treatment of preventable disease) and is subject to severe foreign exchange distortions in international comparisons (see UNDP annual).

Of course, there are MORAL GEOGRAPHIES here constructed around what might be defined as 'goods' and 'bads' in society (a conflict illustrated most readily by the debate over moves towards banning smoking in public places) but the prevailing discourse represented through GNP is that of the overwhelming salience of quantitative economic values in measuring the level, quality and sustainability of social reproduction. RL

References

Murgatroyd, L. and Neuberger, H. 1997: A household satellite account for the UK. *Economic Trends* 527, October: 63–71. · UNDP (United Nations Development Programme) annual: *Human development report*. New York: Oxford University Press.

growth coalitions Simply put, these are groups of individuals and/or organizations that encourage, enable, or maintain local economic DEVELOPMENT. Growth coalitions are frequently called *regimes*, which more generally refers to public–private partnerships between state and market sectors. Given this rather open definition, the nature of economic development (and thus the issues it invokes) can be highly variable from place to place, or over time within a place. Membership in a coalition can also vary by degree, but will likely include: politicians, STATE bureaucrats, local media, utilities, universities, the arts, professional sports, organized labour, small retailers, and local capitalists (Logan and Molotch, 1987). Consequently, the consensus within, and stability of any growth coalition is also an open question. Bargaining, negotiation, brokerage, and compromise therefore are stressed in the literature. Likewise, the success of growth coalitions or the projects they support are by no means given, thus an ongoing, multifaceted interrogation of who wins and who loses is always necessary.

Interest in growth coalitions grew through the 1980s and continues presently, having both empirical and theoretical motivations. Empirically, the retrenchment of the WELFARE STATE and the heightened GLOBALIZATION of capital mobility has meant that the *relative* weight of COLLECTIVE CONSUMPTION issues in city politics has declined relative to a more entrepreneurial, development-oriented agenda. Indeed, Cox (1993) has termed development issues as 'the new urban politics'.

Theoretically, REGIME THEORY has arguably provided more sophisticated understandings of local POWER than previous theories obtained, and enables exploration of not only political actors, but also broader structural issues when explaining local growth politics. Questions about the relative mobility *and* fixity of capital in LOCALES have been raised, for example. Likewise more sophisticated understandings of spatial SCALE have been suggested by Jonas (1994). Towards these aims Lauria's (1997) collection situates regime studies in a REGULATION SCHOOL. A rather different take has come from FEMINIST GEOGRAPHY, which has taken this literature to task for reductionist conceptualizations of public and private spheres in local politics (Staeheli and Clarke, 1995). (See also REGIONAL ALLIANCE.) MPB

References

Cox, K.R. 1993: The local and the global in the new urban politics. *Environmental and Planning D: Society and Space* 11: 433–48. · Jonas, A. 1994: The scale politics of spatiality. *Environmental and Planning D: Society and Space* 12: 257–64. · Lauria, M., ed., 1997: *Reconstruction urban regime theory*. Beverly Hills: Sage. · Logan, J. and Molotch, H. 1987: *Urban fortunes*. Berkeley: University of California Press. · Staeheli, L. and Clarke, S. 1995: Gender, place, and citizenship. In J. Garber and R. Turner, eds, *Gender in urban research*. Beverly Hills: Sage, 3–23.

growth pole A dynamic and highly integrated set of industries organized around a propulsive leading sector or industry ('industrie motrice'). A growth pole is capable of rapid growth and of generating growth through spillover and multiplier effects in the rest of the economy (see MULTIPLIERS).

The growth pole concept, associated with François Perroux (1955), was translated into spatial terms by J.R. Boudeville (1966). On the bases of EXTERNAL ECONOMIES and economies of AGGLOMERATION, Boudeville argued that the set of industries forming the growth pole (or 'pole de croissance') might be clustered spatially and linked to an existing urban area. He also pointed to the regionally differentiated growth that such a spatial strategy might generate. The precise meaning of the term 'growth pole' is difficult to pin down, however, because it is frequently used in a far looser fashion to denote any (planned) spatial clustering of economic activity.

The apparent simplicity of the notion, its suggestion of dynamism and its ability to wed problems of sectorial growth and planning with those of intra- and interregional growth and physical planning led to its ready acceptance and widespread use in URBAN, regional (see REGION) and national planning. However there are several difficulties associated with both the idea and practice of growth poles which fall into three broad groups.

First, there are a number of *technical problems* including: (a) the interdependent decisions to be made on an appropriate location, threshold size and sectorial composition of a growth pole within an urban or regional network of firms. This was not a serious problem for Perroux who defined growth poles around the existence of a single propulsive industry – a dangerous strategy in the longer term – whilst literature based around the idea of INDUSTRIAL DISTRICTS identifies networks of linked industries as central to urban and regional development; (b) the distinction between spontaneous and planned poles with the need, in the latter case at least, for integrated social and physical planning; (c) the nature of the intersectorial and interregional transmission of growth; (d) the facilitative relationship between state-provided services and INFRASTRUCTURE and the success of the growth pole; (e) the relationships between the pole and the existing, unevenly developed, city distributions; and (f) the need for monitoring and management to avoid dis-economies.

Secondly, *the appropriate time span over which to judge success or failure* – say, 15–25 years – may be too long in political terms, as elected governments will wish positive results of policy to be clear over the length of the electoral cycle (which is usually less than four years).

Thirdly, *the success of a growth pole must depend upon the extent to which it conforms to the productive and reproductive demands of the society in which it is located.* The process of production both helps to create and necessarily takes place in an existing LANDSCAPE. As production itself changes, it makes fresh demands upon the landscape – demands which may not be met within its existing dimensions. As a result the landscape must be changed. A growth pole is a planned insertion into this constantly changing landscape. It must, therefore, combine with what is already there in both physical and functional terms as well as provide an appropriate location for the extension or reorganization of production.

In short, growth poles – like any other planned spatial strategy for production – can never be autonomous of the underlying productive dynamic. As a result they may also generate problems relating to UNEVEN DEVELOPMENT. Growth poles provide a particularly clear and direct example of the implication of the STATE in the structure and dynamic of the wider society of which it is an inseparable part.

RL

References

Boudeville, J.R. 1966: *Problems of regional economic planning.* Edinburgh: Edinburgh University Press. · Perroux, F. 1955: Note sur la notion de pôle de croissance. *Économie Appliquée* 7: 307–20.

Suggested Reading

Buttler, F.A. 1975: *Growth pole theory and economic development.* Farnborough/Lexington, MA: Saxon House/Lexington Press. · Dicken, P. and Lloyd, P.E. 1990: *Location in space: theoretical perspectives in economic geography.* New York and London: Harper and Row, ch. 6.

growth theory In the wake of the Second World War, and after the experience of the Marshall Plan in assisting the recovery of war-torn Europe, several economists with direct experience in multilateral institutions and the Marshall Plan turned their attention to the question of economic DEVELOPMENT in the THIRD WORLD. Among these pioneers of development thinking were Finnish economist Ragnar Nurkse, Austrian economist Paul Rodentstein-Rodan, German-born and American-naturalized economist Albert Hirschmann, West Indian Nobel Laureate Sir Arthur Lewis, and American economic historian Walt Rostow. Their ideas were far from identical but they formed a loose school of thought – growth theorists – emphasizing a historically informed and practical approach to economic development, and stood at an angle to the neo-classical models of Solow and others. Rostow was something of an odd man out insofar as his simple stage theory of European industrial replication was both less analytical and less historically sophisticated than the others (cf. ROSTOW MODEL).

The growth theorists were framed by three historical dynamics: *the legacy of the Keynesian revolution* and the experience of international Keynesianism through the European recovery programme; the *political agenda of the USA* in the wake of 1945 and increasingly during the Cold War which turned on the use of Bretton Woods institutions to foster development and fair dealing as President Truman put it in 1949; and the *nationalist developmentalism* (cf. NATIONALISM) associated with the last wave of DECOLONIZATION which also emerged during and after the Second World War. Growth theory in its emphasis on aggregate phenomena and on industrialization bred a predilection for authoritative intervention – in which the STATE was a necessary actor – which involved planning systems, the application of economic growth models and AID mechanisms.

All of the growth theorists shared some sort of affinity for Keynes. They emphasized aggregate economic processes such as rates of saving and rates of investment (cf. NEO-CLASSICAL ECONOMICS). Poor economic performance and lack of aggregate demand were related. They also revealed a preference for INDUSTRIALIZATION as a driving force – indeed they were advocates of what in the 1930s had become import-substituting industrialization – and for short-term state intervention. Markets were means not ends, and like Alexander Gerschenkron (1968 – one of their contemporaries), they realized that late developers required a dirigiste state. However, as growth theorists they presumed that an economy would achieve its best results within a competitive market structure.

Each of the growth theorists is a major intellectual figure in the history of economics but there were important commonalties and points of confluence (if not necessarily agreement) which animated their policy and theory during the 1950s.

There was the concept of *hidden developmental potential* in the less developed nations. As Gerschenkron had argued, there were 'advantages to backwardness', and in these advantages lay hidden COMPARATIVE ADVANTAGES:

- a recognition of *market failures* and the role of positive EXTERNALITIES in creating virtuous circle effects. Rodenstein-Rodan's emphasis on social overhead capital and the role of government was a case in point;
- the *differences and merits of balanced and unbalanced growth* and how each was related to the necessity for a 'big push' to trigger economic growth. Nurkse, like Rodan, emphasized the need for a coordinated increase in the amount of capital utilized in a wide range of industries if industrialization was to be achieved. Hirschmann, while agreeing with Nurkse and others, also argued that unbalanced growth could, through linkage effects, generate innovations created by market responses to shortage and surplus;
- the potential, as Lewis indicated, for *surplus labour as a stimulant to growth* in so-called DUAL ECONOMIES; and
- the *significance of saving* at particular historical moments in order to enter what Rostow called the 'take-off stage' of industrialization.

Growth theory, from the vantage of the NEO-LIBERAL revolution of the 1980s, appears as an instance of Keynesian internationalism in which market failures, planning, social capital, and some aspects of classical POLITICAL ECONOMY (CLASS) are put to the service of 'developing' the poorer nations of the world. All of these growth theorists identified key developmental issues – equilibrium, social overhead capital, planning – which have continued to be objects of debate, and each (perhaps with the exception of Rostow) contributed to both the building of post-war multilateral development institutions and to the idea, which in a way was crushed by the weight of the Cold War, of a sort of liberal developmental internationalism.

MW

References

Gerschenkron, A. 1968: *Continuity in history*. Cambridge, MA: Harvard University Press. · Hirschmann, A. 1958: *The strategy of economic development*. New Haven: Yale University Press. · Lewis, A. 1984: Development economics in the 1950s. In G. Meier and D. Seers, eds, *Pioneers in development*. Oxford: Oxford University Press. · Nurkse, R. 1953: *Problems of capital formation in underdeveloped countries*. New York: Oxford University Press. · Rodenstein-Rodan, P. 1976: The theory of the big push. In G. Meier and D. Seers, eds, *Pioneers in development*. Oxford: Oxford University Press. · Rostow, W. 1960: *Stages of economic growth*. Cambridge: Cambridge University Press.

Suggested Reading

Cypher, J. and Dietz, J. 1997: *The process of economic development*. London: Routledge. · Preston, P. 1996: *Development theory*. Oxford: Blackwell.

H

habitus The human capacity for structured improvisation. 'Habitus' is a term borrowed from classical scholarship by the French sociologist Pierre Bourdieu, as a means of overcoming the opposition between THEORIES that take practice to be solely constituting, as found in individualist approaches like PHENOMENOLOGY, and theories that take practice to be solely constituted, as in most forms of STRUCTURALISM.

For Bourdieu, social life is best understood as the mutual interaction between structures (or what Bourdieu calls social fields), dispositions or orientations to action, and actions themselves. As a term, habitus is present in each of these moments (though it is concentrated in the middle one) since it is the means by which structure is played out as it is captured in particular orientations to action and, at the same time, it is also the capacity for improvisation in actions which, though they will always be structured, are not reducible to structures. Habitus, then, consists of a set of 'general generative schemas' which are durable and transposable (that is, able to be used in a variety of structures) but also allow some free play. That these schemes are able to be both structuring and improvisatory is due, in large part, to the capacities of the BODY, a body that 'believes in what it plays at: it weeps if it mimes grief. It does not represent what it performs, it does not memorise the past, it enacts the past, bringing it back to life' (Bourdieu, 1991, p. 23).

In using the notion of habitus, Bourdieu is often criticized for being a closet STRUCTURALIST, even a neo-Marxist (Alexander, 1995). But though this criticism is clearly unfair, it is true to say that Bourdieu sometimes allows the reader to form this impression because in both his theoretical and empirical work he pays relatively little attention to improvisation (see PERFORMANCE; PERFORMATIVITY).

In human geography, Bourdieu's notion of habitus has been used in three chief ways. In the early 1980s it was an important piece of ammunition in the debate over structure and agency since it seemed to form a bridge between the two poles. In the late 1980s and early 1990s geographers tended to call on Bourdieu to sustain work on CLASS and CONSUMPTION: his book *Distinction* (Bourdieu, 1984) seemed to provide an important key, through concepts like habitus, to a number of issues concerning choice and constraint. Then, in the late 1990s, Bourdieu's emphasis on the body as the crucial element of the habitus has chimed with geographers' attempts to trace out the significance of embodied knowledge. NJT

References

Alexander, J. 1995: *Fin-de-siècle social theory*. London: Verso. · Bourdieu, P. 1984: *Distinction*. London: Routledge and Kegan Paul. · Bourdieu, P. 1990: *The logic of practice*. Cambridge: Polity Press. · Bourdieu, P. 1991: *Language and symbolic power*. Cambridge: Polity Press. · Calhoun, C., Lipuma, E. and Postone, M., eds, 1993: *Bourdieu: critical perspectives*. Cambridge: Polity Press. · Fowler, B. 1997: *Pierre Bourdieu and cultural theory*. London: Sage. · Swartz, D. 1997: *Culture and power. The sociology of Pierre Bourdieu*. Chicago: University of Chicago Press.

Suggested Reading

Bourdieu, P. and Wacquant, L. 1992: *An invitation to reflexive sociology*. Chicago: University of Chicago Press.

hazard, human-made Human-made (or anthropogenic) hazards are products, processes and other conditions that potentially directly threaten individuals and/or their reproduction (in all senses). These hazards are somewhat distinguishable from ENVIRONMENTAL HAZARDS by the direct level of human involvement in their causation. For example, a volcanic eruption is an environmental or natural hazard, whereas radioactive wastes and insecticides such as DDT (see POLLUTION) are human-made hazards. However, the dualism between 'natural' and 'human-made' hazards is built upon a separation of 'humans' and 'NATURE'. This division has collapsed as we understand that humans are part of nature, and have been so for thousands of years (see Willems-Braun, 1997). While it is possible sometimes to distinguish between natural and human-made direct causes of events, the transformation of a natural event into a hazard involves social processes that have left some people vulnerable to the effects of a natural event. This may be due to their initial physical location, lack of viable options for escape, or human activities that exacerbate events with natural causes, e.g. deforestation that leads to increased flooding after heavy rainfall. Human-made hazards relate also to the siting of facilities, the transport of materials and products, the methods of production processes used, and the disposal of products and wastes (cf. ENVIRONMENTAL JUSTICE).

The concept of RISK is very important in understanding vulnerability to both human-made and environmental hazards. *Risk profiling* often identifies discrepancies between people's perceptions of risk of personal harm caused by a particular event, and the statistical probability that such an event will harm them. The statistical evidence is based on the frequency and damage caused by previous events of a similar character and often assists in the development of plans and policies to reduce the initial risk, or managing events if they do occur. However, the notion of risk tends to individualize disaster. It may provide quantitative justification for not addressing particular issues, especially when the most vulnerable people are grouped in a homogenous population so their vulnerability is masked in the statistic. The perception of risk is influenced by personal histories and psychological dispositions, local histories, media reporting of events, experts, institutions, availability of information and other factors which interact to influence people's perceptions and actions in ways that may vary greatly from statistical risk, and may contribute to either increasing or reducing the probability of personal harm.

Research on human-made hazards and risk (e.g. Schrader-Frechette, 1991) often includes nuclear power, toxic substances and biotechnology. Beck (1992) argues that in previous centuries hazards were caused by an undersupply of hygienic technology; now their basis is in industrial overproduction. He defines risk as 'a systematic way of dealing with hazards and insecurities induced and introduced by modernization itself' (Beck, 1992, p. 21). Unlike the often personal hazards of previous eras, contemporary human-made hazards (e.g. human-induced climate change) are often global in threat (cf. GLOBAL WARMING). PM

References

Beck, U. 1992: *Risk society: towards a new modernity*. London: Sage. · Brown, M. 1995: Ironies of distance: an ongoing critique of the gographies of AIDS. *Environment and Planning : Society and Space* 13: 159–83. · Schrader-Frechette, K. 1991: *Risk and rationality: philosophical foundations for popularist reforms*. Berkeley: University of California Press. · Willems-Braun, B. 1997: Buried epistemologies: the politics of nature in (post)-colonial British Columbia. *Annals of the Association of American Geographers* 87 (1) 3–31.

health and health care, geography of A sub-discipline focused on the dynamic, and recursive, relationship between health, health services, and PLACE, and on the impact of both health services and the health of population groups on the vitality of places. In brief, geographies of health and health care must go beyond description and cartography to construct accounts of why place matters to health and health care.

This focus is of a relatively recent origin (e.g. Kearns, 1993) and its development reflects a critique of the extent to which conventional medical geography adopted a biomedical model of disease. Critics argue that a socio-ecological model is needed to replace biomedicine. From such a perspective, analysis focuses on an interactive set of relationships between a population and its social, cultural and physical environment. This contrasts with the linear and unidirectional relationships implied by a biomedical model, with its emphasis on the monocausal origins of disease. Geographies of health thus (implicitly at least) take as their point of departure the World Health Organization's (WHO) emphasis on health as a 'state of complete physical, mental and social well-being, and not merely the absence of disease or infirmity'.

This move away from medical geography has had important analytical consequences for geographies of both health and health care. Crucially, there has been recognition of the importance of supplementing EXTENSIVE, quantitative methods with INTENSIVE, qualitative investigations. The former are methodologically limited, it is suggested, because they cannot distinguish CONTEXTUAL EFFECTS (the difference a place makes) from COMPOSITIONAL effects (what is in a place). Successful accounts of relationships between place and health therefore need to blend extensive and intensive approaches. Secondly, there is a new sensitivity to the BODY. Medical geography's understandings of health and illness have been restricted by defining bodies as sites 'invaded by a disease with a specific aetiology' (Dorn and Laws, 1994). By contrast, recent work suggests that the body is a social construct. Given this view of health and well-being, the deviant body is no longer the product of medical diagnoses, nor does it necessarily require medical intervention (Dyck, 1995). Recent work on DISABILITY exemplifies this. Golledge (1996) argues for the application of traditional geographic skills to enable those with disabilities to navigate their environments safely and overcome physical constraints. Critics of this position suggest that it links the negative experiences of disabled people to individual impairment, rather than resulting from forms of social and political discrimination (Imrie, 1996); however, Golledge suggests that this is a utopian position which will yield little practical improvement in the lives of the disabled.

A third implication for geographies of health is a rather different conception of the subject. In biomedical models, people are simply seen as patients or as hosts to a disease. By contrast geographies of health and health care seek to foreground individuals' subjective experiences, using participatory methods to engage respondents in the process of research (Kearns, 1994); showing how they contest and renegotiate socio-spatial constraints on their daily lives (Dorn and Laws, 1994). This offers scope to redeem medical geography from its genderless and colour-blind past (Mohan, 1989; Matthews, 1993). Studies have shown how social constraints, imposed by GENDER roles, are far more restrictive than spatial constraints, in terms of permitting women to access services. Likewise, lay perceptions of health and illness, and of what enables or constraints healthy lifestyles, should be given more prominence; such beliefs and attitudes are rooted in the characteristics of particular places (a pioneering study was Cornwell, 1984). Such issues have come to the fore in analyses of perceptions of the extent to which ENVIRONMENTAL HAZARDS pose challenges to health, and in work which examines the political construction of healthy and unhealthy environments.

There are also signs of an emerging concern with a wider range of health services. When studied by geographers health care has often been taken to mean either primary care services (to a large degree, the location of general practitioners or family doctors) or hospital care. There have been studies of trends in the spatial organization of health care under a range of social systems and in recent years attention has been devoted to evaluating the geographical consequences of various health service reforms, for example in the former Soviet Union (Curtis and Taket, 1995). But there is recognition of the multifaceted nature of services and of the ways individuals and COMMUNITIES can draw upon a range of services, both formal and informal (Pinch, 1997). As a result, and in the spirit of what social-policy commentators characterize as welfare pluralism, there are increasing numbers of studies of informal and community-based sources of care, and of the interactions between the formal health-care system and alternative therapies. In addition, the role of self-help groups and of initiatives in the voluntary sector is receiving attention (e.g. Brown, 1995).

In this reformed geography of health and health care, there are signs of renewed sensitivity to place. There is acknowledgement, for example, of the therapeutic character of certain places (Gesler, 1992) in contrast to the socially dysfunctional characteristics of others (Wallace, 1990). The extent or otherwise of SOCIAL CAPITAL – dense, informal networks of participation and sociability – can make a significant difference to the extent of social inequalities in health status (Wilkinson, 1996; Gatrell, 1997). There are also accounts of geographies of welfare services which demonstrate the significance of place to collective mobilization to defend or extend health-care facilities. These are showing how SOCIAL MOVEMENTS develop around health-care issues and how these contribute to a wider sense of participatory DEMOCRACY and social cohesion (e.g. Scarpaci, 1991): by raising political consciousness and building new forms of oppositional political movements. Health care is a vehicle for more wider-ranging political change. A third strand of thinking has sought to comprehend the importance of spatial arrangements of services in shaping social life. Often inspired by Foucault, this work looks at the ways individual geographies are shaped by institutions, drawing on disciplinary categorizations and constructions of individuals as unhealthy, mad or dangerous, and therefore requiring confinement. Much of this work is historical, showing how institutional arrangements reflected hegemonic (see HEGEMONY) (or sometimes competing) DISCOURSES – for example, the debate over 'sterilization versus segregation' in the treatment of the mentally handicapped, with consequences for the spatial arrangement and location (as well as internal geography) of institutions (Radford, 1991). One could extend this to the socio-spatial elements of the provision of facilities for the mentally ill in contemporary societies (e.g. Dear and Taylor, 1982; Philo, 1997).

A final implication of all this is whether there is scope for a sub-discipline concerned with geographies of health and health care. The WHO emphasizes the social and political determinants of health and illness, suggesting that progress towards the laudable aim of universal good health is unlikely to be attained short of political or social change. For this reason some have suggested that geographies of health and health care should be subsumed within the broader field of SOCIAL GEOGRAPHY, drawing the wrath of those who still insist that MEDICAL GEOGRAPHY plays a potentially crucial role in integrating many of the intellectual concerns of human geography (see the exchange between Kearns, 1993, 1994 and Mayer and Meade, 1994). JM

References

Brown, M. 1995: Ironies of distance: an ongoing critique of the geographies of AIDS. *Environment and Planning : Society and Space* 13: 159–83. · Cornwell, J. 1984: *Hard-earned lives: accounts of health and illness from East London*. London: Tavistock. · Curtis, S. and Taket, A. 1995: *Changing perspectives on health and society*. London: Arnold. · Dear, M. and Taylor, S.M. 1982: *Not on our street*. London: Pion. · Dorn, M. and Laws, G. 1994: Social theory, body politics and medical geography. *Professional Geographer* 46: 106–10. · Dyck, I. 1995: Hidden geographies: the changing lifeworlds of women with multiple sclerosis. *Social Science and Medicine*, 40: 307–32. · Gatrell, A. 1997: Structures of geographical and social space and their consequences for human health. *Geografiska Annaler* 79B: 141–54. · Gesler, W. 1992: Therapeutic landscapes: medical issues in light of the new cultural geography. *Social Science and Medicine*, 34: 735–46. · Golledge, R.G. 1996: Geography and the disabled: a response to Imrie and Gleeson. *Transactions, Institute of British Geographers* NS 21: 404–11. · Imrie, R. 1996: Ableist geographers, disablist spaces. *Transactions, Institute of British Geographers* NS 21: 397–403. · Kearns, R. 1993: Place and health: towards a reformed medical geography. *Professional Geographer* 45: 139–47. · Kearns, R. 1994: Putting health into place: an invitation accepted and declined. *Professional Geographer* 46: 111–15. · Matthews, S. 1993: Curriculum redevelopment: medical geography and women's health. *Journal of Geography in Higher Education* 17: 91–102. · Mayer, J. and Meade, M. 1994: A reformed medical geography reconsidered, *Professional Geographer* 46: 103–6. · Mohan, J.F. 1989: Medical geography: competing diagnoses and prescriptions. *Antipode* 20: 166–77. · Philo, C. 1997: Across the water: reviewing geographical studies of asylum and other mental health facilities. *Health and Place* 3: 73–90. · Pinch, S. 1997: *Worlds of welfare*. London: Routledge. · Radford, J. 1991: Sterilisation versus segregation: control of the feeble-minded, 1900–38. *Social Science and Medicine* 33: 49–58. · Scarpaci, J. 1991: Primary care decentralisation in the Southern Cone: Shantytown health care as a social movement. *Annals of the Association of American Geographers* 81: 103–26. · Wallace, R. 1990: Urban desertification, public health and public order. *Social Science and Medicine* 31: 801–13. · Wilkinson, R. 1996: *Unhealthy societies: the afflictions of inequality*. London: Routledge.

heartland A geopolitical concept first coined by the British geographer Sir Halford Mackinder in 1904, and later used in Cold War discourse to denote an area of Eurasia roughly synonymous with the boundaries of the Russian Empire/USSR. Mackinder suggested that the Columbian era of sea power, which had given Europe its pivotal role for the past four centuries, was coming to a close and was being eclipsed by the ascendancy of land-based powers and in particular with a new 'geopolitical pivot of history', namely the 'heartland' of 'Eurasia' (Mackinder, 1904, pp. 430–1). For Mackinder, whichever STATE could gain control of this world island would be in an almost unstoppable position to dominate global affairs. The key control of the heartland, Mackinder later argued, lay in eastern Europe, reflecting powerful strains of pre- and post-Versailles geopolitical thinking concerning the need to separate the two land powers of Russia and Germany through the creation of a series of buffer states. Despite the ENVIRONMENTAL DETERMINISM inherent in much of Mackinder's geopolitical writings, the simplicity of the heartland concept was to play an influential part in western geopolitical thinking concerning the image of an expansionist USSR. The term also continues to be used by practitioners of classical geopolitics (e.g. Brezhinski, 1997), recast and applied to a post-Cold War Eurasia to describe the purported tensions concerning the struggle for HEGEMONY over the post-Soviet heartland. GES

References and Suggested Reading

Brezezinski, Z. 1997: *The grand chessboard: American primacy and its geostrategic imperatives*. New York: HarperCollins. · Hauner, M. 1990: *What is Asia to us? Russia Asian heartland yesterday and today*. London: Unwin Hyman. · Mackinder, H.J. 1904: The geographical pivot of history. *Geographical Journal* 23: 421–37. · Mackinder, H.J. 1919: *Democratic ideals and reality: a study of the politics of reconstruction*. London: Constable.

hegemony The capacity of a dominant group to exercise control, not through visible regulation or the deployment of force, but rather through the willing acquiescence of citizens to accept subordinate status by their acceptance of cultural, social, and political practices and institutions that are unequal and unjust. Current use of the term is derived from the prison writings of Antonio Gramsci (1971), incarcerated by the Italian Fascist state between 1928 and 1935. Like other critical intellectuals, including members of the Frankfurt School, who lived through the rise of totalitarian governments in formerly (if weakly) democratic states, Gramsci reflected on the problem of social order, on how citizens might willingly lend their assent to forms of government that curtailed their freedoms and denied other democratic ideals (cf. DEMOCRACY).

Hegemony incorporates more than the IDEOLOGY of a dominant elite, the VALUES and beliefs which it disseminates. It also includes the sedimentation of these values and interests in everyday practices and institutional arrangements. It is, therefore, 'a lived system of meanings and values – constitutive and constituting – which as they are experienced as practices appear as reciprocally confirming' (Williams, 1977, p. 110). Buried in everyday life, hegemonic processes become TAKEN-FOR-GRANTED and 'natural'. As a result, popular CULTURE plays a significant theoretical and political role in the achievement of hegemony – or, indeed, resistance to it.

Members of the Frankfurt School played a key part in disseminating awareness of the hegemonic properties of post-1945 consumer culture (cf. CONSUMPTION, GEOGRAPHY OF). One of the most powerful challenges was presented by Herbert Marcuse (1964) in his influential unveiling of a one-dimensional society, a critique that was a leading manifesto of the student and counter-cultural movements of the 1960s. Equally significant, initially in France, have been the idiosyncratic works of the *Situationists*, a small avant-garde collective who drew attention to, and constantly sought to destabilize, what they saw as the society of the spectacle (Debord, 1969), a totalizing presence of consumer culture and mass media that led, in Orwellian fashion, to the passivity and entrapment of citizens beneath the seductive spells of consumer gratification. 'The spectacle', wrote Debord (1969, para 21) 'is the nightmare of imprisoned modern society which ultimately expresses nothing more than its desire to sleep. The spectacle is the guardian of sleep'. Despairing of the continuing revolutionary potential of the working class, the Marxian intuition that was one of the formative influences upon the Situationists sought other emancipatory moments in street pantomime and cultural interventions to disorient and thereby awaken a critical awareness in receptive members of society. The task of the Situationists to denaturalize an entrenched cultural hegemony in the society of the spectacle has carried over into recent critical assessments of the cultural project of POSTMODERNITY.

Hegemony has growing salience in POLITICAL GEOGRAPHY and GEOPOLITICS, where it similarly refers to the 'dominant representations and practices' (Agnew, 1998, p. 6) of élites and power blocs who maintain the 'dominant story lines' that help to consolidate existing relations of POWER. Geopolitics can be interpreted as a succession of hegemonies where dominant powers, for example, Britain in the nineteenth century and the United States in the twentieth, define and enforce the prevailing 'rules of the game' (Agnew, 1998, p. 7: also Taylor, 1996). This usage, closely aligned with Gramsci's thinking, is replacing an earlier and much looser deployment of the term that included also more conventional expressions of power that were explicit and coercive.

The concept of hegemony has proven valuable more broadly in cultural studies, and in a new CULTURAL GEOGRAPHY examining the reproduction of domination by élite groups. In an interpretation of North American Chinatowns, Anderson (1988, 1991) has noted how the use of RACE as a dominant colonial discourse impregnated the routine practices of the STATE and reproduced the marginal status of 'the oriental'. 'Chinatown' as a category, rather than as a PLACE, was not innocent in the fabrication of this cultural fiction. Indeed there are many rich applications of the concept of hegemony within the colonial project, where rule, though finally undergirded in the force of the military cantonments, was constituted on a daily basis through a never-ending (and never fully successful) practice of training and persuasion (Myers, 1998; cf. Guha, 1997). In a different context, Duncan (1990) has detailed the contribution of a ritualized palace LANDSCAPE and its supportive meanings to sustain royal power in pre-colonial Kandy, Sri Lanka. Resistance to the centralized and often tyrannical role of the king by an oppositional élite proceeded by denaturalizing his building projects. This deconstruction of the king's landscapes was simultaneously a challenge to the king's power and right to rule.

These examples introduce two additional developments of the concept of hegemony. First, although presented by Gramsci primarily in the context of HISTORICAL MATERIALISM with its characteristic focus on CLASS relations, hegemony is applicable to the interpretation of other sources of domination, such as RACISM, COLONIALISM (as we have seen above) and PATRIARCHY. Indeed, at whatever site a dominant culture emerges, the naturalization and routinization of its values and practices provide the ground for the unequal deployment of power. Second, the penetration of dominant values into the 'whole social process' does not mean that its terms are not negotiated, nor indeed resisted. Beginning with the Frankfurt School's uncompromising depiction of the culture industry, and continuing through

Debord's society of the spectacle to current representations of a single and oppressive postmodern culture, there has often been a tendency to treat hegemonic forces as systemic and total, as a static and paralysing presence, with their effects assumed rather than demonstrated. Such a theorization negates Gramsci's view of cultural hegemony as 'a moving equilibrium', dynamic, evolving, yet oscillating around a consensual form. More empirically accountable studies tend to show that the achievement of hegemony requires sacrifice and compromise, vigilance and hard work by elites (Mitchell, 1996; Myers, 1998). One of the contributions of the Birmingham Centre for Contemporary Cultural Studies has been to document the 'rituals of resistance' of a number of working-class, youth sub-cultures to mainstream norms (Hall and Jefferson, 1976). In these instances, resistance has often been symbolic; that is, the subculture has assumed a style of dress or ornament (a safety pin, for example) intended to subvert the pervasive and accepted forms of the dominant culture (Warren, 1996). The rapid onset and departure of many of these sub-cultures underscores the constantly changing and renegotiated nature of cultural forms. Gramsci noted that such fluidity might also exist within the elite itself, a point well-illustrated in the jockeying for power by competing groups in the Kandyan Kingdom. DL

References

Agnew, J. 1998: *Geopolitics: revisioning world politics.* London: Routledge. · Anderson, K. 1988: Cultural hegemony and the race definition process in Chinatown, Vancouver. *Environment and Planning D: Society and Space* 6: 127–49. · Anderson, K. 1991: *Vancouver's Chinatown: racial discourse in Canada, 1875–1980.* Montreal and Kingston: McGill–Queens Press. · Debord, G. 1970: *Society of the spectacle.* Detroit: Black and Red. · Duncan, J. 1990: *The city as text: the politics of landscape interpretation in the Kandyan Kingdom.* Cambridge: Cambridge University Press. · Gramsci, A. 1971: *Selections from the prison notebooks.* London: Lawrence and Wishart. · Guha, R. 1997: *Dominance without hegemony: history and power in colonial India.* Cambridge, MA: Harvard University Press. · Hall, S. and Jefferson, T., eds, 1976: *Resistance through rituals: youth subcultures in postwar Britain.* London: Hutchinson/Centre for Contemporary Cultural Studies. · Marcuse, H. 1964: *One-dimensional man.* Boston: Beacon Press. · Mitchell, K. 1996: Visions of Vancouver: ideology, democracy, and the future of urban development. *Urban Geography* 17: 478–501. · Myers, G. 1998: Intellectual of empire: Eric Dutton and hegemony in British Africa. *Annals of the Association of American Geographers* 88: 1–27. · Taylor, P.J. 1996: *The way the world works: world hegemony to world impasse.* Chichester: Wiley. · Warren, S. 1996: Popular cultural practices in the 'postmodern city'. *Urban Geography* 17: 545–67. · Williams, R. 1977: Hegemony. In *Marxism and literature.* Oxford: Oxford University Press, 108–14.

Suggested Reading

Anderson (1988). · Lears, T.J. 1985: The concept of cultural hegemony: problems and possibilities. *American Historical Review* 90: 567–93.

hermeneutics The study of interpretation and meaning. Hermeneutics derives from the Greek word *hermēneuein* meaning to announce, to clarify, or to reveal (Thompson, 1996, p. 360). In this sense, hermeneutics has been practised since the first stirrings of LANGUAGE. However, its first stirrings as a formal discipline began with its exegesis of biblical texts. Hermeneutical theological scholars used philological methods to clarify the meaning of God's word. They also adjudicated among competing interpretations, which during the Reformation became particularly important as Protestants challenged Rome over biblical interpretation. With the work of F. Schleiermacher (1768–1834), by the end of the eighteenth century hermeneutics had broadened to include the interpretation of historical texts more generally. By suggesting that the interpretation of a TEXT required scrutiny of the very intentions of its author, advocates of hermeneutics implicitly challenged the relevance of the emerging scientific method for the human sciences.

Wilhelm Dilthey's (1833–1911) writings both generalized hermeneutics, and made its critique of natural science explicit. He argued that the human sciences (*Geisteswissenshaften*), because of their subject matter, required a special methodology, hermeneutics, which was very different from the empirical methodology of the natural sciences (*Naturwissenshaften*). In both cases, though, 'objective' knowledge was obtainable. Specifically, Dilthey argued that meaning is found in all kinds of activities and objects: in written texts, certainly, but also in the non-textual, for example, in works of ART, in tools, and in LANDSCAPES. In all of these cases we find meaning because each is an 'objectification of life', to use Dilthey's phrase. The methodology of natural science denies such meanings, however. It examines each by means of an abstract universal vocabulary: laws of physics, chemical formulae, geometrical relations. But in so doing the very object of study of the human sciences is lost, for it is meanings that must be understood.

But how is meaning to be explicated? The hermeneutical model of interpreting a text provides the key. In trying to understand a text we bring to it a whole set of presuppositions. By tacking back and forth both between our presuppositions and the text itself, as well as between individual parts of the text and its whole, we eventually gain meaning and understanding. Known as the *hermeneutic circle*, this same procedure can be used to clarify meanings within the sphere of the non-textual as well, such as for works of art, for tools, and for landscapes. More generally, the hermeneutic method is a creative, progressive and open-ended process of interpretation, that is circular, indeterminate and perspectival (Bohman, 1993, p. 116). It is *circular* because it involves a constant movement from us, the interpreter, to the interpreted, and back again, thereby also implying that every interpretation is itself interpreted. It is *indeterminate* because that loop of interpretation has no end. And it is *perspectival* because interpreters are embedded in their situations which makes their knowledge always partial and incomplete. That said, Dilthey makes clear that interpretation is never just personal whim and fancy, that is, purely subjective. Rather, our interpretations are always made against a set of socially agreed upon canons and texts (albeit interpreted ones), which are themselves publicly accessible in the case of disputations (Rouse, 1987).

In the twentieth century the German philosopher Martin Heidegger took Dilthey's epistemological rendering of hermeneutics and transformed it into an ontological one, that is, he made the focus 'being' rather than 'knowledge' (see ONTOLOGY). The details are very complex, but the gist is that problems of understanding unfold from our 'being in the world'. Just as the hermeneutic circle for Dilthey involved tacking between parts of a text and its whole, for Heidegger it involves a movement between an anticipatory pre-understanding, which comes from our very 'beingness', and our role as knowing subjects with knowledge about objects in the world.

Later Hans-Georg Gadamer (1975) took Heidegger's notion of pre-understanding and showed its relation to notions of prejudice, authority and tradition. Since the ENLIGHTENMENT, argues Gadamer, there has been prejudice against prejudice. For Gadamer, however, 'pre-judgement', or prejudice, is what makes understanding possible. In particular, the prejudices of historical 'traditions' are vital; without immersion in traditions there can be no understanding. Not that traditions are frozen and immutable. Rather, Gadamer's point is that we can never escape traditions and the historical perspective they bring. Historical understanding proceeds by a movement from our prejudices (traditions) to the historical totality and back again, making understanding 'an open and continuously renewed "fusion" of "historical horizons"' (Thompson, 1996, p. 381; cf. CULTURE).

Gadamer's work, in turn, has been picked up by the neo-PRAGMATIST philosophers, Richard Rorty (1979) and Richard Bernstein (1983). Both argue that Gadamer provides an opening into the 'human conversation' which means being ever receptive to new evidence and ideas even though they may not be commensurate with existing ones. Of course, such openness to challenging the old by the new, the known by the unknown, is only another way to restate the importance of the hermeneutic circle. In addition, it also highlights hermeneutics' critical edge. Implied by hermeneutics' openness is a critique of the closed nature of GRAND THEORY and other forms of FOUNDATIONALISM. Here we can also see an affinity between hermeneutics and POST-STRUCTURALISM, for both are engaged in an anti-foundationalist enterprise (a link made explicit by both Rorty and Bernstein).

More broadly, the use of a hermeneutical approach has become widespread across a wide range of disciplines during the last two decades and is found in anthropology (Geertz, 1983), the history and philosophy of science (Rouse, 1987), and economics (Lavoie, 1991). The result is a major challenge to the approach of natural science, and, in particular, the notion that there are fixed methods for revealing the truth.

In geography hermeneutics was originally introduced to contest the EMPIRICISM and POSITIVISM found in SPATIAL SCIENCE. Buttimer's (1974) 'dialogical approach' which involved bringing together inside and outside views was an important early contribution, as was Y.-F. Tuan's (1974) reflexive approach to TOPOPHILIA ('to know the world is to know oneself'). These early forays were codified in the late 1970s under two different rubrics: HUMANISTIC GEOGRAPHY and CRITICAL THEORY. Humanistic geography made human meaning and intentionality the very core of its concern, while critical theory, as proposed by Gregory (1978), attempted to link the hermeneutical approach to a critique of, in particular, traditional HISTORICAL and REGIONAL GEOGRAPHY. This critical impulse was more generally formalized by Harrison and Livingstone (1980) under their presuppositional approach. Since then the explicit working out of the hermeneutical approach has become less important, although there have been significant elaborations of spatial ontology prompted by Heidegger's work (Schatzki, 1991; see SPATIALITY). Nonetheless, the spirit of hermeneutical inquiry, that is, the recognition of the importance of interpretation, open-mindedness, and a critical, reflexive sensibility, is as great as it has ever been, and certainly evident in the discipline's recent CULTURAL TURN and interest in the poetics and politics of representation (see also POST-STRUCTURALISM). TJB

References

Bernstein, R.J. 1983: *Beyond objectivism and relativism: science, hermeneutics and praxis*. Philadelphia: University of Pennsylvania Press. · Bohman, J. 1993: *New philosophy of social science: problems of indeterminacy*. Cambridge, MA: MIT Press. · Buttimer, A. 1974: *Values in geography*. Washington, D.C.: Association of American Geographers, Commission on College Geography, resource paper 24. · Feyerabend, P. 1975: *Against method*. London: Verso. · Gadamer, H.-G. 1975: *Truth and method*. New York: Seabury Press. · Geertz, C. 1983: *Local knowledge: further essays in interpretive anthropology*. New York: Basic Books. · Gregory, D. 1978: *Ideology, science and human geography*. London: Hutchinson. · Harrison, R.T. and Livingstone, D.N. 1980: Philosophy and problems in human geography: a presuppositional approach. *Area* 12: 25–31. · Lavoie, D., ed., 1991: *Economics and hermeneutics*. London: Routledge. · Rorty, R. 1979: *Philosophy and the mirror of nature*. Princeton: Princeton University Press. · Rouse, J. 1987: *Knowledge and power: toward a political philosophy of science*. Ithaca, NY: Cornell University Press. · Schatzki, T. 1991: Spatial ontology and explanation. *Annals of the Association of American Geographers* 81: 665–70. · Thompson, J.B. 1996: Hermeneutics. In A. Kuper, and J. Kuper, eds, *The social science encyclopaedia*. London: Routledge, 360–1. · Tuan, Y.-F. 1974: *Topophilia: a study of environmental perception, attitudes and values*. Englewood Cliffs, NJ: Prentice Hall.

Suggested Reading

Bernstein, R.J. (1983). · Gregory, D. (1978).

heterotopia Literally, 'a place of Otherness'. Originally a medical term, the concept was introduced into the humanities and social sciences by the French philosopher Michel Foucault in a lecture delivered in 1967 that remained unpublished until after his death (Foucault, 1986). Foucault used it to identify sites – in linguistic or physical SPACE – where the incongruous and incommensurable are brought together in tense, unsettling and often transgressive juxtapositions: in shorthand, then, a heterotopia is a space of HYBRIDITY. Several English-language writers have since toyed with the idea – including Genocchio (1995) and also Soja (1996) in his reflections on the radical possibilities opened up by THIRD SPACE – but the most creative empirical deployment of the concept to date is to be found in Hetherington (1997) who redescribes heterotopia as 'spaces of an alternate ordering'. He insists that heterotopia do not exist 'in and for themselves': that the constitution of specific sites as heterotopia depends upon their ambivalent relationship to other sites, and that it is through this relation – of DIFFERENCE and deferral – that alternate orderings are made both visible and concrete through 'spatial play'. He also offers a series of historical case studies (of the Palais Royal, masonic lodges and factories) to illustrate his principal argument, namely that MODERNITY should be considered

> in terms of an ordering that never comes to rest but which vacillates between ideas of freedom and control. This means not only that the space of modernity is inherently open to resistance and difference, but that it is indeed constituted by it. It also means, however, that resistance and marginality cannot be seen as separate from, or opposed to, the process of ordering (p. 139).

DG

References

Foucault, M. 1986: Of other spaces. *Diacritics* 16 (1): 22–7. · Genocchio, B. 1995: Discourse, discontinuity, difference: the question of 'Other' spaces. In S. Watson, and K. Gibson, eds, *Postmodern cities*. Oxford and Cambridge, MA: Blackwell, 35–46. · Hetherington, K. 1997: *The badlands of modernity: heterotopia and social ordering*. London and New York: Routledge. · Soja, E. 1996: *Thirdspace: journeys to Los Angeles and other real-and-imagined places*. Oxford and Cambridge, MA: Blackwell.

Suggested Reading

Hetherington (1997). · Soja (1996), pp. 155–63 and ch. 7.

high seas These constitute all those parts of the ocean and the ocean-floor, including the subsoil beyond the limits of national jurisdictions. Under the terms of the Third United Nations Convention on the Law of the Sea (UNCLOS III), the high seas constitute the common heritage of humankind and rights to their resources are vested in humankind as a whole, with the International Seabed Authority acting on behalf of the global community. When the convention was first published in 1982, the major maritime industrial nations, including France, the UK and the USA, refused to accept an arrangement whereby they ceded their exclusive rights to exploit the resources of the high seas, in particular the seabed. They argued that they alone possessed the technology to do so and that they should be free to reap the economic benefits. A compromise was eventually agreed in 1994, which preserved the concept of the International Seabed Authority but gave the industrial nations disproportionate power to influence its decisions through a weighted voting system.

France and the UK both signed up to the convention in 1997, but the largest global industrial power, the USA, still refuses to do so. The reasons for its reluctance are now becoming abundantly clear. Not only is the technology for exploiting the known mineral resources of the ocean-floor increasingly cost-effective, but new resources, especially those associated with deep sea volcanic outpourings, are also being discovered and in many cases are proving of even greater potential economic value. As a result, the robustness and viability of the provisions for the management of the high seas in the UNCLOS III remain very much open to question (see LAW OF THE SEA). MB

Suggested Reading

Juda, L. 1996: *International law and ocean use management. The evolution of ocean governance*. London and New York: Routledge.

hinterland The tributary (or catchment) area of a port, from which materials for export are collected and through which imports are distributed: its complementary area – connected to the port by ship – is termed the *foreland*. In more general usage, the term refers to the sphere of influence of any settlement (or of an establishment within a settlement): it is the area for which the settlement is the trading nexus (as in the hexagonal hinterlands of CENTRAL PLACE THEORY). RJJ

historical geography A subfield of human geography that is concerned with geographies of the past and their relations with the present. The development of the subfield in Anglo-American geography, and geographers' changing attitudes towards the past, can be divided into three phases, though any classification is bound to be partial.

Between the 1930s and 1960s historical geography was central to the discipline as a whole. Darby (1953) viewed historical geography as a 'pillar' of geography, alongside geomorphology, because both subfields were based on the study of the LANDSCAPE. But he insisted that a properly *historical* geography found its subject matter in the 'borderlands' of geography and history, and thus could not be based on geographical ideas and methods alone. A distinctive feature of British historical geography was its close ties with economic history and meticulous reconstruction of human geographies of the past as cartographic CROSS-SECTIONS that were pieced together from (often individual) historical sources and linked by historical themes in landscape change (see VERTICAL THEMES). Darby's series of *Domesday geographies of England* (1952–77) is a distinguished example of cross-sectional analysis. North American historical geographers tended to take the REGION as their basic unit of analysis and – like geographers from Sauer's BERKELEY SCHOOL – study the development of human–environment relationships. Clark (1954) argued that historical geography and REGIONAL GEOGRAPHY found common ground in the study of 'areal associations and differentiations' (cf. AREAL DIFFERENTIATION); Meinig's *The Great Columbia Plain* (1968) is a meticulous example of regional-historical geography. Yet during this period these differences in emphasis and orientation were circumscribed by a broad orthodoxy: historical geographers on both sides of the Atlantic were concerned with the reconstruction of past geographies and their changes over time.

The importance of an historical perspective in geography was challenged by the QUANTITATIVE REVOLUTION. The promulgation of the discipline as a SPATIAL SCIENCE pushed historical geography towards the margins of the discipline. The search for general theorems of spatial organization was supported by a version of FUNCTIONALISM that left little room for historical modes of inquiry, and model-builders whittled away historical and geographical specificity. These developments spurred a second phase of methodological refinement and philosophical exploration in the sub-field. Some historical geographers found useful ideas and (especially) techniques in spatial science, though few of them embraced the NOMOTHETIC spirit of the times wholeheartedly. Others proceeded as they had for years, subsisting largely on their own 'enthusiasms and insights', as Baker and Gregory (1984) put it. Still others, such as Harris (1971), attacked the logical foundations of 'a science of spatial relations' and argued that geography is a project of regional-historical synthesis that springs from an engagement with human experience and intentionality rather than one of positivist ABSTRACTION (cf. POSITIVISM). Some historical geographers suggested that these two projects were not necessarily at odds – Langton (1972), for example, sketched the purchase of SYSTEMS ANALYSIS – but they skirted around Harris's more sonorous point:

that the emergence of spatial science sharpened 'the confrontation of scientific and humanistic cultures' within geography.

During the 1970s and 80s there was a flurry of writing by human geographers which turned around this confrontation. In the first place, spatial science and orthodox historical geography were not completely dissimilar. Baker (1979) noted that they both cast people as passive witnesses of geographical change (or dumb objects of low-level theoretical propositions) rather than as 'active subjects' who struggled to make geography and history. The development of an avowedly HUMANISTIC GEOGRAPHY concerned with issues of subjectivity rekindled historical geography and reaffirmed geography's historic links with the humanities. Many humanistic geographers focused on the past and did not restrict their enquiries to the annals of the wealthy and powerful, which underpinned many cartographic cross-sections. They probed the multiple layers of human meaning embedded in 'ordinary landscapes' and the symbolic orders of power at work in elite landscapes (see Meinig, 1979; ICONOGRAPHY). These developments may have helped geographers to overcome what Philo (1994) sees as their long-standing 'fear of "the immaterial"', but they did not lead solely into the geography of the mind or entail an unwitting celebration of HUMAN AGENCY. Gregory (1978) and others insisted that the revivification of geography's traditional commitment 'to particular places and the people that live in them' necessitated non-functionalist inquiries into the economic, social and political forces that structure human geographies, and processes of historical-geographical transformation – in short, an engagement with social theory and the social sciences as well as the humanities. Humanistic-historical geography was stimulated by HISTORICAL MATERIALISM as well as IDEALISM, and it wrestled with the causal relations between people, society and space (see SPATIAL STRUCTURE). Interest was shown in STRUCTURATION THEORY because it posited a set of interconnections between human agency and social systems and structures, and sketched their constitution in space and time.

During this period some of the most remarkable work in British historical geography, such as Dennis's survey of English industrial cities and Overton's study of agrarian transformation in early modern England (cf. AGRICULTURAL REVOLUTION; INDUSTRIAL REVOLUTION), brought a range of theoretical sensibilities and quantitative methods to bear on refractory archival materials, and historical geographers more generally stepped away from source-bound EMPIRICISM, which characterized orthodox work in the sub-field, and explored different modes of explanation (see Dodgshon and Butlin, 1900; Green, 1991). In North America, geographers attempted to pool their regional expertise and provide general accounts of the shaping of the continent (e.g. Harris, 1988).

Over the last fifteen years geographical work on the past has become eclectic and no new orthodoxy for historical geography is likely to emerge. Many recent studies are self-consciously inter-disciplinary and some are presented without any sub-disciplinary labels. Such labels still have an institutional purchase and remain important to some self-professed historical geographers, but they make increasingly less sense intellectually. This third phase of eclecticism reflects a frenetic period of creativity – some would say crisis – in the social sciences and humanities which is being shaped by changes in the global economy and is characterized by wide-ranging critiques of the foundational narratives of MODERNITY. From the perspective of historical geography, three interrelated themes stand out:

There is now a general concern with *the historicity of geography*. The discipline of geography does not furnish a transparent or timeless window on to the world. Geographical ideas, methods and knowledges arise from specific settings, privilege particular objects of study and subject positions, and work on assumptions about the nature of society, history and intellectual inquiry that are not universally valid. As such, Driver (1988) noted, 'thinking historically' about geography is not a 'luxury' that should be afforded solely to historical geographers but is 'an essential part of doing human geography'. Historical geographers have been centrally involved in the production of 'contextual' and 'critical' histories of geography which show that 'geography' has meant different things in different times and places (cf. CONTEXTUAL APPROACH), and examine how some geographical ideas, approaches and knowledges came to be seen as central to the discipline and others were ignored or denigrated (see e.g. Withers, 1993; Driver et al., 1995; cf. GEOGRAPHY, HISTORY OF). These sensibilities are informed by the perspectives of POSTMODERNISM and they are affiliated with the 'new CULTURAL GEOGRAPHY', which has a strong historical component and has spawned new links between geography and the interdisciplinary field of cultural studies. Much recent work in cultural and historical geography starts from the premise that geographers create and communicate meaning from partial (limited and situated) vantage points rather than simply reconstruct a prior and separate geographical reality in a more or less accurate and complete fashion. Cosgrove and Domosh (1993) pointed up the androcentric and ethnocentric predilections of much Anglo-American geographical research and writing – particularly the use of gendered metaphors and a western rationalist faith 'the cumulative progression of knowledge' – and urged geographers to think about how their practices of REPRESENTATION are implicated in relationships of POWER. Over the last two decades geographers have explored the ideological duplicity of some key geographical objects and methods of study. Cosgrove (1984), for example, argued that 'landscape' is a historically and culturally specific 'way of seeing' and ordering the world which has served the interests of the propertied classes; Harley (1989) criticized 'the mapping tradition' in historical geography for its insensitivity to the links between CARTOGRAPHY and STATE power; and there is a growing literature on the complicity of geography and empire (e.g. Bell et al., 1995).

This work on the historical geographies embedded in the discipline is linked to a range of work on *the spatiality and temporality of social life and human* IDENTITY. Harvey (1990) argued that analysis of 'the historical geography of concepts of space and time,' the PRODUCTION OF SPACE, and the GEOGRAPHICAL IMAGINATION is central to any critical evaluation of the contemporary world. Harvey has shown that human attachments to PLACE, conceptions of SPACE, and views of cultural difference have been transformed radically over the last 500 years by the dynamics of capitalism (see TIME–SPACE COMPRESSION). Among other things, such insights have raised important questions about the configuration of time in geography. Meinig (1978) noted that orthodox historical geography was more concerned with the description of 'changing geographies' than the interpretation of geographical change *through* time. In a number of books, Pred (e.g. 1995) has drawn on TIME-GEOGRAPHY and tropes of montage to represent the 'multiple (geographical his)stories' inscribed within European modernity and its global outreach. Harvey and Pred work with various strands of Marxism and focus largely on the West, but other theoretical resources and geographical issues have been brought into play. Michael Foucault's haunting GENEALOGY of modernity, feminist critiques of the constitution of the male–European–bourgeois subject as the global norm against which 'others' have been judged and found lacking (see FEMINIST GEOGRAPHIES; GENDER AND GEOGRAPHY), and the perspectives of POST-COLONIALISM thread through a diverse body of scholarship on material and imaginative geographies of power, identity and difference. Geographers are exploring how social divisions and projects of domination developed in spaces of confinement, segregation and SURVEILLANCE (see e.g. Hannah, 1997), and they have become interested in Travel writing, in part, because it underscores the idea that identities are neither eternal nor shaped at one place but are variegated and malleable. Notions of home and belonging, and familiarity and foreignness, were renegotiated as disparate lands and peoples came into contact through processes of capitalist expansion, technological change and COLONIALISM (see e.g. Blunt and Rose, 1994). Other geographers are examining how ideas of diversity and difference have been fixed around SEXUALITY, CLASS and RACE; how visions of social order, historical progress, cultural difference and NATIONAL identity have been created and naturalized by landscape painters, museums and exhibitions (cf. ART, GEOGRAPHY AND); and how the tourist and heritage industries package geography and history for public consumption (see Daniels, 1993; Kearns and Philo, 1993; Lowenthal, 1997). Central to these investigations is the idea that space and time are constructs that both shape and are shaped by economic, cultural and political forces.

Public and political concern over environmental issues is rejuvenating what Williams (1994) calls geography's 'stock-in-trade' interest in *human–environment relationships and human relations with nature*. The terms 'environment' and 'NATURE' have multiple connotations, and human geographers' engagement with them now exceeds historical geographers' orthodox interest in landscape change and human modification of the surface of the earth. New links are being forged between historical geography and environmental history, particularly in North America, where historians are arguably making a more significant contribution to debates about nature and society than geographers (see Walker, 1994). Marxist geographers argue that capitalism has *produced* a specific kind of nature and space, and they have been at the forefront of attempts to explain the historical conditions under which capitalism creates environmental problems. There is an allied and eclectic stream of work which stresses that 'there is no representation of "nature" outside social interests and political agendas' (Castree, 1997) and analyses human relations with nature in different times, places and discourses. Gregory (1998), for example, traces how 'nature,' 'space,' and 'culture' have served as 'foundational constructs' of modernity, and Demeritt (1994) questions the ways in which Green critics derive 'foundational authority' for their work from science and history.

In sum, geographers are reaffirming the importance of historical perspectives in the discipline but the terms 'history' and 'theory' now have different connotations than they did 30 years ago (see Butlin, 1993). These three themes are the building blocks of a critical human geography which looks to the past in order to unsettle understanding of the present.

This third phase does not constitute a wholesale departure from earlier debates in the sub-field, and orthodox work on landscape change, settlement patterns, and FIELD SYSTEMS continues. Clark and Darby stressed that the past and the present cannot be sealed off from one another, and that scholarship is shaped by one's surroundings. Clark spent most of his career trying to figure out the alterations in human–environment relations that stemmed from the meeting of different cultures in the New World and thought of these changing geographies as 'continually changing entities'. And Darby viewed his cross-sections as basic indices of tradition and modernization. Yet historical geographers now have a greater sensitivity to the normative assumptions embedded in their maps of the past and narratives of change, and they have a more hybrid interest in history and social theory.

Carville Earle (1995) criticized the Eurocentric – and often Anglocentric – preoccupations of British historical geography, noted that during the 1980s many historical geographers took an 'involutional path . . . away from substantive problems and toward more philosophical adventures in representation', and called on the sub-field to 'come to grips with the rest of the world'. Yet these 'adventures' made historical geography a more intellectually vibrant and truly 'borderland' field of study, and as a recent geographical scholarship on modernity and colonialism shows, how one approaches 'the world' is not a simple matter. The paths that geographers take into the past are mediated by contemporary issues and processes that themselves have a historical geography and relate *more or less* to specific peoples, places and struggles. Such recognitions now temper theory-building in human geography and forestall the inclination to regulate geographers' diverse political commitments and theoretical concerns in the name of a disciplinary tradition or sub-disciplinary coherence. In recent years geographers have raised profound questions about how one retains a sensitivity to both the particularity of past geographies and the grander forces of historical-geographical transformation with which they are bound up, and about the critical position one adopts on the relations of power embedded in the past and its relations with the present. Scholars in other fields are interested in the geographies in history, and it seems clear that an historical perspective in geography will remain central to the attempt to work out how extraordinary the geographies of the late twentieth-century world might be. The *Journal of Historical Geography*, established in 1975, remains an important forum for debate. DC

References

Baker, A.R.H. 1979: Historical geography: a new beginning? *Progress in Human Geography* 3: 360–70. · Baker, A.R.H. and Gregory, D. 1984: Some *terrae incognitae* in historical geography: an exploratory discussion. In A.R.H. Baker and D. Gregory, eds, *Explorations in historical geography*. Cambridge: Cambridge University Press, 180–94. · Bell, M., Butlin, R.A. and Heffernan, M., eds, 1995: *Geography and imperialism, 1820–1940*. Manchester: Manchester University Press. · Blunt, A. and Rose, G. 1994: *Writing women and space: colonial and postcolonial geographies*. New York: Guilford Press. · Butlin, R.A. 1993: *Historical geography: through the gates of space and time*. London: Edward Arnold. · Castree, N. 1997: Nature, economy and the cultural politics of theory: the 'war against the seals' in the Bering Sea, 1870–1911. *Geoforum* 28: 1–20. · Clark, A.H. 1954: Historical geography. In P.E. James and C.F. Jones, eds, *American geography: inventory and prospect*. Syracuse: Syracuse University Press, 70–105. · Cosgrove, D. 1984: *Social formation and symbolic landscape*. London. · Croom Helm; Cosgrove, D. and Daniels, S., eds, 1988: *The iconography of landscape: essays on the symbolic representation, design and use of past environments*. Cambridge: Cambridge University Press. · Cosgrove, D. and Domosh, M. 1993: Author and authority: writing the new cultural geography. In J. Duncan and D. Ley, eds, *Place/culture/representation*. London and New York: Routledge, 25–38. · Daniels, S. 1993: *Fields of vision: landscape imagery and nation identity in England and the United States*. Cambridge: Polity Press. · Darby, H.C. 1952–77: *The Domesday geography of England*, 7 vols. Cambridge and New York: Cambridge University Press. · Darby, H.C. 1953: On the relations of geography and history. *Transactions, Institute of British Geographers* 19: 1–11. · Demeritt, D. 1994: Ecology, objectivity and critique in writings on nature and human societies. *Journal of Historical Geography* 20: 22–37. · Dodgshon, R.A. and Butlin, R.A., eds, 1990: *An historical geography of England and Wales*, 2nd edn. London: Academic Press. · Driver, F. 1988: The historicity of human geography. *Progress in Human Geography* 12: 497–506. · Driver, F. et al. 1995: Geographical traditions: rethinking the history of geography. *Transactions, Institute of British Geographers* NS 20: 403–22. · Earle, C. 1995: Historical geography in extremis?: splitting personalities on the postmodern turn. *Journal of Historical Geography* 21: 455–9. · Green, D.B., ed., 1991: *Historical geography: A methodological portrayal*. Savage: Rowman & Littlefield. · Gregory, D. 1978: *Ideology, science and human geography*. London: Hutchinson. · Gregory, D. 1998: *Explorations in critical human geography*. Hettner-Lectures 1. Heidelberg: Department of Geography, University of Heidelberg. · Hannah, M. 1997: Space and the structuring of disciplinary power: an interpretive review. *Geografisker Annaler* 79B: 171–80. · Harley, J.B. 1989: Historical geography and the cartographic illusion. *Journal of Historical Geography* 15: 80–91. · Harris, R.C. 1971: Theory and synthesis in historical geography. *Canadian Geographer* 15: 157–72. · Harris, R.C., ed., 1988: *Historical atlas of Canada, vol. 1: From the beginning to 1800*. Toronto: Toronto University Press. · Harvey, D. 1990: Between space and time: reflections on the geographical imagination. *Annals of the Association of American Geographers* 80: 418–34. · Kearns G. and Philo C., eds, 1993: *Selling places: the city as cultural capital, past and present*. Oxford: Pergamon Press. · Langton, J. 1972: Potentialities and problems of adopting a systems approach to the study of change in human geography. *Progress in Geography* 4: 127–79. · Lowenthal, D. 1997: *The heritage industry and the spoils of history*. London and New York: Viking, 1997. · Meinig, D.W. 1968: *The great Columbia plain: a historical geography*. Washington: University of Washington Press. · Meinig, D.W. 1978: Andrew Clark, historical geographer. In J.R. Gibson, ed., *European settlement and development in North America: Essays on geographical change in honour and memory of Andrew Hill Clark*. Toronto: University of Toronto Press, 3–26. · Meinig D.W., ed., 1979: *The interpretation of ordinary landscapes*. New York: Oxford University Press. · Mitchell, R.D. and Groves, P.A., eds, 1987: *North America: the shaping of a changing continent*. Totowa, NJ: Rowman and Littlefield. · Philo, C. 1994: History, geography and the 'still greater mystery' of historical geography. In D. Gregory, R. Martin and G. Smith, eds, *Human geography: society, space and social science*. London: Macmillan, 252–81. · Pred, A. 1995: *Recognising European modernities*. London and New York: Routledge. · Walker R., ed., 1994: William Cronon's *Nature's metropolis*: a symposium. *Antipode* 26. · Williams M. 1994: The relations of environmental history and historical geography. *Journal of Historical Geography* 20: 3–21. · Withers, C.W.J. 1993: Geography in its time: geography and historical geography in Diderot and d'Alembert's *Encyclopédie*. *Journal of Historical Geography* 19: 255–64.

Suggested Reading

Butlin (1993). · Green (1991). · Gregory, D. 1994: *Geographical imaginations*. Cambridge, MA and Oxford: Blackwell.

historical materialism An analytical method that emphasizes the material basis of society, and looks to the historical development of social relations to comprehend societal change. Opposed to IDEALISM, historical materialism is generally associated with Marxism, though the term itself was coined by Engels. Historical-materialist analysis assumes the importance of ideas and argues that 'life is not determined by consciousness, but consciousness by life'. As social beings, men and women develop 'their material intercourse', and thereby alter 'their history and the products of their thinking' (Marx and Engels, 1970, p. 47).

In geographical research, historical materialism rose to prominence in the 1970s but its pedigree in economics, history, literary studies, and sociology is much longer. Historical materialism in geography attempts to explain patterns and processes of spatial and environmental change as the result of the specific social relations of CAPITALISM or other MODES OF PRODUCTION (see MARXIST GEOGRAPHY). While initially somewhat independent from the prevailing PARADIGM in geography (SPATIAL SCIENCE), historical materialist research has more recently integrated with broader social and cultural theory. Historical materialists rejected in particular the self-proclaimed objectivity of LOGICAL POSITIVISM, and more generally the intellectual HEGEMONY of 'bourgeois geography', mainly because both have been complicit more with oppression, IMPERIALISM, and RACISM than with any substantive form of social emancipation (Harvey, 1984). Interest in historical materialist analysis was prodded by the social upheaval of the 1960s in many western nations, but has received a wider acceptance in Europe (rather than North America) where its intellectual and political roots are much older than elsewhere.

Fairly or not, historical materialism has become associated with the BASE-SUPERSTRUCTURE model of society. Although Marx never advocated a base-superstructure model, other Marxists did. Some social theorists reacted negatively to this rigid conception which viewed the mode of production as constitutive of all other societal relations. Yet since most Marxists did not dogmatically accept this framework in the first place, the CULTURAL TURN away from this model has actually served more to enrich contemporary political economy with nuanced cultural analysis than to inspire a recalcitrance among historical materialists.

During the late 1970s and 1980s, POSTMODERNISM posed a significant challenge to traditional historical materialism. If postmodernists argued that the assumptions of ENLIGHTENMENT rationality and MODERNITY were now antiquated, defenders of historical materialism responded that the postmodern cultural efflorescence was itself integrally connected to a new flexibility in economic, political, and social relations (Jameson, 1984; Harvey, 1989). No such independence of CULTURE from ECONOMY was yet achieved, despite capitalist social relations having undergone a significant evolution.

POST-COLONIALISM also served as a critique of historical materialism from the 1970s onward. Post-colonialists argued that historical materialism is EUROCENTRIC and does not adequately reflect the experience of colonized peoples. Historical materialism, to postcolonialists, glosses over the cultural dimension to the colonial project and its aftermath, by using rigid epistemological dichotomies. Like the influence of the cultural turn however, this critique has been absorbed more than resisted by historical materialists interested in COLONIALISM (see for example Blaut, 1993). Polyvocal rather than uni-vocal theorizing about the colonial experience is now more commonplace. NS

References

Blaut, J. 1993: *The colonizer's model of the world : geographical diffusionism and Eurocentric history*. New York: Guilford. · Harvey, D. 1984: On the present condition of geography; an historical materialist manifesto. *Professional Geographer* 36: 11–18. · Harvey, D. 1989: *The condition of postmodernity*. Oxford: Blackwell. · Jameson, F. 1984: Postmodernism or the cultural logic of late capitalism. *New Left Review* 146: 53–92. · Marx, K. and Engels, F. 1970: *The German ideology*, trans. C.J. Arthur. New York: International.

Suggested Reading

Harvey (1984). · Marx, K. 1967: *Capital*, volume I. New York: International. · Marx, K. 1971: Preface. *A contribution to the critique of political economy*. London: Lawrence and Wishart.

historicism Historicism has two main meanings within the humanities and social sciences: (i) critical traditions that insist on the importance of historical context to the interpretation of cultural TEXTS and practices; and (ii) intellectual traditions that assume human history to have an inner logic, overall design or direction ('telos').

These two meanings often work against one another: while the first criticizes interpretations that appeal to trans-historical constants, essences or mechanisms ('human nature' or 'the' human subject), the second invokes trans-historical forces to structure its explanations of human 'progress' (perhaps most clearly in the movement of the world-spirit or *Geist* found in Hegel's philosophical history). In practice, however, the sensitivity to context and the suspicion of trans-historical principles is of much more consequence to contemporary social inquiry: elements of historicism in this sense are activated by HERMENEUTICS and POST-STRUCTURALISM. The appeal of TELEOLOGY – of 'unfolding' models of social change in which a series of social situations is logically and necessarily derived forwards from the first term in the sequence or backwards from its last term – has considerably diminished, and there are few scholars who would now accept that human history is predictable and susceptible to the formulation of universal scientific laws (cf. POSITIVISM). When Karl Popper railed against the 'poverty' of this sense of historicism in 1945, he had a reading of HISTORICAL MATERIALISM as economic determinism squarely in his sights, but modern versions of Marxism offer a much more open-ended view of human history and the spaces for political action and intervention (cf. Popper, 1960).

The importance of historical context and historical specificity is an article of faith in HISTORICAL GEOGRAPHY and underwrote the claim by both D. Whittlesey and H.C. Darby that 'all geography is historical geography'. Such afirmations were attacked – or, rather, ignored – by the reconstruction of modern geography as SPATIAL SCIENCE in the 1960s and 1970s, but the recent formation of a cultural-historical geography with a critical edge has brought much of human geography into engagement with a New Historicism. The parallels have rarely been remarked but they are extremely close.

New Historicism is in fact a label applied to a cluster of approaches to literary and cultural studies which had its origins in the USA in the 1980s. It was most closely associated with Stephen Greenblatt and other scholars who made a series of critical interventions around what they came to call the 'cultural poetics' of the Renaissance. It is often regarded as an American counterpart to British cultural materialism (Wilson, 1995), but in practice has drawn on a variety of both American and European sources. Among others, New Historicism appeals to the THICK DESCRIPTION of Clifford Geertz to establish the importance of a close reading of minor events, the re-telling of anecdotes, in such a way that they reveal the larger situations of which they are a part and to which they can be made to speak; the GENEALOGY of

Michel Foucault to develop an analytics of POWER that can resist 'power's description of itself' by looking to the margins and the peripheries of situations; and the HISTORICAL MATERIALISM of Raymond Williams to capture the materiality of cultural formations and their contradictory constitution.

New Historicism has been the subject of considerable critical debate (Veeser, 1989), but its protocols have influenced the close critical reading of colonial DISCOURSE (see POSTCOLONIALISM) and they have much in common with recent work in CULTURAL GEOGRAPHY and in the development of what has come to be called a 'contextual' approach to the history of GEOGRAPHY. Finally, it should be noted that when Soja (1989, 1996) objects to 'historicism' in the humanities and social sciences and proposes a 'spatial critique' he seems to have in mind simply an aggressive over-valuation of historical explanation and a marginalization, even erasure of a 'spatial imagination': but there are many practitioners of New Historicism who have little or no problem in attending to both the historicity and the spatiality of their objects of inquiry. DG

References

Hamilton, P. 1996: *Historicism*. London: Routledge. · Popper, K. 1960: *The poverty of historicism*. London: Hutchinson; New York: Harper & Row (first published in 1945). · Soja, E. 1989: *Postmodern geographies: the reassertion of space in critical social theory*. London: Verso. · Soja, E. 1996: *Thirdspace: journeys to Los Angeles and other real-and-imagined places*. Oxford and Cambridge, MA: Blackwell. · Veeser, H.A., ed., 1989: *The new historicism*. London and New York: Routledge. · Wilson, S. 1995: *Cultural materialism: theory and practice*. Oxford and Cambridge, MA: Blackwell.

Suggested Reading

Hamilton (1996), pp. 133–204. · Soja (1996), pp. 164–83.

homelessness Definitional problems make it difficult to achieve accurate counts of homeless populations. Historically, the homeless in industrialized societies have tended to be single, white, middle-aged men, often alcoholics, who have elected voluntarily to dissociate themselves from society. During the last three decades, this group has been joined and numerically overwhelmed by the deinstitutionalized mentally disabled, those who have never been institutionalized, substance abusers, women and children (the former often victims of domestic abuse), RACIAL and ETHNIC minorities, runaway and 'throw-away' youth, and war veterans. The demographics of the homeless population provide some indication of how complex the causes of homelessness have become.

Most operational definitions characterize homelessness as the absence of a place where one can sleep and receive mail. But researchers increasingly emphasize the loss of support networks and progressive social disaffiliation that are typical of the descent into homelessness (cf. ALIENATION; ANOMIE). People who become homeless in industrialized societies often pass through an extended sequence of deteriorating circumstances involving, for example, first a move to cheaper rental accommodation, then doubling up with friends and family, and a shift into temporary housing in a hostel or shelter, before ultimately ending up on the street.

The factors causing the enormous increase of 'new' homelessness vary according to national and regional contexts. Nevertheless, most western industrialized nations have experienced: (a) a massive economic RESTRUCTURING, associated with DEINDUSTRIALIZATION and the rise of POST-FORDISM, that caused recession and significant long-term unemployment; (b) a dismantling of the WELFARE STATE that reduced levels of, and eligibility for, public assistance at a time when demand for such assistance was sky-rocketing; and (c) a collapse of government-supported affordable housing programmes (including public housing). These broad trends created a class of 'proto-homeless' – economically and residentially marginalized individuals and families only one or two pay cheques away from the street. At the same time, the availability of alcohol, crack cocaine, and other relatively cheap and highly addictive drugs contributed to the incidence of proto-homelessness.

The rise in the number of homeless people and the withdrawal of welfare-state services produced a number of interrelated consequences: (a) the extensive growth of a not-for-profit service and advocacy sector known as the SHADOW STATE; (b) while the growing numbers of homeless people tended initially to raise public concerns and sympathy, current evidence suggests there is an increasing unwillingness to accept the proximate presence of homeless people and services designed to assist them (the NIMBY phenomenon); (c) COMMUNITY intolerance is often expressed through the enactment of local ordinances that outlaw the behaviours of homeless people, including panhandling and sleeping/sitting in public places, and have the effect of channelling growing numbers of homeless people into the criminal justice system; (d) homeless individuals and service providers have been pushed into ZONES OF DEPENDENCE, or 'GHETTOES' of service-dependent people (see also SKID ROW). The consequent spatial concentration is often a result of deliberate efforts at containment. In the zone of dependence, homeless people often build street-based social networks that (for better or worse) substitute for earlier home-based networks. Service agencies may also benefit from agglomeration economies that derive from the proximity of other service providers in the zone of dependence.

The complexity of homelessness as a social process, plus the growing diversity of homeless populations, has meant that any single policy response to homelessness is unlikely to achieve instant, substantial change. The prevalence of dual, even triple diagnoses (homelessness *plus* psychiatric illness, substance abuse, physical illness or disability) only highlights the shortcomings of single-issue treatment programmes. Getting off the streets permanently may require access to a continuum of housing-, work-, and service-related opportunities, including emergency shelter and services as well as long-term supported housing. In the absence of an integrated network of assistance, many people may move from streets to temporary accommodation and back again, in an on-going cycle of homelessness.

In developing countries, homelessness on a large scale has emerged as one consequence of rapid urban development (cf. URBANIZATION). Large numbers of rural–urban migrants and an expanding urban population have been unable to gain access to formal employment and shelter within the formal housing sector. A widespread response to this crisis of poverty and homelessness has been the growth of SQUATTER SETTLEMENTS and shanty towns, which develop on vacant land within and around cities and comprise a dense patchwork of shelters assembled from available materials. Some estimates suggest that more than 40 per cent of the urban populations of developing countries now live in these informal settlements. Their populations face many challenges including health and sanitation, and outside pressure for clearance and redevelopment. Residents and non-governmental organizations have focused on, among other things, improving the physical infrastructure of settlements, facilitating access to health care and education, and political empowerment. (See also SQUATTING.) MJD

Suggested Reading

Dear, M. and Wolch, J. 1987: *Landscapes of despair: from deinstitutionalization to homelessness*. Princeton, NJ: Princeton University Press. · Wolch, J. and Dear, M. 1993: *Malign Neglect: Homelessness in an American City*. San Francisco, CA: Jossey Bass.

homophobia and heterosexism Though interrelated, these terms accurately refer to different exercises of oppression. Homophobia literally refers to the fear of lesbians, gays or otherwise queer subjects. The term is used vaguely, however, to describe sentiments ranging from the unease to disgust or hatred, and can be directed at others or oneself (see PERFORMATIVITY; PSYCHOANALYTIC THEORY, GEOGRAPHY AND). By contrast, heterosexism refers to the biases in society towards heteronormativity (see QUEER THEORY), signalling the ways that heterosexuality is uncritically assumed (see DISCOURSE) or directly claimed to be the normal, best, or only form of sexuality. Both homophobia and heterosexism can take a wide variety of forms (e.g. feelings, actions, structures, etc.) or magnitudes (from subtle to blatant), and can be witnessed in a wide variety of geographies.

There are at least two ways that geography is implicated by these terms. By the early 1990s a growing number of geographers noticed a reluctance or 'squeamishness' to discuss sexualities (see PRIVATE AND PUBLIC SPHERES), signalling a certain homophobia (where ignorance is equated with fear) in the discipline's research agenda (Knopp, 1992). This point spurred a critique of the discipline's heterosexism even within its more progressive wings (Binnie, 1997). Out of these critiques emerged a substantive and impressively diverse strand of research that shows the importance and diversities of sexualities' relations with space (see DIFFERENCE; SEXUALITY, GEOGRAPHY AND).

A second, and much more disparate relevance has been detected by work that points to homophobia and heterosexism *vis-à-vis* geographers' own sexualities. This theme can be traced through direct harassment (Valentine, 1998), the use of pseudonyms for authors or places in publications (e.g. Jay, 1997), or the relevance of sexuality to the ways geographers and explorers approached the field. Even the momentous decision to close Harvard University's geography department in 1948 was influenced partially by heterosexism and homophobia (Smith, 1987). MPB

References

Binnie, J. 1997: Coming out of geography. *Environment and Planning D: Society and Space* 15: 223–38. · Jay, E. 1997: Domestic dykes: the politics of 'in-difference'. In G. Ingram, A. Bouthillette, A. and Y. Retter, eds, *Queers in space*. Seattle: Bay Press, 163–70. · Knopp, L. 1992: Sexuality and the spatial dynamics of capitalism, *Environment and Planning D: Society and Space* 10: 651–69. · Smith, N. 1987: Academic war over the field of geography. *Annals of the Association of American Geographers* 77: 155–72. · Valentine, G. 1998: Sticks and stones may break my bones. *Antipode* 30: 305–32.

Hotelling model An analysis of the location strategy of two firms competing for market TERRITORY (cf. HINTERLAND). Hotelling was one of the first economists to address the question of the spatial arrangement of competing firms, and his analysis has provided a starting point for a number of illustrative extensions. Hotelling postulated the highly simplified situation of two producers competing to supply identical goods to consumers evenly spread along a linear market. The usual text-book example (though not in Hotelling's original presentation) is of two ice-cream sellers competing to supply people evenly distributed on a beach. Under circumstances such as these, Hotelling deduced the seemingly unlikely conclusion that the two sellers would end up standing back-to-back in the centre of the beach, each supplying his own half of the market (see GAME THEORY). This was then extended into a generalization concerning industrial AGGLOMERATION under certain demand conditions. Hotelling's model is thus an illustration of the useful practice of deductive generalization in spatial economic analysis.

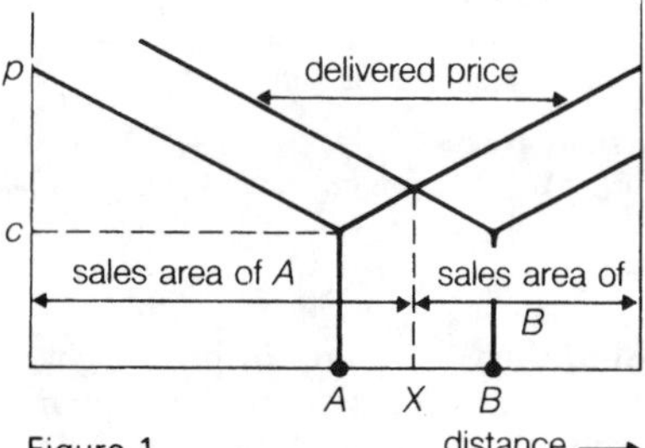

Figure 1

from B
from A
sales area of A
sales area of B
A B

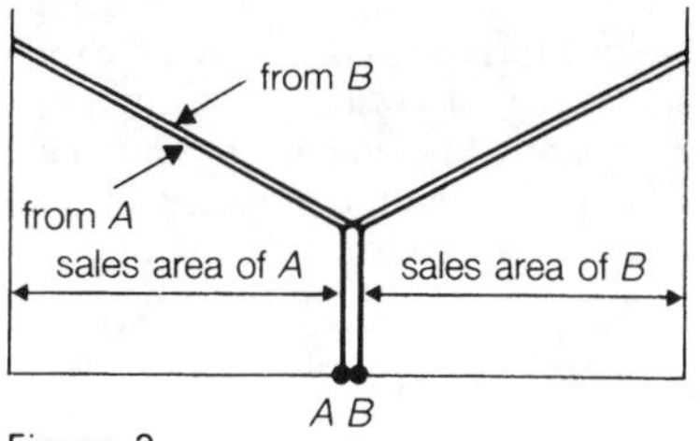

Figure 2

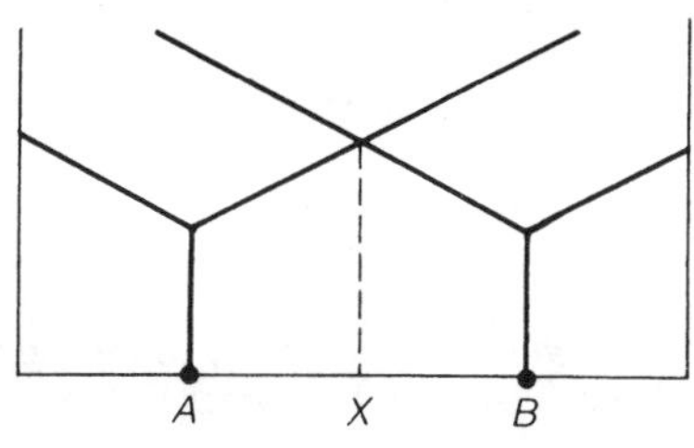

Figure 3

Hotelling model

Hotelling's argument and some of its implications with respect to competition between two firms (duopolists) in space may be illustrated diagrammatically (see figures). Two producers are competing to serve the linear market (a beach) represented by the horizontal axis. Production costs (c) are the same in all locations and the product is sold at a price p reflecting transport cost to the consumer (in the ice-cream case this is the effort of customers walking to the seller's location). In figure 1, firm A locates in the centre of the market; B locates some distance to the right. The respective sales areas split at X where the delivered prices from the two suppliers are the same (see MARKET-AREA ANALYSIS). But under the conditions of infinitely inelastic demand when every consumer will buy one unit of the product in one unit of time irrespective of price (or effort of acquisition), firm B loses nothing by moving to the left, as in figure 2, and taking part of A's sales area, even though this raises the delivered price to customers on the right. Hence the conclusion that B will join A at the centre of the market, where neither firm can gain further sales by relocating. This conclusion holds irrespective of the initial location of the producers, as long as conditions of infinitely inelastic demand exist. The introduction of sensitivity of demand level to price will discourage sales to distant customers and producers seeking to maximize sales will move apart to the so-called 'quartile' positions, as in figure 3. Thus the general deduction is that elasticity of demand will stimulate industrial dispersal.

Hotelling's model has been applied in other competitive situations, as in PUBLIC CHOICE THEORY, and a large literature on the 'spatial theory of voting' developed from Downs'(1957) adaptation of the model for political science. DMS

References

Downs, A. (1957) *An economic theory of democracy*. New York: Harper & Row. · Hotelling, H. 1929: Stabilily in competition. *Economic Journal* 39: 40–57.

Suggested Reading

Smith D.M. 1981: *Industrial location: an economic geographical analysis*, 2nd edn. New York: John Wiley, 91–7.

housing class A group of people characterized by their occupation of a particular housing type, usually defined by tenure. The term was coined by a British sociologist John Rex (1968, 1971) who identified three access routes to housing: possession of capital and credit, thereby allowing entry to the owner-occupier market; a tenancy in a public (social) housing sector; and a tenancy in a private housing rental sector. He identified seven housing classes:

- outright owners;
- mortgagees;
- tenants in purpose-built public housing;
- tenants in publicly-acquired SLUM properties awaiting demolition;
- tenants of whole properties belonging to private owners;
- house-owners who must sublet parts of their properties in order to afford the repayments; and
- lodgers who occupy one or more rooms in a dwelling shared with other households.

Rex developed the concept and classification to appreciate the position of immigrant groups within the British housing market (Rex and Moore, 1967). He showed that access was not a function of socio-economic status alone, because of the discrimination operated by URBAN MANAGERS AND GATEKEEPERS who control access to the various tenures, such as financial institutions which may discriminate in the allocation of mortgages and managers who discriminate in creating and operating the rules for allocating public housing.

The concept was adopted by students of urban residential patterns as providing a better appreciation of how SEGREGATION was produced than models based on the free operation of a property market. It has been criticized as no more than an inductive generalization from a particular case, however (which Rex himself accepted: Rex and Tomlinson, 1979), for its assumption of common value systems regarding the desirability of certain types of housing and housing tenure, and for its confusion of CONSUMPTION sectors within a society with people's CLASS position. Nevertheless, its clarification of the role of constraints as well as choices within urban housing markets made a major contribution to the sophistication of analysis and understanding in this aspect of URBAN GEOGRAPHY and HOUSING STUDIES.

RJJ

References

Rex, J. 1968: The sociology of a zone in transition. In R.E. Pahl, ed., *Readings in urban sociology*. Oxford and New York: Pergamon Press, 211–31. · Rex, J. 1971: The concept of housing class and the sociology of race relations. *Race* 12: 293–301. · Rex, J. and Moore, R. 1967: *Race, community and conflict*. Oxford: Oxford University Press. · Rex, J. and Tomlinson, S.A. 1979: *Colonial immigrants in a British city*. London: Routledge and Kegan Paul.

housing studies Housing is a form of shelter, a refuge, a welfare service, an investment and a gateway to jobs, services and social support. In most societies, housing is available both according to need (in areas where housing provision is an element of social policy) and according to ability to pay (where housing policy is more directly geared to market principles). Housing studies therefore investigate the patterning of both a basic HUMAN RIGHT and a COMMODITY or capital asset.

Whether as state-subsidized shelter or as a saleable commodity, housing is a spatially uneven resource of variable cost and quality. Its variety stems partly from the process of housing production, which itself reflects the changing fortunes of the dwelling construction industry (Ball, 1988). This unevenness is also a consequence of differences in the extent of maintenance, repair and rehabilitation effected by either private individuals or corporate owners. There is, then, a geography of housing production which is one element of the PRODUCTION OF SPACE more generally.

Because qualitative differences in housing character and condition (use value), as well as quantitative price differences (exchange value), vary over space, the geography of housing consumption has a bearing on the study of social inequality (see also INEQUALITY, SPATIAL). This geography of consumption can be explored in several ways.

First, *housing outcomes may be viewed as a spatial reflection of social differentiation.* Access to housing is fundamentally mediated by income and wealth. This is most obvious when examining access to the private sector, which depends on a regular income at a given level to sustain mortgage repayments or market rents in different residential areas. But even in the public sector, where income is supposed to be less important than housing need in mediating access to shelter, economic factors are an important determinant of residential SEGREGATION (Clapham and Kintrea, 1987).

Access to housing is also mediated by other qualities in a way which cannot wholly be explained by financial considerations. Direct and indirect discrimination, effected by individuals, institutionalized within housing allocation systems and inherent in the wider organization of society, underpin the gender, 'race' and health inequalities currently embedded in the organization of residential space (cf. URBAN MANAGERS AND GATEKEEPERS). Such discrimination is found both in the market sector (where access to housing finance may be dictated as much by who people are, what they do, and where they live, as by actual ability to pay), and in the public sector (where the principle of need can be compromised by judgements about who deserves what kind of housing, and where: see Smith and Mallinson, 1996).

Watson (1988), for instance, shows how the operation of the housing system in Britain and Australia reflects and reinforces the PATRIARCHAL character of such societies by marginalizing those 'non-family' households which do not reproduce the traditional family form. Working in the USA, Farley (1995) argues that continuing high levels of residential segregation between white and African-American households cannot be explained by income differences and housing costs alone. Work like this testifies to the persistence of discriminatory barriers to open housing in US cities. There are parallels in Britain, where Henderson and Karn (1987) indicate that, in the allocation of public housing, 'racial' stereotypes become associated with scales of distinction and disrepute which are translated into offers of better tenancies (for 'white' applicants) and worse homes (for their 'black' counterparts). In a related vein, Smith (1990) argues that neither the public nor the private sector of the housing system provides adequate accommodation for people with health problems. Despite their position among the 'deserving' poor, many sick people may be forced into some of the poorest and least healthy homes and, at worst, find themselves disproportionately vulnerable to homelessness.

From this first perspective on housing consumption, *where* people live – whether in the public or the private sector, or in the most or least affluent NEIGHBOURHOOD – is largely a function of who they are. Groups high in the income or status hierarchy tend to benefit most (in terms of the quality and quantity of their living space as well as in the potential to secure returns on housing investment) from prevailing patterns of housing provision. Moreover, in many countries those who are better off reap most benefits from the system of housing subsidies and tax exemptions.

From a second perspective, *housing attainment can be viewed not as an outcome giving spatial expression to social attributes but rather as a resource which itself, in part, determines what characteristics (associated with wealth, status and service availability) residents can acquire.* The attainment of owner-occupation is the best example.

Owner-occupation is the dominant, politically favoured and most widely aspired after tenure sector in Britain, Australia and North America. For homeowners in these nations, dwelling locations – in national, regional and urban space – may be a significant determinant of house price appreciation and of dwelling saleability. Thus where people live affects the exchange value of their home. Over a period of time, this determines owners' ability to make capital gains from their housing investment. The potential to increase personal wealth and social standing through home ownership is therefore geographically uneven.

As a consequence of the differing ability of homes in different locations to hold their price, gain value and store equity, owner-occupation is differentiated and spatially polarized into low- and high-value sectors. Low-income home ownership often denotes a risky investment of limited capital into properties which require high expenditure on maintenance and repair (cf. REDLINING). Higher-income groups can make a better investment into appreciating homes which provide a store of equity and a source of cheap housing services in old age. Nevertheless, significant housing market instability, as experienced towards the end of the twentieth century in Britain, for example, emphasizes the potential riskiness of owner-occupation for all socio-economic classes. Such risks may be unevenly spread. In the British example, mortgage arrears, repossessions and 'negative equity' (where mortgage debt exceeds the sale value of the home) were all particularly marked in the south of the country (Dorling and Cornford, 1995).

For all households – owners and renters alike – housing outcomes also have a bearing on access to jobs, services and social support, as well as to a range of risks and opportunities which are themselves unevenly spread over space. For example, poor-quality housing is often a health hazard (Hunt, 1993), a crime risk (Smith, 1986: see CRIME, GEOGRAPHY OF) and a financial liability when the costs of upkeep and insurance are considered (Karn et al., 1995). Residential location affects access to health services (see HEALTH AND HEALTH CARE, GEOGRAPHY OF), police services (cf. SURVEILLANCE), reasonably priced shopping facilities, and educational and recreational facilities. Selective access to housing has led to the spatial concentration of disadvantaged households (particularly in the least desirable parts of the stock of public housing). The limited access these locations afford to a range of public and private goods, services and employment opportunities, adds a spatial dimension to the process of SOCIAL EXCLUSION (Power, 1987). In the USA these processes, especially those relating to a much-debated spatial mismatch between African-American homes and local employment opportunities, are implicated in the creation of a black UNDERCLASS.

Where people live is not, then, simply a passive product of who they are; it is the factor affecting what they can do and who they can become. Housing attainment is therefore implicated in the structuring of society and in the processes of SOCIAL REPRODUCTION. This occurs through the process of social segregation which reinforces spatial inequalities within tenure sectors; it is implicit in the consumption sector cleavages identified by Saunders (1986) between those able to secure housing in the market place and those reliant on state provisioning (cf. HOUSING CLASS); and it is exemplified in the gulf between those with any kind of permanent home and the growing number of homeless people in virtually all societies in the developed and developing worlds (cf. HOMELESSNESS).

Because housing outcomes not only reflect but also shape social differences and inequality, a third perspective on the geography of housing can be gained from a consideration of *housing policy (see* PUBLIC POLICY, GEOGRAPHY AND*). Housing interventions can affect both the production and consumption of residential space, and they are a key factor determining (either deliberately or inadvertently) the extent to which housing attainment passively reflects or actively moulds the social structure.*

The role and impact of housing policy can be thought of in at least four ways:

Housing interventions may be conceived of as a tool of macro-economic policy. Investment in housing can be made to pump-prime both national and local economies, and to stimulate the construction industry and the finance markets. This may be achieved *either* directly by state subsidies to dwelling production and to the consumption of public housing; *or* it may be achieved indirectly through tax exemptions (which effectively allow the state to subsidize the market), or through the manipulation of interest rates. The trend over most of Europe, North America and Australasia in recent years has been towards the latter practice, completing the cycle of commodification, decommodification and recommodification which is discussed by Dickens et al. (1985; see COMMODITY).

Housing policy may be used as an instrument of urban change and as the motor of NEIGHBOURHOOD *revitalization.* In much of western Europe, for example, area-based housing policies have been a popular alternative to the cycle of SLUM clearance and redevelopment which once displaced and fragmented INNER-CITY communities. *In situ* revitalization policies were designed to facilitate the gradual upgrading and renewal of older urban areas without disturbing the existing social fabric. In some areas, the (generally low) level of grant assistance was sufficient to stimulate the socio-economic changes associated with GENTRIFICATION. In others it was inadequate to halt a spiral of disinvestment and selective out-migration (by young people and white households). Increasingly the target for area regeneration policies has shifted away from inner cities, especially in Britain, where run-down peripheral estates have become impoverished and isolated. Here, public–private partnerships have been developed to tackle housing and environmental improvements, while other policies attempt to increase the access of residents to training and employment opportunities.

Housing policy plays a part in promoting public welfare and may therefore be seen as an element of social policy (Clapham et al., 1990). This is the area of housing consumption in which the STATE has a central role, and can therefore use housing provision to meet health needs, facilitate community care, offset income inequalities and so on. However, most developed societies are now engaged in a process of welfare restructuring, so that SOCIAL WELL-BEING is becoming one of the most neglected aims of housing provision (cf. WELFARE STATE).

The changing role of social housing is exemplified in Britain, where over a million public dwellings were sold into private ownership during the 1980s. These sales were spatially and socially uneven: better quality homes in suburban locations were bought by better-off tenants, leaving a residual sector housing the benefit-dependent poor and other marginalized groups (Forrest and Murie, 1988). Public housing became the welfare arm of the housing system at the moment it was least suited to perform this role – when it had become restricted in its geography and had undergone a decline in overall quality.

Housing policy is increasingly caught up in debates about ENVIRONMENTAL JUSTICE. In the USA, the location of waste management facilities interacts with the geography of residential segregation so that the burden of toxic contamination is borne disproportionately by poor people (see POVERTY, GEOGRAPHY OF), and people of colour (Heiman, 1996). In Britain, plans to accommodate four million new households over the next 20 years has exposed a tension between existing greenbelt policies and residential preferences for ex-urban locations (cf. EDGE CITY; PRIVATE INTEREST DEVELOPMENT). Low-density ex-urban developments imply car dependency and reduced thermal efficiency in buildings, so that a democratic solution to the housing problem (meeting the locational preferences of new households) conflicts with the principle of environmental sustainability.

To summarize, housing studies contribute to many areas of human geography; there is a link between LABOUR MARKETS and the housing system which has a bearing on the pattern of economic restructuring; housing often forms the leading edge of welfare restructuring and so affects the geography of disadvantage; and as well as providing shelter, housing functions as a home – it has a meaning and a symbolism which insert it firmly into the CULTURAL LANDSCAPE. In short, even a few examples indicate that studies of housing policy, production and consumption comprise an important interface between geography and the social sciences.

SJS

References

Ball, M. 1988: *Rebuilding construction: economic change in the British construction industry*. London: Routledge. · Clapham, D. and Kintrea, K. 1987: Rationing choice and constraint: the allocation of public housing in Glasgow. *Journal of Social Policy* 15: 51–67. · Clapham, D., Kemp, P. and Smith, S.J. 1990: *Housing and social policy*. London: Macmillan. · Dickens, P., Duncan, S., Goodwin, M. and Gray, F. 1985: *Housing, states and localities*. London: Methuen. · Dorling, D. and Cornford, J. 1995: Who has negative equity? How house price falls in Britain have hit different groups of house buyers. *Housing Studies* 10: 151–78. · Farley, J.E. 1995: Race still matters: the minimal role of income and housing cost as causes of housing segregation in St. Louis, 1990. *Urban Affairs Review* 31: 244–54. · Forrest, R. and Murie, A. 1988: *Selling the welfare state: the privatisation of public housing*. London: Routledge and Kegan Paul. · Heiman, M.K. 1996: Race, waste and class: new perspectives on environmental justice. *Antipode* 28 (2) (special issue). · Henderson, J. and Karn, V. 1987: *Race, class and state housing*. Aldershot: Gower. · Hunt, S. 1993: Damp and mouldy housing: a holistic approach. In R. Burridge and D. Ormandy, eds, *Unhealthy housing. Research, remedies and reforms*. London: E. and F. Spon, 69–93. · Karn, V., Kemeny, J. and Williams, P. 1985: *Home ownership in the inner city: salvation or despair*. Aldershot: Gower. · Power, A. 1987: *Property before people – the management of twentieth century council housing*. London: Allen and Unwin. · Saunders, P. 1986: *Social theory and the urban question*, 2nd edn. London: Hutchinson. · Smith, S.J. 1986: *Crime, space and society*. Cambridge: Cambridge University Press. · Smith, S.J. 1990: Housing status and the housing system. *Social Science and Medicine* 31: 753–62. · Smith, S.J. and Mallinson, S. 1996: The problem with social housing. *Policy and Politics* 24: 339–67. · Watson, S. 1988: *Accommodating inequality: gender and housing*. Sydney: Allen and Unwin.

Suggested Reading

Ball, M., Harloe, M. and Martens, M. 1988: *Housing and social change in Europe and the USA*. London: Routledge. · Karn, V. and Wolman, H. 1992: *Comparing housing systems: housing performance and housing policy in the United States and Britain*. Oxford: Clarendon Press. · Kemeny, J. 1992: Housing and social theory. London: Routledge. · Morris, J. and Winn, M. 1990: *Housing and social inequality*. London: Hilary Shipman. · Power, A. 1993: *Hovels to high-rise. State housing in Europe since 1850*. London: Routledge.

human agency The capabilities of human beings. Human agency is a central concern of both HUMANISTIC GEOGRAPHY (and humanism in general; Gregory, 1981) and various 'post-humanistic' geographies (and ANTI-HUMANISM in general) (Barnes and Gregory, 1997). As these oppositions and entanglements suggest, concepts of human agency have occasioned a number of major disagreements, including the following:

The relations between agents and human agents. For Cutler et al. (1977), for example, 'an agent is an entity capable of occupying the position of a locus of decision in a social relation' and recognized as such by other potential agents and by law or custom. They explicitly rejected the view that 'to be an agent is to be a subject [and] to act in terms of a will and a consciousness endowed with a faculty of "experience"' and insisted that 'there can be no basis for maintaining that agents must be conceptualised as human subjects'. Indeed, 'there may be agents other than individuals', e.g. companies, corporations and STATES. In response, Giddens (1979) dismissed these views as 'wholly unenlightening':

> They do not address the philosophical problems of agency at all. It is perfectly true that a corporation can be an agent in law. But laws have to be interpreted and applied; it takes human agents to do that, as well as to frame them in the first place.... [N]o approach which ignores the will and consciousness of human subjects is likely to be of much use in social theory.

Even so, the critique of limiting 'agents' to 'human agents' was subsequently radicalized by several contributions to science studies in general (Haraway, 1992) and ACTOR–NETWORK THEORY in particular. 'We do not know who the agents [are] who make up our world', Latour (1988) remarked: 'We must begin with this uncertainty if we are to understand how, little by little, the agents define one another, summoning other agents and attributing to them intentions and strategies'. Both Haraway and Latour thus treat 'agency' as a matter of *attributing the ability to act.* For this reason they prefer to speak of *actants* not actors or agents: 'Non-humans are not actants in the human sense, but they are part of the functional collective that makes up an actant' (Haraway, 1992, p. 331). As this implies, actants can include non-human actors and new couplings of human beings and machines (cf. CYBORG; HYBRIDITY). More radically still, the emphasis on a collectivity means that agency is no longer seen as a purely internal property of discrete individuals, which would include both Cutler et al.'s 'corporate actors' and Giddens's human agents (above). Instead, 'agency is reconfigured as a relational effect generated by a network of heterogeneous, interacting components whose activity is constituted in the networks of which they form a part' (Whatmore 1999, p. 28).

The relations between intentions and actions. For Giddens (1984), for example, although 'it has frequently been supposed that human agency can be defined only in terms of intentions', agency refers 'not to the intentions people have in doing things but to their capability of doing those things in the first place'. Such capabilities, he contends, are logically tied to POWER: 'an agent ceases to be such if he or she loses the capability to "make a difference", that is, to exercise some sort of power' (but see Thompson, 1984). Giddens acknowledged that these practical interventions 'cannot be examined apart from a broader theory of the acting self' and hence elaborated what he called a *stratification model of action* (see figure on p. 352). Not all action is purposive, therefore, in the sense of being directed by definite intentions, but it is purposeful in the sense of being 'reflexively monitored' by actors. Even so, a number of critics claimed that Giddens too often collapsed agency into action: 'what is obscured in [Giddens's] presentation is the claimed status of agency beyond the poles and intentional activity and reactive behaviour' (Dallmayr, 1982).

Here too there has been a more radical objection to Giddens's formulations: to limit the discussion to intentions and actions is to foreclose on the ways in which the *unconscious* enters into human agency. This is scarcely unique to Giddens's programmatic reformulation of social theory. The relationships between social theory and psychoanalytic theory have always been contentious, and the relationships between human geography and psychoanalytic theory have been broached only recently. As Pile (1996) remarks, 'the unconscious has always been a stumbling block for BEHAVIORAL GEOGRAPHY' (p. 73); similarly, most versions of HUMANISTIC GEOGRAPHY and RADICAL GEOGRAPHY emphasize 'visibility, legibility and consciousness' (p. 75). But a number of human geographers have started to explore the implications of psychoanalytic theory – and in particular the play of desire – for the critical understanding of human agency in ways that raise serious questions for social theory and human geography (see FEMINIST GEOGRAPHIES; PSYCHOANALYTIC THEORY, GEOGRAPHY AND).

The relations between agency and structure. One of the central objections of the humanistic project in geography was to those approaches that reified systems and structures: in which actions and outcomes were explained by 'functional imperatives' or 'structural logics' that seemingly determined human actions. This critique was part of a much wider debate staged with a special force within so-called 'English Marxism'. In both STRUCTURAL FUNCTIONALISM and STRUCTURAL MARXISM, for example, socialist-humanist historian E.P. Thompson (1978) complained that 'systems and sub-systems, elements and STRUCTURES, are drilled up and down the pages pretending to be people': human agency was evicted from history other than 'as the "supports" or vectors of ulterior structural determinations' (for a parallel critique in human geography, see Duncan and Ley, 1982). Against this, however, Anderson (1980) noted that 'agency' was such 'a dominant in [Thompson's] vocabulary' that he continually trembled on the edges of a voluntarism. Anderson proposed 'area of self-determination' as a more precise term than agency; even if this has been widening in the last 150 years, Anderson argued, 'it is still very much less than its opposite'. What was at stake here was not simply the deeply sedimented dualism between 'agency' and 'structure' that Giddens's STRUCTURATION THEORY sought to transcend with disputed degrees of success, but the development of an historical or historico-geographical (as opposed to a purely axiomatic) approach that would trace the changing 'curve' of human agency over time and space (see also Thrift, 1983). This is an immensely challenging project, which has involved the development of a CONTEXTUAL APPROACH to social inquiry in general and human geography in particular that pays special attention to the concept of *practice* and to a series of key terms clustered around it (including the BODY; HABITUS; SUBJECT-FORMATION; TRANSGRESSION) (see Thrift, 1996).

These three areas of disagreement intersect with debates about the constitution of human subjects (cf. Hirst and Woolley, 1982). Across the field of the humanities and the social sciences the continued development of anti-humanism and post-humanism has sustained considerable interest in the 'decentring' of the autonomous subject of traditional humanism and humanistic geography. This critique has been driven, in large measure, by various forms of POST-STRUCTURALISM, and revolves around the possibility of identifying multiple and competing subject-positions such that subjectivities are constituted at the intersection of different DISCOURSES (see Smith, 1987). These ideas have had far-reaching consequences. The incorporation of more complex constructions of identity, subjectivity and agency within POST-MARXISM has disrupted the classical Marxist thesis of ALIENATION and identified the salience of social struggles that are not sutured around a singular and coherent CLASS subject. In FEMINIST GEOGRAPHY parallel debates have clarified the ways in which both human agency and human subjects have been tacitly gendered in mainstream ('malestream') geographical inquiry, where typically agency has been coded in masculinist terms and the exemplary human subject has been constructed as both heterosexual and masculine (see MASCULINISM; QUEER THEORY). It has become clear, too, just how far human geography has internalized a conception of human agency that is 'ableist' and thus restricts still further the space for what Chouinard (1997) calls 'disabling differences' (cf. DISABILITY, GEOGRAPHY AND). In addition, dominant conceptions have usually been profoundly ethnocentric, and POST-COLONIALISM has played a vital (though at times, and by virtue of its own theoretical allegiances, an undoubtedly compromised) part in contesting the privileges accorded to Eurocentric concepts of human agency and the collective power of 'the subject of Europe' in hegemonic narratives of historical and geographical change (see also EUROCENTRISM; SUBALTERN STUDIES). Finally, the incorporation of actants other than human beings promises to rethink not only the 'human' in human geography but the 'geography' too: to provide for a much more sensuous, physical 'ecology' of action and agency (Thrift, 1996, ch. 1; see also Wolch, West and Gaines, 1995). The most profound impact of these ideas is likely to be in the braiding of these streams: in seeking to situate agency at the intersection of these different discourses. DG

References

Anderson, P. 1980: *Arguments within English Marxism*. London: Verso. · Barnes, T. and Gregory, D. 1997: Agents, subjects and human geography. In T. Barnes, and D. Gregory, eds, *Reading human geography: the poetics and politics of inquiry*. London: Arnold, 356–63. · Chouinard, V. 1997: Making space for disabling differences: challenging ableist geographies. *Environment and Planning D: Society & Space* 15: 379–87. · Cutler, A., Hindess, B., Hirst, P. and Hussain, A. 1977: *Marx's Capital and capitalism today*. London: Routledge and Kegan Paul. · Dallmayr, F. 1982: The theory of structuration: a critique. In A. Giddens, ed., *Profiles and critiques in social theory*. London: Macmillan, 18–25. · Duncan, J. and Ley, D. 1982: Structural Marxism and human geography: a critical assessment. *Annals of the Association of American Geographers* 72: 30–59. · Giddens, A. 1979: *Central problems in social theory: action, structure and contradiction in social analysis*. London: Macmillan. · Giddens, A. 1984: *The constitution of society*. Cambridge: Polity Press. · Gregory, D. 1981: Human agency and human geography. *Transactions, Institute of British Geographers*. NS 5: 1–16. · Haraway, D. 1992: Promises of monsters: a regenerative politics for 'inappropriate/d others'. In L. Grossberg, C. Nelson, and P. Treichler, eds, *Cultural studies*. New York: Routledge, 295–337. · Hirst, P. and Woolley, J. 1982: *Social relations and human attributes*. London: Tavistock; New York: Methuen. · Latour, B. 1988: *The Pasteurization of France*. Cambridge, MA: Harvard University Press. · Pile, S. 1996: *The body and the city: psychoanalysis, space and subjectivity*. London and New York: Routledge. · Smith, P. 1987: *Discerning the subject*. Minneapolis: University of Minnesota Press. · Thompson, E.P. 1978: *The poverty of theory and other essays*. London: Merlin. · Thompson, J.B. 1984: The theory of structuration: an assessment of the contribution of Anthony Giddens. In J.B. Thompson, ed., *Studies in the theory of ideology*. Cambridge:

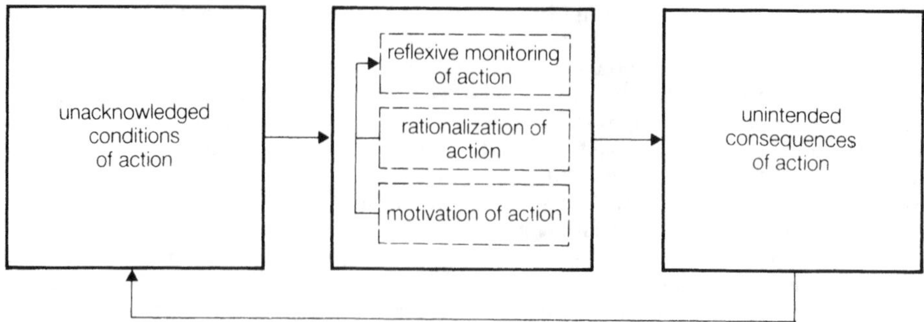

human agency *Stratification model of action* (after Giddens, 1984)

Polity Press. · Thrift, N. 1983: On the determination of social action in space and time. *Environment and Planning D: Society and Space* 1: 23–57. · Thrift, N. 1996: *Spatial formations*. London and New York: Sage. · Whatmore, S. 1999: Hybrid geographies: rethinking the 'human' in human geography. In D. Massey, J. Allen, and P. Sarre, eds, *Human geography today*. Cambridge: Polity Press, 22–39. · Wolch, J., West, K. and Gaines, T.E. 1995: Trans-species urban theory. *Environment and Planning D: Society and Space* 13: 735–60.

Suggested Reading
Pile (1996), ch. 2. · Whatmore (1999), pp. 26–31.

human ecology The extension of concepts drawn from ECOLOGY to the social realm: ecology deals with the relationships between organisms and their environment, and so human ecology studies the relationships between people and their social and physical environments. Steiner and Nauser (1993, p. xxiii) defined the term as 'look[ing] at human lifespaces and at the interplay occurring in those spaces between human beings and the biophysical environment'. Dangana and Tropp (1995, p. 19) wrote:

> Human ecology is concerned with relationship to the global environment. This vast field includes the patterns of development of past and present human societies as they have sought, by regulation and adaptation, to come to grips with a changing world throughout geological and historical time.

The term has a long history and its use highlights some of the important changes in geography during this century. Steiner and Nauser (1993, p. xxiii) note that although 'geography originally set out from the background of a philosophy which stressed the importance of a holistic view of regions and landscapes', it has become internally segmented and divergent. This has meant importing ideas from other disciplines to create sub-disciplines such as URBAN GEOGRAPHY and SOCIAL GEOGRAPHY (cf. URBAN ECOLOGY). Steiner and Nauser (1993, p. xxiii) add that 'geography tends to import theories and methods from the neighbouring disciplines, whereas the latter are largely unconcerned with developments in geography'. This situation has changed to some degree, but the comment remains valid.

The term came to geography via sociology, when a University of Chicago geographer, Harlan Barrows (1923), defined geography as 'the science of human ecology'. This definition gave the term a different sense than that used by the CHICAGO SCHOOL of sociologists, who included Park, Burgess, Thomas and Wirth; they imported concepts and analogies from ecology (such as COMMUNITY, competition, disturbance, climax equilibrium and INVASION AND SUCCESSION: cf. SOCIAL DARWINISM) to develop theories and models on human society but were not explicitly concerned with interrelationships with NATURE. Sociological human ecology has since tended to downplay the urban spatial focus of the Chicago School. Hawley (1986, pp. 2–3) wrote that in contrast to Park's emphasis on measures of distance, the 'more fruitful lesson to be learned from the work of plant and animal ecologists [is that] a workable relationship with the environment is not achieved by individuals or even species acting independently, but by their acting in concert . . .'.

Barrows' focus was on human adjustment to physical environments and promoted a NOMOTHETIC aspect to geography's character that the Chicago School sociologist, Robert Park, would have denied the discipline. The term 'human ecology' was not firmly established in geography thereafter, however, although it appears later in geographies of ENVIRONMENTAL HAZARDS (see also HAZARDS, HUMAN-MADE). Its use increased during the early 1970s, following the United Nations Conference on the

Human Environment (known as Stockholm '72) and has been extended into fields such as design (Papanek, 1984) and economics, which, as currently practised, has been termed 'errant human ecology' (Rees and Wackernagel, 1994). The term has also been used by biologists, e.g. Ehrlich, et al. (1973), to refer to the dwindling naturalness of environments. The contemporary inter-disciplinary journal *Human Ecology* claims to provide 'a forum for papers concerned with the complex and varied systems of interaction between people and their environment'; the named subject areas from which papers are encouraged are anthropology, geography, psychology, biology, sociology and urban planning.

The recent use of the term in geography has been limited. This may be a result of various interacting factors, including the term's vagueness through use in many disciplines and its connotations with ideas that were popular earlier in the twentieth century. Concern about SYSTEMS ANALYSIS, and its use in LIMITS TO GROWTH work in the early 1970s, coincided with Chorley's (1973) attack on human ecology as a futile attempt to regain something natural. Almost simultaneously, David Harvey's *Social justice and the city* (1973) heralded a move away from both systems analysis and human ecology to MARXIST GEOGRAPHY.

PM

References

Barrows, H. 1923: Geography as human ecology. *Annals of the Association of American Geographers* 13: 1–14. · Chorley, R. 1973: Geography as human ecology. In R. Chorley, ed., *Directions in geography*. London: Methuen and Co., 155–69. · Dangana, L. and Tropp, C. 1995: Human ecology and environmental ethics. In M. Atchia and S. Tropp, eds, *Environmental management: issues and solutions*. Chichester: John Wiley and Sons, 19–29. · Ehrlich, P., Ehrlich, A. and Holdren, J. 1973: *Human ecology*. San Francisco and London: W.H. Freeman. · Harvey, D. 1973: *Social justice and the city*. London: Edward Arnold. · Hawley, A. 1986: *Human ecology: a theoretical essay*. Chicago and London: The University of Chicago Press. · Papanek, V. 1984: *Design for the real world: human ecology and social change*, 2nd edn. London: Thames and Hudson. · Rees, W. and Wackernagel, M. 1994: Ecological Footprints and Appropriated Carrying Capacity: Measuring the Natural Capital Requirements of the Human Economy. In A.-M. Jannson et al., eds, *Investing in natural capital: the ecological economics approach to sustainability*. Washington, D.C.: Island Press, 362–90. · Steiner, D. and Nauser, M. 1993: *Human ecology: fragments of anti-fragmentary views of the world*. London and New York: Routledge.

Suggested Reading

Human Ecology: An Interdisciplinary Journal. New York and London: Plenum Press. · Steiner and Nauser (1993).

human geography That part of the discipline of geography concerned with the spatial differentiation and organization of human activity and its interrelationships with the physical environment.

Geography as a formal discipline has a long history; 'geographical knowledge' is much older (see GEOGRAPHY, HISTORY OF). The separation of human from physical geography is relatively recent. Its roots are in both German (cf. ANTHROPOGEOGRAPHY) and French late eighteenth- and early nineteenth-centuries' writings (the latter on *la géographie humaine*), whose influence continued into the early twentieth century, when geography was becoming established in the UK and in North America (Martin, 1985). From then on, however, contacts between the three language realms diminished substantially. Within the English-speaking world, geographers in the UK and the USA were numerically dominant, with British approaches widely adopted throughout the British Empire (not only the original dominions – Australia, Canada, New Zealand, South Africa – but also many other countries, some of which, India and Nigeria for example, have substantial numbers of academic geographers in their universities: initially, many of the geography departments were staffed by British expatriates). French and German approaches developed in substantial isolation from the English-speaking world, and there was considerable fragmentation within both of those realms until relatively recently (on France, see Knafou, 1997). There was also substantial development of a Spanish-language realm (the discipline is now very large in parts of Latin America, especially Argentina), of a Soviet Russia-dominated eastern European realm, and a significant presence (largely Jewish, with strong North American links) in Israel. The remainder of this essay focuses on the English-speaking realm during the twentieth century, within which there have been substantial differences at certain times alongside common strands, representing the many close trans-Atlantic contacts.

In the first decades of the twentieth century most works in English covered both human and physical geography topics, emphasizing human–environment interrelationships and their regional variations, as in the main mid-twentieth century programmatic texts – Hartshorne's (1939) *The nature of geography* in North America and Wooldridge and East's (1951) *The spirit and purpose of geography* in the UK. Nevertheless, specialization by individual workers in either human or, especially, physical geography became more common between 1919 and 1939, although physical geography was substantially downgraded in the United States – Peltier (1954), for example, argued that the study of geography needed information about physical landforms ('what? where? and how much?') but need not incorporate geomorphology, the science of landform genesis, which was an intriguing development given that geography initially developed in the United States within university geology departments. (This lack of attention to 'why?' questions regarding the environment in the USA – though not in Canada too – was not characteristic of UK geography then.) Its absence was marked by the lack of any contribution on physical geography to the volume of essays marking the Association of American Geographers' 75th anniversary in 1979 (although see Marcus, 1979). The situation has since changed and contemporary geography in the USA once again incorporates a substantial volume of work in physical as well as human geography (see also Gaile and Willmott, 1989; NRC, 1997): although the two major branches of the discipline co-exist within the same institutional structures (university departments and learned societies), however, the intellectual links between them are relatively weak and little research involves close collaboration between human and physical geographers.

Human geography was only weakly developed by British geographers before the Second World War. Freeman (1980) suggested a fourfold division of interests then – physical, historical, regional, and human; his review grouped the last two together, concentrating on REGIONAL GEOGRAPHY, LAND-USE SURVEY and the study of settlement types, especially villages. He quoted Fawcett (1934) that:

> We are as yet in the early stages of investigation of the many problems of human geography, and have not reached well-established generalisations. The study is in the stage of collecting facts, and framing and establishing hypotheses, most of which can only mark stages in its development.

Only after 1945 did human geography challenge physical geography in its standing within the discipline in the UK, as regional geography receded in both repute and practice and the sub-disciplines of URBAN, SOCIAL, POLITICAL, and INDUSTRIAL GEOGRAPHY began to attract attention as the foci of individual careers (Johnston and Gregory, 1984), alongside an established strength in HISTORICAL GEOGRAPHY which was substantially different in its approach from that practised in North America.

Stimuli for new work came to the UK from European and North American sources, with the latter acting as an intermediary in some cases, as with the 1960s appreciation of the work of the Swedish geographer Torsten Hägerstrand on MIGRATION and DIFFUSION (Duncan, 1974) and the '(re)discovery' of German developments of CENTRAL PLACE THEORY by geographers at the University of Washington, Seattle (Johnston, 1997). British urban geographers, for example, were influenced by German work – introduced to them by Dickinson (1947) and Conzen (1960) – and other continental European writings stimulated a range of American innovations (see Garrison's, 1959–60, review of work on locational analysis).

During the 1960s and 1970s many human geographers enthusiastically adopted the QUANTITATIVE REVOLUTION and promoted the sub-discipline as LOCATIONAL ANALYSIS or SPATIAL SCIENCE. The main texts (Haggett, 1965; Morrill, 1970; Abler, Adams and Gould, 1971) did not subdivide human geography further. Nor did two pathbreaking books of essays (Chorley and Haggett, 1965, 1967), although the second of those influential volumes – *Models in geography* – included chapters covering demographic models, sociological models, economic development models, models of urban geography and settlement location, models of industrial location, and models of agricultural activity, all under the heading 'Models of socio-economic systems'. Together these presaged the growth of some of the later major systematic specialisms within the discipline (population, social, urban, economic, industrial, agricultural) but not others (political, cultural).

British geographers continued attempts to sustain the links between human and physical geography through shared interests in models and quantitative methods – as illustrated by the two books edited by Chorley and Haggett, their volume on line patterns (Haggett and Chorley, 1969), and Haggett's (1972) major student text, written for the North American as well as the British market, though the last contained less physical than human geography material. By then, however, physical and human geographers were very largely going their separate ways as specialist researchers and though, for political and pedagogical reasons, they remained together in higher education institutions (with some claims that the discipline as a whole integrated material from the natural and social sciences and the humanities: Johnston, 1983) the nature of their research became ever more divorced (Johnston, 1986, 1996b, 1998).

The adoption of spatial science as the dominant PARADIGM for human geography in the 1960s was the basis for disciplinary self-promotion within the social sciences, among which it was largely disregarded until then. In the United States, two reports led to the discipline's acceptance within the funding bodies for scientific research. The first was commissioned because it was considered that 'geography does not have the esteem which it merits by virtue of the importance of its subject matter' (NAS–NRC, 1965). The committee of seven responded that:

> geography is on the threshold of an important opportunity that derives from: (1) the now vital need to understand as fully as possible every aspect of the man–environment system, including spatial distributions, throughout the world; (2) the development of a common interest among several branches of science in the overriding problem and its spatial aspects; (3) the development of a more or less common language for communication for the first time among all the pertinent branches of science through mathematical statistics and systems analysis; (4) the development of far more powerful techniques than ever before for analyzing systems problems, including spatial distributions; and (5) a backlog of spatial experience which geographers have accumulated from their spatial perspective and their past dedication to the study of the man–environment complex.

The eventual outcome was a Geography and REGIONAL SCIENCE Programme within the NAS–NRC (The National Academy of Sciences and the National Research Council), indicating the discipline's acceptance within the national institutional structure for scientific research. The second report, part of a survey of the behavioural and social sciences (Taaffe, 1970), promoted modern geography as the study of spatial organization which promised contributions to 'better solutions to policy and planning decisions'.

This US acceptance of human geography into the country's scientific and social scientific institutions, as spatial science with a strong basis in location theory, was paralleled in the UK where a Social Science Research Council (now the Economic and Social Research Council) was established in the mid-1960s without human geography as one of its component disciplines. This was challenged by the Institute of British Geographers (Steel, 1984) and a report prepared for a committee by Michael Chisholm resulted in the creation of a geography and planning committee responsible for allocating research studentships and grants. The unpublished report also stressed the SPATIAL SCIENCE/LOCATION THEORY elements of modern geography, alongside traditional strengths in area studies and society–environment interrelationships, as did a subsequent survey of current research in human geography (Chisholm, 1971; see also Chisholm and Rodgers, 1972; Chisholm, 1975).

Two main trends characterized human geography in the 1970s and 1980s: internal specialization and philosophical pluralism. *Internal specialization* was partly a consequence of rapid growth in the number of academic geographers (Stoddart, 1967), with scholars seeking to establish their own niches and career trajectories, and in part reflected their wide-ranging links with the literature, if not the practitioners, of other social sciences. (The flows were asymmetrical: geographers quoted other social scientists much more than other social scientists quoted geographers.) Specialist sub-groups were established within the main professional societies to cater for these interests (cf. GEOGRAPHICAL SOCIETIES: each runs its own sections at major conferences, many organize specialist conferences, and some publish their own journals and book series. For analyses of these groups, see Goodchild and Janelle, 1988; Johnston, 1991: Gaile and Willmott's (1989) overview of American geography is based on the AAG's speciality groups). Other specialized journals – both sub-disciplinary (e.g. *Political Geography*; *Journal of Transport Geography, Geographical Analysis*) and inter-disciplinary (such as *Environment and Planning A*) – were launched by commercial publishers to realize the potential of new niche markets, segmenting the discipline's literature (see Johnston, 1996a).

URBAN GEOGRAPHY and ECONOMIC GEOGRAPHY were the initial growth areas within spatial science, with shared interests in locational analysis and quantitative methods. They were later joined by a growing emphasis on SOCIAL GEOGRAPHY, a revived and revised POLITICAL GEOGRAPHY, a restructured CULTURAL GEOGRAPHY, and studies of a range of issues to do with society–nature relationships, such as RESOURCE MANAGEMENT. These shifts in substantive emphasis were paralleled by a growing sophistication of quantitative work by a relatively small group of researchers in the late 1970s and early 1980s (as in work on SPATIAL AUTOCORRELATION) and then the rapid growth of interest in GEOGRAPHICAL INFORMATION

SYSTEMS from the mid-1980s on (see also GEOCOMPUTATION).

Philosophical pluralism reflected geographers' growing involvement with the literature of other social science disciplines and, in the 1990s, some of the humanities. These provided bases for both critiques of current geographical practice (Harvey, 1973, and Gregory, 1978 were seminal early contributors) and attempts to restructure the discipline (e.g. Smith's (1977) volume with its focus on RELEVANCE, inequality and SOCIAL JUSTICE). Critiques of locational analysis and spatial science were launched from two directions in the 1970s: one attacked quantification and POSITIVIST approaches for their derogation of individual humans and their attitudes, values and feelings (as in SENSE OF PLACE) which could not be appreciated through the search for quantitatively stated laws; the other criticized the same work for its implicit acceptance of the political status quo and an inability to match its quantitative descriptions with meaningful understanding as the basis for radical political action. These two strands of work – often termed HUMANISTIC GEOGRAPHY and RADICAL GEOGRAPHY, respectively – meant that geographical scholarship in the 1980s was marked by three very different approaches to the discipline, or parts of it (humanistic geography was particularly associated with cultural and historical geography, for example, and radical geography with urban and economic studies).

These three strands of work became complexly interwoven within the fabric of geographical activity since the 1970s and their coexistence resulted in general rejection of the PARADIGM model of disciplinary development, whereby one approach achieves a HEGEMONIC position, followed by a 'revolutionary episode' in which it is overthrown for an alternative that is considered superior. Meanwhile, geographers have explored other literatures and opened their discipline to new stimuli – empirical, methodological, and philosophical (see, for example, the agenda in Thrift and Johnston, 1993). This exploration involved close engagement with disciplines in the humanities as well as the social sciences (notably literary theory, art history and theory, and history), and geographers are to the fore in a number of new multidisciplinary developments, notably the burgeoning area of Cultural Studies. The breadth of the contemporary discipline and the complex interweaving of various strands reflecting the many influences on what human geographers study, and how, mean that it is now impossible to impose any classificatory order on the discipline's structure and practices: more than ever before it comprises a range of communities exploring the myriad interactions of people, place and environment, with its more recent concerns and interactions illustrated by journals such as *Society and Space*, *Ecumene*, and *Gender, Place and Culture*.

Ideas in POSTMODERNISM attracted initial attention among those rejecting existing approaches in the 1980s (e.g. Dear, 1986; Soja, 1989), who offered it as a basis for reconstructing geographical practice around the main theme of DIFFERENCE. More influential, however, was the rapid expansion of FEMINIST GEOGRAPHY (Women and Geography Study Group, 1984). Arguments over both the role of women within the academy and the many 'silences' about women across a wide range of subject matter studied in a male-dominated discipline alerted geographers, through the breadth of the feminist literature (reviewed by McDowell, 1993a, 1993b), to wider issues of POSITIONALITY and the critiques of GRAND THEORY being developed in POST-COLONIAL and POST-STRUCTURAL approaches to the humanities and social sciences. Increased interest in environmental issues across those disciplines – with the emergence of sub-fields such as environmental history and environmental ethics as well as environmental politics and environmental sociology – stimulated renewed interest in the interactions between SOCIETY and NATURE, which if not bringing a fusion of physical and human geography into an integrated discipline (much of the former has become strongly scientific in recent years, with close links to the natural sciences and to engineering) has at least increased awareness of the social construction of nature.

Alongside these discussions, and stemming from the arguments that particular theoretical stances should not be privileged over others, there has been a CULTURAL TURN within human geography. This has involved challenges to not only the distinction between separate economic and cultural realms within society but also the privileged place allocated to economic mechanisms by some adherents to Marxist and other approaches, coupled with suggestions for embedding the two within each other (as in the essays in Lee and Wills, 1997). This is associated with calls for greater recognition of the role of (spatial) context as both a constraint to and enabler of behaviour: that 'places matter' is pivotal to many geographers' presentations of their discipline's niche within the academy and arguments for the centrality of place in the STRUCTURATION of local responses to GLOBALIZATION processes (e.g. Massey and Allen, 1984). It has led many to reject any search for 'grand theory' as they explore the tensions between various approaches to understanding (as in Gregory, 1994).

Against this trend towards philosophical pluralism and inter-disciplinary hybridization, others have argued for greater attention to a form of APPLIED GEOGRAPHY involving 'selling' geography's RELEVANCE to contemporary, materialist society. Knowledge is becoming more commodified and universities are under pressure to 'sell' their research capabilities (Johnston, 1995). Some have responded to this with calls for a renewed emphasis on spatial science and locational analysis based on the increased analytical power of GIS and associated modelling technologies (Openshaw, 1994). An example is provided by a further report on the nature of geography, designed to consolidate its status within the American scientific community because of a 'well-documented growing perception (external to geography as a discipline) that geography is useful, perhaps even necessary, in meeting certain societal needs'. Entitled *Rethinking geography: new relevance for science and society* (NRC, 1997) it focuses strongly on materialistic *utility*: technical expertise is stressed and the report makes virtually no reference to the great range of methods used by geographers to appreciate people's understanding and construction of the worlds in which they live and act, as well as their transmission of that understanding to others through various textual devices. A statement that 'current trends in geography's techniques suggest a future in which researchers, students, business people, and public policy makers will explore a world of shared spatial data from their desktops' because 'technology now plays a pre-eminent role in a wide range of geographic research' sits very oddly alongside the work discussed in the previous paragraphs (which the report very largely ignored), as does a section on 'geography's relevance to issues for science and society' which stresses two mathematical concepts – complexity and non-linearity.

The report was much influenced by a survey of opportunities for geography graduates and trends in geography faculty appointments in 212 American universities, which listed the main specializations of appointees as:

programs in environmental/resource management, techniques (GIS, cartography, and remote sensing), and urban planning. These tracks appear to be designed to prepare students for the occupations in which geographers have traditionally found work rather than to develop their interests in regional geography or the systematic specialties like urban, economic or physical geography that have traditionally formed the core of the discipline.

Exploration of graduates' employment opportunities led the authors to identify a major shift in the discipline as it was being taught to undergraduates:

> The debate over geography as a broad-based liberal arts discipline or as a technical semiprofessional field ignores the realities of the current labor market. Sponsors told us they want employees who can combine technical skills with a broad-based background. Geography's comparative advantage over other social sciences lies in its ability to combine technical skills with a more traditional liberal arts perspective. Successful geography programs will be those that are able to find the appropriate balance of field-based technical skills like GIS, cartography and air-photo interpretation with competence in literacy, numeracy, decision making, problem solving and critical thinking.

The argument presented in *Rethinking geography* is countered by a growing body of work under the general heading of CRITICAL HUMAN GEOGRAPHY. This stresses the distinction between *is* and *ought*, between observations of what the world is (and has been) like and views of what it should be like, and includes explorations of moral philosophy and related fields (as in Harvey, 1996, and Smith, 1994) – to which Smith (1998) has suggested a particular geographic contribution – and is reflected in the launch of a journal on *Ethics, Place and Environment* (see MORAL LANDSCAPES). Such work has 'applied' goals very different from that promoted in *Rethinking geography*: to increase self- and mutual awareness and to facilitate emancipation – what Buttimer (1993) terms education for responsibility and invitation to discovery (critical, speculative and emancipatory) rather than specifications of appropriate conduct.

There are strong tensions within contemporary human geography, therefore, at least partly stimulated by political pressures (on which see Sheppard, 1995). One set of arguments suggests that in order for their discipline to survive in universities, geographers must both ensure that graduates are taught the sorts of 'transferable skills' necessary for job market success otherwise students will not be attracted to the discipline (these arguments are common in the *Journal of Geography in Higher*

Education) and develop research agenda which allow them to 'sell' their knowledge and skills in the public and private sectors: human geography must prove itself in a relatively narrow, utilitarian sense. On the other hand, there are geographers who promote their discipline as a LOCALE for the development of critical thinking about issues involving the interrelationships among people and nature, in places, without privileging any one approach or interpretation.

Recent books reflect some of the excitement and debate that has characterized two or more decades of internal specialization and philosophical pluralism. Some review the richness of the discipline in all-embracing compendia such as Gaile and Willmott's (1989) 840 pages on *Geography in America*. Peet and Thrift's (1989) two-volume work brought together major reviews of work done in the radical geography mould; Gregory and Urry (1985), Gregory and Walford (1989) and Wolch and Dear (1990) edited volumes promoting new perspectives on the study of spatial structures; Macmillan's (1989) volume was largely prepared, despite some dissenting voices from within, as a defence of the quantitative-dominated approach, as was Haggett's (1990) personal view of 30 years in the discipline; others, such as Kobayashi and Mackenzie (1989) sought accommodations, in their case between the humanistic and radical views and promoting the restructured cultural geography (Jackson, 1989). All of these reflect the rapidity of change within the discipline. In 1973, Chorley invited several authors to consider *Directions in geography*: their essays bear little resemblance to those produced by another group twelve years later in *The future of geography* (Johnston, 1985) – and a further collection only seven years later again once more illustrates the rapidity of disciplinary change (Johnston, 1992), as does comparison of the three previous editions (1981, 1986, 1994) of the present work.

At the end of the 1980s, the Association of American Geographers commissioned what it termed the first comprehensive survey of the discipline for some 30 years, 'written primarily for geographers rather than for readers outside the discipline, and ... focus[ing] on what geographers of all specialties and persuasions had in common': its goals were to 'reintroduce geographers to each other' and 'to highlight the common elements within a discipline whose practitioners are in danger of forgetting their shared heritage and ideals'. *Geography's inner worlds* (Abler, Marcus and Olson, 1992) has four sections – on 'What geography is about', 'What geographers do', 'How geographers think' and 'Why geographers think that way': the five chapters on 'What geographers do', for example, cover 'Observation', 'Visualization', 'Analysis', 'Modeling' and 'Communication', and thereby privilege the ongoing legacy of the 'quantitative and theoretical revolution'. The strongest themes in the editors' retrospect, however, are their admitted failure to bridge the divide between human and physical geography as successfully as they hoped and their concerns about a similar divide developing within human geography – basically between those who can be described as 'spatial scientists' and those who are 'social theorists' – the major tension within contemporary human geography identified above.

In 1978 a senior American geographer edited a special issue of a general social science journal under the title *Human geography: coming of age* (Zelinsky, 1978). In retrospect, he would undoubtedly see that as a premature conclusion. In the following 20 years human geography has certainly not displayed the characteristics of maturity and staidness often associated with coming-of-age but has instead continued to demonstrate the vitality, vibrancy and unpredictability of youth. To some this is unfortunate; to others, it is the basis of their excitement in the discipline. Human geographers are involved with scholars from a wide range of other disciplinary perspectives in the exploration and development of new areas of work – including reinterpretations of the history and politics of their own discipline. Much of their research cannot be constrained by the 'disciplinary containers' of universities. The major advances in all areas of knowledge are multidisciplinary, and yet the institutional structures constrain these developments somewhat – not least in the allocation of resources in universities (on which see Taylor, 1996, 1997) – leading to occasional myopic attempts to impose a disciplinary-based order on what might best be seen as a glorious intellectual anarchy, within which it may be very difficult to perceive 'progress' (on which see Bassett, 1998). Different approaches have been more popular in some places and at some times than others but there is always tension among their protagonists as they seek approval and resources within the academy.

RJJ

References

Abler, R.F., Adams, J.S. and Gould, P.R. 1971: *Spatial organization: the geographer's view of the world*. Englewood Cliffs, NJ: Prentice-Hall. · Abler, R.F., Marcus, M.G. and Olson, J.M., eds, 1992: *Geography's inner worlds: pervasive themes in contemporary American geography*. New Brunswick, NJ: Rutgers University Press. · Bassett, K. 1998: Is there progress in human geography? The problem of progress in the light of recent work in the philosophy and sociology of science. *Progress in Human Geography* 24. · Buttimer, A. 1993: *Geography and the human spirit*. Baltimore: Johns Hopkins University Press. · Chisholm, M. 1971: *Research in human geography*. London: Social Science Research Council. · Chisholm, M. 1975: *Human geography: evolution or revolution*. London: Penguin Books. · Chisholm, M. and Rodgers, H.B., eds, 1972: *Studies in human geography*. London: Heinemann. · Chorley, R.J., ed., 1973: *Directions in geography*. London: Methuen. · Chorley, R.J. and Haggett, P., eds, 1965: *Frontiers in geographical teaching*. London: Methuen. · Chorley, R.J. and Haggett, P., eds, 1967: *Models in geography*. London: Methuen. · Conzen, M.R.G. 1960: Alnwick, Northumberland: a study in town-plan analysis. *Transactions, Institute of British Geographers* 27. · Dear, M.J. 1986: The postmodern challenge: reconstructing human geography. *Transactions, Institute of British Geographers* NS 13: 262–74. · Dickinson, R.E. 1947: *City, region and regionalism*. London: Routledge and Kegan Paul. · Duncan, S.S. 1974: The isolation of scientific discovery: indifference and resistance to a new idea. *Science Studies* 4: 109–34. · Fawcett, C.B. 1934: The Geographical congress at Warszawa. *Geographical Journal* 84: 424–7. · Freeman, T.W. 1980: *A history of modern British geography*. London and New York: Longman. · Gaile, G.L. and Willmott, C.J., eds, 1989: *Geography in America*. Columbus: Merrill Publishing Co.. · Garrison, W.L. 1959–60: Spatial structure of the economy. *Annals of the Association of American Geographers* 49: 238–49; 471–82 and 50: 357–73. · Goodchild, M.F. and Janelle, D.G. 1988: Specialization in the structure and organization of geography. *Annals of Association of American Geographers* 78: 11–28. · Gregory, D. 1978: *Ideology, science and human geography*. London: Hutchinson. · Gregory, D. 1994: *Geographical imaginations*. Oxford: Blackwell. · Gregory, D. and Urry, J., eds, 1985: *Social relations and spatial structures*. London: Macmillan. · Gregory, D. and Walford, R., eds, 1989: *Horizons in human geography*. London: Macmillan. · Haggett, P. 1965: *Locational analysis in human geography*. London: Edward Arnold. · Haggett, P. 1972: *Geography: a modern synthesis*. New York and London: Harper and Row. · Haggett, P. 1990: *The geographer's art*. Oxford: Basil Blackwell. · Haggett, P. and Chorley, R.J. 1969: *Network models in geography*. London: Edward Arnold. · Hartshorne, R. 1939: *The nature of geography*. Lancaster, PA: Association of American Geographers. · Harvey, D. 1973: *Social justice and the city*. London: Edward Arnold. · Harvey, D. 1996: *Justice, nature and the geography of difference*. Oxford: Blackwell. · Jackson, P. 1989: *Maps of mind*. London: Unwin Hyman. · James, P.E. and Jones, C.F., eds, 1954: *American geography: inventory and prospect*. Syracuse: Syracuse University Press. · Johnston, R.J. 1983: Resource analysis, resource management and the integration of human and physical geography. *Progress in Physical Geography* 7: 127–46. · Johnston, R.J., ed., 1985: *The future of geography*. London: Methuen. · Johnston, R.J. 1986: *On human geography*. Oxford: Basil Blackwell. · Johnston, R.J. 1991: *A question of place: exploring the practice of human geography*. Oxford: Basil Blackwell. · Johnston, R.J., ed., 1992: *The challenge for geography: a changing world, a changing discipline*. Oxford: Basil Blackwell. · Johnston, R.J. 1995: The business of British geography. In A.D. Cliff, P.R. Gould, A.G. Hoare and N.J. Thrift, eds, *Diffusing geography: essays for Peter Haggett*. Oxford: Blackwell, 317–41. · Johnston, R.J. 1996a: The expansion and fragmentation of geography in higher education. In R.J. Huggett, M.E. Robinson and I. Douglas (eds.) *Companion Encyclopædia of Geography*. London: Routledge, 794–817. · Johnston, R.J. 1996b: *Nature, state and economy: the political economy of environmental problems*. Chichester: John Wiley. · Johnston, R.J. 1997: *Geography and geographers: Anglo-American human geography since 1945*, 5th edn. London: Edward Arnold; New York: Routledge. · Johnston, R.J. 1998: Fragmentation around a defended core: the territoriality of geography. *Geographical Journal* 168. · Johnston, R.J. and Gregory, S. 1984: The United Kingdom. In R.J. Johnston and P. Claval, eds, *Geography since the Second World War: an international survey*. London: Croom Helm. · Totowa, NJ: Barnes and Noble, 107–31. · Knafou, R., ed., 1997: *L'état de la géographie: Autoscopie d'une science*. Paris: Balin. · Kobayashi, A. and Mackenzie, S. 1989: *Remaking human geography*. Boston: Unwin Hyman. · Lee, R. and Wills, J., eds, 1997: *Geographies of economies*. London: Arnold. · McDowell, L. 1993a: Space, place and gender relations: Part I. Feminist empiricism and the geography of social relations. *Progress in Human Geography* 17: 157–79. · McDowell, L. 1993b: Space, place and gender relations: Part II. Identity, difference, feminist geometries and geographies. *Progress in Human Geography* 17: 305–18. · Macmillan, B., ed., 1989: *Remodelling geography*. Oxford: Basil Blackwell. · Marcus, M.G. 1979: Coming full circle: physical geography in the twentieth century. *Annals of the Association of American Geographers* 69: 521–32. · Martin, G.J. 1985: Paradigm change: a history of geography in the United States, 1892–1925. *National Geographic Research*, Spring 1985: 218–35. · Massey, D. and Allen, J., eds, 1984: *Geography matters! A reader*. Cambridge: Cambridge University Press. · Morrill, R.L. 1970: *The spatial organization of society*. Belmont, CA: Wadsworth. · NAS–NRC, 1965: *The science of geography*. Washington, D.C.: National Academy of Sciences–National Research Council. · NRC, 1997: *Rethinking geography*. Washington, D.C.: National Research Council. · Openshaw, S. 1994: Computational human geography: towards a research agenda. *Environment and Planning A* 26: 499–505. · Peet, R. and Thrift, N.J., eds, 1989: *New models of geography, 2 vols*. Boston: Unwin Hyman. · Peltier, L.C. 1954: Geomorphology. In P.E. James and C.F. Jones, eds, *American geography: inventory and prospect*. Syracuse: Syracuse University Press, 362–81. · Sheppard, E.S. 1995: Dissenting from spatial analysis. *Urban Geography* 16: 283–303. · Soja, E.W. 1989: *Postmodern geographies*. London: Verso. · Smith, D.M. 1977: *Human geography: a welfare approach*. London: Edward Arnold. · Smith, D.M. 1994: *Geography and social justice*. Oxford: Blackwell. · Smith, D.M. 1998: How far should we care? On the spatial scope of beneficence. *Progress in Human Geography* 24. · Steel, R.W. 1984: *The Institute of British Geographers: the first fifty years*. London: Institute of British Geographers. · Stoddart, D.R. 1967: Growth and structure of geography. *Transactions, Institute of British Geographers* 41: 1–19. · Taaffe, E.J. ed., 1970: *Geography*. Englewood Cliffs, NJ: Prentice-Hall. · Taylor, P.J. 1996: Embedded statism and the social sciences: opening up to new spaces. *Environment and Planning A* 28: 1917–29. · Taylor, P.J. 1997: The crisis of boundaries: towards a new heterodoxy in the social sciences. *Journal of Area Studies* 11: 32–43. · Thrift, N.J. and Johnston, R.J. 1993: The futures of *Environment and Planning A*. *Environment and Planning A* (anniversary issue), 83–102. · Wolch, J. and Dear, M.J., eds, 1990: *The power of geography: how territory shapes social life*. Boston: Unwin Hyman. · Women and Geography Study Group, 1984 *Geography and gender: an introduction to feminist geography*. London: Hutchinson. · Wooldridge, S.W. and East, W.G., 1951: *The spirit and purpose of geography*. London: Hutchinson. · Zelinsky, W., ed., 1978: Human geography coming of age. *American Behavioral Scientist* 22: 1–167.

human rights A right is an entitlement embedded in some social or institutional context. To have a right is to expect to be treated in a certain way, which others are under an obligation to fulfil. We say that rights should be 'guaranteed', not 'violated': words which express the force with which we assert a right, as opposed to a mere need or want. Rights are special claims, with respect to the kind of things customarily involved, such as protection from arbitrary arrest, freedom of speech, and life itself. To refer to *human* rights is to stress that they apply to humankind rather than to all living creatures, though this usage can have other implications (considered below).

Rights have certain common features: *strength*, as particularly important interests; *urgency*, in the sense of priority over other interests (e.g. needs and wants); and they are *peremptory* in that they may exclude certain actions such as preventing persons from voting or torturing them. Rights which relate to what people should have are sometimes termed *positive*; those which specify what should not happen to them are *negative*. A distinction is sometimes made between rights as *derivative*, held and respected insofar as they promote some ultimate good (like the right to vote promoting political freedom), and as *foundational* or arising from our humanity.

Rights are sometimes regarded as purely personal attributes: part of what individual citizens are entitled to in a democratic society. However, we do talk of the rights of particular groups in society, such as racial or ethnic minorities, women and political dissidents. In any event, rights can never be entirely individual, because they imply an *obligation* or *duty* on others. This is most obvious in the case of rights with a peremptory character; the requirement not to treat people in a particular way is often stronger than to do something positive for them. Individual rights are central to liberalism, which is criticized in COMMUNITARIANISM as giving insufficient attention to obligations.

A distinction can be made between *legal* and *moral* rights. Legal rights are the more secure, because they can be asserted or defended in the courts. Moral rights may simply express an aspiration, such as votes for blacks in South Africa before this was enshrined in law. A further distinction is between *liberty-oriented* rights, sometimes referred to as civic and political rights, which concern freedom of action, and *security-oriented* rights (or *claim* rights) which refer more to economic and social requirements to protect people's physical and material status, such as unemployment and social security benefits.

Some rights may be held to be *universal*, applying to all people everywhere and at all times, and *inalienable* in that they can neither be given nor taken away. The term *human rights* is often used to refer to those moral rights which are supposed to be universal. That such rights are not universally respected in practice is a matter of common observation, of the (geographical) relativity of actual rights.

The notion of human rights is itself problematic. It is not generally agreed that our common humanity necessarily justifies any rights as *natural* attributes of humankind. Some POSTMODERN attitudes see any definition of human nature as dangerous, because it threatens to devalue or exclude acceptable DIFFERENCES. However, the idea of a range of universal rights, equally attributed to all persons by virtue of their shared humanity, has strong appeal in a world of domination and oppression, even without invoking the proposition that human rights are natural.

A particular attraction of the concept of human rights is that it requires specificity. In claiming or denying a right, it is important to know exactly what someone is or is not entitled to. A formal statement of rights is a useful means of being precise. For example, the *Declaration of Rights of Men and Citizens* enacted by the First French Republic in 1791 asserted that 'Men are born and remain free and equal in rights . . . these rights are liberty, property, security, and resistance to oppression'. The first ten Amendments to the Constitution of the United States (the *Bill of Rights*) specify certain freedoms that people should not be denied, for example freedom of worship and speech, and not to be subject to unreasonable searches and seizures. At the international scale, the United Nations adopted the *Universal Declaration of Human Rights* in 1948, and in 1966 produced its *Covenant on Civil and Political Rights* and *Covenant on Economic, Social and Cultural Rights* which are legally binding on those STATES formally ratifying them. However, such declarations are sometimes criticized as promising more than they can make individuals and nations deliver.

An important geographical issue is whether people can be said to have a right to, literally, a place in the world. That they are was suggested by Thomas Hobbes in his classic *The Elements of Law*, recognizing the right to a place to live among things necessary for life. This is sometimes extended into an argument for the right to private property, in the form of land ownership required to guarantee security of a place to live as a legal right. John Locke proposed a natural law of property, which is an important feature of LIBERTARIANISM. However, a right to own land differs from other commonly enunciated rights, in that it concerns appropriation of the scarce material world, and can impinge on the rights of others to meet such vital needs as food and shelter. At the extreme, private ownership of land, by restricting access, can deprive others of a place to live, even of the right to life. This is an example of how rights can conflict with one another. Land rights, manifest in private ownership or other forms of tenure, are of paramount importance to the link between geography and SOCIAL JUSTICE. (See also CITIZENSHIP; ETHICS, GEOGRAPHY AND.)

DMS

Suggested Reading

Jones, P. 1994: *Rights*. London: Macmillan. · Selby, D. 1987: *Human rights*. Cambridge: Cambridge University Press. · Waldron, J., ed., 1984: *Theories of rights*. Oxford: Oxford University Press. · Waldron, J. 1993: Rights. In R.E. Goodin and P. Pettit, eds, *A companion to political philosophy*. Oxford: Blackwell, 575–85.

humanistic geography An approach to human geography distinguished by the central and active role it gives to human awareness and HUMAN AGENCY, human consciousness and human creativity. Humanistic geography emerged in the Anglo-American discipline during the 1970s and was advertised as offering 'an expansive view of what the human person is and can do' (Tuan, 1976) and as an attempt at 'understanding meaning, value and [the] human significance of life events' (Buttimer, 1979). At the time humanistic geographers often traced the roots of their concerns back to the French school of human geography, but Vidal de la Blache's writings bear many of the hallmarks of FUNCTIONALISM and of what Duncan (1980) called the 'superorganic' that most humanistic geographers would presumably repudiate. Whatever the strength of the French connection, it was claimed that humanistic geography (especially where it was informed by SYMBOLIC INTERACTIONISM) was also heir to the neo-KANTIANISM and PRAGMATISM of Park and the CHICAGO SCHOOL of sociology: 'Park's practical concerns clearly have immense contemporary relevance, offering the basis of a much-needed methodological armoury capable of sustaining the variety of humanistic philosophies currently pervading SOCIAL GEOGRAPHY' (Jackson and Smith, 1984).

However profitably these twin legacies might be invested – and the others that might be discovered: the gentle ANARCHISM of Kropotkin and Reclus, for example, or the sensibilities of Fleure and Herbertson – it is clear that the formalization and advance of humanism in Anglo-American geography sprang from a deep dissatisfaction with the 'new geography' of the 1960s and its concerted reformulation of the discipline as SPATIAL SCIENCE. Humanistic geography shared in the critique of POSITIVISM and was for a time represented as 'a form of criticism' through which 'geographers can be made more self-aware and cognizant of many of the hidden assumptions and implications of their methods and research', rather than as a coherent and serviceable 'methodology for the "postbehavioural revolution" in geography' (Entrikin, 1976).

Yet humanistic geography was always intended as much more than a critical philosophy. Insofar as it was also a rejection of the prevailing geometric PARADIGM in which men and women were assumed to respond passively to the dictates of universal SPATIAL STRUCTURES and abstract spatial logics, it was at the same time a claim for what its architects believed to be a 'truly human geography' concerned with the social construction and experience of place, space and landscape rather than the spatial confinement of peoples and societies (see, e.g., Tuan, 1977). During the next ten years humanistic geography moved far from the base-line plotted by Entrikin, and drew its strength from two main sources.

The first source for humanistic geography was provided by the *humanities*, which Meinig (1983) characterized as 'that special body of knowledge, reflection and substance about human experience and human expression, about what it means to be a human being on this earth'. He had most prominently in mind the study of literature and history, and made much of the interpretative sensibilities of scholars in these disciplines. The favoured methods were usually those of HERMENEUTICS and mainstream historiography: a close and careful reading of TEXTS in which geographers were urged to listen carefully to the murmur of voices in the cultural archive. This style of humanistic geography had such a close interest in the recovery of the sedimented layers of meanings and actions embedded in PLACES and LANDSCAPES that it was in practice intimately associated with HISTORICAL GEOGRAPHY (Harris, 1978; Meinig, 1979). Many of its authors shared a deep concern with particularity and specificity, rather than with general theories of spatial organization, and often preferred to avoid any kind of formalization altogether. This diffidence was perhaps most obvious in humanistic geography's early engagements with literature (Pocock, 1981). Once humanistic geographers had recognized that the humanities could also be 'theoretical' in at least some of their sensibilities, however, many of them started to work with concepts from literary theory and art theory (see ART, GEOGRAPHY AND) to provide sophisticated readings of CULTURAL LANDSCAPES as texts and as images (cf. Daniels, 1985).

The second source for humanistic geography was provided by the *social sciences*, where theoretical self-consciousness was always much more visible. To be sure, many writers insisted that there was literally a world of difference between the high-level abstractions of spatial science and its successor projects – so-called GRAND THEORY – and the more modest, 'grounded' theories that they believed were more appropriate for humanistic inquiry (Ley, 1989). One of their central concerns was the clarification of the 'theoretical attitude' itself through a critical reflection underwritten by PHENOMENOLOGY (Christensen, 1982). Empirical studies were often informed by conceptual frameworks derived from ETHNOMETHODOLOGY and SYMBOLIC INTERACTIONISM; their interpretative methods were typically those of ETHNOGRAPHY (Smith, 1984; Pile 1991). This style of humanistic geography paid close attention to the social construction of places and the incursions of rationalized, even 'placeless' landscapes into the social topographies of the LIFEWORLD and the TAKEN-FOR-GRANTED WORLD, so that it was closely associated with contemporary SOCIAL GEOGRAPHY (see, for example, Ley, 1978; Relph, 1981; Western, 1981; cf. PLACELESSNESS).

Even as they formed, these two streams from the humanities and the social sciences braided into one another (see Ley and Samuels, 1978). One important series of cross-currents emerged in the 1980s out of an interest in historical geographies of CLASS struggle, inspired by E.P. Thompson's avowedly socialist-humanist history and the central credo of HISTORICAL MATERIALISM: namely, people make history (and geography) but not just as they please and not under conditions of their own choosing. Thompson's writings were distinguished by their elegance and attentiveness to the creative capacities of ordinary language to capture the ebb and flow of historical eventuation, and Thompson himself made no secret of his hostility to formal or 'high' theory. And yet within the social sciences a parallel body of social theory was under construction that promised to illuminate the changing intersections between 'agency' (the actions of men and women) and 'structure' (the formations of capitalism). The stage was thus set for an encounter between historical materialism and humanistic geography in which the pivot was provided by what came to be called STRUCTURATION THEORY (Gregory, 1981; Kobayashi and Mackenzie, 1989).

Another series of cross-currents emerged in the 1990s through the construction of a 'new' CULTURAL GEOGRAPHY and the extraordinary growth of an inter-disciplinary 'cultural studies', but these turned out to be much more turbulent for humanistic geography. The so-called 'CULTURAL TURN' has made it immensely difficult to identify a distinctively humanistic geography, so much so that it would now probably be more meaningful to speak of various 'post-humanistic geographies'. There has certainly been no shortage of 'posts-', and many scholars who had been closely associated with the development of humanistic geography were subsequently drawn to POSTMODERNISM and even POST-STRUCTURALISM (see Barnes and Duncan, 1992; Duncan and Ley, 1993). Post-humanism, like the other 'posts-', effectively radicalizes the prior term, so that many of the concerns of humanistic geography have undoubtedly helped to forge a generalized sensibility within the discipline at large. But in doing so those concerns have been subject to critical reflection and reformulation. There have been three main axes of critique:

First, a revivified history of GEOGRAPHY has helped to rewrite the historiography of humanism. This has involved more than new interpretations of Vidal de la Blache or Robert Park (important though these have been). In particular, Cosgrove (1989) traced humanism back to the European Renaissance and showed that it was implicated in the very geometricization of knowledge which, in its modern geographical form, it sought to contest. The sovereign subject of Renaissance humanism was, significantly, European and male, and intellectual historians and literary scholars have provided artful demonstrations of the ways in which these (and other) cultural markings inflected the knowledges produced under its authorizing sign (cf. HISTORICISM). These revisionist historiographies have fed into:

Secondly, a powerful ANTI-HUMANISM which has challenged the concept of the human subject that lies at the heart of humanistic geography. There had been an earlier and largely indecisive tussle over one version of anti-humanism, in which a deeply passionate critique of STRUCTURAL MARXISM in human geography was met with a no less passionate response (Duncan and Ley, 1982; Chouinard and Fincher, 1983). But the rise of POST-STRUCTURALISM has had a far more decisive impact on the discipline. The central charge is that the subject of humanism was a fiction constructed through an IDEOLOGY which suppressed the multiple ways in which human subjects are constructed: these erasures both promoted and privileged a white, masculine, bourgeois, heterosexual subject as the norm (Rose, 1993) (see also EPISTEMOLOGY). It is plainly impossible to found a 'truly human geography' on a series of exclusions, as the critique from FEMINIST GEOGRAPHY has shown, and in order to understand the complexity and heterogeneity of subject-formation many geographers have since been drawn to an exploration of the spaces within which and through which these processes literally take place: hence the project of 'mapping the subject' (Pile and Thrift, 1995) (see also SUBJECT FORMATION, GEOGRAPHIES OF).

Thirdly, humanistic geography is criticized for a superficial understanding of human action. Humanistic geography drew much of its intellectual power from its critique of another fictional subject: 'rational economic man' who was located at the core of mainstream spatial science. Much of the reconstructive work of humanistic geography was predicated on the claim that the creativity and diversity of human agency could not be restricted to the operation of such a narrowly instrumental rationality; the purposes and meanings embedded in human action were not confined to a peculiarly economic, means-ends calculus of UTILITY maximization. In substituting a richer range of motivations and satisfactions, however, humanistic geography typically retained a focus on intentions; even when conceptual space was made for the unintended consequences of action, as it was in structuration theory, it was still assumed that the origins of human action lay in human consciousness. In short, humanistic geography, like human geography more generally, drew back from an engagement with the unconscious. Perhaps this reticence was in part the product of the discipline's earlier forays into behavioural geographies which seemed to differ so little from the mechanistic models of spatial science (see Ley, 1981). Post-humanistic geography is increasingly informed by an interest in PSYCHOANALYTIC THEORY (here too the intersections with FEMINIST GEOGRAPHIES are particularly significant), and thereby seeks to illuminate the ways in which desire and fantasy animate human action (Pile, 1996). DG

References

Barnes, T. and Duncan, J., eds, 1992: *Writing worlds: discourse, text and metaphor in the representation of landscape*. London and New York: Routledge. · Buttimer, A. 1979: Reason, rationality and human creativity. *Geografiska Annaler* 61B: 43–9. · Chouinard, V. and Fincher, R. 1983: A critique of 'Structural Marxism and human geography'. *Annals of the Association of American Geographers* 73: 137–46. · Christensen, K. 1982: Geography as a human science: a philosophical critique of the positivist-humanist split. In P. Gould and G. Olsson, eds, *A search for common ground*. London: Pion, 37–57. · Cosgrove, D. 1989: Historical considerations on humanism, historical materialism and geography. In A. Kobayashi and S. Mackenzie, eds, *Rethinking human geography*. London: Unwin Hyman. · Daniels, S. 1985: Arguments for a humanistic geography. In R.J. Johnston, eds, *The future of geography*. London: Methuen, 143–58. · Duncan, J. 1980: The superorganic in American cultural geography. *Annals of the Association of American Geographers* 70: 181–98. · Duncan, J. and Ley, D. 1982: Structural Marxism and human geography. *Annals of the Association of American Geographers* 72: 30–59. · Duncan, J. and Ley, D., eds, 1993: *Place/culture/representation*. London and New York: Routledge. · Entrikin, J.N. 1976: Contemporary humanism in geography. *Annals of the Association of American Geographers* 66: 615–32. · Gregory, D. 1981: Human agency and human geography. *Transactions, Institute of British Geographers* NS 6: 1–16. · Harris, R.C. 1978: The historical mind and the practice of geography. In D. Ley and M. Samuels, eds, *Humanistic geography: prospects and problems*. London: Croom Helm, 123–37. · Jackson, P. and Smith, S.J. 1984: *Exploring social geography*. London and Boston: Allen & Unwin. · Kobayashi, A. and Mackenzie, S., eds, 1989: *Remaking human geography*. London:

Allen & Unwin. · Ley, D. 1978: Social geography and social action. In D. Ley and M. Samuels, eds, *Humanistic geography: prospects and problems*. London: Croom Helm, 41–57. · Ley, D. 1981: Behavioural geography and the philosophies of meaning. In K. Cox and R. Golledge, eds, *Behavioral problems in geography revisited*. London: Methuen, 209–30. · Ley, D. 1989: Fragmentation, coherence and the limits to theory in human geography. In A. Kobayashi and S. Mackenzie, eds, *Remaking human geography*. London: Allen and Unwin, 223–44. · Ley, D. and Samuels, M., eds, 1978: *Humanistic geography: prospects and problems*. London: Croom Helm. · Meinig, D., ed., 1979: *The interpretation of ordinary landscapes*. New York: Oxford University Press. · Meinig, D. 1983: Geography as an art. *Transactions, Institute of British Geographers* NS 8: 314–28. · Pile, S. 1991: Practising interpretative geography. *Transactions, Institute of British Geographers* NS 16: 458–69. · Pile, S. 1996: *The body and the city: psychoanalysis, space and subjectivity*. London and New York: Routledge. · Pile, S. and Thrift, N.J., eds, 1995: *Mapping the subject: geographies of cultural transformation*. London and New York: Routledge. · Pocock, D., ed., 1981: *Humanistic geography and literature: essays on the experience of place*. London: Croom Helm. · Relph, E. 1981: *Rational landscapes and humanistic geography*. London: Croom Helm. · Rose, G. 1993: *Feminism and geography: the limits of geographical knowledge*. Cambridge: Polity Press. · Minneapolis: University of Minnesota Press. · Smith, S. 1984: Practicing humanistic geography. *Annals of the Association of American Geographers* 74: 353–74. · Tuan, Y.-F. 1976: Humanistic geography. *Annals of the Association of American Geographers* 66: 266–76. · Tuan, Y.-F. 1977: *Space and place: the perspective of experience*. London: Edward Arnold. · Western J. 1981: *Outcast Cape Town*. London: Allen & Unwin.

Suggested Reading

Cloke, P., Philo, C. and Sadler, D. 1991: *Approaching human geography: an introduction to contemporary theoretical debates*. London: Paul Chapman; New York: Guilford Press, ch. 3. · Kobayashi and Mackenzie (1989). · Ley and Samuels (1978). · Pile (1996), 45–70.

hybridity The conceptual boundaries produced by dominant DISCOURSES often depend on binary divisions between an OTHER and a same; hybridity refers to those things and processes that transgress and displace such boundaries and in so doing produce something ontologically new. The term is often used in discussions of the CULTURAL POLITICS of GLOBALIZATION. As (some) people, IMAGES and COMMODITIES move around the world with increasing frequency and speed, it is argued that certain divisions become harder to sustain. In particular, the IDENTITY of the modern NATION-STATE, imagined in terms of a bounded and uniform COMMUNITY, is challenged by acknowledging the POST-COLONIAL practices that rupture its boundary and challenge its apparent uniformity: the complex cultural negotiations of the (post-)colonial contact zone (Pratt, 1992), the SENSES OF PLACE wrought by those migrating from (ex-)colonies to the contemporary western metropolis (Sharp, 1994), and the identities of those never admitted into the imagined community of the western nation (Bhabha, 1994), for example. Bhabha (1994) argues that hybridity is thus a means of challenging particular understandings of same and Other more generally. Specifically, he argues that hybrid selves refute binary understandings, typical of the West, that construct the western self only in relation to stereotyped notions of non-Western peoples. Hybridity is also used in other contexts as a strategy for displacing Western processes of Othering. It can refer to the constitution of new forms of identity in fields other than the post-colonial (Rose, 1994; Smith, 1996). It has also been extended to NATURE as the Other of CULTURE, and to objects and animals as the Other of the human self, in work which explores the agency of the physical environment and of objects, often by drawing on ACTOR–NETWORK THEORY (Battersbury et al., 1997; Whatmore, 1997).

These arguments suggest the need to think of space in particular ways. The spaces of hybridity may be spaces of flows and connections rather than of divided TERRITORIES, for example, and some of these new spaces are perhaps not yet recognizable (Sharp, 1994; Rose, 1995; see also THIRD SPACE). However, hybridity is not necessarily an easy position to occupy and the POWER relations implicit in its geographies are diverse and complex (Rose, 1995). Massey (1994, pp. 157–73), for example, points out that some forms of hybridity are empowering and others disempowering and concludes that hybrid spaces display a 'power-geometry' that demands attention in a critical analysis. Other cautious approaches to hybridity include that of Young (1995), who worries that the term hybrid, with its geneticist overtones, may actually reinstate and naturalize the Other and its opposite even as it claims to displace the distinctions between them.

GR

References

Battersbury, S. et al. 1997: Environmental transformations in developing countries: hybrid research and democratic policy. *Geographical Journal* 163: 126–32. · Bhabha, H. 1994: *The location of culture*. London: Routledge. · Massey, D. 1994: *Space, place and gender*. Cambridge: Polity Press. · Pratt, M.L. 1992: *Imperial eyes: travel writing and transculturation*. London: Routledge. · Rose, G. 1994: The cultural politics of place: local representation and oppositional discourse in two films.

Transactions, Institute of British Geographers NS 19: 46–60. · Rose, G. 1995: The interstitial perspective: a review essay on Homi Bhabha's *The Location of Culture. Environment and Planning D: Society and Space* 13: 365–73. · Sharp, J. 1994: A topology of 'post' nationality: (re) mapping identity in *The Satanic Verses. Ecumene* 1: 65–76. · Smith, F. 1996: Problematising language: limitations and possibilities in foreign language research. *Area* 28: 160–6. · Whatmore, S. 1997: Dissecting the autonomous self: hybrid cartographies for a relational ethics. *Environment and Planning D: Society and Space* 15: 37–53. · Young, R.J.C. 1995: *Colonial desire: hybridity in theory, culture and race*. London: Routledge.

hyperspace A term used by Jean Baudrillard (1986) to denote a space of pure immediacy and surface. Hyperspace is a simulation of a space which is able to be reproduced and reduplicated; no originary space exists: 'we can therefore have the tropical*ness* of a hotel atrium in Los Angeles or Chicago, without the inconvenience of the tropics, 1930s*ness* without the great depression' (Homer, 1998, p. 134). The idea of a space of simulation and simulacra is a crucial element of POSTMODERNISM and the notion of COGNITIVE MAPPING, since both emphasize the delirium of images in which we apparently now exist. NJT

References

Baudrillard, J. 1986: *America*. London: Verso. · Homer, S. 1998: *Fredric Jameson. Marxism, hermeneutics, postmodernism*. Cambridge: Polity Press.

hypothesis A provisional statement which guides empirical work in several scientific EPISTEMOLOGIES: more informally, the term is widely used to embrace a set of guiding ideas about PROCESSES and outcomes.

Within POSITIVISM, a hypothesis is an empirical statement not yet accepted as true: the purpose of the positivist methodology is to test its veracity, establishing the statement's truth through empirical investigation. The hypothesis, derived from a body of THEORY, should be general in its application and not refer to a specific place or event. Hypotheses are therefore the core elements of structured empirical research programmes within this philosophy, which was strongly promoted during geography's QUANTITATIVE REVOLUTION.

Whereas in positivism hypotheses are devised to be verified – i.e. proven – in CRITICAL RATIONALISM they are designed to be refuted – or falsified – rather than validated: science advances, it is argued, not by accumulating evidence of verified hypotheses (because any verification can only be provisional) but by discarding false hypotheses. In PRAGMATISM, too, they are provisional statements which guide action until a superior hypothesis is derived. RJJ

Suggested Reading

Harvey, D. 1969: *Explanation in geography*. London: Edward Arnold. · Newman, J.L. 1973: The use of the term 'hypothesis' in geography. *Annals of the Association of American Geographers* 63: 22–7. · Sayer, A. 1992: *Method in social science: a realist approach*. London and New York: Routledge.

I

iconography The description and interpretation of visual IMAGES in order to disclose and interpret their hidden or symbolic meanings. Iconography was initially applied to religious icons and painted images, and theorized as a methodology within Renaissance art history by the cultural historian Erwin Panofsky. Its impact on geographical study was limited (but cf. Gottman, 1952) until iconography was promoted as a method of LANDSCAPE and CARTOGRAPHIC interpretation in CULTURAL GEOGRAPHY by Daniels and Cosgrove (1988). Landscapes, both on the ground and in their representation through various media such as MAPS, painting and photography, are regarded as deposits of cultural meanings. The iconographic method seeks to address these meanings through describing the form, composition and content of such REPRESENTATIONS, disclosing their symbolism, and interpreting the significances and implications of that symbolism by re-immersing landscapes into their social and historical contexts. Successful iconographic interpretation requires close formal reading, broad contextual knowledge, interpretative sensitivity and persuasive writing skills; it reveals human landscapes as both shaped by and themselves active in shaping broader social and cultural processes, and thus possessed of powerful human significance. Geographical iconography today accepts that landscape meanings are unstable over time and between different groups, always negotiated, and political in the broadest sense. This is exemplified by a significant body of work on landscape images and national or local identities produced by geographers in the early 1990s, (see, e.g., Daniels, 1993; Schama, 1995). See also ART, GEOGRAPHY AND.

DEC

References

Daniels S. 1993: *Fields of vision: landscape imagery and national identity in England and the United States*. Cambridge: Polity. · Daniels, S. and Cosgrove, D. 1988: Iconography and landscape. In D. Cosgrove and S. Daniels, eds, *The iconography of landscape: essays on the representation design and use of past environments*. Cambridge: Cambridge University Press, 1–10. · Gottmann, J. 1952: *La politique des états et leur géographie*. Paris: Armand Colin. · Schama, S. 1995: *Landscape and memory*. London: HarperCollins.

ideal type A theoretical construction proposed by the sociologist Max Weber (1949) as a means of understanding the complexity and variety of social action. It provides a datum against which comparisons can be made to advance the appreciation of particular events. The necessity for ideal types was advanced by Saunders (1986, p. 30) who argued that

> although all social events are historically unique, there is clearly a need for some means whereby social phenomena can be classified in general terms, for only in this way is it possible to understand typical motives and to recognize typical patterns of action. It is, in other words, necessary to generalize in order to explain unique events.

Ideal types are thus mental constructs which isolate the theoretically most salient features of the subject being considered: they may be *generic*, and refer to ahistorical concepts, or *individual*, in Weber's terminology, limited in their scope to particular times, place and contexts, but individual types should be constructed on the basis of generic types 'which are taken to be timeless and spaceless' (Saunders, 1986, p. 294).

Ideal types are created from empirical knowledge, and are necessary, according to Saunders (1986, p. 31) because:

> Social reality is infinite, and we can never know all there is to know about a given phenomenon. When we come to study some aspect of social life, therefore, we are immediately confronted with a chaotic complexity of sense impressions, and the only way to impose order on this chaos in order to distinguish that which is relevant to our concerns from that which is not is through the application of conceptually pure types. Ideal types are the yardsticks by means of which empirical reality can be rendered accessible to analysis.

They are not descriptions, and they are always partial. Different types could be constructed for the same phenomena depending on the reason why they are being studied: they are viewpoints, or diagnostic norms, constructed to aid analysis – 'Social reality does not possess a real essence because it is always capable of being constructed or represented in various different ways' (Parkin, 1982, p. 28: cf. MODEL).

Use of ideal types may involve dichotomies, as in the RURAL–URBAN CONTINUUM, or a set of 'pure' categories, as with CLASS, CITY and bureaucracy (three of Weber's main concerns); they may be employed ideologically, as in the concept of a 'free market', which most critiques of CAPITALISM suggest cannot exist.

According to some versions of PHENOMENOLOGY, ideal types are constructs which individuals use in the creation of their TAKEN-FOR-GRANTED WORLDS – they are means of simplifying reality in order to come to terms with it, as suggested in Sennett's (1973) work on stereotypes. RJJ

References and Suggested Reading

Jackson, P. and Smith, S.J. 1984: *Exploring social geography*. London and Boston: George Allen and Unwin. · Parkin, F. 1982: *Max Weber*. Chichester: Ellis Horwood. · Saunders, P. 1986: *Social theory and the urban question*, 2nd edn. London: Hutchinson. · Sennett, R. 1973: *The uses of disorder*. London: Penguin Books. · Weber, M. 1949: *The methodology of the social sciences*. New York: The Free Press.

idealism Any philosophy which *either* regards reality as residing in or constituted by the mind ('metaphysical idealism') *or* limits understanding to perceptions of external objects ('epistemological idealism'; cf. the materialism of HISTORICAL MATERIALISM in general and MARXIST GEOGRAPHY in particular).

In human geography, however, 'idealism' was also used in the 1970s and early 1980s to connote an approach promoted by Canadian historical geographer Leonard Guelke which sought 'to understand the development of the earth's CULTURAL LANDSCAPES by uncovering the thought that lies behind them' (Guelke, 1974). It was this emphasis on mind, 'on rethinking the thoughts of geographical agents', which Guelke claimed entitled him to represent his programme as an idealist one. His approach was modelled on the example of historian R.G. Collingwood (1946) and his 'crucial' contention that 'all history is the history of human thought' (see Guelke, 1982). On Guelke's reading, therefore, and in contradistinction to the theoretical emphases of SPATIAL SCIENCE and its successor projects, 'the human geographer does not need theories of his [or her] own because he [or she] is concerned with the theories expressed in the actions of the individual being investigated': hence the central object of inquiry ought to be to recover the *rationality* and *intentionality* embedded in human actions (Guelke 1974; see also Guelke, 1971).

Collingwood's original theses had a limited impact on the conduct of historical inquiry, and Guelke's own proposals, though they were advanced with unremitting vigour, were subjected to considerable criticism and failed to command widespread assent within human geography (see Curry, 1982). Subsequent developments broke the tie between 'rational choices' and 'rational consequences' on which Guelke's methodology depended (Barnes and Sheppard, 1992); provided a more comprehensive account of different forms of rationality than he allowed (Miller, 1992); fashioned a more productive – and more materialist – conception of DISCOURSE than he envisaged; and widened the scope of inquiry beyond the domain of human consciousness to address the unconscious (see PSYCHOANALYTIC THEORY, GEOGRAPHY AND). DG

References

Barnes, T. and Sheppard, E. 1992: Is there a place for the rational actor? A geographical critique of the rational choice paradigm. *Economic Geography* 68: 1–21. · Curry, M. 1982: The idealist dispute in Anglo-American geography. *Canadian Geographer* 27: 35–50 [see also responses, pp. 51–9]. · Collingwood, R.G. 1946: *The idea of history*. Oxford: Oxford University Press. · Guelke, L. 1971: Problems of scientific explanation in geography. *Canadian Geographer* 15: 38–53. · Guelke, L. 1974: An idealist alternative in human geography. *Annals of the Association of American Geographers* 66: 168–9. · Guelke, L. 1982: *Historical understanding in geography: an idealist approach*. Cambridge: Cambridge University Press. · Miller, B. 1992: Collective action and rational choice: place, community and the limits to individual self-interest. *Economic Geography* 68: 22–42.

Suggested Reading

Curry (1982). · Guelke (1974).

Identity see SUBJECT FORMATION, GEOGRAPHIES OF

identity politics A concept that refers to SOCIAL MOVEMENTS organized around the politicization of particular cultural identities. It is sometimes used as a synonym for some versions of feminist, anti-racist and anti-heterosexist social movements, to both credit and criticize their effects of fragmenting leftist CLASS politics. Identity politics arose, however, in reaction to the particularisms that were represented as universalist in radical as well as liberal politics (see MASCULINISM). The distinction between class as opposed to identity politics is sometimes conceptualized through a series of dualisms: class politics attend to the economy – identity politics are cultural; class politics address redistributive

TYPES OF REMEDY		
TYPES OF JUSTICE	AFFIRMATIVE	TRANSFORMATIONAL
REDISTRIBUTION	liberal welfare state	socialism
RECOGNITION	mainstream multiculturalism (gay identity politics)	deconstruction (queer politics)

identity politics *Four political orientations* (After Fraser, 1997)

justice – identity politics are about matters of recognition. These are problematic dualisms for two reasons: first, within CULTURAL POLITICS the conceptual and political terrain is more complex than such dualisms suggest – identity politics are potentially at odds with deconstructive anti-identity politics inspired by POST-STRUCTURALISM; and second, a crude distinction between CULTURE AND ECONOMY evades the task of articulating the relations between them (Crang, 1997).

A more nuanced discussion engages with the challenges of creating effective political alliances across social movements. One concern is that identity politics can make this difficult if boundaries are sharply drawn between groups and 'experience' within a group is taken as the only grounds for knowledge and speech; in such a circumstance, there is little basis for communication with those deemed outside the group. Another problem is that struggles around redistributive justice and identity politics sometimes have contradictory aims (see JUSTICE, GEOGRAPHY AND): the first tends to undermine group differentiation and the latter promotes it. (In feminism, this restates the classic equality/difference dilemma: should women seek equality with men or insist on their difference from them?) Fraser attempts to 'finesse' this dilemma through a further distinction among attempts to remedy injustice: between affirmative efforts that seek to correct inequitable outcomes without disturbing the processes that underlie them, and transformative ones that address both outcomes and underlying processes. She thus produces four categories of politics (see figure on p. 368). Fraser distinguishes, for example, between two types of sexual politics: she conceives gay-identity politics as an affirmative politics of recognition that seeks to enhance gay group identity and queer politics as an anti-identity politics that attempts to destabilize all fixed sexual identities, including heterosexual ones (see QUEER THEORY). (See also Kobayashi (1990) for a parallel distinction between MULTICULTURALISM that transforms rather than simply affirms RACE identity.) Fraser's assessment is that both forms of transformational politics complement each other, as do both varieties of affirmative politics, but that it is contradictory to combine affirmative and transformational politics; Fraser favours the latter. This is a coherent resolution that nonetheless sidesteps the psychic and political demands for identification, the problem that anti-identity politics may jar with the lived experience of a coherent stable identity, and the fact that identities can be important political resources (see SUBJECT FORMATION, GEOGRAPHIES OF). Less categorical resolutions of the dilemma of the seemingly contradictory objectives of identity and deconstructive politics are suggested by those who see identity politics as a necessary moment of organizational cohesion before DECONSTRUCTION, or simply as different political objectives that can be drawn upon strategically (Rose, 1993).

Critical geographers continue to debate the challenges of determining which and when particular identities and differences matter (see CRITICAL HUMAN GEOGRAPHY): if 'a thousand flowers are encouraged to bloom under the sign of "critical" [geography], might not the notion of critical lose all meaning as well as grit? Doesn't politics require figuring out which differences matter when?' (Katz, 1998, p. 258). Haraway's suggestive account of SITUATED KNOWLEDGE continues to tantalize: 'In the consciousness of our failures, we risk lapsing into boundless difference and giving up on the confusing task of making partial, real connections. Some differences are playful, some are poles of world historical systems of domination. Epistemology is about knowing the difference.' (1990, pp. 202–3). But which epistemology? This remains a matter of debate (e.g. Harvey, 1996). GP

References

Crang, P. 1997: Cultural turns and the (re)constitution of economic geography. In R. Lee and J. Wills, eds, *Geographies of economies*. London: Arnold, 3–15. · Fraser, N. 1997: *Justice Interruptus: critical reflections of the 'postsocialist' condition*. London: Routledge. · Haraway, D. 1990: A manifesto for cyborgs: science, technology, and socialist feminism in the 1980s. In L. Nicholson, ed., *Feminism/postmodernism*. London: Routledge. · Harvey, D. 1996: *Justice, nature and the geography of difference*. Oxford and Cambridge, MA: Blackwell. · Katz, C. 1998: Lost and found in the posts: addressing critical human geography. *Environment and Planning D: Society and Space* 16: 257–78. · Kobayashi, A. 1990: Racism and the law in Canada: a geographic perspective. *Urban Geography* 11: 447–73. · Rose, G. 1993: *Feminism and geography*. Oxford: Polity Press and Minneapolis: University of Minnesota Press.

ideology The term *idéologie* was originally used by the French Enlightenment philosopher Destutt de Tracy in 1796 both to describe and to recommend a new, rigorous 'science of ideas' which, 'by overcoming religious and metaphysical prejudices, may serve as a new basis for public education'. It was thus profoundly 'positive' (cf. POSITIVISM) and only assumed a negative and indeed pejorative meaning in the course of the nineteenth century. In this transformation of meaning the writings of Karl Marx (1818–83) were instrumental: 'With Marx, the concept of ideology came of age' (Larrain, 1979).

The concept subsequently took on a number of different meanings, so that it is impossible to provide a single definition (within HISTORICAL MATERIALISM alone, see Eagleton, 1991). In the most general terms, most writers who use the term do so in one of two conventional senses, each of which bears the marks of its eighteenth- and nineteenth-century origins. Thompson (1981) distinguished them thus:

(a) 'the lattice of ideas which permeate the social order, constituting the collective consciousness of an epoch', i.e. a generalized system of ideas; and
(b) 'a consciousness which is in some way "false" [and] which fails to grasp the real conditions of human existence', i.e. a distorted system of ideas.

In Thompson's view, neither is satisfactory. He objects to the first 'because it is too wide : by anchoring ideology in the very nature of consciousness, it conceals the specificity of the ideological phenomenon and renders the latter unsurpassable'. He objects to the second 'because it is too narrow: by defining ideology in opposition to science, it precludes the possibility that science itself may be ideological' (cf. Harvey, 1974: 'The use of a scientific method is of necessity founded in ideology, and any claim to be ideology-free is of necessity an ideological claim'; see also Gregory, 1978).

Thompson (1981, 1984) preferred to treat ideology as 'a system of signification which facilitates the pursuit of particular interests' and which sustains specific 'relations of domination' (cf. POWER). This formulation drew on critical social theory and took advantage of the so-called 'linguistic turn' that was prominent in philosophy and social theory in the 1980s:

> For increasingly it has been realized that ideas do not drift through the social world like clouds in a summer sky, occasionally divulging their contents with a clap of thunder and a flash of light. Rather, ideas circulate in the social world as utterances, as expressions, as words which are spoken or inscribed. Hence to study ideology is, in some part and in some way, to study language in the social world. It is to study the ways in which language is used in everyday social life, from the most mundane encounter between friends and family members to the most privileged forms of political debate (Thompson, 1984).

The reflection on language in use – on linguistic practices, language-games and social contexts (see PRAGMATISM) – is significant because it strongly suggests that it is a mistake to think of ideology as merely 'illusion':

> Once we recognize that ideology operates through language and that language is a medium of social action, we must also acknowledge that ideology is partially constitutive of what, in our societies, 'is real'. Ideology is not a pale image of the social world but is part of that world, a creative and constitutive element of our social lives (Thompson, 1984).

This much was widely acknowledged by geographers in the 1980s. There was more or less general agreement on the need to avoid those versions of HEGEMONY and the 'dominant ideology thesis' that over-emphasize the degree of coherence, integration and stability of societies (Abercrombie et al., 1980), and of the importance of recovering the multiple ideologies which inform and are invigorated by diverse social struggles (Eyles, 1981). The interest in ideology extended beyond spoken and written forms of communication to an examination of the constellations of power inscribed in visual images, including maps and paintings (see CARTOGRAPHY), and in the forms and folds of the CULTURAL LANDSCAPE itself.

But these ideas were given new force and new form through an increasing interest in DISCOURSE. As the 1980s turned into the 1990s even Eagleton (1991) conceded that 'ideology is a matter of "discourse" rather than of language'; he suggested that ideology represents 'the points where power impacts upon certain utterances ["knowledges"] and inscribes itself tacitly within them'. The most sustained examinations of discourse in these terms have been conducted under the sign of POST-STRUCTURALISM, where particular interest attaches to the identification of regimes of truth and the conjunction of power-knowledge (see Barrett, 1991). It is thus not surprising that the term 'ideology' fell from favour in the 1990s as geographers, like scholars elsewhere in the humanities and social sciences, were persuaded that all knowledge is SITUATED KNOWLEDGE, partial and imperfect; that there is no pure point of overview, detached from the grubby particulars and power-plays of the world; and that all claims to knowledge are made within and help to shape relations of power. These realizations have not licensed a wild and unconstrained relativism. In recent years the practice of human geography has been made considerably more demanding – ethically and intellectually – by careful and principled critiques of ETHNOCENTRISM, EUROCENTRISM, MASCULINISM, ORIENTALISM and PHALLOCENTRISM. These discussions have been advanced by close, critical readings of TEXTS – of what language does beyond the intentions of its authors – and a probing, almost forensic excavation of 'buried epistemologies' (cf. DECONSTRUCTION). These exercises in what would once have been called 'ideology critique' have shown that all discursive practices are inescapably 'worldly', and that they are engaged with other, profoundly political and thoroughly material social practices (see Willems-Braun, 1997; Barnett, 1998).

DG

References

Abercrombie, N., Hill, T. and Turner, B.S. 1980: *The dominant ideology thesis*. London: Allen & Unwin. · Barnett, C. 1998: Impure and worldly geography: the Africanist discourse of the Royal Geographical Society, 1831–73. *Transactions, Institute of British Geography* NS 23: 239–52. · Barrett, M. 1991: *The politics of truth: from Marx to Foucault*. Stanford: Stanford University Press. · Eagleton, T. 1991: *Ideology: an introduction*. London: Verso. · Eyles, J. 1981: Ideology, contradiction and struggle: an exploratory discussion. *Antipode* 13 (2): 39–46. · Gregory, D. 1978: *Ideology, science and human geography*. London: Hutchinson. · Harvey, D. 1974: Population, resources and the ideology of science. *Economic Geography* 50: 256–77. · Larrain, J. 1979: *The concept of ideology*. London: Hutchinson. · Thompson, J.B. 1981: *Critical hermeneutics*. Cambridge: Cambridge University Press. · Thompson, J.B. 1984: *Studies in the theory of ideology*. Cambridge: Polity Press. · Thompson, J.B. 1990: *Ideology and modern culture*. Cambridge: Polity Press. · Willems-Braun, B. 1997: Buried epistemologies: the politics of nature in (post)colonial British Columbia. *Annals of the Association of American Geography* 87: 3–31.

Suggested Reading

Barrett (1991). · Willems-Braun (1997).

idiographic Concerned with the unique and the particular (cf. NOMOTHETIC). The term originated at the end of the nineteenth century when W. Windelband and N. Rickert made a famous distinction between the nomothetic and idiographic sciences which, they claimed, entitled history to be regarded as radically different from other forms of intellectual inquiry (see KANTIANISM). Their arguments have been challenged by other historians and philosophers of science, but made a forceful entry into geography through the Hartshorne-Schaefer debate over EXCEPTIONALISM, when traditional REGIONAL GEOGRAPHY was represented as essentially idiographic and incapable of contributing towards effective generalization. These claims were subsequently revived during the QUANTITATIVE REVOLUTION: both Bunge (1962) and Haggett (1965) argued that 'one can do little with the unique except contemplate its uniqueness', and although Chorley and Haggett's influential *Models in geography* (1967) did 'not propose to alter the basic Hartshorne definition of geography's prime task', attempts there and elsewhere to establish a model-based PARADIGM nevertheless marked the re-emergence of a nomothetic geography 'after the lapse into ideography' (Burton, 1963). Some geographers would (then and now) reverse this charge, in the belief that a preoccupation with abstract models constituted the real lapse: certainly, the emergence of IDEALISM within geography was accompanied by equally polemical claims that the human geographer 'does not need theories of his [or her] own' (Guelke, 1974). Whatever one thinks of Guelke's specific proposals, a number of traditions which would otherwise contest his philosophy nevertheless agree that 'the avoidance of the unique is not a requirement of science' (Guelke, 1977). From the perspective of HISTORICAL MATERIALISM, for example, Massey (1984) contends that:

> Variety should not be seen as a deviation from the expected; nor should uniqueness be seen as a problem. 'General processes' never work themselves out in pure form. There are always specific circumstances, a particular history, a particular place or location. What is at issue . . . is the articulation of the general with the local (the particular) to produce qualitatively different outcomes in different localities.

It is exactly this issue which is at the very centre of the revival of interest in AREAL DIFFERENTIATION and the reconstruction of a theoretically informed REGIONAL GEOGRAPHY. Thus, Johnston (1985) argues that:

> [R]egional geography must focus on the *unique* characteristics of the place being studied, but must not express them as if they were *singular* [emphasis added]. This means that regions must not be studied solely as separate entities. They are part of a much larger whole . . . . We need a regional geography that finds a middle course between on the one hand the generalising approaches, which allow for no real freedom of individual action, and on the other the singular approaches, which argue that all is freedom of action.

(Cf. CONTEXTUAL APPROACH; STRUCTURATION THEORY.) All of these formulations are simplifications, of course: it is not so much a matter of connecting 'the' general to 'the' particular as one of recognizing the *hierarchy of concepts* which are involved (see REALISM). But they all register a significant advance over the combative opposition of the nomothetic and the idiographic. DG

References

Bunge, W. 1962: *Theoretical geography*. Lund, Sweden: C.W.K. Gleerup. · Burton, I. 1963: The quantitative revolution and theoretical geography. *Canadian Geography* 7: 151–62. · Chorley, R.J. and Haggett, P., eds, 1967: *Models in geography*. London: Methuen. · Guelke, L. 1974: An idealist alternative in human geography. *Annals of the Association of American Geographers* 64: 193–202. · Guelke, L. 1977: The role of laws in human geography. *Progress in Human Geography* 1: 376–86. · Haggett, P. 1965: *Locational analysis in human geography*. London: Edward Arnold; New York: John Wiley. · Johnston, R.J. 1985: The world is our oyster. In R. King, ed., *Geographical futures*. Sheffield: Geographical Association, 112–28. · Massey, D. 1984: Introduction. In D. Massey and J. Allen, eds, *Geography matters! A reader*. Cambridge: Cambridge University Press, 1–11.

Suggested Reading

Harvey, D. 1969: *Explanation in geography*. London: Edward Arnold; New York: St. Martin's Press, 49–54. · Johnston (1985).

image A depiction of something. The term 'image' can be regarded as the product of three processes.

The first of these is the *philosophical critique of* REPRESENTATION. For some time, the concept of representation was often considered to be coincident with a model of pictorial representation summed up by the word 'resemblance'. But this stance has now been all but rejected in favour of a notion that there are many forms of representation – pictorial, linguistic, mental, and so on – which cannot be reduced to one another.

The second process is the *interpretation of images*. Not surprisingly, this process is most often associated with art, which is often considered to be the major archive of images, and makes an appeal to ICONOGRAPHIC traditions (cf. ART, GEOGRAPHY AND). However, other interpretative traditions, such as HERMENEUTICS, can also be drawn upon.

The last process is the *manufacture of images*. Images have been produced in profusion over many centuries. But, increasingly, it has become possible to mass produce them in their thousands and millions through the medium of print, film and television. Whole industries – like advertising and design – have grown up whose purpose is to tend the mass-produced image. In other words, images have increasingly become just another aspect of modern production, rather than something special to be brought out and displayed on high days and holidays (see SITUATIONISTS). Whether they have lost some of their special qualities as a result is a source of impassioned debate.

Perhaps the most important recurring motif in work on images has been suspicion. From Plato's famous analogy of the cave where the unenlightened are confined, through religious icons, to many works of art, the concern has been that images bear false witness, are somehow inauthentic shadows of reality. Modern considerations of the image have increasingly attempted to avoid this kind of stance, opting instead for the notion that images are just one more means of constructing reality – not simply reporting back on it – and as such have a rich and varied history and geography. Images are, in other words, the chief currency of modern visual cultures. But, in a world where photographs can be so easily altered, where reality can be so easily re-imaged, it also becomes imperative to retain a critical edge: images have their own rhetoric which has to be acknowledged (Mitchell, 1994). Nowhere has this been made clearer than in the feminist literature (see, for example, Pollock, 1996) which has had to cope with the damage that images can do to female bodies in cultural arenas as diverse as arts, advertising, and pornography (see FEMINIST GEOGRAPHIES).

These considerations become even more relevant because human geography is itself a provider of potent images which circle and, indeed, have constituted the globe. From early MAPS and atlases through multitudinous graphs and diagrams, to the output from today's GEOGRAPHICAL INFORMATION SYSTEMS, human geography is a discipline which deals in, even lives and dies by, images.

Of, course, not all images are visual. IMAGINATIVE GEOGRAPHIES can be conjured up by words as well, from newspaper headlines to the most intricate novelistic evocation. Some writers would go further again; believing that what is needed is to write new images of thinking itself. For example, the French POST-STRUCTURALIST philosopher Deleuze wants to replace the dominant fixed images of thought with new images of flow and movement like the RHIZOME. NJT

References

Bryson, N. 1992: *Word and image: French painting of the ancien régime*. Cambridge: Cambridge University Press. · Gombrich, E. 1977: *Art and illusion. A study in the psychology of pictorial representation*, 5th edn. Oxford: Phaidon. · Jordanova, L. 1989: *Sexual visions. Images of gender in science and medicine between the eighteenth and twentieth century*. New York: Harvester Wheatsheaf. · Lutz, C.A. and Collins, J.L. 1995: *Reading National Geographic*. Chicago: University of Chicago Press. · Mitchell, W.T.J. 1994: *Picture theory. Essays on verbal and visual representation*. Chicago: University of Chicago Press. · Nead, L. 1997: Mapping the Self: gender, space and modernity in mid-Victorian London. *Environment and Planning A* 29: 659–72. · Pointon, M. 1993: *Hanging the head. Portraiture and social formation in eighteenth century England*. Newhaven, CT: Yale University Press. · Ryan, J. 1998: *Picturing Empire. Photography and the visualisation of the British Empire*. Chicago: University of Chicago Press. · Pollock, G., ed., 1996: *Generations and geographies in the visual arts*. London: Routledge. · Silverman, D. 1997: *Qualitative research. Theory, method and practice*. London: Sage. · Stafford, B.M. 1996: *Good looking. Essays on the virtue of images*. Cambridge, MA: MIT Press. · Schwartz, J.M. 1996: The geography lesson: photographical construction of imaginative geographies. *Journal of Historical Geography* 22: 16–95.

imaginative geographies REPRESENTATIONS of other places – of peoples and LANDSCAPES, CULTURES and 'NATURES' – and the ways in which these images reflect the desires, fantasies and preconceptions of their authors and the grids of power between them and their subjects. The term was proposed by the Palestinian/American cultural and literary critic Edward Said (1978) in his influential critique of ORIENTALISM (see Gregory, 1995a). It is possible to derive from Said's discussion several significant differences between an 'imaginative geography' as he conceived it and the concepts of 'MENTAL MAP', 'behavioural environment' or 'perceived environment' then current in BEHAVIOURAL GEOGRAPHY.

In the first place, Said's emphasis on POWER (in the case that most concerned him, colonial power) was alien to behavioural geography, and drew attention to the 'non-innocence' of any act of representation. In one sense, perhaps, Said's formulation anticipated ideas of the situatedness of knowledge and the POSITIONALITY of the viewing subject (see SITUATED KNOWLEDGE); but he was most concerned to disclose the privileges that European and American authors typically arrogated to themselves when representing other cultures and hence the asymmetric grid of power within which (specifically) 'the West' watches, 'the East' is watched (see also ETHNOCENTRISM; EUROCENTRISM).

In the second place, Said's emphasis on viewing, watching, looking, observing – on VISION AND VISUALITY – drew attention to the cultural construction of the gaze. Unlike 'mental maps' and the other constructs of behavioural geography, imaginative geographies are never the product of purely cognitive operations. Their images are animated by fantasy and the play of desire (though Said himself said rather too little about these issues for those of his critics who are more sympathetic to PSYCHOANALYTIC THEORY) and carry within them comparative valorizations – what Said, following Bachelard (1969) called a 'POETICS of space' – by means of which places are endowed with 'figurative value'.

In the third place, Said claimed that those figurative values enter not only into the production of alterity (see OTHER/OTHERNESS) but also into the identity-formation of the viewing subject. Imaginative geographies sustain images of 'home' as well as images of 'away' or 'abroad', therefore: 'Imaginative geography and history help the mind to intensify its own sense of itself by dramatizing the distance and difference between what is close to it and what is far away' (Said, 1978, p. 55).

In the fourth place, 'dramatization' is not (quite) the same as 'falsification', and Said's discussion undercut the distinction between 'real' and 'perceived' worlds on which behavioural geography depended. This is the most complicated and contentious part of Said's argument. There are certainly passages where he contrasted what he called 'positive knowledge' with imaginative geographies produced under the sign of Orientalism. And yet: if imaginative geographies are 'fictions' in the original Latin sense of *fictio* – something made, something fabricated – this does not mean that they are necessarily without concreteness, substance and, indeed, 'reality'. On the contrary: Said emphasized that imaginative geographies circulate in material forms (including sketches, paintings and photographs – cf. ART AND GEOGRAPHY and 'intelligence' reports, and popular TRAVEL WRITING; and in collections and exhibitions), and they become sedimented over time to form an internally structured and, crucially, self-reinforcing 'archive'. This 'citationary structure' is also in some substantial sense PERFORMATIVE: it shapes and legitimizes the attitudes and dispositions, policies and practices of its collective audience, so that in this way imaginative geographies spiral into and out of a sort of cultural PARADIGM of 'otherness'.

There have been several studies of imaginative geographies that, while they may have been inspired by Said's original formulations, retain at best a loose affiliation with his work: thus, for example, Carter's (1987) project of an avowedly spatial history that seeks to show how the landscape of Australia was brought within the horizon of European intelligibility through a series of explicitly textual practices (see also Ryan, 1996). The concept of an imaginative geography has also been developed in directions that Said's original discussion left largely unremarked: thus, for example, feminist scholars have shown how the production of imaginative geographies intersects with GENDER and SEXUALITY, and the very idea of an 'imagination' has been extended through geographies indebted to various forms of psychoanalytic theory for an understanding of the operations of fantasy, desire and the unconscious. What has been clearly retained from Said's account, in large part a result of his initial debt to Foucault, has been an interest in recovering the imaginative geographies of other 'spaces' produced under the signs of COLONIALISM and POST-COLONIALISM (Jarosz, 1992; Gregory, 1995b; Radcliffe, 1996). But there are indications of an emerging interest in recovering imaginative geographies of other 'natures' too (Sioh, 1998).

It should be noted that there has been a long tradition of reading nominally fictional works as expressive of 'imaginative geographies' in a far more limited sense than Said had in mind. This approach to the TEXT (almost always the novel) has usually been naive in the extreme, with little or no engagement with literary or critical theory and an extraordinarily weak understanding of the work of re-presentation (e.g. Darby, 1948; cf. HERMENEUTICS). But these criticisms are more than methodological; they extend to the very object of such studies. For Said's concept of an 'imaginative geography' is not confined to ostensibly fictional works. On the contrary, there is an important sense in which all geographies are imaginative: even the most formal, geometric lattices of SPATIAL SCIENCE are at once abstractions and cultural constructions, and as such vulnerable to the critical readings proposed by Said and other scholars. DG

References

Bachelard, G. 1969: *The poetics of space*. Boston: Beacon Press. · Carter, P. 1987: *The road to Botany Bay: an essay in spatial history*. London: Faber. · Darby, H.C. 1948: The regional geography of Hardy's Wessex. *Geographical Review* 38: 426–43. · Gregory, D. 1995a: Imaginative geographies. *Progress in Human Geography* 19: 447–85. · Gregory, D. 1995b: Between the book and the lamp: imaginative geographies of Egypt, 1849–50. *Transactions, Institute of British Geographers* NS 20: 29–57. · Jarosz, L. 1992: Constructing the Dark Continent: metaphor as geographic representation of Africa. *Geografisker Annaler* 74B: 105–15. · Mitchell, T. 1988: *Colonising Egypt*. Cambridge: Cambridge University Press. · Radcliffe, S. 1996: Imaginative geographies, postcolonialism and national identities: contemporary discourses of the nation in Ecuador. *Ecumene* 3: 23–42. · Ryan, S. 1996: *The cartographic eye: how explorers saw Australia*. Cambridge: Cambridge University Press. · Said, E. 1978: *Orientalism*. London: Penguin [1995: new edition with Afterword]. · Sioh, M. 1998: Authorizing the Malaysian rainforest: configuring space, contesting claims and conquering imaginaries. *Ecumene* 5: 144–66.

Suggested Reading

Gregory (1995a). · Said (1978), 49–73.

immigration A form of MIGRATION that occurs when people move from one nation-state to another. Immigrants change their permanent dwelling place and are therefore distinct from *sojourners*, who relocate temporarily, usually for employment-related reasons; immigrants also move voluntarily and are therefore distinct from REFUGEES, who are forced to leave their homes because of persecution (see also *GASTARBEITER*). When immigrants settle in a new country without the knowledge and approval of the government in power, they are called 'undocumented', 'illegal', or 'unrecorded' immigrants.

Millions of people immigrate each year, and this form of migration is one of the most significant causes of social change in the world today (Clark, 1986; Sasson, 1996).

There have been several episodes of mass migration in history, but the decades following the Second World War have seen the largest population movements of all time. Immigration, in the sense the term is used today, began after the creation of nation-states and, until recently, was closely associated with colonization (cf. *COLONIALISM*). For example, British subjects migrated to the colonies and created *settler societies*; after colonies gained independence this movement continued in the form of immigration. Others, at first mainly from European countries, joined them and many former colonies, such as Australia, Canada, and the US, consider themselves 'immigrant societies' in the sense that the overwhelming majority of their citizens are either immigrants themselves or the descendants of immigrants. Until recently, virtually all immigrants migrated toward what they believed to be greater economic opportunities. These historic patterns have changed in the last 25 years, in two key ways. First, both source and destination regions have multiplied, and immigration now is more global in scope than at any time in the past (Castles and Miller, 1993). Second, in marked contrast to past periods, a small but highly significant number of today's immigrants are wealthy. These 'designer immigrants' are especially concerned with political issues (i.e. stability) and lifestyle. They are sought by many countries for their entrepreneurial skill and capital, and have significantly changed the way immigrants are perceived in the places they settle (Mitchell, 1993; Skeldon, 1994).

Immigrants, wherever they settle, are usually culturally different from their receiver societies. Often, they are 'visible minorities' (i.e. of a different skin colour than the dominant population). The reception of immigrants varies widely between countries but three types of responses are typical: isolation, ASSIMILATION, and PLURALISM. Some societies believe that immigrants are necessary to fulfil certain functions – e.g. when they face labour shortages – but that they should remain separate from the dominant population and, ideally, leave when no longer needed. This was the case, for example, in many western countries in the period following the Second World War, and many believe it is true of Japan today. Countries that ascribe to this view make it difficult for immigrants to acquire full legal rights and, especially, CITIZENSHIP. Others, such as France and, to a more limited extent, the US, expect immigrants to conform, or assimilate, to a predefined national CULTURE. In this case, full legal rights and citizenship are often granted in stages, in step with the assimilation process. Finally, a few countries, notably Australia and Canada, have enacted legislation enshrining the concept of MULTICULTURALISM, a policy that fosters the co-existence of many forms of cultural expression. These countries typically allow immigrants to become citizens quickly and, acknowledging the complexities of identity, allow individuals to hold dual or multiple legal citizenship(s). Note, though, that the differences between these policies are easily overstated, and that countries rarely follow single immigration policies that are applied to all groups equally.

Traditionally, immigration has been analysed in straightforward terms as a push–pull process: people leave a country to escape problems, such as poverty or political CONFLICT, and are drawn to particular places that offer them a better life. In this conception, people are treated as rational individuals who are willing to cast aside their old identities and loyalties and embrace new ones if they believe it is to their advantage. Settlement is seen as a unidirectional, progressive process where immigrants eventually become indistinguishable from the society that receives them – they become assimilated. This interpretation arose out of the research of the CHICAGO SCHOOL in the early twentieth century and continues to affect immigration research. However, recent work, drawing on different understandings of history, culture and identity, offers an alternate perspective, even in countries such as the United States where assimilation has been assumed. First, migration is seen as a collective process that occurs sequentially and in both directions. Immigrants rarely sever the links between their previous and present places and social contacts, and life in the new country is linked to life in the old (cf. CHAIN MIGRATION). As a result, immigrant culture becomes a melange of practices, and identities are in flux rather than fixed, or in an inexorable progression from old to new. More and more, immigration studies are adopting the view of cultures as DIASPORIC – as scattered but connected across vast distances. This realization has led to the concept of TRANSNATIONALISM, the idea that many people live in societies that stretch across – and perhaps even transcend – national boundaries (see Appadurai, 1996; Van Hear, 1998).

These new understandings of the immigration process are particularly salient given the importance of immigrants in (re)defining contemporary economic, political and cultural systems. For example, within the next five years non-white people will form the majority of the population in the state of California, the first time in history where a white society has voluntarily become a minority in a territory under its control (Maharidge, 1996). Similar cultural transformations are occurring in large cities throughout the western world, which are becoming more multi-ethnic and polyglot than ever before (for example, nearly 200 languages are spoken in the area served by the municipal government of Toronto). There are few studies of the cultural dynamics of living in multi-ethnic cities (though see Jacobs, 1996 and Germain, 1997), but it is clear that these new contexts raise fundamental questions about the meaning of equity, public participation, and even citizenship itself (Jacobson, 1996). DH

References

Appadurai, A. 1996: *Modernity at large: cultural dimensions of globalization.* Minneapolis: University of Minnesota Press. · Clark, W.A.V. 1986: *Human migration.* Beverly Hills: Sage. · Castles, S. and Miller, M.J. 1993: *The age of migration: international population movements in the modern world.* London: Macmillan. · Germain, A. 1997: *Montréal: an experiment in cosmopolitanism within a dual society.* Utrecht: European Research Centre on Migration and Ethnic Relations (ERCOMER). · Jacobs, J.M. 1996: *The edge of empire: postcolonialism and the city.* London: Routledge. · Jacobson, D. 1996: Rights across borders: immigration and the decline of citizenship. Baltimore and London: Johns Hopkins University Press. · Maharidge, D. 1996: *The coming white minority: California's eruptions and America's future.* New York: Times Books. · Mitchell, K. 1993: Multiculturalism, or the united colours of capitalism. *Antipode* 29: 263–94. · Sasson, S. 1996: *Losing control? sovereignty in an age of globalization.* New York: Columbia University Press. · Skeldon, R. 1994: *Reluctant exiles?: migration from Hong Kong and the new overseas Chinese.* Armonk, NY: M.E. Sharpe. · Van Hear, N. 1998: *New diasporas: the mass exodus, dispersal and regrouping of migrant communities.* Seattle: University of Washington Press.

Suggested reading

Burnley, I., Murphy, P. and Fagan, R. 1997: *Immigration and Australian cities.* Sydney: The Federation Press. · Richmond, A.H. 1994: *Global apartheid: refugees, racism, and the new world order.* Toronto: University of Toronto Press. · Segal, A. 1993: *An atlas of international migration.* New Providence, NJ: Hans Zell Publishers.

imperialism The creation and maintenance of an unequal economic, cultural and territorial relationship, usually between STATES and often in the form of an empire, based on domination and subordination. Over the last 500 years imperialism has been a predominantly western project and form of dominance that has been shaped by expansionist – capitalist and latterly communist – systems. Western overseas expansion was initiated by Portuguese and Spanish mariners in the fifteenth century and reached its territorial and ideological climax in the early twentieth century, when many European states were engaged in 'the scramble for Africa', the British Empire spanned the globe, and imperialism was first defined precisely, as an ethos of state expansion and 'civilizing mission'. Imperialism is closely affiliated with COLONIALISM. Both processes are intrinsically geographical dynamics that involve the extension of the SOVEREIGNTY of a ruler or NATION-STATE over the land and lives of an alien people through a mixture of military conquest, colonial settlement, the imposition of direct rule, or the creation of informal empires of trade and political supervision. With the rise of COMMUNISM in the first half of the twentieth century and the dissolution of colonial empires over the last half, 'imperialism' has gained other connotations. The term is now used to describe – variously – the global economic influence of Japan and the USA; the webs of neo-colonial DEPENDENCY spun by MULTINATIONAL CORPORATIONS; the international spheres of intervention cultivated by the USA, the Soviet Union and China during the Cold War; the USA's recent military campaigns in the Middle East and Central America; and the fashioning and management of the THIRD WORLD as subordinate to the West. In Marxist–Leninist thought, 'imperialism' has been used as a synonym for CAPITALISM.

Earlier in the twentieth century, thinkers such as Lenin and Hobson viewed imperialism as a phase of capitalism which would either bring the capitalist world system to its knees or alert states to the need to redistribute wealth to the masses (see Mommsen, 1980). Imperialism has since been subjected to more wide-ranging analysis and critique. It is now usually argued that Europe's rise to global dominance in the nineteenth century stemmed from a longer history of EXPLORATION, trade, warfare and settlement. There has been considerable debate about whether imperialism was fuelled by an overarching will-to-domination or stemmed from a more haphazard – if propitious – set of ventures and circumstances. Some argue that the terms 'imperialism' and 'European overseas expansion' obscure the variety of European approaches to the world and portray European dominance in much too austere a light. Others insist that we need to conceptualize imperialism in general terms – as a logic of power, system of violence, or set of historical tendencies and cultural stances – because its effects are pervasive and thoroughgoing.

Many scholars have tried to clarify the distinctiveness of modern (post-1492) imperialism and generalize about 'how it was done'. Modern European empires were modelled on those of Greece and (especially) Rome, but states such as Spain and Britain built the first truly global empires and they grappled with issues that their predecessors did not. It is important to distinguish between imperial projects of conquest, commerce, settlement and rule, and note, as Elliott (1998) does, that they 'were not always, or necessarily, mutually supportive or... compatible'. But this does not mean that they were ineffectual, and scholars have identified a set of tendencies in Europe's increasing imperial grip on the world: (a) the creation of a 'portmanteau biota' in the temperate areas of the world, which helped Europeans to thrive in distant places where land and resources were generally more plentiful than in Europe but labour was scarce; (b) the development of weapons, military tactics and other 'tools of imperialism' (such as navigational equipment, quinine, steamships and telegraphs), which allowed Europeans to explore, annex and control large and disparate territories; (c) the subordination of the use of violence to the rational and continuous pursuit of profit; and (d) the generation of complex imperial 'imaginaries' (IDEOLOGIES of superiority, visions of empire, and conceptual devices for ordering the world), which gave Europeans the confidence and capacity to bring the world under their imperial sway (see Headrick, 1979; Crosby, 1986; Tracy, 1991; Rabasa, 1993).

In recent years there has been considerable discussion of the cultural geography of imperialism. It is becoming increasingly apparent that modern imperialism was characterized by a tension between the *universalization* and *differentiation* of European culture and power, and that it nourished both EUROCENTRISM and NATIONALISM. Imperialism fostered, and was fuelled by, what Gregory (1998) describes as 'the production of Europe as a sovereign [and composite] subject at the centre of an imaginative grid that positioned all the other continents in [antediluvian times and] subordinate spaces'. Many imperial projects were inspired by the idea that *Europe* was the hearth and pinnacle of civilization – the fulcrum of world 'History' and 'Geography' – and had the special task of completing human development by bringing the rest of the world up to its mark. Imperial expansion was conceived in triumphalist terms, as a universally beneficent agent of progress and an inevitable consequence of European superiority. As Spurr (1993) neatly remarks, Europeans saw the world as their rightful inheritance and represented colonial intervention as a response 'to a threefold calling: that of NATURE, which calls for wise use of its RESOURCES; that of humanity, which calls for universal betterment; and that of the colonised, who call for protection from their own ignorance and violence'. These were compelling fictions that had profound material consequences. The configuration of non-European lands and peoples as uncultivated or backward, and hence in need of domestication and rule, is an intrinsic feature of imperialism.

Diverse national imperial agendas were integrated in a broadly European vision of dominance and, far from simply stretching Europe's power overseas, colonialism was directly involved in the making of European MODERNITY. Said (1978) has shown how the West engaged (and continues to deal with) the East, and justified colonial intervention, by elaborating 'imaginative geographies' of 'us' and 'them', and representing cultural and geographical differences as unchanging essences. The West fabricated binary oppositions between a dynamic/rational/masculine/democratic 'Occident' and an eternal/excessive/feminine/despotic 'Orient' (see ORIENTALISM). Geographers have considered the ways in which travellers, GEOGRAPHICAL SOCIETIES and professional geographers contributed to empire, and how imperial categories of thought and colonial practices have been shaped by explorers, travelwriters, CARTOGRAPHERS, surveyors, photographers and LANDSCAPE artists (see e.g. Smith and Godlewska, 1994; Bell, Butlin and Heffernan, 1995; cf. ART, GEOGRAPHY AND). In short, imperialism can be conceived as what Said (1993) describes as a multifaceted 'struggle over geography', and as Driver (1996) suggests, geography should be treated as both 'a discipline and discourse' of empire: as a set of geographical ideas, institutions and practices that induced and legitimized territorial expansion; and as a dynamic medium through which European attitudes of dominance and metropolitan–colonial relationships were imagined, represented and negotiated.

Yet imperialism was never simply *Eurocentric* and we can think about its geography in other ways. Imperialism also involved processes of *differentiation*. European states were vigorously competitive, developed distinct imperial ideologies and styles of power, dealt with diverse subject peoples, and held different views about what constituted an appealing land and ordered colonial society (see Pagden, 1995). Furthermore, different agents of empire (such as explorers and merchants, armies and engineers, settlers and governors) made the world over in the image of particular interests – those of CLASS, RACE and GENDER – and with culturally specific ideas and practices (see Pratt, 1992; McClintock, 1995). Imperialism was riven by covetous national agendas and implicated in the rise of NATIONALISM. For example, British national IDENTITY was shaped by a range of imperial ideas that revolved around *the utilization of space*. Contemporaries argued that Britain's strength and distinctiveness in Europe and the imperial world rested on principles of property and liberty, and practices of cultivation and international commerce. Imperial differentiation also stemmed from what might be called the intensive and extensive geographies of European movement, interaction and expansion. First, geographers note that 'the physical passage of European travellers through other landscapes and other cultures marked the very process of their writing and their representations of those spaces', and that European identities were often 're-negotiated in the course of the passage' (Gregory, 1995; cf. Blunt and Rose, 1994). Second, Europeans were never supremely self-confident about their imperial endeavours. Their ventures into alien territory and meetings with different peoples created trepidation. Greenblatt (1991), for example, shows that Europe's 'discovery' of the New World created both 'wonder and estrangement', and Guha (1996) argues that in colonial regions such as India, where British rule was imposed upon a huge and diverse land and subject population, the British were 'not at home in empire'. Fear and anxiety were heightened by resistance to colonial incursion. And third, European politicians struggled to administer large, sprawling settler empires and sustain firm metropolitan–colonial bonds. European colonists forged identities that diverged from metropolitan visions of empire and led colonial societies out of empire (see Cooper and Stoler, 1997). Such insights fracture and pluralize stark oppositional models of 'Europe and its (always somehow inferior) others' and prompt us to think about imperialism as a geographically variegated system of power and knowledge.

Much recent work on these tensions of empire is imbued with the perspectives of POST-COLONIALISM and POSTMODERNISM. Critics continue to pay considerable critical attention to the Eurocentric dimensions of imperialism – particularly the nature of colonial DISCOURSE – because they point out that while colonial empires have been largely dissolved, global relations are still structured by imperial attitudes and the affairs of post-colonial societies are still shaped by western frameworks of knowledge. Such recognitions have generated new debates within and beyond geography about the nature of 'otherness', the legacies of colonialism, and how the West continues to engage the world in imperial terms (see Agnew and Corbridge, 1995; cf. DEVELOPMENT; GLOBALIZATION). Post-colonial critics make two important, if potentially self-defeating, critical moves. First, they have deepened appreciation of how formerly colonized peoples were placed under domination and shown how difficult it still is for Western and non-Western cultures to extricate themselves from imperialism and colonialism. But they do so at the risk of homogenizing the imperial and colonial divides that they seek to question, representing non-Western peoples as the hapless victims of (ongoing) Western domination, and underplaying the ways in which imperial and colonial projects were subverted. And second, other critics question the triumphalist spirit of imperialism by pressing the claim that European projects of expansion and rule were frequently anxiety-ridden. Yet if such ideas are pressed too far, and European imperialism is made to collapse under the weight of its own ambivalencies or contradictions, we will lose sight of the violence and misery that Europe visited upon the world (see Loomba, 1998). DC

References

Agnew, J. and Corbridge, S. 1995: *Mastering space: hegemony, territory and international political economy*. London and New York: Routledge. · Bell, M., Butlin, R.A. and Heffernan, M. 1995: *Geography and imperialism, 1820–1940*. Manchester: Manchester University Press. · Blunt, A. and Rose, G. 1994: *Writing women and space: colonial and postcolonial geographies*. New York: Guilford Press. · Cooper, F. and Stoler, A.L., eds, 1997: *Tensions of empire: colonial cultures in a bourgeois world*. Berkeley, Los Angeles and London: University of California Press. · Crosby, A. 1986: *Ecological imperialism: the biological expansion of Europe 900–1900*. Cambridge: Cambridge University Press. · Driver, F. 1996: Histories of the present? The history and philosophy of geography, part III. *Progress in Human Geography* 20: 100–9. · Elliott, J.H. 1998: The seizure of overseas territories by the European powers. In D. Armitage, ed., *Theories of empire, 1450–1800.* Aldershot: Ashgate, 139–58. · Greenblatt, S. 1991: *Marvellous possessions: the wonder of the New World.* Oxford: Clarendon Press. · Gregory, D. 1995: Between the book and the lamp: imaginative geographies of Egypt, 1849–50. *Transactions, Institute of British Geographers* NS 20: 29–57. · Gregory, D. 1998: *Explorations in critical human geography.* Hettner-Lectures, 1. Heidelberg: Department of Geography, University of Heidelberg. · Guha, R. 1996: Not at home in empire. *Critical Inquiry* 23: 482–93. · Headrick, D. 1979: The tools of imperialism: technology and the expansion of European colonial empires in the nineteenth century. *Journal of Modern History* 51: 231–63. · McClintock, A. 1995: *Imperial leather: Race, gender and sexuality in the colonial encounter.* London and New York: Routledge. · Loomba, A. 1998: *Colonialism/postcolonialism.* London and New York: Routledge. · Mommsen, W. 1980: *Theories of imperialism.* Chicago: University of Chicago Press. · Pagden, A. 1995: *Lords of all the world: Ideologies of empire in Spain, Britain and France, c. 1500–c. 1800.* New Haven: Yale University Press. · Pratt, M.L. 1992: *Imperial eyes: Travel writing and transculturation.* London and New York: Routledge. · Rabasa, J. 1993: *Inventing America: Spanish historiography and the formation of Eurocentrism.* Norman, OK and London: University of Oklahoma Press. · Said, E.W. 1978: *Orientalism.* New York: Random House. · Said, E.W. 1993: *Culture and imperialism.* New York: Alfred A. Knopf. · Smith N. and Godlewska A., eds. 1994: *Geography and empire.* Cambridge, MA and Oxford: Blackwell. · Spurr, D. 1993: *The rhetoric of empire: colonial discourse in journalism, travel writing, and imperial administration.* Durham and London: Duke University Press. · Tracy, J. ed., 1991: *The political economy of merchant empires: state power and world trade, 1350–1750.* Cambridge: Cambridge University Press, 161–95.

Suggested Reading

Gregory (1998). · Pagden (1995). · Said (1993).

indeterminacy A wide-ranging concept used in both human and physical geography to describe systems and events which behave in either non-regular, dis-ordered or non-predictable ways. Strictly speaking, indeterminacy is a misnomer since no system or event lacks a cause or determination. Indeterminacy thus describes not the *lack* of determination but its *irregularity, disorderliness* and *unpredictability* in relation to certain human and physical systems and events.

In both human and physical geography the QUANTITATIVE REVOLUTION of the 1950s and 1960s and its POSITIVIST philosophical underpinning led to a search for general theories, laws and models which could explain whole classes of geographical phenomena. Broadly speaking, the assumption was that general processes were ONTOLOGICALLY stable and produced regular, ordered and predictable temporal and spatial outcomes. 'Deviant' outcomes were seen as aberrations or else as 'normal variability', a variability which probabilistic and STOCHASTIC models could account for. Likewise, although the 'initial conditions' in which a given PROCESS occurred could differentially affect its outcome, the assumption was that the process remained more or less invariant. However, over the last three decades a number of theories have called into question whether systems and events behave in a regular way. These theories have weaker and stronger versions. Weaker versions suggest that it is the events – rather than the systems and processes behind them – which are indeterminate. Stronger versions suggest that the systems processes themselves are indeterminate.

In human geography, philosophical REALISM has been perhaps the most forceful of the weaker indeterminacy theories of the last few years. Realism argues that human and physical objects have specific causal powers by virtue of their own nature and their relations with other objects, but that the outcome of these enduring powers is entirely *contingent* upon the specific contexts in which they are actualized (Sayer, 1992: see also ABSTRACTION; CHAOTIC CONCEPTION). Thus, in complex, large-scale, 'open systems' like economies and societies, indeterminacy routinely results from the sheer variety of causal power combinations and contexts of their realization. The insights of realism also fed into the so-called 'LOCALITY debate' in 1980s British human geography in which the nature and differential effects of international economic RESTRUCTURING upon the UK SPACE-ECONOMY were sought. Among other things, the locality debate turned on trying to understand how *general* processes of economic change led to divergent *specific* outcomes in particular localities, depending on the local socio-economic, political and cultural characteristics. In physical geography, some have taken issue with those (e.g. Bennett and Chorley, 1978) advocating SYSTEMS theory as an approach because it fails to appreciate *non-linear complexity* (Kennedy, 1979). More generally, some physical geographers have pointed to times–space *thresholds* in system behaviour (e.g. Schumm, 1979) and to stepped, phased, uneven, and delayed process-form relationships (Brunsden and Thornes, 1979).

In recent years, however, stronger versions of indeterminacy have been proposed in geography and are now beginning to influence research in the discipline. These versions largely originate outside geography in physics, ecology and social theory respectively. In physics the CATASTROPHE THEORY of Prigogine and others suggests that physical processes are constituted in non-determinate and irregular ways (cf. CHAOS). Likewise, a so-called 'new ECOLOGY' proposes that traditional ecological concepts of niche, competition, succession and climax are erroneously based on notions of ECOSYSTEM equilibrium (Botkin, 1985). Finally, social theorist Ulrich Beck's (1992) *Risk society* has unsettled accepted notions of social system order and regularity. According to Beck, social systemic order is increasingly compromised by unintended consequences, wherein social and natural processes interact unpredictably to create new, and often dangerous, configurations.

In both the weaker and stronger versions of indeterminacy, temporal and spatial SCALE is very important. What may seem stable or unstable according to human scales may be unstable or stable when taken at longer temporal and larger geographical natural scales.

NC

References

Beck, U. 1992: *Risk society*. London: Sage. · Bennett, R. and Chorley, R. 1978: *Environmental systems*. London: Methuen. · Botkin, D. 1985: *Discordant harmonies*. Oxford: Oxford University Press. · Brunsden, D. and Thornes, J. 1979: Landscape sensitivity and change. *Transactions, Institute of British Geographers* NS 4: 463–84. · Kennedy, B. 1979: A naughty world. *Transactions, Institute of British Geographers* NS 4: 550–8. · Sayer, A. 1992: *Method in social science*, 2nd edn. London: Routledge. · Schumm, S. 1979: Geomorphic thresholds. *Transactions, Institute of British Geographers* NS 4: 485–515.

indices of segregation Measures of the degree of residential separation of sub-groups within a wider population. The development of meaningful indices of SEGREGATION has been fundamental to the study of social stratification and residential differentiation in urban areas (see also FACTORIAL ECOLOGY; SOCIAL AREA ANALYSIS).

A simple graphical method of showing segregation is the *Lorenz curve*. The figure shows curves for several ETHNIC groups in Great Britain in 1991. The *x* axis indicates the cumulative percentage of each ethnic group and the *y* axis the cumulative percentage of the total population over the districts (in this case wards) into which the country has been divided. A diagonal line indicates no segregation – i.e. the percentage of a group's population within each sub-area is absolutely consistent with its percentage of the city population as a whole. Normally, the segregation line is a curve whose distance from the diagonal indicates the degree of segregation. The figure shows that at least 60 per cent of all of the ethnic-minority groups are found in wards that contain only 30 per cent of the total

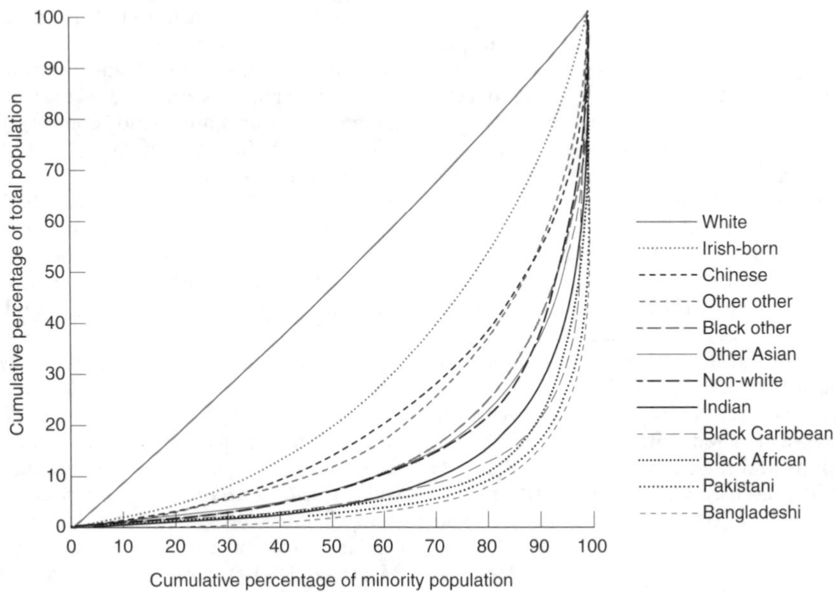

indices of segregation

population and that for the Indians, black Caribbeans, black Africans, Pakistanis and Bangladeshis about 70 per cent are found in wards which contain less than 10 per cent of the total population (Peach, 1996, p. 220). (The Lorenz curve is widely used in other contexts as a general measure of inequalities in distributions.)

Most studies of segregation have used one of two simple indices to summarize differences between two spatial distributions. The indices vary from 0–100 and indicate the percentage redistribution necessary before two groups are similarly distributed over a set of districts. First, the *index of residential dissimilarity* indicates the percentage difference between the distributions of two component groups of population:

$$\mathrm{Id}_{xy} = 1/2 \sum_{i=1}^{k} |x_i - y_i|$$

where x_i represents the percentage of the x population in the ith areal sub-unit, y_i the percentage of the y population in the ith sub-unit, and the summation is given over all the k sub-units making up the given territory, such as a city. Second, the *index of residential segregation* indicates the percentage difference between one group's distribution and that of the rest of the population:

$$\mathrm{IS}_{xn} = \mathrm{Id}_{xn}/[1 - (\textstyle\sum x / \sum n)]$$

where Id_{xn} is the index of dissimilarity between group x and the total population y (including the sub-group), $\sum x$ represents the total number in group x in the city and $\sum n$ represents the total population of the city. For example, in Britain in 1991, the index of dissimilarity for the Bangladeshi population compared to the white population was 73 per cent and the index of segregation for the Bangladeshis was 69, indicating their highly segregated distribution. A further simple measure is the LOCATION QUOTIENT, which shows the relative concentration of a population within any one sub-area.

Variations on these basic measures, and the problems associated with SCALE, the size of sub-groups and the nature of areal units have been much discussed. (See also GHETTO; RACE; RACISM; URBAN GEOGRAPHY.) PEO

Reference

Peach, C. 1996: Does Britain have ghettos? *Transactions, Institute of British Geographers* NS 21: 216–35.

Suggested Reading

Jones, E. and Eyles, J. 1977: *An introduction to social geography*. Oxford and New York: Oxford University Press. · Peach, C., ed., 1975: *Urban social segregation*. London and New York: Longman. · Peach, C., Robinson, V and Smith, S., eds, 1981: *Ethnic segregation in cities*. London: Croom Helm; Athens, GA: University of Georgia Press. · Plane, D.A. and Rogerson, D.A. 1994: *The geographical analysis of population*. New York and Chichester: John Wiley, ch. 10.

indifference curve A plot of combinations of quantities of two things, such that an individual is indifferent as to which combination to choose (see figure). Indifference curves are part of the analytical geometry of NEOCLASSICAL ECONOMICS. In their usual form they show combinations of two commodities which provide consumers with the same level of satisfaction or utility. As consumers move along the curve, they are trading off one commodity for the other; if behaving rationally they would choose the combination which costs least (cf. ALONSO MODEL; VON THÜNEN MODEL). DMS

industrial district A localized region of industrial production characterized by its concentration on a particular range of productive activities and, more tellingly, by close internal linkages based on horizontal and vertical DISINTEGRATION and untraded interdependencies and conventions (Storper, 1997; Storper and Salais, 1997), or taken-for-granted rules, routines and norms between firms constituting the productive organization of the district.

The term is not restricted to manufacturing and, instead, draws on insights relating to the interconnected sequence of processes involved in the transformation and consumption of value. Thus Sarah Whatmore (1995), for example, shows how the analysis of agriculture now goes well beyond the farm gate by looking at the processes of capital ACCUMULATION in the agro-food sector and the associated forms of standardization of diet and consumption embodied in agro-food complexes and in the regulatory programmes attached to it. Central to such analyses are notions of COMMODITY CHAINS which themselves have highly significant but varying geographies organized at SCALES ranging from the local to the global. This dialectic between local and global is central to the formation and development of industrial districts.

The term was coined originally by Alfred Marshall (1919) who referred to Sheffield (cutlery and specialized steel production) and south-east Lancashire (cotton textiles) as

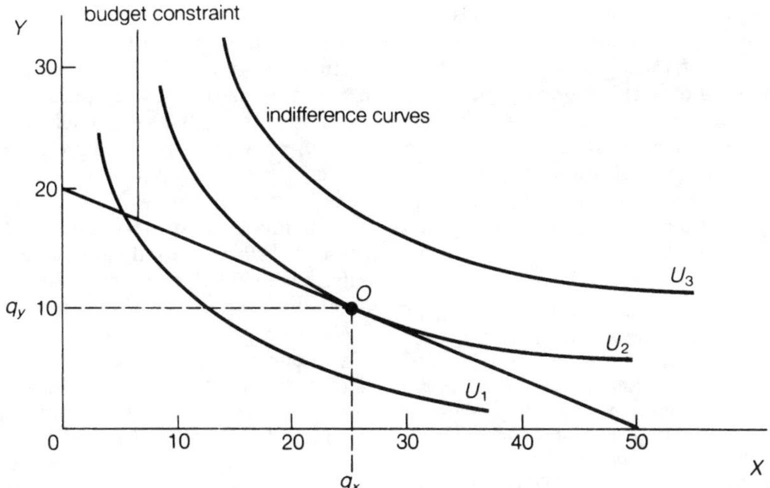

indifference curves *Maximization of consumer satisfaction (at 0) with ten units of Y and 25 of X, where the higher indifference curve just touches the budget constraint representing what the customer has to spend*

examples of industrial districts. He noted the significance of the distinctive characteristics of what he called the 'industrial atmosphere' of such places – a context which provided them with a highly competitive momentum.

A contemporary example is 'motor sport valley' (Henry and Pinch, 1997) – a regional cluster of firms centred around mid-Oxfordshire in and through which has developed the world's major agglomeration of Formula 1 and Indy car engineering. This region is a *community of knowledge* which is sustained by and expands through the rapid production, application and dissemination of knowledge – through observation, gossip and rumour and direct contact – amongst and between the network of highly secretive small and medium-sized enterprises which constitute the region. High rates of new firm formation (itself a source of knowledge) and the movement of knowledge through a mobile workforce operating within a relatively small area (the whole of motor sport valley extends in a 160 km-long crescent about 60 km to the north and west of London) has created a 'knowledge pool . . . on a constant learning trajectory' (Henry and Pinch, 1997, p. 7). The matrix of production here, then, is the socially and industrially constructed region of firms rather than the individual firms which form part of it.

Such an example points to the developmental power of new industrial spaces (Scott, 1988), such as the 'third Italy' and Orange County in California, through which the transmission of impulses around closely integrated but independent firms is seen as both an effective and a flexible means of production – hence the Marshallian argument that the geography of such spaces is a powerful influence upon their productive dynamism and flexibility (Storper and Scott, 1989). This argument is compelling in its SPATIALITY: Storper and Salais (1997), for example, insist in novel and convincing ways on the geographical foundations of economic activity and so place geographical space at the centre of their discourse.

In assessing this work, in part through an illuminating conjunction of two industrial districts – the City of London and Santa Croce in Tuscany – Amin and Thrift (1992) accept that PLACE certainly constitutes social and economic practice but argue that the way in which this constitution takes place is itself shaped by the geographical requirements of social practice. The localization of economic geographies is not an autonomous influence of geography on production but is shaped by the geographical demands of increasingly globally integrated economic geographies. One of the conditions of existence of such geographies is the presence of centres to act as places of representation (*centres of authority*), interaction (*centres of sociability*) and as a means of making sense of data and information (*centres of discourse*). Industrial districts are, in short, doubly geographical: both required for social practice and constitutive of that social practice. However, despite their mutuality, POWER relations (see Massey, 1995) within such districts are asymmetric whilst those that construct their connection to the world economy point up their vulnerability to influences which may overwhelm their internal coherence (expressed in political, social and cultural forms as well as economic) and place severe limits on any notions of determinant autonomy that such coherence may imply. RL

References

Amin, A. and Thrift, N. 1992: Neo-Marshallian nodes in global networks. *International Journal of Urban and Regional Research* 16: 571–87. · Henry, N. and Pinch, S. 1997: *A regional formula for success? The innovative region of motor sport valley*. Edgbaston: University of Birmingham. · Marshall, A. 1919: *Industry and trade*. London. Massey, D. 1995: *Spatial divisions of labour*, 2nd edn. London: Macmillan. · Scott, A.J. 1988: *New industrial spaces: flexible production organisation and regional development in north America and western Europe*. London: Pion. · Storper, M. 1997: Regional economies as relational assets. In R. Lee and J. Wills, eds, *Geographies of economies*, ch. 19. London and New York: Arnold, 248–58. · Storper, M. and Salais, R. 1997: *Worlds of production: the action frameworks of the economy*. Harvard, MA: Harvard University Press. · Storper, M. and Scott, A.J. 1989: The geographical foundations and social regulation of flexible production complexes. In J. Wolch and M. Dear, eds, *The power of geography: how territory shapes social life*. Winchester, MA: Unwin Hyman. · Whatmore, S. 1995: from farming to agribusiness: the global agrofood system. In R.J. Johnston, P.J. Taylor and M.J. Watts, eds, *Geographies of global change. Remapping the world in the late twentieth century*. Oxford and Cambridge, MA: Blackwell, 36–49.

Suggested reading

Henry and Pinch (1997).

industrial geography The study of the spatial arrangement of industrial activity. Industrial geography is a subfield of ECONOMIC GEOGRAPHY and deals with manufacturing or secondary activity. It is distinguished by the fact that the study of industrial location in its early years brought geography and economics closer together than any other branch of geographical inquiry.

Until the quantitative and model-building movement gathered strength in the latter part of the 1950s, the study of industrial geography was largely confined to the verbal description of the distribution of individual manufacturing activities. Explanation tended to emphasize the historical evolution of the patterns and to give undue emphasis to the role of physical-environmental factors, such as the availability of raw materials and natural sources of power. There was little attempt to generalize from the case studies; there was no explicit theoretical framework, and hardly any economic analysis.

In the latter part of the 1950s statistical methods began to be used on the measurement of industrial location patterns (cf. QUANTITATIVE REVOLUTION). Then, as human geography became more interested in THEORY and MODELS, industrial geography was able to benefit from existing work in economics. The birth of modern industrial location theory goes back to 1909, when the German economist Alfred Weber published his *Uber den Standort der Industrien* (translated into English as *Alfred Weber's theory of industrial location* in 1929). This book provided the foundations for VARIABLE COST ANALYSIS, which T. Palander (1935) and E.M. Hoover (1948) had significantly extended by the end of the 1930s. Parallel to this was the development of theory on LOCATIONAL INTERDEPENDENCE, which formed the basis for VARIABLE REVENUE ANALYSIS. This approach grew out of the recognition that firms can derive SPATIAL MONOPOLY advantages from location, contrary to the assumptions of the model of perfect competition in economic theory.

Throughout most of the 1960s the variable cost approach dominated theory in industrial geography. Developments on the revenue side, mainly in MARKET-AREA ANALYSIS, found their most obvious expression in the context of CENTRAL PLACE THEORY. The fusion of the variable cost and variable revenue approaches has proved to be very difficult in theory. The most influential attempts at synthesis in the tradition of spatial economic analysis were those of A. Losch (*The economics of location*, 1954), M.L. Greenhut (*Plant location in theory and in practice*, 1956) and W. Isard (*Location and space economy*, 1956). Important contributions by geographers during this phase of development of industrial location analysis were few, a major exception being E.M. Rawstron's concept of spatial margins to profitability (see VARIABLE COST ANALYSIS).

Geographical contributions became more prominent towards the end of the 1960s, when traditional or 'neo-classical' location theory came under assault during the ascendancy of BEHAVIOURAL GEOGRAPHY. The shift from abstract models based on assumptions of optimizing objectives and capacity on behalf of decision-makers towards observation of actual location practice accorded with the traditionally more empirical predilections of the geographer. The practical application of location theory in the tradition of spatial economic analysis had always proved difficult, by virtue of the data demands of variable cost and variable revenue models. The empirical identification of locational decision-making was easier to undertake.

The 1970s saw two distinct but interconnected themes emerging in the more behaviourally oriented industrial geography. The first focused on the location DECISION-MAKING process. The second theme stressed the role of INDUSTRIAL ORGANIZATION in the location decision and in the spatial organization of industrial activity in general. The perspective gradually broadened, from preoccupation with the location of single-plant firms, through the complexities of giant multi-plant and multi-product firms, to concern with entire spatial industrial systems.

During the 1980s, developments in industrial geograpy reflected the application of MARXIAN ECONOMICS to location problems, in place of the NEO-CLASSICAL ECONOMICS on which traditional location theory was based. The RESTRUCTURING of industrial activity in a spatial context attracted increasing attention, within the broader context of change in the capitalist economy. As FLEXIBLE ACCUMULATION has come to characterize this kind of economy, the small firm has re-emerged as a focus of interest during the 1990s. Increasing attention is also being given to networks of information exchange, which may be replacing traditional concerns such as input costs as factors influencing the location of some industries. There has also been a growing recognition that cultural factors are important in industrial activity, for example in some societies family membership and networks are prominent in the organization and financing of production.

Despite these and other contemporary developments, neo-classical location theory in the space economics tradition still has its adherents. Such considerations as cost minimization and spatial control of markets remain important to firms in a competitive capitalist economy, and the traditional models still have some utility as both predictive and prescriptive devices.

Since the introduction of LOCATION THEORY into industrial geography there has always been an interest in problems of planning industrial development. In the advanced capitalist world the focus has been primarily on problems of economic decline in older industrial regions and on plans to encourage the dispersal of manufacturing firms from prosperous metropolitan centres into the periphery. Attention has also been given to the decline of industry in the INNER CITY. In the underdeveloped world the problem is how to stimulate industrial development in circumstances that may include limitations of resources, CAPITAL and skills, in the general context of dependency on the advanced capitalist world and in circumstances of accelerating GLOBALIZATION.

As with other specialized subfields of ECONOMIC (and HUMAN) GEOGRAPHY, industrial geography finds its independent existence increasingly at variance with the tendency towards integration of subject matter, which was originally stimulated by the quantitative and model-building movements, was further encouraged by the emergence of regional economics and REGIONAL SCIENCE, and is an important feature of the political-economy perspective that seeks a holistic view of society.

DMS

References

Greenhut, M.L. 1956: *Plant location in theory and in practice: the economics of space*. Chapel Hill: University of North Carolina Press. · Hoover, E.M. 1948: *The localtion of economic activity*. New York: McGraw-Hill. · Isard, W. 1956: *Location and space economy: a general theory relating to industrial location, market areas, land use, trade and urban structure*. Cambridge, MA: MIT Press; London: Chapman and Hall. · Losch, A. 1954: *The economics of location*, trans. W.H. Woglom. New Haven: Yale University Press; Oxford: Oxford University Press (first German edition 1940). · Palander, T. 1935: *Beitrage zur Standorts-theorie*. Uppsala: Almqvist and Wiksell. · Weber, A. 1929: *Alfred Weber's theory of the location of industries*, trans. C.J. Friedrich. Chicago: University of Chicago Press. (Reprinted 1971, New York: Russell and Russell; first German edition 1909.)

Suggested Reading

Carr, M. 1983: A contribution to the review and critique of behavioural industrial location theory. *Progress in Human Geography* 7: 386–402. · Chapman, K. and Walker, D. 1991: *Industrial location: principles and policies*, 2nd edn. Oxford: Basil Blackwell. · Corbridge, S., Thrift, N. and Martin, R., eds, 1994: *Money, power and space*. Oxford: Blackwell. · Hayter, R. and Watts, H.D. 1983: The geography of enterprise: a reappraisal. *Progress in Human Geography* 7: 157–81. · Hayter, R. 1997: *The dynamics of industrial location*. Chichester and New York: John Wiley. · Malmberg, A. 1996: Industrial geography: agglomeration and local milieu. *Progress in Human Geography* 20: 392–403. · Malmberg, A. 1997: Industrial geography: location and learning. *Progress in Human Geography* 21: 573–82. · Martin, R. 1994: Economic theory and human geography. In D. Gregory, R. Martin, and G. Smith, eds, *Human geography: society, space and sopcial science*. London: Macmillan, 21–53. · Massey, D. 1984: *Spatial divisions of labour: social structures and the geography of reproduction*. London: Macmillan. · O hUallachain, B. 1989: Industrial geography.

Progress in Human Geography 13: 251–8. · O hUallachain, B. 1991: Industrial geography. *Progress in Human Geography* 15: 73–80. · Scott, A.J. 1988: *New industrial spaces*. London: Pion. · Scott, A. and Storper, M. 1986: *Production, work, territory: the geographical anatomy of industrial capitalism*. London: Unwin Hyman. · Sheppard, E. and Barnes, T.J. 1990: *The capitalist space economy: analysis after Ricardo, Marx and Sraffa*. London: Unwin Hyman. · Smith, D.M. 1981: *Industrial location: an economic geographical analysis*, 2nd edn. New York: John Wiley. · Smith, D.M. 1987: Neoclassical Location Theory. In W. Lever, ed., *Industrial change in the United Kingdom*. London: Longman, 23–37. · Storper, M. and Walker, R.A. 1989: *The capitalist imperative: territory, technology and industrial growth*. Oxford: Basil Blackwell.

industrial inertia The tendency for industry, once established, to remain in its existing location rather than to move with changing economic circumstances. Industrial inertia arises from the fact that many industries will build up local advantages over time as EXTERNAL ECONOMIES, such as skilled labour and ancillary activities. These can be lost if a firm moves away from an area that may have a traditional concentration on the activity in question. Industrial inertia also arises from more general economies associated with AGGLOMERATION and from the relative immobility of fixed CAPITAL in the form of plant and machinery. DMS

industrial location policy The manner in which the STATE seeks to influence the location of industrial activity, generally justified by the pursuit of welfare objectives. Industrial location policy under CAPITALISM is usually directed towards the economic regeneration of declining industrial districts, such as parts of northern England and certain INNER-CITY areas. In the underdeveloped world industrial location policy may be directed towards the initiation of economic development, or MODERNIZATION.

Industrial location policy normally comprises goals, instruments and strategy. The *goals* represent the policy objectives, such as the creation of new jobs or raising local income. The *instruments* are the specific measures adopted to induce industry to become established in the areas in question, which can comprise grants towards the cost of plant and machinery, favourable rates for writing off capital investment, a financial premium for each job created, and tax concessions as well as state-provided industrial premises, industrial estates laid out with the necessary utilities, and general investment in local or regional INFRASTRUCTURE. The *strategy* is the way in which the various measures adopted are related to one another.

An important element in any industrial location policy is the *spatial strategy*. Financial inducements to new industry may be dispersed or concentrated in geographical space. In the latter case, some kind of GROWTH-POLE policy is often adopted, with certain places selected for special consideration by virtue of their apparent growth potential. A further step in the direction of concentration is the creation of a planned industrial complex . Another kind of spatial strategy, favoured by governments committed to the encouragement of market forces, involves local relaxation of constraints on development, for example in an ENTERPRISE ZONE or FREE TRADE AREA.

Under capitalism, the extent to which industrial location policy can succeed is constrained by the profit-seeking objectives of private industry. The inducements that the STATE is able to offer may be insufficient to offset the disadvantages of a relatively high cost location. Under SOCIALISM, industrial location policy is an integral part of national economic and social planning. But there are limits to the freedom of the state to locate industry in pursuit of welfare objectives, for dispersal to high-cost locations can impair overall efficiency – as some eastern European countries discovered.

With the demise of socialist state planning, and the emergence of a neo-liberal economic orthodoxy emphasizing market solutions to local or regional economic problems, interest in industrial location policy has declined in recent years. This is exemplified by the withdrawl of regional policy in England in the 1980s, while continuing in Scotland and Wales. States are now more likely to place their hopes for stimulating industrial development in broader policies of deregulation and flexible labour markets, with the location of new investment less subject to government influence or control. However, some expectations are still vested in industrial development planning, including the designation of free trade zones in the former Soviet Union.

DMS

Suggested Reading

Chapman, K. and Walker, D. 1991: *Industrial location: principles and policies*. Oxford: Basil Blackwell. · Smith, D.M. 1981: *Industrial location: an economic geograpghical analysis*, 2nd edn. New York: John Wiley.

industrial location theory A branch of LOCATION THEORY concerned with manufacturing and providing a theoretical basis for INDUS-

TRIAL GEOGRAPHY. Classical industrial location theory was concerned with VARIABLE COST ANALYSIS, built on the foundations provided by Alfred Weber, to which VARIABLE REVENUE ANALYSIS was added to accommodate the effects of demand and the market. Subsequent developments were concerned with the role of INDUSTRIAL ORGANIZATION and DECISION-MAKING, and with the intepretation of industrial location and change within the broader structure of regional, national and international economic processes (see LAYERS OF INVESTMENT). DMS

industrial organization The structure within which the functions of control and DECISION-MAKING are exercised in the process of industrial production. The impact of industrial organization on the location of economic activity was neglected in the early development of INDUSTRIAL LOCATION THEORY, but subsequently became a major concern. This was partly because of shifts in theoretical perspective and partly because of changes in industrial organization itself.

In the early days of modern industrial development the typical unit of production was organized very simply, with a single owner-operator often exercising complete control. The theory of the firm in economics tended to perpetuate the figure of the individual enterpreneur making all the major production decisions with single-minded dedication to profit maximization. The growing complexity of industrial organization with increasing scale of operation proceeded somewhat ahead of the recognition of this change, both in economics and in location theory. However, a more realistic view subsequently emerged, stimulated by the adoption in location analysis of some concepts from organization theory (which seeks to explain the general behaviour of organizations). The single unit of production run by the individual owner-operator was replaced by the multi-plant, multi-locational firm in which the control functions are much more dispersed (see MULTINATIONAL CORPORATION).

The expansion of industrial production in geographical space had an important bearing on this growing organizational complexity. The simple distinction between parent plant or head office on the one hand and branch or sales outlet on the other requires some division of responsibility. As industrial production become steadily more extensive in scale and in the spatial scope of its operations, a hierarchical structure of control grew up parallel to a hierarchical structure of spatial organization. The major control functions are exercised in major cities or centres of finance, secondary control and coordinating functions will be more dispersed in smaller towns and cities, while production and its day-to-day control will be most dispersed. Such a structure is typical of the modern transnational corporation. It has important implications for the economic DEVELOPMENT of those peripheral territories (generally the THIRD WORLD) that perform the lower-order functions in the organizational hierarchy controlled from elsewhere (generally the advanced capitalist world).

The adoption of more flexible forms of manufacturing, involving less assembly-line mass production and more emphasis on various kinds of subcontracting, has added to organizational complexity and diversity in recent years. This has been accompanied by a resurgence of interest on the part of geographers seeking guidance from organization theories. Reflecting the trend towards DEINDUSTRIALIZATION, attention has been given to industrial restructuring and plant closure, as well as to the more traditional problem of the location of new capacity. DMS

Suggested Reading

Carlton, D. and Perloff, J. 1990: *Modern industrial organization*. Glenview, IL: Scott, Foresman & Co.. · Chapman, K. and Walker, D. 1991: *Industrial location: principles and policies*, 2nd edn. Oxford: Basil Blackwell. · Clark, G.L. and Wrigley, N. 1997: Exit, the firm and sunk costs: reconceptualizing the corporate geography of disinvestment and plant closure. *Progress in Human Geography* 21: 338–58. · Dicken, P. and Thrift, N.J. 1992: The organization of production and the production of organization: why business enterprise matters in the study of geographical industrialization. *Transactions, Institute of British Geographers* NS 17: 279–91. · Hayter, R. 1997: *The dynamics of industrial location*. Chichester and New York: John Wiley. · Smith, D.M. 1981: *Industrial location: an economic geographical analysis*, 2nd edn. New York: John Wiley, ch. 5.

industrial revolution A transformation of the forces of production, centring on (but not confined to) the circuit of industrial capital (see CAPITALISM). The term is most usually applied to the series of changes within the British economy between *c.* 1750 and *c.* 1850, but it has also been used in a number of other contexts. Some writers claim to have identified an 'industrial revolution' in Europe in the sixteenth and seventeenth centuries, based on technical change and the growth of large-scale capitalist organizations (Nef, 1934–35; see Musson, 1978); others speak of a 'Second

Industrial Revolution' at the close of the nineteenth and beginning of the twentieth centuries, in which industrial hegemony passed from Britain, 'the first industrial nation', to Germany and the USA, based on the growth of steel, engineering and electricity and a new scientific' organization of the labour process (TAYLORISM: see Landes, 1969); yet others speak of a further industrial revolution in the late twentieth century, based on the emergence of high-technology, so-called sunrise industries with a new global geography of production (see FLEXIBLE ACCUMULATION; NEW INTERNATIONAL DIVISION OF LABOUR).

However, virtually all of these variant usages take as their point of reference the classical Industrial Revolution in Britain. Most writers attribute the term to Blanqui in 1837: 'Just as the French revolution witnessed great social experiences of earthshaking proportions, England began to undergo the same process on the terrain of industry' (see Tribe, 1981). As the comparison implied, the process was as much social and political as it was economic, but it was far from being as 'revolutionary' as Blanqui and most subsequent commentators assumed. The epic image of the Industrial Revolution as 'Prometheus Unbound' (Landes, 1969) – in Greek mythology Prometheus stole fire from the gods for the benefit of humankind – has been sharply qualified in recent years: it now seems likely that industrial growth started earlier in the eighteenth century (see PROTOINDUSTRIALIZATION), that the industrial sector was then much larger (and its growth more diffuse), and that its expansion later in the eighteenth century was correspondingly less dramatic than conventional accounts allowed (Crafts, 1985). This is not to say that industrialization was a smooth and uninterrupted process, however, and investment in industrial production was often jagged and punctuated by national and regional crises of capital ACCUMULATION and circulation (see CRISIS: Gregory, 1984); industrialization was also uneven over space, and indeed one of the most striking features of the new industrial SPACE-ECONOMY was its heterogeneity (see Langton and Morris, 1986). Over 40 years ago, Dobb (1946) argued that 'the unevenness of development as between different industries' was 'one of the leading features of the period', and later studies have confirmed his views. Marx, whose critique of POLITICAL ECONOMY in *Capital* was centred around an analysis of the Industrial Revolution in Britain, was undoubtedly right to draw attention to the significance of the transformation of the LABOUR PROCESS and in particular in the transition from *manufacture to machinofacture* in the emergence of industrial capitalism (see Dunford and Perrons, 1983); and several geographers have outlined the contributions made by 'heavy industries' such as textiles, coal and iron to the transformation of the manufacturing sector (e.g. Warren, 1976). 'Their growth was connected to important and sometimes dramatic changes – in the resource base of industrialization, and these often excited the imaginations and aroused the fears of those who had to live through them' (Wrigley, 1988; Gregory, 1990). But in so far as capitalism is characterized by a process of UNEVEN DEVELOPMENT it is scarcely surprising that, as Samuel (1977) put it:

> If one looks at the economy as a whole rather than at its most novel and striking features, a less orderly canvas might be drawn – one bearing more resemblance to a Bruegel or even a Hieronymus Bosch than to the geometrical regularities of a modern abstract. The industrial landscape would be seen to be full of diggings and pits as well as tall factory chimneys. Smithies would sprout in the shadows of the furnaces, sweatshops in those of the looms. Agricultural labourers might take up the foreground, armed with sickle or scythe, while behind them troops of women and children would be bent double over the ripening crops in the field ... In the middle distance there might be navvies digging sewers and paviours laying flags. On the building sites there would be a bustle of man-powered activity, with house-painters on ladders and slaters nailing roofs. Carters would be loading and unloading horses, market-women carrying baskets of produce on their heads; dockers balancing weights. The factories would be hot and steamy, with men stripped to the singlet and juvenile runners in bare feet. At the lead works women would be carrying pots of poisonous metal on their heads, in the bleachers shed they would be stitching yards of chlorined cloth, at a shoddy mill sorting rags. Instead of calling [the] picture 'machinery' the artist might prefer to label it 'toil'.

This is indeed to speak of a LANDSCAPE rather than a space-economy, and to conjure up a series of changes in cultural forms and sensibilities that have only recently attracted attention in human geography (see Daniels, 1992). Those sensibilities were, of course, more than aesthetic and they entered into the construction of a vigorous geography of popular CULTURE through which many of the new work-disciplines, their divisions of CLASS and GENDER, and the framing assumptions of the new 'political economy' were sharply contested (see Thompson, 1968; Pinchbeck,

1969). But these have attracted comparatively little attention in geography; where they have been considered, the focus has usually been on contours of class struggle (Gregory, 1984) rather than geographies of GENDER and PATRIARCHY (but see McDowell and Massey, 1984). For the most part, however, discussion has centred on the economic integuments of the REGIONAL GEOGRAPHY of the Industrial Revolution. Indeed, Berg (1985) attributes the 'persistence of traditional forms of organization and labour-intensive techniques' so vividly present in Samuels's vignettes to what she calls 'the different micro-economies of the various sectors and industries' and to 'the *regional and cyclical* pattern of industrialization' (emphasis added). A number of studies have reconstructed the geographies of regional production systems during the Industrial Revolution (e.g. Langton, 1979; Gregory, 1982; Hudson, 1989), but it has also been argued that the Industrial Revolution accentuated the regional specialization of production. The most sustained discussion of the question has been provided by Langton (1984, 1988), who attributed 'the essentially regional structure of the emerging manufacturing economy of the time' to its dependence on canal transportation. Far from forming a coherent system, the canals were disjointed and disarticulated, and long-distance flows along them were interrupted by transfers between one carrier and another. The vast majority of shipments were therefore over short distances, to and from the major ports, and in consequence the canal-based economies 'became more specialized, more differentiated from each other and more internally unified' (Langton, 1984; see also Turnbull, 1987). This growing fragmentation between regions was more than economic; in Langton's view it was repeated in the dissolution of REGIONAL ALLIANCES, in the disunity of social protests and in the dismemberment of trades unions once they reached out from their regional bases. Regional economies found expression in coherent regional cultures. It was not until the coming of the railways, Langton concluded, that 'longterm processes of integration were set in motion'. It was then that 'London again began to exert the sway over national commerce that it had lost to the canal-based regional capitals' (see also Calhoun, 1987).

Against these views, or as a supplement to them, Freeman (1984) argued that Langton 'over-stated the case for economic regionalism during the earlier phases of industrialization and under-stated it for the later ones'. The importance of the canal system is undeniable, Freeman concedes, but much of it was not operational until 1800 and both coastwise shipping and land carriage over the turnpike system ensured that spheres of trade were much less circumscribed than Langton allowed (see Pawson, 1977; Freeman, 1980; Freeman and Aldcroft, 1983). Furthermore, Freeman dismissed 'the view which casts railways as a uniform cohesive agency' as 'a convenient, if widely current fiction'. On the contrary, the railway network was divided 'between a multiplicity of independent companies, sometimes serving highly discrete geographical areas and much of the time operating freight pricing policies which discriminated in favor of the part of the country they served'. The result, Freeman (1984) concluded, was 'to describe for the railways much the same role that Langton conceives for the inland waterway system': that is to say, much rail traffic was also short-haul, 'between consuming or producing areas and major ports', and although this system of flows was evidently part of the internationalization of the Victorian economy it neither required nor resulted in the systematic integration of the space-economy.

However, this exchange revolved around the production and circulation of commodities, and later contributions have focused on *non-commodity forms*. Analyses of the mobility of skilled labour (Southall, 1988, 1991a, b) of the circulation of capital (Black, 1989) and the dissemination of public and private information (Gregory, 1987) have revealed an even more complex picture in which regional differentiation and integration are two sides of the same coin, and in which London acted as a vital commercial and financial pivot between Britain and the world-economy. But it is also important not to lose sight of London's national political and cultural functions (Gregory, 1988). Although there has been considerable interest in municipal government, however, and in the social geographies of industrial towns and cities (Dennis, 1984), historical geographers have paid little attention to the formal domains of national politics – to ELECTORAL GEOGRAPHIES, the geographies of the STATE APPARATUS and its institutions – or to the more subterranean modes of regulating and 'disciplining' the new industrial society: but there are encouraging signs that this is beginning to change (see Driver, 1988, 1993; Ogbom, 1992). In any event, there remain many other geographies of industrialization to be reconstructed and interrogated, and to feed in to debates within the wider discipline. DG

References

Berg, M. 1985: *The age of manufacturers: industry, innovation and work in Britain 1700–1820*. London: Fontana. · Black, I. 1989: Geography, political economy and the circulation of finance capital in early industrial England. *Journal of Historical Geography* 15: 366–84. · Calhoun, C. 1987: Class, place and industrial revolution. In N. Thrift, and P. Williams, eds, *Class and space: the making of urban society*. London: Unwin Hyman, 51–72. · Crafts, N. 1985: *British economic growth during the Industrial Revolution*. Oxford: Clarendon Press. · Daniels, S. 1992: The implications of industry: Turner and Leeds. In T. Barnes, and J. Duncan, eds, *Writing worlds: discourse, text and metaphor in the representation of landscape*. London: Routledge, 38–49. · Dennis, R. 1984: *English industrial cities of the nineteenth century: a social geography*. Cambridge: Cambridge University Press. · Dobb, M. 1946: *Studies in the development of capitalism*. London: Routledge. · Driver, F. 1988: Moral geographies: social science and the urban environment in mid-nineteenth century England. *Transactions, Institute of British Geographers* NS 13: 275–87. · Driver, F. 1993: *An historical geography of the Poor Law in England*. Cambridge: Cambridge University Press. · Dunford, M. and Perrons, D. 1983: *The arena of capital*. London: Macmillan. · Freeman, M. 1980: Road transport in the English industrial revolution: an interim reassessment. *Journal of Historical Geography* 6: 17–28. · Freeman, M. 1984: The industrial revolution and the regional geography of England: a comment. *Transactions, Institute of British Geographers* NS 9: 502–12. · Freeman, M. and Aldcroft, D., eds, 1983: *Transport in the industrial revolution*. Manchester: Manchester University Press. · Gregory, D. 1982: *Regional transformation and industrial revolution: a geography of the Yorkshire woollen industry*. London: Macmillan. · Gregory, D. 1984: Contours of crisis? Sketches for a geography of class struggle in the early industrial revolution in England. In A.R.H. Baker, and D. Gregory, eds, *Explorations in historical geography: interpretative essays*. Cambridge: Cambridge University Press, 68–117. · Gregory, D. 1987: The friction of distance? Information circulation and the mails in early nineteenth-century England. *Journal of Historical Geography* 13: 130–54. · Gregory, D. 1988: The production of regions in England's Industrial Revolution. *Journal of Historical Geography* 14: 50–8. · Gregory, D. 1990: 'A new and differing face in many places': Three geographies of industrialization. In R.A. Dodgshon and R.A. Butlin, eds, *An historical geography of England and Wales*, 2nd edn. London: Academic Press, 351–99. · Hudson, P., ed., 1989: *Regions and industries: a perspective on the industrial revolution in Britain*. Cambridge: Cambridge University Press. · Landes, D. 1969: *The unbound Prometheus: technological change and industrial development in Western Europe from 1750 to the present*. Cambridge: Cambridge University Press. · Langton, J. 1979: *Geographical change and industrial revolution: coal mining in south west Lancashire 1590–1799*. Cambridge: Cambridge University Press. · Langton, J. 1984: The Industrial Revolution and the regional geography of England. *Transactions, Institute of British Geographers* NS 9: 145–67. · Langton, J. 1988: The production of regions in England's Industrial Revolution: a response. *Journal of Historical Geography* 14: 170–4. · Langton, J. and Morris, R.J., eds, 1986: *Atlas of industrializing Britain*. London: Methuen. · McDowell, L. and D. Massey, 1984: A woman's place? In D. Massey, and J. Allen, eds, *Geography matters! A reader*. Cambridge: Cambridge University Press, 128–47. · Musson, A.E. 1978: *The growth of British industry*. London: Batsford. · Nef, J. 1934–5: The progress of technology and the growth of large-scale industry in Britain, 1540–1640. *Economic History Review* 5: 3–24. · Ogborn, M. 1992: Love-state-ego: 'centres' and 'margins' in nineteenth-century Britain. *Environment and Planning D: Society and Space* 10: 287–305. · Pawson, E. 1977: *Transport and economy: the turnpike roads of eighteenth-century Britain*. London: Academic Press. · Pinchbeck, I. 1969: *Women workers and the industrial revolution 1750–1850*. London: Virago. · Samuel, R. 1977: Workshop of the world: steam power and hand technology in mid-Victorian Britain. *History Workshop Journal* 3: 6–72. · Southall, H. 1988: Towards a geography of early unionization: the spatial organization and distribution of early British trade unions. *Transactions, Institute of British Geographers* NS 13: 466–83. · Southall, H. 1991a: The tramping artisan revisited: labour mobility and economic distress in early Victorian England. *Economic History Review* 44: 272–96. · Southall, H. 1991b: Mobility, the artisan community and popular politics in early nineteenth-century England. In G. Kearns and C. Withers, eds, *Urbanising Britain: essays on class and community in the nineteenth century*. Cambridge: Cambridge University Press, 103–30. · Thompson, E.P. 1968: *The making of the English working class*. London: Penguin. · Tribe, K. 1981: *Genealogies of capitalism*. London: Macmillan. · Turnbull, G. 1987: Canals, coal and regional growth during the industrial revolution. *Economic History Review* 40: 537–60. · Warren, K. 1976: *The geography of British heavy industry since 1800*. Oxford: Oxford University Press. · Wrigley, E.A. 1988: *Continuity, chance and change: the character of the Industrial Revolution in England*. Cambridge: Cambridge University Press.

Suggested Reading

Gregory (1990). · Langton (1984). · Langton and Morris (1986). · Samuel (1977).

industrialization The process whereby industrial activity comes to play a dominant role in the economy of a nation or region. Industrialization may take place spontaneously or as a result of some process of development planning. Manufacturing (literally, making by hand) has always been a necessary human activity, ever since the first fashioning of a plough or spear from the branch of a tree. The advantages of DIVISION OF LABOUR eventually created specialist producers of particular types of commodities.

Industrialization as a spontaneous activity refers to the augmentation or replacement of small-scale production for either personal use or a limited local market by a type of activity characterized by a much larger scale of productive unit and by mechanization. Such a change can be stimulated by the growth of the market to such an extent that the pre-existing system of manufacturing cannot maintain an adequate supply; but other necessary conditions exist, such as the accumulation of CAPITAL in quantities required for investment in large plants and the development of a technology appropriate to the task.

The process of industrialization under CAPITALISM involved important changes in the social relations of production. In the early stages of the development of manufacturing industry, apprentices may have been bound to masters in a manner that constrained their mobility and their freedom to sell their labour as they chose. As large-scale industry grew, it was important to have a supply of labour capable of responding to market forces, and this contributed to the breakdown of existing patterns of employment and increased labour mobility.

Industrialization is often considered to be the panacea for the problems of poverty in the underdeveloped world. The process is constrained not only by the shortage of capital but also by the predominance of the role of primary producers assigned to underdeveloped countries in the international division of labour. Industrialization depends to a large extent on the infusion of capital, technology and business organization from outside, and carries the risk of DEPENDENCY. The advent of modern industry may destroy existing manufacturing activity and exacerbate inequality by reinforcing a distinction between those employed in the traditional sector and those in the modern. Planned industrialization forms an important element in the development strategy of most Third World countries. An indigenous process of industrialization under socialist central planning may avoid many of the problems associated with externally induced industrialization, but at the price of limiting access to outside capital and know-how.

Industrialization is no longer regarded as universally beneficial. In addition to some of the negative side-effects observed in the underdeveloped world, there are the ecological implications of indiscriminate resource exploitation and unrestrained POLLUTION of land, sea and air. The continued 'advance' of industrialization also requires sources of energy, the availability or safety of which are no longer assured. Furthermore, as service activities come to dominate many national economies, this sector is viewed as an alternative to industrialization as a source of employment creation. (See also DEINDUSTRIALIZATION; PROTOINDUSTRIALIZATION.) DMS

inequality, spatial The unequal distribution of some particular kinds of attribute among spatially defined population aggregates. Whereas spatial *differentiation* refers to the uneven incidence of any condition, *inequality* refers to those over which moral questions of right or wrong can arise (see ETHICS, GEOGRAPHY AND). It is generally recognized that some differences among individuals do not raise moral questions (for example their height or free choice of leisure activities), whereas differences in their wealth or educational qualifications could be described as inequality. Thus regional variations in topography or the type of goods produced would be differentiation, whereas regional variations in income or health would be inequality.

The geographical expression of inequality was an important element in the WELFARE GEOGRAPHY of the late 1970s and 1980s. Attention was drawn not only to inequality in living standards and elements thereof, but also in spatial accessibility to sources of need satisfaction. Trends in spatial inequality over time can also be useful diagnostic devices, providing clues to the trajectory of society with respect to inequality more generally. However, preoccupation with spatial patterns can obscure inequality by individuals or groups, such as RACE and CLASS, and risks losing sight of the structural basis of inequality. While EQUALITY is an enduring political ideal (see EGALITARIANISM), capable of motivating action, spatial inequality cannot automatically be judged wrong. It might even be approved of, especially among the 'new right', as a reflection of local entitlement to make the most of people's resource holdings (see LIBERTARIANISM). However, it might be asked what moral justification people in particular places have for monopolizing resources to which they have access purely by the good fortune of having been born there.

The crucial and extremely difficult question of SOCIAL JUSTICE concerns the circumstances under which spatial inequality can be justified in some moral sense. In a world with such extreme inequalities as are evident today, the onus may well be on those advocating inequality to justify their position, or at least to explain the morality behind the actual degree of inequality manifest in real life. (See also UNEVEN DEVELOPMENT.) DMS

Suggested Reading

Smith, D.M. 1994: *Geography and social justice*. Oxford: Blackwell.

inference Drawing a conclusion from incomplete evidence. The body of procedures known as inferential statistics has been developed as a means for establishing the degree of certainty with which a statement about a population can be made when data are only available from SAMPLING that population. The degree of certainty is expressed in probabilistic terms – e.g. you can be 95 per cent certain that what has been observed in the sample will hold for the population because under the theory of sampling that conclusion would be drawn from similar analyses of at least 95 out of every 100 samples (see CONFIRMATORY DATA ANALYSIS; PARAMETRIC STATISTICS). RJJ

informal sector Those parts of ECONOMIC GEOGRAPHIES beyond official recognition and record through which people engage in SOCIAL REPRODUCTION outside formal systems of control and remuneration but often in close relationship with formal economic geographies.

The informal sector is, by definition, difficult to pin down and to characterize. It reveals the lack of clear distinction between, say, work and non-work, CULTURE and ECONOMY, legality and illegality. The economic geographies of illegal drugs, for example, are, at all levels of the production and distribution chain, both a means of sustaining and engaging in formal circuits of social reproduction and a subversion of them. Lubell (1991, p.11) is forced into a minimalist position:

> After years of controversy . . . two characteristics have emerged as operational criteria for identifying informal sector enterprises: small size . . . and the extent to which an enterprise avoids official regulations and taxes.

And, for much informal activity a further criterion – its localism – might be added. But, more fundamentally, the question of evaluation is important as much informal activity may be valued in ways which differ in principle as well as in practice from those adopted in the formal economy.

Thus the very nature of the informal sector and its differentiation, between and within different regions of the world, makes a precise and uncontested definition almost impossible. It is a CHAOTIC CONCEPTION in that, although all 'informal' activities have one absence in common – a lack of formal SURVEILLANCE – their diversity and multiple relations with formal economic geographies, themselves subject to frequent but not always well-publicized illegalities, serves to break down any notion of coherence. Enzo Mingione (1991) notes that informal activities may be ranged along various continua: formal–informal; legal–illegal (not provided for in law); monetary–non-monetary; public–private. The informal sector is also characterized by a range of scales of activities from the individual, part-time activity (e.g. taxi driving, do-it-yourself) to small-scale commercial service and manufacturing activities (e.g. window cleaning, prostitution) and takes place throughout the world economy (Pahl, 1984; Portes et al., 1989) although its relative importance in sustaining levels of social reproduction varies.

This diversity points to the wide variety of activities which constitute the material relations of the informal economy. They include handicrafts, shoe repair, machinery repair, street marketing and the bazaar economy, domestic labour, painting and decorating, car-watching, dog-walking, baby- and home-sitting, casual labour, the provision of personal services and, in some Local Exchange and Trading Systems (LETS) which operate with a currency separate from that within the formal economy, the provision of costly professional services or highly skilled labour.

Participation in the informal economy and even within tightly circumscribed components of it may take place for a wide variety of reasons ranging across: considerations of opportunity costs and convenience (it is often easier personally to undertake many tasks of domestic labour than to arrange and pay to consume the services of formal providers); sheer enjoyment in the acts of production, exchange and consumption (see, for example, Crewe and Gregson, 1998 on car boot sales); a need to evade formal controls and surveillance – as in the highly commercialized and sophisticated global production and circulation of illegal drugs (Castells, 1997) or in their local distribution and sale and in the sale and disposal of illegally acquired goods; a wish to develop social contacts and to participate in an autonomous COMMUNITY of interaction (e.g. Lee, 1996); the provision of an outlet for goods and services produced in whole or in part by economies (economic geographies) of regard (Offer, 1997); a means of addressing SOCIAL EXCLUSION from formal economic geographies (e.g. Williams, 1996); or as a means of resistance to, and possible explorations of, alternatives to formal economic geographies (e.g. North, 1999).

More generally, and with special resonance in the THIRD WORLD, the informal sector is seen both as a problem of underdevelopment and as a solution to it (see Portes and Schauffler, 1993 for a review of these arguments). It is associated with the absorption of unemployment highlighted in a series of reports produced by the ILO during the early 1970s (see Lipton, 1982, ch. 4) which prioritized employment over growth and recognized the informal sector as labour-intensive and as a highly flexible sector alongside and in mutual formative relations with formal, often capital intensive, industrialization.

The low PRODUCTIVITY and high labour intensity of most informal activities makes them attractive as a means of absorbing unemployment. Survey evidence (e.g. Gilbert and Gugler, 1982; Lubell, 1991) suggests that between 40 and 70 per cent of the labour force may work in the informal sector in Third World cities where petty trading is the predominant form of informal activity. Clearly, the informal economy contributes substantially to the absorptive capacity of cities (see, e.g. Rogerson, 1992). Local economic geographies, such as the increasingly sophisticated and extensible LETS schemes and their equivalents throughout the developed world, enable some participants to make a living – in part, at least – outside the formal market economy.

Nevertheless, in their 'populist' (Lipton, 1982) reports, the ILO recognized that productivity and hence incomes were low in the informal sector and recommended measures to increase productivity, not least by removing restrictions from the informal sector and advancing credit, organizational and marketing assistance and research and development funding to find technologies that will remove drudgery whilst not replacing labour. There are clear links here with E.F. Schumacher's (1973) advocacy of small-scale, labour-intensive technology whereby conventional notions of DEVELOPMENT – such as productivity, for example – are inserted into models which stress the primacy of people in the development process ('economics as if people mattered' – to quote Schumacher's subtitle) and point to fundamental requirements of SOCIAL REPRODUCTION such as employment, ecological sustainability (SUSTAINABLE DEVELOPMENT) and labour-enhancing (in both senses) intermediate technologies. These notions also infuse local informal alternatives within developed societies.

The wide range of activities within the informal economic geographies is suggestive of close links between the formal and the informal economy. In fact Lubell (1991) reports that backward LINKAGES to formal sector suppliers are relatively strong whereas forward linkages are limited to households and other informal sector producers (see DUAL ECONOMY). But such relationships are extended by bartering between commercial enterprises – a system of exchange designed to reduce transaction costs in the acquisition and sale of intermediate goods – and by payment of wages in kind using the outputs produced by enterprises faced with drastic cash-flow problems in the transitional economies of eastern Europe. But the ambivalent and complex relationships between informal and formal economic geography are also apparent in schemes using use values rather than currency as a means of payment of wages and salaries. In early 1998, for example, Oxfordshire County Council in the UK considered a replication of schemes elsewhere in the formal economy of paying its labour force in part with tokens exchangeable at local supermarkets in order to reduce on-costs of employment – especially National Insurance – and so, notional at least, to redirect flows of money absorbed by *national* social security schemes into the *local* geographies of public service provision and retailing.

Thus, the informal economy straddles most of the dualisms noted by Mingione, dualisms which are useful only in that they point to their inadequacy in describing the informal sector. Very few people would not normally participate in the informal economy on a regular basis and many would, consciously or unconsciously, participate in it in ways considered formally to be illegal. Unpaid domestic labour comprises a major part of the informal sector (Offe and Heinze, 1992) and in the UK its contribution to the social reproduction is estimated at between 40 and 120 per cent of GDP (Murgatroyd and Neuberger 1997).

Thus for Fernand Braudel (1985, pp. 23–4), the informal sector is one of the 'several economies' evolving within the world economy. It is a:

> shadowy zone, often hard to see for lack of adequate historical documents, lying underneath the market economy: this is . . . basic activity which went on everywhere and the volume of which is truly fantastic. This rich zone, like a layer covering the earth, I

> have called... *material life* or *material civilization*. These are obviously ambiguous expressions. But... a proper term will one day be found to describe this infra-economy, the informal other half of economic activity, the world of self-sufficiency and barter of goods within a very small radius.... This layer of activity... has reached sufficient proportions to attract the attention of several economists: some have estimated that it may represent 30 or 40% of the gross national product, which thus lies outside all official accounting, even in industrialised countries.

Given the complexity, scale and motivation of participants in the informal economy it should, perhaps, be considered less as an 'other', defined in terms of formal economic relations – what it is not – than in terms which reflect the highly restricted and uniform notions of the 'economic' emanating from the supposed normality of the formal economy: a discourse with profound significance for surveillance and social control.

Although the total value of its production and consumption can – by definition – only be estimated, one estimate suggests that the so-called *black economy* (which may be defined as paid work without official record or regulation) amounted to between 7 and 16 per cent of the European Union's (EU) GDP in 1998 compared to around 5 per cent in the 1970s. These figures correspond to between 10 and 28 million jobs concentrated largely in labour-intensive sectors with low levels of profitability like agriculture, retailing, construction and catering as well as in modern innovative sectors. The geography of the informal economy is also highly variable. In the EU, for example, between 29 and 35 per cent of GDP is accounted for by the black economy in Greece, whilst in Finland the comparable figures range between 2 and 4 per cent.

However, despite the fact that its growth generates powerful social and political consequences – it is, for example, highly gendered (Waring, 1989; Williams and Windebank, 1998) and unequal (remuneration is often well below official minimum wage levels although the heads of informal enterprises generally receive incomes above such levels (Lubell, 1991)) – the ideological significance of the informal sector for the state is ambiguous (see e.g. Khosa, 1992). One reason for this is that the informal sector not only offers employment but, in so doing, also contributes to a sometimes violent, even murderous form of social control beyond the state in cities throughout the world. This is the informal equivalent of the controls exerted by capitalist markets – the so-called invisible hand or, more accurately – the iron fist in a velvet glove (see, e.g. Watts, 1994). The STATE not only loses tax revenues but also records as informal transactions that take place outside the tax collection and regulatory systems. Thus the ability of state surveillance to define and constrain 'normal' behaviour is threatened with the emergence of informal economic geographies, autonomous economic geographies such as LETS or the appearance of non-standard currencies. It is this potential of informal economic geographies which engenders a suspicion verging on outright opposition by official agencies/states.

The informal economy also poses profound questions about the legitimacy and developmental effectiveness of the formal economy. Nevertheless, one strategy of DEVELOPMENT (see, e.g. Santos, 1979; Dickenson et al., 1983) is to organize the informal economy and integrate it more fully into the formal. More positively, the continuing dynamism of the informal sector points to the demonstrable possibility of the construction of social relations of production and consumption 'beyond the market PARADIGM' (Mingione, 1991). However, as the conclusion (Portes and Itzigsohn, 1997, p. 247) to a series of empirical studies of the informal economy in the Caribbean (Portes, Dore-Cabral and Landolt, 1997) suggests:

> No longer can these activities be conceptualised as a vestige of a pre-capitalist past awaiting incorporation into modern capitalism. Instead, they have themselves become elements of the new stage of capitalist development in the region.... The diversity of informal enterprises... reflects the material and social resources that different groups can bring to bear on the new, unconstrained market. The harsh competition that it creates for urban middle and lower sectors will undoubtedly yield extraordinary entrepreneurial successes, along with exacerbated poverty and suffering.

RL

References

Braudel, F. 1985: *Civilization and capitalism 15th–18th Century*, vol. I: *The structures of everyday life*. London: Fontana Press. · Castells, M. 1997: *End of millennium. The information age, economy, society and culture*. Cambridge, MA and Oxford: Blackwell. · Crewe, L. and Gregson, N. 1998: Tales of the unexpected: exploring car-boot sales as marginal spaces of contemporary consumption. *Transactions, Institute of British Geographers* NS 23: 39–53. · Dickenson, J.P. et al. 1983: *A geography of the third world*. London and New York: Methuen. · Gilbert, A. and Gugler, J. 1982: *Cities, poverty and development: urbanisation in the third world*. Oxford and New York: Oxford University Press. · Khosa, M.M. 1992: Changing state policy and the black taxi industry in

Soweto. In D.M. Smith, ed., *The apartheid city and beyond: Urbanization and social change in South Africa*, ch. 15. London and New York: Routledge, 182–92. · Lee, R. 1996: Moral money? LETS and the social construction of local economic geographies in Southeast England. *Environment and Planning A* 28: 1377–94. · Lipton, M. 1982: *Development and underdevelopment in historical perspective*. London: Methuen. · Lubell, H. 1991: *The informal sector in the 1980s and 1990s*. OECD Development Centre Studies. Paris: OECD. · Mingione, E. 1991: *Fragmented societies: a sociology of life beyond the market paradigm*. Oxford and Cambridge, MA: Basil Blackwell. · Murgatroyd, L. and Neuberger, H. 1997: A household satellite account for the UK. *Economic Trends* 527: 63–71. · North P. 1999: Explorations in heterotopia: local exchange trading schemes (LETS) and the micro-politics of money and livelihood. *Environment and Planning D: Society and Space* 17: 69–86. · Offe, C. and Heinze, R.G. 1992: *Beyond employment: time, work and the informal economy*. Cambridge and Oxford: Polity Press. · Offer, A. 1997: Between the gift and the market: the economy of regard. *Economic History Review* 50 (2): 450–76. · Pahl, R. 1984: *Divisions of labour*. Oxford and Cambridge, MA: Basil Blackwell. · Portes, A. and Itzigsohn, J. 1997: Coping with change. The politics and economics of urban poverty. In A. Portes, C. Dore-Cabral, and P. Landolt, eds, *The urban Caribbean Transition to the new global economy*, ch. 8. Baltimore: Johns Hopkins University Press, 227–252. · Portes, A. and Schaffler, R. 1993: Competing perspectives on the Latin American informal sector. *Population and Development Review* 19 1: 33–60. · Portes, A., Castells, M. and Benton, L.A., eds, 1989: *The informal economy: studies in advanced and less developed countries*. Baltimore: Johns Hopkins University Press. · Portes, A., Dore-Cabral, C. and Landolt, P., eds, 1997: *The urban Caribbean: transition to the new global economy*. Baltimore: Johns Hopkins University Press. · Rogerson, C.M. 1992: The absorptive capacity of the informal sector in the South African city. In D.M. Smith, ed., *The apartheid city and beyond: Urbanization and social change in South Africa*, ch. 13. London and New York: Routledge, 161–71. · Santos, M. 1979: *The shared space*. London and New York: Methuen. · Schumacher, E.F. 1973: *Small is beautiful; economics as if people mattered*. New York: Harper and Row. · Waring, M. 1989: *If women counted: a new feminist economics*. London: Macmillan. · Watts, M.J. 1994: Development II: the privatization of everything? *Progress in Human Geography* 18 (3): 371–84. · Williams, C. 1996: Informal sector responses to unemployment: an evaluation of the potential of Local Exchange and Trading systems (LETS). *Work, Employment and Society* 10: 341–59. · Williams, C.C. and Windebank, J. 1998: *Informal employment in the advanced economies: implications for work and welfare*. London: Routledge.

Suggested Reading

Crewe and Gregson (1998). · Offe and Heinze (1992). · Santos (1979).

information asymmetries A condition in which two economic actors possess, or have access to, different quantities or types of knowledge essential to a transaction. This situation normally confers an advantage upon the agent having the higher level of information. For example, in the field of industrial relations an employer may gain leverage over workers when wages are being bargained if the former has more information concerning the firm's financial position (and, hence, greater knowledge of the maximum wage rate it is able to pay) than do the latter. The concept of information asymmetries has also found application in INDUSTRIAL ORGANIZATION theory where, for example, information asymmetries between two firms may encourage opportunistic behaviour by the firm with more information, thereby undermining the consensual foundations on which subsequent transactions might be based (George et al., 1992). Information asymmetries have also been used to understand the problems associated with the public regulation of privatized utilities (Campbell, 1996) and the origins of obstacles to collective action (Hardin, 1982).

Because information is especially important in supporting financial transactions, information asymmetries are especially significant in this sector of the economy. When a lender is considering whether or not to loan funds to a borrower (or, alternatively, when an investor is considering taking an equity position in a firm through private placement), the major challenge for the lender/investor is to distinguish good customers from bad ones. The ability to determine this depends on the availability of information concerning the borrower's financial health, past credit history, employment history, and personal traits that may influence credit worthiness. Leyshon et al. (1998) argue that while, previously, financial institutions sought to reduce this information asymmetry by collecting the requisite information through face-to-face interaction between bankers and customers (thereby privileging spatial proximity because of its ability to produce trust), more recently this process has become mediated by information and communication technologies that enable such information to be collected 'at-a-distance'. (See also PRISONER'S DILEMMA; SOCIAL CAPITAL.) MSG

References

Campbell, H.E. 1996: The politics of requesting: strategic behavior and public utility regulation. *Journal of Policy Analysis and Management* 15: 395–423. · George, K.D., Joll, C. and Lynk, E.L. 1992: *Industrial organization: competition, growth and structural change*, 4th edn. London: Routledge. · Hardin, R. 1982: *Collective action*. Baltimore: Johns Hopkins University Press. · Leyshon,

A., Thrift, N.J. and Pratt, J. 1998: Reading financial services: texts, consumers, and financial literacy. *Environment and Planning D: Society and Space* 16: 29–56.

information economy A term dating from the late 1960s and early 1970s when it became clear that the production and distribution of information was becoming a key to many of the activities in modern economies. The chief exponents of this idea, authors like Daniel Bell (1973) and Alain Touraine (1969), argued that the new centrality of information processing was resulting in a 'post-industrial' society. The idea has been highly influential across the social sciences, being found in the works of writers as diverse as Lyotard, Giddens, and Castells. (See also CITY; POSTMODERNISM; PRODUCER SERVICES; SERVICES, GEOGRAPHY OF.) NJT

References

Bell, D. 1973: *The coming of post-industrial society*. New York: Basic Books. · Touraine, A. 1969: *La société post-industrielle*. Paris: Denoel.

information society See INFORMATION ECONOMY.

information theory A mathematical approach in communication science which attempts to measure the amount of information or the degree of organization in a SYSTEM. The theory and its associated methods have been used to describe settlement and population distributions in geographical space. Its mathematical formulation exhibits a close relationship to the mathematics of ENTROPY in statistical thermodynamics.

The basic equation is due to Shannon (Shannon and Weaver, 1949):

$$H = \sum x\log(1/x_i) = \sum_{i=1}^{N} -x_i\log x_i$$

Where $\sum_{i=1}^{N} x_i = 1$ and H is the information statistic.

The individual x_is might therefore be the probabilities of N possible outcomes of a stochastic experiment, proportions of a population in N census tracts, proportion of land in N counties, etc. It can be shown, by both example and mathematical proof, that H approaches zero as one of the x_i approaches unity (statistically as one of the outcomes approaches a near certainty). On the other hand if all the x_i are approximately equal (at $1/N$) then H approaches a maximum given by log N.

In information studies these results are used to define an index R:

$$R = 1 - H/H_{\max}$$

which is variously termed a measure of redundancy (Shannon and Weaver, 1949) and order (von Foerster). Ambiguities in interpretation arise in geography because a highly concentrated spatial pattern ($H = 0, R = 1$) and a uniform spatial pattern ($H = H_{\max}, R = 0$) both suggest order, albeit of quite different kinds.

Marchand (1972) pointed out that in CARTOGRAPHY a CHOROPLETH MAP conveys maximum information if each of the class intervals has approximately the same number of mapping units, i.e. H is maximized. He also shows that the maximum amount of information carried by such a map is controlled by the number of mapping units and the number of classes utilized – however much raw data may have been used in the compilation. A similar approach uses the H statistic to partition within group from between group information as an aid to CLASSIFICATION. AMH

References and Suggested Reading

Marchand, B. 1972: Information theory and geography. *Geographical Analysis* 4: 234–57. · Shannon, C.E. and Weaver, W. 1949: *The mathematical theory of communication*. Campaign, IL: University of Illinois Press. · Thomas, R.W. 1981: *Information statistics in geography*. Concepts and techniques in modern geography 31. Norwich: Geo Books.

informational city A term coined by Manuel Castells (1989, 1996) to describe the modern city as the outcome of three linked processes – the RESTRUCTURING of capitalist firms towards more flexible network forms of organization; the growing centrality of the production and management of information in modern societies; and the growth of information technologies – which are reshaping urban time and space. In particular, informational cities both produce and must also live within a 'space of flows' formed by information networks which simultaneously question their existence as places (see WORLD CITY). NJT

References

Castells, M. 1989: *The informational city. Information technology, economic restructuring and the urban-regional process*. Oxford: Blackwell. · Castells, M. 1996: *The rise of the network society*. Oxford: Blackwell.

infrastructure[1] The underlying structure of services and amenities (social overhead capital: SOC) needed to facilitate directly productive activity (DPA). Examples include public services, transport, telecommunications, public utilities, public environmental installations, human capital investment installations and social and community facilities.

Infrastructure tends to be immobile, labour intensive, indivisible, open of access and to have economy-wide effects. There is considerable argument (Hirschman, 1958; Hodder and Lee, 1974) over the extent to which infrastructural investment is a sufficient (or even a necessary) precondition for economic development; whether it should be provided *before* development in the form of excess capacity or whether scarce resources should be devoted primarily to DPA, so allowing bottlenecks to build up as a result of the under-provision of SOC; and whether it should be publicly or privately owned. RL

References and Suggested Reading

Hirschman, A.O. 1958: *The strategy of economic development*. New Haven: Yale University Press. · Hodder, B.W. and Lee, R. 1974: *Economic geography*. London: Methuen, 148–55. · Raviolis, A. and Spence, N. 1998: Promoting regional economic growth in Greece by investing in public infrastructure. *Environment and Planning C*. · Vickerman, R.W. 1991: *Infrastructure and regional development*. London: Pion.

infrastructure[2] Within classical Marxism, a concept which emphasizes the significance of material practice and the structures of the production of material life in giving rise to political and legal systems and in shaping ideas. As such, it contrasts with the Hegelian conception of history in which the 'idea' is seen as the guiding force. (See also SUPERSTRUCTURE.)

The general argument that social action proceeds from social reality, not from abstract categories, intellectual constructs or self-originating and unproblematic ideas, is summarized by Marx:

> It is not the consciousness of men that determines their being, but their social being that determines their consciousness.

But Carver (1982, p. 34) suggests that this is not a deterministic view because the word 'determines' in German is not the same word as 'causes'. More accurate meanings would be given by '"defines", "delimits", "structures" or even "decides"'.

Furthermore, Marx's much quoted relational account (first published in 1859) of infrastructure, base or foundation (*grundlage*) and superstructure (*uberbau*) may suffer in nuance from its translation into English but fails to suggest either that the superstructure is determined by the infrastructure or that consciousness is determined by the superstructure. What it does suggest is that consciousness is not formed directly out of material practice but is a far more complex consequence of the relationships between material, political and legal practices:

> In the social production of their life, men enter into definite relations that are indispensable and independent of their will, relations of production which correspond to a definite stage of development of their material productive forces. The sum total of these relations of production constitutes the economic structure of society, the real foundation, on which rises a legal and political superstructure and to which correspond definite forms of social consciousness. (Marx, 1968, p. 181.)

This passage has been the object of much debate, focusing particularly upon the apparently implied dichotomy between base or infrastructure ('the real foundation') and superstructure, and the determination of the latter by the former. Few would now accept this simple dualism and the passage does not justify such a simplistic interpretation. Furthermore, it is important to realize that Marx refers to this statement as the 'guiding thread' of his studies; it is not a law-full or even law-like statement. It is, rather, a general HYPOTHESIS, a guide (Carver, 1982). Nevertheless, the essentially dialectical (see DIALECTIC) concern for the *relationships* between human labour and ideas in Marxist thought is often interpreted as a *distinction* between infrastructure and superstructure.

The analytical problem is to provide a more satisfactory theorization of the interconnections and indivisibilities between what are otherwise seen as separate and, therefore, conceptually inadequate spheres of social life (see also HISTORICAL MATERIALISM; STRUCTURATION THEORY). Carver (1982, pp. 34–5) makes the following suggestion:

> For a given state of social being (social production of material life within particular relations using material productive forces from which rises a legal and political superstructure) some forms of consciousness (ideas, beliefs, opinions) are likely to be widely held, commonplace, encouraged, etc., and others are likely to be absent, eccentrically held by only a few, discouraged, dismissed, made illegal, etc. '...we do not have the particular elements of our social being that we have because God intended that we should, nor do we have them because man has been consciously or unconsciously striving to realise an idea, such as truth or freedom.... On the contrary, our social being is as it is because of what men have actually accomplished in the economic sphere of material needs and desires.

This may not be adequate for such as E.P. Thompson (1968, pp. 10, 9) who, while accepting that '[T]he class experience is largely determined by the productive relations into which men are born – or enter involuntarily' wishes to distinguish between the CLASS experience and class consciousness: 'If the experience appears as determined, class consciousness does not'. This is because 'the notion of class entails the notion of historical [and, we might add geographical] relationship. . . . Consciousness of class arises in the same way in different times and places, but never in just the same way'.

But the historical and geographical indeterminancy implied here is not pre-determined; it is itself produced. The historical geography of class is not determined through a given and constrained infrastructure (however temporally or geographically varied it may be) of material life but is socially constructed and so brings IDENTITY and material/social life into a duality. Within this duality, identity and social/material life inform and produce each other through both practice and discourse, experience and consciousness embedded, to a greater or lesser extent (both temporally and spatially), in the geographies through and across which they take place and which, in the process, they transform, re-read and re-write. RL

References and Suggested Reading

Carver, T. 1982: *Marx's social theory*. Oxford and New York: Oxford University Press. · Godelier, M. 1978: Infrastructures, societies and history. *New Left Review* 112: 84-96. · Marx, K. 1968 [orig. pub. 1859]: Preface to *A critique of political economy*. In K. Marx, and F. Engels, *Selected works*. London: Lawrence and Wishart. · Thompson, E.P. 1968: *The making of the English working class*. Harmondsworth: Penguin.

inheritance system Rules, either customary or legal, which govern transmission of property (particularly real estate) between generations. Inheritance rules may define the number and gender of heir(s) to whom property should pass, the ways in which property shall be divided between multiple heirs, and the degree to which heirs' claims through inheritance are binding on property holders regardless of their own will.

Geographers have paid particular attention to the effects of different inheritance systems, especially *impartible* (single-heir) versus *partible* (multi-heir) systems: on the physical layout of landholdings; on structures of landholding; on LAND TENURE and the operation of FIELD SYSTEMS; on the ability of local agrarian societies to absorb population growth; and on levels of geographical MOBILITY (generally higher in impartible systems).

Analysts have also sought to explore the relative importance of inheritance systems in channelling property transmission, compared with other means of transfer (by gift, via grants from landlords, or most importantly through landmarkets). The power of market or other mechanisms to offset or over-ride property transfers through inheritance has often been emphasized as a central component of MODERNIZATION, as in debates on the transition from FEUDALISM to CAPITALISM (see BRENNER DEBATE). PG

inner city An ill-defined area close to the CENTRAL BUSINESS DISTRICT in capitalist cities, usually associated with dilapidation, poor housing and economic and social deprivation (cf. CYCLE OF POVERTY; SLUM). In the ZONAL MODEL developed by Chicago sociologists in the 1920s (see CHICAGO SCHOOL), and which informed much writing about urban residential patterns for the next half-century, the inner city was characterized as: (a) the reception area for new migrants to the city, from where they were launched on their search for economic and social improvement and associated moves into the SUBURBS; and (b) a zone in transition whose other residents were either transients or the lowest status, geographically and socially immobile, economic groups.

The term inner city has recently been associated with portions of urban areas suffering substantial economic and social difficulties and requiring programmes of regeneration and revitalization, not least in political rhetoric (as in the British Prime Minister's reference, immediately after her 1987 general election victory, to the work that needed to be done in 'those inner cities': Robson, 1988). A range of policies – such as Model Cities in the US and the Urban Programme in the UK – targeted public money on environmental improvement and job attraction to such areas: academics (see Hall, 1981) pointed out that the inner-city problem could not be appreciated apart from an understanding of the wider forces of UNEVEN DEVELOPMENT which were stimulating COUNTERURBANIZATION and DECENTRALIZATION, however, along with other processes of spatial change which were not favouring congested, run-down, expensive inner-city areas. RJJ

References

Hall, P.G., ed., 1981: *The inner city in context*. London: Heinemann. · Robson, B.T. 1988: *Those inner cities*. Oxford: The Clarendon Press.

innovation The introduction of a new phenomenon – or the new phenomenon itself. Geographical attention to innovations has focused on: (a) *their spatial origins* – are they more likely to emerge in certain areas than others?; and (b) *the spread of innovations* from their original sites (cf. CULTURAL HEARTH) through DIFFUSION. RJJ

input–output An analytical framework developed by the economist Wassily Leontieff to describe and model the inter-industry linkages within the ECONOMY, and to use this information to examine economic and policy impacts. The basic building block is recognition that the production (or outputs) of one sector become the inputs for other sectors. Thus the machine-tools sector uses inputs of energy, steel, metals and other components (all in turn outputs of other sectors) to produce outputs to other industries, such as car and aircraft producers.

Information on inter-industry inputs and outputs is collected by survey or from administrative records, and recorded in an input–output table. The rows and columns represent the different industries or sectors, and the entries or coefficients measure the exchanges between them. Leontieff's innovation was to see that this table could be manipulated as a matrix, and used mathematically. If the final demands of consumers are specified, the input–output matrix can be analysed as a set of simultaneous equations to trace out all the backward linkages involved in producing for those final demands, calculating what each sector must produce. By changing the final demands, we can assess the impact of different policies and economic changes. The model (in its basic form at least) is a comparative equilibrium model: it measures the medium-or long-term adjustments, but does not track the short-run path.

Very detailed input–output models have been constructed for most advanced economies, and the method has been extended to regional and multiregional analyses: examining linkages with a region (e.g. the Philadelphia region) and their dependence on the national economy, and explicitly tracing exchanges between sectors in different regions, using information on commodity flows and transport charges. Full multiregional models have been built for countries such as Japan and the Netherlands, and (with some simplifying adjustments) for the 51 states of the USA. One application of this USA model has been to examine the sectoral and regional impacts of alternative tax policies: tax changes shift the final consumer demands, and the multiregional input–output model computes the effects on industrial production across the regions. Such detailed models are very demanding of data, and so are difficult and expensive to construct. A limitation is that one then has to assume that the coefficients remain stable (or project technical changes by some method).

Recent attention has focused on using the framework to trace the ENERGY use and other activities such as environmental POLLUTION associated with production. Pollution generation can be included as an output, and the costs of pollution abatement or control can be included as an input. Dutch economists have included this in a multiregional framework, so that pollution emissions (to air, river and sea) diffuse into neighbouring regions.

LWH

Suggested Reading

Miller, R.E. and Blair, P.D. 1985: *Input–output analysis: foundations and extensions*. Englewood Cliffs, NJ: Prentice-Hall.

instrumentalism A philosophy of science which directs attention towards (and is in turn legitimated by) the establishment of technical control over the environment; because it is this end-result which matters, the truth or falsity of the theoretical statements which are called upon is never at issue (cf. POSITIVISM) and so they become literally *instruments*, 'computational devices for the generation of successful predictions about observables', which are to be judged solely in terms of their practical utility (Keat and Urry, 1975). Instrumentalism was extremely important during geography's QUANTITATIVE REVOLUTION as a means of qualifying the status of the 'LAWS' of a projected SPATIAL SCIENCE while retaining the commitment to some form of scientific explanation: thus Harvey (1969) argued that the identification of laws in geography is 'partly a matter of our own willingness to regard geographical phenomena *as if* they were subject to universal laws, *even when they are patently not so governed*' (emphasis added). The ability of geography to provide NOMOTHETIC statements in these more restricted terms was translated into empirical studies which were concerned more with the 'goodness of fit' between one spatial pattern and another than with the explication of the processes which produced them (e.g. the surrogates employed in SIMULATION and in SPACE–TIME FORECASTING). Many of these models were clearly capable of generating direct inputs to the formulation of public policy, since they enabled a ready comparison of a range of policy options and their associated outcomes without the need to specify the mechanisms which linked them; but the conception of RELEVANCE which they entailed was evidently a starkly pragmatic one and it was soon vigorously contested by the emergence of other philosophies of science, such as REALISM (Sayer, 1992). DG

References

Harvey, D. 1969: *Explanation in geography*. London: Edward Arnold; New York: St. Martin's Press. · Keat, R. and Urry, J. 1975: *Social theory as science*. London: Routledge and Kegan Paul. · Sayer, R.A. 1992: *Method in social science: a realist approach*, 2nd edn. London: Routledge.

Suggested Reading

Gregory, D. 1978: *Ideology, science and human geography*. London: Hutchinson; New York: St. Martin's Press, 40–2.

integration The creation and maintenance of intense and diverse patterns of interaction and control between formerly more or less separate social spaces. Integration involves the bringing together of different systems of meaning and action founded in different sets of social relations (norms, means of communication, indicators of direction and value, structures of POWER, domination and subordination). At the limit integration implies the obliteration of DIFFERENCE, but it can take place only through social relations capable of being stretched and modified to incorporate other systems of meaning without reaching breaking point – not least in response to resistance to integration. An example would be the chain of production (Dicken, 1998) which integrates the stages of production within or between different corporate structures.

Geography is central to this process. Integration takes place through – not merely across – space. A geography of the links involved in integration (e.g. a political geography of the STATE APPARATUS involved in the GOVERNANCE of integration) must be created and a new geography of integration may emerge. Thus the creation of a space or spaces of integration is central to any form of integration; without such spaces, the social relations which constitute integration cannot themselves be constituted.

The defence of TERRITORY may create separation – the logical pre-condition of integration – which may be broken down forcibly (e.g. via war, annexation), peaceably (via mutually agreed negotiation) or through a mixture of violence and peaceful means. Thus Sidney Pollard (1981), for example, refers to the economic integration of Europe as a process of 'peaceful conquest'. Economic integration may take place via the market, through the circulation of capital, labour and knowledge, through modern processes of IMPERIALISM such as the global integration of consumer practice (which in the case of Coca-Cola is paradigmatic), or through international political economy (via decisions on the conditions of international economic interaction – TRADE, investment, labour MIGRATION and so on).

TIME–SPACE CONVERGENCE (itself driven by the formation of new spaces of interaction) may dynamize integration through distanciation as the influence of once distant and remote others is made more and more insistent through the convergence of space–time. A contemporary example of this process of *distanciation* is the sudden suspension in the light of the crisis in Southeast Asia during 1997/1998 of contemporary discussion of the need to 'easternize' European social practices to compete with the Asian countries of the Pacific Rim.

There are a number of interlinked elements of integration which may be more or less strongly developed in any specific circumstance:

- A *dynamic of integration* – e.g. a geographically expansionary system of material production; an embryonic empire.
- *Integration imagined* – this may involve an ideology, of, for example, an integrated Europe, a European geography. Such IDEOLOGIES, which may in turn act themselves as a dynamic of integration, imply a belief in or desire for particular views of what is being integrated. In the case of European integration, beliefs about the nature of 'Europe', about the space that is thought of as 'Europe' and about the nature of the integrated entity, become very important. Here the question concerns not only the 'definition' of the extent of Europe – where does it begin and end? – but the meaning that we endow upon it and the significance that we attach to it. An example would be the debate within contemporary Europe between those who favour the move towards a federal system and those who wish to retain the existing system of NATION-STATES. This debate reflects highly divergent 'ideologies' of Europe and

quite different views on the importance of Europe in either positive or normative terms.

- *Social construction*: the making of geographies which enable, facilitate, encourage or even demand integration.
- *Processes of integration*: including both formal (negotiated) integrations and informal (socially constructed tendencies) integration such as those emanating from global media (Morley and Robins, 1995) or from globalization within relations of SOCIAL REPRODUCTION.
- *Institutional binding*: institutions/organizations which (help to) bind the (integrated) space together. Economists, for example, recognize several levels of institutional integration: FREE TRADE AREA, customs union, COMMON MARKET, monetary union and economic and political union.
- LANDSCAPES *of integration*: the geography of social life within the integrated space. This would include not merely fixed investments like communication and transport systems as well as processes of interaction like flows of investment and trade and complex structures like city systems but symbolic landscapes of tradition (pre-integration) and change (post-integration) and the struggle – over these landscapes – exemplified by neo-Nazis in an eastern Germany coming to terms with the dislocations of integration into the West by attempting to define and violently to impose their racist and xenophobic notions of place purity within towns and cities in the region.

In an age of electronic landscapes, for example, signs and symbols are both ever-present and ever-changing and rapidly transmitted and absorbed and so cultural boundaries become both fluid and contested. Under such circumstances Morley and Robins (1995, p. 1) explore 'the complex and contradictory nature of contemporary cultural identities and . . . the role of communications media in the reconfiguration of these identities . . . in the context of the relationships between Europe and the significant Others – America, Islam, Japan and the Orient – against which its own identity has been and is now being, defined'.

The objectives of integration are commonly disputed and range from the creation of a unity (e.g. economic and political union – exemplified, for example, by the reunification of Germany in 1990; European Economic and Monetary union (EMU); a takeover of one firm by another; ASSIMILATION), to diversity within some form of unity (e.g. the European Union as a COMMUNITY of NATIONS; a COMMON MARKET; FEDERALISM; MULTICULTURALISM; a joint venture) and links between independent units (e.g. a free trade area; a commonwealth; sub-contracting).

The achievement of unity must involve both *positive integration* (in which new structures and institutions – e.g. a common currency within EMU – are created to replace the extant, more divisive structures and institutions) and *negative integration* (the removal of pre-existing barriers and impediments to integration – e.g. TARIFF barriers). Anything less than the achievement of unity may involve either positive or negative integration or a combination of the two.

Within the sphere of production (see, e.g. Storper and Walker, 1989, ch. 3), integration (or disintegration) may be *vertical* – a process which refers to the extent to which successive stages in production and distribution are placed under the control of a single firm (shaped by internal ECONOMIES OF SCOPE); *horizontal* – the extent to which firms producing related products (competitive, complementary or by-products) operate under central control; or *diagonal*, the corporate integration of firms operating in different sectors and at different stages of the production chain. The disintegration of production is often interpreted as a manifestation of the emergence of flexibility in production (see ECONOMIC GEOGRAPHY; INDUSTRIAL DISTRICT).

Integration may be formal or informal.

Informal integration consists of those patterns of interaction which develop without the impetus of deliberate political decisions, following the dynamics of markets, technology, communications networks and social change.

Thus the economic and social historians Eric Hobsbawm (1962), Sidney Pollard (1973, 1981) and William Ashworth (1974), for example, conceive of European integration during the nineteenth century in terms of the construction of new geographies through which the impulses of industrialization – which greatly extended the geographical and quantitative scale of circuits of SOCIAL REPRODUCTION – might course, thereby transforming Europe which 'at the end of the eighteenth century was very far from being an economic unit' (Ashworth, 1974, p. 296), consisting of 'a conglomeration of small, semi-autarkic markets, each with its own fairly complete array of trades' (Landes, 1969, p. 133), to 'one single macro-development area' (Pollard, 1973, p. 639).

Formal integration consists of those changes in the framework of rules and regulations which encourage – or inhibit, or redirect – informal flows. Informal integration is a continuous process, a flow; it creeps unawares out of the myriad transactions of private individuals pursuing private interests. Formal integration is discontinuous: it proceeds decision by decision, bargain by bargain, treaty by treaty (Wallace, 1990, p. 9).

An example from within the formal political sphere would be the institutional processes which led up to the formation of the European Economic Community and the subsequent widening (extension of geographical SCALE) and deepening (the shift from relatively limited negative integration to more complex and demanding positive integration) involved in the re-formed European Union and EMU.

Marx (1976) distinguishes, too, between the concentration of CAPITAL – 'the increasing concentration of... wealth in the hands of individual capitalists... which grows directly out of accumulation, or rather is identical to it' (p. 776); and the centralization of capital – 'the attraction of capital by capital' (p. 777). Centralization is a process through which one capital takes over another – either in a hostile bid or through mutual agreement; either way, though, formal negotiations must take place and they may be subject to anti-monopoly investigations by the STATE before centralization may proceed.

Helpful as the formal / informal distinction is, it fails to acknowledge that social relations underpin the tendency towards integration and the possibilities of achieving it; it conceives of integration in universal terms. The emergence of CAPITALISM as a dominant set of social relations implies both geographical and quantitative expansion (Smith, 1984, ch. 3; Lee, 1989; see ECONOMIC GEOGRAPHY; WORLD-SYSTEMS ANALYSIS). Integration is, therefore, a tendency accelerated and intensified by capitalism. Thus in the attempt to understand integration within Europe, Lee (1976, p. 12) wished to escape from the narrow view of institutional (formal) approaches to integration:

> Both the supposed dichotomy between economic and political integration and the atomistic concept of the self-determining state are inadequate starting points for the analysis of integration. The international economy is not a simple aggregation of national economies but a total system in which nations are subordinate, but not necessarily subdominant, structures and economic integration is, in fact, a fundamental concept determined by the mode of production.

He went on to outline an historical geography of European integration in terms somewhat less reminiscent of STRUCTURALISM but which, nevertheless, explored the process of STRUCTURATION between economic, political and social processes in the context of the dynamic geography of the CIRCUIT OF CAPITAL (Lee, 1990).

Although the expansionary nature of the capitalist world-economy continuously poses the question of integration, it is important to remember that other forces may resist it. During the sixteenth century 'Islam and Christendom, faced each other along the north–south divide between the Levant and the western Mediterranean, a line running from the shores of the Adriatic to Sicily and then on to the coast of present-day Tunisia' and although 'merchant vessels sailed across it every day' (Braudel, 1985, p. 22), the cultural and social divisions remain highly influential. The integrative world economy is, as Braudel (1985, p. 45) points out, simply 'an order among other orders' and the struggle between integration and distinction remains a powerful determinant of economic, political and social relations.

Of course such a struggle cannot be reduced to this dualism. Integration involves the geographies of the intersection of social relations and their consequent transformation and subsequent re-transformations. Thus there are two ways in which places are said to be endowed with geographical specificity: through an internalized historical geography; and through the construction of

> a particular constellation of social relations, meeting and weaving together at a particular locus... each 'place' can be seen as a particular, unique, point of their intersection. It is indeed a *meeting* place. (Massey, 1991/1996, p. 244).

The implication here is that rather than thinking of PLACES as being constructed in and through their own terms – through some internal dynamic driven by the circumstances within a particular SPACE (an internalized historical geography), places are seen as being constructed through the intersection of local conditions and the perpetually changing relations with the rest of the world. And, of course, the apparently 'internal' characteristics of places will themselves be a mix of external and internal influences. In short there can be no such thing as a bounded place, defined simply in its own terms.

Instead, then, of thinking of places as areas with boundaries around, they can be imagined as articulated moments in networks of social relations and understandings, but where a large proportion of those relations, experiences and understandings are constructed on a far larger scale than what we happen to define for that moment as the place itself, whether that be a street, or a region or even a continent. And this in turn allows a sense of place which is extrovert, which includes a consciousness of its links with the wider world, which integrates in a positive way the global and the local.

It is a sense place, an understanding of 'its character', which can only be constructed by linking that place to places beyond. A progressive sense of place would recognize that, without being threatened by it, what we need, it seems to me, is a global sense of the local, a global sense of place. (Massey, 1996, pp. 244–5.)

Integration is, in short, a permanent but constantly changing process involving the social construction of geographies through which identities and social relations are formed, contested and transformed and social and environmental life can proceed. As such it presents the most profound political challenges. The nature of these challenges may be exemplified by Tom Nairn's (1983, pp. 195–7) account of the counterpoint of integration.

Nairn argues that geographies of disaffection and disintegration parallel those of industrialization and integration in Europe:

The advancing capitalism of the more bourgeois societies bore down upon the societies surrounding them – societies which predominantly appear until the 1790s as buried in feudal and absolutist slumber... polite universalist visions of progress had turned into means of domination.... The spread of free commerce... was turning into the domination of English manufactures – the tyranny of the English 'City' over the European 'country'. In short there was a sort of imperialism built into 'development'. And it had become a prime necessity to resist this aspect of development.

Thus instead of 'continuous diffusion from centre to periphery' and a process whereby the 'metropolis would gradually elevate the rustic hinterland up to its level' uneven development is a means of exploitation so that

progress comes to seem a hammer-blow as well as (sometimes instead of) a prospectus for general uplift and improvement.... So areas of the hinterland, even in order to 'catch up'... are also compelled to mobilise against progress... to demand progress not as it is thrust upon them... by the metropolitan centre, but 'on their own terms'.

'Nationalism' is in one sense only the label for the general unfolding of this vast struggle, since the end of the eighteenth century.

Clearly nationalities, ethnic disputes and nation-states had existed before. And this is not surprising given the diversity and continuous history of Europe (cf. ETHNIC CLEANSING; NATIONALISM; RACISM). But industrialization transformed such features

into the general condition of nationalism after the bourgeois revolutions exploded fully into the world ... and gave them a qualitatively distinct function, an altogether new dynamism for both good and evil.

The political geography of this process follows that of the economic:

In terms of political geography, the contours of the process are familiar. The 'tidal wave' [of modernization and the response of nationalism] invaded one zone after another, in concentric circles. First Germany and Italy.... Almost at the same time, or shortly after, Central and Eastern Europe, and the more peripheral regions of Iberia, Ireland and Scandinavia.

This account should not be taken to imply that the political is a mere reaction to the economic but rather to illustrate the resistance to integration as a process of domination rather than as a discourse of the logic of DEVELOPMENT or MODERNIZATION. RL

References

Ashworth, W. 1974: Industrialisation and the economic integration of nineteenth-century Europe. *European Studies Review* 4: 291–315. · Braudel, F. 1985: *Civilization and capitalism 15th–18th Century*, vol. III: *The perspective of the world.* London: Fontana Press. · Dicken, P. 1998: *Global shift: transforming the world economy*, 3rd edn. London: Paul Chapman Publishing, ch. 1. · Hobsbawm, E.J. 1962: *The age of revolution Europe 1789–1848.* London: Weidenfeld and Nicholson. · Landes, D. 1969: *The unbound Prometheus.* Cambridge: Cambridge University Press. · Lee, R. 1976: Integration, spatial structure and the capitalist mode of production in the EEC. In Lee, R. and Ogden, P.E., eds, *Economy and society in the EEC.* Farnborough: Saxon House, 11–37. · Lee, R. 1989: Social relations and the geography of material life. In D. Gregory and R. Walford, *Horizons in human geography.* London: Macmillan; New York: St. Martin's Press, 152–69. · Lee, R. 1990: Making Europe: towards a geography of European integration. In M. Chisholm and D.M. Smith, eds, *Shared space. Divided space.* London: Unwin Hyman, 235–59. · Marx, K. 1976: *Capital* vol. I. Harmondsworth: New Left Review/Penguin. · Massey, D. 1991: A global sense of place. *Marxism Today*, June: 24–9 [reprinted in Massey, D. 1994: *Space, place and gender.* Cambridge and Oxford: Polity Press, ch. 6, 146–56 and in S. Daniels and R. Lee, eds, 1996: *Exploring human geography.* London: Arnold, 237–45]. · Morley, D. and Robins, K. 1995: *Spaces of identity. Global media, electronic landscapes and cultural boundaries.* London and New York: Routledge. · Nairn, T. 1983: Nationalism and the uneven geography of development. In D. Held et al., eds, *States and societies*, ch. 2.5. Oxford: Martin Robertson, 195–206. · Pollard, S. 1973: Industrialisation and the European economy. *Economic History Review* 26: 636–48. · Pollard, S. 1981: *Peaceful conquest*. Oxford: Oxford University Press. · Smith, N. 1984: *Uneven development*. Oxford and New York: Basil Blackwell. · Storper, M. and Walker, R. 1989: *The capitalist imperative*. New York and Oxford: Basil Blackwell. · Wallace, W. 1990: Introduction: the dynamics of European integration. In Wallace, W. ed., *The dynamics of European integration*. London and New York: Pinter Publishers, 1–24.

Suggested Reading

Lee (1990). · Robins, K. 1995: The new spaces of global media. In R.J. Johnston, M.J. Watts and P.J. Taylor, eds, *Geographies of global change: remapping the world in the late twentieth century*. Oxford and Cambridge MA: Blackwell; Nairn (1983).

intensive agriculture In opposition to extensive forms of agriculture which involve seasonal patterns of transitory land use over large areas, intensive agriculture is characterized by the repeated cultivation and/or grazing of the same area of land using supplementary energy inputs (Simmons, 1996). They are, in other words, land-intensive and require a large number of inputs per hectare to maintain or increase the volume of output year on year. Over the course of the twentieth century these inputs have become increasingly artificial, including chemical fertilizers and pesticides; animal pharmaceuticals; mechanization; and genetic engineering (see, for example, Healey and Ilbery, 1985; Goodman et al., 1987). As these technologies have become established, so the range of soils and environmental conditions amenable to intensive agriculture has increased.

Intensive agricultural practices have become closely associated with growing public concerns about the environmental and food safety problems of industrial systems of production (Clunies-Ross and Hildyard, 1992). These problems range from water pollution caused by agricultural chemical runoff and the loss of biodiversity associated with monocultures, to the incubation and spread of animal diseases like BSE. (See also AGRICULTURAL GEOGRAPHY; EXTENSIVE AGRICULTURE.) SW

References

Goodman, D., Sorj, B. and Wilkinson, J. 1987: *From farming to biotechnology*. Oxford: Basil Blackwell. · Clunies-Ross, T. and Hildyard, P. 1992: *The politics of industrial agriculture*. London: Earthscan. · Healey, M. and Ilbery, B., eds, 1985: *Industrialisation of the countryside*. Norwich: Geobooks. · Simmons, I. 1996: *Changing the face of the earth*. Oxford: Basil Blackwell, ch. 6.

intensive research Research strategies which are concerned to reconstruct the causal chains that connect social structures, social practices and individual agents in particular contexts. Sayer (1992) claims that intensive research typically involves QUALITATIVE METHODS, including ETHNOGRAPHY, and argues that these strategies are particularly appropriate for research conducted under the sign of REALISM. This does not mean that they are 'subjective' or parochial; Sayer makes a detailed comparison with EXTENSIVE RESEARCH (see the figure) and emphasizes that intensive studies can be every bit as 'objective' as extensive studies and that they may well produce 'abstract knowledge [that is] more generally applicable'. DG

Reference and Suggested Reading

Sayer, A. 1992: *Method in social science: a realist approach*, 2nd edn. London: Routledge, 241–51.

interdependence Relations of mutual DEPENDENCE. Human societies are highly influential participants in wider ECOSYSTEMS – so influential in fact that some go beyond the interdependence of SOCIETY and NATURE to recognize nature as a social product (Smith, 1984). Interdependence is applied in a particularly direct way to the understanding of DEVELOPMENT. Here interest lies in the making and extent of interdependence and in the challenge that it poses to monocausal, unilinear explanations of the human condition (Brookfield, 1975).

The contemporary world economy is often presented as a single interdependent whole carrying overtones of STRUCTURAL FUNCTIONALISM and with an emphasis placed on the systemic mechanics rather than the politics of development. The danger of such a conception is that the conflicts and contradictions stemming from the social bases of interdependence are overlooked in the assumption of an ecological unity of purpose (see WORLD-SYSTEMS ANALYSIS).

The emergence of a world economy is the result of the development of social relations capable of conducting human activity at a global scale (see GLOBALIZATION); the social relations of CAPITALISM provide such a basis. They are both further developed by and cause developments in the generalization of the market and the structure and geography of TRADE, flows of CAPITAL and labour, global evaluations of production and exchange and the scale and organization of production. In short, the social relations of production are the language through which interdependence may be realized (see ECONOMIC GEOGRAPHY).

In pre-capitalist societies, interdependence was both highly localized and restricted in

	Intensive	*Extensive*
research question	How does a process work in a particular case or small number of cases? What produces a certain change? What did the agents actually do?	What are the regularities common patterns, distinguishing features of a population? How widely are certain characteristics or processes distributed or represented?
relations	substantial relations of connection	formal relations of similarity
type of groups studied	causal groups	taxonomic groups
type of account produced	causal explanation of the production of certain objects or events, although not necessarily representative ones	descriptive 'representative' generalizations, lacking in explanatory penetration
typical methods	study of individual agents in their causal contexts, interactive interviews, ethnography – qualitative analysis	large-scale survey of population or representative sample, formal questionnaires, standardized interviews – statistical analysis
limitations	actual concrete patterns and contingent relations are unlikely to be 'representative', 'average' or generalizable – necessary relations discovered will exist wherever their relata are present, e.g. causal powers of objects are generalizable to other contexts as they are necessary features of these objects	although representative of a whole population, they are unlikely to be generalizable to other populations at different times and places – problem of ecological fallacy in making inferences about individuals – limited explanatory power
appropriate tests	corroboration	replication

intensive research *Sayer's summary of intensive and extensive research* (Sayer, 1992, p. 30)

scope – although in some cases international trade helped to supply the demand for luxury consumption from an élite. In the contemporary capitalist world economy, interdependence is worldwide. And, in recent years, capitalist social relations have experienced further geographical expansion with the collapse of state SOCIALISM in eastern Europe and the former USSR and the emergence of capitalism in China, now far more closely integrated into the world economic geography than, for example, its frequently cited comparator, India.

The political implications of interdependence are clear: human survival is itself reliant upon social and ecological relations of mutual dependence operating at a world SCALE. Metropolitan economies are as much if not more dependent upon the societies of the so-called periphery as the latter are upon the former (see CORE–PERIPHERY MODEL; DEPENDENCE). In fact, the apparently peripheral societies may have a greater capacity for self-sufficiency and independence, insofar as their social relations of production are characterized by reciprocity rather than by exploitation and their productive use of nature is cooperative rather than exploitative. But in economies and societies organized at a world scale, development may proceed only with the acceptance of mutual interdependence (this was the underlying message of the Brandt Reports – Brandt Commission, 1980, 1983 – in which the argument was that it was in the interests of the developed 'north' to aid the underdeveloped 'south' on the grounds that both would benefit from increased levels of economic activity and interaction) or with their imposition.

But this is to pose the issue of interdependent development only in terms of IDEALISM rather than of the relations between materialism and idealism (see DIALECTIC; HISTORICAL MATERIALISM). All societies need to be able to produce or appropriate a surplus to ensure their material and social reproduction. The expansion of capitalism and the struggle for strategic domination within the capitalist and non-capitalist worlds and between these spheres of influence is a product of this material imperative. The struggle for dominance involves the incorporation and subjugation of formerly independent SOCIAL FORMATIONS. The existence of such a struggle, unproductive as it is, is itself a major cause of UNDERDEVELOPMENT and the violent transformation of societies (see, for example, Watts, 1992/1996). The maintenance of a form of COMMUNISM in China and the abandonment of state socialism in eastern Europe and beyond has led to divergent paths of social pathology with dramatic consequences for the conduct of social life. In Russia, for example, the male LIFE EXPECTANCY has fallen to around 58 years – representing a fall of one year for every year since the collapse of state socialism.

Furthermore, struggle for domination generates a reaction in the form of a countervailing struggle for freedom from domination. Thus, whilst ecological interdependence remains, the question is whether it can withstand the ravages – both social and material – of exploitative modes of production which generate economic, political and ideological conflict throughout the world. It is, perhaps, rather more realistic to speak of an international balance of power based upon the economic geographies of productive capacity and output and cultural geographies of discourse and meaning in which '["W]orlds of comfort" and "worlds of struggle" are interweaved in complicated geographies as they penetrate one another's spaces in ever-increasing ways' (Taylor, Watts and Johnston, 1995, p. 1).

RL

References

Brandt Commission, 1980: *North–south: a programme for survival.* London: Pan Books. · Brandt Commission, 1983: *Common crisis: North–South cooperation for world recovery.* London: Pan Books; Cambridge, MA: MIT Press. · Brookfield, H. 1975: *Interdependent development.* London: Methuen. · Pittsburgh, PA: University of Pittsburgh Press. · Smith, N. 1984: *Uneven development.* Oxford and New York: Basil Blackwell. · Taylor, P.J., Watts, M.J. and Johnston, R.J. 1995: Global change at the end of the twentieth century. In R.J. Johnston, P.J. Taylor and M.J. Watts, eds, *Geographies of global change. Remapping the world in the late twentieth century*, ch. 1. Oxford and Cambridge, MA: Blackwell, 1–10. · Watts, M.J. 1992: The shock of modernity: petroleum, protest and fast capitalism in an industrializing society. In A. Pred and M. Watts, *Reworking modernity: Capitalisms and symbolic discontent*, ch. 2. New Brunswick, NJ: Rutgers University Press [reprinted in Daniels, S. and Lee, R. eds, 1996: *Exploring human geography* ch. 6. London: Arnold, 120–52].

Suggested Reading

Taylor et al. (1995). · Watts (1992/1996).

internal relations Necessary relations between objects or practices; formally, 'a relation *AB* may be defined as *internal* if and only if *A* would not be what it *essentially* is unless *B* is related to it in the way that it is' (Bhaskar, 1979). The relation between landlord and tenant, for example, is an internal relation; in this case each presupposes the other, so that the relation is *symmetrical.* To take a different example: the relation between the STATE and local-authority (or 'social') housing is also an internal relation; in this case, however, the latter presupposes the former but the former does not presuppose the latter (it is perfectly possible to think of a state that makes no provision for social housing), so that the relation is *asymmetrical.* These distinctions are important for the process of rational ABSTRACTION which is the main-spring of the philosophy of REALISM, where they guard against the so-called 'CHAOTIC CONCEPTIONS' which 'combine the unrelated' and 'divide the indivisible' (Sayer, 1982).

Sets of internal relations may be termed *structures*: an example is shown in the figure. Within geography, this terminology was first used by Harvey (1973, pp. 286–314). Drawing upon Ollman's (1971) exegesis of Marx's writings and Piaget's version of STRUCTURALISM, Harvey proposed that a structure be defined 'as a system of internal relations which is in the process of being structured through the

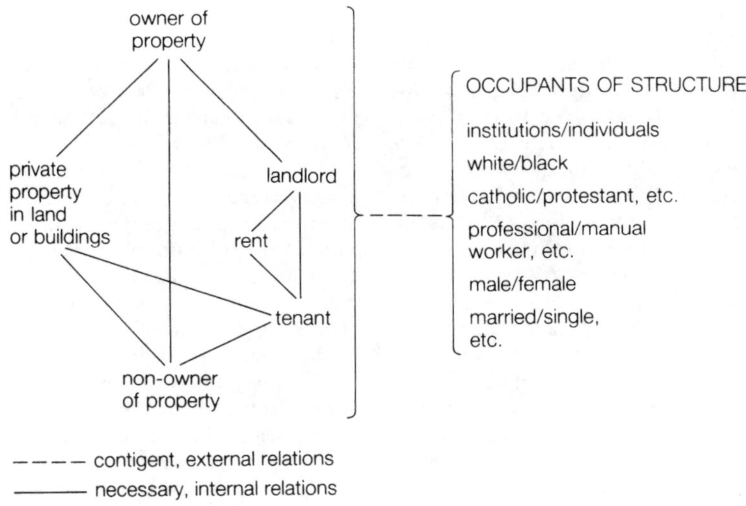

internal relations *Internal relations and structure* (after Sayer, 1984)

operation of its own transformation rules'. This enabled Harvey to pose fundamental questions of ONTOLOGY, to do with the nature of URBANISM, of CAPITALISM and of MODES OF PRODUCTION in general. Thus: 'Should we regard urbanism as a structure which can be derived from the economic base of society (or from superstructural elements) by way of a transformation? Or should we regard urbanism as a separate structure in interaction with other structures?' Harvey's answer was, in fact, to favour the second: 'Urbanism possesses a separate structure – it can be conceived as a separate entity – with a dynamic of its own. But this dynamic is moderated through interaction and contradiction with other structures'. Insofar as he clearly sought to distinguish one structure from another – 'structures may be regarded as separate and differentiable entities when no transformation exists whereby one may be derived from another' – then it is less than fair to say that Harvey somehow *universalized* internal relations 'at the expense of external [or contingent] relations' (Sayer, 1982). In Sayer's view, to do so is to 'nullify' the power of the concept of internal relations: 'If everything is internally related to everything else, then the concept does not help us say anything *particular* about *specific* structures' (emphases added). This may well be so, but such a charge cannot be levelled at Harvey. Indeed, in his later writings Harvey has gone some way beyond Ollman's formulations – which he says allow for conservative and idealist readings – to develop a much more precise and thoroughly materialist determination of internal relations. The concept of internal relations is central to his account of the DIALECTIC, within which 'each moment is constituted as an internal relation of the others within the flow of social and material life' (Harvey, 1996, p. 81).

Sayer's charge of universalizing internal relations may have more force, however, when brought to bear on Olsson's (1980) imaginative investigations of 'thought-and-action'. Like Harvey, Olsson commended Ollman's 'relational' interpretation of Marx, but he came much closer to the exorbitation that Sayer condemned. To Olsson, thought, language and action are internally related:

> Within that philosophy of internal relations, thought is conceived as both being and knowledge of being . . . It follows that internal relations are ontological in its parts. The implication is that truth is a single, all-embracing entity in which each component has its particular place. No component can be separated from any of the others.

'It is a central tenet of this attitude', Olsson continued (and one which is broadly Hegelian), that 'the world and our ideas are so entangled in each other that they cannot be separated'. Hence, so he claimed, we need to see that 'social relations between people [are] like logical relations between propositions' and 'logical relations between propositions [are] like social relations between people': all such relations are internal relations. It is for this reason that Olsson made the so-called '*linguistic turn*' and embarked upon a series of linguistic experiments which took him into the realms of surrealism and beyond: 'We enter a new world by acquiring a new language' (see also IDEOLOGY; PRAGMATISM).

But this very centrality of language, whatever else one might think about such a claim, offers some sort of defence against Sayer's original objection. For Olsson could plausibly insist that Sayer's critique of the universalization of internal relations only 'makes sense' from inside the framework of one *particular* 'language-game' – and Olsson was playing (and continues to play) a very different one (see Olsson, 1991). As a matter of fact Harvey (1996) also pays considerable attention to the *precise and particular* (dialectical) ways in which Marx used language to capture the translations and transformations from one moment to another that take place through the operations of capitalism as a mode of production. DG

References

Bhaskar, R. 1979: *The possibility of naturalism: a philosophical critique of the contemporary human sciences.* Brighton: Harvester; Atlantic Highlands, NJ: Humanities Press. · Harvey, D. 1973: *Social justice and the city.* London: Edward Arnold. · Baltimore, MD: Johns Hopkins University Press. · Harvey, D. 1996: *Justice, nature and the geography of difference.* Oxford and Cambridge, MA: Blackwell. · Ollman, B. 1971: *Alienation: Marx's conception of man in capitalist society.* Cambridge: Cambridge University Press. · Olsson, G. 1980: *Birds in egg/eggs in bird.* London: Pion; New York: Methuen. · Olsson, G. 1991: *Lines of power/Limits of language.* Minneapolis: University of Minnesota Press. · Sayer, A. 1982: Explanation in economic geography: abstraction versus generalization. *Progress in Human Geography* 6: 68–88. · Sayer, A. 1984: *Method in social science: a realist approach.* London: Hutchinson (second edition, 1992, London: Routledge).

Suggested Reading

Harvey (1996) chs 2–4. · Olsson (1980). · Sayer (1982).

interstateness In theories of the STATE the subject matter is usually treated in the singular. Hence we have reasonable understandings of stateness. However, the modern state is not an isolated state; it has a multiple existence but this has been relatively neglected in state theory. Hence we have a rather limited understanding of interstateness. The problem has been an intellectual division of labour between social scientists who study the state and its CIVIL SOCIETY and international relations writers who treat their realm as a sphere of anarchy which is resistant to any theoretical understanding: simple balance of power models is about as far as they go. In geography this simple treatment of interstateness is represented by uncritical GEOPOLITICS.

The existence of all modern states is premised on their SOVEREIGNTY. This includes their control over a designated TERRITORY (*internal sovereignty*) and the recognition of the legitimacy of that control by other states (*external sovereignty*). The latter defines a state of mutuality among states. It is such reciprocity which underpins interstateness. This can be defined as the plural condition of modern states and its general acceptance as a means of organizing politics. This is so embedded in modern ways of thinking that it is usually taken for granted, which is why it has remained unproblematized for so long (but see CRITICAL GEOPOLITICS). Interstateness is associated with internationality and interterritoriality, all three of which define an exhaustive multiplicity of states, NATIONS and territories across the world (Taylor, 1995).

The concept of interstateness is fundamental to defining the historicity of modern states. The development of interstateness culminating in recognition of there being international law at the Treaty of Westphalia in 1648, defines an origin to modern politics (Taylor, 1996a, 1996b). It follows that the demise of modern politics may be detected through the diminishing of interstateness in the growth of new trans-state politics (Taylor, 1995; Risse-Kappen, 1995). PJT

References

Risse-Kappen, T. 1995: *Bringing transnational relations back in.* Cambridge: Cambridge University Press. · Taylor, P.J. 1995: Beyond containers: internationality, interstateness, interterritoriality. *Progress in Human Geography* 19: 1–15. · Taylor, P.J. 1996a: *The Way The Modern World Works.* London: Wiley. · Taylor, P.J. 1996b: The modern multiplicity of states. In E. Kofman and G. Youngs, ed., *Globalization: theory and practice.* London: Pinter.

intervening opportunities A concept developed by the American sociologist S.A. Stouffer (1940) to explain the pattern of human MIGRATION, but subsequently applied in studies of commodity flow, passenger trips, traffic movements, etc. The concept states that the number of movements from an origin to a destination is proportional to the number of opportunities at that destination and inversely proportional to the number of opportunities between the origin and the destination. He also argued that distance of itself has no effect and that any observed decline in the number of movements with distance (see DISTANCE DECAY) is due to the increase in the number of intervening opportunities with distance. AMH

Reference

Stouffer, S.A. 1940: Intervening opportunities: a theory relating mobility to distance. *American Sociological Review* 5: 845–67.

interviewing One of human geography's most widely used FIELDWORK methods. As a key means of data collection in household surveys, face-to-face interviewing forms a cornerstone of the extensive cross-sectional, cohort and panel surveys that underpin large-scale quantitative social science (see QUANTITATIVE METHODS; SURVEY ANALYSIS). Structured QUESTIONNAIRE data are often collected by professional interviewers employed by commercial market research firms who provide varying amounts of project-specific training. The quality of the data can vary enormously from interviewer to interviewer, from study to study (depending on the complexity and sensitivity of the questionnaire and on the character of the target sample), from survey company to survey company (depending on the nature and extent of quality control in the field), from place to place and from time to time.

There are also technical problems related to SAMPLING procedures, response rates, and debates over the nature, use and calculation of inferential statistics, especially for the cluster sampling which forms the basis of so many large-scale surveys (see INFERENCE). Perhaps more crucially, there are important ethical questions related to the storage and analysis of individual computerized records, especially when these are tagged to spatial coordinates (see also ETHICS, GEOGRAPHY AND).

The advantage of the structured questionnaire is that it provides comparability between regions and through history among some key demographic and socio-economic characteristics of large populations. Pieced together, the various national surveys that currently exist already offer a fairly comprehensive map of the social world – at least for the developed countries. The disadvantage of this approach is that it masks individual variety, attributes a consistency and stability to attitudes and opinions that is rarely found in everyday life, and limits the kinds of responses that the interviewees can make. The questions reflect the purposes and presuppositions of the analyst, which respondents have little scope to challenge or augment.

Interview data can, however, also be collected from groups and individuals in less structured settings (see QUALITATIVE METHODS). This approach sacrifices comprehensiveness for intensity, and is less preoccupied with mapping society than with exploring the relationships between society and space. Individual and group interviews have thus been used in geography to explore the relationships between people and their environments providing, among other things, a commentary on the value, utility and safety of ACTIVITY SPACE.

In-depth individual interviews allow researchers to study subjective meanings and motives alongside the more objectifiable attributes and aspirations that can be tapped by structured questionnaires. They are a means of explaining and understanding the kinds of relationships which can only be described by more extensive quantitative approaches. Individual qualitative interviews seem particularly appropriate for documenting life histories, and for charting the route taken by individuals and households through the sets of markets and institutions (LABOUR MARKET, housing system, welfare services, social support networks) that mediate between who people are and where they are positioned (cf. POSITIONALITY). The individual approach may also be appropriate where the subject of the research is highly sensitive or confidential. Wherever they are employed, qualitative interviews offer the subjects of the research much more scope to speak for themselves than do structured questionnaires.

Group interviews take this commitment to the authenticity of everyday life and experience a step further, allowing participants not only to speak for themselves but also to begin to negotiate their own shared views. This can be seen as a contribution to the democratization of the research process: it allows ordinary people to generalize about their lives and futures, rather than relying on the analyst to derive aggregate statements from a set of individual observations.

Group interviewing within geography takes two broad forms: the one-off FOCUS GROUP which was developed as a market research tool (Holbrook and Jackson, 1996); and *in-depth discussion groups*, developed from ideas in psychotherapy, which meet on several occasions in the course of the study (Burgess et al., 1998). During the 1990s, group interviewing virtually became the new orthodoxy for qualitative research in human geography. The distinction between focus groups and group discussions has (for many but not all researchers) become blurred, and as a methodological tool, group interviewing has proved very flexible. Groups may be small (3) or large (*c*.15), pre-existing or purposively assembled, interviewed once or on several occasions, employed on their own, or as one step in a mixed methods approach. The result is a style of interviewing which takes away some (but not all) of the analyst's POWER to define the research agenda, allows those who are being researched to collaborate actively rather than respond passively, and favours a collective approach to the production and negotiation of knowledge. It has even been suggested that group interviews can form the basis of a new politics of knowledge and empowerment, with the potential to democratize GOVERNANCE and service provision (Johnson, 1996).

References

Burgess, J., Limb, M and Harrison, C.M. 1988: Exploring environmental values through the medium of small groups, part one: theory and practice. *Environment and Planning A* 20: 309–26. · Holbrook, B. and Jackson, P. 1996: Shopping around: focus group research in North London. *Area* 28: 136–42. · Johnson, A. 1996: 'It's good to talk': the focus group and the sociological imagination. *The Sociological Review* 44: 517–38.

Suggested Reading

Area 1996, vol. 28 (2) contains six articles on group interviewing.

invasion and succession A term adopted from ECOLOGY to describe a process of NEIGHBOURHOOD change whereby one social group succeeds another in a residential area. The term is particularly associated with the ZONAL MODEL developed by the CHICAGO SCHOOL of sociologists in the 1920s, according to which change was initiated by pressure on INNER-CITY housing, usually from low socio-economic status immigrant groups. They moved into adjacent residential areas, forcing the current occupants to move out into the next zone, stimulating a rippling process of change outwards from the city centre which ended with the highest status groups on the edge of the built-up areas moving to newly built homes on the urban fringe (cf. FILTERING). As with much of the other ecological work of the Chicago School, the concept was influenced by DARWINIAN ideas (Entrikin, 1980; cf. SOCIAL DARWINISM).

The process of invasion and succession, frequently associated with an ETHNIC minority group's movement into an area (cf. BLOCKBUSTING), thus involves changing the characteristics of many of the city's NATURAL AREAS. Its idealized form suggests periods of equilibrium in the urban residential pattern punctuated by episodes of wholesale change, but in most cities the processes are continuous, though substantially speeded-up in some districts at particular times. RJJ

Suggested Reading

Entrikin, J.N. 1980: Robert Park's human ecology and human geography. *Annals of the Association of American Geographers* 70: 615–32. · Knox, P.L. 1995: *Urban social geography: an introduction*, 3rd edn. London and New York: Longman. · Ley, D.F. 1983: *A social geography of the city*. London and New York: Harper and Row.

irredentism The assertion by the government of a country that a minority living across the border in a neighbouring country belongs to it historically and culturally, and the mounting of a propaganda campaign, or even a declaration of war, to effect that claim.

Some of the most violent irredentist conflicts of recent times in Europe flared up as a consequence of the break-up of the former Yugoslavia in the early 1990s. The wars in Croatia and Bosnia Herzogovina were largely about creating a new political framework of states, each of which would be ethnically and politically homogeneous. The conflict erupted further south with the ethnic Albanian majority in Kosovo seeking to switch allegiance to the adjoining state of Albania. MB

Suggested Reading

Chazan, N., ed., 1991: *Irredentism and international politics*. Twickenham: Adamantine.

isolines Lines on a MAP describing the intersection of a real or hypothetical surface with one or more horizontal planes. The configuration of isolines allows map readers to infer relative slope and estimate surface elevation at specific places. Isolines might be either traced on a visible three-dimensional model of the surface, as when a photogrammetrist viewing a stereo-model plots elevation contours, or interpolated from estimated surface elevations, as when a computer program threads contours through a network of observation points or area centroids (Davis, 1986, pp. 353–77). In the latter case, the method of interpolation affects the reliability of individual isolines and their portrayal of slopes, pits and peaks.

MM

Reference

Davis, J.C. 1986: *Statistics and data analysis in geology*, 2nd edn. New York: John Wiley and Sons.

J

justice, geography and Geographical concern with justice tends to fall into two distinct if related fields: *criminal justice* (see CRIME, GEOGRAPHY OF), and a broader concern with societal institutions and their distributional outcomes, or SOCIAL JUSTICE. The difference is sometimes portrayed as between procedural justice and EQUITY, although distributional outcomes are certainly influenced by procedures (such as the law, or the rules and practices of a social security agency used to distribute benefits). Consideration of criminal justice has emerged as a specific topic of interest on the part of a limited number of geographers in recent years (see LAW, GEOGRAPHY OF). DMS

just-in-time production A system of manufacturing in which inputs are supplied and outputs delivered very soon after demand for a finished good has been registered.

Perfected by Japanese automobile producers, and now emulated by North American and European assemblers, this set of practices has also diffused to other industrial sectors such as computer manufacturing. As one objective is to reduce the quantity of producers' capital tied up in inventories of parts and finished products, producers no longer keep large buffer stocks of parts on hand. This has the consequent effect of forcing lower defect rates in parts supplied, and hence improves overall quality. Because suppliers are able to meet buyers' varying requirements (in both number and type) on short notice, the system allows manufacturers to respond more flexibly to changing market demands. Adoption of such practices may exert an agglomerative force bringing buyers and suppliers closer together to facilitate rapid delivery on short notice. (See also COMMODITY CHAIN/FILIÈRE; POST-FORDISM; PRODUCTION COMPLEX; TRANSACTION COSTS.) MSG

K

Kantianism A philosophy developed by Immanuel Kant (1724–1804). The Kantian tradition has been incorporated within contemporary human geography in three main (increasingly interconnected) ways.

Kant's conception of the nature of geography and of its location within the sciences as a whole has provided the basis for a series of major disagreements (see May, 1970). Kant considered that knowledge could be classified in two ways: either logically or physically. 'The logical classification collects all individual items in separate classes according to similarities of morphological features; it could be called something like an "archive" and will lead, if pursued, to a "natural system"' (Büttner and Hoheisel, 1980). In a 'natural system', Kant noted, 'I place each thing in its class, even though they are to be found in different, widely separated places' (cited in Hartshorne, 1939). The physical classification, in contrast, collects individual items which 'belong to the same time or the same space'. In this connection, Kant asserted:

> History differs from geography only in the consideration of time and [space]. The former is a report of phenomena that follow one another (*Nacheinander*) and has reference to time. The latter is a report of phenomena beside each other (*Nebeneinander*) in space. History is a narrative, geography a description.
>
> Geography and history fill up the entire circumference of our perceptions: geography that of space, history that of time (cited in Hartshorne, 1939).

Although Kant's views on geography were broadly similar to those of von Humboldt and Hettner, they appear to have had 'no direct influence' other than 'as a form of confirmation' (Hartshorne, 1958; but cf. Büttner and Hoheisel, 1980). Indeed, they were not explicitly endorsed in any major programmatic statement of the scope of geography (in English) until Hartshorne's account of *The nature of geography* (1939), which accepted that geography's basic task was essentially Kantian:

> Geography and history are alike in that they are integrating sciences concerned with studying the world. There is, therefore, a universal and mutual relation between them, even though their bases of integration are in a sense opposite – geography in terms of earth spaces, history in terms of periods of time.

Others were more sceptical. Blaut (1961) concluded that, for Kant:

> Knowledge about the spatial location of objects is quite distinct from knowledge about their true nature and the natural laws governing them. The latter sorts of knowledge are eternal and universal, are truly scientific . . . [whereas] spatial and temporal co-ordinates are separate and rather secondary attributes of objects, and spatial and temporal arrangement of objects is not a matter for science.

Like Schaefer (1953), therefore, Blaut represented Kant as the originator of an EXCEPTIONALISM which was inimical to the 'explanations' and 'generalizations' (rather than mere 'descriptions') required if geography were to be reconstituted as a SPATIAL SCIENCE. Subsequently, however, Kant's basic distinction was revitalized by Hägerstrand. Although TIME-GEOGRAPHY is evidently predicated on a repudiation of divisions between 'history' and 'geography', 'time' and 'space', the contrast which Hägerstrand drew between a conventional COMPOSITIONAL APPROACH and his own CONTEXTUAL APPROACH paralleled that between 'logical' and 'physical' classifications (cf. Parkes and Taylor, 1975).

Most of the foregoing formulations depend on Kant's early lectures on (physical) geography, but other commentators have drawn attention to Kant's *Critique of pure reason* (1781) and its emphasis on 'the structuring activity of the thinking subject':

> Space is not something objective and real, nor is it a substance or an accident, or a relation, but it is *subjective* and *ideal* and proceeds from the nature of mind by an *unchanging law*, as a schema for co-ordinating with each other absolutely all things externally sensed (Kant, cited in Richards, 1974; emphasis added).

This stress upon 'the epistemic structuring of the world by the human actor [is] the essence of the Kantian heritage', so it is claimed, and 'constitutes the common theme which has, in practice, been distilled from the variety of humanistic philosophies to which geographers of a subjectivist orientation have turned in their endeavour to transcend the dichotomy inherent in subject–object relations' (Livingstone and Harrison, 1981 – see BEHAVIOURAL GEOGRAPHY; HUMANISTIC GEOGRAPHY).

Many of these endeavours might more properly be described as 'neo-Kantian'. *Neo-Kantianism* emerged in Germany in the closing decades of the nineteenth century. Whereas Kant had held the a priori to be 'externally fixed and eternally immutable' – the 'unchanging law' in Richards's quotation above – the neo-Kantians rejected the vision of a unitary scientific method which this allowed. They substituted a distinction between:

- *the cultural and historical sciences* (the *Geisteswissenschaften*), which dealt with an intelligible world of 'non-sensuous objects of experience' which had to be understood (*verstehen*), and which were thus concerned with the IDIOGRAPHIC – this was the focus of the 'Baden school', which included Windelband and Rickert; and
- *the natural sciences* (the *Naturwissenschaften*), which dealt with the 'sensible world of science' which could be explained (*erklaren*), and which were thus concerned with the NOMOTHETIC – this was the focus of the 'Marburg school', which included Cassirer.

Within human geography, neo-Kantianism has been attributed to (*inter alia*) the POSSIBILISM of the French school of human geography (Berdoulay, 1976), to the programme of the CHICAGO SCHOOL of sociology (Park completed a doctoral dissertation under Windelband: see Entrikin, 1980), and to modern HUMANISTIC GEOGRAPHY more generally (see Jackson and Smith, 1984). In a still more fundamental sense, Entrikin (1981) has proposed that Hartshorne's views of the nature of geography (above) incorporated a number of patently neo-Kantian arguments, and that Cassirer's writings might provide a means of reinvigorating (and even bringing together) geography's heterogeneous perspectives upon SPACE (see Entrikin, 1977).

Until recently, most geographers limited their interest in Kant to his lectures on physical geography and his first critique, largely – one suspects – because of their interest in (or objections to) the scientificity of geographies underwritten by POSITIVISM (e.g. SPATIAL SCIENCE). But several writers have since reflected on Kant's second and third critiques. There has been a widespread (if often tacit) acceptance of an essentially Kantian distinction between three forms of knowledge or 'reason'. Following Habermas, for example, many writers associate the ENLIGHTENMENT project inscribed within the project of MODERNITY with the formation of three autonomous spheres:

science	truth and knowledge cognitive–instrumental rationality
morality	norms and justice moral–practical rationality
art	authenticity and beauty aesthetic–expressive rationality

The task of Habermas's version of CRITICAL THEORY is, in part, to bring these three spheres back into balance with one another: to guard against the inflation of 'science' (and the detachment of its 'expert culture' from public scrutiny) which, so he claims, was characteristic of CAPITALISM in the early and middle twentieth century; and, more recently, against the inflation of the aesthetic that he sees within late-twentieth-century POSTMODERNISM (Ingram, 1987). Certainly, Kantian aesthetics have played an extremely important part in discussions of postmodern sensibilities, and particular attention has been paid to the 'aestheticization of politics' which can be found in versions of both MODERNISM and POSTMODERNISM (Harvey, 1989; Eagleton, 1990). DG

References

Berdoulay, V. 1976: French possibilism as a form of neo-Kantian philosophy. *Proceedings of the Association of American Geographers* 8: 176–9. · Blaut, J. 1961: Space and process. *Professional Geographer* 13: 1–7. · Büttner, M. and Hoheisel, K. 1980: Immanuel Kant. *Geographers: Bio-bibliographical Studies* 4: 55–67. · Eagleton, T. 1990: *The ideology of the aesthetic*. Oxford: Blackwell. · Entrikin, J.N. 1977: Geography's spatial perspective and the philosophy of Ernst Cassirer. *Canadian Geographer* 21: 209–22. · Entrikin, J.N. 1980: Robert Park's human ecology and human geography. *Annals of the Association of American Geographers* 70: 43–58. · Entrikin, J.N. 1981: Philosophical issues in the scientific study of regions. In D.T. Herbert and R.J. Johnston, eds, *Geography and the urban environment. Progress in research and applications, volume 4*. Chichester: John Wiley, 1–27. · Hartshorne, R. 1939: *The nature of geography: a critical survey of current thought in the light of the past*. Lancaster, PA: Association of American Geographers. · Hartshorne, R. 1958: The concept of geography as a science of space, from Kant and Humboldt to Hettner. *Annals of the Association of American Geographers* 48: 97–108. · Harvey, D. 1989: *The condition of postmodernity: an enquiry into the origins of cultural change*. Oxford: Blackwell; Ingram, D. 1987: *Habermas and the dialectic of reason*. New Haven: Yale University Press. · Jackson, P. and Smith, S.J. 1984: *Exploring social geography*. London: Allen and Unwin; Livingstone, D.N.

and Harrison, D.T. 1981: Immanuel Kant, subjectivism and human geography: a preliminary investigation. *Transactions, Institute of British Geographers* NS 6: 359–74. · May, J.A. 1970: *Kant's conception of geography and its relation to recent geographical thought*. Toronto: University of Toronto, Department of Geography, Research Publication 4. · Parkes, D. and Taylor, P.J. 1975: A Kantian view of the city: a factorial ecology experiment in space and time. *Environment and Planning A* 7: 671–88. · Richards, P. 1974: Kant's geography and mental maps. *Transactions, Institute of British Geographers* 61: 1–16. · Schaefer, F.K. 1953: Exceptionalism in geography: a methodological examination. *Annals of the Association of American Geographers* 43: 226–49.

Suggested Reading

Büttner and Hoheisel (1980). · Entrikin (1981). · Livingstone and Harrison (1981). · May (1970).

kibbutz Originally, a special type of Israeli agricultural community (plural: *kibbutzim*). The kibbutz movement began in the early twentieth century and was one of the principal means whereby Jews recolonized Palestine (Rayman, 1981). Early proponents combined elements of Zionism (the belief that Jewish people must exercise SELF-DETERMINATION by creating a Jewish-majority NATION-STATE in Palestine) and European SOCIALISM (Mittleberg, 1988). Kibbutzim were established in rural areas both to introduce Jewish settlers to agriculture and to gain territorial control. The new settlements were COLLECTIVES and were autonomous from the surrounding (often hostile) Palestinian-Arab COMMUNITY; many were protected by stockades and watchtowers. Decisions on each kibbutz were collectively reached, meals eaten in common, and children were usually educated, housed and raised in communal facilities. After 1948, the military role of kibbutzim waned and was replaced by a stronger emphasis on mechanization and export-oriented agriculture. Many also established factories to augment their crop and livestock production. Standards of living rose as more land was acquired and a state-controlled water distribution was introduced (a system that privileged kibbutzim). In recent years, this standard has been difficult to maintain, especially after the near economic collapse that occurred in Israel in the 1980s (Warhurst, 1996).

Increasingly, the collectivist IDEOLOGIES of the kibbutz are redefined as more formalized management structures and new income-generating initiatives are introduced (Maron, 1994; Warhurst, 1996). Recent statistics suggest that fewer than half of all children born on kibbutzim remain there, and less than 2.5 per cent of the Israeli population now live a kibbutz lifestyle. Still, new (small-scale) kibbutzim are being created and the movement continues to be a powerful national symbol, both for Israelis and the thousands of tourists who elect to visit and work on kibbutzim each year. DH

References

Maron, S. 1994: Recent developments in the kibbutz: an overview. *Journal of Rural Cooperation* 22: 1–17. · Mittleberg, D. 1988: *Strangers in paradise: the Israeli kibbutz experience*. New Brunswick, NJ: Transaction Books. · Rayman, P. 1981: *The kibbutz community and nation building*. Princeton, NJ: Princeton University Press. · Warhurst, C. 1996: The management of production and the changing character of the Kibbutz as a mode of production. *Economic and Industrial Democracy* 17: 419–45.

Suggested Reading

Palgi, M. 1993: Kibbutz women: gender roles and status. *Israel Social Science Research* 8: 108–21. · Rosolio, D. 1993: The impact of the economic crisis on ideology and life-style of kibbutzim. *Israel Social Science Research* 8: 1–10.

Kondratieff cycles *Long waves* of economic DEVELOPMENT with a wave length of about 40–60 years. Shorter oscillations in the level of business activity may be superimposed upon such long waves but Kondratieff cycles imply fundamental qualitative transformations of economic systems rather than mere quantitative fluctuations. The figure on p. 424 illustrates both the sequence of Kondratieffs since the late eighteenth century (each wave is composed of growth (A) and a stagnation (B) phase) and the range of economic, social and political changes which are thought to accompany them. An assumption of long-wave interpretations of UNEVEN DEVELOPMENT is that, under certain conditions – not least financial and those of economic organization, cooperation and competition (Dicken, 1998) – the dynamics of technical change and its spread through an ECONOMIC GEOGRAPHY is associated with the dynamics of the waves themselves.

Kondratieff waves are named after the Soviet economist N.D. Kondratieff (see, for example, Kondratieff, 1935) who worked during the 1920s on long-term fluctuations in economic activity. Empirical evidence for the existence of long waves is strongly disputed (e.g. Maddison, 1982, 1991) but interest lies in the hypotheses about and insights into the dynamics of capitalist development that have been generated by long-wave theorizing (Freeman et al., 1982) and in the two-way relationships between UNEVEN DEVELOPMENT and the generation and geographical implications of long waves (Marshall, 1987; Allen and Massey, 1988; Hall and Preston, 1988; Kleinknecht et al., 1992).

Ernest Mandel (1980) strongly supports the existence of long waves. He argues that the four waves identified to the present represent segments of the overall history of CAPITALISM that have definite distinguishing characteristics: (a) 1789–1848, the *industrial and bourgeois revolutions* and Napoleonic wars and the constitution of a world market for industrial goods; (b) 1848–93, *free competition*; (c) 1893–1940, IMPERIALISM, the rise of finance CAPITAL and the consequent inter-imperialist wars; and (d) 1940–?, *late capitalism*. For Mandel there are serious technical and economic difficulties facing a capitalist path out of the current decline, which began in the late 1960s after the long post-war boom and, as a result of such difficulties, some even more severe social and political problems.

Maddison (1982) accepts that 'major changes in growth momentum have occurred since 1820'. He argues that these changes have given rise to 'phases of growth' but suggests that their explanation is not to be found in 'systematic long waves, but in specific disturbances of an *ad hoc* character'. Each of Maddison's phases (1870–1914 the *liberal phase*; 1920–38, the *beggar-your-neighbour phase*; 1950–73, the *golden age*; 1973–? the *phase of blurred objectives*) are characterized by quantitative and qualitative characteristics and the latest phase coincides its onset with the contemporary crisis described by long-wave theorists.

A common theme in the analysis of the causes of long waves is the generation and implications of technological change. Schumpeter (1939) and Mensch (1979) point to a bunching of INNOVATIONS. This bunching, Schumpeter suggests, is stimulated by the leadership of pioneering entrepreneurs searching for ways of resuscitating rates of profit during a recession. The innovations create expansionary and transformative systemic effects but, eventually, they too are subject to falling rates of profit. Long waves are therefore distinguished by particular types of technological revolution. Thus the first four Kondratieff waves were associated, respectively, with major innovations in: (a) steampower, cotton and iron; (b) railways and iron and steel; (c) electricity, chemicals and automobiles; and (d) electronics, synthetics and petrochemicals. Speculation continues as to the basis of the fifth Kondratieff, with likely contenders being information technology and telecommunications and biotechnology. Freeman et al. (1982) point rather to the effects of the diffusion of innovations in stimulating change and, like Gordon et al. (1982, 1983), suggest that long waves reflect the social and institutional circumstances (what Gordon et al. call 'the social structure of accumulation') in which technical change is stimulated and diffused as well as the particular characteristics of the technology itself. Certainly, long waves are thought to be associated with the transformation of other features of capitalist society (Knox and Agnew, 1994) such as REGIMES OF ACCUMULATION (see ECONOMIC GEOGRAPHY). This approach to the UNEVEN DEVELOPMENT of capitalism is similar to, but broader in scope than, that propounded by Dunford and Perrons (1983) who point to critical transformations in the LABOUR PROCESS as an explanation of long waves.

Insofar as Kondratieffs are generated by systemic technical change, successive cycles imply quite different geographical conditions of existence for production and, in addition, the associated social, political and regulatory changes themselves present new geographical constraints and possibilities. The geographical implications of Kondratieffs, or rather the complex of changes that they represent, are profound and may be associated with the rise and fall of regions and places of production (see, for example, Hall, 1985; Massey, 1988).

There are broadly two schools of thought on the implications of Kondratieff cycles for geographically uneven development. Peter Hall (1985) adopts a technological-determinist position and argues that places are differentially endowed with respect to the development and growth of new technology, so that uneven development will and should result and that such differences should be intensified in policies for economic growth. By contrast, others (e.g. Freeman et al., 1982; Marshall, 1987; Massey 1988) argue that technical change is facilitative and that places may be adapted to such change. Marshall points out that new or high technology rarely represents a sudden or complete break with the past and that 'low' technology may be modified by high technology via process innovations.

Little attention has been paid to the possibilities of geography being implicated in the generation of technical change (see Allen and Massey, 1988), despite the suggestion that peripheral regions are inherently less hidebound by fixed investment and are, therefore, more open to innovation (see, for example, Dodgshon, 1987). However, insofar as geography

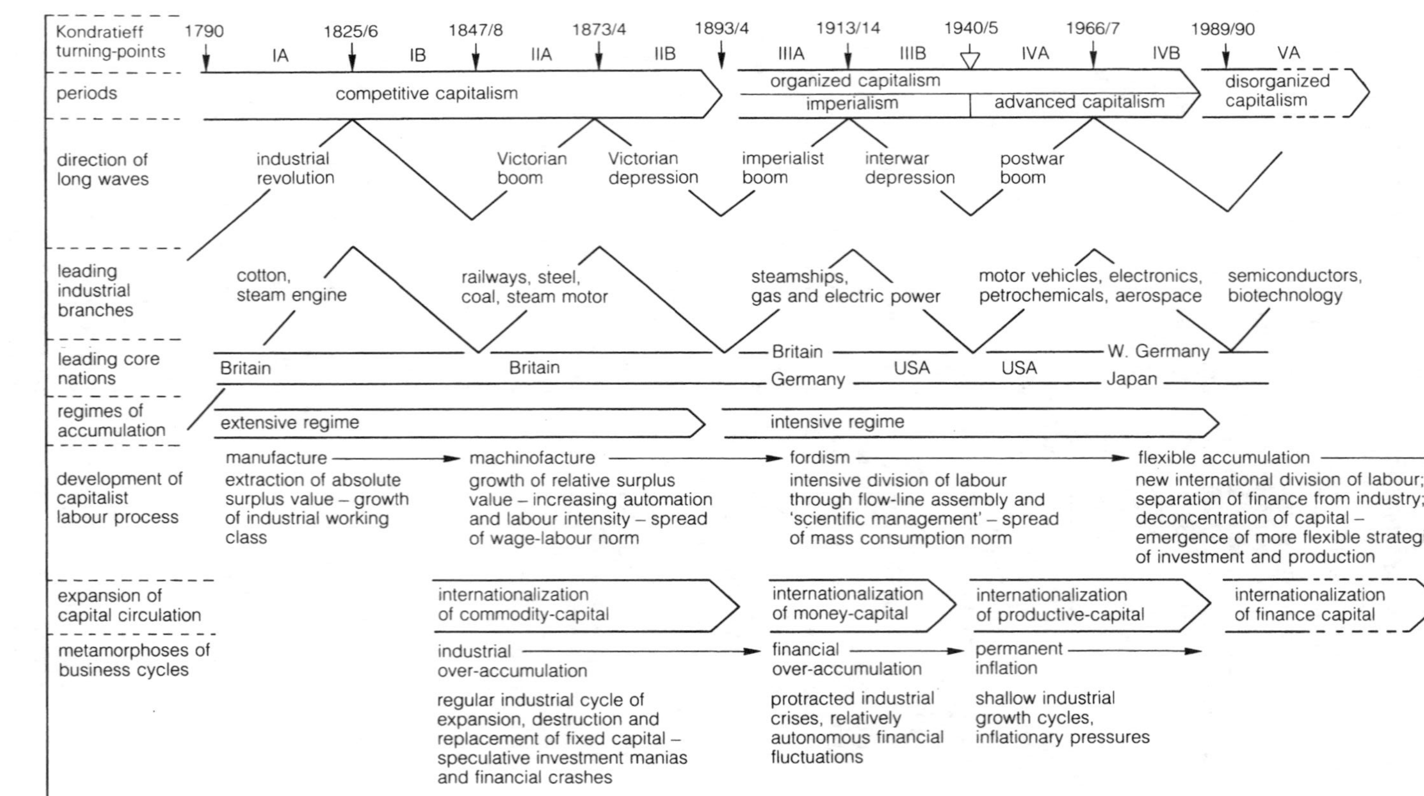

Kondratieff cycles *A schematic representation of the major features associated with long-wave economic cycles* (Knox and Agnew, 1989: adapted from Marshall, 1987)

represents an integral part of the conditions of existence of productive activity, it seems likely that the geography of the generation of long waves is not reducible merely to local conditions of innovation but to contradictions and potentials in the geographical structure of economic development at particular places and points of time to which technical change and innovation may represent a positive response.

It is important to remember, however, that the application of long-wave theory to geographical change remains highly economistic and, indeed, speculative (see, e.g. Dawson, 1994, ch. 3). Avoidance of the catastrophic future in emerging from the fourth Kondratieff predicted by Mandel would depend upon political and social struggle and leadership rather than a resigned acceptance of the inevitability of economically determined and potentially damaging social, cultural and political change.

RL

References and Suggested Reading

Allen, J. and Massey, D., eds, 1988: *The economy in question*. London and Newbury Park, CA: Sage. · Dawson, A. 1994: *A geography of European integration*. London and New York: Belhaven Press. · Dicken, P. 1998: *Global shift: transforming the world economy*, 3rd edn., ch. 5. London: Paul Chapman Publishing; Dodgshon, R.A. 1987: *The European past: social evolution and spatial order*. London: Macmillan; New York: St. Martin's Press. · Dunford, M. and Perrons, D. 1983: *The arena of capital*, ch. 9. London and Basingstoke: Macmillan; New York: St. Martin's Press. · Freeman, C., Clark, J. and Soete, L. 1982: *Unemployment and technical innovation: a study of long waves and economic development*. London: Francis Pinter; Westport, CT: Greenwood Press. · Gordon, D.M., Edwards, R. and Reich, M. 1982: *Segmented work, divided workers*, ch. 2. Cambridge and New York: Cambridge University Press. · Gordon, D.M., Weisskopf, T.E. and Bowles, S. 1983: Long swings and the non-reproductive cycle. American Economic Association, *Papers and Proceedings* vol. 73, no. 2, May: 152–7. · Hall, P. 1985: The geography of the Fifth Kondratieff. In P. Hall and A. Markusen, eds, *Silicon landscapes*, ch. 1. Winchester, MA: Allen and Unwin; Hall, P. and Preston, P. 1988: *The carrier wave: new information technology and the geography of innovation 1846–2003*. London and Winchester, MA: Unwin Hyman. · Kleinknecht, A., Mandel, E. and Wallerstein I. 1992: *New findings in long wave research*. London: Macmillan. · Knox, P. and Agnew, J. 1994: *The geography of the world-economy*, 2nd edn. London and New York: Edward Arnold. · Kondratieff, N. 1935: The long waves in economic life. *Review of Economic Statistics* 17: 105–15. · Maddison, A. 1982: *Phases of capitalist development*, ch. 4. Oxford and New York: Oxford University Press. · Maddison, A. 1991: *Dynamic forces in capitalist development*. Oxford: Oxford University Press; Mandel, E. 1980: *Long waves of capitalist development. The Marxist interpretation*. Cambridge: Cambridge University Press. · Marshall, M. 1987: *Long waves of regional development*. London: Macmillan; New York: St. Martin's Press. · Massey, D. 1988: What's happening to UK manufacturing? In J. Allen and D. Massey, eds, *The economy in question*, ch. 2. London and Newbury Park, CA: Sage. · Mensch, G. 1979: *Stalemate in technology. Innovations overcome the Depression*. New York: Ballinger. · Schumpeter, J.A. 1939: *Business cycles: A theoretical, historical and statistical analysis of the capitalist process*. New York: McGraw-Hill.

L

labour geography An emerging subdiscipline of geography which researches the ways in which broadly political struggles by labour, organized and disorganized, has helped to sculpt the geographical landscape.

Two sources of inspiration led to the development of a labour geography. First, POLITICAL GEOGRAPHY has traditionally been unconcerned with questions of labour while ECONOMIC GEOGRAPHY has tended to examine either the geography 'of' labour – a description of the geographical distribution of different kinds of labour – or to include labour as a factor of production. Marxist analyses went further, insisting that labour was an active agent in the making of economic landscapes, but the overwhelming concern lay with the movements of capital and tended to treat labour as subordinate (Herod, 1997).

Labour geography is centrally concerned with questions of SCALE insofar as the geographical results of labour struggles are not only visible at specific scales but contribute to the moulding and remoulding of specific scales (Herod, 1991; Johns, 1994). Thus labour geography arguably provides a sharper sense than a capital-centred economic geography of the ways in which the geographical differentiation of the economic landscape takes place. While focusing on political struggles, labour geography has developed a broader purview that involves social and cultural as well as political perspectives (Mitchell, 1996; Herod, 1998).

NS

References

Herod, A. 1991: The production of scale in United States labour relations, *Area* 23: 82–8. · Herod, A. 1997: From a geography of labour to a labour geography: labour's spatial fix and the geography of capitalism. *Antipode* 29: 1–31. · Herod, A., ed., 1998: *Organizing the landscape. Geographical perspectives on labour unionism*. Minneapolis: University of Minnesota Press; Johns, R. 1994: *International solidarity: space and class in the US labor movement*. Ph.D. dissertation, Rutgers University, Piscataway, NJ. · Mitchell, D. 1996. *The lie of the land*. Minneapolis: University of Minnesota Press.

Suggested Reading

Herod (1998).

labour market The market through which labour power is exchanged as a commodity and so (re/dis)incorporated into a circuit of SOCIAL REPRODUCTION such as the CIRCUIT OF CAPITAL.

Labour power (the ability to undertake work) is embodied in human beings with multiple corporeal, political, cultural and social determinations and with close emotive and reproductive ties to particular people. Short of out-and-out SLAVERY, labour power cannot, therefore, be reduced to a mere commodity. Thus although capital is able directly to manage and produce other inputs to production in broad conformity with its own dynamics and norms, it is able to do so only within limits in the case of labour power. This is, of course, one reason why the conflict between labour and capital is such a profound and influential contradiction within capitalist systems of social reproduction.

Labour is an active and essential part of the circuit of capital; without labour the circuit is lifeless. But the logic of capital is not the same as the logic of labour. Labour is not reducible to labour power – to its role in the circuit of capital – and the historical geography of CAPITALISM is structured by the contradictory tensions between labour and capital as well as by the expansionary tendencies of capital. Indeed, some argue that the activities of labour in resisting the worst excesses of capital have not only shaped capitalism but sustained it (Urry, 1981).

The conflict between labour and capital is, in part, a conflict over their constitutive geographies. Despite its reliance on place-bound institutions as a critical condition of its existence and expanded reproduction, capital has few if any emotive attachments to PLACE. By contrast, labour requires 'the stability and support of COMMUNITY life' (Peck, 1996, p. 15). It is, in short, exogenous to the circuit of social reproduction under capitalism. Thus for Jamie Peck (1996, pp. 32, 39), 'The distinction between labor and labor-power goes to the heart of the social nature of the labor market'.

The inescapable conclusion is that the spheres of production and social reproduction are both separate and connected. They are separate in the sense that they each have their own structures of dominance, along with their own distinctive rhythms and tendencies, but they are also related in the sense that each conditions and interacts with the other.

And yet, as Antonella Picchio (1992, p. 95) has observed, the imperatives of ACCUMULATION tend to regard labour just like any other inanimate commodity:

> The separation between the processes of production and reproduction hides the ways in which the proportion between the value of production and the costs of reproduction has historically been held within limits compatible with capitalist accumulation. But what is compatible is actually dictated by the rate of profit – by definition historical – and not by natural scarcities or technological dynamics.

Such a separation shuts out the costs of the reproduction of labour from formative influence in the labour market and enables the analysis of labour as if it were an endogenously produced commodity (i.e. produced unproblematically by capitalist systems of production) responding simply to the dictates of demand from production. In such a view, the market for labour is treated like the market for cabbages (Peck, 1996).

So, given the asymmetric relationship of power between labour and capital, one 'solution' to the exogenous nature of labour and its resultant status as a pseudocommodity (Storper and Walker, 1983) is to attempt to force true commodity status onto labour through the unfettered process of labour market discipline. Such strategies have the advantage for capital of driving down the costs of labour by further imbalancing the relations of POWER between capital and labour. However, they also serve to undermine the material and social capacity for work – and thereby demean the reproduction of labour. Not only does this reduce its capacity in production, it alienates and actively dehumanizes labour outside production and reduces its effective demand for commodities, so threatening the realization of the surplus. Thus reliance on the 'naked discipline of the market' (Peck, 1996, p. 29) is profoundly damaging within the circuit of capital and in civil society more generally. And, in any case, they are limited in the extent to which they may be applied by capital.

But attempts to discipline labour begin well before labour power enters the labour market. This imposition is not, as Weber (1976) insisted, reducible simply to the conflict between labour and capital but is associated with the rationalization of social and economic organization and of production. It involves forms of power – residing in bureaucracies – well beyond that of economic power and its contestation in the conflict between labour and capital. One such bureaucracy of rationalization is education. Bowles and Gintis (1976), for example, argue that education should be understood as a response to modern capitalism – providing skills, discipline, respect for authority, rewards for success and penalties for failure. It facilitates cultural reproduction (Bourdieu, 1986, 1988) in perpetuating social and economic inequalities across generations. But, as in the labour market and workplace, this function is not simply imposed on a malleable population. Paul Willis (1977) shows that resistance to and contestation of educational norms is characteristic of many working-class children. They do not simply accept their apparent academic inadequacies and so move into low-grade work as a consequence. Rather they understand the authority system of a school and skilfully resist it for their own ends and the pleasure in conflict. This set of skills is then carried forward into the often mundane blue-collar jobs to which they have access and from which they also expect little direct satisfaction. Nevertheless, material realities begin to intrude as workers in such occupations find themselves trapped in low-paid drudgery from which education might have been an escape.

The lack of control over the nature and volume of its supply relative to the nature and volume of demand for it seems to place labour in a dependent position with respect to capital. But this dependence cuts both ways. On the one hand, labour is dependent upon waged work in order to make a living; it needs to be able to be incorporated into the circuit of social reproduction and cannot, as Jamie Peck (1996, p. 27) remarks, 'wait . . . until conditions are more favourable. In effect, it is thrown onto the labor market and must adjust its expectations to the prevailing (local) conditions.'

This gives capital the decisive advantage. The history of the partial closure of the Rover Group's car plant at Cowley (Hayter and Harvey, 1993) offers a rich account of the forces involved here. But, on the other hand, precisely because neither labour nor capital can regulate the supply of labour, there are places where and times when labour has the upper hand as capital is also dependent upon access to labour to create the surplus. However, a critical difference between capital and labour lies in the former's mobility, which can be expressed geographically, sectorially and in terms of the alternative circuits and fractions of capital through which it may accumulate a surplus. The ability of capital to move increases its power over more place-bound labour.

But this mobility should not be over-exaggerated or over-generalized (see, for example, Cox, 1997). Investment in fixed capital – especially involving the built environment – must, by definition, be fixed in place and represents a substantial commitment, much of which in the form of sunk costs could not be retrieved should the investment fail. Furthermore, the need of capital for certain qualities of labour cannot be satisfied as if the labour market was wholly undifferentiated, in terms of skills for example, and as if it was contained and functioned on the head of a pin. Localized skills and work traditions, to say nothing of the commitment of communities to certain capitals, decrease the mobility of capital and open up a space of power for labour to exploit. Furthermore, the disruptive potential of labour excluded from the controls exerted by participation in regular work and from the ability to participate effectively within civil society as a result of exclusion offers a perpetual threat to the sustained accumulation of capital within the circuit.

The politics of negotiating performance and control between labour and capital in establishing the employment relation (Burawoy, 1985; and see discussion of Willis's, 1977, work above) is reflected in the segmentation of labour markets. Storper and Walker (1989, p. 171) suggest that segmentation is an unintended consequence of the indeterminate politics of 'the conflict between labour and capital within socially- and technically-defined strategic conditions'. Until the mid-1970s, the labour markets of the USA and western Europe were characterized by: an *independent primary segment* in which rewards, security and autonomy were high; a *subordinate primary* sector with reasonably high rewards and stable employment but lower levels of autonomy and higher risks of lay-offs; and a *secondary labour market* characterized by high levels of social control, no autonomy, physical discomfort and low rewards. This segmentation was reproduced and regulated by institutions (including trades unions) within the labour market. Since the mid-1970s, however, transitions within contemporary economies have served to restructure the subordinate, secondary and, to a much lesser extent, the independent primary segments. Fordist production, which was enabled by the development of the former segment, is in decline (in relative if not absolute terms) and productivity increases are essential for maintaining competitiveness. By contrast, subcontracting and outwork are on the increase with conditions (temporary and part-time work, often, thereby, excluded from a range of legal rights of labour) typical of the secondary labour market segment.

Even in the most market-driven circuits of social reproduction, the labour market faces endemic limits. It is hardly surprising, then, that regulation must aim to secure a number of crucial conditions to facilitate the incorporation of labour within the circuit of capital and to control its relationships with the circuit when excluded from it:

- *encourage participation* – rather than merely force participation through material desperation – in the labour market, not least by the pressure of status of participation and the stigma of non-participation;
- *define the limits of non-participation* in the labour market by identifying those (e.g. young children, the elderly) who might legitimately be excused participation and by the maintenance of conditions for the majority whereby non-participation is materially unsustainable. But beyond participants and non-participants, it is also important to define a third component of the labour market:

> Labor markets could not function if the entire [working] population sought actively to participate in waged work or to withdraw [its] labor from the market. (Peck, 1996, p. 33)

There is therefore a need to exert control over exempted labour both to facilitate their inclusion within the circuit of capital if necessary and to avoid their subversive organization against or demands on the circuit. A number of institutions such as the family, the armed forces, prisons, social security programmes, schools and hospitals act as a means of regulating that part of the labour force outside the labour market;

- *sustain an acceptable balance between the waged and unwaged segments* of the population by macro-economic measures designed to deal with cyclical (temporary) imbalances in the demand for labour and putting longer-term conditions in place to cope with structural changes (e.g. those emanating from systematic technical change or from changes in the pattern of demand). These circumstances are especially tricky because their effect is selective and leads to the increasingly systematic exclusion from the labour market of certain groups.

But the regulation of the labour market in sustaining the circuit of social reproduction under capitalism is highly complex and difficult. As Jamie Peck (1996, p. 75) points out

> labor market structures and dynamics do not derive from a fully coherent inner logic... There is not one set of (competitive) labor market rules, embedded within an overarching (market) rationality. Rather, the labor market is a complex, composite structure bearing the imprints of a diverse range of influences.

So, despite the claims of neoclassical theories, labour markets cannot be

> governed by the single, all-pervasive logic of the rationality of the market; in fact, they are places where logics collide.... The conflicting motivations, goals, and strategic practices of different groups in the labor market – which divide not only capital and labor but also social fractions within these aggregates – call for a conception of the labor market as a *socially constructed and politically mediated* structure of conflict between contending forces. (Peck, 1996, p. 2)

The exogeneity of labour which shapes this 'structure of conflict' also points to the crucial significance of geography for an understanding of labour markets. Labour is place-bound not only in terms of limited mobility in relation to capital – which can, therefore, use locational adjustment in the politics of negotiation with labour – but in terms of its own identity and reproduction.

The significance of geographical variation has been conceded primarily in a recognition of nationally differentiated labour markets and in an acceptance that distinctive social relations within national social formations shape the resolution of the tensions between production and reproduction arising from the exogeneity of labour through nationally based systems of regulation. But all labour markets are territorially constituted (again, not least as a result of exogeneity) and, although significant explanatory roles are assigned to national social formations, the formative geographies of labour markets operate at all spatial scales. Furthermore, under conditions of space–time convergence and distanciation, the geographical scales over which labour markets operate become increasingly intertwined and mutually influential (e.g. Cox, 1997). They overlap and interpenetrate in a multi-scalar process of territorial constitution and reconstitution.

Space–time compression is, for example, causing national regulatory systems to examine ways of adjusting to apparently low-cost labour markets and systems of regulation in ways which are conformable with both global competition and the distinctiveness of national social formations. At the same time, international labour markets are being promoted both within economic blocs such as the EU and within corporate circuits of capital. The unevenness of increasingly compressed global geographies of production, realization and HEGEMONY is creating uneven demands for specialized labour in different parts of the world economic geography – within global financial centres, for example – and so are generating mechanisms of, on the one hand, selective local recruitment and, on the other, international labour migration to cope with imbalances in the availability of skilled, specialized and committed labour.

But the direction of causality is not merely from global to local. Local conditions – including, for example, historical geographies, norms, politics, labour relations – shape local labour markets and the possibilities for local change (see, for example, Wills, 1998). Attempts to derive simple cartographies of labour markets miss this point as they posit an influential container which can at best be an almost meaningless geographical average based on arbitrary notions of where the labour markets begin and end in space. As Jamie Peck (1996, ch. 4) expresses it, such concerns are with the edge of labour markets. But the (re/dis)incorporation of labour involves processes operating at the centre and not least the complex social geographies of unionization (e.g. Martin, Sunley and Wills, 1996).

What defines local labour markets are the relationships between workplace, home and residential setting – relationships which open up the most profound influences upon labour markets – and the complex influences of the connections and contradictions between production and reproduction. The construction of gendered labour markets illustrates the complex, two-way relationships between local geographies of labour – including the geographically varied availability of information and supportive networks – and geographies of production as articulated through the geographically conditioned operation of local labour markets (Hanson and Pratt 1995). The geographically uneven gendered supply of labour is a product in part of the local construction of gendered supply as well as of the (current and past) requirements of production (see GENDER AND GEOGRAPHY). The demand from capital is not, therefore, determinant and this relationship offers a further point of leverage to labour in shaping the conditions of its incorporation into the productive process. RL

References

Bourdieu, P. 1986: *Distinction: a social critique of judgements of taste*. London and New York: Routledge. · Bourdieu, P. 1988: *Language and symbolic power*. Cambridge and Oxford: Polity Press. · Bowles, S. and Gintis, P. 1976: *Schooling in capitalist America*. London: Routledge and Kegan Paul. · Burawoy, M. 1985: *The politics of production*. London: Verso. · Cox, K. 1997: Globalization and geographies of workers' struggle in the late twentieth century. In R. Lee and J. Wills, eds, *Geographies of economies*, ch. 14. London and New York: Arnold, 177–85. · Hanson, S. and Pratt, G. 1995: *Gender, work and space*. London and New York: Routledge. · Hayter, T. and Harvey, D., eds, 1993: *The factory and the city. The story of the Cowley automobile workers in Oxford*. London and New York: Mansell. · Martin, R., Sunley, P. and Wills, J. 1996: *Union retreat and the regions: the shrinking landscape of organized labour*. London: Jessica Kingsley. · Peck, J. 1996: *Work-place. The social regulation of labour markets*. New York and London: Guilford Press. · Picchio, A. 1992: *Social reproduction: the political economy of the labour market*. Cambridge: Cambridge University Press. · Storper, M. and Walker, R. 1983: The theory of labour and the theory of location. *International Journal of Urban and Regional Research* 7: 1–41. · Storper, M. and Walker, R. 1989: *The capitalist imperative*, ch. 6. New York and Oxford: Basil Blackwell. · Urry, J. 1981: *The anatomy of capitalist societies*. London: Macmillan; Weber, M. 1976/1904–5: *The protestant ethic and the spirit of capitalism*. London: Allen and Unwin. · Willis, P. 1977: *Learning to labour: how working class kids get working class jobs*. Aldershot: Saxon House. · Wills, J. 1998: A stake in place? The geography of employee ownership and its implications for a stakeholding society. *Transactions of the Institute of British Geographers* NS 23 (1): 79–94.

Suggested Reading

Cox (1997). · Hanson and Pratt (1995). · Hayter and Harvey (1993). · Peck (1996). · Willis (1977).

labour process '. . . a process by which man, through his own actions, mediates, regulates and controls the metabolism between himself and nature' (Marx, 1976). The sexism in this definition reflects the widespread tendency to assume (correctly in some places at some times but far from inherently correct and, in developed industrial economies, increasingly incorrectly) both that participation in the labour process is restricted to wage labour and that males dominate the waged labour force.

The universal characteristics of the labour process include work itself, the object upon which work is undertaken, and the instruments of labour. But human labour is characterized above all by thought and symbolism (Godelier, 1986). Despite the fact that

> a bee would put many an architect to shame by the construction of its honeycomb cells . . . what distinguishes the worst of architects from the best of bees is that the architect builds the cell in his mind before he [sic] constructs it in wax. . . . Man [sic] not only effects a change of form in the materials of nature; he [sic] also realizes his own purpose in those materials. (Marx, 1976)

It is this aspect of the labour process that has been most profoundly modified in capitalist production.

Marx distinguishes between the formal subsumption of labour by CAPITAL, in which labour is subordinated by capital simply by the compulsion for people to sell their labour power in order to survive, and the real subsumption of labour by capital in which capital reorganizes the labour process itself. In the former circumstance, capital has to accept labour as it finds it and so remains dependent upon its workers' bargainable skills and crafts. Under these conditions, the best that can be achieved is the production of absolute surplus value, involving an extension of the working day (see MARXIAN ECONOMICS). With the capitalist transformation of the labour process, the attempt is made formally to subsume labour to capital. But the special nature of labour power as a commodity turns this process into an indeterminate political rather than purely economic or technical dynamic (compare Storper and Walker, 1989 with Dunford and Perrons, 1983; see LABOUR MARKET).

Beginning with the capitalist organization of cooperation between craft workers, capital may secure an ever more rigorous hold over the labour process through the DIVISION OF LABOUR and manufacture, the introduction of machinery, the growth of large-scale industry and the emergence of the factory system (see INDUSTRIAL REVOLUTION). With these developments comes the ability to modify the labour process in order to increase productivity and so to produce relative surplus value (see MARXIAN ECONOMICS). Associated with these changes comes a monumental physical and geographical revolution in production and the re-evaluation of skill.

Not the least significant manifestation of this is the separation of home and work. In pre-industrial societies and for many in the Third World today, home and work are not separate. With the development of modern industry and the rise of the factory system the separation of work and home began and, as the process continued, workers came to be hired on an individualistic rather than a household basis. One response to this was the succession of Factory Acts designed to protect women and children from exploitation and so explicitly gendering the new geographies of labour markets and labour processes (see GENDER AND

GEOGRAPHY). Women's employment outside the home – even if employed in domestic service – remained low until the early part of the twentieth century since when it has risen more or less continuously and markedly so during two world wars.

Today the rate of female (waged) employment is approaching that of male employment in many countries but women are grossly over-represented in poorly paid, routine operations and have moved into such work as technology and organizational change have combined to redefine its status and nature. In 1850 in the UK, for example, 99 per cent of clerks were men; in 1991 nearly 90 per cent of clerical workers and 98 per cent of secretaries in the UK were women (Giddens, 1997). Far more women are in part-time jobs than men and the growth of employment in 'flexible' labour markets like the UK has been fuelled primarily by part-time and often poorly paid female employment. At the other end of the spectrum, women are grossly under-represented in top jobs in the professions and as senior managers and company directors/partners, to say nothing of their rarity as university professors. And, where they are present, they face a range of difficulties emanating from the presumption of such jobs as men's work and from the continuing hegemony and cultural capital established in the nineteenth century (see e.g. McDowell, 1997a, 1997b).

Within the workplace, scientific management, developed from the practices of Henry Ford and the principles of F.W. Taylor (see FORDISM), redefined the nature of work further by the pre-planning and complete specification of every aspect of the labour process. Scientific management further separates the mental and the manual aspects of work and intensifies the demand for management, engineering and design specialists, increases the specialization of skilled and semi-skilled labour and increases the demand for that labour to operate but not control machines. This separation has facilitated the NEW INTERNATIONAL DIVISION OF LABOUR, as capital has been able to separate its productive operations into a hierarchy of activities, with global management at the top of the hierarchy and production at the bottom (see Massey, 1995).

These changes may be summarized (see, for example, Dunford and Perrons, 1983) as four phases of development of the labour process:

- *manufacture*: independent workers gathered together into workshops; rudimentary division of labour;
- *machinofacture*: mechanization, the application of inanimate power and the division of labour extends human labour power and individual production;
- *scientific management and Fordism*: scientific division of work into specialized tasks and the introduction of the moving assembly line;
- *neo-Fordism*: further fragmentation of tasks and increasing automation and mechanization of thought through computer-aided design and production.

Despite this apparent progression of change, the crisis of Fordism is due in large measure to the limitations of its labour process. It is inflexible, capital-intensive, producer-orientated and, notwithstanding its rhetoric of labour control, susceptible to disruption by labour – a contradiction which provided the theme for Charlie Chaplin's 1936 film, *Modern Times*.

Microelectronic technology now allows the complete reintegration of material and information handling (formerly integrated by labour) at the corporate level and so completes the subordination of labour by capital. The crisis of Fordism is thought to be leading not only to the restructuring of the workplace (Meegan, 1988) but of the workforce and labour process too (Harvey, 1989). Functional and numerical flexibility are seen as critical responses to the increasingly intense levels of global competition in an uncertain environment, although the evidence for such changes is far from fully convincing (Allen, 1988).

As always with the labour process, the future is uncertain and far from determined in a simple fashion. It seems likely that specialization, standardization and routinization will continue – with all the implications that such processes may have for the segmentation of labour – and, at the same time, an increasing flexibility of the production process and of the organization of production will develop further. The combined effect of these processes will increase the geographical and sectorial diversity of the labour process. Thus Ray Hudson (1997, p. 303) points to current attempts by capital to experiment with 'high volume production' (HVP) which

> seek to combine the benefits of economies of scope and greater flexibility in responding to consumer demand which are characteristic of small batch production with those of economies of scale characteristic of mass production.

They include JUST-IN-TIME PRODUCTION, lean production, dynamic flexibility, flexible automation and mass customization. Tellingly, his conclusion is that HVP is no more a permanent solution to the sustenance of profitability than was the displacement of craft production by mass production or the once revolutionary innovations of Taylorism–Fordism, due not least to the global differentiation of labour markets.

Labour is far from being a passive element in the development of the labour process (e.g. Wills, 1998): Marx's own account of the course of the Industrial Revolution stresses that point. The development of capitalist production has followed certain tendencies to which labour has responded in a variety of ways, many of which have, paradoxically, tended to stabilize and ensure the reproduction of capitalist production (Urry, 1981). Changes in the forces of production do not deterministically bring forth appropriate changes in the relations of production and the labour force remains influential in the effectivity of production technology. As Halford and Savage (1997) have shown, gender is deeply embodied in organizational RESTRUCTURING and in the deskilling/reskilling processes. Labour is, therefore, able to contest and resist these processes discussed in a more deterministic fashion by Braverman (1974). And resistance to HVP, for example, may come from the possibilities of disrupting production, provided that labour is able to organize across national boundaries.

Thus, neither is geography passive; on the contrary, geography matters. Geography is an active element which shapes the labour process by presenting a diverse range of conditions for production by conditioning production strategies and, through the influence of local social structures and cultures, by influencing the detailed operation of particular processes of production (see, e.g., Herod, 1998). RL

References

Allen, J. 1988: Fragmented firms, disorganized labour? In J. Allen and D. Massey, eds, *The economy in question*. London and Newbury Park, CA: Sage, ch. 5. · Braverman, H. 1974: *Labour and monopoly capital. The degradation of work in the twentieth century*. New York and London: Monthly Review Press. · Dunford, M. and Perrons, D. 1983: *The arena of capital*. London and Basingstoke: Macmillan; New York: St. Martin's Press, part III. · Giddens, A. 1997: *Sociology*, 3rd edn. Cambridge and Oxford: Polity Press. · Godelier, M. 1986: *The mental and the material*. London and New York: Verso. · Halford, S. and Savage, M. 1997: Rethinking restructuring: embodiment, agency and identity in organizational change. In R. Lee and J. Wills, eds, *Geographies of economies*, ch. 9. London and New York: Arnold, 108–17. · Harvey, D. 1982: *The limits to capital*. Oxford: Basil Blackwell; Chicago: University of Chicago Press, ch. 4. · Harvey, D. 1989: *The condition of postmodernity*. Oxford and Cambridge, MA: Basil Blackwell, ch. 9. · Herod, A. 1998: Discourse on the docks: containerization and inter-union work disputes in US ports 1955–1985. *Transactions of the Institute of British Geographers* NS 23. · Hudson, R. 1997: The end of mass production and of the mass collective worker? Experimenting with production and employment. In R. Lee and J. Wills, eds, *Geographies of economies*, ch. 23. London and New York: Arnold, 302–10. · Marx, K. 1976 [orig. pub. 1867]: *Capital*, vol. 1. Harmondsworth: Penguin, ch. 7. · Massey, D. 1995: *Spatial divisions of labour*, 2nd edn. London and Basingstoke: Macmillan. · McDowell, L. 1997a: A tale of two cities? Embedded organizations and embodied workers in the City of London. In R. Lee and J. Wills, eds, *Geographies of economies*, ch. 10. London and New York: Arnold, 118–29. · McDowell, L. 1997b: *Capital culture: gender at work in the city*. Oxford: Blackwell. · Meegan, R. 1988: A crisis of mass production? In J. Allen and D. Massey, eds, *The economy in question*, ch. 4. London and Newbury Park, CA: Sage. · Storper, M. and Walker, R. 1989: *The capitalist imperative*. New York and Oxford: Basil Blackwell, ch. 6. · Urry, J. 1981: *The anatomy of capitalist societies*. London and Basingstoke: Macmillan; Atlantic Highlands, NJ: Humanities Press, ch. 7. · Wills, J. 1998: A stake in place? The geography of employee ownership and its implications for a stakeholding society. *Transactions of the Institute of British Geographers* NS 23: 79–94.

Suggested Reading

Hudson (1997). · McDowell (1997b).

labour theory of value A theory in economics about the origin of value which attributes its entire content to labour. The technical argument is explained in the entry on MARXIAN ECONOMICS: briefly, all the necessary ingredients in the process of production have their origin in the expenditure of labour, which makes the machines (or capital equipment) capable of utilizing raw materials as well as running the factories, farms and so on in which production takes place. It follows that all the VALUE ADDED to otherwise valueless natural resources can ultimately be traced back to labour: hence the reference sometimes made to capital as 'dead labour'.

As well as purporting to describe the technical process of production in a positive manner, the labour theory of value has normative content as contributing to a theory of SOCIAL JUSTICE. Central to this is the concept of *exploitation*, whereby under capitalism those who own the means of production are able to take some of the value which labour has produced, i.e. *surplus value*. That the relationship between exploitation and distributive justice is subject to different interpretations reveals some fundamental issues which arise in linking Marxism to social justice.

Marx conceded that capitalist exchange relations (including the appropriation of surplus value by the capitalist class) are just according to the rules of capitalist society, and its prevailing ideology: they are in accordance with the law in that kind of society. This narrow and relativistic view of social justice has encouraged the interpretation that Marx was not interested in morality except as an aspect of ideology. However, while Marx does not actually describe surplus appropriation as unjust, he does refer to it in such terms as theft, embezzlement and robbery, which amounts to the same thing: to the invocation of universal normative standards. The way capitalists purchase labour-power under the wage contract may be just under 'bourgeois' norms, in that they cover the value of labour-power as determined in the marketplace, but this level of surface appearances obscures what happens when labour is put to use, for it is able to produce something of greater value than what the workers in question are paid, and this surplus accrues to the capitalist. So, what appears to be equal exchange actually enables the capitalist to get something for nothing, the product of unpaid labour.

If exploitation is said to involve capitalist expropriation of what actually belongs to someone else, however, this implies a right or entitlement on the part of labour to the value of what it has produced. Marx is thus asserting a right to the product of natural attributes, which could be thought of as morally arbitrary in the sense of being an outcome of a natural lottery and therefore not a valid basis for desert. Indeed, the claim that people are entitled to realize the value of their holdings, including themselves, is a feature of the conservative philosophy of LIBERTARIANISM. When Marx recognized payment by product as a right, but one which would eventually disappear under communism, he was again alluding to what might be considered just in a particular form of society. In place of 'bourgeois right' as reward according to labour contribution, Marx advocated distribution according to need. Full COMMUNISM was supposed to replace material scarcity with abundance and human selfishness by harmony, so that the axiom of 'from each according to ability and to each according to need' would prevail.

What Marx had proposed implicitly, according to some Marxian scholars, was a conception of justice containing ordered principles. Under CAPITALISM there is exploitation, whereby owners of the means of production take from the value produced by labour. Under the transitional form of SOCIALIST society which replaces capitalism, labour would get the value of its product. When communism finally triumphs, the superior distributional criterion of need comes into play.

The practical issue faced by socialist societies is (or was) how to combine some elements of distribution according to need with the expectation of some reward reflecting value of product so as to provide workers with the incentive to produce in a society still incorporating some individualistic attitudes. This is very similar to the problem faced by governments in liberal societies under capitalism, where criteria of need and contribution are both involved in the distribution of the value of production in the form of public services as well as remuneration. DMS

Suggested Reading

Elster, J. 1985: *Making sense of Marx*. Cambridge: Cambridge University Press. · Geras, N. 1985: The controversy about Marx and justice. *New Left Review* 150: 47–85. · Geras, N. 1992: Bringing Marx to justice: an addendum and rejoinder. *New Left Review* 195: 37–69. · McCarney, J. 1992: Marx and justice again. *New Left Review* 195: 29–36. · Peffer, R.G. 1990: *Marxism, Morality and Social Justice*. Princeton: Princeton University Press. · Smith, D.M. 1994: *Geography and social justice*. Oxford: Blackwell Publishers, 86–98.

Lamarck(ian)ism A non-Darwinian theory of evolutionary change originating with the French naturalist Jean Baptiste de Lamarck. As a doctrine of organic progression, Lamarckism in the pre-Darwinian period differed substantially from its post-Darwinian Neo-Lamarckian successor. Lamarck himself did *not* conceive of evolution as a system of common descent, but rather of 'separate lines progressing in parallel along the same hierarchy' (Bowler, 1989, p. 85). The dynamic behind this organic progress was the active power of NATURE impelling life along predetermined sequences. What facilitated this *tendance de la nature* was the conjoint processes of environmental stimulus and the efforts of organisms to adapt to modified conditions through changed habits and the use and disuse of organs (Burkhardt, 1977).

In the post-Darwinian period it was the Lamarckian insistence on the inheritance of acquired characteristics that provided an alternative mechanism to that of classical Darwinism (Bowler, 1983). In the decades around 1900, when Darwinism itself was in eclipse as a consequence of a series of criticisms within the scientific community, Lamarckian mechanisms achieved considerable support.

These neo-Lamarckians perpetuated certain elements in Lamarck's original system but married them to the principle of natural selection as a secondary mechanism in a distinctively non-Darwinian way.

Particularly in the United States, but also in Britain, this alternative evolutionary theory attracted widespread support during the second half of the nineteenth century (Pfeifer, 1965). Cope and Hyatt spearheaded the movement among paleontologists; LeConte and King added their geological approval; Argyll and Romanes in anthropology and psychology also helped swell the tide. In France, Lamarckian doctrines found institutional expression in the Société Zoologique d'Acclimatation under the direction of Isidore Greffroy St-Hilaire, which systematically investigated the question of environmentally induced hereditary modification – a zoological project that had more or less direct implications for human cosmopolitanism (Osborne, 1994). Even more dramatic was the official endorsement of Lamarckian evolution in the Soviet Union during the 1930s under the influence of T.D. Lysenko; because he was convinced that it fitted more comfortably with Marxist political IDEOLOGY than did classical neo-Darwinism, Lysenko famously erected his theory of agricultural improvement on Lamarckian foundations.

A loose coalition of dissident evolutionary theory was thus available for those with a passion for socializing evolution during the decades around 1900 (Fichman, 1997). Of those conventionally labelled Social Darwinians – not least Spencer himself – many drew more inspiration from neo-Lamarckian dogma than from classical DARWINISM (see also SOCIAL DARWINISM). Thus in neo-Lamarckian evolution, many found grounds for looking to environment as the driving force behind social processes. Others, more taken with the evolutionary significance Lamarckism attributed to mind and will, took a more idealist turn; indeed it was because Lamarckism reserved space for psychic elements in evolution that many sought in it refuge from the 'cultural decay, fatalistic philosophies and genetic determinism' that gripped the end of century *mentalité* (Crook, 1994, p. 73). Either way, Lamarckism could be mobilized to justify the politics of interventionism (Jones, 1980). The ramifications of engaging social Lamarckism were thus many and diverse (Stocking, 1962); it undergirded Herbert Spencer's naturalistic sociology, for example. In the United States Lester Frank Ward found in it the justification for educating his children with the right values for he believed they would then become part of the race's inherited repertoire. Similarly the geologist Joseph Le Conte could only find firm scientific grounds for education in the principles of neo-Lamarckian inheritance (Russett, 1976).

Given these particular conceptual alignments it is not surprising that a number of geographers would find the neo-Lamarckian construal of evolution to their liking, not least because the environment played such a key directive role in the scenario (Campbell and Livingstone, 1983; Livingstone, 1992). In the United States during the late nineteenth and early twentieth centuries, numerous advocates of ENVIRONMENTAL DETERMINISM, such as Shaler, Davis, Semple, Brigham, and Huntington, betray the infiltration of neo-Lamarckism. In one way or another, these environmentalist geographers fastened upon the heritability of environmentally induced modifications both physically and culturally. Similarly, the recapitulationist strains in Turner's FRONTIER THESIS, which portrayed American society as recapitulating the stages of social evolution with each advance of the settlement frontier, drew inspiration from Lamarckian environmentalism (Coleman, 1966). Griffith Taylor in Australia equally found elements of the Lamarckian system attractive, though he did not discount the significance of Mendelian genetics in his elaboration of racial history and ECOLOGY which built on the work of the vertebrate paleontologist, William D. Matthew, whose *Climate and evolution* of 1915 closely connected mammalian evolution with climatic conditions (Christie, 1994).

In late Victorian Britain similar convictions are discernible among those who were drawn to Lamarckism's emphasis on the directive evolutionary significance of consciousness. Geddes, for instance, used it to advocate various URBAN PLANNING and educational reforms; Kropotkin, critical of the cut-throat ethics of capitalist competitive struggle (cf. CAPITALISM), found in Lamarckism the grounds for a more benign social order – an anarchistic humanism – built upon mutual aid (Todes, 1989; cf. ANARCHISM); and Herbertson and Fleure both mobilized the idea in their considerations of REGIONAL GEOGRAPHY. Lamarckian motifs have also been discerned in Vidal de la Blache's *géographie humaine* (see POSSIBILISM) which, while stressing the transforming power of human agency, nonetheless retained strongly naturalistic, ecological, and organicist strains (Archer, 1993).

In more general terms, neo-Lamarckism facilitated geography's transition from a natural theology framework to that of evolutionary naturalism largely due to the ease with which it could be given a teleological reading (Livingstone, 1984). And this, together with its widespread influence on numerous key individuals, demonstrates how profound its impact on the modern geographical tradition has been. DNL

References

Archer, K. 1993: Regions as social organisms: the Lamarckian characteristics of Vidal de la Blache's regional geography. *Annals of the Association of American Geographers* 83: 498–514. · Bowler, P.J. 1983: *The eclipse of Darwinism. Anti-Darwinian evolution theories in the decades around 1900.* Baltimore and London: Johns Hopkins University Press. · Bowler, P.J. 1989: *Evolution. The history of an idea*, 2nd edn. Berkeley, Los Angeles and London: University of California Press. · Burkhardt, R.W. 1977: *The spirit of system: Lamarck and evolutionary biology.* Cambridge, MA and London: Harvard University Press. · Campbell, J.A. and Livingstone, D.N. 1983: Neo-Lamarckism and the development of geography in the United States and Great Britain. *Transactions, Institute of British Geographers* NS 8: 267–94. · Christie, N. 1994: Environment and race: Geography's search for a Darwinian synthesis. In R. MacLeod and P.E. Rehbock, eds, *Darwin's laboratory: evolutionary theory and natural history in the Pacific.* Honolulu: University of Hawaii Press. · Coleman, W. 1966: Science and symbol in the Turner frontier hypothesis. *American Historical Review* 72: 22–49. · Crook, P. 1994: *Darwinism, war and history: the debate over the biology of war from the 'Origin of species' to the first world war.* Cambridge: Cambridge University Press. · Fichman, M. 1997: Biology and politics: defining the boundaries. In B. Lightman, ed., *Victorian science in context.* Chicago: University of Chicago Press, 94–118. · Jones, G. 1980: *Social Darwinism and English thought: the interaction between biological and social theory.* Brighton: Harvester Press; Livingstone, D.N. 1984: Natural theology and Neo-Lamarckism: the changing context of nineteenth century geography in the United States and Great Britain. *Annals of the Association of American Geographers* 74: 9–28. · Livingstone, D.N. 1992: *The geographical tradition. Episodes in the history of a contested enterprise.* Oxford and Cambridge, MA: Basil Blackwell. · Osborne, MA, 1994: *Nature, the exotic, and the science of French colonialism.* Bloomington: Indiana University Press. · Pfeifer, E.J. 1965: The genesis of American Neo-Lamarckism. *Isis* 56: 156–67. · Russett, C.E. 1976: *Darwin in America. The intellectual response 1865–1912.* San Francisco: W.H. Freeman. · Stocking, G.W. Jr. 1962: Lamarckianism in American social science: 1890–1915. *Journal of the History of Ideas* 23: 239–56. · Todes, D.P. 1989: *Darwin without Malthus: the struggle for existence in Russian evolutionary thought.* Oxford: Oxford University Press.

land rights The institutionalized forms of access to, and control over, land, typically understood as a subset of property rights in general. Insofar as land rights express a relation between a thing and persons, these complex social relationships are usually referred to as Land Tenure. Land rights typically constitute land as property which involves some jural entity (individuals, households, lineages, communities, corporations, nations and so on) that has rights and duties over some object (land in this case) against other jural entities (cf. PROPERTY RIGHTS). Land rights are, however, always more complex than public (STATE ownership and transfer) versus private (a jural person is the owner in which a market system of transfer is implied) for the very good reasons that virtually everywhere complex mixtures of group (or communal) and individual (private) control exist.

Rights over land are customarily divided into: *use rights* (grazing, farming, passage, urban construction, collection and so on); *transfer rights* (movement of ownership or possession through inheritance, gift, sale, pledging, lending and so on); and *administrative rights* (the authority to allocate or withdraw land from use, to tax it, collect tribute from it, to arbitrate disputes, regulate transfers, entitle it and so on). Rights over land do not necessarily imply ownership (i.e. there can be rights of use or rental). Similarly communal or COLLECTIVE forms of land management – for example customary land law in Muslim northern Nigeria – may confer substantial 'ownership' security to some individuals; that is to say there are stable and secure use rights in perpetuity. Fully privatized land rights – *fee simple* – in which rights to sell are not proscribed by laws that assign ultimate ownership to the state or to the powers of indigenous COMMUNITIES, are far from universal.

Rights are often divided among different units of aggregation that claim different 'bundles of rights'. Such bundles may be nested or ranked in 'hierarchies of estates' (Glucksman, 1965). But a right of access for one purpose (collecting wood) does not always imply automatic access for another (grazing). Concepts of rights are often rooted in modes of livelihood and their relation to the market. Pastoral communities may have rights to rangeland as a 'common property' system (McCay and Acheson, 1987): this does not mean open access (*res nullius*) but rather complex lineage or confederal systems of regulation which link land and water rights (*res communes*). Foragers may have rights of use rather than ownership.

Typically a distinction is made between systems of rights over land rooted in customary or traditional law, and European systems of property law. African systems of customary law are especially complex and have survived into the post-colonial period (but not without change) as a deliberate artefact of COLONIAL policy to sustain (i.e. not to disrupt radically) local 'tribal' or ethnic institutions (Bassett and Crummey, 1993). Customary law allocates bundles of rights; that is to say the identification of some forms of farmland as family or collective confers particular obligations (everyone must work on them) and disposition (by the male head of household). Personal plots may be for individual gain and use. Allocation of land rights in customary conditions may be through the intermediation of village heads or male heads of households. Women therefore may gain (and lose) access to land rights through marriage. Gender and conjugality are typically important dimensions of land rights allocation in rural African communities which confirms the fact that land rights are not so much about relations between people and things as between people.

Customary law or traditional land rights are often counterpoised against European notions of property. But it should be remembered that custom is dynamic and flexible and was manipulated by colonial states as much as local PEASANTS and headmen during the colonial period as market and other opportunities arose. As a consequence the history of customary land rights is riven with complex struggles and negotiations over bundles of rights and duties, only some of which reached local courts (Berry, 1993). In the post-colonial period, growing commercialization, land scarcity and efforts at state regulation and registration have further deepened these complex material and symbolic struggles over land rights (Carney and Watts, 1990). The possibility of female exclusion is always present in what passes as the MODERNIZATION of customary tenure. If customary land rights are dynamic and complex, European property rights – the exercise of a perpetual, exclusive and absolute right over land – is also far from a piece: English and French legal traditions differ quite substantially, for example.

In family farm systems under freehold or so-called communal or customary land rights, it is often assumed that there are necessarily problems of access to credit (no collateral confirmed by insecure land rights), tenancy regulation, taxation (inchoate senses of ownership) and fragmentation. Land titles and registration are seen as ways of resolving these problems, by reducing the problems of asymmetric information (knowledge and trust is undermined as sales increase between community and non-community buyers and sellers) and providing an institutional framework to facilitate land sales. Such transfers are assumed to enhance efficiency by transferring land from bad to better farmers and by ensuring credit through collateral. In practice, however, various forms of land titling under state auspices (for example in Kenya) have produced greater land concentration, dispossession, and loss of rights by vulnerable groups (especially women: see Downs and Reyna, 1988).

Boserup (1965) has provided an account of the emergence of private rights in land as POPULATION DENSITY increases. Her discussion makes clear that property rights in land are not simple and unrestricted; neither is the process linear. As land becomes scarce, general and inheritable cultivation and grazing rights are complemented by rights to resume cultivating specific plots after fallow, to inherit specific plots not general cultivation rights, to rent out plots, to use them as collateral, and to sell land within the community. When the right to sell includes sales outside the community, the last vestiges of custom disappear and private rights are complete. Much of the work on African land rights – which are some of the most complex in the world – has shown how the Boserup model is too narrowly demographic and obscures the unevenness and irregularity of 'privatization' (Bassett and Crummey, 1993; Berry, 1993). It is precisely because land is a fictitious commodity, embedded in social and cultural relations under customary law, that the process by which land is converted into property will always be contested and a matter of symbolic struggle (Polanyi, 1944).

Titling and registration are ways in which rights and duties over land are changed; that is to say they are instances of land or agrarian reform. Land reform aims at transforming agrarian structure – that is a system of social relations and a system of land tenure/rights. Land reform can have a multiplicity of forms and implications for land rights, however. In some cases reform may involve little more than the regularization and stabilization of tenant rights. In others there may be widespread appropriation of land above specified ceilings, and redistributions of land to landless tenants and semi-proletarians (for example the Land-to-the-Tiller Programmes in Taiwan and Kerala: see Herring, 1980). During the twentieth century, most land reforms within capitalism – unlike the experience of collectivization in the former socialist bloc – were of two broad types: *anti-feudal*, seeking to spur on commercialization and accumulation through a landed elite, a commercial farmer class or peasants; and seeking to create shifts in the dominant rural class from *capitalist landed elites to smallholder or* PEASANT *operations*, or to amplify the reform sector under one of these groups (de Janvry, 1980). Land reform as a way of transforming land rights can therefore fulfil conservative, liberal, populist or radical political impulses. The collectivization of land rights in the name of SOCIALISM has been an object of extraordinary debate, not only over the use and consequences of state violence, but also in terms of the lacks of incentives within agrarian socialist systems (Medvedev, 1980).

Land rights which take the form of rental or tenancy have played a particularly important role in economic and classical political economic theory. The early work on the AGRARIAN QUESTION addressed the issue of the English road to agrarian CAPITALISM in which large landowners actually rented land to an aggressive CLASS of commercial farmers. Debates over the purported parasitic nature of landlords, and of the consequences of land RENT on capitalist ACCUMULATION, have a long pedigree (Harvey, 1982). More recently, tenancy and sharecropping have been explored by institutional economists for whom property right assignments (share-tenancies for example) are 'second best' adaptations of farmers in rural areas of the THIRD WORLD to informational and market imperfections. Communal land rights or SHARECROPPING can be seen as adaptations to high TRANSACTION COSTS or to the imperfections of intertemporal markets (Binswanger and Delinger, 1995). Political economists often see these land rights as sources of exploitation, and focus more on the struggles over the determination of the share or rental agreement. While peasant and Third World agricultures have always been characterized by complex contractual relations and inter-linked markets (land rights for example may be linked to credit), agricultural production in the advanced capitalist states is increasingly characterized by forms of contracting in which private ownership of land and assets is tied to a company which specifies control over the production, price and quality of products (Watts, 1994; cf. AGRIBUSINESS; AGRO-FOOD SYSTEM).

In the wake of the collapse of actually existing socialisms in 1989, and the earlier reforms in China and eastern Europe in the 1960s and 1970s, one of the most important recent reconfigurations of land rights has been the so-called decollectivization of state farms and communes (Szelenyi, 1998). Personal ownership of land in socialist economies was rarely obliterated but the reforms slowly reintroduced various forms of personalized use and *de facto* long-term ownership (for example 99 tenancy types in Vietnam). The variation within the former socialist bloc has been enormous. In some cases (China), the decollectivization witnessed a remarkably egalitarian redistribution of private property rights in land; in others there have been highly contested forms of land restitution (Nicaragua, Hungary); and in others nothing short of administrative chaos (Russia) as the weakened state is incapable of providing an institutional structure in which land can be sold or redistributed with the possibility of effective use (Kitching, 1998). The experience of the socialist states affirms the complex forms of hybrid rights which emerge in the name of land privatization, and the complex struggles – the elasticities as Verdery (1993) calls them – of land rights.

Urban land rights, and especially the workings of city property markets, represent another large literature (Roberts, 1977). In many Third World cities urban land is tightly regulated and is accordingly the source of corruption and substantial rents. At the same time, land invasions are common in which SQUATTERS, if they can resist removal by the state, may be able to *de facto* regularize their claim over waste or state-owned lands (cf. SQUATTER SETTLEMENTS). Land markets in North American and European cities have been the object of substantial research (Harvey, 1989; Castells, 1977), especially in relation to real estates, zoning, REDLINING and city structure more generally. MW

References

Bassett, T. and Crummey, J., eds, 1993: *Land in African agrarian systems*. Madison: University of Wisconsin Press. · Berry, S. 1993: *No condition is permanent*. Madison: University of Wisconsin Press; Binswanger, H. and Delinger, K. 1995: *Towards a political economy of agriculture and agrarian relations*. Washington, D.C.: The World Bank. · Boserup, E. 1965: *The conditions of agricultural growth*. New York: Aldine. · Carney, J. and Watts, M. 1990: Disciplining women? *Signs* 16 (4): 651–81. · Castells, M. 1977: *The urban question*. Oxford: Blackwell. · de Janvry, A. 1980: *The agrarian question in Latin America*. Baltimore: Johns Hopkins University Press. · Downs, R. and Reyna, P., eds, 1988: *Land and society in contemporary Africa*. Hanover: University of New Hampshire Press. · Glucksman 1965: *Politics, law and ritual in tribal society*. Oxford: Blackwell. · Harvey, D. 1982: *Limits to capital*. Oxford: Blackwell. · Harvey, D. 1989: *The urban experience*. Oxford: Blackwell.

· Herring, R. 1980: *Land to the tiller*. New Haven, CT: Yale University Press. · Kitching, G. 1998: The revenge of the peasant. *Journal of Peasant Studies* 26 (1): 43–81. · McCay, B. and Acheson, J., eds, 1987: *The question of the commons*. Tuscon: University of Arizona Press. · Medvedev, R. 1980: *Soviet agriculture*. New York: Norton. · Polanyi, K. 1944: *The Great Transformation*. Boston: Beacon. · Roberts, B.R. 1977: *Cities of peasants*. New York: Sage. · Szelenyi, I., ed., 1998: *Privatizing the land*. London: Routledge. · Verdery, K. 1993: *What was socialism and what comes next*. Princeton NJ: Princeton University Press. · Watts, M. 1994: Life under contract. In P. Little and M. Watts, eds, *Living under contract*. Madison: University of Wisconsin Press.

Suggested Reading

MacPherson, C.B., ed., 1987: *Property*. Oxford: Blackwell. · Waldron, J. 1988: *The right to private property*. Oxford: Clarendon Press.

land tenure The system of ownership of land and of title to its use, generally in agriculture. Land ownership is usually relatively straightforward compared with rights to use land. Types of land tenure may be classified according to their legal basis; the relative rights of landowner and land-user; the conditions and forms of payment from the latter to the former, if any; and the security of tenants (defined either in terms of duration or of predictability). Many forms of tenure involve very complex combinations of use-rights.

The following are the most important types of land tenure:

Owner occupation. This can involve large-scale modern farms, where the owners utilize wage labour alongside their own; family farms; and PEASANT systems. In the last case, land ownership and use may be vested in a family group rather than a single individual. The continuity of owner occupation is affected by INHERITANCE SYSTEMS, whereby partible inheritance may lead to FARM FRAGMENTATION, a problem that occurs less often under tenancy systems.

Tenancy.This is the most complex type of land tenure, embracing a wide variety of conditions. Tenancy involves the tenant repaying the landowner in some way for being granted the right to use land. Most frequently this payment is in one of three forms: (i) *labour supply* for work on land retained by the owners for their personal or institutional use, as in certain forms of FEUDALISM; (ii) *cash payment*; or (iii) some form of *SHARECROPPING*. Often the landowner's return on leasing the land is made up of a blend of these three elements.

Use right. This is characteristic of SHIFTING CULTIVATION, whereby the question of long-run land ownership is of no significance, and where an individual or communal group establishes a right to the land by using it. Many more intensive agricultural systems include elements of use-right over common land, especially for the grazing of animals.

Institutional with wage labour. Under this form of tenure land is owned by an institution, such as a private company, and agricultural production is the result of a contract employment system. The PLANTATION is the commonest example of land held by this form of tenure.

Collectivist. Land is owned by some collectivist interest, such as the state or whole village (e.g. the *ujamaa* village of Tanzania; see also KIBBUTZ), and individuals participate in a communal farming programme; they have shares in either the produce or the revenue from sales.

Land tenure systems, especially considered dynamically, are more complex than this simple classification allows, for five main reasons. First, individual tenures may not fall neatly into just one category. For example, a large landowner may farm some of the land and lease out the remainder. The largest estates held under this system, *latifundia* or *hacienda* estates, often involve the existence of very small tenant holdings, with the part of the estate kept for the landlord's own use being worked by day labourers. Likewise, the STATE farms that dominated agriculture in SOCIALIST countries at certain periods of the twentieth century can be thought of as an intermediate stage between the 'collectivist' and 'institutional with wage labour' systems of tenure: the land is state-owned (i.e. collectivist) but the farm workers are wage earners rather than participants in the produce of the farms (see also COLLECTIVE).

Secondly, many tenure systems are combinations of various tenure types. Thirdly, the relative frequency of different tenure types may not be the most important facet of a tenurial system. For example, Newby (1986) discusses how the legacy of previously dominant property relations can continue to have greater local effects on social and economic change than their contemporary significance might imply. Fourthly, it may be important to distinguish between the formal-legal components of tenurial relationships and the customary components. The latter are the informally accepted 'normal' practices, but may be poorly protected in law at times of stress (Lane, 1998). Finally, agricultural property rights have become divided in new and more complex ways, as in western agriculture during the

1980s, necessitating more sophisticated geographical analyses. In particular, the diverging interests of various fractions of CAPITAL, and the growing indirect involvement of banking capital in landownership, via the accumulation of land as collateral for loans, have produced new interrelations between ownership, occupation, and use rights over agricultural property (Whatmore et al., 1990).

Issues of land tenure feature prominently in debates about both historical and contemporary agrarian change. Compared with earlier debates, however, current work examines land tenure less as a topic in itself than as a component of rural POWER relations in general (Cloke, 1989). Key historical debates concern the relationships between land tenure, ENCLOSURE, and broader social trends (Tawney, 1912; Snell, 1985; Allen, 1992); between land tenure and agricultural PRODUCTIVITY (Campbell and Overton, 1991; Turner, Beckett and Afton, 1997); and between land tenures and the appearance of the agricultural LANDSCAPE.

Active debates on actual or proposed land reform in many less developed countries mostly concern the break-up of very large estates, often focused on export crops, in favour of the redistribution of land to owner-occupiers or secure tenants concentrating on labour-intensive crops, especially food for domestic consumption (Cleary, 1996). Although such changes involve state planning not only of tenure but also of agricultural institutions and INFRASTRUCTURE, there are widely differing views as to the appropriate balance of state and market forces in new tenurial arrangements (Ghose, 1983; Smith, 1989; Harvey, 1990; Christodolou, 1990; Platteau, 1991).

While the preceding discussion draws on instances from around the contemporary world, the land tenures it covers all represent variants within broadly western traditions, and these are not universal or 'natural'. As much geographical work on COLONIALISM has emphasized, colonial encouragement of settler agricultures often imposed Europeanized landscapes, settlements, and tenures on native life which had 'never [been] associated with owned, fenced land and the reduced ecological diversity of cropped fields' (Harris and Demeritt, 1997, p. 219), but for which 'use right' is too simplistic a category (O'Brien, 1997). PG

References

Allen, R.C. 1992: *Enclosure and the yeoman*. Oxford: Clarendon Press. · Campbell, B.M.S. and Overton, M., eds, 1991: *Land, labour and livestock: historical studies in European agricultural productivity*. Manchester: Manchester University Press. · Christodolou, D. 1990: *The unpromised land: agrarian reform and conflict worldwide*. London: Zed Books. · Cleary, M. 1996: *Tradition and reform: land tenure and rural development in south-east Asia*. Oxford: Oxford University Press. · Cloke, P. 1989: Rural geography and political economy. In R. Peet and N. Thrift, ed., *New models in geography: the political economy perspective, volume 1*. London: Unwin Hyman, 164–97. · Ghose, A.K., ed., 1983: *Agrarian reform in contemporary developing countries*. London: Croom Helm. · Goody, J., Thirsk, J. and Thompson, E.P., eds, 1976: *Family and inheritance: rural society in western Europe 1200–1800*. Cambridge: Cambridge University Press. · Harris, C. and Demeritt, D. 1997: Farming and rural life. In C. Harris, *The Resettlement of British Columbia: essays on colonialism and geographical change*. Vancouver: University of British Columbia Press, 219–49. · Harvey, N. 1990: *The new agrarian movement in Mexico, 1979–1990*. London: Institute of Latin American Studies. · Lane, C., ed., 1998: *Custodians of the commons: pastoral land tenure in east and west Africa*. London: Earthscan. · Newby, H.C., 1986: Locality and rurality: the restructuring of rural social relations. *Regional Studies* 20: 209–26. · O'Brien, J. 1997: *Dispossession by degrees: Indian land and identity in Natick, Massachusetts*. Cambridge: Cambridge University Press. · Platteau, J.-P. 1991: *Formalization and privatization of land-rights in sub-Saharan Africa: a critique of current orthodoxies and structural adjustment programmes*. London: Suntory–Toyota International Centre, London School of Economics. · Smith, G.A. 1989: *Livelihood and resistance: peasants and the politics of land in Peru*. Berkeley: University of California Press. · Snell, K.D.M. 1985: *Annals of the labouring poor: social change and agrarian England 1660–1900*. Cambridge: Cambridge University Press. · Tawney, R.H. 1912: *The agrarian problem in the sixteenth century*. London: Allen and Unwin. · Turner, M.E., Beckett, J.V. and Afton, B. 1997: *Agricultural rent in England 1690–1914*. Cambridge: Cambridge University Press. · Whatmore, S., Munton, R. and Marsden, T. 1990: The rural restructuring process: emerging divisions of agricultural property rights. *Regional Studies* 24: 235–45.

Suggested Reading

Whatmore et al. (1990).

landscape A polysemic term referring to the appearance of an area, the assemblage of objects used to produce that appearance, and the area itself. According to Mikesell (1968), during the Middle Ages in England the term referred to the land controlled by a lord or inhabited by a particular group of people. By the early seventeenth century, however, under the influence of the Dutch *landschap* painters, the term landscape came to refer to the appearance of an area, more particularly to the REPRESENTATION of scenery. By the late nineteenth century, as Mikesell points out, the basis for the contemporary definition of landscape took shape as 'a portion of land or

TERRITORY which the eye can comprehend in a single view, including all the objects so seen, especially in its pictorial aspect'.

The term landscape was introduced into American geography in 1925 by Sauer (1963) with the publication of his monograph *Morphology of landscape*. This influential article drew on the concept of LANDSCHAFT developed by German geographers, most prominently Passarge and Schluter. Sauer put forward the concept of landscape as an alternative to the currently popular form of geographical explanation known as ENVIRONMENTAL DETERMINISM. While the latter sought to specify the causal influences of the environment on humans, the landscape approach sought to describe the interrelations between humans and the environment with primary attention given to the human impact on the environment. Sauer downplayed the subjective aspects of the concept of landscape and stressed that landscape was an objective area to be studied scientifically through observation. Although he paid lip service to the subjective in the latter part of *Morphology* it is clear that he envisaged the study of landscape in geography as a scientific endeavour. Under this view the landscape was defined as 'an area made up of a distinct association of forms, both physical and cultural'. Sauer's position was that geographers should proceed genetically and trace the development of a natural landscape into a CULTURAL LANDSCAPE. The difficulty with this methodology, as Sauer himself soon realized, was that it was seldom possible to reconstruct the appearance of the natural landscape, because the human impact on the face of the earth had been pervasive for many millennia. All landscapes had in effect become cultural landscapes. Thus the study of landscapes by Sauer and his students (who constituted the so-called BERKELEY SCHOOL) became the study of culture history.

Beginning in the 1950s two scholars outside of this Berkeley tradition became influential. The first was the English historian W.G. Hoskins who conducted detailed studies of landscape history. The second was J.B. Jackson who founded *Landscape Magazine* in 1951 and went on to write numerous books of essays on the meaning of the American landscape. To a very large extent the intellectual context for landscape studies from the 1960s on was set by the troika of Sauer and his students, Hoskins and Jackson. The single most significant work to emerge during this period was a volume entitled *The interpretation of ordinary landscapes* edited by Donald Meinig (1979). This volume, which explicitly recognized the influence of Sauer, Hoskins and Jackson, contained contributions from such well-known cultural geographers as J.B. Jackson, Pierce Lewis, David Lowenthal, Donald Meinig, David Sopher, and Yi-Fu Tuan. While this work did not for the most part break new ground, it elegantly summarized the work of this period: a geographer who was not included, but whose work fits within this genre and who has been one of the most prolific and insightful interpreters of the American landscape, is Wilbur Zelinsky (1973). This tradition of landscape analysis focusing upon Sauerian themes of artifactual analysis and culture history continues to flourish.

During the 1980s and early 1990s some new directions in landscape interpretation have been charted, associated with what has been termed the *New* CULTURAL GEOGRAPHY. Although this newer work in many instances maintains important connections to the older landscape tradition, it diverges in explicitly applying social and cultural THEORY to landscape interpretation, and showing greater concern for both the socio-cultural and political processes that shape landscapes as well as the role that landscapes play in these processes (Schein, 1997). Cosgrove (1998) has redefined landscape as a 'way of seeing' rather than as an IMAGE or an object. He argued that this way of seeing is IDEOLOGICAL, representing the way in which a particular class has represented itself and its property. Both Cosgrove (1998) and Cosgrove and Daniels (1988) draw upon marxian cultural critics such as Raymond Williams and John Berger to inform their writings, and apply the notion of iconography drawn from art history to landscape interpretation (cf. ART, GEOGRAPHY AND). James and Nancy Duncan (Duncan and Duncan, 1988; Duncan, 1990) have applied post-structural notions of TEXT and intertexuality drawn from literary theory to the landscape, thereby incorporating landscape interpretation into the debate surrounding postmodernism. Another strand of POST-STRUCTURALISM draws inspiration from Baudrillard and explores landscapes as *simulacras* (Clarke and Doel, 1994). A further model of landscape interpretation is that of theatre (Daniels and Cosgrove, 1993). This dramaturgical approach was suggested by the work of Erving Goffman, although Cosgrove and Daniels focus more attention on the visual and painterly than does Goffman. Cresswell (1996) also adopts a dramaturgical approach, and elaborates a performative model of landscape that focuses on marginality.

The 1990s saw an increase in studies of the politics of landscapes. Some have focused on representations through art and literature (Daniels, 1993; Matless, 1994), while others focus on monuments (Johnson, 1995). The 1990s has also seen a rise in interest in feminist (Rose, 1993; Nash, 1996) and marxian approaches to landscape (Mitchell, 1996) (see FEMINIST GEOGRAPHIES; MARXIST GEOGRAPHY).

The thrust of this new landscape work over the past decade has been not only to theorize the concept of landscape but to show how it forms an important part of social, cultural and political systems. How exactly this should be carried out, however, has been the subject of intense debate (Price and Lewis, 1993; Duncan, 1994). JD

References

Baudrillard, J. 1988: *America*. London: Verso; Clarke, D. and Doel, M. 1994: The perfection of geography as an aesthetic of disappearance. *Ecumene* 1: 317–23. · Cosgrove, D. 1998: *Social formation and symbolic landscape*. Madison: University of Wisconsin Press. · Cosgrove, D. and Daniels, S., eds, 1988: *The iconography of landscape*. Cambridge: Cambridge University Press. · Cresswell, T. 1996: *In place/out of place*. Minneapolis: University of Minnesota Press. · Daniels, S. 1993: *Fields of vision: landscape imagery and national identity in England and the United States*. Princeton: Princeton University Press. · Daniels, S. and Cosgrove, D. 1993: Spectacle and text: landscape metaphors in cultural geography. In J. Duncan and D. Ley, eds, *Place/culture/representation*. London: Routledge, 57–77. · Daniels, S. 1989: Marxism, culture, and the duplicity of landscape. In R. Peet and N. Thrift, eds, *New Models in Geography. Vol. 2*. London: Unwin Hyman, 196–220. · Duncan, J. 1990: *The city as text: the politics of landscape interpretation in the Kandyan kingdom*. Cambridge: Cambridge University Press; Duncan, J. 1994: After the civil war: reconstructing cultural geography as heterotopia. In K. Foote et al., eds, *Re-reading cultural geography*. Austin: University of Texas Press. · Duncan, J. and Duncan, N. 1988: (Re)reading the landscape. *Environment and Planning D: Society and Space* 6: 117–26. · Heffernan, M. 1995. Forever England: the western front and the politics of remembrance in Britain. *Ecumene* 2: 293–324. · Hoskins, W.G. 1955: *The making of the English landscape*. London: Hodder and Stoughton. · Jackson, J.B. 1984: *Discovering the vernacular landscape*. New Haven: Yale University Press. · Johnson, N. 1995: Cast in stone: monuments, geography and nationalism. *Environment and Planning D. Society and Space* 13: 51–66. · Kobayashi, A. 1989: A critique of dialectical landscape. In A. Kobayashi and S. Mackenzie, eds, *Remaking human geography*. London: Unwin Hyman, 164–85. · Ley, D. 1987: Styles of the times: liberal and neo-conservative landscapes in inner Vancouver, 1968–86. *Journal of Historical Geography* 13: 40–56. · Lowenthal, D. 1985: *The past is a foreign country*. Cambridge: Cambridge University Press. · Lowenthal, D. and Prince, H. 1964: English landscape tastes. *The Geographical Review* 54: 309–46. · Matless, D. 1994: Moral geography in Broadland. *Ecumene* 1: 127–56. · McCannon, J. 1995: To storm the arctic: Soviet polar exploration and public visions of nature in the USSR 1932–39. *Ecumene* 2: 15–32. · McEwan, C. 1998: Cutting power lines within the palace? Countering paternity and eurocentrism in the 'geographical tradition'. *Transactions, Institute of British Geographers* NS 23: 371–84. · Meinig, D.W., ed., 1979: *The interpretation of ordinary landscapes*. New York: Oxford University Press. · Mikesell, M. 1968: Landscape. In D.L. Sills, ed., *International Encyclopedia of the Social Sciences, vol. 8*. New York: Crowell, Collier and Macmillan, 575–80. · Mitchell, D. 1996: *The lie of the land: migrant workers and the California landscape*. Minneapolis: University of Minnesota Press. · Mitchell, W.J.T., ed., 1994: *Landscape and power*. Chicago: University of Chicago Press. · Nash, C. 1996: Reclaiming vision: looking at landscape and the body. *Gender, Place and Culture* 3: 149–69. · Olwig, K. 1996: Rediscovering the substantive meaning of landscape. *Annals, Association of American Geographers* 86: 630–53. · Price, M. and Lewis, M. 1993: The reinvention of cultural geography. *Annals, Association of American Geographers* 83: 1–17. · Rose, G. 1993: *Feminism and geography: the limits of geographical knowledge*. Cambridge: Polity. · Sauer, C.O. 1963: The morphology of landscape. In J. Leighley, ed., *Land and life: selections from the writings of Carl Ortwin Sauer*. Berkeley: University of California Press, 315–50. · Schein, R.H. 1993: Representing urban America: 19th-century views of landscape, space, and power. *Environment and Planning D: Society and Space* 11: 7–21. · Schein, R.H. 1997: The place of landscape: a conceptual framework for interpreting an American scene. *Annals of the Association of American Geographers* 87: 660–80. · Sharp, J. 1994: A topology of 'post' nationality: (re)mapping identity in Satanic Verses. *Ecumene* 1: 65–76. · Soja, E. 1996: *Thirdspace: journeys to Los Angeles and other real-and-imagined places*. Cambridge, MA: Blackwell. · Zelinsky, W. 1973: *The cultural geography of the United States*. Englewood Cliffs: Prentice-Hall.

Suggested Reading

Cosgrove (1998). · Cosgrove and Daniels (1988). · Duncan (1990). · Duncan and Duncan (1988). · Mikesell (1968).

Landschaft A German word meaning LANDSCAPE, the term is associated with the continental European school of *Landschaftsgeographie*, a tradition which can be traced back to the end of the nineteenth century when German geographers started to define the discipline as 'landscape science'. Viewed in these terms, geography was fundamentally concerned with the form of the landscapes of particular regions (see REGIONALISM), and a number of schemes were proposed to classify landscapes and their elements and to provide for formal procedures of analysis (for a review, see Hartshorne, 1939). Several of these distinguished the natural landscape from the CULTURAL LANDSCAPE and in doing so recognized the importance of HUMAN AGENCY. Many others, however, were circumscribed by a commitment to a genetic MORPHOLOGY that progressively distanced them from human geography altogether.

> Increasingly the trend was to classify on the basis of process, and to trace these forms back to more and more remote forms ... The final step was that some of these specialists lost sight completely of actual land forms and devoted themselves to the construction of theoretical forms deducted from individual physical processes. The defeat of geographic ends was therefore almost complete and such geomorphology became part of general earth science. (Sauer, 1963)

This was not strictly true of British geography, which maintained a strong interest in geomorphology as the 'physical basis' of the subject. Even in the USA, where Sauer's BERKELEY SCHOOL did much to restore the cultural concerns of Passarge's *Landschaftskünde*, an interest in the physical features of the landscape was retained: 'American geography cannot dissociate itself from the great fields of physical geography' (Sauer, 1963). In practice, however, the connections were closer in Britain, where a hegemonic 'landscape school' of HISTORICAL GEOGRAPHY was excavated alongside geomorphology as twin 'foundations' for the rest of the subject (Darby, 1953). Yet here too inquiry was frequently restricted to the morphology of past landscapes treated as assemblies of artefacts; where processes were reconstructed at all, they were often described as VERTICAL THEMES inscribed directly in the landscape: 'clearing the wood', 'draining the marsh', etc.

It is precisely these morphological restrictions that have been challenged by the development of other inquiries which have (a) sought to explain landscape change in terms of social processes and practices, and (b) subjected the cultural construction of the concept of landscape as a 'way of seeing' to searching investigation, often drawing upon aesthetics, art history and cultural studies (Cosgrove, 1985; Daniels, 1992) and feminist theory (Rose, 1993, pp. 86–112) (see also ART, GEOGRAPHY, AND). DG

References

Cosgrove, D. 1985: *Social formation and symbolic landscape*. London: Croom Helm [reprinted with a new introduction, 1998: Madison, WI: University of Wisconsin Press]. · Daniels, S. 1992: *Fields of vision*. Cambridge: Polity Press. · Darby, H.C. 1951: The changing English landscape. *Geographical Journal* 117: 377–98. · Darby, H.C. 1953: On the relations of geography and history. *Transactions, Institute of British Geographers* 19: 1–11. · Hartshorne, R. 1939: *The nature of geography: a critical survey of current thought in the light of the past*. Lancaster, PA: Association of American Geographers. · Rose, G. 1993: *Feminism and geography: the limits of geographical knowledge*. Cambridge: Polity Press. · Sauer, C. 1963: The morphology of landscape. In J. Leighly, ed., *Land and life: a selection from the writings of Carl Ortwin Sauer*. Berkeley: University of California Press, ch. 16.

Suggested Reading

Hartshorne (1939), ch. 5. · Sauer (1963).

land-use survey The investigation and cartographic representation of land use. Large-scale land-use surveys were initiated in Britain by L. Dudley Stamp in the 1930s; they involved field mapping (cf. FIELDWORK), but most surveys now use the technologies of REMOTE SENSING and GEOGRAPHICAL INFORMATION SYSTEMS for data collection, collation and display. Land-use surveys are largely descriptive exercises: their use was long advanced by geographers as the initial stage in the development of land-use plans for urban and rural areas (see APPLIED GEOGRAPHY). RJJ

Suggested Reading

Rhind, D. and Hudson, R. 1980: *Land use*. London and New York: Methuen.

language and dialect, geography of The study of the changing distribution and social usage of language, including the ways in which language within geography is now and has in the past been used to establish and negotiate POWER and IDENTITY.

It is possible to distinguish two main strands in the study of the connections between geography and language. The first embraces the geographical study of language area, has its origins in later eighteenth-century interests in the origins of language and is evident in work on the mapping of language areas and of dialects. The second involves the study of language within and as part of geography's explicit concerns with the politics of power and of knowledge-making (see also CULTURAL POLITICS; DISCOURSE). Whilst it is not helpful to see these two strands either as discrete or as chronologically distinct traditions, since some recent work on the geography of language focuses only on the mapping of language areas (Brice, 1996), work in the second sense represents a significant departure from the mapping of language areas and has close connections with more recent interest in REPRESENTATION and authority within postmodern human geography (see also CULTURE; POSTMODERNISM).

The beginnings of interest in the geographical study of languages are evident in eighteenth-century European debates about the origins of language, the connections between language and national identity (see NATION-STATE), and in discussions about language and social differentiation. In the nineteenth century, several projects mapped the principal European languages in association with ethnic group, projects that were central to the development of ANTHROPOGEOGRAPHY and which provided the impetus to later interest in the mapping of language areas or language groups, either as expressions of CULTURE or CULTURE AREA or as part of POLITICAL GEOGRAPHY, or, indeed, as part of an understanding of PLACE-NAMES as sources for understanding the linguistic history of a given settlement or region. There has been a continuing tradition of language mapping in these ways within western European and North American geography. In Britain, for example, work has been done on the changing geographical extent of the Celtic languages (Withers, 1984). In Canada, the tradition of mapping 'native' languages, notably on the west coast, has considerable contemporary political significance, whilst in the United States, language mapping has concentrated on English and German (Moseley and Asher, 1993).

A related aspect of this concern for the geographic area of certain languages or language forms is *dialect geography*, often termed *linguistic geography*, with its attention to local differentiations within speech areas and the changing geography of particular linguistic forms. Much linguistic geography has been geographical only in the sense that it has been concerned with the spatial distribution of linguistic phenomena, and in Britain and in the United States, most work within this subfield has focused upon internal variation in the geography of English-speaking peoples (Zelinsky and Williams, 1988). It is also possible to identify work in what has from the early 1980s become known as *geolinguistics* where attention has concentrated on the geography of languages as part of the political identity of linguistic minorities and on the politics of language use both within established nation-states and as part of claims to an emergent NATIONALISM (Breton, 1993).

It is likewise possible to discern a strong concern for language as a means to cultural identity in that work which has examined the connections between language, social power and the practice of geography. For Jackson (1989), 'Language is a structure of signification that is reproduced in social practice. Like other practices, however, it does not exist outside social relations of power... There is, in other words, a *politics of language*' (original emphasis: see also CULTURAL POLITICS). He has further noted that 'a revitalised cultural geography must go beyond the mapping of languages and the geography of dialect, towards the study of language itself as the medium through which intersubjective meaning is communicated'.

This recognition within geography of language as a means to social power parallels that wider interest in the 'linguistic turn' in twentieth-century philosophy and its focus on the study of language and the study of thought and, thus, upon the constitution of different realities and ontological theories through language (Carruthers, 1996; Devitt and Sterelny, 1989). Geography's attention to language, reality and power is shared in work on the social history of different forms of language as a means to political power: the authority of one language over another, the power of written languages over oral cultures and the supposed objectivity of the language of scientific discourse (Leith, 1997). Such matters are related, too, to a more widespread interest in the evolution of language as a complex and specialized 'instinct' essential in comprehending and interpreting for others the worlds we live in (Pinker, 1995).

The idea of a politics of language has some connections with that research in geolinguistics which has considered language the basis to political struggle (see also NATIONALISM; POLITICAL GEOGRAPHY), but it has several other rather richer connotations. Language is clearly important in the constitution and negotiation of local meaning. Pred's examination of conflicts of meaning articulated in different language usage in nineteenth-century Stockholm (Pred 1990a) and in other studies (1990b), emphasizes the potential for further study of the locally spoken word. Others have seen geography's 'linguistic turn' as signalling a new beginning for geography's place as a critical social science. Curry (1991), for example, claims that 'the use of language in post-modern works appears to express a radically new view of the nature of the social sciences and of the place of the social scientist in society'. Certainly, others have paid attention to language as intrinsic to the conduct and practice of geography, and, indeed, to the indissoluble connections between authoritative language, the form of knowledge and authorial power (Barnes and Duncan, 1992; Cosgrove and Domosh, 1993). It is clear that there are different languages and voices to be heard (or not) as both an objective and a practice in geography, particularly in relation to questions of ETHNOMETHODOLOGY, and, since all language is spoken from *somewhere*, it is intimately connected with the idea of SITUATED KNOWLEDGE and with what Bourdieu has termed the linguistic HABITUS (Bourdieu, 1990; Crang, 1992).

A key text in recent years was one by Gunnar Olsson (1992). On one level, this is a work of what might be termed *linguistic geometry*, a work concerned to assess what he has called a *cartography of thought* insofar as Olsson's distinctive contribution to geography has been marked by his refusal to limit himself 'to the study of visible things'. On another level, it is concerned with 'questioning the the relations we are talking *in*' rather than considering the object of 'what we are talking about' (Olsson, 1992). Olsson is positing a new linguistic grounding for writing (and thinking) about thought-and-action (in ways which have intriguing connections with the Foucauldian investigation of power and knowledge): the limits of our understanding of our world may indeed be the limits of our language (see also Doel, 1993; Farinelli et al., 1996). Others have also examined the ways in which language is employed within geography to appeal to different audiences and to warrant the 'truth' of what is being claimed (Smith, 1996), and discussed the ways in which deep-seated gender biases in language may permeate the epistemological structures as well as the substantive content of dominant forms of knowledge (Bondi, 1997). In these ways, as Pred noted, 'a vast terrain of enquiry lies open' for continuing research on geography and language. CWJW

References

Barnes, T.A. and Duncan, J.S., 1992: Introduction: writing worlds. In T.A. Barnes and J.S. Duncan, eds, *Writing worlds: discourse, text and metaphor in the representation of landscape*. London and New York: Routledge, 1–17. · Bondi, L. 1997: In whose words?: on gender identities, knowledge and writing practices. *Transactions, Institute of British Geographers* 22: 245–58. · Bourdieu, P. 1990: *In other words: essays towards a reflexive sociology*. Cambridge: Polity Press; Breton, R.J.-L. 1993: *Geolinguistics: language dynamics and ethnolinguistic geography*. Ottawa: University of Ottawa Press. · Brice, W.C. 1996: The geography of language. In I. Douglas, R. Huggett and M. Robinson, eds, *Companion encyclopedia of geography: the environment and humankind*. London and New York: Routledge, 107–19. · Carruthers, P. 1996: *Language thought and consciousness*. Cambridge: Cambridge University Press. · Cosgrove, D.E. and Domosh, M. 1993: Author and authority: writing the new cultural geography. In J. Duncan and D. Ley, eds, *Place/culture/representation*. London and New York: Routledge, 25–38. · Crang, P. 1992: The politics of polyphony: reconfigurations in geographical authority. *Environment and Planning D: Society and Space* 10: 527–50. · Curry, M.R. 1991: Postmodernism, language and the strains of modernism. *Annals of the Association of American Geographers* 81: 210–28. · Devitt, M. and Sterelny, K. 1989: *Language and reality: an introduction to the philosophy of language*. Cambridge, MA: MIT Press. · Doel, M.A. 1993: Proverbs for paranoids: writing geography on hollowed ground. *Transactions, Institute of British Geographers* NS 18: 377–94. · Farinelli, F., Olsson, G. and Reichert, D., eds, 1996: *Limits of representation*. Bologna: Accedo. · Jackson, P. 1989: *Maps of meaning: an introduction to cultural geography*. London: Unwin Hyman. · Leith, R. 1997: *A social history of language*. London and New York: Routledge. · Moseley, C. and Asher, R.E., eds, 1993: *Atlas of the world's languages*. London and New York: Routledge. · Olsson, G. 1980: *Birds in egg/eggs in bird*. London: Pion. · Olsson, G. 1992: *Lines of power/limits of language*. Minneapolis: University of Minnesota Press. · Pinker, S. 1995: *The language instinct*. London: Penguin. · Pred, A. 1990a: *Lost words and lost worlds: modernity and the language of everyday life in late nineteenth-century Stockholm*. Cambridge: Cambridge University Press. · Pred, A. 1990b: In other wor(l)ds: fragmented and integrated observations on gendered languages, gendered spaces and local transformation. *Antipode* 22: 33–52. · Smith, J. 1996: Geographical rhetoric: modes and tropes of appeal. *Annals of the Association of American Geographers* 86: 1–20. · Withers, C.W.J. 1984: *Gaelic in Scotland 1698–1981: the geographical history of a language*. Edinburgh: John Donald. · Zelinsky, W. and Williams, C.H. 1988: The mapping of language in North America and the British Isles. *Progress in Human Geography* 12: 337–68.

Suggested Reading

Barnes, T.A. and Duncan, J.S. eds, 1992: *Writing worlds: discourse, text and metaphor in the representation of landscape*. London and New York: Routledge. · Breton, R.J.-L. 1993: *Geolinguistics: language dynamics and ethnolinguistic geography*. Ottawa: University of Ottawa Press. · Jackson, P. 1989: *Maps of meaning: an introduction to cultural geography*. London: Unwin Hyman. · Olsson, G. 1992: *Lines of power/limits of language*. Minneapolis: University of Minnesota Press.

law (scientific) An integral component of a scientific THEORY, whose nature varies according to the EPISTEMOLOGY.

In POSITIVISM, laws are statements that are universally true, independent of time and place. They represent a constant conjunction – of the form '*if X, then Y*'; given certain antecedent conditions, a particular consequence will necessarily follow (perhaps at some specified level of probability). Laws differ from factual statements, which refer to specific events (times and/or places) only, through their generality: they are produced by the empirical testing of HYPOTHESES and are linked together in coherent theories.

A law in REALISM is a statement of a causal connection: it indicates a necessity in a particular situation but implies neither universality nor regularity. In positivism, laws are frequently produced through the identification of regularities which can be equated with causation (perhaps because the theory posits such a relationship): the implication is that future events can be predicted as further occurrences of the universal regularity – '*if X again, then Y will follow again*'. In realism, on the other hand, causation is identified by an analysis of the circumstances of the event(s) being considered; there is no implication that the conditions will be repeated so the law's validity in those circumstances does not imply that it occurs repeatedly. (Laws identified in positivist science are special cases of those derived in realist science, therefore, since positivism implicitly assumes that circumstances recur, with the same result: see Chouinard, Fincher and Webber, 1984. Realists argue that repeated examples of the same conditions are rare in social science.)

There has been much debate within the social sciences about the relevance of the positivist conception of a law. Realists argue that it is possible to conceive of laws which are particular to a finite domain – as with the marxian law of the falling rate of profit (MARXIAN ECONOMICS) which applies only to capitalist societies. The domain for any law must be precisely specified, however – i.e. it must be a rational ABSTRACTION and not a CHAOTIC CONCEPTION.

Identified laws are frequently descriptive statements only, presenting empirical regularities but no insights into the mechanisms that produce them. Thus realists prefer to focus on uncovering causal connection laws rather than describing unaccounted-for regularities. RJJ

Reference

Chouinard, V., Fincher, R. and Webber, M. 1984: Empirical research in scientific human geography. *Progress in Human Geography* 8: 347–80.

Suggested Reading

Golledge, R.G. and Amedeo, D.W. 1968: On laws in geography. *Annals of the Association of American Geographers* 58: 560–74. · Harvey, D. 1969: *Explanation in geography*. London: Edward Arnold. · Sayer, A. 1992: *Method in social science: a realist approach*, 2nd edn. London: Routledge.

law, geography of The relation between the places and spaces of social life, and the enactment, interpretation and contestation of law, both formal and informal.

There has been a heightened interest in exploring the law–geography link recently, although this should not be seen as unprecedented given an earlier lengthy engagement with legal-geographic questions. Previous research can be broadly divided according to emphasis. An older body of writing, concerned with mapping the *regional diversity of law*, tends towards an account of the geographic environment as a vital structuring agent of law (cf. REGION AND REGIONAL GEOGRAPHY). Another, more recent, literature, inverts the relation, and explores the manner in which *law affects space*. More recently, a 'critical' perspective on law and space has sought to transcend the unilinear causality of both schools by an exploration of the *complex interrelations of the legal, the spatial and the social*.

Although an interest in the regional geography of law can be traced as far back as the sixteenth-century writings of Jean Bodin and the eighteenth-century treatise of Montesquieu, perhaps the first academic treatment was given by John Wigmore who, alerted to the geographic diversity of legal systems by a detailed study of Japanese law, produced a three-volume geographical survey of the world's legal systems (1928). Along with Albert Kocourek, Wigmore also co-edited a three-volume set on legal evolution, one volume of which included papers by sociologists and geographers. These essays vary to the extent that 'race' and the natural environment are assumed to determine spatial variations in law. The geographer Ellen Semple, for example, describes the evolution of the 'land-bond' (defined, broadly, in terms of property relations) that she sees as characteristic of diverse human societies. Evoking naturalistic analogies, she refers to the 'fibres of the land which become woven into the whole fabric of the nation's life. These are the geographic elements constituting the soil in which empires are rooted; they arise in the sap of the nation' (Semple, 1918, p. 223).

In a paper regarded as influential within POLITICAL GEOGRAPHY, Derwent Whittlesey (1935) inverted the law–environment relation by attending to the 'impress of effective central authority upon the landscape'. Although noting that environmental forces may be important, the thrust of his account is clear; 'phenomena engendered by political forces should have a recognized place as elements in the geographic structure of every region' (p. 97). Several laws resulting in 'landscape modification' are identified, including tariffs, property and resource law. As Clark notes (1989), a similar 'spatial impact' emphasis best characterizes a number of recent geographic analyses of law.

These accounts, in tracking the effect that a given law or ruling has on a spatial structure, such as a housing market, are generally applied, pragmatic and non-theoretical, sharing common ground with the orthodox policy-analysis literature.

Although both regional and impact analyses offer useful insights, they were criticized on a number of grounds (Clark, 1989; Blomley, 1994). Most important is the assertion that both perspectives, although with different emphases, assume an analytical separation of law, space and society. The impact analysis literature tends to regard law as acting upon a passive spatial structure, on the assumption that there are two realms, one legal, the other spatial. Similarly, there is a tendency within the regional literature to root law in certain immutable and often naturalized forces. Again, an implicit divide is made between social life and certain non-conditional and asocial legal principles. This is problematic on several counts. For example, the location of law in either an asocial or an aspatial realm, as implied by the impact literature, presents a picture of law as in a higher, 'closed' sphere, beyond the world of local struggle and politics. Not only can this be questioned on certain theoretical grounds (where, for example, is this uniquely legal realm?), but also in political terms. Similarly, the submergence of law beneath the suffocating effects of the geographical environment implies legal immutability and naturalness.

Both impact and regional analyses make implicit assumptions of the determinacy of legal meaning and the operation of power relations. In terms of the former, an extensive post-structuralist literature has argued that legal meaning is deeply ambiguous, even indeterminate, and that legal interpretation must be understood as situated, occurring with reference to certain implicit (and often disempowering) assumptions concerning social and political life (Hutchinson, 1988; see CONTEXTUAL APPROACH; POST-STRUCTURALISM). The categories and vocabulary of LIBERALISM are often assumed to be important in this regard. Rather than focusing on the production of legal meaning, others have paid more attention to the implication of legal discourses and practices in prevailing power relations, including those that centre on the operation of either CLASS domination under CAPITALISM or PATRIARCHY (Chouinard, 1994). Finally, the legal-geographic orthodoxy has been challenged in terms of its account of the effects of law itself. Law, it is argued, is too often understood exclusively as a restrictive and instrumental code. Such a reading, however, underplays the other dimensions of law, including its power to define or constitute the terms of social life, or to empower certain groups. On this account, law is not simply an external imperative, but is in important senses *constitutive* of social and political life (Brigham and Gordon, 1996). Law, in this sense, is not confined to the statute book or the law courts but is seen as a much more pervasive (and important) medium through which society and politics are lived, whether in constrained or liberatory ways.

It is in response to these sorts of assertions that we can understand the rise of what might be termed a 'critical legal geography' over the last decade. Influenced by debates within geographic, social, and legal theory, this perspective has a very different reading of law, space and their mutual relation, with a scepticism of existing legal structures and the social relations they embody. The distinguishing feature of this perspective is its refusal to accept either law or space as pre-political or as the unproblematic outcome of external forces. Both are regarded as deeply social and political. Law is seen both as a site in which competing values, practices and meanings are fought over, and also as the means by which certain meanings and social relations become fixed and naturalized, either in oppressive or potentially empowering ways. Similarly, space is regarded as both socially produced and as socially constitutive, with attention being directed to the 'politics' of SPACE (see SPATIALITY). The relation between law, space and society is redefined and extended in important ways, opening up many new areas to critical geographic enquiry. To date, several areas have been studied, including:

1 The analysis of the manner in which *legal action and interpretation produces certain spaces* (cf. PRODUCTION OF SPACE). This departs from 'impact analysis' by virtue of its attention to such things as the complexities of interpretation and the local context of legal interpretation. The role of the legal apparatus – especially the judiciary – is often given prominence, it being noted that court decisions have profound (and often problematic) effects within local settings in both material and discursive terms, given the manner in which legal categories and discourse can come to frame local debates (see STATE APPARATUS). Examples include Delaney's (1993) examination of restrictive covenants in US cities, or Young's (1997) discussion of British asylum law. The

manner in which such legal evaluations of space are contested by local groups is also receiving attention; see, for example, Cooper's (1996) discussion of law and planning disputes in London and Goodings' (1994) discussion of the politics of spatial naming in US Indian law.

2 The related study of the *situated nature of legal interpretation*, it being argued that legal practice and interpretation is often bound up in the LOCALE in which it occurs. For example, in a careful series of studies in three US towns, Greenhouse, Yngevesson and Engel (1994) reveal the 'place of law and the court in the construction of community and hierarchy' (p. 174), noting not only the manner in which 'COMMUNITY' is locally constructed so as to frequently marginalize those deemed 'outsiders', but also underscoring the manner in which local and extra-local conceptions of law and rights are central to that construction. The study of such local legal cultures has a related political implication. If it is accepted that interpretation – including legal interpretation – is necessarily structured by the diverse spatial and temporal settings of social life, then formal legal interpretation, with its claims concerning the autonomy of the individual legal subject and the balance between universal and particularized legal knowledge, implies an untenuous rejection of the situated contextuality of law. Diverse and contingent legal understandings are presented as 'Law'; a form of higher truth, removed from the vagaries and political and ethical conflicts of 'real life' (see ETHICS, GEOGRAPHY AND). Wesley Pue (1990), in a trenchant critique of the relation between legal discourse and the multiple geographies of social life, argues that law is in this sense 'anti-geographical', to the extent that legal relations are frequently understood within law as existing in a purely conceptual space divorced from the heterogeneity and contextuality of local legal understandings. It follows that an assertion of the spatiality of legal knowledge constitutes, at least implicitly, a powerful critique of certain widely held legal beliefs and concepts of legal 'closure' (Blomley, 1994).

3 The study of the *geographic claims and representations contained within legal discourse*, it being noted that in much the same way that law relies on claims concerning history and time, so it both defines and draws upon a complex range of geographies and spatial understandings. Whilst struggling to make sense of the complexity and ambiguity of social life, legal agents – whether judges, legal theorists, administrative officers or ordinary people – represent and evaluate space in various ways. These juridical representations touch all aspects of legal life – including property, contractual relations, crime and inter-governmental law. The construction of such spaces can be seen, for example, in relation to the designation of boundaries between 'public' and 'private' urban spaces (Mitchell, 1996; see PRIVATE AND PUBLIC SPHERES); struggle over the meanings of ownership and PROPERTY RIGHTS (Blomley, 1996; cf. LAND TENURE); or struggle with the racialized politics of US local autonomy (Ford, 1994).

4 The *politics of the law–space relation*. Recent scholarship has maintained that both law and space – in their strategic use and representation – are deeply political. Rather than being simply 'pre-political' and 'natural', they are both constituted by, and constitutive of, political struggles. A study of their conjunction, then, is revealing. Santos (1995) notes, for example, that the spatial scale at which law is analysed – local, national and supra-national – is not 'innocent', but has profound implications for social life. Other writers have similarly explored the 'geo-politics' of law in terms of local working-class opposition and the delivery of legal services (Chouinard, 1989); as a critique of legal closure (Kobayashi, 1990); or the colonial 'placing' of First Nations in Canada (Peters, 1997).

However useful these insights, recent scholarship on law and geography is still in an undeveloped state. Several issues could profitably be addressed. Most immediately, the theorization of the geographies of law and legal struggles is still undeveloped and somewhat ambiguous. Some have embraced the 'postmodern turn', focusing attention on discourse and the construction of meaning (Clark, 1989). Others have called for this to be supplemented by political-economic and socialist-feminist insights (Chouinard, 1994). The time is ripe for a self-conscious examination of the particular conceptual insights of a 'critical legal geography'. With this in mind, several considerations might be useful.

First, a deeper engagement with legal theory (both in law and in sociology/anthropology) by geographers is needed. Intriguing parallels exist between critical writings in both law and geography. To date, however, little exchange has occurred between the two fields, despite growing interest in questions of space within legal enquiry. Recent legal interest in questions such as resistance or globalization, for example, could be usefully drawn upon. Second, many potential areas of legal/geographic enquiry remain empirically under-explored. For example, detailed empirical accounts of local legal cultures, the legal construction of NATURE, or a consideration of the importance of space within legal discourse and practice demand more sustained exploration. Third, more careful attention could be given to the 'geographies of liberalism', including the legal representation of CITIZENSHIP, property or public and private spaces. Fourth, the connections to other branches of the discipline need to be clarified, such as the geography of crime and policing, recent debates around ethics, or POLITICAL GEOGRAPHY in general (see CRIME, GEOGRAPHY OF; JUSTICE, GEOGRAPHY AND; LAW OF THE SEA; POLICING, GEOGRAPHY OF). Fourth, the historical geographies of law demand more careful attention. For example, it could be argued that real property entails not only certain spatial orderings, but also implies certain claims about past and future (Blomley, 1996). Finally, the 'critical' aspects of this enquiry need to be worked through more carefully (see CRITICAL THEORY). Chouinard (1994, p. 428), in particular, has called for 'meaningful political action in and against the legal system'. Whether this entails intellectual challenges to legal 'closure', or grounded and inclusionary research projects concerning law remains an important question. NB

References

Blomley, N.K. 1989: Text and context: rethinking the law-geography nexus. *Progress in Human Geography* 13 (4): 512–34. · Blomley, N.K. 1994: *Law, space and the geographies of power.* New York: Guilford Press. · Blomley, N.K. 1996: The properties of space: history, geography, and gentrification. *Urban Geography* 18 (4): 286–95. · Brigham, J. and Gordon, D.R. 1996: Law in politics: struggles over property and public space on New York City's Lower East Side. *Law and Social Inquiry* 21 (2): 265–83. · Chouinard, V. 1989: Transformations in the capitalist state: the development of legal aid clinics in Canada. *Transactions of the Institute of British Geographers*, NS 14 (3): 329–49. · Chouinard, V. 1994: Geography, law and legal struggles: which ways ahead? *Progress in Human Geography* 11 (5): 415–40. · Clark, G.L. 1989: The geography of law. In R. Peet and N. Thrift, eds, *The New Models in Human Geography.* London: Unwin Hyman, 310–37. · Cooper, D. 1996: Talmudic territory? Space, law and modernist discourse. *Journal of Law and Society* 23 (4): 529–48. · Delaney, D. 1993: Geographies of judgement: the doctrine of changed conditions and the politics of judgement. *Annals of the Association of American Geographers* 83 (1): 48–65. · Ford, R.T. 1994: The boundaries of race: political geography in legal analysis. *Harvard Law Review* 107 (8): 1841–921. · Gooding, S.S. 1994: Place, race and names: Layered identities in United States v. Oregon, Confederated Tribes of the Colville Reservation, Plaintiff-Intervenor. *Law and Society Review* 28 (5): 1181–229. · Greenhouse, C.J., Yngvesson, B. and Engel, D.M. 1994: *Law and community in three American towns.* Ithaca: Cornell University Press. · Hutchinson, A. 1988: *Dwelling on the threshold: critical essays on modern legal thought.* Toronto: Carswell. · Kobayashi, A. 1990: Racism and the law in Canada: a geographical perspective. *Urban Geography* 11 (5): 447–73. · Mitchell, D. 1996: Political violence, order and the legal construction of public space: power and the public forum doctrine. *Urban Geography* 17 (2): 152–78. · Peters, E. 1997: Challenging the geographies of 'Indianness'; the Batchewana case. *Urban Geography* 18 (1): 56–61. · Pue, W.W. 1990: Wrestling with law: (geographical) specificity vs. (legal) abstraction. *Urban Geography* 11 (6): 566–85. · Santos, B. 1995: *Toward a new common sense: law, science and politics in the paradigmatic transition.* New York: Routledge. · Semple, E.C. 1918: The influences of geographic environment on law, state and society. In A. Kocourek and J.H. Wigmore, eds, *Formative Influences of Legal Development.* Boston: Little, Brown and Company, 215–33. · Whittlesey, D. 1935: The impress of central authority upon the landscape. *Annals of the Association of American Geographers* 25: 85–97. · Wigmore, J. 1928: *A panorama of the world's legal systems*, 3 vols. St Paul Minnesota: West Publishing Company. · Young, C. 1997: Political representations of geography and place in the United Kingdom Asyhum and Immigration Bill (1995). *Urban Geography* 18 (1): 62–73.

Suggested Reading

Blacksell, M., Watkins, C. and Economides, K. 1986: Human geography and law: a case of separate development in social science. *Progress in Human Geography* 10 (3): 371–96. · Clark, G.L. 1985: *Judges and the cities: interpreting local autonomy.* Chicago: University of Chicago Press. · Clark, W.A.V. 1991: Geography in court: expertise in adversarial settings. *Transactions, Institute of British Geographers* NS 16: 5–20. · Frug, G. 1996: The geography of community. *Stanford Law Review* 48: 1047–8. · Herbert, S. 1997: *Policing space; territoriality and the Los Angeles Police Department.* London: University of Minnesota Press.

law of the sea Prior to 1958 most of the law of the sea derived from customary law, but since the late 1950s a series of international conferences sponsored by the United Nations has resulted in three conventions on the Law of the Sea which have had some success in bringing the oceans within a single body of international law. The most recent UNCLOS III was initially agreed on 17 December 1982 at Montego Bay, Jamaica. Although it was signed by the majority of maritime states, the major industrial countries, including France, the UK and the USA, refused, because of the limitations it proposed on their rights to exploit the resources of the HIGH SEAS. This part of the convention was painstakingly renegotiated to try and take account of these countries' objections, and the most important result was the establishment of the International

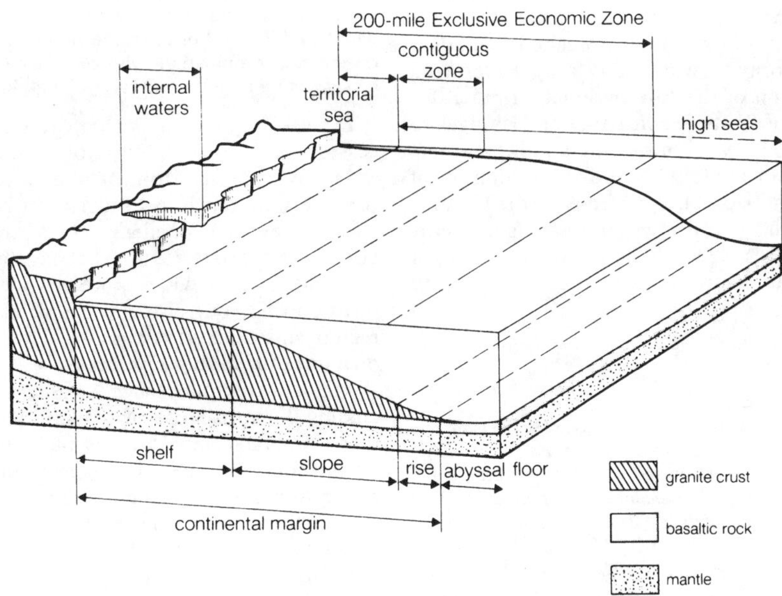

law of the sea *The three-dimensional nature of sea divisions* (after Couper, 1978)

Seabed Authority. The revised version was eventually completed in 1994, but most of the major industrial nations were still reluctant to sign. Since then, France and the UK both acceded to the treaty in 1997, but not the USA which still refuses to contemplate any legal limits on its freedom to exploit the high seas. The convention itself defines seven maritime jurisdictional zones (see the figure):

(a) *Internal waters*: all waters landward of the baseline from which the territorial sea is measured, such as rivers, lakes, bays, ports and any waters landward of the low-tide line.

(b) *The* TERRITORIAL SEA: STATES exercise total SOVEREIGNTY over these waters, except the rights of innocent passage. They extend for 12 nautical miles from the baseline, unless this impinges on the territorial seas of a neighbouring state, when a compromise has to be agreed.

(c) *The* CONTIGUOUS ZONE: an area 12 nautical miles beyond the limit of the territorial sea, within which states are free to apply customs and other national regulations.

(d) *The* CONTINENTAL SHELF: an area extending 200 nautical miles from the baseline, within which states may claim virtually exclusive rights to the seabed resources. It should be noted that that this is the legal and not the physical definition (see the figure). In some instances states are permitted to claim jurisdiction over their continental shelves beyond 200 nautical miles, but such extensions can only be sanctioned by the newly established UN Commission on the Limits of the Continental Shelf.

(e) *Fishing*: most states now claim and exercise exclusive fishing rights up to 200 nautical miles out to sea from their coastal baseline.

(f) *Exclusive Economic Zone*: synonymous with the redefined legal continental shelf described in (d) above.

(g) *The* HIGH SEAS: these include all waters other than those defined in (a)–(f) above, and there is complete freedom of movement within them. However, signatories to the UNCLOS III convention accept that mineral and other seabed resources are an international resource and should be exploited for the benefit of all, not just those countries with the technology to do so.

Finally, all habitable islands are subject to the same regulations as coastal states, but it is not permissible to claim an Exclusive Economic Zone around small, uninhabitable rocks, or artificial structures.

The most notable achievements of the renegotiation of the UNCLOS III Treaty, completed in 1994, was the establishment of the International Seabed Authority to administer the mining of the deep seabed, including the Authority's own mining arm, Enterprise; the creation of the International Tribunal for the Law of the Sea, consisting of 21 judges to settle certain types of dispute about the interpretation of UNCLOS; and the setting up of the Commission on the Limits of the Continental Shelf, to consider submissions concerning the outer edge of the continental margin beyond 200 nautical miles. MB

Reference

Couper, A. 1978: *Geography and law of the sea*. London: Macmillan.

Suggested Reading

Churchill, R.R. and Lowe, A.V. 1988: *The law of the sea*. Manchester: Manchester University Press. · Foreign and Commonwealth Office 1998: *Britain's accession to the United Nations Convention on the Law of the Sea*. Background Brief: *http\\:www.fco.gov.uk/reference/briefs/pdf/lawofsea.pdf*. · Glassner, M.I. 1990: *Neptune's domain: a political geography of the sea*. London: Unwin Hyman. · Juda, L. 1996: *International law and ocean use management. The evolution of ocean governance*. London and New York: Routledge.

layers of investment The successive cycles of economic DEVELOPMENT in particular PLACES or REGIONS. The concept was first developed by Doreen Massey (1978) as a way of characterizing the changing SPATIAL STRUCTURE of the economy.

According to Massey (1984), 'the structure of local economies can be seen as a product of the combination of "layers", of the successive imposition over the years of new rounds of investment, new forms of activity'. With each successive round of investment, the local economy acquires a particular niche in a wider spatial DIVISION OF LABOUR: 'if a local economy can be analysed as the historical product of the combination of layers of activity, those layers also represent in turn the succession of roles the local economy has played within wider national and international spatial structures'. Gregory (1989) has represented the process as a game of cards, in which regions are dealt different cards as a result of the operation of successive rounds of investment to make up a complete, and unique, 'hand' (see the figure).

However, Massey does not see this sort of analysis as an exercise in structural determinism. Rather, the existing character of the area interacts with the new 'layer' in a process of 'mutual determination':

> the internal necessity of a spatial structure does not get 'acted out' in the real world in pure form. What takes place is the interrelation of the new spatial structure with the accumulated results of the old. The 'combination' of layers, in other words, really does mean combination, with each side of the process affecting the other. (Massey, 1984, p. 121)

In seeking to relate the operation of processes of capital ACCUMULATION to the evident AREAL DIFFERENTIATION of the SPACE-ECONOMY, this approach to INDUSTRIAL GEOGRAPHY was an explicit challenge to conventional LOCATION THEORY. Regional change is seen as part and parcel of wider processes of economic restructuring, but also the character of each region and LOCALITY is seen as stamping its own imprint on those processes.

Massey exemplifies her arguments by discussing the impact of new branch-plant investment on the coalfield areas of Britain. The decline of coal, steel and heavy engineering began to break down the existing social structures in these areas. The new factories provided new jobs in areas of high unemployment, but their branch-plant status made the security of employment questionable. Of particular significance was the recruitment of women to work in the factories, often for relatively low wages. The largely male-dominated character of the labour movement in these areas ensured that the new female workforces had little experience of trade-union militancy. These sorts of changes often involved quite deliberate spatial strategies within as well as between regions on the part of firms – as Morgan and Sayer (1985) have shown. (See also SUBURB.)

The causes of new phases of investment have been the subject of some debate. For Harvey (1985) they are a response to successive crises (see CRISIS) in the process of capital accumulation: a product of the 'spatial fix' through which the built-up contradictions of the previous phase of capitalist development are temporarily resolved. Marshall (1987) suggests that they are the result of KONDRATIEFF CYCLES, with each long wave producing a new pattern of UNEVEN DEVELOPMENT (cf. REGIONAL ALLIANCE).

There has also been debate about the nature of the relationship between the layers. Warde (1985) called the idea of layers of investment 'an extended METAPHOR of the geology of social relations' (p. 191) such that 'successive rounds of accumulation deposit layers of industrial sediment in geographical space' (p. 196–7). This characterization of Massey's work quickly became known as the 'geological metaphor' and subsequently it was often assumed that it was a metaphor that Massey herself had developed, or at least endorsed. In fact, as is made clear in the second edition of

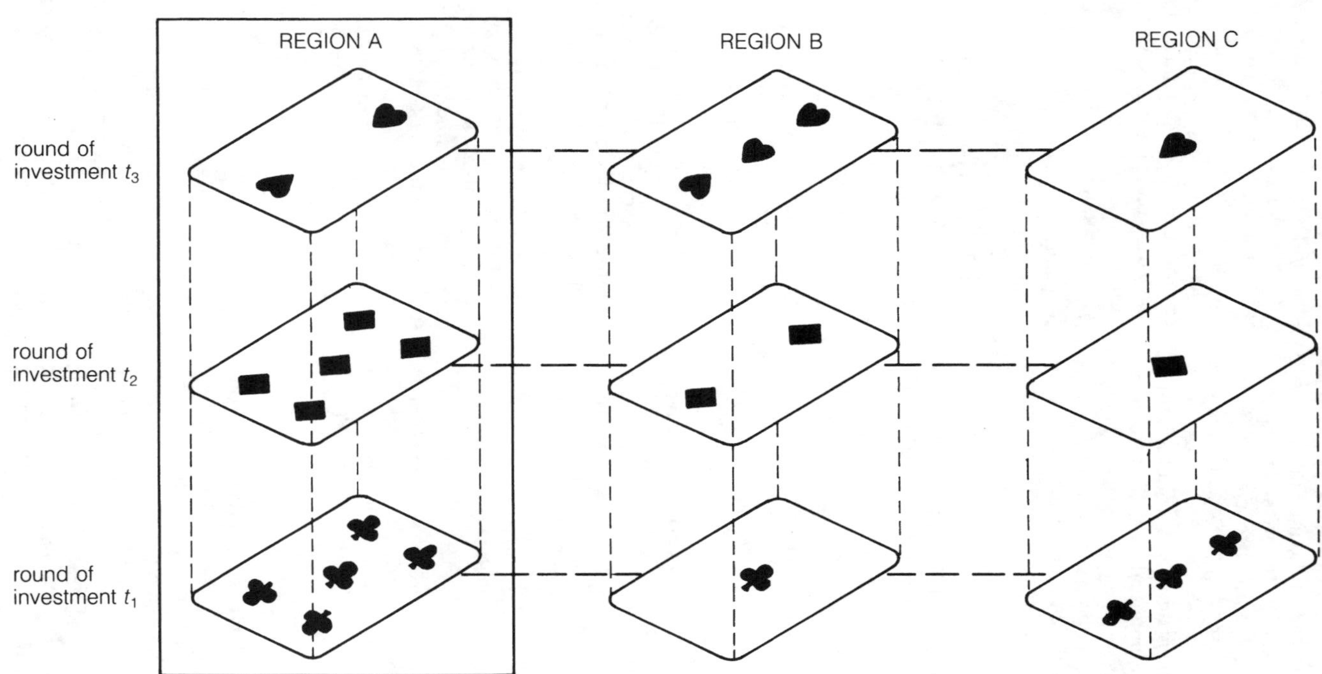

layers of investment *Phases of capital accumulation – translated into a game of cards* (Gregory, 1989)

Spatial Divisions of Labour (Massey, 1995, pp. 320–2), in Massey's view the metaphor of geological sedimentation does not capture the process of layering of rounds of investment. She says that it 'reduces the fluidity, the relational nature, and the fundamental processes of mutual interaction [between layers] and moulding which I wanted to convey. Surely the notion of the *combination* of layers is very ungeological'.

Massey's concept acted as a stimulus both to a wide range of empirical work in INDUSTRIAL GEOGRAPHY and beyond and to considerable debate about the appropriate ways of conceptualizing regional and urban change. (See *Environment and Planning A*, 1989, for examples.) JP

References

Environment and Planning A 1989: Spatial Divisions of Labour in practice. *Environment and Planning A* 21: 655–700. · Gregory, D. 1989: Areal differentiation and post-modern human geography. In D. Gregory and R. Walford, eds, *Horizons in human geography*. London: Macmillan, 67–96. · Harvey, D. 1985: The geopolitics of capitalism. In D. Gregory and J. Urry, eds, *Social relations and spatial structures*. London: Macmillan, 128–63. · Marshall, M. 1987: *Long waves of regional development*. London: Macmillan. · Massey, D. 1978: Regionalism: some current issues. *Capital and Class* 6: 106–25. · Massey, D. 1984: *Spatial divisions of labour*, 1st edn. London: Macmillan. · Massey, D. 1995: *Spatial divisions of labour*, 2nd edn. London: Macmillan. · Morgan, K. and Sayer, A. 1985: A 'modern' industry in a mature region: the remaking of management–labour relations. *International Journal of Urban and Regional Research* 9: 383–403. · Warde, A. 1985: Spatial change, politics and the division of labour. In D. Gregory and J. Urry, eds, *Social relations and spatial structures*. London: Macmillan, 190–212.

Suggested Reading

Environment and Planning A (1989). · Gregory, D. (1989), 75–6. · Massey, D. 1988: Uneven development: social change and spatial divisions of labour. In D. Massey and J. Allen, eds, *Uneven development: cities and regions in transition*. London: Hodder and Stoughton, 250–76. · Massey (1995).

le Play Society A society founded in England in 1930 to promote FIELDWORK and regional survey in sociology and geography. It was named after a nineteenth-century engineer, Frédéric le Play, who published accounts of the places he visited (e.g. *Les ouvriers européen*, 1855) and developed a schema (with strong ENVIRONMENTAL DETERMINISM overtones) of place–work–family to encapsulate the major features of local societies. The Society was disbanded in 1960, having organized 71 major field surveys and published eight monographs during its existence. RJJ

Suggested Reading

Beaver, S.H. 1962: The le Play Society and fieldwork. *Geography* 40: 225–40. · Herbertson, D. 1950: *The life of Frédéric le Play*. Ledbury: le Play House Press.

lead–lag models Statistical models for identifying timing differences ('leads' and 'lags') in the transmission of fluctuations through urban and regional systems. These models have been widely used for studies of REGIONAL CYCLES of economic activity and for studies of spatial DIFFUSION of epidemics such as influenza or measles (cf. MEDICAL GEOGRAPHY). Three types of timing differences can be studied:

- leads/lags between different variables within a region;
- leads/lags between regions or cities;
- leads/lags between a regional series and the national aggregate series.

The models require detailed time-series data for the variables and regions, e.g. unemployment data by month or quarter for Canadian cities.

The lead–lag structure can be defined using lagged CORRELATION (sometimes called cross-correlation). To find the lead–lag between employment cycles in two regions X and Y, the time series for region X is first correlated with that for region Y to give the usual correlation coefficient r. This is then repeated, but with the Y series lagged by one period, i.e. X_t is related to Y_t for $t = 2, 3, \ldots, T$ to give r_{-1}. This is done for several lags, generating r_{-2}, r_{-3}, etc., and then for Y_t related to X lagged by several periods to give r_{+1}, r_{+2}, r_{+3}, etc. The set of cross-correlations r_{+k} to r_{-k} is then examined to find the highest correlation, so identifying the 'best-fit' lead–lag. It is sometimes appropriate then to use such a lead–lag in a lagged REGRESSION model, e.g. when examining local fluctuations in response to national economic cycles. Here Y_t might be local unemployment and X_t the national unemployment series. If k is the best-fit lag, the regression has the form:

$$Y_t = bX_{t-k} + e_t$$

and b measures the cyclical sensitivity of the local economy. It is increasingly recognized, however, that such responses are gradual or distributed, and that accurate modelling requires the incorporation of several lags in the forms of a 'distributed lag' model. SPECTRAL ANALYSIS is also used to examine lead–lags between regions for different types of cycles.

A drawback of lead–lag models is that, like most statistical models, they assume that the relationship is constant across the whole time period under study, e.g. over 12 years and four economic cycles. But each cycle may have very different origins and causes, generating different patterns of leads and lags: downturns may have different timings across space to those of the subsequent upturns, and so it is important to also examine changing relationships, either graphically or by time-varying parameter models. LWH

Suggested Reading

Cliff, A.D., Haggett, P. and Ord, J.K. 1985 *Spatial aspects of influenza epidemics*. London: Pion.

Lebensraum Literally 'living space' or 'the geographical area within which living organisms develop'. In his book on POLITICAL GEOGRAPHY, Ratzel equated a NATION with a living organism and argued that a country's attempts at territorial expansion were similar to a growing organism's search for space in order to survive. Conflict between nations was presented as a contest for TERRITORY within which to expand, with the fittest surviving. The concept was appropriated by the German *Geopolitik* school in the 1920s and 1930s and used to justify the Nazi programme of territorial expansion (cf. ANTHROPOGEOGRAPHY; SOCIAL DARWINISM). RJJ

Suggested Reading

Dickinson, R.E. 1943: *The German lebensraum*. London: Penguin Books. · Parker, G. 1985: *The development of western geopolitical thought in the twentieth century*. London: Croom Helm.

leisure Essentially a state of being, in which a range of activities are undertaken outside work time for the purposes of pleasure, entertainment, knowledge-improvement, and relaxation. Leisure is significantly interconnected with RECREATION and TOURISM. Definitions of leisure have been developed on three principal axes (Glyptis, 1993; Shaw and Williams, 1994). First, leisure is equated with *time*, representing the time remaining when sleeping, working and other 'obligations' have been accounted for. The idea of 'leisure time' is discursively common, yet intrinsically meaningless (Rojek, 1985) since enormous variations occur in the quality of residual time, and in the resources available to individuals during that time. Moreover, leisure is not simply a matter of spare time. For some social groups, for example unemployed and retired people, free time is often enforced rather than self-determined, and can be burdensome rather than leisurely.

In a second defining axis, leisure is equated with particular *activities* which result in 'palpable reward, be it enjoyment, rest and recuperation, diversion, excitement, companionship, escape, or mental recreation' (Glyptis, 1993, pp. 3–4). Here, the overlap with recreation is strongest, and there is a temptation to reduce leisure to a list of measurable pursuits. However, to do so represents a false objectivity. For example in many surveys (see, for example, World Tourism Organization, 1983) eating meals is defined as biological time and therefore excluded from the category 'leisure', whereas going out for a meal is commonly regarded as a leisurely pursuit. Equally, there are activities which will be pleasurable for some and hard work for others, such as shopping, gardening, DIY, walking, and watching particular kinds of television programme.

The third axis defines leisure in terms of the participant's *attitude of mind*. Accordingly, the essence of leisure is found in the meanings ascribed to times and activities rather than in the times and activities themselves. Thus any neat cataloguing of 'work' and 'leisure' needs to be deconstructed to account for the individual subjectivities associated with leisure. So, not only is one person's leisure another person's burden, but for some their work is a kind of hobby/leisure. It is not even possible to regard leisure as something which is always freely chosen and which results in satisfaction or enjoyment. 'Choices' and 'satisfactions' are both permitted and constrained by different living and lifestyle practices associated with social identities such as class, gender and age, all of which will blur any generalized models of activities which are thought to be freely entered into and personally satisfying.

Regardless of these definitional complexities, leisure will usually be a very significant domain of life, and geographies of leisure involve understandings not only of the changing nature of consumption of leisure but also of how changes in consumption have been connected to transformations in urban and rural environments in order to meet the need for new worlds of leisure (cf. CONSUMPTION, GEOGRAPHY OF). There has been a general increase in the quantity of leisure time available to most people living in advanced industrial societies. From a position in the early twentieth century when the ability to engage in leisure was an esteemed position of the 'leisure classes' who were conspicuously exempt from all useful employment, patterns of leisure have become much more complex, with the right to leisure at particular times in the week, or the year, now a presumed characteristic of modern citizenship (Urry, 1995). Indeed, leisure has become embroiled into more general assumptions about health and welfare in these societies. These assumptions have been operationalized in a steady shortening of the working week, and more recently in an increasing flexibility of work time in some sectors. However, there may be evidence that 'working hours' have increased again in recent years, as participation in some office-based service sectors has necessitated working until the task is completed rather than working to fixed time regimes. Flexibility, then, could work both ways and does not automatically lead to an increase in leisure time away from work. Other factors in the increasing importance of leisure include improved levels of personal income mobility (for some), and improved mechanization of household chores through washing machines, dishwashers and so on (again, for some).

The consumption of leisure in contemporary western societies is also rendered complex by the shifting nature of CULTURE, IDENTITY and consumption in postmodern times. Featherstone (1991) suggests that POSTMODERNISM has brought with it a more visual and aesthetic culture which is appreciated in a more everyday and informal manner. Traditionally fixed identities have generally become more open and fluid, and traditionally deeply held and substantive self-identities have become more superficial and one-dimensional. Thus it is argued that 'there is no self beyond appearances, beyond the playful adopting and discarding of multiple life-styles and fashions' (Urry, 1995, p. 216).

Two important trends in leisure interconnect with this superficiality and fragmentation in postmodern consumption. First, leisure has become increasingly *privatized.* During the 1980s and 1990s more time than ever has been spent at home, with an ever-expanding range of virtual pursuits being accessible through the sound system, television, video and personal computer. Participation has declined in most forms of out-of-home leisure which can be replicated or closely substituted by in-home entertainment (Roberts, 1989). Indeed much of the production of leisure spectacles (for example in sport, film and music) will be directed at, and funded by, the potential for home-consumption. Secondly, there has been a growth in the *commercialization* of leisure industries, with very large companies such as Rank and Grand Metropolitan providing for leisure activities across the social spectrum. Commercialization has involved a commodification of heritage, culture, sport, and other leisure foci, both in terms of providing pay-as-you-enter attractions, and in terms of designing and branding clothing, equipment and other paraphernalia which needs to be purchased so that the consumer can be identified with the leisure pursuit in question. Indeed, shopping itself has become the major leisure preoccupation of contemporary western society (Miller et al., 1998; cf. RETAILING, GEOGRAPHY OF).

Postmodern consumption, then, has developed a 'cultural desire' for particular forms and identities of leisure, and indeed for particular kinds of culturally desirable spaces in cities and countrysides. Urry (1995) describes three factors of cultural desirability in TOWNSCAPES and LANDSCAPES: the availability of sites/sights to visit, often involving new forms of capital and organization in specific geographical locations; the visibility of appropriately aesthetic styles of vernacular architecture or of countryside landscapes, often involving specific place promotions which appeal to these cultural desires; and the cultural legitimization of desirable leisure activities, for example the use of literary and artistic figures to render certain countryside (for example Hardy Country, Herriot Country) as tasteful.

Contemporary leisure draws heavily on these cultural desirabilities, with the consumption of signs, or the symbolic aspects of goods becoming a major source of satisfaction derived from leisure. Thus, in urban contexts there is an increasing salience of leisure consumption which focuses on the consuming of experiences and pleasure (notably in these parks, and leisure centres). There is also a move towards recreating traditionally high forms of cultural consumption (such as museums and galleries) into more accessible and enjoyable attractions, emphasizing spectacle, populism and entertainment (cf. SPECTACLE, GEOGRAPHY OF). There is also the growing dominance of these high temples of urban leisure consumption, the shopping malls. In rural contexts, too, themed attractions have become important foci for cultural consumption of heritage, nature and sheer entertainment (Cloke, 1993). Moreover, traditional leisure pursuits such as driving, walking, picnicking and sightseeing have been supplemented by new activities which add a sense of purposeful entertainment, or technological equipment, such as in mountain-biking, off-road vehicle driving, survival and endurance sports and windsurfing.

As is the case with TOURISM, contemporary geographies of leisure have profited from the conceptual understandings emanating from sociology and cultural studies. However, the importance of new and transformed leisure spaces in both urban and rural environments leaves many questions unanswered about how those spaces are (re)constructed and given meaning. Equally, there remain important concerns relating to the inequalities of access to privatized and commercialized leisure, which result in the geography of leisure being an important, and often underestimated component in issues of SOCIAL EXCLUSION. PJC

References

Butler, R. 1998: Rural recreation and tourism. In B. Ilbery, ed., *The geography of rural change*. Harlow: Longman, 211–32. · Cloke, P. 1993: The countryside as commodity: new spaces for rural leisure. In S. Glyptis, ed., *Leisure and the environment*. London: Belhaven, 53–70. · Featherstone, M. 1991: *Consumer culture and postmodernism*. London: Sage. · Glyptis, S., ed., 1993: *Leisure and the environment*. London: Belhaven. · Miller, D., Jackson, P., Thrift, N., Holbrook, B. and Rowlands, M. 1998: *Shopping, place and identity*. London: Routledge. · Roberts, K. 1989: Great Britain: socio-economic polarization and the implications for leisure. In A. Olszewska and K. Roberts, eds, *Leisure and life-style*. London: Sage. · Rojek, C. 1985: *Capitalism and leisure theory*. London: Tavistock; Shaw, G. and Williams, A.M. 1994: *Critical issues in tourism: a geographical perspective*. Oxford: Blackwell. · Urry, J. 1995: *Consuming places*. London: Routledge. · World Tourism Organization 1983: *Development of leisure time and the right to holidays*. Madrid: World Tourism Organization.

Suggested Reading

Rojek, C. 1995: *Decentring leisure, rethinking leisure, theory*. London: Sage. · Urry, J. 1990: *The tourist gaze: leisure and travel in contemporary societies*. London: Sage.

LETS (Local Exchange Trading Systems/ Schemes) Insofar as they are localized sets of transactions based upon local production, exchange and consumption, LETS are local ECONOMIC GEOGRAPHIES. They use a local currency which is not exchangeable with, but which may or may not be closely related in nominal value to, a national currency. Within the USA and Australia such currencies tend to go by the generic term 'green dollars' but in the UK they take on a name associated with the locality – bobbins in Manchester, tales in Canterbury, hops in Tonbridge – thereby indicating their local provenance and circulation. There is no paper money or coinage involved in LETS. Money takes the form of cheque books through which purchases are made. The cheques are then forwarded to the LETS treasurer or accountant who adds the debit or credit the accounts of all individual members. These accounts are made public to all members of the LETS.

The local currency facilitates exchange of services and self-produced or self-earned goods across the network of members within the LETS. Thus, although restricted in geographical scale, exchange within a LETS is not limited to barter (the bilateral exchanges of one good for another). Insofar as information about the LETS network – its members and the commodities that they wish to trade – is kept up-to-date and accurate and is published in the directory of offers and wants provided to all members, the local currency acts as a money network. It offers information not just about the possibility of individual transactions (sale and purchase) but about the extent (diversity, size, geographical range) of those possibilities. In this way, it offers some sense of temporal and spatial continuity, at least insofar as the currency will continue to be a means of engaging in economic activity within a LETS. At the same time, however, the bases of the valuation of transactions may be locally constituted. It is in this sense that LETS cannot be reduced merely to the economic but, like all economic geographies, must be understood as a set of social relations (Lee, 1996).

Thus LETS might equally be categorized as miniature forms of CIVIL SOCIETY in which questions of evaluation may go beyond those associated with use value or exchange value (see MARXIAN ECONOMICS). They might, perhaps, reflect ecologically sustainable values, or enable the foregoing of efficiency and choice, for example, and the acceptance of a lower material standard of living in order to free up time to engage in alternative activities. There is, however, a limit to these alternative values which is set by the inputs necessary to sustain social reproduction. Bowring (1998, p. 106), for example, suggests that:

> [M]aintaining the tension between the micro-social activities of local trading systems and the more efficient and productive functioning of the macro-economic system is . . . crucial to the protection of individual liberties and of the space for innovation, imagination, and experimental change.

Thus, although LETS offer great scope for the practice of alternative values and so open up a range of political possibilities (see North, 1999), there is an uneasy and hotly contested fault line between them and the formal economy. Those who follow Michael Linton, who founded the first LETS on Vancouver Island, British Columbia in 1983, argue that, in order to act as an alternative to the formal economy, LETS must connect with it so as to diversify their potential offerings and to work in ways responsive to the demands of the formal economy. On the other hand, those who advocate LETS primarily as autonomous social alternatives argue that such integration would destroy the very basis of the attraction of LETS as alternatives.

In any event, although LETS have great potential to offer alternative ways of life incorporating values other than those of the formal economic geography, and so to provide a means of regenerating local economic geographies, reintegrating society and promoting SUSTAINABLE DEVELOPMENT, these are possibilities more than capable of subversion by exploitation or by the power of the surrounding formal economic geographies. Thus local firms may gain access to markets, cheap capital and cheap labour, whilst the more affluent and skilled members of a LETS may commit precious little time but acquire large quantities of the time of others. Similarly, LETS will struggle to compete with the efficiency and choice of the formal economic geography and so may be abandoned by the more mobile and lead to a form of currency GHETTOIZATION. At the same time, LETS may be seen as a source of taxable income affecting welfare or may themselves become a form of workfare.

There are ways around such difficulties (see, for example Bowring, 1998), not least through the use of currency units of time which prevent exploitation in the strict Marxist sense, may promote a more egalitarian reconfiguration of value, avoid taxation and benefits traps and maximize the use of time. However, not only is it the case that LETS account for only a tiny proportion of the population even in countries, like Australia and New Zealand, for example, where they are well-developed but they represent only a marginal addition to the material welfare of their members. But such a conclusion is to assert the autonomy of the economic. Perhaps the greatest value of LETS is their very demonstration of alternative conceptions and uses of time and space, less as resources than as processes. RL

References

Bowring, F. 1998: LETS: an eco-socialist initiative? *New Left Review* 232: 91–111. · Lee, R. 1996: Moral money? LETS and the social construction of local economic geographies in southeast England. *Environment and Planning A* 28: 1377–94. · North, P. 1999: Explorations in heterotopia: Local exchange trading schemes (LETS) and the micro-politics of money and livelihood. *Environment and Planning D: Society and Space*, 17, 69–86.

Suggested Reading

Bowring (1998). · Croall, J. 1997: *Lets act locally*. Calouste Gulbenkian Foundation: London; Lee (1996). · North (1999). · Williams, C.C. 1996: The new barter economy: an appraisal of Local Exchange Trading Systems (LETS). *Journal of Public Policy* 16: 85–101.

liberalism An enormously influential western political theory that underpins modern democracy and more. It structures political systems, bureaucracies, our notions of CITIZENSHIP, and self, and is often (though not always) conjoint to CAPITALISM. Liberalism is usually called a protean political theory because its emphasis has changed over the centuries and in different places. Gray (1986), however, has suggested four strands in liberal thought, outlined below. Amidst these themes, its relationship to geographic thought is best characterized as equivocal. On the one hand, there are affirmative links between the two bodies of thought, where the two theoretical domains clearly reflect and reinforce each other (see DISCOURSE). On the other hand, there have been numerous critiques of liberalism in which geographies have participated insightfully.

Individualism. The individual is the principal focus and unit of analysis in liberal thinking. The liberal individual is delimited by the BODY and holds certain inalienable rights, achieves self-worth and knowledge (in other words, his/her idea of 'the good') through exercises of freedom. For liberals, then, individual liberty to pursue the good is the primary social good in SOCIETY (in some strands of liberalism this point is argued to be a natural human condition). In order to argue this point, liberals must hold a certain sceptical and ambivalent attitude toward the STATE. It is a necessary evil: on the one hand guaranteeing freedoms (and this should be its only aim), while on the other constantly threatening other freedoms when it tries to carry this very function! There is deep suspicion of state authority, especially in determining the nature of 'the good'. Politics is conceptualized as a morally neutral arena where individuals seek to maximize their pursuit of the good. This is sometimes summarized as 'the priority of the right over the good' (Mouffe, 1993), meaning that individual rights should trump any broader social, collective definition of 'the good' should the two conflict. By drawing distinctions between PRIVATE AND PUBLIC SPHERES, liberals limit state POWER and force or create forums where individuals' freedoms are guaranteed. Here we can see how liberalism reinforces the hegemony of CAPITALISM, since profit-making and a capacity to sell one's own labour are validated as freedoms.

Emphases on individualism are found at several turns in geographic thought. Neo-classical ECONOMIC GEOGRAPHY's *homo economicus* (see RATIONAL CHOICE THEORY) is informed clearly by this perspective. HUMANISTIC GEOGRAPHY, in a rather different way, also celebrates the integrity and primacy of the individual. In POLITICAL GEOGRAPHY, liberalism influences debates over jurisdictional partitioning's consequences for individual rights and freedoms (GERRYMANDERING; ELECTORAL GEOGRAPHY; DISTRICTING ALGORITHM). Most recently, geographers have been interested in how much public and private spheres are spatialized.

Within political theory, COMMUNITARIANS characteristically criticize liberalism's individualism as socially thin, atomizing, and amoral. They challenge liberalism by declaring 'the priority of the good over the right', thus linking politics and morality at a social, contextual scale. In geography, strains of communitarian thought might be detected paradoxically in both Marxist and Humanistic authors, insofar as both draw broader moral arguments into their understandings of political action. Marxism, however, especially rejects the radical individualism ideological subterfuge (Harvey, 1973; cf. MARXIST GEOGRAPHY), while Humanism depicts a less instrumental, fuller psyche for agents.

Egalitarianism. According to liberal theory, all citizens have equal political standing and moral worth in society. Egalitarianism is a necessary corollary to the liberal individualism, since it would be logically inconsistent to argue for human freedoms but then claim that certain people's freedoms are more vital than others. Geographers interested in SOCIAL JUSTICE have certainly manifested liberalism (Smith, 1994). POST-STRUCTURAL geographers are currently interested in how to sustain egalitarianism while simultaneously appreciating DIFFERENCE and diversity (see RADICAL DEMOCRACY). In the post-war era, some theorists have claimed the rise of NEO-LIBERALISM. While difficult to pin down because it is used quite differently in different places, it signals an endorsement of egalitarian diversity (often depicted as the outcome of SOCIAL MOVEMENTS' struggles since the 1960s), though it is caught in debates over the extent to which the state should pursue (and pay for) this aim. NEO-LIBERALISM seems to underpin *the new middle class* that Ley (1991) associates with GENTRIFICATION.

Universalism. Liberalism argues an overarching, trumping unity to the human species and places historical and geographical social arrangements as secondary or contingent. The ESSENTIALISM of the human subject is echoed in humanistic and neoclassical thinking of course, but geography's IDIOGRAPHIC tendencies have always provided a challenge to this tenet. Most recently, and more sophisticatedly, POSTMODERN geographers of various stripes have worked over this point. Feminists exposed the PATRIARCHY in liberal ideas that are grounded in an exclusively male individual, undermining not only its claims to UNIVERSALISM but egalitarianism as well (Marston, 1990). This sexism not only excludes the subject of women from politics and CITIZENSHIP, but also ignores a priori forms and location of action that may well be considered political. Similar arguments have been made with respect to exclusionary heterosexism. Likewise, a major thrust of POST-COLONIALISM has been directed at the racism and cultural violence of liberal individualism promulgated by IMPERIALISM (e.g. Hyndman, 1997). How, for example, does the UN declaration of HUMAN RIGHTS violate indigenous communal or natural ONTOLOGIES of the self?

Meliorism. Liberalism is an essentially optimistic and progressive worldview, believing fundamentally that political institutions and social arrangements can be improved upon by human effort. Thus the most compelling arguments in early radical (and critical human) GEOGRAPHY work from the liberal assumption that social institutions can be improved, hence the point of critique. Likewise, APPLIED GEOGRAPHY's focus is clearly grounded in this strand of liberalism. This belief, however, has suffered under the more extreme nihilism sometimes associated with postmodernism, since a major consequence of that thinking has been the impossibility of removing oneself from the exercises of power that inevitably cause oppression. Here we might note a series of reflexive essays and editorials in the last decade that have posed questions of meliorism in geographic research (e.g. Barnes and Gregory, 1997). MPB

References

Barnes, T. and Gregory, D., eds, 1997: *Reading human geography*. London: Arnold. · Gray, J. 1986: *Liberalism*. Minneapolis: University of Minnesota Press. · Harvey, D. 1973: *Social justice and the city*. London: Arnold and Baltimore: Johns Hopkins. · Hyndman, J. 1997: Border crossings. *Antipode* 29: 149–76. · Ley, D. 1991: Gentrification and the politics of the new middle class. *Environment and Planning D: Society and Space* 12:

53–74. · Marston, S. 1990: Who are 'the people'? *Environment and Planning D: Society and Space* 8: 449–58. · Mouffe, C. 1993: *The return of the political*. London: Verso. · Smith, D.M. 1994: *Geography and social justice*. Oxford: Blackwell.

Suggested Reading

Gray, J. 1986: *Liberalism*. Minneapolis: University of Minnesota Press. · Kymlicka, W. 1990: *Contemporary political philosophy*. New York: Oxford University Press. · Sandel, M. 1984: *Liberalism and its critics*. New York: New York University Press.

libertarianism A moral and political philosophy which prioritizes individual freedom or liberty. In a libertarian society, as described by Robert Nozick (1974) for example, individuals are entitled to do as they please with their holdings, including their property (providing that it has been acquired justly), and with themselves, so long as they do not infringe the same freedom for others. The role of the STATE is minimal, and should not be extended to taxing some citizens so as to provide for the needs of others. There is no obligation for anyone to do anything for anyone else unless this is their free choice. This form of 'right libertarianism' is sometimes contrasted with ANARCHISM as 'left libertarianism'. DMS

Reference

Nozick, R. 1974: *Anarchy, state, and utopia*. New York: Basic Books.

life expectancy The average number of years to be lived, generally derived from LIFE TABLE calculations, either from birth or from a particular age (usually denoted as e_x, where x is age). *Life expectancy at birth*, e_0, is frequently used as a summary measure of MORTALITY for the whole population; life expectancy generally increases during the first year, because of infant mortality, but thereafter the decline is generally steady. Life expectancy has improved dramatically in most countries during the twentieth century: in the USA, e_0 for the population as a whole was around 76 years in 1996; and in Europe e_0 for males was in the low–middle 70s, and for females well into the 70s or early 80s – e.g. in Sweden, 81.5 years for females in 1996, and 76.2 for males. Much of the developing world has also seen sharp improvements in life expectancy, especially since mid-century, as a consequence of improved nutrition, public health and medical care, whose most important effects are frequently to reduce the level of infant mortality (see HEALTH AND HEALTH CARE, GEOGRAPHY OF; MEDICAL GEOGRAPHY). But life expectancy in Africa, for example, was still only in the mid-50s for both men and women in 1996. PEO

Suggested Reading

Jones, H. 1990: *Population geography*. London: Paul Chapman, ch. 3.

life table A table showing the probability of surviving from one age to any subsequent age, according to the age-specific death rates prevailing at a particular time and place (cf. MORTALITY). It may be assumed for the purposes of calculation, for example, that 100,000 babies are all born on the same day, and the experience of this COHORT is followed until its last surviving member dies: the summary of that experience is the life table. Life tables were first compiled for actuarial purposes in order to calculate for each age group the possibility of dying, the number of deaths, the number of survivors, and the average LIFE EXPECTANCY of the latter, as a basis for life assurance premiums. They may also be used as structural models for studying population growth (see STABLE POPULATION) and projections (see POPULATION PROJECTION) and as a summary of mortality experiences in different countries or regions. PEO

Suggested Reading

Plane, D.A. and Rogerson, P.A. 1994: *The geographical analysis of population*. New York and Chichester: John Wiley, ch. 3. · Woods, R.I. 1979: *Population analysis in geography*. London and New York: Longman, ch. 3.

life-cycle The process of growth, adulthood and old age which human beings experience, each stage being associated with various forms of social, economic and political behaviour. The idea of stage in the life-cycle has been much used in FACTORIAL ECOLOGIES of urban areas. Crucial stages in the life-cycle for many people following childhood include: marriage, a pre-child stage, birth and rearing of children, a post-child stage, and finally family dissolution with the death of one spouse. These stages may affect MOBILITY, income, demand for housing and recreational activities, among other things (see HOUSING STUDIES; LEISURE, GEOGRAPHY OF; RECREATION). The life-cycle is reflected in the AGE AND SEX STRUCTURE of an area's population.

More recently, the term *life course* has been increasingly preferred (Warnes, 1992) in order to recognize the complexity of experiences which may mark an individual's passage from birth to death including, for example, non-heterosexual lifestyles and diverse living arrangements which follow divorce and remarriage. PEO

Reference

Warnes, T. 1992: Migration and the life course. In T. Champion and T. Fielding, eds, *Migration patterns and processes. Volume 1: Research Progress and Prospects*. London and New York: Belhaven, 175–87.

Suggested Reading

Bongaarts, J., Burch, T.K. and Wachter, K.W. 1987: *Family demography. Methods and their application.* Oxford: Clarendon Press.

lifeworld According to Buttimer (1976), 'the culturally defined spatio-temporal setting or horizon of everyday life', lifeworld encompasses the totality of an individual person's direct involvement with the PLACES and environments experienced in ordinary life.

The term originates in German PHENOMENOLOGY as *Lebenswelt*, which signifies a relationship of *intentionality* between a conscious and imaginative human subject and the external world as it is given unreflexively to individual human attention. Thus it incorporates both the conscious projects which shape human existence with respect to the world of experience, as well as a more passive sense of that world impacting upon ourselves, thereby generating the idea of a *field of care*: the meaningful subjectivity of the experienced world in the frame of an individual's life. It is within the lifeworld that meaning is attributed to external phenomena through intuitive experiences and relationships with them. Phenomenological philosophies give attention to the apparently trivial phenomena of a lifeworld, using the possessive pronoun to denote the field of care – *my* embodied experiences, being in *my* birthplace, *my* home. This distinguishes phenomenologically informed explorations of PLACE and SPACE from more POSITIVIST and STRUCTURALIST approaches which, respectively, presuppose such matters but leave them unexamined or regard them as epiphenomenal to more impersonal forces shaping human existence. In the classic phenomenological formulation of the *époché*, close attention to such phenomena, freed as far as possible from a priori presuppositions and as they are constituted in consciousness, gives access to truths about them and about ourselves. This conception of the lifeworld was much studied in HUMANISTIC GEOGRAPHY in the 1970s and 1980s in its concern to understand places and environments without accepting the analytical separation of subject from object (Buttimer and Seamon, 1980). From this perspective, geographic phenomena such as places, environments and COMMUNITIES become understood as material realizations of fields of care.

In geography the concept of the lifeworld has directed attention to the significance of everyday life and the personal, meaningful geographies developed and practised within it (see TAKEN-FOR-GRANTED WORLD). The concept's use denotes opposition to the more distant, analytical and manipulative approaches of SPATIAL SCIENCE and planning spatial organization or behaviour. Thus, from the person-centred perspective of the lifeworld, place is more important than space, and geographical investigation is required to honour the experiences, imagination and attachments of intentional human subjects. More recent geographical studies of place have recognized the dangers of essentializing human experience and identity, and that in shaping the SENSE OF PLACE individual lifeworlds are never entirely disconnected from more structural constraints upon consciousness and action, and have therefore sought to incorporate both into geographical investigation (Pickles, 1987). On the other hand, geographical studies of the subject and its embodied identities since the 1980s have tended to ignore the concept of individually shaped and coherent lifeworlds in favour of more fluid notions of selfhood and place identity (Pile and Thrift, 1995; cf. BODY, GEOGRAPHY AND). DEC

References

Buttimer, A. 1976: Grasping the dynamics of the lifeworld. *Annals, Association of American Geographers* 66: 277–92. · Buttimer, A. and Seamon, D. 1980: *The human experience of space and place*. London: Croom Helm. · Pickles, J. 1987: *Geography and humanism*. Norwich: GeoBooks. · Pile, S. and Thrift, N., eds, 1995: *Mapping the subject: geographies of cultural transformation*. London and New York: Routledge.

Suggested Reading

Rodaway, P. 1994: *Sensuous geographies: body, sense and place*. London and New York: Routledge. · Seamon, D. 1979: *A geography of the lifeworld: movement, rest and encounter*. London: Croom Helm.

limits to growth A phrase introduced in 1972 as a report title by a group called the Club of Rome (Meadows et al., 1972). Researchers for this group used computer modelling of the world system to conclude that humans were likely to overshoot the earth's RESOURCE capacity (cf. CARRYING CAPACITY). According to them, avoiding this scenario necessitated immediate action to achieve global equilibrium between human demands and environmental resources, focusing on the stabilization of population and per capita consumption levels (cf. GLOBAL FUTURES).

The term 'limits to growth' is derived from the writings of Thomas Robert Malthus, John Stuart Mill and Adam Smith. In 1776 Smith suggested that a country which had acquired a full complement of riches and could advance no further would at some point in the future encounter limits to economic growth. However, the report *Limits to growth* is often labelled 'Neo-Malthusian' because it is based on the MALTHUSIAN MODEL's incorporation of a geometric or exponential growth rate of population. This model points either to the need for urgent action because 'problems' are continually doubling or a sense that problems are too entrenched to be effectively addressed. McCormick (1995) discusses the Club of Rome, and other reports of the same era, under the heading 'The Prophets of Doom: 1968–1972'.

The report examined five basic factors that the authors believed 'determine, and therefore ultimately limit, growth on this planet – population, agricultural production, NATURAL RESOURCES, industrial production and POLLUTION' (Meadows et al., 1972, pp. 11–12). Interested in limits, they recast these five factors as 'five major trends of global concern – accelerating INDUSTRIALIZATION, rapid population growth, widespread malnutrition, depletion of non-renewable resources, and a deteriorating environment' (Meadows et al., 1972, p. 21). Their report was heavily criticized for its perceived doomsday tone, its methodology and its focus. From a Marxist perspective, for example, David Harvey followed some of Marx's original critiques of Malthus' 1798 *Essay on the principle of population*, by arguing that questions of overpopulation diverted attention from issues of distribution rather than production and from questions of CLASS. Buttel et al. (1990) claimed that the report's only lasting impact is its localization in the form of NIMBY movements and local growth control politics. However, many authors use the idea of limits. Dobson (1996) recognized that acceptance of the limits to growth thesis in some form (not necessarily that of Meadows et al., 1972) is a distinguishing feature between the more radical ecologism, and less radical ENVIRONMENTALISM (cf. DEEP ECOLOGY).

In a further report, published twenty years after the first, *Beyond the limits: global collapse or a sustainable future*, Meadows et al. (1992) maintained that their 1972 conclusions were still valid, but should be strengthened. They emphasized the challenge facing humanity to achieve sustainability. There are many limits to growth, but the key limit in their book was *throughput* (i.e. the physical flows of ENERGY and materials in extraction, production, consumption and the disposal of waste into nature's sinks). But the context has altered significantly from the early 1970s and Meadows et al.'s radical message appears to have gained little acceptance due to the reformist notion of SUSTAINABLE DEVELOPMENT and the backlash by anti-environmental authors. However, the work of Paul and Anne Ehrlich (1996), addressing some of the myths advanced by growth advocates, has highlighted again the importance of limits. Many scientists and other writers now recognize that the earth is finite, and are prepared to consider limits in some form. PM

References

Buttel, F., Hawkins, A. and Power, A. 1990: From limits to growth to global change: constraints and contradictions in the evolution of environmental science and ideology. *Global Environmental Change* 1: 57–66. · Dobson, A. 1996: *Green political thought: an introduction*, 2nd edn. London: Unwin Hyman; Ehrlich, P. and Ehrlich, A. 1996: *Betrayal of science and reason: how anti-environmental rhetoric threatens our future*. Washington, D.C.: Island Press. · Covelo, California: Shearwater Books. · McCormick, J. 1995: *The global environmental movement*, 2nd edn. Chichester: John Wiley and Sons. · Meadows, D.H., Meadows, D.L., Randers J. and Brehens III, W. 1972: *The limits to growth*. London: Earth Island. · Meadows, D.H., Meadows, D.L. and Randers, J. 1992: *Beyond the limits: global collapse or a sustainable future*. London: Earthscan.

linear programming A mathematical tool for seeking optimal solutions to location problems, devised to identify optimal configurations for whole SYSTEMS in terms of an objective function to be maximized (i.e. a goal to be achieved), subject to constraints. The methods of solution are iterative, converging on the optimum by a series of adjustments from an initial, feasible, solution.

The first task is to define the *objective function*. In economic studies this is usually stated in monetary terms – such as maximizing revenue or minimizing costs – but other quantities may be defined, such as minimizing the total distance travelled to schools from their homes by pupils, minimizing the average distance from a fire station to any potential site of a fire, or maximizing the food output from a farm.

The second step involves setting the *constraints*. These may be either equalities, such as the number of pupils allocated to each school is equal to the number of places there, or inequalities, such as the number of pupils

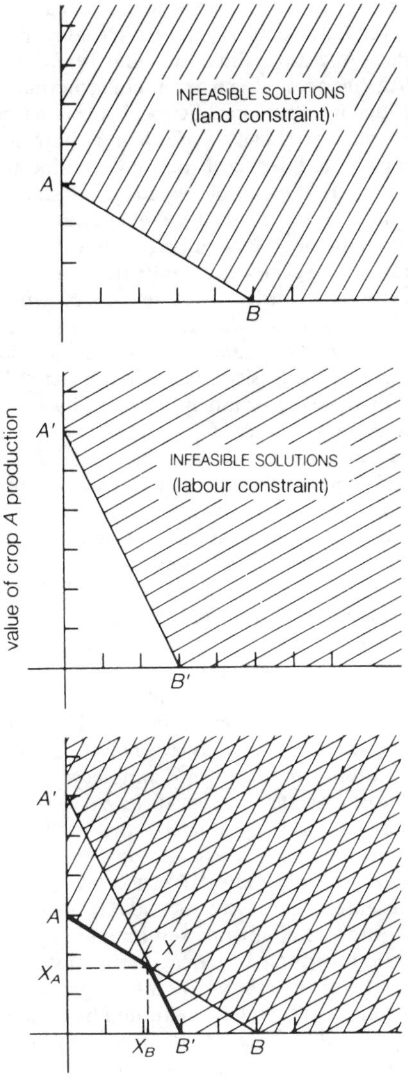

linear programming *The graphical solution to a simple linear programming problem, showing the effect of constraints, the convex set of feasible solutions lying within the convex hull AXB′ and the optimal solution at X*

allocated to a school shall be equal to, or less than, the number of places there. It is assumed that the production functions involved are linear: e.g. that the total amount of travel by the pupils is a function of the number of pupils and the distance travelled.

Simple linear programming problems can be solved graphically. A farmer, for example, may wish to maximize the cash return from two crops A and B (the objective function), subject to the constraints of the amount of land and labour available. The possible combinations of the two crops are plotted on the first graph in the figure, where the axes indicate the amounts of A and B grown: they can vary through monoculture (i.e. only crop A is grown), through various mixes of A and B, to a further monoculture (i.e. only crop B is grown). The amount of land available means that all solutions above and to the right of the line joining A and B are not feasible, whereas any solution below and to the left is sub-optimal, since it does not use up all of the available land. The middle graph in the figure shows a similar analysis using the constraint of available labour. Superimposition of the two graphs (in the lower part of the figure) reveals that some solutions are infeasible because of land constraints whereas others result from labour supply constraints. The maximum yield is achieved with the combination of A and B at X (i.e. X_A of crop A and X_B of crop B). The line AXB' is known as the *convex hull* and the area below it as the *convex set*: all solutions within the set are feasible; all those on the hull employ all of the land and labour resources.

More complex problems, with more than two constraints, have more sides to the hull, which means that solutions have to be found in multi-dimensional space, which is not possible graphically: they have to be approached either by using a *simplex algorithm* or by recasting the problem as a TRANSPORTATION PROBLEM.

Solution of such problems also produces what are known as *shadow prices*. The farmer might, for example, decide to reduce production of crop A below the optimum indicated, but there will be OPPORTUNITY COSTS in so doing: income will be lost because of such sub-optimal behaviour (i.e. RENT will be lost).

Linear programming was originally devised as an approach to solving management problems in, for example, resource allocation but has proved valuable in a wide range of geographical applications such as the planning of agricultural, transport, industrial and warehouse location, the delimitation of school districts and the siting of health-care facilities. Occasionally, linear programming has been used to evaluate the efficiency of actual location decisions – whether the pattern is the most efficient possible – usually with disappointing results: close matches are rarely found, suggesting that the objective functions and constraints applied by decision-makers are too complex to be modelled in this way.

AMH

Suggested Reading

Abler, R.F., Adams, J.S. and Gould, P.R. 1971: *Spatial organization: the geographer's view of the world*. Englewood Cliffs, NJ: Prentice Hall. · Killen, J.E. 1979: *Linear programming: the simplex method with geographical applications*. Norwich: GeoBooks, CATMOG 24. · Vajda, S. 1960: *An introduction to linear programming and the theory of games*. London: Methuen and New York: John Wiley.

linkages The contacts and flows of information and/or materials between two or more individuals. The term is widely used in both INDUSTRIAL GEOGRAPHY and the geography of SERVICES to indicate inter-firm interdependence and its effects on location choice (see AGGLOMERATION). A firm's linkages can be divided into: (1) *backward*, which provide goods and services for its production activities; (2) *forward* – links with customers purchasing its products; and (3) *sideways* – interactions with other firms involved in the same processes. Membership of such networks is increasingly seen as crucial to success and survival for a firm, especially a small firm. (See also INTEGRATION; LOCATIONAL INTERDEPENDENCE.) RJJ

local knowledge A term first coined by the English philosopher Gordon Ryle, and popularized by the American anthropologist Clifford Geertz (1983). Local knowledge now refers to the two-part idea that first, all knowledge is located and geographically and historically bounded, and second, that the local conditions of its manufacture affect substantively the nature of the knowledge produced. Note that local knowledge does not mean knowledge of only a restricted geographical area. Local refers to the context in which knowledge is produced, not the geographical domain to which the knowledge applies. Stephen Hawking's theory of the universe, for example, is a piece of local knowledge even though the theory's explanatory province is infinitely large.

To take in turn the two parts of the definition, by '*located and geographically and historically bounded*' is meant that knowledge is historically constrained, and produced within particular material settings which include, for example, the geographical site, particular kinds of human bodies, and specific types of buildings, machines and equipment. A key word here is 'produced'. As a process, producing knowledge contrasts with the conventional view that knowledge is acquired through discovery (meaning literally 'uncover'). In the discovery view, knowledge is assumed free-floating and pre-existent, for example, as Platonic forms (see UNIVERSALISM), requiring only the right conditions to be revealed. To say that knowledge is produced, however, suggests something different; that there is an active process of creative construction 'on site' according to specific local rules and conditions. Specifically, producing knowledge entails a confluence of the right conditions of production: people, places, ideas and material artefacts (see SITUATED KNOWLEDGE). Examples might be: Marx poring over the records of factory inspectors at the British Museum in the 1860s in order to write *Das Kapital*; or graduate students making vigorous use of large desk calculators in the statistics laboratory at the University of Iowa in the late 1950s, and in so doing producing geography's QUANTITATIVE REVOLUTION.

By '*local conditions affect the knowledge produced*' is meant that the material and historical setting, and the various social interests associated with it, enter into the very lineaments of knowledge itself. The reason is that the production of knowledge is a social activity. Knowledge does not come from the sky, from heavenly inspiration, but from engaging in particular kinds of social practices that are historically and geographically variable. Knowledge is therefore irreducibly social, never innocent, and always coloured by the context of its production. Examples are legion: ENVIRONMENTAL DETERMINISM perfectly expressed (and legitimated) the RACIST and IMPERIALIST impulses of late-nineteenth-century Europe; REGIONAL SCIENCE assiduously represented the INSTRUMENTALIST, MASCULINIST, and economistic sentiments of mid-twentieth-century America; and POSTMODERNISM reflects a late-twentieth-century restless consumer CAPITALISM constituted by flickering images and fabricated identities. All knowledge, then, is local knowledge, born from specific contexts (cf. CONSUMPTION, GEOGRAPHY OF). The important corollary is that universal claims to Truth are unsupportable. All knowledge claims are made inside the circle of local context, with no means of moving outside for 'a God's eye view', as Haraway (1991, p. 193) puts it.

Local knowledge, then, is local in a double sense. First, it is produced in limited geographical and historical settings (and not everywhere), and second, its claims to truth are not inherently universal (see UNIVERSALISM).

There have been two main groups of scholars concerned with local knowledge. First, anthropologists, and especially ETHNOGRAPHERS, have long struggled with the problem of understanding and representing difference; in their case, cultures that are typically vastly different from their own. Early ethnographers dealt with the difficulty by judging the Other according to their own invariably western standards taken as universal. More recently, though, ethnographers, such as Clifford Geertz (1988, p. 137), have argued for the impossibility of 'telling it like it is' because ethnographic accounts are as much about the world of the representer as the world of the represented (and so transparently obvious in those early ethnographies; Geertz, 1988). Ethnographers, then, have come up against the problem of local knowledge. One recent complication, however, is the effect of an increasingly fluid, mobile, and hyperactive world on the very notion of local knowledge. James Clifford (1986, p. 22) writes, 'A conceptual shift, "tectonic" in its implications, has taken place. We ground things, now, on a moving earth. There is no longer any place of overview (mountaintop) from which to map the human ways of life.... [O]ne cannot occupy, unambiguously, a bounded cultural world from which to journey out and analyze other cultures.' Knowledge is still produced at specific sites, but it also travels. Knowledge is now inter-local, though never universal.

A tectonic shift has also occurred in the philosophy and sociology of science since the early 1960s. Prior to Kuhn's (1962) work (see PARADIGM), the 'standard model' of scientific practice was that of the dispassionate scientist systematically applying universal, rational methods to unlock the truths of an inert, material world. But since Kuhn, and the various offspring he in effect spawned (SCIENCE, GEOGRAPHY AND), the standard model has been increasingly criticized (Barnes, 1996, pp. 106–21). The main objection is that science should be conceived as a social activity with all the implied biases, inconsistencies, rationalizations, and divided loyalties. Scientific knowledge, like any knowledge, is shot full of social interests, reflecting the time and place of its manufacture: it is local knowledge. Initially the Edinburgh school, and later feminists, such as Haraway (1989), provided detailed, often historical, studies laying bare those social interests (for example, Shapin and Schaffer's, 1985, study of Boyle's air pump experiments). Later work, such as Latour and Woolgar (1979), concentrated on very specific local sites, such as the laboratory, and concomitant micro practices of research and relations of power that produce knowledge. The point here, as Rouse (1987, p. 72) writes, is that scientists 'go from one local knowledge to another rather than from universal theories to their particular instantiations'. Again, there is a sense of local knowledge travelling; in this case, proceeding hesitantly and provisionally from one particular site and type of practice to another (see also ACTOR–NETWORK THEORY).

Ironically geography's recent past has been dominated by the quest for universal knowledge rather than the local kind. The discipline's post-war history is intimately bound up with the search for GRAND THEORY and attendant universality, ESSENTIALISM and FOUNDATIONALISM. Things are beginning to change, however, with an increasingly POST-STRUCTURAL sensibility. Although the term local knowledge is not always used, the sentiments it expresses are now found in recent works on the history of the discipline (Livingstone, 1992); IDENTITY POLITICS (Pile and Thrift, 1995); the geography of DEVELOPMENT (Slater, 1992; see also EUROCENTRISM); and ECONOMIC GEOGRAPHY (Barnes, 1996). (See also CONTEXTUAL EFFECT; NEIGHBOURHOOD EFFECT.) TJB

References

Barnes, T.J. 1996: *Logics of dislocation: models, metaphors and meanings of economic space*. New York: Guilford. · Clifford, J. 1986: Introduction: partial truths. In J. Clifford, and G.E. Marcus, eds, *Writing culture: the poetics and politics of enquiry*. Berkeley, CA: University of California Press, 1–26. · Geertz. G. 1983: *Local knowledge: further essays in interpretive anthropology*. New York: Basic Books. · Geertz, C. 1988: *Works and lives: the anthropologist as author*. Stanford, CA: Stanford University Press. · Haraway, D.J. 1989: *Primate visions: gender, race and nature in the world of modern science*. New York: Routledge. · Haraway, D.J. 1991: *Simians, cyborgs and women: the reinvention of nature*. New York: Routledge. · Kuhn, T. 1962: *The structure of scientific revolutions*. Chicago: University of Chicago Press. · Latour, B. and Woolgar, S. 1979: *Laboratory life: the construction of scientific facts*. London: Sage. · Livingstone, D.N. 1992: *The geographical tradition: episodes in a contested enterprise*. Oxford: Blackwell. · Pile, S. and Thrift, N.J., eds, 1995: *Mapping the subject: geographies of cultural transformation*. London: Routledge. · Rouse, J. 1987: *Knowledge and power: towards a political philosophy of science*. Ithaca, NY: Cornell University Press. · Shapin, S. and Schaffer, S. 1985: *Leviathan and the air pump: Hobbes, Boyle and the experimental life*. Princeton, NJ: Princeton University Press. · Slater, D. 1992: On the borders of social theory: learning from other regions. *Environment and Planning D: Society and Space* 10: 307–27.

Suggested Reading

Barnes (1996), chs 4 and 8. · Rouse (1987), ch. 4.

local state The set of institutions charged with the maintenance and protection of social relations at the sub-national level (see GOVERNANCE). This set includes local government, local judiciary, licensing authorities and the machinery of local politics, as well as QUANGOS and other local administrative agencies (representative of central government, for instance). The term is most commonly invoked with reference to metropolitan-level governments, although it can also refer to state/provincial, county or regional scales.

The local state is part of the STATE APPARATUS: its existence is predicated on the need for CRISIS avoidance at the local level and it is a vital component in the control of spatially extensive and socially heterogeneous TERRITORIES. No matter what the nature of the state organization (democratic, totalitarian, etc.), SURVEILLANCE and social integration of the populace is facilitated by a decentralized structure of state organs. The local state also has an important political function, in that it legitimates central state actions through such means as party organizations and electoral politics. Local elections are buttressed by an IDEOLOGY of participation or democracy which often insists on the right to local self-determination (cf. TIEBOUT MODEL). Recent years, however, have witnessed various forms of retreat from local electoral politics, ranging from secessionist movements fragmenting local jurisdictions to the partial withdrawal from local state authority, commonly into privatized enclaves invested with their own regulatory powers (see PRIVATE INTEREST DEVELOPMENTS). This atomization of the local state, while increasing self-determination at the local level, has also rendered large metropolitan regions increasingly difficult (perhaps even impossible) to manage.

Conservative and liberal analysts, who simply view the business of government as the provision of PUBLIC GOODS and services, tend to be primarily concerned with efficiency and control of local state operations. Other social theorists have concentrated on the reasons for the existence of a separate local state. For them, the fundamental theoretical question is the authority relationship between central and local states: 'To what extent is the local state autonomous from the central state?' The local state is alternatively viewed as either the Achilles heel of the state or as the creature of the central state. In the former case, it is perceived as the weak and vulnerable gap in the central state's armour, because well-organized local SOCIAL MOVEMENTS may be able to capture the state and, hence, practise a potentially threatening local autonomy. In the latter case, the local state is regarded as simply the puppet of the central agencies.

The question of local autonomy has fundamental political significance, since many pressure groups have attempted to capture the local state. The resolution of the question of the autonomy of the local state is most likely to be achieved only at the empirical level. The degree of autonomy is a function of the extent of local power of initiative, and local immunity from interference by other tiers of the state apparatus. By examining the power and role of significant human agents, such as URBAN MANAGERS AND GATEKEEPERS, it would be possible to determine the value of attempting to capture the local state. (For other views of local urban politics, see COLLECTIVE CONSUMPTION and DUAL THEORY OF THE STATE.)

In the fragmented politics characteristic of POSTMODERN society, the potential for political power at the local level is critically important in the fate of non-class-based social movements, such as those involving women, gays and minorities. This question is presently underscored in many capitalist countries by the contraction of the central state itself, in the process devolving greater administrative responsibility onto the local level. The ramifications of these developments are uncertain. On the one hand, it may be argued that this increasing prominence of the local state affords empowering opportunities for previously under-recognized minority groups, whether long-established, proliferating new immigrant, or newly formed through accelerating processes of cultural 'hybridization'. But it may also be argued that in the absence of a central state presence, the limited scope and scale of the local state's operations, and the growing fragmentation of the local state itself, leaves the local state and the individuals under its jurisdiction increasingly disempowered in relation to supranation-states and transnational enterprises of varying degrees of legitimacy. MJD

Suggested Reading

Castells, M. 1983: *The city and the grassroots*. Berkeley, CA: University of California Press. · Clark, G.L. and Dear, M.J. 1984: *State apparatus: structures and language of legitimacy*. Boston: Allen and Unwin, ch. 3. · Wolch, J.R. 1990: *The shadow state*. New York: The Foundation Center.

locale A setting or context for social interaction. The term was proposed by Anthony Giddens in his development of STRUCTURATION THEORY. Giddens's notion of structuration suggests how the flow of HUMAN AGENCY 'binds' time and SPACE. The social interactions involved in this are integrative. *Social* integration involves individual actors who are

Type of society	Dominant locale organization	Power-container
Tribal societies	band groups or villages	villages(?)
Class-divided societies	symbiosis of city and countryside	cities
Class societies	'the created environment'	nation-states

locale *Dominant locales and time–space distanciation* (Giddens, 1981)

'co-present' in time and space, while *system* integration involves relations between actors, groups and collectivities outside conditions of 'co-presence'. In both cases interactions are situated in time and space, and this setting furnishes the resources on which the actors draw in their interaction. It is this context which Giddens labels 'locale'. In an early (1979) formulation he defines it thus:

> 'Locale' is in some respects a preferable term to that of 'place', more commonly employed in social geography: for it carries something of the connotation of space used as a *setting* for interaction. A setting is not just a spatial parameter, and physical environment, in which interaction 'occurs': it is these elements mobilised as part of the interaction. Features of the setting of interaction, including its spatial and physical aspects... are routinely drawn upon by social actors in the sustaining of communication.

On a number of occasions Giddens refers to locales as the characteristic physical settings associated with different types of collectivities: 'virtually all collectivities have a *locale* of operation, spatially distinct from that associated with others' (1979, pp. 206–7) and 'all collectivities have defined *locales* of operation: physical settings associated with the "typical interactions" composing those collectivities as social systems' (1981, p. 39; cf. COMMUNITY). Thus the typical locale of the school is the classroom; that of the prison, the cell block; that of the bureaucracy, the office; that of the army, the barracks (1987, pp. 153–62).

Moreover, Giddens distinguishes between organizations and social movements and claims that 'unlike organizations, SOCIAL MOVEMENTS do not characteristically operate within fixed locales' (1984, p. 204). Elsewhere, however, he makes it clear that he means the concept of locale to have 'very general applicability' and that it applies in principle to all social interaction (1981, p. 40). The reason for stressing the typical locales of certain types of institutions (barracks, schools etc.) is that *in some cases* locales can take on a fixed physical form, but this form does not completely specify the nature of a locale, and indeed some locales may not have a physical form in that sense at all:

> Locales provide for a good deal of the 'fixity' underlying institutions, although there is no clear sense in which they 'determine' such 'fixity'. It is *usually* possible to designate locales in terms of their physical properties, either as features of the material world or, more commonly, as combinations of those features and human artefacts. But *it is an error to suppose that locales can be described in those terms alone*... A house is grasped as such only if the observer recognises that it is a 'dwelling' with a range of other properties specified by the modes of its utilisation in human activity. (1984, p. 118, emphases added)

However, the idea that 'locale' is applicable to all social interaction introduces a further ambiguity. On the one hand, Giddens (1984, p. 71) implies that interactions situated in locales necessarily involve the 'co-presence' of the actors: on the other, he stresses that 'locales may range from a room in a house, a street corner, the shop floor of a factory, towns and cities, to the territorially demarcated areas occupied by nation states' (1984, p. 118), or to put it, as Nigel Thrift (1983) does, more concisely, 'a locale does not have to be local'. The apparent contradiction here is partially resolved by Giddens' (1984, p. 68) comments on media of communication:

> Although the 'full conditions of co-presence' exist only in unmediated contact between those who are physically present, mediated contacts that permit some of the intimacies of co-presence are made possible in the modern era by electronic communications, most notably the telephone.

However, elsewhere Giddens (1987, p. 137) insists that 'co-presence' must involve literal 'face-to-face' interaction:

> Interaction in contexts of co-presence obviously has characteristics not found in 'mediated' interaction – via the telephone, recordings, the mail and so on.

Although there is a confusion here, it seems fairly clear that Giddens regards a 'locale' as something which can have (potentially considerable) spatial and temporal extension. The interactions for which locales form the setting can therefore in principle be subject to TIME–SPACE DISTANCIATION. This allows for the existence within locales of REGIONS which provide for the 'zoning' of social practices in time and space.

According to Giddens (1981) some locales dominate in particular types of society and form their principal 'power containers' (see the figure).

A number of writers have discussed the relationship between locale and the apparently related concept of LOCALITY. Cooke (1989) sees them as competing alternatives such that acceptance of one would imply the rejection of the other. Favouring the concept of locality, Cooke claims that the idea of locale should be rejected because 'it reproduces the passive connotations of community in the way it refers to setting and context for action rather than as a constituting element in action' (Cooke, 1989, p. 10). Giddens's insistence on the constitutive nature of context shows that this is a misreading, but, as Duncan (1989) points out, locale and locality in any case refer to different things. This is recognized by Massey (1991), who briefly hints that localities could be conceptualized as 'the intersection of sets of locales', while her insistence that localities should be seen as socially constructed applies equally to locales. (See also CONTEXTUAL APPROACH; HABITUS; PLACE; SPATIALITY; TIME-GEOGRAPHY.) JP

References

Cooke, P. 1989: *Localities: the changing face of urban Britain*. London: Unwin Hyman; Duncan, S. 1989: What is locality? In R. Peet and N. Thrift, eds, *New models in geography*, vol. 2. London: Unwin Hyman, 221–52. · Giddens, A. 1979: *Central problems in social theory*. London: Macmillan. · Giddens, A. 1981: *A contemporary critique of historical materialism*, vol. 1, *Power, property and the state*. London: Macmillan. · Giddens, A. 1984: *The constitution of society*. Cambridge: Polity Press. · Giddens, A. 1987: *Social theory and modern sociology*. Cambridge: Polity Press. · Massey, D. 1991: The political place of locality studies. *Environment and Planning A* 23: 267–81. · Thrift, N. 1983: On the determination of social action in space and time. *Environment and Planning D: Society and Space* 1: 23–57.

Suggested Reading

Giddens (1984), esp. ch. 3. · Giddens (1987), ch. 6. · Thrift (1983).

local–global dialectic An understanding of the processes of GLOBALIZATION as the interaction between global processes and local circumstances. There are three possible accounts. On one, global processes leave their footprints on PLACES, allowing these little choice but either to fall into line or be stamped out. On another, local places 'turn' global processes; particularly popular in cultural accounts, this notion of the global–local dialectic sees the world as such a diverse place that global processes can only obtain a purchase by fitting in with local CULTURES. Finally, between these two views, is one which argues for a process of *'glocalization'*, a complex interaction between globalizing and localizing tendencies. Usually left hanging in all these accounts is what is actually meant by the terms 'local' and 'global'. NJT

References

Amin, A. and Thrift, N.J., eds, 1994: *Globalization, institutions and regional development in Europe*. Oxford: Oxford University Press. · Cox, K., ed., 1997: *Spaces of globalisation: reasserting the power of the local*. New York: Guilford. · Daniels, P. and Lever, W., eds, 1996: *The global economy in transition*. Harlow: Longman. · Herod, A., O'Tuathail, G. and Roberts, S., eds, 1998: *Unruly world? globalisation, governance and geography*. London: Routledge.

locality In lay terms, a PLACE or REGION of sub-national spatial SCALE. Despite, or perhaps because of, considerable debate about the concept, there is no consensus concerning its technical meaning within human geography. The origins of the debate lie in attempts in the 1980s to explain the RESTRUCTURING of economies and their SPATIAL STRUCTURES. At a time of significant transformations in the human geography of the UK, Urry (1981) and Massey (1984) argued that an understanding of spatial variations in social, political and economic change was particularly important (see also Massey, 1991).

The UK Government's Economic and Social Research Council (ESRC) translated this concern into substantive research programmes: the 'Changing Urban and Regional System' initiative (CURS), the 'Social Change and Economic Life' initiative (SCELI), and the 'Economic Restructuring, Social Change and the Locality' programme. At the centre of each was a series of studies of the impact of restructuring on particular places or regions. A key concern of these 'locality studies' was to collect detailed empirical evidence to assist the identification of the nature, causes and consequences of spatial differentiation in processes of change.

As well as substantive results (Dickens, 1988; Cooke, 1989a; Bagguley et al., 1990;

Beynon et al., 1994), this research effort raised a series of methodological and theoretical issues which became bound up with wider debates:

The delimitation of localities for research. Despite extensive deliberations on the nature of localities, many studies have in practice used (statistically defined) local LABOUR MARKET areas. By contrast, Massey (1991) argues that 'localities are not simply spatial areas you can easily draw a line around' but should be 'defined in terms of the sets of social relations or processes in question'. Savage et al. (1987) claim to have adopted this sort of approach in defining the localities for the Economic Restructuring, Social Change and the Locality programme.

The relationship between locality research and critical realism. Many writers have explicitly or implicitly linked locality research to the EPISTEMOLOGY of REALISM (e.g. Urry, 1987; Duncan, 1989). From this perspective: (i) localities are the concrete outcome of the contingent combination in particular places of a number of causal PROCESSES; (ii) localities may become causally powerful social objects in their own right, with effects on wider processes (e.g. by influencing STATE policy or the locational decisions of firms); and (iii) locality *studies* are exercises in INTENSIVE RESEARCH which seek to unravel these processes and hence to identify through ABSTRACTION the necessary relations which define social structures (Sayer, 1984). Sayer himself, however, has objected to the ways in which some protagonists in the debate have mistakenly conflated the distinctions of realist philosophy (Sayer, 1991).

The theoretical status of the concept of locality. According to Cooke (1989b, p. 12), 'locality is a concept attaching to a process characteristic of MODERNITY, namely the extension, following political struggle, of civil, political and social rights of citizenship to individuals'. Since there are considerable differences between apparently similarly constituted localities, Cooke argues that this link with CITIZENSHIP forms a basis for local 'pro-activity', with localities 'actively involved in their own transformation' (Cooke, 1989c, p. 296).

Despite the stress on CITIZENSHIP, this formulation leaves unclear the relationship between HUMAN AGENCY and the pro-activity of localities. Cooke asserts that 'localities are not simply places or even COMMUNITIES: they are the sum of social energy and agency resulting from the clustering of diverse individuals, groups and social interests in space' (Cooke, 1989c, p. 296). However, the heterogeneous character of this clustering casts doubt on the possibility of grounding pro-activity in a notion of universal citizenship, and in practice Cooke reduces pro-activity to the policies of the LOCAL STATE.

Duncan, Savage and their co-workers regard the idea that localities are pro-active, causally powerful objects as a worrying return to SPATIAL FETISHISM. They argue that while social processes vary spatially, and are sometimes constituted at the local scale, unique 'locality effects' (such as local political cultures) are extremely unusual (Savage et al., 1987, p. 32). This scepticism leads them to abandon the concept in favour of an existing vocabulary of spatial variation: 'most of the time, instead of writing about "locality" researchers should more simply talk about "case study areas", "towns", "labour market areas", or just "areas", "places" and "spatial variations"' (Duncan and Savage, 1989, p. 192).

Cox and Mair (1991) retain the concept of locality, and like Cooke they argue that localities can have an impact on wider processes. Where they differ is in teasing out in detail the mechanisms through which this operates.

Although they have involved much dissent, these debates have largely been conducted among those engaged in locality studies or otherwise connected with the ESRC programmes. In addition, several writers who have not been directly involved in the empirical research projects have criticized this form of research from a variety of perspectives.

Smith (1987) argued that the 'empirical turn' embodied in the locality studies of the late 1980s ran the risk of neglecting key theoretical and political issues. For Smith, the localities approach seemed to be generating vast amounts of detailed descriptive information on local areas without the necessary conceptual tools to provide explanation and generalization. He also suggested that the significance of the local scale was being assumed, rather than demonstrated theoretically. Although not all critics of the locality idea would endorse Smith's apparent equation of theory with generalization, his reminder about the importance of conceptualization was timely, and subsequent developments paid much more attention to the theoretical status of the locality concept.

Through a study of Poplar in the 1920s, Rose (1989) argues that the theoretical contributions of locality studies have been compromised by their stress on the sphere of waged labour. The radical politics of 1920s Poplar, she suggests, were largely constituted outside the workplace in the home and the community. Jackson (1991) develops this line of argument through his 'cultural critique of locality studies'. He suggests that, notwithstanding frequent references to local cultures and regional traditions, most studies have failed adequately to theorize cultural relations.

By the early 1990s, with the ending of the formal research programmes, the locality concept appeared much less frequently in the research literature. In reflecting on what had by then become known as the 'locality debate', several authors have argued that, with hindsight, the vehemence and occasional acrimony of the discussions appear rather out of proportion to the conceptual developments generated. One effect seems to have been to encourage others to avoid using the term 'locality' in favour of other formulations that may be less contentious and 'loaded'. Two developments during the 1990s may be noted:

A much stronger emphasis on relational and networked concepts of locality and on the links between localities and other spatial scales. Insisting that a focus on localities need not be parochial, Massey (1993) argues that localities should not be seen as coherent entities with tightly drawn boundaries around them, but as 'nets of social relations' (p. 148) and that 'localities [. . .] are always provisional, always in the process of being made, always contested' (p. 149). The idea of localities as constituted through networks of social relations is developed even more explicitly by Murdoch and Marsden (1995) who draw on ACTOR–NETWORK THEORY to suggest that 'localities should be seen as constituted by various networks operating a different scales (p. 368), and that 'localities can now be examined as implicated in sets of cross-cutting networks of relations. They have no single pre-given identity but are tied into wider (i.e. non-local) processes in a multitude of differing ways' (p. 370).

The translation of many of the issues highlighted by the localities debate into new conceptual frameworks. For example, the upsurge of interest in GLOBALIZATION during the 1990s has involved a recasting of the issue of local specificity in terms of global–local relations, while the further development of CULTURAL GEOGRAPHY has seen increasingly sophisticated treatments of the relationships between politics, PLACE and IDENTITY (May, 1996). JP

References

Bagguley, P., Mark-Lawson, J., Shapiro, D., Urry, J., Walby, S. and Warde, A. 1990: *Restructuring: place, class and gender.* London: Sage. · Beynon, H., Hudson, R. and Sadler, D. 1994: *A place called Teesside: a locality in a global economy.* Edinburgh: Edinburgh University Press. · Cooke, P., ed., 1989a: *Localities: the changing face of urban Britain.* London: Unwin Hyman; Cooke, P. 1989b: Locality, economic restructuring and world development. In P. Cooke, ed., *Localities: the changing face of urban Britain.* London: Unwin Hyman, 1–44. · Cooke, P. 1989c: The local question – revival or survival? In P. Cooke, ed., *Localities: the changing face of urban Britain.* London: Unwin Hyman, 296–306. · Cox, K. and Mair, A. 1991: From localised social structures to localities as agents. *Environment and Planning A* 23: 197–213. · Dickens, P. 1988: *One nation? Social change and the politics of locality.* London: Pluto Press. · Duncan, S. 1989: What is locality? In R. Peet and N. Thrift, eds, *New models in geography,* vol. 2. London: Unwin Hyman, 221–52. · Duncan, S. and Savage, M. 1989: Space, scale and locality. *Antipode* 21: 179–206. · Jackson, P. 1991: Mapping meanings: a cultural critique of locality studies. *Environment and Planning A* 23: 215–28. · Massey, D. 1984: *Spatial divisions of labour.* London: Macmillan. · Massey, D. 1991: The political place of locality studies. *Environment and Planning A* 23: 267–81. · Massey, D. 1993: Questions of locality. *Geography* 78: 142–9. · May, J. 1996: Globalization and the politics of place: place and identity in an inner London neighbourhood. *Transactions, Institute of British Geographers* NS 21: 194–215. · Murdoch, J. and Marsden, T. 1995: The spatialization of politics: local and national actor-spaces in environmental conflict. *Transactions, Institute of British Geographers* NS 20: 368–80. · Rose, G. 1989: Locality studies and waged labour: an historical critique. *Transactions, Institute of British Geographers* NS 14: 317–28. · Savage, M., Barlow, J., Duncan, S. and Saunders, P. 1987: 'Locality research': the Sussex programme on Economic Restructuring, Social Change and the Locality. *Quarterly Journal of Social Affairs* 4: 27–51. · Sayer, A. 1984: *Method in social science: a realist approach.* London: Hutchinson. · Sayer, A. 1991: Behind the locality debate: deconstructing geography's dualisms. *Environment and Planning A* 23: 283–308. · Smith, N. 1987: Dangers of the empirical turn: some comments on the CURS initiative. *Antipode* 19: 59–66. · Urry, J. 1981: Localities, regions and social class. *International Journal of Urban and Regional Research* 5: 455–74. · Urry, J. 1987: Society, space and locality. *Environment and Planning D: Society and Space* 5: 435–44.

Suggested Reading

Cooke (1989a, b and c); *Environment and Planning A* 1991: Special issue on new perspectives on the locality debate. *Environment and Planning A* 23 (2). · Massey (1993). · Peet, R. 1998: *Modern geographical thought.* Oxford: Blackwell, 180–93.

localization The forces of GLOBALIZATION are, allegedly, leading to the replacement of a 'space of places' by a 'space of flows' (Castells, 1996); to the 'de-territorialization' of human (especially economic) activity. However, this view is based upon a deep misconception of the nature of social processes, all of which are inherently spatially structured and, most importantly, deeply embedded in PLACE. In a variety of senses, all human activity is localized. At the most basic level, all activities – even those most often depicted as being hypermobile (such as finance; cf. MONEY AND FINANCE, GEOGRAPHY OF) – are 'grounded' in specific places. They require spatial fixedness in order to function, despite the undoubted fact that transport and communications technologies have increased the degrees of spatial freedom of human activity. Many phenomena (including both physical and human resources) are geographically localized, rather than ubiquitous, and have to be used 'in place'.

One important reason for the geographical localization of economic activities is the existence of economies of AGGLOMERATION (the traded interdependencies which may exist between actors in close geographical proximity together with the provision of collectively accessible infrastructures; cf. ECONOMIES OF SCALE; ECONOMIES OF SCOPE). More generally, however, the key localizing force derives from the essential 'socialness' of human activities and the fact that such socialness is facilitated and enhanced by geographical proximity. Such untraded interdependencies are essentially socio-cultural. As Amin and Thrift (1994) point out, geographical localization facilitates three particular processes: (1) face-to-face contact; (2) social and cultural interaction – 'to act as places of sociability, of gathering information, establishing coalitions, monitoring and maintaining trust, and developing rules of behaviour' (p. 13); and (3) enhancement of knowledge and innovation – 'centres are needed to develop, test, and track innovations, to provide a critical mass of knowledgeable people and structures, and socio-institutional networks, in order to identify new gaps in the market, new uses for and definitions of technology, and rapid responses to changes in demand patterns' (p. 13).

Localization is, of course, a dynamic and not a static process. Places develop a specific history which reflects the complex articulation over time of localized cultures, institutions, and practices. Such structures characteristically evolve in a path-dependent manner which implies that, for example, the economy of a particular place becomes 'locked-in' to a pattern of development which is strongly influenced by its particular history. (See, for example, Scott, 1995; Storper, 1997; Storper and Walker, 1989.) Such 'lock-in' may be either a source of continued strength or, if it embodies too much institutional rigidity, a source of weakness. As Scott (1995, p. 57) observes in relation to regional economies:

> the notion of path-dependence also implies the existence of critical branching points representing conjunctures where the regional economy may move in any one of a number of different possible directions (though once it has moved, its future is then to that degree committed) . . . the onward march of development in economically successful regions is always in practice subject to eventual cessation or reversal, not only because there are usually limits to the continued appropriation of external economies, but also because radical shifts in markets, technologies, skills, and so on, can undermine any given regional configuration of production. Indeed, the very existence of lock-in effects means that regions, as they develop and grow, will eventually find it difficult to adapt to certain kinds of external shocks.

One of the most significant 'external shocks' has undoubtedly been that of GLOBALIZATION. Having argued that the localization of human activities remains fundamental even in a globalizing world we must also recognize that such localized clusters are themselves deeply embedded within globalizing processes and structures. Without doubt, what happens in specific places is deeply influenced by processes operating at larger geographical scales. But it is mistake to see this is a one-way, top-down process in which the 'global' determines the 'local'. The scalar relationships are extremely complex and not unidirectional (see Amin and Thrift, 1992; Swyngedouw, 1997a, b). Indeed, we need to grasp the reality of a world made up of a multiplicity of geographical scales which, in extent, range from the global to the local (though not confined to these two extremes) but which are constituted in an intricate, simultaneous, and nested manner (Swyngedouw, 1997b). Swyngedouw has adapted the term *glocalization* to capture this 'rescaling' of human activities. Such a term helps us to appreciate the interrelatedness of geographical scales and, in particular, the idea that while the 'local' exists within the 'global' the 'global' also exists within the 'local' (Massey, 1991). PD

References and Suggested Reading

Amin, A. and Thrift, N. 1992: Neo-Marshallian nodes in global networks. *International Journal of Urban and Regional Research* 16: 571–87. · Amin, A. and Thrift, N. 1994: Living in the global. In A. Amin and N. Thrift, eds, *Globalization, institutions and regional development in Europe*. Oxford: Oxford University Press, 1–22. · Castells, M. 1996: *The rise of the network society*. Oxford: Blackwell. · Massey, D. 1991: A global sense of place. *Marxism Today*, June: 24–9. · Scott, A.J. 1995: The geographic foundations of industrial performance. *Competition and Change* 1: 51–66. · Storper, M. 1997: Territories, flows, and hierarchies in the global economy. In K.R. Cox, ed., *Spaces of globalization: reasserting the power of the local*. New York: Guilford, 19–44. · Storper,

M. and Walker, R. 1989: *The capitalist imperative: territory, technology, and industrial growth*. Oxford: Blackwell; Swyngedouw, E. 1997a: Excluding the other: the production of scale and scaled politics. In R. Lee and J. Wills, eds, *Geographies of economies*. London: Arnold, 167–76. · Swyngedouw, E. 1997b: Neither global nor local: 'glocalization' and the politics of scale. In K.R. Cox, ed., *Spaces of globalization: reasserting the power of the local*. New York: Guilford, 115–36.

location quotient The ratio of a quantitative value for a defined area to a specified norm. Location quotients are used to describe the relative concentration of an activity or group in one section of a larger area, using the formula

$$LQ_i = S_i/A$$

where

S_i is the value for segment *i*;
A is the value for the total area; and
LQ_i is the location quotient for section *i*.

Thus if the percentage voting Labour in the whole of Great Britain was 43.3 whereas in Scotland it was 49.7, the location quotient for Scotland would be

$$49.7/43.3$$
$$= 1.148$$

A quotient over 1.0 indicates that the activity is more concentrated in the segment relative to the whole, whereas one less than 1.0 indicates its relative absence there. RJJ

location theory A body of theories which seek to account for the location of economic activities. An interest in the POLITICAL ECONOMY of location can be traced back to the seventeenth and eighteenth centuries, when several writers attempted to explicate patterns of agricultural land use (see Scott, 1976), and these efforts can now be seen to have culminated in the classical VON THÜNEN MODEL (1826). However, with the growing influence of Ricardo and then Marshall (1890; see Marshall, 1952) time was judged to be 'more fundamental' than space. And ever since Marshall, according to Isard (1956), 'the architects of our finest [economic-] theoretical structures have intensified [his] prejudice'. The cardinal exception to this, as Isard noted, was the German school of location theory, whose contribution – for all their differences – reclaimed and reinvigorated the constructs of an earlier generation and did much to prefigure the general theories of the SPACE-ECONOMY which were Isard's own objective. Especially important here were the formulations of Alfred Weber (1909; see Weber, 1928) with respect to the location of manufacturing activity, and Walter Christaller (1933; see Christaller, 1966) and August Lösch (1944; see Lösch, 1954), who produced theories to explain the location of settlements as market centres (for historical summaries, see Isard, 1956, ch. 2; Smith, 1981, ch. 8; see also REGIONAL SCIENCE).

In geography the significance of the German school was recognized by Hartshorne, whose *The nature of geography* (1939) was based on an exegesis of a primarily German intellectual tradition. However, location theory was not formally admitted into the developing corpus of HUMAN GEOGRAPHY until the early 1960s, mainly through the efforts of Garrison and the Washington school in the USA and, on the other side of the Atlantic, through Haggett's *Locational analysis in human geography* (1965). During this formative period it drew much of its theoretical strength from NEO-CLASSICAL ECONOMICS. In particular, attempts were made to use general equilibrium theory to provide a theory of industrial location capable of integrating VARIABLE COST ANALYSIS and VARIABLE REVENUE ANALYSIS (see Smith, 1981), while UTILITY THEORY was used to reconstruct spatial preference structures within the framework of CENTRAL PLACE THEORY (see Rushton, 1969). Yet location theory encountered formidable problems in translating these formulations into the spatial domain, because 'the working assumptions and abstractions that the neoclassicist uses as a starting point for his analysis could never be justified in a world which recognises the existence of space as well as time' (Richardson, 1973). These special misgivings were reinforced by a growing awareness of the more general critique of neoclassical economics, and together these objections forced a series of responses from location theory. Three main developments can be distinguished.

A long-standing concern with the spatial behaviour of rational *economic man (sic;* see METHODOLOGICAL INDIVIDUALISM) was replaced as the emergence of BEHAVIOURAL GEOGRAPHY allowed for the incorporation of more realistic behavioural assumptions into location theory; in other words, for the construction of what Stafford (1972) called 'the geography of manufactur*es*' rather than 'the geography of manufactur*ing*'. Typical of these various studies, in roughly chronological order, were investigations of SATISFICING BEHAVIOUR, the formalization of Pred's behavioural matrix, and whole series of models of corporate DECISION-MAKING. Indeed in the second edition of *Locational analysis in human geography* (1977), Haggett, Cliff and Frey recorded their optimism about 'major developments in human microgeography' (including ENVIRONMENTAL PERCEPTION, PHENOMENOLOGY and TIME-GEOGRAPHY) which promised to 'enrich' the 'somewhat formal areas of aggregate MODEL-building' with which mainstream location theory continued to be preoccupied.

The single-plant, single-product firm was displaced as the primary object of industrial location theory, and earlier work on industrial AGGLOMERATION and LOCATIONAL INTERDEPENDENCE was extended as the structural context of corporate behaviour gradually became more clearly defined. This was achieved in part through the refinement of the decision-making models referred to above, but more particularly through what has come to be called the '*geography of enterprise*' approach (Keeble, 1979; see also special issue of *Regional Studies*, 1978; McDermott and Taylor, 1982; Hayter and Watts, 1983).

The ahistorical nature of location theory was challenged through a more considered recognition of the historical specificity of the space-economy of CAPITALISM. This had been treated by Weber in summary form (see Gregory, 1981) and it is also latent within both of the previous approaches, but what is distinctive about its explicit acknowledgement is the conjoint denial of any autonomy for location theory: 'spatial development can only be seen as part of the overall development of capitalism' (Massey, 1977: see also Scott, 1980; Harvey 1982; Cooke, 1983a). Most of these discussions depend upon MARXIAN ECONOMICS and POLITICAL ECONOMY. Harvey's (1982) exegesis of classical Marxism – most of all his analysis of the contradictory needs of capital for both spatial fixity and fluidity – provides an essential benchmark. However, as Harvey admits, Marx's original formulations are 'powerful with respect to time but weak with respect to space'. Other approaches in a broadly Marxian vein include theorizations of UNEVEN DEVELOPMENT and of the changing spatial DIVISION OF LABOUR (Clark, 1980; Browett, 1984), theorizations of the differential geographies of different LAYERS OF INVESTMENT (see, e.g., Massey, 1978), of strategies of industrial RESTRUCTURING which transform the LABOUR PROCESS and impact on geographies of both CLASS and GENDER (Walker and Storper, 1981; Storper and Walker, 1983; Massey, 1984; Gregory and Urry, 1985; Scott and Storper, 1986; Clark, 1989), and of the segmentation and differentiation of the LABOUR MARKET and its implications for theories of spatial development (Cooke, 1983b). This stream of studies encompasses three fundamental features:

- the *historical particularity* of different phases of capitalist development – hence the attention paid to 'long waves' (see KONDRATIEFF CYCLES) and other periodizations of capitalism (Webber and Rigby, 1996);
- the *global context* of different phases of capitalist development – hence the attention paid to the NEW INTERNATIONAL DIVISION OF LABOUR, to MULTINATIONAL CORPORATIONS and to the very phenomenon of GLOBALIZATION itself (Dicken, Peck and Tickell, 1997; Dicken, 1998; Schoenberger, 1988); and
- the *structural interdependencies* between commodity production, social reproduction and the URBANIZATION of the space-economy (Cooke, 1983a; Harvey, 1985; see also COLLECTIVE CONSUMPTION).

A broad question receiving much attention within the past decade concerns how economic geography, with its sensitivity to locational variation, might contribute to a reconstruction of the other social sciences (which followed Marshall's advice in privileging time over space). In taking on this project, geographers have, with strange irony, returned to Isard's original mission. However, while their motives may be similar, their approaches are rather different. At least two distinct thrusts are especially noteworthy.

Within *the tradition of analytical political economy*, economic geographers have addressed the more mathematically inclined body of work associated with economists such as Marx, Ricardo, Sraffa, Kalecki and Pasinetti (see Barnes, 1990 and accompanying papers; see also Sheppard and Barnes, 1990; cf. ANALYTICAL MARXISM, GEOGRAPHY AND). Their intent and effect has been to mount a serious challenge to the logical deductions arising from this (as well as more traditional neo-classical) theory when the spatial dimension of the economy is explicitly introduced. In showing how the determinate conclusions of Marxian economics – e.g. that profit rates will tend to fall over time – are thrown into doubt when space is admitted into the analysis, this work has been of key importance in illustrating the contribution of geographical theory to the wider body of economic analysis.

Still within a political-economic tradition, but employing a non-mathematical discourse, other economic geographers have rejected the logical separation between the 'growth question' and the 'location question' implicit in earlier location theory, and have instead sought to demonstrate how the basic theory of economic growth itself can only be properly constructed when it is explicitly couched in spatial terms (Storper and Walker, 1989). In this work, the history of economic change is viewed as the 'inconstant geography of capitalism' and, by invoking the central analytical concept of 'geographical INDUSTRIALIZATION', Storper and Walker demonstrate how the series of major upheavals in this history have each found their origins in the specific physical, economic and social configurations of individual places. Furthermore, the willing acceptance of a priori spatial variation in the cost and availability of factors of production that is so evident within the Weberian tradition of location theory is explicitly rejected here. Thus, the notion of local industrial growth arising 'in passive response to endowment-based local comparative advantages' (see COMPARATIVE ADVANTAGE) is instead conceived of as 'an active shaping of local factor supplies by industry itself' (Gertler, 1991). Notwithstanding the important contributions of this perspective, recent work by Herod (1997), DiGiovanna (1996) and others reminds us that one particular 'factor supply' – that is, labour – is anything but passive in the face of industries' attempts to shape it.

In the most general terms, then, it is clear that since the early 1970s the highly schematic representations of the geometry of space-economy have yielded to much more substantive specifications of the social and political processes (see PROCESS) which produce and reproduce constellations of economic activities in time and space. In effect, an insistence on the importance of careful specification and conceptualization (see ABSTRACTION) evident in the first-generation location theory has provided a basis for both the critique of theoretical approaches underlying the non-Marxian tradition (Sayer, 1982; Clark, Gertler and Whiteman, 1986; Storper and Walker, 1989; Barnes, 1996) as well as the construction of alternative formulations.

As we approach the half-century anniversary of the publication of Isard's *Location and space economy*, location theorists (broadly defined) continue to define new research frontiers in a number of important areas. One major thrust has focused on the study of economic activities whose locational dynamics were for decades considered to be unworthy of geographers' detailed scrutiny. Hence, for example, there is now a significant and growing literature on the locational tendencies of service activities (Wood, 1991; Daniels, 1993) that offers a useful corrective to location theorists' longstanding infatuation with manufacturing and agriculture (but see also Walker, 1985 for a dissenting view). An important subcategory of this work which has attracted considerable attention concerns the geography of financial services. While the popular wisdom asserts that financial activities are, thanks to the widespread use of information and communications technologies, increasingly footloose and dispersing (O'Brien, 1992), geographers have shown that important social and economic forces continue to reproduce strong concentrations of many financial services in the largest metropolitan centres (Corbridge, Martin and Thrift, 1994; Leyshon and Thrift, 1997; McDowell, 1997). In the area of retail services, although a long and continuous tradition extends from the seminal work of Christaller and Lösch to recent syntheses (Jones and Simmons, 1993), the past decade has seen the emergence of much important work seeking to move beyond simply explaining the location of the 'point of sale', to situate retailing within a broader geography of CONSUMPTION (see, e.g., the contributions to Lowe and Wrigley, 1996). More recently still, Scott (1996, 1997) has asserted the importance of another hitherto neglected set of activities constituting the 'cultural economy of cities'. These activities cut across the manufacturing/services divide and bring together the many elements of the 'sign economy' (Lash and Urry, 1993) in which cultural assets are central to the production process and product: film, television and video production, publishing, audio recording, multimedia, animation, advertising, fashion apparel, jewellery, toys, specialty foods and furniture. (See also MONEY AND FINANCE, GEOGRAPHY OF; RETAILING, GEOGRAPHY OF; SERVICES, GEOGRAPHY OF.)

Further evidence of location theory's rising stature comes from recent work in economics by Krugman and his colleagues (Krugman, 1991). This body of work, which is now commonly referred to by economists as the '*new economic geography*', has returned to the formalistic argumentation of Isard in order to produce a general theory of the location of economic activities under conditions of increasing returns to scale (Krugman, 1995). Not surprisingly, an agenda as ambitious as this, pursued with the modeller's normal accompaniment of simplifications and EQUILIBRIUM assumptions (Venables, 1996), has provoked insightful critical responses from geographers themselves (Martin and Sunley, 1996). Nevertheless, the vitality of this and related debates seems to indicate that location theory is still high on the agenda of human geography and related social sciences, although its form may have changed and its ambit broadened substantially in recent years.

MSG

References

Barnes, T.J. 1990: Analytical political economy: a geographical introduction. *Environment and Planning A* 22: 993–1006. · Barnes, T.J. 1996: *Logics of dislocation*. New York: Guilford Press. · Browett, J. 1984: On the necessity and inevitability of uneven spatial development under capitalism. *International Journal of Urban and Regional Research* 8: 155–76. · Christaller, W. 1966: *Central places in southern Germany*. Englewood Cliffs, NJ: Prentice Hall (originally published in German in 1933). · Clark, G.L. 1980: Capitalism and regional inequality. *Annals of the Association of American Geographers* 70: 226–37. · Clark, G.L. 1989: *Unions and communities under siege*. Cambridge: Cambridge University Press. · Clark, G.L., Gertler, M.S. and Whiteman, J.E.M. 1986: *Regional dynamics: studies in adjustment theory*. Boston: Allen and Unwin. · Cooke, P. 1983a: *Theories of planning and spatial development*. London: Hutchinson. · Cooke, P. 1983b: Labour market discontinuity and spatial development. *Progress in Human Geography* 7: 543–65. · Corbridge, S., Martin, R. and Thrift, N., eds, 1994: *Money, space and power*. Oxford: Blackwell. · Daniels, P. 1993: *Service industries in the world economy*. Oxford: Blackwell. · Dicken, P. 1998: *Global shift*, 3rd edn. New York: Guilford Press. · Dicken, P., Peck, J. and Tickell, A. 1997: Unpacking the global. In R. Lee, and J. Wills, eds, *Geographies of economies*. London: Edward Arnold, 158–66. · DiGiovanna, S. 1996: Industrial districts from a Regulation perspective. *Regional Studies* 30: 373–86. · Gertler, M.S. 1991: Review: Storper and Walker's *The capitalist imperative*. *Economic Geography* 67: 361–4. · Gregory, D. 1981: Alfred Weber and location theory. In D.R. Stoddart, ed., *Geography, ideology and social concern*. Oxford: Blackwell. · Gregory, D. and Urry, J., eds, 1985: *Social relations and spatial structures*. London: Macmillan. · Haggett, P. 1965: *Locational analysis in human geography*. London: Edward Arnold. · Haggett, P., Cliff, A.D. and Frey, A.E. 1977: *Locational analysis in human geography*, 2nd edn. London: Edward Arnold. · Hartshorne, R. 1939: *The nature of geography: a critical survey of current thought in the light of the past*. Lancaster, PA: Association of American Geographers. · Harvey, D. 1982: *The limits to capital*. Oxford: Blackwell. · Harvey, D. 1985: *The urbanization of capital*. Oxford: Blackwell. · Hayter, R. and Watts, H.D. 1983: The geography of enterprise: a reappraisal. *Progress in Human Geography* 7: 157–81. · Herod, A. 1997: From a geography of labor to a labor geography: labor's spatial fix and the geography of capitalism. *Antipode* 29: 1–31. · Isard, W. 1956: *Location and space economy*. Cambridge, MA: MIT Press. · Jones, K. and Simmons, J. 1993: *Location, location, location: analyzing the retail environment*, 3rd edn. Toronto: Nelson. · Keeble, D. 1979: Industrial geography. *Progress in Human Geography* 3: 425–33. · Krugman, P. 1991: *Geography and Trade*. Cambridge, MA: MIT Press. · Krugman, P. 1995: *Development, Geography and Economic Theory*. Cambridge, MA: MIT Press. · Lash, S. and Urry, J. 1993: *Economies of signs and space*. London: Sage. · Leyshon, A. and Thrift, N. 1997: *Money space*. London: Routledge. · Lösch, A. 1954: *The economics of location*. New Haven: Yale University Press (originally published in German in 1940). · Lowe, M. and Wrigley, N. 1996: *Retailing, consumption and capital*. Harlow, Essex: Longman. · McDermott, P. and Taylor, M. 1982: *Industrial organization and location*. Cambridge: Cambridge University Press. · McDowell, L. 1997: *Capital culture*. Oxford: Blackwell. · Marshall, A. 1952: *Principles of economics*, 8th edn. London: Macmillan (1st edn 1890). · Martin, R. and Sunley, P. 1996: Paul Krugman's geographical economics and its implications for regional development theory: a critical assessment. *Economic Geography* 72: 259–92. · Massey, D. 1977: Towards a critique of industrial location theory. In R. Peet, ed., *Radical geography: alternative viewpoints on contemporary social issues*. London: Methuen; Chicago: Maaroufa, 181–96. · Massey, D. 1978: Regionalism: some current issues. *Capital and Class* 6: 106–25. · Massey, D. 1984: *Spatial divisions of labour: social structures and the geography of production*. London: Macmillan. · O'Brien, R. 1992: *Global financial integration: the end of geography*. London: Pinter. · *Regional Studies* 1978: Organization and industrial location in Britain. *Regional Studies* 9: part 2. · Richardson, H.W. 1973: *Regional growth theory*. London: Macmillan. · Rushton, G. 1969: Analysis of spatial behavior by revealed space preference. *Annals of the Association of American Geographers* 59: 391–400. · Sayer, R.A. 1982: Explanation in economic geography. *Progress in Human Geography* 6: 68–88. · Schoenberger, E. 1988: Multinational corporations and the new international division of labor: a critical appraisal. *International Regional Science Review* 11: 105–19. · Scott, A.J. 1976: Land and land rent: an interpretative review of the French literature. *Progress in Geography* 9: 101–45. · Scott, A.J. 1980: *The urban land nexus and the state*. London: Pion. · Scott, A.J. 1996: The craft, fashion, and cultural-products industries of Los Angeles: competitive dynamics and policy dilemmas in a multisectoral image-producing complex. *Annals of the Association of American Geographers* 86: 306–23. · Scott, A.J. 1997: The cultural economy of cities. *International Journal of Urban and Regional Research* 21: 323–39. · Scott, A.J. and Storper, M., eds, 1986: *Production, work, territory*. Boston: Allen and Unwin. · Sheppard, E. and Barnes, T.J. 1990: *The capitalist space economy: analysis after Ricardo, Marx and Sraffa*. London: Unwin Hyman. · Smith, D.M. 1981: *Industrial location: an economic geographical analysis*, 2nd edn. New York: John Wiley. · Stafford, H. 1972: The geography of manufacturers. *Progress in Geography* 4: 181–215. · Storper, M. and Walker, R. 1983: The theory of labour and the theory of location. *International Journal of Urban and Regional Research* 7: 1–41. · Storper, M. and Walker, R. 1989. *The capitalist imperative; territory, technology, and industrial growth*. Oxford: Blackwell. · Venables, A. 1996: Equilibrium locations of vertically linked industries. *International Economic Review* 37: 341–59. · Walker, R. 1985: Is there a service economy? The changing capitalist division of labor. *Science and Society* 49: 42–83. · Walker, R. and Storper, M. 1981: Capital and industrial location. *Progress in Human Geography* 5:

473–509. · Webber, M.J. and Rigby, D. 1996: *The golden age illusion*. New York: Guilford Press. · Weber, A. 1928: *Alfred Weber's theory of the location of industries*. Chicago: University of Chicago Press (originally published in German in 1909). · Wood, P. 1991: Flexible accumulation and the rise of business services. *Transactions, Institute of British Geographers* NS 16: 160–72.

Suggested Reading

Cooke (1983a), chs 6–10. · Smith (1981). · Storper and Walker (1989), chs 1–4.

locational analysis An approach to HUMAN GEOGRAPHY focusing on the spatial arrangement of phenomena and on related flow patterns: its usual methodology is that of SPATIAL SCIENCE. The philosophy of POSITIVISM underpins the approach, which is closely linked to the discipline's QUANTITATIVE REVOLUTION.

Work within the locational analysis framework was taken up by several groups of geographers in the US from the late 1950s on, although it had much deeper roots in the work of non-geographer pioneers (Johnston, 1997a): the main initial centres were at the University of Washington, Seattle, the University of Wisconsin, Madison, and the University of Iowa and the ideas were rapidly spread – mainly by graduates from those three centres – to other universities (such as Chicago, Northwestern, and Ohio State): developments at Seattle were significantly influenced by a visiting Swedish pioneer, Torsten Hägerstrand.

The focus of this work was on developing geography as 'the science of locations'. At Seattle, this was strongly influenced by CENTRAL PLACE THEORY and other presentations of regularities in point and line patterns, and in the geography of flows (Garrison, 1959–60); Bunge (1966) generalized on this in his thesis on *Theoretical geography*, based on the premise that 'nearness [is] a candidate for the central problem in geography' and defined geography as the 'discovery of predictive patterns'. Stewart (1956), a physicist who worked at the American Geographical Society, originally a physicist, argued for what he termed *social physics*, which sought mathematical rules describing human behaviour and its spatial outcomes, and which differed from sociology by its 'avoidance of subjective descriptions' (cf. MACROGEOGRAPHY). Others, such as McCarty at Iowa, were strongly influenced by developments in the field of economics, to which they introduced the spatial variable in searches for CORRELATIONS between mapped distributions (as in McCarty and Lindberg, 1966): these links led to the close interrelationships between geographers and regional scientists in the 1960s and 1970s (see REGIONAL SCIENCE), and are illustrated by attempts to build economic geography theories of spatial arrangements (as in Smith, 1981).

Locational analysis was introduced to the UK by geographers who had visited the main centres of innovation in the USA (some were graduate students there). One of them, Peter Haggett, codified the PARADIGM in a textbook – *Locational analysis in human geography* (first published in 1965: see also Haggett, Cliff and Frey, 1977) – which rapidly attained the status of a classic. He established the pedigree of locational analysis by linking its geometrical focus to the work of early Greek cartographers: others argued that 'of the three classic areas of mathematics, geometry would appear to be the most promising for geography' (see also Bunge, 1966) although Sack (1972) doubted whether geometry can be used as a language to explain as well as describe form.

Haggett's appeal to the relatively neglected geometrical tradition within geography was 'placed squarely on asking questions about the order, locational order, shown by the phenomena studied traditionally as human geography'. Such a focus needed:

- to adopt a SYSTEMS approach which concentrates on the patterns and linkages within an assemblage;
- to employ MODELS as the stimuli for understanding (as with his frequent references to Thompson's (1917) *On growth and form*); and
- to use quantitative procedures to make precise statements (generalizations) about locational order (see also MACROGEOGRAPHY).

His book, and its successor (Haggett et al., 1977), was in two main parts: the first dealt with models and the second with methods.

Haggett's major innovation was his framework for classifying models of locational order. (Interestingly, his schema is paralleled by one developed contemporaneously by Cole and King, 1968.) His initial presentation contained five components: the sixth (DIFFUSION) was added in the second edition. Their separate chapters were ordered in what he saw as a logical sequence for the analysis of REGIONS (see figure). The first (a) was concerned with *interactions*, or flows across space; the second (b) analysed the *networks* along which those flows moved; and the third (c) considered the major *nodes*, or organizational centres, on those networks. In the fourth (d) the *hierarchical structure* of the nodal system (see URBAN

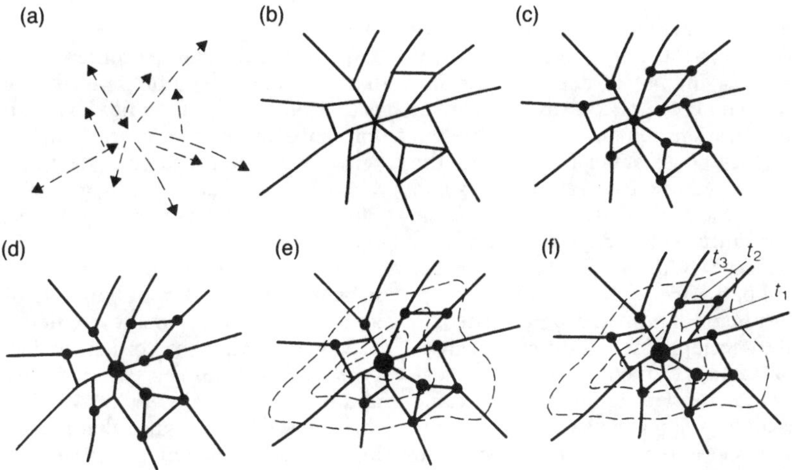

Locational analysis *Stages in the analysis of nodal regional systems: (a) interaction: (b) networks: (c) nodes: (d) hierarchies: (e) surface: (f) diffusion* (Haggett et al., 1977)

systems; CENTRAL PLACE THEORY) was decomposed, whereas in the fifth (e) the focus was the organization of the space between the nodes – the *surfaces*. The final component (f) looked at *diffusion* down the hierarchy, along the networks, and across the surfaces. Haggett decomposed systems, therefore, but – despite his discussion of regions – didn't recombine them into wholes.

Regarding methods, there was a major shift of emphasis between the two editions of Haggett's book. In the first, he accepted the then-conventional view that the methods associated with the GENERAL LINEAR MODEL could be adopted for SPATIAL ANALYSIS without difficulty but a decade later, influenced by his studies of diffusion and the work of his colleague Andrew Cliff on SPATIAL AUTOCORRELATION, he argued that such applications were 'more difficult than might at first appear' so that, for example, conventional REGRESSION procedures were omitted from the book.

From this pioneering conspectus, Haggett explored the component parts of his framework in more detail. A book on network analysis combined human and physical geography (Haggett and Chorley, 1969) but most of his work has focused on aspects of diffusion (Cliff et al., 1975, 1981; see LEAD–LAG MODELS), especially in the context of MEDICAL GEOGRAPHY.

Haggett's major role was as a synthesizer and stimulant, and he promoted both the search for locational order as a major goal of contemporary geography and its adopted positivist philosophy, although he wrote very little himself on the latter. Others followed his lead, providing their own perspectives on the study of what became known as SPATIAL STRUCTURES (Johnston, 1973). Morrill (1970), for example, was also strongly influenced by the geometrical tradition and his text *The spatial organization of society* focused on the 'nearness principle': people, he argued, seek to maximize spatial interaction at minimum cost and so bring related activities into proximity – the result is that 'human society is surprisingly alike from place to place . . . [because of] the predictable, organized pattern of locations and interrelations'. Whereas Morrill concentrated on substantive illustration of his principle (which he later revised somewhat, downplaying the geometrical component: Morrill and Dormitzer, 1979), Abler, Adams and Gould (1971) spent the first third of *Spatial organization* discussing the nature of science and the methods to be used in locational analysis.

Critiques of locational analysis developed during the 1970s, focused initially on the validity of NORMATIVE THEORY in geographical studies, on the grounds that this did not reflect the reality of DECISION-MAKING and so was of little value in predicting locational arrangements. This stimulated growth of the more inductive approach of BEHAVIOURAL GEOGRAPHY which, nevertheless, also assumed that generalizations about spatial behaviour and pattern are feasible. This position was countered in further critiques, located within HUMANISTIC GEOGRAPHY and RADICAL GEOGRAPHY, which argued that locational analysis studies imply an absence of human free will whereas societies comprise individuals with the capacity to remember, learn and promote change. As a consequence, while the study of spatial patterns, the use of relevant quantitative methods and the implied search for laws of spatial organization remain part of human geography, they play a smaller role within the discipline than was the case in the 1960s and early 1970s, when they were presented as geography's entrée to, and niche within, the social sciences (NAS–NRC, 1965; Taaffe, 1970; Chisholm, 1971).

Some historians of human geography debate whether the development of locational analysis in the 1960s reflected the influence of persuasive leaders such as Haggett, whether it came about because of greater awareness of the existence of relevant models and methods in other disciplines, as Pooler (1977) suggests, or whether it was just a general realization that the traditional form of regional analysis was increasingly less suited to study of the contemporary world and needed to be replaced. Cox (1976) argued that until the nineteenth century societies were predominantly local in their orientation and the local physical environment was the main influence on livelihood – hence traditional regional geography and its society–land focus (what Haggett called vertical links). The twentieth-century integration of societies into a global world-economy (see WORLD-SYSTEMS ANALYSIS; GLOBALIZATION) means that spatial interdependence has become much more important (horizontal links) and 'locally experienced environmental dependencies lost their rationale: men [sic] relate less and less to the land on which they stand and more and more to socially-created geographical patterns over a much wider area': recognition of this by geographers led to locational analysis ousting regional analysis as the discipline's dominant paradigm.

Whatever its origins, locational analysis substantially changed the nature of human geography from the mid-1960s on. It presented geography as a positivist social science, concerned to develop precise, quantitatively stated generalizations about patterns of spatial organization, thereby enriching and being enriched by LOCATION THEORY, and to offer models and procedures which could be used in physical planning. By 1978, Haggett could write that:

> the spatial economy is more carefully defined than before, we know a little more about its organization, the way it responds to shocks, and the way some regional sections are tied into others. There now exist theoretical bridges, albeit incomplete and shaky, which span from pure, spaceless economics through to a more spatially disaggregated reality.

Twelve years later, he continued to promote the search for 'scientific generalizations' (Haggett, 1990), while accepting that in the search for spatial order 'the answer largely depends on what we are prepared to look for and what we accept as order': only a minority of geographers now claim that order is the focus of their quest.

Changes in the nature of modern communications and the diminishing role of distance as an influence on many methods of interaction is making the formal models of locational analysis obsolescent according to some authors (Johnston, 1997b, 1997c). Against this, however, it is argued that making optimal location decisions remains crucial to the profitability of many businesses (see APPLIED GEOGRAPHY) and locational analysis models and methods allow an appreciation of earlier societies whose spatial order provides the foundation (such as the urban systems) on which modern societies are built.

Haggett's schema made no mention of 'bounded spaces', divisions of the earth's surface into separate territories at a variety of scales, within which much human behaviour is constrained (cf. TERRITORIALITY). In part this may have been because it proved difficult to develop theories of such spaces, rather than of the point, line and surface patterns which were the focus of locational analysis, but Nystuen's (1963) essay on 'fundamental geographical concepts' identified only three as both necessary and sufficient for the construction of an abstract geography – *directional orientation*, *distance*, and *connectedness* – although he did consider whether BOUNDARY should be included as a further 'geographical primitive'. Space in the locational analysis paradigm was largely continuous in its nature, and boundaries were impediments to its rational use rather than central components of its STRUCTURATION (see Haggett, 1981).

Locational analysis was very firmly set in the spatial science paradigm of geography that emerged in the 1960s, therefore, but it was not the only approach to understanding SPATIAL STRUCTURES and the organization of the SPACE-ECONOMY. Others, stimulated by the work of Harvey (1973, 1982) and Massey (1984), adopted a POLITICAL-ECONOMY approach, whose goal of accounting for changing geographies of capitalist organization eschewed any search for spatial regularities and instead focused on the contingent influence of PLACE-based factors on the general processes of UNEVEN DEVELOPMENT (cf. LAYERS OF INVESTMENT). This latter approach now dominates, and the search for 'spatial order' as set out in Haggett's pioneering conspectus is much less important in contemporary geography: locational analysis as spatial science marked an important turning-point in the discipline's history – according to some it was crucial to its continued presence in the academy and its acceptance within the institutional structure of the social sciences in North America and the UK (it was adopted much later, and in a much more muted form, in the French- and German-speaking realms), and it continues to be promoted as such by some (Johnston, 1998) – but it now barely rates a mention in contemporary presentations of the discipline's contents (e.g. Peet, 1998). RJJ

References
Abler, R.F., Adams, J.S. and Gould, P.R. 1971: *Spatial organization: the geographer's view of the world*. Englewood Cliffs, NJ: Prentice-Hall. · Bunge, W. 1966: *Theoretical geography*. Lund: C.W.K. Gleerup. · Chisholm, M. 1971: *Research in human geography*. London: Social Science Research Council. · Chorley, R.J. and Haggett, P., eds, 1967: *Models in geography*. London: Methuen; Cliff, A.D. et al. 1975: *Elements of spatial structure: a quantitative approach*. Cambridge and New York: Cambridge University Press. · Cliff, A.D. et al. 1981: *Spatial diffusion*. Cambridge and New York: Cambridge University Press. · Cole, J.P. and King, C.A.M. 1968: *Quantitative geography*. London: John Wiley. · Cox, K.R. 1976: American geography: social science emergent. *Social Science Quarterly*. 57: 182–207. · Garrison, W.L. 1959–60: The spatial structure of the economy I, II and III. *Annals of the Association of American Geographers* 49: 238–48 and 471–82, and 50: 357–73. · Haggett, P. 1965: *Locational analysis in human geography*. London: Edward Arnold. · Haggett, P., Cliff, A.D. and Frey, A.E. 1977: *Locational analysis in human geography*, 2nd edn. London: Edward Arnold. · Haggett, P. 1981: The edges of space. In R.J. Bennett, ed., *European progress in spatial analysis*. London: Pion. · Haggett, P. 1978: The spatial economy. *American Behavioral Scientist* 22: 151–67. · Haggett, P. 1990: *The geographer's art*. Oxford and Cambridge, MA: Basil Blackwell. · Haggett, P. and Chorley, R.J. 1969: *Network analysis in geography*. London: Edward Arnold. · Harvey, D. 1969: *Explanation in geography*. London: Edward Arnold. · Harvey, D. 1973: *Social justice and the city*. London: Edward Arnold. · Harvey, D. 1982: *The limits to capital*. Oxford: Blackwell. · Johnston, R.J. 1973: *Spatial structures: introducing the study of spatial systems in human geography*. London: Methuen. · Johnston, R.J. 1997a: *Geography and geographers: Anglo-American human geography since 1945*, 5th edn. London: Edward Arnold. · Johnston, R.J. 1997b: W(h)ither spatial science and spatial analysis. *Futures* 29: 323–35. · Johnston, R.J. 1997c: Geography in a restructuring world. *GeoJournal* 42: 9–16. · Johnston, R.J. 1998: Turning full circle: American geography and the social sciences, 1950–2000. In H.H. McCarty and J.B. Lindberg, *A preface to economic geography*. Englewood Cliffs, NJ: Prentice-Hall. · Massey, D. 1984: *Spatial divisions of labour*. London: Macmillan. · Morrill, R.L. 1970: *The spatial organization of society*. Belmont, CA: Wadsworth. · Morrill, R.L. and Dormitzer, J. 1979: *The spatial order: an introduction to modern geography*. North Scituate, NJ: Duxbury; NAS–NRC 1965: *The Science of Geography*. Washington: National Academy of Sciences–National Research Council. · Nystuen, J.D. 1963: Identification of some fundamental spatial concepts. *Proceedings of the Michigan Academy of Science, Arts and Letters* 48: 373–84. · Peet, R. 1998: *Modern geographical thought*. Oxford: Blackwell; Pooler, J.A. 1977: The origins of the spatial tradition in geography: an interpretation. *Ontario Geography* 11: 56–83. · Sack, R.D. 1972: Geography, geometry and explanation. *Annals of the Association of American Geographers* 62: 61–78. · Smith, D.M. 1981: *Industrial location: an economic geographical analysis*, 2nd edn. New York: John Wiley. · Stewart, J.Q. 1956: The development of social physics. *American Journal of Physics* 18: 99–123. · Taaffe, E.J., ed., 1970: *Geography*. Englewood Cliffs, NJ: Prentice-Hall; Thompson, W. d'Arcy 1917: *On growth and form*. Cambridge: University of Cambridge Press.

locational interdependence The dependence of locational choice on the location chosen by others. The location of any factory will be dependent to some extent on the location of suppliers or consumers, but locational interdependence generally refers to situations where choice of location depends on that of competitors. The locational interdependence approach in INDUSTRIAL LOCATION THEORY is closely associated with the theory of imperfect competition, in which it is recognized that geographical space necessarily introduces imperfections in market competition (see HOTELLING MODEL; MARKET-AREA ANALYSIS; VARIABLE REVENUE ANALYSIS). DMS

location–allocation models Models used to determine the optimal location of central facilities (hospitals, offices, warehouses, etc.) in order to minimize movement and other costs. A public-sector example is the location of two new hospitals in a city: the objectives would be to minimize the aggregate travel cost to patients and to arrive at an optimal assignment of patients to the hospitals. A private-sector example is the location of warehouse facilities between factories and markets in order to minimize total distribution costs.

Unlike TRANSPORTATION PROBLEM models, in which all the locations are fixed and the optimal assignment can be determined by LINEAR PROGRAMMING, in location–allocation models the siting of the central facilities and the assignment of least-cost flows must be determined simultaneously. The choice of location (whether or not to build a hospital at any given location) is a discrete or integer variable, and linear programming only deals with continuous variables. This makes the solution of these models more difficult, and many applications use heuristic or trial-and-error procedures that search for, but cannot be guaranteed to find, the true optimum. The degree of difficulty is a function of the number of unknowns: a two-hospital problem with fixed hospital capacities is much easier than a five-hospital problem with variable hospital sizes.

Two important classes of location–allocation models are distinguished: location on a continuous surface or plane, and location on a NETWORK. The continuous surface form has been widely used in theoretical analysis, and is related to Weber's industrial location model (cf. INDUSTRIAL LOCATION THEORY), but its limitations are increasingly recognized. Straight-line distance is often a poor proxy for real TRANSPORT COSTS, which occur on a route network, and potential locations are usually restricted. Work has increasingly used the network form, where potential locations are defined as nodes and are linked to sources (and destinations in the warehousing case) by a route network. Mixed integer-continuous techniques are now available to find a true optimum for such problems. Recent extensions have very effectively linked location–allocation together with ENTROPY-MAXIMIZING MODELS and GEOGRAPHICAL INFORMATION SYSTEMS to plan both commercial (e.g. car showrooms) and public (e.g. hospital) facilities.

LWH

Suggested Reading

Killen, J.E. 1983: *Mathematical programming for geographers and planners*. London: Croom Helm.

logical positivism A particular development of the philosophy of POSITIVISM which was formulated by the Vienna Circle in the 1920s and 1930s and which in its modern form is usually associated with the writings of Ayer, Hempel and Nagel (among others). Unlike earlier versions of positivism, logical positivism recognized two (and only two) kinds of statement as scientifically meaningful: (a) *empirical (or 'synthetic') statements*, the truth of which had to be established by verification; and (b) *analytical statements* of logic and mathematics, which were judged to be true by definition. Much of the specific critique of logical positivism, as opposed to the more general critique of positivism, has concentrated on the problems posed by this central 'principle of verification' and on the physicalism which it was often supposed to entail. Indeed, Popper (1976) insisted that 'everybody knows nowadays that logical positivism is dead' and declared 'I must admit responsibility'. He believed that his formulation of CRITICAL RATIONALISM in the 1930s, and especially its contrary 'principle of FALSIFICATION', had decisively discredited the claims of logical positivism. Certainly Suppe (1977), from a rather more catholic perspective, reckoned that 'virtually all of the positivistic program for philosophy of science has been repudiated by contemporary philosophy of science' and that today 'its influence is that of a movement historically important in shaping the landscape of a much-changed contemporary philosophy of science'. Even so, according to Guelke (1978), 'from Hartshorne to Harvey geographical writing on philosophy and methodology has to a greater or lesser degree shown the influence of logical positivist ideas'. Its most sharply focused application came during the QUANTITATIVE REVOLUTION:

> In the 1950s and 1960s, many geographers in emphasising the importance of laws, theories and prediction in empirical research implicitly adopted a logical positivist view of science and scientific explanation. The connection between geography and logical positivism was made explicit by Harvey [in his *Explanation in geography* (1969)] who presented a thorough logical positivist analysis of geographical explanation. (Guelke, 1978, p. 46)

Whether or not it is fair to use Harvey's text as an index of human geography as a whole, it is certainly clear that today, as the critique of logical positivism has become more widely known, fewer geographers now cheerfully accept the label and most resist the suggestion that logical positivism represents 'the' scientific method.

DG

References

Guelke, L. 1978: Geography and logical positivism. In D.T. Herbert and R.J. Johnston, eds, *Geography and the urban environment, volume 1*. Chichester: John Wiley, 35–61. · Harvey, D. 1969: *Explanation in geography*. London: Edward Arnold; New York: St. Martin's Press. · Popper, K. 1976: *Unended quest: an intellectual autobiography*. London: Fontana. · Suppe, F., ed., 1977: *The structure of scientific theories*, 2nd edn. Urbana, IL: University of Illinois Press.

Suggested Reading

Guelke (1978).

logistic regression A form of REGRESSION analysis in which the dependent variable is measured on a nominal scale, in binary categories (i.e. the variable can take one of two values only: see LOGIT). Because the transformation process uses natural logarithms, the regression coefficients are multiplicative, and their anti-logs are ratio measures (see MEASUREMENT) of the rate of change in the dependent variable with a unit change in the relevant independent. (Cf. CATEGORICAL DATA ANALYSIS.) RJJ

logit A TRANSFORMATION of a variable to meet the constraints of the GENERAL LINEAR MODEL approach to statistical analysis. Logit transformations are usually performed on binary data (i.e. the variable can only take the values of 0.0 and +1.0), to avoid estimating equations which might produce 'nonsense' estimates of their values outside that range. RJJ

Suggested Reading

O'Brien, L. 1992: *Introducing quantitative geography: measurement, methods and generalised linear models*. London and New York: Routledge.

log-linear modelling Procedures for analysing data measured at the nominal level only. The goal, as in REGRESSION, is to fit an equation which predicts the values in a contingency table (i.e. the entries in each cell) in terms of the values of independent variables (which may also be measured at the nominal level only). The terms in the model, presented in logarithmic form, are the deviations for the relevant cell (defined by the values of the independent variables) from a control value, usually the grand mean for the entire sample. (Cf. CATEGORICAL DATA ANALYSIS.) RJJ

Suggested Reading

O'Brien, L. 1990: *The statistical analysis of contingency table designs. Concepts and techniques in modern geography 51*. Norwich: Environmental Publications. · O'Brien, L. 1992: *Introducing quantitative geography: measurement, methods and generalised linear models*. London and New York: Routledge.

longitudinal data analysis The study of repeated measurements of one or more variables on the same observation units over a period of time. This allows consideration of change without potentially committing a cross-level fallacy (see ECOLOGICAL FALLACY) which might occur if inferring change processes from cross-sectional studies of different samples over time. RJJ

M

macrogeography The search for empirical regularities in spatial distributions as a basis for generalizations about SPATIAL STRUCTURES. The approach was pioneered by a physicist, John Q. Stewart, and developed with William Warntz, who was employed on the American Geographical Society's Macrogeography Project (see Warntz, 1984; Johnston, 1997).

Stewart and Warntz's agenda was similar to that associated with the application of GENERAL SYSTEMS THEORY to geography; they sought SCALE-free generalizations. Their most lasting contribution to SPATIAL ANALYSIS was the concept of POPULATION POTENTIAL, cartographic surfaces which generalize point (and point-in-area) distributions, which underpinned later developments in CLASSIFICATION AND REGIONALIZATION using GEOGRAPHICAL INFORMATION SYSTEMS. (Cf. CENTROGRAPHY.) RJJ

References and Suggested Reading

Johnston, R.J. 1997: *Geography and geographers: Anglo-American human geography since 1945*, 5th edn. London: Arnold. · Warntz, W. 1965: *Macrogeography and income fronts*. Philadelphia: Regional Science Research Institute. · Warntz, W. 1984: Trajectories and coordinates: geography as spatial science. In M. Billinge et al., eds, *Recollections of a revolution*. London: Macmillan.

malapportionment An electoral abuse in which a party promotes its own interests by defining constituencies of differing (population or electorate) sizes. The most successful method involves creating small constituencies for your own party to win and much larger ones for opposition party victories, a strategy that is only potentially successful if the parties' supporters are spatially separated to some extent. Malapportionment was ruled unconstitutional and its practice outlawed in the USA in the 1960s, and British legislation requires the definition of constituencies whose electorates are 'as equal as is practicable' (cf. GERRYMANDERING). RJJ

Suggested Reading

Baker, G.E. 1966: *The reapportionment revolution*. New York: Random House. · Taylor, P.J. and Johnston, R.J. 1979: *Geography of elections*. London: Penguin Books.

Malthusian model The economist Thomas Robert Malthus (1766–1834) published *An essay on the principle of population* in 1798 and it is to his ideas that subsequent thinking on the economic approach to demography may be traced. While he modified his own position (for example between the first essay of 1798 and the second, more detailed and reasoned, account of 1803), and subsequent developments of Malthusian theory are complex, his general view was that population tends to increase faster than the means of subsistence, thus absorbing all economic gains, unless controlled by what he termed 'preventive' and 'positive' checks. He maintained that population, if unchecked, tended to increase at a geometric rate (i.e. 1, 2, 4, 8, 16 . . .) while subsistence increased at an arithmetic rate (1, 2, 3, 4, 5 . . .) and 'in two centuries the population would be to the means of subsistence as 256 to 9; in three centuries as 4096 to 13, and in two thousand years the difference would be almost incalculable'. His 'positive and preventive checks' which occur in human populations to prevent excessive growth relate to practices affecting MORTALITY and FERTILITY respectively. The 'positive' checks included wars, disease, POVERTY and, especially, lack of food; his 'preventive' checks included principally 'moral restraint', or the postponement of marriage, and 'vice', in which he included adultery, birth control and abortion. He saw the tension between population and RESOURCES as a major cause of misery for much of humanity. Malthus was not, however, in favour of contraception, since its use did not generate the same drive to work hard as would a postponement of marriage. He stressed the negative correlation between station in life and number of children and, in order to induce in the lower classes the self-control and social responsibility he saw in the middle classes, Malthus asserted that the poor should be better paid and educated (see CLASS).

Malthus's views have been challenged in a great variety of ways. He certainly established the thesis that population was growing quickly and that people are biological as well as social beings, depending on sexual drive and food. Yet he has been criticized, for example, for confusing moralist and scientific approaches and for being a poor prophet of events. Marx was one of the most powerful critics of Malthus, asserting that poverty is the result of the unjust social institutions of CAPITALISM rather than of population growth. No country of Europe or North America, except possibly Ireland, conformed to the Malthusian prediction. During the nineteenth century economic growth far outdistanced population growth, resulting in rising standards of living; and, despite this, birth-rates declined first in France and Sweden and then more generally. It has also been argued that Malthus's reactionary views impeded the development of demography as a science. Nevertheless, the power of the Malthusian argument lies in its acuity as a system of reasoning and it is for that reason that Malthus's ideas are still debated two centuries after their initial formulation. PEO

Suggested Reading

Coleman, D. and Schofield, R., eds, 1986: *The state of population theory. Forward from Malthus*. Oxford: Blackwell. · Dupâquier, J., Fauve-Chamoux, A. and Grebenik, E., eds, 1983: *Malthus past and present*. London and New York: Academic Press. · James, P. 1979: *Population. Malthus: his life and times*. London and Boston: Routledge and Kegan Paul. · Malthus, T.R. 1970: *An essay on the principle of population and a summary view of the principle of population*, ed. A. Flew. London: Pelican. · Malthus, T.R. 1990: *An essay on the principle of population; or a view of its past and present effects on human happiness; with an inquiry into our prospects respecting the future removal or mitigation of the evils it occasioned: the version published in 1803, with variora of 1806, 1807, 1817 and 1826*, ed. P. James. Cambridge: Cambridge University Press. · Petersen, W. 1979: *Malthus*. London: Heinemann; Cambridge, MA: Harvard University Press. · Wrigley, E.A. 1969: *Population and history*. London: Weidenfeld and Nicolson.

map image and map A graphical representation of all or a portion of the earth or a similarly vast environment. Until the advent of digital computing, this concise definition applied equally well to maps in general, all of which were visible arrangements of labels and graphic symbols. Most discussions of maps in a geographical context still refer to visual compositions, but widespread use of electronic storage often demands a distinction between the structured geographical information in an electronic DATABASE and the map images that might – or might not – be generated to display or analyse data. Although visual analysis is often desirable, some GEOGRAPHICAL INFORMATION SYSTEMS let the user measure and compare maps without looking at them.

All map images have three principal elements: scale, projection, and symbolization. SCALE is defined as the ratio of distance on the map to the corresponding distance on the ground. When recorded as a ratio or fraction, the scale expresses both distances in identical units of measurement, with the map distance reported first as one unit, as in 1:10,000 or 1/10,000, which means that a centimetre on the map represents 10,000 cm on the ground. (A dimensionless number, 1/10,000 also indicates that an inch on the map represents 10,000 inches on the ground.) Scale may be expressed verbally, as in 'one inch represents one mile', which users might find more convenient than the equivalent ratio 1:63,360. Maps often include a graphical scale, on which a carefully measured line, commonly subdivided with appropriately labelled ticks, portrays one or more typical distances. Unlike ratio or verbal scales, a graphical scale remains true if the map is enlarged or reduced on a photocopier.

Fractional representations of scale afford a distinction between large scales, like 1/5,000, and small scales with much larger denominators. At scales of 1/250,000 or smaller, maps that compress huge territories onto small sheets or computer monitors incur a substantial loss of detail especially apparent in the simplification and smoothing of rivers and shorelines (Jenks, 1981). Generalization is particularly severe on page-size world maps with scales of 1/200,000,000 or less. By contrast, scales of 1/10,000 or more can accommodate a wider range of features as well as usefully detailed descriptions of irregular curves and complex patterns. In general, small-scale maps afford a broader geographic scope, whereas large-scale maps can provide a more realistic depiction of the landscape (Goodchild and Proctor, 1997). Whatever its scale, the map serves the geographer much like the microscope serves the biologist, albeit through reduction rather than enlargement.

Only on a globe is scale constant everywhere. Because fitting a curved surface onto a flat map requires stretching or compressing some parts of the globe more than others, scale typically varies with direction as well as from point to point. These distortions are usually negligible on large-scale maps because the stretching required to represent a small city or neighbourhood is far less troublesome than distortions caused by map generalization or the paper's sensitivity to moisture. Not so for small-scale maps of continents and other vast areas. Because of substantial geographical variation in stretching – some maps even stretch the poles into lines as long as the equator – world maps typically omit graphic scales, which invite misleading estimates of distance.

And a ratio scale, if included, refers only to so-called standard lines, at which a hypothetical globe with the stated scale intersects the plane, cylinder or cone onto which the map's PROJECTION transfers coastlines, boundaries and other features.

Map projection is easily understood as a two-stage computational process. In the first stage, the planet is reduced to a globe, which establishes the map's scale. In the second stage, an algorithm transfers meridians, parallels and other geographical features onto a simple geometric surface that is either flat or easily flattened by cutting. A plane, cylinder or cone avoids needless mathematical complexity yet affords flexibility in positioning the projection's standard lines, where the surface meets the globe and around which distortion is comparatively low. Conic projections are particularly suitable for mid-latitude continents like Europe or Australia, for which a single carefully chosen standard parallel can limit overall distortion. Even so, a secant cone, which intersects the globe along two standard parallels, can control distortion more than a tangent cone, which merely touches the globe along a single parallel. For polar regions, the plane provides a realistic view on which meridians converge at the pole, whereas for regions that straddle the equator, like Africa and south Asia, the cylinder affords a secant projection with standard parallels equidistant from the equator. A cylinder secant at 10° N and S, for instance, positions features in Africa closer to a standard line, on average, than would a cylinder tangent at the equator.

Cylindrical projections centred on the equator are widely used for world maps. The simplest cylindrical projection is the plane chart, also called the equirectangular projection, on which evenly spaced straight-line meridians intersect evenly spaced straight-line parallels. North–south scale is constant throughout the map but east–west scale escalates to infinity at the poles, where area and shape are severely distorted. In 1772, mathematician J.H. Lambert proposed a cylindrical equivalent (equal-area) projection, which compensates for the poleward exaggeration of area with ever greater reductions in north–south scale (Snyder, 1993, pp. 85–7). Lambert's solution eliminated areal distortion at the expense of more pronounced east–west stretching in polar regions. Although secant cylindrical projections can achieve equivalence of area with mid-latitude belts of low distortion, these solutions incur marked north–south stretching near the equator. A typical example is the rectangular equal-area projection secant at 45°, devised by Scottish minister James Gall in 1855. In the late 1960s, German historian Arno Peters proposed an identical projection as the first world map to eliminate areal distortions that diminished the apparent importance of developing nations (Vujakovic, 1989; Crampton, 1994).

Another mathematical modification of cylindrical projection attacked the plane chart's poleward distortion of angles and small shapes. In 1599, English mathematician Edward Wright described an equatorially centred cylindrical projection that kept scale constant in all directions at a point – cartographers call this property conformality – and rendered true angles at all points. Wright's name is rarely mentioned because he merely worked out the mathematics for a projection introduced less rigorously thirty years earlier by the famed atlas publisher Gerardus Mercator (Snyder, 1993, pp. 43–9). Although seldom appreciated for its wide use in large-scale topographic mapping, the Mercator projection gained deep respect among mariners. Because straight lines on the Mercator represent lines of constant geographical direction, also called rhumb lines or loxodromes, a navigator need only plot a course's origin and destination, connect the points with a straight line, and measure the angle between the line and a meridian to find the bearing. This benefit has a cost: in achieving conformality, the projection incurs an outrageous poleward distortion of area. But because sailing ships rarely ventured into polar latitudes, map-makers truncated the Mercator world map in northern Greenland and just south of the Shetland Islands, and conveniently ignored the absurdity of poles located at infinity.

Another solution to the areal distortion of the plane chart is the pseudocylindrical projection, so called because its meridians bend inward to compensate for areal exaggeration near the poles (Maling, 1968). This strategy, it turns out, is older than Lambert's clever rearrangement of parallels: in 1570 the mariner Jehan Cossin of Dieppe produced a world map on the sinusoidal projection, characterized by equidistant straight-line parallels and evenly spaced curved meridians (Snyder, 1993, p. 50). In 1805, Karl Mollweide introduced the pseudocylindrical projection that bears his name. With unevenly spaced parallels and semi-elliptical meridians, the Mollweide projection provides a more pleasing equivalent world map than the sinusoidal projection, on which rapidly converging meridians greatly distort shape near the poles. In addition to a standard line at the equator, the sinusoidal and Mollweide projections have low distortion along the central meridian, which remains a straight line. Even so, these projections severely distort shape and angles at places well removed from both the equator and the central meridian.

The compromises and trade-offs of map projection are readily apparent in interrupted projections, which split the world into lobes that meet along the equator (Dahlberg, 1962). By interrupting over water, these composite equal-area projections lessen the distortion of continents and provide a whole-world base map especially useful for phenomena occurring on land. An exemplar is the homolosine equal-area projection of J. Paul Goode (1925), who centred northern lobes on North America and Eurasia, and southern lobes on the South Pacific Ocean, South America, Africa and Australia. To further limit distortion of shape and angles over land, Goode established standard parallels at 40°44'11.8"N and S, where he further conserved shape by dividing each lobe into an equatorial zone represented with a sinusoidal projection and a polar zone with a Mollweide. Although the resulting land-biased map is poor for portraying ocean currents and shipping routes, Goode demonstrated the versatility of composite projections with an oceanic variant, interrupted over land to conserve the continuity of continents.

In a further demonstration of the flexibility of map projection, Arthur Robinson (1974) devised a non-interrupted pseudocylindrical projection that lessened the maximum amount of angular shear as well as the apparent distortion of continental areas. His projection is neither conformal nor equivalent. Using an iterative trial-and-error approach informed by computer plots and measurements of areal and angular distortion, he adjusted the projection's parameters to make the world 'look right'. In 1988, the National Geographic Society adopted the Robinson projection for its physical and political maps of the world. Although the Society's projection is a Euro-centric version centred on the Greenwich meridian, useful variations of the Robinson projection can be centred on East Asia or the Americas.

By relieving the numerical drudgery that impeded the use of customized map projections, COMPUTER-ASSISTED CARTOGRAPHY helps map authors tailor a map's perspective to a specific distribution or part of the world (Robinson and Snyder, 1991). In addition to balancing distortions of angles, area, distance, direction and the gross shape of continents, software users can centre projections on areas of interest and compose maps that engage as well as communicate. Software can also assist in the development of area CARTOGRAMS, which provide base maps focused on population size, wealth or economic clout rather than land area (Dent, 1996, pp. 202–16).

SYMBOLIZATION, the third element of all maps, refers to the graphic codes – pictorial, geometric or verbal – used to portray geographic features and spatial phenomena. Non-verbal symbols rely on one or more visual variables to communicate differences in kind or degree. Jacques Bertin (1983) defined six retinal variables: shape, pattern, hue, orientation, size and graytone value. Of these, shape, hue and pattern are most appropriate for showing qualitative differences; size and value are most suited to quantitative differences; and orientation (as apparent in arrows and ISOLINES) is ideal for showing direction. A mismatch between the data and the retinal variable, such as widely varied hues to show differences in rate or density, can be inefficient if not misleading (Monmonier, 1996, pp. 19–24). Map authors can also misrepresent quantitative data by ignoring the logical links between intensity data (for example, population density, median income and rates of growth) and graytone symbols, as on CHOROPLETH maps, and between count data (for example, number of people, total payroll and amount of increase) and magnitude symbols like graduated circles.

Some map symbols demand a specific kind of projection. A world map of climatic regions, for instance, needs an equivalent projection, which more accurately shows the relative areas of various climatic regions, whereas a world map of weather or individual climatic elements benefits from a conformal projection, which preserves the angles that meridians and isobars make with winds and ocean currents. Similarly, an equivalent projection is essential if a dot-distribution map, on which each dot represents a specified number of people, dairy cattle or tornadoes, is to show worldwide or regional variation in density.

Classifications based on dimensionality and conventional practices do not readily accommodate image maps ranging from black-and-white aerial photographs to colour–infrared satellite imagery (cf. REMOTE SENSING). Distinguished from traditional 'cartographic line maps' by their photo-like tonal variations, these high-altitude portraits of land, oceans and atmosphere reflect nearly a century of progress in optics, aeronautics and electronic image processing. Image maps acquire the trappings of conventional maps through the addition of labels, a grid, coastlines and other cartographic symbols as well as through the removal of geometric distortions characteristic of aerial cameras and orbiting scanners. Orthophotomaps and orthophotoquadrangle maps – geometrically accurate photomaps that capture subtle but significant features like paths and vegetation boundaries – have become a valuable complement to the traditional TOPOGRAPHIC MAP (Thrower and Jensen, 1976).

Image maps are but one of many new cartographic forms. Dynamic maps that incorporate time and motion as visual variables provide animated descriptions of spatial processes, and interactive maps afford point-and-click access to highly customized maps, complementary graphs and diagrams, detailed explanations of data and even the map-maker's raw data, heretofore available largely to other insiders. Especially promising are maps adapted to colour-impaired users (Olson and Brewer, 1997). No longer must all users settle for a single static map.

In addition to radically changing the nature of graphic maps, cartography's digital transition promises to alter fundamentally the relationship between map-maker and map user (Monmonier, 1985). Because of inexpensive personal computers, innovations originally intended only for map-makers are commonplace. And because of the Internet and its worldwide computer-oriented telecommunications network, map users can acquire map images, software and data from a rich variety of institutions and individuals, radical as well as traditional (Peterson, 1997). Despite these promising solutions, the new electronic cartography cannot escape contentious policy issues of public access, privacy, intellectual property and liability (Onsrud and Rushton, 1995).

Equally persistent is the notion that maps are rhetorical communications, readily adapted to the map-maker's agenda and customarily accorded respect, if not awe, by users ill-equipped to question motives or authority (Monmonier, 1996). As a graphic representation, the map acquires persuasiveness from the crispness of its lines, the implied precision of grid and scale, and the self-proclaimed accuracy of basic information the user already knows, or presumes to know. Users who understand the constraints of cartographic generalization and the opportunities for manipulation will approach with caution a map's silences as well as its facts: the history of cartography is rich in examples of maps that reify the territorial assertions of map authors who deliberately suppressed or conveniently ignored competing claims (Harley, 1988; Black, 1998). While electronic cartography seems likely to intensify, not lessen, the use of maps as propaganda, the new media afford broader opportunities for interrogating data and exploring alternative views. MM

References

Bertin, J. 1983: *Semiology of graphics: diagrams, networks, maps*, trans. W.J. Berg. Madison: University of Wisconsin Press. · Black, J. 1998: *Maps and politics*. London: Reaktion Books. · Crampton, J. 1994: Cartography's defining moment: the Peters projection controversy, 1974–1990. *Cartographica* 31(4): 16–32. · Dahlberg, R.E. 1962: Evolution of interrupted map projections. *International Yearbook of Cartography* 2: 36–53. · Dent, B.D. 1996: *Cartography: thematic map design*, 4th edn. Dubuque, Iowa: William C. Brown. · Goodchild, M.F. and Proctor, J. 1997: Scale in a digital world. *Geographical and Environmental Modelling* 1: 5–23. · Goode, J.P. 1925: The homolosine projection: a new device for portraying the earth's surface entire. *Annals of the Association of American Geographers* 15: 119–25. · Harley, J.B. 1988: Silences and secrecy: the hidden agenda of cartography in early modern Europe. *Imago Mundi* 40: 57–76. · Jenks, G.F. 1981: Lines, computers, and human frailties. *Annals of the Association of American Geographers* 71: 1–10. · Maling, D.H. 1968: The terminology of map projections. *International Yearbook of Cartography* 8: 11–64. · Monmonier, M. 1985: *Technological transition in cartography*. Madison, Wisc.: University of Wisconsin Press. · Monmonier, M. 1996: *How to lie with maps*, 2nd edn. Chicago: University of Chicago Press. · Olson, J.M. and Brewer, C.A. 1997: An evaluation of color selections to accommodate map users with color-vision impairments. *Annals of the Association of American Geographers* 87: 103–34. · Onsrud, H.J. and Rushton, G., eds, 1995: *Sharing geographic information*. New Brunswick, NJ: Rutgers University Press. · Peterson, M.P. 1997: Cartography and the Internet: introduction and research agenda. *Cartographic Perspectives* 26: 3–12. · Robinson, A.H. 1974: A new map projection: its development and characteristics. *International Yearbook of Cartography* 14: 145–55. · Robinson, A.H. and Snyder, J.P., eds, 1991: *Matching the map projection to the need*. Rockville, MD: American Congress on Surveying and Mapping. · Snyder, J.P. 1993: *Flattening the earth: two thousand years of map projections*. Chicago: University of Chicago Press. · Thrower, N.J.W. and Jensen, J.R. 1976: The orthophoto and orthophotomap: characteristics, development and application. *The American Cartographer* 3: 39–56. · Vujakovic, P. 1989: Mapping for world development. *Geography* 74: 97–105.

Suggested Reading

Hall, S.S. 1992: *Mapping the next millennium*. New York: Random House. · Keates, J.S. 1996: *Understanding maps*, 2nd edn. London: Longman. · MacEachren,

A.M. 1995: *How maps work: representation, visualization, and design*. New York: Guilford Press. · Monmonier, M. 1993: *Mapping it out: expository cartography for the humanities and social sciences*. Chicago: University of Chicago Press. · Robinson, A.H. et al. 1995: *Elements of cartography*, 6th edn. New York: John Wiley and Sons.

map-reading The psycho-physical, cognitive and intellectual process of decoding cartographic symbols and making sense of features and relationships portrayed on a map (see MAP IMAGE AND MAP). Map-reading is similar to the reading of a book, news report or other literary work insofar as an accurate and efficient interpretation depends on not only a vocabulary shared by author and reader but also a common understanding of how information should be structured for ready communication. Successful map-reading thus relies heavily on the user's experience with cartographic vocabulary (see SYMBOLIZATION), map PROJECTION, map SCALE, and common forms of TOPOGRAPHIC and THEMATIC MAPS – experience at least sufficient to inculcate a belief that map-reading will be informative – as well as some prior understanding of the phenomena portrayed (Eastman and Castner, 1983).

Map-reading differs markedly from verbal reading (Balchin, 1976). Literary TEXTS rely on the vocabulary and grammatical structure of everyday speech, in which words are organized linearly in sentences, grouped in turn into paragraphs and chapters. Within sentences, the familiar sequence of subject–verb–object affords a logical framework for describing who did what to whom. And within paragraphs – at least in well-written works – the topic sentence establishes the context for a coherent sequence of sentences in which the speaker or writer adds new information to what the listener or reader has already been told (Williams, 1990). By contrast, maps often rely on abstract geometric symbols, which few if any readers use with the regularity of verbal language. And even maps consisting largely of pictograms or words must present their symbols in a two-dimensional format unable to dictate the sequence of decoding. Perhaps the closest similarity between maps and literature is the index, which points to specific features or facts with grid coordinates or page numbers.

Semiologist Jacques Bertin (1983) made an important distinction between map viewing and map-reading. Simply put, some maps are made to be read whereas others are made to be seen. In advertising and political propaganda, for example, a map to be seen will blatantly announce the locational convenience of a firm's retail outlets or the unfair threat posed by a small nation's larger neighbours. Although an accurate interpretation demands a minimal appreciation of the map's context and objective, little conscious decoding is required. By contrast, a map to be read imposes a 'mental cost that the viewer must expend to extract information' (MacEachren, 1995, p. 209).

Contrast and similarity among map symbols provide rudimentary guidance for map-readers, who seem proficient in identifying edges and processing information in chunks (Marr, 1982). Evidence suggests that the reader's eyes are attracted more readily to darker symbols, thicker lines and larger labels than to lighter symbols, thinner lines or smaller type (MacEachren, 1995, pp. 51–149). Cartographers and other graphic designers are thus advised to develop and reinforce a graphic hierarchy by concentrating this 'data ink' on the symbols representing the more salient features (Tufte, 1983, pp. 91–105). Equally important is recognition of the variety of map-reading tasks that can be improved or hindered by a specific design or juxtaposition of features (Olson, 1976). Authors must also be wary that a viewer's reaction to the map's aesthetic appearance can enhance or diminish interest and expectations (Wood, 1993).

Animation and interactive electronic multimedia promise more structured cartographic communication insofar as temporal sequences of maps, diagrams, photographs and blocks of text can approximate the linear coherence of a narrative dramatized on film or video (Monmonier, 1992). No less important than graphic sequencing is the potential for adding a sound channel and customizing the presentation to the interests and experience of the 'reader' (see VISUALIZATION). MM

References

Balchin, W.G.V. 1976: Graphicacy. *The American Cartographer* 3: 33–8. · Bertin, J. 1983: *Semiology of graphics: diagrams, networks, maps*, trans. W.J. Berg. Madison: University of Wisconsin Press. · Eastman, J.R. and Castner, H.W. 1983: The meaning of experience in task-specific map reading. In D.R.F. Taylor, ed., *Graphic Communication and Design in Contemporary Cartography*. New York: John Wiley and Sons, 115–48. · MacEachren, A.M. 1995: *How maps work: representation, visualization, and design*. New York: Guilford Press. · Marr, D. 1982: *Vision: a computational investigation into the human representation and processing of visual information*. San Francisco: W.H. Freeman. · Monmonier, M. 1992: Authoring graphic scripts: experiences and principles. *The American Cartographer* 19: 247–60, 272. · Olson, J.M. 1976: A coordinated approach to map communication improvement. *The American Cartographer* 3: 151–9. ·

Tufte, E.R. 1983: *The visual display of quantitative information*. Cheshire, Connecticut: Graphics Press. · Williams, J.M. 1990. *Style: toward clarity and grace*. Chicago: University of Chicago Press. · Wood, M. 1993: The map-user's response to map design. *The Cartographic Journal* 30: 149–53.

Suggested Reading

MacEachren, A.M. 1995: *How maps work: representation, visualization, and design*. New York: Guilford Press. · Muehrcke, P.C. and Muehrcke, J.O. 1997: *Map use: reading, analysis, interpretation*, 4th edn. Madison, Wisc.: JP Publications.

market-area analysis The examination of the conditions under which the market area of a firm is determined. This type of analysis is important both to industrial location and to the provision of services. For any industrial organization, control over a sales territory is of some relevance to locational choice and plant viability. Some further aspects of market-area analysis in industrial location are discussed under HOTELLING MODEL and VARIABLE REVENUE ANALYSIS.

The derivation of a market area for the single plant is explained in the figure. A plant is located at A, in the (one-dimensional) space represented by the horizontal axis. The cost of producing one unit or a given volume of output is represented by C. The commodity is sold to the customers, ranging along the distance axis, at a price that includes production cost and transport costs (represented by t_A). A price p is the most that the consumers are prepared to pay for the commodity, a condition assumed to be constant in space. Under these simple conditions, the market area for the firm located at A will be bounded by the points M_A and M'_A, where delivered price is just equal to the maximum that the consumer is prepared to pay. Introducing the second distance dimension and rotating the edge of the market line about A would generate a circular market area.

Relaxing the assumption of a single firm in isolation and introducing a second plant at B, the figure illustrates the effect of LOCATIONAL INTERDEPENDENCE on market competition. Firm B is able to offer the commodity at a lower delivered price (t_B) than A in the section of A's market area extending from M_A to X. On the assumption that consumers purchase from the cheapest source of supply, this area would now be transferred to the market area of firm B. As other firms enter the industry, space should gradually be filled up and market areas whittled down to the minimum size consistent with profitable operation by a process of competition, as elaborated in the CENTRAL PLACE THEORY associated with Walter Christaller and August Losch.

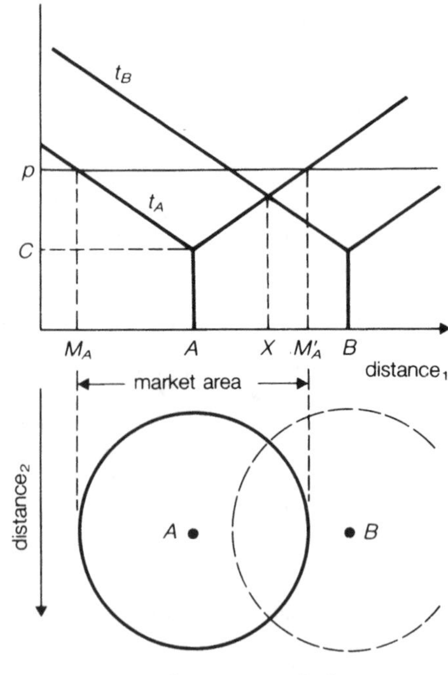

market-area analysis

In reality, market areas will be more complex in both form and derivation than in this simple model, because of the actual nature of consumer preferences, behaviour, pricing policies and competitive practice (cf. HINTERLAND). DMS

Suggested Reading

Smith, D.M. 1981: *Industrial location: an economic geographical analysis*, 2nd edn. New York: John Wiley, chs 4 and 9.

market exchange A system of exchange organized through price-fixing markets. Market exchange was one of three FORMS OF ECONOMIC INTEGRATION identified by Karl Polanyi. When he used it to characterize an entire economy (rather than segments within an economy) Polanyi spoke of a *market economy* thus: 'an economic system controlled, regulated and directed by markets alone; order in the production and distribution of goods is entrusted to this self-regulating mechanism ... [and] ensured by prices alone' (Polanyi, 1957). Three features of market exchange are especially important.

(a) Market exchange depends upon a characteristic SPATIAL STRUCTURE involving the transmission of price signals and the interdependence of markets in time and space. 'Price-making markets are integrative only if they are linked up in a system that tends to spread the effects of prices to markets other than those directly affected' (Polanyi, in Dalton, 1968). Much of mainstream LOCATION THEORY assumed, and on occasion addressed, these matters but attention was usually focused on the pattern of markets – for example, as in Christaller's CENTRAL PLACE THEORY – with comparatively little regard to the diffusion of price signals. Notable empirical exceptions include Losch's (1954, pp. 496–504) suggestive descriptions of 'spatial differences in the movement of commodity prices' and Pred's (1973) reconstruction of the circulation of information (including prices current) through systems of American cities between 1790 and 1840. Most of the theoretical formulations depended upon NEO-CLASSICAL ECONOMICS, however, which assumes: (i) the universality of market exchange; and (ii) its tendency toward equilibrium. Polanyi contested both of these assumptions: see (b) and (c) respectively.

(b) Market exchange is historically specific. Before the INDUSTRIAL REVOLUTION in England, Polanyi argued, 'the economic system was submerged in general social relations; markets were merely an accessory feature of an institutional setting controlled and regulated . . . by social authority'. In pre-industrial societies, therefore, 'the self-regulating market was unknown': and it was precisely because he believed that the emergence of 'the idea of self-regulation was a complete reversal of the trend of development' that Polanyi entitled his celebrated account of the INDUSTRIAL REVOLUTION *The great transformation* (1957). Within geography, the historical specificity of market exchange has been accentuated most sharply by those approaches which have drawn upon MARXIAN ECONOMICS to recognize 'integration through price-fixing markets [as] characteristic of the capitalist mode of production' (Harvey, 1973; see CAPITALISM). Even so, Harvey described the Industrial Revolution in terms which were as close to Polanyi as they were to Marx:

> The slow build-up of the Industrial Revolution in Britain . . . represented a gradual penetration of market exchange into production (as distinct from trade and commerce) through the penetration of land and labour. As the industrial revolution gained momentum, more and more sectors of activity became integrated through market exchange, and distribution and service activities were also drawn in. The circulation of surplus value in its capitalist form finally broke free from the restraining influence of the rank society and then, through its domination of all the key sectors of society became the medium through which the market mode of economic integration gradually bound society into one cohesive economic system. (Harvey, 1973, p. 243)

This slippage between Marx and Polanyi is problematic – Polanyi was not a Marxist and there are important differences between his formulations and those of HISTORICAL MATERIALISM – but Harvey was not alone in seeking to connect them. More recently, Wallerstein's discussions of the formation of the capitalist world-economy and what he calls 'historical capitalism' rely on similar connections and accord a peculiar primacy to systems of (unequal) exchange (see Brenner, 1977; Skocpol, 1977). This is not to argue for an intellectual fideism, of course: Marx's formulations have no necessary privilege over Polanyi's and, indeed, one commentator has claimed that Wallerstein's schema is deficient because it pays *too little* attention to Polanyi's work (Dodgshon, 1977). But the rise of this WORLD-SYSTEMS ANALYSIS has confirmed the continuing significance of Polanyi's writings and has underscored the historical specificity of market exchange.

(c) Market exchange entails relations of CONFLICT. According to Polanyi, 'exchange at fluctuating prices aims at a gain that can be attained only by an attitude involving a distinctive antagonistic relationship between the partners . . . [which] is ineradicable' (Polanyi, in Dalton, 1968). In his first formulations Harvey (1973) thus identified market exchange with stratified societies, but he soon acknowledged that this begged the central question. Giddens (1981) had emphasized that for both Marx and Weber '*the market is intrinsically a structure of power*' (emphasis added) and that for any account seeking to build on either of these foundations 'the problem . . . is not the recognition of the diversity of the relationships and conflicts created by the capitalist market as such, but that of making the *theoretical* transition from such relationships and conflicts to identification of classes as structured forms'. In a later essay Harvey (1974) drew upon Giddens's writings to provide a thumbnail sketch of the connections between class structure and residential differentiation; and although this derived 'primarily from a reading of Marx', it also gave a special prominence to differential 'market capacities' in a way which plainly owed just as much to Weber (see CLASS). There have been a number of developments from this baseline (see, e.g., Cox, 1978) and particular interest has been attached to studies of the relations between housing markets and LABOUR MARKETS (see, e.g. Harvey, 1978; Thorns, 1982; Hamnett, 1984; Saunders, 1984). More recently, the collapse of communism in eastern Europe and the dissolution of the Soviet Union ushered in a new period of so-called 'market triumphalism', but many of the former COMMAND ECONOMIES have experienced considerable problems in making the transition to a market economy, which seems to confirm the conflicts and asymmetries which Polanyi believed to be inherent within market exchange. DG

References

Brenner, R. 1977: The origins of capitalist development: a critique of neo-Smithian Marxism. *New Left Review* 104: 25–92. · Cox, K.R., ed., 1978: *Urbanization and conflict in market societies*. London: Methuen. · Dalton, G., ed., 1968: *Primitive, archaic and modern economies. Essays of Karl Polanyi*. Boston: Beacon Press. · Dodgshon, R.A. 1977: Review symposium; The modern world system by Immanuel Wallerstein. A spatial perspective. *Peasant Studies* 6: 8–19. · Giddens, A. 1981: *The class structure of the advanced societies*, 2nd edn. London: Hutchinson. · Hamnett, C. 1984: The postwar restructuring of the British housing and labour markets. *Environment and Planning A* 12: 147–61. · Harvey, D. 1973: *Social justice and the city*. London: Edward Arnold; Baltimore, MD: Johns Hopkins University Press. · Harvey, D. 1974: Class structure in a capitalist society and the theory of residential differentiation. In R. Peel, M. Chisholm and P. Haggett, eds, *Processes in physical and human geography: Bristol essays*. London: Heinemann, 354–69. · Harvey, D. 1978: Labour, capital and class struggle around the built environment in advanced capitalist societies. In K.R. Cox, ed., *Urbanization and conflict in market societies*. London: Methuen; Chicago; Maaroufa Press, 9–37. · Losch, A. 1954: *The economics of location*. New Haven: Yale University Press. · Polanyi, K. 1957: *The great transformation: the political and economic origins of our time*. Boston: Beacon Press; Pred, A. 1973: *Urban growth and the circulation of information: the United States system of cities 1790–1840*. Cambridge, MA: Harvard University Press. · Saunders, P. 1984: Beyond housing classes. *International Journal of Urban and Regional Research* 8: 202–25; Skocpol, T. 1977: Wallerstein's world capitalist system: a theoretical and historical critique. *American Journal of Sociology* 82: 1075–90. · Thorns, D.C. 1982: Industrial restructuring and changes in the labour and property markets in Britain. *Environment and Planning A* 14: 745–63.

Suggested Reading

Cox (1978). · Harvey (1973), 210–15, 241–5, 261–84. · Polanyi (1957).

market orientation The tendency of an economic activity to locate in proximity to its market. This will be the case where the cost of shipping the product to the consumer accounts for a relatively high proportion of total cost, or where the effort involved in consumers getting to the source of supply, along with the attraction of the good or service, is such that only short distances will be travelled. Market orientation used to apply mainly at the local level, with small-scale producers supplying a local market, while today the pull of the market is rather a factor in the AGGLOMERATION of economic activity in major metropolitan areas. (Compare MATERIAL ORIENTATION.) DMS

market potential model A device for estimating the likely volume of sales attainable from alternative plant locations. It is an application of the general concept of POPULATION POTENTIAL, which also forms the basis of the GRAVITY MODEL. It rests on some very specific assumptions as to the prevailing demand situation: that the level of sales at any market will be proportional to some initial local magnitude there, and that this will decrease with increasing distance from the source of supply. There is thus the implicit assumption of a downward sloping demand curve and an f.o.b. price (whereby the cost of transportation is met by the consumer; see PRICING POLICIES).

The market potential, or estimated volume of sales (M), attainable from any plant location i is given by:

$$Mi = \sum_{j=1}^{n} Qi/Tij,$$

where Q is some initial measure of magnitude of the size of the local market at j, and T some measure of the transfer cost from i to j, or the rise in delivered price with increasing distance from the plant: summation is over all n markets. The magnitude of Q is usually measured by size of local population or by per capita income or retail sales, in the absence of a more accurate basis for the estimation of size of market for the commodity in question. T may be measured by the prevailing TRANSPORT COSTS, but this is more usually taken simply as linear distance between production points and markets.

When M is calculated for a set of possible plant locations, the one with the largest market potential can be identified. Market potential at alternative locations can be used to interpolate a market potential surface. If revenue is expected to be proportional to volume of sales, and if this is actually identified by the market potential formulation, then a market potential surface can act as a revenue surface (see VARIABLE REVENUE ANALYSIS).

The practical application of the concept of market potential is severely limited by the stringency of the assumptions on which its prediction of likely sales is based. These rarely exist in reality. The market potential concept has been used rather indiscriminately in economic geography, often in circumstances where it is not appropriate to the empirical situation. DMS

Suggested Reading

Smith, D.M. 1981: *Industrial location: an economic geographical analysis*, 2nd edn. New York: John Wiley, 275–8.

market socialism The idea of market socialism can be traced at least as far back as the New Economic Policy experiments in the USSR of the 1920s which partially and temporarily restored markets and private ownership. In this sense market socialism as a concept and set of programmes is inexplicable outside the actual or purported failures of socialist theory and practice. According to Roemer (1996, p. 13), market socialism is 'any of a variety of economic arrangements in which most goods including Labor are distributed through the price system and the profits of firms, perhaps managed by workers or not, are distributed equally among the population. By what mechanism profits can be so distributed, without unacceptable costs in efficiency, is the central question.'

Socialist-type economies were characterized by the centrality of the plan over the market as a form of coordination, by STATE over private ownership (cf. CENTRAL PLANNING). More precisely the system of socialist economic planning turned on (i) targets for physical production (the plan); (ii) the absence of price signals for market clearing; and (iii) the absence of bankruptcy (the so-called soft budget constraint). The structural flaws in these sorts of economy – whether China in the 1960s, USSR in the 1940s or Hungary in the 1970s – turned on the conjunction of three characteristics: first, *the allocation of most goods by an administrative apparatus* under which producers did not have to compete with one another; second, *the direct political control of firms*; and third, *non-competitive, non-democratic politics*.

Actually existing socialisms have, as a number of commentators have observed, suffered from a number of ideal–typical dynamics. These included the lack of incentives (the fundamental criterion of the enterprise is the quantity produced determined by negotiation with a central authority), and UNCERTAINTY driven in large measure by (i) the systemic shortage of the right and proper inputs, which is reflected in limited inter-enterprise trade, bartering, hoarding, self-sufficiency, gigantism (the scale of enterprises) and hyper-centralization; and (ii) the deleterious consequences of low prices and a limited role of money (Isachsen, Hamilton and Gylfason, 1992). The brilliant Hungarian economist Janos Kornai (1992) systematized this socialist-type economy and inventoried the sorts of problems (forced consumption, rationing, suction, shortage) which emerge from the logic of the plan and the dominance of political over financial accountability. Kornai spells out in detail the mechanisms of softening the budget constraint (of keeping inefficient enterprises in business): namely, soft subsidies, soft taxation, soft credit, and soft administered prices. In the economics literature these attributes are typically seen to confer problems of information or agency, and of credible commitment on the part of the state (Bardhan, 1993). According to Roemer (1996, pp. 14–15), COMMUNIST economies suffered from three principal–agent problems: manager–worker relations on the collective farm or in the state enterprise; the planner–manager relation; and the public–planner relationship.

Market socialism can be understood as a reformist response to the problems of 'actually existing socialism' which emerged almost from the inception of the project in 1917. As a theoretical model it was developed by Oskar Lane and Abba Lerner in the 1930s (see Temkin, 1996) in response to a critique of SOCIALISM developed largely by Ludwig von Mises in the 1920s – what came to be called the debate on rational economic calculation under socialism (Hayek, 1940). Market socialist ideas have passed through a number of stages since (Bardhan and Roemer, 1993). The first was marked by the realization by socialists that prices must be used for economic calculation under socialism; they could not in other words use some kind of natural unit such as energy or labour (cf. LABOUR THEORY OF VALUE). The second stage involved the use of Walrasian equilibrium theory to calculate the correct prices in a socialist economy by solving simultaneous equations (cf. NEO-CLASSICAL ECONOMICS). The third stage was marked by the realization by Lange and others that markets of some kind would be required to find the socialist equilibrium. Lane's (1938) model was as follows: the socialist economy based on STATE ownership of CAPITAL and land is controlled by a Central Planning Board, which substitutes for the market and its price mechanism and imitates conditions of perfect competition. It creates a quasi-market by setting prices for capital goods and by providing firms with rules of micro-economic behaviour. This model was subsequently the object of intense critique, most notably by Hayek (1940), but was in any case a western theoretical debate that was rejected outright by the USSR.

The fourth stage was associated with the development of the idea of a market socialism by market reforms in Yugoslavia after 1950, in Hungary after 1968, in China after 1978, and in Poland and USSR in the 1980s. Prices were not fully free and the soft budget constraint was typically maintained with the result that so-called incentive compatibility remained a central theoretical conundrum (see Nove, 1983). Finally, the fifth stage was marked by the events of 1989 and the collapse of the socialist bloc. Here the attempt was to construct market socialism as a 'third way' between the socialism of old on the one hand and the market-driven shock therapy on the other. Significantly, much of the work of this stage has been developed by western intellectuals – Roemer (1994), Stiglitz (1994), Blackburn (1991) – and rejected much of Lange's earlier model. In this new work public ownership is essentially abandoned and rather a multiplicity of different kinds of property rights are explored that would provide incentives for profit maximization but would preclude unequal profit distribution. Here the case of China and the dynamism of township and village enterprises (TVEs) characterized by so-called 'hybrid' property rights have attracted much attention (Walder, 1995; Naughton, 1996). The most theoretically elaborate model of market socialism is provided by Roemer (1996).

The debate over market socialism embraces a diversity of programmes and practices which include questions of enterprise self-management, investment policy, incentive compatibility and forms of 'market socialization'. While market socialism is especially associated with the cases of reformist post-socialist states and forms of experimentation (China, Vietnam, Hungary), other scholars include within the market socialist paradigm the Swedish social democratic model, new forms of so-called associative democracy (Hirst, 1994), and the so-called Third Way programmes of Blair and Clinton (Giddens, 1998). MW

References

Bardhan, P. 1993: On tackling the soft budget constraint in market socialism. In P. Bardhan and J. Roemer, eds, *Market socialism*. Oxford: Oxford University Press, 145–56. · Bardhan, P. and Roemer, J., eds, 1993: *Market socialism*. Oxford: Oxford University Press. · Blackburn, R. 1991: *After the fall*. London: Verso. · Giddens, A. 1998: *The third way*. Oxford: Polity Press. · Hayek, J. 1940: Socialist calculation, *Economica* 7: 125–49. · Hirst, P. 1994: *Associative democracy*. Cambridge: Polity. · Isachsen, A., Hamilton, C. and Gylfason, T. 1992: *Understanding the market economy*. Oxford: Oxford University Press. · Kornai, J. 1992: *The socialist system*. Princeton, NJ: Princeton University Press. · Lane, O. 1938/1964: On the economic theory of socialism. In B. Lippincott, ed., *On the economic theory of socialism*. Minneapolis: University of Minnesota Press. · Naughton, B. 1996: *Growing out of the plan*. Cambridge: Cambridge University Press. · Nove, A. 1983: *The economics of feasible socialism*. London: Allen and Unwin. · Roemer, J. 1994: *A Future for Socialism*. Cambridge, MA: Harvard University Press. · Roemer, J. 1996: *Unequal shares*. London: Verso. · Stiglitz, J. 1994: *Whither socialism*. Cambridge, MA: MIT Press. · Temkin, G. 1996: The new market socialism. *Communist and Post Communist Studies* 29/4: 467–78. · Walder, A. 1995: Local governments as industrial firms. *American Journal of Sociology* 101: 263–301.

Markov process (or Markov chain) A type of STOCHASTIC PROCESS: if the probability of being in a state at time t is wholly dependent upon the state(s) at some preceding time(s), it is said to be a Markov process. Where only the immediately preceding state is considered it is said to be a first order Markov process, but higher order processes (i.e. dependence on earlier states) can be modelled. The process is often represented by a transition probability matrix in which the rows and columns represent states and the cells represent the probabilities of movement between states. For example, land-use changes between the categories 'residential', 'commercial', and 'industrial' could be modelled by the matrix:

		State at time t+1:		
		Res.	Comm.	Ind.
State	Res.	0.90	0.06	0.04
at time	Comm.	0.02	0.85	0.13
t	Ind.	0.00	0.10	0.90

The matrix may be interpreted as follows: between time t and time $t + 1$, 90 per cent of the residential land remains in the same use, 6 per cent is transferred to commercial use, and 4 per cent becomes industrial; the second and third rows may be interpreted similarly. Note that each of the rows sums to unity (no land is lost or gained in the conversion process). The repeated operation of such a matrix results in a stable distribution between states, which is independent (in general) of the initial distribution. But for such a repeated operation to be realistic it is necessary to demonstrate (or assume) that the transition matrix is constant over a number of time intervals (referred to as stationary). The Markov model has been used to study the growth of firms (movement between size categories) and the migration of firms and households (movement between geographical locations). AMH

Suggested Reading

Collins, L., Drewett, R. and Ferguson, R. 1974: Markov models in geography. *Statistician* 23: 179–210.

Marxian economics A body of THEORY that seeks to provide an explanation of how an economy functions, derived from the political economy of Karl Marx (1818–83) and from its elaborations and extensions by Friedrich Engels (1820–95). The alternative body of theory is NEO-CLASSICAL ECONOMICS, which forms the basis of the analysis usually accepted in the West, or the capitalist world.

The 1960s and 1970s saw a resurgence of interest in Marxian economics. What Marxists described as 'bourgeois economics' appeared increasingly inadequate as a basis for understanding how a capitalist economy actually functions. Marxian economics provides an alternative and (for Marxists) more persuasive interpretation of how CAPITALISM operates.

Marxian economics does not form a prominent component in conventional textbooks and courses in economics in the capitalist world. This has led to misunderstanding of what Marx was actually trying to do when he addressed himself to economic matters. Marxism is not merely a guide to revolutionary practice, though Marx did make some predictions concerning the demise of capitalism, nor does Marxian analysis offer a blueprint for the operation of a centrally planned socialist economy. The purpose of Marxian analysis is to provide a general historical perspective on economic affairs, focused particularly on laying bare the operation of the capitalist system.

Marxian economics and neo-classical theory share common roots in the so-called classical economics of the late eighteenth and early nineteenth century. The strongest link between Marx and the classical tradition is provided by the LABOUR THEORY OF VALUE, and it is in the treatment of value that the fundamental difference between Marxian economics and the alternative perspective is to be found. In the classical labour theory of value, prices of all goods are seen as derived from the current labour input and from the labour input embodied in the materials of production. In neo-classical economics the role of value theory is similarly to explain relative prices, but with the explicit recognition that capital and land as well as labour make a contribution and are entitled to a return. For Marx, value theory was the key to understanding the nature of capitalist society as a historically specific form of economic organization. Whereas the neo-classical analysis sees value (reflected in prices and income distribution) arising from some almost mechanical process of market determination, Marxian economics uses the concept of value to expose the social (CLASS) relations seen to be at the root of the inequality manifest under capitalism.

Marxian analysis is thus more of a general theory of society than an approach to economics. Indeed, to separate out those notions that might be labelled 'economic' from the rest of Marx's work is contrary to the very spirit of Marxism, with its emphasis on the holistic perspective of POLITICAL ECONOMY. What follows is a highly selective summary of the basics of Marxian analysis as applied to economic processes. Those seeking additional insight may refer to the Suggested Reading listed at the end of this entry, as well as to *Capital* and other writings of Marx himself.

The general perspective of Marxism is sometimes referred to as HISTORICAL MATERIALISM. The emphasis is on identifying those relationships that are of fundamental importance in determining a social system's overall direction of movement and change, as unfolded in history. The economic base or MODE OF PRODUCTION is seen as the key to understanding the complex web of interconnections involving the institutions, patterns of behaviour, beliefs and so on that make up a society. The mode of production consists of the PRODUCTIVE FORCES or capacity to produce (these are labour, resources and instruments of labour) and the RELATIONS OF PRODUCTION whereby people participate in the productive process. The social relations involve CLASS cleavages, as for example between landlords and peasants or capitalists and workers. The base or substructure of the mode of production is connected with the SUPERSTRUCTURE of religion, ethics, laws, mores and institutions via reciprocal cause-and-effect relationships, but the effect of economic base on superstructure is held to be dominant.

Historically, four successive modes of production are recognized before the advent of

SOCIALISM: primitive COMMUNISM, SLAVERY, FEUDALISM and CAPITALISM. As the forces of production develop to increase productive capacity, conflict or tension arises within the prevailing relations of production, which threatens their self-perpetuating tendencies. For example, as long as feudal social relations remained it was impossible to take full advantage of the increased production capacities generated by technological advances that took place prior to the INDUSTRIAL REVOLUTION. The ties of apprentice to master and peasant to landlord prevented the redeployment of labour required for rapid economic growth. The resolution of this type of contradiction is the motive force for change, which can lead to the replacement of one mode of production by another – as in the transition from feudalism to capitalism, during which labour was gradually freed from its old obligations. Capitalist social relations, with the distinctions between labour on the one hand and capital on the other, facilitated the full development of the productive forces in an era of major technological change. This made possible rapid increases in production, and a rise in general living standards that would have been frustrated under feudalism. But capitalism brought its own contradictions, as Marx was able to demonstrate. Crucial to the resolution of contradictions between the forces of production and the social relations of production is the class struggle, under which the CLASS controlling the means of production (i.e. the slave owners, feudal landlords or capitalists) is opposed to the mass of the working people (the 'proletariat'). In Marx's analysis, the proletariat would eventually be driven to overthrow the capitalist ruling class, to create socialism and ultimately the classless communist society (cf. COMMUNISM).

The rise of capitalism not only changed the status of labour but also began to divest it of the means of production (in the form of tools and the land), over which many feudal craftsmen and small farmers had direct control. To sustain itself, this 'freed' labour had to offer its services to those who owned the new means of production – the capitalists. Whereas conventional economics views the sale of labour, like that of other commodities, as part of a system of exchange relationships, Marxian analysis uses the theory of value to reveal the exploitative social relationships of capitalism: the class relations hidden beneath commodity transactions.

This process may be explained by reference to some basic categories and relationships in Marxian economics. It is necessary first to distinguish two concepts of value: *exchange value* (or the value at which a commodity can be exchanged for other commodities) and *use value* (or the usefulness of commodities to their possessor). All economic systems produce things with use value to satisfy human needs; capitalism is distinguished by its emphasis on production for exchange and profit. Marx directed his analysis towards the determination of the exchange value of commodities. According to the labour theory of value, the basis of the exchange of commodities (i.e. their prices) should be the amount of labour time required to produce them under the conditions normally obtaining; the labour thus required is termed *socially necessary labour*. This theory applies to labour itself just as to other commodities: the exchange value of *labour power* (i.e. the commodity that workers sell) is determined by the socially necessary labour required for subsistence, or the cost of production (and reproduction) of labour itself. The exchange value of labour is thus (theoretically) decided independently of the specific job that the labourer might do. Once sold to capital, labour power may be employed to produce something that can be sold at a price greater than the cost of labour reflected in its price in the form of wages paid. Thus the use value of labour to the capitalist exceeds its exchange value. The difference is *surplus value*, which accrues to the capitalist and forms the basis for profit. It is ownership of the means of production that enables the capitalist to engage in *exploitation*, whereby part of the value of the product of labour is appropriated by the capitalist. Value and class relations are thus inextricable elements of the social practice of production under capitalism.

Labour enters into the production process in two forms. One is the direct living labour expended, which is *variable capital* (v) in Marxian terminology. The other is the past or 'dead' labour embodied in the means of production (materials and machinery), known as *constant capital* (c). If surplus value is s, then the total value of a commodity (y) is given by:

$$y = c + v + s.$$

The ratio of variable capital to surplus value defines the *rate of surplus value* (r), or rate of exploitation:

$$r = s/v$$

that is, the higher the surplus value (or difference between exchange value and use value of labour) in relation to exchange value (or wages paid), the higher the rate of exploitation. The *rate of profit* (p) is:

$$p = s/(c + v)$$

which reveals the importance of surplus value itself to the capitalist seeking profits. A final relationship that occupies an important place in Marxian economics is the *organic composition of capital* (q):

$$q = c/(c + v)$$

which in conventional terminology is the capital intensity of production.

MONEY plays a crucial part in the creation of surplus value, and this is explained by some further simple relationships that can be expressed symbolically. The capitalist advances a sum of money (M) for the commodities of materials, machines and labour power (C) and sells the final product for more money (M'). This may be represented by the simple cycle of M–C–M'. The commodities C may be subdivided into labour power (L) for which wages are paid and means of production (MP) purchased or rented from other capitalists, the total expenditure (M) being defined as productive capital (P). The production process now creates new commodities (C') which can be sold for more money than the initial outlay. The source of the difference between M and M' can only be the surplus value created by labour. The additional money or profits accruing to the capitalist can then be advanced again for a second round of production (see figure on p. 484). At the end of each round, labour has 'reproduced' itself; capital has accumulated wealth. The distinction arises from the inequality of POWER in capitalist class relations, manifest in the buying and selling of labour power – hence Marx's stress on value as a social relationship rather than as something merely associated with exchange relations. The Marxist critique of conventional (neo-classical) economics is that exploitive class relations are hidden beneath the technicalities of market pricing, resource allocation, production functions and so on, with the formal abstraction of mathematics obscuring social reality.

This framework for analysing the capitalist system helps to reveal certain imperatives for any economy. The process of material production carries with it certain necessary consumption, required to maintain the productive forces in the form of the producers themselves (met via wages) and the means of production (met via funds set aside for depreciation). However, discretion exists over the disposition of the remaining surplus, accruing as private profits under capitalism. This surplus could be returned to labour in the form of higher wages to support higher living standards. It could all be spent on luxury consumption, e.g. by an extravagant capitalist and landowning elite. Alternatively, it could be invested in new means of production or measures to enhance labour's capacity to produce, so as to develop the productive forces. The proportion that is reinvested (i.e. how much of M' in the figure goes into the next round of production) governs the rate of economic growth. Marx's analysis of *expanded reproduction*, whereby society's productive capacity is increased by reinvestment, anticipated by almost a century the INPUT–OUTPUT growth model that became influential in conventional economics.

An important tenet of Marxian economics is that capitalism will eventually be destroyed by its own internal contradictions. The extraction of surplus value from labour is the starting point of the process of capital accumulation, whereby wealth piles up in growing quantities in the hands of the capitalist class while the working class remains living at a bare subsistence level. Some use must be found for the surplus capital, there being limits to the capacity of the capitalist class for the self-indulgence of luxury consumption. The capital can be recycled into new production, but the masses must have the purchasing power to consume what is produced; it is only when commodities are sold that the capitalist can realize surplus value in its money form. There is thus a basic contradiction under capitalism between the pressure to increase surplus value by keeping wages low and the need for people to purchase commodities from their wages so that surplus value can be realized. Capital can be used to produce more machines to replace living labour, but this contributes to unemployment and immiserization of the proletariat. The inherently competitive nature of capitalism squeezes profits, which creates further pressure to reduce labour costs or substitute machines for labour. As the most successful firms grow and the weak go to the wall, capital becomes steadily more concentrated, until major monopolies confront the impoverished working class. The exploited masses are finally driven to the revolutionary overthrow of capitalism.

While the contradictions identified by Marx are certainly important features of the dynamics of capitalism, the final revolutionary outcome in an advanced industrial society has thus far failed to materialize. Among the more obvious reasons for this has been the growing power of organized labour to bargain with capital for increases in real wages, which capital has been able to concede to some extent by virtue of the great success of the capitalist system in expanding the capacity to produce. It may also be the case that affluence, at least in the advanced capitalist world, has helped to diffuse working-class consciousness – a trend assisted by use of the mass media to stimulate materialistic values and reinforce the prevailing IDEOLOGY of capitalism.

Contemporary Marxism is more concerned with dissecting the actual operation of capitalism in its modern form than with the veracity or otherwise of Marx's prediction of revolutionary change. Of special geographical interest is the general theory of UNEVEN DEVELOPMENT that traces its origins to the works of Lenin and Rosa Luxemburg on IMPERIALISM. Whereas neo-classical economics suggests the convergence of territorial income levels via self-adjusting markets for factors of production, Marxian analysis points to the tendency towards spatial concentration of economic activity under capitalism and to a perpetuation and even exacerbation of spatial inequality. The spatial expansion of capitalism in the search for new investment opportunities, materials and markets has tied up much of the world into a web of interdependencies. Each nation or region plays a role in this international (or regional) DIVISION OF LABOUR, determined not by national interest or local need but by the capital accumulation process itself. The beneficiaries are the affluent of the advanced nations of North America and western Europe, together with the elites in the rest of the capitalist world. The losers are the masses of the Third World poor, together with the less affluent inhabitants of the richer nations. The MULTINATIONAL CORPORATIONS are viewed as major instruments in this process, operating beyond the control of national governments but themselves subject to the imperatives by which the capitalist system operates. Local manifestations of uneven development, such as depressed regions and declining inner-city areas, can be related to the broader structural features of the national and international economy via Marxian economic analysis.

While the basics of Marxian economics are timeless, there have been some extensions and revisions. These include technical aspects of the 'transformation problem' of calculating prices under the labour theory of value. Of more interest to geographers has been the exploration of the KONDRATIEFF CYCLES, which are supposed to represent rather regular fluctuations of a capitalist economy over time and are influential in the study of UNEVEN DEVELOPMENT, including WORLD-SYSTEMS ANALYSIS. The changing nature of the capitalist economy is reflected in attention given to the so-called REGULATION SCHOOL and to the concept of the REGIME OF ACCUMULATION which remains relatively stable over a period of time,

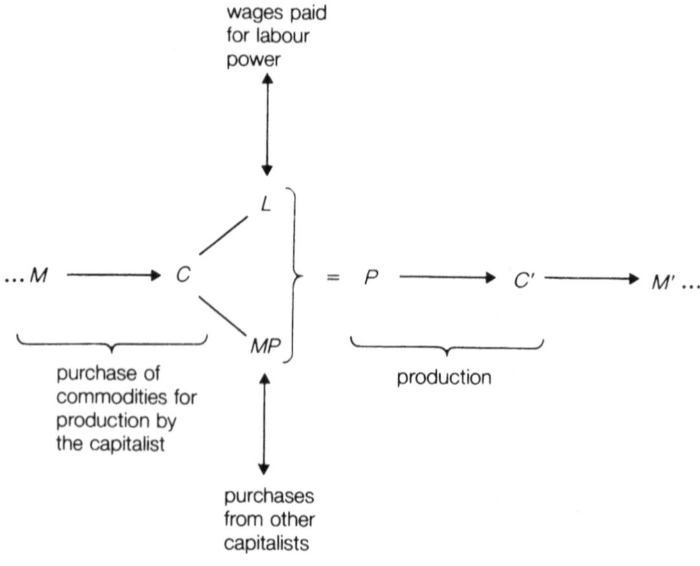

Marxian economics

as well as to the notion of FLEXIBLE ACCUMULATION which is supposed to capture important aspects of contemporary capitalism.

Geographical contributions to Marxian economics have been rare, such is the technical complexity of the field. Most distinctive has been some of the work of David Harvey (1982, 1996) and Neil Smith (1990), who have introduced aspects of the implications of space: a dimension largely ignored in Marxian economics as in NEO-CLASSICAL ECONOMICS. These writers have also introduced nature, or an environmental dimension, similarly given little attention in mainstream economics.

The political-economy perspective derived from Marx and his modern interpreters offers the geographer a general theory in which historically and locationally specific events can be related to one another in a broader context. The danger with Marxian analysis is the tendency of some of its adherents to adopt an unduly dogmatic interpretation in the face of a changing world that requires flexibility on the part of any body of knowledge claiming to facilitate the understanding of human affairs as they actually unfold. The rise of 'new right' thinking and of some strands of POSTMODERNISM, along with the demise of the socialist regimes in eastern Europe, is thought by some to side-line Marxian thinking, but this approach remains of interest to many geographers (see MARXIST GEOGRAPHY; POST-MARXISM).

DMS

References and Suggested Reading

Bottomore, T., ed., 1991: *A dictionary of Marxist thought*, 2nd edn. Oxford: Basil Blackwell. · Cohen, G.A. 1986: Forces and relations of production. In J. Roemer, ed., *Analytical Marxism*. Cambridge: Cambridge University Press. · Desai, M. 1974: *Marxian economic theory*. Oxford: Basil Blackwell and Totowa, NJ: Rowman and Littlefield. · Harvey, D. 1982: *The limits to capital*. Oxford: Basil Blackwell. · Harvey, D. 1996: *Justice, nature and the geography of difference*. Oxford: Blackwell. · Fine, B. 1989: *Marxist economics*, 3rd edn. London: Macmillan. · Kay, G. 1975: *Development and underdevelopment: a Marxist analysis*. London: Macmillan; New York: St. Martin's Press (published as *Development, underdevelopment and the law of value: a Marxist analysis*). · Mandel, E. 1968: *Marxist economic theory*, 2 vols, trans. B. Pearce. London: Merlin Press; New York: Monthly Review. · Mandel, E. 1978: *Late capitalism*, trans. J. de Bres, revised edn. London: Verso Editions; New York: Schocken. · Marx, K. 1976: *Capital*, vol. 1. London: Penguin; New York: International Publishers. · Sheppard, E. and Barnes, T.J. 1990: *The capitalist space economy: analysis after Ricardo, Marx and Sraffa*. London: Unwin Hyman. · Smith, N. 1990: *Uneven development: nature, capital and the production of space*, 2nd edn. Oxford: Blackwell.

Marxist geography The study of geographical questions using the analytical insights, concepts, and theoretical framework of Marxism (see HISTORICAL MATERIALISM; MARXIAN ECONOMICS). Although not inherently limited to one kind of society, Marxist geography has tended to focus on the various geographies of CAPITALISM.

Before the 1960s, geography in North America and western Europe had experienced only a very limited radical critique, and post-war Soviet geography (where, at least outwardly, the influence of Marxism was much greater) was in practice more technocratic than radical (see APPLIED GEOGRAPHY; RADICAL GEOGRAPHY). In the English-speaking world Marxist geography emerged in the early 1970s in response to two sets of events: the critique of 'establishment geography', and in particular its reformulation of geography as a narrowly conceived SPATIAL SCIENCE based on the supposedly 'objective' philosophy of POSITIVISM; and the political struggles and uprisings of the late 1960s in Europe, the Americas and Australia. These struggles took aim at POVERTY, RACISM and the IMPERIALISM of the Vietnam war, and prompted a new generation of ACTIVISM: the civil rights, feminist, environmental and anti-war movements as well as a new left.

Marxists argued that positivist spatial science was flawed in three basic ways. First, insofar as existing geographical relations were treated as spatial patterns rather than the outcome of social processes, ruling social IDEOLOGIES were reaffirmed; geographers might map urban SEGREGATION according to CLASS and RACE, for example, but never interrogate the political and economic processes that produced such unequal geographies. Second, despite its avowed scientific objectivity, spatial analysis was devoted to providing 'socially useful' results that amounted to a 'spatial technology' for capital; LOCATIONAL ANALYSIS sought to identify the most efficient locations for factories, supermarkets and social services, for example, accepting traditional class-based economic definitions of 'efficient location' (Massey, 1973). Third, universal spatial laws of the sort sought by positivist SPATIAL ANALYSIS ignore the historical and geographical variability of spatial arrangements in different societies (Smith, 1979a; Gregory, 1994).

If the emergence of a radical alternative to establishment geography can be dated to 1969, when a group of graduate students and faculty at Clark University published the first volume of *Antipode: A Radical Journal of*

Geography, its consummation came in 1973 with the publication of David Harvey's highly influential *Social justice and the city*. This book traced a personal and political journey from a constellation of unsatisfying liberal assumptions towards a systematic Marxist analysis and demonstrated the ways in which spatial form and urban geographies are integral to an exploitative social and economic system. GHETTO formation, for example, is the result of a housing market that discriminates on the basis of class and race and yet is also a vital urban form through which the costs of social reproduction are minimized. In this light, supposed scientific objectivity seems both unrealistic and politically motivated to endorse rather than criticize the exploitation and oppression inherent to capitalism. A revolutionary geographical theory, Harvey argued, was necessary not just to comprehend current geographies but also to change them, and in the process to change the societies that produced them (Harvey, 1984; Harvey and Smith, 1984).

Marxist geography is a varied and internally differentiated theoretical and political tradition. It can be encapsulated under three (albeit overlapping) headings.

Political economic analyses. POLITICAL ECONOMY explains the geography of capitalism as the outcome primarily of political and economic relationships and processes in the wider society. While therefore borrowing from MARXIAN ECONOMICS, it also attempts to understand capitalist society as spatially and environmentally constituted. Early documentation of spatial inequality and community advocacy (see Bunge, 1971) was superseded by critique and THEORY (Peet, 1977; Harvey, 1982). The urban geographies of capitalism can thereby be understood as resulting from the inherent contradiction between CLASS struggle and ACCUMULATION (Harvey, 1978). URBANIZATION is both the most rational geographical means (for capital) of centralizing productive capital, and at the same time an encouragement to oppositional struggle insofar as it congregates large numbers of people with similar experiences of exploitation and oppression in a single place. Capitalist urbanization represents a further contradiction: on the one hand it brings about an extraordinary economic and geographical fixation of capital in the built environment – as factories, offices and infrastructure – as a condition of economic expansion. Yet at the same time, the changing conditions of production, circulation and realization of capital demand that capital investments be infinitely fluid. Given the long-term fixation of capital investment in the built environment, it is not surprising that economic CRISIS has a particularly sharp effect on urban landscapes.

Suburbanization can thereby be conceived less as a heroic fable of the middle-class consumerism, and more as a distinct geographical form of urban development that expresses the social geography of class inequality and the economic geography of class-based consumption. Suburbanization (see SUBURB) was actively planned and publicly subsidized, and represented a putative solution to the crisis of accumulation in the 1920s and 1930s (Walker, 1978; Chekoway, 1980). At the urban core, GENTRIFICATION can be seen as an economic as well as a social question, resulting as much from geographical patterns of investment and disinvestment in the urban space economy as from consumer choice, and as part of a larger pattern of urban RESTRUCTURING and UNEVEN DEVELOPMENT at the urban scale (Smith, 1979b, 1996a). There is also an intricate connection between class and other social relationships such as GENDER and RACE. Socialist feminists have shown the importance of gender relations in the making of contemporary urban form (McDowell, 1983; Mackenzie, 1989; Pratt, 1989). The requirements of social reproduction, the patterns of women's labour, and class-differentiated ideologies of gender have all shaped capitalist urbanization (McKenzie and Rose, 1983; Marston, 1988; Hanson and Pratt, 1995). Suburbanization was premised on the gender relations of post-war expansion (Seguin, 1989), while gentrification results in part from the changing social and economic roles of women, the changing definitions of family, and the restructuring of the Fordist (see FORDISM) REGIME OF ACCUMULATION (Bondi, 1991).

Regional geographies have been transformed by a similar process, by DEINDUSTRIALIZATION, and by changes in the organization of labour and capital (Massey, 1984; Peck, 1996; Schoenberger, 1996) and technology (Saxenien, 1984). These shifts are integrally connected with economic and social CRISES and bring new geographies of industrial and non-industrial growth, new ensembles of production (Scott, 1989).

At the global SCALE, greatest attention has been paid to the geography of UNDERDEVELOPMENT. Blaut has consistently questioned western versions of the origins of capitalism and capitalist ideologies of NATIONALISM (Blaut, 1976, 1993). How has colonial and imperial expansion led to specific geographical patterns and structures in underdeveloped societies (cf. COLONIALISM)? The answer comes in a number of forms. In environmental terms, underdevelopment has led to a highly destructive social ECOLOGY characterized by chronic FAMINE (Watts, 1983; Blaikie, 1985) and the systematic disruption of the means of social reproduction (Katz, 1991). In social and economic terms, underdevelopment leads to a decentred and imbalanced regional structure that emphasizes communications with the colonial capital and Europe rather than between neighbouring regions (Slater, 1975): thus the fastest way from Mali to neighbouring Niger may still be via Paris. Today the focus has shifted from understanding the ways in which IMPERIAL societies imposed specific geographies toward a more complicated inquiry into the ways that different imperial and local traditions came together to produce different political landscapes in different places (see also POST-COLONIALISM).

The temporal rhythms of capital investment, accumulation and crisis are matched by a geographical logic of economic expansion and decline. Capital seeks a spatial fix for economic crises (Harvey, 1982), whether by disinvesting heavily in one place or investing heavily in another. In Marx's (1973, p. 524) renowned phrase, the accumulation of capital relies upon a highly dynamic 'annihilation of space by time' (see TIME–SPACE COMPRESSION). This implies the simultaneous development of the forces of communication and the cyclical creation of newly built environments for production, consumption and reproduction. But it also implies an equally fervid destruction of capital invested in the built environment, thereby creating new opportunities for expansion. This is the process that Schumpeter (1942), following Marx, later called 'CREATIVE DESTRUCTION'. More broadly, the geography of capitalism is a perpetual maelstrom of construction and destruction that is captured in the general theory of UNEVEN DEVELOPMENT (Smith, 1990; Peet, 1991).

There are of course many debates over all of these issues (see Peet and Thrift, 1989; Peet, 1998), and critiques of political economy approaches have resulted in a broadening and sharpening of Marxist concerns. With the maturation of a social theory tradition in geography, the broader structural analyses of 1970s and early 1980s political economy have been complemented by greater attention to questions of HUMAN AGENCY and resistance, by cultural as well as political economic constructions of LANDSCAPE (Mitchell, 1996), and by attempts to understand the connections between class, gender and race as interwoven sources of socio-spatial difference. In the wake of so-called GLOBALIZATION, a whole range of questions concerning the relationship between global and local have also emerged (Swyngedouw, 1992).

Theories of SPACE. The critique of POSITIVISM and of abstract SPATIAL SCIENCE called into question the conceptions of space employed in geographical discourse. Geography has until recently been dominated by the familiar concept of absolute space – space as a field or container, primordially empty until filled with objects and events. The Marxist critique objected that this was only one of various possible concepts of space, and that when twinned with dubious assumptions of scientific objectivity it encouraged geographers to see abstract spatial forms and processes separate from the concrete social processes that created them. Social processes were disguised within spatial forms and spatial processes, in an ideological move that Marxist geographers identified as SPATIAL FETISHISM (Anderson, 1973). Obviously this conceptual critique intersects with the rationale for a political economic analysis. In concrete terms, it leads to a focus on the SPACE-ECONOMY, but it also encouraged a more philosophical avenue of research.

For a reconstruction of space, Marxist geography looked to physics and beyond – to relative and relational conceptions of space, to the connection of space and time (Thrift, 1983) and to the PRODUCTION OF SPACE (Lefebvre, 1991). Space is seen in relation to material events and processes (social as well as natural), no longer prior to NATURE: material objects do not so much fill up space; rather, their placement *produces* space. Absolute space is not entirely vanquished, but it is rendered relational; the absoluteness of private landed property, for example, represents socially constructed absolute space (Harvey, 1973; Smith, 1990).

We do not know why capitalism has survived since Marx's time, Lefebvre says, but we do know how: by producing space (Lefebvre, 1976, p. 21). Lefebvre argues that a contemporary science of society is necessarily a science of space. In opposition to the homogeneity of abstract space continually imposed by capitalism, he identifies a differential space constructed through opposition to capitalism, class struggle and the actions of emerging SOCIAL MOVEMENTS. The production of differential space is the object of revolutionary theory and practice for Lefebvre, and its agents are class struggle, emerging SOCIAL MOVEMENTS and social ACTIVISM.

Nature and society–nature relations. It is a common misconception that Marx had little to say about NATURE and the environment. His critique of capitalist society was built on an explicit vision of the relationship between society and nature. Rather than assuming that nature and society represent separate realms, Marxist theory posits their fundamental interconnectedness, achieved practically in the performance of social labour. Labour converts naturally occurring material into social commodities, and in transforming the form of nature, simultaneously changes its own (human) nature. Capitalist society produces wealth 'only by sapping' the original sources of all wealth – the soil and the labourer (Marx, 1987, pp. 177, 507).

This has led to the suggestion that geographers ought to develop a 'geographical materialism' comparable to Marx's HISTORICAL MATERIALISM (Peet, 1987; Wittfogel, 1987). Others have suggested a more socially centred vision of nature (Burgess, 1978). But it is also possible to derive from Marx the argument that human societies, and especially capitalism, are involved in the *production of nature* (Redclift, 1987; Smith, 1990; Braun and Castree, 1998). It may sound quixotic to talk about the production of nature since, after all, nature is precisely that which we are used to thinking of as the antithesis of human society and social construction. Yet the strangeness of the idea may belie a persistent bifurcated IDEOLOGY of nature: nature is deemed either external to human society or else as universal, including quite literally everything in the world (Whatmore, 1998). To the extent that the form of the Earth has been entirely altered by productive human activity, however, and no part of the world remains unaffected, the production of nature is a reality. This does not imply that somehow natural laws of gravity or chemical interaction cease to operate, nor that nature is thereby controlled. Control and production are two quite separate issues. It does suggest forcefully that the natural world can no longer be separated conceptually or ONTOLOGICALLY from the social world, and that an environmental politics is a quintessentially social politics (Pulido, 1996; see also Smith, 1996b). This has two results. First, it disqualifies the romantic appeal – from the DEEP ECOLOGIST to CONSERVATIONIST – to a pre-existing, Edenic nature unaffected by social production and social change, to which we ought to return; or the appeal to biological ESSENTIALISM that gives authority to much ECOFEMINISM. Second, it disqualifies the technocratic appeal to 'society–nature interactions' insofar as this perspective also assumes the initial separation of society and nature. As Cosgrove (1984, p. 180) has explained, it 'is not the relationship between human beings and the land that governs their social organization, but ultimately their relations with each other in the course of production'. 'The production of nature' suggests the political question: how do we as a society want to produce nature, and how will these decisions be made?

Marxist analyses of nature–society relations have also focused on more concrete questions. Considerable effort has been aimed at reinterpreting the conventional wisdom on environmental HAZARDS. Where traditional hazard specialists draw a distinction between natural and technological hazards, Marxists have stressed that this distinction perpetuates an ideology of nature separate from society and encourages a belief in natural hazards as inevitable. 'Natural' hazard is in fact a misnomer, since all hazards (as opposed to natural events) are by definition social (O'Keefe et al., 1976). With a clear correlation between on the one side income and social class and on the other vulnerability to hazard, a disproportionate number of deaths due to so-called natural disasters are in the underdeveloped world. By the same token, any given environment has vastly different meanings for different people: a hazard for one population may be a recreational resource for another.

Supposedly natural events, such as the Sahel famine of 1968–74, the wider African famine of the 1980s and 1990s, and certainly GLOBAL WARMING, are now understood as quintessentially social events traceable to the broad structure and specific operation of capitalist social relations (Watts, 1983). Likewise, the Irish starvation of the 1840s, traditionally blamed on potato blight, resulted from the dependence – enforced by British imperialism – of Irish peasants on the potato: as peasants starved, English landlords continued to export large quantities of Irish beef to the English market (Regan, 1980, p. 11). The production of food in general involves an extraordinary appropriation of nature along class lines (Goodman and Redclift, 1991), and the class politics of rainforest destruction are now evident (Hecht and Cockburn, 1990). In the consumption sphere, too, access to nature is privatized (Heiman, 1988), and the disruption of local patterns of social ecology due to capitalist expansion fundamentally disrupts established processes and traditions of SOCIAL REPRODUCTION (Katz, 1991; Peet and Watts, 1996).

A central ideological plank of traditional environmental geography holds that the population and RESOURCES of a place are intricately dependent on each other, and that 'OVERPOPULATION' should be defined in relation to available resources. There is an implicit retention here of MALTHUSIAN assumptions about the separateness and fixity of nature *vis-à-vis* population (Harvey, 1974). But given global economic trade and financial flows, and very unequal patterns of political power, it is doubtful that a place's resources have a determining effect on strictly local population growth or socio-economic development. Resource availability and resource scarcity are themselves socially constructed.

The first phase of Marxist research in geography, lasting until the early 1980s, was concerned, above all else, with demonstrating the ways in which capitalism, as a coherent social system, was responsible for the configuration of specific LANDSCAPES – the URBAN GEOGRAPHY of capitalism, its regional patterns, environmental depredation and underdevelopment at the global scale. The primary intent was to import Marxist ideas and a Marxist framework into geography as a means of analysing questions of traditional geographical concern. This involved a sustained rediscovery of Marx and Marxist ideas and their application to geography, but it was only half the battle; Marxists were no more convinced about geography than most geographers were about Marxism. And yet by the early 1980s, Marxism had come to hold an unprecedented influence within geography, compared to the other social sciences. In part this was a result of uneven intellectual development: in the 1960s, when social theory was dearly needed, geography embodied virtually no social theory beyond the assumptions of positivism. Geographers compensated for this lacuna with such an embrace of Marxism that within 15–20 years, a disproportionate number of the most influential geographers were Marxists (Bodman, 1992).

A second phase of Marxist geography began in the early 1980s and was marked by several shifts. First, the focus was no longer so much on unearthing Marx and Marxism but rather on using them critically and in relation to other emerging social theory. This involved a significant broadening of Marxist geography (Gregory, 1994). But, second it involved an expansion and a corollary of the initial project. It was no longer simply a matter of convincing geographers that Marxism had something to offer – that was already achieved – but rather of taking the case to Marxism that a geographical, and especially a spatial, perspective was vital for Marxism and social theory more broadly. This ambitious 'spatialization of social theory' (Soja, 1989) gathered steam precisely as Marxism itself was subject to increasingly critical analysis by geographers. The second phase of Marxist research also heralded an attempt to rewrite CULTURAL GEOGRAPHY in a radical vein and the reconsideration of 'landscape' as a central geographical concept (Cosgrove, 1984; Daniels, 1989; Gregory, 1994). Mitchell (1996) has taken the argument furthest with an attempt to install labour struggles at the centre of a new political-cultural explanation of landscape formation. This is part of a larger project aimed at developing a LABOUR GEOGRAPHY (Herod, 1997, 1998).

The broadening of Marxist geography in the 1980s and 1990s was the product of internal maturity as well as increasing challenges from outside, as geographers became more versed in social theory and the political climate lurched decisively to the right. These challenges came from several directions. The humanist critique (Duncan and Ley, 1982) tapped a widespread discomfiture with a Marxism portrayed as unnecessarily STRUCTURALIST. It led variously toward a humanist SOCIALISM of the sort advanced by E.P. Thompson or toward the STRUCTURATION THEORY of Anthony Giddens (1979, 1981) which dissected the Marxist DIALECTIC into 'structure' and 'human agency' as a means of investigating their connection. A related argument came from REALISM, some proponents of which argued that Marxism overestimated the range of 'necessary' (i.e. structurally determined) relationships in contemporary capitalism, and that contingent relationships largely accounted for the production of specific geographies (Sayer, 1984).

The feminist engagement with Marxism has a varied history. FEMINIST GEOGRAPHY first emerged in the early 1970s in close connection with radical and socialist analyses, exploring issues of social reproduction, community and women's work, and connecting broader feminist debates with geographical questions, mostly at the urban scale. By the late 1980s, emerging feminist theory took a much more critical approach to Marxism, in part out of frustration that a newly influential Marxism only marginally considered questions of gender. Debate flared around Harvey's (1989) *The condition of postmodernity* (Deutsche, 1991;

Massey, 1991; Harvey, 1992), but a commitment to reintegrating class and gender is already evident (Pratt, 1989; Mackenzie, 1989; Bondi, 1991). Linda McDowell (1991) especially warns that the baby of Marxist insights and class analysis should not be thrown out with the bathwater of a social theory blind to gender differences.

After the late 1980s, the social sciences and humanities underwent a sustained CULTURAL TURN and geography was no exception. If in some quarters the resort to culture became a means of denying the relevance of political economy or of providing an alternative to Marxism, it has quickly become clear that some of the most interesting and innovative work seeks to reintegrate economic and cultural insights depending on Marxist as well as other theoretical traditions.

The inspiration for this cultural turn had various interwoven threads. Attempts to construct feminist theory had already focused away from the logics of economic expansion and crisis toward the relations of social reproduction and daily experiences. POSTMODERN theorists posited that Marxism and positivism, socialism and capitalism were all products of the eighteenth-century ENLIGHTENMENT which valued rationality over irrationality, science over subjectivity, the global over the local, the universal over the partial and fragmented. Arguing that these definitive assumptions of MODERNISM no longer pertain, POSTMODERNISTS generally rejected attempts to read the meaning of contemporary societies from their social and economic structures, focusing instead on cultural systems of signs. Theorists of POST-STRUCTURALISM argue that POWER is expressed and cemented not simply in large-scale social structures but in the fine gauze of daily social interaction, and that social discourse plays a central role in the construction of POWER relations. The critique of discourse therefore marks a vital political intervention.

If Marxism both generated and provoked much of this new generation of political theory, it has also transformed in response to their challenge. Harvey's (1989) critique spearheaded a more critical attitude to postmodernist claims across a number of disciplines, and the sobering economic realities of the late 1990s have encouraged a broad modulation of cultural questions with a revived sense of the importance of economic relations. By the same token, Marxist economic geography has become much more cognisant of the cultural construction of socio-economic relations (Schoenberger, 1996). Treatments of gentrification, regional class ensembles, or human–nature relations in the Marxist tradition now embody a connectedness between cultural and political economic critiques. As Mitchell's (1996) reconstruction of the California landscape makes clear, a concern with political economy is basic to the new cultural geography.

If the challenges to Marxist geography in the 1990s are in part the inevitable result of Marxism's success in academic geography amidst a wider gathering conservatism, they also embody genuine shortcomings to which Marxist research must respond. Ironically, while the defeat of official Communist Parties in the Soviet Union and eastern Europe has given capitalist classes throughout the world a brief cause for jubilation, it also frees Marxist ideas from connection with a particularly oppressive social system which, however much the reality diverged from Marx's own vision of democratic workers' control, nonetheless governed in the name of socialism. Indeed, globalization represents the fruition of capitalist social relations at a global scale, making the world more not less akin to the reality that Marx critiqued (Smith, 1997). In that respect the agenda is open for a re-thought, integrative Marxism, committed still to political action as well as ideas. Perhaps the most salient feature of Marxism in geography at the beginning of the twenty-first century, however, is that its origins in ACTIVISM have largely waned. If history is any measure, a forceful response to the global crisis at the beginning of the new millennium may depend on a revived connection to activism. NS

References

Anderson, J. 1973: Ideology in geography: an introduction. *Antipode* 5: 1–6. · Blaikie, P. 1985: *The political economy of soil erosion in developing countries*. New York: Longman. · Blaut, J. 1976: Where was capitalism born? *Antipode* 8.2: 1–11. · Blaut, J. 1993. *The colonizer's model of the world: geographical diffusionism and Eurocentric history*. New York: Guilford. · Bodman, A. 1992: Holes in the fabric: more on the master weavers in human geography. *Transactions, Institute of British Geographers* NS 17: 21–37. · Bondi, L. 1991: Gender divisions and gentrification: a critique. *Transactions, Institute of British Geographers* NS 16: 190–8. · Braun, B. and Castree, N., eds, 1998: *Remaking reality. Nature at the millennium*. London: Routledge. · Bunge, W. 1971: *Fitzgerald: the geography of a revolution*. Cambridge, MA: Schenkman. · Burgess, R. 1978: The concept of nature in geography and Marxism. *Antipode* 10: 1–11. · Chekoway, B. 1980: Large builders, Federal housing programs, and postwar suburbanization. *International Journal of Urban and Regional Research* 4: 21–44. · Cosgrove, D. 1984: *Social formation and symbolic landscape*. London: Croom Helm. · Daniels, S. 1989: Marxism, culture and the duplicity of landscape. In R. Peet and N. Thrift, eds, *New models in geography*, volume 2. London: Unwin Hyman, 196–220. · Deutsche, R. 1991: Boys town. *Environment and Planning D: Society and Space* 9: 5–30. · Duncan, J. and Ley, D. 1982: Structural Marxism and human geography: a critical assessment. *Annals of the Association of American Geographers* 72: 30–59. · Giddens, A. 1979: *Central problems in social theory*. London: Macmillan. · Giddens, A. 1981: *A contemporary critique of historical materialism*. London: Macmillan. · Goodman, D. and Redclift, M. 1991: *Refashioning nature: food ecology and culture*. London: Routledge. · Gregory, D. 1994: *Geographical imaginations*. Oxford: Blackwell. · Hanson, S. and Pratt, G. 1995: *Gender, work, and space*. London: Routledge. · Harvey, D. 1973: *Social justice and the city*. London: Edward Arnold. · Harvey, D. 1974: Population, resources and the ideology of science. *Economic Geography* 50: 256–77. · Harvey, D. 1978: The urban process under capitalism: a framework for analysis. *International Journal of Urban and Regional Research* 2: 101–30. · Harvey, D. 1982: *The limits to capital*. Chicago: University of Chicago Press. · Harvey, D. 1984: On the history and present condition of geography. *Professional Geographer* 36: 1–11. · Harvey, D. 1989: *The condition of postmodernity*. Oxford: Blackwell. · Harvey, D. 1992: Postmodern morality plays. *Antipode* 25: 300–26. · Harvey, D. and Smith, N. 1984: From capitals to Capital. In B. Ollman and E. Vernoff, eds, *The left academy: Marxist scholarship on American campuses*, volume 2. New York: Praeger, 99–121. · Hecht, S. and Cockburn, A. 1990: *The fate of the forest: developers, destroyers and defenders of the Amazon*. London: Penguin. · Heiman, M. 1988: *The quiet evolution*. New York: Praeger. · Herod, A. 1997: From a geography of labor to a labor geography: labor's spatial fix and the geography of capitalism. *Antipode* 29: 1–31. · Herod, A., ed., 1998: *Organizing the landscape: geographical perspectives on labor unionism*. Minneapolis: University of Minnesota Press. · Katz, C. 1991: Sow what you know: the struggle for social reproduction in rural Sudan. *Annals of the Association of American Geographers* 81: 488–514. · Lefebvre, H. 1976: *The survival of capital*. London: Allison and Busby. · Lefebvre, H. 1991: *The production of space*. Oxford: Blackwell. · McDowell, L. 1983: Toward an understanding of the gender division of urban space. *Environment and Planning D: Society and Space* 1: 59–72. · McDowell, L. 1991: The baby and the bath-water: deconstruction and feminist theory in geography. *Geoforum* 22. · Mackenzie, S. 1989: Women in the city. In R. Peet and N. Thrift, eds, *New models in geography*, volume 2. London: Unwin Hyman, 109–26. · Mackenzie, S. and Rose, D. 1983: Industrial change, the domestic economy and home life. In J. Anderson, S. Duncan and R. Hudson, eds, *Redundant spaces in cities and regions: studies in industrial decline and social change*. London: Academic Press. · Marston, S.A. 1988: Neighborhood and politics: Irish ethnicity in 19th century Lowell, Massachusetts. *Annals of the Association of American Geographers* 78: 414–32. · Marx, K. 1973: *Grundrisse*. London: Penguin. · Marx, K. 1987: *Capital*. New York: International. · Massey, D. 1973: Towards a critique of industrial location theory. *Antipode* 5: 33–9. · Massey, D. 1984: *Spatial divisions of labour: social structures and the geography of production*. London: Methuen. · Massey, D. 1991: Flexible sexism. *Environment and Planning D: Society and Space* 9: 31–57. · Mitchell, D. 1996: *The lie of the land: migrant workers and the California landscape*. Minneapolis: University of Minnesota Press. · O'Keefe, P., Westgate, B. and Wisner, B. 1976: Taking the naturalness out of natural disasters. *Nature* 260, 15 April. · Peck, J. 1996: *Workplace: the social regulation of labor markets*. New York: Guilford. · Peet, R. 1977: *Radical geography: alternative viewpoints on contemporary social issues*. Chicago: Maaroufa. · Peet, R. 1987: The geographical ideas of Karl Wittfogel. *Antipode* 17: 35–50. · Peet, R. 1991: *Global capitalism: theories of social development*. London: Routledge. · Peet, R. 1998: *Modern geographical thought*. Oxford: Blackwell. · Peet, R. and Thrift, N., eds, 1989: *New models in geography*, 2 vols. London: Unwin Hyman. · Peet, R. and Watts, M. 1996: *Liberation ecologies: environment, development, social movements*. London: Routledge. · Pratt, G. 1989: Reproduction, class, and the spatial structure of the city. In R. Peet and N. Thrift, eds, *New models in geography*, volume 2. London: Unwin Hyman, 84–108. · Pulido, L. 1996: *Environmentalism and economic justice: two Chicano struggles in the Southwest*. Tucson: University of Arizona Press. · Redclift, M. 1987: The production of nature. *Antipode* 19: 222–30. · Regan, C. 1980: Economic development in Ireland: the historical dimension. *Antipode* 11: 1–14. · Saxenian, A. 1984: The urban contradictions of Silicon Valley: regional growth and reconstructing in the semiconductor industry. In W. Tabb and L. Sawers, eds, *Sunbelt/Snowbelt*. Oxford: Oxford University Press. · Sayer, A. 1984: *Method and social science*. London: Hutchinson. · Schoenberger, E. 1996: *The cultural crisis of the firm*. Oxford: Blackwell. · Schumpeter, J. 1942: *Capitalism, socialism and democracy*. New York: Harper and Row. · Scott, A. 1989: *New ensembles of production*. London: Pion. · Seguin, A. 1989: Madame Ford et l'espace: lecture féministe de la suburbanisation. *Recherches féministes* 2: 51–68. · Slater, D. 1975: The poverty of modern geographical inquiry. *Pacific Viewpoint* 16: 159–76. · Smith, N. 1979a: Geography, science and post-positivist modes of explanation. *Progress in Human Geography* 3: 356–83. · Smith, N. 1979b: Toward a theory of gentrification: a back to the city movement by capital not people. *Journal of the American Planners Association* 45: 538–48. · Smith, N. 1990: *Uneven development: nature, capital and the production of space*, 2nd edn. Oxford: Blackwell. · Smith, N. 1996a: *The new urban frontier: gentrification and the revanchist city*. New York: Routledge. · Smith, N. 1996b: The production of nature. In G. Robertson et al., eds, *FutureNatural*. London: Routledge 35–54. · Smith, N. 1997: Satanic geographies of globalization: uneven development in the 1990s. *Public Culture* 10 (1) 169–89. · Soja, E. 1989: *Postmodern geographies*. London: Verso. · Swyngedouw, E. 1992: The Mammon Quest: 'glocalisation,' interspatial competition and the monetary order: the construction of new scales. In M. Dunford and G. Kafkalas, eds, *Cities and regions in the new Europe*. New York: Belhaven, 39–67. · Thrift, N. 1983: On the determination of social action in space and time. *Environment and Planning D: Society and Space* 1: 23–57. · Walker, R. 1978: The transformation of urban structure in the nineteenth century and the beginnings of suburbanization. In K. Cox, ed., *Urbanization and conflict in market societies*. Chicago: Maaroufa, 165–211. · Watts, M. 1983: *Silent violence*. Berkeley, CA: University of California Press. · Whatmore, S. 1998: Hybrid geographies: rethinking the 'human' in human geography. In D. Massey, J. Allen and P. Sarre, eds, *Human geography today*. Cambridge: Polity Press, 22–40. · Wittfogel, K. 1987: Geopolitics, geographical materialism and Marxism. *Antipode* 17: 21–34.

Suggested Reading

Harvey (1982, 1989). · Harvey and Smith (1984). · Peet (1998).

masculinism This traces connections between cultures of masculinity, knowledge and POWER. It is frequently located in relation to traditions of western scientific rationality, in particular the dualisms between mind and body and between subject and object, plus the presumption that scientific knowledge can and should be objective and context-free. Masculinist knowledge is criticized for claiming to be exhaustive or universal, while actually ignoring women's existences. Rose (1993) argues that geography is a masculinist discipline and that masculinism determines conventions of what is deemed worthy of geographical investigation, fieldwork practice, theory development, writing and representation, as well as everyday academic life: from conduct in seminars to job searches and promotion. She identifies two masculinities (social scientific and aesthetic) that frame this pervasive masculinism within geography. (See also EPISTEMOLOGY; PHALLOCENTRISM; POST-STRUCTURALISM.) GP

Reference

Rose, G. 1993: *Feminism and geography*. Oxford: Polity Press; Minneapolis: University of Minnesota Press.

material culture The relationships between people and things. The definition of 'human' has often turned on two supposedly unique human capacities: LANGUAGE and tool-using. But whereas the first capacity has been studied almost to distraction and has its own special discipline – linguistics – the second has remained scattered over several different disciplines, often as a minority interest. With the advent of material culture studies, however, this position is changing. An alliance of writers in areas as different as anthropology, archaeology, art history, fashion, social history, psychology – and human geography – has found a common concern and a common cause.

Where were the dominant traditions of material culture studies invented? The first location was anthropology. The fascination with objects as diverse as conch shells and totem poles, pigs and pottery, and houses and henges meant that, from an early point in the history of the discipline, anthropologists lived in a world of things. The second location was archaeology (and ethnology). Archaeologists have often only had things with which to trace the trace of past civilizations. And the third location was the 'semiotic revolution' of the 1960s stimulated by writers like Barthes (1972) which attempted to read consumer objects as TEXTS.

Yet much of the recent history of material culture studies might be interpreted as a reaction against the semiotic model with its emphasis on interpretation and a corresponding desire to give things their proper place and allow them to, in some sense, 'speak back': objects become 'persons' (Gell, 1998). It is also an attempt to capture the virtuosity that is a vital element of the human use of things: they have to be used in *skilled* ways (Hutchins, 1995). Thus, material culture studies link naturally to many recent theoretical currents like ACTOR–NETWORK THEORY and NON-REPRESENTATIONAL THEORY. In particular, material culture studies have interlinked with current work on CONSUMPTION to the point where they are often one and the same thing.

And human geography? This has had a long tradition of work that has emphasized the materiality of CULTURE, from the work of Carl Sauer (see BERKELEY SCHOOL), through the quasi-ethnological work in North America on folk objects like covered bridges, to modern work in Scandinavian countries on aspects of modern life as different as fishing boats and dance pavilions. Yet what is remarkable is how little of this work has intertwined with the wider domain of material culture studies. The real point of contact with human geography has been in the explosion of work on CONSUMPTION. Here there has been – and will continue to be – a high level of interchange and cross-fertilization. NJT

References

Appadurai, A., ed., 1986: *The social life of things. Commodities in cultural perspective*. Cambridge: Cambridge University Press. · Barthes, R. 1972 [orig. pub. 1957]: *Mythologies*. London: Fontana. · Csikzentmihalyi, M. and Rochberg-Halton, E. 1981: *The meaning of things: domestic symbols and the self*. Cambridge: Cambridge University Press. · Gell, A. 1998: *Art and agency*. Oxford: Oxford University Press. · Hutchins, E. 1995: *Cognition in the wild*. Cambridge, MA: Harvard University Press. · Miller, D. 1987: *Material culture and mass consumption*. Oxford: Blackwell.

Suggested Reading

Journal of Material Culture (Sage, London) (Three issues per year). · *Things* (London) (Two issues per year).

material orientation The tendency of an economic activity to locate close to sources of materials. This is likely to be the case where the cost of the material(s) in question forms a large share of total cost and/or where material costs are subject to substantial spatial variations. Historically, the importance of material orientation in industrial location has declined, with a reduction in the use of bulky materials and in transfer costs. Industries that remain predominantly material-oriented are largely confined to primary metal manufacturing and the processing of agricultural products. (Cf. MARKET ORIENTATION.) DMS

mean information field (m.i.f) The representation of a DISTANCE-DECAY pattern by a spatial grid for use in a SIMULATION model, mainly for analyses of the DIFFUSION of an innovation and of MIGRATION. The m.i.f., introduced to geographical study by Torsten Hägerstrand (1967), is usually presented as a 5 x 5 matrix in which the central square represents the origin (e.g. of a migration) and the value in each cell represents the probability of it being the destination. The m.i.f. values may be defined arbitrarily, on the basis of a priori theory, or from prior empirical analyses. RJJ

Reference

Hägerstrand, T. 1967: *Innovation diffusion as a spatial process*, trans. A. Pred. Englewood Cliffs, NJ and London: Prentice-Hall.

measurement A classification of data types for statistical analysis in which four levels are generally recognized:

- *nominal*, in which each individual (member of a population or sample) is allocated to one out of two or more exclusive categories;
- *ordinal*, in which either the individuals or the categories to which they are allocated are rank-ordered on some criterion;
- *interval*, which involves a quantitative assessment of the distance between two observations along a predetermined scale (such as °C); and
- *ratio*, which allows relative quantitative assessment of differences along a scale.

Thus nominal measurement would allocate three million people to Birmingham and nine million to London; ordinal measurement of the same data would say that London is bigger than Birmingham; interval measurement provides the information that London has six million more people than Birmingham; and ratio measurement indicates that London is three times the size of Birmingham. RJJ

media, geography of The media are usually regarded as those technologies of communication which have, over time, produced a sphere of exchange of information and ideas. They therefore include a bewilderingly large range of activities – books, paintings, radio, cinema, television, multimedia, and so on – and a bewilderingly large array of means of COMMUNICATION – print, images, moving pictures, music etc. Given the undoubted POWER of the media in the modern world, the rapid growth of media and communication studies, and the fact that SPACE lies at the heart of many questions about the influence of the media, there has been remarkably little direct work on the media in geography. Although it might be argued that earlier works on DIFFUSION (e.g. Pred, 1977) and TIME–SPACE COMPRESSION (summarized in Thrift, 1990) were important precursors of a geography of media, the fact remains that the first comprehensive edited collection explicitly directed to the topic was only published in 1985 (Burgess and Gold, 1985).

That said, a geography of the media does now exist, albeit in fragmentary form, built upon five main lines of inquiry. First, there are ECONOMIC GEOGRAPHIES of the various media industries. What these geographies reveal is that the media are now a global industry in their own right, dominated by large combines like Fox, Bertelsmann, and Time Warner which stretch across many different means of communication (Sadler, 1997). Second, there are studies which have considered the cultural impacts of the expansion of the media. As the same texts, figures and sounds circulate around the globe (see GLOBALIZATION), they clearly extend western structures of power, not only because much of the media consists of western products but because the media are often saturated with western mores and values (Shohat and Stam, 1994; Morley and Robins, 1995; see POST-COLONIALISM). However, the media can also become a cultural resource, being 'turned' by local populations into new hybrid meanings (Thrift, 1997). Third, there is work on the way in which TEXTS, IMAGES and sounds can produce new geographical sensibilities. Such work can take on a number of forms, from the critical analysis of film and television (Aitken and Zonn, 1994; Clarke, 1998) through the analysis of everyday snapshots (Crang, 1996) to the way that a single satellite image of the globe has been used to foster all kinds of ideas – cultural, political and environmental – that we live in 'one world' (Cosgrove, 1994). But perhaps the most potent example of this kind of work has built on the legacy of writers like Georg Simmel and Walter Benjamin (Caygill, 1998; Gilloch, 1996) and concerns the ways in which our senses of the city have been altered by the media: what we experience in our daily lives is very often mediated. In particular, and fourth, an increasing amount of attention is now being paid to sources other than the visual, most particularly sound (Smith, 1997; Leyshon, Matless and Revill, 1998; cf. MUSIC, GEOGRAPHY OF), but also touch, smell and even taste (after all, it would be possible to argue that many modern restaurant chains have applied media technologies to food; see FOOD, GEOGRAPHY OF). Then, fifthly, there is work on the new digital media and their possible impacts on geography (see CYBERSPACE; VIRTUAL GEOGRAPHIES). Much of this work necessarily remains speculative (Robins, 1996), but it has also clearly had important effects, producing new histories of technologies (see Debray, 1996; Plant, 1997), new metaphors (see CYBORG), and new phenomenological theories about how we apprehend spaces in which instantaneous communication at a distance becomes the norm (Virilio, 1991). NJT

References

Aitken, S.C. and Zonn, L.E., eds, 1994: *Place, power, situation, and spectacle: a geography of film*. Lanham, MD: Rowman and Littlefield. · Burgess, J. and Gold, J., eds, 1985: *Geography, the media and popular culture*. London: Croom Helm. · Caygill, H. 1998: *Walter Benjamin. The colour of experience*. London: Routledge. · Clarke, D., ed., 1998: *The cinematic city*. London: Routledge. · Cosgrove, D. 1994: Contested global visions: one world, whole earth, and the Apollo space photographs. *Annals of the Association of American Geographers* 84: 270–94. · Crang, M. 1996: Envisioning urban histories: Bristol as palimpsest, postcards and snapshots. *Environment and Planning A* 28: 429–53. · Debray, R. 1996: *Mediologies*. London: Verso. · Gilloch, G. 1996: *Myth and metropolis. Walter Benjamin and the City*. Cambridge: Polity Press. · Leyshon, A., Matless, D. and Revill, G., eds, 1998: *The place of music*. New York: Guilford. · Mattelart, A. 1996: *The invention of communication*. Minneapolis: University of Minnesota Press. · Morley, D. and Robins, K. 1995: *Spaces of identity. Global media, electronic landscapes and cultural boundaries*. London: Routledge. · Plant, S. 1997: *Zeros and ones. Digital women and the new technoculture*. London: Fourth Estate. · Pred, A. 1977: *City-systems in advanced economies*. London: Hutchinson. · Robins, K. 1996: *Into the image. Culture and politics in the field of vision*. London: Routledge. · Shohat, E. and Stam, R. 1994: *Unthinking Eurocentrism. Multiculturalism and the media*. New York: Routledge. · Sadler, D. 1997: The global music business as an information industry: reinterpreting economies of culture. *Environment and Planning A* 29: 1919–36. · Smith, S.J. 1997: Beyond geography's visible worlds: a cultural politics of music. *Progress in Human Geography* 21: 502–29. · Thrift, N.J. 1990: Transport and communication, 1730–1914. In R.L. Dodgshon and R.A. Butlin, eds, *A new historical geography of England and Wales*, 2nd edn. London: Academic Press, 453–86. · Virilio, P. 1991: *The lost dimension*. New York: Semiotext(e).

Suggested Reading

Thrift, N.J. 1997: 'Us' and 'Them': re-imagining places, re-imagining identities. In H. Mackay, ed., *Consumption and everyday life*. London: Sage/Open University, 159–212.

medical geography Geographical analyses of health, disease, mortality and health care. The relationships between environment and patterns of ill-health or MORTALITY have long exercised the attention of geographers and the antecedents of this tradition continue to be explored, demonstrating the antiquity of medical geography. The ecology of disease has attracted most attention, providing opportunities for demonstrations of a range of quantitative methodologies for SPATIAL ANALYSIS. In their most basic form such analyses have a strongly cartographic orientation, permitting comparisons of the pattern of disease with the distribution of presumed environmental risks. One of the most famous illustrations is Dr John Snow's map of cholera cases in central London in 1849, which demonstrated a concentration of cholera deaths in households which drew water from a particular pump. Snow suspected that contamination in the water supply might have a relationship to the cholera deaths and shutting off the pump accelerated the decline in the number of new cases of the disease – though, as has often been observed, the decline had begun before the pump was shut off. Quantitative analyses have illustrated the relationships between patterns of material prosperity or deprivation and patterns of mortality, sometimes showing, with the aid of reconstruction of mortality series over time, that areas of high mortality have persisted for many years (Dorling, 1997), and also demonstrating the strength of the gradient in mortality experience between prosperous and poor localities. The complication here is determining precisely what role PLACE has in explaining these patterns: are mortality variations simply a resultant of other patterns of socio-economic disadvantage, or are there independent, CONTEXTUAL EFFECTS of place? Put another way, how do we – for simplicity – disentangle the relationships between area, CLASS and health (McIntyre et al., 1993)?

There is growing acceptance among social scientists that place does make a difference and that it needs to be theorized, conjointly and concurrently with other planes of social division (Popay et al., 1998).

In some circumstances medical geography's traditional emphasis on associations between environment and disease has made valuable contributions, notably in less-developed societies where the connections between environmental influences and disease are relatively transparent (Phillips and Verhasselt, 1994). But there have been considerable achievements elsewhere. Sophisticated methods have been developed, often in parallel with developments in epidemiology, to assess the degree of association between patterns of diseases and associated environmental factors. Three forms of analysis may be mentioned. First, particularly with diseases which occur in small numbers, only point-pattern data are available and so attempts must be made to assess the degree of clustering in spatial distributions; Openshaw's Geographical Analysis Machine was an ambitious attempt to achieve this in the context of debates about 'cancer clusters' in northern England (Openshaw, 1990; cf. GEOCOMPUTATION). Secondly, there have been exercises in modelling the DIFFUSION of diseases such as measles and, more recently, AIDS (Cliff, Haggett and Smallman-Raynor, 1988; Shannon and Pyle, 1989; Gould, 1993). These have been of value in assisting the control of the further spread of such afflictions. Thirdly, recent studies have emphasized the complexity of the relationships between social status and health, seeking to use MULTILEVEL MODELLING techniques to evaluate how individual and area effects interact; such techniques have been used in predictions of health-related behaviour (Duncan et al., 1993).

The foregoing has emphasized geographies of mortality and physical illness. However, geographies of mental illness have also received attention. There are well-known empirical regularities in the distribution of the mentally ill, notably that there are high rates of illness in impoverished areas, but the causal connections are not clear. Are causes to be found in areal characteristics (the 'breeder' hypothesis) or do individuals prone to mental illness gravitate to particular areas (the 'drift' hypothesis)? The debate on this generated one of the best-known examples of the ECOLOGICAL FALLACY: while an association could be demonstrated between high incidence of mental illness and social conditions, quite contradictory inferences could be drawn with respect to causal processes (Giggs, 1973).

Geographical analyses have also been applied to the study of patterns of HEALTH-CARE delivery. Some authors maintain that there are consequently 'two traditions' of medical geography, one focusing on health services, the other addressing mortality and morbidity; there have been persistent calls for the integration of the two (e.g. Mayer, 1982). However, it is not clear that this is a particularly productive debate; more heat than light has been expended on an issue which really amounts to little more than the statement that some medical geographers have rather different objects of study. Few geographers have attempted simultaneously to model geographies of health services with geographies of disease in order to assess the impact of the former on the latter. Instead, rather than assessing variations in the efficacy of services, concern has been focused on the degree of EQUITY in spatial distributions of health services, and on the development and application of techniques for better spatial planning (Joseph and Phillips, 1984; Haynes, 1987). Implicit in this is a judgement that health facilities *per se* are unproblematically beneficial, a judgement which might not be shared by all and which has led to questioning of the biomedical model of health and health care. Following a concern with geographies of human welfare, many studies have analysed the extent of geographical variability in health-care provision and the extent of correspondence with social need. Even within ostensibly egalitarian services, important spatial variations have been identified, and evidence has been provided for Hart's famous '*inverse care law*', which suggests that services allocated under market criteria are inversely related to patterns of need (Powell, 1990). Particularly in health-care systems where they are no financial barriers to use of services, attention has also focused on patterns of utilization, with a view to determining which groups are able to make most use of services and demonstrating the extent to which use of services declines with – and is constrained by – distance from facilities (cf. DISTANCE DECAY). This has been a debate of fundamental importance in resource allocation decisions; some believe that high levels of hospital utilization are a function of the pattern of existing institutions, whereas others suggest that high levels of utilization reflect greater social need (Royston et al., 1990). There are also numerous examples of the application of geographical techniques in health-care planning, such as

LOCATION–ALLOCATION MODELLING, which is used extensively by health-care providers to determine optimum arrangements of services, notably in less-developed societies where health-care systems are still being established (Phillips and Verhasselt, 1994).

These developments in medical geography have not been without their critics. First, the aggregate and ecological approach of many geographies of mortality and illness has been criticized for undertheorizing the social and political determinants of inequalities in health and for failing adequately to link aggregate and individual approaches (which may be partly overcome, using multilevel modelling). Secondly, there has been an overemphasis on the spatial and locational attributes of health-care systems, but this has been criticized for offering a limited understanding of how spatial patterns of services actually evolve, away from the isotropic plain of the spatial analyst, and for an overemphasis on spatial factors to the neglect of social constraints. Finally, in analysing patterns of health and health care, attention has to be given to other social cleavages – RACE, GENDER, DISABILITY, SEXUALITY – as well as to spatial differentiation. For all these reasons, there are growing signs of what some term a '*post-medical geography*', in which the concern is with matters of individual and COMMUNITY identity, and with determining what elements of PLACE shape individuals' health experiences and access to services (see PUBLIC SERVICES, GEOGRAPHY OF). Institutionally, the renaming of the medical geography study groups of the RGS/IBG and the AAG as the 'geography of health and health care' research groups, is indicative of this shift in orientation (see HEALTH AND HEALTH CARE, GEOGRAPHY OF).

The attractions and limitations of conventional approaches to medical geography are well illustrated by a consideration of geographical studies of AIDS. The application of spatial analysis took three forms: modelling the global diffusion of AIDS; tracking the progress of the virus within states; and, on the basis of these analyses, attempting to predict likely future geographies of AIDS (Shannon and Pyle, 1989; Gould, 1993). Such work made an important contribution to understanding likely spatial patterns of diffusion but had less to say about the causes of AIDS and about the experiences of those affected. Brown (1995), in an argument with broader applicability to medical geography, suggests that the focus of diffusion studies is on the virus, which allows a social distance to be maintained between researchers and those affected by, and coping with, AIDS (Kearns, 1996). Studies of the lives of people with AIDS (PWAs) demonstrate a move away from the geometric conception of space of diffusion studies, to an analysis of the importance of place, either in constructing the experience of PWAs, or in shaping community responses to the disease (Wilton, 1996). Constructing knowledge of health and health care thus depends on understanding the meaning and experience of place (Kearns and Joseph, 1993, p. 715). JM

References

Brown, M. 1995: Ironies of distance: an ongoing critique of the geographies of AIDS. *Environment and Planning D: Society and Space* 13: 159–83. · Cliff, A.D., Haggett, P. and Smallman-Raynor, M. 1988: *An atlas of disease distributions*. Cambridge: Cambridge University Press. · Dorling, D. 1997: *Death in Britain*. York: Joseph Rowntree Foundation. · Duncan, C., Jones, K. and Moon, G. 1993: Do places matter? A multilevel analysis of regional variations in health-related behaviour in Britain. *Social Science and Medicine* 37: 725–35. · Giggs, J.A. 1973: The distribution of schizophrenics in Nottingham. *Transactions, Institute of British Geographers* 59: 55–76. · Gould, P. 1993: *The slow plague*. Oxford: Blackwell. · Haynes, R. 1987: *The geography of health services in Britain*. London: Croom Helm. · Joseph, A. and Phillips, D. 1984: *Accessibility and utilisation: geographic perspectives on health care delivery*. London: Longman. · Kearns, R. 1996: AIDS and medical geography: embracing the other? *Progress in Human Geography* 20: 123–31. · Kearns, R. and Joseph, A. 1993: Space in its place: developing the link in medical geography. *Social Science and Medicine* 37: 711–17. · McIntyre, A. et al. 1993: Area class and health: should we be focusing on places or people? *Journal of Social Policy* 22: 213–34. · Mayer, J. 1982: Relations between two traditions of medical geography. *Progress in Human Geography* 6: 216–30. · Openshaw, S. 1990: Automating the search for cancer clusters: a review of problems, progress and opportunities. In R.W. Thomas, ed., *Spatial epidemiology*. London: Pion, 48–78. · Phillips, D. and Verhasselt, Y., eds, 1994: *Health and development*. London: Routledge. · Popay, J. et al. 1998: Theorising inequalities in health: the place of lay knowledge. *Sociology of Health and Illness* 20: 619–44. · Powell, M. 1990: Need and provision in the NHS, an inverse care law. *Policy and Politics* 18: 31–7. · Royston, G. et al. 1990: Modelling the use of health services by populations of small areas to inform the allocation of central resources to larger regions. *Socio-Economic Planning Sciences* 26: 169–90. · Shannon, G. and Pyle, G. 1989: The origin and diffusion of AIDS: a view from medical geography. *Annals of the Association of American Geographers* 79: 1–24. · Shannon, G. et al. 1991: *The geography of AIDS*. New York: Guilford. · Wilton, R. 1996: Diminished worlds? The geography of everyday life with HIV/AIDS. *Health and Place* 2: 69–84.

megalopolis A Greek word (combining the terms for great and city) adapted by Jean

Gottmann (1964) to describe the discontinuous urban complex of the north-eastern seaboard of the US (cf. CONURBATION). RJJ

Reference

Gottmann, J. 1964: *Megalopolis: the urbanized north-eastern seaboard of the United States*. Cambridge, MA: MIT Press.

memory, popular A term used in considerations of the role played by constructions of the past in the present, and generally set against 'official' or 'academic' historical accounts, though these may themselves contribute to the formation of popular memory. Geographers have examined such themes in relation to the study of heritage and tradition, popular geographies, specific LANDSCAPE elements such as MONUMENTS or museums, and issues of PLACE and IDENTITY, whether at a local, regional or national SCALE.

The term popular memory has been employed by historians seeking to understand the power of senses of the past in contemporary cultural and political life. Pierre Nora's multi-volume project *Les lieux de mémoire* (1984–92; for an English translation of the introduction see Nora, 1989) argues that modern society is characterized by the break up of coherent 'real environments of memory' and their replacement by specific 'sites of memory', whose study is essential to understand the place of the past in the present. Work by the Popular Memory Group of the Birmingham Centre for Contemporary Cultural Studies (1982), and by Raphael Samuel (1995), situates popular memory in relation to a series of distinctions concerning forms of historical knowledge: official and unofficial, public and private, dominant and oppositional, academic and popular. For the Popular Memory Group popular memory is both an object of study and a mode of political practice, though in both cases they warn against an uncritical use of the term 'popular', being cautious of a populist assumption that the popular is both unified and unproblematically positive, and recognizing that popular cultural forms may reinforce rather than be resistant to projects of cultural (see CULTURE) HEGEMONY. A critical sense of the presence of the past in everyday life is developed further by Wright (1985), who draws on the work of Agnes Heller as a theoretical basis for his studies of the place of the national past in contemporary British life.

Samuel's (1995) *Theatres of memory* sets popular memory more straightforwardly against 'official' or 'academic' historical knowledge, proposing that we take seriously the 'unofficial knowledge' found in popular sources, including popular myth, oral testimony, popular MEDIA, local lore, PLACE NAMES and other environmental knowledges. The aim in such work is to suggest that history (and by implication geography) as a discipline should be open to considering a more popular range of source material than has traditionally been the case: 'Tapping into popular memory requires a different order of evidence, and a different kind of enquiry' (Samuel, 1995, p. 8). In similar vein Nora suggests that the study of sites of memory can serve to link 'apparently disconnected events' (1989, p. 23), and stresses that historical study itself functions as an important site of memory, and therefore must be aware of its own social and political role. Work on popular histories, often associated in the UK with the History Workshop movement of socialist and feminist historians, has been echoed by recent calls for the study of popular geographies, whether in relation to an expanded sense of the history of geography as a discipline, which includes its popular role, or in terms of popular knowledges of place and environment (see also IMAGINATIVE GEOGRAPHY). Dolores Hayden's *The power of place* (1995) builds on the work of a group of historians and artists in Los Angeles to explore the possibilities of a progressive exploration of memory in the urban landscape. Hayden considers working-class, ethnic and gendered historic landscapes to show how 'places make memories cohere in complex ways' (p. 43).

Popular memory is to be distinguished from the related concept of the 'invention of tradition', coined in Hobsbawm and Ranger's (1983) collection of essays showing the self-consciously invented nature of events and institutions often held to be customary, for example the rituals of monarchy or parliament. Despite Hobsbawm's argument that we should take seriously the capacity of invented traditions to acquire significant cultural power, the term 'invented tradition' has often been taken to imply something fake, lacking cultural authenticity. Such arguments have been extended by critics such as Hewison (1987) to imply that a popular interest in heritage can be put down as trivial, nostalgic, culturally regressive and commercially exploitative, and opposed to a true sense of history as defined by the historian. Samuel (1995) uses popular memory to argue against such a position, suggesting instead that concern for heritage represents a genuine popular and democratic engagement with history. Samuel stresses that in political terms a concern for heritage is by no means confined to conservative movements, and seeks to highlight a tradition of radical and socialist concern for the past.

The political range of popular memory is highlighted in work by geographers on MONUMENTS, whereby contests over memory focus on and are refracted through specific commemorative sites, as in Peet's study of conflicts over the commemoration of an eighteenth-century popular revolt in twentieth-century Petersham, Massachusetts (Peet, 1996). The place of memory in popular geographies is central to work by geographers on the historicity of PLACE, especially in terms of the role of heritage and memory in the production of local, national and ethnic identities. Charlesworth (1994) shows how the former concentration camp at Auschwitz has become a place of contested memory in terms of conflicting commemorations of Jewish, Soviet-Polish and Polish-Catholic suffering. Matless (1993) focuses on the work of English landscape historian W.G. Hoskins to show how academic studies and topographic guides have promoted a particular anti-modern culture of landscape emphasizing local attachment, memory and tradition. Crang shows how the phenomena of heritage can be considered in terms of the PERFORMATIVITY of the past (Crang, 1994), and in a detailed study of the historicity of urban forms of popular memory in Bristol – postcards, old photographs, local displays – shows how an attention to the popular demands a rethinking of the time-spaces of the city (Crang, 1996). The general conclusion to draw from all such work is that the study of popular geographies entails a critical engagement with popular memory. DM

References

Charlesworth, A. 1994: Contesting places of memory: the case of Auschwitz. *Environment and Planning D: Society and Space* 12: 579–93. · Crang, M. 1994: On the heritage trail: maps of and journeys to olde Englande. *Environment and Planning D: Society and Space* 12: 341–55. · Crang, M. 1996: Envisioning urban histories: Bristol as palimpsest, postcards and snapshots. *Environment and Planning A* 28: 429–52. · Hayden, D. 1995: *The power of place: urban landscapes as public history*. Cambridge, MA: MIT Press. · Hewison, R. 1987: *The heritage industry*. London: Methuen. · Hobsbawm, E. and Ranger, T., eds, 1983: *The invention of tradition*. Cambridge: Cambridge University Press. · Matless, D. 1993: One man's England: W.G. Hoskins and the English culture of landscape. *Rural History* 4: 187–207. · Nora, P. 1989: Between memory and history: Les Lieux de Mémoire. *Representations* 26: 7–25. · Peet, R. 1996: A sign taken for history: Daniel Shay's Memorial in Petersham, Massachusetts. *Annals of the Association of American Geographers* 96: 21–43. · Popular Memory Group 1982: Popular memory: theory, politics, method. In R. Johnson, G. McLennan, B. Schwarz and D. Sutton, eds, *Making histories*. London: Hutchinson, 205–52. · Samuel, R. 1995: *Theatres of memory*. London: Verso. · Wright, P. 1985: *On living in an old country: the national past in contemporary Britain*. London: Verso.

Suggested Reading:

Hayden (1995). · Samuel (1995).

mental maps One of the principal concepts of BEHAVIOURAL GEOGRAPHY, referring to the pyschological representation of PLACES as revealed by simple paper and pencil tests. A psychological turn in human geography in the late 1960s directed attention to the central role of ENVIRONMENTAL PERCEPTION as a mediation between the environment and human action. This was a decisive move against determinism, though by this period the offending reduction was to the economic environment rather than the physical environment of earlier decades. To identify a key role for cognition was, then, to relax the micro-economic determinism of LOCATIONAL ANALYSIS with its presupposition of fully rational spatial behaviour. A proliferation of terms was assembled to describe mental configurations of places. In a much-cited project, Lynch (1960) asked residents in several cities to provide him with an image of the downtown district. Downs and Stea (1973) in contrast referred to cognitive maps which they particularly associated with orientation and way-finding behaviour (cf. COGNITIVE MAPPING; IMAGE). Other terminology included spatial cognition, spatial schemata, ACTION SPACE, ACTIVITY SPACE and awareness space (Golledge and Stimson, 1997). All of these concepts implied knowledge of the configuration and structure of SPACE; some of them also included evaluation, that is a concern with the meaning of space (Ley, 1974).

The most influential research was Peter Gould's innovative experiments exploring the content of what he called mental maps (Gould, 1965; Gould and White, 1974). In the initial experiments, students at universities in several American states were asked to rank order the states they would like to live in following graduation. Invariably the results showed the existence of a national preference surface upon which was superimposed a local surface highlighting the desirability of the home region, wherever it might be. The experimental sites were expanded by Gould and his students to Britain, Sweden and Africa, and included consideration of the developmental growth of mental maps by children of different ages, as well as the relation in Africa between the national preference surface and the spatial impress of MODERNIZATION (Gould and White, 1974). The implication of this research programme was that mental maps were not only preference surfaces, but also predictors of future residential choice and MIGRATION. Later American research found that significant relationships did indeed exist between mental maps and the patterning of inter-state migration flows (Lloyd, 1975).

The notion of mental maps has passed from its illustrious and widely-cited origins – including a full page article in *Time* magazine – to a more routinized element in the repertoire of human geography. Work of a more specialized and technical nature continues (e.g. Golledge, Dougherty and Bell, 1995), and, sustaining the old interdisciplinary linkages, there remains a continuing interest in environmental psychology (Kitchin, 1994). Moreover, mental-maps work propelled an ongoing concern with the representation of places that remains as much on the research frontier at the *fin-de-siècle* as it did in Gould's first studies a generation earlier. This is not to say that there have not been immense changes in conceptualization over the past 30 years. Qualitative assessments of the meaning of place were a primary objective of HUMANISTIC GEOGRAPHY, which, working with a range of literary and philosophical styles, demarcated the variable meeting and interpenetration of subject and object, place and IDENTITY (cf. QUALITATIVE METHODS). Currently, work in human geography and beyond, influenced by POST-MODERNISM, POST-STRUCTURALISM, feminism (see FEMINIST GEOGRAPHIES) and POST-COLONIALISM, continues to sustain a keen focus on the REPRESENTATION of places, though, in a move from psychology to social and cultural history, research now more usually sees these representations as constructed through social discourse and practice rather than as individual mental schemata (cf. ORIENTALISM; TRAVEL WRITING, GEOGRAPHY AND). DL

References

Downs, R. and Stea, D., eds, 1973: *Image and environment: cognitive mapping and spatial behavior.* Chicago: Aldine. · Golledge, R.G. and Stimson, R. J. 1997: *Spatial behavior: a geographic perspective*. New York: Guilford Press. · Golledge, R.G., Dougherty, V. and Bell, S. 1995: Acquiring spatial knowledge: survey versus route-based knowledge in unfamiliar environments. *Annals of the Association of American Geographers* 85: 134–58. · Gould, P.R. 1965: *On mental maps*. Discussion paper no. 9. Ann Arbor: Michigan Inter-University Community of Mathematical Geographers. · Gould, P.R. and White, R. 1974: *Mental maps*. London: Penguin. · Kitchin, R. 1994: Cognitive maps: what are they and why study them? *Journal of Environmental Psychology* 14: 1–19. · Ley, D. 1974: *The black inner city as frontier outpost: images and behavior of a Philadelphia neighborhood.* Washington, D.C.: Association of American Geographers, Monograph Series, no. 7. · Lloyd, R. 1975: Cognition, preference and behavior in space. *Economic Geography* 52: 241–53. · Lynch, K. 1960: *The image of the city*. Cambridge, MA: MIT Press.

Suggested Reading

Gould and White (1974).

mercantilist model An approach to the study of URBAN SYSTEMS devised by J.E. Vance Jr. (1970) to counter the dominance of CENTRAL PLACE THEORY. The key models' key urban function is wholesaling and the system's development is founded on the articulation of long-distance trade, especially through GATEWAY and PRIMATE cities. RJJ

Reference

Vance, J.E. Jr. 1970: *The merchant's world: the geography of wholesaling*. Englewood Cliffs, NJ and London: Prentice-Hall.

merit good A particular type of pure PUBLIC GOOD, usually defined as the national minimum standard for its provision. Public policy should ensure that the entire population of the relevant territory obtains at least a specified threshold level of provision of the good in question (such as the purity of a water supply). Any provision above the merit good standard involves the creation of impurely distributed public goods. RJJ

metaphor To use Aristotle's definition, a 'metaphor consists in giving the thing a name that belongs to something else'. Such a practice is rampant in human geography, as in other disciplines: cities are plant biomes (CHICAGO SCHOOL); CULTURAL LANDSCAPES are TEXTS; PLACES are geological strata (LAYERS OF INVESTMENT); and non-renewable RESOURCES take on a LIFE-CYCLE.

While pervasive, metaphors have been seen by some as at best ornamental, and worst obfuscatory and perverted. Plato thought that they made 'trifle points seem important, and important points trifles'; Hobbes believed that they 'deceive others'; and in geography Harvey (1967, p. 551) argued that they 'hinder objective judgement'. In each of these cases, metaphor is attacked because it results in ambiguity, it is 'a sort of extra happy trick with words' as Richards (1936, p. 90) put it. More generally, such misgivings result from a particular view of language held by such critics; that LANGUAGE should be transparent, limpid and utterly dependable, all of which are undermined by metaphor.

In twentieth-century philosophy, however, there is increasing recognition that language takes on none of those characteristics, and concomitantly that metaphors are an indispensable part of both writing and theorizing. Here it is useful to make a distinction between 'large' and 'small' metaphor use (Barnes and Curry, 1992).

Small metaphors are those that pepper individual writing and research projects. As Lakoff and Johnson (1980) argue, our language is full of metaphoric bits and pieces, as when we speak metaphorically of 'attacking' an opponent's argument, or even 'peppering' our prose with metaphors. Metaphors such as these are present from the beginning. They are an 'omnipresent principle of language' (Richards, 1936, p. 92). But effectively mobilizing those small metaphors requires skill and sensitivity, and forms an important component of RHETORIC, the attempt to persuade others of the force of one's argument by using literary tropes such as metaphor. For example, White (1978, p. 114) argues that the writings of the British historian A.J.P. Taylor are so convincing because of his heavy use of 'dead' metaphors that convey OBJECTIVITY.

Large metaphors are those that structure research PARADIGMS, and shape the very explanatory framework offered. Some large metaphors, such as 'organism' or 'mechanism', are so deeply ingrained that they are *'root metaphors'*, to use Pepper's (1942) term, whereas others are temporary, mobilized for a particular use then discarded. However long their durability, all large metaphors operate in the same way, through a process of 'metaphorical redescription' (Hesse, 1980) – that is, transferring meanings and associations of one system in order to redescribe the explanandum (the part of the explanation that does the explaining) of another system. A classic example is Isaac Newton's metaphorical redescription of sound in terms of waves. The practice is ubiquitous, although that doesn't mean it is trivial. For the introduction of large metaphors can be 'potentially revolutionary' (Arib and Hesse, 1986). When Adam Smith coined the metaphor of the 'invisible hand' to describe the efficacy of the market, or when Karl Marx said 'workers have nothing to lose but their chains', or, closer to home, when Bill Bunge (1966, p. 27) asked, 'Why cannot . . . concepts dealing with exotic and dioric streams be applied to highways?', revolutions, albeit of different kinds, rang out.

In philosophical literature three theories have been proposed to explain the force of metaphors. The least satisfactory is the *substitution view* where the literal characteristics of the object of metaphorical comparison are substituted for the characteristics of the object itself; for example, the city is a plant biome in that the former is literally characterized by the features of the latter including competition, niches, invasion and succession, and so on. The problem here is that the new context of the city makes features such as competition and so on, garner meanings that they did not possess in the original biome setting (Barnes and Curry, 1992). Such criticism is avoided in the *interaction approach*, where the meanings associated with both the object of comparison and the object itself are not indelibly fixed, but change in creative ways through interaction producing new meanings. In geography, Livingstone and Harrison (1981) explore this approach through their examination of the metaphor of 'frontier'. The interaction view is criticized for assuming that new meaning takes on a cognitive status; it represents legitimate knowledge. For a third group of philosophers, however, a metaphor can never achieve that kind of status because *a metaphor has no meaning other than its literal one* which is 'usually a patent falsehood or an absurd truth' (Davidson, 1979, p. 41). Rather, the importance of metaphor is not its meaning, but its use, which is changing beliefs through the jolt, or *frisson*, that a novel metaphor can produce. Metaphors, precisely because they are patently false and absurd, cause us to stop and think, leading us sometimes to conjecture in different ways: to conceive the city as a biome, or landscape as text, or human interaction as the force of gravity.

In geography there has been sporadic interest in metaphor since the 1960s when SPATIAL SCIENTISTS first discussed the linkages between models and metaphors (Haggett and Chorley, 1967). But their approach tended towards the now discredited substitution theory. Later HUMANISTIC GEOGRAPHERS, such as Tuan (1978) and Livingstone and Harrison (1981), were drawn to metaphor because it offered a means of illustrating human imagination and creativity, indelible human traits according to them. Most recently, critical attention to metaphor has come from geographers interested in EPISTEMOLOGICAL issues. They argue that users of large metaphors are often not aware of the intellectual freight they carry, and as a consequence are led to positions that either they would not otherwise accept, or which would be contradictory (Pratt, 1992). For this reason it is necessary to 'exhume' dead metaphors that are sometimes unwittingly employed, and inspect them critically for their coherence, consistency and compatibility with the other things that one might also want to say (Barnes, 1996, chs 4 and 5). Doing so often means scrutinizing the historical and material origins of the original metaphor, which shape its meaning. In this sense, taking metaphor seriously means taking the world seriously too (Smith and Katz, 1993). Metaphors require 'worlding'. TJB

References

Arib, M.A., and Hesse, M.B. 1986: *The construction of reality*. Cambridge: Cambridge University Press. · Barnes, T.J. 1996: *Logics of dislocation: models, metaphors and meanings of economic space*. New York: Guilford. · Barnes, T.J., and Curry, M.G. 1992: Postmodernism in economic geography: metaphor and the construction of alterity. *Environment and Planning D: Society and Space* 10: 57–68. · Bunge, W. 1966: *Theoretical geography*. Lund: Gleerup. · Davidson, D. 1979: What metaphors mean. In S. Sacks, ed., *On metaphor*. Chicago: University of Chicago Press, 29–45. · Haggett, P. and Chorley, R.J. 1967: Models, paradigms and the new geography. In R.J. Chorley and P. Haggett, eds, *Models in geography*. London: Methuen, 19–41. · Harvey, D. 1967: Models of the evolution of spatial patterns in human geography. In R.J. Chorley and P. Haggett, eds, *Models in geography*. London: Methuen, 549–608. · Hesse, M.B. 1980: *Revolutions and reconstructions in the philosophy of science*. Brighton: Harvester Books. · Lakoff, G. and Johnson, M. 1980: *Metaphors we live by*. Chicago: University of Chicago Press. · Livingstone, D.N. and Harrison, R.T. 1981: Meaning through metaphor: analogy as epistemology. *Annals of the Association of American Geographers* 71: 95–107. · Pepper, S. 1942: *World hypothesis: a study in evidence*. Berkeley, CA: University of California Press. · Pratt, G. 1992: Spatial metaphors and speaking positions. *Environment and Planning D: Society and Space* 10: 241–4. · Smith, N. and Katz, C. 1993: Grounding metaphor: towards a spatialized politics. In M. Keith and S. Pile, eds, *Place and the politics of identity*. London: Routledge, 67–83. · Richards, I.A. 1936: *The philosophy of rhetoric*. Oxford: Oxford University Press. · Tuan, Y.F. 1978: Sign and metaphor. *Annals of the Association of American Geographers* 68: 363–72. · White, H. 1978: *Tropics of discourse: essays in cultural criticism*. Baltimore, MD: Johns Hopkins University Press.

Suggested Reading

Lakoff and Johnson (1980). · Smith and Katz (1993).

methodological individualism The view that all social events are fully explained by reducing them to the beliefs and actions of only individuals, and the relations among those individuals. For the methodological individualist, *all* macro-scale social entities are ultimately decomposable to the beliefs and actions of indecomposable individuals (cf. STRUCTURATION THEORY). SOCIETY, therefore, is treated as a chimera, something that appears real but which is not. As a perspective, methodological individualism is usefully contrasted with, on the one hand, approaches that accentuate the importance and reality of trans-individual social structures (as found, for example, in STRUCTURAL MARXISM; cf. MARXIST GEOGRAPHY), and approaches that deny the autonomy of individual human subjects altogether (as found, for example, within POST-STRUCTURALISM).

Philosophically, methodological individualism justifies its position on the grounds that a *real* explanation is one that explains by reducing phenomena or events to their most fundamental constituent elements. The model here is natural science, which typically explains by reducing phenomena or events to their most basic cause, for example at the atomic or subatomic level. A similar general approach, suggest methodological individualists, is required for the human world where what is fundamental is individuals and their beliefs, desires, intentions and reasons. All social aggregates and their relationships must be correspondingly reduced to them.

In spite of its seemingly greater explanatory purchase, methodological individualism typically presumes that individuals are governed by the singular motive of RATIONAL CHOICE. Because of this association with the rationality postulate, methodological individualism is found most readily in NEO-CLASSICAL ECONOMICS (and its spatial counterpart REGIONAL SCIENCE), and more recently in ANALYTICAL MARXISM. Also because of that same association, as well as its broader derogation of the social, it is subject to vigorous criticism. TJB

Suggested Reading

Elster, J. 1989: *The cement of society*. Cambridge: Cambridge University Press. · Levine, A., Sober, E. and Wright, E.O. 1987: Marxism and methodological individualism. *New Left Review* 162: 67–84. · Przeworski, A. 1985: Marxism and rational choice. *Politics and Society* 14: 379–409.

metropolitan Often used as an adjectival synonym for a large city, especially, though not exclusively, one with major concentrations of political and cultural power. The term is also used to apply to centres of COLONIAL and IMPERIAL power, both the countries themselves (e.g. France was metropolitan within its empire) and their capital cities (such as Paris and London). RJJ

metropolitan area A general term, originating from the USA, to describe a very large urban settlement. Metropolitan districts were first defined in the 1910 US CENSUS by grouping large central cities (administrative districts) with their contiguous SUBURBS into single data-reporting units. The term was changed to 'Standard Metropolitan Area' in 1950 and to 'Standard Metropolitan Statistical Area' (SMSA) in 1960, when 219 were defined: the criteria for defining SMSAs were population size, population density, and occupational structures, and the basic building blocks were counties. Within SMSAs the US Bureau of the Census also defines 'Urbanized Areas', comprising the built-up portions only. The system was restructured in 1990, creating three types of area:

- *Metropolitan Statistical Areas* (MSAs) are groups of counties (except in New England) comprising a central city with a population of 50,000 or more surrounded by an urbanized area (defined, as before, by population density and occupational structures) whose total population exceeds 100,000;
- *Consolidated Metropolitan Statistical Areas* (CMSAs) are larger than MSAs, with their urbanized areas having populations of at least 1,000,000; and
- *Primary Metropolitan Statistical Areas* (PMSAs) are separate components of CMSAs with distinct characteristics: the Detroit/Ann Arbor CMSA has two PMSAs, for example, focused on the two central cities, whereas the New York/New Jersey/Long Island CMSA is divided into 10 separate CMSAs.

Many countries now have defined metropolitan areas, on widely varying criteria. RJJ

metropolitan labour area (MLA) A term coined by Brian Berry to denote the commuting HINTERLAND of a METROPOLITAN AREA; he showed that nearly all US counties 'exported' at least 5 per cent of their workers to an SMSA and were thus part of at least one MLA. The concept is now widely adopted for reporting CENSUS data (the British term is 'Local Labour Market Area' – LLMA). RJJ

Suggested Reading

Berry, B.J.L., Goheen, P.G. and Goldstein, H. 1969: *Metropolitan area definition: a reevaluation of concept and statistical practice*. Washington, D.C.: US Bureau of the Census. · Coombes, M.G., Dixon, J.S., Goddard, J.B., Openshaw, S. and Taylor, P.J. 1979: Daily urban systems in Britain: from theory to practice. *Environment and Planning A* 11: 565–74.

microsimulation A statistical procedure for estimating the characteristics of individuals from knowledge of the aggregate characteristics of the population to which they belong. For example, a CENSUS may indicate the number of public housing units in a small area, plus the number of single-parent heads of household and the number of households living below the poverty level. Microsimulation estimates the number in the area having all of those characteristics – i.e. the number of single-parent household heads living below the poverty level in a public housing unit. (Cf. ECOLOGICAL FALLACY; ENTROPY-MAXIMIZING MODELS.) RJJ

Suggested Reading

Longley, P.A., Clarke, M. and Williams, H.C.W.L. 1991: Housing careers, asset accumulation and subsidies to owner-occupiers – a microsimulation. *Housing Studies* 6: 57–69.

migrant labour Workers who migrate in order to find employment. MIGRATION may be temporary or permanent and over long or short distances, often involving movement across international frontiers. There are many examples in the contemporary world of economies which have come to rely to a significant extent upon migrant labour. Historically the movement of labour has been crucial to economic growth and cultural change.

Two aspects are important to understanding the distinction between migrant labour and other types of migration. First, for the individual migrant the principal motivation is economic, the search for a better wage and more secure employment. While much migrant labour involves the temporary movement of individuals, more mature streams may lead to permanent settlement of migrants and their families, not least through the process of CHAIN MIGRATION – both women and men play leading roles in stimulating such migrant flows. Thus, migrant labour often becomes a permanent part of the labour force at the point of destination, sometimes indistinguishable from the population at large or, particularly with culturally distinct international migrations, forming distinct ethnic groups (see ETHNICITY). Second, migrant labour may be seen in a wider economic structural context – e.g. in the development of CAPITALISM and DEPENDENCE and the changing DIVISION OF LABOUR.

Since capitalist development is uneven in both time and space, MOBILITY of the labouring population in, for example, nineteenth-

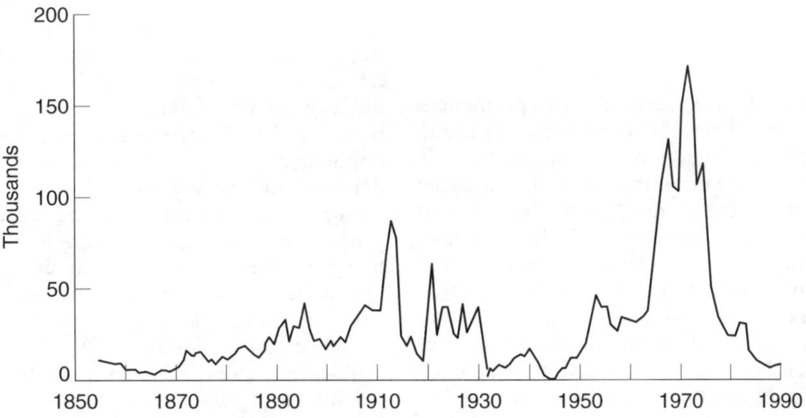

migrant labour *Emigration from Portugal, 1855 to 1988* (Rallu and Blum, 1991)

-century Great Britain was essential for the continuing development of INDUSTRIALIZATION and URBANIZATION (see UNEVEN DEVELOPMENT). Similarly, in north-west Europe after the Second World War, migrant labour became an essential part of economic growth and of urban and industrial concentration and centralization. Thus, countries like the UK, France and West Germany came to rely increasingly upon labour from southern Europe and from the Third World: the UK from the West Indies and South Asia; France from Italy, Spain and Portugal (the figure shows the long-term emigration from Portugal) and from North Africa; West Germany from Greece and Turkey (see *GASTARBEITER*). Equally, in the USA, comparable migration flows came from Mexico and the Caribbean. Labour migrants are found in many other parts of the world and in varying circumstances, e.g. seasonal or periodic migrants in West Africa find employment in both agriculture and industry. Migrant labour was an important feature of the South African economy under APARTHEID. Workers were drawn into 'white' South Africa from the black 'Homelands' on year-long contracts. One advantage of this system, from the perspective of the South African government and relevant capitalists, was that, as elsewhere, the receiving territory was relieved of some of the costs of production and reproduction of the labour which it used, as such costs were borne in the territory of origin where families remained. Migrant labour has been subject to increasing STATE control in most countries and migration policy has frequently proved controversial.

In summarizing the current state of global migration trends and the likely prospects for the immediate future, Castles and Miller (1993, p. 8) have suggested four principal trends. First, the *globalization of migration* refers to the tendency for more and more countries to be affected by migration. A greater diversity of origins means that countries are drawing immigrants from a broad spectrum of economic, social and cultural backgrounds. Second, the *acceleration of migration* – the fact that the volume of movement is increasing in almost all major regions – poses problems for government policies. Third, the *differentiation of migration* indicates that most countries have a broad range of migration movements, not just labour migration. And finally, the *feminization of migration* draws attention to the fact that women play an increasing role in all regions and all types of migration, including labour flows. PEO

References

Castles, S. and Miller, M.J. 1993: *The age of migration: international population movements in the modern world.* Basingstoke: Macmillan. · Rallu, J.-L. and Blum, A., eds, 1991: *European population 1. Country analysis.* London: John Libbey, 396.

Suggested Reading

Chant, S., ed., 1992: *Gender and migration in developing countries.* London: Belhaven. · Cohen, R. 1987: *The new helots. Migrants in the international division of labour.* Aldershot: Gower. · Cohen, R., ed., 1995: *The Cambridge survey of world migration.* Cambridge: Cambridge University Press. · Hatton, T.J. and Williamson, J.G., eds, 1994: *Migration and the international labor market, 1850–1939.* London and New York: Routledge. · King, R., ed., 1993: *Mass migrations in Europe. The legacy and the future.* London: Belhaven. · Miles, R. 1982: *Racism and migrant labour.* London: Routledge and Kegan Paul. · Sassen, S. 1988: *The mobility of labor and capital. A study in international investment and labor flow.*

Cambridge: Cambridge University Press. · Skeldon, R. 1997: *Migration and development: a global perspective*. Harlow: Longman.

migration Permanent or semi-permanent change of residence by an individual or group of people. Migration has been enormously influential in determining cultural and social change at all SCALES, not least the global, and may be fundamental to individual experience.

Geographers have devoted much more attention to the study of migration than to other branches of population study. The collection of statistical data on migration requires a boundary of some sort to have been crossed and a certain length of time to have been spent over that boundary in a new area of residence. The range of migration studies has broadened considerably in recent years to include not only statistical estimates and models but also an appreciation of the impact of migration on places of origin and destination and on the individual. Migration is a key element of BEHAVIOURAL GEOGRAPHY and attempts to understand the meaning and experience of migration for individuals involve the use of qualitative as well as quantitative sources. The process of migration is fundamental to the existence of DIASPORAS. Migration may be a key element in understanding SENSE OF PLACE, COMMUNITY and IDENTITY and for that reason migration studies have been reinforced in recent years as an exciting ingredient in POPULATION and SOCIAL GEOGRAPHY.

Migration, together with FERTILITY and MORTALITY, is a fundamental element determining an area's population growth and structure (see AGE AND SEX STRUCTURE). *Gross migration* includes all flows; *net migration* the balance of moves into and out of an area. MOBILITY is a rather more general term than migration, covering all kinds of territorial movements of whatever distance, duration or degree of permanence. A distinction is sometimes drawn between migration and *circulation*, a term given to short-term, repetitive or cyclical movements. Reviewing the whole process of mobility in history, Wilbur Zelinsky (1971) developed the idea of the 'mobility transition', related to the general model of the DEMOGRAPHIC TRANSITION, in which he hypothesized a relationship between different types of movement and general processes of URBANIZATION, INDUSTRIALIZATION and MODERNIZATION in space and time (see also Potts, 1990; Segal, 1993; Skeldon, 1997). Zelinsky thus related five principal types of migration (international, frontierward, rural–urban, urban–urban and intra-urban, and circulation) to five types of society (pre-modern traditional, early transitional, late transitional, advanced and superadvanced). Changes in intensity of the different migrations were in turn linked to the changes in birth, death and population growth rates associated with the demographic transition.

Migration is an important ingredient in the process of GLOBALIZATION and has been for many centuries through, for example, the operation of the slave trade or through the mass trans-Atlantic migrations of the nineteenth century (Moch, 1992; Hatton and Williamson, 1994; Hoerder and Moch, 1996; see SLAVERY). Migration may also be a crucial symptom of relations of DEPENDENCE between different regions at different times. Equally, there has been a continuing interest in the global significance of migration (Potts, 1990; Castles and Miller, 1993; Skeldon, 1997) and its history (Moch, 1992; Hoerder and Moch, 1996).

SCALE provides an essential criterion for classifying migrations, as specified above. Other classificatory criteria include time (temporary/permanent); distance (long/short); decision-making (voluntary/forced: see also REFUGEES); numbers involved (individual/mass); social organization of migrants (family/clan/individuals); political organization (sponsored/free); causes (economic/social); and aims (conservative/innovative). Different aspects of migration flows are also distinguished: *stepwise migration* generally implies movement through a series of places, e.g. from a village up the urban hierarchy; the related idea of CHAIN MIGRATION links flows to established kinship ties between, for example, rural areas and the city; and *return migration* to the migrants' origin is a feature of many streams. The further notion of *circulation* draws attention to the fact that not all migrations can be neatly classified into permanent movements and that some migration systems depend upon continuous, circular, flows (for seasonal work in agriculture and tourism, for example).

Given the great variety of migrations, it is not perhaps surprising that there is no comprehensive theory of migration. Nevertheless, successful attempts have been made to integrate migration into economic and social theory, spatial analysis and behavioural theory and the body of theory available across the relevant disciplines is now quite substantial (Ogden, 1984). In the late nineteenth century, E.G. Ravenstein formulated what he called 'laws of migration' on which much subsequent work has been based (see Grigg, 1977). These were:

(a) the majority of migrants go only a short distance;
(b) migration proceeds step by step;
(c) migrants going long distances generally go by preference to one of the great centres of commerce or industry;
(d) each migration current produces a compensating counter-current;
(e) the natives of towns are less migratory than those of rural areas;
(f) females are more migratory than males within their country of birth, but males more frequently venture beyond;
(g) most migrants are adults – families rarely migrate out of their country of birth;
(h) large towns grow more by migration than by natural increase;
(i) migration increases in volume as industries and commerce develop and transport improves;
(j) the major direction of migration is from the agricultural areas to the centres of industry and commerce;
(k) the major causes of migration are economic.

These 'laws' have been modified by subsequent research rather than fundamentally disproved.

Geographers have traditionally paid considerable attention to DISTANCE-DECAY relationships in migration patterns. Most studies show the volume of migration to be inversely related to distance and Hägerstrand and others have used regression techniques to describe this relationship, the basis of the idea of the MEAN INFORMATION FIELD. In his formulation of the GRAVITY MODEL, Zipf (1949) demonstrates the relationship between population size, distance and migration. S.A. Stouffer (1940) refined this further by showing that migration was determined by opportunities at origin and destination and by INTERVENING OPPORTUNITIES between the two. Others provided more elaborate multivariate models, relating distance to a variety of other factors (Stillwell and Congdon, 1991) and seeing migration as a component in POPULATION ACCOUNTS.

A more general theory of migration was propounded by Lee (1966), who refined the idea of migration between two places as a response to various 'pushes' at origin and 'pulls' at destination. Another much-quoted effort sought to diminish the simple dualism of origin and destination and instead see migration in terms of a *system* of interlocking and mutually dependent forces, an idea developed in the first instance with reference to rural–urban migration in the developing world (Mabogunje, 1970). The wider understanding of migration flows owes much also to theoretical perspectives from NEO-CLASSICAL ECONOMICS where migration is seen as a response to differences in wage and income levels in different locations. Thus migrants may move from low-wage, high-unemployment regions to high-wage, low-unemployment regions and bring about an equilibrium between the two. A rather different perspective derives from POLITICAL ECONOMY: migrants are seen as an integral part of the working of the capitalist system and reflect capital's search for cheap and exploitable labour. Migration flows may reflect the changing spatial DIVISION OF LABOUR. There is also, however, an increasing awareness that migration needs to be understood not only in terms of economic causation but also as a social process, in relation to, for example, changing family and GENDER relations or changing longevity. Geographers have also begun to use ideas from STRUCTURATION THEORY in order to bridge the gap between the individual and wider structures.

Research has concentrated on both empirical and theoretical aspects of the economic and social causes and consequences of migration; its selectivity by age, sex, marital status, ETHNICITY, education, occupation and stage in the life course; and behavioural aspects of the decision to migrate. Recent developments have emphasized the importance of mixed methods – combinations of quantitative (for example, the population CENSUS) and qualitative sources (for example, in-depth interviews, biographies or creative literature; see King, Connell and White, 1995) – to grasp the full significance and meaning of migration for the individual. Issues such as gender (Chant, 1992), refugees (Black and Robinson, 1993), migration of the highly-skilled (Salt, 1992) and migration policy (Kritz, Lim and Zlotnik, 1992; Kubat, 1993) have also come to the fore, as have the complex links between internal migration and, for example, GENTRIFICATION and COUNTERURBANIZATION (Champion and Fielding, 1992; Stillwell, Rees and Boden, 1992; Geyer and Kontuly, 1996). Studies continue to cover a very broad geographical terrain (see, for example, Skeldon, 1990; King, 1993; Cohen, 1995; Hugo, 1996). PEO

References and Suggested Reading

Black, R. and Robinson, V. 1993: *Geography and refugees: patterns and processes of change*. London: Belhaven.

Boyle, P., Halfacree, K. and Robinson, V. 1998: *Exploring contemporary migration.* Harlow: Longman. · Castles, S. and Miller, M.J. 1993: *The age of migration. International population movements in the modern world.* Basingstoke: Macmillan. · Champion, A. and Fielding, A., eds, 1992: *Migration processes and patterns, volume 1: Research progress and prospects.* London: Belhaven. · Chant, S., ed., 1992: *Gender and migration in developing countries.* London: Belhaven. · Cohen, R. 1987: *The new helots. Migrants in the international division of labour.* Aldershot: Gower. · Cohen, R., ed., 1995: *The Cambridge survey of world migration.* Cambridge: Cambridge University Press. · Geyer, H.S. and Kontuly, T.M., eds, 1996: *Differential urbanisation. Integrating spatial models.* London: Arnold. · Grigg, D.B. 1977: E.G. Ravenstein and the 'laws of migration'. *Journal of Historical Geography* 3: 41–54. · Hatton, T.J. and Williamson, J.G. 1994: *Migration and the international labour market 1850–1939.* London: Routledge. · Hoerder, D. and Moch, L.P., eds, 1996: *European migrants. Global and local perspectives.* Boston: Northeastern University Press. · Hugo, G. 1996: Research review 3: Asia on the move: research challenges for population geography. *International Journal of Population Geography* 2 2: 95–118. · King, R., ed., 1993: *Mass migration in Europe. The legacy and the future.* London: Belhaven. · King, R., Connell, J. and White, P., eds, 1995: *Writing across worlds; literature and migration.* London: Routledge. · Kritz, M.M., Lim, L.L. and Zlotnik, H., eds, 1992: *International migration systems. A global approach.* Oxford: Clarendon Press. · Kubat, D., ed., 1993: *The politics of migration policies. Settlement and integration. The first world into the 1990s.* New York: Center for Migration Studies. · Lee, E.S. 1966: A theory of migration. *Demography* 3 1: 47–57. · McNeill, W.H. and Adams, R.J. 1978: *Human migration: patterns and policies.* Bloomington, Ind. and London: Indiana University Press. · Mabogunje, A.L. 1970: Systems approach to a theory of rural–urban migration. *Geographical Analysis* 2 1: 1–17. · Moch, L.P. 1992: *Moving Europeans. Migration in western Europe since 1600.* Bloomington and Indianapolis: Indiana University Press. · Ogden, P.E. 1984: *Migration and geographical change.* Cambridge: Cambridge University Press. · Potts, L. 1990: *The world labour market. A history of migration.* London: Zed Books. · Salt, J. 1992: Migration processes among the highly skilled in Europe. *International Migration Review* 26 2: 484–505. · Segal, A. 1993: *An atlas of international migration.* London: Hans Zell. · Simon, G. 1995: *Géodynamique des migrations internationales dans le monde.* Paris: Presses Universitaires de France. · Skeldon, R. 1990: *Population mobility in developing countries: a reinterpretation.* London: Belhaven. · Skeldon, R. 1997: *Migration and development: a global perspective.* Harlow: Longman. · Stillwell, J. and Congdon, P., eds, 1991: *Migration models: macro and micro approaches.* London: Belhaven. · Stillwell, J., Rees, P. and Boden, P., eds, 1992: *Migration processes and patterns. Volume 2. Population redistribution in the United Kingdom.* London: Belhaven. · Stouffer, S.A. 1940: Intervening opportunities: a theory relating mobility and distance. *American Sociological Review*: 845–67. · Weiner, M. 1995: *The global migration crisis. Challenge to states and to human rights.* New York: HarperCollins. · White, P.E. and Woods, R.I., eds, 1980: *The geographical impact of migration.* London: Longman. · Zelinsky, W. 1971: The hypothesis of the mobility transition. *Geographical Review* 61: 219–49. · Zipf, G.K. 1949: *Human behavior and the principle of least effort.* New York: Hafner.

mimesis A theory of REPRESENTATION based on the possibility of producing an exact copy of the original. In LANDSCAPE studies, mimetic theories have been challenged by those who emphasize the constructed and partial nature of different 'ways of seeing'. While mimetic representations strive to produce an accurate facsimile of reality, critics stress that 'there is no neutral, univocal, "visible" world out there to match our vision against' (Duncan and Ley, 1993, p. 4). Taussig's study of the 'magic of mimesis' argues that the mimetic faculty is closely tied to Euroamerican colonialism through 'the felt relation of the civilizing process to savagery, to aping' (1993, p. xiv), a point which Bhabha (1994) develops in terms of the ambiguities of the mimic in colonial discourse. PAJ

References

Bhabha, H. 1994: Of mimicry and man. In *The location of culture.* London: Routledge, 85–92. · Duncan, J. and Ley, D., eds, 1993: *Place/culture/representation.* London: Routledge. · Taussig, M. 1993: *Mimesis and alterity.* London: Routledge.

mixed economy A term sometimes applied to an economy which combines private- and state-owned productive activities. As all capitalist economies have some STATE activities and all countries with a centrally planned COMMAND ECONOMY have (or had) some private activity, mixed economy is not a helpful term. It is misleading if taken to describe some intermediate between a fully capitalist and a socialist economic system, because the predominant MODE OF PRODUCTION usually remains capitalist. DMS

mixed farming A pattern of agricultural land-use which combines the production of crops and livestock on the same farm. Until the twentieth century, mixed farming was the staple farming system in most parts of the world. Raising various combinations of domesticated plants and animals provided the basis of more balanced subsistence diets and enabled farmers to spread their market risks across a range of produce. Mixed farming methods also have advantages in the complementary management of resources, for example, by feeding animals on crop waste and fallow land and using animal manure to fertilize crops (Mannion, 1995).

A rapid decline in this pattern of farming in the post-war period, particularly in advanced industrial countries, has been brought about by the industrialization of agriculture (Lawrence, 1987). This has seen an increasing specialization of agricultural land-use at the regional and farm level, with farms becoming larger in size and scale and more intensive in their methods of production (Fitzsimmons, 1986). This shift in the organization of farming practices has been accompanied by changes in the farmed landscape which first aroused public concern about the environmental effects of the industrialization of agriculture (Westmacott and Worthington, 1984). (See also AGRIBUSINESS; AGRICULTURAL GEOGRAPHY; AGRO-FOOD SYSTEM; INTENSIVE AGRICULTURE.) SW

References

Fitzsimmons, M. 1986: The new industrial agriculture: the regional integration of speciality crop production. *Economic Geography* 62: 334–53. · Lawrence, G. 1987: *Capitalism and the countryside: the rural crisis in Australia*. Sydney: Pluto Press. · Mannion, A. 1995: *Agriculture and environmental change*. Chichester: John Wiley, ch. 2. · Westmacott, R. and Worthington, T. 1984: *Agricultural landscapes: a second look*. Cheltenham: Countryside Commission.

mobility A general term which includes all types of territorial movements, including MIGRATION. Strictly, a distinction is necessary between spatial or geographical mobility and social mobility, a term used to cover changes in socio-economic status. Not all forms of spatial mobility may be regarded as migration. The latter usually implies a permanent or semi-permanent change of residence and therefore excludes, for example, commuters, holiday-makers and students moving termly between family home and college (cf. COMMUTING; TOURISM, GEOGRAPHY OF). These forms of mobility are often designated as *circulation*, which covers a 'great variety of movements, usually short-term, repetitive or cyclical in character, but all having in common the lack of any declared intention of a permanent or long-lasting change in residence' (Zelinsky, 1971). PEO

Reference

Zelinsky, W. 1971: The hypothesis of the mobility transition. *Geographical Review* 61: 219–49.

Suggested Reading

Jones, H.R. 1990: *Population geography*, 2nd edn. London: Paul Chapman. · Ogden, P.E. 1984: *Migration and geographical change*. Cambridge: Cambridge University Press, ch. 1.

mode of production The structured social relationships through which human societies organize productive activity, the extraction of surplus value and the reproduction of social life. 'Mode of Production' is a periodizing concept, suggesting the historical development of human societies through a series of such modes.

Although Marx was much more circumspect, orthodox Marxist theory, originating with Engels, identified several different modes of production which are seen, in the broadest terms, to succeed each other: primitive communism, slavery, feudalism, capitalism, socialism and communism. In each of these, different social relationships structure the way in which a society's productive and reproductive activity are organized. The definition of modes of production revolves around who performs the social labour and who reaps the benefit. Under primitive communal societies any means of production (land, tools, etc.) were held in common; these societies had subsistence economies, were egalitarian, and experienced no permanent internal class differences. Typified by hunter-gatherers, they had only the most elementary DIVISION OF LABOUR (often along age and gender lines). In the SLAVERY mode of production, the labourer is owned as a means of production (property), and can therefore be bought and sold, and the benefits of labour accrue entirely to the owner (Marx, 1964). Under FEUDALISM, the labourers are PEASANTS who, while not themselves owned as slaves, remain legally tied to the land as agricultural serfs and servants; a landlord retains the rights to peasants' labour integral with ownership of the land. Peasants own some of the means of production (especially elementary tools) and live on a portion of what they produce, the remainder being retained by the landlord. With the advent of CAPITALISM, the wage labourer is 'freed' from both the land and the means of production and is obliged to sell his/her labour power for a wage. The working class performs the society's work while the capitalist class, by dint of its ownership of CAPITAL, performs no work.

SOCIALISM was envisaged by Marx as transitional. It represents a mode of production in which the capitalist class has been defeated and class distinctions are being broken down through civil as well as state action. COMMUNISM is the mode of production in which egalitarian social relationships have been achieved, CLASS differences have been eroded, and the STATE has withered away in favour of direct popular control of economy, politics and society.

Although modes of production are identified primarily by their distinctive social relationships, there is a clear connection between RELATIONS OF PRODUCTION and forces of production. Each mode of production is identified with a specific range and type of technologies which develop along with the division of labour. Furthermore, each mode of production implies a specific set of social and cultural relationships, and a specific kind of STATE. Whereas feudalism incorporated a legal system that identified different levels of privilege (enforced by the Court) and was buttressed by an IDEOLOGY of knowing one's 'rightful place' in an established hierarchical order, in capitalist societies the legal structure and social ideologies emphasize freedom, DEMOCRACY and EQUALITY, despite the obvious inequality in economic relations between classes which defines capitalism.

A mode of production therefore incorporates not just social relations of production but also a complex of political, economic and cultural relations and institutions. Cohesion between these different elements in a mode of production is vital. Marx argued that under capitalism there developed a systematic disjuncture between the rapidly expanding forces of production and the increasingly antiquated social (class) relations of production such that the creation of greater social wealth depends on the continued impoverishment of a large part of humanity. This situation becomes increasingly untenable as the fundamental class contradiction grows more stark. It brings not only social malaise but also political organization, the threat of revolution and the potential to abandon capitalism in favour of a new mode of production.

There are extensive theoretical and empirical debates concerning 'modes of production'. Whereas the notion of transnational, historical social structures, common to different times and places, makes considerable sense, for example, human history should not be seen as following a tight evolutionary progression of modes of production. Furthermore, this schema of modes of production was constructed largely on the basis of European history as it was understood in the mid-nineteenth century and may not apply more widely. Additional modes of production might be identified: Marx, for example, spoke of an 'Asiatic mode of production' (see Wittfogel, 1957; Peet, 1985).

For geographers, each mode of production can be seen as creating its own distinctive geography, and indeed changing geographies as the mode of production itself develops. Under capitalism, the inequality between capital and labour becomes inscribed in the landscape as the distinction between developed and underdeveloped areas at different scales from the global to the local. UNEVEN DEVELOPMENT is therefore a systematic more than a haphazard aspect of capitalist geographical change. In the twentieth century the geographical unevenness of development has played a central role in defining the fate and directions of capitalist expansions. Likewise, changes in the composition of capitalism have led to a continually transforming geography (Dunford and Perrons, 1983); David Gordon (1984), for example, has shown how the transformation of the US economy from a mercantile to industrial and then to corporate capitalism has involved a parallel transformation in US city structure and spatial form. NS

References

Dunford, M. and Perrons, D. 1983: *The arena of capital*. London: Macmillan. · Gordon, D. 1984: Capitalist development and the history of American crisis. In W. Tabb and L. Sawers, eds, *Marxism and the metropolis*, 2nd edn. New York: Oxford University Press, 21–53. · Marx, K. 1964: *Pre-capitalist economic formations*. London: Lawrence and Wishart. · Peet, R., ed., 1985: The geographical ideas of Karl Wittfogel. *Antipode* 17(1): 35–50. · Wittfogel, K. 1957: *Oriental despotism*. New Haven: Yale University Press.

Suggested Reading

Marx, K. 1964. · Hilton, R. et al. 1976: *The transition from feudalism to capitalism*. London: New Left Books.

model An idealized and structured representation of the real (cf. ABSTRACTION; IDEAL TYPE). Model-building has a long history in many sciences, but its incorporation into geography is of comparatively recent origin. It is usually most closely associated with post-war attempts to establish geography as a SPATIAL SCIENCE. Indeed, scientificity was central to the bench-mark collection of essays edited by R.J. Chorley and P. Haggett as *Models in geography* (1967). They argued that model-building depends on what they called 'analogue theory', which treats models as 'selective approximations which, by the elimination of incidental detail [or 'noise'], allow some fundamental, relevant or interesting aspects of the real world to appear in some generalized form'. The accent on generalization was vital, and it was given a particular inflection by the architects of spatial science. Generalization can take many different forms, but spatial science relied heavily on two strategies: (i) the construction of schematic diagrams to represent geometric schemes in visual terms; and (ii) the formalization of their 'SPATIAL STRUCTURES' as statistical and mathematical models. These twin devices played an important role in the search for general theories of spatial organization that, so it was believed, could underwrite the seemingly endless heterogeneity and differentiation of human LANDSCAPES. Ten years later, P. Haggett, A. Cliff and A. Frey (1977) spoke of 'essential links' between model-building in these terms and the so-called QUANTITATIVE REVOLUTION, and many of the first-generation models were attempts to represent the abstract geometry of an idealized landscape through various transformations of DISTANCE-DECAY functions. Because the itinerary from abstraction through generalization to disclosure was supposed to provide for further extensions and explorations, model-building was seen as a necessary moment in the 'puzzle-solving' activity required for the foundation of a new scientific PARADIGM. It was no accident, therefore, that Chorley and Haggett's advocacy of a model-based paradigm for geographical inquiry should have been based in resolutely Kuhnian terms.

Since Chorley and Haggett wrote, however, the claims and concepts that provided the architecture for their pioneer collection of essays have been re-evaluated on five main levels.

The locational models of spatial science have been subject to a (limited) reformulation. In the second edition of *Locational analysis in human geography* (Haggett, Cliff and Frey, 1977) the authors admitted that 'the present stock of models may be unprepossessing', and a comparison with the first edition (1965) shows that the intervening years had seen remarkably few attempts to construct new locational models, although some of the old ones had been reworked: e.g. Hägerstrand's contagious DIFFUSION model was shown to be a special case of a more general epidemiological model, the classical GRAVITY MODEL was shown to be an instance of a more general class of ENTROPY-MAXIMIZING MODELS and the VON THÜNEN MODEL was recast as the dual of the TRANSPORTATION PROBLEM in LINEAR PROGRAMMING.

This limited advance was, in part, because the autonomy of LOCATION THEORY had been compromised by the construction of more inclusive models of the SPACE-ECONOMY outside the domain of spatial science. Those who continued to work within the conventional modelling framework were more interested in developing statistical and mathematical models that could break open complicated data-sets than with seeking to establish in any direct way the theorems of a general spatial science. Elsewhere in the discipline, however, model-building took radically different directions, and when Peet and Thrift compiled a collection of *New models in geography* (1989) their sub-title identified a tectonic shift in the foundations of model-building: 'the POLITICAL-ECONOMY perspective' signalled a range of different approaches that had a common grounding in forms of critical social theory attached in varying degrees to HISTORICAL MATERIALISM.

Partly as a consequence, the original claim for analytical model-building as the object of geographical inquiry was displaced and efforts were directed towards methods as means rather than as ends in themselves. This effort was originally entangled with the critique of (LOGICAL) POSITIVISM, but the use of analytical methods was subsequently resituated within a wider intellectual landscape that was much more sensitive to the limitations of such methods. So, for example, Sheppard and Barnes (1990) 'recognize that many aspects of society and economy are not subject to analytical treatment, and even those aspects that are may well be more sensitively treated by non-analytical methods'. The same authors direct modelling towards the identification of substantive processes and causal mechanisms rather than mathematical processes and idealized landscapes:

> Distances are not some physical constraint to which all realizations of a process are subject in identical ways, as in the laws of physics, because spatial structures are socially constructed and far more complex than the isotropic and stationary spaces that are generally relied on in [locational] analysis. (Sheppard and Barnes, 1990)

Those reformulations had some impact on conventional modelling, and an international conference held in 1987 to mark the twentieth anniversary of the original *Models in geography* included both revisionists who sought to rethink spatial modelling and dissidents who were sceptical of its ability to address important practical questions. On one side, Harvey claimed that 'those who have stuck with modelling since those heady days [of the late 1960s] have largely been able to do so by restricting the nature of the questions they ask'. To Cosgrove, modelling was a quintessential expression of (high) MODERNISM and the privilege it accorded to abstraction, parsimony and generalization was altogether incapable of responding to the challenges of 'DIFFERENCE' being articulated through a diffuse POSTMODERNISM. On the other side, the conference included a large number of unrepentant spatial scientists who had no time for such concerns, and who reaffirmed their faith in the central importance of formal modelling as a way either of making an accommodation with the New Right (Bennett) or of meeting the demands of the commercial market-place (Openshaw: see Macmillan, 1989). Their priorities have since been boosted by the rapid expansion of GEOGRAPHICAL INFORMATION SYSTEMS and by a robustly contentious statement of the importance of securing human geography as a 'real' science – a computational human geography – that would eschew 'soft methodologies' and incorporate new approaches to modelling at its core (Openshaw 1998).

What most exercised Openshaw was the counter-claim that human geography also had roots in the humanities and the social sciences, and in particular the rapid advance of POST-STRUCTURALISM through the discipline. There is no doubt that post-structuralism calls into question the EPISTEMOLOGY on which conventional model-building relied: the separation between 'the real' and 'REPRESENTATION' (Dixon and Jones, 1998). But its practitioners do none the less provide heuristics – usually in words rather than schematic diagrams or mathematical formulations – and they do offer vignettes that purport to illuminate larger propositions. Openshaw (1998) claimed that these constructions are at once too complicated and too singular: 'difficult-to-read texts' that offer merely 'descriptions of unique experiences that do not generalize'. This appears to reinstate the much misunderstood distinction between IDIOGRAPHIC and NOMOTHETIC approaches, but Sibley (1998) believes that what is really at stake is abjection: 'anxiety about disorder' that is inimical to the model-building enterprise of classical spatial science and its successor projects. 'That there is more order in the world than appears at first sight is not discovered till the order is looked for', Chorley and Haggett (1967) often reminded their readers. Post-structuralism draws attention to the radical non-innocence of just 'looking', and its interventions have unsettling implications not only for the formal modelling of spatial science but also for the 'new models' of political economy and social theory (cf. Sheppard, 1995). DG

References

Chorley, R.J. and Haggett, P., eds, 1967: *Models in geography*. London: Methuen. · Dixon, D. and Jones, J.P. 1998: My dinner with Derrida, or spatial analysis and post-structuralism do lunch. *Environment and Planning A* 30: 247–60. · Haggett, P., Cliff, A. and Frey, A. 1977: *Locational analysis in human geography*, 2nd edn. London: Edward Arnold. · Macmillan, B., ed., 1989: *Remodelling geography*. Oxford: Blackwell. · Openshaw, S. 1998: Towards a more computationally minded scientific human geography. *Environment and Planning A* 30: 317–32. · Peet, R. and Thrift, N., eds, 1989: *New models in geography: the political economy perspective*, 2 vols. London: Unwin Hyman. · Sheppard, E. 1995: Dissenting from spatial analysis. *Urban Geography* 16: 283–303. · Sheppard, E. and Barnes, T. 1990: *The capitalist space-economy*. London: Unwin Hyman. · Sibley, D. 1998: Sensations and spatial science: gratification and anxiety in the production of ordered landscapes. *Environment and Planning A* 30: 235–46.

Suggested Reading

Dixon and Jones (1998); Harvey, D. 1969: *Explanation in geography*. London: Edward Arnold, chs 10–11; Macmillan (1989).

modernism Strategies of REPRESENTATION most closely identified with late nineteenth- and twentieth-century movements in the arts that challenged the conventions of realism and romanticism. Some critics dismiss 'modernism' as the emptiest of labels, and certainly the diversity of modernisms needs emphasis. Even so, Lunn (1985) identifies four major preoccupations of aesthetic modernism in the early twentieth century that provide a useful series of formal coordinates:

- *Aesthetic self-consciousness*. 'Modern artists, writers and composers often draw attention to the media or materials with which they are working', Lunn argues, and in doing so establish the status of their work as a 'fiction' in the literal sense of 'something made': they thus seek to escape from the idea of art as a direct reflection of the world.
- *Simultaneity and juxtaposition*. Modernism often disrupts, weakens or dissolves temporal structure in favour of an ordering based on simultaneity; different perspectives are often juxtaposed within the same frame.
- *Paradox, ambiguity and uncertainty*. Modernism often explores what Lunn calls 'the paradoxical many-sidedness of the world': instead of an omniscient narrator, for example, modernist writers may deploy multiple, limited and partial vantage-points from which to view events.

- *The demise of the centred subject.* Modernism often exposes and disrupts the fiction of the sovereign individual or the 'integrated subject'.

These shifts did not emerge in a vacuum, and many commentators treat modernism – and in particular the avant-garde (Bürger, 1984) – as both a critique of and a response to a protracted series of major crises within capitalist MODERNITY at the turn of the nineteenth and twentieth centuries. Its historico-geographical coordinates include: the explosive growth of modern cities and radical transformations of their built forms, economies and cultures; the restructuring of European CAPITALISM, especially through the Agricultural Depression at the end of the nineteenth century and the intensified technical changes brought about by a new round of INDUSTRIALIZATION; the aggressive advance of European COLONIALISM and IMPERIALISM; and the turbulence of the First World War and the Russian Revolution (see Bradbury, 1976; Anderson, 1984; Timms and Kelley, 1985; Hobsbawm, 1987; Eksteins, 1989).

Even in such an abbreviated form, this cultural mapping has three implications of direct relevance to human geography. First, these episodes brought with them significant changes in conceptions of time and SPACE in the West (Kern, 1983) which also had dramatic repercussions far beyond the shores of Europe and North America (Rabinow, 1989; Wright, 1991) and which were directly implicated in new productions of alterity (see OTHER /OTHERNESS; Torgovnick, 1990). Secondly, the characteristic ways in which these changes were registered in the arts, literature and elsewhere were profoundly gendered and sexualized. 'The territory of modernism', Pollock (1988) reminds us, 'so often is a way of dealing with masculine sexuality and its sign, the bodies of women.' Representations of modern spaces were typically made to revolve around masculine subject-positions – like the mobile figure of the flâneur – and to privilege encounters 'between men who have the freedom to take their pleasures in many urban spaces and women from a class subject to them who have to work in those spaces often selling their bodies to clients or to artists' (Pollock, 1988, p. 54; see also Wolff, 1990). Indeed, Lefebvre's account of the PRODUCTION OF SPACE – which was itself in some part inspired by his own association with early twentieth-century modernism – repeatedly draws attention to the significance of modernism for the triumph of a 'visual-geometric-phallic' space. Thirdly, modernism was connected not only to experimentation in the arts but also to philosophical reflection and the formation of the social sciences, including the critical inquiries of the FRANKFURT SCHOOL (see, e.g. Berman, 1989; Pippin, 1991). Most of these intellectual projects (including human geography) retained the social markings and erasures produced by the racialized, gendered and sexualized processes of othering that were written into modernism's prospectus.

Lunn's characterizations make most sense when applied to modern art and literature – in discussions of movements like surrealism and cubism – and probably have less purchase on modern architecture, which has its own chronologies and concerns (Frampton, 1985; Holston, 1989). These assumed a wider significance in the 1950s and 1960s when a so-called high modernism emerged as a dominant cultural thematic, distinguished by what Bürger (1992) describes as a 'pathos of purity'. 'In the same way as architecture divested itself of ornamental elements', he argues, so 'painting freed itself from the primacy of the representational, and the nouveau roman liberated itself from the categories of traditional fiction (plot and character)'. And in much the same way, and at much the same time, one could see SPATIAL SCIENCE divesting human geography of its interest in DIFFERENCE and differentiation, which became so many 'RESIDUALS' and so much 'noise', in order to reveal the purity of universal geometric form (often, like architecture, cast in terms of a FUNCTIONALISM). It would not be difficult to present other high modern movements in social thought in much the same way: e.g. STRUCTURALISM.

From such a perspective, POSTMODERNISM becomes a critique of high modernism. But equally important are its echoes and filiations with the early twentieth-century avant-garde: connections which, as Lunn (1985) shows, were particularly important for the development of western Marxism. Not for nothing does Berman (1983, 1992) urge the importance of reclaiming that earlier modernism. In fact, he suggests that it has its roots even earlier, in the nineteenth-century writings of Baudelaire and Marx, both of whom (in different ways) sought to come to terms with a world in which 'all that is solid melts into air'. Those most interested in elucidating such connections have often been concerned to establish the ways in which modernism and postmodernism bear on (and yield particular insights into) the production of space and SPATIALITY.

Thus Harvey (1989) sought to elucidate the web of connections between the cultural formations of modernism, the experience of TIME–SPACE COMPRESSION and the changing political economy of twentieth-century CAPITALISM, and this in turn provoked a critique of the ways in which modernist representations like Harvey's work to erase the gendering and sexualization of their maps of modernity (Deutsche, 1996). There have also been explorations of the ways in which the production of modern urban space can be illuminated through the writings of Walter Benjamin (1892–1941) (Gregory, 1994; Savage, 1995; see also Buck-Morss, 1989; Gilloch, 1996), and accounts of the continuities between surrealism and the cultural-political interventions of the SITUATIONISTS in the modern city (Bonnett, 1992; Pinder, 1996). These reflections have had noticeable effects on both the terrain of analysis (objects, methods) and the terrain of representation (strategies, media): most obviously in the carefully and consciously modernist work of US geographer Allan Pred. In particular, his experimental studies of the constellation between commodification, the culture of 'world exhibitions' and the formation of IDENTITIES in the late nineteenth and twentieth centuries make artful use of techniques of visual and verbal montage, and have been freely informed by Benjamin's example (Pred, 1995). Far from eclipsing modernism, therefore, the late twentieth-century rise of postmodernism has prompted many human geographers to provide more critical, constructive and discriminating readings of early twentieth-century modernism. DG

References

Anderson, P. 1984: Modernity and revolution. *New Left Review* 144: 96–113. · Berman, M. 1983: *All that is solid melts into air: the experience of modernity*. London: Verso. · Berman, M. 1992: Why modernism still matters. In S. Lash, and J. Friedman, eds, *Modernity and identity*. Oxford: Blackwell, 33–58. · Berman, R. 1989: *Modern culture and critical theory: art, politics and the legacy of the Frankfurt School*. Madison: University of Wisconsin Press. · Bonnett, A. 1992: Art, ideology and everyday space: subversive tendencies from dada to postmodernism. *Environment and Planning D: Society and Space* 10: 69–86. · Bradbury, M. 1976: The cities of modernism. In M. Bradbury, and J. McFarlane, eds, *Modernism 1890–1930*. London: Penguin, 96–104. · Buck-Morss, S. 1989: *The dialectics of seeing: Walter Benjamin and the Arcades Project*. Cambridge, MA: MIT Press. · Bürger, P. 1984: *Theory of the avant-garde*. Minneapolis: University of Minnesota Press. · Bürger, P. 1992: The disappearance of meaning. In S. Lash and J. Friedman, eds, *Modernity and identity*. Oxford: Blackwell, 94–112. · Deutsche, R. 1996: Men in space. Reprinted in her *Evictions: art and spatial politics*. Cambridge, MA: MIT Press, 195–202. · Eksteins, M. 1989: *The Rites of Spring: the Great War and the birth of the modern age*. Toronto: Lester and Orpen Dennys. · Frampton, K. 1985: *Modern architecture: a critical history*. London: Thames and Hudson. · Gilloch, G. 1996: *Myth and metropolis: Walter Benjamin and the city*. Cambridge: Polity Press. · Gregory, D. 1994: City/commodity/culture: spatiality and the politics of representation. In his *Geographical imaginations*. Cambridge, MA and Oxford: Blackwell, 214–56. · Harvey, D. 1989: *The condition of postmodernity: an enquiry into the origins of cultural change*. Oxford: Blackwell. · Hobsbawm, E. 1987: *The age of empire, 1875–1914*. London: Cardinal. · Holston, J. 1989: *The modernist city*. Chicago: University of Chicago Press. · Kern, S. 1983: *The culture of time and space, 1880–1918*. Cambridge, MA: Harvard University Press. · Lunn, E. 1985: *Marxism and modernism*. London: Verso. · Pinder, D. 1996: Subverting cartography: the situationists and maps of the city. *Environment and Planning A* 28: 405–28. · Pippin, R. 1991: *Modernism as a philosophical problem*. Oxford: Blackwell. · Pollock, G. 1988: Modernity and the spaces of femininity. In her *Vision and difference: femininity, feminism and histories of art*. London and New York: Routledge, 50–90. · Pred, A. 1995: *Recognizing European modernities. A montage of the present*. London and New York: Routledge. · Rabinow, P. 1989: *French modern: norms and forms of the social environment*. Cambridge, MA: MIT Press. · Savage, M. 1995: Walter Benjamin's urban thought: a critical analysis. *Environment and Planning D: Society and Space* 13: 201–16. · Timms, E. and Kelley, D., eds, 1985: *Unreal city: urban experience in modern European literature and art*. Manchester: Manchester University Press. · Torgovnick, M. 1990: *Gone primitive: savage intellects, modern lives*. Chicago: University of Chicago Press. · Wolff, J. 1990: The invisible flâneuse: women and the literature of modernity. In her *Feminine sentences: essays on women and culture*. Berkeley: University of California Press, 34–50. · Wright, G. 1991: *The politics of design in French colonial urbanism*. Chicago: University of Chicago Press.

Suggested Reading

Harvey (1989), ch. 2, 16. · Lunn (1985), ch. 2. · Pollock (1988).

modernity A particular constellation of power, knowledge and social practices whose emergence is usually traced back to Europe in the sixteenth and seventeenth centuries. Those early forms and structures changed over time and extended themselves over space until, by the middle of the twentieth century, modernity was widely supposed to constitute the dominant social order on the planet.

The terms 'modern' and 'modernity' occupy a central position within the DISCOURSE of EUROCENTRISM, which represents Europe as the central axis around which the rest of the world is supposed to revolve. Both terms have a long and complex history. Within Europe 'modern' was repeatedly employed to distinguish a new social order from previous ones. In post-Roman Europe, for example, the Latin *modernus* was used from the late fifth century to distinguish a Christian present from a pagan past, and for centuries the term was used to dramatize a renewed relationship to the ancient world. Relationships with other worlds – and most decisively the so-called 'New World' – began to assume a particular importance after 1492. Indeed, Dussel (1993) claims that it was then, in the wake of the voyages of Columbus, that 'modernity' was born as a concept, since it was then that 'Europe was in a position to pose itself against an other' and to constitute itself as a unified identity 'exploring, conquering, colonizing an alterity that gave back its image of itself' (cf. Greenblatt, 1991).

The first recorded English-language use of 'modernity' as a noun was not until 1627, and many intellectual historians place the origins of modernity as a world-view, as a horizon of meaning and expectation, in the seventeenth century (for a critical review, see Toulmin, 1990). At that time most writers continued to speak of 'our age' when describing their own present, however, but in the course of the eighteenth century many scholars elected to speak of *nova aetas* (the 'new age'). Toward the end of that century the idea of being modern acquired another layer of meaning when it came to be associated not only with 'newness' but also, significantly, with 'looking forward': with a sense of history as a process in which human beings could consciously and creatively intervene. This (new) sensibility is sometimes described as a discourse of *historicity* in which history becomes something that is made by human beings rather than something that merely happens to them. The 'Enlightenment project' was of decisive significance in the formulation of these ideals, with its belief in reason, rationality and progress towards truth, beauty and the just life (see ENLIGHTENMENT, GEOGRAPHY OF). The Enlightenment project had its critics, to be sure, and the violence of European COLONIALISM in the nineteenth century, the experience of two World Wars and a host of other bloody conflicts in the twentieth century left particularly deep marks on what Habermas (1981) identified more generally as the *project of modernity*. Yet common to virtually all post-Enlightenment discussions of modernity is an emphasis on novelty, change and progress. Two major axes of debate concern (a) 'tradition' and 'progress', and (b) 'time' and 'volatility'.

(a) *Tradition and progress*. Although 'the modern' came to be contrasted with – even opposed to – the 'traditional', this marks a site of considerable difficulty. On the one side, 'tradition' turns out to be more complex than most apologists for modernity have allowed. In particular, it would be quite wrong to think of supposedly traditional societies as stagnant (one of the central assumptions of ORIENTALISM) or as 'people without History' (one of the central assumptions of *primitivism*). In any case, modern societies have invented their own traditions (Hobsbawm and Ranger, 1983). On the other side, nominally modern, so-called 'post-traditional' societies have neither mapped a space of sovereign reason nor inaugurated a world of unbounded progress. It may well have been the case that, as Bauman (1991) remarks, 'Empires of unconfined and unchallenged sovereignty, and the truth of unlimited and uncontested universality, were the two arms with which modernity wished to remould the world according to the design of perfect order.' And to its most ardent advocates modernity was indeed an unqualified and unrestricted human good. It promised to enlist Reason to banish ignorance, misery and despotism: to free human beings from myth and superstition, from disease and hunger, from oppression and arbitrary rule. In the middle years of the twentieth century these aspirations culminated in various models of MODERNIZATION, whose development programmes sought to remake the so-called 'THIRD WORLD' in the liberal image of the West. While there have of course been major advances in science and technology, in production and politics, however, the triumph of modernity (if that is what it is) has not been accomplished without attendant violence and its critics have repeatedly insisted that modernity has always also had its dark side. Many of them have argued, in different ways, that modernity has installed novel grids of POWER and SURVEILLANCE that have confined HUMAN AGENCY, consciousness and creativity within what Max Weber once called an 'iron cage' of ABSTRACTION, bureaucracy and regulation. It was within something like this grid – through its networks and spaces – that Michel Foucault (1975, 1977) saw 'the disciplines' (including, centrally, the human sciences) being applied to the distinctively modern constitution of the human body, the human subject and the human population. This critique of a sovereign Reason and its corollary powers has been advanced with particular vigour by scholars working under the sign of POST-STRUCTURALISM. Informed by these ideas, this critique has been given a vital inflection by (i) *feminist theory*, which identifies a persistent and unmarked MASCULINISM and PHALLOCENTRISM at the very centre of modern 'Reason', and by (ii) *post-colonial theory*, which identifies a 'white mythology' within the 'epistemic violence' wrought by the colonizing 'Reason' of the West (see POST-COLONIALISM). But even those writers who have tried to redeem the project of modernity in the face of these criticisms have acknowledged its deformations: hence Habermas's (1987a) claim that the rationalization processes characteristic of modernity have 'over-extended' themselves to such a degree that the ordinary LIFEWORLD is presently being 'colonized' by the abstractions of a constitutively modern SYSTEM (see CRITICAL THEORY).

(b) *Time and volatility*. Closely connected to these remarks, it has become commonplace to connect modernity to a changed consciousness of time. Many of its influential critics have worked within a *cognitive-instrumental analytic* that is predisposed towards time as the measure of the modern (see also TIME, GEOGRAPHY AND). Thus modernity as discontinuity, a punctuation point in human history; modernity as velocity, an acceleration in the speed of social change; and modernity as intensity, a transformation in the regimes of what E.P. Thompson (1967) called 'time-discipline'. All three motifs appear in Marx's critique of POLITICAL ECONOMY, for example, where the construction of CAPITALISM as a MODE OF PRODUCTION is made to revolve around time as embodied in labour, materialized in the COMMODITY and appropriated as surplus value. Indeed, Marx pointed to an essential connection between modernity and the 'creative destruction' of capitalism that issued in a world in which:

> All fixed and fast-frozen relations, with their train of ancient and venerable prejudices are swept away, all new-formed ones become antiquated before they can ossify. All that is solid melts into air. (See Berman (1982) for an extended discussion.)

Other critics of modernity have emphasized an *aesthetic–affective analytic*, and the need to capture the movements of modern time as what the poet Charles Baudelaire described as 'the transient, the fleeting, the contingent'. Baudelaire's views of modernity were more complicated than this implies, but it was none the less that fixation on time, a sense of restless animation, of a break with tradition, of a celebration of the new, that propelled a series of avant-garde movements through the nineteenth and into the early twentieth centuries (see also MODERNISM). Indeed, Habermas treats modernity as 'the epoch that lives for the future, that opens itself up to the novelty of the future' precisely because it is no longer possible (so he says) to appeal to myth or tradition for legitimation:

> Modernity can and will no longer borrow the criteria by which it takes its orientation from the models supplied by another epoch; it has to create its normativity out of itself. Modernity sees itself cast back upon itself without any possibility of escape. (Habermas, 1987b, p. 7)

Giddens (1990, pp. 38–9) similarly regards what he calls *reflexivity* – the constant examination and modification of social practices – as focal to the configuration of modernity. His is not Foucault's reading of the human sciences – although the emergence of these specialized discourses has had an immense bearing on the conduct of social life (Rabinow, 1989) – because he is more interested in the ways in which these processes of monitoring and modification contribute to the volatility of the modern world: 'New knowledge (concepts, theories, findings) does not simply render the social world more transparent, but alters its nature, spinning it off in novel directions' (Giddens, 1990, p. 153). This has reached such a pitch, Giddens argues, that the world is presently in a condition of radicalized modernity.

These twin preoccupations cut in different directions: the first (a) emphasizes a systematic grid of power and a process of rational ordering carried within the project of modernity, while the second (b) emphasizes flux, flow and volatility as intrinsic to the modern world. They find common ground in constructing a threshold – a discontinuity – between the 'pre-modern' and the 'modern'. Both versions have left their mark on the constitution and conduct of human geography, but there are two other sets of issues where a more explicitly 'geographical discourse of modernity' comes directly to the fore (Gregory, 1998). Interestingly, these other sensibilities radically challenge the notion of a 'Great Divide' and substitute a more complex, uneven and foliated process of social change. They are closely connected, suggesting in programmatic ways crucial connections between the 'production of SPACE' and the 'production of NATURE'. These two axes of debate concern (c) 'space' and 'place', and (d) 'CULTURE' and 'nature'.

(c) *Space and place*. Some historians have identified the emergence of modernity with the European colonization of the 'New World' and the formation of a 'modern world system' centred on Europe as early as the sixteenth century (Wallerstein, 1974; cf. WORLD-SYSTEMS ANALYSIS). This series of events established new relations between places – and the possibility of new spaces – and was folded into significant changes in modes of artistic, literary and scientific expression (Albanese, 1996). Other writers have suggested that processes of GLOBALIZATION and TIME–SPACE COMPRESSION subsequently intensified to such a degree in the course of the nineteenth and twentieth centuries that other, still more profound crises of representation ensued. What Jay (1992) described as the dominant 'scopic regime of modernity' – 'Cartesian perspectivalism' – was called into question and constructions of abstract space multiplied endlessly (see PRODUCTION OF SPACE). The production of these new spaces was bound in to new formations of CLASS, GENDER, SEXUALITY and 'RACE', and they could be traced in artistic, literary and scientific registers (Lefebvre, 1992). Many of those that impacted most directly on everyday life have been traced back to the creative destruction of successive regimes of CAPITALISM that restructured landscapes of ACCUMULATION (Harvey, 1989); to the intensified production of colonial forms of spatiality that sought to impose metropolitan, 'rational' spaces over indigenous, supposedly 'non-rational' spaces (Mills, 1996; Berland, 1997); to the physical separation of information transmission from the movement of people (through the development of the telegraph, the radio, television and new electronic media) that produced dramatically new representational spaces (Kern, 1983); and to the experience of modern forms of warfare that shattered established conceptions of landscapes of military conflict (Eksteins, 1989).

These accounts typically flow from and feed back into a scenario in which modernity is realized through the production of an abstract, rational, planned space that characteristically generates a collective alienation from the particularities of PLACE. The theoretical vocabularies differ from one discourse to another: the space of modernity has been described as an optical-geometric-phallocentric space, a panoptical-partitioned-disciplined space, and a measured-directed-standardized space (cf. Harris, 1991). But this is literally a 'master-narrative' that, to some critics, cedes far too much power to a singular and transcendent modernity. Thus Gibson-Graham (1996) can describe all of these characterizations as moments in the discursive production of a 'rape-script' that normalizes an act of non-reciprocal penetration in which non-modern forms inevitably become damaged, violated, fallen; mastered by the spaces of an advancing modernity they are sites of a lack, always and everywhere impending targets for invasion, submission, colonization. Against this one-dimensional narrative, several writers have urged the careful recognition of complex, foliated spaces of TRANSCULTURATION: 'contact zones' of encounter and entanglement in which cultures interpenetrate and interrupt one another. In place of the binary model of the 'Great Divide', for example, Ogborn (1998) treats modernity 'as a matter of the hybrid relationships and connections between places'. He emphasizes that this differentiated and plural understanding of modernity distributes transformations 'across a range of connected sites, scenes and networks' and, equally important, that these 'geographies of connection are moments in the making of modernities rather than being matters of their transfer or imposition' (see also Pred and Watts, 1992; cf. REGIONS AND REGIONAL GEOGRAPHY).

(d) *'Culture' and 'Nature'*. Many accounts of modernity depend upon a Eurocentric opposition between 'culture' and 'nature' that is put in place through two discursive strategies (Gregory, 1998). The first involves the *discrimination of nature*. Thus non-modern cultures are supposed to be 'at one' with nature, creatures of their natures, intimately embedded in and even indistinguishable from their surrounding ecologies, whereas modern cultures are distinguished precisely by their distance from and domination over nature. Claims like these were given a special force in Europe, when 'disordered, active nature' was made to submit to the probes of a new experimental science and a new, mechanical technology. As the slumbering powers of nature were released, harnessed, domesticated and turned to productive account through AGRICULTURAL REVOLUTIONS and INDUSTRIAL REVOLUTIONS, so this aggressively modern culture turned its attention to the colonization of 'other' natures. This activated a second discursive strategy, the *normalization of nature*, in which European, 'temperate' nature was constituted as normal nature from which privileged position all other natures – seductive and terrifying by turns (Arnold, 1996) – were seen as extremes, departures, or deviations. These two discursive strategies had immense politico-ecological consequences, but they also had profoundly important politico-cultural consequences because they were shot through with implications of class, 'race' and gender. Both turned on a process of purification in which the achievement of modernity was signalled through its supposedly triumphant separation of 'culture' from 'nature'.

In Latour's (1993) view, however, this is profoundly mistaken. He insists that the so-called project of modernity rests not only on this acknowledged and sanctioned process of purification but also on its unacknowledged and subversive dual: on a process of translation that creates 'entirely new types of beings, hybrids of nature and culture' (see also Whatmore, 1998). These creations are extraordinarily consequential, Latour agrees, but he insists that their various powers do not reside in any 'modernity': rather, they are released through the production and proliferation of 'networks' (see ACTOR–NETWORK THEORY). Latour accepts some of these networks have become more extensive than others and thereby allowed for the differential accumulation of power and knowledge at particular sites. But he insists that this asymmetry does not sustain any 'Great Divide' between the 'pre-modern' and the 'modern'. On the contrary, Latour argues that 'we have never been modern': from which it logically follows that neither can we have become postmodern (cf. POSTMODERNISM; POSTMODERNITY). DG

References

Albanese, D. 1996: *New science, new world*. Durham: Duke University Press. · Arnold, D. 1996: *The problem of nature*. Oxford and Cambridge, MA: Blackwell. · Bauman, Z. 1991: *Modernity and ambivalence*. Cambridge: Polity Press. · Beck, U. 1992: *Risk society: towards a new modernity*. London: Sage. · Berland, J. 1997: Space at the margins: colonial spatiality and critical theory after Innis. *Topia* 1: 55–82. · Berman, M. 1982: *All that is solid melts into air: the experience of modernity*. New York: Simon and Schuster; London: Verso. · Dussel, E. 1993: Eurocentrism and modernity. *Boundary* 2. · Eksteins, M. 1989: *Rites of spring: the Great War and the birth of the modern age*. Toronto: Lester and Orpen Dennys. · Foucault, M. 1975: *Discipline and punish*. London: Penguin. · Foucault, M. 1977: *The history of sexuality, vol. 1: An introduction*. London: Penguin. · Gibson-Graham, J.-K. 1996: *The end of capitalism (as we knew it): a feminist critique of political economy*. Oxford and Cambridge, MA: Blackwell. · Giddens, A. 1990: *The consequences of modernity*. Cambridge: Polity Press; Stanford, CA: Stanford University Press. · Greenblatt, S. 1991: *Marvellous possessions: the wonder of the New World*. Chicago: University of Chicago Press. · Gregory, D. 1998: The geographical discourse of modernity. In *Explorations in critical human geography*. Heidelberg: University of Heidelberg, 45–67; reprinted in his forthcoming *The colonial present*. Oxford and Cambridge, MA: Blackwell. · Habermas, J. 1981: Modernity versus postmodernity. *New German Critique* 22: 3–14. · Habermas, J. 1987a: *The theory of communicative action, vol. 2: The critique of functionalist reason*. Cambridge: Polity Press. · Habermas, J. 1987b: *The philosophical discourse of modernity*. Cambridge: Polity Press. · Harris, R.C. 1991: Power, modernity and historical geography. *Annals of the Association of American Geographers* 81: 671–83. · Harvey, D. 1989: *The condition of postmodernity: an inquiry into the origins of cultural change*. Oxford and Cambridge, MA: Blackwell. · Hobsbawm, E. and Ranger, T., eds, 1983: *The invention of tradition*. Cambridge: Cambridge University Press. · Horkheimer, M. and Adorno, T. 1974: *Dialectic of Enlightenment*. New York: Seabury. · Jay, M. 1992: Scopic regimes of modernity. In S. Lash and J. Friedman, eds, *Modernity and identity*. Oxford and Cambridge, MA: Blackwell, 178–93. · Kern, S. 1983: *The culture of time and space 1880–1918*. Cambridge, MA: Harvard University Press. · Latour, B. 1993: *We have never been modern*. Cambridge, MA: Harvard University Press. · Lefebvre, H. 1992: *The production of space*. Oxford and Cambridge, MA: Blackwell. · Mills, S. 1996: Gender and colonial space. *Gender, Place and Culture* 3: 125–47. · Ogborn, M. 1998: *Spaces of modernity: London's geographies 1680–1780*. New York: Guilford. · Pred, A. and Watts, M. 1992: *Reworking modernity: capitalism and symbolic discontent*. New Brunswick, NJ: Rutgers University Press. · Rabinow, P. 1989: *French modern: norms and forms of the social environment*. Cambridge, MA: MIT Press. · Thompson, E.P. 1967: Time, work-discipline and industrial capitalism. *Past and Present* 38: 56–97. · Toulmin, S. 1990: *Cosmopolis: the hidden agenda of modernity*. New York: The Free Press. · Wallerstein, I. 1974: *The modern world system: capitalist agriculture and the origins of the European world economy in the sixteenth century*. London: Academic Press. · Whatmore, S. 1998: Hybrid geographies: rethinking the 'Human' in Human Geography. In D. Massey, J. Allen and P. Sarre, eds, *Human Geography today*. Cambridge: Polity Press, 22–39.

Suggested Reading

Gregory (1998). · Harvey (1989), ch. 2. · Ogborn (1998), ch. 1.

modernization A process of social change resulting from the DIFFUSION and adoption of the characteristics of expansive and apparently more advanced societies through societies which are apparently less advanced (see DUAL ECONOMY). Modernization involves social mobilization, the growth of a more effective and centralized apparatus of political and social control, the acceptance of scientifically rational norms and the transformation of social relations (see MODE OF PRODUCTION; Taylor, 1979) and aesthetic forms. The five linear stages of economic growth proposed by Rostow (1960; 1978; see ROSTOW MODEL) point to the importance of the Cold War as a crucial formative context in which notions of modernization were developed. Indeed, the sub-title of Rostow's book – *a non-communist manifesto* – makes this connection directly whilst Peet (1991) demonstrates the links between notions of modernization and structural FUNCTIONALISM.

As Hobsbawm (1979) pointed out, however, DISCOURSES of modernization such as those promoted by Rostow also offer an ideological framework within which the idea and practice of DEVELOPMENT may be interpreted – not least the notion that underdevelopment is a consequence of conditions internal to the underdeveloped society. However, such an IDEOLOGY abstracts from the deeper and wider tendency towards modernization and a postmodern world (Harvey, 1989) associated with the 'remarkable . . . historical geography of capitalism' (Harvey, 1982, p. 373) and its dramatic transformation of VALUES, SOCIETIES and LANDSCAPES across the globe (see POSTMODERNISM). In a passage written at the same time, and remarkably similar to Harvey's, Marshall Berman (1982, p. 16) refers to the 'social processes that bring this maelstrom into being, and keep it in a state of perpetual becoming', as 'modernization'. This is connected with but distinguished from MODERNISM – which Berman refers to as

> the amazing variety of visions and ideas that aim to make men and women the subjects as well as the objects of modernization, to give them the power to change the world that is changing them to make their way through the maelstrom and make it their own

and from 'MODERNITY' seen as

> a mode of vital experience – experience of space and time, of the self and others, of life's possibilities and perils – that is shared by men and women all over the world today.

These distinctions point up Rostowian-inspired discourses of modernization and development as exercises in objectification.

The translation of modernization into a geography of development was closely associated with the 'new' geography of spatial organization and locational analysis of the mid- to late-1960s (e.g. Soja, 1968; Gould, 1970; Riddell, 1970; Soja and Tobin, 1972; cf. LOCATIONAL ANALYSIS; SPATIAL SCIENCE). It conceived of modernization as the creation and spread of a network of urban GROWTH POLES orientated to external markets and through which INNOVATIONS and so development would diffuse throughout a nationally based central place hierarchy (see CENTRAL PLACE THEORY). Modernization is seen as a recursive process as the social and environmental changes induced by it redefine the framework within which it continues to take place.

Like all models of change based upon the stages of growth, modernization emphasizes the temporally uneven nature and complexity of social change. However, the notion also implies a unilinear and teleological process of change (see TELEOLOGY). Modernization is an apparently unproblematic process of social adoption throughout a universal society. The outcome is known in advance: modernization is defined in Eurocentric terms (Hettne, 1990) and the process and direction of change are therefore predetermined. Notions of empowerment and disempowerment (see UNDERDEVELOPMENT) and the contested establishment of particular forms of social and environmental relations are ignored. The modernizing society is, apparently, infinitely pliable and may be pulled and stretched to conform with the parameters of modernization. The implication of modernization is that its subject societies have no history, CULTURE or developed set of social or environmental relations. This is an example of a profoundly culturally racist view of the world (see Blaut, 1992).

Furthermore, modernization is often conceived as an autonomous process of change rather than as the product of the integration of pre-existing societies and their subsequent disintegration and restructuring in line with the tenets of modernization. One consequence of such a view and of its influence upon policy and the legitimation of economic and social action is the generation of underdevelopment. For example, industrialization is still often seen as the path to modernity but, as Knox and Agnew (1998) point out, this view implies the existence of apparently limited multiplier effects in agriculture (see MULTIPLIERS), the notion that agriculturalists are inherently conservative, and the belief that only industry is productive in terms of its potential for PRODUCTIVITY increases, and increasing marginal returns through ECONOMIES OF SCALE. The valuable locally based, often environmentally sensitive, systems of production are thus replaced and their practitioners displaced by a process of change which leads to unsustainable social, environmental and geographical disruption and polarization.

In short, modernization is more than an abstraction, a 'comfortable myth' (Brookfield, 1975, p. 76), which denies the concrete and complex processes of change and struggle in real social formations. It is an environmentally and socially destructive ideology (Blaikie, 1985; Blaikie and Brookfield, 1987; Watts, 1992/96; Watts and McCarthy, 1997) which still retains a power to shape trajectories of economic development within which sustainability is problematic (Adams, 1995). And it is still more than that: as a global set of social relations providing the predominant conditions of existence in the struggle to make a living, capitalism provides the immensely powerful social and material commonality in which postmodern struggles and conflicts are played out. RL

References

Adams, W. 1995: Sustainable development? In R.J. Johnston, M.J. Watts and P.J. Taylor, eds, *Geographies of global change. Remapping the world in the late twentieth century*, ch. 21. Oxford and Cambridge, MA: Blackwell, 354–373. · Berman, M. 1982: *All that is solid melts into air: the experience of modernity.* New York: Simon and Schuster. · Blaikie, P.M. 1985: *The political economy of soil erosion in developing countries.* London: Longman. · Blaikie, P. and Brookfield, H., eds, 1987: *Land degradation and society.* London and New York: Methuen. · Blaut, J.M. 1992: Fourteen ninety-two. *Political Geography* 11: 335–86. · Brookfield, H. 1975: *Interdependent development.* London: Methuen; Pittsburgh, Pa.: University of Pittsburgh Press. · Gould, P. 1970: Tanzania 1920–63: the spatial impress of the modernisation process. *World Politics* 22 2: 149–70. · Harvey, D. 1982: *The limits to capital.* Oxford and Cambridge, MA: Blackwell. · Harvey, D. 1989: *The condition of postmodernity.* Oxford and Cambridge, MA: Blackwell, ch. 5, 99–112. · Hettne, B. 1990: *Development theory and the three worlds.* Harlow: Longman. · Hobsbawm, E.J. 1979: The development of the world economy. *Cambridge Journal of Economics* 3: 305–18. · Knox, P. and Agnew, J. 1998: *The geography of the world economy*, 3rd edn. London and New York: Arnold. · Peet, R. 1991: *Global capitalism: theories of societal development.* London: Routledge. · Riddell, J.B. 1970: *The spatial dynamics of modernisation in Sierra Leone: structure, diffusion and response.* Evanston, Ill.: Northwestern University Press. · Rostow, W.W. 1960: *The stages of economic growth: a non-communist manifesto.* Cambridge: Cambridge University Press. · Rostow, W.W. 1978: *The world economy: history and prospect.* London: Macmillan. · Soja, E.W. 1968: *The geography of modernization in Africa.* Syracuse: Syracuse University Press. · Soja, E.W. and Tobin, R.J. 1972: The geography of modernisation: paths, patterns and processes of spatial change in developing countries. In R. Brunner and G. Brewer, eds, *A political approach to the study of political development and change.* Beverly Hills, CA: Sage Publications. · Taylor, J.G. 1979: *From modernisation to modes of production: a critique of the sociologies of development and underdevelopment.* London: Macmillan; Atlantic Highlands, NJ: Humanities Press. · Watts, M. 1992: The shock of modernity: petroleum, protest and fast capitalism in an industrializing society. In A. Pred and M. Watts, *Reworking modernity: capitalisms and symbolic discontent*, ch. 2. New Brunswick, NJ: Rutgers University Press; reprinted in S. Daniels and R. Lee, eds, 1996: *Exploring human geography.* London: Arnold, ch. 6, 120–52. · Watts, M.J. 1993: Development I: power, knowledge, discursive practice. *Progress in Human Geography* 17 2: 257–72. · Watts, M. and McCarthy, J. 1997: Nature as artifice, nature as artefact: development, environment and modernity in the late twentieth century. In R. Lee and J. Wills, eds, *Geographies of economies*, ch. 6. London and New York: Arnold, 71–86;

Suggested Reading

Corbridge, S. 1986: *Capitalist world development.* London: Macmillan, ch. 1. · Corbridge, S. 1995: *Development studies: a reader.* London and New York: Arnold, section one. · Hobsbawm (1979). · Peet (1991), ch. 3. · Routledge, P. 1995: Resisting and reshaping the modern: social movements and the development process. In R.J. Johnston, M.J. Watts and P.J. Taylor, eds, *Geographies of global change: remapping the world in the late twentieth century*, ch. 16. Oxford and Cambridge, MA: Blackwell, 263–79. · Watts (1992/96). · Watts and McCarthy (1997).

modifiable areal unit problem A particular form of ECOLOGICAL FALLACY associated with the aggregation of data into areal units for geographical analysis.

Most geographical data refer to points in space – such as individual dwellings and workplaces – but many CENSUSES and other sources aggregate these into spatial units (such as CENSUS TRACTS) in order to preserve anonymity. Those spatial units form the 'individuals' used in geographical analysis, from which INFERENCES may be drawn about the individuals within the units: Robinson's classic exposé of the ecological fallacy, for example, showed that a high correlation between two variables at a particular spatial aggregation (in his case, between percentage black and percentage illiterate at the State scale in the US) should not imply a similar correlation at the individual level (that blacks are more likely to be illiterate).

Openshaw (1977, 1984) extended Robinson's work by showing that when data are aggregated spatially the ecological fallacy can be decomposed into two effects. With the *scale effect*, the larger the unit of aggregation the larger on average is the CORRELATION between two variables. There is also an *aggregation effect* because of the very large number of different ways in which, for example, the 500,000 or so residents of the city of Sheffield could be grouped into 29 wards, each comprising a contiguous block of territory and containing about 17,000 residents. Openshaw has shown that if you construct a large number of the possible aggregations for such a situation, you obtain a FREQUENCY DISTRIBUTION for the correlation between two variables across those aggregation units which, although it may be leptokurtic and have most of its values around the distribution mean, could cover the full range of possible values from −1.00 to +1.00 (hence the title of Openshaw and Taylor, 1987).

Openshaw's arguments regarding scale and aggregation effects caution against inferring individual relationships from one aggregation only. To the extent that the spatial division used is arbitrary and unrelated to the nature of the phenomena being analysed, therefore, Openshaw's findings counsel care in data analysis and interpretation. (They also suggest that researchers wanting to produce a particular result could do so by evaluating the many possible optional aggregations open to them until they find one that 'fits'!)

The development of computer programs for assessing the extent of the modifiable areal unit problem (i.e. by generating the frequency distribution for the correlation under consideration) has also allowed advances in the evaluation of procedures for aggregating smaller areal units into larger ones. In the UK, for example, Parliamentary constituencies are constructed by grouping contiguous electoral wards. Johnston and Rossiter (1982) showed that in many parts of England the relative success of the two main political parties can be substantially influenced by the particular aggregation selected by the neutral Parliamentary Boundary Commission whereas in the USA Cirincione and Gurrieri (1997) have suggested the use of similar computer-intensive methods as a means of evaluating allegations of racial GERRYMANDERING in the definition of Congressional Districts. RJJ

References

Cirincione, C. and Gurrieri, G. 1997: Computer-intensive methods in the social sciences. *Social Science Computer Review* 15: 83–97. · Johnston, R.J. and Rossiter, D.J. 1982: Constituency building, political representation and electoral bias in urban England. In D.T. Herbert and R.J. Johnston, eds, *Geography and the urban environment: progress in research and applications*, volume 5. Chichester and New York: John Wiley, 113–55. · Openshaw, S. 1977: A geographical study of scale and aggregation problems in region-building, partitioning and spatial modelling. *Transactions, Institute of British Geographers*. NS 2: 459–72. · Openshaw, S. 1984: *The modifiable areal unit problem*. Concepts and techniques in modern geography 38. Norwich: Geo Books. · Openshaw, S. and Taylor, P.J. 1979: A million or so correlation coefficients: three experiments on the modifiable areal unit problem. In R.J. Bennett, N.J. Thrift and N. Wrigley, eds, *Statistical applications in the spatial sciences*. London: Pion Ltd.

Suggested Reading

Duncan, O.D., Cuzzort, R.P. and Duncan, B. 1961: *Statistical geography*. Glencoe, IL: The Free Press; King, G. 1997: *A solution to the ecological inference problem: reconstructing individual behavior from aggregate data*. Princeton, NJ: Princeton University Press.

money and finance, geography of The study of the relationships between money, space and place. Compared with other social science disciplines, human geography was slow to recognize the importance of money and finance in the unfolding of social life. There were hardly any attempts to write geographies of money before the 1980s (for exceptions, see Kircher, 1961; Code, 1971; Conzen, 1975, 1977), but an important new sub-field of geographical research has since emerged (Leyshon and Thrift, 1997); this is conveniently divided into four main areas, each of which corresponds to a particular SCALE of geographical analysis.

The first area of research has focused upon the systemic implications of money and finance at the scale of the economic system as a whole, best exemplified by David Harvey's (1982, 1989) work. As part of his MARXIST analysis of the geographical dynamics of CAPITALISM, Harvey draws attention to the central role played by the financial system in the capitalist economy which revolves around money; money delivers social power to those who possess it, so that capitalism may be interpreted as a system for the generation of money and, in turn, social power. The social power of money gives those individuals and institutions that possess it in abundance a privileged place within capitalism, so that over time the structure of the capitalist economy may be seen to be bending in line with the interests of money and finance. One of the outcomes of this process is TIME–SPACE COMPRESSION, whereby the speed of economic life accelerates as money and finance is moved about the economy in a continuous effort to reduce the turnover time of capital, dislocating the rest of the economic and political system as it does so (Harvey, 1989). The rise of ever more efficient information and communication technologies, combined with the introduction of more permissive national regimes of financial regulation during the 1980s and 1990s, has made money increasingly mobile globally. While these developments have not brought about the 'end of geography' for money and finance which has been heralded by some (for example, see O'Brien, 1992; cf. Martin, 1994), they have made governments more sensitive to the vagaries of increasingly powerful international financial markets. This has led some commentators to argue that at a systemic level the capitalist economy is subject to a system of

'GOVERNANCE without government', which ultimately is in thrall to the imperatives of the international financial system (Gill, 1992; Thrift and Leyshon, 1994).

The second area of research has focused upon the regional effects of money and finance, especially financial services industry restructuring. Informed by the theories of NEO-LIBERALISM, leading economies in North America, Europe and Southeast Asia have, since the 1970s, sought to re-regulate their financial services industries to improve efficiency and increase competition (Moran, 1984, 1991). During the 1980s, these developments brought about a general increase in retail financial service employment, and human geographers documented and explained the uneven geographies of growth (Leyshon, Thrift and Tommey, 1989; Gentle, Marshall and Coombes, 1991; Marshall, Gentle, Raybould and Coombes, 1992). During the 1990s, the industry underwent a more profound process of restructuring, as competition intensified and new technologies and forms of organization, such as telephone call centres, credit scoring systems and customer databases, were installed; geographers have documented the causes and outcomes of this more uncertain period for the retail financial services industry (Lord, 1992; Leyshon and Thrift, 1993; Marshall and Richardson, 1996; Wills, 1996; Leyshon, Thrift and Pratt, 1998).

The third area of research has focused upon the urban dynamics of money, comprising two main strands. The first seeks to explain the success and persistence of financial centres, which are spatially constrained and transaction-intensive places of monetary exchange. Geographers have sought to explain why, in a world of time–space compression and increasingly mobile money, financial centres such as the City of London, New York and Tokyo continue to control the majority of the world's financial activity (Thrift, 1994; Thrift and Leyshon, 1994). The answer is to be found in the ways financial centres facilitate close interpersonal contact through episodes of co-presence. This facilitates the rapid generation, capture, interpretation and representation of business information (Boden, 1994; Boden and Moltoch, 1995), including financial information (Pryke, 1991; Allen and Pryke, 1994). The financial centre may therefore be seen as a collective way of coping with the vast amount of monetary information which circulates within the global economy. It is a centre of financial expertise founded in a 'complex division of labour embodied in the skills of the workforce, in machines, texts and so on' (Thrift, 1994, p. 375), and which collectively generates and disseminates financial information as well as interpretations and narratives about what this information actually means. This is the reason why it is unlikely that financial centres 'will simply melt away into a generalised "space of flows"... leaving money obligations to speed their way along the cables and through the aether (sic), to and from many different terminals located in many different places' across the global economy (Thrift, 1994, p. 327). The second area of research on the urban dynamics of money focuses upon spaces of FINANCIAL EXCLUSION, those places where poor and disadvantaged groups are directly and indirectly excluded from the financial system and denied access to mainstream retail financial services (Leyshon and Thrift, 1995; Dymski and Veitch, 1996).

The fourth and final area of research has analysed money at the institutional and individual scale, with particular attention being paid to the bodies that perform tasks in service of the monetary and financial system. This work has focused in the main upon the changing 'gender cultures' of financial institutions (Jones, 1997), such as the overthrow of cultures of paternalistic masculinity within British retail banking (Halford and Savage, 1995, 1997) and analyses of labour market segregation within the City of London, and the ways in which highly paid jobs in corporate finance and dealing are implicitly and explicitly coded as masculine (McDowell and Court, 1994a, b, c; McDowell, 1994a, 1997). AL

References

Allen, J. and Pryke, M. 1994: The production of service space. *Environment and Planning D: Society and Space* 12: 453–75. · Boden, D. 1994: *The business of talk: organizations in action*. Cambridge: Polity Press. · Boden, D. and Molotch, H. 1995: The compulsion of proximity. In R. Friedland and D. Boden, eds, *Now/here: time, space and modernity*. Berkeley: University of California Press. · Code, W.R. 1971: *The spatial dynamics of financial intermediaries: an interpretation of the distribution of financial decision-making in Canada*. Ph.D. dissertation, Berkeley, University of California. · Conzen, M.P. 1975: Capital flows and the developing urban hierarchy: state bank capital in Wisconsin, 1854–1895. *Economic Geography* 51: 321–38. · Conzen, M.P. 1977: The maturing urban system in the United States, 1840–1910. *Annals of the Association of American Geographers* 67: 88–108. · Dymski, G. and Veitch, J. 1996: Financial transformation and the metropolis: booms, busts, and banking in Los Angeles. *Environment and Planning A* 28: 1233–60. · Gentle, C.J.S., Marshall, J.N. and Coombes, M.G. 1991: Business reorganization and regional development: the case of the British building societies movement. *Environment and Planning A* 23: 1759–77. · Gill, S. 1992: Economic globalisation and the internationalisation of authority: limits and contradictions. *Geoforum* 23: 269–83. · Halford, S. and Savage, M. 1995: Restructuring organisations, changing people: gender and restructuring in banking and local government. *Work, Employment and Society* 9: 97–122. · Halford, S. and Savage, M. 1997: Rethinking restructuring: embodiment, agency and identity in organizational change. In R. Lee and J. Wills, eds, *Geographies of economies*. London: Arnold, 108–17. · Harvey, D. 1982: *The limits to capital*. Oxford: Blackwell. · Harvey, D. 1989: *The condition of postmodernity*. Oxford: Blackwell. · Jones, A. 1997: (Re)producing gender cultures: theorising gender in investment banking recruitment. *Geoforum*. · Kircher, H.B. 1961: *The geography of financial agglomeration in the United States*. Ph.D. dissertation, Clark University. · Leyshon, A. and Thrift, N. 1993: The restructuring of the financial services industry in the 1990s: a reversal of fortune. *Journal of Rural Studies* 9: 223–41. · Leyshon, A., and Thrift, N. 1995: Geographies of financial exclusion: financial abandonment in Britain and the United States. *Transactions, Institute of British Geographers* NS 20: 312–41. · Leyshon, A., and Thrift, N. 1997: *Money/space: geographies of monetary transformation*. London: Routledge. · Leyshon, A., Thrift, N. and Pratt, J. 1998: Reading financial services: texts, consumers and financial literacy. *Environment and Planning D: Society and Space* 16: 29–55. · Leyshon, A., Thrift, N. and Tommey, C. 1989: The rise of the British provincial financial centre. *Progress in Planning* 31(3): 151–229. · Lord, J.D. 1992: Geographic deregulation of the U.S. banking industry and spatial transfers of corporate control. *Urban Geography* 13: 25–48. · Marshall, J.N., Gentle, C.J.S., Raybould, S. and Coombes, M. 1992: Regulatory change, corporate restructuring and the spatial development of the British financial sector. *Regional Studies* 26: 453–67. · Marshall, J.N. and Richardson, R. 1996: The impact of 'telemediated' services on corporate structures: the example of 'branchless' retail banking in Britain. *Environment and Planning A* 28: 1843–58. · Martin, R. 1994: Stateless monies, global financial integration and national economic autonomy: the end of geography? In S. Corbridge, N. Thrift and R. Martin, eds, *Money, power and space*. Oxford: Blackwell, 253–78. · McDowell, L. 1994: Social justice, organizational culture and workplace democracy: cultural imperialism in the City of London. *Urban Geography* 15: 661–80. · McDowell, L. 1997: *Capital culture: gender at work in the city*. Oxford: Blackwell. · McDowell, L. and Court, G. 1994a: Gender divisions of labour in the post-Fordist economy: the maintenance of occupational sex segregation in the financial services sector. *Environment and Planning A* 26: 1397–418. · McDowell, L. and Court, G. 1994b: Missing subjects: gender, power, and sexuality in merchant banking. *Economic Geography* 70: 229–51. · McDowell, L. and Court, G. 1994c: Performing work: bodily representations in merchant banks. *Environment and Planning D: Society and Space* 12: 727–50. · Moran, M. 1984: *The politics of banking: the strange case of competition and credit control*. London: Macmillan. · Moran, M. 1991: *The politics of the financial services revolution: the USA, UK and Japan*. London: Macmillan. · O'Brien, R. 1992: *Global financial integration: the end of geography*. London: Pinter. · Pryke, M. 1991: An international city going 'global': spatial change in the City of London. *Environment and Planning D: Society and Space* 9: 197–222. · Thrift, N. 1994: On the social and cultural determinants of international financial centres: the case of the City of London. In S. Corbridge, N. Thrift and R. Martin, eds, *Money, power and space*. Oxford: Blackwell, 327–55. · Thrift, N. and Leyshon, A. 1994: A phantom state? The de-traditionalization of money, the international financial system and international financial centres. *Political Geography* 13: 299–327. · Wills, J. 1996: Uneven reserves: geographies of banking trade unionism. *Regional Studies* 30: 359–72.

Suggested Reading

Leyshon and Thrift (1997). · McDowell (1997). · Thrift (1994).

monuments Built memorials, usually in the form of public statuary or other symbolic architecture, are designed and constructed to commemorate a sense of national or local identity and symbolize a collective memory of events or persons. Public monuments have been used in this way largely since the nineteenth century, to cultivate national identity, to present in 'heroic' form figures of national historical importance and, thus, to commemorate a sense both of place and of significant historical events. Geographers have only relatively recently turned to study public monuments as a way of understanding the ways in which cultural identity, at national and local SCALES, is constructed or resisted at the popular level (see also NATION; NATIONALISM). Harvey's (1979) study of the Basilica of the Sacre Coeur in Paris was a pioneering paper in this respect, in which he documented the contested political meaning of the building and its site in Montmartre for conservatives and communards alike in nineteenth-century Paris and demonstrated the ways in which the monument could be read as a way of understanding French national politics. More recent work has been concerned with the role of monuments in negotiating national identity and with the politics of commemoration as revealed through war and other memorials (see also CULTURE).

Some work on monuments, commemoration and national identity discusses the idea of the built form and design of cities as itself expressive of 'the spirit of the age', monumental expressions of a national character. It is possible to concede, too, that other LANDSCAPES – such as Monument Valley in southern Utah, USA, or, for England, the Stour Valley immortalized by John Constable – have enduring iconic significance as a nation's view of itself (Daniels, 1993; Johnson, 1995) (see also MORAL LANDSCAPES). Most studies have concentrated, however, upon individual monuments or public statuary as a means to explore, for example, issues of nationalism, local IDENTITY, CLASS allegiance and the collective memory of war. In national commemoration these uses of monuments have been shown to be gendered in several ways: through the allegorical use of the female form as the representation of Liberty or Virtue or 'Motherland'; through the fact that most figures commemorated are male; and because women, whilst active in some ways, were often marginalized from the processes of negotiation involved in the organization and construction of commemorative statues (Nora, 1984–92; Gillis, 1994; Johnson, 1995). If monuments are, then, figurative representations of national sentiments and of myths 'cast in stone' as part of the ways in which national 'imagined communities' are structured (see also IMAGINATIVE GEOGRAPHY and ICONOGRAPHY), it is also the case that monuments may subvert the claims of authority, that they may become a symbol of local meaning and the focus not of a collective memory but of disputed renditions of the past (Withers, 1996). Johnson has shown for Ireland, for example, how public statuary has been used to construct and mythologize a heroic past for Ireland, a national identity forged in opposition to English authority yet one never itself fixed and monolithic but one always being reshaped as an ideological contest between Republican and Unionist traditions (Johnson, 1995).

War memorials as monuments of commemoration have been the focus of a wide range of work, by historians interested in the politics of remembrance and in sites of memory and by political and cultural geographers exploring the connections between place, landscape and political meaning (see POPULAR MEMORY). The politics of memory and meaning of Great War memorials in Britain, for example, has been shown to be highly contested (Heffernan, 1995). More recently, the meanings attaching to the Vietnam Veterans' Memorial in Washington, D.C., have been differently defined by the values of the military, of non-military personnel and by grieving relatives, and, not least, by its stark non-triumphalist architecture in a central site of the capital city of the USA (MacCannell, 1992). Attention has also been paid to the contested memorialization of Auschwitz and other concentration camps of the Second World War. In these ways, monuments are a central part of what Young has called 'the objects of a people's national pilgrimage' (Young, 1993, p. 2), and offer considerable potential for further geographical research. CWJW

References

Daniels, S. 1993: *Fields of vision: landscape imagery and national identity in England and the United States*. Cambridge: Polity Press. · Gillis, R., ed., 1994: *Commemorations: the politics of national identity*. Princeton, NJ: Princeton University Press. · Harvey, D. 1979: Monument and myth. *Annals of the Association of American Geographers* 69: 362–81. · Heffernan, M. 1995: For ever England: the western front and the politics of remembrance in Britain. *Ecumene* 2: 293–324. · Johnson, N. 1995: Cast in stone: monuments, geography, and nationalism. *Environment and Planning D: Society and Space* 13: 51–65. · MacCannell, D. 1992: The Vietnam memorial in Washington, DC. In D. MacCannell, ed., *Empty meeting grounds*. London: Routledge, 280–2. · Nora, P. 1984–92: *Les lieux de mémoire*, 3 vols. Paris: Arthaud. · Withers, C.W.J. 1996: Place, memory, monument: memorializing the past in contemporary highland Scotland. *Ecumene* 3: 325–44. · Young, J.E. 1993: *The texture of memory: holocaust memorials and meaning*. London and New Haven, CT: Yale University Press.

Suggested Reading

Gillies, R., ed., 1994: *Commemorations: the politics of national identity*. Princeton, NJ: Princeton University Press. · Johnson, N. 1995: Cast in stone: monuments, geography, and nationalism. *Environment and Planning D: Society and Space* 13: 51–65.

moral geographies The study of the interrelationship of moral and geographical arguments. Work has focused on the ways in which the conduct of particular groups or individuals in particular spaces may be judged appropriate or inappropriate, and the ways in which assumptions about the relationship between people and their environments may both reflect and produce moral judgements. Both forms of study further the Social and Cultural Geography Study Group Committee's (1991, p. 26) suggestion that: 'human geography must engage with the articulation of the moral and the spatial'. Smith (1998) sees moral geographies as one of six possible research areas linking geography and moral philosophy, the others being the historical geography of moralities, issues of inclusion and exclusion in bounded spaces, the moral significance of distance and proximity, questions of SOCIAL JUSTICE, and environmental ETHICS (see also MORAL LANDSCAPES; MORAL ORDER; RELIGION, GEOGRAPHY OF).

Driver (1988) uses moral geographies to consider nineteenth-century social scientific studies of the city in terms of their alliance of 'ENVIRONMENTALISM and moralism', whereby environmentalist forms of social science assumed a relationship between the conduct of populations and their habitat: 'Moral science was . . . a science of conduct and its relationship to environment, both moral and physical' (p. 279). Driver argues that such moral geographies 'permitted the birth of social science in England' (p. 276), the implication being that subsequent work by academic geographers may itself have contributed to such moral geographies by drawing on moralistic assumptions concerning environment and society. Livingstone (1992, pp. 221–31) thus shows how geographical accounts of the relationship of climate and society in the late nineteenth and early twentieth centuries worked through 'moral assumptions concerning racial character and levels of civilisation'. Matless (1994) discusses such issues in relation to geographical discussions of the use and misuse of land, and also develops the theme of moral geographies of conduct by considering how the geography of a particular region, the Norfolk Broads in eastern England in this case, can be understood in terms of competing formulations of appropriate behaviour in the LANDSCAPE, TOURISM, nature study, wildfowling etc. Moral geographies are here shown to be constituted through assumptions concerning CLASS and the relations between locals and outsiders, themes extended in a wider discussion of moral geographies of LEISURE and the BODY in twentieth-century England (Matless, 1997).

Work on moral geographies echoes work on *geographies of exclusion and* TRANSGRESSION in highlighting the basis on which people may be labelled as in or out of place. Cresswell (1996) shows how a consideration of events and groups labelled as transgressive of a dominant MORAL ORDER, such as travelling groups, peace camps and graffiti artists, can reveal the TAKEN-FOR-GRANTED assumptions underlying the use of everyday space. Moral codes are revealed when their limits are transgressed. Sibley's (1995) study of the geographies of exclusion suggests that to understand such moral judgements we might look to PSYCHOANALYTIC THEORY, specifically those theories which highlight the role played by senses of purification and dirt in the human psyche. Sibley shows how the social exclusion of groups such as gypsies, and more general processes of RACISM, can be understood in terms of the labelling of groups as being out of place, a polluting threat to a dominant social order in their deviance from a norm, whether in terms of ETHNICITY, NOMADISM or specific cultural practices.

With some exceptions (Birdsall, 1996), the term moral geographies has not been used in a prescriptive way. Geographers are generally not seeking to moralize. Smith (1998, p. 14) indeed has referred to such moral geographies as 'geographical exercises in descriptive ethics', but it would be wrong to assume that such studies seek a position of moral neutrality. Rather, work on moral geographies has been informed by a philosophical and political assumption that senses of MORAL ORDER are produced through environmental and spatial practices which are always bound up with relations of POWER. The connection of the moral and the spatial in moral geographies is therefore often bound up with a suspicion regarding any claim to be able to define morality, and with a critical attitude to the social power of the moral.

The reader should therefore be aware that different meanings of the term moral geography may apply according to the approach to 'morality' taken by any one author. As in other areas of philosophical and political debate the definition of terms is crucial. Care should also be taken to establish the way in which an author may be distinguishing between the 'moral' and the 'ethical'. In some accounts the two are interchangeable, while in others they carry precise and different meanings. What is defined as 'ethical' by one writer may be defined as 'moral' by another. The key point is to remember that the distinction between morality and ethics is a fluid one, and that understanding an author's argument will demand a clear sense of the terms upon which that argument is being made. DM

References

Birdsall, S. 1996: Regard, respect and responsibility: sketches for a moral geography of the everyday. *Annals of the Association of American Geographers* 96: 619–29. · Cresswell, T. 1996: *In place/out of place: geography, ideology and transgression*. Minneapolis: University of Minnesota Press. · Driver, F. 1988: Moral geographies: social science and the urban environment in mid-nineteenth century England. *Transactions, Institute of British Geographers* NS 13: 275–87. · Livingstone, D. 1992: *The geographical tradition*. Oxford: Blackwell. · Matless, D. 1994: Moral geography in Broadland. *Ecumene* 1: 127–55. · Matless, D. 1997: Moral geographies of English landscape. *Landscape Research* 22: 141–55. · Sibley, D. 1995: *Geographies of exclusion*. London: Routledge. · Smith, D. 1998: Geography and moral philosophy. *Ethics, Place and Environment* 1: 7–34. · Social and Cultural Geography Study Group Committee 1991: De-limiting human geography: new social and cultural perspectives. In C. Philo, ed., *New words, new worlds:*

reconceptualising social and cultural geography. Lampeter: Social and Cultural Geography Study Group, 14–27.

Suggested Reading

Driver (1988). · Matless (1994).

moral landscapes The association of particular LANDSCAPES with schemes of moral value (see also MORAL GEOGRAPHIES). Tuan (1989) reviews the wide-ranging historical and geographical association of particular moral values with the landscapes of city, country and garden. A moral–spatial DIALECTIC may also be identified whereby moral landscapes both reflect and reproduce senses of MORAL ORDER. Work has focused on such processes in the geography of institutions, in the use of architecture and landscape design to promote particular moral principles, and in the production of consciously 'alternative' social spaces.

The institution as moral landscape is considered in Ploszajska's (1994) work on the Victorian reformatory school as an 'environment of moral reform'. Such moral landscapes are one element of a growing geographical interest in relations of SPACE and POWER, whereby spatial organization is shown to be not only reflective of but central to the workings of power. Daniels' (1982) study of the 'morality of landscape' in the work of Georgian landscape gardener Humphry Repton shows how aesthetic values of landscape design were at the same time moral values concerning social harmony, plebeian deference and aristocratic responsibility. The theme of moral landscapes thereby connects to aesthetic, social, political and economic issues, indeed all of those categories are shown to be mutually constitutive.

Studies of moral landscapes may also address the ways in which moral value is located in particular environments. Associations of morality and NATURE, whereby moral order may be equated with a sense of natural order, serve to enable particular groups or individuals to claim a moral landscape close to nature, as in Bell's contemporary study of the southern English village of 'Childerley' (Bell, 1994). Locating the moral in the natural is a common trope of certain forms of ENVIRONMENTALISM, which cultivate an ecological morality or environmental ethic around an assumed moral community of the human and non-human. Such work differs from much of the work discussed above (see also MORAL GEOGRAPHIES) in operating with a strongly normative sense of morality. A normative use of the term moral landscape is also found in Ley's (1993) work on cooperative housing in Canada, presented as embodying moral principles of COMMUNITY and individuality through an oppositional POSTMODERN architectural style. Such work asserts a particular landscape as an embodiment of what is moral. One could suggest that a converse normative geography runs through Cresswell's (1996) studies of the 'heretical geography' embodied in the self-consciously alternative landscapes of hippy convoys, peace camps, and graffiti artists, where landscapes labelled by others as immoral are upheld as pointers towards the production of alternative SOCIAL SPACE. DM

References

Bell, M. 1994: *Childerley: nature and morality in a country village*. Chicago: University of Chicago Press. · Cresswell, T. 1996: *In place/out of place: geography, ideology and transgression*. Minneapolis and London: University of Minnesota Press. · Daniels, S. 1982: Humphry Repton and the morality of landscape. In J. Gold and J. Burgess, eds, *Valued environments*. London: Allen and Unwin, 124–44. · Ley, D. 1993: Co-operative housing as a moral landscape: re-examining the postmodern city. In J. Duncan and D. Ley, eds, *Place/culture/representation*. London: Routledge, 128–48. · Ploszajska, T. 1994: Moral landscapes and manipulated spaces: gender, class and space in Victorian reformatory schools. *Journal of Historical Geography* 20: 413–29. · Tuan, Y.-F. 1989: *Morality and imagination: paradoxes of progress*. Madison: University of Wisconsin Press.

moral order The outcome of the operation of shared moral assumptions concerning right and wrong in human action. Two broad philosophical approaches to the study of moral order can be identified. One is concerned to formulate principles through which one might judge different actions or values as being moral or immoral. Sack (1997, p. 24) thus emphasizes the inherently geographical nature of moral actions in order to develop a framework through which we might improve ourselves as moral geographical subjects: 'Thinking geographically heightens our moral concerns; it makes clear that moral goals must be set and justified by us in places and as inhabitants of a world.' Sack's work, like that of Tuan (1989), recognizes the complex variations of morality between different times and places, but the aim, in common with the general tenor of HUMANISTIC GEOGRAPHY, is to seek a normative framework for being human; for being, in Sack's (1997) terms, a 'geographical self' (cf. SUBJECT FORMATION, GEOGRAPHIES OF).

A second broad approach begins from the assumption not only that moral values are relative to specific histories and geographies but also that claims to morality and definitions of moral order are an effect of relations of power. This approach, which informs a number of the studies of MORAL GEOGRAPHIES inspired by the work of Michel Foucault and is associated philosophically with the 'genealogy of morality' developed by the late nineteenth-century German philosopher Friedrich Nietzsche (Nietzsche, 1994), does not seek a position from which to make moral judgement but aims to problematize the moral in relation to the political, the economic, the cultural, the aesthetic etc. (cf. PROBLEMATIC). By showing the contingency of seemingly universal moral values it becomes possible to trace an HISTORICAL GEOGRAPHY of morality. The implications for the study of moral order of such a rejection of the universal and transhistorical (often associated with the term POSTMODERNISM) are explored in the work of sociologist Zygmunt Bauman (1995) in relation to issues of morality, ETHICS and the relations of self and OTHER.

In this second approach the term 'moral order' can almost appear pejorative, with its suggestion of a regulatory ethical framework produced through specific local power relations. However, for a geographer such as Jackson (1984) 'moral order' takes on a positive meaning precisely because of its geographical relativity. Jackson's account of the work of the early twentieth-century CHICAGO SCHOOL of urban sociologists highlights the way in which social geographical inquiry is able to reveal the existence of a moral order in those parts of the city labelled by many outsiders as socially disorganized and therefore immoral. In Jackson's work the study of moral order as relative to its location therefore leads not to a criticism of moral order *per se*, but to a highlighting of other forms of moral order which 'underlie apparent social disorganization' (p. 178), and which therefore enable a critique of conventional moralistic assumptions concerning life in the modern city. DM

References

Bauman, Z. 1995: *Life in fragments: essays in postmodern morality*. Oxford: Blackwell. · Jackson, P. 1984: Social disorganization and moral order in the city. *Transactions, Institute of British Geographers* NS 9: 168–80. · Nietzsche, F. 1994 [orig. pub. 1887]: *On the genealogy of morality*. Cambridge: Cambridge University Press. · Sack, R.D. 1997: *Homo geographicus: a framework for action, awareness and moral concern*. Baltimore: Johns Hopkins University Press. · Tuan, Y.-F. 1989: *Morality and imagination: paradoxes of progress*. Madison: University of Wisconsin Press.

morphogenesis Evolutionary or revolutionary change in form. There have been two main areas of application in human geography.

The transformation of a LANDSCAPE. Sauer established such a concern as focal to HISTORICAL GEOGRAPHY in his essay on *The morphology of landscape* (1925), when he emphasized that 'we cannot form an idea of landscape except in terms of its time relations as well as of its space relations'. This approach has been especially prominent in American and European studies of the rural landscape (see, e.g. Helmfrid, 1961) but there are also classical counterparts for the urban landscape (in particular, Conzen, 1960) which have provided impetus for modern and more theoretically informed studies of changing urban morphologies (Whitehand, 1987; Vance, 1990). (See also MORPHOLOGY; SEQUENT OCCUPANCE; TOWNSCAPE; VERTICAL THEME.)

The transformation of a SYSTEM. Biology has been an especially important source of inspiration for many morphogenetic studies within this tradition, providing both informal, typically 'organic' analogies of the Earth, its REGIONS and STATES (see Stoddart, 1967), and much more formal methods and models, most of which usually acknowledge a debt to D'Arcy Thompson's celebrated *On growth and form*, first published in 1917 (see Tobler, 1963). Thus, Bunge's *Theoretical geography* (1962) hailed Thompson's work as 'most suggestive' and Haggett's *Locational analysis in human geography* (1965) found 'common ground' in its focus on 'movement and geometry'. In many ways, CATASTROPHE THEORY represents a radical development of this tradition.

The connections between these two were explored in an early essay by Harvey (1967), which was much more concerned with the elucidation of the PROCESSES which sustained morphogenesis rather than with the changing forms themselves. Many subsequent attempts at SYSTEMS ANALYSIS reflected Maruyama's (1963) distinction between a 'first cybernetics' which studies *morphostasis* – '"deviation counteracting" mutual causal processes', i.e. negative FEEDBACK – and a 'second cybernetics' which studied *morphogenesis* – '"deviation amplifying" mutual causal processes', i.e. positive feedback. The distinction between positive and negative feedback is more complicated than this implies, however, and involves no necessary correspondence with instability and stability (see, e.g. Bennett and Chorley, 1978, pp. 41–3). DG

References

Bennett, R.J. and Chorley, R.J. 1978: *Environmental systems: philosophy, analysis and control*. London: Methuen. · Bunge, W. 1962: *Theoretical geography*. Lund: C.W.K. Gleerup. · Conzen, M. 1960: Alnwick:

Northumberland: a study in town plan analysis. *Transactions, Institute of British Geographers* 27. · D'Arcy Thompson, W. 1942: *On growth and form*. Cambridge: Cambridge University Press. · Haggett, P. 1965: *Locational analysis in human geography*. London: Edward Arnold. · Harvey, D. 1967: Models of the evolution of spatial patterns in human geography. In R.J. Chorley and P. Haggett, eds, *Models in geography*. London: Methuen, 549–608. · Helmfrid, S. 1961: Morphogenesis of the agrarian landscape. *Geografiska Annaler* 43: 1–328. · Maruyama, M. 1963: The second cybernetics: deviation-amplifying mutual causal processes. *American Scientist* 51: 164–79. · Sauer, C. 1925: The morphology of landscape. In J. Leighly, ed., *Land and life: a selection from the writings of Carl Ortwin Sauer*. Berkeley, CA: University of California Press (reproduced 1963). · Stoddart, D.R. 1967: Organism and ecosystem as geographical models. In R.J. Chorley, and P. Haggett, eds, *Models in geography*. London: Methuen, 511–48. · Tobler, W. 1963: D'Arcy Thompson and the analysis of growth and form. *Papers of the Michigan Academy of Science, Arts and Letters* 48: 385–90. · Vance, J. 1990: *The continuing city: urban morphology and Western civilization*. Baltimore, MD: Johns Hopkins University Press. · Whitehand, J. 1987: *The changing face of cities: a study of development cycles and urban form*. Oxford: Blackwell.

Suggested Reading

Harvey (1967). · Helmfrid (1961).

morphology Strictly the science of form but often used as a synonym for form itself: for example, 'geomorphology' is both 'the science of landform study' and a synonym for 'landform'.

Some social scientists have used morphology as a synonym for 'structure', as in Halbwachs's (1960) *Morphologie sociale* which is concerned with society's demographic and socio-economic structure: Halbwachs drew on Durkheim's writings, which also influenced French geography through Vidal de la Blache. Durkheim identified geographers' proper role as the study of social morphology, of 'the mass of individuals who comprise the society, the manner in which they are disposed upon the earth, and the nature and configuration of objects of all sorts which affect collective relations'.

In human geography, the term's classic use is Sauer's (1925) statement on *The morphology of landscape*. He argued that morphologic method is a particular form of synthesis, an inductive procedure for identifying the major structural (form) elements in the landscape and arranging them in a developmental sequence (their morphogenesis). He emphasized that study of CULTURAL LANDSCAPES involved: (a) general geography, or the study of the form-elements themselves (what today is called systematic geography); (b) regional geography, or comparative morphology; and (c) HISTORICAL GEOGRAPHY, which studies the development sequence, as in SEQUENT OCCUPANCE.

The study of elements of the TOWNSCAPE is frequently referred to as the study of urban morphology (see FRINGE BELT). RJJ

References

Halbwachs, M. 1960: *Morphologie sociale*, trans. O.D. Duncan and H.W. Pfautz. Glencoe, IL: The Free Press. · Sauer, C.O. 1925: *The morphology of landscape*. Berkeley, CA: University of California Publications in *Geography* 2: 19–54.

Suggested Reading

Leighly, J., ed., 1963: *Land and life: a selection from the writings of Carl Ortwin Sauer*. Berkeley and Los Angeles, CA: University of California Press.

mortality Together with FERTILITY and MIGRATION, death is an essential determinant of population structure and growth. Geographers are interested in the role of mortality in population change; in the influences of environment on mortality (see HEALTH AND HEALTH CARE, GEOGRAPHY OF); in the ways in which particular diseases are diffused (cf. DIFFUSION); and in the relationship between mortality and economic and social conditions.

Mortality is measured in a number of ways. The simplest is the *crude death rate*, the number of deaths in a specific period per 1000 of the population. Like the crude birth rate (see FERTILITY) this simple measure is severely distorted by age-structure variations which are obviously fundamental to determining overall mortality (see AGE AND SEX STRUCTURE). *Age-specific mortality rates* express the number of deaths of persons of a certain age per 1000 of the population in that age group. In order to produce single-number indicators of mortality, *standardized mortality rates* may be calculated which take into account variations in age structure and make comparisons possible between regions or countries. Mortality rates may also be related to causes, which can be most informative about the incidence of disease in different age groups and different areas. LIFE TABLES and the measures derived from them (e.g. LIFE EXPECTANCY) provide the most detailed and sophisticated measures of mortality and are widely used in population models.

A most important group of measures relates to *infant mortality*, often given special attention because of its sensitivity to social and environmental conditions. The most frequently used *infant mortality rate* is the number of deaths of infants under one year old per 1000 live births in a given year. More precise measures include *neonatal mortality*, defined as those deaths occurring during the first four weeks of life, and *post-neonatal mortality*, those occurring within the remainder of the first year. There is also an important distinction in the causes of infant mortality between endogenous and exogenous mortality. The former refers to deaths from congenital malformations or delivery complications and the latter to deaths from infections or poor care. Improvements in modern medicine, health services, nutrition and maternal care have brought the most dramatic decline in infant mortality. General reductions in infant mortality are usually the first stage in overall mortality decline. In some underdeveloped countries and in past centuries in the presently developed world, infant mortality might account for 30 per cent or more of all deaths. In most developed states, the number is now very low: the graph shows the decline in infant mortality in Finland from 1750–1990.

The decline in general mortality levels in the developed world has been fairly constant during the twentieth century, with the result that fertility has generally been more important than mortality in determining short-term fluctuations in population. In the developing world, however, mortality has often been reduced dramatically over a few years, producing very rapid population growth. Mortality decline is an essential element in the DEMOGRAPHIC TRANSITION model. Ascribing causes to mortality decline is not as simple as it may seem. Many of the worst diseases have certainly either disappeared or been greatly reduced, and FAMINE and subsistence crises are now less influential as the world's social and economic environment has improved. Causes of death have changed dramatically (Mercer, 1990): plague, smallpox, cholera and tuberculosis are not the killers they once were and in developed countries mortality is now associated more with cancer, heart disease and road accidents. Nevertheless, mortality may still surprise, as the geography of AIDS has demonstrated in both the developed and the developing worlds (Gould, 1993; see AIDS, GEOGRAPHY OF).

The major argument about causes of the general decline in mortality centres around the conflict between the role of medicine and the general improvements in standards of living. Techniques of diagnosis and surgery, inoculation and the development of drugs were undoubtedly influential, but more so in recent decades in the THIRD WORLD than in nineteenth- and early twentieth-century Europe. For it has been shown that general

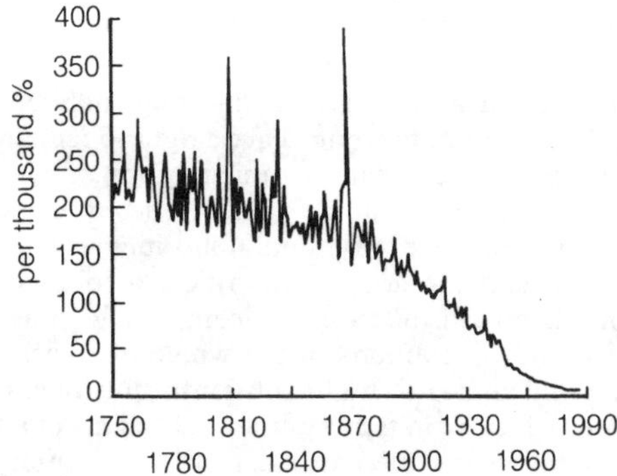

mortality *Infant mortality in Finland, 1750–1990* (Rallu and Blum, 1991)

increases in living standards – improvements in the quantity and quality of food, better sanitation, hygiene and housing conditions – were just as important as changes in medical care. Research has also concentrated on the varying susceptibility of sections of the population to disease and death: differential mortality rates may be calculated to show the influence of racial or ethnic background, education, income and social or occupational status, sex and rural or urban residence. (See also MEDICAL GEOGRAPHY.) PEO

References

Gould, P. 1993: *The slow plague: a geography of the AIDS pandemic.* Oxford: Blackwell. · Mercer, A, 1990: *Disease, mortality and population in transition.* Leicester: Leicester University Press. · Rallu, J.-L. and Blum, A., eds, 1991: *European population. I. Country analysis.* London: John Libbey, 153.

Suggested Reading

Cliff, A. and Haggett, P. 1992: *Atlas of disease distributions.* Oxford: Blackwell. · Cliff, A., Haggett, P. and Smallman-Raynor, M. 1993: *Measles. An historical geography of a major human viral disease. From global expansion to local retreat 1840–1990.* Oxford: Blackwell. · Daugherty, H.G. and Kammeyer, K.C.W. 1995: *An introduction to population*, 2nd edn. New York and London: Guilford Press, ch. 7. · Howe, G.M. 1976: *Man, environment and disease in Britain; a medical geography of Britain through the ages.* London: Penguin; New York: Barnes and Noble. · Jones, H.R. 1990: *Population geography*, 2nd edn. London: Paul Chapman. · Livi-Bacci, M. 1997: *A concise history of world population*, 2nd edn. Oxford: Blackwell. · Lopez, A.D., Caselli, G. and Valkonen, T., eds, 1995: *Adult mortality in developed countries: from description to explanation.* Oxford: Clarendon Press. · Lutz, W., ed., 1990: *Future demographic trends in Europe and North America.* London: Academic Press, part 1. · McKeown, T. 1976: *The modern rise of population.* London: Edward Arnold; New York: Academic Press. · Schofield, R.S., Reher, D.R. and Bideau, A., eds, 1991: *The decline of mortality in Europe.* Oxford:

Clarendon Press. · Woods, R.I. 1979: *Population analysis in geography*. London and New York: Longman.

multiculturalism The belief that different cultural or ethnic groups have a right to remain distinct rather than assimilating to 'mainstream' norms. Though often restricted to the cultural practices of ethnic minorities in education and the arts, more critical theories of multiculturalism strive to encompass the practices and institutions of the whole of society. The dilemmas of multiculturalism for 'liberal democracies', in terms of the equal rights of all citizens versus the particular needs of minorities, are outlined by Taylor (1992 and subsequent commentaries). Liberal theories of multiculturalism risk depoliticizing or commodifying the term, reducing it to 'the united colors of CAPITALISM' (Mitchell, 1993; cf. LIBERALISM). More critical theories have therefore attempted to identify oppositional forms of multiculturalism as well as narratives of authenticity, genealogy and heterogeneity (Lowe, 1996). The idea of 'multiculture' has also been introduced to undermine the belief in homogeneous CULTURES and IDENTITIES on which liberal theories of multiculturalism depend. (See also ETHNICITY; DIFFERENCE.) PAJ

References

Lowe, L. 1996: Imagining Los Angeles in the production of multiculturalism. In A.F. Gordon and C. Newfield, eds, *Mapping multiculturalism*. Minneapolis: University of Minnesota Press, 413–23. · Mitchell, K. 1993: Multiculturalism, or the united colors of capitalism. *Antipode* 25: 263–94. · Taylor, C. 1992: *Multiculturalism and 'The politics of recognition'*, ed. A. Gutman. Princeton: University of Princeton Press.

multi-dimensional scaling (MDS) Methods for simplifying and replicating a matrix showing the distances between a set of points (n), while as far as possible retaining the relative ordering of those distances. MDS locates the points in a smaller number of dimensions than n, and so reduces a multi-dimensional representation to more comprehensible proportions. It can also be used to transform MAPS, basing them, for example, on the time-distance between places rather than the crow-flies distance. RJJ

Suggested Reading

Gatrell, A.C. 1983: *Distance and space: a geographical perspective*. Oxford and New York: Clarendon Press.

multi-level modelling A method of statistical analysis developed by educational researchers for examining the nature of a relationship at several spatial SCALES. In educational work, for example, children's examination performance within a town may be related to: (a) their personal and home characteristics (level 1); (b) the class they are taught in (level 2); (c) the school which they attend (level 3); (d) the neighbourhood within which the school is located (level 4); and (e) the territory of the education authority which funds and directs the school (level 5). Area, school and classroom contexts are all presented as important influences on performance, in addition to individual ability (Goldstein, 1987).

The multi-level modelling strategy has many potential applications in geography, reflecting the contention that there are NEIGHBOURHOOD and CONTEXTUAL EFFECTS operating on individuals. The strategy is much superior to conventional ecological analyses using REGRESSION methods to investigate the conjoint influences of individual and areal characteristics. (See also ECOLOGICAL FALLACY; MODIFIABLE AREAL UNIT PROBLEM.) RJJ

References and Suggested Reading

Goldstein, H. 1987: *Multilevel models in educational and social research*. London: Charles Griffin. · Jones, K. 1991: *Multi-level models for geographical research*. Concepts and techniques in modern geography 54. Norwich: Environmental Publications; Theme issue on Multilevel modelling, 1997: *Environment and Planning A*, 29: 581–658.

multinational corporation (MNC) A firm with the power to coordinate and control operations in several countries, even if it does not own those operations (Dicken, 1998). This is a more restricted term than TNC, which refers merely to operations in more than one country (see also TRANSNATIONAL CORPORATION; TRANSNATIONALISM). RL

Reference

Dicken, P. 1998: *Global shift: transforming the world economy*. London: Paul Chapman Publishing.

multiple nuclei model A model of intra-urban land-use distributions developed by Harris and Ullman (1945; see Harris, 1997a, 1997b), which combines the features of the earlier ZONAL and SECTORAL MODELS and shows urban residential districts organized around several nodes and not just the one CENTRAL BUSINESS DISTRICT (see figure). RJJ

References

Harris, C.D. 1997a: 'The nature of cities' and urban geography in the last half-century. *Urban Geography* 18: 15–35. · Harris, C.D. 1997b: Diffusion of urban models:

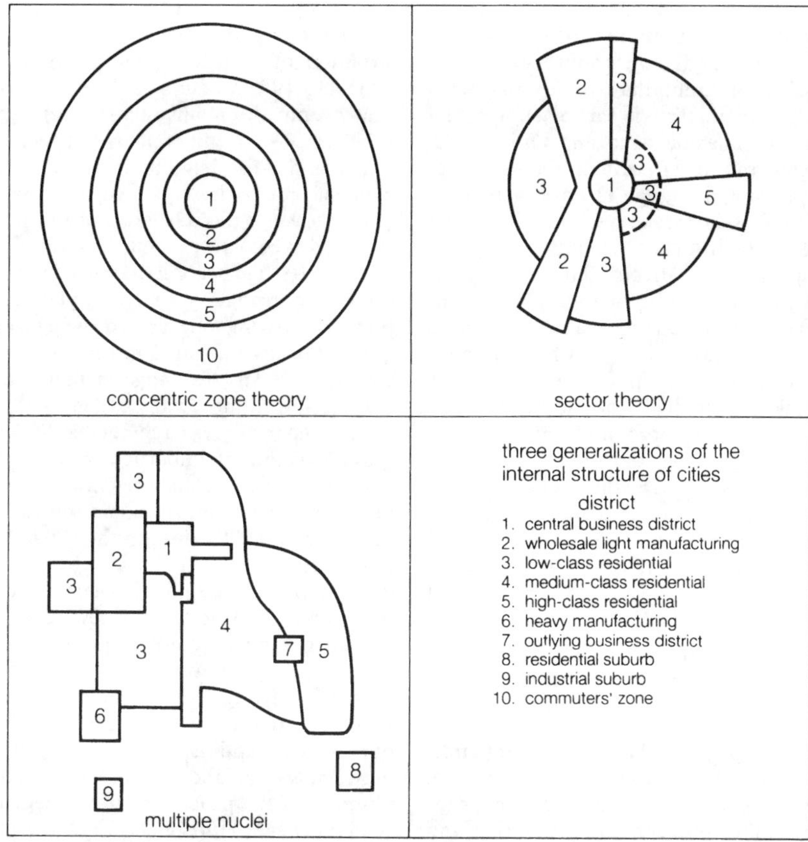

multiple nuclei model *Generalization of the internal structure of cities. The concentric-zone theory is a generalization for all cities. The arrangement of the sectors in the sector theory varies from city to city. The diagram for multiple nuclei represents one possible pattern among innumerable variations* (Harris and Ullman, 1959)

a case study. *Urban Geography* 18: 49–67. · Harris, C.D. and Ullman, E.L. 1945: The nature of cities. *Annals of the American Academy of Political and Social Science* 242: 7–17.

multipliers It is widely observed that a new basic primary or secondary economic activity in an area, such as the development of a mine or the establishment of a car plant, triggers off additional economic activities nearby, especially in the local tertiary sector which provides services to the new industry and/or to its employees and their households. This is termed a multiplier effect, and the multiplier is an attempt to measure its magnitude, which has great potential importance, for high multipliers would indicate to planners the places and activities where investment would create, both directly and indirectly, the greatest amount of new economic activity (see GROWTH POLE).

The exact method for estimating multipliers depends on the theoretical base of the researcher and the data available. The simplest multiplier calculations depend on ECONOMIC BASE THEORY, but in other cases multipliers can be derived from INPUT–OUTPUT analysis. There are two fundamental distinctions in such studies. The first is between *employment multipliers* where the focus is on jobs created, and *income multipliers* where the extra economic activity is treated in value of activities generated. The second is between aggregate and incremental multipliers. The *aggregate multiplier* is the ratio between total regional economic activity and its economic base: the *incremental multiplier* focuses on the ratio between the incremental change in basic economic activity and the consequent change in overall activity. The first is the easier to measure: the latter is more correct theoretically but extremely difficult to measure.

The value of multiplier studies has been called in question. First it can be shown that multipliers are unstable over time, and that the incremental multipliers differ according to whether the initial change in basic activity is an increase or a decrease. Secondly it is clear that (like ECONOMIC BASE THEORY) multipliers deal with short-run effects. Thirdly there is evidence that the results of multiplier estimates are very sensitive to the size, shape, and location of the study region. Very small regions tend to have low multipliers because many effects leak across their boundaries: much larger regions have large multipliers simply because they are larger and more services are provided internally. A US study suggested that multipliers are around 1.5 to 2.0 for smaller cities, greater than 2.0 for cities like Cincinnati and Denver, and over 3.0 for New York city.

AMH

Suggested Reading

Smith, D.M. 1981: *Industrial geography: an economic geographical analysis*, 2nd edn. Chichester and New York: John Wiley.

music, geography of The cultural organization of sounds and silences; the civilization of noise. Music is an artwork and a cultural product, like architecture, literature, painting and film (cf. TEXT). It is also a performance and consumption practice, like dance, theatre and fashion.

The BERKELEY SCHOOL of cultural geography inspired some early work on music, in which musical performances, music association memberships, musical listening, musicians' birthplaces and so on took their place alongside a variety of other cultural artefacts DIFFUSING across space, trickling down hierarchies, attaching themselves to LANDSCAPES and REGIONS and mapping out CULTURE AREAS (Ford, 1971). This 'traditional' approach to the geography of music is exemplified in Carney (1994).

The relevance of music more broadly within human geography has taken longer to establish, for at least two reasons. First, music was the last of the arts to be approached critically within social science – a delay which initially compromised its position within a geography of CULTURAL POLITICS. Second, geography has traditionally been a visually oriented discipline (see VISION AND VISUALITY) whose methodological emphasis has been on observation, mapping and textuality rather than on listening, sensing and PERFORMATIVITY. However, as the role of senses other than sight in the construction of knowledge has been recognized (Pocock, 1993), sound and music have been drawn onto the mainstream research agenda. Likewise, as the differences between silence, music and noise have been accepted as markers of wider POWER struggles in society (Attali, 1977), the relevance of music to POLITICAL, ECONOMIC, SOCIAL and CULTURAL GEOGRAPHY has become more obvious. At the same time struggles over space, place and position are proving relevant to a new, critically and politically informed musicology (cf. POSITIONALITY). All this suggests that the spaces and placing of music will be of growing interest in sociological research generally, and in human geography in particular.

A range of ideas for broadening the agenda of geographies of music is laid out in Leyshon et al. (1995, 1998) and Smith (1994, 1997). It has been argued that music provides a useful critique of the discipline's visual IDEOLOGIES; that popular music adds a new dimension to the geography of cultural politics generally, and to the social construction of IDENTITY in particular (Kong, 1995); and that there is an ECONOMIC GEOGRAPHY of music which informs our understanding of the relationships between global and local affairs, and which illuminates the process of urban regeneration (Cohen, 1991; Hudson, 1995).

On the one hand, music has been analysed as an integral part of the production, reproduction or 'elaboration' of CIVIL SOCIETY (Said, 1991). It is part and parcel of everyday life; and nothing that happens in the social world can be understood without taking this into account. Sound is as important as vision, listening as critical as looking, hearing on a par with seeing, and music as central as the visual arts in the study of social life. This suggests that research on the history and geography of listening practices, on the cultural construction of ways of hearing, and on the politics and POETICS of musical performances, contains important clues to the socio-economic and political organization of, and the power struggles being waged within, the places in which music is made and heard (Johnson, 1995). On the other hand the production and consumption of music has an economics and a sociology of its own. Music is important among the culture industries; the management of music is a significant strand of cultural policy; and music-making has been harnessed to processes of place-marketing and the practice of URBAN

RENEWAL. As a result of this growing interest in every facet of the musical landscape, the sound of music is reinvigorating the study of society and space; and the place of music is reorientating the musicological imagination. SJS

References

Attali, J. 1977: *Noise. The political economy of music*, trans. B. Massumi, 1985. Manchester: Manchester University Press. · Carney, G.O. 1994: *The sounds of people and places: a geography of American folk and popular music*, 3rd edn. London: Rowman and Littlefield. · Cohen, S. 1991: Popular music and urban regeneration: the music industries of Merseyside. *Cultural Studies* 5: 332–46. · Ford, L. 1971: Geographic factors in the origin, evolution and diffusion of rock and roll music. *Journal of Geography* 70: 455–64. · Hudson, R. 1995: Making music work? Alternative regeneration strategies in a deindustrialised locality: the case of Derwentside. *Transactions, Institute of British Geographers* NS 20: 460–73. · Johnson, J.H. 1995: *Listening in Paris*. Berkeley: The University of California Press. · Kong, L. 1995: Popular music in geographical analyses. *Progress in Human Geography* 19: 183–98. · Leyshon, A., Matless, D. and Revill, G. 1995: The place of music. *Transactions, Institute of British Geographers 20* (4) (special issue). · Leyshon, A., Matless, D. and Revill, G. 1998: *The place of music*. New York: Guilford Press. · Pocock, D. 1993: The senses in focus. *Area* 15: 11–16. · Said, E. 1991: *Musical elaborations*. London: Vintage Books. · Smith, S.J. 1994: Soundscape. *Area* 26: 232–40. · Smith, S.J. 1997: Beyond geography's visible worlds: a cultural politics of music. *Progress in Human Geography* 21: 502–29.

Suggested reading

Leyshon et al. (1998). · Smith (1997).

N

nation A COMMUNITY of people whose members are bound together by a sense of solidarity rooted in an historic attachment to a homeland and a common CULTURE, and by a consciousness of being different from other nations (cf. DIFFERENCE; OTHER/OTHERNESS). The term is frequently but misleadingly used interchangeably with both STATE and NATION-STATE on the assumption that every state is a nation and vice versa, although nationalist writings generally hold that they are destined for each other because neither is complete without the other (see NATIONALISM). Anderson (1990) considers the nation to be above all else an 'imagined community' for four reasons: (a) despite the limited bounds of an individual's activities, the nation is associated with *a larger sense of communion* than that of his or her local environment; (b) it is imagined as *limited* in geographical reach by finite, if elastic, boundaries beyond which lie other nations; (c) it is imagined as *sovereign* and thus the ideal is freedom in a sovereign state (cf. SOVEREIGNTY); and (d) it is imagined as *community* based on a territorial relationship which subsumes other community cleavages and divisions (cf. TERRITORY; TERRITORIALITY). GES

References and Suggested Reading

Anderson, B. 1990: *Imagined communities*. London: Verso. · Billig, M. 1996: *Banal nationalism*. London: Sage. · Gellner, E. 1983: *Nations and nationalism*. Oxford: Blackwell; Ithaca, NY: Cornell University Press. · Smith, A. 1998: *Nationalism and modernity*. London: Routledge.

national parks Areas placed under national government protection for their natural significance: many federal systems of government (e.g. USA, Canada, Germany, etc.) have state or provincial parks. The International Union for the Conservation of Nature defines national parks as areas of protection and restricted access containing 'ECOSYSTEMS not materially altered by human exploitation and occupation', of 'special scientific, educational and recreational interest', or 'containing a natural landscape of great beauty'. The concept is applicable at other scales. Some World Heritage Areas have similar attributes, but are considered exceptional on a world scale. The definition, on a broad meaning, could include national forests, game preserves and nature reserves that are not classified as national parks in the strict sense.

In 1864, a US Act of Congress transferred Yosemite Valley and the Mariposa Grove of Big Trees to the State of California on the condition that they be held inalienably for 'public use, resort and recreation' (in McCormick, 1995, p. 13). In 1872, another Act designated an area in Wyoming as Yellowstone National Park, establishing the first designated national park in the world. The creation of national parks there fitted with the idea of democratizing NATURE, which enabled the young USA to distinguish itself from the old Europe. It was possible to designate national parks in areas that were perceived as WILDERNESS, despite habitation for thousands of years by indigenous people. It is important to note that contemporary national parks are not wilderness areas (large areas of public lands untrammelled by human settlement), but may contain wilderness areas within their boundaries while endeavouring to make other areas accessible for human use. National parks were also very popular with railway companies, and the promotion of rail-based TOURISM coincided with the construction of high-class resort facilities by railway companies in some national parks in North America. The original idea of an 'environmental experience' in a national park was not necessarily about environmental PRESERVATION.

Numerous countries created national parks prior to the First World War, although the British system only began with the passing of the *National Parks and Access to the Countryside Act* in 1949 (which covered England and Wales only). The influence of British ideas had been felt in colonial East Africa at least 20 years earlier, however; where conservationists, many based in London, were influential in establishing national parks which dislocated tens of thousands of PEASANTS and pastoralists (Neumann, 1995, 1996).

National parks were often created for their scenic appeal, which was constructed through promotional material, showing mountains, rivers and gorges. Rarely are national parks found in so-called developed countries in areas that are suitable for agriculture or other uses. The initial tourist appeal of national parks has been amplified by changes in transport technology, leisure time and cultural values. This places increasing strain upon the existing national parks, and raises conflict about their role in preservation and CONSERVATION. An additional issue is the desired approach, e.g. environmental management by humans or to let nature decide without further human input. Fires in Yellowstone National Park in the USA in 1988 added to the debate about management processes in national parks. In some countries, the discovery of NATURAL RESOURCES within national park boundaries has caused concern. Uranium mining occurs within the world heritage area of Kakadu in the north of Australia.

While the label 'national park' may be universal, its meaning varies spatially and temporally. The World Resources Institute (1994) estimated that in 1993 the global extent of 'protected natural areas' of all types was 792 million hectares, or 5.9 per cent of the world's land surface. PM

References

McCormick, J. 1995: *The global environmental movement*, 2nd edn. Chichester: John Wiley and Sons. · Neumann, R. 1995: Local challenges to global agendas: conservation, economic liberalization and the pastoralists' rights movement in Tanzania. *Antipode* 27 4: 363–82. · Neumann, R. 1996: Dukes, Earls and ersatz Edens: aristocratic nature preservationists in colonial Africa. *Environment and Planning D: Society and Space* 14 1: 79–98. · World Resources Institute 1994: *World resources 1994–95*. New York and Oxford: Oxford University Press.

nationalism (1) A feeling of belonging to the NATION and (2) a corresponding political IDEOLOGY which holds that the territorial and national unit should be allowed to co-exist in an autonomously congruent relationship. Nationalism is chameleon-like, for it can accommodate itself to such diverse socio-territorial backgrounds and contrasting environments as authoritarian collectivism (e.g. fascism and far right-wing movements) and democratic movements struggling against domination by another nation, STATE or empire. Consequently, it is not necessarily 'emancipatory', although its central claim rests on its goal of securing SOCIAL JUSTICE through attaining SOVEREIGNTY over its own political homeland (Buchanan, 1991). Thus, nationalism draws upon the doctrine of SELF-DETERMINATION, in which the nation considers itself to have a natural right to GOVERNANCE over its own affairs. However, an important political issue to emerge is whether the right to national self-determination can be secured without impinging upon the rights of those who do not belong to, or identify with, the NATION that wishes to secede from a larger polity (Smith, 1999).

As Gellner (1983) has argued, nationalism is a phenomenon connected not so much with INDUSTRIALIZATION or MODERNIZATION but rather with their uneven DIFFUSION. Originating in western Europe with the consolidation of NATION-STATES, it later brought about the reorganization of the nineteenth- and twentieth-century maps of Europe, and has been the prime force in the political awakening of the THIRD WORLD. However, nationalism takes a variety of forms, differing in their relationships to the nation and to those objective conditions which determine its opportunity to achieve or maintain the aim of home rule. On the one hand, there is a *state nationalism*, which reinforces or even exalts the idea of the nation-state. On behalf of the homeland-nation's myths and ICONOGRAPHIES, state actions can be legitimized in both the domestic and the international arena by appealing to 'national unity' and 'national interests'. On the other hand, there is a variety of minority or *substate nationalisms* including: *irredentist* – borderland people striving for secession and unity with co-nationals in an adjacent state (see IRREDENTISM); *anti-colonial* – in which nationalist demands are based primarily, although not exclusively, on an ethnically heterogeneous people's common response to, and rejection of, colonial rule (see COLONIALISM); and *ethnic causes* – where shared experience, CULTURE and often language legitimize demands for home rule. The last category is associated particularly with the European experience (see also SUBSIDIARITY).

Until recently, conventional academic wisdom held that ethnic nationalism was destined to dissolve in the acid bath of MODERNITY as a consequence of both the successful spatial spread of the centralized and uniform state and the homogenizing forces associated with modern society. However, far from being a spent force, the persistence of ethnic-based regional differences and their politicization has in a number of cases threatened the stability of many well-established western-democratic states and, in the case of state socialist federations, their very existence (see PLURALISM; FEDERALISM). The reasons offered for ethnic nationalism have tended to follow one of three lines of explanation.

The first emphasizes *the importance of cultural markers* – based on language, religion, ethnic background, kinship patterns etc. – as providing the automatic reference point for ethnoregional communities seeking security, survival and regeneration under conditions of socio-economic and political pressure to conform to a state-wide, nationalizing process. But this line of reasoning is too ready to assume that, for the ethnic region, cultural differences provide the most compelling basis upon which such politicization might occur, although there is no doubt that threats to COMMUNITY and the increased impersonalization of growing centralized and bureaucratic states can fuel the engines for political action.

The second approach, which has found much sympathy in Marxist writings, sees *the politicization of ethnoregions as a reaction to historically formed peripheral predicaments*, in which the spatial logic of CAPITALISM generates discontinuous and disruptive patterns or waves, conferring advantages on some regions (see UNEVEN DEVELOPMENT), while relegating minority ethnoregional communities to a marginal and subordinate status. Hechter (1975), for instance, sees ethnic regions as conditioned by the historical development of a culturally backward and economically exploited *internal colony*, while the state 'core' ethnoregion, by accumulating capital from and inhibiting its flow into these regions, develops a more advanced and diversified economic base. Such CORE–PERIPHERY differences become institutionalized into a coextensive cultural DIVISION OF LABOUR, forming a basis for political mobilization along ethnoregional lines. Besides underestimating the emotional and cultural appeal of nationalism and its capacity to serve human needs better than instrumental groups and satisfactions, such a view does not account for the revival of nationalism in Europe since the 1960s: nor does it explain why ethnic nationalism can propel both relatively prosperous (e.g. Catalans, Basques, Croats, Latvians and Scots) and relatively poor (e.g. Kosovo Albanians, Kazakhs) peoples alike into political action.

The third perspective focuses on *the spearheading role played by the ethnic intelligentsia* in the 'discovery' and politicization of the homeland nation. Their changing expectations in a state which may no longer be able to meet their material and status aspirations thrusts them to the forefront of the manufacture, organization and mass mobilization of nationalism. On this basis, time- and place-specific mechanisms and events (e.g. the potential for regional development, a flagging core economy or increased remoteness from government, the opening up of political opportunities to challenge the state) not only help us to understand why the ethnic intelligentsia are usually at the forefront but also highlight the key role that they play in popularizing the nationalist cause throughout the ethnoregion. GES

References and Suggested Reading

Buchanan, A. 1991: *Secession. The morality of political divorce from Port Sumter to Lithuania and Quebec*. Boulder, CO: Westview Press. · Brubaker, R. 1996: *Nationalism reframed. Nationhood and the national question in the New Europe*. Cambridge: Cambridge University Press. · Gellner, E. 1983: *Nations and nationalism*. Oxford: Blackwell. · Hechter, M. 1975: *Internal colonialism: the Celtic fringe in British national development 1536–1966*. London: Routledge and Kegan Paul. · Kymlicka, W., ed., 1999: *Citizenship and diversity: theory and practice*. Oxford: Oxford University Press. · Hobsbawm, E. 1995: *Nations and nationalism since 1780: programme, myth, reality*. Cambridge: Cambridge University Press. · Millar, D. 1995: *On nationality*. Oxford: Oxford University Press. · Smith, A. 1998: *Nationalism and modernity*. London: Routledge. · Smith, G.E., ed., 1995: *Federalism: the multiethnic challenge*. London: Longman. · Smith, G.E. 1999: Sustainable federalism, democratisation and distributive justice. In W. Kymlicka, ed., *Citizenship and diversity; theory and practice*. Oxford: Oxford University Press. · Smith, G.E., Law, V., Wilson, A. and Bohr, A. 1998: *Nation-building in the post-Soviet borderlands. The politics of national identities*. Cambridge: Cambridge University Press. · Tamir, Y. 1993: *Liberal nationalism*. Princeton: Princeton University Press.

nation-state A complex array of modern institutions involved in GOVERNANCE over a spatially bounded TERRITORY which enjoys monopolistic control over the means of violence (cf. SOVEREIGNTY). It is still considered to be the most important form of spatial governance.

There are two central components to nation-state formation. First, the process of *state-building* is bound up with the territorialization of state POWER, a set of centralizing processes which, to paraphrase Mann (1984), can be defined as the capacity of the STATE to penetrate CIVIL SOCIETY, and to implement logistically political decisions throughout its territory (cf. TERRITORIALITY). Such infrastructural powers would include the collection and storage of information (what Giddens (1985) calls the SURVEILLANCE aspect of state power), imposition of an administrative-territorial order, the regulation of movements of ideas, goods and people across national boundaries, and the growth of a centralized bureaucracy to coordinate and carry out increasingly complex functions within its territorial realm. Second, there is *nation-building*, which in classic nation-states was facilitated by state-building and the development of industrial CAPITALISM. Nation-state building involves, in particular, the utilization of the NATION by state elites in which a sense of territorial or homeland IDENTITY and of belonging to a national CULTURE is important, aided by the spread of a common vernacular and national educational system. Nation-building is therefore also bound up with creating citizens and citizen identities (cf. CITIZENSHIP). In one sense, the nation-state is an IDEAL TYPE, for there are few cases in which state boundaries are coextensive with a national community within which all citizens possess an identical culture. It is particularly problematic when the territorial boundaries of the state exceed national identified boundaries and in this sense, historically, the nation-state has often been a *conquest state*.

Processes of GLOBALIZATION, in the form of both the internationalization of capital and the growth of global and regionalized forms of spatial governance, challenge the ability of the nation-state effectively to practise its claim to a sovereign monopoly over its bounded space and to protect its citizens from external incursion. Thus the rise of transnational forms of governance, in particular, are not only challenging the power and authority of the nation-state but contributing to its deterritorialization as new, more globalized, scales of governance emerge. There is, however, a general consensus amongst political theorists that while the powers of the state have been eroded as a consequence, it is a myth to claim that the state has no influence over the impact of such globalizing processes. GES

References and Suggested Reading

Archiburgi, D., Held, D. and Kohler, M., eds, 1998: *Re-imagining political community: studies in cosmopolitan democracy*. Oxford: Polity Press. · Biersteker, T. and Weber, C., eds, 1996: *State sovereignty as social construct*. Cambridge: Cambridge University Press. · Camilleri, J. and Falk, R. 1993: *The end of sovereignty? The politics of a shrinking and fragmenting world*. London: Edward Elgar. · Dunn, J. 1995: *Contemporary crisis of the nation-state*. Oxford: Basil Blackwell. · Giddens, A. 1985: *The nation-state and violence*. Oxford: Polity Press. · Hirst. P. and Thompson, G. 1996: *Globalisation in question*. Oxford: Polity. · Mann, M. 1984: The autonomous power of the state: its origins, mechanisms and results. *Archives européennes de sociologie* 25: 185–213 (reprinted in Agnew, J., ed., 1997: *Political geography: a reader*. London: Arnold, 58–80). · Smith, G. 1994: Political theory and political geography. In D. Gregory, R. Martin and G. Smith, eds, *Human geography; society, space and the social sciences*. London: Macmillan, 54–77.

natural area A residential district within an urban area characterized by its physical individuality and, especially, its inhabitants' cultural and other characteristics. The concept was introduced by the sociologists of the 1920s CHICAGO SCHOOL, who presented natural areas as the outcome of an unplanned spatial sorting process of similar people through the operations of the housing market, though some adherents to the HUMAN ECOLOGY perspective saw them as statistical constructs rather than homogeneous outcomes of ecological sorting. (See SEGREGATION.) RJJ

Suggested Reading

Hatt, P.K. 1946: The concept of natural area. *American Sociological Review* 11: 423–7. · Zorbaugh, H.W. 1926: The natural areas of the city. *Publications of the American Sociological Society* 20: 188–97.

natural resources Parts of the physical environment that are considered useful for satisfying human needs and wants. They exist independently of humankind, and in varying, but usually physically finite, quantities. People identify particular properties, substances and organisms in NATURE as a 'RESOURCE'. Their value, scarcity and usefulness are also socially defined; as Zimmerman (1951) noted, 'Resources are not; they become.' Human needs and wants change through time, therefore the means of satisfying these needs and wants must also change. Additionally, changes in technology and knowledge can lead to what Zimmerman (1951) called the 'neutral stuff' of nature being identified as a resource, e.g. rubber became a resource after Charles Goodyear discovered the vulcanization process in 1839. The opposite of resources are what Zimmermann (1951) identified as 'resistances', which includes pests and weeds. Recent work in the geography of plants and animals looks at the construction of 'pests', and their treatment by humans intent on preserving resources (Thorne, 1998). A perspective of '*resourcism*' (i.e. viewing the world as resources to be used by humans) may overlook the importance of the ECOSYSTEM in which the 'natural resources' are embedded. This could lead to policies that recognize the importance of the natural resource, but little else, i.e. the fish without the water.

While the terms 'natural resources' and 'resources' are often used interchangeably, sometimes a distinction is made between them, with resources being defined more broadly to include things such as technology, human labour and ingenuity. It is on this basis that Julian Simon (1994) argues against ideas of resource depletion and notions that there are LIMITS TO GROWTH. It is difficult to justify resources as being 'natural' when increasingly they are being planted, bred or managed by people, e.g. plantation forestry, fish farming.

A distinction is sometimes made between 'stocks' (natural resources that have taken millions of years to form and are considered *non-renewable*, e.g. minerals and fossil-fuels) and 'flows' (natural resources that are naturally *renewable* within a short timespan, e.g. solar radiation and tidal power). Rees (1989) posits a Natural Resources Continuum ranging from exhaustible to infinitely renewable natural resources. The middle ranges of this continuum include natural resources that are renewable dependent on the use levels and human investment, i.e. RESOURCE MANAGEMENT. The term 'natural assets' is sometimes used, e.g. Rees and Wackernagel (1994), by which the authors include material resources (e.g. petroleum, forests) but also process resources (e.g. photosynthesis, waste assimilation) for which MacNeill et al. (1991) use the term '*ecological capital*'.

Recent work in the broadly defined field of SUSTAINABLE DEVELOPMENT has sometimes seen the use of the term '*natural capital*' instead of 'natural resources' (Pearce et al., 1991; Jannson et al., 1994). Natural capital is a financial metaphor that treats the earth like a bank account, and suggests it is wise for humans to live off the natural interest (i.e. renewable resources) and not deplete or degrade our natural capital (i.e. non-renewable resources). This approach to CONSERVATION is favoured by some people, but is criticized by others for extending a financial perspective onto human relationships with aspects of NATURE that are seen as intrinsically valuable (i.e. valued for their own sake).

Pearce et al. (1991) and Rees and Wackernagel (1994), among others, argue that to achieve sustainable development we need to maintain 'constant capital'. One important difference between their two approaches is that Pearce et al. (1991) consider this capital to be both human-made and 'environmental assets', whereas Rees and Wackernagel (1994, p. 367) argue that 'each generation should inherit an adequate stock of natural assets *alone* no less than the stock of such assets inherited by the previous generation' (emphasis in original). They allow for the depletion of non-renewable natural resources to be compensated for through investment in renewable natural resources. The notion of 'natural capital' being 'constant' contains issues such as the location and costs of extraction of constant quantities of natural resources. Emel and Bridge (1995) note that one key feature of resource extraction, e.g. petroleum and gas, has been the marked shift in the northern hemisphere of production sites to colder regions at higher latitudes. In the case of oil and gas, this may also involve drilling in deeper seas. The ability to 'recover' resources is increasingly dependent on greater technological and resource inputs, a process that is incompatible with some concepts of sustainable development. PM

References

Emel, J. and Bridge, G. 1995: The earth as input: resources. In R. Johnston, P. Taylor and M. Watts, eds, *Geographies of global change: remapping the world in the late twentieth century*. Oxford and Cambridge, MA: Blackwell, 318–32. · Jannson, A.-M. et al., eds, 1994: *Investing in natural capital: the ecological economics approach to sustainability*. Washington, D.C.: Island Press. · MacNeill, J., Winsemius, P. and Yakushiji, T. 1991: *Beyond interdependence: the meshing of the world's economy and the earth's ecology*. New York: Oxford University Press. · Pearce, D. et al., eds, 1991: *Blueprint 2: greening the world economy*. London: Earthscan. · Rees, J. 1989: Natural resources, economy and society. In D. Gregory and R. Walford, eds, *Horizons in human geography*. Basingstoke and London: Macmillan, 364–94. · Rees, W. and Wackernagel, M. 1994: Ecological footprints and appropriated carrying capacity: measuring the natural capital requirements of the human economy. In A.-M. Jannson et al., eds, *Investing in natural capital: the ecological economics approach to sustainability*. Washington, D.C.: Island Press, 362–90. · Simon, J. 1994: More people, greater wealth, more resources, healthier environment. *Economic Affairs* 14 3: 22–9. · Thorne, L. 1998: Kangaroos – the non issue. *Society and Animals*. · Zimmerman, E. 1951: *World resources and industries*, rev. edn. New York: Harper and Row.

Suggested Reading

Emel and Bridge (1995). · Rees, J. 1991: *Natural resources: allocation, economics and policy*, 2nd edn. London and New York: Routledge.

naturalism 'The thesis that there is (or can be) an essential unity of method between the natural and the social sciences' (Bhaskar, 1979). Put like that, one might expect naturalism to have played an important part in the history of geography in making possible a conversation between physical geography and human geography. Certainly, those geographers who worked with philosophies of science like CRITICAL RATIONALISM, (LOGICAL) POSITIVISM OR REALISM accepted a (sometimes modified) version of naturalism. But the situation is more complicated than this implies, for two reasons which work in different directions. On the one side are those human geographers who are suspicious of social science, not least because of the shadows which naturalism casts over them, and who prefer to think of themselves as working within the humanities. Their central concern is with questions of intention, interpretation and VALUES as these emerge within a world that is intrinsically meaningful to the beings who inhabit it, and this situation (so they suppose) has no direct counterpart in the natural sciences. This was one of the central planks of an avowedly HUMANISTIC GEOGRAPHY, but the rise of POST-STRUCTURALISM and its critique of EPISTEMOLOGY has produced a more robustly critical view of the cultural construction of nominally scientific inquiries. On the other side, therefore, are those who would insist that all 'sciences' involve questions of intention, interpretation and value; that their texts and traces are always vulnerable to critical DECONSTRUCTION; that their findings are always the product of situated practices that are carried out in specific archival, field, library and laboratory settings; and that the dissemination and generalization of their constitutively 'local knowledges' means that they simply cannot avoid issues of HERMENEUTICS, POWER and RHETORIC (Rouse, 1987, 1996; Woolgar, 1988). There is no doubt that in recent years the 'CULTURAL TURN' in both the humanities and social sciences, and the related development of cultural studies of science ('science studies'), have had a considerable impact on human geography and its understandings of (the cultural construction of) NATURE and natural science (Demeritt, 1994; Barnes, 1996; see SCIENCE, GEOGRAPHY AND). It remains to be seen how successful these interventions will be in radically revising the 'essential unity' between the natural sciences and social sciences originally posited by the proponents and critics of naturalism: but they do seem to suggest that many of the most powerful commonalities between the two rest not on the once unquestionable 'objectivity' of the natural sciences but on the myriad relations between 'power' and 'knowledge' that capture the human and social sciences.

DG

References

Barnes, T. 1996: Probable writing: Derrida, deconstruction and the Quantitative Revolution in economic geography. In his *Logics of dislocation: models, metaphors and meanings of economic space*. New York: Guilford, 161–84. · Bhaskar, R. 1979: *The possibility of naturalism: a philosophical critique of the contemporary human sciences*. Brighton: Harvester. · Demeritt, D. 1994: Ecology, objectivity and critique in writings on nature and human societies. *Journal of Historical Geography* 20: 22–37. · Rouse, J. 1987: *Knowledge and power: toward a political philosophy of science*. Ithaca, NY: Cornell University Press. · Rouse, J. 1996: *Engaging science*. Ithaca, NY: Cornell University Press. · Wooolgar, S. 1988: *Science: the very idea*. London: Tavistock.

Suggested Reading

Bhaskar (1989). · Demeritt (1994). · Woolgar (1988).

nature A term with three main meanings:

- The essence of something (as in 'it's in his nature');
- Areas unaltered by human action, i.e. nature as a realm external to humanity and society; and
- The physical world in its entirety, perhaps including humans, i.e. nature as a universal realm of which humans, as a species, are a part.

These three meanings often overlap (particularly the first and third) and are at times contradictory. In each, 'nature' can also be invoked as either a barrier to human action (e.g. RESOURCES have 'natural limits' which cannot be exceeded) or else as a normative standard of value (e.g. an activity may be deemed to be 'unnatural' and thus perverse). In practice, the three meanings of nature have appeared in everything from everyday speech to literature to science. More specifically, each meaning has been used in an immense variety of ways. As Neil Smith (1984, pp. 1–2) notes:

> Nature is material and it is spiritual, it is given and made, pure and undefiled; nature is order and it is disorder, sublime and secular, dominated and victorious; it is a totality and a series of parts, woman and object, organism and machine. Nature is the gift of God and it is a product of its own evolution; it is a universal outside history and also the product of history, accidental and designed, wilderness and garden.

This polysemism has led cultural critic Raymond Williams to make three important observations. The first is that 'nature is perhaps the most complex word in the language' (Williams, 1988, p. 221). The second is that '[W]hat is usually apparent [when reference is made to nature] is that it is selective, according to the speaker's general purpose' (Williams, 1980, p. 70). And Williams' third observation is that 'any full history of the uses of nature would be a history of a large part of human thought' (Williams, 1988, p. 223).

The first meaning of nature has both prosaic and specialist uses. In *everyday speech* nature is a commonplace which is invoked in a variety of contexts ('she's naturally generous'; 'it's a natural event'). In more specialist uses the first meaning of nature is often linked to deep claims about the nature of the world or its ONTOLOGY. For instance, the REALIST philosophy of science developed by Roy Bhaskar makes a set of claims about 'natural necessity', that is, fundamental causal imperatives inherent in things. Such specialist invocations of nature as the essence of something have also been used to political ends. For instance, one major strand of LIMITS TO GROWTH thinking in population and RESOURCE MANAGEMENT is a neo-Malthusianism which argues that resources have inherent natural limits which people must adapt to (e.g. through birth control) or else perish (e.g. through starvation) – see MALTHUSIAN MODEL.

The second meaning of nature – *areas unaltered by and external to human action* – is as old as it is familiar. Today it is central to the ENVIRONMENTAL MOVEMENT, particularly at the 'deep green' end of the movement which, among other things, is concerned to protect one of the last vestiges of this nature – namely, WILDERNESS – from further destruction by humanity. This notion of an external, non-human, 'first nature' is so ingrained in western cultures as to seem obvious and unquestionable. However, historian of ideas Michel Foucault (1970) has suggested that it is an historically specific notion which only emerged during the period of the European ENLIGHTENMENT. Prior to this time, he argues, Europeans in the Middle Ages linked nature directly to God insofar as they believed it had been made by Him for humanity's perfection. Building on this, Fitzsimmons (1989) and Grove (1995) suggest rather different reasons why nature became separated out as an external realm in Euro-American thought during the Enlightenment period. For Fitzsimmons this separation was bound up with rapid capitalist INDUSTRIALIZATION and URBANIZATION during the early nineteenth century. As formerly unoccupied LANDSCAPES were developed, she argues, a series of stark contrasts were developed between nature and SOCIETY, the RURAL and the URBAN, and the country and the city. For Grove, by contrast, the invention in thought of an unhumanised nature coincided with the imperial outreach of the European powers into tropical islands like Mauritius. Compared with the increasingly dessicated landscapes back home, Grove argues, these islands appeared as 'tropical Edens' or paradises.

These processes of Euro-North American industrialization, urbanization and IMPERIAL outreach went hand in hand with an ambivalent valorization of nature in western thinking. On the one hand, as industrialization proceeded the 'conquest of nature' became an ideological and practical project. Thus, areas of nature that remained 'untamed' were often regarded with fear and suspicion, as was the case with the early American settlers who often demonized the temperate forests of the eastern seaboard (Williams, 1989). However, on the other hand, as nature succumbed to settlement and economic DEVELOPMENT on a scale unprecedented in world history, concern began to be expressed that this 'domination of nature' (Leiss, 1972) was going too far. Not surprisingly, then, the modern environmental movement began life in western Europe and North America, where the defence of nature became an increasing preoccupation leading to today's widespread ENVIRONMENTALISM.

Aside from this negative and positive valorization, the separation of nature from humanity also gave rise to three predominant views of human–nature relationships: humankind in harmony with nature; humankind dominated by nature; and humankind dominating nature (Glacken, 1967). As noted, the third of these has been the predominant reality in the modern world, while many environmentalists have argued for a shift toward the first. However, some have also argued that if humanity does not alter its socio-economic modes of appropriating nature, nature will takes its 'revenge' and once again dominate humanity as it did in pre-industrial times (Hardin, 1996).

In its third meaning as *the physical world in its entirety*, nature has also been a long-standing concept. In its more general meaning as the physical world including human beings it also has a long history. Harking back to pre-Enlightenment notions of a Great Chain of Being linking God and even the lowliest species into an organic whole, this notion of a universal nature is today most strongly articulated by deep greens, like Gaians. Drawing on James Lovelock's (1979) work, the Gaia hypothesis is that the biosphere is a self-regulating superordinate whole of which humans are but one part. However, more diluted notions of a universal nature can be found even in more technocentric forms of environmentalism, like that articulated by US Vice-President Al Gore. His *The earth in balance* (1992) argues that humanity should recall that it is steward – not master – of the planet lest nature discipline its upstart child.

Given that geography has, among other things, been defined as the study of human–environment relations, it is not surprising that geographers have made a number of contributions to understanding of the three predominant meanings of nature, particularly the second and third. With regard to nature as that which is unaltered by humanity, geographers have made four contributions. One is to describe and explain how this notion of an external nature came about (Simmons, 1993), whereas another is to examine the process of the destruction and disappearance of this 'first nature' (Thomas, 1956). A third, more popular early in the twentieth century than today, is to analyse how nature affects humanity (e.g. Semple, 1911; see ENVIRONMENTAL DETERMINISM). A fourth contribution, more critical, is to question whether it is in fact practically possible to talk of an external nature anymore (Smith, 1984: this is discussed further below). With regard to nature as the physical world, by definition physical geographers have long studied that world. They, and several human geographers, have also studied nature in the wider sense of the physical world including humans. For instance, both SYSTEMS theory in geography (Chorley and Kennedy, 1971) and HUMAN ECOLOGY in different ways sought to understand people as key parts of wider natural complexes.

It should be clear from all of the above that nature is as much an idea or concept as it is a material reality. In recent years critics within and outside geography have sought to show how nature in both these forms is *both* a SOCIAL CONSTRUCTION *and* an instrument of social POWER. The notion of nature as a social construction seems perverse insofar as nature in its second and third meanings is separate from or superordinate to humanity respectively. However, critics argue that nature is anything but separate from or superordinate to humanity and suggest that it is constructed both discursively/linguistically and materially. In geography the notion of the discursive construction of nature (see DISCOURSE) is associated with MARXIST and CULTURAL GEOGRAPHY respectively. Marxist geographer Neil Smith (1984) argued that the notions of nature as either external or universal formed an Enlightenment IDEOLOGY of nature associated with the bourgeoisie. More recently, cultural geographers have argued that particular social groups in society construct IMAGES of nature according to their interests and desires (e.g. Henderson, 1994). In both cases these images are argued to have real power in structuring societal views of nature such that they come to stand for the reality they represent (see REPRESENTATION). If sceptics have found the notion of nature as discursive construct difficult to accept, the idea that it is also a material construct has seemed heretical. After all, nature is supposed by definition to be beyond human intervention. However, both Marxist geographers and geographical critics of science suggest that in an era when everything from the genetic manipulation of food to the cloning of sheep has become reality, nature is increasingly remade according to human dictates. Thus Smith (1984) argues that modern CAPITALISM 'produces nature' (see PRODUCTION OF NATURE), while Demeritt (1998) identifies an '*artifactual constructionism*' in which modern science and technology are increasingly able to intervene in nature at the most basic level.

These various forms of the social construction of nature are, it has been argued, equally forms of social power. Rose (1993), for example, suggests that in western culture – including geography – notions of nature have been feminized such that the domination of nature parallels the domination of women in society (see FEMINIST GEOGRAPHIES). Similarly, Willems-Braun's (1997) investigation of modern forestry struggles in British Columbia, Canada, shows that western ideas of nature as wilderness embody a CULTURAL POLITICS which serves to obscure and marginalize native First Nations' COMMUNITIES. In addition to these forms of discursive power, the material construction of nature has been seen by Goodman and Redclift (1991) as part and parcel of the profitability strategies of large MULTINATIONAL CORPORATIONS operating within AGRO-FOOD SYSTEMS whose activities on world markets affect the livelihoods of smaller farmers and consumers. More controversially, Latour (1993) suggests that the material separation between humanity and nature is an illusion which has served to empower those laying claim to expert knowledge of nature, while all the while humanity and nature have long materially interfused as hybrids.

The social construction of nature arguments suffer two drawbacks. First, because they are all drastically anthropocentric, they may over-emphasize the powers of human societies (*hyper-constructionism*) and underplay the material powers and capacities of the 'natural' entities supposedly constructed. At a time of so-called 'environmental crisis', such hyper-constructionism ignores the powers of nature at its peril. Second, because they are so anthropocentric, social constructionist arguments also risk ignoring any aesthetic, moral or spiritual VALUE nature might have in its own right or for humans. However, this said, social constructionist views clearly have the advantage over naive realist positions of nature as either external or universal, for at some level nature undoubtedly is constructed discursively and materially and is undoubtedly implicated in the exercise of social power.

Much of the debate over nature in geography has focused on western – and specifically Anglophone – ideas and practices. However, it is important to understand non-western concepts of and interventions in nature. There is an important history of commonality and difference here. On the one hand, imperial outreach into the New World and beyond from the sixteenth century onwards led to successive waves of the export and import of ideas and natural objects to and from the Americas, Asia and Africa. This traffic was often tied to processes of COLONIALISM and imperial violence involving the discursive racialization and feminization of nature as part of ORIENTALISM, the material appropriation of natural commodities by imperial powers (everything from rubber to gold to timber) and the transfer of disease and other natural health hazards from Europe to indigenous peoples. On the other hand though, many non-western ideas and practices concerning nature survived colonial conquest and remain today in various original or hybrid forms in countries as different as China and Iraq where they form an important part of everyday social, economic, cultural and often religious life. NC

References

Chorley, R. and Kennedy, B. 1971: *Physical geography: a systems approach*. Englewood Cliffs, NJ: Prentice-Hall. · Demeritt, D. 1998: Science, social constructivism and nature. In B. Braun and N. Castree, eds, *Remaking reality: nature at the millennium*. London and New York: Routledge, 173–93. · Fitzsimmons, M. 1989: The matter of nature. *Antipode* 21: 106–20. · Foucault, M. 1970: *The order of things*. New York: Vintage Books. · Glacken, C. 1967: *Traces on the Rhodian shore*. Berkeley, CA: University of California Press. · Goodman, D. and Redclift, M. 1991: *Refashioning nature*. London: Routledge. · Gore, A. 1992: *The earth in balance*. New York: Earthscan. · Grove, R. 1995: *Green imperialism*. Cambridge: Cambridge University Press. · Hardin, G. 1996: *Living within limits*. New York: Oxford University Press. · Henderson, G. 1994: Romancing the sand: constructions of capital and nature in arid America. *Ecumene* 1: 235–55. · Latour, B. 1993: *We have never been modern*. Cambridge, MA: Harvard University Press. · Leiss, W. 1972: *The domination of nature*. New York: George Braziller. · Lovelock, J. 1979: *Gaia*. New York: Oxford University Press. · Rose, G. 1993: *Feminism and geography*. Cambridge: Polity. · Semple, E.C. 1911: *Influences of geographic environment*. New York: H. Hold. · Simmons, I.G. 1993: *Interpreting nature*. London: Routledge. · Smith, N. 1984: *Uneven development*. Oxford: Blackwell. · Thomas, W.L., ed., 1956: *Man's role in changing the face of the earth*. Chicago: Chicago University Press. · Willems-Braun, B. 1997: Buried epistemologies: the politics of nature in (post)colonial British Columbia. *Annals of the Association of American Geographers* 87: 3–31. · Williams, M. 1989: *Americans and their forests*. Cambridge: Cambridge University Press. · Williams, R. 1988: *Keywords*. London: Fontana. · Williams, R. 1980: *Problems of materialism and culture*. London: Verso.

Suggested Reading

Glacken (1967). · Soper, K. 1996: *What is nature?* Oxford: Blackwell.

nearest neighbour analysis A method for comparing the distribution of points in an area with a theoretical norm based on their random distribution within the same area. The theoretical distribution gives an expected average distance between all pairs of nearest neighbours, which is compared with the observed distribution for the mapped pattern. The test statistic R_n is derived by dividing the observed by the expected average distance, and ranges from 0.0 (indicating that the observed distribution is more clustered than expected from a random allocation of the points in that space), through 1.0 (a random distribution), to 2.149 (a more uniform distribution than expected): the scale of values is not linear, however (i.e. a value of 0.4 doesn't imply a distribution twice as clustered as that shown by a value of 0.8), which creates interpretative difficulties. The size of R_n for any set of points is also influenced by the size of the area analysed: what is clustered at one SCALE may be uniform at another. RJJ

Suggested Reading

Aplin, G.J. 1983: *Order-neighbour analysis*. Concepts and Techniques in Modern Geography 36. Norwich: Geo Books.

neighbourhood A district within an urban area. Although the term was coined to describe an area comprising a COMMUNITY of individuals it is frequently applied in general usage for any small residential district irrespective of the degree of social integration there. A neighbourhood *sensu stricto* is a defined area within which there is an identifiable subculture to which the majority of its residents conform (cf. NEIGHBOURHOOD EFFECT). RJJ

Suggested Reading

Ley, D. 1983: *A social geography of the city*. New York and London: Harper and Row.

neighbourhood effect A process by which the characteristics of people's local social milieux influence the ways in which they think and act. Neighbours present individuals with MODELS of attitudes and behavioural patterns, which may either: (a) conform to their own, and thus reinforce their self-identity and behaviours; or alternatively (b) contradict them and thus influence some local residents to modify their own attitudes and behaviour in order to be consistent with those of their local peer groups (cf. CONTEXTUAL EFFECT).

The neighbourhood effect has been used to account for certain geographical patterns – of attitudes towards educational achievement, for example, and of voting (see ELECTORAL GEOGRAPHY) – which indicate greater spatial concentration of an attitude than anticipated from knowledge of the characteristics of their area's residents alone. The inference drawn from the ecological relationships identified, but rarely tested (thus potentially committing an ECOLOGICAL FALLACY), is that people initially predisposed to a minority view within an area will be influenced by the majority opinion there: since this influence comes about through interpersonal interaction it is sometimes termed 'conversion through conversation'. RJJ

Suggested Reading

Burbank, M.J. 1997: The psychological basis of contextual effects. *Political Geography* 14: 621–35.

neighbourhood unit A relatively self-contained residential area. Most identified neighbourhood units are in planned residential developments, either suburban districts or NEW TOWNS and comparable settlements.

The neighbourhood unit concept, first used in Chicago in 1916 and formally enunciated by Clarence Perry in 1929, suggested the importance of SCALE in planning residential districts. Each new district should be of a sufficient size that it was socially self-contained for regular activities – such as daily and weekly shopping, the provision of primary schools and health-care facilities, and so on – and thus would develop as an integrated COMMUNITY (or balanced neighbourhood). British GARDEN CITIES were planned for units containing about 5000 persons each, and the pattern of roads and public transport was arranged to maximize the perceived gains from their separation, with the unit populations living within walking distance of all unit facilities and segregated from motorized traffic as far as possible.

The validity of the assumption that people wished to live in such bounded communities and would constrain their activities and spatial movements largely within them has led to criticisms of the concept, but much urban planning continues to promote such a cellular division of residential space. RJJ

Suggested Reading

Hall, P.G. 1988: *Cities of tomorrow: an intellectual history of urban planning and design in the twentieth century*. Oxford and New York: Basil Blackwell.

neo-classical economics Economics has been defined as the study of the allocation of scarce means among alternative ends. In other words, it is concerned with how human needs and wants are satisfied in a world of limited resources, where everyone cannot have as much as he or she wants of everything. Neo-classical economics forms the basis of the view of how economic activity functions, as conventionally adopted in capitalist society. It represents the refinement and extension of ideas from the formative or classical phase of economics as an academic discipline. The classical period of economics is usually defined by the publication of Adam Smith's *Wealth of nations* in 1776 and John Stuart Mill's *Principles of political economy* in 1848. It was dominated by the work of David Ricardo (see NEO-RICARDIAN ECONOMICS), who developed a theory of relative prices based on costs of production in which labour cost played the dominant role. The LABOUR THEORY OF VALUE was taken up by Karl Marx, to become a central feature of MARXIAN ECONOMICS. The classical economists placed great emphasis on the ability of *laissez faire* to resolve conflicting self-interest in a manner that would benefit the community as a whole, via the 'invisible hand' of market competition recognized by Adam Smith. It was the liberalism of the classical economists rather than the labour theory of value that characterized the neo-classical perspective. A view of human affairs that stressed individualism, *laissez faire* and reverence for market mechanisms (see MARKET EXCHANGE) was more in accordance with the prevailing ethics of CAPITALISM than one which attributed all value produced to the expenditure of labour.

The classical conception of an economy was one composed of many small enterprises, none of which could exercise a significant influence on market prices or on the total quantity of goods sold. The actions of any firm were dictated by consumer tastes as expressed in the marketplace and by the competition of innumerable other small firms seeking consumer expenditure. The UTILITARIANISM of Jeremy Bentham provided a concept whereby consumer satisfaction could be represented. As this framework became formalized in mathematics, the new school of neo-classical

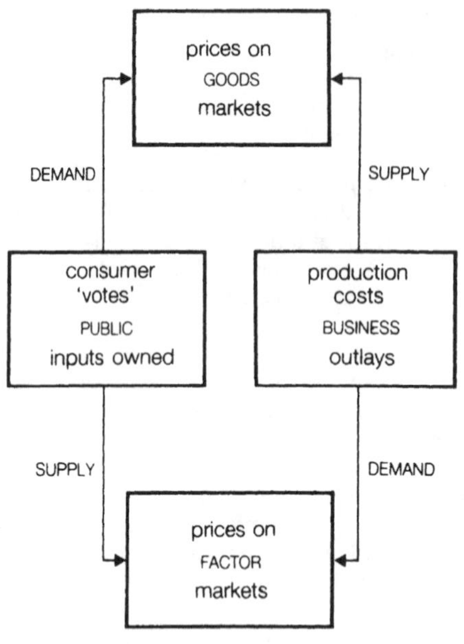

neo-classical economics

economists emerged from the tradition of classical liberalism.

The rise of neo-classical economics is closely associated with three well-known texts published in the early 1870s: William Stanley Jevons's *The theory of political economy*, Karl Menger's *Grundsatze der Volkswirtschaftslehre* and Leon Walras's *Eléments d'économie politique*. Although there were differences between their analyses, the basic approach and content of these works was similar: the framework set down is still highly influential in economics and ECONOMIC GEOGRAPHY.

Neoclassical theory portrays an economy comprising a large number of small producers and consumers without the power to influence the operation of the market significantly. Firms purchase or hire FACTORS OF PRODUCTION (land, labour and capital) which they utilize in the production process in such a way as to maximize their profits. The prices of factors and of finished goods sold are taken as given, and beyond the control of the firm. The decisions facing the firm are the productive process to be adopted (combination of factors) and the volume of output (or scale); plant location is disregarded. Households sell the factors of production that they possess: their land and capital if they have some, otherwise just their labour. They accept the given market price and use the resulting income to purchase goods and services in quantities selected so as to maximize individual satisfaction or *utility*. The entire system is regulated by the interaction of supply and demand in the marketplace, which serves both to allocate resources and to distribute income through the determination of prices for goods and factors of production.

This is essentially how conventional economics textbooks see the operation of a capitalist free-enterprise system. For example, Paul Samuelson's *Economics* (1998) portrays the competitive price system solving the basic economic problem of what to produce, how and for whom, in a manner summarized in the figure. Two groups of participants in the economy are recognized – 'the public' and 'business'. The markets for goods and for factors of production set the prices at which things are exchanged. The public offer their labour, land and capital goods for sale to business, and the interaction of supply and demand in the factor markets determines the prices paid as wages, rent and interest, i.e. it determines the distribution of income. The public takes its income onto the markets for consumer goods, expressing its preferences in the form of what Samuelson refers to as 'dollar votes'. (The implicit analogy with the electoral process evokes the principles of democracy in support of free-market mechanisms: see PLURALISM.) Consumer demand interacts with the costs at which business is able to supply goods, to determine their prices.

All the elements of the economy represented in the figure are related to one another, so that a change in one will have repercussions for others. Thus a change in the willingness of either capital owners or labour to offer their services will affect prices on the factor markets, which will affect the cost of production, the price of goods, and the willingness of the public to consume them. Markets are supposed to adjust automatically to these changes, tending towards the restoration of a state of EQUILIBRIUM at a price that brings supply and demand into balance. It is this self-regulating property that gives free-market mechanisms much of their attraction as means of allocating factors among alternative uses and of distributing returns among the various participants in the productive process.

The consumption and production sides of the economy are themselves the subject of elaborate and sophisticated theory, formalized by the use of algebra and simple geometrical models. The concept of utility is crucial to the theory of consumer behaviour. Consumers are held to possess a *utility function* incorporating their tastes and preferences. They alone know what suits them best: this is the principle of 'consumer sovereignty'. Consumers allocate their expenditure among alternative 'bundles of goods' so as to maximize utility, subject to the 'budget constraint' represented by income and to the prevailing set of prices. For a long time utility was assumed to be measurable, at least on an ordinal scale, but even this was found unnecessary as the level of abstraction from reality became such that consumer behaviour could be analysed without any empirical frame of reference. Economists of the neo-classical school went to great lengths to minimize the ethical content of their theories, which meant avoiding any reference to the actual specification of the utility function. The objective was to identify the general necessary and sufficient conditions for the maximization of utility, irrespective of the actual goods involved and the magnitude of the utility to be derived from their consumption in specific combinations. Consumers maximize utility when the utility derived from the last (or marginal) unit consumed, expressed as a ratio over the price of that commodity, is an equal proportion for all commodities. In other words, marginal utility per unit of expenditure should be the same for all goods or services consumed, otherwise there is additional utility still to be gained by the reallocation of expenditure from things offering low marginal utility to things offering more (cf. UTILITY THEORY).

This analysis is then extended into the collective consumption of an entire community. Individual utility functions are aggregated into a *social welfare function* expressing community preferences for various goods and services. Resources and technology available create certain production possibilities (the community equivalent of the budget constraint), which place limits on what can actually be made available for consumption. COMMUNITY welfare is maximized through the maximization of the individual utility functions. This simple exposition of welfare theory in neo-classical economics (welfare economics) has been the subject of much development and debate, including some geographical extensions (see PARETO OPTIMALITY; WELFARE GEOGRAPHY).

The neo-classical analysis of the operation of the firm on the business side of the figure is analogous to that of consumer behaviour. To maximize profits, the firm operates at the highest level of efficiency in its use of resources and hence produces at the lowest possible cost. It purchases factors of production up to the point where the contribution to production of the last (marginal) unit of each factor, expressed as a ratio over the price of the factor, is an equal proportion for all factors. Thus the last unit of expenditure on each factor should yield the same increase in production, otherwise additional output could be achieved by reallocating outlays among factors or inputs (just as in the consumer's attempt to maximize utility). When production and consumption are brought together, resources are allocated among alternative goods and services in such a way that no reallocation is possible without diminishing the total value of production of the entire economy and the overall utility or welfare derived from it. Income is distributed according to the prevailing marginalist principles, each factor being paid according to its marginal productivity.

Although neo-classical economics traditionally ignores geographical space, attempts have been made to overcome this obvious defect through regional economics (see REGIONAL SCIENCE). For the most part, this is a repetition of the conventional neo-classical formulations. For example, a strict interpretation of the notion of factors of production being allocated according to marginalist principles requires labour to move to places of shortage from places of surplus, and for capital to do the same, until no further addition to output can be achieved by spatial reallocation. This leads to a prediction that market forces will tend to equalize factor returns, and hence incomes, in geographical space. The Swedish economist Bertil Ohlin published a book *Interregional and international trade* in 1933, which showed how specialization and TRADE would lead to regional equality, given certain assumptions which he acknowledged would not necessarily be fulfilled in reality. The truth is that imperfect mobility of factors prevents the instantaneous adjustment that the market is supposed to achieve. The fact that the FRICTION OF DISTANCE is an important impediment to factor mobility makes the neo-classical perspective especially inappropriate as a general theory of how the SPACE-ECONOMY actually functions. However, the rise of regional economics had some benefit for both geography and conventional economics, with the recognition that space is neither non-existent nor neutral in economic processes.

Regional growth theory in the neo-classical tradition has had an important influence on spatial economic planning. Albert Hirschman in *The strategy of economic development* (1958) argued that the selective development of particular sectors of the economy is the most effective way of promoting the interregional transmission of growth. This was similar to François Perroux's argument (1950) for the stimulation of propulsive industry as a GROWTH POLE, a concept which was translated geographically into that of the growth point or location selected for investment. Selective spatial development strategies depend on how effectively growth is transmitted from one place to another, or what Hirschman termed the 'trickle down' effect.

Brian Berry (1970) and others have elaborated a view of 'growth impulses' spreading down the urban hierarchy, rather like the DIFFUSION of an innovation. The tendency towards equalization may be frustrated by 'polarization' effects arising from efficiency advantages maintained where growth was initiated. Gunnar Myrdal's (1957) concept of circular and cumulative causation suggests that the 'spread' effects would be counteracted by 'backwash' effects, thus perpetuating uneven development or regional inequality. Particularly important is the process of CONCENTRATION AND CENTRALIZATION, which implies continuing growth in the core region of a metropolis at the expense of the periphery, as external economies are built up and capital generated in the periphery is transferred back as returns to investors in the core.

Neoclassical economic theory has some obvious attractions. It provides an elegant general theory, in the sense that all aspects of economic activity can be brought together in a set of statements that define the necessary and sufficient conditions for social welfare to be maximized. The association of all this with a market-regulated, free-enterprise system provides what can appear to be objective scientific support for the capitalist system. What is produced, how and for whom, can be conveyed as something ultimately depending on the 'democratic' sanction of the people as they spend their money votes in the marketplace. Thus, however perverse the structure of consumption may appear to be, and however unequal the distribution of rewards, these can be traced logically to the free expression of popular preference and to the response of business under the discipline of the marketplace. Government intervention will merely impede the operation of processes which, if left to themselves, will adjust to change and resolve all conflict in the general interest.

Neoclassical theory is obviously at variance with reality in some important respects. Some of the defects have been addressed in subsequent modifications. For example, it is recognized that buyers and sellers may be large enough to affect prices, so competition is not perfect. In fact, there is a tendency in the competitive process for inefficient firms to be eliminated to the extent that monopoly, or something close to it, can develop. This in its turn distorts or constrains the very competition on which efficient reproduction is supposed to depend. Thus anti-monopoly laws usually form part of the attempt by the STATE to regulate a capitalist economy.

In addition to the monopolistic tendencies conventionally considered, SPATIAL MONOPOLY is a source of market imperfection. Another refinement includes the introduction of the category of PUBLIC GOODS which do not lend themselves to supply under market conditions and for which society usually accepts collective responsibility even under capitalism, e.g. defence, certain social services and aspects of INFRASTRUCTURE. Social costs and EXTERNALITIES (unpriced benefits and burdens) are also seen as major distortions of the free-market model.

More fundamental defects of neo-classical theory have also been recognized. The existing pattern of factor ownership and income distribution is taken as given and its legitimacy is unquestioned. Social institutions characteristic of CAPITALISM, such as the private ownership of land and capital, are portrayed as the natural order of things. The analysis of consumer behaviour is highly individualistic, emphasizing freedom of choice at the expense of examining the origins of personal preference and of the budget constraint. For all their formal elegance (or because of it) the analytical devices of neo-classical theory are confined to technical matters and ignore social relationships, such as those among classes under capitalism.

Much of the criticism of neo-classical theory has come from within mainstream economics itself. J. de V. Graaff's *Theoretical welfare economics* (1957) originally laid bare the long and restrictive list of assumptions necessary for a competitive, free-market capitalist economy to realize the optimally efficient and welfare-maximizing outcomes with which it is credited. J.K. Galbraith (1975) was responsible for a sustained critique on the grounds of the changed nature of business organization and control, while E.J. Mishan (1969) pointed to problems in welfare economics arising from such considerations as the negative externalities of economic growth.

Different lines of critique have been followed by radical and Marxist economists. The ideological content of neo-classical theory has been exposed by M. Dobb (1973) and others, who see the perpetuation of the self-regulating, free-market model with its welfare-maximizing properties, in the face of such evident logical flaws and discordance with reality, as attributable in part to its role in supporting the capitalist system. As seen from the Marxist perspective, the focus on purely technical relationships diverts attention from the exploitive nature of capitalism. Furthermore, capitalism is inherently cyclical (see KONDRATIEFF CYCLES), leading to considerable fluctuations in prosperity over time and with great hardship generated by periods of 'downturn'. The repeated crises of recession/depression, inflation, industrial unrest, business scandals, etc., do little to improve confidence either in the capitalist system as a benign, self-regulating mechanism or in the control capacity of those professional economists who claim to understand it (and whose training tends to be in the neo-classical tradition).

The critique of neo-classical theory can be overdone, however. As a theory of how capitalism (or indeed any economic system) actually operates, it is clearly defective. But the analytical devices used to demonstrate optimality in resource allocation in pursuit of efficiency and even the maximization of social welfare do have some practical applicability if adopted with sensitivity to their limitations. Central planning of the kind at one time followed in eastern Europe and the former Soviet Union used some neo-classical devices in the pursuit of allocational optimality, though the actual operation of these societies frustrated its achievement.

The 1980s and 1990s have seen a resurgence of interest in 'free market' processes. This came first in the West, in Reagan's United States and Thatcher's Britain, for example, and then in eastern Europe with the collapse of SOCIALISM and central planning. While market mechanisms do have the capacity to improve economic efficiency in certain circumstances, their adoption in both West and East is often a matter of political ideology and faith rather then an outcome of careful understanding. The very specific conditions required for markets to work in reality as they are supposed to in theory are frequently overlooked in the enthusiasm of free-market fanatics to implement their favoured panacea.

DMS

References and Suggested Reading

Berry, B.J.L. 1970: City size and economic development. In L. Jacobson and V. Prakash, eds, *Urbanization and national development*. Beverly Hills: Sage Publications, 111–56. · Dobb, M. 1973: *Theories of value and distribution since Adam Smith: ideology and economic theory*. Cambridge: Cambridge University Press. · Galbraith, J.K. 1975: *Economics and the public purpose*. London: Penguin; New York: New American Library. · Graaff, J. de V. 1957: *Theoretical welfare economics*. Cambridge: Cambridge University Press. · Hirschman, A.O. 1958: *The strategy of economic development*. New Haven: Yale University Press. · Mishan, E.J. 1969: *The cost of economic growth*. London: Penguin; New York: Praeger. · Myrdal, G. 1957: *Economic theory and underdeveloped regions*. London: Duckworth. · Ohlin, B. 1933: *Interregional and international trade*. Cambridge, MA: Harvard University Press. · Perroux, F. 1950: Economic space, theory and applications. *Quarterly Journal of Economics* 64: 89–104. · Samuelson, P.A. 1998: *Economics: an introductory analysis*, 18th edn. New York: McGraw-Hill. · Smith, D.M. 1977: *Human geography: a welfare approach*. London: Edward Arnold; New York: St. Martin's Press.

neo-colonialism A means of economic and political control articulated through the powerful STATES and capitals (see TRANSNATIONAL) of developed economies (notably the USA, Japan and, collectively, the member states of the EU) over the economies and societies of the underdeveloped world (see DEVELOPMENT; UNDERDEVELOPMENT). The dominated states are apparently independent – there is no formal or direct rule (see COLONIALISM), they exhibit the outward trappings of independence and they are possibly able to participate in a practice and discourse of POST-COLONIALISM. But their economic and political systems remain closely controlled from outside (see DEPENDENCE).

This control may be exerted in a variety of ways. The presence of foreign industrial and finance capital (Radice, 1975; Dicken 1998) does not merely have an effect upon the external economic relations of the neo-colonial societies but, in addition, serves to restructure their CLASS relations and exerts foreign domination by the maintenance of a comprador bourgeoisie (see NEW INTERNATIONAL DIVISION OF LABOUR). Participation in special commercial relations such as those linking France with its West African dependencies and those within the Sterling Area helps not only to tie underdeveloped to developed economies by means of TRADE and investment but also to enforce an internal economic discipline upon the policies of the underdeveloped economies. The Lomé conventions negotiated between the EU and 60 or so African, Caribbean and Pacific states develop the techniques of neo-colonialism by means of AID, trade and investment agreements (Kirkpatrick, 1979). At an even more extensive multilateral scale, the International Monetary Fund enforces a form of capitalist discipline upon the states of those underdeveloped societies which turn to it for help – as debates around the efficacy of the Fund's involvement in South-East Asia in the late 1990s reveal. Political control may also be manipulated more directly and carried out covertly by agencies such as the US Central Intelligence Agency (Agee, 1975).

More generally neo-colonialism is sustained and developed through DISCOURSE (Said, 1978; cf. ORIENTALISM). The construction of (neo)colonial 'others' is sustained by, for example, representations such as 'emerging markets'. These discursive constructions and reconstructions are made daily in the global financial press, which construct the characteristics of such markets (including their construction *as* 'markets') in terms salient to the needs/interests of portfolio and foreign direct investors. This discourse shapes constructions of development and dependence as the possibilities for and problems to be overcome by 'emerging markets' become those relevant to finance capital, whilst the descriptive representations of 'emerging markets' reflect the competitive challenge presented by fear and loathing of, and disgust and desire for risk in, such 'markets' amongst those articulating flows of capital into and out of them. Such fear and desire was central to the violent contradictions embedded in the geographies of the colonial world.

The colonial world is a world cut in two. The dividing line, the frontiers, are shown by barracks and police stations.

> On one side of the divide,
>
> The settler's town is a strongly-built town; the streets are made of stone and steel. The settler's town is a well fed town, an easy-going town; its belly is always full of good things. The settler's town is a town of white people, of foreigners.
>
> And, on the other side,
>
> The town belonging to the colonized people, or at least the native town, the Negro village, the medina, the reservation, is a place of ill fame, peopled by men of evil repute. They are born there, it matters little where or how; they die there, it matters not where, or how. It is a world without spaciousness . . . The native town is a hungry town, . . . a crouching village, . . . a town of niggers and dirty arabs. The look that the native turns on the settler's town is a look of lust, a look of envy; it expresses his dreams of possession – all manner of possession: to sit at the settler's table, to sleep in the settler's bed, with his wife if possible. . . . The colonized man is an envious man. And this the settler knows very well. (Fanon 1967/1961, p. 30)

Frantz Fanon's study of the Algerian revolution combines not merely the economic and political materialities of colonialism – the contradictions which made and make it unsustainable – but the representations of otherness and of absence; the native town is represented in orientalist terms, down to the conditional possibilities of possession.

Faced with these contradictions of colonialism, the various practices of neo-colonialism serve to keep the dominated societies secure within the wider sphere of neocolonial influence, definition and assessment. Its origins and continued sustenance lie in IMPERIALISM – classically associated with the spread of Euro-American expansion during the latter part of the nineteenth century – driven by RACISM, religious expansionism, economic opportunity and geopolitical power (cf. GEOPOLITICS). But for radicals – despite all their differences of emphasis – 'theories of imperialism have essentially the same logic . . . to relieve contradictions internal to the capitalist system' (Peet, 1991, p. 135). With the GLOBALIZATION of contemporary economic geographies – based traditionally upon trade, the internationalization of production and access to raw materials but now related as much to flows of finance capital – the attempt to maintain this security will be intensified. As a result, neo-colonialism, with its associated unproductive and high costs of maintenance and inherent potential for conflict along with the intensification of discipline and chaos exerted through globalized financial markets, is likely to grow and extend. It will thereby contribute directly as well as indirectly to the continued development of underdevelopment. RL

References

Agee, P. 1975: *Inside the company: C.I.A. diary*. London: Penguin; New York: Bantam Books. · Dicken, P. 1998: *Global shift: transforming the world economy*, 3rd edn. London: Paul Chapman Publishing, ch. 13. · Fanon, F. 1967/1961: *The wretched of the earth*. Harmondsworth: Penguin. · Kirkpatrick, C. 1979: The renegotiation of the Lomé Convention. *National Westminster Bank Quarterly Review* May: 23–33. · Peet, R. 1991: *Global capitalism: theories of societal development*. London and New York: Routledge. · Radice, H., ed., 1975: *International firms and modern imperialism*. London: Penguin. · Said, E. 1978: *Orientalism*. London: Routledge.

Suggested Reading

Buchanan, K.M. 1972: *The geography of empire*. Nottingham: Spokesman Books. · Dicken (1998), ch. 13. · Fanon (1967/1961). · Frobel, F., Heinrichs, J. and Kreye, O. 1980: *The new international division of labour*. Cambridge and Paris: Cambridge University Press and Editions de la maison des sciences de l'homme. · Peet (1991) ch. 8.

neo-liberalism A congerie of ideas and theories associated with the rise of the New Right in the North Atlantic economies during the 1980s and with the desirability of the market as the central plank for the organization of social, economic and political life (Hayek, 1981). As the name implies, neo-liberalism traces some of its lineages to particular interpretations of eighteenth- and early nineteenth-century LIBERALISM. In spite of the frequency with which the name of Adam Smith is invoked by neo-liberal theorists and politicians, the logic of the New Right position and of neo-liberal thinking departs substantially from much of what Smith actually argued in *The wealth of nations*. During the industrial transition in England (1750–1840) a group of political economists gravitated around the idea of the Olympian merits of laissez-faire capitalism. Thomas Malthus, Adam Smith, the so-called Manchester Liberals and David Ricardo, among others (see Hirschmann, 1992; McNally, 1993), argued, in a variety of often incompatible ways, for the radical diminution of constraints to market behaviour. Economic liberalism receded during the nineteenth century, and its defeat was in a sense sealed by the Keynesian revolution of the 1930s which overshadowed the monetarist and Austrian Schools of economic analysis. The crises of the 1970s – inflation, instability in global commodity markets, business cycles – prompted a so-called liberal counter-revolution (Toye, 1987), triggered by the political hegemony of Mrs Thatcher (1979–90) in the UK and Ronald Reagan (1980–8) in the US (Krieger, 1986; Jessop et al., 1988). These two figures and their theorists became the vanguard through which laissez-faire thinking entered the realm of DEVELOPMENT thinking. At the Cancun Conference in 1981, Reagan and Thatcher directly attacked the Keynesian notion of a New International Economic Order (NIEO), expressing a distaste for enhanced foreign assistance and commodity stabilization (two planks of the NIEO). The call for free markets and liberal reforms was given a further push by the debt crisis of 1982 and the growing dominance of the IMF and the IBRD in their STRUCTURAL ADJUSTMENT programmes. In its earliest iteration, the ideas favoured by the New Right were *monetarist*, in which Milton Friedman (1962) figured centrally. Abhorring forms of government regulation they advocated a minimalist role for the STATE. The monetarists were subsequently dubbed neo-liberals since the New Right policies went beyond the monetarist strategy, which was narrowly fiscal. Neo-liberalism had by the 1980s come to describe 'the predominantly laissez faire, market driven economic policies sweeping across the globe' (Cypher and Dietz, 1997, p. 208). Francis Fukuyama's book (1992) *The End of History and the last Man* celebrated the demise of SOCIALISM as the final triumphalist victory for the free market.

The theorists of the New Right offer a stark account of neo-liberalism. The overarching claim is that free markets maximize human welfare: economically, markets efficiently distribute knowledge and resources; socially, liberal individualism will maximize moral worth; and politically, liberalism maximizes political freedoms since it rests on the most efficient (PARETO-OPTIMAL) distribution of resources and wealth. The core of neo-liberalism turns on the functioning of the free market, which comprises 'atomistic individuals who know their own autonomously arising needs and wants and who make contracts with other individuals through the mechanisms of the marketplace to satisfy those wants and needs' (Preston, 1996, p. 253). The market is in all respects neutral and its effective functioning demands a minimum state machinery to provide basic legal and social security to underwrite individualism, private property, and political stability. The pro-market position of neo-liberalism has informed development theory and practice through the multilateral regulatory institutions (GATT, IMF, IBRD). Here the work of Deepak Lal (1985) is important: government failure, in varying ways and degrees, is seen as central to poor economic performance, whether in China or Nigeria. Conversely free trade is read into any success story, whether Taiwan or the US (World Bank, 1994).

Curiously, there is little in Adam Smith (1776), or indeed other of the early liberals, which approximates the sloganeering and free market triumphalism of the neo-liberals. Indeed Smith himself feared the consequences of the unregulated market and of unfettered ACCUMULATION (desire let loose). Such a society would indeed tear itself apart and it was only something like CIVIL SOCIETY that could restrain the impulses and destructive urges of the market, and indeed the corruption and authoritarianism of the state. MW

References

Cypher, J. and Dietz. J. 1997: *The process of economic development*. London: Routledge. · Friedman, M. 1962: *Capitalism and freedom*. Chicago: University of Chicago Press. · Fukuyama, F. 1992: *The end of History and the last Man*. New York: Free Press. · Hayek, F. 1981: *The political order of a free people*. Chicago: University of Chicago Press. · Hirschmann, A. 1991: *The rhetoric of reaction*. Cambridge, MA: Harvard University Press. · Jessop, B. et al. 1988: *Thatcherism*. Cambridge: Polity. · Krieger, J. 1986: *Reagan, Thatcher and the politics of decline*. Cambridge: Polity. · Lal, D. 1985: *The failure of development economics*. Oxford: Oxford University Press. · McNally, D. 1993: *Against the market*. London: Verso. · Preston, D. 1996: *Development theory*. Oxford: Blackwell. · Smith, A. 1776: *The wealth of nations*. New York: Modern Library. · Toye, J. 1987: *Dilemmas of development*. Oxford: Blackwell. · World Bank 1994: *The East Asian miracle*. Washington, D.C.: The World Bank.

Suggested Reading

Gray, J. 1993: *Beyond the New Right*. London: Routledge.

neo-Ricardian economics A school of economics that provides criticisms of, and an alternative to, NEO-CLASSICAL and MARXIAN ECONOMICS by drawing upon the ideas of the English classical economist David Ricardo (1772–1823). Although the historical antecedents of neo-Ricardianism include the Russian economist V. Dmitriev and the Prussian statistician L. von Bortkewicz (both writing at the beginning of the twentieth century), it was an Italian economist working at Cambridge University, Piero Sraffa (1898–1983), who established the school in 1960 with the publication of his slim monograph, *The production of commodities by means of commodities*.

Sraffa's model of the ECONOMY consists of two components (see figure):

The technical conditions of production are represented by a series of fixed, linear input–output production equations, thereby eliminating the effects of demand. Following the classical economic tradition, Sraffa conceives of production as a circular and interdependent process where the output in one production period is used as an input for the next production period. Peculiar to Sraffa's analysis is the absence of any fundamental entity determining relative prices. In contrast, Ricardo, and later Marx, grounded their analysis in the LABOUR THEORY OF VALUE, the idea that the price of a good is fixed by the amount of labour time required to produce it. In Sraffa's scheme there is no such ultimate price determinant: the price of a good in one period is determined by the prices of all goods produced in the previous period, where those prices themselves were determined by the prices of all goods produced in the production period before that, and so on back to the beginning of time. At no point are prices derived from a final source such as labour values.

When outputs exceed inputs, a 'surplus' exists that forms the basis of the social conditions of distribution. The surplus represents the pool from which each social CLASS draws its respective income share. In common with other proponents of the circular view of production, Sraffa demonstrates that at least one of the income shares must be given from outside the system of production in order to derive a determinate set of prices. This is important because it means that, unlike orthodox neo-classical economics, neo-Ricardianism is compelled theoretically to refer to non-economic relations. The effect is to redraw the traditional boundaries of economics so as to include the wider array of social, political and cultural institutions that bear on income distribution. Furthermore, because the surplus is finite, the relationship among social classes is necessarily adversarial: one class's gain is another's loss.

Significantly Sraffa's book is subtitled *Prelude to a critique of economic theory*. While Sraffa does not engage in the critique himself, his model provided the basis for subsequent systematic criticisms of both standard neoclassical and Marxist theories. These criticisms were first taken up in the *capital controversy*, where neo-classical marginal productivity theory was attacked, and later in the *value controversy*, where the Marxist labour theory of value came under scrutiny.

The *capital controversy* raged during the 1960s. It was initiated by Joan Robinson's (1953) query about the definition of capital within the neo-classical aggregate production function, that is, the formally defined relation between the two inputs, labour and 'capital', and the resulting output. It was not until Sraffa's demonstration of 'capital reswitching' and 'capital reversing' that a decisive assault on neoclassicism was made, however. According to neo-classical theory, the income accruing to a FACTOR OF PRODUCTION is equal to its marginal product; the output of the last unit of that factor hired. Assuming that marginal PRODUCTIVITY falls as more of a factor is used (a result of diminishing returns), neoclassicism derives a negative relationship between the rate of profit (the marginal product of capital) and the amount of capital employed (measured as capital intensity). More broadly, this negative relationship implicitly justifies profit as the consequence of capital scarcity: when capital is scarce, and hence marginal productivity high, profits are high, and vice versa when capital is abundant. In this sense, the relationship between the scarcity of capital and its

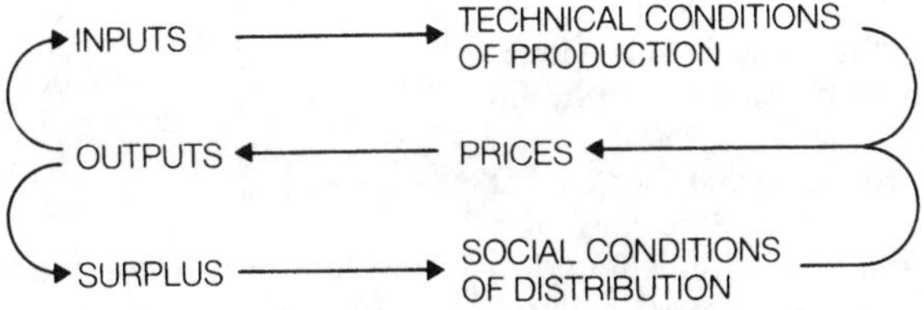

neo-Ricardian economics

price (the rate of profit) seems no different in kind than for any other commodity.

While this neo-classical 'parable' appears intuitively plausible, Sraffa's findings of capital reswitching and reversing rebut it. The details are complex, but both capital reswitching and reversing negate the supposed negative relationship between the rate of profit and the amount of capital employed, thus also undermining the neo-classical marginal productivity theory which is its basis. In so doing, the critique opens the way for a new interpretation of the meaning and justification of profit, in this case, one that treats the price of capital as set by social, not technical, relations.

The *value controversy* began in the mid-1970s. Identified in particular with Ian Steedman (1977), the debate on Marx's labour theory of value centred around the 'transformation problem', that is, finding a correct procedure to convert labour values into a set of consistent prices. Steedman argues that for a number of reasons Marx's original solution to the problem was incorrect. This failing, however, is not simply due to Marx's poor arithmetic, but is a result of employing labour values in the first place. Following Sraffa, Steedman shows that prices can be determined independently of labour values. Steedman's critique is not meant as a sweeping dismissal of the whole of Marxist economics, however. Rather, neo-Ricardians believe that a coherent and logically consistent theory of CAPITALISM can only be elaborated once metaphysical entities such as labour values are expunged from that tradition.

Neo-Ricardianism, in its turn, has been criticized often by Marxists. The complaints include: that neo-Ricardianism is empty formalism, without social or historical grounding; that it contains no theory of history or change; that it draws upon Weber's class categories, which for Marxists at least are inadequate because they are insufficiently rooted in relations of production; that it provides no discussion of the labour process; that it emphasizes market over production relationships; that it is a theory based upon commodity fetishism; and that it smuggles in its own form of ESSENTIALISM (Roosevelt, 1974). In response, the supporters of neo-Ricardianism argue that such criticisms miss the point of Sraffa's work. Sraffa is not concerned with constructing a GRAND THEORY to explain everything. Instead, he offers a *contextual* approach (Barnes, 1996a, ch. 7; cf. CONTEXTUAL APPROACH), concerned with a few precisely defined issues within political economy, but saying nothing about broader questions that are resolvable only within the context at hand.

The question, though, is whether such a minimalist approach satisfies. Judging by the paucity of publications within the neo-Ricardian tradition over the 1990s, it appears that it doesn't. There remains continued interest in Sraffa as a twentieth-century intellectual, but neo-Ricardianism as a school is increasingly dormant. Even former acolytes of the movement, such as Steedman and Hodgson, now pursue historical and methodological studies rather than high theory. (Hodgson's (1988) account of his 'conversion' to institutional economics is especially illuminating.) While Sraffa's logic might be impeccable, it has proven no match against an ostensibly less logical, neo-classical and Marxist economics which has barely registered his objections. The likely problem is that Sraffa's logic is too pure: 'a double distilled elixir' as Joan Robinson (1953, p. 7) once described it. Such purity always required besmirching by the world, and because it wasn't, it lost out to other logics that were.

Economic geographers have made some use of neo-Ricardian economics. The work begins with Scott's (1976) pioneering paper linking Sraffa's model of production with VON THÜNEN'S MODELS of agricultural rent. More recently, other topics within economic geography examined from a neo-Ricardian perspective include: agricultural land use (Huriot, 1981), interregional TRADE (Barnes,

1985), spatial reswitching (Pavlik, 1990), and urban fixed capital (Sheppard and Barnes, 1990, ch. 7). To date there has been no direct empirical application of Sraffa's work in economic geography, however. Rather, as in economics, neo-Ricardianism has been most effective as a logical critique, especially of a number of theories and propositions found in the neo-classical-inspired REGIONAL SCIENCE movement, and offshoots such as the new urban economics. In making those critiques, however, it was found that the introduction of geography into Sraffa's work produces indeterminacy in his otherwise determinant aspatial conclusions (for example, with respect to technical change and trade; Sheppard and Barnes, 1990). While those indeterminacies might be resolved through empirical study, what has happened, as in economics, is the increasing abandonment of neo-Ricardianism by former proponents in favour of other approaches that deal more directly with the world, for example, in Scott's (1988) use of Regulation theory, or in Barnes's (1996b) application of the STAPLES model with its strong links to NEW INSTITUTIONAL ECONOMICS. It might turn out that economic geography is too base a discipline to practise Sraffa's high-minded logic. TJB

References

Barnes, T.J. 1985: Theories of interregional trade and theories of value. *Environment and Planning A* 17: 729–46. · Barnes, T.J. 1996a: *Logics of dislocation: models, metaphors and meanings of economic space*. New York: Guilford. · Barnes, T.J. 1996b: External shocks: regional implications of an open staples economy. In J.N.H. Britton, ed., *Canada and the global economy: the geography of structural and technological change*. Montreal and Kingston: McGill-Queens, 48–68. · Hodgson, G.M. 1988: *After Marx and Sraffa: essays in political economy*. Basingstoke: Macmillan. · Huriot, J.M. 1981: Rente foncière et modèle de production. *Environment and Planning A* 13: 1125–49. · Pavlik, C. 1990: Technical switching: a spatial case. *Environment and Planning A* 22: 1025–34. · Robinson, J.V. 1953: The production function and the theory of capital. *Review of Economic Studies* 21: 81–106. · Roosevelt, F. 1974: Cambridge economics as commodity fetishism. *Review of Radical Political Economy* 7: 1–32. · Scott, A.J. 1976: Land use and commodity production. *Regional Science and Urban Economics* 6: 147–60. · Scott, A.J. 1988: Flexible production systems in regional development: The rise of new industrial spaces in North America and Western Europe. *International Journal of Urban and Regional Research* 15: 171–86. · Sheppard, E. and Barnes, T.J. 1990: *The capitalist space economy: geographical analysis after Ricardo, Marx and Sraffa*. London: Unwin-Hyman. · Sraffa, P. 1960: *Production of commodities by means of commodities*. Cambridge: Cambridge University Press. · Steedman, I. 1977: *Marx after Sraffa*. London: New Left Books.

Suggested reading

Barnes (1996a), ch. 7. · Rowthorn, R. 1974: Neo-classicism, neo-Ricardianism and Marxism. *New Left Review* 86: 63–87. · Wolff, R.P. 1982: Piero Sraffa and the rehabilitation of classical political economy. *Social Research* 49: 209–38.

networks and graph theory In human geography the term network is mainly used to refer to a transport network either of permanent facilities (road, rail, canal) or of scheduled services (bus, train, airlines). It has however been extended to cover many other types of line or linkage patterns including administrative boundaries, social contacts (see SOCIAL NETWORK), and telecommunications.

The representation of a network for purposes of description and analysis has been tackled in a number of ways. CARTOGRAPHIC representations often required the compiler to discard significant amounts of information in order to portray their salient features. This was taken one step further by using *graph theory* (a branch of mathematics), which represented the network as a series of nodes (or vertices) and the links (or edges) between them, with each node or vertex having an equal weighting of unity. This was in turn capable of being represented by a binary matrix. Both the graph and the binary matrix were then susceptible to a range of mathematical analyses which identified salient characteristics of the network, but the loss of information (even distortions) occasioned by the reduction of a network to a graph raised doubts about the validity of the approach in geography. The development of high-speed computers and GEOGRAPHICAL INFORMATION SYSTEMS has resolved the problem to some extent, because it is now possible to store and retrieve highly detailed descriptions of networks within such systems without resorting to abstraction, but there remain problems of arriving at satisfactory ways of summarizing that wealth of information.

However the network is represented, a number of characteristics of networks are of importance to geography – *density, connectedness, and orientation*. Network *density* (most simply, length of network per unit area) is important because it bears a mathematical and empirical statistical relationship with the average distance of points in an area from their nearest route or node, thus having implications for ACCESSIBILITY. Network *connectedness* (sometimes referred to as connectivity) identifies whether movements can be made between locations on the network, and how directly such movements may be made. In measuring the latter property, use is made of the ratio between route distance and geodetic distance (often referred to as the route factor): high ratios suggest a poorly connected network, but may also reflect the indirectness of individual routes (for example as a consequence of rugged terrain). Empirical work suggests that route factors are typically higher for rail networks (around 1.8) than for road networks (1.3 to 1.4). *Connectedness* is usually seen as a characteristic of the whole network, but it may also be seen as a characteristic which differentiates between locations or nodes (some are well-connected to other places, but others are not). It is therefore linked to the third concept – *orientation*: a network may be structured in such a way that some directions of movement are better served than others so that, for example, a radial network may favour movements to and from a central point in contrast to circumferential movements, while a grid network will favour two directions (the orientation of the grid) against diagonal movements.

In addition to such descriptive and analytic studies geographers have attempted to explain the form of networks. Such explanation may focus on the decisions to construct and maintain individual network elements (ports, airports, road, rail or canal links) or on the way whole network characteristics are associated with other variables (date of construction, political conditions, population density, terrain etc.). AMH

Suggested Reading

Chorley, R.J. and Haggett, P. 1974: *Network analysis in geography*, 2nd edn. London: Edward Arnold. · New York: St. Martin's Press.

new institutional economics An umbrella term describing a set of interrelated theoretical approaches that emphasize the centrality of social, cultural, and political *institutions*, and their interaction, in the constitution and maintenance of the ECONOMY. Typically inclined towards a form of POLITICAL ECONOMY, the new institutional economics is a third way lying between, on the one hand, the more politically driven and theoretically closed MARXIAN ECONOMICS, and, on the other, the more abstract and formal NEO-CLASSICAL ECONOMICS with its often uncritical belief in the beneficence of the market.

Institutional economics originally arose with the work of the American maverick economist Thorstein Veblen (1857–1929). Reacting against both the increasing dominance of an imported European neo-classical economic theory, with its celebration of *homo economicus* (parodied by Veblen, 1919, p. 73, as a 'homogeneous globule of desire'), and a domestic industrial system that spawned massive inequalities in levels of wealth and consumption, Veblen constructed a made-in-America theory of his own time and place, institutional economics. But theory travels. The cultural-historical sensibility Veblen brought to the analysis of economic life, along with his specific emphasis on the close relationship between behaviour and evolving institutions (defined as 'settled habits of thought'; Veblen, 1919, p. 239), subsequently shaped the character of four contemporary new institutionalist approaches, each of which have influenced economic geographers to different degrees.

The most direct legacy of Veblen's work is found in Hodgson's (1988) and Mirowski's (1989) *methodological criticisms of neo-classical economics*, and especially of that school's representation of markets and value. They argue that neither markets nor value are spectral phenomena, the result of respectively an 'invisible hand' or abstract 'n-dimensional consumer preference maps', but they are a direct consequence of human institutions and their instantiated power. In addition, contemporary institutional economics remains vigorously empirical, examples of which are found in the school's flagship journal, *Journal of Economic Issues*. In geography, Martin (1994) discusses the applicability of Veblen's work, and Barnes (1997) Hodgson's and Mirowski's.

Evolutionary economics stems from Veblen's use of DARWINIAN theory; indeed, he labelled his work 'post-Darwinian economics'. Drawing upon the Darwinian triad of individual variation, inheritance of characteristics, and natural selection, Nelson and Winter (1982) developed an influential evolutionary theory of the firm centring on technological choice. This work was subsequently refined by a number of writers who have emphasized the 'lock-in' characteristic of such choice, and resulting 'path dependency' (Arthur, 1989). In economic geography, Rigby and Essletzbichler (1996) draw directly on evolutionary economics in their discussion of technical change in the US, and Storper (1997) discusses and elaborates the ideas of technological 'lock-in' and 'path dependency' in a 'regional world'.

Socio-economics or the new economic sociology is linked to Veblen's work by its emphasis on the social (and cultural) embeddedness of the economy. Initiated by Granovetter's (1985) now classic paper, socio-economics contends that all economic action is social action and socially situated, and that therefore all economic institutions are social institutions. Amin and Thrift (1995) provide geographical case studies.

A final approach, and different from the previous three, but the one for which the label 'the new institutional economics' was originally coined, is Williamson's work on *Markets and hierarchies* (1975). Williamson's argument is that *firms which operate in imperfect markets, a result of inherent uncertainty and bounded rationality* (see SATISFICING BEHAVIOUR), strive to minimize TRANSACTION COSTS by institutionally internalizing them through such strategies as establishing interior GOVERNANCE structures and hierarchies. In turn, according to Williamson, such strategies become the driving force behind the rise of large vertically integrated firms, the dominant form of business organization in the post-war period (cf. INTEGRATION). On institutional structure Williamson's work is more subtle than conventional economic theory, which reduces it simply to the sum of individual decision-makers (METHODOLOGICAL INDIVIDUALISM). But there is still a strong sense in his work that governance structures and hierarchies are arrived at by RATIONAL CHOICE, a supposition that would have been anathema to Veblen. In economic geography, the most well-known exponent of Williamson's work is Scott (1988) who makes it foundational for his 'post-Weberian' LOCATION THEORY. TJB

References

Amin, A. and Thrift, N.J. 1995: Institutional issues for European regions: from markets and plans to socioeconomics and powers of association. *Economy and Society* 24: 41–66. · Arthur, W.B. 1989: Competing technologies, increasing returns, and lock-in by historical events. *Economic Journal* 99: 116–31. · Barnes, T.J. 1997: Theories of accumulation and regulation: bringing life back into economic geography. In R. Lee and J. Wills, eds, *Geographies of economies*. London: Arnold, 231–48. · Granovetter, M.S. 1985: Economic action and social structure: the problem of embeddedness. *American Journal of Sociology* 91: 481–510. · Hodgson, G. 1988: *Economics and institutions: a manifesto for a modern institutional economics*. Cambridge: Polity. · Martin, R.L. 1994: Economic theory and economic geography. In D. Gregory, R. Martin, and G. Smith, eds, *Human geography: society, space and social science*. London: Macmillan, 21–53. · Mirowski, P. 1989: *More heat than light. Economics as social physics, physics as nature's economics*. Cambridge: Cambridge University Press. · Nelson, R.R., and Winter, S.G. 1982: *An evolutionary theory of economic change*. Cambridge, MA: Harvard University Press. · Rigby, D.L., and Essletzbichler, J. 1996: Evolution, process variety and regional trajectories of technological change in US manufacturing. *Economic Geography* 73: 269–84. · Scott, A.J. 1988: *Metropolis: From division of labor to urban form*. Berkeley, CA: University of California Press. · Storper, M. 1997: *The regional world: territorial development in a global economy*. New York: Guilford. · Veblen, T. 1919: *The place of science in modern civilization and other essays*. New York: B.W. Huebsch. · Williamson, O. 1975: *Markets and hierarchies*. New York: Free Press.

Suggested Reading

Amin and Thrift (1995). · Barnes (1997).

new international division of labour (NIDL) An emergent form of the worldwide DIVISION OF LABOUR associated with the internationalization of production and the spread of INDUSTRIALIZATION, especially in a number of rapidly growing newly industrializing countries (NICs). Although apparently 'new', the NIDL is more accurately understood as a manifestation of the perpetual geographical restructuring of capital at a global SCALE – a restructuring that has been in process for centuries – intensively so since the end of the nineteenth century (see IMPERIALISM; NEOCOLONIALISM).

The term has been used most explicitly by Fröbel et al. (1980) in their account of the DEINDUSTRIALIZATION of the old industrial countries. It is associated with the outflow of investment as CAPITAL operating on a global scale and taking advantage of transportation and communications technology and the fragmentation and locational separability of the productive process, to tap the global reserve army of labour and to seek out cheap production sites in order better to face competitive pressures. An alternative interpretation suggests that MULTINATIONAL CORPORATIONS are pushed out of highly industrialized economies by the falling rate of profit. The implication is that the NIDL is one strategic response to the continuous imperative of ACCUMULATION in CAPITALISM. TRANSNATIONAL CORPORATIONS (TNCs) – the major agents of the NIDL – reorganize the geography of their productive structure in order to enhance profitability and so stimulate the growth of industrial production in the NICs and elsewhere. However, the resultant industrialization process within the host economies is limited in its effects:

> Only rarely do developing countries end up with the establishment of reasonably complex industrial branches... And even in the very few developing countries where such centres of partial industrialization have been established there are no signs that they are being supplemented by a wider industrial complex which would enable them to free themselves from their dependency on the already industrialised

countries for imports of capital and other goods, and for the maintenance of their industrial installations ... Instead, industrial production is confined to a few highly specialized manufacturing processes ... in world market factories ... with no connection to the local economy except for their utilization of extremely cheap labour and occasionally some local inputs. (Fröbel et al., 1980, p. 6)

A central feature of such accounts is the stress upon the role of multinational capital (Schoenberger, 1988) in shaping the world economy, especially in the expansion/relocation of production:

One form of this relocation ... is the closing down of certain types of manufacturing operations ... in the industrial nations and the subsequent installation of these parts of the production process in foreign subsidiaries of the same company. (Fröbel et al., 1980)

The NIDL is, in this view, the result of the multinational RESTRUCTURING of production. Only incidentally would the interests of MNCs coincide with the build-up of an integrated and complex industrial structure in a developing country. The countries remain passive and *dependent* (see DEPENDENCE).

Less critical than this dependency view of the NIDL is that presented by the *diffusionist* theorists (e.g. see Chisholm, 1982; see also Corbridge, 1986; cf. DIFFUSION). Here most emphasis is placed upon the leading forces within the industrializing economies to mobilize available resources and to develop distinctive patterns of COMPARATIVE ADVANTAGE in exploiting the opportunities for development presented by the international environment. The primacy of multinational capital is supplemented in this account by the practice of NATION-STATES, assisted by an assumed and unspecified, but apparently beneficent, transfer of developmental resources from the core nations to those of the periphery.

While it is right to move away from determinist accounts of the emergence of the NIDL and to point out that NATIONS need not necessarily be passive, it is also necessary to situate the process in the overarching context of the structure and dynamics of the world economic geography (see WORLD-SYSTEMS ANALYSIS for one interpretation) and to inquire into the national politics and potential for national resistance to the dominant forces of international development. It is in this context that Chisholm's entirely appropriate insistence upon the significance of geographical variations from place to place in the working out of the development process should be, but is not, most apparent.

The central importance of international CAPITAL in shaping the NIDL is clearly apparent in the recognition that only a very small number of developing countries have developed a significant level of industrialization (Dicken, 1998). It is also apparent in the tendency of investment to switch back to the old industrial economies as computer-aided production and other information and biotechnologies increase the capital intensity of the LABOUR PROCESS and so reassert the significance of the production of relative, as opposed to absolute, surplus value (see MARXIAN ECONOMICS). Indeed, a critique of the NIDL thesis focuses upon its almost exclusive attention on the significance of absolute surplus value as a determinant of the geography of production. However, the production of relative surplus value may allow and even require that production locations – especially those based on high value, high productivity and high levels of skill – are based in regions associated with an 'old' division of labour. The new international division of labour could, thereby, itself soon become old.

Such dynamics have, according to Manuel Castells (1996, pp. 106, 136), already created the 'newest international division of labour' within the global economy emerging from informational-based production and competition and

characterised by its *interdependence*, its *asymmetry*, its *regionalization*, the *increasing diversification within each region*, its *selective inclusiveness*, its *exclusionary segmentation* and ... extraordinarily *variable geometry* that tends to dissolve historical, economic geography

in which, for example, 'most of Africa ceased to exist as an economically-viable entity'. Such dramatic transformations and processes of UNEVEN DEVELOPMENT are the latest representations of the geographical shifts driven and exploited by capital in its search for surplus value. They raise fundamental questions about the nature of and strategies for development and the criteria and time frames used to define and evaluate them. RL

References

Castells, M. 1996: *The rise of the network society, volume I: The information age: economy, society and culture*. Cambridge, MA and Oxford: Blackwell, ch. 2. · Chisholm, M. 1982: *Modern world development*. London: Hutchinson; Ottawa, NJ: Barnes and Noble. · Corbridge, S. 1986: *Capitalist world development*. London: Macmillan, ch. 4. · Dicken, P. 1998: *Global shift: the internationalisation of economic activity*, 3rd edn. London: Paul Chapman Publishing, ch. 6. · Fröbel, F., Heinrichs, J. and Kreye, O. 1980: *The new international division of labour*. Cambridge and New York: Cambridge University Press. ·

Knox, P. and Agnew, J. 1994: *The geography of the world economy*. London and New York: Arnold, ch. 3. · Schoenberger, E. 1988: Multinational corporations and the new international division of labour: a critical appraisal. *International Regional Science Review* 11: 105–19.

Suggested reading

Castells (1996). · Fröbel, Heinrichs and Kreye (1980).

New Town A planned free-standing, urban centre, added to an existing settlement system. In this sense any planned settlement of substantial size is a 'new town'; including, for example, the *bastides* of medieval Europe, company towns built by enlightened industrialists for their workers, settlements of colonial powers in overseas empires, and 'artificial' capital cities in independent states. In Britain the phrase refers to the post-Second World War overspill solution to excessive conurbation growth, itself a natural successor of Howard's GARDEN CITY concept (indeed, Welwyn Garden City became one of the first London New Towns). These also showed other defining characteristics of minimal COMMUTING and maximum social balance. Some of these New Towns were also intended to serve as instruments of REGIONAL POLICY.

So the world's first industrial nation became the first also to respond to the economic and social pressures of dysfunctional metropolitan growth in this way. Abercrombie's influential 1944 Greater London Plan advocated ten New Town reception areas for London overspill beyond a GREEN BELT, and the New Towns Act two years later established the necessary administrative and financial structures, including their management by non-elected development corporations. In total, 14 New Towns were designated in the UK in a frenzy of activity from 1947 to 1950, of which 8 served London overspill, and a further 17 have been designated since, none around London.

While the general principles of economic self-containment, social balance, landscaping, recreation and high-quality transport provision have been followed, Britain's New Towns have also undergone detailed changes in their half-century of achievement. Their planned eventual size has risen tenfold, the amount of private development incorporated has increased, and the NEIGHBOURHOOD UNIT principles in the early schemes were abandoned in some of the later ones. Finally, the intended transfer of New Town assets to local government with the 'wind up' of their development corporations became complicated by the PRIVATIZATION programme of public assets, leading to a wider mix of housing tenure than originally envisaged.

The concept has been widely admired and copied: Osborn and Whittick (1977) list parallel developments in 67 countries. Those in France (notably, to accommodate Paris overspill), Sweden and the USA are particularly significant in advanced economies, although their experience differs from Britain's (Cervero, 1995).

In the USA, for example, the oldest of its over 140 New Towns pre-dates the British experiment (i.e. Radburn, designed in 1928). Private development is more to the fore (for example, Reston, Virginia); and free-standing locations are less commonplace (such as the 'town within a town' at Cedar-Riverside, to revitalize downtown Minneapolis/St. Paul). Equally, neither self-containment nor social balance is sacrosanct: Soul City, North Carolina, is designed to house poor blacks while many others are avowedly middle-class, and use ZONING ordinances to remain so.

In the latest phase of the New Town story the spotlight has switched to Japan and the THIRD WORLD, as correctives to PRIMATE CITY dominance, as through new capitals in Brazil and Nigeria or Egypt's programme of desert cities as counterweights to the economic pull of the Nile Delta (Stewart, 1996). AGH

References

Cervero, R. 1995: Planned communities, self-containment and commuting – a cross-national perspective. *Urban Studies* 32: 1135–61. · Osborn, F.J. and Whittick, A. 1977: *New Towns*, 3rd edn. London: Leonard Hill; Boston: Routledge and Kegan Paul. · Stewart, D.J. 1996: Cities in the desert – the Egyptian New Town program. *Annals of the Association of American Geographers* 86: 459–80.

NIMBY The acronym for Not-In-My-Back-Yard, an attitude typical of individuals resisting the siting of a source of negative EXTERNALITIES next to their homes and campaigning for its location elsewhere (cf. CONFLICT). RJJ

nodal region A REGION whose defining characteristic is the links between its various parts and one or more focal points. Nodal regions are usually defined using flow data, such as those on COMMUTING (see HINTERLAND; METROPOLITAN LABOUR AREA), and form the core of Haggett's LOCATIONAL ANALYSIS schema. RJJ

nomadism A high degree of spatial MOBILITY or wandering as a basis for a particular way of life (Salzman, 1980). Nomadism implies no or very limited reliance upon sedentary cultivation. In general, nomadism is presumed to be synonymous with livestock rearing and the movements of herds (animal husbandry), especially in the semi-arid tropics and in montane regions (Johnson, 1969). But hunter-gatherers who typically have no domesticated livestock are also defined by their 'nomadic style' (for example the San peoples of the Kalahari desert). Nomadism in both of these cases is distinguished from the very limited seasonal movements of animals associated with sedentary agriculture (see TRANSHUMANCE). Nomadism is often classified in terms of the degree of spatial mobility. So-called *full or true nomads* have no permanent dwellings and practise no agriculture, though they participate in exchange relations to acquire grain (e.g. the Wodaabe of the West African Sahel). *Semi-nomads* practise wet season agriculture but are usually mobile during the dry season (e.g. the Masai of East Africa) as they search for pasture and water with their herds (see PASTORALISM). MW

References

Johnson, D. 1969: *The nature of nomadism: a comparative study of pastoral migrations in Southeast Asia and Northern Africa*. Chicago: University of Chicago, Department of Geography Research Paper #118. · Salzman, P. 1980: Is nomadism a useful concept? *Nomadic Peoples* 6: 1–7.

nomothetic Concerned with the universal and the general. The term derived from neo-Kantian EPISTEMOLOGY, and most notably from an 1894 address by the philosopher Windelband, who used it to signify one of two possible goals of concept formation:

> The theoretical interests associated with nomothetic concept formation highlight those common qualities of objects of experience that lead to the formulation of general laws of nature. The process is one of continual ABSTRACTION in which the special qualities of an object are filtered out and the object is seen as a general type that exists with certain relations to other, general types. (Entrikin, 1991)

Windelband contrasted this with IDIOGRAPHIC concept formation, which is concerned to achieve a complete understanding of the *individual* case (see also KANTIANISM).

The term gained currency in geography after the middle of the twentieth century, in the wake of the Hartshorne–Schaefer exchange over EXCEPTIONALISM, when the proponents of SPATIAL SCIENCE claimed that geography should be directed towards the formulation (rather than simply the application) of scientific THEORIES and LAWS. Guelke (1977) saw that mid-century debate as being 'of crucial importance in changing the direction of research... away from any consideration of the unique' and towards the search for general laws of spatial organization (see Golledge and Amedeo, 1968). Much of that search, itself part of the formalization of POSITIVISM within geography, took place within the existing framework of LOCATION THEORY; but its rapid extension into the very centre of the discipline and its displacement of more traditional objectives soon produced a host of claims that geography should be concerned with intrinsically spatial theory if it was to be a distinctive science. Harvey's *Explanation in geography* (1969) thus concluded that 'by our theories you shall know us'. The status of many of these laws and theories was often qualified (see INSTRUMENTALISM), and their autonomy was challenged by those who thought that 'the spatial position's aim of prying apart a subject matter from the systematic sciences by arguing for spatial questions and spatial laws does not seem viable' (Sack, 1974a, 1974b). Even so, these efforts were a vitally important input to the development of SPACE–TIME FORECASTING and also a formative influence on the growth of a greater theoretical awareness within the subject. Today that awareness rarely hinges on any ideographic–nomothetic distinction: interest in the philosophy of REALISM and in the development of various forms of a CONTEXTUAL APPROACH to human geography, together with a critique of GRAND THEORY and an interest in SITUATED KNOWLEDGES, has produced a much more nuanced understanding of both the powers and the limits of 'theory'. DG

References

Entrikin, J.N. 1991: *The betweenness of place: towards a geography of modernity*. London: Macmillan. · Golledge, R.G. and Amedeo, D. 1968: On laws in geography. *Annals of the Association American Geographers* 58: 760–74. · Guelke, L. 1977: The role of laws in human geography. *Progress in Human Geography* 1: 376–86. · Harvey, D. 1969: *Explanation in geography*. London: Edward Arnold. · Sack, R. 1974a: Chorology and spatial analysis. *Annals of the Association of American Geographers* 64: 439–52. · Sack, R. 1974b: The spatial separatist theme in geography. *Economic Geography* 50: 1–19.

Suggested Reading

Entrikin (1991), 93–8. · Guelke (1977).

non-parametric statistics A family of statistical procedures (also referred to as distribution-free statistics) used to analyse data at either the nominal or ordinal level of MEASUREMENT; PARAMETRIC STATISTICS are used with interval and ratio level data. The most popular non-parametric statistical test is the CHI SQUARE. RJJ

non-representational theory A theory of mobile practices. Non-representational theory, a term coined by Thrift (1996), is a radical attempt to wrench the social sciences and humanities out of their current emphasis on representation and interpretation by moving away from a view of the world based on contemplative models of thought and action towards theories of practice which amplify the potential of the flow of events.

Taking its line from early protagonists like Dewey, Wittgenstein and Bakhtin, as well as more recent writers like Shotter, Irigaray and Butler, non-representational theory depends upon a single question: how would the social sciences and humanities go on if they were to take practices seriously? But the answer to this seemingly simple question demands a number of reformulations. First, the world must be seen as momentary, as always in the making of *now*. Second, 'SOCIETY' becomes a set of more or less durable networks of heterogeneous actors – or, more properly, '*actants*' (see ACTOR–NETWORK THEORY) – who are able to produce more or less durable moments by forging connections. However, this durability arising out of difference requires something more than the simple conjunction of actors, it also requires the expressive power offered by embodiment and the other capacities of actors or the moment cannot be made afresh and active. Third, and relatedly, the world cannot be counted as a primarily discursive phenomenon. Many capacities arise from interaction between elements, without any explicit discursive formulation (rather as TIME-GEOGRAPHY attempted to argue but without the rigidities of that approach's graphic trails). Fourth, non-representational theory is based on a notion of time and SPACE (or, rather, times and spaces) as the effects of the commotion arising from the manifold possibilities of interconnection produced by network-building. This is a world in which the 'and' of the connection between actors defines the actors' times and spaces and not vice versa. Places therefore became 'the effect of the folding of spaces, times and materials together into complex topological arrangements that perform a multitude of differences' (Hetherington, 1997, p. 197). Fifth, this sense of the world entails the production of a new theoretical style. The old EPISTEMOLOGY-driven technologies of THEORY, and the notions of theory that underpin them, are replaced by a more modest anti-epistemological style of work which is both determinedly political (in that it requires active engagement with the world) and determinedly partial (in that it no longer aims to encompass the world).

What does all this mean for human geography? So far as the discipline is concerned, non-representational theory challenges the increasingly anaemic and predictable HEGEMONY of current CULTURAL GEOGRAPHY. In particular, much cultural geography, with its commitment to REPRESENTATION, is seen as reproducing elitist intellectual practices whilst arguing the opposite. So far as methodology is concerned, non-representational theory obtains much of its inspiration from the performing arts – theatre, dance, music, performance art, and the like – because they have to negotiate the non-discursive and because they are committed to notions of PERFORMANCE and PERFORMATIVITY which foster the new. They have therefore developed a whole series of technologies for refiguring times and spaces upon which it is possible to call. Then, so far as politics is concerned, non-representational theory is an attempt to move off onto new ground where the witness *must* become an observant participant rather than a participant observer. Through its emphasis on the intensity of commitment and the commitment of intensity, non-representational theory allows of no hiding place. You must be in it. NJT

References

Hetherington, K. 1997: In place of geometry: the materiality of place. In K. Hetherington, and R. Munro, eds, *Ideas of difference. Social spaces and the labour of division*. Oxford: Blackwell, 183–99. · Thrift, N.J. 1996: *Spatial formations*. London: Sage. · Thrift, N.J. 1997: The still point: expressive embodiment and dance. In S. Pile and M. Keith, eds, *Geographies of resistance*. London, Routledge, 124–51.

Suggested Reading

Rose, G. and Thrift, N.J., eds, 2000: Special issue on performance and performativity. *Environment and Planning D. Society and Space*, 18(4). · Thrift, N.J. 1999: Steps to an ecology of place. In J. Allen, D. Massey and Sarre, P., eds, *Human geography today*. Cambridge: Polity Press.

normal distribution A theoretical FREQUENCY DISTRIBUTION whose identifying characteristic is its bell-shaped symmetry around the three measures of its central tendency – mean, median and mode (see figure). As with all theoretical distributions, it has a smooth shape based on a histogram for an infinitely large population of values. Using the two major measures of its form (its mean and standard deviation – sd) it is possible to identify the exact location of an individual value within it – i.e. how far that value is from the mean in sd units.

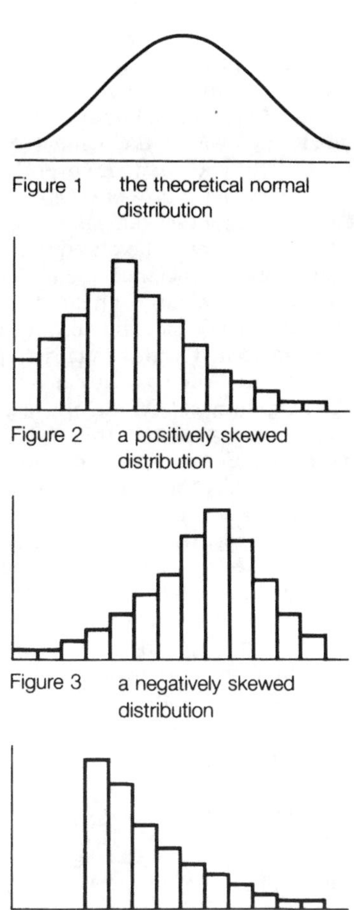

Figure 1 the theoretical normal distribution

Figure 2 a positively skewed distribution

Figure 3 a negatively skewed distribution

Figure 4 a truncated positively skewed distribution

normal distribution

Many of the test statistics used in CONFIRMATORY DATA ANALYSIS have normal distributions, which allow precise statements of the probability of an observed value being obtained from a random allocation procedure (e.g. the probability of getting a CORRELATION coefficient, *r*, of 0.67 with a random allocation of the values across that number of observations). Thus the normal distribution is central to much PARAMETRIC STATISTICAL analysis.

Deviations from the normal distribution involve *skewness* (in which the mean and the median are not the same value) and *kurtosis*. A positively skewed distribution has a longer right-hand than left-hand tail, for example, with the reverse for a negatively skewed distribution: a truncated distribution lacks one of the tails (see figure). Regarding kurtosis, a platykurtic distribution is 'flatter' than the normal (i.e. has a relatively large sd) and a leptokurtic distribution is more 'peaked' (has a relatively small standard deviation). RJJ

Suggested Reading

Gardiner, V. and Gardiner, G. 1978: *Analysis of frequency distributions*. Concepts and Techniques in Modern Geography 19. Norwich: Geo Books.

normative theory A THEORY which 'concerns what ought to be'. Unlike '*positive theory*', which 'concerns what is, was, will be', normative theory cannot be adjusted by 'an appeal to the facts' but depends instead on the disclosure of competing VALUE systems (Lipsey, 1966). This distinction was of some importance to ECONOMIC GEOGRAPHY, where Chisholm (1978) drew on Lipsey's NEOCLASSICAL ECONOMICS and the philosophy of POSITIVISM which underwrote it to argue that the 'greatest casualty' of geography's QUANTITATIVE REVOLUTION was the mistaken belief that 'positive theory would lead to normative insights'. Hence 'to criticise normative theory because it fails to yield positive results is to tilt at windmills' (Chisholm, 1975). On this reading it was illegitimate to attempt an empirical validation of most of classical LOCATION THEORY since its constructions were for the most part explicitly normative: 'The question of the best location is far more dignified than the determination of the actual one' (Lösch, 1954). In his own *Geography and economics* (1966) Chisholm used neo-classical concepts to sketch the outlines of a 'positive' economic geography, and subsequently turned to welfare economics to suggest a new 'normative' basis for location theory (Chisholm, 1971; see also WELFARE GEOGRAPHY).

However, Smith (1977) argued that the distinction had been irredeemably blurred during geography's RELEVANCE revolution: the critique of positivism had demolished claims for a 'value-free geography' and it was no longer tenable to assume that an 'appeal to the facts' was as straightforward as these views supposed. One might think that normative questions would have loomed large in post-positivist human geography, but most attention has been directed towards what Benhabib (1985) calls more generally an explanatory-diagnostic moment – particularly to the critique of modern CAPITALISM – and there has been considerably less attention paid to an anticipatory-utopian moment: to detailed discussions of what ought to be and, indeed, could be (cf. CRITICAL THEORY). Even so, Smith's central point remains as sharp as ever, because both moments are underwritten by implicit normative claims.

DG

References

Benhabib, S. 1985: *Critique, norm and utopia: a study of the foundations of critical theory*. New York: Columbia University Press. · Chisholm, M. 1966: *Geography and economics*. London: Bell. · Chisholm, M. 1971: In search of a basis for location theory: micro-economics or welfare economics. *Progress in Geography* 3: 111–34. · Chisholm, M. 1975: *Human geography: evolution or revolution?* London: Penguin. · Chisholm, M. 1978: Theory construction in geography. *South African Geographical Journal* 6: 113–22. · Lipsey, R.G. 1966: *An introduction to positive economics*. London: Weidenfeld and Nicolson. · Lösch, A. 1954: *The economics of location*. New Haven: Yale University Press. · Smith, D.M. 1977: *Human geography: a welfare approach*. London: Edward Arnold.

north–south North is a rather loose, portmanteau term for the wealthy advanced industrial countries, both SOCIALIST and CAPITALIST. In this sense it is roughly synonymous with the term *First World* which is employed widely in political economic analyses (see DEVELOPMENT; CORE–PERIPHERY). The 'South' corresponds to those poor, largely non-industrial, and ex-colonial states that are seen to constitute a THIRD WORLD (mostly in Africa, Asia and Latin America), a term which arose in the post-war period emerging from the *Non-Aligned Movement* (see COLONIALISM; DECOLONIZATION: the term *Second World* was used for the countries of the former Soviet bloc where COMMUNISM was practised). The language of First and Third Worlds or North and South is often conspicuously absent among the major multilateral and national development agencies (for example the World Bank or the International Monetary Fund) which stratify STATES according to income (low, middle and so on). The average per capita income of the South is currently about 50 times less than that of the industrialized North.

North–South is a dichotomous term used in macro-POLITICAL ECONOMY to identify one of the most pervasive bipolar divisions in the current global system (Evans and Newnham, 1999). *North–South* was the title of an influential book which became popularly known in the 1980s as the *Brandt Report* after its Chairman, the former West German Chancellor (Brandt, 1980). It signalled divisions between rich and poor NATIONS in contradistinction to the East–West divide of the Cold War (cf. GEOPOLITICS): the events of the late 1980s, including the collapse of many state socialisms, made the East–West divide increasingly irrelevant. The Brandt Report sought to address the growing economic, political and military polarities at the beginning of a decade during which the material circumstances of the Third World were to deteriorate seriously. The North–South dialogue was part of ongoing political debates within the United Nations during the 1970s and elsewhere over the need for a *New International Economic Order*.

The single greatest difficulty with the North–South concept is the question of economic and political coherence. While it might be argued that the collapse of many state socialisms has produced a more homogenous capitalist core associated with capitalist regional TRADE blocs, the South is extremely diverse and becoming more so. On the one hand, the *newly industrializing countries* (the NICs) such as Taiwan and South Korea are no longer primary commodity producers and, on the other, the South has rarely had a unified political position even within the Non-Aligned Movement. The appearance of a *Fourth World* of extreme POVERTY (the so-called FAMINE belt), particularly in Africa, suggests a growing economic polarization within the South coeval with a deepening polarization between North and South.

MW

Reference

Brandt, W. 1980: *North–South: a program for survival*. London: Pan. · Evans, G. and Newnham, J. eds. *Dictionary of International Relations*. Harmondsworth, Penguin, 1999.

nuptiality The extent to which a population marries. Marriage is important in determining demographic behaviour, particularly FERTILITY (see MALTHUSIAN MODEL) and family formation. The simplest nuptiality rate expresses the number of marriages celebrated (or the total number of persons marrying) in a given year as a ratio of the average number of persons alive in that year, expressed in parts per 1000. Consideration must also be given to two fundamental aspects of the marriage pattern: the intensity of nuptiality, expressed as the proportion of the population that is single at any one time and in certain age groups; and the precocity of marriage, expressed as age at first marriage for both sexes. Historical research has demonstrated the importance of marriage patterns in determining fertility changes and in influencing and being influenced by wider social and economic trends (Hajnal, 1965).

The contemporary world has seen fundamental changes in attitudes towards marriage, especially in the developed world. The availability of contraceptive methods, the acceptability of living alone after leaving the parental home and the financial ability to do so, the rise of cohabitation and of divorce, and changing economic and POWER relationships between men and women have radically altered marriage behaviour. This in turn affects the pattern of household formation with a greater variety of living arrangements and higher rates of transition from one household type to another (cf. HOUSING STUDIES). From the 1970s onwards marriage rates declined in all European countries, for example, and the average age of marriage rose. In many countries, marriage is no longer the necessary precursor to bearing children, though there is a great deal of variation: by 1991, some 30 per cent of births in the UK and France and 48 per cent in Sweden were non-marital compared with 9 per cent in Spain and 17 per cent in Ireland. PEO

Reference and suggested reading

Hajnal, J. 1965: European marriage patterns in perspective. In D.V. Glass and D.E.C. Eversley, eds, *Population in history*. London: Arnold, 101–43. · Hall, R. 1995: Households, families and fertility. In R. Hall and P. White, eds, *Europe's population. Towards the next century*. London: UCL Press, 34–50. · Pressat, R. 1972: *Demographic analysis*. London: Edward Arnold; Chicago: Aldine, ch. 7.

O

objectivity A word that only became widely used in English in the nineteenth century. It took on three distinct meanings which still persist today. The first derives from a distinction between objectivity and subjectivity. To be subjective means to exercise personal judgements based upon individual taste or preference. *To be objective, however, is to eliminate reference to the personal altogether*, and to appeal to some higher guarantor of truthfulness. Typically, that appeal is to a particular methodology, such as the scientific method, or philosophy, such as POSITIVISM. The consequence is that personal bias is purged, resulting in an objective view. The second meaning is *neutrality or disinterestedness*. In this definition the opposite of objectivity is not subjectivity, but something like political advocacy or social judgement. An additional argument sometimes made here is that the social sciences, because of their very subject matter, necessitate VALUE judgements, while the natural sciences, because of their 'objective' subject matter, do not. The final meaning of objectivity, and emerging particularly with the work of American PRAGMATIST philosophers, is *communal judgement*. Inquiry is not objective because it employs a particular method, or is value-free, but because it is collectively agreed upon by a community of scholars.

Each of these three meanings has been elaborated over the course of the twentieth century, sometimes generating heated debate. Furthermore, they can be correlated with specific movements in post-war human geography.

The first meaning – *objectivity as a special method* – was especially prominent in the first part of the twentieth century, and was associated with the celebration of scientific practice and concomitant philosophies such as POSITIVISM and LOGICAL POSITIVISM. This meaning of objectivity became critical to human geography during the late 1950s and early 1960s when there was an attempt to remake the discipline in the likeness of natural science. One of the means to do so was through the use of mathematical and statistical techniques (see QUANTITATIVE REVOLUTION). As David Harvey (1969, p. 179) put it, mathematical 'systems provide an objective and universal language for discussing geographical problems'. The difficulty by the early 1970s, though, was that many of those geographical problems were increasingly expressed in a value-laden language – urban RACISM, rural POVERTY, SLUM housing – that could not be easily accommodated within a formalized vocabulary. As hard as people tried, value judgements kept creeping in.

This leads to the second meaning – *objectivity as neutrality*. While neutrality continues to be a goal in the physical sciences, its attainment in the social sciences has been seen as increasingly problematic. The argument, first made by philosophers such as Ludwig Wittgenstein and Michael Polanyi, is that knowledge, experience, practice and value judgement are indissolubly linked within the realm of the social. As a consequence, even the basic vocabulary of the social sciences is soaked in moral and political imperatives – goods seem good, equilibrium sounds harmonious, class appears divisive, place is comforting, but space rather cold and bleak (see MORAL GEOGRAPHIES). Human geographers first mounted a systematic critique of objectivity as neutrality during the 1970s, which was often associated with RADICAL GEOGRAPHY. In particular, the infusion of Marxism sharpened the discussion of objectivity by geographers in two ways (see MARXIST GEOGRAPHY). First, it introduced the idea of IDEOLOGY, the notion that all inquiry (except the Marxist one) is biased. Second, it insisted that all practitioners of the social sciences are engaged in an advocacy project whether they know it or not. On the political Left the goal is to change the system, and on the political Right to keep the status quo.

The third meaning, associated with PRAGMATISM, has become increasingly important in geography with the growing interest in POST-MODERNISM and POST-STRUCTURALISM. In this view *objectivity is socially constructed within a specific community of a given time and place*. Rather than lying outside human practices, objectivity is produced within them through dialogue, forming strategic allies, and exerting power. Objectivity is not something final and fixed, but provisional and in process. For critics of this view the result is intellectual anarchy, a world bereft of reliable truths (see RELATIVISM). For proponents, however, nothing of the sort eventuates. We continue the same practices, and believe the same truths, except we realize that the objectivity in which we put our trust is fallible and human-made, and not, as Haraway (1991, p. 193) puts it, 'a God's eye view' (see LOCAL KNOWLEDGE and SITUATED KNOWLEDGE). TJB

References

Haraway, D.J. 1991: *Simians, cyborgs and women: the reinvention of nature*. London: Routledge. · Harvey, D. 1969: *Explanation in geography*. London: Edward Arnold.

Suggested Reading

Bernstein, R.J. 1983: *Beyond objectivism and relativism: science, hermeneutics and praxis*. Philadelphia: University of Pennsylvania Press, part 1. · Haraway (1991), ch. 9.

Occidentalism The systematic construction of REPRESENTATIONS of 'the West' ('the Occident') as a more or less unified entity. Occidentalism is often treated as the inverse of ORIENTALISM: just as western cultures systematically construct(ed) stereotypes of 'the Orient', so non-western cultures produce(d) their own stereotypes of 'the Occident' (for a collection of these, see Carrier, 1995). Hence scholars have described Occidentalism as an inversion of the western imaginary, 'the world turned upside down' (Carrier, 1992), or as a 'counter-discourse' to Orientalism (Xiao-me Chen, 1995).

Against these seemingly commonsensical readings, however, Edward Said, one of the principal architects of the modern critique of Orientalism as a system of power-knowledge, insisted that 'no one is likely to imagine a field symmetrical to [Orientalism] called Occidentalism' precisely because the images produced by non-western cultures were not bound into a system of power-knowledge comparable to the tensile strength and span of western COLONIALISM and IMPERIALISM (Said 1978, p. 50). For Said, the distinctive quality of the DISCOURSE of Orientalism was thus its implication in globalizing projects of domination and dispossession. Hence Coronil (1996) explains that

> The study of how 'Others' represent the 'Occident' is an interesting enterprise in itself that may help counter the West's dominance of publicly circulating images of difference. Calling these representations 'Occidentalist' serves to restore some balance and has relativizing effects. Given Western hegemony, however, opposing this notion of 'Occidentalism' to 'Orientalism' runs the risk of creating the illusion that the terms can be equalized and reversed, as if the complicity of power and knowledge entailed in Orientalism could be countered by an inversion.

For this reason Coronil prefers to treat Occidentalism not as 'the reverse of Orientalism but [as] its condition of possibility, its dark side (as in a mirror)'. Accordingly, he defines Occidentalism as 'the conceptions of the West' that underwrite its representations of non-western cultures, a tactic that switches attention to the ways in which 'Occidentalist' modalities of representation simultaneously construct and privilege the West-as-Subject (see EUROCENTRISM). Coronil claims that this change of focus reveals the asymmetries of power that tie together western conceptions of its 'others' and its own self-conception, and hence shows how these modalities of representation 'present as the internal and separate attributes of bounded entities what are in fact historical outcomes of connected peoples' (see also POST-COLONIALISM).

These considerations suggest a further important qualification. Occidentalism in any of the senses described above constructs 'the West' as a unified entity, but the existence of connections between diverse peoples maps a heterogeneous space in which diverse conceptions of 'the West' originate from multiple positions inside and outside its contours, so that, at the limit, 'the West' becomes not so much a bounded, centred and homogeneous physical space as an imaginative space of dispersion. DG

References

Carrier, J.G. 1992: Occidentalism, the world turned upside down. *American Ethnologist* 19: 195–212. · Carrier, J., ed., 1995: *Occidentalism: images of the West*. Oxford and New York: Clarendon Press. · Coronil, F. 1996: Beyond Occidentalism: toward nonimperial geohistorical categories. *Cultural anthropology* 11: 51–87. · Said, E. 1978: *Orientalism*. London: Penguin; Xiao-me Chen 1995: *Occidentalism: a theory of counter-discourse in post-Mao China*. New York: Oxford University Press.

ontology Theories – sometimes called 'meta-theories' – which seek to answer 'the question of what the world must be like for knowledge to be possible' (Bhaskar, 1978; cf. EPISTEMOLOGY). Bhaskar contends that 'every account of science presupposes an ontology' and distinguishes three broad ontological traditions within the philosophy of science:

Classical EMPIRICISM, in which 'the ultimate objects of knowledge are atomistic events'. From this perspective, Bhaskar claims, 'knowledge and the world may be viewed as surfaces whose points are in isomorphic correspondence':

there is a direct, one-to-one relation between them (see also POSITIVISM).

Transcendental IDEALISM, in which the ultimate objects of knowledge are artificial constructs – models and idealizations – imposed upon the world. From this perspective, 'knowledge is seen as a structure rather than a surface', but a structure which is constituted by the thinking subject (see also KANTIANISM).

Transcendental REALISM, which regards the ultimate objects of knowledge as 'the structures and mechanisms that generate phenomena' and which are intransitive in the sense that 'such objects exist and act independently of their identification'.

Bhaskar himself endorses the third and claims that a concept of ontological depth – of 'the multi-tiered stratification of reality' – is indispensable for the natural, the social and the human sciences (Bhaskar, 1979). An outline example is given in the first figure: thus analysis conducted under the sign of realism is directed towards the elucidation of structures which possess specific 'causal powers'; these powers are realized under specific conditions through mechanisms that generate a pattern of empirical events. This is the barest of skeletons, however, and Keat and Urry (1981) emphasize that a realist philosophy in this general sense does not provide 'a ready-made social ontology and a set of substantive theoretical propositions about the social world'. One possible – and still highly simplified – mapping of this model is shown in the second figure (Gregory, 1985). It is important to understand that, from this perspective, 'it is not the character of science that imposes a determinate pattern or order upon the world; but the order of the world that, under certain determinate conditions, makes possible the cluster of activities that we call "science"' (Bhaskar, 1978; see also Bhaskar, 1986).

Although Bhaskar intended to explore the possibility of NATURALISM within the human and social sciences, and in this sense moves in a radically different direction from Husserl and his followers, a recognition of the fundamental and foundational role of ontology is also the starting-point for PHENOMENOLOGY. Within human geography Pickles (1985) has drawn upon Husserl's writings to indicate the importance of regional ontologies for the 'grounding' of empirical inquiry. These 'regions' are not those of REGIONAL GEOGRAPHY: the object of the exercise is to identify, through philosophical reflection, spaces ('regions') in which particular knowledges are made possible. Pickles particularly wanted to challenge research programmes that 'impose constructions on phenomena without the careful and necessary prior clarification, through descriptive phenomenology, of the domain of the phenomenon under consideration'. In the case of human geography, so he claimed, those who were committed to SPATIAL SCIENCE had 'unreflectively adopted an ontology of physical nature as the fundamental and underlying logic of geographical DISCOURSE and inquiry'. In his

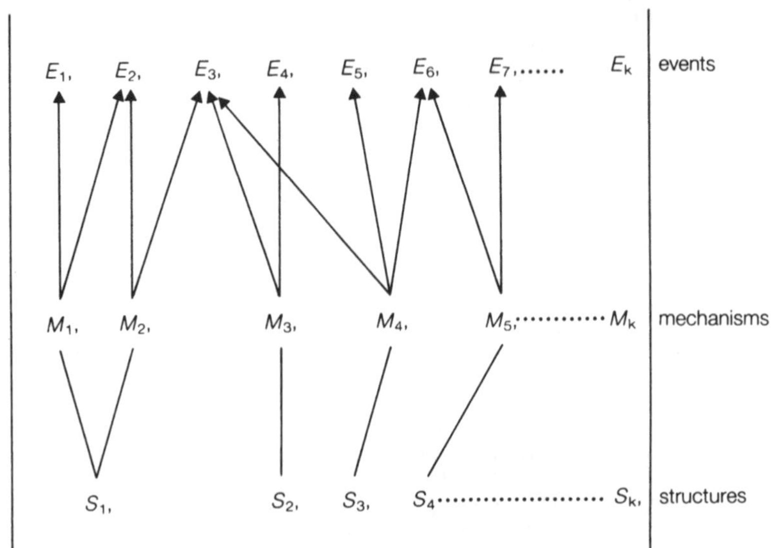

ontology *1: A realist ontology: structures, mechanism and events* (after Sayer, 1984)

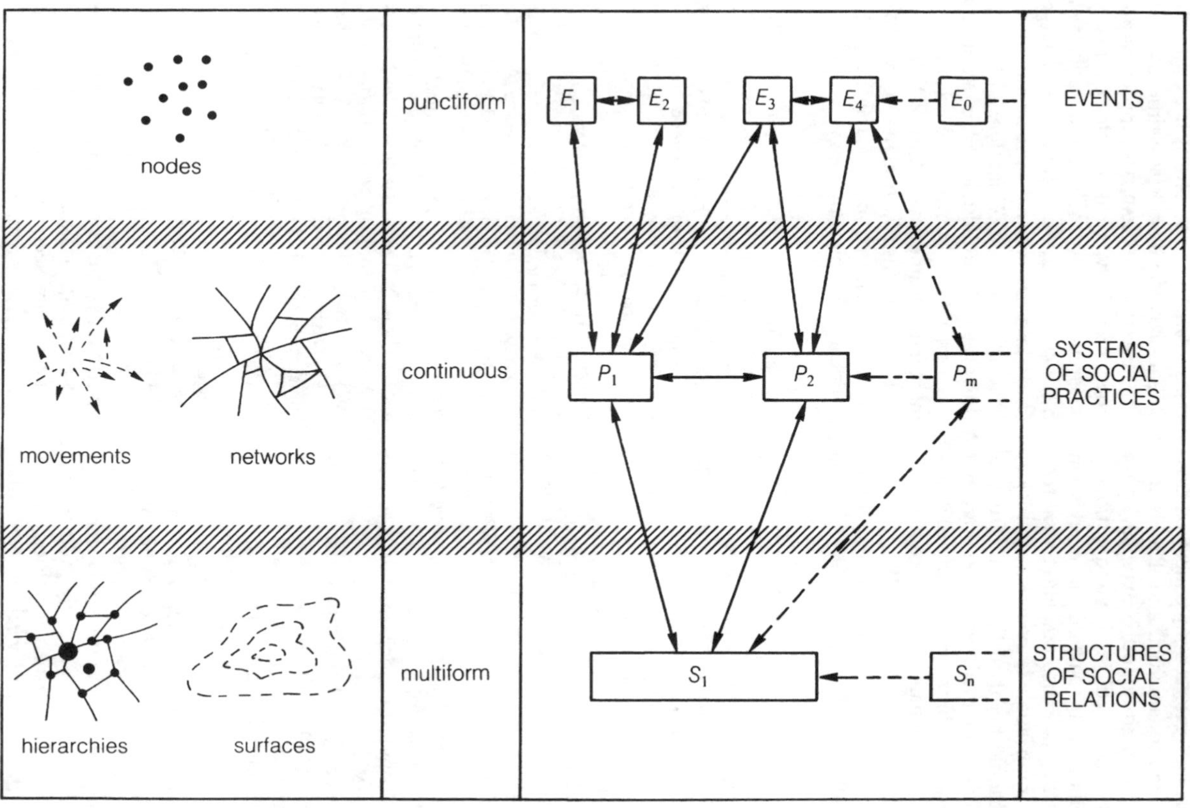

ontology *2: Realism and strategies for geographical enquiry* (Gregory, 1985, p. 72)

view, this physical ontology was derived from a KANTIANISM which stood in the closest of associations to Newtonian conceptions of space, and for this reason took 'human SPATIALITY to be the same as, or a modification (or distortion) of, the spatiality appropriate to the physical world'. Pickles accepted that 'if spatial organization and interaction, conceived geometrically, are fundamental, and if the ontology of material nature and Newtonian space on which they are predicated is unquestioned, then modelling such spaces is an exercise in SOCIAL PHYSICS' (see also MACROGEOGRAPHY). But if this implication is rejected, as Pickles insisted it should be, then 'it becomes necessary to rethink not merely methodology but also ontology: to fashion a place-centred ontology of human spatiality for a geographical human science'.

It is precisely this task that was taken up by Pickles's colleague Schatzki (1991) in his account of 'spatial ontology'. He drew on Heidegger (rather than Husserl) to distinguish between objective space (which is composed by or contains 'objects' including human beings) and social space, which he conceived as the opening and occupation of sites for human existence: of places which are the preconditions for particular human activities to (literally) take place. This is a profoundly ontological claim, for Schatzki is arguing that 'human existence ipso facto constitutes a space', that 'human agency is always embedded within a space which it shapes and is shaped by', and it is within this social space (not 'objective space') that overlapping and hierarchical webs of interconnection are inscribed to constitute 'social reality' (see also EXISTENTIALISM).

Other writers have been equally critical of spatial science and made similar claims about the importance of social space and SPATIALITY, but by no means all of them would accept the foundational claims advanced above: in particular, POSTMODERNISM, POST-STRUCTURALISM and PRAGMATISM have all encouraged a profound scepticism towards FOUNDATIONALISM. Perhaps the most provocative departure from the 'depth ontologies' proposed by Bhaskar and Sayer, and from the distinctively 'human and social' spatialities pursued by Pickles and Schatzki, is the so-called weak ontology that Thrift (1996) places at the centre of NON-REPRESENTATIONAL THEORY. It is only a departure of sorts; as Thrift concedes, it owes something to Bhaskar's more recent writings and to Heidegger's phenomenology of 'dwelling', and works – subversively – in the space between them. Its implications, in consequence, may turn out to be extremely radical and far-reaching. Unlike realism, for example, it provides a 'flattened' ontology and so underwrites a new analytics of the surface: non-representational theory, Thrift (1998) explains, is anchored in an -irreducible ontology of fluid encounters, juxtapositions and divergences, a fibrous, thread-like, capillary space-time. And unlike HUMANISTIC GEOGRAPHY's appropriations of phenomenology, weak ontology replaces the separations between 'CULTURE' and 'NATURE' by incorporating non-human actants of all kinds into the world in which human beings have to go on. As Whatmore (1998) shows, this project is nothing less than an attempt to 're-cognize' the human by fabricating – both intellectually and practically – 'hybrid geographies' (see also ACTOR–NETWORK THEORY): but it is also an attempt to establish an avowedly political and ethical ontology. DG

References

Bhaskar, R. 1978: *A realist theory of science*. Brighton: Harvester. · Bhaskar, R. 1979: *The possibility of naturalism: a philosophical critique of the human sciences*. Brighton: Harvester. · Bhaskar, R. 1986: *Scientific realism and human emancipation*. London: Verso. · Gregory, D. 1985: People, places and practices: the future of human geography. In R. King, ed., *Geographical futures*. Sheffield: Geographical Association. · Keat, R. and Urry, J. 1981: *Social theory as science*, 2nd edn. London: Routledge. · Pickles, J. 1985: *Phenomenology, science and geography: spatiality and the human sciences*. Cambridge: Cambridge University Press. · Sayer, A. 1984: *Method in social science: a realist approach*. London: Hutchinson. · Schatzki, T. 1991: Spatial ontology and explanation. *Annals of the Association of American Geographers* 81: 650–70. · Thrift, N. 1996: *Spatial formations*. London: Sage. · Thrift, N. 1998: Steps to an ecology of place. In D. Massey, J. Allen and P. Sarre, eds, *Human geography today*. Cambridge: Polity Press, 295–322. · Whatmore, S. 1998: Hybrid geographies: rethinking the 'human' in human geography. In D. Massey, J. Allen and P. Sarre, eds, *Human geography today*. Cambridge: Polity Press, 22–39.

Suggested Reading

Bhaskar (1979). · Pickles (1985). · Schatzki (1991); Whatmore (1998).

opportunity costs An important concept in NEOCLASSICAL ECONOMICS, where the costs of an action are seen in terms of opportunities forgone. For example, if rural land is set aside as a nature reserve there will be costs to the society and the landowner in terms of the net value of the agricultural products not produced. Similarly a commuter may see the cost of travel time as earnings forgone. The concept can therefore be used in explanations of the allocation of productive resources between competing activities, especially where those resources are in short supply. It plays an important role in theories of RENT and COMPARATIVE ADVANTAGE, and in LINEAR PROGRAMMING. AMH

optimization models Models, many of them adapted from mathematics and operational research, which search for the optimal solution to a problem.

Common to these models is their definition of a quantity (in some cases quantities) to be either minimized or maximized: this is often termed the model's *objective function*. For example, the goal may be to maximize food production in an agricultural system or to minimize the total transport costs involved in an industrial location decision (see INDUSTRIAL LOCATION THEORY). Most problems will also have *constraints* which limit the range of solutions – parameters within which the solution must lie if it is to be either or both acceptable and feasible: the amount of agricultural production may be limited by fertilizer and labour availability, for example, whereas the capacity of certain transport links may constrain the industrial location decision. The optimum solution for the SYSTEM as a whole may differ from the optima for individual actors – the solution which maximizes agricultural production throughout a system may not be the best for each individual farmer.

The methods of modelling and solving optimization problems vary substantially: a few are capable of direct mathematical, or even graphical, solution, but most involve iterative stepwise search algorithms which converge on the optimum (see LINEAR PROGRAMMING). Some models assume that the system being analysed is entirely predictable, but an important group of methods (based on GAME THEORY) assumes that there is some UNCERTAINTY in the environment. In such cases, the objective function may have to be made conditional – for example, farm output is to be optimized in the agricultural system such that land is allocated to various uses so as to maximize the minimum output in the most unfavourable weather conditions that might occur.

The scope of such models is very wide, covering industrial location issues, agricultural location (see VON THÜNEN MODEL), retail location, transport network development, transport flows (see TRANSPORTATION PROBLEM) and the definition of legislative districts (see DISTRICTING ALGORITHM). There are three main types: explanatory, normative-critical, and prescriptive. In a few cases it can be claimed that the model is a realistic representation of the 'real-world' causal processes, and so the model can be used as an *explanatory device* for how decisions are made. More generally, however, models may be used to demonstrate the inadequacies of existing solutions – hence these are *normative-critical*. And in some applications, when the model fully represents both the system and its constraints, they can be used as *prescriptive devices*, to suggest what should be. AMH

optimum city size A city size below which the benefits of further growth outweigh the costs but above which costs exceed benefits. Some analysts believe that URBANIZATION has seen the optimum city size exceeded in many cases but – as is often the situation where society's best interests and those of its members individually are not met by unregulated market operations (see TRAGEDY OF THE COMMONS) – no mechanism exists to restrain growth beyond the desirable level. (For example, an additional 10,000 people in a city of 1,000,000 may lead to a 10 per cent increase in traffic congestion but the extra individuals share the additional costs with those already there – which comes to only 0.01 per cent each.) Some argue that planning policies are needed to identify the optimum and ensure that it is not breached, but supporters of a free-market approach argue that when the optimum is reached then urbanization will halt – hence the COUNTERURBANIZATION recently experienced in several parts of the world and, perhaps, the reduced concern about the issue at the end of the twentieth century. RJJ

Suggested Reading

Richardson, H.W. 1973: *The economics of urban size*. Farnborough: Saxon House. · Lexington, MA: Lexington Books.

optimum population The number of people that produces the maximum return, in relation to given economic, military or social goals. The idea of population optima has long been discussed, especially in relation to OVERPOPULATION and the general notions of the MALTHUSIAN MODEL. Very difficult to define with any precision, it has most often been seen in economic terms of total production or real income per head, its definition and usefulness being hotly disputed by each generation of economists. (See also OPTIMUM CITY SIZE.) PEO

Suggested Reading

Sauvy, A. 1969: *General theory of population*, trans. C. Campos. London: Weidenfeld and Nicolson; New York: Basic Books, ch. 4.

Orientalism 'Orientalism' has at least three meanings. The first two involve (i) the scholarly study of the Orient, and (ii) a more general (and especially aesthetic or cultural) interest in the Orient; but neither of them pays close attention to the ways in which the object of their interest – 'the Orient' – is itself a predominantly European and American construction produced within a grid of POWER, knowledge and geography. This is the focus of the third, critical definition proposed by the Palestinian/American cultural critic Edward Said (1978): Orientalism as (iii) both a discursive formation and a 'corporate institution' for the production and domination of 'the Orient' (p. 3).

Said acknowledged that in this latter sense Orientalism has a long and tangled history within western thought, but his specific focus was on the distinctively modern apparatus of Orientalism that started to emerge at the end of the eighteenth century with the short-lived Napoleonic occupation of Egypt and its visual and textual inventory constructed in the '*Description de l'Egypte*' (see Godlewska, 1995). Said's emphasis on Orientalism as an 'institution' – the materiality of its constellation of power-knowledge – is also highly significant: while he was keenly interested in the production and circulation of IMAGINATIVE GEOGRAPHIES of 'the Orient' he insisted that Orientalism was not 'an airy European fantasy about the Orient, but a created body of theory and practice in which, for many generations, there has been considerable material investment' (p. 6). What gave Orientalism its peculiar power – and also confounded its constructions – was its exteriority: from the perspective of Orientalism, 'what gave the Oriental's world its intelligibility and identity was not the result of his own efforts but rather the whole complex series of knowledgeable manipulations by which the Orient was identified by the West' (p. 40). It was this, above all else, that so deeply implicated the discourse of Orientalism in a constellation of colonizing power: it made 'the Orient' appear as 'an essentialized realm originally outside and untouched by the West, lacking the meaning and order that only COLONIALISM can bring' (Mitchell, 1992, p. 313, emphasis added; see also Mitchell, 1988).

To specify these 'knowledgeable manipulations' and the series of absences that Orientalism construed as constitutive of 'the Orient', Said drew upon the work of the French philosopher Michel Foucault and made creative appropriations of both his 'archaeology' (which was concerned with 'spaces of knowledge') and his GENEALOGY (which mixed in a concern with 'spaces of power': see Gregory, 1995). Said thus characterized the DISCOURSE of Orientalism in terms of a series of binary oppositions between the positivities of the 'West' and the corresponding absences that constituted the 'East'.

'WEST'/'OCCIDENT'	'EAST'/'ORIENT'
'positive'/'presence'	*'negative'/'absence'*
masculine	feminine
rational	irrational
democratic	despotic
progressive	timeless

Said's characterization and critique of Orientalism had its origins in his personal political commitment to the Palestinian cause (Gregory, 1995; Kasbarian, 1996), and while his work has met with vigorous criticism – from both Right and Left – it has also proved to be of the utmost importance to the political-intellectual corpus of POST-COLONIALISM. The critical interrogation and development of Said's work has taken several directions. Many critics have explored the internal architecture of Orientalism (and of Said's subsequent work): they have been exercised, among other issues, by the conjunction of Said's avowed humanism with the ANTI-HUMANISM of Foucault (Clifford, 1988); by the complicated and sometimes fraught relationship between Said and HISTORICAL MATERIALISM (Ahmad, 1992; cf. Parry, 1993); and by Said's seeming inability to break out from the dualistic structure of Orientalism itself: his account remains confined within the binary distinctions that are the very object of his critique (Young, 1990).

Much of this critical discussion comprises variations on the theme of ESSENTIALISM: Said is typically charged with reducing the complexity of European and American engagements with non-western cultures to a single, totalizing 'essence'. Other scholars (including Said himself) have sought to engage with this objection by developing a more nuanced analysis of Orientalism. Their key propositions include the following:

Orientalism is not a synonym for colonial discourse in general. There are overlaps between its practices and other colonial discourses, but scholars have recovered the construction of other imaginative geographies for other places and periods. Said (1993) has extended his own inquiries to the wider relations between CULTURE and IMPERIALISM, and many writers have directed their attention to imaginative geographies of (for example) Africa, Australia and South America. Others have considered the relations between 'NATURE' and imperialism and, inspired by Said's example, have drawn attention to the production of concepts of 'environmental OTHERNESS'. Thus Arnold (1996, p. 142) argues that 'we need to understand the tropics as a conceptual and not just physical space', and proposes a critical mapping of the concept of tropicality.

The focus of Said's original inquiry was not so much 'the Orient' at large but Egypt and Palestine in particular. It is perhaps easier to see how the 'exteriority' of Orientalism came to assume such power in those regions where European and American powers declared a colonizing interest than in (say) Japan or China where different discursive formations were developed; but even in colonial India Orientalism assumed different forms. This has prompted a recognition of the ways in which the discourses of Orientalism discriminated, however imperfectly, between the different geographies of 'the Orient' (see, for example, Breckenridge and van der Veer, 1993; Jewitt, 1995).

There were also significant differences between the collective authors of Orientalism, and scholars have sought to trace the historical curve of Orientalism in more detail and to map its cultural geographies by distinguishing between the discourses of (for example) British and French Orientalisms (Lowe, 1991) and showing the heterogeneity of Orientalisms in the USA (Schueller, 1998).

Mapping the complexity of Orientalism's discursive terrain has also qualified the exteriority of Orientalism. It is misleading to imply that power – including the power of representation – lay entirely with the colonizer, and this has produced a more nuanced view of cross-cultural exchanges – of mimicry, HYBRIDITY, and TRANSCULTURATION – and of the achievements of anti-colonial resistance.

Said recognized that Orientalism was a gendered and sexualized discourse, but he was always much more interested in its metaphorical codings ('the Orient as feminine'), and feminist scholars have paid much closer attention to the gendered and sexualized experiences, practices and representations of Orientalist travellers, artists and writers (Lewis, 1996; Melman, 1992; Yegenoglu, 1998).

Much of Said's work was concerned with the written TEXTS of high culture, and scholars have paid increasing attention to other modes of representation (including art and photography) and to more mundane cultural practices like TRAVEL WRITING (Gregory, 1999).

Much of this revisionist work has been broadly historical in nature, and the emergence of the interdisciplinary field of POSTCOLONIALISM has sparked considerable debate over the relations between literary and cultural studies on the one side and the discipline of history on the other. Said has often become the talismanic figure through which the contending parties identify themselves (MacKenzie, 1995; cf. Gregory, 1997). But it is important to recognize that Orientalism is by no means confined to the past; on the contrary. Here too there is the same complexity of terrain: from the Orientalist stereotypes deployed to represent Iraq during the Gulf War of 1991 to the signs of what Morley and Robins (1992) have called a 'Techno-Orientalism' directed against Japan and other Asian societies. (See also OCCIDENTALISM.) DG

References

Ahmad, A. 1992: Orientalism and after: ambivalence and metropolitan location in the work of Edward Said. In his *In theory: classes, nations, literatures*. London: Verso, 159–219. · Arnold, D. 1996: *The problem of nature: environment, culture and European expansion*. Oxford and Cambridge, MA: Blackwell. · Breckenridge, C. and van der Veer, P., eds, 1993: *Orientalism and the postcolonial predicament: perspectives on South Asia*. Philadelphia: University of Pennsylvania Press. · Clifford, J. 1988: On Orientalism. In his *The predicament of culture: twentieth-century ethnography, literature and art*. Cambridge, MA: Harvard University Press, 255–76. · Godlewska, A. 1995: Map, text and image: the mentality of enlightened conquerors. A new look at the Description de l'Egypte. *Transactions, Institute of British Geographers* NS 20: 5–28. · Gregory, D. 1995: Imaginative geographies. *Progress in Human Geography* 19: 447–85. · Gregory, D. 1997: Orientalism re-viewed. *History workshop journal* 44: 269–78. · Gregory, D. 1999: Scripting Egypt: Orientalism and cultures of travel. In J. Duncan and D. Gregory, eds, *Writes of passage*. London and New York: Routledge, 114–50. · Jewitt, S. 1995: Europe's 'Others'? Forest policy and practices in colonial and postcolonial India. *Environment and Planning D: Society and Space* 13: 67–90. · Kasbarian, J.A. 1996: Mapping Edward Said: geography, identity and the politics of location. *Environment and Planning D: Society and Space* 14: 529–58. · Lewis, R. 1996: *Gendering Orientalism: race, femininity and representation*. London and New York: Routledge. · Lowe, L. 1991: *Critical Terrains: British and French Orientalisms*. Ithaca: Cornell

University Press. · MacKenzie, J. 1995: *Orientalism: history, theory and the arts*. Manchester: Manchester University Press. · Melman, B. 1992: *Women's Orients: English women and the Middle East, 1718–1918*. Ann Arbor, MI: University of Michigan Press. · Mitchell, T. 1988: *Colonising Egypt*. Cambridge: Cambridge University Press. · Mitchell, T. 1992: Orientalism and the exhibitionary order. In N. Dirks, ed., *Colonialism and culture*. Ann Arbor, MI: University of Michigan Press, 289–317. · Morley, D. and Robins, K. 1992: Techno-Orientalism: futures, foreigners and phobias. *New formations* 16: 136–56. · Parry, B. 1993: A critique mishandled. *Social Text* 35: 121–33. · Said, E. 1978: *Orientalism*. London: Penguin. · Said, E. 1993: *Culture and imperialism*. New York: Alfred A. Knopf. · Schueller, M.J. 1998: *U.S. Orientalisms: race, nation and gender in literature 1790–1890*. Ann Arbor, MI: University of Michigan Press. · Yegenoglu, M. 1998: *Colonial fantasies: towards a feminist reading of Orientalism*. Cambridge: Cambridge University Press. · Young, R. 1990: *White mythologies: writing History and the west*. London: Routledge.

Suggested Reading

Prakash, G. 1995: Orientalism now. *History and Theory* 34: 199–212. · Said (1978). · Sprinker, M., ed., 1993: *Edward Said: a critical reader*. Oxford and Cambridge, MA: Blackwell.

other/otherness In her classic text *The second sex*, Simone de Beauvoir (1949) charts the ideological tradition of treating 'woman' as always *Other* to man (cf. IDEOLOGY). According to de Beauvoir, 'otherness is a fundamental category of human thought . . . as primordial as consciousness itself' (1972, pp. 16–17). De Beauvoir insists that to be the Other is the basic trait of woman: 'To decline to be the Other, to refuse to be a party to the deal – this would be for women to renounce all the advantages conferred upon them by the alliance with the superior caste' (p. 21). The female is used by the male as his 'Other'; she remains the object, unable to become a subject in her own right. Though de Beauvoir's work has been criticized for 'idealist universalism' and 'latent biologism' through her association of women with NATURE and men with CULTURE (Okely, 1996, pp. 12–13), her concept of Otherness has subsequently been extended to many different contexts where the Self is defined in contrast to various socially significant Others.

The duality of Self and Other is a recurrent feature of the politics of knowledge. In his exploration of the psychology of COLONIALISM, for example, Frantz Fanon (1967) shows how the 'exotic' colonial Other simultaneously provided a source of fascination and fear, evoking contradictory emotions of desire and dread in the mind of the colonizer. Similarly, Edward Said's (1978) work on ORIENTALISM demonstrates how 'the Orient', as a cultural construction, has provided Europeans with their deepest and most enduring sense of the Other.

Geographers have applied these ideas to studies of racialization (e.g. Anderson, 1991), the stigmatization of the disabled, homeless and mentally ill (e.g. Dear and Wolch, 1987) and other forms of socio-spatial exclusion (e.g. Sibley, 1995). While critical studies such as these clearly have emancipatory potential, recent developments in ETHNOGRAPHY and cultural studies (see CULTURE) have been criticized for their obsessive fascination with otherness: 'where the "Other" is always made object, appropriated, interpreted, taken over by those in power, by those who dominate' (hooks, 1990, p. 125).

As projections of the dominant imagination, constructions of otherness raise fundamental questions about POSITIONALITY. Drawing on feminist theory and psychoanalysis, recent work in FEMINIST GEOGRAPHY has shown how the Same–Other structure of masculinist discourse reveals the limits of geographical knowledge (Rose, 1993), leading to an inability to recognize DIFFERENCE. PAJ

References

Anderson, K.J. 1991: *Vancouver's Chinatown*. Montreal and Kingston: McGill-Queen's University Press). · Beauvoir, S. de 1949: *The second sex*. Harmondsworth: Penguin (1972 edition). · Dear, M.J. and Wolch, J.R. 1987: *Landscapes of despair*. Cambridge: Polity Press). · Fanon, F. 1967: *Black skin, white masks*. New York: Grove Press). · hooks, b. 1990: *Yearning: race, gender, and cultural politics*. Toronto: Between the Lines; Okely, J. 1996: *Own or other culture*. London: Routledge). · Rose, G. 1993: *Feminism and geography*. Cambridge: Polity Press). · Said, E.W. 1978: *Orientalism*. London: Routledge. · Sibley, D. 1995: *Geographies of exclusion*. London: Routledge.

overpopulation An excess of population in an area in relation to RESOURCES or to other broader economic or social goals. Since Malthus first propounded his ideas on population, economists and demographers have tried to refine the concepts of overpopulation, underpopulation and OPTIMUM POPULATION, often with little success. Overpopulation may exist at rural, regional or national levels and today is most frequently seen in underdeveloped rural areas where the outstripping of resources by population growth may be evident in undernourishment or underemployment. Some Marxists deny the possibility of overpopulation in a socialist society, attaching more importance to the distribution of resources in a population than to the rate of population growth itself (Harvey, 1974). (See also CARRYING CAPACITY; MALTHUSIAN MODEL; SUSTAINABLE DEVELOPMENT.) PEO

Reference

Harvey, D. 1974: Population, resources and the ideology of science. *Economic Geography* 50: 256–77.

Suggested Reading

Sauvy, A. 1969: *General theory of population*, trans. C. Campos. London: Weidenfeld and Nicolson). · New York: Basic Books, ch. 23.

overurbanization A concept used in comparisons of URBANIZATION rates and levels in the contemporary THIRD WORLD with those in the First World (the 'advanced industrial countries') at similar levels of DEVELOPMENT. In the 1950s and 1960s it was argued that many Third World cities had too many residents relative to their industrial base, which led to proposals for the return of recent inmigrants, especially the residents of SQUATTER SETTLEMENTS, to the countryside. Later analyses claimed that it was invalid to compare nineteenth-century European urbanization, based on labour-intensive factory industries, with the current Third World situation, in which outmigration from the countryside is needed to promote an efficient agricultural sector and cities absorb new residents not into capital-intensive manufacturing industries but rather into labour-intensive service industries (Sovani, 1964). Crucial to such analyses is not the size of the city but whether it is parasitic on its HINTERLAND or stimulates growth there (Hoselitz, 1955). RJJ

References

Hoselitz, B.F. 1955: Generative and parasitic cities. *Economic Development and Cultural Change* 3). · Sovani, N.V. 1964: The analysis of overurbanization. *Economic Development and Cultural Change* 12: 113–22.

P

Pacific Rim A geographic REGION that is generally considered to include Japan, Australia, the coastal cities of East Asia and the westernmost cities of North America, as well as selective smaller islands in between. The 'selectivity' as to which cities and which islands are generally included in this regional formation is not based on any kind of geographical logic or integrity, but rather on their position within a RESTRUCTURED economic order that promotes and reproduces new kinds of 'cross-Pacific' trade and financial linkages. The recent intensification of these interlinked areas indicates a movement away from Cold War allegiances and rivalries and the formation of a powerful new economic domain, also known as the Asia Pacific. The establishment of the Asia-Pacific Economic Cooperation (APEC) in 1989 heralded the increased interest of Canada and the United States in participating in this primarily 'Asian' economic engine, and in guiding its growth and development.

The burgeoning political and economic interest in the Pacific Rim has spurred a voluminous scholarly literature on the area. Numerous theories purporting to explain the reasons for the region's recent economic success have appeared, often employing widely diverse analytical frameworks. These include studies extolling the vindication of laissez-faire markets, those emphasizing the key role of the STATE (see e.g. Johnson, 1982; Appelbaum and Henderson, 1992), and others reflecting on topics such as neo-traditionalism, Confucianism, and the vital impact of Chinese business networks operating across the Pacific (e.g. Hamilton, 1996; Deyo, 1987; Redding, 1990).

The literature on this region has employed so much hyperbole (e.g. the 'Asian Miracle' and the 'Pacific Century') that a number of scholars have begun to argue that the 'region' is itself merely a literary creation – one that has served the economic agendas and geopolitical visions of a largely Euro-American audience (see also CRITICAL GEOPOLITICS; GEOPOLITICS). The critique of Pacific Rim as 'Region' ties into larger debates in POST-STRUCTURALISM and POST-COLONIALISM concerning the social construction of PLACE and IDENTITY, and most particularly of the social (re)construction of Asia (see also ORIENTALISM). The intensity of the Pacific Rim's creation, its rapid growth as hegemonic discourse (cf. HEGEMONY) and its new-found role as 'geo-political imaginary' has prompted cultural critics such as Wilson and Dirlik (1995, p. 2) to ask, 'whose "Asia-Pacific" are we talking about, whose interests are being served, and when and how did this discourse of knowledge and power historically emerge?'

In this critical view, the idea of the Pacific Rim that has energized western politicians and scholars in recent years has taken shape as something abstracted away from the actual economic, social and cultural processes occurring in daily interactions and in particular, contingent spaces within and between this clearly defined and essentialized formulation. Wilson and Dirlik have argued that the emphasis on the region as an abstract, yet all-encompassing economic space, 'whose circumference is everywhere and center nowhere', has led to the complete elision of local cultural politics and anything that may be potentially oppositional to the production and ongoing reproduction of the region as economic miracle. They argue further that the focus on contemporary military–economic ties has blinded both scholars and policy-makers to the temporal fluidity of transcultural innovation and to the socio-cultural networks that have existed in the region for thousands of years.

The impact of the severe financial recession in East and Southeast Asia beginning in 1997 has yet to be analysed by either the region's economic boosters or those determined to reframe the area with a focus on its micropolitics and resistant cultures. KM

References

Appelbaum, R. and Henderson, J., eds, 1992: *States and development in the Asian Pacific rim*. London and New Delhi: Sage. · Deyo, F., ed., 1987: *The political economy of the new Asian industrialism*. Ithaca and London: Cornell University Press. · Hamilton, G., ed., 1996: *Asian business networks*. Berlin and New York: Walter de Gruyter. · Johnson, C. 1982: *MITI and the Japanese miracle*. Stanford: Stanford University Press. · Redding, S. 1990: *The spirit of Chinese capitalism*. Berlin: Walter de Gruyter. · Wilson, R. and Dirlik, A. 1995: Introduction. In R. Wilson and A. Dirlik, eds, *Asia/Pacific as space of cultural production*. Durham and London: Duke University Press.

Suggested Reading

Dirlik, A., ed., 1993: *What is in a rim? Critical perspectives on the Pacific region idea*. Boulder: Westview. · Palat, R.A., ed., 1993: *Pacific-Asia and the future of the world-system*. Westport, Conn.: Greenwood Press. · Winchester, S. 1991: *Pacific rising: the emergence of a new world culture*. New York: Prentice-Hall.

paradigm The working assumptions, procedures and findings routinely accepted by a group of scholars, which together define a stable pattern of scientific activity; this in turn defines the community which shares in it (cf. PROBLEMATIC). The term comes from Kuhn (1962, 1970), who argued that *'normal science'* proceeds uninterrupted through the cumulative sedimentation of theoretical systems and empirical materials, until it begins to be disrupted by a cluster of *'anomalies'* which cannot be explained away or subsumed within the existing framework; the pressure is temporarily accommodated by what Kuhn called *'extraordinary research'* which, if successful, eventually produces a *'revolution'*, i.e. a *'paradigm shift'*, which inaugurates the emergence of a new disciplinary matrix.

Criticisms of the concept have been registered at two levels. First, and most generally, Kuhn's original formulation is questionable; even though he modified his views between the first and second editions, his usages remained unclear (e.g. Mastermann, in Lakatos and Musgrave, 1970, recorded 21 different meanings of 'paradigm' in his work) and yet at the same time overbold, e.g. the consensus within any one science is seldom complete and stable, and the negotiation of systems of concepts is not an autonomous activity carried out entirely within the confines of a particular discipline or discourse (see Mulkay, 1979). Indeed, Karl Popper – whose *The logic of scientific discovery* (1959) has been a formative influence on many philosophers and historians of science, including Kuhn – thought that 'one ought to be sorry for' Kuhn's 'normal' scientist because, as a matter of empirical record, any scientist worthy of the name is necessarily engaged in 'extraordinary research': in short, normal science is not so normal. His objections to the THEORY of paradigms as 'the myth of the framework' (see also CRITICAL RATIONALISM) were extended and refined by Imre Lakatos (in Lakatos and Musgrave, 1970), who claimed that science in fact advances (and, prescriptively, that it ought to advance) through progressive 'problemshifts'. A series of propositions is judged as 'theoretically progressive' if 'each new theory has some excess empirical content over its predecessors, i.e. if it predicts some novel, hitherto unexpected fact', and as 'empirically progressive' if 'some of this empirical content is also corroborated', i.e. if each new theory leads us to the discovery of some new fact (see also Wheeler, 1982; Chouinard et al., 1984). Against these various objections, however, Kuhn has himself acknowledged that he 'made unnecessary difficulties for many readers'. In writing *The structure of scientific revolutions*, he recalled:

> [P]aradigms took on a life of their own, largely displacing the previous talk of consensus. Having begun simply as exemplary problem solutions, they expanded their empire to include, first, the classic books in which these accepted examples initially appeared and, finally, the entire global set of commitments shared by members of a particular scientific community. The more global use of the term is the only one most readers of the book have recognized, and the inevitable result has been confusion: many of the things said there about paradigms apply only to the original sense of the term. Though both senses seem to me important, they do need to be distinguished, and the word 'paradigm' is appropriate only to the first. (Kuhn, 1977, pp. xix–xx)

Hence, the 'more fundamental' (localized) sense of paradigm is what Kuhn now refers to as an *exemplar*; the other (global) sense of paradigm is what Kuhn now calls a *disciplinary matrix*. He attaches considerable importance to the empirical identification of scientific communities and to the scrutiny of the disciplinary matrix in which their members share because this is 'central to the cognitive operation of the group' (emphasis added): in other words, Kuhn's model is descriptive, not prescriptive. It is this central point which most of Kuhn's critics have missed (see Barnes, 1982).

Second, and more specifically, the application of the concept of a paradigm (in either sense) to geography is open to objection. Kuhn himself restricted his account to the natural sciences – indeed, one of the reasons he formulated the notion of 'paradigms' in the first place was his perception of deep-rooted disagreements about basic premises that seemed to him to characterize social science but not natural science: except in certain phases of transformation – so it is hardly surprising that attempts to apply Kuhn to the history of human geography should be so unsuccessful (Johnston, 1997). Most of the early applications of Kuhn, however, were prescriptive rather than descriptive. Chorley and Haggett, for example (in their *Models in geography*, 1967), drew on Kuhn to argue that the QUANTITATIVE REVOLUTION represented the establishment of a 'model-based paradigm' for geography, but their usage was at best polemical (Stoddart, 1981; but cf. Stoddart, 1967). Certainly, they did not identify any 'anomalies' in the Kuhnian sense within the framework of traditional REGIONAL GEOGRAPHY, and insofar as they sought to overthrow the regional 'paradigm' and replace it with a ('revolutionary') model-based SPATIAL SCIENCE, then their use of Kuhn was patently as prescriptive as most of Kuhn's critics. What is more, Kuhn's whole conception of science was irredeemably non-positivist (cf. Marshall, 1982) and there is something perverse in using his writings to legitimize the rise of a largely positivist geography (see POSITIVISM; Billinge et al., 1984). Kuhn's project has much more in common with HERMENEUTICS (Bernstein, 1983), and more recent investigations of the history of human geography which have focused on communication between members of particular 'communities' (e.g. Gatrell, 1984) and on the wider and intrinsically societal contexts in which this takes place (e.g. Barnes and Curry, 1983) come much closer to reclaiming the spirit of that hermeneutic tradition. (See also SCIENCE, GEOGRAPHY AND.) DG

References

Barnes, B. 1982: *T.S. Kuhn and social science*. London: Macmillan. · Barnes, T. and Curry, M. 1983: Towards a contextualist approach to geographical knowledge. *Transactions, Institute of British Geographers* NS 8: 467–82. · Bernstein, R.J. 1983: *Beyond objectivism and relativism: science, hermeneutics and praxis*. Oxford: Blackwell. · Philadelphia: Pennsylvania University Press. · Billinge, M., Gregory, D. and Martin, R.L. 1984: Reconstructions. In M. Billinge, D. Gregory and R.L. Martin, eds, *Recollections of a revolution: geography as spatial science*. London: Macmillan; New York: St. Martin's Press, 1–24. · Chorley, R.J. and Haggett, P., eds, 1967: *Models in geography*. London: Methuen. · Chouinard, V., Fincher, R. and Webber, M. 1984: Empirical research in scientific human geography. *Progress in Human Geography* 8: 347–80. · Gatrell, A. 1984: The geometry of a research speciality: spatial diffusion modelling. *Annals of the Association of American Geographers* 74: 437–53. · Johnston, R.J. 1991: *Geography and geographers: Anglo-American human geography since 1945*, 5th edn. London: Edward Arnold; New York: John Wiley. · Kuhn, T.S. 1962 and 1970: *The structure of scientific revolutions*, 1st and 2nd edns. Chicago: University of Chicago Press. · Kuhn, T.S. 1977: *The essential tension: selected studies in scientific tradition and change*. Chicago: University of Chicago Press. · Lakatos, I. and Musgrave, A., eds, 1970: *Criticism and the growth of knowledge*. Cambridge: Cambridge University Press. · Marshall, J.D. 1982: Geography and critical rationalism. In J.D. Wood, ed., *Rethinking geographical inquiry*. Downsview, Ontario: Department of Geography, Atkinson College, York University, 75–171. · Mulkay, M. 1979: *Science and the sociology of knowledge*. London: Allen and Unwin; Popper, K. 1959: *The logic of scientific discovery*. New York: Basic Books. · Stoddart, D.R. 1967: Organism and ecosystem as geographical models. In R.J. Chorley and P. Haggett, eds, *Models in geography*. London: Methuen, 511–48. · Stoddart, D.R. 1981: The paradigm concept and the history of geography. In D.R. Stoddart, ed., *Geography, ideology and social concern*. Oxford: Blackwell, 70–80. · Wheeler, P.B. 1982: Revolutions, research programmes and human geography. *Area* 14: 1–6.

Suggested Reading

Bernstein (1983), part 2; Johnston (1991), chs 1 and 7. · Kuhn (1977), ch. 12; Mair, A. 1986: Thomas Kuhn and understanding geography. *Progress in Human Geography* 10: 345–70.

parametric statistics A family of statistical procedures (including those associated with the GENERAL LINEAR MODEL) that can be applied to interval and ratio data (see MEASUREMENT), providing that they meet certain criteria, most of which assume that the data are normally distributed (see NORMAL DISTRIBUTION). These criteria are much more stringent than those which apply to NON-PARAMETRIC STATISTICS. If parametric procedures are applied to non-normally distributed data, the estimated parameters (e.g. of a REGRESSION equation) are likely to be either biased or inefficient (or both), in which case that data should either be transformed to meet the criteria (see TRANSFORMATION OF VARIABLES) or subjected to non-parametric tests only. RJJ

Pareto optimality A situation in which it is impossible to make some people better off without making others worse off. This criterion of 'economic efficiency' was devised by the economist and sociologist V.F.D. Pareto, and is an important element in NEO-CLASSICAL ECONOMICS. The Pareto criterion may be applied to efficiency of RESOURCE allocation, optimality being achieved when it is impossible to reallocate resources to produce an outcome that would increase the satisfaction of some people without reducing the satisfaction of others. A more direct application to distributional issues would be to recognize as Pareto optimal a distribution of income that cannot be changed in favour of one individual or group without taking some income from another individual or group.

The attainment of Pareto optimality is illustrated in the figure. Resources are available to

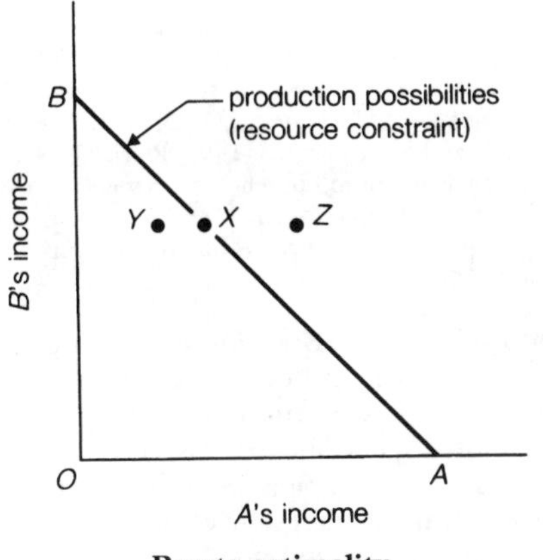

Pareto optimality

generate a certain amount of income, which may be distributed among *A* and *B* – these could be individuals, groups of people or even the inhabitants of two different territories. The line *AB* indicates the possible distributions of the maximum total income available, ranging from all going to *A* and none to *B* (at point *A*) to all going to *B* (at *B*). Point *X* is a position of Pareto optimality, where any redistribution in the direction of either *A* or *B* (along the line) will make the other party worse off. In fact, any starting position on the line is Pareto-optimal. It would be impossible to increase *A*'s share from *X* to *Z* (thus leaving *B* in the same position) because this conflicts with the resource constraint. However, point *Y* inside the triangle *ABO* is suboptimal by the Pareto criterion because available resources are not fully utilized and it is possible to increase *A*'s income to *X*, for example, without taking anything away from *B*. Such a move would be a 'Pareto improvement'.

The Pareto criterion figures prominently in traditional welfare economics, where it is argued that acceptance of Pareto optimality as a rule for allocative efficiency or distributive equity involves minimal ethical content. However, adoption of the Pareto criterion carries some important implications that tend to strengthen the status quo. Once society has reached the limit of production possibilities, i.e. there is no more growth, then the poor cannot be made better off without conflicting with the Pareto criterion, for any such move would be at the expense of others (the rich). Thus however badly off the poor may be, they can be made better off only if more income (or whatever) is produced. In practice, the application of the Pareto criterion in a no-growth economy would prevent redistribution in the direction of the poor, no matter how unequal the existing distribution. (Cf. WELFARE GEOGRAPHY.) DMS

participant observation Originating in anthropological research on so-called 'traditional' societies, participant observation is one of the principal QUALITATIVE METHODS for conducting ETHNOGRAPHY. Based on prolonged and intensive first-hand FIELDWORK, participant observation involves a conscious and systematic attempt to understand the way of life of a group of people or a LOCALITY that is often significantly different from the researcher's own (Jackson, 1983). Participant observation frequently entails a year or more 'in the field' (Burgess, 1982) and may require learning another language.

As the method has increasingly been applied in contemporary urban settings, studies using participant observation have become more common in sociology and geography (Cook, 1997; Walsh, 1998). Debates about the method have focused on whether participant observation is merely a *technique* that can be applied like any other, whether (and, if so, how) it is appropriate to use participant observation in association with more QUANTITATIVE METHODS such as social surveys (cf. SURVEY ANALYSIS), and on a wide range of associated ethical and moral issues (Spradley, 1980; see ETHICS, GEOGRAPHY AND).

Participant observation endeavours to interpret other CULTURES from a participant's perspective. This normally involves living with the people being studied and engaging as thoroughly as possible in their lives. Those employing the method usually keep a field diary (Sanjek, 1990), recording observations in a systematic fashion, constantly mediating between their 'insider' and 'outsider' roles. As with other ethnographic methods, participant observation is caught up in current debates about the politics of REPRESENTATION, including issues of ethnographic authority and POSITIONALITY. PAJ

References

Burgess, R.G. 1982: *In the field*. London: Allen and Unwin. · Cook, I. 1997: Participant observation. In R. Flowerdew and D. Martin, eds, *Methods in human geography*. London: Harlow, 127–50. · Jackson, P. 1983. Principles and problems of participant observation. *Geografiska Annaler* 65B: 39–46. · Sanjek, R., ed., 1990: *Fieldnotes*. Ithaca: Cornell University Press. · Spradley, J.P. 1980: *Participant observation*. New York: Holt, Rinehart and Winston. · Walsh, D. 1998:

Doing ethnography. In C. Seale, ed., *Researching society and culture*. London: Sage, 217–32.

participatory action research is a research process that emerged out of FEMINIST and HUMANISTIC GEOGRAPHY, for which the goal is not just to describe social reality but to change it (see ACTIVISM AND THE ACADEMY; QUALITATIVE METHODS). The researcher is aligned with a social group working for change, and the research is done *with* rather than *for* this group. This partnership ideally involves cooperation over the design and implementation of the research project. One of the researcher's goals may be to share research skills so that the group can conduct research on their own in the future. Participatory action research can be extremely difficult in practice: inequities in material resources can pose challenges for equalizing DECISION-MAKING and contradictions may arise from the fact that the research emerges at the intersection of institutions (e.g. universities, government funding agencies, and community groups) that may have different priorities. GP

part-time farming A situation in which farmers engage in some other regular occupation from which they derive income to enhance their standard of living and/or underwrite their farming activities (Gasson, 1988). This livelihood strategy was instigated by falling real incomes amongst farmers in advanced industrial countries in the 1970s. Since then there has been a dramatic rise in the incidence of part-time farming in western Europe, North America and Australasia (Cavazzani and Fuller, 1982). It takes many forms and involves the diversification of several, sometimes overlapping, dimensions of farm organization (see also FARMING, TYPES OF). These include the use of farm land, buildings and other capital assets for other business ventures; multiple job-holding; multiple sources of income; and new divisions of labour within farming households (MacKinnon, et al., 1991). Such activities have been promoted by farm 'diversification' policies in many countries and have become so commonplace that the more comprehensive term 'pluriactivity' is now widely used to describe them (Marsden, 1990; Evans and Ilbery, 1993). SW

References

Cavazzani, A. and Fuller, A. 1982: International perspectives on part-time farming: a review. *GeoJournal*, 6/4: 383–9. · Evans, N. and Ilbery, B. 1993: The pluriactivity, part-time farming, and farm diversification debate. *Environment and Planning A* 25: 945–59. · Gasson, R. 1988: *The economics of part-time farming*. London: Longman. · MacKinnon, N., Bryden, J., Bell, C., Fuller, A. and Spearman, M. 1991: Pluriactivity, structural change and farm household vulnerability in Western Europe. *Sociologia Ruralis* 31: 58–71. · Marsden, T. 1990. Towards a political economy of pluriactivity. *Journal of Rural Studies* 6: 375–82.

pastoralism The breeding and rearing of certain domesticated herbivorous animals and ruminants as a primary means to provide food, clothing and shelter. Pastoral production involves an interaction between land, water and mineral resources, livestock and labour. Livestock as a capital good serves as a technology to transform otherwise unpalatable cellulose into consumable products. Pastoralism embraces both commercial livestock rearing (e.g. commercial stockrearing on the Argentinian pampas) and 'traditional' pastoral NOMADISM which combines livestock husbandry and spatial mobility for the largely SUBSISTENCE production of animal products. The variety of animals raised by pastoral nomads is quite small (there are six widely-distributed species: sheep, goats, camels, cattle, horses, donkeys) and is associated with seven distinctive zones (high latitude sub-Arctic, Eurasian steppe, montane Southwest Asia, Saharan and Arabian deserts, sub-Saharan savannas, the Andes, and Asian high altitude plateaux). Pastoral nomadism is internally differentiated with respect to its dependence on agricultural production, forms of pasture ECOLOGY, and the animals herded. A common pastoral taxonomy distinguishes between flat/mountainous land, large/small animals and the relationship to agriculture (i.e. pure pastoralists versus semi-pastoralists). Like PEASANTS, pastoralists exhibit significant differences in terms of household structure, property rights, sexual DIVISIONS OF LABOUR, patterns of consumption and exchange and LABOUR PROCESSES (Galanty and Johnson, 1990). Pastoralism is, however, a distinctive form of ecological and cultural adaptation to specific sorts of ECOSYSTEMS (see CULTURAL ECOLOGY) in which humans and animals live in a symbiotic COMMUNITY typified by a fierce independence and SELF-DETERMINATION. MW

Reference

Galanty, J. and Johnson, D. 1990: *The world of pastoralism: herding systems in comparative perspective*. New York: Guilford.

patriarchy A system of social structures and practices through which men dominate, oppress and exploit women. A distinction is made between classic or *paternal patriarchy*, a form of household organization in which the father dominates other members of an extended kin network (including younger men) and controls the economic production of the household, and *fraternal patriarchy* in which men dominate women within CIVIL SOCIETY; the latter provided the key focus for feminist theorizing and organizing through the 1960s and 1970s. By the 1980s the utility of the concept was in doubt; critics saw it as ahistorical and insensitive to cross-cultural variation. Efforts to theorize patriarchy in relation to CAPITALISM seemed to collapse into FUNCTIONALISM, or leave the relations between the two systems unresolved. And if partriarchy operates autonomously from capitalist relations, as posited by dual systems theory, did this not leave the patriarchal relations of capitalism undertheorized? In geography efforts were made by Foord and Gregson (1986) to resolve these dilemmas through REALISM; Walby (1989) criticized their model for neglecting paid work, the state and male violence (see GENDER AND GEOGRAPHY and Women and Geography Study Group (1997) for reviews of critical reactions within geography), and herself posited a dual systems theory of patriarchy at three levels of abstraction: system, structure and practice. Patriarchy, according to Walby, is composed of six structures: the patriarchal mode of production, male violence, and patriarchal relations in paid work, the state, sexuality and cultural institutions. But in Acker's view (1989) the moment of theorizing patriarchy in this way had passed; the object of feminism had moved from patriarchy as a system to gender relations (and heteronormativity). Interest had also moved away from delineating the *cause(s)* of patriarchal relations to understanding the diversity of *effects*. As early as 1980 Barrett had suggested that patriarchy is better conceived as an adjective than as a noun. The term is still used as a noun, but typically in the plural: Grewal and Kaplan (1994, pp. 17–18) urge the need 'to address the concerns of women around the world in the historicized particularity of their relationships to multiple patriarchies as well as to international economic hegemonies' but their concern is to compare 'multiple, overlapping, and discrete oppressions' and not to construct 'a theory of hegemonic oppression under the unified sign of gender' (that is, under the sign of patriarchy).

GP

References

Acker, J. 1989: The problem with patriarchy. *Sociology* 23: 235–40. · Barrett, M. 1980: *Women's oppression today: problems in Marxist feminist analysis.* London: Verso. · Foord, J. and Gregson, N. 1986: Patriarchy: towards a reconceptualisation. *Antipode* 18: 186–211. · Grewal, I. and Kaplan, C., eds, 1994: *Scattered hegemonies: postmodernity and transnational feminist practices.* Minneapolis: University of Minnesota Press. · Walby, S. 1989: Theorising patriarchy. *Sociology* 23: 213–34. · Women and Geography Study Group 1997: *Feminist geographies: explorations in diversity and difference.* Harlow: Addison Wesley Longman.

peasant The term was in common use in English from the fifteenth century referring to individuals working on the land and residing in the countryside. By the nineteenth century 'peasant' was employed as a term of abuse (for example, by Marx on the idiocy of rural life) and in the recent past it has been imbued with heroic and revolutionary connotations (as in Maoism, for example). In modern usage peasants are on family farms (farming households) which function as relatively corporate units of production, consumption and reproduction (Chayanov, 1966). The particular social structural forms of the domestic unit (nuclear families, multi-generational extended families, intra-household sexual DIVISIONS OF LABOUR and property systems), the social relations between households within peasant COMMUNITIES, and the ecological relations of production (the peasant ecotype) are, however, extremely heterogeneous (Wolf, 1966). The terms peasant and peasantry have often been employed loosely to describe a broad range of rural producers as generic types characterized by certain social, cultural or economic traits: the backward or anti-economic peasant, the rational and moral peasant, the uncaptured peasant. These and other terms such as traditional, subsistence, or smallholder, detract however from the important analytical task of situating peasants as specific social producers in concrete, historically specific political economies with their own dynamics and laws of motion.

Peasants are distinguished by direct access to their means of production in land, by the predominant use of family labour and by a high degree of self-sufficiency (see SUBSISTENCE AGRICULTURE). Nonetheless, all peasants are by definition characterized by a partial engagement with markets (which tend to function with a high degree of imperfection) and are subordinate actors in larger POLITICAL ECONOMIES in which they fulfil obligations to holders of political and economic POWER. Peasants as forms of household enterprise rooted primarily in production on the land have a distinctive LABOUR PROCESS (the unity of the domestic unit and the productive group) and a unique combination of labour and property through partial market involvement. Peasants stand between those social groups who have lost all or most of their productive assets (proletarians or semi-proletarians), on the one hand, and farming households which are fully involved in the market (so-called petty or simple commodity producers), on the other. Seen in this way peasants have existed under a variety of economic, political and cultural circumstances (FEUDALISM, CAPITALISM; state SOCIALISM) spanning vast periods of history and are 'part societies'. Peasant societies are often seen as transitional – they 'stand midway between the primitive tribe and industrial society' (Wolf, 1966, p. vii) – and yet are marginal or outsiders, 'subordinate to a group of controlling outsiders' (Wolf, 1966, p. 13) who appropriate surpluses in a variety of forms (RENT, interest, unequal exchange).

In many THIRD WORLD societies in which peasants constitute an important and occasionally dominant stratum, a central question pertains to the fate of the peasantry in relation to growing STATE and market involvement. Peasants are invariably the victims of MODERNITY (Moore, 1966). The question of growing commercialization and mechanization of peasant production and of the growth of off-farm income (MIGRATION, craft production, local wage labour), is reflected in the long-standing concern with internal differentiation among peasantries and hence their long-term survival (hence the debates over peasant persistence, de-peasantization, and captured peasants). It is probably safe to say that the period 1950–75 witnessed an epochal shift in which the peasantry became for the first time a global minority.

The proliferation of peasant studies in the last 30 years has been the source of important theoretical innovations in political economy speaking to questions of commoditization, CLASS formation, resistance and rebellion (Shanin, 1988). The study of peasants was also key to the evolution of CULTURAL ECOLOGY and POLITICAL ECOLOGY insofar as peasant knowledge and practice is an indispensable starting point for the understanding of household management of resources, and hence the processes of ecological change and rehabilitation (Watts, 1983; Blaikie and Brookfield, 1987).

In the context of the transitions to and from capitalism, the role of the peasantry is central. Barrington Moore (1966) argued that the relations between landlord and peasantry are fundamental in understanding the various routes of DEMOCRACY and dictatorship in the modern world. Peasant revolutions in Mexico, Algeria and China for example – the antithesis of the idea of apolitical or tradition-laden peasantries – have fundamentally shaped the twentieth century (Skocpol, 1980). Kautsky (1899) referred to the AGRARIAN QUESTION in western Europe in the nineteenth century to underscore the political ramifications of the new forms of differentiation and proletarianization associated with growing commercialization, and the political and strategic questions which arose from peasant protest and struggle. One of the major features of the period since 1989 and the decollectivization of agriculture in the former socialist bloc (cf. COLLECTIVE), has been the re-emergence of millions of peasant households (re-peasantization) in China, Russia and eastern Europe. The role of peasants in post-socialist transitions has been a crucial part of the political landscape in these parts of the world and they represent intriguing cases for the study of new forms of agrarian capitalist trajectories (see Verdery, 1996; Selenyi, 1998). MW

References

Blaikie, P. and Brookfield, H.C. 1987: *Land degradation and society*. London: Methuen. · Chayanov, A.V. 1966: *The theory of peasant economy*, ed. D. Thorner, B. Kerblay and R.E.F. Smith and trans. R.E.F. Smith. Homewood: American Economic Association (first Russian edition, 1912). · Kautsky, K. 1899: *The agrarian question*. London: Zwan. · Moore, B. 1966: *The social origins of dictatorship and democracy*. Boston: Beacon. · Shanin, T., ed., 1988: *Peasants*. London: Blackwell. · Selenyi, I., ed., 1998: *Privatizing the land*. London: Routledge. · Skocpol, T. 1980: *States and social revolutions*. Cambridge, MA: Harvard University Press. · Verdery, K. 1996: *What was socialism and what comes next?* Princeton: Princeton University Press. · Watts, M. 1983: *Silent violence*. Berkeley: University of California Press. · Wolf, E. 1966: *Peasants*. New York: Prentice-Hall.

peasant-workers A social category that includes households constituted by persons who are *both* PEASANTS *and* wage-workers. Typically peasant-workers appear in the literature as part-time farmers, cottage industrialists, outworkers or simply as day labourers. The distinctiveness of peasant-workers, often classified as either peasants or workers, resides in the fact that they are both, simultaneously and serially. In the face of industrial CAPITALISM, peasant households are invariably drawn into a multiplicity of wage work (*proletarianization*) which may include MIGRATION, local farm work, or working for industrial firms. But the process of proletarianization is discontinuous, ragged and often incomplete, with the result that many farming families are simultaneously involved in industrial wage work.

The contradictions between property and the wage relation are contained within the household, which gives the peasant-workers their social coherence and cultural character. Holmes (1987) shows in the case of northern Italy, for example, how peasant-workers represent a complex and politically distinct segment of Italian society which draws upon both the traditions of small-scale cultivation, indigenous Catholicism and the Weberian world of industrial wage work. Increasing mobility of transnational capital has contributed to the proliferation of industrial enterprises in THIRD WORLD rural locations (for example electronics sub-assembly in Indonesia or agro-food processing in Kenya) with the result that peasants (often young and female) are drawn into industrial wage work. Wolf (1990) has shown how young Javanese peasant girls working in rural electronics plants face struggles and CONFLICTS within the household over gender and personal autonomy as their wage packet begins to represent a significant proportion of household income. The contradiction and tensions between two different forms of political and cultural economy – the household enterprises and industrial wage work – often play themselves out within cultural arenas, and this is a unique aspect of what Holmes (1987) calls the liminal, transitional and phantom aspects of the lived experiences of worker-peasants. MW

References

Holmes, D. 1987: *Cultural disenchantments*. Princeton: Princeton University Press. · Wolf, D. 1990: *Factory daughters*. Berkeley: University of California Press.

performance The art of producing the now. Performance is currently one of the key metaphors in the social sciences and humanities, and is inevitably making its way into human geography (e.g. Schechner, 1988; Phelan, 1994, 1998; Campbell, 1996; Dening, 1996; Frith, 1996; Hetherington, 1998; Hughes-Freeland, 1998; Abercrombie and Longhurst, 1998; Thrift, 2000).

Performance can be thought of on two levels. On one, performance is a means of *theorizing the day-to-day improvisations* which are the means by which the now is produced. Arising especially out of the expressive powers of the body, these improvisations enable each moment to be open to possibility even if, as Judith Butler (1997) makes clear in her account of PERFORMATIVITY, they often fall back into, indeed often form a part of, the normative. At another level, performance is the *practical means by which these improvisatory skills are brought out* and used to construct performances of various kinds. At this level, performance includes the vast archive of work in the performing arts – theatre, dance, music – which has honed these skills through the centuries.

Performance offers human geography five things. First, it provides a means of communication which moves away from the purely textual and, in so doing, provides new means of expression and new communities to reach out to. Second, it provides a new set of QUALITATIVE METHODS which can be used to expand human geographers' currently very limited (and often elitist) repertoire of ETHNOGRAPHY, FOCUS GROUPS, in-depth INTERVIEWS and the like. Third, it provides a political instrument. Since the 1960s, performance has become a mainstream of much political protest, both in its ability to stage events and in its corresponding ability to involve the media for progressive ends. Fourth, it provides a spur to theory since, by emphasizing creativity, it moves back to Aristotelian ideas of phronesis, of the production of practical wisdom, and then strikes out on an alternative track which stresses many of the same non-representational skills and institutions that are to be found in NON-REPRESENTATIONAL THEORY and similar bodies of work (Thrift, 2000). And fifth, performance gains many of its effects through the speculative manipulation of space and time. It is therefore inherently and intimately geographical. NJT

References

Abercrombie, N. and Longhurst, B. 1998: *Audiences*. London: Sage. · Butler, J. 1997: *Excitable speech*. London and New York: Routledge. · Campbell, P., ed., 1996: *Analysing performance*. Manchester: Manchester University Press. · Dening, C. 1996: *Performances*. Chicago: University of Chicago Press. · Frith, S. 1996: *Performing rites*. Oxford: Oxford University Press. · Hetherington, K. 1998: *Expressions of identity. Space, performance, politics*. London: Sage. · Phelan, P. 1994: *Unmarked. The politics of performance*. New York: New York University Press. · Phelan, P., ed., 1998: *The ends of performance*. New York: New York University Press. · Schechner, R. 1988: *Performance theory*. London: Routledge. · Thrift, N.J. 2000: Afterwords. *Environment and Planning D: Society and Space* 19. · Hughes-Freeland, F., ed., 1998: *Ritual, performance, media*. London: Routledge.

Suggested Reading

Performance Research (three times a year), Routledge: ISSN 1352–8165.

performativity Geographers have used this term in at least three ways. First, it is used to refer to *practices such as music and dance* (see PERFORMANCE). Considerations of these practices not only expand the substantive reach of the discipline; they emerge from and extend critiques of VISION AND VISUALITY and representational theory (see MUSIC, GEOGRAPHY OF; NON-REPRESENTATIONAL THEORY). Second, studies have been made of the *scripted performances* demanded by/in particular workplaces (Crang, 1994; McDowell, 1995). Gregson and Rose (2000) distinguish this use, which assumes that the self exists anterior to these scripted performances, from a third one, derived from Butler's concept of performativity. Culler (1997) traces the genealogy of this third sense of 'performative' from Austin's distinction between constative and *performative utterances*, the latter (famously exemplified by the statement: 'I pronounce you . . .' uttered at the marriage ceremony) is itself an act that performs the action to which it refers. The performative 'brings to centre stage an active, world-making use of language' (Culler, 1997, pp. 97–8).

Butler's (1990, 1993a, 1993b, 1997; see QUEER THEORY) concept of performativity provides a model for thinking about not only language but also social processes more generally. First, in arguing that gender is a performance without ontological status (gender is not what one is, but what one does), she is outlining a theory of SUBJECT FORMATION in which she attempts to mediate the extremes of ESSENTIALISM and social constructivism (see GENDER AND GEOGRAPHY). She also attempts to hold PSYCHOANALYSIS in tension with DISCOURSE analysis insofar as she argues that identities are not simply performed on the surface of the body; what is performed always operates in relation to what cannot be performed or said (notably homosexual relations), mediated by the unconscious. Second, Butler's discussion of performativity articulates a theory of the individual's relation to social norms. Performances are not freely chosen roles; Butler argues that norms of compulsory heterosexuality dictate that the subject cannot exist outside gender. Performances are also historically embedded; they are 'citational chains' and their effect is dependent on conventions (i.e. previous utterances). But, third, norms and identities are instantiated through repetitions of an ideal (e.g. the ideal of 'woman' or 'man'). Since we never quite inhabit the ideal, there is room for disidentification and agency (see HUMAN AGENCY). Geographers have been drawn to Butler's concept of performativity as a model for thinking about sexual (Bell, Binnie, Cream and Valentine, 1994) and gender (Lewis and Pile, 1996) identities. Gregson and Rose (2000) argue that geographers have tended to misapply Butler's theory of performativity, sometimes conceiving performances as voluntaristic roles chosen by already formed subjects. As yet, the spatiality of Butler's theorizing of performativity also lies relatively unexplored. Certainly Butler points to the importance of geographical context when she insists that 'subversiveness is the kind of effect that *resists calculation*' but it is a complicated, entwined relation insofar as 'the demarcation of context is . . . already a prefiguring of the result' (1993b, p. 29); Gregson and Rose (2000) begin to explore these 'performative spatialities'. GP

References

Bell, D., Binnie, J., Cream, J., Valentine, G. 1994: All hyped up and no place to go. *Gender Place and Culture* 1: 31–48. · Butler, J. 1990: *Gender trouble: feminism and the subversion of identity*. London and New York: Routledge. · Butler, J. 1993a: *Bodies that matter: on the discursive limits of 'sex'*. London and New York: Routledge. · Butler, J. 1993b: Critically queer. *GLQ* 1: 17–32. · Butler, J. 1997: *Excitable speech*. London and New York: Routledge. · Crang, P. 1994: It's showtime: on the workplace geographies of display in a restaurant in South east England. *Environment and Planning D: Society and Space* 12: 675–704. · Culler, J. 1997: *Literary theory: a very short introduction*. Oxford: Oxford University Press. · Gregson, N. and Rose, G. 2000: Taking Butler elsewhere: performativities, spatialities and subjectivities. *Environment and Planning D: Society and Space*. · Lewis, C. and Pile, S. 1996: Woman, body, space: Rio Carnival and the politics of performance. *Gender Place and Culture* 3: 23–41. · McDowell, L. 1995: Body work: heterosexual gender performances in city workplaces. In D. Bell and G. Valentine, eds, *Mapping desire: geographies of sexualities*. London: Routledge, 75–95.

periodic market systems The provision of retail and other service functions in a settlement on a particular day or days of the week only. These may be all of the functions assembled there, as in some current West African periodic markets, or they may complement a permanent set available throughout the week, as in British market towns. Research into these systems was stimulated by analogies with CENTRAL PLACE THEORY; in situations with relatively low ranges and high thresholds, a system of traders moving around a set cycle of markets might overcome the problem of insufficient demand to support a permanent establishment at any one place. The movement of the traders to be near their customers on set occasions is more efficient than the customers travelling long distances to permanent markets much less frequently. Detailed research has identified considerable variability in the ways in which traders work within such systems, however: each system must be analysed as a particular local cultural phenomenon. (See also MARKET EXCHANGE.) RJJ

Suggested Reading

Bromley, R.F. 1980: Trader mobility in systems of periodic and daily markets. In D.T. Herbert and R.J. Johnston, eds, *Geography and the urban environment: progress in research and applications*, volume 3. Chichester and New York: John Wiley, 133–74.

phallocentrism Placing man at the centre; a masculine way of representing and approaching the world that some theorists root in male genitalia and a masculine libidinal economy. It is characterized by a unified, self-controlled, and distanced drive towards a singular truth or goal (i.e. a notion of progress). Cixous (1980) argues that it is intertwined with *logocentrism* (the fixing of meaning in concepts), such that meaning is fixed in a set of hierarchized and sexualized binary oppositions (hence the term *phallogocentrism*). Culture/nature is a central organizing dichotomy within phallogocentric thought, with CULTURE conceived as masculine and active, and NATURE as feminine and passive. Many critiques of phallocentrism have roots in PSYCHOANALYSIS. They have led French feminists such as Cixous and male philosophers such as Lacan and Derrida to explore feminine (more open and multiple) ways of writing and reading, an exploration that Jardine (1985) terms *gynesis* and evaluates with some suspicion.

Geography intersects with phallocentrism in a number of ways. Jardine (1985) attributes the critiques of phallocentrism (e.g. the disbelief in origins, master narratives, humanism, and progress) that have been developed throughout the twentieth century to the end of European imperial domination, as well as to the growing influence of feminist voices (see FEMINIST GEOGRAPHIES). She interprets *gynesis*, the 'solution' to phallocentrism proposed by male philosophers, as a working out of male paranoia: men began to desire to be women as a way to avoid becoming the object of female desire. (The frequent feminization of non-European countries is especially interesting in the context of this interpretation: see ORIENTALISM.) Critiques of phallogocentrism also intersect with conceptions of NATURE insofar as they are tied to attempts to displace 'man' from the controlling centre and to refigure nature in active, equal terms. To the extent that humanism and phallocentrism are intertwined, the critiques of that latter extend to HUMANISTIC GEOGRAPHY. Framed through the analogous concept of MASCULINISM, Rose (1993) claims that elements of phallocentrism pervade geography as a discipline. (See also SEXUALITY AND GEOGRAPHY.) GP

References

Cixous, H. 1980: Sorties. In E. Marks and I. de Courtivron, eds, *New French feminisms*. Amherst: The University of Massachusetts Press, 90–8. · Jardine, A. 1985: *Gynesis: configurations of women and modernity*. Ithaca: Cornell University Press. · Rose, G. 1993: *Feminism and geography*. Oxford: Polity Press and Minneapolis: University of Minnesota Press.

phenomenology A continental European philosophy which is founded on the importance of reflecting on the ways in which the world is made available for intellectual inquiry: this means that it pays particular attention to the active, creative function of language in making the world intelligible. One of phenomenology's main concerns is 'to disclose the world as it shows itself before scientific inquiry, as that which is *pre-given* and *presupposed* by the sciences' (Pickles, 1985; emphases added). As such, phenomenology provides a powerful critique of POSITIVISM, which disavows any such reflection as meaningless metaphysics and, by virtue of its commitment to EMPIRICISM, assumes that there is no need to say anything at all about the preconceptions on which its various objectifications depend. Against this, phenomenology claims that 'observation' and 'objectification' are never the simple exercises which conventional forms of science assume them to be (cf. ABSTRACTION). Indeed, it rejects any assumption of the separation of subject ('the observer') and object ('the observed'), and insists instead that 'we exist primordially not as subjects manipulating objects in the external, "real", physical world, but as beings in, alongside and toward the world' (Pickles, 1985; cf. EXISTENTIALISM).

This contradicts our seemingly commonsensical views, but that is precisely the point. Edmund Husserl (1859–1938), one of the principal architects of phenomenology, called these common-sense views the *natural attitude*, by which he meant a set of views in which the possibility of cognition is simply taken for granted. For Husserl, the task of a truly rigorous and radical philosophy was to interrogate the natural attitude in order to show 'from what perspective things in the world are taken by the sciences and how the objects of each science are constituted' (Pickles, 1985).

Husserl argued that this intrinsically critical examination could be achieved through an act of pure philosophical reflection which he called the *epoché*, or the 'phenomenological reduction' (see Johnson, 1983). This method involves:

- suspending one's taken-for-granted presuppositions;
- reflecting 'not upon the objects of our perception but on the way in which they are originally given ... [on] the way in which we grasp the corresponding experiences' (Pickles, 1985) (Husserl called these experiences *phenomena*); and
- disclosing the very essence (*eidé*) of the phenomena.

Seen in this way, *phenomen*-ology becomes an *eidetic science* – not only a critique of positivism (Entrikin, 1976) but also an *alternative* to it (Gregory, 1978) – and it is in this double sense that phenomenology attracted the attention of many human geographers in the 1970s and 1980s. Phenomenology's central purpose is to establish, through the disclosure of 'essences', what Husserl called *regional ontologies* (see ONTOLOGY), in other words to 'ground' the thematic frameworks of the various empirical sciences by revealing the really essential nature of the objects and concepts which constitute their empirical domains (cf. PRAGMATISM):

> The purpose of a regional ontology is to describe the domain of entities appropriate to that science. This purpose is achieved through an ontological description of the a priori theoretical framework posited by a science when it engages in empirical work. Such a description lays out precisely the origin, the meaning and the functions of the concepts, principles and methods of a particular framework which has been assumed before that science can establish facts, develop hypotheses, or build theory. (Christensen, 1982)

This makes it necessary to distinguish between:
(a) *descriptive phenomenology*, which deals with the 'essential structures' underlying and governing the facts of the various empirical sciences – with 'the a priori framework of meaning adopted by a particular empirical science'; and
(b) *transcendental phenomenology*, which deals with the 'essential structures' of intentionality itself – with 'that realm which gives rise to the possibility of scientific reflection in the first place' (Pickles, 1985).

In human geography, however, the distinctions between (a) and (b) were often erased. Readings of Husserl were frequently closed around his transcendental phenomenology and, much more seriously, misrepresented to underwrite a patently 'subjectivist' critique of SPATIAL SCIENCE. To reinstate descriptive phenomenology is *not* to arrive at subjective constructions of 'the world naively given':

> We do not arrive at 'phenomenological description' of everyday activities such as going to the mailbox [cf. Seamon, 1979]. Descriptive phenomenology provides us with formal and abstract universal structures through methodically conscious performance of the eidetic reduction. (Pickles, 1985)

As an empirical science then, clearly, human geography is susceptible to interrogation by descriptive phenomenology: to the clarification of what Relph (1970) called 'the phenomenological basis of geography' through a systematic reflection on 'the elements and notions which characterize the nature of an entity within its empirical domain'. It is through procedures of this sort, in fact, that Pickles (1985) sought 'to retrieve two basic concepts of geographic concern – place and space – for a viable and vital regional ontology of the geographical, on the grounds of which geographical inquiry as a human science of the world can be explicitly founded' (see SPATIALITY).

But what about those 'everyday activities' (above)? Christensen (1982) claimed that:

> The *descriptive* component of given human science cannot guarantee that the theoretical framework of meaning employed by the empirical component is adequate and relevant to the lived world. This can be guaranteed only by an *interpretive* component to science which accounts critically for the meanings held by the agents in their lived world. (emphases added)

Indeed, Husserl himself once complained that the scientist 'does not make it clear to himself that the constant foundation of his admittedly subjective thinking activity is the environing world of life. This latter is constantly presupposed as the basic working area, in which alone his questions and his methodology make sense.' And again: 'The sciences build upon the life-world as taken-for-granted in that they make use of whatever in it happens to be necessary for their particular ends. But to use the life-world in this way is not to know it scientifically in its own manner of being' (Husserl, 1954). According to Pickles (1985), however, the task of phenomenology is to clarify the *universal and general* structure of the LIFEWORLD – what he calls the '*universal a priori of the lifeworld*' – and *not*, 'contrary to the claims of much "geographical phenomenology", [to] be a capturing of the everyday lifeworld as it is lived'.

Others disagreed with this objective and insisted upon the importance of the 'interpretative component' identified by Christensen (1982). She associated the interpretative, above all, with the writings of Alfred Schutz, whose ideas 'align more comfortably with the tradition of Heidegger than with the tradition of Husserl', but which are also indebted to Weber's interpretative sociology (see Gorman, 1977). This necessitates a further distinction: (c) *constitutive phenomenology*, which deals with the structures of social meaning – with frames of reference and systems of typification – which constitute the 'multiple realities' embedded in the lifeworld.

It is only in this context that it makes sense to speak of 'a plurality of worlds' (Relph, 1970; see also Tuan, 1971). It was certainly not Husserl's intention to license 'a multiplicity of different frames of reference; on the contrary, he made it perfectly clear that the purpose of the *epoché*, was to ensure that the world could be 'identically reconstituted in each individual through a similar reflective procedure' (Gregory, 1978). Insofar as Husserl's supposed 'preoccupation with the individual' was contrasted with the 'fundamentally social' focus of Schutz (Jackson, 1981), then constitutive phenomenology informed – Pickles (1985) would say '*mis*informed' – several studies in HUMANISTIC GEOGRAPHY. 'Rather than stressing experiences', Relph (1981) observed, such 'phenomenological studies can emphasize the phenomena of the geographical lifeworld'. This is not how Husserl understood 'experiences' and 'phenomena' (see above), and when Relph cites as examples his own *Place and placelessness* (1976) and Tuan's *Space and place* (1977) it should be noted that neither of these texts draws upon Husserl at all. In the course of the 1970s and 1980s other studies moved still further beyond 'the letter of the phenomenological law' to explore the dynamism of the LIFEWORLD (Buttimer, 1976) and the constitution of the TAKEN-FOR-GRANTED WORLD in ways which directly intersected with STRUCTURATION THEORY and SYMBOLIC INTERACTIONISM (Ley, 1977; Warf, 1986).

In the 1990s, however, other human geographers returned not only to Husserl but also (rather more emphatically) to the writings of Martin Heidegger (1889–1976) to offer critical readings of the concepts of space and SPATIALITY embedded within the phenomenological tradition (Schatzki, 1991; Strohmayer, 1998). It is noticeable that these readings are much more sensitive to the play of power within the phenomenological tradition: Heidegger's own political sympathies have been the subject of considerable debate, and so too have the political implications of his ideas about 'dwelling', PLACE and space (cf. Harvey, 1996, pp. 299–304, 313–16). DG

References

Buttimer, A. 1976: Grasping the dynamism of the lifeworld. *Annals of the Association of American Geographers* 66: 277–92. · Christensen, K. 1982: Geography as a human science: a philosophic critique of the positivist–humanist split. In P. Gould and G. Olsson, eds, *A search for common ground*. London: Pion, 37–57. · Entrikin, J.N. 1976: Contemporary humanism in geography. *Annals of the Association of American Geographers* 66: 615–32. · Gorman, R.A. 1977: *The dual vision: Alfred Schutz and the myth of phenomenological social science*. London: Routledge and Kegan Paul. · Gregory, D. 1978: The discourse of the past: phenomenology, structuralism and historical geography. *Journal of Historical Geography* 4: 161–73. · Harvey, D. 1996: *Justice, nature and the geography of difference*. Oxford and Cambridge, MA: Blackwell. · Husserl, E. 1954: *The crisis of European sciences and transcendental phenomenology*. Evanston, IL: Northwestern University Press. · Jackson, P. 1981: Phenomenology and social geography. *Area* 13: 299–305. · Johnson, L. 1983: Bracketing lifeworlds: Husserlian phenomenology as geographical method. *Australian Geographical Studies* 21: 102–8. · Ley, D. 1977: Social geography and the taken-for-granted world. *Transactions, Institute of British Geographers* NS 2: 498–512. · Pickles, J. 1985: *Phenomenology, science and geography: spatiality and the human sciences*. Cambridge: Cambridge University Press. · Relph, E. 1970: An inquiry into the relations between phenomenology and geography. *Canadian Geographer* 14: 193–201. · Relph, E. 1976: *Place and placelessness*. London: Pion. · Relph, E. 1981: Phenomenology. In M.E. Harvey and B.P. Holly, eds, *Themes in geography thought*. London: Croom Helm. · New York: St. Martin's Press; Schatzki, T. 1991: Spatial ontology and explanation. *Annals of the Association of American Geographers* 81: 650–70. · Seamon, D. 1979: *A geography of the life-world*. London: Croom Helm; New York: St. Martin's Press; Strohmayer, U. 1998: The event of space: geographic allusions in the phenomenological tradition. *Environment and Planning D: Society and Space* 16: 105–22. · Tuan, Y.-F. 1971: Geography, phenomenology and the study of human nature. *Canadian Geographer* 15: 181–92. · Tuan, Y.-F. 1977: *Space and place*. London: Edward Arnold; Minneapolis: University of Minnesota Press. · Warf, B. 1986: Ideology, everyday life and emancipatory phenomenology. *Antipode* 18: 268–83.

Suggested Reading

Christensen (1982). · Pickles (1985). · Schatzki (1991).

Phillips curve The relationship between the percentage change in money wages and the level of unemployment. Phillips (1958)

showed that the lower the unemployment, the higher the rate of change of wages. As the rate of increase in wages influences the rate of inflation, the Phillips curve suggests that the lower the level of unemployment the higher the rate of inflation. This implies that the aims of low unemployment and a low rate of inflation may be inconsistent. The change in Britain from low unemployment and high inflation in the 1970s to high unemployment and a reduced rate of inflation in the 1980s and 1990s represents a shift along the Phillips curve. DMS

Reference

Phillips, A.W.H. 1958: The relation between unemployment and rate of change in money wage rate in the UK, 1861–1957. *Economica* 25: 283–99;

Pirenne thesis With the publication of *Medieval cities* in 1925, Belgian historian Henri Pirenne (1862–1935) advanced a theory of medieval URBANIZATION that has only recently been superseded. According to Pirenne, the Islamic conquest of North Africa, Sicily and Spain in the eighth century finally closed the Mediterranean to TRADE between Europe and the Middle East. In the absence of systematic international trade, Europe fragmented into parochial REGIONS with largely self-sufficient economies. As a result cities became both unnecessary and unsupported, and were abandoned for some 200 years until east–west commerce was revived through Venice and Scandinavia. The reurbanization of Europe in the tenth century was led by merchants creating trade-based SUBURBS on the peripheries of ecclesiastical or military centres. Relations characteristic of FEUDALISM did not apply in these suburbs, which became progenitors of 'free labour' and a mercantile legal system.

Recent evidence drawn from archaeology, lexicology, topography, and numismatics has shown that Pirenne underestimated the level of international trade during the Carolingian period and the connections between agricultural and urban economies. He also overlooked the critical role played by the church in establishing ecclesiastical centres. The reurbanization of Europe is now interpreted as the result of internal population growth and an increased agricultural surplus which together underpinned a revival of both local and international trade. New interpretations of medieval urbanization seek to reveal the interdependence between city and countryside and no longer see these as separately functioning economic and social systems. DH

Reference and Suggested Reading

Pirenne, H. 1925: *Medieval cities: their origins and the revival of trade*, trans. Frank D. Halsey. Princeton: Princeton University Press. · Hodges, R. and Whitehouse, D. 1983: *Mohammed, Charlemagne and the origins of Europe: archaeology and the Pirenne thesis*. London: Duckworth. · Nicholas, D. 1997: *The growth of the medieval city from late antiquity to the early fourteenth century*. London and New York: Duckworth.

pixel A 'picture element', or the primitive element in a digital image composed of a rectangular RASTER of uniform elements. In Earth observation by REMOTE SENSING the size of an image pixel determines the image's spatial resolution, and is normally expressed in units of length on the ground. For example, the pixel size of the Landsat Thematic Mapper is 30 m, which is sufficient to allow crops to be identified in large fields, but not detailed enough to identify individual dwellings in many parts of the world. The images created by computer monitors are composed of pixels, as are the images captured by digital cameras. MG

place A portion of geographic SPACE. Space is organized into places often thought of as bounded settings in which social relations and IDENTITY are constituted (cf. TERRITORY; TERRITORIALITY). Such places may be officially recognized geographical entities or more informally organized sites of intersecting social relations, meanings and collective memory. The concept of place, the uniqueness of particular places and place-based identities are hotly contested concepts in the contemporary context of increasing GLOBALIZATION and the perceived threat of growing PLACELESSNESS.

Place, SENSE OF PLACE, and placelessness were some of the key concepts used in HUMANISTIC GEOGRAPHY during the 1970s to distinguish its approach from positivist geography, whose principal focus was space (see POSITIVISM). Place was seen as more subjectively defined, existential and particular, while space was thought to be a universal, more abstract phenomenon, subject to scientific LAW. The humanistic concept of place, largely drawn from PHENOMENOLOGY (e.g. Relph, 1976; Tuan, 1977), was concerned with individuals' attachments to particular places and the symbolic or metonymic quality of popular concepts of place which link events, attitudes, and places to create a fused whole. It was concerned with meaning and contrasted the experienced richness of the idea of place with the detached sterility of the concept of space. Humanistic approaches to place continued into the 1980s in the work of such authors as Black, Kunze and Pickles (1989). Entrikin (1991) mediated between positivist and phenomenological notions of place by arguing that '(t)o seek to understand place in a manner that captures its sense of totality and contextuality is to occupy a position that is between the objective pole of scientific theorising and the subjective pole of empathetic understanding'. He is opposed to the tendency to reduce geometric space to existential place and vice versa.

During the 1980s interest in the concept of place began to grow outside humanistic geography. Economic geographers such as Massey and Allen (1984) sought to theorize place as manifesting specificity within the context of general processes (see LOCALITY; PRODUCTION OF SPACE). Historical geographers such as Pred (1984), drawing on the STRUCTURATION THEORY of sociologist Anthony Giddens, saw place as an integral part of the structuration process: both constitutive of, and constituted by, social relations. Agnew (1987) and Johnston (1991) have argued that place should be one of the cornerstones of POLITICAL GEOGRAPHY. Agnew (1987) identifies three major elements of place as 'LOCALE, the settings in which social relations are constituted (these can be informal institutional); location, the geographical area encompassing the settings for social interaction as defined by social and economic processes operating at a wider scale; and sense of place, the local structure of feeling'. Like Entrikin's, his definition of place also mediates between the objective and subjective.

More recently arguments have been made for the importance of studying place and place specificity in the face of increasing globalization, TIME–SPACE COMPRESSION and CONVERGENCE, and the geographically uneven effects of these processes. Nostalgia for stable, homogeneous place-based COMMUNITIES, new NATIONALISMS, and other place-based IDENTITY POLITICS (the most extreme cases resulting in APARTHEID or even ETHNIC CLEANSING) are all seen by geographers as evidence of the importance of a critical perspective on place.

Harvey (1989) argues that a concern with place and place specificity is apt to lead to aestheticization in the form of nostalgic myths of community and reactionary politics. Feminist geographers such as Rose (1993) also worry that romantic notions of place, particularly homeplaces, as stable and secure may ignore unequal constructions of gender. In fact, she argues, the social organization of homeplaces is highly patriarchal and oppressive for many (see GENDER AND GEOGRAPHY; PATRIARCHY).

Massey (1997a) acknowledges these various dangers, but sees the possibility of a normative concept of place that avoids the implications of boundedness, homogeneity and exclusion. She argues that studying places does not always mean fetishizing them. On the contrary, studying large-scale processes as they vary between places reveals much that is otherwise undetectable. Massey says that a focus on place variation is an excellent basis for understanding diversity and difference and the inequality generated by effects of various types of large-scale RESTRUCTURING. Massey (1997a, 1997b) points out that a concern with the specificity or uniqueness of places in no way precludes theorization and that recognizing place specificity does not imply ignoring processes operating at a global scale. In fact, adequate theorization of such wider processes would recognize uneven effects caused by the peculiarities of specific places and their unique histories within larger regions.

Concern with adding richness of place-specific detail to ECONOMIC GEOGRAPHY resonates with calls for attention to DIFFERENCE and fragmentation associated with POSTMODERNISM. However, Massey is at pains to point out that there is a major difference between saying that 'place matters' in the contemporary era of POSTMODERNITY and her transhistorical claim that 'place matters' and always has. Nevertheless an argument can be made that the intensity of attachment to place varies among people and with changing historical conditions (e.g. increasing globalization or westernization). Massey's progressive concept of place recognizes the open and porous BOUNDARIES of places as well as the myriad interlinkages and interdependencies among places. It also acknowledges that the lives of some types of people are highly interconnected into a global network (e.g. the INTERNET) while others lead severely circumscribed lives. The progressive concept of place is normative as well as descriptive. It assumes social and cultural heterogeneity within places rather than assimilation to a national or local norm. Any given place is materially and imaginatively constructed by many different types of people. The dynamic tension created by the co-presence of all these people results in each lending different dimensions to those places. Other normative definitions of place that emphasize heterogeneity and fluidity of boundaries can also be found in Penrose (1993) and Young (1990).

Cresswell (1996) offers a critical view of place that sees the organization of places as ideological in the sense that it constrains practices in the interests of maintaining established hierarchies. 'A place for everything and everything in its place' is a deeply engrained sentiment in many cultures. Spatial divisions constrain as much as enable action. The common-sense organization of space into places lends a degree of stability to a society allowing people to know what behaviours to expect in which places. Such structures are relatively stable, but changing and contested, never rigid. Cresswell suggests that CRITICAL HUMAN GEOGRAPHY focus its attention on the RESISTANCE to, and TRANSGRESSION of, this mapping of cultural norms onto space. When actions, events and people are deemed to be 'out of place' by dominant groups in society, they are transgressive (in the spatial as well as the social sense of the term). (Skelton and Valentine (1998) also show how the spatial behaviour of youth can be transgressive and enabling in their struggles to redefine the often oppressive spatial order of society.)

Like Entrikin and Agnew, Cresswell seeks to show the interaction between the subjective and objective or material, between ideas and practices, and between cultural and economic geography through the concept of place which itself is both material and abstract. And like Massey, he has a normative concept of place that challenges common-sense beliefs about the classification of people, practices and objects according to their 'natural' location within a system of places. He states that 'the materiality of place gives it the aura of "NATURE". The nature of place can thus be offered as a justification of what is good, just and appropriate.'

Anderson (1991), Davis (1990), Sibley (1995) and Jackson and Penrose (1993) present a variety of studies of the racialization of place, exclusion and spatial oppression (cf. SOCIAL EXCLUSION). Jackson and Penrose (1993) argue that 'place contextualises the construction of "race" and nation generating geographically specific ideologies of RACISM and NATIONALISM'. The apparent 'naturalness' of race blends with the apparent 'naturalness' of rootedness in place, resulting in a powerful basis for identity politics. Such racialization of place can also lead to complacency about place-based structures of inequality. Social and cultural geographers have exposed the spurious basis for the legitimacy of race and racial segregation by deconstructing its naturalized links to place. Jackson and Penrose take this analysis further, showing how the 'strategic ESSENTIALISM' of place-based identity politics can lead to an unintentional endorsement of racist ideology (1993, p. 205). JD

References

Agnew, J. 1987: *Place and politics: the geographical mediation of state and society*. Boston: Allen and Unwin. · Anderson, K. 1991: *Vancouver's Chinatown: racial discourses in Canada, 1875–1980*. Montreal: McGill-Queens University Press. · Black, D.W., Kunze, D. and Pickles, J. 1989: *Commonplaces: essays on the nature of place*. New York: University Press of America. · Cresswell, T. 1996: *In place/out of place: geography, ideology and transgression*. London: University of Minnesota Press. · Davis, M. 1990: *City of quartz*. London: Verso. · Entrikin, J.N. 1991: *The betweenness of place: towards a geography of modernity*. Baltimore: Johns Hopkins. · Harvey, D. 1989: *The condition of postmodernity*. Oxford: Basil Blackwell. · Jackson, P. and Penrose, J., eds, 1993: *Constructions of race, place and nation*. London, UCL Press. · Johnston, R.J. 1991: *A question of place: exploring the practice of human geography*. Oxford: Blackwell. · Massey, D. 1997a: A global sense of place. In T. Barnes and D. Gregory, eds, *Reading human geography: the poetics and politics of inquiry*. London: Arnold, 315–23. · Massey, D. 1997b: The political place of locality studies. In L. McDowell, ed., *Undoing place? A geographical reader*. London: Arnold. · Massey, D. and Allen, J., eds, 1984: *Geography matters! A reader*. Cambridge: Cambridge University Press. · Penrose, J. 1993: Reification in the name of change. In P. Jackson and J. Penrose, eds, *Constructions of race, place and nation*. London: UCL Press, 27–49. · Pred, A. 1984: Place as historically contingent process: structuration and the time geography of becoming places. *Annals of the Association of American Geographers* 74: 279–97. · Relph, E. 1976: *Place and placelessness*. London: Pion. · Rose, G. 1993: *Feminism and geography: the limits of geographical knowledge*. Cambridge: Polity. · Sibley, D. 1995: *Geographies of exclusion: society and difference in the west*. London: Routledge. · Skelton, T. and Valentine, G., eds, 1998: *Coolplaces: geographies of youth cultures*. London: Routledge. · Tuan, Y.-F. 1977: *Space and place: the perspective of experience*. Minneapolis: University of Minnesota. · Young, I.M. 1990: *Justice and the politics of difference*. Princeton: Princeton University Press.

Suggested Reading

Cresswell (1996). · Entrikin (1991). · Johnson (1991); Massey (1997a). · Relph (1976).

place names As objects of philological study, the names of settlements, localities, fields, and LANDSCAPE features (both natural and cultural), may provide evidence of environmental, settlement, and social conditions at the time the name was coined. This is possible because many place names are composed of elements which have topographic, habitative or social meanings, and they can be approximately dated. Obviously, the utility of place names is limited mainly to periods at which names were being coined, and varies with the volume of other sources of information.

In western Europe, thousands of surviving place names were coined in pre- or early-medieval periods which are otherwise very poorly documented. For these periods, syntheses of evidence on place names and their distribution with palaeo-environmental work underlie important work on the geography of settlements (e.g. Cameron, 1975); on woodland clearance and expanding agriculture (e.g. Hooke, 1989); on territorial organization (e.g. Fellows-Jensen, 1985); and on inter-settlement relations (e.g. Jones, 1990).

Geographical analysis of place names faces four main problems. First, the earliest recording of a name may occur several centuries after its coining, and place names were subject to prevailing linguistic transformations and developments (Fellows-Jensen, 1990). For example, many English place names are first recorded in the *Domesday Book*, but may have been coined as early as the sixth century (Cox, 1975): their original form, the identification of their elements, and hence their meaning, all have to be inferred from their later forms and known patterns of linguistic change. Secondly, the interpretation of particular elements is disputed or uncertain. For example, it is often difficult to distinguish the habitative term 'ham' from the topographic term 'hamm', yet they have different implications. Thirdly, in dating the original coining of a place name, it may be important to know whether the feature of landscape or society to which the name relates is a long-run or an ephemeral one, the former being in general much more informative than the latter. Lastly, the name may not originally have been that of the settlement, field or feature which now bears it. The phenomenon of the mobile village in the Dark Ages is now widely recognized (Taylor, 1983, 1989), and if mobile settlements retained their previous name, they may no longer be located at the place to which they refer, a particular problem when dealing with topographic elements.

In areas settled much later, naming evidence relating to dominant cultural groups is much more accessible, and analysis centres on the cultural context and symbolism of naming. Particular attention has been paid to COLONIAL contexts, where indigenous names have been lost with the deaths of native populations, or deliberately suppressed. Re-naming, along with new cartography, formed part of European appropriations of native peoples' lands and contributed to European portrayals of such land as 'empty' (Harley, 1988), a reminder of the political nature of naming places. PG

References

Cameron, K., ed., 1975: *Place-name evidence for the Anglo-Saxon invasion and Scandinavian settlements*. Nottingham: English Place Names Society. · Cox, B. 1975: The place-names of the earliest English records. *Journal of the English Place-Names Society* 8: 12–66. · Fellows-Jensen, G. 1985: Scandinavian settlement in England: the place-name evidence. In H. Bekker-Nielsen and H. Frede-Nielsen, eds, *Vikingesymposium, Odense Universitet 1982*. Odense. · Fellows-Jensen, G. 1990: Place-names as a reflection of cultural interaction. *Anglo-Saxon England* 19: 13–21. · Gelling, M. 1988: Towards a chronology for English place-names. In D. Hooke, ed., *Anglo-Saxon settlements*. Oxford: Clarendon Press. · Harley, J.B. 1988: Silences and secrecy: the hidden agenda of cartography in early modern Europe. *Imago Mundi* 40: 111–30. · Hooke, D. 1989: Pre-conquest woodland: its distribution and usage. *Agricultural History Review* 37: 113–29. · Jones, G.R.J. 1990: Celts, Saxons and Scandinavians. In R.A. Dodgshon and R.A. Butlin, eds, *An historical geography of England and Wales*, 2nd edn. London: Academic Press, 45–68. · Taylor, C.C. 1983: *Village and landscape: a history of rural settlement in England*. London: George Philip & Son. · Taylor, C.C. 1989: Whittlesford: the study of a river-edge village. In M. Aston et al., eds, *The rural settlements of medieval England: studies dedicated to Maurice Beresford and John Hurst*. Oxford: Basil Blackwell, 207–27.

Suggested Reading

Gelling, M. 1997: *Place-names in the landscape*, 3rd edn. London: Dent.

place utility A concept used in BEHAVIOURAL GEOGRAPHY to measure an individual's satisfaction with a given location. The term was introduced to assist studies of MIGRATION concerned with people's evaluations of available options (Wolpert, 1965), including their current homes. Having decided to investigate the possibility of a move, a household would search within its ACTION SPACE for available dwellings (cf. SEARCH BEHAVIOUR) and evaluate each against their criteria for assessing desirability. Such evaluations provide the measures of place utility which determine whether to move (the place utility of the existing home may be higher than that of any other identified) and which of the potential destinations is the best. RJJ

Reference and Suggested Reading

Brown, L.A. and Moore, E.G. 1970: The intra-urban migration process: a perspective. *Geographical Analysis* 52B: 1–13. · Wolpert, J. 1965: Behavioral aspects of the decision to migrate. *Papers [and Proceedings] of the Regional Science Association* 15: 159–69.

placelessness The existence of relatively homogeneous and standardized LANDSCAPES which diminish the local specificity and variety of PLACES that characterized pre-industrial societies. In the 1970s this term was associated with HUMANISTIC GEOGRAPHY, particularly the work of Relph (1976) who, drawing upon Heidegger (1962), argues that in the modern world, the loss of place diversity is symptomatic of a larger loss of meaning – the 'authentic' attitude which characterized pre-industrial and handicraft CULTURES and produces the 'SENSE OF PLACE' that some claim has now been largely lost and replaced with an 'inauthentic' attitude. Relph offers as examples of placelessness and the 'inauthentic' attitude which produces them: tourist landscapes, commercial strips, NEW TOWNS and SUBURBS and the international style in architecture. Entrikin (1991) pointed out that while some meanings are indeed lost when places become increasingly homogenized, others are gained. To speak solely of loss, therefore, is to adopt the values of conservationists and preservationists who seek to preserve cultural artefacts and places.

With the influence of POSTMODERNISM in geography during the 1980s and 1990s, authenticity came to be considered a highly problematic concept. Soja (1996), Duncan and Duncan (1992) and other geographers, who were influenced by the writings of French thinkers such as Baudrillard and Barthes, began to take a more critical and sociological approach to the notion of authentic places. Rather than offering expert judgements about landscapes according to such criteria as placelessness, inauthenticity or authenticity, they began to critique popular versions of these notions.

Interest in POSTMODERNITY as an era, however, has led geographers to focus on GLOBALIZATION and TIME–SPACE COMPRESSION. While some assume that globalization has homogenizing effects, reducing the particularity of places and increasing placelessness, others point to its uneven effects across the globe and the defensive reaction which seeks to maintain or recover place differences. Massey (1997) however, argues that the notion of sense of place (as needing a single, essentialized identity) is reactionary and that the persistent identification of place with COMMUNITY is a mistaken romanticism. Any single LOCATION can be many very different places to different types of people. The notion of a sense of place or of placelessness has to be rethought in light of highly complex constellations of social relations linking a place to other places beyond that produce a highly particularized, but nevertheless global, sense of the local. JD

References

Duncan, J. and Duncan, N. 1992: Ideology and bliss: Roland Barthes and the secret histories of landscape. In T. Barnes and J. Duncan, eds, *Writing worlds: discourse, text and metaphor in the representation of landscape*. London: Routledge. · Entrikin, J.N. 1991: *The betweenness of place: towards a geography of modernity*. Baltimore: Johns Hopkins Press. · Heidegger, M. 1962: *Being and time*. New York: Harper and Row. · Massey, D. 1997: A global sense of place. In T. Barnes and D. Gregory, eds, *Reading human geography: the poetics and politics of inquiry*. London: Arnold. · Relph, E. 1976: *Place and placelessness*. London: Pion. · Soja, E. 1996: *Thirdspace: journeys to Los Angeles and other real-and-imagined places*. Cambridge, MA: Blackwell.

Suggested Reading

Porteous, J.D. 1988: Topicide: the annihilation of place. In J. Eyles and D.M. Smith, eds, *Qualitative methods in human geography*. Cambridge: Polity, 75–93. · Seamon, D. and Mugerauer, R., eds, 1985: *Dwelling, place and environment: towards a phenomenology of person and world*. Dordrecht: Martinus Nijhoff.

place/space tensions A concept for integrating geographical concern for PLACE and SPACE. It draws on Yi-Fu Tuan's (1977) work in which place is interpreted as *humanized space*. Any locality can be transformed from place to space or vice versa; for instance, the passing of the FRONTIER marks a transformation from unknown space to settled place. It is a tension when different persons treat the same LOCALITY in different ways – a city is viewed as a place by its inhabitants but it is a space to plan, for urban planners. In POLITICAL GEOGRAPHY the rise of the NATION-STATE can be interpreted as the conversion of a space (sovereign TERRITORY; cf. SOVEREIGNTY) into a place (national homeland) (Taylor, 1999). Such tensions arise at all SCALES, from home (place) and household (space), to GLOBALIZATION (space) and global ECOSYSTEM (place). PJT

References

Taylor, P.J. 1999: Places, spaces and Macy's: place–space tensions in the political geography of modernities. *Progress in Human Geography* 23: 7–26. · Tuan, Y.-F. 1977: *Space and place*. London: Arnold.

plantation The meaning of plantation has changed over time. Originally a plot of ground with trees, it came to mean a group of settlers or their political units during British overseas expansion (e.g. the Ulster Plantation; see COLONIALISM). Later, plantation came to mean a large farm or landed estate especially associated with tropical or subtropical production of 'classical' plantation crops such as sugar, coffee, tobacco, tea, cocoa, bananas, spices, cotton, sisal, rubber and palm oil (Thompson, 1975; see FARMING, TYPE OF). Most plantations combined an agricultural with an industrial process but technologies, labour processes, property rights and INFRASTRUCTURE have varied enormously across space and time making a generic definition of plantation impossible (see AGRIBUSINESS). Plantations have witnessed historical transformations in labour relations between slave, feudal, migratory, indentured and free wage labour, and many plantations in Latin America operated on a mixture of these labour forms (see LABOUR PROCESS).

All definitions of plantation tend to differentiate it from other agricultural forms of production by size, authority structure, crop or labour force characteristics (low skills, work gangs, various forms of servility). The theory of plantations has a long lineage that can be traced back to David Ricardo and John Stuart Mill in the nineteenth century through to H.J. Nieboer and Edgar Thompson in the twentieth. An important distinction has been made between old and new style plantations in which the former (e.g. the *hacienda* in Central America) were essentially pre-capitalist with surpluses directed at conspicuous consumption, while the latter were capitalist enterprises driven by the rigours of capitalist ACCUMULATION (see FEUDALISM and CAPITALISM).

Recent work has seen plantations as 'totalizing institutions' whose historical connections with RACISM and SLAVERY have fundamentally shaped entire social and political structures (as in the Caribbean and the US South) but have also acted as powerful agents of UNDERDEVELOPMENT. Plantations and plantation economies and societies cannot be understood in terms of the narrow logic of production of the enterprise alone, however. The enormously diverse forms and circumstances in which the plantation has persisted and transformed itself must be rooted in the historical forms and rhythms of capitalist accumulation under specific land, labour and capital markets. MW

References

Beckford, G. 1972: *Persistent poverty: underdevelopment in plantation economies of the Third World*. London: Oxford University Press. · Thompson, E. 1983: *Plantation society*, Durham: Duke University Press.

plural society Coined by the British economist and colonial administrator J.S. Furnivall on the basis of his experience in Southeast Asia, the term was originally applied to colonial societies in which an alien minority ruled over an indigenous majority (cf. COLONIALISM). In his classic study of Burma and the Dutch East Indies, Furnivall used the term to describe those SOCIETIES in which different sections of the COMMUNITY live side by side, but separately, within the same political unit: 'Each group holds by its own religion, its own culture and language, its own ideas and ways. As individuals they meet, but only in the market place, in buying and selling' (Furnivall, 1948, pp. 304–5). Though now rather dated, the concept has since been applied to a variety of post-colonial societies in Africa and the Caribbean (Smith, 1965; Kuper and Smith, 1969; see POST-COLONIALISM). More recently, the term has been extended even more widely to encompass societies such as Britain, Canada and the United States which, in Furnivall's terms, have plural elements but are not strictly plural societies (Clarke et al., 1984). When used in this broader sense, most contemporary societies have some elements of PLURALISM and the term may lose its specificity in applying to colonial societies ruled by an ethnically distinct minority. The term has some affinities with liberal notions of MULTICULTURALISM in its acceptance of plurality as opposed to an insistence on ASSIMILATION. Like multiculturalism, however, it has been criticized for implying a degree of equality between different sections within such societies, obscuring the existence of deeply structured inequalities between them. PAJ

References

Clarke, C.G., Ley, D. and Peach, C., eds, 1984: *Geography and ethnic pluralism*. London: Allen and Unwin. · Furnivall, J.S. 1948: *Colonial policy and practice*. Cambridge: Cambridge University Press. · Kuper, L. and Smith, M.G., eds, 1969: *Pluralism in Africa*. Berkeley: University of California Press. · Smith, M.G. 1965: *The plural society in the British West Indies*. Berkeley: University of California Press.

pluralism A concept that has two distinct meanings:

(a) A descriptive term signifying *cultural diversity in a society* (which may then be referred to as a PLURAL SOCIETY), the three most common criteria for division being RACE, LANGUAGE and RELIGION. Since cultural diversity is often associated with social CONFLICT, Dahl terms this *conflictual pluralism*, which has been a major theme in CULTURAL and SOCIAL GEOGRAPHY (Clarke et al., 1984) and POLITICAL GEOGRAPHY (Kliot and Waterman, 1983). Today much of what went under the rubric of pluralism is studied as DIFFERENCE.

(b) A theory of POWER in society associated with the work of Robert Dahl, which he has termed *organizational pluralism*. The theory asserts that power is diffused and balanced in modern societies so that there is no one group or CLASS able to dominate DECISION-MAKING in government. A high degree of consensus is assumed such that 'conflicts' are not fundamental but can be dealt with pragmatically in the political marketplace. Decisions are ultimately legitimized through the electoral process. The institutions of the STATE take on the role of umpire, adjudicating among competing interest groups. The theory was applied by Dahl (1961) to an urban area in order to disprove the conclusion of COMMUNITY power studies that American cities were run by local elites. The debate surrounding this study has been important for URBAN GEOGRAPHY. The major attempt to refute pluralism is still that of Miliband (1969), who argues that the theory takes as resolved the major questions concerning the nature of political power in capitalist society. He reasserts class domination of the state and sets out to show that pluralism 'far from providing a guide to reality, constitutes a profound obfuscation of it'. Lukes (1974) provides a theoretical discussion of POWER in which pluralism is designated a 'one-dimensional view' because it is limited to considering observable behaviour as a study of decision-making. Today, the pluralist theory of power is best viewed as one of political science's major contributions to the 'optimistic' American social science which dominated world social studies in the period 1945–70 (Taylor, 1996, ch. 3). PJT

References

Clarke, C., Ley, D. and Peach, C., eds, 1984: *Geography and ethnic pluralism*. London. · George Allen and Unwin. · Dahl, R.A. 1961: *Who governs?* New Haven: Yale University Press. · Kliot, N. and Waterman, S., eds, 1983: *Pluralism and political geography*. London: Croom Helm. · New York: St. Martin's Press. · Lukes, S. 1974: *Power: a radical view*. London: Macmillan. · Miliband, R. 1969: *The state in capitalist society*. London: Quartet. · Taylor, P.J. 1996: *The way the modern world works: world hegemony to world impasse*. Chichester: Wiley.

poetics of geography A set of linguistic resources and a particular literary and theoretical sensibility to cope with problems of geographical REPRESENTATION. In the conventional view of LANGUAGE, known as *naive* REALISM, 'words are felt to link up with their thoughts or objects in essentially right and incontrovertible ways' (Eagleton, 1983, p. 134). The task of writing, of representing the world, is simply the mechanical one of lining up words in the right order. This view of language and writing, however, has been severely criticized in twentieth-century philosophy on the grounds that words are not mirrors of the world. Instead, the two are in a much more complex relation involving social power, cultural norms, interpretive and RHETORICAL strategies, and, to use Wittgenstein's phrase, a people's very 'form of life'. To signal that complexity, researchers in a number of fields in the humanities and social sciences have paid special attention to the process of *inscription*. Note that the issue is as much about a new theoretical and critical attitude to writing as it is about writing per se. It is devising different narrative strategies, novel tropes, and alternative vocabularies to represent a set of new critical theoretical goals such as reflexivity, or openness and inclusivity, or the denaturalization of commonly accepted relations (Culler, 1997). The heightened CRITICAL THEORETICAL sensibility towards, and experimentation with, geographical writing constitute the poetics of geography.

The term 'poetics' was first popularized in the sense described above in an important collection of ETHNOGRAPHIC essays, *Writing culture* (Clifford and Marcus, 1986). There contributors wrestled with the problem of including in their representations the wider contexts of POWER, constraint, heterogeneity, historical rupture, and even redemption, that bear on both their subjects and themselves as authors. Lining up words mechanically in the right order does not work because there is no right order. This is the importance of poetics. It makes readers and authors acutely aware of both the difficulties and possibilities of writing (Barnes and Gregory, 1997, pp. 3–6). Note that poetics is not equivalent to purple prose, or the unfettered use of language, quite the opposite. It is about treating words with respect, recognizing their power, passion and potential, and using them with precision and consequence. To practise poetics is not to distance oneself from the world, but to take the world utterly seriously. Words are all that we have. 'Language goes all the way down', as the American philosopher Richard Rorty puts it, and we must be keenly aware in deploying it.

In geography the issue of how to write is increasingly important, and found particularly in CULTURAL GEOGRAPHY in studies around IDENTITY POLITICS and SEXUALITY, and in recent FEMINIST GEOGRAPHIES. Olsson (1980, 1992) is perhaps the best-known experimenter within the English language, which is remarkable given that it is not his native tongue. Pred (1990) has also been acutely conscious of the power of words, both of others (discussed in his historical studies of Stockholm) and of his own. TJB

References

Barnes, T.J. and Gregory, D., eds, 1997: *Reading geography: the poetics and politics of inquiry*. London: Arnold. · Clifford, J. 1986: Introduction: partial truths. In J. Clifford and G.E. Marcus, eds, *Writing culture: the poetics and politics of ethnography*. Berkeley, CA: University of California Press, 1–26. · Clifford, J. and Marcus, G.E., eds, 1986: *Writing culture: the poetics and politics of ethnography*. Berkeley, CA: University of California Press. · Culler, J. 1997: *Literary theory: a very short introduction*. Oxford: Oxford University Press. · Eagleton, T. 1983: *Literary theory: an introduction*. Minneapolis, MN: University of Minnesota Press. · Olsson, G. 1980: *Birds in egg/eggs in bird*. London: Pion · Olsson, G. 1992: *Lines of power/limits of language*. Minneapolis, MN: University of Minnesota Press. · Pred, A. 1990: *Lost words and lost worlds: modernity and language in everyday life in nineteenth century Stockholm*. Cambridge: Cambridge University Press.

Suggested Reading

Barnes and Gregory (1997), 1–9. · Clifford and Marcus (1986).

policing, geography of Policing refers to a set of activities involving the use of SURVEILLANCE and the threat of sanctions for discovered deviance, intended to ensure the security of a particular social order (Reiner, 1997). These activities are carried out by a variety of agencies but most research has focused on the public police who are defined by their specific mandate of crime control and order maintenance; their specific powers of the right to use coercive force within the STATE's domestic territory; and their specific form of accountability to the law. Geographical interest in policing has developed around several overlapping themes. Initially there was concern that many studies of the geography of crime (see CRIME, GEOGRAPHY OF) failed to address the possible impact of police practices on the spatial distribution of crime. Different crime recording procedures between police forces can have a significant impact on regional variations in 'official' crime rates, while at a local level proactive policing of so-called victimless crimes, such as prostitution and offences involving illegal drugs (where there is no specific victim to report an incident to the police), can have an important influence on the location of these crimes (see Lowman, 1992). In terms of the role of the police in reducing crime, the generally limited effectiveness of police patrols has been shown to be enhanced when these patrols are spatially targeted on so-called 'hot spots', locations such as street intersections, retail or residential areas which generate disproportionately high numbers of calls for police attention.

This research on policing and crime control has helped focus attention on the more general importance of the spatiality of police practices. The use of TIME-GEOGRAPHY (Fyfe, 1992) and studies of police TERRITORIALITY (Herbert, 1997) highlight how the power of the police to secure social order depends crucially on their control of space. The police routinely draw on their coercive powers to define and enforce BOUNDARIES between public and private space, to restrict people's mobility and to disperse gatherings of people in locations where such activity is seen as threatening to public order. Shaping this use and control of space are a variety of wider influences relating to police subcultures, the bureaucratic organization of police forces, and the law (see LAW, GEOGRAPHY OF). These studies of the spatiality of public policing have a much wider relevance within human geography. The local actions of police officers are bound up with the POLITICAL GEOGRAPHY of state power given that the cumulative effect of officers' actions is to support the central state's administrative and disciplinary efforts and so contribute to processes of 'internal pacification'. Of course, this does not occur without conflict and both historical (see Ogborn, 1993) and contemporary (see Smith, 1986; Blomley, 1994, ch. 5) geographical studies have explored the tensions that can exist between the policing priorities of local communities and the broader policing agenda set by central state interests. The study of police territoriality also establishes connections between policing and SOCIAL GEOGRAPHY by revealing the contours of those images of the city (see MENTAL MAPS) held by police officers which equip them with sets of expectations about what is normal or typical activity for a location at a certain time. Particular attention has focused on the policing of so-called 'no-go' areas in US and UK cities, where conflict between the police and local, often ethnic minority, communities has become routine (see Keith, 1993).

Although research into policing has focused mainly on the public police, policing is not a public monopoly. In many metropolitan areas policing is performed by a mix of public organizations and private agencies and individuals (see Fyfe, 1995). Two forms of private policing are of particular geographical interest:

self-policing (also referred to as responsible or active CITIZENSHIP), which involves private individuals taking responsibility for the surveillance of public spaces, like the street, and the security of private spaces, such as the home, via local neighbourhood or block watch schemes; and

private security policing, which has grown rapidly in the post-1945 period due to the expansion in privately-owned but publicly-accessible spaces like shopping malls, industrial estates and university campuses, where security is provided by private police personnel and video-surveillance systems. (See also PRIVATE INTEREST DEVELOPMENTS.)

Compared with public policing, research into private policing is in its infancy but given that in both Britain and North America private police personnel now outnumber their counterparts in public policing, the activities of private police in regulating behaviour and maintaining order in privately owned 'public' spaces is of growing importance. Indeed, against the background of a growing debate about the impact of increasing social control and surveillance for the 'destruction of any truly democratic urban space' (Davis, 1992, p. 155), the roles of both public and private police deserve continuing critical geographical scrutiny.

While local urban communities provide the focus for most research on public and private policing, the exercise of surveillance at other geographical scales and in new and different environments is also of growing significance. At an international level, for example, the increasing globalization of crime means that patrolling the 'global village' involves national security organizations like MI5 and federal law enforcement agencies like the FBI or DEA operating alongside more established global policing and suveillance organizations like Interpol, MI6 and the CIA to tackle problems of international terrorism, drug trafficking or cross-border fraud. In terms of new environments, the policing of virtual communities in CYBERSPACE, where so-called 'cybercrimes' such as espionage, theft of intellectual property, and pornography are a growing problem, poses a significant challenge for traditional police organizations and surveillance methods in the twenty-first century (see Wall, 1997). NRF

References

Blomley, N.K. 1994: *Law, space and the geographies of power*. New York: Guilford Press. · Davis, M. 1992: Fortress Los Angeles: the militarization of urban space. In M. Sorkin, ed., *Variations on a theme park: the new American city and the end of public space*. New York: Hill and Wang, 154–80. · Fyfe, N.R. 1992: Space, time and policing: towards a contextual understanding of police work. *Environment and Planning D: Society and Space* 10: 469–86. · Fyfe, N.R. 1995: Policing the city. *Urban Studies* 32: 759–78. · Herbert, S. 1997: *Policing space: territoriality and the Los Angeles Police Department*. Minneapolis: University of Minnesota Press. · Keith, M. 1993: *Race, riots and policing: lore and disorder in a multi-racist society*. London: UCL Press. · Lowman, J. 1992: Police practices and crime rates in the lower world: prostitution in Vancouver. In D.J. Evans, N.R. Fyfe and D.T. Herbert, eds, *Crime, policing and place: essays in environmental criminology*. London: Routledge, 233–54. · Ogborn, M. 1993: Ordering the city: surveillance, public space and the reform of urban policing in England 1835–56. *Political Geography* 12: 505–21. · Reiner, R. 1997: Policing and the police. In M. Maguire, R. Morgan and R. Reiner, eds, *The Oxford handbook of criminology*, 2nd edn. Oxford: Clarendon Press, 997–1049. · Smith, S.J. 1986: Police accountability and local democracy. *Area* 18: 99–107. · Wall, D. 1997: Policing the virtual community: the Internet, cyberspace and cyber-crime. In P. Francis, P. Davies and V. Jupp, eds, *Policing futures: the police, law enforcement and the twenty-first century*. London: Macmillan, 208–36.

Suggested reading

Fyfe, N.R. 1991: The police, space and society: the geography of policing. *Progress in human geography* 15: 249–67. · Herbert, S. 1997: *Policing space: territoriality and the Los Angeles Police Department*. Minneapolis: University of Minnesota Press.

political ecology An approach to, but far from a coherent theory of, the complex metabolism between NATURE and SOCIETY (see Blaikie, 1985; Blaikie and Brookfield, 1987). The expression itself emerged in the 1970s in a variety of intellectual contexts – employed by the journalist Alex Cockburn, the anthropologist Eric Wolf, and the environmental scientist Graheme Beakhurst – as a somewhat inchoate covering term for the panoply of ways in which environmental concerns were politicized in the wake of the ENVIRONMENTALIST wave which broke in the late 1960s and early 1970s. In its academic, and specifically geographical, usage political ecology has a longer and more complex provenance – which both harkens back to HUMAN and CULTURAL ECOLOGY and to an earlier history of relations between Anthropology and Geography in the 1940s and 1950s and incorporates a more recent synthetic and analytical deployment in the early 1980s associated with the work of Piers Blaikie (1985), Michael Watts (1983, 1986), and Suzanna Hecht (1985). In the 1990s the core empirical concerns of political ecology – largely rural, agrarian and THIRD WORLD – were properly expanded, and the theoretical horizons have deepened the original concerns with the dynamics of RESOURCE MANAGEMENT (see Peluso, 1992; Zimmerer, 1996; Neumann,

1999). Political ecology has also splintered into a more complex field of political ecologies which embraces environmental history (Grove, 1995), science studies (Demerit, 1998; see SCIENCE, GEOGRAPHY AND), ACTOR–NETWORK THEORY (Braun and Castree, 1998), gender theory (Aggarwal, 1998; cf. GENDER AND GEOGRAPHY), discourse analysis (Escobar, 1995) and a reinvigorated Marxism (O'Connor, 1997; Leff, 1995; cf. MARXIST GEOGRAPHY).

Two geographical monographs – *The political economy of soil erosion* (1985) by Piers Blaikie and *Land degradation and society* (1987) edited by Harold Brookfield and Piers Blaikie – provided the intellectual and theoretical foundation stones for the formalization of political ecology as such. What Blaikie achieved in *The political economy of soil erosion* was to systematize the growing confluence between three theoretical approaches: cultural ecology (Nietschmann, 1973) in geography, rooted in ECOSYSTEMS approaches to human behaviour; ecological anthropology, grounded in cybernetics and the adaptive qualities of living systems (see Rappaport, 1967); and the high tide of Marxist-inspired POLITICAL ECONOMY, and PEASANT studies in particular, of the 1970s. A number of people contributed to this intersection of ideas – Richards' (1985) work on peasant science, Hecht's (1985) analysis of rent seeking, inflation and deforestation in eastern Amazonia, Grossman (1984) on subsistence in Papua New Guinea, and Watts (1983) on the simple reproduction squeeze and drought in Nigeria – but Blaikie pulled a number of disparate themes and ideas together, drawing in large measure on his own South Asian experiences. In rejecting the COLONIAL model of soil erosion which framed the problem around environmental constraints, mismanagement, OVERPOPULATION, and market failure, Blaikie started from the resource manager and specifically households from whom surpluses are extracted 'who then in turn are forced to extract "surpluses" from the environment ... [leading] to degradation' (1985, p. 124). The analytical scaffolding was provided by a number of key middle-range concepts – marginalization, proletarianization and incorporation – which permitted geographers to see the failure of soil conservation schemes in CLASS or social terms, namely the POWER of classes affected by soil erosion in relation to STATE power, the class-specific perception of soil problems and solutions, and the class basis of soil erosion as a political issue. Blaikie was able to drive home the point that POVERTY could, in a dialectical way, cause degradation – 'peasants destroy their own environment in attempts to delay their own destruction' (1985, p. 29) – and that poverty had to be understood not as a thing or a condition, but as the social RELATIONS OF PRODUCTION which are realms of possibility and constraint.

In this work political ecology came to mean a combination of 'the concerns of ECOLOGY and a broadly defined political economy' (Blaikie and Brookfield, 1987, p. 17), the latter understood as a concern with effects 'on people, as well as on their productive activities, of on-going changes within society at local and global levels' (1987, p. 21). This is a broad definition – an approach rather than a theory – which was adopted by the editors in the inaugural issue of the *Journal of Political Ecology* in 1995. Political ecology has three essential foci.

The first is interactive, contradictory and DIALECTICAL: society and land-based RESOURCES are mutually causal in such a way that poverty, via poor management, can induce environmental degradation which itself deepens poverty. Less a problem of poor management, inevitable natural decay or demographic growth, land degradation is seen as *social* in origin and definition. Analytically, the centrepoint of any nature–society study must be the 'land manager' whose relationship to nature must be considered in a historical, political and economic context.

Second, political ecology argues for regional or spatial accounts of degradation which link, through 'chains of explanation', local decision-makers to spatial variations in environmental structure (stability and resilience as traits of particular ecosystems in particular). LOCALITY studies are, thus, subsumed within multi-layered analyses pitched at a variety of regional scales.

Third, land management is framed by 'external structures' which for Blaikie meant the role of the state and the CORE–PERIPHERY model.

If political ecology was not exactly clear what political economy implied, beyond a sort of 1970s DEPENDENCY THEORY, it did provide a number of principles and mid-range concepts. The first is a refined concept of marginality in which its political, ecological and economic aspects may be mutually reinforcing: land degradation is both a result and a cause of social marginalization. Second, pressure of production on resources is transmitted through social relations which impose excessive demands on the environment (i.e. surplus extraction). And third, the inadequacy of environmental data of historical depth linked to a chain of explanation analysis compels a plural approach. Rather than unicausal theories one must, in short, accept 'plural perceptions, plural definitions... and plural rationalities' (Blaikie and Brookfield, 1987, p. 16).

Political ecology had the advantage of seeing land management and environmental degradation (or SUSTAINABILITY) in terms of how political economy shapes the ability to manage resources (through forms of access and control, through forms of exclusion, and through forms of exploitation), and through the lens of cognition (one person's ACCUMULATION is another person's degradation). But in other respects political ecology was demonstrably weak: it often had an outdated notion of ECOLOGY and ecological dynamics (including an incomplete understanding of ecological agency: Zimmerer, 1994); it was often remarkably silent on the politics of political ecology; it had a somewhat voluntarist notion of human perception, and not least it did not provide a theoretically derived set of concepts to explore particular environmental outcomes or transformations. These weaknesses, coupled with the almost indeterminate and open-ended nature of political ecology, not unexpectedly produced both a deepening and a proliferation of political ecologies in the 1990s (see Hecht and Cockburn, 1989; Peet and Watts, 1996; Bryant and Bailey, 1997). A number of studies address the question of politics, focusing especially on patterns of resistance and struggles over access to and control over the environment, and how politics as policy is discursively constructed (Leach and Mearns, 1996; Moore, 1995; Pulido, 1996; Neumann, 1999; see environmental justice). Others have taken the political economy approach in somewhat differing directions: one takes the poverty–degradation connection and explores outcomes with the tools of institutional economics (Das Gupta, 1993) and entitlements, whereas another returns to Marx to derive concepts from the second contradiction of capitalism (O'Connor, 1998). Much work has addressed the original silence of political ecology on questions of GENDER (Aggarwal, 1998). And still others, often drawing upon discourse theory and social studies of science (cf. SCIENCE, GEOGRAPHY AND), examine environmental problems and policies – often outside the THIRD WORLD – in terms of ecological MODERNIZATION, RISK, and GOVERNMENTALITY (see Keil et al., 1998; Leach and Mearns, 1996; Braun and Castree, 1998).

Political ecology has in a sense almost dissolved itself over the last 15 years as scholars have sought to extend its reach. At the same time it has met up with the proliferations of forms of environmental study emerging from history, science studies, POST-STRUCTURALISM, and new SOCIAL MOVEMENTS. Much of this work continues to struggle with the dialectical relations between nature and society that the early political ecology identified (see Harvey, 1996), however, and which continues to provide the central conundrum for what is now a hugely expanded and polyglot landscape of political ecology. MW

References

Aggarwal, B. 1998: The gender and environment debate. In R. Keil et al., eds, *Political ecology*. London: Routledge, 193–220. · Blaikie, P. 1985: *The political economy of soil erosion*. London: Longman. · Blaikie, P. and Brookfield, H.C., eds, 1987: *Land degradation and society*. London: Methuen. · Braun, B. and Castree, N., eds, 1998: *Remaking reality*. London: Routledge. · Bryant, R. and Bailey, S. 1997: *Third World political ecology*. London: Routledge. · Das Gupta, P. 1993: *An inquiry into well being and destitution*. Oxford: Clarendon. · Demeritt, D. 1998: Science, Social Constructivism and Nature. In B. Brown and N. Castree, eds, *Remaking reality*: Nature at the millennium. London: Routledge, 173–93. · Escobar, A. 1995: *Encountering development*. Princeton: Princeton University Press. · Fairchild and Leach 1996: *Misreading the African landscape*. Cambridge: Cambridge University Press. · Grossman, L. 1984: *Peasants, subsistence ecology and development in the highlands of Papua New Guinea*. Princeton: Princeton University Press. · Grove, R. 1995: *Green imperialism*. Cambridge: Cambridge University Press. · Harvey, D. 1996: *Justice, nature and the geography of difference*. Oxford: Blackwell. · Hecht, S. 1985: Environment, development and politics. *World Development* 13: 663–84. · Hecht, S. and Cockburn, A. 1989: *The fate of the forest*. London: Verso. · Keil, R. et al., eds, 1998: *Political ecology*. London: Routledge. · Leach, M. and Mearns, M., eds, 1996: *The lie of the land*. London: Heinemann. · Leff, E. 1995: *Green production*. New York: Guilford. · Moore, D. 1995: Marxism, culture and political ecology. In R. Peet and M. Watts, eds, *Liberation ecologies*. London: Routledge, 125–47. · Neumann, R. 1999: *Imposing wilderness*. Berkeley: University of California Press. · Nietschmann, B. 1973: *Between land and water*. New York: Academic Press. · O'Connor, J. 1998: *Natural causes*. New York: Guilford. · Peet, R. and Watts, M., eds, 1996: *Liberation ecologies*. London: Routledge. · Peluso, N. 1992: *Rich forests, poor people*. Berkeley: University of California Press. · Pulido, L. 1996: *Environmentalism and economic justice*. Tucson: University of Arizona Press. · Rappaport, R. 1967: *Pigs for the ancestors*. New Haven, CT: Yale University Press. · Richards, P. 1985: *Indigenous agricultural revolution*. London: Hutchinson. · Watts, M. 1983: *Silent violence: food, famine and peasantry in Northern Nigeria*. Berkeley: University of California Press. · Watts, M. 1986: Drought, environment and food security. In M. Glantz, ed., *Drought and hunger in Africa*.

Cambridge: Cambridge University Press, 171–212. · Zimmerer, K. 1994: Integrating the new ecology in human geography, *Annals of the Association of American Geographers* 84: 108–25. · Zimmerer, K. 1996: *Changing fortunes*. Berkeley: University of California Press.

Suggested Reading

Adam, B. 1998: *Timescapes of modernity*. London: Routledge. · Faber, D., ed., 1998: *The struggle for ecological democracy*. New York: Guilford. · Demeritt 1998. · Fairhead, J. and Leach, M. 1998: *Reframing deforestation*. London: Routledge. · Guha, R. and Martinez-Alier, J. 1997: *Varieties of environmentalism*. London: Earthscan. · Hajer, M. 1995: *The politics of environmental discourse*. Oxford: Oxford University Press. · Kuletz, V. 1998: *The tainted desert*. London: Routledge. · Moore, D. 1996: Culture and Political Economy. In R. Peet and M. Watts, *Liberation Ecologies*. London: Routledge, 125–48.

political economy The term was first used in the early eighteenth century and referred to government policy. The English classical economists Adam Smith (1723–90), and especially David Ricardo (1772–1823), later took up political economy as a term, but redefined it in terms of two theoretical emphases: first, the production and accumulation of wealth; and second, the distribution of the 'surplus' so produced. It is especially the stress on distribution that accounts for the political part of political economy. Questions of apportioning the surplus among social CLASSES necessarily pushed inquiry beyond the purely economic and into social and political spheres.

In the mid-nineteenth century Karl Marx (1818–83) also fixed upon the same two emphases, and creatively wedded them to both a theory of revolutionary change and a new science. Revolutionary change would occur because of inherent contradictions within the spheres of production and distribution (see MARXIAN ECONOMICS and HISTORICAL MATERIALISM). And a new science was necessary, he thought, to probe beneath the surface of CAPITALISM that hid those contradictions from general view. This last point requires elaboration. Marx argued that the kind of exploitation and oppression found in pre-capitalist societies required no special scientific investigation because it was so transparent. In contrast, under capitalism exploitation and oppression are concealed under the veil of seemingly free exchange. In such an obfuscatory setting they can only be exposed by a new science, Marxian political economy.

More generally, Marx's writings were a critical reaction to Smith and Ricardo, whom he judged at least half right. NEO-CLASSICAL ECONOMICS, however, which began to gain ascendancy from 1870 onwards, Marx found wholly wrong. Exclusively emphasizing the noun in political economy, neo-classical economics was not so much a science as an IDEOLOGY. By celebrating market exchange, neoclassicism acclaimed the very source of capitalism's mystification. It was 'vulgar economics', to use Marx's phrase.

Vulgar or not, it took hold, and at least in the western academy neoclassicism's dominance pushed political economy into an underground existence until the late 1950s. It was then, particularly through the work of the American Marxist Paul Baran (1957), that political economy began enjoying a revival, which continues to the present.

Political economy is now a vibrant and variegated theoretical tradition consisting of at least five different strains:

- fundamental Marxists who keep to the letter of Marx (Meiksins Wood, 1996);
- REGULATIONISTS who analyse the regulatory apparatus of capitalism in order to understand its continued existence in spite of Marx's best predictions of its demise (Boyer, 1990);
- NEO-RICARDIANS who provide a minimalist account of both politics and economics following Sraffa (1960);
- ANALYTICAL MARXISTS who employ RATIONAL CHOICE THEORY to scrutinize analytically, and reconstruct logically, Marx's essential insights (Roemer, 1988); and
- POST-MARXISTS who draw upon a wide range of often POST-STRUCTURAL writers (Gibson-Graham, 1996).

Ironically, also during the late 1950s the radical libertarian right from the University of Chicago appropriated the term 'political economy'. Focusing on the problem of choosing among alternatives, the group examined all facets of human life – literally from birth to death – in terms of the tenets of rational choice theory. The nature of the STATE, political choice and DECISION-MAKING are similarly examined by them, giving rise to PUBLIC CHOICE THEORY.

In human geography, political economy first emerged in the late 1960s with RADICAL GEOGRAPHY, and later with a fully-blown MARXIST GEOGRAPHY associated, in particular, with Harvey's (1973, 1982) writings on URBANISM and later his close, geographical reading and theoretical interpretation of Marx's texts. Initially, the focus was on urban and regional issues, but since the early 1980s political economy has become both more diffuse and more pervasive. It has directly or indirectly influenced at least five major debates since the mid-1980s

(Peet and Thrift, 1989): (1) on structure and agency (seen, for example, in Duncan and Ley's, 1982, criticisms of structural Marxism's treatment of HUMAN AGENCY; see also STRUCTURATION THEORY); (2) around REALISM (Sayer, 1984, argues that Marx's work best exemplifies the critical realist approach); (3) in the LOCALITY debates (Cooke, 1987, was challenged among other things about the political economic credentials of his locality project; Smith, 1987); (4) around CULTURAL LANDSCAPES (Cosgrove, 1984, in one of the first substantive works within the new CULTURAL GEOGRAPHY, maintained that cultural landscapes must be understood as the product of specific political economic formations); and (5) discussions about POSTMODERNISM (seen in Deutsche's, 1991, and Morris's, 1992, criticisms of Harvey's, 1989, *The condition of postmodernity*).

Most recently, within ECONOMIC GEOGRAPHY there have been a number of discussions around the possibility of integrating political economy with CULTURAL POLITICS and POSTSTRUCTURALISM (Gibson-Graham, 1996; Lee and Wills, 1997).

Only a single common thread seems to connect the many uses of political economy within geography: the belief that the political and the economic are irrevocably linked; a sentiment not so unlike that held by the originators of the term. TJB

References

Baran, P.A. 1957: *The political economy of growth*. New York: Monthly Review Press. · Boyer, R. 1990: *The regulation school: a critical introduction*. New York: Columbia University Press. · Cooke, P. 1987: Clinical inference and geographical theory. *Antipode* 19: 69–78. · Cosgrove, D. 1984: *Social formation and symbolic landscape*. London: Croom Helm. · Deutsche, R. 1991: Boy's town. *Environment and Planning D: Society and Space* 9: 5–30. · Duncan, J.S. and Ley, D.F. 1982: Structural Marxism and human geography: a critical assessment. *Annals of the Association of American Geographers* 72: 30–59. · Gibson-Graham, J.K. 1996: *The end of capitalism (as we knew it). A feminist critique of political economy*. Oxford: Blackwell. · Harvey, D. 1973: *Social justice and the city*. London: Edward Arnold; Harvey, D. 1982: *The limits to capital*. Chicago: Chicago University Press. · Harvey, D. 1989: *The condition of postmodernity: an enquiry into the origins of cultural change*. Oxford: Blackwell. · Lee, R. and Wills, J., eds, 1997: *Geographies of economies*. London: Arnold. · Meiksins Wood, E. 1996: A chronology of the new left and its successor, or: who's old fashioned now? In L. Panitch, ed., *Socialist Register*. London: Merlin Press, 22–49. · Morris, M. 1992: The man in the mirror: David Harvey's 'The condition of postmodernity'. *Theory, Culture and Society* 9: 253–79. · Peet, R. and Thrift, N.J. 1989: Political economy and human geography. In R. Peet and N.J. Thrift, eds, *New models in geography: the political-economy perspective*. London: Unwin-Hyman, 1–29. · Roemer, J. 1988: *Free to lose: an introduction to Marxist economic philosophy*. Cambridge, MA: Harvard University Press. · Sayer, A. 1984: *Method in social science: a realist approach*. London: Hutchinson (2nd edn, published 1992). · Smith, N. 1987: Dangers of the empirical turn: some comments on the CURS initiative. *Antipode* 19: 59–68. · Sraffa, P. 1960: *The production of commodities by means of commodities*. Cambridge: Cambridge University Press.

Suggested Reading

Barnes, T.J. 1995: Political economy I: 'the culture, stupid'. *Progress in Human Geography* 19: 423–31. · Peet and Thrift (1989).

political geography It has been conventional to divide the subject matter of HUMAN GEOGRAPHY into three sub-disciplines dealing with economic, political and social events respectively. This is by no means original but merely mimics the standard division of modern social science into economics, political science and sociology. Hence, we may define what currently goes under the title of political geography as simply 'political studies carried out by geographers using the techniques and ideas associated with their spatial perspectives' (Burnett and Taylor, 1981). More recently, Dear (1988, p. 270) has argued that this tripartite division is more than a convention and reflects 'the three *primary processes* which structure the time–space fabric'. From this position he defines political geography more formally as 'the analysis of the systems of CLASS/group CONFLICT over time and space'. But the history of political geography is much more problematic than this contemporary division of human geography suggests.

Although it has recently been considered the weakest of those three divisions of human geography, political geography actually pre-dates both ECONOMIC and SOCIAL GEOGRAPHY and has traditionally attracted the most prominent geographers to its subject matter. Before the emergence of modern geography as a generally accepted academic discipline, the term political geography was applied generally to 'human' aspects of geography: physical geography was an adjunct of geology, political geography the equivalent adjunct of history. With the establishment of geography in universities, human aspects of geography were given new names, indicating the creation of sub-disciplines. In this way a 'new' political geography was created alongside colonial geography and COMMERCIAL GEOGRAPHY. This particular trilogy of human geographical knowledge reflects the concerns of the late nineteenth-century society in which the 'new' geography was being developed (see IMPERIALISM). Political geography was established as a sub-discipline by the publication in 1897 of Friedrich Ratzel's *Politische Geographie*. Ratzel is remembered today for his organic theory of the STATE and the concept of LEBENSRAUM or living space in which vigorous societies could expand. But Ratzel's political geography was much more than this. In keeping with the geography of his era he defined a broadly based environmental approach to political geography very different from the more narrow 'political studies' currently in vogue (see ANTHROPOGEOGRAPHY).

The establishment of political geography cannot be discussed without mention of Sir Halford Mackinder's 'geographical pivot of history' (1904) which later developed into the HEARTLAND theory. This initiated a geostrategic tradition in political geography that continued to provide a framework for strategic thinking throughout the period of the Cold War in international relations. The first major opportunity for Mackinder to apply his ideas came with the First World War and its aftermath. Mackinder and many other geographers were government advisors at Versailles where the task of redrawing the map of Europe brought geography and geographers into public view. This marks the heyday of traditional political geography both academically and in practice, epitomized by the publication in 1921 of *The new world: problems in political geography* by the chief geography advisor to the American government, Isaiah Bowman.

We now come to a very controversial episode in political geography: *geopolitik* or German GEOPOLITICS. Drawing on ideas from Ratzel, Mackinder and others, Karl Haushofer attempted to develop a special kind of political geography as a policy tool for the German state. His links with the Nazi leadership made him notorious during the Second World War. Some contemporary writers saw in Haushofer's work the blueprint for German conquests and Allied geographers were very strong in their condemnation of this embarrassing skeleton in their cupboard. In hindsight it now seems improbable that Haushofer had as much influence as contemporary enemies imagined; he was in effect a convenient and colourful bogeyman. Nevertheless, memories are long and the aftermath of *Geopolitik* has been hotly debated. It was obviously a negative factor for the image of political geography, so much so that it has often been blamed for the subsequent decline of the sub-discipline. Once again this position has now been revised so that political geography's fortunes are seen to be based on much broader criteria than any one particular episode in its history (Claval, 1984).

In the immediate aftermath of the Second World War, political geography retreated into the safer realm of study at the scale of the individual STATE. Although publicly overshadowed by the more spectacular geostrategic studies, state-scale analyses had always been a major component of political geography, the most notable pre-Second-World-War example of this genre being Derwent Whittlesey's *The earth and the state* of 1939. By the early 1950s we see a quickening of the trend towards shedding some of the environmental baggage of political geography and making the sub-discipline more narrowly systematic in character. Important papers of the period (e.g. Hartshorne, 1950) attempted to provide a new rigorous framework for analysing the geography of political areas and the modern state in particular. Basically, these amounted to a theory of the geographical integration of states as a balance between CENTRIFUGAL AND CENTRIPETAL FORCES. It was from this point, until about 1970, just after Brian Berry's (1969) oft-quoted remark about political geography being 'a moribund backwater', that the sub-discipline seemed to lose its way. As a 'logical' division of human geography it continued to be widely taught in universities but there was a dearth of research to back up the teaching. Just as human geography as a whole was going through a major and exciting expansion phase usually referred to as the QUANTITATIVE REVOLUTION, political geography was failing to attract its share of the latest 'new' geographers. It seemed to many to be stodgy and old-fashioned. Textbooks consisted of the geography of different bits of politics – BOUNDARIES, capital cities, TERRITORY, administrative areas, elections, geostrategy, etc. – but with no particular coordination of these parts. In shedding its environmental basis, traditional political geography would seem to have lost its coherence (Cox, 1979). This was the real cause of the post-war demise of political geography (Claval, 1984).

Although political geography was in the doldrums in the 1960s this was certainly not true of its related social science, political science. Hence the most obvious solution to political geography's problems seemed to be to follow the example of human geography's other sub-disciplines and borrow heavily from the theories of the relevant social science. This approach was adopted in the most ambitious textbooks of the period (e.g. Kasperson and Minghi, 1969) but without the expected success. Quite simply, political science was not able to furnish any LOCATION THEORY equivalent to that available in economics and sociology. Furthermore, political geography's continued emphasis at the scale of the state was out of step with the intra-state and largely urban concerns of the new human geography (Claval, 1984). Systems theory became widely advocated but rarely applied in a constructive manner (Burnett and Taylor, 1981, p. 46) and in the end the sub-discipline's revival came about more because of external influences than through the efforts of the political geographers themselves.

The momentous political events of the late 1960s in Europe and USA – anti-Vietnam War demonstrations, city riots and student rebellions – had a profound effect on all social science. In human geography it brought the political dimension to the fore. This was expressed in three distinctive ways. First, ECONOMIC and SOCIAL GEOGRAPHY included political considerations in their analyses and interpretations. Second, as geography became more politicized RADICAL GEOGRAPHY was created, firmly establishing a MARXIST GEOGRAPHY. Third, there was the revival of political geography. The first two trends are important for understanding modern political geography because very often they covered subjects which were also dealt with in political geography itself, producing, as it were, 'Political Geographers' and 'political Geographers'. The distinctions between the sub-disciplines of human geography were becoming extremely fuzzy in the wake of the criticism of POSITIVISM in geography.

Initially two main research areas came to dominate the growing political geography of the 1970s. First, urban conflicts became a very common topic in human geography generally and, in political geography, location of 'goods' and 'bads' with their respective EXTERNALITIES became an important part of a new urban political geography (Cox, 1973). This has developed into a WELFARE GEOGRAPHY approach to political geography (Cox, 1979). The second growth was ELECTORAL GEOGRAPHY where the techniques of the quantitative revolution were, at last, comprehensively applied in political geography (Taylor and Johnston, 1979). But this research growth did not overcome the uncoordinated nature of political geography; if anything it enhanced the lack of coherence. The general reaction was to order political geography information into three separate SCALES for teaching and research: international/global, national, and intra-national/urban. This framework became almost ubiquitous among political geographers of all persuasions.

There has been a remarkable resurgence in political geography since about 1980, reflected in the establishment of the journal *Political Geography Quarterly* in 1982, which has subsequently outgrown its quarterly title (it is now just *Political Geography*). Reynolds and Knight (1989, p. 582) have identified another 'new' political geography in which 'there is now a concern for social theory and a readiness to examine afresh such central concepts as STATE, SOCIETY, NATIONALISM, PLACE and SPACE'. In addition, in the 1990s, political geographers have even problematized the political (Taylor, 1991) and 'political geography' itself (Painter, 1995).

Today political geography is a vibrant subdiscipline making important contributions both to understanding contemporary affairs and to the development of geography as a whole. The former is represented by recent studies of new multi-ethnic conflicts and FEDERALISM (Smith, 1995) and political geographic analyses of the restructuring of the US state in the wake of GLOBALIZATION (Staeheli, Kodras and Flint, 1997). Globalization is related more broadly to questions of SOVEREIGNTY and ENVIRONMENTALISM and these and other contemporary issues are tackled by political geographers (Demko and Wood, 1994; Agnew and Corbridge, 1995). Political geographers have contributed to debates on the influence of globalization at other scales. In particular, contributors to Cox (1979) emphasize the geographical scale implications of globalization with reference to local politics. Also Taylor (1994, 1995) has investigated the changing nature of the territorial state with specific reference to the conundrum of how you identify the demise of the state when the institution is always changing; his solution is to concentrate on the changing balances between INTERSTATENESS and trans-state processes. Generally, political geography is moving away from its state-centred heritage towards concern for broader frameworks such as GOVERNANCE.

In terms of contributions to geography, Agnew (1997) illustrates how contemporary political geography equates with the general development of geography by illustrating the SPATIAL ANALYSIS, the POLITICAL ECONOMY and the POSTMODERNISM/POST-STRUCTURALISM theoretical viewpoints. The latter two are most notably represented by WORLD-SYSTEMS ANALYSIS in political geography, which is based on a critical treatment of scale (Taylor and

Flint, 1999), and CRITICAL GEOPOLITICS (O'Tuathail, 1996) respectively. However, the sub-discipline has still yet to meet the challenge of FEMINIST GEOGRAPHY whose concerns for POWER in place and space from a GENDER perspective have only appeared intermittently in contemporary political geography. The study of PLACE/SPACE TENSIONS may be one way of integrating feminist geographical concerns into political geography (Taylor, 1999). PJT

References

Agnew, J., ed., 1997: *Political geography: a reader*. London: Arnold. · Agnew, J. and Corbridge, S. 1995: *Mastering space*. London: Routledge. · Berry, B.J.L. 1969: Review of Russett, B.M. International regions and the international system. *Geographical Review* 59: 450–1. · Bowman, I. 1921: *The new world: problems in political geography*. New York: World Books. · Burnett, A.D. and Taylor, P.J., eds, 1981: *Political studies from spatial perspectives*. Chichester: John Wiley. · Claval, P. 1984: The coherence of political geography: perspectives on its past evolution and its future relevance. In P.J. Taylor and J.W. House, eds, *Political geography: recent advances and future directions*. London: Croom Helm, 8–24. · Cox, K.R. 1973: *Conflict, power and politics in the city: a geographic view*. New York: McGraw-Hill. · Cox, K.R. 1979: *Location and public problems. A political geography of the contemporary world*. Chicago: Maaroufa. · Oxford: Basil Blackwell. · Cox, K.R. 1997: *Spaces of globalization: reasserting the power of the local*. New York: Guilford. · Dear, M.J. 1988: The postmodern challenge: reconstructing human geography. *Transactions, Institute of British Geographers* NS 13: 262–74. · Demko, G.J. and Wood, W.B., eds, 1994: *Reordering the world: geopolitical perspectives on the 21st century*. Boulder: Westview. · Hartshorne, R. 1950: The functional approach to political geography. *Annals of the Association of American Geographers* 40: 95–130. · Kasperson, R.E. and Minghi, J.V., eds, 1969: *The structure of political geography*. Chicago: Aldine. · Mackinder, H.J. 1904: The geographical pivot of history. *Geographical Journal* 23: 421–42. · O'Tuathail, G. 1996: *Critical geopolitics*. Minneapolis: University of Minnesota Press. · Painter, J. 1995: *Geography, politics and 'political geography'*. London: Arnold. · Ratzel, F. 1897: *Politische Geographie*. Munich: Oldenburg; Reynolds, D.R. and Knight, D.B. 1989: Political geography. In G.L. Gaile and C.J. Willmott, eds, *Geography in America*. Columbus: Merrill. · Smith, G., ed., 1995: *Federalism: the multiethnic challenge*. London: Longman; Staeheli, L.A., Kodras, J.E. and Flint, C., eds, 1997: *State devolution in America*. Thousand Oaks: Sage. · Taylor, P.J. 1991: Political geography within world-systems analysis. *Review* 14: 387–402. · Taylor, P.J. 1994: The state as container: territoriality in the modern world-system. *Progress in Human Geography* 18: 151–62. · Taylor, P.J. 1995: Beyond containers: internationality, interstateness, interterritoriality. *Progress in Human Geography* 19: 1–15. · Taylor, P.J. 1999: Places, spaces and Macy's: place–space tensions in the political geography of modernities. *Progress in Human Geography* 23: 1–26. · Taylor, P.J. and Johnston, R.J., eds, 1979: *Geography of elections*. London: Penguin. · Taylor, P.J. and Flint, C. 1999: *Political geography, world-economy, nation-state and locality*, 4th edn. London: Longman. · Whittlesey, D. 1939: *The earth and the state. A study of political geography*. New York: Holt.

Suggested Reading

Agnew (1997). · Muir, R. 1997: *Political geography: a new introduction*. London: Macmillan. · Painter (1995). · Taylor and Flint (1999).

pollution A substance, released into an environment, that causes harm either to living organisms or built structures. The substance may be human-made or natural (see HAZARD, HUMAN-MADE; ENVIRONMENTAL HAZARD) and causes harm when the receiving environment cannot easily assimilate the type or quantity of substance released. One aspect of environmental management is establishing criteria for acceptable and unacceptable levels of particular forms of pollution. This means that pollution is now defined in relation to impacts and in relation to an index of acceptable levels: sometimes there appear to be significant discrepancies between these two.

The effects of pollution range from aesthetic nuisance through to economic loss, health damage, death and long-term environmental degradation. The release of pollution may be sudden (as in Bhopal, India, in 1984), or it may involve a slow accumulation of substances, as in the concentration of heavy metals, herbicides and pesticides in food chains (i.e. bioaccumulation). The impacts of pollution may also be gradual or sudden, short-lived or maintained over a long time period. The impact is also spatial; it may be local, widely dispersed, or far from the source of the pollution (see ACID RAIN). Sometimes the earth is polluted, but this is not noticed until humans re-occupy the already polluted site (e.g. Love Canal, USA). Pollution may be described by its medium (e.g. air or water pollution), by its character (e.g. noise pollution and acid rain) or by its source (e.g. industrial pollution).

Pollution may be regarded as an 'accident', or it may be understood as the deliberate and inevitable consequences of production processes. Sections of the ENVIRONMENTAL MOVEMENT have strongly criticized production processes that generate pollution as being undesirable. Their concerns are partly being heeded because increasingly efforts are being made to 'close the circle' by using former wastes from processes as inputs into new production processes, in what is known as '*industrial ecology*'. This is sometimes identified with '*ecological modernization*', and is regarded as one form of SUSTAINABLE DEVELOPMENT.

Due to pollution regulations and the need for corporations to maintain a positive public image, there are almost always economic advantages for corporations to adopt this approach. Regulations are being enforced to prevent the deliberate emission of pollution that is considered unacceptable. Sometimes the pollutant must be treated to a set standard before it is emitted but the setting of standards is not uniform throughout the world, partly because the receiving environments are different, and partly because of concern not to deter economic growth.

The history of pollution is very long. Lead pollution in the water supplies is alleged to have been responsible for madness in Ancient Rome. Cities have always had pollution of some form, such as contamination of water supplies, the pollution of air by industrial processes, the pollution that affects specific occupations (e.g. hatters becoming mad due to the mercury they used), or the emissions from transport (including both manure from horses and exhaust fumes from automobiles). However, contemporary concern with pollution increased dramatically after the smog that killed about four thousand people in London in December 1952, and after the publication of *Silent spring* by Rachel Carson in 1962 (the book was serialized in *The New Yorker*, and became a major-seller). Kates (1995) situates the London smog in the longer term and observes that the sharp decrease in pollution following the passing of Britain's Clean Air Act of 1956 was part of a longer trend to improve air quality, resulting from the displacement of coal as a source of ENERGY. While older pollutant sources were being phased out, Rachel Carson identified further dangers, those caused by the insecticide DDT. Her book was the forerunner for concerns about many other human-produced substances, ranging from pesticides through to the products of the nuclear industry. Continental and global-scale pollutants such as CFC emissions, acid rain and pollutants that contribute to GLOBAL WARMING, have caused most concern for governments, the environmental movement and citizens in so-called developed countries. However, in areas said to be in a state of UNDERDEVELOPMENT, it is often the results of local forms of pollution, such as the inability to obtain clean drinking water, that are of the greatest immediate concern.

Pollution has been an issue in human geography through the literature on DEVELOPMENT. It is increasing in importance as an aspect of ENVIRONMENTAL JUSTICE (Bowen, et al., 1995; Harvey, 1996; Low and Gleeson, 1997), particularly in the United States where pollution and other differences in environmental quality are seen as intentional acts of discrimination. These acts are often referred to as 'environmental racism'. PM

References

Bowen, W. et al., 1995: Toward environmental justice: spatial equity in Ohio and Cleveland. *Annals of the Association of American Geographers* 85 4: 641–63. · Carson, R. 1962: *Silent spring*. Boston: Houghton Mifflin Company. · Harvey, D. 1996: *Justice, nature and the geography of difference*. Oxford: Blackwell. · Kates, R. 1995: Labnotes from the Jeremiah Experiment: hope for a sustainable transition (Presidential Address). *Annals of the Association of American Geographers* 85 4: 623–40. · Low, N. and Gleeson, B. 1997: Justice in and to the environment: ethical uncertainties and political practices. *Environment and Planning A* 29: 21–42.

Suggested Reading

Newson, M. 1995: The earth as output: pollution. In R. Johnston, P. Taylor and M. Watts, eds, *Geographies of global change: remapping the world in the late twentieth century*. Oxford and Cambridge, MA: Blackwell, 333–53. · Pulido, L., et. al. 1996: An archaeology of environmental racism in Los Angeles. *Urban Geography* 17: 419–39.

population accounts A form of spatial demographic analysis which takes fully into account MIGRATION between regions, FERTILITY and MORTALITY. In the past, population analysis and projections have typically been carried out for a single region only, connected via net MIGRATION to the outside world, but 'accounting' methods allow the building of population models for multiregional systems within which gross migration can be represented explicitly. The life histories of people are accounted for by demographic 'states' which must include all those in which people can originate (for example birth and existence in a region) and all those to which people can move over a specified time period (for example survival or death). These states may be further broken down, depending on the purpose of the analysis, into a variety of different socio-economic categories such as sex, age, race, occupation or educational attainment. Accounting has great potential for integrating SPATIAL ANALYSIS and demography, thus serving as a vital part of models of urban and regional systems, as a basis for population projection, and as a basis for estimating demand for facilities of all kinds. PEO

Suggested Reading

Rees, P.H. and Wilson, A.G. 1977: *Spatial population analysis*. London: Edward Arnold; New York: Academic Press. · Woods, R. and Rees, P. 1986: *Population structures and models. Developments in spatial demography*. London: Allen and Unwin.

population density The number of people in relation to the SPACE that they occupy. The simplest measure, crude density of population, is the number of people per square kilometre or other unit area and is most useful for small units such as counties or parishes rather than countries or continents, where internal environmental conditions vary markedly. More refined density measures may be calculated by relating numbers to cultivated or cultivable land or to other economic measures such as national income. Equally, for urban areas, measures such as persons per room or per house are useful refinements. PEO

Suggested Reading

Clarke, J.I. 1972: *Population geography*, 2nd edn. Oxford and New York: Pergamon, ch. 4. · Plane, D.A. and Rogerson, P.A. 1994: *The geographical analysis of population*. Chichester and New York: Wiley, ch. 2.

population geography The study of the ways in which spatial variations in the distribution, composition, MIGRATION and growth of population are related to the nature of places. A concern with spatial variation has been the geographer's distinctive contribution to population studies and comparison is frequently made with demographers, who are much more interested in patterns of birth, death and marriage *per se*, neglecting the influence of migration and spatial variations in general. Within the wider discipline of geography, population study has long ranked prominently, research at a variety of SCALES covering a very wide scope. Many university departments offer a separate course in population geography, and much relevant research and teaching is also subsumed under URBAN, SOCIAL or HISTORICAL GEOGRAPHY. Yet increasingly, and encouragingly, the boundaries between geography and other disciplines interested in population matters – economics, sociology, history, psychology and biology as well as demography – are blurred. Thus, it is no longer accurate to think of the population geographer as being concerned exclusively with distribution and description, since recent years have seen an interest in, for example, theory and explanation in regional and national levels of FERTILITY and MORTALITY, detailed patterns of disease DIFFUSION and advanced modelling of interregional population growth. Nevertheless, there is still more concern with migration and spatial variation than with other matters. The field has recently been enriched by the publication of the new *International Journal of Population Geography* (from 1995), though work related to population geography has appeared regularly in all major geographical journals.

The study of population has a long, varied and distinguished history (see MALTHUSIAN MODEL) and the evolution of population geography as a sub-branch of the discipline reflects changes in the focus and methodology of geography itself, as well as in the nature of demography and population studies more generally, and also reflects a number of different national traditions. The origins of population geography date back to the German and French schools of human geography of the second half of the nineteenth and early twentieth centuries (Kosinski, 1984). There was a particular concern with population mapping and with the relationship between population and the environment. It was not, however, until after the Second World War that the sub-discipline began to take shape fully, following the publications of George (1951) in France (reflecting that country's renewed emphasis on demographic research more generally) and Trewartha (1953) in the United States. Other countries such as Germany, where demography had been discredited by its association with Nazi policy, were slower to follow though there was significant progress in the Soviet Union, Japan, India and elsewhere (see Clarke, 1984). Trewartha's paper (1953) in particular is usually seen as something of a bench-mark, since he expressed a 'conviction that the neglect of population geography constitutes a fundamental weakness in the general approach to modern geography'. For him, 'population is the point of reference from which all the other elements are observed and from which they all, singly and collectively, derive significance and meaning. It is population which furnishes the focus' (Trewartha, 1953, pp. 6 and 14). His 'tentative system of content and organisation' for population geography defined the field broadly, including historical population geography, the dynamics of population growth, distribution, migration, population structure and socio-economic characteristics.

The post-war resurgence, which was also a reflection of the increased availability of demographic sources and of the very obvious relevance of population issues in both the developed and the less developed worlds, spawned a number of texts between the late 1950s and early 1970s (for example, Beaujeu-Garnier, 1956–8; Clarke, 1965; Demko, Rose and Schnell, 1970) which gave population geography a firm place in the university curriculum in many countries. Geographers took a broad view of the importance of population with a particular, though by no means exclusive, emphasis on patterns of population change and structure and their global diversity. Migration played a central role. The field was bolstered by an improved institutional environment, including the activities sponsored by the Commission on Population Geography of the International Geographical Union (especially from the late 1950s), the Population Geography Study Group of the Institute of British Geographers (from 1963) and the Population Specialty Group of the Association of American Geographers (from 1980). Population geographers have had some, though more limited, involvement with multi-disciplinary groups such as the International Union for the Scientific Study of Population.

These early geographical approaches were quite different from (and indeed had rather little effect upon) demography itself and from the 1970s it was increasingly argued that geographers needed to focus more clearly on, and benefit from, demographic method. Thus texts such as Woods (1979) and later Woods and Rees (1986) began to focus on *spatial demography* with much more emphasis on the central demographic phenomena of FERTILITY and MORTALITY and rather less on migration. For Woods (1979, p. 3) the intention was 'to merge spatial demography and population geography' around a core of theory derived from demography (Woods, 1982). This coincided with the greater use of quantitative methods in human geography with texts such as Rees and Wilson (1977) focusing on the use of POPULATION ACCOUNTS and models for spatial demographic analysis and Congdon and Batey (1989) bringing geographers, demographers, planners and statisticians together in the pursuit of *regional demography*. For some this attachment to the methods of demography represented a narrowing of the field, although standard texts such as Jones (1981) and Noin (1979) still drew a wide canvas and publication in the field was both buoyant and very varied throughout. Nevertheless, when reviewing the available texts, Clarke (1984, p. 2) considered that they did not reflect 'the immense variety of peoples, cultures and countries as well as of approaches, attitudes and policies to population phenomena'.

For Findlay and Graham (1991, p. 150) the consequence of the narrower focus on demographic measures had been to lessen the impact of population geography on the discipline as a whole and to remove it from some of the debates current in human geography in the 1980s and 1990s: 'debates about gender, humanism, realism and postmodernism, which are so much part of human geography at the present time, have only the faintest of echoes in population geography'. There has thus been a call for a greater awareness of social theory in population geography (White and Jackson, 1995) which mirrors calls for a wider theoretical and empirical base in demography itself, with a more critical view of established data sources and theories (Ogden, 1998). Thus Greenhalgh (1996, p. 27) notes that 'reflexivity about the politics of demographic praxis is notably lacking in the field . . . Neither the global political economies of the 1970s, nor the POSTCOLONIALISM and postcolonialities of the 1980s and 1990s, nor the feminisms of any decade have had much perceptible impact' (see FEMINIST GEOGRAPHIES; POST-COLONIALISM). There is also a conscious attempt to provide a more robustly critical approach to sources and to reinforce a 'mixed methodology' that combines, for example, the quantitative data from the population CENSUS with qualitative analysis from in-depth interviews or other non-statistical sources.

However geographers have chosen to define the scope of the field at particular moments, fertility, mortality and migration are at the root of any studies of population growth and composition. So for any area:

$$\mathrm{p}^{t+n} = \mathrm{p}^{t} + \mathrm{B}^{t,t+n} - \mathrm{D}^{t,t+n} + \mathrm{NM}^{t,t+n}$$

where given a population at time $t(p^t)$, that population after a period of time t to $t+n(p^{t+n})$ will be the result of increase due to births during the period ($B^{t,t+n}$), decrease due to deaths ($D^{t,t+n}$) and either increase or decrease due to net migration ($NM^{t,t+n}$). The study of overall population growth has concerned geographers working at a number of scales and it is worth remembering that world population grew from 2500 million in the early 1950s to 6000 million in October 1999. Some have been interested in, for example, the history of world population growth and the relative prospects for both developing and developed countries; others have devoted attention to the experience of individual countries and regions. Patterns of growth through space and time (see DEMOGRAPHIC TRANSITION) have always been considered fundamental to the understanding of the wider geographical processes of URBANIZATION, INDUSTRIALIZATION and the use of RESOURCES. There has been a continuing interest in the links between the physical and human environments, for example the impact of disasters. The study of the principal elements in the demographic equation, fertility and mortality, has not been neglected (see MEDICAL GEOGRAPHY). Attention has been devoted in particular to highlighting the spatial dimension of patterns and their links with environmental or social conditions, e.g. the study of the spatial incidence of mortality and disease (see Howe, 1976; Cliff and Haggett, 1992) or fertility (see Gould and Brown, 1996) or combining demography and geography to produce persuasive portraits of countries (for example, Coleman and Salt, 1992) or continents (Noin and Woods, 1993; Hall and White, 1995). Demographers themselves have taken an interest in international and national patterns of demographic change which have clear geographical implications (for example, Coale and Watkins, 1986). Geographers have also taken an interest in historical population geography (though this is a field which deserves much fuller attention, see Ogden, 1986), reconstructing patterns of fertility and mortality, as well as household and family formation, through techniques such as FAMILY RECONSTITUTION and the detailed manipulation of past census, registration and ecclesiastical records (Woods, 1992).

Yet the element in the above equation to which geographers have given most attention is MIGRATION: estimating net and gross flows at all scales; looking at relationships of direction and distance (see DISTANCE DECAY); building models of interregional flows (Stillwell and Congdon, 1991); and analysing economic and social causes and consequences. Studies of migration have included international movements, rural–urban, urban–urban and intra-urban flows as well as seasonal and diurnal movements. Migration has further been seen as an integral part of the study of the SOCIAL GEOGRAPHY of the city (see URBAN GEOGRAPHY), though the study of the consequences of migration, for example issues connected with ETHNICITY (Peach, 1996) and COMMUNITY, have increasingly tended to be treated outside the confines of population geography *sensu stricto*. Geographers have also sought to make contributions to migration theory and method. They have made use of myriad statistical sources and become competent statisticians; and their concern with recent and contemporary conditions has led them to rely greatly on, and make sophisticated use of, national censuses. Geographers have looked at migration in a broader perspective, using for example creative literature (King et al., 1995) or a renewed (though not new) biographical approach through questionnaires or in-depth interviews to establish the meaning of migration and the experience for the individual.

The resultant patterns of population distribution and density have long been an object of geographical inquiry. Densities have been discussed in relation not only to general environmental conditions but also with respect to agriculture and economic potential (see POPULATION DENSITY). At a broad scale there has been concern with population growth, distribution and resources, e.g. in the countries of the Third World, and increasingly with projections of these relationships. Population geography has also spread its net more widely to encompass population composition and structure. This ranges from studies of AGE AND SEX STRUCTURE (Rodgers, 1992) and its implications for demographic and economic change, to studies of marital status, occupation, education and religious beliefs. The importance of gender relations has been explicitly recognized (for example, Chant, 1992; see GENDER AND GEOGRAPHY). The contemporary analysis of population change and structures has been discussed by geographers specifically in the context of public policy (see Champion, 1993, for Britain) and a recent text (Plane and Rogerson, 1994) has the specific sub-title 'with applications to planning and business'. Yet, much of social, economic and CULTURAL GEOGRAPHY neglects population issues: some social geography of the city, for example, shows too little awareness of the profound changes taking place in the way people live in terms of family, household, patterns of sexual partnership, morbidity and MOBILITY in particular areas. The interest in, for example, the world city or in issues of IDENTITY and SEXUALITY would benefit from a better understanding of the wider demographic processes at work in contemporary society and their geographical diversity across the globe (Ogden, 1998). At least some of these issues are not new but their importance needs reasserting.

The opportunities and challenges for population geography in the new millennium are threefold: first, building on a sound grasp of demographic principles to strengthen population geography by engaging more fully in wider methodological and theoretical debates in human geography; second, not far removed from Trewartha's statement of nearly 50 years ago (though expressed in a different vocabulary and against the background of a hugely expanded literature in social theory), to demonstrate to other branches of human geography a renewed awareness of the extent to which demographic phenomena underpin social structure and change; and third, to communicate a heightened appreciation of the importance of a spatial perspective to other disciplines concerned with population issues. PEO

References and Suggested Reading

Alonso, W., ed., 1987: *Population in an interacting world*. Cambridge, MA and London: Harvard University Press. · Beaujeu-Garnier, J. 1956–8: *Géographie de la population*, 2 vols. Paris: Presses Universitaires de France. · Champion, A., ed., 1993: *Population matters: the local dimension*. London: Paul Chapman Publishing. · Champion, A. and Fielding, A., eds, 1992: *Migration processes and patterns, volume 1: Research progress and prospects*. London: Belhaven. · Chant, S., ed., 1992: *Gender and migration in developing countries*. London: Belhaven. · Clarke, J.I. 1965: *Population geography*. Oxford: Pergamon (2nd edn., 1972). · Clarke, J.I., ed., 1984: *Geography and population – approaches and applications*. Oxford and New York: Pergamon. · Cliff, A. and Haggett, P. 1992: *Atlas of disease distributions*. Oxford: Blackwell. · Coale, A.J. and Watkins, S.C., eds, 1986: *The decline of fertility in Europe. The revised proceedings of a conference on the Princeton European Fertility Project*. Princeton, NJ: Princeton University Press. · Coleman, D. and Salt, J. 1992: *The British population. Patterns, trends and processes*. Oxford: Oxford University Press. · Congdon, P. and Batey, P. 1989: *Advances in regional demography. Information. Forecasts. Models*. London: Belhaven. · Daugherty, H.G. and Kammeyer, K.C. 1995: *An introduction to population*, 2nd edn. New York and London: Guilford. · Demko, G.J., Rose, H.M. and Schnell, G.A. 1970: *Population geography: a reader*. New York: McGraw-Hill. · Findlay, A.M. and Graham, E. 1991: The challenge facing population geography. *Progress in Human Geography* 15 2: 149–62. · Gentileschi, M.-L. 1991: *Geografia della popolazione*. Rome: La Nuova Italia Scientifica. · George, P. 1951: *Introduction à l'étude géographique de la population du monde*. Paris: Institut D'Etudes Démographiques. · Gould, W.T.S. and Brown, M.S. 1996: Research review 2: fertility in sub-Saharan Africa. *International Journal of Population Geography* 2 1: 1–22. · Greenhalgh, S. 1996: The social construction of population science: an intellectual, institutional and political history of twentieth-century demography. *Comparative Studies in Society and History* 38: 26–66. · Hall, R. and White, P., eds, 1995: *Europe's population. Towards the next century*. London: UCL Press. · Howe, G.M. 1976: *Man, environment and disease in Britain: a medical geography of Britain through the ages*. London: Penguin; New York: Barnes and Noble. · Jones, H.R. 1981: *Population geography*, 2nd edn 1990. London: Paul Chapman. · King, R., Connell, J. and White, P., eds, 1995: *Writing across worlds. Literature and migration*. London: Routledge. · Kosinski, L. 1984: The roots of population geography. In J.I. Clarke, ed., 1984: *Geography and population – approaches and applications*. Oxford and New York: Pergamon, 11–24. · Lutz, W., ed., 1990: *Future demographic trends in Europe and North America*. London and New York: Academic Press. · Noin, D. 1979: *Géographie de la population*. Paris: Masson. · Noin, D. and Woods, R. 1993: *The changing population of Europe*. Oxford: Blackwell. · Ogden, P.E. 1986: Historical demography. In M. Pacione, ed., *Historical geography: progress and prospect*. London: Croom Helm, 217–49. · Ogden, P.E. 1998: Population geography. *Progress in Human Geography* 22 2: 105–14. · Peach, C., ed., 1996: *Ethnicity in the 1991 census. Volume 2. The ethnic minority populations of Great Britain*. London: HMSO. · Plane, D.A. and Rogerson, D.A. 1994: *The geographical analysis of population. With applications to planning and business*. New York and Chichester: Wiley. · Rees, P.H. and Wilson, A.G. 1977: *Spatial population analysis*. London: Edward Arnold. · Rodgers, A., ed., 1992: *Elderly migration and population redistribution. A comparative study*. London: Belhaven; Stillwell, J. and Congdon, P., eds, 1991: *Migration models: macro and micro approaches*. London: Belhaven. · Trewartha, G.T. 1953: A case for population geography. *Annals of the Association of American Geographers* 43 2: 71–91. Reprinted in Demko, G.J., Rose, H.M. and Schnell, G.A. 1970: *Population geography: a reader*. New York: McGraw-Hill, 5–26. · White, P. and Jackson, P. 1995: Research review 1: (Re)theorising population geography. *International Journal of Population Geography* 1 2: 111–23. · Woods, R.I. 1979: *Population analysis in geography*. London and New York: Longman. · Woods, R.I. 1982: *Theoretical population geography*. London and New York: Longman. · Woods, R.I. 1992: *The population of Britain in the nineteenth century*. Basingstoke: Macmillan. · Woods, R. and Rees, P., eds, 1986: *Population structures and models. Developments in spatial demography*. London and Boston: Allen and Unwin.

population potential A measure of the nearness or ACCESSIBILITY of a given mass of people to a point. The term is derived from SOCIAL PHYSICS and the concept is closely related to the GRAVITY MODEL, in that it relates mass (population) to distance, but whereas the gravity model deals with the separate relationships between pairs of points, population potential encompasses the influence of all other points on a particular one. The potential exerted on a point (V_i) is defined as:

$$V_i = \sum_{j=1}^{k} P_j/d_{ij}, \ j \neq i$$

where P_j is the population at the jth point, d_{ij} is the distance between points i and j, and summation is over all k points. (Most measures of potential include P_i and estimate d_{ij} where $i = j$.) The population potential at point i is thus the sum of the ratios of populations at all points to the distances from i to those points (d_{ij} may be raised to some power to incorporate the FRICTIONS OF DISTANCE; see DISTANCE DECAY). Isopleth maps of population potentials have been produced at various scales, to indicate spatial variations in general accessibility (see ISOLINES). Population may be replaced by, for example, purchasing power (P_j becomes PP_j) to give a measure of the market potential – accessibility to customers – at point i. PEO

Suggested Reading

Stewart, J.Q. and Warntz, W. 1968: The physics of population distributions. In B.J.L. Berry and D.F. Marble, eds, *Spatial analysis: a reader in statistical geography*. Englewood Cliffs, NJ and London: Prentice-Hall, 130–46.

population projection An estimate of future population size or composition based on the extrapolation of past demographic trends. A distinction may be drawn between a projection and a FORECAST; the latter is the term used when demographic variables are set in a more general socio-economic framework. The simplest form of projection is that based on extrapolation of the past growth of the total population, but modern projections tend to take into account detailed trends in FERTILITY, MORTALITY and MIGRATION. PEO

Suggested Reading

Lutz, W. 1996: *The future population of the world. What can we assume today?* Laxenburg, Austria: International Institute for Applied Systems Analysis. · Plane, D.A. and Rogerson, P.A. 1994: *The geographical analysis of population*. New York and Chichester: Wiley, ch. 6.

population pyramid A diagrammatic representation of the AGE AND SEX STRUCTURE of a population (see figure). The vertical axis represents age groups – with males on the left and females on the right – and the horizontal axis indicates the numerical or percentage distribution for each sex. The population pyramid is a reflection of past and current demographic trends and also provides some indication of future demographic structures. A population whose pyramid has a broad base and narrows quickly upwards, for example, is young and highly fertile. The figure for France is more typical of populations of the developed world. It shows the general influence of ageing, which, because of lower male LIFE EXPECTANCY, produces a strong excess of women in the over 70 age groups. The recent decline in birth rates is also evident in the shortfall in those aged under 25 years. The demographic consequences of war are also apparent in the pyramid, e.g. the sharp decline

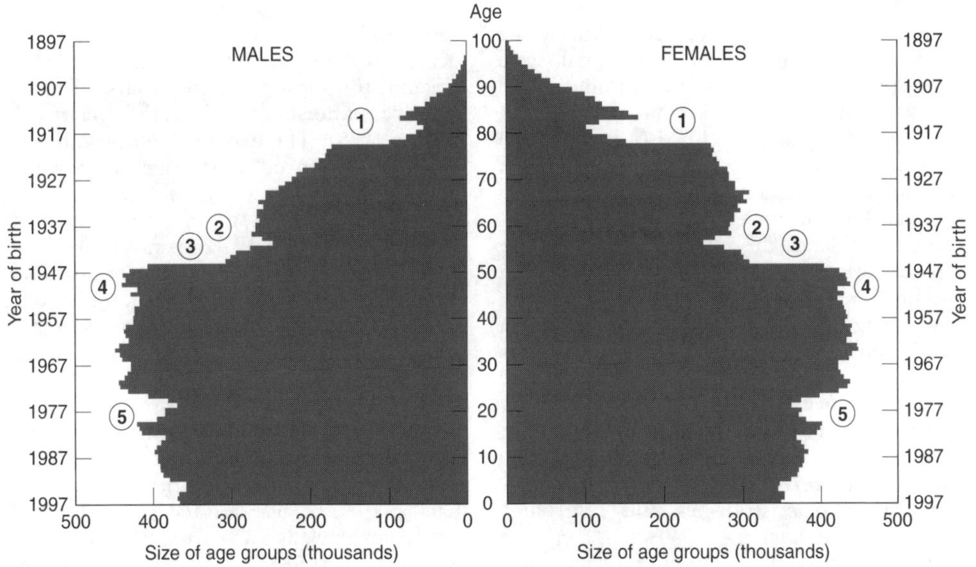

Population Pyramid *France, 1897–1997* (Lévy, 1998, p.4).

in births during the First World War is reflected in the shortfall in the numbers of people in their late 70s and early 80s. In countries of the developing world, population pyramids are more steep-sided, reflecting higher fertility, which adds people to the base of the pyramid, and higher MORTALITY through the life course, which steadily removes them. The DEPENDENCY RATIO is one measure that may be derived from the study of age–sex pyramids. Pyramids may also be constructed for sub-groups within a population, reflecting distinctive demographic structures associated with particular geographical areas (for example, INNER CITIES or remote rural districts) or with ETHNICITY or other characteristics. PEO

Reference

Lévy, M.L. 1998: La population de la France, 1995–1997. *Population et Sociétés* 333: 1–4.

Suggested Reading

Daugherty, H.G. and Kammeyer, K.C.W. 1995: *An introduction to population*, 2nd edn. New York and London: Guilford, ch. 5. · Petersen, W. 1975: *Population*, 3rd edn. London and New York: Collier-Macmillan, ch. 3.

populism An enormously complex term which refers to both political IDEOLOGIES and economic DEVELOPMENT strategies that are bound up with notions of the ordinary, the people, anti-industrialism and small-scale enterprise ('small is beautiful'). Populism as practice can be seen as a counter-current, a minority DISCOURSE, to the rise of industrial CAPITALISM. While certain lines of populist thinking can be traced to pre-industrial Leveller and Digger movements of seventeenth-century England, the intellectual origins are typically traced to Sismondi and the Ricardian socialists (Kitching, 1982).

Kitching notes that there are two senses in which populism is employed. One turns on its *opposition to large-scale urban manufacture* and its promotion of small-scale, moral, efficient enterprises, and the other on a particular sort of *politics in which an effort is made to manufacture a national-collective will* (see also NATIONALISM). Populist political strategies and RHETORICS reside in what Laclau (1977) calls a double articulation: first, the creation of a stable bloc consisting of the people and powerful classes, and second, the discourses by which 'the people's' interests are configured with those of other classes (see CLASS and STATE). Populist movements can, for example, encompass farmer radicalism, agrarian SOCIALISM, populist dictatorship (Peronism), populist DEMOCRACY, and URBAN SOCIAL MOVEMENTS (Canovan, 1981; see also SQUATTER SETTLEMENT). Populist, or neo-populist, development strategies can include peasant COOPERATIVES, the informal sector, land reform and THIRD WORLD flexible specialization (Kitching, 1980). A powerful line of populist thinking in development geography and agrarian studies includes the work of Chayanov (see PEASANT). MW

References and Suggested Reading

Canovan, M. 1981: *Populism*. London: Junction Books. · Kitching, G. 1982: *Development and underdevelopment in historical perspective*. London: Methuen. · Laclau, E. 1977: *Politics and ideology in Marxist theory*. London: Verso. · Watts, M. 1995: A new deal for the emotions. In J. Crush, ed., *Power of development*. London: Routledge, 44–62.

pork barrel An American term for the unequal distribution of PUBLIC GOODS in order to promote a party's or a candidate's re-election prospects. Although not exclusively American, the activity is particularly common there because of the individual nature of much campaigning for Congressional office: the term is also applied more generally to describe any apparent government favouritism of certain areas. RJJ

positionality The notion that 'where we are located in the social structure as a whole and which institutions we are in . . . have effects on how we understand the world' (Hartsock, 1987, p. 188). The debate about positionality has been advanced most rigorously within feminist theory, rejecting the HEGEMONY of 'abstract MASCULINISM' and challenging its epistemological claims to universality (see FEMINIST GEOGRAPHIES). In her work on *Feminism and methodology* (1987), Sandra Harding reverses the charge that feminist research is flawed by an inherent RELATIVISM. Rather than accepting the criticism that feminist research is invalidated because it is politically 'biased', she argues that declaring the position from which one writes may lead to more sound analyses, rooted in the authority of experience, than apparently disinterested research which fails to acknowledge its partiality. Drawing on Hartsock's (1983) work, Harding distinguishes between a *standpoint* and a *perspective*. Unlike a 'perspective' which anyone can claim, a feminist standpoint has to be struggled for, to be earned. It is 'not something anyone can have by claiming it, but an achievement' (1987, p. 185). Similar arguments have been made by those who claim that the 'margins' may offer a privileged position from which to view the 'centre' (hooks, 1990) and by the insistence that all forms of knowledge are situated (Haraway, 1988). The idea that one's positionality can be easily identified and readily acknowledged, described by Rose (1997) as 'transparent reflexivity', has also been criticized, requiring a thorough examination of the ambiguities and uncertainties of research practice.

While it has been developed most strongly in feminist theory, the debate about positionality applies more widely to questions of REPRESENTATION, where it is increasingly accepted that all ways of seeing are partial (in the dual sense of incomplete and rarely, if ever, disinterested). The argument about positionality has been successful in forcing dominant groups to acknowledge their particular angle of vision, to accept, in Stuart Hall's words, that we are *all* ethnically located, rather than seeing 'ETHNICITY' as something that only applies to minority groups: 'We all speak from a particular place, out of a particular history, a particular experience, a particular culture, without being contained by that position' (1992, p. 258). A politics of position is therefore particularly appropriate as a challenge to all forms of ETHNOCENTRISM (cf. IDENTITY POLITICS).

A politics of position demands that attention be paid to the structures of POWER that privilege certain (typically white, male, middle-class) voices, sanctioning some points of view while silencing others (typically black, female, working-class). Some authors have reached pessimistic conclusions about the prospects for retrieving oppressed and subordinated voices, arguing that there is currently 'no space from which the sexed subaltern subject can speak' (Spivak, 1988, p. 307; see SUBALTERN STUDIES) without their voices being distorted and misappropriated by those with greater powers of representation. Others are more optimistic, including Hartsock herself, who argues that 'We need to develop our understanding of DIFFERENCE by creating a situation in which hitherto marginalized groups can name themselves, speak for themselves, and participate in defining the terms of interaction' (1987, p. 189).

The debate about positionality raises complex issues about speaking positions, about silencing and giving voice, especially for social scientists who have a vested interest in representing those who may be culturally different from ourselves. For, as Bourdieu has argued in his study of academic politics, 'it is not, as is usually thought, political stances which determine people's stances on things academic; but their positions in the academic field which inform the stances they adopt on political issues in general' (Bourdieu, 1988, pp. xvii–xviii). As Hartsock's argument about earning rather than claiming a standpoint suggests, positionality involves more than merely stating one's position ('writing as a white, middle-class man . . .' etc.). It requires us to examine how we are ourselves positioned in relation to various contexts of power and how such power can be channelled in politically progressive ways. Rather than simply adding new voices to pre-existing debates without altering their underlying terms, a politics of position has the potential to transform the nature of those debates. Through such fundamental questioning, the crisis of representation can move forward from arguments about 'good' versus 'bad' images to challenge the very grounds on which such judgements are made and the social relations that lead to the empowerment of some representations while disempowering others. (See also SITUATED KNOWLEDGE.) PAJ

References

Bourdieu, P. 1988: *Homo academicus*. Cambridge: Polity Press. · Hall, S. 1992: New ethnicities. In J. Donald and A. Rattansi, eds, *'Race', culture and difference*. London: Sage, 252–9. · Haraway, D. 1988: Situated knowledges: the science question in feminism and the privilege of partial perspective. *Feminist Studies* 14: 575–99. · Harding, S., ed., 1987: *Feminism and methodology*. Milton Keynes: Open University Press. · Hartsock, N. 1983: The feminist standpoint. Reprinted in Harding, S., ed., 1987: *Feminism and methodology*. Milton Keynes: Open University Press, 157–80. · Hartsock, N. 1987: Rethinking modernism: minority versus majority theories. *Cultural Critique* 7: 187–206. · hooks, b. 1990: *Yearning: race, gender, and cultural politics*. Toronto: Between the Lines. · Rose, G. 1997: Situated knowledges: positionality, reflexivities and other tactics. *Progress in Human Geography* 21: 305–20. · Spivak, G.C. 1988: Can the subaltern speak? In C. Nelson and L. Grossberg, eds, *Marxism and the interpretation of culture*. Urbana, IL: University of Illinois Press, 271–313.

Suggested Reading

Harding (1987). · Rose (1997).

positive discrimination Policies designed to favour disadvantaged groups within society, in order to reduce if not eliminate inequalities. Some of these policies are targeted at particular areas, either because the service is delivered on an areal basis (e.g. a NEIGHBOURHOOD school) or because it is the most effective way of reaching the target group (e.g. defining those eligible for house improvement grants as all households in a specified area). Spatial targeting often means that some of the intended beneficiaries receive no advantage, because they live outside the defined areas, whereas residents of the targeted areas do benefit whether or not they are deserving cases. RJJ

positivism A philosophy of science originally proposed by the French philosopher and sociologist Auguste Comte (1798–1857) whose primary purpose was to distinguish science from both metaphysics and religion. Comte drew upon the earlier ideas of the French social reformer the Comte de Saint-Simon (1760–1825), and presented his own ideas in a series of lectures which were codified in *The course of positivist philosophy* (6 vols, 1830–42). The subsequent history of positivism in both philosophy and the sciences is complex, and there are several different versions of positivism (Bryant, 1985; Kolakowski, 1972). In the most general terms, however, Comtean positivism determined the scientific status of its statements through five steps:

(1) Scientific statements were to be grounded in a direct, immediate and empirically accessible experience of the world, and observation statements were therefore privileged over theoretical ones (see EMPIRICISM): observations of events were the leading particulars of scientific inquiry and as such, observation statements could be made independently of any theoretical statements that might subsequently be constructed around them.

(2) Scientific observations had to be repeatable, and their generality was to be ensured by a unitary scientific method that was accepted and routinely drawn upon by the scientific community as a whole.

(3) Science would advance through the formal construction of THEORIES which, if empirically verified, would assume the status of scientific LAWS.

(4) Those scientific laws would have a strictly technical function, in that they would reveal the effectivity or even the necessity but emphatically not the desirability of specific conjunctions of events: in other words, they had to take the form '*If A, then B*' (laws of constant conjunction or 'Humean laws': for example, 'If somebody receives favourable information about an innovation, then they will decide to adopt it'; see DIFFUSION).

(5) Scientific laws would be progressively unified and integrated into a single system of knowledge and truth (or, rather, Truth).

The founders of the modern discipline of geography often relied on conceptions of science which were denied by positivism: Humboldt rejected the brute empiricism on which Comte's system was built, for example, and elaborated a sophisticated philosophical system in its place (Bowen, 1979). Yet much of the subsequent history of geography was dominated by the (often tacit) acceptance of some or all of these assumptions, so that when they were formalized during the QUANTITATIVE REVOLUTION of the 1950s and 1960s the so-called 'New Geography' that resulted was 'less of a radical departure than a logical extension of ideas which were already generally accepted by many geographers' (Guelke, 1978; see also Gregory, 1978). Insofar as these were in any sense philosophically novel, they derived their originality from a commitment to LOGICAL POSITIVISM. The introduction of the prefix 'logical' signalled a break with the classical Comtean model which had been made by the Vienna Circle, a group of philosophers, mathematicians and natural scientists that met regularly in Vienna in the 1920s and 1930s and whose manifesto – *The scientific conception of the world: the Vienna Circle* – was published in 1929. The basis of logical positivism was a distinction between:

(a) *analytic statements*: a priori propositions whose truth was guaranteed by their internal definitions and connections. These constituted the domain of the *formal sciences*, logic and mathematics, which (strictly speaking) had no place in a Comtean model that required all scientific statements to rely on empirical verification; and

(b) *empirical or synthetic statements*: statements about things of all kinds whose truth had to be established empirically through hypothesis testing. This 'principle of verification' was supposed to be the hallmark of the *factual sciences*, but it was soon challenged by Popper's principle of FALSIFICATION. Instead of making every effort to prove an hypothesis, Popper believed that the scientist's task was to try to disprove it: if it stood up, then the hypothesis could be accepted, but only for the time being (see CRITICAL RATIONALISM).

These revisions provided empirical inquiry with a more secure basis than the classical Comtean model, and the 'New Geography' was readily accommodated within their framework: the philosophical highpoint of this tradition was David Harvey's *Explanation in geography* (1969). The major omission within this conception of geography was the development of deductive-nomological explanation and a considered recognition of the importance of Popper's proposals for the business of hypothesis testing: certainly, much of the early work in SPATIAL SCIENCE depended on inductive-statistical rather than deductive-mathematical methods (Wilson, 1972). Even so, the overriding concern with the derivation, validation and integration of general theories of spatial organization was an unequivocally positivist project (see LOCATION THEORY). The debate over EXCEPTIONALISM had established the legitimacy of a NOMOTHETIC conception of geography, and the search for models of SPATIAL STRUCTURE and methods of SPATIAL ANALYSIS was soon widened by the incorporation of MODELS and techniques drawn from other sciences that were also predicated on an unflinching positivism, e.g. classical mechanics and NEO-CLASSICAL ECONOMICS. When research effort in human geography moved on from spatial form towards the study of generative PROCESS, much of its energy was still contained within the positivist tradition: e.g. the development of BEHAVIOURAL GEOGRAPHY. But the discipline eventually broke through those bounds to confront a series of rival philosophical systems.

The critique of positivism that followed was both fierce and decisive: 'almost every aspect of the prescribed method can be shown to be open to question' (Bowen, 1979; cf. Hay, 1979). And yet it needs to be emphasized that the relation between positivism as a philosophy and the evolving empirical method of human geography has remained contentious. Harvey's (1969) philosophical codification of spatial science and spatial analysis was largely retrospective: much of the innovative groundwork had already been done by geographers (including Harvey himself) who at the time had little interest in or even knowledge of philosophy, and *Explanation in geography* consistently referred to 'the' scientific method rather than to positivism. In any case, empirical methods are constituted by more than philosophical warrants, and a revisionist historiography of geography informed by 'science studies' is beginning to uncover the complex cultural history in which the QUANTITATIVE REVOLUTION was embedded (Barnes, 1998; Hepple, 1998). Whether 'quantitative' is an effective summary description of the 'revolution' of the 1950s and 1960s is itself open to question, but there are also serious issues surrounding the connection between positivism and quantitative methods: positivists are not required to make use of formal mathematical or statistical methods, and neither does the use of quantitative techniques immediately identify (or condemn) an inquiry as incorrigibly positivist. None of this protects spatial science from the critique of positivism, but it does help to explain why so many quantitatively minded geographers were left unmoved by the philosophical interrogation of their work (Flowerdew, 1998). If, as Flowerdew says, the practice of quantitative geography continues to thrive, there is nevertheless no doubt that the critique of positivism had and continues to have a series of major effects on the contemporary discipline.

That critique has involved an assault on four plans of the positivist platform: empiricism, exclusivity, autonomy, and universality.

Empiricism: The relationship between observation statements and theoretical statements has been shown to be much more problematic than positivism allowed. The belief that 'the facts' could speak for themselves was called into question in several ways. Within quantitative geography alternative modes of statistical inference were deployed in order to allow for varying degrees of theoretical co-determination, e.g. Bayesian theory. A recognition of the constitutive importance of 'theory' reached far beyond formal analytical methods, however, and human geographers developed a much greater sensitivity to the importance of theoretical critique – to the clarification of concepts and categories – which prompted them to engage with theoretical systems that promised to provide a more incisive exposure of the structures of social life in time and space. In the first instance these theoretical systems were underwritten by foundational epistemologies like REALISM, but in the second instance non-foundational epistemologies like POST-STRUCTURALISM have risen to prominence. Post-structuralism has redoubled the significance of a critical interrogation of concepts and categories, but it is no theoreticism: it requires a close and careful reading of empirical materials to disclose their silences and erasures and their assumptions and ambiguities (cf. DECONSTRUCTION).

Exclusivity: The assumption that the 'objective' methods of the natural sciences could be extended into the domain of the humanities and the social sciences to provide a self-sufficient and unitary system of inquiry has been challenged. On the one side, the application of QUALITATIVE METHODS showed the importance of recovering meanings, intentions and values as an essential moment in human geographical inquiry: 'data' could thus not reasonably be limited to the computational and enumerative (see HUMANISTIC GEOGRAPHY; PHENOMENOLOGY). It would in any case be a mistake to think in terms of a simple binary opposition between the quantitative and the qualitative. It is possible to work with qualitative materials in thoroughly positivist ways and, equally, the rigorous use of quantitative methods can (and usually does) require a careful and critical understanding of the qualitative matrix in which they are embedded. On the other side, therefore, such supposedly 'subjective' concerns were found to be important in the constitution and conduct of the natural sciences too, whose inquiries also involve difficult questions of meaning, interpretation and RHETORIC (see NATURALISM; SCIENCE, GEOGRAPHY AND). The privileges accorded to 'the' scientific method were thus comprehensively compromised, and the natural sciences – whose power and importance was not in question – came to be seen in new, more complex and more interesting ways that nonetheless removed them from the pedestal on which positivism had placed them.

Autonomy: It was no longer possible to claim that science was (or should be) insulated from social life, offering 'neutral' and 'value-free' knowledge, and the embeddedness of scientific inquiry in social life was seen to require an explicit reflection on the ETHICS and politics of human geography: on its various 'regimes of truth' and the ways in which they are imbricated in wider relations of power and knowledge (see CRITICAL THEORY; DISCOURSE; EPISTEMOLOGY; IDEOLOGY).

Universality: Even the natural sciences could be shown to be context-dependent in various ways, so that the extension and generalization of their findings becomes a precarious, negotiated achievement and not a given (Rouse, 1987). The same applied *a fortiori* to the humanities and social sciences, and in consequence human geography has been obliged to recognize that explanations and understandings arrived at in one setting cannot be transferred to other settings without critical scrutiny and often substantial reconstruction (cf. TRAVELLING THEORY). Human geographies are always 'LOCAL KNOWLEDGES' (cf. Barnes, 1989), even when they address global issues, and the recognition of all geographies as forms of SITUATED KNOWLEDGE means that it is vitally important to attend to the play of different interests from different positions and in different voices (see POSTMODERNISM).

What these philosophical counter-claims amounted to was a reinstatement of the social foundations and responsibilities of intellectual inquiry and a refusal to separate 'science' from DISCOURSE more generally. Many human geographers no doubt continue to think of themselves as social scientists; many do not (the connections between human geography and the humanities are now probably stronger than at any time since the Second World War). In either case, however, probably very few count themselves as positivists. The continued exploration of post-positivist geographies has: (a) dimmed the old enthusiasm for the unrestrained application of quantitative techniques as ends in themselves (though analytical methods continue to be important in many areas of non-positivist geography); (b) reinvigorated a number of areas which had hitherto been characterized by an unreflective positivism; and (c) helped to open up new avenues of inquiry throughout the discipline and beyond (e.g. FEMINIST GEOGRAPHIES; POST-COLONIALISM). In retrospect, it seems clear that, in the most general terms, the critique of positivism at once shook the sense of certainty that the conjunction of positivism and spatial science had promised human geography – replacing it with a pervasive 'cartographic anxiety' (Gregory, 1994) – and, since so much of physical geography remained largely unaffacted by and indifferent to these arguments, also made the connections between the disciplines of human geography and physical geography much more tenuous.

DG

References

Barnes, T. 1989: Place, space and theories of economic value: contextualism and essentialism in economic geography. *Transactions, Institute of British Geographers* NS 14: 299–316. · Barnes, T. 1998: A history of regression: actors, networks, machines and numbers. *Environment and Planning A* 30: 203–23. · Bowen, M.J. 1979: Scientific method – after positivism. *Australian Geographical Studies* 17: 210–16. · Bryant, C. 1985: *Positivism in social theory and research*. London: Macmillan. · Flowerdew, R. 1998: Reacting to *Ground Truth*. *Environment and Planning A* 30: 289–301. · Gregory, D. 1978: *Ideology, science and human geography*. London: Hutchinson. · Guelke, L. 1978: Geography and logical positivism. In D.T. Herbert and R.J. Johnston, eds, *Geography and the urban environment*, vol. 1. New York: John Wiley, 35–61. · Harvey, D. 1969: *Explanation in geography*. London: Edward Arnold. · Hay, A.M. 1979: Positivism in human geography: response to critics. In D.T. Herbert and R.J. Johnston, eds, *Geography and the urban environment*, vol. 2. New York: John Wiley, 1–26. · Hepple, L. 1998: Context, social construction and statistics: regression, social science and human geography. *Environment and Planning A* 30: 225–34. · Kolakowski, L. 1972: *Positivist philosophy: from Hume to the Vienna Circle*. Harmondsworth: Penguin. · Rouse, J. 1987: *Knowledge and power: toward a political philosophy of science*. Ithaca: Cornell University Press. · Wilson, A.G. 1972: Theoretical geography: some speculations. *Transactions, Institute of British Geographers* 57: 31–44.

possibilism A thesis about the relationship between human CULTURE and the natural environment which claims that the human species has the capacity to choose between a range of possible responses to physical conditions. The doctrine is primarily associated with the French School of Geography as articulated in the writings of Vidal de la Blache and, perhaps even more especially, the historian Lucien Febvre (Buttimer, 1971). It also found favour elsewhere; in Britain possibilist strains are detectable in the early twentieth-century work of Patrick Geddes and H.J. Fleure, while in the United States Carl Sauer's insistence on the transforming power of human culture evinces similar influences (cf. BERKELEY SCHOOL).

On the surface at least, possibilism stands in direct contrast to ENVIRONMENTAL DETERMINISM. Febvre, for example, inaugurated his magisterial treatise, *A geographical introduction to history*, by expanding on the tradition of geographical necessitarianism and contrasting Vidal's *genres de vie* and Michelet's earlier historical sketches with what he took to be the rigid and illusory determinism of such figures as Montesquieu, Ratzel and – not without a good deal of philosophical caricature – Victor Cousin. Such schemes, he considered, amounted to little more than formulaic catechisms conducive to an 'attitude of routine and mechanical conservatism' (Febvre, 1932, p. 27). As he put it in a now justly renowned credo that celebrated the power of HUMAN AGENCY: 'There are no necessities, but everywhere possibilities; and man, as master of the possibilities, is the judge of their use. This, by the reversal which it involves, puts man in the first place – man, and no longer the earth, nor the influence of climate, nor the determinant conditions of localities' (Febvre, 1932, p. 237). In part at least, Febvre's concerns arose from the sense that, in environmental determinist mode, geography as a discipline became an 'impudent interloper on ground reserved to economists and sociologists' disclosing an expansive arrogance based on sweeping but facile declarations of environmental causation (Febvre, 1932, p. 34). The polemical character of this work meant that misrepresentations abounded, not least of which was a persistent failure to appreciate the intellectual subtlety of Victor Cousin (Davie, 1994).

Abstracted from the actual writings of key personalities, the contrast between these two doctrines seems stark. But when the original texts are read it quickly becomes clear that such a theoretical bifurcation is sustainable only insofar as these systems of thought are treated as IDEAL TYPES. Thus while Patrick Geddes could at times write of the central importance of consciousness and will in the human transformation of the earth, his celebrated Valley Section – which umbilically connected geographical position with settlement cultures – was redolent with the necessitarianism of Edmond Demolins, which was, in turn, derived from Frédéric le Play's sociology (cf. LE PLAY SOCIETY). And again H.J. Fleure was inclined to interpret evolutionary theory in such a way as to allow for the possibility of environmentally induced, hereditary modifications. Indeed much the same can be said for supposedly archetypal environmental determinists. Thus Ellen C. Semple, while emphasizing the determining power of NATURE in the shaping of human history and SOCIETY, could also speak of the cultural persistence of racial types in radically different environmental milieux, not least among the Anglo-Saxons of the Kentucky Mountains who displayed what she called in 1901 an 'inextinguishable excellence'. Even among the possibilists of the classical French School, there was, as Henri Berr (in the foreword to Lucien Febvre's *La terre et l'évolution humaine*) insisted, no denial of the 'direct action of the environment on the physical and psychical nature of man' (p. vi). And Vidal himself, as Berdoulay has demonstrated, sought a scheme for understanding the interaction of nature and culture that eschewed both environmental determinism and what he calls 'radical possibilism' (Berdoulay, 1976).

All of this is indicative of the conceptual turmoil surrounding the genesis of *géographie humaine* in turn-of-the-century France (Friedman, 1996). For it was in dialogue with, and in opposition to, the sociological writings of Emile Durkheim and his disciples that the distinctive character of Vidalian geography was constituted – a conversation that rotated around the determinism inherent in Ratzel's *Anthropogéographie* and Durkheim's judgement that social MORPHOLOGY, as a division of sociology, exhausted the scope of human geography (Andrews, 1984). The contextual circumstances within which possibilism can be located, however, cannot be reduced to the academic-political manoeuvrings of the Vidalians and the Durkheimians. Thus Berdoulay, for example, has argued that French possibilism was essentially a neo-Kantian (see KANTIANISM) solution to the seeming dichotomy between the human and the environmental. The Kantian insistence on the human mind's creative structuring of an external world, it is claimed, resonated with Vidal's concerns to maintain human freedom within certain ontological limits (Berdoulay, 1976, 1988). Again, Lukermann (1965) sought to situate the early École Française in the context of developments in probability theory associated with Henri Poincaré and A.-A. Cournot. The idea of what elsewhere has been dubbed 'bounded contingency' (Gregory, 1981) was thus mediated to Brunhes and Vallaux through such writers as Bourtrous, Borel and Meyerson.

More recently, Archer (1993) has made a strong case for placing Vidalian possibilism within the sphere of Lamarckian biology (see LAMARCK(IAN)ISM). This reading has the merit of taking seriously the natural science aspirations that Vidal had for *géographie humaine* – he spoke, for example, of 'the biological method' (Vidal, 1903) – and the naturalistic emphasis on human agency that Febvre saw as the crucial influence of Buffon on the tradition. Here, Vidal's organicism is seen to correlate closely with Lamarck's ideas about spontaneous generation, multiple environmental stimuli, and the directive significance of will and consciousness in organic modification. Whether or not this account is altogether persuasive, it has the advantage of redrawing attention to Vidal's belief in the scientific status of human geography, an aspiration not always sufficiently acknowledged by those who have used the Vidalian tradition as a resource for more recent humanistic programmes (cf. HUMANISTIC GEOGRAPHY). It also serves to recall attention to the ecological cast of Vidal's *Principles of human geography* (see also Robic, 1993) which, bereft of the kind of epistemological manoeuvrings typical of a disciplinary manifesto, proceeds on a much more inductive basis. DNL

References

Andrews, H.F. 1984: The Durkheimians and human geography: some contextural problems in the sociology of knowledge. *Transactions, Institute of British Geographers* NS 9: 315–36. · Archer, K. 1993: Regions as social organisms: the Lamarckian characteristics of Vidal de la Blache's regional geography. *Annals of the Association of American Geographers* 83: 498–514. · Berdoulay, V. 1976: French possibilism as a form of Neo-Kantian philosophy. *Proceedings of the Association of American Geographers* 8: 176–9. · Berdoulay, V. 1988: Le discours géographique et les orientations Kantiennes et dynamiques. In *Des mots et des lieux: la dynamique de discours géographique*. Paris: Editions du Centre National de la Recherche Scientifique (CNRS), ch. 3. · Buttimer, A. 1971: *Society and milieu in the French geographic tradition*. Chicago: Rand McNally; Davie, G.E. 1994: Victor Cousin and the Scottish philosophers. In *A passion for ideas: essays on the Scottish Enlightenment*, vol. II. Edinburgh: Polygon, 70–109. · Febvre, L. 1932: *A geographical introduction to history*. London: Kegan Paul, Trench, Trübner (originally published in 1922 as *La terre et l'évolution humaine*). · Friedman, S.W. 1996: *Marc Bloch, sociology and geography*. Cambridge: Cambridge University Press. · Gregory, D. 1981: Human agency and human geography. *Transactions of the Institute of British Geographers* NS 6: 1–18. · Lukerman, F. 1965: The 'calcul des probabilités' and the Ecole Française de Géographie. *Canadian Geographer* 9: 128–37. · Robic, Marie-Claire, 1993: L'invention de la 'géographie humaine' au tournant des années 1900: les Vidalians et l'écologie. In Paul Claval ed., *Autour de Vidal de la Blache: la formation de l'école française de géographie*. Paris: Centre National de la Recherche Scientifique (CNRS), 137–47. · Vidal de la Blache, P. 1903: La géographie humaine: ses rapports avec la géographie de la vie. *Revue de Synthèse Historique* 7: 219–40.

Suggested Readings

Andrews (1984); Archer (1993). · Buttimer (1971). · Friedman (1996). · Montefiore, A.G. and Williams, W.M. 1955: Determinism and possibilism: a search for clarification. *Geographical Studies* 2: 1–11. · Spate, O.H.K. 1957: How determined is possibilism? *Geographical Studies* 4: 3–12.

Postan thesis A theoretical explanation of economic and social change in medieval England, formulated and developed by the medievalist and economic historian Michael Postan (1966, 1973; Postan and Hatcher, 1978). Postan sought to replace earlier linear models of western medieval economy based on the growth of international TRADE, arguing instead that medieval European societies needed to be analysed first and foremost in terms of their agrarian bases. He took the critical component of the agrarian base to be the ability of PEASANT households to produce sufficient to support themselves and their social superiors, in the case of the latter through rents, tithes and taxes (see LAND TENURE).

While Postan's work involved comparative analysis of England and the continent, he drew mainly on empirical material from southern England, especially from large ecclesiastically owned estates such as those of the Bishop of Winchester, for which extensive records survive. His chief inferences were based on evidence of population trends, land use, new colonization or abandonment of arable land, prices, wages, rents, grain yields, and livestock numbers.

The Postan thesis holds that medieval England moved inexorably towards an agrarian CRISIS. Population growth during the eleventh, twelfth and thirteenth centuries put increasing strain on the ECOLOGICAL base of peasant production. Pastures, woodlands and wastes were converted to arable use, but scope for such expansion was finite, and peasant family landholdings became increasingly sub-divided. The rate at which this impoverishment occurred varied between areas according to their resource base, settlement history, and population density. Eventually, population growth outstripped both the availability of new land to bring under arable cultivation, and the ability of farmers to maintain or increase PRODUCTIVITY per cropped acre. Much arable land was abandoned (Baker, 1973). Land abandonment and falling yields precipitated chronic food crises, causing population to fall, with a significant demographic turning point in the early fourteenth century (Kershaw, 1973). Compared with earlier arguments, Postan played down the significance of the Black Death as a *turning point*, arguing that it accelerated a population decline already underway.

For Postan, the tendency towards ecological crisis built into medieval agrarian society was twofold: 'People found that they had reached the limits of the land's productivity; not only because they were reclaiming new, poor soils but also because they had been cultivating old land for too long' (Postan, 1973, p. 15). Thus medieval husbandmen faced a double bind. Yields were falling on old-cultivated land (Titow, 1972), because the emphasis on arable was so extreme that diminished livestock populations could no longer provide sufficient dung to maintain soil fertility. On newly colonized areas of marginal land, yields were initially high but could not be maintained as accumulations of soil nutrient stores became depleted. (For analysis of the Postan thesis in terms of soil productivity, see Shiel, 1991; Clark, 1992; Newman and Harvey, 1997).

Among many areas of critical debate, five are of particular significance to historical geographers. First, many have argued that Postan underestimates the significance of feudal social relations as a cause of peasant hardship, and a constraint on agricultural technology (see FEUDALISM; BRENNER DEBATE). What is at issue here is not so much whether there was a general medieval agrarian crisis, as whether its ultimate causes were social rather than techno-ecological. Secondly, others dispute the notion that the crisis was general and sustained (Hallam, 1989; Harvey, 1991), crediting at least some regional agrarian economies with a greater capacity to make technical innovations and increase productivity than does Postan (Langdon, 1986; Campbell, 1991, 1995a and b; Campbell and Overton, 1995). In part, it appears that the Postan thesis draws too heavily on evidence from atypically conservatively managed estates. However, even within the Winchester estates, later work has ascribed geographical variations in land productivity to differing levels of labour inputs (Thornton, 1991). Third, peasant agriculture may have been generally more dynamic than the seigneurial cultivation which provides most of the available evidence; this seems to be the case, for example, in the use of horses and the cultivation of legumes (Langdon, 1986). Postan's focus on arable production also marginalizes pastoral agriculture, which Biddick (1989) sees as a dynamic sector. Debates on all these topics highlight geographical variations in rural life. So too, fourthly, has the growing realization of the extent of commercialization on patterns of agricultural production, especially around London. Whereas Glasscock wrote in 1973 that 'technology and exchange had not progressed far enough by the early fourteenth century to allow much regional [agricultural] specialisation', recent work identifies substantial spatial differentiation in agricultural systems, and ascribes this to widespread processes of commercialization (Campbell and Power, 1989; Britnell, 1996).

Finally, Postan's concept of the geographical margin has been extended and refined. There were several senses in which land might be marginal: soil quality, climate, location, topography, tenure (Bailey, 1989a and b; Dyer, 1989). Postan conflated these senses, thereby oversimplifying the geography of expansion and contraction in settlement and cultivation. As Bailey observes with respect to the Norfolk and Suffolk Brecklands, 'the profitability of land depended as much upon its location, and upon institutional factors, as it did upon its quality' (1989b, p. 320). The relationships between different dimensions of marginality were contingent rather than necessary, and the classic Postanian marginal decline was largely restricted to areas which were marginal in several respects simultaneously.

In all these debates, much revision has taken the form of refining or elaborating the Postan thesis, rather than rejecting it outright. There is no current uniformity of opinion as to whether geographical differences in agrarian systems are better understood as exceptions to (or disproofs of) the Postan thesis, or as different regional development trajectories within the same fundamental set of constraints. Likewise, debate continues about the peak level of medieval population (Campbell, 1995a, argues for not more than 5 million, rather than the more widely accepted 6 to 6.5

million), and about whether undoubtedly severe crisis conditions in the early fourteenth century persisted in the 1330s and 1340s (Jordan, 1997; Bailey, 1998). But whether the Postan thesis is seen as crumbling or as becoming more complicated, Langdon's (1991, p. 209) view 'that a more comprehensive view of the medieval English economy is being developed' remains apposite. PG

References

Bailey, M. 1989a: *A marginal economy? East Anglian Breckland in the later middle ages*. Cambridge: Cambridge University Press. · Bailey, M. 1989b: The concept of the margin in the medieval English economy. *Economic History Review* 42: 1–18. · Bailey, M. 1998: Peasant welfare in England, 1290–1348. *Economic History Review* 51: 223–51. · Baker, A.R.H. 1973: Evidence in the '*Nonarum Inquisitiones*' of contracting arable land in England during the fourteenth century. *Economic History Review* 2nd series 19: 518–32. · Biddick, K. 1989: *The other economy: pastoral husbandry on a medieval estate*. Berkeley: University of California Press. · Brenner, R. 1976: Agrarian class structure and economic development in pre-industrial Europe. *Past and Present* 70: 30–75. · Britnell, R. 1996: *Commercialisation in Medieval England*, 2nd edn. Manchester: Manchester University Press. · Campbell, B.M.S. 1991: Land, labour, livestock, and productivity trends in English seignorial agriculture, 1208–1450. In B.M.S. Campbell and M. Overton, eds, *Land, labour and livestock: historical studies in European agricultural productivity*. Manchester: Manchester University Press, 144–82. · Campbell, B.M.S. 1995a: Ecology versus economics in late-thirteenth and early-fourteenth century English agriculture. In D. Sweeney, ed., *Agriculture in the Middle Ages: technology, practice and representation*, Philadelphia: University of Pennsylvania Press, 75–108. · Campbell, B.M.S. 1995b: Progressiveness and backwardness in thirteenth- and early fourteenth-century English agriculture: the verdict of recent research. In J.-M. Duvosquel and E. Thoen, eds, *Peasants and townsmen in medieval Europe*. Gent: Snoeck-Docaju and Zoon, 541–59. · Campbell, B.M.S. and Overton, M. 1995: A new perspective on medieval and early modern farming: six centuries of Norfolk farming *c*.1250–*c*.1850. *Past and Present* 141: 38–105. · Campbell, B.M.S. and Power, J. 1989: Mapping the agricultural geography of medieval England. *Journal of Historical Geography* 15: 24–39. · Clark, G. 1992: The economics of exhaustion, the Postan thesis, and the agricultural revolution. *Journal of Economic History* 52: 61–84. · Dyer, C. 1993: *Standards of living in the later middle ages*, 2nd edn. Cambridge: Cambridge University Press. · Dyer, C. 1989: The retreat from marginal land: the growth and decline of medieval rural settlements. In M. Aston et al., eds, *The rural settlements of medieval England: studies dedicated to Maurice Beresford and John Hurst*. Oxford: Basil Blackwell, 45–57. · Hallam, H.E., ed., 1989: *The agrarian history of England and Wales, volume II, 1042–1350*. Cambridge: Cambridge University Press. · Harvey, B. 1991: Introduction: the 'crisis' of the early fourteenth century. In B.M.S. Campbell, ed., *Before the Black Death: studies in the 'crisis' of the early fourteenth century*. Manchester: Manchester University Press, 1–24. · Jordan, W.C. 1997: *The Great Famine: Northern Europe in the early fourteenth century*. Princeton, NJ: Princeton University Press. · Kershaw, I. 1973: The agrarian crisis in England 1315–1322. *Past and Present* 59. · Langdon, J. 1986: *Horses, oxen and technological innovation: the use of draught animals in English farming from 1066–1500*. Cambridge: Cambridge University Press. · Langdon, J. 1991: Bringing it all together: medieval English economic history in transition. *Journal of British Studies* 30: 209–16. · Newman, E. and Harvey, P. 1997: Did soil fertility decline in medieval English farms? Evidence from Cuxham, Oxfordshire, 1320–1340. *Agricultural History Review* 46: 119–36. · Postan, M.M. 1966: Medieval agrarian society in its prime: England. In M.M. Postan, ed., *Cambridge economic history of Europe, volume 1: The agrarian life of the middle ages*. Cambridge: Cambridge University Press, 549–632. · Postan, M.M. 1973: *Essays on medieval agriculture and general problems of the medieval economy*. Cambridge: Cambridge University Press. · Postan, M.M. and Hatcher, J. 1978: Population and class relations in feudal society. *Past and Present* 78: 24–37. · Shiel, R.S. 1991: Improving soil productivity in the pre-fertilizer era. In B.M.S. Campbell and M. Overton, eds, *Land, labour and livestock: historical studies in European agricultural productivity*. Manchester: Manchester University Press, 51–77. · Smith, R.M. 1991: Demographic developments in rural England, 1300–1348: a survey. In B.M.S. Campbell, ed., *Before the Black Death: studies in the 'crisis' of the early fourteenth century*. Manchester: Manchester University Press, 25–78. · Thornton, C. 1991: The determinants of land productivity on the Bishop of Winchester's demesne of Rimpton, 1208–1403. In B.M.S. Campbell and M. Overton, eds, *Land, labour and livestock: historical studies in European agricultural productivity*. Manchester: Manchester University Press, 183–210. · Titow, J.Z. 1972: *Winchester yields: a study in medieval agricultural productivity*. Cambridge: Cambridge University Press.

Suggested Reading

Bailey (1998). · Campbell and Overton (1995). · Clark (1992). · Newman and Harvey (1997). · Postan (1966). · Smith (1991).

post-colonialism A critical politico-intellectual formation that is centrally concerned with the impact of COLONIALISM and its contestation on the cultures of both colonizing and colonized peoples in the past, and the reproduction and transformation of colonial relations, REPRESENTATIONS and practices in the present. Historically, there have been many colonialisms, but the idea of writing 'post' – 'after', 'against the grain of' and 'in the knowledge of' – colonialism in such a way that our understanding of the present is transformed means that post-colonial studies have usually been concerned with the period between the sixteenth and twentieth centuries, which has been marked by the expansion and contraction of European empires, the consolidation of a capitalist world-economy and the formation of a colonial, colonizing MODERNITY (cf. WORLD-SYSTEMS ANALYSIS). Historically, there have also been many studies that sought to make critical contributions to our knowledge of the colonial past and to draw attention to the shadows it still casts over the present, including colonial/imperial history and studies of 'the development of UNDERDEVELOPMENT' carried out within radical POLITICAL ECONOMY (see DEVELOPMENT). But the emergence of post-colonialism in the 1980s and 1990s signalled two linked departures from these established traditions of inquiry: first, an explicit theoretical sensibility (which was largely foreign to mainstream history); and secondly, an attempt to recover the political significance of CULTURE and the 'epistemic violence' of colonialism (which was largely foreign to political economy).

Conceived thus, post-colonialism had its origins in literary and cultural studies, where it received a decisive impetus from Edward Said's (1978) critique of ORIENTALISM. This influential text depended on a tense conjunction of humanism and ANTI-HUMANISM to expose the forms through which European and North American representations of 'the Orient' had been produced and circulated, but the subsequent development of post-colonialism has usually been much more critical of western humanism and has involved a much closer engagement with POST-STRUCTURALISM, especially the work of Derrida, Foucault and Lacan (Young, 1990). Most recent surveys of post-colonialism have drawn their interpretative contours around the theoretical claims registered by the contrasting figures of Said, Homi Bhabha and Gayatri Chakravorty Spivak, all of whom are located within literary and cultural studies (e.g. Childs and Williams, 1997; Moore-Gilbert, 1997). Such an intellectual cartography reflects the disciplinary origins of post-colonialism, and its analytical power has been registered in several important contributions to cultural-historical geography, the history of cartography (see CARTOGRAPHY, HISTORY OF) and the history of geography (see GEOGRAPHY, HISTORY OF) (Huggan, 1989; Barnett, 1998; Clayton, 1999). Even so, this sketch-map does little to register the intersections between scholars in literary and cultural studies and the contributions made to what has become an interdisciplinary field by scholars from other traditions of anthropology, history, sociology and human geography. To be sure, there have been sharp disagreements and constructive engagements across these disciplinary frontiers (Kennedy, 1996), but in this expanded sense post-colonialism takes the following propositions as axiomatic for the critical analysis of colonialism and its successor projects (e.g. NEO-COLONIALISM).

An understanding of colonialism and its successor projects has to involve a close and critical reading of colonial discourse. This is much more than an appeal to the TEXTS and records of colonialism; indeed, the appeal to DISCOURSE is a way of registering the interpretative problems that inhere within the colonial archive (see Barnett, 1997). A crucial focus of inquiry is on the way in which colonialism constructs its objects by incorporation, projection and erasure. Approaching colonial POWER in this way has the double effect of allowing us 'to see how power works through LANGUAGE, literature, culture and the institutions which regulate our daily lives' (Loomba, 1998, p. 47) and of making possible a fuller understanding of the multiplicity of ways in which the exactions and impositions of colonialism are resisted by colonized peoples in cultural as well as political registers (Thomas, 1994). In this connection, colonial spaces are seen as heterogeneous spaces, and colonial discourse theory draws attention to the significance of mimicry, HYBRIDITY and TRANSCULTURATION in the co-production of subjectivities and SPATIALITIES (cf. Bhabha, 1994) (see also IDENTITY POLITICS; SUBJECT-FORMATION, GEOGRAPHIES OF). Some critics continue to be alarmed at the possibility that this interest in the cultures and discursive formations of colonialism has been achieved at the expense of an older, still vital interest in the political economy of CAPITALISM and that, at the limit, a concern with colonial texts and colonial subjectivities licenses a textualism and a subjectivism that are complicit with the new global regimes of capital accumulation (Dirlik, 1997).

An understanding of colonialism and its successor projects has to grasp the complicated and fractured histories through which colonialism passes from the past into the present. This has been a special concern of the SUBALTERN STUDIES project, which has sought to decolonize Indian history in order to illuminate the predicaments of contemporary Indian politics (Chakrabarty, 1992; Prakash, 1994). Some scholars have claimed that the general attempt to chart the cultural displacements of colonialism into the present threatens to destabilize the term 'post-colonialism' itself. McClintock (1992) has argued that post-colonialism is haunted by the very figure it seeks to displace, as it continues to privilege Europe as the central subject of History by reorienting the world around the single axis of the colonial/post-colonial (see EUROCENTRISM). Neither the history of colonizing societies nor the history of colonized societies is fully and exhaustively defined by colonialism and its afermath. But Hall (1996) has suggested that the post-colonial is more productively seen as marking an uneven and serialized process of decolonization that calls into question the binary form in which the colonial encounter has conventionally been represented.

An understanding of colonialism and its successor projects has to map the ways in which metropolitan and colonial societies are drawn together in webs of affinity, influence and dependence. It has become a commonplace to remark colonialism's dependence on dispossession through a series of intrinsically spatial strategies (Gregory, 1994, pp. 168–81), but these strategies were by no means confined to nominally colonized societies and there were vital interpenetrations and articulations of metropolitan and colonial societies: neither can be treated as self-contained entities. Thus (post-)colonial spaces are complex, fractured and foliated, and can rarely be reduced to any simple binary geometry (Low, 1996; Mills, 1996). In a major study of culture and IMPERIALISM, Said (1993) proposed a method of what he called 'contrapuntal reading' as a way of revealing the overlapping and intertwining geographies that appear in the margins and between the lines of the cultural archive. Strangely, there is not the same tradition of comparative inquiry within human geography, but a similar impetus animates Jacobs's (1996) doubled readings of London (UK) and Brisbane and Perth (Australia) as 'edges of empire', and Driver and Gilbert's (1998) account of the LANDSCAPES of imperial London as being symptomatic of 'less the heart of empire than just another of its limbs' (p. 26). These concerns converge around GLOBALIZATION and TRANSNATIONALISM, a terrain on which 'the local' and 'the global' interpenetrate in new and often unsettling geographies, where compound identities and marginalities are under construction, and where 'difference is encountered in the adjoining neighbourhood [and] the familiar turns up at the ends of the earth' (Clifford, 1988; see also Appadurai, 1996).

An understanding of colonialism and its successor projects has to be a history of the present that is sensitive to the political implications of its constructions. Post-colonialism ought not to license a 'retreat' into texts but instead force a recognition of the materiality and PERFORMATIVITY of texts; post-colonialism ought not to collapse into a culturalism but instead expose the articulations between 'the cultural' and 'the economic'; and post-colonialism ought not to become a premature celebration of the 'end' of colonialism but instead act as a forceful and unsettling reminder of the constitution of our own colonial present (cf. Jackson and Jacobs, 1996) (see also EUROCENTRISM; RACISM; WHITENESS). DG

References

Appadurai, A. 1996: *Modernity at large: cultural dimensions of globalization.* Minneapolis: University of Minnesota Press. · Barnett, C. 1997: 'Sing along with the common people': politics, postcolonialism and other figures. *Environment and Planning D: Society and Space* 15: 137–54. · Barnett, C. 1998: Impure and worldly geography: the Africanist discourse of the Royal Geographical Society, 1831–73. *Transactions, Institute of British Geographers* NS 23: 239–51. · Bhabha, H. 1994: *The location of culture.* London and New York: Routledge. · Chakrabarty, D. 1992: Postcoloniality and the artifice of history: Who speaks for 'Indian' pasts? *Representations* 37: 1–26. · Childs, P. and Williams, W. 1997: *An introduction to post-colonial theory.* London and New York: Prentice-Hall. · Clayton, D. 1999: *Islands of truth.* Vancouver, BC: University of British, Columbia Press. · Clifford, J. 1988: *The predicament of culture: twentieth-century ethnography, literature and art.* Cambridge, MA: Harvard University Press. · Dirlik, A. 1997: *The postcolonial aura: Third World criticism in the age of global capitalism.* Boulder, CO and Oxford: Westview Press. · Driver, F. and Gilbert, D. 1998: Heart of empire? Landscape, space and performance in imperial London. *Environment and Planning D: Society and Space* 16: 11–28. · Gregory, D. 1994: *Geographical imaginations.* Oxford and Cambridge, MA: Blackwell. · Hall, S. 1996: When was 'the post-colonial'? Thinking at the limit. In I. Chambers and L. Curti, eds, *The Post-colonial question: common skies, divided horizons.* London and New York: Routledge, 242–60. · Huggan, G. 1989: Decolonizing the map: post-colonialism, post-structuralism and the cartographic connection. *Ariel* 20: 115–31. · Jacobs, J. 1996: *Edge of empire: postcolonialism and the city.* London and New York: Routledge. · Jackson, P. and Jacobs, J. 1996: Postcolonialism and the politics of race. *Environment and Planning D: Society and Space* 14: 1–3. · Kennedy, D. 1996: Imperial history and post-colonial theory. *Journal of Imperial and Commonwealth History* 24: 345–63. · Loomba, A. 1998: *Colonialism/Postcolonialism.* London and New York: Routledge. · Low, G.C.-L. 1996: The city of dreadful night. In her *White skins, black masks: representation and colonialism.* London and New York: Routledge. · McClintock, A. 1992: The Angel of Progress: Pitfalls of the term 'Post-colonialism'. *Social Text* 31: 84–92. · Mills, S. 1996: Gender and colonial space. *Gender, Place and Culture* 3: 125–47. · Moore-Gilbert, B. 1997: *Postcolonial theory: contexts, practices, politics.* London and New York: Verso. · Prakash, G. 1994: Subaltern Studies as postcolonial criticism. *American Historical Review* 99: 1475–90. · Prakash, G., ed., 1995: *After colonialism: imperial history and postcolonial displacements.* Princeton: Princeton

University Press. · Said, E. 1978: *Orientalism*. London: Penguin (reprinted 1995). · Said, E. 1993: *Culture and imperialism*. New York: Alfred A. Knopf. · Scott, D. 1995: Colonial governmentality. *Social Text* 45: 191–215. · Thomas, N. 1994: *Colonialism's culture: anthropology, travel and government*. Cambridge: Polity. · Young, R. 1990: *White mythologies: writing History and the West*. London and New York: Routledge.

Suggested Reading

Barnett (1998). · Childs and Williams (1997), 1–25. · Jacobs (1996), 13–37. · Rattansi, A. 1997: Postcolonialism and its discontents. *Economy and Society* 26: 480–500.

post-development A term coined in the 1990s to denote both the failure of conventional post-1945 DEVELOPMENT, and the alternatives to it. The first international meeting organized under the term was held in Geneva in 1991 and involved a number of key figures in the post- or alternatives to development movement (Rist, Rahnema and Esteva, 1992). Post-development expresses the idea of development as failed MODERNITY, as a set of practices, DISCOURSES and strategies institutionalized in the multilateral development institutions which emerged after the Second World War and which have overseen the growing polarization between North and South. Development is a mirage and a hoax predicated upon development discourses which construct POVERTY and its solutions in particular ways (non-political, technocratic) (Escobar, 1995). As Rahnema puts it, 'under the banner of development and progress, a tiny minority of local profiteers and their foreign patrons ... waged war against the age-old traditions of communal solidarity' (1997, p. xi). If development consists of a set of HEGEMONIC western practices, the alternatives reside in the resistance to global CAPITALISM provided by a panoply of SOCIAL MOVEMENTS, people's organization and NGOs rooted in SUBALTERN knowledge, local forms of practice and alternative forms of livelihood (see Shiva, 1991; Sachs, 1992; Rahnema, 1997; cf. GLOBALIZATION). MW

References

Escobar, A. 1995: *Encountering development*. Princeton: Princeton University Press. · Rahnema, M., ed., 1997: *The post-development reader*. London: Zed Books. · Rist, G., Rahnema, M. and Esteva, G. 1992: *Le Nord perdu; Repères pour l'après-développement*. Lausanne: Editions d'en bas. · Sachs, W., ed., 1992: *Global ecology*. London: Zed Books. · Shiva, V. 1991: *The violence of the green revolution*. London: Zed Books.

post-Fordism A collection of workplace practices, modes of industrial organization, and institutional forms identified with the period since the mid-1970s, following the era referred to as Fordist (see FORDISM). It is characterized by the application of production methods considered to be more flexible than those of the Fordist era (see Gertler, 1988). These may include more versatile, programmable machines, labour that is more flexibly deployed (in terms of both quantity and tasks performed), vertical disintegration of large corporations (cf. INTEGRATION), greater use of inter-firm relations – such as subcontracting, strategic alliances and JUST-IN-TIME PRODUCTION – and a closer integration of product development, marketing, and production. Accompanying these changes in production and industrial organization is a new set of enabling institutions to restructure labour–management relations, labour training, competition law, and financial markets. Post-Fordism may also be conceived as a response to the CRISIS conditions that developed toward the end of the Fordist period (a rupture of the post-war compromise between owners and workers, a breaking of the link between wages and productivity gains, and a lack of balance between the aggregate productive capabilities of the economy and the aggregate purchasing power of workers as consumers). Consequently, the classic geographical pattern of economic activity associated with Fordist production (particularly the spatial separation of product development from the actual production of standardized goods) may be contrasted with a post-Fordist geography characterized by strong AGGLOMERATION tendencies, to facilitate interaction between vertically disintegrated functions.

An increasingly common alternative appearing in the geographical literature is the term 'after-Fordism'. Peck and Tickell (1994) adopt this term because, in their view, a coherent REGIME OF ACCUMULATION (in which the most important contradictions of the late Fordist period have been resolved successfully) has not yet emerged. They emphasize further that capitalist societies face a collective political choice concerning which of several possible alternative paths they wish to follow. (See FLEXIBLE ACCUMULATION; PRODUCTION COMPLEX; TRANSACTIONAL ANALYSIS.) MSG

References

Gertler, M.S. 1988: The limits to flexibility: comments on the post-Fordist vision of production and its geography. *Transactions, Institute of British Geographers* NS 13: 419–32. · Peck, J. and Tickell, A. 1994: Searching for a new institutional fix: the after-Fordist crisis and the global–local disorder. In A. Amin, ed., *Post-Fordism: a reader*. Oxford: Blackwell, 280–315.

post-industrial city A city with an employment profile focused on advanced services – that is, jobs in the professions, management, administration, and skilled technical sectors. Its profile is materialized in a downtown skyline of office towers, arts and leisure sites, and political institutions. Its middle-CLASS ambience may be reflected in a distinctive politics charged with 'a responsible social ethos . . . the demand for more amenities, for greater beauty and a better quality of life in the arrangement of our cities' (Bell, 1973, p. 367).

Against this somewhat jaunty representation, more recent research has identified the problem of income polarization in the post-industrial city, resulting from the dual LABOUR MARKET of a service economy, which includes a number of poorly paid and often racialized service workers (Mollenkopf and Castells, 1991; Waldinger, 1996; see SERVICES, GEOGRAPHY OF). The working poor and unemployed are particularly disadvantaged in a city geared to middle-class consumption, for example in the housing market, where an expanding downtown (cf. CBD), GENTRIFICATION, and inflating land values may contribute to serious problems of housing affordability.

For many authors, the post-industrial city has been used as a conceptual term without necessarily testing its empirical status on the ground (cf. Savitch, 1988). For others again, the term is used casually in a discussion of WORLD CITIES or the 'information city'. But there is evidence that the post-industrial city is an empirical object as well as a conceptual one, and that its scope extends well beyond labour market profiles. Canadian studies have shown that the gender and family characteristics of a city with a post-industrial employment profile are markedly different from those of a city whose economic base is in manufacturing, over such domains as family size, level and age of marriage, and women's income and education relative to men's (Ley, 1996). Such cities are also associated with distinctive attitudinal and cultural associations. For example, post-industrial city status is a sharper predictor of disaffiliation from mainstream religious belief than more conventional explanatory variables (Ley and Martin, 1993). This lifestyle LIBERALISM is also frequently projected into support for left-liberal political programmes; Boston, San Francisco and Seattle, cities with well-defined post-industrial identities, are also among the very few in the United States to be characterized by liberal political regimes in recent years (Stone et al., 1991). Like the thesis of POST-INDUSTRIAL SOCIETY, it seems that the intellectual possibilities of the concept of the post-industrial city are greater than was once thought. DL

References

Bell, D. 1973: *The coming of post-industrial society.* New York: Basic Books. · Ley, D. 1996: *The new middle class and the remaking of the central city.* Oxford: Oxford University Press. · Ley, D. and Martin, B. 1993: Gentrification as secularisation: the status of religious belief in the post-industrial city. *Social Compass: International Review of Sociology of Religion* 40: 217–32. · Mollenkopf, J. and Castells, M. 1991: *Dual city: restructuring New York.* New York: Russell Sage Foundation. · Savitch, H. 1988: *Post-industrial cities: politics and planning in New York, Paris and London.* Princeton, NJ: Princeton University Press. · Stone, C., Orr, M. and Imbroscio, D. 1991: The reshaping of urban leadership in U.S. cities: a regime analysis. In M. Gottdiener and C. Pickvance, eds, *Urban life in transition.* Newbury Park, CA: Sage, 222–39. · Waldinger, R. 1996: *Still the promised city? African-Americans and new immigrants in post-industrial New York.* Cambridge, MA: Harvard University Press.

post-industrial society A concept widely used, and now often lacking the specificity of its original formulation by Daniel Bell (see below). At its current and general level, post-industrial society describes an occupational transformation, noted first in the United States, toward a white-collar, service-oriented workforce in advanced nations, with specialized information (and information technology) playing a key role in the shaping of ECONOMY and SOCIETY. Some authors see the development of post-industrial society in an evolutionary context with nations passing through successive economic and social phases dominated first by the extraction of raw materials (agriculture, logging, fishing, mining), second by the processing of raw materials (manufacturing), and finally by the provision of services of a wide variety. The privileging of western, specifically American, trends in such a schema has been challenged; in addition, due to automation and increasing productivity, occupational transformation may not be followed by an equal diminution in the importance of raw materials or manufacturing in national economies (see SERVICES, GEOGRAPHY OF).

Around this basic set of propositions, there are several more or less related theoretical departures. In the early 1970s, coinciding with the initial dissemination of the concept, Alaine Touraine (1971) proposed that the holders of specialized information were becoming a *class in ascendancy*, a technocracy extending its alienating control over ever-expanding domains of everyday life. Touraine's views repeat a good deal of the intellectual and political preoccupation of the French student movement of the 1960s and its antagonism toward over-centralized and inaccessible STATE bureaucracies. In North America these antipathies were directed at the 'military-industrial complex', one of the early manifestations of private–public partnerships. The critique of the rationalization of society also has a strong tradition in German literature, and the work of Touraine's contemporaries, Habermas (1970) and Marcuse (1964), carried forward Max Weber's pessimistic portrait of the 'iron cage' of bureaucracy. A second theoretical departure discusses more centrally the emergence of a *new middle class* of professional and managerial workers who hold in common their deployment of theoretical knowledge, though, including both the intelligentsia and professionals in the private sector, they occupy several political positions and hold varying shares of economic and cultural capital (Gouldner, 1979; Bourdieu, 1984). More recently, this group has been highlighted because of its substantial contribution to new job creation over the past 25 years. Hamnett (1994) has emphasized the *professionalization* of the workforce in large European cities, and the same trend is observable in North America (Ley, 1996). In Canada, for example, the professional-managerial sector added more than 3 million jobs between 1961 and 1991 and rose from 12.6 to almost 30 per cent of all employment. The metropolitan concentration of the new middle class has led to their identification in a number of contemporary forms of urban RESTRUCTURING, and notably in GENTRIFICATION (Sassen, 1991; Ley 1996). A third theoretical departure is represented by a range of authors who have posited the pervasive part played by the generation and transmission of electronic information in advanced societies; perhaps Castells (1989, 1997) has carried the possible theoretical implications of this transition the furthest in his discussion of a society shaped by nodes and flows of information. (Cf. INFORMATION ECONOMY.)

The most influential writer on post-industrial society has been Daniel Bell (1973) who, if he did not coin the term, is certainly responsible for its wide dissemination. In an ambitious synthesis, Bell attempted to chart the forward trajectory of advanced societies, primarily the United States, in the three interlocking domains of social structure, culture and politics. Bell envisaged theoretical knowledge to be the driving force in production in post-industrial society, so that the R&D laboratory and the university became its central institutions, replacing the factory, the dominant institution of the industrial era. Moreover (and here Bell and Habermas seem to be in agreement), a knowledge theory of value replaces a LABOUR THEORY OF VALUE (cf. CRITICAL THEORY). Consequently (and its best recognized characteristic) a post-industrial society shows a tendency toward service employment and the growth of a knowledge class in the privileged professional-managerial employment sector. In the political realm, Bell both anticipated and hoped for the maturation of the public household, with a managed economy and GOVERNANCE that favoured communal rather than individualistic social policy. In contrast, in the realm of culture he was pessimistic of antinomian tendencies he identified both in the arts and in popular culture (Bell, 1976). Indeed, part of the complexity of his argument, which is too rarely observed by critics, is the disjuncture he discerns between a steadily more disciplined economy and a regressively less disciplined culture. This asymmetry extends to his own position, as he describes himself as a liberal in economics, a socialist in politics, and a conservative in culture.

The breadth and influence of Bell's treatise has inevitably attracted considerable commentary. During the 1970s much of that commentary was critical. Writers challenged his labour force projections, his optimism concerning a middle-class future, and his anxieties about the condition of American culture. He was labelled unproblematically as a neo-conservative (albeit as Habermas, 1989, observed, a neo-conservative to be taken seriously) – although it was the centralizing imperatives of neo-conservatism in the 1980s that undid both his prediction and his predilection for the public household. Nonetheless if the post-industrial thesis is a good deal more subtle than its critics often imply, Bell's original thesis, like all social theory, was also a child of its times. Published in the year that the post-war boom ended, it is written from an optimistic middle-class and western perspective, where CONFLICT and scarcity do not provide too serious a deflection of a vision of upward social mobility. Ironically, in these terms the thesis is not nearly sociological enough.

In contrast to its initial critical reception, the past decade has seen a significant rehabilitation of the post-industrial thesis and renewed respect for its breadth and foresight. Bell's frequently despised review of the state of public culture now concurs with the views of critics of the POSTMODERN condition. David Harvey, for example, finds Bell's treatment of American culture in the 1970s 'probably more accurate than many of the left attempts to grasp what was happening' (1989, p. 353). So too his labour force projections have aged far better than the opposing deskilling thesis of the 1970s favoured by Braverman, Wright and others. In a re-examination of employment data in the 1980s, Wright admitted the superiority of Bell's forecast (Wright and Martin, 1987), while a second investigation showed that in Canada during the 1961–81 period 'skilled jobs expanded at an accelerating rate', while 'a significant part of this upgrading was a result of growth in new middle-class professional and managerial occupations' (Myles, 1998). Though it may not always be credited, and its insights are far from complete, the post-industrial thesis has proven a seminal source for subsequent research; as a heuristic it is now routinely alluded to in discussions of social, economic and urban restructuring (e.g. Clement and Myles, 1994; Waldinger, 1996). (See also POST-INDUSTRIAL CITY.) DL

References

Bell, D. 1973: *The coming of post-industrial society*. New York: Basic Books. · Bell, D. 1976: *The cultural contradictions of capitalism*. New York: Basic Books. · Bourdieu, P. 1984: *Distinction*. Cambridge, MA: MIT Press. · Castells, M. 1989: *The informational city*. Oxford: Blackwell. · Castells, M. 1997: *The power of identity*. Oxford and Cambridge, MA: Blackwell. · Clement, W. and Myles, J. 1994: *Relations of ruling: class and gender in postindustrial societies*. Montreal: McGill-Queen's University Press. · Gouldner, A. 1979: *The future of intellectuals and the rise of the new class*. New York: Seabury Press. · Habermas, J. 1970: *Toward a rational society*. London: Heinemann. · Habermas, J. 1989: *The new conservatism*. Cambridge, MA: MIT Press. · Hamnett, C. 1994: Socio-economic change in London: professionalisation not polarisation. *Built Environment* 20: 192–203. · Harvey, D. 1989: *The condition of postmodernity*. Oxford: Blackwell. · Ley, D. 1996: *The new middle class and the remaking of the central city*. Oxford: Oxford University Press. · Marcuse, H. 1964: *One-dimensional man*. Boston: Beacon Press. · Myles, J. 1988: The expanding middle: some Canadian evidence on the deskilling debate. *Canadian Review of Sociology and Anthropology* 25: 335–64. · Sassen, S. 1991: *The global city: New York, London, Tokyo*. Princeton: Princeton University Press. · Touraine, A. 1971: *The post-industrial society*. New York: Random House. · Waldinger, R. 1996: *Still the promised city? African-Americans and new immigrants in post-industrial New York*. Cambridge, MA: Harvard University Press. · Wright, E. and Martin, B. 1987: The transformation of the American class structure, 1960–1980. *American Journal of Sociology* 87: 1–29.

Suggested Reading

Bell (1973).

post-Marxism This is not so much a movement or a theoretical position as a reference point for the various efforts over the last two decades to overcome what are seen by some as the debilitating limitations of 'conventional', 'traditional' or 'classical' Marxism as social theory, as politics, and as practice (see MARXIAN ECONOMICS; MARXIST GEOGRAPHY). This 'crisis of Marxism' was thrown into relief by the waning role of organized revolutionary parties in continental Europe in the 1970s and by the rise of Eurocommunism, and more recently by the collapse of state SOCIALISMS in the Soviet Union and eastern Europe. On a theoretical plane, various POST-STRUCTURALISMS associated with the work of Michel Foucault, Ernesto Laclau and Jacques Derrida – and more generally with the ascendancy of cultural studies and feminisms of many hues (Brantlinger, 1990) – have been critical of Marxism for its grand vision (its 'totalizing discourse'), for its crude economic determinism, and its CLASS reductionism. In this sense, the IDENTITY POLITICS and new SOCIAL MOVEMENTS of the 1980s, the rise of DISCOURSE theory and what Perry Anderson (1983) called the absolutization of language, and the genesis of debates within the political Left over Marxist practice (reflected, for example, in the appearance of the journal *Marxism Today* in Britain and the debate over 'New Times' and 'new true socialisms') are all part and parcel of what some see as post-Marxism and hence of a crisis of Marxism itself.

Post-Marxism is a loose, portmanteau term typically used to refer to wide-ranging debates over causality, determinism, HUMAN AGENCY and POWER from a variety of often incompatible theoretical positions (Laclau and Mouffe, 1985; Geras, 1987). A fundamental line of post-Marxist critique points to the inherent deficiencies of identifying CAPITALISM's logic or 'laws of motion'; it is, in short, a rationalist and evolutionary discourse steeped in late nineteenth-century concepts and TELEOLOGY. Marxism is thus mechanistic – history is simply a succession of stages and MODES OF PRODUCTION – and suffers from an enormous overdose of what Laclau and Mouffe (1985) call economism and class reduction. In this view, Marxism reduces the polity directly and unequivocally to the economy; Hindess and Hirst (1977) call this the 'economic monist causality of Marxism'. Booth (1985) and Corbridge (1989), for example, have launched similar critiques of Marxism and neo-Marxism as they have addressed THIRD WORLD development and DEVELOPMENT geography, emphasizing what they see as the pitfalls of capital-logic reasoning and of the epistemological weaknesses of 'rationalism and structural causality'. Efforts during the 1970s to upgrade Marxism theoretically – the project of Althusser and Balibar (1970), for example – are seen as interesting failures (see STRUCTURAL MARXISM).

Post-Marxist theory has developed in several (non-unitary) directions. First are the efforts by John Roemer, John Elster, Adam Przeworski, Pranab Bardhan and others (see Roemer, 1986; Carling, 1986) to make the philosophical and methodological basis of Marxism more rigorous scientifically (so-called *analytical Marxism*), a project which endeavours to fuse Marxism with rational choice and METHODOLOGICAL INDIVIDUALISM (see ANALYTICAL MARXISM, GEOGRAPHY AND). Second, Barry Hindess and Paul Hirst (1977), Chantal Mouffe and Ernesto Laclau (1985), Stuart Hall (1988) and others emphasize the fact that there is no necessary correspondence between economics and politics, and hence between the working class and socialism. The *relative autonomy of the political and* IDEOLOGICAL *planes* produces a concern with a multiplicity of popular struggles around universal human goals and an attendant concern with discourse and non-class practices (for example, IDENTITY POLITICS – sexuality, the environment, RACE; cf. SEXUALITY, GEOGRAPHY AND; ENVIRONMENTALISM). This post-Marxism rests, then, on a different notion of causality and on a presumption that capitalism requires conditions of existence that are not simply determined by the RELATIONS OF PRODUCTION. A third approach is associated with the so-called REGULATION SCHOOL which attempts to avoid teleology and ESSENTIALISM by focusing on meso-level concepts, and in particular on the historically specific institutional configurations of capital, labour and the STATE which give rise to distinctive, but unstable, regimes of accumulation (Lipietz, 1987). A confluence between regulation theory – and its concerns with forms of institutional compromise – and convention theory (Boltanski and Thevenot, 1991) has produced some interesting post-Marxist explorations in the field of industrial and economic organization (Boyer and Allaire, 1995; Salais and Storper, 1997).

Corbridge (1989) has, with a very substantial number of caveats, attempted to outline the lineaments of post-Marxism. It shares with classical Marxism a 'materialist ontology', a commitment to causal analysis and to a concept of determination. But it departs from this tradition insofar as it rejects the idea of exclusivism, in other words that Marxism is epistemologically privileged and that primacy must be lent to the economic. Opposed to FUNCTIONALIST accounts of power, the state and CIVIL SOCIETY, post-Marxism draws insights from non-Marxism (feminism, discourse theory, neo-Weberianism) and wishes to advance Marxism in terms of a compelling scientific methodology.

The 'crisis of Marxism' approach has naturally produced an enormous, wide-ranging and at times abusive debate. For Geras (1987), Anderson (1983), and Wood (1986), the post-Marxism of Laclau and Mouffe represents a vast misreading of the textured and open-ended tradition of Marxist theory, and installs in its place a world of contingent discourses, slippery causality, in short a social science without necessity or reason. A post-Marxist world rests, as Perry Anderson (1983) put it, on a foundation without a vantage point. In much of the acrimonious debate, there has often been a great deal of heat but little light and a tendency to vastly simplify and caricature both classical Marxism and post-Marxisms. What needs to be emphasized is the following:

First, the so-called crisis of Marxism, for better or worse, is part of a larger intellectual landscape of the crisis of Grand Theory – 'a crisis of REPRESENTATION' – which speaks to the rise more generally of a POSTMODERN sensibility (Harvey, 1989). The crisis of Marxism in this view, like other grand theories, is deeply flawed by its totalizing framework, its dogma and its canonic terminology (Fischer and Marcus, 1986).

Second, to the extent that post-Marxism is a catch-all for the important debates, in- and outside of Marxism, over causality, EPISTEMOLOGY, determination and so on, one should be very wary of assuming that post-Marxism has any theoretical unity whatsoever (or indeed that it signifies the end of anything).

Third, and most crucially, the 'crisis talk' is not a recent phenomenon in Marxism but, as Althusser noted long ago, the very history of Marxism is a long succession of crises and transformations. Indeed, one of the strengths of Marxism is that it can be seen historically as a research enterprise which has expanded and deepened its core theoretical postulates through successive problem-solving innovations driven by the anomalies and practical problems it has been compelled to address. The tradition of theorizing from Marx to Luxemburg to Lenin to Trotsky to Gramsci represents a series of 'crises' in which post-Marxisms have arisen from the debates of specific historical conjunctures (Watts, 1988). CRISIS does not mean collapse and death but signals the liberation of something vital and alive. Almost a decade after the fall of the Berlin Wall and the devastation wrought by two decades of high NEO-LIBERALISM, there are signs of some sort of rejuvenation of Marxism which has witnessed none other than Jacques Derrida (1997) – the high guru of deconstructionism – call for the centrality of Marx in social theory (see also Gibson-Graham, 1996).

References

Althusser, L. and Balibar, E. 1970: *Reading capital*. London: Verso. · Anderson, P. 1983: *In the tracks of historical materialism*. London: Verso. · Aronson, D. 1996: *After Marxism*. New York: Guilford. · Boltanski, L. and Thevenot, L. 1991: *De la justification*. Paris: Gallimard. · Booth, D. 1985: Marxism and development sociology: interpreting the impasse. *World Development* 13: 761–87. · Boyer, R. and Allaire, G., eds, 1995: *La grande transformation*. Paris: Institute Nationale de Recherche Agronomique (INRA). · Brantlinger, P. 1990: *Crusoe's footprints: cultural studies in Britain and America*. London: Routledge. · Carling, A. 1986: Rational choice Marxism. *New Left Review* 160: 24–62. · Corbridge, S. 1989: Marxism, post-Marxism and the geography of development. In R. Peet and N. Thrift, eds, *New models in geography*, volume 1. London: Unwin Hyman, 224–56. · Derrida, J. 1997: *Specters of Marx*. London: Routledge. · Fischer, M. and Marcus, G. 1986: *Anthropology as cultural critique: an experimental moment in the human sciences*. Chicago: University of Chicago Press. · Geras, N. 1987: Post-Marxism? *New Left Review* 163: 40–82. · Gibson-Graham, K. 1996: The end of capitalism (as we knew it). Oxford: Blackwell. · Hall, S. 1985: Authoritarian populism. *New Left Review* 151: 110–25. · Hall, S. 1988: The toad in the garden. In C. Nelson and L. Grossberg, eds, *Marxism and the interpretation of culture*. Urbana: University of Illinois Press, 35–7. ·Harvey, D. 1989: *The condition of postmodernity*. Oxford: Blackwell. · Hindess, B. and Hirst, P. 1977: *Mode of production and social formation*. London: Macmillan. · Laclau, E. and Mouffe, C. 1985: *Hegemony and socialist strategy*. London: Verso. · Lipietz, A. 1987: *Mirages and miracles: the crisis of global Fordism*. London: Verso. · Roemer, J., ed., 1986: *Analytical Marxism*. Cambridge: Cambridge University Press. · Salais, M. and Storper, M. 1997: *Worlds of production*. Cambridge, MA: Harvard University Press. · Watts, M. 1988: Deconstructing determinism. *Antipode* 20/2: 142–68. · Wood, E. 1986: *The retreat from class: a new 'true' socialism*. London: Verso.

Suggested Reading

Aronson (1996) Callinicos, A. 1989: *Against postmodernism: a Marxist critique*. Cambridge: Polity Press. · Elliot, G. 1987: *Althusser: the detour of theory*. London: Verso. · Jameson, F. 1990: *Late Marxism*. London: Verso. · McCarney, J. 1990: *Social theory and the crisis of Marxism*. London: Verso.

postmaterialism A term coined by Inglehart (1977) for societies in which there has been a 'cultural shift' in political attitudes away from issues of production and distribution. The combination of affluence and a strong WELFARE STATE erodes the salience of CLASS-based politics (see CLEAVAGE), which are replaced by approaches reflecting environmental concerns along with what Inglehart terms 'orientations towards work, fertility, and consumption patterns'. RJJ

Reference

Inglehart, R. 1977: *The silent revolution: changing values and political styles*. Princeton, NJ: Princeton University Press.

Suggested Reading

Inglehart, R. 1997: *Modernisation and postmodernisation: cultural, economic and political change in 43 societies*. Princeton, NJ: Princeton University Press.

postmodernism A movement in philosophy, the arts, and the social sciences characterized by scepticism towards the grand claims and GRAND THEORY of the modern era with its privileged EPISTEMOLOGICAL vantage point for the artist, theorist, or observer (decried by Rorty as the God's eye view), and bearing an equal suspicion of changeless, foundational relationships that escape the contingencies of time and SPACE (cf. FOUNDATIONALISM). Instead, interpretations and the authority of the observer are regarded as socially constituted, contingent, and partial, so that postmodern positions stress an openness to a range of voices and perspectives in social inquiry, artistic experimentation, and political empowerment (Lyotard, 1984). PLURALISM, then, is endemic to postmodernism, and the term is often used generically to refer loosely to a series of more specific perspectives (such as POST-STRUCTURALISM, POST-COLONIALISM, and even feminism; see FEMINIST GEOGRAPHIES) that share these anti-foundational features. Consequently, while this much may be said, there is agreement about little else (though for classificatory attempts, see Hassan, 1985, and Jencks, 1993). The babble of voices around postmodernism is also intensified by the extraordinary disciplinary reach of the movement, ranging through philosophy, theology, the arts, and the social sciences. Indeed there is even a postmodern position in such apparently rational enlightenment fields as accounting and CARTOGRAPHY.

Nor in some fields is the break between modern and postmodern genres all that clear (cf. MODERNISM). If collage, for example, is a central feature of postmodernism as many in the arts assert (citing, perhaps, the works of David Salle) then it is salient to recall that collage was also part of the experimentation of the modern avant garde (Kern, 1983; Pred, 1995). So too the collision of disparate elements in postmodern pastiche is calculated to impart the same strangeness to the familiar as was attempted by the modern tactic of defamiliarization. Even the stability of a fixed perspective, a God's eye view, was disrupted in the perspectival pluralism of the cubists. A fixation with these and other lines of continuity (for example a constant sense of disorientation before rapid change, cited by Berman, 1982) have led some theorists to deny any significant break between modernism and postmodernism.

But fixing upon other dimensions, the discontinuities come into focus. Dear (1986) classifies postmodernism into three components: style, method, and epoch (for which see POSTMODERNITY). In *style*, architecture has become the PARADIGMATIC art, and is often a point of departure in discussions of postmodernism more generally, if only because its forms are both visible and public (Jameson, 1984). Postmodern architecture commonly shows some combination of the following features: it should be contextual, reflecting regional traditions and perhaps the forms of adjacent buildings; it should be at a human scale, or if a necessarily large structure, should show a sympathetic frontage to the street, with its bulk broken into diverse forms and surfaces; it should pay attention to social life and the needs of users, even including them in the design process; it should include a recognizable symbolic content to confirm local memories and identities; and decoration should be part of its aesthetic programme (Ley, 1993; Ellin, 1996). In these features there would be a conscious rejection of the abstraction, universalism, and historical erasure brought to architecture and design by the modern movement.

There has been much controversy around the qualities of such an architecture. Some critics, enamoured perhaps by Le Corbusier's battle cry, 'architecture or revolution', have expected more of architecture than it can possibly deliver. Others have forgotten that virtue does not rest in forms alone but also in the intentions that animate them. Like all innovation, postmodern styles can move through the creative phase of invention to the much blander stage of mimicry and duplication. So too, as has long been recognized, good ideas may be subverted to less noble ends, a fate of much architecture during the entrepreneurial years of the 1980s and 1990s with their celebration of consumer CULTURE, even if these structures were sometimes approached with a sense of parody – as in the suburban box stores designed by the New York-based site team. Postmodernism, then, includes examples that are both accommodating and critical of existing patterns of URBANISM, though interestingly this diversity is rarely recognized by critics, who, both on the political Right and the Left, defensive of their own grand narratives, commonly engage in undifferentiated search and destroy missions. Symptomatic of the approach from the Left is Harvey's (1989) rejection of postmodern culture as an art of surfaces that simply masks a more fundamental POLITICAL ECONOMY. In response, Deutsche (1996) has demonstrated how the work of some postmodern artists is not a reflection of surfaces but an interrogation of them. Cindy Sherman's generic images of women, far from upholding superficial stereotypes, challenge the very act of social construction that reduces subjects to limited social roles. One can see the same attention to a more fluid and contingent treatment of identity in such authors as Margaret Atwood or Michael Ondaatje (Hutcheon, 1991).

Constructionism is also at the heart of the second of Dear's categories, postmodern *method*. The recognition that reality, including knowledge, is a social product achieved by subjects with distinctive subject positions, encourages a strategy of deconstruction, a mode of critical interpretation that seeks to demonstrate how the (multiple) positioning of an author (or reader) in terms of CLASS, CULTURE, RACE, GENDER, etc. has influenced the writing (and reading) of a TEXT (cf. POSITIONALITY). The destabilization of meaning, of fixed interpretations, throws into doubt both the ONTOLOGICAL certitude of reality and also the authority claims of interpreters. Positively, it prises loose alternative readings of texts, whether these take the form of literature, cartography, or LANDSCAPES. In human geography, Olsson (1980, 1991) was the earliest exponent of deconstruction and remains its most innovative and skilful practitioner. However, negatively, Olsson's work also shows the methodological weaknesses of a RELATIVISM that knows few limits. Given the uncertain (or at least contingent) ground upon which the observer stands, the scholar's claim to provide an adequate understanding of other people and places must be slender indeed. This crisis of representation has been a major concern in recent theoretical writing on ETHNOGRAPHY (Clifford, 1988), and has given rise to the notion of ethnographies as fictions, that is, productions in which are embedded the unseen subjectivities of the author. How then does it become possible to represent the OTHER when the shaping of that representation is so utterly contaminated by the author's own socialization?

It is at this stage that the epistemological challenges of postmodernism's radical perspectivalism become for many intolerable, and perhaps untenable. Radical perspectivalism or the strong constructionist programme appears to lead to an intellectual dead end, where entrapment within a socially constructed world allows little confidence in reaching beyond its borders for understanding (cf. Barnes, 1996). In this (over)socialized domain, the closure effected by internalized actions, VALUES and (especially) LANGUAGE refutes any meaningful knowledge of the other and thus also any meaningful politics. The strong programme may also encourage, ironically, its own ESSENTIALISM with attributes assigned to 'all men' or 'all gays' or 'all whites' on the basis of a single socialized standpoint. Bonnett (1996), for example, has identified this serious weakness in a number of anti-racist sources that, in their eagerness to expose RACISM, duplicate the mind of the racist in ascribing invariant characteristics to the homogeneous category of whiteness. The limitations of strong constructionism have been recognized by many authors, some of whom prefer a weak constructionism, much closer to the historic position of HERMENEUTICS. For while hermeneutics acknowledges the collision between the author and the data as an inescapable element in the production of knowledge, it is a realization that generates not paralysis but a series of best practices to limit and contain authorial distortions. This weaker position recognizes both the materiality and contingency of the world and readings of it; however, for foundationalists even the weaker form can be a betrayal of both science and politics (cf. Yapa, 1996, 1997; Shrestha, 1997). DL

References

Barnes, T. 1996: *Logics of dislocation*. New York: Guilford. · Berman, M. 1982: *All that is solid melts into air: the experience of modernity*. New York: Simon and Schuster. · Bonnett, A. 1996: Anti-racism and the critique of white identities. *New Community* 22: 97–110. · Clifford, J. 1988: *The predicament of culture*. Cambridge, MA: Harvard University Press. · Dear, M. 1986: Postmodernism and planning. *Environment and Planning D: Society and Space* 4: 367–84. · Deutsche, R. 1996: *Evictions: art and spatial politics*. Cambridge, MA: MIT Press. · Ellin, N. 1996: *Postmodern urbanism*. Cambridge, MA: Blackwell. · Harvey, D. 1989: *The condition of postmodernity*. Oxford: Blackwell. · Hassan, I. 1985: The culture of postmodernism. *Theory, Culture and Society* 2(3): 119–32. · Hutcheon, L. 1991: *Splitting images: contemporary Canadian ironies*. Toronto: Oxford University Press. · Jameson, F. 1984: Postmodernism, or the cultural logic of late capitalism. *New Left Review* 146: 53–92. · Jencks, C. 1987: *What is postmodernism?* New York: St. Martin's Press. · Jencks, C., ed., 1992: *The postmodern reader*. London: Academy Editions. · Kern, S. 1983: *The culture of time and space 1880–1918*. Cambridge, MA: Harvard University Press. · Ley, D. 1993: Co-operative housing as a moral landscape: re-examining 'the post-modern city'. In J. Duncan and D. Ley, eds, *Place/culture/representation*. London: Routledge, 128–48. · Ley, D. and Mills, C. 1992: Can there be a postmodernism of resistance in the urban landscape? In P. Knox, ed., *The restless urban landscape*. Englewood Cliffs, NJ: Prentice-Hall, 255–78. · Lyotard, J. 1984: *The postmodern condition*. Minneapolis: University of Minnesota Press. · Olsson, G. 1980: *Birds in egg: eggs in bird*. London: Pion. · Olsson, G. 1991: *Lines of power/limits of language*. Minneapolis: University of Minnesota Press. · Pred, A. 1995: *Recognizing European modernities: a montage of the present*. New York: Routledge. · Shrestha, N. 1997: A postmodern view or denial of historical integrity? The poverty of Yapa's view of poverty. *Annals of the Association of American Geographers* 87: 709–16. · Yapa, L. 1996: What causes poverty? A postmodern view. *Annals of the Association of American Geographers* 86: 707–28. · Yapa, L. 1997: Reply: why discourse matters, materially. *Annals of the Association of American Geographers* 87: 717–22.

Suggested Reading

Best, S. and Kellner, D., eds, 1991: *Postmodern theory: critical interrogations*. New York: Guilford. · Harvey (1989). · Jencks (1992). · Ley and Mills (1992). · Relph, E. 1987: *The modern urban landscape*. Baltimore: Johns Hopkins University Press. · Rosenau, P. 1992: *Post-modernism and the social sciences*. Princeton, NJ: Princeton University Press.

postmodernity In contrast to POSTMODERNISM, postmodernity is usually regarded as the historic period when the social and economic processes associated with the postmodern turn have taken place. For a number of authors this periodization goes on to include its own content, so that postmodernity becomes not just an era but also the shorthand for the dominant processes of that period writ large in SOCIETY and SPACE. David Lyon, for example, writes 'Postmodernity ... has to do with putative social changes. Either a new kind of society is coming into being, whose contours can already be dimly perceived, or a new stage of CAPITALISM is being inaugurated' (Lyon, 1994, p. 7). In his controversial interpretation, David Harvey selects the latter option: the condition of postmodernity is explained as the social and cultural forms flowing directly from the 'CRISIS of overaccumulation' in the capitalist economy that came to a head in 1973 (Harvey, 1989, pp. 327–8). About timing there is more general agreement; Jencks (1984) dates the rise of an aesthetic postmodernism in architecture to the disillusionment with modern URBANISM symbolized by the demolition of the Pruitt-Igoe housing complex in St. Louis in 1972, a project built in the post-war idiom of high modernism and celebrated as such with awards upon its construction in the 1950s. The postmodern period, then, was born during the decade between 1965 and 1975.

What are the 'putative social changes' of the postmodern era? Undoubtedly there are some linkages here with other transition theories, notably POST-FORDISM and that of POST-INDUSTRIAL SOCIETY (Rose, 1991; Ley, 1996). For example, if both FORDISM and MODERNISM extolled the mass production factory as the 'spirit of the age', both POST-FORDISM, with its emphasis on the fragmentation of the mass market into niches, and postmodernism with its emphasis on the consumer, including Baudrillard's (1975) insights on the production of consumption, have reversed that emphasis. There are also clear links with Bell's view of the role of specialized information in post-industrial society and the postmodern emphasis upon electronic communication (Lyotard, 1984; Lyon, 1994). However, the most persistent theme in the literature is the creation of an image society, where style, fashion, the simulacrum, the SPECTACLE, all point to an ephemeral world of mirrors and deceits, of unredeemable lightness and insubstantial surfaces. For most authors, whatever their theoretical perspective, the culture of CONSUMPTION is the central motif of postmodernity, and the world of Disney is its most exemplary expression (Harvey, 1989; Featherstone, 1991; Lyon, 1994). From this interpretation, we can readily understand also the recent fixation with CULTURE – in all its forms – in shaping urban LANDSCAPES. Together these elements help assemble the outline of postmodern urbanism, a condition that several authors have located unambiguously in Los Angeles (Soja, 1996; Dear and Flusty, 1998).

From here some authors move toward a fatalism where identities are shaped by the spin doctors of marketing and the media. But there may well be too much of an Anglocentricity in such a view. Reacting against the North American view of a pervasive neo-conservatism, continental European writers have noted the continuity of the WELFARE STATE, if in weakened form, in many countries of western Europe, introducing a more plural ideological armature to the postmodern era than the free market alone is willing to support. Indeed, in eastern Europe, the postmodern era is contrasted with the severe MODERNITY of the Soviet empire. The DEMOCRACY movements at the end of the 1980s, dissolving a particularly inflexible iron cage where STATE brutalism took many forms, introduce an entirely different symbolic content to postmodernity. They perhaps point to a more generalized movement concerned to introduce individual autonomy and semantic thickness over against a modernity that suffered from a poverty of meaning and that justified individual oppressions through an ontology of the masses. Of course the culture of consumption represents a singular distortion of that movement, where individualism means freedom to consume and meaning is reduced to the symbolism of the product. But in the rush to condemn consumer society, we should not reduce postmodernity to a discursive monologue, nor ignore the lessons of its own geographical differentiation (Ley, 1996). Resistant forms of postmodernity bear more careful theoretical, as well as political, examination, pointing as they do to a widely felt deficit of meaning and emancipation in the modern project.

DL

References

Baudrillard, J. 1975: *The mirror of production*. St. Louis: Telos Press. · Dear, M. and Flusty, S. 1998: Postmodern urbanism. *Annals of the Association of American Geographers* 88: 50–72. · Featherstone, M. 1991: *Consumer culture and postmodernism*. Beverly Hills, CA: Sage. · Harvey, D. 1989: *The condition of postmodernity*. Oxford: Blackwell. · Jencks, C. 1984: *The language of post-modern architecture*. New York: Rizzoli. · Ley, D. 1996: *The new middle class and the remaking of the central city*. Oxford: Oxford University Press. · Lyotard, J. 1984: *The postmodern condition*. Minneapolis: University of Minnesota Press. · Lyon, D. 1994: *Postmodernity*. Minneapolis: University of Minnesota Press. · Rose, M. 1991: *The postmodern and the postindustrial: a critical analysis*. Cambridge: Cambridge University Press. · Soja, E. 1996: *Thirdspace: journeys to Los Angeles and other real-and-imagined places*. Oxford and Cambridge, MA: Blackwell.

Suggested Reading

Lyon (1994).

post-Soviet states Those STATES which emerged from the geopolitical disintegration of the Soviet Union in 1991. They comprise Russia, the south-western borderland states (Ukraine, Belarus, Moldova), the Baltic republics (Estonia, Latvia, Lithuania), and the post-Soviet south (Azerbaijan, Armenia,

Georgia, Kazakstan, Kyrgyzstan, Tajikistan, Turkmenistan, Uzbekistan). Their geographical transformation has tended to be viewed through the prism of *transition theory*. However, any understanding of what the post-Soviet states are in transition to must recognize three things. First, contrary to a number of theories, their transition to either or both of CAPITALISM and DEMOCRACY should not be considered as predetermined or automatic. Secondly, it is important to acknowledge that any understanding of the post-Soviet transition must first examine where they have come from (see SOCIALISM). And finally, we need to recognize that they are not necessarily all travelling in the same path: they are in effect assuming multiple trajectories.

Accordingly, the post-Soviet transition can be best considered as part of a fourfold process (Smith, 1999).

First, *DECOLONIZATION* (the transition from COLONIALISM to POST-COLONIALISM). While there is considerable debate as to whether the Soviet Union constituted an empire, there is little doubt that for the post-Soviet borderland states, their supposed status as colonies of a Russian-dominated Soviet Union continues to inform their attitudes and policies towards Russia and in particular towards the large Russian DIASPORA located throughout the borderland states. As Brubaker (1996) has also noted, although having secured NATION-STATEHOOD in 1991, to varying degrees the new titular NATIONS in power in these borderland states aspire to create political homelands in which the titular language, CULTURE and people are elevated to a central place (see NATIONALISM). In contrast, for Russians, the relationship between establishing a post-colonial IDENTITY is complicated by their identification association with the legacy of being part of a bigger homeland, the Soviet Union and earlier the former tsarist empire. Crudely put, for Russians the choice of identity is often seen as between focusing either on democratic state-building or on empire rebuilding, the latter including the re-colonization of the post-Soviet borderlands.

Second, *democratization* (the transition from totalitarian to post-totalitarian rule). While the post-Soviet states have all made the successful transition from the highly centralized totalitarian state that was the Soviet Union, some are in the process of establishing proto-democracies by taking on the features usually associated with the western democratic state (e.g. Baltic states, Ukraine), while others have slid with relative ease into authoritarian forms of GOVERNANCE (e.g. many of the post-Soviet states of the south).

Thirdly, *economic liberalization* ('from Marx to the Market'). Moving from state ownership of the means of production and a centrally planned economy (cf. CENTRAL PLANNING) towards introducing price liberalization, the de-nationalization of former state-owned economic enterprises (see PRIVATIZATION), the end of the state monopoly over trade and of securing new property rights for citizens (cf. CITIZENSHIP), continues to be fraught with problems, not least in terms of social dislocation, and of the way in which crime syndicates have seized upon the opportunities of change to challenge the rule of law.

Finally, GLOBALIZATION (from exclusion to inclusion within the world economy). As Przeworski (1995) has noted, while the Soviet regime pursued a policy of *MODERNIZATION without internationalization*, the post-Soviet states are all to varying degrees committed to pursing paths towards *modernization via internationalization*. Besides having to compete as late entrants on the margins of the world economy, other globalizing processes are also shaping their economies, polities and societies as a result of the liberalization of international trade, foreign investment and more liberal methods of policing state borders. GES

References and Suggested Reading

Aarnason, J. 1993: *The future that failed. Origins and destinies of the Soviet model.* London: Routledge. · Bradshaw, M., ed., 1997: *Geography and transition in the post-Soviet republics.* London: Wiley. · Brubaker, R. 1996: *Nationalism reframed.* Cambridge: Cambridge University, Press. · Dawisha, K. and Parrot, B. 1994: *Russia and the new states of Eurasia: the politics of upheaval.* Cambridge: Cambridge University Press. · Elster, J., Offe, C. and Preuss, U. 1998: *Institutional design in Post-Communist Societies. Rebuilding the ship at sea.* Cambridge: Cambridge University Press. · Pickles, A. and Smith, A., eds, 1998: *Theorising transition: the political economy of post-communist transformation.* London: Routledge. · Przeworski, A. 1995: *Sustainable democracy.* Cambridge: Cambridge University Press. · Rubin, B. and Snyder, J. 1998: *Post-Soviet political order. Conflict and state-building.* London: Routledge. · Smith, G.E., ed., 1996: *The nationalities question in the post-Soviet states,* 2nd edn. London: Longman. · Smith, G.E. 1999: *The post-Soviet states. Mapping the politics of transition.* London: Arnold. · Smith, G.E., Law, V., Wilson, A. and Bohr, A. 1998: *Nation-building in the post-Soviet Borderlands. The politics of national identities.* Cambridge: Cambridge University Press. · Starvakis, P., De-Bardeleben, J. and Black, J., eds, 1997: *Beyond the monolith: the emergence of regionalism in Post-Soviet Russia.* Baltimore and London: Johns Hopkins University Press. · Webber, M. 1996: *The international politics of Russia and the successor states.* Manchester: Manchester University Press.

post-structuralism A term used most commonly in English-speaking countries since the early 1970s to draw a line of affinity around several French theorists who may themselves (have) reject(ed) the designation; this group includes Derrida, Lacan, Foucault, Deleuze, Baudrillard, Lyotard and Kristeva. In Poster's (1989) view, the validity of the term post-structuralism derives from the fact that these thinkers were all influenced by and rejected the formalism of structuralist linguistics and its (at least implicit) epistemological subject. In addition, they all first adhered to Marxist theory of one variety or another and later wrote in opposition to the French Communist Party. The chronological marker ('post') is, however, complicated by the complex relationship between post-structuralist, pre-structuralist (especially Hegel, Husserl, Heidegger, Freud, Marx, and Nietzsche) and structuralist thought.

Post-structuralists draw on and extend important insights of STRUCTURALISM, especially (a) Saussurian linguistics and (b) Althusser's critique of the humanist subject.

(a) *Language is seen as the medium for defining and contesting social organization and subjectivity.* Saussure is credited with the understanding that meaning is produced within rather than reflected through LANGUAGE; language is therefore constitutive rather than reflective of social reality. He argued that there is no necessary fixed relation between signifier (sound or written image) and signified (the concept it serves to evoke). The meaning of a signifier is derived from its difference from and relation to other signifiers; IDENTITY is created through DIFFERENCE.

(b) Post-structuralists also helped to formulate and absorb *an anti-humanist critique of a unified, knowing and rational subject*, instead interpreting subjectivity as continually in process, as a site of disunity, conflict, and contradictions, and hence potential political change (see ANTI-HUMANISM; see Gregory, 1997, for Althusser's debts to Lacan). They diverge from Althusser in seeing the production of subjectivity as a discursive rather than ideological effect. The distinction is an important one: while Althusser represented his critique of the subject as a scientific exposé (and thus never broke fully with the humanist knowing subject), post-structuralist writers maintain that there is no 'real' outside of cultural systems. The subject is thus rid of the last traces of ESSENTIALISM; a real or essential CLASS consciousness is no longer anticipated on the basis of an individual's material conditions.

In different ways, post-structural thinkers opened up to contingency and indeterminacy what had been conceived as relatively closed (although not static) linguistic, economic and social systems. In literary theory, structuralism had refocused analysis away from the intentionality of the author but then stabilized meaning construction within the TEXT; by calling attention to the multiplicity and indeterminacy of reader interpretations, Barthes released the text from this interpretative closure. By arguing that meaning is never fully present but emerges from undecidable presence–absence, Derrida foregrounded the instability of language. Foucault's historical analyses of POWER as networks of local power relations, and DISCOURSE as polyvalent and productive, had the same effect on social theory, as did Lacan's concept of libidinal instability (see PSYCHOANALYTIC THEORY, GEOGRAPHY AND) and Deleuze's release of the production of desire from the Oedipal narrative, re-conceptualized by Deleuze as incessant flux.

A second characteristic of post-structuralist theorizing is its anti-foundationalism; theories of language and the subject were turned onto the production of truth and knowledge itself. Different post-structural thinkers have different targets of knowledge production: for Baudrillard, the media; Foucault, the human sciences and the state; Derrida, the western philosophical tradition. Derrida criticizes western philosophy for its logocentricism (see MASCULINISM and PHALLOCENTRICISM). He argues that our beliefs in reason are built through a series of unequally valued binaries (e.g. mind/body, literal/metaphorical, man/woman, positive/negative); the first term assumes priority and the second, inferior, term 'marks a fall' and is conceived in relation to the former as 'a complication, a negative, a manifestation, or a disruption of the first' (Culler, 1983, p. 93). Derrida's method of DECONSTRUCTION involves demonstrating that presence (the priorized term) requires the absent (inferior) term. Post-structuralists thus expose the foundations and limits of theory, and the extent to which western reason is associated with a subject configured as autonomous and implicitly male (and western). Theory and claims to truth regulate the terms of reality; as systems of regulation they are enmeshed in relations of power and domination.

This forces self-contextualization and reflexivity onto the post-structuralist theorist, in an effort to understand the will to power behind and within his or her own truth claims. Truth, as a thoroughly social process, as a medium and effect of a truth/power regime, loses its foundational status and its capacity to ground politics (see EPISTEMOLOGY). The challenge for the theorist is to generate a discourse 'whose power effects are limited as much as possible to the subversion of power' (Poster, 1989, p. 30). Foucault thus generated his discourses about the proliferation of excluded and marginalized subjects (e.g. the pervert, the insane, the homosexual, the hysterical woman) to clarify the positions of the oppressed, but refrained from laying down a political programme. (His troubled relations with feminists in part reflect this difference in epistemology, along with his related refusal of the categories of gender or sexualized crime – i.e. rape.) In their own texts, post-structuralists attempt to instantiate a non-oppressive politics by avoiding characteristics of logocentric texts: they avoid interpretive closure, unsettle categories, resist binary oppositions (in their own formulations and in their engagement with other theories), and explore new connective modes of theorizing (see ACTOR–NETWORK THEORY; NON-REPRESENTATIONAL THEORY; RHIZOME). Whether these interpretative strategies are effective (and whether they are political) are matters of debate (see Morris, 1996, on the necessity of contextualizing an opposition to binaries). Post-structuralists negotiate the charge of relativism, sometimes through the concept of SITUATED KNOWLEDGE.

Epistemological and anti-ontological concerns of post-structuralists flow into substantive analyses; we can see their influence in the topics that geographers have chosen to study in the 1980s and 1990s. Critiques of categories and binaries have led to intense interest in boundary formation and a revaluing of undervalued terms in oppositional binaries – for example: the animal (Wolch and Emel, 1995); the emotional (Rose, 1993); and the body (see BODY, GEOGRAPHY AND). Rejection of the humanist subject has directed attention to processes of subject formation (see SUBJECT FORMATION, GEOGRAPHIES OF), to both boundary formation and identification (see GENDER AND GEOGRAPHY; RACE) and processes of disruption (e.g. across the male/female, hetero-sexual/homosexual, human/animal, body/machine, and NATURE/CULTURE divides; see PERFORMATIVITY; QUEER THEORY; SEXUALITY, GEOGRAPHY AND).

A post-structuralist understanding that conceptualization both frames and regulates social reality – literally brings reality into being – profoundly disrupts the distinction between REPRESENTATION and a pre-discursive reality. Post-structuralists are sometimes criticized for reducing the world to language, but this misses the messiness of the relations they posit between the material and discursive, which are seen as fully imbricated, one in the other (see DISCOURSE). This has immense implications for our understanding of time and space (see POSTMODERNISM). Poster (1989, p. 9) remarks that 'linearity and causality are the spatial and temporal orderings of a now-bypassed modern era', an era when individuals believed in a stable world that existed apart from representations of it. 'Today language increasingly intervenes in a different configuration, which resists linear and causal framing. Words in our culture shamelessly point to themselves, like television newscasters who brashly admit their role in shaping the news, not simply repeating it. This self-referentiality of signs upsets the representational model of language' (Poster, 1989, p. 10). It also upsets representations of SPACE and CARTOGRAPHY (see IMAGINATIVE GEOGRAPHIES; VISION AND VISUALITY; also Natter and Jones, 1993; Gregory, 1994; Doel, 1999). This has provoked an examination of the world-making capacities of cartographies that fashion fragments into coherent, exclusionary visual narratives (Harley, 1989; Gregory, 1994; Sparke, 1998), and to a fuller appreciation of the PRODUCTION OF SPACE as a social process and to the SPATIALITY of social life, from the constitution of the individual subject to international geopolitics (Smith, 1993). Geographers influenced by post-structural theory strive to produce new cartographies and ways of writing (e.g. Massey, 1997; Pred, 1997). GP

References

Culler, J. 1983: *On deconstruction: theory and criticism after structuralism*. London: Routledge and Kegan Paul. · Doel, M. 1999: *Poststructuralist geographies: The diabolical art of spatial science*. Edinburgh: Edinburgh University Press. · Gregory, D. 1994: *Geographical imaginations*. Oxford and Cambridge, MA: Blackwelll. · Gregory, D. 1997: Lacan and geography: the production of space revisited. In G. Benko and U. Strohmayer, eds, *Space and social theory: interpreting modernity and post-modernity*. Oxford and Cambridge, MA: Blackwell, 203–311. · Harley, B. 1989: Deconstructing the map. *Cartographica* 26: 1–201. · Massey, D. 1997: Spatial disruptions. In S. Golding, ed., *The eight technologies of otherness*. London: Routledge, 218–251. · Morris, M. 1996: Crazy talk is not enough. *Environment and Planning D: Society and Space* 14: 384–941. · Natter, W. and J.P. Jones III 1993: Signposts toward a poststructuralist geography. In J.P. Jones III, W. Natter and T.R. Schatzki, eds, *Post-modern contentions: epochs, politics, space*. New York: Guilford, 165–2031. · Poster, M. 1989: *Critical theory and post-structuralism: in search of a context*. Ithaca: Cornell University Pressl. · Pred, A. 1997: Re-Presenting the extended present moment of danger: a meditation on hypermodernity, identity and the montage form. In G. Benko and U. Strohmayer, eds, *Social theory: interpreting modernity and postmodernity*. Oxford and Cambridge, MA: Blackwell, 117–40l. · Rose, G. 1993: *Feminism and geography*. Oxford: Polity Pressl. · Minneapolis: University of Minnesota Pressl. · Smith, N. 1993: Homeless/global: scaling places. In J. Bird, B. Curtis, T. Putnam, G. Robertson and L. Tickner, eds, *Mapping the futures: local cultures, global change*. London: Routledge, 87–119l. · Sparke, M. 1998: Mapped bodies and disembodied maps: (dis)placing cartographic struggle in colonial Canada. In H. Nast and S. Pile, eds, *Places through the body*. London: Routledge, 305–36l. · Wolch, J. and Emel, J. 1995. Bring the animals back in. *Environment and Planning D: Society and Space* 13: 632–6.

Suggested Reading

Best, S. and Kellner, D. 1991: *Postmodern theory: critical interrogations*. New York: Guilford. · Sarup, M. 1993: *Introductory guide to post-structuralism and postmodernism*. Athens, GA: University of Georgia Press.

poverty gap Poverty is conventionally measured in terms of an Absolute Poverty Line expressed in monetary terms: it is the income or expenditure below which a minimum nutritionally adequate diet plus essential non-food requirements are no longer affordable (for example spending per capita of less than US$1.00 per day which is the World Bank absolute poverty line). A poverty line distinguishes, then, the poor from the non-poor (Ravallion, 1995; UNDP, 1998). Poverty estimates are typically based on data from actual household budget or income/expenditure surveys. In this way a proportion of a country's population or an absolute number of persons or households can be designated as living in absolute poverty; this is the *Head Count Index*. Currently, for example, it is estimated that 47 per cent of the population of Yemen live in absolute poverty. Using this absolute poverty line it is possible to calculate what proportion of the GDP of a country would be required to lift those in absolute poverty above the poverty line (i.e. what proportion of Nigeria's GDP will it require to lift the millions who are absolutely poor to a condition in which their basic needs are fulfilled). This is the *Poverty Gap*: the poorer the country and the larger the number of people in poverty, the greater the Gap (i.e. the resources which must be devoted to raise those in poverty). The *Poverty Gap Index* refers to additional money the average poor person would have to spend (in aggregate or as a proportion of total consumption) in order to reach the poverty line. The Poverty Gap for India is currently 4 per cent, for China 1 per cent and for eastern Europe 0.1 per cent. *The Poverty Severity Index* measures the distribution of welfare of those below the poverty line (i.e. between the poor and the ultra-poor). MW

References

Ravallion, M. 1995: *Poverty comparisons*. London: Harwood. · UNDP 1998: *Human development report 1998*. London: Oxford University Press.

poverty, geography of Poverty is a condition experienced by many people who have a shortage of financial and other resources, and it means that they are likely to face difficulties in obtaining and maintaining sufficient nutrition, adequate accommodation and long-term good health. While attempts are sometimes made to define *absolute* levels of poverty linked into the basic bodily requirements of all human beings, most social scientists prefer a *relative* concept which assesses the extent of 'poverty' present within a given SOCIETY relative to its prevailing norms and expectations: thus, 'it is apparent that the poverty of an Indian peasant who may today die of starvation is a qualitatively different state from that which afflicts those who may be called poor in European countries or in North America' (Wedderburn, 1974, p. 1). One implication is that poverty should be thought of geographically, with understandings, definitions and measurements of the phenomenon being allowed to vary depending on the particular parts of the world under study. Such a realization has rarely been explicit in the literature, though, and for the most part the geographical aspect of poverty research has involved taking specific indicators of poverty (e.g. the percentage of households earning below a specified income) and mapping these out across spatial units such as nation-states, planning regions or electoral wards.

Geographers have long been interested in such an approach to poverty, as is evident from this observation by Brunhes (1920, p. 576): 'A study of poverty should mean not simply statistics but an attempt at precise localisation. Since to fix the topographical distribution of poverty is a means of knowing it more exactly, it is doubtless also a means of relieving it and curing it in a less abstract and more efficacious manner.' Some earlier geographers addressed the associations of given regions with dimensions of poverty, as in Fleure's (1919) references to 'regions of hunger', 'regions of debilitation' and 'regions of lasting difficulty', while others – ones involved in establishing the foundations of SOCIAL GEOGRAPHY – paid considerable attention to areal variations in 'social aspects of life' including relative levels of wealth, welfare and housing quality. Watson's study of Hamilton, Ontario warrants mention in this respect, since he used a variety of sources to demonstrate 'a remarkable concentration of unemployment, neglect, desertion and delinquency in [what he termed] the city's shatter zones' (Watson, 1951, p. 495), and also began to unpick the various processes leading to the appearance of poverty in certain areas of the city rather than in others. In addition, he stressed the *contrast* between wealthy areas and poor areas, and talked of the 'social Himalayas' perceived locally to exist between populations resident in adjacent wealthy and poor areas.

Watson's work encapsulates much that was subsequently to be expanded upon by geographers interested in poverty, particularly in the post-1970 emergence of versions of human geography hostile to the seeming *lack* of social concern displayed by practitioners of SPATIAL SCIENCE. At the heart of WELFARE GEOGRAPHY was a wish to expose the spatial correlates of social inequalities, although studies in this vein often adapted the standard empirical and statistical techniques of spatial science (e.g. Coates and Rawstron's 1971 mapping of direct and indirect measures of income across the regions and cities of Britain). Other welfare geographers, meanwhile, began to think more conceptually about the connections between welfare, (in)JUSTICE, poverty and PLACE (e.g. Smith, 1979, 1994). Similarly, central to RADICAL GEOGRAPHY was a clearly stated concern for the geography of poverty, as was apparent from an early *Antipode* special issue (1970) tackling geographical aspects of American poverty. Unsurprisingly, as radical geography became increasingly identified with MARXIST GEOGRAPHY, significant advances were made in deploying Marxist political-economic analyses of poverty to illuminate its varying spatial manifestations at all scales from the global to the local. This orientation was explicit in Peet's (1975, p. 564) attempt to synthesize 'the Marxist principle that inequality and poverty are inevitably produced by capitalist societies' with 'the social-geographic idea that inequality may be passed on from one generation to the next via the environment of opportunities and services into which each individual is implanted at birth'. Writing more recently, and yet in many respects echoing Peet's line, Kodras (1997, p. 69) portrays poverty as 'a component of [the] interactive linkage between political-economic change and alterations in the social order of places'. Within Marxist political-economic scholarship the explanation of poverty has remained a prominent concern, and many key debates here – about spatial aspects of the LABOUR PROCESS, the LABOUR MARKET and the LABOUR THEORY OF VALUE; about the workings of land and housing markets in relation to urban RENT surfaces; about the necessarily UNEVEN DEVELOPMENT of CAPITALISM – have all had important ramifications for how best to understand the production of poverty's complex geographies.

During the 1990s it has sometimes been complained that poverty has disappeared from the agendas of geographers inspired by more fashionable trends within social theory and cultural studies (see POSTMODERNISM; POST-STRUCTURALISM; DECONSTRUCTION). The claim is that questions of 'IDENTITY' now prevail over ones to do with 'inequality', and that poverty as more a structural category than a politicized identity ceases to come under scrutiny. Indeed, Leyshon (1995) made this point when reflecting on the absence of an entry on 'poverty' from the third edition of the *Dictionary of Human Geography*, while Yapa's (1996) attempt to offer a postmodern theorization of how DISCOURSE constitutes the object of poverty met with the hostile response that his 'postmodern discursive approach (and solution) to poverty amounts to little more than an open surrender to . . . moral bankruptcy, social irresponsibility and political expediency' (Shrestha, 1997, p. 715). This view arguably misses the subtlety of Yapa's position, failing to appreciate that excavating the discursive construction of a 'poverty problem' does not deny the material processes productive of grounded hardship for particular peoples and places. Rather, Yapa's approach seeks to expose the implicatedness here of certain 'poverty discourses', as tied up with certain development and MODERNIZATION discourses, which often obscure the grounded hardships, diagnose them inappropriately and inform either inaction or unhelpful responses (see also Yapa, 1997, 1998).

More generally, there are signs that poverty *has* returned to greater prominence on the geographical agenda. Yapa's work is testimony to this, but so too are the following: surveys documenting basic empirical geographies of poverty, inequality and social division (Green, 1994; Philo, 1995); statements about how such documentation provides a powerful tool for critiquing interpretations which simplistically blame individuals and 'sub-cultures' for allowing themselves to slide into poverty (Philo, 1995; Kodras, 1997); inquiries into not just the urban but also the rural dimensions of poverty, tracing out the hidden geographies of poverty in localities whose 'idyllic' images commonly deflect such attention (Cloke, 1997); examinations of the connections between the UNDERCLASS, HOMELESSNESS, service-dependent populations and impoverished urban places (Dear and Wolch, 1987); studies into the processes of 'financial exclusion' being endured by, and in part productive of, many poor parts of western cities (Leyshon and Thrift, 1995); studies into not only the structural causes of 'poor places' but also the ways in which such places are lived and experienced on a daily basis by local people (Rollinson, 1990); and studies into the situated GENDER and RACE dimensions of poverty (Jones and Kodras, 1990; and, although not by an academic geographer, see Campbell's 1993 provocative account of differential responses by women and men to the poverty of Britain's 'dangerous places'). This is just a sample of ongoing research, the cumulative effect of which suggests that geographers have not abandoned a commitment to studying poverty, even if deploying a wider range of conceptual lenses to do so than previously. In addition, this work continues to echo Brunhes (1920) in its conviction that geographical research on poverty can and should contribute valuably to the formulation of anti-poverty strategies involving state interventions, voluntary activities and 'grassroots' COMMUNITY initiatives (e.g. several chapters in Philo, 1995). CP

References

Antipode 1970: Special theme issue on 'The geography of American poverty'. *Antipode* 2(2). · Brunhes, J. 1920: *Human geography: an attempt at a positive classification – principles and examples*. London: George G. Harrap. · Campbell, B. 1993: *Goliath: Britain's dangerous places*. London: Methuen. · Cloke, P. 1997: Poor country: marginalisation, poverty and rurality. In P. Cloke and J. Little, eds, *Contested countryside cultures: otherness, marginalisation and rurality*. London: Routledge, 252–71. · Coates, B.E. and Rawstron, E.M. 1971: *Regional variations in Britain: studies in economic and social geography*. London: B.T. Batsford; Dear, M. and Wolch, J. 1987: *Landscapes of despair: from deinstitutionalisation to homelessness*. Oxford: Polity Press. · Fleure, H.J. 1919: Human regions. *Scottish Geographical Magazine* 35: 94–105. · Green, A.E. 1994: *The geography of poverty and wealth*. Coventry: University of Warwick, Institute for Employment Research. · Jones, J.P. and Kodras, J.E. 1990: Restructured regions and families: the feminisation of poverty in the United States. *Annals of the Association of American Geographers* 80: 163–83. · Kodras, J.E. 1997: The changing map of American poverty in an era of economic restructuring and political realignment. *Economic Geography* 73: 67–95. · Leyshon, A. 1995: Missing words: whatever happened to the geography of poverty? *Environment and Planning* 27: 1021–8. · Leyshon, A. and Thrift, N.J. 1995: Geographies of financial exclusion: financial abandonment in Britain and the United States. *Transactions, Institute of British Geographers* NS 20: 312–41. · Peet, R. 1975: Inequality and poverty: a Marxist-geographic theory. *Annals of the Association of American Geographers* 65: 564–71. · Philo, C., ed., 1995: *Off the map: the social geography of poverty in the UK*. London: Child Poverty Action Group. · Rollinson, P.A. 1990: The everyday geography of poor elderly residents in Chicago. *Geograpiska Annaler* 72B: 47–57. · Smith, D.M. 1979: *Where the grass is greener: living in an unequal world*. Harmondsworth, Middlesex: Penguin; Smith, D.M. 1994: *Geography and social justice*. Oxford: Blackwell. · Watson, J.W. 1951: The sociological aspects of geography. In G. Taylor, ed., *Geography in the twentieth century: a study of growth, fields, techniques, aims and trends*. London: Methuen. · Wedderburn, D. 1974: Introduction. In D. Wedderburn, ed., *Poverty, inequality and class structure*. Cambridge: Cambridge University Press, 1–12. · Yapa, L. 1996: What causes poverty? A postmodern view. *Annals of the Association of American Geographers* 86: 707–28. · Shrestha, N. 1997: A postmodern view or denial of historical integrity? The poverty of Yapa's view of poverty. *Annals of the Association of American Geographers* 87: 709–16. · and Yapa, L. 1997: Reply: why discourse matters, materially. *Annals of the Association of American Geographers* 87: 717–22. · Yapa, L. 1998: The poverty discourse and the poor in Sri Lanka. *Transactions, Institute of British Geographers* NS 23: 95–115.

Suggested reading

Campbell (1993). · Kodras (1997). · Philo (1995). · Yapa (1996, 1998).

power The ability to achieve certain ends. Strictly speaking, power is an absolute concept but it is often treated as a synonym for *influence*: the concept may refer to the relationship between an individual or group and the natural world (see NATURE) but it is more frequently used to characterize inter-personal and inter-group relationships, including those between STATES.

Allen (1997) has identified three different conceptions of power. In the first, *power is an inscribed capacity*, something possessed by an individual, group or organization as inherent to a position occupied within a network. It is a potential to 'control, command or direct the actions of others' which may or may not be exercised: when it is, how and why is contingent on the particular circumstances. The second conception is of *power as a resource*, the 'power to' rather than the 'power over' which characterizes the first conception; it is mobilized to achieve desired objectives. Finally, there is the conception of *power as strategies, practices and techniques*, an approach usually associated with Foucault's work (Driver, 1985).

Power is exercised at all SCALES and levels of society, from within the individual household to the entire world-economy (see WORLD-SYSTEMS ANALYSIS). It is rarely symmetrical: x's power over y usually exceeds that of y over x (perhaps by many orders of magnitude). Such asymmetry is characteristic of many social structures such as PATRIARCHY (see GENDER AND GEOGRAPHY) and most MODES OF PRODUCTION. Power (other than power over nature, which is usually a technological relationship) can be achieved and sustained in a variety of ways, among which the most usual are: *force* (including mental and physical – both violent and non-violent); *manipulation*; *persuasion* and the creation of consensus; and *authority*. It is most readily exercised if its source is recognized as legitimate by those subject to it (see SOVEREIGNTY): legitimation may be achieved through appeal to tradition, the charisma of the powerful, or its institutionalization in societal structures, especially those of the STATE APPARATUS.

Much of the exercise of power involves spatial techniques and strategies, hence the interest among geographers in Foucault's work, and also in TERRITORIALITY. Allen argues that all three conceptions have their own spatial vocabularies: the inscribed capacity varies between and works across places; the network conception involves organizing space in the drive to achieve desired objectives; and many of the techniques for applying power are spatial in their character, as illustrated by Foucault's work on the spatial organization of prisons (see SURVEILLANCE).

Under CAPITALISM, for example, power is unevenly distributed because of the unequal distribution of ownership of the means of production, and thus of the ability to bargain over prices. Those with greatest power have most control over society's organization of production, distribution and exchange (including their spatial organization), plus the allocation of the benefits that follow: this unequal power is reflected in the social relations between CLASSES and is the foundation of much social, economic and political CONFLICT. The more successful the legitimation of the resulting inequality within a society (see HEGEMONY; IDEOLOGY) the less the need for explicit coercion and the fewer the challenges to class power: where legitimation is weak, however (see CRISIS), the greater the demands on, and problems for, the STATE, one of whose crucial functions is the exercise of power in order to legitimate existing social relations (Held, 1987; Johnston, 1992).

Much work on the ownership and exercise of power thus focuses on the state, which has a range of inscribed capacities, is at the centre of a vast array of networks, and employs a variety of strategies, many of them spatial, to achieve its goals. The state infiltrates and regulates most aspects of contemporary economic and social life. In capitalist states, for example, some of the bourgeoisie's power over labour is transferred to the state apparatus, in part to aid its legitimation and in part to ensure the continued reproduction of the mode of production (Jessop, 1990): the state, for example, regulates a wide range of workplace practices in order to sustain profitability.

The nature of state power is theorized in a variety of ways (see Alford and Friedland, 1985; and Dunleavy and O'Leary, 1987). According to liberal theories of democracy, for example, power is evenly distributed through the population and can be exercised on its behalf only if those controlling the state have majority popular support (see PLURALISM). According to Marxian theories, on the other hand, state power is not independent of class power, although the state can act autonomously because of its particular status as a territorially defined institution (Mann, 1984). The state, according to this view, exists to promote the capitalist mode of production and advance the interests of the dominant forces in the local SOCIAL FORMATION; the interests of other groups within society are only advanced to the extent that this is perceived as in the whole society's, and thus the dominant class's, interests too. (For example, some states have granted liberal democratic participatory privileges through a universal franchise, as part of the ideological bulwark to legitimation of inequality: Johnston, 1989.)

A major feature of state power is its territorial expression and the TERRITORIALITY strategies employed (Johnston, 1991a, 1991b). A state's sovereignty involves it being recognized as the locus of authority within a defined territory, and it is usually the sole repository of coercive (military and police) force there. Within its territory the state, according to Mann, exercises both *despotic power* (actions taken without prior negotiation with the population, as under totalitarianism) and *infrastructural power*, whereby it infiltrates most aspects of life with (implicit) consent, as under capitalism: under FEUDALISM, the state is relatively weak on both power dimensions. Mann argues that a state is necessary for anything other than a primitive society (though see ANARCHISM), and that one exercising a very wide range of infrastructural powers is necessary under capitalism.

Geography is crucial if the capitalist state is to be effective. State power is exercised from a central place over a unified territorial reach, and involves the mobilization of four types of potential power resources – economic, ideological, military and political. For each, the existence of a territory within which the power applies is fundamental. The interest groups associated with the four types of power all need to have their activities regulated over defined territories: economic interests are provided with a single currency and a uniform set of laws of contract, for example; ideological interests are advanced through the association of the state and its society with a defined territory (see NATION; NATIONALISM); military interests are provided with clearly defined boundaries to defend; and political interests are given an arena within which to mobilize support and gain legitimation. Thus, as Mann expresses it: 'the state is merely and essentially an arena, a *place* . . . '.

Power resides and is realized in all parts of a society, therefore, and the associated spatial practices are widely applied. The creation of spatial structures, including but not limited to bounded spaces (see LOCATIONAL ANALYSIS), is thus deeply implicated in a vast range of social, economic, cultural and political practices: whereas much academic and popular attention is given to those practices as applied by the state, whose inscribed capacities and resources far exceed those of most other individuals, groups and institutions, nevertheless the exercise of power at all levels is a crucial element in the making and remaking of geographies. RJJ

References

Alford, R.R. and Friedland, R. 1985: *Powers of theory: capitalism, the state and democracy*. Cambridge and New York: Cambridge University Press. · Allen, J. 1997: Economies of power and space. In R. Lee and J. Wills, eds, *Geographies of economies*. London, Arnold, 59–70. · Driver, F. 1985: Power, space and the body: a critical assessment of Foucault's *Discipline and punish*. *Environment and Planning C: Society and Space* 3: 425–46. · Dunleavy, P. and O'Leary, B. 1987: *State theory: the politics of liberal democracy*. London: Macmillan. · Held, D. 1987: *Models of democracy*. Cambridge: Polity Press. · Jessop, B. 1990: *State theory: putting capitalist states in their place*. Cambridge: Polity Press. · Johnston, R.J. 1989: Individual freedom in the world-economy. In R.J. Johnston and P.J. Taylor, eds, *A world in crisis? Geographical perspectives*, 2nd edn. Oxford and Cambridge, MA: Basil Blackwell, 200–28. · Johnston, R.J. 1991a: The territoriality of law: an exploration. *Urban Geography* 12: 548–65. · Johnston, R.J. 1991b: *A question of place: exploring the practice of human geography*. Oxford and Boston: Basil Blackwell. · Johnston, R.J. 1992: The internal operations of the state. In P.J. Taylor, ed., *The state in the twentieth century*. London: Belhaven Press. · Mann, M. 1984: The autonomous power of the state; its origins, mechanisms, and results. *European Journal of Sociology* 25: 185–213. · Sack, R.D. 1986: *Human territoriality: its theory and history*. Cambridge and New York: Cambridge University Press.

Selected Reading

Claval, P. 1978: *Espace et pouvoir*. Paris: Presses Universitaires de France. · Giddens, A. 1984: *The constitution of society*. Cambridge: Polity Press. · Giddens, A. 1985: *The nation state and violence*. Cambridge: Polity Press.

power-geometry The more or less systematic and usually highly uneven ways in which different individuals and groups are positioned within networks of time–space flows and connections. These variable positions derive from the intimate connections that exist between productions of POWER and productions of SPACE: thus spatial modalities of power are differentially engaged such that different actors have different degrees of freedom. The basic idea was proposed by Doreen Massey (1993) in a critique of David Harvey's concept of TIME–SPACE COMPRESSION. In her view, Harvey (1989) had emphasized the importance of CLASS positions to such an extent that he failed to acknowledge the wider range of social positions that were involved, including GENDER: time–space compression 'needs differentiating socially'. Similarly, Gregory (1994, p. 414) argued that the process needed to be differentiated spatially: there is a complex geography to time–space compression. The concept of a 'power-geometry' speaks to these twin concerns.

Massey's intervention was intended as a feminist critique of Harvey's MASCULINISM, and yet her illustration-sketches were by no means free of a masculinist imaginary. She introduced the idea of a 'power-geometry' by appealing to what Donna Haraway (1991) called a 'God-trick', thus:

> Imagine for a moment that you are on a satellite, further out and beyond all satellites; you can see 'planet earth' from a distance and, rare for someone with only peaceful intentions, you are equipped with the kind of technology that allows you to see the colours of people's eyes and the number on their number-plates. You can see all the movement and tune-in to all the communication that is going on, Furthest out are the satellites, then aeroplanes, the long haul between London and Tokyo and the hop from San Salvador to Guatemala City. Some of this is people moving, some of it is physical trade,

> some is media broadcasting. There are faxes, e-mail, film-distribution networks, financial flows and transactions. Look in closer and there are ships and trains, steam trains slogging laboriously up hills somewhere in Asia. Look in closer still and there are lorries and cars and buses and on down further and somewhere in sub-Saharan Africa there's a woman on foot who still spends hours a day collecting water... Different social groups and different individuals are placed in very distinct ways in relation to these flows and interconnections. (Massey, 1993, p. 61)

In her subsequent writings, however, Massey (1998, 1999) has moved to a more open and situated account of the variable power-geometries of contemporary GLOBALIZATION that refuses these totalizing images and transparent spaces. As she develops the concept of a power-geometry, so Massey now weaves it into a web of affiliations and solidarities that speaks much more directly to Haraway's vision of a SITUATED KNOWLEDGE. Thus she treats power-geometries as being centrally involved in processes of identity formation and in the possibilities of political action within the project of a RADICAL DEMOCRACY:

> 'Identities', in this formulation, are temporary... constellations, always interrelationally hybrid but none the less, and to varying degrees, with viably different stories to tell... What is (or could be) at issue politically is the power relations through which such identities are constituted and those through which they interact with each other and the wider world. It is the fact of their plurality and interrelation which keeps the future open for politics. (Massey, 1999, p. 291)

Seen like this, the idea of a power-geometry is not only vitally involved in contemporary reformulations of conceptions of space in human geography (see SPACE, HUMAN GEOGRAPHY AND): it is also of considerable moment in any politics of space. DG

References

Gregory, D. 1994: *Geographical imaginations*. Oxford and Cambridge, MA: Blackwell. · Haraway, D. 1991: Situated knowledges: the science question in feminism and the privilege of partial perspective. In *Simians, cyborgs and women: the reinvention of nature*. London: Routledge, 183–201. · Harvey, D. 1989: *The condition of postmodernity: an enquiry into the origins of cultural change*. Oxford and Cambridge, MA: Blackwell. · Massey, D. 1993: Power-geometry and a progressive sense of place. In J. Bird, B. Curtis, T. Putnam, G. Robertson, and L. Tickner, eds, *Mapping the futures: local cultures, global change*. London and New York: Routledge, 59–69. · Massey, D. 1998: Imagining globalisation: power-geometries of time-space. In A. Brah, M.J. Hickman and M. MacanGhaill, eds, *Future Worlds: migration, environment and globalization*. London: Macmillan. · Massey, D. 1999: Spaces of politics. In D. Massey, J. Allen and P. Sarre, eds, *Human geography today*. Cambridge: Polity Press, 279–94.

Suggested Reading

Massey (1993), (1998).

pragmatism An American philosophical tradition that emerged in the late nineteenth century and is associated with John Dewey (1859–1952), William James (1842–1910), George Herbert Mead (1863–1931), and Charles Sanders Peirce (1839–1914). The movement is perhaps best known for the idea that what counts as knowledge is determined by its usefulness. As James (1987, p. 578) wrote, 'the true is the name of whatever proves itself to be good in the way of belief'. After enjoying widespread popularity in the first half of the twentieth century, pragmatism fell out of favour after the Second World War following the ascendancy of empirical social science and especially analytical philosophy, a narrowly conceived, often technically recondite form of philosophy concerned with assessing the coherence, consistency and precise meaning of an argument. The publication of Richard Rorty's (1979) *Philosophy and the mirror of nature* revived pragmatism's fortunes, however. As an ex-analytical philosopher, Rorty diagnosed with forensic precision the pathology of modern philosophy, prescribing as cure a large dose of American pragmatism, now found in a range of humanities and social sciences. The rehabilitation of pragmatism is also a consequence of the wider interest in POST-STRUCTURALISM and POSTMODERNISM, movements with which it shares common interests.

James coined the name pragmatism in 1898 to describe the movement, but there were always strong differences among its proponents. At one point, for example, Peirce minted his own neologism, 'pragmaticism', to mark off what he was doing from his colleagues. Bernstein (1992, appendix) usefully characterizes pragmatism by five features:

- anti-FOUNDATIONALISM, the belief that there are no secure anchor points either in the world or in the mind that hold and guarantee the permanency of true knowledge;
- fallibilism, the belief that no truth is ever final, and that knowledge should always be subject to further investigation, critical scrutiny, and questioning;
- communal enquiry, the notion that scholarship takes place within a wider community involving trust, conversation, and shared norms and responsibilities;

- radical contingency, the belief stemming partly from Darwin's theory of evolution that change is propelled by chance and accident, that the only certainty is uncertainty (and for this reason humans must always be ready to expect the unexpected, to cultivate a 'reflective intelligence' as Dewey put it); and
- 'radical pluralism', the belief that neither bits of the world nor of philosophy coherently fit together all of piece. Radical pluralism, as James (1977, p. 26) writes, is a 'turbid, muddled, Gothic sort of affair without a sweeping outline and little pictorial nobility': but for James it is all we have.

The rise of analytical philosophy in America from the 1940s brought with it everything that pragmatism formerly shunned – FOUNDATIONALISM, certainty, individual rationality, necessity, and monism. Consequently, pragmatism was pushed, and sometimes shoved aside. After his death Dewey, for example, was regarded by one analytical philosopher as 'a nice old man who hadn't the vaguest conception of real philosophical rigor or the nature of a real philosophical problem' (Gouinlock, 1972, p. xi). Analytical philosophy's hold on the profession was relatively short-lived, however, and by the 1980s it was vigorously challenged by a new group of pragmatists including Richard Rorty (1931–) and Richard Bernstein (1932–).

Rorty, drawing upon the writings of Dewey and James, seeks, first, to dismantle from the inside out – to DECONSTRUCT – the edifice of contemporary analytical philosophy, especially the variant known as REALISM and, second, to substitute for it a neo-pragmatic alternative which he calls, possibly tongue-in-cheek, 'postmodernist liberal bourgeois irony'. Very briefly, Rorty argues that the problems of analytical philosophy stem from its appropriation of an inappropriate METAPHOR, vision or sight or 'occularism'. The metaphor mistakenly convinced philosophers that it was possible for the mind to mirror the world. In contrast, Rorty, following the pragmatists, argues for a different central metaphor, 'conversation'. Under this model there are no fixed end points, strict rules, or necessary logics. This is evident by unpacking the terms of Rorty's eccentrically labelled alternative: '*postmodernist*', because Rorty doesn't believe in the grand meta-narratives of MODERNISM that supposedly make everything commensurable (cf. GRAND THEORY); '*liberal*' because for the conversation to continue there must be freedom of expression and DEMOCRACY (thereby echoing Dewey's concerns); '*bourgeois*' because Rorty thinks that LIBERALISM has so far only been possible under CAPITALISM; and '*ironic*' because for the conversation to continue we need to affirm certain beliefs even though there are no firm philosophical foundations for them. Here Rorty often quotes Joseph Schumpeter to the effect that although he recognized the relative validity of all of his beliefs he nonetheless stood by them 'unflinchingly'.

While sympathetic to many of Rorty's ideas, Bernstein (1992, ch. 8) is searingly critical of his economic conservatism, and his disengagement from questions of unequal POWER and resources. In contrast, Bernstein deals with those absences by joining to pragmatism various strands of continental European philosophy, producing what he calls 'the new constellation' (Bernstein, 1992). An important component within Bernstein's mix are poststructural writers such as Foucault and Derrida, and in no small part the renaissance of American pragmatism is a result of its resonance with their concerns.

In geography there have been sporadic but neither consistent nor concerted attempts to draw upon pragmatist writers. Jackson and Smith (1984) utilize Mead's more applied prescriptions in their portrayal of SOCIAL GEOGRAPHY; Wescoat (1992) describes the relation between Gilbert White's environmental outlook, and particularly Dewey's ideas; both Barnes (1996, chs 2 and 5) and Gibson-Graham (1996) make use of Rorty's work in countering ESSENTIALISM in ECONOMIC GEOGRAPHY; and Sunley (1996) takes the ideas of another ex-analytical-philosopher-turned-pragmatist, Hilary Putnam, and puts them to work in a discussion of the relationship between the NEW INSTITUTIONAL ECONOMICS and economic geography. TJB

References

Barnes, T.J. 1996: *Logics of dislocation: models, metaphors and meanings of economic space*. New York: Guilford. · Bernstein, R.J. 1992: *The new constellation: the ethical political horizons of modernity/postmodernity*. Cambridge, MA: MIT Press. · Gibson-Graham, J.K. 1996: *The end of capitalism (as we knew it). A feminist critique of political economy*. Oxford: Blackwell. · Gouinlock, J. 1972: *John Dewey's philosophy of value*. New York: Humanities. · Jackson, P. and Smith, S.J. 1984: *Exploring social geography*. London: Allen and Unwin. · James, W. 1977: *A pluralistic universe*. Cambridge, MA: Harvard University Press. · James, W. 1987: *Writings, 1902–1910*, ed., B. Kuklick. New York: Library of America. · Rorty, R. 1979: *Philosophy and the mirror of nature*. Princeton, NJ: Princeton University Press. · Sunley, P. 1996:

Context in economic geography: the relevance of pragmatism. *Progress in Human Geography* 20: 338–55. · Wescoat, J. 1992: Common themes in the work of Gilbert White and John Dewey: a pragmatic appraisal. *Annals of the Association of American Geographers* 82: 587–607.

Suggested Reading

Barnes (1996). · Bernstein (1992).

prediction The creation of an expected value, or estimate, for an observation involved in the generation of the estimating equation (cf. FORECAST). RJJ

pre-industrial city All cities prior to the INDUSTRIAL REVOLUTION, plus those in non-industrialized regions today. The term reflects the THEORY, initially advocated by Gideon Sjoberg (1960; SJOBERG MODEL), that all pre-industrial cities, regardless of their time, place, or cultural backdrop, share similar reasons for existence, social hierarchies, and internal SPATIAL STRUCTURES. The term is now rarely used, as few researchers believe that the variety of urban forms created by pre-industrial and non-industrialized societies have enough in common to be considered as variations of a single category. DH

Reference

Sjoberg, G. 1960: *The pre-industrial city, past and present*. New York: The Free Press.

preservation The saving of relict features in the human LANDSCAPE, typically in the built environment. It complements CONSERVATION, which is generally concerned with protecting environmental features. Preservation involves maintaining the feature in a state of good repair: *restoration* aims to bring it back to its original condition, whereas *revival* reproduces past features. RJJ

pricing policies The arrangements whereby the prices at which commodities are offered to consumers are determined. In spatial economic analysis the important distinguishing feature of pricing policies is the extent to which price varies with distance from the origin or source of the commodity. There are two major alternative policies. The first is known as the *f.o.b. (free on board)* price system, under which there is a basic price at origin and the consumer pays the TRANSPORT COST involved in getting the commodity to the point of purchase. The second is the *c.i.f. (cost, insurance, freight)* price system, under which the producer adds insurance and shipping costs to the production cost and offers the commodity at a uniform delivered price irrespective of distance from origin. The distinction between these two policies is important, for commodities sold c.i.f. should have no bearing on COMPARATIVE (LOCATIONAL) ADVANTAGE for productive activities requiring them as inputs; similarly, distance from origin should not affect the level of demand for goods offered on a c.i.f. basis (other things being equal). There is an increasing tendency for commodities to be sold at a uniform delivered price.

Various alternative pricing policies may be implemented. An f.o.b. system does not necessarily have minor incremental increases in price for small increases in distance; more often the prevailing FREIGHT RATES on which delivered price is based will be constant over broad zones. There may be forms of spatial price discrimination, under which customers in some areas are charged a high price (perhaps because the supplier has a local monopoly) so as to subsidize the price charged in a more competitive market elsewhere. A well-known variant is the *basing point price policy*, whereby customers are charged as if the commodity originated at a certain (base) point; this can be used to protect producers in the basing point location, for commodities actually produced elsewhere will cost more. The operation of some pricing policies may involve collusion on the part of producers to maintain an artificially high price in the industry as a whole – an increasing tendency in the advanced capitalist world. DMS

primate city, the law of the An empirical regularity identified by Mark Jefferson (1939) in the relationship of the populations of a country's three largest cities. He noted that the ratio of the three populations approximated the sequence 100:30:20 in many cases (i.e. the third largest is one-fifth the size of the largest), which he attributed to the largest city's pre-eminence in economic, social and political affairs. The sequence he identified is now largely ignored but the concepts of primacy and a primate city are still widely referred to. Accounts usually relate a primate city's predominance to the small size of the country, the export orientation of its trade, and a recent colonial past (see also CITY-SIZE DISTRIBUTION; MERCANTILIST MODEL; RANK-SIZE RULE). RJJ

Reference

Jefferson, M. 1939: The law of the primate city. *Geographical Review* 29: 226–32.

principal components analysis (pca) A statistical procedure for transforming an (observations by variables) data matrix so that the variables in the new matrix are uncorrelated. Unlike FACTOR ANALYSIS, there are as many new variables (termed components) in the transformed as in the original matrix.

The components are extracted by an iterative averaging procedure. The first principal component occupies a position as close to (i.e. as highly correlated with) all of the original variables as possible. The second is as close as possible to the residual variation from the first, and so on until all have been extracted.

The output of a pca (which normally takes only a few seconds on modern computers, with many standard packages available) comprises three important sets of information. The *eigenvalues* are measures of the relative importance of each component (i.e. the proportion of the variation in the original variables accounted for by each); the greater the value of an eigenvalue, the greater the commonality among the original variables. The *component loadings* show the CORRELATIONS between the original variables and the new ones, thus identifying which groups of variables have common patterns. Finally, the *component scores* are values for the observations on each of the new variables.

Principal components analysis has been used by geographers: (a) to identify groups of inter-correlated variables, in an inductive search for common patterns; (b) to simplify a data set by removing redundant information resulting from inter-correlated variables; (c) to reorganize a data set by removing COLLINEARITY (see REGRESSION; GENERAL LINEAR MODEL); and (d) to test hypotheses. RJJ

Suggested Reading

Johnston, R.J. 1978: *Multivariate statistical analysis in geography: a primer on the general linear model.* London and New York: Longman.

prisoner's dilemma An application of GAME THEORY which illustrates the benefits of cooperative behaviour in certain situations. In the classic example, two men are arrested on charges of car theft and armed robbery. The first offence is readily proven, but the other will not be unless at least one of them confesses and implicates the other. The suspects know that if they both stay silent, each will be found guilty of the theft and sentenced to one year in jail; they also know that if both confess to the armed robbery they will get eight years each. They are interrogated separately, and not allowed to consult, let alone collude. Each is offered a deal: if you confess and as a result your accomplice is found guilty of the armed robbery you will be freed and he will get ten years. The four possible joint outcomes to their separate decisions whether or not to confess are given in the following payoff matrix in which the left-hand value in each cell indicates A's punishment at that outcome, and the right-hand value indicates B's punishment (thus if A doesn't confess and B does, A will get ten years and B will get released):

	Suspect B	
Suspect A	Not Confess	Not Confess
Not Confess	1,1	10,0
Confess	0,10	8,8

Both prisoners have to evaluate the possible consequences of each action, which can be done by rank-ordering the outcomes according to their relative desirability. (In this ranking, NC = not confess, and C = confess, so that the top left-hand cell of the above matrix is [NC,NC]. > indicates 'is preferable to'.) For A the ordering (with A's decision first) is

[C,NC] > [NC,NC] > [C,C] > [NC,C]

and for B (also with A's decision first) it is

[NC,C] > [NC,NC] > [C,C] > [C,NC]

Thus each determines that to confess is the best option, because if he does not and the other does, then the worst outcome will eventuate. Neither dare stay silent, for fear that the other will confess. So both confess, and both get eight years. If each could have been sure of the other's silence (and also sure that he wouldn't accept a police claim that his companion had already confessed) then both would have stayed silent and got a one-year sentence. Because neither can guarantee the other's behaviour, however, they fail to select the optimal strategy, which they surely would have done if they had been able to cooperate.

This dilemma has been used to illustrate not only how selfish behaviour may not be in the individual's best interest but also that it is not in a person's interest to be unselfish unless everybody else is (cf. TRAGEDY OF THE COMMONS). In most cases, it is argued, unselfish behaviour by all can only be guaranteed if enforced by an external authority, which argument is taken to provide a convincing case for the existence of the STATE to promote both the collective and the individual good. There are many other situations in which cooperation is sensible and promotes the general good without state involvement, however. RJJ

Suggested Reading

Brams, S.J. 1975: *Game theory and politics.* New York: The Free Press. · Laver, M. 1997: *Private desires, political action: an invitation to the politics of rational choice.* London: Sage Publications. · Poundstone, W. 1992:

Prisoner's dilemma. New York: Doubleday. · Taylor, M. 1987: *The possibility of cooperation*. Cambridge and New York: Cambridge University Press.

private and public spheres Discursively constructed, contested categories that define boundaries between households, market economies, the state and political participation. The boundary between public and private is drawn and functions differently in different political theories (see Benhabib, 1992); Deutsche (1996) reviews how a variety of these political theories have figured in debates about urban public space.

Habermas's account of the relations among various spheres of public and private life in early and WELFARE STATE capitalist societies (see CAPITALISM; CRITICAL THEORY) and his concept of the bourgeois public sphere have been particularly influential. Early capitalist societies were organized into four institutional spheres: family-consumer (private), market economy (private), the state (public) and citizen-political participation (public) (see figure); Habermas identifies the last as the bourgeois public sphere. As both a historical phenomenon and a normative ideal, the bourgeois public sphere functioned as a counterweight to the state. This liberal model of the public sphere was never fully achieved, however, and in welfare state capitalist societies the separation between STATE and ECONOMY, between public and private, dissolves and family-consumer and citizen roles are transformed, the latter declining in importance and changing form (from citizen to passive recipient of publicity and social welfare client). Habermas's account is suggestive to geographers; he analyses landscape changes that concretize and reinforce both the rise and decline in active public debate (for example, coffeehouses and nineteenth-century urban culture, and the SUBURB, respectively; Habermas, 1989). Howell (1993) nonetheless criticizes the universalism of Habermas's theorizing and his lack of sensitivity to context and SCALE, and Gregory (1994) draws out both the centrality of geographical context for Habermas's social theory and its EUROCENTRISM. Critics argue that Habermas idealizes the bourgeois public sphere and that CLASS, GENDER and RACIAL exclusions were constitutive of, and not simply incidental to, it (Howell, 1993; Fraser, 1997).

The notion of a public sphere is nonetheless central to democratic theory and practice (see RADICAL DEMOCRACY), and there have been numerous attempts to rethink it in contemporary contexts. Fraser (1997) does this by questioning four of Habermas's assumptions, including the liberal assumption that private interests are antagonistic to the public sphere (this reflects a feminist scepticism about the ways in which concepts of 'privacy' often protect dominant (male) interests and legitimate the oppression of women in the 'private' sphere: what counts as private and public is itself the result of political struggle), and that one cohesive public sphere (rather than multiple public spheres) is the ideal. Fraser gestures towards the SPATIALITY of these multiple public spheres: 'they consist in culturally specific institutions – for example, the fora of textual exchange, including various journals and the Internet; and social geographies of urban space, including cafes, public parks, and shopping malls' (1997, p. 83). Deutsche (1996) takes up public space in relation to a less stable process of SUBJECT FORMATION. Following Lefort, she theorizes public space in relation to the image of the empty space that founds democracy, namely the absence of foundational POWER (beyond 'the people', which is a category that has no essential identity). To fill this empty space, DEMOCRACY 'invents' public space, which is where the meaning and unity of the social (i.e. 'the people') is negotiated. The social identities constituted within public space are always and necessarily constituted by designating an outsider/non-citizen. Public space is only democratic insofar as these exclusions are taken into account and open to contestation.

Geographers have asked whether such theorizing uses space simply as a metaphor: 'is public space simply the space of politics . . . Are the terms "public space" and "public sphere" interchangeable as they often seem to be in much of the literature?' (Mitchell, 1996, p. 127). While the terms may not be interchangeable (Staeheli, 1996), it is nonetheless the case that '[a]ctivists do not dance on the head of a pin' (Mitchell, 1996, p. 127) and a number of empirical studies document, not only the increasing privatization of public space (Davis, 1990), but the racial, gender, age, heterosexist and class exclusions of existing, material public spaces (Ruddick, 1996; Valentine, 1996), so as to demonstrate that radical democracy remains an ideal that we strive towards, in and through the construction and use of public space. GP

References

Benhabib, S. 1992: *Situating the self*. Oxford: Polity. · Davis, M. 1990: *City of quartz: excavating the future in Los Angeles*. London: Verso. · Deutsche, R. 1996:

Early Capitalism

	PRIVATE		PUBLIC	
LIFEWORLD	Family	linked by money exchange, channeled through roles as worker and consumer	Citizen	linked through state administrative system, channeled through roles as citizen and client (the bourgeois public sphere)
SYSTEM	Market Economy		State	

Welfare State Capitalism

	PRIVATE		PRIVATE	
LIFEWORLD	Family–Consumer	consumer role enchanced	Client–Citizen	citizen role declines, channeled through social welfare client role
SYSTEM	Market Economy		State	

public and private spheres *in early and welfare capitalist societies* (adapted from Fraser, 1989: Habermas, 1987)

Evictions: art and spatial politics. Cambridge, MA: MIT Press. · Fraser, N. 1989: *Unruly practices: power, discourse and gender in contemporary social theory*. Minneapolis: University of Minnesota Press. · Fraser, N. 1997: *Justice Interruptus: critical reflections of the 'postsocialist' condition*. London and New York: Routledge. · Gregory, D. 1994: *Geographical imaginations*. Oxford and Cambridge, MA: Blackwell. · Habermas, J. 1987: *The theory of communicative action, vol. 2: Lifeworlds and system: a critique of functionalist reason*, trans. T. McCarthy. Boston: Beacon Press. · Habermas, J. 1989: *The structural transformation of the public sphere: an inquiry into a category of bourgeois society*, trans. T. Burger. Cambridge, MA: MIT Press. · Howell, Philip 1993: Public space and the public sphere: political theory and the historical geography of modernity. *Environment and Planning D: Society and Space* 11: 303–22. · Mitchell, D. 1996: Introduction: public space and the city. *Urban Geography* 17: 127–31. · Ruddick, S. 1996: Constructing difference in public spaces: race, class, and gender as interlocking systems. *Urban Geography* 17: 132–51. · Staeheli, L. 1996: Publicity, privacy, and women's political action. *Environment and Planning D: Society and Space* 14: 601–19. · Valentine, G. 1996: Children should be seen and not heard: the production and transgression of adults' public space. *Urban Geography* 17: 205–20.

Suggested Reading

Fraser (1997).

private interest developments (pids) Communal housing projects in the USA (also known as *community interest developments* and *common interest communities*) in which the property is held in common, residents must be members of the Homeowners' Association, and that Association's constitution governs a wide range of aspects of land and property use. The Association usually provides and manages open spaces, including gardens, parking facilities and garbage removal; more than half provide a swimming pool and a meeting place. Association regulations on behaviour within their territories – which extend to such issues as the minimum age for a resident, the size of dogs which may be kept, and even whether kissing in cars parked on the street is permissible – in effect mean that they operate as 'private governments' separate from the state apparatus, although decisions have been challenged through the court systems.

The original pids were associated with condominium developments but the form of GOVERNANCE has spread rapidly in recent years, involving a wide range of developments, comprising detached housing as well as townhouses and apartments. There were less than 500 registered Homeowners' Associations in 1964 but 150,000 by 1992, with the latter covering 32 million residents and over 11 per cent of all housing in the USA: the main concentrations are in California (20,000 Associations in 1992) and Florida (15,000). Associations are governed by elected Boards of about five members, so that in California alone some 100,000 people are involved in the governance of these separate communities.

Most pid residents are relatively affluent, for whom the Associations are, in effect, 'independently-policed GHETTOES' – a further example of the use of TERRITORIALITY strategies in the spatial structuring of social life. (Knox, 1994, termed pids 'an ideology of hostile privatisation . . . [creating] a caste society with utter social separation of the rich'; Harvey, 1996, called them a 'form of contracted fascism'.) RJJ

References and Suggested Reading

Barton, S.E. and Silverman, C.J., eds, 1994: *Common interest communities: private governments and the public interest.* Berkeley, CA: Institute of Local Government Studies, University of California. · Harvey, D. 1996: Cities or urbanization? *City* 1–2: 38–61. · Knox, P.L. 1994: The stealthy tyranny of community spaces. *Environment and Planning A* 26: 170–3. · McKenzie, E. 1994: *Privatopia: Homeowner Associations and the rise of residential private government.* New Haven, CT: Yale University Press.

privatization The sale or transfer of public assets to the private sector. This should not be confused with deregulation, which concerns the reduction or elimination of STATE regulation on activities that may already be privately owned. The case for privatization is usually grounded in claims that efficiency will be increased, but the aim may also be to raise revenue for the state, to spread share ownership and to de-politicize decision-making. That private production is actually more efficient than state enterprise is hard to demonstrate, and depends crucially on the competitive process. Thus, the privatization of state monopolies (like public utilities and transport systems; cf. PUBLIC GOODS) carries no guarantee of greater efficiency passed on as benefits for the consumer, unless strong competition can be introduced. This is very difficult, if not impossible, in circumstances of natural monopoly where there is only one possible source of the commodity in question (like water), or when geographical circumstances make the duplication of facilities impracticable (as in the privatization of British Rail). Then, the public interest may have to be protected via some form of state regulation of prices and/or quality of service, which somewhat contradicts the principle of private ownership and control.

Privatization is generally part of a broader political agenda intended to inculcate or strengthen positive attitudes towards the free enterprise system associated with CAPITALISM, as in Britain under the Thatcher government and in post-socialist eastern Europe. In the post-socialist world privatization has sometimes led to those who controlled state assets becoming the main private owners, which has tended to discredit the process – especially where this form of 'insider privatization' is perceived to have taken place by dubious means. The term reprivatization is used to describe the process of returning to the original private owners, or their descendants, property expropriated by the state with the advent of socialism, as in Poland. DMS

probabilism The view that although the physical environment does not uniquely determine human actions, it does nevertheless make some responses more likely than others. The term was proposed for the terrain midway between a stark ENVIRONMENTAL DETERMINISM and a radical POSSIBILISM: human action was represented as 'not so much a matter of an all-or-nothing choice or compulsion, but a balance of probabilities' (Spate, 1957). This view was in fact perfectly compatible with the original Vidalian conception (see Lukermann, 1964), but in any event it was not long before geographers sought 'to use the probability calculus as well as rely on its philosophical connotations', and probability theory came to be regarded as an essential component of geographical analysis since it provided 'a common mode of discourse' for 'scientific study of the landscape' (Curry, in House, 1966). DG

References

House, J.W., ed., 1966: *Northern geographical essays in honour of G.H.J. Daysh.* Newcastle-upon-Tyne: University of Newcastle-upon-Tyne, Department of Geography. · Lukerman, F. 1964: Geography as a formal intellectual discipline and the way in which it contributes to human knowledge. *Canadian Geography* 8: 167–72. · Spate, O.H.K. 1957: How determined is possibilism? *Geographical Studies* 4: 3–12.

Suggested Reading

Spate (1957).

probability map A MAP describing spatial variation in the likelihood of an event. The symbols might depict likelihood directly, as on a map showing probability of burglary or arson (MacEachren, 1992), or the map might hold likelihood constant and describe spatial variation in the magnitude of an event with that likelihood. The latter strategy is common on maps of environmental HAZARDS such as floods, earthquakes and volcanic eruptions. For example, a map of the 100-year flood (with an annual probability of 0.01) might not only delineate the flood zone but describe the expected inundation in feet or metres. MM

Reference

MacEachren, A.M. 1992: Visualizing uncertain information. *Cartographic Perspectives* 13: 10–19.

problematic A framework which determines the ways in which problems are identified within a DISCOURSE, and which thereby 'appears' in the concepts and evidences through which they are realized. The term comes from Jacques Martin, but it gained prominence through Louis Althusser's 'symptomatic' reading of Marx, in which he tried to uncover the system of concepts at work behind the evident form of the various TEXTS and, in particular, to identify an epistemological break in which Marx was supposed to have made the transition from IDEOLOGY to science (see STRUCTURAL MARXISM). As such, the concept owes much to modern STRUCTURALISM, so that while there are a number of superficial similarities between them it is in fact very different from the Kuhnian concept of a PARADIGM. Although the term is widely used as a convenient shorthand, particularly in Marxist theory, Althusser's particular usage has been subject to several criticisms, and most especially for a conflation of the external processes, through which a discourse is produced, and its own internal structure of dependence and connection (see, e.g. Hindess, 1977). DG

Reference

Hindess, B. 1977: *Philosophy and methodology in the social sciences.* Brighton: Harvester. · Atlantic Highlands, NJ: Humanities Press

Suggested Reading

Glucksmann, M. 1974: *Structuralist analysis in contemporary social thought.* London: Routledge and Kegan Paul, 3–10.

process A flow of events or actions which produces, reproduces or transforms a system or structure.

It was not until the 1960s that modern geography was alerted to the complexity of the concept of a process. Blaut (1961) insisted that the standard distinction between SPATIAL STRUCTURE and temporal process derived from a KANTIANISM which had been discredited by what he called 'the relativistic revolution'. It was now clear, so he claimed, that 'nothing in the physical world is purely spatial or temporal; everything is process . . . '. In Blaut's view, therefore, 'structures of the real world' were simply 'slow processes of long duration'. Although most formalizations of geography as a SPATIAL SCIENCE appeared to accept such a claim – Golledge and Amedeo (1968) and Harvey (1969) endorsed the central importance of 'process laws' in their general accounts of explanation in geography (see POSITIVISM) – in practice many studies used distance as a surrogate for process (hence 'spatial processes') and thereby confirmed the geometric cast of much of LOCATIONAL ANALYSIS and SPATIAL ANALYSIS (see DISTANCE DECAY).

Many of these models depended upon *formal language systems*, i.e. language systems the elements of which have *unassigned meanings*. The *x*s and *y*s in their equations or the points and lines in their diagrams could thus refer to anything – they were empty of concrete content – and so analysis was governed by the relations between these abstract elements in the language system itself: by the laws of geometry, the calculus of probability theory or the mathematical theory of STOCHASTIC PROCESSES, rather than by 'the things we are talking *about*' (Olsson, 1974). These models were reviewed in Cliff and Ord (1981).

The past 20 years, however, have seen the resurgence of geographies based on *ordinary language systems*, the elements of which have assigned meanings. These have allowed much more *substantive* conceptions of process to be utilized., e.g. cognitive and DECISION-MAKING processes in BEHAVIOURAL GEOGRAPHY, the LABOUR PROCESS and the dynamics of capital ACCUMULATION in ECONOMIC GEOGRAPHY, and processes of STRUCTURATION in SOCIAL GEOGRAPHY, and this has in turn required a careful reworking of some of the most basic theorems of the other human and social sciences (see Gregory, 1985). For, as Harvey (1973) recognized: 'An understanding of space in all its complexity depends upon an appreciation of social processes . . . [and] an understanding of the social process in all its complexity depends upon an appreciation of spatial form.' One of his most pressing concerns was thus 'to heal the breach' between the 'sociological' and the 'GEOGRAPHICAL IMAGINATION'. (See also CONTEXTUAL APPROACH.)

The distinction between 'formal' and 'substantive' definitions of process is cross-cut by a second distinction drawn by Hay and Johnston (1983) between the following:

Process as sequence in space and/or time. This view of process is characteristic of the VERTICAL THEMES of traditional HISTORICAL GEOGRAPHY and of more modern SPACE–TIME FORECASTING MODELS. In both cases, the account is usually descriptive: compare Darby's (1951) identification of the processes which changed the English landscape ('clearing the wood', 'draining the marsh', etc.) with Bennett's simple (1978) typology of barrier, hierarchy, network and contiguity processes (see the figure).

Process as mechanism. This view of process is most closely associated with SYSTEMS ANALYSIS, in which the 'central concept' of diachronic analysis is held to be 'that of process' (Langton,

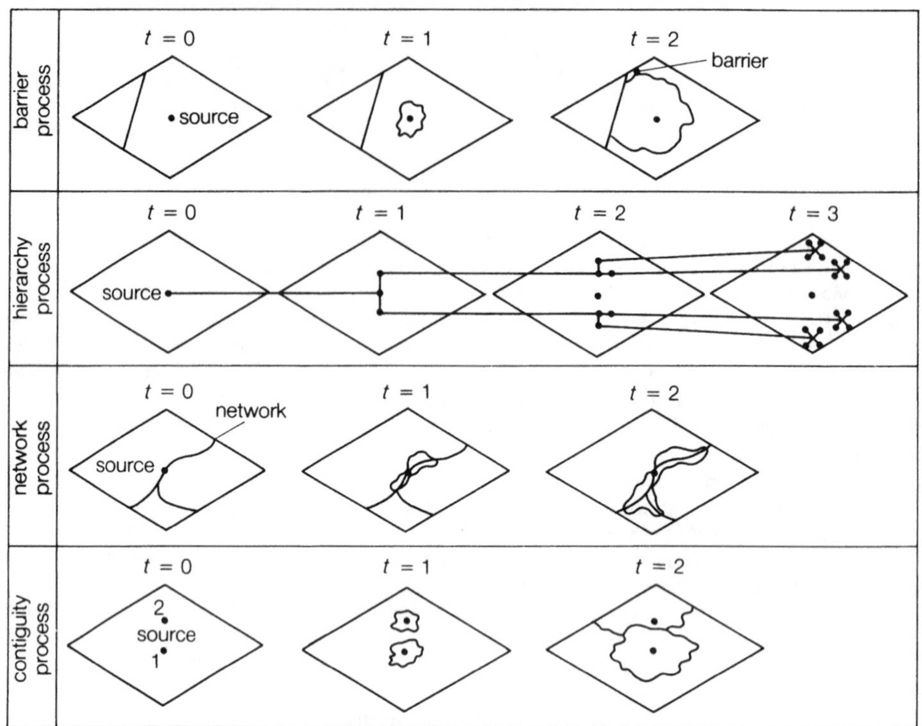

process *Spatial patterns produced through time (t) by barrier, hierarchy, network and contiguity processes* (after Bennett, 1978)

1972, pp. 137–56), and more recently with those geographies which have been influenced by philosophies of REALISM, which require the identification of the relations between the 'causal powers' of structures and their realizations (Sayer, 1984, pp. 94–107). In both cases, the account is *explanatory*: it seeks to show how – by what means – something happens.

Hay and Johnston (1983) integrate (a) and (b) as follows:

> A process study seeks to identify the rules which govern spatio-temporal sequences, in such a form that the rules are interpretable in terms of the results of the sequence, in terms of the exogenous variables which influence the sequence, and in terms of the mechanisms by which exogenous and endogenous influences give rise to the results which the sequence itself records.

Although this formulation is explicitly restricted to quantitative studies in human geography, its emphasis on *interpretation* registers an important advance over most early spatial models (particularly those concerned with replication and SIMULATION) and it opens the door for translation between the two distinctions drawn above. DG

References

Bennett, R.J. 1978: *Spatial time series: analysis, forecasting and control*. London: Pion. · Blaut, J. 1961: Space and process. *Professional Geographer* 13: 1–7. · Cliff, A.D. and Ord, J.K. 1981: *Spatial processes: models and applications*. London: Pion. · Darby, H.C. 1951: The changing English landscape. *Geographical Journal* 117: 377–94. · Golledge, R. and Amedeo, D. 1968: On laws in geography. *Annals of the Association of American Geographers* 58: 760–74. · Gregory, D. 1985: People, places and practices: the future of human geography. In R. King, ed., *Geographical futures*. Sheffield: Geographical Association, 56–75. · Harvey, D. 1969: *Explanation in geography*. London: Edward Arnold, 419–32. · Harvey, D. 1973: *Social justice and the city*. London: Edward Arnold, 22–49. · Hay, A.M. and Johnston, R.J. 1983: The study of process in quantitative human geography. *L'espace géographique* 12: 69–76. · Langton, J. 1972: Potentialities and problems of adopting a systems approach to the analysis of change in human geography. *Professional Geographer* 4: 125–79. · Olsson, G. 1974: The dialectics of spatial analysis. *Antipode* 6: 50–62. · Sayer, A. 1984: *Method in social science: a realist approach*. London: Hutchinson.

Suggested Reading

Cliff and Ord (1981). · Harvey (1973). · Hay and Johnston (1983).

producer services Services which are supplied to businesses and governments, rather than directly to individual (or 'end') consumers (cf. CONSUMER SERVICES). Such services, often characterized as those which provide 'intermediate' inputs into the process of production, include economic activities as diverse as financial services, research and development, computer services, marketing and advertising, and certain kinds of transport and communication. Producer services have economically important consequences and often quite distinctive geographies because: (i) there needs to be no spatial coincidence between the demand for these services and their supply; and (ii) they are often only partially dependent upon the level of economic activity in a city or region. The study of these geographies has become an increasing visible part of ECONOMIC GEOGRAPHY. As clusters of interconnected activity, they are also increasingly regarded as an important determinant in the formation of REGIONAL POLICY. (See also SERVICES, GEOGRAPHY OF; MONEY AND FINANCE, GEOGRAPHY OF; CONSUMPTION, GEOGRAPHY OF.) NJT

References

Daniels, P.W., ed., 1991: *Services and metropolitan development: international perspectives*. London: Routledge. · Daniels, P.W. 1993: *Service industries in the world economy*. Oxford: Blackwell. · Daniels, P.W. and Lever, W., eds, 1996: *The global economy in transition*. Harlow: Longman. · Marshall, J.N. and Wood, P.A. 1995: *Services and space: key aspects of urban and regional development*. Harlow: Longman.

product life cycle A concept used to understand the changing locational needs of an industry based on a characteristic process of maturation of its principal good over time, often referred to simply as 'product cycle'. The idea is conventionally attributed to Vernon (1966), although its antecedents are actually considerably older (Kuznets, 1930; Burns, 1934). Vernon's classic study of the economy of the New York metropolitan region (Vernon, 1963), and especially his appraisal of that region's ability to retain manufacturing functions that had already begun to disperse to new locations, provided the original empirical foundation for his product cycle theory. However, by the time his 1966 article was written, Vernon's research interests had shifted to the MULTINATIONAL CORPORATION and the international economy (cf. GLOBALIZATION). His motivation was to show that investment decisions taken by manufacturers on an international scale were driven by considerations far more complex than simple COMPARATIVE COST ANALYSIS with its focus on geographical differences in factor and transportation costs. Instead, he posited that products tend to undergo a series of transitions through three distinct stages of their life cycle, and that firms choose different production locations to suit these characteristics as they change over time.

'New products' are, by their nature, somewhat unstable since their design is still being modified and perfected, as are the accompanying processes required to produce them. There is also likely to be considerable iterative interaction between the producing firm and the market as successive modifications are introduced, test-marketed, and appraised. Consequently at this early stage, producers require ready access to customers but also to a diverse and deep pool of suppliers, since inputs are likely to be modified as the product's design changes. As Vernon notes (1966, p. 195), 'the need for swift and effective communication on the part of the producer with consumers, suppliers, and even competitors is especially high at this stage'. Such requirements are most likely to be met in major industrialized countries, especially in major metropolitan economies.

At the second stage, the *'maturing product'* undergoes a process of increasing standardization and expansion of production scale as demand for the product grows. Hence, the need for flexibility that was so evident earlier is now greatly reduced, as uncertainties about the product's design and marketability diminish. At this stage, minimizing production costs becomes the foremost concern for manufacturers, who will select locations outside the most heavily industrialized countries in search of lower labour costs.

By the time a product has reached the third stage of *'standardized product'*, Vernon contends (p. 202), 'at an advanced stage in the standardisation of some products, the less-developed countries may offer competitive advantages as a production location'. This is especially likely for products that are labour-intensive, have a high price elasticity of demand, and are only weakly dependent on EXTERNAL ECONOMIES for their production.

Although Vernon's ideas were important in shaping research on international business (see, for example, Wells, 1972), product cycle theory enjoyed its most intensive application at the sub-national scale. An early exponent of Vernon's ideas at the interregional scale was Wilbur Thompson, whose classic paper (Thompson, 1968) recast the Vernon hypothesis in the form of a 'filtering-down' theory of urban economic change. According to this approach, new products would originate in the largest metropolitan regions at the top of the urban hierarchy because of the concentration of highly educated scientific and technical workers, as well as universities and other research institutions found there. The earliest commercial production of such innovations would occur in the same regions for the reasons outlined by Vernon. With increasing standardization of the product and the production process, the tie to such highly skilled labour would weaken and cost considerations would drive manufacturers to seek out locations in intermediate-sized urban centres where semi- and unskilled workers would be available in plentiful supply and at substantially lower wage rates. As products reached the point of advanced maturity, their production would shift to the smallest urban centres at the bottom of the urban hierarchy (or even to rural locations). Although this shifting investment would bring employment opportunities to relatively depressed areas with high unemployment rates, Thompson's assessment of the long-term prospects for such regions was clear and unequivocal (p. 56): 'their industrial catches come to them only to die'.

At the time when Vernon and Thompson first began work on the product cycle concept, the long-term dominance of established industrial regions such as the Manufacturing Belt of the US Midwest and Northeast was unchallenged. For Thompson, the decline of such regions was unthinkable because of their proven ability over the long run to continue to generate new products. For this reason, the loss of certain manufacturing functions to more peripheral regions through the filtering-down process, while inevitable, was little cause for concern. A scant decade later, however, the assumptions supporting Thompson's analysis came into question as a major shift in economic activity between the regions of the United States became evident. It is therefore hardly surprising that scholars such as Rees (1979) and Thomas (1980) used the work of Vernon and Thompson as a conceptual framework with which to explain the decline of the Manufacturing Belt (which was then coming to be known as the 'Frostbelt' or even the 'Rustbelt') and the rise of the 'Sunbelt' states of the US South and West (cf. SUNBELT/SNOWBELT). For them, the decline of the Frostbelt could be explained by the accelerated rate of decentralization of production activities, as intensified foreign competition from offshore, newly industrializing countries heightened the importance of cost reduction for US-based manufacturers. Moreover, in contrast to Thompson's views, Rees and Stafford (1986) advanced the proposition that previously 'peripheral' areas such as the US Southeast could eventually achieve a critical mass once a sufficient volume of capital had been invested in production facilities in the region. At this point, they argued, the 'incubator' functions (generating new products and firms) traditionally associated exclusively with the largest metropolitan regions in the Northeast and Midwest could take root in these once-peripheral locations. Such arguments, which implied an even more fundamental challenge to the economic supremacy of the largest urban regions, were supported by the empirical work of Pred (1977), which demonstrated that many of the largest industrial firms in the United States were shifting some of their highest-order activities (especially research and development) away from their original headquarter locations to urban centres considerably further down the hierarchy.

More recently the product life cycle concept has been criticized for its excessive determinism and ESSENTIALISM, especially the argument implicit in the theory that all products naturally follow a similar trajectory over time (Storper, 1985; Taylor, 1986). Critics have pointed out that even standardized and mature products can be rejuvenated through innovation in later stages of a product's 'life cycle'. A case in point is the automobile, which, while hardly a new product, has been continuously modified and improved over time. It has also been argued that many products never achieve the status of cheap, standardized, mass-produced goods – especially those which, under a regime of FLEXIBLE ACCUMULATION, exhibit a high degree of variability, customization, and qualitative differentiation. (See also PROFIT LIFE CYCLE.) MSG

References

Burns, A.F. 1934: *Production trends in the United States*. New York: Bureau of Economic Research. · Kuznets, S. 1930: *Secular movements in production and prices*. Boston: Houghton Mifflin. · Pred, A.R. 1977: *City-systems in advanced economies*. New York: Halsted Press. · Rees, J. 1979: Technological change and regional shifts in American manufacturing. *Professional Geographer* 31: 45–54. · Rees, J. and Stafford, H.A. 1986: Theories of regional growth and industrial location: their relevance for understanding high technology complexes. In J. Rees, ed., *Technology, regions and policy*. Totowa, NJ: Rowman and Littlefield, 23–50. · Storper, M. 1985: Oligopoly and the product cycle: essentialism in economic geography. *Economic Geography* 61: 260–82. · Taylor, M.J. 1986: The product cycle model: a critique. *Environment and Planning A* 18: 751–61. · Thomas, M.D.

1980: Explanatory frameworks for growth and change in multiregional firms. *Economic Geography* 56: 1–17. · Thompson, W.R. 1968: Internal and external factors in urban economies. In H.S. Perloff and L. Wingo, eds, *Issues in urban economics*. Baltimore: Johns Hopkins University Press and Resources for the Future, 43–62. · Vernon, R. 1963: *Metropolis 1985: an interpretation of the findings of the New York metropolitan region study*. Garden City, NJ: Doubleday. · Vernon, R. 1966: International investment and international trade in the product cycle. *Quarterly Journal of Economics* 80: 190–207. · Wells, L.T., ed., 1972: *The product life cycle and international trade*. Boston: Harvard Business School Press.

Suggested Reading

Malecki, E.J. 1991: *Technology and economic development: the dynamics of local, regional, and national change*. Harlow: Longman.

production complex A spatial cluster of specialized, interrelated economic activities bound together by the creation and exploitation of EXTERNAL ECONOMIES (Scott, 1988). Such clusters offer producers the ability to establish, and easily realign, transactional LINKAGES with other local buyers and suppliers, thereby encouraging the development and maintenance of a social division of labour (see JUST-IN-TIME PRODUCTION; TRANSACTION COSTS; TRANSACTIONAL ANALYSIS). They also provide a local labour market specialized to match the needs of local producers. They are further sustained by the existence of public and quasi-public institutions developed to support specialized local economic activity and to foster non-market forms of interaction and interdependencies between local economic actors. (See AGGLOMERATION; COMMODITY CHAIN/FILIÈRE; INDUSTRIAL DISTRICT.)

MSG

Reference

Scott, A.J. 1988: *Metropolis*. Berkeley: University of California Press.

production of nature The social production of nature by human societies. The phrase derives from Neil Smith (1984), whose *Uneven development* provides the clearest explanation of how nature is produced within CAPITALISM. The idea of the production of nature seems quixotic. After all, NATURE is usually defined as the non-human or that which is beyond human control. Against this, Smith argued that such a notion of nature as 'external' to society is an IDEOLOGY which in fact obscures nature's real nature under capitalism. Specifically, he used MARXIAN ECONOMICS to argue that capitalism has replaced a non-human 'first nature' with a socially produced 'second nature'. From new agricultural LANDSCAPES to managed fisheries, nature is thus for Smith materially transformed by capitalism.

The 'production of nature' argument is easy to misinterpret in at least two ways. The first misinterpretation overstates the power of capitalist production by assuming that Smith argued that production occurs right down to the last atom (Castree, 1995). Here, nature becomes a mere *tabula rasa* – or blank slate – for capitalism. Yet this is clearly an untenable position and one Smith distanced himself from. For instance, even the genetically modified foods produced by large MULTINATIONAL CORPORATIONS require sunshine, water and soil minerals to grow. The second mistake is to assume that production equates only to what occurs in the LABOUR PROCESS (e.g. in the factory or on the farm). However, against this rather narrow definition of production, Smith argued that it involves the whole system of capitalist economic relations, including exchange, distribution and competition. In this way he drew attention to the systematicity and extended scale of nature's production under capitalism. Perhaps the finest empirical exemplification of Smith's arguments is *Nature's metropolis* (1991), authored, ironically, by non-Marxist William Cronon (Cronon rejects Marx's LABOUR THEORY OF VALUE among other things).

The 'production of nature' thesis has three strengths. First, by registering the redundancy of thinking of nature as an external realm, it undermines the arguments of those ENVIRONMENTALISTS – like neo-Malthusians (cf. LIMITS TO GROWTH; MALTHUSIAN MODEL) – who would impose social sanctions on people in the name of a nature to be 'protected' or 'saved' (cf. CONSERVATION; PRESERVATION). Second, by insisting that nature is produced, not given, it reveals how capitalism makes nature into an instrument of ACCUMULATION. Nature thus becomes subordinated to the profit imperative. Finally, though, insisting on nature's production also opens up the liberating possibility and politics of producing nature along more socially and ECOLOGICALLY progressive lines associated with SOCIALISM.

In recent years, the 'production of nature' argument has been modified and extended. As awareness of a 'global environmental crisis' has grown, it has been recognized that Smith failed to theorize the ways in which capitalism actively produces environmental problems. Harvey (1996, part II) has thus sought to demonstrate how produced nature has a materiality which can be ecologically and economically deleterious for capitalism. At the same time, Swyngedouw (1997) has tried theoretically and empirically to show how Smith's arguments feed into a Marxist urban POLITICAL ECOLOGY in which economic and ecological change are but sides of the same coin and in which nature reflects and refracts POWER relations between dominant and subordinated groups in society. Finally, Harvey (1998) has recently suggested that the human body is becoming increasingly commodified as an 'accumulation strategy' (see BODY, GEOGRAPHY AND). NC

References

Castree, N. 1995: The nature of produced nature. *Antipode* 27: 12–48; Cronon, W. 1991: *Nature's metropolis*. New York: W.W. Norton. · Harvey, D. 1996: *Justice, nature and the geography of difference*. Oxford: Blackwell. · Harvey, D. 1998: The body as an accumulation strategy. *Environment and Planning D: Society and Space*. · Smith, N. 1984: *Uneven development*. Oxford: Blackwell. · Swyngedouw, E. 1997: Power, nature and the city. The conquest of water and the political ecology of urbanisation in Guayaquil, Ecuador: 1880–1990. *Environment and Planning A* 29: 311–32.

production of space The social production of the spaces within which social life takes place. The term derives from the writings of the French Marxist philosopher Henri Lefebvre (1901–91), who explored the concept in a number of texts, most notably in *La production de l'espace* (1991; see Kofman and Lebas, 1996, for an intellectual biography). This book is a dense and complex TEXT which has been subject to many different readings – there is no single route through its passages – but it is the single most important source for understanding Lefebvre's ideas about social space. He was writing within a broadly humanist tradition of HISTORICAL MATERIALISM, and for this reason he was deeply critical of the ascendancy of ANTI-HUMANISM in the 1960s and 1970s, and in particular the rise of STRUCTURALISM, STRUCTURAL MARXISM and POST-STRUCTURALISM within the intellectual firmament of French culture. He took particular exception to their use of spatial metaphors by means of which, so he said, 'the philosophico-epistemological notion of space is fetishized and the mental realm comes to envelop the social and physical one'. This is a contentious claim; post-structuralism does not conceive of the relationship between discursivity and materiality in such idealist terms (see Gibson-Graham, 1966, pp. 74–5; 81–2). Still, in place of these spatial metaphors Lefebvre proposed a concept of socially produced space – SPATIALITY – as a way of registering both 'mental space' and 'material space'.

Lefebvre's argument drew critically and creatively on Marx, Hegel and Nietzsche. He provided what could be called an historical geography of the present – an argumentation-sketch intended to illuminate the present LANDSCAPE and its conjunctures in new and unsettling ways – which was, in effect, a critical account of 'the rise of the West' that was particularly sensitive to the modalities of violence that were involved in the formation and extension of CAPITALISM both inside and outside Europe (though Lefebvre himself said remarkably little in any detail about the production of space under COLONIALISM). He mapped the trajectory of capitalism not only in terms of CLASS struggle and capital ACCUMULATION – meat and drink to conventional Marxian accounts – but also as the inscription of masculine POWER ('phallic brutality') on social life and social space. This involved Lefebvre in a subterranean critique of PSYCHOANALYTIC THEORY that nonetheless activated many of its central concerns (Gregory, 1997): so much so, in fact, that Blum and Nast (1996) argue that his sketch is not founded on the primacy of class struggle at all 'but on the construction of alterity itself' through a projected PHALLOCENTRISM.

In outline, Lefebvre sketched an historical series of representations of space, each connected to a specific MODE OF PRODUCTION, through which social space had been progressively 'de-corporealized': the advance of capitalism thus depended not only on a logic of accumulation but also on a logic of visualization through which human spatiality bore less and less relation to the human BODY (see the first figure; cf. Gregory, 1994). This was not intended to be a detailed historico-geographical reconstruction, of course, but its architecture has been criticized on grounds other than the purely empirical. Blum and Nast (1996) argue that its activating logic is shot through with a MASCULINISM and a heterosexism in which the paternal is identified with the operative logic of history – 'activity is that which materially inscribes the body in history' and which is equated with 'the phallic' – so that feminine bodies are rendered 'passive' and 'invisible'. Pile (1996, pp. 146–75; 211–17) concedes the force of these objections, but believes that even as Lefebvre sets these 'masculinist presumptions' in motion he also struggles to negate them through 'an explicit critique of masculine space, ruled by the deathly phallus'. Certainly, the temporary terminus of Lefebvre's narrative was the installation of an abstract space – which he described

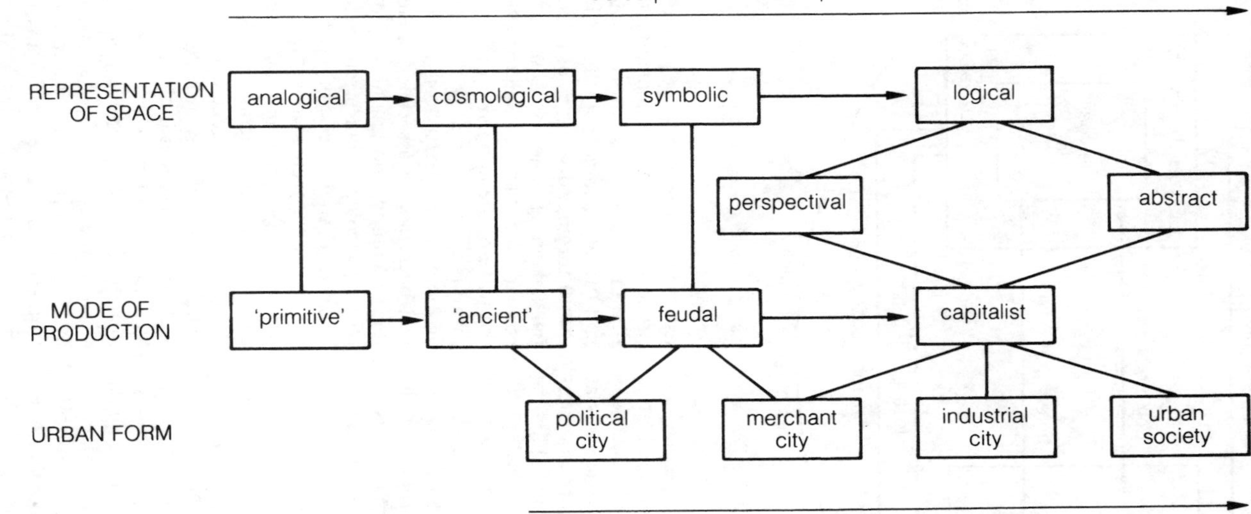

production of space *1: The production of space* (Gregory, 1993; after Lefebvre)

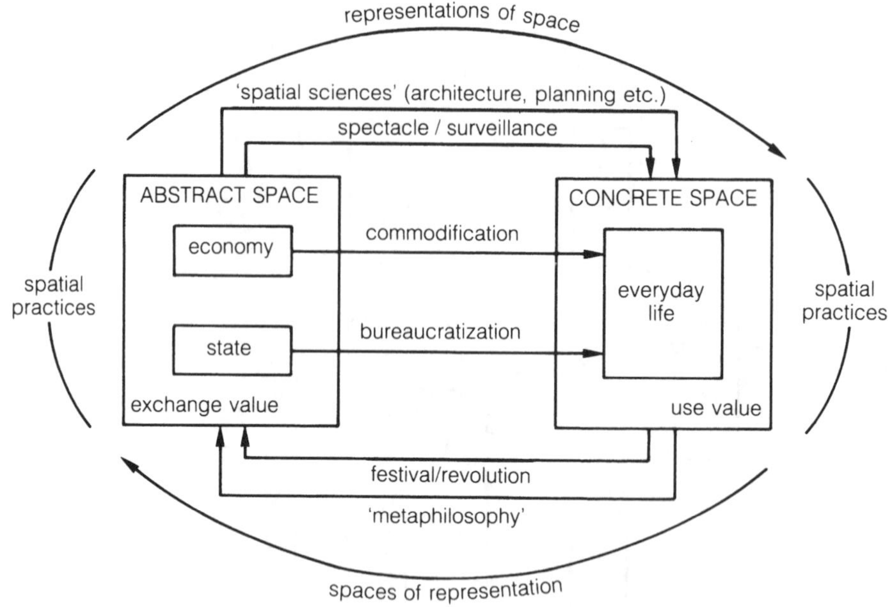

production of space *2: The colonization of concrete space* (Gregory, 1993)

as a 'visual-geometric-phallic space' – in which 'space had no social existence independent of an aggressive and repressive visualization' (see VISION AND VISUALITY). Abstract space was at once symptomatic of and constitutive of capitalist MODERNITY: it was a fragmented, differentiated and aggressively expanding social space, whose contradictions disclosed the unstable constitution of GLOBALIZATION. Moving back to a more familiar materialist terrain, Lefebvre argued that the STATE played a crucial role in attempting to manage the contradictions of abstract space by provisionally 'fixing' territorial configurations that could underwrite landscapes of capital accumulation. The production of abstract space was thus also a process of the production of spatial SCALE, articulating the relations between globalization, territorialization and URBANIZATION (see Brenner, 1997, and TERRITORIALITY). In the course of these hierarchical productions, which were also deformations, Lefebvre argued that abstract space 'colonized' everyday life and atrophied its roots in an older, historically sedimented concrete space (see also Lefebvre, 1971, 1992; cf. CRITICAL THEORY).

As indicated in the second figure, Lefebvre suggested that this process of colonization had been effected through: (i) multiple *spatial practices* of bureaucratization and commodification, which relied on the production and extension of spatial grids of power (an unstable process of territorialization and reterritorialization in both political and economic registers); and (ii) *representations of space* which were produced through discourses of urban and regional planning and SPATIAL SCIENCE, and strategies of SPECTACLE and SURVEILLANCE. In the wake of the popular uprisings and student protests in France in May 1968, and the interventions of the SITUATIONISTS with whom he had been closely associated, Lefebvre hoped that a counter-movement would emerge to resist the colonization of concrete space and to reclaim the spaces of everyday life. He believed that such a movement would work through (iii) *spaces of representation*, whose countervailing productions would be informed by a series of insurgent counter-DISCOURSES, including Lefebvre's own 'metaphilosophy', and critical practices in the arts, which would feed into a series of spontaneous struggles ('festivals'). Spaces of representation had their origin in the concrete spaces of everyday life – in the memories and residues of an older, 'authentic' human existence inscribed within the TAKEN-FOR-GRANTED WORLD – and many of them depended on restoring an essential connective between human SPATIALITY and the human body (see also Lefebvre, 1973, 1992).

Although Lefebvre's major theses were written in the 1960s and early 1970s, many commentators have insisted on their continuing and contemporary significance. Indeed, so prescient were Lefebvre's ideas about the production of space to both Dear (1997) and Soja (1989) that they claimed them for a critical POSTMODERNISM, though there have been dissenting voices (Gregory, 1994; Kofman and Lebas, 1996). These tussles are much less important than Lefebvre's central thesis about the production of space, which Dear (1997) glosses thus: 'Space is, in a manner of speaking, nature's way of preventing everything from happening in the same place.' If this one-liner is taken literally, it opens up two avenues of inquiry in human geography. The first concerns the relations between 'space' and 'place'. Following Lefebvre, Merrifield (1993) treats SPACE and PLACE as different aspects of a dialectical unity within which 'space' is constituted through and conceptualized as a 'rootless, fluid reality of material flows' that congeals and fixes itself in 'place'. Soja (1996), however, noted that Lefebvre rarely used the concept of 'place' in his writings since – so he said – its richest meaning is conveyed through the dense constellation crystallized around lived space, everyday life and concrete space. Instead of a DIALECTIC between space and place, therefore, Soja proposed what he called a TRIALECTICS of spatiality that transcends the oppositions between 'material' and 'mental' spaces that had so forcefully attracted Lefebvre's attention and which, in Soja's terms, embeds the subversive production of 'spaces of representation' in the insurgent possibilities of a THIRD SPACE, a differential space within which ordinary people might freely claim what Lefebvre called 'the right to DIFFERENCE'. (See also PLACE/SPACE TENSIONS.) The second avenue concerns the 'place' of NATURE within Lefebvre's corpus and thus the connections between the production of space and the production of nature. This problematic was much less developed in Lefebvre's writings. While he concedes that the production of abstract space has been achieved through the domination of nature – a commonplace of conventional historical materialism – he said remarkably little about the orderings of nature and the emancipatory 'politics of nature' that should also presumably have their place within any 'third space'. For in the end, Smith (1998, p. 67) declares, 'it is spatialized nature rather than naturalized space that provides the banal substance of everyday life, and the fruition of Lefebvre's ambition – politically and intellectually – requires an adjustment to the politics of the production of nature'.

Lefebvre's ideas are an immensely provocative source for thinking about the politics and productions of space, but it remains to be seen how far they will succeed in informing empirical research and political practice (cf. Allen and Pryke, 1994), and how well they will survive a renewed critique from a human geography seemingly increasingly sympathetic to post-structuralism. DG

References

Allen, J. and Pryke, M. 1994: The production of service space. *Environment and Planning D: Society and Space* 12: 453–75. · Blum, V. and Nast, H. 1996: Where's the difference? The heterosexualization of alterity in Henri Lefebvre and Jacques Lacan. *Environment and Planning D: Society and Space* 14: 559–80. · Brenner, N. 1997: Global, fragmented, hierarchical: Henri Lefebvre's geographies of globalization. *Public culture* 10 (1): 135–67. · Dear, M. 1997: Postmodern bloodlines. In G. Benko and U. Strohmayer, eds, *Space and social theory: interpreting modernity and postmodernity.* Oxford and Cambridge, MA: Blackwell, 49–71. · Gibson-Graham, J.K. 1966: *The end of capitalism (as we knew it): a feminist critique of political economy.* Cambridge, MA and Oxford: Blackwell. · Gregory, D. 1994: *Geographical imaginations.* Oxford and Cambridge, MA: Blackwell. · Gregory, D. 1997: Lefebvre, Lacan and the production of space. In G. Benko and U. Strohmayer, eds, *Space and social theory: interpreting modernity and postmodernity.* Oxford and Cambridge, MA: Blackwell, 203–31. · Kofman, E. and Lebas, E. 1996: Lost in transposition: Time, space and the city. Editorial introduction to H. Lefebvre, *Writing on cities.* Oxford and Cambridge, MA: Blackwell, 3–60. · Lefebvre, H. 1970: *La révolution urbaine.* Paris: Gallimard. · Lefebvre, H. 1971: *Everyday life in the modern world.* New York: Harper. · Lefebvre, H. 1972: *Espace et politique.* Paris: Anthropos [reprinted in Lefebvre, 1996]. · Lefebvre, H. 1973: *The survival of capitalism.* London: Allison and Busby. · Lefebvre, H. 1991: *The production of space.* Oxford and Cambridge, MA: Blackwell (orig. pub. in French as *La production de l'espace*, 1974). · Lefebvre, H. 1992: *Critique of everyday life.* London: Verso. · Lefebvre, H. 1996: *Writings on cities.* Oxford and Cambridge, MA: Blackwell. · Merrifield, A. 1993: Place and space: a Lefebvrean reconciliation. *Transactions, Institute of British Geographers* NS 18: 516–31. · Pile, S. 1996: *The body and the city: psychoanalysis, space and subjectivity.* London and New York: Routledge. · Smith, N. 1998: Antinomies of space and nature in Henri Lefebvre's *The Production of Space.* In A. Light and J. Smith, eds, *Philosophy and Geography, vol. II: The production of public space.* London and Boulder, CO: Rowman and Littlefield, 49–69. · Soja, E. 1989: *Postmodern geographies: the reassertion of space in critical social theory.* London: Verso. · Soja, E. 1996: *Thirdspace: journeys to Los Angeles and other real-and-imagined places.* Oxford and Cambridge, MA: Blackwell.

Suggested Reading

Blum and Nast (1996). · Gregory (1994), ch. 6; Lefebvre (1991). · Soja (1996), ch. 1.

productive forces The interaction of the means of production and labour, from which arises a society's capacity to produce. The means of production comprise the objects of labour and the means or instruments of labour. The *objects of labour* are all the things to which human labour is applied: they can be found as natural resources in the form of minerals, virgin timber, etc., or they can be objects to which some labour has already been applied such as components and crops cultivated or harvested. The *means of labour* are the things that people use to transform the objects of labour. These can vary from a stick with which one may knock an apple from a tree to the complex plant used to produce pig iron from iron ore. The development of the LABOUR PROCESS and its capacity to generate a greater volume of output is crucially dependent on technological advances in the means of labour. Thus means of production created by human labour (such as machines) become steadily more important compared with natural objects of labour.

The means of production cannot themselves produce anything without the application of labour. The special status of labour in the productive forces is expressed in its capacity both to activate and to produce means of production. The advancement of labour skills and PRODUCTIVITY contributes critically to the development of the productive forces.

The level of development of the productive forces is an indication of society's capacity to make use of nature. A territory well endowed with NATURAL RESOURCES will be able to generate things useful to people only to the extent that the other productive forces of human labour and the instruments at its disposal are also available. At any particular time and place, the further development of the productive forces may be crucially dependent on advances in either the means of labour or the capacity of labour itself, given the limits of natural resources, though these advances may themselves open up possibilities for using new resources. This emphasizes the importance of interdependence among the productive forces (see also INFRASTRUCTURE; MODE OF PRODUCTION). DMS

productivity A measure of output relative to input, usually expressed as the ratio of the returns from sales to the costs of production. The term was developed in analyses of the efficiency of manufacturing industry, where it is equivalent to the rate of surplus value or rate of exploitation in MARXIAN ECONOMICS. The higher the amount of VALUE-ADDED in the production process relative to the costs incurred (of labour, materials and fixed capital), the greater the productivity. In primary industries, however, productivity usually implies the ratio of production per unit area of land rather than to its (imputed) cost.

With the growth of service industries in advanced capitalist societies, attempts have been made to measure productivity in sectors other than manufacturing – not least in higher education! – though the concept of value added is not readily applied in many such situations. RJJ

professional ethics Moral standards concerning professional conduct, specifying what is right or wrong practice. 'Medical ethics' involves a set of rules governing the conduct of doctors, for example: making sexual advances to patients is unethical, as is breaching the confidentiality of the doctor–patient relationship. Standards of professional ethics are likely to be adopted and observed very widely, if not universally, in societies sharing the same broad culture and code of morality. Unresolved ethical issues in medicine and health can generate heated public debate, for example euthanasia, and the cloning of animals for human spare parts.

Ethical issues arise in academic research, the more so when the subject is humankind. Some rules of conduct are clear-cut: it is unethical to engage in plagiarism (i.e. to present the work of others as one's own), to invent data and to falsify results. Such conduct is different from doing 'bad' research in a technical sense, however. For example, fitting a linear trend through a curvilinear relationship is incorrect, but not unethical unless the result is knowingly misrepresented.

More difficult ethical questions arise in survey research, especially QUALITATIVE METHODS (cf. SURVEY ANALYSIS). Should research workers always reveal their true identity and reasons for seeking information, for example, if this could prejudice the inquiry by making informants less forthcoming (researchers sometimes pose as prospective job applicants or house purchasers, in order to test whether their race has a bearing on how they are treated)? Should interviews be tape-recorded without the subject's knowledge? There is also the broader question of whether it is right to use people for research from which they may gain nothing.

Research on politically contentious topics is sometimes accompanied by charges of unethical conduct. An example is Jewish Israeli settlement of Palestine, the analysis of which has been involved in accusations of bias and distortion of evidence (e.g. papers in the *Political Geography Quarterly*, 10:3, 1991).

There are lively debates on professional ethics within geography. These have been prompted in part by the changing societal context within which academic workers are required to operate, including increased competition for resources along with the commercialization and commodification of knowledge. The importance of having one's personal or institutional name on a publication raises questions of intellectual property rights, for example, such as who is entitled to claim the results of research, and the right to publish or realize any commercial advantage to be derived from new knowledge? Is it right to seek research grants or publish particular kinds of work in order to boost departmental or personal performance indicators such as external income or citation ratings? Such questions are helpful in raising awareness of the moral basis of choice in academic activity.

Innovations in the collection, display and dissemination of information, such as GEOGRAPHICAL INFORMATION SYSTEMS and the Internet, pose ethical issues, at least for some of their users. The more traditional devices of the map and photograph have been found to contain moral messages. How 'we' scholars represent the lives of 'others' is increasingly a matter of critical reflection. Thus, the construction (or production) of geographical knowledge is now widely regarded as part of our problematic. DMS

Suggested Reading

Corry, M.R. 1991: On the possibility of ethics in geography. Writing, citing and the construction of intellectual property. *Progress in Human Geography* 15: 125–47. · Crampton, J. 1995: The ethics of GIS. *Cartography and Cartographic Information Systems* 22: 84–9. · Hay, I. 1998: Making moral imaginations. Research ethics, pedagogy, and professional human geography. *Ethics, Place and Environment* 1: 55–75. · Kirby, A. 1991: On ethics and power in higher education. *Journal of Geography in Higher Education* 15 1: 75–7 (and the papers following). · Rose, G. 1997: Situating knowledge: positionality, reflexivities and other tactics. *Progress in Human Geography* 21: 305–20. · Smith, D.M. 1994: On professional responsibility to distant others. *Area* 26: 359–67. · Winchester, H.P.M. 1996: Ethical issues in interviewing as a research method in human geography. *Australian Geographer* 2: 117–31.

profit cycle A sectional approach to understanding changes experienced by regional economies, developed as an alternative to the PRODUCT LIFE CYCLE model. Instead of focusing on regularities in the changing scale of output or changes in the qualitative characteristics of a product and its production process over time, Markusen (1985) argues that the economic variable most crucial to determining industrial change is the rate of profit. Drawing her inspiration from Schumpeter and Marx, she asserts that change within an industry should be understood in terms of two central processes, each of which is pursued by firms to increase market power and, hence, profit rates: innovation and imperfect competition. She posits a five-stage model through which industries are argued to move.

In the stage where new industries are born and core products are being designed, '*zero profit*' best describes the state of the sector.

Once an innovation has proved to be commercially successful, and so long as its production is concentrated in the hands of a single (monopoly) firm, the industry will enjoy '*super profit*' levels.

As patents expire and/or imitation and innovation diffusion facilitates entry into the industry by new firms, the market power once held by the monopoly firm dissipates. Profit rates then decline to '*normal profit*' levels, as the industry moves towards market saturation. It is only at this stage that competitive conditions in the industry come to resemble perfect competition.

The fourth stage is the least determinate of the five. If a small number of firms are able to increase their market shares through mergers and acquisitions, this move toward oligopoly will raise profit rates to '*normal-plus*' levels. If, instead, the industry evolves along a path of predatory pricing and excessive competition, profit rates will be squeezed to '*normal-minus*' levels.

Finally, once the sector matures to a state of obsolescence, '*negative profit*' rates will ensue.

Moreover, Markusen argues that 'distinct spatial tendencies also accompany each stage of a sector's passage through the profit cycle' (p. 24). Corresponding to the five stages described above are: concentration, agglomeration, dispersion, relocation and abandonment. MSG

Reference

Markusen, A.R. 1985: *Profit cycles, oligopoly, and regional development*. Cambridge, MA: MIT Press.

projection A geometric transformation that portrays a spherical world on a flat map (see MAP IMAGE AND MAP). The alternative – a globe – is cumbersome, expensive to reproduce and useless to viewers eager to look from place to place at will, without lifting or turning a bulky three-dimensional model. Unless viewed

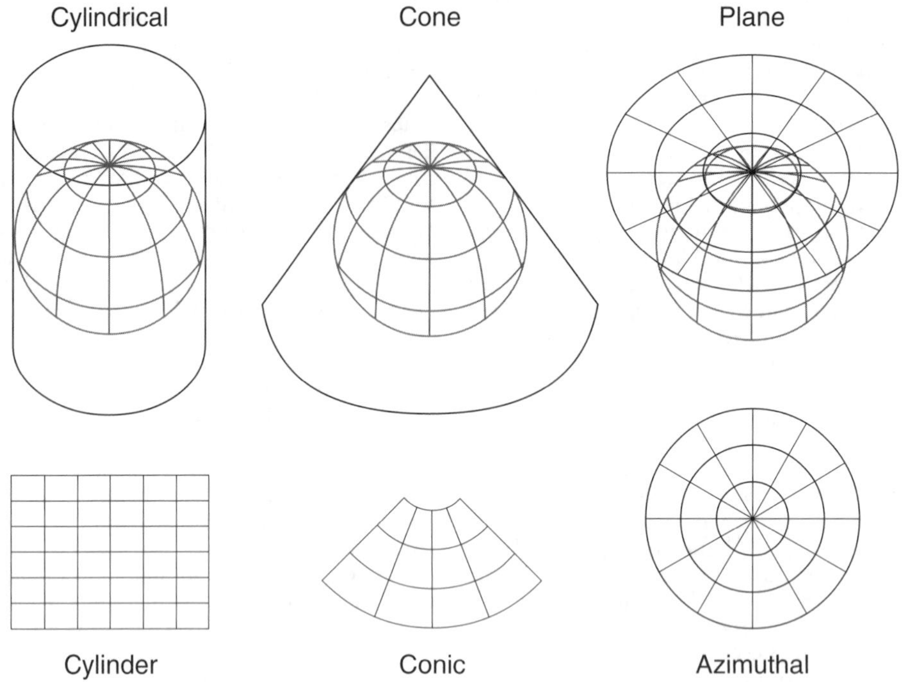

projection *principal developable surfaces (above) generate distinctive projection grids (below)*

directly, a globe also distorts the relative appearance of size, shape, distance and direction.

Map projection is readily understood as a two-stage process. In stage one, shrinking the world to a hypothetical globe establishes the map's stated scale (Maling, 1992, pp. 82–3). In stage two, placing this globe in contact with a plane, cone or cylinder allows the mathematical transfer of meridians, parallels, coasts and boundaries onto a flat or flattenable surface (see figure). In some projections a third stage readjusts locations and shapes, as when the sinusoidal projection corrects for the enlarged poleward areas on the equirectangular projection by bending meridians inward toward a central meridian.

Flattening a globe distorts distances. SCALE is no longer the same everywhere and in all directions away from all points. In general, a projection maintains its stated scale only at the point (for projection onto a plane) or line of contact (for a cone or cylinder). Moreover, distortion grows with increased distance from the tangent point or standard line. Allowing the projection surface to penetrate the globe affords a broader, more balanced pattern of distortion by providing a circular band of low distortion in the case of a plane or two bands of low distortion on a cone or cylinder. A cartographer can tailor a projection to a specific country or region by carefully selecting the projection surface and its orientation to the globe (Robinson and Snyder, 1991).

Because of many possible perspectives and orientations, map projection is a source of frustration as well as insight (Snyder and Voxland, 1989). Although all projections distort most distances, an equidistant projection might preserve true distance from the equator or from a pole or another point of interest. Similarly, an equivalent projection can preserve the true relative areas of countries and continents, whereas a conformal projection, which preserves small shapes as well as angles around points, is especially useful on large-scale maps of small areas. Unfortunately, equidistance, equivalence and conformality are mutually exclusive properties.

Projections can be controversial (Monmonier, 1995, pp. 1–44). The Mercator projection, a conformal mapping onto a cylinder, is valuable to navigators because straight lines are lines of constant geographical direction. But as a general view of the world, the Mercator map diminishes the size and presumably the importance of developing nations, nearer than most developed countries to the map's low-distortion zone along the equator. By contrast, the Gall-Peters map, an equivalent projection proposed as 'fair to all peoples', accurately portrays relative area but grossly distorts the shapes of Africa and Latin America (Snyder, 1993, pp. 164–6). Although other projections offer a more balanced treatment of area and shape, authors eager to focus on people, not land area, can map socio-economic data on a cartogram on which area represents population. MM

References

Maling, D.H. 1992: Coordinate systems and map projections, 2nd edn. Oxford: Pergamon Press. · Monmonier, M. 1995: Drawing the line: tales of maps and cartocontroversy. New York: Henry Holt. · Robinson, A.H. and Snyder, J.P., eds, 1991: Matching the map projection to the need. Rockville, Md.: American Congress on Surveying and Mapping. · Snyder, J.P. 1993: Flattening the earth: two thousand years of map projections. Chicago: University of Chicago Press. · Snyder, J.P. and Voxland, P.M. 1989: An album of map projections, Professional Paper 1453. Washington: US Geological Survey.

property rights An *enforceable* claim made against others to the use or benefit of something (and thus distinguishable from property more generally, which need not entail enforceability). Usually, that enforcing body is understood to be the STATE. Legal scholars tend to see property rights as residing in the 'jural relations' between individuals, rather than in the thing itself. Thus, if I have a property right in a thing (such as land), what is really being asserted is that I can exclude you from access to it (MacPherson, 1978).

Usually, property rights are seen as identical with a private property regime, where the right to exclude is central. The implicit linkage between property rights and capitalist market relations is often explicit in the economics literature, where there is frequently assumed to be a linkage between private property rights and economic efficiency. Hence arguments about PRIVATIZATION and resource use (cf. Hardin's metaphor of the TRAGEDY OF THE COMMONS) and the more recent fascination with extending a privatized property regime to the formerly communist countries of eastern Europe.

Given its historical development under a liberal capitalist society (cf. LAND TENURE), many critics have cast property rights in a negative light, pointing to the manner in which privatized property rights instrumentally and ideologically underpin class rule in CAPITALISM, PATRIARCHY and COLONIALISM (see LAND RIGHTS). However, recent years have seen an attempt to revisit property rights in a more favourable light. For example, in her exploration of rent control, Radin (1993) privileges 'personal' property rights – such as that of a tenant to her apartment – over commodified 'fungible' property rights – such as that of her landlord to the same apartment. The distinction largely turns on the personal significance of the object of property – in this case, the apartment – to the respective parties. When a holding is fungible, she suggests, the value to the holder lies in its exchange value, rather than the object *per se*. For the tenant, however, a particular apartment could become an extension of her personhood and, as such, morally valuable.

Geographic writing on property rights and property more generally is surprisingly undeveloped. The politics embodied in real property rights, for example, are deeply geographical to the extent that they entail conflicts over the meanings and uses of space, both 'social' and 'natural'. Some suggestive exceptions include discussions of property rights in relation to IDEOLOGIES of homeownership (Agnew, 1981), GENTRIFICATION (Blomley, 1997), and conflicts over NATURAL RESOURCES (Wescoat, 1997). NB

References

Agnew, J. 1981: Homeownership and the capitalist social order' In M. Dear and A. Scott, eds, *Urbanization and urban planning in capitalist societies*. London and New York: Methuen, 457–80. · Blomley, N.K. 1997: Property, pluralism and the gentrification frontier. *Canadian Journal of Law and Society* 12 2: 1–32. · MacPherson, C.B. 1978: *Property: mainstream and critical positions*. Toronto: University of Toronto Press. · Radin, M.J. 1993: *Reinterpreting property*. Chicago: University of Chicago Press. · Wescoat, J. 1997: Toward a modern map of Roman water law. *Urban Geography* 18 2: 100–5.

protoindustrialization A term coined by the economic historian Franklin Mendels to describe 'the first phase' which both 'preceded and prepared for' the INDUSTRIALIZATION of the capitalist SPACE-ECONOMY through 'the rapid growth of traditionally organised but market-oriented, principally rural industry' (Mendels, 1972). The emergence of industries in the countryside was a commonplace of European HISTORICAL GEOGRAPHY, but since Mendels reopened the debate the process has been formalized in various ways which seek to contest conventional assumptions of a marked ('revolutionary') discontinuity between pre-industrial and industrial economies and to elucidate the regional specificity of the transformation. Two main models have been proposed, and although their substantive connections have stimulated a series of cross-fertilizations, they can nevertheless be located within two distinctive theoretical traditions:

(1) *Ecological-functionalist models.* These note that labour in an agrarian economy is

intrinsically seasonal so that 'the adoption of industry by a growing number of PEASANTS . . . meant that labour previously unemployed or underemployed during a part of the year [could be] put to work on a more continuous basis' (Mendels, 1972). Such a logic would locate protoindustrialization in the arable regions, of course, whereas in her classic essay on 'Industries in the countryside' Thirsk (1961) drew attention to the importance of pastoral regions. Her argument was based on daily rather than seasonal 'time-budgets', however, and so there seems little reason to promote one logic over the other and to expect any simple relationship between proto-industrialization and the agrarian economy. Even so, many writers have accentuated the DIVISION OF LABOUR between the corn-growing arable regions and the cloth-making pastoral regions, and have explained its emergence in terms of 'COMPARATIVE ADVANTAGES' (Jones, 1968). This was achieved through the co-ordinating functions performed by merchants in the towns, who thus became foci of capital ACCUMULATION.

(2) *Economic-structural models*. These suggest that the pace and pattern of protoindustrialization was determined by the relations between two basic circuits:

(a) *Petty commodity production*: at the micro-level, the artisan household strove to maintain a precarious balance between production and consumption and its labour discipline was thus oriented towards use-values. When prices fell, therefore, the system was peculiarly vulnerable because production was stepped up to boost the shortfall in receipts, thereby deepening and widening the recession; and

(b) *Mercantile capitalism*: at the macro-level, the products of the domestic labour process were consigned to distant (often overseas) markets by merchants who were oriented towards exchange-values. When prices rose, therefore, the system was peculiarly vulnerable because artisan households could satisfy their immediate needs most easily and production slowed down – at the very moments at which opportunities from mercantile profits were at their greatest.

The contradiction between these two was supposedly resolved by merchants seizing hold of production and taking the first steps towards the mechanization of the LABOUR PROCESS and the formation of a factory system (see Kriedte et al., 1981, 1986).

One of the most serious weaknesses of both models is an unstated appeal to a transcendent logic of CAPITALISM. Thus:

> the major weakness of the comparative advantage model of regional specialization is its assumption of individual and social rationality in the various farming regions, and the implication that production will always adjust to comparative advantage in the long run. In reality, regional specialization was fundamentally affected by custom and tradition, embodied in the motivations and practices of economic actors, and in the variety of institutional environments. (Berg et al., 1983)

The importance of 'custom' and 'tradition' is recognized by Medick and his collaborators, but usually confined to the artisan household where the pursuit of profit is hedged around by the precepts of a 'moral economy' (see Thompson, 1974). The merchant is reduced to the status of rational 'economic man', closed in the cloth-hall and the counting-house and the 'bearer' of the immanent logic of capitalist rationality. There is little room for the complex social and political affiliations which, in some instances, prompted merchants to set themselves against the incursions of the factory system (Wilson, 1971; Du Plessis and Howell, 1982; Gregory, 1982).

Both models also find common ground in their emphasis on the demographic consequences of protoindustrialization, and in particular on the creation of a labour-surplus economy (Levine, 1987; see also AGRICULTURAL INVOLUTION). Here too, however, the complexity of the situation belies the simplicity of most of the explanations which have been offered: the ways in which a labour-*surplus* economy 'prepared for' labour-*saving* technical change needs careful elucidation of the contingent features of the regional settings in which protoindustrialization took place (Hudson, 1981, 1983; see Berg, 1985). (See also INDUSTRIAL REVOLUTION.) DG

References

Berg, M. 1985: *The age of manufacturers: industry, innovation and work in Britain, 1700–1820*. London: Fontana. · Berg, M., Hudson, P. and Sonenscher, M. 1983: Manufacture in town and country before the factory. In M. Berg, P. Hudson and M. Sonenscher, eds, *Manufacture in town and country before the factory*. Cambridge: Cambridge University Press, 1–32. · Du Plessis, R. and Howell, M.C. 1982: Reconsidering the early modern urban economy: the cases of Leiden and Lille. *Past and Present* 94: 49–84. · Gregory, D. 1982: *Regional transformation and Industrial Revolution: a geography of the Yorkshire woollen industry*. London: Macmillan. · Minneapolis: University of Minnesota Press. · Hudson, P. 1981: Proto-industrialisation: the case of the West Riding textile industry. *History Workshop Journal* 12: 34–61. · Hudson, P. 1983: From manor to mill: the West Riding in transition. In M. Berg, P. Hudson and M. Sonenscher, eds, *Manufacture in town and country before the factory*. Cambridge: Cambridge University Press, 124–44.

· Jones, E.L. 1968: The agricultural origins of industry. *Past and Present* 40: 128–42. · Kriedte, P., Medick, H. and Schlumbohm, J. 1981: *Industrialization before industrialization: rural industry in the genesis of capitalism*. Cambridge: Cambridge University Press. · Kriedte, P., Medick, H. and Schlumbohm, J. 1986: Protoindustrialization on test with the guild of historians: response to some critics. *Economy and Society* 15: 254–72. · Levine, D. 1987: *Reproducing families: the political economy of English population history*. Cambridge: Cambridge University Press. · Mendels, F.F. 1972: Proto-industrialization: the first phase of industrialization. *Journal of Economic History* 32: 241–61. · Thirsk, J. 1961: Industries in the countryside. In F.J. Fisher, ed., *Essays in the economic and social history of Tudor and Stuart England*. Cambridge: Cambridge University Press, 70–88. · Thompson, E.P. 1974: Patrician society, plebeian culture. *Journal of Social History* 7: 382–405. · Wilson, R.G. 1971: *Gentlemen merchants: the merchant community in Leeds, 1700–1830*. Manchester: Manchester University Press.

Suggested Reading

Houston, R. and Snell, K.D.M. 1984: Protoindustrialization? Cottage industry, social change and industrial revolution. *History Journal* 27: 473–92. · Hudson (1981, 1983).

psychoanalytic theory, geography and

Psychoanalysis is a theory and a therapy of human subjectivity developed and modified by Sigmund Freud (1856–1939) and later writers and practitioners. Working mostly with middle-class patients, often women, Freud was concerned with the fraught processes through which children separate from their caregivers to become relatively autonomous subjects, and with the complicated legacies of that process for their subsequent senses of BODY, self, OTHER and self–Other relations. Geographers have been particularly concerned with the spatialities of these dynamics (Rose, 1995; Sibley, 1995; Blum and Nast, 1996; Pile, 1996; Aitken and Herman, 1997).

Freud assumes that all humans begin life in an undifferentiated relationship with their mother. He locates the break from the mother and the beginning of subjecthood with the intervention of the father. (Heterosexual) masculinity is constituted by the boy-child feeling threatened by the father with castration if he does not give up his closeness to the mother (a threat made effective by the sight of the mother's genitalia as apparently lacking); (heterosexual) femininity, in ways less convincingly theorized by Freud, is produced by girl-children seeing themselves as lacking and transferring their attachment from the mother to the father. This process – the castration crisis or Oedipus complex – represses the child's profound drives and desires and thus produces the unconscious. The unconscious is not accessible to the subject but its dynamics persistently intervene in more conscious dreams, thoughts, speech and practices. Already, then, psychoanalysis offers a very different notion of subjectivity from that of BEHAVIOURAL GEOGRAPHY and from geographers' accounts of HUMAN AGENCY. Subjectivity here is in part unknowing and unknowable, always unstable and relational (Pile, 1992); it is also always gendered and sexualized. These points have been utilized in relation to QUALITATIVE METHODS in geography, with discussion focusing on the complexity and partial unknowability of relations between and among researcher and researched (Burgess, Limb and Harrison, 1988a, 1988b; Pile, 1991; Rose, 1997).

The subsequent developments in psychoanalytic theory used by geographers have been diverse. They include the work of Jacques Lacan for whom the intervention of the father is also the intervention of the cultural (what Lacan called the Symbolic); it is the moment when signs and symbols (mostly) replace the pre-Symbolic (or the Real, in Lacan's terminology). Lacan argues that this substitution is always felt as such and that there is therefore always a sense of loss, of lack, of uncertainty, in human subjectivity. Lacan also insisted on the importance of the 'mirror stage' to a child's sense of self, which is the moment when a child recognizes an image in a mirror as a coherent and bounded self which can comprehend Others. In contrast, the work of Melanie Klein depends less than Lacan or Freud on the father and more on the child's own agency in establishing the DIFFERENCE between its self and Others, while Julia Kristeva's notion of abjection examines the construction of Others both as intensely, somatically repulsive and as necessary to the subject. Finally, there is Donald Winnicott's emphasis on a more fluid and recursive relation between self and Others, articulated through what he termed a 'transitional space' in which clear boundaries between self and Other can be blurred.

Utilizing any of these psychoanalytic positions in the social sciences is complicated and controversial (Craib, 1990; Elliott, 1992). Psychoanalysis has been accused of essentializing anatomical difference, of universalizing from a very specific social and cultural location (the bourgeois, European, white, nuclear family), and of naturalizing gendered difference and heterosexuality. Not surprisingly then, Sibley (1995) argues strongly that psychically charged articulations of difference can only be understood through the particularities of their social and cultural contexts. Given this caveat, however, several geographers have drawn on psychoanalytic arguments as means of exploring both the geographies of subjectivities and the subjectivity of geography as a discipline.

Sibley's (1995) aim in drawing on the work of Klein and Kristeva, among others, is to understand the geographies of the exclusion of marginalized groups. He insists that there are psychic as well as social and cultural processes at work in these acts of exclusion, and argues that the dominant western sense of a 'purified' self depends on a range of historically variable and culturally mediated stereotypes of Others. He traces both the placing of those Others into spaces separate and distinct from dominant social groups and the ambiguity and instability of their borders, which he describes as liminal, abject zones of intense anxiety and even violence (see also O'Tuathail, 1994; Pile, 1996). Sibley is therefore rather sceptical about claims that the contemporary world is now dominated by processes of boundary-displacing HYBRIDITY. Aitken and Herman (1997), on the other hand, use Winnicott's work to suggest that transitional space may allow a more positive relation between self and Others. A child's play produces transitional space, in which dominant social and cultural values may be reiterated but also in which a child may develop new understandings of the relation between the self and the environment. Despite their important differences, psychoanalytic arguments produce for these geographers a similar sense of space and place as very complex: as contradictory, multiple, and always becoming.

Feminist revisions of psychoanalysis have also been deployed in some FEMINIST GEOGRAPHIES to initiate a critique of the PHALLOCENTRISM of academic geography. Bondi (1997) and Rose (1993, 1995, 1996) argue that such phallocentrism is deeply embedded in the structures of its knowledge. Deutsche (1991) and Rose (1993, 1995) have both utilized Mulvey's (1989) feminist reworking of Lacan's mirror-stage in order to understand why MASCULINIST geography has so much difficulty in seeing the world as radically different from its self. Mulvey re-describes the IMAGE seen during the mirror-stage as a mirage of an autonomous, mastering and masculine self; the geographer perceiving the world through its dynamics can thus see the world only as a reflection of his self or as his Other (see also Sparke, 1994). But Lacan's insistence on the lack structuring all subjectivity has also been drawn on by Bondi (1997) and Rose (1993, 1995) to argue for the persistent possibility of critique and change. As Bondi (1997, p. 254) notes, no-one is immune from the uncertainties of subjectivity.

This last point explains why, despite its dangers, psychoanalytic theory is being used by some geographers as a critical tool to re-interpret and reconfigure different kinds of geographies. For it demands that interpretation seeks fracture, uncertainty and partiality, and admits to these things as part of its self; 'it is the differences within these ostensibly self-identical edifices that offer maps as to where we might find difference without them' (Blum and Nast, 1996, p. 579). GR

References

Aitken, S.C. and Herman, T. 1997: Gender, power and crib geography: transitional spaces and potential places. *Gender, Place and Culture* 4: 63–88. · Blum, V. and Nast, H. 1996: Where's the difference? The heterosexualization of alterity in Henri Lefebvre and Jacques Lacan. *Environment and Planning D: Society and Space* 14: 559–80. · Bondi, L. 1997: In whose words? On gender identities, knowledge and writing practices. *Transactions, Institute of British Geographers* NS 22: 245–58. · Burgess, J., Limb, M. and Harrison, C.M. 1988a: Exploring environmental values through small groups. Part one: theory and practice. *Environment and Planning A* 20: 309–20. · Burgess, J., Limb, M. and Harrison, C.M. 1988b: Exploring environmental values through small groups. Part two: illustrations of a group at work. *Environment and Planning A* 20: 457–76. · Craib, I. 1990: *Psychoanalysis and social theory*. Amherst, MA: Massachusetts University Press. · Deutsche, R. 1991: Boys town. *Environment and Planning D: Society and Space* 9: 5–30. · Elliott, A. 1992: *Social theory and psychoanalysis in transition: self and society from Freud to Kristeva*. Oxford: Basil Blackwell. · Mulvey, L. 1989: Visual pleasure and narrative cinema. In L. Mulvey, *Visual and other pleasures*. London: Macmillan, 14–26. · O'Tuathail, G. 1994: Critical geopolitics and development theory: intensifying the dialogue. *Transactions, Institute of British Geographers* NS 19: 228–38. · Pile, S. 1991: Practising interpretive geography. *Transactions, Institute of British Geographers* NS 16: 458–69. · Pile, S. 1992: Human agency and human geography revisited: a critique of 'new models' of the self. *Transactions, Institute of British Geographers* NS 18: 122–39. · Pile, S. 1996: *The body and the city: psychoanalysis, space and subjectivity*. London: Routledge. · Rose, G. 1993: *Feminism and geography: the limits of geographical knowledge*. Cambridge: Polity. · Rose, G. 1995: Distance, surface, elsewhere: a feminist critique of the phallocentric space of self/knowledge. *Environment and Planning D: Society and Space* 13: 761–81. · Rose, G. 1996: As if the mirrors had bled: masculine dwelling, masculinist theory and feminist masquerade. In N. Duncan, ed., *BodySpace: destabilizing geographies of gender and sexuality*. London: Routledge, 56–74. · Rose, G. 1997: Situating knowledges: positionality, reflexivities and other tactics. *Progress in Human Geography* 21: 305–20. · Sibley, D. 1995: *Geographies of exclusion: society and difference in the west*.

London: Routledge. · Sparke, M. 1994: Escaping the herbarium: a critique of Gunnar Olsson's 'Chiasm of thought and action'. *Environment and Planning D: Society and Space* 12: 207–20.

Suggested Reading

Grosz, E. 1990: *Jacques Lacan: a feminist introduction*. London: Routledge. · Pile (1992).

public administration, geography of Studies of spatial variations in the management of the STATE APPARATUS and geographical contributions to that management. Early works focused on the LOCATIONAL ANALYSIS approach and what that PARADIGM could offer to understanding 'the influence of space and location on the provision of public services' (Massam, 1975, 1993). Massam's text concentrated on: (a) the size and shape of the administrative areas used in the delivery of public services; (b) interactions among those areas; and (c) the spatial allocation of public services among and within areas (see LOCATION–ALLOCATION MODELS). Later work has been more widely concerned with the administration of urban areas, especially those with fragmented local government structures (Barlow, 1991), with restructuring local governments (including issues of SCALE: Johnston, Pattie and Rossiter, 1997) and the definition of constituencies for a variety of electoral systems. In addition, Bennett (1989) has argued for geographical involvement in determining what should be delivered as a public service, through the transfer of resources from rich to poor (both people and areas) by the state, and what should be placed in the 'free market'. RJJ

References

Barlow, M. 1991: *Metropolitan government*. London: Routledge. · Bennett, R.J. 1989: Whither models and geography in a post welfarist world? In B. Macmillan, ed., *Remodelling geography*. Oxford and Cambridge, MA: Basil Blackwell, 273–90. · Johnston, R.J., Pattie, C.J. and Rossiter, D.J. 1997: The arithmetic or the organic: independent commissions and the redrawing of the UK's administrative maps. *Regional Studies* 31: 337–49. · Massam, B.H. 1975: *Location and space in social administration*. London: Edward Arnold. · Massam, B.H. 1993: *The right place: shared responsibility and the location of public facilities*. London and New York: Longman.

public choice theory Deriving from Duncan Black's (1958) pioneering work, public choice theory considers topics normally covered by political science, such as voting behaviour (cf. ELECTORAL GEOGRAPHY), the bureaucracy, party politics, and the theory of the STATE, but examines them using the analytical techniques of NEO-CLASSICAL ECONOMICS. In particular, it is assumed that all agents within the political sphere act out of a narrow self-interest, maximizing their own individual welfare through RATIONAL CHOICE. For example, politicians enact only those policies that ensure their re-election, voters remain deliberately ignorant because of the disproportionate costs of learning about election issues, and bureaucrats do whatever is necessary to please their superiors in order to gain promotion.

Within public choice theory a number of core theoretical concerns are recognizable. First, there are the problems attending aggregating individual choices in maximizing some social welfare function; that is, the difficulties of deriving consistent policy goals by examining the individual preferences of constituents. Second, there is a range of issues that stem from the introduction of PUBLIC GOODS and market failure. Specifically, because of its monopoly POWER, government tends to extend public ownership and administration beyond that warranted by market efficiency. Third, there is the issue of party competition. With two vote-maximizing parties, the equilibrium result is of two parties that are virtually identical; only with three parties is policy variability introduced (cf. HOTELLING MODEL). Fourth, there is the difficulty of organizing interest groups because of the free rider problem (see GAME THEORY). Finally, a number of complexities are entailed by treating PUBLIC FINANCE as a rational exchange among citizens.

Public choice models have been widely tested empirically (Mueller, 1979). They show that the government rarely maximizes general social welfare, but is much more concerned with its own particular welfare. As a branch of NEO-CLASSICAL ECONOMICS, public choice theory is subject to all the standard objections raised against that school. Specifically, its supposition of rational choice has been severely criticized. Within geography Cox and Johnston (1982) explore the issue of public goods and market failure, and Bennett (1980) the topic of public finance. TJB

References

Arrow, K.K 1951: *Social choice and individual values*. New York: John Wiley. · Bennett, R.J. 1980: *The geography of public finance*. London: Methuen. · Black, D. 1958: *The theory of committees and elections*. Cambridge: Cambridge University Press. · Cox, K. and Johnston, R.J., eds, 1982: *Conflict, politics and the urban scene*. New York: St. Martins Press. · Mueller, D.C. 1979: *Public choice*. Cambridge: Cambridge University Press.

Suggested Reading

Archer, J.C. 1981: Public choice paradigms in political geography. In A.D. Burnett and P.J. Taylor, eds, *Political studies from spatial perspectives*. New York: John Wiley, 73–90. · Mueller (1979).

public finance, geography of Studies of geographical variations in the incidence of public sector income and expenditure. Bennett (1980) suggested that its particular focus should be the spatial imbalance between the geographies of revenue raising and public expenditure, producing a sub-discipline concerned with

> how burdens and expenditure incidence vary as a function of geographical location. Who gets what benefits, and bears what burdens as a function of where they live: *who gets what, where, at what cost?* (p. ix)

Such a focus is required within the broader study of public finance, Bennett argued, because needs, costs and preferences for various PUBLIC GOODS vary spatially, among individuals and the local governments which provide them (cf. COLLECTIVE CONSUMPTION), and if geographical redistribution is not undertaken to correct for such variations then spatial polarization of rich and poor (again, both individuals and local governments) will occur (cf. POSITIVE DISCRIMINATION).

Bennett's detailed evaluation of the equity issues involved in tackling such differentials (according to him, 'Public finance in general and in its geographical components in particular, is aimed at eliminating, or at least reducing, the unequal treatment of individuals in society'), and empirical studies of British local government finance mechanisms (Bennett, 1985), have been countered by later arguments that equity in the distribution of public goods is unattainable and their provision by the STATE APPARATUS should be much reduced (Bennett, 1989). RJJ

References and Suggested Reading

Bennett, R.J. 1980: *The geography of public finance: welfare under fiscal federalism and local government finance*. London and New York: Methuen. · Bennett, R.J. 1985: *Central grants for local governments*. Cambridge and New York: Cambridge University Press. · Bennett, R.J. 1989: Whither models and geography in a post-welfarist world? In B. Macmillan, ed., *Remodelling geography*. Oxford and Cambridge, MA: Basil Blackwell, 273–90. · Pinch, S. 1997: *Worlds of welfare: understanding the changing geographies of social welfare provision*. London: Routledge.

public goods Goods and services that are either freely available to all, such as unpolluted air, or those provided equally to all citizens of a defined TERRITORY. Public goods are generally provided by the STATE, and fall into three main categories:

- *Pure public goods*, which are freely and equally available to all people throughout a state's territory. Although ideally all public goods should fall within this category, few do, because of difficulties – impossibilities in many cases – in ensuring their equal provision. One of the few goods which normally falls into this category is national defence;
- *Impure public goods*, which are provided either at fixed locations (such as health centres and parks) or along fixed routes (such as public transport services). These are more accessible to some people than others, and because usage tends to decline with distance from a facility (cf. DISTANCE DECAY) the closer people live to them the greater their (potential) benefit. As a consequence, there is likely to be social and political CONFLICT over the location of such facilities (cf. TURF POLITICS); and
- *Public goods impurely distributed*, because of decisions to vary the density of provision. Many public services are provided by local governments, which may differ in how much is spent on a service (or even whether it is provided), thus producing a geography of uneven provision. In addition there may be variations in the density of provision above a certain norm (cf. MERIT GOOD) within one (local) government's territory, perhaps reflecting political decisions on the greater 'need' of some areas relative to others (cf. PORK BARREL). RJJ

Suggested Reading

Bennett, R.J. 1980: *The geography of public finance*. London and New York: Methuen. · Cox, K.R. and Johnston, R.J., eds, 1982: *Conflict, politics and the urban scene*. London: Longman; New York: St. Martin's Press. · Pinch, S. 1997: *Worlds of welfare: understanding the changing geographies of social welfare provision*. London: Routledge.

public policy, geography and Geographical study of and involvement in the creation, implementation, monitoring and evaluation of public policies. Work in this area has increased in recent years in capitalist countries because of: (a) the growing importance of the STATE in economic and social affairs, offering enhanced opportunities for such work; (b) increased governmental recognition of environmental and spatial problems awaiting resolution; (c) the desire among individual geographers to contribute to attacks on such problems; and (d) the perceived need for geographers to demonstrate the RELEVANCE of their field and so promote their discipline's claim for resources within higher education institutions in increasingly materialist situations.

Most geographical analyses have been concerned with evaluating policies addressed at identified 'spatial problems of environment, economy and society' (House, 1983) and with assessment of their 'geographical impact and degree of effectiveness': in the volume of essays that he edited on *United States public policy*, he commented:

> Critique stops short of prescription but there is some attempt to look ahead and also, in some cases, to set the problems within a theoretical, as well as an operational, framework. (pp. v–vi)

He saw the benefits of such work as twofold:

> to non-geographical academic or lay audiences . . . [it reflects] a particular set of perspectives on some urgent problems which face policy-makers in our very critical times. To geographers in training, the relevance of applications of the discipline should be a major concern, whether to add practical purpose to their studies, or to point in the direction of possible professional careers outside the education field. (p. 6)

House identified the discipline's technocratic skills and its practitioners' ability to synthesize the many component parts of a complex problem as the geographical perspectives most valuable to public policy study (see his survey of early British contributions in House, 1973); later promotions of geographers' utility have stressed their technical skills, such as those associated with GEOGRAPHICAL INFORMATION SYSTEMS (GIS) (see NRC, 1997). Others, such as Smith (1988), suggest that because many social problems are exacerbated, if not created, by environmental, time, place and circumstance contexts (cf. CONTEXTUAL EFFECT), then changing those contexts, through the geography of service provision and delivery, can be as influential as moves to solve the problems.

The nature of geographers' applied contributions has been largely pragmatic, reflecting the available opportunities and the ability of geographers to capitalize on them with their technocratic skills, hence the current promotion of REMOTE SENSING and GIS (Openshaw, 1989). Whereas some geographers claim that such involvement is necessary for the discipline's survival (Berry, 1970; Abler, 1993), others have queried this by pointing to the role of much public policy as sustaining, if not enhancing, the inequalities and exploitation that are inherent to CAPITALISM, hence Harvey's (1974) question 'What kind of geography for what kind of public policy?' (cf. APPLIED GEOGRAPHY). RJJ

References and Suggested Reading

Abler, R.F. 1993: Desiderata for geography. In R.J. Johnston, ed., *The challenge for geography. A changing world: a changing discipline*. Oxford and Cambridge, MA: Basil Blackwell. · Berry, B.J.L. 1970: The geography of the US in the year 2000. *Transactions, Institute of British Geographers* 51: 21–53. · Harvey, D. 1974: What kind of geography for what kind of public policy? *Transactions, Institute of British Geographers* 63: 18–24. · House, J.W. 1973: Geographers, decision takers and policy makers. In M. Chisholm and B. Rodgers, eds, *Studies in human geography*. London: Heinemann, 272–301. · House, J.W., ed., 1983: *United States public policy: a geographical view*. Oxford: The Clarendon Press. · NRC 1997: *Rethinking geography: new relevance for science and society*. Washington, D.C.: National Research Council. · Openshaw, S. 1989: Computer modelling in human geography. In B. Macmillan, ed., *Remodelling geography*. Oxford: Basil Blackwell, 273–90. · Smith, C.J. 1988: *Public problems: the management of urban distress*. New York and London: Guilford Press.

public services, geography of The study of geographical aspects of the provision and utilization of public services, understood as services provided by (or on behalf of) the STATE according to non-MARKET criteria. Although the boundary between public and private service provision has varied historically, in general services are provided collectively because reliance solely on the market or the non-profit sector would be inefficient or inequitable. Studies of public services have concentrated largely on those providing for individual welfare – HEALTH CARE, EDUCATION, HOUSING, and social security – but there has also been work on the provision of utilities and INFRASTRUCTURE, particularly in the context of recent PRIVATIZATION initiatives. Within what might be seen as a narrow geographical tradition of SPATIAL SCIENCE, there are three reasons for a geographical perspective on public services: the phenomenon of jurisdictional partitioning, or the fragmentation of TERRITORY into jurisdictions which vary considerably in the provision of services; tapering effects, which means that the utility of public services to individuals is a function of distance from them (cf. DISTANCE DECAY); and EXTERNALITY effects, which means that locating services has unpriced impacts on NEIGHBOURHOODS, impacts which also decline with distance.

Much work was stimulated by Teitz's (1968) influential article. He proposed some elementary models of public facility systems, although they differed only marginally from their private-sector counterparts in INDUSTRIAL LOCATION. Initially, distance-minimization techniques were employed; these were subsequently refined in various ways, for example by the incorporation of SPATIAL INTERACTION concepts (Beaumont, 1980). There have been numerous efforts to refine such

MODELS and apply them in planning (e.g. Massam, 1992). Such techniques offer useful aids to DECISION-MAKING and are used extensively in evaluating the consequences of alterations in the locational arrangements of public services. Much debate has focused on efforts to achieve solutions to locational problems which attempt a trade-off between 'the opposing forces of ECONOMIES OF SCALE and the advantages of dispersion' (Teitz, 1968, p. 42) – in other words, a trade-off between EQUITY and efficiency.

With the development of models based on efficiency criteria came a realization that the implicit centralization of services had adverse consequences for ACCESSIBILITY, and that the distributive consequences of public service location required investigation. There was also a realization that despite the achievements of the WELFARE STATE in providing comprehensive welfare services, considerable geographical variations remained at a more local scale. Studies therefore began to focus on the question of TERRITORIAL JUSTICE, seeking to identify whether, and to what extent, patterns of public service provision were distributed in relation to need. There are obvious difficulties in agreeing on a concept of need, but such work was able to demonstrate important variations. In geographies of health care, for example, the so-called 'inverse care law', which postulated that service distributions were negatively correlated with need, received considerable attention (Joseph and Phillips, 1984). The impacts of jurisdictional partitioning and of FEDERALISM on geographies of public services attracted much attention in the USA (e.g. Kodras and Jones, 1990).

In addition to studies of accessibility, there has been a focus on the externality effects of public services. Taking up Harvey's (1971) point that much of urban politics can be interpreted as conflicts over who is to bear the costs – externalities – of public decisions, there have been many investigations of the effects associated with waste disposal facilities, community care centres and so on. These have often demonstrated the distance-decay patterns evident in such externality fields. There has also been work on locational conflicts over proposals to locate such facilities (Cox, 1980; Dear and Taylor, 1982). Such work offers a useful corrective to the often spaceless view of the welfare state presented in other social science disciplines.

Mapping patterns of service distribution, or offering technical advice on how to improve them, offer a rather restrictive view of geographical perspectives on public services. In particular, explanations of patterns of provision have been weakly developed. Quantitative studies of public service distributions have investigated links between local economic and political indicators and the variations in service provision between jurisdictions. Such studies usually demonstrate some degree of association, after controlling for demography, between provision and party control, but like much extensive, quantitative social science, such studies have been criticized for producing little more than broad generalizations and associations. A further difficulty is that decision-making is treated as a black box, so that conflict and negotiation between competing interests is not analysed explicitly (Pinch, 1985).

Such difficulties led Dear (1978) to propose a much greater engagement with social theory and POLITICAL ECONOMY as a way of explaining patterns of service distribution. A geography of public services required a 'theory of society' and, in particular, consideration of the state. This has been attempted at various levels. Managerialist studies have drawn attention to the discretion available to urban managers in allocating scarce resources; critics have argued that the constraints on the autonomy of managers, and on the resources available to them, need to be theorized explicitly (Leonard, 1982; cf. URBAN MANAGERS AND GATEKEEPERS). This requires explicit theorization of the role of the state, and in geography this has generally meant drawing on political-economy perspectives. Such perspectives are also important because the boundary between public and private service provision is not fixed. Welfare services may be delivered in a number of ways – by the family, charitable/voluntary organizations (Wolch, 1990; cf. SHADOW STATE), the state or the market – and the balance between them varies between states and over time.

There is increasing recognition of the diversity of welfare state arrangements, with several implications for the geography of public services. First, processes of restructuring are mediated in different ways by political and social structures, and welfare policies are played out on an increasingly fragmented socio-political terrain; for instance, growing social polarization may be undermining collective support for comprehensive welfare systems. There have consequently been efforts to chart the geographical outcomes of this restructuring process (e.g. Dear and Wolch, 1987; Mohan, 1995), paying particular attention to the interactions between global and national processes and their local outcomes. In the context of debates about the (putative) transition from FORDISM to POST-FORDISM, REGULATION THEORISTS have postulated the emergence of a Schumpeterian Workfare State, in which patterns of welfare provision would be subordinate to the dictates of competitiveness, and in which, as a consequence, heightened geographical disparities would be evident (Jessop, 1993). Secondly, as the public–private divide is redrawn, attention will need to be paid to geographies of privatization and their implications for access to services and for employment (Feigenbaum et al., 1998; Scarpaci, 1989; Laws, 1988). Privatization is also associated with a transition in the *modus operandi* of the state, away from direct provision of services towards a more regulatory role; this is part of a 'hollowing-out' of state structures. Thirdly, the expansion of the welfare state led some commentators to place social rights – access to a package of services simply by virtue of one's membership of a national community – alongside civil and political rights as a dimension of CITIZENSHIP. Contemporary developments in the welfare state are calling into question the social rights of citizenship and much work is being done on the associated political geographies of citizenship (Smith, 1989; Pierson, 1991; Painter and Philo, 1995). JM

References

Beaumont, J.R. 1980: Spatial interaction models and the location–allocation problem. *Journal of Regional Science* 20: 37–51. · Cox, K.R. 1980: *Location and public problems*. Oxford: Blackwell. · Dear, M. 1978: A paradigm for public facility location theory, *International Regional Science Review* 3: 93–112. · Dear, M.J. and Taylor, S.M. 1982: *Not on our street*. London: Pion; Dear, M. and Wolch, J. 1987: *Landscapes of despair*. Oxford: Polity. · Esping-Andersen, G. 1990: *The three worlds of welfare capitalism*. Oxford: Polity. · Feigenbaum, H., Henig, J. and Hamnett, C. 1998: *Shrinking the state: the political underpinnings of privatisation*. Cambridge: Cambridge University Press. · Harvey, D. 1971: Social processes, spatial form and the redistribution of real income in the urban system. In M. Chisholm, A.E. Frey and P. Haggett, eds, *Regional forecasting*. London: Butterworth, 267–300. · Jessop, B. 1993: Towards a Schumpeterian workfare state? *Studies in Political Economy* 40: 7–39. · Joseph, A. and Phillips, D. 1984: *Accessibility and utilisation: geographical perspectives on health care delivery*. London: Longman. · Kodras, J. and Jones, J.P., eds, 1990: *Geographic dimensions of US social policy*. London: Edward Arnold. · Laws, G. 1988: Privatisation and the local welfare state. *Transactions, Institute of British Geographers*, NS 13: 449–65. · Leonard, S. 1982: Urban managerialism: a period of transition. *Progress in Human Geography* 6: 190–215. · Massam, B. 1992: *The right place: shared responsibility and the location of public facilities*. London: Longman. · Mohan, J.F. 1995: *A National Health Service? The restructuring of health care in Britain since 1979*. London: Macmillan. · Painter, J. and Philo, C. 1995: Spaces of citizenship. *Political Geography* 14: 107–20. · Pierson, C. 1991: *Beyond the welfare state?* Oxford: Polity. · Pinch, S. 1985: *Cities and services*. London: Routledge. · Pinch, S. 1997: *Worlds of welfare*. London: Routledge. · Powell, M. and Boyne, G. 1993: Territorial justice and Thatcherism. *Environment and Planning C: Government and Policy* 11: 35–54. · Scarpaci, J., ed., 1989: *Health services privatisation in industrialised societies*. New Brunswick, NJ: Rutgers University Press. · Smith, S.J. 1989: Society, space and citizenship: a human geography for the 'new times'? *Transactions, Institute of British Geographers* NS 14: 144–56. · Teitz, M. 1968: Towards a theory of urban public facility location, *Papers, Regional Science Association* 21: 35–53. · Wolch, J. 1990: *The shadow state: government and voluntary sector in transition*. New York: Foundation Center.

Q

quadtree A scheme of hierarchical representation of the contents of an image or a RASTER data set. It is often disadvantageous to assign uniform cells to every part of an image, because this strategy fails to take advantage of uniformity in some parts of the image, and cannot respond to more rapid variation in other parts. A quadtree is constructed by beginning with the entire image, and dividing it into four quadrants. If the image in any of the quadrants shows variation, it is divided again into four. The process continues until no variation exists within any quadrant; or until the process reaches some limit of resolution. The result is a 'tree', every branching having four shoots, and all branches terminating in a 'leaf'. Quadtrees can be very efficient for storing certain types of geographic information, and have been widely implemented in geographical information systems. MG

qualitative methods A set of tools developed to pursue the epistemological mandate of the philosophies of meaning (see EPISTEMOLOGY). Qualitative methods have been developed through a variety of research traditions and in a range of disciplinary contexts. They became popular within geography as the QUANTITATIVE REVOLUTION gave way to more humanistic concerns (see HUMANISTIC GEOGRAPHY). They signal a recognition of what Cloke et al. (1991) call 'the peopling of human geography'. This recognition quickly gained currency among the research community and has also been the subject of enthusiastic debate on the teaching curriculum (Lee, 1992; Gerber and Williams, 1996).

Qualitative methods are concerned with how the world is viewed, experienced and constructed by social actors. They provide access to the motives, aspirations and POWER relationships that account for how places, people, and events are made and represented. Such methods include: (i) in-depth open-ended INTERVIEWS with groups and individuals (see also FOCUS GROUP); (ii) direct engagement with subjects and their LIFEWORLD through PARTICIPANT OBSERVATION and related ethnographic techniques (see ETHNOGRAPHY), which may be implemented by individuals or teams of researchers; and (iii) the interpretation of a variety of 'TEXTS' including LANDSCAPES, archival materials (diaries, reports, minutes of meetings), maps, literature and visual images.

Qualitative interviews may be used to elicit personal life histories, COMMUNITY biographies and a range of information that is relevant to the understanding of human action and experience. The aim is not to collate typical responses to pre-defined questions from a random SAMPLE, or to generalize about the views of a population, but rather to record in complex detail the opinions and ideas of a relatively small number of individuals or groups who may have been selected systematically for the light they can cast on a particular area of sociological concern. Such in-depth interviews are normally taped and transcribed, prior to analysis. A debate has, however, developed over the pros and cons of using computer-assisted methods for coding and retrieving the results (Crang et al., 1997).

There are several software packages capable of formalizing, summarizing and abstracting information from machine-readable text data. These provide a way of categorizing and manipulating qualitative data without losing the texture and detail of what was actually said. They reduce dependence on researchers' memories; facilitate the involvement of analysts who were not present at the interview or coding stage; and provide convenient access to the spread of ideas within the data set. Critics, however, question the motivation and justification for objectifying qualitative materials in this way, arguing that such procedures reproduce the problems of formalization and decontextualization which qualitative methods were designed to overcome.

Methods of engagement and encounter range from passive observation and personal reflection on a series of events or a social situation, through routine participation to active intervention in the life and work of an individual or community (see Cook and Crang, 1995). These approaches regard the social world not as something pre-existing and awaiting discovery, but as something dynamic and changeable, always in the process of becoming – of being constructed through a web of cultural, political and economic relationships (see SYMBOLIC INTERACTIONISM). The emphasis is on the importance of understanding lived experience and of reflecting on the meanings associated with everyday life. Such approaches include descriptive ethnography as well as the more rigorous case study methods discussed by Mitchell (1983).

There is some debate as to whether analysts should attempt to minimize their intrusion into the ACTIVITY SPACE of their subjects (emphasizing the role of onlooker that is implicit at one extreme of the strategy of PARTICIPANT OBSERVATION), or whether they should abandon attempts to achieve this neutrality and instead engage more fully in a form of PARTICIPATORY ACTION RESEARCH which allows them to translate their own, and their subjects', normative theories into practice. There is also a question over whether the goal of ethnographic research is one of complete empathy (which involves identifying with one's subjects to the extent that one can effectively speak on their behalf), or whether the aim is for a dialogue, driven forward precisely because there can never be a full understanding between analysts and their subjects, because ideas and ideals differ, and because there are always more questions to ask (Folch-Serra, 1990). Additionally, and crucially, there is the growing challenge to analysts to acknowledge the power of POSITIONALITY, and to recognize the moral and ontological shortcomings of approaches which 'presume to speak for or about peoples and nations as if they were outside of the contemporary world system, refusing to recognize that our ability to construct them as such is rooted in a larger system of domination' (Katz 1992, p. 495; cf. ETHICS, GEOGRAPHY AND).

It has been argued that the distinction between observation and intervention is to an extent immaterial, because any changes resulting from strategies of encounter are likely to have less effect on the studied community than on the analyst's 'self' (Smith, 1988). This has prompted geographers to step beyond the philosophies of meaning towards the practice of psychoanalysis in order to exploit the full potential of qualitative research (see PSYCHOANALYTIC THEORY, GEOGRAPHY AND). Certainly, an understanding of how 'selves' relate to 'others' is crucial to our handling of the 'double hermeneutic' which provides qualitative methods with their most formidable challenge (i.e. with the challenge of recognizing that the end-point of qualitative research is an analyst's construction of other people's constructions of the meaning systems within which they operate – a problem which is perhaps best, if rather unconventionally, illustrated by Mitchell, 1974).

The interpretation of texts has an important place in the lexicon of qualitative methods. Texts need to be interpreted because what we read and what we see are REPRESENTATIONS rather than realities. MAPS, for example, usually appear to be scientific abstractions of geographical facts. However, as Harley (1988) and others have shown, by reflecting on the content of maps and on the circumstances in which they are produced, it very quickly becomes clear that maps are ways of representing, interpreting, commenting on, and indeed exercising POLITICAL GEOGRAPHY.

'Fictional' texts may be equally important in the production of geographical knowledge. Said (1993) alerts us to the way in which struggles over space and resources are also struggles to control the collective imagination. Literature, therefore, may be fictional, but interpreted critically, it is exposed as a key force shaping a received wisdom or shared common sense about the ordering of society and space – a common sense which powerful groups have an interest in manipulating. Story-telling, like mapping, exerts a powerful influence on metageographical knowledge. Other cultural products can similarly be interrogated for what they reveal about the power struggles that shape knowledge and understanding about the world. The use of LANGUAGE, for example, has a role in making places (Tuan 1991); studies of painting, photography and film direct attention towards a growing range of visual methods (see VISION AND VISUALITY); and a relatively new culturally and politically informed interest in musical texts demands an appreciation of the history, geography and social production of listening practices (see MUSIC, GEOGRAPHY OF). Ways of seeing, ways of speaking, ways of writing and ways of hearing are culturally coded and contain important clues to the political and economic circumstances of the societies that produced them. Methods for interpreting images, words, writings and sounds provide a gateway into these cultural codes and into the political economies they permeate.

Reflecting on the power of the text has impacted not only on methods of accessing the world, but also on methods of communicating the results of the encounter. Recognizing that textual representations create rather than reflect the world of experience, some analysts adopt textual strategies which are explicitly designed to get a particular message across. Allan Pred's (1995) use of literary montage – the juxtaposition of verbal and visual fragments to tell the story of European MODERNITIES – is one example. He calls his work 'heretical EMPIRICISM' which he claims 'brings the past into tension-filled constellation with the present moment' in a way which 'speaks to the here and now in strikingly unexpected but potentially meaningful and politically charged ways' (p. 24).

The various qualitative methods outlined above have some things in common. Their common theme is a preoccupation with shared systems of meaning; their common project is subjective understanding rather than statistical description; and their primary goal is an ability to empathize, communicate and (in some cases) emancipate, rather than to generalize, predict and control. Generally, there is a dynamic relationship between THEORY-building and empirical inquiry wherein observable/ sense-able facts are neither wholly independent of theory nor wholly determined by it. Most qualitative approaches therefore depend on INTENSIVE empirical RESEARCH, but recognize that there is no 'real' world that exists independently of the relationships between researchers and their subjects. These relationships are a prerequisite for achieving the intersubjectivity which leads to an appreciation of the constitution of social life. They also provide a basis for the clarification and interpretation of meaning, thus linking qualitative methods to the project of HERMENEUTICS.

Despite these similarities, the means and ends of the various qualitative approaches to human geography do vary. This is one consequence of the diverse philosophies that the field embraces (see EXISTENTIALISM; IDEALISM; MARXIST GEOGRAPHY; PHENOMENOLOGY; POST-COLONIALISM; POST-STRUCTURALISM; PRAGMATISM). However, although purists might argue that any one philosophy has its own ONTOLOGICAL presumptions, its distinctive epistemological mandate and its particular methodological toolbox, the majority of qualitative research in human geography has always mixed its methods. In recent years this 'mixed methods' approach has received renewed and explicit attention (Rocheleau, 1995). Research which combines different qualitative methods and exploits the complementarity of qualitative and quantitative findings looks poised to gain a new respectability within the discipline. This respectability, however, is tempered by a well-established, if rapidly growing, concern about the standards by which qualitative research should be executed and judged (Smith, 1984). A new preoccupation with standards for evaluating qualitative research has been particularly notable in health services research (Popay et al., 1998; cf. HEALTH AND HEALTH CARE, GEOGRAPHY OF), and is likely to become of increasing importance for qualitative human geography (Baxter and Eyles, 1997). SJS

References

Baxter, J. and Eyles, J. 1997: Evaluating qualitative research in social geography: establishing 'rigour' in interview analysis. *Transactions, Institute of British Geographers* NS 22: 505–25. · Cloke, P., Philo, C. and Sadler, D. 1991: *Approaching human geography*. London: Paul Chapman. · Cook, I. and Crang, M. 1995: *Doing ethnographies*. Concepts and Techniques in Modern Geography no. 58. Norwich: Geo Books. · Crang, M.A., Hudson, A.C. and Reimer, S.M. 1997: Software for qualitative research: 1. Prospectus and overview. *Environment and Planning A* 29: 771–87. · Folch-Serra, M. 1990: Place, voice, space: Mikhail Bakhtin's dialogical landscape. *Environment and Planning D: Society and Space* 8: 255–74. · Gerber, R. and Williams, M. 1996: *Qualitative research in geographical education*. Armidale: University of New England Press for the IGU Commission on Geographical Education. · Harley, J.B. 1988: Maps, knowledge and power. In D. Cosgrove and S. Daniels, *The iconography of landscape*. Cambridge: Cambridge University Press, 277–312. · Katz, C. 1992: All the world is staged: intellectuals and the projects of ethnography. *Environment and Planning D: Society and Space* 10: 495–510. · Lee, R., ed., 1992: Teaching qualitative geography: a JGHE written symposium. *Journal of Geography in Higher Education* 16 (2) Special issue: 123–84. · Mitchell, J.C. 1974: Perceptions of ethnicity and ethnic behaviour: an empirical exploration. In A. Cohen, ed., *Urban ethnicity*. London: Tavistock, 1–35. · Mitchell, J.C. 1983: The logic of the analysis of social situations and cases. *Sociological Review* 31: 187–211. · Popay, J., Rogers, A. and Williams, G. 1998: Rationale and standards for the systematic review of qualitative literature in health services research. *Qualitative Health Service Research* 8: 341–51. · Pred, A. 1995: *Recognising European modernities. A montage of the present*. London and New York: Routledge. · Rocheleau, D.E. 1995: Maps, numbers, text and context: mixing methods in feminist political ecology. *The Professional Geographer* 47: 458–66. · Said, E. 1993: *Culture and imperialism*. London: Chatto and Windus. · Smith, S.J. 1984: Practising humanistic geography. *Annals of the Association of American Geographers* 74: 353–74. · Smith, S.J. 1988: Constructing local knowledge: the analysis of self in everyday life. In J. Eyles and D.M. Smith, eds, *Qualitative methods in human geography*. Cambridge: Polity Press, 17–38. · Tuan, Y.-F. 1991: Language and the making of place: a narrative–descriptive approach. *Annals of the Association of American Geographers* 81: 684–96.

Suggested Reading

Baxter and Eyles (1997). · Cook and Crang (1995). · Lee (1992).

quality of life The state of SOCIAL WELL-BEING of individuals or groups, either as they perceive it or as it is identified by 'observable indicators'. Most 'quality of life' studies concentrate on aspects of the human condition. Geographical studies have largely focused on mapping indicators for the populations of defined areas, with the potential for the ECOLOGICAL FALLACY to be committed.

RJJ

quango An acronym, coined by a British political scientist Tony Barker, for *q*uasi-*a*utonomous-*n*on-*g*overnmental-*o*rganizations, bodies to which public functions have been assigned and whose appointed members are not directly accountable to the electorate. The number of quangos in the UK has increased very significantly since the 1970s, as part of the drive to reduce the size and direct power of the STATE APPARATUS and to introduce 'market disciplines' to the provision of public services – as with the ability for schools to 'opt out' of local government control and receive grants directly from central government, to be managed by appointed governors. (Cf. PRIVATIZATION; URBAN ENTREPRENEURIALISM.)

RJJ

quantitative methods The use of mathematical techniques, theorems, and proofs in understanding geographical forms and relations. Two main types of application exist: *statistical methods*, which are employed in generating and testing hypotheses using empirical data, and pure *mathematical modelling*, which is employed when deriving formal models from a set of initial abstract assumptions. The two types come together in *calibration*: statistical methods are used to estimate, and test the significance of, various parameters associated with a given mathematical model, e.g. the FRICTION OF DISTANCE coefficient of the GRAVITY MODEL.

Statistical methods first began to be generally adopted by geographers in the 1950s (Burton, 1963). Consisting initially of descriptive statistics, there were also attempts at HYPOTHESIS testing, using, for example, CHI SQUARE. Bivariate REGRESSION analysis was also tried, but it was not until the 1960s that the GENERAL LINEAR MODEL was fully explored (e.g. in FACTORIAL ECOLOGY). Since then much attention has been paid to a set of very sophisticated dynamic linear (e.g. SPACE–TIME FORECASTING MODELS) and non-linear (e.g. spectral analysis) statistical techniques, including those that bear peculiarly upon geographical problems (e.g. SPATIAL AUTOCORRELATION).

More generally, since the first flush of enthusiasm back in the early 1960s, the history of statistics within geography has been one of trying to overcome the biased results that non-spatial statistics produce. Non-spatial statistical techniques, such as chi square and those based on the general linear model, produce bias when used on spatial data because of the effects of SPATIAL AUTOCORRELATION; that is, sample points which are spatially proximate will tend to have similar values because of that proximity, and as a result will not be statistically independent of one another. After forty years of work, however, geographers have now developed a number of methods for correcting those biases, and for performing distribution-free tests on spatial data (Griffith, 1988; Haining, 1990).

Mathematical modelling. Inspiration for this second use of quantitative methods came most immediately from three sources:

- SOCIAL PHYSICS, which focused on SPATIAL INTERACTION among a set of discrete points and was represented initially by the GRAVITY MODEL, and later by the ENTROPY-MAXIMIZING MODEL;
- NEO-CLASSICAL ECONOMICS, which was concerned with OPTIMIZATION MODELS around RATIONAL CHOICE THEORY, and influencing geography principally through the REGIONAL SCIENCE movement and LOCATION THEORY; and
- NETWORKS AND GRAPH THEORY, a branch of mathematics concerned with topological diagrams, and initially used to represent route networks in TRANSPORT GEOGRAPHY, but later utilized in some of geography's most abstract theorizing in CENTRAL PLACE THEORY.

Most recently, a number of spatial theorists and modellers have turned to the analysis of complex SYSTEMS and large data sets (see GEOCOMPUTATION). Stemming from long-standing criticisms made in human geography about the paucity of equilibrium frameworks, spatial complexity theory explicitly builds into its analysis non-linear dynamics and interaction (cf. CATASTROPHE THEORY; CHAOS). Such mathematical models allow for such useful properties as path dependence, short-term unpredictability, and sensitivity to initial conditions and external perturbations (for more details and examples, see National Research Council, 1997, pp. 92–3).

In these various applications, the use of mathematics has been justified on a variety of grounds, but they amount to the same basic claim: that the world itself and the world of mathematics are fundamentally ordered according to the same arithmetic logic. As Galileo puts it, 'mathematics is nature's own language' (Barnes, 1994).

But since the first heady days of the QUANTITATIVE REVOLUTION, geographers have become increasingly leery of quantitative methods in particular and their broader intellectual justification in general. In the first backlash, both RADICAL and HUMANISTIC GEOGRAPHERS argued during the 1970s that many questions asked by human geographers could not be effectively answered using mathematics – as Harvey (1973, p. 128) famously put it: 'The quantitative revolution has run its course, and diminishing marginal returns are setting in.' Such scepticism was bound up with a more general philosophical critique of POSITIVISM within human geography occurring at the same time. That argument in its most unsophisticated form was that because mathematics is the principal language of science, and because science is undergirded by the flawed philosophy of positivism, mathematics should be rejected. Such a position, however, established neither that geographers using quantitative methods ever practised positivism nor, even if they did, that positivism is a necessary justification for the use of mathematics.

More recently, from a POST-STRUCTURAL perspective, a different kind of argument has been put forward that attacks the very logocentric ambitions of mathematics, that is, its belief in a fundamentally ordered world (Barnes, 1994; see DECONSTRUCTION). Related also is work stemming from science and cultural studies that sees the use of mathematics, and statistical methods, as an effective vocabulary for social surveillance and control (Barnes, 1998; see also ACTOR–NETWORK THORY; SCIENCE, GEOGRAPHY AND). Mathematics and quantitative methods are not inherently ordered by some transcendental logic, but it can create order and discipline when applied to the social world.

Perhaps a more measured opinion of quantitative methods, then, is that like any specialized language they are very useful in answering some questions but not all questions (Pratt, 1989). Furthermore, the social entailments of the questions they do answer require continual scrutiny. (See also LOCATIONAL ANALYSIS; SPATIAL ANALYSIS; SPATIAL SCIENCE.) TJB

References

Barnes, T.J. 1994: Probable writing: Derrida, deconstruction and the quantitative revolution in human geography. *Environment and Planning A* 26: 1021–40. · Barnes, T.J. 1998: A history of regression: actors, networks, numbers and machines. *Environment and Planning A* 30: 203–23. · Burton, I. 1963: The quantitative revolution and theoretical geography. *Canadian Geographer* 7: 151–62. · Griffith, D.A. 1988: *Advanced spatial statistics: special topics in the exploration of quantitative spatial data series.* Dordrecht: Kluwer. · Haining, R. 1990: *Spatial data analysis in the social and environmental sciences.* Cambridge: Cambridge University Press. · Harvey, D. 1973: *Social justice and the city.* London: Edward Arnold; National Research Council 1997: *Rediscovering geography: new relevance for science and society.* Washington, D.C.: National Academy Press. · Pratt, G. 1989: Quantitative techniques and humanistic–historical materialist perspectives. In A. Kobayashi and S. MacKenzie, eds, *Remaking human geography.* Boston: Unwin Hyman, 101–15.

Suggested Reading

Burton (1963). · Macmillan, B., ed., 1988: *Remodelling geography.* Oxford: Basil Blackwell.

quantitative revolution The 'radical transformation of spirit and purpose' (Burton, 1963, p. 151) which Anglo-American geography underwent in the 1950s and 1960s following the widespread adoption of both inferential statistical techniques and abstract models and theories. In the process, an old IDIOGRAPHIC geography characterized by a focus on AREAL DIFFERENTIATION and REGIONAL GEOGRAPHY was displaced by a new NOMOTHETIC discipline, SPATIAL SCIENCE. As in most revolutions, tracts were written (such as Ian Burton's, 1963, quoted above), slogans coined (e.g. Harvey's, 1969, 'By our models you shall know us'), heroes lionized (the gendering is appropriate in this case), and villains vilified. All of which attests to the fact that the revolution was as much social as it was intellectual.

In many ways both the adjective and the noun in 'quantitative revolution' are misnomers. The noun is wrong because geography has been quantitative since its formal institutionalization as a discipline in the nineteenth century. The widespread use of formal statistical techniques from the 1950s onwards therefore represented *evolution* rather than revolution (Chisholm, 1975). The adjective is

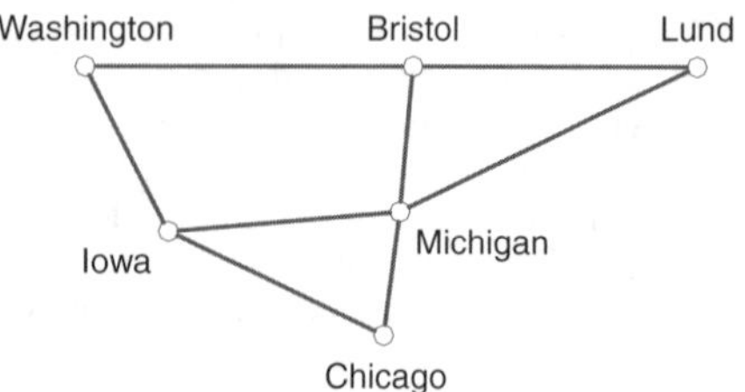

quantitative revolution *Quantgeog Airlines flight plan* (from P. J. Taylor, 1997, p. 15)

wrong because what was so significant about the 1950s was the introduction of theory not numbers; it was a theoretical revolution. Indeed, the new-found theoretical sensibility has been the period's most enduring legacy. Initially it secured the discipline's membership within the social sciences but also, and perhaps more importantly, prepared it for the inordinate range of theoretical 'isms' that were to come – including, ironically, many 'isms' that were diametrically opposed to the original conception of THEORY proffered at the time. (Note that Burton's, 1963, paper did link the 'quantitative revolution' to 'theoretical geography' – clearly getting the order of the adjectives wrong but illustrating the contemporary emphasis placed on quantification.)

As a discipline that is descriptive and practical, it is not surprising that geographers have a long history of using numbers. In Britain, the Royal Geographical Society (RGS; cf. GEOGRAPHICAL SOCIETIES) founded in 1830 was a classic 'centre of calculation' (Latour, 1987) providing resources for foreign expeditions, the products of which were sorted, sifted, displayed and presented back in London in the form of maps, tables, and figures (Livingstone, 1992, ch. 5). Similarly, in the US between 1852 and 1871 the American Geographical (AGS) and Statistical societies were formally twinned, and even when they went their separate ways, the mandate of the AGS remained 'the collection, classification and scientific arrangement of statistics and their results' (quoted in Berry and Marble, 1968, p. 1). The point, then, is that geographers have always been numerate. Even within the discipline's reputedly least numerate PARADIGM which preceded the quantitative revolution, areal differentiation, Richard Hartshorne (1959, p. 161) still affirmed that 'scientific knowing . . . and objectivity . . . can best be accomplished . . . by quantitative measurements . . . through the logic of mathematics'.

When the quantitative revolution began in the mid-1950s it was as a series of local affairs crystallized around one or two key individuals (see Johnston, 1997, pp. 62–73). In America the Department of Geography at the University of Washington, Seattle, was pivotal, as was the University of Iowa, Iowa City. At Washington, the presence of Edward Ullman, and especially William Garrison, was key. In 1954 Garrison gave the first advanced course in statistical methodology in a US Department of Geography, and in an early advertisement for the Department, the Head, Donald Hudson (1955), boasted about the departmental use of an IBM 604 digital computer, also a national first. The first cohort of graduate students from that department, which included Brian Berry, Michael Dacey, Arthur Getis, Richard Morrill, John Nystuen, and Walter Tobler, was critical in diffusing the Washington message, which they did by quickly establishing themselves and their research agenda at several prestigious US universities including Chicago, Northwestern and Michigan. At Iowa, the work of Harold McCarty was central. Again, he attracted a number of graduate students, including some from Australia and New Zealand (such as Leslie King and Reginald Golledge), all of whom were to prove vital in spreading the word about numbers. Outside the US, the University of Toronto became important in the mid-to-late 1960s, while Peter Haggett and Richard Chorley in the UK (the 'terrible twins' of British geography) and Torsten Hägerstrand in Sweden were crucial in establishing a European beachhead. The influence of Chorley and Haggett on British school teachers through the Madingly Hall lectures and concomitant publications was especially important sociologically (Chorley and Haggett, 1965, 1967). Those lectures brought pressure for change from those entering the discipline at the bottom, making the message of quantification more deeply entrenched in the educational hierarchy than in the US.

By the mid-1960s a network of quantification (and symbolized by Taylor's, 1977, fictional Quantgeog Airlines flight plan – see figure) was in place that connected researchers and universities on both sides of the Atlantic. The network was both *literal* and *figurative*. It was literal because individuals, as well as reprints, data sets, and mimeographs ceaselessly moved among its nodes. Faculty and graduate students travelled to workshops (such as the Michigan Interuniversity Community of Mathematical Geographers: MICMOG), seminars and special conferences were organized, and papers circulated for discussion and criticism.

It was figurative because the network was associated with two new sets of geographical practices: technique-based and theory-based. The new techniques included computerization (reading computer FORTRAN manuals, writing programs, interpreting printouts), and the study and application of ever more complex statistical methods (PARAMETRIC and NON-PARAMETRIC, linear and non-linear, static and dynamic; for details, see Gould, 1969, and QUANTITATIVE METHODS). The theory-based practices involved thinking about SPACE and location in rigorously abstract terms (cf. LOCATIONAL ANALYSIS). Before the 1950s human geography was resolutely atheoretical. With the quantitative revolution, however, a flood of theoretical models from other disciplines were imported and applied. There were several sources: from physics came GRAVITY and later ENTROPY-MAXIMIZING MODELS (and associated with MACROGEOGRAPHY and SOCIAL PHYSICS); from economics, often by way of REGIONAL SCIENCE, came the holy trinity of VON THÜNEN's MODEL, Weber's location triangle (cf. INDUSTRIAL LOCATION THEORY), and Losch's and Christaller's hexagonal CENTRAL PLACE THEORY; from sociology came the CHICAGO SCHOOL, urban FACTORIAL ECOLOGY, and the RANK-SIZE RULE; and from geometry came NETWORKS AND GRAPH THEORY and the analysis of topological forms which were incorporated into TRANSPORTATION MODELS. More generally the quantitative revolution was defined by an innovative set of geographical practices that stemmed from a distinct set of technical and theoretical competencies. In the process human geography moved from a field-based, craft-form of inquiry to a technical, desk-bound one where places were analysed from afar.

Whether these practices represented a self-consciously new philosophical approach, POSITIVISM, is unclear. Reflecting on what they had done, many of the early proponents of the quantitative revolution speak of their work in terms of a revolution of technique not of philosophical conviction (discussed in several reflections on the revolution in *Urban Geography*, vol. 14, 1993). Few had any philosophical training, and most had never heard of positivism before the 1970s; Richard Morrill (1993, p. 443), for example, in recalling his experiences as a graduate student at the University of Washington, said 'I never met a positivist'. Rather, when people turned to positivism, such as Harvey (1969), it was in effect an *ex post* rationalization of quantification, and then, ironically, just as the movement was beginning its slow arc of decline.

Much more clearly marked than positivism was the role of sociological processes in both maintaining and extending the quantitative revolution. Most immediately the revolution required that the message be spread. This occurred through: establishing new journals (e.g. *Geographical Analysis* in 1969); hiring the 'right' people (the Department of Geography at Ohio State was transformed following Edward Taaffe's appointment as Chair in the mid-1960s); securing funding to carry out research (mainly from the National Science Foundation (NSF) and the US Office of Naval Research: see NAS–NRC, 1965); and training the wider discipline to think in a new vocabulary (carried out under the auspices of NSF-funded summer workshops on quantitative methods beginning in 1961).

In all of this, circumstances, particularly in the US, were propitious. Higher education was expanding, the social sciences were burgeoning, and the broader instrumental, 'can-do' attitude of the time resonated perfectly with the new geographical models and techniques (cf. INSTRUMENTALISM). The old-style geography of regional description was being swept away by the new broom of the quantitative revolution. Peter Gould (1978), in fact, labelled the era 'The Augean period' after the mythic Augean stables which after 30 years of neglect were cleaned all of a piece by Hercules.

Equating the quantitative revolutionaries with Hercules, and an earlier non-quantitative geography with unkempt, filthy Augean stables, also speaks to other sociological processes around the revolution that typically are not acknowledged. First, Gould's portrayal of the revolution in heroic terms, whether he wanted to or not, points to its MASCULINIST nature. This is true in a number of senses: that its initial proponents and expositors were all men; that there were virtually no substantive studies of women carried out by that group; and that the disembodied, totalized knowledge proponents sought matched what later feminists would describe as PHALLOCENTRIC (see SITUATED KNOWLEDGE). Second, Gould's Augean METAPHOR also illustrates the extent to which quantifiers were desperately keen to separate themselves from the past. Clearly the main reason was intellectual, but, as Taylor (1976) argues, another was for internal sociological reasons within the academy. For in order to get ahead, to secure early promotion and academic status, it was, and still is, necessary to be original, and to do something different. For a group of very bright, ambitious and competitive young scholars emerging from graduate school, the quantitative revolution was the perfect vehicle to achieve such career goals.

At some point in the late 1960s, or early 1970s, these once-compelling sociological reasons began to slip, and with them the grip of the quantitative revolution on the discipline. There were at least two broad reasons for change. First, a different kind of world was emerging that was more restless, less innocent than before. Great debates were happening around issues of poverty, civil rights, the environment, gender and racial equality and war, but the quantitative revolution seemed unable or unwilling to address them. The ensuing RELEVANCE debate of the early 1970s left quantifiers flat-footed (cf. RADICAL GEOGRAPHY). As Harvey (1973, p. 129) damningly put it, 'There is an ecological problem, an urban problem, an international trade problem, and yet we seem incapable of saying anything of depth or profundity about any of them. When we do say something, it appears trite and slightly ludicrous. In short, our paradigm is not coping well. It is ripe for overthrow.' Second, an academic generation had already passed since the first quantifiers, and the time was once more ripe for change. So yet a new vocabulary was forged to mark off the old from the new, in this case, one principally derived from Marxism (Harvey, 1973), and its later successor projects. But the important point, and why the quantitative revolution remains a watershed in geography's recent history, is that Marxism and the various intellectual movements that followed persisted with a *theoretical* vocabulary. Certainly since that time the meaning of theory has altered, but the continuity of some kind of theoretical vocabulary has proven more important in subsequently shaping the discipline than any rupture. TJB

References

Berry, B.J.L. and Marble, D.F., eds, 1968: *Spatial analysis: a reader in statistical geography*. Englewood Cliffs, NJ: Prentice-Hall. · Burton, I. 1963: The quantitative revolution and theoretical geography. *Canadian Geographer* 7: 151–62. · Chisholm, M. 1975: *Human geography: evolution or revolution*? Harmondsworth: Penguin. · Chorley, R.J. and Haggett, P., eds, 1965: *Frontiers in geographical teaching*. London: Methuen. · Chorley, R.J. and Haggett, P., eds, 1967: *Models in geography*. London: Methuen. · Gould, P. 1969: Methodological developments since the fifties. *Progress in Geography* 1: 1–49. · Gould, P. 1978: The Augean period. *Annals of the Association of American Geographers* 69: 139–51. · Hartshorne, R. 1959: *Perspective on the nature of geography*. Chicago: Rand McNally. · Harvey, D. 1969: *Explanation in geography*. London: Edward Arnold. · Harvey, D. 1973: *Social justice and the city*. London: Edward Arnold. · Hudson, D. 1955: University of Washington. *Professional Geographer* 7(4): 28–9. · Johnston, R.J. 1997: *Geography and geographers: Anglo-American human geography since 1945*, 5th edn. London: Arnold. · Latour, B. 1987: *Science in action: how to follow scientists and engineers through society*. Cambridge, MA: Harvard University Press. · Livingstone, D.N. 1992: *The geographical tradition: episodes in a contested enterprise*. Oxford: Blackwell. · Morrill, R. 1993: Geography, spatial analysis and social science. *Urban Geography* 14: 442–6. · NAS–NRC, 1965: *The science of geography*. Washington, D.C.: NAS–NRC. · Taylor, P.J. 1976: An interpretation of the quantification debate in British geography. *Transactions, Institute of British Geographers* NS 1: 129–42. · Taylor, P.J. 1977: *Quantitative methods in geography: an introduction to spatial analysis*. Boston: Houghton Mifflin.

Suggested Reading

Barnes, T.J. 1998: The history of regression: actors, networks, numbers and machines. *Environment and Planning A* 30: 203–23. · Gould (1978).

queer theory An intellectual movement developed in the 1990s that centres on the significance of sexuality and gender and their interrelationships. This definition is necessarily broad because the term adamantly resists easy characterization. Above all, 'queer theory' draws on both senses of its adjective: lesbian/gay/pan-sexual identity and desire (see PSYCHOANALYTIC THEORY, GEOGRAPHY AND); and odd or strange: in the sense of challenging norms of sexuality (De Lauretis, 1991; Jagose, 1996).

Two rather general uses of the term can be noticed, however. First, queer theory is a term often used loosely to describe any work in gay and lesbian studies. Second, and more precisely, queer theory challenges the dominance and ubiquity of hetero-normativity (the presumption that heterosexuality is the normal or best form that sexuality can take; cf. HOMOPHOBIA AND HETEROSEXISM). It also constantly destabilizes our taken-for-granted ideas by rejecting any fixed or stable notions of sexuality and gender, their characterizations or effects (see ESSENTIALISM; GENDER AND GEOGRAPHY; PERFORMATIVITY). Here, it is interesting that the target of its critique is not just other research orientations, but also gay and lesbian studies, politics, and even queer theory itself (Jagose, 1996).

The problem with any dictionary definition of the term is that it is meant to refuse fixing or defining, because such a move logically excludes facets of sexualities, or strategies that rethink them (see POST-STRUCTURALISM; POSTMODERNISM). This dilemma reflects the tendency of dominant discourses to incorporate and diffuse any moves to stand outside and challenge them. Thus, queer theory is quite ambivalent about the growing normalization of gays and lesbians in society (which is even reflected in its first definition given above).

Queer theory's relationship with geography is two-way, with one increasingly recognizing the implications of the other. Simply put, queer theory demands that geographers recognize how hetero-normativity can blatantly or subtly taint the geographies that we write and research. Here sexuality's implications for exploring new and/or different geographies is highlighted (Ingram, Bouthillette and Retter, 1997; cf. SEXUALITY, GEOGRAPHY AND). Geographers and architects conversely have pointed out queer theory's penchant for historicity, language, and literary texts while ignoring the SPATIALITY of those representations, even when they are analysed explicitly (Bell et al., 1996; Betsky, 1997). MPB

References

Bell, D., Binnie, J., Cream, J. and Valentine, G. 1996: All hyped up and no place to go. *Gender, Place, and Culture* 1: 31–48. · Betsky, A. 1997: *Queer space*. New York: William Morrow & Company; De Lauretis, T. 1991: Queer theory: lesbian and gay sexualities: an introduction. *Differences* 3: 1–10. · Ingram, G., Bouthillette, A. and Retter, Y. 1997: *Queer in spaces*. Seattle: Bay Press; Jagose, A. 1996: *Queer theory*. New York: New York University Press.

questionnaire An instrument used for the data collection segment of a SURVEY ANALYSIS, comprising a carefully structured and ordered set of questions designed to obtain the needed information without either ambiguity or bias. Every respondent answers the same questions, asked in the same way and in the same sequence, which contrasts with the more open-ended formats used in INTERVIEWS and other QUALITATIVE METHODS for obtaining information from individuals. The questionnaire may be administered by a trained person, either in a face-to-face meeting or by telephone, or it may be self-administered.

Questionnaires are devised to obtain a variety of data. The simplest are the factual, ascertaining information such as age, place of birth etc. Others are attitudinal, for which questions are designed to probe people's values, attitudes and opinions. (These must be carefully pre-tested and piloted to ensure their validity.) Such data may be obtained through open-ended questions, with the 'free' responses recorded and later categorized, but more common are specially designed scaling instruments for measuring different types of attitude (personality, political ideology, etc.): some are generally applicable but many are specific to a particular study, reflecting the local cultural situation and context. (*Likert scales, repertory grid analysis*, and *semantic differential* are scaling instruments widely used in the social sciences.)

Production of questionnaires is sometimes assumed to be a straightforward task and undertaken in a rather cavalier manner. For collecting all but the simplest of factual information, however, great care is needed to ensure the absence of ambiguity (recalling that the questions may be asked of people from a wide range of backgrounds), so that all respondents will interpret them in the same way. (If a respondent has to ask what a question means, then the questioner's answer will potentially introduce bias, especially if not all respondents ask.) With a self-administered questionnaire, the problems of varying interpretations of an unclear question are very substantial and may invalidate any analysis of the data obtained.

RJJ

Suggested Reading

Dixon, C.J. and Leach, B. 1976: *Questionnaires and interviews in geographical research*. Concepts and Techniques in Modern Geography 18. Norwich: Geo Books.

R

race Although its value as a scientific concept has long since been repudiated (e.g. Gould, 1984), the idea of race continues to be employed as a popular (and sometimes as a social scientific) marker of human DIFFERENCE, based on physical criteria such as skin colour, nose shape and type of hair. Coming into English usage in the sixteenth century, race took on its current problematic range of meanings in the nineteenth century, when writers such as Thomas de Gobineau began to confuse classifications of human beings based on physical criteria with value judgements about social status and moral worth. Further confusions followed from debates about SOCIAL DARWINISM in which the idea of human evolution as a competitive struggle was extended from the biological realm (where it referred to relations *between* species) to the sociological realm (where it was held to apply to relations *within* a single species, *homo sapiens*). Ideas of racial superiority (and their discriminatory consequences) quickly followed, paralleling Europe's imperial expansion overseas (cf. IMPERIALISM).

The belief that human beings can be readily divided into a series of discrete races is now widely regarded as fallacious (though attempts to reinstate the biological basis of human difference occasionally resurface, e.g. Hernstein and Murray, 1994). Instead, races are now widely regarded as a political and social construction rather than a biological fact, the product of RACISM rather than of human genetics (Jackson and Penrose, 1993). Racial IDEOLOGIES have underpinned some of the most repressive political regimes of the twentieth century including Nazism and APARTHEID (Smith, 1992; Robinson, 1995). In recent years, geographers have turned from mapping and measuring patterns of ethnic and racial SEGREGATION, to investigating (spatially and temporally specific) processes of racialization (Bonnett, 1996). Attention now also focuses on constructions of 'WHITENESS' as well as on the social geographies of so-called 'minority' groups. (See also HYBRIDITY; SOCIAL EXCLUSION.) PAJ

References

Bonnett, A. 1996: Constructions of 'race', place and discipline: geographies of 'racial' identity and racism. *Ethnic and Racial Studies* 19: 864–83. · Gould, S.J. 1984: *The mismeasure of man*. London: Penguin. · Hernstein, R.J. and Murray, C. 1994: *The bell curve: intelligence and class structure in American life*. New York: Free Press. · Jackson, P. and Penrose, J., eds, 1993: *Constructions of race, place and nation*. London: UCL Press. · Robinson, J. 1995: *The power of apartheid*. London: Butterworth-Heinemann. · Smith, D.M., ed., 1992: *The apartheid city and beyond*. London: Routledge.

racial districting An aspect of REDISTRICTING in the USA designed to ensure that racial minorities do not suffer discrimination, such as GERRYMANDERING (intentional or otherwise), which has been outlawed by the *Voting Rights Acts* (first passed in 1965). This requirement normally involves ensuring sufficient 'minority–majority' districts in each State so that, for example, if 30 per cent of a State's population is black, then 30 per cent of its Congressional Districts should contain a majority of black residents, although there are continued legal disputes over whether this is an absolute requirement. RJJ

Suggested Reading

Grofman, B., Handley, L.R. and Niemi, R.G., eds, 1992: *Minority representation and the quest for voter equality*. Cambridge and New York: Cambridge University Press.

racism An IDEOLOGY of DIFFERENCE whereby social significance is attributed to culturally constructed categories of RACE. Racism is 'an ideology which ascribes negatively evaluated characteristics in a deterministic manner... to a group which is additionally identified as being in some way biologically... distinct' (Miles, 1982, p. 78). Such ideological distinctions invariably lead to discrimination and racialized inequality. Racism can take various forms, from the 'scientific' racism of the nineteenth century to the 'cultural' racism of today (Blaut, 1992) where the emphasis is on supposedly 'inherent' cultural differences rather than on innate biological differences. Discourses of 'race', like ideologies of GENDER, attempt to ground themselves in nature though they are both socially constructed (Kobayashi and Peake, 1994). Geographical studies have highlighted the territorial basis of various forms of racism including the institutionalization of radicalized inequality in housing markets (see

HOUSING CLASS; HOUSING STUDIES; TERRITORIALITY). PAJ

References

Blaut, J.M. 1992: The theory of cultural racism. *Antipode* 24: 289–99. · Kobayashi, A. and Peake, L. 1994: Unnatural discourse: 'race' and gender in geography. *Gender, Place and Culture* 1: 225–43. · Miles, R. 1982: *Racism and migrant labour*. London: Routledge and Kegan Paul.

Suggested Reading

Miles, R. 1989: *Racism*. London: Routledge.

radical democracy A POSTMODERNIST or POST-STRUCTURALIST rethinking of modern democratic theory influenced by Mouffe (1992), Trend (1995) and Lummis (1996). It takes a decentred, or unfixed perspective on CITIZENSHIP (the capacity to 'be political' in a DEMOCRACY). Centrally, it challenges two fixed characterizations of the citizen. Rather than locating the citizen as one identity alongside and mutually exclusive to others (LIBERALISM), or elevating it as the principal identity of the individual (COMMUNITARIANISM), radical democracy views citizenship as a potential moment of any identity when it becomes politicized or contested (Mouffe, 1993). Thus people can be acting on or embodying democratic principles of freedom, justice, or EQUALITY through their very 'being' or 'doing' a particular CLASS, ETHNICITY, gender, sexuality, etc. (see GENDER AND GEOGRAPHY; JUSTICE, GEOGRAPHY AND; PERFORMATIVITY; SEXUALITY, GEOGRAPHY AND; STRUCTURATION THEORY; SUBJECT FORMATION, GEOGRAPHIES OF).

Radical democracy obviously has consequences for POLITICAL GEOGRAPHY. Geographers' interest in this body of thought can be seen as part of a broader theoretical turn that political geographers called for in the 1980s (e.g. Painter, 1995). Further, it insists that political geography cannot remain solely focused on the STATE as the prime location for politics (Brown, 1997). Deutsche (1997), for instance, places the access and control over urban public space at the very heart of democratic theory. How do different aspects of individuals' identities enable or constrain their access to a public sphere allegedly open to everyone in a democracy? (See PRIVATE AND PUBLIC SPHERES.)

Radical democracy also has implications for SOCIAL and CULTURAL GEOGRAPHY, given its emphasis on social meanings of identities. Since it rejects ESSENTIALISM, radical democracy implores a sensitivity to the openness and fluidity in people's multi-faceted identities. How are different facets of identity enabled or constrained geographically for people; how are places constituted on the basis of identity formation (Massey, 1995; Moss and Jones, 1995), for example? Most provocatively, radical democracy challenges the will to either fixate on a single aspect of identity at the expense of others (see IDENTITY POLITICS; SOCIAL MOVEMENT) or assume a hierarchy of different oppressions (Mouffe, 1995).

Radical democracy, therefore, is appealing to geographers in a number of ways. It encourages us to see politics in new or hybrid locations (see HYBRIDITY). It gives us a more democratic sense of how identity and subjectivity are always mediated geographically. Finally, it provides an intellectual framework for practising political solidarity between and within places that is truly democratic. MPB

References

Brown, M. 1997: *RePlacing citizenship: AIDS activism and radical democracy*. New York: Guilford. · Deutsche, R. 1997: *Evictions*. Cambridge: MIT Press. · Lummis, C. 1996: *Radical democracy*. Ithaca: Cornell University Press. · Massey, D. 1995: Thinking radical democracy spatially. *Environment and Planning D: Society and Space* 13: 283–8. · Moss, P. and Jones, J.P. 1995: Guest editorial: Democracy, identity, space. *Environment and Planning D: Society and Space* 13: 253–8. · Mouffe, C. 1992: *Dimensions of radical democracy*. London: Verso. · Mouffe, C. 1993: *The return of the political*. London: Verso. · Mouffe, C. 1995: Post-Marxism: democracy and identity. *Environment and Planning D: Society and Space* 13: 259–65. · Painter, J. 1995: *Politics, geography, and political geography*. London: Edward Arnold. · Trend, D., ed., 1995: *Radical democracy: identity, citizenship, and the state*. London: Routledge.

radical geography A term introduced in the 1970s to describe the increasing volume of geographical writing critical of SPATIAL SCIENCE and of POSITIVISM as the philosophy which dominated the discipline's research methods then. The critique began within the contemporary liberal concerns of society, but later coalesced around a belief in the power of Marxian analyses (Peet, 1998; see MARXIAN ECONOMICS; MARXIST GEOGRAPHY) and focused on the pages of *Antipode: a radical journal of geography* (founded in 1969 but with little Marxist material in its earliest issues, and with more focus on RACE than CLASS).

By the late 1980s, Walker (1989a, p. 620) concluded that what he termed 'left geography' had 'edged towards the mainstream' of the discipline's work: it can, he contends, 'claim a good deal of credit for broadening the intellectual respectability of the geographic enterprise outside the discipline in recent years, and can claim a measure of intellectual leadership and even hegemony within certain geographic subfields': according to Peet (1998, p. 109), 'Radical and Marxist geography responded to the political events of the 1960s and early 1970s in ways which transformed the discipline.'

Origins of the radical geography movement can be traced to concern in the late 1960s, especially in the USA, over three political issues – the Vietnam war, civil rights (especially of American blacks) and continued pervasive POVERTY and inequality at all spatial scales, all of which were stimulating social unrest. Out of these evolved a more general critique of CAPITALIST society, so that radical geography developed largely as 'a negative reaction to the established discipline' (Peet, 1977): it promoted the study of topics such as poverty, hunger, health and crime by human geographers, who had previously largely ignored them. Led by Harvey (1973) and others, that critical stance was incorporated into a theoretical base which sought, again quoting Peet, to create a 'radical science, which seeks not only to explain what is happening but also to prescribe revolutionary change': Marxism was the favoured theoretical structure (Harvey, 1982), and CLASS analysis the preferred approach to a wide range of topics covering virtually the whole of the discipline (as Walker's, 1989a, review shows).

Much of the radical critique of the mainstream human geography of the 1960s and 1970s became fairly widely accepted within the discipline, even if the radicals' revolutionary goals were not, so that, according to Peet and Thrift (1989), by the 1980s it had become less combative, for four reasons: (a) Marxist thought was itself subject to powerful critiques; (b) the failure of socialist-inspired states made the revolutionary goals less certain; (c) the discipline had become more professional and less accepting of radicals; and (d) a number of the 1960s–1970s radicals had joined the disciplinary 'establishment'. Other lines of radical critique were being developed, however, notably in FEMINIST GEOGRAPHY, only parts of which were allied to the traditional 'left-wing' causes (McDowell, 1993a, 1993b) and which has also stimulated significant transformations within the discipline, and in studies stimulated by the POST-COLONIALISM literature, which focus on a particular aspect of capitalist society and have a strong base in the humanities as well as the social sciences (cf. IMPERIALISM).

By the end of the 1980s, various authors were relabelling radical geography – Peet and Thrift termed it 'the POLITICAL-ECONOMY perspective', for example – whereas others (notably Harvey) pressed for a continued commitment to a Marxist perspective and theoretical foundation, which he, unlike many others, did not find antithetical to the criticisms of attempts to develop 'GRAND THEORY' coming from the adherents to POSTMODERNISM (on which see Harvey, 1989, and the debate in *Environment and Planning D: Society and Space* 1987, stimulated by his critique of British urban studies: Harvey, 1987). The fall of the STATE APPARATUS practising SOCIALISM in the USSR and eastern Europe at the end of the decade also caused some to reconsider (e.g. Walker, 1989b); Sayer and Folke (1991) concluded that whereas some people interpret the events of 1989–91 as 'the final victory for capitalism', for them 'For decades all discussions in our part of the world about socialism have been marred by the bureaucratic and oppressive character of the "real, existing socialism". Now the slate is clean. Let us try a fresh start!'

This 'fresh start' has involved a number of strategies. Sayer (1995), for example, has explored new directions for radical political economy in the understanding of various modes of production, whereas others have promoted what has been termed critical human geography, which questions the foundations of contemporary societies (arguing that *what is* should not be equated with *what ought to be*). Similarly, the CULTURAL TURN is promoting new paths to understanding and shares the 'radical tradition' of questioning how society is structured and organized and individuals are treated within it. Together, these new trends have directed attention away from *oppression* within capitalist society and into wider concerns of IDENTITY POLITICS (cf. ACTIVISM AND THE ACADEMY; POSITIONALITY).

RJJ

References

Harvey, D. 1973: *Social justice and the city*. London: Edward Arnold. · Harvey, D. 1982: *The limits to capital*. Oxford: Basil Blackwell. · Harvey, D. 1987: Three myths in search of a reality in urban studies. *Environment and Planning D: Society and Space* 5: 367–76. · Harvey, D. 1989: *The condition of postmodernity*. Oxford: Basil Blackwell. · McDowell, L. 1993a: Space, place and gender relations: Part I. Feminist empiricism and the geography of social relations. *Progress in Human Geography* 17: 157–79. · McDowell, L. 1993b: Space, place and gender relations: Part II. Identity, difference, feminist geometries and geographies. *Progress in Human Geography*. 17: 305–18. · Peet, R. 1977: *Radical geography: alternative viewpoints on contemporary social issues*. Chicago: Maaroufa; London: Methuen. · Peet, R. 1998: *Modern geographic thought*. Oxford and Boston: Blackwell. · Peet, R. and Thrift, N.J. 1989: Political economy and human geography. In R. Peet and N.J. Thrift, eds, *New models in geography*, volume 1. Boston and London: Unwin Hyman, 3–29. · Sayer, A. 1995: *Radical political economy*. London: Routledge. · Sayer, A. and Folke, S. 1991: What's left to do? Two views from Europe. *Antipode* 23, 240–8. · Walker, R.A. 1989a: Geography from the left. In G.L. Gaile and C.J. Willmott, eds, *Geography in America*. Columbus: Merrill Publishing Co., 619–50. · Walker, R.A. 1989b: What's left to do. *Antipode* 21: 133–65.

rank-size rule An empirical regularity in the CITY-SIZE DISTRIBUTIONS of countries and regions. In its most general form, if the cities are rank-ordered according to their populations from the largest (*1*) to the smallest (*n*), then the population of the city ranked *k* can be derived from:

$$P_k = P_1/k$$

where P_k is the population of the city ranked *k* and P_1 is the population of the largest city. The form of the relationship between P_k and *k* is J-shaped, but is linear if both are transformed logarithmically (see TRANSFORMATION OF VARIABLES).

The precise relationship is usually identified empirically using REGRESSION analysis of the form:

$$\log P_k = \log P_1 - b(\log k)$$

The larger the value of *b*, the steeper the slope and thus the larger the city P_1 relative to all others. (In the 'pure' formulation, $b = 1.0$.)

No convincing explanation for the existence of the relationship has been developed, despite the frequency with which it is observed. Nor are there convincing explanations for the varying size of *b* (see also PRIMATE CITY, THE LAW OF THE). RJJ

Suggested Reading

Carroll, G.R. 1982: National city-size distributions: what do we know after 67 years of research? *Progress in Human Geography* 16: 1–43.

raster A scheme for storing a digital representation of a map, image, or other two-dimensional distribution. A rectangular area is divided into an array of rows and columns to form cells or PIXELS. Each cell's contents are then summarized as a single number, class, or measure, and stored in a predetermined sequence, normally row by row from the top left. Their fixed spatial resolution makes rasters more suitable for certain kinds of geographic data, notably data from REMOTE SENSING (but see QUADTREE). Rasters are a popular choice for GEOGRAPHICAL INFORMATION SYSTEM applications in resource management, but VECTOR DATA are more popular in other applications. Difficulties arise in applying rasters to the curved surface of the Earth, but recent research has identified several promising ways of subdividing the planet systematically and hierarchically. MG

rational choice theory Rational choice theory is a NORMATIVE THEORY of individual DECISION-MAKING that claims that human action is motivated by getting the most for the least. On the one hand, individuals strive to achieve an unlimited set of ends where each end is associated with a different level of UTILITY but, on the other hand, they possess only limited means to realize those ends. The role of the rationality postulate is to ensure that the best ends are chosen given the constraint of limited means. Often couched in terms of the mathematics of constrained maximization, the problem of making the best choices is formally shown to reduce to a formal set of consistency requirements (Hahn and Hollis, 1979). Those requirements define rationality in the sense that if any one of them is contravened the choice is not rational.

The historical antecedents of rational choice theory are with the British classical economists, but it is now most closely associated with their successor, NEO-CLASSICAL ECONOMICS, and even more recently with a maverick strain of Marxism (ANALYTICAL MARXISM). Not surprisingly, among human geographers the use of rational choice theory is found most frequently in ECONOMIC GEOGRAPHY, and in particular, in the formal location models associated with REGIONAL SCIENCE. Its role there was to impose a determinant order on spatial arrangements, one allowing the theorist to make scientific claims to precision, exact inference and predictability (cf. LOCATION THEORY; LOCATIONAL ANALYSIS).

Criticisms of the rationality assumption are vast, and frequently focus on the patently unrealistic characteristics attributed to the rational actor: perfect knowledge; egoism; independent preferences; the ability and desire to maximize utility (minimize costs); and pursuit of a single goal (see SATISFICING BEHAVIOUR). Barnes (1996, chs 2 and 3) argues, however, that such criticisms are moot because the rationality postulate by its very construction is empirically untestable, and therefore charges of unrealism have no purchase. A more convincing critique derives from Mirowski's (1989) work which uses biographical and historical sources to argue that the rational choice postulate is based on an inappropriate physical METAPHOR taken by economists from physicists in the late nineteenth century. While that metaphor has provided its users with power and prestige in an age of science, its concomitant physicalist assumptions mitigate any isomorphism with the social world it supposedly explains, and it is now simply a piece of out-dated theoretical physics. TJB

References

Barnes, T.J. 1996: *Logics of dislocation: models, meanings and metaphors of economic space*. New York: Guilford. · Hahn, F. and Hollis, M., eds, 1979: Introduction. In *Philosophy and economic theory*. Oxford: Oxford University Press, 1–17. · Mirowski, P. 1989: *More heat than light. Economics as social physics: physics as nature's economics*. Cambridge: Cambridge University Press.

Suggested Reading

Barnes (1996), chs 2 and 3.

realism A philosophy of science that uses ABSTRACTION to identify the specific causal powers and liabilities of specific structures that are realized under specific conditions. This is a complicated sentence, but in order to understand its repeated emphasis on specificity – in sharp contrast to the philosophy of POSITIVISM – we need to begin by considering realism's view of causation.

Realism makes a fundamental distinction between:

- *the identification of causal mechanisms*, which is typically the concern of so-called INTENSIVE RESEARCH: the key question here is 'how does something happen?'; and
- *the identification of empirical regularities*, which is typically the concern of so-called EXTENSIVE RESEARCH: the key question here is 'how widespread is something?'

Realism distinguishes between these two forms of research because 'what causes something to happen has nothing to do with the number of times it happens' (Sayer, 1985a). Yet in the 1960s and 1970s much of mainstream human geography effectively erased this distinction. SPATIAL SCIENCE was preoccupied with the identification of empirical regularities, with a search for 'order' and 'pattern', and this tradition of extensive research was continued in the prediction of empirical regularities using SPACE–TIME FORECASTING MODELS. All of these projects were tacitly informed by the philosophy of positivism. But they faced a serious barrier, because the empirical regularities that they detected could only approach the status of the scientific LAWS envisaged by positivism – could only be regarded as laws of constant conjunction – provided both the mechanism capable of generating them and the conditions under which they were produced were held constant. These requirements can only be satisfied, however, if research is confined to a *closed* SYSTEM. The problem, as Chouinard et al. (1984) explained, was this: all of the cases with which human geography and the other human and social sciences are centrally concerned are *open systems*.

On the basis of this equation between the identification of empirical regularities, the conduct of extensive research and the existence of closed systems, realism makes three critical interventions:

(a) The success of different sciences in identifying and predicting empirical regularities is determined in large measure by their ability to devise either empirically or (more usually) experimentally closed systems. In open systems it is not possible to guarantee the symmetry of explanation and prediction required by positivism. (Sayer, 1984a)

(b) The analysis of open systems requires the elaboration of a stratified and differentiated ONTOLOGY, and it is here that realism makes its strongest and most strategic claim (Yeung, 1997). Both EMPIRICISM and positivism assume that the world is made up of *events*: these are the 'empirical particulars' of science, and so their observation is accorded a special privilege as the leading edge of scientific discovery. In opposition to such 'atomism', realism provides a multi-tiered ontology in which the world is made up not only of events but also of *mechanisms* and *structures* (see the figure). The connection between the last two is crucial. 'Structures' are seen as sets of INTERNAL RELATIONS that have characteristic ways of acting: more formally, they possess 'causal powers and liabilities', which are seen as *constitutive* because they possess these powers and liabilities by virtue of what they *are*. Precisely because these powers and liabilities enter fundamentally into the constitution of structures they are thus held to be *necessary*. Whether they are activated or not, however, is *contingent*: less technically, whether they are put into practice through the 'mechanisms' of the structure (or not) depends on the circumstances. Seen like this, the task of a realist science is to tease out the causal chains that situate specific events within specific mechanisms and structures. The technical term for this procedure is the recovery of *ontological depth*: whereas positivism collapses the world into a single plane pockmarked by the space–

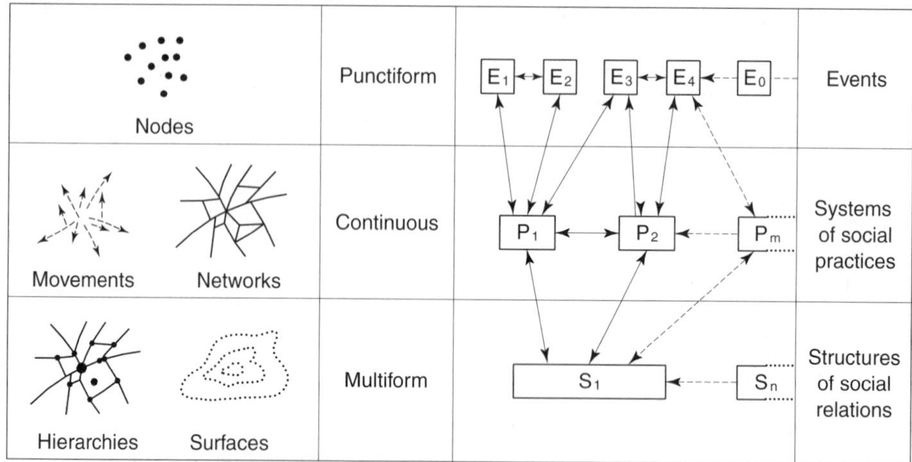

realism *and strategies for geographical inquiry* (Gregory, 1985a, p. 72)

time incidence of events, realism seeks to recover the connective tissue between the differentiated, foliated domains of events, mechanisms and structures.

(c) The identification and recovery of the various mechanisms and structures that make up the world is far from straightforward, because they are not immediately inscribed in the taken-for-granted categories which we draw upon in our everyday, 'common-sense' discourse. Their disclosure thus requires a process of *abstraction* that is progressive, reflexive and essentially iterative (Yeung, 1997). In other words, realism relies on a research strategy in which theoretical categories inform and are in turn informed by empirical materials. Rather than privilege supposedly 'theory-free' observations, realism places a premium on theoretical work: both on the *critique* of theoretical systems and on the *co-determination* of theoretical and empirical systems (Hesse, 1974; Gregory, 1978).

These three interventions can be used to underwrite both the natural sciences and the human and social sciences. Although physical geography did not engage with realism in any systematic fashion until the 1990s (see Richards, 1990a, 1990b), realist perspectives were opened up across the spectrum of the human and social sciences in the early 1980s: in history (e.g. McLennan 1981), in sociology (e.g. Keat and Urry, 1981), and in human geography (e.g. Williams, 1981; Sayer, 1982, 1985a; Chouinard et al., 1984). Within the human and social sciences the 'mechanisms' that are the mainsprings of realism were usually identified with systems of social practices: indeed, Williams (1981) insisted that 'in a fundamental sense the concept of practice lies at the heart of the realist account'. Many thinkers sought to establish filiations between realism and both HISTORICAL MATERIALISM and STRUCTURATION THEORY, and in doing so were led to a view of social practices as (i) being dependent upon knowledgeable and capable human subjects (although not reducible to them) and as (ii) having their effects determined in some substantial degree by contingent features of the settings in which they occur (Gregory, 1985). Double-edged claims of this sort sparked two major debates around realism in human geography.

(d) The appeal to 'knowledgeable and capable human subjects' was intended to distance realism from ESSENTIALISM (the belief that there is an essential reality lying 'behind' the surface particulars of the world) and from STRUCTURALISM (which displaces the human subject altogether). If this appeal is taken seriously, however, then it has to be allowed that the human and social sciences confront a world that is *pre-interpreted*, and that those interpretations are of basic importance to any explanatory account. As Keat and Urry (1981) recognized, this makes the abstractions of realism insufficient. For the fact is that most of us most of the time do not make sense of the world through the clean and clinical abstractions that lie at the centre of the realist account; our 'lay' constructions must not be severed from the 'scientific' explanations provided by realism. As Sayer (1985b) put it:

> In real life we live in conjunctures whose boundaries are arbitrary; they haphazardly cut across structures and causal relations, and unless we devote considerable energy to their understanding, we only disentangle such conjunctures sufficiently for us to cope with everyday tasks. As theorists, however, we seek to understand the world by making rational abstractions which isolate unified objects, structures or groups, and we try to conduct concrete research by starting from such abstraction.

Elsewhere Sayer (1984b) argued that the separation of these two facets, which he called the 'expressive' and the 'objective' respectively, had serious consequences for the social sciences and for social policy.

(e) The appeal to 'contingent features' of the 'settings' in which social practices occur – in other words, to their conditions of operation – was intended to prise realism away from any determinism. In contrast to positivism, realism regards scientific 'laws' as statements of necessity not universality. Sayer illustrated the difference between the two by a simple thought experiment. Consider gunpowder: it has the (necessary) causal power to explode, *yet it does not do so anywhere and everywhere.* Whether it does so depends on (contingent) circumstances: it 'depends on it being in the right conditions – in the presence of a spark, etc. So although causal powers exist necessarily by virtue of the nature of the objects which possess them, it is contingent whether they are activated or exercised.' By extension, too, their effects 'depend on the presence of certain contingently related conditions'. What this means, Sayer concluded, is that in 'concrete research' – in the examination of the exercise and effect of causal powers – SPACE (or, more accurately, spatial configuration) 'makes a difference':

> In closed system ... science the contingencies of spatial form are either rendered constant or a matter of indifference where they concern spatial relation between objects which do not causally interact. ... In [open] systems we have a continually changing jumble of spatial relations, not all of them involving objects which are causally indifferent to one another. So even though concrete studies may not be interested in spatial form per se, it must be taken into account if the contingencies of the concrete and the differences they make to outcomes are to be understood. (Sayer 1984a; see also 1985b)

This was an important conclusion for the human and social sciences as a whole, not just human geography, because it effectively undermined the possibility of any aspatial social science. But some critics regarded it as the weak version of a much stronger thesis. In their view spatial configurations are important not only for concrete research but also for 'abstract research'. To use Sayer's own example: gunpowder is constituted as gunpowder, and hence possesses its specific causal powers, by virtue of the time–space relations which exist between its elements. This means that its constitution cannot be accounted for either by its time–space relations alone (the error of SPATIAL SCIENCE) or by its elements alone (the error of any COMPOSITIONAL approach): they must be considered together. This turned out to be of decisive importance in providing an ontology for a socio-spatial science. As Urry (1985) put it, 'the social world should be seen as comprised of space–time entities having causal powers which may or may not be realised depending on the patterns of spatial–temporal interdependence [between them]' (see also Bhaskar, 1986).

Realism was a powerful presence in human geography in the 1980s, but its star seemed to wane in the 1990s. In part, perhaps, this was a result of the connections made between realism and HISTORICAL MATERIALISM and between realism and STRUCTURATION THEORY. The retreat from (or advance beyond) these formulations seems to have gone hand in hand with a displacement of realism from the central position it had assumed within post-positivist human geography (cf. Harvey, 1987; Pratt, 1995). In part, perhaps, this was also the result of a profound uncertainty about how accounts conducted under the sign of realism were to be written. Here one needs to remember that 'realism' refers not only to a twentieth-century philosophy but also to a mode of REPRESENTATION in the visual arts and literature which was particularly prominent in Europe and North America in the nineteenth century. This is not to say that realist philosophies require a realist aesthetics – they almost certainly do not – but simply to note that the attentiveness to theoretical work which realism succeeded in making so important for *analysis* during the 1980s was, in the next decade, extended to equally searching theoretical reflection on *description* (cf. Sayer, 1989). This 'crisis of representation' called into question not only realist methodologies – the almost forensic precision of its 'rational abstractions' was increasingly seen as problematic – but also, in the eyes of some critics, realist ontologies. Some forms of POSTMODERNISM made 'ontological depth' yield to 'depthlessness', for example, while the rise of POST-STRUCTURALISM induced considerable suspicion towards the sort of 'structures' envisaged by realism and also fostered the development of a new 'analytics of the surface' (see also NON-REPRESENTATIONAL THEORY). DG

References

Bhaskar, R. 1975: *A realist theory of science*. Leeds: Leeds Books; reprinted 1978, Brighton: Harvester. · Bhaksar, R. 1979: *The possibility of naturalism: a philosophical critique of the contemporary human sciences*. Brighton: Harvester. · Bhaskar, R. 1986: *Scientific realism and human emancipation*. London: Verso. · Chouinard, V., Fincher, R. and Webber, M. 1984: Empirical research in scientific human geography. *Progress in Human Geography* 8: 347–80. · Gregory, D. 1978: *Ideology, science and human geography*. London: Hutchinson; New York: St. Martin's Press. · Gregory, D. 1985: People, places and practices: the future of human geography. In R. King, ed., *Geographical futures*. Sheffield: Geographical Association. · Harvey, D. 1987: Three myths in search of a reality in urban studies. *Environment and Planning D: Society and Space* 5: 367–76. · Hesse, M. 1974: *The structure of scientific inference*. London: Macmillan; Berkeley, CA: University of California Press. · Keat, R. and Urry, J. 1981: *Social theory as science*, 2nd edn. London: Routledge. · McLennan, G. 1981: *Marxism and the methodologies of history*. London: Verso; New York: Schocken. · Pratt, A. 1995: Putting critical realism to work: the practical implications for geographical research. *Progress in Human Geography* 19: 61–74. · Richards, K.S. 1990a: 'Real' geomorphology. *Earth Surface Processes and Landforms* 15: 195–7. · Richards, K.S. 1990b: 'Real' geomorphology revisited. *Earth Surface Processes and Landforms* 19: 277–81. · Sayer, A. 1982: Explanation in economic geography: abstraction versus generalization. *Progress in Human Geography* 6: 66–88. · Sayer, A. 1984a: *Method in social science: a realist approach*. London: Hutchinson (2nd edn. 1992, London: Routledge). · Sayer, A. 1984b: Defining the urban. *GeoJournal* 9: 279–85. · Sayer, A. 1985a: Realism in geography. In R.J. Johnston, ed., *The future of geography*. London: Methuen, 159–73. · Sayer, A. 1985b: The difference that space makes. In D. Gregory and J. Urry, eds, *Social relations and spatial structures*. London: Macmillan, 49–65. · Sayer, A. 1989: The 'new' regional geography and problems of narrative. *Environment and Planning D: Society and Space* 7: 253–76. · Urry, J. 1985: Social relations, space and time. In D. Gregory and J. Urry, eds, *Social relations and spatial structures*. London: Macmillan, 20–48. · Williams, S. 1981: Realism, Marxism and human geography. *Antipode* 13 (2): 31–8. · Yeung, H.W.-E. 1997: Critical realism and realist research in human geography: a method or a philosophy in search of a method? *Progress in Human Geography* 21: 51–74.

Suggested Reading

Lawson, V. and Staeheli, L. 1990: Realism and the practice of geography. *Professional Geographer* 42: 13–19. · Pratt (1995). · Sayer (1984a) [1992]. · Yeung (1997).

reciprocity A system of mutual exchange, reciprocity was one of three FORMS OF ECONOMIC INTEGRATION identified by Karl Polanyi and linked with a characteristic spatial pattern: 'Reciprocity denotes movements between correlative points of symmetrical groupings' (in Dalton, 1968). This emphasis on symmetry was intended to distinguish reciprocity from other forms of exchange, notably REDISTRIBUTION, and was repeated by Harvey (1973) in his equation of reciprocity with egalitarian societies which were incapable of sustaining the concentration of a surplus required for the emergence of urbanism. But other versions of exchange theory have emphasized that reciprocity need not entail consensus (see Lebra, 1975), and indeed *exchange theory* – the modern development of which is usually attributed to Homans (1961) and Blau (1964) – has provided a much more elaborate typology of transactions than Polanyi's original sketches. DG

References

Blau, P. 1964: *Exchange and power in social life*. New York: John Wiley. · Dalton, G., ed., 1968: *Primitive, archaic and modern economics: essays of Karl Polanyi*. Boston: Beacon Press. · Harvey, D. 1973: *Social justice and the city*. London: Edward Arnold; Baltimore, MD: Johns Hopkins University Press. · Homans, G. 1961: *Social behaviour: its elementary forms*. London: Routledge and Kegan Paul. · Lebra, T. 1975: An alternative approach to reciprocity. *American Anthropologist* 77: 550–65. · Sahlins, M. 1974: *Stone age economics*. London: Tavistock; Chicago: Aldine, ch. 5.

Suggested Reading

Ekeh, P. 1974: *Social exchange theory: the two traditions*. London: Heinemann.

recreation Any pursuit, activity (or even inactivity) which is undertaken voluntarily during leisure time primarily for the purposes of pleasure, enjoyment and satisfaction. There is considerable overlap between studies of recreation, LEISURE and TOURISM. Indeed, in many cases the activities involved are the same, although the location, duration and consumer motivations of each can be very different. As Butler et al. (1998) suggest, 'in recent years the differences between recreation and tourism in particular, except at a philosophical level, have become of decreasing significance and distinctions [have become] increasingly blurred' (p. 4).

Studies of recreation have tended to categorize recreational activities according to three principal lines of division (Patmore, 1983). First, *active recreation* is differentiated from passive, according to the degree of physical exercise involved. Here there are connections, for example, with geographies of sport. To play in a football match is active; to watch is passive. Certain forms of active recreation, particularly those relating to health and leisure clubs and to a range of outdoor sports, have become increasingly popular over recent years (Urry, 1990). Equally, passive recreation relating to the production of spectacular events has been in tune with trends of postmodern consumption. Secondly, *formal recreation* is differentiated from informal, according to the degree to which participation is organized. There is a trend towards increased formality of recreation, either through the organization of enthusiasts or through increasing commodification of recreational venues or practices. Thirdly, *resource-based recreation* is differentiated from user-orientated, according to the degree to which activities rely on the natural environment or on planned facilities and attractions. This distinction is often viewed as a contrast between rural (resource-based) and urban (user-orientated) locations. Rural issues therefore commonly relate to potential conflicts with other land uses, and to the sustainability (see SUSTAINABLE DEVELOPMENT) of multi-functional uses of rural space. Urban issues by contrast tend to relate to the planned provision of facilities. However, the rural–urban distinction tends to cloak the different recreational uses of different spaces. Parklands and riversides in cities, for example, represent essential sites of resource-based recreation which add to more formal leisure centres in the urban environment. Moreover, informal recreation in the open countryside is nowadays strongly complemented by commodified, pay-as-you-enter attractions, ranging from traditional heritage sites to more recent farm parks and theme parks (see Cloke, 1993).

Demand for recreation is usually disaggregated in terms of factors such as disposable income, personal accessibility, and social characteristics of age, health, class and education. Ideally, however, recreation implies a universally available experience of restoring and refreshing the mind and the body, and policy-makers have indeed often viewed recreation as a social service for which public provision should be made within processes of RURAL PLANNING and URBAN planning. The take-up of recreational opportunities, then, will also depend on the success with which the recreational ideal is borne out in the implementation of planning policies. There are fears that with the privatization of previously public-sector activities, the provision of recreation sites and facilities will become more unevenly distributed. Indeed, Mike Davis's (1991) account of Los Angeles – the City of Quartz – charts the virtual abandonment of public recreation, with parks being encouraged to operate as businesses based on user-fees. He describes the result as 'recreational apartheid', with a drastic deterioration of public space in the poorest inner-city areas where parks have become increasingly run-down, unsupervised and dangerous. Geographies of recreation, therefore, need to be linked with a wider appreciation both of contemporary consumption and of the changing nature of the production of urban and rural space. PJC

References

Butler, R., Hall, C.M. and Jenkins, J., eds, 1998: *Tourism and recreation in rural areas*. Chichester: Wiley. · Cloke, P. 1993: The countryside as commodity: new spaces for rural leisure. In S. Glyptis, ed., *Leisure and the environment*. London: Belhaven. · Davis, M. 1991: *City of quartz*. London: Verso. · Patmore, J.A. 1983: *Recreation and resources: leisure patterns and leisure places*. Oxford: Blackwell. · Urry, J. 1990: *The tourist gaze: leisure and travel in contemporary societies*. London: Sage.

Suggested Reading

Rojek, C. 1995: *Decentring leisure, rethinking leisure theory*. London: Sage. · Urry (1990).

recycling A process that reuses the materials and ENERGY components of an item to create another product. It is often seen as the third level of environmental action after reducing consumption and reusing an existing item. Recycling may reduce waste and reduce the need for raw materials in production processes. It may be either 'horizontal' (e.g. aluminium cans into aluminium cans) or it may be 'vertical' (e.g. bond paper to lesser-quality newspaper). Recycling was widely used during the two World Wars, but not for environmental reasons. Although contemporary recycling may be undertaken solely for economic reasons (if recycled materials cost less than raw ones), it is usually represented as an action of environmental concern. PM

red light district A district, usually within an urban area, where activities associated with commercialized sex, such as prostitution, are concentrated. RJJ

redistribution A system of transfer from one group or place to another, usually articulated by a mediating institution or group of institutions (e.g. the STATE). Redistribution is one of the general concerns of WELFARE GEOGRAPHY and its examination played a central role in Harvey's preliminary, so-called 'liberal' formulations of the relationships between social justice and spatial systems (Harvey, 1973, chs 2 and 3). But as Harvey subsequently recognized in his 'socialist' reformulations (especially ch. 6), redistribution was, more specifically, one of three FORMS OF ECONOMIC INTEGRATION identified by Karl Polanyi and linked with a characteristic spatial pattern. Thus, 'redistribution designates appropriational movements toward a centre and out of it again' (Polanyi, in Dalton, 1968). These centrifugal and centripetal flows were supposed to be in marked contrast to other forms of exchange, notably RECIPROCITY, because they allowed for the concentration of a surplus. Hence, Harvey identified redistribution with hierarchical, rank societies and, following Wheatley (1971), claimed that 'the conditions that enabled the transformation from reciprocity to redistribution were crucial for the emergence of URBANISM; they were instrumental in concentrating surplus product in a few hands and in a few places' (Harvey, 1973). Much of the debate over URBAN ORIGINS accepts the crucial importance of this transformation, but controversy continues over the nature of its 'conditions'. Wheatley (1971) emphasizes the formative significance of religion, while Harvey regards it as 'super-structural' and instead accentuates the classical Marxian 'BASE' in the ECONOMY itself (Harvey, 1973, p. 227; see also Harvey, 1972). But redistribution is not confined to the distant past and, returning to his original theme of SOCIAL JUSTICE, Harvey (1973, pp. 274–84) drew attention to reciprocity and redistribution as 'countervailing forces to market exchange in the contemporary metropolis'. He was writing before the rise of the New Right, however, and as he subsequently acknowledged, the 1970s and 1980s witnessed a 'political attack on redistributive politics' throughout the West and, eventually, the articulation of a 'post-welfare geography' (see Bennett, 1989): one of the most pervasive features of what he now described as the post-Keynesian transition was thus inter-urban competition for redistribution (Harvey, 1985, p. 218). (See also AID.)

DG

References

Bennett, R. 1989: Whither models and geography in a post-welfarist world? In B. Macmillan, ed., *Remodelling geography*. Oxford: Blackwell, 274–90. · Dalton, G., ed., 1968: *Primitive, archaic and modern economies: essays of Karl Polanyi*. Boston: Beacon Press. · Harvey, D. 1972: Review of Paul Wheatley's Pivot of the four quarters. *Annals of the Association of American Geographers* 62: 509–13. · Harvey, D. 1973: *Social justice and the city*. London: Edward Arnold; Baltimore, MD: Johns Hopkins University Press. · Harvey, D. 1985: *The urbanization of capital*. London: Blackwell. · Wheatley, P. 1971: *The pivot of the four quarters*. Edinburgh: Edinburgh University Press; Chicago: Aldine.

Suggested Reading

Harvey (1973), chs 2 and 6. · Wheatley, P. 1975: Satyantra in Suvarnadvipa: from reciprocity to redistribution in ancient S.E. Asia. In J.A. Sabloff and C.C. Lamberg-Karlovsky, eds, *Ancient civilization and trade*. Albuquerque, NM: University of New Mexico Press, ch. 6.

redistricting The term used in the USA for redrawing the boundaries of electoral districts, such as the Congressional Districts used for the election of members of the House of Representatives and the districts which return members of State legislatures: the British term is *redistribution*.

The process of redistricting can involve both MALAPPORTIONMENT and GERRYMANDERING, whereby those political interest groups (usually parties) within the STATE APPARATUS responsible for the task promote their own electoral interests. To prevent this, the US Supreme Court ruled in the 1960s that malapportionment is unconstitutional; in the 1980s it also sought to reduce gerrymandering, including gerrymandering against racial minorities. In the light of these decisions, partisan domination of redistricting in many states has been removed and replaced by either bi-partisan or multi-partisan procedures: as a consequence redistricting is now needed in most States every decade, after publication of the Census count, because of either or both of malapportionment as a result of differential population changes, and changes in the State's entitlement to Representatives. Such procedures cannot prevent 'unintentional gerrymandering', however, because (as Gudgin and Taylor, 1979, showed in a seminal work) 'most redistrictings are likely to favour one party's interests over its opponents'.

Most countries which have legislatures elected from single-member constituencies undertake regular, non-partisan redistrictings. In the UK, this is done by four independent Boundary Commissions, but their work almost invariably results in 'biased' election results (against a norm of proportional representation for parties: Rossiter, Johnston and Pattie, 1999). The nature of the problem, fitting a map of bounded territories (i.e. constituencies) onto a map of population distribution subject to certain constraints (such as the allowed population variation between constituencies) could be undertaken using GEOGRAPHICAL INFORMATION SYSTEMS, but although technically feasible this is not politically desirable to most participants in the process (cf. RACIAL DISTRICTING).

RJJ

References and Suggested Reading

Courtney, J.C., MacKinnon, P. and Smith, D.E., eds, *Drawing boundaries: legislatures, courts, and electoral values*. Saskatoon: Fifth House Publications. · Grofman, B., ed., 1990: *Political gerrymandering and the courts*. New York: Agathon Press. · Gudgin, G. and Taylor, P.J. 1979: *Seats, votes and the spatial organization of elections*. London: Pion Ltd. · McLean, I. and Butler, D.E., eds, 1996: *Fixing the boundaries: defining and redefining single-member electoral districts*. Aldershot: Dartmouth. · Rossiter, D.J., Johnston, R.J. and Pattie, C.J. 1999: *The Boundary Commissions: redrawing the United Kingdom's map of Parliamentary constituencies*. Manchester: Manchester University Press.

redlining The delimitation by financial institutions of residential districts within a city as being in decline and thus not sensible areas for mortgage lending. Such policies discriminate against potential borrowers (most of them low-income households) who can only afford to live in low-cost areas. The existence of such districts is often denied by institutions but there is little doubt that redlining is widely practised. More recently, decisions by financial institutions, such as banks, building societies and savings and loans associations, to close branches in low-income areas have generated concerns that various socio-economic groups are suffering 'FINANCIAL EXCLUSION' – a further example of the changing geographies of UNEVEN DEVELOPMENT: this is being countered to some extent by the creation of new elements in the financial structure, such as credit unions and local economic trading systems (LETS). RJJ

Suggested Reading

Bassett, K. and Short, J.R. 1980: *Housing and residential structure: alternative approaches*. London: Routledge and Kegan Paul. · Leyshon, A. and Thrift, N.J. 1995: Geographies of financial exclusion: financial abandonment in Britain and the United States. *Transactions, Institute of British Geographers* NS 20: 312–41.

reductionism The methodological strategy of explaining some phenomenon or event by means of an often simpler, but presumed more fundamental, entity. The strategy is especially prominent in the natural sciences that strive to decompose a phenomenon or event into its most basic constituents or causes, for example, sub-atomic particles or forces. Reductionism implies that facts that are apparently important are really dispensable because they can be reduced to a more basic set of elements. For example, rather than to talk about genes, it is better to speak about strands of DNA molecules, or rather than talk about lightning, it is better to speak about an electrical discharge or even more fundamentally the flow of electrons.

Reductionism is also found in the social sciences, including human geography. One of its most common forms is METHODOLOGICAL INDIVIDUALISM. Here the complexities of human behaviour are reduced to the single fundamental cause of individual RATIONAL CHOICE. While it might appear that the diverse decisions involved around, say, setting up a new home, or going to war with another country, or relocating an old factory, have nothing to do with one another, in reality, say methodological individualists, they all obey the same fundamental logic of rational DECISION-MAKING. The facts and circumstances of each particular case can be eliminated because they are reducible to a more elementary set of axioms.

While reductionism as a methodological strategy appears enormously powerful and productive, yielding seemingly ever more secrets of nature and social life, it has been criticized on a number of grounds.

- That some entities, such as human motivations and creativity, are simply not divisible into constituent parts; that there is always a 'ghost in the machine' to use Arthur Koestler's phrase. Humans can never be reduced to Pavlovian salivating dogs or Skinnerian rats in a maze.
- That some phenomena or events are characterized by the property of *emergence*; that is, the interaction of constituent elements produces an effect that cannot be predicted by examining the properties of the individual elements themselves. As a result, reductionism as a strategy is ineffective (see also COMPOSITIONAL THEORY; CONTEXTUAL APPROACH).
- That there is often something important in the original facts and setting that is lost when it is reduced to a different vocabulary. Translations are never perfect, and important contextual factors useful in explanation may be lost when reductionism is applied.

In human geography reductionism was most strenuously applied during the period of the QUANTITATIVE REVOLUTION and SPATIAL SCIENCE. Then the complexities of geographical LANDSCAPES were reduced to supposedly more fundamental entities such as the postulates of geometry or the actions of *homo economicus*. Even after this period reductionism remained important within the discipline. RADICAL GEOGRAPHY, for example, was often characterized by *economism*, that is, the reduction of spatial relationships to economic ones. Historically, however, the discipline has always emphasized the importance of context, attempting to keep geographical facts intact rather than reducing them to something else. This sensibility has taken on greater theoretical momentum in the wake of POST-STRUCTURALISM and POSTMODERNISM, movements entering geography in the 1980s and associated with an explicitly anti-reductionist agenda. Critiques of reductionism, and attempts to develop non-reductionist research strategies, are now found in FEMINIST GEOGRAPHY (Hanson and Pratt, 1996), CULTURAL GEOGRAPHY and ECONOMIC GEOGRAPHY (Gibson-Graham, 1996). TJB

References

Gibson-Graham, J.K. 1996: *The end of capitalism (as we knew it). A feminist critique of political economy*. Oxford: Blackwell. · Hanson, S. and Pratt, G. 1996: *Gender, work and space*. London: Routledge.

Suggested Reading

Gibson-Graham (1996).

reflexive modernization A term coined by the British sociologist Anthony Giddens (1990, 1991), to describe the tendency in western industrial societies to continually revise most aspects of social activity, arising out of the proliferation of organizations and technologies which generate new information or knowledge. This continual revision is not incidental to modern social institutions but is constitutive of them because the certainty of the knowledge they must utilize is constantly being undermined by new knowledge. In turn, this process of continual revision leads to the generation of new ways of life that are able to cope with this condition of uncertainty (and most especially new forms of reflexive individualism) and equally to new risks to society that are constantly being generated by the application of specialized knowledges which can only ever have partially understood consequences.

Such a depiction of MODERNITY has much in common with Ulrich Beck's notion of a RISK SOCIETY which also utilizes the notion of reflexive modernization (see especially Beck, Giddens and Lash, 1996). NJT

References

Beck, U. 1992: *Risk society. Towards a new modernity*. London: Sage. · Beck, U., Giddens, A. and Lash, S. 1996: *Reflexive modernisation*. Cambridge: Polity Press. · Giddens, A. 1990: *The consequences of modernity*. Cambridge: Polity Press. · Giddens, A. 1991: *Modernity and self-identity*. Cambridge: Polity Press.

refugees Displacement, banishment and exodus are as old as human history but the legal concept of refugee was not formulated until the twentieth century inter-war period (1919–39). Two basic statutes (the UN Convention relating to the Status of Refugees, 1951 and the UN Protocol, 1967) extend international protection to refugees, defined as persons who, owing to a well-founded fear of persecution for reasons of RACE, RELIGION, nationality, membership of a particular social group or political opinion, are outside the country of their nationality and either unable or unwilling to return. This broad definition encompasses refugees who are conventionally classified according to their desire or possibility of returning to their homeland (so-called *majority-identified*, *events-alienated* and *self-alienated* refugees). The Convention/Protocol definition does not include internally displaced persons and victims of repressive military or economic policies, however, and there are at least 5 million such persons according to UNHCR (1998; refugees are often defined situationally – Harrell-Bond, 1986). At present there are almost 15 million refugees; two-thirds are in Africa and Asia with the African continent accounting for about half (6 million) of the world's refugees (UNHCR, 1998).

Although many displaced persons and refugees may experience only limited geographical relocation – for example the current (turn-of-the-century) crisis in Central Africa illustrates how many thousands of people shuttle back and forth across borders and in and out of refugee camps in response to the civil wars and ethnic strife in Congo, Rwanda and Burundi – one important feature of the twentieth-century refugee landscape has been the global relocations. Many thousands of Albanian refugees have arrived on Italian shores, for example, in the same ways that very large populations of Cambodian and Laotian refugees reside in the Central Valley of California, and huge Somali populations in rural and small-town Minnesota. Just as there are many practical problems associated with rehabilitating refugees from camps into sustainable livelihoods in Africa and Southeast Asia, so there are equally compelling problems of ASSIMILATION and cultural adaptation associated with the arrival of THIRD WORLD refugees in the advanced capitalist states. Problems of ALIENATION, unemployment, and exploitation surround these refugee COMMUNITIES, and raise difficult questions about the extent to which such populations can attain something like citizen status or whether they are socially excluded (ILO, 1995; cf. CITIZENSHIP). Not all refugees are poor or marginalized, of course; some political refugees flee persecution as well-placed (and wealthy) politicians and activists who continue their political and oppositional work from afar. Some of the key figures in the Iraqi, Kashmiri and Somali movements – whether NATIONALIST, SECESSIONIST or ETHNIC – are based in London, Toronto and New York, which has led some commentators to refer to refugee communities as the source of 'fax nationalism'. MW

References

Harrell-Bond, B. 1986: *Imposing aid: emergency assistance to refugees*. Oxford: Oxford University Press. · ILO 1995: *Social exclusion*. Geneva: International Labor Organization. · UNHCR 1998: *The state of the world's refugees*. Oxford: Oxford University Press.

Suggested Reading

Malkki, L. 1995: *Purity and exile*. Chicago: University of Chicago Press.

regime of accumulation A concept from the REGULATION SCHOOL of POLITICAL-ECONOMIC theory, referring to an extended period of relative stability or growth within the capitalist economy. Adherents to the Regulation approach accept Marx's basic proposition that CAPITALISM is characterized by certain fundamental contradictions (such as the collective tendency for capitalists to economize on workers' wages, thus ultimately reducing the effective demand for manufactured goods), and that these must be resolved, suppressed, or controlled in order for successful ACCUMULATION to occur. Hence, regulation theorists contend that different solutions to this problem have been arrived at through time and across space. As a noted member of this school asserts, 'My central hypothesis is, in fact, that the overall reproduction of the system can take different forms. It then becomes essential to make a precise analysis of the changes, both qualitative and quantitative, that have been necessary for the maintenance of capitalist relations in general in the long run' (Boyer, 1990). Therefore Regulation theorists interpret capitalist history as consisting of a series of relatively stable periods, during which the organization of private productive activity is in some general state of balance with the organization of consumption (the level and stability of wages, and the distribution of purchasing power within society). Each regime ends in a crisis period of major instability or stagnation, and a new regime begins when new ways of organizing production are developed, supported by an appropriate new set of public and private institutions and societal norms to structure labour markets and workplace practices. (See also FLEXIBLE ACCUMULATION; FORDISM; POST-FORDISM.) MSG

Reference

Boyer, R. 1990: *The Regulation school: a critical introduction*. New York: Columbia University Press.

Suggested Reading

Amin, A. 1994: Post-Fordism: models, fantasies and phantoms of transition. In A. Amin, ed., *Post-Fordism: a reader*. Oxford: Blackwell, 1–39.

regime theory An approach to international relations that focuses on cooperation among STATES and non-governmental organizations, as in a range of institutions established to tackle regional and global environmental problems which are beyond the purview of any one state. According to Vogler (1995) a regime is

> an institution, or more precisely, a set of norms, principles, rules and decision-making procedures that govern a particular issue area, such as trade, money or more relevantly the use of the global commons.

A regime thus involves more than inter-state legal arrangements and international organizations and can embrace a wide range of accepted behaviours and norms (including informal practices) with regard to the use of COMMON POOL RESOURCES. The oceans, the Antarctic continent, the atmosphere, and outer space are the main examples of such resources in which international regimes operate. (See also GOVERNANCE; LAW OF THE SEA; PRISONER'S DILEMMA; TRAGEDY OF THE COMMONS.) RJJ

Reference

Vogler, J. 1995: *The global commons: a regime analysis*. Chichester and New York: John Wiley.

regional alliance A treaty signed by a group of neighbouring STATES agreeing to a system of collective security, whereby an attack on any one of them by an external aggressor is deemed to be an attack against them all (as with NATO). RJJ

regional class alliance A coherent response by members of a region's different CLASSES (notably labour, capital, and the local STATE APPARATUS) to economic problems there. Such a compromise is agreed by parties who otherwise might be in CONFLICT, in order both to promote profitability (for capital) and to ensure the continued availability of jobs (for labour) – and thereby also sustaining the STATE's legitimacy. According to Harvey (1985), such alliances are necessary to the continued reproduction of CAPITALISM in a LOCALITY: 'if regional structures and class alliances did not already exist, then the processes at work under capitalism would necessarily create them'. (See also URBAN ENTREPRENEURIALISM.) RJJ

Reference

Harvey, D. 1985: The geopolitics of capitalism. In D. Gregory and J. Urry, eds, *Social relations and spatial structures*. London: Macmillan, 128–63.

regional cycles Fluctuations or cyclical waves in the level of economic activity in a region, usually measured by industrial output or unemployment rates. Such fluctuations can be very long-term, as with KONDRATIEFF CYCLES, or shorter-term, reflecting both seasonal variations in the demand for labour and the regional impact of national business cycles of expansion and recession. Descriptive studies of regional cycles, measuring and comparing their amplitudes, and the timings of peaks for different regions, were done in the early years of REGIONAL SCIENCE, but the major work was done in the 1970s and later.

There have been two main approaches. The first (mainly by economists) has involved building regional (e.g. the State of California) or multiregional (e.g. the States of the USA) *econometric models*. These relate macroeconomic variables of output, expenditure and employment at the regional level to each other, parallel to the development of national Keynesian econometric models, and they also relate regional variables to national and other-region variables (cf. NEO-CLASSICAL ECONOMICS). Such models now exist for many countries and regions. The second approach (mainly by geographers) has focused on the *statistical modelling* of the magnitude and spatial DIFFUSION of regional cycles, mainly using unemployment rates, and comparing the timing and cyclical amplitude for different cities and regions. The regional and urban time series are related to each other using the REGRESSION methods of LEAD–LAG MODELS, SPACE–TIME FORECASTING and also SPECTRAL ANALYSIS to look separately at seasonal and business-cycle effects. Differences in magnitude and timing can then be linked to regional industrial structure and the hierarchical and spatial diffusion of the cycles. The techniques for regional cycles have also been applied to the geography of epidemics.

LWH

Suggested Reading

Glickman, N.J. 1997: *Econometric analysis of regional systems: explorations in model building and policy analysis*. New York and London: Academic Press.

regional geography See REGIONS AND REGIONAL GEOGRAPHY

regional policy Policy directed at problems arising from UNEVEN DEVELOPMENT between regions. How then does geographically uneven development arise and how does it take on the character of problems?

Geographically uneven development under CAPITALISM is a consequence of

- the market conditions (see REGULATION SCHOOL) under which, and the criteria on which, capital moves through successive rounds of ACCUMULATION (see DIVISION OF LABOUR); and hence on
- the choice of investment (e.g. here vs. there, direct vs. indirect portfolio/securities) and sphere of capital (reproduction vs. production vs. realization); and
- the geographical requirements (and hence location and SPATIAL STRUCTURE) of that investment.

Thus capital investment in retailing (sphere of realization), for example, under conditions of loose planning control, creates new geographical forms and sites of production for consumption (clearly apparent in the rise of large-scale super- and hypermarkets located on the edge of towns where land is more plentiful and relatively cheap and vehicular access easier) and abandons others, such as town centres (see CONSUMPTION, GEOGRAPHY OF; RETAILING, GEOGRAPHY OF). At a much larger scale, the single European market Economic and Monetary Union (EMU) will change the market conditions (e.g. through the convergence of once widely divergent short-term national interest rates, and price convergence enhanced by the greater transparency of market relations) and the criteria underpinning the circulation of capital in Europe, with potentially significant consequences for uneven development. EMU will both increase the geographical range over which a greater number of investment decisions may be made, thereby increasing the rigour by which alternative locations are evaluated and, at the same time, greatly reduce the possibilities for national economic interventions in the face of uneven development (through, e.g. monetary policy, exchange rate adjustments, fiscal policy).

Although the area-based nature of regional policy sets it apart from other policies which may have pronounced regional effects (e.g. the Common Agricultural Policy of the EU or federal defence expenditure in the USA), the definition of what constitutes a *regional* problem as distinct from a geographical pattern of DEVELOPMENT deriving from other stimuli (e.g. Massey, 1979) makes the precise specification of regional policy extremely difficult. An underlying reason for this difficulty is the complexity of the nature of regional differences (see Markusen, 1987). But another complication is the practical meaning of what constitutes a regional *problem* (e.g. Lee, 1989). 'Regional problems' may derive from geographical unevenness in the distribution of income and welfare (see WELFARE GEOGRAPHY), in the conditions of effective production or in the level and effectiveness of regional cultural integrity or political representation. Whatever the origin of such unevenness, however, it becomes problematic for the established social order when it begins to undermine economic, political or moral legitimacy and so threaten the SOCIAL REPRODUCTION of the prevailing social order (see CRISIS).

If the effect of a single currency, for example, is to exacerbate regional unevenness in Europe then, without the degree of the mobility of labour or the possibility of recourse to the kinds and levels of federal redistribution characteristic of the economic geography of the USA, for example, the resultant inequalities and adjustments to the new conditions might become associated with much-feared fundamentalist and xenophobic political and social reactions of the kind already observed in Eastern Germany and other parts of the former state socialist countries.

Thus economic INTEGRATION may be responsible for helping to stimulate the growth of regional consciousness and the drive to regional separatism or even independence. Such has been the historical geography of the Basque province in northern Spain since the inflow of capital and people associated with the development of heavy industry in an agricultural region as a result of the INDUSTRIAL REVOLUTION. The regional problem may be based in strongly felt and long-held cultural distinctions – as in the case of the Québécois in Canada. Although such distinctions may be long-dormant, they may be exploited (and misrepresented) for wider political objectives, as in the rapid rise of the right-wing Northern or Lombard Leagues in Italy in the belief that the DEPENDENCE of the south of Italy is stultifying the development and threatening the political purity of the north.

From the perspective of the STATE (see, e.g. Johnston, 1986), regional problems arise when uneven development threatens political stability and presents the possibility of the break-up of the state system (e.g. Nairn, 1981). Similarly, when looked at from the perspective of the economy as a whole, the regional problem arises when uneven development acts as a barrier to capital ACCUMULATION. Indeed, the 'regional' problem may simply be a geographical dimension of the wider problems of DEVELOPMENT (Massey, 1979).

Given the multi-faceted nature and complex provenance of the regional problem, it is hardly surprising that regional policy has varied over time and space in terms of its determinants, formal content, relative significance and objectives. This variation reflects not only the policy perception of the problem but the prevailing ideology of state involvement in the functioning of the ECONOMY or CIVIL SOCIETY. Thus regional policy may need to address the regional structure of the STATE APPARATUS itself in response to demands for greater self-government, autonomy or even dependence.

Thus regional policy may be founded on:

Intervention in the market conditions under which investment decisions are made (see, for example, Allen et al., 1998). Two distinct stances have prevailed here: on the one hand, market forces have been overridden or constrained by interventions – including public ownership, pricing policies, state-directed investment strategies (designed to achieve particular objectives such as the preservation of jobs or a particular geography of investment) and the provision of subsidies on investment such as tax breaks or investment incentives; and, on the other, markets have been deregulated in the belief that the intensification of competition and the increased freedom of capital which results – from privatization, for example – will generate growth.

Attempts to encourage inward investment during the 1980s and 1990s as a basis for national and regional development were founded on a curious mix of market regulation (including, for example, a wide range of inducements to mobile capital – often creating interregional competition in inducements on offer) and deregulation (most notably of LABOUR MARKETS and URBAN AND REGIONAL PLANNING). Attempts to encourage (dis)investment from/in particular kinds of economic activities may be made by allowing or stimulating decline or RESTRUCTURING (through PRIVATIZATION, for example, or the targeting of particular sectors or specialized regions for retraining) and through the provision of risk and venture capital.

The provision and improvement of a wide range of INFRASTRUCTURE ranging through: physical infrastructure (e.g. telecommunications); research and development (R&D) and technology DIFFUSION; education and training;

support for the diffusion and dissemination of locally applicable knowledge around, and assistance in assessing new markets throughout, regional networks of firms engaged in particular types of production; housing and transportation to encourage direct investment in general, and investment in particular regions; and responding to contemporary requirements of production by creating a culturally and environmentally attractive and efficient geography for investment and the encouragement of a social, scientific and built environment – in the form, for example, of science parks – intended to encourage the transformation of pure into applied science and technology and the creation of an innovative industrial atmosphere.

The role of infrastructure in regional policy is contested, with one view suggesting that it provides the basis for development and another arguing that scarce resources should be allocated to the provision of infrastructure only when present provision is demonstrably overloaded and holding back accumulation (see Hirschmann, 1958; Vickerman, 1991).

Spatial restructuring aimed at the large-scale modification of a regional geography with restricted potential for accumulation. This may be addressed by regional policy through attempts to induce a locational shift which corresponds to a more effective economic geography for production. Much of the rationale for regional policy in the UK advanced in the influential Barlow Report of 1944, for example, was of this kind, arguing in particular that the geographical concentration of the economy in and around London was not only economically inefficient but also, under wartime conditions, strategically dangerous. On an intra-regional scale, the building of the post-war NEW TOWNS represented an attempt to create a built environment more amenable to the locational requirements of space-consuming industries and to the enhancement of the demand for their products (e.g. household appliances and the car).

Redistribution directed at the amelioration of unevenness in levels of living (see QUALITY OF LIFE; SOCIAL WELL-BEING). Such direct redistributive intervention is normally aimed at individuals and groups and is undertaken through the WELFARE STATE at the national level, albeit with pronounced regional effects.

Regional policy is rarely, if ever, definable in either purely economic terms (e.g. as a means of facilitating accumulation) or purely political terms (e.g. as a means of buying off regional political discontent). The links between the geography of IDEOLOGY, accumulation, CLASS and politics in the evolution not only of the formal existence and content of regional policy but also of its determinants, objectives and measures of 'success' are extremely complex. And, more fundamentally – as Richard Walker (1997) shows in the case of California – the power of class and RACE in the making of acceptable geographies cannot be subjugated merely by a particular ideology of GOVERNANCE – manifest, perhaps, in 'regional' policies of repression and development. Regional policy cannot, therefore, be reduced to a separate, 'geographical' sphere of policy-making and implementation. Like the making of geographies, regional policy is an intrinsic, though variable, part of the process of social reproduction and is subject to the struggles over the establishment of acceptable social relations and the POWER that flows through them. RL

References

Albrechts, L., Moulaert, F., Roberts, P. and Swyngedouw, E. 1989: *Regional policy at the crossroads: European perspectives*. London: Jessica Kingsley. · Allen, J., Massey, D., Cochrane, A. et al. 1998: *Rethinking the region: spaces of neo-liberalism*. London: Routledge. · Dunford, M. 1997: Divergence, instability and exclusion: regional dynamics in Great Britain. In R. Lee and J. Wills, eds, *Geographies of economies*, ch. 20. London and New York: Arnold, 259–77. · Hirschman, A.O. 1958: *The strategy of economic development*. New Haven: Yale University Press. · Johnston, R.J. 1986: The state, the region, and the division of labour. In A.J. Scott and M. Storper, eds, *Production, work, territory. The geographical anatomy of industrial capitalism*. Winchester, MA and London: Allen and Unwin, 265–80. · Knox, P. and Agnew, J. 1994: *The geography of the world-economy*. London and New York: Arnold. · Lee, R. 1989: Urban transformation: From problems in to the problem of the city. In D.T. Herbert and D.M. Smith, eds, *Social problems and the city*, ch. 4. Oxford: Oxford University Press, 60–77. · Markusen, A. 1986: Neither ore, nor coal, nor markets: A policy-oriented view of steel sites in the USA. *Regional Studies* 20 5: 449–61. · Markusen, A. 1987: *Regions. The economics and politics of territory*. Totowa, NJ: Rowman and Littlefield. · Massey, D. 1979: In what sense a regional problem? *Regional Studies* 13 2: 233–43. · Massey, D. 1995: *Spatial divisions of labour*. London and Basingstoke: Macmillan; New York: Methuen, ch. 6. · Nairn, T. 1981: *The break-up of Britain crisis and neo-nationalism*. London: Verso. · Vickerman, R.W. 1991: *Infrastructure and regional development*. London: Pion. · Walker, R. 1997: California rages: regional capitalism and the politics of renewal. In R. Lee and J. Wills, eds, *Geographies of economies*, ch. 27. London and New York: Arnold, 345–56.

Suggested Reading

Allen et al. (1998). · Dunford (1997). · Massey (1979). · Walker (1997). · Wannop, U. 1995: *The regional imperative: regional planning and governance in Britain, Europe and the United States*. London: Jessica Kingsley.

regional science A hybrid discipline originating in the early 1950s which employs formal NEO-CLASSICAL ECONOMIC theory and rigorous statistical techniques to examine spatial issues in economics, geography, and planning. The boundaries between regional science and cognate disciplinary concerns of LOCATION THEORY, regional economics and planning models, are blurred. This lack of definition has meant that while regional science has become a convenient rubric under which to group methodologically similar pursuits, it has not obtained the disciplinary, and hence institutional, standing its initial proponents perhaps envisaged.

Regional science was the vision of a single man, the American economist Walter Isard (1919– : for details, see Barnes, 1996, pp. 130–6). Having published several papers during the 1940s that both lambasted the assumption of the pin-head ECONOMY found in standard economic theory, and provided an alternative reconstruction based upon the work of several German location theorists, Isard convened the first meeting of the Regional Science Association in Detroit in December 1954. In particular, by adding transportation inputs to neo-classical models, early regional scientists added a spatial plane to the hitherto 'wonderland of no dimensions' (Isard, 1956, p. 25). In the formative years of the Association, the *Papers and Proceedings* (1954–present), and later the *Journal of Regional Science* (first published in the autumn of 1958), were the principal fora for debate and dissemination of research. Also early on, Isard solidified the embryonic discipline with two major pieces of writing: *Location and space economy* (1956), and four years later the collective tome, *Methods of regional analysis* (1960).

Using the literal translation of the German word *Raumwirstschaft* ('SPACE-ECONOMY') as his leitmotif, Isard (1956) in *Location and space economy* synthesized a number of disparate location theories into one general doctrine. Using the idea of a 'substitution framework' that applied to transportation inputs, Isard showed how each of the classical location theories could be restated, and hence integrated, in terms of the same fundamental logic. When scrutinized, that logic was none other than neo-classical RATIONAL CHOICE THEORY, which in many ways continues to be the tie that binds within regional science. By 1960 Isard (1960, p. vii) had recognized that his earlier 'general theory of location was of little direct use in treating the concrete problems of reality', and so the second volume became a primer on all the operational techniques a fully fledged regional scientist would ever need to know when confronting the 'real' world. Together these two volumes provided the twin foundations for regional science; a combination of formal neo-classical theory and sophisticated techniques for manipulating empirical data.

Those foundations were sufficient for Isard to establish the first Department of Regional Science in 1958 at the University of Pennsylvania, subsequently followed by one at Cornell University. The growth of regional science departments has since slowed. When it exists at all, regional science is typically an interdisciplinary programme rather than a department. The same disciplinary diversity also applies to the members and participants of the various Regional Science Congresses that occur around the world (for example, the annual European one that was first held in the Hague in 1961). They tend to be condensation points for researchers originating in very different disciplines, rather than those who are regional scientists *per se*. Certainly this promotes an exchange of ideas, but it makes defining the core of regional science problematic.

Regional science had a very important effect on the reconstruction of human geography as SPATIAL SCIENCE. During the 1960s it provided an umbrella under which the early quantifiers and spatial theorists in human geography could work (on those links, see Berry, 1995). In particular, it exposed human geographers to the competitive equilibrium models of neo-classical economics and their associated techniques of OPTIMIZATION. For this reason some of the classic papers on, for example, CENTRAL PLACE THEORY, INPUT–OUTPUT modelling, LINEAR PROGRAMMING, the GRAVITY MODEL, and urban RENT theory, were published by geographers in regional science journals during this heyday of the QUANTITATIVE REVOLUTION. In addition, regional science was one of the vehicles by which the ideas of SOCIAL PHYSICS were brought to human geography. In fact, such was the blurred nature of boundaries that social physics' main popularizer, William Warntz, moved effortlessly among the trio of regional science, human geography and social physics during this period. Again, this indicates that what is holding regional science together is not its subject matter, but its methodology, one ultimately rooted in POSITIVISM. In fact, this was the main attraction of regional science for some geographers. It provided a justification for prosecuting an extreme form of positivism, admittedly a tendency long latent in human geography.

It was inevitable that when those positivist tendencies were criticized during the 1970s by both RADICAL and HUMANISTIC GEOGRAPHERS the influence of regional science on human geography waned. For radical geographers regional science failed because its vocabulary of equilibrium and optimization denied the social conflict and injustice that they saw as endemic to CAPITALISM. For humanistic geographers the rational actor of regional science was only the palest reflection of a fully sentient and emotionally complex human being. Perhaps the strongest criticisms, though, were internal and came from those who turned regional science's creed against itself. Olsson (1980) brilliantly deconstructed the gravity model equation to illuminate the internal contradictions of regional science's broader methodology; Sack (1973) used the very language of science to show that spatial relations cannot have the properties ascribed to them by the models of regional science; and Holland (1976) undercut regional science's pretensions to realism by demonstrating the tenuous relation of its models to the 'real world' (Isard's work came in for particular opprobrium). More recently, regional science was countered by researchers from the political left who used sophisticated mathematical models and statistical techniques, first, to demonstrate rigorously some of the errors of conventional regional science (see NEO-RICARDIAN ECONOMICS), and second, to reconstruct a formal POLITICAL-ECONOMY alternative (Sheppard and Barnes, 1990).

Against the backdrop of two decades of critique, regional science has increasingly moved to the intellectual margins of human geography, and the social sciences more generally. Indicative of this trend was the closure in 1994–5 of Isard's founding Regional Science Department at the University of Pennsylvania. If there is a spark of hope for regional science in North America it is found: first, in the continued enthusiasm of its proponents (seen in the two-part special issue of the *International Regional Science Review*, volumes 17 (1995) and 18 (1996), celebrating the 40th anniversary of the movement); and second, in the interest of some economic geographers in the work of the economist Paul Krugman who draws upon, and extends, the results of regional science (Martin and Sunley, 1996). Given both regional science's stubborn resistance to change and the massive shifts recently occurring in economic geography (Barnes, 1996), the chances of that spark being fanned into life within geography appear very slim, however. TJB

References

Barnes, T.J. 1996: *Logics of dislocation: models, metaphors and meanings of economic space.* New York: Guilford. · Berry, B.J.L. 1995: Whither regional science? *International Regional Science Review* 17: 297–306. · Holland, S. 1976: *Capital versus the region.* London: Macmillan. · Isard, W. 1956: *Location and space economy.* New York: John Wiley. · Isard, W. et al. 1960: *Methods of regional analysis: an introduction to regional science.* Cambridge, MA: MIT Press. · Martin, R. and Sunley, P. 1996: Paul Krugman's geographical economics and its implications for regional development theory: a critical assessment. *Economic Geography* 72: 259–92. · Olsson, G. 1980: *Birds in egg/eggs in bird.* London: Pion. · Sack, R.D. 1973: A concept of physical space in geography. *Geographical Analysis* 5: 16–34. · Sheppard, E. and Barnes, T.J. 1990: *The capitalist space economy: geographical analysis after Ricardo, Marx and Sraffa.* London: Unwin-Hyman.

Selected Reading

Barnes (1996). · Isserman, A.M. 1995: The history, status and future of regional science: an American perspective. *International Regional Science Review* 17: 249–96.

regionalism A political or cultural movement which seeks to politicize the territorial predicaments of its regions with the aim of protecting or furthering regional interests. An important distinction should be drawn between *functional regionalism*, in which the STATE is responsible for regional demarcation, such as administrative and planning regions, and a *regional movement* with feelings of collective identity that are not necessarily rooted in an officially defined region but emanate from a grassroots or homeland IDENTITY, although its politicization can often be strengthened by such an arrangement (see REGIONAL ALLIANCE). Regionalism can also involve ethnic regions (see ETHNICITY; NATIONALISM), for all regionalisms have in common a counter-culture, aims of autonomy and local POWER, and a political rhetoric and self-assertiveness based on a deep-seated mistrust of what is commonly perceived to be a remote and overly centralized state. Despite local economic and social RESTRUCTURING, regional identities have proved highly malleable; both ethnic and non-ethnic-based regionalisms have emerged over the past decade in particular to play a part both in engaging in a politics with new forms of continental (e.g. European Union) and global GOVERNANCE, and in relation to the global economy through bypassing the formal structures of the NATION-STATE and establishing links with other globalizing regions (cf. GLOBALIZATION). Many regions in Europe now aspire to being part of a more federated form of European governance (e.g. the Basque Country, Catalonia, Scotland). (See FEDERALISM.) GES

Suggested Reading

Loughlin, J. 1996: 'Europe of the Regions' and the federalisation of Europe. *Publius* 26 (4): 141–62. · Le Gales, P. and Lequesene, C. 1998: *Regions in Europe.* London: Routledge. · Smith, G.E. 1985: Nationalism, regionalism and the state. *Environment and Planning C: Government and Policy* 3 (1): 3–9. · Smith, G.E., ed., 1995: *Federalism. The multiethnic challenge.* London: Longman. · Taylor, P.J. 1991: A theory and practice of the regions. The case of Europe. *Environment and Planning D: Society and Space* 9: 183–95.

regions and regional geography In most conventional usages a *region* is defined as a more or less bounded area possessing some sort of unity or organizing principle(s) that distinguish it from other regions. This view can be traced back at least as far as the ancient worlds of Greece and Rome (see CHOROLOGY), but in its modern form it has been circulated through two general, sometimes overlapping and sometimes antagonistic discourses.

In the eighteenth century a European geographical imaginary placed a particular construction of 'Europe' at the centre of its grid and installed 'Africa', 'Asia' and 'America' in distinctive positions within this matrix of DIFFERENCE and deferral (Gregory, 1998). These cardinal orientations then structured the production of regional stereotypes: these were in the main the products of European projects of EXPLORATION whose results were circulated to a wider public through exhibitions, illustrations and accounts of travel. In fact, TRAVEL WRITING has been a vital source for the discursive production of regions as bounded spaces. Within this genre, regions are typically represented as distinctive zones set off from other regions, whose essential nature – at once a matter of 'identity' and 'authenticity' – is to be conveyed through both a narrativization of space (plotting the author's tracks) and an aestheticization of LANDSCAPE (the author's word-pictures). Their IMAGINATIVE GEOGRAPHIES became deeply sedimented over time, so much so that many late twentieth-century travel writings by European and North American authors continue to sustain an elaborate textualization of regions as zones that reinscribe eighteenth- and nineteenth-century stereotypes: 'the tropics' as a zone of excess, of primeval nature and human abjection; 'the Orient' as a liminal zone of eroticism, seduction and even transgression (cf. ORIENTALISM); 'the South Seas' as a zone of allure, plenitude and freedom; and 'the Arctic' as a limit-zone of solitude, silence and extremity (Holland and Huggan, 1999, ch. 2; see also Lutz and Collins, 1993). These are not (and never were) innocent representations, and similar ways of dividing up the world into regions and identifying their supposedly characteristic natures are activated within other public discourses: think, for example, of the images that have been associated with 'India' or 'Japan', 'the Middle East' or 'Central America', or the partitional vocabularies of 'BALKANIZATION', 'ENCLAVES' and 'DOMINOES' mobilized within contemporary GEOPOLITICS and reports from global media organizations.

In the course of the nineteenth and early twentieth centuries the academic discipline of Geography was drawn to the region as its central object. 'Object' is exactly the word: the region was widely seen as one of the basic 'building-blocks' of geographical inquiry. This METAPHOR clearly conveys the common sense of regionalization as both partitional (the world can be exhaustively divided into bounded spaces) and aggregative (these spaces can be fitted together to form a larger totality). This sensibility applied both to traditional *regional geography* and to the successor projects of SPATIAL SCIENCE. In the regional monographs written by French geographer Paul Vidal de la Blache at the turn of the nineteenth and twentieth centuries, for example, the regions (*pays*) of France owed their identity (or 'personality') to the local CULTURES that impressed themselves on the local LANDSCAPES ('differentiation') and to their connections with other places within the larger system of the French NATION (*'circulation'*: see also AREAL DIFFERENTIATION). In the austere lexicon of LOCATIONAL ANALYSIS regions were seen as cells within spatial grids. Thus Grigg (1965) argued that 'regionalization is similar to classification', and his account of the logic of regional taxonomy provided the basis for a series of formal region-building algorithms in which regions were treated as combinatorial, assignment and DISTRICTING problems: in effect as the product of purely technical procedures. To Haggett, Cliff and Frey (1977), therefore, the region was simply 'one of the most logical and satisfactory ways of organizing geographical information' (see also CLASSIFICATION AND REGIONALIZATION).

The most important entanglements and disassociations between these two discourses concerned the description of regions. In the first place, and in contradistinction to spatial science, both travel writing and traditional regional geography placed a premium on field experience as the ground for evocative prose, so much so that Hart (1982) hailed regional geography as 'the highest form of the geographer's art'. How many regional monographs ever reached those commanding heights remains an open question, but Lewis (1985) observed that even if few academic geographers were trained as painters or poets there was no reason to boast about it. Spatial science found its own aesthetic in the elegance of formal analytical methods and models, and represented regions as little more than convenient ordering devices within an overwhelmingly abstract space. In the second place, both travel writing and traditional regional geography sought to convey descriptions of physical and cultural landscapes. To return to Vidal de la Blache, he assumed an intimacy between culture, landscape and region – in particular between *paysan, paysage* and *pays* in rural France – that placed great demands on the sensibilities and skills of the geographer. In contrast, spatial science was largely preoccupied with *functional regions* or regional systems in which the central organizing principle was to be found within a society largely severed from its physical landscape (see NODAL REGION). Immediately after the Second World War, for example, R.E. Dickinson (1947) had proposed a focus on the city region as 'an area of interrelated activities, kindred interests and common organizations, brought into being through the medium of the routes which bind it to urban centres', and ten years later A.K. Philbrick (1957) argued that 'the functional organization of human occupance in area' should be analysed '*independent of the natural environment*' (emphasis added) through a series of intrinsically spatial concepts: focality, localization, interconnection and discontinuity. These proposals formed a springboard for the subsequent leap towards the formal SPATIAL ANALYSIS of regions as 'open SYSTEMS' (Haggett, 1965, pp. 18–19).

Running in the depths of these different literatures and transgressing the boundaries they drew around regions was a sub-text that threatened to interrupt and prise open the compartments and closures of such DISCOURSES. The journeys of explorers and traveller-writers, the capillary circulations that coursed through regions, and the thematization of regions as 'open systems' all spoke to the porosity of regional formations (the networks of connection between places) and to the POETICS of regional description (the conventional nature of boundary delimitation). These twin issues have since received explicit and substantial critical attention.

Even at its height regional geography was criticized for its closures. Vidal de la Blache's celebrated *Tableau de la géographie de la France* was a portrait – some commentators have said a painting – of the individual regions of pre-revolutionary France produced through a style and a method that critics claimed had little purchase on the post-revolutionary world. 'The region is an eighteenth-century concept', declared G.H.T. Kimble (1951), whereas in the modern world 'it is the links in landscapes . . . rather than the breaks' that matter. Similarly, E.A. Wrigley (1965) argued that the intimacy of the bonds between 'CULTURE' and 'NATURE' celebrated by regional geography was 'admirably suited to the historical geography of Europe before the Industrial Revolution' but 'with the final disappearance of the old, local, rural, largely self-sufficient way of life the centrality of regional work to geography has been permanently affected'. These twin objections were marked by their common origins (see EUROCENTRISM), and by an unusually superficial understanding of INDUSTRIALIZATION and of the dynamics of the capitalist SPACE-ECONOMY more generally (which in fact produces regional differentiations rather than erases them: see Langton, 1984; more generally, Storper and Walker, 1989).

Recent attempts to situate regional formations and transformations as constellations or condensations within more extensive networks have been far more attentive to such concerns (for example, Agnew, 1987; Dixon, 1991; Becker and Egler, 1992). These projects have been distinguished by a much greater sense of historicity – of PLACE and region as historically contingent process (Pred, 1984; see also Gilbert, 1988) – which has in turn made the 'bounded spaces' and 'building blocks' of conventional regional genres seem much less solid. To talk in this way is not merely to invoke Marx's description of capitalist MODERNITY as a world in which 'all that is solid melts into air', important though that is, because the tensions between 'fixity' and 'motion' that spasmodically interrupt and restructure regional formations are not the exclusive preserve of CAPITALISM and hence are not contained by its history alone. Our present understanding of regions suggests that they have never been closed, cellular, bounded spaces: indeed, much of 'traditional' regional geography may turn out to have been about inventing a 'traditional' world of supposedly immobile, introspective and irredeemably localized cultures. Many anthropologists, geographers, historians and others now accept that non-capitalist worlds have also always been actively engaged in other worlds, and that they have also always been constituted through their involvement in trans-local and trans-regional 'POWER-GEOMETRIES'.

In order to develop historical geographies of regional formation that are open to these possibilities it is not enough to locate regions within progressively larger global frameworks or to identify the 'regional' as one level within an interlocking system of scalar coordinates. One of the persistent difficulties of such approaches is that regions become products of processes that are located 'on the outside' – in the absolute spaces of the containing frameworks and coordinate systems – so that regions become surfaces that can only register the impacts of GLOBALIZATION, of successive rounds of the DIVISION OF LABOUR, or of TIME–SPACE COMPRESSION that are seen as enframing them. Against these ways of figuring the world, many scholars now argue that such processes are also 'on the inside' – indeed, that the demarcations between 'outside' and 'inside' are deeply problematic and that, if they are to be drawn at all, they cannot be plotted in absolute space (see SPACE, HUMAN GEOGRAPHY AND). There is presently an emerging consensus within human geography that regional formations are more or less impermanent condensations of institutions and objects, people and practices that are intimately involved in the operation and outcome of local, trans-local and trans-regional processes. For much the same reason, even though the 'regional' has constantly been hypostatized as the quintessential SCALE of geographical analysis, many writers have become much more attentive to the ways in which these scalar distinctions have been historically produced and hence enmeshed in constellations of POWER, knowledge and SPATIALITY (see Brenner, 1998). It is through these productions, at once material and discursive, that regional structures have become sedimented in imaginative geographies, in physical landscapes, and in public policy.

The theorization of regional formations as partial, porous and hybrid condensations of entangled networks of social relations, each of different spans and with inconstant geometries, raises difficult questions of REPRESENTATION. How are these ideas and concepts to be redeemed in the fabrication of regional accounts? Part of the problem concerns the need to find ways of conveying these theoretical constructs in empirical solution: as Pudup (1988) observed, 'Anyone trying to mesh theory with empirical description [in regional geography] soon learns that the movement among abstract concepts and empirical description is like performing ballet on a bed of quicksand' (see also Sayer, 1989). To Thrift (1998) the metaphor of dance is peculiarly appropriate: one implication of his presentation of NON-REPRESENTATIONAL THEORY is that all human geographies need to become much more physically sensuous, much more expressive in their poetics. In the specific case of regional geography, there is clearly much to learn from careful, critical readings of imaginative literature and from contemporary travel writings that have tried to come to terms with – to find the terms for – the complex interpenetrations of cultures: what Pico Iyer (1989) epigrammatically described as 'Video night in Kathmandu' (cf. TRANSCULTURATION). In doing so, novelists and travel-writers have wrestled with some of the same demons that haunted traditional regional geography, and above all with a sense of belatedness – a sort of elegy for 'the worlds we have lost' – that, on occasion, too readily modulates into what Rosaldo (1993) calls 'imperial nostalgia' whereby 'people mourn the passing of what they themselves have transformed' (cf. COLONIALISM; IMPERIALISM).

These issues are thus not confined to regional geography, and they admit of no easy solution. They also indicate the importance of developing an ETHICS of regional description capable of addressing both the subjects and the audiences of such accounts. The authors of regional geographies have an obligation to respond to questions of adequacy, accountability and authorization: what are their responsibilities to the people whose lives they write about? And they also have an obligation to convey places, regions and LANDSCAPES as something more than the lifeless parade of categories and the endless tabulations of statistics that loom so large in many textbooks in regional geography. There is a genuine need to represent places and their inhabitants in ways that compel their audiences to care about them: which is why the 'openness' of regions – the sense of trans-local and trans-regional engagement and interconnection – is important not only intellectually but also politically. Whatever else contemporary regional geography is about, it ought surely to be about disclosing our involvement with what Michael Ignatieff (1984) called 'the needs of strangers'.

DG

References

Agnew, J. 1987: *The United States in the world-economy: a regional geography*. Cambridge: Cambridge University Press. · Becker, B.K. and Egler, C. 1992: *Brazil: a new regional power in the world-economy: a regional geography*. Cambridge: Cambridge University Press. · Brenner, N. 1998: Between fixity and motion: accumulation, territorial organization and the historical geography of spatial scales. *Environment and Planning D: Society and Space* 16: 459–81. · Dickinson, R.E. 1947: *City region and regionalism: a geographical contribution to human ecology*. London: Kegan Paul, Trench Trübner. · Dixon, C. 1991: *South-East Asia in the world-economy: a regional geography*. Cambridge: Cambridge University Press. · Gilbert, A. 1988: The new regional geography in English and French speaking countries. *Progress in Human Geography* 12: 208–28. · Gregory, D. 1998: Power, knowledge and geography. In *Explorations in critical human geography*. Heidelberg: Department of Geography, Karl-Ruprechts Universität, 9–40. · Grigg, D. 1965: The logic of regional systems. *Annals of the Association of American Geographers* 55: 465–91. · Haggett, P. 1965: *Locational analysis in human geography*. London: Edward Arnold. · Haggett, P., Cliff, A. and Frey, A. 1977: *Locational analysis in human geography*, 2nd edn. London: Edward Arnold. · Hart, J.F. 1982: The highest form of the geographer's art. *Annals of the Association of American Geographers* 72: 1–29. · Holland, P. and Huggan, G. 1999: *Tourists with typewriters: critical reflections on contemporary travel writing*. Ann Arbor, MI: University of Michigan Press. · Ignatieff, M. 1984: *The needs of strangers*. London: Chatto and Windus. · Iyer, P. 1989: *Video nights in Kathmandu*. London: Abacus. · Kimble, G.H.T. 1951: The inadequacy of the regional concept. In L.D. Stamp and S.W. Wooldridge, eds, *London essays in geography*. London: Longman. · Langton, J. 1984: The industrial revolution and the regional geography of England. *Transactions, Institute of British Geographers* NS 9: 145–67. · Lewis, P. 1985: Beyond description. *Annals of the Association of American Geographers* 75: 465–78. · Lutz, C.A. and Collins, J.L. 1993: *Reading National Geographic*. Chicago: University of Chicago Press. · Philbrick, A.K. 1957: Principles of areal functional organization in regional human geography. *Economic Geography* 33: 299–336. · Pred, A. 1984: Place as historically contingent process: structuration and the time-geography of becoming places. *Annals of the Association of American Geographers* 74: 279–97. · Pudup, M.-B. 1988: Arguments within regional geography. *Progress in Human Geography* 12: 369–90. · Sayer, R.A. 1989: The 'new' regional geography and problems of narrative. *Environment and Planning D: Society and Space* 7: 253–76. · Storper, M. and Walker, R. 1989: *The capitalist imperative: territory, technology and industrial growth*. Oxford and Cambridge, MA: Blackwell. · Thrift, N. 1998: The still point: resistance, expressive embodiment and dance. In S. Pile and M. Keith, eds, *Geographies of resistance*. London: Routledge, 124–51. · Wrigley, E.A. 1965: Changes in the philosophy of geography. In R.J. Chorley and P. Haggett, eds, *Frontiers in geographical teaching*. London: Methuen, 3–24.

Suggested Reading

Gilbert (1988). · Pudup (1988). · Thrift, N.J. 1994: Taking aim at the heart of the region. In D. Gregory, R. Martin and G. Smith, eds, *Human geography: society, space and social science*. London: Macmillan, 200–31.

regression A PARAMETRIC statistical technique for identifying the relationship between a dependent variable and one or more independent variables. The data employed in regression analyses should be at the interval or ratio level of MEASUREMENT (though nominally measured independent variables, known as *dummy variables*, may be included).

The technique fits a straight-line plane to the trend in a scatter of points in *n* dimensions (where *n* is the total number of variables being investigated). It is best visualized in the two-dimensional case (i.e. with one independent variable only), in which the plane is represented by a straight line (see figure) whose parameters are determined by the formula:

$$Y = a + bX \pm e$$

where X is the independent (or causal) variable, Y is the dependent (or effect) variable, *b* is the slope of the line (often termed the *regression coefficient*), *a* is its *intercept* (where the regression line crosses the vertical axis – i.e. the value of Y when X = 0.0: it is also termed the *constant*) and *e* is the error term for the RESIDUALS (cf. SIGNIFICANCE TEST).

A multiple regression equation contains more than one independent variable and has the general form:

$$Y = a + b_1X_1 + b_2X_2 \pm e$$

In this each value of *b* (termed a *partial regression coefficient*) indicates the change in the value of Y with a unit change in the value of the relevant X variable, assuming no change in the values of the other X (i.e. they are 'held

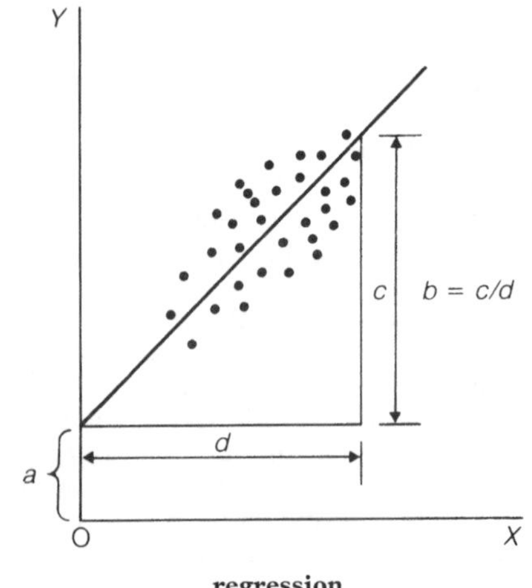

regression

constant' in the technical jargon). The intercept coefficient (*a*) indicates the estimated value of Y when all of the X variables are set to 0.0.

The goodness-of-fit of a regression line (i.e. its closeness to all of the points in the scatter) is measured by a CORRELATION coefficient. The goodness-of-fit for each separate variable in a multiple regression is termed the partial correlation coefficient.

Regression analysis, like other techniques within the GENERAL LINEAR MODEL, makes a variety of assumptions about the data used. If these are not met in a data set being analysed, then the coefficients are likely to be either or both inefficient and biased. RJJ

Suggested Reading

Barnes, T.J. 1998: A history of regression. *Environment and Planning A* 30: 203–23. · Johnston, R.J. 1978: *Multivariate statistical analysis in geography: a primer on the general linear model.* London and New York: Longman. · O'Brien, L. 1992: *Introducing quantitative geography: measurement, methods and generalised linear models.* London and New York: Routledge.

Regulation school A group of French POLITICAL-ECONOMIC theories developed to explain the structure of capitalist economies and how these change over time. Born out of an explicit rejection of market equilibrium as the organizing force within CAPITALISM, the Regulation approach instead posits societal reproduction as the central imperative underlying capitalist dynamics. Such reproduction is said to be achieved through the 'mode of regulation' – a set of STATE and private institutional forms, social practices, habits, and norms (such as those governing wage determination), which induce private individuals to act in the interests of achieving overall economic stability. Regulation theorists place particular importance on the balancing of national production and consumption (via the mode of regulation) in order to ensure the reproduction of capitalism. Distinctive historical periods of long-run expansion or relative stability (see REGIME OF ACCUMULATION) are seen to culminate in CRISIS (stagnation, instability) when such balance is no longer achieved by the existing mode of regulation. A new period of stability will arise only if successful ways of reorganizing production and/or consumption, or effective new institutions and social practices, are found. Because they are seen as being produced through active human struggle, many different modes of regulation can, in theory, support a given regime of accumulation. Modes of regulation will thus vary over time within the same national economy, and will also vary from country to country at any point in time.

Although Regulation theorists have tended to emphasize the NATION-STATE as the key scale of GOVERNANCE at which the mode of regulation is shaped, geographers have argued that there is a strong link between regulation processes and the spatial-economic and social variation *within* each nation-state. Early on, Scott (1988) argued that particular regimes, and the mode of regulation historically associated with them, have each favoured a particular set of industries and production locations. Similarly, Storper and Walker (1989) asserted that successive eras of capitalist competition have each produced their own distinctive geography of 'winner' and 'loser' regions within countries such as the United States, creating an 'inconstant geography of capitalism'. More recently, geographers have replaced this passive view of space with a more active conception in which the very production of regimes and modes of regulation is seen as being fundamentally grounded in the histories and socio-political dynamics of particular places (Tickell and Peck, 1992). As Goodwin and Painter (1997, p. 21) argue, 'the geography of regulation is not an optional extra or final complicating factor. On the contrary, the process of regulation is constituted geographically. Its unevenness is inherent.' Empirical demonstrations of this argument can be found in DiGiovanna's (1996) analysis of the local historical processes leading to the creation of particular elements of the mode of regulation. (See also FLEXIBLE ACCUMULATION; FORDISM; POST-FORDISM.) MSG

References

DiGiovanna, S. 1996: Industrial districts from a Regulation perspective. *Regional Studies* 30: 373–86. · Goodwin, M. and Painter, J. 1997: Concrete research, urban regimes, and regulation theory. In M. Lauria, ed., *Reconstructing urban regime theory.* Thousand Oaks, CA: Sage, 13–29. · Scott, A.J. 1988: *New industrial spaces.* London: Pion. · Storper, M. and Walker, R.A. 1989: *The capitalist imperative.* Oxford: Blackwell. · Tickell, A. and Peck, J. 1992: Accumulation, regulation and the geographies of post-Fordism: missing links in regulationist research. *Progress in Human Geography* 16: 190–218.

Suggested Reading

Boyer, R. 1990: *The Regulation school: a critical introduction.* New York: Columbia University Press.

reification The ascription of human qualities – such as the ability to reason – to non-humans, both animate and inanimate. RJJ

Reilly's law A method derived by a market researcher for estimating the relative flow of trade from a place to each of two towns (Reilly, 1931). Built on the same foundations as the GRAVITY MODEL, the law states that 'two cities attract trade from an intermediate town in the vicinity of the breaking point approximately in direct proportion to the populations of the two cities and in inverse proportion to the squares of the distances from these two cities to the intermediate town'. Algebraically this is represented as:

$$T_a/T_b = (P_a/P_b) \times (d_b/d_a)^2$$

where T_a and T_b are the proportions of the trade (T) going to towns a and b respectively, P_a and P_b are the populations of a and b respectively, and d_a and d_b are the distances from the place being considered to a and b. All other things being equal, more trade will go to the larger cities and to the closer places. (Note that in CENTRAL PLACE THEORY all trade goes to the closest centre, whatever its size.) RJJ

Reference

Reilly, W.J. 1931: *The law of retail gravitation*. New York: Knickerbocker Press.

relational database One of several design models for databases. Databases allow users to store and access complex information without needing to know the details of the information's arrangement in storage. In the relational model, all information is expressed in the form of rectangular tables. The rows of tables correspond to instances of a particular type of record, and the columns to variables. For example, an airline's reservation database might include tables of flights, aircraft, passengers, and crew; each table would include the appropriate attributes (for flights, the departure airport and time, arrival airport and time, aircraft assigned to the flight, number of seats etc.). Tables are linked by 'common keys'; for example, flight numbers would link flight data to passenger data. The relational model is well-suited to statistical data, such as those collected and disseminated by a CENSUS; and to GEOGRAPHICAL INFORMATION SYSTEMS (GIS), where its use has been identified with the term *georelational model*.

The relational model was originally described by Date (1975). In recent years numerous limitations of the model have led to interest in *object-oriented databases* (Cattell, 1994), although the relational model still dominates in many applications, including GIS. Object-oriented databases can include many features not found in relational databases, including the ability of objects to 'inherit' properties from other objects, and the ability to define new types of objects, and many of these are of potential value in GIS. But object-oriented databases are largely limited to research prototypes at this time. MG

References

Cattell, R.G.G. 1994: *Object data management: object-oriented and extended relational database systems*. Reading, MA: Addison-Wesley. · Date, C.J. 1975: *An introduction to database systems*. Reading, MA: Addison-Wesley.

relations of production The manner in which participants in the productive process relate to one another, sometimes referred to as the social relations of production. In MARXIAN ECONOMICS, relations of production correspond to a definite stage in the development of the PRODUCTIVE FORCES. The social relations of SLAVERY involved producers owning workers; under FEUDALISM there existed rights whereby landowners could appropriate some of the production of others; while under the social relations of CAPITALISM workers sell their labour on the open market. The tension between the forces of production and the social relations of production is held by Marxists to be responsible for changes in the MODE OF PRODUCTION. (See also CLASS.) DMS

relativism The idea that knowledge is produced and justified in terms of the social practices of the time and place in which it arises. As Protogoras, possibly the first reported relativist, said, 'man [sic] is the measure of all things'. Note, though, that relativism is not equivalent to *subjectivism*, the idea that beliefs are mere personal opinion, taste or whim. The force of the relativist position lies precisely in its recognition that beliefs are socially and not merely individually variable. It further follows that because knowledge is dependent upon its social context, truth itself is relative. To put it in different terms, knowledge that we believe as true is accepted not because it is correct, or corresponds to rigorous, context-independent epistemological standards; it is deemed true because we believe it.

Opposed to relativism ever since Plato (who mocked Protogoras), is *rationalism*, which asserts that true knowledge is grounded in some foundation that transcends particular practices and contexts (cf. FOUNDATIONALISM). Rationalism guarantees that true knowledge really is true, and not just because we happen to believe it, and is characterized by four beliefs:

- that rationality provides a set of universal rules and procedures that if followed lead directly to the truth;
- that those same rules and procedures are ineluctable in that they necessarily draw their users along like 'invisible rails which reach ahead . . . giving guidance' (Bloor, 1988, p. 69);
- that rationality is a final arbiter ensuring commensurability in cases where there are initial disagreements; and
- that rationality is the only means to understand disciplinary or individual successes or failure.

For example, while Newton's undiluted rationality brought him success as a physicist, his irrationality brought him failure as a closet alchemist. In every *context*, then, one can appeal to a set of non-locally specific, neutral rules and procedures – rationality – to resolve the issue at hand (cf. CONTEXTUAL APPROACH).

In contrast, relativists argue it is never possible to know such rules and procedures because we can never stand outside of our particular local context – history, geography, GENDER, CLASS, ethnic heritage, CULTURE, and so on. That context forms the very basis of all our claims to knowledge: it enters into its very pores. For that reason rationality's claim to universality, to ineluctability, to commensurability, and to arbitrate success, is misplaced (or more precisely out of place; it is 'the view from nowhere' as Haraway, 1991, p. 191, writes; see SITUATED KNOWLEDGE). If rationality is believed, it is only because the context of its espousal makes it seem credible.

There are a number of different forms of relativism, among which the most important are: *perceptual* (everyone experiences the world differently); *moral* (my good might be your evil); *aesthetic* (beauty is in the eye of the beholder); *cultural* (when in Rome, do as the Romans); and, the one already discussed, *epistemological or cognitive* (it is true for you but not necessarily for me). Of the five, the last has met the greatest resistance, at least within the academy. Portrayed as the view that there are no grounds for choosing among competing truth claims, it is then dismissed by critics on the basis of self-refutation; for any statement about the impossibility of truth claims is itself a truth claim. This form of relativism, called naive or radical, however, has 'except for the occasional freshman' few adherents (Rorty, 1982, p. 166).

There exist, though, much more sophisticated versions of relativism that are not so easily dismissed, and are found in a number of disciplines. In the sociology of knowledge ('a notorious black spot for fatal accidents', Hesse, 1980, p. 30), there is Barnes and Bloor's (1982, p. 23) strong programme (see SCIENCE, GEOGRAPHY AND): 'all beliefs are on par with one another with respect to the causes of their credibility'. In anthropology Geertz (1984) has long practised a form of relativism ('anti anti-relativism' as he calls it), which he thinks must be the stock and trade of any ETHNOGRAPHER recording cultural difference – 'if we wanted home truths, we should have stayed at home' (Geertz, 1984, p. 276). In philosophy there is the work of the PRAGMATIST philosopher Richard Rorty (1982), who seeks to evade the standard objection to relativism by arguing that it is only a problem in the first place because of the traditional FOUNDATIONALIST vocabulary in which philosophy couches it. Change that vocabulary, and the difficulty evaporates. Finally, in science studies, there is the work of Woolgar (1988) and Ashmore (1989) who seek to develop a radical form of relativism by using the conception of reflexivity, in this case, the idea that a relativist perspective should be applied to the very belief in relativism.

Relativism since the early 1970s while 'beg[inning] as a trickle, has swelled . . . into a roaring torrent' (Bernstein, 1983, p. 13). A lot of that popularity is due to the success of anti-foundationalist and anti-ESSENTIALIST approaches associated with POST-STRUCTURALISM and POSTMODERNISM. There remain, however, energetic and committed critics of relativism who span traditional political and intellectual divides. For them the idea that there is nothing more fundamental anchoring our beliefs than a set of contingent social practices is akin to intellectual nihilism and moral irresponsibility. As Geertz (1984, p. 264) describes it, 'to suggest that "hard rock" foundations for cognitive, aesthetic, or moral judgements may, in fact, not be available . . . is to find oneself accused of disbelieving in the physical world, thinking pushpin as good as poetry, regarding Hitler as a fellow with unstandard tastes, or having . . . no politics at all'. Here critics, from the far Left, such as the physicist Alan Sokal (1996) who criticizes the relativism of science studies (see SCIENCE, GEOGRAPHY AND), to those on the far Right, such as US Senator Jesse Helms's interventions in various projects funded by the National Endowment of the Humanities, are equally convinced that relativism heralds the beginning of the end, that, as Yeats put it, 'mere anarchy is loosed upon the world'.

Even writers who seemingly align themselves with a post-structural sensibility are not always comfortable with relativism, for example, in FEMINISM, POST-MARXISM or POST-COLONIALISM. This is because writers in those traditions, while recognizing the importance of social context, also want to hold to progressive and critical political views that are seemingly undermined by strict forms of relativism (e.g. upholding the constants of patriarchy or class oppression or racism). In such cases, a third way is sought, as in Haraway's (1991) idea of SITUATED KNOWLEDGE, or Gibson-Graham's (1996) use of *overdetermination*, or Said's 'IMAGINATIVE GEOGRAPHY' (Gregory, 1995).

Given geography's historical concern of understanding different PLACES in the same way that anthropologists study different cultures, it is remarkable that relativism has not been more widely discussed in the discipline. When theory began entering the discipline from the 1960s onwards, it tended toward FOUNDATIONALISM and ESSENTIALISM, such as found in rationalism, Marxism, PHENOMENOLOGY or Humanism. As a result, relativism was a non-starter. With recent interest in POST-STRUCTURALISM, POSTMODERNISM and social constructionism, and associated with some types of feminism, CULTURAL GEOGRAPHY, and even ECONOMIC GEOGRAPHY, there have been tentative explorations of relativism. Given the politicized nature of current human geography, however, there is a reluctance to push relativism very far (Jones, Natter et al., 1994). To do so would blunt the discipline's critical edge (an issue that is raised explicitly by Harvey, 1987, in his critiques of the 'formless relativism' sometimes found in postmodernism and even REALISM, and also central to the debate between Barnes 1993, 1994, and Bassett, 1994, 1995). TJB

References

Ashmore, M. 1989: *The reflexive thesis: wrighting sociology of scientific knowledge*. Chicago: University of Chicago Press. · Barnes, B. and Bloor, D. 1982: Relativism, rationality and the sociology of knowledge. In M. Hollis and S. Lukes, eds, *Rationality and relativism*. Cambridge, MA: MIT Press, 21–47. · Barnes, T.J. 1993: Whatever happened to the philosophy of science? *Environment and Planning A* 25: 301–4. · Barnes, T.J. 1994: Five ways to leave your critic: a sociological scientific experiment in replying. *Environment and Planning A* 26: 1653–8. · Bassett, K. 1994: Whatever happened to the philosophy of science? Some comments on Barnes. *Environment and Planning A* 26: 337–42. · Bassett, K. 1995: On reflexivity: further comments on Barnes and the sociology of science. *Environment and Planning A* 27: 1527–31. · Bernstein, R.J. 1983: *Beyond objectivism and relativism: science, hermeneutics and practice*. Philadelphia, PA: University of Pennsylvania Press. · Bloor, D. 1988: Rationalism, supernaturalism, and the sociology of knowledge. In I. Hronsky, M. Feher and B. Dajka, eds, *Scientific knowledge socialised*. Budapest: Akedemiai Kiado, 55–74. · Geertz, C. 1984: Anti anti-relativism. *American Anthropologist* 86: 263–78. · Gibson-Graham, J.-K. 1996: *The end of capitalism (as we knew it)*. Oxford: Blackwell. · Gregory, D. 1995: Imaginative geographies. *Progress in Human Geography* 14: 447–85. · Haraway, D.J. 1991: *Simians, cyborgs, and women: the reinvention of nature*. New York: Routledge. · Harvey, D. 1987: Three myths in search of a reality in urban studies. *Environment and Planning D: Society and Space* 5: 367–76. · Hesse, M.B. 1980: *Revolutions and reconstructions in the philosophy of science*. Brighton: Harvester Wheatsheaf. · Jones, J.P., Natter, W. and Schatzki, T., eds, 1994: *Postmodern contentions: epochs, politics and space*. New York: Guilford. · Rorty, R. 1982: *The consequences of pragmatism*. Minneapolis, MN: University of Minnesota Press. · Sokal, A.D. 1996: Transgressing the boundaries: towards a transformative hermeneutics of quantum gravity. *Social Text* 46/47: 217–52. · Woolgar, S. 1988: *Science: the very idea*. London: Tavistock.

Suggested Reading

Barnes and Bloor (1982). · Jones et al. (1994).

relevance Concerns over the relevance of their work surfaced among geographers during the late 1960s as they realized that their adoption of SPATIAL SCIENCE had not led to their discipline making substantial contributions to the resolution of what were perceived as the major social problems. As Prince put it (1971, p. 152):

> Many geographers were deeply frustrated by a sense of failure, conscious that the knowledge they already possessed was not being put to good use, that much had been learned about ways and means of reducing hunger, disease and poverty, but little had been achieved, that educated people had not been instrumental in stopping a barbarous war [in Vietnam] and that, within their own universities, they had failed to bring about overdue reforms.

Many associated these feelings with a critique of spatial science, which was recognized as offering technical solutions to some problems (such as transport planning) but ignored major long-term issues.

This general feeling of malaise and unimportance was represented in two very separate directions within the discipline. One argued that geographers had much to offer, but that they were largely ignored by decision-makers (see PUBLIC POLICY, GEOGRAPHY AND). Steel (1974, p. 200), for example, claimed in his Presidential Address to the British Geographical Association that:

> As geographers we often get hot under the collar over the number of theoretical economists who are

called on to advise the governments of developing countries. We comment on how much better World Bank surveys of countries would be if they were prepared, at least in part, by geographers . . . We wonder why university departments of geography are not engaged on a consultancy basis more often than they are, and we marvel that the Overseas Development Administration in London has only a handful of geographers on its staff where, we feel, an army would be more appropriate.

Out of such concerns came arguments that geographers should more actively promote the relevance of their knowledge and the applicability of their methods, albeit in particular contexts in which they could operate as detached, 'value-free' scientists (see APPLIED GEOGRAPHY). This was accentuated in the 1980s, in part as a response to the pressures for universities to become more focused in their work on society's problems (see Johnston, 1995) and to raise greater shares of their research income from private as well as public sector sources. In pressing this case within the discipline, many promoted the rapidly expanding technologies such as REMOTE SENSING and GEOGRAPHICAL INFORMATION SYSTEMS. Longley (1995, p. 129), for example, argued that training in GIS provides students with saleable skills in contemporary labour markets, providing 'clear testimony that quantitative spatial analysis is most certainly not preoccupied with techniques that do not work to analyse problems that do not matter'. (See also GEODEMOGRAPHICS.)

For some the need to be relevant is closely linked to disciplinary survival in materialist societies. For example, Ron Abler (1993), Executive Director of the Association of American Geographers, argued for a refocusing of American geography on what he termed a 'priority for the practical': currently 'too many geographers still preoccupy themselves with what geography is: too few concern themselves with what they can do for the societies that pay their keep'. These attitudes were strongly reflected in a report to the US National Research Council on *Rethinking geography* (NRC, 1997), which was commissioned because of a 'well-documented growing perception (external to geography as a discipline) that geography is useful, perhaps even necessary, in meeting certain societal needs' which the committee that prepared it took as an invitation to provide a showcase for geography's strengths as 'good science and societally relevant science'. In 'selling geography' to the US scientific community and potential 'buyers' in the country's public and private sectors, this committee chose to emphasize the spatial science approach within the discipline and significantly under-play that (assumed irrelevant or, at least, less relevant) based on social theory (the dichotomy is Sheppard's, 1995; cf. HUMAN GEOGRAPHY).

The second set of responses to the 'relevance malaise' developed through the contemporary critique of spatial science and POSITIVISM. It emphasized both the poverty of the theory that geographers were employing in their searches for explanation and the relative insignificance of many of the topics that they were studying. This was typified by Harvey's (1973, p. 129) statement that:

The quantitative revolution has run its course, and diminishing marginal returns are setting in. . . . There is a clear disparity between the sophisticated theoretical and methodological framework which we are using and our ability to say anything meaningful about events as they unfold around us. There are too many anomalies between what we purport to manipulate and what actually happens. There is an ecological problem, an urban problem, an international trade problem, and yet we seem incapable of saying anything in depth or profundity about any of them.

Although many followed Harvey's lead by seeking understanding in Marxist theory, 16 years later he wrote a similar, more trenchant, critique (Harvey, 1989, pp. 212–13):

I accept that we can now model spatial behaviours like journey-to-work, retail activity, the spread of measles epidemics, the atmospheric dispersion of pollutants, and the like, with much greater security and precision than once was the case. And I accept that this represents no mean achievement. But what can we say about the sudden explosion of third world debt in the 1970s, the remarkable push into new and seemingly quite different modes of flexible accumulation, the rise of geopolitical tensions, even the definition of key ecological problems? What more do we know about major historical-geographical transitions (the rise of capitalism, world wars, socialist revolutions, and the like)?

Harvey was not alone in pointing to a myopic condition among geographers. Stoddart, from a very different position within the discipline, has also been highly critical. In 1986 he recognized and regretted

the fact that for many people the geographer has long since appeared to have surrendered to other specialists his catholic concern for the diversity of the natural world. We have too long accepted the artificial constructions of the bookmen about what geography is, what it should be concerned with and how it is done . . . so many retreat into increasingly restrictive and esoteric specialities, where they protect themselves with secret languages and erudite techniques.

A year later, he not only extended that case, claiming that geography has collapsed into a series of specialisms, each with 'its own technical expertise . . . its own theoretical constructs', with the result that 'we speak separate languages, do very different things' and 'Many have abandoned the possibility of communicating with colleagues working not only in the same titular discipline but also in the same department' (Stoddart, 1987, p. 330), but also proclaimed that:

> Quite frankly . . . I cannot take seriously those who promote as topics worthy of research subjects like geographic influences in the Canadian cinema, or the distribution of fast-food outlets in Tel Aviv. Nor have I a great deal more time for what I can only call the chauvinist self-indulgence of our contemporary obsession with the minutiae of our own affluent and urbanized society – housing finance, voting patterns, government subsidies for this and that, and how to get most from them. We cannot afford the luxury of putting so much energy into peripheral things. Fiddle if you will, but at least be aware that Rome is burning all the while. (Stoddart, 1986, p. ix)

For him, like Harvey, geographers should focus on 'the big questions, about man, land, resources, human potential' but unfortunately

> We no longer ask these questions, but the questions remain. It is largely people other than geographers who are asking – and answering – them now. It is astonishing that it is Ladurie and the *Annales* school who have commandeered the whole field of the relations of climate and history. Braudel writes what is in effect geography (though without maps) and calls it history: the historical geographers tag along in dutiful homage. (Stoddart, 1987, p. 330)

Harvey's means of focusing on the 'big questions' is based on a very different view of the purpose of relevant work from that of *Rethinking geography*'s authors. For him, theoretical advance and the greater appreciation of the world that this provides is a crucial applied task, leading to the emancipation that a successful 'people's geography' will bring (Harvey, 1984): this then enables the enhancement, through education, of people's awareness of how their current condition has been created and so allows them to take control of their own lives: social change comes about through an 'informed revolution'.

These wider issues of relevance than those linked to the narrow conceptions of APPLIED GEOGRAPHY associated with Stamp and his successors are illustrated by geographers' recent engagement with ethical issues (cf. ETHICS, GEOGRAPHY AND). Moral questions regarding justice and equality, and whether all conceptions of what is 'good' and 'bad', 'right' and 'wrong', are relative rather than absolute are now central concerns in geographical debate – with reference not only to research and its application but also to teaching and the role of 'authority' in construction of the 'learning experience'. Work characterized as the CULTURAL TURN and CRITICAL HUMAN GEOGRAPHY is promoting awareness of how all knowledge is produced and situated in particular contexts and then used to promote privileged positions for some forms over others – MASCULINISM, EUROCENTRISM, and COLONIALISM are just three examples of such positions. Geographers' concerns with the philosophy of science are seen as of lesser importance than those with knowledge-construction, as part of critical engagements with capitalism, imperialism and the production of inequality. Such work is highly relevant to the creation and maintenance of humane societies, but because it transcends the narrow utilitarianism that characterizes much of modern geography, especially its institutional structures (both professionally and within the universities, many of whose leaders have embraced that utilitarianism), many seek to marginalize it from the disciplinary project.

Geography is a fragmented discipline, necessarily so (Johnston, 1998). Workers in the various fragments seek to establish their relevance in very different ways, which occasionally stimulates debates over what should be privileged in disciplinary promotional activities: for too long, the concept of relevance has been narrowly construed. RJJ

References and Suggested Reading

Abler, R.F. 1993: Desiderata for geography: an institutional view from the United States. In R.J. Johnston, ed., *The challenge for geography. A changing world: a changing discipline?* Oxford: Blackwell, 215–38. · Buttimer, A. 1993: *Geography and the human spirit.* Baltimore: Johns Hopkins University Press. · Harvey, D. 1973: *Social justice and the city.* London: Edward Arnold. · Harvey, D. 1984: On the history and present condition of geography: an historical materialist manifesto. *Professional Geographer* 36: 1–11. · Harvey, D. 1989: From models to Marx: notes on the project to 'remodel' contemporary geography. In B. Macmillan, ed., *Remodelling geography.* Oxford: Blackwell. · Johnston, R.J. 1986: *On human geography.* Oxford: Basil Blackwell. · Johnston, R.J. 1995: The business of British geography. In A.D. Cliff, P.R. Gould, A.G. Hoare and N.J. Thrift, eds, *Diffusing geography: essays for Peter Haggett.* Oxford: Blackwell. · Johnston, R.J. 1998: Fragmentation around a defended core: the territoriality of geography.

Geographical Journal 164. · Longley, P.A. 1995: GIS and planning for businesses and services. *Environment and Planning B* 22: 127–9. · National Research Council 1997: *Rethinking geography: new relevance for science and society*. Washington, D.C.: NRC. · NAS–NRC, 1965: *The science of geography*. Washington, D.C.: NAS–NRC. · Prince, H.C. 1971: Questions of social relevance. *Area* 3: 150–3. · Sheppard, E.S. 1995: Dissenting from spatial analysis. *Urban Geography* 16: 283–303. · Steel, R.W. 1974: The Third World: geography in practice. *Geography* 59: 189–207. · Stoddart, D.R. 1986: *On geography, and its history*. Oxford: Basil Blackwell. · Stoddart, D.R. 1987: To claim the high ground: geography for the end of the century. *Transactions, Institute of British Geographers* NS 12: 327–36.

religion, geography of A sub-field of CULTURAL GEOGRAPHY, and variously concerned with the description and interpretation of the spatial relationships, LANDSCAPES, and places of sacred phenomena and religious practices (Park, 1994). The geography of religion is consequently most fully developed where cultural geography is also prominent, notably the United States and Germany. However, this pattern is changing, as the CULTURAL TURN has led to the broader DIFFUSION of interest in all manner of cultural phenomena and institutions, including religion and spirituality. At the same time the geographical study of religion is also beginning to engage the sociology of religion and indeed social theory more generally. In this respect, as will be noted below, there are also some important initiatives by theologians to undertake critical assessments of EPISTEMOLOGY and THEORY in the social sciences.

Earlier reviews noted both a 'lack of coherence' (Sopher, 1981) and that the sub-field is 'in disarray' (Tuan, 1976). The earliest and still the largest number of studies are concerned with the patterning of religious phenomena, either as map distributions or as MORPHOLOGICAL features of the CULTURAL LANDSCAPE. The distribution of religious denominations in the United States, for example, has been used to demarcate *cultural regions* (Zelinsky, 1961), while descriptive studies have itemized such visible landscape elements as cemeteries, sacred places, or the landscapes of distinctive groups such as the Mormons. Much of this work is descriptive, IDIOGRAPHIC in nature, and with limited attempts at explanation or theorization. Its concept of CULTURE is 'superorganic', that is of a monolithic and pre-existing entity that incorporates a weak sense of human agency. More analytical or interpretive studies of religious adherence (Doeppers, 1976), or of a religious event such as the diffusion of the Reformation (Hannemann, 1975), are indicative of more ambitious attempts to place religious phenomena in a wider explanatory context.

An important question for human geographers who seek more than a descriptive approach to the geography of religion is both knowledge of the literature of religious studies and also familiarity with the nature of religious experience (Buttner, 1980). Tuan (1976) has pressed this position further, arguing for a PHENOMENOLOGY of religious experience, a HUMANISTIC perspective to which he has made important contributions. Sharing this orientation is Tanaka's (1977) detailed interpretation of the symbolic meaning of 36 landscape elements of Buddhist religious sites, an effort that may be replicated in other places, such as palaces or classical gardens. Also concerned with sacred places, but at a less experiential level, is work on pilgrimages (Sopher, 1968), and Ben-Arieh's (1984) immense historical geography of Jerusalem (cf. SACRED AND PROFANE SPACE).

Such work is closely related to studies exploring the relationship between religious cosmology or world-view and the meaning of the land. The cities of early civilizations were frequently laid out as a microcosm of the cosmological order, with the king's palace a MIMETIC representation of the holy of holies at the centre of the universe (Wheatley, 1971; Duncan, 1990). Cosmologies also present a strong symbolic bond to the land; the belief in the promised land, such a central tenet of Judaism (Houston, 1978), has propelled the twentieth-century reinvention of the Jewish STATE. Not least, and controversial, has been the debate over the implications of the Judaeo-Christian traditions in the constitution of NATURE. The earlier emphasis on a dominion mandate and its destructive implications for environmental use, is now much tempered, as a countervailing argument has identified the ethic of environmental stewardship in Biblical sources (Kay, 1989). Discussions of this type are likely to grow with the rising normative interest in ETHICS in human geography. A related development has occurred in the literature on missionary endeavours, where an earlier critical (indeed sometimes hostile) genre of work that fully implicated the church with the project of empire has more recently been revised to a more nuanced view of the differential impact of national and even denominational missions, some of which practised not only significant humanitarian works in education and health care and intervened to block the grosser intrusions of IMPERIALISM, but also held a view of 'the native' at odds with the hierarchical tropes of Eurocentrism (Sanneh, 1993; cf. Comaroff and Comaroff, 1991, 1997).

A productive literature has explored the role of religious belief and practice in the construction of local geographies. Too little of this work, as yet, has been institutional, though informative exceptions include an assessment of the church as a landholder (Hamnett, 1987) and as a service provider (Pacione, 1990). With the immense international MIGRATIONS of recent decades, another promising field is examination of the role of the immigrant church, temple, and gurdwara in providing services and also in staking out models for cultural integration and thereby for the remaking of IDENTITIES (cf. ASSIMILATION). More common than this institutional perspective has been examination of the practices of adherents as a group and their contribution to a distinctive SENSE OF PLACE. A Catholic predisposition to wine-making, for example, has introduced marked variations in agricultural land use between adjacent Catholic and Protestant parishes (Geipel, 1978), whereas in Belfast similar ethnic characteristics demarcate the boundaries of mutually hostile TERRITORIES (Boal, 1969). In PLURAL SOCIETIES, religious adherence sometimes marks the division between more or less entitled citizens; the status of Jew and Arab (whether Muslim or Christian) is a case in point (Romann and Weingrod, 1991). A significant group of studies has considered the effects of religious dietary practices and associated regimes of agriculture (Simoons, 1960).

The recent interest in cultural politics has led to several innovative studies. Harvey's (1979) materialist reading of the Basilica of Sacré-Coeur in Paris regards the building as a political symbol intended to restore a conservative politics, following the insurrection of the Paris Commune. This attempt to achieve HEGEMONY through the built environment was resisted by Republican Parisians. In a quite different setting, and with an alternative set of heuristics, Duncan (1990) has told much the same story. In pre-colonial Sri Lanka, the monarchy of the Kandyan kingdom sought to expand and legitimate its control in a series of ritualized building programmes. The new construction followed specific protocols laid out in sacred texts. The designs were intended to rebuild the cosmological order in microcosm, but the larger political imperative was to legitimate the rule of the king. In a seminal volume, Duncan has made several advances, and brought new intellectual vitality to the task of recording the presence of religious phenomena in the landscape. Religious traits are not merely described MORPHOLOGICALLY, but are read as symbolic entries, authored by identifiable agents from a received tradition, and directed by them to a larger political purpose. To accomplish this objective, the study includes a sophisticated knowledge of the sacred texts themselves as well as a literary strategy of intertextuality that relates the holy books to the landscape, itself conceived as a TEXT.

A final genre of work was labelled by Sopher (1981) as confessional, that is, it offered geographical interpretations premised upon a religious cosmology. While such an interpretation is most usually drawn from the tradition of a religious world-view (Ley, 1974; Aay and Griffioen, 1998; Wallace, 1998), Sopher suggests that it may equally be derived from a secular cosmology, and he cites the conclusion of Harvey (1979), with the author 'coming forward, as it were, for Karl Marx'. This nexus between knowledge and social interests is one that has been pursued by theologians and a few geographers in examining the treatment of religious themes by secular authors. In an eloquent critique, Livingstone (1998) has demonstrated some particular lacunae in the history of geography, notably the erasure of religious influences, such as natural theology, upon the construction of geographical knowledge. This work connects with an expansive project in the sociology of religion, where John Milbank (1990) has shown how repeatedly the undeclared work of social science has been to erase and distort religious modes of knowledge, to engage in an unstated metaphysical move against metaphysics. This revelation of the policing of the domains of religion by social science is only one of a number of recent interventions by sociologists of religion and theologians that are opening up some extremely interesting lines of engagement around theoretical and epistemological concerns. Other examples include Thiselton's (1992) review of hermeneutics that bridges the humanities, theology and the social sciences, and Pasewark's (1993) theological challenge to a Foucauldian view of POWER as domination (also Milbank, 1990). This is part of a broader unease with the entire edifice of the POST-STRUCTURAL hermeneutics of suspicion, and the posing of other starting points, such as a hermeneutics of trust.

Such work projects the geography of religion into far more refined intellectual spaces. It provides the intellectual counterpart to the historical revitalization of religious questions occasioned by such developments as the rise of militant forms of Islam, the role of the Catholic Church in DEMOCRACY movements in Latin America and elsewhere, the political mobilization of conservative Christians in the USA, and GLOBALIZATION forces which are creating far more heterogeneous national religious COMMUNITIES. In short, the emergence of religious forces which significantly constitute new regional geographies coincides with theoretical and epistemological advances. Together they provide considerable momentum to press forward Kong's (1990) hope for 'more room for geographical exploration (of religion) than has thus far been attempted'. DL

References

Aay, H. and Griffioen, S., eds, 1998: *Geography and worldview: a Christian reconnaissance*. Lanham, MD: University Press of America. · Ben-Arieh, Y. 1984: *Jerusalem in the nineteenth century*. New York: St. Martin's Press. · Boal, F. 1969: Territoriality on the Shankill–Falls divide, Belfast. *Irish Geography* 6: 30–50. · Buttner, M. 1980: On the history and philosophy of the geography of religion in Germany. *Religion* 10: 86–119. · Comaroff, J. and Comaroff, J. 1991, 1997: *Of revelation and revolution: Christianity, colonialism and consciousness in South Africa*, 2 vols. Chicago: University of Chicago Press. · Doeppers, D. 1976: The evolution of the geography of religious adherence in the Philippines before 1898. *Journal of Historical Geography* 2: 95–110. · Duncan, J. 1990: *The city as text: the politics of landscape interpretation in the Kandyan kingdom*. Cambridge: Cambridge University Press. · Geipel, R. 1978: The landscape indicators school in German geography. In D. Ley and M. Samuels, eds, *Humanistic geography*. London: Croom Helm, 155–72. · Hamnett, C. 1987: The church's many mansions: the changing structure of the Church Commissioners' land and property holdings. *Transactions, Institute of British Geographers* NS 12: 465–81. · Hanneman, M. 1975: *The diffusion of the Reformation in southwestern Germany, 1518–1534*. Chicago: University of Chicago, Department of Geography, Research paper no. 167. · Harvey, D. 1979: Monument and myth. *Annals of the Association of American Geographers* 69: 362–81. · Houston, J. 1978: The concepts of 'place' and 'land' in the Judaeo-Christian tradition. In D. Ley and M. Samuels, eds, *Humanistic geography*. London: Croom Helm, 224–37. · Kay, J. 1989: Human dominion over nature in the Hebrew Bible. *Annals of the Association of American Geographers* 79: 213–32. · Kong, L. 1990: Geography and religion: trends and prospects. *Progress in Human Geography* 14: 355–71. · Ley, D. 1974: The city and good and evil: reflections on Christian and Marxian interpretations. *Antipode* 6: 66–74. · Livingstone, D. 1998: Geography and the natural theology imperative. In H. Aay and S. Griffioen, eds, *Geography and worldview: a Christian reconnaissance*. Lanham, MD: University Press of America, 1–17. · Milbank, J. 1990: *Theology and social theory: beyond secular reason*. Oxford: Blackwell. · Pacione, M. 1990: The ecclesiastical community of interest as a response to urban poverty and deprivation. *Transactions, Institute of British Geographers* NS 15: 193–204. · Park, C. 1994: *Sacred worlds: an introduction to geography and religion*. London: Routledge. · Pasewark, K. 1993: *A theology of power: being beyond domination*. Minneapolis: Fortress Press. · Romann, M. and Weingrod, A. 1991: *Living together separately: Arabs and Jews in centemporary Jerusalem*. Princeton: Princeton University Press. · Sanneh, L. 1993: *Encountering the west: Christianity and the global cultural process*. London: Marshall Pickering. · Simoons, F. 1960: *Eat not this flesh*. Madison: University of Wisconsin Press. · Sopher, D. 1968: Pilgrim circulation in Gujarat. *Geographical Review* 58: 392–425. · Sopher, D. 1981: Geography and religions. *Progress in Human Geography* 5: 510–24. · Tanaka, H. 1977: Geographic expression of Buddhist pilgrim places in Shikoku Island, Japan. *Canadian Geographer* 21: 111–32. · Thiselton, A. 1992: *New horizons in hermeneutics*. Grand Rapids, MI: Zondervan. · Tuan, Y.-F. 1976: Humanistic geography. *Annals of the Association of American Geographers* 66: 266–76. · Wallace, I. 1998: A Christian reading of the global economy. In H. Aay and S. Griffioen, eds, *Geography and worldview: a Christian reconnaissance*. Lanham, MD: University Press of America. · Wheatley, P. 1971: *The pivot of the four corners*. Chicago: Aldine. · Zelinsky, W. 1961: An approach to the religious geography of the United States: patterns of church membership in 1952. *Annals of the Association of American Geographers* 51: 139–93.

Suggested Reading

Kong (1990). · Milbank (1990). · *Social Compass: International Review of Sociology of Religion*, 1993: The geography of religions. 40 (2), whole issue.

remote sensing The practice of collecting data by observing at a distance; the term is most often applied to observation of the Earth's surface from above, from either an aircraft or a satellite. The history of remote sensing extends back to the early days of photography, but the field received a major impetus during both World Wars, when very extensive use was made of aerial photography for reconnaissance. Photographs were taken from aircraft, often flying at high altitude to avoid enemy fire, then developed and interpreted on the ground. The science of air photo interpretation developed as an effort to systematize the detection of features from high-altitude aerial photography. Remote sensing received another boost during the Cold War, as instruments were developed to obtain high-resolution images from satellites flying above the Earth's atmosphere. Much of the imagery collected by the US using these systems in the 1960s has now become available to researchers.

Modern remote sensing uses digital instruments attached to satellites or aircraft. Passive systems measure the radiation received by the satellite in various parts of the electromagnetic spectrum, while active systems generate radiation of microwave or radar wavelengths and measure the proportion reflected from below. The radiation detected in a small area known as the instantaneous field of view (IFOV) is integrated, and recorded. A complete image is assembled as a two-dimensional array of PIXELS, and the spatial resolution of the image is determined by the linear dimensions of each pixel on the Earth's surface. Some early satellite systems recorded images on film, which was then ejected from the satellite and caught by an aircraft; but these systems were largely abandoned in favour of radio transmission of images in digital form to a ground receiving station. Early systems required several ground receiving stations, in order to ensure that at least one was in direct view of the satellite; modern systems either store images until the receiving station is in view, or relay the signal via a second satellite.

Applications of remote sensing can be divided into two broad categories, depending on the eventual use of the data. Some systems are designed to provide data that can be treated as measurements of some significant variable, and analysed directly, or used as input to simulation models; the so-called 'Ozone Hole' over Antarctica was detected by such a system. Other systems are used primarily for mapping, in which case the image is used to identify and locate various types of features on the Earth's surface, such as growing crops, roads, urban development, or sea ice. In these latter cases the relationship between radiation and feature may be complex, and largely empirical. Remote sensing systems are now widely used to observe and forecast weather events; measure the precise elevation of the land and ocean surfaces; identify crops and forecast yields; evaluate timber resources; and a host of other practical applications. Low-altitude imagery from aircraft platforms is used to provide a source of higher accuracy to validate satellite-derived estimates; and there is increasing use of miniature remote-controlled aircraft for both civilian and military applications.

Of the hundreds of remote sensing systems now in Earth orbit, only a few are of significance for mapping applications. Much use has been made of the US Landsat series of satellites, which produce images in several visible and near-infrared areas of the spectrum at spatial resolutions down to 30 m. The French SPOT instruments have spatial resolutions down to 10 m. Several companies have been authorized to launch instruments with 1m resolution, beginning in 1998; and it seems likely that the products of high-resolution military satellites will also become increasingly available.

Over the past three decades much effort has gone into finding applications of remote sensing in social and economic domains, though the vast majority of applications address issues in the physical sciences and in natural RESOURCE MANAGEMENT. A ground resolution of 30 m is sufficient to detect clearing and settlement in the Amazon basin, for example, or urban growth around Mexico City. But many other variables of interest to human geographers are simply invisible from above the surface of the Earth. Imagery from the new 1 m satellites may have potential for human geography, but has not yet been evaluated. It seems, however, that such imagery will be of great value for applications in urban infrastructure management, and for construction of geographic DATABASES describing urban form.

Although it is not possible to count people from satellite imagery, good results have been obtained in studies that have used imagery to estimate small-area demographic statistics, and particularly housing statistics, by disaggregating large-area counts. For example, Langford, Maguire and Unwin (1991) demonstrated the use of these techniques for Leicestershire; Deichmann (1996) has used them to build a world population map at high spatial resolution; and Clarke, Hoppen and Gaydos (1997) have used them to calibrate spatial models of urban growth in the San Francisco Bay area.

The use of remote sensing for social and economic research raises a host of technical and social issues. The visible part of the spectrum, which is most useful for mapping applications, is obstructed by cloud, and certain areas of the Earth's surface, particularly in the tropics, are almost never totally cloud-free. Certain types of features and land-cover classes are easily differentiated, but others are not; remote sensing thus inevitably favours things that can be differentiated from space over things that cannot. Issues of SURVEILLANCE and invasion of privacy arise when satellites fly over foreign countries, or when high spatial resolutions make it possible to detect and possibly to identify vehicles. While not normally associated with the term, modern technologies that make it possible to identify vehicle licence numbers from imaging devices at the roadside are also a form of remote sensing, and constitute collection of information about individuals without their informed consent. MG

References

Clarke, K.C., Hoppen, S. and Gaydos, L. 1997: A self-modifying cellular automaton model of historical urbanization in the San Francisco Bay area. *Environment and Planning B: Planning and Design* 24: 247–61. · Deichmann, U. 1996: A *review of spatial population database design and modeling*. Technical Report 96–3. Santa Barbara, CA: National Center for Geographic Information and Analysis. · Langford, M., Maguire, D. and Unwin, D. 1991: The areal interpolation problem: estimating population using remote sensing in a GIS framework. In I. Masser and M. Blakemore, eds, *Handling geographic information*. Harlow: Longman, 55–77.

Suggested Reading

Lillesand, T.M. and Kiefer, R.W. 1994: *Remote sensing and image interpretation*. New York: Wiley. · Ryerson, R.A., ed., 1996: *Manual of remote sensing*, 3rd edn. Bethesda, Maryland: American Society for Photogrammetry and Remote Sensing.

rent Formally defined, rent is any payment to a FACTOR OF PRODUCTION over and above that necessary to keep it in its present use. Under this definition, pieces of industrial machinery, professors of geography, and plots of land are all potentially capable of accruing rent. However, ECONOMIC GEOGRAPHY, the sub-discipline most concerned with rent, has exclusively studied it as a payment for a plot of land. Rent to economic geographers, then, means exclusively land rent (and typically not even housing rent). There is one other definitional wrinkle: because land exists irrespective of remuneration – it cost nothing to produce and freely exists – then from the initial definition, all of a payment going to land is rent. So, unlike other factors of production, e.g. industrial machinery or geography professors, where part of their remuneration is non-rental, in the case of land its recompense is defined as wholly rental.

But what determines the precise level of rent on any specific tract of land? Two broad factors are recognized: differences in land characteristics, and differences in social POWER around the ownership of land. Note that these two factors are associated with two quite different theoretical traditions investigating land rent (and found in economic geography): NEO-CLASSICAL and MARXIAN ECONOMICS. Neo-classical economics begins with land as part of a pristine NATURE that is inherently differentiated and scarce, which through the forces of supply and demand translates into specific rental levels. Because landowners are conceived as passive, ownership itself is irrelevant to the precise rental level set; the only important factor is the differential characteristics of the plots of land themselves. In contrast, Marxians begin with nature socially transformed from the outset, with scarcity, and thereby rental levels established by a set of broader social relations, of which the most important is the active power invested in land owners (Barnes, 1988). While land characteristics play a role, they are always subordinate to social relations.

Differences in land characteristics, the first of the factors, and most associated with the neo-classical scheme, produce what is called *differential rent*, which arises because of two separate causes. The first is locational, and is garnered because of unequal distances between different plots of land and some common fixed point such as a market place (Chisholm, 1962). Seen in VON THÜNEN'S MODEL, which assumes that agricultural crops are cultivated at varying distances around a town, which is also their sole market, crops grown closer to town will make savings in terms of TRANSPORT COSTS compared with crops cultivated farther out. Those savings, in turn, through a competitive process among farmers, are eventually bid away in the form of differential rents: closer plots of land command higher rents than more distant ones because of greater transportation savings. Here, rent acts as a rationing device in ensuring that each plot of land is used in the best possible way. For only those farmers growing crops that make the best use of a given location (that is, maximize transportation savings) are able to outbid all the others and capture the desired plot of land (Chisholm, 1962).

The second cause of *differential rent* is differential land PRODUCTIVITY, which, following the English classical economist David Ricardo (1772–1823), arises because of both natural and human-made differences in the land. Ricardo distinguishes two forms of differential rent: *extensive differential rent*, where all plots of land have equal amounts of capital investment, and *intensive differential rent*, where investments are unequal (Barnes, 1988). In both cases, differential rent is determined by the difference in cost between any productive (technically the 'intramarginal') plot of land, and the so-called marginal plot. The marginal plot is land so unproductive that the cost of producing a crop there is equal to its market price, thereby leaving no room for rent. Note too, that an equivalent to the marginal land exists in von Thünen's model: land located so far from the market that transportation savings are zero, and hence rent too.

Marxists recognize counterparts to Ricardo's extensive and intensive differential rents, which they call respectively differential rents (DR) I and II. They are calculated in a similar manner to their Ricardian equivalents (although see Ball's, 1977, unorthodox analysis of DR II). Quite different, though, is the rationale for differential rent. In the neoclassical interpretation of Ricardo and von Thünen, differential rent is portrayed as an index of natural scarcity whether of locations or differentially fertile lands, while in the Marxist account, such as Katz's (1986, p. 67), it is an expression of the 'monopoly power of capital as a whole': CAPITALISM is the culprit, not a niggardly nature.

In the case of land, one group, the landowners, has an overwhelming monopoly power, which, according to Marx, they use to demand two additional forms of rent beyond DR I and II: absolute and monopoly rents. *Absolute rent* is the difference between the labour value (see LABOUR THEORY OF VALUE) of a crop and its price of production (see MARXIAN ECONOMICS), and occurs because of the power of landowners as a CLASS to prevent new capital investment in agriculture. By keeping the capital/labour ratio artificially low, labour values and prices necessarily diverge to the advantage of the landowner (Sheppard and Barnes, 1990, pp. 129–32). *Monopoly rent* represents the most naked form of landowner power occurring when owners hold back land, not leasing it until they receive a positive return above some minimum threshold level beyond DR I and II (Harvey, 1974).

These classic theorizations of rent are all set within an agricultural context, but there have been extensions to the urban realm. The neoclassical ALONSO MODEL of urban land rent is based upon the VON THÜNEN MODEL, and subsequently refined in countless ways by the new urban economics, an extension of REGIONAL SCIENCE. Harvey (1973, 1974) has also refashioned Marx's rental categories for the city, especially the idea of monopoly rent. In addition, Harvey's student, Neil Smith (1979), developed his own Marxist-inspired analysis of rent, the RENT GAP, although some claim it is based upon the neo-classical concept of opportunity cost. Finally, there have been attempts to analyse rents that stem from fixed capital within the city, i.e. buildings and structures that have a 'life' of more than a year. Formal modelling of this type of rent is very complex, however, involving the intricacies of joint products, and generally has not been pursued (Sheppard and Barnes, 1990, ch. 7). TJB

References

Ball, M. 1977: Differential rent and the role of landed property. *International Journal of Urban and Regional Research* 1: 380–403. · Barnes, T.J. 1988: Scarcity and agricultural land rent in light of the capital controversy: three views. *Antipode* 20: 207–38. · Chisholm, M. 1962: *Rural settlement and land use: an essay in location*. London: Hutchinson. · Harvey, D. 1973: *Social justice and the city*. London: Edward Arnold. · Harvey, D. 1974: Class monopoly rent, finance capital, and the urban revolution. *Regional Studies* 8: 239–55. · Katz, S. 1986: Towards a sociological definition of rent: notes on David Harvey's *Limits to capital*. *Antipode* 18: 64–76. · Sheppard, E. and Barnes, T.J. 1990: *The capitalist space economy: geographical analysis after Ricardo, Marx and Sraffa*. London: Unwin Hyman. · Smith, N. 1979: Toward a theory of gentrification: a back to the city movement by capital not people. *Journal of the American Planners Association* 45: 538–48.

Suggested Reading

Ball (1977). · Scott, A.J. 1976: Land and land rent: an interpretive review of the French literature. *Progress in Geography*, vol. 9: 101–46. London: Edward Arnold. · Sheppard, E. and Barnes, T.J. (1990), ch. 6.

rent gap The rent gap describes the discrepancy between actual rent attracted by a piece of land ('capitalized ground rent') and the rent that could be gleaned under a higher and better use ('potential ground rent'). The rent gap is a central element in explanations of GENTRIFICATION (Smith, 1979, 1996; Clark, 1995). To the extent that disinvestment in the built

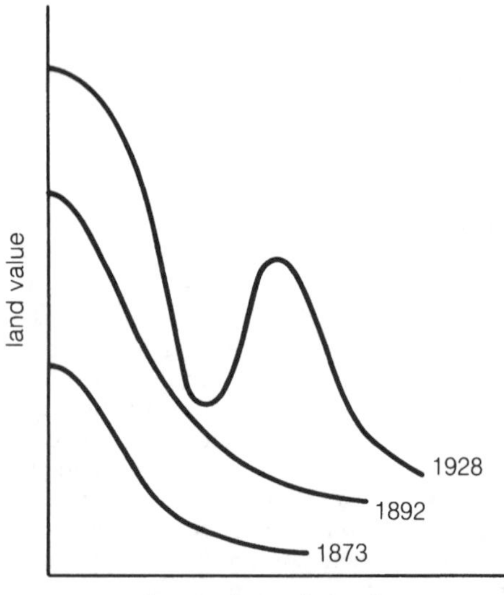

rent gap *The evolution of land values in Chicago* (after Hoyt, 1933)

environment brings about a reciprocal decline in ground rent for the land on which structures sit, the rent gap expands and the opportunities for reinvestment increase. Geographically, the rent gap has emerged in INNER-CITY areas where disinvestment was not sufficiently compensated by reinvestment, and a distinct valley in land values resulted (see the figure). Empirically, the rent gap has been identified in cities on three continents (Clark, 1987; Badcock, 1989) as a precursor to gentrification. Although subjected to some criticism (Beauregard, 1990; Hamnett, 1991), the rent gap, in the light of 1990s gentrification tied closely to economic swings, remains a theoretical linchpin in explanations of gentrification. NS

References

Badcock, B. 1989: Smith's Rent Gap Hypothesis: an Australian view. *Annals of the Association of American Geographers* 79: 125–45. · Beauregard, R. 1990. Trajectories of neighborhood change: the case of gentrification. *Environment and Planning A* 22: 855–74. · Clark, E. 1987: *The rent gap and urban change: case studies in Malmo, 1860–1985*. Lund: Lund University Press. · Clark, E. 1995. The rent gap re-examined. *Urban Studies* 32: 1489–503. · Hamnett, C. 1991: The blind men and the elephant: the explanation of gentrification. *Transactions, Institute of British Geographers* NS 16: 173–89. · Smith, N. 1979: Toward a theory of gentrification: a back to the city movement by capital not people. *Journal of the American Planners Association* 45: 538–48. · Smith, N. 1996: *The new urban frontier*. London: Routledge.

replacement rates Measures of the extent to which a given population is replacing itself. Natural increase, the simple balance of births over deaths, is too strongly influenced by age structures to give a real measure of replacement of generations (see AGE AND SEX STRUCTURE). Three single-number indicators are frequently used instead: the *total fertility rate*, the *gross reproduction rate* and the *net reproduction rate* (see FERTILITY). The last of these (NRR) is most used. Devised by R.R. Kuczynski (1935), it measures the average number of daughters produced by a woman during her reproductive life-time, taking into account MORTALITY. If the NRR is less than 1 then the population will ultimately decline; if it equals 1 then the population is stationary. PEO

Reference

Kuczynski, R.R. 1935: *The measurement of population growth: methods and results*. London: Sidgwick and Jackson; New York: Oxford University Press.

Suggested Reading

Woods, R.I. 1979: *Population analysis in geography*. London and New York: Longman, ch. 5.

representation A set of practices by which meanings are constituted and communicated. Such representational practices produce and circulate meanings among members of social groups and these meanings can be defined as CULTURE. Such shared meanings are based on representations of the world. Representations not only reflect reality, but they help to constitute reality. People make sense of their worlds and are positioned within social worlds through representations. Some representations are imposed on them from the outside but these are also contested by representations generated from within the culture. Thus imagined geographies are contested by 'rival' geographies (Smith and Godlewska, 1994).

Spivak (1988) makes a useful distinction between two interrelated definitions of the term representation: speaking of and speaking for. Representation (re-presentation) is a description or depiction of some aspect of reality. If that reality is a cultural reality or understanding that in some sense belongs to a cultural group other than that of the representer, then EPISTEMOLOGICAL and ETHICAL issues of rights and responsibilities to speak on behalf of OTHERS may be raised. Geography and other fields, particularly anthropology, have experienced what is referred to as a 'crisis of representation' brought about by post-colonial and feminist critiques which challenge the ETHNOCENTRISM and MASCULINISM of grand narratives of western theorists (Barnett, 1997; see also FEMINIST GEOGRAPHIES; POST-COLONIALISM; SUBALTERN STUDIES).

Issues of representation have come into prominence in geography mainly through CULTURAL GEOGRAPHY (Schein, 1993; Pred, 1997), post-structural CARTOGRAPHY (Harley, 1992), CRITICAL GEOPOLITICS (O'Tuathail, 1994), and post-positivist feminism (Gibson-Graham, 1997). The principal influences in these subfields have been SOCIAL CONSTRUCTIONISM, POST-COLONIALISM and POST-STRUCTURALISM. Although there are profound differences among such theoretical traditions (principally on issues of REALISM versus anti-FOUNDATIONALISM), all reject simple reflective or 'mimetic' theories of representation. All support the idea that language and other forms of cultural representation are to some degree constitutive of the reality they represent.

The realist or Marxian version of social constructionism suggests that representations can often affect or even help to constitute the realities which they refer to. REIFICATIONS are representations that have become alienated or naturalized in the sense that their social origins are forgotten (Ollman, 1971; see MARXIST GEOGRAPHY). On the other hand the most extreme anti-FOUNDATIONALIST positions deny the very possibility of representing an external reality. From such a point of view, representations are necessarily flawed attempts to represent the 'unpresentable' (Derrida, 1981).

If one accepts that representation is an active, constitutive practice, then it follows that knowledge cannot be neutral or innocent of POWER relations. For example, ORIENTALISM is implicated in the history of western IMPERIALISM (Said, 1977, 1993): the tropes and METAPHORS used in orientalist DISCOURSE can be deconstructed to reveal and destabilize the binary oppositions that structure representations of Asia and Asians into a hierarchical world-view. Western geographers have tended to marginalize or effectively silence cultural Others through universalizing theories and models of human behaviour. They have presumed an authority to speak on the behalf of cultural others (Duncan and Sharp, 1993; Barnett, 1997). When cultural differences *are* represented, homogenizing and excluding dichotomies are often employed to essentialize and exoticize difference (see ESSENTIALISM). The use of binary oppositions to define the western self in contrast to non-western Others leads inevitably to the devaluation of the Other. The goal of many contemporary geographers is to replace unitary representations with plural and complexly intersecting understandings.

Post-colonial theorists have sought to refine the starkness of Said's self–other analysis with ideas of HYBRIDITY, THIRD or interstitial SPACES, sites of resistance, complicity, TRANSCULTURATION, scattered HEGEMONIES and internally differentiated politics of colonial knowledge.

The politics and POETICS of geographical representation have come under intense scrutiny in recent work by geographers who have initiated a more self-critical approach to the tropes and rhetorical strategies of academic geography itself (Barnes and Gregory, 1997; Pratt, 1992; Duncan, 1996). Travel literature as geographical knowledge has also been the focus of much recent discussion (see TRAVEL WRITING, GEOGRAPHY AND). The pleasures of the masculine gaze underlying geographical representations of landscape have come under attack (Rose, 1993; Sparke, 1996).

Representations are not only TEXTS, words, and pictures, but may include material culture such as LANDSCAPES as well. Although not referential in the simple one-to-one sense of expressing a prior reality, landscapes communicate multiple and heterogeneous messages and stimulate highly active although not necessarily conscious readings (King, 1996; Barnes and Duncan, 1992). People select, appropriate, recompose and particularize the meanings of such material, cultural phenomena as landscapes.

Lefebvre makes a distinction between sensuous lived 'representational spaces' and the more dispassionately articulated 'representations of space' (Lefebvre, 1991) (see PRODUCTION OF SPACE). Landscapes *re*-present and often reify cultural values; but landscapes as representations can be dereified as well. Often people react in their everyday spatial practices to the culturally specific meanings of their lived environments in ways they may not be able to articulate. They may uncritically accept cultural ideas and social relations embedded in landscapes because landscapes are taken for granted as material facts of life, as non-ideological. Alternatively people may intentionally resist and subvert the dominant readings of their landscapes, thereby creating new representations of space (Cresswell, 1996). JD

References

Barnes, T. and Gregory, D., eds, 1997: *Reading human geography*. London: Arnold. · Barnes, T. and Duncan, J., eds, 1992: *Writing worlds*. London: Routledge. · Barnett, C. 1997: Sing along with the common people: politics, postcolonialism and other figures. *Environment and Planning D: Society and Space* 15: 137–54. · Cresswell, T. 1996: *In place/out of place: geography, ideology and transgression*. Minneapolis: University of Minnesota Press. · Derrida, J. 1981: *Positions*. Chicago: Chicago University Press. · Duncan, J. 1996: Me(trope)olis: or Hayden White among the urbanists. In A. King, ed., *Re-presenting the city*. London: Macmillan. · Duncan, N. and Sharp, J. 1993: Confronting representation(s). *Environment and Planning D: Society and Space* 11: 473–86. · Gibson-Graham, J.K. 1997: Postmodern becomings. In G. Benko and U. Strohmayer, eds, *Space and social theory*. Oxford: Blackwell. · Harley, J.B. 1992: Deconstructing the map. In T. Barnes and J. Duncan, eds, *Writing worlds*. London: Routledge. · King, A., ed., 1996: *Re-presenting the city*. London: Macmillan. · Lefebvre, H. 1991: *The production of space*. London, Blackwell. · Ollman, B. 1971: *Alienation: Marx's conception of man in capitalist society*. Cambridge: Cambridge University Press. · Ó'Tuathail, G. 1994: (Dis)placing geopolitics. *Environment and Planning D: Society and Space* 12: 525–46. · Pratt, G. 1992: Spatial metaphors and speaking positions. *Environment and Planning D: Society and Space* 10: 241–4. · Pred, A. 1997: Re-presenting the extended present moment of danger. In G. Benko and U. Strohmayer, eds, *Space and social theory*. Oxford: Blackwell. · Rose, G. 1993: *Feminism and geography: the limits of geographical knowledge*. Cambridge: Polity. · Said, E. 1977: *Orientalism*. New York: Phaidon. · Said, E. 1993: *Culture and imperialism*. New York: Alfred Knopf. ·

Schein, R. 1993: Representing urban America: nineteenth century views of landscape, space, power. *Environment and Planning D: Society and Space* 11: 7–21. · Smith, N. and Godlewska, A., eds, 1994: *Geography and empire*. Oxford: Blackwell. · Sparke, M. 1996: Displacing the field is fieldwork: masulinity, metaphor and space. In N. Duncan, ed., *Body Space* destabilizing geographier of gender and sexuality. London: Routledge, 212–33. · Spivak, G. 1988: Can the subaltern speak? In C. Nelson and L. Grossberg, eds, *Marxism and the interpretation of culture*. London: Macmillan, 217–313.

Suggested Reading

Barnes and Duncan (1992). · Barnett (1997).

residual The difference between the estimated and actual value for an observation on the dependent variable in a REGRESSION equation: a positive residual is where the observed value exceeds that estimated for it; a negative value is where the estimate is larger. The largest residuals indicate where the estimating equation has relatively failed and Haggett (1965) suggested that advances in geographical research can be achieved by mapping residual values to inaugurate a search for new causal variables. Maps of residuals are used to test whether SPATIAL AUTOCORRELATION is present. RJJ

Reference and Suggested Reading

Haggett, P. 1965: *Locational analysis in human geography*. London: Edward Arnold. · Johnston, R.J. 1978: *Multivariate statistical analysis in geography: a primer on the general linear model*. London and New York: Longman.

resistance This has two distinctive meanings in geography: *political resistance*, the more common usage, refers to resistance to domination or oppression; *psychic resistance* refers to unconscious attempts to maintain repressions of traumatic or dangerous memories (see PSYCHOANALYTIC THEORY, GEOGRAPHY AND). Pile and Keith (1997) discuss how the two concepts work in relation to each other.

Debates about political resistance crystallize key trends in critical geography. MARXIST GEOGRAPHY has a long tradition of studying collective organizing and everyday resistance to CLASS exploitation, and struggle against PATRIARCHY is well articulated in FEMINIST GEOGRAPHY. Resistance places emphasis on the creativity, ingenuity and resilience of non-dominant groups and individuals. But what Loomba and Kaul (1994, p. 3, quoted in Moore, 1997) described as a 'tropology of resistance and hybridity' emerged through the 1980s. It was part of the CULTURAL TURN, reflecting the influence of IDENTITY and CULTURAL POLITICS. The frame of politics was enlarged to include a myriad everyday symbolic and material practices that contest not only class exploitation but also gender, racial, sexual (and other) forms of domination and oppression. James Scott's *Weapons of the weak* was a key text in which he identified as everyday resistance:

> foot dragging, dissimulation, desertion, false compliance, pilfering, feigned ignorance, slander, arson, sabotage, and so on. These Brechtian – or Schweikian – forms of class struggle have certain features in common. They require little or no coordination or planning; they make use of implicit understandings and informal networks; they often represent a form of individual self-help; they typically avoid any direct, symbolic confrontation with authority. (1985, p. xvi)

Concern was soon raised that that concept of resistance had become both too encompassing and too weak. When almost every action is conceptualized as resistance, critical distinctions between effective and ineffective political resistance, and commitments to collective organizing and the coordination across different forms of domination, may be lost (Pile and Keith, 1997).

Spatial vocabulary has been important for conceptualizing the relations between resistance and POWER. James Scott is credited with conceiving resistance outside domination, in the sense that resistant subjects are conceived as authoring their identities outside and beyond the reach of dominant groups, in spaces of relative autonomy (for a review of criticisms of Scott's text, see Moore, 1997). Those influenced by Foucault's version of POST-STRUCTURALISM reject this spatialization; from a Foucauldian perspective, resistance is neither inside nor outside but 'present everywhere in the power network' (1990, p. 95). This is in part because subjectivity, resistant or otherwise, emerges in relation to dominant discourse (see SUBJECT FORMATION, GEOGRAPHIES OF). To cite a familiar example, if the term 'queer' now functions as a critique and a means of destabilizing heteronormativity, it first emerged as a mechanism to effect the opposite: to stabilize both heteronormativity and bourgeois class superiority; it is inextricably intertwined with dominant CULTURE (see QUEER THEORY). De Certeau's vocabulary of *tactics* of resistance (as opposed to strategies of power) evokes a similar spatial imagery: a tactic 'cannot count on a "proper" (a spatial or institutional) localization . . . A tactic insinuates into the other's place' (1984, p. xix). A third spatial relation emerged out of an appreciation of the complexity of identity formation, in terms of both the multiplicities of identities negotiated by each individual and the HYBRIDITY of cultures; this locates resistance in spaces in between varying systems of oppression (see THIRD SPACE; Pile and Keith, 1997).

This spatial vocabulary is more than metaphorical; there is a rich body of writing about the geographies in which resistance develops and the ways that resistance is mobilized through space. Pile and Keith (1997) urge that resistance cannot, however, be easily located in particular spatial practices and warn against assumptions that resistance is aligned with, for example, mobility, the permeability of boundaries, or the local. In the latter case, recent theorizing points to the ways in which the production of SCALE is itself an outcome of political struggle (Smith, 1993; Massey, 1998) and new models for organizing resistance globally attempt to build networks that respect local specificity (Grewal and Kaplan, 1994). GP

References

de Certeau, M. 1984: *The practice of everyday life*. Berkeley: University of California Press. · Foucault, M. 1990: *The history of sexuality, volume I: an introduction*, trans. R. Hurley. New York: Vintage. · Grewal, I. and Kaplan, C., eds, 1994: *Scattered hegemonies: postmodernity and transnational feminist practices*. Minneapolis: University of Minnesota Press. · Loomba, A. and Kaul, S. 1994: Introduction: location, culture, post-coloniality. *Oxford Literary Review* 16: 3–30. · Massey, D. 1998: The spatial construction of youth cultures. In T. Skelton and G. Valentine, eds, *Cool places: geographies of youth cultures*. London: Routledge, 121–9. · Moore, D. 1997: Remapping resistance: 'ground for struggle' and the politics of place. In S. Pile and M. Keith, eds, *Geographies of resistance*. London: Routledge, 87–106. · Pile, S. and Keith, M., eds, 1997: *Geographies of resistance*. London: Routledge. · Scott, J. 1985: *Weapons of the weak: everyday forms of peasant resistance*. New Haven: Yale University Press. · Smith, N. 1993: Homeless: global: scaling places. In J. Bird, B. Curtis, T. Putnam, G. Robertson and L. Tickner, eds, *Mapping the futures: local cultures, global change*. London: Routledge, 87–119.

resource A concept used to denote sources of human satisfaction, wealth or strength. Labour, entrepreneurial skills, investment funds, fixed capital assets, technology, knowledge, social stability and cultural and physical attributes may be referred to as the resources of a country (or household, corporation, region and even the world – e.g. attempts under the rubric of SUSTAINABLE DEVELOPMENT to represent the Amazon rainforest as a global resource). Resources may be used for both desirable and undesirable means, e.g. to wage war.

In a RESOURCE MANAGEMENT context, the term is usually restricted to NATURAL RESOURCES, which are substances, organisms and properties of the physical environment that are valued for their perceived ability to satisfy human needs and wants. People, acting through CULTURE, evaluate NATURE and decide that certain of its elements are 'resources' while others may be either disregarded or perceived as a pest, weed or danger. This *perceived resource set* alters markedly over time and space to reflect variations in knowledge, technology, social structures, economic conditions and political systems. The expansion of the resource base to include more elements of nature, e.g. through ecotourism, causes concern among many ENVIRONMENTALISTS who believe humans should 'tread lightly' on the earth. The notion of 'resource' is human centred, and assumes that nature is available to satisfy human wants and needs (see ECOLOGY; ENVIRONMENTALISM). Viewing the entire world as resources for human consumption is known as '*resourcism*'.

The question of whether there are LIMITS TO GROWTH is based on the perception of available resources and the relative importance given to specific resources: for example, Julian Simon (1994) emphasizes the importance of human ingenuity whereas Meadows et al. (1992) stress the finite aspect of resources (materials and ENERGY) in throughput (i.e. the extraction, production, consumption and the disposal of wastes into nature's sinks, e.g. air, water). Meadows et al. (1992) saw the extraction of resources and the disposal of wastes so as not to deplete our resource base, as important problems that could not simply be overcome by the application of new technology. This represents a change in their position: previously they, and other authors such as Paul Ehrlich, had suggested that human beings would overexploit important resources, thereby leading to shortages and increased resource prices. However, these claims ignored the POLITICAL ECONOMY of global TRADE (see Zacher, 1993; cf. GLOBALIZATION). Wealthy countries can ensure a supply of cheap resources from developing countries that are burdened with debt, and are competing on international markets with each other, thereby driving down prices. These authors also underestimated technological changes to identify and extract previously unknown, or unrecoverable, resources, and ignored the secrecy aspect of corporations not willing to release knowledge about the full extent of their 'resource reserves'.

In many ways, resources are increasingly being managed for sustainable development through a process of CONSERVATION. This may involve reducing use, but more often involves reusing or RECYCLING products to reduce both material and energy consumption. Given the laws of thermodynamics and particularly the second law (the ENTROPY law), infinite recycling is impossible; the act of recycling also uses some additional energy and materials. There will continue to be a demand for resources to satisfy human needs and wants, but the distribution of resources, access to resources and the pattern of resource use are highly contingent upon social processes. Current resource use patterns are an issue in ENVIRONMENTAL JUSTICE. It is apparent that there are not enough material resources in the world for everybody to have the same material standard of living as is currently enjoyed by people in developed countries. Many authors (including the World Resources Institute, 1994) have suggested that changes must take place in the wealthier countries if we are to have sustainable development in the world.

However, there are also changing conceptions of what is a resource. This includes the patenting of BIODIVERSITY, mainly from countries in the developing world, by corporations from countries in the developed world, in an act that Shiva (1997) has labelled '*biopiracy*'. This raises questions of whose resource is it, who will have access to it, at what price, and how will resource exploitation be avoided? As Shiva (1997) notes, the structures promoting international trade are increasingly making it an infringement to deny TRANSNATIONAL CORPORATIONS access to these materials (i.e. there is the enclosure of the global commons by private property rights: cf. TRAGEDY OF THE COMMONS). The management of resources that have suddenly become (potentially) economically valuable in the wealthy countries calls into question the implementation of conservation and sustainable development. PM

References

Meadows, D.H., Meadows, D.L. and Randers, J. 1992: *Beyond the limits: global collapse or a sustainable future*. London: Earthscan. · Shiva, V. 1997: *Biopiracy: the plunder of nature and knowledge*. Toronto: Between the Lines. · Simon, J. 1994: More people, greater wealth, more resources, healthier environment. *Economic Affairs* 14 3: 22–9. · World Resources Institute 1994: *World resources 1994–95*. New York and Oxford: Oxford University Press. · Zacher, M., ed., 1993: *The international political economy of natural resources*, 2 vols. Aldershot and Brookfield, Vermont: Edward Elgar Publishing Limited.

Suggested Reading

Emel, J. and Bridge, G. 1995: The earth as input: resources. In R. Johnston, P. Taylor and M. Watts, eds, *Geographies of global change: remapping the world in the late twentieth century*. Oxford and Cambridge, MA: Blackwell, 318–32. · Rees, J. 1991: *Natural resources: allocation, economics and policy*, 2nd edn. London and New York: Routledge.

resource economics A branch of RESOURCE MANAGEMENT which uses economic instruments to prevent or ameliorate the over-exploitation of resources. Like ENVIRONMENTAL ECONOMICS, resource economics sees an absent or uncorrected market as largely responsible for resource over-exploitation. Two main classes of economically induced resource problems are recognized. Following economist Harold Hotelling (1931), the first problem, *discounting the future*, is particularly applicable to non-renewable resources like oil, coal and copper. Although historically few non-renewable RESOURCES have been exploited to the point of absolute scarcity, many have been exploited to the point of social scarcity. Discounting partly explains this. It describes a situation where, because of the nature of economic interest rates and people's social preferences, 'people prefer a benefit today or this year to one tomorrow or next year: a social time preference exists for the present over the future' (Chapman and Mather, 1995, p. 33). Thus resources are used heavily in the present rather than being exploited with a view to the future and future generations. The second class of economically induced resource problem, following economist H. Scott Gordon (1954), concerns *common – or unowned/open-access – resources* and is particularly applicable to renewable resources, like oceanic fish stocks. The problem arises because open-access encourages a free-for-all in which producers scramble for a share of the resource before their rivals take it, leading ultimately to resource over-exploitation – as has happened for several species of whales and, recently, for the Newfoundland cod fishery (see TRAGEDY OF THE COMMONS).

For resource economics the solution to these problems is not (as one might suppose) to abandon the market but to 'correct' it so that it is more eco-friendly. From being eco-villain, the market is thus proposed as eco-saviour. This is achieved through a variety of so-called 'economic instruments' which 'decouple' economic growth from resource/environmental exhaustion and degradation. First, discounting the future can be averted by governmental intervention to either alter interest rates or else impose sustainable use policies (e.g. through a resource depletion tax) in specific resource sectors (cf. SUSTAINABLE DEVELOPMENT). Second, the common resource problem can be averted by either PRIVATIZING the resource or else imposing a government ceiling on resource take.

Although resource economics has enjoyed some success in reducing resource use, in practice it is subject to a number of technical problems (Rees, 1990, ch. 9). In addition, more radical economists associated with POLITICAL ECONOMY argue, first, that resource economics deals only with the symptom of resource problems – the market – and not the real cause – CAPITALISM – and, second, that it ignores questions of the social distribution of resource problems. Finally, ecocentrists, like Greenpeace, worry that it is anthropocentric, putting humans – rather than NATURE – first. (See also: ENVIRONMENTALISM.) NC

References

Gordon, H.S. 1954: The economic theory of a common-property resource: the fishery. *Journal of Political Economy* 62: 124–42. · Hotelling, H. 1931: The economics of exhaustible resources. *Journal of Political Economy* 39: 137–75. · Mather, A.S. and Chapman, K. 1995: *Environmental resources*. Harlow: Longman. · Rees, J. 1990: *Natural Resources*, 2nd edn. London: Routledge.

resource evaluation A generic term for assessments which attempt to decide either the value (physical, economic or perceptual) of a RESOURCE, or the consequences and adequacy of RESOURCE MANAGEMENT strategies. Generalizing, the concept has been applied to five main areas of work:

Ascertaining the quantity and quality of resource supplies. This includes both renewable and non-renewable NATURAL RESOURCES, and identifying the 'recoverable' resources, i.e. those that are potentially economically feasible to extract given physical conditions and levels of technology. The availability of resources is dynamic, depending upon past use patterns and investment or CONSERVATION decisions.

Ascertaining the value of a resource. Value may include actual use value (the current benefits derived from using a particular resource), option value (anticipation of benefits derived from potential future use, which is influenced by factors such as technological change and a decline in the availability of substitutes) and intrinsic value (see ENVIRONMENTALISM). These values may be decided by market prices, set government prices, opportunity costs, labour value (cf. MARXIAN ECONOMICS), social indicators, ENERGY accounting, public preferences and ecological (intrinsic) values (see ENVIRONMENTAL PERCEPTION; WELFARE GEOGRAPHY). Work by Pearce (1994) highlights some issues in the so-called 'environmental values debate'.

Ascertaining the capacity of ECOSYSTEMS to support human life and development over time (see SUSTAINABLE DEVELOPMENT). This includes the CARRYING CAPACITY of land and water, the assimilative capacity of land, water and air to assimilate wastes (see POLLUTION) and the 'ecological footprint' of the population (see Wackernagel and Rees, 1996).

Assessing the likely consequences of proposed resource programmes, projects, policies and administrative changes (see COST–BENEFIT ANALYSIS; ENVIRONMENTAL AUDIT; ENVIRONMENTAL IMPACT ASSESSMENT).

Assessing the adequacy and/or effectiveness of existing resource management strategies. The evaluation criteria used are crucial to the results of any assessment. Possible criteria for evaluation may include meeting stated policy objectives, economic efficiency, equity of distribution of resources and benefits, employment generation, creating wider accessibility to a region, or achieving sustainable development. PM

References and Suggested Reading

Pearce, D. 1994: The great environmental values debate. *Environment and Planning A* 26: 1329–38. · Wackernagel, M. and Rees, W. 1996: *Our ecological footprint: reducing human impact on the earth*. Gabriola Island, British Columbia: New Society Publishers.

resource management (1) A broad multidisciplinary area or programme of study focusing on the management of NATURAL RESOURCES. This includes both renewable and non-renewable RESOURCES that are managed by private enterprise, public-sector agencies or community-based forms of management. It seeks to:

- explain the processes (physical, socio-economic, cultural and political) involved in resource supply, exploitation and consumption;
- analyse the allocation of resource products and services over space and time;
- evaluate management systems, policies, programmes and practices; and
- develop alternative management strategies and evaluatory tools.

Although issues of resource management have a long history (see CONSERVATION), the recognition of resource management as a distinct area of inquiry has occurred largely since the 1960s with the growth of ENVIRONMENTALISM. It is sometimes seen as a sub-field of *environmental management*, and sometimes the terms appear to be used interchangeably.

Contemporary resource management is linked closely to the notion of SUSTAINABLE DEVELOPMENT. It is often seen as part of the technocratic approach to looking at human–NATURE relationships and is sometimes opposed by environmentalists who believe that humans should manage themselves and their consumer lifestyles, rather than attempting to manage nature as a resource for human purposes. Nesmith and Wright (1995) emphasize the GENDER dimensions of resource management, and argue that women have played key roles, over many years, in moving towards more participatory forms of resource management and towards sustainability. Wolfe-Keddie (1995) and Aplin (1998) highlight the importance of indigenous people in resource management over many years.

Despite these conceptual changes, the multidisciplinary field of resource management sometimes fails to address the complex interrelationships between physical, social, economic and political systems. This is particularly the case when resource management is seen as the application of scientific fact (often ignoring cultural considerations), and when the field becomes very specialized into the management of specific resources, e.g. water management. Geographers have participated in the field of resource management primarily through resource analysis, but increasingly there is work on environmental VALUES and perceptions of resources (Nesmith and Wright, 1995).

Johnston (1983) investigated the potential for integration of human and physical geography through this field, but found that the case for links across the human/physical divide remained weak in comparison to links with related disciplines, e.g. sociology. The attempt to unite human and physical geography by using aspects of the environment (as done by Manning, 1990, in relation to sustainable development) has been a recurring theme in the discipline of geography, but has to date met with little success.

resource management (2) A process or system of DECISION-MAKING about the use, CONSERVATION and future of what has been labelled as a RESOURCE. The SCALE of resource management may range from a single resource, e.g. fish, through to the global ecosphere. Resource management may be conducted through a rational, scientific–technical ends–means approach, or it may explicitly incorporate VALUES (More et al., 1996). *Ends–means management* involves meeting clearly defined objectives by devising appropriate administrative structures, selecting and employing appropriate management tools and creating effective implementation strategies: in this context, environmental problems are generally seen as results of inadequate or inappropriate management structures, rather than from values, ETHICS, IDEOLOGY and POWER relationships.

Resource management involves the interrelationship of many decisions by private sector organizations, government bodies, environmental groups, community groups and individual householders. The choices for resource management structures range from the currently unfashionable STATE-SOCIALISM model of eastern Europe and other countries, through to no STATE 'interference', as advocated by self-labelled Free Market Environmentalists (e.g. Julian Simon, 1981) and the Wise Use Movement in western North America. Resource management structures generally include some form of state–private sector interaction. Sometimes this is formalized into partnerships, as in the Landcare groups in Australia (Curtis and De Lacy, 1996), but often it involves governments funding programmes and subsidizing activities that are left to the individual landholder or consumer to follow through. There has been a trend, in countries such as New Zealand (see May et al., 1996), for the public sector management of resources to be handled at the local, rather than national, level of government. However, this is not the case throughout the world for resources that are considered critical to a country's 'national interest'. Within the public sector, resource management also includes legislating and managing state-owned resources or resource-using industries. This latter role is still important, but in the 1990s has been eroded due to the PRIVATIZATION strategies of many governments who have attempted to make such industries attractive for private ownership. The requirement of corporate profitability necessitates new regulatory or monitoring approaches to ensure that natural-resource management does not neglect crucial environmental and social considerations. The issues of who should regulate, and how, have become important. Business groups often favour self-regulation, but this is deemed unacceptable by many environmental, COMMUNITY and left-wing political groups.

Academic work on resource management has also included critiques from POLITICAL-ECONOMY perspectives and the BEHAVIOURAL GEOGRAPHY approach to analysing decision-making behaviour within firms, with some academics and practitioners working on the integration of these in the development of effective resource management strategies. However, unlike some political-economy approaches, they often favour economic incentives over regulation as effective resource management tools, a difference that can be traced back to deep ideological divides between STRUCTURALISM and PLURALISM. The resource management approaches favoured by authors such as Pearce and Turner (1990) and Turner (1995) focus on the creation of new markets to permit trade in resource and POLLUTION permits, for example. This approach is often favoured where ECOSYSTEMS are threatened by the successful CONSERVATION of a particular species, e.g. elephants, and some form of culling is considered desirable, but is controversial.

Recent work in environmental management has focused on the establishment of international standards by the International Organization for Standardization, a non-government organization based in Geneva. ISO 14000 relates to the standardization of environmental management systems and their components, e.g. ENVIRONMENTAL AUDITS. This is both a management process, and a yardstick for more localized processes. While this aspect of resource and environmental management is supported by many people, governments and businesses, many parts of the ENVIRONMENTAL MOVEMENT see it as tokenism in relation to the size and character of environmental issues. While the two are not necessarily separate, the division between managing resources (or the wider term 'environments'), and humans managing themselves as part of NATURE, is a key division that will not be easily overcome. The concept of SUSTAINABLE DEVELOPMENT attempted to address this division, but has been criticized for the manner in which it was done. PM

References

Aplin, G. 1998: *Australians and their environment.* Oxford and New York: Oxford University Press. · Curtis, A. and De Lacy, T. 1996: Landcare in Australia: beyond the expert farmer. *Agriculture and Human Values* 13 1: 20–31. · Johnston, R. 1983: Resource analysis, resource management and the integration of physical and human geography. *Progress in Physical Geography* 13: 127–46. · Manning, E. 1990: Presidential Address: sustaining development, the challenge. *The Canadian Geographer* 34 4: 290–320. · May, P. et al. 1996: *Environmental management and governance: intergovernmental approaches to hazards and sustainability.* London and New York: Routledge. · More, T., Averill, J. and Stevens, T. 1996: Values and economics in environmental management: a perspective and critique. *Journal of Environmental Management* 48: 397–409. · Nesmith, C. and Wright, P. 1995: Gender, resources and environmental management. In B. Mitchell, ed., *Resource and environmental management in Canada: addressing conflict and uncertainty.* New York and Toronto: Oxford University Press, 80–98. · Pearce, D. and Turner, R.K. 1990: *The economics of natural resources and the environment.* Hemel Hempstead: Harvester Wheatsheaf. · Simon, J. 1981: *The ultimate resource.* Princeton, NJ: Princeton University Press. · Turner, R.K. 1995: Environmental economics and management. In T. O'Riordan, ed., *Environmental science for environmental management.* Essex: Longman, 30–44. · Wolfe-Keddie, J. 1995: Gender, resources and environmental management. In B. Mitchell, ed., *Resource and environmental management in Canada: addressing conflict and uncertainty.* New York and Toronto: Oxford University Press, 55–79.

Suggested Reading

Aplin (1998). · May, P. et al. 1996: Devolution and co-operation: resource management in New Zealand. *Environmental management and governance: intergovernmental approaches to hazards and sustainability.* London and New York: Routledge, 43–68. · Mitchell, B., ed., 1995: *Resource and environmental management in Canada: addressing conflict and uncertainty.* New York and Toronto: Oxford University Press. · Turner (1995).

restructuring Change(s) in and/or between the constituent parts of a circuit of SOCIAL REPRODUCTION emanating from the dynamics of the circuit itself or from contradictions and crises within it.

Such changes may represent a response to changed conditions induced, for example, by TIME–SPACE COMPRESSION, technical change, conflicts between labour and CAPITAL in the workplace or transmitted through the competitive conditions endemic to CAPITALISM. The inherently competitive social relations of capitalism generate a permanent tendency to transformation or restructuring but the term has come to be more widely used since the end of the long boom in the late 1960s and early 1970s (see CRISIS; MODERNITY). For some it is a process closely associated with the transition from one KONDRATIEFF CYCLE to another or from one REGIME OF ACCUMULATION to another or with the speed of the circulation of capital and the increasing GLOBALIZATION of the world economic geography.

As such, restructuring may be thought to be synonymous with DEVELOPMENT (Streeten, 1987), or at least with certain forms of development. But it goes beyond that. Thus Laurence Harris (1988, p. 10) points out that although there is 'no easy, obvious way to distinguish structural from other changes in the abstract . . . some periods seem to see greater and more significant shifts than others'. He identifies four such periods in the UK since the early nineteenth century: the 1830s and 1840s; the 1880s and 1890s;

the 1930s and 1940s; and the 1970s and 1980s. But what marks these out as periods of restructuring? Apart from certain specific and system-wide components of changes (e.g. those identified by Harris, pp. 11–14), restructuring involves not just quantitative change but pronounced qualitative transformations of the ways in which consumption, production and exchange take place and relate to each other. Furthermore, as a set of essentially qualitative changes operating on the circuit of social reproduction, restructuring necessarily involves transformations of the conditions in which such circuits create and find their conditions of existence.

At an extreme of structural change such as occurred in the transformation of the former state-socialist societies during the late 1980s, the social relations through which the dynamic, direction and mode of evaluation of social reproduction are shaped are themselves transformed and the circuit of social reproduction comes to operate on completely different principles often associated with profound economic disruption and profound social pathologies. The parallels between *perestroika* in the former Soviet Union during the middle 1980s and capitalist restructuring are marked:

> *Perestroika* is inevitable when existing economic conditions do not respond to . . . the needs of development of society and the demands of the future. Here it is necessary to change the economic system, to transform and renew it fundamentally. For this transformation restructuring is necessary not just of individual aspects and elements, but of the whole economic system. (Anganbegyan, 1988, p. 6)

This strategy for development – fatefully for Soviet SOCIALISM – presumed *uskorenie*, an acceleration of economic growth, and *glasnost*, or openness, to be achieved by the spread of DEMOCRACY and local self-management.

The more insidious, continuous and widespread social and political consequences of restructuring driven by the imposition of capitalist social relations and the norms, directions and criteria of evaluation that go with them within the THIRD WORLD are dramatically illustrated in Michael Watts's (1992/1996) harrowing account of 'fast capitalism' and the exploitation of petroleum in Nigeria.

Less dramatic but still profound changes may occur within the dynamics of particular forms of social reproduction such as capitalism (e.g. Harris, 1988). Manuel Castells (1989, pp. 21–8) suggests that certain transformations of the capitalist mode of production on a global scale during the twentieth century are structural in form. Certainly, they serve to exemplify the point that restructuring is qualitative as well as merely quantitative. The Great Depression of the late 1920s and early 1930s and the associated disruption of the Second World War 'triggered a restructuring process that led to a new form of capitalism very different from the laissez-faire model of the pre-Depression era' (p. 21). The new model relied on restructured relations between capital and labour whereby stability in capitalist production was exchanged by the recognition of union rights, rising wages and the development of welfare states; Keynesian regulation and intervention in circuits of capital articulated primarily at the national scale; and the creation of a new set of international regulatory institutions around the International Monetary Fund underwritten by the POWER of the economy of the USA.

The limits of this model manifest, for example, in rampant inflation, increases in returns to labour and FISCAL CRISES of the STATE, were formative influences (for an attempt to assess the articulation of these formative processes see Yergin and Stanislaw, 1998) on the creation and imposition of a restructured model of the circuit of capital involving the appropriation of an increased share of the surplus by capital based around increases in productivity, changes in the LABOUR PROCESS and restructuring of LABOUR MARKETS in terms of: deregulation and reductions in the power of trades unions; a shift in the role of states from intervention to facilitation of capital accumulation; and further deregulation and opening up of local and national spaces to global competitive processes – not least through the increasing significance of globally sensitive and active spheres of reproduction (see ECONOMIC GEOGRAPHY) acting through global financial centres.

Restructuring may involve one or more of a number of transformations:

- STRUCTURAL ADJUSTMENT, which Streeten (1987, p. 1469) defines as 'adaptation to sudden or large, often unexpected changes' to an economic geography. Such changes may, however, be forced by powerful institutions like the World Bank in, for example, making AID dependent on profound changes in macro-economic policy. Structural adjustment programmes have been designed to open up underdeveloped economies to the global economic geography in order to maximize their potential for development. In this sense they may be viewed as a means through which the social relations of capitalism may be spread through the underdeveloped world in ways which make them secure for the future by insisting, for example, on

- transformations in the modes of coordination and exchange within circuits of social reproduction (by, for example, opening up economies to the pressures of market forces and international competition) with the objective of removing local rigidities and reducing vulnerability to shock through means such as increasing the flexibility of markets, the provision of productive INFRASTRUCTURE and the development of institutions orientated to export markets;
- switches of capital between forms of investment (direct/indirect), sphere of circulation of capital (reproduction/production/realization – see ECONOMIC GEOGRAPHY) and sector (e.g. DEINDUSTRIALIZATION);
- geographical switches of capital (here/there – see LAYERS OF INVESTMENT; NEW INTERNATIONAL DIVISION OF LABOUR; UNEVEN DEVELOPMENT). Such changes clearly have substantial implications for the UNEVEN DEVELOPMENT of places (re/dis)incorporated from CIRCUITS OF CAPITAL (see Allen and Massey, 1988; Allen et al., 1998).

More narrowly, the restructuring of production (e.g. Graham et al., 1988) may have significant consequences well beyond production itself:

- changes in the process of production as a consequence of ECONOMIES OF SCALE, the concentration of centralized capital (see MARXIAN ECONOMICS) or transitions from one regime of accumulation to another (see REGULATION SCHOOL);
- changes in the organization of production along the production chain (see Dicken, 1998, ch. 1);
- changes in corporate organization – such as those associated with forms of INTEGRATION within production, multidivisional organization and decentralization in the attempt to combine corporate size whilst maximizing entrepreneurial initiative within the organization;
- the development of tasking flexibility in production, based, for example, upon ECONOMIES OF SCOPE or temporal flexibility resulting from just-in-time forms of supply along the production chain;
- a redefinition of a firm's core activities so redefining its sphere of activities, with profound implications for the size and status of its labour force;
- a repositioning of the firm along the production chain to deal with downstream service functions;
- a geographical reconfiguration to redefine the role and functioning of individual productive units; and
- an organizational restructuring involving a redefinition of the firm's internal and external boundaries.

The restructuring of production in these ways has implications for, or may be undertaken through, changes in the labour process or the DIVISION OF LABOUR, but it relates to wider processes of change within which labour is necessarily caught up and over which it has less direct influence than changes in the immediate conditions of work.

Although restructuring is a term applied mainly to economic transformation and is frequently driven by and is obviously manifest in the activities of individual firms and capitals, it cannot be restricted to the economic sphere. It involves, and so is predicated upon, responsiveness elsewhere in SOCIETY. Nor is restructuring reducible merely to economic dynamics. It frequently requires the support and/or restructuring of the STATE or, as in the case of *perestroika* or the market-based restructuring around the discourses of monetarism in the US ('Reaganomics') and, to a more dramatic extent, the UK ('Thatcherism') or New Zealand ('Rogernomics') SOCIAL FORMATIONS, is driven by the transformation of regulatory practices instituted by the state and so generates a range of ideological and political relationships and struggles (see, for example, Walker 1997). RL

References

Aganbegyan, A. 1988: *The challenge: economics of perestroika*. London: Hutchinson. · Allen, J. and Massey, D. 1988: *The economy in question*. London and Newbury Park, CA: Sage. · Allen, J., Massey, D., Cochrane, A. et al. 1998: *Rethinking the region; spaces of neo-liberalism*. London: Routledge. · Castells, M. 1989: *The informational city*. Oxford and Cambridge, MA: Blackwell. · Dicken, P. 1998: *Global shift: transforming the world economy*, 3rd edn. London: Paul Chapman Publishing. · Graham, J., Gibson, K., Horvath, R. and Shakow, D. 1988: Restructuring in US manufacturing: the decline of monopoly capitalism. *Annals of the Association of American Geographers* 78: 473–90. · Harris, L. 1988: The UK economy at the crossroads. In J. Allen and D. Massey, eds, *The economy in question*, ch. 1. London and Newbury Park, CA: Sage, Open University, 7–44. · Streeten, P. 1987: Structural adjustment: a survey of the issues and options. *World Development* 15: 1469–82. · Walker, R. 1997: California rages: regional capitalism and the politics of renewal. In R. Lee and J. Wills, eds, *Geographies of economies*, ch. 27. London and New York: Arnold, 345–56. · Watts, M.J. 1992/1996: The shock of modernity: petroleum, protest, and fast capitalism in an industrializing society. In A. Pred and M.J. Watts, *Reworking modernity: capitalisms and symbolic discontent*, ch. 2. New Brunswick, NJ: Rutgers University Press, 21–63; reprinted in S. Daniels and R. Lee, eds, *Exploring human geography*. London: Arnold, 120–52. · Yergin, D. and Stanislaw, J. 1998: *The commanding heights: the battle between government and the market place that is remaking the modern world*. New York: Simon and Schuster.

Suggested Reading

Allen, Massey, Cochrane et al. (1998). · Castells (1989), ch. 1. · Corbridge, S. 1995: *Development studies: a reader*. London and New York: Arnold, section 5. · Walker (1997); Watts (1992/1996).

retailing, geography of Conventionally defined as the study of the interrelations between the spatial patterns of retail location and organization, on the one hand, and the geography of retail consumer behaviour on the other. Retail geography is often situated at the overlap of related sub-fields, including ECONOMIC GEOGRAPHY, the geography of SERVICES (Daniels, 1995), and URBAN GEOGRAPHY.

Work within retail geography follows one of two broad trajectories. The historically dominant perspective is somewhat more applied and neo-classical in orientation. Since the late 1980s a self-defined 'new' retail geography has emerged, in clear opposition to the former. This has been influenced initially by POLITICAL-ECONOMY perspectives, being subsequently responsive to developing debates within CULTURAL GEOGRAPHY (see Clarke, 1996, for an overview).

Mainstream retail geography has certain general characteristics. Broadly speaking, NEO-CLASSICAL ECONOMIC principles predominate, with considerable emphasis placed upon the structuring role of individual consumer decisions. This can be seen in the continuing influence of CENTRAL PLACE THEORY (cf. Parr, 1995), the refinement of which played an important role in the QUANTITATIVE REVOLUTION of the 1960s. With strong links to marketing (Jones and Simmons, 1993), retail geography is also applied in its emphases (APPLIED GEOGRAPHY), with an historically well-developed attention to the geographic concerns of retail management or in relation to planning (Wrigley, 1988). Retail geography has conventionally adopted a specific spatial focus, with inquiry usually directed at the intra-urban and, occasionally, at the regional scale. The geographies of consumer behaviour and retail organization are also frequently theorized as some function of distance, actual or perceived (see DISTANCE DECAY; SPATIAL SCIENCE). Retail geography continues to develop; of special importance are recent developments in GEOGRAPHICAL INFORMATION SYSTEMS (Benoit, 1995).

It is the geography of retail consumption that appears to be the most well-developed sub-field (CONSUMPTION, GEOGRAPHY OF). One historically important perspective draws from general SPATIAL INTERACTION theory, and its family of GRAVITY MODELS, to simulate and forecast consumer spatial behaviour which is assumed to be some response to distance minimization and utility maximization on the part of the consumer. From the 1960s, cognitive-behavioural perspectives were introduced, with consequent developments in consumer spatial cognition, perception and spatial learning. This proved important to the wider field of BEHAVIOURAL GEOGRAPHY.

The emphasis on consumer demand accounts for the relatively limited attention given to the geography of retail capital. One important stream of analysis, however, drawn from the early pioneering work of Berry, has classified and analysed both the morphology of urban commercial structures and the central place hierarchy in line with principles derived from CENTRAL PLACE THEORY. Spatial changes in retailing – such as the relation between decentralized retail investment and traditional city centre retailing – have also received attention. Recent important developments include the importation of 'institutional' accounts of retail organization and spatial change (Brown, 1987). Again, the 'applied' focus of much research in this field is much in evidence, as witnessed by the level of development of fields such as store location and MARKET-AREA ANALYSIS (e.g. Thill, 1995).

Despite its many insights, this perspective has come under challenge in the last decade, as political economic and cultural perspectives have been brought to bear on retail geography. Initial insights were drawn from the allied field of INDUSTRIAL GEOGRAPHY which saw the import of Marxist perspectives into spatial-economic analysis in the 1980s. One influential analysis by Ducatel and Blomley (1990), drawing from Marxist insights into economic structure, sought to re-theorize retail capital both as a vital component of a larger capitalist system and as characterized by its own internal logic (see CIRCUIT OF CAPITAL).

Although this re-theorization has been criticized (Fine and Leopold, 1993), the call for a political economic perspective on retail capital generated a response, particularly in the United Kingdom, which has seen some striking changes in both the organization and importance of retail capital over the past two decades. The 'new economic geographies of retailing', as Wrigley and Lowe (1996) style them, have paid particular attention to the phenomenon of retail restructuring. For Wrigley and Lowe (1996, p. 7), six themes are prominent: (a) the reconfiguration of corporate retail structures; (b) the reconfiguration of retailer–supplier chain interfaces; (c) the organizational and technological transformations in retail distribution; (d) the reconfiguration of labour practices and social relations of production within retailing; (e) the spatial penetration, manipulation and switching of retail capital; and (f) the regulation of retail restructuring. Several of the essays in their book are instructive on these issues, as are related papers (e.g. Sparks, 1996). The geography of retail change, not surprisingly, has received special attention, as witnessed by the attention given re-configured 'consumption spaces', such as the 'mega-mall', and shifts in both the intra-urban and international location of retail capital (Hallsworth, 1992).

The 'new retail geography' has recently become more attentive to the cultural geographies of retailing, as well as the economic geographies (cf. CULTURAL TURN). In line with a more generalized recognition that economic processes are culturally coded, retail geographers have again become attentive to questions of consumption. However, consumption is not seen simply as the unproblematic expression of consumer demands, but is understood as a critical site for the expression, reproduction and contestation of various identities. One question, in this regard, is the way in which gender roles are formed in 'retail spaces' (see GENDER AND GEOGRAPHY). Certain retail spaces – notably the department store and the mall – have received particular attention (Blomley, 1996). However, it is interesting to see other retail sites coming under scrutiny (e.g. Gregson and Crewe, 1997).

As Glennie and Thrift (1996) note, academic treatments of consumption have often been semiotic in focus, that is, the images invoked by retail capital and retail spaces are given special attention (cf. Shields, 1992). Such analyses also tend to fall into two camps. On the one hand, contemporary forms of consumption are seen negatively, as inducing fragmentation, ANOMIE and superficiality (compare Hopkins' 1990 treatment of the 'PLACELESSNESS' of mall design). On the other hand, consumption is seen as offering possibilities – albeit faint – for more redemptive futures where contemporary forms of consumption, associated with retail capital, allow for creative reworkings of the self.

While still rooted in an applied and largely empiricist paradigm, retail geography seems to have evidenced an opening up in the 1980s. For a long time retail geography has been largely immune from broader theoretical debates within human geography. With a partial willingness to embrace some of these questions, it will be interesting to see what the next decade will bring. Perhaps insights from POST-COLONIAL theory might be applicable (cf. Smith, 1996). Also, recent discussions concerning GLOBALIZATION might be relevant, particularly given an interest in international capital flows within the retail sector.

One important question relates to the treatment of space within retail geography. The applied, modelling-based perspective seems to treat space either as a neutral container or as an independent variable. Conversely, the 'new retail geography' sees the relation between space and retail activity as reciprocal and mutually constitutive. Thus, for example, retail capital can structure space in particular ways, yet is itself configured by socio-spatial processes, such as nation-specific 'corporate cultures' (Shackleton, 1996). However, the specific importance of SPATIALITY to retail activity awaits a self-conscious examination. Knotty conceptual issues such as SCALE, the politics of space, or the construction of PLACE need to be more systematically unravelled in relation to retail geography.

Finally, the bifurcation of retail geography into applied and social-theoretic streams begs some important questions. The former seems largely indifferent to the latter, which has attempted to consciously distinguish itself. While there are some evident differences, this need not obscure the possibilities for productive exchanges. For example, more conscious critical reflection on some of the assumptions that underpin 'mainstream' retail modelling might be productive. Alternatively, some recent insights from marketing, such as Butner's (1992) discussion of 'servicescapes', might be of interest to critical retail geographers. More generally, the degree of *actual* difference between the two perspectives, or the possibilities of other 'new retail geographies', demand more careful consideration. NB

References

Benoit, D. 1995: Using GIS for retail location analysis of United Kingdom supermarkets. *Geo Info Systems* 5 9: 46–51. · Blomley, N.K. 1996: I'd like to dress her all over: masculinity, power and retail space. In N. Wrigley and M. Lowe, eds, *Retailing, consumption and capital: towards the new retail geography*. London: Longman, 238–57. · Brown, S. 1987: Institutional change in retailing. *Progress in Human Geography* 11 2: 181–206. · Butner, M.J. 1992: Servicescapes: the impact of physical surroundings on customers and employees. *Journal of Marketing* 56: 57–71. · Clarke, D.B. 1996: The limits to retail capital. In N. Wrigley and M. Lowe, eds, *Retailing, consumption and capital: towards the new retail geography*. London: Longman, 284–301. · Daniels, P.W. 1995: Services in a shrinking world. *Geography* 80 2: 97–110. · Ducatel, K.J. and Blomley, N.K. 1990: Rethinking retail capital. *International journal of urban and regional research* 14 2: 207–27. · Fine, B. and Leopold, E. 1993: *The world of consumption*. New York: Routledge. · Glennie, P. and Thrift, N.J. 1996: Consumption, shopping and gender. In N. Wrigley and M. Lowe, eds, *Retailing, consumption and capital: towards the new retail geography*. London: Longman, 221–37. · Gregson, N. and Crewe, L. 1997: The bargain, the knowledge and the spectacle: making sense of consumption in the space of the car-boot sale. *Environment and Planning A: Society and Space* 15 1: 87–112. · Hallsworth, A.H. 1992: *The new geography of consumer spending*. London: Belhaven Press. · Hopkins, J.A. 1990: West Edmonton Mall: Landscape of myths and elsewhereness. *Canadian Geographer* 34 1: 2–17. · Jones, K. and Simmons, J. 1993: *Location, location, location: analyzing the retail environment*. Toronto: Methuen. · Parr, J.B. 1995: Alternative approaches to market area structure in the urban system. *Urban Studies* 32 8: 1317–29. · Shackleton, R. 1996: Retailer internationalization: a culturally constructed phenomenon. In N. Wrigley and M. Lowe, eds, *Retailing, consumption and capital: towards the new retail geography*. London: Longman, 137–56. · Shields, R., ed., 1992: *Lifestyle shopping: the subject of consumption*. London: Routledge. · Smith, M.D. 1996: The empire filters back: consumption, production, and the politics of Starbucks coffee. *Urban Geography* 17: 502–24. · Sparks, L. 1996: Space wars: Wm Low and the 'auld enemy'. *Environment and Planning A* 28: 1465–84. · Thill, J.-C. 1995: Modelling store choices with cross-sectional and pooled cross-sectional data: a comparison. *Environment and Planning A* 27 8: 1303–15. · Wrigley, N. 1988: Retail restructuring and retail analysis. In N. Wrigley, ed., *Store choice, store location and market analysis*. London: Routledge, 3–34. · Wrigley, N. and Lowe, M., eds, 1996: *Retailing, consumption and capital: towards the new retail geography*. London: Longman.

Suggested Reading

Berry, B.J.L. and Parr, J. 1988: *Market centers and retail location: theory and applications*. Englewood Cliffs, NJ: Prentice-Hall. · Hollinshead, G. 1996: Retailing: historical patterns and future trends. *Plan Canada* 36 6: 12–18. · Potter, R. 1982: *The urban retailing system*. Aldershot: Gower. · Reekie, G. 1993: *Temptations: sex, selling and the department store*. Sydney: Allen and Unwin. · Shields (1992).

retroduction A mode of inference (particularly associated with REALISM) in which events are explained by postulating (and then identifying) the mechanisms by which they are produced. Those mechanisms realize causal powers, the potential causes of events which have to be activated (as with the striking of a match and the creation of fire): those powers may not be observable (as with gravity) and their existence has to be retroduced from appreciation of observed events. RJJ

Suggested Reading

Sayer, A. 1992: *Method in social science: a realist approach*, 2nd edn. London: Routledge.

retrogressive approach A method of working towards an understanding of the past by an examination of the present (cf. RETROSPECTIVE APPROACH). The term gained its currency from Maitland's *Domesday Book and beyond* (1897) and achieved a wide circulation through the work of Marc Bloch. He insisted that the analysis of past landscapes required the prior analysis of the present LANDSCAPE, 'for it alone furnished those comprehensive vistas without which it was impossible to begin'. Likening history to a film, Bloch argued that 'only the last picture remains quite clear' so that 'in order to reconstruct the faded features of others' it is first necessary 'to unwind the spool in the opposite direction from that in which the pictures were taken' (see Friedman, 1996). DG

References

Friedman, S. 1996: *Marc Bloch, sociology and geography*. Cambridge: Cambridge University Press. · Maitland, F.W. 1897: *Domesday Book and beyond*. Cambridge: Cambridge University Press.

Suggested Reading

Baker, A.R.H. 1968: A note on the retrogressive and retrospective approaches in historical geography. *Erdkunde* 22: 243–4.

retrospective approach The study of the past for the light it throws on the present (cf. RETROGRESSIVE APPROACH). The approach would make HISTORICAL GEOGRAPHY a prerequisite – or, as Darby once claimed, an essential foundation – for contemporary geography. Its most explicit advocate was Roger Dion, who believed that a consideration of the present LANDSCAPE poses problems that can only be solved by a search for their origins; but the approach can evidently be extended beyond the analysis of the landscape and has much in common with 'genetic' or 'historical' explanations (cf. FUNCTIONALISM). DG

Suggested Reading
Gulley, J.L.M. 1961: The retrospective approach in historical geography. *Erdkunde* 15: 306–9.

revealed preference analysis Statistical methods, many of them based on MULTI-DIMENSIONAL SCALING, for deriving an aggregate set of decision rules from a series of individual decisions (e.g. in the choice of which shopping centre to patronize). The individual observed choices are termed *behaviour in space*; the general rules (unconstrained by any particular spatial arrangements of alternatives) are called the rules of *spatial behaviour* (Rushton, 1969). RJJ

Reference
Rushton, G. 1969: Analysis of spatial behavior by revealed space preference. *Annals of the Association of American Geographers* 59: 391–400.

rhetoric Originating in the fifth century BC with the sophists, rhetoric is the study of persuasive discourse; of how words 'influence men's [sic] souls' as Plato put it. Rhetoricians suggest that researchers in *all* forms of inquiry employ a multitude of different stylistic devices (tropes) to convince others of the plausibility of their arguments. Metaphors, ironic asides, equations, jokes, citations, and anecdotes are all part of the same attempt to establish authority and persuade one's audience. Rhetoric is counterposed to EPISTEMOLOGY, which attempts to establish truth on the basis of a set of a priori, abstract criteria. For rhetoricians, however, truth emerges only within specific practices of persuasion on the ground. Epistemology tells us what people ought to say, whereas for students of rhetoric it is what people actually do say that is critical. For example, POSITIVIST epistemologists would claim that they uphold the DISTANCE-DECAY effect because it was established using the most rigorous of statistical techniques. Yet for most, the plausibility of the distance-decay effect comes from a set of convincing tropes: from *self-inspection* (what would I do?), from *thinking about others* (what would they do?), from *authority* (some very famous geographers believe in it), from *analogy* (if it works for planetary masses, it should work for humans), and from *a sense of parsimony* (one equation explains everything). In short, what is persuasive is far wider than the official rhetoric admits, thereby casting doubt on the official rhetoric itself.

With the recent CULTURAL TURN in the social sciences since the 1980s there has been an increasing critical appreciation of rhetoric. For that cultural turn problematizes all representations, from those of high-energy physics (cf. SCIENCE, GEOGRAPHY AND) to those of CULTURAL GEOGRAPHY. In each case, it is suggested, REPRESENTATIONS are not mirror copies of the world but cultural constructions infused by both politics and poetics, and which are made substantial and powerful by, among other things, specific rhetorical manoeuvres and devices (cf. POETICS OF GEOGRAPHY). In geography rhetoric has been explored by Barnes (1989) and Curry (1996), and most systematically by Smith (1996). TJB

References
Barnes, T.J. 1989: Rhetoric, metaphor, and mathematical modelling. *Environment and Planning A* 21: 1281–4. · Curry, M.R. 1996: *The work in the world: geographical practice and the written word.* Minneapolis: University of Minnesota. · Smith, J.M. 1996: Geographical rhetoric: modes and tropes of appeal. *Annals of the Association of American Geographers* 86: 1–20.

Suggested Reading
Nelson, J.S., Megill, A. and McCloskey, D. 1987: *The rhetoric of the human sciences: language and argument in scholarship and public affairs.* Madison: University of Wisconsin Press. · Smith (1996).

rhizome A term used by Gilles Deleuze, a French Professor of Philosophy, and Felix Guattari, a French psychotherapist and political activist, to suggest a new IMAGE of thought, one which thinks of the world as a network of multiple and branching roots 'with no central axis, no unified point of origin, and no given direction of growth' (Grosz, 1994, p. 199). Instead, then, of a world of coagulations of entities which have to be held in thought, rhizomatics is about lines of flow and flight, processes of territorialization, deterritorialization, and reterritorialization, networks of partial and constantly changing connections.

What this means is that Deleuze and Guattari are not interested in models of knowledge which search for hidden depths beneath a manifest surface. Rather, like proponents of ACTOR–NETWORK THEORY and NON-REPRESENTATIONAL THEORY (with which they have much in common), they are interested in connections and interrelations that are never hidden. For example, instead of looking for a connection between a TEXT and its meaning, they look for the connections between a text and other objects, how it connects with other things. In other words, they turn the logic of REPRESENTATION on its head.

Grosz (1994) argues that rhizome is therefore based upon five elements. First, it is based on connection between diverse fragments.

Second, it is therefore irrevocably committed to heterogeneity, to the bringing together of diverse objects, functions, domains, effects, aims. Third, it is also therefore committed to multiplicity, understood as a constant proliferation as unexpected connections are made, rather like the wanderings of NOMADS from place to place. Fourth, and relatedly, it is based on ruptures, breaks and discontinuities; any connection can be broken, bringing about new possibilities of different connections. Fifth, its model is the MAP, understood not as some Cartesian plane but rather as a folded and refolded topology which can be 'torn, reversed, adapted to any kind of mounting, reworked by an individual, group or social formation' (Deleuze and Guattari, 1987, p. 12).

'Rhizomatics' is, in other words, both a method and an objective. It names a contingent world of acentred and partial connections and it is also a means of doing things with that world by making new connections. It is a form of pragmatics – concerned with what can be done, put to work, made to do things, connected up; 'liberation occurs through addition' (Goodchild, 1996, p. 2).

In human geography, this intrinsically connective practice of rhizomatics has made three main linkages. First, it has been used by a number of POST-COLONIAL theorists to find new ways of imagining LANDSCAPE, which move away from the fixed cartographies of colonial regimes of representation (e.g. Carter, 1996). Second, it has been used by non-representational theorists to bolster the argument that the real is not represented, it is performed (Thrift, 1996; see PERFORMANCE; PERFORMATIVITY). Third, it is used as a general technology for undermining fixity and shaking up certainty by jesters whose jokes are always serious (Doel, 1996, 1999). NJT

References

Boundas, C.V., ed., 1993: *The Deleuze reader.* New York: Columbia University Press. · Boundas, C.V. and Olkowski, D., eds, 1994: *Gilles Delueze and the theater of philosophy.* New York: Routledge. · Carter, P. 1996: *The lie of the land.* London: Faber and Faber. · Deleuze, G. and Guattari, F. 1987: *A thousand plateaus. Capitalism and schizophrenia.* Minneaopolis: University of Minnesota Press. · Deleuze, G. and Guattari, F. 1994: *What is philosophy?* London: Verso. · Doel, M. 1996: A hundred thousand lines of flight: a machinic introduction to the normal thought and scrumpled geography of Gilles Deleuze and Felix Guattari. *Environment and Planning D: Society and Space* 14: 421–40. · Doel, M. 1999: *Postmodern geographies.* Edinburgh: Edinburgh University Press. · Goodchild, P. 1996: *Deleuze and Guattari. An introduction to the policy of desire.* London: Sage. · Grosz, E. 1994: A thousand tiny sexes: feminism and rhizomatics. In C. Boundas and D. Olkowski, eds, *Gilles Deleuze and the theater of philosophy.* New York: Routledge, 187–210. · Thrift, N.J. 1996: *Spatial formations.* London: Sage.

Suggested Reading

Deleuze, G. 1997: What children say. In G. Deleuze, *Gilles Deleuze. Essays critical and clinical.* Minneapolis: University of Minnesota Press, 61–7. · Marks, J. 1998: *Gilles Deleuze. Vitalism and multiplicity.* London: Pluto Press.

ribbon development Urban SPRAWL along the main roads leading from a built-up area, which may generate the creation of a CONURBATION. Locations on such routes usually offer businesses relatively cheap but accessible sites plus potential custom from passers-by. Within built-up areas, the term is often used to describe strings of commercial land uses along the main roads leading into major centres, which offer the same advantages. RJJ

risk The likelihood of a range of possible outcomes resulting from a decision or course of action. Strictly speaking, risk exists when known probabilities can be assigned to these outcomes. Risk is thus distinguished from UNCERTAINTY, under which probabilities cannot be established. Businesses tend to prefer working with risk rather than uncertainty, because of the calculable nature of risk. DMS

risk society A term invented by the German sociologist, Ulrich Beck (1992), to describe a fundamental shift in western industrial societies towards a dependence upon scientific and technical knowledge that in turn produces RISKS and HAZARDS which can reach across large swathes of space and time and whose consequences are accordingly difficult to assess (as in the case of nuclear power). The culture of scientism would attempt to combat these risks by the application of further scientific and technical solutions but Beck argues that in SOCIETY at large the population finds different ways of coping, based upon a REFLEXIVE MODERNIZATION which is a combination of the availability of reflexive critiques, which can lay claim to a morality equal to that of science (as in the principles of the Green movement), and an increasing individualization, which is the outcome of an expanding field of knowledge forcing people to reflexively fashion their biographies on the basis of knowledgeable choices.

This conception of MODERNITY has much in common with that of Anthony Giddens (see especially Beck, Giddens and Lash, 1996) and has important links to the German tradition of CRITICAL THEORY. NJT

References

Beck, U. 1992: *Risk society. Towards a new modernity*. London: Sage. · Beck, U., Giddens, A. and Lash, S. 1996: *Reflexive Modernisation*. Cambridge: Polity Press. · Franklin, J., ed., 1998: *The politics of the risk society*. Cambridge: Polity Press.

rural Areas which are dominated (either currently or recently) by extensive land uses such as agriculture or forestry, or by large open spaces of undeveloped land; which contain small, lower-order settlements demonstrating a strong relationship between buildings and surrounding extensive landscape, and which are perceived as rural by most residents; and which are thought to engender a way of life characterized by a cohesive identity based on respect for the environment, and behavioural qualities of living as part of an extensive landscape. In practice, rural areas vary considerably, from those which may still be defined functionally (by land use and geographical location) to those closer to urban centres where 'rural' is more of a socially and culturally constructed and therefore contested category. PJC

Suggested Reading

Cloke, P. and Park, C. 1985: *Rural resource management*. London: Croom Helm, ch. 1. · Pratt, A. 1996. Rurality: loose talk or social struggle. *Journal of Rural Studies* 12: 69–78.

rural community A collection of socially interacting people living in a rural area, and often sharing one or more common ties. As with rurality (see RURAL and RURAL GEOGRAPHY), COMMUNITY has been defined in widely different ways: G.A. Hillery's (1955) study revealed 94 specific definitions.

Geographers have leaned heavily on the work of anthropologists and sociologists in their evolving understanding of rural community. Early STRUCTURAL-FUNCTIONALIST studies portrayed rural communities as resilient in the face of change and distinctively different from their urban counterparts. Tönnies' (1955) concept of *Gemeinschaft* was adopted to describe close kinship relations linked to a particular rural place leading to cooperative action for the common good (see RURAL–URBAN CONTINUUM). It was soon extended to cover actual social structures resulting in particular settlement forms, and this extension has been heavily criticized (see Harper, 1989).

Two different strands of rural community study emerged from this critique. The first consists of new rural ETHNOGRAPHIES which address the question of whether people are 'truly rural' in their lived worlds and whether there is an 'essence' in the emerging place of a village. A key theme here is *centredness* (Harper, 1987). It is argued that centred rural people will confine most of their physical, social and symbolic relationships to one rural place, and that centred rural places occur when the majority of their inhabitants are centred rural people. Truly rural communities will thus reflect centred people in centred places (see Bell, 1994).

The second strand of study stresses the use of community as a mechanism for interpreting wider organizations and social relations. Fred Buttel in the USA and Howard Newby in the UK have both investigated the agricultural power relations which underlie changes in rural communities (Newby, 1977; Newby et al., 1978; Buttel et al., 1990). As in-migrant middle classes have exerted greater influence, so studies of the interrelations between new CLASS fractions and rural communities have become increasingly important. Here the notion of *cultural competences* helps the understanding of how in-migrants do/do not fit into the community (Cloke et al., 1998). The recognition of social groups who are being marginalized by wider economic and social changes has also become important (see Cloke et al., 1997).

There is still little common ground in the conceptualization of community in rural studies, and the term is still frequently used simply to denote a collection of people in a particular place. This is especially so when used in the context of RURAL PLANNING, in which the discourses of community analysis, community development and community renewal continue to infer the need for cooperative good. Here community is often merged with sustainability (see SUSTAINABLE DEVELOPMENT) to suggest long-term strategies for development in rural communities. PJC

References

Bell, M.M. 1994: *Childerley: nature and morality in a country village*. Chicago: Chicago University Press. · Buttel, F.H., Larson, O.F. and Gillespie, G.W. 1990: *The sociology of agriculture*. New York: Greenwood. · Cloke, P., Goodwin, M. and Milbourne, P. 1997: *Rural Wales, community and marginalisation*. Cardiff: University of Wales Press. · Cloke, P., Goodwin, M. and Milbourne, P. 1998: Inside looking out; outside looking in. Different experiences of cultural competence in rural lifestyles. In P. Boyle and K. Halfacree, eds, *Migration into rural areas*. Chichester: Wiley, 134–50. · Harper, S. 1987: A humanistic approach to the study of rural populations. *Journal of Rural Studies* 3: 309–20. · Harper, S. 1989: The British rural community: an overview of perspectives. *Journal of Rural Studies* 5: 161–84. · Hillery, G.A. 1955: Definitions of community: areas of agreement. *Rural Sociology* 20: 111–23. · Newby, H. 1977: *The deferential worker*. London: Allen Lane. · Newby, H., Bell, C., Rose, D. and Saunders, P. 1978: *Property, paternalism and power*. London: Hutchinson. · Tonnies, F. 1955 [orig. pub. 1887]: *Community and society*. New York: Harper & Row.

Suggested Reading

Cloke, P. and Thrift, N. 1990: Class change and conflict in rural areas. In T. Marsden, P. Lowe and S. Whatmore, eds, *Rural restructuring: global processes and their responses*. London: David Fulton. · Cloke, P., Phillips, M. and Thrift, N. 1995: The new middle classes and the social constructs of rural living. In T. Butler and M. Savage, eds, *Social change and the middle classes*. London: University College Press, 220–40. · Murray, M. and Dunn, L. 1996: *Revitalizing rural America: a perspective on collaboration and community*. Chichester: Wiley. · Urry, J. 1995: A middle-class countryside? In T. Butler and M. Savage, eds, *Social change and the middle classes*. London: University College Press, 205–19.

rural geography The study of people, places and environments in RURAL areas, with special reference to society, economy, politics and culture in the developed world, although such study can also be applied to THIRD WORLD contexts. Rural geographers have widely differing interests, and are often closely associated with interdisciplinary research in rural areas with sociologists, economists and agricultural specialists. Indeed, in the USA there is little evidence of a specific sub-discipline called 'rural geography'.

Rural areas have traditionally been important to geography. The studies of rural settlement patterns by Paul Vidal de la Blache and Albert Demangeon, and the ensuing concern for agricultural land use and settlement systems, stemming in part from the classical models of von Thünen and Christaller, ensured that most human geographers would be familiar with aspects of rural space (see VON THÜNEN MODEL). With the demise of REGIONAL GEOGRAPHY, however, rural areas were relatively neglected in geography until a distinctly demarcated subject area of 'rural geography' emerged in the 1970s. Prompted by Hugh Clout's (1972) book *Rural geography: an introductory survey*, the agricultural focus of rural work was expanded to cover aspects of society, economy and land, and the literature of rural geography burgeoned in the 1970s and 1980s; covering, for example, ACCESSIBILITY, agriculture, employment, housing, land use, RECREATION and RURAL PLANNING (see Cloke, 1985). Initially, there was a phase of resurgence for rural geography, particularly in parts of Europe, Canada and Australasia, but by the 1980s the band-wagon was again losing momentum. The general appetite for new information on the changing rural milieu had been satiated, and new challenges were required in order to generate fresh energy. In particular, rural geographers were urged to be more policy-orientated and more theoretically informed.

During the early 1980s much of rural geography was characterized by a form of 'applied POSITIVISM'. In this way rural geographers began to tackle issues relating to problems of policy and planning in rural areas, and yet were unwilling to replace their technical role with one which engaged directly with politics and ideology. In some cases, rural geography was therefore seen to be 'broadly theory-free' (Gilg, 1985, p. 172), while others saw the sub-discipline as 'tinkering with existing socio-economic conditions in order to weaken the impress of malevolent trends [while failing] to recognise that the process which brought about current maldistributions ... are inherent in policy procedures' (Hoggart and Buller, 1987, p. 267).

This perceived bankruptcy of explanations of change grounded in NEO-CLASSICAL ECONOMICS and positivist recording of trends provided a significant impulse to the wider acceptance of POLITICAL-ECONOMIC concepts in the understanding of socio-spatial phenomena. In the late 1980s and early 1990s, with the strong backing of progress being made by critical rural sociologists, there was a greater willingness to develop a research agenda founded on a series of key themes: the role of *economic restructuring* in bringing about UNEVEN DEVELOPMENT; the recognition that RESTRUCTURING does not occur in a social vacuum and that *social recomposition* occurs both as a shaping mechanism for restructuring, and in response to it; the equally valid – yet less publicized – recognition that economic restructuring and social recomposition do not occur in an environmental vacuum, and that *environmental recomposition* is also relevant; and the role of the STATE in mediating or organizing change (see Cloke, 1990). With this agenda, rural geographers began to address several crucial questions: How attractive are particular areas to capital accumulation under contemporary modes of regulation? How and why are particular areas attractive to people seeking a 'rural experience', and how does the structuring and experience of rural lifestyle differ according to GENDER, age, ETHNICITY and localism?

What public intervention is necessary for CONSERVATION purposes in processes of environmental recomposition? How and why does the state intervene to make rural places more attractive? These themes encompass both the traditional emphasis of rural geography on the agricultural sector (dealing particularly with issues of pluriactivity, diversification, environmental and LANDSCAPE impacts, the international food chain and policies of deregulation) and the broader task of bringing together a range of economic, social and political considerations in rural areas (including INDUSTRIALIZATION and the service sector, commodification, PRIVATIZATION, settlement rationalization, COUNTERURBANIZATION, GENTRIFICATION, POVERTY, ACCESSIBILITY and CITIZENSHIP).

Most recently, geographers have been seeking to bring POSTMODERN, POST-STRUCTURAL, and a-modern understandings of society–space, structure–agency, nature–society and self–other to bear on rural issues. Rurality is increasingly being recognized as a series of socio-cultural constructs, with 'rural' thus being increasingly interpreted as a world of social, moral and cultural values in which both rural dwellers and others participate. Social spaces of rurality are no longer seen necessarily to overlap with geographical spaces of rurality, as cultural constructs of the rural pervade various aspects of REPRESENTATION and CONSUMPTION in wider society (Halfacree, 1993). This bifurcation has been regarded by some as constituting a 'post-rural' condition (Murdoch and Pratt, 1993).

Equally, there has been a championing of difference within these rural worlds, with a particular focus on rural others (Cloke and Little, 1997; cf. OTHER/OTHERNESS). There has, however, been considerable disagreement over how to handle the IDENTITY POLITICS of otherness in rural areas, with the wish for other voices to 'speak for themselves' being set against a wish to identify and challenge the power relations which bring about political and cultural discrimination against others (see Philo, 1992, 1993; Murdoch and Pratt, 1993, 1994). The CULTURAL TURN has brought many new insights to rural geography, but there remains a strong inclination to set these insights alongside political-economic understandings of marginalization and social exclusion. PJC

References

Cloke, P. 1985: Whither rural studies? *Journal of Rural Studies* 1: 1–10. · Cloke, P. 1990: Rural geography and political economy. In R. Peet and N. Thrift, eds, *New models in geography*, vol. 1. London: Unwin Hyman. · Cloke, P. and Little, J., eds, 1997: *Contested countryside cultures: otherness, marginalization and rurality*. London: Routledge. · Clout, H. 1972: *Rural geography: an introductory survey*. Oxford: Pergamon. · Gilg, A. 1985: *An introduction to rural geography*. London: Edward Arnold. · Halfacree, K. 1993: Locality and social representation: space, discourse and alternative definitions of the rural. *Journal of Rural Studies* 9: 23–38. · Hoggart, K. and Buller, H. 1987: *Rural development: a geographical perspective*. London: Croom Helm. · Murdoch, J. and Pratt, A. 1993: Rural studies: modernism, postmodernism and the post-rural. *Journal of Rural Studies* 9: 411–28. · Murdoch, J. and Pratt, A. 1994: Rural studies of power and the power of rural studies: a reply to Philo. *Journal of Rural Studies* 10: 83–8. · Philo, C. 1992: Neglected rural geographies: a review. *Journal of Rural Studies* 8: 193–208. · Philo, C. 1993: Post-modern rural geography? *Journal of Rural Studies* 9: 429–36.

Suggested Reading

Cloke, P. 1997: Country backwater to virtual village? Rural studies and 'the cultural turn'. *Journal of Rural Studies* 13: 367–76. · Flora, C.B., Flora, J.L., Spears, J.D., Swanson, L.E., Lapping, M.B. and Weinberg, M.L. 1992: *Rural communities: legacy and change*. Boulder, CO: Westview. · Ilbery, B., ed., 1998: *The geography of rural change*. Harlow: Longman. · Marsden, T., Murdoch, J., Lowe, P., Munton, R. and Flynn, A. 1993: *Constructing the countryside*. London: University College London Press. · Phillips, M. 1998: The restructuring of social imaginations in rural geography. *Journal of Rural Studies* 14: 121–53.

rural planning The attempt to identify problems, organize resources and generate action in RURAL areas, often with the stated aims of diversifying the economic base, seeking a pluralistic social order and maintaining a healthy (and where necessary, conserved) environment. Policy-making and implementation occur at different scales of government and are often functionally discrete, such that it is possible for one arm of planning (e.g. agricultural improvement) to conflict with another (e.g. LANDSCAPE; CONSERVATION). Rural planning is usually studied in the developed world, although rural development strategies are also relevant in a THIRD WORLD context. Planning covers a wide diversity of land uses and socio-economic processes, including: agriculture and FORESTRY, CONSERVATION, employment and training, ENERGY, HOUSING, RECREATION (e.g. HEALTH and EDUCATION; TOURISM; transport).

The geography of rural planning has focused particularly on attempts to bring a number of these planning functions together. This may reflect particular rural LOCALES, where the need is either to generate economic development to provide jobs, services and homes, or to control development or resource use so as to protect the area's character. For example, key settlement policies (Cloke, 1979) have been used to concentrate resources into planned service centres, which can then serve the settlements in their rural HINTERLANDS. Planning has also been integrated in particular rural areas (e.g. rural Wales and rural Scotland in the UK and Appalachia in the USA) where specific regional planning agencies have been established to deal with areas with special needs. More rarely, socio-economic land-use and landscape planning are all involved in specially designated zones such as NATIONAL PARKS.

There has been a widespread acceptance of *rational* concepts in planning in rural areas, such that until recently the place of planning in wider social and political relations has been little questioned. However, interest in the relative inability to implement policies with which to secure many planning aims in rural areas has led some researchers to view planning as an activity in the wider context of the STATE (see Cloke, 1987). If planning is part of the STATE APPARATUS then it will also be subject to the constraints imposed by the form and function of the state. It may, for example, be better suited to aiding elements of production rather than consumption, and it may generate consistent biases in favour of dominant fractions of capital and class (Cloke and Little, 1990). Moreover, as the relationship between state, society and government changes, so too do the politics, decision-making mechanisms, aims and resources associated with rural planning. For example, many aspects of rural planning in the UK have been Europeanized, particularly in terms of fitting development schemes to the requirements of bids for competitive EU funding. More generally, geographers have turned to concepts of GOVERNANCE (Marsden and Murdoch, 1998) in their understanding of new partnerships between public-sector agencies, voluntary organizations, and private-sector concerns in the pursuit of development or planning objectives. PJC

References

Cloke, P. 1979: *Key settlements in rural areas*. London: Methuen. · Cloke, P., ed., 1987: *Rural planning: policy into action?* London: Harper & Row. · Cloke, P. and Little, J. 1990: *The rural state? Limits to planning in rural society*. Oxford: Oxford University Press. · Marsden, T. and Murdoch, J., eds, 1998: Rural governance and community participation – Special issue. *Journal of Rural Studies* 14: 1–118.

Suggested Reading

Buller, H. and Wright, S., eds, 1990: *Rural development: problems and practices*. Aldershot: Avebury. · Flora, C.B. and Christenson, J.A., eds, 1991: *Rural policies for the 1990s*. Boulder, CO: Westview Press. · Lapping, M.B., Daniels, T.L. and Keller, J.W. 1989: *Rural planning and development in the United States*. New York: Guilford. · Murdoch, J. and Marsden, T. 1994: *Reconstructing rurality: class, community and power in the development process*. London: UCL Press. · Winter, M. 1996: *Rural politics. Policies for agriculture, forestry and the environment*. London: Routledge.

rural–urban continuum A continuous gradation of ways of life between the two poles of truly rural COMMUNITY and truly urban SOCIETY. The concept suggests that the way of life is best understood in terms of the type of settlement that people live in, and it has been used both to distinguish between URBAN and RURAL extremes, and as a theory of social change which emphasizes the transformations from one pole to another. The characteristics of urban and rural polarities were drawn from Redfield's (1941) 'folk–urban continuum', Wirth's (1938) 'urbanism as a way of life' and Tönnies' (1955) differentiation between *Gemeinschaft* (the community built round kinship, attachment to place and cooperative action) and *Gesellschaft* (the association or society of industrialized populations, where impersonal relationships are founded on formal contract and exchange).

A series of studies (see Frankenberg, 1966, in the UK; also Fischer, 1976; Glenn and Hill, 1977, in the USA) have reflected the continuum concept in their descriptions of differences in economic, family, religious, political and social characteristics between rural community and urban society. Yet the question here is not whether such differences occur, but whether 'rural' or 'urban' are causal factors in these differences. The continuum has been heavily criticized not only for its western ETHNOCENTRISM but also because studies clearly showed different elements of 'urban' and 'rural' in the same community (Gans, 1962). Thus the revelation of village communities in cities and urban societies in supposedly rural areas (Pahl, 1965) seriously undermined the concept. Indeed, Ray Pahl is commonly credited with demolishing the concept of a rural–urban continuum, finding its use simplistic and overgeneralized and, more crucially, arguing against the formulation of a sociological definition of any settlement type (Pahl, 1966). He preferred to describe the rural–urban relationship as 'a whole series of meshes of different textures superimposed on each other, together forming a process which is creating a much more complex pattern' (p. 321).

More recently, geographers have recognized that rural–urban relations have become increasingly blurred, fragmented and renegotiated in POSTMODERN times (see RURAL GEOGRAPHY). Attention has, therefore, been focused on how social and cultural constructions of rurality have interconnected with HUMAN AGENCY, lifestyles and LIFEWORLDS to form 'experiences from within' of the rural. Geographers have also been interested in how these experiences have been structured or mediated 'from the outside', and have sought to map out the impacts in rural areas of wider social, economic and political changes. PJC

References

Fischer, C. 1976: The metropolitan experience. In A.H. Hawley, and V. Rock, eds, *Metropolitan America in contemporary perspective*. New York: Halstead, 201–34. · Frankenberg, R. 1966: *Communities in Britain*. London: Pergamon. · Gans, H. 1962: *The urban villagers*. Glencoe, IL: Free Press. · Glenn, N.D. and Hill, L. 1977: Rural–urban differences in attitudes and behaviour in the United States. *Annals of the American Academy of Political and Social Science* 429: 36–50. · Pahl, R.E. 1965: *Urbs in rure*. London: Weidenfeld and Nicolson. · Pahl, R.E. 1966: The rural–urban continuum. *Sociologia Ruralis* 6: 299–327. · Redfield, R. 1941: *The folk culture of Yucatan*. Chicago: University of Chicago Press. · Tonnies, F. 1955 [orig. pub. 1887]: *Community and society*. New York: Harper and Row. · Wirth, L. 1938: Urbanism as a way of life. *American Journal of Sociology* 44: 1–24.

rural–urban fringe A zone of transition between the continuously built-up URBAN and SUBURBAN areas of the central city and rural HINTERLAND (Pryor, 1968). This area displays a changing mix of land-use, social and demographic characteristics, and is an arena in which issues of the siting of large-scale urban amenities (such as airports and sewage works), the problems of 'fringe' agriculture, the acquisitions of land banks for later development, and the social integration of commuters have all been prominent (see Errington, 1994). The idea of a fringe is problematic (see FRINGE BELT), both because particular mixes of characteristics may be sedimented in some places (for example, by strict planning controls on urban development – see GREEN BELT), and because views on the extent of the fringe vary from a tightly drawn girdle around a city to a much wider area containing socio-economic features of the fringe which have migrated away from a city-edge location. PJC

References

Errington, A. 1994: The peri-urban fringe: Europe's forgotten rural areas. *Journal of Rural Studies* 10: 367–75. · Pryor, R.J. 1968: Defining the rural–urban fringe. *Social Forces* 47: 202–15.

Suggested Reading

Bryant, C.R. and Johnston, J.R.R. 1992: *Agriculture in the city's countryside*. London: Frances Pinter. · Bryant, C.R., Russwurm, L.H. and McLellan, A.G. 1982: *The city's countryside: land and its management in the rural–urban fringe*. New York: Longman. · Herington, J. 1984: *The outer city*. London: Harper and Row. · Roberts, R. 1995: Rural conflict and change – Special issue. *Journal of Rural Studies* 11: 239–350.

S

sacred and profane space A distinction drawn in the study and experience of religion between PLACES and sites that are imbued with a transcendent spiritual quality and those that are not. In the course of pilgrimage there is frequently said to be, as in the PARADIGMATIC case of *Pilgrim's progress*, a sense of movement toward the sacred and away from the profane (Graham and Murray, 1997). In Eliade's original terms, *sacred space* is oriented around a fixed point, a centre, while *profane space* is homogeneous and neutral. The symbolism of the cosmic centre is projected MIMETICALLY in the construction and consecration of sacred places; 'where the sacred manifests itself in space, *the real unveils itself*... [and] communication with the transmundane is established' (Eliade, 1959; also Duncan, 1990). (See also RELIGION, GEOGRAPHY OF.) DL

References

Duncan, J. 1990: *The city as text: the politics of landscape interpretation in the Kandyan Kingdom.* Cambridge: Cambridge University Press. · Eliade, M. 1959: *The sacred and the profane*. New York: Harcourt, Brace and World. · Graham, B. and Murray, M. 1997: The spiritual and the profane: the pilgrimage to Santiago de Compostela. *Ecumene* 4: 389–409.

sampling The selection of a subset from a defined population to provide needed information (as in a SURVEY ANALYSIS), used when the population is too large for a complete enumeration of all individuals (i.e. a CENSUS).

Sampling theory has been developed by statisticians so that conclusions about a population's characteristics can be inferred from those of the selected sample; the inferred values lie within error limits, whose size is known from the theory. The selection of the sample members must follow certain rules if valid INFERENCES regarding the population characteristics are to be drawn; if these rules are violated the sample is likely to be biased and the conclusions unreliable. In general, the larger the sample (in absolute terms, not as a percentage of the population) the greater its likely accuracy as a representation of the population.

The most common selection procedure is *random sampling*: the population is enumerated and a sample of predetermined size taken, usually employing a table of random numbers. To reduce effort, and also to counter problems if the size of the population is unknown, a *systematic sample* may be taken (e.g. of every tenth person entering a shopping centre). The investigator must be sure that this will not introduce bias because of some periodicity in the population (e.g. every tenth shopper is more likely to be a male than are the other nine!). *Stratified sampling* is used when the researcher wants to ensure a representative selection from two or more subgroups within the population. (If it is known that 20 per cent of all theatre-goers are male, for example, then to get an equal number of male and female respondents every fourth male and every sixteenth female entering the theatre might be questioned.) A *quota sample* (frequently used in opinion polling) is a variant on the stratified form: the investigator uses either random or systematic sampling procedures to obtain a set of respondents with a particular profile of characteristics and selection continues until the desired profile is achieved, with unneeded respondents discarded. (For example, a sample of ten may have to include six females, five individuals aged under 40, seven in white-collar occupations etc. Once the sampling procedure delivers five persons aged under 40 in a survey of shoppers, that part of the profile will be complete. It may be necessary to interview more than ten persons before all of the criteria are met, however, so that more than five respondents aged under 40 are interviewed in order to obtain a satisfactory sample on the other variables.)

In geographical studies, the standard procedures may be varied to ensure spatial coverage. Methods of random, systematic and stratified sampling of points on a map have been devised using coordinate systems, for example, as have methods of selecting transects (line samples) across an area.

Analyses of sample data make statements about the population as a whole, using SIGNIFICANCE TESTS based on theoretical FREQUENCY DISTRIBUTIONS. They involve statements regarding the range of values around the sample statistic within which the population characteristic will probably be found at a specified significance level: the most frequently used of these is the *standard error*. For example, the standard error around a sample mean may be four percentage points: thus if the observed percentage of shoppers purchasing shoes at a suburban centre is 23, then in 67 per cent of all samples the population value will lie between 19 and 27 per cent. The size of the standard error is a function of the sample size (cf. QUANTITATIVE METHODS). RJJ

Suggested Reading

Berry, B.J.L. and Baker, A.M. 1968. Methods of spatial sampling. In B.J.L. Berry and D.F. Marble, eds, *Spatial analysis: a reader in statistical geography*. Englewood Cliffs, NJ and London: Prentice-Hall, 91–100. · Dixon, C.J. and Leach. B. 1977: *Sampling methods for geographical research*. Concepts and Techniques in Modern Geography 17. Norwich: Geo Books. · Walford, N. 1995: *Geographical data analysis*. Chichester and New York: John Wiley.

satisficing behaviour Originating with Herbert Simon (1956), satisficing was developed as an alternative to RATIONAL CHOICE THEORY and its presumption of OPTIMIZATION. In contrast to the optimizer, a satisficer chooses among alternatives on the basis of whether they meet or exceed a certain minimum threshold, and not whether they are the best. Conceptually linked to satisficing is *bounded rationality*, the notion that DECISION-MAKERS choose among a narrowly defined set of options, rather than as in rational choice theory among every possible option. Two kinds of circumstances are especially germane to the applicability of both ideas: (1) either when it is logically impossible to calculate an optimal solution, or when the costs, time and expertise necessary to make such a calculation are too great; and (2) when the very choices among which the individual chooses are either in conflict with one another (see PRISONER'S DILEMMA) or incommensurable.

In geography, the best-known use of the satisficing concept and bounded rationality is found in Allan Pred's (1969) *behavioural matrix* (see figure), and defined by the twin axes of ability to use information and its availability. Any particular industrialist seeking an optimal location for their factory can be positioned on the matrix. Traditional *homo economicus* is in the bottom right-hand corner, and industrialists who are both stupid and ignorant at the top left-hand corner. Satisficers and bounded rationalists are somewhere in the middle, their precise position affecting their eventual proximity to the optimal site. Pred's work was subsequently incorporated into various BEHAVIOURAL GEOGRAPHIES of the firm,

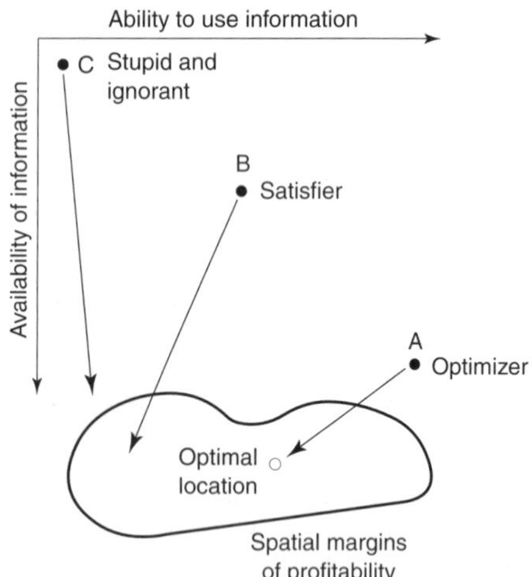

satisficing behaviour

but was also criticized for not recognizing that the two axes of the matrix are interdependent. TJB

References

Pred, A. 1967 and 1969: *Behavior and location: foundations for a geographic and dynamic location theory*, 2 vols. Lund: C.W.K. Gleerup. · Simon, H.A. 1956: Rational choice and the structure of the environment. *Psychological Review* 63: 129–38.

Suggested Reading

Pred (1967) (1969).

scale Scale refers to one or more levels of REPRESENTATION, experience and organization of geographical events and processes. There are three discernible meanings of scale in geographical research: the cartographic, methodological and what can be called geographical scale.

Cartographic scale refers to the level of abstraction at which a map is constructed. A map drawn to scale 1:50,000 means that 1 cm on the map represents 50,000 cm (0.5 km) in real space. The scale at which a map is drawn therefore colours the level and kind of detail that can be shown: a small-scale map shows a large area but at the expense of considerable detail; a large-scale map generally shows greater detail but over a more restricted terrain. Cartographic scale is therefore crucial in determining what is included and excluded in a map and the overall image a map conveys.

Methodological scale is closely related. This refers to the choice of scale made by a researcher in the attempt to gather information aimed at answering a research problem. Thus a geographer wishing to know where the wealthiest 5 per cent of a city's population lived might resort to data gathered at the level of the *census tract*. The choice of scale is largely determined by some compromise between the research problem (what kind of answer is anticipated), the availability of data, and the cost of data-acquisition and processing. Data gathered at the level of wards or community districts may be too coarse, while a block-by-block mapping of wealth in the city may be too expensive in terms of data purchase and analysis.

If these first two definitions refer to conceptualizations of scale – cartographic and methodological – *geographical scale* is of a different order. 'Geographical scale' refers to the dimensions of specific landscapes: geographers might talk of the regional scale, the scale of a watershed, or the global scale, for example. These scales are also of course conceptualized, but the conceptualization of geographical scale here follows specific processes in the physical and human LANDSCAPE rather than conceptual abstractions lain over it. The URBAN scale, for example, differs from that of census tracts insofar as the former purports to capture something about the extent of city living under given historical and geographical conditions, while the latter is imposed as an administrative convenience.

In human geography until the 1980s, the methodological and geographical meanings of scale were not systematically distinguished. Geographical scale was largely taken as either the product of the researcher's methodology or else as unproblematically given. Thus although there may be periodic conflicts over BOUNDARIES and the extent of included TERRITORY may vary widely, the scale of the NATION-STATE as such was not questioned. This was a pattern of response established after debates on REGIONAL GEOGRAPHY between the 1920s and 1950s. Some of the best works of SPATIAL SCIENCE began to insist that scale was more than a methodological choice and might inhere in spatial processes themselves (Cliff and Ord, 1981). With the rise of MARXIST GEOGRAPHY and social theory in the 1980s and 1990s, however, the question of scale has become a major research concern and the object of energetic theorization.

Proposing that all politics is at root spatial, Henri Lefebvre (1990) exhorted that a research focus on SPACE *per se* fuelled a bureaucratic agenda aimed at spatial control and spatial policy. The appropriate focus, he argued, lay in an understanding of the PRODUCTION OF SPACE. This argument found a receptive audience during the 1980s and 1990s when so many established spatial configurations of POWER and social interchange – from the local to the global – were dramatically reorganized. With such an emphasis on the fluidity and pliability of geographical space – 'the space of flows' as Castells (1996) has called it – it is also important to theorize the ways in which space is redifferentiated into recognizable PLACES, social units and groupings of places (Smith and Dennis, 1987).

A crucial insight emerging from scale research, therefore, is that geographical scale is in no sense natural or given. There is nothing inevitable about global, national or urban scales, for instance. These are specific to certain historical and geographical locations, they change over time, sometimes rapidly sometimes slowly, and in some cases a scale that operates in one society may fail to appear in another. Accordingly, nation-states are a very powerful scale of social organization today, even if their power is threatened, but nation-states were rare before the seventeenth century in Europe.

Geographical scale, then, is a central organizing principle according to which geographical differentiation takes place. It is a metric of spatial differentiation; it arbitrates and organizes the kinds of spatial differentiation that frame the landscape. As such it is the production of geographical scale rather than scale *per se* that is the appropriate research focus (Smith, 1992a). Thus Taylor (1981) has proposed that there is a 'POLITICAL ECONOMY of scale' specific to capitalist society. The specific forms taken by different scales may be constantly transforming but there is a central necessity, inherent to the logic of capitalist expansion, for the differentiation of some system of absolute spaces as particular scales of social activity (Smith, 1984). In the broadest terms, specific geographical scales can be conceived as platforms for specific kinds of social activity. They are platforms of absolute space in a wider sea of relational space.

It is therefore possible to recognize a loose hierarchy of geographical scales, from that of the BODY, the home and the COMMUNITY through the local, regional, national and global. The importance of recognizing this somewhat nested hierarchy of scales is to begin to provide a stable, theoretically derived language for analysing scale where none previously existed. It expresses the fact that the *production of scale* in capitalist society is not arbitrary or voluntaristic but is to a considerable degree ordered.

Viewed from a parallel perspective, geographical scale can be seen as a means of both containment and empowerment. A political movement which conquers urban politics in the attempt to challenge national government is empowered by its hold on politics at the urban scale, while an embattled national government may attempt to contain the political challenge at the urban scale. This was precisely the predicament in Britain in the early 1980s when Labour Party control of several metropolitan governments provided a political base from which to challenge Margaret Thatcher's national Conservative government.

According to this perspective, the construction of geographical scale is a process of profound political importance. '*Scaling places*' – the establishment of geographical differences according to a metric of scales – etches a certain order of empowerment and containment into the geographical landscape. Thus the response by the Thatcher government was to abolish metropolitan governments, erasing the geographical scale of metropolitan governance as a means of defeating political opposition. Conversely, this suggests that a central means of political power comes from a process of 'jumping scales' whereby political claims and power established at one geographical scale can be expanded to another (Smith, 1992b). Inherently contested, the establishment of geographical scale is equally a spatial means of arbitrating the social and economic contradiction between cooperation and competition: to the extent that certain scales are accepted as natural, responsibility for SOCIAL inclusion and EXCLUSION can be displaced to geography.

The nested hierarchy of scales proposed above, from the global to the body, is of course an analytical schema. In reality there is rarely if ever such a precise differentiation or nesting of scales, nor such a unilinear path through the hierarchy. The overthrow of Indonesian President Suharto in 1998 was simultaneously a community event insofar as the major uprisings were concentrated in specific parts of Jakarta (and other cities) and yet at the same time the political uprising resulted directly from regional (East Asian) economic collapse and contributed to wider global events (the global economic crisis of 1998). The interflow between bodily, global and intervening scales is neither smooth nor regular, and specific events may embody destructions and reconstructions of various scales at the same time. This simultaneity of scales, especially in times of economic crisis or major political conflict, demonstrates precisely the socially constructed nature of geographical scale and the vulnerability of power hardened as geographical scale. The collapse of scale is often the collapse of certain forms of political power in favour of others.

Burgeoning empirical research on geographical scale is beginning to document the powerful but highly variegated connections between geographical scale and politics. Marston (2000) has shown that early twentieth-century American women explicitly constructed various scales of resistance to CLASS and GENDER oppression – from the body to the STATE – and refused the imposed boundaries of scale differences. The current unification of Europe has prompted considerable attention to the restructuring of scale by Helga Leitner, John Agnew (Italy) and Neil Brenner (Germany) (all in Delaney and Leitner, 1997a), as have GLOBALIZATION (Brenner, 1997; Smith, 1997) and deindustrialization (Smith and Dennis, 1987; Miller, 1997).

In order to distinguish geographical scale from the conceptual schemas implied by cartographic and methodological notions of scale, the emphasis has been placed here on the produced materiality of geographical scale. Geographical scales may not be tangible or visible but they are real. As Delaney and Leitner (1997b) insist, 'scale exists not simply in the eye or political consciousness of the beholder'. Yet scale is simultaneously a conceptual product. In social science research scale is indeed a methodological device and the choice of scale at which to pursue specific research questions, and the choice of concepts of scale, is simultaneously a choice of conceptual and political abstraction (Cox and Mair, 1989). As Delaney and Leitner put it, 'scale emerges . . . in the fusion of ideology and practice' (p. 97).

Thus another strand of empirical work concerning scale develops the political intent inherent in the notion of 'jumping scales', and the connections to ACTIVISM. In his examination of telecommunications in various political struggles, Adams (1996) suggests that 'protest' *is* 'a scale politics'. As part of a concerted attempt to develop a LABOUR GEOGRAPHY, Herod has argued that the conquest of geographical scale represents a crucial strategy for organized labour. The political geography of union organizing involves a barrage of choices about whether specific labour contracts, establishing wage levels and work conditions, should be forged at the local, national or international scales (Herod, 1991, 1998). The scales at which class struggles are waged are crucial in forging the spatial compromises that emerge as recognizable scales of socio-economic activity in the geographical landscape.

As questions of space and geography become an increasingly keen focus of research in the social sciences and humanities, very much as an expression of the remaking of world geography from the local to the global level and everywhere in between, it will be of increasing importance to understand how this extraordinary fluidity of social relations also finds stability in a dramatic fixity of certain relations in the landscape, and how certain fixations of social assumption can be fought for over others (Swyngedouw, 1997). The question of scale will become one of mounting theoretical and practical relevance. NS

References

Adams, P.A. 1996: Protest and the scale of telecommunications. *Political Geography* 15: 419–41. · Brenner, N. 1997: Global, fragmented, hierarchal: Henri Lefebvre's geographies of globalization. *Public Culture* 10.1: 135–67. · Castells, M. 1996: *The information age, vol. 1: The rise of the network society*. Oxford: Basil Blackwell. · Cliff, A.D. and Ord, J.K. 1981: *Spatial processes*. London: Pion. · Cox, K. and Mair, A. 1989: Levels of abstraction in locality studies. *Antipode* 21: 121–32. · Delaney, D. and Leitner, H. 1997a: Issue on Scale. *Political Geography* 16.2. · Delaney, D. and Leitner, H. 1997b: The political construction of scale. *Political Geography* 16: 93–7. · Herod, A. 1991: The production of scale in United States labour relations. *Area* 23: 82–8. · Herod, A., ed., 1998: *Organizing the landscape: geographical perspectives on labour unionism*. Minneapolis: University of Minnesota Press. · Lefebvre, H. 1990: *The production of space*. Oxford: Basil Blackwell. · Marston, S. 2000: The social construction of scale. *Progress in Human Geography*, forthcoming. · Miller, B. 1997: Political action and the geography of defense investment: geographical scale and the representation of the Massachusetts Miracle. *Political Geography* 16: 171–82. · Smith, N. 1984: *Uneven development: nature, capital and the production of space*. Oxford: Basil Blackwell. · Smith, N. 1992a: Geography, difference and the politics of scale. In J. Doherty, E. Graham and M. Malek, eds, *Postmodernism and the social sciences*. London: Macmillan, 57–79. · Smith, N. 1992b: Contours of a spatialized politics: homeless vehicles and the production of geographical scale. *Social Text* 33: 54–81. · Smith, N. 1997: Satanic geographies of globalization: uneven development in the 1990s. *Public Culture* 10.2: 169–89. · Smith, N. and Dennis, W. 1987: The restructuring of geographical scale: coalescence and fragmentation of the northern core region. *Economic Geography* 63: 160–82. · Swyngedouw, E. Neither global nor local: globalization and the politics of scale, 1997: In K. Cox, ed., *The Global and the Local*. New York Guilford. · Taylor, P.J. 1981: Geographical scales in the world systems approach. *Review* 5: 3–11.

Suggested Reading

Delaney and Leitner (1997a). · Smith (1992a, 1992b).

science park A particular form of GROWTH POLE established by property developers to promote technology transfer and investment in new industries, usually in conjunction with a higher education institution and sometimes with local governments also. The goal is to capitalize on the available local scientific and technological expertise by ensuring that INNOVATIONS are developed locally, generating jobs for the local economy and contributing to the higher education institution's costs (see also SEED BED LOCATION). RJJ

Suggested Reading

Massey, D., Quintas, P. and Wield, D. 1991: *High-tech fantasies: science parks in society, science and space*. London: Routledge.

science, geography and (including science studies) The history of the relationship between geography and science has been complex, multifaceted, and asymmetrical. Since its formal institutionalization, geography has usually identified with science, sometimes reacted against it, but never ignored it. In contrast, modern science has all but ignored geography.

Identification with science was there from the beginning, or even before the beginning according to Livingstone (1992, ch. 2). Renaissance mapmakers were central to early European geographical explorations, which, in turn, formed 'the very roots of modern science' (Livingstone, 1992, p. 61; cf. CARTOGRAPHY, HISTORY OF). One outcome of those explorations was European IMPERIALISM, and here too geography was closely linked. Livingstone (1992, p. 190) calls 'geography... the science of imperialism *par excellence*'. The 'new geography' of the nineteenth century, and its associated scientific skills of topographic and social surveying (cf. SURVEY ANALYSIS), CARTOGRAPHY, and regional resource inventory techniques, was made for the colonial project (Hudson, 1977; see COLONIALISM; COMMERCIAL GEOGRAPHY).

A different form of identification between geography and science emerged in the late 1950s when some in the discipline began explicitly to adopt its techniques, methods, and philosophy (see QUANTITATIVE REVOLUTION and SPATIAL SCIENCE). Coming to dominate human geography by the late 1960s, the culmination of scientific geography was David Harvey's (1969) celebratory tome *Explanation in geography*, a primer on everything anyone might want to know about science and spatial relations. In retrospect, the timing of Harvey's book could scarcely have been worse (a fact Harvey in effect acknowledged by his disavowal of traditional, 'bourgeois' ideological science just four years after its publication for a different definition of science altogether, scientific Marxism: see MARXIAN ECONOMICS; MARXIST GEOGRAPHY). First, science had nothing to say about a range of vexing social issues (e.g. chronic POVERTY or SLUM housing), and about which geographers were increasingly concerned (the so-called 'RELEVANCE debate' which was a precursor to Harvey's full-blown Marxism). Second, and of more enduring effect although never really taken up by Harvey himself, were the increasing number and severity of criticisms made by historians and sociologists of science of the very philosophical justification of the scientific method based upon rationality, objectivity, and truth seeking.

The origins of those criticisms are in Thomas Kuhn's (1922–97) work on the history of science in which he argued that the PARADIGMS in which scientific theories are embedded are:

- *incommensurable with one another* because their core values and assumptions cannot by their very nature be compared; and
- *incapable of final empirical validation* because facts are not independent of the theories that they are used to test (Kuhn, 1962).

Therefore, science cannot be conceived as Harvey and others originally suggested. Science does not progress towards ultimate objective truth because scientific theories can be neither directly compared nor proven (cf. TELEOLOGY). Kuhn's work, in turn, shaped subsequent research, first, by giving 'a new respect for scientists, not as impersonal automata but simply as human individuals participating in a culture common to all' (Richards, 1987, p. 201), and second, by its implicit RELATIVISM, the idea that knowledge is produced and accepted according to local, contextual circumstances, and not on the basis of iron-clad, universal rules.

Whether Kuhn liked it or not (and the indications are that he didn't), later researchers developed and deepened both points, creating what has become *science studies*. A cross-disciplinary endeavour involving historians, sociologists, philosophers, cultural theorists, and recently human geographers, in science studies treats science as a particular kind of social practice, and assesses it accordingly. Specifically, through detailed empirical case studies, proponents of science studies argue that scientific theories are socially constructed, reflecting the political and IDEOLOGICAL interests, unequal relations of POWER and uneven resource ownership that are found in SOCIETY at large. They are not the precipitate of some universal, ineluctable, rational method.

Science studies has burgeoned and fragmented from its inception in the early 1970s. Three main variants are recognizable. The earliest was the *Edinburgh School*, or *strong programme*, which emerged intellectually from the already existing sub-discipline of the sociology of science. Bloor (1976), in particular, provided trenchant criticisms of science's supposed rational method ('the force of reason... is the force of society mislocated and mystified'; Bloor, 1988, p. 70), as well as furnishing a set of research principles (causality, impartiality, symmetry and reflexivity) for determining how a given social interest causes a particular scientific theory (e.g. how Robert Boyle's theological beliefs determined his corpuscular theory of nature; Bloor, 1976). The Edinburgh School was largely concerned with examining the effect of broad social interests. A number of sympathetic critics, however, subsequently suggested that much of the social construction of science occurs in micro-level activities, and at particular sites such as the laboratory. Latour and Woolgar's (1979) detailed, ETHNOGRAPHIC work carried out at the Salk Institute in California, pioneered what became known as the *constructionist approach*, later modified and developed by Latour as ACTOR–NETWORK THEORY. The latter suggests that the problem of science is the creation and maintenance of order which is achieved through the marshalling of a network of resources, both human and non-human. Once in place, that network is very hard to dislodge, and so the knowledge with which it is associated – the model of DNA, a computer, a book called *The dictionary of human geography* – form 'black boxes', the legitimacy of which are rarely questioned (Latour, 1987). While Latour's work has received much attention, he was criticized for not recognizing effects of social power. In contrast, feminists within science studies have consistently pointed to them (Harding, 1987), the works of whom have become central to the third sub-genre, the *cultural studies of science* (Rouse, 1996, ch. 9). Here, Haraway's (1991, 1997) writings, and especially her notion of SITUATED KNOWLEDGE, have been important in delineating the effects of patriarchy and racism on the construction of scientific theory. Rouse's (1987) work, which applies Foucault's idea of disciplinary power to laboratory practices, and which makes use of the notion of LOCAL KNOWLEDGE hesitantly but cumulatively spreading from one local site to another, has also been important, especially in its geographical resonances. It is this latest variant of science studies that has attracted the greatest attention and criticism, and has become known as 'the science wars'. (See *Social Text*, volumes 46/47, 1996.)

In geography, Kuhn's work, but not its radical implications, was picked up relatively early (Haggett and Chorley, 1967). Strangely it was used to justify SPATIAL SCIENCE, not disable it. With Harvey's Marxist renunciation of traditional scientific methods in the early 1970s, interest in the whole topic waned, and was not revived until the early 1990s when there was both a philosophical and substantive interest in science studies. The philosophical interest was prompted by wider discussions around POST-STRUCTURALISM, feminism, CULTURAL POLITICS and NATURE where issues of social constructionism, power, and practice were central. Barnes (1996), for example, draws on the Edinburgh school, Thrift (1996) on actor–network theory, Gregory (1994) on the writings of Haraway and Rouse, and Demeritt (1996) on social constructionism more generally.

The substantive interest derives from two sources. First, it comes from geographers interested in the history of their own discipline which, as already noted, was historically tethered to science. Livingstone's (1992, especially ch. 1) work is formative, although he has misgivings about the attendant RELATIVISM of science studies. More recently, Livingstone (1995) has begun systematically to explore the geographies of science from the spatial configuration of the laboratory to the global circulation of scientific data and knowledge. Secondly, some geographers critical of GEOGRAPHICAL INFORMATION SYSTEMS have drawn upon the science studies tradition in mounting their critique (Pickles, 1995). TJB

References

Barnes, T.J. 1996: *Logics of dislocation: models, metaphors, and meanings of economic space*. New York: Guilford. · Bloor, D. 1976: *Knowledge and social imagery*. London: Routledge, Kegan & Paul. · Bloor, D. 1988: Rationalism, supernaturalism, and the sociology of knowledge. In I. Hronsky, M. Feher and B. Dajka, eds, *Scientific knowledge socialised*. Budapest: Akedemiai Kiado, 55–74. · Demeritt, D. 1996: Social theory and the reconstruction of science and geography. *Transactions, Institute of British Geographers* NS 21: 483–504. · Gregory, D. 1994: *Geographical imaginations*. Oxford: Blackwell. · Haggett, P. and Chorley, R.J. 1967: Models, paradigms and the new geography. In R.J. Chorley and P. Haggett, eds, *Models in geography*. London: Methuen, 19–41. · Haraway, D.J. 1991: *Simians, cyborgs, and women: the reinvention of nature*. New York: Routledge. · Haraway, D.J. 1997: *Modest-Witness@second-millennium. FemaleMan© Meets_OncoMouse TM: Feminism and Technoscience*. New York: Routledge. · Harding, S. 1987: *The science question in feminism*. Ithaca, NY: Cornell University Press. · Harvey, D. 1969: *Explanation in geography*. London: Edward Arnold. · Hudson, B. 1977: The new geography and the new imperialism: 1870–1918. *Antipode* 9: 9–18. · Kuhn, T. 1962: *The structure of scientific revolutions*. Chicago: University of Chicago Press. · Latour, B. 1987: *Science in action: how to follow scientists and engineers through society*. Cambridge, MA: Harvard University Press. · Latour, B. and Woolgar, S. 1979: *Laboratory life: the construction of scientific facts*. London: Sage. · Livingstone, D.N. 1992: *The geographical tradition: episodes in a contested enterprise*. Oxford: Blackwell. · Livingstone, D.N. 1995: The spaces of knowledge: contributions towards a historical geography of science. *Environment and Planning D: Society and Space* 13: 5–34. · Pickles, J. 1995: *Ground truth: the social implications of geographic information systems*. New York: Guilford. · Richards, S. 1987: *Philosophy and the sociology of science*. Chicago: Chicago University Press. · Rouse, J. 1987: *Knowledge and power: towards a political philosophy of science*. Ithaca, NY: Cornell University Press. · Rouse, J. 1996: *Engaging science: how to understand its practices philosophically*. Ithaca, NY: Cornell University Press. · Sokal, A.D. 1996: Transgressing the boundaries: towards a transformative hermeneutics of quantum gravity. *Social Text* 46/47: 217–52. · Thrift, N.J. 1996: *Spatial formations*. London: Sage.

Suggested Reading

Livingstone (1995). · Rouse (1996).

search behaviour The process of seeking out and evaluating alternatives in spatial decision-making, as in the selection of potential MIGRATION destinations. Search behaviour normally occurs within the constraints of an ACTION SPACE, that segment of all possible locations which are known to the searcher. (See also PLACE UTILITY; BEHAVIOURAL GEOGRAPHY.) RJJ

secession The transfer of one part of a state's area and population to another new or existing STATE. There are many instances of groups that wish to secede and such movements are invariably very disruptive politically, leading to war and guerrilla conflicts. The establishment of the Irish Free State in Ireland in 1922 is an example of a successful secessionist movement, but most claims are frustrated by opposition from established states which stand to lose TERRITORY. Secessionist movements can take several forms: sub-state NATIONALISM, where a minority wishes to set up a separate independent state; unification nationalism, where minorities spread throughout a number of neighbouring states desire political unity; and IRREDENTISM, where the aim is to effect the transfer of territory from one state to another. MB

Suggested Reading

Chazan, N., ed., 1991: *Irredentism and international politics*. Twickenham: Adamantine.

second home A property owned or rented on a long lease as the occasional residence of a household that usually lives elsewhere. Second homes come in different shapes and sizes, from luxury houses to mobile homes and boats, and are more numerous in some nations than others: there are, for example, nearly one million 'dachas' located around Moscow. Although accurate data are difficult to construct, over 20 per cent of households in France and Sweden have access to a second home, whereas the equivalent figure in the USA, Canada and UK is around 4 per cent. Second homes may bring economic advantages to a rural area, but they are sometimes viewed as a symbol of outsiders' involvement in the cultural and material take-over of local RURAL COMMUNITY. With trends of COUNTERURBANIZATION some households now have their main residence in a rural area, and keep a 'second home' close to the urban workplace. PJC

Suggested Reading

Coppock, J.T. 1977: *Second homes: cures or blessing?* Oxford: Pergamon. · Shucksmith, M. 1983: Second homes: a frame-work for policy. *Town Planning Review* 54: 174–93.

secondary data analysis The use of a data set for research projects other than that for which it was originally collected. Increasingly data sets, such as those obtained through CENSUSES and QUESTIONNAIRES, are stored in computer databases and housed in archives from where they are made available to other researchers. This further use of data allows both efficiency in data collection and the conduct of comparative studies (across space and time) that otherwise would be impossible: increasingly, researchers funded by public bodies are required to deposit their data in archives (such as the Data Archive at the University of Essex, which has been operating since 1967). RJJ

Suggested Reading

Hakim, C. 1982: *Secondary analysis in social research: a guide to data, sources and methods with examples*. London: George Allen and Unwin.

section A territorial division of a country associated with an electoral CLEAVAGE created when a party mobilizes the majority of that area's population around a particular economic or social issue. The classic sectional cleavage occurred in the southern States of the USA for most of the century following the end of the American Civil War; the great majority of white voters were mobilized by the Democratic party to block the achievement of equality of civil rights granted to blacks constitutionally by the ending of SLAVERY. RJJ

Suggested Reading

Archer, J.C. and Taylor, P.J. 1981: *Section and party: a political geography of American Presidential elections from Andrew Jackson to Ronald Reagan*. London and New York: John Wiley.

sectoral model A model of intra-urban land-use patterns developed by Homer Hoyt (1939) using housing rental and value data. From observations of over 200 US cities in the 1930s, Hoyt argued that the common residential pattern involves housing of different quality and value segregated into sectors radiating out along major routeways from the CENTRAL BUSINESS DISTRICT. The wealthy occupied the most desirable sector, which usually had the most attractive physical environment, and the lowest-income groups occupied land adjacent to the main industrial districts. Changes in a district's characteristics were produced by the FILTERING process, with the affluent moving further out along their sector and releasing their former homes, closer to the city centre, for slightly lower income groups.

Hoyt's model was presented as an alternative to Burgess's ZONAL MODEL, and was later incorporated with it in a MULTIPLE NUCLEI MODEL (see figure for that entry). RJJ

Reference

Hoyt, H. 1939: *The structure and growth of residential neighborhoods in American cities*. Washington, D.C.: Federal Housing Administration.

Suggested Reading

Johnston, R.J. 1971: *Urban residential patterns: an introductory review*. London: George Bell and Sons.

seed bed location An area whose characteristics encourage the establishment and growth of new firms there. Initially, such areas were associated with the fringe of the CENTRAL BUSINESS DISTRICT, where relatively small, cheap and easily converted older properties offered favourable conditions for people wishing to set up their own businesses: in recent years, URBAN RENEWAL policies have restricted the availability of such properties. Various public policies have been experimented with to stimulate the development of new businesses in planned seed bed locations, as with ENTERPRISE ZONES and SCIENCE PARKS. RJJ

segmented labour market A LABOUR MARKET divided into two or more separate segments between which movement is difficult. A dual labour market, for example, may comprise one segment for skilled labour and the other for unskilled, with people in the latter unable to compete for jobs in the former (which may itself be further divided according to the skills involved). Spatially, a country may be divided into a large number of separate labour markets between which movement is difficult for some people because of the costs of either COMMUTING or MIGRATION. Such segmentation makes for particular difficulties during periods of RESTRUCTURING, when available labour supply does not match demand. RJJ

Suggested Reading

Cooke, P.N. 1983: Labour market discontinuity and spatial development. *Progress in Human Geography* 7: 545–66.

segregation Associated with the ecological ideas of the CHICAGO SCHOOL of urban sociology, the concept of segregation refers both to *processes* of social differentiation (usually at the urban scale) and to the spatial *patterns* that result from such processes. According to the Chicago sociologists, ethnic groups in American cities went through a series of stages from contact and competition to CONFLICT and eventual ASSIMILATION. Social geographers and 'spatial sociologists' argued that patterns of residential segregation could be taken as an index of that process. INDICES OF SEGREGATION were calculated and refined (Peach, 1975; Peach et al., 1981), often with the implication that some form of dispersal (voluntary or induced) would be a desirable policy response. Studies have focused on the high levels of segregation in American cities, particularly among African-American and Hispanic minorities (e.g. Massey and Denton, 1993), and on whether similar GHETTOES exist elsewhere (e.g. Peach, 1996). The balance between voluntary and involuntary forces of residential clustering has been vigorously debated (often theorized in terms of 'choice' and 'constraint'). Attention has also focused on the potential role of residential segregation in CLASS formation and the growth of COMMUNITY consciousness within and between segregated NEIGHBOURHOODS. As attention has turned to the structures and institutions underlying patterns of residential segregation, geographers have addressed the role of housing markets and mortgage finance in the racialization of minority groups, exploring the political links between RACE and residence (Smith, 1989; Cross and Keith, 1993). (See also HOUSING CLASS; HUMAN ECOLOGY; SOCIAL AREA ANALYSIS; URBAN ECOLOGY; URBAN GEOGRAPHY.) PAJ

References

Cross, M. and Keith, M., eds, 1993: *Racism, the city and the state*. London: Routledge. · Massey, D.S. and Denton, N. 1993: *Apartheid American style*. Cambridge, MA: Harvard University Press. · Peach, C., ed., 1975: *Urban social segregation*. London: Longman. · Peach, C. 1996: Does Britain have ghettos? *Transactions, Institute of British Geographers* NS 21: 216–35. · Peach, C., Robinson, V. and Smith, S., eds, 1981: *Ethnic segregation in cities*. London: Croom Helm. · Smith, S.J. 1989: *The politics of 'race' and residence*. Cambridge: Polity Press.

self-determination The right of a group with a distinctive territorial identity to determine its own destiny. The concept, similar to that of NATIONALISM, is generally applied to the claims of indigenous populations living within territories occupied by others, such as American Indians and New Zealand Maori (cf. COLONIALISM). Such groups claim self-determination rights according to the statement in the United Nations' Charter that:

> All people have the right to self-determination; by virtue of that right they may freely determine their political status and freely pursue their economic, social and cultural development.

RJJ

Suggested Reading

Johnston, R.J., Knight, D.B. and Kofman, E., eds, 1988: *Nationalism, self-determination and political geography*. London and New York: Croom Helm.

sense of place Originating in studies of the physical characteristics and qualities of geographical locations as appropriated in human experience and imagination, sense of place has increasingly been examined in human geography as an outcome of interconnected PSYCHOANALYTIC, social and environmental processes, creating and manipulating quite flexible relations with physical place. Geographers have thus examined both the character intrinsic to a PLACE as a localized, bounded and material geographical entity, and the sentiments of attachment and detachment that human beings experience, express and contest in relation to specific places. In terms of the second approach, place may have no visible, material expression but may emerge and become articulated in and through social interaction (McDowell, 1997).

Certain physical locations seem to generate similarly powerful responses from quite different people over sustained historical periods through their distinctive or memorable qualities. This may result from unique topographical characteristics, as in the case of Mount Royal in Montreal (Debarbieux and Petit, 1997), the Sugar Loaf at Rio de Janeiro or

Table Mountain at the Cape of Good Hope, visible as landmarks over great distances. Geographical distinctiveness may also result from long-term human occupance and physical shaping of a TERRITORY, as in the case of Tuscany in Italy (Greppi, 1990, 1991, 1993) or Rutlandshire in England (Cosgrove, Roscoe and Rycroft, 1996). It may alternatively be associated with significant events which have occurred and left their mark in social memory at a location, as in the case of battlefields, locations of great tragedy or evil such as Auschwitz in Poland (Charlesworth, 1994), or of epiphany (the eruption of the sacred into secular space), for example Temple Mount in Jerusalem, Delphi in Greece or Lourdes in south-west France. Finally, a powerful sense of place may be projected onto entirely mythical locations such as the Mountains of the Moon, believed from Classical times to hide the source of the River Nile. Such places become known and familiar to large numbers who may never have visited them personally, constituent parts of their IMAGINATIVE GEOGRAPHIES, constructed in and through stories, paintings, photographs and media images, often as exotic or 'other' places through which the identity of the home place is normalized and reinforced. TRAVEL WRITING and guide books play a critical role in creating and enhancing such imagined senses of place, reporting and promoting travel pilgrimage and tourism (Gregory, 1995; Graham and Murray, 1997; Gilbert, 1999; see also ART, GEOGRAPHY AND).

Whether physically distinctive or not, sense of place is profoundly connected to individual human and social processes producing deep emotional connections with specific locations. PHENOMENOLOGIES of place have tended to emphasize positive feelings of attachment, particularly in the case of 'home' places, psychological satisfaction or spiritual elevation, but the experience of place may equally be one of fear, disgust or sadness (Relph, 1976). Places of fear and danger have also been studied, as in the case of women's effective exclusion from certain urban places and districts through fear of CRIME (Valentine, 1989). The most commonly examined aspect of this sense of place within HUMANISTIC GEOGRAPHY has been of the experience of 'home', where one feels oneself 'in one's place' within a familiar locale. The social struggles and negotiations through which the personal sense of home place is realized have been the subject of study, as have the various expressions of HOMELESSNESS, transience and being 'out of place' (Cresswell, 1996). Because the sense of attachment and significance in place always draws upon memory, desire and experience of other people, it is as much social as personal, and a product of interaction between people at a specific location as much as of the physical properties of that location. Recent studies have concentrated on examining the ways that material expression is given to these complex senses of place and how both social memory and political struggle become expressed and concretized in place. This may find material expression in various markers, from the physical construction of memorials and MONUMENTS (Withers, 1996) to the more subtle indicators of social inclusion and exclusion within neighbourhoods (Western, 1993). A notable example is the case of war, where battlefield memorials may become the only material signifier of events which provided locations with a deep sense of place and social connection for people otherwise spatially and culturally disconnected from them and where there may be conflict over where and how to memorialize war dead: at 'home' or in a 'corner of a foreign field' (Heffernan, 1995).

In sustaining a sense of place, the measurable and visible features of a place are thus conflated with the subjective aspects of human experience, direct or indirect, and with social solidarity at that place, giving to places the characteristic of 'betweenness' explored by Entrikin (1990). Entrikin emphasizes the significance of such social relations as family and COMMUNITY over the visible, physical features of material locations. A critical concern which has paralleled the whole history of modernization – expressed in much humanistic geographical writing in the 1970s – is that an 'authentic' sense of place to which traditional forms of social solidarity gave rise (the village or small town for example) was becoming disrupted by processes of economic and social change, uprooting people from enduring local attachments and relocating them in less permanent, apparently anonymous and alienating, mass-produced places deemed to lack the necessary preconditions for developing a sense of place (cf. RURAL–URBAN CONTINUUM). In the 1980s this concern was recast within geography in the critique of POSTMODERN places as commodified, alienated and dangerous by comparison with the more secure sense of place in the immediate post-war world (Eyles, 1985). The sense of place thus always seems to entail a dimension of nostalgic yearning.

Some geographers have sought to develop a more sophisticated theorizing of human connections to place. Doreen Massey has described 'a global sense of place', a progressive rather than nostalgic and conservative sense, in which places are no longer regarded as fixed in scale or bounded in space and time, but as 'articulated moments in networks of social relations and understandings' (Massey, 1993, p. 66). In a sensitive evocation of her own city NEIGHBOURHOOD, she describes how expressions of intense localism such as newspapers carrying news of small, geographically distant rural locations in Ireland are to be found on a busy inner-London street in Kilburn, a district occupied by a rich variety of ethnic and language groups and over which intercontinental airlines visibly inscribe connections to global destinations. Local intimacy, distance, movement and memory combine to produce a complex but not necessarily contradictory sense of place, a specific and local realization of multiple processes, connections and networks that are global in scope and range. The rapid evolution of electronic modes of COMMUNICATIONS, particularly the Internet, has also allowed the social connections formerly associated with face-to-face communication and thus a localized sense of place, to be realized at a global scale and in virtual space (Mattelart, 1996). A *virtual sense of place* may already exist for many regular users of these technologies, as for those participating vicariously in the imagineered places of TV soap operas, although these have only recently begun to be systematically explored by human geographers.

Place remains powerfully important in framing and sustaining individual and collective IDENTITIES. In the contemporary context of mobile, flexible and contingent senses of place, various agencies seek to fix and control place meanings and identity, and thus materialize an 'official' sense of place. Much of CONSERVATION and heritage activity is concerned to achieve and sustain a singular and univocal sense of place through controlling change in the physical landscape. GENTRIFICATION of villages and inner-city communities, and NIMBY attitudes among those with fixed economic and emotional investments in place are popular expressions of the same urge to resist change and flexibility in the sense of place, although, ironically, many who are most vociferous in defending a localized and univocal sense of place are also tightly connected into the networks that construct place's more global expression. The consequential marginalization of groups with respect to place, such as sexual non-conformists, homeless people, travellers and formerly institutionalized individuals have been the subject of geographical explorations of alternative senses of place (Shields, 1991; Sibley, 1995; Cresswell, 1996). Here, 'knowing one's place' takes on a less comfortably secure and domestic resonance, as questions of identity, 'OTHERING' and exclusion point to the connections between power and place. A number of geographers have drawn upon de Certeau's distinction between strategies and tactics in everyday social life to explore the power relations constituted in place through the impositions and resistances of a distanciated, synoptic view of place and a more intimate knowledge of its quotidian workings (Stewart, 1996).

The conscious creation and manipulation of place images through advertising, architectural coding, place promotion and naming strategies have become distinguishing features of planning and representing place, particularly in the context of CONSUMPTION spaces, as for example in 'themed' areas within large shopping malls, designed to resemble stereotypes of places familiar through cultural conventions and media images (Goss, 1997). The supposed 'authenticity' of former production spaces (docklands and textile mills for example) and heritage centres is both emphasized by conserving their physical form and deployed to promote altered uses, while new places are created which draw upon iconic references to other localities to enhance their own identity. There is much to suggest that most users of such places, far from being unconsciously duped by such manipulations of the senses of place, are actually knowing participants in this charade of place-making, suggesting that the human sense of place is highly sophisticated and flexible, and therefore most accurately theorized in terms of contingent connections and understandings. The shift in geographical studies of sense(s) of place from a concern with the physical qualities of location to their social construction has perhaps underemphasized the continuing significance of the aesthetic, sensual and visceral aspects of the sense of place, most powerfully expressed in rituals of death and burial (Foster, 1998). There are signs however of a revived interest in the materialities of place, stimulated by the focus within CONSUMPTION studies on the signifying role of material culture, and of studies of embodiment on the physical presence of the gendered, aged, sexed, sensitized and variously abled human body within physical space (Imrie, 1996). DEC

References

Charlesworth, A. 1994: Contesting places of memory: the case of Auschwitz. *Environment and Planning D: Society and Space* 12: 579–93. · Cosgrove, D., Roscoe, B. and Rycroft, S. 1996: Landscape and identity at Ladybower Reservoir and Rutland Water. *Transactions, Institute of British Geographers* NS 21: 534–51. · Cresswell, T. 1996: *In place/out of place: geography, ideology and transgression*. Minneapolis and London: University of Minnesota Press. · Debarbieux, B. and Petit, E. 1997: Receuillement et déambulation, ailleurs et même au-delà. Façonnement et usages des cimetières du Mont Royal, Montréal: 1850–1996. *Géographie et Cultures* 23: 23–50. · Entrikin, N. 1990: *The betweenness of place: towards A geography of modernity*. Basingstoke: Macmillan. · Eyles, J. 1985: *Senses of place*. Warrington: Silverbrook. · Foster, J. 1998: John Buchan's 'Hesperides': Landscape rhetoric and the aesthetics of bodily experience on the South African highveld, 1901–1903. *Ecumene* 5: 323–47. · Gilbert, D. 1999: London in all its Glory – or how to enjoy London: representations of Imperial London in its guidebooks. *Journal of Historical Geography* 25. · Goss, J. 1997: The 'magic of the mall': an analysis of form, function and meaning in the contemporary retail built environment. In L. McDowell, ed., *Undoing place? A geographical reader*. London: Arnold, 265–83. · Graham, B. and Murray, M. 1997: The spiritual and the profane: the pilgrimage to Santiago de Compostela. *Ecumene* 4: 389–409. · Gregory, D. 1995: Between the book and the lamp: imaginative geographies of Egypt, 1849–50. *Transactions, Institute of British Geographers* 20: 29–57. · Greppi, C., ed., 1990, 1991, 1993: *Paesaggi dell'Appennino toscano*; *Paesaggi delle colline toscane*; *Paesaggi della costa toscana*. Venezia: Marsilio. · Heffernan, M. 1995: For ever England: the Western Front and the politics of remembrance in Britain. *Ecumene* 2: 293–324. · Imrie, R. 1996: *Disability and the city: international perspectives*. London: Paul Chapman. · McDowell, L., ed., 1997: *Undoing place? A geographical reader*. London: Arnold. · Massey, D. 1993: Power-geometry and a progressive sense of place. In J. Bird, et al., eds, *Mapping the futures: local cultures, global change*. London and New York: Routledge, 59–69. · Mattelart, A. 1996: *The invention of communication*. Minneapolis and London: University of Minnesota Press. · Relph, E. 1976: *Place and placelessness*. London: Pion. · Shields, R. 1991: *Places on the margin: alternative geographies of modernity*. London and New York: Routledge. · Sibley, D. 1995: *Geographies of exclusion: society and difference in the West*. London and New York: Routledge. · Stewart, K. 1996: *A space on the side of the road: cultural poetics in an 'other' America*. Princeton: Princeton University Press. · Valentine, G. 1989: The geography of women's fear. *Area* 21: 385–90. · Western, J. 1993: Ambivalent attachments to place in London: twelve Barbadian families. *Environment and Planning D: Society and Space* 11: 147–70. · Withers, C.W.J. 1996: Place, memory and monument: memorializing the past in contemporary Highland Scotland. *Ecumene* 3: 325–44.

Suggested Reading

Daniels, S. 1992: Place and the geographical imagination. *Geography* 337: 310–22. · McDowell, L., ed., 1997: *Undoing place? A geographical reader*. London: Arnold. · Oakes, T. 1997: Place and the paradox of modernity. *Annals of the Association of American Geographers* 87: 509–31.

sequent occupance 'The view of geography as a succession of stages of human occupance . . . which establishes the genetics of each stage in terms of its predecessor' (Whittlesey, 1929; cf. SETTLEMENT CONTINUITY). Whittlesey's scheme owed much to HUMAN ECOLOGY, but although he knew that 'the analogy between sequent occupance in CHOROLOGY and plant succession in botany will be apparent to all', he insisted that his own conception was more 'intricate'. While 'human occupance of area, like other biotic phenomena, carries within itself the seed of its own transformation' (cf. DIALECTIC(S)), such uninterrupted or 'normal' progressions were 'rare, perhaps only ideal, because extraneous forces are likely to interfere with the normal course, altering either its direction or rate, or both' and 'breaking or knotting the thread of sequent occupance'. These detailed qualifications were vital, but Whittlesey was also determined to distance himself from 'the physiographic cycle of erosion', an evolutionary scheme, with similar disclaimers – although few of those who followed in his wake displayed an equal caution or an equivalent subtlety (see Mikesell, 1975). The most successful applications of the concept (especially Broek, 1932) in fact departed from the series of stable CROSS-SECTIONS envisaged by Whittlesey and linked them with deliberately dynamic VERTICAL THEMES, so that his projected systematization of the 'relatively few sequence patterns that have ever existed' was never realized. DG

References

Broek, J.O.M. 1932: *The Santa Clara Valley, California: a study in landscape changes*. Utrecht: Oosthock. · Mikesell, M.W. 1975: The rise and decline of sequent occupance. In D. Lowenthal and M. Bowden, eds, *Geographies of the mind: essays in historical geography in honour of John Kirkland Wright*. New York: Oxford University Press. · Whittlesey, D. 1929: Sequent occupance. *Annals of the Association of American Geographers* 19: 162–6.

Suggested Reading

Mikesell (1975).

services, geography of The study of the geography of service industries. Services are usually defined as 'activities which are relatively detached from material production and which as a consequence do not directly involve the processing of physical materials. The main difference between manufacturing and service products seems to be that the expertise provided by services relies much more directly on work-force skills, experience, and knowledge than on physical techniques embodied in machinery or processes' (Marshall et al., 1988, p. 11). But general statements of this kind have proved very difficult to convert into clear working definitions of services and, in reality, the definition is often made by a process of exclusion; services are not agricultural, mining or industrial production. Only recently have complex and partly satisfactory definitions of services been made, usually on the basis of binary distinctions such as PRODUCER and CONSUMER SERVICES, public and private services, tradeable and non-tradeable services, office-based and non-office-based services, and so on (see Petit, 1986; Marshall, Damesick and Wood, 1987; cf. ABSTRACTION; CHAOTIC CONCEPTION).

The study of services has clearly become a pressing task as these industries have become a more and more prominent part of all developed economies (in terms of both output and, more particularly, employment). As the absolute and proportional importance of services has become clear so the debates over their actual economic importance have become more intense. On the one hand, there has been growing debate over whether service industries are dependent on manufacturing industry, for example, and over the apparently lower levels of PRODUCTIVITY in many service industries (although measuring productivity in service industries is itself a vexed topic). On the other hand, some commentators (for example, Dicken and Thrift, 1992; Sayer and Walker, 1992) have suggested that many of these problems only arise because service industries are seen as discrete entities rather than as links in extended COMMODITY CHAINS or '*filières*', and because it is too often forgotten that service industries themselves produce tangible, traded commodities (whether these are wills, pieces of software, or instructional videotapes). Again, the success of manufacturing industry is often nowadays associated with intangible factors, many of which turn out to be associated with the quality of services provided either from within or from outside the manufacturing firm (Marshall, 1989).

Given these problems, it is no surprise that the geography of services remains a very diverse area of research. Certain service industries (like PRODUCER SERVICES and RETAILING) are comparatively well studied. Others, like TOURISM and many PUBLIC SERVICES, are only now being given their due (Pinch, 1989; Mohan, 1991; cf. HEALTH AND HEALTH CARE, GEOGRAPHY OF). What seems certain is that there is no one geography of services. Rather, there is a whole set of different geographies of services which vary according to the characteristics of the specific industry (Allen, 1988). It may still be possible to make some generalizations about the geography of services as a whole, because certain types of service industry are still concentrated in very large metropolitan centres, others are growing in intermediate cities, or major provincial cites, and others still are growing in small towns and rural areas (Glasmeier and Borchard, 1989; O'hUallachain and Reid, 1991) but whether the results repay the effort can be questioned.

There are currently six discernible tendencies in the study of the geography of services.

The first is an increasing emphasis on large services firms as service industries have become increasingly centralized (cf. CONCENTRATION AND CENTRALIZATION).

The second tendency is a natural development of the first: service firms are becoming more and more international in scope. The past 20 years have seen the growth of the services MULTINATIONAL CORPORATION in industries as diverse as financial services, retailing, and tourism (Daniels, 1993; O'Farrell, Wood and Zheng, 1996; Bryson and Daniels, 1998a, 1998b; Dicken, 1998). The study of these large services MULTINATIONAL CORPORATIONS involves research into many of the same strategies as those found in other sectors of the world economy, including merger and takeover franchising, strategic alliances, and the full range of flexible labour force and production possibilities (see FLEXIBLE ACCUMULATION).

The third tendency, one that is both counterposed and linked to the previous ones, is the growing interest in the role of small and medium-sized service firms. Small and medium-sized firms in the service industries have been relatively neglected in favour of their larger cousins. This exclusive emphasis is now changing as it has been increasingly realized that such firms can, under certain circumstances, become dynamic elements of urban and regional economies (Keeble, Bryson and Wood, 1991; Wood, Bryson and Keeble, 1993).

A fourth tendency has been to take more account of the rise of service industries as a function of the production and distribution of knowledge. Business schools, management consultancies, lawyers, accountants, and the like all have one chief characteristic: the construction of knowledge for economic gain.

Neglected in the past, these *knowledge industries* are now seen to be at the centre of any geography of services (Thrift, 1997, 1998).

A fifth focus of study has been on the often vital role of advances in telecommunications, both in allowing services to internationalize and in making many services more tradeable. It is important to remember that without modern telecommunications many modern services firms and products could not exist (Brunn and Leinbach, 1991; Graham and Marvin, 1995; Mitchelson and Wheeler, 1994). (See COMMUNICATIONS, GEOGRAPHY OF; INFORMATION ECONOMY; WORLD CITY.)

Finally, the nature of service industries' workforces is now seen as vital. In particular, much more attention has been paid to the exact role of managerial and professional workers, and especially their intense patterns of interaction, often at the world scale (Beaverstock, 1991, 1995). Equally, attention is being paid to service industry labour processes and, especially, to the vital role that planned and increasingly taught human interaction plays within them (Crang, 1995, 1997). Then, because service industries are relatively more feminized than other industries, considerable attention has also been paid to issues of the social construction of gendered jobs in services, and the consequent struggles to redefine these jobs in terms of pay, conditions and status (Pringle, 1988; Crompton and Jones, 1990; McDowell, 1997). (See also GENDER AND GEOGRAPHY.)

As a result of increasing interest in how service industries are 'performed', the economic geography of services has begun to take a markedly CULTURAL TURN (see Thrift and Olds, 1996; Lee and Wills, 1997). NJT

References

Allen, J. 1988: The geographies of service. In D. Massey and J. Allen, eds, *Uneven redevelopment: cities and regions in transition*. London: Hodder and Stoughton, 124–41. · Beaverstock, J. 1991: Skilled international migration analysis of international secondments within large accountancy firms. *Environment and Planning A* 23: 1087–22. · Brunn, S. and Leinbach, T., eds, 1991: *Collapsing space and time: geographic aspects of communication and information*. London: HarperCollins. · Bryson, J. and Daniels, P.W., eds, 1998a: *Service industries in the global economy, volume 1: Service theories and service employment*. Cheltenham: Edward Elgar. · Bryson, J. and Daniels, P.W., eds, 1998b: *Service industries in the global economy, volume 2: Services, globalisation and economic development*. Cheltenham: Edward Elgar. · Coffey, W. 1995: Producer services research in Canada. *Professional Geographer* 47: 74–81. · Crang, P. 1995: It's showtime: on the workplace geographies of display in a restaurant in South-East England. *Environment and Planning D: Society and Space* 15: 87–112. · Crang, P. 1997: Performing the tourist product. In R. Rojek and J. Urry, eds, *Touring cultures. Transformations of travel and theory*. London: Routledge, 137–54. · Crompton, R. and Jones, R. 1990: *Gendered jobs and social change*. London: Unwin Hyman. · Daniels, P. 1993: *Service industries in the world economy*. Oxford: Blackwell. · Daniels, P. 1995: Producer services research in the United Kingdom. *Professional Geographer* 47: 82–7. · Daniels, P. and Lever, W.F., eds, 1996: *The global economy in transition*. Harlow: Longman. · Dicken, P. 1998: *Global shift: transforming the world economy*, 3rd edn. London: Sage. · Dicken, P. and Thrift, N.J. 1992: The organisation of production and the production of organisation: why enterprises matter in the study of geographical industrialisation. *Transactions, Institute of British Geographers* NS 17: 279–91. · Glasmeier, A. and Bochard, G. 1989: From branch plants to back offices: prospects for rural services growth. *Environment and Planning A* 21: 1565–83. · Graham, S. and Marvin, S. 1995: *Telecommunications and the City. Electronic spaces, urban spaces*. London: Routledge. · Harrington, J. 1995: Empirical research on producer service growth and regional development: international comparisons. *Professional Geographer* 47: 66–9. · Keeble, D., Bryson, J. and Wood, P. 1991: Small firms, business services growth and regional development in the UK. *Regional Studies* 25: 439–54. · Lee, R. and Wills, J., eds, 1997. *Geographies of economies*. London: Arnold. · Macpherson, A. 1997: The role of producer service outsourcing in the innovation performance of New York State manufacturing firms. *Annals of the Association of American Geographers* 87: 52–71. · Marshall, J.N. 1989: Corporate reorganisation and the geography of services. *Regional Studies* 23: 139–50. · Marshall, J.N. et al. 1988: *Services and uneven development*. Oxford: Oxford University Press. · Marshall, J.N., Damesick, P. and Wood, P. 1987: Understanding the location and role of producer services in the UK. *Environment and Planning A* 19: 575–95. · McDowell, L. 1997: *Capital culture*. Oxford: Blackwell. · Mitchelson, R.L. and Wheeler, J.O. 1994: The flow of information in a global economy: the role of the American urban system in 1990. *Annals of the Association of American Geographers* 81: 254–71. · Mohan, J. 1991: The internationalisation and commercialisation of health care in Britain. *Environment and Planning A* 23: 853–68. · Noyelle, J.J. 1997: Business services and the economic performance of the New York metropolitan region. *Federal Reserve Bank of New York Economic Policy Review* 3: 79–82. · O'Farrell, P., Wood, P.A. and Zheng, J. 1996: Internationalization of business services: an inter-regional analysis. *Regional Studies* 30: 101–18. · O'hUallachain, B. and Reid, N. 1991: The location and growth of business and professional services in American metropolitan areas. *Annals of the Association of American Geographers* 81: 254–70. · Petit, D. 1986: *Slow growth and the service economy*. London: Frances Pinter. · Pinch, S. 1989: The restructuring thesis and the study of public services. *Environment and Planning A* 21: 905–26. · Pringle, R. 1988: *Secretaries' work*. London: Verso. · Sayer, A. and Walker, R. 1992: *The new social economy*. Oxford: Blackwell. · Thrift, N.J. and Olds, K. 1996: Refiguring the economic in economic geography. *Progress in Human Geography* 20:

311–37. · Thrift, N.J. 1997: The rise of soft capitalism. *Cultural Values* 1: 29–57. · Thrift, N.J. 1998: Virtual capitalism: the globalization of reflexive business knowledge. In J. Carrier and D. Miller, eds, *Virtualism. A new political economy*. Oxford, Berg, 161–86. · Wood, P.A., Bryson, J. and Keeble, D. 1993: Regional patterns of small firm development in the business services: evidence from the United Kingdom. *Environment and Planning A* 25: 677–700.

Suggested Reading

Marshall, N. and Wood, P. 1995: *Services and space: key aspects of urban and regional development*. Harlow: Longman.

settlement continuity The maintenance of (typically rural) settlement sites, settlement systems and territorial structures across a period of major societal transformation (cf. SEQUENT OCCUPANCE). In Great Britain, a fundamental question of continuity arises over the fabric of rural settlement during the collapse of the Roman occupation and the beginnings of Anglo-Saxon colonization (*c*. AD 400–1110). The two extremes were posed by Finberg as 'Continuity or cataclysm?' (1964) and 'Revolution or evolution?' (1972). Within British HISTORICAL GEOGRAPHY, these two poles are conventionally represented by: Darby, who once wrote that 'As far as there ever is a new beginning in history, the coming of the Angles, Saxons and Jutes was such a beginning' (Darby, 1964) and that, even though 'the Anglo-Saxons did not come into an empty land, and . . . many contributions from pre-Saxon days have entered into the making of England', nevertheless 'with the coming of the Anglo-Saxons, a new chapter in the history of settlement and land utilisation was begun' (Darby, 1973); and Jones, for whom 'the roots of the Saxon settlements were planted while Britain was still part of the Roman Empire' (Jones, 1978). Jones proposed a *multiple estate model* to summarize his thesis. Multiple estates were groups of townships whose tenants 'were subject to the jurisdiction of the territorial lord and [who], in return for their lands, paid rents in cash or kind and performed various services on his behalf' (see FEUDALISM). 'A network of obligations linked even the most distant settlements on each estate to the lord's' (Finberg, 1972). Multiple estates have been identified in Northumbria, Wales and south-east England and, so Jones claims, have a common pre-Saxon origin. He also argues that 'the multiple structure of these ancient estates appears to have conditioned the evolution of the constituent settlements', with some growing into villages or even market towns and the multiple structures breaking up or being re-sorted. Jones (1976) concludes that:

> to arrive at an adequate understanding of the colonization of England it is essential to look beyond unitary settlements. Rather it is necessary to adopt as a model the multiple estate: for this provides the most meaningful of all frameworks for unravelling the complex interrelationships between society, economy and habitat involved in the process of colonization.

Whatever the rights and wrongs of Jones's specific thesis (see Gregson, 1985, for a commentary and Jones's response), most scholars would endorse his emphasis on the complexity of the situation – Roberts (1979) declares that the answer to Finberg's questions (above) 'is to be found, not only between the two extremes, but varying spatially across the complex and intricate landscape varieties within these small islands – and would probably, on balance, favour continuity rather than cataclysm (Fowler, 1976). For, as Jones (1978) notes, 'the chief sufferers from the Saxon conquest . . . were British kings and nobles'. As Taylor (1983) puts the matter:

> the Saxons came not to a new and relatively untouched country but to a very old one, a country where most of the 'best' places had already been occupied not once but many times . . . All this activity took place within clearly marked territories or estates, often grouped together under the control of large landowners.

When the Roman Empire began to collapse, all that happened was that the protection of the Imperial army was removed and the sophisticated central government system was taken away. But the great mass of the population stayed on, as they had to, in their homes and on their land, to face up to what were to be increasingly difficult times both socially and economically. DG

References

Darby, H.C. 1964: Historical geography: from the coming of the Anglo-Saxons to the Industrial Revolution. In J. Wreford Watson, ed., *The British Isles: a systematic geography*. London: Nelson, 198–220. · Darby, H.C. 1973: The Anglo-Scandinavian foundations. In H.C. Darby, ed., *A new historical geography of England*. Cambridge: Cambridge University Press, 1–38. · Finberg, H.P.R. 1964: Continuity or cataclysm? In H.P.R. Finberg, ed., *Lucerna: studies of some problems in the early history of England*. London, 1–20. · Finberg, H.P.R. 1972: Revolution or evolution? In H.P.R. Finberg, ed., *The agrarian history of England and Wales, volumes I and II*. Cambridge: Cambridge University Press, 385–401. · Fowler, P.J. 1976: Agriculture and rural settlement. In D.M. Wilson, ed., *The archaeology of Anglo-Saxon*

England. London: Methuen, 23–48. · Gregson, N. 1985: The multiple estate model: some critical questions. *Journal of Historical Geography* 11: 339–51. · Jones, G.R.J. 1972: The multiple estate as a model framework for tracing early stages in the evolution of rural settlements. In F. Dussart, ed., *L'habitat et les paysages ruraux d'Europe*. Liege: University of Liege, 255–62. · Jones, G.R.J. 1976: Multiple estates and early settlement. In P.H. Sawyer, ed., *Medieval settlement: continuity and change*. London: Edward Arnold, 15–40. · Jones, G.R.J. 1978: Celts, Saxons and Scandinavians. In R.A. Dodgshon and R.A. Butlin, eds, *An historical geography of England and Wales*. London: Academic Press, 57–79. · Jones, G.R.J. 1985: Multiple estates perceived. *Journal of Historical Geography* 11: 352–63. · Roberts, B.K. 1979: *Rural settlement in Britain*. London: Hutchinson. · Taylor, C. 1983: *Village and farmstead: a history of rural settlement in England*. London: George Philip.

Suggested Reading

Finberg (1972). · Gregson (1985). · Jones (1976).

sexuality, geography and Studies of how sexualities and space are mutually constituted focusing particularly on the SPATIALITY of the construction of sexual identities and the sexuality of SPACE. The earliest work on sexuality and geography focused on heterosexual prostitution (e.g. Symanski, 1974). In the 1990s a significant body of research developed, firstly, on the geographies of lesbians and gay men, and latterly, on queer geographies (Bell and Valentine, 1995). This was facilitated by the development of POSTMODERN thought within human geography which promoted a sensitivity to DIFFERENCE and the voice of 'the OTHER'. As a result of the impact of this work, the study of sexuality and geography is often assumed to be synonymous with the study of sexual dissidents, yet there is also a growing interest in geographies of heterosexualities, and sexuality is important in geographical writing on PSYCHOANALYSIS. The complex theoretical links between sexuality and GENDER, most notably in feminist theory, mean that the two are commonly discussed in tandem (Duncan, 1996).

Work on sexuality and geography has been most prolific within the sub-disciplinary areas of URBAN, SOCIAL and CULTURAL GEOGRAPHY but it is also gradually spilling out into other parts of the discipline including ECONOMIC GEOGRAPHY, POLITICAL GEOGRAPHY and MEDICAL GEOGRAPHY, in the form of research on the pink economy, sexual CITIZENSHIP and HIV/AIDS respectively (e.g. Binnie, 1997). The main strands of writing on sexuality and geography can be summarized as:

Geographies of lesbian and gay men. Lesbians and gay men lead distinct lifestyles – defined to a lesser or greater extent by their sexuality and others' reactions to it – which have a variety of spatial expressions creating distinct social, political and cultural landscapes in some contemporary western cities. A number of studies have attempted to map these neighbourhoods and to examine gay commercial districts as sites of international lesbian and gay tourism. Knopp's (1992) work on GENTRIFICATION by gay men has particularly contributed to analysing the role of sexuality within the spatial dynamics of CAPITALISM.

In a famous study of lesbian and gay space in San Francisco, Castells (1983) argued that such NEIGHBOURHOODS and institutions are dominated by men and that lesbians lack similar territorially based forms of COMMUNITY. This provoked a number of studies of lesbian space which suggest that women do create spatially concentrated communities but that these have a quasi-underground character (e.g. Adler and Brenner, 1992). While much of the work on the geographies of lesbians and gay men is located in the urban, there is an upsurge in interest in the structural limitations experienced by those living in RURAL areas, and the attempts of sexual dissidents to establish utopian rural 'communities' (cf. TERRITORIALITY).

The heterosexuality of everyday space. Studies (e.g. Valentine, 1993) have highlighted the fact that everyday spaces are commonly taken for granted as heterosexual, and have explored the processes through which spaces are produced in this way. For example, McDowell's (1995) research in merchant banks examines the disciplinary practices that regulate the performance of sexuality within the workplace. Other research has focused on the discrimination and violence experienced by sexual dissidents in *heterosexual space*.

Geographies of HIV/AIDS. Mapping the transmission of the HIV virus has been at the heart of medical geographers' attempts to trace its origins and establish global typologies. This work has been criticized by sexual dissidents as irrelevant and politically dangerous. Brown (1995) has played a key role in re-focusing geographical research on AIDS (GEOGRAPHY OF) onto understanding sexual relations and issues of HEALTH AND HEALTH CARE promotion.

Queer geographies represent a reaction against the early work on geographies of lesbian and gay men which adopted an uncritical, all-embracing conceptualization of lesbian and gay identity. Drawing heavily on social theory from outside the discipline, queer geographies have attempted to scrutinize the desirability of IDENTITY POLITICS and to challenge notions of fixed identities, in particular by employing the concept of PERFORMATIVITY. Attempts have also been made to utilize the theoretical insights of QUEER THEORY to think about the production of space (Bell et al., 1994).

Geographies of heterosexualities are most evident in work on prostitution which has looked at the role of moral representations, social DISCOURSES and practices in determining RED LIGHT DISTRICTS and marginalizing commercial sex workers (Hubbard, 1998). Geographical writing based on PSYCHOANALYTIC THEORY has drawn on accounts of psychosexual development, sexual differences and desire, while also challenging the heterosexism evident in the writing of authors such as Lacan.

Critiques of the Discipline. Geographers working on sexuality share many of the concerns of feminist geographers about the MASCULINISM, heteronormative and disembodied heritage of the discipline and about the operation of POWER within the academy (Chouinard and Grant, 1995; cf. FEMINIST GEOGRAPHIES). GV

References

Adler, S. and Brenner, J. 1992: Gender and space: lesbians and gay men in the city. *International Journal of Urban and Regional Research* 16: 24–34. · Bell, D. and Valentine, G. 1995: *Mapping desire: geographies of sexualities*. London: Routledge. · Bell, D., Binnie, J., Cream, J. and Valentine, G. 1994: All hyped up and no place to go. *Gender, Place and Culture: a Journal of Feminist Geography* 1: 31–47. · Binnie, J. 1997: Invisible Europeans: sexual citizenship in the new Europe. *Environment and Planning A* 29: 237–48. · Brown, M. 1995: Ironies of distance: an ongoing critique of geographies of AIDS. *Environment and Planning D: Society and Space* 13: 159–83. · Castells, M. 1983: *The city and the grassroots*. Berkeley, CA: University of California Press. · Chouinard, V. and Grant, A. 1995: On being not even anywhere near the project: ways of putting ourselves in the picture. *Antipode* 27: 137–66. · Duncan, N., ed., 1996: *BodySpace: destabilizing geographies of gender and sexuality*. London: Routledge. · Hubbard, P. 1998: Sexuality, immorality and the City: red-light districts and the marginalisation of female street prostitutes. *Gender, Place and Culture: a Journal of Feminist Geography* 5: 55–76. · Knopp, L. 1992: Sexuality and the spatial dynamics of capitalism. *Environment and Planning D: Society and Space* 10: 651–69. · McDowell, L. 1995: Bodywork. In D. Bell and G. Valentine, eds, *Mapping desire: geographies of sexualities*. London: Routledge. · Symanski, R. 1974: Prostitution in Nevada. *Annals of the Association of American Geographers* 64: 357–77. · Valentine, G. 1993: (Hetero)sexing space: lesbian perceptions and experiences of everyday spaces. *Environment and Planning D: Society and Space* 11: 395–413.

Suggested Reading:

Bell and Valentine (1995). · Binnie, J. and Valentine, G. 1998: Geographies of sexuality: a review of progress. *Progress in Human Geography*.

shadow state A para-STATE APPARATUS comprised of voluntary non-profit organizations providing a variety of collective goods and services. Although administered outside traditional democratic politics or avenues of accountability, the voluntary organizations of the shadow state are publicly subsidized and regulated, enabling their ability to provide services but limiting political activism. Voluntary groups can thus become tools of state policy, providing services, legitimating the STATE, and maintaining the status quo. Simultaneously, however, shadow state organizations can transform society. They can provide new opportunities for democratic participation, and orchestrate social change efforts. Collective provision through voluntary organizations can thus decentralize political power and decision-making, undermine state hegemony and challenge the existing social order.

Since the Second World War, the shadow state has grown relative to the WELFARE STATE in many western capitalist democracies, stimulated by a popularity that spans the political spectrum. For the Right, voluntary groups protect freedom and individual liberty; the Left emphasizes their ability to decentralize power and pursue social change; and the pragmatic centre focuses on voluntary organization flexibility and efficiency. Voluntarism can thus become a rallying cry for a wide range of constituencies seeking alternatives to the bureaucratic state. In contrast, for democratizing nation-states of the former Soviet bloc, the shadow state can take on a decidedly different social and political role, becoming the 'CIVIL SOCIETY sector'. In such contexts, where institutions of civil society have long been repressed, new voluntary organizations are essential to state formation. They also serve to reweave a political fabric of traditional interest groups and new constituencies.

The voluntary sector is not uniform over time or space. Strong national contrasts as well as local conditions lead to uneven development of the shadow state. At the national level, prevailing ideological positions on the utility of government in general, and social policy specifically, along with convictions concerning the appropriate locus of service funding and provision within the state hierarchy, all shape prospects for the shadow state. At the local level, economic structure and dynamics; political ideologies of local elites; traditions of charitable giving; and historical divisions of service responsibilities between government and the voluntary sector, and the behaviour of key local agents, strongly influence the rates and outcomes of shadow state formation in specific geographic locales.

Shadow state status both enables and constrains voluntary group action. In the United States, for example, where institutional interdependence between voluntary groups and government is long-standing, many voluntary organizations gained resources through purchase-of-service contracting and garnered political power by becoming integral to the welfare state during periods of welfare programme contraction and devolution. Such organizations are, however, increasingly subject to state regulation through accountability requirements, resource dependence, and legal restrictions on political activism, reflecting a deepening penetration by the state into everyday life. JW

Suggested Reading

Kramer, R. 1981: *Voluntary agencies in the welfare state*. Berkeley: University of California Press. · Lipsky, M. and Smith, S.R. 1993: *Nonprofits for hire: the welfare state in the age of contracting*. Cambridge, MA: Harvard University Press. · Salamon, L.M. and Anheier, H.K. 1996: *Defining the nonprofit sector: a cross-national analysis*. Manchester: Manchester University Press. · Wolch, J.R. 1990: *The shadow state: government and voluntary sector in transition*. New York: The Foundation Center. · Wolpert, J. 1993: *Patterns of generosity in America*. New York: Twentieth Century Fund.

sharecropping A form of land tenure in which the landowners' returns take the form of a share of the farmers' produce rather than a cash or farm rent, also known by the French term *métayage* (Wells, 1984). Sharecropping arrangements involve short-term contracts for the annual cycle of production of a specific crop in which crop raising is contracted out to labouring households, individuals or work gangs who thereby take on the large part of the economic risks of production. These arrangements have been widely assumed to belong to the agricultural past and interpreted as feudal or pre-capitalist in nature (e.g. Marx, 1964), but they remain significant in contemporary agriculture, even in the West. Sharecropping takes many forms in different contexts, but all tend to be associated with highly concentrated patterns of landownership and exploitative labour relations; for example, in the cotton South of the USA between white landowners and black farmers (Mann, 1984), or, between landowners and Mexican migrant workers in California's strawberry industry (Wells, 1996). SW

References

Mann, S. 1984: Sharecropping in the cotton South: a case of uneven development in agriculture. *Rural Sociology* 49: 412–29. · Marx, K. 1964: *Pre-capitalist economic formations*. London: Lawrence and Wishart. · Wells, M. 1984: The resurgence of sharecropping: historical anomaly or political strategy? *American Journal of Sociology* 90/1: 1–29. · Wells, M. 1996: *Strawberry fields: politics, class and work in California agriculture*. Ithaca and London: Cornell University Press.

shifting cultivation Minimally, shifting cultivation is an agricultural system characterized by a rotation of fields rather than of crops, by discontinuous cropping in which periods of fallowing are typically longer than periods of cropping, and by the clearing of fields (usually called swiddens) through the use of slash and burn techniques. Known by a variety of terms (including field–forest rotation, slash and burn, swiddening), shifting cultivation is widespread throughout the humid tropics, but was also practised in temperate Europe (Conklin, 1962). It is estimated that there are over 250 million shifting cultivators world-wide, 100 million in South-east Asia alone. Shifting cultivation is enormously heterogeneous and subtypes can be distinguished according to crops raised, crop associations and successions, fallow lengths, climatic and edaphic conditions, field technologies, soil treatment and the mobility of settlement. Many distinguish between *integral* (shifting cultivation as an integral part of SUBSISTENCE) and *partial* (shifting cultivation as a technological expedient for cash cropping, see PEASANTS) forms of shifting cultivation (Conklin, 1962). In all shifting cultivation systems the burning of cleared vegetation is critical to the release of nutrients, which ensures field productivity. Shifting cultivation by definition is land-extensive and is threatened by population growth and expanding land settlement (see CARRYING CAPACITY; INTENSIVE AGRICULTURE). MW

Reference

Conklin, H. 1962: An ethnoecological approach to shifting cultivation. In P. Wagner and M. Mikesell, eds, *Readings in cultural geography*. Chicago: University of Chicago Press, 457–64.

shift-share model A technique for assessing the relative importance of different components in regional employment growth or decline. Regional employment growth may be due to the REGION having a high concentration of industries that are growing nationally (such as micro-electronics), or it may be due to locational shifts within industries or differential regional trends within an industry. Shift-share models try to disentangle and measure these effects using simple algebraic manipulation of growth rates.

Let E_{ij0} be the level of employment in industry i in region j in the initial time period 0, and let E_{ijt} be the level in the next period t. Then the total employment in region j at time 0 is

$$E_{j0} = \sum_i E_{ij0}$$

total national employment in industry i is

$$E_{i0} = \sum_j E_{ij0}$$

and total national employment is

$$E_0 = \sum_i \sum_j E_{ij0}$$

The figures for time t are then obtained in the same way. The total shift (TS) is then the difference between actual regional employment growth and that which would have occurred if the region had grown at the overall national rate:

$$TS = E_{jt} - E_{j0} \times (E_t / E_0)$$

This total shift can then be divided into a proportionality shift (or 'composition effect') and a differential shift. The *proportionality shift* (PS) measures change due to regional concentration in slow- or fast-growing sectors, and is calculated by applying to each industry a growth factor that is the difference between the actual industrial growth rate and the overall national rate. For industry i, this factor is:

$$G_i = E_{it}/E_{i0} - E_t/E_0$$

and the proportionality shift for region j is $PS = \sum_i G_i E_{ij0}$. The *differential shift* (DS) is the shift due to locational changes within industries and is obtained as $DS = TS - PS$.

The technique is purely descriptive, and does not explain why certain sectors are growing or declining or why locational shifts are taking place, but the data are easily obtained, and it gives a useful starting point for further inquiry. The method is very dependent on the level of sector aggregation (more sectors produces lower differential shifts), and it takes no account of LINKAGES or MULTIPLIERS. Limitations of the technique, especially the way it overlooks the need to standardize industry growth rates for their regional mix effects, have led to the construction of 'multifactor partitioning' by Ray (1990), which overcomes this problem and also identifies interaction effects and an allocation effect. These extensions complicate the formulae but can readily be programmed. LWH

Reference

Ray, M. 1990: *Standardising employment growth rates of foreign multinationals and domestic firms in Canada: from shift-share to multifactor partitioning*. Multinational Enterprises Programme: Working Paper No. 62. Geneva: International Labour Office.

Suggested Reading

Armstrong, A. and Taylor, J. 1978: *Regional economic policy and its analysis*, 2nd edn. Deddington, Oxford: Philip Allan, 300–8.

significance test A statistical procedure for identifying the probability of an observed event having occurred by chance. Most statistics, such as CHI SQUARE and the CORRELATION coefficient (r), have an associated sampling distribution of possible values with its own mean and standard error (the latter is equivalent to the standard deviation of a FREQUENCY DISTRIBUTION). For example, a 3×3 matrix will have a large number of possible sets of cell values for a given set of row and column totals, each of which will produce a different value of chi square when compared with the observed distribution (see also ENTROPY-MAXIMIZING MODELS). Because the frequency distribution of chi square is known for every table size (i.e. numbers of rows and columns, the product of which – less one in each case – is the *degrees of freedom* for the test), then the probability of getting an observed value can be obtained readily from the relevant statistical table.

Significance tests are used in two ways. In CONFIRMATORY DATA ANALYSIS they assist the testing of HYPOTHESES about the characteristics of a population, undertaken through a study of a properly selected sample (see SAMPLING). For example, a chi-square test may be conducted to see if the age structure of two counties varies (i.e. if they are both samples of the same population). If, according to the frequency distribution, the observed value of chi square would occur very frequently for samples of that size, given the degrees of freedom, it is concluded that the two counties do not differ significantly. The usual criterion for 'very frequently' is more than one test in 20 (normally stated as at the 95 per cent or 0.05 level). If the observed value occurs only rarely in the frequency distribution, then it is unlikely that the observed value has occurred by chance and it is concluded that the difference between the two samples is almost certainly present in the population from which they were drawn (i.e. the two county populations combined).

In EXPLORATORY DATA ANALYSIS the significance test is not used to draw a conclusion about a population from a sample (see INFERENCE) but rather to indicate the likely importance of an observed result. Again, the comparison is with what would happen if the only influences were random; if the observed value of the statistic falls in one of the tails (the extreme values) of the theoretical frequency distribution it is concluded that what has been observed is so unlikely to have occurred by chance that it must be 'real' and worthy of further investigation. RJJ

Suggested Reading

O'Brien, L. 1992: *Introducing quantitative geography: measurement, methods and generalised linear models*. London and New York: Routledge. · Hay, A.M. 1985: Statistical tests in the absence of sample: a note. *Professional Geographer* 37: 334–8.

simulation A heuristic device for solving theoretically intractable mathematical and statistical problems. Simulation is used either to model a 'real world' process or to create an empirical FREQUENCY DISTRIBUTION on which a SIGNIFICANCE TEST may be based.

Many simulation models use what are known as Monte Carlo procedures, involving the drawing of random numbers, as in Hägerstrand's work on the DIFFUSION of INNOVATIONS, which used an empirically observed MEAN INFORMATION FIELD as the framework allocating the random numbers. (See also MICROSIMULATION; STOCHASTIC PROCESS.)

Other simulation methods include the construction of analogue models, as in the Varignon frame used in the Weber model for investigating industrial location problems. RJJ

Suggested Reading

Board, C. 1967: Maps as models. In R.J. Chorley and P. Haggett, eds, *Models in geography*. London and New York: Methuen, 671–726. · Morgan, M.A. 1967: Hardware models in geography. In R.J. Chorley and P. Haggett, eds, *Models in geography*. London and New York: Methuen, 727–74.

situated knowledge A term coined by the feminist cultural critic of science Donna Haraway (1991, p. 188), to denote 'a doctrine of embodied objectivity that accommodates paradoxical and critical feminist science projects'. Situated knowledge replaces the traditional conception of scientific practice as the pursuit of a disembodied, inviolable and neutral OBJECTIVITY with an alternative formulation that stresses embodied physicality, social construction, and cultural politics. It is also an agenda for political action, and subsequently a key term in the 'science wars' (see *Social Text*, volumes 46/47, 1996).

Haraway argues that vision or sight has been a guiding METAPHOR for western scientists in carrying out their work: they see the world and write down its truths. But in so doing they write themselves out of their own stories; their role is solely as 'modest witness' (Haraway, 1997, ch. 1). That presumption of modesty, Haraway argues, is a direct consequence of the starting point of visuality. It creates the illusory possibility of a disembodied science. She calls this illusion a 'god trick', the idea that it is possible to have 'vision from everywhere and nowhere' (Haraway, 1991, p. 191). Moreover, it is just such a trick that is the basis of one of science's most cherished ideas, objectivity, the belief in the possibility of a single, final, detached, and unblemished rendering of the world.

For Haraway the 'gaze from nowhere' (Haraway, 1991, p. 188), as she calls objectivity, is really a kind of front, or RHETORICAL move, that hides and protects the interests of those who propose and most benefit from it, typically white western males. As Haraway (1997, p. 23) writes, 'modesty pays off... in the coin of epistemological and social power'. In this sense, being a modest witness turns out not to be very modest at all. It is a strategy to promulgate a particular kind of knowledge which is often MASCULINIST and RACIST. (Specific illustrations are found in Haraway's, 1989, critical examination of primate research.)

Scientific practices that masquerade under the cloak of objectivity are labelled 'fetishistic' by Haraway (1997, ch. 4) because knowledge is conceived as a thing rather than a social process. Fetishism would not occur if it was recognized from the outset that all knowledge is embodied and partial, that is, 'situated'. Indeed, only with that recognition does it become possible 'to construct a usable, but not an innocent doctrine of objectivity' (Haraway, 1991, p. 189; see also SPATIAL FETISHISM).

Take in turn the two definitional components of situated knowledge. By *embodiment* Haraway means not just the literal definition of that word. While it is important to recognize the organic embodiment of vision in particular kinds of human bodies, each of which make a difference to what is seen, embodiment is also technological. Machines, like humans, are not passive observers, but in their very construction record the world from a particular slant. For example, the software used in the computer programs of GEOGRAPHICAL INFORMATION SYSTEMS come with a systematic set of biases, hidden assumptions, and aporias. Print-outs are not mirror copies of the world, 'the view from nowhere', but always the view from somewhere. Furthermore, embodiment means recognizing the collective nature of inquiry involving interaction, difference, and debates over meanings and responsibilities: 'feminist embodiment . . . is not about fixed location in a reified body . . . but about nodes in fields, inflections in orientations, and responsibility for differences in material-semiotic fields of meaning' (Haraway, 1991, p. 195).

By *partial knowledge* Haraway means the recognition that no one, except omniscient Gods and Goddesses, ever has full (objective) knowledge. Instead, there are only partial perspectives, a consequence of our own circumscribed subject location that makes us who we are, and what we know. As Haraway writes, 'The knowing self is partial in all its guises, never finished, whole, simply there and original; it is always constructed and stitched together imperfectly.'

While embodiment and partiality might seem like difficult conditions under which to acquire knowledge, for Haraway they are pregnant with political possibility. They are also the only hope of achieving an attainable, as opposed to a mythical, objectivity, for the partiality of individual knowledge necessitates that people reach out and construct networks of affiliation, to engage in discussion, to recognize difference but also common beliefs and shared responsibilities. It is then through these 'shared conversations in EPISTEMOLOGY' that it is possible to forge 'solidarity in politics' (Haraway, 1991, p. 191). Not that the end result is unanimity, or even a trajectory towards some final end point of agreement. That was the problematic assumption of the old type of objectivity. Rather, 'shared conversations' are open-ended, varied, sometimes inconsistent and paradoxical. Most importantly, conversation is social intercourse, and for Haraway a necessary condition for both political projects, such as feminism, and epistemological ones, such as objectivity.

In sum, and returning to Haraway's original definition, situated knowledge is embodied in that it is grounded in the physicality of specific human bodies and their artefacts. Knowledge does not 'come from above, from nowhere, from simplicity', but from ground level, from somewhere and from complexity (Haraway, 1991, p. 195). As a result, the traditional notion of objectivity must be recast, conceived as an incomplete process, not a final outcome. Specifically, objectivity is the process of working out of difference and commonality, of struggling epistemologically and politically to make connections, affiliations, and alliances. Consequently, situated knowledge is often paradoxical, but always containing the possibility of critical engagement. Those possibilities for critical engagement are picked up in geography by Gregory (1994) and Harvey (1996) and in a sustained case study by Merrifield (1995). In addition, Rose (1997) has added an important qualifier: that anyone claiming to fully situate their own knowledge is practising precisely the same kind of God trick that they criticize in others. All situated knowledge is partial, including the situated knowledge we have of our own knowledge about ourselves. (See also BODY, GEOGRAPHY AND.)

TJB

References

Gregory, D. 1994: *Geographical imaginations*. Oxford: Blackwell. · Haraway, D.J. 1989: *Primate visions: gender, race, and nature in the world of modern science*. New York: Routledge. · Haraway, D.J. 1991: *Simians, cyborgs, and women: the reinvention of nature*. New York: Routledge. · Haraway, D.J. 1997: *Modest-Witness@second-millennium.FemaleMan©Meets_OncoMouse TM: Feminism and Technoscience*. New York: Routledge. · Harvey, D. 1996: *Justice, nature and the geography of difference*. Oxford: Blackwell. · Merrifield, A. 1995: Situated knowledge through exploration: reflections on Bunge's 'Geographical Expeditions'. *Antipode* 27: 49–70. · Rose, G. 1997: Situating knowledges: positionality, reflexivities and other tactics. *Progress in Human Geography* 21: 305–20.

Suggested Reading

Gregory (1994); Haraway (1991), ch. 9.

situationists/situationism The Situationist International was a small group of European ultra-radical left-wing thinkers who existed in various fragile combinations from 1957 until 1972. Their most famous participant was Guy Debord, whose book *Society of the Spectacle* (Debord, 1970) might have been regarded – by a less fractious group – as its manifesto.

Situationism's artistic roots lay in surrealism, and its philosophical ones in EXISTENTIALISM (though Debord spat on both). That it has been influential in human geography is chiefly because the situationist analysis of CAPITALISM put SPACE at its centre and accordingly looked to space as one of its chief means of (a fleeting) liberation. For the situationists, the market economy had reached an apogee, including whole areas of everyday life once left out of social and cultural contention: 'There remains nothing which has not been transformed and polluted according to the means and interests of modern industry' (Debord, 1970). In particular, the production and consumption of things has given way to the production and consumption of images. Hence 'the society of the SPECTACLE'; 'the spectacle is capital accumulated until it becomes an image' (Debord, 1970). But it was possible to fight back against this all-consuming monster by creating pockets of disorder and dissonance in the fabric of everyday life which could show the masses their torpid, image-drugged state: 'revolution is the critique of human geography through which individuals and communities have to create places and events suitable for the appropriation of their own history' (Debord, 1970, p. 23). Thus the situationists developed a number of 'psychogeographic' technologies like the *dérive* ('drifting') which could produce, however briefly, subversive and irreverent anti-authoritarian spaces in cities by turning art into life, rather than life into art. In other words, they would actively construct 'situations' (hence 'situationist').

Though the situationists' activities were on the political margins, many of their concepts (which were themselves heavily influenced by the work of writers like Breton, Sartre and Lefebvre) and artistic conceits (and, most especially, their slogans, artwork and urban architecture) were incorporated into later analytical frameworks (see COGNITIVE MAPPING). They have therefore proved more influential beyond their time than in it. NJT

References

Blazwick, I. 1989: *An endless passion: an endless banquet. A situationist scrapbook*. London: Verso. · Bonnett, A. 1989: Situationism, geography and post of mutualism. *Environment and Planning D: Society and Space* 7: 131–46. · Debord, G. 1970: *Society of the spectacle*. Detroit: Black and Red. · Debord, G. 1997: *Panégyriques*. Paris. · Gonzalvez, S. 1997: *Guy Debord ou la Beauté du Négatif*. Paris: Mille et une Nuits. · Marcus, G. 1992: *Lipstick traces. A secret history of the twentieth century*. London: Secker and Warburg. · Pinder, D.A. 1996: Subverting cartography: the situationists and maps of the city. *Environment and Planning A* 28: 405–28. · Plant, S. 1992: *The most radical gesture. The situationist international in a postmodern age*. London: Routledge. · Sussmann, E. 1989: *On the passage of a few people through a rather brief moment in time. The Situationist International 1957–1972*. Cambridge, MA: MIT Press.

Sjoberg model A model of social and spatial order of the PRE-INDUSTRIAL CITY, first expressed in Gideon Sjoberg's (1960) book of the same title. Sjoberg's model arises from his desire to provide a critique of, and alternative to, the concentric ZONAL MODEL of the city offered by Ernest Burgess and, more generally, of HUMAN ECOLOGY as applied by prominent members of the CHICAGO SCHOOL. As such, Sjoberg's work was part of a larger project, initiated by Walter Firey (1947), to replace HUMAN ECOLOGY with STRUCTURAL FUNCTIONALISM as the central PARADIGM of urban sociology (p. 12). The major factors used to explain urban MORPHOLOGY in Sjoberg's model are social structure and technology.

Sjoberg begins by differentiating between non-URBAN, FEUDAL, and industrial societies. He is concerned with the second of these: societies that utilize animate sources of energy, and are literate and urbanized, including all world civilizations prior to the INDUSTRIAL REVOLUTION as well as non-industrialized contemporary societies. He argues that feudal, or pre-industrial, societies everywhere, and through time, are characterized by similar technological achievements and a three-tiered CLASS structure that includes a small ruling class, a large lower class, and outcaste groups. The ruling class, comprised of those in religious and administrative authority, establishes a social order that reproduces its control over succeeding generations; URBANIZATION is both the outcome of social stratification and a means whereby HEGEMONY is perpetuated. The morphology of pre-industrial cities reflects this interdependence between social and spatial order: POWER is consolidated by the ruling class through its residential location in the city centre, the most protected and most accessible district. Here, residents forge a social solidarity based on their literacy, access to the surplus (which is stored in the central area of the city), and shared upper-class CULTURE that includes distinctive manners and patterns of speech. Elite clustering in the city centre is reinforced by the lack of rapid transportation.

The privileged central district is surrounded by haphazardly arranged NEIGHBOURHOODS housing the lower class. Households in these areas are sorted by occupation/income (merchants near the centre, followed by minor bureaucrats, artisans, and finally the unskilled), ethnic origin, and extended family networks. Merchants are generally not accorded elite status, since power is achieved through religious and military control while trade is viewed with suspicion. The model is less clear on the residential placement of outcaste groups (typically SLAVES and other conquered peoples): some of these perform service roles and are intermingled with the rest of the urban population, while others live at the extreme periphery of the city – frequently beyond its walls.

In formulating this model, Sjoberg reverses the logic used by Burgess – who placed commercial activities at the centre of the city, and a succession of residential districts, from poor to wealthy, around it. Sjoberg notes that the Burgess model is applicable only to industrial cities, where production and commerce propel economic growth and where capitalists are accorded high social standing. Further, he argues that human ecology incorrectly treats urbanization as an independent social force, when in reality urban growth should be seen as a 'dependent variable', as it depends on the distribution of social power and available technology. Empirical investigations of the Sjoberg model have been generally supportive, but caution that the model cannot account for the intricate details of urban development across different cultural contexts. Others have criticized the theoretical content of Sjoberg's work, especially his stress on the role of technology and uncritical view of social power. Sjoberg's FUNCTIONALIST logic (which blurs distinctions between causes and consequences), however, remains largely unnoticed and unchallenged. DH

References

Firey, W. 1947: *Land use in central Boston*. Cambridge, MA: Harvard University Press. · Sjoberg, G. 1960: *The pre-industrial city, past and present*. New York: The Free Press. (Two chapters are co-authored with Andrée F. Sjoberg.)

Suggested reading

Carter, H. 1983: *An introduction to urban historical geography*. London: Edward Arnold. · Langton, J. 1975: Residential patterns in pre-industrial cities. *Transactions, Institute of British Geographers* NS 8: 1–27. · Ley, D. 1983: *A social geography of the city*. New York: Harper and Row. · Morris, A.E.J. 1994: *History of urban form: before the industrial revolutions*. New York: Wiley. · Radford, J.P. 1979: Testing the model of the pre-industrial city. *Transactions, Institute of British Geographers* NS 12: 392–410. · Wheatley, P. 1963: What the city is said to be. *Pacific Viewpoint* 2: 163–88.

skid row A run-down section of an urban area, usually close to the city centre, where transient populations are concentrated; many of the individuals are on the margins of economic survival (i.e. 'on the skids') and suffer a variety of complaints, such as alcoholism. Skid rows are especially characteristic of North American cities, where they offer temporary homes in poor-quality rental accommodation for transient male visitors; they now also house permanent residents without access to conventional homes. In the ZONAL MODEL of urban residential structure skid row occupies part of the zone in transition. (See also ANOMIE; HOMELESSNESS; INNER CITY.) RJJ

Suggested Reading

Rowley, G. 1978: Plus ça change . . . a Canadian skid row. *Canadian Geographer* 22: 211–24.

slavery A MODE OF PRODUCTION within which labour is controlled through non-economic compulsion. The individual slaves, plus other members of their households in many cases, are privately-owned 'commodities' denied any control over either their own labour or their own reproduction (i.e. there is no CIVIL SOCIETY under slavery); this complete control differentiates the slave from the condition of the serf under FEUDALISM. The Greek and Roman empires provided the paradigm exemplars of slavery, but many other societies have contained elements of it, such as the American South prior to the Civil War: the legal and cultural systems that have regulated and legitimated slavery have varied considerably both historically and geographically, however. RJJ

Suggested Reading

Hindess, B. and Hirst, P.Q. 1975: *Pre-capitalist modes of production*. London: Routledge and Kegan Paul.

slum An area of overcrowded, dilapidated and usually old housing occupied by people who can afford only the cheapest dwellings available in the urban area, generally in or close to the INNER CITY. The term usually implies a poverty-ridden population, an unhealthy environment, and a district rife with crime and vice (see also CYCLE OF POVERTY), and is often associated with concentrations of people in certain ETHNIC groups, although the terms GHETTO and slum should not be used as synonyms. RJJ

social area analysis A theory and technique developed by two American sociologists, Eshref Shevky and Wendell Bell (1955), linking changing urban social structure and residential patterns to economic DEVELOPMENT and URBANIZATION processes (which they termed the 'increasing scale' of society).

According to Shevky and Bell, increasing scale involves three interrelated trends:

- *Changes in the range and intensity of social relations* produced by a greater DIVISION OF LABOUR, as reflected in the distribution of skills and their rewards within society – Shevky identified this trend with the construct that he termed 'social rank', though Bell preferred the term 'economic status';

- *An increasing differentiation of functions within society and its constituent households*, which generates new lifestyles and household forms – a construct Shevky termed 'urbanization' and Bell 'family status'; and
- *The concentration of people from different cultural backgrounds in cities* – producing 'SEGREGATION' for Shevky and 'ETHNIC status' for Bell.

This theory of changing urban society was linked to residential differentiation within urban areas although, as critics pointed out (e.g. Timms, 1971), the link was far from clear. Shevky and Bell's empirical work identified three dimensions to the residential differentiation of Los Angeles and San Francisco which were consistent with the three trends, though their statistical procedures involved selecting variables to represent the three, suggesting that the theory may have been 'invented' inductively to account for their empirical mapping rather than as the source for a study of district socio-economic differences.

Shevky and Bell's technique for analysing urban residential differentiation used US CENSUS TRACT data. Variables were selected to represent the three constructs – occupation and schooling for social rank; fertility, women at work and households in single-family dwelling units for urbanization; and population in certain ethnic and immigrant groups for segregation. These were combined to produce three standardized indices, and used to create residential area categories – such as high social rank, high urbanization, and low segregation (i.e. tracts with many well-educated, white-collar workers living in apartments with low fertility levels and many adult women employed in the workforce, and with few members of ethnic groups).

Further work by Bell tested the validity of the constructs in other cities and used the classification as a SAMPLING framework for investigating differences in social behaviour within cities (see Johnston, 1971). The technique was largely replaced by the more technically sophisticated inductive procedure of FACTORIAL ECOLOGY, and the absence of a clear theoretical base meant that this initial stimulus to work in URBAN GEOGRAPHY soon became little more than an important historical reference. RJJ

References

Johnston, R.J. 1971: *Urban residential patterns: an introductory review*. London: George Bell and Sons. · Shevky, E. and Bell, W. 1955: *Social area analysis: theory, illustrative application and computational procedures*. Stanford, CA: Stanford University Press. · Timms, D.W.G. 1971: *The urban mosaic: towards a theory of residential differentiation*. Cambridge: Cambridge University Press.

social capital Those characteristics of social structure or social relations that facilitate collaborative action and, as a result, enhance economic performance. The term has been popularized by Robert Putnam (1993), a political scientist, who emphasizes key aspects of social organization 'such as trust, norms, and networks' (p. 167). However, the original usage of the term is normally attributed to Coleman (1990), a sociologist, whose definition is somewhat broader. As Foley and Edwards (1997) note, 'for Coleman, social capital is to be found in any sort of social relation that provides a resource for action' (p. 552). The 'action' in question may be individual or collective, and may or may not have any direct economic significance.

It is only with Putnam's work that the concept of social capital came to be closely linked to social action leading to improved economic performance. In his classic study, the concept of social capital emerged as the central explanatory variable in his analysis of the factors underlying the economic success of the north-eastern regions of Italy relative to the rest of the country. In a manner strongly consistent with the earlier work of Piore and Sabel (1984) and economic geographers such as Storper and Scott (1989) and Sayer and Walker (1992), Putnam argued that the economic prosperity of Emilia-Romagna and surrounding regions in the 1970s and 1980s could be attributed to the prevalence of certain norms of reciprocity, trust and 'civic engagement', widespread amongst local economic actors, that encouraged cooperation and collaboration. Moreover, this collaborative behaviour was crucial to the region's economic success (Putnam, 1993, p. 161):

> Typically singled out as essential for the success of industrial networks, in Italy and beyond, are norms of reciprocity and networks of civic engagement. Networks facilitate flows of information about technological developments, about the credit-worthiness of would-be entrepreneurs, about the reliability of individual workers, and so on. . . . Social norms that forestall opportunism are so deeply internalized that the issue of opportunism at the expense of community obligation is said to arise less often here than in areas characterized by vertical and clientelistic networks. What is crucial about these small-firm industrial districts, conclude most observers, is mutual trust, social cooperation, and a well-developed

sense of civic duty – in short, the hallmarks of the civic community.

While Putnam's arguments may have added little new insight to the pre-existing work by geographers and others on the importance of social processes and associative behaviour to the performance of firms in INDUSTRIAL DISTRICTS, perhaps his unique contribution has been to encapsulate a set of complex arguments within a single term – social capital. Within the field of political economy, Putnam's emphasis on *regional and civic institutions* and their economic consequences represents an important complement to the analyses of institutional economists such as Hodgson (1988) and North (1990), who had already begun to revive interest in the impact of *national social institutions* on relative economic performance.

The increasingly widespread use of the concept of social capital can also be understood within the context of growing interest, across a number of social sciences, in the fundamental connections between economic and social or cultural phenomena. Reviving the much earlier arguments of Veblen (1919) and Polanyi (1944) that central economic institutions such as those governing MARKET EXCHANGE are the product of active social construction, a growing number of contributors to the field of 'socio-economics' have adopted the view that 'the social' and 'the economic' are inextricably intertwined (see, for example, Granovetter and Swedberg, 1992; Barnes, 1995; Gertler, 1995; Thrift and Olds, 1996; Schoenberger, 1997).

As might be expected of such a seductively simple term, Putnam's conception of social capital has been the subject of considerable critical commentary. One strand of criticism takes issue with Putnam's analysis of civic politics – even in those societies with a large stock of social capital – as being unrealistically devoid of conflict and contestation. Seen in this light, Putnam's model becomes rather static and lifeless. As Amin argues (1996, p. 327):

> Putnam's definition of civic virtue . . . represents a kind of paradise on earth, with citizens, state and economic networks intertwined in civilized harmony and mutual regard. Putnam's good citizenship ends up, perhaps inadvertently, as a denial of civil society as an arena of social contestation.

Instead, Amin contends, societies should aspire to fostering 'a new civic politics . . . as an arena of social contestation', enabling the civic sphere to function dynamically 'as a source of democratic change' (p. 328).

Another strand of critique notes that the theory of social capital is mute on the crucial issues of why some regions or nations appear to have an abundance of social capital while others have little, as well as which institutions matter most in the production of social capital. While Putnam rhapsodizes about the virtues of bowling clubs and choral societies as local institutions that build social capital by fostering social interaction, others argue that macro-regulatory institutions governing labour markets, industrial relations, corporate governance, industrial organization and investment exert a much more important influence on the degree to which firms engage in collaborative behaviour (Christopherson, 1993; Gertler, 1997). (See also NEW INSTITUTIONAL ECONOMICS.) MSG

References

Amin, A. 1996: Beyond associative democracy. *New Political Economy* 1: 309–33. · Barnes, T.J. 1995: Political economy I: 'the culture, stupid'. *Progress in Human Geography* 19: 423–31. · Christopherson, S. 1993: Market rules and territorial outcomes: the case of the United States. *International Journal of Urban and Regional Research* 17: 274–88. · Coleman, J. 1990: *Foundations of social theory*. Cambridge, MA: Belknap Press of Harvard University Press. · Foley, M.W. and Edwards, B. 1997: Escape from politics? Social theory and the social capital debate. *American Behavioral Scientist* 40: 550–61. · Gertler, M.S. 1995: 'Being there': proximity, organization and culture in the production and use of advanced manufacturing technologies. *Economic Geography* 71: 1–26. · Gertler, M.S. 1997: The invention of regional culture. In R. Lee and J. Wills, eds, *Geographies of economies*. London: Edward Arnold, 53–64. · Granovetter, M. and Swedberg, R., eds, 1992: *The sociology of economic life*. Boulder, CO: Westview Press. · Hodgson, G.M. 1988: *Economics and institutions*. Cambridge: Polity Press. · North, D. 1990: *Institutions, institutional change and economic performance*. Cambridge: Cambridge University Press. · Piore, M.J. and Sabel, C. 1984: *The second industrial divide*. New York: Basic Books. · Polanyi, K. 1944: *The great transformation*. Boston: Beacon Hill Press. · Putnam, R.D. 1993: *Making democracy work*. Princeton, NJ: Princeton University Press. · Sayer, A. and Walker, R. 1992: *The new social economy*. Oxford: Blackwell. · Schoenberger, E. 1997: *The cultural crisis of the firm*. Oxford: Blackwell. · Storper, M. and Scott, A.J. 1989: The geographical foundations and social regulation of flexible production complexes. In J. Wolch and M. Dear, eds, *The power of geography: how territory shapes social life*. London: Unwin Hyman, 21–40. · Thrift, N.J. and Olds, K. 1996: Refiguring the economic in economic geography. *Progress in Human Geography* 20: 311–37. · Veblen, T.B. 1919: *The place of science in modern civilization and other essays*. New York: B.W. Huebsch.

social construction The idea that the social context of inquiry, rather than the world which is investigated, determines – constructs – knowledge. Knowledge, therefore, is always *relative* to its social setting (there are no absolutes), and the outcome of an active process of fabrication rather than the discovery of a reality pre-existent and fully formed. As a result, social constructionism is both RELATIVIST and anti-REALIST.

While intellectual antecedents of social constructionism can be found as far back as Plato, who recognized a link between a citizen's knowledge and their place in society, it was Karl Marx (1818–83) who established an intellectual agenda with his claim about the powerful role of social interests in shaping dominant beliefs (IDEOLOGY). As Marx famously put it: 'It is not the consciousness of men [sic] that determines their social being, but, on the contrary, their social being that determines their consciousness.'

During the twentieth century, social constructionism emerged most systematically in studies around the sociology of knowledge. In particular, the American sociologists Peter Berger and Thomas Luckmann, in their 1966 book *The social construction of reality*, were the first to make critical use of the term: they wrote that (1966, p. 3) 'insofar as all human "knowledge" is developed, transmitted and maintained in social situations ... *the sociology of knowledge is concerned with the analysis of the social construction of reality*'. Using the example of religion, Berger and Luckmann argued that social knowledge becomes real and takes on causative powers when people start believing it, and allow it to enter into their everyday life routines (cf. TAKEN-FOR-GRANTED WORLD). Furthermore, socially derived concepts are believed in part because of powerful reinforcing institutions, in this case the church (which is itself socially constructed).

Making the social constructionist argument for religion or other social 'facts' such as GENDER, RACE or even PLACE is now common, but making the same argument for the facts of nature such as rocks and water, or more exotically, black holes and quarks, meets greater resistance. NATURE appears fixed and constant, to be permanently 'out there', and therefore not dependent upon the social beliefs of a given time and place. Since the early 1970s, however, sociologists of scientific knowledge have argued that even nature is socially constructed by scientists (see ACTOR–NETWORK THEORY; LOCAL KNOWLEDGE; SCIENCE, GEOGRAPHY AND). In brief, the argument is that the activities of scientists are no different from those of anyone else. Their practices are thoroughly social, and as a consequence so is the knowledge that they produce, even about black holes and quarks. This is not to say that socially constructed scientific knowledge is wrong, or irrelevant. What is wrong, though, is to think that scientists have some special method that allows them to escape their social setting. Note that in making this claim sociologists of scientific knowledge are *not* saying that the material world is a social construction, that it is all in our heads. That view leads only to a paralysing solipsism. Rather, it is the set of scientific terms in which nature is expressed that is socially constructed, not brute reality itself. But because brute reality cannot express itself in its own terms, we have only the representations of the scientists and the social world which they inhabit.

In human geography Berger and Luckmann's work on social constructionism was picked up and elaborated during the 1970s and 1980s by SOCIAL GEOGRAPHERS prosecuting SYMBOLIC INTERACTIONISM, the view that meaning is constituted by and through social interaction. Special attention was paid to the role of everyday life routines, and which also formed a component of TIME-GEOGRAPHY. The influence of the sociologists of scientific knowledge came later, and is also partly associated with the movement in human geography towards POSTMODERNISM and POST-STRUCTURALISM. Social constructionism is now found in studies around NATURE (Demeritt, 1994); GENDER (Rose, 1993); RACE (Jackson, 1987); and the ECONOMY (Gibson-Graham, 1996). TJB

References

Berger, P.L. and Luckmann, T. 1966: *The social construction of reality: a treatise in the sociology of knowledge*. New York: Doubleday. · Demeritt, D. 1994: Ecology, objectivity and critique in writings on nature and human societies. *Journal of Historical Geography* 20: 22–37. · Gibson-Graham, J.K. 1996: *The end of capitalism (as we knew it). A feminist critique of political economy*. Oxford: Blackwell. · Jackson, P., ed., 1987: *Race and racism: essays in social geography*. London: Unwin. · Rose, G. 1993: *Feminism and geography: the limits of geographical knowledge*. Cambridge: Polity Press.

Further Reading

Sismondo, S. 1993: Some social constructions. *Social Science Studies* 23: 515–53.

Social Darwinism The application of Darwinian evolution to socio-economic and political affairs. Generally speaking Social Darwinism tends to be regarded as a 'pejorative tag' (Moore, 1986), and for this reason is typically used to label opponents. Yet this judgement has served to disguise how 'social' DARWINISM itself was from the start (Greene, 1959, 1977; Williams, 1973) and to permit a too comfortable critique of the doctrine as a 'distortion' of pure biology (Shapin and Barnes, 1979; La Vergata, 1985; Moore, 1991). Thus to conceive of Social Darwinism as an *extension* of Darwinism is likely to be a misconception. On the contrary, MALTHUSIAN demographic principles and a range of presumptions about racial type, for example, were part of Darwin's intellectual furniture as he devised his grand biological theory. Besides, that quintessential Darwinian pursuit – biogeography – has been shown to have long engaged imperial vocabulary and projected imperial values (Browne, 1996; cf. IMPERIALISM).

It was under the influence of Richard Hofstadter's (1959) classic study that the term came to describe almost any evolutionary model of SOCIETY – particularly if it was pernicious. Here the dangers of manufactured history assert themselves. For as Donald Bellomy (1984) has shown, the *term* Social Darwinism itself did not achieve currency in the English-speaking world until the early years of the twentieth century. Since then much debate about the issue has revolved around the question of definitions and labels. The emphasis of figures like Hofstadter, moreover, tended to obscure alternative biological sources of social evolution, like LAMARCKISM, and to ignore the substantial body of social evolutionary literature conceived quite independently of biology (Burrow, 1966). In its most vulgar form, Social Darwinism is generally portrayed as an attempt 'to justify the competitive ethos of Victorian capitalism in terms of the struggle for existence' (Bowler, 1984).

In this vein, championed by Herbert Spencer and his disciples, social evolution could be used to justify laissez-faire economic policies, nationalistic aggression and ideas of racial supremacy (see NATIONALISM; RACISM). At the same time, as Jones has made clear, certain forms of Social Darwinism were equally compatible with the traditional LIBERALISM that sought to curb the power of the aristocracy which 'by awarding social status for reasons of birth rather than achievement, protected the idle and unproductive in society' (Jones, 1980). Opposition to the laissez-faire construal of Social Darwinism was also forthcoming from those advocates of eugenics who felt that Darwinian evolution sanctioned a breeding programme for the human species in order to combat racial degeneration and ensure the best eugenic mixtures (Haller, 1963; Mackenzie, 1982; Kevles, 1985). The militaristic construal of social Darwinism as the doctrine's major legacy, moreover, has recently been challenged by Crook (1994) who urges that, whatever its internal dissonances, a much neglected discourse of 'peace biology' emanated from the ecological holism that pervaded Darwin's writings (cf. ECOLOGY). Besides this, the assumption that Social Darwinism was commonly embraced as an explicit economic philosophy has been questioned by Wyllie (1959) and Bannister (1979). At the same time, beyond the business community, the social implications of Lamarckian evolution became attractive to many. If organisms could adapt themselves to their environments and pass on the benefits to succeeding generations, then this model could give biological support to social interventionism, whether by educational initiatives or environmental improvement. It is not surprising, therefore, that it was its congruence with SOCIALISM that made Lamarckism attractive to so many reformers. Plainly, Social Darwinism was a far from coherent system of ideas; at most it provided a rhetorical lexicon under which a suite of naturalistic political philosophies could shelter (Fichman, 1997; Hawkins, 1997).

The strains of social evolutionary thought, whether derived from Darwinism or Lamarckism, are clearly detectable in the works of numerous geographers during the late nineteenth and early twentieth centuries (Livingstone, 1985, 1992). Ratzel's POLITICAL GEOGRAPHY, for example, with its attendant concept of the *LEBENSRAUM*, was grounded in the (Lamarckian) evolutionary outlook of figures like Haeckel and Wagner (Stoddart, 1966; Bassin, 1987; see ANTHROPOGEOGRAPHY). The racialized geographies of Shaler, Gilman, Huntington, Taylor and Fleure all display various appropriations of evolutionary vocabulary. For some, as with Huntington (who retained a long-standing interest in the anatomical researches of Paul Kammerer) and Taylor (for whom William Diller Matthew's work on palaeo-climates was crucially significant), climate, MIGRATION and natural selection were the key ingredients (Livingstone, 1991; Christie, 1994) – an emphasis disclosing the geographical community's long-standing concern with questions to do with the role of acclimatization in imperial affairs (Livingstone, 1987). Indeed Kuklick (1996, p. 628) has claimed that the basic elements of the Darwinian schema 'were the constituent components of acclimatization analyses' and that interest 'in the outcomes of encounters between indigenes and colonial invaders of every variety – plants, animal, and human – was not marginal to Darwinian inquiry, but occupied its very center'. For others, as with Fleure, it was in the interplay of racial type, evolutionary mechanisms, anthropometric localization, and psycho-social factors that were of central importance (Campbell, 1972; Gruffudd, 1994). Again, the necessitarian cast of Mackinder's early geography *and* his later disquiet over a resigned laissez-faire show traces of social Lamarckism, as do the deterministic geographies of Brigham, Semple, Davis and Huntington (see ENVIRONMENTAL DETERMINISM). Socializing evolution, of course, was also to be found among geographers of a more radical outlook. Kropotkin, for instance, found in biological Lamarckism the grounds for championing collectivism, opposing Spencerian individualism, and connecting up the philosophy of natural science with ANARCHISM. Here we encounter a biologization of political categories akin to that of Patrick Geddes who found in the same intellectual source inspiration for his planning and educational initiatives (Campbell and Livingstone, 1983). The POSSIBILISM that lay at the heart of the French School of Geography, particularly as expressed by Vidal de la Blache, has also been interpreted as embracing a range of evolutionary motifs derived from Lamarckism and of cultivating an ecologistic *géographie humaine* (Archer, 1993).

Social evolutionary doctrines were thus used by geographers in a variety of ways: for some it was the idea of struggle that energized their geographical theorizing; for some it was a version of cultural evolution derived from anthropology that informed their writing of historical geography (Newson, 1976); for others, as Herbst (1961) puts it, 'environmental determinism . . . became the geographer's version of Social Darwinism'; for still others it was the idealist thrust of vitalistic evolution that undergirded a more possibilist outlook. Indeed there is much to be said for the view that it was in a social evolutionary rendering of the relations between NATURE and CULTURE that the cognitive content of professional geography, within a specializing academy, was originally sought (Livingstone, 1992).

More recently, with the rise of socio-biology, the legitimacy of transferring biological categories to the social order has again become the subject of debate. Darwinian motifs have thus, in one form or another, persistently resurfaced in new incarnations (Degler, 1991). Within the field of human geography, the issues raised by Social Darwinism are still in need of resolution (see also HUMAN ECOLOGY). DNL

References

Archer, K. 1993: Regions as social organisms: the Lamarckian characteristics of Vidal de la Blache's regional geography. *Annals of the Association of American Geographers* 83: 498–514. · Bannister, R.C. 1979: *Social Darwinism: science and myth in Anglo-American social thought.* Philadelphia: Temple University Press. · Bassin, M. 1987: Friedrich Ratzel 1884–1904. *Geographers. Biobibliographical Studies* 11: 123–32. · Bellomy, D. 1984: 'Social Darwinism' revisited. *Perspectives in American History* NS 1: 1–29. · Bowler, P.J. 1984: *Evolution. The history of an idea.* Berkeley: University of California Press. · Browne, J. 1996: Biogeography and empire. In N. Jardine, J.A. Secord and E.C. Spary, eds, *Culture of natural history.* Cambridge: Cambridge University Press, 305–21. · Burrow, J.W. 1966: *Evolution and society. A study in Victorian social theory.* Cambridge: Cambridge University Press. · Campbell, J. 1972: *Some sources of the humanism of H.J. Fleure.* Oxford: School of Geography, University of Oxford, Research Paper, no. 2. · Campbell, J.A. and Livingstone, D.N. 1983: Neo-Lamarckism and the development of geography in the United States and Great Britain. *Transactions, Institute of British Geographers* NS 8: 267–94. · Christie, N. 1994: Environment and race: Geography's search for a Darwinian synthesis. In R. MacLeod and P.E. Rehbock, eds, *Darwin's laboratory: evolutionary theory and natural history in the Pacific.* Honolulu: University of Hawai'i Press. · Crook, P. 1994: *Darwinism, war and history: the debate over the biology of war from the 'Origin of species' to the first world war.* Cambridge: Cambridge University Press. · Degler, C.N. 1991: *In search of human nature: the decline and revival of Darwinism in American social thought.* New York: Oxford University Press. · Fichman, M. 1997: *Biology and politics: defining the boundaries.* In Lightman, B., ed., *Victorian science in context.* Chicago: University of Chicago Press, 94–118. · Greene, J.C. 1959: Biology and social theory in the nineteenth century: August Commute and Herbert Spencer. In Marshall Claret, ed., *Critical problems in the history of science.* Madison, Wis: University of Wisconsin Press, 419–46. · Greene, J.C. 1977: Darwin as a social evolutionist. *Journal of the History of Biology* 10: 1–27. · Gruffudd, P. 1994: Back to the land: historiography, rurally and the nation in interior Wales. *Transactions, Institute of British Geographers* NS 19: 61–77. · Haller, M.H. 1963: *Eugenics: hereditarian attitudes in American social thought.* New Brunswick, NJ: Rutgers University Press. · Hawkins, M. 1997: *Social Darwinism in European and American thought, 1860–1945: nature as model and nature as threat.* Cambridge: Cambridge University Press. · Herbst, J. 1961: Social Darwinism and the history of American geography. *Proceedings of the American Philosophical Society* 105: 538–44. · Hofstadter, R. 1959: *Social Darwinism in American thought*, rev. edn. New York: George Braziller. · Jones, G. 1980: *Social Darwinism and English thought: the interaction between biological and social theory.* London: Harvester Press; Atlantic Highlands, NJ: Humanities Press. · Kevles, D.J. 1985: *In the name of eugenics. Genetics and the uses of human heredity*. Harmondsworth: Penguin. · Kuklick, H. 1996: Islands in the Pacific: Darwinian biogeography and British anthropology. *American Ethnologist* 23: 611–38. · La Vergata, A. 1985: Images of Darwin. A historiographic overview. In D. Kohn, ed., *The Darwinian heritage*. Princeton: Princeton University Press, 901–75. · Livingstone, D.N. 1985: Evolution, science and society: historical reflections on the geographical experiment. *Geoforum* 16: 119–30. · Livingstone, D.N. 1987: Human acclimatization: perspectives on a contested field of inquiry in science, medicine and geography. *History of Science* 25: 359–94. · Livingstone, D.N. 1991: The moral discourse of climate: historical considerations on race, place and virtue. *Journal of Historical Geography* 17: 413–34. · Livingstone, D.N. 1992: *The geographical tradition. Episodes in the history of a contested enterprise*. Oxford: Blackwell. · Mackenzie, D. 1982: *Statistics in Britain, 1865–1930: the social construction of scientific knowledge*. Edinburgh: Edinburgh University Press; New York: Columbia University Press. · Moore, J.R. 1986: *Socialising Darwinism: historiography and the fortunes of a phrase*. In L. Levidow, ed., *Science as Politics*. London: Free Association Books, 38–80. · Moore, J.R. 1991: Deconstructing Darwinism: the politics of evolution in the 1860s. *Journal of the History of Biology* 24: 353–408. · Newson, L. 1976: Cultural evolution: a basic concept for human and historical geography. *Journal of Historical Geography* 2: 239–55. · Shapin, S. and Barnes, B. 1979: Darwin and Social Darwinism: purity and history. In B. Barnes and S. Shapin, eds, *Natural order: historical studies of scientific culture*. Beverley Hills: Sage Publications, 125–42. · Stoddart, D.R. 1966: Darwin's impact on geography. *Annals of the Association of American Geographers* 56: 683–98. · Williams, R. 1973: Social Darwinism. In J. Benthall, ed., *The limits of human nature*. London: Allen Lane; New York: Dutton, 115–30. · Wyllie, I. 1959: Social Darwinism and the businessman. *Proceedings of the American Philosophical Society* 103: 629–35.

Suggested Reading

Bannister (1979). · Bellomy (1984). · Hawkins (1997). · Jones (1980). · Moore (1986).

social distance The separation of two or more social groups, either by mutual desire or by discrimination involving one or more against the others. Social distance is usually identified through the amount of interaction between the groups – as in rates of intermarriage: it is rarely complete (except in caste and similar societies; cf. APARTHEID) but is represented by a range of distances from totally integrated groups at one extreme (see ASSIMILATION) to those which live almost entirely separate lives (usually within the same urban areas) at the other (see GHETTO). The social distance between two groups may be related – as both cause and effect – to the spatial distance between them within an urban area, as argued in a classic paper by Park (1926; cf. CHICAGO SCHOOL): the greater the social distance between two groups the less they would be mixed together within the same residential area (see INDICES OF SEGREGATION). RJJ

Reference

Park, R.E. 1926: The urban community as a spatial pattern and a moral order. In E.W. Burgess, ed., *The urban community*. Chicago: University of Chicago Press.

social exclusion A situation in which certain members of a society are, or become, separated from much that comprises the normal 'round' of living and working within that society. While often envisaged in abstractly social terms, relative to the levels of material resources, well-being and social activity typical of most citizens within a society, exclusion can also be thought of as a situation which is simultaneously social and spatial. Indeed, excluded individuals will tend to slip outside, or even become unwelcome visitors within, those spaces which come to be regarded as the loci of 'mainstream' social life (e.g. middle-class SUBURBS, up-market shopping malls, prime public space).

The notion of 'social exclusion' has recently been popularized in a policy sense, initially through its widespread use in a European context and more recently through the establishment by the British government of a Social Exclusion Unit. The working definition favoured in policy circles becomes: 'the outcome of processes and/or factors which bar access to participation in CIVIL SOCIETY' (Eisenstadt and Witcher, 1998, p. 6). The emphasis goes beyond conventional income-based indicators of poverty, and incorporates additional issues such as 'access to legal justice, the labour market and political processes'. (Criticisms have arisen from those who regard this new emphasis on 'the socially excluded' as simply revising older, prejudicial notions such as the UNDERCLASS and the 'undeserving poor': e.g. Samers, 1998.) Interestingly, policy analysts and others are noting that '[s]ocial exclusion may have a geographical dimension', leading them to highlight the experiences of individuals, groups and communities who are socially and spatially 'isolated' in one way or another. (See POVERTY, GEOGRAPHY OF; and also Philo, 1995.) There are important links here to academic work on 'FINANCIAL EXCLUSION', which stresses the growing withdrawal of financial assistance from certain peoples and places as a result of an insistent 'restructuring for profit' by banks, building societies, insurance agencies and other financial services (see Fuller, 1998; Leyshon and Thrift, 1995).

An academic geographical concern for socio-spatial exclusion predates the current upshot of policy interest, though, and can be traced to Sibley's innovative *Outsiders in urban societies* (Sibley, 1981). Through substantive studies of 'Gypsies', 'travellers' and the North American Inuit, Sibley anticipated a new tradition of research into excluded minority ('other') social groupings which has greatly enlarged the purview of SOCIAL GEOGRAPHY (Philo, 1986). All manner of peoples who stand outside of the socio-spatial 'mainstream', on whatever grounds, have now had their 'exclusionary geographies' traced, critiqued and theorized (and perhaps alternatives suggested): and it is hence possible to identify works in this vein tackling women, people of colour, sexual 'dissidents', children and elderly people, disabled and chronically ill people, unemployed and homeless people, people with particular religious, political and other world-views, and many others. Commonly, these are peoples who suffer stigmatization because of who they are, what they do and how they look, and who are thereby positioned on socio-spatial margins, both through their own choices (to avoid hostility) and because of wilful pressures on them to do so (as exerted by an unaccommodating 'mainstream'). Various attempts have been made to conceptualize the forces underlying such socio-spatial exclusion, notably Sibley's (1995) *Geographies of exclusion*, which deploys psychoanalytic arguments about the inherent will of the 'self' to distance itself from all that it perceives as 'other' (as alien, impure, polluting and 'abject'). Sibley speculates that such psychodynamics, as fostered in individual psyches, then translate into wider socio-spatial configurations which set up lines of socio-spatial exclusion between 'selves' who reckon themselves to be essentially similar ('the same') and those identified as fundamentally 'other' (and who suffer from being 'othered'). (See also PSYCHOANALYTIC THEORY, GEOGRAPHY AND; also Wilton, 1998.) A recent theme issue of *Geoforum* (Sibley, 1998) brings together many of these substantive and conceptual themes, as well as referencing the recent policy interest in social exclusion. CP

References

Eisenstadt, N. and Witcher, S. 1998: Social exclusion and poverty. *Outlook: The Quarterly Journal of the National Council of Voluntary Child Care Organisations*, no. 1: 6–7. · Fuller, D. 1998: Credit union development: financial inclusion and exclusion. *Geoforum* 29: 145–58. · Leyshon, A. and Thrift, N.J. 1995: Geographies of financial exclusion: financial abandonment in Britain and the United States. *Transactions, Institute of British Geographers* NS 20: 312–41. · Philo, C. 1986: *'The Same and the Other': on geographies, madness and 'outsiders'*. Loughborough: Loughborough University of Technology, Department of Geography, Occasional Paper, no. 11. · Philo, C., ed., 1995: *Off the map: the social geography of poverty in the UK*. London: Child Poverty Action Group. · Samers, M. 1998: Immigration, 'ethnic minorities' and 'social exclusion' in the European Union: a critical perspective. *Geoforum* 29: 123–44. · Sibley, D. 1981: *Outsiders in urban societies*. Oxford: Blackwell. · Sibley, D. 1995: *Geographies of exclusion: society and difference in the west*. London: Routledge. · Sibley, D., ed., 1998: Theme issue on 'Social Exclusion'. *Geoforum* 29: no. 2. · Wilton, R.D. 1998: The constitution of difference: space and psyche in landscapes of exclusion. *Geoforum* 29: 173–85.

social formation The specific combination of class relations, institutions and relations of social oppression within society at a particular time and place.

Whereas the MODE OF PRODUCTION specifies a society's class relations in the most general terms, identifying the central class relationships involved in the production of surplus value, the concept of social formation refers to concrete forms of social relations at a specific conjuncture. It takes account of relict social relations and forms that survive and operate in later societies, as well as specific patterns of social oppression, whether based on RACE or ETHNICITY, gender or nationality (see NATIONALISM). The important question in discussions of any formation is how these different specific experiences 'articulate' with the dominant class structure.

The concept of social formation was primarily derived from a reading of Marx's *Capital* undertaken in the 1960s and early 1970s by a group of French scholars associated with the Marxist philosopher Louis Althusser (see STRUCTURAL MARXISM). These scholars sought to translate between the generalities of mode of production and the concreteness of everyday life (Poulantzas, 1973). 'Social formation' provides a middle-level conceptualization which aids in connecting the general economic rationale of the ACCUMULATION of CAPITAL with specific forms and relations, as well as STATE institutions. 'Social formation' has, therefore, been used as a means of relating different forms of existence (Cosgrove, 1984) and is thus similar to what Gramsci (1971) has termed an 'historic bloc'. In either usage, the idea of social formation calls attention to the need for a close material and conceptual analysis of social relations within a given place at a given time. NS

References

Cosgrove, D.E. 1984: *Social formation and symbolic landscape*. Totowa, NJ: Barnes and Noble. · Gramsci, A. 1971: *Selections from the prison notebooks*, ed. and trans. Q. Hoare and G. Nowell Smith. London: Lawrence and Wishart; New York: International. · Poulantzas, N. 1973: *Political power and social classes*. London: New Left Books.

Suggested Reading

Cosgrove (1984). · Hindess, B. and Hirst, P. 1977: *Mode of production and social formation*. London: Macmillan.

social geography The study of social relations and the SPATIAL STRUCTURES that underpin those relations, social geography has been transformed over the last 20 years by its encounter with social theory and the so-called 'CULTURAL TURN' across the human sciences (Philo, 1991; Chaney, 1994). Even before these developments, some observers suggested that social geography was suffering from an 'identity crisis' (Cater and Jones, 1989, p. viii). The product of 1960s radicalism, social geography expanded dramatically in the 1970s until it was virtually synonymous with the whole field of human geography (cf. RADICAL GEOGRAPHY). Since then, especially in the UK, social geography has tended to be subsumed by the rapid development of CULTURAL GEOGRAPHY blurring its boundaries as a separate sub-discipline. As a result, some critics have detected an evacuation of 'the social' in social geography, leading to an over-emphasis on meaning, IDENTITY, REPRESENTATION and IDEOLOGY to the neglect of structured inequalities based on socially significant differences of gender, class, race, sexuality, (dis)ability etc. (Gregson, 1995).

Writing in the mid-1960s, Ray Pahl defined social geography as concerned with 'the theoretical location of social groups and social characteristics, often within an urban setting' (1965, p. 82). His emphasis on LOCATION THEORY was typical of the contemporary dominance of SPATIAL SCIENCE, as was his distinctly URBAN emphasis. In fact, social geography's intellectual roots extend much deeper and are more complex. The nineteenth-century French tradition of *la géographie humaine*, for example, is an important precursor of recent developments in social geography, particularly in its more humanistic aspects (e.g. Ley, 1983). With its emphasis on the complex relationship between landscapes (*pays*) and way of life (*genre de vie*), the 'French school' represented a sharp break from predominant forms of ENVIRONMENTAL DETERMINISM, reasserting the significance of HUMAN AGENCY against the claims of an all-constraining physical environment. Similarly, there are important precedents for social geography's radical orientation in the anarchist tradition associated with the work of Peter Kropotkin (1842–1921) and Elisée Reclus (1830–1905) (see ANARCHISM). There are also continuities with the URBAN ECOLOGISTS of the 'CHICAGO SCHOOL' and with the development of the German 'LANDSCAPE indicators' tradition. Indeed, though it is often regarded as an Anglo-American tradition, a more international perspective on social geography is to be welcomed (Eyles, 1986).

That social geography's intellectual agenda has rarely been divorced from its wider political context is suggested by Gilbert and Steel's (1945) confident assertion at the end of the Second World War of social geography's continuing place in colonial studies. These connections persist, though now in more critical form, via social geography's current engagement with POST-COLONIALISM (Jacobs, 1996). Despite passing references to the sociological aspects of geography during the 1950s, social geography's period of most rapid growth did not take place for another ten years, associated with the turbulent events of the 1960s. Informed by current developments in Marxism and French sociology (Castells, 1977), a more politicized social geography developed, emphasizing spatially differentiated social inequalities and leading to both liberal and radical approaches to questions of SOCIAL JUSTICE (Harvey, 1973) (see also WELFARE GEOGRAPHY).

The 1970s also saw the development of an explicitly HUMANISTIC GEOGRAPHY (Ley and Samuels, 1978) with a renewed emphasis on human subjectivity, including an emphasis on understanding 'the patterns which arise from the use social groups make of space as they see it, and . . . the processes involved in making and changing such patterns' (Jones, 1975, p. 7). Despite the growth of Weberian, Marxist and humanistic approaches (Jackson and Smith, 1984), social geography maintained a strongly empirical tradition, particularly regarding the mapping and measuring of patterns of residential SEGREGATION. Geographers then began to develop a more critical concern with the social construction of 'RACE' and the politics of RACISM (Jackson, 1987) and with other forms of DIFFERENCE including the geographies of GENDER (WGSG, 1984), SEXUALITY (Bell and Valentine, 1995) and DISABILITY (Imrie, 1996). The emergence of an explicitly FEMINIST GEOGRAPHY (Rose, 1993; WGSG,

1997) has also been particularly evident within social geography.

Today, social geography covers a wide range of empirical work, informed by a variety of theoretical perspectives (Hamnett, 1996). It encompasses studies of CRIME and POVERTY, HEALTH AND HEALTH CARE, as well as the variety of SOCIAL MOVEMENTS that are struggling for social and political change. Though they are still concerned to analyse the spatial incidence of social problems, social geographers have become increasingly interested in understanding the importance of SPACE in the constitution of social life and in examining the spatial structures that underpin social relations (Gregory and Urry, 1985). A reassertion of the importance of space in social theory is also characteristic of geographical studies of MODERNISM and POSTMODERNISM (Harvey, 1989; Soja, 1989).

Following the cultural turn, social geography's agenda has moved closer to CULTURAL GEOGRAPHY, via studies of the iconography of LANDSCAPE and the CULTURAL POLITICS of SPACE and PLACE. Current research in social geography is also beginning to acknowledge the cultural significance of our embodiment and corporeality, and (via research on genetic engineering and the refashioning of NATURE) to emphasize the social construction of our most TAKEN-FOR-GRANTED categories. Within social geography (as elsewhere), conventional distinctions between the 'economic' and the 'cultural', between 'nature' and 'society', are being increasingly undermined as disciplinary boundaries across the social sciences are themselves transcended. PAJ

References

Bell, D. and Valentine, G., eds, 1995: *Mapping desire: geographies of sexualities*. London: Routledge. · Castells, M. 1977: *The urban question*. London: Edward Arnold. · Cater, J. and Jones, T. 1989: *Social geography: an introduction to contemporary issues*. London: Edward Arnold. · Chaney, D. 1994: *The cultural turn*. London: Routledge. · Eyles, J.D., ed., 1986: *Social geography: an international perspective*. London: Croom Helm. · Gilbert, E.W. and Steel, R.W. 1945: Social geography and its place in colonial studies. *Geographical Journal* 106: 118–31. · Gregory, D. and Urry, J., eds, 1985: *Social relations and spatial structures*. London: Macmillan. · Gregson, N. 1995: And now it's all consumption? *Progress in Human Geography* 19: 135–41. · Hamnett, C., ed., 1996: *Social geography: a reader*. London: Arnold. · Harvey, D. 1973: *Social justice and the city*. Oxford: Blackwell. · Harvey, D. 1989: *The condition of postmodernity*. Oxford: Blackwell. · Imrie, R. 1996: *Disableism and the city*. London: Paul Chapman. · Jackson, P., ed., 1987: *Race and racism*. London: Allen and Unwin. · Jackson, P. and Smith, S.J. 1984: *Exploring social geography*. London: George Allen and Unwin. · Jacobs, J.M. 1996: *Edge of empire: postcolonialism and the city*. London: Routledge. · Jones, E., ed., 1975: *Readings in social geography*. Oxford: Oxford University Press. · Ley, D. 1983: *A social geography of the city*. New York: Harper and Row. · Ley, D. and Samuels, M.S., eds, 1978: *Humanistic geography*. London: Croom Helm. · Pahl, R.E. 1965: Trends in social geography. In R.J. Chorley and P. Haggett, eds, *Frontiers in geographical teaching*. London: Methuen, 81–100. · Philo, C., ed., 1991: *New words, new worlds*. IBG Social and Cultural Geography Study Group. · Rose, G. 1993: *Feminism and geography*. Cambridge: Polity Press. · Soja, E.W. 1989: *Postmodern geographies*. London: Verso. · WGSG (Women and Geography Study Group) 1984: *Geography and gender*. London: Hutchinson. · WGSG (Women and Geography Study Group) 1997: *Feminist geographies*. London: Longman.

Suggested Reading

Cater and Jones (1989). · Gregson, N. 1992: Beyond boundaries: the shifting sands of social geography. *Progress in Human Geography* 16: 387–92. · Sibley, D. 1995: *Geographies of exclusion*. London: Routledge.

social justice The distribution of society's benefits and burdens, and how this comes about. Social justice is the concern of various disciplines, in particular moral philosophy and political philosophy. The scope of the field, and the variety of perspectives adopted, is illustrated in a number of overviews, for example Arthur and Shaw (1991), Kymlicka (1990) and Sterba et al. (1995). There has been a resurgence of interest in social justice in geography in recent years. Geographical perspectives on social justice are informed by work in other disciplines, but there is also a specifically geographical interest in distribution among populations defined by the places in which they live, i.e. TERRITORIAL JUSTICE. A separate but related field concerns geographical aspects of the implementation of justice in the procedural and especially legal sense (see JUSTICE, GEOGRAPHY AND).

In the first volume of his *Treatise on social justice*, Brian Barry (1989) states that 'a theory of social justice is a theory about the kind of social arrangements that can be defended'. While social justice is a very broad concept, attention is often focused on the distribution of income and other sources of need satisfaction on which the material conditions of a population depend. To echo Barry, it is *in*equality or *un*equal treatment that requires justification. People's common humanity and capacity for pleasure and pain is a plausible starting point for EGALITARIANISM, with such individual differences as strength, skill, intellect, family, race or place of birth being regarded as fortuitous and hence morally irrelevant to the way people should be treated.

However, it does not follow that there are no grounds on which different and unequal treatment can be justified. Some people may be deemed to deserve more or less of what there is to distribute, for example if they produce more than others or occupy positions of special responsibility. Greater or lesser contribution to the common good is often built into the justification of unequal rewards in relation to quantity or quality of work performed. Need is another frequently invoked criterion for unequal treatment, some people being in greater need than others (e.g. for certain services).

A common point of entry into the question of what specific conditions justify unequal treatment is to try to identify an initial state of affairs which can be agreed to be just, and to argue that any outcome will be just, providing that it arises from a just process. An example can be found in the LIBERTARIANISM of Robert Nozick (1974). If peoples' holdings of property (such as land and natural resources) have been justly acquired, for example by settling land that belongs to no one else or purchasing it by mutual agreement, and if they subsequently use this property justly to acquire further wealth, for example by free trade or mutually agreed employment of others, then the distributional consequences can be justified, no matter how unequal. In short, a distribution is just if it arises from a just prior distribution by just means: a process sometimes termed 'clean accumulation'. There is thus no particular pattern to which a just distribution should conform. Such an argument is sometimes used to justify the distribution generated by free market forces, assumed to embody a just process, though the justice of the prior distribution (including how people actually acquired their property in the first place) may not be closely scrutinized.

An alternative starting point is to be found in social contract theory, the best-known contribution to which is the work of John Rawls (1971). Although subject to extensive subsequent critique, Rawls's theory of justice is still extremely influential, and figures prominently in some subsequent texts on social justice (e.g. Barry, 1989) as well as in a persuasive attempt to sketch out a theory of human need (Doyal and Gough, 1991). The approach adopted by Rawls was to try to deduce the social contract to which people would subscribe in particular circumstances. He began with an 'original position' or 'state of nature', in which people would have to approve of institutions under a 'veil of ignorance' as to their social position, e.g. whether they would belong to the rich or poor. Not knowing who, and where, they would be in society, most people would be prepared to entertain only a narrow range of life chances, if any inequality at all, because they could end up among the worst-off (though a few might be prepared to take the risk of ending up very poor for the sake of the chance of being very rich). Rawls's statement of principles runs as follows (Rawls, 1971, p. 302):

> *First Principle*
> Each person is to have an equal right to the most extensive total system of equal basic liberties compatible with a similar system of liberty to all.
> *Second Principle*
> Social and economic inequalities are to be arranged so that they are both:
> (a) to the greatest benefit of the least advantaged, consistent with the just savings principle [required to respect the claims of future generations], and
> (b) attached to offices and positions open to all under conditions of fair equality of opportunity.

The central distributional points here are that inequality can be justified, providing that society's poorest benefit from this, and that there are equal opportunities to acquire the positions of advantage. Rawls's formulation represents a strengthening of the familiar principle that contribution to the common good justifies favourable treatment: it is contribution to the well-being of the poorest that matters.

An interesting elaboration of Rawls's original theory has been provided by Peffer (1990), writing from a Marxian perspective. He departs from the position, common among Marxists, that morality and social justice are ideological constructs deployed by a ruling class to legitimate their position of privilege, to recover what he sees as the moral theory implicitly (for the most part) in Marx's voluminous and occasionally contradictory writings. He concludes with a modification of Rawls's theory, which is claimed to entail Marx's moral principles but to be more complete and adequate. The main effect is to prioritize peoples' rights to security and subsistence, to make more specific certain liberties and opportunities which should prevail, and to further constrain the permissible degree of inequality by requiring that this should not exceed that which would seriously undermine equal worth of liberty or self-respect. However, some Marxists are suspicious of any suggestion that Marxism and liberal egalitarianism may share such common ground, preferring to maintain the critical edge of Marx's critique of capitalist social relations (or CLASS) as the fundamental source of injustice.

Works addressing social justice in geography with some rigour have been rare. By far the most influential early treatment was by Harvey (1973), who argued that a just territorial distribution of income (broadly defined) would be such that: the needs of the people of each territory would be met; resources would be allocated so as to maximize interterritorial multiplier effects, thus rewarding contribution to national economic good; and extra resources would be allocated to help overcome special difficulties stemming from the physical and social environment, which could be considered as cases of merit. He also proposed that, in a just distribution justly arrived at, the prospects of the least advantaged territory would be as great as possible: a clear echo from John Rawls. Smith (1977) subsequently reviewed a range of perspectives that might be applied to the task of judging distributions as better or worse.

Until quite recently, preoccupation with distribution characterized much, if by no means all of the discourse of social justice in moral and political philosophy as well as in geography. The implications are explained by Young (1990, p. 25) as:

> The distributive paradigm implicitly assumes that social judgements are about what individual persons have, how much they have, and how that amount compares with what other persons have. This focus on possession tends to preclude thinking about what people are doing, according to what institutionalized rules, how their doings and havings are structured by institutionalized relations that constitute their positions, and how the combined effect of their doings has recursive effects on their lives.

To Young, social injustice concerns the domination and oppression of one group or groups in society by another, not merely the distributional outcomes. This involves not only formal institutions, but also the day-to-day practices whereby subordination and exclusion are realized and reproduced in the form of what is sometimes termed cultural imperialism. Democracy is central to social justice, but formal political rights conceived merely as 'one person one vote' are not sufficient for the full democratization of society. She argues that we require real participatory structures in which actual people, with their geographical, ethnic, gender and occupational differences, assert their perspectives on social issues within institutions that encourage the representation of their distinct voices.

Other critiques of mainstream ('liberal') theories of social justice, with their emphasis on distribution, come from COMMUNITARIANISM and feminism. The former asserts the good of community, which should render justice a remedial virtue to be called upon when collective ethics fail, while the latter has generated a critique of the emphasis on justice in moral philosphy by proposing an 'ethic of care' (see ETHICS, GEOGRAPHY AND).

While direct consideration of social justice in geography remained muted for much of the 1980s, interest in such issues as discrimination on grounds of RACE and GENDER raised relevant questions. However, at the beginning of the 1990s geographers began to return to the more explicit discussion of social justice. Something of the diversity of geography's re-engagement with social justice is indicated in Laws (1994), in papers on substantive issues such as population migration (Black, 1996) and disability (Gleeson, 1997), and in treatments of theoretical topics (Gleeson, 1996; Smith, 1997). There is also work in the established tradition of territorial social justice (e.g. Boyne and Powell, 1991, 1993).

Central questions in contemporary social justice concern the possibility (or otherwise) of reconciling alternative theoretical positions, and the possibility (or otherwise) of transcending the specificity of historical–geographical circumstances. Working out questions of social justice in particular situations, such as post-socialist eastern Europe and post-apartheid South Africa, might be considered exercises in the contextual thickening of a thin theory with claims to universality, after the fashion suggested earlier. Social justice as a process of moving towards equality, constrained by Rawls's difference principle, has been proposed as such a theory (Smith, 1994).

Providing rigorous foundations for a general theory remains a major challenge, which Harvey (1996) still finds daunting in the face of POSTMODERN attitudes. However, he remains committed to FOUNDATIONALISM: 'the task of critical analysis is not, surely, to prove the impossibility of foundational beliefs (or truths), but to find a more plausible and adequate basis for the foundational beliefs that make interpretation and political action meaningful, creative, and possible'. Hence: 'We need critical ways to think about how differences in ecological, cultural, economic, political, and social conditions get produced . . . and we also need ways to evaluate the justice/injustice of the differences so produced.' Harvey poses the tension between particularity and universality, asking whether it is possible to talk about justice 'as anything other than a contested effect of power within a particular place at a particular time', but recognizes that 'Justice appears to be a foundational concept that is quite indispensable in the regulation of human affairs.' He sees signs of discontent with the impasse generated by the relativism of particularity, leading to attempts to resurrect general principles of social justice which nevertheless acknowledge the force of POST-STRUCTURALIST critiques of universalizing theories, exemplified by Young (1990). Harvey emphasizes the importance of human similarity (rather than difference) in alliance formation among seemingly disparate groups. He concludes:

> Only through critical re-engagement with political-economy, with our situatedness in relation to capital accumulation, can we hope to re-establish a conception of social justice as something to be fought for as a key value within an ethics of political solidarity built across different places.

The incorporation of NATURE in Harvey's revisitation of social justice reflects an emerging interest in ENVIRONMENTAL JUSTICE as part of a movement involving geography with environmental ethics (see ETHICS, GEOGRAPHY AND), or what Low and Gleeson refer to as political ecology. A major concern is the uneven distribution of hazards generated by waste disposal, industrial plants and other noxious facilities or processes. Cutter (1995) makes a distinction between environmental equity and ENVIRONMENTAL JUSTICE. 'Environmental equity is a broad term that is used to describe the disproportionate effects of environmental degradation on people and places', which implies an ideal of equal sharing of risk burdens; environmental justice is a more politically charged term relating to policy, connoting some remedial action to correct an injustice imposed on a specific group of people. The environmental justice movement represents a shift in focus from the 'white upper-class environmental rhetoric' surrounding the preservation of distant pristine habitats to a more localized strategy of environmental improvements closer to the homes of affected residents, who are usually those of lower socio-economic status and belonging to ethnic minorities (cf. NIMBY).

It is important to bear in mind the distinction between justice as broad sets of social institutions and their outcomes, on the one hand, and specific practices on the other. Gleeson (1996) notes the opportunity for confusion between concerns for due legal process (*procedural justice*; see JUSTICE, GEOGRAPHY AND) and a range of perspectives on *social fairness* (social justice). He argues that notions of social justice have been deeply problematized by neo-liberal and postmodern critiques, with the latter encouraging political equivocation: 'The "meta-silence" of the academy contrasts with the chorus from the global political grassroots which is proclaiming market injustice, manifested as socio-spatial polarisation and environmental degradation. . . . It is really postmodernism which most imperils our journey back to justice in geography.' His attempt to provide pointers towards a meta-ethics of justice for geography underlines the importance of the search for more rigorous foundations for effective critique of local practices which invite the judgement of injustice.

Some fundamental questions are being raised in geography's return to social justice, more closely connected to theoretical work in philosophy than before. But there is still scope for new empirical research revealing the injustice actually experienced, by almost any notion of fairness, in such day-to-day problems as spatial access to sources of need satisfaction and unequal exposure to such hazards as environmental pollution. As market relations become almost universal in the organization of human economic and social life, it is especially important to continue to subject their outcomes to rigorous interrogation, and to deploy the discourse of social justice in devising and creating a better world. DMS

References

Arthur, J. and Shaw, W.H., eds, 1991: *Justice and economic distribution*, 2nd edn. Englewood Cliffs, NJ: Prentice-Hall. · Barry, B. 1989: *Theories of justice*. London: Harvester-Wheatsheaf. · Black, R. 1996: Immigration and social justice: towards a progressive European immigration policy? *Transactions, Institute of British Geographers* NS 21: 64–75. · Boyne, G. and Powell, M. 1991: Territorial justice: a review of theory and evidence. *Political Geography Quarterly* 10: 263–81. · Boyne, G. and Powell, M. 1993: Territorial justice and Thatcherism. *Environment and Planning C: Government and Policy* 11: 35–53. · Cutter, S.L. 1995: Race, class and environmental justice. *Progress in Human Geography* 19: 111–22. · Doyal, L. and Gough, I. 1991: *A theory of human need*. London: Macmillan. · Gleeson, B. 1996: Justifying justice. *Area* 28: 229–34. · Gleeson, B. 1997: Community care and disability: the limit to justice? *Progress in Human Geography* 21: 199–224. · Harvey, D. 1973: *Social justice and the city*. London: Edward Arnold. · Harvey, D. 1996: *Justice, nature and the geography of difference*. Oxford: Blackwell. · Kymlicka, W. 1990: *Contemporary political philosophy: an introduction*. Oxford: Clarendon Press. · Laws, G., ed., 1994: Special issue: Social (in)justice in the city: theory and practice two decades later. *Urban Geography* 15(7). · Low, N. and Gleeson, B. 1998: *Justice, society and nature: an exploration of political ecology*. London and New York: Routledge. · Nozick, R. 1974: *Anarchy, state, and utopia*. New York: Basic Books. · Peffer, R.G. 1990: *Marxism, morality, and social justice*. Princeton: Princeton University Press. · Rawls, J. 1971: *A theory of justice*. Cambridge, MA: Harvard University Press. · Smith, D.M. 1977: *Human geography: a welfare approach*. London: Edward Arnold. · Smith, D.M. 1994: *Geography and social justice*. Oxford: Blackwell. · Sterba, J.P., Machan, T.R., Jagger, A.M., Galston, W.A., Gould, C.C., Fisk, M. and Solomon, R.C. 1995: *Morality and social justice: point/counterpoint*. London: Rowman Littlefield. · Young, I.M. 1990: *Justice and the politics of difference*. Princeton: Princeton University Press.

Suggested Reading
Harvey (1996). · Smith (1994).

social movement Social movements are the organized efforts of multiple individuals or organizations, acting outside formal STATE or economic spheres, to pursue political goals within society. They may be organized around either particular *groups* – e.g. the working class – or particular *goals* – e.g. access to HEALTH CARE. Their demands may be focused on the state (e.g. the passage of new laws), on economic actors (e.g. wage demands), on society as a whole (e.g. the changing of norms relating to RACE or SEXUALITY), or on any combination of these. Social movements present methodological difficulties because, as informal, voluntary associations, they are inherently mutable objects of study. Moreover, it is difficult to measure their effects, or to predict whether, when, and how one will arise from a given set of social contradictions or problems (Rochon and Mazmanian, 1993; Peet and Watts, 1996).

Social movements are best understood within a broader framework of social analysis. Thus, social movement theory understands them as phenomena within CIVIL SOCIETY – one of the three major arenas of action and conflict in modern societies, alongside the state and the ECONOMY. Classical POLITICAL ECONOMY began to conceive of civil society as a sphere distinct from, but complementary to, the state and the market. It is thus a concept inseparable from the evolution of capitalist liberal DEMOCRACIES and the modern NATION-STATE, and corresponding ideas of CITIZENSHIP. After Hegel and Marx, civil society came to be understood as the *sphere of reproduction*, and of the informal norms and institutions necessary to the ongoing reproduction of the economy and the state. It also became a catch-all category to refer to forms of social participation and difference not strictly tied to economic class or legal citizenship status, such as voluntary associations and race, ETHNICITY, gender, religion, etc. (see Urry, 1981).

For much of the nineteenth and early twentieth centuries, most social sciences focused on the state and market, and paid relatively little attention to civil society. As a result, most theories of social movements developed before the mid-twentieth century were largely derived from theories of the state and the economy: social movements were understood as expressions of CONFLICTS rooted in those spheres, and were believed to be composed *of* and *for* already-given groups within society. Thus, the labour movement was believed to be a direct result of the structural conflict between capital and wage workers; the latter pursued their evolving interests through conflict with other groups in society. Similar interpretations were applied to agrarian social movements and others. The discipline of sociology was an exception: it made civil society and collective action central objects of study from the early twentieth century on. Sociologists attempted to explain social movements in terms of the need for individuals and groups in the rapidly shifting geographies and economies of modern capitalist societies to continually rebuild informal norms and institutions, to create new relationships, and to bring their material existences and expectations into alignment. All of these theories were broadly functionalist (cf. FUNCTIONALISM).

By the mid-twentieth century, the continued failure of Marxist theories of revolution to fulfil themselves in practice led social theorists to look beyond the state and market, in order to understand how consent and HEGEMONY were both created and resisted in modern societies. This heightened attention to the operations of CULTURE and IDEOLOGY, led by the work of Italian Marxist Antonio Gramsci in the 1930s (Gramsci, 1971), made civil society and social movements central to post-war social theory.

The first major new approach to theorizing social movements in the post-war period was *resource mobilization theory* in the late 1960s and 1970s (Olson, 1965; Oberschall, 1973; Tilly et al., 1975). It argued that the successes and failures of social movements were best understood via reference to what resources – both material and symbolic – they were able to mobilize for their cause. It treated social movements as the products of rational individuals acting in their self-interest, and thus drew more from neo-classical than Marxist theory (cf. MARXIAN ECONOMICS; NEO-CLASSICAL ECONOMICS). Resource mobilization theory has been heavily criticized for incorporating METHODOLOGICAL INDIVIDUALISM and liberal models of public action: in short, it is extremely unclear whether and how rational individuals would ever make the requisite calculations regarding their participation in social movements.

Since the 1960s, a variety of what have come to be known as *new social movements* (NSMs) have appeared and grown around the world, first in advanced capitalist countries and subsequently in the 'Third World'. They include modern ENVIRONMENTALISM, feminism, and the peace movement, among others. NSMs seemingly defy much existing social movement theory, and so new theories have been developed to account for them. Most begin with attempts to specify what is new about NSMs. A consensus has developed that, compared with 'old' social movements such as organized labour, NSMs are more issue-specific, cut across class lines to represent larger segments of the populations, use a wider variety of unconventional tactics, contain elements expressive of meaning and identity beyond purely instrumental goals, and often focus on issues that cannot be understood in terms of zero-sum conflict models of society, such as the threat of nuclear war (see Buttel, 1992). NSMs also operate more outside the organized political sphere, being less likely than previous social movements to turn to established political parties and channels to achieve their goals.

These new elements in the composition and functioning of NSMs may be indicative of broader shifts in the functioning of post-war civil society. Some authors have argued that their emergence is functionally related to the breakdown of many FORDIST, CORPORATIST institutional arrangements in advanced capitalist countries and the resurgence of neo-liberalism since the mid-1970s (Scott, 1990; Buttel, 1992). Others have argued that NSMs represent a positive recognition of the complexity of modern society, demonstrating that individuals cannot be reduced to a single subject position dictated by their place in society, but instead may participate in multiple combinations of social movements, reflecting different facets of their shifting social IDENTITIES and concerns (Laclau, 1985). These analyses are valuable but risk reverting to functionalism in the first case, and underestimating the continued relevance of class politics to NSMs in the second.

Attention to social movements has grown rapidly in recent years. Following the break-up of the Soviet Union and widespread democratization in the Third World, civil society has emerged as a critical arena for contemporary social change and social theory. And social movements are perhaps the major institutions or modes of action within civil society, particularly when organized into networks of Non-Governmental-Organizations. The growth of social movements in the contemporary neo-liberal climate is often interpreted as a response to diminished state capacity or legitimacy: many of the regulatory and social welfare functions of the post-war state are now being shunted to civil society. In this light, recent celebrations of NSMs in the Third World as offering 'alternatives to development' (e.g. Escobar, 1995), need to be greeted cautiously (see Watts and McCarthy, 1997). JMC

References

Buttel, F. 1992: Environmentalization. *Rural Sociology* 57/1: 1–27. · Escobar, A. 1995: *Encountering development*. Princeton: Princeton University Press. · Gramsci, A. 1971: *Selections from the prison notebooks*. New York: International Publishers. · Laclau, E. 1985: New social movements and the plurality of the social. In D. Slater, ed., *New social movements and the state in Latin America*. Amsterdam: Centro de Estudios y Documentación Latinoamericanos (CEDLA). · Oberschall, A. 1973: *Social conflicts and social movements*. Englewood Cliffs, NJ: Prentice-Hall. · Olson, M. 1965: *The logic of collective action*. Cambridge, MA: Harvard University Press. · Peet, R. and Watts, M. 1996: Liberation ecology: development, sustainability, and environment in an age of market triumphalism. In R. Peet and M. Watts, eds, *Liberation ecologies: environment, development, social movements*. London: Routledge. · Rochon, T. and Mazmanian, D. 1993: Social movements and the policy process. *Annals of the American Academy of Political and Social Science* 528: 75–87. · Scott, A. 1990: *Ideology and the new social movements*. London: Unwin Hyman. · Tilly, C., Tilly, L. and Tilly, R. 1975: *The rebellious century: 1830–1930*. Cambridge, MA: Harvard University Press. · Urry, J. 1981: *The anatomy of capitalist societies: the economy, civil society, and the state*. London: Macmillan. · Atlantic Highlands. · Watts, M. and McCarthy, J. 1997: Nature as artifice, nature as artefact: development, environment and modernity in the late twentieth century. In R. Lee and J. Wills, eds, *Geographies of Economies*. London: Arnold.

social network The kin, neighbours and friends to whom an individual is tied socially, usually by shared values, attitudes and aspirations. Such networks may be spatially concentrated, as both cause and effect: people choose to live close to others in their network, thereby maximizing the potential for contact and interaction; and people join networks with their neighbours, reflecting the influence of

DISTANCE DECAY on social interaction (cf. COMMUNITY). RJJ

Suggested Reading

Ley, D. 1983: *A social geography of the city*. New York and London: Harper and Row.

social physics An approach that suggests aggregate human interaction over space can be explained and predicted using physical theories and laws. Implicit within such a view is theoretical monism, one where a single explanatory principle holds for both physical and social processes alike.

H.C. Carey (1858) first codified social physics when he proposed that use be made '. . . of the great law of molecular gravitation as the *indispensable* condition of . . . man [sic]'; a suggestion that was subsequently empirically supported by E.G. Ravenstein's (1885) early work on MIGRATION. W.J. Reilly (1931) presented the first mathematical formulations in his study of retail trade areas (cf. APPLIED GEOGRAPHY; HINTERLAND; RETAILING, GEOGRAPHY OF), but it was primarily J.Q. Stewart (1950), professor of astronomy and physics at Princeton University, who systematically worked through the analogy between interacting particles and interacting humans. During the late 1950s, Stewart, along with W. Warntz (1965), prosecuted social physics under the rubric of MACROGEOGRAPHY, a short-lived movement but one that paved the way for the subsequent success of SPATIAL SCIENCE within human geography (exemplified by the QUANTITATIVE REVOLUTION and REGIONAL SCIENCE).

The GRAVITY MODEL remains the best-known exemplar of social physics. Drawing an analogy with Newton's law of gravitation, it is assumed that humans interact over space as do heavenly bodies in the celestial system. In this formulation, interaction between places is directly proportional to the product of their masses (usually measured by population size) and inversely proportional to some function of the distance between them. The gravity model, along with other social physical analogies such as POPULATION POTENTIAL, DIFFUSION, and ENTROPY-MAXIMIZATION MODELS, have been extensively tested. They often give good empirical fits, but are less satisfactory in their predictions, and even worse in providing explanations.

The lack of explanatory purchase, as Lukermann (1958) pointed out in an early critique of social physics, is because the assumptions made in the physical models are not met in the human realm: 'the lacuna is of the order of two worlds' (Lukermann, 1958, p. 2). There is nothing wrong with analogies *per se*, but for them to succeed there must be certain core similarities between the analogy and the analogized. For many critics of social physics the similarities between human and celestial movements are not just hard to find, they are simply not there to be found. TJB

References

Carey, H.C. 1858: *Principles of social science*. Philadelphia: J.B. Lippincott. · Lukermann, F. 1958: Towards a more geographic economic geography. *Professional Geographer* 10: 2–10. · Reilly, W.J. 1931: *The law of retail gravitation*. New York: W.J. Reilly. · Ravenstein, E.G. 1885: The laws of migration. *Journal of the Royal Statistical Society* 48: 167–235. · Stewart, J.Q. 1950: The development of social physics. *American Journal of Physics* 18: 239–53. · Warntz, W. 1965: *Macrogeography and income fronts*. Philadelphia: Regional Science Research Institute.

Suggested Reading

Barnes, T.J. 1996: *Logics of dislocation: models, metaphors and meanings of economic space*. New York: Guilford, chs 4 and 5. · Lukermann, F. and Porter, P.W. 1960: Gravity and potential model in economic geography. *Annals of the Association of American Geographers* 50: 493–504; Stewart (1950).

social reproduction The interdependent reproduction both of the social relations within which, and the material and discursive means through which, social life is premised, sustained and transformed over space and time (see DEVELOPMENT; ECONOMIC GEOGRAPHY; SOCIETY). Engagement within sustainable circuits of social reproduction is a critical prerequisite for, and a condition of existence of, social life. Questions of the existence and significance of any distinction – as well as of the substantive and interpretative relationships – between biological and social reproduction have been debated within FEMINIST GEOGRAPHY (e.g. Butler, 1998).

The processes and circumstances of social reproduction are of critical significance in understanding both the making of geographies and histories, and the possibilities for and constraints upon their transformation. The analysis of such geographies cannot be (but all too often is) abstracted from the conditions and practices of social reproduction, which is ongoing and in constant flux and movement. Thus, as a condition of the continued existence of social life, social reproduction, shapes the path dependency of what, in economic geography for instance, are but fleeting moments of production, consumption and exchange, the nature of which is shaped by their place in what is always a dynamic and more (or less) conflict-ridden process of social reproduction which varies over space and time.

Social reproduction is both a material and a social process: material in that the consumption, exchange and production of value is central to it; social in that it is dependent upon the maintenance and minimally disruptive transformation of social relations which give direction and purpose to the dynamics of material life. This duality is recognized (rather narrowly and with an all-too-easy invitation to slip into materially deterministic interpretations) in Marxist accounts of the tendency of the dynamics of productive forces to challenge the continued legitimacy of social relations.

But social reproduction involves not only the reproduction of the relations and forces of production involved in the production and consumption of value but the sustenance and development of (from a modernist perspective) hegemonic dominance (see HEGEMONY) and IDEOLOGIES which frame ways of thinking about the world or (from a perspective of postmodernism) of the practices of POWER/knowledge which both construct identity and so define value through discursive practice and thereby serve to challenge the prior significance of social relations in discourse.

Discursive formations may become dominant – and thereby stable, for a time and a space – in a struggle with alternative DISCOURSES and so may then be thought of as regimes of truth (Foucault, 1980). But here truth is defined in terms of the discourse itself: a dominance of power/knowledge rather than social or material veracity or prior logic, which, in this view, are themselves merely part of the discourse. In such ways, SOCIETIES and processes of social reproduction are conceived in terms of socially constructed, deconstructed and reconstructed discourse (see POSTMODERNISM) which define identity and so shape social relations.

Clearly the question of the social becomes highly problematic in such a conception of social reproduction. Does it have any meaning other than power/knowledge – or rather is power/knowledge merely another term for (socially constructed) social relations? And does the social have any historical geography or is it always immediate and forgetful? If (socially constructed, deconstructed and reconstructed) social relations amount to something more than power/knowledge, then remembering becomes a powerful social force – a form of power/knowledge in itself, and identity is constructed out of more than discourse. But discourse is itself a social and material process hardly left untouched by the practical circumstances of social reproduction. The struggle between discourses is not merely discursive and regimes of truth are sustained in part by a discursive legitimacy derived from the materiality and sociality of social reproduction.

Thus the maintenance of social reproduction depends on a practice of social relations (Godelier, 1986) which become widely accepted without the expenditure of a great deal of materially expensive and discursively disruptive force, and/or a transformation of social relations without material breakdown. Breakdown may result from the debilitating effects of the excessive amount of force or violence involved in enabling transformation or may, as was the case in the decade or more after the collapse of state socialism in eastern Europe and, more especially, in the former Soviet Union, result from the profound social pathologies generated by the sudden reorientation of social relations. More generally, breakdown may result from processes of UNDERDEVELOPMENT and exclusion from circuits of social reproduction exemplified over the past two decades or so by the widespread and devastating famines in various regions of Africa.

In one sense at least, social reproduction is irredeemably non-reductive: it 'refers to how societies "keep going" over time' (Giddens, 1997, p. 6), and (crucially) in and through space. If social reproduction is to be sustained, the activities of consumption, production and the transactions which link them together must be combined in continuous, if ever-changing, circuits of social reproduction involving the consumption, production and exchange of values (see figure).

But these circuits are dependent not merely upon material flows of value but upon a discursive acceptance of the nature and direction of such flows. So, although in material terms, social reproduction involves the continued production and consumption of *value* or worth, the practical meaning of value is itself socially constructed through the social

→ ec → Cn → el → P → ec → Cn → el → P → ec →

where P = production
Cn = necessary consumption
ec = exchange of produced use values
el = exchange of labour power

social reproduction *A circuit of social reproduction*

experience of its consumption and production and in the transactions and exchanges involved in its circulation through the material sustenance of social life.

Social reproduction may be

- *static*, involving the sustenance of social relations and the production of quantities of value sufficient for subsistence. Production must be capable of meeting the needs of consumption, so enabling the reproduction of the labour involved in production, and the replacement of other inputs (like tools, for example) used up in the process of production;
- *expanded*, involving the sustenance and/or transformation of social relations in the face of the production of a material surplus and its use in the quantitative expansion of the practices of social reproduction. The surplus may be used to expand the circuit quantitatively and/or geographically, to improve quality and techniques of production and/or to enter new spheres of production, in the development of new productive activities or, more generally, to extend the provision of public goods and infrastructure or the production and distribution of social welfare; and
- *complex*, involving increasingly unconstrained choice through the critical assessment and displacement of dominant meanings and norms to reveal and make possible new, possibly even autonomous, systems of consumption, exchange and production.

In order to make a living, people must be able to engage with a system of social reproduction in order to gain access to the *use values* – 'things which serve to satisfy needs of one kind or another' (Marx, 1976, p. 283; see MARXIAN ECONOMICS). One measure of the value of use values is their effectiveness in providing and continuing to provide the material means of social reproduction. Access to such use values involves the establishment of processes of production and consumption coordinated by exchange. So, without access to circuits of social reproduction, human life cannot be sustained whilst the failure of such circuits – a failure often induced by social action rather than by some apparently autonomous conjunctural circumstances but rarely, if ever, without unintended consequences – imperils the reproduction of material life.

The collapse of COMMUNISM in eastern Europe and the former Soviet Union at the end of the 1980s provides an example of the complexity of social reproduction and the causes of its breakdown as revealed in the consequences of its failure – material, political and discursive – and in the resultant breakdown of a regime of truth. Again, however, the use of the word 'and' here slides over the question of whether material and discursive failure are additive, whether they are two quite different perspectives on the world or whether they are mutually constitutive and, if so, how. The tortuous process of rebuilding those societies into the new millennium also reveals the difficulty of reconstructing new circuits of social reproduction and new regimes of truth as well as the continued significance of the social (as revealed, for example in all the manifestations of social pathology within these societies) in the path dependency of identity formation, social reproduction and social understanding. This tortuous process of change confirms the complexity of the relations between materiality, sociality and discourse in directing and sustaining social and material life and the variable ways in which they may combine in social reproduction. What it does not reveal – as the inadequacy of the multitude of alternative discourses and practices implemented within the region demonstrate – is the nature of the relations between them, relations which are themselves continuously moving and in socially constructed flux. RL

References

Butler, J. 1998: Merely cultural? *New Left Review* 227: 33–44. · Foucault, M. 1980/1977: *Power/knowledge*. Brighton: Harvester Press. · Giddens, A. 1997: *Sociology*, 3rd edn. Cambridge: Polity Press. · Godelier, M. 1986/1984: *The mental and the material*. London: Verso. · Gunn, C. and Gunn, H.D. 1991: *Reclaiming capital: democratic initiatives and community development*. Ithaca and London: Cornell University Press. · Lee, R. 1989: Social relations and the geography of material life. In D. Gregory and R. Walford, eds *Horizons in human geography*, ch. 2.4. London: Macmillan; New York: St. Martin's Press. · Marx, K. 1976: *Capital*, vol. I. Harmondsworth: Penguin.

Suggested Reading

Daniels, S. and Lee, R., eds, 1996: *Exploring human geography*. London: Arnold, part 1. · Gunn and Gunn (1991), chs 1 and 2. · Lee (1989). · McDowell, L. 1995: Understanding diversity: the problem of/for 'theory'. In R.J. Johnston, P.J. Taylor and M.J. Watts, eds, *Geographies of global change. Remapping the world in the late twentieth century*, ch. 17. Oxford and Cambridge, MA: Blackwell. · Rose, G. 1993: *Feminism and geography*. Oxford: Polity Press.

social space Space as it is perceived and used by social groups. (Space as perceived and used by individuals is usually termed *personal space*.)

As introduced by Buttimer (1969), the term closely approximated the definitions of both COMMUNITY and NATURAL AREA: a portion of an urban residential mosaic occupied by a homogeneous group whose members are identifiable not only by their socio-economic and demographic characteristics but also by their shared values and attitudes, leading to common behaviour patterns. Such spaces are defined and given meaning by the group, however, and so are not readily identified from quantitative indicators alone, such as those used in SOCIAL AREA ANALYSES. (See TERRITORIALITY; TERRITORY.) RJJ

Reference

Buttimer, A. 1969: Social space in interdisciplinary perspective. *Geographical Review* 59: 417–26.

social well-being The degree to which a population's needs and wants are being met. A well society based on MARKET EXCHANGE, for example, is one in which all people have sufficient income to meet their basic needs, where all are treated with equal dignity and have equal rights (cf. HUMAN RIGHTS), where they have reasonable access to their needed range of services, and where their opinions are heard and respected. The quality of a society can be measured by its success on variables reflecting such desiderata, as can variations within a society.

Mapping the geography of social well-being was taken up in the 1970s, as part of a general acceptance of the need for TERRITORIAL SOCIAL INDICATORS with which to chart and understand spatial variations in the quality of life. RJJ

Suggested Reading

Smith, D.M. 1973: *A geography of social well-being in the United States*. New York: McGraw-Hill.

socialism A body of writings, ideas and beliefs on SOCIAL JUSTICE and EQUALITY which, in its most generally understood form, envisages a social system based on common ownership of the means of production and distribution. In communist writings, it is considered as a necessary precondition to achieving full COMMUNISM, from which it is also generally distinguished by an emphasis on the difference between common and STATE ownership. In many other socialist writings, however, socialism is regarded as a system in which only a significant proportion of the means of production is owned and run by the state.

As a response to nineteenth-century industrial CAPITALISM, nineteenth-century socialism encompassed a number of different socialist movements, the most important being utopian socialism, Marxian socialism and democratic socialism. All three shared the following characteristics:

- each contained an economic and social-humanist critique of the social and territorial injustices of the capitalism of its time;
- each had a comprehensive and integrated programme based on a better organized and more just society; and
- each was to change the human geography of state activity.

But there were also vital differences between them.

Utopian socialists saw the self-contained small community as the ideal form for future society, based on the principle of cooperation (cf. ANARCHISM). Land was to come under public ownership, while the daily economic and social life of the COMMUNITY was to be part of a well-planned and human distributive system in which basic needs would be met by the COLLECTIVE. Some utopians expressed in their ideas a yearning for the vanished past of rural life, while few had much faith in an impersonal urban society based on materialism and competition. Many of these ideas found expression in the communities founded by the early nineteenth-century social reformer Robert Owen, and in the later GARDEN CITY movement (see also KIBBUTZ).

Marxian socialism, however, saw such ideas as unrealizable and unscientific because they were not rooted in the historical realities of CLASS struggle and the structural necessities of capitalist production. According to Marx, social reforms cannot change the nature of society and the systems of property relations, for nothing short of an urban proletarian-led revolution could eradicate social injustices and the obstacles to the further development of productive forces (see MARXIAN ECONOMICS). It was only on the basis of collective ownership of the means of production, and through CENTRAL PLANNING, that town–country and other CLASS-based inequalities would be resolved.

In contrast, *democratic socialists* contended that revolution was unnecessary, and that socialism could be achieved through the ballot box. For them the bourgeois state of turn-of-the-century Great Britain and Germany did aid economic progress and had initiated social-welfare programmes for workers (see WELFARE STATE). On this basis, it was believed that democratic socialism could build and prosper through essentially reformist measures.

Many of today's democratic socialists would argue that the experiences of post-1945 parliamentary industrial societies show that their path was right and Marx was wrong, for government could reform capitalism and was not simply the agent of a capitalist ruling class – as instrumental theories of the state contend: nor are all capitalist states the same, and politics simply an instrument of the prevailing mode of production.

State socialism is a term popularized in the West to describe societies whose dominant values are those of Marxism–Leninism, with a character of SOCIETY based on the determining influence of class forces operating through the laws of historical and dialectical materialism (cf. HISTORICAL MATERIALISM). The dominant institution is the Communist Party, the territorial power of which is assured through state control of the means of production (cf. TERRITORIALITY). Central planning is also an important hallmark of state socialism. To varying degrees, such societies set themselves the task of ensuring that differences between town and country, state and collective forms of property, types of labour and ethnoregional distinctions would be overcome, if not eradicated. However, the inability of modern-day state socialism to deliver living standards comparable to those offered by advanced capitalist societies, and to secure social justice and liberties for its peoples, led to popular revolutions between 1989 and 1991 throughout eastern Europe and the former Soviet Union (cf. POST-SOVIET STATES), a process also precipitated, at least initially, by the end of the Cold War. Rejection of state socialism has led to an acceptance of the market as the alternative for ensuring economic growth and the struggle for reincorporation into the capitalist world economy. GES

Suggested Reading

Callinicos, A. 1991: *The revenge of history: Marxism and the East European revolutions*. Oxford: Polity Press. · Giddens, A. 1998: *The Third Way*. Oxford: Polity Press. · Kornai, J. 1990: Socialist transformation and privatization: shifting from a socialist system. *East European Politics and Societies* 4 Spring: 255–304. · Pierson, C. 1995: *Socialism after communism*. Cambridge: Cambridge University Press. · Smith, G.E. 1989: *Planned development in the socialist world*. Cambridge: Cambridge University Press.

society 'There is', a former British prime minister once famously claimed, 'no such thing as society.' This remarkable assertion had at least two ideological goals. One was the refusal to accept anything other than the nature and behaviour of individuals as explanations for human action; another was the displacement of socially constructed forms of SOCIAL REPRODUCTION through distinctive and formative sets of social relations as a significant influence upon the trajectory of human society. The intersection of individuals, tainted only by their internal nature, through markets was seen as the dynamic of a liberal and free society: the world is all agents and one structure – the market formed in the liberal view simply through the free interaction of those agents.

And yet human being is impossible outside some form of society (e.g. Lee, 1989) – even non-human society. Society is both an identifiable cluster of socially constructed individuals, institutions, relationships, forms of conduct, material and social practices and DISCOURSES that are reproduced and reconstituted across time and space, and the condition under which such phenomena are formed. The stress here upon relationships, institutions and conduct underlines the point that societies are far more than the individuals which comprise them but it does not imply that they are unitary or determinant totalities. For one thing, the social relations which give direction and evaluative norms to practices of social reproduction are difficult, if not impossible, to resist – at least in the short term and over all but the most restricted geographical spaces – and, for another, Foucauldian notions of regimes of truth (McDowell, 1995) refer to the temporary and partial geographies of stabilization of discursive formations, the nature of which are definable only in terms of their own power/knowledge.

At least four levels of meaning may be ascribed to society: (a) human (or non-human) society in general; (b) historically distinct types of society, e.g. feudal society (see FEUDALISM), capitalist society (see CAPITALISM), defined in terms of a particular set of social relations; (c) particular instances of society, e.g. national societies – sometimes thought of as national SOCIAL FORMATIONS – Arabian society, Christian society; and (d) particular interest groups (e.g. GEOGRAPHICAL SOCIETIES) which represent and proselytize the significance of discourses related closely to the narrow confines of their specific interest. The formative relationships between (a) and (c) are problematic and highly complex and involve intersections between these different instances.

Human life is necessarily social in organization, if only for the most basic reason that it could not be reproduced outside society (Lee, 1989). Equally, human life is necessarily part of NATURE, and nature and society are conjoined in the LABOUR PROCESS (Gregory, 1978). But material production is rarely merely instinctive. It cannot somehow predate systems of meaning or significance. Systems of meaning direct and endow significance upon material practice. Even in the most desperate circumstances of material deprivation, human beings respond emotionally as well as physiologically to their plight and try to make sense of or protest at the nonsense of their predicament. Social being certainly determines consciousness but whether material production determines social being is another matter altogether (see ECONOMIC GEOGRAPHY). Similarly, the question of 'social being' itself is problematic in that it may presuppose nothing more than adherence to a particular discourse or regime of truth.

Society is always in a process of becoming as a result of the conscious actions of human beings – including their representations of their own circumstances. Indeed, the term social formation carries with it the notion that society is an ever-changing process. Human actions are informed by society itself, by the understandings held of society – which may be no more than acceptance of particular discourses – although these are social practices which presuppose, therefore, some prior social, if only competing, discourses, and by the relationships between society and its knowledgeable participants. This means that the study of society cannot be reduced to the simplicities of natural or physical science. We cannot divorce subject and object and alternative societies are always possible if we choose to construct them.

Human beings create societies at the same time as they are created by them, and they are knowledgeable participants in this double process of creation (see STRUCTURATION THEORY). Indeed, Godelier (1986, p. 1) argues (italics in original) that

> human beings, in contrast to other social animals, do not just live in society, they *produce society in order to live*. In the course of their existence, they invent new ways of thinking and acting – both upon themselves and upon the nature which surrounds them. They therefore produce culture and create history...

and he should have added that the production of CULTURE and history is predicated upon the making of geographies as an essential condition of human existence.

An alternative view (Mann, 1986, p. 14) of the relationship between people and society is that whilst human beings 'need to enter into social power relations, ... they do not need social totalities'. Here the very notion of society as 'a bounded and patterned social totality' is questioned whilst, at the same time, the inherent sociability of human beings is acknowledged in the recognition of the inherency of social relations (Lee, 1989). Michael Mann (1986, p. 5) describes the relationship between people and society thus:

> Human goals require both intervention in nature – a material life in the widest sense – and social cooperation. It is difficult to imagine any of our pursuits or satisfactions occurring without these. Thus the characteristics of nature and the characteristics of social relations become relevant to, and may indeed structure, motivations. They have *emergent* properties of their own.

Resnick and Wolff (1987) also shy away from the idea of a patterned social totality in their rejection of determinist and essentialist forms of analysis (cf. ESSENTIALISM). They stress instead the multiple determinations involved in the complex of interactions between natural, economic, political and cultural processes, each of which may be subdivided into what they call class (production, appropriation and distribution of surplus production) and the wide (almost limitless) range of non-class processes (e.g. commodity exchange, friendship, social intercourse).

However, it would be a profound mistake to conclude from such arguments that human beings are not influenced in a quite fundamental fashion by the societies into which they are born and in which they live. Norms and values, direction and purpose are social constructs and the social relations which articulate such constructs and enable individuals to engage with them are inescapable for human involvement in society even if they become nothing other than the object of opposition. But again such norms and values and so on, are socially constructed not merely through social and material practice but through discursive practice which endows the social and the material with meaning and purpose.

The systems of meanings to which people refer help to define the society to which they, in practice, belong. In one sense, societies are the means and the consequence of communication between human subjects. The breakdown of communication signals the breakdown of society in time and space and so offers one means of defining particular societies. However, it follows that no pure form of society can exist and that no clear social boundaries based upon a particular set of criteria may, realistically, be drawn (see TIME–SPACE DISTANCIATION).

Even societies defined in terms of production relations never exist in a pure state. They are always mixed with other forms of social relations (see SOCIAL FORMATION). And even within, say, capitalist societies there is great scope for cultural, political, moral and ideological differentiation. The struggle for HEGEMONY – for sustainable regimes of truth which in turn reside in practice and in the social relations through which people attempt to make sense of their lives (Lee, 1989) – is, therefore, a fundamental driving force in human society. An alternative interpretation which assumes social determination and closure and treats society as a SYSTEM with clearly defined boundaries is associated with the writings of Talcott Parsons (see FUNCTIONALISM).

Distinctions may be drawn between ECONOMY, STATE and society. The intention of so doing is to try to separate the idea of an association of free individuals from the coercion of economic imperatives or state power. John Urry (1981), for example, refers to 'CIVIL SOCIETY' and defines it as 'that set of social practices outside the relations and forces of production in which agents are both constituted as subjects and which presuppose the actions of such subjects' in struggling to sustain their conditions of existence. This is a helpful concept because it recognizes the interdependence but extreme variability of social practices which both make up and transform society (Bauman, 1991).

Society remains a contested concept. Some fear the implication that to admit to society means to accept a form of social determinism, the denial of individual responsibility in the making of geography and history or, in opposition to such a view, the failure to recognize that 'an individual subject is constructed through a grid of discourse and practice' (McDowell, 1995, p. 288) which, nevertheless and by definition, accepts the existence of the social even if it is only ever constructed instantly and fleetingly. Others object to the possibility that society implies a form of totalizing discourse taking place, somehow, behind the backs of knowing subjects. As an example, Peter Jackson (1989, p. 18) notes that Carl Sauer adopted a super-organic approach to culture which asserts that 'culture is an entity at a higher level than the individual, that it is governed by a logic of its own and that it actively constrains human behaviour' (see BERKELEY SCHOOL). Such an approach 'severely limits the questions that may be asked' as the answer is offered before the question is posed. Questions of the formation of identity and social practice through discourse become irrelevant. But notions of super-organicism do force the issue of memory and the path dependency of historical geographies – socially constructed as they always are.

Paradoxically, NEO-CLASSICAL ECONOMICS, that most asocial of social theory, makes massive assumptions about the sociability of people. Communication is assumed to be perfect, instantaneous and unproblematic in the market economy. If ever there was a totalizing discourse which limits questioning, it is this doctrine so beloved of liberal champions of individual freedom. RL

References

Bauman, Z. 1991: *Intimations of post modernity*. London and New York: Routledge. · Godelier, M. 1986: *The mental and the material*. London and New York: Verso. · Gregory, D. 1978: *Ideology, science and human geography*. London: Hutchinson. · Jackson, P. 1989: *Maps of meaning*. London and Winchester, MA: Unwin Hyman. · Lee, R. 1989: Social relations and the geography of material life. In D. Gregory and R. Walford, *Horizons in human geography*. London: Macmillan; New York: St. Martin's Press, 152–69. · Mann, M. 1986: *The sources of social power*, volume I: *A history of power from the beginning to A.D. 1760*. Cambridge and New York: Cambridge University Press. · McDowell, L. 1995: Understanding diversity: the problem of/for 'theory'. In R.J. Johnston, P.J. Taylor and M.J. Watts, eds, *Geographies of global change: remapping the world in the late twentieth century*, ch. 17. Oxford and Cambridge, MA: Blackwell. · Resnick, S.A. and Wolff, R.D. 1987: *Knowledge and class: a Marxian critique of political economy*. Chicago and London: University of Chicago Press. · Urry, J. 1981: *The anatomy of capitalist societies*. London and Basingstoke: Macmillan; Atlantic Highlands, NJ: Humanities Press.

Suggested reading

Giddens, A. 1982: *Sociology: a brief but critical introduction*. London and Basingstoke: Macmillan; New York: Harcourt Brace Jovanovich, ch. 1. · Giddens, A. 1996: *Sociology*. 2nd edn, Oxford: Polity Press, ch. 2. · Lee (1989). · McDowell (1995).

sovereignty A condition of final and absolute authority in a political COMMUNITY. Originally conceived as a singular universal attribute of pre-modern empires, in the modern world the concept has been turned on its head to define a situation of multiple political authority (Taylor, 1996, ch. 1). Hence, since the Treaty of Westphalia (1648) which codified this modern international politics, sovereignty has been invested in STATES, which have authority over the land and people in their TERRITORIES. This organization of states as political containers (Taylor, 1994) may be interpreted as the last political vestige of the age of absolutism (Taylor, 1997).

The emergence of states based upon territorial sovereignty created an inter-state system, first in Europe and then worldwide, that is the heart of POLITICAL GEOGRAPHY. This sovereignty implies two political processes. First, *internal sovereignty* means that outside powers cannot intervene in the domestic politics of a state unless invited to by the legitimate government. This is usually considered to be the first law of international relations. Second, *external sovereignty* means mutual recognition among sovereign states. Sovereignty cannot be simply proclaimed, it is a reciprocal relation. As such it acts as the ground rule for international relations, by defining who is and who is not a member of the inter-state system. For instance, the creation of black 'states' as part of South Africa's APARTHEID system failed to produce sovereign states because not one other state recognized the new political units as members of the inter-state system. Since 1945 the main way in which new states have confirmed their sovereignty has been by joining the United Nations.

Although an integral part of international law for providing an order to international relations, in practice state sovereignty has been a source of CONFLICT. Unlike earlier polities and their FRONTIERS, sovereign states have to be precisely delimited by BOUNDARIES. Disputes over boundaries have been the major cause of wars in the inter-state system. Originally, such territorial claims by one state on another were mainly dynastic or simply opportunistic in nature, but contemporary claims are usually based upon either historical–cultural arguments (national self-determination, e.g. Pakistan's claims to Kashmir) or spatial integrity (proximity, e.g. Spanish claims to Gibraltar) (Murphy, 1990).

Contemporary conflicts over claims to sovereignty are by no means limited to surface land areas. Theoretically, a state's sovereignty extends downwards to the centre of the Earth, defining a cone in which the state has claim to all subterranean resources. Similarly, sovereignty extends upwards, as a 1919 convention gave states the right to prevent their territory being overflown. The problem is defining the upper limit of this sovereignty; established practice is a limit defined by the operational ceiling of conventional aircraft, leaving everything above this level – satellites, for instance – free from sovereignty restrictions (therefore, spy satellites are legal, spy planes are not). Lateral extensions of sovereignty over the adjacent seas of coastal states are covered by the LAW OF THE SEA. Basically sovereignty has been extended from 'territorial waters', a narrow zone with primarily a defensive function, to large economic zones where states have authority over sea and seabed resources.

Finally, it should be noted that territorial sovereignty features in current debates concerning the nature of GLOBALIZATION. Given that the latter is premised upon trans-state processes (see INTERSTATENESS), it is sometimes argued that globalization marks the end of the state as a sovereign entity (Camilleri and Falk, 1992). But this is to take too formal a view of sovereignty (Murphy, 1994). Sovereignty as an absolute source of power is a myth; there have always been trans-state processes operating throughout the history of the modern world-system (Taylor, 1995). Contemporary globalization represents one of several periods of more intense trans-stateness tendencies. We do not yet understand what the influence of globalization will be on the future of territorial sovereignty. PJT

References

Camilleri, J.A. and Falk, J. 1992: *The end of sovereignty.* London: Edward Elgar. · Murphy, A.B. 1990: Historical justifications for territorial claims. *Annals of the Association of American Geographers* 80: 531–48. · Murphy, A.B. 1994: International law and the sovereign state: challenges to the status quo. In G.K. Demko and W.B. Wood, eds, *Reordering the world.* Boulder: Westview. · Taylor, P.J. 1994: The state as container: territoriality in the modern world-system. *Progress in Human Geography* 18: 151–62. · Taylor, P.J. 1995: Beyond containers: internationality, interstateness, interterritoriality. *Progress in Human Geography* 19: 1–15. · Taylor, P.J. 1996: *The way the modern world works: world hegemony to world impasse.* Chichester: Wiley. · Taylor, P.J. 1997: Territorial absolutism and its evasions. *Geographical Research Forum.*

Suggested Reading

Hinsley, F.A. 1986: *Sovereignty.* London: Watts. · James, A. 1984: Sovereignty: ground rule or gibberish? *Review of International Studies* 10: 1–18.

space, human geography and The production of geographical knowledge has always involved claims to know 'space' in particular ways. Historically, special importance has been attached to the power to fix the locations of events, places and phenomena on the surface of the earth and to represent these on maps. The extension of these capacities involved a series of instrumental, mathematical and graphical advances, but these innovations were also political technologies that were implicated in the production of particular constellations of POWER. As such they carried within them highly particular conceptions of space that were always more than purely technical constructions (see also CARTOGRAPHY, HISTORY OF). This recognition of an intricate connection between power, knowledge and geography has transformed the ways in which the contemporary discipline of human geography has conceptualized space. A suite of concepts has been developed to address what Allen (1997, 1999) calls 'spatial assemblages of power'. These elaborations have significant repercussions for concepts like LOCATION, PLACE, REGION and TERRITORY, but in what follows attention is directed towards 'plenary' concepts of space within which these more specific concepts may be convened.

Richard Hartshorne's influential inquiry into *The nature of geography* (1939) occupies a strange position within modern geographical discourses about space. To Hartshorne AREAL DIFFERENTIATION was the pivot and pinnacle of geographical inquiry, and he treated geography as a 'correlative discipline' whose research methodology involved making comparisons between maps in order to disclose 'the functional integration of phenomena' over space. Yet Hartshorne's original text provided little or no systematic discussion of the concept of space on which his prospectus depended, and even his subsequent genealogy of geography as one of the 'spatial sciences' (with astronomy and geophysics) failed to elucidate the conceptual basis of his claim. What preoccupied Hartshorne (1958) was the recovery of a line of descent from Kant through Humboldt to Hettner, and by implication its culmination in his own work, and yet the ways in which these writers *conceptualized* space was never allowed to become a problem. Like most of his peers within the discipline, Hartshorne simply took it for granted that space (like time) was a universal of human existence, an external coordinate of reality, an empty grid of mutually exclusive points, 'an unchanging box' *within which objects exist and events occur*: all of which is to say that he privileged the concept of *absolute space* (Smith, 1984, pp. ix, 67–8; see also KANTIANISM).

While it became commonplace to treat space as 'the basic organizing concept of the geographer' (Whittlesey, in James and Jones, 1954), in North American and British geography at any rate, Hartshorne's critics fastened on the way in which he had taken a specific concept of space and elevated it into a single and supposedly universal concept of space. Although Schaefer (1953) objected to the EXCEPTIONALISM of Hartshorne's views, he none the less agreed that 'spatial relations are the ones that matter in geography and no others'. The significant difference for most of Hartshorne's critics was that 'spatial relations' were now to be defined *between objects and events* (not between the fixed points of a coordinate system) and thereby made relative to the objects and events that constituted a spatial system or spatial structure. This substituted a concept of *relative space* whose elucidation required a more complex geometry, and for this reason SPATIAL ANALYSIS – the preferred research methodology of many of Hartshorne's critics – involved a process of ABSTRACTION in which 'physical space [was] superseded by mathematical space' (Smith, 1984, pp. 68–73). This intellectual project promised to turn geography into a truly formal SPATIAL SCIENCE in the prosecution of which many geographers seemed to accept Sigwart's claim: 'That there is more order in the world than appears at first sight is not discovered *till that order is looked for*' (cited in Haggett, 1965, p. 2). This was used to demarcate a new research frontier – a 'new geography' – whose explorer-scientists were animated by the conviction that there was an intrinsically and essentially spatial order to the world: that spatial science made it possible to disclose – to make visible – the spatiality of the natural and the social in ways that were literally overlooked by the other sciences. At the limit, some of the principal architects of spatial science held out the tantalizing prospect of an autonomous science of the spatial in which physical geography and human geography would be articulated around the central place of geometry: as Bunge (1962) wrote in his *Theoretical geography*, 'The science of space [geography] finds the logic of space [geometry] a sharp tool.'

Yet many human geographers became increasingly uncomfortable at these claims for what some critics called SPATIAL FETISHISM – treating social relations as purely spatial relations – and what Sack (1974) called a SPATIAL SEPARATISM. The subsequent critique of spatial science was many-stranded, but most of the original objections can be made to revolve around Olsson's (1974) deceptively simple claim that the statements of spatial science revealed more about the language its protagonists were talking *in* than the world they were talking *about*. Criticism of this kind licensed a general retreat from *formal language systems* like geometry (whose elements have unassigned meanings: in principle the points and lines and surfaces can refer to anything) towards *ordinary language systems* (whose elements have assigned meanings). This movement involved an interrogation of the substantive processes that were inscribed on and which operated through the production of spatial systems and spatial structures. In this way geography reclaimed its classical etymology – 'earth-writing' – by exploring the process-domains of (for example) political economy and social theory, and by tracing the marks that these social processes left on the surface of the earth. From such a perspective, concepts of space were not to be adjudicated by appeals to the courts of Philosophy or Science but through the conduct of social practices. As Harvey (1973, p. 14) put it, 'The question "what is space?" is therefore replaced by the question "how is it that different human practices create and make use of distinctive conceptualizations of space?"' This trades on a somewhat different concept of 'relative space'. Critical of the objectivism that characterized spatial science, this approach developed what is sometimes called a *relational* concept of space in which space is 'folded into' *social relations through practical activities* (see Harvey, 1996).

Harvey's original question admitted no single answer. Some geographers chose to consider the production of 'material, concrete spaces' while others were more interested in the production of 'imagined, symbolic spaces' (the reason for those quotation marks will become clear below). For all these differences, however, there was a general convergence on the *socialization of spatial analysis* and, hard on its heels, the *spatialization of social analysis*: like simultaneous equations, each was seen to require the other (Gregory and Urry, 1985; see also Cox, 1995; Sheppard, 1995).

Many of the first and formative attempts to reconceptualize space in these terms owed much to a (re)reading of HISTORICAL MATERIALISM which sought to show how Marx's POLITICAL ECONOMY of CAPITALISM depended on the production of a SPACE-ECONOMY that he himself never explicitly theorized (Harvey, 1982). Harvey described this project as an 'historico-geographical materialism', which to Soja (1989, p. 78) implied a *socio-spatial dialectic* between 'the vertical and horizontal dimensions of the mode of production'. Soja's formulations were derived, in part, from Lefebvre's theses about the PRODUCTION OF SPACE, which were also the inspiration for another DIALECTIC proposed between 'space' and 'place' (cf. Tuan, 1977). Following Lefebvre (1991), Merrifield (1993) treated *space under capitalism* as 'the realm of dispassionate "objects" rationally "ordered in space"', as 'the realm of flows of capital, money, commodities and information', which Lefebvre called the *realm of the conceived*, whereas *place under capitalism* 'comprises the locus and a sort of stopping of these flows', which Lefebvre called the *realm of the lived* (cf. Castells, 1983).

These contributions to a MARXIST GEOGRAPHY emphasized the importance of constructing a materialist history of space that was capable of grounding specific concepts of space in specific social formations. So, for example:

> The emergence of capitalist social relations in Europe brought a very specific set of social and political shifts that established absolute space as the premise of hegemonic social practices. The inauguration of private property as the general basis of the social economy, and the division of land into privately held and demarcated plots; the juridicial assumption of the individual body as the basic social unit; the progressive, outward expansion of European hegemony through the conquest, colonization and defence of new territories; the division of global space into mutually exclusive nation-states: these and other shifts marked the emerging space-economy of capitalism from the sixteenth century onwards and represented a powerful enactment of absolute space as the geographical basis for social intercourse. (Smith and Katz, 1993, p. 75)

In his landmark study of UNEVEN DEVELOPMENT, Smith (1984, pp. 69–90) had described capitalism as a continuous but jagged process of expansion into 'absolute space' – through the advances of COLONIALISM and IMPERIALISM – until those absolute spaces were differentiated and transformed within the production of a larger and highly unstable 'relative space'. What Smith and Katz (1993) now emphasized was the way in which these material productions were elaborated in ideological registers, thereby forging a powerful connection between 'material' and 'metaphorical' spaces.

These were all significant ideas, but these theorizations of space were interrupted, extended and reworked through other politico-intellectual traditions. Some thinkers were suspicious of the ways in which accounts deriving from historical materialism seemed to privilege capitalism as their explanatory locus – in particular its economic structures and its grid of CLASS relations – and so failed to properly register the ways in which the production of space was caught up in the production of 'RACE', GENDER and SEXUALITY (see, for example, FEMINIST GEOGRAPHIES). Others were critical of classical Marxism's reluctance to recognize the significance of cultural formations, cultural practices and cultural politics in the production, interpretation and transformation of space (see CULTURAL GEOGRAPHY). For this reason many critics turned to other philosophical traditions to clarify the practical importance of language and meaning, of experience and subjectivity, and the ways in which space is embedded within all of them: that is, the 'spaces of being-in-the-world' (Strohmayer, 1998; see also Pickles, 1985; Schatzki, 1991; cf. PHENOMENOLOGY). So-called 'western Marxism' was always much more responsive to these considerations, but its avowed 'westernness' made theorizations of space conducted under its sign vulnerable to charges of EUROCENTRISM (Slater, 1992).

Through these intersecting contributions and debates many of the assumptions underwriting both spatial science and its successor projects summarized in the previous paragraphs have been revisited and substantially revised. The international journal *Society and Space* was founded in 1983 to foster the multiple, interdisciplinary conversations that were emerging in the discursive spaces between the socialization of spatial analysis and the spatialization of social analysis. The most significant contributions to re-theorizing space in these terms have concerned both (a) EPISTEMOLOGY and (b) ONTOLOGY.

(a) *Human geographers have become much more interested in the ways in which claims to knowledge about space have been registered.*

In the first place, rather than passing over the visual preoccupations and privileges of spatial science ('looking for order'), human geographers have returned to them and sought to understand the cultural construction of vision as visuality (see VISION AND VISUALITY). They have filed nuanced accounts of the connections between claims to knowledge and the metaphorics of vision ('observation', for example, or 'evidence' from the Latin *videre*, 'to see'); of the constitution of the grids of power and political technologies through which particular visual practices are socially structured and legitimized ('scopic regimes'); and of the ways in which gender, sexuality and desire are implicated in visual appropriations of the world. These contributions have been centrally concerned with the production of spaces within which the world is made visible from specific vantage points in specific ways: with the connections between scopic regimes and the formation of *spaces of constructed visibility* (Rajchman, 1991) and with the *geographies of presence and absence* that they make possible (Strohmayer, 1997). Ideas like these have revised traditional conceptions of the ways in which LANDSCAPE and MAPS function as representations – as orderings – of space, redescribing their naturalization as the product of cultural practices, and more generally have called into question the systems of power written into the discipline's claims to know the world by rendering it as a *transparent space*. Critics have argued that this epistemology involves human geography in analytical gestures that install – through a particular, highly partial conception of space – both a colonizing 'white mythology' and a MASCULINISM (see Rose, 1993; Gregory, 1994; cf. SITUATED KNOWLEDGE).

In the second place, rather than enforcing the radical separation between 'words' and 'things' that was central to Olsson's critique of spatial science, many human geographers have instead tried to understand the 'object-constituting' and performative dimensions of DISCOURSE. Drawing on the POST-STRUCTURALISM of Foucault, Deleuze and Guattari and others, and on the PSYCHOANALYTIC THEORY of Lacan, Irigaray and others, much of this work has sought to show how the production of spaces enters into the co-production of human subjects (see SUBJECT FORMATION, GEOGRAPHIES OF). These themes were not inimical to Lefebvre's (1991) theorizations of the production of space – though he was critical of both post-structuralism and psychoanalytic theory (Pile, 1996; Gregory, 1997) – but they have been developed in ways that interrupt and undo the dualisms around which any 'dialectics of space' revolves. It is perfectly true that constellations of power and knowledge are typically elaborated through a spatial system of inclusions and exclusions: most generally, through the demarcation of a 'space of the Same' from which 'the Other' is supposedly excluded (Foucault, 1975; see also Philo, 1992). But a common critical response is now to call these boundary-making and boundary-marking exercises to account – to denaturalize them by disclosing their cultural constitution and consequences – and at the same time to break open (literally to 'de-limit') the 'space of the Same'. *This involves recognizing the presence of the Other within the space of the Same*: the ways in which the geographical knowledges brought 'home' by European explorers relied on and appropriated indigenous knowledges, for example, or the ways in which the racialized, gendered and supposedly 'pure' spaces of colonialism were routinely disrupted and transgressed (Mills,

1996). *But it also involves imagining a 'somewhere else'*, what is sometimes called a *paradoxical space* that somehow 'straddles the space of representation and unrepresentability' (Rose, 1993, pp. 153–4). For Rose this possibility is central to a feminist imaginary, whereas other writers have drawn attention to the emancipatory recognition of similarly hybrid spaces under the signs of POST-COLONIALISM and TRANSCULTURATION. Soja (1996) has convened many of these contributions within a plenary THIRD SPACE, which he describes as a way of thinking about and (crucially) being in the world that values the production of heterogeneous spaces of 'radical openness' (see also HETEROTOPIA; HYBRIDITY).

(b) *Human geographers have also called into question the ways in which space has been conceptualized, and they have done so by destabilizing three sets of oppositions that formed the axis around which spatial science and its early critiques were articulated*:

The dualism of 'time' and 'space'. Conventional social science privileged the first term – so that time was seen as the source of change, movement and history – and marginalized the second, so that space was identified as the site of a lack of these 'ordering' processes. Massey (1993) argued that this dualism effectively masculinized the concept of time and feminized the concept of space, but Gregory (1994) suggests that this is unduly restrictive: colonial productions of space typically feminized 'nature', for example, and sought to establish a mappable, transparent space whose planning and production were identified with a masculinist Reason. Even so, Massey's central point remains a sharp one, and while she develops it through an explicitly feminist critique it plainly also owes much to her continuing interest in historical materialism. In Massey's view, and that of many others, an effective human geography must abandon the project of an autonomous science of the spatial by deploying a concept of space–time capable of elucidating the production of what she calls a POWER-GEOMETRY, that is, uneven and asymmetric constellations of power that are constituted through their 'binding together' of space and time in differential ways (see also REGIONS AND REGIONAL GEOGRAPHY).

The dualism of 'absolute space' and 'relative space'. According to Gibson-Graham (1996) the concept of absolute space presupposes a *stable spatial ontology* within which 'objects are fixed at an absolute location', whereas the concept of relative space requires a *fluid spatial ontology*, 'continually under construction by the force-fields established between objects'. Gibson-Graham argues that *both* concepts invoke the image of space as 'ground' which relies in its turn on a metaphysics of presence, the bête-noire of post-structuralism, and seeks to contest this through a rhizomatics derived from the work of Deleuze and Guattari (see also Doel, 1996; cf. RHIZOME).

The dualism between 'real, material, concrete space' and 'non-real, imagined, symbolic space'. Rose (1996) claims that these oppositions constitute the performances of normative power within a masculinist geographical imaginary:

> [Real space] is simultaneously concrete and dynamic, yet both these qualities signify the masculine; the non-real is simultaneously fluid and imprisoning, but always engendered as feminine. Material real space could thus be re-described as the effect of masculinist power, its very materiality also its particular masculinity; but non-real space is also the effect of masculinist power, its lack of reality the sign of its feminization.... [T]he distinction is a dualism which reiterates the constitutive relation between the masculine Same and the feminine Other. Through trying to fix difference, they fix the same. (p. 59)

Three basic propositions have emerged from these intertwined reformulations (all of which owe much to feminist theory and feminist geography).

First, *space and time (or space–time) are now seen as being 'produced' or 'constituted' through action and interaction*. According to this view, space and time are not neutral, canonical grids that exist 'on the outside', separate from and so enframing and containing everyday life, but are instead folded into the ongoing flows and forms of the world in which we find ourselves. This is the central motif of any CONTEXTUAL APPROACH. These ideas are focal to historico-geographical materialism, but they have also been developed in other ways through other theoretical vocabularies. Thus Thrift (1996, 1999) draws on ACTOR–NETWORK THEORY to talk of *spatial formations*, thereby seeking to figure a sensuous ontology of practices and encounters between diverse, distributed bodies and things (see also Hetherington, 1997). This is a thoroughly materialist account, but one which operates through an analytics of the surface rather than the 'depth models' of mainstream Marxism, and which refuses the oppositions between 'culture' and 'nature' on which historical materialism is predicated. Similarly, but not identically, Rose (1999) draws on feminist theory to think of space as 'a doing'. In contradistinction to concepts of TIME–SPACE COMPRESSION or

TIME–SPACE DISTANCIATION, she insists that space is not a pre-existent void or a terrain 'to be filled or spanned or constructed' but is instead practised and performed (see PERFORMANCE).

Secondly, *space and time cannot be held fast in fixed compartments, measured intervals or regular geometries*. Both spatial science and conventional social theory are now seen to have made too much of pattern and systematicity, labouring to solve what they usually called 'the problem of order', without recognizing the multiple ways in which life on earth evades and exceeds those orders. This is a much more radical claim than – for example – de Certeau's (1981) distinction between the *strategies* of dominant powers (which inhere within *productions* of space that seek to confine 'others' to their 'proper' places) and the *tactics* of those who seek to resist such enclosures 'on the wing' through their 'insurgent' and 'guerrilla' *consumptions* of space. To be sure, space is not infinitely plastic: 'certain forms of space tend to recur, their repetition a sign of the power that saturates the spatial' (Rose, 1999). And yet, while modalities of power often work to condense particular spatialities as 'natural' outcomes – and thus to sanction 'strategies' – Massey (1999) insists that *space is not a coherent system of discriminations and interconnections*, a grid of 'proper places'. It is important to understand that this argument does not turn on reducing spatial structures to some central generating mechanism that provides for both 'surface' variability and 'deep' systematicity, because this is where Massey departs most substantially from historico-geographical materialism. On the contrary: insofar as space is formed and transformed through countless productions, practices and performances, Massey suggests that *space necessarily entails plurality and multiplicity*. It follows that spatial formations involve (and invite) 'happenstance juxtapositions' and 'accidental separations', so that space ought to be conceived as a turbulent field of constellations and configurations: a world of structures and solidarities, disruptions and dislocations that provides for 'the possibility of the emergence of genuine novelty'. Far from space being the fixed and frozen – the 'dead', as one of Foucault's astringent critics once claimed – it is now more usually and more constructively theorized *as being fully involved in the modulations of tension and transformation*.

Thirdly, *productions of space are inseparable from productions of* NATURE (Smith, 1984). Spatial science had supposed that 'space' and 'nature' could be reconciled through their geometries, but there is now a gathering stream of important work that seeks to show how these productions are folded into one another through practices. This was an important theorem of historico-geographical materialism, but some of the most imaginative contributions to the delimitation of these mobile, fluid 'hybrid geographies' have been made by actor–network theory (see, e.g. Whatmore, 1999; see also GEOGRAPHICAL IMAGINATION). DG

References

Allen, J. 1997: Economies of power and space. In R. Lee and J. Wills, eds, *Geographies of economies*. London and New York: Edward Arnold, 59–70. · Allen, J. 1999: Spatial assemblages of power: from domination to empowerment. In D. Massey, J. Allen, and P. Sarre, eds, *Human geography today*. Cambridge: Polity Press, 194–218. · Bunge, W. 1962: *Theoretical geography*. Lund: C.W.K. Gleerup. · Castells, M. 1983: *The city and the grassroots*. London: Edward Arnold. · Cox, K. 1995: Concepts of space, understanding in human geography, and spatial analysis. *Urban Geography* 16: 304–26. · De Certeau, M. 1981: *The practices of everyday life*. Berkeley: University of California Press. · Doel, M.A. 1996: A hundred thousand lines of flight: a machinic introduction to the nomad thought and scrumpled geography of Gilles Deleuze and Félix Guattari. *Environment and Planning D: Society and Space* 14: 421–39. · Foucault, M. 1975: *Discipline and punish*. London: Penguin. · Gibson-Graham, J.K. 1996: *The end of capitalism (as we knew it)*. Oxford and Cambridge, MA: Blackwell. · Gregory, D. 1994: *Geographical imaginations*. Oxford and Cambridge, MA: Blackwell. · Gregory, D. 1997: Lacan and geography: the production of space revisited. In G. Benko and U. Strohmayer, eds, *Space and social theory: interpreting modernity and postmodernity*. Oxford and Cambridge, MA: Blackwell, 203–31. · Gregory, D. and Urry, J., eds, 1985: *Social relations and spatial structures*. London: Macmillan; Minneapolis, MN: University of Minnesota Press. · Haggett, P. 1965: *Locational analysis in human geography*. London: Edward Arnold. · Hartshorne, R. 1939: *The nature of geography: a critical survey of current thought in the light of the past*. Lancaster, PA: Association of American Geographers. · Hartshorne, R. 1958: The concept of geography as a science of space from Kant and Humboldt to Hettner. *Annals of the Association of American Geographers* 48: 97–108. · Harvey, D. 1973: *Social justice and the city*. London: Arnold (new edition, Oxford and Cambridge MA: Blackwell). · Harvey, D. 1982: *The limits to capital*. Oxford: Blackwell. · Harvey, D. 1996: *Justice, nature and the geography of difference*. Oxford and Cambridge, MA: Blackwell. · Hetherington, K. 1997: In place of geometry: the materiality of place. In K. Hetherington and R. Munro, eds, *Ideas of difference: social spaces and the labour of division*. Oxford: Blackwell, The Sociological Review, 183–99. · James, P.E. and Jones, C.F., eds, 1954: *American geography: inventory and prospect*. Syracuse, NY: Syracuse University Press. · Lefebvre, H. 1991: *The production of space*. Oxford and Cambridge, MA: Blackwell. · Massey, D. 1993: Politics and space/time. In M. Keith and S. Pile, eds, *Place and the politics of identity*. London: Routledge, 141–61 [and in *New Left Review* 196: 65–84]. · Massey, D. 1999: Spaces of politics. In D. Massey, J. Allen and P. Sarre, eds, *Human geography today*. Cambridge: Polity Press, 279–94. · Merrifield, A. 1993: Place and space: a Lefebvrian reconciliation. *Transactions, Institute of British Geographers* NS 18: 516–31. · Mills, S. 1996: Gender and colonial space. *Gender, place and culture* 3: 125–47. · Olsson, G. 1974: The dialectics of spatial analysis. *Antipode* 6 (3): 50–62. · Philo, C. 1992: Foucault's geography. *Environment and Planning D: Society and Space* 10: 137–62. · Pickles, J. 1985: *Phenomenology, science and geography: spatiality and the human sciences*. Cambridge: Cambridge University Press. · Pile, S. 1996: *The body and the city: psychoanalysis, space and subjectivity*. London and New York: Routledge. · Rajchman, J. 1991: Foucault's art of seeing. In his *Philosophical events: essays of the 80s*. New York: Columbia University Press, 68–102. · Rose, G. 1993: *Feminism and geography: the limits of geographical knowledge*. Cambridge: Polity Press; Minneapolis, MN: University of Minnesota Press. · Rose, G. 1996: As if the mirrors had bled: masculine dwelling, masculinist theory and feminist masquerade. In N. Duncan, ed., *Bodyspace: destabilizing geographies of gender and sexuality*. London and New York: Routledge, 56–75. · Rose, G. 1999: Performing space. In D. Massey, J. Allen and P. Sarre, eds, *Human geography today*. Cambridge: Polity Press, 247–59. · Sack, R.D. 1974: The spatial separatist theme in geography. *Economic Geography* 50: 1–19. · Sack, R.S. 1980: *Conceptions of space in social thought*. London: Macmillan; Minneapolis, MN: University of Minnesota Press. · Schaefer, F.K. 1953: Exceptionalism in geography: a methodological examination. *Annals of the Association of American Geographers* 43: 226–49. · Schatzki, T. 1991: Spatial ontology and explanation. *Annals of the Association of American Geographers* 81: 650–70. · Sheppard, E. 1995: Dissenting from spatial analysis. *Urban Geographer* 16: 283–303. · Slater, D. 1992: On the borders of social theory: learning from other regions. *Environment and Planning D: Society and Space* 10: 307–27. · Smith, N. 1984: *Uneven development: nature, capital and the production of space*. Oxford and Cambridge, MA: Blackwell (2nd edn, 1990). · Smith, N. and Katz, C. 1993: Grounding metaphor: towards a spatialized politics. In M. Keith and S. Pile, eds, *Place and the politics of culture*. London: Routledge, 67–83. · Soja, E. 1989: *Postmodern geographies: the reassertion of space in critical social theory*. London: Verso. · Soja, E. 1996: *Thirdspace: journeys to Los Angeles and other real-and-imagined places*. Oxford and Cambridge, MA: Blackwell. · Strohmayer, U. 1997: Technology, modernity and the restructuring of the present in historical geographies. *Geografiska Annaler* 79B: 155–69. · Strohmayer, U. 1998: The event of space: geographic allusions in the phenomenological tradition. *Environment and Planning D: Society and Space* 16: 105–21. · Thrift, N. 1996: *Spatial formations*. London: Sage. · Thrift, N. 1999: Steps to an ecology of place. In D. Massey, J. Allen and P. Sarre, eds, *Human geography today*. Cambridge: Polity Press, 295–322. · Tuan, Y.-F. 1977: *Space and place: the perspective of experience*. London: Edward Arnold. · Whatmore, S. 1999: Hybrid geographies: rethinking the 'human' in human geography. In D. Massey, J. Allen and P. Sarre, eds, *Human geography today*. Cambridge: Polity Press, 22–39.

Suggested Reading

Allen (1997). · Massey (1999). · Sheppard (1995).

space-economy The SPATIAL STRUCTURE of an economy. The term is a direct translation of the German word *Raumwirtschaft*, and is originally associated with a distinctive German school of LOCATION THEORY. Popularized during the 1950s and 1960s by Walter Isard (1919–), the founder of the NEO-CLASSICAL ECONOMICS-inspired REGIONAL SCIENCE movement, space-economy became associated with a distinctive style of economic geography that emphasized QUANTITATIVE METHODS and theoretical abstraction (Isard, 1956). As a term it was later deployed by geographers operating within a framework of POLITICAL ECONOMY, but with the recent CULTURAL TURN in ECONOMIC GEOGRAPHY the expression has become increasingly dated.

The idea of a space-economy has always been underwritten by theoretical assumptions. Initially space was treated abstractly and unproblematically as something to be filled, as an empty container to be stuffed with various economic activities. Those activities could be examined at a variety of geographical SCALES – farm, city, region, nation, globe. Of particular interest were the ordered geographical patterns that emerged, for example, concentric rings of land use (ALONSO MODEL; VON THÜNEN MODEL), or a hexagonal distribution of urban production sites (CENTRAL PLACE THEORY). Both in the original German location school's use of the term, and later in Isard's too, those geographical patterns were formally derived from the postulate of economic rationality in combination with assumptions about TRANSPORT COSTS (the means by which space was introduced into the analysis). Links with neo-classical economics resulted also in an equilibrium approach that stressed optimal spatial arrangements, for example, ones that maximized profit for industrialists, or retailing choice for consumers.

Even in this idealised space-economy various intractable mathematical and theoretical problems arose because of the very inclusion of space as a variable (Massey, 1973). Partly as a response to these technical problems (see SPATIAL AUTOCORRELATION), but mainly as part of a much broader social critique, some economic geographers from the early 1970s onwards attempted to recast the space economy in the theoretical terms of POLITICAL

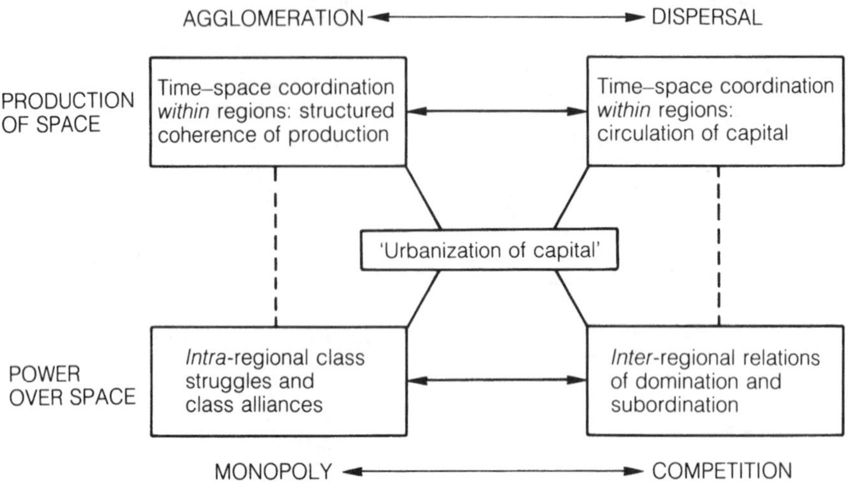

space-economy *Fundamental tensions in the landscape of contemporary capitalism (Source: Gregory, 1989)*

ECONOMY. Harvey's (1982, 1985) work from a MARXIAN ECONOMIC perspective was formative. Rather than the ordered, optimal and tranquil LANDSCAPES suggested by Isard et al., Harvey postulated a space-economy riven by CRISIS, always in motion, and relentlessly driven by the capitalist imperative to ACCUMULATE. In particular, key for Harvey was a fundamental contradiction between fixity and mobility – between agglomeration in place and dispersion over space – which is then implicated in the constitution of place-based CLASS alliances (cf. REGIONAL ALLIANCE) and subject to 'the fires of open and escalating competition with others' (see the figure).

After Harvey's initial work space-economy as a term became less used. In part it is because of Doreen Massey's (1984) writings on LAYERS OF INVESTMENT, and the subsequent LOCALITY studies, that emphasized PLACE rather than space. And in part it is because of a different style of theorizing, one that is less abstract, less all-encompassing (see GRAND THEORY). Indeed, the recent cultural turn in economic geography (Lee and Wills, 1997) has accentuated and developed both lines of development, resulting in the further marginalization of space-economy as a term. When it is used it tends to be by those mobilizing an analytical approach either on the political Left (such as Sheppard and Barnes, 1990; Webber and Rigby, 1996), or on the political Right (represented by neo-classical analysis, and given a recent boost by the work of Paul Krugman; see Martin and Sunley, 1996). TJB

References

Harvey, D. 1982: *The limits to capital*. Oxford: Blackwell. · Harvey, D. 1985: *The urbanization of capital*. Oxford: Blackwell. · Isard, W. 1956: *Location and space economy*. New York: John Wiley. · Krugman, P. 1991: *Geography and trade*. Cambridge, MA: MIT Press. · Lee, R. and Wills, J., eds, 1997: *Geographies of economies*. London: Arnold. · Martin, R. and Sunley, P. 1996: Paul Krugman's geographical economics and its implications for regional development theory: a critical assessment. *Economic Geography* 72: 259–92. · Massey, D. 1973: A critique of industrial location theory. *Antipode* 5 (3): 33–9. · Massey, D. 1984: *Spatial divisions of labour*. London: Macmillan. · Sheppard, E. and Barnes, T. 1990: *The capitalist space economy: geographical analysis after Ricardo, Marx and Sraffa*. London: Unwin. · Webber, M. and Rigby, D. 1996: *The golden age illusion*. New York: Guilford.

Suggested Reading

Harvey (1985), ch. 2.

space–time forecasting models Statistical models that attempt to forecast the evolution of variables over both time and space (sets of regions). These models are of the general REGRESSION form, and they forecast the value of a variable and an observation-unit in terms of (a) its own past values, (b) lagged spatial DIFFUSION effects, and (c) lagged exogenous or explanatory variables. The simplest form is (a), where a variable (such as population) in region j at time t is predicted by regression on its own earlier values (the 'autoregressive', or memory, effect) and also perhaps by its delayed response to the impact of random shocks e_{jt}, e_{jt-1} and e_{jt-2} (the moving average coefficients b_1 and b_2):

$$p_{jt} = a_1 p_{jt-1} + a_2 p_{jt-2} + e_{jt} + b_1 e_{jt-1} + b_2 e_{jt-2}$$

This is the well-known time-series autoregressive-moving average (or ARMA) model. It is a 'black-box' model in that it does not explain the population changes *causally*, but models and extrapolates them *statistically*. Such models can have quite good short-term forecasting ability.

Space–time forecasting models extend the single-region ARMA model to include (b), spatial diffusion between regions, so that p_{jt} is also dependent on population changes in nearby regions and hence trends in population change diffuse across the map. Defining the average (or weighted average) of population for regions adjacent to region j at time t as Lp_{jt}, the space–time ARMA model (STARMA) can be written (using only one-lag terms) as:

$$p_{jt} = a_1 p_{jt-1} + c_1 Lp_{jt-1} + e_{jt} + b_1 e_{jt-1} + d_1 Le_{jt-1}$$

The final term allows random shocks to spill over between regions also. DISTANCE DECAY can also be built into the definition of the weights L. The STARMA model is still a black-box model, and the introduction of (c), lagged exogenous variables (such as employment opportunities, *EMP*), is essential for a causal model:

$$p_{jt} = a_1 p_{jt-1} + c_1 Lp_{jt-1} + f_1 EMP_{jt-1} + g_1 LEMP_{jt-1} + \ldots$$

The exogenous variable *EMP* then has to be itself extrapolated (which is possible by STARMA) before population can be forecast more than one period ahead. However, STARMA models have not proved as useful as first hoped, mainly because of their black-box structure (the same criticism is made of such black-box models in forecasting for macroeconomic policy), and modellers have found form (c) the most relevant, allowing conditional forecasts to be made based on different assumptions about the exogenous variables. LWH

Suggested Reading

Bennett, R.J. 1979: *Spatial time series*. London: Pion.

spatial analysis The quantitative procedures employed in LOCATIONAL ANALYSIS, and sometimes used as a synonym for that portion of the discipline. Unwin (1981) presents spatial analysis as the study of the arrangements of points, lines, areas and surfaces on a MAP. Whereas many geographers merely apply techniques derived from the GENERAL LINEAR MODEL, others have argued that spatial data analysis poses particular statistical problems (such as SPATIAL AUTOCORRELATION), which means developing procedures specifically designed to counter them (Haining, 1990). The development of GEOGRAPHICAL INFORMATION SYSTEMS is facilitating advances in spatial analysis and the greatly increased power of computers has very significantly increased geographers' ability to work with large data sets and complex models (cf. GEOCOMPUTATION). RJJ

References and Suggested Reading

Bailey, T.C. and Gatrell, A.C. 1995: *Interactive spatial data analysis*. London: Longman. · Haining, R.P. 1990: *Spatial data analysis in the social and environmental sciences*. Cambridge: Cambridge University Press. · Unwin, D.J. 1981: *Introductory spatial analysis*. London and New York: Methuen.

spatial autocorrelation The presence of spatial pattern in a mapped variable due to geographical proximity. The most common form of spatial autocorrelation is where similar values for a variable (such as county income levels) tend to cluster together in adjacent observation-units or regions, so that on average across the map the values for neighbours are more similar than would occur if the allocation of values to observation-units were the result of a purely random mechanism. More general and complicated forms of autocorrelation can also be defined. The presence of spatial autocorrelation is very widespread, and violates a basic assumption (that the observations be 'independent' or non-autocorrelated) of many standard PARAMETRIC STATISTICAL tests (cf. GENERAL LINEAR MODEL). A variety of tests for spatial autocorrelation in raw data and regression residuals is available, and a group of techniques known as 'spatial econometrics' has been developed to allow the inclusion of autocorrelation in statistical models. These techniques are now being employed in many different social sciences. LWH

Suggested Reading

Anselin, L. 1988: *Spatial econometrics*. Dordrecht and Boston: Kluwer Academic. · Bailey, T.C. and Gatrell, A.C. 1995: *Interactive spatial data analysis*. Harlow, Essex: Longmans. · Haining, R. 1990: *Spatial data analysis in the social and environmental sciences*. Cambridge: Cambridge University Press.

spatial decision support systems Systems that assist their users in the solution of ill-structured spatial problems. Spatial decision support systems are a special form of decision support system (Bonczek, Holsapple and Whinston, 1981). A spatial problem can be defined as one whose solution is embedded in a space, usually geographic space; examples include selection of sites for particular uses, or determination of the best routes between given origins and destinations. Such problems are ill-structured if it is impossible to know in advance the full set of criteria or constraints that will ultimately affect the solution (Hopkins, 1984). Frequently, additional criteria only become apparent once a tentative solution has been identified, or through involvement of additional stakeholders in the DECISION-MAKING process. In such cases decision-making may extend over a substantial period of time, and the criteria and constraints may change repeatedly before the final solution is determined.

A spatial decision support system (SDSS) must be iterative, producing tentative solutions that can then be used as one basis for the revision of criteria and constraints, in a FEEDBACK process that may occur many times during the solution of a problem. With each iteration the problem becomes better-defined, and more inclusive of the views of all of the stakeholders. An SDSS is thus also participative, because the decision-makers and stakeholders play active roles in defining the problem, carrying out analyses and evaluating the outcomes; it would not be appropriate for these functions to be given to a specialized analyst. Finally, an SDSS must be integrative because value judgements that materially affect the final outcome are made by decision-makers who have expert knowledge that must be integrated with the quantitative data in the models.

There are strong similarities between SDSS and GEOGRAPHICAL INFORMATION SYSTEMS (GIS), and GIS often form the base on which SDSS are constructed. Although many practical SDSS have been built for special purposes (Gould and Densham, 1991), it has proven difficult to develop general-purpose software, or to minimize the effort involved in constructing an SDSS for a specific purpose. Thus the concept remains largely elusive, and is best treated as a model of decision-making practice rather than an accurate characterization. MG

References

Bonczek, R.H., Holsapple, C.W. and Whinston, A.B. 1981: *Foundations of decision support systems*. New York: Academic Press. · Gould, M.J. and Densham, P.J. 1991: *Spatial decision support systems: a bibliography*. Technical Paper 91-6. Santa Barbara, CA: National Center for Geographic Information and Analysis; Hopkins, L. 1984: Evaluation of methods for exploring ill-defined problems. *Environment and Planning B: Planning and Design* 11: 339–48.

spatial fetishism A term of criticism applied to approaches that accord SPACE a separate and substantial reality with its own distinctive powers (cf. SPATIAL SEPARATISM): the term has been most forcefully applied to LOCATIONAL ANALYSIS and SPATIAL SCIENCE, in particular their treatment of the so-called FRICTIONS OF DISTANCE as a causal mechanism. Space *per se* is contentless and only important when given status by human agents, as also occurs with NATURE. RJJ

Suggested Reading

Sayer, A. 1985: The difference that space makes. In D. Gregory and J. Urry, eds, *Social relations and spatial structures*. London: Macmillan, 49–66.

spatial interaction A term coined by Edward Ullman (1980) to indicate interdependence between geographical areas, which he saw as complementary to the people–environment interactions which take place *within* each individual area. The study of spatial interaction was thus presented as a major focus of geographical inquiry, covering the movements of goods, people, money and information between places. The concept was similar to the '*géographie de circulation*' developed by French geographers at the beginning of the twentieth century.

The strength of Ullman's concept was that it recognized that many different forms of spatial interaction are themselves interdependent: a migrant flow may stimulate subsequent flows (or backflows) of trade, tourists and information, for example (see CHAIN MIGRATION). Furthermore, Ullman's proposed bases of interaction (COMPLEMENTARITY, INTERVENING OPPORTUNITIES and TRANSFERABILITY), conceived initially as an explanation of patterns of commodity flow, can also be applied to the study of other movements – of people and of ideas, for example. This unity has been underlined by the application of similar models (such as the GRAVITY MODEL and ENTROPY-MAXIMIZING MODELS) to studies of not just commodity flows but also migrations and telephone traffic. Ullman clearly hoped that this unity would provide the basis for a wide appreciation of geography as the study of spatial interaction, but this has not occurred: TRANSPORT GEOGRAPHY has become a separate subfield; MIGRATION is normally studied within POPULATION GEOGRAPHY; and much study of information DIFFUSION was incorporated within CULTURAL GEOGRAPHY.

More recently, the term has been used in a more restricted sense to cover two types of study: some authors have used it to describe studies of *spatial flows*; a few have extended it to cover sociological concepts of social interaction, thereby defining spatial interaction as the *spatial dimension of social contacts*. AMH

Reference

Ullman, E.L. 1980: *Geography as spatial interaction*. Seattle: University of Washington Press.

Suggested Reading

Hay, A.M. 1979: The geographical explanation of commodity flow. *Progress in Human Geography* 3: 1–12.

spatial monopoly Monopolistic control over a market by virtue of location. The usual meaning of monopoly is that one firm or individual sells the entire output of some commodity or service. This is normally the final outcome of a competitive process taking place under capitalist market conditions, in which one supplier is able to produce and sell the commodity at a price favourable enough to consumers to force other suppliers out of business. Spatial monopoly is a special case, in which distance from competitors or ways of bounding space give a producer monopolistic control over a section of the market.

Spatial monopoly can arise when a producer is distributing a commodity from its point of origin, and also when consumers travel to the point of origin. In the first case, the operation of an f.o.b. pricing policy, whereby the cost of transportation is passed on to the consumer (see PRICING POLICIES), will increase delivered price with distance from the production point, so that consumers close to the production point can purchase the commodity relatively cheaply, i.e. more cheaply than from alternative suppliers. The greater the elasticity of demand, or the sensitivity of the consumer to price, the greater the likelihood of local monopoly. The area within which monopoly control exists (assuming that consumers buy from the cheapest source) is bounded by a locus of points where delivered price from the supplier in question is equal to the price charged by a competitor (see MARKET-AREA ANALYSIS). In the second case, consumers will tend to travel to the production point which is closest in time, effort or cost. In this case, too, the area of monopoly control will be bounded by a locus of points of consumer indifference as to whether to purchase from one point or another.

Spatial monopoly can also arise from collusion between otherwise competing firms, who may agree to a 'carve-up' of the market among themselves. As in other situations of spatial monopoly, this will enable suppliers to raise prices and exact above-normal profits in the area over which they exert exclusive control. Distance provides no absolute protection of a market, however, for some consumers may choose to purchase from high-cost sources or to travel to more distant outlets, out of preference, ignorance or other behavioural considerations.

There may be other strategies for protecting space over which monopoly control is exerted. These include the imposition of tariffs, and restriction on the use of means of transportation: suppliers may use coercion to prevent competitors from entering a particular city to sell their goods, for example, as has happened in the former Soviet Union since the collapse of socialism.

In some instances, spatial monopoly may be a case of so-called natural monopoly, where the market in question is best served by a single firm because of the nature of the production process. Some public utilities are of this kind: for example, local water supply. Such public spatial monopoly may be turned into private monopoly by PRIVATIZATION.

DMS

Suggested Reading

Smith, D.M. 1981: *Industrial location: an economic geographical analysis*, 2nd edition. New York: John Wiley.

spatial science The presentation of human geography as that component of the social sciences which focuses on the role of SPACE as a fundamental variable influencing both society's organization and operation and the behaviour of its individual members (e.g. Cox, 1976). It was formulated during the QUANTITATIVE REVOLUTION and is usually closely associated with the philosophy of POSITIVISM (cf. LOCATIONAL ANALYSIS).

Berry and Marble (1968) expressed the goal of spatial science as 'building accurate generalizations with predictive power by precise quantitative description of spatial distributions, SPATIAL STRUCTURE and organization, and spatial relationships': Nystuen (1968) claimed that such generalizations could be based on just three fundamental spatial concepts – *directional orientation*, *distance* and *connectedness* (or relative position).

Criticisms of spatial science focused on its attempt to construct human geography as an autonomous science of the spatial – on its SPATIAL FETISHISM and SPATIAL SEPARATISM – and emphasized the importance of incorporating social relations and processes into spatial analysis. Many have also called for a recognition of human geography's links to the humanities as well as the social sciences. RJJ

References

Berry, B.J.L. and Marble, D.F. 1968: Introduction. In B.J.L. Berry and D.F. Marble, eds, *Spatial analysis: a reader in statistical geography*. Englewood Cliffs, NJ and London: Prentice-Hall, 1–9. · Cox, K.R. 1976: American geography: social science emergent. *Social Science Quarterly* 57: 182–207. · Nystuen, J.D. 1968: Identification of some fundamental spatial concepts. In B.J.L. Berry and D.F. Marble, eds, *Spatial analysis: a reader in statistical geography*. Englewood Cliffs, NJ and London: Prentice-Hall, 35–41.

Suggested Reading

Haggett, P. 1980: *The geographer's art*. Oxford: Blackwell. · Sack, R.D. 1981: *Conceptions of space in social thought*. London and New York: Macmillan.

spatial separatism A term coined by Sack (1974) to describe the view, which he contested, that geography should focus on the independent role of space as an influence on human behaviour. He was explicitly criticizing Bunge's (1973) claim that geometry provided geography with a formal language facilitating spatial prediction – as in CENTRAL PLACE THEORY and the VON THÜNEN MODEL. Sack's position was that geometry could be used to describe but not to explain since it could not encapsulate human decision-making processes (cf. SPATIAL FETISHISM; SPATIAL SCIENCE). RJJ

References

Bunge, W. 1973: Spatial prediction. *Annals of the Association of American Geographers* 63: 566–8; Sack, R.D. 1974: The spatial separatist theme in geography. *Economic Geography* 50: 1–19.

spatial structure The orderings through which space is implicated in the operation and outcome of cultural–natural processes. 'Ordering' has several different meanings that have been activated in different and overlapping phases in the history of Anglo-American human geography since the Second World War.

In the course of the post-war critique of REGIONAL GEOGRAPHY it was claimed that 'spatial relations' were 'the only ones that mattered' to a properly constituted, nominally scientific geography, and that geographical inquiry should be directed towards the search for an intrinsically spatial order to the world. For F.K. Schaefer (1953) this necessarily involved the discovery of spatial patterns – 'morphological laws' (see MORPHOLOGY) – while to William Bunge (1962) the project of a theoretical geography turned on a dualism between 'spatial process' ('movements over the earth's surface') and 'spatial structure' ('the resulting arrangement of phenomena on the earth's surface'). Although Bunge thus widened Schaefer's prospectus, he none the less strongly agreed that 'spatial structure' could be defined 'most sharply by interpreting "structure" as "geometrical"': from which it followed, so he said, that 'the science of space [geography] finds the logic of space [geometry] a sharp tool'. The revival of this classical geometric tradition (cf. CHOROGRAPHY) was a central feature of LOCATIONAL ANALYSIS in human geography and the constitution of geography as a SPATIAL SCIENCE (Haggett, 1965; Harvey, 1969). From this perspective 'spatial structure' was often translated into purely formal conceptions of sequences in mathematical or statistical spaces rather than concrete outcomes of causal mechanisms or substantive processes. Within this tradition, 'ordering' implied spatial orders in geometrical–mathematical–statistical domains characterized by degrees of symmetry, regularity and predictability.

In the second phase, in contrast, there was a movement towards the assignment of substantive rather than surrogate processes to the production and reproduction of particular spatial structures. In the course of this intellectual transition – the critique of spatial science – spatial structure came to be seen as literally superficial: *either* as a 'codification' by the human subject *or* as a 'reflection' of human society. Explanations of spatial structure were sought within the COMPOSITIONAL approach of the various humanities and social sciences (most commonly psychology, cultural anthropology, political economy and sociology). Within human geography, therefore, the debates of most moment came to pivot around whether social life ought to be conceived in terms of either the human subject or the structures of society, a dualism that was traced both within and between HUMANISTIC GEOGRAPHY and MARXIST GEOGRAPHY in particular. To simplify, the temporary result was two human geographies, one preoccupied with intentions and meanings and another preoccupied with systems and structures. At best, spatial structuring was marginal to these exchanges; at worst, it was condemned as an irrelevant distraction that ran the real risk of confusing 'deeply social' relations with merely 'geometrical' ones (see SPATIAL FETISHISM). From this perspective, 'ordering' had intrinsically social connotations: no matter how varied and various CULTURAL LANDSCAPES seemed to be on the surface, they could be 'structured' by appealing to various 'depth models' that disclosed the ordering capacities of human subjects and social structures.

During the third phase many of the attempts that were made to overcome the dualism between 'agency' and 'structure' – a dualism which reappeared in many other fields – made the substantive connections between social relations and spatial structures a central focus for inquiry not only within human geography but across the spectrum of the humanities and social sciences (Gregory and Urry, 1985; Gregory, 1994, ch. 2). Human geographers who were drawn to the development of STRUCTURATION THEORY, for example, often continued to invoke concepts of spatial structure to capture the interpenetrations of 'presence' and 'absence' within the conduct of social life: both the time–space routines traced by individuals in their daily lives (see TIME-GEOGRAPHY) and the stretching of social relations over time and space (see TIME–SPACE DISTANCIATION) were seen as structured – or 'ordered' – through the 'binding' of time and space into the conduct of social life. These contributions intersected with the emergence of 'postmodern geographies' and the continued development of historico-geographical materialism, which, in similar ways, also insisted on the 'reassertion of space in critical social theory' and refined concepts of spatialization and SPATIALITY to capture what Soja (1989) identified (in the case of late twentieth-century Los Angeles) as 'an economic order, an instrumental nodal structure, an essentially exploitative spatial division of labour' (p. 248; see also POSTMODERNISM).

During the present, nominally fourth phase, the emphasis on 'structure' and 'order' that runs through the previous three paragraphs has come to be seen as unduly restrictive by a number of human geographers and others (see SPACE, HUMAN GEOGRAPHY AND). They have been prompted by POST-STRUCTURALISM and/or ACTOR–NETWORK THEORY to reconceptualize spatial structure *not as an 'order' but as an ordering*. This subsumes the claim advanced by structuration theory in particular that the structures of social life are not installed through the realization of some abstract, transcendental Order or Structure: that they are instead rooted in the flow of everyday life as a *stream of situated practices and performances*. But the emphasis on 'ordering' directs analytical attention towards 'foldings' of time and space into the operation of cultural–natural processes in contingent, fluid and sensuous ways. This implies, crucially, both a recognition of the ways in which practices and performances *evade and exceed* the symmetrical and/or logical orders proposed by mainstream social theory and human geography ('the problem of order') and also a recognition of couplings and engagements *between human and non-human actors* (or 'actants'; see HUMAN AGENCY) such that 'the "material" and the "social" intertwine and interact in all manner of promiscuous combinations' (Thrift, 1996, p. 24). From this perspective, and in contradistinction to those views that treat 'order' or 'structure' as a thing rather than a process, ordering becomes

> not something fixed but a mobile process full of uncertainty, heterogeneity and contradiction. Just as the process of social ordering creates positions of uncertainty, so those positions of uncertainty are implicated in processes of ordering and re-ordering. Ordering and disordering go together, as do centres and margins, in ways that are tangled, uncertain and topologically complex. (Hetherington, 1997a, p. 7; see also Hetherington, 1997b; cf. HETEROTOPIA; THIRD SPACE)

The sense that runs through these last sentences of fluidity and promiscuity – of orderings that cannot be reduced to any single Order – is of vital importance not only for the analysis of 'heterogeneous engineerings' and 'impure geographies' but also for the activation of an emancipatory and empowering *politics of space* (see also SPACE, HUMAN GEOGRAPHY AND). DG

References

Bunge, W. 1962: *Theoretical geography*. Lund: C.W.K. Gleerup. · Gregory, D. and Urry, J., eds, 1985: *Social relations and spatial structures*. London: Macmillan. · Gregory, D. 1994: *Geographical imaginations*. Oxford and Cambridge, MA: Blackwell. · Haggett, P. 1965: *Locational analysis in human geography*. London: Edward Arnold. · Harvey, D. 1969: *Explanation in Geography*. London: Edward Arnold. · Hetherington, K. 1997a: *The badlands of modernity: heterotopia and social ordering*. London and New York: Routledge. · Hetherington, K. 1997b: In place of geometry: the materiality of place. In K. Hetherington and R. Munro, eds, *Ideas of difference: social spaces and the labour of division*. Oxford and Cambridge, MA: Blackwell, 183–99. · Schaefer, F.K. 1953: Exceptionalism in geography: a methodological examination. *Annals of the Association of American Geographers* 43: 226–49. · Soja, E. 1989: *Postmodern geographies: the reassertion of space in critical social theory*. London and New York: Verso. · Thrift, N. 1996: *Spatial formations*. London: Sage.

Suggested Reading

Barnes, T. and Gregory, D. 1997: Space, spatiality and spatial structure. In T. Barnes and D. Gregory, eds, *Reading human geography: the poetics and politics of inquiry*. London: Arnold, 232–43. · Hetherington (1997b).

spatiality There are four main senses in which 'spatiality' has been used in human geography to connote the human and social implications of space (see also SPACE, HUMAN GEOGRAPHY AND). Each of them derives from a distinctive intellectual tradition.

Drawing upon EXISTENTIALISM and PHENOMENOLOGY, and in particular the writings of Heidegger and Husserl, Pickles (1985) proposed human spatiality as the fundamental basis on which 'geographical inquiry as a human science of the world can be explicitly founded'. Pickles's primary concern was ONTOLOGY: with understanding 'the universal structures characteristic of [human] spatiality as the precondition for any understanding of places and spaces as such'. In particular, Pickles objected to those views which regard 'the physical space of physics [as] the sole genuine space'. This sort of thinking is typical of SPATIAL SCIENCE but, in Pickles's view, is wholly inappropriate for a genuinely human geography. He urges in its place a recovery of our 'original experiences prior to their thematization by any scientific activity', i.e. a rigorous exposure of the TAKEN-FOR-GRANTED WORLD assumed (but unexplicated) by spatial science. One of its essential characteristics is what Pickles calls 'the structural unity of the "in-order-to"'. Our most immediate experiences are not cognitive abstractions of separate objects, Pickles contends, but rather 'constellations of relations and meaning' which we encounter in our everyday activities – what Heidegger termed 'equipment' – and which are 'ready-to-hand'. Such a perspective reveals the human significance of *contextuality*. For human spatiality is related 'to several concurrent and non-concurrent equipmental contexts' and 'cannot be understood independently of the beings that organise it'. Spatiality thus has the character of a 'situating' enterprise in which we 'make room' for and 'give space' to congeries of equipment. Put in this way, one can perhaps hear distant echoes of TIME-GEOGRAPHY, but Pickles is evoking an intellectual tradition antithetical to the physicalism of Hägerstrand's early writings and which fastens not on 'objective space' but on social space (see Schatzki, 1991; cf. Hägerstrand, 1984).

Drawing upon STRUCTURAL MARXISM, a number of Francophone Marxists suggested that concepts of spatiality identify the connections and correspondences between social structures (MODES OF PRODUCTION or SOCIAL FORMATIONS) and SPATIAL STRUCTURES. Althusser had argued that different concepts and constructions of time ('temporalities') could be assigned to different levels of modes of production – 'economic time', 'political time', 'ideological time' – and that they had to be constructed out of the concepts of the different social practices within these domains. But if, as Althusser claimed, the distinctions between these temporalities are essential for any properly theoretical ('scientific') history, then, as one historian reminded him, history is not only an interlacing of times but of spaces as well (Vilar, 1973). In much the same way, therefore, it was argued that different concepts of space (or 'spatialities') could also be assigned to the different levels of modes of production. According to Lipietz (1977), for example, the concept of spatial structure is dependent on and so must be derived from a concept of social structure. From his perspective, spatiality consists of a correspondence between 'presence–absence' in space and 'participation–exclusion' in the particular system of social practices contained within each level. Each of these correspondences is supposed to have its own topology, so that 'one can speak, for example, of the *economic* space of the capitalist mode of production . . . or of the *legal* space which is superimposed upon it'. Spatial structure then becomes the articulation of the spatialities of these different levels, at once a 'reflection' of different systems of social practices and a 'constraint' upon them. In his early writings, Castells (1977) presented the most detailed analysis of spatial structure in these terms (see figure), but he concluded that it made more sense to theorize concepts of temporality and concepts of spatiality conjointly and to speak instead of space–times:

> From the social point of view . . . there is no space (a physical quantity yet an abstract entity) . . . [only] an historically defined space–time, a space constructed, worked, practised by social relations. . . . Socially speaking space, like time, is a conjuncture, that is to say, the articulation of concrete historical practices. (Castells, 1977)

Drawing upon Lefebvre's vision of a critical Marxism, and in particular his account of the PRODUCTION OF SPACE, Soja (1985) used the term spatiality 'to refer specifically to socially produced space, the created forms and relations of a broadly defined human geography'. 'All space is not socially produced', Soja continued, 'but all spatiality is'. In the course of his work as a whole Lefebvre provided critiques of existentialism and phenomenology and of structuralism and structural Marxism, and for this reason Soja insists that his 'materialist interpretation of spatiality' cannot be

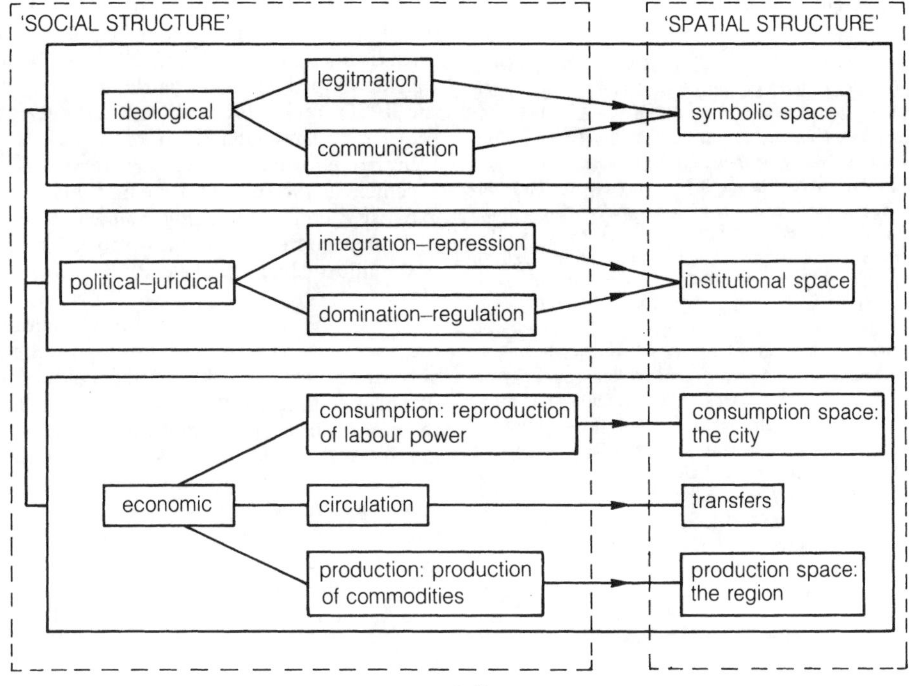

spatiality

assimilated to either of the two traditions summarized above. For to speak of 'the production of space' in the spirit of Lefebvre (1991) is to accentuate spatiality as 'both the medium and the outcome' of situated HUMAN AGENCY and systems of social practices in a way which is, so Soja claimed at the time, broadly consonant with STRUCTURATION THEORY. Hence:

> Spatiality and temporality, human geography and human history, intersect in a complex social process which creates a constantly evolving sequence of spatialities, a spatio-temporal structuration of social life which gives form not only to the grand movements of social development but also to the recursive practices of day-to-day activity. (Soja, 1985)

Transcending his earlier claims for a 'socio-spatial dialectic' (Soja, 1980), he concluded that 'spatiality is society, not as its definitional or logical equivalent, but as its concretisation, its formative *constitution'*. And it is precisely this realization, he subsequently argued, that is characteristic of POSTMODERNISM and its reassertion of space – of spatiality – in critical social thought (Soja, 1989; see also THIRD SPACE; TRIALECTICS). Other writers have registered similar claims, though without the post-modern inflection. In his later writings, for example, Castells (1983) repudiated the monolithic structuralism of his previous formulations and declared that 'space is not a "reflection" of society, it is society'. Giddens (1984) also rejected the possibility of a distinctive social science of space predicated on the belief that 'space has its own intrinsic nature'. 'In human geography spatial forms are always social forms', he asserted, and 'spatial configurations of social life' – spatialities – 'are just as much a matter of basic importance to social theory as are the dimensions of temporality'.

Drawing upon POST-STRUCTURALISM, and in particular the work of Deleuze and Foucault, a number of writers use spatiality to indicate the ways in which constellations of power-knowledge are inscribed in space and through which particular subject-positions are constituted and particular identities fabricated (see Gregory, 1994).

For all the differences between these four traditions, they are united in their opposition to the conventional separations between 'space' and 'society' (which can be traced to a persistent KANTIANISM) and in this sense can be read as four moments in the movement towards an exploration of what Smith (1990) calls 'deep space': that is to say, 'quintessentially social space...physical extent fused through with social intent'. DG

References

Castells, M. 1977: *The urban question*. London: Edward Arnold. · Castells, M. 1983: *The city and the grassroots*. London: Edward Arnold. · Giddens, A. 1984: *The constitution of society*. Cambridge: Polity Press. · Gregory, D. 1994: *Geographical imaginations*. Oxford and Cambridge, MA: Blackwell. · Hägerstrand, T. 1984: Presence and absence: a look at conceptual choices and bodily necessities. *Regional Studies* 18: 373–80. · Lefebvre, H. 1991: *The production of space*. Oxford: Blackwell. · Lipietz, A. 1977: *Le capital et son espace*. Paris: Maspero. · Pickles, J. 1985: *Phenomenology, science and geography: spatiality and the human sciences*. Cambridge: Cambridge University Press. · Schatzki, T. 1991: Spatial ontology and explanation. *Annals of the Association of American Geographers* 81: 650–70. · Smith, N. 1990: *Uneven development: nature, capital and the production of space*, 2nd edn. Oxford: Blackwell. · Soja, E. 1980: The socio-spatial dialectic. *Annals of the Association of American Geographers* 70: 207–27. · Soja, E. 1985: The spatiality of social life: towards a transformative retheorisation. In D. Gregory and J. Urry, eds, *Social relations and spatial structures*. London: Macmillan, 90–122. · Soja, E. 1989: *Postmodern geographies: the reassertion of space in critical social theory*. London: Verso. · Vilar, P. 1973: Histoire marxiste, histoire en construction: essai de dialogue avec Althusser. *Annales ESC* 28: 165–98.

Suggested Reading

Pickles (1985). · Smith (1990), Afterword. · Soja (1989).

spectacle, geography of A social or cultural event, usually of a temporary nature, attracting a mass audience through its dramatic and sensuous staging. The term is typically attached to heavily imagineered and marketed events such as cultural festivals, world's fairs, the Olympic Games, and other sports jamborees, but may be extended to permanently staged sites such as theme parks or other places of mass LEISURE. The labelling of a spectacle is not a neutral designation, but is frequently part of a larger negative critique of the marketing of consumption in the theoretical realm of POSTMODERNITY (Harvey, 1989; cf. CONSUMPTION, GEOGRAPHY OF).

There is a certain irony to this theoretical niche for the spectacle, for key events such as the Olympics and world exhibitions were firmly established during the last half of the nineteenth century, the era of MODERNITY, while Disneyland, the most referenced site of POSTMODERN spectacle, derives from the post-war period of high modernity. Authors such as Brantlinger (1983) have reminded us that the work of the spectacle may be traced back several millennia to the courts of kings and emperors. The theoretical history of the concept is equally promiscuous. Allusions to the spectacle were made prior to the 1960s by members of the FRANKFURT SCHOOL, while the most influential exposition by Guy Debord was developed in avant-garde media during the 1950s and 1960s, although the English translation came later (Debord, 1973). It was Debord who most forcefully rendered the spectacle as the site of false consciousness, an expansive empire inducing political slumber, that made contemporary mass society immune to the injustice and HEGEMONY of its corporate elites.

The theme of passivity before the allure of the spectacle has survived into a number of current theoretical works. However, another perspective that is rather more accountable to the empirical record is sceptical of such passivity, arguing instead for a more active popular culture, so that people bring their own goals and objectives when viewing a spectacle (Ley and Olds, 1988). Indeed, ETHNOGRAPHIES suggest that even the world of Disney is negotiated on the terms of its visitors, and that its hegemonic achievements should not be overstressed (Warren, 1996) (cf. VISION AND VISUALITY). DL

References

Brantlinger, P. 1983: *Bread and circuses: theories of mass culture as social decay*. Ithaca, NY: Cornell University Press. · Debord, G. 1973: *Society of the spectacle*. Detroit: Black and Red. · Harvey, D. 1989: *The condition of postmodernity*. Oxford: Blackwell. · Ley, D. and Olds, K. 1988: Landscape as spectacle: world's fairs and the culture of heroic consumption. *Environment and Planning D: Society and Space* 6: 191–212. · Warren, S. 1996: Popular cultural practices in the 'postmodern city'. *Urban Geography* 17: 545–67.

spectral analysis A technique for examining the oscillations and patterns in a time series by calculating the relative importance of different wavelengths, periodicities or 'frequency bands' (just as a prism analyses light in terms of colours of the spectrum). The method is an extension of classical *Fourier analysis*: it does not analyse in terms of exact periodic waves (e.g. 12 months or 2.5 years), but uses frequency bands of specified width (e.g. 11–13 months and 2.25–2.75 years). This is more appropriate for socio-economic fluctuations, which are not exactly periodic. Major applications in human geography have been to REGIONAL CYCLES and LEAD–LAG MODELS of regional and urban unemployment, and to the geography of epidemics such as measles. Cross-spectral analysis between two or more time series allows the calculation of different CORRELATION and REGRESSION coefficients for each frequency band. Spectral analysis can also be applied to transects across space and to two-dimensional patterns, although examples are rare in human geography. LWH

Suggested Reading

Bennett, R.J. 1979: *Spatial time series*. London: Pion.

spontaneous settlement A residential district developed by its inhabitants, often after illegally occupying the land, in which both the housing and the public facilities are constructed outside the usual market and public sector mechanisms. The term spontaneous implies that there is no 'forethought' or 'planning' prior to occupation of the land, although increasingly such clandestine settlements, including a basic infrastructure, are the result of 'planned invasions' by their initial occupants (cf. SQUATTER SETTLEMENT). RJJ

sport, geography of The study of spatial variations in the pursuit of various sports and of the impact of sporting activities on the landscape. Interest in these topics is growing, given the increased use of RECREATION and LEISURE in many societies, as evidenced by the launching of a specialized journal – *Sport Place*.

Bale (1989) identified three main components to work on the geography of sport, in the first general text on the subject:

- Study of the *changing spatial pattern of sports activity*, as, for example, with the DIFFUSION of a new sport from its origin, and the study of sporting regions, areas identifying with particular sports (cf. LOCALITY);
- Study of the *'sports landscape'* and how it changes, as in the design and visual impact of stadia and golf courses; and
- Prescriptions for *changing the spatial organization* of sport and sporting landscapes.

Most studies have been of the first type – as in Rooney's (1974) work on various aspects of American sports. RJJ

References

Bale, J. 1989: *Sports geography*. London and New York: E.F. and N. Spon. · Rooney, J.F. 1974: *A geography of American sport: from Cabin Creek to Anaheim*. Reading, MA: Addison-Wesley.

sprawl A term often used pejoratively to describe the unplanned extension of relatively low density urban land uses into rural areas, usually alongside main roads (see RIBBON DEVELOPMENT). Sprawl implies little control of land sub-division (see ZONING), so that conversion of plots to urban uses creates enclaves of agricultural land in which farmers may suffer negative EXTERNALITIES through the impact of neighbouring activities. Much planning legislation, especially in heavily populated countries, includes policies to reduce sprawl – as with GREEN BELTS. RJJ

squatter settlement A general term for residential districts created by the illegal occupation of land. Such settlements are mainly found in THIRD WORLD cities where conventional housing markets cannot cope with the demand created through rapid URBANIZATION. The land occupied is either on the urban fringe or in the interstices of existing development (as in deep gullies in Caracas, on steep hillsides in Rio, and alongside railway tracks in Mexico City). The occupation may be entirely unplanned and piecemeal (see SPONTANEOUS SETTLEMENT), but most recent squatter settlements result from planned 'invasions' by groups living elsewhere in the city, and are targeted on unused land whose ownership is uncertain and where occupation is unlikely to be resisted by the STATE.

Many squatter settlements – variously termed BARRIOS, bidonvilles, bustees, favelas, kampongs, ranchos and shanty towns – lack a basic INFRASTRUCTURE (public utilities such as running water, electricity, and sewage and garbage removal) and the housing is of poor quality. Stokes (1962) introduced an important distinction between two main types of settlement, however: *slums of despair*, in which the residents have little expectation of material advancement and make few improvements to their homes; and *slums of hope*, where self-help movements promote both investments in the infrastructure and improvements to individual dwellings (often over a considerable time period, as resources allow: as a consequence, many homes are incomplete).

Squatter settlements were for a long time viewed by urban elites as major irritants, not only landscape eyesores but also sources of potential health hazards and the breeding places for radical social movements: in such contexts, governments sought to eradicate them, even if they were unable to provide alternative housing for their low-income residents. From the 1960s on, however, some housing specialists argued that the settlements offered viable solutions to chronic housing supply problems in rapidly-growing cities with large low-income populations. Conventional housing provision (both private and public sector) cannot match the demand, and the available capital is better spent on other projects. Squatter settlements involve people investing in their own homes and neighbourhoods, and if encouraged they may invest more. Thus the settlement process has been aided in many cities by assisting groups to identify land on which to found their settlements, helping with their planning, ensuring a basic infrastructure of utilities to the sites, and in some cases providing basic 'core dwellings' around which growth can occur as the 'owner' wishes. RJJ

References and Suggested Reading

Gilbert, A.G. 1998: *The Latin American city*. London: Latin American Research Bureau. · Hardoy, J. 1989: *Squatter citizen: life in the urban Third World*. London: Earthscan. · Lloyd, P.C. 1979: *Slums of hope: shanty towns in the Third World*. London: Penguin. · Stokes, C.J. 1962: A theory of slums. *Land Economy* 38: 127–37. · Ward, P., ed., 1982: *Self-help housing: a critique*. Oxford: Mansell.

squatting The illegal occupation of land and dwellings. In advanced industrial societies it is usually associated with the occupation of empty, possibly dilapidated, dwellings awaiting demolition, by individuals and groups who are either unable to afford (or choose not to afford) homes through conventional market mechanisms or are ineligible for the allocation of public housing. Some countries' laws give a degree of security of occupation – known as 'squatter's rights' – making eviction of squatters difficult for the legal owners. Most squatting occurs in INNER-CITY areas, especially districts characterized as SLUMS. (See also SQUATTER SETTLEMENT.) RJJ

stable population A population in which age-specific FERTILITY and MORTALITY are assumed to be constant and to and from which no MIGRATION takes place. The concept was first developed in a series of papers by Alfred Lotka (see, for example, Lotka, 1922) and is much used in demographic analysis. He showed how such a population tends towards a constant age distribution which increases at a constant rate. A *stationary* population, a special case of a stable population, is one where fertility and mortality are equal and the age distribution is the LIFE TABLE distribution. PEO

Reference

Lotka, A. 1922: The stability of the normal age distribution. *Proceedings National Academy of Sciences* 8: 339–45.

Suggested Reading

Woods, R.I. 1979: *Population analysis in geography*. London and New York: Longman, ch. 8.

stages of growth A five-stage sequence of economic and social DEVELOPMENT postulated by the American economic historian Walt W. Rostow (1971) through which, he argued, all societies may pass (see figure). The stages represent an attempt to generalize 'the sweep of modern history'. Their elaboration in book form is described by its author as *a non-communist manifesto*, written in deliberate opposition to what were perceived to be Karl Marx's views on the relationships between economic and non-economic behaviour (see HISTORICAL MATERIALISM; MARXIAN ECONOMICS) and, more immediately, to the perceived threat to capitalist HEGEMONY posed by the Cold War.

The first of the five stages – the *traditional society* – is characterized by 'primitive' technology, hierarchical social structures (the precise nature of which is not specified) and behaviour conditioned more by custom and accepted practice than by what Rostow takes to be 'rational' criteria. These characteristics combine to place a ceiling on production possibilities. Outside stimuli to change (including, for example, COLONIALISM and the expansion of CAPITALISM) are admitted in the transitional second stage – the *preconditions for take-off*. This stage emphasizes a rise in the rate of productive investment, a start on the provision of social and economic INFRASTRUCTURE, the emergence of a new, economically based elite and an effective centralized national STATE. Again, no specification of social relations is given. However, the opportunities for profitable investment presented by the preconditions for take-off are unlikely to be ignored by CAPITAL and they pave the way for the third stage: *'take-off' into sustained growth*. This is described by Rostow as 'the great watershed in the life of modern societies'. It is a period of around 10–30 years, during which growth dominates society, the economy and the political agenda (although the social relations which facilitate this dominance are not described) and investment rises, especially in the leading sectors of manufacturing industry. Self-sustaining growth results in the *drive to maturity* (stage 4), characterized by diversification as most sectors grow, imports fall and productive investment ranges between 10 and 20 per cent of national income. The increasing importance of consumer goods and services and the rise of the WELFARE STATE indicate that the final stage of the *age of high mass-consumption* has been reached (see POST-INDUSTRIAL SOCIETY).

The insistence within the model upon placing growth in a wider historical and social

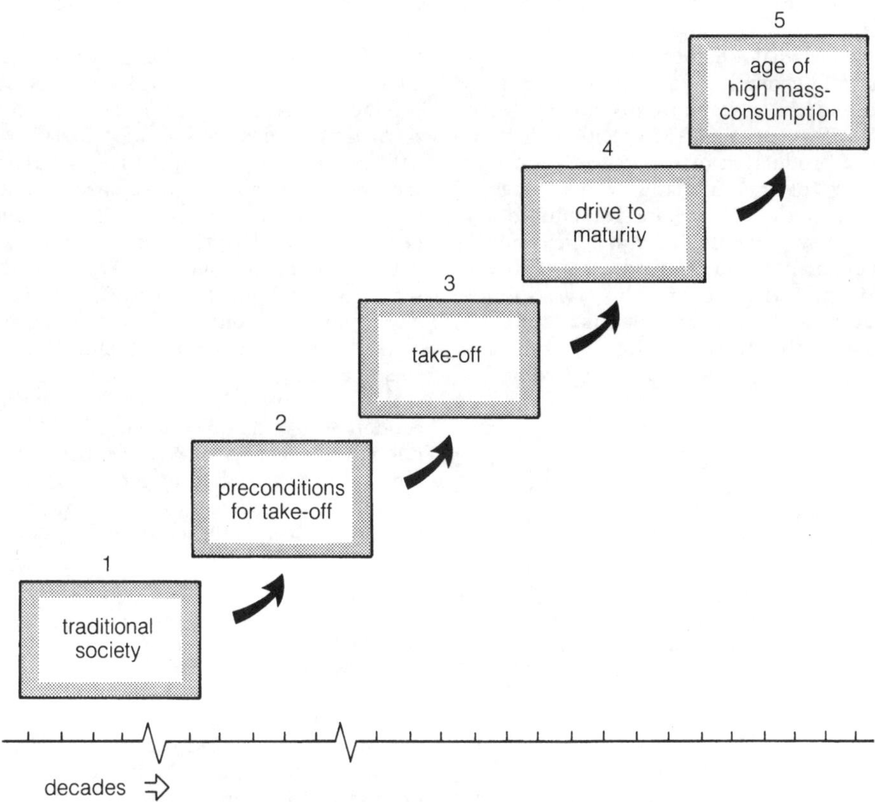

stages of growth *Rostow's stages theory of economic development* (after Keeble, 1967, p. 250)

context and upon a disaggregated approach which reflects the UNEVEN nature of DEVELOPMENT marks a substantial advance upon abstracted and formal theories of economic growth. But at the same time these characteristics expose its socially universal and ahistoric features.

The model of economic development derived from the stages is teleological, mechanical, ahistorical and ethnocentric:

- *teleological* in the sense that the end result (stage 5) is known at the outset (stage 1) and derived from the historical geography of 'developed' societies which are then simply used to form the template for the 'underdeveloped', which are thereby denied a historical geography;
- *mechanical* in that, despite the claim that the stages have an inner logic 'rooted in a dynamic theory of production', the underlying motor of change is not explained, so that as a result the stages become little more than a classificatory system based on data for fifteen countries only, plus outline data for others;
- *ahistorical*, in that notions of path-dependency are ignored, so that it can be assumed that the historical geographies of the underdeveloped countries are unaffected by that of the dependent, and so the intervention of the latter into the former is simply an irrelevance – this position is also profoundly a-geographic as it is incapable of recognizing that geographical relationships are continuously formed and re-formed across the world economic and political geographies; and
- *deliberately ethnocentric* in espousing a future for the world based on American history and aspiring to American norms of high mass-consumption: the Other is to be made the Self, thereby making the world safe for the American dream.

Thus the strategic implications are clear: history does not change but repeats itself across space and time. Capitalist society is, following Rostow's logic, a necessary consequence of development (see CAPITALISM). All societies that are not currently capitalist in form will become so: there is no alternative. Such underlying implications are not made explicit. By concealing the specific social relations of production of the stages – and most especially of the first and second stages – capitalist societies may be reproduced and extended by apparently neutral policies advocating apparently universal processes of growth. This is the true meaning of Rostow's subtitle. If it were to read 'a capitalist manifesto', its ideological objectives (see IDEOLOGY) would be revealed and their achievement limited or subverted. RL

Reference

Rostow, W.W. 1971: *The stages of economic growth: a non-communist manifesto*, 2nd edn. Cambridge: Cambridge University Press.

Suggested Reading

Baran, P.A. and Hobsbawm, E.J. 1961: The stages of economic growth. *Kyklos* 14: 324–42. · Foster-Carter, A. 1985: *The sociology of development*. Ormskirk: Causeway. · Keeble, D.E. 1967: Models of economic development. In R.J. Chorley and P. Haggett, eds, *Models in geography*. London and New York: Methuen, 248–54. · Peet, R. 1991: *Global capitalism: theories of societal development*. London and New York: Routledge, ch. 3. · Rostow (1971).

staple A principal item of TRADE or consumption produced and/or consumed by a SOCIETY. The potato was the staple commodity of consumption in Ireland before the famine of the 1840s. Production failures during the 1840s coupled with the absence of alternative strategies as a consequence of the UNDERDEVELOPMENT of Irish agriculture, conditioned largely by its connections with the British economy and land-ownership, led to widespread famine, emigration and the decimation of the rural population. Rice Is the staple foodstuff of many parts of South-East Asia today in the sense that, like the potato in pre-famine Ireland, it forms the central contribution to diet.

Heavy DEPENDENCE upon staple items of trade leaves economies vulnerable to fluctuations in demand and price and to the long-term fall in demand for naturally produced products as they are replaced by industrial alternatives. Even in more diversified and industrialized economies, the process of UNEVEN DEVELOPMENT may lead to the emergence of a dominant staple commodity, with critical implications for sustained growth. Conversely, staples of local consumption frequently face competition from more commercial, export-orientated users of land with harmful consequences (such as those in Ethiopia during the 1980s and 1990s) for local food production and food supplies as well as for the possibilities of SUSTAINABLE DEVELOPMENT.

Dependence upon staples is not restricted to the less economically developed countries. Cotton products accounted for over 50 per cent by value of British exports in 1830 (36 per cent in 1870). Such a heavy dependence serves to condition the possibilities of future development not only because alternatives are squeezed out but also because of the formative socio-economic influence of a distinctive DIVISION OF LABOUR. Even in highly developed economies like that of Canada where the production and export of resource-based staples are central to growth, they generate distinctive patterns and processes of development (Hayter and Barnes, 1990; see STAPLES THEORY). RL

Reference

Hayter, R. and Barnes, T. 1990: Innis' staple theory, exports and recession: British Columbia, 1981–86. *Economic Geography* 66 2: 156–73.

staples theory A theory which suggests that national economic and social development is based upon the export of unprocessed or semi-processed primary resources (STAPLES). Although the theory has long historical antecedents, and different, frequently truncated, versions of it have been presented (e.g. ECONOMIC BASE THEORY), staples theory is most closely associated with the work of the Canadian economic historian Harold A. Innis (1894–1952).

In Mel Watkins's (1963, p. 144) classic exposition of Innis's staples model, exports of primary resources function as 'the leading sector of the economy, and set the pace for economic growth'. In the optimistic version of the theory (particularly associated with NEO-CLASSICAL ECONOMICS), this sector then stimulates diversification through its various linkages, eventually leading to full INDUSTRIALIZATION (Baldwin, 1956). In the pessimistic account, and one now associated with the so-called Canadian school of POLITICAL ECONOMY, the economy is ensnared in a staples trap (Williams, 1983). That is, diversification is blocked for reasons such as an export mentality among producers, the domination of the ECONOMY by a few, large and often foreign-owned MULTINATIONAL CORPORATIONS, and a truncated industrial branch-plant structure that minimizes the development of higher order control and research functions (Britton and Gilmour, 1971). The result, to use Innis's terminology, is that staples-producing regions become HINTERLAND economies, the fates of which are strongly tied to events in more powerful foreign metropoles (cf. MERCANTILIST MODEL). Of these two different accounts, it is the pessimistic version that is most persuasive (Clement and Williams, 1989).

A principal task of researchers supporting the pessimistic version has been to establish the causal relations between the nature of staples production, on the one hand, and the economic instability and dependency found within staples regions, on the other. Four principal connections have been noted. First, that *the market for staple commodities approximates more closely perfect competition than that for manufactured goods*. As such, staples regions are price-takers in a market where price volatility is the norm and, in particular, the bulk of crude exports that are the basis of most staples regions tend to be very vulnerable to demand shifts in markets that are both highly competitive and price-elastic. Second, *because domestic sales of staples are relatively small, international market volatility has direct and strong impacts*, thereby producing the characteristic boom and bust economy of resource-producing regions. Third, for a variety of reasons (technological advances that reduce resource inputs for production, the growth of synthetic substitutes, and low long-run income elasticities of demand), the *TERMS OF TRADE* for primary commodities are increasingly less favourable to staples-producing areas. Finally, *resource production tends to be undertaken by big, often foreign-owned, multinational corporations*. Spry (1981) argues that this is a direct consequence of the large capital expenditures and production indivisibilities associated with staples. However, the presence of foreign multinational firms in staples regions creates a number of potential problems including: the appropriation of economic RENTS because of the undervaluing of resources by the LOCAL STATE, and done to induce local investment (see REGIONAL ALLIANCE); the failure to process the resource prior to export because resource extraction is only one stage within a vertically integrated corporation that often prefers for reasons of internal control to process elsewhere (cf. INTEGRATION); the low levels of technological innovation and development; the lack of local control; and finally, a weakened ability to control trade through explicit policy because of the high degree of intra-corporate transfers.

In sum, there is a very direct relationship between the type of TRADE in which a staples region engages, and its level of social and economic development. Note that this is not a connection that traditional (neo-classical) economic theory would ever make. It would say that staples nations, such as Canada, most benefit from specializing and trading in those commodities for which they have a COMPARATIVE ADVANTAGE, primary resources. But in drawing upon this theory, as Innis (1956, p. 3) wrote in the late 1920s, orthodox economists 'attempt to fit their analysis of new economic facts into . . . the economic theory of old countries . . . The handicaps of this process are obvious, and there is evidence to show that [this is] . . . a new form of exploitation with dangerous consequences'.

To circumscribe such exploitation, Innis developed his staples theory in such a way that it was peculiarly suited to the 'new economic facts' (Barnes, 1996, ch. 8). That theory brought together three types of concerns: geographical/ecological, institutional and technological. In turn, this triad became the basis for a theory of *staples accumulation*, one that begins with the metropole and the dominant technology found there in production, communications and transportation. That technology, in turn, determines the type of resources demanded by the metropole, and those sites within the periphery that are potentially exploitable. In fact, the centrality of *technology* to Innis's scheme has led some commentators to conclude that 'methodologically, [the] staple approach was more technological history writ large than a theory of economic growth in the conventional sense' (Watkins, 1963, p. 141). This cannot be entirely true because it is also necessary that the right kind of *geography* be present on which that technology can gain purchase. Unless, say, quantities of a resource are found at a location, or the site is accessible, no resource will be extracted regardless of the technology. As Innis (1946, p. 87) wrote: 'Geography provides the grooves which determine the course and to a large extent the character of economic life.' This is not geographical determinism, however, because geography and technology work together. Moreover, they can only work together provided that the third leg of the triad is also present, an appropriate *institutional structure*. Investing in staples production in the periphery requires large amounts of capital expenditure because of the high 'minimum indivisible cost[s] that must be met if production is to be undertaken at all' (Spry, 1981, pp.

155–6: cf. CORE–PERIPHERY MODEL). Only two institutional forms are capable of raising sufficient funds to cover such costs, the STATE, which provides basic INFRASTRUCTURE, and large corporations which meet the immediate costs of plant and capital equipment.

When the right technology comes together with the right geography and the right institutional structure, the result is ACCUMULATION of 'cyclonic' frenzy. In this way virgin resource regions are transformed and enveloped within the produced spaces of the capitalist periphery. Such intense accumulation, however, never lasts, and because of the very instabilities of staples production, sooner rather than later investment shifts to yet other staples regions, leaving in its wake abandoned resource sites and communities. Studies of staples economies have been mostly carried out in Canada, and often bring together issues of the physical environment, local community development, and global economics (see LOCAL–GLOBAL DIALECTIC; and essays in Britton, 1996; and Barnes and Hayter, 1997). TJB

References

Baldwin, R.E. 1956: Patterns of development in newly settled regions. *Manchester School of Economics and Social Studies* 24: 161–79. · Barnes, T.J. 1996: *Logics of dislocation: models, metaphors and meanings of economic space*. New York: Guilford. · Barnes, T.J. and Hayter, R., eds, 1997: *Troubles in the rainforest: British Columbia's forest economy in transition*. Victoria, BC: Western Geographical Press. · Britton, J.N.H., ed., 1996: *Canada and the global economy: the geography of structural and technological change*. Montreal and Kingston: McGill-Queen's University Press. · Britton, J.N.H. and Gilmour, J.M. 1971: *The weakest link: a technological perspective on Canadian industrial underdevelopment*. Background study 43. Ottawa: Science Council of Canada. · Clement, W. and Williams, G., eds, 1989: *The new Canadian political economy*. Montreal and Kingston: McGill-Queen's University Press. · Innis, H.A. 1946: *Political economy in the modern state*. Toronto: Ryerson. · Innis, H.A. 1956: The teaching of economic history in Canada. In M.Q. Innis, ed., *Essays in Canadian economic history*. Toronto: University of Toronto Press, 3–16 (first published in 1929). · Spry, I.M. 1981: Overhead costs, rigidities of productive capacity and the price system. In W.H. Melody, L. Salter and P. Heyer, eds, *Culture, communication, and dependency. The tradition of H.A. Innis*. Norwood, NJ: Ablex, 155–66. · Watkins, M.H. 1963: A staple theory of economic growth. *Canadian Journal of Economics and Political Science* 29: 141–58. · Williams, G. 1983: *Not for export: towards a political economy of Canada's arrested industrialization*. Toronto: McClelland and Stewart.

Suggested Reading

Barnes (1996), ch. 8. · Drache, D. 1995: Celebrating Innis: the man, the legacy, and our future. In D. Drache, ed., *Staples, markets, and cultural change: selected essays of Harold A. Innis*. Montreal and Kingston: McGill-Queen's University Press, xiii–lix. · Watkins (1963).

state Traditionally regarded as an area of land (or land and water) with relatively well-defined, internationally recognized, political BOUNDARIES. Within this TERRITORY resides a people presumed to have an independent political identity, usually referred to as NATIONALISM. This traditional use of the term is perhaps better confined to the notion of a NATION-STATE; another use of the term is common in the literature and refers to the *theory of the state*.

The nation-state has long been a major focus in POLITICAL GEOGRAPHY. The Greek philosopher Aristotle wrote about the ideal state in the third century BCE, and its relevance in geography can be found in the writings of Carl Ritter and Friedrich Ratzel in the nineteenth century. The evolution of the nation-state is usually traced through four broad phases: pre-agrarian, agrarian, industrial and post-industrial. In pre-agrarian societies, tribal loyalties predominated. Hunting and gathering bands were typically too small and isolated to allow for, or require, the existence of an independent political institution. In contrast, agrarian societies were mostly state-endowed. The emergence of literacy and a specialized clerical class made possible the centralized organization and storage of records, rules and culture. However, COMMUNITIES remained isolated, and the clerisy could not dominate beyond localized territories.

A crucial transitional phase in this conventional sequence was the absolutist state, in which a single monarchy displaced prior feudal arrangements and decentralized fiefdoms (see FEUDALISM), and created such key precursors of the nation-state as standing armies, uniform tax structures and bureaucracies. Industrial society permitted a specialized division of labour and the emergence of a high culture. In such a complex society, a centralized state agency takes over the roles of socialization, education and authority, commonly rationalizing these functions throughout the national territory. In the POST-INDUSTRIAL SOCIETY, the state has grown to play a dominant role in social relations. A new world political organization is evidenced in the development of supranation-states, based on such things as trade and defence agreements (see COMMON MARKET). Parallel to this, however, has been a series of developments questioning the extent to which a new world organization will be state-dominated, or even organized at all. The activities of non-state economic institutions, ranging in formal legitimacy from TRANSNATIONAL CORPORATIONS to networks of money laundering and narcotics trafficking overseen by assorted transnationalizing criminal organizations, have been undermining the authority of the state while rendering the boundaries of the nation-state ever more porous. In some instances, organized criminal activity has insinuated itself into the state proper by capturing the STATE APPARATUS, thus engendering 'gangster nations'. Simultaneously, growing volumes and ranges of MIGRATION have led to a process of widespread diasporization (cf. DIASPORA), whereby peoples previously associated as 'culturally of' a given nation-state may now be found with increasing variety in numerous nation-states, and in contact between nation-states. The resulting destabilization of prescribed national culture and bounded nation-state authority plays a significant role in the resurgence of local NATIONALISMS, which have encouraged a splintering of nation-states into smaller units based on sentiments of ETHNICITY, RACE or local separatist sentiments. Thus, the vulnerability of the nation-state to numerous transnational forces (see TRANSNATIONALISM) has served to dissolve territorial borders while simultaneously fragmenting the political terrain within, challenging the continued viability of existing nation-states. In the process, border regions once considered marginal to the nation-state are reconstituted as centres of economic and cultural focus, acting not as dividers of distinct national populations but as generators of 'hybrid' identities and societies.

Needless to say, not all nation-states necessarily develop as a consequence of the four-stage model. Different patterns of nation-state evolution have been observed in, for example, the socialist states of eastern Europe and the military/authoritarian states of South America. Further, given that the very idea of the nation-state in its present form can be seen to have originated in western Europe of the eighteenth century (as in Herder's writings), it has been observed that in some LOCALES the present-day system of nation-states is an imposed and ill-fitting alien overlay, most notably for those regions of the world that formed as nation-states (or had the form imposed upon them) during DECOLONIZATION following the Second World War.

More generally, a *theory of the state* focuses on the state as a set of institutions for the protection and maintenance of SOCIETY. These institutions include government, politics, the judiciary, armed forces, etc., and guarantee the reproduction of social relations in a way that is beyond the capability, or commonly the opposition, of any individual or single social group (cf. SOCIAL REPRODUCTION). The theory of the state is driven by a profoundly important question: 'Why is it necessary to constitute in society a separate agency called the state?' Contemporary discussions of this question usually trace their roots back to Hobbes and Locke, who advanced a vision of human existence as a 'war of all against all' resulting in lives that could only be 'nasty, brutish and short' unless SOVEREIGNTY was invested in the body of an overarching temporal authority. Liberal democrats such as Mill and Bentham elaborated upon these ideas, seeing the state as integral to the maximization of human happiness by overcoming problems of social coordination (see PRISONER'S DILEMMA; TRAGEDY OF THE COMMONS) through the establishment and enforcement of a social contract. Later social theorists like Kropotkin, Marx and Weber dissented from these positions, however, by re-envisioning the state as more akin to 'a body of armed men' largely operating to ensure the perquisites of privileged minorities. Weber, along with Ratzel, was also central to arguments emphasizing the spatial dimension of the state, arguing that it is within a given territory that the state administers POWER and holds a monopoly on the use of legitimized force. These thinkers have touched on many enduring themes, including the design of a minimalist state, legitimacy and public accountability in a democracy, the potentially repressive nature of state control, and the bureaucratization of the state.

Current analyses of the state typically draw the distinction between state *form*, state *function* and state *apparatus*. The question of form examines how a specific state structure is constituted by, and evolves within, a given SOCIAL FORMATION. (A capitalist society should, in principle, give rise to a distinctively capitalist state.) The issue of function refers to those activities undertaken in the name of the state; in other words, what the state actually 'does'. Finally, STATE APPARATUS refers to the mechanisms through which these functions are executed.

Liberal political thought isolates four views of the state as: (a) supplier of PUBLIC GOODS and services; (b) regulator and facilitator of the economy; (c) social engineer with an agenda of its own; and (d) arbiter between the many groups which compose society (cf. PLURALISM). Structuralist thought has focused on the links between the state elite and the ruling class. A popular view of the present-day state, which is common to theorists of many persuasions, presents it as a 'crisis-manager'. According to this perspective, the state acts to contain the political repercussions of the socio-economic system, operating (in effect) as an input–output mechanism. State outputs consist of administrative decisions taken in the interest of diverse social groups; their inputs are constituent demands and mass loyalty. If the outputs do not satisfy the various constituencies, a 'rationality crisis' results, in which the state's viability is brought into question. This could lead to a 'legitimation crisis' if mass loyalty to the state is withdrawn. (See also CRISIS; CRITICAL THEORY.)

The LOCAL STATE is a key instrument of crisis management, as is the trend towards CORPORATISM, involving an institutionalized form of group or CLASS conflict in which formal avenues of CONFLICT and compromise are established and maintained in order to minimize the risk of unpredictable crises. The expansion of the state apparatus has been an important manifestation of contemporary corporatist relations, although recent retreats from the state and its operations have prompted countervailing contractions of the state apparatus.

The theory of the state is of vital importance in the rebirth of political geography. Some analysts question whether we need a theory of the state. Others suggest that at some point in the near future there may not be conventionally understood states left to theorize about. But still others claim that a theory of the state is of fundamental, central significance to a properly constituted POLITICAL GEOGRAPHY. Part of the difficulty in this latter task is the fact that state theory is a highly contested topic of scholarly debate. There are a great many *theories* of the state, each with a claim to privileged insight within its 'home domain', but most contemporary theorists recognize the significance of territory/geography in the creation and re-creation of states. MJD

Suggested Reading

Alford, R.R. and Friedland, R. 1985: *Powers of theory: capitalism, the state, and democracy*. New York: Cambridge University Press. · Brown, Michael P. 1997: *Replacing citizenship: AIDS activism and radical democracy*. New York: Guilford. · Clark, G.L. and Dear, M.J. 1984: *State apparatus: structures and language of legitimacy*. Boston: Allen and Unwin. · Dalby, S. Ó 'Tuathail, G. and Routledge, P., eds, 1997–8: *A geopolitics reader*. London: Routledge. · Gellner, E. 1983: *Nations and nationalism*. Oxford: Blackwell. Ithaca, NY: Cornell University Press. · Held, D. et al. 1983: *States and societies*. New York: New York University Press. · Mann, M. 1986: *The sources of social power, volume 1: A history of power from the beginning to A.D. 1760*. New York: Cambridge University Press; Ó Tuathail, G. 1996: *Critical geopolitics: the politics of writing global space*. Minneapolis: University of Minnesota Press. · Painter, J. 1965: *Politics, geography and political geography: a critical perspective*. London: Edward Arnold. · Taylor, P.J. 1991: Political geography within world-systems analysis. *Review, Fernand Brandel Center XIV*: 387–402.

state apparatus The set of institutions and organizations through which STATE power is exercised. Analysis of the state apparatus is important because: (a) the apparatus is an imperfect, at times obsolescent, manifestation of changing social relations; (b) the apparatus acts as a medium through which the exercise of state POWER is 'filtered' and inevitably transformed; and (c) because it is manifest as a concrete set of institutions, the apparatus offers the potential for strategic intervention by powerful social groups.

The state apparatus consists of various kinds of sub-apparatus, as follows:

- *political*, the set of parties, elections, governments and constitutions;
- *legal*, the mechanisms which allow peaceful mediation between conflicting social groups (cf. LAW, GEOGRAPHY OF);
- *repressive*, the mechanisms of internal (intra-national) and external (international) enforcement of state power, including civilian police and armed forces (cf. SURVEILLANCE);
- *production*, the range of state-manufactured and state-distributed goods and services (cf. PUBLIC GOODS);
- *provision*, whereby the state contracts with other agencies for the production and distribution of goods and services;
- *treasury*, fiscal and monetary arrangements for regulating internal and external economic relations;
- *health, education and welfare*, basic services for the promotion of population well-being (cf. WELFARE STATE);
- *information*, state-sponsored or state-controlled mechanisms for information and disinformation dissemination;
- *communications and media*, licensed and regulated but usually relatively autonomous information-dissemination channels, including telecommunications and print;
- *administration*, a sub-apparatus designed to ensure the overall compatibility and operation of all the various state sub-apparatuses; and

- *regulatory*, agencies created to organize and extend state intervention into non-state activities, including family and industrial relations.

The various state apparatuses are vital in achieving the three functions of the modern capitalist state: (a) *to secure social consensus* by guaranteeing acceptance of the prevailing social contract by all groups within a society; (b) *to secure the conditions of production* by regulating social investment to increase production in the public and private sectors, and social consumption to ensure the reproduction of the labour force; and (c) *to secure social integration* by ensuring the welfare of all groups in society.

The state apparatus exhibits a propensity for seemingly autonomous self-perpetuation, producing an adaptability whereby the structure and practices of the state apparatus can alter dramatically according to the vicissitudes of the political climate. This has been demonstrated recently in capitalist societies by increasing pressures for selective deregulation and state austerity, resulting in the roll-back of the state and leaving the state apparatus vulnerable both to corruption through infiltration of criminal activity and to PRIVATIZATION. In the latter, the functions of the state apparatus are transferred to private enterprises or to CIVIL SOCIETY, giving rise to a SHADOW STATE, falling levels of state employment (most notably in the health, education and welfare sector), and growing inequities in the delivery of services. (See also LOCAL STATE.) MJD

Suggested Reading

Clark, G.L. and Dear, M.J. 1984: *State apparatus: structures and language of legitimacy*. Boston: Allen and Unwin, ch. 3. · Kammerman, S.B. and Kahn, A.J., eds, 1989: *Privatization and the welfare state*. Princeton, NJ: Princeton University Press. · Wolch, J.R. 1990: *The shadow state*. New York: The Foundation Center.

stochastic process A mathematical–statistical MODEL describing the sequence of outcomes from a series of trials in probability terms. Some authorities distinguish between a *probabilistic model*, in which the outcome of individual trials is predicted, and a *stochastic model*, in which the development of a series of outcomes is modelled (cf. PREDICTION); a stochastic model may therefore include situations in which the outcome of a specific trial is in some way dependent upon the outcome of previous trials. The same PROCESS can produce an infinite (or at least very large) number of realizations – a sequence of 50 throws of a die, for example, can produce very many different sequences of the numbers 1 to 6 – so that a stochastic process is very different from a deterministic one, which can realize only a single outcome from a given set of inputs.

Geographers have applied the concept of a stochastic process to both temporal (such as crop yields and commodity prices) and spatial sequences, and in some cases have combined the two (as in studies of epidemics; cf. DIFFUSION). The underlying time scale may be either discrete or continuous, and the stochastic element is included because the process involved is believed to include either a purely random element or a large number of minor causal factors whose net effect is a quasi-random disturbance of the outcomes.

One geographical usage of these ideas involves the proposal that a point pattern (of settlements or factories, for example) has resulted from a quasi-random process in which each geographical unit of a given size (such as a *quadrat*) has an equal probability of being the chosen location for such a point. The process can be modelled using a Poisson distribution (cf. FREQUENCY DISTRIBUTION), which assumes that the location decisions are independent of each other, but if the positioning of one point in an area changes the probability of a further point being placed there (cf. AGGLOMERATION), then the process is stochastic and should be modelled accordingly using an alternative frequency distribution (such as the negative binomial).

Analysis of time series within this approach has focused on three main types of stochastic process: in *autoregressive* models the value at time t is highly correlated with the values at t-1, t-2 etc., but with a random component; in moving average models, the value at t is determined as a weighted average of preceding and subsequent values; and in MARKOV PROCESSES there is no random element – each value is a deterministic function of previous values. If the process proceeds slowly (as, for example, in the evolution of a settlement pattern), two problems may arise: it may be necessary to infer the process from the pattern at just a single or, at best, a small number of cross-sections on the time scale; and most models assume *stationarity* – that the process operates constantly over either or both of time (temporal stationarity) or space (spatial stationarity). Where these assumptions regarding stationarity are valid, it may be possible to filter the data (i.e. to remove temporal or spatial trends); where they are not, sophisticated analytical procedures are required (as in the *expansion method*: Jones and Casetti, 1991).

AMH

Reference

Jones, J.P. and Casetti, E., eds, 1991: *Applications of the expansion method*. London: Routledge.

Suggested Reading

Bennett, R.J. 1979: *Spatial time series*. London: Pion. · Hoel, P.G., Port, S.C. and Stone, C.J. 1972: *Introduction to stochastic processes*. Boston: Houghton Mifflin.

structural adjustment A policy package, prompted by balance of payment crises, inflation and the disarray of state finances, associated with the two multilateral regulatory institutions of contemporary capitalism: the International Monetary Fund (IMF) and the World Bank (IBRD) (Mosley et al., 1991). The increasing number of structural adjustment programmes adopted by (some would say forced upon) THIRD WORLD economies since 1980 – sometimes referred to as stabilization programmes, sometimes as neo-liberal reforms – is a measure of what has been called the 'counter-revolution' (Toye, 1987) in DEVELOPMENT thinking, and specifically the global influence of New Right IDEOLOGY and the new global HEGEMONY of NEO-LIBERALISM. While structural adjustment has come to mean the agreements between Third World governments and the multilateral development institutions – quite standard deflationary packages involving exchange rate reform, PRIVATIZATION of STATE enterprises and service provision, and social austerity programmes – most of the North Atlantic developed economies experienced some form of adjustment during the 1980s led by the governments of Ronald Reagan, Margaret Thatcher and Helmut Kohl. Structural adjustment, both as a set of economic practices and as an ideology grounded in a set of theoretical propositions, emerged from the eclipse of the post-1945 WELFARE STATE settlement (sometimes referred to as FORDISM) as the North Atlantic economies slid into economic CRISIS during the 1970s. The origins and genesis of the crisis are complex and vary substantially across national economies. Nonetheless it is widely agreed that the US devaluation in 1973 which effectively ended the Bretton Woods system (established in 1944, in which the IMF and IBRD were the central products), which itself was rooted in the costs of the Vietnam war, was a key moment in the process by which the Fordist compromise – the liberal or social-democratic orthodoxy – was dismantled. The New Right theorists who came to political POWER on the backs of Reagan, Thatcher and so on offered a stark and brutal refashioning of economic liberalism and the centrality of the market. Milton Friedman (1962) was an important popular figure in the rise of laissez-faire economics, but the key ideas derived from the power of the market (efficiency, EQUITY, liberal individualism, political freedom) were taken up in the sphere of development economics by the likes of Peter Bauer, Deepak Lal and Anne Kreuger.

The IMF and the IBRD were established at Bretton Woods in 1944 and gradually emerged as two of the most powerful regulatory institutions in the global economy (cf. GLOBALIZATION; MONEY AND FINANCE, GEOGRAPHY OF). Both are dominated by US veto power, and have always been the mouthpieces of the Group of 7. While the IMF's role was as the lender of last resort for national economies, and the IBRD was a vehicle for project development in the Third World, in actual fact there has been a confluence in their activities, precipitated in part by the financial crisis and the debt problems of the early 1980s. Now both institutions are in the business of facilitating capital flows, of dealing with external debt problems and with macro-economic management of economies which are seen to have structural weaknesses (the balance of payments crisis simply being the most convenient measure of these weaknesses). To understand the structural adjustment package of the IMF and IBRD presupposes a particular economic architecture: the idea of a national economy, of particular endowments and entitlements, of a balance of payments (and the current account deficit), and patterns of state activity associated with investment, consumption and service provision. During the 1970s and early 1980s, many Third World governments borrowed heavily from private commercial banks (flush with oil dollars) in order to cover short-term deficits associated with the oil crisis, declining commodity prices and economic recession. By 1982 a number of key borrowers – Brazil, Mexico, Nigeria among them – were in effect bankrupt and unable to pay interest payments or cover key imports (cf. FISCAL CRISIS); a number of these governments suffered from inflation and state collapse. Many of these indebted Third World states had also adopted import-substituting INDUSTRIALIZATION policies and limited their so-called openness to the global economy, to protect infant industries. In this sense free trade, and sometimes export promotion, was limited. In keeping with the nationalist developmentalism of the 1950s, most states were interventionist, at the level both of production (state-owned enterprises), of the market (State Marketing Boards, tariffs and protectionism) and service provision (public education and health). Against this background, the fiscal (and therefore political) crisis of many Third World states in the early 1980s was, in the view of the IMF/IBRD, a function of state overspending, of state mismanagement (and of its anti-market mentality) and of waste and corruption. To the extent that there was endemic government failure, the market could not work its wonders. Economic growth – meaning export-led growth – was stifled. What was needed was a complete overhaul of the macro-political economy (cf. GROWTH THEORY). This is the heart and soul of structural adjustment. It rests on a particular reading and interpretation of the crisis – the Berg Report (World Bank, 1981) on Africa published in 1980 is one of the earliest and most influential neo-liberal accounts of the African, and by implication, the Third World's misfortunes – and provides a neat blueprint: what by the mid-1980s was called the 'Washington consensus' or the New Realism.

The structural adjustment package – the majority of Third World economies have signed some sort of agreement with the IMF or the IBRD since 1980 – endeavours to cure the problem not through adjustment by expansion (this was in fact the solution to the balance of payments crises of the 1970s as commodity price falls compelled governments to borrow, i.e. expand) but through austerity and contraction. The cure is to redress state action through two reform processes: reforms to compel the state to restructure its own taxation and social provision (to cut back on social expenditures and to raise more revenue), and reforms of how the state regulates prices and intervenes in the market (to create 'a favourable climate for investment'). For the former, public expenditures are to be cut back (including food and other subsidies which are seen to be wasteful and sources of rent) and user fees charged for necessary service provision. The market reforms turn on 'getting the prices right' and on exchange rate reform (the principle being that most currencies are overvalued). The main policy measures are devaluation of the currency, raising interest rates (to prevent inflation and put enterprises to the test of competition), the abolition of price controls and subsidies, and the abolition of barriers to foreign competition and foreign investment. Devaluation makes exports cheap and compels belt-tightening through a more prudent use of imports; interest rates restrain spending; and subsidy abolition redresses distorted prices (and waste). The entire adjustment package seeks to open up the national economy to world market competition, to promote export-led growth and to restrain domestic spending. Growth will be encouraged and its benefits will trickle down.

The structural adjustment package has been the subject of enormous debate, both within policy circles and among Third World leaders (Pastor, 1987; Killick, 1995; World Bank, 1994). Opposition to adjustments cites the limits of a standard blueprint and its authoritarian, top-down and imposed nature. Markets can of course fail just like governments, and the costs of this failure for the poor and vulnerable (women, children, peasants and urban poor) can be, and have been, enormous. A group of scholar-activists in fact brought a case to the World Court against the IMF in the 1980s for crimes against humanity. Adjustment in the short term necessarily involves the bankruptcy of enterprises, falling employment and real wages, cuts in public provisioning and rising food prices. The political costs of this adjustment may be substantial. On the one hand, many governments withdraw from IMF/IBRD agreements, others adopt authoritarian and anti-democratic practices to quell social instability, and still others face what have been called 'IMF food riots' (Walton and Seddon, 1990) as the popular classes (informal sector workers, students, trades unions and so on) organize against adjustment which is seen as anti-democratic, undermining national SOVEREIGNTY and a 'new' form of IMPERIALISM. To the extent that adjustment often involved the placement of IMF/IBRD personnel in key ministries and government offices, there is a good deal of truth to these popular claims. Adjustment has always been politically charged, but it is clear that there is no simple relation between economic liberalism and political democratization, as Milton Friedmann (1962) suggests.

Structural adjustment has without question been costly in social and political terms. Indeed, since 1989 the formerly SOCIALIST bloc has experienced an enormously painful adjustment ten years after Africa and Latin America. The rising levels of child mortality and morbidity, the declining standards of living, and the reduced access to heath and education, all speak of the legacies of adjustment. A key question is whether the package contributed to economic growth (since Left critics are the first to admit that some economic and politic reforms were necessary in the 1980s even if the form imposed by the IMF/IBRD was unconscionable). Here the record is at best ambiguous, and at worst grim (World Bank, 1994). The much vaunted turnaround in Africa has been slow and some of the World Bank success stories (Ghana, Ivory Coast) look frail at best. Some of the growth in India and Brazil is dramatic but how much can be attributed to adjustment is an open question. Conversely the case of Mexico, which was the neo-liberal touchstone in the 1980s, has experienced withering economic crises throughout the 1990s. By the late 1980s opposition to the costs of structural adjustment was sufficiently great that UNICEF called for adjustment 'with a human face' which focuses on the protection of the most vulnerable groups (UNICEF, 1990).

To the extent that structural adjustment is about attempting to improve peoples lives through a growing economic pie, it is doubtless laudable. But long-term investment in people is essential, as is a responsive, accountable and efficient state. It is within these realms of state capacity, empowerment and participation, and democracy that the IMF/IBRD recipes are sorely lacking. MW

References

Friedmann, M. 1962: *Capitalism and freedom*. Chicago: University of Chicago Press. · Killick, T. 1995: *IMF programmes in developing countries*. London: Routledge. · Mosley, P. et al. 1991: *Aid and power* (2 volumes). London: Routledge. · Pastor, M. 1987: The effects of IMF programs in the Third World. *World Development*, 15: 24–62. · Toye, J. 1987: *Dilemmas of development*. Oxford: Blackwell. · UNICEF 1989: *The state of the world's children*. New York: UNICEF. · Walton, J. and Seddon, D. 1990: *Free markets and food riots*. Oxford: Blackwell; World Bank 1981: *Accelerated development in Sub Saharan Africa*. Washington, D.C.: The World Bank. · World Bank 1994: *Adjustment in Africa*. Washington, D.C.: The World Bank.

Suggested Reading

Wuyts, M., Mackintosh, M. and Hewitt, T., eds, 1992: *Development policy and public action*. Oxford: Oxford University Press.

structural functionalism A tradition of social theory most closely associated with the writings of the American sociologist Talcott Parsons (1902–79), whose central proposition is that the structure of any social SYSTEM cannot be derived from 'the actor's point of view' but must instead be explained by the ways in which four 'functional imperatives' necessary for the survival of any social system are met (see also FUNCTIONALISM). These functions are:

> *Adaptation* [which] refers to the problem of obtaining enough resources or facilities from the system's external environment, and their subsequent distribution in the system.
>
> *Goal attainment* [which] refers to the features of an action system which serve to establish its goals, and to motivate and mobilize effort and energy in the system towards their achievement.
>
> *Integration* [which] refers to the problem of maintaining coherence or solidarity, and involves those elements which establish control, maintain co-ordination of subsystems and prevent major disruption in the system.
>
> *Latency* [which] refers to the processes by which motivational energy is stored and distributed to the system, [and] involves two interlinked problems: pattern-maintenance, the supply of symbols, ideas, tastes and judgements from the cultural system, and tension-management, the resolution of internal strains and tensions of actors. (Hamilton, 1983, p. 108)

The most detailed account of this 'A–G–I–L' schema is provided in Parsons's *The social system* (1951). This is often contrasted with his early account of *The structure of social action* (1937), which is usually assumed to be 'voluntarist' in its overarching concern with developing an action theory around the so-called 'unit act'. But there are some basic continuities between the two formulations, and Parsons himself subsequently rejected descriptions of his work as STRUCTURAL FUNCTIONALISM and reinstated the earlier term 'action theory'.

Parsons insisted that the analysis of any social system requires the conjunction of static ('structure') and dynamic ('function') components and he constantly accentuated the need to grasp the dynamics of social systems. Hence he attributed crucial importance to the interchanges between the systems and sub-systems and, in order to sharpen the focus still further, in his later formulations he developed a more formal cybernetic model of society. This drew upon biology and GENERAL SYSTEMS THEORY as much as it did upon classical social theory and was primarily concerned with interchanges of information and ENERGY and with modelling the evolution of societies 'as an extension of biological evolution' (Giddens, 1984, pp. 263–74; Parsons, 1971).

Although Parsons's views have been subjected to a sustained and at times devastating critique, his influence on modern social theory has been quite extraordinary. Not only has there been a series of striking developments of systems theory – including Alexander's (1983) vigorously constructive appraisal of Parsons's ideas; Luhmann's innovative extensions of Parsons's original schema (Luhmann,

1979, 1981); and Wallerstein's WORLD-SYSTEMS ANALYSIS, which Cooper (1981) calls 'Parsonianism on a world scale' (see Aronowitz, 1981) – but even those seemingly distant from Parsons have often made a series of critical appropriations of his ideas (see, e.g., Giddens, 1977; Habermas, 1987).

For all this, however, Parsons's shadow over human geography has been much shorter. This is partly the result of the atheoretical cast of traditional SOCIAL GEOGRAPHY – Parsons described himself as 'an incurable theorist' – but even the more theoretical exercises in social geography that followed (where they addressed such issues at all) concerned themselves with general models of social systems rather than Parsons's specific formulations. Interestingly, however, many of the criticisms which were made of STRUCTURAL MARXISM within human geography (e.g. Duncan and Ley, 1982) mimic exactly those objections which have been most frequently registered against STRUCTURAL FUNCTIONALISM (DiTomaso, 1982; Gregory, 1980; see also HUMAN AGENCY). The more recent arrival of the 'posts-' has driven more nails into Parsons's coffin. Both POSTMODERNISM and POST-STRUCTURALISM have underwritten a scepticism towards totalizing claims to knowledge and 'foundational' epistemologies (see FOUNDATIONALISM) which makes it highly unlikely that Parsons's version of GRAND THEORY will attract a sympathetic audience in human geography in the immediate future. And the interest in POST-COLONIALISM reinforces the critique of Parsons's scheme as an intellectual imperialism: many commentators have seen STRUCTURAL FUNCTIONALISM as another attempt to construct a general model of society out of what is in fact a highly particular reading of the United States of America. DG

References

Alexander, J. 1983: *Theoretical logic in sociology, vol. 4: The modern reconstruction of social thought: Talcott Parsons*. Berkeley: University of California Press. · Aronowitz, S. 1981: A metatheoretical critique of Immanuel Wallerstein's *The modern world-system*. *Theory and Society* 9: 503–20. · Cooper, F. 1981: Africa and the world economy. *African Studies Review* 14: 1–86. · DiTomaso, N. 1982: 'Sociological reductionism' from Parsons to Althusser: linking action and structure in social theory. *American Sociological Review* 47: 14–28. · Duncan, J. and Ley, D. 1982: Structural Marxism and human geography: a critical assessment. *Annals of the Association of American Geographers* 72: 30–59. · Giddens, A. 1977: *Studies in social and political theory*. London: Hutchinson. · Giddens, A. 1984: *The constitution of society*. Cambridge: Polity Press. · Gregory, D. 1980: The ideology of control: systems theory and geography. *Tijdschrift voor Economische en Sociale Geografie* 71: 327–42. · Habermas, J. 1987: *The theory of communicative action, vol. 2: Lifeworld and system: a critique of functionalist reason*. Cambridge: Polity Press. · Hamilton, P. 1983: *Talcott Parsons*. London and New York: Tavistock. · Luhmann, N. 1979: *Trust and power*. New York: John Wiley. · Luhmann, N. 1981: *The differentiation of society*. New York: Columbia University Press. · Parsons, T. 1937: *The structure of social action*. New York: Free Press. · Parsons, T. 1951: *The social system*. London: Routledge and Kegan Paul. · Parsons, T. 1971: *The system of modern societies*. Englewood Cliffs, NJ: Prentice-Hall.

Suggested Reading

Alexander (1983). · Hamilton (1983).

structural Marxism A modern school of Marxism most closely associated with the work of the French philosopher Louis Althusser (1918–90). His ideas went through a series of reformulations and autocritiques, but most critical attention fastened on his work during the 1960s and 1970s (see Elliott, 1987). His project was ambitious and complex, but in general Althusser proposed a fundamental distinction (an 'epistemological break') between Marx's 'early' writings, which were still close enough to Kantian and particularly Hegelian philosophy to represent a humanism, and Marx's 'mature' writings, which supposedly broke so completely with Hegelian philosophy that they could be judged a 'science' (Althusser, 1969; Althusser and Balibar, 1970).

Two issues are woven together in these claims: on the one hand, the distinction between the work of the young Marx (1840–4) and the mature Marx (1857–83); and on the other hand, the opposition between an early humanism that was still 'ideological' (see IDEOLOGY) and a subsequent ANTI-HUMANISM that was supposed to provide a secure foundation for the construction of a truly critical 'science'. Both manoeuvres were contested by critics. In the first place, even when separated by the hybrid and 'transitional' works of 1845–57 – which include the *Grundrisse*, the notebooks Marx composed in preparation for *Das Kapital* – most intellectual historians insisted that it was extremely difficult to divide Marx's writings into such clinical stages. In the second place, Althusser's vision of modern Marxism as a science of MODES OF PRODUCTION which focuses on the structures of CAPITALISM, exposes the ideology of liberal humanism and seemingly evicts HUMAN AGENCY from historical eventuation, was attacked by humanist scholars who objected to the unwelcome shadow of STRUCTURALISM falling over HISTORICAL MATERIALISM.

The debate was especially vigorous within Anglophone Marxism, particularly among social historians, where it was sparked off by E.P. Thompson's (1978) polemic against Althusser and by Richard Johnson's (1978) survey of the limits of Thompson's own position. A barrage of exchanges then appeared in *History Workshop Journal* and the debate was eventually joined by, among others, Hirst (1979) – who had collaborated with a number of others in a series of critical engagements with Althusser that went some considerable way beyond Althusser's own positions (Hindess and Hirst, 1975, 1977; Cutler, Hindess, Hirst and Hussain, 1977, 1978) – and Anderson (1980), who had played a large part in opening Anglophone Marxism to other traditions of Continental European Marxism and who had himself produced two distinguished Althusserian accounts of European history (Anderson, 1975, 1976). For some scholars, the result of all this was a vindication of humanist inquiry, while for yet others Althusser's anti-humanism continued to offer the prospect of a 'renewal' of Marxian theory (Resch, 1992). But in Francophone circles the arguments over structural Marxism – which were equally passionate and politicized – radicalized Althusser's thought and were drawn into the formation of what came to be called POST-STRUCTURALISM.

In human geography, the exchanges in the 1970s and early 1980s were more muted than they were in many other disciplines (Chouinard and Fincher, 1963; Duncan and Ley, 1982) – perhaps because Althusser's ideas never had the constituency they enjoyed elsewhere – and the interest in post-structuralism emerged correspondingly later. But in the 1990s it has become clear that the legacy of Althusser is much greater than this suggests, and includes the following:

(1) A well-established rejection of EMPIRICISM and a recognition of the basic importance of theoretical work (see also PROBLEMATIC). In human geography this took the form of a critique of SPATIAL SCIENCE which depended, at least in part, on an engagement with structural Marxism (Gregory, 1978, pp. 105–20); it has since been developed most extensively within different – but nonetheless related – approaches like post-structuralism and REALISM.

(2) A more complex view of the architectonics of CAPITALISM than the base–superstructure model to be found in Marx's original writings ('classical Marxism'). Althusser distinguished between the economic, political and ideological levels of a SOCIAL FORMATION, and argued that different levels would dominate different social formations (the political or ideological in FEUDALISM, for example, and the economic in capitalism); the dominant level would in each case be determined by the economic level. This was intended to militate against an ESSENTIALISM and reductionism in which explanations are immediately and directly reduced to a single and supposedly 'essential' level: instead structural Marxism treated causality as a question of overdetermination. In human geography this sort of topography eventually became something of a commonplace in two main streams of thought. On the one side were those political and economic geographers drawn to the REGULATION SCHOOL and its attempts to elaborate the highly complex overdeterminations of the process of capital ACCUMULATION (see Gibson-Graham, 1996, pp. 24–45). On the other side were those cultural and social geographers seeking a more sophisticated conceptualization of the social location of CULTURE. This did not require Althusser's formal apparatus: Cosgrove's *Social formation and symbolic landscape* (1984, 1998) was exemplary in its appeal to the concept of a social formation to secure the integrity of cultural production without once invoking Althusser. More formal expressions of Althusser's schema could be found in the work of those geographers who drew on Fredric Jameson's (1991) account of POSTMODERNISM as the 'cultural dominant' in the social formation of late twentieth-century capitalism.

(3) The assignment of distinctive 'times' and 'spaces' to each of the levels of the social formation. The social construction of these times and spaces was an important counter to the abstract geometries of Anglo-American spatial science, but the theoretical elaboration of SPATIALITY in this sense derived from Francophone work in urban sociology (Castells, 1977), political economy (Lipietz, 1977) and political philosophy (Poulantzas, 1980). It subsequently fed into an interest in the PRODUCTION OF SPACE, where it joined with work undertaken outside the framework of structural Marxism (cf. Lefebvre, 1992; Gregory, 1994).

(4) A recognition of the social constitution of the human subject. The autonomous, sovereign and 'centred' subject of liberal humanism has been displaced from many analyses as human geographers have been drawn to various versions of anti-humanism. Althusser's concept of *interpellation* has proved to be of particular importance in clarifying the differ-

ent ways in which human subjects are constituted over space and through time and in elaborating concepts of multiple and competing subject-positions (cf. Smith, 1989; Castree, 1995). DG

References

Althusser, L. 1969: *For Marx*. London: Verso. · Althusser, L. and Balibar, E. 1970: *Reading Capital*. London: New Left Books. · Anderson, P. 1975: *Passages from antiquity to feudalism*. London: New Left Books. · Anderson, P. 1976: *Lineages of the absolutist state*. London: New Left Books. · Anderson, P. 1980: *Arguments within English Marxism*. London: Verso. · Benton, T. 1984: *The rise and fall of structural Marxism: Althusser and his influence*. London: Macmillan. · Castells, M. 1977: *The urban question: a Marxist approach*. London: Edward Arnold. · Castree, N. 1995: Theory's subject and subject's theory: Harvey, capital and the limits to classical Marxism. *Environment and Planning A* 27: 269–97. · Chouinard, V. and Fincher, R. 1963: A critique of 'Structural Marxism and human geography'. *Annals of the Association of American Geographers* 73: 137–46. · Cosgrove, D. 1984: *Social formation and symbolic landscape*. London: Croom Helm; reprinted 1998, Madison: University of Wisconsin Press. · Cutler, A., Hindess, B., Hirst, P.Q. and Husain, A. 1977: *Marx's capital and capitalism today*, 2 vols. London: Routledge. · Duncan, J. and Ley, D. 1982: Structural Marxism and human geography. *Annals of the Association of American Geographers* 72: 30–59. · Elliott, G. 1987: *Althusser: the detour of theory*. London: Verso. · Gibson-Graham, J.K. 1996: *The end of capitalism (as we knew it): a feminist critique of political economy*. Oxford and Cambridge, MA: Blackwell. · Gregory, D. 1978: *Ideology, science and human geography*. London: Hutchinson. · Gregory, D. 1994: *Geographical imaginations*. Oxford and Cambridge, MA: Blackwell. · Hindess, B. and Hirst, P.Q. 1975: *Pre-capitalist modes of production*. London: Routledge. · Hindess, B. and Hirst, P.Q. 1977: *Mode of production and social formation*. London: Macmillan. · Hirst, P. 1979: The necessity of theory. *Economy and Society* 8: 417–45. · Jameson, F. 1991: *Postmodernism, or the cultural logic of late capitalism*. Durham: Duke University Press. · Johnston, R. 1978: Edward Thompson, Eugene Genovese and socialist-humanist history. *History Workshop Journal* 6: 79–100. · Lefebvre, H. 1992: *The production of space*. Oxford: Blackwell. · Lipietz, A. 1977: *Le Capital et son espace*. Paris: Maspero. · Poulantzas, N. 1980: *State, power, socialism*. London: Verso. · Resch, R. 1992: *Althusser and the renewal of Marxist social thought*. Berkeley: University of California Press. · Smith, P. 1989: *Discerning the subject*. Minneapolis: University of Minnesota Press. · Thompson, E.P. 1978: *The poverty of theory and other essays*. London: Merlin.

Suggested Reading

Anderson (1980). · Benton (1984). · Gregory (1978), 105–20. · Gibson-Graham (1996), 24–45.

structuralism A set of principles and procedures originally derived from linguistics and linguistic philosophy which involve moving 'beneath' the visible and conscious designs of active human subjects in order to expose an essential logic which is supposed to bind these designs together in enduring and underlying structures that can be exposed through a series of purely intellectual operations. Structuralism was a dominant current in post-war French philosophy, where it owed much to the pioneering contributions of Roland Barthes in literary theory, Claude Lévi-Strauss in anthropology and Jean Piaget in psychology. It had an important (though contentious) impact on the development of STRUCTURAL MARXISM (particularly the work of Louis Althusser and Etienne Balibar) and on the rise of POST-STRUCTURALISM (including the work of Jacques Derrida and Michel Foucault): but it cannot be mapped directly onto either of these fields (see Merquior, 1986; Harland, 1987).

In the 1970s structuralism was extended, in a loose and for the most part programmatic fashion, into Anglophone human geography as part of the critique of EMPIRICISM and POSITIVISM that characterized modern SPATIAL SCIENCE (Tuan, 1972; Harvey, 1973; Marchand, 1974; Sayer, 1976; Gregory, 1978). In general, and in part in consequence, most human geographers came to recognize the importance of clarifying the theoretical status of the constructs with which they worked: there was a widespread acknowledgement that the 'facts' did not 'speak for themselves' and that all empirical inquiry required a keen theoretical sensibility. That sensibility often entailed a suspicion about voluntarism – many geographers doubted that social life could be explained in terms of the unbounded capacities of HUMAN AGENCY – and this was given a political edge by those who believed that structures of various sorts constrained and shaped the outcomes of human actions over space. For this reason, many human geographers adopted various 'depth models' of LANDSCAPES, SPACE-ECONOMIES and spatial SYSTEMS in order to look 'beneath' the taken-for-granted categories by means of which social life was usually comprehended. As the 1970s turned into the 1980s, however, these inquiries increasingly relied on the philosophy of REALISM rather than structuralism, and the most common theoretical tools used to dissect the surfaces of the social world were probably drawn from POLITICAL ECONOMY rather than literary theory, anthropology or psychology. It was not until the end of the 1980s and the beginning of the 1990s that those three fields assumed a greater prominence, largely as a result of the rise of a FEMINIST GEOGRAPHY and the reinvigoration of CULTURAL GEOGRAPHY, both of which have been informed by versions of post-structuralism which, even as they seek to move beyond structuralism, nonetheless typically retain that tradition's deep interest in language and DISCOURSE and its profound suspicion of humanism (see ANTI-HUMANISM).

DG

References

Gregory, D. 1978: *Ideology, science and human geography.* London: Hutchinson, 81–122. · Harland, R. 1987: *Superstructuralism: the philosophy of structuralism and post-structuralism.* New York: Methuen. · Harvey, D. 1973: *Social justice and the city.* London: Edward Arnold, 286–314. · Marchand, B. 1974: Quantitative geography: revolution or counter-revolution? *Geoforum* 17: 15–24. · Merquior, J. 1986: *From Prague to Paris: a critique of structuralist and post-structuralist thought.* London: Verso. · Sayer, R.A. 1976: A critique of urban modelling: from regional science to urban and regional political economy. *Progress in Planning* 6: 3. · Tuan, Yi-Fu 1972: Structuralism, existentialism and environmental perception. *Environment and Behaviour* 3: 319–31.

Suggested reading

Gregory (1978), 81–105. · Merquior (1986).

structuration theory An approach to social theory developed by the British sociologist Anthony Giddens (b. 1938) that seeks to elucidate the intersections between knowledgeable and capable human agents and the wider social systems and structures in which they are implicated.

Giddens identified the central problem in modern social theory as a dualism between 'agency' and 'structure' that recurs across the whole field of the humanities and the social sciences (cf. Chouinard, 1997). He also proposed an explanation for the chronic failure to reconcile the two: the mistake, so he said, was to treat 'structure' as establishing the parameters within which 'agency' was able to exercise its independent discretion. Giddens argued that structure was instead implicated in every moment of action – that it was at once constraining and enabling – and that, conversely, structure was an 'absent' order of differences, 'present' only in the constituting moments of interaction through which it was itself reproduced or transformed. These ideas were formalized in a model of the duality – not dualism – of structure that depended upon three fundamental concepts:

Reflexivity: the production and reproduction of social life is a skilled accomplishment on the part of knowledgeable and capable human subjects (see HUMAN AGENCY) rather than an autonomic response to any transhistorical 'logic' or 'functional imperative' (cf. FUNCTIONALISM).

Recursiveness: social life goes forward under conditions that are neither fully comprehended nor wholly intended by social actors but which nonetheless enter directly into the production and reproduction of the stream of social practices in which actors are involved: more technically, 'structure' – which Giddens conceives as sets of rules and resources made available by structures of signification, domination and legitimation (see figure 1) – is both the medium and the outcome of the social practices constituting social systems.

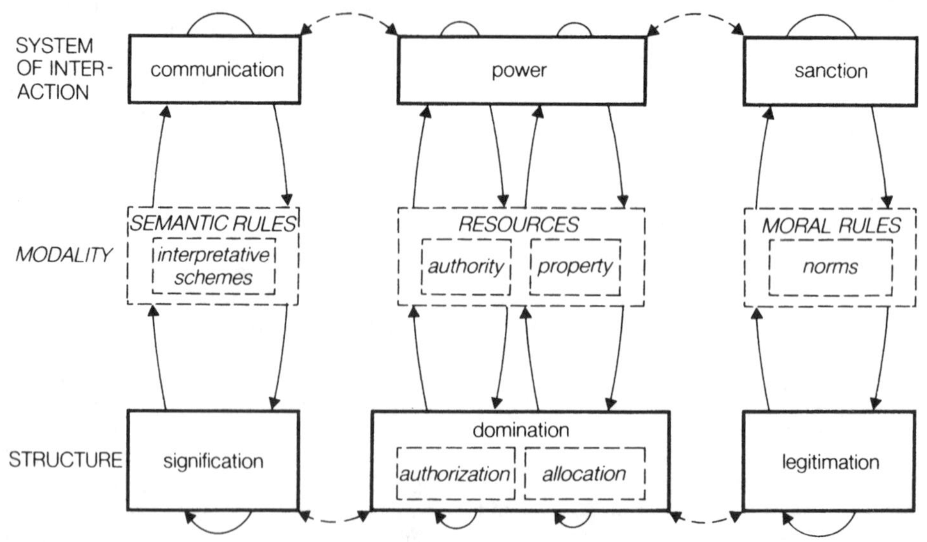

structuration theory *1: System and structure*

Regionalization: the continuity of social life depends both on interactions between actors who are co-present in time and/or space and on relations that reach beyond the 'here and now' to constitute interactions with others who are absent in time and/or space. These two dimensions – time–space routinization and TIME–SPACE DISTANCIATION – entail the articulation of 'presences' and 'absences' through modes of regionalization that channel social life into and out of sites/LOCALES/domains (see figure 2; see also TIME-GEOGRAPHY).

Giddens argued that these propositions made it possible to explicate the interconnection of routinized and repetitive conduct between actors or groups of actors with long-term, large-scale institutional development in a depth which is denied to both conventional social theory and HISTORICAL MATERIALISM (see Giddens, 1979, 1981, 1984, 1985). Several human geographers agreed that Giddens's ideas had much to offer studies of historico-geographical change, but most of them were much more reserved than Giddens about distancing themselves from historical materialism (Gregory, 1982; Harris, 1991; Pred, 1990; Thrift, 1983). In any event, in his later writings Giddens was markedly less interested in fleshing out his arguments about the genealogy of CLASS societies and CAPITALISM with any empirical sophistication, than in using some of the basic ideas of structuration theory as what he preferred to call 'sensitizing devices' that enabled him to offer a generalized, highly schematic argumentation-sketch of the constitution of late twentieth-century 'high modernity' (see Giddens, 1990, 1991, 1994) (see also MODERNITY). Of most interest to human geography have been Giddens's claims that, in the course of the twentieth century, and intensifying since the end of the Second World War:

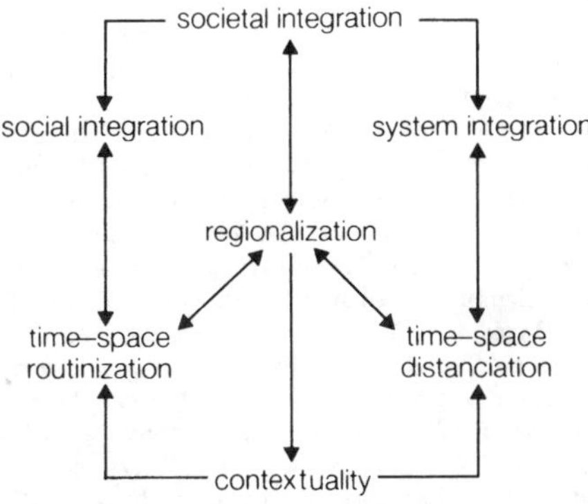

structuration theory *2: Time–space relations*

(1) The proliferation and circulation of information and knowledge in late twentieth-century societies has not only sustained 'reflexivity' but also heightened uncertainty in a process of REFLEXIVE MODERNIZATION;

(2) The generalized 'disembedding' of spheres of social life through processes of time–space distanciation has dissolved many of the ties that once held the conditions of daily life in place (as localized condensations of social practices) and recombined them across much larger tracts of time–space to issue in the GLOBALIZATION of social life on a continuous and systematic basis.

Structuration theory attracted considerable attention not only in human geography but in the social sciences more generally; but several criticisms of structuration theory in particular and Giddens's project in general made its status much less secure as the 1980s turned into the 1990s.

First, Giddens's advertisement of structuration theory as a critique of historical materialism was held to be suspect. While most of his critics conceded that his work was a serious engagement with Marx's writings, they objected to the 'almost complete absence of any serious examination of the theory or history of Marxism after Marx' (Gane, 1983) and were often puzzled as to why his own account of social change, 'with its stress on changing modes of surplus-extraction', should be regarded 'as in any sense critical of or an alternative to Marxism' (Callinicos, 1985; Sayer, 1990). Indeed, Wright (1989) concludes that Giddens's propositions are 'largely compatible with most of the substantive claims of both classical and contemporary Marxism'. Many human geographers were persuaded of the affinities between structuration theory and historical materialism, but for this precise reason some Marxist geographers (particularly those who were attracted to Marx's own work) could see no good grounds to change their theoretical vocabularies.

Secondly, Giddens was charged with eclecticism. It is impossible, so many critics argued, to bring together such radically discrepant theoretical traditions and rework them into some new synthesis. This charge might have lost some of its force in recent years, since there are probably few geographers who now situate their work under the sign of a single '-ism' or '-ology': but this does not mean that intellectual work can evade the responsibilities of discrimination and judgement. Indeed, Mestrovic (1998) insists that there are profound political and ethical dangers in Giddens's syncretic project, which, so he says, elevates ambivalence into virtue. Again, this is an argument familiar to human geographers who have had to negotiate a passage between ESSENTIALISM and FOUNDATIONALISM on the one side and RELATIVISM on the other.

Thirdly, Giddens was supposed to have retained the very dualism he sought to transcend. According to Archer (1990), structuration theory 'oscillates between the two divergent images it bestrides, between (a) the hyperactivity of agency, whose corollary is the innate volatility of society, and (b) the rigid coherence of structural properties associated with the essential recursiveness of social life'. In fact Giddens has consistently advocated a methodological bracketing that allows for either the analysis of strategic conduct or the analysis of institutions. Insofar as this manoeuvre merely transposes the dualism between 'agency' and 'structure' from a theoretical to a methodological level, it is perhaps scarcely surprising that there should have been so few empirical exemplifications of structuration theory inside or outside human geography (Gregson, 1989).

Fourthly, Giddens's conceptions of both 'agency' and 'structure' have been attacked: the former for collapsing agency into action, for tying agency too closely to everyday conduct understood as 'doing' (Dallmayr, 1982), and the latter for collapsing structure into rules and resources, and thereby driving the notion of structure back into the concrete and 'depriving it of autonomous [objective] properties which govern conduct quite independently of the creative and constituting capacities of actors' (Layder, 1981). Certainly many human geographers have become highly sceptical of the account of human agency offered by structuration theory: its emphasis on 'rational action' leaves no conceptual space for passion and desire, considerations that have animated human geography's contemporary interest in subjectivity and processes of SUBJECT FORMATION; and much of this developing work has been informed by a POST-STRUCTURALISM with which Giddens has little sympathy. Indeed, Thrift (1996, pp. 54–5) has argued that most of the lacunae in structuration theory can be traced back to Giddens's limited encounter with post-structuralism. He suggests that this includes its anaemic version of 'structure': 'Giddens over-emphasizes action as individual and never fully considers the ghost of networked others that continually informs that action' (cf. ACTOR–NETWORK THEORY).

Fifthly, and closely connected to the foregoing, Giddens is seen to have an unusually weak understanding of CULTURE. Critics have argued that not only does this contract the generalized contours of structuration theory but it also impoverishes Giddens's understanding of modernity, 'POSTMODERNITY' and the politics of POSTMODERNISM (Gregory, 1994, pp. 123–4; Thrift, 1996, p. 55; Mestrovic, 1998, pp. 25, 221). And it is perhaps the absence of culture – more than anything else – that accounts for the coincidence between the eclipse of Giddens's star in human geography in the 1990s and the rise of a critical CULTURAL GEOGRAPHY to a new prominence within the discipline. DG

References

Archer, M. 1990: Human agency and social structure: a critique of Giddens. In J. Clark, C. Modgil and S. Modgil, eds, *Anthony Giddens: consensus and controversy*. Brighton: Falmer Press, 73–84. · Callinicos, A. 1985: Anthony Giddens: a contemporary critique. *Theory and Society* 14: 133–66. · Chouinard, V. 1997: Structure and agency: contested concepts in human geography. *Canadian Geographer* 41: 363–77. · Dallmayr, F. 1982: The theory of structuration: a critique. In A. Giddens, *Profiles and critiques in social theory*. London: Macmillan, 18–25. · Gane, M. 1983: Anthony Giddens and the crisis of social theory. *Economy and Society* 12: 368–98. · Giddens, A. 1979: *Central problems in social theory*. London: Macmillan. · Giddens, A. 1981: *A contemporary critique of historical materialism, vol. 1: Power, property and the state*. London: Macmillan. · Giddens, A. 1984: *The constitution of society*. Cambridge: Polity Press. · Giddens, A. 1985: *A contemporary critique of historical materialism, vol. 2: The nation-state and violence*. Cambridge: Polity Press. · Giddens, A. 1990: *The consequences of modernity*. Stanford: Stanford University Press. · Giddens, A. 1991: *Modernity and self-identity*. Cambridge: Polity Press. · Giddens, 1994: *Beyond Left and Right: the future of radical politics*. Cambridge: Polity. Stanford, CA: Stanford University Press. · Gregory, D. 1982: *Regional transformation and industrial revolution*. London: Macmillan; Minneapolis: University of Minnesota Press. · Gregory, D. 1989: Presences and absences: time–space relations and structuration theory. In D. Held and J.B. Thompson, eds, *Social theory of the modern societies: Anthony Giddens and his critics*. Cambridge: Cambridge University Press, 185–214. · Gregory, D. 1994: *Geographical imaginations*. Oxford and Cambridge, MA: Blackwell. · Gregson, N. 1989: On the (ir)relevance of structuration theory to empirical research. In D. Held and J.B. Thompson, eds, *Social theory of the modern societies: Anthony Giddens and his critics*. Cambridge: Cambridge University Press, 235–48. · Harris, R.C. 1991: Power, modernity and historical geography. *Annals of the Association of American Geographers* 81: 671–83. · Layder, D. 1981: *Structure, interaction and social theory*. London: Routledge. · Mestrovic, S. 1998: *Anthony Giddens: the last modernist*. London and New York: Routledge. · Pred, A. 1990: *Making histories and constructing human geographies*.

Boulder, CO: Westview Press. · Sayer, D. 1990: Reinventing the wheel: Anthony Giddens, Karl Marx and social change. In J. Clark, C. Modgil, and S. Modgil, eds, *Anthony Giddens: consensus and controversy*. Brighton: Falmer, 235–50. · Thrift, N. 1983: On the determination of social action in space and time. *Environment and Planning D: Society and Space* 1: 23–57. · Thrift, N.J. 1996: *Spatial formations*. London: Sage. · Wright, E.O. 1989: Models of historical trajectory: an assessment of Giddens's critique of Marxism. In D. Held and J.B. Thompson, eds, *Social theory of the modern societies: Anthony Giddens and his critics*. Cambridge: Cambridge University Press, 77–102.

Suggested Reading

Bryant, C.G.A. and Jary, D. 1991: *Giddens' theory of structuration: a critical appreciation*. London: Routledge, chs 4–5. · Giddens (1984). · Gregory (1994), 109–24. · Thrift (1996), 53–61.

subaltern studies Originally 'Subaltern Studies' identified a radical project in contemporary Indian history. The Subaltern Studies collective had its origins in the early 1980s, and owed much to the energies and skills of Ranajit Guha. It set its face against two dominant and, so its architects convincingly claimed, imperial intellectual traditions: (i) a modern secular history, in which the Indian subcontinent was ushered from tribalism, petty brigandage and FEUDALISM into capitalist MODERNITY under the benign tutelage of the Raj; and (ii) a NATIONALIST historiography, that cast a native Indian elite in an heroic role, wresting the STATE APPARATUS from the IMPERIALISTS in order to complete a political trajectory that had nonetheless been inaugurated by the British. The subaltern historians argued that both histories erased the presence – and the POWER – of various subaltern groups, and they produced a rich stream of case studies which were issued as a series (Subaltern Studies): a selection of these has been gathered together in two synoptic collections (Guha and Spivak, 1988; Guha, 1997).

The term 'subaltern' was derived from the work of the Italian Marxist Antonio Gramsci, and 'subaltern studies' also has much in common with the socialist-humanist history of the British historian E.P. Thompson who was deeply interested in writing 'history from below' and recovering the collective agency of exploited, oppressed and marginalized groups. The subaltern historians have retained their affinities with HISTORICAL MATERIALISM; but, in part through their increasing engagement with literary and cultural studies, many of them have also been drawn towards feminism and POST-STRUCTURALISM. These moves have attracted considerable critical discussion, centring on the place of CAPITALISM in their revisionist historiography, on the relations between resistance and accommodation among subaltern groups, and on the compound, fractured constitution of subaltern subjectivities: it is these immensely challenging issues that have brought their work to the attention of audiences outside the specialized circles of Indian historiography, including anthropology (Sivaramakrishnan, 1995) and geography (Gregory, 1994, pp. 183–94).

This wider interest in subaltern studies has involved both theoretical interrogation and empirical development. Particular theoretical interest has been attached to the ways in which the figure of 'the subaltern' exposes the limitations imposed on the recovery of subaltern voices through readings of TEXTS produced under the sign of COLONIALISM (Spivak, 1988): this argument has implications not only for POST-COLONIALISM but for the understanding of HUMAN AGENCY across the field of the humanities and social sciences (Barnett, 1997). Empirical development that has attracted the special interest of human geographers includes an extensive engagement with ecological politics and subaltern groups, often inspired by the work of Ramachandra Guha (Guha, 1989; see also Corbridge and Jewitt, 1997), and a richer understanding of the SPATIALITIES of resistance and accommodation. The work of the subaltern historians has also encouraged similar inter-disciplinary projects on other continents (Rabasa, Sanjines and Carr, 1994). DG

References

Barnett, C. 1997: 'Sing along with the common people': politics, postcolonialism and other figures. *Environment and Planning D: Society and Space* 15: 137–54. · Corbridge, S. and Jewitt, S. 1997: From forest struggles to forest citizens? Joint Forest Management in the unquiet woods of India's Jharkhand. *Environment and Planning A* 29: 2145–64. · Gregory, D. 1994: *Geographical imaginations*. Cambridge, MA and Oxford: Blackwell. · Guha, Ramachandra 1989: *The unquiet woods: ecological change and peasant resistance in the Himalaya*. Delhi: Oxford University Press. · Guha, Ranajit, ed., 1997: *A subaltern studies reader 1986–1995*. Minneapolis: University of Minnesota Press. · Guha, Ranajit and Spivak, G.C., eds, 1988: *Selected subaltern studies*. New York: Oxford University Press. · Rabasa, J., Sanjines, J. and Carr, R., eds, 1994: Subaltern studies in the Americas. A special issue of *Dispositio/n*, 19 (46) [published 1996]. · Sivaramakrishnan, K. 1995: Situating the subaltern: history and anthropology in the Subaltern Studies Project. *Journal of Historical Sociology* 8: 395–429. · Spivak, G. 1988: Can the subaltern speak? In C. Nelson and L. Grossberg, eds, *Marxism and the interpretation of culture*. Urbana: University of Illinois Press, 271–313.

Suggested Reading

Barnett (1997). · Guha (1997). · Shurmer-Smith, P. and Hannam, K. 1994: Subaltern geographies. In their

Worlds of desire, realms of power: a cultural geography. London: Arnold, 124–39.

subject formation, geographies of Subject formations ground our understanding of who we are, as well as our knowledge claims. All geography presumes some theory of subjectivity; even 'objective' SPATIAL SCIENCE rests on a theory of subjectivity as a foundation for 'objective' knowledge. But different theories of the subject provoke different geographical narratives (and vice versa). Harvey reads the subject of CAPITALISM through 'the interlocking concepts of money, society, time and space' (Castree, 1995, p. 287), and Marxist assumptions about CLASS identification have prompted studies of homeownership, residential segregation, and suburbanization, many aimed at understanding the dissolution of class consciousness in Anglo-American countries in the twentieth century. HUMANISTIC GEOGRAPHY, with its emphasis on the ethical responsibility for human agency, invites studies of the social construction of meanings in different LANDSCAPES, and the inauthenticity/authenticity of particular landscapes. Until recently, much of SOCIAL GEOGRAPHY involved locating stable, coherently formed identities (such as ETHNICITY or RACE) in particular places; this was the objective of SOCIAL AREA ANALYSIS. The influences of IDENTITY POLITICS and POST-STRUCTURALISM from the mid-1980s led geographers to be attentive to a wider range of identifications (e.g. GENDER, SEXUALITY, DISABILITY) and problems of overgeneralization. Within FEMINIST GEOGRAPHY, for example, there is now more sensitivity to how the experiences of different groups of women vary. From the perspective of post-structural theories of the subject, this focus on multiplicity is not enough; identity politics (which receive partial credit for the proliferation of politicized identifications) is criticized for taking the fact and stability of identities for granted and for failing to problematize the processes through which identities are created and differentiated.

Debates about the human subject are vast; they lie at the heart of twentieth-century western philosophy; they are difficult to summarize (see Pile and Thrift, 1995, for one attempt). One organizational device is to distinguish between humanist and anti-humanist conceptions of subjectivity (Soper, 1986; see ANTI-HUMANISM). In geography this distinction is often articulated through debates about agency and structure (see STRUCTURATION THEORY). Emphasizing agency, humanist/phenomenological versions of subject formation take identity as given in experience. 'Man' (some feminists argue that the gendering of this term is by no means incidental; see MASCULINISM; PHALLOCENTRISM) is at the centre of the world and, in order to be fully human, has the ethical responsibility to act autonomously, to claim his agency (e.g. Ley and Samuels, 1978; see ETHICS, GEOGRAPHY AND). Anti-humanists decentre the subject insofar as they interpret subjectivity as a regulatory idea and question the capacity and the authority of individuals to direct their actions self-consciously and autonomously. In the most influential anti-humanist *structuralist* account of subjectivity, Althusser argued that subjectivity, especially notions of individuality and citizenship, are ideological constructs (see IDEOLOGY; STRUCTURAL MARXISM). In geography this argument often has been read as economistic, but in cultural studies, particularly film studies, Althusser is credited with exactly the opposite, for opening a realm for ideology separate from the ECONOMY. Drawing on psychoanalysis, Althusser posited a more psychologically complex subject for Marxist theory.

There is considerable variation among post-structuralist theories of subject formation, but they have two broad characteristics: they view subject formation as an effect of POWER relations, and posit the boundaries that define identity as intertwined with processes of disidentification, such that the effect of identification is a fragile and contradictory achievement. To give a sense of the former, in Foucault's post-structuralist anti-humanist history of western subjectivity, subject positions are seen to be constructed within and through DISCOURSE. He argues that, from the eighteenth century, discourses of SEXUALITY and individual rights have altered our perceptions of subjectivity and society, and have acted as media of disciplinary control. They introduced new identities (e.g., the homosexual, the pervert, the hysterical woman), territorialized bodily pleasures as sexual, and brought the individual into new relations with the social through BIOPOWER.

The intertwined processes of identification and disidentification work differently in different theories. Psychoanalytical theories have offered rich resources for thinking about the difficulties of recognizing DIFFERENCE, traced from a young child's initial difficulties of registering sexual difference from a loved parent. From the perspective of POST-COLONIALISM, theorists such as Homi Bhabha have drawn on Freud's notion of the fetish (which functions as a mechanism for both recognizing and disavowing sexual difference) as a way of interpreting the ambivalences of colonial discourse and relations between colonized and colonizer. The concept of *abjection*, which describes the process by which what is reviled in oneself is denied and relocated in another, offers another means for theorizing stigmatizing discourses of ORIENTALISM, racism, ablism and heterosexism. If psychoanalytic theories draw our attention to the processes whereby what is unbearable or disallowed in oneself and our loved ones is cast outside and used to stigmatize others (but imperfectly: our identity is constantly haunted and destabilized by what is disavowed or abject), DECONSTRUCTION offers a reverse perspective, of the way in which identity is always defined in relation to and inhabited by what it is not (the constitutive outside). Recognizing the exclusions that found every identity and the necessity of keeping this process of boundary construction in view have been important ideas for recent theorizing about CITIZENSHIP and RADICAL DEMOCRACY (see also PRIVATE AND PUBLIC SPHERES).

Anti-humanist accounts have been criticized for closing off the possibilities and responsibilities of agency, rights, ethics, and politics. Four responses suggest the opposite. First, discourses are polyvalent; they structure identities without determining them. The identity of 'homosexual' can become a resource for persons thus identified when they demand rights in the name of this identity. So too, the meaning of the term 'queer' has been reworked, from a stigmatizing identity to a critique of heteronormativity (see QUEER THEORY). Second, *individuals are subject to multiple discourses and subject positions* and it is at the disjuncture between various subject positions that agency can be located (Smith, 1988). Third, Butler's theory of PERFORMATIVITY, which posits identities as performative repetitions of an ideal, opens *possibilities for variation and change through repetition*, ones that are closed off by positions that see identities as stable. A fourth response is that psychoanalytic theories that explore the effects of the unconscious widen responsibilities insofar as they call into question our *responsibilities for actions of which we are not conscious*, such as racism and heterosexism (Culler, 1997).

A key area of contemporary theorizing explores the possibilities for new processes of subject formation whereby we come to understand ourselves and others without creating stigmatized others and hierarchies of difference (in which some groups are seen to be superior to others), that is, a critical MULTICULTURALISM. The concepts of CYBORG and HYBRIDITY are two ways of disrupting ideas of pure identities and rigid boundaries. Theorists of radical democracy, such as Mouffe, are sceptical about such a possibility and place emphasis instead on a continual questioning of the process of boundary construction that must, they argue, necessarily exclude. To evade these exclusions is impossible but we can insist on a public sphere in which the lines that discriminate inclusion from exclusion are contestable.

If theories of the subject have always informed geography, what is perhaps new is the extent to which geography is now woven into theories of the subject. Where one is located is constitutive of (and not incidental to) perceptions of self. Thus for Foucault (1990) the designs of European schools and homes are both reflective of and instrumental in creating the sexualized nuclear family. And one may see oneself differently in different PLACES; Blunt (1994) has argued that nineteenth-century British bourgeois women travellers were defined predominantly in terms of (a rather frail) femininity at home, but in their travels, in Africa for example, their gendered identity receded (and their health improved), and their RACE and CLASS positions came to the fore. The constructions of coherent places and identities are intertwined social processes; Anderson (1991) describes how the construction of Chinatown as a stigmatized place apart from the rest of Vancouver was instrumental in cohering a white British Columbian identity. Non-essentialist readings of identity, in which identities are conceived as the outcome of power-laden social (not natural) processes, have thus been read back into the PRODUCTION OF SPACE (Massey, 1994; Sibley, 1995; Natter and Jones, 1997). Places are conceived as open-ended sites of social contestation, and spatial politics involve attending to the moments of closure whereby the identities of places are stabilized and particular social groups claim a natural right to that space. This can involve a dense layering of different identities; Anderson (1996) reworks her earlier argument by considering how gender discourses underwrote discourses of NATION and race in early twentieth-century British Columbia.

Geographies are also at the centre of recent efforts to think about new subject formations of hybridity and flexible borders. Spatial metaphors of nomad, mobility, travel, borderland, THIRD SPACE, and paradoxical space have been used to conceptualize these subjectivities. In some of these discussions, geography functions only as METAPHOR, but the prevalence of geographical terminology in discussions of identity also reflects processes of TRANSNATIONALISM and GLOBALIZATION, and increasingly complex geographies of subject formation, which may lead to pluri-local identifications (distributed across and located in different places) or, ironically, the intensification of localized identities (Watts, 1991).

Theories of identity have led geographers to rethink methodology and theory (see NON-REPRESENTATIONAL THEORY). Calls for reflexivity reflect the understanding that knowledge is a social construct contingent on social location; theories of the unconscious indicate the limits of self-reflexivity (Rose, 1997). Theories of mobile, fragmented identities have encouraged different mapping and writing strategies (Massey, 1997; Pred, 1997). GP

References

Anderson, K. 1991: *Vancouver's Chinatown: racial discourse in Canada, 1875–1980.* Montreal: McGill-Queen's University Press. · Anderson, K. 1996: Engendering race research. In N. Duncan, ed., *BodySpace.* London: Routledge, 197–211. · Blunt, A. 1994: *Travel, gender, and imperialism: Mary Kingsley and West Africa.* New York: Guilford. · Castree, N. 1995: On theory's subject and subject's theory: Harvey, capital, and the limits to classical Marxism. *Environment and Planning A* 27: 269–97. · Culler, J. 1997: *Literary theory: a very short introduction.* Oxford: Oxford University Press. · Foucault, M. 1990: *The history of sexuality, volume 1: An introduction,* trans. R. Hurley. New York: Vintage Books. · Ley, D. and Samuels, M., eds, 1978: *Humanistic geography: prospects and problems.* Chicago: Maaroufa. · Massey, D. 1994: *Space, place and gender.* Oxford: Polity. · Massey, D. 1997: Spatial disruptions. In S. Golding, ed., *The eight technologies of otherness.* London: Routledge, 218–25. · Natter, W. and J.P. Jones III 1997: Identity, space, and other uncertainties. In G. Benko and U. Strohmayer, eds, *Social theory: interpreting modernity and postmodernity.* Oxford: Blackwell, 141–61. · Pile, S. and Thrift, N, eds, 1995: *Mapping the subject: geographies of cultural transformation.* London: Routledge. · Pred, A. 1997: Re-presenting the extended present moment of danger: a meditation on hypermodernity, identity and the montage form. In G. Benko and U. Strohmayer, eds, *Social theory: interpreting modernity and postmodernity.* Oxford: Blackwell, 117–40. · Rose, G. 1997: Situating knowledges: positionality, reflexivities and other tactics. *Progress in Human Geography* 21: 305–20. · Sibley, D. 1995: *Geographies of exclusion.* London: Routledge. · Smith, P. 1988: *Discerning the subject.* Minneapolis: University of Minnesota Press. · Soper, K. 1986: *Humanism and anti-humanism: problems in modern European thought.* London: Hutchinson. · Watts, M. 1991: Mapping meaning, denoting difference, imagining identity: dialectical images and postmodern geographies. *Geografiska Annaler* 73B: 7–16.

Suggested Reading

Culler (1997). · Pile and Thrift (1995).

subsidiarity The principle that a central authority has a subsidiary function, performing only those tasks which cannot be performed effectively at a more immediate or local level. Although not a new concept, subsidiarity has come to prominence in Europe with the growing political significance of the European Union. It was present in embryonic form in the Treaty of Paris that established the European Coal and Steel Community in 1952 and was implicit in the Treaty of Rome in 1956, but it was spelled out explicitly in the Single European Act in 1986, with specific reference to the environment and EU environment policy. Since the Treaty on European Union in 1992, it has become an increasingly important guiding principle for all areas of EU decision-making. Before any function may be handed over to the EU centrally, it must be demonstrated that it can no longer be satisfactorily carried out by any of the levels of decision-making within Member States. However, any transfer of powers must have due regard for national identity and the powers of the regions. For their part, Member States are required to actively facilitate the achievement of EU objectives, as set out in the Treaty on European Union and the other founding treaties. MB

subsistence agriculture A subsistence agricultural system is a complex of functionally related resources and human practices through which a group (a household, a village, a SOCIETY) secures FOOD for its reproduction through its own effort, typically by the direct exploitation of the environment (Nietschmann, 1973). The primary objective is food, whether from hunting, fishing, horticulture or agriculture. Subsistence normally refers to production for use (i.e. use values) as opposed to production for exchange but food may circulate within social networks for ritual, ceremonial and reciprocal exchange purposes, and some food may be sold on the market (i.e. exchange values; see MARXIAN ECONOMICS; NEO-CLASSICAL ECONOMICS). Subsistence agriculture without market involvement of any sort is referred to as a tribal or 'primitive' economy; household subsistence producers with some form of production for sale, and some degree of surplus production over needs, are PEASANTS. Subsistence agriculture is often seen as a form of cultural adaptation by which social groups adapt to and regulate the ECOSYSTEMS of which they are part (see CULTURAL ECOLOGY). Self-sufficient, internally regulated subsistence systems are rare in the modern world as the expansion of the market and production for exchange erodes 'pure subsistence' and what is seen by many as the ecological stability and rational utilization of complex tropical ecosystems. MW

Reference

Nietschmann, B. 1973: *Between land and water: the subsistence ecology of the Miskito Indians, Eastern Nicaragua.* New York: Seminar Press.

substitutionism The products of agriculture present special obstacles and barriers for industrial production. Food, with its necessary links to health, well-being, sociability and CULTURE, represents impediments to the simple notion of the replacement of foodstuffs by industrial products (see APPROPRIATIONISM). But the growth and maturity of the food industry has witnessed a discontinuous but permanent process to achieve the industrial production of food. Goodman, Sorj and Wilkinson (1987, p. 2) refer to the rising proportion of VALUE-ADDED attributable to industrial production in the food system and the gradual replacements of agricultural by non-agricultural products (for example sugar derived from sugar cane, by synthetic sugars) as the twin characteristics of what they call substitutionism (see AGRARIAN QUESTION; AGRO-FOOD SYSTEM). MW

Reference

Goodman, D., Sorj, B. and Wilkinson, J. 1987: *From farming to biotechnology*. Oxford: Blackwell.

suburb An outer district lying within the commuting zone of an urban area, often as a separate political jurisdiction (see COMMUTING). The concept has debatable utility because it is used to describe a wide range of communities and LANDSCAPE forms. Silverstone (1997, p. 4) nevertheless claims that each suburb is the 'embodiment of the same ideal': 'the attempt to marry town and country, and to create for middle classes middle cultures in middle spaces in middle America or Britain or Australia'.

Some suburban differences reflect varying stages of suburban development. In many industrialized countries construction of suburban elite residential environments, distanced from the crowding and pollution of industrial cities, began in the early nineteenth century. By the late nineteenth and early twentieth centuries, suburbanization became a mass phenomenon, as middle- and skilled working-class families moved into residential communities located some distance from paid employment. After the Second World War, this trend was magnified in many countries by freeway construction and governmental restructuring of mortgage financing, which put a single-family house on a small plot of land within the reach of a larger number of households. Post-war suburbanization was buttressed by public policy and media images to resocialize women into the home.

In a number of countries, including Australia, Canada and the United States, the post-war suburb is conceived as a residential, privatized, automobile-oriented, consumerist landscape, which houses a homogeneous grouping of white, middle-class nuclear families. In FEMINIST GEOGRAPHY both the representation and reality of this suburban form have been explored and contested: it has been argued that what is represented as a place of consumption is also a site of production and reproduction, and that the actual landscape form restricts women's access to services and paid employment (England, 1991). Women living in post-war suburbs nevertheless negotiate long commutes to paid employment and the care of their children through carefully-tended informal networks of other mothers (Dyck, 1996).

In MARXIST GEOGRAPHY the construction of the post-war suburban environment has been viewed as a means of staving off an ACCUMULATION crisis and as a mechanism of ideological incorporation (Walker, 1981). In HUMANISTIC GEOGRAPHY suburban landscapes have been criticized as PLACELESS environments, devoid of authentic meaning and opportunities to invest identity in PLACE (Relph, 1981). Contemporary cultural critics are more likely, however, to view suburbs as creative spaces of popular CULTURE. In Silverstone's (1997, p. 6) words: 'Levittown has now become a passable model of postmodern individuality, as standardized houses have been transformed, trees and gardens planted, and the basic structure of the grid and lot have been overlaid by other designs and other models of suburban architecture.' The racialization of US suburbs remains a continuing concern within SOCIAL GEOGRAPHY, although there is some evidence that middle-class African-American households are more prevalent in suburbs in the American north-east and south-east and Asian households more numerous in western US suburbs than in the 1960s

(Frey, 1993). Winddance Twine (1996) underlines the continuing effects on RACE identification of the middle-class ideology of liberal consumerist individualism that she detects in affluent white suburbs; she found that it was only after leaving their suburban family homes that young women of African descent reinterpreted themselves, from white to black.

It has become clear, however, that there is a considerable variability even within the post-war suburban model. In other national contexts, public, non-profit, as well as private, multi-family housing has been constructed in suburban contexts that are, in some cases, well served by public transit (see Popenoe, 1977, for a comparison of American and Swedish suburban environments: see also HOUSING STUDIES). Strong-Boag (1991) doubts that Canadian post-war suburbs were ever as socially homogeneous (in terms of class and ethnicity) as those portrayed in accounts of US suburbs.

Certainly the post-war suburban model provides a poor description of many contemporary suburbs, including those in the US, given the suburbanization of a variety of types of employment, the growing diversity of housing forms and the variety of age groups, household types, CLASSES, and racial and ethnic groups living in them. In Beauregard's words: 'The urban is constantly seeping into the nonurban' (1995, p. 716). Edge cities and gated communities, and neo-traditional towns, are forms that have received considerable attention. EDGE CITIES have been defined by Garreau (1991) by their distinctive clustering of office and retail space and their large numbers of high-waged, white-collar jobs; they are, then, much more than residential and consumption spaces; their residential landscapes tend to be represented as common-interest developments (CIDs: see PRIVATE INTEREST DEVELOPMENTS), such as gated communities (Beauregard, 1995).

Neotraditional towns are defined against this and an earlier suburban model. The 'picture window' of the post-war suburban home has been used to symbolize the decline of both the PRIVATE AND PUBLIC SPHERES (Silverstone, 1997). Conceived as an antidote to this house form and a sprawling, automobile-oriented, privatized suburban landscape, architects of neo-traditional towns (the Miami-based architectural team of Duany and Plater-Zyberk are typically credited with the neo-traditional planning movement) proclaim 'the second coming of the American small town' (quoted in McCann, 1995, p. 213). Drawing upon the early ideas of the urban planner Jane Jacobs (among others), they attempt to reinvigorate COMMUNITY and public life in suburban areas through developments designed with narrow walking paths, short grid-patterned streets, small yards with shallow front yards and short picket fences, and houses with open front porches; all aimed to increase pedestrian traffic and sociability. Social diversity is encouraged through a mix of housing types and tenures. Critics are sceptical about whether this social utopianism amounts to more than a marketing tool and explore how exclusivity and claims to the virtues of neo-traditional suburbs are now drawn, not only against negative images of the city (Till, 1993), but against the traditional suburb, which now may be seen as too socially diverse (Dowling, 1998). GP

References

Beauregard, R. 1995: Edge cities: peripheralizing the center. *Urban Geography* 16: 708–21. · Dowling, R. 1998: Neotraditionalism in the suburban landscape: cultural geographies of exclusion in Vancouver, Canada. *Urban Geography* 19: 105–22. · Dyck, I. 1996: Mother or worker? Women's support networks, local knowledge and informal child care strategies. In K. England, ed., *Who will mind the baby?* London: Routledge, 123–40. · England, K.V.L. 1991: Gender relations and the spatial structure of the city. *Geoforum* 22 2: 135–47. · Frey, W.H. 1993: The new urban revival in the United States. *Urban Studies* 30: 741–74. · Garreau, J. 1991: *Edge city: Life on the new frontier.* New York: Doubleday; McCann, E. 1995: Neotraditional developments: the anatomy of a new urban form. *Urban Geography* 16: 210–33. · Popenoe, D. 1977: *The suburban environment.* Chicago: University of Chicago Press. · Relph, E. 1981: *Rational landscapes and humanist geography.* London: Croom Helm. · Silverstone, R. 1997: *Visions of suburbia.* London: Routledge. · Strong-Boag, V. 1991: Home dreams: women and the suburban experiment in Canada, 1945–60. *Canadian Historical Review* 72 4: 471–504. · Till, K. 1993: Neotraditional towns and urban villages: the cultural production of a geography of otherness. *Environment and Planning D: Society and Space* 11: 709–32. · Walker, R.A. 1981: A theory of suburbanization: capitalism and the construction of urban space in the United States. In M. Dear and A.J. Scott, eds, *Urbanization and urban planning in capitalist society.* London: Methuen, 383–429. · Winddance Twine, F. 1996: Brown skinned white girls: class, culture and the construction of white identity in suburban communities. *Gender, Place and Culture* 3: 205–24.

sunbelt/snowbelt A popular term polarizing the main growing and declining regions of the US economy in recent decades: the contrast is between the older industrial districts of the country's north-east (the snowbelt – sometimes termed either the *frostbelt* or the *rustbelt*) and the rapidly expanding parts of the south and west (the sunbelt). This major shift is usually accounted for by a combination of:

- The increasing COMPARATIVE ADVANTAGE of the sunbelt states, based on their agricultural and energy resources, relatively cheap and non-unionized labour, and attractive environments;
- The processes of regional RESTRUCTURING involved in the creation of a new spatial DIVISION OF LABOUR to counter the low productivity in the traditional industries during economic recession; and
- The substantial volume of federal investment in the southern states, reflecting the politics of the PORK BARREL. The major industries of the sunbelt – aerospace, microprocessors, etc. – are termed the 'sunrise' industries.

The term is now frequently applied in other countries: the expanding industrial corridor along the M4 motorway to the west of London – including Reading, Swindon and Bristol – is sometimes referred to as Britain's sunbelt. RJJ

Suggested Reading

Boddy, M., Lovering, J. and Bassett, K. 1986: *Sunbelt city: a study of economic change in Britain's M4 growth corridor*. Oxford: Clarendon Press. · Hall, P.G. et al. 1987: *Western sunrise: the genesis and growth of Britain's major high-tech western corridor*. London: George Allen and Unwin. · Markusen, A.R. 1987: *Regions: the economics and politics of territory*. Totowa, NJ: Rowman and Littlefield.

sunk costs In production systems, a form of costs which cannot be recovered once committed. Baumol and Willig (1981) are responsible for introducing the concept of sunk costs into formal economic analysis. Recent application of the idea by economic geographers stems from the observation that 'sunk costs represent a nonrecoverable commitment to production in an industry; sunk costs are irrevocably committed to a particular use, and therefore are not recoverable in the case of exit' (Mata, 1991, p. 52). Hence, Clark and Wrigley (1995, 1997) use the concept to enrich their analysis of corporate strategy with respect to the geography of investment, disinvestment, plant closure, and exit from an industry. They note how the existence of significant sunk costs (for example, investments in physical plant that cannot be resold, or continuing liabilities to cover the future cost of pensions for former employees) imposes a degree of immobility on large, multilocational corporate actors. Taking such costs into consideration, options such as firm exit and plant closure are 'extreme decisions' (Clark and Wrigley, 1997), pursued only after many other possibilities have been tried or rejected, since the firm will suffer a significant financial setback. In this sense, the acknowledgement of sunk costs introduces an important complication into the analysis of spatial investment decisions, improving upon simpler theories based on ideas from NEO-CLASSICAL ECONOMICS (Romans, 1965) in which CAPITAL is assumed to be perfectly or near-perfectly mobile. In addition to creating potential barriers to exit from an industry, sunk costs can also produce barriers to entry. If firms are aware that high sunk costs exist in a particular industry, this may discourage them from entering the market in the first place. In this way, as Baumol and Willig originally pointed out, the existence of sunk costs can create the conditions for sustaining monopoly or oligopoly. (See also COST STRUCTURE; DECISION-MAKING; ECONOMIES OF SCALE; RESTRUCTURING.) MSG

References

Baumol, W. and Willig, R. 1981: Fixed costs, sunk costs, entry barriers, and the sustainability of monopoly. *Quarterly Journal of Economics* 95: 405–31. · Clark, G.L. and Wrigley, N. 1995: Sunk costs: a framework for economic geography. *Transactions, Institute of British Geographers* NS 20: 204–23. · Clark, G.L. and Wrigley, N. 1997: Exit, the firm and sunk costs: reconceptualizing the corporate geography of disinvestment and plant closure. *Progress in Human Geography* 21: 338–58. · Mata, J. 1991: Sunk costs and entry by small and large plants. In P.A. Gerosky and J. Schwalbach, eds, *Entry and market contestability*. Oxford: Blackwell, 49–62. · Romans, J.T. 1965: *Capital exports and growth among US regions*. Middletown, CT: Wesleyan University Press.

superstructure A relational notion attempting to locate and signify ideational aspects of SOCIETY (see also INFRASTRUCTURE). In arguing for such a relational interpretation, Marx was, *contra* Hegel, attacking the view that politics and social practice are products simply of ideas and beliefs unrelated to the technical, productive and economic conditions in society. Marx (1968, p. 181) argues instead that 'a legal and political superstructure . . . to which correspond definite forms of social consciousness' rises on 'the real foundation' of the 'relations of production' which constitute the 'economic structure of society'.

A common reading of this argument is that immaterial social, political and cultural conditions are directly determined by the material; the social by the economic. Such a reading not only presupposes that there is an unproblematic distinction between the material (e.g. the economy) and the non-material (e.g. the law) despite the fact that both are based on ideas in practice and both must be produced and reproduced in material forms, but ignores the fact that Marx's suggestion is, in any case, more complex. It refers not only to the general question of material:non-material (infrastructure:superstructure) links/distinctions but also to the related links/distinctions between superstructure and consciousness.

However, the suggestion of a direct determinism seems to be given greater credence by Marx's (1968, p. 182) distinction between the economic conditions of production, which can be determined with the precision of natural science, and the legal, political, religious, aesthetic or philosophic – in short, ideological forms which together form 'the entire immense superstructure'.

Terrell Carver (1982, p. 29) argues that Marx

> was not committed to the view that everything (including consciousness, ideas etc.) is ultimately material or is in principle explicable in wholly material terms, nor was he committed to a view that the realm of ideas is in some sense less real than material things.

The *existence* of material phenomena and consciousness and their combination in people does not presuppose a *dichotomy or dualism* between them. Carver suggests that the distinction being drawn by Marx was that between the *results* rather than the *constituents* of activity: goods and services as distinct from ideas, beliefs and opinions. But in a world in which the symbolic value of consumption is increasingly important, where the ownership of intellectual property is expensively contested, and where the commodification of medical care, religion and the arts becomes increasingly systematic, even this distinction is difficult to sustain (see MODERNISM; POSTMODERNISM). The question of the distinction between the primacy of the material and/or the non-material then shifts back to that concerning the contested relationships between consciousness and matter.

However, it is important not to slip back into a dualistic position here. Marx's presupposition is a triune: living individuals, their activities and the material conditions that they find and hand on to others (Carver, 1982). In this context, the question of the abstract separation between superstructure and infrastructure is less important than their practical overlap and lack of distinction in social practice. Thus CONFLICT and change in the 'infrastructure' are taken up in the 'superstructure' where 'men (sic) become conscious of this conflict and fight it out' (Marx, 1968, p. 182). Under such circumstances, any insistence on determination or complete distinction between infrastructure and superstructure is impossible to maintain. Individuals do not have two forms of consciousness corresponding to whether they are inside or outside the factory gate or office door. And it is in such a context of practice, with all the intended and unintended consequences which result from it, that the legal and political superstructure may be said to arise from the conditions of existence of the relations of production.

In this view, superstructure comes close to the concept of civil society derived from Gramsci (1971) and developed recently by John Urry (1981; see figure in the entry for CIVIL SOCIETY). Civil society forms an integral part of capitalist SOCIAL FORMATIONS overlapping both the ECONOMY and the STATE. It is connected to the former via circulation of capital and to the latter by the law. As well as providing the location for struggle, civil society also provides the location for the production and reproduction of labour. As such, civil society is the primary focus for state planning (see URBAN AND REGIONAL PLANNING), which attempts to cope with the dynamics of social conflict and to rationalize the LANDSCAPE of production within and beyond the factory gate or office door (Cooke, 1983). But even this notion involves a kind of schematic dualism.

E.P. Thompson (1968, p. 9) once wrote: 'We cannot have love without lovers, nor deference without squires and labourers'. Love and deference may be deep structures but the relationship of love and deference must always be embodied in real people and in a real context.

The involvement of real people and real contexts is not insignificant because experience defines the meaning of love and deference, which is, thereby, changed for others. The apparent dualism of infrastructure and superstructure is, in social practice, a duality in which both exist in dialectical relationship (see DIALECTIC(s)). Social existence and practice is, therefore, a practice of multiple determinations through STRUCTURATION rather than a mere conflict between superstructure and infrastructure. It is in such a context that the correspondence between consciousness and superstructure may be grasped. The institutions of the law and formal politics help sustain certain beliefs and desires and to suppress others – which do not, however, disappear.

Such a view may be exemplified within geography by Peter Jackson's (1989) arguments for a materialist CULTURAL GEOGRAPHY. The contested system of shared beliefs, social actions and material representations that constitute CULTURE are grounded in materiality but not in a narrow or determinist fashion. Following Raymond Williams, Jackson suggests (p. 35) that 'the idea of "determination" as "the setting of limits"' effectively restores 'an active conception of human agency but one which is subject to "very definite conditions"' and is thoroughly appropriate for a 'reconstituted cultural geography'. The implication here is that the making of culture may struggle to attempt to transcend those conditions in asserting that there are always political and ideological alternatives notwithstanding the materiality of culture.

Such a reading insists that the superstructure is an integral part of social life – the place where consciousness is developed and struggles occur. It follows from this that the superstructure is neither a free-floating, nor a determined and structured set of ideas but rather a complex of practices conditioned (Marx's word) by the MODE OF PRODUCTION of material life. The distinction between infrastructure and superstructure is, then, an ABSTRACTION from rather than a reflection of reality. RL

References

Carver, T. 1982: *Marx's social theory*. Oxford and New York: Oxford University Press. · Cooke, P. 1983: *Theories of planning and spatial development*. London: Hutchinson. · Cosgrove, D. 1983: Towards a radical cultural geography: problems of theory. *Antipode* 15: 1–11. · Cosgrove, D. 1984: *Social formation and symbolic landscape*. London: Croom Helm. · Gramsci, A. 1971: *Selections from prison notebooks*. London: Lawrence and Wishart. · Jackson, P. 1989 *Maps of meaning*. London and Winchester, MA: Unwin Hyman. · Marx, K. 1968 [orig. pub. 1859]: Preface to *A contribution to the critique of political economy*. In K. Marx and F. Engels, *Selected works*. London: Lawrence and Wishart. · Thompson, E.P. 1968: *The making of the English working class*. Harmondsworth: Penguin. · Urry, J. 1981: *The anatomy of capitalist societies*. London and Basingstoke: Macmillan. · Williams, R. 1973: Base and superstructure in Marxist cultural theory. *New Left Review* 82: 3-16.

Suggested Reading

Jackson, P., Cosgrove, D., Duncan, J. and Mitchell, D. 1996: Exchange. There's no such thing as culture? *Transactions, Institute of British Geographers* NS 21: 572–82. · Mitchell, D. 1995: There's no such thing as culture: towards a reconceptualization of the idea of culture in geography. *Transactions, Institute of British Geographers* NS 20: 102–16.

surface A three-dimensional model of a spatial variable, defined as a single-valued function of either latitude and longitude or grid coordinates. Although geographical surfaces can be represented and analysed as three-dimensional solid objects, cost and convenience usually dictate display in two dimensions, as on a paper map (see MAP IMAGE AND MAP) or computer monitor.

The most common geographical phenomenon treated as a surface is elevation, typically portrayed on TOPOGRAPHIC MAPS by contour lines (see ISOLINES). In most instances elevation contours are captured by a photogrammetrist who traces the intersections of a three-dimensional, stereoscopic model of terrain with horizontal planes of constant elevation (Moffitt and Mikhail, 1980, pp. 335–417). The elevations of these planes and their corresponding contour lines are integer multiples of a fixed contour interval, chosen to strike an appropriate balance between information and clutter. Although elevation is a continuous variable, which in principle can be measured anywhere within the horizontal plane, the contour map is a generalization that reflects the relief and complexity of the terrain, the scale of the photogrammetrist's original map, and the reliability of the aerial photography and plotting instruments.

Many surfaces are estimated from discrete measurements at representative or conveniently accessible sample points. In meteorology and climatology, for instance, configurations of surfaces representing temperature, pressure and other atmospheric variables are interpolated from sparsely scattered observations, either manually or by computer. Although the informed intuition of a trained meteorologist can reflect predictable effects of land cover as well as avoid conceptual inconsistencies in the patterns of isotherms and isobars, interpolation by computer allows precise inverse-distance weighting and the consistent treatment of local trends (Lam, 1983). Interpolation can also generate isoline maps for population density, per capita income and other area data assigned to presumably representative points within census tracts or counties.

Computational statistics offers several specialized estimation methods. TREND SURFACE ANALYSIS yields generalized maps of salient trends. Kriging, a geostatistical technique developed to estimate the grade and tonnage of ore deposits, affords potentially insightful interactive solutions (Oliver and Webster, 1990). FRACTAL surface simulation can generate hypothetical surfaces useful in testing interpolation algorithms and describing theoretical landscapes (Lam and De Cola, 1993).

Surfaces coded for electronic display and analysis are usually represented as either (1) matrices of elevation points aligned along the rows and columns of a uniform grid, or (2) lists of point coordinates describing the location and shape of individual contour lines. Array storage as a digital elevation model allows the ready calculation of slope, aspect and other measures of surface geometry and promotes the ready integration of elevation and slope with other data in a GEOGRAPHICAL INFORMATION SYSTEM.

Oblique views of terrain and other surfaces that mimic solid three-dimensional models can be revealingly dramatic (see VISUALIZATION). Although taller, closer parts of surfaces often hide shorter, more distant features, high-interaction graphics workstations can provide the rotation and tilt needed for a more complete picture as well as cross-sectional and dynamic fly-by views. MM

References

Lam, N. 1983: Spatial interpolation methods: a review. *The American Cartographer* 10: 129–49. · Lam, N.S-N. and De Cola, L. 1993: Fractal simulation and interpolation. In N.S-N. Lam and L. De Cola, eds, *Fractals in geography*. Englewood Cliffs, NJ: Prentice-Hall, 56–83. · Moffitt, F.H. and Mikhail, E.M. 1980: *Photogrammetry*, 3rd edn. New York: Harper and Row. · Oliver, M.A. and Webster, R. 1990: Kriging: a method of interpolation for geographical information systems. *International Journal of Geographical Information Systems* 4: 313–32.

surveillance The institutionalized monitoring of individuals, events and actions. Surveillance typically relies on the production of a time–space grid that segments its field of observation, and for this reason human geography has become interested and involved in the process in two main ways.

On the one side has been a largely technical or instrumental interest, expressed through the collection and analysis of official statistics, often sponsored by STATE or corporate institutions. This interest has been intensified by the development of GEOGRAPHICAL INFORMATION SYSTEMS (GIS) which have considerably enhanced the capacity of those powerful enough to have access to them to maintain routinized and often publicly unaccountable surveillance (see Pickles, 1995).

On the other side, and mirroring those practices, has been a critical interest which has been inspired by the French philosopher Michel Foucault's *Discipline and punish* (1975; trans., 1977; see Driver, 1985). This extraordinarily influential text was ostensibly a history of the modern French prison, but Foucault used those materials to provide an ambitious GENEALOGY of a distinctively modern form of POWER which he called 'disciplinary power'. His analysis had two stages.

In the first instance, disciplinary POWER depended on the installation of geographies of partition: it operated within closed institutions like prisons, where it partitioned and subdivided internal spaces, assigned individuals to their 'proper' places, and subjected them to regular and routinized monitoring (cf. Philo, 1989; Robinson, 1990; Driver, 1993; Crush, 1994). To illustrate his ideas, Foucault used Bentham's eighteenth-century model of the ideal prison – the Panopticon – within whose confines inmates were isolated in their cells where they were constantly liable to visual inspection from a central watchtower. The point of this example was to dramatize the intimacy of the connections between the segmentation of space, VISION AND VISUALITY, and the operation of disciplinary power. Foucault's most controversial claim was that, within a disciplinary apparatus of this kind, the inmates would regulate their own conduct: never knowing whether they were under surveillance or not, they would come to act as though they always were:

> He who is subjected to a field of visibility, and who knows it, assumes responsibility for the constraints of power; he makes them play spontaneously upon himself; he inscribes in himself the power relations in which he simultaneously plays both roles; he becomes the principle of his own subjection.

By such means the regulation of space provided for the 'normalization' of the subject.

In the second instance, Foucault provided an argumentation-sketch in which disciplinary power slowly emerged from these peripheral locations and 'swarmed' towards the centre until, at the limit, the whole surface of society was punctuated with centres of observation. Seen thus, surveillance was indispensable to the formation of what he called *disciplinary society*:

> Our society is one not of spectacle but of surveillance; under the surface of images, one invests bodies in depth; behind the great abstraction of exchange, there continues the meticulous, concrete training of useful forces; the circuits of communication are the supports of an accumulation and centralization of knowledge; the play of signs defines the anchorages of power; it is not that the beautiful totality of the individual is amputated, repressed,

altered by our social order, it is rather that the individual is carefully fabricated in it, according to a whole technique of forces and bodies.

These claims speak directly to the connections between the production and segmentation of space, the BODY and the formation of subjectivities (see SUBJECT FORMATION, GEOGRAPHIES OF). But they also insist on the productive capacities of surveillance and disciplinary power, a sort of operative agency, in contrast to what Foucault took to be the passivity of visual technologies like the SPECTACLE: 'We are neither in the amphitheatre nor on the stage,' he insisted, 'but in the panoptic machine, invested by its effects of power, *which we bring to ourselves since we are part of its mechanism*' (emphasis added).

Many contemporary analyses of 'the surveillance society' have drawn productively on Foucault's theses. They have qualified the diagram of the Panopticon in suggestive and important ways: the reproduction of 'normal' social life takes place within a system of 'imperfect Panopticism' (Hannah, 1997); dispersed and networked systems of surveillance have produced no single, central watch-tower – a masculinized 'Big Brother' – but rather 'a widening, deepening, and broadening range of "Little Brothers"' (Lyon, 1994; Graham, 1998); and the development of new technologies is intimately connected to the production of new spatial practices and new material geographies (Lyon, 1994; Graham, 1998). DG

References

Crush, J. 1994: Scripting the compound: power and space in the South African mining industry. *Environment and Planning D: Society and Space* 12: 301–24. · Driver, F. 1985: Power, space and the body: a critical assessment of Foucault's *Discipline and punish*. *Environment and Planning D: Society and Space* 3: 425–46. · Driver, F. 1993: *Power and pauperism: the workhouse system 1834–1884*. Cambridge: Cambridge University Press. · Foucault, M. 1977: *Discipline and punish: the birth of the prison*. London: Allen Lane. · Graham, S. 1998: Spaces of surveillant simulation: new technologies, digital representations and material geographies. *Environment and Planning D: Society and Space* 16. · Hannah, M. 1997: Imperfect Panopticism: envisioning the construction of normal lives. In G. Benko and U. Strohmayer, eds, *Space and social theory: interpreting modernity and postmodernity*. Oxford and Cambridge, MA: Blackwell, 344–59. · Lyon, D. 1994: *The electronic eye: the rise of surveillance society*. Minneapolis: University of Minnesota Press. · Philo, C. 1989: Enough to drive one mad: the organisation of space in nineteenth-century lunatic asylums. In J. Wolch and M. Dear, eds, *The power of geography*. London: Unwin Hyman, 258–90. · Pickles, J., ed., 1995: *Ground truth: the social implications of Geographic Information Systems*. New York: Guilford. · Poster, M. 1990: *The mode of information: post-structuralism and social context*. Cambridge: Polity Press. · Robinson, J. 1990: 'A perfect system of control?' State power and native locations in South Africa. *Environment and Planning D: Society and Space* 8: 135–62.

Suggested Reading

Crush (1994). · Dandeker, C. 1990: *Surveillance, power and modernity*. Cambridge: Polity Press. · Foucault (1977). · Lyon (1994).

survey analysis The various procedures involved in the collection and analysis of data from individuals, almost invariably using QUESTIONNAIRES.

A survey involves several stages. The first is definition of the research problem, including the formulation of HYPOTHESES and identification of the needed information. The second includes determining the population to be studied, which includes deciding whether SAMPLING will be necessary and, if so, how the sample will be taken. The next stage involves deciding how the hypotheses will be tested (including the analytical techniques to be employed), and is followed by development of a questionnaire (which should include pretest stages and pilot investigations).

After administration of the questionnaires, either by the researchers themselves or contracted to a specialist market research company, the data are prepared for analysis: quantitative data are readily dealt with; qualitative information (such as reported occupations and responses to open-ended questions) has to be handled through the development of coding schemes, increasingly through the use of sophisticated computer software for textual analysis. The data are then usually entered into a computer database and checked for consistency ('cleaning' the data set) before the analyses are conducted, although increasingly the responses are entered directly to a computer by the interviewer (whether at a face-to-face interview or in an interview by telephone) (cf. SECONDARY DATA ANALYSIS). RJJ

Suggested Reading

Dixon, C.J. and Leach, B. 1978: *Questionnaires and interviews in geographical research*. Concepts and techniques in modern geography 18. Norwich: Geo Books. · Sheskin, I.M. 1985: *Survey research for geographers*. Washington, D.C.: Association of American Geographers.

surveying The technology and practice of measuring and recording exact locations or boundaries. As a profession and a technology, surveying has several levels of application and accuracy. At its most precise level, geodetic surveying, or geodesy, focuses on the exact measurement of the earth and other heavenly bodies. At an intermediate level, control surveying establishes a network of monuments and control points with precisely estimated locations that enable cartographers to add meridians and parallels to air photos and large-scale maps (see TOPOGRAPHIC MAP). At the local and least precise level, land surveys provide legal descriptions of real property and help contractors mark the alignments of roads, pipelines and other transport facilities. In addition, hydrographic surveys use depth soundings to identify underwater hazards and delineate navigation channels, and aerial surveys provide earth scientists, foresters and planners with maps and measurements derived from aerial photography or satellite imagery (see REMOTE SENSING).

Although the simplifying assumption of a spherical earth is adequate for small-scale maps (see MAP IMAGE AND MAP), a systematic series of large-scale quadrangle maps with minimal scale error requires that the PROJECTION accommodate a planet with an equatorial axis roughly 1/300 longer than its polar axis. Geodesists acknowledge this flattening at the poles by rotating an ellipse about the earth's axis (Jackson, 1980). The resulting ellipsoid is a practicable compromise between a sphere and the highly complex, largely theoretical geoid. Calibrated to coastal measurements of mean sea level, the ellipsoid provides a reference elevation for inland areas. Geodesists have calculated separate ellipsoids for Europe, North America and other continents as well as global standards such as the WGS 84 (World Geodetic System) ellipsoid, presented in 1984 (Snyder, 1987, pp. 11–13).

Because geodetic measurement is costly and time-consuming, control surveyors rely on networks of triangles anchored by a few highly accurate estimates of length and position. Triangulation based on carefully measured angles and trigonometric tables can carry across a continent the precision of a single carefully measured base line ten miles long. Similar efficiencies accrue to the direct astronomical and chronometric determination of latitude and longitude at a small number of first-order control stations. Triangulation also allows topographic and property surveyors to 'tie into' and share the benefits of more precise, higher-order surveys. Land surveyors, who typically describe a parcel's boundary with a series of lengths and angles, use trigonometry to estimate the error of closure.

Technological advances have reduced the need to measure angles. In the 1970s, electronic distance measurement (EDM) equipment afforded direct measurement of distances and the adoption of trilateration, which bases network calculations on the sides, not the angles, of triangles (Bird, 1989). In the 1990s, increased civilian access to the constellation of geodetic satellites placed in orbit by the United States Department of Defense encouraged widespread use of GLOBAL POSITIONING SYSTEMS (GPS), which provide direct estimates of latitude, longitude and elevation (Hofmann-Wellenhof, 1997). In addition, electronic computing allows surveyors to assess and adjust for errors associated with individual measurements (Mikhail and Gracie, 1981).

MM

References

Bird, R.G. 1989: *EDM traverses: measurement, computation and adjustment*. Harlow, Essex: Longman Scientific and Technical. · Hofmann-Wellenhof, B. 1997: *Global positioning system: theory and practice*, 4th edn. Vienna: Springer-Viennaerlag. · Jackson, J.E. 1980: *Sphere, spheroid and projections for surveyors*. New York: John Wiley and Sons. · Mikhail, E.M. and Gracie, G. 1981: *Analysis and adjustment of survey measurements*. New York: Van Nostrand Reinhold. · Snyder, J.P. 1987: *Map projections – a working manual*. Professional Paper 1395. Washington, D.C.: US Geological Survey.

sustainable development A term that was first used in 1980 in the *World conservation strategy*, but was popularized by the World Commission on Environment and Development (WCED, 1987) in *Our common future*. The term attempts to incorporate various strands of intellectual thought on LIMITS TO GROWTH, NATURE, DEVELOPMENT and POVERTY. Fowke and Prasad (1996) identified at least eighty *definitions* of 'sustainable development', with the most widely known being the WCED's (1987, pp. 8 and 43): 'development that meets the needs of the present without compromising the ability of future generations to meet their own needs'. However, there are also numerous *interpretations* of this definition, plus various terms which sound similar, e.g. 'sustainability', 'sustainable growth', 'sustainable economic growth', 'sustainable economic development' and, as used in Australia, 'ecologically sustainable development' (ESD).

The idea of sustainable development can be traced to the CONSERVATION work of Gifford Pinchot in the United States in the late nineteenth and early twentieth centuries. Pinchot advocated the use of RESOURCES to enable prosperity for current and future generations. This strand of thought informed a number of African-based conferences in the mid-1960s. To achieve conservation of wildlife on game reserves there, it was apparent that adjacent lands had to provide food to overcome rural poverty to assist efforts to prevent hunting of endangered species for food (O'Riordan, 1993). The International Union for the Conservation of Nature and Natural Resources (IUCN) in 1969 defined conservation as the 'management ... of air, minerals, and living species including man, so as to achieve the highest sustainable quality of life' (McCormick, 1995, p. 53). In 1972 this concept was introduced by Maurice Strong to the United Nations Conference on the Human Environment as '*eco-development*'. This term had stronger connotations of self-reliance; its key features are the provision of basic needs starting with the poorest, participation for the COMMUNITY and the use of appropriate technology (O'Riordan, 1993).

The *World conservation strategy* introduced the term 'sustainable development', but it was not widely adopted. In 1987, almost one year to the day after the Chernobyl nuclear catastrophe in the former Soviet Union, the WCED released their report in London. The WCED, popularly known as 'the Brundtland Commission' after its Norwegian chair, Mrs Gro Harlem Brundtland, immediately succeeded in changing the terminology and the terrain for debates about the environment. While the term 'sustainability' had been used in literature that advocated the existence of limits to growth, the Brundtland Commission recognized limits as being 'not absolute limits but limitations imposed by the present state of technology and social organisation on environmental resources and by the ability of the biosphere to absorb the effects of human activities' (WCED, 1987, p. 8). The GLOBAL FUTURE advocated from this analytical base was a form of '*green accumulation*' which involved improving the efficiency of economic growth so that it used less NATURAL RESOURCES, and redistributing the costs and benefits of increased growth with increased EQUITY. The approach is sometimes recognized as a form of '*ecological modernization*'. It includes both *intergenerational* and *intra-generational* equity and equity between so-called 'developed' and 'developing' countries, and also called for equity across CLASS and GENDER barriers.

Our common future had high political acceptability because of its timing, because it built on the work of previous reports such as *Common crisis* and *Our threatened future* (the Palme Report), because it offered a positive message rather than environmental doom and because it provided something for many competing groups. Wealthy countries could continue to have economic growth, but do so more efficiently. *Qualitative* improvements would enable this change to be called 'development', unlike the *quantitative* increases known as growth. They could ignore limits-to-growth thinking that had been influential in the 1970s, and had the potential to regain influence in the late 1980s. Poorer countries could have economic development to overcome poverty, and to achieve some of the material benefits of the wealthy countries. The WCED called for a 'five-to-ten-fold expansion of world industrial output by the time world population stabilises (at twice the present level) sometime in the next century' (WCED, 1987, p. 213). Much to the annoyance of many environmentalists, business groups could use the term 'sustainable', and either replace 'development' with 'growth', or use development to mean growth. This tendency would be less likely to occur if the Australian term 'ecologically sustainable development' (ESD) was adopted and implemented: it is defined as (Commonwealth of Australia, 1992, p. 6):

> using, conserving and enhancing the community's resources so that ecological processes, on which life depends, are maintained, and the total quality of life, now and in the future, can be increased.

This gives greater emphasis to the maintenance of ECOLOGICAL processes, whereas the WCED definition emphasizes development. In the Australian definition there is little doubt about what must be sustained.

The WCED's call for increased economic growth was strongly criticized by more radical environmentalists. The Brundtland Commission report was seen as a technocratic extension of global management. The concerns of Redclift (1987) that 'sustainable development' is an oxymoron were shared by many authors, including feminists and authors writing about DEVELOPMENT (as in Sachs, 1993a). The report's inadequate attempt to address population growth, and the lack of political analysis focusing on the role of TRANSNATIONAL CORPORATIONS (TNCs) in promoting unsustainable practices, were also criticized. Some environmentalists complained that business got the noun (development) and they were left with the supporting adjective (sustainable). Sachs (1993b) was strongly critical of the notion that development should be sustained, because this form of exploitation by wealthy countries was considered the problem. The shift in the term 'sustainable development' to mean 'sustaining development' (rather than sustaining NATURE, ECOSYSTEMS or the earth's life support systems) was encapsulated in a 1992 World Bank report which asked; 'What is sustainable? Sustainable development is development that lasts' (Sachs, 1993b, p. 10). In 1994, the World Bank Group published a report, *Making development sustainable*, which highlights the importance of the question: What is being sustained?

The Brundtland Commission changed the terrain for debate and decision-making. In the period 1987 to 1992, the literature on sustainable development appeared either to focus on the forthcoming follow-up conference (e.g. MacNeill et al., 1991), or to critique the notion of sustainable development from a variety of perspectives (see McManus, 1996). From within ENVIRONMENTAL ECONOMICS, some authors distinguished between different forms of sustainability from a narrow economic focus on capital, with the ability to substitute human-made capital for natural capital (see NATURAL RESOURCES) being the primary distinction between 'very weak', 'weak', 'strong' and 'very strong' forms of sustainability (in Johnston, 1996).

The five-year follow-up to the Brundtland Commission, the 1992 United Nations Conference on Environment and Development (UNCED, sometimes known as the Earth Summit) in Rio de Janeiro, Brazil, was the largest environmental conference ever held. It included representatives from 172 countries (including over 100 heads of state) and more than 8000 media representatives. As Finger (1993, p. 39) recognized: 'Above all, the UNCED process must be seen as an attempt by nation-states and their governments to rehabilitate themselves as pertinent and legitimate actors in the eyes of their citizens.' In Rio, at the same time as UNCED, there were approximately 28,000 participants at the International Non-governmental Organization Forum (INGOF or the Global Forum). The differences in the perspectives of the two conferences can be seen from the documents developed at each. UNCED produced five key documents: *The Framework Convention on Climate Change*, the *Convention on Biological Diversity*, *Agenda 21*, *The Rio Declaration* and *The Forest Principles* (see Grubb et. al., 1993). The Global Forum produced a *People's Earth Declaration*, the *Rio de Janeiro Declaration* and an *Earth Charter*. The Global Forum material contains a greater sense of urgency, calls for more fundamental changes to be made to achieve sustainability and is very critical of both TNCs and international institutions such as the World Bank and the International Monetary Fund.

UNCED did not criticize the role of TNCs. Instead it praised their role and that of business in general in achieving the economic growth that was needed to overcome poverty. The Secretary-General of UNCED, Maurice Strong, was closely advised by the Swiss millionaire Stephan Schmidheiny and the organization he created to influence the UNCED agenda, the Business Council for Sustainable Development (BCSD). Schmidheiny and the BCSD's 1992 publication, *Changing course*, advocated open markets, economic incentives rather than regulation, and economic growth to achieve sustainable development (see Eden, 1996). Rowell (1996) documents the links between the BCSD and the transnational public relations firm Burson–Marsteller, and demonstrates the deliberate way in which they succeeded in influencing the UNCED agenda. Middleton et al. (1993) demonstrate how the notion of sustainable development changed from Brundtland to Rio, with greater emphasis on 'global issues' in Rio. These so-called global issues (such as BIODIVERSITY and greenhouse gases) were the issues that most interested northern hemisphere businesses and governments. The move from eco-development (beginning with the needs of the poorest) through to a business-oriented notion of sustainable development was apparent at UNCED.

The events of 1992 may be interpreted differently depending upon the viewer's ideological perspective. Some see UNCED and the notion of sustainable development as being successful and desirable. They are working within the new PARADIGM of economy plus environment, rather than seeing economic development (often meaning growth) as contrary to ecological futures. Since 1992 there has been less media salience for environmental issues, but more focused activity at local, regional, national and global SCALES. Many local authorities throughout the world are engaged in preparing and implementing *Local Agenda 21* (see Selman, 1996). Many projects which previously would have been identified as environmental protection, or ENERGY-saving, are now presented under the banner of 'sustainable development'. It is sometimes difficult to distinguish between new projects and activities, and those existing projects and activities that have been 'window-dressed' in the latest fashionable term. At the global scale, to the dismay of many environmentalists, the financial leveraging power was gained by the World Bank through their joint management of the Global Environmental Fund. Organizations such as the Commission for Sustainable Development (CSD), the Earth Council and Mikhail Gorbachev's 'Green Cross' continue to operate, but the aspirations of many people at UNCED have not been met. The 1995 United Nations Climate Change Convention in Berlin highlighted the lack of significant changes following UNCED (see GLOBAL WARMING AND GREENHOUSE EFFECT). Small island states protested about their vulnerability to sea-level rises, but the oil producing and consuming countries (almost the remainder of the world) did not address this issue with the integrity they desired, a situation which continued at the Kyoto conference in 1997 in Japan.

The 1997 United Nations General Assembly Special Session (UNGASS, or Earth Summit 2) held in New York City saw over 4000 diplomats, journalists and lobbyists reviewing the progress of the UNCED process: 173 countries, including over 60 heads of state, attended the conference. The small island states recognized that despite all the talk at Rio, and some action towards achieving reductions in greenhouse gas emissions, the wealthy countries were not going to meet their targets and the small island states were still as vulnerable as they had been in the early 1990s. The President of the United Nations General Assembly said achievements since Rio had been 'paltry'. Since the Rio conference in 1992, POLLUTION has been increasing, NATURAL RESOURCES have been decreasing or degraded, BIODIVERSITY continues to decline markedly and POVERTY still threatens over a billion people.

These issues have been studied by geographers for many years before the term 'sustainable development' became fashionable. The early 1990s saw the entry of the term into a number of presidential addresses at geography conferences. This was partly due to media salience, recognition of skills and knowledge within geography, the rejection of some reductionist work on sustainable development emanating from other disciplines, and the possibility that geographers might miss the research funding if they did not get aboard the sustainable development 'gravy train'. Work by Middleton et al. (1993), Kirkby et al. (1995), Eden (1996), Adams (1995), Johnston (1996) and McManus (1996) are just a few examples of geographers addressing sustainable development. Many geographers write in areas that intersect sustainable development, including RURAL GEOGRAPHY and CRITICAL GEOPOLITICS (Dalby, 1996).

Sustainable development is an important concept for the future of the world, and for developments in geography. It will spawn more literature on implementation, critiques of how it is being implemented or diverted from its original meaning, critiques that reject the basic assumptions contained in the term, and give rise to alternative conceptions of how we should relate to nature. Geographers have much to contribute to these debates. The idea of sustainable development is a bridge between geography and compatible disciplines. Beyond that, it is a conduit through which geographers can contribute to a positive future for life on earth. In doing so, geographers are well-positioned to address the most important question in sustainable development: What is being sustained? PM

References

Adams, W. 1995: Sustainable development. In R. Johnston, P. Taylor and M. Watts, eds, *Geographies of global change: remapping the world in the late twentieth century*. Oxford and Cambridge, MA: Blackwell, 354–73; Commonwealth of Australia 1992: *National strategy for ecologically sustainable development*. Canberra: Commonwealth of Australia. · Dalby, S. 1996: Reading Rio, writing the world: the *New York Times* and the 'Earth Summit'. *Political Geography* 15 6–7: 593–613. · Eden, S. 1996: *Environmental issues and business: implications of a changing agenda*. Chichester: John Wiley and Sons. · Finger, M. 1993: Politics of the UNCED Process. In W. Sachs, ed., *Global ecology – a new arena of political conflict*. London and New Jersey: Zed Books, 36–48. · Fowke, R. and Prasad, D. 1996: Sustainable development, cities and local government. *Australian Planner* 33 2: 61–6. · Grubb, M. et al., eds, 1993: *The Earth Summit agreements: a guide and assessment*. London: Earthscan. · Johnston, R. 1996: *Nature, state and economy: a political economy of the environment*, 2nd edn. Chichester: John Wiley and Sons. · Kirkby, J., O'Keefe, P. and Timberlake, L., eds, 1995: *The Earthscan reader in sustainable development*. London: Earthscan. · MacNeill, J., Winsemius, P. and Yakushiji, T. 1991: *Beyond interdependence: the meshing of the world's economy and the earth's ecology*. New York: Oxford University Press. · McCormick, J. 1995: *The global environmental movement*. Chichester: John Wiley and Sons. · McManus, P. 1996: Contested terrains: politics, stories and discourses of sustainability. *Environmental Politics* 5 1: 48–71. · Middleton, N., O'Keefe, P. and Moyo, S. 1993: *The tears of the crocodile: from Rio to reality in the developing world*. London: Pluto Press. · O'Riordan, T. 1993: The politics of sustainability. In R.K. Turner, *Sustainable environmental economics and management: principles and practice*. London: Belhaven. · Redclift, M. 1987: *Sustainable development: exploring the contradictions*. London: Methuen. · Rowell, A. 1996: *Green backlash: global subversion of the environment movement*. London and New York: Routledge. ·

Sachs, W., ed., 1993a: *Global ecology – a new arena of political conflict*. London and New Jersey: Zed Books. · Sachs, W. 1993b: Global ecology and the shadow of 'development'. In W. Sachs, ed., *Global ecology – a new arena of political conflict*. London and New Jersey: Zed Books, 3–21. · Selman, P. 1996: *Local sustainability: managing and planning ecologically sound places*. London: Paul Chapman Publishing Limited. · Schmidheiny, S. and the Business Council for Sustainable Development 1992: *Changing course: a global business perspective on development and the environment*. Cambridge, MA: MIT Press. · World Commission on Environment and Development (WCED) 1987: *Our common future*. Oxford: Oxford University Press.

Suggested Reading

Adams (1995). · Kirkby, O'Keefe and Timberlake (1995). · McManus (1996). · Sachs (1993a). · Selman (1996).

symbolic interactionism A diffuse tradition of social theory which regards the social world as a social product, the meanings of which are constituted in and through social interaction. Craib (1984, p. 72) claims that symbolic interactionism conceives of social life as a conversation: 'the social world shows the same qualities of flow, development, creativity and change as we would experience in a conversation... [and] the world is made up of conversations, internal and external'. Other analogies can be equally salient, however, and Geertz (1983, ch. 1) speaks of a 'refiguration of social thought' around the interpretation of social life variously conceived as a game, as a drama and as a TEXT. Whatever the difficulties of unambiguously characterizing symbolic interactionism – Rock (1979) speaks of its 'deliberately constructed vagueness' – most commentators would have agreed that it had its origins in the CHICAGO SCHOOL of sociology in the1920s (see PRAGMATISM). Contrary to the conventional wisdom of much mainstream URBAN GEOGRAPHY, the Chicago School was not uniquely concerned with the development of a HUMAN ECOLOGY based on brute Darwinian competition (cf. DARWINISM; SOCIAL DARWINISM): Park and Thomas in particular treated communication as 'fundamental to the existence of society' (see Jackson and Smith, 1984, pp. 79–80). Important though these foundations were, however, the principal architect of symbolic interactionism is usually taken to be Mead. It was his *Mind, self and society*, composed posthumously from students' lecture notes and published in 1934, which was used – particularly by one of his students, Blumer, who coined the term 'symbolic interactionism', whereas Mead himself always referred to his 'social psychology' – to formalize its fundamental tenets. According to Craib (1984, p. 73; see also Blumer, 1969), these are as follows:

- Human beings act towards things on the basis of the meanings that the things have for them;
- These meanings are the product of social interaction in human society; and
- These meanings are modified and handled through an interpretative process that is used by each individual in dealing with the signs each encounters.

Craib claims that these three postulates roughly correspond to the three sections of *Mind, self and society*, but that it is now clear that such a summary does considerable violence to the integrity of Mead's work. Joas (1985) has warned that:

> [Symbolic interactionism] cannot be regarded as the authoritative interpretation of Mead's thought. For this theory's understanding both of social organization and of human needs, its reduction of the concept of action to that of interaction, its linguistic attenuation of the concept of meaning, and its lack of any consideration of evolution and history are enormous deviations from Mead's positions and, furthermore, achieved by means of an extremely fragmentary appropriation of Mead's work. Only those aspects of Mead's thought that are completely ignored by symbolic interactionism make it possible to correct this tradition's 'subjectivist' features. (pp. 6–7)

Within human geography, interactionist perspectives have opened up three progressively wider avenues of inquiry. First, a number of authors have continued the ethnographic tradition of the Chicago School to provide compelling accounts of the social construction of specific milieux (for a review, see Jackson, 1985; cf. ETHNOGRAPHY). Second, a more formal thematization of the social construction of PLACE has been proposed. Hence, for example, Ley (1981) identifies a major focus of HUMANISTIC GEOGRAPHY as a recovery of 'the relationship between landscape and identity'. In some part following Mead, Ley argues, its central argument is that: '[P]lace is a negotiated reality, a social construction by a purposeful set of actors. But the relationship is mutual, for places in turn develop and reinforce the identity of the social group that claims them.' Third, and spiralling away from propositions of this sort, is a series of more inclusive theorems about the constitution of society. Elements of interactionism can be found, in their most general form, in Schutz's constitutive PHENOMENOLOGY and in Giddens's

STRUCTURATION THEORY, both of which had a major impact on the development of post-positivist human geography, but it was undoubtedly Berger and Luckmann's *The social construction of reality* (1967) which provided at once the most comprehensive and the most focused engagement of human geography with interactionism. Acutely critical of what elsewhere he calls the 'superorganic' (see Duncan, 1980), Duncan (1978) notes that:

> Interactionism... posits no separation between the individual and society; individual selves are socially constructed. The self is largely a product of the opinions and actions of others as these are expressed in interaction with the developing self... With interactionism there is no need for a transcendental object such as an abstract notion of culture [or] society... to mediate between the individual and society. (p. 269)

(See also Ley, 1982; for a critique, see Gregory, 1982.)

These social constructions constitute a TAKEN-FOR-GRANTED WORLD, Duncan continues, and this is, at least in part, 'dependent on one's relation to a place and the persons associated with that place'. Although Berger and Luckmann said nothing about such relations, Duncan shows how such a place-specific perspective on 'the stranger' or 'the outsider' prompts a recognition of what he calls 'the social construction of *un*reality' (emphasis added). What Berger and Luckmann (1967) do acknowledge, however, is the importance of routinized and repetitive social conduct to the continuity of social life: 'The reality of everyday life maintains itself by being embodied in routines, which is the essence of institutionalisation. Beyond this, however, the reality of everyday life is ongoingly reaffirmed in the individual's interaction with others' (p. 169). This makes it possible to rework their formulations to incorporate the time–space paths traced out in Hägerstrand's TIME-GEOGRAPHY. Although Berger and Luckmann regard the 'spatial structure' of everyday life as 'peripheral to our present considerations', therefore, Pred (1981, p. 7) regards this as a serious mistake:

> [W]hat is wanting, among other things, in the Berger–Luckmann formulation is a spelling out of the detailed means whereby the everyday intersections of individual biographies with institutional activities, at specific times and places, are rooted in previous intersections, at specific times and places, yet simultaneously serve as the roots of future intersections between particular individuals and institutional activities.

Using time-geography in this way, Pred claims, it is possible to expose 'the workings of society'. (See also PRAGMATISM.) DG

References

Berger, P. and Luckmann, T. 1967: *The social construction of reality*. London: Doubleday. · Garden City, NY: Anchor Books. · Blumer, H. 1969: *Symbolic interactionism: perspectives and method*. Englewood Cliffs, NJ: Prentice-Hall. · Craib, I. 1984: *Modern social theory: from Parsons to Habermas*. Brighton: Wheatsheaf; New York: St. Martin's Press. · Duncan, J.S. 1978: The social construction of unreality: an interactionist approach to the tourist's cognition of environment. In D. Ley and M. Samuels, eds, *Humanistic geography: prospects and problems*. London: Croom Helm; Chicago: Maaroufa, 269–82. · Duncan, J.S. 1980: The superorganic in American cultural geography. *Annals of the Association of American Geographers* 70: 181–98. · Geertz, C. 1983: *Local knowledge: further essays in interpretative anthropology*. New York: Basic Books. · Gregory, D. 1982: A realist construction of the social. *Transactions, Institute of British Geographers* NS 7: 254–6. · Jackson, P. 1985: Urban ethnography. *Progress in Human Geography* 9: 157–76. · Jackson, P. and Smith, S.J. 1984: *Exploring social geography*. London: Allen and Unwin. · Joas, H. 1985: *G.H. Mead: a contemporary reexamination of his thought*. Cambridge: Polity Press, see especially ch. 5. · Ley, D. 1981: Behavioural geography and the philosophies of meaning. In K.R. Cox and R.G. Golledge, eds, *Behavioural problems in geography revisited*. London: Methuen, 209–30. · Ley, D. 1982: Rediscovering man's place. *Transactions, Institute of British Geographers* NS 7: 248–53. · Mead, G.H. 1934: *Mind, self and society*. Chicago: Chicago University Press. · Pred, A. 1981: Social reproduction and the time-geography of everyday life. *Geografiska Annaler* 63B: 5–22. · Rock, P. 1979: *The making of symbolic interactionism*. London: Macmillan. · Totowa, NJ: Rowman and Littlefield.

Suggested Reading

Anderson, K. 1987: The idea of Chinatown: the power of place and institutional practice in the making of a racial category. *Annals of the Association of American Geographers* 77: 580–98. · Craib (1984), ch. 5. · Duncan (1978). · Jackson and Smith (1984), 79–86.

symbolization The graphic codes that represent similarities and differences among features and data values on a map. In addition to making visible the otherwise inconspicuous scaled-down versions of geographic features, map symbols help viewers identify patterns and relationships not readily apparent in written accounts or numerical tables (Tufte, 1997, pp. 29–35).

Map symbols usually reflect the dimensionality of the features portrayed. For example, radio towers and accident sites are commonly represented as points, railways and political boundaries as lines, and counties and countries as areas. Map SCALE and context play an important role, though, in determining whether a city or an airport is generalized as a point or an area.

Feature and symbol can differ in dimension. Because solid three-dimensional models are expensive to construct and reproduce, map-makers usually portray terrain and other SURFACES either with contours (ISOLINES) or as perspective block diagrams consisting largely of line symbols. Moreover, because area symbols varying in intensity or pattern are less suited to showing magnitudes than point symbols varying in size, map-makers often portray the populations of countries and provinces with graduated circles centred within their borders. Cartographic animation, which adds time as an active dimension, affords symbols adept at portraying the order, duration and rate of events (DiBiase et al., 1992).

Jacques Bertin (1983) identified six retinal variables that affect the efficiency with which viewers decode map symbols. Because size is most suited for showing variation in magnitude, proportional point symbols are ideal for mapping population size and other count data. And because graytone value is most appropriate for showing variation in intensity, CHOROPLETH maps are effective for mapping growth rates, median income, population density and other intensity measures. Similarly, symbols that vary in hue, shape or pattern, all of which connote difference in kind rather than quantity, are most suited to mapping qualitative differences, whereas orientation symbols like contours, arrows and flow lines provide concise descriptions of directional trends.

Colour is common on TOPOGRAPHIC MAPS, which exploit cultural associations of blue with water and green with vegetation. Pictorial symbols rich in shape cues are especially helpful for general users, most of whom readily associate tiny picnic benches with picnic areas. On orienteering maps, weather maps and other cartographic genres too complex for readily decoded pictorial symbols, efficient MAP READING benefits from standardized symbols familiar to frequent users (MacEachren, 1995, pp. 290–2).

Typographic labels are another important element of cartographic symbolization. As a link between graphic marks and written language, words on maps help users locate specific features and obviate a litany of highly abstract symbols. Because typography has its own visual variables, map authors use the size and style of labels to describe or reinforce similarities or differences among features (Monmonier, 1993, pp. 106–9).

Large or bold labels thus point out a map's more important features, whereas italic type underscores the geographic kinship of rivers, lakes and other hydrographic phenomena.

MM

References

Bertin, J. 1983: *Semiology of graphics: diagrams, networks, maps*, trans. W.J. Berg. Madison: University of Wisconsin Press. · DiBiase, D. et al. 1992: Animation and the role of map design in scientific visualization. *Cartography and Geographic Information Systems* 19: 201–14, 265–6. · MacEachren, A.M. 1995: *How maps work: representation, visualization, and design*. New York: Guilford. · Monmonier, M. 1993: *Mapping it out: expository cartography for the humanities and social sciences*. Chicago: University of Chicago Press. · Tufte, E.R. 1997: *Visual explanations*. Cheshire, Connecticut: Graphics Press.

system A group of elements organized such that each one is in some way interdependent (either directly or indirectly) with every other element: in addition, many analysts also require that the system have a function, goal or purpose (if only the maintenance of the system itself), although this does not imply either conscious goals or deliberate intent (cf. TELEOLOGY), so that systems ideas are akin to those of FUNCTIONALISM. Identification of a system involves delimiting its boundaries, identifying its constituent elements, and defining its function. Some systems may have clear, objective existence (as with a domestic hot-water system or a car engine), but in many geographical studies isolation of a system involves a fairly arbitrary ABSTRACTION of a part from a whole in order to facilitate study: unwise abstractions involve studying CHAOTIC CONCEPTIONS, from which few valid conclusions can be drawn.

Studies of systems have to address four main issues:

- *Whether the system is open or closed.* A closed system has no links to or from a surrounding environment whereas open systems (much more common in geography) have, and interact with their milieux;
- *Whether the system can be divided into subsystems*, clusters of interdependent elements which are only weakly-linked to the remainder of the system;
- *Whether the links involve flows, causal relationships or 'black-box' relationships* (in which the consequence of the link is known – i.e. if A in element x then B in element y – but the causal factors are not); and
- *Whether there is* FEEDBACK *in the system*, such that change in x may stimulate change in y, and this in turn will have an impact on x,

either negative or positive. The interval between a disturbance to a system and the return to an equilibrium state is known as the *relaxation time*.

In geography, the concept of a system is sometimes used relatively loosely to stress the interdependence of phenomena (as in the concept of an ECOSYSTEM), but some analysts (especially physical geographers) have used formal SYSTEMS ANALYSIS methods to examine interdependent phenomena. AMH

Suggested Reading

Bennett, R.J. and Chorley, R.J. 1978: *Environmental systems: philosophy, analysis and control.* London: Methuen; Chapman, G.P. 1977: *Human and environmental systems.* London: Academic Press; Huggett, R.J. 1980: *Systems analysis in geography.* Oxford: Clarendon Press.

systems analysis A mathematical approach to the modelling of SYSTEMS, using techniques developed in control engineering to investigate systems behaviour in response to external stimuli. In their simplest forms, such models include an input (X_t), an output at a later time (Y_{t+n}), and a transfer function S which links the two such that

$$Y_{t+n} = S(X_t)$$

There is an important distinction between models that refer to continuous time and those in which the inputs and outputs occur (or are observed to occur) at discrete time scales: the latter are most common in geography, as in studies using LEAD–LAG MODELS.

Such models can be used to examine the likely behaviour of systems, and their impacts on their environments, even where the transfer function S is derived inductively without any knowledge of the causal mechanisms involved (as in work on LIMITS TO GROWTH; cf. GLOBAL FUTURES and work on urban dynamics: Forrester, 1969).

A particular application of systems thinking which attracted some geographers in the 1960s and 1970s was GENERAL SYSTEMS THEORY, an attempt pioneered by von Bertalanffy (1968) to develop general statements about the common properties of superficially different systems (the search for *isomorphisms*): such searches were exemplified by Woldenberg and Berry (1967), but dismissed as 'an irrelevant distraction' by Chisholm (1967). AMH

References

Chisholm, M. 1967: General systems theory and geography. *Transactions, Institute of British Geographers* 42: 45–52. · Forrester, J.W. 1969: *Urban dynamics.* Cambridge, MA: MIT Press. · von Bertalanffy, L. 1968: *General systems theory: foundation, development, applications.* New York: G. Brazillier; London: Allen Lane. · Woldenberg, M.J. and Berry, B.J.L. 1967: Rivers and central places: analogous systems? *Journal of Regional Science* 7: 129–40.

Suggested Reading

Bennett, R.J. and Chorley, R.J. 1978: *Environmental systems: philosophy, analysis and control.* London: Methuen. · Wilson, A.G. 1981: *Geography and the environment: systems analytical methods.* Chichester and New York: John Wiley.

T

taken-for-granted world Usually a synonym for LIFEWORLD, the term gained currency in human geography through an influential essay by Ley (1977), in which he argued for a recognition of the importance of ordinary, everyday, 'mundane experience' and hence for the incorporation into HUMANISTIC GEOGRAPHY of the intersubjective meanings and intentions that gave shape and direction to 'the contours of the lifeworld'. Ley claimed that the appropriate methodology could be derived from (constitutive) PHENOMENOLOGY – thus 'the phenomenological method provides a logic for understanding the lifeworld' – and in this he followed, among others, Schutz and Merleau-Ponty. A common criticism of their work has been that it pays insufficient attention to the constellations of POWER that are involved in the production and reproduction of social life, and in order to meet these objections Warf (1986) extended Ley's ideas in the direction of STRUCTURATION THEORY. But the taken-for-granted assumed a deeper significance in Husserl's transcendental phenomenology, and his writings were used by Pickles (1985) to clarify 'the pre-theoretical character of the lifeworld and its pre-givenness in relation to all the sciences', i.e. its foundational role (see EPISTEMOLOGY). Pickles saw this as an important corrective to those who would limit so-called 'geographical phenomenology' to 'a capturing of the everyday lifeworld as it is lived'.

Elucidation of the taken-for-granted world is not the unique preserve of phenomenology, however, and the French philosopher Henri Lefebvre provided an important discussion of what he called *everyday life* which intersects with both of these traditions. He treats the taken-for-grantedness of everyday life in the modern world as a product of its 'colonization' by the abstract space of CAPITALISM (see IDEOLOGY; PRODUCTION OF SPACE); but he also sees the everyday as the site of resistance, as the source of an authentic (and in this sense 'foundational') mundanity that has remained untouched by the corrosions of capitalist modernity (Lefebvre, 1991). A different politico-intellectual reading of the taken-for-granted world and its spatiality was provided by another French philosopher, Michel de Certeau (1984), who sought to elucidate the everyday social practices – the myriad informal tactics – through which ordinary people are able to resist the encroachments and strategies of formal, institutionalized apparatuses of power. Neither of these contributions is phenomenological, but they join Ley in accentuating the creativity (rather than passivity) that inheres within everyday life and the supposedly taken-for-granted world, and in this way the concept is given a distinctly subversive cast. DG

References

de Certeau, M. 1984: *The practice of everyday life*. Berkeley: University of California Press. · Lefebvre, H. 1991: *Critique of everyday life*. London: Verso. · Ley, D. 1977: Social geography and the taken-for-granted world. *Transactions, Institute of British Geographers* NS 2: 498–512. · Pickles, J. 1985: *Phenomenology, science and geography: spatiality and the human sciences*. Cambridge: Cambridge University Press. · Warf, B. 1986: Ideology, everyday life and emancipatory phenomenology. *Antipode* 18: 268–83.

Suggested Reading

de Certeau (1984). · Ley (1977). · Pickles (1985), 114–20.

tariff A tax on the value of imported commodities intended to increase their cost to the domestic consumer. Tariffs, the rate of which tend to rise with the stage of processing, are normally designed to regulate imports for a variety of reasons of STATE economic policy. These may include a concern for the balance of payments, the protection of infant industries, strategic sectors and sectors suffering from competition from imports, and retaliation against and protection from dumping. Tariffs may be preferential (favouring some importers over others) or non-discriminatory (extending the treatment of the most favoured nation to all trading partners).

Although it may be implemented on a bilateral basis, trade policy is set within the international context of the General Agreement on Tariffs and Trade (GATT) which began in 1947 with 23 members and, since January 1995, of the World Trade Organisation (WTO) with 123 members then covering more than 90 per cent of world trade. The objectives of the WTO/GATT are to reduce tariffs, to remove other non-tariff barriers (NTBs) which are probably more important than tariffs in influencing the level and composition of international trade and to eliminate trade restriction. Reciprocity and non-discrimination based upon the most favoured nation clause underpin the working of GATT which since its formation in 1948 set out to achieve its objectives via a series of eight negotiating rounds (the latest being the Uruguay Round completed in 1994) and rules governing trade relations emanating from these rounds. Whilst the average level of tariffs was around 40 per cent in 1940, the level in 1995 was about 4 per cent. RL

Suggested Reading

Dicken, P. 1998: *Global Shift: transforming the world economy*, 3rd edn. London: Paul Chapman Publishing, ch. 3.

Taylorism A set of workplace practices developed from the principles of 'scientific management' set out by Frederick W. Taylor (1911), arising from his classic time-and-motion studies of work processes in American factories. Fundamental concepts include the fragmentation of production activities into their simplest constituent components, and the linking together of these fragmented activities into precisely coordinated and closely supervised sequences. Designed to enhance overall efficiency by reducing the scope of activity of individual workers and optimizing the performance of individual tasks, these practices (by their reliance on close supervision) also accentuate the separation of conception and execution of tasks in the workplace.

For this reason, analysts such as Braverman (1974) have associated the widespread introduction of Taylorist principles with the 'deskilling' or 'degradation' of work. The result is a distinctive occupational DIVISION OF LABOUR, in which unskilled workers execute simple, repetitive shop-floor fabrication functions while skilled technical and managerial workers perform functions related to research, product design, process and quality control, coordination, finance and marketing. The economic outcomes for workers under such production systems depend to a large extent on the nature of the wider social and political context in which they are embedded. For example, under the terms of classical FORDISM as it existed within countries such as the USA, the array of institutions governing collective bargaining and wage determination increased the likelihood that even unskilled workers might earn a decent living and enjoy tolerable working conditions. On the other hand, the application of Taylorist work principles in the developing economies of Asia, Africa and Latin America were not normally accompanied by such institutional frameworks, leading to a more 'primitive Taylorization' based on the 'bloody exploitation' of labour (Peck and Tickell, 1994, pp. 286–7).

As Clark (1981) and others have observed, during the post-war period in which Taylorist principles gained their widest acceptance, large firms organized along Taylorist lines would often segregate skilled and unskilled functions in separate plants, producing a spatial division of labour defined by the pre-existing geography of labour supply, wage rates and social relations. The more recent methods of work organization associated with POST-FORDISM are generally regarded as having reversed the task fragmentation and separation of conception and execution characteristic of Taylorism. However, Schoenberger (1997) and others suggest that organizational innovations such as JUST-IN-TIME PRODUCTION were developed by eliminating wasted time in production through the use of precisely the same tools of time-and-motion study pioneered by Taylor himself. MSG

References

Taylor, F.W. 1911: *The principles of scientific management*. New York: Harper and Brothers. · Braverman, H. 1974: *Labor and monopoly capital*. New York: Monthly Review Press. · Clark, G.L. 1981. The employment relation and the spatial division of labor. *Annals of the Association of American Geographers* 71: 412–24. · Peck, J. and Tickell, A. 1994. Searching for a new institutional fix: the after-Fordist crisis and the global–local disorder. In A. Amin, ed., *Post-Fordism: a reader*. Oxford: Blackwell, 280–315. · Schoenberger, E. 1997: *The cultural crisis of the firm*. Oxford: Blackwell.

teleology A theory that events can be accounted for as stages in the movement towards a pre-ordained end which may be determined by those involved, as in various forms of planning, or may be externally defined, as in many religions. (See also FUNCTIONALISM; STAGES OF GROWTH.) RJJ

terms of trade Ratios of prices, volumes, values, or productivities of factors of production embodied within goods traded in exchange. Modifications may be made to indices to distinguish between price changes resulting from changes in costs and changes in demand, and to indicate the effect of the volume of trade upon national income. Improvements/deteriorations in the terms of trade are said to occur when the indices favour goods being sold/bought.

Contrary to notions of TRADE based on theories of COMPARATIVE ADVANTAGE whereby technical change in the core countries would reduce the price of industrial exports so enabling primary exporters to buy larger and larger quantities of industrial imports with given levels of primary exports, the Prebisch–Singer hypothesis states that long-run terms of trade tend to move against primary producers (see, e.g. Mathur, 1991). This is due in part to the low income elasticity of demand for primary products, along with relatively sluggish growth in demand for them, especially in comparison with manufactures and services; technical progress concentrated in industrialized regions enabling reductions in demand for primary commodities; and competitive conditions of supply facing monopsonistic tendencies of demand. Furthermore, the prices of primary products tend to fluctuate over greater amplitudes than those of manufactures because the price elasticity of supply is also low. Such relationships tend to hold back the development of primary producers and lead to policy prescriptions to increase the amount of value added to commodities – to retain or add more of the chain of production within the regions of their production – and so to INDUSTRIALIZATION within the primary producing regions.

However, although classically applied to the economic characteristics of different kinds of *commodities*, a pronounced *geography of power* also shapes terms of trade. The political economy of the geography of the globalizing CIRCUIT OF CAPITAL not only underpins quantitative imbalances in control over supply and demand for commodities but promotes norms of evaluation founded upon capitalist rationalities applied to sectors of economic activity in the cores which are then imposed upon peripheries (see CORE–PERIPHERY MODEL) and their economic activities. Such manoeuvres shape discourses of developmentalism (see DEVELOPMENT) and urban/rural bias (see, e.g. Corbridge, 1982) in developmental strategies as one, largely unquestioned but highly specific, set of concepts of development, is spread through the 'logic' of market exchange and so constrains both thought and practice. RL

References

Corbridge, S. 1982: Urban bias, rural bias and industrialization: An appraisal of the work of Michael Lipton and Terry Byres. In J. Harriss, ed., *Rural development: theories of peasant economy and agrarian change*. London: Hutchinson. · Mathur, P.N. 1991: *Why developing countries fail to develop*. London: Macmillan.

territorial justice The application of principles of SOCIAL JUSTICE (see WELFARE GEOGRAPHY) to territorial units. As such, it may be a principle of the application of area-based policies (see REGIONAL POLICY). But social justice must take account both of the conditions of production of wealth and SOCIAL WELL-BEING and of their distribution. It can, therefore, be given meaning only in the context of a particular set of social relations (see ECONOMIC GEOGRAPHY).

Need must be a primary variable in determining territorial justice and should be complemented by contribution to the common good. However, the problem of measuring such variables in the implementation of territorially based programmes of social justice is complicated by the ECOLOGICAL FALLACY and the appropriateness of the spatial definition of the territorial units. Furthermore, the achievement of territorial justice may exacerbate other forms of injustice. RL

Suggested Reading

Boyne, G.A. and Powell, M. 1993: Territorial justice and Thacherism. *Environment and Planning C: Government and Policy* 11: 35–53. · Herbert, D.T. and Smith, D.M., eds, 1979: *Social problems and the city*. Oxford and New York: Oxford University Press. · Smith, D.M. 1994: *Geography and social justice*. Oxford and Cambridge, MA: Blackwell.

territorial sea The area of sea, beyond its coast and inland waters, over which a STATE claims exclusive jurisdiction. Coastal states have made such claims since classical times, but until the Third UN Convention on the Law of the Sea was fully ratified in 1994, setting the extent of territorial seas at 12 nautical miles, there was no universally accepted definition.

From the late eighteenth century, most coastal states claimed three nautical miles, sufficient for the defence of the realm and for protecting access to inshore fisheries, but a minority laid claim to more extensive tracts. Following the lead of the USA, and later the former USSR, more and more states began to lay claim to 12 nautical mile territorial seas in the first half of the twentieth century. One of the main tasks on the agenda of the Third UN Conference on the Law of the Sea was to broker the agreement that ultimately emerged.

The SOVEREIGNTY of a state extends to the airspace above its territorial seas, as well as to the seabed and the subsoil below. Indeed, its jurisdiction is identical in all but one respect to that exercised over its land: the sole exception is the right of innocent passage through territorial seas granted to international shipping.

Not all states have yet exercised their rights to claim territorial seas up to 12 nautical miles, while others, such as Chile and Ecuador, claim up to 200 nautical miles, but there is a growing acceptance of the UN norm (see LAW OF THE SEA). MB

Suggested Reading

Glassner, M.I. 1990: *Neptune's domain: a political geography of the sea*. Boston: Unwin Hyman.

territorial social indicator A measure of SOCIAL WELL-BEING in a defined territory, referring to either a broad concept or a specific condition – such as health status.

The social indicator movement developed during the 1960s, initially in the USA, in response to growing concern over a wide range of social problems: it was argued that governments should collect and publish social indicators to chart trends in society's social health, alongside well-established economic indicators. Within this movement, geographers argued that territorial social indicators should be developed, so that spatial variations and trends in the country's well-being could be assessed and, if necessary, policies developed to counter identified disparities.

Although an earlier paper by Lewis (1968) extended the related concept of a *'level of living' index* developed by rural sociologists, the seminal geographical work was by Smith (1973), who selected seven sets of indicators to represent different aspects of social well-being: income, wealth and employment; the living environment, including housing; physical and mental health; education; social order; social belonging; and recreation and leisure. Available quantitative indicators were analysed using PRINCIPAL COMPONENTS ANALYSIS to identify the extent and nature of spatial variations across States, across metropolitan areas, and across residential areas within cities. Similar work was reported for England and Wales by Knox (1975) and later studies investigated spatial variations at a variety of scales (e.g. Coates, Johnston and Knox, 1977; Smith, 1977, 1979).

Although the approach has been subject to a number of criticisms, on the selection and nature of the data and the problems of the ECOLOGICAL FALLACY in spatial analyses, for example, the case for mapping spatial variations in social welfare has been widely accepted as a desirable monitoring tool – as indicated by the British 'booming towns studies' (Green and Champion, 1991). A wider range of variables has been incorporated in later studies, including subjective perceptions of the quality of life (Rogerson et al., 1989).

The social indicators movement has substantially fulfilled its original mission (it has its own literature, including the journal *Quantitative Social Indicators*) and the case for territorial disaggregation has also largely been accepted: mapping spatial variations in social well-being is now a standard activity and attention increasingly focuses on understanding their causes and consequences (as in Herbert and Smith, 1989) as well as developing a rigorous theoretical framework for understanding spatial variations in welfare (cf. WELFARE GEOGRAPHY). RJJ

References and Suggested Reading

Coates, B.E., Johnston, R.J. and Knox, P.L. 1977: *Geography and inequality*. Oxford: Oxford University Press. · Green, A.E. and Champion, A.G. 1991: The 'Booming Towns' studies: methodological issues. *Environment and Planning A* 23: 1393–408. · Herbert, D.T. and Smith, D.M., eds, 1989: *Social problems and the city: new perspectives*, 2nd edn. Oxford: Oxford University Press. · Knox, P.L. 1975: *Social well-being: a spatial perspective*. Oxford: The Clarendon Press. · Lewis, G.M. 1968: Levels of living in the north-eastern United States c.1960: a new approach to regional geography. *Transactions, Institute of British Geographers* 45: 11–37. · Rogerson, R.J., Findlay, A.M., Morris, A.S. and Coombes, M.G. 1989: Indicators of quality of life: some methodological issues. *Environment and Planning A* 21: 1655–66. · Smith, D.M. 1973: *A geography of social well-being in the United States*. New York: McGraw-Hill. · Smith, D.M. 1977: *Human geography: a welfare approach*. London: Edward Arnold. · Smith, D.M. 1979: *Where the grass is greener: living in an unequal world*. London: Penguin.

territoriality The assignment of persons and social groups to discrete areas through the use of boundaries. In socio-biology the division of space into discrete areas (TERRITORY) is seen as an evolutionary principle, a way of fostering competition such that the territorially successful will have more surviving offspring. The literature on animal behaviour or ethology offers little more than analogical reasoning for understanding human territoriality, however. More typically, therefore, human territoriality is viewed as the strategy used by individuals, groups and organizations to exercise power over a portion of SPACE and its contents (Sack, 1986. · Vandergeest and Peluso, 1995; Agnew, 1997). This exercise of power can range from the bubble of personal space of an individual person to the spaces associated with membership in different groups, through patterns of territorial regionalism (as, for example, in FEDERALISM) to the division of world-space into territorial NATION-STATES. Beyond its capacity for enabling a space for individual action, territoriality is a relatively efficient way of maintaining centralized control at the same time that a service or activity is provided to a localized population.

Sack (1986) shows how this is done by a variety of organizations, from states and churches to charities and businesses, at a range of geographical SCALES from that of the workplace to the world as a whole. Space is partitioned into territorial cells or units that are grouped together in hierarchical sequence from the basic unit in which work, administration or some other activity is controlled or supervised through intermediate levels at which many managerial and supervisory functions are located, to the top-most level at which central control is concentrated. In this way power is both diffused and controlled at one and the same time to increase administrative efficiency yet maintain centralized control.

There are important cultural and historical dimensions to human territoriality. In different societies the average size of personal space varies from a relatively large envelope (as in Scandinavia) to a very small one (as in Mediterranean Europe). Some churches (such as the Roman Catholic Church) and some STATES (such as the United States) have more complex forms of territorial organization than do others, although all organizations operating over large areas tend to take a territorial form. In the past, churches and polities (states, empires, federations, etc.) were perhaps the most important agents of formal territorial organization but today transnational and global businesses erect territorial hierarchies that cross-cut existing political and religious ones. Subsidiaries and branch plants, plus the flows between them and their suppliers, are organized within such territorial frameworks (Amin and Thrift, 1997). Even as one type of territoriality (that of churches or states, for example) might fade in importance, therefore, another (such as transnational business) emerges to replace it. Though varying in form and complexity, territoriality is always with us.

Territoriality is put into practice through the following mechanisms: (1) popular acceptance of *classifications* of space (e.g. 'ours' versus 'yours'); (2) *communication* of a SENSE OF PLACE (where territorial markers and BOUNDARIES have meaning); and (3) *enforcing control* over space (by means of SURVEILLANCE, POLICING and legitimation). The mixture of consent and coercion in strategies of territoriality is often referred to as HEGEMONY. JAA

References and Suggested Reading

Agnew, J.A. 1997: *Political geography: a reader*. London: Edward Arnold, section two: The spatiality of states, 31–92. · Amin, A. and Thrift, N. 1997: Globalization, socio-economics, territoriality. In R. Lee and J. Wills, eds, *Geographies of Economies*. London: Edward Arnold, 147–57. · Sack, R.D. 1986: *Human territoriality: its theory and history*. Cambridge: Cambridge University Press. · Vandergeest, P. and Peluso, N. 1995: Territorialization and state power in Thailand. *Theory and Society* 24: 385–426.

territory A general term used to describe a portion of space occupied by a person, group, local economy or STATE. When associated with the state the term has two specific connotations. The first is of territorial SOVEREIGNTY, whereby a state claims exclusive legitimate control over a given area defined by clear boundaries. The second is of an area not fully incorporated into a state, as with a colonial territory (British Antarctic Territory) or a frontier region (Northern Territory in Australia). More generally, territory refers to the bounded SOCIAL SPACE occupied and used by different social groups as a consequence of following strategies of TERRITORIALITY. Sometimes territory is used as equivalent to such spatial concepts as PLACE and REGION, conveying the sense of a clustering or concentration of people or activities (e.g. Storper, 1997). It also finds increasing use as a metaphor; as, for example, in the 'territory' of the geographer, with reference to the academic division of labour, or the 'territory' of the imagination, to symbolize both an inner psychological 'terrain' and personal ownership of it. This latter metaphor betrays the modern origins of the term as associated with state sovereignty: in the definition of private property rights guaranteed by the state and the modern 'self' owning or investing exclusively in its territory (Wikse, 1977; Agnew, 1994). JAA

References and Suggested Reading

Agnew, J.A. 1994: The territorial trap: the geographical assumptions of international relations theory. *Review of International Political Economy* 1: 53–80; Storper, M.J. 1997: Regional economies as relational assets. In R. Lee and J. Wills, eds, *Geographies of Economies*. London: Edward Arnold, 248–58; Wikse, J.R. 1977: *About possession: the self as private property*. University Park, PA: Penn State University Press.

text A set of signifying practices commonly associated with the written page but over the past several decades increasingly broadened to include other types of cultural production such as LANDSCAPES, MAPS, paintings as well as economic, political and social institutions (Cosgrove and Daniels, 1988; Duncan and Duncan, 1988; Harley, 1991; Benko and Strohmayer, 1997; cf. ART, GEOGRAPHY AND). Since the nineteenth century, textual analysis has been associated with the HERMENEUTIC method of Wilhelm Dilthey and others. According to this method, an interpretation is produced which results from the interaction between the text being studied and the intellectual framework of the interpreter. Throughout the twentieth century, competing methods of textual analysis have been put forward such as STRUCTURALISM, which would include semiotics, and POST-STRUCTURALISM, which includes DISCOURSE analysis and DECONSTRUCTION. These textual methods of analysis, once largely confined to such fields as literature, religion, and history within the humanities, have diffused as part of the 'linguistic turn' within the social sciences. An important consequence of this DIFFUSION is that the humanities have become an important source of method and theory for the social sciences, and as a consequence the oft-noted divide between the social sciences and the humanities has become blurred.

Once the notion of text has been expanded to include types of cultural production other than writing then the assumption is made that these productions, whether they be landscapes or political institutions, have a text-like quality. There is also recent literature in critical CARTOGRAPHY on maps as cultural texts (Harley, 1991; Jarvis, 1998). Ricoeur (1971) attempts to demonstrate that this assumption has merit by first posing two questions: is the model of the text a good PARADIGM for social science?, and is the textual method of interpretation relevant? He offers four reasons why the answer to both questions should be yes. First he argues that the principal characteristics of written discourse also describe social life. For example, as meaning in written discourse is concretized through inscription, so recurrent behaviour in the built environment becomes concretized. Second, just as within written works an author's intentions and the reception of the text often fail to coincide, so institutionalized patterns of action are frequently detached from their collective agents. Third, as written texts are reinterpreted in the light of changing circumstances, similarly social events are subject to continual reinterpretation. Fourth, while the meaning of a text is unstable due to its dependence upon the interpretations of its different readers, so social action and institutions are open to a range of interpretations.

It is probably within anthropology that we find the most developed notion of social action as text. Geertz (1973, 1988) was the first anthropologist to systematically develop the notion that CULTURE is a text. He interprets culture as a text to be read by an ethnographer as one might read written material. He further argues that it is not simply ethnographers who read cultures, rather such reading is practised by all those who live within a culture. Hermeneutic and post-structural notions of text have served to problematize the notion of REPRESENTATION in ETHNOGRAPHY and geography (Marcus and Fischer, 1986; Pred, 1990; Barnes and Duncan, 1991). There are important EPISTEMOLOGICAL and ETHICAL issues surrounding the notion of representation. One is the question of the translatability of cultural difference and another is the question of the morality of speaking for others (Spivak, 1988; Duncan and Sharp, 1993; McEwan, 1998). Some of the closest readings of texts in the recent geographical literature occur in the study of travel writing and in particular the gendered nature of travel writing. Blunt and Rose (1994) and McEwan (1998) argue against ESSENTIALIST notions of women's travel writing (see TRAVEL WRITING, GEOGRAPHY AND).

There is an ongoing debate in geography about the nature and usefulness of the text METAPHOR. Some have argued that it leads to IDEALISM and away from concerns with the material world (Mitchell, 1995). Others have argued that written texts and other cultural productions with text-like qualities such as landscapes are material realities and that it is unnecessary and unhelpful to separate texts (or even ideas and discourses) from other aspects of reality (Duncan and Duncan, 1996; Schein, 1997).

Another concept of importance is *intertextuality*, the textual context of a literary work. Tyler (1987) has argued that although most empirical work is portrayed as objectivist it can be better described as intertextual, that is, mediated by a traditional corpus of monographs and theories. Furthermore, it is not simply academic accounts of the world which are intertextual; the world itself is intertextual. PLACES are intertextual sites because texts and discursive practices based upon texts are (re)inscribed in social practices, institutions and landscapes (Duncan, 1990; Duncan and Duncan, 1997). JD

References

Barnes, T. and Duncan, J., eds, 1991: *Writing worlds: discourse, text and metaphor in the representation of landscape*. London: Routledge. · Blunt, A. and Rose, G., eds, 1994: *Writing women, writing space: colonial and post colonial geographies*. New York: Guilford. · Benko, G. and Strohmayer, U., eds, 1997: *Space and social theory*. London: Blackwell. · Cosgrove, D. and Daniels, S., eds, 1988: *The iconography of landscape: essays on the symbolic representation, design and use of past environments*. Cambridge: Cambridge University Press. · Duncan, J. 1990: *The city as text: the politics of landscape interpretation in the Kandyan kingdom*. Cambridge: Cambridge University Press. · Duncan, J. and Duncan, N. 1988: (Re)reading the landscape. *Environment and Planning D: Society and Space* 6: 117–26. · Duncan, J. and Duncan, N. 1997: Deep suburban irony. In R. Silverstone, ed., *Visions of suburbia*. London: Routledge. · Duncan, J. and Duncan, N. 1996: Reconceptualizing the concept of culture in geography. *Transactions, Institute of British Geographers* NS 21: 572–82. · Duncan, N. and Sharp, J. 1993: Confronting (re)presentations. *Environment and Planning D: Society and Space* 11: 473–86. · Geertz, C. 1973: *The interpretation of cultures*. New York: Basic Books. · Geertz, C. 1988: *Works and lives: the anthropologist as author*. Cambridge: Polity Press. · Harley, B. 1991: Deconstructing the map. In T. Barnes and J. Duncan, eds, *Writing worlds: discourse, text and metaphor in the representation of landscape*. London: Routledge, 231–47. · Jarvis, B. 1998: *Postmodern cartographies*. London: Pluto Press. · Marcus, G.E. and Fischer, M.M.J. 1986: *Anthropology as cultural critique: an experimental moment in the human sciences*. Chicago: Chicago University Press. · McEwan, C. 1998: Cutting power lines within the palace: countering paternity and eurocentricism in the geographical tradition. *Transactions, Institute of British Geographers* NS 23: 371–84. · Mitchell, D. 1995: There's no such thing as culture. *Transactions, Institute of British Geographers* NS 20: 102–16. · Pred, A. 1990: *Lost words and lost worlds: modernity and the language of everyday life in late nineteenth century Sweden*. Cambridge: Cambridge University Press. · Ricoeur, P. 1971: The model of the text: meaningful action considered as text. *Social Research* 38: 529–62. · Schein, R. 1997: The place of landscape. *Annals of the Association of American Geographers* 87: 660–80. · Spivak, G. 1988: Can the Subaltern Speak? In C. Nelson and L. Grossberg, eds, *Marxism and the interpretation of culture*. London: Macmillan. · Tyler, S. 1987: *The unspeakable: discourse, dialogue and rhetoric in the postmodern world*. Madison: University of Wisconsin Press.

Suggested Reading

Barnes and Duncan (1991). · Blunt and Rose (1994). · Duncan (1990). · Ricoeur (1971). · Schein (1997).

thematic map A special-purpose map (see MAP IMAGE AND MAP) presenting a single category of information, as on a map of geology, land use, mortality, trade routes or vegetation. In depicting similar features or facts, thematic maps are functionally different from general-purpose or reference maps, which juxtapose unlike features, such as cities, political boundaries, rivers, roads and terrain. Thematic maps, which began to appear in the late seventeenth century, address spatial structure, rather than the mere existence or location of geographical phenomena (Robinson and Petchenik, 1976, pp. 116–20). MM

Reference

Robinson, A.H. and Petchenik, B.B. 1976: *The nature of maps: essays toward understanding maps and mapping*. Chicago: University of Chicago Press.

theory A set of connected statements used in explanation. The nature and status of theories differ among philosophies of social science (cf. EPISTEMOLOGY).

Within POSITIVISM, a theory comprises a set of hypotheses and constraining conditions which, if validated empirically, assume the status of LAWS, so that the theory structures understanding of the relevant portion of the empirical world. These linked coherent statements, which are assumed to be universal in their application, stimulate future research: deduction and speculation from the known (the validated theory) to the unknown (the HYPOTHESIS) guide production of future knowledge.

Within IDEALISM there are no universals, only the individual theories resident in each person's mind which are used to guide action and which may be refined, even changed, according to its outcome (see also PRAGMATISM). In this context, human action is directed by personal theories not external ones. Various forms of STRUCTURALISM and POSTMODERNISM contend that since understanding is contextually achieved, usually through interpersonal interaction and shared cultural appreciations, then theories are outlooks shared by people from the same position within society (cf. POSITIONALITY; SITUATED KNOWLEDGE).

In REALISM a theory is a means of conceptualizing reality which provides a mental framework for its apprehension; the test of a theory is not its validation against empirical evidence, therefore, but rather its coherence and, especially, its practical adequacy. A theory is adequate for an individual if the understanding that it provides is sufficient for a satisfactory life; for the social scientist, it must provide a basis for understanding and, potentially, changing society. Realists argue that because societies are open systems in which the same conditions are rarely reproduced, theories cannot, as positivists contend, be used to predict the future; they can only illuminate the past and the present and provide guidance to an appreciation of the future. RJJ

Suggested Reading

Harvey, D. 1969: *Explanation in geography*. London: Edward Arnold. · Keat, R. and Urry, J. 1981: *Social theory as science*, 2nd edn. London and Boston: Routledge and Kegan Paul. · Sayer, A. 1992: *Method in social science: a realist approach*, 2nd edn. London: Routledge.

thick description A term coined by the philosopher Gilbert Ryle and introduced into social science by Clifford Geertz (1973), referring to ETHNOGRAPHIC descriptions based on intensive investigations of informants' actions and their interpretations of their own actions placed within a specific cultural context. Thick description is contrasted with 'thin description' based on the tenets of behaviourism or on survey research (cf. BEHAVIOURAL GEOGRAPHY; SURVEY ANALYSIS), where a detailed description of the informants' meaning system and broader social context is not always considered necessary. Thick description is a type of HERMENEUTIC rather than PHENOMENOLOGICAL method in that it represents the researcher's interpretation of her or his informants' interpretations. JD

References

Geertz, C. 1973: *The interpretation of cultures*. New York: Basic Books.

Thiessen polygon A polygon including a single data point, or node, and bounded by line segments equidistant between the included point and nearby nodes. All locations within the polygon lie closer to the included data point than to any other node, and its sides are the perpendicular bisectors of lines connecting nearby nodes. In addition to delineating areas of dominance around points, Thiessen polygons (also called Voronoi polygons) provide a framework for the triangulated irregular network (TIN) data structure, which describes a three-dimensional terrain SURFACE based on elevations measured at irregularly spaced data points (Peucker and Chrisman, 1975). MM

Reference

Peucker, T.K. and Chrisman, N. 1975: Cartographic data structures. *The American Cartographer* 2: 55–69.

third space Third space is a space produced by those processes that exceed the forms of knowledge that divide the world into binary oppositions. Bhabha (1990) argues that third space is a consequence of HYBRIDITY, for example; he suggests that certain forms of POST-COLONIAL knowledges challenge the division of the world into the West and the rest by producing third spaces in which new IDENTITIES can be enacted. For Bhabha (1994, p. 39), third space is a position from which it may be possible 'to elude the politics of polarity and emerge as others of ourselves'. Some geographers have used the term to displace oppositional categories in geographical analysis; Routledge (1996) has used the term to displace the opposition between academic theorizing and political activism, for example (see also Pile, 1994; cf. ACTIVISM AND THE ACADEMY). Soja (1996), drawing on Lefebvre (1991), offers the most sustained discussion of the status of this SPACE. He argues that it involves a notion of space which displaces many of the binary oppositions through which geographers have often conceptualized space itself: for example, this space is simultaneously material and symbolic, and it also eludes the distinction Soja detects in much Western philosophy between dynamic time and static space. For Soja (1996, p. 11), 'thirdspace' is 'simultaneously real and imagined and more'. This 'more' is where Soja locates the critical potential of third space. Third space is more because it both contains binary ways of thinking about space but also exceeds them with a lived intractibility to interpretive schemas that allows for a potentially emancipatory practice. In third spaces, new things happen and this disrupts old and dominant ways of thinking and doing. Thus discussions of third space aim to reconceptualize ways of thinking about space in order to remake understandings of the world. (See also DIALECTIC(S).) GR

References

Bhabha, H. 1990: Interview with Homi Bhaba: the third space. In J. Rutherford, ed., *Identity: community, culture, difference*. London: Lawrence and Wishart, 207–21. · Bhabha, H. 1994: *The location of culture*. London: Routledge. · Lefebvre, H. 1991: *The production of space*, trans. D. Nicholson-Smith. Oxford: Basil Blackwell. · Pile, S. 1994: Masculinism, the use of dualistic epistemologies and third spaces. *Antipode* 26: 255–77. · Routledge, P. 1996: The third space as critical engagement. *Antipode* 28: 399–419. · Soja, E.W. 1996: *Thirdspace*. Oxford: Basil Blackwell.

Third World A term coined by French social scientists in the 1950s to denote the growing number of non-aligned STATES reluctant to take sides in the Cold War. As a category, it was intended 'to designate the embattled territory between the two superpowers' (Sachs, 1992, p. 3). During the late 1950s and early

1960s, the term came increasingly to be used as a way of representing an alternative mode of social development and of distinguishing societies engaged in often violent anti-colonial struggles and in resisting the NEO-COLONIALISM of the USA and former colonial powers.

Although institutionalized by the Bandung Conference of 1955 at which the main influence was that of Jawaharlal Nehru (Ahmad, 1992), Berger (1994, p. 259) argues that 'none of the ways in which the term has subsequently been used are easily extrapolated from the meeting itself' which involved clearly aligned states, no government from Latin America or Oceania (yet to experience decolonization) and not all the Asian and African countries. Soviet and Chinese variants of Third Worldism emerged and political links were formed with the new left in North America, Europe and Japan. Not surprisingly, the Vietnam war, exemplifying and represented as a national struggle for liberation from imperialist powers (see IMPERIALISM), proved to be a decisive influence on the geopolitical relations of the USA in the Third World and in ways of theorizing UNDERDEVELOPMENT.

Although the term has a meaning associated with the struggles of a diversity of countries to liberate themselves from external oppression and control, it is also frequently used more loosely to denote underdeveloped countries in general – in Africa, Asia and Latin America. But even countries like China, never ruled from Europe, were subject – primarily for economic reasons – to European military force from the seventeenth century onwards and so were severely influenced by colonial relations. Used in this way, the term represents a form of Orientalist thinking (Said, 1985; see ORIENTALISM): the imposition of a discourse on others.

Such a representation facilitates theories of MODERNIZATION – including military modernization theory, involving the development of a powerful élite to see through development programmes, the politics of order approach exemplified by the Brandt Commission's (1980) *North-South* report and, more recently, neo-liberal notions based on the operation of the 'free market' (with its freedom sustained of course by the intervention of the IMF and the World Bank and programmes of structural adjustment imposed upon many countries seeking western aid) – which both accepts underdevelopment as a DISCOURSE and as a homogeneous condition and sees it as an internal problem to be solved by adopting Western models of DEVELOPMENT (see, e.g. ROSTOW MODEL) assisted, notionally at least, by a Brandt-style opening up of Western markets.

Given the colonial histories of many countries in the Third World, it is, however, not surprising that the political systems of many of them are founded on the European model of the NATION-STATE. But Orientalist thought also influences more radical theories like DEPENDENCE and even those placing state and CLASS or MODE OF PRODUCTION at the centre of analysis which see underdevelopment as an essentially homogeneous and externally driven condition so denying internal historical geographies either as formative influences, or as formative alternatives.

Despite the designation of up to five 'worlds', the notion of worlds is misleading (see, e.g. Hettne, 1990) for at least four reasons. First, it implies a degree of separation between them in a globalizing world already influenced by imperialism and neocolonialism which have left their political, economic and cultural marks on both subjugated and imperial nations. However, a form of separation does exist as the links between the advanced economies of the world intensify at the expense of the Third World and as the contacts between the former and the latter become increasingly selective. Secondly, despite efforts to stimulate and sustain Third World unity in the struggle for liberation, nationalist conflicts – not least those between Vietnam, Cambodia and China in the late 1970s – undermined international solidarity and action. Thirdly, the increased degree of polarization within a global world ECONOMIC GEOGRAPHY, along with the collapse of state SOCIALISM and the insertion of capitalist social relations even in a communist state like China, suggests not a reduction of worlds but a multiplication including the production of material conditions characteristic of Third World societies within the USA, Western Europe and Japan. Fourthly – and relatedly – the emergence of the newly industrializing countries (NICs; see NEW INTERNATIONAL DIVISION OF LABOUR) in Latin America, Eastern Europe and, most symptomatically, in South-East Asia represents a form of dependent development (but see Corbridge, 1986, ch. 4; Harris, 1987) which is, nevertheless – and notwithstanding the financial crisis in Asia which began in 1997 and was caused primarily by the relationships between financial capital in developed economies and borrowers in the NICs – a further differentiation of the global economic geography. Singapore, for example, is emerging as a global financial centre and countries like South Korea, Malaysia and Taiwan were (before the financial crisis) becoming significant overseas investors and the base of some major Transnational Corporations.

The highly diverse (see Krugman, 1989) countries of the loosely designated Third World contain over 70 per cent of the population of the world. At one extreme are the members of OPEC and, at the other, countries such as Kampuchea, Bangladesh, Lao PDR, Bhutan and Ethiopia – the poorest of the poor.

Not only are the variations in well-being between developing countries much greater than those between industrialized countries but also variations between *different parts of the same developing country* tend to be much greater. In particular the differential between urban and rural areas is especially great (Dicken, 1998, p. 446).

The United Nations has abstracted the 25 least developed countries as a separate group. Today this group is rapidly becoming known as the 'Fourth World' or, if the OPEC group is also considered separately, as the 'Fifth World'. The World Bank distinguishes between low-income countries, lower and upper middle-income countries – including the dozen or so Newly Industrializing Countries, high income industrialized countries, capital-surplus oil exporters and the former centrally planned economies. The average per capita income of the high income industrialized countries is over 60 times greater than that of the 51 low-income countries identified by the World Bank.

Dominance in the global economic geography is constantly under competitive threat: 'the new, global economic system is . . . highly dynamic, highly exclusionary, and highly unstable in its boundaries' (Castells, 1996, p. 102). This dynamism, argues Castells, reflects global evaluations of four geographically uneven sources of competitiveness:

- technological capacity (the science–technology–industry–society (STIS) system;
- access to a large, integrated affluent market;
- differential between production costs and market prices; and
- political capacity of institutions to steer growth strategy of regions/countries.

On such bases, 'developed Asia' (NICs plus Japan) will account for 30 per cent of world manufacturing by 2000 (western Europe 25 per cent; USA 18 per cent).

The crisis of 1997/1998 in South-East Asia will slow this process but the inclusion of China magnifies its effects. Castells suggests that the Asian Pacific economic geography is segmented amongst five distinct networks of economic power:

- Japanese corporations;
- Korean corporations;
- long-established US corporations in electronics and finance;
- the 'China circle': ethnic Chinese capital linking Hong Kong, Taipei, Singapore; and
- 'overseas' Chinese, all with direct links to China, including Chinese central government and local states.

Thus he concludes (1996, p. 112):

> The emergence of Asian Pacific fast-growth capitalism is, with the end of the Soviet Empire and the process of European unification, one of the most important structural changes taking place in the world at the turn of the century.

At the other end of the spectrum of development (defined by Castells as the simultaneous improvement in living standards, structural change in production and increased competitiveness)

> some rural regions of China, India and Latin America, entire countries around the world [especially in sub-Saharan Africa], and large segments of the population everywhere are becoming irrelevant (*from the perspective of dominant economic interests*) in the new pattern of international division of labor, and thus they are being socially excluded. (Castells, 1996, p. 113; emphasis in original)

Castells (1996) points to the increased polarization within the world economic geography and suggests that GLOBALIZATION has already led to the 'end of the Third World' and 'the rise of the Fourth World' (Castells 1997). This represents a geography of SOCIAL EXCLUSION – to the point of redundancy especially in Africa (but see Agnew and Grant, 1997) – at a global scale. It asks the most profound and critical questions of the point of development. At the same time, it queries analyses of development and underdevelopment which are not capable of recognizing local and global influences on the idea of development. The assumption of universal notions of development prevents an escape both from deterministic models and from doctrines of development (see DEVELOPMENT) imposed on the Third World:

> Most of the disciplines and organisations concerned with the study . . . and generation of polices related to, the 'Third World', continue to be shaped by a set of assumptions that flow from a conception of history [which, it might be added, has no geographies]

as linear progression from a condition of political and economic 'underdevelopment' and 'tradition', to a state of liberal democratic industrialism and modernity. The 'Third World' and its history [and geography!] has been created and understood primarily in terms of the failure of the countries of Latin America, Africa, Asia and Oceania to become idealised industrial democracies of North America and Western Europe. (Berger, 1994, p. 266)

The task, therefore, is to reinsert the geography, to begin to allow people to make their geographies in conditions of their own choosing. RL

References

Agnew, J. and Grant, R. 1997: Falling out of the world economy? Theorising 'Africa' in world trade. In R. Lee and J. Wills, eds, *Geographies of economies*, ch. 18. London and New York Arnold, 219–28. · Ahmad, A. 1992: *In theory: classes, nations, literatures*. London: Verso. · Berger, M.T. 1994: The end of the 'Third World'? *Third World Quarterly* 15 (2): 257–75. · Brandt, W. 1980: *North–South: a programme for survival. Report of the Independent commission on international development issues*. London: Pan. · Castells, M. 1996: *The rise of the network society. The information Age: Economy, society and culture*, vol. I. Cambridge, MA and Oxford: Blackwell. · Castells, M. 1997: *End of millennium. The information age: economy, society and culture*, vol. III. Cambridge, MA and Oxford: Blackwell. · Corbridge, S. 1986: *Capitalist world development. A critique of radical development geography*. Houndmills: Macmillan. · Dicken, P. 1998: *Global shift: transforming the world economy*, 3rd edn. London: Paul Chapman Publishing. · Harris, N. 1987: *The end of the third world*. Harmondsworth: Penguin. · Hettne, B. 1990: *Development theory and the three worlds*. Harlow: Longman. · Krugman, P.R. 1989: Developing countries in the world economy. *Daedalus* 118: 183–203. · Sachs, W. 1992: Introduction. In W. Sachs, ed., *The development dictionary. A guide to knowledge as power*. Johannesburg: Witwatersrand University Press; London and New Jersey: Zed Books, 1–5. · Said, E. 1985: *Orientalism*. London: Penguin.

Suggested Reading

Berger (1994). · Crow, B., Thomas, A. et al. 1983: *Third world atlas*. Milton Keynes and Philadelphia: Open University Press.

Tiebout model An argument for a large number of competing local government units in an area, offering a range of 'service-taxation packages'. According to Tiebout (1956), large local governments are inefficient because they cannot react to the great diversity of demand for locally provided public services (see PUBLIC GOODS) and the willingness to pay for them. Fragmentation of local government is thus more efficient (especially within an urban area) because each unit can tailor its service provision and tax requirements to meet a particular set of demands and consumers (householders and/or other land users) can choose to locate in that unit which is closest to their preferences. Consumer mobility will ensure that provision and preferences are matched (see FISCAL MIGRATION), and a local government unit that fails to attract residents will have to change its service-tax package to ensure viability.

Tiebout's model provides a theoretical justification for local government and underpins aspects of the 'consumer sovereignty' arguments promoted strongly during the 1980s by the 'New Right'. It is based on strong assumptions regarding consumer information and mobility, however, and its validity as a guide to policy has been questioned by those who point to the constraints on mobility which many people suffer. To them the fragmented local government system in most US metropolitan areas is seen not as a paradigm example of the model in action but rather as a device for the affluent and powerful in society to create 'tax havens' from which, through exclusionary ZONING practices, those less well-off than themselves are excluded. RJJ

Reference

Tiebout, C.M. (1956) A pure theory of local expenditures. *Journal of Political Economy* 64: 416–24.

Suggested Reading

Johnston, R.J. 1984: *Residential segregation, the state and constitutional conflict in American urban areas*. London and New York: Academic Press. · Whiteman, J. 1983: Deconstructing the Tiebout hypothesis. *Environment and Planning D: Society and Space* 1: 339–54. · Zodrow, G.R., ed., 1983: *Local provision of public services: the Tiebout model after twenty-five years*. New York and London: Academic Press.

time-geography An approach to human geography that treats time and space as resources that enter directly into the constitution of social life. The basic ideas were developed by the Swedish geographer Torsten Hägerstrand and his associates at the University of Lund ('the Lund School') in the 1960s, 1970s and early 1980s. Time-geography is at once a development of a longstanding view of geography as HUMAN ECOLOGY (Hägerstrand described time-geography as a 'situational ecology') and an attempt to advance human geography and the other social sciences in the direction of CONTEXTUAL theory. Accordingly, Hägerstrand's ideas emphasize the continuity and connectedness of sequences of events that take place in situations bounded in time and space and whose outcomes are thereby mutually modified by their common localization (Hägerstrand, 1976, 1984).

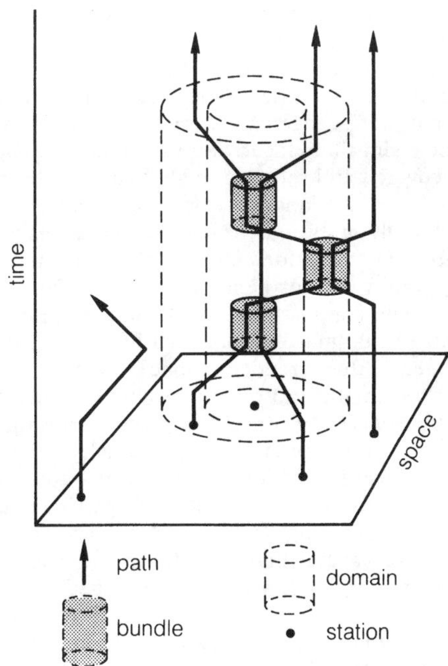

time-geography *Hägerstrand's web model*

Although the first formal discussions of time-geography appeared in the 1960s, it had its origins in an earlier investigation of what Hägerstrand called the 'population archaeology' of Åsby in central southern Sweden. It was then that he thought of depicting individual biographies as paths in time and space; but he was unable to devise a notation capable of describing the intricacies of a 'forest' of time–space paths and so turned instead to the exploration of generalized SOCIAL NETWORKS. It was this investigation which culminated in his models of spatial DIFFUSION and, in particular, in the concept of the MEAN INFORMATION FIELD (Gregory, 1985). But Hägerstrand returned to his original problem and eventually developed an elementary time–space notation from standard Lexis–Becker diagrams used in demography.

His basic framework can be represented as a web model (see figure) spun across four basal propositions:

(1) Space and time are resources on which individuals have to draw in order to realize projects.

(2) The realization of any project is subject to three constraints:

Capability constraints, which limit the activities of individuals through their own physical capabilities and/or the facilities which they can command. These constraints define individual prisms, which contains sets of feasible time–space paths flowing through a constellation of accessible stations, e.g. farms, factories, schools, shops.

Coupling constraints, which define where, when and for how long an individual has to join with other individuals, tools and materials in order to produce, transact or consume. Coupling constraints define time–space bundles.

Authority or 'steering' constraints, which impose conditions of access to and modes of conduct within particular time–space domains.

(3) These constraints are interactive rather than additive, and together they delineate a series of possibility boundaries which mark out the paths available for individuals or groups to fulfill particular projects. These boundaries correspond to an underlying and evolving 'logic' or 'structure' whose disclosure requires a way of 'dealing with POWER in space–time terms of considerable conceptual precision' (Hägerstrand, 1973).

(4) Within these structural templates, competition between projects for 'free paths' and 'open space–times' is usually the 'central problem for analysis' and is mediated by specific institutions which seek to maintain an essential time–space coherence (Hägerstrand, 1973, 1975).

These claims have been read in different ways. A number of writers, including Hägerstrand himself, have attributed a profound NATURALISM to time-geography. Certainly, Hägerstrand's (1973) belief that the human being can be considered 'a central elementary particle' and that human geography can, in consequence, be reconstructed around the systematic time–space recording of events in a LANDSCAPE something like 'the bubble-chamber of the physicist' reveals a deliberate physicalism; and his debt to the biological sciences is disclosed in his desire 'to incorporate certain essential biotic and ecological predicates' within human geography and the social sciences more generally. Other writers have represented time-geography as another STRUCTURALISM: the distinction between a repertoire of *possible* time–space paths and a concrete configuration of trajectories *realized* within these structural templates was supposed to be formally equivalent to Saussure's distinction between *langue* (language) and *parole* (speech) (Carlstein, 1982). Both naturalism and structuralism displace human subjects from their formulations, and in fact one of the most consistent criticisms of Hägerstrand's model has been its relegation of HUMAN AGENCY in the broadest of senses. Hägerstrand describes the realization of projects with compelling originality but he says little about their constitution or accomplishment by knowledgeable and skilled actors (Buttimer, 1976). The relegation of the human subject in this way reduces social life to a form of what Sartre called seriality, in which subjects regard themselves and others as objects, and critics have claimed that this limits Hägerstrand's spatial ONTOLOGY to objective rather than a fully 'social' space (Schatzki, 1991). More particularly, Rose (1993, p. 28) criticized time-geography's erasure of 'the emotional, the passionate, the disruptive, and the feelings of relations with others'.

Some geographers have sought to develop more socialized versions of time-geography. In the 1980s many writers drew attention to the immanent convergence between time-geography and STRUCTURATION THEORY, and claimed that Hägerstrand's graphical representations made visible the 'material logic' of structuration: the 'cement' binding individuals and institutions into a coherent matrix (Pred, 1981; Thrift, 1983). Perhaps the two most ambitious empirical attempts to work with these ideas were Pred's studies of agrarian change and urban change in Sweden (Pred, 1986, 1990), which made effective use of time-geographic diagrams to illustrate a series of propositions about the restructuring of economic and social life. Pred was interested in more than mapping paths and projects, however, and in both cases he sought to show how these changing routines fed into and out of the production, negotiation and contestation of social meaning. Similar concerns animated Dyck's (1990) important time-geographic study of mothering, which demonstrated how conceptions of IDENTITY, self-esteem and mothering were constructed through regular relationships with other women in a diversity of LOCALES. 'Woman' and 'motherhood' thus emerged from her study as categories whose meanings are situationally defined, and the social construction of space was shown to involve much more than the logistical exercise conveyed in time-geography's vocabulary of time–space budgets, time–space packing and the like: Dyck was able to show how the production and reproduction of routines in time and space entered directly into the construction of social meaning.

Much of this work sought to harness the methodological power of time-geography; but the 1990s have seen the development of two streams of criticism that have taken the conceptual bases of time-geography in altogether more novel directions.

On the one side, critics charged conventional time-geography with a MASCULINISM. The claim that Hägerstrand's diagrams finally uncovered and revealed in all their complexity the 'inner workings' of social life is an extraordinarily ambitious, even imperial assertion: 'There are no hidden corners into which time-geography cannot penetrate' (Rose, 1993, p. 38). The supposed power of time-geography rests on its 'mastery' of social life by a visual strategy that renders space transparent, unproblematic and fully knowable (see VISION AND VISUALITY). From this perspective it is thus entirely appropriate that Hannah (1997) should use Hägerstrand's graphical system to illustrate the SURVEILLANCE of life-paths within a system of panopticism. But Rose's objections go much farther than this, for at the heart of time-geography is what she identified as the 'imaginary body': a body whose social and cultural markings by 'RACE', GENDER and SEXUALITY are wilfully erased by mapping it as 'an elementary' – and, by implication, a 'universal' – 'particle'. Critiques of this kind have fed into a developing stream of work on the BODY. Many of these recent studies owe little or nothing to time-geography, but some of them have drawn on Hägerstrand's ideas to 'map the logic of corporeality' and illuminate the ways in which human subjects are constituted through situated social practices (Pile and Thrift, 1995).

On the other side are those geographers who have been unimpressed by Hägerstrand's diagrams for quite other reasons. Far from seeing such graphical representations as methodologically powerful, these critics have noted that most of the empirical work that has been carried out under the aegis of time-geography has been confined to the small-scale, short-term and essentially individual level; that it typically focuses on the time–space intersections of individual paths and institutional projects, with little regard for the changing structural templates and station configurations that make them possible. Identifying a substantial gap between theoretical ambition and empirical achievement, Hoppe and Langton (1988, 1994) have thus sought to develop the conceptual base of time-geography in such a way that it can help 'to produce a coherent account of how individuals, society and milieu combine into processes operating over longer time spans and at larger geographical scales'.

Their rich empirical analysis of the transition to capitalism in western Ostergötland in Sweden centred on the concept of a 'livelihood position'. They defined a livelihood position as 'the set of resources, divisible or indivisible, owned or otherwise acquired, which sustains the livelihood of an individual or household'. These sets could never be satisfied at a single location in space, Hoppe and Langton argued, but they elected to focus less on the webs between different stations at a point in time (what Pred (1977) called 'the choreography of existence') and more on the ways in which people moved through a sequence of livelihood positions over the course of their lifetimes. A study of this kind clearly makes considerable demands of archival sources and requires sophisticated methods of nominal linkage, but it is much more than a longitudinal social history. Its purpose is to recover the movement of people through livelihood positions as an intrinsically geographical process. Thus Hoppe and Langton do not treat 'stations' as points on a plane – the classical logic of LOCATION THEORY – but instead conceptualize them as 'structured bundles of partial livelihood positions'. They then use the livelihood positions maintained by a project at a station to define its 'production structure', which enables them to show – empirically – how the change from a peasant society to capitalism in western Ostergötland was expressed 'in the production structures which represent the projects through which the economic system is sustained and organised'. They also show how the suite of stations on which livelihood positions depended both increased and changed into new, more complex configurations as capitalist MODERNIZATION proceeded. DG

References

Buttimer, A. 1976: Grasping the dynamism of the lifeworld. *Annals of the Association of American Geographers* 66: 277–92. · Carlstein, T. 1982: *Time resources, society and ecology*. London: Allen and Unwin. · Dyck, I. 1990: Space, time and renegotiating motherhood: an exploration of the domestic workplace. *Environment and Planning D: Society and Space* 8: 459–83. · Gregory, D. 1985: Suspended animation: the stasis of diffusion theory. In D. Gregory and J. Urry, eds, *Social relations and spatial structures*. London: Macmillan, 296–336. · Hägerstrand, T. 1973: The domain of human geography. In R.J. Chorley, ed., *Directions in geography*. London: Methuen, 67–87. · Hägerstrand, T. 1975: Space, time and human conditions. In A. Karlqvist, L. Lunqvist and F. Snickars, eds, *Dynamic allocation of urban space*. Farnborough: Saxon House, 3–14. · Hägerstrand, T. 1976: Geography and the study of interaction between society and nature. *Geoforum* 7: 329–34. · Hägerstrand, T. 1978: Survival and arena: on the life-history of individuals in relation to their geographical environment. In T. Carlstein, D. Parkkes and N. Thrift, eds, *Timing space and spacing time. Vol. 2: Human activity and time-geography*. London: Edward Arnold, 122–45. · Hägerstrand, T. 1982: Diorama, path and project. *Tijdschrift voor Economische en Sociale Geograpie* 73: 323–56. · Hägerstrand, T. 1983: In search for the sources of concepts. In A. Buttimer, ed., *The practice of geography*. Harlow: Longman, 238–56. · Hägerstrand, T. 1984: Presence and absence: a look at conceptual choices and bodily necessities. *Regional Studies* 18: 373–80. · Hannah, M. 1997: Imperfect panopticism: envisioning the construction of normal lives. In G. Benko and U. Strohmayer, eds, *Space and social theory: interpreting modernity and postmodernity*. Cambridge, MA and Oxford: Blackwell, 344–59. · Hoppe, G. and Langton, J. 1988: Time-geography and economic development: the changing structure of livelihood positions on farms in nineteenth-century Sweden. *Geografiska Annaler* 68B: 115–37. · Hoppe, J. and Langton, G. 1994: *Peasantry to capitalism: western Ostergötland in the nineteenth century*. Cambridge: Cambridge University Press. · Pile, S. and Thrift, N.J., eds, 1995: *Mapping the subject: geographies of cultural transformation*. London: Routledge. · Pred, A. 1977: The choreography of existence: some comments on Hägerstrand's time-geography and its effectiveness. *Economic Geography* 53: 207–21. · Pred, A. 1981: Social reproduction and the time-geography of everyday life. *Geografiska Annaler* 63B: 5–22. · Pred, A. 1986: *Place, practice and structure: space and society in Southern Sweden 1750–1850*. Cambridge: Polity Press. · Pred, A. 1990: *Lost words and lost worlds: modernity and the language of everyday life in late nineteenth-century Stockholm*. Cambridge: Cambridge University Press. · Rose, G. 1993: *Feminism and geography: the limits of geographical knowledge*. Cambridge: Polity. · Schatzki, T. 1991: Spatial ontology and explanation. *Annals of the Association of American Geographers* 81: 650–70. · Thrift, N. 1983: On the determination of social action in space and time. *Environment and Planning D: Society and Space* 1: 23–57 [reprinted in Thrift (1996)]. · Thrift, N.J. 1996: *Spatial formations*. London: Sage.

Suggested Reading

Dyck (1990). · Hägerstrand (1973). · Hoppe and Langton (1994), 41–6, 334–8.

time–space compression 'Processes that so revolutionize the objective qualities of space and time that we are forced to alter, sometimes in quite radical ways, how we represent the world to ourselves' (Harvey, 1989). Consistent with his vision of historico-geographical materialism, Harvey treats time–space compression primarily as the product of what Marx (and other nineteenth-century writers) identified as the compulsion to 'annihilate space by time' under CAPITALISM, shaped by the rules of commodity production and capital ACCUMULATION. Harvey explained that he deliberately used the word 'compression' because 'a strong case can be made that the history of capitalism has been characterized by speed-up in the pace of life, while so overcoming barriers that the world sometimes seems to collapse in upon us'. As this suggests, the concept of time–space compression is intended to have an experiential dimension that is missing from concepts of TIME–SPACE CONVERGENCE and TIME–SPACE DISTANCIATION. Harvey pays particular attention to the ways in which time–space compression dislocates the HABITUS that gives social life its (precarious) coherence: implicated in a crisis of representation, its consequences are alarming, disturbing, threatening; a 'maelstrom' and a 'tiger', time–space compression under the sign of capitalist modernity induces 'foreboding', 'shock', a 'sense of collapse' and, ultimately, 'terror' that translates into a 'crisis of identity' (Harvey, 1989, 1990, 1996, pp. 242–7).

Harvey's description of the experience of time–space compression in these terms conjures up the sublime. The sense of being overwhelmed by the scale and sheer power of the world was a persistent motif in modern Western aesthetics in the eighteenth and nineteenth centuries: in the sublime 'we are forcibly reminded of the limits of our dwarfish imaginations and admonished that the world as infinite totality is not ours to know' (Eagleton, 1990, p. 89). The sublime reappears in late twentieth-century postmodern thought, wherein the Marxist critic F. Jameson (1991) memorably despairs at 'the suppression of distance' and the 'perceptual barrage of immediacy from which all sheltering layers and intervening mediations have been removed'.

This synoptic account radicalizes an argument proposed by the conservative critic Daniel Bell in *The cultural contradictions of capitalism* (1978). In his view, 'physical distance' was 'compressed' by new systems of transportation and communication at the turn of the nineteenth and twentieth centuries, and what he called 'aesthetic distance' was in its turn compressed by a corresponding stress on 'immediacy, impact, sensation and simultaneity' that he took to be characteristic and indeed constitutive of the cultural formations of MODERNISM. Harvey's account takes this two steps further, by (i) wiring such crises of REPRESENTATION to basal crises of capital accumulation; and (ii) reading the cultural formations of POSTMODERNISM as symptoms of the heightened intensity of a new round of time–space compression produced by a regime of FLEXIBLE ACCUMULATION at the close of the twentieth century (see Gregory, 1994, pp. 406–14).

These are undoubtedly suggestive theses, and it is vitally important to understand that Harvey intends the concept of time–space compression as a contribution to more than academic debate: it is also a political construct, whose implications extend far beyond a radical critique of postmodernism and POSTMODERNITY into a series of propositions about political struggle and political organization in the face of the exploitations and oppressions of contemporary capitalist GLOBALIZATION (Harvey, 1995). And it is on both these grounds – political and intellectual – that his original formulation has been subject to critical attention, extension and reformulation by other scholars. Analytically it is possible to distinguish two lines of engagement, but these distinctions are matters of convenience and it will be obvious that each stream braids into the other. On one side is a series of reflections on Harvey's representation of time–space compression. In particular, why do so many intellectuals like Harvey feel threatened when their 'normal' maps of the world fail them? Is their 'cartographic anxiety' symptomatic of a challenge to the supremacy of an all-seeing masculinist subject-position and its ability to render space as transparent and fully knowable ('mappable')? (Deutsche, 1996; see also O'Tuathail, 1996). On the other side is a series of arguments about Harvey's explanation of time–space compression. In particular, is it possible to understand time–space solely in terms of CLASS relations and capitalism? How is it possible to reinstate the multiple and compound geographies of time–space compression that seem to disappear from Harvey's account? (see Gregory, 1994, pp. 413–14). These twin streams are articulated around the pivotal METAPHOR of 'compression': what does it imply, and what does it leave unsaid and unseen?

Major interventions include the following:

(1) Time–space compression cannot be reduced to the logic of capital accumulationand the circulation of money. To be sure, capital circulation is a highly significant structural dimension of contemporary time–space compression, but it is not the only one (Massey, 1993). In the longer term, time–space compression has been instrumental in the production of systems of COLONIALISM and IMPERIALISM – in articulating political and cultural as well as economic relations between metropolitan societies and colonial societies, and in the formation of transnational public spheres – in ways that are not reducible to the imperatives of capital accumulation. They are also inextricably connected to global questions of GEOPOLITICS (O'Tuathail, 1996) and TRANSCULTURATION.

(2) Time–space compression is socially differentiated. Thus Massey (1993) insisted that groups and individuals are differentially positioned in relation to flows and circulations: some people are able to intervene in the process of time–space compression and so shape its direction and intensity, while others are marginalized and even excluded. Massey acknowledged the importance of subject-positions constituted through CLASS relations, consistent with the emphasis of Harvey's theorization, but drew attention to the ways in which subject-positions were also constituted through relations of GENDER, SEXUALITY and 'RACE'. Her comments conjured up a comprehensive grid of agency and affect, of position and power, which she called 'the POWER-GEOMETRY of time–space compression'. But to Bridge (1997) the concept of a power-geometry remained 'strangely elusive', and he provided a more detailed series of topological theorizations drawing on social exchange theory, social network analysis and ACTOR–NETWORK THEORY that could, so he said, provide a more substantial access to the connections between positionality and subjectivity.

(3) Harvey's treatment of time–space compression undertheorizes not only social relations but also social practices. Kirsh (1995) argued that the original metaphor of time–space compression drew attention away from the social processes and practices involved in the colonization of 'lived space' by 'abstract space'. In particular, the technologies that sustained the annihilation of space are also implicated in the production of new kinds of social space (cf. PRODUCTION OF SPACE). ACTOR–NETWORK THEORY was again advertised as a means of disclosing what Kirsch called 'the technics of spatialization'. In a parallel series of essays that centred on the technical tranformations in the circulation of money that lie at the heart of Harvey's own theses, Thrift successfully established that 'new forms of electronic detachment have produced new forms of social involvement': that contemporary processes of time–space compression still depend on the intimacy of interpersonal contact (Thrift, 1997).

(4) Time–space compression treats PLACE as passive: the physical metaphor of time–space compression thematizes places as bounded sites whose 'essential identity' is crushed and 'hollowed out' by the powerful forces of time–space compression. Gibson-Graham (1996) suggested that this scenario erects a 'rape script' that 'normalizes an act of non-reciprocal penetration': all non-capitalist forms are construed as 'sites of potential invasion, envelopment, accumulation', victims waiting their violation by capitalist globalization. This evidently militates against the very politics that Harvey is concerned to advance (but cf. Harvey, 1996, pp. 291–326). DG

References

Bell, D. 1978: *The cultural consequences of capitalism.* New York: Basic Books. · Bridge, G. 1997: Mapping the terrain of time–space compression: power networks in everyday life. *Environment and Planning D: Society and Space* 15: 611–26. · Deutsche, R. 1996: Boys town. In her *Evictions: art and spatial politics.* Cambridge, MA: MIT Press, 203–44. · Eagleton, T. 1990: *The ideology of the aesthetic.* Oxford and Cambridge, MA: Blackwell. · Gibson-Graham, J.-K. 1996: Querying globalization. In J.-K. Gibson-Graham, *The end of capitalism (as we knew it): a feminist critique of political economy.* Oxford and Cambridge, MA: Blackwell, 120–47. · Gregory, D. 1994: *Geographical imaginations.* Oxford and Cambridge, MA: Blackwell. · Harvey, D. 1989: *The condition of postmodernity: an enquiry into the origins of cultural change.* Oxford: Blackwell. · Harvey, D. 1990: Between space and time: reflections on the geographical imagination. *Annals of the Association of American Geographers* 80: 418–434. Harvey, D. 1995: Globalization in question. *Rethinking Marxism* 8 (4): 1–17. · Harvey, D. 1996: *Justice, nature and the geography of difference.* Cambridge, MA and Oxford: Blackwell. · Jameson, F. 1991: *Postmodernism, or the cultural logic of late capitalism.* London: Verso; Durham: Duke University Press. · Kirsch, S. 1995: The incredible shrinking world? Technology and the production of space. *Environment and Planning D: Society and Space* 13: 529–55. · Massey, D. 1993: Power-geometry and a progressive sense of place. In J. Bird, B. Curtis, T. Putnam, G. Roberston and L. Ticker, eds, *Mapping the futures: local cultures, global change.* London: Routledge, 59–69. · O'Tuathail, G. 1996: Visions and vertigo. Postmodernity and the writing of global space. In his *Critical geopolitics.* Minneapolis: University of Minnesota Press, 225–56. · Thrift, N.J. 1995: A hyperactive world. In R.J. Johnston, P.J. Taylor and M.J. Watts, eds, *Geographies of global change: remapping the world in the late twentieth century.* Oxford and Cambridge, MA: Blackwell, 18–35. · Thrift, N.J. 1997: New urban eras and old technological fears: reconfiguring the good will of electronic things. In A. Leyshon and N.J. Thrift, *Money/Space: geographies of monetary transformation.* London: Routledge, 323–54.

Suggested Reading

Harvey (1989), chs 15–17. · Massey (1993). · Thrift (1995).

time–space convergence A decrease in the FRICTION OF DISTANCE between places (see DISTANCE DECAY). As the definition suggests, the concept originated within SPATIAL SCIENCE. It was first formulated by D. Janelle (1968), who defined the convergence rate between two places as the average rate at which the time needed to travel between them decreases over

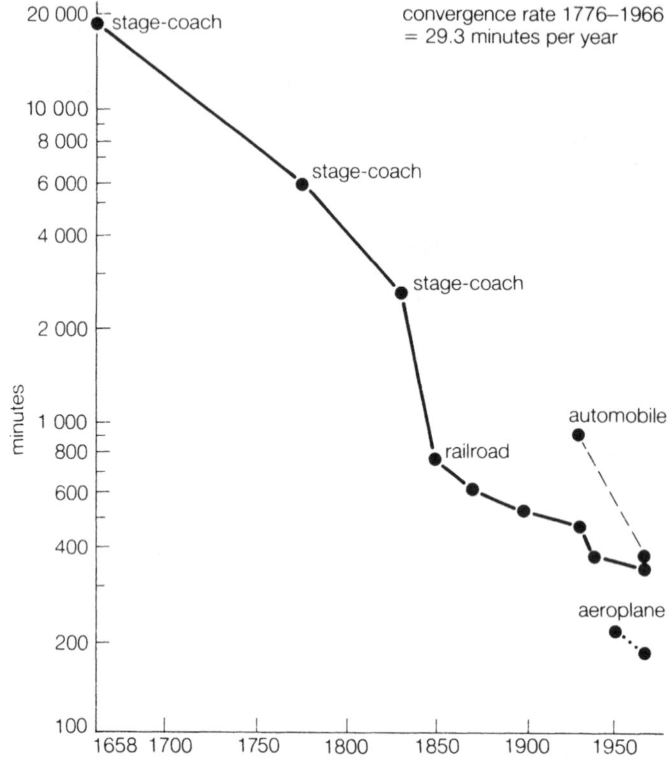

time–space convergence *1: Edinburgh to London, 1658–1966* (after Janelle, 1968)

time: the measure was supposed to be 'mathematically analagous to velocity as defined by the physicist'. In a subsequent, more extensive essay, Janelle (1969) attributed time–space convergence to technical change: 'as a result of transport innovation, places approach each other in time–space'.

Janelle showed that time–space convergence is usually both discontinuous in time – hence the convergence curve in figure 1 is not smooth but jagged – and also uneven over space: 'any transport improvement will tend to be of greatest advantage to the highest-ordered centre that it connects' (Janelle, 1968). Forer (1974) noted that the converse is also true – that time–space convergence is partly a function of the hierarchical structure of settlement – so that Janelle's (1969) model of 'spatial reorganization' entailed 'cyclic causality' in which 'places define spaces' and spaces in turn progressively 'redefine' places.

The concept was extended by Abler (1971), still largely within the framework of spatial science, who distinguished distance-convergence from an equally important cost-convergence: taken together, these were supposed to be 'two basic determinants of human spatial behavior'. Abler identified a pervasive tendency in the modern world for the friction of distance to decrease (cf. MODERNITY; MODERNIZATION). And since the friction of distance is a fundamental postulate of classical LOCATION THEORY, CENTRAL PLACE THEORY and DIFFUSION THEORY – it is, after all, what makes the identification of regular patterns possible – then time–space convergence 'scrambles' and 'plays havoc' with these standard geometric models (see also Falk and Abler, 1980). Hence time–space convergence has been wired to a concept of plastic space: 'a space defined by separation in time or cost terms, a space which the progressions and regressions of technology make one of continuous flux' (Forer, 1978).

Forer (1978) also noted a 'lack of response to Janelle's ideas', and attributed this in part to their links with 'the larger canvas of economic history and the long-term development of society'. Ironically, however, it is precisely those links that turned out to be most

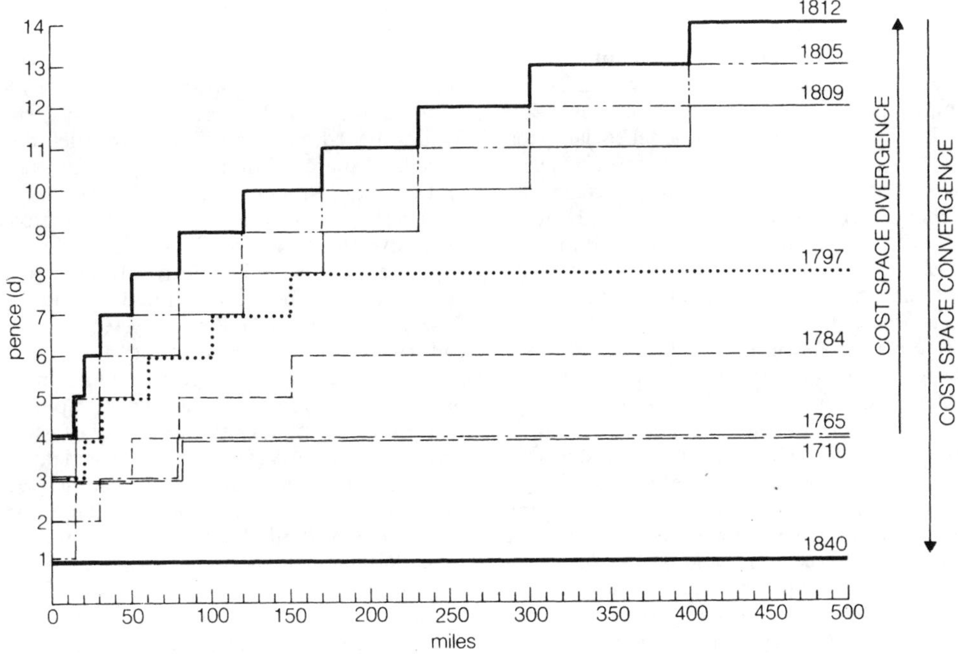

time–space convergence *2: Cost–space divergence: postal rates in Great Britain, 1710–1840*

important. Pred (1973) had already provided an exceptionally imaginative reconstruction of the changing time-lags within the circulation of public information through major newspapers published on the eastern seaboard of the United States between 1790 and 1840. Although his studies mapped the geography of time–space convergence and its hierarchical structure, and made explicit reference to Janelle's contributions, Pred was plainly as interested in the politico-economic and cultural implications of time–space convergence as he was in the geometric structures that preoccupied the original architects of the concept. Some of them eventually moved in a similar direction to explore the wider implications of contemporary time–space convergence for capitalist GLOBALIZATION (see Janelle, 1991). For precisely this reason, calibrations of time–space convergence are now more likely to be situated within the conceptual fields of TIME–SPACE COMPRESSION or TIME–SPACE DISTANCIATION that speak directly to such concerns.

DG

References

Abler, R, 1971: Distance, intercommunications and geography. *Proceedings of the Association of American Geographers*. 3: 1–4. · Falk, T. and Abler, R. 1980: Intercommunications, distance and geographical theory. *Geografisker Annaler* 62B: 59–67. · Forer, P. 1974: Space through time. In E.L. Cripps, eds, *Space–time concepts in urban and regional models*. London: Pion, 22–45. · Forer, P. 1978: A place for plastic space? *Progress in Human Geography* 2: 230–67. · Janelle, D. 1968: Central place development in a time–space framework. *Professional Geographer* 20: 5–10. · Janelle, D. 1969: Spatial reorganisation: a model and concept. *Annals of the Association of American Geographers* 59: 348–64. · Janelle, D. 1991: Global interdependence and its consequences. In S.D. Brunn and T. Leinbach, eds, *Collapsing space and time: geographic aspects of communications and information*. London: HarperCollins, 49–81. · Pred, A. 1973: *Urban growth and the circulation of information: the United States system of cities 1790–1840*. Cambridge, MA: MIT Press.

Suggested Reading

Janelle (1968, 1991). · Pred (1973).

time–space distanciation A term proposed by the British sociologist Anthony Giddens to describe the 'stretching' of social systems across time and space. The term is used in STRUCTURATION THEORY to describe what Giddens called system integration – interaction with people who are absent in time or space – which (historically) has entailed 'the expansion of interaction over space and its contraction over time' (Giddens, 1981, 1984).

The basic idea is scarcely foreign to human geography: the concept has obvious and close affinities with both TIME–SPACE COMPRESSION and TIME–SPACE CONVERGENCE. But Giddens argued that the concept has two important implications for social theory more generally.

In the first place, conventional social theory has been strongly influenced by forms of FUNCTIONALISM which assume that societies are coherent and bounded SYSTEMS, and by models of social change which presume that the basic structural dimensions of societies are internal ('endogenous') to those systems. Giddens rejects these propositions: 'The nexus of relations – political, economic or military – in which a society exists with others is usually integral to the very nature of that society' and, indeed, 'to what "societies" are conceived to be' (Giddens, 1981). At the limit, he implies, the time–space constitution of social life dislocates most of the 'totalizing' ambitions of conventional social theory (cf. Mann, 1986; see also Gregory, 1990).

In the second place, Giddens uses the concept to offer an outline sketch of the historical trajectory of time–space distanciation which is also an analytical map of different societies. In this scheme 'tribal societies' are characterized by low levels of time–space distanciation (most interactions are localized) and by little substantive distinction between 'authoritative' and 'allocative' resources (between 'political' and 'economic' power). With the emergence of so-called CLASS-divided societies like those of European FEUDALISM the level of time–space distanciation increases, largely through the powers extended by 'authoritative resources' to the STATE. The transition to the class societies of CAPITALISM is measured by the much greater prominence accorded to 'allocative resources', especially through INDUSTRIALIZATION, and is marked by much higher levels of time–space distanciation. In his early texts Giddens (1981, 1984) drew attention to the historical importance of systems of writing, recording and SURVEILLANCE and systems of monetization and commodification in underwriting this genealogy of MODERNITY. In his later texts Giddens (1990, 1991) became much more interested in the constitution of late twentieth-century 'high' modernity and the generalization of processes of time–space distanciation. He now distinguished between (i) *expert systems*, which 'bracket time and space through deploying modes of technical knowledge which have validity independent of the practitioners and clients who make use of them', and (ii) *symbolic tokens*, which are 'media of exchange which have standard value and thus are interchangeable across a plurality of contexts'. Together these constitute abstract systems which, so Giddens argued, penetrate all aspects of everyday life and in doing so undermine local practices and local knowledges; they dissolve the ties that once held the conditions of daily life in place and recombine them across much larger tracts of space (see ABSTRACTION; GLOBALIZATION; REFLEXIVE MODERNIZATION).

Giddens's scheme has been subject to several criticisms. The most common objection is to the generality of Giddens's system of concepts which lack sufficient historical and geographical specificity (Gregory, 1990). In its original form Giddens's genealogy of capitalist modernity accentuates the centrality of CLASS and fails to accord (for example) PATRIARCHY the same importance. Indeed, in treating space as a gap to be overcome and describing how time–space is 'bound in' to the conduct of social life, Giddens represents space as a barrier to interaction and as a void to be transcended, incorporated and subjugated. In doing so, he repeats the characteristic movement of Western master-narratives more generally, which has been to recover what eludes them as lacunae, margins, 'blank spaces' on the map' (Gregory, 1994, p. 129). This intersects with other objections to the ETHNOCENTRISM of Giddens's formulations. Hirst (1982) claims that the trajectory of time–space distanciation outlined by Giddens 'harbours an idea of the immediate and intimate and our movement away from them'. 'If we take the categories of non-Western societies seriously,' he contends, this is simply a myth. It is also a myth if we take the categories of Western societies seriously (see Mestrovic, 1998). Finally, Giddens's theorization of time–space distanciation is conducted in the language of domination, and fails to explore the ways in which signification and legitimation, supposedly equally important axes of social structuration, are implicated in the cultural formations that are centrally involved in historical and contemporary processes of globalization (cf. MEDIA, GEOGRAPHY OF). DG

References

Giddens, A. 1981: *A contemporary critique of historical materialism. Volume 1: Power, property and the state*. London: Macmillan. · Giddens, A. 1984: *The constitution of society*. Cambridge: Polity Press. · Giddens, A. 1985: *A contemporary critique of historical materialism. Volume 2: The nation-state and violence*. Cambridge: Polity Press. · Giddens, A. 1990: *The consequences of modernity*. Stanford: Stanford University Press. · Giddens, A. 1991:

Modernity and self-identity. Cambridge: Polity Press. · Gregory, D. 1990: 'Grand maps of history': structuration theory and social change. In J. Clark, C. Modgil and S. Modgil, eds, *Anthony Giddens: consensus and controversy*. Basingstoke: Falmer Press, 217–33. · Gregory, D. 1994: *Geographical imaginations*. Oxford: Blackwell. · Hirst, P. 1982: The social theory of Anthony Giddens: a new syncretism? *Theory, culture and society* 1 (2) 78–82. · Mann, M. 1986: *The sources of social power. Volume 1: A history of power from the beginning to AD 1760*. Cambridge: Cambridge University Press. · Mestrovic, S. 1998: *Anthony Giddens: the last modernist*. London and New York: Routledge. · Wright, E.O. 1989: Models of historical trajectory: an assessment of Giddens's critique of Marxism. In D. Held and J.B. Thompson, eds, *Social theory of modern societies: Anthony Giddens and his critics*. Cambridge: Cambridge University Press, 77–102.

Suggested Reading

Giddens (1984), chs 4 and 5. · Giddens (1991). · Kilminster, R. 1991: Structuration theory as world view. In C.G.A. Bryant, and D. Jary, eds, *Giddens' theory of structuration: a critical appreciation*. London: Routledge, 74–115. · Wright (1989).

topographic map A large- or intermediate-scale map (see map image or map) describing the salient physical and cultural features of a place or region. Derived from the Greek words *topos* (place) and *graphein* (to write), the word topographic originally referred to the work of landscape illustrators, whose pictorial treatment of terrain evolved from more primitive symbolic representations (Harvey, 1980). Contemporary topographic maps – the products of land survey (the third phase of topographic mapping) – typically describe the shape of the land with contour lines (see ISOLINE) and use varied abstract symbols (see SYMBOLIZATION) to represent roads, railways, political boundaries and hydrographic features such as rivers, streams and lakes (Keates, 1972). These maps also contain *toponyms* (place names), which usually reflect traditional local usage. If SCALE permits, topographic maps might show individual buildings and other large structures as well as woodland, marshland and other types of land cover that might hide troops or impede their movement. Because national defence is a primary use, totalitarian regimes often severely restrict the distribution of detailed maps that might prove useful to insurgents or invaders.

Modern topographic maps are the outgrowth of systematic national surveys initiated in the eighteenth and nineteenth centuries, when advances in measurement technology coincided with recognition by central governments that a detailed, geometrically precise cartographic inventory was essential for efficient civil administration (Konvitz, 1987). Trigonometric surveying (see SURVEYING) enabled topographers to construct *planimetric maps*, which show reliable distances between locations projected perpendicularly onto a horizontal reference plane, or datum. After measuring or calculating differences in elevation, topographers described the three-dimensional land surface with either hachures (short strokes running uphill and representing relative slope by variations in width or spacing) or contours (lines of constant elevation). For those who understand how to read them, contours afford a concise description of the terrain's shape and elevation. For less 'savvy' users, cartographers occasionally incorporate hill shading or other dramatic pictorial enhancements (Imhof, 1982).

Because of the need for myriad details, topographic maps are rarely published at scales smaller than 1:250,000. In the developed world, where scales of 1:50,000 or larger are common, they provide a cartographic base for geological, soils and planning maps, and occasionally for cadastral maps, which describe property boundaries. More generally, topographic maps serve as source materials for compiling physical–political reference maps at smaller scales.

Aerial photography proved an enormous boon to topographic mapping. Although air photos are perspective views with appreciable distortion of horizontal distances in areas of moderate or high relief, a pair of overlapping photos provides a stereoscopic image of terrain useful for identifying features on the ground and measuring differences in elevation. Photogrammetric plotting substantially reduced the need for direct measurement and field observation, and aerial photographic interpretation afforded an efficient method of compiling and updating topographic maps. In the 1970s, efficient automated removal of horizontal distortion encouraged production of orthophotomaps – geometrically accurate images of terrain that complement the traditional but comparatively abstract topographic 'line map' (Thrower and Jensen, 1976). MM

References

Harvey, P.D.A. 1980: *The history of topographical maps: symbols, pictures and surveys*. London: Thames and Hudson. · Imhof, E. 1982: *Cartographic relief representation*. Berlin: Walter de Gruyter. · Keates, J.S. 1972: Symbols and meaning in topographic maps. *International Yearbook of Cartography* 12: 168–81. · Konvitz, Josef W. 1987: *Cartography in France, 1660–1848: science, engineering, and statecraft*. Chicago: University of Chicago Press. · Thrower, N.J.W. and Jensen, J.R. 1976: The orthophoto and orthophotomap: characteristics, development and application. *The American Cartographer* 3: 39–56.

topology In mathematics, a property that is invariant under spatial distortion. For example, if a line is drawn on a rubber sheet, it is impossible to stretch the sheet so as to make the line into a point; thus the property of being a line, rather than a point (a one-dimensional object rather than a zero-dimensional object) is a topological property. In GEOGRAPHICAL INFORMATION SYSTEMS (GIS) the term applies similarly to those aspects of a database that survive geometric distortion of objects; such aspects include adjacency and connectivity between objects, and the distinction between points, lines and areas. One major distinction between GIS and much computer-assisted design (CAD) and COMPUTER-ASSISTED CARTOGRAPHY software is the ability to handle topology, since topological properties such as relationships between objects are central to many forms of SPATIAL ANALYSIS, and thus to the role of GIS in implementing such methods.

In DIGITIZING a map, it is virtually impossible to ensure that there is perfect closure between the two ends of a loop representing an area's boundary, or between two lines that should meet at a point. Software is used to detect near-intersections, and to make perfect closures. Because this process results in a transformation of lines into perfectly closed areas it is referred to loosely in GIS as 'building topology' (e.g. Demers, 1997, p. 109). MG

References

DeMers, M.N. 1997: *Fundamentals of geographic information systems*. New York: Wiley.

topophilia A term coined by Yi-Fu Tuan (1974) in his book by the same title to refer to 'the affective bond between people and place...' (1974, p. 4; cf. SENSE OF PLACE). He argues that this bond may vary greatly in intensity from individual to individual and that there is cultural variation in its expression. And yet there is also a biological component of attachment to place. Topophilia often takes the form of an aestheticizing of a PLACE or LANDSCAPE. This suggests that the aesthetic is a major way in which many people relate to their environment. Another major form of topophilia is attachment to home place which can vary in SCALE from the NATION to the home. Tuan suggests that such attachment can be based upon memories, or pride of ownership or creation. Topophilia, therefore, is not only a response to place but actively produces places for people. The term is associated with the HUMANISTIC GEOGRAPHY of the 1970s and with QUALITATIVE and PHENOMENOLOGICAL research. It was contrasted to the supposed alienation produced by many modern environments that induced PLACELESSNESS. In this work, attachment to place and the aesthetic were rarely seen as anything but benign and admirable qualities to be encouraged. While interest continues in attachment to place, it now takes a rather different form. Current researchers are more likely to speak of place-based identity and to an IDENTITY POLITICS, both positive and negative, which is based upon attachment to place (Jackson and Penrose, 1993). Likewise researchers have shown the dark side of national attachment and its celebration in the landscape (Johnson, 1995). In addition the CLASS and gender biases of an aesthetic appreciation of place have been scrutinized (Mitchell, 1996; Rose, 1993) (see GENDER AND GEOGRAPHY). JD

References

Jackson, P. and Penrose, J., eds, 1993: *Constructions of place, race and nation*. London: UCL Press. · Johnson, N. 1995: Cast in stone: monuments, geography and nationalism. *Environment and Planning D: Society and Space* 13: 51–66. · Mitchell, D. 1996: *The lie of the land: migrant workers and the California landscape*. Minneapolis: University of Minnesota Press. · Rose, G. 1993: *Feminism and geography: the limits of geographical knowledge*. Cambridge: Polity. · Tuan, Y.-F. 1974: *Topophilia: a study of environmental perception, attitudes, and values*. Englewood Cliff, NJ: Prentice-Hall.

tourism, geography of Tourism has been defined as 'the activities of persons travelling to and staying in places outside their usual environment for not more than one consecutive year for leisure, business and other purposes' (World Tourism Organization, 1993). Such a definition is, however, inherently problematic on at least two counts. First, it fails to encapsulate any distinct sphere of social practice, thus permitting tourism, LEISURE, RECREATION, hobbying, CULTURE and so on to elide uncritically. Secondly, it fails to capture the relationships between tourism and its 'other'. MacCannell (1992) argues that a tourist is someone who leaves home in order to experience some kind of 'otherness', and although the nature of tourism will change as sought-after othernesses change, the common denominator for tourists is an escape from the 'normal' experiences of home and work, and a search for experiences of otherness.

Tourism has now been heralded as the world's biggest industry, having overtaken petroleum and motor vehicles as the leading export earner in the world in 1994 (Youell, 1998). It makes a significant contribution to global economic development, and generates wealth and employment on an international scale, with many nations, regions and people relying on tourism for their social and economic well-being. Equally tourism has been responsible for the packaging of entire cultures and environments for tourists. In some cases, tourist places have been transformed through such packaging, and in others places have been created specifically for tourist consumption. Tourist places are not only experienced *in situ*, through advances in the technology of travel which have shrunk the world, but also virtually, through exposure in a wide range of media and advertising. Tourism, therefore, has been directly implicated in both the changing nature of PLACE, and in shaping GEOGRAPHICAL IMAGINATIONS and experiences of place on a global scale.

Geographers have taken a long-standing interest in tourism, but geographies of tourism have blossomed during the 1990s as a wider range of concepts and issues have been opened up as part of the CULTURAL TURN. Foundational studies in the geography of tourism have focused on four phenomena, and the connections between them: the *places* that groups of people leave, visit and pass through; the *people* so travelling; those *organizers* who make these trips possible; and the *people* who are encountered along the way (Pearce, 1995). Such studies have often taken the form of locational analysis of tourist flows and movements, and attempts to model the evolution of particular tourist resorts. Critics of these studies (see Britton, 1991; Shaw and Williams, 1994) have suggested that more nuanced geographies of tourism should involve greater theoretical understandings both of the dynamics of the tourism industry and of the social practices involved. Spatial characteristics, it is argued, should not merely be seen as providing the environment within which the social activities of tourism happen to take place. Rather, the places and practices of tourism are integrally interconnected, and more recent geographies of tourism have leaned heavily on the sociological and anthropological contributions of Erik Cohen, Dean MacCannell and John Urry to chart these interconnections in the ways in which tourist places are produced, represented and consumed.

The places of tourism are now usually set in a global culture of tourism, which can result in a trip to a destination which not only seems to resemble every other tourist destination, but which can also increasingly resemble the tourist's home. Tourism is often characterized by industrial standardization, with airports, planes, restaurants, tour buses, hotels, shopping malls, theme parks, beach resorts and so on acquiring characteristics of uniformity which can render a particular place as in some ways 'placeless' (cf. PLACELESSNESS). Ritzer and Liska (1997) describe this phenomenon as 'McDisneyization'. Tourism, then, has reproduced places, and in some cases (such as the Disney resorts themselves) created places from scratch, in such a way as to conform to a universal 'architecture of pleasure'. The specificity of the destination thus becomes eroded, and the presentation of the 'authentic' place is often reduced to a replication of previous ways of living and working or of other cultures for consumption by tourists. Thus local tradition and culture becomes tourist spectacle, and the resultant tourist culture represents particular fragments of local culture which tourism itself has helped to destroy (see SPECTACLE, GEOGRAPHY OF).

With underlying processes of standardization, and attempts to authenticate local distinctiveness through the production of cultural spectacle, the representations of tourist places and practices can become more 'real' than the places themselves. Take, for example, MacCannell's (1996) account of tourism in Switzerland:

> Certain spots in Switzerland have become a theme park or cartoon image of its idealized former self. The mountains and lakes are not merely natural, but 'scenery' organized by official viewing points; there is an elaborate transportation system of mountain trains for the exclusive use of sightseers; the national dish, fondue, is exclusively a party dish; former peasants have obligingly agreed to wear picturesque outfits and use picturesque equipment, Heidi and William Tell costumes, Alpine horns and oversized cowbells, long after other European peasants abandoned their colourful ways; one of the main industries turns out what are two of the most stable souvenirs not just of Switzerland but of Western Europe, music boxes and cuckoo clocks; 'Swiss' chalets are the model of mountain recreation homes throughout the Western world. 'Switzerland' is everywhere and also, in a sense, it no longer exists in Switzerland. (p. 11)

Representations of tourist places are central to the cultural practice of tourism. The distribution of tourist images is worldwide, and for most people the images in brochures, magazines or calendars, or on television or video, establish anticipatory expectations of the tourist places concerned. Places are given meanings in such images, and tourists will expect to see these place-images and experience these place-meanings when they visit (Goss, 1993). The importance of how places are represented then, lies not only in the construction of expectation through place promotion (Selwyn, 1996), but also in the presentation of a place as a picture-perfect image of itself, which the tourist will take back in some form, only with themselves at the centre of it.

The consumption of tourist places will depend on the varying 'gaze' (Urry, 1990) of the tourist, who as a receiver of the signs and symbols of produced tourist culture is not necessarily structured by those signs, but can assemble and destroy the realities of tourist places and practices in the free play of the imagination (MacCannell, 1989). There are commonly thought to be two different types of tourist: those who seek pleasure, entertainment, relaxation and often clement weather, for whom the specific destination is not of vital importance; and those who deliberately choose to avoid destinations frequented by the first group of tourists, seeking instead a travel experience that can be conveyed as real or authentic (Zurich, 1995). These categories are neither mutually exclusive nor entirely bound up with matters of class, wealth or income (May, 1996), although these may be important. Thus 'pleasure-seeking' tourists frequent cheap and cheerful domestic holiday camps as well as expensive and exclusive Caribbean club-resorts, and seekers after authenticity may be young hitch-hikers on a low budget as well as consumers of expensively micro-packaged adventures in exotic places.

Even within these categories, different tourists will have different ways of seeing and experiencing tourist places. Domosh's (1991) work on gender, and Munt's (1994) work on class, for example, have opened up some of these differences. More generally, the tourist gaze can be seen to have shifted over time, rendering particular types of places more or less interesting to visit. Thus in Britain, the seaside holiday has tended to wane in importance in comparison with rural, cultural and heritage sites. Tourists seem more inclined to seek out 'authenticity' through these choices, even though they realize just how inauthentic these authenticities are. The shifting tourist gaze is at least in part a product of the close linkages between commodification, consumption and tourism. Tourism has become a commodity which is marketed and sold, and even those who seek to escape the excesses of commodified tourism are catered for in the niche-marketing of tourism commodities.

Some commentators now believe that we are in the age of the 'post-tourist' (Feifer, 1985), an idea with three principal elements:

- the post-tourist can increasingly gaze on tourist sites without leaving home, by using virtual technology and media;
- post-tourism has become an eclectic pastiche of niched interests; and
- post-tourists play games – playing at and with tourism and recognizing that there is no such thing as authentic experience.

However, as Rojek (1993) has shown, even post-tourists are incorporated within the commodification of tourist places and practices, and they are drawn to the signs and significations of tourism just as 'other' tourists are. Post-tourists, then, offer yet more interesting geographies of the changing nature and gaze of tourism.

Finally, it should be emphasized that geographies of tourism have a number of inherent contradictions to deal with. First, with the increasingly spectacular and uniform nature of 'placeless' tourism, there is a realization that *virtual* experiences of spectacular places are often superior to the real experience. Secondly, it is becoming increasingly difficult to provide innovative places or practices with which to satisfy the discerning post-tourist. Every niched packaging of adventurous or exotic place-experience has the effect of narrowing the scope of tourisms which are yet to be encountered. The portfolio of 'been there done that', or even worse 'others have been there done that' is ever-widening, making further innovation problematic, and reducing the remnants of non-globalized cultures. Even the repackaging of existing destinations – such as the promotion of adventure tourism to provide embodied thrills in scenic locations in a place like New Zealand (Cloke and Perkins, 1998) – involves continual innovation in order to present yet more adventurous pursuits for tourists. Thirdly, and perhaps most importantly, much of contemporary tourism raises crucial questions about sustainability, in that by its very nature it tends to ruin the very places and cultures which tourists come to see. As Connell (1993) has shown in the case of Bali, tourism represents a means by which the other is both made dependent, and exploited (Cf. RECREATION; LEISURE, GEOGRAPHY OF). PJC

References

Britton, S. 1991: Tourism, capital and place: towards a critical geography of tourism. *Environment and Planning D: Society and Space* 16: 185–218. · Cloke, P. and Perkins, H. 1998: 'Cracking the canyon with the 'Awesome Foursome': representations of adventure tourism in New Zealand. *Environment and Planning D: Society and Space* 16: 185–218. · Connell, J. 1993: Bali revisited: death, rejuvenation and the tourist cycle. *Environment and Planning D: Society and Space* 1: 641–61. · Domosh, M. 1991: Towards a feminist historiography of geography. *Transactions, Institute of British Geographers* NS 16: 95–104. · Feifer, M. 1985: *Going Places*. London: Macmillan. · Goss, J.D. 1993: Placing the market and marketing place: tourist advertising of the Hawaiian Islands 1972–1992. *Environment and Planning D: Society and Space* 11: 663–88. · MacCannell, D. 1989: *The tourist*, 2nd edn. London: Macmillan. · MacCannell, D. 1992: *Empty meeting grounds: the tourist papers*. London: Routledge. · MacCannell, D. 1996: *Tourist or traveller?* London: BBC Education. · May, J. 1996: In search of authenticity off and on the beaten track. *Environment and Planning D: Society and Space* 14: 709–36. · Munt, I. 1994: The 'other' postmodern tourism. Culture, travel and the new middle class. *Theory, Culture and Society* 11: 101–23. · Pearce, D. 1995: *Tourism today: a geographical analysis*, 2nd edn. Chichester: Wiley. · Ritzer, G. and Liska, A. 1997: 'McDisneyization:' and 'Post-Tourism': complementary perspectives on contemporary tourism. In C. Rojek and J. Urry, eds, *Touring cultures: transformations of travel and theory*. London: Routledge. · Rojek, C. 1993: *Ways of escape: modern transformations in leisure and travel*. London: Macmillan. · Selwyn, T. 1996: *The tourist image: myths and myth making in tourism*. Chichester: Wiley. · Shaw, G. and Williams, A.M. 1994: *Critical issues in tourism: a geographical perspective*. Oxford: Blackwell. · Urry, J. 1990: *The tourist gaze: leisure and travel in contemporary societies*. London: Sage; World Tourism Organization 1993: *Recommendations on tourism statistics*. Madrid: World Tourism Organization. · Youell, R. 1998: *Tourism: an introduction*. Harlow: Longman. · Zurich, D. 1995: *Errant journeys*. Austin: University of Texas Press.

Suggested Reading

MacCannell, D. 1989: *The tourist*, 2nd edn. London: Macmillan. · Squire, S.J. 1994: Accounting for cultural meanings: the interface between geography and tourism studies re-examined. *Progress In Human Geography* 18: 1–16.

Urry (1990). · Urry, J. 1995: *Consuming places*. London: Routledge. · Urry, J. and Rojek, J., eds, 1997: *Touring cultures: transformations of travel and theory*. London: Routledge.

town A general name for an urban place, usually a settlement exceeding a prescribed minimum population threshold. No specific size range is generally accepted to distinguish a town from either a CITY or a village, however, and practices differ significantly. (Cf. NEW TOWN.) RJJ

townscape A central term in an approach to URBAN GEOGRAPHY that emphasizes classification and mapping of the observable units of urban form. In its early decades, urban geography was principally the study of MORPHOLOGY, that is, the pattern of land uses and built forms, and morphogenesis, the historic stages of land use development including a significant concern with URBAN ORIGINS. Though scarcely noticed, this focus upon genesis, growth, and form was consistent with a widespread SOCIAL DARWINISM in the social sciences prior to the Second World War.

More recently, this work has been extended, particularly in Britain, in the work of Conzen (1969), Whitehand (1992) and their students. Study of the town plan, its land-use units, and architectural forms together comprised an understanding of the townscape. From an essentially descriptive and classificatory project, work has now expanded to include the roles of the agents and institutions who have shaped the townscape, including property owners, developers, architects and planners, and also strategic planning questions such as urban CONSERVATION (Larkham, 1996). The focus of this work has become associated particularly with Jeremy Whitehand at the University of Birmingham, and has increasingly become institutionalized through international conferences, their proceedings (Whitehand and Larkham, 1992) and the launch of the journal, *Urban Morphology*, in 1997, which has confirmed the interdisciplinary trajectory of this research tradition to include architects and urban planners.

Outside Britain, similar research has been conducted by students of the CULTURAL LANDSCAPE, notably in Germany and the United States; of this genre, a widely cited example is the interpretation of New Orleans by Peirce Lewis (1976). But there has also occurred a separate development, sometimes associated with the rubric of the 'new cultural geography'. Influenced more closely by developments in social and cultural theory, notably precedents in anthropology and literary theory, this work has paid more attention to the HERMENEUTICS of the urban LANDSCAPE. It has explored the METAPHOR, and the method, of landscape as a TEXT which may be read to reveal the ideas, practices, interests, and contexts of the SOCIETY that created it (Ley, 1987; Knox, 1991; Pred, 1995). Moreover, such landscapes are not simply products, but may themselves be fully implicated in the ongoing reproduction of society (Duncan, 1990). DL

References

Conzen, M.R.G. 1969: *Alnwick, Northumberland; a study in townplan analysis*. London: Institute of British Geographers, Publication no. 27. · Duncan, J. 1990: *The city as text: the politics of landscape interpretation in the Kandyan kingdom*. Cambridge: Cambridge University Press. · Knox, P. 1991: The restless urban landscape: economic and socio-cultural change and the transformation of metropolitan Washington, D.C. *Annals of the Association of American Geographers* 81: 181–209. · Larkham, P. 1996: *Conservation and the city*. London: Routledge. · Lewis, P. 1976: *New Orleans: the making of an urban landscape*. Cambridge, MA: Ballinger. · Ley, D. 1987: Styles of the times: liberal and neoconservative landscapes in inner Vancouver, 1968–1986. *Journal of Historical Geography* 10: 40–56. · Pred, A. 1995: *Recognizing European modernities: a montage of the present*. London: Routledge. · Whitehand, J. 1992: *The making of the urban landscape*. Oxford: Blackwell. · Whitehand, J. and Larkham, P., eds, 1992: *Urban landscapes: international perspectives*. London: Routledge.

Suggested Reading

Whitehand and Larkham (1992).

trade A flow of commodities from producers to consumers. In terms of the CIRCUIT OF CAPITAL, trade takes place within the sphere of realization and represents the conversion of CAPITAL in the form of commodities back into its money form, so enabling the realization of surplus value (see ECONOMIC GEOGRAPHY; MARXIAN ECONOMICS).

Conventionally trade is considered as an aggregate set of flows of one or more commodities between one or more urban, regional, national or international economies – hence the distinction between intra- and inter-urban, intra- and interregional, and intra- and international trade. However, as production is itself organized increasingly on a global basis, a growing proportion of international trade takes place within TRANSNATIONAL CORPORATIONS (TNCs). Such intra-firm trade accounts for at least one third of international trade (Dicken, 1998) and the economic and political circumstances under which commodities flow across geographical space within firms are very different from those in which firms trade across an international market: the pressures, constraints and controls of an external market simply do not apply. One consequence of intra-firm international trade is the phenomenon of *transfer pricing* whereby a TNC may set internal prices for commodities – subject to audit by tax authorities – in order to optimize the achievement of corporate goals. Thus pricing may be set in order to maximize tax advantages in the corporate balance sheet so that relatively low profits are represented as being 'made' in areas with high levels of corporate taxation and high levels of profits 'made' in areas with low levels of taxation. The incentive to indulge in such practices tends to increase the greater the differences in levels of taxation and so transfer pricing – which is widely practised – is itself a powerful influence helping to reduce differences in the tax regimes of different countries, so causing them to tend to converge on a global norm.

Two broad schools of thought exist on the reasons for trade. First, following the classical analysis of David Ricardo, are those who start from pre-existing natural or historically created differences between areas. For Paul Krugman (1991), however, comparative advantage is socially constructed and takes the form, for example, of the clustering of production into distinct geographical areas held together by external economies of scale. Trade is then explained in terms of the law of COMPARATIVE ADVANTAGE (see Dicken, 1998). This law suggests that only a relative advantage, measured in terms of opportunity costs, is necessary to make trade of benefit to all participants and thereby to the economic system as a whole. The exploitation of relative advantage may help to shift the PRODUCTIVE FORCES from higher to lower cost activities and hence to increase total productivity. Such a consequence is explicit in the explanation of comparative advantage advanced by the *Heckscher–Ohlin principle*. This states that comparative advantage stems from geographical variations in the endowment of FACTORS OF PRODUCTION between places. Given the (unrealistic) assumption of invariant production functions (the quantitative relationship between inputs and outputs in production) between places, trade will enable its participants to export commodities which are intensive in factors in which they are well-endowed and to import commodities intensive in those factors in which they are less well-endowed.

Second, there are those who explain trade in terms of the exchange relationships within and between MODES OF PRODUCTION. Thus the limited amount of trade under FEUDALISM – limited, that is, in relation to the value of total feudal production – was made possible and encouraged by the profits to be made by merchants who were able to exploit the spatially parcellized SOVEREIGNTY of feudal society by buying commodities cheaply and selling them elsewhere at much higher prices. By contrast the emergence of CAPITALISM increased the total value and volume of production and reduced its unit price through large-scale production, thereby expanding the market for the commodities. In addition, the inherently competitive social relations of capitalism constantly drive it to seek new markets for the realization of surplus value and sources of supply. Thus the volume and extent of trade was greatly increased both between capitalist economies and between pre-capitalist and capitalist economies. In the same way the restrictions on trade initially imposed by the emergence of state-socialist economies were penetrated by the internal and external pressure of demands for inputs and outlets.

These two schools of thought come together as the integrated system of production and exchange embodied within modes of production is projected upon a network of national economies. Differences between countries in the level of DEVELOPMENT or capital intensity of the PRODUCTIVE FORCES and in the availability and unionization of labour may enable a larger surplus to be appropriated in developed economies by exchanging goods at prices above their value for goods, originating in economies having inferior productive facilities and large, unorganized labour reserves which help to keep prices low, priced below value. Such a process of *unequal exchange* (Emmanuel, 1972) may be intensified by a dependence upon a limited number of commodities or a limited number of markets, or both. Unequal exchange may help to maintain a permanent inability to gain from trade by the systematic extraction of value from underdeveloped economies and by the development of a permanent technology gap. This may not only result in the increased penetration of imports into the developed economies but may also undermine traditional modes of production and intensify technological DEPENDENCE in the underdeveloped economies. This is, however, only one aspect of the more general condition of social dependence which results from the penetration of traditional economies by developed ones.

In fact the majority of world trade flows between the developed economies, as a result of the technologically induced division of labour between them. The realization of surplus value through sale and exchange remains a problem however – hence the long-standing and increasing interest in developing the underdeveloped countries to serve as a market not merely for consumer goods but also for capital goods. Similarly food, raw materials and energy are still produced in large quantities by the underdeveloped countries and so it is vital for the reproduction of developed economies that they maintain a hold upon supplies by strategic and commercial means (see NEOCOLONIALISM).

The flow of commodities across international frontiers enables its regulation by national and international agencies although this is not so easy in the case of intra-firm trade and transfer pricing. During the twentieth century, two periods, the first between 1929 and 1933 and the second during the period of reconstruction after the Second World War, have witnessed the erection of barriers to trade. TARIFFS, import quotas and more covert measures such as marginal adjustments to national standards may be used singly or together as barriers to trade.

The General Agreement on Tariffs and Trade (GATT, which began operations in 1947 and became the World Trade Organization (WTO) in 1994) was one response to the post-war period of protectionism: it meets regularly to reduce trade barriers through the design and implementation of eight successive rounds of negotiation (the latest being the Uruguay Round completed in 1994). The United Nations Conference on Trade and Development (UNCTAD) was first convened in 1964 with the objectives of reorganizing the institutional arrangements affecting world trade and of prompting the redesign of trade policies in the developed economies in order to encourage trade with and development of the underdeveloped world through a generalized system of preferences within GATT. Control is also exerted by international agreements on particular commodities such as sugar and fibres. Regionally based organizations such as the EU, NAFTA (North American Free Trade Agreement), LAFTA (Latin American Free Trade Association) and ASEAN (Association of South-East Asian Nations) have been established in part to encourage the growth of trade between their members.

In so far as economic growth is stimulated by such arrangements, external trade may also be encouraged. But the erection of external tariffs around such FREE TRADE AREAS, customs unions or COMMON MARKETS may have the effect of reducing world trade. In practice, however, little more than 30 per cent of US and Japanese trade is with the rest of the Americas and the ASEAN group, respectively, despite recent moves to establish free trade areas in both regions. Furthermore, only about 17 per cent of US GDP and 18 per cent of Japanese GDP is traded. By contrast, nearly three-quarters of the trade of the member countries of the EU is within Europe whilst the average proportion of GDP accounted for by trade in the member states of the EU is nearly 50 per cent. The external trade of the EU as a whole amounts to less than 19 per cent of its total Community GNP.

The volume of world trade at any point in time reflects the global level of output and production and the restrictions – social, geographical and institutional – upon the exchange of this output. The emergence of capitalist social relations both stimulated output and reduced barriers to trade. This stimulus has been intensified during the present century by the rapid development of state-socialist economies and their consequently increased capacity for trade within and beyond COMECON (Council for Mutual Economic Aid). The collapse of COMMUNISM in eastern Europe and the former USSR has led to dramatic declines in the trade of the region and rapid increases in the negative balance of its international trade.

One of the most characteristic features of the post-war development of the world economy – what Peter Dicken (1998, p. 25) calls the 'roller-coaster of world merchandise production and trade' – has been the rapid but dramatically fluctuating growth of output of especially from the 1950s and the even faster growth, but with slightly less fluctuation, of international trade in almost every year. The implication of this relationship is not only that the world economic geography has become more integrated but that production anywhere is subjected to more intense competition and evaluation and to globally transmitted cycles of growth and decline from around the world economic geography.

Participation in trade remains uneven – three-quarters of all manufactured exports are generated by the developed market economies of the world economy and about 60 per cent of such exports are to other developed market economies. One effect of the growth of international trade has been a systematic decline of the share of underdeveloped economies in world trade – most especially from Africa (with a very low proportion of exports accounted for by manufactures) and Latin America. To some extent this has been compensated for by the increasing share in manufactured exports from developing market economies but this emanates largely from South-East Asia (with very high shares of manufactured exports in total exports) and is due mainly to the newly industrializing countries. Western Europe, Asia (especially Japan) and North America dominate world trade in tradable services although the concentration of trade amongst the leading exporters is not as great as with manufactures.

The beginnings of a world economic geography became apparent from the middle of the fifteenth century with the expansion of international trade which remains major force of GLOBALIZATION (see also WORLD-SYSTEMS ANALYSIS). Increasingly, however, and despite the dramatic growth of international trade, its relative significance has fallen as foreign direct and indirect investment, the global reorganization of production and the emergence of increasingly international capital markets have grown to comparative levels of influence. RL

References

Dicken, P. 1998: *Global shift; transforming the world economy*, 3rd edn. London: Paul Chapman Publishing. · Emmanuel, A. 1972: *Unequal exchange: a study of the imperialism of trade*. New York: Monthly Review Press. · Krugman, P. 1991: *Geography and trade*. Leuven: Leuven University Press.

Suggested Reading

Agnew, J. and Grant, R. 1997: Falling out of the world economy? Theorising 'Africa' in world trade. In R. Lee and J. Wills, eds, *Geographies of economies*, ch. 18. London and New York Arnold, 219–28. · Dicken (1998), ch. 2. · Harvey, D. 1975: The geography of capitalist accumulation. *Antipode* 2: 9–21.

tragedy of the commons A METAPHOR used to illustrate and account for situations in which the depletion of natural resources occurs because individual and collective interests do not coincide and no individual or institution has the power to ensure that they do.

Hardin's (1968) classic paper defining the metaphor gives the example of graziers using common land and continually adding to their herds for so long as the marginal return from the additional animal is positive, even though this means that the average return per animal is falling and the resource is being depleted. Indeed, he argues that graziers will be impelled to follow the example of all others and add to their herds in order to maintain overall returns, given the fall in average yield that follows the addition of every further animal. Efficient use of the resource requires its rationing through limitations on herd size but individuals will not altruistically limit their herd sizes unless they know that all others will also (see PRISONER'S DILEMMA); to ensure that all do requires an external organization (such as the STATE) with the power to enforce optimal use, thereby ensuring the best interests of both the individuals and the collective.

Hardin's metaphor has been extended to a wide range of situations, such as population control (Hardin, 1974). Others have argued that the metaphor's applicability depends on the resource in question. Laver (1984, 1986) identified three possible solutions to the problem specified: (a) *privatization* of the commons, with owners protecting the natural resource in ways that collective owners could not; (b) *collective agreements* among the users, enforced without the need for external power (as illustrated by Ostrom, 1990); and (c) *regulation by an external body*. The extent to which the first two are viable strategies for the long-term conservation of the earth's natural resources is doubted by many. (Cf. REGIME THEORY.) RJJ

References

Hardin, G. 1968: The tragedy of the commons: the population problem has no technical solution; it requires a fundamental extension in morality. *Science* 162: 1243–8. · Hardin, G. 1974: Living on a lifeboat. *Bioscience* 24: 561–8. · Laver, M. 1984: The politics of inner space: tragedies of three commons. *European Journal of Political Research* 12: 59–71. · Laver, M. 1986: Public, private and common in outer space. *Political Studies* 34: 359–73. · Ostrom, E. 1990: *Governing the commons: the evolution of institutions for collective action*. Cambridge and New York: Cambridge University Press.

transaction costs The costs associated with effecting an economic transaction, either through MARKET EXCHANGE between two or more legally distinct economic actors, or internally within a single economic organization (firm or, more generally, 'hierarchy'). Costs for market-mediated transactions might include: the cost of gathering information concerning the availability, price and quality of particular commodities (goods or services); the costs associated with identifying potential customers for one's output; the cost of determining the reliability of a supplier or the credit worthiness of a purchaser; the costs associated with negotiating the terms of a particular exchange, including price, delivery date, and terms of payment (and of setting these out in the form of an agreed contract); and the cost of completing a transaction (i.e. making or collecting payment). Costs will also accompany non-market transactions taking place within a single firm – i.e. the costs of organizing and coordinating complex, multi-step production processes in-house. TRANSPORT COSTS associated with moving goods between transacting parties (whether within the same firm or in different firms) are one form of transaction cost that has traditionally received special attention from ECONOMIC GEOGRAPHY (cf. TRANSPORT GEOGRAPHY). However, as is evident in the following discussion, other forms of transaction cost have recently attracted considerably more interest within INDUSTRIAL GEOGRAPHY.

Williamson (1975, 1985) is generally credited with developing the comprehensive economic analysis of transaction costs, extending the pioneering work by Coase (1937) in his classic paper on the nature and *raison d'être* of the firm. Williamson's (1975) original motivation is clear (pp. 1–2): 'to achieve a better understanding of the origins and functions of various firm and market structures – stretching from elementary work groups to complex modern corporations'. Instead of relying on technological arguments based on concepts such as indivisibilities or non-separabilities for explaining why two or more functions might be performed within the same firm (organizational hierarchy), Williamson takes another approach: 'I focus on transactions and the costs that attend completing transactions by one institutional mode rather than another': he contends that 'transactional considerations, not technology, are typically decisive in determining which mode of organization will obtain in what circumstances and why'. Most goods will require a number of semi-finished or intermediate inputs for their production. They will also require a number of discrete, separate functions to be performed as part of the overall production process. The extent to which all of these operations will be performed within a single ('vertically integrated') firm (cf. INTEGRATION), versus the alternative approach in which some or all of the required inputs are produced by other firms and then acquired through some form of market transaction, depends (according to Williamson's analysis) on which mode of organization best succeeds at minimizing transaction costs (p. 8): 'whether a set of transactions ought to be executed across markets or within a firm depends on the relative efficiency of each mode'. Generally, the more difficult or expensive the task of coordination or 'GOVERNANCE' of the production process, the greater the likelihood that production will be vertically integrated within a single internal hierarchy.

The geographical significance of transaction costs (other than transportation costs) was first made clear by Scott (1988) who demonstrated, both theoretically and empirically, that the spatial clustering of firms often serves to reduce the cost of transactions occurring between them. Under such conditions, firms will find it easier and cheaper to acquire the requisite information concerning potential buyers and suppliers nearby. Moreover, because such firms may be managed by individuals who have come into contact with one another repeatedly over extended periods of time, they may have built up a high degree of familiarity and trust between them which serves to facilitate the sharing of information and the successful achievement of non-routine transactions (Harrison, 1992) – what Storper (1997) describes as 'untraded interdependencies'. When such circumstances prevail, Scott argued, one should expect to find a much more fully articulated social DIVISION OF LABOUR, in which individual firms specialize in the production of a relatively small number of goods and/or services and trade actively with one another. Such arrangements are likely to be especially useful in industries for which market tastes are changing rapidly, and in which PRODUCT LIFE CYCLES are short. Since input requirements for such goods will also change rapidly, spatial concentration will reduce the transaction costs associated with producers finding and assessing the performance characteristics of potential new suppliers. Similarly, when the product is complex or highly customized, it is advantageous for producers and users to interact frequently and easily. Possibilities for achieving this are enhanced when the user and producer are close to one another, thereby reducing the cost of such a complex transaction (Lundvall, 1988).

Hence, as Storper (1997) has observed (pp. 34–5), this kind of analysis demonstrates 'that geography figures in transaction costs in general, and hence influences the boundaries of the firm and production system': he also concludes that 'the geography of transaction costs helps explain agglomeration and spatial divisions of labour'. However, the transaction cost approach has been criticized for its rather reductionist analysis of industrial organization – for its 'exclusive focus on the transaction rather than the relationship' (Powell, 1990, p. 323) and for its tendency to ignore the influence of the public sector in shaping the institutions (such as markets) which mediate exchange (Harrison, 1997). (See also ECONOMIES OF SCALE; ECONOMIES OF SCOPE; INDUSTRIAL DISTRICT; INDUSTRIAL ORGANIZATION; JUST-IN-TIME PRODUCTION; SOCIAL CAPITAL.)

MSG

References

Coase, R. 1937: The nature of the firm. *Economica* 4: 386–405. · Harrison, B. 1992: Industrial districts: old wine in new bottles? *Regional Studies* 26: 469–83. · Harrison, B. 1997: *Lean and mean*. New York: Guilford: Lundvall, B.-A. 1988: Innovation as an interactive process: from user-producer interaction to the national system of innovation. In G. Dosi, C. Freeman, R. Nelson, G. Silverberg and L. Soete, eds, *Technical change and economic theory*. London: Pinter, 349–69. · Powell, W.W. 1990: Neither market nor hierarchy: network forms of organization. In B. Straw and L. Cummings, eds, *Research in organizational behavior*. Greenwich, CT: JAI Press, 295–336. · Scott, A.J. 1988: *New industrial spaces*. London: Pion. · Storper, M. 1997: *The regional world*. New York: Guilford. · Williamson, O.E. 1975: *Markets and hierarchies*. New York: The Free Press. · Williamson, O.E. 1985: *The economic institutions of capitalism*. New York: The Free Press.

transactional analysis An approach to understanding how the number of firms in an industry, and the nature of exchanges between such firms, is determined. It is based on the fundamental proposition 'that the economic institutions of capitalism have the main purpose and effect of economizing on transaction costs' (Williamson, 1985, p. 17). To this end, a firm may judge it cheaper to produce a commodity within its internal organization (or 'hierarchy'), perhaps to exploit internal ECONOMIES OF SCOPE or to reap internal ECONOMIES OF SCALE. Alternatively, the firm may judge it cheaper to acquire the same commodity through an external transaction (e.g. market purchase, subcontracting), the cost of making this transaction perhaps having been reduced by the clustering of suppliers near to the firm. This type of analysis illuminates one of the forces said to propel the AGGLOMERATION of productive activities in urban centres. (See LOCATION THEORY; PRODUCTION COMPLEX; TRANSACTION COSTS.) MSG

Reference

Williamson, O.E. 1985: *The economic institutions of capitalism*. New York: The Free Press.

transculturation The term was originally employed by Latin American sociologists, ETHNOGRAPHERS and literary critics to refer to the creative appropriation by colonized or SUBALTERN groups of cultural material and forms received from dominant or IMPERIAL cultures (cf. COLONIALISM). The term was used in an attempt to supplant the overly reductive concept of *acculturation* (see ASSIMILATION). The term is also associated with Mary Louise Pratt's (1992) analysis of the *contact zone* of colonial encounter in which subordinated groups selected and transformed European knowledge and modes of REPRESENTATION (see also Morin, 1998). While imperial relations of POWER and knowledge are largely asymmetrical, disruption, destabilization and mutations of various modes of representation can sometimes be successful as forms of resistance.

The concept of transculturation depends upon a recognition of heterogeneous reception and the impossibility of authorial control over reception of cultural material. It is closely allied to those of HYBRIDITY and *mimicry* (Bhabha, 1994) in that it is formulated to escape from unitary identities and binary oppositions of colonized and colonizer. Examples of transculturation offered by Pratt (1992, ch. 8) include selective uses by Creole élites of von Humboldt's aestheticized descriptions of primal America (*Views of Nature* and *Views of the Cordilleras and Monuments of the Indigenous Peoples of the America*). Humboldtian tropes are reformulated as sites of resistance and improvised self-invention directed towards Latin American independence and NATION building.

Transculturation as a form of undermining imperial HEGEMONY is not nearly as pessimistic a concept as Spivak's notion of the *epistemic violence* of colonial discourse whereby a passive native is effectively silenced (Spivak, 1988). Transculturation instead posits a process whereby the colonial or post-colonial SUBALTERN can interrogate and 'answer back' if only within the circumscribed spaces of various dominant modes of representation. The emphasis on modes of representation such as transculturation are characteristic of the 'discursive turn' in geography, anthropology and other social sciences. This emphasis can underplay the economic and political structures and geographies within which such discursive and cultural practices occur (Mitchell, 1997). However, calls for the grounding of discursive approaches in material or institutional 'realities' can equally underplay the role discursive forms play in constituting transnational IDENTITY (Fanon, 1967). JD

References

Bhabha, Homi K. 1994: *The location of culture*. London: Routledge. · Fanon, F. 1967: *Black skin, white masks*. New York: Grove. · Mitchell, K. 1997: Different diasporas and the hype of hybridity. *Environment and Planning D: Society and Space* 15: 533–53. · Morin, K.M. 1998: British women travellers and constructions of racial difference across the nineteenth century American west. *Transactions, Institute of British Geographers* NS 23: 311–30. · Pratt, M.L. 1992: *Imperial eyes: travel writing and transculturation*. London: Routledge. · Spivak, G. 1988: Can the subaltern speak?. In C. Nelson and L. Grossberg, eds, *Marxism and the interpretation of culture*. London: Macmillan, 217–313.

transfer pricing The setting of transfer prices for products (goods and services) moving between semi-autonomous divisions (cost or profit centres) within large organizations. The practice is most often associated with TRANS-NATIONAL CORPORATIONS (TNCs) which respond to variable corporate tax regimes, TARIFF and other barriers to TRADE and exchange rates by setting prices for internal transactions between establishments located in different national locations in ways which minimize costs or maximize gains. For example, firms may charge high prices for semi-finished products moving for further processing to plants located in countries with high rates of tax in such a way as to reduce the tax take on profits generated by the work of such plants.

As the GLOBALIZATION of investment, production and trade proceeds, the possibilities for and, thereby, the extent of transfer pricing is likely to increase. Peter Dicken (1998, p. 347) points out that

> [I]n general, the greater the differences in levels of corporate taxes, tariffs, duties, exchange rates, the greater will be the incentive for the TNC to manipulate its transfer prices.

TNCs have a strong incentive to engage in transfer pricing and the very large, highly centralized, global TNC has the strongest potential for doing so. The problem, he goes on, is that

> it has proved extremely difficult for governments (and researchers) to gather evidence on its . . . extent.

Transfer prices are set by and within firms and are, at one level, purely managerial – having to do with the monitoring and control of individual cost and profit centres. But at another level, the judicious use of internal transfer pricing facilitates the avoidance of tax and the costs of trade barriers. Firms can optimize their financial relations with the geographies in which they are located and so minimize payment of tariffs, for example, or shift accounted profits from locations with high tax regimes to locations with low rates of corporate taxation. TNCs can also get around difficulties associated with fluctuating exchange rates which, on the open market, might tend to the over- or under-pricing of products in transactions taking place between establishments of the same TNC located in different currency spaces. By disembedding themselves in such ways, TNCs are able to reduce their costs and increase their profitability at the expense of the locations in which they operate. RL

Reference and Suggested Reading

Dicken, P. 1998: *Global shift: transforming the world economy*, 3rd edn. London: Sage, ch 8.

transferability One of the bases for SPATIAL INTERACTION identified by E.L. Ullman (1956); it covers both (a) the TRANSPORT COSTS, which reflect the characteristics of the transport system and the commodity being moved, and (b) the ability of the commodity to bear those costs. Precious metals have high transferability, for example, because they are easy to handle and transport costs are small (per unit weight) relative to their total value; plate glass has low transferability because it is difficult to handle and has relatively low value.
AMH

Reference

Ullman, E.L. 1956: The role of transportation and the bases for interaction. In W.L. Thomas, ed., *Man's role in changing the face of the Earth*. Chicago: University of Chicago Press, 862–80.

transformation of variables Procedures used in PARAMETRIC STATISTICAL analysis to replace one set of numbers by some function of it, such as their logarithms or their square roots.

In EXPLORATORY DATA ANALYSIS transformations are used to improve the descriptive accuracy of statements. The GENERAL LINEAR MODEL assumes that relationships between pairs of variables are linear, for example, so that fitting a straight line to a curvilinear relationship describes it inefficiently. Transformation of either or both of the independent and the dependent variable may 'linearize' the relationship, and thus justify the use of REGRESSION analysis. (The figure shows two examples of such a transformation. In the first, a curvilinear relationship is made linear by transforming the x variable – on the horizontal axis – to x^2. In the second, the x variable is transformed into its square root.)

In CONFIRMATORY DATA ANALYSIS, involving testing HYPOTHESES according to the rules of statistical INFERENCE, transformations ensure that the requirements of the general linear model are met. If this is not done, the estimated coefficients are inefficient and valid inferences cannot be drawn from the sample taken.

A common transformation, which alters neither the form of the FREQUENCY DISTRIBUTION for a variable nor the shape of a relationship between two variables, but puts the data into a universal metric, expresses each value in a data set as a Z-score, where

$$Z_i = (x_i - x)/sd_x$$

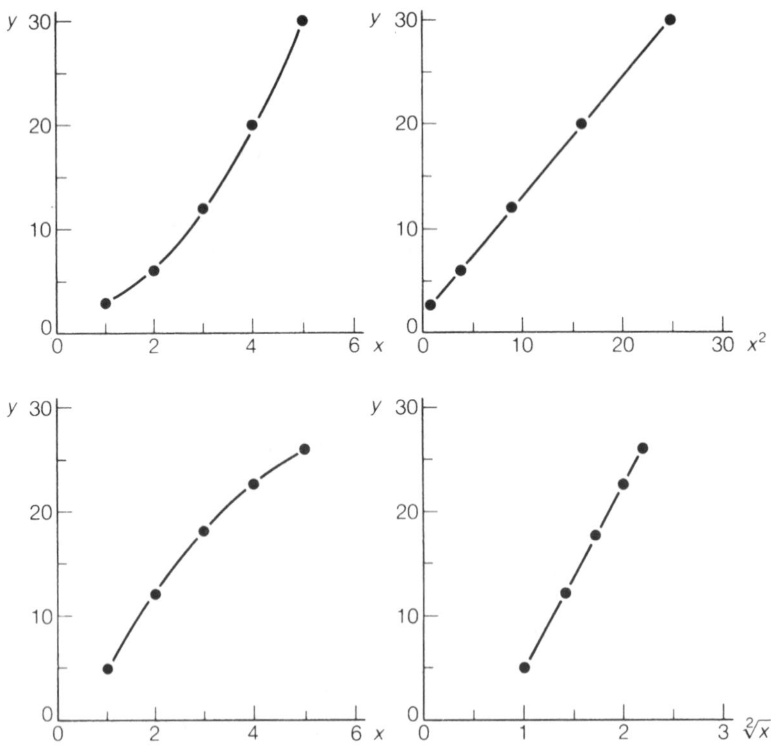

transformation of variables *Transformation from non-linear to linear relationships*

The original value (x_i) is transformed into its distance from the mean for all values of x, divided by the standard deviation (sd) of that mean, to produce the Z-score, Z_i. With a NORMAL DISTRIBUTION, the location of each individual value in the data set can then be identified, relative to the location for the same observation on a different variable. (For example, we may have data for the percentage voting Labour in a set of Parliamentary constituencies – mean 30.0, *sd* 15.0 – and the percentage of households in each living in rented dwellings – mean 35.0, *sd* 8.0. A constituency with 45 per cent voting Labour and 39.0 per cent living in rented dwellings would have Z-scores of +1.0 for the first variable [(45–30)/15] and +0.5 [(39–35)/8] for the second, indicating that it was above average on both variables, but substantially more so on the first.) Such transformations are central to the computational work involved in the techniques grouped under the rubric of the general linear model. RJJ

Suggested Reading

Johnston, R.J. 1978: *Multivariate statistical analysis in geography: a primer on the general linear model.* London and New York: Longman. · O'Brien, L. 1992: *Introducing quantitative geography: measurements, methods and generalised linear models.* London and New York: Routledge.

transgression Transgression involves the interrogation of boundaries, crossing lines that are not meant to be crossed, the infraction of binary structures that organize psyches, bodies, geographic spaces and social orders into high and low, inside and outside, normal and deviant. Writings by Bakhtin (1968), Foucault (1977) and Stallybrass and White (1986) have been particularly influential in foregrounding transgression as an analytical category.

Stallybrass and White (1986) theorize transgression in relation to the identity formation of the bourgeois classes in Renaissance Europe (see SUBJECT FORMATION, GEOGRAPHIES OF) through the interplay of psychic, cultural, social and political processes. Identities are constructed in relation to categories of disidentification: 'cultural identity is inseparable from its limits, it is always a boundary phenomenon and its order is always constructed around the figures of its territorial edge' (Stallybrass and White, 1986, p. 200). But what is explicitly excluded from European bourgeois identity produces new objects of desire. The political and psychic imperative to denigrate and expel the low or outsider is in conflict with the desire for this Other (see ORIENTALISM). This 'constitutive ambivalence' toward the low or the Other creates the conditions for transgression: for the bourgeoisie and middle classes, transgression can be a ritual or symbolic practice that allows them temporary access to their taboo desires, a 'delirious expenditure of the symbolic capital accrued (through the regulation of the body and the decathexis of HABITUS) in the successful struggle of bourgeois HEGEMONY' (Stallybrass and White, 1986, p. 201). Hence Stallybrass and White's phrase, 'the poetics' of transgression, and Eagleton's characterization of some forms of transgression (e.g. carnivals) as 'licensed' release (1981, p. 148).

Transgression also has a radical potential; this is to criticize and potentially denaturalize the existing social order by offering a 'temporary retextualizing of the social formation that exposes its "fictive" foundations' (Eagleton, 1981, p. 149). Hebdige (1979) posits two ways of incorporating trangressions that threaten to transform the social order: the commodification of the transgressive activity and labelling the transgressive group as deviant. Cresswell (1996) demonstrates the use of both of these strategies through case studies of graffiti artists in New York, anti-nuclear protest at Greenham Common and trespass at Stonehenge.

Geographic metaphors (boundaries, borders) are integral to the meaning of transgression, but the geographies of transgression go beyond this. At the micro-scale, Stallybrass and White (1986) argue that the body is a privileged site of transgression; the grotesque, polluted and deviant body is often the site for articulating transgression (BODY, GEOGRAPHY AND). Geographic spaces are also coded in terms of social binaries (e.g. safe/unsafe; private/public; clean/polluted) and transgressions of established socio-spatial orderings (matter out of place) are highly visible and can be especially disruptive. Cresswell argues that, in contrast to RESISTANCE (which implies intentionality), transgression is distinguished by its effects – be it the temporary release of sublimated desire, or rendering visible and open to criticism existing binarized hierarchies of bodies, spaces and cultures. GP

References

Bahktin, M. 1968: *Rabelais and his world*, trans. H. Iswolsky. Cambridge, MA: MIT Press. · Cresswell, T. 1996: *In place/out of place; geography, ideology and transgression.* Minneapolis: University of Minnesota Press. · Eagleton, T. 1981: *Walter Benjamin: Towards a revolutionary criticism.* London: Verso. · Foucault, M. 1977: *Language/counter-memory/practice*, ed., D.F. Bouchard, trans. D.F. Bouchard and S. Simon. Ithaca: University Cornell Press. · Hebdige, D. 1979: *Subculture: The meaning of style*. London: Routledge. · Stallybrass, P. and White, A. 1986: *The Politics and Poetics of Transgression*. Ithaca: Cornell University Press.

transhumance The practice by some pastoralists and pastoral farmers of moving herds of animals seasonally or periodically to exploit locally specific ECOSYTEMS, typically seasonal pastures (see MIXED FARMING; PASTORALISM). Transhumance was first used in a precise sense to describe the spatially limited patterns of animal movement in Alpine Europe among people who were primarily agrarian and who identified with a permanent settlement rather than a pastoral encampment (Johnson, 1969). Farmers who normally occupy permanent dwellings in one ecotype typically move animals, and often a proportion of household members, *vertically* from mountain to valley pastures between summer and winter months. Pastoral nomads who are periodically sedentary (for example, around dry season water holes) but who rely primarily upon animal products, may also engage in seasonal patterns of movements of animals and people, typically a *horizontal* search for pasture associated with spatial variation in monsoonal rainfall (cf. NOMADISM). MW

Reference

Johnson, D. 1969: *The nature of nomadism: a comparative study of pastoral migrations in Southeast Asia and Northern Africa*. Chicago: University of Chicago, Department of Geography Research Paper #118.

transnational corporation (TNC) 'A firm which has the power to coordinate and control operations in more than one country, even if it does not own them' (Dicken, 1998, pp. 8, 177). This definition implies that, although TNCs generally do own the assets that they use, 'they are also typically involved in a spider's web of collaborative relationships with other legally independent firms across the globe' (Dicken, 1998, p. 8) and in the ways in which they coordinate and control transactions throughout the production chain. TNCs cannot, therefore, be reduced merely to foreign direct investment. The more restrictive term MULTINATIONAL CORPORATION (MNC) implies operations in more than two countries.

No longer integrated (see INTEGRATION) merely by flows of merchant CAPITAL and TRADE or by finance capital and indirect (portfolio) investment, or even by the internationalization of industrial capital (see ECONOMIC GEOGRAPHY) and the global evaluation of bond markets, the world economic geography is increasingly tied together by the corporate organization of large enterprises which operate at a worldwide scale and account for the transfer of a high proportion of knowledge and (often specialized) labour in global circulation (see GLOBALIZATION). According to Peter Dicken (1998, p. 177):

> [M]ore than any other single institution it is the Transnational Corporation which has come to be regarded as the primary shaper of the global economy.

The growth of TNCs/MNCs has now gone beyond their mere spatial expansion (including their origins and the ever-increasing diversity of the geography of their investments); instead it is characterized by the intensification of corporate control over the global operating environment. Between one-fifth and one-quarter of total world production in market economies is undertaken by TNCs/MNCs. Electronic communications and management systems allow the centralization of information and decision-making and the decentralization of operations, while the freeing of national controls over the international movement of finance capital and the establishment of international capital markets and financial systems combine to increase the international mobility of capital.

This combination of centralization, decentralization and global structure facilitates locational flexibility and the reduction of risk, as corporate strategy is able to respond quickly with the use of what are, in corporate terms, ephemeral branch plants and national subsidiaries, to changes in the world economy, without destabilizing the organization as a whole. However ephemeral such investments may be for the corporation, for the host nation they often represent a significant part of the national economy over which local interests may have little or no control.

TNCs/MNCs are now multinational in their origin as well as their destination: many American corporations are now outstripped in size by Japanese and even by Western European TNCs/MNCs and, although generally small in size, TNCs/MNCs are now emerging from the leading newly industrializing countries. There is, as a result, an increase in the interpenetration of capital around the world which serves to break down the possibilities for integrated and locally controlled indigenous development in particular economies. However, over 89 per cent of the world's largest TNCs/

MNCs are based in the USA (32 per cent), the EU (31 per cent) and Japan (25 per cent).

There is 'little evidence of TNCs having the share of their activities outside their home country which might be expected if they are global firms' (Dicken, 1998, p. 196) although the largest TNCs/MNCs are enormous: each of the top 50 TNCs has an annual turnover greater than the GNP of many of the world's smaller LDCs, whilst the largest (such as Mitsubishi, Mitsui, Itochu, General Motors, Sumitomo, Ford and Exxon) rival countries like South Africa, Norway, Portugal and Greece (Knox and Agnew, 1998). And, through their profit-making interest in national currency differentials articulated through the multinational network of banking corporations, they are capable of both the stimulation and destabilization of national economic geographies. Furthermore, TNCs/MNCs dominate world TRADE with over 50 per cent of the total trade of Japan and the USA accounted for by intra-firm trade. They are also able to indulge in the largely invisible practice of TRANSFER PRICING. This is an accounting practice which enables the allocation of costs and the pricing of goods moving within the corporation to be made in the most profitable fashion in response to local conditions of regulation, regardless of the accuracy of the costs, the prices or their allocation.

The increasingly multinational origin of TNCs has been accompanied by a diversification of forms of organization with significant cultural and economic consequences. The *chaebol* in South Korea, modelled on the Japanese *zaibatsu* (the giant family-owned firms which dominated the pre-Second World War development of the Japanese economic geography) were at the heart of the crisis of the Korean economy during the late 1990s because of their close, state-articulated links with the financial sector and their significance for the economy as a whole. One response to the crisis was a fundamental restructuring of the *chaebol* to make their financial relations far more transparent. But such a transformation not only reduces diversity in the population of TNCs but exposes the Korean economy to the vicissitudes of financial capital controlled primarily in Western Europe, the USA and Japan.

Networks of relationships also characterize the Japanese *keiretsu* which, Dicken (1998) remarks, are characterized by transactions conducted through highly symbolic alliances of affiliated companies based around long-term relationships within 'families' of related firms and founded on highly complex links – financial, personal and commercial. *Keiretsu* may be horizontal – organized around a core bank and a general trading company (*sogo shosha*) which carries out a variety of commercial functions for the *keiretsu* (examples include Mitsubishi, Mitsui and Sumitomo), or vertical – organized around a large parent company in a particular industry such as Toshiba, Toyota and Sony. But a highly complex network of links also exists between horizontal and vertical *keiretsu* which serve further to bypass purely market-based relationships within 'industries' but also to make a flexible response to change rather difficult.

The counterfactual problem of assessing the balance sheet of advantages and disadvantages of TNCs/MNCs is difficult (TNCs/MNCs have social, cultural and political effects as well as environmental and economic consequences). The bottom line is far from clear for the CIRCUIT OF CAPITAL as a whole (its overall efficiency and responsiveness to change and the potential for change), for the various forms of CAPITAL around the circuit, or for the places caught up in the influence of TNCs/MNCs. Judged from the perspective of DEVELOPMENT, their influence is malign insofar as at the same time that they connect economies into the global circuit of capital and so increase supply lines and markets and introduce new technology (which has both positive and negative developmental effects), they displace control over the making of history and geography from people struggling to make their living and define their identity in such economic geographies by imposing a particular understanding and measure of value and progress.

RL

References

Dicken, P. 1998: *Global shift: the internationalization of productive activity*, 3rd edn. London: Paul Chapman Publishing. · Knox, P. and Agnew, J. 1998: *The geography of the world economy*. London and New York: Arnold.

Suggested Reading

Dicken (1998).

transnationalism An ongoing series of cross-border movements in which immigrants develop and maintain numerous economic, political, social and cultural links in more than one NATION (see also NATION-STATE). Unlike earlier theories of MIGRATION and IMMIGRATION, which generally characterized a movement across borders as one of either permanent rupture followed by assimilation in a new society, or as one of temporary 'sojourning' followed by a return home, transnationalism describes a migration pattern of simultaneous connection to two or more nations.

Many scholars have linked this type of migration process with changes in the nature of CAPITALISM (see, e.g. Blanc, Basch and Glick Schiller, 1995; Ong and Nonini, 1997; Smith and Guarnizo, 1998; cf. GLOBALIZATION). With the increased flexibility of production and finance in the global economy of POST-FORDISM, the use of both labour and capital has shifted dramatically in the last three decades. The rapid growth of TRANSNATIONAL CORPORATIONS and the organization of production on a worldwide scale has affected the flows of immigrants across national borders, and has led to a transformed CULTURE of migration and to new kinds of strategies by the migrants themselves. These strategies involve both greater flexibility in terms of national and cultural allegiances, and greater fixity in the establishment and maintenance of a social field that crosses formerly regulated borders (cf. BOUNDARY; FRONTIER).

One of the key components of transnationalism is the 'multiplicity of involvements that transmigrants sustain in both home and host societies' (Basch, Glick Schiller and Blanc, 1996, p. 7). In numerous case studies immigrants have been shown to construct an intricate, multi-webbed network of ongoing social relations that span their country of origin and their country (or countries) of settlement (see e.g. Rouse, 1991; Soguk, 1995; cf. CHAIN MIGRATION). These continuous social relations, moreover, have major implications for both the immigrants and their host societies. Migrant labourers have boosted the economies of many developing countries through their remittances to friends and family; the growing importance of this source of economic hard currency for the state has, in turn, led to more generous laws and policies governing the rights of the new transmigrants. In some cases, the state's attempt to capture these migrants and their capital remittances has extended as far as granting them property rights, health and welfare benefits, voting rights, and even dual CITIZENSHIP (Guarnizo, 1994).

For transmigrants of the wealthy classes, often called the 'transnational elite', the movements and allegiances formed across borders have had major implications for both international business and state policy. Transnational citizens, a new cosmopolitan CLASS with passports to at least two countries, are occasionally able to manipulate local laws and cultures in ways that can greatly influence both business opportunities and the philosophical foundations of local and national cultural norms. Their impact can be felt in areas as divergent as NEIGHBOURHOOD struggles over ZONING, and federal laws regulating the disclosure of overseas assets (Hannerz, 1990; Mitchell, 1997a).

Both transnational labourers and the transnational élite have influenced current debates on the meaning of citizenship and on the viability of STATE control over the new global flows characteristic of late CAPITALISM. The concept of transnationalism itself is often invoked by those seeking a middle ground between proclamations of the death of the state and exaggerated claims of its ongoing vitality. Its conceptual position as a site of fluidity, HYBRIDITY and 'in-betweenness' (in-between nations and in-between theoretical positions) has made it a dominant leitmotif in POST-COLONIALISM, where many theorists have written of the liberatory potential of positions of transience, hybridity and ambiguity (e.g. Bhabha, 1994). This, in turn, has led to greater calls for empirically grounded research in which the actual geographies of transnationalism are made manifest (Mitchell, 1997b).

KM

References

Bhabha, H. 1994: DissemiNation: time, narrative and the margins of the modern nation. *The location of culture*. New York: Routledge, 139–70. · Basch, L., Glick Schiller, N. and Blanc, C. 1996: *Nations unbound: transnational projects, postcolonial predicaments and deterritorialized nation-states*. New York: Gordon and Breach. · Blanc, C., Basch, L. and Glick Schiller, N., eds, 1995: Transnationalism, nation-states and culture. *Current Anthropology* 36 (4): 683–6. · Guarnizo, L. 1994: Los Dominicanyorks: the making of a binational society. *Annals of the American Academy of Political and Social Science* 533: 70–86. · Hannerz, U. 1990: Cosmopolitans and locals in world culture. *Theory, Culture and Society* 7: 2–3. · Mitchell, K. 1997a: Conflicting geographies of democracy and the public sphere in Vancouver, B.C. *Transactions, Institute of British Geographers* NS 22: 162–79. · Mitchell, K. 1997b: Transnational discourse: bringing geography back in. *Antipode* 29 (2): 101–14. · Ong, A. and Nonini, D., eds, 1997: *Ungrounded empires: the cultural politics of modern Chinese transnationalism*. New York and London: Routledge. · Rouse, R. 1991: Mexican migration and the social space of postmodernism. *Diaspora*, Spring: 8–34. · Smith, P.S. and Guarnizo, L., eds, 1998: *Transnationalism from below*. New Brunswick: Transaction Publishers. · Soguk, N. 1995: Transnational/transborder bodies: resistance, accommodation, and exile in refugee and migration movements on the U.S.–Mexican border. In M. Shapiro and J. Alker, eds, *Challenging boundaries: global flows, territorial identities*. Minneapolis: University of Minnesota Press, 285–323.

Suggested Reading

Ang, I. and Stratton, J., eds, 1996: Asianing Australia: notes toward a critical transnationalism in cultural studies. *Cultural Studies* 10 (1): 16–36. · Lavie, S. and Swedenburg, T. 1996: *Displacement, diaspora, and geographies of identity*. Durham: Duke University Press. · Wilson, R. and Dissanayake, W., eds, 1996: *Global/local: cultural production and the transnational imaginary*. Durham and London: Duke University Press.

transport costs The total costs involved in moving between two places, which in the case of goods movements involves not only the FREIGHT RATE but also the costs of documentation, packaging, insurance and inventory. Transport costs are a central element in most classical LOCATION THEORIES, being presented as a primary determinant of both agricultural land use (see VON THÜNEN MODEL) and INDUSTRIAL LOCATION THEORIES: they were at the heart of arguments for geography as SPATIAL SCIENCE, or as a 'discipline in distance' (Watson, 1955; cf. LOCATIONAL ANALYSIS).

AMH

Reference

Watson, J.W. 1955: Geography: a discipline in distance. *Scottish Geographical Magazine* 71: 1–13.

transport geography The study of the role of transport in geography, including the provision of transport systems, the use of those systems for the movement of people and goods, and the relationships between transport and other geographical phenomena.

Nineteenth-century geographers (e.g. F. Ratzel and A. Hettner) recognized the importance of transport as providing features of the LANDSCAPE and as an agent of geographic change. In the early twentieth century leading French geographers (e.g. P. Vidal de la Blache and J. Brunhes) developed the geographical study of transport as part of the 'geography of circulation', which studied not only the permanent landscape features associated with transport but also the transient movements of goods and people. The sub-discipline developed little until the 1950s, when studies of individual transport modes were initiated (ports, airports and railways). Then, in the 1960s North American geographers led by E.L. Ullman, W.L. Garrison, E.J. Taaffe and others, demonstrated the applicabiliity of quantitative techniques for transport studies. As a result there was a rapid expansion of studies in transport geography (often with direct or indirect planning applications). But this whole approach came under critique because in its attachment to QUANTITATIVE METHODS and POSITIVISM it seemed to emphasize spatial patterns and spatial associations at the expense of a fuller theoretically based understanding of transport phenomena in a broader economic and social perspective.

The first and most persistent feature of transport geography has nevertheless been the study of transport phenomena in their own right. Five categories of work can be identified:

NETWORK studies attempt to describe the *geographical pattern of transport networks* (roads, railways, canals, etc.), and to explain these patterns either at the level of the whole network or by reference to individual links, including an account of how these patterns have changed over time by the growth and decay of networks.

Studies of transport nodes and terminals have concentrated chiefly on ports and airports, describing not only the MORPHOLOGY of individual facilities and their evolution over time, but also of whole SYSTEMS of competing ports and airports. Some authors have attempted to systematize these studies in the form of idealized sequences or models.

Studies of the *provision of scheduled services* (by train, bus and air) complement the study of physical networks and terminals. Some of the descriptive studies use the same concepts and techniques as are applied to networks, but more successful measures incorporate reference to frequency of scheduled services in time as well as their spatial pattern. Recent studies have focused especially on the changes in patterns occasioned by the trend toward national and international deregulation. In all this work attention also needs to be paid to the mobility problems of those (in both rural and urban areas) who are dependent upon scheduled services, and the inequities between them and those who have access to private transport.

Studies of the movement of commodities have often been hindered by the absence of reliable and complete data, but where such data are available techniques (including FACTOR ANALYSIS) have been developed to identify the distinctive structures within a complex set of flows (for example, the existence of hierarchies and subsystems). Explanations in terms of the geography of places have often used Ullman's bases for SPATIAL INTERACTION, while operational models have used been based upon LINEAR PROGRAMMING and GRAVITY MODELS. Attention has also been paid to the issue of modal split (see TRANSPORTATION CHOICE MODELS). In recent years there has been a greater emphasis on the link between commodity flows and the organizational and behavioural characteristics of the commercial corporations as the initiators and agents of commodity movements.

The *movement of people* is studied at all geographical scales (within regions, between regions, and internationally). Once again complete and accurate data sets are difficult to collect, especially where large numbers of trips are made by private transport. Early descriptive studies have now largely been replaced by analytical or explanatory studies which attempt to account: first, for the number of movements originating in or terminating in a geographical area; second, for the levels of flow between areas; and third, for the allocation of these trips between competing modes. Earlier studies used aggregate travel models, the most successful of which were GRAVITY MODELS but other models (e.g. INTERVENING OPPORTUNITIES) have their champions. From the 1980s onwards criticisms of the weak behavioural basis of such models led to an increased interest in various TRANSPORTATION CHOICE MODELS in which the behaviour of individuals is related to the perceived utility of alternative destinations.

A second common theme in transport geography is the role of transport as an agent or facilitator of geographic change. The geographical pattern of transport networks can often be correlated with urban growth and the location of manufacturing and service industry. Such spatial associations provide casual evidence that transport changes induce geographic change. But attempts to verify this claim stumble over two problems. The first is circular causation: although transport developments can lead to urban growth, urban growth itself may be the cause of transport expansion. The second is that the transport induced changes are often inextricably linked to concurrent changes induced by other causes.

The third area of interest has become more dominant in the 1990s. It is increasingly evident that the transport sector is a major consumer of ENERGY and source of atmospheric POLLUTION. The emission of hydrocarbons, additives, the products of the combustion of fossil fuels (particulates, oxides of nitrogen, carbon dioxide) has raised questions about the long-term sustainability of current transport systems, and two consequential problems for geography. First, if the use of transport has to be reduced for environmental reasons what new geographical patterns will emerge? Conversely, what new geographical patterns of economic and social activity, and what new patterns of transport provision will best facilitate such a reduction?

All these central concerns of transport geography have potential importance for transport planning: it is therefore unsurprising that transport geography has forged close links with the cognate of transport planning and traffic engineering. AMH

Suggested Reading

Eliot Hurst, M.E., ed., 1974: *Transportation geography: comments and readings*. New York: McGraw-Hill. · Hanson, S., ed., 1986: *The geography of urban transportation*. New York: Guilford. · Hanson, S. 1998: Off the road? Reflections on transportation geography in the information age. *Geoforum* 6: 241–9. · Hoyle, B.S. and Knowles, R.D. 1992: *Modern transport geography*. London: Belhaven; *Journal of Transport Geography* 1993. Exeter: Elsevier Science. · McKinnon, A.C. 1989: *Physical distribution systems*. London: Routledge. · White, P. 1995: *Public transport*, 3rd edn. London: UCLPress.

transportation choice models A range of statistical and mathematical procedures used to model the ways in which individuals choose between discrete alternatives. The models, which collectively are known as *discrete choice models*, can be applied to a variety of choice situations – such as a home, mode of transport for a journey, and a holiday destination.

When applied to choice of travel mode, journey type and destination, such models operate at the level of the individual (hence they are often known as *disaggregate travel demand models* and *modal split models*). They assume that people choose that option which provides them with the greatest utility (cf. UTILITY THEORY). The models are usually tested using LOGISTIC REGRESSION methods (see also LOGIT) and include such criteria as price, speed, comfort and safety in the assessment of alternative travel modes and routes which are used in assessing utility (including subjective evaluations of those criteria). AMH

Suggested Reading

Bruton, M.J. 1985: *Introduction to transportation planning*, 3rd edn. London: Hutchinson. · Hensher, D.A. 1981: *Applied discrete choice modelling*. London: Croom Helm. · Pipkin, J.S. 1986: Disaggregate travel models. In S. Hanson, ed., *The geography or urban transportation*. New York: Guilford, 179–206.

transportation problem A special case of LINEAR PROGRAMMING, dealing with the least-cost supply of goods from N origins to M destinations. If the amounts available at N are known, together with the demand at M and the TRANSPORT COSTS between each N–M pair of locations, solution of the transportation problem yields the least-cost pattern of flows between the origins and destinations.

Solution of the problem is normally iterative, beginning with a feasible solution (i.e. one consistent with the supplies at all *N* points and the demands at all *M*) and converges upon the optimum (or one of the optima if there are more than one). The iteration procedure operates by establishing relative prices at the origins and destinations, and converges on an optimal set of prices by solving two problems simultaneously: (a) a *primal problem*, which involves establishing an optimal pattern of flows which minimizes transport costs; and (b) a *dual problem*, which establishes a pattern of prices that maximizes the value-added in transportation.

The basic procedure can be adapted to more complex situations. A capacitated network may restrict the flow on certain links in the SYSTEM, for example, and a dummy (or dump) destination may be used to absorb (at nil transport costs) supplies available at, at least some, of the *N* origins which are additional to demand. Even where transport is not involved, as in the allocation of *M* plots of agricultural land to *N* crops with a minimum expenditure on fertilizers, it is possible to structure the problem in terms of the transportation model.

The technique has been applied in geography in two main ways. First, it has been used in attempts to explain flow and/or production patterns, to show that they are consistent with the model's least-cost basis; these are rarely successful, as 'real-world' situations normally find more of the *N–M* links being used than solution of the transportation problem suggests. Secondly, it may be used to evaluate the relative efficiency of an actual flow pattern, but the latter usually involves more constraints and heterogeneities than can be accounted for in the model. AMH

Suggested Reading

Hay, A.M. 1977: *Linear programming: elementary geographical applications of the transportation problem.* Norwich: Geo Books CATMOG 11. · Taaffe, E.J. and Gauthier, H.L. 1973: *Geography of transportation.* Englewood Cliffs, NJ: Prentice-Hall.

travel writing, geography and One possible meaning of 'geo-graphy' is 'earth-writing', and so one might expect there to be a close association between geography and 'travel writing'. Yet one of the great ironies of the modern discipline is that, at the very moment when the sensibilities of traditional REGIONAL GEOGRAPHY had been eclipsed by the rise of a formal and abstract SPATIAL SCIENCE and its successor projects, most of which showed little or no concern for the representation of other places and other people, there was an extraordinary surge of public interest in the imaginative accounts and popular geographies provided by travel writing.

Modern geography's interest in the academic study of travel writing is equally recent, and has several interrelated sources. First, a revivified history of GEOGRAPHY has installed a greatly expanded sense of what constitutes 'geography': no longer circumscribed by the genealogy of geography as a science or a formal discipline, scholars have become much more attentive to the production of geographical knowledge in a variety of forms and from a variety of subject-positions and social locations that had no place in conventional histories. Secondly, a new interest in historical geographies of COLONIALISM and IMPERIALISM has opened up the records of scientific expeditions and the journals of explorers and ordinary (and not-so-ordinary) travellers to a critical interrogation that seeks to recover not only their production of 'spaces of knowledge' but also their entanglements in 'spaces of POWER' (cf. EXPLORATION). Thirdly, the 'new CULTURAL GEOGRAPHY' has placed questions of representation at the very heart of geographical inquiry, and the study of travel writing has an important part to play in illuminating the POETICS and politics involved in the production and reception of IMAGINATIVE GEOGRAPHIES, in revealing the reciprocities between identity-formation and the construction of alterity (see OTHER/OTHERNESS), and in teasing out the complexities and entailments of HYBRIDITY and TRANSCULTURATION.

The boundaries between 'fact' and 'fiction' are called into question (or at any rate blurred) by these developments. While geographers have offered critical readings of nominally fictionalized accounts of travel (e.g. Cresswell, 1993; Phillips, 1997), much of the interest in travel writing has centred on using the apparatus of CRITICAL THEORY and POST-COLONIALISM to offer readings of ostensibly factual travel accounts. Geographers are not alone in these predilections, and the academic study of such travel writing has attracted scholars in anthropology and sociology, cultural and literary studies, and cultural history and the history of science. Neither has it been confined to written texts – to 'travel writing' in the narrow sense – and there have been important cross-fertilizations with the history of art, the history of cartography, the history of photography and the history of 'collecting' (e.g. Stafford, 1984; Smith, 1985; see also ART, GEOGRAPHY AND; CARTOGRAPHY, HISTORY OF). The study of travel writing has been concerned less with the routine documentation and record-keeping produced in the course of political administration or commercial affairs – although the conduct of both has involved and continues to involve extensive travel – than with the texts produced in the course of travel conducted under the signs of Reason and Pleasure. Those two well-springs flow into and out of one another, and they are hardly without political or economic implications, so that any (conventional) distinction between 'exploration', 'travel' and 'TOURISM' is far from stable or secure. For analytical purposes, however, it is possible to list a series of prominent themes under those three – loose – headings:

Cultures of exploration and enumeration: images of other cultures and landscapes on the occasions of European 'discovery' and colonial dispossession (e.g. Carter, 1987; Campbell, 1988; Greenblatt, 1991; Clayton, 1999); images of other 'natures', the cultural formation of natural history and the conduct of European scientific expeditions (e.g. Jardine, Secord and Spary, 1996; Miller and Reill, 1996); regional surveys and regional geographies (e.g. Godlewska, 1995; Naylor and Jones, 1997).

Cultures of travel: imaginative geographies produced by independent, 'extra-scientific' travellers and the 'imperial stylistics' of travel writing (e.g. Pratt, 1992; Gregory, 1995); gendered geographies and women travellers (e.g. Mills, 1991; Melman, 1992; Blunt, 1995; McEwen, 1996; Morgan, 1996); the intersections of cultures of travel, transgression and sexuality (e.g. Porter, 1991; Aldrich, 1993; Boone, 1995).

Cultures of tourism: the connections between imaginative geographies, the formation of national identities and the consolidation of bourgeois culture (e.g. Pemble, 1987; Andrews, 1989; Ousby, 1990; Buzard, 1993).

The study of travel writing is thus not a narrow textualism in which the circle of interest is drawn tightly around the author and the TEXT. Duncan and Gregory (1999) have urged scholars to recover both the spaces of REPRESENTATION and the spaces of travel that enter into the production of travel writings: on the one side, to attend to the multiple sites at which representation takes place, the different means by which travellers record their experiences, and the ways in which travel writing works as an act of translation to produce (and authorize) a tense 'space in-between'; on the other side, to attend to the spatiality of travel by registering travel writings and other travel texts as productions by corporeal subjects physically moving through material landscapes. It is also important to consider the effects of travel writing: both its domestic reception and its non-domestic PERFORMATIVITY (i.e. its effects on subsequent travellers and local inhabitants) (Gregory, 1999).

The study of travel writing and geography threads out into a wider interest in the connections between travel and the cultural formations of modernity. It is noticeable that much of this work has been concerned with historical rather than contemporary writings (cf. Holland and Huggan, 1998) and that it has been dominated by studies of European and North American travellers (cf. Burton, 1996, 1998; Yarid, 1996; see also OCCIDENTALISM). These are significant lacunae; but it also remains to be seen whether the gap identified in the opening paragraph will be closed, and whether the study of travel writing will eventually enliven the practice of 'earth-writing': whether it will license more critically aware, more imaginative and more effective geographical descriptions that succeed in attracting a wider public audience than the enumerations (rather than evocative descriptions) found in the standard regional geographies. DG

References

Aldrich, R. 1993: *The seduction of the Mediterranean: writing, art and homosexual fantasy*. London: Routledge. · Andrews, M. 1989: *The search for the picturesque: landscape aesthetics and tourism in Britain 1760–1800*. Stanford: Stanford University Press. · Boone, J. 1995: Vacation cruises, or the homoerotics of Orientalism. *Public Modern Language Association* 110: 89–107. · Blunt, A. 1995: *Travel, gender and imperialism*. New York: Guilford. · Burton, A. 1996: Making a spectacle of Empire: Indian travellers in fin-de-siècle London. *Historical Workshop Journal* 42: 127–46. · Burton, A. 1998: *At the heart of empire: Indians and the colonial encounter in late Victorian Britain*. Berkeley: University of California Press. · Buzard, J. 1993: *The beaten track: European tourism, literature and the ways to 'culture' 1800–1918*. Oxford: Clarendon Press. · Campbell, M. 1988: *The witness and the other world: exotic European travel writing 400–1600*. Ithaca: Cornell University Press. · Carter, P. 1987: *The road to Botany Bay*. London: Faber. · Clayton, D. 1999: *Islands of truth*. Vancouver: University of British Columbia Press. · Cresswell, T. 1993: Mobility as resistance: a geographical reading of Kerouac's *On the road*. *Transactions, Institute of British Geographers* NS 18: 249–62. · Duncan, J. and Gregory, D. 1999: Writes of passage: reading travel writing. In J. Duncan and D. Gregory, eds, *Writes of passage*. London and New York: Routledge, 1–13. · Godlewska, A. 1995: Map, text and image: The mentality of enlightened conquerors. A new look at the *Description de l'Egypte*. *Transactions, Institute of British Geographers* NS 20: 5–28. · Greenblatt, S. 1991: *Marvellous possessions: the wonder of the New World*. Chicago: University of Chicago Press. · Gregory, D. 1995: Between the book and the lamp: imaginative geographies of Egypt, 1849–50. *Transactions, Institute of British Geographers* NS 20: 29–57. · Gregory, D. 1999: Scripting Egypt: Orientalism and the cultures of travel. In J. Duncan and D. Gregory, eds, *Writes of passage*. London and New York: Routledge, 114–50. · Holland, P. and Huggan G. 1998: *Tourists with typewriters: critical reflections on contemporary travel writing*. Ann Arbor: University of Michigan Press. · Jardine, N., Secord, J.A. and Spary, E.C., eds, 1996: *Cultures of natural history*. Cambridge: Cambridge University Press. · McEwan, C. 1996: Paradise or pandemonium? West African landscapes in the travel accounts of Victorian women. *Journal of Historical Geography* 22: 68–83. · Melman, B. 1992: *Women's Orients: English women and the Middle East 1718–1918*. London: Macmillan. · Ann Arbor, MI: University of Michigan Press. · Miller, D. and Reill, P., eds, 1996: *Visions of empire: voyages, botany and representations of nature*. Cambridge: Cambridge University Press. · Mills, S. 1991: *Discourses of difference: an analysis of women's travel writing and colonialism*. London and New York: Routledge. · Morgan, S. 1996: *Place matters: gendered geography in Victorian women's travel books about Southeast Asia*. New Brunswick, NJ: Rutgers University Press. · Naylor, S. and Jones, G.A. 1997: Writing orderly geographies of distant places: the Regional Survey Movement and Latin America. *Ecumene* 4: 273–99. · Ousby, I. 1990: *The Englishman's England: travel, taste and the rise of tourism*. Cambridge: Cambridge University Press. · Pemble, J. 1987: *The Mediterranean passion: Victorians and Edwardians in the South*. Oxford: Oxford University Press. · Phillips, R. 1997: *Mapping men and Empire: a geography of adventure*. London and New York: Routledge. · Porter, D. 1991: *Haunted journeys: desire and transgression in European travel writing*. Princeton, NJ: Princeton University Press. · Pratt, M.L. 1992: *Imperial eyes: travel writing and transculturation*. London and New York: Routledge. · Smith, B. 1985: *European vision and the South Pacific*. New Haven: Yale University Press. · Stafford, B. 1984: *Voyage into substance: art, science, nature and the illustrated travel account 1760–1840*. Cambridge, MA: MIT Press. · Yarid, N. 1996: *Arab travellers and Western civilization*. London: Saqi Books.

Suggested Reading

Duncan and Gregory (1999). · Holland and Huggan (1998). · Pratt (1992).

travelling theory Intellectual ideas that circulate from discipline to discipline and from situation to situation. The term has its origins in the writings of the Palestinian/American cultural critic Edward Said (1983), who acknowledged the existence of a general 'transplantation, transference, circulation and commerce of theoretical ideas': 'The movement of ideas and theories from one place to another is both a fact of life and a usefully enabling condition of intellectual activity'. This is a generalized condition of all contemporary intellectual work: laboratory scientists are drawn into a global traffic of ideas as much as scholars labouring in the archives. To make such distinctions is to be reminded that this 'inter-disciplinary space' is not homogeneous, and Said draws particular attention to the existence of interruptions and irregularities that fracture the planes of the humanities and social sciences. He might also have noticed the striations and circuits that channel flows of ideas in particular directions: most often, at least in the humanities and social sciences, from the HEGEMONIC sites of the Western academy to sites elsewhere in the world. Other critics have taken Said at his word: they argue that the 'commerce' of theoretical ideas to which he refers is increasingly valorized through a generalized commodification of knowledge in which universities have become TRANSNATIONAL CORPORATIONS and theory (including CRITICAL THEORY) has been turned into another form of 'symbolic capital' (cf. Dhareshwar, 1990; Gregory 1994, pp. 181–3). This bears directly on Said's larger concerns – the critique of ORIENTALISM and the politics of POST-COLONIALISM – and there has been a lively and anguished debate about the possibilities (or otherwise) of calling upon European 'high theory' to subvert EUROCENTRISM (cf. Young, 1990).

These are vitally important concerns, but Said's original point was a different – though no less critical – one. In the humanities and the social sciences, he proposed, 'theory is a response to a specific social and historical situation of which an intellectual occasion is a part' (p. 237). Such a claim intersects with arguments about SITUATED KNOWLEDGE and, anticipating those discussions, Said welcomed the possibilities for alliance, affinity and solidarity opened up by the mutual exchange of ideas. But he also sounded a serious caution: he warned that powerful ideas, simply because they are so powerful, run the risks of being reduced to narrowly dogmatic, closed and irreflexive versions of their original forms or of being inflated to imperial, exorbitant and arrogant versions of their original forms (p. 239). For this reason, Said urged the need for what he called a 'critical consciousness', 'a sort of spatial sense' that would be capable of grasping the historico-geographical circumstances out of which particular theories have emerged and the distances that intervene and leave their marks when such theories are set in motion (pp. 241–2). Only then, Said believed, would it be possible to keep theory open: to treat theory as always partial, always unfinished: 'No theory exhausts the situation out of which it emerged or to which it is transported' (p. 242).

Seen thus, for Said and for many others, 'travelling' can become a way of resisting the imperial ambitions of theory, of making those who work with it accountable for its movements, and of challenging the politics of closure. The origins of travelling theory need to be scrupulously acknowledged, therefore, since it will always be freighted with assumptions and dispositions which may not – and often should not – survive the journey intact. Talcott Parsons's sociology produced a supposedly general model of 'the social system' that turned out to be a highly partial model of post-war US society (see STRUCTURAL FUNCTIONALISM); Jürgen Habermas developed a programmatic account of the project of MODERNITY that was in substantial degree a response to the predicament of post-war Germany coming to terms with the Holocaust (see CRITICAL THEORY). This does not mean that such formulations are inescapably context-bound; and both these examples draw on sources from a wide range of other sites, so that their 'local knowledge' is conspicuously not 'local' even in its originating versions. Said's point, rather, is that the multiple local geographies written into any theory need to be opened up for inspection.

And yet other critics continued to be worried by Said's root METAPHOR. Images of travel – of movement and mobility, of tours and visits, of nomadic theory (see RHIZOME) and 'travelling theory' – have become commonplaces of contemporary theorization. But the metaphor of travel comes with its own cultural and political baggage, and when that is opened up and inspected it reveals much about the privileges accorded to 'cosmopolitan intellectuals' within the Western academy and about the situated and highly unequal freedoms of Western intellectual culture more generally within the global production and dissemination of ideas (cf. Wolff, 1993; Kaplan, 1996; Clifford, 1997). DG

References

Clifford, J. 1997: *Routes: travel and translation in the late twentieth century.* Cambridge, MA: Harvard University Press. · Dhareshwar, V. 1990: The predicament of theory. In M. Kreiswirth and M. Cheetham, eds, *Theory between the disciplines: Authority, vision, politics.* Ann Arbor, MI: University of Michigan Press, 231–50. · Gregory, D. 1994: *Geographical imaginations.* Oxford and Cambridge, MA: Blackwell. · Kaplan, C. 1996: *Questions of travel: postmodern discourses of displacement.* Durham: Duke University Press. · Said, E. 1983: Travelling theory. In his *The word, the text and the critic.* Cambridge, MA: Harvard University Press; London: Faber (1984 publication), 226–47. · Wolff, J. 1993: On the road again: metaphors of travel in cultural criticism. *Cultural Studies* 7: 224–39. · Young, R. 1990: *White mythologies: writing History and the West.* London and New York: Routledge.

Suggested Reading

Gregory (1994), 9–14, 181–3. · Kaplan (1996), 101–42.

trend surface analysis A technique for fitting a generalized SURFACE to a set of geographical point data. The method also encompasses evaluating the degree of fit, representing the surface with ISOLINES, and mapping the RESIDUALS, that is, the vertical deviations between the observed data values and the best-fit surface. Because identification and removal of an obvious trend can yield a more meaningful map, the residuals are often of greater interest than the trend surface itself (Chorley and Haggett, 1965).

Trend surface analysis is usually a form of multiple REGRESSION in which dependent variable Z is a function of orthogonal geographical coordinates X and Y (Swan and Sandilands, 1995, pp. 290–300). The simplest configuration is the linear trend surface, a plane represented by the equation:

$$Z = b_0 + b_1X + b^2Y$$

in which b_0 is the Z intercept and slope coefficients b_1 and b^2 describe the plane's inclination along the X and Y axes. Trend surfaces are easily mapped because the polynomial can be evaluated readily at any point. If the contour interval is constant, a linear trend surface yields a map of parallel, uniformly spaced straight-line contours. Multiple regression measures the degree of fit with the coefficient of determination R2, which ranges from 0.0 for data with no discernible trend to 1.0 for a surface passing through every data point.

Addition of quadratic, cubic or higher-order terms affords a more flexible surface and a better fit (see figure). The quadratic polynomial

$$Z = b_0 + b_1X + b^2Y + b^3X^2 + b_4XY + b_5Y^2$$

allows a single warp, which can represent a single peak, pit, ridge or valley, whereas the cubic polynomial

$$Z = b_0 + b_1X + b^2Y + b^3X^2 + b_4XY + b_5Y^2 + b_6X^3 + b_7X^2Y + b_8XY^2 + b_9Y^3,$$

provides a second warping, which can accommodate a peak and a pit. Still higher orders of trend surface are possible, at least in theory, as long as the number of terms in the polynomial does not exceed the number of data points. In practice, rounding error and other computational difficulties obviate the

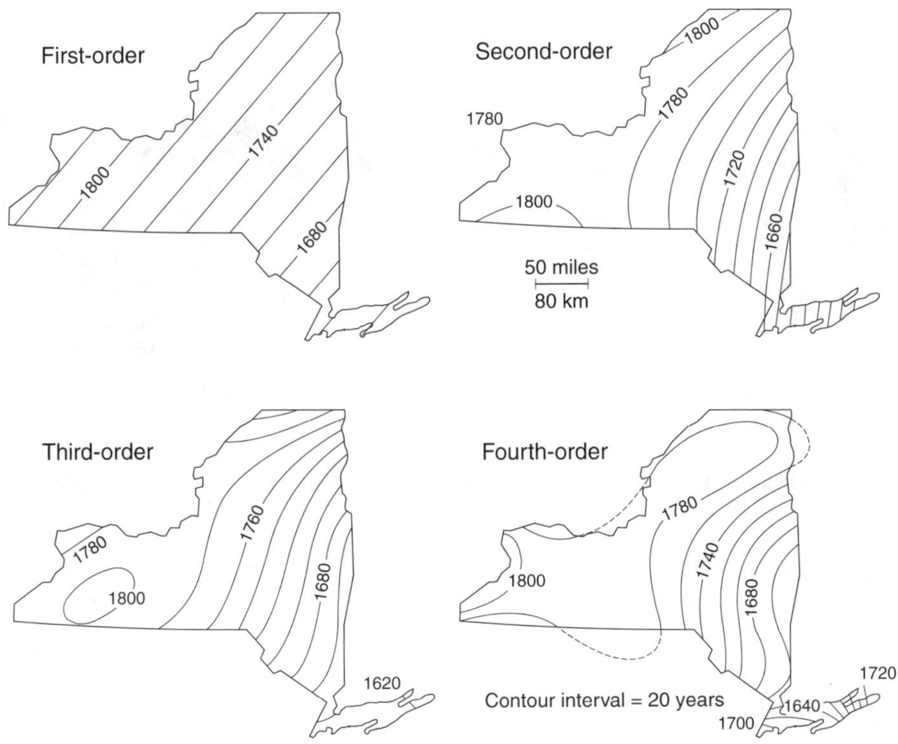

trend surface analysis four orders of trend surface, based on the date of arrival of each country's first settler, describe the generalized advance of the settlement frontier in New York State

exact fit of higher-order trend surfaces to large data sets (Unwin, 1975).

Trend surface analysis supports hypotheses testing as well as exploratory pattern analysis. Whereas a researcher using trend surface analysis as a confirmatory tool might specify the order or number of warpings – for example, a quadratic surface to model a phenomenon declining uniformly with distance from a single peak – the analyst looking for interesting patterns (see EXPLORATORY DATA ANALYSIS) might examine the relationship between flexibility and fit for a range of trend surfaces. As a rule of thumb, a surface merits visual examination if the number of data points is at least three times greater than the number of terms in the polynomial and the fit represents a marked improvement over the next lower-order surface. Researchers willing to ignore underlying assumptions of inferential statistics might use the analysis of variance to assess a surface's statistical significance (see SIGNIFICANCE TEST). Geographers who base trend surfaces on area data can use Monte Carlo SIMULATION to explore the effects of representing areal units by arbitrarily assigned data points. MM

References

Chorley, R.J. and Haggett, P. 1965: Trend surface mapping in geographical research. *Transactions, Institute of British Geographers* 37: 47–67. · Swan, A.H.R. and Sandilands, M. 1995: Introduction to geological data analysis. Oxford: Blackwell. · Unwin, D.J. 1975: An introduction to trend surface analysis, Concepts and techniques in modern geography, no. 5. Norwich: Geo Abstracts Ltd.

trialectics A term proposed by the American geographer E. Soja (1996) as 'a mode of dialectical reasoning that is more inherently spatial than the conventional temporally-defined dialectics of Hegel or Marx' (p. 10). As this suggests, 'trialectics' depends on the transcendence of conventional DIALECTICS: it does so by identifying three moments (not two), each of which contains the others. Soja's purpose is to insist on the importance of the 'third term' in any trialectic in order 'to defend against any form of binary reductionism or totalization' (cf. DECONSTRUCTION).

This is more than an abstract exercise in logic, and Soja proposes two basic trialectics (see the figure on p.862). The first is primarily concerned with ONTOLOGY: Soja (1996,

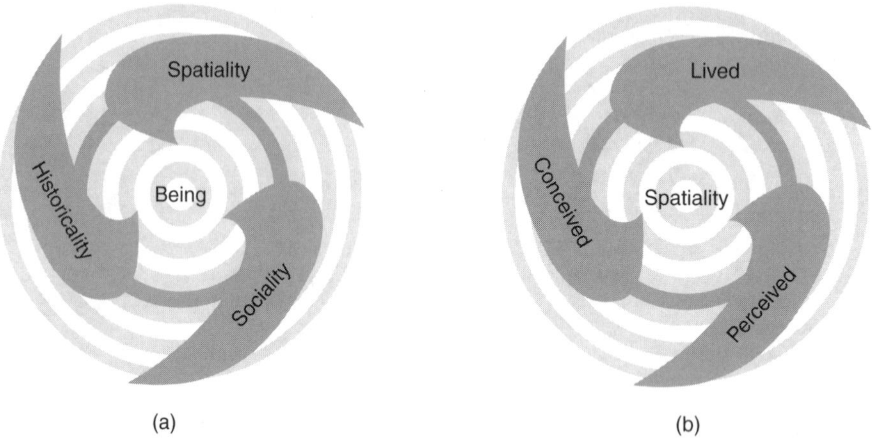

trialectics (a) Ontology: 'trialectics of being'; (b) Epistemology: 'trialectics of spatiality'

pp. 71–3) describes this as the *trialectics of being*, and uses it to diagram the production of time, being in the world and space: his argument turns on the claim that the 'third term', space, is characteristically erased in conventional critical theory (cf. Soja, 1989).

The second is primarily concerned with EPISTEMOLOGY: Soja (1996, pp. 73–82) describes this as the *trialectics of spatiality*, and uses it to diagram three approaches to SPATIALITY which he derives from H. Lefebvre's (1991) thematization of the PRODUCTION OF SPACE. In Soja's reading of Lefebvre, most discussions of spatiality have been confined to the realms of either (i) 'spatial practices', a space of objectivity and object-ness that Soja terms 'Firstspace' or (ii) 'representations of space', a space of signification and subject-ness that Soja terms 'Secondspace'. Again, it is the force of the 'third term' that Soja seeks to release: (iii) 'spaces of representation', where REPRESENTATION carries both political and cultural connotations, and whose animation corresponds to the subversive, radical and even revolutionary potential of 'Thirdspace' (see THIRD SPACE). DG

References

Lefebvre, H. 1991: *The production of space*. Oxford and Cambridge, MA: Blackwell. · Soja, E. 1989: *Postmodern geographies: the reassertion of space in critical social theory*. London: Verso. · Soja, E. 1996: *Thirdspace: journeys to Los Angeles and other real-and-imagined places*. Oxford and Cambridge, MA: Blackwell.

Suggested Reading

Soja (1996), 53–82.

turf politics Political activity by a NEIGHBOURHOOD's residents involved in resisting proposed changes to their locality. Such activity is usually very local in scale and involves responses to changes in either the built environment (e.g. a new road through a suburb – see NIMBY) or an area's socio-economic characteristics (cf. INVASION AND SUCCESSION). RJJ

Suggested Reading

Cox, K.R. 1989: The politics of turf and the question of class. In J. Wolch and M.J. Dear, eds, *The power of geography: how territory shapes social life*. Boston: Unwin Hyman, 61–90.

U

uncertainty The possibility of more than one outcome resulting from a particular course of action, the form of each possible outcome being known but the chance or probability of one particular outcome being unknown. Uncertainty differs from RISK, in that under conditions of risk it is possible to know the probability of a particular outcome. For example, in tossing a coin the probability of heads coming up is 50 per cent, so betting on the toss of a coin is a risk. Playing Russian roulette is a risk if the pistol is known to be loaded; with a bullet in one of the six chambers there is a one-in-six probability of death with any shot. However, if it was not known whether the gun was loaded, this would be a situation of uncertainty.

Uncertainty is part of the environment within which location (and other) decisions are made. This greatly limits the practical value of theories and models that assume perfect knowledge. For example, the firm setting up a new factory or service outlet in a new territory cannot know what the reaction of competitors is likely to be. They may follow suit with new facilities of their own, they may find an alternative competitive strategy, or they may choose not to compete: there is no way of calculating the probability of each option. Residential choice is similarly made under conditions of uncertainty – for example, with respect to the stability of the neighbourhood or the sociability of the neighbours. DMS

underclass Multiply deprived individuals – typically members of visible minority groups, and women and children in single-parent families – who experience a form of poverty from which there is virtually no escape (cf. CYCLE OF POVERTY). Those facing long-term poverty usually lack higher education, skills that are in demand, and any apparent means of achieving upward mobility; most depend on social assistance for their livelihood. The underclass suffer from *spatial mismatch*, in that they live in areas of concentrated poverty with few job opportunities, but they are too poor to afford the transportation and child-care costs associated with finding work in other, more distant areas. These problems are compounded by discrimination against women and minorities in LABOUR MARKETS (see GENDER AND GEOGRAPHY).

While liberal and radical analysts emphasize the structural causes of poverty (the nature of CAPITALISM, PATRIARCHY and RACISM – Wilson, 1987; Gans, 1995), conservative authors concentrate on the personal characteristics and lifestyles of the disadvantaged (Auletta, 1982). This latter view usually draws upon the *culture of poverty* thesis outlined by Oscar Lewis (1959) in his anthropological studies of Latin American SLUMS during the 1950s and 1960s. Lewis argued that the very poor share behavioural patterns that on the one hand allow them to cope with poverty, but on the other hand reproduce their disadvantage (e.g. a sceptical attitude towards education that is passed on to children). Because of the frequent association of the term underclass with this conservative view, many critical scholars refuse to use it.

The size of the underclass appears to be growing in North America and Europe as governments reduce the scope and universality of social programmes, and as mental health patients are deinstitutionalized. PUBLIC POLICY in Western countries tends to oscillate between liberal/radical and conservative views on poverty and the underclass, sometimes targeting structural problems (e.g. the 'war on poverty' of the 1970s in the US; the creation of the Social Exclusion Unit in 1997 in the UK: see SOCIAL EXCLUSION), while at other times attempting to change the behaviour of the poor by reducing welfare payments ('welfare reform' of the 1990s in the US) and/or providing additional funds to those who are entrepreneurially inclined. DH

References

Auletta, K. 1982: *The underclass*. New York: Random House. · Gans, H.J. 1995: *The war against the poor: the 'underclass' and antipoverty policy*. New York: Basic Books. · Lewis, O. 1959: *Five families: Mexican case studies in the culture of poverty*. New York: Basic Books. · Wilson, W.J. 1987: *The truly disadvantaged: the inner city, the underclass, and public policy*. Chicago: University of Chicago Press.

Suggested Reading

Fainstein, N. 1993: Underclass: over class, race and inequality. *Urban Affairs Quarterly* 29: 340–7. · Mingione, E., ed., 1996: *Urban poverty and the underclass*. Oxford: Blackwell.

underconsumption A concept of particular importance in MARXIAN ECONOMICS where it refers to a persistent shortfall in demand frequently explained in terms of inadequate purchasing power. This is one manifestation of the CRISIS of over-accumulation in which the surplus of labour and CAPITAL which CAPITALISM needs to sustain its own reproduction can no longer be absorbed. Harvey (1982, p. 195) notes the following manifestations of over-accumulation: an over-production of commodities, a surplus of inventories, idle capital within the production process, surplus money capital, surpluses of labour power (un- and under-employment), falling rates of return on capital.

These conditions point to a contradiction in capitalist societies which undermines the notion attributed to J.B. Say that supply creates its own demand as a result of the circular flow of income (rents, wages, profits) to land, labour and capital in production, which must equal the total price of goods produced. Extra production involves extra income and so there can be no general tendency to underconsumption.

The consumption of goods by labour certainly forms an important component of aggregate demand for the total output of the economy. But, at the same time, the consumption of labour is, in part, merely a moment in the process of circulation of capital as ACCUMULATION is the objective of the CIRCUIT OF CAPITAL. Competition between capitalists as measured by the rate of profit tends to force perpetual revolution in the PRODUCTIVE FORCES, often involving aggregate downwards pressure on wages – in real if not nominal terms – and on the incorporation of variable capital (labour) into the production process. Thus the benefits of increasing PRODUCTIVITY and technical change cannot all flow to labour because of the antagonistic social relations of reproduction between labour and capital and the competitive relations between capitals which constantly threaten the rate of profit. One consequence is the increasing inability of labour to consume the commodities produced.

Capitalists may respond to this contradiction by switching capital to different forms of production and by encouraging consumption – not least though the provision of credit – and the STATE may respond through the provision of the means of COLLECTIVE CONSUMPTION. Equally, advertising can shape consumption by labour in both quantitative and qualitative terms and so help to make consumption rather more rational with respect to the ongoing process of accumulation.

Strictly speaking, underconsumption refers only to consumption goods. But there are other, related, components of demand in the economy. The consumption of constant capital is more directly under the control of capital than is the consumption of variable capital. However, when constant capital is particularly lumpy or characterized by substantial externalities, investment is frequently undertaken by the state. This does not mean that the state can solve the problem of underconsumption, for it, too, is dependent upon the capitalist economy for resources. However, the state can help to annihilate time by borrowing and so may contribute to the management of demand (see NEO-CLASSICAL ECONOMICS).

There remains the problem of where the demand for the surplus value produced but not yet realized through exchange, is to come from. The capacity of luxury consumption as a solution to this problem is self-limiting. Another solution is the geographical expansion of the market, a process closely connected with IMPERIALISM. Again, clearly, there are limits to this possibility. However, it is not so much the expansion of markets that is served by geographical extension as the conversion of money into capital through the further exploitation of labour power. Thus, the solution to the problem of the realization of surplus value through exchange is resolved by the further exploitation of labour power in production (Harvey, 1982, p. 95). Perpetual accumulation provides the solution and so, of course, simply intensifies the problem. RL

Reference

Harvey, D. 1982: *The limits to capital.* Oxford: Basil Blackwell, 75–97.

underdevelopment Underdevelopment is, clearly, a comparative lack – the lack of DEVELOPMENT. It is, therefore, usually regarded as a negative. At its coarsest but – following Adorno (1993/1951, pp. 156–7, quoted in Cowen and Shenton 1996, p. 476) – also most tender, it is hunger and a future of hunger. And these are indubitably a product of CAPITALISM which 'stands between' (Cowen and Shenton, 1996, p. 474) the possibilities of the idea of development – movement and fluidity, a process of becoming, whereby 'none shall go hungry anymore' (Adorno, in Cowen and Shenton, 1996) – and doctrines of development – the intention to develop as a form of policy. Doctrines of development ignore the implications of underdevelopment as a comparative geographical adjective, the use of which is founded on presumptions of 'oneness,

cially when the specificities of capitalism as an especially powerful form of economic valuation are also obscured in the process. The spread of capitalism across the world did not take place across an isotropic plain, nor did it encounter an undifferentiated or politically unstructured social vacuum; rather it was confronted with a geographically diverse range of more or less well-developed sets of social and environmental relations and processes of social reproduction, the distinctions between which served to differentiate SOCIAL FORMATIONS (e.g. Sahlins, 1972). So the response to the spread of capitalism was by no means uniform (Larrain, 1989) and the paths from underdevelopment towards development must be equally diverse – notwithstanding the universal need to disengage from capitalist accumulation as the highly dangerous and amoral arbiter of development.

Such transformations may be enabled only through social struggle which, it is increasingly apparent, must take place from below (Friedmann, 1992). Unless people can succeed in creating humane conditions of existence, underdevelopment must remain the normal human condition. But, as Corbridge (1989, 1991) has pointed out, it is one thing to mount a critique of an exploitative system based upon the crucial recognition of inequalities in relations of power, and quite another to imagine and to practise an alternative (or more appropriately a geographically diverse range of alternatives) based upon rights and participation as well as upon needs and equality and, above all, on a refusal to subordinate the social to the economic notwithstanding the material necessities of consumption, exchange and production for social reproduction. What is needed, however, is the freeing of the idea of development from doctrines of development and their trustees (Cowen and Shenton, 1996). RL

References

Adorno, T.W. 1993/1951: *Minima moralia*. London: Verso. · Beenstock, M. 1984: *The world economy in transition*. London and Winchester MA: George Allen and Unwin. · Brenner, R. 1986: The social basis of economic development. In Roemer, J. ed., *Analytical Marxism*, ch. 2. Cambridge: Cambridge University Press; Editions de la Maison des Sciences et de l'Homme, 23–53. · Castells, M. 1996: *The rise of the network society. The information Age: Economy, society and culture*, vol. I. Cambridge, MA and Oxford: Blackwell. · Corbridge, S. 1989: Marxism, post-Marxism and the geography of development. In R. Peet and N. Thrift, eds, *New models in geography*, ch. 9. Boston and London: Unwin Hyman, 224–54. · Corbridge, S. 1991: Third world development. *Progress in Human Geography* 15 3: 311–21. · Cowen, M.P. and Shenton, R.W. 1996: *Doctrines of development*. London and New York: Routledge. · Dicken, P. 1998: *Global shift; transforming the world economy*, 3rd edn. London: Paul Chapman Publishing. · Esteva, G. 1992: Development. In W. Sachs, ed., *The development dictionary: the guide to knowledge as power*. London and New Jersey: Zed Books, 6–25. · Friedmann, J. 1992: *Empowerment: the politics of alternative development*. Oxford and Cambridge, MA: Oxford University Press. · Harrison, P. 1981: *Inside the third world: an anatomy of poverty*. London: Penguin. · Harvey, D. 1982: *The limits to capital*. Oxford and Cambridge, MA: Blackwell. · Larrain, J. 1989: *Theories of development*. Cambridge: Polity Press. · Maddison, A. 1982: *Phases of capitalist development*. Oxford: Oxford University Press. · Peet, R. 1991: *Global capitalism: theories of societal development*. London and New York: Routledge. · Sahlins, M. 1972: *Stone age economics*. New York: Aldine. · Thrift, N. 1989: The geography of international economic disorder. In R.J. Johnston and P.J. Taylor, eds, *A world in crisis?* Oxford and Cambridge, MA: Basil Blackwell; UNDP (United Nations Development Programme) annual *Human development report*. New York: Oxford University Press. · Watts, M. 1992: The shock of modernity: Petroleum, protest and fast capitalism in an industrializing society. In A. Pred and M. Watts, *Reworking modernity: capitalisms and symbolic discontent*, ch. 2. New Brunswick, NJ: Rutgers University Press. · reprinted in S. Daniels and R. Lee, eds, 1996: *Exploring human geography*. London: Arnold, ch. 6, 120–152. · Watts, M.J. 1993: Development I: power, knowledge, discursive practice *Progress in Human Geography* 17 2: 257–72.

Suggested Reading

Castells, M. 1997: *End of millennium. The information age: economy, society and culture*, vol. III. Cambridge, MA and Oxford: Blackwell. · Corbridge, S., ed., 1996: *Development studies: a reader*. London: Arnold; Esteva (1992). · Peet (1991). · Watts (1992).

uneven development A systematic process of economic and social development that is uneven in space and time, and endemic to CAPITALISM. Uneven development is a basic geographical hallmark of the capitalist MODE OF PRODUCTION. It reflects far more than simply the lack of geographical evenness in capitalist growth; rather, it comprises an integral aspect of capitalist development, combining the opposed but connected processes of DEVELOPMENT and UNDERDEVELOPMENT.

Marx argued that 'capital grows in one place to a huge mass in a single hand because it has in another place been lost by many' (1987, p. 586). More broadly, this implies that underdevelopment is not simply the result of neglect but is actively produced (Frank, 1967), and that uneven development is closely bound up with the logic of capital ACCUMULATION. There is a geographical as much as an economic logic to capitalist development and underdevelopment and this is captured in theories of uneven development, which takes place at different geographical SCALES; indeed the same processes of centralization and development, and DECENTRALIZATION and underdevelopment that create geographically uneven development are also largely responsible for producing geographical scale in the first place (Smith, 1990).

In the classic case, capitalist development is concentrated in the so-called 'First World' of Europe and North America, while the THIRD WORLD has been underdeveloped. The former contains the majority of the world's industrial production and accounts for most of its consumption, while the latter has become a supplier of cheap raw materials and labour power. While the developed world enjoys a balanced, self-centred mode of accumulation, the Third World is continually dependent on the First World for markets, CAPITAL and technology (Amin, 1976). This same pattern of development and underdevelopment is repeated at other scales, as capital is agglomerated in one place in favour of another. Within Britain for example, the rapid development of the south-east in the post-war economy contrasted sharply with growth elsewhere. And at the urban scale, the disjuncture between INNER CITY and SUBURB is equally a product of uneven development.

Uneven development is highly dynamic, however, and the patterns of unevenness are continually transformed as the mode of production itself evolves. At the global scale, the economies of Japan and the German-led EU threaten to supersede the power of the USA, much as the USA superseded the UK in the early decades of the twentieth century (cf. KONDRATIEFF CYCLES). And a NEW INTERNATIONAL DIVISION OF LABOUR in the late twentieth century (NIDL; see Frobel et al., 1980) has led to the INDUSTRIALIZATION of the newly industrializing countries (NICs) such as Taiwan, South Korea and Malaysia, which were previously underdeveloped. Sub-Saharan Africa, by contrast, is virtually REDLINED in the global economy and is experiencing the most intensely debilitating effects of uneven development. At the regional scale, some previously developed regions, such as northern England or the upper Midwest of the USA, have experienced rapid DEINDUSTRIALIZATION, while other long deindustrialized regions have experienced significant economic redevelopment associated with a new regime of FLEXIBLE ACCUMULATION (e.g. Central Scotland and New England). At the urban scale, the relative underdevelopment of the central and inner cities of the First World is partially offset by GENTRIFICATION and RESTRUCTURING, while the suburbs are experiencing the growth of integrated urban functions. At each of these scales, different political-economic variables, such as the price and productivity of labour, the availability and cost of INFRASTRUCTURE, political stability, and ground rent, mediate the geographical mobility of capital between different places.

From these empirical trends, as well as from Marx's general theory of capital accumulation, it is possible to derive a theory of uneven development which describes the geography of development and underdevelopment under capitalism. In the process of developing a particular place or region, capital creates some of the very conditions that can mitigate against future development: wages and ground rent levels rise, while the AGGLOMERATION of large numbers of labourers working under similar conditions encourages political organization in opposition to the social relations of capitalism. By contrast, underdevelopment produces the conditions that are likely to encourage development: lowered wage rates and ground rent levels, unemployment, and defeated working-class organizations. In so far as underdevelopment creates the conditions for its opposite, and vice versa, there is a tendency for CAPITAL to oscillate geographically from places of development to those of underdevelopment and back again (see CONVERGENCE, REGIONAL; EQUILIBRIUM). This see-saw movement can be observed in recent patterns of uneven development, especially at the subnational scale, but can also be derived theoretically as the geography of capital accumulation (Smith, 1990).

Marx grasped only some of the importance of uneven development. He expected that the world market would largely homogenize global levels and conditions of development, a position furthered by Rosa Luxemburg (1968) who expected that when the capitalist system had expanded into every geographical corner of the Earth its expansion would necessarily end and SOCIALISM would follow. That geographical expansion of capital was effectively ended by the beginning of the twentieth century – the end of colonial expansion, the end of FRONTIER – was recognized by geographers such as Alexander Supan in Germany, Halford Mackinder in Britain and Isaiah Bowman in the USA, as well as by Cecil Rhodes, the British imperialist, who argued the importance of the colonies as a safety valve for political discontent at home. It was Lenin, however, who most explicitly recognized the advent of uneven development proper when he argued that, henceforth, economic expansion would not take place in consort with territorial expansion (COLONIALISM), but as an internal re-differentiation of an already conquered world (Lenin, 1975). The spatial constitution of global capitalism was definitively altered.

From the early part of the twentieth century, uneven development came to characterize the geography of capitalism. This dramatic shift in the spatial constitution of capitalism, from continued external expansion to internal uneven development, came at the same time that concepts of space and time were being revolutionised in art and physics (Kern, 1983). However, the recognition of the importance of uneven development was stunted. First, the Russian revolution of 1917 put more immediate political issues on the agenda, especially of course in Russia but also in Western nations like Italy and Germany whose radical factions watched the events in Russia with eager anticipation. Second, rather than deal with the radical implications of the recognition of uneven development, orthodox geographers veered away from such global issues and either focused on local and regional questions or took a technocratic approach to geographical problems. Orthodox geographers generally prescribed to the hopeful precepts of NEO-CLASSICAL ECONOMICS which saw the uneven landscape as little more than a temporary phase in an ultimately equilibrating process. Nevertheless, in the 1920s Leon Trotsky proposed a 'law of uneven and combined development', which explored the political possibilities and constraints of constructing SOCIALISM directly out of FEUDAL society (Trotsky, 1969; Lowy, 1981). The rediscovery of uneven development in its geographical and economic as well as political guises took place in the 1970s in connection with a resurgence of interest in Marxist theory (see MARXIST GEOGRAPHY), but also as a result of the evident RESTRUCTURING of the geography of capitalism at all spatial scales that began at the same time.

The contours of uneven development are again changing rapidly, as part of the protracted crisis of capital accumulation (and responses to it) that emerged after the late 1960s and more recently with volatility in global stock markets since the early 1990s recession. Despite having been 'global' for several centuries, this latest phase of uneven development has been championed (and lamented) as 'GLOBALIZATION' (Smith, 1997). Although the NATION-STATE continues to function in several different guises, globalization has largely been described as a process wherein global capital has dissolved national boundaries, thereby eroding the level of national autonomy from the tentacles of the world economy – the ultimate expression of global uneven development. MULTINATIONAL CORPORATIONS, on the other hand, appear to be pulling the strings of global capital with increasing autonomy from regulatory oversight. This has, not surprisingly, exacerbated uneven development at various scales. Several multi-nation territorial agglomerations have sprung up during this period (e.g. NAFTA) in order to regulate this market-driven uneven development. NS

References

Amin, S. 1976: *Unequal development*. New York: Monthly Review Press. · Frank, A. 1967: *Capitalism and underdevelopment in Latin America*. New York: Monthly Review Press. · Frobel, F., Kreye, O. and Heinrichs, J. 1980: *The new international division of labour*. Cambridge: Cambridge University Press. · Kern, S. 1983: *The culture of time and space 1980–1918*. London: Weidenfeld and Nicolson. · Lenin, V. 1975: *Imperialism, the highest stage of capitalism*. Beijing Foreign Languages Press. · Lowy, M. 1981: *The politics of combined and uneven development*. London: Verso. · Luxemburg, R. 1968: *The accumulation of capital*. New York: Monthly Review Press. · Marx, K. 1987: *Capital, volume 1*. New York: International. · Smith, N. 1990: *Uneven development: nature, capital and the production of space*, 2nd edn. Oxford: Blackwell. · Smith, N. 1997: Satanic Geographies of globalization: uneven development in the 1990s. *Public Culture* 10 (1): 169–89. · Trotsky, L. 1969: *Permanent revolution and results and prospects*. New York: Pathfinder.

universalism The idea that certain characteristics of phenomena or certain moral, aesthetic or EPISTEMOLOGICAL truths hold for all times and places. Such supposed universal characteristics and truths are then frequently made the basis of wider practices and conceptual schemes, the justification for which is given by their universal starting point. For example, the truths of mathematics are universal in that $2 + 2 = 4$ irrespective of when and where the calculation is made. Mathematical truths are as good in ancient Egypt for carrying out pyramid building as they are in mid-twentieth-century America for undertaking SPATIAL SCIENCE. A feature of universalism, then, is that one cannot imagine the situation as otherwise: there are no alternative worlds where $2 + 2 \neq 4$.

A distinction made in philosophy since Plato is between universals and particulars. Universals are characteristics such as the colour 'red' that potentially an infinite number of different objects can take. Any red object is an 'instant' of the universal 'redness'. In contrast, particulars cannot be instantiated; they are one of kind. What, though, is the status of universals? Plato thought they have an independent existence: somewhere there exists fundamental 'redness' of which British pillar boxes and tunics of Canadian Mounties are pale copies. EMPIRICISTS, in contrast, argue that universals do not exist in themselves but are lodged in the mind of the perceiver. Finally, nominalists contend that there are no universals such as redness, only general words like red that are applied to a number of objects such as pillar boxes and Mountie tunics. The nominalist approach, especially when reinforced by Wittgenstein's idea of 'family resemblances', attracts the greatest support among contemporary philosophers. It suggests that we as humans, in the language we use and its associated practices, determine what counts as universal.

In the recent history of human geography (and associated with ENLIGHTENMENT thinking), Platonic universals have dominated. They are present in discussions over REGIONAL GEOGRAPHY, RATIONAL CHOICE, QUANTITATIVE METHODS, and the nature of humanness in HUMANISTIC GEOGRAPHY. In each case, the issue is the exact form that the universal takes. For example, what is the universal form of the region of which any specific region is an example? The fact that, in this case, there has never been agreement about the nature of a universal region points to a pervasive problem, the semantic difficulty in defining universals. Furthermore, argue critics, when there is seeming agreement about universals it is the power and social status of the definer that makes them stick, not their inherent universality. Just as history is written by victors, so definitions of the universal are written by the powerful in their own interests. For example, the ostensibly universal characteristics defining man and woman and set by men has led to systematic PATRIARCHY; and the apparently universal characteristics defining RACE and established in the West has led to systematic racism. Here a nominalist approach to universals, when combined with a POST-STRUCTURAL sensibility toward power and language, is an important critical foil. In geography that combination has been mobilized around FEMINIST writings about gender, around studies of SEXUALITY, around race and POST-COLONIALISM, and around the 'economic' part of economic geography. TJB

Suggested Reading

Barnes, T.J. 1996: *Logics of dislocation: models, metaphors and meanings of economic space*, ch. 1. New York: Guilford.

urban Relating to TOWNS and CITIES. If URBANIZATION is treated as a demographic phenomenon only, urban places are those which exceed the thresholds of population size and/or density frequently used in CENSUS definitions. If urbanization is also considered as both a structural and a behavioural process, however, then urban places are those above a certain size and density, performing particular economic functions within the spatial DIVISION OF LABOUR and with their own particular life styles.

The study of urban places is central to many social sciences, including geography, because of their importance not only in the distribution of population within countries but also in the organization of economic production, distribution and exchange, in the structuring of social reproduction and cultural life, and in the exercise of political power. Sub-fields of the different social science disciplines were established in the decades after the Second World War to study these separate components, such as urban anthropology, economics, geography, politics, and sociology; later attempts were made to integrate these under the umbrella title of urban studies.

Urban and RURAL places are distinct in a number of ways according to some arguments, a distinction formalized by scholars through the concept of a RURAL–URBAN CONTINUUM which suggested that as the size of a place changed so did its residents' characteristics, Wirth's (1938) classic paper on URBANISM defined those characteristics, and there was a strong tradition, extending back to Jefferson's anti-urban and pro-rural sentiments in the United States, promoting the 'idyllic rural' myth and denigrating the urban. The association of particular lifestyles with different settlement sizes has been substantially criticized more recently, however: 'rural-like' COMMUNITIES have been 'discovered' in INNER CITIES (cf. URBAN VILLAGE) while the concept of COUNTERURBANIZATION indicates a DIFFUSION of the urban way of life into remote rural areas: in this sense, the concept of urban appears redundant because it cannot be negated – wherever we live, we are all urban now (Saunders, 1986). Such claims regarding the concept of a separate urban realm are not entirely new, however: in the nineteenth century both Durkheim and Marx argued that towns and cities played a distinct role in the transition from FEUDALISM to CAPITALISM but then became a part of that universal mode of organization with no independent identity or function. To study urban places separately was thus, in modern language, to draw upon CHAOTIC CONCEPTIONS.

Major stimuli to reinterpreting the nature of the urban was provided in the 1970s by David Harvey's (1973) *Social justice and the city* and Manuel Castells's (1977) *The urban question*. Harvey set out on what he considered the impossible task of constructing a general urban theory, and concluded that urbanism has a separate structure with its own dynamic set within the larger forces of capitalism. His later essays continue the attempt: *The limits to capital* (1982) is introduced as his reworking of Marxist economic theory en route to a 'theory of urbanization'; the essays in The *urbanization of capital* (1985a) explore how capitalism creates a 'physical landscape of roads, houses, factories, schools, shops and so forth' as part of the process of creating space (see also Lefebvre, 1991); and in *Consciousness and the urban experience* (1985b) he focuses on the experience of living in such places and the resulting social relations and forms of political consciousness. He concluded the last of those volumes with the emancipatory case (see APPLIED GEOGRAPHY) that 'If the urbanization of capital and of consciousness is so central to the perpetuation and experience of capitalism,... then we have no option but to put the urbanization of revolution at the center of our political strategies'.

Castells's book also attempted to reinterpret what was already known – 'in order to detect the distorting ideological mechanisms and to reread in a new light the empirical discoveries made'. Like Harvey, he argued that social scientists were failing to understand 'urban problems' because of ideological blinkers which obstructed the development of a THEORY that could inform practice. This was because of the widespread belief in a separate urban realm, which Castells showed was a wrong ABSTRACTION: urban problems are problems of societies, not of particular types of place, however defined, thus (p. 454)

> there is no cultural system linked to a given form of spatial organization;... the social history of humanity is not determined by the type of development of the territorial collectivities; and the spatial environment is not the root of a specificity of behaviour and representation.

The processes that characterize late capitalism are general: its economic forms are as apparent in AGRIBUSINESSES as in city-based manufacturing industries, and ideologies and attitudes are shared by people in similar socio-economic positions whatever their home location. Nevertheless, Castells did argue that under capitalism urban places are the spatial units within which COLLECTIVE CONSUMPTION, the processes of reproducing labour power and social relations, is grounded: indeed, he suggests that this is their *raison d'être*.

These two books were part of a major trend in social science to redefine urban in other than spatial/territorial terms (and thus to end its treatment as a form of SPATIAL FETISHISM), and to create a theory of the role of urban places in capitalist society – a theory that would not only advance understanding but also inform political practice and lead to a restructuring of society.

The concept of a separate urban realm is still widely used in general language and much social science, however. Two areas have been advanced where this is particularly valid: (a) in historical investigations, which illustrate the role of urban places as the motor for capitalist development (Sutcliffe, 1983); and (b) in parts of the world where capitalism has not fully penetrated all areas and aspects of life so that urban and rural stand out as unique in certain respects. Nevertheless, the relative decline of a distinctively URBAN GEOGRAPHY in recent years in North America and the United Kingdom may be associated with the critiques launched by Harvey and Castells. RJJ

References

Castells, M. 1977: *The urban question: a marxist approach*. London: Edward Arnold; Cambridge, MA: MIT Press. · Harvey, D. 1973: *Social justice and the city*. London: Edward Arnold. · Harvey, D. 1982: *The limits to capital*. Oxford: Basil Blackwell. · Harvey, D. 1985a: *The urbanization of capital*. Oxford: Basil Blackwell. · Harvey, D. 1985b: *Consciousness and the urban experience*. Oxford: Basil Blackwell. · Lefebvre, H. 1991: *The production of space*. Oxford: Basil Blackwell. · Saunders, P. 1986: *Social theory and the urban question*, 2nd edn. London: Hutchinson. · Sutcliffe, A.R. 1983: In search of the urban variable: Britain in the later nineteenth century. In D. Fraser and A.R. Sutcliffe, eds, *The study of urban history*. London: Edward Arnold, 234–63. · Wirth, L. 1938: Urbanism as a way of life. *American Journal of Sociology* 44: 1–24.

Suggested Reading

Pahl, R.E. 1983: Concepts in context: pursuing the urban of 'urban' sociology. In D. Fraser and A.R. Sutcliffe, eds, *The study of urban history*. London: Edward Arnold, 371–87. · Saunders, P. 1985: Space, the city, and urban sociology. In D. Gregory and J. Urry, eds, *Social relations and spatial structures*. London: Macmillan, 67–89. · Smith, M.P. 1979: *The city and social theory*. Oxford: Basil Blackwell; New York: St. Martin's Press. · Smith. M.P. 1988: *City, state and market: the political economy of urban society*. Oxford: Basil Blackwell.

urban and regional planning At a purely technical level the meaning of urban and regional planning is quite straightforward. Peter Hall (1974) considers planning first as 'a general activity . . . the making of an orderly sequence of action that will lead to the achievement of a stated goal or goals'. In this view, planning is an ahistoric, universal process common to all thinking beings and it is essentially technical: its 'main techniques', Hall goes on, 'will be written statements, supplemented as appropriate by statistical projections, mathematical representations, quantified evaluations and diagrams illustrating relationships between different parts of the plan. It may, but need not necessarily, include exact physical blueprints of objects'.

From this perspective, urban and regional planning is simply 'a special case of general planning' which incorporates 'spatial representation' (Hall, 1974). But this is a tenuous distinction. City planning 'immediately embraces regional economic planning, which is logically inseparable from national economic planning' (Hall, 1996, p. 6). Peter Hall's 'more-or-less arbitrary boundary line' between economic and urban and regional planning has a substantive foundation in the geography that is so often omitted from economics of 'places' like nations (but which actually cannot be omitted see ECONOMIC GEOGRAPHY) and is not omitted from urban and regional planning which deals with the geographies through which human, animal and plant life is constructed.

Thus urban and regional planning may be understood as a rational process of forethought set in motion by the need to resolve urban and regional problems. Hall (1996, p. 7), for example, finds 'that twentieth-century city planning, as an intellectual and professional movement, essentially represents a reaction to the evils of the nineteenth-century city'. It was first carried out by 'practical men dealing with practical matters' who were, nevertheless, influenced by 'thinkers about the urban problem'. Similarly, regional planning arose, according to Hall, in the regional economic problem of the 1930s. Post-war planning was quite different, being dominated by the creation of the 'post war planning system' which was strongly influenced in its formation by follow-up studies to the Barlow Report of 1940 which 'brought together the urban and regional economic elements as two aspects of a single problem'.

But this view of urban and regional planning as a set of ideas, procedures and responses – albeit under dramatically transformed institutional conditions – a transformation which itself reflects prevailing understandings of the dynamics of society – fails to address the relationship between planning and the society being planned nor does it address the nature of the relationships between planning and POWER. Urban and regional planning are seen in technical terms as a rational response to a set of self-evident problems. The objectives or goals of planning – the definition of what is 'rational' seem to be unproblematic, as does the definition of the nature of the problems themselves. Even the power relations of the institutions carrying out urban and regional planning are left largely unexplored.

Allen Scott's (1980, p. 238) comments on this state of affairs coming at the end of his own attempt to connect the dynamics of capitalist production, the urban land nexus and the state in a critique of planning and planning theory, are especially pertinent:

> Mainstream planning theory presents itself to the world as a system of ideas that is no doubt internally coherent and logical. However, it fails dramatically to reflect and explain an underlying historical reality. On the contrary, it interposes identifiable barriers to a global understanding of the real universe of urbanization and urban planning. It is, in the fullest sense of the term, an ideology.

Planning law is introduced by the STATE and agencies of the state are primarily responsible for its implementation. But the state is an integral part of the wider society (see Held, 1983) and planning both grows out of and contributes towards socially distinctive processes of SOCIAL production and REPRODUCTION (see SOCIETY). Looked at in this way, urban and regional planning becomes a material, political and economic process rather than a mere technical exercise (Ambrose, 1986). It is, according to Cooke (1983), part of the 'civilizing process, performed by the state through the medium of the law . . . not only to rationalise the external physical configuration of production, but to sustain the . . . forms of social relations that have developed' (see CAPITALISM; SOCIAL REPRODUCTION). It is, in short, an exercise in power and in social reproduction.

But, insofar as the objectives are made explicit, it is an exercise which may be contested both by those who suffer the consequences (e.g. Rose, 1992) and it is an exercise of imagination by those who set up the suffering. Whilst it is 'a statement of the blindingly obvious' that (planning)

> ideas do not suddenly emerge, by some kind of immaculate conception, without benefit of worldly

> agency. . . . Equally, human beings . . . are almost infinitely quirksy and creative and surprising; therefore the real interest in history . . . lies in the complexity and variability of the human reaction. The anarchist fathers (of planning) had a magnificent vision of the possibilities of urban civilization which deserves to be remembered and celebrated: Le Corbusier, in contrast represents the counter-tradition of authoritarian planning, the evil consequences of which are ever with us. (Hall, 1996, pp. 4–5.)

Thus, urban and regional planning cannot be understood merely on the basis of their content. Rather, they must connect with the processes of physical, social and economic development characteristic of the particular societies in which planning is being carried out (Ambrose, 1986; Murdoch and Marsden, 1995; Short, 1996) and the imaginations of those who try to frame the carrying out. As the significance of church and state as formative institutions within contemporary society shifts to that of business and capital, a move away from the autonomy of the plan towards the complex processes of urban change involves an understanding of the intersections of economics, culture, power and aesthetics in understanding urban and regional transformations. Susan Fainstein (1994, p. x), for example, stresses 'the factors influencing the dynamic of real-estate development and, in turn, the influence of that dynamic on the prosperity and attractiveness of urban areas' in her study of 'city builders'.

The way in which such processes operate is profoundly political (Brindley, Rydin and Stoker, 1989; Thornley, 1990). Planning involves the attempt to shape prevailing social and economic dynamics to achieve particular developmental ends. And those ends may well include the discourse of development as well as development itself. A planning system which emphasizes the power of the market and so aims to remove restrictions on the allocation of investment or aims to enhance the rewards flowing from urban and regional development presents a quite different discourse on the nature of society than one which replaces the market with expert systems or state bureaucracies (see Beck, 1992).

These points may be illustrated by a brief consideration of the history of planning controls on retail development in the UK over the 20 years or so from 1979. This history demonstrates:

- the significance of DISCOURSE in shaping planning policy (here of individualism and the place of consumption and of property investment and the wisdom of a deregulated market for investment);
- the effect that particular policies may have on the structure and location of investment (large-scale, decentralized locations which tie in with prevailing economic geographies of retailing and the use of the car as a means of consumption); and
- the consequences that flow from such investments (such as the retail evacuation of town centres) for urban and regional systems.

The re-regulation of development from the middle of the 1990s with controls aimed at recolonizing brown-field sites in or near existing shopping centres, reflects concerns both about the over-use of cars and the social pathologies associated with urban abandonment.

This example demonstrates the complex influences on the urban and regional planning process emanating not merely from straightforward state control but reflecting a reading of the economic geographies involved (e.g. Lee, 1992) as well as prevailing views on appropriate urban and regional landscapes. Debates around the notion of the sustainability of cities (e.g. Breheny, 1995; Owens/Breheny, 1995) and the significance of environmental influences on the production of urban and regional landscapes tell a similar story of the inseparability of planning from prevailing discourses of and the material relations involved in social reproduction (see, e.g. Harrison and Burgess, 1994; Healey and Shaw, 1994; Owens, 1994; Breheny, 1995; Owens/Breheny, 1995).

The existence and activities of urban and regional planning asks some profoundly geographical questions about the nature of the discourses and dynamics of society, the significance of UNEVEN DEVELOPMENT and the relations, central and local, between the political and the economic. It poses some crucial issues concerned not merely with the acceptability or otherwise of the techniques of implementation of planning (which for the people affected by them are of signal importance) but with the role and potential of state and of planning in developing alternatives in urban and regional development within the constraints posed by the practicalities of social reproduction and the discourses of power which shape such practicalities. (See also REGIONAL POLICY.) RL

References

Ambrose, P. 1986: *Whatever happened to planning?* London and New York: Methuen. · Beck, U. 1992: *Risk society: towards a new modernity*. London and Newbury Park: Sage. · Breheny, M. 1995: The compact city and transport energy consumption. *Transactions, Institute of British Geographers* 20: 81–101. · Brindley, T., Rydin, Y. and Stoker, G., eds, 1989: *Remaking planning: the politics of urban change in the Thatcher years*. New York and London: HarperCollins. · Cooke, P. 1983: *Theories of planning and spatial development*. London: Hutchinson. · Fainstein, S. 1994: *The city builders Property, politics and planning in London and New York*. Cambridge, MA and Oxford: Blackwell. · Hall, P. 1974: *Urban and regional planning*. Harmondsworth: Penguin. · Hall, P. 1996: *Cities of tomorrow*. Oxford and Cambridge, MA: Blackwell. · Harrison, C.M. and Burgess, J. 1994: Social constructions of nature: a case study of conflicts over the development of Rainham Marshes. *Transactions, Institute of British Geographers* 19: 291–310. · Healey, P. and Shaw, T. 1994: Changing meanings of the 'environment' in the British Planning system. *Transactions, Institute of British Geographers* 19: 425–38. · Held, D. 1983: Central perspectives on the modern state. In D. Held et al., eds, *States and societies*. Oxford: Martin Robertson. · Lee, R. 1992: 'London Docklands: the exceptional place'? An economic geography of inter-urban competition. In P.E. Ogden, ed., *London Docklands: the challenge of change*. Cambridge: Cambridge University Press. · Murdoch, J. and Marsden, T. 1995: The spatialization of politics: local and national actor spaces in environmental conflict. *Transactions, Institute of British Geographers* 20: 368–80. · Owens, S. 1994: Land limits and sustainability: a conceptual framework and some dilemmas for the planning system. *Transactions, Institute of British Geographers* 19: 439–58. · Owens, S. and Breheny, M. 1995: Exchange: The compact city and transport energy consumption. *Transactions, Institute of British Geographers* 20: 381–86. · Rose, G. 1992: Local resistance to the LDDC: community attitudes and action. In P. Ogden, ed., *London docklands: The challenge of development*, ch. 5. Cambridge: Cambridge University Press, 32–42. · Scott, A.J. 1980: *The urban land nexus and the state*. London: Pion. · Short, J.R. 1996: *The urban order. An introduction to cities, culture and power*. Cambridge, MA and Oxford: Blackwell. · Thornley, A. 1990: *Urban planning under Thatcherism: the challenge of the market*. New York and London: Routledge.

Suggested Reading

Ambrose (1986). · Hall (1996). · Owens (1995). · Wannop, U. 1995: *The regional imperative. Regional planning and governance in Britain, Europe and the United States*. London: Jessica Kingsley.

urban ecology A term applied by later adherents of the CHICAGO SCHOOL of sociologists to their study of the social and spatial organization of urban society. Although urban ecologists have paid some attention to URBAN SYSTEMS at national and regional scales, most of their attention has focused on the internal structure of large cities.

Berry and Kasarda (1977) show that traditional urban ecology, represented by Hawley's classic (1950) text, concentrated on three areas of study:

- adoption of concepts from animal and plant ECOLOGY to study of the human COMMUNITY – as in the Chicago School's work (see INVASION AND SUCCESSION);
- detailed descriptions of the NATURAL AREAS of cities; and
- investigations of the geography of social problems (such as crime and vice) in the context of those natural areas, hence use of the term *ecology* because the individual elements were being investigated in the context of their local societal whole.

The focus since the 1960s, they argued, has been a concern with 'how a population organizes itself in adapting to a constantly changing yet restricting environment'.

This contemporary urban ecological approach assumes that urban societies are constantly responding to shocks to their socio-spatial arrangements by seeking to re-establish an equilibrium which encompasses the area's functional, demographic and spatial structures. Theorists such as Duncan (1959) and Schnore (1965) identified what they termed the *ecological complex* comprising four interrelated variables which characterize the urban realm:

- *population*, a functionally integrated and structured collectivity;
- *organization*, the system of relationships which allows a population to sustain itself within its physical and built environment;
- *environment*, characterized by Berry and Kasarda as 'the least well conceptualized of the variables ... it has been broadly defined as all phenomena, including other social systems, that are external to and have influence upon the population under study'; and
- *technology*, comprising the artefacts and techniques developed by the community to assist in its sustenance.

All four are interdependent, with a change in each having an impact on the other three. Urban ecology thus differs from traditional URBAN GEOGRAPHY, which focuses more exclusively on spatial arrangement as both a causal and a dependent variable in the study of evolving social systems.

Berry and Kasarda (1977) note that all of the programmatic statements for contemporary urban ecology were written during the late 1950s and early 1960s but 'their *raison d'être* no longer prevails'. Sociologists had moved from macro-to micro-concerns, and the purpose of their 1977 book was to remind the 'sociological audience' that 'all principles of sociological organization could not be reduced to individualistic concepts'. The four variables in the ecological complex are necessary to an appreciation of patterns and processes of social and spatial organization, which they illustrate with a SYSTEMS ANALYSIS approach.

Work continues to be done in the ecological tradition, especially focusing on patterns of population change (such as DECENTRALIZATION and suburbanization within METROPOLITAN AREAS), but the area is not in the mainstream of contemporary urban sociology. RJJ

References

Berry, B.J.L. and Kasarda, J.D. 1977: *Contemporary urban ecology*. New York and London: Macmillan. · Duncan, O.D. 1959: Human ecology and population studies. In P.M. Hauser and O.D. Duncan, eds, *The study of population*. Chicago: University of Chicago Press; Cambridge: Cambridge University Press, 678–716. · Hawley, A.H. 1950: *Human ecology: a theory of community structure*. New York: Ronald Press. · Schnore, L.F. 1965: On the spatial structure of cities in the two Americas. In P.M. Hauser and L.F. Schnore, eds, *The study of urbanization*. New York and London: John Wiley, 347–98.

urban entrepreneurialism The promotion of local economic development by urban governments in alliance with private capital and unions (cf. REGIONAL CLASS ALLIANCE; GOVERNANCE). Urban area governments have typically played restricted roles in the promotion of their local economy involving only the provision of physical INFRASTRUCTURE plus small amounts of advertising. With the shift from FORDISM to FLEXIBLE ACCUMULATION during the crisis of the 1970s and 1980s, however, local governments have been impelled to extend away from their managerial role and functions within the WELFARE STATE (cf. DUAL THEORY OF THE STATE; URBAN MANAGERS AND GATEKEEPERS) and to adopt 'more initiatory and... "entrepreneurial"... forms of action' (Harvey, 1989, p. 4), a common trend throughout the advanced capitalist world.

Central to urban entrepreneurialism is the concept of 'public–private partnerships' through which public money is used as leverage to attract private investment to an area. This process is encouraged by national governments, as with the Development Corporations established in the UK to promote economic regeneration in depressed areas (such as the Liverpool and London Dockland Development Areas), though outside local government control. Such bodies are known in the UK as QUANGOS (quasi-autonomous non-governmental organizations) which are not democratically accountable to the local population; they are playing an increasing role in the restructuring of labour markets as well as environmental regeneration and the attraction of inward investment.

Urban entrepreneurialism (often termed '*urban boosterism*' in the USA) involves local governments and related bodies competing for economic growth. To promote their cities' COMPARATIVE ADVANTAGES, many become involved in image-development and image-enhancement strategies, exemplified by major investments in leisure facilities and 'world events', such as the Seville World Fair, the Barcelona Olympic Games in 1992, and the Millennium Dome at Greenwich in London's Docklands (see SPECTACLE, GEOGRAPHY OF). These are promoted as potential profit-making activities (as with the 1984 Olympic Games in Los Angeles), but many make losses, and leave the local population with large long-term debt repayments to be met from local taxes, as with the 1991 *Universiade* (incorporating the World Student Games) in Sheffield. As more cities invest in such facilities and events, so the competitive edge that they gain is increasingly transitory and the public debt can grow while mobile capital rapidly moves on to reap the advantages of new partnerships elsewhere: as Harvey points out, the outcome may be that the public sector takes the risks while the private sector reaps the benefits. RJJ

Reference

Harvey, D. 1989: From managerialism to entrepreneurialism: the transformation in urban governance in late capitalism. *Geografiska Annaler* 71B: 3–17.

Suggested Reading

Bennett, R.J., ed., 1990: *Decentralization, local government and markets: towards a post-welfare agenda*. Oxford: Clarendon Press. · Cox, K.R. 1998: Spaces of dependence, spaces of engagement and the politics of scale, or: looking for local politics. *Political Geographer* 17: 1–24. · Cox, K.R. and Mair, A.J. 1988: Locality and community in the politics of local economic development. *Annals of the Association of American Geographers* 78: 307–25. · Hausner, V.A. ed., 1986: *Critical issues in urban economic development, Volume 1*. Oxford: Clarendon Press. · Logan, J.R. and Molotch, H.L. 1987: *Urban fortunes: the political economy of place*. Berkeley: University of California Press. · Marston, S.A., ed., 1990: Review symposium. *Urban Geography* 11: 176–208. · Seyd, P. 1990: Radical Sheffield: from socialism to entrepreneurialism. *Political Studies* 38: 325–44.

urban geography The geographical study of URBAN areas. The literature on urban geography in English was small until the 1940s, with the first textbook appearing in 1946. There was then a major surge of interest, and scholars who termed themselves urban geographers were in the vanguard of geography's QUANTITATIVE REVOLUTION during the 1960s and 1970s.

Early studies reflected the currently dominant PARADIGM. The importance of ENVIRONMENTAL DETERMINISM in the 1920s and 1930s, for example, stimulated a focus on the role of physical features – site and situation – as determinants of urban foundations and growth, and the subsequent growth of REGIONAL GEOGRAPHY saw attention switch to the regional relations of towns and to identifying morphological regions within them – see MORPHOLOGY and TOWNSCAPE. (All of these topics are illustrated in Taylor's, 1946, pioneering text, and in Dickinson's, 1949, work on URBAN ECOLOGY, the latter influenced by both German and North American sources.) During the 1950s, 1960s and 1970s the growing number of those who identified themselves as urban geographers were attracted to developments in LOCATION THEORY and LOCATIONAL ANALYSIS, though Berry's (1964) programmatic essay indicated the continued (rhetorical at least) importance of defining formal and functional REGIONS to the expanding sub-discipline. (Berry was on the committee which prepared the 1965 NAS–NRC report on *The science of geography*, which incorporated urban geography into the wider field of 'location theory studies'. The later BASS report – Taaffe, 1970 – had 'urban studies' as one of the four research directions selected to illustrate the 'growing research interests in contemporary geography'.)

Urban geographers' adoption of locational analysis, the philosophy of POSITIVISM, and the methodology and goals of SPATIAL SCIENCE was illustrated by two main strands of work in the late 1950s and early 1960s, much of it stimulated by pioneering studies undertaken at the University of Washington, Seattle (Johnston, 1997). The first concentrated on the pattern of urban settlement in a country or region, treating towns and cities as points on a map; the second, which dominated in the 1970s, focused on the internal structure of cities – treating them as areas with internal spatial structures rather than as points. In both, the goal was to identify the laws which it was believed governed the observed spatial arrangements: as Harris and Ullman expressed it in their classic (1945) paper on 'The nature of cities' (see MULTIPLE NUCLEI MODEL):

> Each city is unique in detail but resembles others in function and pattern. What is learned about one helps in studying another. Location types and internal structures are repeated so often that broad and suggestive generalizations are valid.

The study of URBAN SYSTEMS devoted much attention to testing the applicability of CENTRAL PLACE THEORY, especially the work of Walter Christaller. The concept of a spatially structured hierarchy attracted many empirical investigations: for example, of shopping centres within urban areas as well as of towns as central places, as exemplified in Berry's (1967; Berry and Parr, 1988) classic text. Studies of the functional structure and spatial arrangements of central places were complemented by investigations of shopping behaviour, to see whether people adhered to the theory's distance-minimizing principles (cf. RETAILING, GEOGRAPHY OF).

The study of the internal structure of urban areas initially concentrated on commercial districts but attention increasingly shifted to the residential areas. The main stimuli came from the URBAN ECOLOGY literature, especially the CHICAGO SCHOOL's models of land-use patterns (see ZONAL MODEL), which suggested not only that various social groups lived in separate residential areas but also that those areas were arranged in a particular spatial order. Geographers tested hypotheses derived from those models, analysing CENSUS TRACT data with multivariate statistical methods (see FACTORIAL ECOLOGY; SOCIAL AREA ANALYSIS): the seminal statement (by Berry and Rees, 1969) applied these methods to Calcutta, and was the first of a range of attempts seeking to impose models developed in North America on cities in other cultural realms, with later work exploring the differences between different contexts (e.g. Johnston, 1972) and then promoting models developed specifically for them (e.g. Ford, 1996).

Many of these empirical studies, both inter-urban and intra-urban, identified disparities between the observed and expected patterns: the models did not appear very realistic, although they remained the foundations for further exploration. Their assumptions, especially those concerning spatial behaviour, came under close scrutiny, and behaviourist approaches were introduced as an alternative, much more inductive, foundation.

Research in BEHAVIOURAL GEOGRAPHY at that time was not critical of the positivist philosophy and shared its goal of theory development premised on the existence of laws of spatial behaviour (as illustrated in King and Golledge's, 1978, text). Data were collected on the DECISION-MAKING which underpins the creation of the observed patterns of central places and residential segregation: initially, they only described the outcomes (as with work on intra-urban MIGRATION) but increasingly the choice decisions were explored.

Urban geography was linked then to the study and practice of URBAN AND REGIONAL PLANNING, built on the premise that well-ordered and efficient cities and regions could be engineered by applying the uncovered laws of spatial behaviour and organization. By the end of the 1960s, however, the continued prevalence of issues such as poverty, deprivation, and inequality led to a questioning of that apparently rational process (cf. RELEVANCE). Urban geographers were drawn into investigating why this was so: initially, they refocused their work onto the roles of URBAN MANAGERS AND GATEKEEPERS as controllers of the spatial structuring of urban areas, recognizing that location decisions are made in contexts not vacuums, and that constraints are as important as choices in determining where, for example, people migrated to.

This broadening of empirical studies was followed by further realization that those who managed urban areas, and thereby constrained choices, were themselves operating in a constrained context within which their degrees of freedom were limited. Attention shifted to the nature of those wider contexts, as part of the general reaction against POSITIVISM and SPATIAL SCIENCE, and urban geographers were led by the writings of Harvey (1973), Castells (1977) and others into the field of POLITICAL ECONOMY, especially those parts of it dominated by Marxian thought (see also MARXIST GEOGRAPHY; RADICAL GEOGRAPHY; URBAN); many accepted at least part of the thrust of these writings and the suggested general processes within which particular outcomes were realized (see REALISM).

The predominant focus of this era of urban geography was on the towns and cities of the First World. McGee (1971) pioneered work on THIRD WORLD cities, arguing for models sympathetic to their cultural and historical backgrounds rather than attempts to apply 'western', mainly Anglo-American, models (White's, 1984, book on west European cities illustrated how Anglocentric those models were: see also Gugler, 1988). On the Second World of the now ex-socialist states see French and Hamilton (1979), Forbes and Thrift (1987) and Thrift and Forbes (1986). (Cf OVERURBANIZATION.)

The position of urban geography at the forefront of innovative work within the discipline declined somewhat after the 1970s. Many still call themselves urban geographers, as illustrated by the size of the relevant groups within the main GEOGRAPHICAL SOCIETIES; there is a thriving journal of *Urban Geography*; and the sub-discipline is still widely taught. But many of the concerns formerly encapsulated within urban geography are now studied under different banners: the revival of POLITICAL GEOGRAPHY and the expansion of both SOCIAL GEOGRAPHY and CULTURAL GEOGRAPHY have attracted workers whose empirical focus is mainly urban (intriguingly, RURAL GEOGRAPHY has prospered during the same period), and studies of topics such as COUNTERURBANIZATION are now as likely to be found under the title of POPULATION GEOGRAPHY as within urban geography. To some extent urban geographers now respond to trends elsewhere in the discipline, refashioning their investigations of particular areas, as well as reacting to new urban issues identified by society at large; for example. Leitner's (1992) review identified urban geographers as responding to the challenges of either 'new urban problems' (such as RACISM) or 'new developments in social theory', such as POST-STRUCTURALISM and POSTMODERNISM.

Part of the reason for the declining of the vitality of urban geography is shown in the conspectus of *Geography in America*. The chapter entitled 'The urban problematic' (Marston et al., 1989) begins by noting that 'over three-quarters of the American population is now urban (employing standard definitions), and almost any empirical analysis, and much theoretical conjecture, must in some way touch upon the realities or urban life' (p. 651): everything is now urban. In addition, the sub-discipline was presented as suffering from a 'crippling historical legacy' of outmoded approaches; in response it was 'developing a historical consciousness, has sophisticated analytical skills, and is moving into new and challenging areas of substantive research' (p. 669). (Similarly, in the autumn 1998 issue of its Newsletter, the Urban Geography Study Group of the Royal Geographical Society – with the Institute of British Geographers – noted a 'lack of identity of urban geographers, particularly in the UK, and the lack of ability of geographers to agree on what constitutes urban geography'.) The changed orientations of urban geographers' research is illustrated both by recent editions of well-established textbooks – compare Short (1984) and Short (1996) – and by newly-conceived volumes (such as Hall, 1998): the spatial science material is almost entirely absent now.

The period during which urban geography flourished so strongly coincided with the dominance of what Buttimer (1993) termed the mosaic and machine metaphors in human geography, which emphasized the establishment of generalizations regarding urban patterns and the assumed processes that generated them. As these, with their associated goal of explanation via generalization, decayed somewhat in importance, to be replaced by the search for understanding through the organism and arena metaphors (stressing contextual understanding), urban areas changed their roles within geography: rather than being the focus of attention *per se*, they became the contexts within which cultural, economic, social and political processes and conflicts were played out. Thus, although some work published in the journal *Urban Geography* follows traditional themes, such as the mapping of racial residential segregation, this is rarely set in the context of a search for general laws about such topics. Rather, urban geographers concentrate on the particular features of specific places within a general appreciation of URBANIZATION and the role of urban places in the contemporary world, studies which embrace a wide range of subject matter covering the cultural, social and political dimensions of urban life alongside the economic. No longer are urban geographers driven by what Agnew (1997) terms the 'urge to simplify cities into discrete types': their concerns are with 'the landscape complexity' of cities, its structuration and consequences for individual and group well-being. RJJ

References

Agnew, J. 1997: Commemoration and criticism: fifty years after the publication of Harris and Ullman's 'The nature of cities'. *Urban Geography* 18: 4–6. · Berry, B.J.L. 1964: Approaches to regional analysis: a synthesis. *Annals of the Association of American Geographers* 54: 2–11. · Berry, B.J.L. 1967: *The geography of market centers and retail distribution*. Englewood Cliffs, NJ: Prentice-Hall. · Berry, B.J.L. and Parr, J.L. 1988: *The geography of market centers and retail distribution*, 2nd edn. Englewood Cliffs, NJ: Prentice-Hall. · Berry, B.J.L. and Rees, P.H. 1969: The factorial ecology of Calcutta. *American Journal of Sociology* 74: 445–91. · Buttimer, A. 1993: *Geography and the human spirit*. Baltimore: Johns Hopkins University Press. · Castells, M. 1977: *The urban question: a marxist approach*. London: Edward Arnold; Cambridge, MA: MIT Press. · Dickinson, R.E. 1947: *City, region and regionalism*. London: Routledge and Kegan Paul. · Forbes, D. and Thrift, N.J., eds, 1987: *The socialist Third World: urban development and territorial planning*. Oxford: Basil Blackwell. · Ford, L.R. 1996: A new and improved model of Latin American city structure. *Geographical Review* 86: 437–40. · French, R.A. and Hamilton, F.E.I., eds, 1979: *The socialist city: spatial structure and urban policy*. Chichester and New York: John Wiley. · Gugler, J. 1988: *The urbanization of the Third World*. Oxford: Clarendon Press. · Hall, T. 1998: *Urban geography*. London: Routledge. · Harris, C.D. and Ullman, E.L. 1945: The nature of cities. *Annals of the American Academy of Political and Social Science* 242: 7–17. · Harvey, D. 1973: *Social justice and the city*. London: Edward Arnold; Baltimore: Johns Hopkins University Press. · Johnston, R.J. 1972: Towards a general model of intra-urban residential patterns: some cross-cultural comparisons. In C. Board et al., eds, *Progress in Geography* 4: 83–124. · Johnston, R.J. 1997: *Geography and geographers: Anglo-American human geography since 1945*, 5th edn. London: Edward Arnold. · King, L.J. and Golledge, R.G. 1978: *Cities, space and behavior: the elements of urban geography*. Englewood Cliffs, NJ: Prentice-Hall. · Leitner, H.A. 1992: Urban geography: responding to new challenges. *Progress in Human Geography* 16: 105–18. · McGee, T.G. 1971: *The urbanization process in the Third World: explorations in search of a theory*. London: George Bell and Sons. · Marston, S.A., Towers, G., Cadwallader, M. and Kirby, A. 1989: The urban problematic. In G.L. Gaile and C.J. Willmott, eds, *Geography in America*. Columbus: Merrill Publishing Company, 651–72. · NAS–NRC, 1965: *The science of geography*. Washington, D.C.: NAS–NRC. · Short, J.R. 1984: *An introduction to urban geography*. London: Routledge. · Short, J.R. 1996: *The urban order: an introduction to cities, culture and power*. London: Routledge. · Taaffe, E.J., ed., 1970: *Geography*. Englewood Cliffs, NJ: Prentice-Hall. · Taylor, T.G. 1946: *Urban geography*. New York: E.P. Dutton. · Thrift, N.J. and Forbes, D.N. 1986: *The price of war: urbanization in Vietnam, 1954–1985*. London: George Allen and Unwin. · White, P.E. 1984: *The West European city: a social geography*. London: Longman.

Suggested Reading

Carter, H. 1995: *The study of urban geography*, 5th edn. London: Edward Arnold; New York, John Wiley. · Hartshorn, T.A. 1991: *Interpreting the city: an urban geography*, 2nd edn. New York: John Wiley. · Johnston, R.J. 1989: *City and society: an outline for urban geography*. London: Unwin Hyman. · Knox, P.L. 1994: *Urbanization: an introduction to urban geography*. Englewood Cliffs, NJ: Prentice-Hall.

urban managers and gatekeepers Professionals and bureaucrats whose decisions influence the internal SPATIAL STRUCTURE of urban areas through their control of, for example, access to public housing and the allocation of mortgages. Bureaucrats who work in parts of the STATE APPARATUS are normally termed *urban managers* whereas professionals engaged in the private sector (such as real estate agents) are called *gatekeepers*.

Identification of the important role of managers and gatekeepers in the structuring of urban areas is generally associated with the works of Pahl (1975) and Rex (1968; cf. HOUSING CLASS), who demonstrated their importance in constructing and operating the constraints to choice in access to key resources, such as housing. Their writing stimulated considerable research by urban geographers in the 1970s (as in the special issue of the *Transactions, Institute of British Geographers* published in 1976), but later developments in RADICAL GEOGRAPHY directed attention away from the managers and their operations towards the constraints on their activities posed by the demands of the capitalist political economy (Williams, 1982; cf. URBAN). RJJ

References and Suggested Reading

Pahl, R.E. 1975: *Whose city? and further essays on urban society*. London: Penguin. · Rex, J. 1968: The sociology of a zone in transition. In R.E. Pahl, ed., *Readings in urban sociology*. Oxford and New York: Pergamon Press, 211–31. · Saunders, P. 1986: *Social theory and the urban question*, 2nd edn. London: Hutchinson. · Williams, P.R. 1982: Restructuring urban managerialism. *Environment and Planning A* 14: 95–105.

urban origins The origins of URBANISM are as problematic as its definition, but four broad explanations have been proposed:

Ecological models, which typically associate urbanism with the production and concentration of a 'surplus' of some kind through, in particular, the construction of large-scale irrigation schemes (see URBAN ECOLOGY).

Economic models, which, although they typically focus on changing FORMS OF ECONOMIC INTEGRATION and, in particular, on the transition from RECIPROCITY to REDISTRIBUTION, are especially concerned with the ways in which such systems of exchange are 'embedded' in non-economic institutions. Most of these models are indebted to Polanyi's substantivist anthropology but Harvey (1973) has attempted to give them a Marxian gloss and to elucidate the concentration of a socially designated surplus product, defined via the labour theory of value, 'in a few hands and in a few places'. In his view, urbanism may arise with the emergence of redistribution, necessarily arises with the emergence of MARKET EXCHANGE, and in both cases is causally connected to the ALIENATION of the surplus.

Cultural models, which typically examine the formative influence of religion on urban genesis. 'The religious component is almost alone', Wheatley (1971) argued, 'in having left in several of the realms of nuclear urbanism [see figure 1] a more or less continuous success of surviving material traces through . . . to fully evolved urban life.' In his view, 'the earliest foci of power and authority took the form of ceremonial centres, with

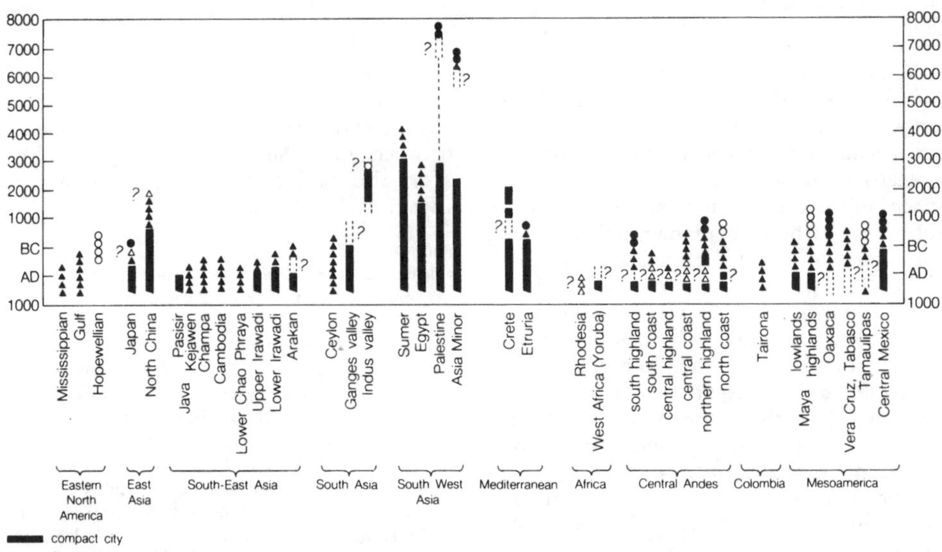

urban origins *1: Urban genesis in space and time* (after Wheatley, 1971: Carter, 1983)

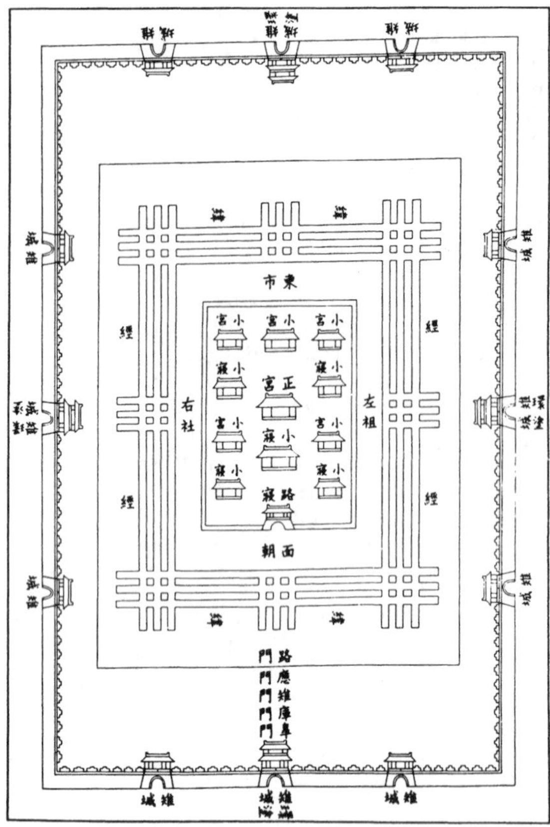

urban origins *2: The ancient Chinese city as the pivot of the four quarters* (after Wheatley, 1971)

religious symbolism imprinted deeply on their physiognomy and their operation in the hands of organised priesthoods'. Wheatley made much of the cosmo-magical symbolism or ICONOGRAPHY of the ancient city, which 'projected images of the cosmic order on to the plane of human experience, where they could provide a framework for [and legitimation] of social action' (see figure 2; and see also Sack, 1980).

Politico-military models, which typically conceive of the first cities as both fortresses and refuges. Many of these models are, of course, compatible with the arguments of the previous paragraphs – the supposed conjunction between 'hydraulic society' and 'Oriental despotism', for example, or the centring of 'political and military power . . . first in theocratic and later in monarchical control' (Giddens, 1981; see also Giddens, 1985) – but they usually go beyond those claims to emphasize the decisive importance of military power exercised through a grid of cities for the creation of empires.

Most modern debates, at least in geography, have fastened on the relations between the second and third of these, but the relations between urbanism and the origins of the STATE also mark out the fourth as an arena of considerable interest. DG

References

Carter, H. 1983: *An introduction to urban historical geography*. London: Edward Arnold, 1–17. · Giddens, A. 1981: *A contemporary critique of historical materialism, volume 1, Power, property and the state*. London: Macmillan. · Giddens, A. 1985: *A contemporary critique of historical materialism, volume 2, The nation-state and violence*. Cambridge: Polity Press. · Harvey, D. 1973: *Social justice and the city*. London: Edward Arnold; Baltimore, MD: Johns Hopkins University Press. · Sack, R.D. 1980: *Conceptions of space in social thought: a geographic perspective*. London: Macmillan; Minneapolis: University of Minnesota Press. · Wheatley, P. 1971: *The pivot of the four quarters: a preliminary inquiry into the origins and character of the ancient Chinese city*. Edinburgh: Edinburgh University Press; Chicago: Aldine.

Suggested Reading

Adams, R.Mc.C. 1966: *The evolution of urban society.* Chicago: Chicago University Press. · Carter, H. 1977: Urban origins: a review. *Progress in Human Geography* 1: 12–32. · Kostof, S. 1985: *A history of architecture: settings and rituals.* New York: Oxford University Press, chs 3–5. · Wheatley (1971), part two. · Wheatley, P. 1972: Proleptic observations on the origins of urbanism. In R.W. Steel and R. Lawton, eds, *Liverpool essays in geography.* London: Longman, 315–45.

urban renewal Both the process, and the result, of large-scale redevelopment of the built environment in downtown (cf. CENTRAL BUSINESS DISTRICT) and older INNER-CITY neighbourhoods, typically on a massive scale, and undertaken by the STATE, or more recently in the strategic form of a public–private partnership. The story of urban renewal is usually dated from the 1950s, though the spirit of the process may be seen in earlier huge projects like the Haussmannization of Paris, or the construction of Vienna's *Ringstrasse,* or some of the vast public works of Robert Moses in New York – and that spirit has much to do with the Promethean vision of MODERNITY (cf. Berman, 1982). By the 1950s, conditions were propitious for a sweeping MODERNIZATION of the urban LANDSCAPE in Western Europe and North America. Ageing infrastructure and decaying NEIGHBOURHOODS had seen little improvement in some cities since the 1920s; the post-war boom, the rapid URBANIZATION that accompanied it, the leadership of the emergent WELFARE STATE, and in Europe (both east and west) reconstruction following wartime damage, all conspired to sustain a vigorous rebuilding spree. The process was highly centralized and bureaucratized, and in its corporate execution and allegiance to Le Corbusier-style MODERNISM represented a formidable version of municipal FORDISM (Ley, 1996).

Its public works were massive, as Berman (1982) noted with pathos in his autobiographical essay on the Cross-Bronx Expressway in New York, or again as Fyfe (1996) has described in his innovative account of renewal in Glasgow. The state's deployment of POWER and authority in the city were remarkable, the power of its categories to shape reality, absolute. Designation of a district as a SLUM was a forensic diagnosis that led directly (and often in these terms) to the operation of surgical excision. Responses by citizens counted for nothing. This form of state despotism began to be challenged intellectually in the early 1960s, in part as a result of an ETHNOGRAPHIC study of urban renewal in Boston's West End that revealed the human consequences of forced relocation (Gans, 1962). Simultaneously, Jane Jacobs' remarkably precise diatribe against modern planning and its dire consequences widened the indictment across the United States (Jacobs, 1961; cf. URBAN AND REGIONAL PLANNING).

By the end of the 1960s, government began a fundamental re-assessment of the urban renewal programme in face of a brush fire of citizen opposition and intellectual critique. A strategic withdrawal was sounded, and through the 1970s the softer hand of the state was seen in policies that emphasized not *le grand récit* of 'slash and build' renewal, but rather *le petit récit* of rehabilitation, neighbourhood enrichment, and degrees of local empowerment, including decentralized neighbourhood planning and 'third sector' housing built and managed by non-profit societies. The move away from renewal was abrupt. In Canada in 1971, the entire federal urban budget was given over to renewal policies; by 1977, 96 per cent of a much larger budget was committed to PRESERVATION and enrichment (cf. Smith and Moore, 1993).

The 1980s saw the paling of incrementalism and the return of renewal by another name – *private–public partnerships* (Frieden and Sagalyn, 1989). Typically these projects have included a generous contribution to urban conviviality as the sugar coating on the pill of massive urban change. A number of cities (for example, Montreal, Knoxville, and Brisbane) have used the SPECTACLE of a world's fair, or major sporting event, as the cover for major infrastructure development. Others have employed the softer touch of James Rouse style urban redevelopment perfected in Boston's Faneuil Hall-Quincy Market, and Baltimore's Inner Harbor, where a festival market in conjunction with LEISURE venues, preferably in a waterfront setting, can become the symbolic and material anchor of wider private and public redevelopment. In this manner a leisure, or in more refined cases, an arts or cultural strategy (Zukin, 1995), can provide a palatable *entrée* for contemporary urban renewal. DL

References

Berman, M. 1982: *All that is solid melts into air: the experience of modernity.* New York: Simon and Schuster. · Frieden, B. and Sagalyn, L. 1989: *Downtown Inc.: how America rebuilds cities.* Cambridge, MA: MIT Press. · Fyfe, N. 1996: Contested visions of a modern city: planning and poetry in Glasgow. *Environment and Planning A* 28: 387–403. · Gans, H. 1962: *The urban villagers.* New York: Free Press. · Jacobs, J. 1961: *The death and life of great American cities*. New York: Random House. · Ley, D. 1996: *The new middle class and the remaking of the central city*. Oxford: Oxford University Press. · Smith, P. and Moore, P. 1993: Cities as a social responsibility: planning and urban form. In L. Bourne and D. Ley, eds, *The changing social geography of Canadian cities*. Montreal: McGill–Queen's University Press, 343–66. · Zukin, S. 1995: *The cultures of cities*. Cambridge, MA: Blackwell.

urban social movement Defined broadly as protest challenging state provision of urban social services and/or environmental regulation, such as popular movements against expressways, to preserve NEIGHBOURHOODS threatened by redevelopment, or squatters' rights movements. The term originates in the work of Manual Castells (1977) who linked the definition of urban SOCIAL MOVEMENTS to his conception of the city and its place within CAPITALISM (cf. URBAN). Critical of all previous theories of the city, especially the legacy of the CHICAGO SCHOOL, Castells argued that urban sociologists should embrace a marxist approach where the city is seen as a spatial expression of a unit of labour power that must be continuously reproduced for capitalism to survive. Basic social services, such as education and public transportation, must be provided by the STATE because corporations find these activities unprofitable (cf. COLLECTIVE CONSUMPTION; WELFARE STATE). However, it is virtually impossible for the state to deliver PUBLIC GOODS and services evenly across an entire urban population; moreover, in recent decades LOCAL STATES have found it difficult to maintain the level of service provision achieved in the 1960s. The capacity of the state to protect urban environments is also limited in a society geared to profit maximization. CONFLICTS over the provision of public services, or to strengthen environmental regulations, are therefore inevitable. In his early work Castells argued that these struggles should be classified as urban social movements only when they have the potential to improve the CLASS position of workers *vis-à-vis* the bourgeoisie. He asserted that the escalation of these movements, in conjunction with other forms of conflict (e.g. labour–capital), will lead to a 'ruptural unity' and transform capitalism. In later work Castells (1978, 1983) broadened his definition of urban social movements to include struggles to maintain cultural identity and to achieve more decentralized urban government as well as conflicts over public services. In the process he began to recognize the importance of feminism as a social movement and, more generally, the need to understand the motivations and beliefs of actors involved in protest movements.

Subsequent research has explored the nature of urban social movements in a variety of national contexts; much of this is reported in *The International Journal of Urban and Regional Research*. Key issues are the identification of factors that encourage or impede the mobilization process (Lustiger-Thaler and Maheu, 1995), the role of women in initiating and maintaining protest, state responses to urban social movements, and cross-cultural comparisons of these movements (Lowe, 1986). Critical appraisals of the concept focus on the imputed linkages between social structure and political behaviour. R.E. Pahl (1989), among others, believes that theorists of urban social movements have yet to reveal how people acquire a consciousness of structured inequities and how they transform this consciousness into political action. Ironically, although the concept of urban social movements continues to have much salience, Castells has abandoned it in his more recent work.

DH

References

Castells, M. 1977: *The urban question: a marxist approach*. London: Edward Arnold. · Castells, M. 1978: *City, class and power*. London: Macmillan. · Castells, M. 1983: *The city and the grassroots*. London: Edward Arnold. · Lowe, S. 1986: *Urban social movements: the city after Castells*. New York: St. Martin's Press. · Lustiger-Thaler, H. and Maheu, L. 1995: Social movements and the challenge of urban politics. In N.J. Ramapo Coll, ed., *Social movements and social classes: the future of collective action*. London: Sage, 151–68. · Pahl, R.E. 1989: Is the emperor naked? Some questions on the adequacy of sociological theory in urban and regional research. *International Journal of Urban and Regional Research* 13: 709–20.

urban system A set of interdependent urban places. The term was introduced by Berry (1964) as part of his application of SYSTEMS ANALYSIS and GENERAL SYSTEMS THEORY to the study of CENTRAL PLACE THEORY.

National territories are organized, according to proponents of the urban systems approach, as a set of urban-centred regions – towns and cities plus their HINTERLANDS – which together exhaust the land area and are articulated into a working system through networks along which goods, services, ideas, capital and labour flow (cf. LOCATIONAL ANALYSIS). Economic functions are distributed such that each urban centre and its associated hinterland has a prescribed set of roles within the whole (i.e. within the functional DIVISION OF LABOUR): over time roles change and the relative functions of places vacillate. With the increasing integration of the capitalist world-economy (cf. WORLD-SYSTEMS ANALYSIS), urban systems are developing which transgress national boundaries, as implied by the concept of a WORLD CITY.

Description of the organization, operation and change in a system involves much data analysis (as in FUNCTIONAL CLASSIFICATION OF CITIES), but empirical studies have not been matched by theoretical advances that have demonstrated the value of the terminology and concepts of systems theory, other than as very general descriptive devices. RJJ

Reference

Berry, B.J.L. 1964: Cities as systems within systems of cities. *Papers [and Proceedings] of the Regional Science Association* 13: 147–63.

urban village A residential district, usually in either the INNER CITY or the zone in transition of the ZONAL MODEL, containing people with a common cultural background and forming a COMMUNITY. Early studies in URBAN ECOLOGY suggested that cities were characterized by weak community ties, in contrast to rural areas (cf. CHICAGO SCHOOL; RURAL–URBAN CONTINUUM) – by *Gesellschaft* (association) rather than *Gemeinschaft* (community) in Tönnies's classic dualism – though Wirth's study of the GHETTO contradicted this claim (cf. URBANISM). The identification of urban villages is often associated with Gans's (1962) detailed PARTICIPANT OBSERVATION of an area of inner Boston where he found an Italian community brought together there through CHAIN MIGRATION and remaining to assist with assimilation into the host society, to defend the migrants' culture, and to ensure the provision of services – such as food shops – oriented to their market alone. RJJ

Reference

Gans, H.J. 1962: *The urban villagers: group and class in the life of Italian-Americans*. New York: Free Press of Glencoe.

Suggested Reading

Anderson, K. 1991: *Vancouver's Chinatown: racial discourse in Canada, 1875–1980*. Montreal: McGill University Press. · Johnston, R.J. 1988: Living in America. In P.L. Knox et al., *The United States: a contemporary human geography*. London and New York: Longman, 237–59. · Ley, D.F. 1974: *The black inner city as frontier outpost*. Washington, D.C.: Association of American Geographers.

urbanism A way of life associated with residence in an urban area. The concept was introduced in a classic essay by a sociologist of the CHICAGO SCHOOL, Louis Wirth (1938), who was concerned with social problems in urban areas; he identified the URBANIZATION process as leading to the erosion of the moral order of society because of the concomitant decline of COMMUNITY. The complexity of social and economic organization and the fine-grained division of labour in urban areas fragment the individual's life: much social interaction involves transactions with 'unknown others' and is thus transitory and superficial, in contrast to the situation of strong extended family ties and communities believed to be characteristic of rural areas and small settlements. Thus, Wirth presented the social disorganization of cities as stemming from their size, density and heterogeneity, his three criteria for distinguishing urban places (cf. RURAL–URBAN CONTINUUM).

Wirth's thesis typified studies that identified the URBAN as a separate spatial realm with its own contextual influences on individuals. It contradicted much of the other work of the Chicago School, however (including his own on the GHETTO), which identified strong communities within urban areas (cf. URBAN VILLAGE) and failed to locate the processes of urbanization within the wider political economy of CAPITALISM.

Within the literature of POSTMODERNISM and POSTMODERNITY many writers use the term urbanism as a synonym for the entire *built environment* of an urban area. RJJ

Reference

Wirth. L. 1938: Urbanism as a way of life. *American Journal of Sociology* 44: 1–24.

Suggested Reading

Smith, M.P. 1979: *The city and social theory*. Oxford: Basil Blackwell; New York: St. Martin's Press.

urbanization The process of becoming urban: in general usage, urbanization refers to the relative concentration of a territory's population in towns and cities (i.e. relative urban growth).

As a *demographic process*, which is the commonest use of the term, urbanization involves towns and cities growing in relative size within a space-economy through, first, an increasing proportion of the population living in urban places and, second, their concentration in the larger urban settlements. The end of the sequence is an almost completely urbanized society, with the great majority of its population living in just a few large places (but see COUNTERURBANIZATION).

Linked to these demographic processes (with MIGRATION the main contributor to urban growth) are the structural changes in society consequent upon the development of CAPITALISM (i.e. *structural urbanization*). Cities are the foci of the production, distribution and exchange processes at the heart of this MODE OF PRODUCTION, because of the ECONOMIES OF SCALE and SCOPE from AGGLOMERATION: urbanization is a necessary component of INDUSTRIALIZATION and DEVELOPMENT (though see OVERURBANIZATION).

Finally, there is *behavioural urbanization*. Urban areas, especially the larger ones, are centres of social change: values, attitudes and behaviour patterns are modified in urban milieux (cf. URBANISM), and new forms (which may be reflected in the TOWNSCAPE, as with architectural styles) then spread through the URBAN SYSTEM by DIFFUSION processes. (On the role of particular cities as centres of economic, social, political and cultural change, see Hall, 1998.)

This three-part model of urbanization has demographic change as a dependent variable within a process driven by structural imperatives. As a model it is particularly suited to analysis of modern CAPITALISM. It has been demonstrated, for example, that substantial urban growth and urbanization occurred in other parts of the world, notably Asia, long before the INDUSTRIAL REVOLUTION and rapid urbanization of the North Atlantic area in the nineteenth and twentieth centuries. City growth is not a feature of industrial societies alone and large settlements have characterized other FORMS OF ECONOMIC INTEGRATION; similarly, rapid urban growth is occurring in many parts of the contemporary THIRD WORLD as migrants flock to cities with aspirations for both better economic and social conditions than found in smaller places. Thus, as the arguments over counterurbanization and overurbanization also show, demographic urbanization can occur in a variety of contexts and what is typical of one time and place may not be typical of others. RJJ

References and Suggested Reading

Hall, P. 1998: *Cities in civilization*. London: Weidenfeld and Nicolson. · Johnston, R.J. 1989: *City and society: an outline for urban geography*. London: Unwin Hyman. · Knox, P.L. 1994: *Urbanization: an introduction to urban geography*. Englewood Cliffs, NJ: Prentice-Hall. · Taylor, P.J. 1989: The error of developmentalism in human geography. In D. Gregory and R. Walford, eds, *New horizons in human geography*. London: Macmillan, 303–19.

utilitarianism A moral theory which proposes the maximization of human well-being (utility or welfare) as the goal of life. It originated in the work of the eighteenth-century philosopher Jeremy Bentham and his nineteenth-century successor John Stuart Mill (see Mill, 1962). Utilitarianism was a radical ENLIGHTENMENT challenge to the prevailing beliefs in divine will, aristocratic authority and superstition as the principle guides to how people should act. It still has its followers, and is deeply implicated in some contemporary understandings of economic and social affairs.

Utilitarianism proposes that the only sound basis for normative appraisal is the promotion of human well-being. Other terms may be substituted for well-being, and take on special meaning in some versions of utilitarianism, e.g. pleasure, happiness, utility and welfare (cf. UTILITY THEORY). Utilitarianism finds application in the appraisal of political and economic institutions and public policies, as well as guiding individual conduct.

A distinction is made between *act utilitarianism*, which concerns the direct link between an individual action and the good it generates, and *rule utilitarianism*, which concerns the rules or institutions which mediate between action and their consequences with respect to human welfare. Utilitarianism is a *consequentialist* theory, with acts judged by their good or bad consequences in the promotion or otherwise of human well-being. Utilitarianism requirs *impartiality*, giving the same weight to each person's well-being and asking each to consider everyone else equally with themselves in deciding what to do. A further important property is to *maximize*, i.e. to achieve or promote as much aggregate or total well-being as possible, subject to some constraint such as personal budget or society's available resources.

In classical utilitarianism what was to be maximized was pleasure, or the absence of pain. More contemporary versions of utilitarianism are closely related to NEO-CLASSICAL ECONOMICS and its welfare theory (see WELFARE GEOGRAPHY). The focus here is on individual (consumer) preferences, the satisfaction of which yields *utility*. People act so as to get as much utility as possible from their limited resources, within the general structure of market exchange. While this notion is often confined to commodities acquired by spending money, it is in principle capable of generalization to all things from which people derive satisfaction, either positive or negative. The aggregate of individual utility is *welfare*, which is what society is supposed to maximize.

With respect to SOCIAL JUSTICE, whatever distribution maximizes welfare is deemed to be just.

The concept of utility and the utilitarian calculus are replete with problems The most obvious is the unreality of the behaviour postulated: real human beings do not engage in precise calculations of how to maximize their satisfaction. The difficulty of measuring utility is compounded when moving beyond market transactions to all things from which we derive satisfaction. Other problems arise with the interpersonal comparisons of utility required to aggregate individual experience into collective welfare. And to assert that whatever distribution maximizes aggregate welfare is socially just, no matter how unequal, is open to serious objections. DMS

Reference

Mill, J.S. 1962: *Utilitarianism*, ed. M. Warnock. London: Collins.

Suggested Reading

Brown, A. 1986: *Modern Political Philosophy: theories of the just society*. Harmondsworth: Penguin, ch. 2. · Kymlicka, W. 1990: *Contemporary Political Philosophy: an introduction*. Oxford: Clarendon Press, ch. 2. · Smith, D.M. 1994: *Geography and social justice*. Oxford: Blackwell, 58–64.

utility theory The basis of NEO-CLASSICAL ECONOMICS, which rests on the doctrine of consumer sovereignty and an ideological belief in both individualism and libertarianism – that individuals are the best judges of their own needs. A consumer's utility function is identified based on either assumed or revealed preferences and predicts choices, constrained within the available budget (cf. REVEALED PREFERENCE ANALYSIS). Utility theory has provided the base for much work on travel behaviour and the choice of shopping centre to patronize, referring to destination, modal split (choice of travel mode), and choice of route. RJJ

Suggested Reading

Golledge, R.G. and Timmermans, H. 1990: Applications of behavioural research on spatial problems I: cognition; and II: preference and choice. *Progress in Human Geography* 14: 57–100 and 311–44.

V

value-added A process which adds value (as reflected in price) to some commodity. Typically, value is added when labour is applied to a material, transforming it into something more useful (cf. MARXIAN ECONOMICS). Value can be added sequentially, at different stages in the production process, as material is turned into a component, which is added to others to make a finished article, which is then packaged and marketed, for example. A value-added tax usually applies a fixed percentage to the price of a good or service; this discriminates against poorer people, who pay the same tax as the rich when they purchase the same thing. DMS

values A set of beliefs and ideas which inform assessments (evaluations) of worthiness. The implications of this interpretation is that value – the measure of worth – and values are defined through socially constructed material and discursive practices (e.g. Harvey, 1996, Introduction). Although theoreticians of management have, apparently, just realized that consumption is as productive of value as destructive of it (e.g. Ramirez, 1998), economic geographies which recognize the significance of SOCIAL REPRODUCTION as a process sustained in time and across space conceive of value in just such a way (see ECONOMIC GEOGRAPHY). Consumption of value is a vitally necessary part – even a precondition of – production.

Values are socially specific; they derive from the concepts that we use to legitimate society. To take values seriously implies far more than the liberal manoeuvre of presenting different points of view about the same set of circumstances (e.g. is nuclear power good or bad?) or even of evaluating between alternative sets of circumstances, e.g. is this distributive outcome better or worse than that one? Rather, the issue is to relate these assessments, perfectly valid in their own right, to the wider social framework and discourses which set the parameters (e.g. profitability, human needs, ecological sustainability) within which measures of worth are defined. And it is important to recognize (as have, for example, Storper and Salais, 1997, drawing on the work of Boltanski and Thevenot, e.g. 1991) that the dualism of structure and agency leaves aside action and the negotiation of meaning (e.g. worth) through action (e.g. in conventions).

For example, in pointing to fundamentals, the expression 'the bottom line' is both offensive and realistic. It is *offensive* in its assumption that values measured in a particular form of market economy are somehow elemental; but it is *realistic* if it represents a response to the imperatives of capitalist society (see CAPITALISM). However, it is *particularly offensive* when the latter usage is simply assumed as unproblematic and beyond debate – most especially in a context in which critical thought might be a reasonable expectation.

Consider the diminution of geography implied in the following assertions:

> The need for theory still exists but only to the extent that it will be used if it can be shown to deliver 'better' working models or is otherwise useful . . . if geographers are not prepared to meet these emerging needs . . . [they] will be left with no other course of action other than to become social theorists in the style of Harvey and Scott. (Openshaw, 1989, p. 74)

Usefulness is here contrasted with knowledge, categorized as 'useless' if

> the questions being asked relate to the pursuit of knowledge rather than more pressing [*sic*!] applied matters of contemporary relevance and public concern. (Openshaw, 1986, p. 143)

However, there is some compensation for looking at the world from such a narrow perspective; it opens up a more 'valuable' alternative:

> There are vast potential new markets if geographers are able to sell themselves, merchandise their products, and adopt a less (*sic*!) restrictive *modus operandi*. (Openshaw, 1989, p. 88)

Again, it is one thing to make the legitimate, if value-laden, claim that the 'key aspect' for the future health of geography as an academic discipline 'is a better understanding of the structure of economic incentives and rights, rather than CLASS' (Bennett, 1989, p. 289). But it is quite another if this is taken to mean that a concern for 'class' is not relevant to issues like '"choice" conceptions of rights which promote autonomy, freedom, self-determination, and human development' (Bennett, 1989, p. 289) on the grounds that

> capitalism has become seen as the means of creating and distributing the good things of life ... [as] ... the spirit of market freedom of individuals has heralded a consumer and service economy which has offered the release from the least attractive toils and labours, and has seemed to offer the potential to satisfy many of people's most avaricious dreams. (p. 286)

Not only does the conclusion (issues such as class are no longer relevant to geography) not follow from the premise (capitalism produces and generates the good things of life – a view which is, in any case, hotly contested) but – and much more importantly from the point of view of this discussion – there is an unquestioned assumption that 'the bottom line' may be *unproblematically* defined in terms of 'avaricious dreams'. The assumption of a particular measure of value could hardly be more clear.

One of the major contributions of RADICAL GEOGRAPHY was its demonstration of the social construction of value and, by implication, the possibility of changing values. In parallel fashion, HUMANISTIC GEOGRAPHY pointed to the often contested and limiting prior definitions of the objects of research implied in particular methodologies – notably those like EMPIRICISM – which rest upon a limited perception and narrow definition of 'facts' (Buttimer, 1974).

Unless it is literally true that 'facts' are both unproblematic and, always and everywhere, speak for themselves, a value-free geography is impossible. How, for example, do we value the environment – in monetary terms? – a socially relative, and geographically and historically uncertain measure if ever there was one; in ecological terms – but then what about the social construction of science?; or in political terms which recognize that human beings are part of nature but are social (and socially constructed) entities too and so actively contest the meaning of the environment and their engagement with it? (see ECONOMIC GEOGRAPHY).

If we accept the need for the political resolution of such problems (and it is difficult to see how we may proceed without so doing despite the fact that the formal practice of politics itself is far from unproblematic) then we must accept that NATURE itself is a social construct and so reject in no uncertain terms the notion geography is nothing more than an uncontested 'space-time data model' or 'huge integrated GIS' (see GEOGRAPHICAL INFORMATION SYSTEMS) (Openshaw, 1991, pp. 622 and 627). And we must go further for geographers cannot merely *contemplate* alternative social constructions of values for they are themselves *participants* in the process of the production and reproduction of values. The question of ETHICS goes well beyond the important matter of *conducting* and *reporting* research. It asks questions about the *moral purposes* of research. But it can never be enough merely to assert

> a moral duty to help society and the world to unlock and understand the key patterns and relationships that may exist encrypted in ... [GIS] ... data bases. (Openshaw, 1991, p. 625.)

It is not enough because, despite the phenomenal but geographically highly uneven power of GISS to generate data, the very notion of *the key* patterns and relationships implies a set of values founded in a particular discourse which cannot be assumed away or ignored. Thus David Smith (1997, pp. 586–7), for example, distinguishes between *meta-ethics* which 'concerns the meaning of such terms as good and bad, right and wrong, ought or should, i.e. the language of moral discourse', *descriptive ethics* (actual moral beliefs and practices) and *normative ethics*. Whilst it may well be 'true' that 'truth' resides solely in discourse, discourse resides in social practice and, in particular, in the social relations through which social beings try to make sense of their circumstances (Lee, 1989). So regimes of truth founded on temporally and geographically uneven dominant competitive discourses may be established and may indeed be imagined and transcend the particular but they are themselves socially constructed, changeable and open to contestation (McDowell, 1995); they cannot be free-floating otherwise they would be meaningless and so, quite simply, there cannot be unproblematic significance.

Values and ethics force geographers to reconsider questions of, for example, social justice and ethics as well as 'economic incentives and rights' not merely as states to be measured or defined but as the bases for the purpose of their labours. And the labour of geographers ('to examine the contextual thickening of moral concepts in the particular (local) circumstances of differentiated human being' (Smith, 1997, p. 587)) is made the more complex by the varied formative geographies (themselves socially constructed) in and through which such notions are constructed, contested and given meaning. RL

References

Bennett, R.J. 1989: Whither models and Geography in a post-welfarist world? In B. Macmillan, ed., *Remodelling Geography*. Oxford and Cambridge, MA: Basil Blackwell, 273–90. · Boltanski, L. and Thevenot, L. 1991: *De la justification*. Paris: Gallimard. · Buttimer, A. 1974: *Values in Geography*. Association of American

Geographers Commission on College Geography, Resource Paper number 24. Washington, D.C.. · Harvey, D. 1996: *Justice, nature and the geography of difference*. Cambridge, MA and Oxford: Blackwell. · Lee, R. 1989: Social relations and the geography of material life. In D. Gregary and R. Walfard, eds, *Horizons in human geography*, ch. 2.4. Houndmills: Macmillan, 152–69. · McDowell, L. 1995: Understanding diversity: the problem of/for 'theory'. In R.J. Johnston, P.J. Taylor and M.J. Watts, eds, *Geographies of global change Remapping the world in the late twentieth century*, ch. 17. Oxford and Cambridge, MA: Blackwell, 280–94. · Ramirez, R. 1998: Unchaining value in a new global age. *Mastering global Business*. Part 4 *The Financial Times*, 12–13. · Openshaw, S. 1986: Modelling relevance. *Environment and Planning A* 18: 143–7. · Openshaw, S. 1989: Computer modelling in geography. In B. Macmillan, ed., *Remodelling Geography*. Oxford and Cambridge, MA: Basil Blackwell, 70–88. · Openshaw, S. 1991: A view of the GIS crisis in geography, or, using GIS to put Humpty-Dumpty back together again. *Environment and Planning A* 23: 621–8. · Smith, D.M. 1997: Geography and ethics: a moral turn? *Progress in Human Geography* 21: 583–90. · Storper, M. and Salais, R. 1997: *Worlds of production*. Cambridge, MA and London: Harvard University Press.

Suggested Reading

Buttimer, A. and Lee, R. 1997: Classics in human geography revisited: 'Values in geography'. *Progress in Human Geography;* McDowell (1995). · Taylor, P.J., Watts, M.J. and Johnston, R.J. 1995: Remapping the world: What sort of map? What sort of world? In R.J. Johnston, P.J. Taylor and M.J. Watts, eds, *Geographies of global change. Remapping the world in the late twentieth century*, ch. 22. Oxford and Cambridge MA: Blackwell, 377–85.

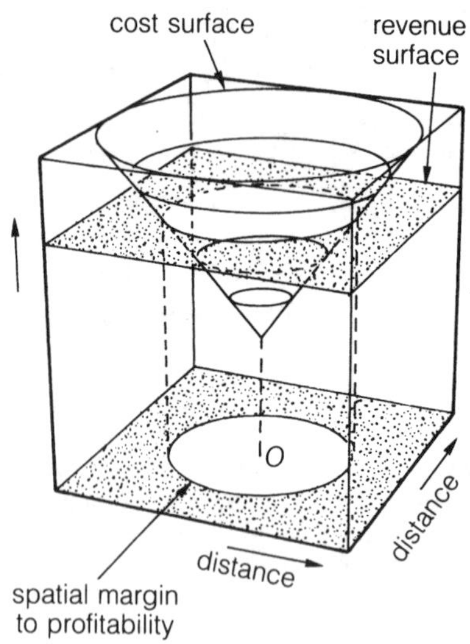

variable cost analysis

variable cost analysis An approach to industrial location (or the location of facilities in general) concerned with spatial variations in production costs. This is one of two major alternative theoretical approaches to industrial location in the classical tradition, the other being VARIABLE REVENUE ANALYSIS.

The variable cost model in its simplest form may be expressed as follows:

$$TC_i = \sum_{j=1}^{n} Q_j U_{ij}$$

where TC_i is total cost of producing a given volume of output at location i, Q_j is the input coefficient or required quantity of input j and U_{ij} is the unit cost of the input in question at location i. Total cost is simply the summation over n inputs of the product of required quantity and unit cost.

As the expression above shows, total cost (for a given output) depends on two major considerations: the input coefficients and spatial variations in input cost. The *input coefficients* arise from the technique adopted in manufacturing the goods in question: they may vary from place to place, within the technical constraints that may require certain minimum quantities, as the quantity of a particular input used increases where its cost is low relative to that of other inputs. The capacity to substitute among inputs, along with the fact that input combinations may also vary with scale of output, greatly increases the complexity of variable cost analysis in both theory and practice.

The *unit cost* of the required input will vary in geographical space in obvious ways. For many materials these will be a reflection of TRANSPORT COSTS (see also PRICING POLICIES), but for other inputs all manner of complications can arise to influence the spatial cost pattern. For example, the cost of labour per unit of output can vary with actual wage rates, fringe benefits paid, training costs and welfare facilities provided by the firm, as well as with the PRODUCTIVITY of labour. The intricacy of modern systems of INPUT–OUTPUT linkages, as manufacturing processes become more sophisticated technically, is a major complication in calculating input costs. Added to this is the difficulty of incorporating more general EXTERNAL ECONOMIES and advantages arising from AGGLOMERATION.

Variable cost analysis proceeds under one or other of two assumptions concerning the incidence of alternative locations: that they are discrete points or that a continuous surface exists.

The assumption of relatively few discrete points is the more realistic, in the sense that actual location practice generally involves the evaluation of a small number of alternatives: this is the usual framework for COMPARATIVE COST ANALYSIS. However, INDUSTRIAL LOCATION THEORY often proceeds on the implicit assumption that those locations actually considered and costed are selected from an infinite number of possible locations. Total cost is thus conceived of as a continuous spatial variable.

The concept of a *cost surface* is central to variable cost analysis. A cost surface depicts spatial variations in the cost of production as a three-dimensional surface, with distance along the two horizontal axes and cost in pecuniary units on the vertical axis (see figure). Cost surfaces are typically portrayed by the pecuniary equivalent of contour lines. The surface may represent spatial variations in the cost of single inputs, such as labour, land or individual materials. It may also represent total operating costs at a given scale, though this is more difficult to identify empirically.

The cost surface reveals, in effect, the topography of cost of production, any section through which can be depicted as a *space cost curve*, or plot of spatial variations in production cost along one distance dimension. This is the spatial analogy of the cost curve of conventional production theory in economics which depicts the relationship between cost of production and volume of output. The space cost curve can portray single-input costs or total costs at a given scale. The form of the space cost curve – whether it is steep or shallow – can give some indication as to the degree of restriction likely to be imposed on locational choice if plant viability is to be achieved. With appropriate assumptions as to the form of the *revenue surface* (see VARIABLE REVENUE ANALYSIS), an optimal or profit-maximizing location can be identified, along with the *spatial margins to profitability* constraining freedom of choice of location.

The spatial margin is the locus of points where the total cost of producing a given volume of output is equal to the total revenue obtainable from selling that output. This defines the area within which profitable operation is possible. The concept of the spatial margin to profitability was introduced by E.M. Rawstron (1958), as one of the few really original spatial-economic concepts devised by a geographer. Its derivation from the cost and revenue surfaces is shown in the figure. The significance of the spatial margin is that it permits the incorporation of sub-optimal decisions into a theoretical framework previously directed towards searching for the single optimal profit-maximizing location (*O* in the figure). Anywhere within the margin offers some profit, so a firm would be able to exercise freedom of choice within these limits, trading-off profits for personal or other considerations. Within the margin a firm can locate in total ignorance yet still survive. The shape and extent of the spatial margin will vary with the prevailing cost and revenue surfaces. Some industries operate within wide margins, while others will be confined by tight and localized limits to viability. The margins can vary with the nature of the industrial organization – they may be wider for highly skilful entrepreneurs than for the less able, for example.

If revenue is assumed to be a spatial constant, then the optimal location for the profit-maximizing firm will be where total cost is minimized, i.e. at the lowest point on the total cost surface. How this point arises and how it may be identified are the problems around which Alfred Weber (1929) built his classical approach to industrial location theory. Much of the work of later exponents of the variable cost approach, such as T. Palander (1935) and E.M. Hoover (1948), was greatly influenced by Weber's theory. For almost half a century the variable cost model constituted the core of industrial location theory, but its lack of realism resulted in a broadening perspective with more attention given to revenue and decision-making considerations. Nevertheless, variable cost analysis is still highly relevant to actual location practice, from the small unit of production to the multinational firm. Cost of production is still very important to locational viability. And in the field of industrial development planning, variable cost analysis still provides a useful framework for the design of spatial strategy. DMS

References

Hoover, E.M. 1948: *The location of economic activity*. New York: McGraw-Hill. · Palander, T. 1935: *Beitrage zur Standortstheorie*. Uppsala: Almqvist and Wiksell. · Rawstron, E.M. 1958: Three principles of industrial location. *Transactions, Institute of British Geographers* 25: 132–42. · Weber, A. 1929: *Alfred Weber's theory of the location of industries*, trans. C.J. Friedrich. Chicago: University of Chicago Press. (Reprinted 1971, New York: Russell and Russell; first German edition, 1909.)

Suggested Reading

Smith, D.M. 1981: *Industrial location: an economic geographical analysis*, 2nd edn. New York: John Wiley. · Smith, D.M. 1987: Neoclassical location theory. In W. Lever, ed., *Industrial change in the United Kingdom*. London: Longman, 23–37.

variable revenue analysis An approach to INDUSTRIAL LOCATION THEORY concerned with spatial variations in revenue. It concentrates on the demand side of the industrial location problem, as opposed to the cost side addressed in VARIABLE COST ANALYSIS.

Total revenue may be defined as the product of the quantity of goods sold and the price obtainable for them. Revenue in alternative locations is thus:

$$TR_i = \sum_{j=1}^{n} Q_j P_j$$

where TR_i is revenue that can be earned by a plant located at i, Q_j is the quantity of goods that can be sold at market j and P_j is the price at j: summation is over all n markets. This expression is a first step to opening up the various determinants of revenue, operating through quantity sold and price charged respectively.

On the quantity (demand) side, sales expectations in any market j will be influenced by a number of variables. The most obvious is population: the more people the greater the demand, other things being equal. Among those other things (which seldom, if ever, are equal) are people's incomes and their tastes or preferences, which influence the propensity to consume. Demand generally rises with income but it can fall (which is the case for the so-called 'inferior goods' that people tend to buy in smaller quantities as they become better off). Tastes may vary with income, but they are also subject to spatial variations in accordance with CULTURE, custom and so on. Another influence on the local level of demand for a good is the availability and price of substitutes.

The other variable in the expression above – price – is discussed under PRICING POLICIES. There are various ways in which goods can be priced, and this choice will determine whether price varies from place to place and the pattern that such variations might take. As price falls, more of a good should be consumed, subject to limits on capacity to consume and on the ability of some goods to attract additional sales as price rises, e.g. goods where status is gained by the purchase of things that are expensive. Price and quantity are thus related to each other in determining volume of revenue.

MARKET-AREA ANALYSIS forms an important component of the variable revenue approach. The revenue that a firm can earn may be proportional to the market size or areal extent of the territory over which control can be exerted (see HINTERLAND). However, the same area may yield different levels of revenue, because of the operation of the variables described above relating to the nature of the local population and its demand characteristics.

The analysis of market areas is closely bound up with LOCATIONAL INTERDEPENDENCE. The location of one unit of production is seen as dependent on the strategy of competitors, as they seek SPATIAL MONOPOLY or control over market areas. Specific analyses of how firms locate in competition with one another under variable revenue conditions include the HOTELLING MODEL and its extensions, which incorporate alternative assumptions as to the elasticity of demand. The variable revenue approach has arisen as much from the development of the theory of imperfect competition in economics as from the realization that the effect of the market on plant location goes further than the cost of distribution (as approached via the AGGREGATE TRAVEL MODEL).

The graphic device of the *revenue surface* portrays spatial variations in the revenue to be derived from the sale of a given volume of output, depicted as a three-dimensional surface with distance along the two horizontal axes and revenue in pecuniary units on the vertical (see figure illustrating VARIABLE COST ANALYSIS, where it is a spatial constant and thus depicted an a horizontal plane). A section through a revenue surface is a *space revenue curve*, i.e. a plot of the revenue to be earned from a given volume of sales, in one distance dimension. Revenue surfaces are extremely difficult to identify empirically, and the revenue likely to be earned from alternative locations is normally estimated less directly.

The variable revenue approach is prone to both conceptual and practical difficulties. Although cost variations among alternative locations need not be disregarded completely (for example, they can be built into delivered price from alternative suppliers), the reciprocal relationship of unit cost to price via ECONOMIES OF SCALE is extremely difficult to handle. If unit cost varies with volume of sales, and this is dependent on price which, in its turn, is influenced by unit costs, then the problem of the optimal location is impossible to resolve. This is why industrial location theory makes such stringent assumptions on either the cost or the demand side.

At a practical level the variable revenue approach is more difficult to apply than variable cost analysis, because it is hard to identify consumer demand schedules. Hence the adoption of alternatives, notably the MARKET POTENTIAL MODEL. Further complications arise from the actual practice of DECISION-MAKING under the conditions of UNCERTAINTY characterizing real market competition. The unpredictability of consumer behaviour in choosing which outlet to patronize is a further complication. DMS

Suggested Reading

Smith, D.M. 1981: *Industrial location: an economic geographical analysis*, 2nd edn. New York: John Wiley. · Smith, D.M. 1987: Neoclassical location theory. In W. Lever, ed., *Industrial change in the United Kingdom*. London: Longman, 23–37.

vector data A form of geographic data in which primitive objects (points, lines, and areas) are represented using coordinates, connected as necessary by straight lines (vectors). Vector representations are commonly seen as alternatives to RASTER, and GEOGRAPHICAL INFORMATION SYSTEMS can be broadly divided into these two types, although most now have some aspects of both. A vector representation of an area is a polygon, and by extension a representation of a line is termed a *polyline*. Vector representations often appear more accurate than raster representations, because the latter have fixed spatial resolution determined by the size of each cell, but such accuracy is often illusory, since it fails to reflect the real positional uncertainty of each object. MG

vertical theme The teasing out and tracing through of a distinctive PROCESS operating in a society and (particularly) its LANDSCAPE over time. The establishment of 'vertical themes' is characteristic of studies of landscape change in classical HISTORICAL GEOGRAPHY (see MORPHOGENESIS; cf. CROSS-SECTION). Within that tradition, the model is usually taken to be H.C. Darby's (1951) account of the changing English landscape, which identified six 'vertical themes': clearing the wood, draining the marsh, reclaiming the heath, the changing arable, the landscape garden, and urban-industrial growth. These themes are described in conventional narrative form and often summarized as a progressive sequence of thematic maps. Darby reaffirmed his belief in such a procedure as an attempt to deal with the problem of combining historical and geographical description some ten years later (Darby, 1962), and the schema has been adopted by a number of his students and others (see, e.g. Williams, 1974). DG

References

Darby, H.C. 1951: The changing English landscape. *Geographical Journal* 117: 377–98. · Darby, H.C. 1962: The problem of geographical description. *Transactions, Institute of British Geographers* 30: 1–14. · Williams, M. 1974: *The making of the South Australian landscape: a study in the historical geography of Australia*. London and New York: Academic Press.

virtual geographies As computer networks have spread across the globe, and as computers have acquired increasing visualization capacities, so it has become clear that the ability of human beings and machines to imagine the world (and each other) has been extended in significant new ways. Though these extensions have been the subject of much ill-judged hyperbole, it seems undeniable that four different but related processes are occurring.

First, the ability to produce detailed, moving three-dimensional environments is reaching the point where these environments are becoming significant supplements to the landscape around us, or even new kinds of LANDSCAPE (rather as film altered our perception of the city in times past).

Second, through the power of computer SIMULATION, it is becoming possible to extend the range of 'would-be worlds' it is possible to think of (Casti, 1996): filmic special effects, computer games like 'Sim City', and various outputs from geographical information systems are only the tip of the technological iceberg (Mitchell, 1995).

Third, computer VISUALIZATION is re-inscribing the visual domain, perhaps to the point where we 'may be returning to an oral–visual culture. Animation, virtual reality, fibre-optic video, laser disks, computer modelling, even e-mail, are part of a new vision and visionary art-science' (Stafford, 1994, p. xxv).

Then, finally, this power to represent in new ways has heralded an era in which there is considerable uncertainty about what counts as 'real' and what counts as 'virtual'. When using computers it is possible to alter images and produce new ones at the drop of a hat, so that the world can sometimes seem as though it is built on shifting sands (Wark, 1994). But, more likely, we are entering a period rather like that which heralded the introduction of print or film when we are having to gain new kinds of skills, new cultural apprehensions of the digital realm and new cultural appreciations of what can and cannot be: a new virtual 'literacy', if you like. What we can be sure of is that this process of settling in is clearly not yet complete (Turkle, 1996).

Geography is intimately bound up with each and every one of these processes, both in the sense that new geographies of the imagination are being produced and that new geographies of production are being established – in places like Boston and Los Angeles – from which these new IMAGINATIVE GEOGRAPHIES can venture out into the world. NJT

References

Casti, J. 1996: *Would-be worlds*. New York: Wiley. · Crang, M. and May, J., eds, 1998: *Virtual geographies*. London: Routledge. · Cubitt, S. 1998: *Digital aesthetics*. London: Sage. · Graham, S. and Marvin, S. 1996: *Telecommunications and the city. Electronic spaces, urban places*. London: Routledge. · Mitchell, W.T.J. 1995: *City of bits. Space, place and the infobahn*. Cambridge, MA: MIT Press. · Stafford, B. 1994: *Artful science. Enlightenment entertainment and the eclipse of visual education*. Cambridge, MA: MIT Press. · Stafford, B. 1996: *Good looking. Essays on the virtue of images*. Cambridge, MA: MIT Press. · Thrift, N.J. 1996: New urban eras and old technological fears: reconfiguring the goodwill of electronic things. *Urban Studies* 33: 1463–93. · Turkle, S. 1996: *Life on the screen. Identity in the age of the internet*. London: Weidenfeld and Nicolson. · Wark, M. 1994: *Virtual geography*. Bloomington: Indiana University Press.

virtual reality Recreation of aspects of sensory experience through the use of digital technology. Virtual reality (VR) technologies include head-mounted displays that project images directly in front of each eye, and modify the images as the head moves to create the illusion of sensory immersion in a real physical setting; systems for feeding sound to the ears; and systems for detecting movements of the user's hands and simulating appropriate visual effects (for a review of VR technology, see Burdea and Coiffet, 1994). The term *augmented reality* is used when technology adds to or enhances perception of surroundings.

Virtual and augmented realities have found applications in several areas relevant to human geography, although the technology remains largely exploratory. The concept of a virtual field course, in which some aspects of the field experience are recreated in virtual environments, has been explored in several projects (Raper, 1997). Golledge et al. (1991) have developed systems to augment the reality of visually impaired people, to help them navigate through unfamiliar spaces. Systems that display information in the peripheral vision of field workers are being adopted to enhance the effectiveness of FIELDWORK.

The idea of virtual geographic reality raises a host of interesting questions, and reveals our lack of understanding of how people perceive and record field experiences. No virtual reality can ever fully replace 'being there'; the challenge is rather to find aspects of reality that can be recreated virtually, and that have value in aiding research or interpretation. MG

References

Burdea, G. and Coiffet, P. 1994: *Virtual reality technology*. New York: Wiley. · Golledge, R.G., Loomis, J.M., Klatzky, R.L., Flury, A. and Yang, X.L. 1991: Designing a personal guidance system to aid navigation without sight: progress on the GIS component. *International Journal of Geographical Information Systems* 5: 373–95. · Raper, J. 1997: Progress towards spatial multimedia. In M. Craglia and H. Couclelis, eds, *Geographic information research: bridging the Atlantic*. London: Taylor and Francis, 525–43.

vision and visuality Geographical knowledges are very often conveyed visually, and geographers, like those in other social science disciplines, are beginning to pay some attention to the specifically visual dynamics of this process (see also FILM, GEOGRAPHY OF; IMAGINATIVE GEOGRAPHY; MEDIA, GEOGRAPHY OF; SPECTACLE, GEOGRAPHY OF). The starting point for much of this work is that, like any other cultural TEXT, an IMAGE draws on particular signifying conventions in order to make its meaning. These conventions – what Foster (1988) calls culturally specific 'visuality' in an uneasy distinction from the 'vision' of human corporeal optics – might be described as ensembles of visual practices which structure what is visible and invisible. These are at work in both the visual content of an image – what it shows – as well as its visual and spatial organization – how it shows it and what position that may invite an audience to take in relation to it.

Geography as a discipline has traditionally used a wide range of visual technologies and genres – maps of course (Harley, 1992), but also topographic painting, lantern slides, photography (Ryan, 1997), film, and more recently GEOGRAPHICAL INFORMATION SYSTEMS, among others – and has often assumed that such images show, not a geographer's REPRESENTATION of the world, but some true aspect of the object under observation. It is only recently that many geographers have begun to argue that the visuality inherent in all these sorts of images must be critically examined (cf. ART, GEOGRAPHY AND).

Daniels and Cosgrove (1988), for example, advocate the use of ICONOGRAPHY to unpack the meanings carried by visual symbols, and geographers have paid some attention to the ways in which certain conventions of visuality produce and reproduce visible signs of social difference. Thus the construction of images of classed, gendered and racialized IDENTITY through particular visualisations of SPACE, PLACE, NATURE, LANDSCAPE, the BODY, the NATION-STATE and the URBAN has been examined. In this work, the significance of a visual image is understood as a consequence of social processes of meaning-making at work in both the production and interpretation of an image. Somewhat similar approaches adopted by other geographers include rather general claims that particular visual images are given meaning by their historically and geographically specific social, economic, cultural and political 'context' (Schwartz, 1996; see also CONTEXTUAL APPROACH), or the argument that it is an image's embeddedness in DISCOURSE which gives it its meanings (Harley, 1992). In the MARXIST tradition of GEOGRAPHY, meanwhile, Harvey (1989) argues that various films and photographs reflect changes in the time–space organization of contemporary capitalism, while Cosgrove (1985) offers a rather less reductionist account of landscape painting as a bourgeois way of seeing (see also Daniels, 1989).

In his work, Cosgrove (1985) utilizes Berger's (1972) notion of 'ways of seeing' to suggest that a particular tradition of visualizing LANDSCAPE offers a viewing position to the spectator which is also a social position: the bourgeois, white masculine owner of land. This notion of a 'way of seeing' in which image and spectator may produce each other (although this complicity is never guaranteed; see Burgess, 1990), has been reworked and used extensively in FEMINIST GEOGRAPHIES. Many historians have explored the importance of apparently accurate and objective vision to dominant Western scientific modes of knowledge (Haraway, 1991), and the analytical language of the social sciences remains structured by a highly visual vocabulary which constructs perspectives, points of view and foci even when no visual images are under discussion. In geography, some work has begun to explore the effects of this visualizing of knowledge. It has been argued that the MASCULINISM of much geography depends in part on what Haraway (1991, p. 191) calls the 'god-trick': that is, the production of an invisible critic who nonetheless claims to see others fully. Haraway makes it clear that to (attempt to) remain invisible while claiming to see clearly is to occupy a discursive position that remains unaccountable for its own specificity and partiality. Thus feminist geographers have critiqued those geographical accounts of the URBAN (Deutsche, 1991) or of LANDSCAPE (Nash, 1996; Rose, 1993) which claim omniscience while remaining blind to other visions.

This critique has found a response in some attempts to see geographical knowledges differently, by offering partial, multiple or fragmented views (Allen and Pryke, 1994; Seager and Olson, 1997). It also suggests that a critical geography of vision and visuality may need to pay more attention to its methodology (Rose, 1996) and to the specificities of its own ways of seeing. GR

References

Allen, J. and Pryke, M. 1994: The production of service space. *Environment and Planning D: Society and Space* 12: 453–75. · Berger, J. 1972: *Ways of seeing*. London: BBC and Penguin. · Burgess, J. 1990: The production and consumption of environmental meanings in the mass media. *Transactions, Institute of British Geographers* NS 15: 139–61. · Cosgrove, D. 1985: Prospect, perspective and the evolution of the landscape idea. *Transactions, Institute of British Geographers* NS 10: 45–62. · Daniels, S. 1989: Marxism, culture and the duplicity of landscape. In R. Peet and N. Thrift, eds, *New models in geography (volume two)*. London: Unwin Hyman, 196–220. · Daniels, S. and Cosgrove, D. 1988: Introduction: the iconography of landscape. In D. Cosgrove and S. Daniels, eds, *The iconography of landscape: essays on the symbolic representation, design and use of past environments*. Cambridge: Cambridge University Press, 1–10. · Deutsche, R. 1991: Boys town. *Environment and Planning D: Society and Space* 9: 5–30. · Foster, H., ed., 1988: *Vision and visuality*. Seattle: Bay Press. · Haraway, D. 1991: *Simians, cyborgs and women: the reinvention of nature*. London: Free Association Books. · Harley, J.B. 1992: Deconstructing the map. In T.J. Barnes and J.S. Duncan, eds, *Writing worlds: discourse, text and metaphor in the representation of landscape*. London: Routledge, 231–47. · Harvey, D. 1989: *The condition of postmodernity: an enquiry into the origins of cultural change*. Oxford: Basil Blackwell. · Nash, C. 1996: Reclaiming vision: looking at landscape and the body. *Gender, Place and Culture* 3: 149–70. · Rose, G. 1993: *Feminism and geography: the limits of geographical knowledge*. Cambridge: Polity Press, ch. 5. · Rose, G. 1996: Teaching visualised geographies: towards a methodology for the interpretation of visual materials. *Journal of Geography in Higher Education* 20: 281–94. · Ryan, J. 1997: *Picturing Empire: photography and the visualisation of the British Empire*. London: Reaktion Books. · Schwartz, J. 1996: The geography lesson – photographs and the construction of imaginative geographies. *Journal of Historical Geography* 22: 16–45. · Seager, J. and Olson, A. 1997: *The state of women in the world atlas*, 2nd edn. London: Penguin.

Suggested Reading

Mirzoeff, N., ed., 1998: *The visual culture reader*. London: Routledge.

visualization The technical and cognitive processes of displaying, manipulating, viewing and understanding quantitative measurements representing the behaviour of complex systems. As a physiological–cognitive response to patterns of light, human vision accounts for much of the sighted person's knowledge of the environment. Data graphics and computer display extend the eye's reach beyond quantitative measurements to abstract concepts not viewable with ease, if at all. In providing an efficient, high-capacity link between mind and data – a link credited with numerous serendipitous discoveries, including continental drift and the relationships among air pressure, wind and storms – computer graphics and the eye–brain system help scientists cope with vast amounts of information generated by electronic monitoring, computer simulation and prodigious data collection by government agencies and private firms. Although the phenomena involved range in scale from subatomic to intergalactic, spatio-temporal relationships are a common denominator and paramount concern (Hall, 1992).

In the 1980s recognition of the potential of high-speed interactive graphic display fuelled emerging interdisciplinary interest in 'Visualization in Scientific Computing', often identified by the acronym ViSC. As a focus for symposia and collaborative research, scientific visualization attracted scholars in computer science, cognitive psychology, statistics and cartography, as well as investigators in earth science, physics, biology and other fields eager for efficient exploration of large data sets. In the 1990s geographers interested in both the semiotic foundations and the cognitive processes of a 'new cartography' embraced geographic visualization (GVis) as a distinct research focus and began to plan for highly realistic, fully manipulable 'virtual geographies' (Batty, 1997; MacEachren and Kraak, 1997).

As applied to mapping, scientific visualization embodies technological and policy issues ranging from data standards and storage formats to software compatibility across diverse computing environments. More enigmatic are the challenges and prospects of high-speed, high-memory workstations able to offer GEOGRAPHICAL INFORMATION SYSTEMS at least a minimal sense of virtual reality's three-dimensional interactivity. Although large geographic data sets might be slow to benefit from the stereo-vision helmet, data glove and three-dimensional mouse, enhanced realism seems destined to increase the persuasiveness, if not the insight, of cartographic simulations.

By raising new issues as well as developing new analytical techniques, geographic visualization is radically altering how geographers look at their data. By compressing and transforming time – in essence doing for time what conventional maps do for space – animations and other dynamic maps offer new insights to diurnal, seasonal and other temporal effects (DiBiase et al., 1992). By affording simultaneous exploration of the geographic space of the map and the attribute space of the scatterplot (see EXPLORATORY DATA ANALYSIS), multiple linked windows and 'geographic brushing' promote an integrated understanding of spatial and statistical relationships (Monmonier, 1989). In complementing traditional cartographic views, which often emphasize patterns in sparsely inhabited areas, customized population CARTOGRAMS offer researchers more reliable insights to population-related distributions (Dorling, 1995). By trolling mortality data for potentially meaningful patterns, intelligent pre-screening systems like the Geographical Analysis Machine (GAM) can make visual exploration more efficient as well as more reliable (Openshaw et al., 1990). And by providing a graphic and conceptual framework for addressing uncertainty in geographical data, interactive decision support systems grounded in fuzzy set theory offer a more reliable approach to exploratory spatial analysis (Hootsmans, 1996). Geographic visualization extends well beyond zooming in, panning around, and clicking on highlighted labels.

No less important than computational solutions are human-factors investigations of the behaviour and limitations of the eye–brain system. Especially promising are subject-testing studies of the varied reliability of diverse colour schemes for quantitative data, including sequences adapted to personal preferences or impaired colour vision (Brewer et al., 1997). Equally relevant are the different strategies and requirements of experts and novices (McGuinness, 1994). For geographic visualization to confer its full benefits upon all users, software designers must accommodate both the real and the perceived needs of individual viewers. MM

References

Batty, M. 1997: Virtual geography. *Futures* 29: 337–52. · Brewer, C.A. et al. 1997: Mapping mortality: evaluating color schemes for choropleth maps. *Annals of the Association of American Geographers* 87: 411–38. · DiBiase, D. et al. 1992: Animation and the role of map design in scientific visualization. *Cartography and Geographic Information Systems* 19: 201–14, 265–6. · Dorling, D. 1995: The visualisation of local urban change across Britain. *Environment and Planning B* 22: 269–90. · Hall, S.S. 1992: *Mapping the next millennium.*

New York: Random House. · Hootsmans, R. 1996: *Fuzzy sets and series analysis for visual decision support in spatial data exploration*. NGS no. 202. Utrecht: Netherlands Geographical Studies. · MacEachren, A.M. and Kraak, M.-J. 1997: Exploratory cartographic visualization: advancing the agenda. *Computers and Geosciences* 23: 335–43. · McGuinness, C. 1994: Expert/novice use of visualization tools. In A.M. MacEachren and D.R.F. Taylor, eds, *Visualization in modern cartography*. London: Pergamon, 185–99. · Monmonier, M. 1989. Geographic brushing: enhancing exploratory analysis of the scatterplot matrix. *Geographical Analysis* 21: 81–4. · Openshaw, S., Cross, A. and Charlton, M. 1990: Building a prototype geographical correlates exploration machine. *International Journal of Geographical Information Systems* 4: 297–311.

Suggested Reading

Hearnshaw, H.M. and Unwin, D.J., eds, 1994: *Visualization in geographical information systems*. Chichester: John Wiley and Sons. · MacEachren, A.M. and Taylor, D.R.F., eds, 1994: *Visualization in modern cartography*. London: Pergamon.

von Thünen model A model for analysing agricultural location patterns based on the pioneering work of a Prussian landowner, Johann Heinrich von Thünen (1966: originally published in 1826). His goal was to explain variations in farm product prices and the way they influenced the use of agricultural land. He envisaged a single market for the products and, by simplifying his analysis to a small number of variables only, suggested that distance from that market would be a prime determinant of the geography of agricultural land use. His model was a statement of what the contemporary distribution of land uses should be, given certain assumptions, and it has been widely used as a norm against which actual patterns are compared – thereby accepting that the assumptions are largely valid (Chisholm, 1979).

The model is constructed around the concept of RENT and assumes that all farmers will produce that commodity which yields the 'highest' rent in order to maximize their net returns. Their net profit is land rent (L), whose value is determined by the production costs per unit of the commodity (a), its market price (p), the yield per unit of land (E), and the distance from the market to the production point (k). These are combined to give (Dunn, 1954):

$$L = E(p - a) - Efk$$

Land rent in this context differs from economic rent because it takes no account of OPPORTUNITY COSTS and ignores what might be earned from alternative uses.

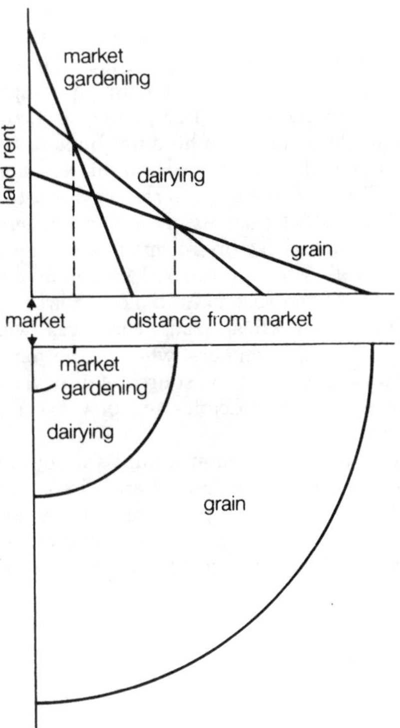

von Thünen model *Land rent variations and land-use patterns*

In the model's simplest applications only transport costs vary (i.e. prices, production costs and yields are held constant for each commodity): rates per unit of distance are highest for bulky and/or perishable items such as dairy products and timber. Thus land rent declines away from the market point where the net returns are greatest (cf. DISTANCE DECAY), but the rate of decline differs by commodity. The result is a family of land rent slopes, as shown for three commodities in the figure. If the distance-decay curves are translated from one- to two-dimensional space, they describe a zonal pattern of land use organization around the market point.

Although geographers have focused on the distance variable in von Thünen's model, each of the others can be allowed to vary, generating idealized land-use patterns which reflect differences in land productivity, for example. Similarly, price changes and/or changes in production costs can be introduced, to illustrate how the zonal pattern might change as a consequence – on the assumption that farmers respond rationally to those changes (cf. RATIONAL CHOICE THEORY).

Geographers were particularly attracted to the zonal component of von Thünen's model, having 'discovered' it when LOCATIONAL ANALYSIS was a dominant paradigm, and its validity has been evaluated at a range of spatial scales from the global (Peet, 1969) to the individual village and farm holding (Blaikie, 1971; Chisholm, 1979): it also stimulated similar modelling of zonal patterns of intra-urban land use (cf. ALONSO MODEL). This concentration on spatial factors meant less recognition of the role of environmental factors as determinants of land-use patterns: only part of von Thünen's analytical framework was widely adopted by geographers, whereas the remainder was considered the source of a 'deviation' from the basic principles of LOCATIONAL ANALYSIS.

As with most economic models, von Thünen's simplifies the 'real world' in order to understand it. The processes of DECISION-MAKING by farmers are considerably oversimplified, for example, and the elements of RISK and UNCERTAINTY are ignored (see GAME THEORY and Wolpert, 1964). Its spatial component is thus no more than an IDEAL TYPE, therefore, whereas its analytical framework has much wider applicability. RJJ

References

Blaikie, P.M. 1971: Spatial organization of agriculture in some north Indian villages. *Transactions, Institute of British Geographers* 52: 1–40, 53, 15–30. · Chisholm, M. 1979: *Rural settlement and location*, 3rd edn. London: Hutchinson; Atlantic Highlands, NJ: Humanities Press. · Dunn, E.S. 1954: *The location of agricultural production*. Gainesville: University of Florida Press. · Peet, J.R. 1969: The spatial expansion of commercial agriculture in the nineteenth century: a von Thünen explanation. *Economic Geography* 45: 283–301. · Thünen, J.H. von 1966: *Isolated state, an English translation of der isolierte staat*, trans. C.M. Wartenberg, ed. P. Hall. Oxford and New York: Pergamon Press. · Wolpert, J. 1964: The decision process in spatial context. *Annals of the Association of American Geographers* 54: 337–58.

Suggested Reading

Grotewöld, A.A. 1959: Von Thünen in retrospect. *Economic Geography* 35: 346–55.

W

welfare geography An approach to human geography that emphasizes questions of inequality (see INEQUALITY, SPATIAL) and SOCIAL JUSTICE. The welfare approach emerged from the radical reaction to the quantitative and model-building preoccupations of the 1960s, which were thought to be insufficiently concerned with contemporary social issues (see RADICAL GEOGRAPHY). The 1970s saw a major redirection of human geography towards such welfare problems as POVERTY, hunger, CRIME, racial discrimination (cf. RACISM) and access to PUBLIC SERVICES (e.g. HEALTH CARE and EDUCATION). This corresponded to a major shift in societal concern, from narrow economic criteria of development or progress to broader aspects of the 'QUALITY OF LIFE'.

Distributional issues assume special importance under conditions of slow economic growth, when policies of redistribution in favour of the poor or socially deprived can be implemented only at the expense of the rich or better-off members of a society (see PARETO OPTIMALITY). Dramatic political and social change, of the kind which has taken place in Eastern Europe and South Africa since 1990 (see APARTHEID; POST-SOVIET STATES) also highlights distributional issues with a spatial dimension. For example, PRIVATIZATION of state assets such as housing and industrial enterprises in Eastern Europe has generated new forms of inequality, as some people in some places are better able than others elsewhere to benefit from post-socialist society.

As originally formulated (Smith, 1977), the basic focus of the welfare approach is on '*who gets what, where and how?*'.The 'who' refers to the population of the area under review (a city, region or nation, or even the entire world), subdivided into groups on the basis of CLASS, RACE, GENDER or other relevant characteristics. The 'what' refers to the various goods (and bads) enjoyed or endured by the population, in the form of commodities, services, environmental quality, social relationships and so on. The 'where' reflects the fact that living standards differ according to area of residence. The 'how' refers to the process whereby the observed differences arise.

The initial task posed by the welfare approach is descriptive. The present state of society, with respect to who gets what where, may be represented by extension of the abstract formulations of welfare economics, and the practical objective is to give these empirical substance. In a spatially disaggregated society, the general level of welfare may be written as:

$$W = f(S_1 \ldots S_n)$$

where S is the level of living or social well-being in a set of n territorial subdivisions. In other words, welfare is some function of the distribution of goods and bads among groups of the population defined by area of residence. Social well-being may be defined in terms of what the people actually get, as follows:

$$S = f(X_1 \ldots X_m)$$

where X represents the quantity of the m goods and bads consumed or experienced. SOCIAL WELL-BEING may also be expressed in terms of the distribution within the area in question:

$$S = f(U_1 \ldots U_k)$$

where U is the level of well-being, satisfaction or *utility* of each of the k population subgroups (cf. UTILITY THEORY). In all the above expressions, the terms may be weighted differentially and combined according to any function, to represent the combination of territorial levels of well-being, goods and bads or group well-being that maximizes the objective function (W or S).

The empirical identification of inequality in territorial distribution involves developing TERRITORIAL SOCIAL INDICATORS (see INEQUALITY, SPATIAL). These may combine particular elements of social well-being in a composite measure. Conditions that might be included are income, wealth, employment, housing, environmental quality, health, education, social order (i.e. absence of crime, deviancy and other threats to social stability and security), social participation, recreation and leisure. Alternatively, the focus may be on individual aspects of social well-being, such as inequalities in access to health care or the differential experience of a nuisance such as noise, air pollution and so on (see ENVIRONMENTAL JUSTICE).

Descriptive research of this kind was initially justified on the grounds that it provided information on aspects of life hitherto neglected in geography (e.g Smith, 1979, 1988). It also provides a basis for evaluation, whereby the existing state is judged against an alternative (past, predicted or planned) according to some criteria of welfare improvement. Thus the impact of alternative plans for facility location or closure (e.g. of hospitals) could be judged by the criterion of which would most equally (or least unequally) distribute the benefits (such as access to health care) among the populations of various subdivisions of the area under review. This raises the question of rules of distributive justice (see SOCIAL JUSTICE), and the manner in which they are actually applied (explicitly or otherwise) in the political process.

The early preoccupation with descriptive research in welfare geography subsequently gave way to more process-oriented work on the question of how inequality arises. The abstract formulation of welfare problems based in NEO-CLASSICAL ECONOMICS was found impotent as a basis for explanatory analysis, and alternatives such as MARXIAN ECONOMICS have become useful sources of guidance. Explanation tends to be sought at two different levels.

The first involves understanding the operation of the economic–social–political system as an integrated whole in order to reveal its general tendencies (see MODE OF PRODUCTION; SOCIAL FORMATION). Thus a broad examination of CAPITALISM shows that the generation of inequality is inevitable because it is endemic to the system; UNEVEN DEVELOPMENT is its spatial consequence. SOCIALISM as actually practised may have its own inbuilt tendencies towards inequality, apparently similar in spatial expression to some of those observed under capitalism but with different origins and probably with less extreme manifestations among regions and within the city.

The second level of explanation is concerned with details of how specific elements of an economic–social–political system operate. Examples might be the differential distribution of public services in a city, how the location of health-care facilities benefits some people in some places and disadvantages others elsewhere, or how the housing market (under capitalism) or administrative allocation process (under socialism) differentially bestow shelter according to who and where people are. Attention might also be given to how people mobilize locally to prevent the location of facilities perceived to generate nuisance (see EXTERNALITIES; NIMBY).

Although originally proposed as an alternative framework for human geography (Smith, 1977), the welfare approach soon merged with other lines of critical inquiry within geography directed towards the fundamental problem of inequality (cf. CRITICAL HUMAN GEOGRAPHY). The issues in question extend beyond the limits of a single discipline, and in fact render disciplinary boundaries increasingly irrelevant. The welfare approach requires a holistic social science perspective, incorporating economic, social and political factors and also consideration of the moral philosophy which unederpins conceptions of SOCIAL JUSTICE (see ETHICS, GEOGRAPHY AND). Although the term welfare approach is seldom used in human geography today, in this rapidly changing world where new political and economic institutional arrangements can benefit populations unequally, there is continuing interest in the issues raised by the welfare approach. DMS

References

Smith, D.M. 1977: *Human geography: a welfare approach*. London: Edward Arnold; New York: St. Martin's Press. · Smith, D.M. 1979: *Where the grass is greener; living in an unequal world*. London: Penguin. · Baltimore: Johns Hopkins University Press; New York: Barnes and Noble (published as *Geographical perspectives on inequality*). · Smith, D.M. 1988: *Geography, inequality and society*. Cambridge: Cambridge University Press.

Suggested Reading

Herbert, D.T. and Smith, D.M., eds, 1989: *Social problems and the city: new perspectives*. Oxford: Oxford University Press. · Pinch, S. 1997: *Worlds of welfare: understanding the changing geographies of social welfare provision*. London: Routledge. · Smith, D.M. 1988: A welfare approach to human geography. In J. Eyles, ed., *Research in human geography: problem, tactics and opportunities*. Oxford: Basil Blackwell, 139–54. · Smith, D.M. 1989: *Urban inequality under socialism: case studies from Eastern Europe*. Cambridge: Cambridge University Press (*Update* series). · Smith, D.M. 1994: *Geography and social justice*. Oxford: Blackwell. · Smith, D.M. 1996: The quality of life: human welfare and social justice. In I. Douglas, R. Huggett and M. Robinson, eds, *Companion encyclopedia of geography: the environment and humankind*. London: Routledge, 772–90.

welfare state Those parts of the STATE APPARATUS involved in the provision of public services and benefits: it is generally assumed that the welfare state involves redistribution of income and wealth in favour of the poorer income groups within society, though empirical analyses have suggested that the more affluent frequently benefit most from at least some public services (such as education and health care).

Growth of the welfare state was especially rapid in the countries of the First World after the depression of the 1930s. Many elements of the British welfare state were introduced by the Labour government elected in 1945, for example, based on the case made in William Beveridge's 1942 paper, *Social insurance and allied services*, commissioned by the wartime government. Beveridge identified five 'scourges' of contemporary society – want, disease, ignorance, squalor and idleness – and proposed a programme of social insurance to tackle three of them, later introduced through a comprehensive social security system and the National Health Service. (Ignorance was countered by the compulsory education service and squalor by housing and town planning policies.)

The size and extent of the welfare state came under considerable attack in most countries as part of the 'New Right' formulation of policies to counter the recession of the 1970s and 1980s, and this case has since been accepted by the 'centre left' too. The size and expansion of the welfare state was presented as the dominant cause of the FISCAL CRISIS of the state, with the volume of its tax demands and public borrowing acting as major influences on inflation and interest rates as well as forming constraints to enterprise and initiative. Welfare states were substantially dismantled in some countries, not least New Zealand which had one of the most extensive, and the provision of PUBLIC SERVICES is increasingly being either privatized or subject to market conditions, with the state's role reduced to guaranteeing a threshold provision only (cf. MERIT GOOD).

RJJ

Suggested Reading

Johnston, R.J. 1992: The rise and decline of the corporate-welfare state: a comparative analysis in global context. In P.J. Taylor, ed., *Political geography of the twentieth century: a global analysis*. London: Belhaven Press, 115–70. · Kelsey, J. 1995: *Economic fundamentalism*. London: Pluto Press. · Pinch, S. 1997: *Worlds of welfare: understanding the changing geographies of social welfare provision*. London: Routledge. · Timmins, N. 1995: *The five giants: a biography of the welfare state*. London: HarperCollins. · Westergaard, J. and Resler, H. 1975: *Class in a capitalist society: a study of contemporary Britain*. London: Heinemann.

whiteness Informed by recent work in media and cultural studies (e.g. Dyer, 1997), geographers and other social scientists have begun to attend to cultural constructions of 'whiteness' as well as to the racialization of more 'visible' ethnic minorities. Often regarded as an unmarked category, the apparent invisibility of whiteness is a direct product of its privileged position within a hierarchy of radicalized POWER. Recent interest in whiteness is part of a more general reflexive moment in the social sciences in which other dominant categories such as masculinity and heterosexuality are being critically re-examined. Rather than simply adding whiteness to existing studies of black and ethnic minorities, however, recent work (Jackson, 1998) has sought to repudiate the binary logic of all such radicalized ways of thinking. As Bonnett (1997) has argued, geographers need to examine the multiple ways in which 'white' identities are constituted in different places and at different times, and in relation to other socially constituted differences of GENDER, CLASS and NATION. Such intersections have been explored in historical research on the colonial encounter (McClintock, 1995), highlighting the mutual constitution of RACE, GENDER and SEXUALITY. While it is important to examine different versions and sub-categories of whiteness (Irish, Jewish, English, etc.), the particularity of whiteness as a category of radicalized power should not be neglected. Cultural constructions of whiteness also have political significance in contexts where the assertion of a 'white' identity is usually associated with extreme right-wing groups. Geographers have therefore begun to consider the extent to which white identities can be articulated within a more progressive and explicitly anti-racist politics (Bonnett, 1996).

PAJ

References

Bonnett, A. 1996: Anti-racism and the critique of white identities. *New Community* 22: 97–110. · Bonnett, A. 1997: Geography, race and Whiteness: invisible traditions and current challenges. *Area* 29: 193–99. · Dyer, R. 1997: *White: essays on race and culture*. London: Routledge. · Jackson, P. 1998: Constructions of whiteness in the geographical imagination. *Area* 30: 99–106. · McClintock, A. 1995: *Imperial leather: race, gender and sexuality in the colonial encounter*. London: Routledge.

wilderness Literally a wild or untamed part of NATURE. The word derives from the Anglo-Saxon *wildeor*, denoting wild or savage beasts, and has a long history of usage in Western CULTURE. In Biblical references wilderness is an uncultivated or unhumanized LANDSCAPE, while in early European meanings it indicates places in a savage condition. Until the mid-nineteenth century, wilderness had a largely negative connotation in the Euro-American imaginary, as an area to be feared if left unconquered. Such an attitude, for instance, was strong among the early European settlers in the eastern USA when confronted with the seaboard's expanses of temperate forest. However, in the modern era wilderness has taken on far more positive meanings. Historically this coincided with large-scale human transformation of environment and the birth of an early ENVIRONMENTAL MOVEMENT. In the US, the latter took the forms of preservationism, and a less pro-environmental conservationism (see CONSERVATION; PRESERVATION), as thinkers like John Muir and Gifford Pinchot decried the ECOLOGICAL destructiveness of American INDUSTRIALIZATION. In particular, Muir and romantics like Henry David Thoreau in the late nineteenth century, and nature photographers like Ansell Adams of the Sierra Club in the early twentieth century, were responsible for revalorizing wilderness in a positive way in North America and beyond.

In the late twentieth century this has fed into a widespread desire within the environmental movement to protect wilderness from the predations of humanity. In particular, many 'DEEP ECOLOGISTS' argue that the last vestiges of wilderness on the planet must be saved for their inherent beauty and moral worth. Such arguments have proved important in securing the survival of wilderness areas, like the old growth trees in Clayoquot Sound, British Columbia (see Willems-Braun, 1997). However, in recent years some critics have suggested that there is more to the notion of wilderness than there seems.

Such criticism begins with the observation that since the meanings of wilderness have altered historically then wilderness is as much an *idea* as it is a brute reality (Oelschlaeger, 1991). Some have taken this further to suggest that wilderness in a 'cultural construction' (Cronon, 1996, p. 81). While this argument does not deny that there is a natural world, it does emphasize the fact that this world is always interpreted and appraised through specific cultural categories. By constructing wilderness is this way rather than that, the argument goes, such categories can decisively affect people's views while pretending to merely mimic or objectively represent a mute wilderness 'out there' in the world. A failure to recognize that wilderness is a specific cultural category is arguably problematic. For instance, Guha (1994) suggests that wilderness is a peculiarly Western, middle-class construction in its modern form, one based on the desire to escape from URBANISM and industrialization. More particularly, he argues, it is a construction which ignores the fact that most supposed 'wilderness' has long been inhabited by indigenous peoples. In turn, Willems-Braun (1997) shows how this can translate into an environmental politics and practice which erases First Nations' LAND RIGHTS. London (1998), however, has recently argued that some western environmental organizations are now beginning to deconstruct the notions of wilderness which have hitherto underpinned their political beliefs and actions. NC

References

Cronon, W. 1996: The trouble with wilderness. In W. Cronon, ed., *Uncommon ground: toward reinventing nature*. New York: W.W. Norton: 69–90. · Guha, R. 1994: Radical American environmentalism and wilderness preservation: a Third World critique. In L. Gruen and D. Jamieson, eds, *Reflecting on nature*. New York: Oxford University Press, 241–51. · London, J.K. 1998: Common roots and entangled limbs: Earth First! and the growth of post-wilderness environmentalism on California's north coast. *Antipode* 30: 155–76. · Oelschlaeger, M. 1991: *The idea of wilderness*. New Haven: Yale University Press. · Willems-Braun, B. 1997: Buried epistemologies: the politics of nature in (post)colonial British Columbia. *Annals of the Association of American Geographers*. 87: 3–31.

world city A term coined by Patrick Geddes (1915) for 'certain great cities in which a quite disproportionate part of the world's most important business is conducted' (Hall, 1984, p. 1). Hall identified eight such cities, centres of both economic and political power (though he later referred to them as 'giant metropolises').

Within the global organization of the capitalist world-economy, world cities have been presented as the major foci. Friedmann's (1986) seminal paper, presented as 'a framework for research . . . neither a theory nor a universal generalization about cities, but a starting point for political inquiry' linked URBANIZATION processes to global economic forces through a 'series of loosely joined statements' or 'interrelated theses':

> The form and extent of a city's integration with the world economy, and the functions assigned to the city in the new spatial division of labour, will be decisive for any structural changes occurring within it.
>
> Key cities throughout the world are used by global capital as 'basing points' in the spatial organization and articulation of production and markets. The resulting linkages make it possible to arrange world cities into a complex spatial hierarchy.
>
> The global control functions of world cities are directly reflected in the structure and dynamics of their production sectors and employment.
>
> World cities are major sites for the concentration and accumulation of international capital.
>
> World cities are points of destination for large numbers of both domestic and/or international migrants.

World city formation brings into focus the major contradictions of industrial capitalism – among them spatial and class polarization.

World city growth generates social costs at rates that tend to exceed the fiscal capacity of the state.

Much research has been undertaken in the context of these theses, focusing especially on identification of hierarchies of world cities and (largely through comparative studies) the degree of social and economic polarization in the largest (especially London and New York): much of this is summarized in Knox and Taylor (1996).

Ten years after his original statement, Friedmann (1996) reviewed the subsequent literature, and concluded that there were 'five agreements' regarding the 'conceptual object' – the world city:

World cities articulate regional, national, and international economies into a global economy. They serve as the organizing nodes of a global economic system.

A space of global capital accumulation exists, but it is smaller than the world as a whole. Major world regions and their populations are, at present, virtually excluded from this space, living in a permanent subsistence economy.

World cities are large urbanized spaces of intense economic and social interaction.

World cities can be arranged hierarchically, roughly in accord with the economic power they command. They are cities through which regional, national, and international economies are articulated within the global capitalist system of accumulation. A city's ability to attract global investments ultimately determines its rank in the order of world cities.

The controlling world city strata constitute a social class that has been called the transnational capitalist class. Its interests are the smooth functioning of the global system of accumulation; its culture is cosmopolitan; and its ideology is consumerist. Its presence gives rise to often severe conflict between itself and the subaltern classes who have more locally defined territorial interests and whose rise into the transnational class is blocked.

These agreements are woven together into what Friedmann terms a meta-narrative, which is able

to synthesize what would otherwise be disparate and diverging researches – into labour markets, information technology, international migration, cultural studies, city-building processes, industrial location, social class formation, massive disempowerment, and urban politics.

For the future, the relationships between these economic centres of a global economy and the system of territorial nation-states will be a major elements of the world geopolitical system. (See also GEOPOLITICS, GLOBALIZATION.) RJJ

References and Suggested Reading

Geddes, P. 1915: *Cities in evolution*. London: Benn. · Friedmann, J. 1986: The world city hypothesis. *Development and Change* 17 (1): 69–84. · Friedmann, J. 1996: Where we stand: a decade of world city research. In P.L. Knox and P.J. Taylor, eds, *World cities in a world system*. Cambridge: Cambridge University Press. · Hall, P. 1984: *The world cities*, 3rd edn. London: Weidenfeld and Nicolson. · Knox, P.L. and Taylor, P.J., eds, 1996: *World cities in a world system*. Cambridge: Cambridge University Press. · Sassen, S. 1993: *The global city. New York, London, Tokyo*. Princeton: Princeton University Press.

world-systems analysis A materialist approach to the study of social change developed by Immanuel Wallerstein (1974, 1979, 1980, 1983, 1984a). The approach builds upon three research traditions: the study of DEPENDENCE; the ANNALES SCHOOL; and Marxist theory and practice (see HISTORICAL MATERIALISM). The product is a unidisciplinary study of SOCIETY combining economic, political and social aspects with history in a holistic historical social science. The main application of this approach to geography has been in POLITICAL GEOGRAPHY (Flint and Shelley, 1996; Taylor and Flint, 1999).

Wallerstein argues that historically there have only been three basic ways in which societies have been organized to sustain production and reproduction, which he terms MODES OF PRODUCTION. The *reciprocal-lineage* mode describes a society in which production is largely differentiated by age and gender and exchange is simply reciprocal. The *redistributive-tributary* mode occurs when a society is class-based, with production carried or by a large majority of agriculturists who pay tribute to a small ruling class. The *capitalist* mode of production is also class-based but the distinguishing characteristic is ceaseless capital ACCUMULATION operating through a market logic where prices and wages are set through supply and demand mechanisms (Chase-Dunn, 1989) (see CAPITALISM; NEO-CLASSICAL ECONOMICS).

To discover which mode prevails in any society one must first define the real bounds of that society, as indicated by the DIVISION OF LABOUR in production. There are, therefore, just three types of society: *mini-systems* encompassing the reciprocal-lineage mode; *world-empires* defined by the redistributive-tributary mode; and *world-economies* which are capitalist (see FORM OF ECONOMIC INTEGRATION; SCALE). The latter two describe societies whose divisions of labour are larger than any one local grouping and so are designated 'world-systems'. There have been 'countless' mini-systems in the evolution of humankind, and numerous world-empires since the Neolithic Revolution but only one successful capital-expanding world-economy, which originated in Europe after 1450 and spread to cover the whole world by about 1900. This is the *modern world-system*. Related work on pre-modern systems has attempted to be both more specific with particular concern for patterns of Eurasian development (Abu-Lughod, 1989) and more general by producing an overview of the rise and demise of all types of system (Chase-Dunn and Hall, 1997). This wider work has led to a major debate on the nature of world-systems (Frank and Gills, 1993).

World-systems analysis of the current situation treats our world as a single entity, the *capitalist world-economy* or modern world-system (the two terms are synonymous in world-systems analysis). The primary message of this approach is, therefore, that any meaningful study of social change cannot proceed country by country, but must incorporate the whole world-system. This is the single-society assumption which replaces the multiple-society assumption of most social science. In world-systems terms the latter commit the fundamental *error of developmentalism* (Taylor, 1989a). Wallerstein identifies this error as being dominant in liberal studies of DEVELOPMENT and in orthodox Marxist analyses, both of which envisage individual countries progressing through stages (see ROSTOW MODEL). In world-systems analysis countries do not develop autonomously but rather they have trajectories through the space–time entity, the modern world-system, which is the scale at which development unfolds.

The capitalist world-economy has three fundamental structural features. First, there is *one world market*, the logic of which permeates economic decisions throughout the system (cf. GLOBALIZATION). Second, there is a *multiple -state system* in which no one STATE is able to dominate totally; it is this political competition which gives economic decision-makers a room for manoeuvre which is not available in unitary world-empires. Finally, there is a *three-tier structure of stratification* throughout the system which prevents polarization by the existence of middle groupings between the extremes. One representation of this structure is to be found in the spatial organization of the world-economy where Wallerstein adds a *semi-periphery* category between the commonly recognized *core* and *periphery* (see CORE–PERIPHERY MODEL). The semi-periphery is political in nature, as a stabilizing force between the economic-geographical extremes. It plays a key role in the dynamics of the world-economy, since it is in the semi-periphery where the most acute CLASS struggle occurs, particularly when it becomes the focus of periodic RESTRUCTURING, as represented by Latin America and Eastern Europe in the 1980s. In Wallerstein's scheme, core and periphery are not geographically static but are continually changing, with a few selected countries moving up and down through the semi-periphery. Furthermore this process does not occur at a constant rate. Wallerstein recognizes that the goal of ceaseless accumulation produces consecutive periods of stagnation and growth. Long waves (KONDRATIEFF CYCLES and logistic curves) are interpreted as the basic rhythm of our world-system (Wallerstein, 1984b), with the stagnation providing the necessary conditions for restructuring the world-economy, heavily involving the semi-periphery.

The capitalist world-economy is defined concretely by its integrated and hierarchical DIVISION OF LABOUR. This operates through myriad interlocking COMMODITY CHAINS which connect every point of initial extraction of raw material to every final point of consumption (Gereffi and Korzeniewicz, 1994). Each chain is made up of numerous nodes of production where value is added to the commodity on its way up the chain. The social relations at each node will vary depending on the roles of the four basic institutions of the system at the node (Wallerstein, 1984a). These institutions are households, classes, peoples and states, which reproduce labour, capital, consent and order, respectively. The operation of these institutions varies immensely between the core, semi-periphery and periphery to reproduce UNEVEN DEVELOPMENT.

Finally, since Wallerstein (1983) claims to be following 'the spirit of Marx if not the letter', it is important to identify his differences with orthodox Marxism. As well as the error of developmentalism, there are three other key differences.

First, in terms of MODE OF PRODUCTION, Wallerstein uses a broader definition, resulting in his identification of capitalism not being reliant on the existence of 'free labour'. Hence, both 'feudal-like' social relations which have existed in parts of the 'Third World' and 'socialist-like' social relations which have existed in the 'Second World' are both deemed to have been part of a single division of labour which is the capitalist world-system (Wallerstein, 1979; Chase-Dunn, 1982).

Second, Wallerstein proposes an alternative 'meta-history' which is also related to his identification of fewer modes of production. Orthodox Marxists share with liberals a progressive theory of history, so that, for instance, the transition from feudalism to capitalism is interpreted by both as a victory of 'advanced' bourgeois forces over 'backward' feudal forces. In stark contrast, Wallerstein identifies this transition as a regression, in that capitalism was the European, feudal ruling classes' solution to the crisis of their world-system – feudal Europe. The ruling class remained largely intact as the mode of production changed to provide new means of exploitation (Wallerstein, 1983).

Third, Wallerstein (1991a) interprets the cultural dimension (notably the faith in progress), not as a SUPERSTRUCTURE, but as the 'underside' of the system. This *geoculture* is the more opaque part of the modern world-system and is therefore more difficult to analyse. World HEGEMONY has been the main tool used to unravel geoculture (Taylor, 1996a, 1996b).

Wallerstein (1991b) has been especially concerned with the contemporary 'crisis of the sciences', in particular in terms of the future of social science (Wallerstein et al., 1996). This is integral to his interpretation of future transition derived from his meta-history: Wallerstein is at one with Marxist analysis in not view capitalism as eternal. In world-systems analysis, the 'rhythm' of the system is accompanied by secular trends which are asymptotic and, as these run their course, so the world-economy enters its generalized CRISIS phase. According to Wallerstein (1983) we are just entering this phase. The next transition will be towards either a more egalitarian system which we may term 'socialism' or a new mode of production will again be invented to perpetuate inequalities (Taylor, 1996a, ch. 6). World-systems analysis was created as a contribution towards making the former more likely but the future remains to be won. PJT

References

Abu-Lughod, J. 1989: *Before European hegemony: the world system* AD *1250–1350*. New York: Oxford University Press. · Chase-Dunn, C., ed., 1982: *Socialist states in the world-system*. Beverly Hills: Sage. · Chase-Dunn, C. 1989: *Global formation*. Oxford: Blackwell. · Chase-Dunn, C. and Hall, T.D. 1997: *Rise and demise: comparing world-systems*. Boulder: Westview. · Flint, C. and Shelley, F.M. 1996: Structure, agency and context: the contributions of geography to world-systems analysis. *Sociological Inquiry* 66: 494–508. · Frank, A.G. and Gills, B.K. eds, 1993: *The world system: five hundred years or five thousand?* London: Routledge. · Gereffi, G. and Korzeniewicz, M. eds, 1994: *Commodity chains and global capitalism*. Westport: Praeger. · Polanyi, K. 1944: *The great transformation*. Boston: Beacon Press. · Taylor, P.J. 1989a: The error of developmentalism in human geography. In R. Walford and D. Gregory, eds, *New horizons in human geography*. London: Macmillan. · Taylor, P.J. 1996a *The way the modern world works: world hegemony to world impasse*. Chichester: Wiley. · Taylor, P.J. 1996b: What's modern about the modern world-system? Introducing ordinary modernity through world hegemony. *Review of International Political Economy* 3: 260–86; Taylor, P.J. and Flint, C. 1999: *Political geography: world-economy, nation-state and locality*, 4th edn. London: Longman. · Wallerstein, I. 1974: *The modern world system. Capitalist agriculture and the origins of the European world-economy in the sixteenth century*. New York: Academic Press. · Wallerstein, I. 1979: *The capitalist world-economy*. Cambridge: Cambridge University Press. · Wallerstein, I. 1980: *The modern world system II. Mercantilism and the consolidation of the European world-economy, 1600–1750*. New York: Academic Press. · Wallerstein, I. 1983: *Historical capitalism*. London: Verso. · Wallerstein, I. 1984a: *The politics of the world-economy*. Cambridge: Cambridge University Press. · Wallerstein, I. 1984b: Long waves as capitalist process. *Review* VII: 4: 559–76. · Wallerstein, I. 1991a: *Geopolitics and geoculture*. Cambridge: Cambridge University Press. · Wallerstein, I. 1991b: *Unthinking social science. The limits of nineteenth century paradigms*. Cambridge: Polity Press. · Wallerstein, I. et al. 1996: *Open the social sciences*. Stanford: Stanford University Press.

Suggested Reading

Chase-Dunn and Hall (1997). · Hall, T.D. ed. 1996: Special section. The world-system perspective: a small sample from a large universe. *Sociological Inquiry* 66: 440–508. · Taylor, P.J. 1989b: The world-systems project. In R.J. Johnston and P.J. Taylor, eds, *A world in crisis? Geographical perspectives*. Oxford: Basil Blackwell. · Taylor (1996a). · Wallerstein (1983).

Z

zero population growth (ZPG) The tendency of a population to become stationary (see STABLE POPULATION). The likelihood of achieving ZPG, and its advantages and disadvantages, have been discussed increasingly both as a result of the marked decline in FERTILITY in many developed countries and as a possible long-term aim for the developing world. ZPG has direct implications in the short term for AGE AND SEX STRUCTURE, and economic and social policy, but long-term relationships, especially with economic growth, are problematical. PEO

Suggested Reading

Spengler, J.J. 1978: *Facing zero population growth: reactions and interpretations, past and present*. Durham, NC: Duke University Press.

zonal model A model of urban spatial organization created by E.W. Burgess (1924, 1927), a leading member of the CHICAGO SCHOOL of sociologists. His main research

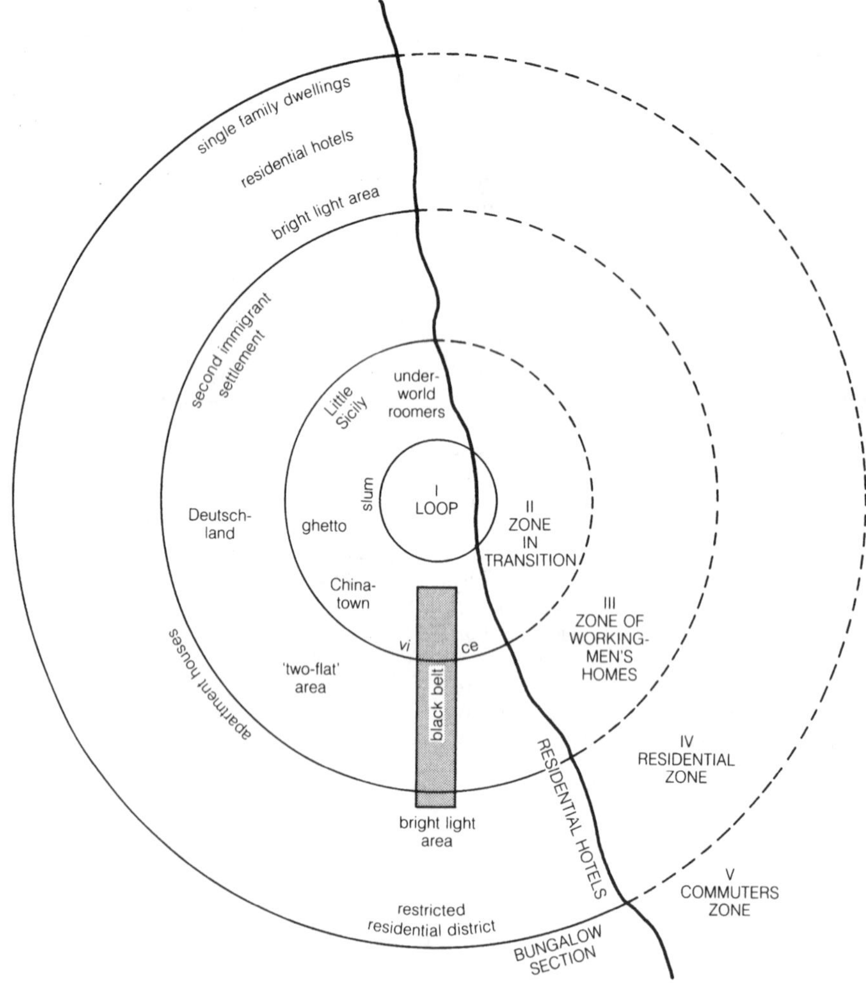

zonal model *Burgess's zonal model* (Park et al., 1925)

interest was the determinants of urban social problems, such as vice and crime, and his maps of their occurrence within Chicago indicated their concentration in certain type areas only. To appreciate their nature, he developed a model of the socio-spatial organization of the entire city comprising five major zones (see figure).

The dominant feature of this zonal structure is the positive correlation between the socio-economic status of residential areas and their distance from the CENTRAL BUSINESS DISTRICT: the most affluent urban residents live in the outer suburbs, a finding which Burgess's followers generalized from Chicago to all American cities (see Schnore, 1965). Growth within the city was propelled from the centre through the process of INVASION AND SUCCESSION whereby new immigrants occupied the lowest quality homes in the zone in transition and pressed longer-established groups to migrate outwards towards the suburbs.

Burgess's model has been tested empirically many times, and subject to a variety of criticisms. Hoyt, for example, proposed an alternative, SECTORAL MODEL and Harris and Ullman combined the two into their MULTIPLE NUCLEI MODEL. In addition, invasion and succession was presented as a special case of the FILTERING process which underpinned Hoyt's model. These models were popular with urban geographers in the 1960s and 1970s (Johnston, 1971), but are widely considered obsolete now. RJJ

References

Burgess, E.W. 1924: The growth of the city: an introduction to a research project. *Publications of the American Sociological Society* 18: 85–97. · Burgess, E.W. 1927: The determination of gradients in the growth of the city. *Publications of the American Sociological Society* 21: 178–84. · Johnston, R.J. 1971: *Urban residential patterns: an introductory review*. London: George Bell and Sons. · Park, R.E., Burgess, E.W. and Mackenzie, R.T. 1925: *The city*. Chicago: University of Chicago Press. · Schnore, L.F. 1965: On the spatial structure of cities in the two Americas. In P.M. Hauser and L.F. Schnore, eds, *The study of urbanization*. New York: John Wiley, 347–98.

Suggested Reading

Burgess, E.W. and Bogue, D.J., eds, 1965: *Urban sociology*. Chicago: University of Chicago Press.

zone of dependence The spatial clustering or 'ghettoization' of human service clients and the facilities designed to serve them in the INNER CITY (also referred to as the service-dependent population GHETTO). Forces producing the zone of dependence are numerous and complex and can be linked to broader debates about the processes of social exclusion which isolate certain groups from mainstream social and economic opportunities on the basis of dimensions of oppression like 'RACE', CLASS, GENDER, SEXUALITY and DISABILITY. In the recent past, one of the most prominent has been the trend toward deinstitutionalization, whereby many groups with mental and physical disabilities were discharged from institutional environments into an inadequate system of community-based care.

The deinstitutionalization of people from psychiatric facilities is typical of the experience of many such groups. Their ghettoization following discharge can be seen as the result of a number of factors. For instance, the inner city is the place where there are: large properties available for conversion to community facilities; an established supply of cheap rental accommodation; and established support networks, both personal and those associated with formal support services. Former psychiatric-hospital patients gravitated towards core areas in search of housing opportunities, such movements often occurring over large distances and including rural–urban MIGRATION. They were also referred by professionals to core-area housing and service opportunities.

The original plans for deinstitutionalization envisaged a spatially dispersed system of care that would successfully mainstream previously stigmatized client groups. At least two factors worked to prevent the realization of this goal. First, deinstitutionalization was often used as an opportunity to cut budgets for funding services to the extent that it was impossible to provide the comprehensive systems of assistance needed to ensure successful community-based care. Second, there has been continued and widespread community opposition to the placement of facilities in residential and commercial districts beyond the zones of dependence, particularly in suburban locations (see NIMBY). Public intolerance is sparked by fear and uncertainty, and perpetuated by a lack of knowledge about and familiarity with disabled people, intensified by a conservative turn in national politics during recent decades and reflecting what Galbraith terms a 'culture of contentment' among the privileged. Neighborhood concern is often manifest as a range of material concerns relating to (for instance) anticipation of diminished property values, or reduced neighbourhood amenity. The force of the opposition is often so intense that planners and facility operators have attempted to avert conflict by seeking out non-controversial sites for community-based facilities. These have typically been found in low-income, inner-city neighbourhoods. Such areas have often become saturated with human service facilities, giving rise to a call for a 'fair-share' policy of facility location within metropolitan areas.

Those discharged from psychiatric institutions have been joined in zones of dependence by a variety of other populations, including the dependent elderly, the developmentally disabled, the physically disabled, runaway youth, parolees, and people with drug and alcohol addictions. Many in these groups also experienced deinstitutionalization, but a growing proportion now come from a 'never-institutionalized' category. Economic, political and socio-cultural changes in the past three decades have produced an unprecedented concentration of these populations in the inner city. Often, the growing numbers of people in need has overwhelmed existing social service networks, contributing to the ongoing crisis of HOMELESSNESS.

Intolerance and community opposition continue to play a major role in containing service-dependent populations in zones of dependence. However, there are significant variations in public attitudes toward the different groups. A number of dimensions determine levels of public acceptance, including the perceptions of personal culpability, unpredictability and dangerous behaviour, and the extent to which disabilities interfere with accepted social conventions. Efforts to facilitate the siting of facilities in neighbourhoods beyond existing zones of dependence illustrate how variations in acceptance arise (see ZONING). For example, neighbours may be willing to tolerate the presence of board-and-care homes for the elderly, but they are likely to oppose efforts to establish transitional housing for the homeless, or residential drug and alcohol treatment programmes. Such reactions are a consequence of a complex mix of factors, including the characteristics of the neighbours themselves, plus their perceptions of the potential facility, and the kind of clients it is designed to serve.

As an urban phenomenon, the zone of dependence represents an enduring feature of inner-city morphology. As a social welfare phenomenon, the zone continues to act as a reservoir of potential clients and as a reception area for individuals in search of assistance; for them, the inner city has become a coping mechanism, especially since they lack the power to radically change their situation. As more and more needy people arrive, so increasing numbers of services are established to care for them. The new services themselves act as a catalyst to attract yet more clients, and so a self-reinforcing cycle of ghettoization and dependency is established. MJD

Suggested Reading

Dear, M., Gaber, S., Takahashi, L. and Wilton, R. 1997: Seeing people differently: the social and spatial construction of disability. *Environment and Planning D: Society and Space* 15: 455–80. · Dear, M. and Wolch, J. 1987: *Landscapes of despair: from deinstitutionalization to homelessness*. Princeton, NJ: Princeton University Press. · Dear, M., Wolch, J. and Wilton, R. 1994: *The Service Hub Concept in Human Services Planning*. London: Pergamon Press. · Wolch, J. and Dear, M. 1993: *Malign Neglect: Homelessness in an American City*. San Francisco, CA: Jossey Bass.

zoning The general process of subdividing geographical space for some purpose, especially for implementing public space-use policy. Zoning can be applied to a wide range of geographical contexts and purposes, such as allocating land uses to hazardous environments like flood plains and the reconciliation of competing commercial and recreational uses of water bodies. Whatever the context, individual tracts, or zones, are identified with some preferred uses(s) either by positive designation (for example, low-cost housing or community recreation) or the negative exclusion of undesirable ones. Zoning represents a regulatory rather than discretionary approach to land-use planning.

In North American cities, where the term is most widely applied today, decisions on what is allowed where, are taken in advance of particular applications, through zoning ordinances. In the USA zoning is 'the most influential public technique for controlling private land use ... in the 20th century' (Ervin, 1977, p. 6). Its first appearance in Boston in about 1904 was followed by the first zoning ordinance for an entire community, in New York City in 1916. A landmark decision in the US Supreme Court a decade later upheld the constitutional basis of zoning regulations, since when they have extended to specifying the height, density and size of urban construction, as well as permitted uses. Thwarted developers can challenge zoning ordinances through the Courts. The resulting complexity makes zoning systems prime candidates for the application of GEOGRAPHICAL INFORMATION SYSTEMS to track zoning codes and development permits.

For zoning's proponents it offers protection against undesirable EXTERNALITIES (for example, polluting, noisy or otherwise dangerous activities), constrains costs of supplying municipal services, and encourages the efficient provision of PUBLIC GOODS. Its opponents emphasize the negative effects of slowing or preventing development and maintaining the status quo, by eliminating 'undesirable' activities (for example, low-income housing) and others making heavy calls on local taxes for support services. Exclusionary zoning was seen at its most extreme form in the intra-urban racial geography of South African cities, under APARTHEID.

Generation of zoning regulations is very much part and parcel of LOCAL STATE politics within US municipalities. Most, although not all, operate under the aegis of state enabling legislation, which allows for a variety of municipality-level responses. However, determining the impact of urban zoning is far from straightforward, notably over the establishment of a credible COUNTERFACTUAL EXPLANATION (Pogodzinski and Sass, 1991). In some cases zoning may largely follow market trends, but elsewhere it can prove inflexible over growing urban needs, such as housing for the elderly and attempts at stimulating public over private transport. More generally, zoning plays a part in the emergence of a sense of COMMUNITY and the visible, cultural landscape of NEIGHBOURHOODS in US cities (Schein, 1997). As an interesting exception, Houston has developed with no zoning regulations at all.

In other national contexts the significance of zoning in public land allocation policy is both different from the US context, and has evolved more over time. Thus in the complex case of the United Kingdom, the first tranche of local scale Development Plans, prepared under the 1947 Town and Country Planning Act, identified existing land use arrangements, and preferred future ones within the plan period, for mapped parcels of land. These were detailed both in their geographical boundaries and land use classification, and were the template against which subsequent planning applications would be judged. This close adherence to zoning principles is less evident in the more recent wave of Development Plans, where planning policy identifies preferred land use dispositions, based on underlying planning criteria. Such plans have to be 'in conformity' with Structure Plans prepared at a larger geographical scale, following legislation of 1971, which offer strategic guidance on land-use policy, rather than specific zoning-based descriptions and prescriptions. AGH

References

Ervin, D.E. et al. 1977: *Land use control: evaluation economic and political effects*. Cambridge, MA: Ballinger. · Pogodzinski, J.M. and Sass, T.R. 1991: Measuring the effects of municipal zoning regulations: a survey. *Urban Studies* 28: 587–621. · Schein, R.H. 1997: The place of landscape: a conceptual framework for interpreting an American scene. *Annals of the Association of American Geographers* 87: 660–80.

INDEX

Note: This index aims to provide a guide to the complex interconnections within human geography. References to particular topics will be found most easily by looking up that particular topic, but extensive sets of subheadings also indicate the various aspects of more general headings. In addition a network of *see* and *see also* references indicates alternative headings and related topics. For example, all references to gentrification will be found directly under the specific heading 'gentrification', but readers who have approached the topic less directly will find that they are guided to it by cross-references or subheadings under headings such as 'housing' and 'inner city'. Alphabetical arrangement is word-by-word: 'central place theory' therefore precedes 'centralization', for example. Words such as 'and', 'in', 'by', 'through', etc. are ignored in the arrangement of subheadings. References to particular authors are included only where their work is quoted or discussed in some detail. Page numbers in **bold** type indicate the main discussion of a topic which is also treated in less detail on the other pages cited. Page numbers in *italics* refer to diagrams.

Index compiled by Ann Kingdom (formerly Barham)